REGISTER
OF
DEFUNCT
COMPANIES

REGISTER
OF
DEFUNCT
COMPANIES

STOCK
EXCHANGE PRESS

M
MACMILLAN
PUBLISHERS

This Register of Defunct Companies is published by
Macmillan Publishers Limited under licence from the
International Stock Exchange.
The Stock Exchange Press is an imprint of the International
Stock Exchange of the United Kingdom and the Republic of
Ireland Limited who own all proprietary rights to the name
'Stock Exchange Press'. Independent publishers are licensed
by the Exchange to use the imprint for approved commercial
projects relating to topics of City and general financial
interest.

Second edition first published by
MACMILLAN PUBLISHERS LTD (Journals Division), 1990

Distributed by Globe Book Services Ltd
Brunel Road, Houndmills
Basingstoke, Hants RG21 2XS

British Library Cataloguing in Publication Data

Register of defunct companies. – 2nd ed.
  1. Defunct companies
  I. Stock Exchange Publications
  338.7'4

  ISBN 0-333-51529-3

Typeset and printed in Great Britain

FOREWORD

The 1989–90 edition of the *Register of Defunct Companies* is the first separate annual volume to be published since the 1979–80 edition. Since that date the Register of Defunct and Other Companies has been published as a cumulative section in *The International Stock Exchange Official Yearbook* to supplement the 1979–80 edition.

This edition contains over 25,000 notices of companies removed from *The International Stock Exchange Official Yearbook* and its predecessors since 1875. The majority of these are defunct companies removed following liquidation, dissolution or winding up. There are, however, many others which may be defunct that have been removed either due to their securities listed in London having been redeemed or for similar reasons.

It is the only official reference publication giving authoritative information about defunct companies and will prove invaluable for member firms, institutions, banks, solicitors and accountants for purposes of valuation and winding up of deceased estates.

The Editor would like to express his appreciation to all those who have given their valuable assistance in the preparation of this edition.

October 1989

Gavin Fryer

Director of Quotations
The International Stock Exchange

INTRODUCTORY NOTES

It may be helpful to readers to explain terms used in the text by setting out briefly the steps involved in bringing a company registered under the Companies Act to its end. This can be effected by a winding-up, removal from the Register under the provisions of Section 652 of the Companies Act, 1985, whereby the Registrar has jurisdiction to strike off the Register the names of companies believed to be defunct, or by dissolution by Order of the Court in connection with a reconstruction under Section 427 of the Act.

The different kinds of winding-up are:
   (1) by the Court—more usually called **compulsory winding-up;**
   (2) **voluntary**—which may be either a members' voluntary winding-up or a creditors' voluntary winding-up; or
   (3) **subject to the supervision of the Court**—a mode which may be adopted in the case of either kind of voluntary winding-up;
of these the most common is the voluntary winding-up.

The provisions applicable to companies which commenced their liquidation since 1 July 1948 are contained in Part XX of the Companies Act, 1985.

A **compulsory winding-up** by Order of the Court is initiated on a petition either by the company or by one or more creditors or contributories, or, where a company is being wound-up voluntarily or subject to the supervision of the Court in England, by the Official Receiver [Companies Act, 1985, S. 519 (6)]. Upon a Winding-up Order being made the control of the company passes to the Official Receiver or liquidator with a view to the realisation and distribution of assets.

A compulsory winding-up in England is subject to a considerable measure of control by the Department of Trade and Industry, and an account of the liquidator's receipts and payments must be rendered to that Department every six months. When the account has been audited by the Department a duplicate copy is filed with the Court and is 'open to the inspection of any person' [Companies Act, 1985, S. 543]. All moneys received by the liquidator must be paid into the *Companies' Liquidation Account* at the Bank of England, or, if so authorised by the Department of Trade and Industry, into an account with any other bank. In the latter event dividends unclaimed for six months and funds unclaimed or undistributed at the conclusion of the winding-up must, however, be paid into the *Companies' Liquidation Account.* Claimants in respect of unclaimed dividends or funds should in all cases apply to the Department of Trade and Industry for an order for payment.

Where a company is registered in Scotland the undistributed balances at the conclusion of the winding-up are paid into an account in the name of the Accountant of the Court at any joint stock bank of issue, claimants should apply to the Accountant; subsequently the funds are transferred to the Queen's and Lord Treasurer's Remembrancer, who makes payments on an Order of the Court.

Upon completion of a compulsory winding-up the Court can make an order dissolving the company; in practice, however, such an order is seldom made. The Registrar subsequently strikes the name of the Company off the Register under Section 652.

The process of a **voluntary winding-up** is instituted by the passing of appropriate resolutions. The winding-up is known as a *members' voluntary winding-up* when the passing of these resolutions is preceded by a majority of the directors making and filing with the Registrar of Companies a statutory declaration to the effect that they have made a full enquiry into the affairs of the company, and that having done so they have formed the opinion that the company will be able to pay its debts in full within a period not exceeding twelve months; in such a case shareholders appoint the liquidator and control the liquidation. Where this Declaration of Solvency has not been made the winding-up is known as a *creditors' voluntary winding-up*; a meeting of creditors is held after the meeting of the company for the passing of the necessary resolutions, and the creditors and company may each nominate a liquidator but (subject to an application to, and subsequent order of, the Court) the nomination of the creditors will prevail; the creditors further have the right to appoint a committee of inspection.

In either type of voluntary winding-up the liquidator then takes steps to realise the assets, to ascertain and settle claims against the company, and thereafter to distribute any surplus funds by way of return of capital among the members. If the winding-up is not completed within one year after its commencement a statement as to the proceedings in and position of the winding-up must be filed with the Registrar of Companies [Companies Act, 1985, S. 641]. These statements which are kept at the Companies Registry are open to inspection by any person [Companies Act, 1985, S. 709 and S. 710].

During the course of the winding-up in England certain balances must be paid into the *Companies' Liquidation Account*, and at the conclusion of the winding-up the unclaimed or undistributed funds must be paid into that account; claimants to the undistributed funds should apply to the Department of Trade and Industry for an order for payment.

When a company is registered in Scotland, the undistributed balances at the conclusion of the winding-up are paid into an account, in the name of the Accountant of the Court at any joint stock bank of issue, claimants having to apply to the Accountant; subsequently the funds are transferred to the Queen's and Lord Treasurer's Remembrancer who makes payments on an Order of the Court.

On conclusion of the liquidation in a members' voluntary winding-up an account of the winding-up must be prepared by the liquidator and laid before a general meeting of the company, and a return of that meeting with a copy of the account sent to the Registrar [Companies Act, 1985, S. 585]. In a creditors' voluntary winding-up an account is required to be laid before a general meeting of the company and a meeting of creditors, and a return of the meetings, with a copy of the account, must be sent to the Registrar [Companies Act, 1985, S. 595]. These particulars are kept at the Companies Registry and are open to inspection by any person. Three months after the registration of the return of the final meeting or meetings the company is deemed to be dissolved.

When a resolution to wind-up voluntarily has been passed by a company, the Court on the application of the company or any creditor or contributory, may make an order directing that the winding-up shall continue, but **subject to the supervision of the Court** [Companies Act, 1985, S. 606]. Since the Companies Act, 1900, creditors have had the right to apply to the Court to determine any question arising in a voluntary winding-up, this provision being re-enacted by Section 602 of the Act of 1985; consequently a Supervision Order is not frequently sought. Subject to the directions made by the Supervision Order which in England usually requires a report to be filed with the Court every three months, the procedure, in practice, is similar to the case of a voluntary winding-up, although an order for winding-up subject to Supervision is deemed to be an order for winding-up by the Court, except as provided by Section 610 and the Eighteenth Schedule of the Act of 1985.

The Court has power to order a stay of any mode of winding-up. It is interesting to note that in addition the law provides machinery for applications to the Court for restoration to the Register of a company which has been fully wound-up and dissolved. This important provision enables application to be made for the purpose, for example, of realising a newly discovered asset. There is a time limit within which the application to the Court must be made; in some cases it is two years from the date of dissolution, in others it is twenty years (Companies Act, 1985, S. 651 and S. 653).

REGISTER OF DEFUNCT AND OTHER COMPANIES

REMOVED FROM
THE STOCK EXCHANGE OFFICIAL YEAR-BOOK

The volume referred to is that in which particulars of the undermentioned companies, &c., last appeared in Burdett's Official Intelligence (1882 to 1898), The Stock Exchange Official Intelligence (1899 to 1933), The Stock Exchange Year-Book (1875 to 1933), or The Stock Exchange Official Year-Book (1934 and since), being the different titles under which the publication has appeared.

The term "Regd." is used only in connection with companies formed under the Companies Acts of Great Britain or Northern Ireland.

The expression "Removed from Register", used in the case of certain companies dissolved in or before 1914, relates to removal of the name either as a defunct company or upon dissolution following the filing of the notice of final meeting.

The significance of the "Companies' Liquidation Account" and (in the case of Companies registered in Scotland) "Accountant of the Court" mentioned in many of the entries is explained in the Introductory Notes.

A

A. A. Stuart & Sons (Contractors) Ld. *See* Stuart (A. A.) & Sons (Contractors) Ld.

A. A. Stuart (Carmyle) Ld. *See* Stuart (A. A.) & Sons (Contractors) Ld.

A. A. Stuart & Sons (Glasgow) Ld. *See* Stuart (A. A.) & Sons (Contractors) Ld.

A. A. Syndicate Ld. Regd. 1901. Reconstructed 1904 as Amalgamated Mining and Exploration Co. Ld., in which company shareholders were entitled to 2 shares of 5s. (credited with 3s. 6d. paid) and 3 fully-paid shares of 5s. for each share of £1 held. Removed from Register 1905 .... **1905**

A. & M. Rubber Syndicate Ld. Regd. 1926. Vol. liq. (members') 4 Aug. 1937. Undertaking and assets were acquired by Hevea (Burma) Co. Ld. for 50,000 fully-paid shares of 2s. Final meeting return regd. 18 May 1938 .... **1938**

A. V. Ld. Regd. 1930 as Automatch & Vester Ld.; name changed 12 Sept. 1934. Vol. liq. (creditors') 1 Aug. 1941. No capital returned. Final meeting return regd. 3 Oct. 1941 .... **1943**

A. B. C. Cab Co. Ld. Regd. 1908. Vol. liq. 18 Aug. 1910. Final meeting return regd. 13 Jan. 1915 .... **1911**

A. B. C. Motors (1920) Ld. Regd. 1920. Court Order to wind up 31 July 1923. Struck off Register Apr. 1929 **1930**

ABM Brierley & Sons (1904) Ld. *See* Brierley (ABM) & Sons (Holdings) Ld.

A. C. C. Holdings Ld. Regd. 1910 as Grand Canary, Teneriffe & Atlantic Coaling Co. Ld.; name changed to Atlantic Coaling Co. Ld. 17 Dec. 1912 and as above on 22 Apr. 1938. Vol. liq. (members') 1 July 1938. Certain assets were distributed in specie. Capital returned to contributories—9s. 1·2975d. per share of £1. Final meeting return regd. 28 Aug. 1945 **1938**

A. C. (Acèdés) Cars, Ld. Regd. 1927. Receiver appointed 13 Feb. 1930; ceased to act 13 Oct. 1931. Vol. liq. (creditors') 28 Feb. 1930. Undertaking acquired by company of same name (later A. C. Cars Ld.). Assets realised sufficient to pay debenture holders approximately 9s. in £. Final meeting return regd. 11 Dec. 1931 .... ***1931**

A. C. Cars Ld. Regd. 1911 as Auto-Carriers (1911) Ld.; name changed to Auto-Carriers Ld. in Jan. 1920 and as above in Nov. 1922. Struck off Register Feb. 1931 **1931**

A. D. C. Aircraft Ld. Regd. 1920 as Aircraft Disposal Co. Ld., name changed July 1925. Receiver appointed 4 Mar. 1931 ceased to act 23 Oct. 1933. Struck off Register 17 Dec. 1935 .... **1925**

A. G. E. Electric Motors Ld. *See* Bull Motors Ld.

A. & H. Meltzer (Holdings) Ld. *See* Meltzer (A. & H.) (Holdings) Ld.

A. I. P. Trust Ld. Regd. 1925 as Graphic & Bystander Ld.; name changed 15 Dec. 1926. Vol. liq. 2 Apr. 1927. Final meeting return regd. 30 Dec. 1927 .... ***1928**

(A. I. R.) Aviation Investment & Research Ld. Regd. 1910. Vol. liq. 15 Nov. 1911. Final meeting return regd. 21 Mar. 1916 .... **1912**

A. & J. Main & Co. Ld. *See* Main (A. & J.) & Co. Ld.

A. N. Z. Gr. Hldgs. Ld. Inc. Victoria Apr. 1976. Under scheme of arrangement effective 30 Sept. 1977 shares were cancelled and holders received 1 $A1

share in Australian and New Zealand Banking Gr. Ld. for each $A1 share held. Company dissolved without winding up on 19 Sept. 1977 .... **1978-9**

A1 Biscuit Co. Ld. Regd. 1888. Vol. liq. 1897. Final meeting return regd. 21 Oct. 1899 .... **1898**

A. U. Alcock Electric Light & Motive Power Co. Ld. Undertaking acquired by Melbourne Electric Supply Co. Ld. from 1 Jan. 1899 .... **1937**

A. W. Consolidated Stock Trust Ld. Regd. 1929. 42⅜% of 5% income debenture stock was repaid at par in July 1935 and a final repayment of 74⅞% in Aug. 1938. Struck of Register 26 Sept. 1939 .... **1940**

A.W. Second Stock Trust Ld. Regd. 1929. Vol. liq. (members') 22 Sept. 1938. Capital returned to contributories—£187 1s. per £100 stock held. Final meeting return regd. 1 Aug. 1939 .... **1940**

A. W. (Securities) Ld. Regd. 1936 as Associated Weavers Ld; name changed 1957. All capital owned by Chaltard Ld. Dissolved 29 Dec. 1980............ **1974–5**

Aabada Trust Ld. Regd. 1912. Vol. liq. July 1922. Struck off Register Oct. 1931 .... **1932**

Aabosica Gold Mining Co. Ld. Regd. 1901. Removed from Register 1915 .... **1940**

Aamosen, Ld. Regd. 1912. Vol. liq. (members') 16 Dec. 1946. Capital returned to contrubutories —6s. 3·3d. per preference shares of £1. Final meeting return regd. 12 Dec. 1947 .... **1948**

Aarons Reefs, Ld. Regd. 1890. Vol. liq. 30 May 1893. Undertaking acquired by Victoria & Altamira Ld. Final meeting return regd. 17 June 1897.......... **1894**

Aawin Syndicate Ld. Regd. 1901. Removed from Register 1903.................... **1904**

Aawudwa Mines Syndicate Ld. Regd. 1901. Vol. liq. July 1908. Removed from Register 1909 .... **1909**

Ab-Intra Bootmaking Process Co. Ld. Regd. 1887. Vol. liq. Nov. 1890. Final meeting return regd. 15 Dec. 1892 .... **1891**

Abaco (Selangor) Rubber, Ld. Regd. 1913. Vol. liq. (members') 6 Nov. 1953. Capital returned to contributories—£1 0s. 0·3d. per share of £1. £306 19s. 6d. was paid into Companies' Liquidation Account. Final meeting return regd. 30 Aug. 1956 **1957**

Abang Rubber Co. Ld. Regd. 1927. Vol. liq. (creditors') 7 May 1934. No capital returned to contributories. Final meeting return regd. 4 Aug. 1934 .... **1935**

Abara Syndicate Ld. Regd. 1901. Reconstructed 1904 as Amalgamated Mining and Exploration Co. Ld., in which company shareholders were entitled to 2 shares of 5s. (credited with 3s. 6d. paid) and 3 fully-paid shares of 5s. for each share of £1 held. Removed from Register 1905 .... **1905**

Abaris Mining Corporation Ld. Regd. 1891. Struck off Register 26 Oct. 1900 .... **1901**

Abbassi (Wassau) Gold Mines Ld. Regd. 1901. The properties were abandoned. Struck off Register 18 Feb. 1936 .... **1936**

Abbaye Consolidated Ld. Regd. 1930. Vol. liq. (creditors') 25 Apr. 1933. No capital returned to contributories. Final meeting return regd. 3 Dec. 1936...... **1934**

Abbaye Development Co. Ld. Regd. 1928. Vol. liq. (members') 14 Jan. 1930 for reconstruction under title of Abbaye Consolidated Ld. Shareholders were entitled to receive 1 share of 1s. (credited with 8d.

VOL. FOR

for each preference share and every 8 ordinary shares held. Dissolved under Sect. 208 of Companies Act. 1948 on 31 Jan. 1966 .... **1967**

Aberdeen Jute Co. Ld. Regd. Edinburgh 1873 Vol. liq. (creditors') 17 Oct. 1932. No capital returned to contributories. Final meeting return regd. 11 Jan. 1934 .... **1933**

Aberdeen, Leith and Moray Firth Steam Shipping Co. Ld. Regd. Edinburgh 1881. Vol. liq. June 1914. Final meeting return regd. 6 June 1915 .... **1915**

Aberdeen Music Hall Co. Ld. Regd. Edinburgh 1858. Vol. liq. Mar. 1928. Final meeting return regd. 20 Dec. 1928 .... **1929**

Aberdeen Newspapers Ld. Regd. Edinburgh 1922. Vol. liq. Oct. 1928. Undertaking and assets acquired by Aberdeen Journals Ld. Final meeting return regd. 2 Aug. 1929 .... **1929**

Aberdeen Preserving Co. Ld. Regd. Edinburgh 1907 as Aberdeen Salt Fish Curing (Home and Export) Co. Ld.; name changed June 1908. Vol. liq. July 1920. Final meeting return regd. 5 Nov. 1920 .... **1921**

Aberdeen Preserving Co. Ld. Regd. Edinburgh 1920. Vol. liq. (creditors') 18 Oct. 1933. Assets realised insufficient to pay creditors in full. Final meeting return regd. 10 Oct. 1934 .... **1934**

Aberdeen Salt Fish Curing (Home and Export) Co. Ld. See Aberdeen Preserving Co. Ld.

Aberdeen Steam Trawling and Fishing Co. Ld. Regd. Edinburgh 1899. Vol. liq. (members') 26 Dec. 1942. Capital returned to contributories—20s. per preference share of £1; £5 9s. 5d. per ordinary share of £1; certain assets were distributed in specie. Final meeting return regd. 11 Dec. 1943 .... **1945**

Aberdeen Suburban Tramways Co. Inc. by Provisional Order 1899. Liquidated 1927 .... **1928**

Aberdeen Theatre and Opera House Co. Ld. Regd. Edinburgh 1872. Vol. liq. May 1897. Final meeting return regd. 22 Sept. 1897 .... **1898**

Aberdeen Town & County Banking Co. See Town & County Bank.

Aberdeen Town & County Property Co. Ld. Regd. Edinburgh 1897. Vol. liq. June 1904. Court Order; to continue winding up under supervision Oct. 1904; to dissolve 28 Oct. 1907 .... **1905**

Aberdeen Trust Co. Ld. Regd. Edinburgh 1911. Undertaking acquired on 23 Nov. 1962 by Aberdeen & Canadian Investment Trust Ld. (now Aberdeen Trust Ld.) in which company shareholders were entitled to receive £29 5s. fully paid ordinary capital for every £25 ordinary stock and £9 fully-paid preference capital for every £8 preference stock held plus a cash payment (as compensation for loss of preference voting rights) of 7d. per £1 preference stock held. Liability to holders of deposits of this company was assumed by the amalgamated company. Dissolved under Sec. 208 of Companies Act, 1948 31 Dec. 1962 .... **1964**

Aberfeldy Gas Light Co. Ld. Regd. in Edinburgh 1919. Dissolved 1 May 1949. undertaking being vested in Scottish Area Gas Board under Gas Act 1948. Holders of ordinary shares (of £1) were entitled to receive £2 18s. British Gas 3% guaranteed stock 1990–95 for each share held **1952**

Aberfoyle Slate Quaries Co. Ld. Regd. in Edinburgh 1882. Vol. liq. 25 Aug. 1947; undertaking acquired by Scottish Slate Industries Ld. Share holders were entitled to 15 fully-paid ordinary shares of 10s. for every share (of £10) held and an allotment of fully-paid 5% preference shares of 10s. in new company, estimated at 4 such shares for every share (of £10) held. Final meeting return regd. 28 May 1948 ..... **1949**

Aberlady & Gullane Gas Co. Ld. Regd. in Edinburgh 1911. Dissolved 1 May 1949, undertaking being vested in Scottish Area Gas Board under Gas Act 1948. Holders of shares (of £5) were entitled to receive £10 British Gas 3% guaranteed stock 1990–95 for each share held **1952**

Aberlady, Gullane & North Berwick Railway Co. Inc. by Special Act 1893. North British Railway Co, purchased undertaking 1 Aug. 1900. Holders of the £33,000 ordinary stock and of the £33,000 preference stock received an amount of North British Rly. 3% consolidated lien stock and holders of the £22,000 4% debenture stock an amount of North British Rly. 3% debenture stock 1883 on basis of equal income **1901**

Abernethy Gas Co. Ld. Regd. in Edinburgh 1911. Dissolved 1 May 1949, undertaking being vested in Scottish Area Board under Gas Act 1948. Holders of shares (of £5) were entitled to receive £10 British Gas 3% guaranteed stock 1990–95 for each share held.................. **1952**

VOL. FOR

Aberystwyth & Chiswick Electricity Supply Corporation Ld. See Chiswick Electricity Supply Corporation Ld.

Aberystwyth Gas Co. Inc. by Special Act 1873. Dissolved 1 May 1949, undertaking being vested in Wales Area Gas Board under Gas Act 1948. Holders of securities were entitled to receive British Gas 3% guaranteed stock 1990–95 as follows in respect of each £10 unit, unless otherwise stated, of security held:

	£	s.	d.
Ord shares (10% stand.)	30	0	0
New shares (7% stand.)	22	0	0
5% pref.shares	11	4	0
4% red. deb. stock (per £100)	101	0	0

1952

Abford Estates Ld. Regd. 1927. Vol. liq. (members') 22 May 1933. Undertaking was acquired by Aerated Bread Co. Ld. Capital returned to contributories—£28,008 18s. 1d. Final meeting return regd. 27 Feb. 1936 .... **1934**

Abingdon Cafe Co. Ld. Regd. 1879. Vol. liq. 1890. Final meeting return regd. 25 Sept. 1891 .... **1891**

Abingdon-Ecco Ld. See Abingdon Works Ld. regd. 1906.

Abingdon Electric Supply Co. Ld. Regd. 1912. Vol. liq. (members') 15 Feb. 1938. Capital returned—£5 5s. per preference share of £5; £1 9s. 2½d. per preferred ordinary or ordinary share of £1. Final meeting return regd. 30 June 1938 .... **1939**

Abingdon Gas-Light and Coke Co. Ld. Regd. 1863. By Special Order of 1930 the undertaking was acquired by Oxford & District Gas Co. For every A share of £12 10s. held shareholders were entitled to £15 consolidated stock in acquiring company plus 10s. in cash; for every B share of £12 10s. held shareholders were entitled to £11 5s. consolidated stock in acquiring company plus 10s. in cash. Holders of 5% perpetual debentures were entitled to an equal amount of 5% perpetual debenture stock. Vol. liq. (members') 27 June 1930. £14 11s. 10d. was paid into Companies' Liquidation Account. Final meeting return regd. 29 Aug. 1930 .... **1931**

Abingdon Railway Co. Inc. Special Act 1855. In July 1904 undertaking was transferred to Great Western Railway which took over the mortgage bonds. Shareholders received 5% consolidated preference stock in acquiring company as follows: £100 for each share of £100 held; £8 for each B share of £10 held; £20 for each ordinary share of £10 held **1905**

Abingdon Works Ld. Regd. 1896. Vol. liq. 27 Sept. 1906. Reconstructed as Abingdon-Ecco Ld. (later Abingdon Works Ld.) in which company shareholders were entitled to 1 ordinary share of £1 (credited as fully paid) for every 2 ordinary shares of £1 held or to 1 fully-paid preference share of £1 for each preference share of £1 held. Final meeting return regd. 24 Sept. 1907 .... **1907**

Abingdon Works Ld. Regd. 1906 as Abingdon-Ecco Ld., name changed Dec. 1919. Vol. liq. (members') 3 June 1931. Capital returned—9d. per preference share of £1. £78 9s. 2d. was paid into Companies Liquidation Account for unclaimed dividends. Final meeting return regd. 20 July 1932 .... **1932**

Abinger Investment Trust Ld. Regd. 1946. Vol. liq. (members') 15 Mar. 1957. Final meeting return regd. 11 May 1957 .... **1953**

Abompeh Syndicate Ld. Regd. 1900. Vol. liq. May 1908. Removed from Register 1912 .... **1909**

Abosso Gold Mining Co. Ld. Regd. 1901. Vol. liq. 13 Feb. 1923 for reconstruction as Taquah & Abosso Consolidated Ld., in which company shareholders were entitled to 2 fully-paid shares of 5s. for every share of £1 held. Final meeting return regd. 13 Mar. 1924 .... **1924**

Aboukir Bay Treasure Recovery Co. Ld. Regd. 1889. Court Order to wind up 19 July 1890. Removed from Register 1907 .... **1891**

Aboukir Co. Ld. Regd. 1888 Control was transferred to Egypt 5 Dec. 1945. Under Decree of 1 Mar. 1960, company was authorised to continue its activity as an Egyptian Company under title of Aboukir Land Co. S.A.E. and shareholders were entitled to exchange their shares for shares of that company. Struck off Register 28 Sept. 1962 .... **1960**

Abram Coal Co. Ld. Regd. 1892. Vol. liq. (members') 23 Feb. 1933 for amalgamation with Ackers, Whitley & Co. Ld., in which company shares were received in exchange for shares held. Final meeting return regd. 30 Sept. 1933 .... **1934**

Abrochere Syndicate Ld. Regd. 1901. Removed from Register 29 May 1906 .... ***1904**

Absolute Life Assurance Co. Ld. Regd. 1894. Removed from Register 1912 .... **1903**

See Stock Exchange Year-Book.

Abu Tin Co. Ld. Regd. 1913. Vol. liq. 1 Mar. 1921. Final meeting return regd. 27 Feb. 1923 .... **1922**

Abundancia (Mexico) Mining & Milling Co. Ld. Regd. 1902. Removed from Register 1915 .... **1908**

Abyssinia Corporation Ld. Regd. 1918. Vol. liq. 13 Apr. 1926. Final meeting return regd. 30 Apr. 1927...... **1927**

Abyssinian Exploration (Parent) Co. Ld. Regd. 1901. Court Order to wind up 6 Feb. 1902. Removed from Register 1911 .... **1903**

Abyssinian Gold Jewellery Co. Ld. Regd. 1897. Vol. liq. Sept. 1909. Capital returned to contributories—3s. per preference share of £1; further payments (if any) not known. Removed from Register 1912 .... **1910**

Acadia Pulp & Paper Mill Co. Ltd. Inc. Nova Scotia 1897. Receiver and Manager appointed Aug. 1903 **1906**

Acadia Sugar Refining Co. Ld. Regd. Edinburgh 1893. Vol. liq. May 1926. Undertaking and assets transferred to a Canadian company of same name, preference shareholders were entitled to 75 preference shares of $5 or £1 in new company for every 100 shares of £1 held and ordinary shareholders to 25 ordinary shares of $5 or £1 for every 100 shares of £1 held. Final meeting return regd. 28 Dec. 1928 ...... **1927**

Acadia Sugar Refining Co. Ld. Inc. Nova Scotia 1926. Assets sold 31 Oct. 1939 to company of same name (inc. Ontario). Shareholders on Glasgow register received 21s. 8·97d. per preference and 20s. 7·92d. per ordinary share; further payments (if any) not known **1940**

Acaténe Cycle Co. Ld. Regd. 1896. Removed from Register 1902 .... **1903**

Accident Death Insurance Co. See Accident Insurance Co. Ld.

Accident Insurance Co. Ld. Established as Accident Death Insurance Co. Regd. as City Accident Insurance Co. Ld. 1870; name changed Mar. 1870. Vol. liq. 14 Jan. 1907. Business was acquired by Commercial Union Assurance Co. Ld. Final meeting return regd. 9 Dec. 1907 .... **1907**

Accles Ld. Regd. 1896. Removed from Register 1904 **1900**

Accra Consolidated Corporation Ld. Regd. 1901. Vol. liq. 26 Oct. 1906. Final meeting return regd. 26 Apr. 1917 .... **1907**

Accrington Corporation Steam Tramways Co. Regd. 1885. Inc. by Special Act 1887. Vol. liq. 30 June 1908. Lines taken over by local authorities **1909**

Accrington District Gas & Water Board. See below.

Accrington District Water Board. Inc. by Special Act 1894 as Accrington District Gas & Water Board; name changed 10 Apr. 1951. Undertaking vested in Calder Water Board and this Board dissolved on 1 Apr. 1963 .... **1964**

Accumulator Industries Ld. Regd. 1900. Vol. liq. 22 July 1914. Final meeting return regd. 25 July 1924 ..... **1915**

Acetate & Acetate Products (Foreign Rights) Ld. Regd. 1928. Vol. liq. (creditors') 8 Dec. 1932. No capital returned to contributories. Final meeting return regd. 27 Nov. 1933 .... **1933**

Acetate Products Corporation Ld. Regd. 1928. Vol. liq. (members') 20 July 1931. Capital returned to contributories—11½d. per ordinary share of £1. Final meeting return regd. 11 Aug. 1934 .... **1932**

Acetex Safety Glass Ld. Regd. 1928. Vol. liq. (members') 26 Sept. 1934. Capital returned to preferred shareholders—8d. per share of 5s. Final meeting return regd. 14 May 1937 .... **1935**

Acetylene Beacon Light Co. Ld. Regd. 1898. Removed from Register 1901 .... **1902**

Acetylene Equipment Co. Ld. Regd. 1895 as Acetylene Illuminating Co. Ld.; name changed Jan. 1918. Vol. liq. 16 Aug. 1919. Business sold to Dissolved Acetylene Co. Ld. Final meeting return regd. 2 Dec. 1920 .... ***1920**

Acetylene Illuminating Co. Ld. See above.

Achilles Gold Mines Ld. Regd. 1898. Reconstructed 1899 as company of same name. Shareholders were entitled to 1 share 2s. 6d. (credited with 2s. paid) in new company for each share of 2s. 6d. held. Removed from Register 1901 .... **1902**

Achilles Gold Mines Ld. Regd. 1899. Removed from Register 1904 .... **1903**

Achilles Goldfields Ld. Regd. 1893. Vol. liq. 1898. Reconstructed as Achilles Gold Mines Ld., in which company shareholders were entitled to 1 share of 2s. 6d. (credited with 1s. 6d. paid) for each share of 2s. 6d. held. Final meeting return regd. 1 June 1900 **1899**

Acklington Coal Co. Ld. Regd. 1899. Vol. liq. 13 July 1910. Final meeting return regd. 7 Oct. 1910 ...... ***1911**

Ackroyd (William) & Brothers Ld. Regd. 1893. Removed from Register 1906 .... **1903**

Ackworth Coal Syndicate Ld. Regd. 1906. Removed from Register 1914 .... **1911**

Ackworth, Featherstone, Purston & Sharlston Gas Co. Inc. by Special Act 1880. Dissolved 1 May 1949,

undertaking being vested in North Eastern Area Gas Board under Gas Act 1948. Holders of securities were entitled to receive British Gas 3% guaranteed stock 1990–95 as follows in respect of each £10 unit, unless otherwise stated, of security held:

	£	s.	d.	
Orig. A shares (10% stand.)	24	10	0	
Addit. B shares (7% stand.)	18	10	0	
6% red. pref. stock (per £100)......	110	0	0	
4% deb. stock (tax-free) (per £100)	140	0	0	**1952**

Ackworth Light Railway Co. Inc. (under Light Railways Act 1896) by order of Light Railway Commissioners confirmed by Board of Trade 1907. At 4 Nov. 1909 no capital had been issued **1910**

Acme Insurance Co. Ld. Regd. 1896. Vol. liq. 10 May 1901. Certain insurance business was acquired by Law Accident Insurance Society Ld. Removed from Register 1903 .... **1902**

Acme Pullman Services Ld. See London General Omnibus Co. Ld.

Acme Wood Flooring Co. Ld. Regd. 1889. Removed from Register 1905 .... **1905**

Acol Collieries (Natal) Ld. Regd. 1897. Removed from Register 1910 .... **1905**

Acorn Gold Mines Ld. Regd. 1911. Struck off Register 3 June 1921 .... ***1916**

Acorn Securities Company Ld. Regd. as private company 26 Aug. 1959; converted to public company 10 Jan. 1963. Vol. liq. (members') 14 Jan. 1981. Holders of capital shares received, as first liquidation payment, either 133p cash per share or 2·1018 units of Britannia Shield Trust per share, and as second and final payment either 6·92338p cash per share or 0·12657 units. Alternatively they received as first and final payment 5·05 ordinary shares of 10p of London and Liverpool Trust Ld. per share. Holders of income shares received either 50p cash per share or 1·8 ordinary shares of 10p of London and Liverpool Trust Ld. per share. Final meeting held 15 Sept. 1982. Amounts paid into Companies' Liquidation Account—£1,264 in respect of unclaimed dividends and £2,798 in respect of unclaimed distributions. **1984–5**

Acorn Trust Ld. Regd. 1903. Vol. liq. 28 June 1928. Final meeting return regd. 2 Nov. 1928 .... ***1929**

Acquisition & Development Co. Ld. Regd. 1895. Removed from Register 1908 .... **1900**

Acton's Swaziland Concession Ld. Regd. 1889. Vol. liq. Dec. 1909. Struck off Register June 1932 .... **1933**

Adam Steamship Co. Ld. Regd. Edinburgh 1883. Vol. liq. Mar. 1920. Capital returned to contributories— £2 per share of £2 10s. in Mar. 1920; further payments (if any) not known. Final meeting return regd. 24 Nov. 1925 .... **1921**

Adamansu Syndicate Ld. Regd. 1901. Removed from Register 1911 .... **1910**

Adamant & Asphalte Ld. Regd. 1888 as Adamant Cement Co. Ld.; name changed to Adamant Co. Ld. in Sept. 1888 and as above in Jan. 1907. Vol. liq. Dec. 1911. Final meeting return regd. 11 Mar. 1915 **1912**

Adamant Cement Co. Ld. See Adamant & Asphalte Ld.

Adamant Co. Ld. See Adamant & Asphalte Ld.

Adams British Columbia Co. Ld. Regd. 1897. Undertaking acquired by Adams Investment Syndicate Ld., in which company shareholders were entitled to 1 ordinary share of 2s. for each share of £1 held. Removed from Register 1902 .... **1903**

Adams Investment Syndicate Ld. Regd. 1900. Removed from Register 1906 .... **1904**

Adams Patent Suspension Co. Ld. Regd. 1926. Vol. liq. (members') 16 Apr. 1934. Direct controlling interest held by Rubber Roadways Ld. Final meeting return regd. 2 Apr. 1935 .... **1935**

Adams Randall Telephone Patents Co. Ld. Regd. 1899. Removed from Register 1910 .... **1910**

Adams (Thomas) & Co. Ld. Regd. 1865. Reconstructed 1904 as Thomas Adams Ld. in which company shareholders were entitled to 1 ordinary share of £5 for each ordinary share of £20 (£2 10s. paid) or 1 preference share of £20 for each preference share of £20 held. Removed from Register 1912 .... **1904**

Adams (Thomas) & Sons Ld. Regd. 1889. Removed from Register 1911 .... **1911**

Adansi Consolidated Mines Ld. Regd. 1902. Vol. liq. June 1907. Removed from Register 1908 .... **1908**

Adansi Goldfields Ld. Regd. 1899. Undertaking acquired by New Adansi Goldfields Ld. for £100,000 in cash. Removed from Register 1903 .... **1903**

Addie (Robert) & Sons' Collieries, Ld. Regd. 1893. Vol. liq. (members') 8 Jan. 1952. Final meeting return regd. 21 Mar. 1961 .... **1925**

VOL. FOR

Addlestone Linoleum Co. Ld. Regd. 1877. Dissolved by Order of Court 27 June 1891 .... ***1882**

Addressograph Ld. Regd. 1901. Vol. liq. 15 Oct. 1909. Final meeting return regd. 12 Jan. 1912 .... **1938**

Adelaide Electric Supply Co. Ld. Regd. 10 Apr. 1905. As from 1 Mar. 1921 the control and management were transferred from London to Adelaide. Under Electricity Trust of South Australia Act 1946 undertaking of company, except assets situated outside South Australia, was vested in Electricity Trust of South Australia on 1 Sept 1946. On "settlement day" (1 June 1947) each capital stockholder of company was entitled to be satisfied in cash at market value (in Australian currency) of holder's capital as at 1 Aug. 1945 *plus* (*a*) in respect of ordinary capital interest at 4% p.a. on amount of that market value for period commencing 1 Mar. 1946 and ending on "settlement day" and additional payment of 1*s*. 6*d*. per £1 nominal capital to be deemed, for purposes of Act, part of market value of capital and (*b*) in respect of all classes of preference capital interest at 4% p.a. on amount of that market value commencing 1 Sept. 1946 and ending on "settlement day". Any capital stockholder could accept 4% debentures issued by the trust at par in satisfaction of all or part (in multiples of £10) of market value. The market value (in Australian currency) of each £1 of stock as at 1 Aug. 1945 was as follows:

	Adelaide Register			London Register		
8% B pref.stock	1	19	0	1	19	0
6¼% C pref. stock	1	12	6	1	5	6
6% pref. stock	1	10	0	1	5	0
5% A pref.stock...............	—			1	8	0
5% D pref.stock...............	1	6	2	1	6	2
Ordinary stock.................	1	16	6	1	16	6

The liability in respect of debenture stocks of company was assumed by the trust **1948**

Adelaide Star Mines Ld. Regd. Edinburgh 1897. Vol. liq. Dec. 1914. Final meeting return regd. 28 Dec. 1916 .... **1915**

Adelaide Steamship Co. Ld. *See* Eryldon Steamship Co. Ld.

Adeline Mines Ld. Regd. 1902. Removed from Register 1911 .... **1910**

Adeline Syndicate Ld. Regd. 1897. Undertaking acquired in 1902 by Adeline Mines Ld. for £3,000 in cash and £20,000 fully-paid shares of £1. Removed from Register 1905 .... **1908**

Adelphi Bank Ld. Regd. 1862. Vol. liq. 13 Feb. 1899. Undertaking transferred to Lancashire & Yorkshire Bank Ld., in which company shareholders were entitled to 1 share of £20 (credited with £10 paid) *plus* £3 in cash for every 2 shares of £20 (£10 paid) held. Final meeting return regd. 6 May 1901 ...... **1900**

Adelphi Theatre Ld. Regd. 1901 as Adelphi Theatre Co. Ld.; name changed Sept. 1901 to Century Theatre Ld. and as above in Mar. 1902. Vol. liq. May 1908. Removed from Register 1911 .... **1909**

Adepton Ld. *See* Williams Hudson Group Ld.

Adie & Lovekin Ld. Regd. 1889. Vol. liq. 24 Mar. 1925. Assets employed in silversmith business carried on by the company were sold to Adie and Lovekin (1925) Ld., the remaining assets being realised. Final meeting return regd. 16 Mar. 1926 .... **1926**

Adisham Colliery Ld. Regd. 1913. Vol. liq. 27 May 1924. Final meeting return regd. 25 June 1925 .... ***1925**

Adjah Bippo Deep Ld. Regd. 1902. Vol. liq. 19 Feb. 1906. Assets acquired by Wassau (Gold Coast) Mining Co Ld. Removed from Register 1907 ...... **1906**

Adler's Consolidated Mining & Land Corporation Ld. Regd. 1895. Majority of assets were acquired in 1904 by Consolidated Mining and Investment Corporation Ld for £75.000 in shares of 10*s*. Removed from Register 1908 .... **1908**

Adrar Syndicate Ld. Regd. 1902. Struck off Register May 1929.. **1930**

Adrar Trading Corporation Ld. Regd. 1902. Struck off Register May 1929.. **1930**

Adulessa Syndicate Ld. Regd. 1901. Vol. liq. June 1908. Removed from Register 1910 .... **1909**

Advance Australia Prospectors Ld. Regd. 1896. Removed from Register 1908 .... **1900**

Advance Australia Prospectors Ld. Regd. 1899. Removed from Register 1911 .... **1904**

Advance Corporation Ld. Regd. 1888. Vol. liq. Aug. 1925. Final meeting return regd. 1 Dec. 1927 .... **1926**

Adventurers (Ashanti & Wassan) Ld. Regd. 1901. Removed from Register 1911 .... **1908**

Adventurers of British Columbia Ld. Regd. 1897. Vol. liq. 26 Mar. 1908. Final meeting return regd. 4 May 1908 .... ***1909**

VOL. FOR

Advertising Match & Spill Works Ld. Regd. 1886. Removed from Register 1906 .... **1888**

Ægean Trust Ld. Regd. 1927. Vol. liq. (creditors') 8 July 1932. No capital returned to contributories. Final meeting return regd. 5 June 1936 .... **1933**

Ægis Investment Co. Ld. Regd. 1894. Vol. liq. 10 June 1898. Final meeting return regd. 8 Feb. 1899 ...... **1899**

Aeolian Co. Ld. Regd. 1912 as Orchestrelle Co. Ld.; name changed July 1921. Vol. liq. (creditors') 16 May 1939. No capital returned to contributories. Final meeting return regd. 3 Nov. 1955 .... **1956**

Aeonic Radio Ld. Regd. 1928. Vol. liq. (creditors') 16 June 1930. Shareholders were entitled to 3 shares of 2*s*. 6*d*. (credited with 2*s*. per share paid) in Electrical & Radio Products Ld for every 5 shares held. Final meeting return regd. 8 Nov. 1937 .... **1931**

Aeonic Wireless Co. Ld. Business acquired in 1928 by Aeonic Radio Ld. **1929**

Aerated Beverage & Buffet Co. Ld. Regd. 1889. Vol. liq. 5 Jan. 1891. Reconstructed as company of same name. Shareholders were entitled to 2 ordinary shares of £1 (credited with 15*s*. paid) in new company for each ordinary share of £1 10*s*. held or 1 preference share of £1 10*s*. (credited as fully paid) for each preference share of £1 10*s*. held. Final meeting return regd. 30 Apr. 1897 .... **1899**

Aerated Beverage & Buffet Co. Ld. Regd. 1891. Reconstructed 1895 as New Aerated Beverage and Buffet Co. Ld. Shareholders were offered shares in new company. Removed from Register 1904 .... **1899**

Aerated Cream & Dairy Co. Ld. Regd. 1903. Court Order to wind up 1905. Removed from Register 1910 .... **1906**

Aerators Ld. Regd. 1896. Reconstructed 1900 as company of same name. Preference shareholders were entitled to 3 shares of 10*s*. (credited with 6*s*. paid) for every 2 preferenee shares of £1 held; ordinary shareholders were entitled to subscribe for shares not taken by preference shareholders. Holders of debentures were entitled to an equal amount of debentures in new company. Struck off Register 8 Apr. 1938 .... **1939**

Aerators, Ld. Regd. 1900. Vol. liq. 1 Sept. 1919. Undertaking and assets were acquired by Sparklets Ld. in which company shareholders were entitled to receive 1 1/16 fully-paid share for each preferred ordinary or 8 ordinary shares held. Struck off Register 4 May 1948. .... **1949**

Aero-Glydas Ld. Regd. 1923. Struck off Register 1927 ***1925**

Aeronautical Corporation of Great Britain Ld. Regd. 1936. Vol. liq. (creditors') 5 Nov. 1937. No capital returned to contributories. Final meeting return regd. 1 Mar. 1941 .... **1938**

Afex Corporation Ld. Inc. in Zimbabwe 28 June 1924 as Rhodesian Mining Corporation Ld.; name changed 29 Dec. 1924 to Rhodesian Corporation Ld. and to present title 6 Feb. 1981. Vol. liq. (members') 16 Sept. 1982 under S.223 Co's Act (Ch 190) of Zimbabwe—holders received 1 share of $US1·50 of Afex Corporation SA for each 16⅔p share **1984–5**

Affiliated Oilfields Ld. Inc. in Canada 1928. The Charter was surrendered and the company dissolved as from 24 April 1953 .... **1954**

Affoh Gold Mining Syndicate Ld. Regd. 1910. Vol. liq. 12 Dec. 1924. Final meeting return regd. 21 Oct. 1925 .... **1925**

Afortunada Copper Mines Ld. *See* Rio Rimal Copper Co. Ld.

Afric Corporation Ld. Regd. 1920. Vol. liq. (members') 21 Dec. 1933. Final meeting return regd. 4 May 1934 **1934**

Afric Gold Corporation Ld. Regd. 1934. Vol. liq. (members') 10 Sept. 1936. Undertaking and assets were acquired by West African Mines & Estates Ld. Shareholders were entitled for each share of £1 held, to 4 fully-paid shares of 2*s*. 6*d*. in West African Mines & Estates Ld., 2 fully-paid shares and 2 shares of 5*s*. (credited with 2*s*. 6*d*. paid) in Bramansu Gold Corporation Ld. Final meeting return regd. 5 Mar. 1937 .... **1937**

Africa Trust Consolidated & General Exploration Co. Ld. Regd. 1898. Vol. liq. 3 Feb. 1905. Reconstructed as Africa Trust Ld., in which company shareholders were entitled to 1 share of £1 (credited with 12*s*. 6*d*. paid) for each share of £1 held. Removed from Register 1910. .... **1950**

Africa Trust Ld. Regd. 1895. Vol. liq. 28 Apr. 1898. Business and properties were transferred to Africa Trust Consolidated & General Exploration Co. Ld., in which company shareholders were entitled to 82 shares of £1 (credited as fully paid) for every 100 fully-paid shares of £1 held or 41 fully-paid shares of £1 for every 100 shares of £1 (10*s*. paid) held. Removed from Register 1909 .... **1899**

VOL. FOR

Africa Trust Ld. Regd. 1905. Vol. liq. Dec. 1908. Removed from Register 1910 .... **1909**

African Adventurers Ld. Regd. 1919. Struck off Register July 1931 .... **1932**

African Alluvial Gold Mines Ld. Regd. 1895. Vol. liq. 19 Apr. 1898. Final meeting return regd. 20 July 1899 **1899**

African & Australian Co. Ld. Regd. 1902. Struck off Register 9 Dec. 1930 .... **1931**

African & Australian Goldfields Syndicate Ld. Regd. 1895. Struck off Register 23 July 1901 .... **1902**

African & Colonial Co. Ld. Regd. 1896. Removed from Register 1913 .... **1914**

African & European Agency Ld. Properties were acquired in 1901 by New Buffels Land and Mining Co. Ld. (later Transvaal Proprietary Ld.) for £206,500 .... **1904**

African & General Exploration Co. Ld. Regd. 1903. Removed from Register 1911 .... **1908**

African & General Exploring Co. Ld. Regd. 1889. Removed from Register 23 July 1901 .... ***1896**

African & United Colonies Supply & Cold Storage Ld. Regd. 1902. Vol. liq. 28 July 1905. The 6% 1st mortgage debenture stock was repaid at 112½%. Shareholders were entitled to 45,000 fully-paid ordinary shares of £1 in McArthur Atkins & Co. Ld. (35,000 to preference shareholders and 10,000 to ordinary shareholders). Removed from Register 1906 .... **1906**

African Asbestos Trust Ld. Inc. Union of South Africa 1928. Vol. liq. July 1933 .... **1934**

African Banking Corporation Ld. Regd. 1890. Vol. liq. Nov. 1920. Undertaking and assets were acquired by Standard Bank of South Africa Ld. (later Standard Bank Ld.) In which company shareholders were entitled to 2 shares of £20 (credited with £5 paid) *plus* £1 0s. 3d. cash for every 3 shares of £10 (£5 paid) held **1921**

African British Columbia Corporation Ld. Regd. 1897. Vol. liq. 15 Feb. 1909. Final meeting return regd. 7 Dec. 1918 .... ***1910**

African City Properties Trust Ld. Regd. 1889. Vol. liq. 11 May 1894. Reconstructed as company of same name. Shareholders were entitled to 3 fully-paid shares of £1 for every 4 ordinary shares of £1 (15s. paid) held or 1 fully-paid share of £1 for each fully-paid ordinary share of £1 held or 50 fully-paid shares of £1 for each founders' share of £1 held. Final meeting return regd. 26 Oct. 1896 .... **1898**

African City Properties Trust Ld. Regd. 1894. Vol. liq. (members') 22 May 1953. Final meeting return regd. 8 Mar. 1955 .... **1956**

African Claim & Land Co. Ld. Inc. Transvaal 1902. London office was closed in 1907 and later information was unobtainable **1907**

African Coal & Exploration Co. Ld. Regd. 1894. Assets and liabilities acquired in 1907 by African Freehold Coal Lands Ld., in which company shareholders were offered shares of 5s. (credited with 4s. 6d. paid). Removed from Register 1910 .... **1908**

African Concessions Syndicate Ld. Regd. 1895. Vol. liq. 25 May 1909. Final meeting return regd. 14 July 1914 .... ***1910**

African Concessions Syndicate (1920) Ld. Regd. 1920. Vol. liq. 29 Dec. 1949. All capital owned by Victoria Falls & Transvaal Power Co. Ld. Final meeting return regd. 19 Apr. 1951 .... **1952**

African Concessions Trust Ld. Regd. 1889. Removed from Register 1894 .... ***1892**

African Consolidated Investment Co. Ld. Regd. 1899. Vol. liq. 3 July 1905. Removed from Register 1913 **1906**

African Consolidated Land & Trading Co. Ld. Regd. 1894. Assets and liabilities acquired in 1907 by African Freehold Coal Lands Ld. in which company shareholders were offered shares of 5s. (credited with 4s. 6s. paid). Removed from Register 1910 .. **1908**

African Contracts Corporation Ld. Regd. 1895. Removed from Register 28 July 1899 .... ***1898**

African Diamond Farms Ld. Regd. 1903. Struck off Register 13 Oct. 1908 .... **1909**

African Estate Co. Ld. Inc. South Africa Republic 1895. Undertaking and assets were acquired by Estate, Finance and Mines Corporation Ld., in which company shareholders were entitled to 1 new share for each share held **1908**

African Estates & Mining Co. Ld. Regd. 1897 as South African Estates and Mining Co. Ld.; names changed Aug. 1898. Vol. liq. 28 Aug. 1908 for reconstruction as Mining and General Investment Ld., in which company shareholders were entitled to 1 fully-paid share of 1s. for each share of 10s. held. Final meeting return regd. 10 May 1911 .... **1909**

African Exchequer Gold Mining & Prospecting Co. Ld. Regd. 1888. Vol. liq. 30 May 1890. Capital returned to contributories—10s. per share of £1 in June 1890;

VOL. FOR

further payments (if any) not known. Final meeting return regd. 26 June 1891 .... **1891**

African Exploration & Investment Co. Ld. Regd. 1889. Vol. liq. 22 Feb. 1894. Capital returned to contributories—3s. 2d. per fully-paid share of £1; further payments (if any) not known. Final meeting return regd. 13 May 1898 .... **1896**

African Farms Ld. Regd. 1902. Removed from Register 1914 .... **1907**

African Farms Ld. Inc. Transvaal 1902. Vol. liq. Dec. 1919. Amalgamated with South African Townships Mining and Finance Corporation Ld. which company acquired undertaking and assets for 319,831 shares of £1 .... **1920**

African Freehold Coal Lands Ld. Regd. 1907. Vol. liq. 20 Nov. 1917. Undertaking and assets transferred to Vaalbank (Transvaal) Colliery Ld., in which company shareholders were entitled to 1 ordinary, preference or priority share of 5s. (credited with 1s. paid) for every ordinary, preference or priority share of 5s. respectively held; debenture holders were entitled to an equal amount of similar debentures in the purchasing company. Final meeting return regd. 13 July 1923 .... **1918**

African General Syndicate Ld. Regd. 1901. Struck off Register 8 Aug. 1905 .... **1906**

African Gold Coast Ld. Regd. 1901. Reconstructed 1902 as Gold Coast United Ld. Removed from Register 1904 .... **1903**

African Gold Coast Syndicate Ld. Regd. 1882. Struck off Register 20 Mar. 1906 .... **1907**

Afrcan Gold Concessions & Development Co. Ld. Regd. 1894. Vol. liq. 30 Dec. 1896. Final meeting return regd. 4 May 1900 .... **1897**

African Gold Dredging & Mining Concessions Ld. Regd. 1902. Vol. liq. Nov. 1909. Undertaking was acquired by Ancobra Exploration and Dredging Co. Ld., in which company shareholders were entitled to 1 fully-paid share of 2s. for each fully-paid share of £1 held. Removed from Register 1910 .... **1910**

African Gold Properties Ld. Regd. 1895. Vol. liq. 20 Jan. 1898. Removed from Register 1903 .... **1898**

Alrican Gold Recovery Co. Ld. Regd. 1891. Vol. liq. 28 Dec. 1910 for reconstruction under same name. Shareholders were entitled to 1 share of 10s. (credited with 7s. 6d. paid) in new company for each share of £1 held. Final meeting return regd. 17 Feb. 1930 .... **1911**

African Gold Recovery Co. Ld. Regd. 1911. Vol. liq. 9 July 1915. Final meeting return regd. 15 Feb. 1930 **1916**

African Gold Share Investment Co. Ld. Regd. 1889. Vol. liq. 14 Sept. 1892. Certain assets were acquired by Consolidated Gold Fields of South Africa Ld. (later Consolidated Goldfields Ld.) for 63,500 fully-paid shares of £1 and an option (since expired) over further shares at par. Final meeting return regd. 12 Feb. 1894 .... **1892**

African Indent Merchants Ld. Regd. 1902. Vol. liq. 31 May 1922. Final meeting return regd. 13 Dec. 1924 **1923**

African India-Rubber, Mahogany & Development Co. Ld. Regd. 1897. Struck off Register 26 Oct. 1900 **1901**

African International Corporation Ld. Regd. 1918 as Liberian International Corporation Ld.; name changed Aug. 1922. Struck off Register 1927 .... **1924**

African International Flotilla & Transport Co. Ld. Regd. 1892. Vol. liq. May 1906. Undertaking and assets were acquired by Oceana Consolidated Co. Ld. Removed from Register 1907 .... **1907**

African Investment Corporation Ld. Regd. 1887. Vol. liq. 19 Apr. 1895. Capital returned to conributorles—£11 19s. 7d. per share with £7 10s. paid; further payments (if any) not known. Removed from Register 1906 .... **1896**

African Joint Stock Co. Ld. Regd. 1896. Vol. liq. 30 July 1902. Final meeting return regd. 3 Feb. 1933 .... **1903**

African Metals Co. Ld. Regd. 1895. Vol. liq. 25 June 1897. Reconstructed as Consolidated Mines Selection Co. Ld. Final meeting return regd. 2 May 1898 **1897**

African Mineral Estates Ld. Inc. Transvaal 1895. Secretary stated (10 Dec. 1907) "the company is practically defunct" **1908**

African Mines Ld. Regd. 1905. Vol. liq. Dec. 1908 for reconstruction under the same name. Shareholders were entitled to 2 shares of 5s. (credited with 4s. 4d. paid) in new company for each share of 10s. held. Removed from Register 1909 .... **1909**

African Mines Ld. Regd. 1909. Vol. liq. 2 Oct. 1913 for reconstruction as African Mines (1913) Ld., in which company shareholders were entitled to 1 share of 5s. (credited with 4s. paid) for each fully-paid share of 5s. held. Final meeting return regd. 19 Dec. 1914 .... **1914**

African Mines (1913) Ld. Regd. 1913. Struck off Register 7 Dec. 1937 .... **1938**

See Stock Exchange Year-Book.

VOL. FOR

African Mining Trust Ld. Regd. 1901. Removed from Register 1909 .... **1903**

African Ore Concentration Syndicate Ld. Regd. 1905. Vol. liq. 2 Jan. 1920. Final meeting return regd. 20 May 1921 .... **1920**

African Pioneers Co. Ld. Regd. 1894. Removed from Register 27 Oct. 1905 .... ***1899**

African Plantations Ld. Regd. 1906. Vol. liq. 5 Oct. 1914. Final meeting return regd. 12 Jan. 1921 .... **1915**

African Produce Co. Ld. Regd. 1909. Vol. liq. (creditors') 3 Nov. 1931. No capital returned to contributories. Final meeting return regd. 31 July 1936 .... **1932**

African Railway Finance Co. Ld. Regd. 1926. Vol. liq. 27 May 1949. All shares were owned by Tanganyika Concessions Ld. Final meeting return regd. 20 Nov. 1948 .... **1949**

African Rubber Co. Ld. Regd. 1905. Receiver appointed Oct. 1912; property since sold. Struck off Register 1922 .... **1914**

African (Sefwi) Gold Mining Co. Ld. Regd. 1893. Removed from Register 1908 .... **1898**

African Selection Trust Ld. Regd. 1922. Vol. liq. (members') 31 Mar. 1931. Undertaking was acquired by Consolidated African Selection Trust Ld. Capital returned to contributories—£23,049 7s. 1d. Final meeting return regd. 30 Mar. 1935 .... ***1932**

African Steam Ship Co. Inc. by Royal Charter 1852. Court Order to wind up 13 July 1936. Undertaking was acquired by Elder Dempster Lines Holdings Ld. (later Liner Holdings Ld.). Holders of 6% debenture stock were entitled to an equal amount of 3% convertible non-cumulative income debenture stock of acquiring company **1937**

African Timber & Trading Co. Ld. *See* Lingham Timber & Trading Co. Ld.—regd. 1905 .... **1905**

African Tin Ld. Regd. 1911. Vol. liq. 11 Nov 1920. Final meeting return regd. 25 May 1921 .... ***1921**

African Transcontinental Telegraph Co. Ld. Regd. 1892. Vol. liq. 20 Dec. 1911. Final meeting return regd. 28 Jan. 1928 .... **1912**

African Ventures Syndicate Ld. Regd 1903. In May 1905 undertaking was acquired by Central Mining and Investment Corporation Ld., in which company shareholders were entitled to shares equal to nominal amount of holdings. Removed from Register 1905 .... **1905**

Africana Ld. Regd. 1895. Vol. liq. 8 Sept. 1896. Reconstructed as Oceana Consolidated Co. Ld., in which company shareholders were entitled to 1 fully-paid share of £1 for every 2 shares of £1 held. Final meeting return regd. 28 Nov. 1896 .... **1896**

Africander Alliance & General Syndicate Ld. Regd. 1900. Removed from Register 1908 .... **1925**

Africander Deep Levels Ld. Regd. 1895. Removed from Register 1902 .... **1903**

Afrikander Gold Mining Co. Ld. Regd. 1892. Reconstructed 1897 as company of same name. Shareholders were entitled to 1 share of £1 (credited with 14s. paid) in new company for each share of £1 held. Removed from Register 1901 .... **1898**

Afrikander Gold Mining Co. Ld. Regd. 1897. Reconstructed 1898 as New Afrikander Gold Mining Co. Ld., in which company shareholders were entitled to 1 share of £1 (credited with 15s. paid) for each share of £1 held. Removed from Register 1901 .... **1902**

Afrikander Gold Mining Co. (1902) Ld. Regd. 1902 Removed from Register 1910 .... **1909**

Agamemnon Ld. Regd. 1897. Removed from Register 1901 .... **1900**

Agency & Exploration Co. of Australasia Ld. Regd. 1889. Vol. liq. 24 Aug. 1893. Final meeting return regd. 21 July 1894 .... **1894**

Agency, Land & Finance Co. of Australia Ld. Regd. 1889. Vol. liq. 9 July 1902. Proceedings stayed Dec. 1902. Vol. liq. 3 Nov. 1910. Final meeting return regd. 18 Feb. 1915 .... **1911**

Agger Consolidated Mines Ld. Regd. 1906. Dissolved before 1949 .... **1909**

Agilete Lagos Rubber Estates Ld. Regd. 1910. Vol. liq. 23 July 1915. Final meeting return regd. 30 Sept. 1918 .... **1916**

Agnes Block Ld. Regd. 1892. Removed from Register 1907 .... **1897**

Agra Bank Ld. Inc. 1833. Regd. 1866. Vol. liq. 30 Apr. 1900. Capital returned to contributories—£5 per share of £6 at Oct. 1900; further payments (if any) not known. Removed from Register 1902 .... **1901**

Agrarna i Komercijalna Banka (of Sarajevo). In July 1928 the bank was absorbed by Jugoslavenska Idruzena Banka D.D. **1929**

Agricultural & General Engineers Ld. Regd. 1919. Court Order to wind up Apr. 1932. Struck off Register 1 Sept. 1936 .... **1937**

VOL. FOR

Agricultural Bank of Cyprus Ld. Inc. Cyprus 1925. The outstanding 5% sterling bonds were redeemed at par on 2 Jan. 1939 .... **1939**

Agricultural Bank of Egypt (Société Anonyme)—1937 Inc. by Khedival Decree 1902. Vol. liq. 20 June 1936. Capital returned to contributories—£8 13s. · 1½d. per ordinary share of £5; £873 per deferred share of £5 ....

Agricultural Co. of Mauritius Ld. Regd. 1874. Vol. liq. 2 Apr. 1906. Final meeting return regd 27 June 1921 **1919**

Agricultural Hotel Co. Ld. Regd. 1863. Struck off Register 1916 .... **1910**

Agricultural Industries Ld. Regd. 1919. Winding-up order 6 Nov. 1950. Returns to contributories—4s. 7·547298d. per preference share (of £1) and 1·7617206d. per ordinary share (of 2s). Liquidator released 3 May 1961. Struck off register 29 Oct. 1963 **1962**

Agricultural Savings & Loan Co. (of London, Ontario). Est. Canada 1872 as Agricultural Investment Society & Savings Bank; name changed 1877. Amalgamated with Ontario Loan and Debenture Co. in which company shareholders were entitled to 9 fully-paid shares of $50 for every 10 fully-paid shares of $50 held **1913**

Agricultural Tractors (United Kingdom) Ld. Regd. 1919. Vol. liq. 9 June 1920. Final meeting return regd. 14 Dec. 1922 .... **1921**

Agua Santa Coffee Co. Ld. Regd. 1913. Vol. liq. (creditors') 8 Dec. 1938. No capital returned to contributors. Final meeting return regd. 12 July 1945 .... **1946**

Agua Santa Nitrate & Railway Co. Inc. Chile 1890. The outstanding 5% Mortgage Debentures (Bearer) were redeemed 1 July 1919 .... **1918**

Agua Suja Mining Co. Ld. Regd. 1903. Vol. liq. Feb. 1911 for reconstruction as Agua Suja Mining Co. (1910) Ld. Holders of income bonds were entitled to 3 fully-paid shares of £1 in new company for each £1 bond held; holders of shares were entitled to 1 fully-paid share for every 30 shares of £1 held. Removed from Register 1912 .... **1911**

Aguas Blancas Nitrate Co. Ld. Regd. 1909. Vol. liq. 26 Mar. 1928 for reconstruction as Aguas Blancas Nitrate Co. (1928) Ld., in which company shareholders were entitled to 1 share of 5s. (credited with 3s. paid) for each share of 5s. held. Debenture holders were entitled to 60 fully-paid shares of 5s. and £100 income debentures for every £100 debenture held. Struck off Register 26 Jan. 1934 .... **1929**

Aguas Blancas Nitrate Co. (1928) Ld. Regd. 1928. Vol. liq. (members') 24 Apr. 1931. Undertaking and assets acquired by Nitrate Corporation of Chile, which corporation assumed liability in respect of debentures. Shareholders were to receive fully-paid series B shares of 100 pesos (either ordinary or 7% cumulative preferred) in new Corporation in proportion of 194 shares for every 10,000 shares held. Final meeting return regd. 2 June 1936 .... **1934**

Aguas Blancas Railway. Inc. Chile 1908. The outstanding 4½% 1st mortgage debenture stock was redeemed 1 Jan. 1947 .... **1947**

Aguna Rubber & Trading Co. Ld. Regd. 1910. Struck off Register 1918 .... **1917**

Agwi Oil Marketing Co. Ld. Regd. 1922. In Jan. 1926 British Mexican Petroleum Co. Ld. offered £1 of 5¼% 10-year bonds in exchange for each A share of £1 held. Vol. liq. 26 Oct. 1926. Final meeting return regd. 22 Apr. 1927 .... **1927**

Agwi Petroleum Corpn. Ld. Regd. 1920. Vol. liq. 20 Aug. 1947. Undertaking and assets taken over in specie by sole shareholder, Anglo American Oil Co. Ld. (later Esso Petroleum Co. Ld.) Final meeting return regd. 1 Feb. 1952 .... **1953**

Aheaba Ld. Regd. 1919. Vol. liq. 10 Apr. 1922. Undertaking and assets transferred to Akoko Main Reef Ld., in which company shareholders were entitled to 2 fully-paid shares of 1s. for every share of 5s. held. Final meeting return regd. 16 Aug. 1923 **1923**

Aibheel Tea Co. Ld. Regd. 1896. Vol. liq. Mar. 1920 for reconstruction under same name. Shareholders (preference and ordinary) were entitled to 3 fully-paid shares of £1 in new company for each share of £1 held. Final meeting return regd. 20 Aug. 1920 **1921**

Aigburth Picture House Ld. Regd. 1920. Vol. liq. 2 Aug. 1928. Properties were purchased by Denman Picture Houses Ld. Final meeting return regd. 13 Dec. 1928 .... **1940**

Aiheabah Concession Ld. Regd. 1901. Reconstructed 1904 as New Nimrod Co. Ld. in which company shareholders were entitled to 1 fully-paid share of £1 for every 4 shares of £1 held. Removed from Register 1905 .... **1905**

Ain Zeft Oil Co. Ld. Regd. 1914. Vol. liq. 14 July 1925. Capital returned to contributories—12s. per share of

See Stock Exchange Year-Book.

VOL. FOR

£1; further payments (if any) not known. Final meeting return regd. 11 Aug. 1927 .... **1926**

Ainibak Gold Concessions of West Africa Ld. Regd 1901. Removed from Register 1910 .... **1910**

Ainsworth Brothers & Co. Ld. Regd. 1920. Vol. liq. (members') 31 Aug. 1944. All capital was owned by Crosses & Heaton Ld. Final meeting return regd. 12 July 1945 .... **1946**

Ainsworth (W. & C.) Ld. Regd. 1920. Vol. liq. (members') 31 Aug. 1944. All capital was owned by Crosses & Heaton Ld. Final meeting return regd. 12 July 1945 .... **1946**

Aircraft Disposal Co. Ld. *See* A. D. C. Aircraft Ld.

Aircraft Industries Corporation Ld. Regd. 1935. Court order to wind up was made on 18 Oct. 1937; liquidator released in Sept. 1949. No capital return to contributories. Struck off Register 16 Feb. 1954 **1950**

Aircraft Manufacturing Co. Ld. Regd. 1912. Vol. liq. 23 Dec. 1920. Final meeting return regd. 3 Aug. 1929 **1921**

Airdrie & Coatbridge Tramways Co. Inc. by Special Act 1900. Under Act of 1921 the tramways were sold to Airdrie & Coatbridge Tramways Trustees for £82,250 .... **1922**

Airdrie & Coatbridge Water Co. Inc. by Special Act 1846. The undertaking was transferred on 1 June 1903 to Airdrie, Coatbridge and District Water Trustees for £396,638. Shareholders received £17 3s. 3·65d. per original share (10% maximum) of £5 or ordinary share (5%. maximum) of £10; £20 11s. 11·58d. per 6% preference share of £10; £17 3s. 3.65d. per 5% preference share of £10; further payments (if any) not known **1904**

Aire & Calder Navigation (The Undertakers of The). Inc. by Special Act as Undertakers of the Navigation of the Rivers of Aire and Calder in the West Riding of the County of York; name changed 1899. Dissolved 3 June 1949; undertaking vested from 1 Jan. 1948 in British Transport Commission under Transport Act 1947. Holders of securities were entitled to receive British Transport 3% guaranteed stock 1978–88 as follows in respect of every £100 of old security held:—

	£	s.	d.
Ordinary stock	66	10	0
Terminable loans	100	0	0
3½% irred. debenture stock	100	0	0
4% red. debenture stock	109	0	0

1949

Airedale Collieries Ld. Regd. 1919. Vol. liq. (members') 17 July 1950 the collieries &c. having vested in National Coal Board. Capital returned to contributories—£2 7s. 0·39d. per 10s. stock. £357 paid to Companies Liquidation Account. Final meeting return regd. 23 Jan. 1956 .... **1957**

Airedale Gas Co. Inc. by Special Act 1870. Undertaking sold to Bradford Corporation. Holders received £310 for each £100 10% stock and £217 for each £100 7% stock (or shares) **1903**

Airey's Brewery Ld. Regd. 1906. A subsidiary of Northwestern Brewery Investments Ld. Vol. liq. (members') 30 Sept. 1955. Final meeting return regd. 18 Feb. 1959 .... **1940**

Airspeed Ld. Regd. 1934 as Airspeed (1934) Ld., name subsequently changed. Vol. liq. 1951. A subsidiary of De Havilland Aircraft Co. Ld. Final meeting return regd. 3 Feb. 1955 .... **1949**

Airways (Africa) Ld. Regd. 1929 as Imperial Airways (South Africa) Ld.; name changed Nov. 1930 to Imperial Airways (Africa) Ld. and as above in Apr. 1940. Vol. liq. (members') 1 Nov. 1940. Capital returned to contributories—£1 4s. 9d. per share of £1. Final meeting return regd. 21 July 1941 .... **1940**

Airways (Atlantic) Ld. *See* British Airways (Atlantic) Ld.

Airways (Bermuda) Ld. *See* British Airways (Bermuda) Ld.

Aitchee's Luck Gold Mining Co. Ld. Regd. 1891. Vol. liq. 4 Feb. 1897. Final meeting return regd. 21 June 1897 .... **1898**

Aix-les-Bains & Mont Revard Railway Co. Ld. Regd. 1892. Removed from Register 1906 .... **1894**

Ajaka Alluvial Mining Co. Ld. Regd. 1904. Vol. liq. 24 Oct. 1905. Removed from Register 1906 .... **1906**

Ajax Fraction Development Syndicate Ld. *See* Monitor & Ajax Fraction Ld.

Akabo (Wassau & Ashanti) Exploration Co. Ld. Regd. 1901. Vol. liq. May 1907. Removed from Register 1910 .... **1908**

Akankoo (Gold Coast) Mining Co. Ld. Regd. 1881. Reconstructed as New Akankoo (Gold Coast) Mining Co. Ld., in which company shareholders were entitled to 1 share of £1 (credited with 17s. 6d. paid) for each stare of £1 held. Removed from Register 1907 .... **1890**

VOL. FOR

Akankoo Gold Mining Co. Ld. Regd. 1890. Removed from Register 1907 .... **1892**

Akim Concessions Ld. Regd. 13 Sept. 1948. Vol. liq. (members') 18 July 1972. Return of final meeting regd. 5 June 1984. Dissolved 7 Sept. 1984. Distributions per (ordinary share of 25p): 15p in Oct. 1973, 6p in Dec. 1981 and final of 4·5p in Jan. 1984; (deferred share of 10p): first and final of 10·208125p in Jan. 1984. Amounts paid into Companies' Liquidation Account in respect of unclaimed distribution was £4,570 for deferred shares and £1,027 for ordinary shares **1985–6**

Akim Alluvials Ld. Regd. 1920. Vol. liq. 5 Jan. 1922 for reconstruction as Akim Ld., in which company snareholders were entitled to 1 fully-paid ordinary share of £1 for every 4 shares of 5s. held. together with an option (since expired) to subscribe for preference shares at par. Final meeting return regd. 29 July 1926 .... **1922**

Akim Cocoa & Rubber Estates Ld. Regd. 1902 as Akim Gold Fields Ld. Struck off Register 1916. .... **1907**

Akim Corporation Ld. Regd. 1901. Vol. liq. 17 Aug. 1904. Undertaking acquired by Atomé Extended Mines Ld., in which company shareholders were entitled to 1 share of 5s. (credited with 3s. paid) for each share of £1 held plus 1 fully-paid share of 5s. for every 4 shares held. Removed from Register 1913 **1905**

Akim Diamond Fields Ld. Regd. 1920. Vol. liq. 5 Jan. 1922 for reconstruction as Akim Ld. in which company shareholders were entitled to 1 fully-paid ordinary share of £1 for every share of £1 held and an option (since expired) to subscribe for preference shares at par. Final meeting return regd. 29 July 1926 .... **1922**

Akim Gold Fields Ld. *See* Akim Cocoa & Rubber Estates Ld.

Akim Ld. Regd. 1922. Vol. liq. 8 Nov. 1928 for reconstruction as Akim (1928) Ld., in which company shareholders were entitled to 8 fully paid shares of 2s. 6d. for every preference, share of £1 held or 1 fully-paid share of 2s. 6d. for every ordinary share of £1 held. Final meeting return regd. 13 Nov. 1931 .... **1929**

Akim (1928) Ld. Regd. 1928. Vol. liq. (members') 17 Mar. 1939. Undertaking and assets were acquired by National Mining Corporation Ld. now N.M.C. Investments Ld. in which company shareholders were entitled to 3 fully-paid shares of 2s. 6d. for every 2 shares of 2s. 6d. held and an option (since expired) over further shares. Final meeting return regd. 24 May 1941 .... **1940**

Akinassi Syndicate (Ashanti) Ld. Regd. 1900. Vol. liq. Jan. 1902. Reconstructed as company of same name. Shareholders were entitled to 10 fully-paid shares of £1 in the new company for each share of £1 held. Removed from Register 1902 .... **1908**

Akinassi Syndicate (Ashanti) Ld. Regd. 1902. Receivers for debenture holders appointed June 1908. Struck off Register 1919 .... **1911**

Akoko Gold Mines & Estates Ld. Regd. 1911. Vol. liq. 8 Oct. 1918. Property acquired by Akoko Main Reef Ld., in which company shareholders received 1 fully-paid share of 1s. for every 2 shares of 5s. held. Final meeting return regd. 3 Oct. 1921 .... **1919**

Akoko Gold Mines Ld. Regd. 1901. Vol. liq. 1 Sept. 1905. Reconstructed as African Mines Ld., in which company shareholders were entitled to 2 shares of 10s. (credited with 8s. paid) for each share of £1 held. Removed from Register 1906 .... **1906**

Akoko Gold Mines Ld. Regd. 1925. Vol. liq. May 1927 for reconstruction as New Akoko Ld. No capital returned to contributories, but they had preferential rights to subscribe for shares in new company. Struck off Register June 1932 .... **1933**

Akoko Investment Trust Ld. Regd. 1924. Vol. liq. 22 Mar. 1928. Final meeting return regd. 2 Mar. 1931 **1929**

Akoko Main Reef Ld. Regd. 1913. Vol. liq. 27 Jan. 1925. Undertaking and assets were sold to Akoko Gold Mines Ld., in which company shareholders were entitled to 3 shares of 1s. (credited with 8d. per share) for every 2 shares of 1s. held. Final meeting return regd. 17 Mar. 1928 .... **1926**

Akrill (C.) Ld. Regd 1902. Vol. liq. Jan. 1951. Final meeting return regd. 14 Dec. 1951 .... **1949**

Akriporisu (Ashanti) Syndicate Ld. Regd. 1900. Vol. liq. 26 Sept. 1904. Removed from Register 1906 .... **1905**

Akrokerri (Ashanti) Mines Ld. Regd. 1900. Removed from Register 1912 .... **1910**

Akropong (Ashanti) Mines Ld. Regd. 1901. Removed from Register 1904 .... **1904**

Akropong Concessions Ld. Regd. 1901. Removed from Register 1902 .... **1903**

Akropong Gold Mining & Exploration Co. Ld. Regd. 1900. Removed from Register 26 July 1912 .... *****1910**

See Stock Exchange Year-Book.

VOL. FOR

Akroyd (James) & Son Ld. Regd. 1883. Vol. liq. 28 June 1893. Final meeting return regd. 5 May 1900 ..... **1896**

Akroyd (James) & Son Ld. Regd. 1893. Vol. liq. (members') 4 Dec. 1931. Capital returned to contributories—£9 5s. 2¾d. per share of £10. Final meeting return regd. 31 Aug. 1932 .... **1932**

Aktiebolaget Uniononbanken. Inc. Helsingfors 1924. Amalgamated 1931 with Helsingfors Aktiebank, in which company shareholders were entitled to 3 shares of F. mk 100 for every 4 shares of F. mk 100 held *plus* F. mk 4¼ per share **1932**

Aktieselskabet Burmeister & Wain's Maskinog Skibsbyggeri. *See* Burmeister and Wain, Engineers and Shipbuilders Ld.

Aktieselskabet Risor Traemassefabriker. All capital was acquired by Standard Wood Pulp Co. Ld. in 1928 **1939**

Akwara Tin Trust of Nigeria Ld. Regd. 1912. Vol. liq. 15 May 1914. Final meeting return regd. 18 May 1920 **1915**

Alabama Coal, Iron, Land & Colonization Co. Ld. Regd. 1882. Vol. liq. (members') 19 June 1947. Capital returned to contributories—5s. 7d. per share of 2s. Final meeting return regd. 9 Sept. 1948 .... **1949**

Alabama Great Southern Railway Co. Ld. Regd. 1877. Vol. liq. Dec. 1905. Shareholders were entitled to an equal amount of shares in Alabama Great Southern Railroad Co. Liability for funded certificates was assumed by that company. Debenture holders were to be repaid in cash at par. Removed from Register 1907 .... **1906**

Alabama Midland Railway Co. Organised Alabama and Georgia 1888. Acquired in 1901 by Savannah, Florida & Western Railway Co. which company assumed liability for 1st guaranteed gold bonds 1928 **1901**

Alabama Portland Cement Co. Ld. Regd. 1900. Vol. liq. 11 Jan. 1909. Final meeting return regd. 6 May 1909 ***1909**

Alabama Traction. Light & Power Co. Inc. Canada. Undertaking and assets were acquired by Southeastern Power & Light Co., in which company shareholders were entitled to 1 7% preferred share of no par value for each 6% preferred share held or 2 common shares of no par value for each common share held. Bondholders were entitled to an equal amount of 6% gold debentures in purchasing company and an option warrant to purchase certain shares **1926**

Aladdin Cobalt Ld. Regd. Apr. 1913. Vol. liq. Sept. 1919 for purpose of forming new company, Kirkland Lake Proprietary (1919) Ld., in which company shareholders were entitled to receive 2 new shares of £1 for every 7 held. Final meeting return regd. 27 Aug. 1920 .... **1920**

Aladdin Polish Co. Ld. Regd. 1915. Vol. liq. 1 Jan. 1923. Controlling interest held by Hargreaves Bros. & Co. Ld. Final meeting return regd. 10 May 1924 .... **1923**

Aladdin Renew Electric Lamp Corporation Ld. Regd. 1919. Vol. liq. 26 July 1921 for reconstruction as Aladdin Renew Electric Lamp Corporation (1921) Ld. Final meeting return regd. 13 Feb. 1924........ **1922**

Aladdin's Lamp Gold Mining Co. Ld. Regd. 1892. Vol. liq. 8 Jan. 1906. Undertaking acquired by Australasian Share Trust Ld. Shareholders were given the opportunity to subscribe for shares in Mines & Smelting Co. Ld. at 3s. 4d per share of 5s. Struck off Register 30 Apr. 1946 .... **1947**

Alagoas Railway Co. Ld. Regd. 1881. Line purchased by Brazilian Government from July 1902. Holders of debentures and debenture stock were entitled to either repayment at par or £140 in 4% railway guaranteed rescission bonds for every £110 held. Shareholders were entitled to £20 in bonds *plus* £2 6s. in cash for each share of £20 held. Removed from Register 1904 .... **1904**

Alameda Oil Co. Ld. Regd. 1902. Vol. liq. Feb. 1907. Removed from Register 1911 .... **1908**

Alamillos Co. Ld. Regd. 1863. Reconstructed 1904 as company of same name. Shareholders were entitled to 2 fully-paid shares of 10s. and 8 shares of 10s. (credited 7s. paid) for every 5 shares of £2 held. Removed from Register 1905 .... **1907**

Alamillos Co. Ld. 1904. Reconstructed 1907 as company of same name. Shareholders were entitled to 1 fully-paid share of £1 in new company for every 7 shares of 10s. paid. Removed from Register 1909 .... **1908**

Alamillos Co. Ld. Regd. 1907. Vol. liq. Sept. 1909. Undertaking acquired by Linares Lead Mining Co. Ld., in which company shareholders were entitled to 1 fully-paid share of £1 for every 4 shares of £1 held. Removed from Register 1911 .... **1910**

Alangoua & Comoé Goldfields Ld. Regd. 1903. Vol. liq. 18 Dec. 1907. Final meeting return regd. 20 Mar. 1920 .... **1908**

Alaska Consolidate Mines Ld. Regd. 1904. Removed from Register 1913 **1913**

VOL. FOR

Alaska Exploration Co. Ld. Regd. 1911. Vol. liq. 19 May 1913. Final meeting return regd. 20 May 1922 .... **1914**

Alaska Gold Dredging Co. Ld. Regd. 1928. Vol. liq. (members') 28 Apr. 1930. Capital returned to contributories—9s. 8⅜d. per share of £1. Final meeting return regd. 21 Jan. 1931 .... **1931**

Alaska Goldfields Ld. Regd. 1897. Vol. liq. 3 Mar. 1925. Capital returned to contributories 2s. 3¼d. per share of 9d. Final meeting return regd. 1 July 1935 ..... **1926**

Alaska Mexican Gold Mining Co. Inc. Minnesota 1892. Shareholders were entitled to 1 share of Treadwell Yukon Corporation Ld. for every 4·4 shares held. Dissolved Feb. 1938 .... **1939**

Alaska Mill & Mining Co. The mines were acquired in 1895 by Alaska United Gold Mining Co. Shareholders were entitled to 1 share of $5 for each share of $100 held **1908**

Alaska Rodman Bay Co. Ld. Regd. 1902. Vol. liq. 16 Dec. 1908. Final meeting return regd. 15 Apr. 1921 **1909**

Alsaka Steam Coal & Petroleum Syndicate Ld. Regd. 1900. Vol. liq. 7 July 1904. Property acquired by Pacific Coal and Oil Co. Ld., in which company shareholders were entitled to £1 debenture stock and £5 in common stock for each share of £1 held. Final meeting return regd. 25 Apr. 1922 .... **1905**

Alaska Syndicate Ld. Regd. 1899. Vol. liq. 1903. Property was acquired by Klondyke Estates Corporation Ld., in which company shareholders were entitled to 1 share of £1 (credited as fully paid) for every 2 shares of £1. held. Removed from Register 1907 .... **1904**

Alaska Treadwell Gold Mining Co. Inc. Minnesota 1890. Shareholders were entitled to 2 shares of Treadwell Yukon Corporation Ld. and 2·8 cents in cash for each share held. Dissolved Feb. 1938.................... **1939**

Alaska United Gold Mining Co. Inc. West Virginia 1895. Shareholders received 1·8 cents per share in cash. Dissolved Jan. 1938 .... **1939**

Alaska Whitworth Ld. *See* Whitworth Finance & Mining Corporation Ld.

Albanian National Brewery Ld. Regd. 1929. Court Order to wind up Dec. 1929. Struck off Register 24 Oct. 1939 .... **1940**

Albany Land Corporation Ld. Regd. 1896. Vol. liq. 9 Jan. 1907. Final meeting return regd. 14 Mar. 1921 **1907**

Albany Mill (Holdings) Ld. Regd. as Albany Spinning Co. (1920) Ld. Name changed 1951 to Albany Spinning Co Ld. and 1953 to above title. Vol. liq. 16 Dec. 1980. Final meeting return regd. 15 Dec. 1981 **1956**

Albany Shipping Co. Ld. Regd. 1882. Vol. liq. Nov. 1907. Removed from Register 1908 .... **1908**

Albany Spinning Co. Ld. *See* Albany Mill (Holdings) Ld.

Albemarle Jewellers, Ld. Regd. as Garrard & Co., Ld., 1909; name changed 3 June 1952. Vol. liq. (members') 3 June 1952, the goodwill and certain assets having been acquired by the Goldsmiths' & Silversmiths' Co. Ld. (later Garrard & Co. Ld.). Capital returned to contributories—preference shares (of £1), £1; ordinary shares (of 2s.), 4s. 11·648d. £258 paid into Companies' Liquidation Account in respect of unclaimed dividends or distributions. Final meeting return regd. 12 Aug. 1954 .... **1955**

Albert Dock (Riverside) Cold Storage Co. Ld. Regd. 1907. Removed from Register 1912 .... **1912**

Albert Eadie Chain Co. Ld. *See* Ecco Works Ld.

Albert Exhibition Palace Ld. Regd. 1882. Buildings were acquired in 1884 by Albert Palace Association Ld., for £145,000 in shares of £5. Removed from Register 1906 .... **1886**

Albert Mills Co. Ld. Regd. 1875. Vol. liq. 18 July 1879. Final meeting return regd. 7 May 1880 .... ***1880**

Albert Mine Ld. Inc. South Africa 1886. Vol. liq. **1895**

Albert Mines Syndicate Ld. Regd. 1895. Removed from Register 1901 .... **1900**

Albert New Mill Co. Ld. Regd. 1874. Vol. liq. 21 June 1920. Final meeting return regd. 9 Dec. 1920 .... ***1881**

Albert Palace Association Ld. Regd. 1884. Court Orders; to wind up 19 Mar. 1887; to dissolve 19 Feb. 1895 .... **1887**

Albert Railway Co. of New Brunswick. Inc. New Brunswick 1864 by Special Act. Reconstructed as Salisbury and Harvey Railway Co. (inc. 1889), in which company holders of 1st mortgage bonds received 1 share for every £200 held **1891**

Alberta & British Columbia Exploration Co. Ld. Regd. 1900. Vol. liq. (members') 23 July 1947. Final meeting return regd. 2 Oct. 1950 .... **1909**

Alberta & Great Waterways Railway Co. Inc. Albeta 1909 by Special Act. The undertaking was acquired jointly by Canadian National Railways and Canadian Pacific Railway Co. and transferred to a new company (Northern Alberta Railways Co.) The Province of Alberta assumed liability for the 5% 1st mortgage gold debenture bonds **1930**

VOL. FOR

Alberta Irrigation Co. *See* Canadian North West Irrigation Co.

Alberta Land Co. Ld. Regd. 1906. Vol. liq. 14 Aug. 1917. Reconstructed in 1919 as Port Arthur (Ontario) Developments Ld. Final meeting return regd. 12 June 1926 .... **1919**

Alberta Land Co. Ld. Inc. Canada 1911. Vol. liq. 1917 for amalgamation with 2 other companies under title of Canada Land and Irrigation Co. Ld. Holders of 5% debenture stock received £1 in 6% debenture stock and 1 fully-paid share of £1 in new company for each £2 stock held; shareholders received 2 fully-paid shares of £1 and 5 shares of £1 (credited with 16*s*. paid) for every 10 shares held **1918**

Alberta Pacific Grain Co. Ld. Inc. Canada 1926. Undertaking was purchased in June 1943 by Algoma Grain Securities Ld. (which changed its name to Alberta Pacific Grain Co. (1943) Ld.) **1944**

Alberta Railway & Coal Co. Inc. Canada 1889 by Special Act. Amalgamated with 2 other companies 20 July 1904 under title of Alberta Railway and Irrigation Co. The ordinary shares were extinguished, preference shareholders received 50% of their holdings in new capital stock; holders of A debenture stock $5 of new prior lien debenture stock for every £1 held and holders of B debenture stock $2½ of new 5% debenture stock and $2½ of new capital stock for every £1 held and a payment of 2½% in cash upon their respective holdings **1908**

Alberta Railway & Irrigation Co. Inc. Canada by Special Act 1904. Lines were leased to Canadian Pacific Railway Co. which company held majority of capital stock and all 4% 1st mortgage bonds **1921**

Albion Bank & Discount Co. Ld. Regd. 1871 as Albion Loan & Banking Co. Ld.; name changed in 1883. Court Orders; to wind up 20 Dec. 1886: to dissolve 27 Oct. 1893 .... **1888**

Albion Brewery Co. Ld. Regd. 1872. Vol. liq. 25 Nov 1920. Final meeting return regd. 21 July 1921 ..... **1921**

Albion Brewery, Leeds, Ld. Regd. 1897. Vol. liq. (members') 8 Apr. 1943. Capital returned to contributories—20*s*. per preference share of £1; £1 8*s*. 11·216*d*. per ordinary share of £1. Final meeting return regd. 20 Apr. 1944 .... **1945**

Albion (Burton-on-Trent) Brewery Ld. Regd. 1896. Vol. liq. 2 Mar. 1903. Final meeting return regd. 20 Dec. 1916 .... **1904**

Albion Fire Insurance Association Ld. Regd. 1880 as Fire Insurance Association Ld.; name changed Apr. 1893. Vol. liq. 16 Jan. 1894. Business acquired by Manchester Assurance Co. Final meeting return regd. 12 Mar. 1896 .... **1904**

Albion Gold Mines Ld. Regd. 1892. Vol. liq. 31 May 1895. Reconstructed as Albion (Transvaal) Gold Mines Ld., in which company shareholders were entitled to 16 shares of 10*s*. (credited with 8*s*. paid) for every 5 preference shares of £1 held or 8 shares of 10*s*. (credited with 8*s*. paid) for every 5 ordinary shares of £1 held. Final meeting return regd. 28 Dec. 1897 .... **1897**

Albion Greyhounds (Glasgow) Ld. Regd. Edinburgh 1927. Vol. liq. Feb. 1934. Reconstructed as Glasgow Albion Racing Co. Ld. in which company shareholders were entitled to 1 ordinary share of 5*s*. or 1 deferred share of 1*s*. (credited as fully paid) for each ordinary share of 5*s*. or deferred share of 1*s*. respectively held. Final meeting return regd. 9 Feb. 1935 .... **1934**

Albion Greyhounds (Stoke) Ld. Regd. 1932. Vol. liq. (members') 29 Sept. 1954. Capital returned to contributories—20*s*. per preference share (of £1) and 2*s*. 3½*d*. per ordinary share (of 2*s*. 6*d*.). £148 2*s*. was paid into Companies' Liquidation Account. Final meeting return regd. 18 Dec. 1956 .... **1957**

Albion Hotel, Manchester, Ld. Regd. 1896. Vol. liq. 21 Dec. 1900. Final meeting return regd. 19 Nov. 1902 ***1902**

Albion Life Assurance Society. Regd. 1863. Court Orders: to wind up 11 Mar. 1878. to dissolve 2 Feb. 1891 .... ***1879**

Albion Loan & Banking Co Ld. *See* Albion Bank & Discount Co. Ld.

Albion Steam Coal Co. Ld. Regd. 1891. Vol. liq. (creditors') 12 Feb. 1931. Debenture holders were repaid £23,943; no capital returned to contributories. Final meeting return regd. 12 Dec. 1934 .... **1931**

Albion (Transvaal) Gold Mines Ld. Regd. 1895. Vol. liq. 26 Feb. 1897 for reconstruction as company of same name. Shareholders were to receive 1 share of 10*s*. (credited with 7*s*. 6*d*. paid) for each share of 10*s*. held. Final meeting return regd. 28 Dec. 1897 ..... **1908**

Albion (Transvaal) Gold Mines Ld. Regd 1897 Vol. liq. Mar. 1908. Winding up continued under supervision of Court. Reconstructed as New Albion Transvaal Gold Mines Ld in which company shareholders were entitled to 1 share of 5*s*. (credited with 3*s*. paid) for each share of 10*s*. held. Removed from Register 1914 .... **1909**

Albo-Carbon Light Co. Ld. Regd. 1878. Vol. liq. 26 Sept. 1892. Final meeting return regd. 28 Apr. 1893..... **1893**

Albrighton Gas Co. Ld. Regd. 1934. Dissolved 1 May 1949, undertaking being vested in West Midland Area Gas Board under Gas Act 1948. Holders of ordinary shares (of £1) were entitled to receive £1 10*s*. British Gas 3% guaranteed stock 1990–95 for each share held **1952**

Alby United Carbide Factories Ld. Regd. 1905 as Sun Gas Co. Ld.: name changed Oct. 1906. Struck off Register 1 Sept. 1936 .... **1937**

Alcock (A. U.) Electric Light & Motive Power Co. Ld. *See* A. U. Alcock Electric Light & Motive Power Co. Ld.

Alcock Pottery Ld. Undertaking and assets acquired by Cauldon Potteries Ld. **1924**

Alcock (Ralph) & Sons. Ld. Regd. 1929. Vol. liq. Aug. 1932. Struck off Register 9 Mar. 1954 .... **1933**

Alcohol Fuel Corporation Ld. Regd. 1920. Vol. liq. (members') 31 Oct. 1930. Capital returned to contributories—£5,861 1*s*. 5*d*. A further £209 was paid to Companies' Liquidation Account in respect of unclaimed dividends. Final meeting return regd. 7 Sept. 1932 .... **1931**

Alcudia Lead Mines Ld. Regd. 1903. Vol. liq. May 1910. Struck off Register 15 Aug. 1944 .... **1945**

Alda Copper Mines Ld. Regd. 1900. Vol. liq. 9 May 1906. Removed from Register 1912 .... **1907**

Aldeburgh Electric Supply Co. Ld. Regd. 1911. Dissolved 1 Apr. 1948. undertaking being vested in the British (later Central) Electricity Authority and Eastern Area Board under the Electricity Act 1947. Ordinary shareholders were entitled to receive £1 11*s*. 2*d*. British Electricity 3% guaranteed stock (1968–73), for each share (of £1) held **1949**

Aldeburgh Gas Light Co. Ld. Regd. 1856. Dissolved 1 May 1949, undertaking being vested in Eastern Area Gas Board under Gas Act 1948. Holders of 5% preference shares (of £10) were entitled to receive £11 4*s*. British Gas 3% guaranteed stock 1990–95 for each share held **1952**

Aldeburgh Waterworks Co. Ld. Regd. 1870. Under Act of 1901, the undertaking was required by Aldeburgh Corporation. Removed from Register 1903 .... **1902**

Alder Spinning Co. (1920) Ld. Regd. 1920. undertaking acquired by Combined Egyptian Mills Ld. (later Combined English Mills (Spinners) Ld.). Struck off Register 1938 .... ***1930**

Alderley & Wilmslow Electric Supply Ld. Regd. 1893. Undertaking transferred to Alderley Edge & Wilmslow Electricity Board in Dec. 1928. Vol. liq. (members') 3 Jan. 1930. Capital returned—£2 8*s*. 2⅔*d*. per ordinary share of £1. Final meeting return regd. 11 Nov. 1930 .... **1930**

Alderley Mining Co. Ld. Regd. 1911. Struck off Register 17 Dec. 1915 .... ***1915**

Aldershot & Farnborough Light Railway Co. Inc. (under Light Railways Act 1896) by order of Light Railway Commissioners confirmed by Board of Trade 1902. Powers expired 1905 .... **1903**

Aldershot & Farnborough Light Railway Co. Inc. (under Light Railways Act 1896) by order of Light Railway Commissioners confirmed by Board of Trade 1909 **1911**

Aldershot Brewery Co. Ld. Regd. 1882. Removed from Register 1906 .... ***1883**

Aldershot Gas & Water Co. *See* Mid-Southern Utility Co.

Aldershot Gas, Water & District Lighting Co. *See* Mid-Southern Utility Co.

Aldine Publishing Co. Ld. Regd. 1895. Vol. liq. (members') 28 Dec. 1932. Debenture holders repaid £3,000. No capital returned to contributories. Final meeting return regd. 20 Mar. 1936 .... **1933**

Aldridge Colliery Co. Ld. Regd. 1874. Vol. liq. (members') Nov. 1930. Undertaking and assets were acquired by Aldridge Brick, Tile & Coal Co. Ld. Capital returned to contributories—£50 per fully-paid ordinary share of £20; £37 10*s*. per ordinary share of £20 (£15 paid); £8 15*s*. per preference share of £10 (£3 10*s*. paid); 10*s*. per deferred share of 10*s*.; no unclaimed balance. Final meeting return regd. 31 July 1931 .... **1931**

Aldwych Engineering Co. Ld. Regd. 1928. Vol. liq. (creditors') 26 May 1931. Assets realised insufficient to meet claims of creditors in full. Final meeting return regd. 23 June 1938 .... **1931**

Aldwych House Estates Ld. Regd. 1927. Vol. liq. (members') 14 Sept. 1934. Capital returned to contributory—£6,953 15*s*. 1*d*. (by release of debt). Final meeting return regd. 24 June 1935 .... **1935**

VOL. FOR

Aldwych Industrial Trust Ld. Regd. 1929. Vol. liq. (creditors') 26 May 1931. No capital returned to contributories. Final meeting return regd. 23 June 1938 .... **1932**

Alexander & Shepheard Ld. Regd. 1907. Vol. liq. 18 Mar. 1920. Amalgamated with Wyman & Sons Ld. (later Wyman & Marshall Ld.) in which company shareholders were entitled to 1 preference share of £1 for each share of £1 held. Final meeting return regd. 4 Aug. 1920 .... **1921**

Alexander Brothers Ld. Regd. 1886. Vol. liq. 23 Nov. 1904. Removed from Register 1905 .... **1905**

Alexander (H.) & Co. Ld. Regd. 1918. Vol. liq. 20 May 1921. Final meeting return regd. 19 Nov. 1925..... ***1922**

Alexander (James & Thomas) Ld. Regd. Edinburgh 1895. Vol. liq. 25 Oct. 1926. Final meeting return regd. 26 Dec. 1929 .... **1920**

Alexander (R. F. & J.) & Co. Ld. Regd. Edinburgh 1892. Vol. liq. (members') 20 Apr. 1950. Final meeting return regd. 23 Apr. 1951 .... **1940**

Alexander Stanley Linings (Manchester) Ld. *See* Stanley Linings Ld.

Alexandra Estate & Gold Mining Co. Ld. Inc. Cape of Good Hope 1889. Vol. liq. Dec. 1909. Undertaking sold to Paardekraal Estates Ld. in which company shareholders were to receive 1 share of 2s. fully-paid for each fully-paid share of £1 .... **1910**

Alexandra Furnishing Co. Ld. Undertaking and assets were acquired by Hackney Furnishing Co. (1928) Ld. **1929**

Alexandra Hotel & Hydro Co. (Bridlington) Ld. Regd. 1905. Struck off Register 1923 .... ***1917**

Alexandra Hotel Co. Ld. Regd. 1863. Vol. liq. 28 Jan. 1948. Capital returned to contributories—£28 19s. 1d. per share of £10. £145 was paid into Companies' Liquidation Account. Final meeting return regd. 22 Sept. 1948 .... **1949**

Alexandra (Newport & South Wales) Docks & Railway Co. Inc. by Special Act 1865 as Alexandra (Newport) Dock Co.; name changed by Act of 1882. In 1922 the undertaking was merged into the Great Western Railway Co., in which company stockholders were entitled to stock as follows:

For each £100 held		G.W.R.	
4% Debenture	£100	4% Debenture	
4½% 1st Pref. Cons.			
"A"	£90	5% Cons. Pref.	
4½% 2nd Pref. Cons.			
"B"	£90	5% Cons. Pref.	
Cons. Ordinary	£45	5% Cons. Pref.	
	£45	Cons. Ordinary	

£581,963 4% Redeemable Debenture Stock issued as security for a temporary loan was replaced with an equal amount of Great Western 4% Debenture Stock **1924**

Alexandra Palace & Park Co. Ld. Regd. 1887. Court Orders: to wind up 13 Mar. 1890; to dissolve 13 Aug. 1894 .... ***1890**

Alexandra Palace Co. Ld. Regd. 1866. Court Orders: to wind up 7 Nov. 1876; to dissolve 20 June 1887.... ***1878**

Alexandra Theatre & Opera House Co. Ld. Regd. 1864. Vol. liq. 11 Mar. 1896. Final meeting return regd. 22 Sept. 1896 .... **1897**

Alexandria & Ramleh Railway Co. Ld. Regd 1883. Struck off Register 11 Aug. 1961 .... **1962**

Alfloc, Ld. Regd. 1931. Vol. liq. (members') 31 Dec. 1942. All shares owned by I.C.I. (Alkali) Ld. Final meeting return regd. 12 Aug. 1943 .... **1943**

Alford Gas Co. Inc. by Special Act 1875. Dissolved 1 May 1949, undertaking being vested in East Midland Area Gas Board under Gas Act 1948. Holders of securities were entitled to receive British Gas 3% guaranteed stock 1990–95 as follows:

	£ s. d.	
Orig. shares & stock (10% max.) (per £10)	5 0 0	
4% debs. (per £100)	100 0 0	**1952**

Alfred Clough Ld. *See* Grindley of Stoke (Ceramics) Ld.

Alfreton Gas Act Inc. by Special Act 1900. Dissolved 1 May 1949, undertaking being vested in East Midland Area Gas Board under Gas Act 1941. Holders of securities were entitled to receive, in respect of each £100 held, British Gas 3% guaranteed stock 1990–95 as follows:

	£ s. d.	
10% orig. stock	210 0 0	
7% additional stock	150 0 0	
6% pref. stock	127 10 0	**1952**

Algeciras (Gibraltar) Railway Co. Ld. Regd. 1888. Vol. liq. July 1913. Undertaking was acquired by Andaluces Railway Co. Prior lien debenture holders received £105 in cash for each £100 debentures held;

VOL. FOR

holders of 6% mortgage debentures were repaid at par; holders of 5% new (income) debenture stock were to receive two and a half 4½% bonds of 500 pesetas in the purchasing company and £2 10s. in cash for every £100 held; preference shareholders were to receive £1 10s. per share of £10 and ordinary shareholders received 10s. per share of £10. Removed from Register 1914 .... **1914**

Algemeene Bankvereeniging N. V. Inc. Louvain 1928 as Algemeene Bankvereeniging en Volksbank van Leuven; name changed Oct. 1931. Undertaking absorbed by Kredietbank voor Handel en Nijverheld **1936**

Algemeene Bankvereeniging (S. A.). Inc. Antwerp 1921. Assets and liabilities transferred to a new bank Algemeene Bankvereeniging en Volksbank van Leuven (later Algemeene Bankvereeniging N. V.) **1929**

Alger Spinning Co. Ld. Regd. 1899 as Curzon Mill Co. Ld.; name changed Dec. 1911. Vol. liq. (members') 26 Aug. 1941. Capital returned to stockholders—£1 2s. 7·84d. per 10s. stock. Final meeting return regd. 26 June 1942 .... **1943**

Algeria Consolidated Oil Estates Ld. Regd. 1913 as Gouria Consolidated Oil Estates Ld.; name changed June 1914. Vol. liq. 12 Mar. 1924. Final meeting return regd. 27 Sept. 1929 .... ***1925**

Algerian Esparto Grass Co. Ld. Regd. 1910. Vol. liq. 2 Feb. 1923. Final meeting return regd. 30 Sept. 1924 .... **1924**

Algerian Oilfields Ld. Regd. 1910. Undertaking (except its holding in Trinidad Esmeralda Co.) was acquired by African Investment Trust Ld. Vol. liq. 30 May 1927. Final meeting return regd. 8 Jan. 1930........ **1937**

Algoma Central Terminals Ld. Inc. Canada 1912. The outstanding sterling bonds and stock were redeemed on 31 Dec. 1949. Charter surrendered from 30 Nov. 1955. .... **1951**

Algoma Consolidated Corporation Ld. Inc. Canada 1930. Scheme for liquidation, Apr. 1937, provided (inter alia) for (a) holders of 5% income debenture stock and bonds to receive $40 5% 1st mortgage income debenture stock of Algoma Central & Hudson Bay Railway Co., (now Algoma Central Railway) voting trust certificates representing 309,255 his share in 214,445 common shares of the Railway Company and cash payment estimated at not less than $3 in respect of every $30 stock or bonds held. (b) The remaining assets, except 2nd mortgage bonds of Railway Co., which are to be cancelled, to be distributed to holders of preference stock, such holders thus receiving, apart from their proportion of the 8,889½ shares of the Northern Ontario Lands Corpn. Ld., about 20 cents for every $5 preference stock held, and (c) no distribution to be made to holders of common shares **1938**

Algoma Eastern Railway Co. Inc. Canada 1900 as Manitoulin & North Shore Railway Co.; name changed 1911. The outstanding 5% 1st mortgage 50-year gold bonds were redeemed on 1 Mar. 1947 ... **1947**

Algoma Land Co, Ld. Regd. 1913. Vol. liq. 24 Oct. 1924. Final meeting return regd. 22 Sept. 1928 .... **1925**

Algoma Steel Corporation Ld. Inc. Ontario 1907 as Lake Superior Iron & Steel Co. Ld.; name changed 1912. Undertaking, assets and certain liabilities were acquired by company of same name. Holders of 5% purchase money bonds were entitled to $50 in preference stock for every $100 bonds held; holders of 1st and refunding mortgage bonds were entitled to 1 common share of no par value for every $200 bonds held **1935**

Alhambra (Blackpool) Ld. Regd. 1897. Vol. liq. 22 Nov. 1902. Undertaking and assets were acquired by Blackpool Tower Co. Ld. Only 1st mortgage debenture stockholders were expected to receive any return of capital. Removed from Register 1909 ... **1904**

Alhambra Co. Ld. Regd. 1865. Vol. liq. (members') 22 Jan. 1937. Capital returned to contributories—£100,461 1s. 8d. Final meeting return regd, 9 Mar. 1938 .... **1937**

Alhambra Theatre (Attercliffe) Sheffield, Ld. Regd. 1897. Vol. liq. (members') 4 June 1963. Final meeting return regd. 2 Mar. 1964 .... **1919**

Alianza Co. Ld. Regd. 1895. Reconstructed in 1903 as company of same name. The 200,000 shares of £5 were exchanged for 100,000 shares of £5 and £500,000 4½% debentures in new company. Removed from Register 1908 .... **1909**

Alianza Co. Ld. Regd. 1903. Vol. liq. (members') 3 June 1931. Undertaking and assets acquired by Nitrate Corporation of Chile. Shareholders were to receive fully-paid Series B shares of 100 pesos (either ordinary or 7% cum. preferred) in new corporation in proportion of 173 shares for every 100 held. Final meeting return regd. 24 Aug. 1938 .... **1932**

VOL. FOR

Alicante Waterworks Ld. Regd. 1883. Removed from Register 1901 1895

Alice Proprietary Mines (Rhodesia) Ld. Regd. 1899. Vol. liq. 2 Feb. 1910. Final meeting return regd. 13 Mar. 1916 1910

Alicia Gold Mine Ld. Regd. 1899. Removed from Register 1903 1903

Alicoombe Estates Ld. Regd. 1929. Receiver appointed 3 July 1940. Properties were sold and 5% 1st Mortgage debenture stock was repaid at par plus distribution in respect of interest at 5% p.a. for 5¾ years. Liquidator released 10 Dec. 1951. Struck off Register 9 Dec. 1960 1958

Aligarh Co. Ld. In liquidation. Direct controlling interest was held by West's Patent Press Co. Ld. 1939

All Blue Transport Ld. See Neath Omnibus Co. Ld.

All British Car Co. Ld. Regd. Edinburgh 1906. Vol liq. Nov. 1907. Court Orders: to continue winding up under supervision Dec. 1907: to dissolve 19 Oct. 1910 1908

All British Oil Co. Ld. Regd. 1921 as All British Oil Syndicate Ld.; name changed Sept. 1922. Struck off Register Feb. 1932 1932

All Nations Gold Mines Ld. Regd. 1896. Vol. liq. 14 Dec. 1897. Final meeting return regd. 25 May 1898 1898

All Red Route Investments Ld. See British & Allied Investments Corporation Ld.

All Saints' Brewery Co. Ld. Regd. 1896. Vol. liq, (members') 14 June 1954. Undertaking transferred to Ind Coope & Allsopp Ld. (later Ind Coupe Ld.) which company owned all capital. Final meeting return regd. 13 Oct. 1954 1955

All Seas Marine & Salvage Co. Ld. Regd. 1919. Vol. liq. 8 Mar. 1926. Final meeting return regd. 2 Aug. 1926 1927

Allagar Rubber Estates Ld. Regd. 1909. Vol. liq. 7 Nov. 1921. Reconstructed as Allagar Rubber Plantations Ld., in which company shareholders were entitled to 1 share of 2s. (credited with 1s. 3d. paid) for each share of 2s. held. Final meeting return regd. 22 July 1922 1922

Allagar Rubber Plantations Ld. Regd. 21 Nov. 1921. All capital owned or controlled by Warren Rubber Holdings Ld. Dissolved 15 Mar. 1981 1962

Allan Bros. & Co. (U. K.) Ld. Regd. 1898 as Allan Brothers & Co. Liverpool & London, Ld.; name changed Nov. 1909. Vol. liq. (members') 28 Feb. 1930. Capital returned to contributories—9 ll·695d. per share of £1 (10s. paid). Final meeting return regd. 26 Jan. 1931 .... *1917

Allan Brothers & Co. (Liverpool & London) Ld. See above.

Allan (J. & R.), Ld. Regd. Edinburgh 1897. Vol. liq. (members') 30 Jan. 1953. All ordinary capital was owned by House of Fraser Ld. to which company the undertaking and assets were transferred as distribution. £20 1s. 9d. was paid into Companies Liquidation Account in respect of unclaimed dividends and £17 3s. 10d. in respect of unclaimed distributions. Final meeting return regd. 15 Mar. 1965 1966

Allan Line Steamships Co. Ld. Regd. Edinburgh 1897. Vol. liq. (members') 28 Feb, 1930, Capital returned to contributories—£62 6s. 8·503d. per share of £10. Final meeting return regd. 28 Jan. 1931 1931

Allansons Stores, Ld. Regd. 1934. All ordinary capital was owned by James Beattie Ld. Vol. liq. (members') 9 Aug. 1965. Final meeting return regd. 14 Oct. 1965 1964

Allatini Mines Ld. Regd. 1927. Vol. liq. 18 July 1958. 7½% debentures repaid at par. Capital returned to contributories—9s. 8·1d. per preferred ordinary share of £1. £6,170 14s. 4d. was paid into Companies Liquidation Account. Final meeting return regd. 13 Sept. 1958 1961

Alldays & Onions Ld. Regd. 1889 as Alldays and Onions Pneumatic Engineering Co. Ld.; name changed Jan. 1919. Assets sold to New Alldays & Onions Ld.; proceeds were insufficient to make any return to shareholders. The Receiver stated that Court had funds in hand to pay 1st debentures in full. Struck off Register 1927 1926

Allegheny Valley Railway. Organised Pennsylvania 1892; undertaking acquired in 1910 by Pennsylvania Railroad Co 1934

Allen & Simmonds (Reading) Ld. Regd. 1920. Court Order to wind up 5 Feb. 1924. Struck off Register 1931 1925

Allen (David) & Sons (Holdings) Ld. Regd. 1897 as David Allen & Sons, Ld.; name changed in 1946. Vol. liq. (members') 1 July 1955. Final meeting return regd. 25 Feb. 1956 1946

Allen (David) & Sons. Ld. See above.

VOL. FOR

Allen (David) & Sons Theatres (1925) Ld. Regd. 1925. Vol. liq. (members') 31 Dec. 1956. Final meeting return regd. 9 Sept. 1957 1940

Allen (Frederick) & Sons Ld. Regd. 1901. Struck off Register 30 Nov. 1917 1906

Allen-Liversidge Ld. Regd. 1910 as Allen-Liversidge Portable Acetylene Co. Ld.; name changed Apr. 1917. Vol. liq. (members') 16 Oct. 1933. Undertaking and assets were acquired by British Oxygen Co. Ld. Final meeting return regd. 19 Dec. 1933 1934

Allen-Liversidge Portable Acetylene Co. Ld. See Allen-Liversidge Ld.

Allerton Estates (Ceylon) Ld. Regd. 1917. Vol. liq. 21 Nov. 1927. Final meeting return regd. 16 Apr. 1928 *1928

Allgemeine Depositen-Bank. Inc. Vienna 1871. The business was being carried on by a Receiver in 1925 1925

Allgemeine Verkehrsbank. In 1927 the Bank amalgamated with Allgemeine Osterreichische Boden-Credit-Anstalt, in which company shareholders were entitled to 1 share of 50 schillings for every 33 shares held 1928

Allgemeine Oesterreichische Boden-Credit-Anatalt Inc. Vienna 1863. In 1929 the assets and liabili ties were transferred to Oesterreichitche-Credit Anstalt für Handel und Gewerbe (later Creditanstalt Bankverein) in which company shareholders were entitled to 1 share of 40 schillings for every 4 shares of 50 schillings held 1930

Allhallows-On-Sea Estate Ld. Regd. 1930. Court order to wind up 16 Jan. 1939. liquidator released 20 Mar. 1953. Struck off Register 8 Sept. 1972 1954

Alliance Aluminium Co. Ld. Regd. 1888. Vol. liq. 7 Apr. 1892. Final meeting return regd. 27 June 1893 1893

Alliance Artificial Silk Ld. Regd. 1928. Court Order to wind up 8 Oct. 1934. Struck off Register 24 Aug. 1943 1944

Alliance Bank Ld. Regd. 1862. Vol. liq. 26 June 1871 for reconstruction as company of same name. Final meeting return regd. 11 Jan. 1878 1892

Alliance Bank Ld. Regd. 1871. Reconstructed 1892 as Parr's Banking Co. and the Alliance Bank Ld. (later Parr's Bank Ld.), in which company shareholders were entitled to 1 share of £100 (credited with £20 paid) plus £10 in cash for every 5 shares of £25 (£10 paid) held 1893

Alliance Bank of Simla Ld. Inc. British India 1874. Vol. liq. May 1923 1924

Alliance Cinemas Ld. Regd. 1936. Vol. liq. (creditors') 25 Apr. 1938. All shares held by Union Cinemas Ld. Final meeting return regd. 7 Aug. 1941 1939

Alliance Cold Storage Co. Ld. Regd. 1898 as Union Cold Storage Co. of Blackfriars Ld.; name changed 11 Mar. 1914. Vol. liq. (members') 10 Nov. 1938. Undertaking acquired by Union Cold Storage Co. Ld. Final meeting return regd. 18 Jan. 1939 1941

Alliance Consolidated Securities Ld. Regd. 1916 as Alliance Trading Co. Ld.; name changed 18 Sept. 1936. Final meeting return regd. 26 Mar. 1962 1947

Alliance Dairy Co. Ld. See W. & E. Long (Dairy Farmers) Ld.

Alliance Electrical Co. Ld. Regd. 1898. Removed from Register 1911 1911

Alliance Estates & Development Co. Ld. Regd. 1907. Vol. Liq. 4 May' 1922. Struck off Register 16 Feb. 1954 1955

Alliance Exploring & Finance Corporation Ld. Regd. 1896. Removed from Register 1905 1900

Alliance Film Corporation Ld. Regd. 1919. Vol. liq. 30 Dec. 1922. Final meeting return regd. 2 Sept. 1933 1923

Alliance Financial Corporation Ld. Regd. 1889. Court Order to wind up 3 Sept. 1895. Removed from Register 1906 1896

Alliance House and Property Trust Ld. Regd. 1902. Vol. liq. 8 June 1912. Final meeting return regd. 20 Apr. 1928 .... *1913

Alliance Land & Dwellings Co. Ld. Regd. 1884 as National Conservative Industrial Dwellings Association Ld.; name changed Mar. 1890. Removed from Register 1913 1911

Alliance Marine & General Assurance Co. Ld. Founded 1824. Regd. 1881 as Alliance Marine Assurance Co. Ld.; name changed Jan. 1892. Vol. liq. 7 Dec. 1905. Business was acquired by Alliance Assurance Co. Ld. Shareholders were entitled to either 5 fully-paid shares of £1 in new company or £65 in cash for each share of £100 (£25 paid) held. Final meeting return regd. 5 Oct. 1916 1906

Alliance Marine Assurance Co. Ld. See Alliance Marine & General Assurance Co. Ld.

Alliance Mining Corporation Ld. Regd. 1927 as Overseas Minerals & General Finance Co. Ld.; name changed 1934. Struck off Register 30 June 1959 ... 1938

Alliance Mortgage & Investment Co. Ld. Regd. 1890. Vol. liq. 15 Nov. 1921. All the capital was repaid

VOL. FOR

leaving a surplus to be distributed. Final meeting return regd. 16 Oct. 1925 .... **1922**

Alliance Motor Bus Co. Ld. Regd. 1906. Court Order to wind up 15 Oct. 1907. Removed from Register 1913 **1908**

Alliance Phosphate Co. Ld. Regd. 1878. Vol. liq. 23 Jan. 1895. Final meeting return regd. 17 Oct. 1895 ...... ***1882**

Alliance Trust & Investment Co. Ld. Regd. 1887. Struck off Register 31 Dec. 1895 .... **1899**

Alliance Vegetable Co. Ld. Regd. 1915. Vol. liq. 5 Nov. 1920. Final meeting return regd. 10 Mar. 1922..... **1921**

Allied British Airways Ld. *See* British Airways Ld.

Allied Cement Manufacturers Ld. Regd. 1911 as Stanlow Works Estate Ld.; name changed to Ship Canal Portland Cement Manufacturers Ld. in Sept. 1912 and as above in Aug. 1929. Court Order to wind up 7 Dec. 1931. Debenture stockholders were entitled to repayment at 103% No return to shareholders was anticipated. The works were sold to Associated Portland Cement Manufacturers Ld. Liquidator released 3 June 1935. Struck off Register 18 Feb. 1938 .... **1932**

Allied Colloids Ld. Regd. 1935 as Allied Colloids (Bradford) Ld.; name changed 31 Mar. 1960. Vol. liq. (members') 11 Mar. 1966. Shareholders (other than Badishe Anilin & Soda Fabric A.G.) were entitled to receive fully paid ordinary shares (of 2s.) of Allied Colloids Manufacturing Co. Ld. for every 2 ordinary shares (of 2s.) and cash distributions as follows—6s. per ordinary share held by public and 2s. 5·7218d. per B share (ordinary shares held by certain directors) £185 15s. paid into Companies Liquidation Account. Final meeting return regd. 17 June 1968 .... **1969**

Allied Finance & Insurance Services Ld. Regd. 11 Feb. 1964 as Allied Insurance Brokers ld.; name changed 16 Oct. 1969. Vol. liq. (creditors') 23 July 1975. Final meeting return regd. 23 Dec. 1985 .... **1986–7**

Allied Insurance brokers ld. *See* Allied Finance & Insurance Services Ld.

Allied Investors' Corporation Ld. Regd. 1909. Removed from Register 1913 .... **1912**

Allied Produce Co., Ld. Regd. 1920 as Harris (Calne) and the General Produce Co. Ld.; name changed Oct. 1922. Winding-up Order 24 July 1967. Struck off Register 22 Oct. 1971 .... **1965**

Allied Properties Co. Ld. Business was acquired in 1925 by London County Freehold and Leasehold Properties Ld **1935**

Allied Road Transports Ld. Regd. 1919. Vol. liq. 13 June 1921. Final meeting return regd. 24 June 1922 ..... **1922**

Allied Road Transports (Southern) Ld. Regd. 1919 as London & Midland Transport Co. Ld.; name changed June 1920. 95% of share capital was owned by Allied Road Transports Ld. Vol. liq. 6 July 1921. Final meeting return regd. 28 June 1922. Court Order declaring dissolution void Dec. 1922. Final meeting return regd. 20 July 1923 .... **1921**

Allied Securities Ld. Regd. 1935. Vol. liq. (member's) 15 Sept. 1966. Capital returned to contributories—11s. 8·04d. per ordinary share of 5s. Final meeting return regd. 31 Jan. 1970 .... **1970**

Allied Steam Navigation Co. Ld. Regd. 1920. Vol. liq. 10 Aug. 1923. Final meeting return regd. 18 Oct.1923 ***1924**

Allied Suppliers (Holdings) Ld.*See* Cavenham Ld.

Allied Traders' Insurance Co. Ld. Regd. 1920. Vol. liq. 3 Sept. 1925. Undertaking and assets were acquired by Eagle Star & British Dominions Insurance Co. Ld. (later Eagle Star Insurance Co. Ld.) Final meeting return regd. 3 Oct. 1929 .... **1926**

Alliston & Co. Ld. Regd. 1904. Vol. liq. Nov. 1927. Undertaking was acquired by Pawsons and Leafs Ld. Struck off Register Dec. 1932 .... **1933**

Alloa Railway Co. Inc. by Special Act 1879. Under Caledonian Railway Co. (No. 1) Act 1884 the line was merged into that company **1885**

Allsopp (Samuel) & Sons Ld. Regd. 1887. Vol. liq. (members') 29 July 1935. Undertaking was acquired by Ind Coupe & Allsopp Ld. [later Ind Coupe Ld.] which company owned all shares acquired by offer of 5 fully-paid ordinary shares of £1 for every 8 ordinary shares of £1 held or 110 fully-paid 6½% preference shares of £1 for every £100 preference stock held. Final meeting return regd. 22 Aug. 1939 **1936**

Allsop's Birmingham General Omnibus Co. Ld. Regd. 1878. Vol. liq. Jan. 1886. Capital returned to contributories—£9 3s. 5d. per share of £10, fully paid; £5 3s. 5d. per share of £10 (£6 paid). Final meeting return regd. 19 May 1888 .... **1887**

Alluta Rubber & Produce Co. Ld. Regd. 1910. Vol. liq. (members') 4 Aug. 1936. The assets were sold to Kepitigalla Rubber Estates Ld., in which company shareholders were entitled to 4 shares of 2s. (credited as fully paid) for each share of £1 held. £22 1s. 3d.

VOL. FOR

was paid into Companies' Liquidation Account. Final meeting return regd. 19 May 1938 .... **1937**

Alluvial & General Mining Co. Ld. Undertaking was acquired in 1929 by Viborita Gold Mines Ld. **1945**

Alluvial Diamonds (Gold Coast) Ld. Regd. 1927. Vol. liq. (creditors') 16 Dec. 1931. No capital returned to contributories. Final meeting return regd. 12 Mar. 1932 .... **1932**

Alluvial Tin Co. (Nigeria) Ld. Regd. 1911. Vol. liq. June 1913. Struck off Register Apr. 1929 .... **1930**

Alluvial Tin Fields of Africa Ld. Regd 1912. Vol. liq. 11 Nov. 1920. Final meeting return regd. 25 May 1921 **1922**

Almada & Tirito Co. Ld. Regd. 1897. Vol. liq. 8 July 1898. Final meeting return regd. 20 Apr. 1899...... **1899**

Almagam Ld. Regd. 1910. Vol. liq. 26 Jan. 1915 Struck off Register 4 May 1948 .... **1949**

Almagro Gold Syndicate Ld. Regd. 1902. Vol. liq. 1 June 1905. Removed from Register 1907 .... **1906**

Almaraz Tin Mining & Smelting Co. Ld. Regd. 1896. Removed from Register 1908 .... **1900**

Almeida Accumulators Ld. Regd. 1927. Receiver appointed 8 Feb. 1933; ceased to act 30 July 1934: assets realised insufficient to cover receivership expenses. Struck off Register 2 July 1935............... **1936**

Almeria & Alhamilla Railway Co. Ld. Regd. 1891. Removed from Register 1897 .... **1901**

Almeria Mines Ld. Regd. 1896. Vol. liq. 12 July 1916. Final meeting return regd. 26 Mar. 1917 .... **1917**

Alnery No. 152 p.l.c. *See* Porvair p.l.c.

Alnwick Gas Co. Inc. by Special Act 1881. All shares were acquired in 1945 by exchange of stock of Newcastle-upon-Tyne & Gateshead Gas Co **1911**

Alor Pongsu Amalgamated Estates Ld. Regd. 1931. Vol. liq. (members') 1 June 1962. Capital returned to contributories—4s. 8¼d. per 2s. stock. £1,891 16s. 2d. was paid into Companies Liquidation Account in respect of unclaimed distributions. Final meeting return regd. 27 Oct. 1965............... **1967**

Alor Pongsu Rubber Estate Ld. Regd. 1909. Vol. liq. (members') 16 Dec. 1931. Undertaking and assets were acquired by Alor Pongsu Amalgamated Estates Ld. in which company shareholders were entitled to 10 shares of 2s. (credited as fully paid) for each share of £1 held, £22 19s. 11d. was paid into Companies' Liquidation Account. Final meeting return regd. 1 Dec. 1932 .... **1932**

Alperton Rubber Co. Ld. Regd. 1910 as Crude Rubber Washing Co. Ld.; name changed Dec. 1914. Court Order to wind up Mar. 1916. Struck off Register 1925 .... **1916**

"Alpha" Air Horse Collar & Saddlery Co. Ld. Regd. 1889. Removed from Register 1907 .... **1892**

Alpha Cement Co. Ld. *See* Rodmell Works Ld.

Alpha Petroleun Co. Ld. Regd. 1911. Vol. liq. 25 Nov. 1912. Part of the assets were acquired by Premier Oil and Pipe Line Co. Ld. Final meeting return regd. 12 July 1928 .... **1913**

Alpha (Rand) Gold Mines Ld. Regd. 1895. Removed from Register 1906 .... **1899**

Alpha (Rand) Syndicate Ld. Regd. 1895. Removed from Register 8 Aug. 1905 .... ***1904**

Alpha (Westralia) Syndicate Ld. Regd. 1895. Removed from Register 8 Aug. 1905 .... ***1904**

Alsing & Co. Ld. Regd. 1887. Vol. liq. 20 Aug. 1914. Final meeting return regd. 11 Oct. 1930 .... **1915**

Alsop Flour Process (1906) Ld. Regd. 1906. Vol. liq. 30 Dec. 1910. Final meeting return regd. 20 April 1911 ***1912**

Alston, Arhuthnot & Harrisons Ld. Regd. 1919. Vol. liq. 28 Mar. 1924. Final meeting return regd. 29 Jan. 1925 .... ***1925**

Alston Gas Co. Ld. Regd. 1911. Dissolved 1 May 1949, undertaking being vested in Northern Area Gas Board under Gas Act 1948. Holders of securities were entitled to receive British Gas 3% guaranteed stock 1990–95 as follows:

	£	s.	d.
Ord. shares (of £1)	10	0	0
5% pref. shares (of £5)	3	0	0

1952

Alston Moor Mining Co. Ld. Regd. 1873. Vol. liq. 18 Nov. 1887. Final meeting return regd. 24 June 1892 **1888**

Altai Gold Concessions Ld. Regd. 1908. Court Order to wind up Apr. 1910. Struck off Register 1916 .... **1911**

Altifund p.l.c. Regd. as private company 2 Mar. 1966; converted public company 7 Mar. 1966. Vol. liq. (members') 12 Dec. 1986. Return of final meeting regd. 7 Dec. 1987. First and final distribution of 7·1p per share made 27 Aug. 1987. Amount paid into Companies' Liquidation Account in respect of (a) unclaimed dividends £2,167·71, (b) distributions £4,875 .... **1988–9**

Alton & Co. Ld. Regd. 1888. Vol. liq. 21 July 1899 for reconstruction as company of same name [later Ind Coope (North West) Ld.]. Final meeting return regd. 27 Dec. 1899 .... **1899**

See Stock Exchange Year-Book.

VOL. FOR

Alton & District Gas Co. Ld. Inc. by deed 1847 as Alton Gas & Coke Co. Undertaking was acquired from 31 Dec. 1928 by Farnham Gas & Electricity Co. **1909**

Alton Battery Co. Ld. *See* Porvair p.l.c.

Alton Court Brewery Co. Ld. Regd. 1865. All capital was owned by Stroud Brewery Co. Ld. Vol. liq. (members') 1 May 1961. Final meeting return regd. 7 Jan. 1964 .... **1957**

Alton District Electricity Co. Ld. Regd. 1926. Dissolved 1 Apr. 1948. undertaking being vested in the British (later Central) Electricity Authority and Southern Area Board under the Electricity Act 1947. Ordinary shareholders were entitled to receive £2 10*s.* British Electricity 3% guaranteed stock (1968–73) for each share (of £1) held **1949**

Alton Gas & Coke Co. *See* Alton & District Gas Co. Ld.

Altrincham Electric Supply, Ld. Regd. 1894. Dissolved 1 Apr. 1948, undertaking being vested in British (later Central) Electricity Authority and North Western Area Board under the Electricity' Act 1947. Holders of securities were entitled to receive British Electricity 3% guaranteed stock (1968–73) as follows in respect of each £1 unit of capital held:

	£	s.	d.
6% 1st preference shares	1	10	0
7% 2nd preference shares	1	13	0
Participating ordinary shares	2	1	0
Deferred shares	3	10	0

1949

Altrincham Gas Co. Inc. by Special Act 1872. Dissolved 1 May 1949, undertaking being vested in North Western Area Gas Board under Gas Act 1948. Holders of securities were entitled to receive British Gas 3% guaranteed stock 1990–95 as follows in respect of each £10 unit of security held:

	£	s.	d.
Orig. shares (9¼% max.)	18	10	0
New ord. shares (7% max.)	14	8	0
4% red. pref. shares	10	2	9

Liability in respect of certain mortgage loans assumed by the Board **1952**

Alturas Gold Ld. Regd. 1886. Vol. liq. 19 Feb. 1889. Reconstructed as Elmore Gold Co. Ld., in which company shareholders were entitled to 1 share of £1 (credited with 17*s.* paid) for each share of £1 held. Final meeting return regd. 19 Mar. 1895 .... **1891**

Aluminium Co. Ld. Regd. 1887. Vol. liq. 23 Aug. 1900. Undertaking and certain assets were acquired by Castner-Kellner Alkali Co. Ld., in which company shareholders were entitled to 3 shares of £1 (credited as fully paid) for each share of £1 held. Debenture stockholders were entitled to an equal amount of 4½% debenture stock of acquiring company. Removed from Register 1901 .... **1901**

Aluminium Corporation Ld. Regd. 1907. Vol. liq. Dec. 1908 for reconstruction under same name. Shareholders were entitled to 1 ordinary share of £1 (credited with 14*s.* 6*d.* paid) in new company for each 2 ordinary shares of £1 held; holders of each preference share of £1 with £1, 15*s.* or 10*s.* paid were entitled to 1 ordinary share of £1 (credited with 14*s.* 6*d.*, 9*s.* 6*d.* or 4*s.* 6*d.* respectively paid). Removed from Register 1912 .... **1910**

Alves Braga Rubber Estates & Trading Co. Ld. Regd. 1909. Struck off Register 1923 .... ***1912**

Alves Fuel Economisation Syndicate Ld. *See* British Fuel Economiser & Smoke Preventer Ld.

Alyth Gas Light Co. Ld. Regd. in Edinburgh 1937. Dissolved 1 May 1949, undertaking being vested in Scottish Area Gas Board under Gas Act 1948. Holders of ordinary shares (of £5) were entitled to receive £6 British Gas 3% guaranteed stock 1990–95 for each share held **1952**

Amac Ld. Regd. 1903 as Aston Motor Accessories Co. Ld.; name changed Aug. 1918. Vol. liq. 1 Nov. 1928. All capital acquired by Amal Ld. Final meeting return regd. 3 Aug. 1929 .... **1936**

Amador Gold Mine Ld. Regd. 1889, Vol. liq. 19 Apr. 1893. Undertaking acquired by Jackson Goldfields Ld. Removed from Register 21 June 1907 .... ***1894**

Amalgamated Asbestos Corporation Ld. Inc. Canada 1909. In 1912 the Trustee for the Bondholders sold the assets to Asbestos Corporation of Canada Ld. Bondholders were entitled to $250 5% bonds, $500 preferred stock and $250 common stock in new company for each $1,000 bond held **1913**

Amalgamated Bruas Rubber Estates Ld. Regd. 1937. Vol. liq. (members') 20 Jan. 1961. Capital returned to contributories—14*s.* 3¼*d.* per 2*s.* stock. Paid into Companies' Liquidation Account £42 5*s.* 6*d.* in respect of unclaimed dividends and £499 17*s.* 2*d.* in respect of unclaimed distributions. Final meeting return regd. 18 Nov. 1964 .... **1966**

VOL. FOR

Amalgamated Cinematograph Theatres Ld. Regd. 1910. Vol. liq. 23 Mar. 1921. Final meeting return regd. 9 Oct. 1922 .... **1922**

Amalgamated Copper Co. Inc. New Jersey 1899. In June 1915 steps were taken to dissolve company and the assets, 3,327,937 shares of $25 of Anaconda Copper Mining Co. (later Anaconda Co.) were distributed **1916**

Amalgamated Dairies Co. Ld. Regd. 1889. Vol. liq. 30 Mar. 1894. Final meeting return regd. 19 Oct. 1894. **1895**

Amalgamated Denaby Collieries Ld. Regd. 1936. Vol. liq. (members') 29 Apr. 1953. Final meeting return regd. 2 Feb. 1956. Dissolution declared void 28 Apr. 1958 and company restored to Register. Final meeting return regd. 31 May 1961. .... **1962**

Amalgamated Dinas Silica Works Ld. Regd. 1921. Receiver appointed May 1927. Struck off Register 16 Jan. 1936 .... **1936**

Amalgamated Finance Co. Ld. Regd. 1924 as Amalgamated (Rubber) Finance Co. Ld.; name changed Nov. 1927. Vol. liq. 7 Oct. 1929 for reconstruction as Amalgamated Finance Co. (1929) Ld., in which company shareholders were to receive 1 fully-paid share of 1*s.* for every share of 2*s.* held. Final meeting return regd. 7 Mar. 1930 .... **1930**

Amalgamated Finance Co. Ld. Regd. 1931. Vol. liq. (members') 23 July 1937. Capital returned to contributories—8$\frac{7}{20}$*d.* per share of 4*d.* £130 3*s.* 4*d.* was paid to Companies' Liquidation Account in respect of unclaimed dividends. Final meeting return regd. 30 Nov. 1937 .... **1938**

Amalgamated Finance Co. (1929) Ld. Regd. 1929. Vol. liq. (members') 22 May 1931 for reconstruction as Amalgamated Finance Co. Ld. Share holders were entitled to apply for 1 share of 1*s.* (credited with 6*d.* per share paid) in the company for every share held. Final meeting return regd. 30 Mar. 1932 .... **1932**

Amalgamated Fixed Trust Ld. Regd. 1934. Vol. liq. (members') 15 May 1941. Capital returned to contributories—18*s.* 4¾*d.* per share. Final meeting return regd. 13 May 1943 .... **1942**

Amalgamated Fruiterers Ld. Regd. 1928. Vol. liq. 26 Oct. 1939. No capital returned to contributories. Final meeting return regd. 6 Dec.1948 .... **1949**

Amalgamated Glass Bottle Works Ld. Regd. 1920. Vol. liq. 10 Mar. 1922. Final meeting return regd. 27 June 1924 .... **1923**

Amalgamated Gold Mines Ld. Regd. 1900. Vol. liq. 1903. Assets acquired by Field's Reward Gold Mines Ld., in which company shareholders were entitled to 4 shares of 10*s.* (credited with 8*s.* paid) for every 5 shares of 10*s.* held. Removed from Register 1904 .... **1904**

Amalgamated Gowns Ld. Regd. 1937. A winding-up order was made on 18 Nov. 1940. In Nov. 1945 the liquidator stated, 'The claim of the debenture holder has not been discharged in full and there is no prospect of any payments either to creditors or contributories". Struck off register 7 Oct. 1949. ... **1950**

Amalgamated Industrials Ld. Regd. 1919 Struck off Register Feb. 1934 .... **1934**

Amalgamated Investment & Financial Trust Ld. Regd. 1909 as Mercantile & General Trust Ld.; name changed Apr. 1909. Struck off Register 1916 .... **1912**

Amalgamated Investments Ld, Regd. 1922. Vol. liq. (members') 23 July 1935. All shares owned by London Freehold & Leasehold Property Co. Ld. Final meeting return regd. 9 Sept. 1936 .... **1936**

Amalgamated Land & Mortgage Companies of Winnipeg Ld. Inc. Manitoba 1912. In Nov. 1926 it was stated that company had been declared wound up by Courts of Manitoba **1927**

Amalgamated London Properties Ld. Regd. 1931 as C.M.L. Properties Ld.; name changed Aug. 1931. Vol. liq. (members') 13 Dec. 1938. Capital distributions were made in cash and specie. Final meeting return regd. 15 Aug. 1942 .... **1939**

Amalgamated Mining & Exploration Co. Ld. Regd. 1904. Vol. liq. 18 Dec. 1906. Removed from Register 1909 .... **1907**

Amalgamated Mining Trust Ld. Regd. 1898 as Gold Coast Amalgamated Mines Ld.; name changed Mar. 1927. Vol. liq. (members') 11 June 1930. Undertaking and assets acquired by Consolidated Gold Fields of South Africa Ld., (later Consolidated Gold Fields Ld.) in which company shareholders were to receive 3 fully-paid ordinary shares of £1 for every 5 shares of £1 held. Final meeting return regd. 27 June 1931 .... **1931**

Amalgamated Motor Bus Co. Ld. Regd. 1906. Vol. liq. 31 Mar. 1910. Final meeting return regd. 30 Sept. 1910 .... ***1911**

Amalgamated Oil Fields (Maikop) Ld. Regd. 1911. Vol. liq. 26 Nov. 1914. Final meeting return regd. 30 Dec. 1916 .... **1915**

**See Stock Exchange Year-Book.*

VOL. FOR

Amalgamated Oil lands of Ruumania Ld. Regd. 1922. Vol. liq. (creditors') 18 Nov. 1935. No capital returned to contributories. Final meeting return regd. 19 June 1940 .... **1936**

Amalgamated Oil Pipe-Lines of Galicia Ld. Regd. 1911. Vol. liq. 16 Oct. 1912. Undertaking was acquired by Premier Oil and Pipe line Co. Ld., for £546,875 in £100,000 fully-paid preference shares and £446,875 fully-paid ordinary shares. Final meeting return regd. 29 Oct. 1914 .... **1913**

Amalgamated Oxides Ld. Regd. 1935. Vol. liq. (creditors') 2 Mar. 1939. No capital returned to contributories. Final meeting return regd. 10 Apr. 1940 ... **1940**

Amalgamated Pictorials Ld. Regd. 1910. Vol. liq. Jan. 1911. Part of the business was sold to John Bull Ld., for 320,000 shares of 2s. 6d. (credited with 1s. 3d. paid). Removed from Register 1913 .... **1911**

Amalgamated Pneumatic Tyre Cos. Ld. Regd. 1897. Reconstructed 1900 as New Amalgamated Tyre Co. Ld., in which company shareholders were entitled to 4 shares of 2s. 6d. (credited with 2s. paid) for every 10 shares of £1 held. Debenture stockholders were entitled to 50% of holding in debentures in new company *plus* 120 fully-paid shares of 2s. 6d. for every £100 stock held. Removed from Register 1902 **1904**

Amalgamated Press Ld. Regd. 1896 as Harmsworth Brothers Ld.; name changed Dec. 1901. Vol. liq. 26 June 1922 for reconstruction as Amalgamated Press (1922) Ld. Holders of preference shares received 1 fully-paid preference share of £1 in new company for each share held; holders of ordinary shares received 4 fully-paid ordinary shares of new company, 1 5% preference share of 10s. in Imperial Paper Mills Ld., 3 8% preference shares of $1 in Anglo-Newfoundland Development Co. Ld. and 2s. in cash for each share of £1 held. Final meeting return regd. 24 Mar. 1923 .... **1923**

Amalgamated Press (1922) Ld. Regd. 1922. Vol. liq. 21 Feb. 1927. Undertaking and assets were acquired by Amalgamated Press Ld. (later Fleetway Publications Ld.) Shareholders were entitled to £1 in debenture stock and £2 6s. 8·771d. per ordinary share of £1 held or £1 4s. in cash per preference share of £1 held. Final meeting return regd. 4 Nov. 1927 **1928**

Amalgamated Properties of Rhodesia Ld. Regd. 1909. Vol. liq. 29 July 1913 for reconstruction as Amalgamated Properties of Rhodesia (1913) Ld. Shareholders were entitled to 1 new share of 4s. (credited with 3s. paid) in new company for each share of 5s. held. Final meeting return regd. 22 Feb. 1918 .... **1914**

Amalgamated Properties of Rhodesia (1913) Ld. Regd. 1913. Vol. liq. 9 July 1917 for reconstruction as Rhodesia Exploration Co. Ld., in which company shareholders were to receive 1 share of 3s. (credited with 2s. paid) for each share of 4s. held. Final meeting return regd. 15 July 1919 .... **1918**

Amalgamated Rubber & General Estates Ld. Regd. 1919 as Amalgamated Rubber Estates Ld.; name changed June 1926. Vol. liq. 6 Jan. 1928. Undertaking and assets were acquired by United Serdang (Sumatra) Rubber Plantations Ld. in which company shareholders were entitled to 1 share of 2s. (credited as fully paid) for every 2 shares of 2s. held. Debenture stockholders were entitled to either repayment at 21s. or 4 fully-paid shares in acquiring company per £1 stock held. Final meeting return regd. 9 Oct. 1930 .... **1928**

Amalgamated Rubber and Industrial Products Ld. *See* Amalgamated Transport Services Ld.

Amalgamated (Rubber) Development Co. Ld. Regd. 1923. Vol. liq. 6 Jan. 1928. Undertaking and assets were acquired by United Serdang (Sumatra) Rubber Plantations Ld., in which company shareholders were entitled to 1 share of 2s. (credited as fully paid) for every 2 shares of 2s. held. Final meeting return regd. 7 Dec. 1928 .... **1928**

Amalgamated Rubber Estates Ld, *See* Amalgamated Rubber & General Estates Ld.

Amalgamated (Rubber) Finance Co. Ld. See Amalgamated Finance Co. Ld.

Amalgamated Slate Association Ld. Regd. 1918. Vol. liq. (creditors') 9 Jan. 1931. 2nd debenture holders were repaid £4,664 12s. 10d. No capital returned to contributories. Final meeting return regd. 12 Dec. 1933 .... **1931**

Amalgamated Smelters Ld. Regd. 1923. Vol. liq. 27 Mar. 1927. Final meeting return regd. 1 Nov. 1927....... **1928**

Amalgamated Tin Properties of Nigeria Ld. Regd. 1912. Struck off Register 1924 .... **1922**

Amalgamated Tyre & Rubber Co. Ld. Regd. 1923. Vol. liq. (members') 16 Nov. 1932. Direct controlling interest was held by North British Rubber Co. Ld. [later Uniroyal Ld.]. Final meeting return regd. 5 May 1933 .... **1933**

VOL. FOR

Amalgamated Trade Publications Ld. Regd. 1919. Vol. liq. Dec. 1926. Capital returned to contributories— £3 10s. per share of £1 at Jan. 1927; further payments (if any) not known. Final meeting return regd. 3 Aug. 1927 .... **1927**

Amalgamated Transport Services Ld. Regd. 3 Nov. 1909 as Java Amalgamated Rubber Estates Ld.; name changed 7 Feb. 1958 to Amalgamated Rubber and Industrial Products ld. and to present title on 26 Nov. 1969. Vol. liq. (creditors') on 3 Nov. 1971. Final meeting held 5 Nov. 1984 .... **1985–6**

Amalgamated Wallpaper Mills Ld. Regd. 1928. Court Order to wind up Feb. 1932. Struck off Register 1943 .... **1933**

Amalgamated Water-Gas Co. Ld. Regd. 1893. Vol. liq. 31 Jan. 1898. Removed from Register 1902 .... **1898**

Amalgamated Zinc (De Bavay's) Ld. Inc. Victoria 1909. Vol. liq. 5 July 1938. Shareholders were entitled to 2½ fully-paid shares of 4s. in Zinc Investments Ld. and 1s. 2⅝d. in cash for each share of 8s. held **1940**

Amana (Wentworth) Gold Mining Co. Ld. Regd. 1892. Struck off Register 14 May 1897 and restored 31 July 1897. Vol. liq. 29 Feb. 1904. Final meeting return regd. 2 Oct. 1909 .... **1905**

Amari (Nigeria) Tin Mines Ld. Regd. 1924. Vol. liq. (members') 22 Dec. 1930. Reconstructed as Amari (Nigeria) Tin Mines (1931) Ld. [later Amari Ld.], in which company shareholders were entitled to 1 share of 2s. (credited with 1s. 8½d. paid) for each share of 2s. held. Final meeting return regd. 27 May 1933 .... **1931**

Amarilla Gold Mines Ld. Regd. 17 Nov. 1932. Vol. liq. (creditors') 18 July 1938 .... **1983–4**

Amatongaland Exploration Co. Ld. Regd. 1889. Vol. liq. 18 Jan. 1905. Removed from Register 1909 .... **1905**

Amatongaland Rubber Corporation Ld. Regd. 1910. Vol. liq. 25 Apr. 1916. Final meeting return regd. 7 Nov. 1916 .... **1916**

Amazon River Steam Navigation Co. (1911) Ld. Regd. 1911. Struck off Register 1941 .... **1937**

Amazon Steam Navigation Co. Ld. Regd. 1872. Vol. liq. 4 May 1911. Final meeting return regd. 27 Nov. 1924 .... **1911**

Amazon Telegraph Co. Ld. Regd. 1895. Vol. liq. (members') 19 Sept. 1945. Capital returned to contributories—£2 13s. 7½d. per share of £10. £91 12s. was paid into Companies' Liquidation Account. Final meeting return regd. 22 Dec. 1949 .... **1951**

Amazonas Rubber Estates Ld. Regd. 1898. Struck off Register 2 Aug. 1904 .... **1905**

Amazonia Rubber & Trading Co. Ld. Regd. 1899. Removed from Register 1909 .... **1904**

Ambassador Super Cinema Ld. Regd. 1927. Vol. liq. (members') 28 June 1965. Final meeting return regd. 18 Mar. 1966 .... **1947**

Ambergate, Nottingham, Boston and Eastern Junction Railway. *See* Nottingham and Grantham Railway and Canal Co.

Amble & Warkworth Gas Light & Coke Co. Ld. Regd. 1865. Dissolved 1 May 1949, undertaking being vested in Northern Area Gas Board under Gas Act 1948. Holders of securities were entitled to receive British Gas 3% guaranteed stock 1990–95 as follows:

	£	s.	d.
Ordinary shares of £5	2	0	0
4½%. Mort. Deb. loan (£100)	100	10	0	**1952**

Amble Ferro-Concrete Co. Ld. See Amble Shipbuilding Co. Ld.

Amble Shipbuilding Co. Ld. Regd. 1918 as Amble Ferro-Concrete Co. Ld.; name changed Sept. 1920. Vol. liq. (creditors') 3 Apr. 1935. Assets realised insufficient to pay creditors in full. Final meeting return regd. 11 Oct. 1935 .... **1936**

Amdic Hardware Supplies Ld. Regd. 1922. Struck off Register 1930 .... **1929**

Amelia Nitrate Co. Ld. Regd. 1896. Vol. liq. 17 Apr. 1925. Undertaking and assets sold to Aguas Blancas Nitrate Co. Ld. After repayment of preference capital, ordinary shareholders received 35s. per share at Nov. 1925; further payments (if any) not known. Final meeting return regd. 5 Dec. 1929 ... **1926**

American Association Ld. Regd. 1961. All capital owned by J. M. Huber Corpn. Outstanding 5% debentures redeemed at par on 5 Apr. 1979. Dissolved 6 jan. 1981 .... **1979–80**

American & British Securities Co. Ld. Regd. 1900. Vol. liq. 29 Apr. 1910. Capital returned to contributories—£3 10s. per share of £10; further payments (if any) not known. Final meeting return regd. 13 Feb. 1919 .... **1911**

See Stock Exchange Year-Book.

VOL. FOR

American & Continental "Sanitas" Co. Ld. Regd. 1886. Vol. liq. 20 Aug. 1897. Final meeting return regd. 19 May 1898 .... **1898**

American & Dominions Unbreakable Records Ld. Regd. 1928. Struck off Register 29 Oct. 1935 .... **1936**

American and General Mortgage and Investment Corporation Ld. Regd. 1889. Reconstructed 1905 as American English and General Trust Ld., in which company shareholders were entitled to 10 shares of £1 for each preferred share of £10 held or 2½ shares of £1 for each special share of 1s. held. The deferred shareholders received nothing. Removed from register 1907 .... **1908**

American Association Inc. Inc. Kentucky 1895. In 1962 the undertaking and assets were sold to American Association Ld. for 158,475 fully-paid shares of £1 of that company which were distributed (share for share) to shareholders, and this company was subsequently dissolved. American Association Ld. also assumed liability of the B income debentures **1964**

American Association Ld. Regd. 1887. Vol. liq. 27 Oct. 1893. Reconstructed as company of same name. Debenture holders were entitled to an equal amount of B debentures and 35% of holding in common stock in new company. Shareholders subscribing for A debentures received a bonus of 100% in common stock. Final meeting return regd. 6 May 1897 ..... **1896**

American Austin Car Co. Inc. Inc. Delaware 1929 as Austin Car Co. of America Inc.; name changed May 1929. Company was liquidated **1936**

American Automatic Weighing Machine Co. Ld. Regd. 1899. Vol. liq. 1903. Undertaking and assets were acquired by National Automatic Weighing Machine Co. of New York, in which company shareholders were entitled to an equal number of shares of same class. Removed from Register 1904 **1904**

American Belle Mines Ld. Regd. 1890. Removed from Register 1902 .... **1899**

American Bemberg Corpn. Inc. in Delaware 1925. In 1949 stockholders approved the merger with the parent company (Beaunit Mills Inc.) and the dissolution of the corporation. Holders of both classes of preferred stock were repaid at $110 per share. Common stockholders were entitled to receive one share (of no par value) of $1·25 cumulative convertible preferred stock of Beaunit Mills Inc. for each common share of the corporation held **1950**

American Breweries & General Securities Trust Ld. Regd. 1889. Vol. liq. 7 May 1897. Capital returned to contributories—£6 per founders share of £10; holders of preferred and deferred stock received 32½% of holding in May 1897 and a further 32½% was anticipated. Removed from Register 1901 .... **1898**

American, British & Continental Corporation. Inc. Delaware 1926. Amalgamated with Equity Corporation in Sept. 1935, in which company holders of 1st preferred shares received ⁷⁄₁₀ths of a share of $3 preferred stock and 3 shares of common stock for each preferred share held; holders of common shares received ¼ share of common stock for each common share held. Liability in respect of 5% gold debentures were assumed by Equity Corpn. **1936**

American, Canadian & General Investment Trust Ld. Regd. 1931 as Coleridge Financial Trust Ld.; name changed 1954. Vol. liq. (members') 11 June 1964. All capital was acquired by Tor Investment Trust Ld. Ordinary stock holders receiving either 15s. ordinary stock in that company or 43s. cash for each £1 stock held and debenture holders receiving like amounts of identical stocks. Final meeting return registered 6 June 1968 .... **1970**

American Chemical & Metallurgical Corporation Ld. Regd. 1920. Struck off Register Feb. 1933 .... **1933**

American Cotton Oil Co. Inc. New Jersey 1889. In Sep. 1923 a plan was submitted for the exchange of the stock of this company for stock (of no par value) of the Gold Dust Corporation **1924**

American Deposit & Loan Co. See Equitable Trust Co. of New York.

American "E. C." & Schultze Gunpowder Co. Ld. Regd. 1897. Vol. liq. Feb. 1911. Removed from Register 1912 .... **1911**

American "E. C." Powder Co. Ld. Regd. 1890 as Anglo American "E. C." Powder Co. Ld.; name changed Jan. 1893. Vol. liq. 5 Mar. 1897. Final meeting return regd. 4 Mar. 1898 .... **1897**

American, English & General Trust Ld. Regd. 1905. Vol. liq. Mar. 1910. Undertaking and assets sold to Mercantile Investment and General Trust Co. Ld. [later Mercantile Investment Trust Ld.] in which company holders of every £100 stock received 100 shares of £1 (converted into £50 preferred and £50 deferred stock). Removed from Register 1911 ..... **1911**

VOL. FOR

American, English, Scottish & Irish Trust Ld. Regd. 1891. Court Order to wind up 15 May 1895. Removed from Register 1907 .... **1896**

American Exchange in Europe Ld. Regd. 1880. Court Orders; to wind up 9 June 1888; to dissolve 10 Nov. 1893 .... ***1889**

American Exploration & Development Corporation Ld. Regd. 1890. Removed from Register 1911 .... **1899**

American Express Bank & Trust Co. Undertaking was acquired in 1931 by Chase National Bank of The City of New York (later The Chase Manhattan Bank) **1942**

American Fisheries Co. Inc. New Jersey 1898. Reorganised 1900 as Fisheries Co. of New Jersey, in which company ordinary shareholders were entitled to 1 common share of $100 (credited with $95 paid) for every 160 shares of $5 held. Preference shareholders were entitled, on subscribing for $25 bonds, to 1 fully-paid preference share of $100 for every 20 preference shares of $5 held **1915**

American Fisheries Co. Ld. Regd. 1898. Reconstructed 1900 as Fisheries Co. of New Jersey, U. S. A., in which company shareholders were entitled to 1 common share of $100 (credited with $95 paid) for every 160 ordinary shares of $5 held. Preference shareholders were entitled to 1 fully-paid preference share of $100 for every 20 preference shares of $5 held after subscribing for $25 bonds. Struck off Register 1902 .... **1903**

American-Foreign Oil Corporation. Inc. Virginia 1920. It is understood that the charter was forfeited in 1933 .... **1939**

American Founders Corporation. Inc. Maryland 1928. Merged with a new company (American General Corporation) in Oct. 1935, in which company holders of 1st preferred stock (series A and B) were entitled to 1⅕th shares of preferred stock ($2 dividend series) and ⅕th common share for every share of $50 held; holders of 1st preferred stock (series D) were entitled to 1⅕th shares of preferred stock ($2 dividend series) for every share of $50 held; holders of common stock were entitled to ₇⁄₂₅ths of a share of common stock for each share of $1 held **1936**

American Freehold-Land Mortgage Co. of London Ld. Regd. 1879. Vol. liq. 8 Feb. 1921. After repaying the debenture debt and preference shares, the ordinary shareholders received £3 17s. 3d. per share of £5 (£1 paid); further payments (if any) not known. Final meeting return regd. 14 Feb. 1922 .... **1922**

American Investment and General Trust Co. Regd. 1879 as American Investment Trust Co. Ld.; name changed Apr. 1919. In 1959, securities of the company were exchanged for those of Foreign & Colonial Investment Trust Co. Ld. on the basis of £104 ordinary per £100 deferred; £110 preference per £100 preferred; and £1 4½% debenture stock 1982–7 per £1 4% or 4½% debenture stock held. The company was dissolved 23 May 1960 .... **1961**

American Investment Co. Inc. Iowa 1885. A receiver was appointed in June 1894 .... **1897**

American Investment Trust Co. Ld. See American Investment & General Trust Co. Ld.

American Land and Colonization Co. of Scotland. Regd. Edinburgh 1881. Vol. liq. 2 Aug. 1886. A bonus of 5s. per share out of reserve fund was made in Aug. 1886; further payments (if any) not known. Final meeting return regd. 22 Dec. 1906 .... **1887**

American Lumber Co. Ld. Regd. Edinburgh 1882. Vol. liq. 21 Jan. 1884. Final meeting return regd. 27 Feb. 1888 .... **1885**

American Mortgage Co. of Scotland Ld. Regd. Edinburgh 1877. Vol. liq. June 1906 for reconstruction under same name. Holders of 10 ordinary shares of £10 (£2 paid) were entitled to 25 fully-paid ordinary shares of £1; holders of 10 ordinary shares of £2 fully-paid were entitled to 21 fully-paid ordinary shares of £1. The preference stock was paid off in cash. Final meeting return regd. 10 Sept. 1919 .... **1908**

American Mortgage Co. of Scotland Ld. Regd. Edinburgh 1906. Vol. liq. Nov. 1921. Final meeting return regd. 9 Mar. 1922 .... **1922**

American Mortgage Trust Ld. Regd. 1889. Vol. liq. 15 Jan. 1896. Final meeting return regd. 22 Dec. 1898 **1896**

American Pastoral Co. Ld. Regd. 1884. Vol. liq. 16 Nov. 1915. Final meeting return regd. 17 Nov. 1916 .... **1916**

American Produce Importers Co. Ld. Regd. 1887 as Metropolitan Trading Association Ld.; name changed Mar. 1894. Removed from Register 1910 **1926**

American Quick Service Restaurants Co, Ld. Regd. 1903. Court Order wind up to 1905. Removed from Register 1911 .... **1906**

American River Syndicate Ld. Regd. 1889. Vol. liq. 15 Aug. 1892. Final meeting return regd. 1 June 1896 **1893**

See Stock Exchange Year-Book.

VOL. FOR

American Stove & Furnace Co. Ld. Regd. 1890. Vol. liq. 8 June 1891. Final meeting return regd. 16 July 1900 — 1892

American Trust Co. Ld. Regd. Edinburgh 1899. Vol. liq. Aug. 1902. Capital was repaid in full. Final meeting return regd. 31 Jan. 1903 1904

American Water Works & Electric Co. (Inc.). Organised Virginia 1914. Undertaking and assets were acquired by company of same name. (Inc. Delaware). Holders of shares of common stock of $20 were entitled to 2 shares of common stock of no par value for each share of common stock held. Holders of 7% preferred stock were entitled to repayment at 110% or to 1 1st preferred share of no par value *plus* $11 in cash for every $100 preferred share held 1927

American Water Works and Electric Co. (Inc.). Inc. in Delaware 1927. Company was dissolved in 1947 under a reorganisation plan approved by Securities & Exchange Commission on 17 Feb. 1947 and by United States District Court on 19 Mar. 1947, which provided (inter alia) for this company (a) to transfer to American Water Works Co. Inc. its interests in waterworks properties for cash and subscription warrants entitling holders to purchase a total of 2,343,105 common shares of that company (in Sept.) 1947 common stockholders were given the right to subscribe at $8 per share for these shares), (b) to retire its preferred stock at $100 per share *plus* accrued interest (distribution of $100·25 cash was made 15 Oct. 1947), (c) West Penn Electric Co. to assume all remaining liabilities of this company and (d) all common shares of West Penn Electric Co. held by this company to be distributed to common stockholders of this company (this was done in Jan. 1948 on a share for share basis and completed the dissolution) 1948

American Waterworks & Guarantee Co. Inc. New Jersey 1891. Property acquired Apr. 1914 by American Waterworks & Electric Co. (inc. 1914). Preferred stockholders were entitled in respect of every share held by them, (a) to $50 participating preferred stock on paying an assessment of $5 per share held, or (b) to $40 first preferred stock and $100 participating preferred stock on subscribing $35. Common stockholders were entitled in respect of every share held by them. (a) to $10 common stock on paying an assessment of 50 cents per share so held, or (b) to $10 first preferred stock and $70 common stock on subscribing $10 1915

Americas & Orient Trust Co. Ld. Regd. 1911. Struck off Register 1917 — 1917

Amersham, Beaconsfield & District Water Co. Regd. 1895 as Amersham, Beaconsfield & District Waterworks Co. Ld.; inc. by Special Act 1933 and name changed. Undertaking acquired by Rickmansworth & Uxbridge Valley Water Co. in 1951. Ordinary stockholders were entitled to 1½ fully-paid 4½% Rickmansworth preference shares for every £10 stock held. Liability for mortgage debentures and debenture stock was assumed by the Rickmansworth Co. Dissolved under Special Act with effect from 20 Oct. 1952 1954

Ames Holden McCready Ld. Inc. Canada 1911. Undertaking and assets were acquired by new company of same name in Sept. 1922 — 1924

Ames Holden McCready Ld. Inc. Canada 1922. Court Order to wind up 5 May 1925 1926

Amexway Ld. *See* Euroflame Holdings p.l.c.

Amherst Estates (Selangor) Rubber Co, Ld. Regd. 1911. Vol. liq. (members') 30 Jan. 1961. Capital returned to contributories—5s. 2¼d. per share of 2s. Final meeting return regd. 15 Dec. 1962 1964

Amistad Rubber Plantations & Estates Ld. Regd. 1910. Court Order to wind up Feb. 1911. Struck off Register 1925 — 1912

Amlwch Gas Co. Reconstructed as East Anglesey Gas Co. 1938

Amman Valley Gas Light & Coke Co. Ld. Regd. 1905. Undertaking acquired by Ammanford Gas Co. Struck off Register 1917 — 1910

Ammanford Gas Co. Inc. by Special Act 1919. Dissolved 1 May 1949, undertaking being vested in Wales Area Gas Board under Gas Act 1948. Holders of ordinary shares of £1 (8% max.) were entitled to receive £1 10s. British Gas 3% guaranteed stock 1990–95. Liability in respect of 5% 1st debentures was assumed by the Board 1952

Ammonal Explosives Ld. Regd. 1903. Vol. liq. Feb. 1908 for reconstruction as Ammonal Explosives (1908) Ld., in which company shareholders were entitled to 1 share of £1 (credited with 18s. paid) for each share of £1 held. Removed from Register 1909 1909

Ammonal Explosives (1908) Ld, Regd. 1908. Vol. liq. 25 June 1913. The undertaking was acquired by Roburite & Ammonal Ld. for £21,900 (payable as to

£20,000 in ordinary and £1,900 in preference shares). Final meeting return regd. 29 Jan. 1916 . — 1914

Ammonia Gas Purifying & Alkali Co. Ld. Regd. 1881. Vol. liq. 6 Apr. 1898. Final meeting return regd. 30 Sept. 1898 — 1899

Ammonia Soda Co. Ld. Regd. 1908. Vol. liq. 15 Sept. 1919. Final meeting return regd. 12 Oct. 1921 1920

Ammoniaphone Co. Ld. Regd. 1886. Vol. liq. June 1887. Final meeting return regd. 11 Oct. 1887 1889

Ammonium Finance Syndicate Ld. Regd. 1911. Vol. liq. 17 Jan. 1927. Final meeting return regd. 11 July 1928 1927

Amo (Nigeria) Tin Mines Ld. Regd. 1912. Removed from Register 1914 1913

Amoor River Navigation Co. Constituted by Russian Imperial Government decree 1871. In Nov. 1913 it was stated that liquidation of company in Russia had been formally completed 1914

Ampang (Perak) Tin Dredging Ld. Regd. 1926. Vol. liq. (creditors') 31 Mar. 1930. No capital returned to contributories. Final meeting return regd. 15 May 1934 1931

Ampat Tin Dredging Ld. Regd. 27 Oct. 1933. Vol. liq. (members') 29 Apr. 1971. Distributions per share (of 2½)—10p in July 1971, Mar. 1975 and a final distribution of 4·31p on 31 July 1984 1985–6

Ampico Ld. Regd. 1926. Vol. liq. (members') 28 June 1932. Capital returned to contributories—1s. 5d. per preference share of £1. Final meeting return regd. 9 Sept. 1933 1931

Amsterdam Hill Water Co, Inc. Holland 1851. Undertaking acquired by Municipality for Fl. 12,000,000 2½% bonds 1897

Anamalai Coffee Co. Ld. Regd. 1877. Vol. liq. 9 June 1922. Capital returned to contributories—£4 per share of £10; further payments (if any) not known. Final meeting return regd. 12 Mar. 1923 1923

Anantapur Gold Field Ld. Regd. 1906. Vol. liq. 19 Mar. 1929. Capital returned to contributories—3s. per preference share of £1 *plus* distribution of investments in specie: further payments (if any) not known. Final meeting return regd. 17 Dec. 1930 — 1930

Anapa Liquid Fuel & Petrol Co. Ld. Regd. 1900. Removed from Register 1912 — 1910

Anatolia Co. Ld. Regd. 1911. Struck off Register Feb. 1931 — 1931

Anatolia Copper Co. Ld. *See* Tigon Mining & Finance Corporation Ld.

Anatolia Serdjiller Syndicate Ld. Regd. 1914. Vol. liq. 14 July 1925. Final meeting return regd. 1 July 1931 — 1926

Anatolian Exploration Co. Ld. Regd. 1927. Vol. liq. (members') 31 Dec. 1931. No capital returned to contributories. Final meeting return regd. 17 Nov. 1932 1932

Anchor Consolidated Gold Mines (W. A.) Ld. Regd. 1900. Vol. liq. 10 Dec. 1906. Removed from Register 1907 — 1907

Anchor Diamond Mines Ld. Regd. 1907. Vol. liq. 25 Feb. 1919. Final meeting return regd. 12 Jan. 1924 — 1919

Anchor Line (Henderson Brothers) Ld. Regd. 1899. Court Order to wind up 13 May 1935. Fleet and other assets were transferred to Anchor Line (1935) Ld. (later Anchor Line Ld.) for £792,000 in cash. No return to shareholders was anticipated. Liquidator released 8 Aug. 1944. Struck off Register 25 Feb. 1947 — 1936

Anchor Spinning Co. (1920) Ld. Regd. 1920. Receiver had sold machinery at Nov. 1935. Struck off Register 21 Apr. 1939 — 1940

Anchor Tin Mine Ld. Regd. 1895. Reconstructed 1902 as company of same name. Removed from Register 1903 — 1908

Anchor Tin Mine Ld. Regd. 1902. Vol. liq. Dec. 1908 for reconstruction. Removed from Register 1912........ 1909

Anchor Tin Mine Ld. Regd. 1909. Vol. liq. 11 July 1918. Final meeting return regd. 28 June 1919 1919

Anciens Etablissements George Whitechurch Ld. In liquidation. Practically all shares were owned by Whitechurch (George) Ld. 1935

Ancobra Exploration & Dredging Co. Ld. Regd. 1909. Vol. liq. 23 July 1914. Final meeting return regd. 5 Apr. 1922 1915

Ancomansi Syndicate Ld. Regd. 1902. Struck off Register 13 Jan. 1905 1905

Ancon Oil Co. of Ecuador Ld. Regd. 1910. Vol. liq. 18 Oct. 1917. Final meeting return regd. 5 Mar.1918 — 1918

Ancona Sulphur Ld. Regd. 1929. Vol. liq. (creditors') 20 May 1931. No capital returned to contributories. Final meeting return regd. 17 Oct. 1934 1932

Andalucia Lead & Silver Mining Co. Ld. Regd. 1902. Removed from Register 1912 — 1910

Andalusia Water Co. Ld. Regd. 1912. Vol. liq. (members') 23 Feb. 1955. 6% and 5% debentures were redeemed at par plus arrears of interest. Capital

VOL. FOR

paid) and 1 fully-paid ordinary share of £3 for each share of £5 held. Removed from Register 1905 ... **1889**

Anglo-American Cattle Co. Ld. Regd. 1879. Removed from Register 1905 .... *****1882**

Anglo-American Cold Storage Co. Ld. Regd. 1909. Receiver appointed May 1912. Court Order to wind up Nov. 1912. Struck off Register 1919 .... **1913**

Anglo-American Commercial Corpn. Ld. Regd. 1919. Vol. liq. 20 July 1923. Struck off Register 2 Feb. 1954 .... **1924**

Anglo-American Debenture Corpn. Ld. Regd. 1890. All capital was owned by Anglo-American Securities Corpn. Ld. Vol. liq. (members') 14 June 1963. Final meeting return regd. 22 Jan. 1965 .... **1961**

Anglo-American "E. C." Powder Co. Ld. *See* American "E. C." Powder Co. Ld.

Anglo-American Exploration & Development Co. Ld. Regd. 1888. Removed from Register 1895 .... *****1896**

Anglo-American Exploration Co. of Western Australia Ld. Regd. 1895. Reconstructed 1897 as Venture Corporation Ld., in which company shareholders were entitled to 79 fully-paid shares of £1 for every 100 ordinary shares of £1 (15s. paid) held or 6⅞ fully-paid shares of £1 for each deferred share of £1 (15s. paid) held. Removed from Register 1901 .... **1903**

Anglo-American Fresh Meat Supply Co. Ld. See Mexican National Land Mortgage and Investment Co. Ld.

Anglo-American Land Mortgage & Agency Co. Ld. Regd. 1882. The real estate and mortgages were acquired by Anglo-American Assets Co. Ld. Capital returned to contributories—£2 15s. per share of £10. Removed from Register 1909. .... **1906**

Anglo-American Patent Bottle Co. Ld. Regd. 1913. Vol. liq. 4 Feb. 1920. Final meeting return regd. 2 Aug.1922 .... **1921**

Anglo-American Telegraph Co. Ld. Regd. 1866. Vol. liq. (members') 10 Dec. 1968. Amount returned to contributories (per £100 stock)—£14 5s. Final meeting return regd. 20 Oct. 1970 .... **1971**

Anglo-Arabian & Persian Steamship Co. Ld. Regd. 1892. Vol. liq. 20 June 1905 Final meeting return regd. 1 May 1908 .... *****1905**

Anglo-Argentine Bank Ld. Regd. 1889 as London & Argentine Bank Ld.; name changed June 1889. Vol. liq. 6 Feb. 1901 for amalgamation with Bank of Tarapaca & Argentina Ld. (later Anglo-South American Bank Ld.) in which company shareholders were to receive 1 share of £10 (credited with £5 paid) and £1 10s. in cash for each share of £9 (£7 paid). Final meeting return regd.21 June 1904 ..... **1901**

Anglo-Argentine Live Stock & Produce Agency Ld. Regd. 1895. Removed from Register 1903 .... *****1902**

Anglo-Argentine Shipping Co. Ld. Regd. 1906. Receiver appointed Feb. 1908. Court Order to wind up Mar. 1908. Struck off Register 1916 .... **1909**

Anglo-Argentine Tramways Co. Ld. Regd. 1876. Vol. liq. 18 Nov. 1887. Reconstructed as company of same name. Shareholders were entitled to 2 shares of £5 in new company for every share of £5 held. Final meeting return regd. 9 Mar. 1892 .... **1888**

Anglo-Asiatic Rubber & Finance Trust Ld. Regd 1910. Removed from Register 1914 .... **1913**

Anglo-Asiatic Syndicate Ld. Regd. 1889. Struck off Register 18 Nov. 1902. .... **1909**

Anglo-Asiatic Syndicate Ld. Regd. 1906. Vol liq. Jan. 1909. Removed from Register 1910 .... **1909**

Anglo-Australasian Land Mortgage Co. Ld. Regd. 1884. Vol. liq. 18 Jan. 1898. Final meeting return regd. 12 July 1898 .... **1892**

Anglo-Australasian Steam Navigation Co. Ld. Regd. 1883. Vol. liq. 20 Oct. 1916. Business was acquired by Commonwealth & Dominion Line Ld. (later Port Line Ld.) Final meeting return regd. 3 May 1921 **1917**

Anglo-Australian Assets Co. Ld. Regd. 1893. A bonus of £5 per share of £8 was made in May 1910. Vol. liq. May 1910. Capital returned to contributories—£23 3s. 1d. per share at Feb. 1911; further payments (if any) not known. Removed from Register 1911 .... **1911**

Anglo-Australian Exploration Ld. Regd. 1894. Reconstructed 1897 as company of same name. Shareholders were entitled to 2 fully-paid shares of £1 in new company for each ordinary share of £1 (10s. paid) held or 5 fully-paid shares of £1 for each deferred share of £1 held. Removed from Register 1913 ... **1908**

Anglo-Australian Exploration Ld. Regd. 1897. Vol. Liq. Feb. 1913 for reconstruction as Anglo-General Exploration Ld. Removed from Register 1913 ...... **1913**

Anglo-Australian Gold Development Ld. Regd. 1933. Vol. liq. (members') 4 Sept. 1941. Winding-up Order 27 Nov. 1945. Capital returned to contributories— 5½d. per share of 5s. liquidator released 12 Nov. 1954. Struck off Register 22 Mar. 1961 .... **1955**

VOL. FOR

Anglo-Australian Investment, Finance & Land Co. Ld. Established Australia 1880. Vol. liq. Anglo-Australian Assets Co. Ld., was formed to take over the assets in 1893 .... **1894**

Anglo-Austrian Bank. Inc. Austria 1863. Business wound up under Trading with the Enemy (Amendment) Act 1916. Reconstituted as Anglo-Austrian Bank Ld. **1926**

Anglo-Austrian Bank Ld. Regd. 1922. Vol. liq. 11 Feb. 1927. Undertaking and assets were acquired by Anglo-International Bank Ld., in which company shareholders were entitled to 1 share of £1 (credited as fully-paid) for every 4 ordinary shares of £1 held **1927**

Anglo-Austrian Brush Electrical Co. Ld. *See* International Electric Co. Ld.

Anglo-Austrian Exploration Co. of Western Australia Ld. Regd. 1895. Reconstructed 1897 as Venture Corporation Ld., in which company shareholders were entitled to 78 shares of £1 (credited as fully-paid) for every 100 ordinary shares of £1 (15s. paid) held or to 1⅓ shares for each deferred share of £1 (15s. paid) held. Removed from Register 1901 .... **1903**

Anglo-Austrian Petroleum Co. Ld. Regd. 1897. Removed from Register 1910 .... **1907**

Anglo-Austrian Printing & Publishing Union Ld. Regd. 1889. Removed from Register 1907 .... **1892**

Anglo-Baltic & Mediterranean Bank Ld. Regd. 1919. Vol. liq. 26 Jan. 1925. Final meeting return regd. 20 Feb. 1930 .... **1938**

Anglo-Bauchi Tin Dredging Co. Ld. Regd. 1927. Vol. liq. (members') 15 Jan. 1930. Undertaking and assets were acquired by London Tin Corporation Ld., in which company shareholders were entitled to 1 fully-paid share of £1 for every 16 shares of 5s. held. Final meeting return regd. 18 July 1931 .... **1930**

Anglo-Bavarian Steel Ball Co. Ld. Regd. 1897. Vol. liq. 7 Feb. 1900. Undertaking was acquired by Steel Balls Ld. in which company shareholders were entitled to 1 share of £1 for every 6 shares of £1 held. Removed from Register 1907 .... **1900**

Anglo-Belgian Exploration Co. of Western Australia Ld. Regd. 1895. Reconstructed 1897 as Venture Corporation Ld., in which company shareholders were entitled to 78 shares of £1 (credited as fully-paid) for every 100 ordinary' shares of £1 (15s. paid) held or to 1⅓ shares for each deferred share of £1 (15s. paid) held. Removed from Register 1901 .... **1903**

Anglo-Belgian Petroleum Co. Ld. Regd. 1925. Struck off Register 1934 .... **1940**

Anglo-Belgian Safety Horseshoe Co. Ld. Regd. 1888. Removed from Register 1906 .... **1891**

Anglo-Belgian (Sierra Leone) Corporation Ld. *See* Mid-African & Overseas Properties Ld.

Anglo-Belgian Sugar Trust Ld. Regd. 1898. Struck off Register 1929 .... **1905**

Anglo-Belgian Tanning Co. Ld. Regd. 1898. Removed from Register 1905 .... **1904**

Anglo-Belgian Welsbach Incandescent Gas Light Co. Ld. Regd. 1899. Acquired by Société Belge de Chaleur et Lumiere, in which company shareholders were entitled to 1 fully-paid obligation share of Frs. 250 for every 10 preference shares of £1 held or to 1 fully-paid share of Frs. 250 for every 10 preference shares of £1 held or to 1 fully-paid share of Frs. 250 for every 10 ordinary or 10 deferred shares of £1 held. Removed from Register 1903 .... **1901**

Anglo-Belgique Shipping Co. Ld. Regd. 1916. Bankers, as mortgages, had seized and sold the assets. As assets realised insufficient to discharge liability no funds were available for cost of liquidation. Struck off Register Sept. 1933................................... **1934**

Anglo-Bibao Steel Ore Co. Ld. Regd. 1881. Court Orders: to wind up 10 Feb 1883: to dissolve 16 Dec. 1895 .... **1884**

Anglo-Bolivian Rubber & Trading Co. Ld. Regd. 1921. Vol. liq. 23 Aug. 1928 for reconstruction as Asbestos and General Trust Ld., in which company shareholders were entitled to 1 preferred ordinary share of 5s. credited with 4s. paid) for every 4 shares of 1s. held and an option (since expired) to subscribe for further shares. Final meeting return regd. 17 Dec. 1936 .... **1929**

Anglo-Bolivian Rubber Estates Ld. Regd. 1910' Vol. liq. 6 June 1921. The undertaking and assets were acquired by Anglo-Bolivian Rubber & Trading Co. Ld., in which company shareholders were entitled to 6 shares of 1s. (credited with 8d. per share paid) for every 5 shares of 1s. held. Final meeting return regd. 31 Jan. 1930 .... **1922**

Anglo-Brazilian Commercial & Agency Co. Ld. Regd. 1918. Vol. liq. 31 July 1929, An interest held by British Trade Corporation Ld. Final meeting return regd. 25 Sept. 1929 .... **1925**

See Stock Exchange Year-Book.

Anglo-Brazilian Exploration & Trading Co. Ld. Regd. 1920. Struck off Register July 1929 .... **1930**

Anglo-Brazilian Gold Syndicate Ld. Regd. 1899. Struck off Register 19 Mar. 1907 .... **1908**

Anglo-Brazilian Line Ld. Regd. 1912. Vol. liq. 18 Mar. 1919. Final meeting return regd. 30 Aug. 1921 .... **1919**

Anglo-Brazilian Meat Co. Ld. Regd. 1912. Struck off Register 1919 .... **1917**

Anglo-Brazilian Stores Ld. Regd. 1913 as Mappin Stores (Brazil) Ld.; name changed May 1940. Vol. liq. (members') 21 Aug. 1962. Capital returned to contributories—25s. 2·326d cash and 7 ordinary shares (of 1s.) of Polycell Holdings Ld. per A ordinary share of £1 or B ordinary share of 1s. £923 19s. 10d. paid into Companies Liquidation Account. Final meeting return regd 22 Dec. 1964 .... **1965**

Anglo-Bulgarian Oilfields Ld. See Anglo-Hellenic Oil-fields Ld.

Anglo-Burma Oil Co. Ld. Regd. 1910. Court Order to wind up 19 Jan. 1924. Struck off Register Jan. 1933 ... **1933**

Anglo-Californian Bank Ld. Regd. 1873. Vol. liq. 30 Mar. 1909. Shareholders were entitled to 1 share of $100 in Anglo & London Paris National Bank for every 2 shares of £20 (£10 paid) held. Removed from Register 1911 .... **1910**

Anglo-Californian Oil Syndicate Ld. Regd. 1905. Vol. liq. 17 Jan. 1921. Final meeting return regd. 11 Apr. 1922 .... **1922**

Anglo-Canadian Asbestos Co. Ld. Regd. 1889. Removed from Register 1901 .... **1900**

Anglo-Canadian Explorers Ld. Regd. 1922. Vol. liq. 26 July 1927. Undertaking and assets (except certain shares) were acquired by Anglo-Canadian Explorers (1927) Ld., in which company shareholders were entitled to 2 fully-paid shares of 4s. for every share of £1 held, plus 3 fully-paid shares of $1 in Central Manitoba Mines Ld. for every share held. Final meeting return regd. 18 July 1928 .... **1928**

Anglo-Canadian Explorers (1927) Ld. Regd. 1927. Vol. liq. (members') 17 Dec. 1936. Shareholders were to receive 17 shares of $1 in Central Manitoba Mines Ld. for every 20 shares of 4s. held; a cash payment of 4$\frac{7}{10}$d. per share was also made. Unclaimed and undistributed shares were lodged with Court by Order of 12 Dec. 1938. Final meeting return regd. 19 Sept. 1938. Court Order deferred dissolution until 16 Mar. 1939 .... **1937**

Anglo-Canadian Finance Co. Ld. Regd. 1906. Vol. liq. Dec. 1911 for reconstruction under same name. Shareholders were entitled to 2$\frac{1}{2}$ fully-paid shares of 10s. in new company for each ordinary share of £1 or 1$\frac{1}{2}$ shares of 10s. for each deferred share of 1s. held. Removed from Register 1914 .... **1912**

Anglo-Canadian Finance Co. Ld. Regd. 1912. Vol. liq. 29 Dec. 1922. Final meeting return regd. 4 Sept. 1928 **1923**

Anglo-Canadian Gold Estates Ld. Regd. 1899. Removed from Register 1906 .... **1904**

Anglo-Canadian Graphite Syndicate Ld. Regd. 1904. Vol. liq. 8 Oct. 1905. Removed from Register 1907 **1906**

Anglo-Canadian Hotels Ld. Regd. 1911. Vol. liq. (members') 11 May 1949. Capital returned to contributories—10s. per share of 10s. £234 was paid into Companies' Liquidation Account. Final meet-ing return regd. 15 Aug. 1950 .... **1951**

Anglo-Canadian Insurance Co. Ld. Regd. 1909 as Anglo-Scottish Assurance Corporation Ld.; name changed Sept. 1929. Vol. liq. (members') 26 Jan. 1943. Capital returned to contributories—£1 8s. 9·4157d. per share of £1. Final meeting return regd. 25 Jan. 1944 .... **1944**

Anglo-Canadian Lands Ld. Regd. 1910. Vol. liq. Aug. 1912 for reconstruction as Anglo-Canadian Lands (1912) Ld. Shareholders were entitled to 1 share of £1 (credited with 10s. paid) in new company for each share of £1 held. Final meeting return regd. 4 Mar. 1930 .... **1913**

Anglo-Canadian Lands (1912), Ld. Regd. 1912. Vol. liq. 1929; final meeting return regd. 4 Mar. 1930, but dissolution deferred to 31 Dec. 1930 and 1931 by orders of the Court and declared void by order of the Court of 22 Feb. 1932. All assets were realised and, in respect of 6% 1st mortgage deb. stock. principal was satisfied at 105% and interest paid to 22 Apr. 1918. Final meeting return regd. 23 Apr. 1949 .... **1950**

Anglo-Canadian Lead Syndicate Ld. Regd. 1899. Re-moved from Register 1913 .... **1911**

Anglo-Canadian Phosphate Co. Ld. Regd. 1886. Struck off Register 1924 .... **1907**

Anglo-Canadian Securities Corporation. Inc. Quebec 1931. In Nov. 1943 it was stated that company was in process of winding up **1944**

Anglo-Canadian Timber Co. of British Columbia Ld. Regd. 1911. Struck off Register 1925 .... **1925**

Anglo-Celtic Shipping Co. Ld. Regd. 1920. Vol. liq. (creditors') 5 Dec. 1935. No capital returned to contributories. Final meeting return regd. 5 Jan. 1954 .... **1955**

Anglo-Celtic Trust. Regd. 1925. Undertaking and assets acquired by Rio Claro Investment Trust Ld. (later Raeburn Investment Trust Ld.) in which company stockholders were entitled to receive 112 ordinary stock units of 5s. for every 100 stock units held and £1 5% preference stock per £1 preference stock held. The 3$\frac{1}{2}$% and 4$\frac{1}{4}$% debenture stocks and 4$\frac{1}{2}$% convertible unsecured loan stock were ex-changed for like amounts of similar stocks in the acquiring company. The company will be dissolved under Section 208 of the Companies Act 1948...... **1970**

Anglo-Central American Commercial Bank Ld. Regd. 1914. Vol. liq. 8 Oct. 1936. Capital returned to contributories—11$\frac{3}{4}$d. per founders' share of 1s.; 19s. 4$\frac{2}{3}$d. per ordinary share of £1. Final meeting return regd. 26 May 1939... **1937**

Anglo-Chilean Nitrate & Railway Co. Ld. Regd. 1888. Vol. liq. 15 Apr. 1925. Undertaking and assets acquired by Anglo-Chilean Consolidated Nitrate Corporation; both classes of shareholders received £4 of debenture stock in that company plus 2s 3·9d. in cash per share of £1. Final meeting return regd. 27 Apr. 1926.. **1926**

Anglo-Chilean Pastoral Co. Ld. Regd. 1904. Vol. liq. 15 June 1921. Final meeting return regd. 13 Nov. 1924 **1922**

Anglo-Colombian Development Co. Ld. Regd. 1911. Vol. liq. (members') 2 July 1954. All shares owned by South American Gold & Platinum Co. Final meeting return regd. 7 Dec. 1954 .... **1920**

Anglo-Colombian Investment Co. Ld. Regd. 1903. Undertaking acquired in 1904 by company of same name, for £33,733 in ordinary shares of £1. Removed from Register 1906 .... **1908**

Anglo-Colombian Investment Co. Ld. Regd. 1904. In 1909 assets and properties were acquired by Anglo-Colombian Mines Ld. Debenture stock was ex-changed for ordinary shares in that company. Vol. liq. Dec. 1912. Stuck off Register Apr. 1929......... **1930**

Anglo-Colombian Mines Ld. Regd. 1909. Vol. liq. Dec. 1912. Struck off Register Apr. 1929.......................... **1930**

Anglo-Colorado Exploration Syndicate Ld. Regd, 1896. Removed from Register 1910 .... **1909**

Anglo-Continental Corporation of Western Australia Ld. Regd. 1895. Vol. liq. 1897. Capital returned to contributories—15s. 3d. per share of £1, fully paid. Struck off Register 1929 .... **1898**

Anglo-Continental Gas Lamp Co. Ld. See Wenham & Co. Ld.

Anglo Continental Glassworks Ld. Regd. 1909. Re-moved from Register 27 Sept. 1912 .... ***1911**

Anglo-Continental Gold Reefs ot Rhodesia Ld. Regd. 1900. Removed from Register 1906 .... **1904**

Anglo-Continental Gold Syndicate (1899) Ld. Regd. 1899. Vol. liq. Dec. 1909. Reconstructed as Anglo-Continental Mines Co. Ld., in which company shareholders were entitled to 1 share of 10s. (credited as fully paid) and 5s. in debenture stock for each fully-paid share of £1 held. Removed from Register 1912 .... **1910**

Anglo-Continental Gold Syndicate Ld. Regd. 1895. Reconstructed 1899 as Anglo-Continental Gold Syndicate (1899) Ld., in which company sharehold-ers were entitled to 1 share of £1 for each ordinary share of £1 held or 20 shares of £1 for each founders' share of £1 held. Removed from Register 1901 ... **1908**

Anglo-Continental Grape Products Ld. Regd. 1928. Vol. liq. (members') 9 May 1932. Undertaking and assets were acquired by Vine Products Ld. for £26,000. Capital returned to contributories—1s. 3·8d. per preference share of £1. Final meeting return regd. 4 Feb. 1933 .... **1933**

Anglo-Continental Guano Works, Ld. Regd. 1916. Vol. liq. (members') 29 Jan. 1946, the undertaking and assets having been acquired by Fisons Ld. which company owned all ordinary shares. Preference shareholders were offered (a) exchange of their holdings into an equal number of 4$\frac{1}{2}$% cumulative preference shares in Fisons Ld., or (b) repayment at par with interest up to 21 Feb. 1946, plus 2s. 6d. per share premium; holders of 489,934 shares ex-changed their holdings and holders of 10,066 shares were paid out in cash. The outstanding debenture stock was redeemed at par on 5 Feb. 1946 plus an additional 3 months' interest in lieu of notice of redemption. Remaining assets have been distribut-ed in specie. £21 was paid into Companies' Liquidation Account. Final meeting return regd. 1 May 1952 .... **1953**

Anglo-Continental Investment & Finance Co. Ld. Regd. 1897 as Pekin Syndicate Ld.; name changed 1961.

VOL. FOR

All capital owned by Genberale Occidentale Ld. Outstanding $9\frac{1}{2}\%$ debenture stock 1982 & Six month rate debenture stock 1974–83 were redeemed at par 30 Sept. & 31 Dec. 1982, respectively Vol. liq. 17 mar. 1986 .... **1983–4**

Anglo-Continental Mines Co. Ld. Regd. 1909. Vol. liq. (members') 19 Nov. 1945. Capital returned to contributories—6s. $6\frac{3}{4}d$. per share of 10s. £3,880 9s. 5d. was paid into Companies' liquidation Account. Final meeting return regd. 1 Oct. 1946 .... **1947**

Anglo-Continental Supply Co. Ld. Regd. 1910. Vol. Liq. 30 Aug. 1922. Undertaking was acquired by Société Anonyme des Establissements an Planteur de Caiffe. Final meeting return regd. 1 Sep. 1928 .... **1940**

Anglo-Cuban Asphalt & Bitumen Ld. Regd. 1927 at Oil Trust (1927) Ld.; name changed Nov. 1928. Vol. liq. (creditors') 20 Nov. 1931. No capital returned to contributories Final meeting return regd. 5 Dec. 1932 .... **1932**

Anglo-Cuban Mercantile Co. Ld. Regd. 1912. Struck off Register 1917 .... **1915**

Anglo-Cuban Oil, Bisumen & Asphalt Co. Ld. Regd. 1911. Court Order to wind up Nov. 1912. Struck off Register Apr. 1934 .... **1935**

Anglo-Dutch East Indies Tin Syndicate Ld. Regd. 1925. Vol. liq. 7 June 1927. Shareholders received 2 fully-paid shares in Ampang (Perak) Tin Dredging Ld., and 3 fully-paid shares in British Malayan Tin Syndicate Ld. for every 6 shares of £1 held. Final meeting return regd. 10 Mar. 1928 .... **1928**

Anglo-Dutch Exploration Co. Ld. Regd. 1895. Removed from Register 1913 .... **1908**

Anglo-Dutch Petroleum Exploration Ld. Regd. 1899. Vol. liq. 12 Sept. 1904. Removed from Register 1905 **1905**

Anglo-Dutch Tobacco Co. Ld. Regd. 1889. Vol. liq. 18 Nov. 1892. Final meeting return regd. 27 Oct. 1896 **1893**

Anglo-Dutch Trading Co. (Amsterdam-Holland) Regd. 1911. Vol. liq. June 1914. Struck off Register Mar. 1929 .... **1930**

Anglo-Dutch Utilities Co. Ld. Regd. 1924. Vol. liq. (members') 9 Feb. 1937. Capital returned—$9\frac{1}{2}d$. (approx.) per share of £1. Final meeting return regd. 7 Dec. 1937 .... **1937**

Anglo East African Cotton Co. Ld. Regd. 1925. Struck off Register 19 Dec. 1947 .... **1948**

Anglo-East African Rubber Plantations Ld. Regd. 1910. Vol. liq. 2 Apr. 1919. Final meeting return regd 28 May 1925 .... **1919**

Anglo-East African Trading Co. Ld. Regd. 1919. Vol. liq. Dec. 1922. Struck off Register 2 Apr. 1943 ... **1923**

Anglo-Eastern Tin Ld. Regd. 1928. Vol. liq. (creditors') 30 Dec. 1949. Debenture holders were repaid to the extent of 3s. $2\frac{3}{4}d$. (per £1). Final meeting return regd. 28 Aug. 1951 .... **1952**

Anglo-Egyptian Bank Ld. Regd. 1864. Vol. liq. Mar. 1867. Final meeting return regd. 21 Mar. 1870 .... **1897**

Anglo-Egyptian Bank Ld. Regd. 1887. Vol. liq. Nov. 1925. Undertaking and assets transferred to Barclays Bank D.C.O., in which company shareholders received 5 fully-paid preference shares of £1 and $7\frac{1}{2}$ A shares of £1 for each share of £15 (with £5 paid) held. Struck off Register 6 Dec. 1963 .... **1926**

Anglo-Egyptian Banking Co. Ld. Regd. 1867 Reconstructed 1887 as Anglo-Egyptian Bank Ld., in which company shareholders were entitled to 1 share of £20 (credited with £10 paid) for each fully-paid share of £20 held., Removed from Register 1902 **1897**

Anglo-Egyptian Commercial Co. Ld. Regd. 1907. Vol. liq. 9 July 1915. Final meeting return regd. 1 July 1921 .... **1916**

Anglo-European Steamship Co. Ld. Regd. 1919 as Anglo-European Steamship, Coal & Pitwood Co. Ld.; name changed July 1919. Vol. liq. 15 Aug. 1929. Final meeting return regd. 9 Oct. 1929 .... **1930**

Anglo-Foreign Banking Co. Ld. Regd. 1872. Vol. liq. May 1913. Undertaking and assets acquired by Société Générale de Belgique. Shareholders were entitled to £8 10s. per share of £7. Removed from Register 1913 .... **1914**

Anglo-Foreign Mortgage Corpn. Ld. Regd. 1927. Struck off Register 1934 .... *****1932**

Anglo-Foreign Oil & General Trust Ld. Regd. 1928. Struck off Register 8 Dec. 1939 .... **1940**

Anglo-Foreign Pulp Co. Ld. Regd. 1926. Court Order to wind up Oct. 1930. Struck off Register 17 July 1942 **1943**

Anglo-Foreign Securities Corporation Ld. Regd. 1910. Vol. liq. (members') 29 June 1931. Undertaking and assets were acquired by Anglo-Canadian Securities Corporation in which company shareholders were entitled to 1 preference share of $100 and 10 common shares of no par value for every 40 shares of £1 held. Final meeting return regd. 27 July 1932 **1943**

Anglo-Franco Belgian Quarries of Oran Ld. Regd. 1890. Removed from Register 15 Aug. 1893 .... *****1892**

VOL. FOR

Anglo-French China Corporation Ld. Regd. 1912. Vol. liq. (members') 17 Nov. 1938. Capital returned—1s. 1d. per preferred share. Final meeting return regd. 1 Nov. 1939 .... **1939**

Anglo-French Colonial Mining Trust Ld. Regd. 1895. Vol. liq. 5 Feb. 1897. Undertaking was acquired by Colonial Estates & Investment Co. Ld. Court Orders: to continue winding up under supervision 22 Feb. 1897; to dissolve from 21 Apr. 1902. Final meeting return regd. 31 Jan. 1907 .... **1902**

Anglo-French Colonial Syndicate Ld. Regd. 1904 Vol. liq. Oct. 1907. Removed from Register 1908 .... **1908**

Anglo-French Exploration Co. of Western Australia Ld. Regd. 1895. Reconstructed 1837 as Venture Corporation Ld. in which company shareholders were entitled to 103 fully-paid shares of £1 for every 100 ordinary shares of £1 (15s. paid) held or to 38 fully-paid shares of £1 for each deferred share of £1 (15s. paid) held. Removed from Register. 1901 .... **1903**

Anglo-French Fire Insurance Co. Ld. See Lion Fire Insurance Co. Ld.

Anglo-French General Finance Co. Ld. Regd. 1904. Vol. liq. Mar. 1908 for reconstruction as New Anglo-French General Finance Co. Ld. in which company shareholders were entitled to 1 share of £1 (credited with 10s. paid) for each share of of £1 held. Removed from Register 1910 .... **1909**

Anglo-French Gold Fields of Australasia Ld. Regd. 1896. Vol. liq. 30 Mar. 1900. A distribution of 1 fully-paid ordinary share of £1 in Arnheims Land Exploration Co. Ld., for every 2 shares held was expected. Removed from Register 1913 .... **1901**

Anglo-French Gold Mining Syndicate Ld. See London & Johannesburg Syndicate Ld.

Anglo-French Greyhound Association Ld. Regd. 1927. Court Order to wind up June 1929. Struck off Register 15 Oct. 1935 .... **1936**

Anglo-French Guinea Syndicate Ld. Regd. 1909. Vol. liq. 9 June 1913. Final meeting return regd. 11 Nov. 1913 .... *****1914**

Anglo-French Herald Motor Co. Ld. Regd. 1906. Vol. liq. May 1907. Removed from Register 1909 .... **1908**

Anglo-French Klondyke Syndicate Ld. Regd. 1898. Removed from Register 1902 .... **1902**

Anglo-French Land Co. of the Transvaal Ld. Inc. Transvaal 1895. Vol. liq. Oct. 1928. Properties were acquired by New Transvaal Gold Farms Ld. (now Waverley Gold Mines Ld.) Capital returned to contributories—5s. per share of 11s. at Dec. 1928 further payments (if any) not known **1929**

Anglo-French Matabeleland Co. Ld. Regd. 1895. Vol. liq. 22 Aug. 1927. Final meeting return regd. 26 Oct. 1934 .... **1928**

Anglo-French Mercantile & Finance Corporation Ld. Regd. 1910. Vol. liq. Feb. 1914. Undertaking was acquired by Imperial and Foreign Corporation Ld. in which company shareholders were entitled to 2 ordinary and 2 preference shares of £1 (credited as fully paid) for every 5 shares of £1 held. Holders of option certificates were entitled to subscribe (until 31 Dec. 1944) for one ordinary share or £1 at 30s. for every 4 options held. Struck off Register 7 July 1939 **1940**

Anglo-French Middle East Development Corporation, Ld. See Middle East Development Corporation Ld.

Anglo-French Motor Carriage Co. Ld. Regd. 1896. Removed from Register 1903 .... **1899**

Anglo-French Nickel Co. Ld. Regd. 1899. Vol. liq. (members') 10 Jan. 1933. Capital returned—20s. per preference share of £1; 20s. 7d. (approx.) per ordinary share of £1. Final meeting return regd. 2 Aug. 1933 .... **1933**

Anglo French Oilfields Ld. Regd. 1914. Struck off Register 1918 .... *****1915**

Anglo-French Pacific Syndicate Ld. Regd. 1905. Vol. liq. 19 Jan. 1914. Final meeting return regd. 26 Mar. 1924 .... **1914**

Anglo-French Pneumatic Compensation Cycle Co. Ld. Regd. 1897. Vol. liq. 11 Oct. 1897. Final meeting return regd. 24 Oct. 1898 .... **1898**

Anglo-French Public Works Co. Ld. Regd. 1907. Removed from Register 1911 .... **1910**

Anglo-French Quicksilver & Mining Concession (Kweichau Province) of China Ld. Regd. 1899. Vol. liq. 25 Jan 1906 Reconstructed as company of same name. Shareholders were entitled to 1 share of £1 (credited with 17s. 6d. paid) in new company for each preference share of £1 held or for every 4 founders' shares of £1 held or for every 5 ordinary shares of £1 held. Final meeting return regd. 11 July 1917 ...... **1906**

Anglo-French Quicksilver & Mining Concession (Kweichau Province) of China Ld. Regd. 1906. Vol. liq. 23 Mar. 1916. Final meeting return regd. 11 July 1917 **1916**

Anglo-French Syndicate Ld. See Syndicat du Yunnan Ld.

See Stock Exchange Year-Book.

VOL. FOR

Anglo-French Textile Co. Ld. Regd. 1898. Control transferred to French India in 1951. Vol. liq. (members') 19 Aug. 1955. Final meeting return regd. 23 Feb. 1960 1952

Anglo-French Ticapampa Silver Mining Co. Ld. Regd. 1903. Vol. liq. (members') 5 Apr. 1968. Amount returned to contributories—U.S.$0·7937 per share (of 10s.). £6,185 was paid into Companies' Liquidation Account in respect of unclaimed distributions and £2,333·22 in respect of unclaimed dividends. Final meeting return regd. 8 Sept. 1971 1972

Anglo-French Tramways Co. Ld. Regd. 1882. Removed from Register 1884 1882

Anglo French Transvaal Navigation Coal Estate Ld. *See* Transvaal Navigation Coal Estates Ld.

Anglo-French (Verdun) Artificial Silk Ld. Regd. 1928. Vol. liq. (members') 9 Apr. 1936. No capital returned to contributories. Final meeting return regd. 24 June 1956 1937

Anglo Galieian Naphtha Syndicate Ld. *See* Romana Petroleum Co. Ld.

Anglo-Galician Oil Co. Ld. Regd. 1899. Reconstructed 1903 as Anglicia Petroleum Co. Ld., in which company shareholders were entitled to 1 fully-paid preference share of £1 for every 2 preference shares of £1 held or 1 fully-paid ordinary share of £1 for every 5 ordinary shares of £1 held. Removed from Register 1910 1908

Anglo-General Exploration Ld. Regd. 1913. Vol. liq. 28 Nov. 1924. Final meeting return regd. 1 Jan. 1932 1925

Anglo-German Exploration Co. Ld. *See* Minerals Exploration Co. Ld.

Anglo-German Exploration Co. of Western Australia Ld. Regd. 1895. Reconstructed 1897 as Venture Corporation Ld., in which company shareholders were entitled to 82 fully-paid shares of £1 for every 100 ordinary shares of £1 (15s. paid) held or to 29½ fully-paid shares of £1 for each deferred share of £1 (15a. paid) held. Removed from Register 1901 1903

Anglo-German Trust Ld. Regd. 1921. Vol. liq. (members') 25 Jan. 1935. No capital returned to contributories. Final meeting return regd. 11 June 1935 ... 1935

Anglo Greek Financial Co. Ld. Regd. 1923. Vol. liq. (members') 3 July 1939. Capital returned to contributories—£1 per preference share of £5 (£1 paid) plus interest in lieu of accrued dividend from 11 Nov. 1932 to Feb. 1946 and £1 6s. 3d. per 20 ordinary shares of £5. Final meeting return regd. 29 Mar. 1946 1947

Anglo-Greek Magnesite Co. Ld. Regd. 1902. Vol. liq. (members') 30 Nov. 1960. Capital returned to contributories—11s. 8d. plus 2·5p. per ordinary share of £1 and 7d. plus 0·125p per deferred share of 5p. £38·57 was paid into Companies Liquidation Account in respect of unclaimed dividends. Final meeting return regd. 4 Apr. 1972 1972

Anglo-Hellenic Oilfields Ld. Regd. 1910 as Anglo Ottoman Oilfields Ld.; name changed to Anglo Bulgarian Oilfields Ld. in Jan. 1915, and as above in Oct. 1920. Receiver appointed Sept. 1928. Assets realised insufficient to satisfy claims of debenture holders. Struck off Register Jan. 1932 1932

Anglo-Hungarian Petroleum Co. Ld. Regd. 1910. Vol. liq. 19 July 1912 for reconstruction as Hungarian National Petroleum Co. Ld., in which company shareholders were entitled to 1 fully-paid share of £1 for each share of £1 held. Final meeting return regd. 2 Oct. 1915 1913

Anglo-India Jute Mills Co. Ld. Regd. Edinburgh 1895. Vol. liq. Dec. 1916. Final meeting return regd. 21 Jan. 1920 1917

Anglo-International Bank Ld. Regd. 1926. Vol. liq. (members') 19 Oct. 1951. Capital returned to contributories—2s. 2¼d. per share of 15s. £1,268 3s 2d. was paid into Companies' Liquidation Account. Final meeting return regd. 8 Nov. 1962 1964

Anglo-International Securities Corporation, Ld. Regd. 1921. Directly controlled by African Consolidated Investments Corpn. Ld. Vol. liq. (members') 25 May 1955. Final meeting return regd. Dec. 1955 1953

Anglo-Investment Corporation Ld. Regd. 1906. Vol. liq. 8 Feb. 1909. Struck off Register 16 July 1915 ......

Anglo-Israel Securities Ld. *See* Transatlantic and General Investments p.l.c.

Anglo-Italian Bank Ld. Regd. 1866. Removed from Register 1913 1910

Anglo-Italian Chemical & Mineral Co. Ld. Regd. 1898. Vol. liq. 14 Nov. 1906. Removed from Register 1909 1907

Anglo-Italian Concentrated Produce Co. Ld. Regd. 1882. Vol. liq. Jan. 1884. Removed from Register 1890 1885

Anglo-Italian Petroleum Co. Ld. Regd. 1909. Struck off Register 1918 1913

Anglo-Japanese Bank Ld. *See* Commercial Bank of London Ld.

VOL. FOR

Anglo-Java Rubber & Produce Co. Ld. Regd. 1910. Vo 1. lid. (members') Feb. 1934. Reconstructed as Anglo-Java Rubber Co. Ld. (later Anglo-Asian Rubber Plantations Ld.) in which company shareholders were entitled to 1 ordinary share of 1s. (credited with 9d. paid) for each ordinary share of 2s. held, or 1 fully-paid ordinary share of 1s. for each preference share of 2s. held. Debenture stockholders were entitled to £50 in income debenture stock and 1,000 fully-paid ordinary shares of 1s. for every £100 stock held. Final meeting return regd. 15 Oct. 1935 1934

Anglo-Johore Consolidated Rubber Estates Ld. Regd. 1921. Vol. liq. (members') 24 Jan. 1934 for reconstruction as Anglo-Johore Rubber Estates Ld. (regd. 1934), in which company shareholders were entitled to 1 share of 1s. (credited with 10½d paid) for each share held; debenture holders were satisfied by repayment at par with interest at 10% p.a. and bonus of 25% in fully-paid shares of new company. Capital return of 1½d. per share to shareholders who did not take up their rights. £131 15s. 7d. was paid to Companies' Liquidation Account. Final meeting return regd. 24 Jan. 1935. 1934

Anglo-Johore Rubber Estates Ld. Regd. 1910. Vol. liq. 10 Jan. 1921. Undertaking and assets acquired by Anglo-Johore Consolidated Rubber Estates Ld., in which company shareholders were entitled to 4 shares of 2s. (credited with 1s. 3d. per share paid) for every 3 shares of 2s. held and an option (since expired) over further shares at par. Final meeting return regd. 1 Apr. 1926 1921

Anglo-Johore Rubber Estates Ld. Regd. 1934. Vol. liq. (members') 12 Apr. 1937. Reconstructed as company of same name. Shareholders were entitled to 1 share of 1s. (credited as fully paid) in new company for every 2 shares of 1s. held. Final meeting return regd. 1 Dec. 1938 1938

Anglo-Johore Rubber Estates, Ld. Regd. 1937. Vol. liq. (members') 30 June 1947 for reconstruction as Anglo-Johore Rubber Plantations Ld. in which company stockholders were entitled to receive 1 share of 1s. (credited with 9d. paid) for every 1s. stock held; stockholders not taking up these shares were entitled to 0·84d. per 1s. stock. Holders of the 6% convertible debenture stock received a like amount of a similar 6% stock in the new company. Final meeting return regd. 7 Dec. 1956 1958

Anglo-Klondyke Mining Co. Ld. Regd. 1900. Vol. liq. 15 June 1906. Capital returned to contributories—6s. 7¾d. per ordinary share of £1; further payments (if any) not known. Removed from Register 1907 1907

Anglo-Lautaro Nitrate Corpn. *See* Compania Salitrera Anglo-Lautaro.

Anglo-Levantine Banking Co. Ld. Regd. 1908. Struck off Register 1924 1924

Anglo-Maikop Corporation Ld. Regd. 1909. Vol. liq. May 1911 for reconstruction under same name. Shareholders were entitled to 1 fully-paid share of £1 in the new company for each ordinary share of £1 held or 5 fully-paid shares for every 4 B deferred shares of 1s. held. Removed from Register 1912 . 1912

Anglo-Maikop Corporation Ld. Regd. 1911. Struck off Register 17 Jan. 1950 1951

Anglo-Malay Investment Trust Ld. Regd. 1910. Struck off Register Jan. 1932 1932

Anglo-Malay Rubber Co. Ld. Regd. 1905. Vol. liq. 9 Apr. 1920 for reconstruction under same name. Shareholders were entitled to 1 share of £1 (credited as fully paid) in the new company for every 4 shares of 2s. held. Final meeting 1921 return regd. 15 Feb. 1922 1921

Anglo-Malay Rubber Co. Ld. Regd. 1920. Vol. liq. (members') 27 Feb. 1953. Undertaking and assets acquired as from 1 Nov. 1952 by Paalling Rubber Estates Ld. Stockholders were entitled to receive 40 fully-paid shares (of 2s.) in respect of every £13 stock held. £5 7s. 6d. was paid into Companies' Liquidation Account. Final meeting return regd. 11 Nov. 1953 1955

Anglo-Maltese Hydraulic Dock Co. Ld. Regd. 1869. Removed from Register 1902 1885

Anglo-Manchurian Bank Ld. Regd. 1923. Struck off Register 1931 .... *1925

Anglo-Marine Insurance Co. Ld. Regd. 1918. Struck off Register 26 Jan. 1940 1940

Anglo-Mersing Rubber Estates Ld. Regd. Apr. 1920. Vol. liq. Dec. 1920. Undertaking and certain assets acquired by Anglo-Johore Consolidated Rubber Estates Ld., in which company shareholders were entitled to 2 shares of 2s. (credited with 1s. 3d. per share paid) for every 5 shares of 2s. held, and an option (since expired) over further shares at par. Final meeting return regd. 1 Apr. 1926 1921

See Stock Exchange Year-Book.

VOL. FOR

Anglo-Mexican Colonization & Trading Co. Ld. Regd. 1896. Vol. liq. 6 Apr. 1906. Removed from Register 1908 .... **1907**

Anglo-Mexican Electric Co. Ld. Regd. 1906. Vol. liq. 28 Apr. 1922. Final meeting return regd. 29 Mar. 1923 **1923**

Anglo-Mexican Mining Co. Ld. Regd. 1883. Removed from Register 1903 .... **1901**

Anglo-Mexican Oil & Shipping Co. Ld. Regd. 1909 as Bowring Petroleum Co. Ld.; name changed to Lubricants Producers Ld. 26 Jan. 1921; to Cerais Petroleum Co. Ld., 7 Sept. 1928 and as above 29 Nov. 1929. Vol. liq. 1 Jan. 1931. Undertaking acquired by Eagle Oil & Shipping Co. Ld., in which company shareholders were entitled to 10 7% preference shares of £1 for each 6% or 8% preference share held and 10 preferred ordinary shares of £1 for each ordinary share of £10 held. Final meeting return regd. 1 Jan. 1932 .... *****1921**

Anglo-Mexican Oilfields Ld. Regd. 1907. Vol. liq. 23 Dec. 1924. Final meeting return regd. 11 Apr. 1925 **1925**

Anglo-Mexican Properties Ld. Regd.' 1896. Removed from Register 1906 .... **1905**

Anglo-Montana Mining Co. Ld. Regd. 1896. Court Orders: to wind up 25 July 1888; to dissolve 29 Dec. 1892 .... **1889**

Anglo-Netherland Sugar Corporation Ld. Regd. 1911. Vol. liq. 9 Feb. 1916. The English assets were acquired by English Beet Sugar Corporation Ld. (regd. 1916), in which company shareholders received 1 fully-paid share of £1 for every 4 shares of £1 held; holders of debentures received an equal amount of debentures in purchasing company. Final meeting return regd. 9 Nov. 1916 .... **1916**

Anglo-Netherlands Exploration Co. of Western Australia Ld. Regd. 1895. Reconstructed 1897 as Venture Corporation Ld., in which company shareholders were entitled to 82 fully-paid shares of £1 for every 100 ordinary shares of £1 (15s paid) held or to 3 fully-paid shares of £1 for each deferred share of £1 (15s. paid) held. Removed from Register 1901 .... **1903**

Anglo-Newfoundland Development Co. Ld. Inc. Newfoundland 1905. Vol. liq. June 1933 for reconstruction under same name. The 6% 2nd mortgage bonds were repaid at 103% in cash. Holders of ordinary shares were entitled to 1 share of $5 in the new company for each ordinary share held; holders of cumulative preference and 2nd preference shares were repaid at par and received an option (since expired) to purchase shares **1934**

Anglo-Nigerian Corporation Ld. Regd. 1929. Vol. liq. 29 Jan. 1934. Reconstructed as Gold & Base Metal Mines of Nigeria Ld., in which company shareholders were entitled to 1 share of 2s. 6d (credited with 1s. 6d. paid) for each share of 5s. held. Debenture holders were entitled to an equal amount of 5% debentures in new company; arrears of interest were payable in cash and fully-paid shares. Final meeting return regd 28 Feb. 1936 .... **1934**

Anglo-Nigerian Exploration Ld. Regd. 1912. Val. liq. 3 June 1925. Controlled by Niger Co. Final meeting return regd. 12 Oct. 1925 .... **1925**

Anglo-Nigerian Tin Mines Ld. Regd. 1923. Vol. liq. (members') 12 Dec. 1929. Undertaking acquired by Anglo-Nigerian Corporation Ld in which company shareholders were entitled to 1 share of 5s. for each share of 5s. held. Final meeting return regd. 19 Dec. 1934 .... *****1931**

Anglo-Norwegian Aluminium Co. Ld. Regd. 1907. Vol. liq. June 1913. Capital returned to contributories—preference shares were repaid at par; 4s. per ordinary share of £1; further payments (if any) not known. Removed from Register 1914 .... **1914**

Anglo-Norwegian Kieselguhr Co. Ld. Regd. 1898. Removed from Register 1903 .... **1903**

Anglo-Orient Syndicate Ld. Regd. 1905. Vol. liq. 2 Dec. 1929. Controlling interest held by Siberian Syndicate Ld. Final meeting return regd. 27 June 1930 **1929**

Anglo-Oriental Financial Trust Ld. Regd. 1911. Court Order to wind up Dec. 1912. Struck off Register 1919 .... **1913**

Anglo-Oriental Mining Corporation Ld. Regd. 1928 as Anglo-Oriental Corporation Ld.; name changed 14 Mar. 1928. Undertaking and assets acquired by London Tin Corporation Ld. in which company shareholders received 16 ordinary shares of 4s. for every 5 preference shares of £1 and 13 ordinary of 4s. for every 30 ordinary shares of 5s. held. Dissolved under Sec. 154 of Companies Act 1929 on 13 Mar. 1937 .... **1938**

Anglo-Oriental Plantations Ld. Regd. 1958 as G. & H. Plantations Ld.; name changed Jan. 1959. Vol. liq. (members') 14 Jan. 1969. Capital returned to contributories (per share of 1d.)—4s. 2¼d. Final meeting return regd. 12 Apr. 1979 ....**1979–80**

VOL. FOR

Anglo-Oriental Produce Co. Ld. Regd. 1886. Removed from Register 1906 .... **1882**

Anglo-Ottoman Oilfields Ld. See Anglo Hellenic Oilfields Ld.

Anglo-Ottoman Tobacco Co. Ld. Regd. 1912. Struck off Register 25 Mar. 1938 .... **1939**

Anglo-Pacific Exploring Syndicate. Ld. Regd. 1895. Vol. liq. 20 May 1897. Final meeting return regd. 4 Jan. 1898 .... **1898**

Anglo-Pacific Trading Corporation Ld Regd 1916. Vol. liq. 20 Jan. 1926. Final meeting return regd. 28 Jan. 1927 .... **1927**

Anglo-Pacific Trust & Loan Co. Ld. Regd. 1874. Vol. liq. 1883. Capital returned to contributories—£4 4s. per share of £20 at 30 Nov. 1883; further payments (if any) not known. Removed from Register 1901 .... **1884**

Anglo-Paraguayan Co. Ld. Regd. 1894. Vol. liq. July 1909. Struck off Register 1914 .... **1910**

Anglo-Paraguayan Land Co. Ld. Regd. 1888 as Paraguay Land Co. Ld.; name changed Oct. 1889. Reconstructed 1894 as Anglo-Paraguayan Co. Ld. Holders of debenture stock received fully-paid shares in new company at par for both principal and interest. Removed from Register 1904 .... **1908**

Anglo-Parisian Automobile Ld. Regd. 1911 as Automobiles Rolls Royce (France) Ld.; name changed Jan. 1932. All capital owned by Rolls Royce Ld. Vol. liq. (members') 6 Dec. 1933. Final meeting return regd. 6 Dec. 1934 .... **1934**

Anglo-Peninsular Mining & Chemical Co. Ld. Regd. 1896. Vol. liq. (members') 9 July 1947. Final meeting return regd. 29 Dec. 1947 .... **1906**

Anglo-Polish Bank Ld. See Bank Anglilsko-Polski Sp. Ack.

Anglo-Portuguese Collieries Ld. Regd. 1907. In Oct. 1913 holders of shares and debentures sanctioned sale of properties in Portugal for £9,000. Struck off Register 1923 .... **1915**

Anglo-Portuguese (East Africa) Concessions Ld. Regd. 1913. Vol. liq. 10 Feb. 1932 for reconstruction as Rand & East African Corporation Ld. Shareholders were to receive in new company 2 ordinary or 3 preferred ordinary shares of 2s. 6d. (credited with 2s. per share paid) for every 5s. ordinary or preferred capital held respectively £542 8s. 9d. was distributed to shareholders in respect of proceeds of sale of unclaimed shares. Final meeting return regd. 8 Feb. 1935 .... **1932**

Anglo-Portuguese Gas & Water Co. Ld. Regd. 1887. Vol. liq. 21 Jan 1926. All assets were realised and proceeds were in hands of Receiver for debenture holders. Final meeting return regd. 31 Oct. 1930 **1926**

Anglo-Portuguese Motor & Machinery Co. Ltd. Regd. 1910. Vol. liq. 10 Feb. 1919. Final meeting return regd. 14 Sept. 1921 .... *****1920**

Anglo-Portuguese Petroleum Co. Ld. Regd. 1908. Removed from Register 1912 .... **1912**

Anglo-Portuguese Tin Co. Ld. Regd. 1912. Vol. liq. 5 Aug. 1927. Final meeting return regd. 21 Aug. 1928 **1928**

Anglo-Rhenich Syndicate Ld. Regd. 1904. Vol. liq. 30 Oct. 1906. Final meeting return regd. 26 Mar. 1909 *****1906**

Anglo-Rhodesia Development Co. Ld. Regd. 1910 as Yorkshire & Rhodesia Development Co. Ld.; name changed 1911. Struck off Register 1925 .... **1925**

Anglo-Rhodesian & General Investment Co. Ld. Regd. 1929. Vol. liq. 27 Mar. 1957. Final meeting return regd. 24 Dec. 1957 .... **1955**

Anglo-Rhodesian Tobacco Co. Ld. See Rhodesian Tobacco Estates Ld.

Anglo-Romano Gas Co. See Elettricita e Gas di Roma.

Anglo-Roumanian Finance & Trading Co. Ld. Regd. 1898. Removed from Register 1904 .... **1902**

Anglo-Roumanian Oil & General Trust Ld. Regd. 1910. Struck off Register 7 Dec. 1937 .... **1938**

Anglo-Roumanian Petroleum Co. Ld. Regd. 1908. Vol. liq. (members') 28 Feb. 1936. Final meeting return regd. 28 Apr. 1936 .... **1937**

Anglo-Roumanian Produce Co. Ld. Regd. 1906. Struck off Register 28 Feb. 1939 .... **1940**

Anglo-Russian Contract Co. Ld. Regd. 1898. Removed from Register 1904 .... **1902**

Anglo-Russian Flour Mills Ld. Regd. 1889. Removed from Register 1911 .... **1905**

Anglo-Russian Petroleum Co. Ld. Regd. 1897. Vol. liq. June 1902 for reconstruction as company of same name. Removed from Register 1914 .... **1908**

Anglo-Russian Petroleum Cu. Ld. Regd. 1902. Struck off Register Dec. 1931 .... **1932**

Anglo-Russian Platinum Mining Co. Ld. Regd. 1903. Removed from Register 1911 .... **1925**

Anglo-Russian Shipping & Investment Co. Ld. See Aurochs Investment Co. Ld

Anglo-Russian Shipping Co. Ld. See Aurochs Investment Co. Ld

See Stock Exchange Year-Book.

VOL. FOR

Anglo-Russian Trust Ld. Regd. 1909. Vol. liq. 9 Aug. 1922. Final meeting return regd. 10 Dec. 1924 .... **1923**

Anglo-Sardinian Antimony Co. Ld. Regd. 1887. Court Order to wind up 14 Nov. 1891. Removed from Register 1906 .... **1892**

Anglo-Saxon Gold Mining Syndicate Ld. Regd. 1887. Removed from Register 1906 .... **1894**

Anglo-Saxon Trust Co. Ld. Regd. 1912 as Anglo-Saxon Trust & Loan Co. Ld.; name changed Sept. 1913. Struck off Register 1918 .... **1915**

Anglo-Scandinavian Exploration Co. of Western Australia Ld. Regd. 1895. Reconstructed 1897 as Venture Corporation Ld., in which company shareholders were entitled to 80 fully-paid shares of £1 for every 100 ordinary shares of £1 (15s. paid) held or to 2 fully-paid shares of £1 for each deferred share of £1 (15s. paid) held. Removed from Register 1901 .... **1903**

Anglo-Schodnica Oil Fields Ld. Regd. 1912. Vol. liq 6 Aug. 1912. Undertaking and assets were sold to Schodnica Consolidate Oil lands Ld. Final meeting regd. 22 Aug. 1924 .... **1915**

Anglo-Scottish Beet Sugar Corporation, Ld. Regd. Edinburgh 1924. Vol. liq. (members') 6 Aug. 1946. Under the provisions of the Sugar Industry (Reorganisation) Act 1936 the undertaking and assets of this company and its subsidiaries [Second Anglo-Scottish Beet Sugar Corpn. Ld. and West Midland Sugar Co. Ld.] were acquired by British Sugar Corp. Ld. in 1936, this company receiving in all 1,205,266 shares of £1 in that company, of which 750,000 were transferred to H. M. Treasury in 1946 in satisfaction of indebtedness. Shareholders were entitled to receive shares of British Sugar Corpn. Ld. equivalent to a total of 13s. 9d. plus 7.11d. cash for every share of £1 held. Final meeting return regd. 17 Dec. 1947 .... **1948**

Anglo-Scottish Finance Corporation Ld. Regd. 1919. Court Order to wind up Nov. 1926. Struck off Register Oct. 1933 .... **1934**

Anglo-Scottish Securities Ld. Regd. 1928. Court Order to wind up 2 June 1930. Struck off Register 10 May 1935 .... **1936**

Anglo-Scottish Tin Corporation Ld. Regd. 1927. Vol. liq. (creditors') 10 July 1931. No capital returned to contributories. Final meeting return regd. 1 July 1938 .... **1932**

Anglo-Scottish Trust Ld. Regd. 1920. Vol. liq. 5 Oct. 1925. Reconstructed as Anglo-Scottish Amalgamated Corporation Ld. in which company shareholders were entitled to 2 ordinary shares of £1 and 1 deferred share of 1s. (credited as fully-paid) for every 3 shares of £1 held. Final meeting return regd. 23 July 1927 .... **1926**

Anglo-Servian Gold Dredging Co. Ld. Regd. 1913. Vol. liq. 23 May 1918. Final meeting return regd. 17 Apr. 1924 .... **1919**

Anglo-Servian Trading Co. Ld. Regd. 1910. Receiver appointed Apr. 1913. Struck off Register 1916...... **1914**

Anglo-Siberian Co. Ld. Regd. 1906. Vol. liq. Apr. 1912. Shareholders were entitled to 5 fully-paid shares of £1 in Russo-Asiatic Corporation Ld., for every 9 shares of £1 held, £100 debenture in Kyshtim Corpn. Ld. for every 200 shares held and 9s. 2·4d. per share in cash. Removed from Register 1912 .... **1913**

Anglo-Sicilian Sulphur Co. Ld. Regd. 1896. Vol. liq. Oct. 1907. Capital returned to contributories—20s. per preference share of £1; 5s. 6d. per ordinary share of 1s. at Feb. 1908; further payments (if any) not known. Removed from Register 1911 .... **1908**

Anglo-South American Agency Ld. Regd. 1878. Vol. liq. 4 Mar. 1892. Capital returned to contributories— £60 15s. per fully-paid share of £50. Final meeting return regd. 30 July 1892 .... **1893**

Anglo-South American Bank Ld. Regd. 1888 as Bank of Tarapaca & London Ld; name changed to Bank of Tarapaca and Argentina Ld., in Dec. 1900 and as above in Jan. 1907. In 1932 assets amounting to about £7,500,000 connected with the nitrate industry were transferred to Chilnit Ld., the shares of which were subscribed for by the Bank of England and a group of important banks; 1,000,000 new preference shares were also taken up by the new company to which was transferred a sight-liability of the bank equal to the amount of the said assets and shares, the nominal value of the assets (plus interest at a low rate) being guaranteed by the bank, such guarantee to rank after all the bank's liabilities to its clients, present and future. In July 1936 the assets (excluding uncalled capital and any rights under the agreement of 1932 with Chilnit Ld.) were agreed to be transferred to Bank of London & South America Ld. for 100,000 of its fully-paid shares of £5 and the discharge, by the bank, of the liabilities (excluding those under the agreement of 1932) of

VOL. FOR

this bank; the 100,000 shares of Bank of London & South America Ld. were thereafter transferred to Chilnit Ld. in consideration of the rescission of agreement of 1932. Vol. liq. (members') 13 Aug. 1936. The liquidators have stated that no call will be made in respect of the uncalled liability on the shares of £10 each, £5 paid. Final meeting return regd. 27 Nov. 1961 .... **1937**

Anglo-South American Oilfields Ld. Regd. 1919. Court Order to wind up 28 July 1920. Struck off Register 1928 .... **1921**

Anglo-South American Real Property Co. Ld. Regd. 1910. Vol. liq. 31 Mar. 1938. No capital returned to contributories. Final meeting return regd. 31 Oct. 1945 .... **1946**

Anglo-Spanish "Brush" Electric Light & Power Co. Ld. Regd. 1882. Vol. liq. Apr. 1885. Final meeting return regd. 14 Mar. 1887 .... **1886**

Anglo-Spanish Coaling Co. Ld. Regd. 1913. Vol. liq. 20 Dec. 1928. Final meeting return regd. 8 Mar. 1930 **1929**

Anglo-Spanish Construction Co. Ld. Regd. 1924. Vol. liq. (creditors') 1 May 1952. No capital was returned to contributories. Final meeting return regd. 12 Feb. 1963 .... **1963**

Anglo-Spanish Copper Co. Ld. Regd. 1907. Vol. liq. Nov. 1909. Struck off Register 1919. .... **1911**

Anglo-Spanish Gas Co. Ld. Regd. 1886. Vol. liq. 25 Jan. 1910. Debenture holders received 15s. in £ at 5 Feb. 1914; further payments (if any) not known. No capital returned to contributories. Final meeting return regd. 26 Jan. 1916 .... **1914**

Anglo-Spanish Tartar Refineries Ld. Regd. 1920. Vol. liq. 25 Feb. 1926. Final meeting return regd. 28 May 1926 .... **1927**

Anglo-Straits Rubber & General Trust Ld. Regd. 1910. Vol. liq. 31 Mar. 1927. Capital returned to contributories—6s. 11d. per share of £1 plus 1⅔ shares of $1 in Kong Sang Rubber Co. Ld., for each share held. Final meeting return regd. 23 Apr. 1929 .... **1928**

Anglo-Sumatra Tobacco Co. Ld. Regd. 1889. Court Order to wind up 16 Jan. 1892. Removed from Register 1906 .... **1893**

Anglo-Swazi Co. Ld. Regd. 1890. Vol. liq. (members') 12 Jan. 1945. Capital returned to contributories-£23 10s. per share of £50. £164 10s. was paid into Companies' Liquidation Account. Final meeting return regd. 28 Dec. 1945 .... **1947**

Anglo-Swedish Steel Tube Co. Ld. Regd. 1896. Vol. liq. 20 July 1899. Removed from Register 1904 .... **1900**

Anglo-Swedish Trust Ld. Regd. 1912. Vol. liq. 26 Apr. 1915. Final meeting return regd. 20 May 1916 .... **1916**

Anglo-Swiss Asbestos Co. Ld. Regd. Vol. liq. Dec. 1912. Struck off Register 1916 .... **1911**

Anglo-Terek Petroleum Co. Ld. Regd. 1901. Vol. liq. 19 Nov. 1918. Final meeting return regd. 19 Nov. 1924 **1919**

Anglo-Texas Oil Co. Inc. Inc. Delaware about 1920. All shares owned by Caltex Oil Co. **1939**

Anglo-Transvaal Development Co. Ld. Regd. 1902. Vol. liq. 24 Nov. 1913. Final meeting return regd. 25 Feb. 1921 .... **1914**

Anglo-Transvaal Gold Mining Exploration Co. Ld. Regd. 1889. Vol. liq. 22 Feb. 1892. Final meeting return regd. 5 May 1896 .... ***1893**

Anglo-Transvaal Land & Exploration Co. Ld. Regd. 1902. Vol. liq. 15 Dec. 1905. Undertaking was acquired by Transvaal Mines Ld. (inc. Transvaal), in which company shareholders were entitled to approximately an equal number of shares. Removed from Register 1911 .... **1906**

Anglo-Transvaal Mines Ld. Regd. 1905. Vol. liq. 6 Dec. 1906. Removed from Register 1908 .... **1907**

Anglo-Transvaal Prospecting Co. Ld. Vol. liq. 21 Jan. 1891. Final meeting return regd. 14 Dec. 1891 .... ***1892**

Anglo-Transvaal Rhodesian Trust Ld. Regd. 1910. Vol. liq. 2 Apr. 1928. Undertaking and assets were acquired by Rhodesian Corporation Ld., in which company shareholders were entitled to 1 share of 5s. (credited as fully paid) for every 2 shares of 5s. held. Final meeting return regd. 7 Aug. 1930 .... **1929**

Anglo-United Oilfields Ld. Regd. 1919. Vol. liq. 5 Nov. 1921 for reconstruction as Anglo-United Oilfields (1921) Ld., in which company shareholders were entitled to 1 share of 10s. (credited with 7s. paid) for each share of £1 held. Final meeting return regd. 2 Mar. 1923 .... **1922**

Anglo-United Oilfields (1921) Ld. Regd. 1921. Vol. liq. 11 Aug. 1922. Shareholders were entitled to 1 share of $5 in Derby Dome (Wyoming) Oil Co., for every 2 shares of £1 held. Final meeting return regd. 23 May 1925 .... **1923**

Anglo-Universal Bank Ld. Regd. 1879. Vol. liq. May 1882. Court Order to continue winding up under supervision May 1882. Final meeting return regd. 26 Sept. 1887 .... **1883**

*See Stock Exchange Year-Book.

VOL. FOR

Anglo-Vasco Navarro Railway Co. Ld. Regd. 1886. Removed from Register 1902 .... **1891**

Anglo-Venezuelan Gold Mining Co. Ld. Regd. 1883. Struck off Register 22 June 1894 .... **1901**

Anglo-Venezuelan Oil Trust Ld. Regd. 1925. Vol. liq. (creditors') 8 Mar. 1937. Capital return to contributories—6d. per share of 1s. British Controlled Oilfields Ld. waived their right. Final meeting return regd. 6 Sept. 1939 .... **1938**

Anglo-Welsh Investments Ld. Regd. 1959. All capital was owned by Anglo-Welsh Investment Trust (Continuation) Ld. Vol. liq. (members') 2 Feb. 1967; all assets and liabilities being transferred to parent company. Final meeting return regd.4 Aug. 1967 **1969**

Anglo-Welsh Investment Trust (Continuation) Ld. Regd. 1964 as Inter-city Investment Co. Ld.; name changed Sept. 1964 to Christopher Spence Investment Co. Ld.; in Mar. 1965 to Dynamic Income Investment Trust ld. and in Apr. 1966 to above title. Vol. liq. (members') 28 Sept. 1977. Capital returned to contributories—80p per preference share (of 50p) and 69·541p per ordinary share (of 50p). £1,253 was paid into Companies' Liquidation Account in respect of unclaimed dividends and distributions. Dissolved Oct. 1978 ....**1979–80**

Anglo-West Australian Agency Ld. Regd. 1895. Vol. liq. 27 May 1897. Amalgamated with British Australian Mines Agency Ld., in which company shareholders were entitled to 1 fully-paid share of £1 for each share of £1 held. Final meeting return regd. 20 Nov. 1899 .... **1898**

Anglo-Westphalian (Chislet, Kent) Colliery Ld. See Chislet Colliery Ld.

Angla-Westphalian Copper Co. Ld. Regd. 1904. Removed from Register 1913 .... **1911**

Anglo-Westphalian Kent Coal Syndicate Ld. See North Kent Coalfield Ld.

Anglo-Westphalian Kent Coalfield Ld. See North Kent Coalfield Ld.

Anglo-Westralian & General Exploration Co. Ld. Regd. 1897. Vol. liq. 11 Jan. 1899. Final meeting return regd. 16 Dec. 1899 .... **1899**

Anglo-Westralian Development Syndicate Ld. Regd. 1900. Vol. liq. 18 Oct. 1904. No capital return to contributories was expected. Removed from Register 1907 .... **1905**

Anglo-Westralian Share & Investment Syndicate Ld. Regd. 1896. Removed from Register 1902 .... **1901**

Anglowest Ld. regd. 1967. name changed to Westminster Investment Group Ld. in 1977. Vol. liq. (creditors') 26 July 1977. Final meeting held 31 Jan. 1985 .... **1986–7**

Angola Estates Ld. Regd. 1922. Vol. liq. (creditors') 23 Apr. 1941. No capital returned to contributories. Final meeting return regd. 26 Dec. 1941 .... **1942**

Angola Exploration Syndicate Ld. Regd. 1910. Vol. liq. 23 Sept. 1914. Final meeting return regd. 7 June 1915 .... **1915**

Angola Holdings Ld. Regd. 1919 as Walford Lines Ld.; name changed 1955. Vol. liq. 31 Mar. 1966. Shareholders received 2s. 7d. cash per share (of 1s.) and 1·02 share in Companhia de Combustiveis de Lobito per 15 shares held. £1,619 unclaimed dividends and £1,092 unclaimed distributions paid into Companies' Liquidation Account. Final meeting return regd. 18 Sept. 1970 .... **1970**

Angola Oilfields Ld. Regd. 1921. Vol. liq. 22 Mar 1928. Final meeting return regd. 24 Apr. 1929 .... **1929**

Angostura Bitters (Dr. J. G. B. Siegert & Sons) Ld. Regd. 1909. Vol. liq. 5 Sept. 1921 for reconstruction as company of same name (formed in Trinidad). Shareholders were entitled to 1 ordinary and 1 preference share of new company for each ordinary and preference share held respectively. Final meeting return regd. 19 Apr. 1923 .... **1922**

Angular-Hole Machine Co. Ld. Regd. 1894. Vol. liq. 18 June 1901. Final meeting return regd 16 June 1903 ***1902**

Angus Electric Light & Power Co. Ld. See North of Scotland Electric Light & Power Co. Ld.

Angus Shipping Co. Ld. Regd. Edinburgh 1903. Vol. liq. Sept. 1916. Final meeting return regd. 19th June 1917 .... **1917**

Anibiri Wassau Exploration Ld. Regd. 1901. Vol. liq. 18 Dec. 1905. Removed from Register 1908 .... **1906**

Animal Charcoal Co. Ld. Regd. 1865. Removed from Register 1907 .... **1899**

Ankobra River Power Co. Ld. Regd. 1949. Vol. liq. (members') 30 Oct. 1967. Final meeting return regd. 9 May 1969 .... **1962**

Ankobra Rubber Estates Ld. Regd. 1910. Court Order to wind up Nov. 1911. Struck off Register 1923........ **1912**

Ankobra (Taquah & Abosso) Development Syndicate Ld. Regd. 1901. Vol. liq. May 1907. Undertaking and assets were sold to Taquah Mining and Exploration

VOL. FOR

Co. Ld., in which company shareholders were entitled to 2 fully-paid shares of £1 for every 5 shares of £1 held. Removed from Register 1908 .... **1908**

Ankola Tea & Rubber Co. Ld. Regd. 1911. Vol. liq. (members') 27 Nov. 1957. All shares were owned by Harrisons & Crosfield Ld. £89 was paid into Companies' Liquidation Account. Final meeting return regd. 20 Mar. 1958 .... **1958**

Annan Gas Co. Ld. Regd. in Edinburgh 1899. Dissolved 1 May 1949, undertaking being vested in Scottish Area Gas Board under Gas Act 1948. Holders of securities were entitled to receive, in respect of each £1 unit held. British Gas 3% guaranteed stock 1990—95 as follows:

	£	s.	d.
Ord.shares	1	12	0
6% pref. shares	1	6	6	**1952**

Annan Waterfoot Dock & Railway Co. Inc. by Special Act 1881. Undertaking abandoned under Caledonian Railway Act 1889 .... **1890**

Annapolis Iron Co. Ld. Inc. Nova Scotia 1905. Undertaking and properties acquired by Canada Iron Corporation Ld., in which company bondholders received £200 in 6% 1st mortgage sterling bonds for each $1,000 bond held. Holders of shares of common stock received an equal number of shares of common stock in purchasing company **1909**

Annexe Ld. See Nicholls, Nagle & Co. Ld.

Annfield Plain & District Gas Co. Inc. by Special Act 1907. Dissolved 1 May 1949, undertaking being vested in Northern Area Gas Board under Gas Act 1948. Holders of securities were entitled to receive British Gas 3% guaranteed stock 1990–95 as follows in respect of each £100 unit, unless otherwise stated, of security held:

	£	s.	d.
Ord. shares (7% stand.) (of £10)	0	5	0
5% pref. shares (of £10)	2	0	0
4½% perp. deb. stock	100	0	0
5% red. deb. stock 1960	100	0	0
4½% red. deb. stock	100	0	0
5% red. deb.stock	100	0	0	**1952**

Anning Steamship Co. Ld. Regd. 1903. Vol. liq. 10 Aug. 1915. Final meeting return regd. 16 Jan. 1918 ..... ***1916**

Anona Mining & Mahogany Co. Ld. Regd. 1895. Court Order to wind up May 1911. Struck off Register 1918 .... **1912**

Ansell & Sons Ld. Regd. 1889. Malting and brewery business was acquired by Ansell's Brewery Ld. for £232,747 in cash, £200,000 in ordinary shares, £120,000 in preference shares and £200,000 in debentures. Preference shareholders were entitled to either £150 in cash or 1 debenture of £100 and 10 fully-paid preference shares of £5 in new company for every 10 preference shares of £10 held. Debenture holders were entitled to £105 either in cash or in new debentures plus £6 in cash. Removed from Register 1902 .... **1901**

Anstruther & St. Andrews Railway Co. Inc. by Special Act 1880. Under North British Rly. Act 1897 the undertaking was amalgamated with that company. Holders received : £133 6s. 8d. 3% debenture stock of the North British Rly. for each £100 of 4% debenture stock held; an equal amount of 3% consolidated lien stock for each 5% preference share held; £3 10s. in cash for each ordinary share of £10 **1898**

Answers Publications Ld. Regd. 1893 as Answers Ld.; name changed Mar. 1896. Vol. liq. 9 Dec. 1896. Acquired by Harmsworth Brothers Ld. (later Amalgamated Press Ld.). Preference shareholders were entitled to 1 ordinary share in new company plus £1 in cash for each share held; ordinary shareholders were entitled to 4 ordinary shares plus £3 in cash for every 3 shares held. Final meeting return regd. 10 Feb. 1898.. **1897**

Antelope Gold Mine (Rhodesia) Ld. Regd. 1908. Vol. liq. 6 Jan. 1920. Final meeting return regd. 13 May 1921 **1920**

Antenior (Matabele) Gold Mines Ld. Regd. 1896. Removed from Register 1911 .... **1910**

Anti-Dazzle Screens (Canada) Ld. Regd. 1928. Vol. liq. (creditors') 20 Dec. 1929. No capital returned to contributories. Final meeting return regd. 11 Feb. 1933 .... **1930**

Anti-Dazzle Screens Ld. Regd. 1928. Court Order to wind up July 1929. Struck off Register 20 Mar. 1936 **1937**

Antigua Sugar Factory Ld. Regd. 1920. Vol. liq. (members') 26 Oct. 1967. Assets were purchased by Government of Antigua. Amount returned to contributories (per share of £1) 6s. 8½d. Final meeting return regd. 30 Oct. 1970 .... **1971**

Antimony-Gold & Complex Ores Extraction Co. Ld. Regd. 1896. Removed from Register 1908 .... **1900**

Antioquia (Frontino) Co. Ld. Regd. 1874. Vol. liq. 16 Nov. 1904. Final meeting return regd. 20 Oct. 1920 **1905**

VOL. FOR

Antofagasta Nitrate Co. Inc. Chile 1872. Vol. liq. Aug. 1925. Undertaking and assets were acquired by Lautaro Nitrate Co. Ld. Shareholders were entitled to 1 fully-paid share of £5 in acquiring company for every 3¾ shares of $50 held. Holders of debentures and debenture stock were entitled to either repayment at 102% or an equal amount of debenture stock *plus* 2% premium in cash **1926**

Antonio (Bilbao) Iron Ore Co. Ld. Regd. 1890. Vol. liq. 10 Dec. 1891. Final meeting return regd. 31 Dec. 1894 .... **1892**

Antrim Iron Ore Co. Ld. Regd. Dublin 1872. Vol. liq. Mar. 1891. Reconstructed under same name......... **1910**

Antwerp & Rotterdam Railway Co. Inc. Belgium 1852. Lines purchased by Belgian Government in June 1897. Fcs, 850 per ordinary share and fcs. 600 per action de dividende of no capital value were returned to holders in 1898 in 3% Belgian rentes.. **1899**

Antwerp Coal Co. (London) Ld. Regd. 1919. Vol. liq. (members') 26 Jan. 1955. Final meeting return regd. 25 Oct. 1955 .... **1938**

Antwerp Tivoli Brewery Ld. Regd. 1888. Vol. liq. 26 Jan. 1905. Removed from Register 1905 .... **1905**

Antwerp Tramways Co. Ld. Regd. 1874. Vol. liq. 14 Feb. 1877. Final meeting return regd. 19 Mar. 1878 ..... *1876

Anty-Sag Parent Co. Ld. See Furniture Appliances Ld.

Aosta Central Mining Co. Ld. Regd. 1907. Struck off Register 1915 .... **1910**

Aowin Rubber & Produce Co. Ld. Regd. 1910. Court Order to wind up Oct. 1911. Struck off Register 1923 **1912**

Apex (British) Artificial Silk Ld. Regd. 1925. Vol. liq. (members') 19 Dec. 1930. Capital returned to contributories—£3,613 4s. 8d. Final meeting return regd. 10 May 1933 .... **1931**

Aplite Syndicate Proprietary Ld. Inc. Victoria. In liquidation. All capital was owned by New Broken Hill Consolidated Ld. **1940**

Apollo (Black Reef) Gold Mining Co. Ld. Regd. 1895. Reconstructed 1902 as Klip River Estate & Gold Mines Ld. Removed from Register 1909 .... **1906**

Apollo Player & Piano Co. Ld. Regd. 1922. Court Order to wind up 18 Nov. 1924. Struck off Register Apr. 1929 .... **1930**

Apollo Tea & Rubber Trust Ld. Regd. 1926. Struck off Register 14 Jan. 1936 .... **1936**

Aporoma Goldfields Ld. Regd. 1910. Vol. liq. 22 Dec. 1926 for reconstruction as Aporoma Land & Minerals Ld., in which company shareholders were entitled to 3 shares of 5s. (credited with 3s. 9d. paid) for each share held. Holders of debentures agreed to cancellation of their holdings. Final meeting return regd. 24 Dec. 1930.. **1928**

Aporoma Land & Minerals Ld. Regd. 1927. Struck off Register 23 Sept. 1938 .... **1939**

Apostle's Bread Co. Ld. Regd. 1905. Receiver appointed 21 May 1910; ceased to act 30 Sept. 1911. Vol. liq. 30 Apr. 1909. Final meeting return regd. 7 May 1912 *1909

Apostoloff Automatic Telephone Parent Syndicate Ld. Regd. 1895. Assets were acquired in 1897 by Automatic Telephone Co. Ld. for £2,000 in cash and £73,000 in fully-paid shares. Removed from Register 1906 .... **1902**

Appalachian Exploring Co. Ld. Regd. 1895. Reconstructed 1897 as Appalachian Tin Mine Ld. in which company shareholders were entitled to 1 share of 2s. (credited with 1s. 9d. paid) for each share of 2s. held. Removed from Register 1901 .... **1898**

Appalachian Ld. Regd. 1889. Vol. liq. 29 Dec. 1891. Reconstructed 1895 as Appalachian Exploring Co. Ld. Final meeting return regd. 24 Apr. 1895 .... **1897**

Appalachian Tin Mine Ld. Regd. 1897. Undertaking was acquired by Minerals Assets Co. Ld. Removed from Register 1901 .... **1899**

Appankran Consolidated Mines Ld. Regd. 1903. Vol. liq. Dec. 1908. Removed from Register 1913. .... **1909**

Appantoo Consolidated Ld. Regd. 1910. Vol. liq. 18 Jan. 1917. Final meeting return regd. 4 July 1919 ...... **1917**

Appantoo Gold Mining Co. Ld. Regd. 1893. Vol. liq. 27 Jan. 1897. Property was acquired by W. A. P. Syndicate Ld. Final meeting return regd. 5 Jan. 1899 **1898**

Appantoo Mines Ld. Regd. 1900. Vol. liq. July 1910. Property was acquired by Appantoo Consolidated Ltd. Holders of every 40 shares of £1 were entitled to 8 fully-paid shares in Prestea Block A Ltd. and 5 fully-paid shares of £1 in purchasing company and an option (since expired) over further shares. Removed from Register 1914 .... **1911**

Appleby Brothers Ld. Regd. 1886. Vol. liq. 22 Mar. 1889. Court Order to continue winding up under supervision Apr. 1889. Final meeting return regd. 9 May 1895 .... **1890**

Appleby Gas Light & Coal Co. Inc. by Special Act 1837. Undertaking was transferred on 2 Jan. 1905 to

VOL. FOR

Appleby Corporation for £5,000 *plus* liquidation expenses **1906**

Appleby Iron Co. Ld. Reconstructed as Appleby Frodingham Steel Co. Ld. **1936**

Appleby (Joseph) Ld. Regd. 1896. Removed from Register 1905 .... **1905**

Appleby's (Alfred) Twin Roller Chain Ld. Regd. 1897. Vol. liq. 22 July 1907. Final meeting return regd. 9 Nov.1908 .... *1908

Appleton, French & Scratten Ld. Regd. 1890. Vol. liq. 27 Jan. 1898. Removed from Register 1907 .... **1892**

Appollonia Concessions Ld. Regd. 1900. Vol. liq. July 1907. Removed from Register 1908 .... **1908**

Appollonia Gold Fields Ld. Regd. 1901. Vol. liq. (members') 23 June 1938. Undertaking and assets were acquired by London & African Mining Trust Ld., [later London & Associated Investment Trust Ld.] in which company shareholders were entitled to 1 share of 1s. (credited as fully-paid) for every 3 shares of 1s. held. Final meeting return regd. 1 May 1941 .... **1939**

Approponsu (Ashanti) Syndicate Ld. Regd. 1901 Removed from Register 1912 .... **1907**

Aqueous Works & Diamond Rock-Boring Co. Ld. Regd. 1879. Vol. liq. 2 Jan. 1890. Final meeting return regd. 1 Apr. 1892 .... **1890**

Aqueous Works & Diamond Rock-Boring Co. Ld. Regd. 1891. Vol. liq. 7 Jan. 1921. Final meeting return regd. 27 Nov. 1923 .... **1922**

Aragon & Catalonia Railway Co. Ld. See Construction & Investment Co. Ld.

Aramayo Francke & Co. Ld. See Aramayo Francke Mines Ld.

Aramayo Francke Mines Ld. Regd. 1906 as Aramayo Francke & Co. Ld.; name changed Jan. 1912. Vol. liq. Jan. 1921. Undertaking and assets were acquired by Aramayo Mines in Boliva Co. in which company shareholders were entitled to 1 share of Fr. 25 for each share of £1 held. Final meeting return regd. 4 Oct. 1927 .... **1922**

Aramecina Gold & Silver Mining Co. Ld. Regd. 1889. Vol. liq. 29 June 1908. Final meeting return regd. 5 Jan. 1926 .... **1909**

Aramo Copper Mines Ld. Regd. 1897. Vol. liq. 15 Sept. 1919. Final meeting return regd. 14 July 1936 ...... **1920**

Aranka Gold Co. Ld. Regd. 1922. Vol. liq. 15 June 1926. Final meeting return regd 21 Mar. 1929 .... **1927**

Araraquara (San Paulo) Railway Co. Inc. Brazil 1896. The 6% sterling 1st mortgage debentures were repaid in 1911 .... **1911**

Arauco Co. Ld. Regd. 1886. Vol. liq. Aug. 1920. Compania de Lota y Coronel of Chili owned 97% of shares. The 5% 1st mortgage and 6% 2nd mortgage debenture stocks were repaid on 6 Sept. 1920. Struck off Register 1923 .... **1921**

Arbroath and Forfar Railway Company. Inc. by Special Act 1836. In 1923 the undertaking was merged into the London Midland & Scottish Railway Co. Holders of every £100 of Arbroath Stock of any class were entitled to £146 L.M.S. 4% debenture stock . **1924**

Arbroath & London Steamship Co. Ld. Regd. Edinburgh 1882. Vol. liq. Dec. 1887. Capital returned to contributories—£7 per share; further payments (if any) not known. Final meeting return regd. 6 Jan. 1888 .... **1888**

Arbroath Electric Light & Power Co. Ld. Regd. 1908. Vol. liq. 18 July 1946. Final meeting return regd. 27 Dec. 1946 .... **1945**

Arbuthnot Latham Holdings p.l.c. Regd. as a private company on 15 Apr. 1969; converted into public company 22 July 1969;re-regd. as p.l.c. in 1981. Dissolved on 14 Dec. 1984 .... **1982–3**

Arc & General Equipment Ld. Regd. 1895 as Jandus Arc Lamp & Electric Co. Ld.; name changed Sept. 1917. Vol. liq. 19 Aug. 1921. Final meeting return regd. 2 July 1924 .... **1922**

Arc Lamps Ld. Regd. 1901. Vol. liq. Apr. 1911. Property and assets sold to Engineering & Arc Lamps Ld. Removed from Register 1912 .... **1912**

Arcas Plating Co. Ld. Regd. 1892. Vol. liq. 19 Dec. 1894. Final meeting return regd. 7 May 1896 ...... **1895**

Archangel Matrine Insurance Co. Ld. Regd. 1873. Vol. liq. 28 Dec. 1880. Taken over by Commercial Union Assurance Co. Ld. Final meeting return regd. 25 Sept. 1885 .... *1882

Archway Investment Co. Ld. Regd. 1959. Vol. liq. (members') 30 Nov. 1970. Assets transferred to Archway Capital Fund and Archway Income Fund, shareholders receiving 1 unit per share. Final meeting return regd. 3 Nov. 1972 .... **1973–4**

Arcos Banking Corporation Ld. See Bank for Russian Trade Ld.

Ardath Tobacco Co. Ld. Regd. 1912. Vol. liq. 30 June 1926. Undertaking and assets sold to company of

VOL. FOR

same name. Preference shareholders received either 1 preference share of £1 in new company for each preference share of £1 held or cash payment at par. Final meeting return regd. 21 Dec. 1926 .... **1927**

Ardilla Copper Mines Ld. Regd. 1899. Vol. liq. Feb. 1908. Removed from Register 1908 .... **1909**

Ardrossan Gas & Water Co. Ld. Regd. Edinburgh 1874. Under Act of 1886 works were sold to the commissioners for £18,411 and company dissolved **1890**

Ardrossan, Saltcoats & District Tramways Co. Inc. by Special Act 1906. No portion of the lines had been completed at 1 Mar. 1911, nor any capital issued **1911**

Ards Railways Co. Inc. by Special Act 1908 .... **1916**

Ardwick Picture Theatre Ld. Regd. 1920. Vol. liq. 14 May 1928. Capital returned to contributories—8*s.* per share of 10*s.*; further payments (if any) not known. Final meeting return regd. 21 Mar. 1931 **1929**

Argenta Falls Silver Mining Co. Ld. Regd. 1883. Vol. liq. 5 Mar. 1889. Final meeting return regd. 5 June 1891 ***1887**

Argentella Mines Ld. Regd. 1890. Removed from Register 1906 .... **1896**

Argentina Electric Traction Co. Ld. Regd. 1899. Vol. liq. 11 Apr. 1904. Final meeting return regd. 2 Aug. 1905 .... ***1905**

Argentine Borax Co. Ld. Regd. 1899. Court Order to wind up 9 Mar. 1901. Removed from Register 1910 **1902**

Argentine Colonization & Land Co. Ld. Regd. 1888. Vol. liq. 26 Apr. 1905. Capital returned to contributories—£6 15*s.* per share of £8 at Nov. 1905; further payments (if any) not known. Removed from Register 1908. .... **1906**

Argentine Co. Ld. Regd. 1875. Removed from Register 1885 .... ***1878**

Argentine Concessions Ld. Regd. 1899. Struck off Register May 1929 .... **1930**

Argentine Crédit Foncier Ld. Removed from Register 1898 .... **1895**

Argentine Eastern Land Co. Ld. Regd. 1910. Vol. liq. (members') 17 Nov. 1938. Capital returned to contributories—2*s.* 1⅓*d.* per share of 1*s.* £22 3*s.* 6*d.* was paid to Companies' Liquidation Account. Final meeting return regd. 3 May 1940 .... **1940**

Argentine Farmers' Bank Ld. *See* Land & Banking Agency Ld.

Argentine Great Western Railway Co. Ld. Regd. 1887. Vol. liq. (members') 1 Apr. 1948. The undertaking was acquired by Argentine Government as from 1 July 1946. The 4% 1st and 4% 2nd debenture stocks were repaid at par. with interest to 30 Sept. 1947 and 5% debenture stock at 110% (arrears of interest being cancelled); capital returned to contributories £37 10*s.* per £100 5% preferred, £65 per £100 6% guaranteed preference and £17 10*s.* per £100 ordinary stock. £5,065 paid into Companies Liquidation Account. Final meeting return regd. 7 Apr. 1954 .... **1955**

Argentine Gulf Oil Syndicate Ld. Regd. 1910. Court Order to wind up Jan. 1913. Struck off Register 1919 **1913**

Argentine Hardwoods & Lands Co. Ld. Regd. 1910. Receiver appointed for holder of debentures and debenture stock Apr. 1922; ceased to act June 1930. In 1927 the property was sold for $200,000. Struck off Register July 1931 .... **1932**

Argentine Iron & Steel Co. (Pedro Vasena E. Hijos) Ld. Regd. 1912. Court Order to wind up 19 Feb. 1924. Struck off Register 1936 .... **1925**

Argentine Lands & Industries Ld. *See* Tokengate Investment Co. Ld.

Argentine Meat Preserving Co. Ld. Regd. 1889. Undertaking was acquired in 1903 by Liebig's Extract of Meat Co. Ld. for £50,000 in cash. Removed from Register 1905 .... **1905**

Argentine-Montezuma Investment Corporation. Inc. Colorado 1910. It is understood that company was advertised as defunct in 1916 .... **1913**

Argentine National & Provincial Lands Ld. Regd. 1911. Vol. liq. 25 Oct. 1929. Capital returned to contributories—10*s.* per share of 5*s.*; further payments (if any) not known. Final meeting return regd. 25 July 1933 .... **1930**

Argentine Navigation Co. Mihanovich Ld. Inc. Argentine 1930. Undertaking sold to an Argentine financial group; resolution approving premature dissolution and liquidation passed 5 Nov. 1942. The outstanding 5½% 1st mortgage debenture were repaid at 103% on 1 Dec. 1942. Shareholders received $m/n 22·71 per 10% participating preference, $m/n 22·07 per participating preference or $m/n 30·41 per ordinary share **1943**

Argentine Navigation Co. (Nicholas Mihanovich) Ld. Regd. 1909. Vol. liq. (members') 31 Mar. 1931. Undertaking and assets were sold to Argentine Navigation Co. Mihanovich Ld. Shareholders received 22*s.* 6*d.* per preference share of £1; and 25*s.* 7½*d.* per ordinary share of £1. £578 2*s.* 6*d.* was paid to Companies' Liquidation Account. A further £877 6*s.* 4*d.* unclaimed in respect of dividends, bonds, etc., which fell due before liquidation was also paid to Companies' Liquidation Account. Final meeting return regd. 19 Sept. 1933 .... **1942**

Argentine North Eastern Railway Co. Ld. Regd. 1887. Vol. liq. (members') 31 Mar. 1948. the undertaking having been sold to the Argentine Government as from 1 July 1946. Capital returned to contributories—£17 13*s.* 4*d.* per £100 ordinary stock. £18,453 was paid into Companies Liquidation Account. Final meeting return regd. 27 June 1957 .... **1958**

Argentine Northern Land Co. Ld. Regd. 1905. Vol. liq. June 1908 for reconstruction under same name. Shareholders were entitled to 16*s.* 8*d.* in shares of new company and £1 1*s.* 8*d.* in cash for each share of £1 (13*s.* paid) held. Removed from Register 1909 **1909**

Argentine Oilfields Ld. Regd. 1922. Vol. liq. 24 Nov. 1926. Final meeting return regd. 14 Mar. 1935 .... **1927**

Argentine Railway Co. Inc. Maine 1912. In May 1920 certain assets were transferred to South American Assets Co. Ld. (later Share & Assets Investments Ld.) in which company noteholders were entitled to £40 1st debenture stock, £23 6*s.* 8*d.* 2nd debenture stock and 5 fully-paid ordinary shares of £1 *plus* £55 in cash for every £100 6% notes held **1921**

Argentine Railway Loan Co. Ld. Inc. Argentine 1905. The outstanding 5% Advance Certificates (to bearer) were repayable on 1 Nov. 1914 .... **1914**

Argentine Refinery Co. Inc. Province of Buenos Aires 1886. Outstanding debentures were repaid on 17 June 1937 .... **1938**

Argentine Republic Land & Trust Co. Ld. Regd. 1889. Removed from Register 1906. .... **1901**

Argentine Stone & Brick Co. Ld. Regd. 1909. Struck off Register 1922 .... **1921**

Argentine Sugar Estate & Factories Ld. Regd. 1883. Removed from Register 1909 .... **1890**

Argentine Timber & Estates Co. Ld. Regd. 1915. A receiver was appointed on behalf of debenture holders in Mar. 1922. Vol. liq. 10 Oct. 1922. Final meeting return regd. 13 Aug. 1935 .... **1923**

Argentine Tobacco Co. Ld. Regd. 1911. Vol. liq. 9 Feb. 1920. Undertaking and assets were acquired by Sociedad Anonima Manufactura de Tabacos, Piccardo & Cia. Ltda. of Buenos Aires, in which company shareholders were entitled to $16·265454 in preference shares of m/n 100 for each preference share of £1 held or $0·789223 in preference shares and $2·360755 in ordinary shares for each ordinary share of 10*s.* held or $0·572729 in ordinary shares of m/n 100 for each deferred share of 1*s.* held. Final meeting return regd. 18 Mar. 1922 .... **1921**

Argentine Tramways & Power Co Ld. Regd. 1912. In June 1923 Argentine Light & Power Co. Ld. (later Atlas Electric & General Trust Ld.), acquired over 99% of ordinary shares of £1, all preference shares of £1 and all debenture stock by exchanging 1 ordinary share of £1 and 1 preference share of £1 for each ordinary and preference share held respectively; debenture stockholders received £85 in 6% debenture stock for each £100 of 5% stock held. Vol. liq. (members') 16 Apr. 1931. Final meeting return regd. 5 Jan. 1932 .... **1930**

Argentine Tramways Co. Ld. Regd. 1871. Taken over by Anglo-Argentine Tramways Co. Ld. Removed from Register 1884 .... ***1878**

Argentine Transandine Holdings Ld. Regd. 1939. Vol. liq. (members') 20 June 1946. Holders of outstanding C stock were satisfied by cash payment in Aug. 1946 equal to 66% of holdings. Capital returned to contributories—2*s.* 5*d.* per share of 1*s.* Paid into Companies' Liquidation Account—(1) unclaimed dividends £1,075 15*s.* 2*d.*; (2) distributions £426 17*s.* 0*d.* Final meeting return regd. 3 Mar. 1960 .... **1961**

Argentine Transandine Railway Co. Ld. Regd. 1886 as Buenos Aires and Valparaiso Transandine Railway Co. Ld.; name changed Dec. 1904. In July 1937 the railway undertaking was sold to the Argentine Government. Holders of 5% (Government bond) debenture stock were entitled to an equal nominal amount of Argentine 5% sterling bonds. The remaining assets were sold to Argentine Transandine Holdings Ld., in which company holders of 4% A and 4% B debenture stocks were entitled to equal amounts of similar stock *plus* 80% and 20% respectively of their holdings in C stock; holders of preferred shares were entitled to £8 C stock and 12 shares of 1*s.* for each preferred share of £20 held; holders of deferred shares were entitled to 20 shares of 1*s.* for each deferred share of £20 held. Court Order to dissolve 30 Apr. 1940 .... **1940**

**See Stock Exchange Year-Book.*

VOL. FOR

Argentine Tunnel Railway Co. Practically all capital was held by Argentine-Montezuma Investment Corporation 1913

Argentine Union Railway Co. Ld. Regd. 1910. Vol. liq. 16 Mar. 1915. Final meeting return regd. 28 Mar. 1924 1915

Argentine (Western) Petroleum Syndicate Ld. Regd. 1909. Removed from Register 1912 1912

Arghan Co. Ld. Regd. 1919. Vol. liq. 29 Aug. 1924. Final meeting return regd. 16 Apr. 1927 1925

Argo Mining & Tunnel Co. Inc. Delaware 1908. The properties were in the hands of the bondholders in Mar. 1927 1931

Argo Transportation & Tunnel Co. Ld. Regd. 1905. Vol. liq. Sept. 1908. Properties and assets were sold to Argo Mining and Tunnel Co. Shareholders were entitled to subscribe at par for $50 6% Bonds in new company for every 100 shares held and a bonus of fully-paid shares of an equivalent amount. Removed from Register 1910 1909

Argo Tunnel & Mining Co. Ld. Regd. 1899. Reconstructed 1905 as Argo Transportation and Tunnel Co. Ld., in which company shareholders were entitled to 1 share of 10s. (credited with 7s. paid) for each share of £1 held. Removed from Register 1909 1908

Argonaut Corporation Ld. Regd. 1928 as Argonaut Salvage Corpn. Ld.; name changed 1933. Struck off Register 16 Mar. 1951 1938

Argonaut Marine Insurance Co. Ld. Regd. 1 Feb. 1917. Court Order to wind up 7 July 1930. Liquidator released 15 Dec. 1942. Struck off Register 21 Aug. 1945 1946

Argonaut Salvage Corpn. Ld. See Argonaut Corporation Ld.

Argonauts Ld. Regd. 1895. Vol. liq. 4 Nov. 1920. Shareholders received 18 fully-paid shares of £1 in Pniels Ld., for every 100 shares of £1 held; further distributions (if any) not known. Final meeting return regd. 7 Oct. 1921 1921

Argonite Non-Flammable Celluloid Co. Ld. Regd. 1911. Vol. liq. 17 Mar. 1913. Final meeting return regd. 31 Dec. 1914 1914

Argosy and Sundial Libraries Ld. Regd. 1935. Vol. liq. (members') 3 Nov. 1964. Capital returned to contributories—2s. 1d. per preference share of 10s. £63 14s. was paid into Companies Liquidation Account in respect of unclaimed returns of capital and £675 in respect of unclaimed distributions. Final meeting return regd. 29 Apr. 1966 1967

Argosy Investment Trust Ld. Regd. 1920. Vol. liq. (creditors') 17 June 1937. No capital returned to contributories. Final meeting return regd. 9 Sept. 1939 1938

Argus Concessions Ld. Regd. 1926. Vol. liq. (members') 28 May 1937. Certain investments were distributed in specie. Final meeting return regd. 28 June 1941 1938

Argus Financial Co. Ld. Regd. 1893. Vol. liq. 8 Feb. 1897. Capital returned to contributories—£1 0s. 4½d per share of £1 at 17 Sept. 1897; further payments (if any) not known. Final meeting return regd. 6 Nov. 1897 1898

Argus Life Assurance Co. Inc. by Special Act 1833. Policies were taken over by Imperial Life Insurance Co., in 1888 1889

Argus Printing Co. Ld. Regd. 1897. Vol. liq. 1 Jan. 1925. Undertaking and assets were acquired by Argus Press Ld. Capital returned to contributories—£2 in cash per share of £1 held. Final meeting return regd. 3 Feb. 1926 1926

Argus Tin Corporation Ld. Regd. 1924. Vol. liq. (members') 5 Nov. 1937 for reconstruction under same name (later Argus Tin & Securities Corporation Ld.). Shareholders were to receive 1 share of 2s. (credited with 1s. 8d. paid) in new company for every 4 shares held. Final meeting return regd. 16 July 1942 1938

Argyle Assets Co. Ld. Regd. Edinburgh 1906 as Stewart & McDonald Ld.; name changed Apr. 1925. Vol. liq. Dec. 1932. Business was acquired by Csmpbells and Stewarts & Macdonald Ld. Final meeting return regd. 8 June 1935 1933

Argyll Cotton Spinning Co. (Holdings) Ld. Regd. 1920 as Argyll Cotton Spinning Co. Ld.; name changed Mar. 1953. Vol. liq. (members') 30 Sept. 1955. All assets transferred to Lancashire Cotton Corpn. Ld. which owned all capital of this company. £706 6s. paid into Companies' Liquidation Account. Final meeting return regd. 20 June 1956 1957

Argyll Furnishing Co. Ld. Regd. 1929 as Bed Settees Ld.; name changed Apr. 1931. Vol. liq. (members') 6 Mar. 1936. £44 10s. 2d. was paid to Companies' Liquidation Account in respect of unclaimed dividends. Final meeting return regd. 11 May 1937 1937

VOL. FOR

"Argyll Motors" Ld. Regd. Edinburgh 1905. Vol. liq. July 1908 for reconstruction as Argylls Ld., in which company debenture stockholders were entitled to 12s. debenture stock for every £1 held; shareholders were entitled to 1 preference share of 10s. (credited with 6s. 4d. paid) for every £1 of preference shares held and 1 ordinary share of 10s. (credited with 6s. 4d. paid) for every ordinary share of £1 held. Struck off Register 9 Apr. 1937 1909

Argylls Ld. Regd. Edinburgh 1909. Vol. liq. June 1914. Court Order to continue winding up Aug. 1914. Struck off Register 26 Sept. 1933 1915

Ariadne Steamship Co. Ld. Regd. 1891. Vol. liq. 15 Nov. 1927. Final meeting return regd. 30 Mar. 1929 1917

Arica and Tacna Railway Co. Inc. Peru 1857. In 1942 the Peruvian Government took over the line. Vol. liq. July 1944. Capital returned to contributories—4s. 11d. per share of £20 1945

Ariel Motors (1906) Ld. Regd. 1906. Removed from Register 1913 1910

Ariel Pram Wheel Works Ld. Regd. 1897 as Littlewood's Ariel Wheel Works Ld.; name changed 1906. Removed from Register 1914 1914

Arigna Colliery Extension Railway. Under terms of Irish Free State Railways Act 1924, the undertaking was absorbed by Great Southern Railways Co. from 1 Jan. 1929 1945

Arinem Tea Co. Ld. Regd. Edinburgh 1912. Vol. liq. Dec. 1923. Final meeting return regd. 25 June 1924 1924

Arinis (Roumania) Oilfields Ld. Regd. 1923. Struck off Register 1933 .... *1933

Ariston Gold Mines Ld. Regd. 1927. Vol. liq. 22 Aug. 1929 for reconstruction as Ariston Gold Mines (1929) Ld. in which company shareholders were entitled to receive 5 shares (credited with 2s. 6d. paid) for every 4 shares held and noteholders were entitled to receive 1 note for every 1 note held. Final meeting return regd. 18 Dec. 1935 1931

Ariston Gold Mining Syndicate Ld. See New Ariston Gold Mining Co. Ld.

Arizona Consolidated Copper Mines Ld. Regd. 1899. Vol. liq. 16 Jan. 1922. Reconstructed as Bellingwe Gold Reefs Ld., in which company shareholders were entitled to 12 shares of 2s. 6d. (credited with 1s. 8d. paid) for each share of £1 held. Final meeting return regd. 17 May 1939 1922

Arizona Copper Co. Ld. Regd. Edinburgh 1882. Vol. liq. 23 July 1884. Business and property acquired by company of same name. Final meeting return regd. 13 Apr. 1892 1908

Arizona Copper Co. Ld. Regd. Edinburgh 1884. Vol. liq. Apr. 1929. Capital returned to contributories—£2 3s. 5¾d. per share of 5s. at July 1929; further payments (if any) not known. Practically all assets were acquired by Phelps Dodge Corporation. Dissolution deferred to 21 Aug. 1930 by Order of Court 1930

Arizona-Morenci Copper Co. Inc. Arizona 1909. The London office was closed in May 1913 1913

Arizona Power Company. Inc. Maine 1908. Under plan of reorganization of 24 July 1934 all property and assets were transferred on 1 Oct. 1935 to Arizona Power Corporation 1936

Arizona Trust & Mortgage Co. Ld. Regd. Edinburgh 1883. Vol. liq. Dec. 1894. Court Order to continue winding up under supervision Mar. 1895. Shareholders were entitled to £2 6s. 6d. "A" debenture stock in Arizona Copper Co. Ld. for each share of £3 (£1 paid); holders of fully-paid shares received back the £2 paid in advance of calls either in cash or in 5% debentures at par. Final meeting return regd. 19 July 1895. Court Order to dissolve 30 Oct. 1895 1895

Arizona Western Oil Co. Ld. Inc. Arizona 1900. Undertaking and property transferred to British California Oil Co. Ld., in which company shareholders received an equal number of shares. 1903

Arizu Estates. Inc. Province of Mendoza 1907. The outstanding debentures were redeemed on 1 Oct. 1943 at 102% 1944

Arkansas Valley Land & Cattle Co. Ld. Regd. 1882, Vol. liq. 29 Jan. 1891. Final meeting return regd. 25 Mar. 1896 1891

Arkell Bros. Ld. Regd 1900. Court Order to wind up 1906. Removed from Register 1911 1908

Arkikilie (Wassau) Gold Mining Co. Ld. Regd. 1900. Vol. liq. 2 Oct. 1902. A capital return to contributories of 5s. 3d. per share of £1 was anticipated. Removed from Register 1904 1903

Arklow Manure Co. Ld. Regd. Dublin 1886 to acquire business of Wicklow Copper Mine Co. In liquidation in 1888 1888

Armadale Gas Co. Ld. Regd. in Edinburgh 1918. Dissolved 1 May 1949, undertaking being vested in Scottish Area Gas Board under Gas Act 1948.

*See Stock Exchange Year-Book.

VOL. FOR

Holders of 3½% mort. deb. stock were entitled to receive £100 British Gas 3% guaranteed stock 1990–95 for every £100 stock held **1952**

Armdale Gold Mining Co. Ld. Regd. 1896. Court Order to wind up 23 Feb. 1898. Removed from Register 1908 .... **1899**

Armagh & Keady Light Railway Co. Ld. Regd. Dublin 1883. Removed from Register 1892. .... **1893**

Armitage & Ibbetson Ld. Regd. 1898. Removed from Register 1912 .... **1911**

Armitage (Sir Elkanah) & Sons Ld. Regd. 1890. Vol. liq. 16 Dec. 1980. Final meeting return regd. 15 dec. 1981 .... **1960**

Armitstead & Co. Ld. Regd. 1923. Vol. liq. (members') 5 Dec. 1930. Capital returned to contributories-£9 3s. 6·816d. per share of £10. Final meeting return regd. 28 Jan. 1931 .... **1931**

Armstrong & Co. Ld. Regd. 1885. Vol. liq. 1889. Removed from Register 1892 .... **1890**

Armstrong & Siddle Motor Services Ld. Regd. 1928. Vol. liq. 18 Sept. 1929. Direct controlling interest held by Ribble Motor Services Ld. Final meeting return regd. 27 Mar. 1930 .... **1930**

Armstrong Propeller Co. Ld. Regd. 1895. Struck off Register Aug. 1904 .... **1905**

Armstrong (Sir W.G.) & Co. Ld. *See* Armstrong Whitworth Securities Co. Ld.

Armstrong (Sir W.G.), Mitchell & Co. Ld. Regd. 1882. Undertaking was acquired by Armstrong Whitworth Securities Co. Ld. in 1896. Struck off Register Aug. 1929 .... **1943**

Armstrong (Sir W. G.) Whitworth & Co. Ld. *See* Armstrong Whitworth Securities Co. Ld.

Armstrong (Sir W. G.) Whitworth & Co. (Shipbuilders) Ld. Regd. 1929. Vol. liq. (members') 9 Jan 1956. All capital owned by National Shipbuilders Security Ld. Final meeting return regd. 28 Nov. 1956 ...... **1940**

Armstrong Whitworth Securities Co. Ld. Regd. 1896 as Sir W.G. Armstrong & Co. Ld., name changed to Sir W.G. Armstrong Whitworth & Co. Ld. in Mar. 1897. and as above in July 1929. Vol. liq. (members') 16 Sept. 1943. Capital returned to contributories—1·872d. per A ordinary share of 1s. and 3s. 0·695805d. per B ordinary share of 10s. Final meeting return regd. 6 Nov. 1945; Court Order deferring dissolution until 1 Nov. 1948 .... **1947**

Armstrongs & Main Ld. *See* Main (A. & J.) & Co. Ld.

Army & Navy Auxiliary Co-operative Supply Ld. Regd. 1886. Vol. liq. 16 June 1919. Undertaking was acquired by Army and Navy Co-operative Society Ld. (later Army and Navy Stores Ld.) in which company shareholders were entitled to 3 shares of 1s. (credited as fully-paid) for each share of £1 held. Debenture holders were offered redemption at par or 5% debentures of new company. Final meeting return regd. 22 June 1921 .... **1920**

Army & Navy Co-operative Bread Co. Ld. Regd. 1886. Vol. liq. 16 Jan. 1888. Final meeting return regd. 9 Dec. 1892 .... **1899**

Army & Navy Co-operative Breweries Ld. Regd. 1895. Removed from Register 1902 .... **1901**

Army & Navy Depository Ld. Regd. 1885. Removed from Register 1902 .... **1889**

Army & Navy Furnishing & General Supply Co. Ld. Regd. 1883 as Army & Navy House Furnishing Co. Ld.; name changed Mar. 1914. Vol. liq. 22 Jan. 1927. Final meeting return regd. 15 Aug. 1927 .... **1911**

Army & Navy Hotel Co. Ld. Regd. 1880. Court Orders: to wind up 5 Mar. 1886; to dissolve 9 Apr.1889 .. **1887**

Army & Navy House Furnishing Co. Ld. *See* Army & Navy Furnishing & General Supply Co. Ld.

Army and Navy Investment Co. Ld. Regd. 1887. Under scheme of 1 May 1964 the undertaking and assets were acquired by Bankers' Investment Trust Ld. in which company ordinary shareholders were entitled to receive a like amount of fully-paid ordinary capital, and preference stockholders £10 fully-paid preference capital for every £9 of preference held. The outstanding £400,000 4% perpetual debenture stock was cancelled, holders receiving a like amount of 4% perpetual debenture stock in exchange. Dissolved 31 Aug. 1964 under Sect. 208 of the Companies Act, 1948 .... **1965**

Army, Navy & Civil Service Co-operative Society of India Ld. Regd. 1890. Vol. liq. 29 June 1893. Court Order to wind up 9 Aug. 1893. Removed from Register 1897 .... **1894**

Army, Navy & Civil Service Co-operative Society of South Africa Ld. *See* Naval, Military & Civil Service Co-operative Society of South Africa.

Arnakal Tea Estates Ld. Regd. 1926. Vol. liq. (members') Jan. 1944. Capital returned to contributories—39s. 10·9d. per share of £1. Final meeting return regd. 9 July 1947 .... **1948**

Arnheim's Land Exploration Co. Ld. Regd. 1899. Removed from Register 1911 .... **1909**

Arnhemsche Petroleum Mij. In liquidation. Controlling interest was held by Phoenix Oil & Transport Co. Ld **1936**

Arnhold Bros. & Co. Ld. (China). Business was acquired in Mar. 1923 by Arnhold & Co. Ld. **1937**

Arniston Coal Co., Ld. Regd. Edinburgh 1874. Vol. liq. (members) 30 Sept. 1952. Capital returned to contributories—51s. 0·80194d. per 1s. ordinary stock. Final meeting return regd. 14 Oct. 1960 .... **1961**

Arnoya Mining Co. Ld. Regd. 1907. Vol. liq. Aug. 1915. Struck off Register Mar. 1933 .... **1934**

Aroa Mines Ld. Regd. 1896. Removed from Register 1910 .... **1900**

Aroha Gold Mines Ld. Regd. 1896. Removed from Register 1901 .... **1899**

Arrol (Archibald) & Sons Ld. Regd 1895. Vol. liq. (members') 27 Aug. 1951. Undertaking acquired by Ind Coope & Allsopp Ld. [later Ind Coope Ld.] which company formerly owned direct controlling interest. £1,056 8s. 7d. was paid into Companies' Liquidation Account. Final meeting return regd. 12 Aug. 1952 .... **1953**

Arrol-Johnston & Aster Engineering Co. Ld. Regd. Edinburgh 1912 as Arrol-Johnston Ld.; name changed May 1927. Vol. liq. July 1929. Final meeting return regd. 21 July 1939 .... **1930**

Arrol (Sir William) & Co. (Swansea) Ld. Regd. 1922. Vol. liq. 15 Jan. 1929. Final meeting return regd. 18 Dec. 1929 .... *****1929**

Arrow Brownbill Gold Mining Co. Ld. Regd. 1898. Removed from Register 1904 .... **1903**

Arrow Fuel Co. Ld. Regd. 1920. Vol. liq. (members') 12 Sept. 1930. Capital returned to contributories—£6,591 17s. 1d. *plus* certain investments which were distributed as specie. Works, plant, &c. were acquired by British Briquettes Ld. Final meeting return regd. 16 Mar. 1931 .... **1931**

Arrow Proprietary Gold Mines (Western Australia) Ld. Taken over by New Arrow Proprietary Gold Mines (W.A.) Ld. Removed from Register 1911 .... *****1898**

Arrow Shipping Co. Ld. Regd. 1881. Vol. liq. 8 Nov. 1899. Final meeting return regd. 17 Aug. 1900 .... **1900**

Art Photogravure Co. Ld. Regd. 1930. Vol. liq. (members') 19 May 1931. Capital returned to contributories—1s. 2¼d. per share. Final meeting return regd. 6 June 1933 .... **1932**

Arthur (Robert) Theatres Co. Ld. Regd. 1897. Vol. liq. (members') 9 Apr. 1941. Undertaking acquired by Howard & Wyndham Ld., in which company shareholders were entitled to 1 fully-paid 5% preference share of £1 for every 3 preference shares of £1 held *plus* 4s. 5d. per share in cash. Ordinary shareholders were entitled to 3d. per ordinary share of £1 held. £618 1s. 4d. was paid into Companies' Liquidation Account. Final meeting return regd. 26 May 1942 .... **1942**

Artificial Silk Spinning Co. Ld. Regd. 1896. Vol. liq. 28 June 1899. Undertaking was acquired by New Artificial Silk Co. Ld. Final meeting return regd. 12 Jan. 1900 .... **1899**

Artisans Free Homes, Land, Investment & General Insurance Co. Ld. Regd. 1905. Court Order to wind up 21 June 1904. Liquidator released 7 Sept. 1910. Removed from Register 6 June 1913 .... **1905**

Artizans' Land & Mortgage Corporation Ld. Regd. 1892. Vol. liq. 1903. Capital returned to contributories—1s. 3d. per share of 10s. in July 1903; further payments (if any) not known. Removed from Register 1904 .... **1904**

Aruba Gold Concession Ld. Regd. 1899. Vol. liq. Apr. 1908. Removed from Register 1909 .... **1909**

Aruba Island Gold Mining Co. Ld. Regd. 1872. Removed from Register 1903 .... **1901**

Arundel Gas Co. Inc. by Special Act 1897. Dissolved 1 May 1949, undertaking being vested in South Eastern Area Gas Board under Gas Act 1948. Holders of 4½% irred. deb. stock were entitled to receive £113 British Gas 3% guaranteed stock 1990—95 for every £100 stock held **1952**

Arvon Shipping Co. Ld. Regd. 1876. Vol. liq. Oct. 1887. Final meeting return regd. 12 Dec. 1883 .... **1884**

Asahan (Sumatra) Rubber Estates Ld. Regd. 1910. Vol. liq. 18 Aug. 1913. Reconstructed as Asahan Rubber Estates Ld. in which company shareholders were entitled to 4 shares of 10s. (credited with 7s. paid) for every 3 shares of £1 held. Final meeting return regd. 27 Apr. 1914 .... **1914**

Asam Kumbang Tin Dredging Ld. Inc. Federated Malay States 1920. Vol. liq. 11 Feb. 1939. Undertaking and assets were acquired by Austral Amalgamated Tin Ld., in which company shareholders were entitled to 580 shares of 5s. (credited as fully-paid) for every 100 shares of £1 held **1940**

VOL. FOR

Ashby's Staines Brewery Ld. Regd. 1899. Vol. liq. (members') 1 Oct. 1936. Undertaking was acquired by H. & G. Simunds Ld., in which company shareholders were entitled to £1 preference stock for each preference share of £1 held. Holders of 4½% and 5½% debenture stocks were entitled to either repayment at 110% or 105% respectively on 7 Nov 1936 or 110% or 105% of holding in 3½% debenture stock in purchasing company *plus* 1% in cash. Final meeting return regd. 22 June 1937 1937

Ashford Gas & Coke Co. Ld. Regd. 1865. Vol. liq. 13 Dec. 1897. Undertaking was acquired by Ashford Urban District Council. Final meeting return regd. 22 June 1898 1899

Ashley Gardens Properties Ld. Regd. 19 May 1896. Vol. liq. (creditors') 3 nov. 1975. Return of final meeting regd. 22 Nov. 1983. Struck off register Feb. 1984 1985–6

Ashley Wireless Telephone Co. Ld. Regd. 1922 Vol. liq. 8 July 1924. Final meeting return regd 6 Apr.1925 *1925

Ashley's Patent (Machine-made) Bottle Co. Ld. Regd. 1888. Receiver was appointed in Sept. 1894. Vol. liq. 2 Oct. 1894. Removed from Register 1898 1895

Ashover Light Railway Co. Liq. by order of Court 26 July 1950. Final meeting return regd. 2 Feb. 1951 1953

Ashton & Oldham Canal Co. Inc. by Special Act. Under an Act of 1883 the guaranteed annuity from the Manchester, Sheffield and Lincolnshire Railway Co., was converted into 4½% debenture stock 1884

Ashton & Parsons Ld. Regd. 1898. Vol. liq. (members') 14 Feb. 1930. Capital returned to contributories— 20s. per preference share of £1; £37 12s. 6½d. per ordinary share. Final meeting return regd. 2 July 1930 1935

Ashton (F. W.) & Co. Ld. Regd. 1896. Undertaking was acquired by Calico Printers' Association Ld. Removed from Register 1901 1900

Ashton Gas Co. Inc. as Ashton-under-Lyne Gas & Waterworks Co.; reinc. by Special Act 1847 as above. Dissolved 1 May 1949, undertaking being vested in North Western Area Gas Board under Gas Act 1948. Holders of securities were entitled to receive British Gas 3% guaranteed stock 1990–95 as follows:

	£	s.	d.
10% stand. shares (of £30)	90	0	0
5½% perp. deb. stock (per £100)	130	0	0

1951

Ashton, Higgin & Co. Ld. Regd. 1909. Vol. liq. (members') 30 Dec. 1938. Undertaking acquired by I.C.I. (Salt) Ld. Capital returned to contributories— £10 0s. 9·9d. per preference or ordinary share of £10. Final meeting return regd. 2 Aug. 1939 1943

Ashton Moss Colliery Co. Ld. Regd. 1922. Vol. liq. 30 July 1928. Final meeting return regd. 17 Apr. 1929 1929

Ashton, Stalybridge, Hyde and Glossop Bank Ld. Regd. 1884. Vol. liq. 26 July 1900. Business sold to Parr's Bank Ld. for 1,250 shares of £100 (credited with £20 paid) and £6,250 in cash 1901

Ashton-Under-Lyne Gas & Waterworks Co. See Ashton Gas Co.

Ashwell (Oakham) Farming Co. Ld. Regd. 1921. Struck off Register 19 Mar. 1937 1938

Ashworth (Geo. l.) & Bros. Ld. Undertaking and assets acquired by Cauldon Potteries Ld. 1924

Asia Mill (Holdings) Ld. Regd. 1920 as Asia Mill (1920) Ld.; name changed July 1942 to Asia Mill Ld. and as above Mar. 1953. Vol. liq. 11 Apr. 1957. Final meeting return regd. 28 Sept. 1959 1955

Asia Mill Ld. See above.

Asia Mill (1920) Ld. See above

Asia Minor Co. Ld. Regd. 1892. Struck off Register Mar. 1929 1930

Asia Minor Co. Ld. Regd. 1896. Removed from Register 1911 1910

Asia Minor Mining Co. Ld. Reconstructed 1892 as Asia Minor Co. Ld., in which company shareholders were entitled to 1 ordinary share of 10s. (credited with 7s. 6d. paid) for each share held. The debenture holders were entitled to an equal amount of fully-paid preference shares of 10s. in the new compsny 1896

Asiakwa Alluvial Syndicate Ld. Regd. 1911. Vol. liq. 26 June 1919. Undertaking was acquired by Goldfields of Eastern Akim Ld. Final meeting return regd. 27 Apr. 1920 1920

Asiakwa Hydraulicking & Mining Corporation Ld. Regd. 1900. Vol. liq. May 1908. Removed from Register 1912 1909

Asiatic Industries Ld. Regd. 1914. Vol. liq. 2 Mar. 1920. Undertaking acquired by Pernambang Rubber Estates Ld. Final meeting return regd. 3 Feb. 1921 *1921

Asiatic Trading Corporation Ld. Regd. 1921. Struck off Register 14 Dec. 1951 1940

Asikam Bibiani Goldfields Ld. Regd. 1901. Vol. liq. 30 Jan. 1906. Removed from Register 1906 1907

VOL. FOR

Askern Coal & Iron Co. Ld. Regd. 1910. A subsidiary of S. Instone & Co. Ld., Vol. liq. 5 Nov. 1953. Final meeting return regd. 28 Mar. 1956 1949

Askham Bros. & Wilson Ld. Regd. 1880. Removed from Register 1906 .... *1886

Askrigg & Reeth Electric Supply Co. Ld. Regd. 1930. Dissolved 1 Apr. 1948, undertaking being vested in the British (later Central) Electricity Authority and North-Eastern Area Board under the Electricity Act 1947. Ordinary shareholders were entitled to receive £1 18s. 6d. British Electricity 3% guaranteed stock (1968–73) for each share (of £1) held 1949

Asolvesby Steamship Co. Ld. Regd. 1905. Removed from Register 1913 1910

Asp Gold Mining Co. Ld. Inc. Southern Rhodesia 1911. Vol. liq. Mar. 1928 1929

Aspatria Gas Light Co. Ld. Regd. 1895. Dissolved 1 May 1949, undertaking being vested in Northern Ares Gas Board under Gas Act 1948. Holders of ordinary shares (of £5) were entitled to receive £8 6s. 8d. British Gas 3% guaranteed stock 1990–95 for each share held. 1952

Asphaltic Wood Pavement Co. Ld. Regd. 1874. Wound up by Order of Court 14 Mar. 1883 .... *1884

Aspinall's Enamel Ld. Regd. 1891. Court Order to wind up 23 Apr. 1934. Struck off Register 24 Oct. 1939 1940

Aspinall's Ticket Machines Ld. Regd. 1925. All shares owned by Automatic Equipments Ld. Struck off Register 1936 1930

Aspley Guise & Woburn Sands Gas Co. Ld. Regd. 1868. Dissolved 1 May 1949, undertaking being vested in Eastern Area Gas Board under Gas Act 1948. Holders of securities were entitled to receive British Gas 3% guaranteed stock 1990–95 as followers in respect of each £5 unit, unless otherwise stated, of securty held:

	£	s.	d.
Ord. shares	5	0	0
6% pref. shares	6	6	6

1952

Assam-Bengal Railway Co. Ld. Regd. 1892. Vol. liq. (members') 1 Jan. 1942. Capital returned to contributories—£100 10s. 6d. per £100 stock held. £90 was paid into Companies Liquidation Account. Final meeting return regd. 27 Apr. 1945 1946

Assam Co. Ld. Inc. by Special Act 1865; regd. as limited Nov. 1923. Vol. liq. 21 Dec. 1923 for reconstruction under same name. Shareholders received 100 fully-paid shares of £1 in new company for each share of £20 held. Final meeting return regd. 10 Apr. 1929 1924

Assam Development Co. Ld. Regd. 1923. Vol. liq. 2 July 1925. Final meeting return regd. 18 June 1927 ..... *1926

Assasiodum-Tarkwa Gold Mines Ld. Regd. 1901. Removed from Register 1911 1907

Assets & Debenture Securities Corporation Ld. Regd. 1889. Vol. liq. 12 June 1895. Final meeting return regd. 9 Mar. 1896 1896

Assets Co. Ld. Regd. in Edinburgh 1882. Vol. liq. (members') 18 Jan. 1955. Capital returned to contributories—41s. 6½d. per 10s. stock. Final meeting return regd. 4 Oct. 1956 1957

Assets Founders' Share Co. Ld. Regd. 1890. Vol. liq. 1903. Capital returned to contributories—£1 10s. per share of £4; further payments (if any) not known. Removed from Register 1904 1904

Assets Realisation Co. Ld. Regd. 1883. Vol. liq. 1 July 1924. Undertaking was acquired by Debenture Corporation Ld. Final meeting return regd. 13 June 1927 1925

Assheton Mining Co. Ld. Regd. 1869. Vol. liq. 16 Aug. 1881. Undertaking acquired by Assheton United Mining Co. Ld. Final meeting return regd. 25 Apr. 1882 1883

Assin & Ashanti Syndicate Ld. Regd. 1901. Removed from Register 1905 1905

Assin Fesu & Gold Coast Syndicate Ld. Regd. 1901. Struck off Register 24 Jan. 1936 1936

Associated Anglo-Atlantic Corporation Ld. Regd. 1923. Court Order to wind up 24 Feb. 1930. Struck off Register 13 Dec. 1938 1939

Associated Bakeries & General Investment Co. Ld. Regd. in Edinburgh 1928. All capital was owned by Associated British Foods Ld. Vol. liq. 29 Mar. 1963. Final meeting return regd. 27 Jan. 1964 1961

Associated Belting Companies Ld. Regd. 1920. Vol. liq. (members') 8 Oct. 1962. Capital returned to contributories—preference, 10s. per share (of 10s.); ordinary, 10s. 6d. per share (of 10s.). Final meeting return regd. 20 Aug. 1963 1964

Associated Brick & Tile Works Ld. Regd. 1927 as Associated Facing Brick & Tile Works Ld.; name changed Sept. 1930. Vol. liq. (creditors') 23 July 1937. No capital returned to contributories. Final meeting return regd. 16 July 1938 1938

See Stock Exchange Year-Book.

VOL. FOR

Associated Canners Ld. Regd. 1930. Vol. liq. (members') 29 Jan. 1959. Final meeting return regd. 11 Aug. 1959 .... **1940**

Associated Clay Industries Ld. Regd. 1925 as Associated Fireclay Companies Ld; name changed as above July 1935. Payments to 1st mortgage debenture stockholders on account of principal and premium amounted to 31$\frac{3}{5}$%. Struck off Register 14 May 1965 **1965**

Associated Coal Consumers Ld. Regd. 1910. Vol. liq. 15 Feb. 1929. Final meeting return regd. 20 Jan. 1931 **1930**

Associated Companies. Organised Massachusetts by Agreement & Declaration of Trust 1903 as Mackay Companies; name changed Jan. 1938. All shares acquired by Postal Telegraph Inc........ **1943**

Associated Consols Ld. Regd. 1899. Removed from Register 1902........ **1901**

Associated Electric Theatres Ld. Regd. 1910. Vol. liq. 31 Dec. 1919. Final meeting return regd. 20 Dec. 1920 **1921**

Associated Enamellers Ld. Regd. 1916. Vol. liq. (members') 1 July 1938. Capital returned to preference shareholders £13,877. Final meeting return regd. 18 Feb. 1939 .... **1939**

Associated Estancias, Ld. Regd. 1919. Vol. liq. (members') 21 May 1947. Capital returned to contributories—£6 1*s*. 1*d*. per share of £10. Final meeting return regd. 27 Nov. 1953 .... **1954**

Associated Exhibitors' Film Co. Ld. Regd. 1921. Vol. liq. 30 Dec. 1922. Final meeting return regd. 29 June 1925 .... **1923**

Associated Facing Brick & Tile Works Ld. *See* Associated Brick & Tile Works Ld.

Associated Financial Corporation Ld. Regd. 1903. Reconstructed 1904 as Joint Stock Trust & Finance Corporation Ld., in which company shareholders were entitled to 1 share of 5*s*. (credited with 3*s*. 6*d*. paid) for each share of 5*s*. held. Removed from Register 1910 .... **1906**

Associated Fireclay Companies Ld. *See* Associated Clay Industries Ld.

Associated Garages Ld. Regd. 1927. Vol. liq. 13 Aug. 1931. All capital owned by London General Cab Co. Ld. (later Transport Group Holdings Ld.). Final meeting return regd. 19 Feb. 1934 .... **1932**

Associated Gas & Electric Co. Inc. New York 1906. Under a plan of Jan. 1940 the company's securities were to be exchanged for securities of Associated Gas & Electric Corporation **1941**

Associated Gas & Water Undertakings Ld. Regd. 1933. Dissolved 1 May 1949, undertaking being vested in Gas Council under Gas Act 1948. Holders of securities were entitled to receive British Gas 3% guaranteed stock 1990–95 as follows in respect of each £1 unit, unless otherwise stated, of security held:

	£	s.	d.	
4½% red pref. stock	1	1	5	
4% red pref. stock	1	0	6	
4% irred. pref. stock		19	6	
Ord stock	1	3	7	
Defd. stokc	1	4	0	
3½% deb. stock (per £100)	100	10	0	**1952**

Associated Gold Mines of Western Australia (New) Ld. Regd. 1925. Vol. liq. 30 Nov. 1934. Amalgamated with Associated Mining and Finance Co. Ld. in which company shareholders were entitled to 1 share of 8*s*. (credited as fully-paid) for every 2 shares of 4*s*. held *plus* 2*s*. per share in cash. £44 15*s*. was paid into Companies' Liquidation Account in respect of unclaimed proceeds from sale of fractions; £413 2*s*. in respect of unclaimed returns of capital. Final meeting return regd. 1 Oct. 1937..... **1935**

Associated Greyhound Racecourses Ld. Regd. 1927. Court Order to wind up 7 May 1935. Struck off Register 17 July 1942 .... **1943**

Associated Lead Manufacturers, Ld. Regd. 1919. Dissolved in 1930 under Section 154 of Companies Act 1929, the undertaking having been acquired by Goodlass. Wall & Lead Industries Ld. under an amalgamation scheme sanctioned by the Court in 1930. Shareholders were entitled to receive 6 fully-paid preference shares of acquiring company for every 7 preference shares held and 18 fully-paid ordinary shares of acquiring company for every 16 ordinary shares held; the preference shareholders also received a cash payment equivalent to 6% p.a. on such shares from 30 June to date of transfer, and the ordinary shareholders received a cash payment of 9*d*. per share **1931**

Associated London Properties, Ld. Regd. 1927. All capital was owned by Land Securities Investment Trust (regd. 1931). Vol. liq. (members') 17 Nov. 1961. Final meeting return regd. 3 Feb. 1965 .... **1955**

VOL. FOR

Associated Mineowners Ld. Regd. 1879. Vol. liq. July 1885. Final meeting return regd. 22 Dec. 1886 .... **1886**

Associated Mines of Gippsland Ld. Regd. 1898. Vol. liq. 1908. Removed from Register 1910 .... **1909**

Associated Mining & Finance Co. Ld. Regd. 1925. Vol. liq. (members') 7 Dec. 1944. Capital returned to contributories—12s. 2¾*d*. per share of 8*s*. £7,937 was paid into Companies' Liquidation Account. Final meeting return regd. 6 Aug. 1947........ **1948**

Associated Motor Cycles Ld. Regd. 1928 as Matchless Motor Cycles (Colliers) Ld.; name changed 12 Oct. 1937. In Sept. 1966 goodwill, undertaking and certain assets acquired by Manganese Bronze Holdings Ld. Debenture stocks repaid 26 Jan. 1967. No capital returned to ordinary shareholders. Struck off Register 7 Sept. 1973. .... **1970**

Associated Mount Jackson Gold Mines (W. A.) Ld. Regd. 1897. Struck off Register 13 Oct. 1908 ...... **1909**

Associated Murchison Gold Mines Ld. Regd. 1899. Reconstructed 1900 as Murchison Associated Gold Mines Ld., in which company shareholders were entitled to 1 share of 10*s*. (credited with 8*s*. paid) for each share of 10*s*. held. Removed from Register 1901 .... **1901**

Associated Nigerian Tin Mines Ld. Regd. 1919. Vol. liq. 3 June 1921. Undertaking and assets acquired by Keffi Consolidated Tin Co. Ld. in which company shareholders were entitled to 1 share of 5*s*. for each share of 5*s*. held. Final meeting return regd. 28 Feb. 1922 .... **1922**

Associated Northern Blocks (W. A.) Ld. Regd. 1899. Vol. liq. (members') 11 Oct. 1935. 350,000 fully-paid shares of 5*s*. of Great Boulder Mining & Finance Ld. were distributed to contributories. Final meeting return regd. 13 Sept. 1938 .... **1935**

Associated Oil Co. Inc. California 1901. In Nov. 1936 company was merged with Tide Water Associated Oil Co., in which company shareholders received 2¼ shares of common stock for each share held **1937**

Associated Omnibus Co. Regd. 1900. Vol. liq. Dec. 1918. Undertaking and assets were acquired by London General Omnibus Co. Ld. Capital returned to contributories—2*s*. 9*d*. per ordinary share of 5*s*. Struck off Register May 1929 .... **1930**

Associated Printers Ld. Regd. 1921. Vol. liq. (members') 14 June 1933. Reconstructed as William Brown & Charles Knight Ld. (later Brown, Knight & Truscott Ld.) in which company shareholders were entitled to 11 B preference shares of £1 for every 10 preference shares of £1 held or 1 ordinary share of 10*s*. for each ordinary share of £1 held. Final meeting return regd. 28 June 1934 .... **1934**

Associated Proprietors in the Royal Swedish Railway Co. Ld. Regd. 1883. Vol. liq. 5 Nov. 1896. The 5% debenture stock was repaid on 20 Dec. 1897. Final meeting return regd. 1 Oct. 1897........ **1898**

Associated Provincial Picture Houses Ld. Regd. 1914. Vol. liq. (members') 15 June 1950. Capital returned to contributories: 1*s*. per preference share (of 1*s*.) and £2 8*s*. 9*d*. (approx.) per ordinary share (of £1). £369 paid into Companies Liquidation Account. Final meeting return regd. 4 June 1973 .... **1974-5**

Associated Queensland Mines Ld. Inc. Queensland 1903. It was stated in 1916 that the assets were transferred to Atlas Corporation Ld. and the London Office closed........ **1916**

Associated Reinsurers Ld. Regd. 1919. Vol. liq. (members') 1 Sept. 1932. Capital return to contributories—3*s*. 7½*d*. per share of £1 (10*s*. paid). £54 1*s*. 9*d*. was paid to Companies' Liquidation Account. Final meeting return regd. 22 May 1942........ **1933**

Associated Rhodesian Gold Estates Ld. Regd. 1897. Court Order to wind up 16 Jan. 1902. Removed from Register 1909 .... **1902**

Associated Rubber Manufacturers Ld. Regd. 1913. Vol. liq. (creditors') 7 May 1935. No capital returned to contributories. Final meeting return regd. 4 Mar.1937 .... **1936**

Associated Share & Investment Co. Ld. *See* New Eastern Investment Co. Ld.

Associated Shipbuilders Ld. *See* Swan Hunter Group p.l.c.

Associated Southern Gold Mines (W. A.) Ld. Regd. 1899. Vol. liq. 7 Nov. 1904. Undertaking was acquired by Corona Consolidated Ld., in which company shareholders were entitled to 1 share of 5*s*. (credited with 3*s*. 6*d*. paid) for each share of £1 held. Removed from Register 1910 .... **1905**

Associated Tamworth Mines Ld. Regd. 1899. Vol. liq. Jan. 1909 for reconstruction as Central Killham Tin Mines Ld., in which company shareholders were entitled to 1 fully-paid ordinary share of 1*s*. for each share of 5*s*. held. Removed from Register 1911 ... **1909**

**See Stock Exchange Year-Book.*

VOL. FOR

Associated Tea Planters Ld. Regd. 1889. Vol. liq. 24 July 1891. Final meeting return regd. 5 July 1892 .... **1892**

Associated Tin Mines of Nigeria Ld. Regd. 1926. Vol. liq. (members') 31 Mar. 1939. Undertaking and assets were acquired by Amalgamated Tin Mines of Nigeria Ld., in which company shareholders were entitled to 1 share of 5s. (credited as fully-paid) for each share of 5s. held. Final meeting return regd. 12 Feb. 1941 .... **1940**

Associated Utilities Ld. Regd. 1923. Dissolved 1 May 1949, undertaking being vested in Gas Council under Gas Act 1948. Holders of securities were entitled to receive British Gas 3% guaranteed stock 1990–95 as follows in respect of each £1 unit, unless otherwise stated, of security held:

	£	s.	d.
Ord shares	1	1	0
4% pref.shares	1	0	0
3½% deb. stock (per £100)	100	0	0

1952

Associated Weavers Ld. *See* A. W. (Securities) Ld.

Association of Land Financiers Ld. Regd. 1870. Court Order to wind up 8 Nov. 1878. Removed from Register 1930 .... ***1878**

Assurance Compagniet Baltica A/S. Inc. Denmark 1915. Ceased to have place of business in Great Britain 1948 .... **1948**

Assurance Finance Trust Ld. Regd. 1932. Vol. liq. (creditors') 18 Dec. 1939. No capital returned to contributories. Final meeting return regd. 3 June 1941 .... **1941**

Assurances Trust Corporation Ld. Regd. 1890. Vol. liq. 23 July 1896. Reconstructed as Guarantee and General Trading Corporation Ld., in which company shareholders were entitled to 1 preference share and 2 ordinary shares of £1 (credited as fully-paid) for each share of £10 held. Final meeting return regd. 20 Apr. 1897 .... **1900**

Aster Engineering Co. (1913) Ld. Regd. 1913. Vol. liq. 16 Mar. 1927. Undertaking acquired by Arrol-Johnston Ld. (later Arrol-Johnston & Aster Engineering Co. Ld.). Final meeting return regd. 17 July 1939 **1928**

Aster Shipping Co. Ld. Regd. 1919. Vol. liq. (creditors') 26 Jan. 1933. No capital returned to contributories. Final meeting return regd. 14 Oct. 1933 .... **1933**

Astley & Tyldesley Coal & Salt Co. Ld. *See* Astley & Tyldesley Collieries Ld.

Astley & Tyldesley Collieries Ld. Regd. 1864 as Astley & Tyldesley Coal & Salt Co. Ld.; name changed 1900. Undertaking was acquired in 1929 by Manchester Collieries Ld., in which company shareholders were entitled to 27 ordinary and 18 preference shares of £1 for every 40 ordinary shares of 15s. held. Preference shareholders were entitled to £1 3s. per preference share of £1 held. Struck off Register Oct.1934 .... **1935**

Aston Brass and Engineering Co. Ld. *See* Aston Brass Co. Ld.

Aston Brass Co. and Whitehouse Ld. *See* Aston Brass Co. Ld.

Aston Brass Co. Ld. Regd. 1904 as Aston Brass and Engineering Co. Ld.; name changed Oct. 1909 to Aston Brass Co. and Whitehouse Ld. and as above in July 1919. Vol. liq. (members') 20 Apr. 1932. Undertaking was acquired by Valor Co. Ld. Final meeting return regd. 20 Nov. 1933 .... **1935**

Aston Coal Co. Ld. Regd. 1900. Under Mining Industrial Act of 1926 the undertaking was acquired in 1927 by Sheffield Coal Ld. and company dissolved **1940**

Aston Construction Co. Ld. Regd. 1911. All capital owned by Smith Walker Ld. Vol. liq. (members') 21 Feb. 1961. Final meeting return regd. 2 May 1962 **1956**

Aston Motor Accessories Co. Ld. *See* Amac Ld.

Astor Alliance Mines Ld. Regd. 1886. Vol. liq. 18 Apr. 1888. Court Order to continue winding up under supervision 5 July 1888. Final meeting return regd. 9 Sept. 1891 .... ***1889**

Astral Shipping and Investment Co. Ld. Regd. 1899 as Astral Shipping Co. Ld.; name changed 1935. Vol. liq. (members') 21 Mar. 1951. Capital returned to contributories (per share of £5) £14 6s. 8d. in cash and £16 15s. in specie. Final meeting return regd. 16 June 1952 .... **1953**

Astrop Patent Co. Ld. Regd. 1886. Removed from Register 1906 .... **1891**

Astyra Mining Co. Ld. Regd. 1888. Vol. liq. 4 May 1893. Final meeting return regd. 28 Oct. 1897 .... **1894**

Asuncion Tramway, Light & Power Co. Ld. Regd. 1912. Vol. liq. 31 July 1918. Final meeting return regd.8 July 1938 .... **1919**

Atal Tea Co. Ld. Inc. India. Undertaking acquired by Saikowah (Assam) Tea Co. Ld. **1942**

VOL. FOR

Atbasar Copper Fields Ld. Regd. 1906. Vol. liq. 1913. Undertaking and assets acquired by Spassky Copper Mine Ld., in which company shareholders received 1 fully-paid share of £1 for every 2 shares of £1 held. Struck off Register 15 Aug. 1944 .... **1945**

Atchison, Topeca & Santa Fe Railroad Co. Organised Kansas 1863. Reorganised 1895 as company of same name. Holders of securities were entitled to securities in new company as follows—$100 common and $10 preferred stock after payment of assessment of $10 for every $100 capital stock held; $750 general mortgage bonds and $400 adjustment bonds *plus* $10 in cash for every $1,000 4% general mortgage bond held; $1,130 preferred stock, after payment of assessment of 4% for every $1,000 second mortgage bonds class A held; $1,180 preferred stock, after payment of assessment of 4% for every $1,000 second mortgage bond class B held; the guarantee fund notes and equipment trust series A were to be exchanged, if necessary into prior lien bonds **1896**

Athahasca Gold Mine Ld. Regd. 1900. Removed from Register 1912 .... **1902**

Athanasu Concessions Ld. Regd. 1901. Removed from Register 1909 .... **1908**

Athenry & Ennis Junction Railway Co. Inc. by Special Act 1860. Undertaking purchased by Waterford and Limerick Railway Co. (later Waterford, Limerick & Western Railway Co.,) for £180,000 4% debenture stock **1901**

Athenry and Tuam Extension to Claremorris Railway Co. Ld. Inc. by Special Act 1891. In 1925 the undertaking was merged into the Great Southern Railways Co. Holders of Baronial Guaranteed Share capital were entitled to an equal amount of Great Southern Railways 4% Preference Stock; the other shares were to be cancelled **1925**

Athenry & Tuam Railway Co. Inc. by Special Act 1858. Under Waterford & Limerick Railway Act 1893 the undertaking was acquired by that company (later Waterford, Limerick & Western Railway Co.), for £79,000 in cash **1901**

Atherfield (Hevea) Rubber Estates Ld. Regd. 1910. Vol. liq. 14 July 1913. Court Order to continue winding up under supervision 14 Oct. 1913. Final meeting return regd. 8 Feb. 1917 .... **1914**

Atherstone Gas Light & Coke Co. Ld. Regd. 1906 Dissolved 1 May 1949, undertaking being vested in West Midland Area Gas Board under Gas Act 1948. Holders of ordinary shares (of £1) were entitled to recieve £1 10s. 6d. British Gas 3% guaranteed stock 1990-95 for each share held **1952**

Atherton Mills Ld. Regd. 1919. Vol. liq. (members') 30 Sept. 1957 for reconstruction under same name. Undertaking and assets (excluding £100,000 cash which was distributed to shareholders) transferred to new company in which shareholders were entitled to receive 4 fully-paid shares of £1 for every 5 shares of £1 held. £82 17s. paid into Companies' Liquidation Account. Final meeting return regd. 2 Apr. 1959 .... **1960**

Atholl Investments Ld. Inc. in Isle of Man 1902 as Manx Electric Railway Co. Ld.; name changed 1 June 1957. Vol. liq. (members') 16 Sept. 1957, the railway assets having been sold to the Manx Government. Under scheme of distribution ordinary shareholders were entitled to receive 6d. per share of 10s. and debenture stockholders were entitled to receive £59 15s. 5d. per £100 stock held. £246 15s. 9d. was paid into Companies' Liquidation Account. Final meeting held 27 Aug. 1958 .... **1960**

Athy-Wolfhill Colliery Railway. Under terms of Irish Free State Railways Act 1924 the undertaking was acquired by Great Southern Railways Co. from 1 Jan. 1929 .... **1945**

Atkins Filter & Engineering Co. Ld. Regd. 1884. Removed from Register 1905 .... **1890**

Atkins Water Softening & Purifying Co. Ld. Regd. 1881 as Water Reform Co. Ld.; name changed 3 Jan., 1882. Business acquired by Atkins Filter & Engineering Co. Ld. Removed from Register 17 June 1898 .... ***1889**

Atkinson Brothers Ld. Regd. 1897. Removed from Register 1914 .... **1914**

Atlanta Gold & Silver Consolidated Mines Ld. Regd. 1897. Removed from Register 1905 .... ***1902**

Atlantic & Danville Railway Co. Organised Virginia 1882. Reorganised 1894 as company of same name. An assessment of 25% on 1st mortgage 6% coupon gold bonds was made and holders were entitled to 1st mortgage bonds in new company at par for amount of assessment *plus* 60% of holding in preferred shares and 40% in deferred shares **1894**

VOL. FOR

Atlantic & Eastern Steamship Co. Ld. Regd. 1885. Vol. liq. 19 Apr. 1923. Final meeting return regd. 2 Oct. 1925 1924

Atlantic and Great Western Railroad, Organised 1871. After default in 1874 the property was purchased under foreclosure in 1880 by New York, Pennsylvania & Ohio Railroad Co. 1896

Atlantic and Great Western Railway. Formed in 1865. Succeeded in 1871 by Atlantic and Great Western Railroad 1896

Atlantic Coaling Co. Ld. See A. C. C. Holdings Ld.

Atlantic Copper Mining Co. Regd. 1880. Removed from Register 1888 .... *1883

Atlantic Finance Corporation Ld. Regd. 1900. Struck off Register 1915 1911

Atlantic Leased Lines Ld. Regd. 1880 as Atlantic First Leased Lines Rental Trust Ld.; name changed 17 Dec. 1925. Vol. liq. (members') 3 Jan. 1940. Capital returned to stockholders £138 19s. 8d%. An unspecified amount was paid to Companies' Liquidation Account. Final meeting return regd. 5 Feb. 1941 ... 1942

Atlantic Merthyr Collieries Ld. Regd. 1905. Vol. liq. June 1910. Undertaking was sold to Locket's Merthyr Collieries (1894) Ld. for £30,000 in cash and £120,000 5% 1st mortgage debenture bonds. Removed from Register 1911 1911

Atlantic Oil Syndicate Ld. Regd. 1919. Struck off Register Feb. 1926 1926

Atlantic Oyster Fisheries Co. Ld. Regd. 1899. Struck off Register 13 Oct. 1908 1909

Atlantic Patent Fuel Co. Ld. Regd. 1879. Vol. liq. Jan. 1921. Struck off Register Nov. 1932 1933

Atlantic, Quebec & Western Railway Co. Inc. by Special Act of Province of Quebec 1901. In 1929 the undertaking was sold to Canadian National Railways. 1st mortgage debenture bonds were repaid at par. 2nd mortgage debentures received 10% of nominal value 1931

Atlantic Transport Co. Ld. Regd. 1880. Vol. liq. 7 May 1889. Capital returned to contributories—£46 10s. per share of £50. Final meeting return regd. 27 June 1890 1890

Atlantic Trust Ld. Regd. 1910 as Atlantic Oil & Rubber Trust Ld.; name changed June 1916. Vol. liq. 5 Oct. 1925. Reconstructed as Anglo Scottish Amalgamated Corporation Ld., in which company shareholders were entitled to 5 ordinary shares of £1 and 2½ deferred shares of 1s. (credited as fully-paid) for every 80 shares of 2s. held. Final meeting return regd. 23 July 1927 1926

Atlas Artificial Silk Processes Ld. Regd. 1929. Court Order to wind up June 1931. Struck off Register 27 Oct. 1942 1943

Atlas Banking Corporation Ld. Regd. 1907 as International Concessions Ld.; name changed 17 Sept. 1907. Court Order to wind up 13 Oct. 1907. Liquidator released 10 Sept. 1914. Struck off Register 14 Feb. 1919 .... *1910

Atlas Cement of South Africa Ld. Regd. 1935. Vol. liq. (members') 12 Jan. 1937. Undertaking and assets were acquired by Anglo Alpha Cement Ld. for 880,000 fully-paid shares and an option (since expired) over further shares; these shares were to be distributed to shareholders. Debenture stockholders were entitled to £350,000 5% convertible debenture stock and an option over further shares in acquiring company in exchange for holdings. Final meeting return regd. 24 Nov. 1937 1937

Atlas Corporation Ld. Inc. Queensland 1904 as Elmslie (Australia) Ld.; name changed Mar. 1907 to Elmslie Ld. and as above in July 1913. Vol. liq. Jan. 1920 for reconstruction under same name. Shareholders were entitled to 1 share of 2s. (credited with 1s. paid) in new company for each share held 1921

Atlas Corporation Ld. Inc. Queensland 1920. Vol. liq. 2 July 1947. Capital returned to contributories—3s. 3·6d. per share of £1. Dissolved 3 Sept. 1949 1951

Atlas Gold Mines Co. Ld. Regd. 1900 as Atlas Gold Mine Ld. Reconstructed 1904 as company of same name. Shareholders were entitled to 1 share of £1 (credited with 17s. paid) in new company for each share of £1 held. Removed from Register 1906 ... 1908

Atlas Gold Mines Co. Ld. Inc. 1904 under Laws of Western Australia. In Jan. 1909 the Secretary stated "the company has long since ceased to exist" 1909

Atlas Investment Trust Ld. Regd. 1889. Vol. liq. 27 Oct. 1898. Reconstructed as Atlas Trust Ld. Stockholders were entitled to 80 fully-paid preference shares and 20 fully-paid ordinary shares of £1 for every £100 preferred stock held or to 15 fully-paid ordinary shares of £1 for every £100 deferred stock held. Debenture holders were entitled to an equal amount of debenture stock in new company. Final meeting return regd. 16 Feb. 1900 1899

VOL. FOR

Atlas Loan Co. Inc. 1887 under Canadian Laws and by Special Act of Dominion Parliament 1898. In liquidation in 1904 1904

Atlas Mill Company Ld. Regd. 1898. Vol. liq. 14 April 1920; undertaking and assets were acquired by Atlas Mills Ld. Final meeting return regd. 8 Jan. 1921. Court Order declared dissolution void 6 Apr. 1923. Final meeting return regd. 3 Oct. 1933 1921

Atlas Mills Ld. Regd. 1920. Court Order to wind up 31 Mar. 1931. Liquidator ceased to act 17 Jan. 1944. Struck off Register 26 July 1946 1947

Atlas Securities Co. Ld. Regd. 1906. Vol. liq. 11 Mar. 1929. Undertaking and assets were acquired by Dwa Plantations Ld., in which company shareholders were entitled to 6½ ordinary shares of 2s. (credited as fully-paid) for each share of £1 held. Final meeting return regd. 21 Sept. 1937 1930

Atlas Tin Mining Co. Ld. Regd. 1889. Removed from Register 1914 1895

Atlas Trust Ld. Regd. 1898. Vol. liq. Mar 1911. Investments and assets were acquired by Trust Union Ld. Debenture stockholders were entitled to an equal amount of debenture stock in acquiring company; ordinary stockholders to an equal amount of preference shares; preference stockholders to £46 debenture stock and £50 in preference shares for every £100 preference stock held. Removal from Register 1912 1912

Atlin Lake Co. Ld. Regd. 1899. Removed from Register 1909 1908

Atlin Mining Co. Ld. Regd. 1900. Vol. liq. Nov. 1909. The undertaking was acquired by an American company—Pittsburgh-British Gold Co.—for 80,000 fully-paid shares of $1. Removed from Register 1913 ... 1910

Atmospheric Nitrogen Co. Ld. Regd. 1897. Removed from Register 1902 1902

Atomé Extended Mines Ld. Regd. 1902. Vol. liq. Oct. 1909 for reconstruction as Gold Coast Consolidated Lands Ld., in which company shareholders were entitled to 1 share of 5s. (credited with 4s. paid) for each share of 5s. held. Removed from Register 1911 1910

Atomé Mines Ld. Regd. 1901. Undertaking was acquired by United Gold Mines of West Africa Ld in which company shareholders were entitled to 1 share of 5s. (credited as fully-paid) for each fully-paid share of 5s. held. Removed from Register 1905 ... 1904

Atta Gold Co. Ld. Regd. 1925. Vol. liq. 19 June 1928. Reconstructed as Atta Gold Co. (1928) Ld. Shareholders were entitled to receive 1 share of 2s. (credited with 1s. paid) in new company for every share of 5s. held. Final meeting return regd. 19 Nov. 1930 1929

Atta Gold Co. (1928) Ld. Regd. 1928. Vol. liq. (members') 16 April 1952. Capital returned to contributories—7·7d. per share of 2s. £1,597 5s. 8d. was paid into Companies' Liquidation Account. Final meeting return regd. 11 Feb. 1953 1954

Attapadi Tea & Rubber Co. Ld. Regd. 1907. Vol. liq. 11 Sept. 1912. Final meeting return regd. 5 Nov.1914 1913

Attasi & Bokitsi Development Co. Ld. Regd. 1901. Reconstructed 1905 as Attasi Mines (1905) & Railway Ld., in which company shareholders were entitled to 105,000 shares of 10s. (credited with 1s. paid). Removed from Register 1914 1909

Attasi Concessions Ld. Regd. 1899. Removed from Register 1905 1903

Attasi Goldfields Ld. Regd. 1901. Reconstructed as Attasi Mines (1905) & Railway Ld. in which company shareholders were entitled to 140,000 shares of 10s. (credited with 2s. 9d. paid). Removed from Register 1909 1906

Attasi Mines Ld. Regd. 1900. Reconstructed 1905 as Attasi Mines (1905) & Railway Ld., in which company shareholders were entitled to 200,000 fully-paid shares of 10s. and £23,275 in cash. Debenture holders were entitled to an equal amount of debentures in new company. Removed from Register 1913 1906

Attasi Mines (1905) & Railway Ld. Regd. 1905. Vol. liq. 15 Feb. 1907. Removed from Register 1913 1907

Attleborough Gas Co. Ld. Regd. 1903. Controlling interest held by British Gas Light Co. Ld. 1909

Attractive Cinema (West Kensington) Ld. Regd. 1923. Vol. liq. 16 Mar. 1928. Properties were purchased by Denman Picture Houses Ld. Final meeting return regd. 25 May 1928 1940

Aublet, Harry & Co. Ld. Regd. 1897. The laundry machinery manufacturers' business was acquired in 1924 by Baker Perkins Ld. (later Baker Perkins Holdings Ld.). Vol. liq. (members') 19 Mar. 1934. Final meeting return regd. 14 Nov. 1934 1934

Auchen Steam Shipping Co. Ld. Regd. Edinburgh 1899. Vol. liq. Oct. 1916. Final meeting return regd. 23 Apr. 1918 1917

See Stock Exchange Year-Book.

VOL. FOR

Auchinblae Distillery Co. Ld. Regd. Edinburgh 1896. Vol. liq. June 1916. Final meeting return regd. 7 July 1917 .... **1917**

Auchinleck Gas Light Co. Ld. Regd. in Edinburgh 1859. Dissolved 1 May 1949, undertaking being vested in Scottish Area Board under Gas Act 1948. Holders of securities were entitled to receive, in respect of each 10s. unit held, British Gas 3% guaranteed stock 1990-95 as follows:

	£	s.	d.
Ord shares	1	1	0
5% cum. ord. shares	11	0	**1952**

Auchterarder Gas Light Co. Ld. Regd. in Edinburgh 1926. Dissolved 1 May 1949, undertaking being vested in Scottish Area Gas Board under Gas Act 1948. Holders of ordinary shares (of £1) were entitled to receive £1 17s. British Gas 3% guaranteed stock 1990-95 for each share held **1952**

Auchtermuchty Gas Co. Ld. Regd. in Edinburgh 1939. Dissolved 1 May 1949, undertaking being vested in Scottish Area Gas Board under Gas Act 1948. Holders of securities were entitled to receive British Gas 3% guaranteed stock 1990-95 as follows:

	£	s.	d.
Ord. shares (of £1)	1	8	0
4% red. debs. (of £10)	10	0	0	**1952**

Auchtertool Distillery Co. Ld. Regd. Edinburgh 1921. Vol. liq. Jan. 1926. Final meeting return regd. 18 Apr. 1927 .... **1927**

Auckland Agricultural Co. Ld. Regd. 1881. All debentures were paid off. Removed from Register 1901. **1897**

Auckland Electric Tramways Co. Ld. Regd. 1899. Vol. liq. 19 Feb. 1923. Undertaking sold to Auckland Corporation. Debenture stock was redeemed at 105%. Capital returned to contributories—20s. per preference share of £1; £1 4s. 3d. per ordinary share of £1. Final meeting return regd. 5 Aug. 1924 ..... **1924**

Auckland Park Real Estate Co. Ld. Regd. 1902. Vol. liq. 16 Aug. 1921. Undertaking and assets were acquired by South African Townships Mining & Finance Corporation Ld. in which company shareholders were entitled to 1 share of 10s. (credited as fully-paid) for each share of £1 held. Final meeting return regd. 4 June 1929 .... **1922**

Auction Mart Ld. Regd. 1864. Vol. liq. 20 Mar. 1896. Reconstructed as company of same name. Each holding of £25 was converted into 5 ordinary and 5 preference shares of £5 in new company. Final meeting return regd. 1 Apr. 1897 .... **1908**

Auction Mart Co. Ld. Regd. 1896. Vol. liq. 3 Apr. 1919. Final meeting return regd. 3 Sept. 1919 .... **1919**

Audible Filmcraft Ld. Regd. 1930. Vol. liq. (creditors') 3 Aug. 1932. No capital returned to contributories. Final meeting return regd. 5 Jan. 1937 .... **1933**

Augusta Tea Estates Co. Ld. Regd. 1896. Vol. liq. (members') 10 June 1942. Capital returned to contributories—£5 per preference share of £5: £1 6s. 3d. per ordinary share of £1. Final meeting return regd. 15 Feb. 1945 .... **1946**

Auriferous Properties Ld. Regd. 1895. Court Order to wind up 19 Dec. 1896. Removed from Register 1908 **1897**

Aurochs Investment Co. Ld. Regd. 1920 as Anglo-Russian Shipping Co. Ld.; name changed in Jan. 1926 to Anglo-Russian Shipping & Investment Co. Ld. and in Aug. 1926 as above. Vol. liq. (members') 17 June 1955. Ordinary shareholders were entitled to 1s. cash and 1 ordinary share of 1s. 6d. in Aurochs Finance Co. Ld. (now Anglo-African Finance Co. Ld.) per share of 4s. held. Final meeting return regd. 7 Dec. 1956 .... **1958**

Aurora Gold Mining Co. Ld. Formed in South Africa 1886. Undertaking absorbed in 1892 by New Aurora West Gold Mining Co. Ld., in which company shareholders received 67 shares for every 100 shares held **1898**

Aurora West United Gold Mining Co. Ld. Inc. Transvaal 1895. Vol. liq. Mar. 1928. Capital returned to contributories—3s. 8d. per share of 10s. further payments (if any) not known **1929**

Aurum Co. Ld. Regd. 1889. Removed from Register 1911 .... **1891**

Austen (Gwelo) Development Syndicate Ld. *See* Central Rhodesian Reefs Ld.

Austin Car Co. of America Inc. *See* American Austin Car Co. Inc.

Austin (E. J.) International Ld. Regd. 1964 as Exoteric Transport Ld. Nmae changed to E. J. Austin Contractors Supply Ld. in 1965 and to present title 1969. Winding-up order 11 Dec. 1972. First and final dividend of 11·4p in the £ paid on 31 Mar. 1981. Final meeting held early 1982 .... **1986-7**

Austin Friars Finance Syndicate Ld. Regd. 1895. Vol. liq. 21 Nov. 1898. Undertaking and assets were

---

VOL. FOR

acquired by Standard Exploration Co. Ld., for 60,000 fully-paid shares. Removed from Register 1903.......... **1899**

Austin Friars Investment Trust Ld. *See* Aylesbury Trust Ld.

Austin Friars Trust Ld. Regd. 1927 as Aylesbury Trust Ld.; name changed June 1927. Court Order to wind up 15 Oct. 1929. Struck off Register 27 Oct. 1942 **1943**

Austin Gold Mines Ld. Regd. 1894. Vol. liq. 4 Sept. 1895. Reconstructed as New Austin Gold Mines Ld. Final meeting return regd. 4 Nov.1897 .... **1897**

Austin (James) & Sons Ld. *See* Hartley Crosland Group Ld.

Austin Motor Co. Ld. Regd. 1905. Vol. liq. 17 Sept. 1914. Business was acquired by Austin Motor Co. (1914) Ld. (later Austin Motor Co. Ld.) for £399,993 in ordinary shares. Final meeting return regd. 9 Mar. 1915 .... **1929**

Austin Syndicate Ld. Regd. 1895. Vol. liq. 23 Mar. 1898. Final meeting return regd. 9 Dec. 1898 .... **1899**

Austin Veneer & Panel Co. Ld. Regd. 1936. Vol. liq. (members') 14 Mar. 1949. Assets sold as follows:— (a) manufacturing section of business to Edmonton Panel Co. Ld. and (b) the group of companies (except Avco Ld.) hitherto controlled by company to A.V.P. Industries Ld. Ordinary shareholders received a cash payment of 1s. 6d. for each share held plus 9 fully-paid ordinary shares of 6s. 8d. each in A.V.P. Industries Ld. for every 8 ordinary shares of 2s. held. Preference shareholders received 1 fully-paid 5½% redeemable preference share of £1 for each redeemable preference share held. £529 paid into Companies' Liquidation Account. Final meeting return regd. 29 May 1951 .... **1952**

Austral-African & General Gold Trust Ld. Regd. 1895. Vol. liq. 6 May 1897. Reconstructed as Austral-African Exploration Co. Ld., in which company shareholders were entitled to 3 ordinary shares of £1 (credited with 15s. paid) for every 2 ordinary shares of £1 held, or 1 deferred share of £1 (credited with 15s. paid) for each deferred share of £1 held. Final meeting return regd. 6 May 1898 .... **1899**

Austral-African Co. Ld. Regd. 1895. Vol. liq. 8 Sept. 1896. Reconstructed as Oceana Consolidated Co. Ld., in which company shareholders were entitled to 1 share of £1 (credited as fully-paid) for each share of £1 held. Final meeting return regd. 28 Nov. 1896 **1896**

Austral-African Exploration Co. Ld. Regd. 1897. Vol. liq. 21 Mar. 1899. Reconstructed as Nannine Goldfields Ld., in which company shareholders were entitled to 1 fully-paid share and 2 shares of 10s. (credited with 7s. 6d. paid) for each ordinary share of £1 held and 6 fully-paid shares and 12 shares of 10s. (credited with 7s. 6d. paid) for each deferred share of £1 held. Final meeting return regd. 2 Aug. 1899 .... **1902**

Austral Cycle Agency Ld. Regd, 1896. Removed from Register 1903 .... **1900**

Austral Gold Explorers Ld. Regd. 1895. Removed from Register 1903 .... **1903**

Australasian Agency & Banking Corporation Ld. Inc. Australia 1877. In Sept. 1881 business and property were taken over by R. Goldsbrough and Co. Ld., in which company shareholders were entitled to 1 share of £10 (£1 paid) for each share of £10 (£1 paid) held **1883**

Australasian Alkaline Reduction & Smelting Syndicate Ld. Regd. 1889. Court Order to wind up 19 Dec. 1891. Removed from Register 1907 .... **1892**

Australasian Electric Light, Power & Storage Co. Ld. Regd. 1882. Vol. liq. 14 Feb. 1890. Undertaking was acquired by Brush Electrical Engineering Co. Ld. (later Hawker Siddeley Industries Ld.) for 5,500 fully-paid preference shares of £2 and 5,500 fully-paid ordinary shares of £3. Final meeting return regd. 27 July 1893 .... **1890**

Australasian Fresh Meat Co. Ld. Regd. 1882. Court Order to wind up under supervision 4 Apr. 1884. Final meeting return regd. 18 Aug. 1885 .... **1885**

Australasian Gold & Finance Corporation Ld. Regd. 1896. Removed from Register 1901 .... **1901**

Australasian Gold Extracting Co. (Pollok Patents) Ld. Regd. Edinburgh 1890. Vol. liq. Jan. 1903. for reconstruction as West of Scotland Mines Trust Ld. Holders of fully-paid shares were entitled to 1s. 3d. per share of £1 in cash or 1 share in purchasing company; holders of shares of £1 (17s. 6d. paid) had option (since expired) of paying 1s. 3d. per share as full settlement of their liability or paying 2s. 6d. and receiving 1 fully-paid share for each share held. Struck off Register 26 Sept. 1933 .... **1908**

Australasian Gold Mining Co. Ld. Regd. 1897. Removed from Register 1912 .... **1911**

See Stock Exchange Year-Book.

VOL. FOR

Australasian Gold Trust Ld. Regd. 1895. Removed from Register 1904 .... **1900**

Australasian Investment Co. Ld. Regd Edinburgh 1884. Vol. liq. June 1912. Capital returned to contributories—6d. per share. Final meeting return regd. 4 Mar. 1913 .... **1913**

Australasian Mines Investment Co Ld. Regd 1873. Vol. liq. 13 July 1888. Final meeting return regd. 2 Oct. 1894 .... **1889**

Australasian Mining Co. Ld. Regd. 1887 as Gympie Great Eastern Gold Mining Co. Ld.; name changed 1893. Vol. liq. 3 Aug. 1897. Final meeting return regd. 25 July 1898 .... **1908**

Australasian Mining Ventures Ld. Regd. 1898. Removed from Register 1902 .... **1900**

Austrslasian Mortgage and Agency Co. Ld. Regd. Edinburgh 1880. Vol. liq. Dec. 1911. Final meeting return regd. 27 Dec. 1911 .... **1912**

Australasian Motor Cab Co. Ld. Regd. 1910. Vol. liq. 6 Nov. 1914. Final meeting return regd. 22 Sept. 1915 .... **1915**

Australasian Ore Concentration Syndicate Ld. Regd. 1903. Vol. liq. 25 Feb. 1915. Final meeting return regd. 29 Oct. 1915 .... **1916**

Australasian Prospecting Syndicate Ld. Regd. 1900. Vol. liq. 10 Jan. 1906. Removed from Register 1906.... **1906**

Australia United Mining Co. Ld. Regd. 1896. Vol. liq. 2 Dec. 1901. A capital return to contributories of 1s. 6d. per share of £1 was anticipated. Removed from Register 1902 .... **1902**

Australian Alliance Mining & Finance Co. Ld. Regd. 1896. Vol. liq. 15 May 1897. Final meeting return regd. 23 Dec. 1897 .... **1898**

Australian Alluvial Gold Syndicate Ld. Regd. 1903. Vol. liq. 4 Apr. 1906. Removed from Register 1906..... **1907**

Australian Alum Co. Ld. Regd. New South Wales 1905. Vol. liq. Sept. 1929 .... **1930**

Australian & General Asbestos Co. Ld. Regd. 1928. Court Order to wind up 17 Oct. 1932. Struck off Register 14 May 1943 .... **1933**

Australian and International Trust Ld. regd. as private company 26 June 1961 as Trans Australia Investment Trust Ld., converted into public company 14 July 1961. Name changed 9 nov. 1971. Vol. liq. (members') 18 Mar. 1981. Holders received 3 units of Schroder Australian Fund per ordinary share of 50p. Final meeting held 6 Sept. 1984 .... **1984–5**

Australian and New Zealand Mortgage Co. Ld. Regd. 1879. Removed from Register 1912 .... **1912**

Australian Bank of Commerce Ld. Inc. New South Wales 1909. Vol. liq. Nov. 1931. Undertaking and assets were acquired by Bank of New South Wales, in which company shareholders were entitled to 1 share of £20 (credited as fully-paid) for every 34½ shares of £1 held **1932**

Australian Broken Hill Consols Ld. Regd. 1888. Vol. liq. 15 May 1896. Reconstructed as New Australian Broken Hill Consols Ld., in which company shareholders were entitled to 1 ordinary share of £1 (credited with 19s. paid) for each share of £1 held. Final meeting return regd. 3 July 1897.......... **1907**

Australian Cities Investment Corporation Ld. Regd. 1890. Reconstructed 1899 as company of same name. Shareholders were entitled to 1 share of £1 for each ordinary or founders' share of £10 held. Removed from Register 1902 .... **1908**

Australian Cities Investment Corporation Ld. Regd. 1899. Vol. liq. Mar. 1908. Capital returned to contributories—20s. per share of £1 in Nov. 1908; further payments (if any) not known. Removed from Register 1909 .... **1909**

Australian Coking & By-Products Co. Ld. Regd. 1909. Vol. liq. 21 Dec. 1923. Final meeting return regd. 4 May 1934 .... **1925**

Australian Commonwealth Fuels & Oils Ld. Regd. 1905 as Australian Commonwealth Mines Ld.; name changed Feb. 1907. Winding-up order 5 Feb. 1934. 9½d. in the £1 was paid to creditors. Liquidator released 30 Apr. 1955. Struck off Register 21 Feb. 1958 .... **1957**

Australian Commonwealth Mines Ld. *See* above.

Australian Commonwealth Trust Ld. Regd. 1903. Vol. liq. Nov. 1907. Reconstructed as Australian Deep Leads Trust Ld., in which company shareholders were entitled to 5 shares of 4s. (credited with 3s. paid) for each share of £1 held. Removed from Register 1910 .... **1908**

Australian Co. Ld. Regd. 1881. Vol. liq. May 1888. Final meeting return regd. 30 May 1889 .... **1889**

Australian Cotton Growing Association (Queensland) Ld. *See* British Australian Cotton Association Ld.

Australian Cycle & Motor Co. Ld. Regd. 1896. Removed from Register 1903 .... **1900**

Australian Deep Leads Trust Ld. Inc. New South Wales 1907. Vol. liq. May 1910. Undertaking was acquired

VOL. FOR

by Australian Maikop Oil Co. Ld in which company shareholders were entitled to 1 fully-paid share of 2s. for each fully-paid share of 4s. held **1911**

Australian Deposit & Mortgage Bank Ld. Inc. Melbourne 1874. Reconstructed under same name in 1892 .... **1909**

Australian Deposit & Mortgage Bank Ld. Inc. Melbourne 1892. Deposit receipts were paid off 13 Sept. 1918. The London agency was terminated 31 Dec. 1918 .... **1918**

Australian Development & Finance Co. Ld. Regd. 1895. Vol. liq. 19 Mar. 1900. Final meeting return regd. 19 Feb. 1901 .... **1901**

Australian Diamond Fields Ld. Regd. 1898. Vol. 4. 14 Jan. 1901. Removed from Register 1905 .... **1901**

Australian Explosives & Chemical Co. Ld. Regd. 1875 as Australian Lithofracteur Co. (Krebs' Patent) Ld.; name changed Oct. 1888. Vol. liq. 11 May 1926. Indirect controlling interest held by Nobel Industries Ld. Final meeting return regd. 20 Dec. 1927 **1926**

Australian Gold Leases Development Co. Ld. Regd. 1898. Reconstructed 1900 as company of same name. Shareholders were entitled to 1 share of £1 (credited with 18s. paid) in new company for each share of £1 held. Removed from Register 1903.... **1901**

Australian Gold Leases Development Co. Ld. Regd. 1900. Reconstructed 1901 as Jourdie Hills Gold Mining Co. Ld., in which company shareholders were entitled to 2 ordinary shares of 10s. (credited with 8s. 6d. paid) for each ordinary share of £1 held or 2 fully-paid preference shares of 10s. for each preference share of £1 held. Removed from Register 1903 .... **1903**

Australian Gold Recovery Co. Ld. Regd. 1892. Reconstructed 1901 as Australian Mining & Gold Recovery Co. Ld., in which company shareholders were entitled to 1 fully-paid share of 10s. *plus* 5s. in cash for each share of £1 held. Removed from Register 1914 .... **1901**

Australian Gold Reefs Corporation Ld. Regd. 1934. Vol. liq. (members') 16 Mar. 1938. All capital owned by Nigel Van Ryn Reefs Ld. (later Nigel Finance & Investment Ld.) Final meeting return regd. 25 Aug. 1939 .... **1939**

Australian Ice Co. Ld. Regd. 1878. Removed from Register 1906 .... **1890**

Australian Joint Stock Bank Ld. Est. 1852. Inc. by Act of Council 1853. Reincorporated 1893 under Companies Act of New South Wales. Vol. liq. Jan. 1910. The liquid assets were sold to Australian Bank of Commerce Ld. **1911**

Australian Jones Rock Drill Co. Ld. Regd. 1897. Vol. liq. 2 Nov. 1899. Final meeting return regd. 11 July 1900 .... **1900**

Australian Lithofracteur Co. (Krebs' Patent) Ld. *See* Australian Explosives & Chemical Co. Ld.

Australian Maikop Oil Co. Ld. Regd. 1910. Vol. liq. 21 Dec. 1920. Final meeting return regd. 19 July 1922 **1921**

Australian Midas Gold Estates Ld. Regd. 1909. Vol. liq. 1912 for reconstruction as Creswick Gold Mines Ld., in which company shareholders were entitled to 2 shares of 2s. 6d. (credited with 1s. 9d. paid) for each share of 5s. held. Struck off Register 1 Feb. 1944 .... **1944**

Australian Mines Agency Ld. Regd. 1896' Vol. liq. 4 Apr. 1906. Removed from Register 1910 .... **1907**

Australian Mines Agency Ld. Inc. Australia 1896. Properties and assets were acquired by company of same name (regd. England 1896) **1899**

Australian Mining & Gold Recovery Co. Ld. Regd. 1901. Vol. liq. Mar. 1912. Capital returned to contributories—2s. 6d. per share of 3s.; further payments (if any) not known. Removed from Register 1914 .... **1913**

Australian Mining Co. Regd. 1845. Inc. by Royal Charter 1855. The amount paid up per share of £20 was £7 7s. 6d., but returns of capital (representing 18s. 3d. per share) were made out of proceeds of old materials and land sales; further returns (if any) not known. Reconstructed 1902 as Australian Mining Co. Ld in which company shareholders were entitled to an equal number of shares **1902**

Australian Mining Co. Ld. Regd. 1902. During 1906 £2 15s. per share was returned to shareholders. Vol. liq. Mar. 1908. Removed from Register 1909 .... **1909**

Australian Mutual Shipping Co. Ld. Regd. 1886. Vol. liq. 27 Dec. 1916. Final meeting return regd. 3 Sept.1917 .... **1917**

Australian Oil Co. Ld. *See* British Australian Oil Co. Ld.

Australian Prospecting Co. Ld. Regd. 1895. Vol. liq. 11 May 1905. Removed from Register 1907 .... **1906**

Australian Search Syndicate Ld. Regd. 1896. Vol. liq. (creditors') 25 June 1930. No capital returned to contributories. Final meeting return regd. 22 Apr. 1932.......... **1931**

See Stock Exchange Year-Book.

VOL. FOR

Australian Shale Syndicate Ld. Regd. 1895. Undertaking acquired by British Australian Oil Co. Ld. Removed from Register 1911 1911

Australian Sheep Farms Ld. Regd. 1925. Vol. liq. (members') 23 Dec. 1937. Capital returned to contributories—£3 1s. 4¾d. per share of £5. Final meeting return regd. 21 Mar. 1940 1941

Australian South African Gold Exploration Co. Ld. Regd. 1895. Vol. liq. 18 Mar. 1898. Final meeting return regd. 28 Sept 1898 1899

Australian Syndicate Ld. Regd. 1894. Vol. liq. 13 Apr. 1896. Final meeting return regd. 9 Sept. 1896 ..... *1897

Australian Trans-Continental Railway Syndicate Ld. Regd. 1881. Removed from Register 1905 1890

Australian Tri-Metallic Co. Ld. Inc. Queensland 1908. 59,990 shares were owned by Metals Extraction Corporation Ld. in 1931 1932

Australian Wine Importers Ld. Regd. 1887. Vol. liq. 14 Nov. 1892. Final meeting return regd. 10 May 1893 1893

Australis Investment Co. Ltd. Inc. in New South Wales 1959. Vol. liq. 13 Aug. 1974. Net assets transferred to The Darling Fund. Stockholders received 89·03 units of The Darling Fund for every $A100 stock held 1975-6

Austrian Central Land Credit Bank. See Oesterreichische-Central-Boden-Credit.

Austrian Co. for Industrial Credit Ld. See Oesterreichische industriekredit.

Austrian Incandescent Share Co. Ld. Regd. 1895. Vol. liq. 4 Dec. 1897. Acquired by Welsbach Incandescent Gas Light Co. Ld., for £533,325 in cash, £51,155 in preference shares and £164,365 in deferred shares. Removed from Register 1901 1898

Austrian Laenderbank. See K.K. Privilegirte Osterreichsiche Laenderbank.

Austrian National Bank. See Oesterreichische Nationalbank.

Austro-African Estates Ld. Regd. 1908. Wound up in 1916 under Trading with the Enemy Amendment Act, 1916 .... *1918

Austro-Bavarian Lager Brewery & Crystal Ice Factory Ld. Regd. 1881. Vol. liq. Jan. 1886. Final meeting return regd. 24 Aug. 1887 1887

Austro-Hungarian Bank. Certain assets of the Austrian section were acquired by Austrian National Bank 1926

Austro-Hungarian Z.I.G. Taxi-Cab Co. Ld. Regd. 1910. Vol. liq. 8 May 1914. Final meeting return regd. 4 May 1937 1915

Austro-Rhodesian Development Co. Ld. Regd. 1899. Vol. liq. Apr. 1908. Removed from Register 1909 1909

Authors' Co-operative Publishing Co. Ld. See Tarstow, Denver & Co. Ld.

Auto-Bulbs Ld. Business acquired by Sphinx Electric Ld., for £47,000 in cash, 770,000 ordinary shares of 1s. and 10,000 preference shares of 5s. all fully-paid 1930

Auto-Carriers Ld. See A.C. Cars Ld.

Auto-Carriers (1911) Ld. See A. C. Cars Ld.

Auto-Dore Ld. Regd. 1929. Vol. liq. (creditors') 23 July 1930. No capital returned to contributories. Final meeting return regd. 8 Oct. 1935 1931

Auto-Electric Devices Ld. Regd. 1928. Vol liq. (members') 22 Dec. 1931. Capital returned to contributories—⅓ of one penny per share of 1s. Final meeting return regd. 26 Oct. 1932. 1932

Auto-Made Sales Ld. Regd. 1928. Court order to wind-up 11 May 1931. No capital returned to contributories. Liquidator released 22 Feb. 1955. Struck off Register 1 Sept. 1967 1956

Auto-Portraits Ld. Regd. 1928. Court Order to wind up Sept. 1930. Struck off Register 20 Mar. 1936 1937

Auto-Rides Ld. See General Amusements Corporation Ld.

Autoboys Ld. Regd. 1928. Directly controlled by British Chewing Sweets Ld. Struck off Register 1936 1936

Automat Sales Ld. Regd. 1928. Vol. liq. (members') 2 July 1931. Capital returned to contributories—⅟₄₆ of one penny per share of 1s. Final meeting return regd. 16 Oct. 1936 1932

Automatch & Vester Ld. See A. & V. Ld.

Automatic & Horton Ices Ld. Regd. 1893. Vol. liq. 30 July 1894. Reconstructed as Horton Ices Co. Ld. in which company shareholders were entitled to 1 share of £1 (credited with 15s. paid) for each share of £1 held. Final meeting return regd. 7 Apr. 1897 .. 1908

Automatic Bottle Makers Ld. Regd. 1923. Court Order to wind up 13 Oct. 1925. Struck off Register Aug. 1932 1933

Automatic Coal-Gas Retort Co. Ld. Regd. 1890. Vol. liq. 3 Aug. 1899. Final meeting return regd. 11 Aug. 1900 1900

Automatic Confections Ld. Regd. 1929. Receiver was appointed Nov. 1930. Struck off Register 15 Oct. 1935 1936

VOL. FOR

Automatic Cycle Rack Ld. Regd. 1897. Removed from Register 1901 1900

Automatic Development Ld. Regd. 1929. Directly controlled by General Engineering Development Trust Ld. Struck off Register 2 June 1944 1944

Automatic Electric Co. Ld. Regd. 1911 as Automatic Telephone Manufacturing Co. Ld.; name changed Jan. 1932. Vol. liq. (members') 1 Oct. 1934. Struck off Register 23 Feb. 1954 1937

Automatic Electrical & Mechanical Controls Ld. Regd. 1934. Vol. liq. (creditors') 15 Dec. 1937. Business was sold as going concern. Debentures were paid off in full: no return of capital to contributories. Final meeting return regd. 2 Mar.1938 1938

Automatic Equipments Ld. Regd. 1928. Vol. liq. (creditors') 28 Nov. 1929. Capital return to contributories—2s. 3½d. per ordinary share of 5s. Final meeting return regd. 4 May 1935 1930

Automatic Fire-proof Curtain Co. Ld. Regd. 1888. Court Order to wind up 1 Apr. 1890. Removed from Register 1892 1891

Automatic Gas Meter (1895) Corporation Ld. Regd. 1895. Undertaking was acquired by Meters Ld. in 1897. Removed from Register 1903 1899

Automatic Glass Blowing Patents Syndicate Ld. Regd. 1898. Receiver appointed 1905; ceased to act 17 Sept. 1913. Removed from Register 8 Jan. 1915 .. *1901

Automatic Light Controlling Co. Ld. Regd. 1898. Goodwill was acquired by British, Foreign and Colonial Automatic Light Controlling Co. Ld. Vol. liq. 11 June 1906. Final meeting return regd. 14 Sept. 1907 1940

Automatic Lock Nut Co. Ld. Regd. 1909. Receiver was appointed 4 Mar. 1912. Struck off Register 1915 . 1913

Automatic Machines (Haydon & Urry's Patents) Ld. Regd. 1900. Removed from Register 1907 1903

Automatic Match Supply Co. Ld. Regd. 1887. Removed from Register 1906 .... *1889

Automatic Photograph Co. Ld. Regd. 1890. Court Order to wind up 11 Mar. 1893. Removed from Register 1907 1894

Automatic Photograph (Foreign & Colonial) Co. Ld. Regd. 1890. Court Order to wind up 8 Aug. 1891. Removed from Register 1907 1892

Automatic Records Player Ld. Regd. 1929. Vol. liq. (creditors') 10 May 1938. No capital returned to contributories. Final meeting return regd. 20 July 1938 1939

Automatic Refreshment Supply Co. Ld. Regd. 1901. Removed from Register 1905 1905

Automatic Safety Lock Brake Co. Ld. Regd. 1890. Struck off Register 5 May 1896 1890

Automatic Services Ld. Regd. 1927. Vol. liq. (members') 22 July 1930. All shares owned by British Automatic Co. Ld. Final meeting return regd. 12 Jan. 1931 1931

Automatic Sight Testing & Optical Supply Co. Ld. See Key Lens Optical Co. Ld.

Automatic Supply Co. Ld. Regd. 1899. Vol. liq. 9 Nov. 1901. The business was sold to satisfy ordinary creditors. Final meeting return regd. 18 May 1915 1904

Automatic Telephone Co. Ld. Regd. 1897 Vol. liq. 29 Dec. 1902. Reconstructed as Automatic Telephone Co. (1903) Ld., in which company shareholders were entitled to 2 shares of 2s. 6d. (credited with 2s. paid) for each share of 5s. held. Struck off Register 16 July 1915 1903

Automatic Telephone Co. (1903) Ld. Regd. 1903. Court Order to wind up 15 Mar. 1904. Removed from Register 1910 1905

Automatic Telephone Manufacturing Co. Ld. See Automatic Electric Co. Ld.

Automatic Trade Mark Machine Co. Ld. Regd. 1929. Vol. liq. (creditors') 8 Dec. 1932. No capital returned to contributories. Final meeting return regd. 10 Feb. 1938 1933

Automatic Trading Co. Ld. Regd. 1887. Court Orders: to wind up 31 July 1889; to dissolve 27 June 1891 .. 1890

Automatic Weighing Machine Co. Ld. Regd. 1888. Vol. liq. 14 Nov. 1893. Undertaking acquired by Sweetmeat Automatic Delivery Co. Ld. (later British Automatic Co. Ld.) for £4,500 in cash and 93,000 fully-paid shares of £1. Final meeting return regd. 21 Nov. 1894 1909

Automatic Wheel Phonographs Ld. Regd. 1906. Removed from Register 1911 1908

Automobile Cab Co. Ld. Regd. 1905. Vol. liq. Aug. 1907. Removed from Register 1910 1908

Automotor Finance Ld. Regd. in Edinburgh 1929. Vol. liq. 31 Aug. 1964. Final meeting return regd. 27 Apr. 1965 1953

Autosales Gum & Chocolate Co. Inc. New York State 1911 1913

Aux Classes Laborieuses, Ld. Regd. 1897. Vol. liq. (members') 29 June 1948. Capital returned to

VOL. FOR

contributories—2·9*d.* per share (of 1*s.*). £5,244 6*s.* 6d. was paid into Companies' Liquidation Account in respect of unclaimed distributions. Final meeting return regd. 21 Nov. 1957 .... **1958**

Auxiliary Associated Gold Mines (W. A.) Ld. Regd. 1897. Removed from Register 1907 .... **1905**

Auxiliary Stores Ld. *See* Industrial Contract Corporation Ld.

Avala Quicksilver Mines Ld. Regd. 1889. Vol. liq. 29 Dec. 1894. Final meeting return regd. 26 July 1895 **1895**

Avenue Super Cinema Ld. Regd. 1927. Vol. liq. (members') 30 Sept. 1930. Certain assets were distributed in specie. Capital returned to contributories—2*s.* 11½*d.* per ordinary share of 5*s.* Preference shares were repaid in full. Final meeting return regd. 17 Jan. 1931 .... ***1931**

Avery (John) & Co. Ld. Regd. Edinburgh 1884. Vol. liq. (members') 15 Feb. 1954. All capital was owned by Aberdeen University Press Ld. Capital returned to contributories—preference repaid at par; 15*s.* 5*d.* per £1 ordinary. £23 was paid into Companies' Liquidation Account in respect of unclaimed dividends or distributions. Final meeting return regd. 11 Apr. 1958 .... **1959**

Aviation & General Insurance Co. Ld. Regd. 1919. Vol. liq. 19 Jan. 1928. Final meeting return regd. 19 Jan. 1935 .... **1928**

Avino Mines Ld. Regd. 1909. Vol. liq. Apr. 1923 for reconstruction as company of same name in which company shareholders were entitled to 2 shares of 1*s.* (credited with 7½*d.* paid) for each priority share of 1*s.* held or 1 share of 1*s.* (credited with 6*d.* paid) for each ordinary share of 1*s.* held. Struck off Register June 1932 .... **1933**

Avino Mines Ld. Regd. 1923. Struck off Register June 1932 .... **1933**

Avino Mines of Mexico Ld. Regd. 1899. Vol. liq. Jan. 1903. Reconstructed as company of same name. Shareholders were entitled to 1 share of £1 (credited with 17*s.* 6*d.* paid) for every share of £1 held. Removed from Register 1903 .... **1908**

Avino Mines of Mexico Ld. Regd. 1903. Vol. liq. with a view to reconstruction Dec. 1908. Removed from Register 1910 .... **1909**

Avon Manure Co. Ld. Regd. 1893. Vol. liq. (creditors') 6 Apr. 1944. All capital owned by Fisons Ld. Final meeting return regd. 29 Sept. 1944 .... **1945**

Avondale Hotel & Restaurant, & Hatchett's Restaurant Ld. Regd. 1898. Receiver was appointed in Dec. 1911. Struck off Register 1917 .... **1913**

Avondale Property Co. Ld. Regd. 1917. Vol. liq. 31 May 1920. Final meeting return regd. 19 Nov. 1920..... **1921**

Avoniel Distillery Ld. Inc. Dublin 1892. Vol. liq. Mar. 1930. The debenture stock and preference shares of £10 were repaid at par; further payments (if any) not known **1931**

Avonmouth Colliery Ld. Regd. 1900. Vol. liq. 21 Nov. 1904. Removed from Register 1906. .... **1905**

Avonmouth Light Railway Co. Inc. (under Light Railways Act 1896) 1903. Undertaking was transferred to London Midland & Scottish Railway and Great Western Railway Companies jointly **1928**

Avonside Engine Co. Ld. Regd. 1864. Vol. liq. 31 May 1879. Court Orders: to continue winding up under supervision June 1879; to wind up July 1881; to dissolve 6 Apr. 1887 .... **1883**

Avonvale Bread Co. Ld. Regd. 1899. Receiver was appointed Aug. 1907. Assets were acquired by Borough Flour Mills Evesham Ld. Removed from Register 1913 .... **1910**

Avreboo Rubber Estates Ld. Regd. 1909. Court Order to wind up June 1913. Struck off Register 1918 .... **1914**

Axe Vale & Thames Valley Creameries Ld. Regd. 1918. Vol. liq. (members') 22 Dec. 1933. Capital returned to contributories—20*s.* per preference share of £1; 3*s.* 4*d.* per ordinary share of £1. Final meeting return regd. 28 Dec. 1934 .... **1934**

Axholme Joint Railway Committee. Dissolved 2 Apr. 1949; undertaking vested 1 Jan. 1948 in British Transport Commission under Transport Act 1947 **1949**

Axim & Tarkwa Goldfields Ld. Regd. 1900 as Lo Magundi Central Ld.; name changed 1909. Court Order to wind up 1913. Struck off Register 1919.. **1913**

Axim Mahogany Co. Ld, Regd. Edinburgh 1913. Vol. liq. Sept. 1916. Struck off Register 15 Oct. 1937... **1938**

Axim Mines Ld. Regd. 1897. Vol. liq. Aug. 1908 for reconstruction as New Axim Co. Ld., in which company shareholders were given an option (since expired) to apply for shares. Removed from Register 1910 .... **1909**

Axminster & Lyme Regis Light Railway Co. Inc. (under Light Railways Act 1896) by order of Light Railway Commissioners confirmed by Board of Trade 1899. Undertaking purchased by London and South Western Railway in Jan. 1907, in which company holders of general capital stock received an equal amount of 3½% preference stock. The preference stock, which was held by purchasing company, was cancelled **1907**

Ayan Corporation Ld. Regd. 1921. Vol. liq. (creditors') 29 Nov. 1929. £18,924 was returned to debenture holders. No capital returned to contributories. Final meeting return regd. 16 July 1931 .... **1930**

Ayer Hitam Tin Dredging Ld. Regd. 1926. All capital acquired by Ayer Hitam Tin Dredging Malaysia Bhd. under scheme of arrangement effective 1 Nov. 1976. Vol. liq. 1 July 1978. Final meeting return regd. 3 Nov. 1981 .... **1977–8**

Ayer Kuning (F.M.S.) Rubber Co. Ld. Regd. 1910. Vol. liq. (members') Sept. 1946. Undertaking and assets acquired by Highlands & Lowlands Para Rubber Co. Ld. in which company stockholders were entitled to 1 fully-paid share of £1 for each £1 stock held. Final meeting return regd. 3 Oct. 1947 .... **1948**

Aylesbury & Buckingham Railway Co. Inc. by Special Act 1860. Under Metropolitan Railway Act 1890 the undertaking was acquired by that company. for £100,000 3% guaranteed stock **1892**

Aylesbury Dairy Co. Ld. Regd. 1868. Vol. liq. 22 Jan. 1926. Final meeting return regd. 4 Feb. 1927 ...... **1927**

Aylesbury Gas Co. Regd. as limited 1861; inc. by Special Act 1905. Dissolved 1 May 1949, undertaking being vested in Southern Area Gas Board under Gas Act 1948. Holders of securities were entitled to receive British Gas 3% guaranteed stock 1990-95 as follows in respect of each £100 unit, unless otherwise stated, of security held:

	£	s.	d.	
Cons. ord. stock (5% stand.)	112	0	0	
6% pref. stock	133	0	0	
5½% red. pref. stock	114	0	0	
5% red. pref. stock	107	0	0	
4% red. pref. stock	101	16	5	
3½% red. deb. stock	100	10	0	
4% debs. (per £50)	50	0	0	
6% irred. deb stock	149	0	0	**1952**

Aylesbury Trust Ld. Regd. 1925 as Austin Friars Investment Trust Ld.; name changed June 1927. Vol. liq. 7 Dec. 1928. Final meeting return regd. 31 Dec. 1935 .... **1929**

Aylesbury Trust Ld. *See* Austin Friars Trust Ld.—regd. 1927.

Aylsham Gas Co. Ld. Regd. 1856. Vol. liq. (members') 26 Oct. 1938. Undertaking and assets acquired by British Gas Light Co. Ld., which company held direct controlling interest. Capital returned to contributories—£10 per share of £10. £20 was paid into Companies' Liquidation Account on account of capital and £27 4*s.* 4*d.* in respect of unclaimed dividends. Final meeting return regd. 23 Feb. 1939 **1939**

Ayr & District Motor Services Ld. Regd. Edinburgh 1927. Vol. liq. (members') Dec. 1932; the undertaking and assets were transferred to Western S.M.T. Co. Ld. Capital returned to contributories—20*s.* per preference share of £1; 10*s.* 1½*d.* per ordinary share of £1. Final meeting return regd. 14 Dec. 1933 ... **1933**

Ayr & Maybole Junction Railway Co. Inc. by Special Act 1854. Amalgamated with Glasgow and South Western Railway Co., in Feb. 1912. Holders of each £10 share received £17 10*s.* 4% debenture stock of purchasing company **1912**

Ayr Gas Co. Ld. Regd. in Edinburgh 1935. Dissolved 1 May 1949, undertaking being vested in Scottish Area Gas Board under Gas Act 1948. Holders of ordinary shares (of £1) were entitled to receive £1 18*s.* British Gas 3% guaranteed stock 1990-95 for each share held **1952**

Ayr Harbour Trust. Constituted by Special Act 1855. Under Act of 1919 the undertaking was vested in Glasgow and South Western Railway Co. Stockholders were entitled to £81 18*s.* 6*d.*, £67 8s., or £45 11*s.* 7*d.* debenture stock of the railway company for every £100 "A", "B" or "C" debenture stock held respectively **1920**

Ayr Picture Houses Ld. Regd. Edinburgh 1919. Vol. liq. Apr. 1923. Court Orders: to continue winding up under supervision 6 Oct. 1925; to dissolve 18 July 1930 .... **1924**

Ayrshire & Wigtownshire Railway Co. Inc. by Special Act 1887. Under Glasgow and South Western (Ayrshire and Wigtownshire Railway and Bridge St. Joint Station, Glasgow) Act 1892 the line was purchased for £235,000 in cash **1893**

Ayrshire Gold Mine & Lomagunda Railway Co. Ld. Regd. 1901. Vol. liq. Feb. 1908 for reconstruction as Ayrshire Gold Mine Ld., in which company shareholders were entitled to 1 fully-paid share of £1

**See Stock Exchange Year-Book.*

See Stock Exchange Year-Book.

VOL. FOR

Bacon (G. W.) & Co. Ld. Regd. 1890. Vol. liq. 11 Dec. 1913 for reconstruction as company of same name. Shareholders were entitled to 1 fully-paid ordinary share of 12s. 6d. in new company for each ordinary share of £1 held or 1 fully-paid preference share of £1 for each preference share of £1 held. Final meeting return regd. 29 Nov. 1915 1915

Bacon (G. W.) & Co. Ld. Regd. 1913. Vol. liq. (creditors') 31 May 1945. Goodwill and certain assets were acquired by W. & A. K. Johnston Ld. & G. W. Bacon Ld. Capital returned to contributories—10s. per preference share of 10s.; 7s. 7d. per ordinary share of 12s. 6d.; £299 was paid into Companies' Liquidation Account. Final meeting return regd. 5 Jan. 1954 1954

Badams & Co. Ld. *See below.*

Badams & Slyth Ld. Regd. 1913 as Badams & Co. Ld.; name changed July 1930. Vol. liq. (members') 25 July 1932. Capital returned to contributories— £2,327 12s. Final meeting return regd. 25 Jan. 1940 1941

Baddow Brewery Co. Ld. Undertaking was acquired in 1927 by Seabrooke & Sons Ld. 1934

Badek Rubber Estate, Ld. Regd. 1910. Vol. liq. (members') 20 Dec. 1954. Undertaking transferred to Bradwall (F.M.S.) Rubber Estate Ld. for 1,010,192 fully-paid 2s. shares in that company in ratio of 8 2s. shares for £1 stock. Capital returned to contributories—1s. 6d. per £1 stock. Final meeting return regd. 8 Feb. 1956 1957

Badenoch Rubber Estate Ld. Regd. 1936. Vol. liq. (members') 29 Sept. 1961. All capital was owned by Straits Rubber Ld. Final meeting return regd. 3 May 1963 1964

Badminton Cycle & Components Co. Ld. Regd. 1897. Court Order to wind up 20 Dec. 1899. Removed from Register 1909 1900

Bagan Serai Co. Ld. Regd. 1909. Vol. liq. 29 Dec 1919. Reconstructed as company of same name. Shareholders were entitled to 3 fully-paid shares of £1 in new company for each share of £1 held. Final meeting return regd. 24 Sept. 1921 1921

Bagan Serai Co. Ld. Regd. 1919. Vol. liq. (members') 15 Aug. 1935 for reconstruction as Bagan Serai Rubber Estates Ld., in which company shareholders were entitled to 1 share of £1 (credited as fully-paid) and 5s. in cash for every share of £1 held. Final meeting return regd. 3 Aug. 1936 1935

Bagan Serai Rubber Estates Ld. Regd. 1935. Vol. liq. (members') 29 Sept. 1961. All capital was owned by Straits Rubber Ld. Final meeting return regd. 3 May 1963 1964

Bagillt Coal Co. Ld. Regd. 1904. Vol. liq. 12 Oct. 1911. Final meeting return regd. 6 Mar. 1924 1913

Bagilt Zinc Smelting Co. Ld. Regd. 1882. Removed from Register 1890 .... *1885

Bagley & Wright Manufacturing Co. (1919) Ld. Regd. 1919. Scheme of Arrangement sanctioned by Court 16 Oct. 1930. Vol. liq. (creditors') 7 Nov. 1930. Assets acquired by Lancashire Cotton Corpn. Ld.; in which corporation shareholders were to receive 33·802 fully-paid deferred shares of 1s. for every £100 paid up and, in addition, 1 fully-paid deferred share for every 2s. 6d. of the half of the capital called up, but not paid, acquired by the Corporation as and when such capital is received by the Corporation. Final meeting return regd. 19 Oct. 1938 1931

Bagley (M. S.) & Co. Ld. Regd. 1898. Vol. liq. 4 Sept. 1901. Undertaking acquired by Sociedad Anonima M. S. Bagley y Companie Limitada. Shareholders were entitled to par value, either in cash or shares in respect of their holdings. Final meeting return regd. 8 Jan. 1902 1903

Bagnall (John) & Sons Ld. Regd. 1873. Wound up by Order of Court 11 Aug. 1882 .... *1882

Bagot Pneumatic Tyre Co. Ld. Regd. 1896. Removed from Register 1903 1903

Bagot, Shakes & Lewis Ld. In July 1924 the undertaking was acquired by Goldsbrough, Mort & Co 1934

Bagots, Hutton & Co. Ld. Inc. Dublin 1894. Vol. liq. Aug. 1927. Undertaking and assets acquired by Henry Pattison & Co. Ld., in which company shareholders were entitled to £4 in 6½% income notes for each preference share of £5 held and £1 in 7% income notes for each ordinary share of £5 held... 1928

Bagshaw & Morris Ld. Regd. 1951. All ordinary capital was owned by Grafton Industrial Securities Ld. Vol. liq. (members') 28 Jan. 1966. Struck off Register 22 Sept. 1970 1963

Bagshawes Ld. Regd. 1897. Debenture holders took possession of assets at end of 1899. Struck off Register 23 July 1901 1902

Bahamas (Inagua) Sisal Plantation Ld. Regd. 1894. Removed from Register 1911 1910

VOL. FOR

Bahia & San Francisco Railway Co. Ld. Regd. 1851. Vol. liq. 24 July 1901. Lines were acquired by Brazillian Government on 1 July 1901. Each share of £20 in main line undertaking was entitled to £25 in 4% Government bonds *plus* £1 per share in cash: further payments (if any) not known. Each share of £20 in Timbo Branch undertaking was entitled to £11 17s. in 4% Government bonds *plus* 6s. per share in cash. Removed from Register 1903 1902

Bahia-Blanca & North Western Railway Co. Ld. Regd. 1889. Vol. liq. (members') 2 Apr. 1948, the undertaking together with all other British-owned railways in the Argentine, having been sold to Argentine Government as from 1 July 1946. The 4% 1st and 4½% 2nd debenture stocks were repaid at par. Capital returned to contributories—£90 per £100 guaranteed stock. £2,667 paid into Companies' Liquidation Account. Final meeting return regd. 28 Mar. 1956 1956

Bahia-Blanca Gas Co. Ld. Regd. 1907. Vol. liq. 15 Dec. 1927. Agreement was entered into for sale of all assets at price which provided for purchase of debenture stock at 50% of nominal value. A shares of £5 at 1s. per share and B shares of £1 at 1¼d. per share. Final meeting return regd. 6 Mar. 1929 1928

Bahia-Blanca Gas Works (Construction) Syndicate Ld. Regd. 1906. Vol. liq. Nov. 1907. Shareholders were entitled to 2 fully-paid Ordinary "A" shares of £5 and 5 ordinary "B" shares of £1 fully-paid in Bahia Blanca Gas Co. Ld. for every 10 ordinary shares of £1 held or 5 fully-paid ordinary "B" shares of £1 for every 5 shares held. Removed from Ragister 1910 1908

Bahia-Blanca Water Works Co. Ld. Regd. 1906. Vol. liq. (members') 2 Apr. 1948. The undertaking was sold to the Argentine Government as from 1 July 1946. Preference shareholders were entitled to receive (per share of £1) £1 on account of principal and 15s. 3·25d. on account of arrears of dividend. Final meeting return regd. 19 Mar. 1957 1958

Bahia Central Sugar Factories Ld. Regd. 1882. The properties were sold on behalf of debenture holders. Removed from Register 1909 1909

Bahia Gas Co. Ld. Regd. 1860. Removed from Register 1905 1895

Bahia Proprietary Mines Ld. Regd. 1911. Removed from Register 30 Oct. 1941 1942

Bahia Rubber & Fibre Plantation Ld. *See* British Brazilian Rubber Planters & Manufacturers Ld.

Bahia Steam Navigation Co. Ld. Regd. 1861. Vol. liq. 8 June 1881. Final meeting return regd. 12 Apr. 1882 *1881

Bahia Tramway, Light & Power Co. Inc. Maine 1905 Undertakings sold to muncipality in 1913. Holders of 5% 1st mortgage debentures were entitled to distributions of 12% in Sept. 1930 and £1 17s. 1d. per $100 (final) in Aug. 1948 1952

Bahru Selangor Rubber Co. Ld. Regd. 1912. All capital was owned by Seafield Amalgamated Rubber Co. Ld. Vol. liq. (members') 13 Jan. 1961. Final meeting return regd. 4 Jan. 1964 1960

Bai Rubber & Cocoa Estates Ld. Regd. 1910. Vol. liq. (members') 12 Apr. 1948. Final meeting return regd. 2 May 1953 1921

Bailey (Charles S.) Ld. Regd. 1902. Court Order to wind up 1906. Removed from Register 1911 1908

Bailey, Nokes & Co. Ld. Regd. 1888. Receiver was appointed Apr. 1891. Removed from Register 1894 1892

Bain (William) Ld. Regd. Edinburgh 1885. Vol. liq. May 1894. Final meeting return regd. 7 Feb. 1895 1895

Baines & Co. Ld. Regd. 1901. Vol. liq. (members') 19 Feb. 1937. Capital returned to contributories— £10,792 6s. 5d. Final meeting return regd. 9 Oct. 1937 1938

Baines & Sons (Croydon) Ld. *See* Henry Ridgway & Sons (Provision Merchants) Ld.

Baines (H. R.) & Co. Ld. See Graphic Publications Ld.

Baird International Television Ld. *See* Baird Television Ld.

Baird Television Development Co. Ld. Regd. 1927. Scheme of Arrangement for Amalgamation with Baird International Television Ld. (later Baird Television Ld.) under Sect. 154 Companies Act 1929. Company deemed dissolved 4 Oct. 1930 1931

Baird Television Ld. Regd. 1928 as Baird International Television Ld.; name changed June 1930. Under scheme of arrangement sanctioned by the Court on 17 Dec. 1940, the undertaking and assets were acquired by Cinema Television Ld. (later Bush & Rank Cintel Ld. later Rank Radio & Television Ld.). Loan stockholders received an equal amount of fully-paid participating preference shares in Cinema Television Ld. at par in satisfaction of the principal (premium and accrued interest being cancelled); unsecured creditors received fully-paid redeemable preference shares in respect of their

VOL. FOR

claims; and preferred ordinary and deferred ordinary shareholders received 1 fully-paid deferred share of 6d. for every 10 shares held. Dissolved under section 154 of the Companies Act 1929 on 25 Mar. 1946 .... **1947**

Baird (William) & Co. Ld. Regd. Edinburgh 1893. Vol. liq. (members') 27 June 1939. Stockholders were entitled to 1 ordinary share of £1 in William Baird & Co. Ld. (regd. 1939) taken at a premium of 6s. 8d. per share for every £1 stock held. Debenture stockholders were entitled to an equal amount of 5% debenture stock in new company. Final meeting return 29 June 1942 .... **1940**

Bairds & Dalmellington, Ld. Regd. Edinburgh 1931. Vol. liq. (members') 31 Dec. 1953. Capital returned to contributories—£3 5s. 10·8d. per 5s. ordinary stock. £49 12s. 9d. was paid to Accountant of Court. Final meeting return regd. 27 Dec. 1957; dissolution declared void 15 Mar. 1960 and company restored to register 22 Mar. 1960. Final meeting return regd. 2 July 1962 .... **1963**

Baiss Bros. & Co. Ld. Regd. 1900 as Baiss Bros. & Stevenson Ld.; name changed Sept. 1916. Vol. liq. 21 Sept. 1922. Undertaking and assets were acquired by company of same name. No return had been made to shareholders at 22 Oct. 1923. Final meeting return regd. 5 Jan. 1926........................ **1924**

Baiss Brothers & Co. Ld. Regd. 1922. Struck off Register 14 Sept. 1951 .... **1937**

Bakap Rubber Plantations Ld. Regd. 1909. Assets were taken over by debenture holders and realised insufficient to make distribution to shareholders. Struck off Register Feb. 1935 .... **1935**

Baker (Albert) & Co. (1898) Ld. Regd. 1898. Vol. liq. (members') 29 Dec. 1939. Undertaking and assets were acquired by Finlay & Co. Ld. Capital returned to contributories—£2 2s. 0·54d. per share of £1. Final meeting return regd. 10 Aug. 1940.............. **1941**

Baker Brothers Ld. Regd. 1887. Struck off Register 1918 **1897**

Baker, Duncombe & Co. Ld. Regd. 1905. Vol. liq. (members') 18 Oct. 1933. Capital returned to contributories—£5 per A share of £5; £18 11s. 2¾d. per B share of £5. Final meeting return regd. 21 Mar. 1934 .... **1934**

Baker (John) & Bessemer Ld. Regd. 1920 as John Baker & Co. (Rotherham) 1920 Ld.; name changed Oct. 1929. Vol. liq. (members') 3 Apr. 1964. Distributions (per share of £1): preference 20s.; ordinary £164 8s. 4¾d. Final meeting return regd. 17 Nov. 1970 .... **1971**

Baker (John) & Co. (Rotherham) 1920 Ld. See Baker (John) & Bessemer Ld.

Baker Street and Waterloo Railway Company. Inc. by Special Act 1893. Amalgamated with Great Northern Piccadilly and Brompton Railway Co. (later London Electric Railway Company). Debenture stockholders received an equal nominal amount of debenture stock in the amalgamated company. preference shareholders an equal nominal amount of preferred stock, "A" ordinary shareholders 75% of preference stock, and "B" ordinary shareholders £17 12s. 4½d. preference stock and £82 7s. 7½d. ordinary shares for every £100 held **1911**

Bakhtiari Oil Co. Ld. Regd. 1909. Vol. liq. 30 Mar. 1925. A controlling interest was held by Anglo-Persian Oil Co. Ld. (later Anglo-Iranian Oil Co. Ld later British Petroleum Co. Ld.). Final meeting return regd. 24 Nov. 1925 .... **1925**

Bakrobe Mine Ld. Regd. 1901. Vol. liq. 1903. Undertaking was acquired by United Gold Mines of West Africa Ld in which company shareholders were entitled to 1 fully-paid share of 5s. for each share of 5s. held. Removed from Register 1905 .... **1904**

Baku Consolidated Oilfields Ld. Regd. 1919. Winding-up order 8 Nov. 1943. Capital returned to contributories—3s. 6½d. per A preferred ordinary share of £1. Liquidator released 21 June 1955 .... **1955**

Baku-London Oil Co. Ld. Regd. 1921. Struck off Register 1942.................... **1940**

Baku-Russian Petroleum Co. Ld. Regd. 1898. Vol. liq. 1909. Reconstructed as Baku Russian Petroleum Co. (1909) Ld. in which company shareholders were entitled to 1 share of 10s. (credited with 5s. paid) for each ordinary or preference share of £1 held, plus 10s. in profit sharing certificates for each share subscribed by preference shareholders or 5s. in profit sharing certificates for each share subscribed by ordinary shareholders. Final meeting return regd. 3 Jan. 1917 .... **1910**

Baku-Russian Petroleum Co. (1909) Ld. Regd 1910. Vol. liq. 1 Sept. 1919, undertaking acquired by Baku Consolidated Oilfields Ld. Debenture holders were entitled to receive 50% of the nominal value of their holdings in fully-paid A preferred ordinary shares of

VOL. FOR

£1 and 50% in fully-paid B ordinary shares of £1. Shareholders were entitled to receive 2 fully-paid B ordinary shares for every 9 shares of 10s. held and right to subscribe for 1 A preferred ordinary share (credited with 2s. 6d. paid) for every 4 shares held. Holders of profit-sharing certificates were entitled to receive 1 fully-paid B ordinary share for every 40 certificates of 5s. held. Struck off Register 13 Dec. 1955 .... **1955**

Bala & Dolgelly Railway Co. Inc. by Special Act 1862. Undertaking vested in Great Western Railway Co. 1 Aug. 1877. Ordinary stockholders received £80 Great Western Railway 5% consolidated stock for every £100 held **1882**

Bala & Festiniog Railway Co. Inc. by Special Act 1873. Under Act of 1910 the Great Western Railway Co. purchased the undertaking. Debenture stockholders received an equal amount of 4% Great Western Railway debenture stock and ordinary stockholders £95 consolidated guaranteed stock and deferred certificates for every £100 stock held.................... **1911**

Balaghât Gold Mines Ld. Regd. 1919. Vol. liq. (members') 3 Oct. 1932. Certain assets were sold to Nundydroog Mines Ld. for £40,000 in cash. Capital returned to contributories—14s. 9·1d. per ordinary or preference share of 10s. Final meeting return regd. 28 Aug. 1935 .... **1933**

Balaghât Gold Mining Co. Ld. Regd. 1896. Vol. liq. 17 Oct. 1919. Reconstructed as Balaghât Gold Mines Ld., in which company shareholders were entitled to 1 ordinary share of 10s. (credited with 6s. paid) for each ordinary share of £1 held or 1 fully-paid preference share of 10s. for each preference share of £1 held. Final meeting return regd. 29 Mar. 1921 **1920**

Balaghât-Mysore Gold Mines Ld. Regd. 1890. Reconstructed 1894 as Balaghât-Mysore Mines Ld. in which company shareholders were entitled to 1 share of £1 (credited with 15s. paid) for each share of £1 held. Removed from Register 1901 .... **1894**

Balaghât-Mysore Gold Mining Co. Ld. Regd. 1886. Reconstructed 1890 as Balaghât-Mysore Gold Mines Ld., in which company shareholders were entitled to 1 share of £1 (credited with 15s. paid) for each share of £1 held. Removed from Register 1901 **1891**

Balaghât-Mysore Mines Ld. Regd. 1894. Vol. liq. 3 Dec. 1896 for reconstruction as Balaghât Gold Mining Co. Ld., in which company shareholders were entitled to 1 new share of £1 (credited with 15s. paid) for each share of £1 held. Debenture holders were entitled to an equal amount of preference shares of £1 in new company. Final meeting return regd. 19 Mar. 1901 .... **1908**

Balakhany Oil Co. Ld. See below.

Balakhany Black Sea Oil Co. Ld. (The). Regd. 1910 as The Balakhany Oil Co. Ld.; name changed May 1913. Vol. liq. (members') 15 May 1956. The undertaking and assets were sold to Balakhany Ld. in which company shareholders were entitled to 1 fully-paid share (of 2s.) for every 3 shares (of 2s.) of this company held. Final meeting return regd. 14 Oct. 1958 .... **1960**

Balata & Rubber Corporation Ld. Regd. 1908. Vol. liq. 6 Jan. 1911. Undertaking acquired by Consolidated Rubber & Balata Estates Ld. Final meeting return regd. 11 Dec. 1911 .... ***1910**

Balaton Palace Hotel & Casino Ld. Regd. 1912. Struck off Register 26 Mar. 1915 .... ***1915**

Balbardie Colliery Co. Ld. Regd. Edinburgh 1896. Vol. liq. Aug. 1906. Capital was returned to contributories in full; certain funds were in hand for further payments, though details of such payments are not known. Final meeting return regd. 22 Oct. 1907 .. **1907**

Balcobo Tin Mines Ld. Regd. 1911. Court Order to wind up Oct. 1912. Struck off Register Mar. 1929 .... **1930**

Baldwin (J. & J.) & Partners Ld. Regd. 1900. Vol. liq. 13 Apr. 1920. Undertaking and assets were acquired by Paton & Baldwins Ld. in which company shareholders were entitled to 1 preference share of £1 for each preference share of £1 held or £4 11s. 6d. in preference and ordinary shares for each ordinary share of £1 held. Debenture stockholders were entitled to an equal amount of 5% 1st mortgage debenture stock in acquiring company. Final meeting return regd. 13 Jan. 1921 .... **1921**

Baldwins (Holdings) Ld. Regd. as Baldwins Ld.; name changed 5 Jan. 1945. Vol. liq. (members') 11 May 1957. Capital returned to contributories—preference stocks (per £1): 1st, 21s., A. £1, & B, £1; ordinary stock (per 4s.); 3s. 3·256215d. in cash and 10s. British Iron & Steel 3½% guaranteed stock 1979-81. Final meeting return regd. 1 May 1956 .... **1967**

Baldwins Ld. See above.

Balfour Boardman & Co. Ld. Regd. 1926 as Harris, Forbes & Co. Ld.; name changed to Chase, Harris,

VOL. FOR

Forbes Ld. in July 1931 and as above in June 1933. Vol. liq. (members') 8 May 1939. Capital returned to contributories—£16 11s. 7·578d. per share of £20; as to £44,328 15s. 1d. in specie and £154,227 10s. 5d. in cash. Final meeting return regd. 11 July 1946 ..... **1948**

Balfour Darwins Ld. Regd. 1961 as Balfour & Darwins Ld.; name changed 1969. Vol. liq. (members') 24 Feb. 1977. Final meeting return regd. 2 Aug. 1980 **1981–2**

Baling Road Rubber Co. Ld. *See* Paloh Plantations Ld.

Baling Rubber Estates Ld. Regd. 1925. Vol. liq. 28 Aug. 1928. Undertaking and assets were transferred to North Malay Rubber Estates Ld., in which company shareholders were entitled to 8 fully-paid shares of 2s. for every 10 shares of 2s. held. Final meeting return regd. 19 Oct. 1929 **1929**

Balkan Co. Ld. Regd. 1895. Removed from Register 1901 **1900**

Balkan Copper Corporation Ld. Regd. 1899. Removed from Register 1912 **1911**

Balkis Co. Ld. Property was acquired in 1885 by Balkis Consolidated Co. Ld. in which company shareholders were entitled to 1 share of £1 (credited with 18s. paid) for every 5 shares held **1892**

Balkis Consolidated Co. Ld. Regd. 1885. Vol. liq. 24 May 1892. Undertaking disposed of partly to Balkis Land Co. Ld. and partly to Balkis Eersteling Ld. Final meeting return regd. 13 Aug. 1896 .... ***1893**

Balkis Eersteling Ld. Regd. 1892. Reconstructed 1896 as New Balkis Eersteling Ld. in which company shareholders were entitled to 1 share of 10s. (credited with 7s. 9d. paid) for each share of 10s. held. Struck off Register 1935 **1902**

Balkis Land Co. Ld. Regd. 1892. Vol. liq. 13 Dec. 1898. Reconstructed as company of same name (later Balkis Ld.). Shareholders were entitled to 1 share of 10s. (credited with 9s. paid) in new company for each share of 10s. held. Final meeting return regd. 17 Aug. 1899 **1899**

Balkis Land Co. Ld. *See next page*

Balkis Ld. Regd. 1898 as Balkis Land Co. Ld., name changed May 1905. Vol. liq. (members') 31 Mar. 1944. Ordinary stock was repaid at par. Capital returned to deferred shareholders—£2 15s. 7d. per share of £1. £162 16s. 6d. was paid into Companies' Liquidation Account on account of unclaimed dividends and £6,276 2s. 2d. on account of unclaimed distributions. Final meeting return regd. 17 June 1954 **1955**

Balla Balla Copper Mines Ld. Regd. 1899 as Westralian Copper Mines Ld.; name changed Feb. 1899. Vol. liq. 2 May 1901 for reconstruction as New Balla Balla Copper Mines Ld. in which company shareholders were entitled to 1 share of £1 (credited with 17s. 6d. paid) for each share of £1 held. Final meeting return regd. 10 Jan. 1913 **1908**

Ballaarat (Steigitz District) Gold Mines Ld. Regd. 1895. Struck off Register 26 Oct. 1900 **1901**

Ballachulish Slate Quarries Co. Ld. Regd. Edinburgh 1893. Vol. liq. Aug. 1907. Court Order to dissolve 29 Apr. 1911 **1908**

Ballarat & Lyell Mines Ld. Regd. 1903. Vol. liq. June 1908. Removed from Register 1908 **1909**

Ballarat & Prince Oscar Co. Ld. Regd. 1903. Receiver for debenture holders was appointed July 1907. Struck off Register 31 Oct. 1916. **1909**

Ballarat & Prince Oscar Syndicate Ld. Regd. 1897. Vol. liq. 15 May 1903 for reconstruction as Ballarat and Prince Oscar Co. Ld., in which company shareholders were entitled to 1 new share of 5s. (credited with 4s. 3d. paid) for each ordinary share of 5s. held or 2 shares of 5s. (one fully-paid and one credited with 4s. 3d. paid) for each preferred share of 5s. held. Struck off Register 27 Aug. 1907 **1908**

Ballarat Gold Fields Ld. Regd. 1895. Court Order to wind up 17 Oct. 1922. Struck off Register 1928 ... **1923**

Ballard & Co. Ld. Regd. 1898. Vol. liq. (members') 1 Nov. 1938. Undertaking and assets were acquired by Page & Overton's Brewery Ld., which company owned all ordinary and preference shares. Holders of 4½% 1st mortgage debenture stock were entitled to repayment at 110% on 1 Apr. 1939 or an equal amount of 4½% 1st mortgage debenture stock in purchasing company. Final meeting return regd. 2 Feb. 1929 **1939**

Ballina & Killala Railway & Harbour Co. Inc. by Special Act 1883. Undertaking abandoned by Act of 1889 **1890**

Ballinascarthy and Timoleague Junction Light Railway Co. Ld. Regd. 1883. In 1925 the undertaking was merged into the Great Southern Railways Co. Shareholders were entitled to £125 Great Southern Railways 4% Preference Stock for every £100 shares held. **1925**

Ballincolig Royal Gunpowder Mills Co. Ld. Regd. 1888 as Gunpowder Co. Ld.; name changed Aug. 1889.

VOL. FOR

Vol. liq. 1 Feb. 1899. Undertaking acquired by Curtis's & Harvey Ld. Final meeting return regd. 6 June 1901 **1940**

Ballinrobe and Claremorris Light Railway Co. Ld. Regd. 1885, under the Tramways and Public Companies (Ireland) Act, 1883. In 1925 the undertaking was merged into the Great Southern Railways Co. Shareholders were entitled to £125 Great Southern Railways 4% Preference Stock for every £100 shares held **1925**

Bally Paper Mills Co. Ld. Regd. 1874. Vol. liq. Aug. 1907. Shareholders were entitled to 20·458 ordinary shares and 26·391 6% cumulative preference shares of Titaghur Paper Mills Co. Ld. and 12·782 ordinary shares of £5 of Barnagore Jute Factory Co. Ld., for every 100 shares of £10 held. A final cash payment of 1s. 6½d. per share was made in Aug. 1908. Removed from Register 1908 **1909**

Ballycastle Railway Co. Inc. by Special Act 1878. By act of 1925 the undertaking was acquired by London Midland & Scottish Railway Co. for £12.500 in cash **1926**

Ballyclare, Ligoniel & Belfast Junction Railway Co. Inc. by Special Act 1881. Line abandoned in 1885 ..... **1886**

Ballymena & Larne Railway Co. Inc. by Special Act 1874. Under Belfast and Northern Counties and Ballymena and Larne Railway Co. Amalgamation Act 1889 the undertaking was dissolved and absorbed into the Northern Counties system. Holders of ordinary shares received £35 Northern Counties ordinary stock for every £100 held; holders of £100 4% preference shares, debenture stock or 4½% debenture stock received £87 10s., £93 15s. or £87 10s. 4% Northern Counties debenture stock respectively **1890**

Ballymena & Portglenone Railway Co. Inc. by Special Act 1879. Abandoned by Act of 1886 **1888**

Ballymena, Cushendall & Red Bay Railway Co. Inc. by Special Act 1872. Under the Belfast and Northern Counties Railway Act 1884 the undertaking was purchased by that company **1885**

Balmenacb-Glenlivet Distillery Ld. Regd. Edinburgh 1897. Vol. liq. Aug. 1922. Distillery was sold to company of same name. Struck off Register 27 Sept. 1932 **1923**

Balmoral Hotel, Edinburgh Ld. Regd. 1897. Vol. liq. Mar. 1917. Struck off Register 22 Sept. 1936 ...... **1937**

Balmoral Main Reef Gold Mining Co. Ld. Inc. Transvaal 1898. Court Order to wind up 13 Apr. 1905.. **1906**

Baltic & Mediterranean Corporation Ld. Regd. 1919 as British-Baltic Commercial Corporation Ld.; name changed Jan. 1923. Vol. liq. (members') 14 Feb. 1930. Capital returned to contributories—8s. 11·317d. per share of £1. Final meeting return regd. 16 Apr. 1930 **1930**

Baltic Co. Ld. Regd. 1857. Vol. liq. 14 Sept. 1899. Final meeting return regd. 28 Dec. 1900 **1901**

Baltic Lead Mines Ld. Regd. 1912. Struck off Register 1917 **1916**

Baltimore & Potomac Railroad Co. Consolidated with Philadelphia. Wilmington & Baltimore Railroad Co. to form Philadelphia, Baltimore and Washington Railroad Co. **1911**

Baltimore Breweries Co. Ld. Regd. 1889. Vol. liq. 21 Nov. 1898. Reconstructed as Baltimore Breweries Ld., in which company shareholders were entitled to 5 preference shares of £1 for each preference share of £10 held or 3 ordinary shares of £1 for each ordinary share of £10 held. Final meeting return regd. 3 Jan. 1900 **1900**

Baltimore Breweries Ld. Regd. 1898. Vol. liq. 3 Mar. 1902. Struck off Register 4 Mar. 1910 **1900**

Baltimore Electric Co. In 1927 the properties and assets were transferred to Consolidated Gas Electric Light and Power Co. of Baltimore (later Baltimore Gas & Electric Co.) **1928**

Baltimore Extension Railway Co. Ld. Regd. 1888. In 1925 the undertaking was merged into the Great Southern Railways Co. All the stocks of this company were cancelled **1925**

Bamber Bridge Engineers Ld. Regd. 1925 as Russell Edwards & Co. Ld.; name changed Jan. 1937. Vol. liq. (members') 3 May 1937. Undertaking was acquired by Thomas Blackburn & Sons Ld. Capital returned to contributories—£850 11s. 2d. plus 1·4 shares in purchasing company for each share of £1 held. Final meeting return regd. 3 Oct. 1939 .... **1946**

Bamboo Consolidated Gold Mines Ld. Regd. 1895. Struck off Register 23 July 1901 **1902**

Bamboo Creek Gold Mining Co. Ld. Regd. 1895. Removed from Register 1898 **1897**

Bamboo Cycle Co. Ld. Regd. 1894. Vol. liq. 30 Dec. 1897. Final meeting return regd. 10 Nov. 1898 .... **1898**

"Bamboo Queen" & "Reward" Mines Ld. Regd. 1896. Removed from Register 1908 **1899**

See Stock Exchange Year-Book.

VOL. FOR

Bambrakelly (Ceylon) Tea & Rubber Co. Ld. Regd. 1908. Vol. liq. 14 June 1926. Estates and certain assets were acquired by Lunuva (Ceylon) Tea & Rubber Estates Ld. in which company shareholders were entitled to 1 share of £1 (credited as fully-paid) *plus* 1s. 6d. in cash for each share of £1 held and an option (since expired) over further shares. Final meeting return regd. 29 Mar. 1927...................... **1927**

Banbury & Cheltenham Direct Railway Co. Inc. by Special Act 1873. Under Act of 1897 the undertaking was amalgamated with Great Western Railway Co. Holders of 1873 and 1879 debenture stock received an equal amount of G. W. Rly. 5% debenture stock and 2½% debenture stock respectively. Holders of £100 1881 debenture stock, 1877 debenture stock, 1883 debenture stock, 5% preference stock, preferred stock, ordinary stock or deferred stock received £20, £10, £3, £2 10s., £2, £2 or £2 respectively in cash **1898**

Banbury Gaslight & Coke Co. Estd. 1833. Inc. by Special Act 1866. Dissolved 1 May, 1949, undertaking being vested in Southern Area Gas Board under Gas Act 1948. Holders of securities were entitled to receive British Gas 3% guaranteed stack 1990–95 as follows in respect of each £10 unit, unless otherwise stated, of security held:

	£	s.	d.
Orig. ord. shares (10% max.).................	20	10	0
New ord. shares (7% max.)...................	14	10	0
4½% pref. stock (per £100)...................	109	0	0
4½% perp. deb. stock (per £100)	112	10	0

1952

Banbury Water Company. Inc. by Special Act 1865. As from 1 Jan. 1947 the undertaking was transferred to Banbury Corporation. Members received 4% Corporation stack in exchange for their holdings at following rates—for each ordinary share (10% maximum), £25 stock; for each 5% preference share £12½ stock; for each 4½% preference share, £11¼ stock; for each 4% preference share, £10 stock; for every £100 ordinary stock (5% maximum), £125 stock. The liability for outstanding mortgages was assumed by Corporation **1947**

Banca Bergamasca di Deposit e Conti Convent. Inc. Bergamo 1873. Bank went into liquidation Jan. 1933 **1934**

Banca Chrissoreloni S. A. R. *See* Banque Chrissoreloni S.A.R.

Banca di Genova. *See* Credito Italiano.

Banca di Sconto Svizzera. *See* Banque d' Escompte Suisse.

Banca Franco-Romana de Comert si Industrie. *See* Banca Franco-Romana (S.A.).

Banca Franco-Romana (S.A.). Inc. Bucharest 1914 as Banca Franco-Romana de Comert si Industrie; name changed Mar. 1928. Bank suspended payment 1929 .... **1931**

Banca Italo-Britannica. Certain assets were taken over by B. I. Holding Co. Ld. in 1929 .... **1941**

Banca Nazionale di Credito. Est. Italy 1922. Absorbed in Mar. 1930 by Credito Italiano, in which company shareholders received 1 share for each share held **1931**

Banchory Gas Light Co. Ld. Regd. in Edinburgh 1879. Dissolved 1 May 1949, undertaking being vested in Scottish Area Gas Board under Gas Act 1948. Holders of ordinary shares (of £1 with 19s. paid) were entitled to receive £1 4s. British Gas 3% guaranteed stock 1990–95 for each share held....... **1952**

Banco Central. Established Bogotá 1905. In Apr. 1928 the assets and liabilities were transferred to Banca de Bogotá.. **1929**

Banco Colonial e Agricola Portuguez. Inc. Lisbon 1924. Undertaking was acquired in 1928 by Banco da Agricultura **1928**

Banco Colonial Portuguez. In 1924 amalgamated with Banca Nacional Agricola to form Banco Colonial e Agricola Portuguez **1925**

Banco Commercial de Lisboa. Inc. Portugal 1875. Amalgamated with Banca Espirito Santo, in 1937 the undertaking was transferred to Banco Espirito Santa e Commercial de Lisboa **1938**

Banco Commercial de Nicaragua Ltdo. Business was acquired by Anglo-Central American Commercial Bank Ld **1936**

Banco de Burgos. Absorbed by Banco Espanal de Credito in 1929 .... **1940**

Banco de Oviedo. Absorbed by Banco Espanol de Credito in 1929 .... **1940**

Banco del Comercio Ferrocarriles Unidos de la Habana y Almacenes de Regla. The outstanding 5% mortgage bonds 1890 were redeemed at par in July 1930 .... **1931**

Banco del Ecuador (C. A.). Inc. Guayaquil 1868. Bank suspended payment May 1931 and went into liquidation **1932**

Banco del Peru y Londres. Inc. Peru 1897. In liquidation in 1931 .... **1932**

VOL. FOR

Banco di Roma (Espana) S,A. Inc. Spain 1926. Absorbed in 1930 by Banco Espanol de Credita .. **1940**

Banco Espirito Santo. Established Portugal 1879, as Silva, Beirao, Pinto & Co.; name changed 1916 to Espirito Santa Silva & Co., and as above in 1920. Amalgamated with Banco Commercial de Lisboa; the undertaking was transferred to Banco Espirito Santo e Commercial de Lisboa............................ **1938**

Banco Gijones de Credito. Absorbed by Banca Espano. de Credita in 1929 .... **1940**

Banco Hipotecario de Bogota. Inc. Colombia 1925. Liability for external bonds (including 7% sterling bonds) was assumed by Agricultural Mortgage Bank of Colombia **1934**

Banco Hipotecario de Colombia. Inc. Colombia 1910. Liability for external bonds was assumed by Agricultural Mortgage Bank of Colombia **1934**

Banco Internacional do Brazil. Established 1886. Incorporated into Banca Nacional do Brazil **1893**

Banco Internacional e Hipotecario de Mexico. Established Mexico 1883 (under concession of 24 Apr. 1882) as Banco Hipotecario Mexicane; reconstituted under present title under concession of 31 Aug. 1888. Vol. liq. Aug. 1933 .... **1934**

Banco Nacional Agricola. In 1924 amalgamated with Banca Colonial Portuguez to form Banco Colonial e Agricola Portuguez **1925**

Banco Nacional de la Republica Oriental del Uruguay. *See* National Bank of Uruguay.

Banco Nacional do Brazil. Established 1889. In 1894 stated to be defunct **1894**

Banco Sud Americano de Buenos Aires. [South American Bank of Buenos Aires.] Established 1888. London agency was closed on 30 June 1893 .... **1894**

Bancourt Mine Ld. Regd. 1902. Vol. liq. 25 Oct. 1904. Final meeting return regd. 9 Apr. 1906 .... **1905**

Banda Syndicate Ld. Regd. 1901. Vol. liq. 9 July 1907. Final meeting return regd. 9 July 1908 .... **1908**

Bandijarsarie (Java) Rubber Co. Ld. Regd. 1908. Vol. liq. (members') 16 Aug. 1948. Capital returned to contributories—7s. 5·6d. per £1 stock. £46 17s. 6d. was paid into Companies Liquidation Account. Final meeting return regd. 25 July 1956 .... **1957**

Banff & Macduff District Gas Co. Ld. Regd. in Edinburgh 1925. Dissolved 1 May 1949, undertaking being vested in Scottish Area Gas Board under Gas Act 1948. Holders of ordinary shares (of £1) were entitled to receive £2 2s. British Gas 3% guaranteed stock 1990—95 for each share held..... **1952**

Bangawan Rubber Estates Ld. Regd. 1930. Vol. liq. (members') 16 Nov. 1934. Reconstructed as Bangawan Estates Ld. Holders of convertible debenture stock were entitled to repayment at 105%, preference shareholders were entitled to repayment at par with arrears of dividend. Holders of ordinary shares were entitled to an equal number of fully-paid ordinary shares in new company. All share and stockholders were entitled to subscribe for shares in new company. Final meeting return regd. 26 Sept. 1935 .... **1935**

Bangawan Rubber Ld. Regd. 1909. Vol. liq. (members') 5 Aug. 1930; undertaking and assets acquired by Bangawan Rubber Estates Ld. in which company shareholders were entitled to receive 1 share of 2s. (with 1s. 8d. credited as paid up) for every share of 2s. held. Final meeting return regd. 1 Oct. 1931 .. **1931**

Bangwaketsi Concession Co. Ld. Regd. 1895. Undertaking absorbed by Balkis Land Co. Ld. Removed from Register 1903 .... ***1902**

Banir Rubber Estates Ld. Regd. 1925. Vol. liq. (members') 30 June 1961. Capital returned to contributories—5s. 3½d. per 2s. stock. Final meeting return regd. 4 Mar. 1969 .... **1970**

Bank Angielsko-Polski Sp. Akc. Inc. Warsaw 1920. Amalgamated with Bank Handlowy w Warszawie in May 1935. Shareholders received a like number of shares in that bank **1936**

Bank dla Handlu i Przemyslu w Warzawie. *See* Bank for Commerce & Industry in Warsaw.

Bank for Commerce & Industry in Warsaw, Inc. Warsaw 1909. In 1925 the undertaking was placed in hands of supervisor appointed by Polish Court **1926**

Bank for Russian Trade Ld. Regd. 1923 as Arcos Banking Corporation Ld.; name changed Apr. 1925. Vol. liq. (members') 31 Dec. 1931. Undertaking and assets were acquired by Moscow Narodny Bank Ld. Final meeting return regd. 9 Feb. 1934 **1932**

Bank für Deutsche Industrie-Obligationen (Bank for German Industrial Debentures) **1932**

Bank für Handel und Industrie. In 1922 amalgamated with Nationalbank für Deutschland to form Darmstadter und Nationalbank K.A.A. **1929**

Bank für Textilindustrie A.G., Berlin. *See* Textile Traders Corpn. Berlin.

See Stock Exchange Year-Book.

VOL. FOR

Bank Holdings Ld. Regd. 1923. Vol. liq. 20 Oct. 1926. Final meeting return regd. 14 Feb. 1927 .... **1927**

Bank Kredytowy w Warszawie. In 1924 the assets and liabilities were acquired by Bank for Commerce and Industry in Warsaw Ld. for 1,200,000 fully-paid shares................. **1925**

Bank of Abyssinia. Constituted with limited liability by Khedival Decree 30 May 1905. Vol. liq. Oct. 1930. Business was transferred to Banque d'Ethiopie on 10 Oct. 1931. Capital returned to contributories—25s. per share of £5 (£1 5s. paid) in Dec. 1931 further payments (if any) not known. **1932**

Bank of Africa Ld. Regd. under English Companies Acts 1879 and under Cape of Good Hope Acts No. 6 of 1864, 19 of 1865 and 11 of 1879. Vol. liq. Apr. 1912. Undertaking and assets acquired by National Bank of South Africa Ld.; shareholders were entitled to £7 16s. 3d. for each share of £18 15s. (£6 5s. paid) **1913**

Bank of America National Association. Established U. S. A. 1112 as Bank of America; name changed Mar. 1928. Absorbed by National City Bank of New York (later First National City Bank of New York Ld.) in Nov. 1931 .... **1932**

Bank of Athens. Inc. in Greece by Royal Decree 30 Nov. 1893. Merged by Royal Decree of 26 Feb. 1953 with Ethniki Trapeza Tis Ellados as National Bank of Greece and Athens S.A. (later National Bank of Greece S.A.). Shareholders were entitled to receive 1 share of the new bank for every 12$\frac{5}{10}$ shares held **1954**

Bank of Australasia Ld. Inc. by Royal Charter 1835; regd. as limited 1951. Vol. liq. 29 Sept. 1951, all assets and liabilities having been taken over by Australia & New Zealand Bank Ld. in which company shareholders were entitled to 5 shares of £2 (£1 paid) for every share of £5 held **1969**

Bank of Bengal. Established 1809. In Jan. 1921 undertaking and business was transferred to Imperial Bank of India in which company shareholders were entitled to share of Rs.500 (credited as fully paid) and 2 shares of Rs.500 (credited with Rs.125 paid) for each share of Rs.500 held. Shareholders were entitled to Rs.308.5.4 per share in cash **1922**

Bank of Bolton Ld. Regd. 1879, Amalgamated 1897 with Manchester and County Bank Ld. Capital returned to contributories—£12 10s. per share of £20 (£8 10s. paid); £9 per share of £20 (£5 paid); £7 10s. per share of £20 (£3 10s. paid). Removed from Register 1904 .... **1898**

Bank of Bombay. Inc. India. In Jan. 1921 undertaking and business was transferred to Imperial Bank of India in which company shareholders were entitled to 1 fully-paid share and 2 shares of Rs.500 (credited with Rs.125 paid) for every 2 shares of Rs.500 held. Shareholders were entitled to Rs.756.10.6 per share in cash **1922**

Bank of British Columbia. Inc. by Royal Charter 1862. Business was taken over in 1900 by Canadian Bank of Commerce, in which company shareholders were entitled to 4 fully-paid shares of $50 plus £6 8s. 3d. in cash for every 3 fully-paid shares of £20 held **1901**

Bank of British North America. Established 1836. Inc. by Royal Charter 1840. Vol. liq. Nov. 1918. Business was acquired by Bank of Montreal Ld. in which company shareholders were entitled to either 2 shares of $100 (credited as fully-paid) or £75 in cash for each share of £50 held **1919**

Bank of Calcutta Ld. Established Calcutta 1895. Undertaking and assets were acquired by Mercantile Bank of India Ld. (later Mercantile Bank Ld.), in which company shareholders were entitled to 1 B share of £25 (credited with £12 10s. paid) for each share of £25 held **1907**

Bank of China & Japan Ld. Regd. 1894. Vol. liq. 23 Apr. 1902. Capital returned to contributories—£2 per ordinary share of £8 (£4 paid) at 2 June 1902; further payments (if any) not known. Final meeting return regd. 12 Jan. 1904 .... **1908**

Bank of China, Japan & the Straits Ld. Regd. 1889 as Trust & Loan Co. of China, Japan & the Straits Ld.; name changed Mar. 1891. Reconstructed as Bank of China & Japan Ld. in which company shareholders were entitled to 1 ordinary share of £8 (credited with 5s. paid) for each ordinary share of £10 held. Holders of founders' shares were entitled to 1 fully-paid deferred share of £1 for each founders' share of £1 held. Removed from Register 1903................. **1902**

Bank of Commerce in New York. Inc. New York 1839 as National Bank of Commerce in New York; name changed Apr. 1929. Merged into Guaranty Trust Co. of New York (later Morgan Guaranty Trust Co. of New York) in which company shareholders were entitled to 1 share of $100 for each share of $100 held **1930**

VOL. FOR

Bank of Commerce, United Railways of Havana & Regla Warehouses Co. Inc. Havana 1889. The railway system, warehouses and certain lands were acquired in 1898 by United Railways of the Havana and Regla Warehouses Ld. **1898**

Bank of Constantinople. Constituted Constantinople under statute Apr. 1872. Undertaking was taken over by Société Ottomane de Change et de Valeurs, in which company shareholders received 4 shares for every 5 shares of £10 (£6 paid) held **1895**

Bank of Egypt Ld. Inc. 1856. Regd. 1887. Court Order to wind up 17 Oct. 1911. Struck off Register 1925 .... **1912**

Bank of Ethiopia. Inc. Ethiopia 1931. Stated to be placed in liquidation (under martial law) in June 1936 .... **1937**

Bank of Liverpool. See Martins Bank Ld.

Bank of Liverpool & Martins Ld. See Martins Bank Ld.

Bank of London Ld. Regd. 1904. Vol. liq. (members') 7 Mar. 1936. Court Order to continue winding up under supervision 14 May 1936. Liquidator released 21 Aug. 1940. Struck off Register 1 May 1953 ..... **1937**

Bank of Madras. Inc. by Charter 1843. In Jan. 1921 undertaking and business were acquired by Imperial Bank of India, in which company shareholders were entitled to 1 share of Rs.500 (credited as fully-paid) for each share of Rs.500 held and, after payment of Rs.225 per share to subscribe for 2 shares of Rs.500 (credited with Rs.125 paid) **1922**

Bank of Manchester Ld. See Consolidated Bank Ld.

Bank of Mauritius Ld. Regd. 1894. Vol. liq. 3 May 1916. The goodwill and substantial part of assets were acquired by Mercantile Bank of India Ld. (later Mercantile Bank Ld.) for £234,535. A return of £18 15s. per share of £10 was anticipated. Final meeting return regd. 18 Jan 1918 .... **1916**

Bank of New Zealand Estates Co. Ld. Regd. 1890. Vol. liq. 11 Nov. 1927. Final meeting return regd. 23 Apr. 1928 .... **1908**

Bank of Nicaragua Ld. See London Bank of Central America Ld.

Bank of Nigeria Ld. Regd. 1899 as Anglo African Bank Ld.; name changed Mar. 1905. Vol. liq. June 1912. Undertaking was acquired by Bank of West Africa Ld. (later Standard Bank of West Africa Ld.) in which company shareholders were entitled to 1 share of £10 (credited with £4 paid) for every 9 shares of £1 held. Removed from Register 1913 .. **1913**

Bank of North America & Trust Co. Inc. Pennsylvania 1894 as the Commercial Trust Co.; name changed Mar. 1923. Merged into Pennsylvania Co. on 1 June 1929 .... **1930**

Bank of North Queensland Ld. Inc. Queensland 1888. Business acquired by Bank of Queensland Ld....... **1918**

Bank of Oldham. See Manchester & Oldham Bank Ld.

Bank of Port Elizabeth Ld. Regd. 1881. Removed from Register 1888 .... **1883**

Bank of Queensland Ld. Inc. Queensland 1917. Vol. liq. Jan. 1922. Undertaking and assets were acquired by National Bank of Australasia Ld. Capital returned to contributories—£11 11s. per share of £10 .... **1923**

Bank of Roumania Ld. Inc. 1866 under a Roumanian Charter as Bank of Roumania. Regd. (in London) as limited 17 Apr. 1903. Vol. liq. (members') 28 July 1948. Capital returned to contributories—£4 3s. 4d. per share of £6. £7,813 was paid into Companies' Liquidation Account. Final meeting return regd. 9 Sept. 1952. Final dissolution deferred until 9 Oct. 1970 by Order of Court in Oct. 1963; restored to register 14 Oct. 1964............ **1953**

Bank of South Australia Ld. Established 1841. Inc. by Royal Charter 1847. Regd. 1884. Certain assets were acquired by Union Bank of Australia Ld. Vol. liq. Apr. 1892. Court Order to wind up 6 Dec. 1894. Liquidator released 27 Nov. 1899. Court Order to dissolve 31 Dec. 1899 .... **1892**

Bank of Tarapaca & Argentina Ld. See Anglo-South American Bank Ld.

Bank of Tarapaca & London Ld. See Anglo-South American Bank Ld.

Bank of Toronto. Inc. in Ontario 1855. In 1955 amalgamated with Dominion Bank as Toronto-Dominion Bank. Shareholders received 4 shares of $10 of the new bank for every 3 shares of £10 held **1956**

Bank of Victoria Ld. Inc. Victoria 1889. Assets and liabilities were acquired by Commercial Banking Co. of Sydney Ld., in which company shareholders were entitled to 1 share of £25 (credited with £12 10s. paid) plus £25 in cash for every 5 ordinary shares of £10 (£5 paid) held or 2 shares of £25 (credited with £12 10s.) plus £50 in cash for every 5 preference shares of £10 held. **1928**

Bank of Westmorland Ld. In 1893 business was acquired by London & Midland Bank Ld. (later Midland Bank Ld.) Shareholders received £34 per share plus

See Stock Exchange Year-Book.

VOL. FOR

surplus value of investments as appeared in balance sheet 1894

Bank of Whitehaven. Established 1837. Regd. 1866. Vol. liq. 1 Feb. 1916. Business was acquired by Manchester and Liverpool District Banking Co. Ld. (later District Bank Ld.) for £216,766 in cash; equivalent to £22 per share of £30 (£10 paid) held. Shareholders were given option to subscribe for shares in absorbing company. Struck off Register 3 July 1953 1916

Bankers Guarantee Trust. Established 1865 as Bankers Guarantee and Trust Fund. Inc. by Special Act 1910 and name changed. Under Act of 1919 the business was transferred to Alliance Assurance Co. Ld 1902

Bankers Industrial Development Co. Ld. Regd. 15 Apr. 1930. Vol. liq. (members') 22 Aug. 1945. Capital returned to contributories—£30 per share of £10. Final meeting return regd. 5 Jan, 1946 1946

Banket Exploration Co. Ld. Regd. 1906. 60,000 fully-paid shares of £1 were held by "K" Exploration Co. Ld. In liquidation in 1908. Removed from Register 1912 1908

Banket Reefs of West Africa Ld. Regd. 1901. Removed from Register 1913 1910

Bankfoot Light Railway Co. Inc. (under Light Railways Act 1896) by order of Light Railway Commissioners, confirmed by Board of Trade 1898. Acquired by Caledanian Railway Co. on and from 1 Feb. 1912 1913

Bankhall Oil & Chemical Works Ld. Regd. 1866. Vol. liq. 14 Mar. 1890. Removed from Register 1902... 1891

Bankhaus J. F. Schreder. See Norddeutsche Kreditbank A.G.

Bankside Finance & Industries Ld. See below.

Bankside Investment Trust Ld. Regd. 1920 as Bankside Finance & Industries Ld.; name changed 1928. Vol. liq. (members') 17 Nov. 1950. Capital returned to contributories—£10 9s. 0·816d. Final meeting return regd. 12 Dec. 1952 1954

Banner Gold Mine Ld. Regd. 1895. Vol. liq. 10 Mar. 1897. Reconstructed as Consolidated Gold Mines of California Ld., in which company shareholders were entitled to 1 share of £1 (credited with 17s. paid) for each share of £1 held. Final meeting return regd. 6 Dec. 1897 1898

Bannerman (Henry) & Sons Ld. Regd. 1899. Vol. liq. Mar. 1929 for reconstruction as company of same name (later Henry Bannerman (Holdings) Ld.) Final meeting return regd. 21 June 1930 1930

Bannerman Mills Co. Ld. Regd. 1899. Vol. liq. 12 Mar. 1923 for amalgamation with Henry Bannerman & Sons Ld. Final meeting return regd. 21 June 1930 1924

Banque Belge pour l'Etranger, S.A. See Compagnie Beige pour l'Etranger, S.A.

Banque Chrissoreloni S.A.R. Inc. in Roumania in June 1920. In Sept. 1948 it was stated that bank had been liquidated by Decree of 13 Aug. 1948 1949

Banque Commerciale de Bale. Inc. Switzerland 1863. All assets and liabilities not affected by transfer restrictions were acquired by Swiss Bank Corporation from 31 July 1945 1946

Banque Continentale de Paris Ld. Regd. 1893. Vol. liq. 7 Aug. 1907. Final meeting return regd. 1 Dec. 1917 1908

Banque Co-operative de Transit. See Co-operative Transitbank.

Banque de Bruxelles (inc. 1871). See Société de Bruxelles pour la Finance et l'Industrie.

Banque de Calamata. In 1924 amalgamated with J. F. Costopulo to form Credit Commercial Hellenique S.A. 1926

Banque de Crédit Foncier et Agricole de Santa Fé. Created by law of 1886. In June 1895 bondholders decided to exchange their bonds for shares of Société de Crédit Foncier de Santa Fé at the rate of 1½ shares of 100 piastres for each obligation of $m/n 100. Shareholders were to receive 20,000 shares .. 1896

Banque de Crédit Industriel de Grèce. Established 1873. Vol. liq. 10 June 1906. Undertaking acquired by Bank of Athens in which bank shareholders were entitled to 2 shares of Dr. 100 for every 3 shares of Dr. 100 held 1907

Banque de Depôts et de Crédit. Amalgamated with Banque d'Escompte Suisse (see below) in 1933 1934

Banque d'Escompte Suisse. Inc. Switzerland 1931. Amalgamated with Banque de Depots et de Crédit in 1933 1934

Banque de l'Union de Varsovie. See Union Bank of Warsaw.

Banque d'Outremer. Absorbed in 1928 by Société Générale de Belgique 1936

Banque de Suez (U. K.) Ld. Reg'd. private company 1926 as British & Continental Banking Co. Ld.; converted public company 1938; name changed 1973; merged with Banque de l'Indochine (London); dissolved 22 Mar. 1979 1977-8

VOL. FOR

Banque Française de l'Afrique S.A. Inc. Paris 1904 as Banque Française de l'Afrique Equatoriale; name changed 1924. Suspended payment in Nov. 1930 .. 1931

Banque Francaise de l'Afrique Equatoriale. See Banque Francaise de l'Afrique S.A.

Banque Francaise de l'Afrique du Sud. In liquidation in 1902. Amalgamated with another company under the title of Banque Francaise pour le Commerce et l'Industrie 1902

Banque Française pour le Commerce et l'Industrie. Inc. France 1901. Vol. liq. Sept. 1922. Undertaking and assets were transferred to Banque Nationale de Crédit, on 1 Aug. 1921, in which bank shareholders were entitled to 4 fully-paid shares of frs.500 and frs.100 in cash for every 5 shares of frs.250 held .. 1923

Banque Franco-Belge de Bulgarie S.A. See Banque Franco. Bulgare, S.A.

Banque Franco-Belge et Balkanique, S.A. See Banque Franco-Bulgare, S.A.

Banque Franco-Bulgare, S. A. Inc. Bulgaria 1923 as Banque Franco-Belge de Bulgarie S.A.; name changed to Banque Franco-Belge et Balkanique S.A. in Feb. 1929 and as above in Mar. 1938. Placed in voluntary liquidation 10 Aug. 1944 1947

Banque Générale de Bulgarie S.A. Inc. Bulgaria 1906. In Mar. 1938 the undertaking was acquired by Banque Franco-Bulgare S.A. in which bank shareholders were entitled to 1 share of L.200 for every 40 shares of L.250 held 1939

Banque Générale de Grèce. See Geniki Trapeza tis Hellados

Banque Hongroise-Bulgare. See Ungarisch Bulgarische Bank

Banque Hongroise des Rentes et du Credit Agricole S.A. See Hungarian Land Mortgage Bank

Banque Internationale de Paris. In liquidation in 1903. Amalgamated with another company under title of Banque Française pour le Commerce et l'Industrie 1903

Banque J. Allard & Cie. Established Paris 1901. Undertaking acquired by Banque Belge pour l'Etranger in 1921 1936

Banque Littlejohn Ld. Regd. 1926. Struck off Register 1936 .... *1931

Banque Nationale de Credit. Established France 1913. Vol. liq. Feb. 1932. Reconstructed as Banque Nationale pour le Commerce et l'Industrie 1933

Banque Nationale de Turquie. See National Bank of Turkey.

Banque Nationale Ethiopienne. See Bank of Ethiopia.

Banque Parisienne, Established 1874. Reconstructed 1904 as Banque de l'Union Parisienne Société Anonyme 1908

Banque pour le Commerce et l'Industrie a Varsovie. See Bank for Commerce & Industry in Warsaw.

Banque Rhétique. Absorbed by Crédit Suisse in 1930 1934

Banque Russe pour le Commerce Etranger. See Russian Bank for Foreign Trade

Banque Russo-Asiatique. Inc. Russia 1910. English Court Order to wind up 14 Dec. 1926. Assets realised insufficient to meet claims of creditors. A 1st and final dividend to creditors was paid in Mar. 1955 1927

Banque Sino Belge (S.A.). See Compagnie Belge pour l'Etranger S.A.

Bansu Properties Ld. Regd. 1901. Vol. liq. 7 Jan. 1903. Undertaking was acquired by Gold Coast Exploration and Trading Co. Ld. in which company shareholders were entitled to 1 fully-paid share of £1 for every 10 shares of £1 held or to 1 share of £1 (credited with 12s. 6d. paid) for each shares of £1 (7s. 6d. paid) held. Final meeting return regd. 7 Sept. 1903 1904

Bansu Tarkwa Syndicate Ld. Regd. 1901. Vol. liq. 15 Apr. 1908. Final meeting return regd. 20 July 1908 1909

Bantardawa Rubber Estates, Ld. Regd. 1910. Vol. liq. (members') 11 June 1953. Capital returned to contributories-6½d. per 2s. share. £690 2s. 7d. was paid into Companies' Liquidation Account in respect of unclaimed distributions. Final meeting return regd. 30 Oct. 1970 1971

Banten (Selangor) Rubber Estates Ld. Regd. 1907. Vol. liq. 28 Aug. 1962. Final meeting return regd. 25 June 1964 1960

Banties Consolidated Mines Ld. Inc. Transvaal 1895. Vol. liq. May 1922. Capital returned to contributories—6s. per share of £1 at Feb. 1923; further payments (if any) not known 1923

Banties Deep Ld. Inc. Transvaal 1896. Application was made in 1906 to Johannesburg Court to wind up . 1907

Banties Reef Gold Mining Co. Ld. Inc. Transvaal 1887. Reconstructed 1895 as Banties Consolidated Mines Ld. Shareholders were entitled to 5 fully-paid shares of £1 for every 4 shares held 1908

See Stock Exchange Year-Book.

Bantry Extension Railway. Inc. by Special Act 1878. In 1925 the undertaking was merged into the Great Southern Railway Co. in which company stock-holders were entitled to stock as follows:

For each £100 held   G.S.R.
5% Debenture ....£125   4% Debenture
A or Baronial Gtd. Extn.   £20 Ordinary
B or Ordinary Extn.*   £20 Ordinary
*Stock held by Great Southern Railways Co. was to be cancelled   **1925**

Baoulé (Ivory Coast) Consolidated Mines Ld. Regd. 1902. Vol. liq. 11 Nov. 1904. Shareholders were entitled to 1 fully-paid share of £1 in Kokumbo (Ivory Coast) Co. Ld. for each share of £1 held. Removed from Register 1908   **1905**

Bar-Lock Typewriter Co. Ld. Regd. 1908. Receiver was appointed Sept. 1923. Assets realised insufficient to satisfy claims of 6% debenture holders. Struck off Register Jan. 1932   **1932**

Barancannes Copper Mining Co. Ld. Regd. 1883. Reconstructed 1885 as company of same name. Final meeting return regd. 15 June 1888 ....   **1891**

Barancannes Copper Mining Co. Ld. Regd. 1885. Reconstructed 1887 as company of same name. Final meeting return regd. 16 Oct. 1888 ....   **1891**

Barancannes Copper Mining Co. Ld. Regd. 1888. Vol. liq. 26 Jan. 1891. Final meeting return regd. 29 Oct. 1894   **1891**

Barangah Oil Refining Co. Ld. Regd. 1877. Court Orders: to wind up 25 July 1885; to dissolve 4 July 1891 ....   ***1885**

Barbados Electricity Supply Corporation Ld. Regd. 1909. Vol. liq. (members') 14 Oct. 1960. Capital returned to contributories—21s. per preference share of £1 and 47s. 5·85d. per ordinary share of £1. Paid into Companies' Liquidation Account—(1) unclaimed dividends £46 0s. 1d.; (2) distributions £814 4s. 5d. Final meeting return regd. 19 May 1961   **1962**

Barbados Railway Co. Ld. Regd. 1879. Line was sold to bondholders under Court Order for £50,000. Removed from Register 1901   **1899**

Barbados Water Supply Co. Ld. Regd. 1886. Vol. liq. 24 Mar. 1896. Undertaking was acquired by Government of Barbados. Final meeting return regd. 11 May 1896   **1897**

Barber & D'Ambrumenil Ld. Regd. 1925. Vol. liq. (members') 26 July 1935. Undertaking amalgamat-ed with Robert Gardner, Mountain & Co. Ld. Capital returned to contributories—£53.437 5s. 3d. Final meeting return regd. 2 June 1938 ....   **1936**

Barber (J. Lionel) & Co. Ld. Regd. 1912. Vol. liq. 8 Mar. 1921. Certain assets transferred to Lionel Barber (1921) Ld. Final meeting return regd. 16 Jan. 1934   **1922**

Barber [Lionel] (1921) Ld. Regd. 1921. Vol. liq. (creditors') 19 Feb. 1930. Assets realised insufficient to pay creditors in full. Final meeting return regd. 23 Sept. 1940   **1931**

Barberton Consolidated Gold Fields Ld. Regd. 1896. Removed from Register 1905 ....   **1901**

Barberton Estates and Gold Mining Co. Ld. Inc. South African Republic 1895. In liquidation in 1899 .....   **1899**

Barberton Exploring & Development Co. Ld. Regd. 1903. Reconstructed 1906 as company of same name. Shareholders were entitled to 4 shares of 10s. in new company (credited with 8s. 6d. paid) for every 3 shares of 10s. held. Removed from Register 1909 ....   **1908**

Barberton Exploring & Development Co. Ld. Regd. 1906. Removed from Register 1912 ....   **1912**

Barberton Gold Fields (South) Ld. Regd. 1895. Struck off Register 2 Aug. 1904 ....   **1905**

Barberton Gold Mines Ld. Regd. 1887. Vol. liq. Dec. 1889. Reconstructed as Barberton Gold Mining Co. Ld. Final meeting return regd. 4 Feb. 1892 ....   **1890**

Barberton Reefs Ld. Regd. 1895. Vol. liq. 31 Oct. 1898. Final meeting return regd. 11 Aug. 1899 ....   **1900**

Barbour (John) & Co. Ld. Regd. Dublin 1906. Trans-ferred to Belfast 1920. Vol. liq. 14 Mar. 1960. All capital was owned by Herdmans Ld. Final meeting return regd. 4 July 1962 ....   **1959**

Barcelona (Besos) Waterworks Co. Ld. Regd. 1892. Vol. liq. 30 Nov. 1905. Final meeting return regd. 29 Aug. 1907 ....   ***1896**

Barcelona Tramways Co. Ld. Regd. 1872. Vol. liq. 13 Dec. 1905. Undertaking was acquired by Société Financiére de Transports et d' Entreprises. Capital returned to contributories—£10 per preference share of £10: £13 per ordinary share of £10; further payments (if any) not known. The 4½% debenture stock was repaid at 105%; the 5% debentures were repaid at par. Removed from Register 1907 ....   **1906**

Barclay & Sons Ld. Regd. 1888. Vol. liq. 25 June 1896. Reconstructed as company of same name. Share-holders were entitled to 1 ordinary share of £1 in new

company for every 3 ordinary shares of £1 held or 1 preference share of £1 for each preference share held. Final meeting return regd. 17 June 1897 .....   **1908**

Barclay Ross & Hutchison Ld. Regd. Edinburgh. Vol. liq. (members') 30 June 1943. All shares were held by Scottish Agricultural Industries Ld. Final meet-ing return regd. 24 Jan. 1945 ....   **1945**

Bard Cycle Manufacturing Co. Ld. Regd. 1896. Re-moved from Register 1904 ....   **1904**

Barfield & Sible Hedingham Light Railway Co. Inc. (under Light Railways Act 1896) by order of Light Railway Commissioners confirmed by Board of Trade Nov. 1901 ....   **1903**

Bardoc Gold Mines Ld. Regd. 1895. Removed from Register 1905 ....   **1904**

Baring Estate Co. Ld. Regd. 1894. Vol. liq. 31 Mar. 1898. Debentures were repaid by 1 Apr. 1898. Final meeting return regd. 24 Mar. 1899 ....   **1899**

Barium Consolidated Ld. Regd. 1927. Vol. liq. (credi-tors') 31 May 1937. Assets realised insufficient to pay creditors in full. Final meeting return regd. 24 Aug. 1938 ....   **1938**

Barker Bros. Silversmiths Ld. *See* Norvic Securities Ld.

Barker Ellis Silver Co Ld. *See* Norvic Securities Ld.

Barker (H. & S.) & Co. Ld. Regd. 1872. Vol. liq. 22 Feb. 1897. Final meeting return regd. 18 Feb. 1898 ....   **1925**

Barker, Son & Co, (Hull) Ld. Regd. 1917. Vol. liq. 20 May 1921. Reconstructed as Barkers & Lee Smith Ld. Final meeting return regd. 7 Oct. 1921 ....   **1940**

Barking Gas Co. Established 1839; inc. by Special Act 1867. Under Act of 1911, the undertaking was acquired by Gas Light & Coke Co., in which company shareholders were entitled to £215 ordi-nary stock *plus* £30 in cash for every 10 10% maximum orginal shares of £10 or £150 ordinary stock for every 10 7% maximum ordinary' shares of £10 held. Holders of preference shares and deben-ture stock were entitled to £200 and £133 6s. 8d. respectively in 3% debenture stock for every £100 held **1912**

Barking Jute Factory Ld. Regd. 1889. Vol. liq. 27 Aug. 1891. Final meeting return regd. 1 Aug. 1896 ......   **1892**

Barlow & Jones Ld. Regd. 1874. Reconstructed 1900 as company of same name. Holders of every £100 paid-up capital were entitled to £56 5s. preference shares, £56 5s. ordinary shares and £17 10s. in 4% debenture stock. Removed from Register 1903 ....   **1908**

Barlow & Jones Ld. Regd. 1900. Vol. liq. (members') 17 June 1963 for purpose reconstruction as Barlow and Jones Holdings Ld. [name subsequently changed to Barlow and Jones Ld. (regd. 1963)]. Shareholders received 10 fully-paid shares (of 5s.) of John Myers & Co. Ld. and 4 fully-paid shares (of 10s.) of Barlow and Jones Ld. (regd. 1963) for every 5 ordinary shares (of 10s.) held. £9,230 14s. 2d. was paid into Companies Liquidation Account in respect of unclaimed proceeds of shares sold. Final meeting return regd. 14 Jan. 1966 ....   **1966**

Barlow Brothers & Greenwood Ld. Regd. 1949 as Barlow Brothers & Greenwood (Holdings) Ld.; name changed 31 Mar. 1953. Vol. liq. (members') 31 Mar. 1960. Capital returned to contributories—20s. per preference share of £1 and 3s. 11·4d. per ordinary share of 1s. Final meeting return regd. 19 Feb. 1962   **1962**

Barlow (Samuel) & Co. Ld. *See* Stakehill & Co. Ld.

Barlow, Taylor & Co. Ld. Regd. 1923. All capital acquired by Phillips Furnishing Stores Ld. Dis-solved 22 Mar. 1982. ....   **1958**

Barlows Ld. *See* Stakehill & Co. Ld.

Barmer Bank-Verein Hinsberg, Fischer & Comp. K.A.A. Inc. Barmen 1867. Absorbed by Commerz-und-Privat Bank A.G. Bank cancelled its holding of R.M.23,500,000 of its own shares and the remaining R.M.12,500,000 of shares were exchanged for a like amount in purchasing company..............................   **1933**

Barmouth Gas Co. Ld. Regd. 1893. Dissolved 1 May 1949, undertaking being vested in Wales Area Gas Board under Gas Act 1948. Holders of securities were entitled to receive British Gas 3% guaranteed stock 1990–95 as follows:

	£	s.	d.
Ord. shares (of £10)................	21	10	0
4% deb. stock (per £100)............	101| 0	0	**1952**

Barnard, Bishop & Barnards Ld. Regd. 1887. Court Order to wind up 8 Aug. 1894. Removed from Register 1908 ....   **1895**

Barnard Castle Gas Co. Inc. by Deed of Settlement 1834. Dissolved 1 May 1949, undertaking being vested in Northern Area Gas Board under Gas Act 1948. Holders of securities were entitled to receive in respect of each £100 unit held, British Gas 3% guaranteed stock 1990–95 as follows:

	£	s.	d.
Orig. cons. stock (7% max.)	5	0	0

		VOL. FOR
New ord. stock (5% max.)	3 15 0	
5% red. debs	100 5 0	**1952**

Barnato Consolidated Mines Ld. Inc. Transvaal 1895. Undertaking was acquired in 1905 by Johannesburg Consolidated Investment Co. Ld., in which company shareholders were entitled to 1 share of £1 for each share of £1 held ... **1906**

Barnes (E.) & Sons Ld. Regd. 1899. Removed from Register 1911 ... **1910**

Barnes District Water Co. Inc. by Special Act 1872 as Barnes District Gas & Water Co.; name changed 1950. Undertaking vested in Lee Valley Water Co. from 1 Apr. 1960. Stockholders received capital stocks in new company (per £1 stock held) as follows:

Ordinary (7% maximum), £1 8*s*. 5% ordinary; 4½% preference, £1. 3*s* 6*d*, 4% preference; 4% preference £: 4% preference. Outstanding debenture stock of this company became debenture stock of new company. This company was dissolved 28 Oct. 1964 ... **1966**

Barnoldswick Railway Co. Inc. by Special Act 1867. Under Act of 1899 the Midland Railway Co. purchased the undertaking for £52,500. On 5 Jan. 1900 shareholders received £19 2*s*. 8½*d*. per fully-paid share of £10 or half that amount on shares of £10 (£5 paid) ... **1900**

Barnsley Banking Co. Ld. Regd. 1883. Vol. liq. 14 Jan. 1897. Amalgamated with York City and County Banking Co. Ld. Capital returned to contributories—£4 11*s*. per share of £25 (£5 paid). Final meeting return regd. 3 May 1898 ... **1898**

Barnsley Gas Co. Established 1922. Inc. by Special Act 1852. Undertaking was acquired by Sheffield Gas Co. (later Sheffield and District Gas Co.) in 1937. Capital returned to contributories-£190 per £100 general capital stock; £11 10*s*. per C preference share of £10; £13 per D, E or G ordinary share of £10; £19 per F ordinary share of £10 ... **1938**

Barnsley Smokeless Fuel Co. Ld. Regd. 1914. Under scheme of arrangement of July 1926 the undertaking was amalgamated with Low Temperature Carbonisation Ld. [later Coalite & Chemical Products Ld.]. 1st mortgage debenture holders were entitled to 14 ordinary shares of 2*s*. in acquiring company and 14*s*. in a new Tully Gas Plant company for every £10 bond held. Vol. liq. 6 Dec. 1926. Final meeting return regd 20 Dec. 1927 ... **1927**

Barnstaple Gas Co. Estd. 1812; inc. by Special Act 1869. Dissolved 1 May 1949, undertaking being vested in South Western Area Gas Board under Gas Act 1948. Holders of securities were entitled to receive British Gas 3% guaranteed stock 1990–95 as follows, in respect of each £10 unit, unless otherwise stated, of security held:

	£ s. d.	
A shares (10% stand.)	25 0 0	
B shares (7% stand.)	17 10 0	
4% red. pref. shares	10 2 0	
4½% red. pref. shares	10 6 0	
4% irred. deb. stock (per £100)	102 10 0	
3¾ red. deb. stock (issued since 31 Dec. 1945—per £100)	106 0 0	
3¾% red. deb. stock (issued before 1 Jan. 1946—per £100)	102 0 0	**1952**

Barnstaple Water Co. Inc. by Special Act 1858. In Jan. 1946 the undertaking was transferred to North Devon Water Board, in which Board shareholders were entitled to £26 4% stock for each original 10% maximum share of £10 held, or to £17 10*s*. 4% stock for each new ordinary 7% maximum share of £10 held. The outstanding mortgages became charge on Board. Company has been dissolved ... **1946**

Barnum & Bailey Ld. Regd. 1899. Vol. liq. Dec. 1907. Undertaking was sold to Ringling Brothers for £82,000 in cash. Capital returned to contributories—9*s*. 1½*d*. per ordinary or deferred share of £1; further payments (if any) not known. Removed from Register 1909 ... **1909**

Baron Cigarette Machine Co. Ld. Regd. 1896. Removed from Register 1913 ... **1910**

Baron Liebig's Cocoa & Chocolate Works Ld. Regd. 1882 as Baron Liebig's Malto-Legumine Cocoa & Chocolate Works Ld.; name changed July 1885. Court Orders: to wind up 19 July 1886; to dissolve 11 June 1888 ... **1887**

Barr (Thomas) Ld. Regd. Edinburgh 1898. Vol. liq. Dec. 1917. Final meeting return regd. 3 June 1924. Court Order deferred dissolution till 3 Nov. 1924 **1918**

Barramia Mining & Exploration Ld. Regd. 1909. Vol. liq. 30 Mar. 1920. Final meeting return regd. 14 Mar. 1921 ... **1921**

Barranca Mines & Exploration Co. S.A. Inc. in Mexico in 1922 as Barranca Mines, Mexico, S.A.; name subsequently changed. In 1931 it was stated that the company's property has been lost owing to revolution and that a claim had been filed against the Mexican Government for compensation ... **1931**

Barranca Mines (Mexico) Ld. Regd. 1906. Vol. liq. Nov. 1921. Undertaking and assets were acquired by Barranca Mines and Exploration Co. S.A. (inc. Mexico), in which company shareholders were entitled to 2 fully-paid shares of 10*s*. after payment of 2*s*. per share for each ordinary share of £1 held or to 1 fully-paid share of 10*s*. for each preference share of 5*s*. held. Struck off Register 12 Mar. 1935 ... **1936**

Barratt (J. H.) & Co. Ld. Regd. 1903. Vol. liq. Barratt (J. H.) & Co. (1927) Ld. Final meeting return regd. 3 Jan. 1928 ... **1940**

Barrenechea Nitrate Co. Ld. Regd. 1903. Vol. liq. 22 Feb. 1929. The oficina, nitrate grounds and plant and stocks in Chile were sold for £25,000 in cash. Final meeting return regd. 2 Sept.1929 ... **1929**

Barreto Gold Mines Syndicate Ld. Regd. 1893. Struck off Register 1920 ... **1900**

Barrett & Elers Ld. *See* Elerbar Ld.

Barrett Bros. Ld. Regd. 1927. Vol. liq. (members') 14 May 1931. Capital returned to contributories—£39 11*s*. 3*d*. Final meeting return regd. 9 July 1931 ... **1930**

Barrett Gold Mining Co. Ld. Regd. 1885. Vol. liq. Oct. 1887. Reconstructed as company of same name. Shareholders were entitled to 1 share of £1 (credited with 18*s*. paid) for each share of £1 held. Final meeting return regd. 11 July 1888 ... **1892**

Barrett Gold Mining Co. Ld. Regd. 1887. Vol. liq. 7 Mar. 1892 for reconstruction as company of same name, in which company shareholders were entitled to 1 share of 10*s*. (credited with 8*s*. paid) for each share of £1 held. Final meeting return regd. 8 Dec. 1892 ... **1908**

Barrett Gold Mining Co. Ld. Regd. 1892. Vol. liq. 21 Mar. 1923. Capital returned to contributories—2⅛*d*. per share of 10*s*. at Sept. 1923; further payments (if any) not known. Final meeting return regd. 18 Oct. 1924 ... **1924**

Barrett Samuel & Sons Ld. *See* Decca Gramophone Co. Ld.

Barrett's Brewery & Bottling Co. Ld. Regd. 1886. Vol. liq. Mar. 1907. Reconstructed as Plowman, Barrett & Co. Ld., later Culley-Plowman Ld. in which company shareholders were entitled to 1 preference share of £1 *plus* 8*s*. in cash for each preference share of £2 10*s*. held or 5*s*. in preference shares, *plus* 2*s*. in cash for each ordinary share of £2 10*s*. held. Removed from Register 1908 ... **1908**

Barrhead Gas Co. Ld. Regd. in Edinburgh 1899. Dissolved 1 May 1949, undertaking being vested in Scottish Area Gas Board under Gas Act 1941. Holders of securities were entitled to receive, in respect of each £1 unit held, British Gas 3% guaranteed stock 1990–95 as follows:

	£ s. d.	
Ord. shares (fully paid)	3 15 0	
Ord. shares (15*s*. paid)	2 16 3	**1952**

Barrier & General Finance Co. Ld. Regd. 1924 as Barrier & General Trust (1924) Ld.; name changed Apr. 1927. Vol. liq. 12 Nov. 1928. Shareholders were entitled to fully-paid shares of 5*s*. in Associated Tin Mines of Nigeria Ld., and an option (since expired) over further shares at 15*s*. 6*d*. per share of 5*s*. Final meeting return regd. 9 July 1929 ... **1929**

Barrier South Ld. Regd. 1913. Vol. liq. (members') 31 Dec. 1937. Assets were acquired by New Broken Hill Consolidated Ld. Capital returned to contributories—£1 10*s*. 2*d*. per preference share of £1; 4½*d*. per ordinary share of 2*s*.; £1,061 8*s*. 10*d*. was paid into Companies' Liquidation Account. Final meeting return regd. 20 May 1939 ... **1938**

Barrmill & Kilwinning Railway Co. *See* Lanarkshire and Ayrshire Railway Co.

Barro Equities Ld. Regd. as private company 9 Sept. 1959; converted into public company 30 Sept. Vol. liq. (members') 31 Mar. 1966. Distributions per share (of £1)—18*s*. in Apr. 1967, 7*s*. in Feb. & 6*s*. in Nov. 1968, 3*s*. in May 1969, 1*s*. 6*d*. in Sept. 1970, 5p in Dec. 1972, 7·5p in Jan. 1974, 7·5p in Apr. 1975 & Apr. 1976, 10p in Jan. 1977, 8p in June 1978 and 1·8p in June 1984 (final). Final meeting held 15 June 1984 ... **1985–5**

Barro Investments Ld. Regd. 1959. Vol. liq. (members') 24 Feb. 1965. Capital returned to contributories—30*s*. 1½*d*. per share (of £1). £102 4*s*. 8*d*. was paid into Companies' Liquidation Account (£12 6*s*. 10*d*. unclaimed dividends; £89 17*s*. 10*d*. distributions). Final meeting return regd. 17 May 1965 ... **1965**

Barrow Haematite Steel Co. Ld. Regd. 1864. Vol. Liq. (creditors) 16 Mar. 1964. 52.74p in £1 returned to creditors. Final meeting return regd. 12 Dec. 1974 **1975-6**

**See Stock Exchange Year-Book.*

VOL. FOR

Barrow-in-Furness Tramways Ld. Regd. 1883. Removed from Register 1904 .... **1897**

Barrow Salt Co. Ld. Regd. 1896. Removed from Register 1906 .... **1903**

Barrow Ship Building Co. Ld. Regd. 1871. Vol. liq. 21 Mar. 1899. Final meeting return regd. 2 Aug.1899 ***1888**

Barrow-upon-Humber Gas Co. Ld. Regd. 1877. Dissolved 1 May 1949, undertaking being vested in East Midland Area Gas Board under Gas Act 1948. Holders of ordinary shares (of £5 with £3 10s. paid) were entitled to receive £2 5s. British Gas 3% guaranteed stock 1990–95 for each share held **1952**

Barrowfield Ironworks Ld. Regd. Edinburgh 1922. Vol. liq. (members') 10 June 1936. Directly controlled by Whessoe Foundry and Engineering Co. Ld. (later Whessoe Ld.) Capital returned to contributories—£9,562 11s. 1d. Final meeting return regd. 21 June 1937 .... **1937**

Barry & Cadoxton Gas & Water Co. Inc. by Special Act 1886. Undertaking purchased by local board for £152,000. The debenture stock was taken over **1894**

Barry Docks & Railways Co. See Barry Railway Co.

Barry Estate Co. Ld. Regd. 1889. Vol. liq. (members') 29 May 1957. Final meeting return regd. 12 June 1963 .... **1955**

Barry New Dry Docks Ld. See Severn Dry Docks Co. Ld.

Barry Railway Co. Inc. by Special Act, 1884 as Barry Docks & Railways Co.; name changed by Act of 1891. In 1922 the undertaking was merged into the Great Western Railway Co., in which company stockholders were entitled to stock as follows:

For each £100 held		G.W.R.	
3% Cons. Deb.	£75	4% debenture	
5% Preference.................	£100	5% Cons. Pref.	
4%Con Pref.	£80	5% Cons. Pref.	
4% Third Preference	£80	5% Cons. Pref.	
Ordinary..........................	£80	5% Cons. Guar.	
(Undivided).............	£140	5% Cons. Pref.	
Prefd. Conv. Ord.	£80	5% Cons. Guar.	
Defd. Conv. Ord.	£140	5% Cons. Guar.	**1924**

Barsi Light Railway Co. Ld. Regd. 1895. Railway taken over by Government as from 1 Jan. 1954 Vol. liq. (members') 23 Nov. 1955. Capital returned to contributories: £2 13s. 8½d. per £1 ordinary stock. Final meeting return regd. 9 July 1963 .... **1964**

Bars Ld. Regd. 1902. Vol. liq. (creditors') 28 July 1933. All shares held by Atkinsons Brewery Ld. Final meeting return regd. 21 Oct. 1933 .... **1934**

Bartholomay & General Trust Ld. Regd. 1889 as Bartholomay Brewing Co. (of Rochester) Ld.; name changed June 1931. Vol. liq. (members') 10 Nov. 1941. The outstanding debenture stack was redeemed at 125% on 24 Mar. 1941. Capital returned to contributories—£15 17s. 3d. per share of £10. £2,877 8s. 6d. was paid into Companies' Liquidation Account. Final meeting return regd. 15 Dec. 1943 **1945**

Bartholomew Investment Trust Ld. Regd. 1924. Vol. liq. (members') 10 June 1931. The main assets were distributed in specie. Capital returned to contributories 5d. per share of £1. Final meeting return regd. 21 Jan. 1932 .... ***1932**

Bartica Co. Ld. Regd. 1929. Struck off Register 1934 **1932**

Bartie Corporation Ld. Regd. 1902. Receiver was appointed Apr. 1906. Struck off Register 1914 .... **1910**

Bartie Gold Syndicate Ld. Regd. 1900. Undertaking and assets were acquired in 1902 by Bartie Corporation Ld., in which company shareholders were entitled to 6 shares of £1 (credited with 19s. paid) for every share of £1 held. Removed from Register 1903..... **1908**

Bartissol Gold Mining Co. Ld. Regd. 1899. Vol. liq. 21 Nov. 1902. Struck off Register 10 Oct. 1916 .... **1903**

Barton & Immingham Light Railway Co. Inc. (under Light Railways Act 1896) by order of Light Railway Commissioners confirmed by Board of Trade 1908. Under Great Central Railway Act of 1912 the undertaking was transferred to Humber Commercial Rly. & Dock Co. **1913**

Barton & London Ld. See New Beestan Rim & Components Co. Ld.

Barton Estate Co. Ld. Regd. 1887. Reconstructed 1901 as Barton Vineyard Co. Ld. Holders of 1st debentures were entitled to either 70% of holding in cash or 70% of holding in debentures in new company plus 15,000 fully-paid preferred shares of £1 subject to provision of new capital. Holders of 2nd debentures were entitled to 5,000 preferred shares of £1; holders of preference shares were entitled to 2 deferred shares of £1 in new company for each preference share of £5 held. Removed from Register 1901 .... **1901**

Barton Gas Co. Regd. as unlimited 1856. Dissolved 1 May 1949, undertaking being vested in East Midland Area Gas Board under Gas Act 1948.

VOL. FOR

Holders of securities were entitled to receive, in respect of each £2 unit held, British Gas 3% guaranteed stock 1990–95 as follows:

	£	s.	d.	
Orig. ord. shares........................	4	5	0	
New ord. shares issued before 1 Jan. 1946).............................	4	5	0	
New ord. shares (issued since 31 Dec. 1945).............................	3	0	0	
5% guar. pref. shares..................	2	5	0	
5% 1st pref. shares	2	15	0	**1952**

Barton-on-Humber Electric Supply Co. Ld. Regd. 1913. Vol. liq. (members') 20 July 1936, the undertaking was transferred to North Lincolnshire & Howdenshire Electricity Co. Ld. Capital returned to contributories—£503 10s. 1d. Final meeting return regd. 21 Oct. 1936 .... **1937**

Barton Vineyard Co. Ld. Regd. Edinburgh 1901. 1 Vol. liq. Mar. 1907 for reconstruction as company of same name. Final meeting return regd. 12 Sept. 1907 **1908**

Barton Vineyard Co. Ld. Regd. Edinburgh 1907. Vol. liq. Aug. 1920. Final meeting return regd. 17 Jan. 1921 .... **1921**

Bartram (W. & G.) Ld. Regd. 1894. Undertaking and assets were acquired in 1902 by Dartford Brewery Co. Ld., in which company shareholders were entitled to 2 fully-paid shares of £5 for each share of £10 held. Debenture stockholders were entitled to an equal amount of debenture stock in acquiring company. Removed from Register 1903 .... **1903**

Bartrum Harvey & Co. Ld. (See below)

Bartrum Harvey Realisations Ld. Regd. 1928 as Bartrum Harvey & Co. Ld.; name changed 18 Jan. 1957. Capital returned to contributories 1s. 7¼d. per preference share of £1. Final meeting return regd. 2 Feb. 1961 .... **1961**

Baryta Ld. Regd. 1911. Vol. liq. Sept. 1917 for reconstruction as Cassio Ld., in which company shareholders were entitled to 1 ordinary share of 10s. (credited with 7s. 6d. paid) for each share of £1 held, and an option (since expired) over preference shares. Debenture holders were entitled to bonds in new company. Struck off Register Mar. 1930 ...... **1931**

Basic Investment Trust Ld. See Northern Stockholders Investment Trust Ld.

Basingstoke Gas Co. Estd. 1834; inc. by Special Act 1887. Dissolved 1 May 1949, undertaking being vested in Southern Area Gas Board under Gas Act 1948. Holders of securities were entitled to receive, in respect of each £100 unit held, British Gas 3% guaranteed stock 1990–95 as follows:

Cons. ord. stock (5% stand.)	130 0 0	
6% red. pref. stock	115 0 0	
4% perp. deb. stock.............................	101 0 0	**1952**

Basle Mission Trading Co. In 1919 business was acquired by Commonwealth Trust Ld. In 1929 certain buildings were to be returned for £55,000 **1929**

Basler Handelsbank. See Banque Commerciale de Basle.

Baslow Hydropathic Co. Ld. Regd. 1880. Struck off Register 20 Nov. 1908 .... **1909**

Bass & Flinders Gold Mining Co. Ld. Regd. 1895. Court Order to wind up 18 Feb. 1899. Liquidator released 26 Nov. 1903. Struck off Register 10 July 1908 ... **1900**

Bass, Ratcliff & Gretton Ld. Regd. 1880. Vol. liq. 9. Jan. 1888. Reconstructed as company of same name. Shareholders received 13,600 ordinary and 13,600 preference shares of £100 and £450,000 debenture stock in new company. Final meeting return regd. 26 Feb. 1891 .... **1887**

Bassam Oil Syndicate Ld. Regd. 1908. Vol. liq. Dec. 1912. Struck off Register Feb. 1932 .... **1932**

Bassano (Alexander) Ld. Regd. 1891. Vol. liq. 29 Oct. 1894. Final meeting return regd. 29 Dec. 1897 ***1895**

Basset Mines Ld. Regd. 1896. Vol. liq. 31 Dec. 1918. Final meeting return regd. 29 July 1921............... **1919**

Bassett (D.) and Sons (Gorseinon) Ld. See Bassett Enterprise Ld.

Basset Enterprise Ld. Regd. 1932 as D. Bassett & Sons (Gorseinan) Ld.; name changed Oct. 1935. Vol. liq. (members') 10 Sept. 1940. Undertaking acquired by United Welsh Services Ld. All capital held by Red & White United Transport Ld. (later United Transport Co. Ld.) Final meeting return regd. 18 Dec. 1940 .... **1941**

Basted (Holdings) Ld. Regd. 1886 as Basted Paper Mills Co., Ld.; name subsequently changed. All capital was owned by Wiggins, Teape & Co. (1919) Ld. (later Wiggins, Teape & Co. Ld.) Vol. liq. (members') 28 May 1954. Final meeting return regd. 18 Dec. 1957.. **1940**

Basted Paper Mills Co. Ld. (See above)

VOL. FOR

Bastian Meter Co. Ld. Regd. 1897 as Penny-in the-Slot Electric Supply Synd. Ld. Struck off Register 19 Dec. 1950 .... **1949**

Batak Rabit Rubber Estate, Ld. Regd. 1910. Vol. liq. (members') 3 July 1947, undertaking and assets having been acquired by Straits Rubber Co. Ld. in which company shareholders were entitled to receive 12 fully-paid shares of £1 for every 10 shares of £1 held. Final meeting return regd. 11 Sept. 1950. £31 was paid into Companies' Liquidation Account **1951**

Batang Malaka Rubber Estates Ld. Regd. 1909. Vol. liq. Apr. 1920. Undertaking and assess acquired by Batang Consolidated Rubber Estates Ld. [later Batang Properties Ld.] in which company shareholders were entitled to recieve 2½ fully-paid shares of 2s. for each share of 2s. held. Struck off Register 30 Apr. 1946. Dissolution declared void by Order of Court 25 May 1948. Restored to Register 25 May 1948. Final meeting held 24 Nov. 1950. Struck off Register 3 July 1953 .... **1953**

Batang Selangor Co. Ld. Regd 1910. Vol. liq. 4 Feb. 1920. The undertaking and assets were sold to Compagnie du Selangor for 40,000 fully- paid shares of Frs. 100, and an option (since expired) over further shares. Final meeting return regd. 30 Sept. 1925 .... **1921**

Batavia & General Plantations Trust Ld. Regd. 1917. Court Order to wind up 24 June 1924. Struck off Register June 1932 .... **1932**

Batavia (Kerkhoven) Rubber & Tea Estates Ld. Regd. 1925. Vol. liq. (members') 9 Dec. 1932; undertaking and assets acquired by Batavia (Kerkhoven) Rubber & Tea Estates (1933) Ld. (later Batavia Rubber and Tea Estates Ld., later Batavia Investment Co. Ld.) in which company shareholders were entitled to apply for 1 share of 2s. (credited with 1s. 1d. paid) for each ordinary share held or to receive 1 fully-paid share of 2s. for every 4d. paid up on each preference share held. Final meeting return regd. 17 Dec. 1936 .... **1933**

Batavia Oilfields Ld. Regd. 1913. Vol. liq. 15 Oct. 1924. Undertaking and assets were sold to Oilfields Ld., in which company shareholders were entitled to 1 share of 2s. (credited with 1s. 6d. paid) for each preference share of 2s. held or 3 shares of 2s. (credited with 1s. 6d. paid) for each ordinary share of 5s. held. Final meeting return regd. 20 Sept. 1928 **1925**

Batavia Plantation Investments Ld. Regd. 1912. Vol. liq. 6 Feb. 1917 for reconstruction as Batavia and General Plantations Trust Ld. in which company shareholders were entitled to 2 fully-paid shares of £1 for each share of £1 held. Final meeting return regd. 6 Mar. 1917 .... **1918**

Batchelar & Son Ld. Regd. 1896. Vol. liq. (members') 31 Jan. 1931. Undertaking and assets were acquired by Kennards Ld. Preference shareholders were paid in full; Kennards Ld. held all ordinary shares, and received surplus assets in specie. Final meeting return regd. 4 Dec. 1931 .... **1931**

Bates (Edward) & Sons (Holdings) Ld. Regd. 17 Aug. 1966. Winding-up order 28 Nov. 1977 .... **1983–4**

Batey and Co., Ld. Regd. 1886. All capital was owned by Charrington & Co. Ld. Vol. liq. (members') 4 Aug. 1965. Final meeting return regd. 18 Nov. 1965 .... **1953**

Bath & Bristol Theatres of Varieties, Ld. Regd. 1895. Removed from Register 4 Oct. 1898 .... ***1897**

Bath & District Light Railway Co. Ld. Inc. (under Light Railways Act 1896) by order of Light Railway Commissioners, confirmed by Board of Trade 1901. Regd. 1903. Undertaking was acquired in 1903 by Bath Electric Tramways Ld., which company paid liquidation expenses. Vol. liq. (members') 24 June 1940. Final meeting return regd. 12 July 1940 ...... **1941**

Bath & Lansdown Light Railway Co. Inc. (under Light Railways Act 1896) by order of Light Railway Commissioners, confirmed by Board of Trade 1906 **1910**

Bath Brewery Ld. Regd. 1889. Vol. liq. 5 Nov. 1923. Certain assets were acquired by Bristol Brewery, Georges & Co. Ld. for £160,000 in cash. Final meeting return regd. 7 Nov. 1925 .... **1924**

Bath Gas Co. Estd. 1818; reinc. as Bath Gas Light & Coke Co. by Special Act 1856; name changed 1927. Dissolved 1 May 1949, undertaking being vested in South Western Area Gas Board under Gas Act 1948. Holders of securities were entitled to receive British Gas 3% guaranteed stock 1990–95 as follows in respect of each £100 unit unless otherwise stated, of security held:

	£ s. d.
Cons. ord. stock (5% basic) (of £1)	124 0 0
5% perp. deb. stock	127 0 0
4% perp. deb. stock	103 0 0

1952

Bath Grand Pump Room Hotel Co., Ld. (The). Regd. 1914. Vol. liq. (members') 31 July 1946. The lease,

VOL. FOR

goodwill and licences were sold to Great Western Railway Co. Capital returned to contributaries—£1 per preference share (of £1) and £1 0s. 6d. per ordinary share (of £1). £738 was paid into Companies' Liquidation Account. Final meeting return regd. 9 Apr. 1948 .... **1948**

Bath Hydropathic Co. Ld. See Bath Spa Hotel Co. Ld.

Bath Rubber Mills Ld. Regd. 1923. Vol. liq. (members') 21 Aug. 1934. All capital owned by Peradin Ld. Final meeting return regd. 5 Dec. 1935 .... **1935**

Bath Spa Hotel Co. Ld. Regd. as Bath Hydropathic Co. Ld. Vol. liq. (members') 22 May 1950. Final meeting return regd. 11 May 1951 .... **1947**

Bath Tramways Co. Ld. Regd. 1880. Vol. liq. 10 July 1884. Properties were acquired by Patent Cable Tramways Corporation Ld. Final meeting return regd. 3 June 1885 .... **1885**

Bathampton Steam Navigation Co. Ld. Regd. 1915. Vol. liq. 20 July 1926. Final meeting return regd. 28 Apr. 1928 .... **1927**

Batheaston Trading Co. Ld. Regd. 1917. Vol. liq. (creditors') 20 Dec. 1932. No capital returned to contributories. Final meeting return regd. 2 May 1935 .... **1934**

Bathgate Gas Co. Ld. Regd. in Edinburgh 1903. Dissolved 1 May 1949, undertaking being vested in Scottish Area Gas Board under Gas Act 1948. Holders of ordinary shares (of £1) were entitled to receive £2 9s. British Gas 3% guaranteed stock 1990–95 for each share held **1952**

Bathurst Gold Mines Ld. Regd. 1895. Vol. liq. 23 Sept. 1896. Reconstructed as McDonald Gold Mines Ld. Final meeting return regd. 26 Apr. 1898 .... **1897**

Batley Syndicate Ld. Regd. 1895. Removed from Register 1911 .... **1901**

Batoe Doelang Rubber Estates Ld. Regd. 1930. The assets, consisting of shares of a Dutch company, were applied in satisfying the claims of holders of 8% debenture stock. Struck off Register Mar. 1934 **1935**

Batopilas Mining, Smelting & Refining Co. Ld. Regd. 1909. Vol. liq. 14 Aug. 1913. Final meeting return regd. 10 Dec. 1913 .... **1914**

Battalgalla Estate Co. Ld. Regd. 1889. Vol. liq. (members') 30 Dec. 1957. Company's property in Ceylon was transferred to Poonagalla Valley Ceylon Co. Ld. (which company owned all shares); a cash distribution of 11s. 7·922d. per share of £1 was also made. Final meeting return regd. 25 May 1959 ... **1960**

Batten, Carne & Carne's Banking Co. Ld. Regd. 1890. Amalgamated in 1896 with Bolitho, Williams, Foster, Coode, Grylls & Co. Ld. Removed from Register 1905 .... **1898**

Battery Reef Gold Mining Co. Ld. Regd. 1888. Vol. liq. 31 July 1891. Absorbed by Luipaards Vlei Estate & Gold Mining Co. Ld. Final meeting return regd. 5 July 1893 .... **1892**

Battle Gas & Coke Co. Ld. Undertaking was acquired by Hastings and St. Leonards Gas Co. for £4,750 in cash **1929**

Battlefields (Rhodesia) Ld. Inc. Southern Rhodesia 1904. Vol. liq. Dec. 1914 for amalgamation with New Rhodesia District Development Co. Ld., in which company shareholders were entitled to 2 fully-paid ordinary shares of £1 for every 5 shares of £1 held **1915**

Battrum Oil & Refinery Co. Ld. Regd. 1910. Vol. liq. (members') 23 Jan. 1930. No capital returned to contributories. Final meeting return regd. 13 Jan. 1931 .... **1930**

Batu Caves Rubber Co. Ld. Regd. 1904. Vol. liq. 27 Jan. 1920. Reconstructed as company of same name. Shareholders were entitled to 8 fully-paid shares of £1 in new company for each share of £1 held. Final meeting return regd. 31 Dec. 1921 .... **1920**

Batu Caves Rubber Co. Ld. Regd. 1920. Vol. liq. (members') 7 Aug. 1958. Undertaking and assets acquired by Seafield Amalgamated Rubber Co. Ld., in which company stockholders received 10 fully-paid shares (of 2s.) plus 4s. cash per £1 stock, £222 15s. 11d. paid into Companies' Liquidation Account. Final meeting return regd. 6 Nov. 1961 .... **1963**

Batu Caves Tin Dredging Co. Ld. Inc. Straits Settlements 1927. In Dec. 1933 undertaking and property were acquired by Ampat Tin Dredging Ld., for 507,500 fully-paid shares of 4s. Vol. liq. Jan. 1934 **1934**

Batu Kawan Rubber & Coconut Plantations Ld. Regd. 1909. Vol. liq. (members') 31 Aug. 1971. Undertaking and assets acquired by Batu Kawan Bhd. in which company stockholders received 5 shares for each stock unit of (10p.) and £0·00024287 cash per 10p. capital. £2,187·46 was paid into Companies Liquidation Account. Final meeting return regd. 5 Feb. 1974 .... **1974-5**

See Stock Exchange Year-Book.

VOL. FOR

Batu Lintang Ld. In 1920 the undertaking and assets were acquired by Batu Lintang Rubber Co. Ld. for £875,000 in fully-paid shares 1927

Batu Matang Rubber Plantations Ld. Regd. 1910. Vol. liq. (members') 29 Nov. 1932. Undertaking and assets transferred to Batu Matang Rubber Plantations (1932) Ld., in which company shareholders were entitled to 6 shares of 2s. (credited with 1s. 9d. paid) for each share of £1 held. Final meeting return regd. 25 May 1934 1935

Batu Pahat Coffee Co. Ld. Regd. 1881 as Johore Tea Co. Ld.; name changed to Johore Fibre & Planting Co. Ld. in 1886. Struck off Register 4 Oct.1898 1901

Batu Tiga (Selangor) Rubber Co. Ld. Regd. 1906. Vol. liq. (members') 31 Aug. 1962. Capital returned to contributories—6s. per 2s. stock. Following sale of goodwill and assets to Glenmarie Estates Ld. in 1963, stockholders were entitled to receive 3 shares of M$1 in that company for every 2s. stock held. £927 5s 1d. was paid into Companies Liquidation Account in respect of unclaimed dividends and £228 16s. in respect of unclaimed distributions. Final meeting return regd. 30 Dec. 1965 1967

Batura Monguna Tin Ld. Regd. 1923. Vol. liq. (members') 19 Dec. 1935. Undertaking and assets were acquired by Gold & Base Metal Mines of Nigeria Ld., in which company shareholders were entitled to 1 share of 2s. 6d. (credited as fully-paid) for every 10 shares of 5s. held. Final meeting return regd. 19 Feb. 1937 1936

Bauxite Refining Co. Ld. See International Aluminium Co. Ld.

Bavarian Lead Co. Ld. Regd. 1887. Vol. liq. 6 Dec. 1890. Final meeting return regd. 4 Apr. 1892 1891

Bavarian Lead Mining Co. Ld. Regd. 1879. Vol. liq. Aug. 1886. Undertaking and assets were acquired in 1887 by Bavarian Lead Co. Ld. for £12,000 in cash and £70,000 in ordinary shares. Final meeting return regd. 3 Mar. 1888 1890

Bawdwin Syndicate Ld. Regd. 1914. Vol. liq. 17 Jan. 1921. Final meeting return regd. 15 Feb. 1923 1921

Bawtry & Trent Railway Dock Co. Inc. by Special Act 1882. Line abandoned in 1885 1886

Bay of Havana & Matanzas Railroad. See Railway of the Bay of Havana.

Bay State Gas Co. of New Jersey. Organised New Jersey 1889. Known in England by the issue of the Boston United Gas 5% sinking fund trust bonds (1st series), which bonds have, under a scheme of reorganisation, (a) been repaid in cash, or (b) been replaced by preferred stock of the Massachusetts Gas Cos. 1904

Bay State Street Railway Co. Originally known as Lynn & Boston Railroad. In 1919 the undertaking and assets were acquired by Eastern Massachusetts Street Railway Co. 1929

Bayerische Glanzstoff-Fabrik. Undertaking acquired by Vereinigte Glanzstoff-Fabriken in 1928 1937

Bayley (Thomas) & Co. Ld. Regd. 1904. Vol. liq. (members') 28 July 1931; undertaking and assets acquired by Thomas Bayley & Co. (1931) Ld. Capital returned to contributories—£5 per preference share of £5; 19s. 0½d. per ordinary share of £1. Final meeting return regd. 19 Nov. 1932 1932

Bayley's Gold Mines Ld. Regd. 1901. Reconstructed 1903 as Bayley's Mines Ld., in which company shareholders were entitled to 1 share of 5s. (credited with 4s. paid) for each share of 5s. held. Removed from Register 1907 1904

Bayley's Golden South Ld. Regd. 1894. Removed from Register 1908 1897

Bayley's Mines Ld. Regd. 1903. Vol. liq. May 1907. Removed from Register 1908 1908

Bayley's No. 2 South Gold Mining Co. Ld. Regd. 1895. Vol. liq. 14 Jan. 1898. Final meeting return regd. 12 Nov. 1898 1898

Bayley's Reward Claim Gold Mining Co. N.L. In 1894 the undertaking was acquired by Bayley's Reward Claim Gold Mining Co. Ld., in which company shareholders received 20 shares of £1 for each share held............................. 1896

Bayley's Reward Claim Gold Mining Co. Ld. Inc. Victoria 1894. Reconstructed 1896 as Bayley's United Gold Mines Ld., in which company shareholders were entitled to 1 share of 5s. (credited with 3s. 9d. paid) for each share of £1 held 1901

Bayley's Reward No. 1 South Gold Mining Co. Ld. Inc. Australia 1894. Reconstructed in 1896 as Bayley's United Gold Mines Ld., in which company shareholders were entitled to 1 share 1 of 5s. (credited with 3s. 9d. paid) for each share of £1 held 1901

Bayley's United Gold Mines Ld. Regd. 1896. Reconstructed 1901 as Bayley's Gold Mines Ld., in which company shareholders were entitled to 1 share of 5s.

VOL. FOR

(credited with 3s. 9d. paid) for each share of 5s. held. Removed from Register 1902 1903

Bayley's West Extended Ld. Regd. 1894. Struck off Register 16 Aug. 1901 1902

Bayley's West Gold Mining Co. Ld. Regd. 1894. Struck off Register 26 Oct. 1900 1901

Bayliss & Abbott Ld. Regd. 1925. Controlled by Mermac Ld. Struck off Register 1930 1928

Bayliss, Thomas & Co. Ld. Regd. 1896. Vol. liq. 30 Dec. 1904. Struck off Register 1925 1905

Bayliss (William), Ld. Regd. 1920. Vol. liq. (members') 6 Jan. 1955. Capital returned to contributors—41s. 6-05d. per share (of £1). Final meeting return regd. 5 Jan. 1956 1956

Baynes Lake Land Co. Ld. Regd. 1912 as Southern British Columbia Land Co. Ld.; name changed Feb. 1913. Struck off Register 12 July 1929 1945

Baytree Mills Ld. Regd. 1903. Vol. liq. (members') 14 Mar. 1960. Capital returned to contributories—19s. 10d. per 10s. ordinary stock. Final meeting return regd. 19 Mar. 1963 1964

Bazaloni Tea Co. Ld. Regd. 9 Dec. 1936. Struck off register 11 Nov. 1986. All capital acquired by Bazaloni Holdings Ld. in Nov. 1970 1971

Beach Tin Deposits Ld. Regd. 1928. Vol. liq. (creditors') 25 Jan. 1939. Debenture holders received a total of £810 14s. Final meeting return regd. 27 June 1942 1939

Beacon Brown Flour Co. Ld. Regd. 1929. Vol. liq. (members') 6 July 1936. Final meeting return regd. 13 May 1937 1937

Beacon Gold Mines Ld. Regd. 1896. Vol. liq. 9 Aug. 1899. Final meeting return regd. 27 Sept. 1900 1900

Beacon Hotel Crowborough Ld. Regd. 1906. Court Order to wind up 19 July 1937. Struck off Register 17 July 1942............................. 1943

Beaconsfield Diamond Mining Co. Ld. Regd. 1895. Removed from Register 1906 1897

Beaconsfield Trust Ld. Regd. 1928. Vol. liq. (members') 5 Feb. 1930. All creditors were paid in full. Final meeting return regd. 5 Aug. 1933............................. *1931

Beaconsfield, Uxbridge & Harrow Railway Co. Inc. by Special Act 1882. Abandoned by Act of 1886 1888

Beadle Brothers Ld. Regd. 1890. Removed from Register 1901 .... *1897

Bean Cars Ld. Regd. 1901 as A. Harper & Sons Ld.; name changed Oct. 1907 to A. Harper Sons & Bean Ld. and as above in June 1926. Assets were acquired by Hadfields Ld., who subsequently transferred them to Bean Industries Ld.; proceeds were insufficient to meet claims of debenture stockholders. Struck off Register 29 Oct. 1935 1936

Bear Brand Ld. Regd. 1927 as Howard Ford & Co. Ld.; name changed 15 Feb. 1960. Vol. liq. (creditors') 1 Sept. 1976. No capital returned to contributories or unsecured creditors. Final meeting return regd. 30 Aug. 1977 1978-9

Bear Creek Alluvial Gold Co. Ld. Regd. Edinburgh 1896. Vol. liq. Jan. 1898. Struck off Register 13 Feb 1903............................. 1899

Bear Creek Gold Ld. Regd. 1890. Vol. liq. 16 May 1891. Property was acquired by Poorman Mines Ld., for 100,000 shares of 5s. Final meeting return regd. 24 Oct. 1891 1892

Bear River Irrigation & Ogden Waterworks Co. Company went into liquidation May 1898. Bear River Valley Land Co. was incorporated on behalf of bondholders to realise the properties and distribute the proceeds amongst the original bondholders. $140 per $1,000 bond was paid in Aug. 1906; further payments (if any) not known............................. 1908

Bear River Mountain Ld. See Prince John Mining Co. Ld.

Beardmore Taxicab Co. Ld. Regd. 1925. Vol. liq. (members') 14 Jan. 1943. Capital returned to contributories—£71,156 13s. 10d. Final meeting return regd. 14 Aug. 1943 1943

Bearpark Coal and Coke Co Ld. Regd 1872. Vol. liq. (members') 6 Dec. 1954. Capital returned to contributories—34s. 3⅜d. per share of £1. Final meeting return regd. 10 Aug. 1955 1956

Bear's Paw Restaurant Ld. Regd. 1891. Court Order to wind up 7 Oct. 1924. Struck off Register June 1931 1922

Beaton (W. G.) & Co. Ld. Regd. 1894 as Coal Co-operative Socy. Ld.; name changed Dec. 1933. Vol. liq. (members') 8 Oct 1934. Struck off Register 7 July 1939 1911

Beatrice (Rhodesia) Co. Ld. Regd. 1899. Vol. liq. 9 Dec. 1908. Final meeting return regd. 7 Apr. 1911......... 1909

Beau Sejour (Ceylon) Tea & Rubber Co. Ld. Regd. 1910. Vol. liq. 21 June 1921. Undertaking and assets were acquired by Beau Sejour Rubber Co. Ld., in which company shareholders were entitled to 1 preference share of 2s. (credited as fully-paid) for each preference share of 2s. held or 1 ordinary share of 2s.

*See Stock Exchange Year-Book.

VOL. FOR

(credited with 1s. 3d. paid) for each ordinary share of 2s. held. Final meeting return regd. 7 Jan. 1927 — **1922**

Beaufort Motor Co. Ld. Regd. 1906. Removed from Register 1911 — **1910**

Beauly Electric Supply Co. Ld. Regd. Edinburgh 1912. Vol. liq. (members') 28 Sept. 1939. Capital returned to contributories—£1 17s. 9·0185d. per share of £1. Final meeting return regd. 29 Dec. 1939 — **1940**

Beaumont Brothers Ld. Regd. 1898. Vol. liq. 27 Aug. 1928. Final meeting return regd. 21 May 1929 — **1929**

Beaumont Compressed-air Locomotive Co. Ld. Regd. 1880. Vol. liq. 1885. Business transferred to Mechanical Tramways Co. Ld. Removed from Register 1903 — **1887**

Beaumont (Texas) Petroleum & Liquid Fuel Co. Ld. Regd. 1902. Vol. liq. 22 May 1905. Removed from Register 1910 — **1906**

Beauparc Copper Mines (1909) Ld. Inc. Dublin 1909. Court Order to wind up Mar. 1913 — **1914**

Beaver Consolidated Mines Ld. See Northern Canada Mining Corporation Ld.

Beccles Water & Gas Co. Inc. by Special Act 1854. Dissolved 1 May 1949, undertaking being vested in Eastern Area Gas Board under Gas Act 1948. Holders of securities were entitled to receive, in respect of each £10 unit held, British Gas 3% guaranteed stock 1990–95 as follows:

	£	s.	d.
A shares (10% max.)	15	0	0
B shares (8% max.)	12	0	0
C shares (8% max.)	12	0	0
D shares (8% max.)	12	0	0
E shares (8% max.)	12	0	0
4% perp. debs.	10	2	6

— **1952**

Bechuanaland Copper Co. Ld. Regd. 1909. Vol. liq. 28 Nov. 1919. Final meeting return regd. 10 Oct. 1922 — **1920**

Bechuanaland Farms Ld. Regd. 1907. Vol. liq. (members') 16 Dec. 1938. All capital held by African & European Investment Co. Ld. Final meeting return regd. 1 Feb. 1939 — **1939**

Bechuanaland Railway Trust Ld. Regd. 1895. Vol. liq. 8 Aug. 1899. Amalgamated with Rhodesia Railways Trust Ld., in which company shareholders were entitled to 5 shares of 1s. for every 8 shares of £1 held. Final meeting return regd. 29 Mar. 1900 — **1900**

Bechuanaland Trading Association Ld. Regd. 1891. Vol. liq. (members') 11 Mar. 1932. Capital returned to contributories—1s. 5·42d. per ordinary share of 10s. Final meeting return regd. 30 May 1934 — **1933**

Beciu (Roumania) Oil Fields Ld. Regd. 1910 as Central Roumanian Oil Fields Ld.; name changed Oct. 1910. Vol. liq. (members') 7 Jan. 1935. Capital returned to contributories—0·9685055d. per share of £1. Final meeting return regd. 1 Apr. 1935 — **1935**

Beck Flame Lamp Ld. Regd. 1907. Removed from Register 1912 — **1912**

Becker & Co. Ld. Regd. 1908. Receiver for 1st debenture stock and secured notes appointed Oct. 1923. Vol. liq. 31 Dec. 1923. Undertaking was acquired by company of same name. Final meeting return regd. 18 July 1931 — **1924**

Becker Process Gold Extraction Ld. Regd. 1897. Vol. liq. 6 Dec. 1898. Final meeting return regd.4 Apr.1900 — **1900**

Beckett (T. W.) & Co. Ld. Inc. Transvaal 1890. The outstanding debentures were redeemed Mar. 1934. All capital held by directors and friends — **1934**

Beckman Mines Ld. Regd. 1902. Undertaking was acquired in May 1903 by Parral Mines Ld., in which company shareholders were entitled to 1 fully-paid share for each share held. Removed from Register 1904 — **1904**

Bed Settees Ld. See Argyll Furnishing Co. Ld.

Bedale Gas Co. (1942) Ld. Regd. 1942. Dissolved 1 May 1949, undertaking being vested in Northern Area Gas Board under Gas Act 1948. Holders of ordinary shares (of £1) were entitled to receive £1 British Gas 3% guaranteed stock 1990–95 for each share held — **1952**

Bede Metal & Chemical Co. Ld. Regd. 1872. Vol. liq. (creditors') 23 Sept. 1957. Assets did not realise sufficient to meet claims of unsecured creditors in full and consequently no capital was returned to contributories. Final meeting return regd. 19 Mar 1959 — **1960**

Bedford & Mill Lane Spinning Co. (1920) Ld. Regd. 1920. Undertaking and assets were acquired by Combined Egyptian Mills Ld. (later Combined English Mills (Spinners) Ld.). Struck off Register 1 Feb. 1944 — **1944**

Bedford & Northampton Railway Co. Inc. by Special Act 1865. Under Midland Railway (Additional Powers) Act 1885 the line was sold to that company. 4% debenture stockholders received an equal amount of Midland Railway 4% debenture stock, preferred

VOL. FOR

stockholders £112 10s. 4% preference stock for each £100 stock held, and deferred stockholders either £25 4% preference stock or £21 ordinary stock for each £100 stock held — **1886**

Bedford Brewing & Malting Co. Ld. See George Shaw & Co. Ld.

Bedford Brewery (Plymouth) Ld. Regd. 1900. Struck off Register 1922 — ***1910**

Bedford Brick Co. Ld. Regd. 1935. Vol. liq. (members') 7 Jan. 1936. Undertaking was sold to London Brick Co. Ld., for £420,000 in cash. Capital returned to contributories—20s. per preference share of £1; 2s. 9·967d. per ordinary share of 2s. Final meeting return regd. 30 Mar. 1938 — **1937**

Bedford District Gas Co. Estd. 1833; inc. by Special Act 1864 as Bedford Gas Light Co.; name changed 1924. Dissolved 1 May 1949, undertaking being vested in Eastern Area Gas Board under Gas Act 1948. Holders of securities were entitled to receive, in respect of each £100 unit held, British Gas 3% guaranteed stock 1990–95 as follows:

	£	s.	d.
Cons. ord. stock (3½% stand.)	122	0	0
6% pref. stock	133	0	0
B 6% pref. stock	133	0	0
4% red. pref. stock	100	0	0
4% perp. deb. stock	102	0	0
4½% perp. debs.	112	10	0
5% perp. deb. stock	125	0	0
4½% red. deb. stock	102	0	0

— **1952**

Bedford Motors Ld. See General Motors Ld.

Bedford Music Hall Ld. Regd. 1920. All capital held by Theatre Securities Ld. Struck off Register 5 Jan. 1945 — **1944**

Bedford Park Ld. Regd. 1881. Vol. liq. 27 Aug. 1886. Final meeting return regd. 15 Dec. 1892 — **1887**

Bedford United Mining Co. Ld. Regd. Truro 1877. Vol. liq. 22 Aug. 1889. Final meeting return regd. 8 Jan. 1891 — **1890**

Bedfordshire, Cambridgeshire & Huntingdonshire Electricity Co. Incorporated by Special Act 1925. Dissolved 1 Apr. 1948, undertaking being vested in British (later Central) Electricity Authority and Eastern Area Board under Electricity Act 1947 — **1949**

Bedlington Gas Light Co. Ld. Under Act of 1913 the undertaking was acquired by Blyth Gas Co., from 20 May 1914 for £7,500 in cash plus certain capital expenditure — **1914**

Bedouin Steam Navigation Co. Ld. Regd. 1880. Removed from Register 1913 — ***1886**

Bedrock Syndicate Ld. Regd. 1897. Struck off Register Apr. 1929 — **1930**

Bedwas Navigation Colliery Co. Ld. Regd. 1908. Vol. liq. 7 Feb. 1921. Final meeting return regd. 24 Apr. 1923 — **1922**

Bedwas Navigation Colliery Co. (1921) Ld. Regd. 1921. All shares owned by S. Instone & Co. Ld. Vol. liq. 5 Nov. 1953. Final meeting return regd. 28 Mar. 1956 — **1939**

Bee Hive Spinning Co. Ld. Regd. 1937. Vol. liq. (members') 28 Mar. 1968. Capital returned to contributories—2s. 9d. per share of 2s. Final meeting return regd. 3 July 1969 — **1970**

Bee Land & House Property Investment Co. Ld. Regd. 1881. Vol. liq. 16 Nov. 1892. Final meeting return regd. 23 Apr. 1896 — **1893**

Bee Spinning Co. (Royton) Ld. Regd. 1920. Vol. liq. (members') 26 Feb. 1964. Amount returned to contributories—5s. 3d. per share of 1s. £311 14s. 4d. paid into Companies' Liquidation Account in respect of unclaimed distribution. Final meeting return regd. 2 Sept. 1969 — **1970**

Beeby's Brick Co. Ld. Regd. 1897. Vol. liq. (members') 30 Oct. 1936. The undertaking was acquired by London Brick Co. Ld., which company owned all shares. The assets were distributed in specie. Final meeting return regd. 27 Sept. 1946 — **1947**

Beecham Food Products Ld. See Beechport Ld.

Beecham Overseas Ld. See Beechport Ld.

Beecham Trust Ld. Regd. 1917. Court Order to wind up 12 July 1927. Struck off Register 20 Mar. 1936 — **1937**

Beechcliffe Investment Co. Ld. Regd. 1896 as Harrison & Camm Ld.; name changed June 1927. Vol. liq. (creditors') 30 Dec. 1930. No capital returned to contributories. Final meeting return regd. 17 Mar. 1931 — **1931**

Beechport Ld. Regd. 1946 as Beecham Food Products Ld.; name changed 24 Nov. 1954 to C. & E. Morton Ld. and subsequently to Beecham Overseas Ld. and Beechport Ld. A former subsidiary of Beecham Group Ld. Vol. liq. (members') 4 Sept. 1962. Final meeting return regd. 21 Feb. 1968 — **1955**

Beechworth Goldfields Ld. Regd. 1898. Removed from Register 1906 — **1901**

See Stock Exchange Year-Book.

Beefex Ld. Regd. 1926. Vol. liq. (members') 5 Feb. 1934. Capital returned to contributories—£558,500. Final meeting return regd. 12 Aug. 1935.............. 1934

Beer (G.) Ld. Regd. 1903. Vol. liq. 26 July 1926. Undertaking and assets were transferred to Maison Beer in which company shareholders were entitled to 1 B share of Fr. 100 for every 12 ordinary shares of £1 held, or 2 parts bénéficiaires, Fr. 200 debenture and 1 A share of Fr. 100 for every 12 preference shares of £1 held. Final meeting return regd. 31 Oct. 1928 1927

Beer (George) and Rigden Ld. Regd. 1919 as George Beer & Co. Ld. name changed May 1922. Vol. liq. 31 Jan. 1950; undertaking acquired by Fremlins Ld., which company owned all the capital. Final meeting return regd. 6 May 1952.............. 1953

Beeston Cycle Co. Ld. Regd. 1897. Removed from Register 1902 1901

Beeston Motor Co. Ld. Regd. Nov. 1897. Removed from Register 1901 1901

Beeston Pneumatic Tyre Co. Ld. Regd. 1895. Vol. liq. 3 Sept. 1897. Undertaking was acquired by Amalgamated Pneumatic Tyre Companies Ld. Final meeting return regd. 13 Feb. 1900 1898

Beet Sugar Development Co. of England Ld. Regd. 1910. Struck off Register 1914 1911

Beet Sugar Founders Ld. Regd. 1910. Struck off Register 1923 1911

Begel (Bauchi) Tin Ld. Regd. 1912. Court Order to wind up Oct. 1913. Struck off Register 1921 1914

Behrens (Louis) & Sons Ld. Regd. 1927. Vol. liq. (creditors') 17 Dec. 1931. Assets realised insufficient to meet claims of creditors in full. Final meeting regd. 2 Oct. 1936 .... *1932

Beighton Ovens Ld. Regd. 1919. Vol. liq. 21 July 1927. Undertaking acquired by Sheffield Coal. Co. Ld. Final meeting return regd. 28 Dec. 1927 1940

Beilby (E. L.) & Co. Ld. Regd. 1928. Vol. liq. (members') 30 June 1932. All shares owned by Wiggins, Teape & Alex. Pirie (Merchants) Ld. The assets were distributed in specie. Final meeting return regd. 30 Oct. 1933 1933

Beira Alta Railway Co. of Portugal. *See* Companhia dos Caminhos de Ferro Portugueses da Beira Alta.

Beira Junction Railway (Port Beira to Fontesville) Ld. Regd. 1895. Vol. liq. (members') 17 June 1930. Undertaking and assets were acquired by Beira Railway Co. Ld. The debentures and preference shares were repaid at par. Ordinary shareholders were entitled to 2 ordinary shares in Beira Railway Co. Ld., for every 5 ordinary shares held. Final meeting return regd. 8 Nov. 1935........................ 1931

Beira Railway Co. Ld. Regd. 1892 as company limited by guarantee. Vol. liq. (members') 31 May 1949. Sold rights in Africa to Portuguese Government and she Savoy Hotel to Mozambique Co. Shares held in trust by British South Africa Co. and Mozambique Co. were distributed to holders of certificate of title. 1st debenture stock redeemed at par 1 July 1949. Capital returned to contributories—£3 0s. 0·538d. per "share". Final meeting return regd. 20 Jan. 1959 1960

Beira Rubber & Sugar Estates Ld. Regd. 1909. Vol. liq. 6 May 1914. The property and assets were sold by the receiver for £130,000. Final meeting return regd. 1 Feb. 1916 1915

Beira Works Ld. Regd. 8 Jan. 1926. Vol. liq. (members') 21 Mar. 1951. Capital returned to contributories— 12s. 0·032d. per share of 14s. 6d. Final meeting return regd. 2 July 1955 1957

Beith Gas Light Co, Ld. Regd. in Edinburgh 1889. Dissolved 1 May 1949, undertaking being vested in Scottish Area Gas Board under Gas Act 1948. Holders of ordinary shares (of £10) were entitled to receive £16 13s. 4d. British Gas 3% guaranteed stock 1990—95 for each share held 1952

Bekoh Rubber Estates Ld. Regd. 1912. Vol. liq June 1920. Undertaking and assets acquired by Bekoh Consolidated Rubber Estates Ld. in which company shareholders were entitled to receive 2½ fully-paid shares of 2s. for each share of 2s. held. Struck off Register 30 Apr. 1946. Dissolution declared void by Order of Court 25 May 1948. Restored to Register 25 May 1948. Final meeting held 24 Nov. 1950. Struck off Register 3 July 1953 1954

Belbridge Property Trust Ld. Regd. 1933. Vol. liq. (members') 31 Oct. 1945. Capital returned to contributories—0·634d. per ordinary share of £1. Final meeting return regd. 1 Nov. 1950.............. 1951

Belcher Consolidated Gold Mining Co. Ld. Regd. 1888 as Italian Gold Mining Co. Ld.; name changed Nov. 1890. Removed from Register 1910..................... 1895

Belcher Ld. *See* Silver Fox Electrical Co. Ld.

Beldam Tyre Co. (1920) Ld. Regd. 1920. Vol. liq. 19 Nov. 1924. Receiver appointed 19 Aug. 1925; ceased to act 4 Nov. 1927. Final meeting return regd. 14 Nov. 1927........................ *1925

Belfast & County Down Railway Co. Inc. by Special Act 1846. Dissolved 25 Nov. 1950 the undertaking having vested, as from 1 Oct. 1941 in the Ulster Transport Authority under terms of Transport Act (Northern Ireland) 1948. Holders of securities received, in respect of every £100 held, cash as follows—ordinary stock-£6 1s. 3d.; 4% preference stock £6 15s.; 4½% A preference stock £53 16s. 3d.; 5% preference stock £31 1s. 3d. 3% Baronial guaranteed shares £100; 4% debenture stock £87 13s 9d and 3% debenture stock £93 7s. 6d. 1953

Belfast & North East Ireland Electricity & Power Gas Co. Inc. by Special Act 1904........................ 1911

Belfast & Northern Counties Railway Co, Inc. by Special Act 1845 as Belfast & Ballymena Railway Co.; name changed by Act of 1860. Under Act of 1903 the undertaking was amalgamated with Midland Railway Co. (of England). Holders of 4% debenture stock received £160 2½% debenture stock for every £100 stock held; holders of each £100 4% consolidated preference stock, 3% preference stock or ordinary stock received £160, £120 or £220 consolidated preference stock respectively 1904

Belfast Banking Co. Ld. Inc. 1865. Regd. (in Dublin) 1883; transferred to Belfast under Government of Ireland Act 1920. Undertaking transferred to Northern Bank Ld. from 1 July 1970 under the Northern Bank Act (Northern Ireland) 1970 which also provided for eventual dissolution of this bank 1971

Belfast Central Railway Co. Inc. by Special Act 1864. Under Belfast Central Railways (Sale) Act 1885 the undertaking was transferred to Great Northern Railway Co. (Ireland) for £127,500 1887

Belfast City and District Water Commissioners. Under the Local Government Act (Northern Ireland) 1972, the Commissioners were dissolved on 1 Oct. 1973 and the assets and liability for the loan indebtedness transferred to the Ministry of Finance, Northern Ireland 1974-5

Belfast Commercial Buildings Ld. Inc. Dublin 1885. Vol. liq. Sept. 1919 1920

Belfast Discount Co. Ld. Inc. Dublin 1865. Vol. liq. Sept. 1926 1927

Belfast Gold Mining Co. Ld. Regd. 1899. Reconstructed 1902 as company of same name. Final meeting return regd. 14 May 1910 1906

Belfast Gold Mining Co. Ld. Regd. 1902. Removed from Register 1909 1906

Belfast, Holywood & Bangor Railway Co. Inc. by Special Act 1860. Under Belfast and County Down Railway Act of 1884 the undertaking was transferred to that company for £138,000 debenture stock aad £53,397 preference stock........................ 1885

Belfast Mineral Water Co. Ld. Inc. Dublin 1884. Vol. liq. June 1929 1930

Belfast Omnibus Co. Ld. Regd. 1927. Vol. liq. (members') 24 Apr. 1936. Undertaking acquired by Northern Ireland Road Transport Board 1 Oct. 1935 by compulsory powers under Section 1 of Road and Railway Transport Act (Northern Ireland) 1935. The outstanding £89,660 5% prior lien debenture stock was repaid on 30 Apr. 1936 at £101%. Ordinary shareholders received £1 11s. 6½d. in Northern Ireland Transport B stock *plus* 5s. 0·125d. in cash per ordinary share of £1. Deferred shareholders received 3s. 4·96d. Northern Ireland Transport B stock *plus* 1s. 1·5211d. per deferred share of 1s. Final meeting return regd. 25 Nov. 1937 1940

Belfast Plate Glass Insurance Co. Ld. Regd. Belfast. Finally wound up in 25 Jan. 1944 1944

Belfast Plaza, Ld. Regd. Edinburgh 1926. Vol. liq. Jan. 1959. Final meeting return regd. 29 Oct. 1959 1939

Belfast, Strandtown & High Holywood Railway Co. Inc. by Special Act 1881. Line abandoned in 1885 1886

Belfast Street Tramways Co. Inc. by Special Act 1872. The tramways were taken over by Belfast Corporation under Act of 1904. The debentures were to be redeemed by the Corporation on due date (1 Sept. 1907). Ordinary shareholders received £11 per share of £10, further payments (if any) not known......... 1906

Belfast Warehouse Co. Ld. Inc. Dublin 1874. Removed from Register 1908 1895

Belgian Corporation Ld. *See* Joint Industries Ld.

Belgian Date Coffee Co. Ld. Regd. 1881. Removed from Register 1901 1883

Belgian Eastern Junction Railway Co. Inc. Belgium. The Belgian Government was in possession of the line in 1890 1890

Belgian Finance Co. Ld. *See* Phoenix Finance Co. Ld.

VOL. FOR

Belgian Mills Co. Ld. Regd. 1873. Vol. liq. 30 Jan. 1920. Capital returned to contributories—£12 per share of £3; further payments (if any) not known. Final meeting return regd. 3 June 1920 1921

Belgian Mills Co. Ld. Regd. 1920. Vol. liq. (creditors') 17 Mar. 1932. Assets realised insufficient to repay creditors in full. Final meeting return regd. 29 Apr. 1937 1933

Belgian Mining Trust of South Africa Ld. Inc. Brussels 1895. The undertaking was sold to Compagnie Générale de Mines 1904

Belgrano (Buenos Aires) Gas Co. Ld. Regd. 1878. Vol. liq. 3 Jan. 1898. Business was acquired by River Plate Gas Co. Ld., for 22,500 fully-paid shares of £10. Final meeting return regd. 23 Mar. 1899 1899

Belgrave Mansions Co. Ld. Regd. 1865. Vol. liq. 24 June 1920. Final meeting return regd. 15 July 1922 1921

Belgrave Mills Co. Ld. Regd. 1907. Vol. liq. Apr. 1926. Scheme of arrangement sanctioned in Mar. 1926 provided (*inter alia*)—(1) for sale of undertaking and assets to the Belgrave Mills Company (1926), Ld. [later Belgrave Mills (Holdings) Ld.], (2) for payment of the uncalled liability on the ordinary shares of £5, (3) for allotment of 1 fully-paid share of 5s. in new company and 5 shares of 5s. (credited with 2s 6d. paid) for every 10 preference shares of £1 held, (4) for the allotment of 1 fully-paid share in the new Company for every 5 ordinary shares of £5 held and 1 share (credited with 2s. 6d. paid) and/or 1 share (credited with 6d. paid) for each ordinary share with £1 paid or every 4 ordinary shares with £4 paid, (5) for cancellation of 25% of uncalled liability on ordinary shares on application being made for all the 5s. shares with 6d. paid to which each holder was entitled. Struck off Register Dec. 1932 1933

Belgrave Standard Tyres Ld. Regd. 1920, Vol. liq. 24 Nov. 1924. Final meeting return regd. 21 Jan. 1932 1925

Belgravia Bakery Co. Ld. Regd. 1887. Vol. liq. 13 Feb. 1906. Removed from Register 1907 1907

Belgravia Dairy Co. Ld. Regd. 1881. Vol. liq. (members') 28 Sept. 1934. Debenture holders were repaid at 102%. Capital returned to contributories-£96,349 17s. £195 15s. 9d. was paid into Companies' Liquidation Account. Final meeting return regd. 31 Mar. 1936 1935

Belgravia Hotels Co. Ld. Regd. 1897. Removed from Register 1904 1902

Belhaven Engineering & Motors Ld. Regd. Edinburgh 1907. Vol. liq. July 1912. Final meeting return regd. 13 Dec. 1918 1913

Belingwe Development Syndicate Ld. Regd. 1895. Struck off Register 1915 1911

Belingwe Gold Reefs Ld. Regd. 1897. Vol. liq. 16 Jan. 1922. Reconstructed as company of same name. Shareholders were entitled to 12 shares of 2s. 6d. (credited with 1s. 8d. paid) in new company for each share of £1 held. Final meeting return regd. 17 May 1939 1922

Belingwe Gold Reefs, Ld. Inc. in Southern Rhodesia 1922. In July 1956 the Registrar of Companies, Southern Rhodesia stated that he had been unable to trace the company's whereabouts and that it was "obviously defunct" 1947

Bell Brothers Ld. Regd. 1899, Vol. liq. 2 May 1923. Undertaking and assets were acquired by Dorman Long & Co. Ld., which company held all ordinary shares. Preference shareholders were offered 110 preference shares of £1 in acquiring company for every 10 preference shares of £10 held. Debenture stockholders were entitled to an equal amount of 5½% debenture stock in acquiring company *plus* £15 in cash or repayment in cash at 110%. Final meeting return regd. 17 May 1935 1924

Bell Graphite Co. Ld. Regd. 1923. Vol. liq. 1 June 1920. Final meeting return regd. 16 Mar. 1926 1921

Bell (J. & F.) Ld. Regd. Edinburgh 1895. Vol. liq. Apr. 1904. Final meeting return regd. 7 Dec. 1907 1905

Bell (John) & Co. Ld. Regd. 1897. Vol. liq. 9 Apr. 1902. Undertaking was acquired by Thomas Salt & Co. Ld. Debenture stockholders were entitled to an equal amount of 4% A mortgage debenture stock (Bell issue). Final meeting return regd. 19 Aug. 1902 1903

Bell (John) & Croyden Ld. Regd. 1921. Vol. liq. 4 Mar. 1927. Undertaking was acquired by Savory & Moore Ld. Final meeting return regd. 21 Dec. 1928 1928

Bell (John) & Sons Ld. Regd. 1888. Vol. liq. 8 Aug. 1889. Taken over by Eastman's Ld. Final meeting return regd. 21 Nov. 1891 .... *1890

Bell Organ & Piano Co. Ld. Regd. 1890. Vol. liq. 14 Sept. 1898. Reconstructed 1899 as company of same name. Shareholders were entitled to 2 ordinary shares of £1 credited with 16s. paid in new company for each ordinary share of £5 held, or 5 preference shares of £1 (credited with 16s. paid) for each

VOL. FOR

preference share of £5 held. Debenture holders were entitled to £100 5% 1st mortgage debenture stock, 25 fully-paid ordinary shares of £1 and cash for each £100 debentures held. Final meeting return regd. 20 Sept. 1900 1899

Bell Piano & Organ Co. Ld. Regd. 1899 as Bell Organ & Piano Co. Ld.; name changed Nov. 1903. Vol. liq. (creditors') 5 May 1931. No capital returned to contributories. Final meeting return regd. 12 Sept. 1931 1932

Bell Piano Co. Ld. Regd. 1929 as Piano & Gramophone Co. Ld.; name changed 9 June 1931. Vol. liq. 21 Apr. 1933. All capital owned by S. D. H. Pianos Ld. Final meeting return regd. 25 July 1935 1933

Bell (R.) & Co. Ld. Regd. 1887. Vol. liq. 22 Dec. 1922. Undertaking and assets were acquired by Bryant & May Ld. Final meeting return regd. 14 Jan. 1925 1924

Bell Reef Development Co. Ld. Regd. 1910. Vol. liq. 13 June 1917. Final meeting return regd. 7 Apr. 1920 1918

Bell Stone Slate Quarries Co. Ld. Regd. 1881. Removed from Register 22 June 1894 .... *1886

Belle Steamers Ld. Regd. 1887 as London Woolwich & Clacton-on-Sea Steamboat Co. Ld.; name changed Jan. 1896. Undertaking was acquired by Coast Development Co. Ld. Removed from Register 1901 1905

Belle Vale Tube Co. Ld. Regd. 1896. Removed from Register 1908 1901

Bellevue Consolidated Ld. Regd. 1899. Vol. liq. 7 Feb. 1902. Property was acquired by Bellevue Proprietary Ld. Final meeting return regd. 22 Jan. 1903 1907

Bellevue Ld. Inc. Western Australia 1907. In voluntary liquidation in 1914 1914

Bellevue Proprietary Ld. Regd. 1896. Reconstructed 1899 as Bellevue Consolidated Ld., in which company shareholders were entitled to 1 share of £1 (credited with 17s. paid) for each share of £1 held. Removed from Register 1909 1900

Bellevue Proprietary Ld. Regd. 1902. Assets were to be acquired by Bellevue Ld. (inc. Western Australia), in which company shareholders were entitled to 1 share of 10s. (credited with 8s. paid) for each share of 10s. held. Removed from Register 1909 1907

Bellingham & Co. Ld. Regd. 1887. Vol. liq. 2 Jan. 1929. Final meeting return regd. 16 July 1929 1929

Bellis (T. K.) Turtle Co. Ld. Regd. 1902. Removed from Register 1913 1913

Bellite Explosive Ld. Regd. 1889. Removed from Register 1903 1893

Bell's Asbestos Co. Ld. *See* Bell's United Asbestos Co. Ld.

Bell's Heat Appliances Ld. Regd. 1931. Vol. liq. (members') 12 Mar. 1934. Undertaking acquired by Aga Heat Ld., in which company shareholders were entitled to 2½ fully-paid shares of 5s. for each share held. Final meeting return regd. 14 Dec. 1937 1940

Bell's Heat Appliances (Africa Proprietary) Ld. Undertaking acquired by Aga Heat Ld. 1937

Bell's Stores Ld. Regd. 1904 as Bell's Stores (1902) Ld.; name changed June 1905. Vol. liq. Oct. 1908. Removed from Register 1910 1909

Bell's United Asbestos Co. Ld. Regd. 1888 as Bell's Asbestos Co. Ld.; name changed May 1910. Vol. liq. 31 Dec. 1928. Undertaking and assets were acquired by Turner & Newall Ld., in which company shareholders were entitled to 1 ordinary share of £1 for each ordinary share of £1 held or 1 preference share of £1 for each preference share of £1 held. Turner & Newall Ld. agreed to discharge liabilities including repayment of debentures. Final meeting return regd. 2 Oct. 1934 1929

Bellway Holdings Ld. Regd. 1960 as North British Properties Ld.; name changed Nov. 1973. Vol. liq. (members') 18 May 1979 for reconstruction. Shareholders received 1 share in Bellway Ld. and 1 share in North British Properties Ld. for every 2 shares held. Final meeting return regd. 21 Jan. 1981 1981–2

Belmore Hill Amalgamated Gold Mines Ld. Regd. 1896. Vol. liq. 2 Dec. 1896. Final meeting return regd. 23 Mar. 1897 1897

Belper Waterworks Co. Established 1860. Undertaking was purchased by local board 1895

Belseri-Chardwar Tea Estates Ld. Regd. 1924. Vol. liq. (members') 4 Jan. 1934. Reconstructed as company of same name (later Belseri Tea Co. Ld.). Shareholders were entitled to 10 preference shares of 5s. (credited with 3s. 6d. paid), 1 fully-paid preference share and 1 fully-paid ordinary share of 5s. in new company for every 5 preference shares of £1 held or 2 ordinary shares of 5s. (credited with 2s. 6d. paid) for each ordinary share of £1 held. Mortgagees were satisfied by allotment of 24,000 fully-paid preference and 24,000 fully-paid ordinary shares and £3,092 in cash. £112 7s. was paid into Companies'

See Stock Exchange Year-Book.

VOL. FOR

Liquidation Account in respect of unclaimed dividends. Final meeting return regd. 5 Jan. 1935 ...... **1934**

Belsize Motors Ld. Regd. 1906. Vol. liq. Apr. 1925. Struck off Register July 1934 .... **1938**

Belt Copper Mines Ld. Regd. 1882. Vol. liq. Aug. 1887. Final meeting return regd. 31 Jan. 1896............. **1888**

Beltim Land & Irrigation Co. Ld. Regd. 1880. Removed from Register 1901 .... **1902**

Belvedere Estate Co. Ld. Regd. 1894. Vol. liq. 28 Apr. 1926. Final meeting return regd. 29 Oct. 1926 ...... **1927**

Belvedere Printing & Publishing Co. Ld. Regd. 1911. Vol. liq. Mar. 1912. Shareholders were entitled to £12 5s. 6d. per share of £3, satisfied in part by the allotment of debentures in another company, not specified. Struck off Register 1919 .... **1913**

Bembesi District Gold Claims Ld. Regd. 1895. Struck off Register 25 Feb. 1910. Restored to Register July 1913. Vol. liq. 9 Jan. 1914. Final meeting return regd. 10 Aug. 1914 .... **1915**

Bembesi Gold Reefs. Development Ld. Regd. 1895. Reconstructed 1897 as Associated Rhodesian Gold Estates Ld., in which company shareholders were entitled to 1 share of 10s. for each share of 10s. held. Removed from Register 1909 .... **1898**

Bembesi Goldfields of Rhodesia Ld. Regd. 1908. Struck off Register 1915 .... **1911**

Bembesi Syndicate Ld. Regd. 1894. Undertaking was acquired by Zambesia Exploring Co. Ld. for 13,377 fully-paid shares of £1. Vol. liq. 11 Jan. 1898. Final meeting return regd. 10 Sept. 1900 .... **1899**

Benar (Selangor) Rubber Estates Ld. Regd. 1911. Vol. liq. 9 Aug. 1929. Estate was acquired by Lenggeng Rubber Co. Ld. for 21,000 fully-paid shares of £1. 10,791 were allotted to ordinary shareholders and 10,209 to preference shareholders. Final meeting return regd. 7 Oct. 1930 .... **1931**

Bence Motor Services Ld. Regd. 1930. Vol. liq. (members') 1 July 1936. Undertaking acquired by Bristol Tramways & Carriage Co. Ld. Capital returned to contributories—£1 8s. 9d. per share of £1. Final meeting return regd. 18 Dec. 1936............ **1937**

Bendigo Consols Ld. Regd. 1895. Vol. liq. 3 June 1897. Reconstructed as conpany of same name. Shareholders were entitled to 1 share of 10s. (credited with 9s. paid) in new company for each share of 10s. held. Final meeting return regd. 4 Jan. 1898 .... **1900**

Bendigo District Gold Mines of Victoria Ld. Regd. 1895, Vol. liq. 4 Oct. 1897. Final meeting return regd. 3 Oct. 1898 .... **1898**

Bendigo Gold Mining Co. Ld. Regd. 1891. Struck off Register 12 Apr. 1901 .... **1902**

Bendigo Goldfields Ld. Regd. 1895. Vol. liq. 14 Sept. 1896. Reconstructed as company of same name. Shareholders were entitled to 1 share of £1 in new company for every 4 ordinary shares of 5s. held or for each deferred share of £1 held. Final meeting return regd. 12 Apr. 1900 .... **1899**

Bendigo Goldfields Ld. Regd. 1896. Vol. liq. 10 Apr. 1899. Undertaking and assets were acquired by Goldfields of Victoria Ld., in which company shareholders were entitled to 2 shares of 10s. (credited with 8s. 6d. paid) for each share of £1 held. Final meeting return regd. 23 Apr. 1900 .... **1900**

Bendigo Mines Ld. Inc. Victoria 1934. Vol. liq. 21 May 1937. Undertaking was sold to Bendigo Mines No Liability, in which company shareholders were entitled to 1 share of 15s. (credited with 10s. paid) for each share of 10s. held **1941**

Bendigo Mines No Liability. Inc. Victoria 1937. Vol. liq. 22 Feb. 1940. .... **1941**

Benedictine Order. In Jan. 1945 holders of oulstanding Rio de Janeiro 5% Benedictine Order Gold Loan 1909 were repaid 70% of nominal value in full satisfaction of principal and interest **1945**

Bengal & North Western Railway Co. Ld. Regd. 1882. Vol. liq. members') 31 Dec. 1942. Capital returned to contributories-preference and 2nd preference 100%; £386 11s. 1d for each £100 ordinary stock held. Final meeting return regd. 25 Jan. 1946 ..... **1946**

Bengal Baragunda Copper Co. Ld. Regd. 1883. Vol. liq. 1 Oct. 1891. Final meeting return regd. 29 May 1893 *****1892**

Bengal Central Flotilla Co. Ld. Regd. 1883. Vol. liq. 30 Apr. 1897. Undertaking was acquired by India General Steam Ship Navigation Co. Ld. and Rivers Steam Navigation Co. Ld. Capital returned to contributories—£2 15s. 9d. per share with £2 paid. Final meeting return regd. 29 Oct. 1897 .... **1898**

Bengal Central Railway Co. Ld. Regd. 1881. Vol. liq. 14 June 1905 Secretary of State terminated contracts on 30 June 1905. Capital returned to contributories— £5 2s. 10½d. per share of £10 (£5 paid). Removed from Register 1906.................................... **1906**

Bengal Dooars Railway Co. Ld. Regd. 1891. Vol. liq. (members') 2 Jan. 1941 Preference stock was repaid

VOL. FOR

at par on 3 Jan. 1941. Capital returned to ordinary stockholders—£250 1s. 6d. %. £1,263 was paid into Companies' Liquidation Account in respect of unclaimed ordinary capital, £300 in respect of unclaimed preference capital and £71 in respect of unclaimed dividends. Final meeting return regd. 16 Nov. 1945.. **1946**

Bengal Indigo Manufacturing Co. Ld. Regd. 1889. Removed from Register 1904 .... **1904**

Bengal Iron & Steel Co. Ld. Regd. 1889. Vol. liq. 4 Dec. 1919. Reconstructed as Bengal Iron Co. Ld. Ordinary shareholders were entitled to 5 fully-paid ordinary shares of a £1 cash payment of 6s. 1½d. and option to subscribe for a further share at par for each ordinary share of £1 held. Preference shareholders were entitled to 10 fully-paid preference shares of £1 for each preference share of £10 held or to cash at par. The debenture stock was redeemed at cash at 102%. Final meeting return regd. 31 Oct. 1929..... **1920**

Bengal Iron Co. Ld. Regd. 1919. Vol. liq. (members') 2 Dec. 1936. Undertaking acquired by Indian Iron & Steel Co. Ld. Shareholders were entitled to receive: 1 ordinary share in the Indian company for every 3 ordinary shares held or 5s. cash for each ordinary share held; and £5 4% convertible 2nd debenture stock and 2 ordinary shares in the Indian company for every 5 preference shares held or 26s. cash for each preference share held. Holders of 7% 1st debentures were offered conversion of their holdings into an equal amount of 4% 1st mortgage debentures of the Indian company with cash payment of £7% (plus £3 12s. 6d. for accrued interest); debentures not thus exchanged were redeemed at 105%. In 1963 the liquidator stated "that as far as this liquidation is concerned the only thing outstanding is the transfer of the leases and other title deeds to the Indian Iron & Steel Co. Ld., but this cannot be done in the foreseeable future" **1968**

Bengal Mills Co. Ld. Regd. 1872. Vol. liq. Apr. 1918. Undertaking was sold to an Indian company. Capital returned to contributories—Rs. 93 per ordinary or preference share of £10; further payments (if any) not known. Struck off Register 1922 **1919**

Bengal-Nagpur Railway Co. Ld. Regd. 1887. Vol. liq. 2 Oct. 1944. Capital returned to contributories-£124 8s. 7·5d. per £100 capital stock. Final meeting return regd. 11 Dec. 1948 .... **1949**

Bengal Telephone Corporation Ld. Inc. India 1922. In vol. liq. from 1 Apr. 1943. Undertaking acquired by Government of India and operated by Indian Posts and Telegraph Department. Government Telephone Board Ld. acquired all share capital at Rs. 19·7 per ordinary share of Rs.10 and Rs.12·4 per preference share of Rs.10 .... **1945**

Benguella Estates Ld. Regd. 1928. Vol. liq. (members') 24 Oct. 1942. A direct controlling interest was held by Zambesia Exploring Co. Ld. Capital returned to contributories—£2 5s. 2d. per share of £1. Final meeting return regd. 7 July 1945........................ **1943**

Benhar Coal Co. Ld. Regd. Edinburgh 1872. Undertaking was acquired in 1882 by Niddrie and Benhar Coal Co. Ld., for £97,500. Court Order to wind up 26 Apr. 1892 .... **1882**

Beni-Felkai Mining Co. Ld. Regd. 1907. Vol. liq. Dec. 1925. Capital returned to contributories—5s. per preference share of £1. Struck off Register 14 Apr. 1959 .... **1957**

Benin River Produce Co. Ld. Regd. 1897. Removed from Register 1914 .... **1912**

Benn (Joseph) & Sons Ld. Regd. 1901. Vol. liq. 22 Mar. 1921. Final meeting return regd. 5 May 1922 .... *****1922**

Bennett & Wood Ld. Regd. 1919. Vol. liq. (members') 18 Dec. 1931. All shares owned by Morgan (Charles) & Co. Ld. Final meeting return regd. 18 Mar. 1932 **1932**

Bennett Lake & Klondyke Navigation Co. Ld. Regd. 1898. Taken over by Klondyke Corporation Ld. Removed from Register 1903 .... *****1901**

Bennett (Sir John) Ld. Regd. 1894. Vol. liq. (members') 18 July 1940. Capital returned to contributories—8s. 9½d. per share of 10s. £512 2s. 4d. was paid into Companies' Liquidation Account. Final meeting return regd. 19 July 1941............................... **1941**

Bennett Steamship Co. Ld. Regd. 1890. Vol. liq. (members') 27 Sept. 1945. Capital returned to contributories—£11 11s. 4d. per share of £10. £238 11s. 4d. (amounts unclaimed by shareholders) was paid into Companies' Liquidation Account. Final meeting return regd. 12 Jan. 1953...................... **1954**

Bennett (William), Sons & Co. Ld. Regd. 1907. Vol. liq. 13 Sept. 1929. Indirect controlling interest held by Imperial Chemical Industries Ld. Final meeting return regd. 2 May 1930 .... **1923**

See Stock Exchange Year-Book.

VOL. FOR

Bennett's Dairies Ld. Regd. 1889 as West London Dairy Co. Ld. name changed Jan. 1919. Vol. liq. (members') 21 Jan. 1931. Capital returned to contributories—£26,593 8s. 7d. £83 8s. was paid into Companies' Liquidation Account. Final meeting return regd. 25 Jan. 1934 ......   **1931**

Bennetts Ld. Regd. 1897. Reconstructed 1899 as Manchester Timber Importers Ld., in which company shareholders were entitled to 10½ fully-paid preferred shares of £1 for each preference share of £10 held or to 10 deferred shares of £1 for each ordinary share of £10 held. Removed from Register 1913 ......   **1902**

Bennett's Moss Litter Co. Ld. Regd. 1888. Vol. liq. 1 Oct. 1891. Struck off Register Mar. 1929 ......   **1930**

Benoist (V.) Ld. Regd. 1900. Vol. liq. 17 Apr. 1909. Final meeting return regd. 2 Dec. 1914 ......   **1901**

Benoni Claim Gold Mining & Exploration Syndicate Ld. Inc. South African Republic 1893. £7 12s. 6d. in cash per share of £100 was distributed; shareholders were also entitled to 65 shares in New Kleinfontein Co. Ld., 163 shares in Benoni Gold Mines Ld. (later Benoni Consolidated Gold Mines Ld.) 37 shares in Chimes West Ld., and 16 shares in Kleinfontein Central Gold Mines Ld., for each share of £100 held   **1900**

Benoni Consolidated Gold Mines Ld. Inc. Transvaal 1895 as Benoni Gold Mines Ld.; name changed Jan. 1909. Vol. liq. Mar. 1914. Assets and liabilities were sold to New Kleinfontein Co. Ld., for 31,540 shares of £1 (credited as fully-paid) **1915**

Benoni Gold Mines Ld. See Benoni Consolidated Gold Mines Ld.

Benoni Outcrops Ld. Regd. 1909. Practically all capital owned by Silati Co. Ld. Struck off Register 1940 .   **1932**

Benrinnes-Glenlivet Distillery Ld. Regd. 1896. Vol. liq. 5 Oct. 1926. Dissolved before 1931 ......   **1923**

Benskin's Watford Brewery Ld. Regd. 1894. Vol. liq. 25 Jan. 1898. Reconstructed as company of same name. Final meeting return regd. 17 Jan. 1899 .....   **1898**

Benson and Hedges (Canada) Ld. Inc. Canada 1917. The outstanding 8¼% guaranteed 1st mortgage debenture stock was redeemed at par on 16 July 1928 ......   **1928**

Bent Colliery Co. Ld. Regd. Edinburgh 1920. Vol. liq. (members') 10 July 1952. Colliery vested in National Coal Board as from 1 Jan. 1947. Capital returned to contributories—6s. 8·175d. per share of 3s. 6d. £48 12s. 6d. paid to Accountant of Court in respect of unclaimed distributions. Final meeting return regd. 15 Feb. 1961 ......   **1962**

Bent Ley (Holdings) Ld. Regd. 1890 as Bent Ley Silk Mills Ld.; name changed Feb. 1955. Vol. liq. (members') 23 Mar. 1955, the undertaking and assets having been transferred to a new company (Bent Ley Silk Mills Ld.). Preference shares were repaid at par, but holders were given the right to apply for an equal number of preference shares (of £1) in the new company. Ordinary shareholders received £1 cash, £1 4% unsecured loan notes and 1 fully-paid ordinary share in the new company for each share (of £1) held. £821 13s. 9d. was paid into Companies' Liquidation Account. Final meeting return regd. 31 Oct. 1955 ......   **1956**

Bent Ley Silk Mills Ld. Regd. 1955. Vol. Liq. (members') 10 May 1963. Capital returned to contributories—2Os. per preference share (of £1); 24s. 4·2d. per ordinary share (of £1). Paid into Companies' Liquidation Account £280 10s. 9d. in respect of unclaimed dividends and £241 14s. 11d. in respect of unclaimed distributions. Final meeting return regd. 13 Sept. 1965 ......   **1966**

Bent Ley Silk Mills Ld. (regd. 1890) see Bent Ley (Holdings) Ld.

Bentham Gas Co. Ld. Regd. 1888. Dissolved 1 May 1949, undertaking being vested in North Western Area Gas Board under Gas Act 1948. Holders of securities were entitled to receive British Gas 3% guaranteed stock 1990–95 as follows:

	£	s.	d.	
Ord. shares (of £5)......	7	0	0	
6% red. debs. (of £100)......	100	5	0	**1952**

Bentley (Henry) & Co. Ld. Regd. 1880. Vol. liq. 30 Nov. 1893. Business was acquired by Henry Bentley and Company and Yorkshire Breweries Ld. (later Bentley's Yorkshire Breweries Ld.). Final meeting return regd. 10 Mar. 1896......   **1892**

Bentong "Straits Tin" Co. Ld. Regd 1888. Vol. liq. 22 Sept. 1891. Reconstructed as New Bentong Co. Ld., in which company shareholders were entitled to 1 share of £1 (credited with 17s. 6d. paid) for each share of £1 held. Final meeting return regd. 23 Feb. 1893 ......   **1893**

Benue (Northern Nigeria) Tin Mines Ld. Regd. 1915. Vol. liq. 29 May 1922. Capital returned to contributories—2s. 6d. per share of 10s. at June 1922; further

---

VOL. FOR

payments (if any) not known. Final meeting return regd. 10 Mar. 1931 ......   **1923**

Benzies Consolidated Gold Mines of South Africa Ld. Regd. Edinburgh 1903 as Glasgow Rhodesian & Transvaal Mining Synd. Ld.; name changed Feb. 1905. The properties were sold by the receiver for the debenture-holders. Struck off Register 20 Dec. 1907 ......   **1908**

Benzol & By-Products Ld. Regd. 1920. Vol. liq. (members') 4 July 1955. Capital returned to contributories—31s. 10·918d. per preference share of 20s. and 21s. 7d. per ordinary share of 10s. £329 17s. 3d. was paid into Companies' Liquidation Account in respect of unclaimed dividends and £5,849 6s. 11d in respect of distributions. Final meeting return regd. 17 June 1957......   **1958**

Beranang (Selangor) Rubber Plantations Ld. Regd. 1910. Vol. liq. (members') 25 June 1954. Estates sold to Brooklands Selangor Rubber Co. Ld. for £26,600. Capital returned to contributories—11·85d. per 2s. stock. £4,006 2s. 8d. was paid into Companies' Liquidation Account. Final meeting return regd. 29 Nov. 1955   **1957**

Berca Petroleum Co. Ld. Regd. 1899. Removed from Register 1903......   **1902**

Berehaven Copper Mines Ld. Regd. 1902. Vol. liq. June 1908. Removed from Register 1911......   **1909**

Berehaven Mining Co. Ld. Inc. Dublin 1870. Removed from Register 1889 ......   **1885**

Berenguela Tin Mines Ld. Regd. 1905. Vol. liq. (creditors') Mar. 1930. Capital returned to contributories—7₁₁d. per share of 4s. Final meeting return regd. 5 July 1938 ......   **1931**

Beresford Cinema Ld. Regd. 1921. Vol. liq. 2 Aug. 1928. Properties purchased by Denman Picture Houses Ld. Final meeting return regd. 13 Dec. 1928 ......   **1940**

Berg & Metallbank. See Metallgesellschaft A. G.

Bergen Steamship Co. Inc. Norway 1851. The outstanding debenture stock was repaid on 15 Feb. 1937...   **1937**

Bergenske Damfshibsselskab. See Bergen Steamship Co.

Bergvik Co. Ld. Regd. 1888. Vol. liq. 26 Sept. 1916. Capital returned to contributories—£15 per preferred share of £10; deferred shareholders received either 1½ shares of Kr.180 in a Swedish company or £40 per deferred share of £10. Final meeting return Regd. 3 Nov. 1919   **1917**

Berkeley Gas Works Ld. Regd. 1891. Dissolved 1 May 1949, undertaking being vested in South Western Area Gas Board under Gas Act 1948. Holders of securities were entitled to receive British Gas 3% guaranteed stock 1990–95 as follows:

	£	s.	d.	
Ord. shares (of £1)......	1	2	0	
4½% debs.(of £100)......	100	0	0	**1952**

Berkeley Syndicate Ld. Regd. 1926. Vol. liq. (members') 9 Aug. 1937. Direct controlling interest held by General Theatre Corporation Ld. Final meeting return regd, 7 Feb. 1928.   **1938**

Berkeley Vale Shorthorn Dairy Co. Ld. Regd. 1882. Vol. liq. Aug. 1885. Final meeting return regd. 7 Oct. 1886   **1887**

Berkhampstead Gas Co. Inc. by Special Act 1905. Dissolved 1 May 1949, undertaking being vested in Eastern Area Gas Board under Gas Act 1948. Holders of securities were entitled to receive, in respect of each £100 unit held, British Gas 3% guaranteed stock 1990–95 as follows:

	£	s.	d.	
Orig. stock (10% stand.)......	288	0	0	
Orig. stock (7% stand.)......	202	0	0	
Addit. stock (7% stand.)......	202	0	0	
4% debs	101	0	0	**1952**

Berks & Hants Extension Railway Co. Inc. by Special Act 1859. Amalgamated with Great Western Railway Co. Holders of ordinary shares of £10 received £87 10s. consolidated ordinary stock in acquiring company for every £100 held......   **1883**

Berkshire & General Investment Trust Ld. Undertaking and assets were acquired by London and County Stockholders Investment Trust Ld. (later London Stockholders' Investment Trust Ld.) for £120,000 in fully-paid ordinary shares **1929**

Berlanga Silver-Lead Mining Co. Ld. Regd. 1876. Vol. liq. July 1884. Final meeting return regd. 22 Aug. 1887 ......   **1885**

Berlin Phosphate Sewage & Manure Co. Ld. Regd. 1872. Removed from Register 1904 ......   **1887**

Berlin Proprietary Mines Ld. Regd. 1905. Vol. liq. 16 Feb. 1928. Final meeting return regd. 13 Apr. 1928   **1929**

Bermuda Development Co. Ld. Inc. Bermuda 1920. The outstanding 4% gteed. 1st mtge. debentures were redeemed in Aug. 1947 at 101%......   **1948**

Bermuda Railways Investment Co. Ld. Regd. 1928 as Bermuda Traction Ld., name changed Mar. 1931.

---

*See Stock Exchange Year-Book.

VOL. FOR

Vol. liq. (members') 19 Oct. 1949. The debenture stock was repaid to the extent of 40% in 1946 and a further £3 1s.% in 1950. No capital returned to contributories, £21 7s. was placed in Companies' Liquidation Account. Final meeting return regd. 22 Mar. 1950 .... **1951**

Bermuda Traction Ld. See above.

"Berna" Lorries Ld. Regd. 1920. Vol. liq. 4. Feb. 1922. Struck off Register 1926 .... **1923**

Bernard Oppenheimer Diamond Works Ld. See National Diamond Factories (Bernard Oppenheimer) Ld.

Berne Land Co. Ld. Regd. 1881. Vol. liq. 29 Aug. 1893. Reconstructed as company of same name. Shareholders were entitled to 1 fully-paid share of £17 in new company for each share of £17 held. Final meeting return regd. 7 Mar. 1894 .... **1895**

Berne Land Co. Ld. Regd. 1893. Vol. liq. (members') 23 June 1931. Capital returned to contributories—£2 0s. 9d. per share of £1. Final meeting return regd. 16 June 1932 .... **1932**

Bernhard-Kean Production Ld. Regd. 1925. Vol. liq. (members') 3 Apr. 1930. All shares owned by Union Cinema Co. Ld. Final meeting return regd. 22 Dec. 1933 .... **1931**

Bernhard, Scholle & Co. Ld. Regd. 1922. Vol. liq. (members') 26 Aug. 1935. Capital returned to contributories—15s. 0¼d. per share of £1. Securities valued £8,189 19s. 7d. were distributed in kind in Mar. 1939. £326 10s. 10d. paid into Companies' Liquidation Account in respect of customers' unclaimed balances. Final meeting return regd. 10 June 1954 .... **1955**

Bernheim (Mazoe) Gold Mines Ld. Regd. 1903 Vol. liq. Feb. 1909. Removed from Register 1911 .... **1909**

Bernstein [William] (Furriers) Ld. Regd. 1928. Vol. liq. (members') 25 Aug. 1932. Capital returned to contributories—£18,922 18s. 4d. Final meeting return regd. 19 Dec. 1933 .... **1933**

Bernstein (William) Ld. Business acquired in Apr. 1928 by Bernstein (William) (Furriers) Ld for 20,000 fully-paid preferred ordinary shares and 50,000 fully-paid deferred shares of £1 .... **1929**

Berrida (Nigeria) Tin Fields Ld. Regd. 1912. Vol. liq. 12 Apr. 1926. Final meeting return regd 2 Nov.1926 **1927**

Berrington (H.) & Co. Ld. Regd. Dublin 1908; transferred to Belfast under Government of Ireland Act 1920. Vol. liq. 1933 .... **1934**

Berrisford Engineering Co. Ld. Regd. 1928. Receiver appointed by Court Order 22 July 1938; ceased to act 12 June 1940. Struck off Register 8 June 1945 **1934**

Berry Construction Co. Ld. Regd. 1906. Vol. liq. Apr. 1912 for amalgamation with British Electric Transformer Co. Ld. Removed from Register 1913 ...... **1913**

Berry-Glengower Goldfields Ld. Regd. 1900. Struck off Register 1915 .... **1904**

Berry (Thomas) & Co. Ld. Regd. 1874. Vol. liq. 1 July 1924. All capital held by Tennant Brothers Ld. Final meeting return regd. 4 June 1926 .... **1925**

Berry United Deep Leads Ld. Regd. 1906. Removed from Register 1911 .... **1911**

Bertram Extended Rubber Co. Ld. Regd. 1919. Vol. liq. (members') 16 Mar. 1931. Shareholders were entitled to 2 fully-paid shares of 2s. in Bertram Consolidated Rubber Co. Ld., for every 7 shares of 2s. held. Final meeting return regd. 9 Nov. 1932 **1931**

Bertram Luipaard's Vlei Gold Mining Co. Ld. Regd. 1889. Winding-up Order 27 Feb. 1892. Removed from Register 1906 .... **1893**

Bertrams Ld. Regd. Edinburgh 1888. Vol. liq. June 1898 for reconstruction as company under same name. Final meeting return regd. 23 Nov. 1898 .... **1908**

Berwick & Tweedmouth Gaslight Co. Ld. Regd. 1856. Dissolved 1 May 1949, undertaking being vested in Northern Area Gas Board under Gas Act 1948. Holders of securities were entitled to receive British Gas 3% guaranteed stock 1990–95 as follows:

	£	s.	d.
Ord. shares (of £10)	12	16	0
5% red. debs. (of £100)	107	0	0

1952

Beryl Gold Corporation Ld. Regd. 1934. Vol. liq. (members') 4 Sept. 1941. Winding-up Order 11 Mar. 1946. Capital returned to contributories—2d. per share of 5s. Liquidator released 12 Nov. 1954. Struck off Register 22 Mar. 1961 .... **1955**

Besley (F. J.) & Co. Ld. Regd. 1887. Court Order to wind up 10 Nov. 1888. Reconstructed 1889 as Botolph and Nicholson's Wharves Co. Ld., in which company shareholders were entitled to 1 share of £10 (credited with £6 10s. paid) for each share of £10 held. Court Order to dissolve 5 Aug. 1895 .... **1896**

Bessbrook & Newry Tramway Co. Inc. 1884 under Tramways & Public Cos. (Ireland) Act 1883 and an Order of Irish Privy Council. Under Act of 1900 the

VOL. FOR

undertaking was purchased by Newry, Keady and Tynan Railway Co **1918**

Bessemer (Henry) & Co. Ld. Regd. 1877. Vol. liq. 11 Mar. 1892 for reconstruction as company of same name. Shareholders were offered shares in new company at rate of 1 preference share of £10 at a premium of 10s., and 1 ordinary share of £1 at a premium of £3 10s. for each share of £10 held. Final meeting return regd. 23 Mar 1893 .... **1908**

Bessemer (Henry) & Co. Ld. Regd. 1892. Vol. liq. (members') 6 Mar. 1952. Final meeting return regd. 22 Apr. 1953 .... **1904**

Bessie Mining Co. Ld. Regd. 1892. Absorbed by South East Rand Extension Ld. (inc. Transvaal) for 30,007 fully-paid shares. Vol. liq. 23 Sep. 1895. Final meeting return regd. 29 June 1897 .... **1896**

Beassler, Waechter & Co. Ld. Regd. 1904. Vol. liq. 31 Dec. 1925. Business was sold to company of same name. Final meeting return regd. Jan. 1931 .... **1927**

Beassler, Waechter & Co. Ld. Regd. 1926. Vol. liq. (members') 24 Apr. 1934. Undertaking acquired by company of same name. Capital returned to contributories—£1 4s. 10·332d. per preference share of £1; 7s. 4·028d. per ordinary share of £1 plus certain investments which were distributed in specie. Final meeting return regd. 20 Feb. 1935 ... **1935**

Bestwood Coal & Iron Co. Ld. Regd. 1872. Vol. liq. (members') 10 Dec. 1948. The assets (less £270,000 cash) were transferred to Bestwood Co. Ld., in which company shareholders were entitled to receive 1 fully-paid preference share of £100 plus £100 cash for every preference share of £100 held and 1 fully-paid ordinary share of £1 plus £1 cash for every ordinary share of £1 held. Final meeting return regd. 6 Nov. 1949 .... **1950**

Bethal Syndicate Ld. Regd. 1903. Vol. liq. Jan. 1908. Removed from Register 1913 .... **1909**

Bethanga Goldfields Ld. Regd. 1895. Properties were acquired by Bethanga Goldfields (1901) Ld. The original vendors were entitled to 150,000 fully-paid shares of £1 and 150,000 shares of £1 (credited with 16s. paid). Removed from Register 1910 .... **1902**

Bethanga Goldfields (1905) Ld. Regd. 1901. Reconstructed as Bethanga Goldfields Ld., in which company shareholders were entitled to 1 share of £1 (credited with 18s. paid) for every 4 shares of £1 held. Removed from Register 1911 .... **1906**

Bethanga Goldfields Ld. Regd. 1905. Vol. liq. 30 May 1906. Struck off Register 11 Feb. 1910 .... **1907**

Bethel Diamond Mines Ld. Regd. 1904. Vol. liq. Aug. 1908. Removed from Register 1910 .... **1909**

Bethlehem Steel Co. Inc. Pennsylvania 1899. The outstanding 1st lien & refunding mtge. 5% 30-year gold bonds were redeemed on 1 Nov. 1937 at 105% **1939**

Bethlehem Steel Corporation. Inc. New Jersey 1904. Amalgamated in 1936 with 3 subsidiaries into Bethlehem Steel Corporation (inc. Delaware). Preferred stockholders were entitled to 1 share of 7% preferred stock and 1 share of 5% preferred stock in amalgamated company plus $1 in cash for every $100 preferred stock held; holders of common stock were entitled to 1 share of common stock in that company for each common share held. Liability for the funded debt was also assumed by that company **1937**

Betsileo Exploring Co. Ld. Regd. 1895. Vol. liq. July 1907. Removed from Register 1908 .... **1908**

Betteshanger Boring Co. Ld. Regd. 1912. Vol. liq. 28 July 1922. Final meeting return regd. 1 Feb. 1923 **1939**

Betteshanger Holding Co. Ld. Regd. 1922. Vol. liq. (members') 27 Feb. 1952. Capital returned to contributories—7s. 2¾d. £258 15s. 1d. was paid into Companies' Liquidation Account. Final meeting return regd. 3 July 1953 .... **1954**

Bettisfield Colliery Ld. Regd. 1903 as Pontybodkin Colliery Co. Ld.; name changed 21 Oct. 1905 to Mold Collieries Ld., and as above 2 Oct. 1915. Receiver appointed 12 Feb. 1934; ceased to act 16 July 1940. Struck off Register 21 Apr. 1944 .... *1915

Betts British Foil Factories Ld. Regd. 1915. Vol. liq. (members') 4 Apr. 1945. Direct controlling interest was held by Betts and Co. Ld. Final meeting return regd. 5 Nov. 1945 .... **1946**

Bettws-y-Coed Slate Quarry Co. Ld. Regd. 1895. Receiver for debenture holders appointed May 1906. Struck off Register 1915 .... **1910**

Betz (John F.) & Son's Brewery Ld. Regd. 1888. Struck off Register 9 Jan. 1931 .... **1925**

Beuno Consols Co. Ld. Regd. 1881. Removed from Register 1888 .... *1885

Bevan, Churchill & Co. Ld. Regd. 1920. Vol. liq. 21 Jan. 1924. Final meeting return regd. 25 May 1926...... *1925

Beverley & East Riding Railway Co. Inc. by Special Act 1889. Undertaking abandoned by Act of 1891 ..... **1892**

*See Stock Exchange Year-Book.

VOL. FOR

Beverley Tea & Rubber Estates Ld. Regd. 1910. Vol. liq. (creditors') 15 Nov. 1932. Undertaking and assets were acquired by Beverley Tea & Rubber Estates (1932) Ld., in which company shareholders were entitled to 1 share of 2s. (credited with 1s. 8d. paid) for each share of 2s. held. Debenture stockholders were entitled to £105 7% convertible debenture stock for every £100 7% debenture stock held. Final meeting return regd. 28 Mar. 1934 .... **1933**

Beverley Tea & Rubber Estates (1932) Ld. Regd. 1932. Vol. liq. (members') 30 Apr. 1936. Capital returned to contributories—1s. 4$\frac{7}{13}$d. per ordinary stock unit of 2s. £1,534 16s. 5d. was paid into Companies' Liquidation Account. Final meeting return regd. 3 Nov. 1948 .... **1950**

Beverley Waterworks Co. Inc. by Special Act 1881. Court Order to wind up 12 Mar. 1907. Undertaking was taken over by Beverley Corporation for £20,850 in Mar. 1907 .... **1908**

Bewdley Gas Co. Ld. Regd. 1907. Dissolved 1 May 1949, undertaking being vested in West Midland Area Gas Board under Gas Act 1948. Holders of securities were entitled to receive British Gas 3% guaranteed stock 1990—95 as follows:

	£	s.	d.
Ord shares (of £1)	2	1	0
6% mort. debs. (of £100)	109	0	0	**1952**

Bexhill & Rotherfield Railway Co. Inc. by Special Act 1899. Construction authorised to be abandoned by Act of 1902 .... **1903**

Bexhill Water & Gas Co. Inc. by Special Act 1885. Under Bexhill Corporation Act 1925 the undertaking was purchased by that Corporation for £191,196 in cash and the assumption of all debts and liabilities, including the debenture stocks. Preference shares were to be repaid at par. The net residue was divisible so that holder of each additional ordinary share of £10 received $\frac{7}{10}$th of amount received by holder of each original ordinary share of £10 .... **1926**

Bexley Heath Railway Co. Inc. by Special Act 1883. Under South Eastern Railway Act of 1900 the undertaking was transferred to that company, in which holders of 3% debenture stock received an equal amount of 3% debenture stock and holders of guaranteed shares an equal amount of 3½% preference stock; holders of ordinary shares received £7 10s. per share in cash **1901**

Beynon (T.) & Co. Ld. See *T. B.* & Co. (Holdings) Ld.

Beyrouth Waterworks Co. Ld. Regd. 1873. Vol. liq. June 1909. Undertaking and assets were acquired by Messrs. Sebbag & Co. for £100,000 in cash which was distributed £60,000 among debenture holders, £30,000 among income bondholders and £10,000 among shareholders. Struck off Register May 1929 .... **1930**

Bhadra Valley Estates Ld. Regd. 1926. Estate sold in 1950. Vol. liq. (members') 19 Dec. 1950. Capital returned to preference shareholders—15s. 3d. per share (of £1). No return to ordinary shareholders. Final meeting return regd. 3 Dec. 1952 .... **1954**

Bhubrighat Tea Co. Ld. Regd. Edinburgh 1903. Vol. liq. (members') 28 Apr. 1947. Capital returned to contributories—£3 17s. 1¾d. per share of £1. Final meeting return regd. 1 Nov. 1952 .... **1954**

Biafra Syndicate Ld. Regd. 1901. Vol. liq. 10 Aug. 1906. Capital returned to contributories—2s. 8d. per share of £1; further payments (if any) not known. Removed from Register 1907 .... **1907**

Bibiani Gold Fields Ld. Regd. 1900. Vol. liq. Mar. 1908. Property sold to Bibiani Ld., in which company shareholders were entitled to 1 share of £1 (credited with 15s. paid) for each share of £1 held. Debenture holders were entitled to an equal amount of debentures (50% A 50% B) in new company. Removed from Register 1909 .... **1909**

Bibiani Ld. Regd. 1908. Vol. liq. 28 Nov. 1913. Struck off Register 18 Jan. 1921 .... **1914**

Bibi. Eybat Petroleum Co. Ld. Regd. 1900. Vol. liq. 3 Feb. 1913. Reconstructed as Bibi-Eybat Oil Co. Ld. in which company shareholders were entitled to 5 shares of 10s. (credited with 5s. paid) for every 4 shares of £1 held. Debenture holders were entitled to 50% of holding in debentures in new company and 25% in income notes. Final meeting return regd. 4 Mar. 1914 .... **1913**

Bickford Smith & Co. Regd. 1888. Vol. liq. (members') 31 Dec. 1942. All capital held by I.C.I. (Explosives) Ld. Final meeting return regd. 25 May 1946 .... **1943**

Bicol (Lincoln) Ld. Regd. 1924. Vol. liq. (members') 6 Apr. 1944. All capital was owned by Fisons Ld. Final meeting return regd. Sep. 29 1944 .... **1945**

Bideford & Clovelly Railway Co. Inc. by Special Act. 1898. Construction authorised to be abandoned by Act of 1901 .... **1902**

VOL. FOR

Bideford Black Ld, Regd. 1928. Vol. liq. (creditors') 12 Dec. 1935. Assets realised a sum insufficient to meet debenture holders' claims. Final meeting return regd. 15 Dec. 1938 .... **1936**

Bideford Gas & Coke Co. Ld. Estd. 1835; regd. as limited 1870; statutory powers 1892. Dissolved 1 May 1949, undertaking being vested in South Western Area Gas Board under Gas Act 1948. Holders of securities were entitled to receive British Gas 3% guaranteed stock 1990–95 as follows in respect of each £10 unit, unless otherwise stated, of security held:

	£	s.	d.
Orig. ord. shares (10% stand.)	26	4	0
5% pref. shares	11	0	0
4½ red. debs. (per £100)	101	0	0	**1952**

Bideford, Westward Ho & Appledore Railway Co. Inc. by Special Act. 1896. Vol. liq. May 1929 .... **1930**

Bidor Rubber Estates Ld. Regd. 1909. Vol. liq. (members') 31 Oct. 1961. Capital returned to contributories—57s. 9d. per share of £1. Final meeting return regd. 3 Jan. 1963 .... **1964**

Bieckert Investment Trust Ld. Regd. 1930 as Bieckert's Brewery Investment Co. Ld.; name changed 8 Jan. 1957. Vol. liq. (members') 31 May 1960, assets transferred to holding company Imperial Colonial Investment Trust Ld. Final meeting return regd. 12 May 1962 .... **1963**

Bieckert's Brewery Co. Ld. Regd. 1889. Vol. liq. 8 Nov. 1900. Reconstructed as Bieckert's Brewery Co. (1900) Ld. Shareholders were entitled to 1 fully-paid preference share of £5 and 1 ordinary share of £5 (credited with £4 15s. paid) for each share of £20 held. Holders of 1st debenture stock were entitled to £57 10s. in 1st debenture stock and £50 in 2nd debenture stock in new company for every £100 bond held; holders of 2nd debenture stock were entitled to £106 in 2nd debenture stock for every £100 bond held. Final meeting return regd. 22 Jan. 1901 .... **1905**

Bieckert's Brewery Co. (1900) Ld. Regd. 1900. Vol. liq. (members') 6 Mar. 1930. Undertaking and certain assets were acquired by Bieckert's Brewery Investment Co. Ld. (later Bieckert Investment Trust Ld.) and the Argentine assets by Cerveceria Bieckert, Sociedad Anonima. The outstanding 4% debenture and 5% debenture stocks were redeemed on 30 June 1930, at 105% and 112½% respectively. £20,888 preference stock was cancelled and the balance (£290,272) was repaid at par in Mar. 1930. Ordinary stockholders received 1 share in Bieckert's Brewery Investment Co. Ld. for each £1 stock held and 10 shares of $5 in Cerveceria Bieckert, Sociedad Anonima for each £10 stock held, fractions being satisfied at the rate of 25s. per £1. £613 18s. 4d. was paid into Companies' Liquidation Account in respect of unclaimed dividends. Final meeting return regd. 9 Jan. 1931 .... **1931**

Bieckert's Brewery Investment Co. Ld. See Bieckert Investment Trust Ld.

Big Block Gold Mining Co. Ld. Regd. 1895. Vol. liq. 1 Apr. 1897. Final meeting return regd. 4 Dec. 1897 .... **1898**

Big Blow Gold Mines Ld. Regd. 1894. Vol. liq. 27 July 1896. Reconstructed as Big Blow Ld., in which company shareholders were entitled to 1 share of £1 (credited with 17s. paid) for each share of £1 held. Final meeting return regd. 30 June 1897 .... **1899**

Big Blow Ld. Regd. 1896. Court Order to wind up 18 Jan. 1899. Removed from Register 1909 .... **1899**

Big Creek Mining Co. Ld. Regd. 1891. Struck off Register 1931 .... **1889**

"Big Four" Pari-Mutual Ld. Regd. 1922. Struck off Register 1926 .... ***1922**

Big Golden Quarry Ld. Regd. 1896. Reconstructed 1901 as Cuadro Ld., in which company shareholders were entitled to 1 share of 1d. (credited as fully-paid) for each share of 2s. held. Removed from Register 1902 .... **1903**

Big Golden Quarry Mining & Water Power Co. Ld. Regd. 1887. Vol. liq. 28 Feb. 1889. Property and assets were acquired by Big Golden Quarry Mining Co. Ld. Removed from Register 1903 .... **1890**

Big Gold Quarry Mining Co. Ld. Regd. 1889. Vol. liq. 18 Nov. 1896. Reconstructed at Big Golden Quarry Ld. Final meeting return regd. 15 Nov. 1897 .... ***1897**

Big Reef Gold Mining Co. Ld. Regd. 1890. Vol. liq. 29 Dec. 1893. Final meeting return regd. 8 Jan. 1896 .... **1894**

Big Valley Creek Gold Mines Ld. Regd. 1898. Vol. liq. 22 Dec. 1905. Removed from Register 1908 .... **1906**

Bigger Gas Co. Ld. Regd. in Edinburgh 1930. Dissolved 1 May 1949, undertaking being vested in Scottish Area Gas Board under Gas Act 1948. Holders of ordinary shares (of £1) were entitled to receive £1 8s. British Gas 3% guaranteed stock 1990–95 for each share held **1952**

Bignells Ld. Regd. 1937. Vol. liq. (creditors') 27 Feb. 1964. No capital returned to contributories. £2 16s. 2d. paid into Companies' Liquidation Account in respect of unclaimed dividends. Final meeting return regd. 24 Apr. 1969 1970

Bigrigg Mining Co. Ld. Regd. 1904. Vol. liq. (members') 29 Mar. 1940. Capital returned to contributories—£49,352 11s. 9d. Final meeting return regd. 28 June 1940 1941

Bigwood (Joshua) & Son Ld. Regd. 1937. Winding-up order 7 Feb. 1986. All capital acquired by B. & S. Massey & Sons Ld. 1966

Bikam Rubber Estate Ld. Regd. 1909. Vol. liq. (members') 27 Feb. 1953. Undertaking and assets acquired as from 1 Nov. 1952 by Patalling Rubber Estates Ld. Stockholders were entitled to receive 40 fully-paid shares (of 2s.) in respect of every £7 stock held. £14 3s. 3d. was paid into Companies' Liquidation Account. Final meeting return regd. 11 Nov. 1953 1955

Bila (Sumatra) Rubber Lands Ld. Regd. 1910. Vol. liq. (members') 16 Dec. 1938. Undertaking and assets were acquired by Bah Lias Rubber Estates Ld., in which company shareholders were entitled to 1 share of £1 (credited as fully-paid) for every £2 stock held. Final meeting return regd. 1 Aug. 1939 1938

Billinghay & Metheringham (Light) Railway Co. Inc. by Act of 1883 and abandoned by Act of 1888 1889

Bilbao Iron Ore Co. Ld. See below.

Bilbao River & Cantabrian Railway Co. Ld. Regd. 1871 as Bilbao Iron Ore Co. Ld.; name changed 1883. Vol. liq. (members') 6 May 1937. Capital returned to contributories—28s. 3½d. per £1 stock. £2,370 16s. was paid into Companies' Liquidation Account. Final meeting return regd. 23 May 1947 1948

Billingsley Colliery Co. Ld. Regd. 1910. Struck off Register 1919 1917

Billiter Street Offices Co. Ld. Regd. 1882. Court Orders: to wind up Nov. 1889; to dissolve 1 Sept. 1900.... 1890

Bilson & Crump Meadows Collieries Co. Ld. Regd. 1874. Removed from Register 1885 1886

Bilston Gas Light & Coke Co. Ld. Inc. by Special Act 1846; regd. as limited 1937. Dissolved 1 May 1949, undertaking being vested in West Midland Area Gas Board under Gas Act 1948. Holders of securities were entitled to receive British Gas 3% guaranteed stock 1990–95 as follows in respect of each £5 unit, unless otherwise stated, of security held:

	£	s.	d.
A shares (10% stand.)	10	10	0
B shares (7% stand.)	7	16	0
5½% red. deb. stock (per £100)	104	10	0
4% red. deb. stock (1954) (per £100)	100	0	0
4% red. deb. stock (1958) (per £100)	100	10	0
			1952

Bilston Foundries Ld. Regd. 1939. Vol. liq. (members') 24 June 1963. Final meeting return regd. 23 Mar. 1964 1961

Bilston Iron Sheet & Galvanizing Co. Ld. Regd. 1919. Vol. liq. 8 Oct. 1921. Final meeting return regd. 10 June 1924 .... *1922

Bindley & Co. Ld. Regd. 1888. Vol. liq. (members') 5 Sept. 1945. All shares were owned by Ind Coope & Allsopp Ld. [later Ind Coope Ld.]. Final meeting return regd. 20 Jan. 1947 1948

Bingara Diamond Fields Ld. Inc. Guernsey 1904. In Dec. 1907 the Secretary stated "the company is now dead, having lost its 'leases' " 1908

Bingham Gas Light & Coke Co. Ld. Regd. 1856. Dissolved 1 May 1949, undertaking being vested in East Midland Area Gas Board under Gas Act 1948. Holders of ordinary shares (of £10) were entitled to receive £28 British Gas 3% guaranteed stock 1990–95 for each share held 1952

Binks (C.) (1920) Ld. Regd. 1920. Vol. liq. 1 Nov. 1928. Final meeting return regd. 3 Aug. 1929 1936

Bintan Rubber Estate Ld. Regd. 1926. Receiver was appointed May 1932. Certain assets were taken over by Dutch Government; proceeds of remaining assets were insufficient to meet claims ranking prior to debentures. Struck off Register Mar. 1934 1935

Bio Trust Ld. Regd. 1907. Vol. liq. 27 Aug. 1919. Shareholders were repaid at par; further expected payments not known. Final meeting return regd. 12 July 1920 1920

Biograph Theatres Ld. Regd. 1908. Vol. liq. 4 May 1922. Final meeting return regd. 15 Dec. 1922 1923

Bippo Gold Mining Co. Ld. Regd. 1900. Vol. liq. 1904. Undertaking was acquired by Gold Coast Exploration and Trading Co. Ld., in which company shareholders were entitled to 1 fully-paid share of £1 for every 2 shares of £1 held. Removed from Register 1905 1905

Bipposu Mines Ld. Regd. 1902. Vol. liq. Oct. 1907. Removed from Register 1909 1908

Bipposu Mines Ld. Regd. 1902. Removed from Register 1909 1908

Bipsine Ld. Regd. 1909. Court Order to wind up 30 May 1911. Liquidator released 16 May 1913. Struck off Register 10 Oct. 1916 1912

Birchall (Charles) Ld. Regd. 1900. Vol. liq. (members') 24 Mar. 1933 for reconstruction as Charles Birchall & Sons Ld., in which company shareholders received 1 fully-paid preference share of £1 for each preference share of £1 held and 1 fully-paid ordinary share of £1 plus £1 6s. in cash for each ordinary share of £1 held. Final meeting return regd. 26 May 1934 1934

Birchenwood Colliery Co. Ld. Regd. 1892. Vol. liq. 2 May 1925. A debenture for £251.750 and a controlling interest was held by Heath (Robt.) & Low Moor Ld. Receiver appointed 2 May 1925; ceased to act 20 Dec. 1928. Final meeting return regd. 22 Dec. 1928 1926

Birchington Bay Freehold Land & Estate Co. Ld. Regd. 1881. Removed from Register 1902 .... *1886

Birchley Rolling Mills Ld. Regd. 1919. Vol. liq. (members') 29 July 1955, the undertaking having been acquired by Wolverhampton & Birchley Rolling Mills Ld. Final meeting return regd. 7 May, 1956 1957

Bird & Co. (Africa) Ld. Inc. in Kenya 1920. Tanganyika assets vested in Tanzania Sisal Corpn. from 27 Oct. 1967. Vol. liq. 15 Dec. 1978. Capital returned to contributories (per 25p ordinary stock)—13·25p. Final meeting held 5 Mar. 1981 1981–2

Bird (Alfred) & Sons Ld. Regd. 1900. Vol. liq. 31 Jan. 1925. Reconstructed as private company of same name. Capital returned to contributories—£6 per preference share of £5; payments (if any) to ordinary shareholders not known. Final meeting return regd. 22 Jan. 1926 1926

Bird in Hand Gold Co. Ld. Regd. 1895. Court Order to wind up 16 Mar. 1898. Liquidator released 29 Jan. 1901. Struck off Register 10 July 1908 1899

Bird's Swaziland Concession Ld. Regd. 1889. Vol. liq. 5 Dec. 1910. Struck off Register 10 Oct. 1916 1911

Birdseye Creek Gold Mining Co. Ld. Regd. 1871. Vol. liq. 21 Jan. 1890. Capital returned to contributories—2s. 6d. per share of £4; further payments (if any) not known. Final meeting return regd. 24 Feb. 1891 1891

Birkbeck Bank. Established 1851. Liquidated 8 June 1911 1911

Birkbeck Property Investment Trust. Inc. 1874. By 1901 the certificates had been repaid and the reversionary certificates paid off 1901

Birkbeck Share & Debenture Trust. Established by Deed of Trust 1888. Under Act of 1912 the property and assets were transferred to Rock Investment Co. Ld. Holders of debenture stock, preferred shares and deferred shares were entitled to an equal nominal amount of debenture stock, preference shares and ordinary shares respectively in acquiring company. Holders of founders' shares were entitled to 5 fully-paid ordinary shares of £10 for each founders' share of £10 held 1913

Birkdale & Southport Tramways Co. Ld. Regd. 1870. Removed from Register 1902 .... *1885

Birkdale District Electric Supply Co. Ld. Regd. 1901. Vol. liq. (members') 15 Apr. 1942. Undertaking acquired by Southport Corporation. Capital returned to contributories—£74,842 10s. Final meeting return regd. 25 Apr. 1944 1942

Birkdale Park, Southport, Smedley Hydropathic Co. Ld. See below.

Birkdale Smedley Hydro Hotel, Ld. Regd. 1876 as Birkdale Park, Southport, Smedley Hydropathic Co. Ld.; name changed Sept. 1936. Vol. liq. (members') 29 Dec. 1948. Final meeting return regd.3 Jan. 1950 1950

Birkenhead & District Omnibus & Carriage Co. Ld. Regd. 1883. Vol. liq. 25 July 1890. Final meeting return regd. 12 Aug. 1891 .... *1886

Birkenhead, Lancashire & Cheshire Junction Railway Co. See Birkenhead Railway Co.

Birkenhead Railway Co. Amalgamation under Act of 1847 of Birkenhead, Lancashire & Cheshire Junction and Chester & Birkenhead Railway Cos.; above title assumed under Act of 1859. Railway conveyed, under Act of 1861 to London & North Western (later London Midland & Scottish) Railway Co. and Great Western Railway Co. whose undertakings were vested 1 Jan. 1948 in British Transport Commission under Transport Act 1947. Dissolved 2 Apr. 1949; holders of securities were entitled to receive British Transport 3% guaranteed stock 1978–88 as follows in respect of every £100 of

VOL. FOR

old security held:

	£	s.	d.	
Consolidated stock	112	3	9	
4½% preference stock	124	10	0	1949

Birkenhead Shipping Co. Ld. Regd. 1880. Vol. liq. 12 June 1899. Final meeting return regd. 29 Dec. 1899 ... **1900**

Birkenhead Tramways Co. Inc. by Special Act 1877. In liquidation in 1889 ... **1889**

Birmingham Alliance Life Assurance Co. Ld. *See* London & Birmingham Assurance Co. Ld.

Birmingham & Aston Tramways Co. Ld. Regd. 1881. Vol. liq. 1903. Undertaking was acquired by Aston Urban District Council. Capital returned to contributories—£9 12s. 6d. per share of £5; further payments (if any) not known. Removed from Register 1904 ... **1904**

Birmingham & District Tramways Co. Ld. Regd. 1871. Vol. liq. 6 Apr. 1876. Taken over by Birmingham Tramways & Omnibus Co. Ld. Final meeting return regd. 3 Oct. 1878 ... ***1876**

Birmingham & General Loan & Deposit Co. Ld. *See* Birmingham Financial Co. Ld.

Birmingham & Henley-in-Arden Railway Co. Inc. by Special Act 1884. Under Great Western Railway Act of 1900 the line was purchased by that company. Holders of 4% debenture stock were repaid at par and holders of ordinary shares received £7 in cash per share of £10 ... **1901**

Birmingham & Manufacturing Co. Ld. Regd. 1897 as Perambulata Ld.; name changed 19 Mar. 1901. Vol. liq. 11 June 1902. Final meeting return regd. 18 May 1904 ... ***1898**

Birmingham & Mid. Counties Transport Co. Ld. Regd 1914. Vol. liq. 6 July 1921. 95% of share capital held by Allied Road Transports Ld. Final meeting return regd. 24 June 1922. Court Order declaring dissolution void 5 Dec. 1922. Final meeting return regd. 16 July 1923 ... **1921**

Birmingham & North West Mutoscope Co. Ld. Regd. 1899. Removed from Register 1910 ... **1905**

Birmingham & Suburban Tramways Co. Ld. *See* Birmingham Central Tramways Co. Ld.

Birmingham & Warwickshire "Brush" Electric Light & Power Co. Ld. Regd. 1882. Vol. liq. Jan. 1814. Absorbed in Hammond Electric Light and Power Supply Co. Ld., in which company shareholders were entitled to 1 fully-paid share of £1 for every 6 shares of £2 held. Final meeting return regd. 7 July 1884 ... **1884**

Birmingham Banking Co. Ld. *See* Metropolitan Bank (of England & Wales) Ld.

Birmingham Breweries Ld. Regd. 1896. Removed from Register 1903 ... **1900**

Birmingham, Bristol & Thames Junction Railway Co. *See* West London Railway Co.

Birmingham Cab Co. Ld. Regd. 1885. Court Orders: to wind up 11 June 1887; to dissolve 1 Dec. 1891 ... **1888**

Birmingham Canal Navigations (Co Of Proprietors Of The). Inc. by Special Act 1835. Dissolved 3 June 1949; undertaking vested from 1 Jan. 1948 in British Transport Commission under Transport Act 1947. Holders of consolidated stock and 4% perpetual debenture stock were entitled to receive £103 15s. and £105 British Transport 3% guaranteed stock 1978–88 in respect of each £100 held respectively ... **1949**

Birmingham Central Tramways Co. Ld. Regd. 1883 as Birmingham & Suburban Tramways Co. Ld.; name changed Jan. 1883. Vol. liq. 5 Aug. 1896. Undertaking was acquired by City of Birmingham Tramways Co. Ld. The debentures and preference shares were repaid at par. Ordinary shareholders received a bonus of £1 per share. Final meeting return regd. 27 Apr. 1897 ... **1897**

Birmingham City Collieries Syndicate Ld. Regd. 1898. Vol. liq. Dec. 1908. Removed from Register 1909 ... **1909**

Birmingham Coal Co. Ld. Regd. 1904. Vol. liq 7 June 1909. Final meeting return regd. 25 Oct 1909 ... ***1910**

Birmingham Compressed Air Power Co. Inc. by Special Act 1884. Court Order to wind up 19 Dec. 1891 ... **1892**

Birmingham Concert Halls Ld. Regd. 1890. Court Orders; to wind up 19 Apr. 1890; to dissolve 13 Feb. 1893 ... **1891**

Birmingham Criterion Engineering Co. Ld. Regd. 1897. Vol. liq. 21 Feb. 1899. Final meeting return regd. 12 Sept. 1900 ... **1900**

Birmingham "Daily Times" Ld. Regd. 1889. Removed from Register 1906 ... **1891**

Birmingham Deposit Co. Ld. *See* Birmingham Financial Co. Ld.

Birmingham District & Counties Banking Co. Ld. *See* United Counties Bank Ld.

Birmingham, Dudley & District Banking Co. Ld. *See* United Counties Bank Ld.

VOL. FOR

Birmingham Electric Supply Co. Ld. Regd. 1889. By Special Act of 1899 Birmingham Corporation acquired undertaking for £420,000 (equivalent to £10 10s. cash for each £5 share) and company dissolved on 31 Dec. 1899 ... **1900**

Birmingham Empire Palace Ld. Regd. 1893. Reconstructed 1899 as Moss Empires Ld. (later M. E. Theatres Ld.). in which company shareholders were entitled to 9 preference and 9 ordinary shares of £5 (all fully paid) for every 10 shares of £5 held, subject to payment of £2 10s. Removed from Register 1909 ... **1900**

Birmingham Financial Co. Ld. Regd. 1883 as Birmingham & General Loan & Deposit Co. Ld.; name changed to Birmingham Deposit Co. Ld. and as above in 1912. Vol. liq. (members') 19 Sept. 1945. Capital returned to contributories—17s. 6d. per share of 10s. Final meeting return regd. 12 July 1946 ... **1947**

Birmingham Foundries Ld. Regd. 1920. All shares held by Midland Electric Manufacturing Co. Ld. Struck off Register 28 Apr. 1944 ... **1945**

Birmingham Gaiety Theatre of Varieties Ld. Regd. 1897. Receiver was appointed Jan. 1909. Removed from Register 1913 ... **1910**

Birmingham General Cemetery Co. Established 1835 and incorporated 1856. In voluntary liquidation in 1889 ... **1889**

Birmingham General Cemetery Co. Ld. Regd. 1888. Vol. liq. (members') 12 Mar. 1953. Final meeting return regd. 21 Sept. 1953 ... **1939**

Birmingham General Omnibus Co. Ld. Regd. 1897. Receiver was appointed May 1899. Assets were acquired by British Electric Traction Co. Ld. The 1st debentures were expected to be paid in full. Removed from Register 1904 ... **1905**

Birmingham Great Western Arcade Co. Ld. Regd. 1875. Vol. liq. (members') 7 Apr. 1936. Capital returned to contributories—£75 18s. 1d. per share of £25 (£22 paid). Final meeting return regd. 21 July 1937 ... **1937**

Birmingham Great Western Hotel Co. Ld. Regd. 1864. Removed from Register 1905 ... **1905**

Birmingham Hotel & Restaurant Co. Ld. Regd. 1896. Receiver was appointed June 1910. Struck off Register 1916 ... **1911**

Birmingham Household Supply Association Ld. Regd. 1874. Vol. liq. (members') 16 Apr. 1936. Capital returned to contributories—£1 5s. per ordinary share of £1; £12 10s. per preference share of £10. £877 was paid into Companies' Liquidation Account. Final meeting return regd. 21 Oct. 1937 ... **1937**

Birmingham Insurance Co. Ld. Regd. 1922. All shares owned by Lancashire & General Assurance Co. Ld. Struck off Register 1930 ... **1927**

Birmingham Joint Stock Bank Ld. Regd. 1861. Undertaking was absorbed by Lloyds Bank Ld. Vol. liq. 4 Apr. 1889. Final meeting return regd. 15 Nov. 1895 ... **1891**

Birmingham Metal & Munitions Co. Ld. Regd. 1897. Vol. liq. 18 Dec. 1920. Final meeting return regd. 2 Aug. 1923 ... **1922**

Birmingham Mutual Fire & General Insurance Association Ld. *See* Central Insurance Co. Ld.

Birmingham, North Warwickshire & Stratford-upon-Avon Railway Co. Inc. by Special Act 1894. Powers transferred to Great Western Railway Co. by Act of 1900 ... **1901**

Birmingham Pneumatic Tyre Syndicate Ld. Regd. 1896. Removed from Register 1911 ... **1910**

Birmingham Racecourse Co. Ld. Regd. 1894. Racecourse sold to Birmingham Corpn. in 1964. Vol. liq. (members) 13 Aug. 1965: Capital returned to contributories–£2 10s. per share of £1. £3,438 9s. 10d. was paid into Companies' Liquidation Account. Final meeting return regd. 24 May 1966 ... **1967**

Birmingham Shearardizing Co. Ld. Regd. 1905. Vol. liq. 14 Jan. 1911. Struck off Register 16 July 1915 ... **1913**

Birmingham Small Arms & Metal Co. Ld. Regd. 1873. Vol. liq. 22 Sept. 1896 for reconstruction as Birmingham Small Arms Co. Ld., in which company shareholders were entitled to 1 ordinary and 1 preference share of £5 for each share of £5 held. Final meeting return regd. 20 Feb. 1901 ... **1908**

Birmingham Tramways & Omnibus Co. Ld. Regd. 1876. Vol. liq. Dec. 1885. Undertaking was acquired by Birmingham Central Tramways Co. Ld., for £24,500. Final meeting return regd. 9 June 1887 ... **1886**

Birmingham Trust Ld. Regd. 1890. Vol. liq. 20 July 1914. In July 1914 £6 per fully-paid preference share of £10 was returned, thus leaving all preference shares with £4 paid. In Mar. 1915 £1 per preference share of £10 (£4 paid) was returned; further payments (if any) not known. Final meeting return regd. 8 Oct. 1931 ... **1915**

Birmingham Vinegar Brewery Co., 1897, Ld. later **Birmingham Vinegar Brewery Co. Ld.** *See* Sauce Holdings Ld.

See Stock Exchange Year-Book.

Birnbaum (B.) & Son Ld. Regd. 1890. Receiver appointed for debenture holders in Jan. 1906. Vol. liq. 5 Mar. 1906. A first payment of £25 per 1st mortgage debenture was made on 1 May 1906; further payments (if any) not known. Removed from Register 1909 1907

Birnbaum (B.) & Son Ld. Regd. 1913. Vol. liq. 16 Nov. 1926. Undertaking acquired by Zambrene Ld. (later Sinclair Tailored Clothes Ld.). Final meeting return regd. 31 Mar. 1937 1945

Birrim Dredging Co. Ld. Regd. 1905. Vol. liq. Aug. 1908. Removed from Register 1913 1909

Birrim Valley Gold Mining & Dredging Co. Ld. Regd. 1900. Reconstructed 1905 as Birrim Dredging Co. Ld., in which company shareholders were entitled to 1 fully-paid share of 3s. for every 2 shares of £1 held. Removed from Register 1913 1908

Birthday Amalgamated of Western Australia Ld. Regd. 1895. Reconstructed 1899 as Homeward Bound Mine Ld., in which company shareholders were entitled to 1 share of 10s. (credited with 8s. paid) for each share of 10s. held. Removed from Register 1903 1906

Bishop Auckland District Gas Co. Inc. by Special Act 1877. Dissolved 1 May 1949, undertaking being vésted in Northern Area Gas Board under Gas Act 1948. Holders of securities entitled to receive, in respect of each £10 unit held, British Gas 3% guaranteed stock 1990—95 as follows:

	£	s.	d.
Orig. shares (10% stand.)	24	0	0
Addit. shares (7% stand.)	19	0	0

.... 1952

Bischof White Lead Corporation (1900) Ld. *See* Brimsdown Lead Co. Ld.

Bishop's Castle & Montgomery Railway Co. Inc. by Special Act 1884. Abandoned by Act of 1887 1888

Bishop's Castle Railway Co. Inc. by Special Act 1861. In 1893 the line was administered by a Receiver and Manager 1910

Bishop's Creek Gold Mining Co. Ld. Regd 1888. Court Orders: to wind up 26 Mar. 1890; to dissolve 26 Nov. 1891 1891

Bishop's Stortford, Epping & District Gas Co. Estd. 1834; regd. 1871 as Bishop's Stortford & District Gas Co. Ld.; Inc. by Special Act 1904; reinc. as Bishop's Stortford, Harlow & Epping Gas & Electricity Co. by Special Act 1910; name changed as above by Special Order 1934. Dissolved 1 May 1949, undertaking being vested in Eastern Area Gas Board under Gas Act 1948. Holders of securities were entitled to receive, in respect of each £100 unit held, British Gas 3% guaranteed stock 1990–95 as follows:

	£	s.	d.
A ord. stock (5% stand.)	140	0	0
B ord. stock (5% stand.)	130	0	0
5% C pref. stock	112	0	0
4% D pref. stock	100	10	0
5½% pref. stock	122	0	0
4⅝%-perp. deb. stock	101	0	0
3½% perp. deb. stock	98	0	0

.... 1952

Bishop's Waltham Gas & Coke Co. Ld. Regd. 1862. Vol. liq. 11 July 1932. Undertaking acquired by Gosport District Gas Co. Capital returned to contributories—£1 10s. per share of £5. Final meeting return regd. 29 Dec. 1932 1936

Bishop's Waltham Light Railway Co. Inc. (under Light Railways Act 1896) by order of Light Railway Commissioners confirmed by Board of Trade 1900. Powers expired in 1903 1911

Bishop's Waltham Waterworks Co. Ld. Regd. 1893. Vol. liq. 4 Feb. 1914. Undertaking acquired by South Hants Waterworks Co. by Act of 1913 for £11,212 10s. *plus* capital expenditure in excess of issued capital on 31 Dec. 1911. Final meeting return regd. 7 Apr. 1914 1914

Bismec Group Ld. *See* Business Computers Ld.

Bissagos Oil Palm & Cotton Plantations Ld. Regd. 1911. Vol. liq. 6 Oct. 1913. Final meeting return regd. 8 Aug. 1918 1914

Bissenberger Gold Mining Co. Ld. Regd. 1894. Vol. liq. 10 May 1895. Amalgamated with White Feather Main Reef Gold Mining Co. Ld., in which company shareholders were entitled to similar shares. Final meeting return regd. 26 Jan. 1898 1896

Biting Rubber Estates Ld. Regd. 1920. Vol. liq. (members') 29 May 1934. Undertaking and assets were acquired by company of same name. Shareholders were entitled to 1 preference share of 2s. (credited as fully-paid) in new company for each preference share of 2s. held or 1 fully-paid ordinary share of 1s. for every 2 ordinary shares of 2s. held. Final meeting return regd. 24 Aug. 1934 1935

Bitter Creek Prospectors Ld. *See* Roumanian Consolidated Oilfields Ld.

Bitumuls (U. K.) Ld. Regd. 1926. Vol. liq. 11 Apr. 1929. Undertaking acquired by British Bitumen Emulsions Ld. Struck off Regiser 29 Dec. 1942............. 1940

Blaauwbosch Diamonds Ld. Inc. Orange Free State 1908 as Blaauwbosch Diamond & Development Syndicate Ld.; name changed Apr. 1910. In liquidation in 1925 1925

Black & White Publishing Co. Ld. Regd. 1890. Vol. liq. Oct. 1911. Struck off Register 1916 1912

Black Ball Coal Mining Co. of New Zealand Ld. Regd. 1892. Reconstructed 1898 as Blackball Coal Co. Ld. Shareholders were entitled to 15,000 shares of £1 in new company; debenture holders were entitled to debentures in new company. Removed from Register 1901... 1899

Black Country Tramways Estates Ld. (The). Regd. 1900 as Wolverhampton District Electric Tramways Ld.; name changed 15 Sept. 1930. Vol. liq. (members') 12 June 1947. Final meeting return regd. 18 Nov. 1947 ... 1948

Black Eagle Gold Mining Co. Ld. Regd. 1901. Removed from Register 1911 1909

Black Flag Central Gold Mines Ld. Regd. 1896. Removed from Register 1904 1901

Black Flag Consolidated Gold Mines Ld. Regd. 1895. Vol. liq. 29 Sept. 1897. Reconstructed as New Flag Gold Mining Co. Ld., in which company' shareholders were entitled to 1 share of £1 (credited with 18s. 6d. paid) for each share of £1 held. Final meeting return regd. 15 Mar. 1898 1898

Black Flag Proprietary Co. Ld. Regd. 1895. Vol. liq. 15 Jan. 1897 for reconstruction as company of same name. Shareholders were entitled to 1 share of £1 (credited with 15s. paid) in new company for every 4 shares of £1 held. Final meeting return regd. 16 July 1898 1908

Black Flag Proprietary Co. Ld. Regd. 1897. Struck off Register 1921 1914

Black Horse & Sandstone Gold Reefs Ld. Regd. 1895. Vol. liq. 24 June 1897. Reconstructed as company of same name in which company shareholders were entitled to 1 share of 5s. (credited with 2s. 6d. paid) for each share of £1 held. Final meeting return regd. 19 June 1899 1900

Black Horse & Sandstone Gold Reefs Ld. Regd. 1897. Vol. liq. 16 Mar. 1900. Capital returned to contributories—½d. per share of 5s. further payments (if any) not known. Final meeting return regd.5 Jan. 1901 1901

Black Horse Extended Proprietary Syndicate Ld. Undertaking acquired by Black Horse and Sandstone Gold Reefs Ld., in 1895 for 28,292 fully-paid shares of £1 1896

Black (James) & Co. Ld. Regd. Edinburgh 1898. Absorbed by Calico Printers' Association Ld. Vol. liq. June 1900. Preference shareholders and debenture holders received par value and debenture stockholders 10% premium, in respect of their holdings. Final meeting return regd. 27 Mar. 1901 ... 1901

Black Lion Brewery Co. Ld. Regd. 1890. Vol. liq. 26 Oct. 1898. Final meeting return regd. 15 July 1899 1899

Black Mountain Silica Co. Ld. Regd. 1907. Vol. liq. 30 Nov. 1928. Final meeting return regd. 3 Dec. 1929 ... 1929

Black Reef Proprietary Co. Ld. Inc. Transvaal 1895. Vol. liq. 1905 1906

Black Sea Amalgamated Oilfields Ld. Regd. 1915. Struck off Register 17 Jan. 1950 1951

Black Sea Oilfields Ld. Regd. 1909. Vol. liq. 17 Mar. 1915 for purpose of amalgamation with Maikop New Producers Ld., and Maikop Victory Oil Co. Ld., under title of Black Sea Amalgamated Oilfields Ld., in which company shareholders were entitled to receive 7 fully-paid shares of 10s. for every 10 ordinary- shares of £1 held or 3 fully-paid shares of 10s. for every 2 preferred shares of £1 held. Struck off Register 22 Jan. 1957 1955

Black Sea Telegraph Co. Ld. Regd. 1873. Vol. liq. 26 July 1912. Absorbed by Eastern Telegraph Co. Ld. Final meeting return regd. 25 Feb. 1913 .... *1879

Black Swan Gold Mine Ld. Regd. 1896. Removed from Register 1906 1899

Blackball Coal Co. Ld. Regd. 1898. Vol. liq. May 1923. Final meeting return regd. 14 May 1924 1923

Blackball Coal Mining Co. of N. Z. Ld. Regd. 1892. Removed from Register before 1901 1898

Blackburn Aeroplane & Motor Co. Ld. Regd. 1914. Vol. liq. (members') 6 Nov. 1936. Undertaking was acquired by Blackhurn & General Aircraft Ld. Final meeting return regd. 23 Aug. 1939.............. 1937

Blackburn & Over Darwen Tramways Co. Inc. by Special Act 1879. Undertaking was sold to Corporations of Blackburn and Darwen. Holders of each share of £10 received £10 0s. 3d. in cash 1900

VOL. FOR

Blackburn Bank Ld. Regd. 1875 as Blackburn Discount Investment and Loan Co. Ld.; name changed Feb. 1877. Vol. liq. 13 June 1906. Undertaking acquired by Union Bank of Manchester Ld. Final meeting return regd. 15 Nov. 1907 1940

Blackburn Brewery Co. Ld. Undertaking and assets were acquired in 1928 by Dutton's Blackburn Brewery Ld. [later Dutton's Brewery] for £375,000 in cash and £200,000 5% debenture stock.................. 1929

Blackburn Corporation Tramways Co. Ld. Regd. 1886. Undertaking taken over by Blackburn Corporation. Removed from Register 1901 1899

Blackburn Discount Investment and Loan Co. Ld. See Blackburn Bank Ld.

Blackburn, Whalley & Padiham Light Railway Co. Inc. (under Light Railways Act 1896) by order of Light Railway Commissioners confirmed by Board of Trade 1901 1910

Blackett's Claim Gold Mining Co. Ld. Regd. 1894. Vol. liq. 22 June 1896. Reconstructed as Blackett's Gold Mines Ld., in which company shareholders were entitled to 1 share of £1 (credited with 17s. paid) for each share of £1 held. Final meeting return regd. 23 May 1898 1897

Blackett's Gold Mines Ld. Regd. 1896. Vol. liq. 16 Nov. 1897. Reconstructed as Blackett's Mines Ld., in which company shareholders were entitled to 1 share of £1 (credited with 17s. paid) for each share of £1 held. Final meeting return regd.4 Apr.1900...... 1899

Blackett's Mines Ld, Regd. 1897. Reconstructed 1899 as company of same name, in which company share-holders were entitled to 2 shares of 10s. (credited with 8s. paid) for each share of £1 held. Removed from Register 1901 1901

Blackett's Mines Ld. Regd. 1899. Undertaking and assets were acquired in May 1901 by Amalgamated Gold Mines Ld., in which company shareholders were entitled to 1 share of 10s. (credited with 8s. 6d. paid) for each share of £1 held. Removed from Register 1902 1902

Blackfriars Type Foundry Ld. Regd. 1906. Struck off Register 1 Sept. 1942 1943

Blackheath & Greenwich District Electric Light Co. Ld. See South Metropolitan Electric Light & Power Co. Ld.

Blackheath (Birmingham) Blue Brick Works. Ld. Regd. 1897. Removed from Register 1903 .... *1902

Blacklock & Macarthur Ld. Regd. 1914. Vol. liq. (members') 31 Dec. 1948, undertaking being trans-ferred to Imperial Chemical Industries Ld. Final Meeting return regd. 22 Feb, 1951 1951

Blackman & Conrad Ld. Regd. as private company 2 July 1946.;converted into public company 1 May 1947. Winding-up order 17 May 1982 1984–5

Blackman Air Propeller Ventilating Co. Ld. Regd. 1882. Vol. liq. 30 June 1890. Business and patents were acquired by Blackman Ventilating Co. Ld. (later Keith Blackman Ld). Final meeting return regd. 14 Jan. 1891 1890

Blackmore, Leconte & Co. Ld. Regd. 1896. Removed from Register 1901 1900

Blackpool & Fleetwood Tramroad Co. Inc. by Special Act 1896. Undertaking and certain assets were transferred to Corporation of Blackpool for £248,758. During 1920 holders of each share of £10 received £18 12s. 6d. in cash, further payments (if any) not known. The Corporation assumed liability for debentures 1921

Blackpool & Fylde Light Railway Co. Inc. as Blackpool & Garstang Light Railway Co. (under Light Railways Act 1896) by order of Light Railway Commissioners, confirmed by Board of Trade 1901; name changed 1905 1908

Blackpool & Lytham Railway Co. Inc. by Special Act 1861. Under Lancashire and Yorkshire Railway (Various Powers) Act of 1904 the outstanding shares were converted into 3% debenture stock of the Lancashire and Yorkshire Railway and London and North Western Railway Companies...................... 1905

Blackpool Assembly & Concert Rooms Co. Ld. Regd. 1866. Vol. liq. 13 June 1896. Capital returned to contributories—£10 15s. 8d. per share of £5. Final meeting return regd. 13 Oct. 1896 1897

Blackpool Electric Tramway Co. Ld. Regd. 1885. Vol. liq. 15 Oct. 1892. Undertaking was acquired by Blackpool Corporation. Final meeting return regd. 4 May 1893 1893

Blackpool Electric Tramways (South) Ld. Regd. 1901. Vol. liq. July 1908. The company's holding of 80,598 ordinary shares, 35,513 preference shares and £150,000 debenture stock in Blackpool, St. Anne's and Lytham Tramways Co. Ld., were to be distributed amongst the holders of ordinary and

preference shares and debenture stock. Struck off Register 1922.. 1909

Blackpool Entertainments (1920) Ld. Regd. 1920. All ordinary capital was owned by Associated British Picture Corpn. Ld. Vol. liq. (members) 24 Apr. 1963. Final meeting return regd. 4 Dec. 1963 1952

Blackpool Gigantic Wheel Co. Ld. Regd. 1896. Vol. liq. 18 Jan. 1916. Property and assets were acquired by Blackpool Winter Gardens and Pavilion Co. Ld. Final meeting return regd. 7 Oct. 1916 1916

Blackpool Greyhound Stadium & Racecourse Ld. Regd. 1932. Vol. liq. (members') 3 Jan. 1936. Capital returned to contributories—1½d. per share of 2s. Final meeting return regd. 5 Oct. 1937 1936

Blackpool Land, Building & Hotel Co. Ld. Regd. 1863. Vol. liq. 7 Feb. 1925. Shares were reduced from £3 to 10s. by repayments of capital. Final meeting return regd. 6 May 1925.. 1901

Blackpool Passenger Steamboat Co. Ld. Regd. 1894. Vol. liq. 29 July 1924. In 1924 it was stated that the shares would be repaid at slightly over par. Final meeting return regd. 6 Nov.1924.............................. 1925

Blackpool, St. Anne's & Lytham Tramways Co. Ld. Regd. 1898. Under St. Anne's-on-the Sea Urban District Council Act of 1920 the undertaking was transferred to that Council for £140,000. The debentures were to be repaid at par with a payment on account of arrears of interest. A payment of 2s. per preference share of 18s. and 1s. per ordinary share of 16s. was authorised by debenture stock-holders. Struck off Register 1924 1921

Blackpool Trocadero Ld. Regd. 1920. Court Order to wind up 7 Dec. 1925. Struck off Register June 1931 1932

Blackpool Water Chute Ld. Regd. 1907. Vol. liq. 5 Dec. 1919. Struck off Register 12 July 1935 1920

Blackpool Winter Gardens and Pavilion Co. Ld. Regd. 1875. All capital was owned by Blackpool Tower Co. Ld. Vol. liq. (members') 29 Mar. 1966. Final meeting return regd. 6 July 1966 1951

Blackwater Mines Ld. Regd. 1906. Vol. liq. (creditors') 30 Nov. 1951. Creditors received 18s. 10d. in the £1. Final meeting return regd. 15 May 1957 1958

Blackwell Colliery Co. Ld. Regd. 1871. Reconstructed 1945 as N. H. & B. Collieries Ld., in which company siockholders were entitled to an equal amount of ordinary stock. Court Order to dissolve 1 Jan. 1945 1946

Blackwood Coffee Co. Ld. Regd. 1879. Vol. liq. 26 May 1920. Certain assets were sold to Estates Co. of Uva Ld. Capital returned to contributories-£10 per share at Sept. 1920; further payments (if any) not known. Final meeting return regd. Mar. 1921 1921

Blaenavon Co. Ld. Regd. 1890. Vol. liq. (members') 21 June 1957. Capital returned to contributories—preference shares repaid at par; ordinary shares (of 5s.); 4s. Final meeting return regd. 30 Mar. 1961 1962

Blagdon & Pensford Light Railway Co. Inc. (under Light Railways Act 1896) 1906. No capital raised at 31 Dec. 1909 1911

Blagrove's Freehold Gold Mining Co. Ld. Regd. 1899. Vol. liq. 20 May 1901. Reconstructed as Tarkwa Proprietary Ld., in which company shareholders were entitled to 1 share of 10s. (credited with 8s. paid) for every 8 shares of 2s. 6d. held. Final meeting return regd. 19 July 1904................................ 1902

Blaina & Raven Anthracite Collieries Ld. Regd. 1924 as Raven Anthracite Collieries Ld.; name changed May 1925. Undertaking acquired in 1928 by Henderson's Welsh Anthracite Collieries Ld. Struck off Register 16 Dec. 1949 1940

Blainscough Colliery Co. Ld. Regd. 1891. Vol. liq. (members') 16 May 1949. Final meeting return regd. 11 Nov. 1957 1916

Blair & Co. (Alloa) Ld. Regd. Edinburgh 1936. All capital was owned by United Breweries Ld. Vol. liq. (members') 3 Jan. 1962. £1,616 15s. paid to Companies' Liquidation Account. Final meeting return regd. 25 Jan. 1963 1964

Blair & Co. Ld. Regd. 1900. Vol. liq. 19 May 1925. All preference and ordinary shares owned by Gould Steamships & Industrials, Ld. Struck off Register 18 Mar. 1930 1925

Blair & Co. (London) Ld. Regd. 1922. Vol. liq. (members') 11 Oct. 1941; dissolved before 1952 .. 1940

Blairgowrie Gas Light Co. Ld. Regd. in Edinburgh 1886. Dissolved 1 May 1949, undertaking being vested in Scottish Area Gas Board under Gas Act 1948. Holders of ordinary shares (of £10) were entitled to receive £16 British Gas 3% guaranteed stock 1990—95 for each share held 1952

Blaisdell Pencils (1901) Ld. Regd. 1901. Removed from Register 1905 1904

Blake & Knowles Steam Pump Works Ld. Regd. 1890. Undertaking acquired, in 1903, by Blake & Knowles

See Stock Exchange Year-Book.

VOL. FOR

Steam Pump Works (of America), in which shareholders received 1 preference share of $48·50 for each preference share of £1 held, and 1 ordinary of $48·50 for each ordinary share of £1 held. Debenture holders received $485 6% debentures in new company for every £100 debentures held. Struck off Register 1905 .... **1905**

Blake & Richards Estates Ld. Regd. 1934. All capital was owned by Second Covent Garden Property Co. Ld. Vol. liq. (members') 25 Mar. 1966. Final meeting return regd. 25 Nov. 1968 .... **1953**

Blake Boiler Wagon & Engineering Co. Ld. Regd. 1905. Struck off Register 30 Sept. 1949 .... **1940**

Blake Development Co. Ld. Regd. 1922. Vol. liq. Dec. 1929. Struck off Register 30 Apr. 1946.............. **1947**

Blake Properties Ld. Regd. 1897 as S. & T. N. Blake & Co. Ld.; name changed 5 Jan. 1927. Vol. liq. 9 Oct. 1941. All share capital was owned by Brickwood & Co. Ld. (later Brickwoods Ld.). Debentures were repaid in full and surplus assets transferred to Brickwood & Co. Ld. Final meeting return regd. 4 Mar. 1943 .... **1945**

Blake (S. & T. N.) & Co. Ld. *See above.*

Blandford Gas Co. Ld. Regd. 1909. Dissolved 1 May 1949, undertaking being vested in Southern Area Gas Board under Gas Act 1948. Holders of securities were entitled to receive, in respect of each £1 unit held, British Gas 3% guaranteed stock 1990–95 as follows:

	£	s.	d.
Ord. shares	2	1	0
5% pref. shares	1	2	8

.... **1952**

Blane Valley Railway Co. Inc. by Special Act 1861. Under North British Railway Co.'s Act of 1891 the undertaking was amalgamated with that company, in which holders of 4½% preference shares received an equal amount of 4½% preference stock 1891; ordinary shares were repaid at par.................... **1892**

Blattner (Ludwig) Picture Corporation Ld. Regd. 1928. Court Order to wind up 6 Feb. 1933. Liquidator released 29 Nov. 1943. Struck off Register 8 May 1953 .... **1933**

Blaydon Manure & Alkali Co. (1877) Ld. Regd. 1877. Vol. liq. 20 June 1947. undertaking acquired by Fisons Ld. Final meeting return regd. 21 Apr. 1948 **1901**

Blayney Copper Mines & Smelting Co., No Liability. Inc. Victoria 1907. London office was closed in 1915... **1915**

Blee (Lindsay) & Co. Ld. *See* L. B. (Clundel) Ld.

Blencowe (William) & Co. Ld. Regd. 1889. Vol. liq. 8 Feb. 1926. Undertaking was acquired by W. Butler & Co. Ld. The 4% 1st mortgage debenture stock was redeemed at 105% in 1925. Capital returned to contributories—£28 0s. 9d. per ordinary share of £10 at Dec. 1926; further payments (if any) not known. Final meeting return regd. 31 Jan. 1927 .. **1927**

Blenheim Engineering Co. Ld. Regd. 1900. Vol. liq. 16 May 1901. Final meeting return regd. 18 Nov. 1918 **1903**

Bleriot Manufacturing Aircraft Co. Ld. Regd. 1915. Court Order to wind up 19 Nov. 1916. Liquidator released 17 Jan. 1920. Struck off Register 24 July 1923 .... ***1917**

Blessington & Poulaphouca Steam Tramway Co. Inc. by Order in Council 1889. Winding-up Order Feb. 1931 **1932**

Bletchley Flettons Ld. Regd. 1934. Vol. liq. (members') 6 Feb. 1951. Undertaking sold to London Brick Co. Ld. Capital returned to contributories— 7s. 11½d. per preference share of £1. £1,004 2s. 2d. was paid into Companies' Liquidation Account. Final meeting return regd. 23 Jan. 1957.................... **1957**

Blevin's Find Gold Mining Co. Ld. Regd. 1897. Removed from Register 1901 .... **1901**

Blinkpoort Syndicate Ld. Regd. 1903. Vol. liq. Dec. 1907. Final meeting return regd. 17 May 1938 .... **1908**

Bloch & Behr Ld. Regd. 1901. Vol. liq. 31 Dec. 1912. Reconstructed as company of same name. Shareholders were entitled to 1 fully-paid preference share of £1 in new company for each preference share of £1 held or 1 fully-paid ordinary share of £1 for every 4 ordinary shares of £1 held. Final meeting return regd. 23 Dec. 1914.................... **1913**

Block A Randfontein Gold Mining Co. Ld. Inc. Transvaal 1895. Vol. liq. Mar. 1907. The undertaking was acquired by Randfontein Central Gold Mining Co. Ld., in which shareholders were entitled to 1 share of £1 for every 2 shares of £1 held **1903**

Block B., Langlaate Estate Gold Mining Co. Ld. Inc. Transvaal 1889. Vol. liq. Sept. 1909. Undertaking was acquired by Langlaate Estate & Gold Mining Co. Ld., in which company shareholders were entitled to 40 ordinary shares of £1 (credited as fully-paid) for every 100 ordinary shares of £1 held or 1 ordinary share of £1 (credited as fully-paid) for every 3 preference shares of £1 held **1910**

VOL. FOR

Block Light Ld. Regd. 1906. Vol. liq. Feb. 1908. Removed from Register 1912 .... **1909**

Block 14 (Torrington). No Liability. Inc. Victoria 1911. London office closed in Feb. 1921 .... **1922**

"Block 32" Hampton Plains Estate Ld. Regd. 1896. Removed from Register 1907 .... **1901**

"Block 40" Hampton Plains Estates Ld. Regd. 1896. Vol. liq. 30 Dec. 1898. Undertaking was acquired by Hampton Properties Ld., in which company shareholders were entitled to 1 fully-paid share of £1 for each share of £1 held. Final meeting return regd. 27 Mar. 1900 .... **1899**

"Block 42" Hampton Plains Ld. Regd. 1895. Vol. liq. Oct. 1907. Removed from Register 1909 .... **1908**

"Block 45" Hampton Plains Estate Ld. Regd. 1895. Vol. liq. 30 Dec. 1898. Undertaking was acquired by Hampton Properties Ld., in which company shareholders were entitled to 1 fully-paid share of £1 for each share of £1 held. Final meeting return regd. 22 Mar. 1900 .... **1899**

"Block 50" Hampton Plains Estate Ld. Regd. 1896. Vol. liq. 29 Dec. 1898. Undertaking was acquired by Hampton Properties Ld., in which company shareholders were entitled to 1 fully-paid share of £1 for each share of £1 held. Final meeting return regd 5 Jan. 1900 .... **1899**

Bloomfield Bakery Ld. Regd. Dublin 1894; transferred to Belfast under Government of Ireland Act 1920. Vol. liq. July 1933. Preference shareholders received first distribution of £2 per share of £10 in Oct. 1933 and second distribution of £4 per share in Dec. 1933 **1934**

Blot (G. R.) & Co. Ld. Regd. 1897. Removed from Register 1901 .... **1900**

Blue Asbestos Ld. Regd. 1910. Struck off Register 5 Feb. 1915 .... **1912**

Blue Bells Gold Mines Ld. Regd. 1899. Struck off Register 1921 .... **1918**

Blue Bird Coaches (Skewen) Ld. Regd. 1931 as Thomas Williams & Co. (Skewen) Ld.; name changed Apr. 1935. Vol. liq. 10 Sept. 1940. Undertaking acquired by United Welsh Services Ld. All shares held by Red & White United Transport Ld. [later United Transport Co. Ld.] Final meeting return regd. 18 Dec. 1940.................... **1941**

Blue Bird Holdings Ld. Regd. 1928. Court Order to wind up 4 June 1929. Liquidator released 29 May 1943. Struck off Register 5 Oct. 1945 .... **1946**

Blue Bird Motor Co. (1924) Ld. Regd. 1924. Court Order to wind up 4 June 1929. Liquidator released 9 Nov. 1942. Struck off Register 16 Mar. 1945........ **1945**

Blue Bird Oil Importers Ld. Regd. 1927. Court Order to wind up 14 May 1929. Liquidator released 16 Jan. 1943. Struck off Register 1 May 1945.................... **1946**

Blue Bird Petrol (Foreign) Ld. Regd. 1928. Court Order to wind up 4 June 1929. Liquidator released 16 Jan. 1943. Struck off Register 1 May 1945.................... **1946**

Blue Bird Petrol Ld. Regd. 1928. Court Order to wind up 13 May 1929. Liquidator released 29 Nov. 1943. Struck off Register 26 July 1946 .... **1947**

Blue Cross Line Ld. Regd. 1931. Court Order to wind up Feb. 1932. Struck off Register 18 Feb. 1938........ **1939**

Blue Hill Mine. A winding-up order was made at Truro on 30 July 1891 .... **1899**

Blue Printers Ld. Regd. 1934. All capital was owned by St. Michael's Securities Ld. Vol. liq. (members') 7 May 1965. Final meeting return regd. 15 Dec. 1967 **1961**

Blue Spur & Gabriel's Gully Consolidated Gold Co. Ld. Regd. 1888. Removed from Register 1913 .... **1913**

Bluebell Proprietary Co. Ld. Regd. 1895. Vol. liq. 5 Jan. 1900. Final meeting return regd. 10 Sept. 1900..... **1900**

Blumberg & Co. Ld. Regd. 1883. Court Orders; to wind up 5 June 1886; to dissolve 29 Aug. 1896 .... **1887**

Blundell, Spence & Co. Ld. Regd. 1874. Vol. liq. 19 Mar. 1889 for reconstruction under same name. Shareholders received 1 ordinary and 1 preference share of £10 for each ordinary share of £10 held. Final meeting return regd. 15 May 1889.................... **1909**

Blunt & McCormack Films Ld. Regd. 1900. Vol. liq. (creditors') 8 June 1932. No capital returned to contributories. Final meeting return regd. 31 Mar. 1933.................... **1938**

Blunt & McCormack Ld. Regd. 1928. Vol. liq. (members') for reconstruction 6 Oct. 1930 as Blunt & McCormack Films Ld. in which company' shareholders were to receive 1 share of 5s. (credited with 2s. paid) for every 5 ordinary or deferred shares of 1s. held. Final meeting return regd. 25 Aug. 1932 **1931**

Blyderbos Syndicate (Proprietary) Ld. In liquidation. All capital was owned by Eastern Transvaal Consolidated Mines Ld. **1939**

Blyth Dry Dock Co. Ld. Regd. 1885. Vol. liq. 5 Apr. 1900. Property and goodwill were acquired by Blyth Shipbuilding Co. Ld. Removed from Register 1902 **1910**

*See Stock Exchange Year-Book.

VOL. FOR

Blyth Gas Co. Regd. as Blyth & Cowpen Gas Light Co. Ld. in 1852; inc. as Blyth & Cowpen Gas Co. by Special Act 1887: name changed 1913. Dissolved 1 May 1949. undertaking being vested in Northern Area Gas Board under Gas Act 1948. Holders of securities were entitled to receive, in respect of each £100 unit held, British Gas 3% guaranteed stock 1990–95 as follows:

	£	s.	d.	
Ord stock (5% stand.)	140	0	0	
4½% deb. stock	105	0	0	1952

Blyth Harbour & Dock Co. Undertaking was vested in 1882 in Blyth Harbour Commissioners 1941

Blyth Harbour Commissioners. Inc. by Special Act 1882. Outstanding 5½% mortgage redeemable debenture stock 1940–62 was redeemed 31 Dec. 1939 1941

Blyth Shipbuilding & Dry Docks Co. Ld. Regd. 1883 as Blyth Shipbuilding Co. Ld.; name changed. Vol. liq. 26 Nov. 1926. Final meeting return regd. 3 Sept. 1932 1927

Blythe River Iron Mines Ld. Inc. Victoria 1900. Vol. liq. June 1926 1927

Blythe & Berwick Ld. Regd. 1919. Vol. liq. 3 Apr. 1928. Omnibus and coach business acquired by West Yorkshire Road Car Co. Ld. Final meeting return regd. 10 Dec. 1929 1935

Blyton & Frodingham Light Railway Co. Inc. (under Light Railways Act 1896) 1906 1912

Boar Lane Properties. Ld. Regd. 1905 as Marsh, Jones & Cribb Ld., name changed Oct. 1923. Vol. liq. (members') 12 July 1949. Final meeting return regd. 29 Apr. 1950 1947

Boardman's Breweries Ld. Regd. 1895. Reconstructed 1896 as Boardman's United Breweries Ld. The 4½% 1st mortgage debenture stock was exchanged for a similar amount of 4½% perpetual 1st mortgage debenture stock in new company. Removed from Register 1904 1896

Boardman's United Breweries Ld. Regd. 1896. Vol. liq. (members') 2 May 1946. Capital returned to contributories—£10 10*s*. 4*d*. per preference share of £10 and 17*s*. 3⅝*d*. per ordinary share of £1. The outstanding £268,446 4½% 1st Mortgage debenture stock was repaid at par. Final meeting return regd. 24 Oct. 1947 1948

Boddy Life-Saving Appliances (1914) Ld. Regd. 1914. Vol. liq. 23 May 1923. Final meeting return regd. 2 Dec. 1925 .... *1924

Bode Rubber Estates Ld. Regd. 1910. Vol. liq. 4 May 1914. Reconstructed as Bode Rubber Estates (1914) Ld., in which company shareholders were entitled to 4 shares of 2*s*. (credited with 1*s*. 6*d*. paid) for every 3 shares of 2*s*. held. The debenture stock was exchanged for debenture stock in new company at par. Final meeting return regd. 8 Sept. 1919 1915

Bode Rubber Estates (1914) Ld. Regd. 1914. Receiver was appointed July 1930; ceased to act Aug. 1933. Assets realised insufficient to repay sums borrowed by receiver. Struck off Register Jan. 1935 1935

"Bodega" Co. Ld. Regd. 1881. Undertaking was acquired in Dec. 1928 by Slaters and Bodega Ld. (later Forte's (Holdings) Ld.) for £240,000 in ordinary shares of £1, £100,000 in 2nd preference shares of £1 and £15,000 in cash. Final meeting return regd. 31 July 1929 1928

Boden (Edwin) & Co. Ld. Regd. 1875. Removed from Register 1907 .... *1886

Bodenkreditbank A.-G. *See* Földhitelbank Reszvenytarsasag.

Bodjong Bseh Tea Co. Ld. Regd. Edinburgh 1910. Vol. liq. Feb. 1923. Final meeting return regd. 7 Apr. 1926 1924

Bodmin & Wadebridge Railway Co. Inc. 1832; reincorporated in 1865.. 1886

Bodmin Electric Light & Supply Co. Ld. Regd. 1919. Vol. liq. (members') 8 Oct. 1936. Capital returned to contributories—12*s*. 8½*d*. per share of £1. Final meeting return regd. 14 May 1937 1937

Bodmin Gas Consumers' Co. Ld. Regd. 1865. Dissolved 1 May 1949, undertaking being vested in South Western Area Gas Board under Gas Act 1948. Holders of ordinary shares (of £1) were entitled to receive £1 19*s*.6*d*. British Gas 3% guaranteed stock 1990–95 for each share held 1952

Bodmin Waterworks Co. Inc. by Special Act 1866. The undertaking vested in the North Cornwall Water Board from 1 Jan. 1961 under provisions of the Order of 6 Dec. 1960. Shareholders were entitled to receive £13 and £10 5*s*. for every ordinary or preference share of £10 held respectively 1911

Boekit Boendar Rubber Co. Ld. Regd. 1916 as Tamiang Planting Syndicate Ld; name changed 1919. Vol. liq. 2 Mar. 1921. Undertaking and assets were acquired by Tamiang Rubber Estate 1*d*., in which company shareholders were entitled to 1 fully-paid share of £1 for every 2 shares of £1 held. Debenture holders were entitled to an equal amount of convertible debenture stock in new company. Final meeting return regd. 16 Nov. 1921 1921

Bogabagh Tea Co. Ld. Regd. 1927. Vol. liq. (members') 24 Feb. 1936 for reconstruction under same name. 7% debenture holders were satisfied by allotment of 4 fully-paid preference shares of £1 and 4 fully-paid ordinary shares of £1 in new company for each £8 debenture held. Shareholders received 1 fully-paid ordinary share of the new company for every 8 shares of £1 held. Final meeting return regd. 4 June 1937 1937

Bogahagh Tea Co. Ld. Regd. 1936 in reconstruction of company of same name. Vol. liq. (members') 23 July 1947, the undertaking and assets having been acquired by Grob Tea Co. Ld. (inc. in India). Ordinary shareholders were entitled to receive ·6316 of an "A" ordinary share (of Rs. 10) and ·2491 of a "B" ordinary share (of Rs. 5) in Grob Tea Co. Ld. for each share (of £1) held. Final meeting return regd. 21 Nov. 1949 1951

Bognor & District Gas & Electricity Co. Regd. as limited 1865; reinc. as Bognor Gas Light & Coke Co. by Special Act 1908. name changed to Bognor Gas & Electricity Co. in 1927 and as above in 1940. The electricity undertaking was vested on 1 Apr. 1948 in British (later Central) Electricity Authority and Southern Area Electricity Board. Dissolved 1 May 1949, the remaining undertaking being vested in Southern Area Gas Board under Gas Act 1948. Holders of securities were entitled to receive, in respect of each £100 unit held, British Gas 3% guaranteed stock 1990—95 as follows:

	£	s.	d.	
Cons. ord stock A (5% stand.)	171	0	0	
Orig. ord. cons. stock B (5% stand.)	194	10	0	
New cons. stock (7% max.)	160	10	0	
4½% pref. stock	110	0	0	
4½% perp. deb. stock	114	0	0	
5½% red. deb. stock	105	10	0	
4½% red. deb. stock (1954)	106	0	0	
4½% red. deb. stock (1949)	102	10	0	1952

Bognor Water Co. Inc. by Special Act 1891. Under Act of 1928, Bognor Urban District Council acquired undertaking from 1 Apr. 1929. Shareholders were entitled to 5% Bognor Corporation stock as follows: for each ordinary (10% maximum) share of £10—£20; for each ordinary (7% maximum) share of £10—£14; for each 5½% preference share of £10—£11; for each 5% preference share of £10—£10. £8,850 in cash was to be distributed among ordinary shareholders for arrears of dividends. Debenture stockholders had option of having their debenture stock (*a*) taken over by Council as debenture stock, (*b*) converted into Corporation stock at 80% for the 4% stock and 110% for the 5½% stock, or (*c*) repaid in cash at 80% and 110% respectively 1929

Bogosu Gold Mines Ld. Regd. 1903. Struck off Register 7 Dec. 1937 1938

Bogota Telephone Co. Ld. Regd. 1900. Struck off Register 23 Oct. 1942 1943

Bohemian Breweries Ld. Regd. 1889. Vol. liq. June 1907. Assets realised insufficient to meet claims of secured creditors. Removed from Register 1907................ 1908

Bohemian Mining Corporation Ld. Regd. 1906. Receiver for debenture holders was appointed Sept. 1908. Removed from Register 1911 1910

Bohmische Kommerzialbank. Inc. Prague 1920. Absorbed by Prague Credit Bank in Apr. 1930. Shareholders received 1 share of kc. 400 for every 10 shares of kc. 200 held 1931

Böhnsdalen Mills Ld. Regd. 1900. Removed from Register 1911 1911

Böhnsdalen Wood Pulp & Paper Mills Ld. Regd. 1889. Removed from Register 1903 1900

Boiler Insurance & Steam Power Co. Ld. Regd. 1865. Reconstructed 1880 as company of same name. Removed from Register 1902 1897

Boiler Insurance and Steam Power Co. Ld. Regd. 1880. Reconstructed 1896 as Vulcan Boiler & General Insurance Co. Ld. Removed from Register 1905 .. 1897

Boinsu Rubber Co. Ld. Regd. 1910. Court Order to wind up Oct. 1913. Struck off Register 1914 1914

Bokitsi Goldfields Ld. Regd. 1900. Removed from Register 1910 1905

Bokitsi (West Africa) Syndicate Ld. Regd. 1899. Vol. liq. 1 Dec. 1909. Final meeting return regd. 14 Mar. 1910 .... *1908

**See Stock Exchange Year-Book.*

VOL. FOR

Boksburg Gold Mines Ld. *See* New Boksburg Gold Mines Ld.

Bolckow Vaughan & Co. Ld. Regd. 1864. Vol. liq. Nov. 1929. Amalgamated with Dorman Long & Co. Ld., in which company shareholders were entitled to 11 preferred ordinary and 46 ordinary shares of £1 for every 100 ordinary shares of £1 held or 155 preference shares of £1 for every 10 preference shares of £20 held. Holders of debentures received 5½% debenture stock in Dorman Long & Co. Ld. as follows: for every £100 8% debentures held—£106; for every £100 7% debentures held—£104; for every £100 6% debentures held—£91 10*s*. £30 4*d*. 3*d*. was paid into Companies' Liquidation Account. Final meeting return regd. 17 May 1935 .... **1930**

Bolitho, Williams, Foster, Coode, Grylis & Co. Ld. Regd. 1889 as Bolitho, Foster, Coode & Co. Ld. Vol. liq. 21 Aug. 1905. Business was acquired by Barclay & Co. Ld. (later Barclays Bank Ld.), in which company shareholders were entitled to 6 shares of £20 (credited with £8 paid) for every 5 shares of £50 (£10 paid) held *plus* 12*s*. per share in cash. Final meeting return regd. 15 Nov. 1915 .... **1941**

Bolivar Concessions Ld. Regd. 1913. Vol. liq. 15 Nov. 1917. Final meeting return regd. 28 June 1919 ..... ***1916**

Bolivar Concessions (1917) Ld. Regd. 1917. Vol. liq. 10 Mar. 1920. Shareholders received 4 preferred shares of $5 in British Controlled Oilfields Ld., for each share of £1 held. Final meeting return regd. 12 Apr. 1923 .... **1921**

Bolivar Railway Co. Ld. Regd. 1872. Vol. liq. 28 June 1883. Amalgamated with New Quebrada Co. Ld., to form Quebrada Railway Land and Copper Co. Ld., the railway of the latter company was acquired by Bolivar Railway Co. Ld., in 1896. Shareholders were entitled to 5 fully-paid shares of £10 in Quebrada Railway Land and Copper Co. Ld., for every 4 shares of £10 held. Debenture holders were entitled to an equal amount of debentures in new company. Final meeting return regd. 13 Feb. 1892 .... **1884**

Bolivar Railway Co. Ld. Regd. 1896. Vol. liq. (members') 11 Oct. 1951. Capital returned to contributories on following basis:

5% prior lien deb. stock	120%
5% A and 2% B deb. stocks	100%
6% C deb. stocks	87·44%
preference stocks	5%
ordinary stocks	2½%
Non-interest bearing funding certs.	10%

Final meeting return regd. 4 Aug. 1953 .... **1954**

Bolivar Venezuela Gold Mines Ld. Regd. 1927. Vol. liq. June 1930. Undertaking and assets were acquired by New Goldfields of Venezuela Ld., in which company shareholders were entitled to 1 share of 5*s*. (credited as fully paid) for each share of £1 held **1934**

Bolivia Concessions Ld. Regd. 1926. Court Order to wind up 1931. Struck off Register 1944 .... **1945**

Bolivia Trading Corporation Ld. Regd. 1928. Struck off Register 19 June 1936 .... **1937**

Bolivian General Enterprise Ld. Regd. 1903 as Bolivian Rubber & General Enterprise Ld.; name changed Dec. 1915. Vol. liq. (members') 3 Mar. 1953. Capital returned to contributories—1*s*. 4.64*d*. per share (of 2*s*.). £806 was paid into Companies' Liquidation Account. Final meeting return regd. 7 Mar. 1966 **1967**

Bolivian Silver Co. Ld. Regd. 1888. Removed from Register 1903 .... ***1893**

Bolnore Trust Ld. Regd. 1920. Vol. liq. 10 June 1947. Final meeting return regd. 13 Dec. 1948 .... **1949**

Bolsom Bros. (1928) Ld. Regd. 1928. Court Order to wind up 22 Jan. 1940. No capital returned to contributories. Liquidator released 6 Nov. 1951. Struck off Register 11 May 1954 .... **1952**

Bolsover & District Water Co. Ld. Regd. 1903. Vol. liq. 15 Aug. 1923. Final meeting return regd. 17 Apr. 1924 .... **1924**

Bolsover Billposting Co. Ld. Regd. 1920. Vol. liq. (members') 18 July 1933. Capital returned to contributories—£3,815 12*s*. Final meeting return regd. 18 Oct. 1933 .... **1934**

Bolsover Colliery Co. Ld. Regd. 1890. The Collieries &c. vested in National Coal Board as from 1 Jan. 1947. Vol. liq. (members') 3 Apr. 1952. Capital returned to contributories, per 1*s*. stock—1st preference, 5*s*.; 2nd preference. 7*s*. 6*d*.; ordinary, £3 9*s*. 9·2*d*. Final meeting return regd. 25 May 1956 .... **1957**

Bolsover Gas Light & Coke Co. Ld. Regd. 1859. Dissolved 1 May 1949, undertaking being vested in East Midland Area Gas Board under Gas Act 1948. Holders of securities were entitled to receive, in respect of each £5 unit held, British Gas 3% guaranteed stock 1990–95 as follows:

VOL. FOR

	£	s.	d.	
Orig. ord shares (10% stand.)	4	5	0	
Addit. ord. shares (7% stand.)	3	0	0	**1952**

Bolton Cotton Trade Mutual Fire Insurance Co. Ld. Regd. 1876. Vol. liq. (members') 10 Aug. 1931. Return of deposit of £1 per share paid 24 Aug. 1931. Final meeting return regd. 4 Aug.1932 .... **1932**

Bolton Employers' Mutual Insurance Co. Ld. Regd. 1898. Vol. liq. (members') 10 July 1930. Final meeting return regd. 12 Mar. 1932 .... **1931**

Bolton Insurance Co. Ld. Regd. 1922. All shares owned by Lancashire & General Assurance Co. Ld. Struck off Register 1929 .... **1927**

Bolton Textile Mill Co. Ld. (The). Regd. 1893 as Bolton Textile Mill Co. Ld.; name changed to Bolton Textile (Holdings) Ld. 11 Mar. 1953 and as above 4 May 1956. Vol. liq. (members') 14 Nov. 1957. Undertaking and assets were acquired by Bolton Textile Mill Co. Ld., in which company stockholders were entitled to receive 1 fully-paid share of 5*s*. plus 3*s*. 3*d*. cash for each 10*s*. stock held. £874 12*s*. 6*d*. was paid into Companies' Liquidation Account in respect of unclaimed distributions. Final meeting return regd. 2 Apr. 1959 .... **1960**

Bolton Textile (Holdings) Ld. *See above*.

Bolton Theatre & Entertainments Co. Ld. Regd. 1889. Vol. liq. (members') 27 Feb. 1963. Capital returned to contributories—£2 2*s*. 3¾*d*. per share of £1. Paid into Companies' Liquidation Account—£38 16*s*. 10*d*. in respect of unclaimed dividends and £74 1*s*. in respect of unclaimed distributions. Final meeting return regd. 11 Dec. 1963 .... **1964**

Bolton's Mutual Films Ld. *See* Wardour Films Ld.

Bolus (W.) & Co. Ld. Regd. 1904. Vol. liq. 16 Feb. 1921. Final meeting return regd. 4 Apr. 1928 .... **1922**

Boma (Nigeria) Tin Co. Ld. Regd. 1912. Vol. liq. 1 Oct. 1913. Final meeting return regd. 5 Jan. 1917 .... **1914**

Bombay, Baroda & Central India Railway Co. Inc. by special Act 1855; reconstituted by Special Act 1906. The working of the undertaking was taken over by the Governor-General of India in Council as from 1 Jan. 1942, and by Act of 1942 the directors were appointed to wind up the company. Capital returned to contributories—£117 15*s*. per £100 capital stock. The affairs of the company were declared to be wound up on 25 Sept. 1947 .... **1948**

Bombay Electric Supply & Tramways Co. Ld. Regd. 1905. Vol. liq. Sept. 1920. Reconstructed as company of same name. Shareholders were entitled to 5 ordinary shares of Rs.50 (credited as fully-paid) for each ordinary share of £10 held and 3 fully-paid preference shares of Rs. 50 for each preference share of £10 held. The debenture stock and debentures were redeemable at 105% and 101% respectively on 1 Nov. 1920. Final meeting return regd. 9 May 1922 **1921**

Bombay Electric Supply & Tramways Co. Ld. Inc. in India 1920. Vol. liq. 15 Dec. 1947. Undertaking acquired by Municipality. Capital returned to contributories—per share of Rs. 50—ordinary. RS.142·7; preference Rs.50. Rs4606,00 paid into Companies Liquidation Account. Final meeting return regd. 15 Apr. 1959 .... **1960**

Bombay Fire & Marine Insurance Co. Ld. Inc. India 1896. London office closed. Business was acquired by General Accident Assurance Corporation [later General Accident Fire & Life Assurance Corporation Ld.] **1905**

Bombay Tea Co. Ld. Regd. 1898. Removed from Register 1905 .... **1905**

Bombay Telephone Co. Ld. A substantial interest was acquired by the Government of India **1941**

Bon-Accord Distillery Co. Ld. Regd. Edinburgh 1876. Vol. liq. 22 July 1896. Final meeting return regd. 12 Oct. 1898 .... **1897**

Bon-Accord Gold Mining Co. Ld. Regd. 1895. Reconstructed 1898 as Beechworth Goldfields Ld., in which company shareholders were entitled to 1 share of £1 (credited with 17*s*. paid) for each share of £1 held. Removed from Register 1906 .... **1898**

Bon-Accord Hotel Co. Ld. Regd. Edinburgh 1902. Vol. liq. Jan. 1909. Final meeting return regd. 27 July 1911 .... **1909**

Bon-Accord Steam Fishing Co. Ld. Regd. Edinburgh 1901. Vol. liq. (members') 22 May 1939. Capital returned to contributories—£1 10*s*. 8½*d*. per share of £1. Final meeting return regd. 4 Dec. 1939 .... **1940**

Bon-Accord Steam Laundry Co. Ld. Regd. Edinburgh 1884. Vol. liq. (members') 12 Apr. 1945. Undertaking and assets were acquired by Scottish Cooperative Wholesale Society Ld. Capital returned to contributories—£6 16*s*. 2⅔*d*. per share of £1 10*s*. (15*s*. paid). Final meeting return regd. 17 Oct. 1947 .... **1948**

Bon Marché (Brixton) Ld. *See* Bon Marché Ld.

Bon Marché, Ld. Regd. 1892 as Bon Marché (Brixton) Ld.; name changed Jan. 1894. Vol. liq. (members')

**See Stock Exchange Year-Book.*

VOL. FOR

17 Sept. 1947. The land and buildings were acquired by Suburban & Provincial Stores Ld., which company owned all ordinary capital, and the other trading assets were transferred to Cole Brothers Ld. Holders of the 90,586 8% preference shares of £1 not held by Suburban & Provincial Stores Ld. were offered exchange into 3½% 1st mortgage debenture stock of that company at approx. 33*s*. 2*d*. stock per share held: holders of preference shares who did not ex change their holdings were repaid at 32*s*. 6*d*. per share. The outstanding £90,672 4½% 1st mortgage debenture stock was repaid at 112% on 31 Oct. 1947; £9,328 stock was converted into 3½% 1st mortgage debenture stock of the Suburban company at approx. £114 for every £100 held. £1,055 was paid into Companies' liquidation Account. Final meeting return regd. 14 Sept. 1953 1954

Bonanza Gold Mines Ld. Regd. 1893. Removed from Register 1906 1896

Bonanza Ld. Inc. Transvaal 1894. Vol. liq. May 1907. Shareholders received 7*s*. 4*d*. per share of £1 at Aug. 1908; further payments (if any) not known 1909

Bonaventure Association Ld. Regd. 1896. Vol. liq. 10 Mar. 1898. Undertaking was acquired by Firm Syndicate Ld. (later Central Mono-motapa Ld.) for £14,521 fully-paid shares of £1. Final meeting return regd. 2 May 1898 1899

Bonaventure Mines Trust Ld. Regd. 1898 as Irish Proprietary Oilfields of Gaspe Canada Ld.; name changed to Oilfields of Gaspe Canada Ld. in 1900, to Oilfields of Bonaventure Ld. in 1912 and as above in Apr. 1924. Vol. liq. (creditors') 28 Dec. 1934. No capital returned to contributories. Final meeting return regd.13 Jan.1937 1935

Bonbright (William P.) & Co. Regd. 1933. Vol. liq. (members') 27 July 1938. Capital returned to contributories—£57,933 6*s*. 11*d*. to preference shareholders and £37,957 12*s*. 8*d*. to ordinary shareholders. Final meeting return regd. 2 Oct. 1942 1939

Bond & Share Investment Trust Ld. Regd. 1914. Vol. liq. 12 Oct. 1922. Final meeting return regd. 16 Oct. 1923 1923

Bond's (Bristol) Brewery Ld. Regd. 1890, Removed from Register 1905 1904

Bond Street Fabrics Ld. Regd. as private company on 25 July 1957; converted into public company 11 Mar. 1965 then re-regd. as private company under Companies Act 1980. Voluntary winding-up 28 sept. 1984 1983–4

Bond Worth Holdings Ld. *See* Worth (Bond) Hldgs Ld.

Bonecourt Surface Combustion Ld. Regd. 1912. Vol. liq. 20 May 1919. Final meeting return regd. 31 Mar. 1920 1919

Bonecourt Waste Heat Boiler Co. Ld. Regd. 1914. Vol. liq. 6 June 1928. Patent rights acquired by Spencer-Bonecourt Ld. (later Spencer-Bone court-Clarkson Ld.). Final meeting return regd. 30 July 1928 1940

Bo'ness Gas Light Co. Ld. Regd. in Edinburgh 1896. Dissolved 1 May 1949, undertaking being vested in Scottish Area Gas Board under Gas Act 1948. Holders of ordinary shares (of £5) were entitled to receive £15 British Gas 3% guaranteed stock 1990–95 for each share held 1952

Bongwelli (Nigeria) Tin Syndicate Ld. Regd. 1913. Vol. liq. 25 July 1924. Final meeting return regd. 17 Oct. 1925 1925

Bonmahon Copper Mines Development Syndicate Ld. Regd. 1905. Court Order to wind up Aug. 1907. Removed from Register 1913 1908

Bonnaud Waterproof, Textiles and Papers Ld. Regd. 1904 as Bonnaud Paper Co. Ld.; name changed 1905. Vol. liq. 29 Oct. 1906. Undertaking and assets were acquired by Vevril-Bonnaud Ld. Removed from Register 1907 1907

Bonnick & Co. Ld. Regd. 1890. Vol. liq. 20 July 1896. Business acquired by Riley Cycle Co. Ld. (later Riley (Motors) Ld.). Struck off Register 21 June 1907 1938

Bonnie Dundee Gold Mines Ld. Regd. 1892. Reconstructed 1899 as company of same name. Shareholders were entitled to 1 share of £1 (credited with 14*s*. paid) in new company for each ordinary share of £1 held. The preference shares were redeemed at par *plus* accrued dividend. Removed from Register 1907 1904

Bonnie Dundee Gold Mines Ld. Queensland 1899. Vol. liq. 2 Nov. 1905. Undertaking sold to company of same name. Shareholders were entitled to 1 share of £1 (credited with 15*s*. paid) in new company for each share of £1 held 1908

Bonnie Dundee Gold Mines Ld. Inc. Queensland 1906. Vol. liq. for reconstruction under same name. Shareholders were entitled to 1 share of 6*s*. (credited with 1*s*. paid) in new company for each share of £1 held 1914

VOL. FOR

Bonnie Dundee Gold Mines Ld. Inc. Queensland 1913. London office was closed 30 June 1915 1916

Bonnie Dundee Gold Mining Co. Ld. Regd. 1886. Vol. liq. 13 Dec. 1892. Reconstructed at Bonnie Dundee Gold Mines Ld., in which company shareholders were entitled to 1 ordinary share of £1 (credited with 16*s*. paid) for each ordinary share of £1 held or 1 fullypaid preference share of £1 for each preference share of £1 held. Final meeting return regd. 8 Aug.1893 1899

Bonoproof Ld. Regd. 1903. Vol. liq. 14 July 1905. Removed from Register 1907 1906

Bonsor Gold Mining Co. Ld. Regd. 1897. Vol. liq. Feb. 1910. The assets were acquired by Willoughby's Consolidated Co. Ld., in discharge of a debt. Removed from Register 1910 1911

Bonta Syndicate (West Africa) Ld. Regd. 1901. Vol. liq. Mar. 1908. Removed from Register 1909 1909

Bonvalet Co. Ld. Regd. May 1894. Court Order to wind up 15 Aug. 1894. Struck off Register 1931 1896

Bonville's Court Coal & Iron Co. Ld. Regd. 1873. Vol. liq. 16 Dec. 1875. Final meeting return regd. 4 July 1877 .... *1878

Bookless Brothers Steam Trawling & Fishing Co. Ld. Regd. 1906. Vol. liq. 20 Nov. 1912. Final meeting return regd. 29 Nov. 1913 .... *1912

Boot (Sir Jesse) Property & Investment Co., Ld. Regd. 1920. Struck off Register 27 Apr. 1951. 1935

Boothmans Ld. Regd. 1890. Removed from Register 1901 .... *1894

Booth's United Gold Mines Ld. Regd. 1898. Struck off Register 16 Nov. 1906 1907

Booysen Land & Mining Co. Ld. Regd. 1888. Vol. liq. 27 June 1894. Undertaking was acquired by Consolidated Gold Fields of South Africa Ld. (later Consolidated Gold Fields Ld.) in which company shareholders were entitled to 1 fully-paid share of £1 for every 2 shares of £1 (12*s*. paid) held. Final meeting return regd. 19 Jan. 1897 1895

Borax Co. Ld. Regd. 1887. Vol. liq. Apr. 1913. Shareholders were entitled to shares in Borax Consolidated Ld. [later Borax (Holdings) Ld.] *plus* 4·105*d*. per share in cash. Removed from Register 1913 1914

Borax Properties Ld. Regd. Feb. 1908. Removed from Register 1912 1911

Bordeaux Tramways & Omnibus Co. Ld. Regd. 1880. Undertaking was acquired in 1898 by Compagnie Francaise des Tramways Electriques et Omnibus de Bordeaux S. A. Removed from Register 1902 1941

Bordon & District Gas Co. Regd. 1910 as East Hants Gas Co. Ld. Inc. by Special Act 1912. Undertaking was acquired by Farnham Gas & Electricity Co. Capital returned to contributories—5*s*. per share of £1. Liability for debentures was assumed by acquiring company 1936

Borjam Tea Co., Ld. Regd. 1895. Vol. liq. 1 July 1963. Preference shares repaid at par on 22 July 1963. Capital returned to contributories—30*s*. 7·1*d*. per ordinary share of £1. Final meeting return regd. 11 Sept. 1967 1968

Borjuli Tea Co. Ld. Regd. 1894. Vol. liq. 12 Oct. 1896. Final meeting return regd. 20 Dec. 1897 1897

Borneo Minerals Co. Ld. Regd. 1893. Vol. liq. 30 Dec. 1899. Removed from Register 1902 1899

Borneo Proprietary Estates Ld. Regd. 1888 as Tobacco Co. of British North Borneo Ld.; name changed Apr. 1910. Vol. liq. 9 Nov. 1914. Struck off Register 24 July 1923 1915

Borneo Rubber & Trading Co. Ld. Regd. 1906. Removed from Register 1913 1912

Borneo Rubber Estates Ld. Regd. 1925. Vol. liq. (members') 9 Dec. 1929; undertaking and assets were acquired by Batoe Doelang Rubber Estates Ld., in which company shareholders were to receive 1 fully-paid share of 2*s*. for every 4 shares of 2*s*. held. Final meeting return regd. 26 June 1930 1930

Boro Tin Mines Ld. Regd. 1923. Court Order to wind up 10 Mar. 1930. Struck off Register 16 Aug. 1938 1939

Boroid Ld. Regd. 1910. Receiver was appointed in 1915. Vol. liq. Nov. 1923. Struck off Register 1 Feb. 1944 1944

Borough Bakeries (Burnley) Ld. Vol. liq. 25 May 1921. Final meeting return regd. 1 Dec. 1921 .... *1922

Borough of Portsmouth (Kingston, Fratton & Southsea) Tramways Co. Inc. by Special Act 1883. Undertaking was sold to Provincial Tramways Co. Ld., on 28 June 1892 1893

Borrowdale Plumbago Mines & Manufacturing Co. Ld. Regd. 1887. Vol. liq. 16 June 1891. Final meeting return regd. 16 Sept. 1892 1892

Borth & Ynyslas Electric Supply Co. Ld. Regd. 1932. Dissolved 1 Apr. 1948, undertaking being vested in the British (later Central) Electricity Authority and Merseyside & North Wales Area Board under the

*See Stock Exchange Year-Book.

VOL. FOR

Electricity Act 1947. Holders of ordinary shares and 5% debentures were entitled to receive British Electricity 3% guaranteed stock 1968–73, as follows: £1 1s. stock for each £1 ordinary capital held and £50 stock for each £50 debenture capital held **1949**

Borth Valley Gold Mining Co. Ld. Regd. 1905. Vol. liq. Apr. 1908. Removed from Register 1909 .... **1909**

Bosanska Banka d.d. (of Belgrade). Absorbed in July 1928 by Jugoslavenska Udruzena Banka d.d......... **1929**

Boschfontein Gold Mines Ld. Regd. 1917. Struck off Register 16 Oct. 1936 **1937**

Boson Oil Co. Ld. Regd. Edinburgh 1884. Vol. liq. Sept. 1888. Shares in Fréjus Oil Co. Ld. were allotted to shareholders. Final meeting return regd. 25 Feb. 1890 .... **1889**

Bostock & Co. Ld. Regd. 1896. Removed from Register 1908 .... **1902**

Bostock (Edwin) & Co. Ld. Regd. 1898. Vol. liq. 3 July 1919. Undertaking was acquired by Lotus Ld., in which company shareholders were entitled to 10 preference shares of £1 (credited as fully-paid) for each preference share of £10 held, or 57 ordinary shares of £1 for each ordinary share of £10 held or 53 ordinary shares of £1 for each deferred share of £10 held. Final meeting return regd. 20 Nov. 1920 .... **1920**

Bostock (Frederick) Ld. Regd. 1912. Vol. liq. 2 July 1919. Undertaking was acquired by Lotus Ld., in which company shareholders were entitled to 1 preference share of £1 for each preference share of £1 held, or 252 ordinary shares of £1 for every 100 ordinary shares of £1 held. Final meeting return regd. 20 Nov. 1920 .... **1920**

Boston & Albany Railroad Co. Line was leased in 1900 to New York Central and Hudson River Railroad Co. for 99 years... **1908**

Boston & Maine Railroad. Established 1835. Organised Massachusetts, New Hampshire and Maine. The 6% sterling certificates (Eastern Railroad Co. of Massachusetts) fell due for redemption on 1 Sept. 1906 .... **1906**

Boston Consolidated Copper & Gold Mining Co. Ld. Regd. 1898. Vol. liq. 23 Feb. 1910. The assets were sold to Utah Copper Co., in which company shareholders were entitled to 0·395 share of $10 for each share of £1 held. Final meeting return regd. 17 Feb. 1911. Court Order declared dissolution void. Final meeting return regd. 28 Feb. 1912 .... **1910**

Boston Gas Light & Coke Co. Inc. by Special Act 1825. Dissolved 1 May 1949, undertaking being vested in East Midland Area Gas Board under Gas Act 1949. Holders of securities were entitled to receive British Gas 3% guaranteed stock 1990–95 as follows in respect of each £10 unit, unless otherwise stated, of security held:

	£	s.	d.
Ord. shares (8½% stand.).....................	22	5	0
New ord. shares 7% stand.).................	18	15	0
4% perp. deb. stock (per £100).............	101	0	0

1952

Boston (Henry) & Sons Ld. Regd. 1915. Vol. liq. 27 Aug. 1926. Final meeting return regd. 3 Sept. 1930....... **1927**

Boston Spa Gas Co. Regd. 1865. Inc. by Special Act 1907 .... **1909**

Boston Tanneries Ld. Regd. 1921. Struck off Register 27 June 1950.... **1947**

Boston Waterworks Co. Inc. by Special Act 1846. Under Boston Corporation Act 1930 undertaking was acquired by that Corporation for £70,000 in cash *plus* compensation to directors. **1931**

Bosun Mines Ld. Regd. 1899. Vol. liq. 26 Mar. 1906. Undertaking was acquired by Monitor and Ajax Fraction Ld., for 26,000 ordinary shares of £1 and 6,600 deferred shares of 1s., all fully-paid. Final meeting return regd. 19 June 1925 .... **1906**

Botallack Ld. Regd. 1911. Vol. liq. 27 Aug. 1914. Final meeting return regd. 17 Feb. 1915 .... **1915**

Botallack Mines Ld. Regd. 1906. Vol. liq. 23 Jan. 1911. Reconstructed as Botallack Ld. in which company shareholders were entitled to 1 share of £1 (credited with 5s. paid) for every 2 ordinary shares of £1 held or 1 fully-paid share of £1 for every 4 "A" shares of 5s. held. Noteholders were entitled to an equal nominal amount of fully-paid shares. Final meeting return regd. 17 June 1912 .... **1911**

Botanic Gardens Picture House Ld. Regd. Edinburgh 1922. Court Orders: to wind up 19 June 1929; to dissolve 21 July 1933 .... **1930**

Botha's Reef Gold Mining Co. Ld. Regd. 1888. Undertaking acquired in 1893 by George and May Gold Mining Co. Ld., in which company shareholders were entitled to 1 share of £1 for every 4 shares held **1895**

Bothwell & Uddingston Gas Co. Ld. Regd. Edinburgh 1858; inc. by Special Act 1902. Vol. liq. May 1922. Undertaking purchased by Lanarkshire County Council 30 Apr. for 1921 £210,000, under the

VOL. FOR

Council's Order Confirmation Act of 1922. Both 10% and 7% shares received £5 15s. 2¾d. per share of £1 and the £10,000 5% perpetual debentures were paid off. Final meeting return regd. 18 Dec. 1922 **1923**

Boti-Offin Gold & Trading Co. Ld. Regd. 1900. Vol. liq. 29 July 1912. Final meeting return regd. 26 Mar. 1919 .... **1913**

Botolph & Nicholson's Wharves Co. Ld. Regd. 1889. Vol. liq. 20 Dec. 1895. Reconstructed as Nicholson's Wharves Ld. Final meeting return regd. 7 July 1896 **1896**

Botolph Mining & Exploring Co. Ld. Regd. 1895. Vol. liq. 26 Mar. 1912. Final meeting return regd. 16 June 1916 .... **1913**

Bottle Seal Co. Ld. Regd. 1890, Removed from Register 1902............ **1902**

Bottomley (J. R.) & Co. Ld. Regd. 1897. Business was acquired in 1898 by Bentley's Yorkshire Breweries Ld. Vol. liq. 18 Nov. 1898. Final meeting return regd. 18 Feb. 1899 .... **1899**

Boudard Peveril Gear Co. Ld. Regd. 1894. Struck off Register 23 July 1901 .... **1902**

Bouillon Fleet Ld. Regd. 1889. Assets realised insufficient to pay debenture holders. Removed from Register 1903 .... **1904**

Boulder Bonanza Gold Mining Co. Ld. Regd. 1897. Undertaking was acquired by Boulder Deep Levels Ld., in which company shareholders were entitled to 1 share of £1 (credited with 17s. paid) for every 2 shares of £1 held. Removed from Register 1904 ... **1904**

Boulder Consolidated Investment Corporation Ld. Regd. 1899. Vol. liq. 13 June 1902. Final meeting return regd. 20 Aug. 1902 .... **1903**

Boulder Deep Levels Ld. Regd. 1903. Vol. liq. 17 Sept. 1906 for reconstruction as Boulder Deep Levels (1907) Ld., in which company shareholders were entitled to 1 share of £1 (credited with 17s. paid) for each share of £1 held. Removed from Register 1908 **1907**

Boulder Deep Levels (1907) Ld. Regd. 1907. Vol. liq. Oct. 1909 for reconstruction as Hannan's Star Consolidated Ld., in which company shareholders were entitled to 1 share of 4s. (credited with 1s. paid) for each share of £1 held. Removed from Register 1910 .... **1910**

Boulder Golden Eagle Mines Ld. Regd. 1905. Removed from Register 1910 .... **1908**

Boulder Half-Mile South Gold Mining Co. No Liability. Inc South Australia 1901. In liquidation in 1903 .. **1903**

Boulder Junction Mines Ld. Regd. 1898. Removed from Register 1901............ **1901**

Boulder Perseverance Ld. Regd. 1923. Vol. liq. (members') 10 May 1955. All shares owned by Gold Mines of Kalgoorlie (Aust.) Ld. Struck off Register 8 Feb. 1963 .... **1959**

Boult (Leonard) & Co. Ld. Regd. 1879, Vol. liq. 8 Mar. 1893. Final meeting return regd. 14 Aug. 1900 ..... **1895**

Boulton Bros. & Co. London Ld. Regd. 1921. Vol. liq. 1924. No capital was returned to contributories. Final meeting return regd. 15 Nov. 1945 .... **1946**

Bourne & Grant Electricity Supply Co. Ld. See Chiswick Electricity Supply Corporation Ld.

Bourne End and District Electricity Corporation Ld. See Cookham & District Electricity Corporation Ld.

Bourne Hall Ld. Regd. 1890. Vol. liq. 25 Mar. 1895. Final meeting return regd. 26 Mar. 1898 .... **1896**

Bourne Valley Light Railway Co. Inc. (under Light Railways Act 1896) 1900 .... **1905**

Bournemouth Airport Ld. Regd. 14 Feb. 1935. Vol. liq. (members') 15 July 1955. Final meeting return regd. 27 Oct. 1956 .... **1939**

Bournemouth & Poole Electricity Supply Co. Ld. Regd. 1897. Dissolved 1 Apr. 1948. undertaking being vested in British (later Central) Electricity Authority and Southern Area Board under Electricity Act 1947. Holders of securities were entitled to receive British Electricity 3% guaranteed stock (1968–73) as follows in respect of each £1 unit of capital held:

	£	s.	d.
4½% preference shares...........................	1	6	0
6% 2nd preference shares.....................	1	16	9
Ordinary stock.....................................	3	6	8
3½% redeemable debenture stock...........	1	0	5¾

1949

Bournemouth & Southampton Stadiums Ld. Regd. 1932 Vol. liq. (members') 24 Aug. 1937. Undertaking acquired by Southern Sporting Promotions Ld. Capital returned to contributories—8·27d. per share of 1s. Final meeting return regd. 23 Sept 1938 .... **1938**

Bournemouth, Exeter & Plymouth Bioscope Theatre Ld. Regd. 1910. Court Order to wind up 21 May 1911. Liquidator released 29 Mar. 1913. Struck off Register 10 Oct. 1916 .... ***1912**

Bournemouth Hydropathic Establishment Ld. Regd. 1905. Winding-up Order 6 Oct. 1952. Struck off the Register 20 May 1958 .... **1939**

See Stock Exchange Year-Book.

VOL. FOR

Bournemouth Imperial & Grand Hotels, Ld. Regd. 1898. The Grand Hotel was sold in 1962, the remaining assets and liabilities were transferred to a new company, Bournemouth Imperial Hotel Ld. Vol. liq. (members') 30 June 1962. 5% cumulative preference, 6% B non-cumulative preference, 6% B non-cumulative preference and ordinary shares of £1 were repaid at par. Former holders of 5% preference and ordinary shares were also entitled to receive A and B ordinary shares (of 5*s.*) of the new company as follows: 9 A ordinary for every 8 5% preference, and 3 A ordinary and 5 B ordinary for every 2 ordinary held. £102 13*s.* 10*d.* was paid into Companies' Liquidation Account. Final meeting return regd. 2 Feb. 1965 **1965**

Bournemouth, Swanage & Poole Steam Packet Co. Ld. Regd. 1881. Removed from Register 1905 ***1896**

Bourton-on-the-Water Gas Co. Regd. 1940. Dissolved 1 May 1949, undertaking being vested in South Western Area Gas Board under Gas Act 1948. Holders of ordinary shares (of £1) were entitled to receive £2 British Gas 3% guaranteed stock 1990–95 for each share held **1952**

Bousfield (J. R.) & Co. Ld. Regd. 1899. Vol. liq. 30 Jan. 1923. Final meeting return regd. 30 Aug. 1926 **1924**

Bouvet Whaling Co. Ld. *See* Viking Investment Trust Ld.

Bovril Ld. Regd. 1889. Vol. liq. 21 May 1896. Undertaking and assets were acquired by company of same name for £2,500,000 in cash. Final meeting return regd. 24 Mar. 1898 **1897**

Bow, McLachlan & Co. Ld. Regd. Edinburgh 1900. Vol. liq. Jan. 1920. Final meeting return regd. 5 Sept. 1924 **1919**

Bow, McLachlan & Co. Ld. Regd. Edinburgh 1920. Vol. liq. (creditors') 26 Apr. 1932. No capital returned to contributories. Final meeting return regd. 15 Dec. 1936 **1933**

Bowater-Eburite Ld. Regd. 1922 as Eburite Paper Co. Ld.; name changed 1931 to Eburite Corrugated Containers Ld. and as above 1956. All capital was owned by Bowater Paper Corpn. Ld. Vol. liq. (members') 30 June 1960. Final meeting return regd. 12 Feb. 1963 **1964**

Bowater-Lloyd Newfoundland Ld. Regd. 1938. Vol. liq. (members') 13 June 1947. Undertaking acquired by The Bowater Paper Corpn. Ld., which formerly held all the capital. Final meeting return regd. 17 Mar. 1950 **1951**

Bowater (W.V.) & Sons Ld. Regd. 1910. Vol. liq. 19 Jan. 1926. Reconstructed as W. V. Bowater & Sons (1926) Ld. (later Bowaters Sales Co. Ld.). Final meeting return regd. 15 Mar. 1927 **1926**

Bowater's Lloyd Pulp and Paper Mills Ld. Regd. 1890 as Edward Lloyd Ld.; name changed 25 Sept. 1948. Vol. liq. (members') 16 Nov. 1955. Holders of 7% preference stock received 4 fully-paid 5½% preference shares of Bowater Paper Corpn. Ld. for every £3 stock held and holders of 5½% preference stock 1 fully-paid 5½% preference share plus 6*d.* cash for every £1 held. Final meeting return regd. 16 Dec. 1957 **1958**

Bowater's Mersey Paper Mills Ld. Regd. 1929. Vol. liq. (members') 16 Nov. 1955. Holders of 5½% preference stock received 1 fully-paid 5½% preference share of Bowater Paper Corpn. Ld. plus 6*d.* cash for every £1 held. Final meeting return regd. 16 Dec. 1957 **1958**

Bowden Brake Co. Ld. Regd. 1901. Receiver was appointed 25 Oct. 1929. Assets realised insufficient to meet claims of debenture holders. Struck off Register 4 Oct. 1935 **1936**

Bowdens Ld. Regd. 1899. Struck off Register 25 Oct. 1948 **1912**

Bowery & East River National Bank. In 1928 merged into Bank of America National Association **1929**

Bowes (John) & Partners Ld. Regd. 1886. Vol. liq. (members') 27 May 1953. Capital returned to contributories—£3 2*s.* 6·85*d.* per stock unit of 10*s.* Final meeting return regd. 24 Feb. 1955 **1956**

Bowhill Coal Co. Fife Ld. Regd. Edinburgh 1894. Vol. liq. June 1909. Undertaking and assets sold to Fife Coal Co. Ld., in which company shareholders were entitled to 10 fully-paid ordinary shares of £1 for each share of £10 held. Final meeting return regd. 14 Oct. 1914 **1910**

Bowley Pneumatic Tyre & Cycle Co. Ld. Regd. 1896. Vol. liq. 8 Apr. 1897. Final meeting return regd. 11 July 1899 **1898**

Bowling Co. Ld. Regd. 1903. Vol. liq. 29 Nov. 1921. Final meeting return regd. 19 Jan. 1928 **1922**

Bowling Iron Co. Ld. Regd. 1870. Reconstructed 1903 as Bowling Co. Ld. Shareholders were entitled to 4 shares of £1 and £15 debenture stock in new company and £15 in cash for each share of £50 held. Removed from Register 1904 **1908**

Bowmaker Ld. Regd. as private company 31 Oct. 1927; converted into public compaby 14 May 1934. Voluntary winding-up 11 Sept. 1986. All capital acquired by C. T. Bowring & Co. LD. in 1969 **1970**

Bowman, Thompson & Co. Ld. Regd. 1891. Undertaking acquired in 1900 by Brunner Mond & Co. Ld. (later I. C. I. (Alkali) Ld.) Debenture holders were entitled in respect of each £100 bond held to £105 in cash, preference shares, ordinary shares or partly in each; ordinary shareholders were entitled in respect of each £8 paid share held to £10 in ordinary or preference shares or partly in each; preference shareholders were entitled in respect of each £10 share held to £11 in ordinary or preference shares or partly in each; ordinary shares in acquiring company were valued at £5 per share of £1 and preference shares were valued at £17 per share of £10. Removed from Register 1901 **1901**

Bown (William) Ld. Regd. 1893. Removed from Register 1904 ***1902**

Bowness Estates Ld. Regd. 1912. Vol. liq. 10 Dec. 1924. Final meeting return regd. 14 Mar. 1930 **1925**

Bowring Petroleum Co. Ld. *See* Anglo-Mexican Oil & Shipping Co. Ld.

Box (W. R.) & Co. Ld. Regd. Dublin 1897. Removed from Register 1906 **1904**

Boy Messengers & Electric Call Co. Regd. 1891. Vol. liq. 9 May 1893. Undertaking was sold to District Messengers Service and News Co. Ld. (later Theatre Tickets and Messengers Ld.) for 5,000 ordinary shares of £5, fully-paid and 15.000 preference shares of £1 (13*s.* 4*d.* paid). Final meeting return regd. 15 July 1896 **1894**

Boyer (Paul) Ld. Regd. 1898. Removed from Register 1908 **1901**

Boyle (Robert) & Son Ld. Regd. 1885. Removed from Register 1904 ***1904**

Boyne Weaving & Finishing Co. Ld. *See* Greenmount & Boyne Ld.

Bracken (T. H.) & Co. Ld. Regd. 1888. Vol. liq. 29 Oct. 1923. Final meeting return regd. 22 June 1928 **1924**

Brackenhill Light Railway Co. Inc. (under Light Railways Act 1896) by order of Light Railway Commissioners confirmed by Board of Trade 1901. In 1923 this undertaking was merged into the London & North Eastern Railway Company. The issued capital (£1,250) was not in the hands of the public **1924**

Brackla Distillery Co. Ld. Regd. Edinburgh 1897. Vol. liq. May 1919. Distillery, stock of whiskey and plant were sold. Capital returned to contributories—£11 5*s.* 3*d.* (including arrears of dividend) per preference share of £10; no capital returned to ordinary shareholders. Final meeting return regd. 19 Dec. 1919 **1920**

Brackley Gas Co. Ld. Regd. 1912. Dissolved 1 May 1949. undertaking being vested in Southern Area Gas Board underGas Act 1948. Holders of securities were entitled to receive, in respect of each £5 unit held. British Gas 3% guaranteed stock 1990–95 as follows:

	£ s. d.
Ord. shares	6 10 0
4½% pref. shares	5 5 0

1952

Bradbury & Co. Ld. Regd. 1874. Receiver for debenture holders appointed Nov. 1923. Struck off Register May 1929 **1930**

Bradbury, Son & Co., Ld. Regd. 1920 as Bradbury, Son & Co. (1920) Ld., name changed Mar. 1934. Vol. liq. (members') 31 Dec. 1948. Final meeting return regd. 13 Jan. 1949 **1940**

Bradbury's Patent Drill Sharpener Ld. Regd. 1898. Removed from Register 1910 **1910**

Bradbury's World Patent Drill Sharpener Co. Ld. Inc. South African Republic 1895. Reconstructed 1898 as Bradbury's Patent Drill Sharpener Ld., in which company shareholders were entitled to 1 share of £1 (18*s.* paid) for each share of £1 held **1903**

Braden Copper Mines Co. Inc. Delaware 1909. Absorbed into Kennecott Copper Corporation in 1915. Shareholders were entitled to $15 in cash for each share or 1 share in purchasing company for every 3¼ shares held; bondholders were entitled to $1,500 in cash for each bond held or 30 (approx.) shares in purchasing company for each bond held **1917**

Bradford & District Tramways Co. Ld. Regd. 1888. Receiver appointed Apr. 1891. Removed from Register 1899 **1894**

Bradford & Shelf Tramways Co. Ld. Regd. 1884. Vol. liq. 17 Mar. 1902. Lines were acquired by Bradford Corporation. Removed from Register 1902 **1903**

**See Stock Exchange Year-Book.*

Bradford Banking Co. Ld. Established 1827. Regd. 1880. Vol. liq. 10 Jan. 1910. Undertaking and assets were acquired by London City and Midland Bank Ld. (later Midland Bank Ld.), in which company shareholders were entitled to 11 shares of £60 (credited with £12 10s. paid) for every 10 shares of £10 (£3 paid) held **1910**

Bradford Brick & Tile Co. Ld. Regd 1868. Removed from Register 1902 .... ***1886**

Bradford Brick & Tile Co. Ld. Regd 1900. Vol. liq. (members') 24 June 1930. Capital returned to contributories—20s. per preference share of £1; 16s. 6d. per ordinary share of £1. Final meeting return regd. 26 May 1934 .... **1931**

Bradford Coffee Tavern Co. Ld. Regd. 1878. Removed from Register 1907 .... **1904**

Bradford Commercial Joint-Stock Banking Co. Ld. Regd. 1880. Vol. liq. 18 Jan. 1904. Certain assets were transferred to Bradford District Bank Ld., and the remaining assets were acquired by Knightsbridge & Bradford Estate Co. Ld. (later Knightsbridge Mansions Ld.) Shareholders were entitled to £6 in cash and £7 in debenture stock and 1 fully-paid share of £7 in Knightsbridge & Bradford Estate Co. Ld. for each share of £10 held. Removed from Register 1907 .... **1907**

Bradford District Bank Ld. Regd. 1862. Vol. liq. Jan. 1919. Amalgamated with National Provincial and Union Bank of England Ld. (later National Provincial Bank Ld.), in which company shareholders were entitled to 2 shares of £60 (credited with £12 paid) for every 5 shares of £10 (£4 paid) held; fractions were payable at £14 per share in cash **1919**

Bradford District Steam Tramways Ld. Regd. 1885. Removed from Register 1906 .... **1888**

Bradford Exchange Co. Ld. Regd. 1862. Bradford Corpn. purchased the Wool Exchange for £375,000. Vol. liq. (members') 10 Nov. 1964. £13 11s. 1½d. (per share of £1) was returned to contributories. Final meeting return regd. 11 Nov. 1965 .... **1966**

Bradford Manufacturing Co. Ld. Regd 1890. Vol. liq. (members') 29 Oct. 1954. Capital returned to contributories—5s 4 22/23 d. per share of 1s. £80 3s. 6d. (unclaimed dividends) and £702 6s. 4d. (distributions) was paid into Companies' Liquidation Account. Final meeting return regd.6 June 1957 ...... **1958**

Bradford Old Bank Ld. Regd. 1864. Vol. liq. Jan. 1907. Undertaking acquired by United Counties Bank Ld., in which company shareholders were entitled to 3½ shares of £20 (£4 paid) for every share of £50 (£20 paid) held. **1908**

Bradford-on-Avon Gas Co. Inc. by Special Act 1902. Dissolved 1 May 1949, undertaking being vested in South Western Area Gas Board under Gas Act 1948. Holders of orig. ord. stock (9% stand.) were entitled to receive £210 British Gas 3% guaranteed stock 1990–95 for each £100 stock held. Liability in respect of certain mortgage loans assumed by the Board **1952**

Bradford Steamship Co. Ld. Regd. 1909. Vol. liq. 1 June 1917 for amalgamation with St. Just Steamship Co. Ld. (later Reardon Smith Line Ld.) Final meeting return regd. 7 Dec. 1917 .... **1918**

Bradford Tramways & Omnibus Co. Ld. Regd. 1882. Vol. liq. 3 May 1902. Capital returned to contributories—£13 per share of £10 at 29 Nov. 1902; further payments (if any) not known. Removed from Register 1905 .... **1903**

Bradford Victoria Hotel Co. Ld. Regd. 1864. Vol. liq. 25 Mar. 1892. Hotel was acquired by Great Northern Railway Co. Final meeting return regd. 6 Feb. 1893 **1893**

Brading Harbour & Railway Co. Inc. by Special Act 1874. By Act of 1896 the word "Improvement" was omitted from the title. By Isle of Wight Railway Company's Act of 1898 the undertaking was transferred in consideration of £16,500................. **1899**

Bradley (Thomas & Isaac) Ld. Regd. 1935. Vol. liq. (members') 30 June 1945. Direct controlling interest held by Bradley & Foster Ld. Final meeting return regd. 5 Nov. 1945 .... **1946**

Bradley Williams Ore Treatment Co. (1910) Ld. Regd. 1910. Vol. liq. 17 Dec. 1913. Final meeting return regd. 27 July 1918 .... **1914**

Bradleys (Chepstow Place) Ld. Regd. 23 Oct. 1912. Vol. liq. (members') 2 Feb. 1953. Capital returned to contributories-preference stock repaid at par; ordinary stock (per £1 unit): 40s. 2¾d. Final meeting return regd. 23 July 1954 .... **1955**

Bradmola Mills Ld. See B. M. Realisations Ld.

Braendlin Armoury Co. Ld. Regd. 1871. Vol liq.q. 22 Mar. 1888. Final meeting return regd. 12 Mar. 1889 ***1882**

Braime's Tadcaster Breweries Ld. Regd. 1895. Vol. liq. Dec. 1908. Freehold properties were acquired by

Leeds City Brewery Ld. Removed from Register 1913 .... **1909**

Braintree & Bocking Gas Co. Ld. Constituted by Deed of Settlement 1849; regd. as unlimited 1860 and as limited 1914. Dissolved 1 May 1949, undertaking being vested in Eastern Area Gas Board under Gas Act 1948. Holders of Addit. ord. shares (7% max.) were entitled to receive £13 British 3% guaranteed stock 1990–95 for each share (of £10) held **1952**

Braithwaite Mining Co. Ld. Regd. 1887. Removed from Register 1906 .... **1890**

Brakfontein Concessions Syndicate Ld. Regd. 1907. Vol. liq. Mar. 1910. Struck off Register 1923 .... **1911**

Brakpan Mines Ld. Inc. Transvaal 16 Feb. 1903. Vol. liq. (members') Mar. 1964. Ro·47½ distributed per share. Final meeting held 24 Jan. 1975 .... **1975-6**

Bramansu Gold Corporation Ld. Regd. 1936. Vol. liq. (members') 9 Apr. 1940. Undertaking and assets acquired by West African Mines & Estates Ld., in which company shareholders were to receive 2 ordinary shares of 2s. 6d. for each preferred share of 5s. and 1 ordinary share for each deferred of 5s. held. Final meeting return regd. 12 Nov. 1940 .... **1941**

Brampton Brothers Ld. Regd. 1897. Vol. liq. (members') 7 Jan. 1936. Undertaking was acquired by Renold and Coventry Chain Co. Ld. which company owned all share capital. Final meeting return regd. 21 Dec. 1936 .... **1936**

Brampton Gas Light & Coke Co. Regd. as unlimited 1872. Dissolved 1 May 1949. undertaking being vested in Northern Area Gas Board under Gas Act 1948. Holders of ordinary shares (of £5) were entitled to receive £6 10s. British Gas 3% guaranteed stock 1990–95 for each share held **1952**

Brancepeth Gas & Coke (Strakers & Love) Ld. Regd. 1935. Vol. liq. (members') 16 Dec. 1949. Undertaking and assets acquired by National Coal Board. Outstanding £35.000 5% 14-year registered debentures due for redemption 31 Dec. 1949 were redeemed at par on 31 July 1949 with interest to 31 Dec. 1949 and remaining assets were distributed to shareholders in specie. Final meeting return regd. 12 Mar. 1954 .... **1955**

Branch (John) (Parent Co.) Ld. Regd. 1896 as John Branch Ld.; name changed Dec. 1935. Vol. liq. (members') 10 Apr. 1962. Final meeting return regd. 25 Dec. 1967. .... **1939**

Brand Kumalu Syndicate Ld. Regd. 1895. Undertaking was acquired by Rhodesia Mines Ld. for 30,462 shares of £1 (credited with 15s. paid) and 32,538 fully-paid shares. Removed from Register 1906 ... **1899**

Brand Powdered Fuel System Ld. Regd. 1928. Vol. liq. (creditors) 26 Jan. 1931. Assets realised insufficient to pay creditors in full. Final meeting return regd. 5 Feb 1932 .... **1931**

Brandes Ld. Regd. 1924. Undertaking acquired by Kolster-Brandes Ld. Struck off Register Sept. 1946 **1938**

Brandley Mining Co. Ld. Regd. 1883. Vol. liq. 20 Feb. 1891. Final meeting return regd. 26 Jan. 1894 ...... **1892**

Brandon's Putney Brewery Ld. Regd. 1896. Vol. liq. 25 Aug. 1949. Capital returned to contributories—£12 per preference share of £10. Final meeting return regd. 20 July 1950 .... **1951**

Brandt (Arthur H.) & Co. Regd. (as unlimited) 1924. Vol. liq. Dec. 1930. Struck off Register 2 Oct. 1953 **1931**

Brandts (Wm.) Investment Trust Ld. Regd. 1891 as Rotherham Investment Trust Ld.; name changed Apr. 1972. Vol. liq. 6 June 1974. Shareholders received units in Brandts Income Fund to a value of 41·5p or 41·5p cash per income share of 20p and accumulation units in Brandts Capital Fund to a value equal to the net asset value of the company per issued capital share or 37·89p cash per capital share of 20p. £399 paid into Companies' Liquidation Account. Final meeting return regd. 24 Sept. 1975 **1976-7**

Brandy Distillers Co. Ld. Regd. 1891. Court Order to wind up 6 Mar. 1901. Removed from Register 1907 **1902**

Branon p.l.c. Regd. as private 9 June 1980; converted public 15 Sept. 1980. Vol. liq. 15 May 1986. Shareholders received in Oct. 1983 1 ordinary share in Taddale Investments p.l.c., or 30p cash for each ordinary share held **1984-5**

Bransom, Kent & Co. Ld. Regd. 1896. Vol. liq. (creditors') 23 July 1930. Assets realised insufficient to pay unsecured creditors in full. Final meeting return regd. 14 Jan. 1933 .... **1931**

Bransom, Kent & Co. (1930) Ld. Regd. 1930. Vol. liq. (creditors') 25 Oct. 1937. Assets realised insufficient to pay creditors in full. Final meeting return regd. 24 Oct. 1938 .... **1938**

Branston Artificial Silk Co. Ld. See St. Martin Preserving Co. Ld.

Bratsberg Copper Co. Ld. Regd. 1888. Vol. liq. 28 Nov. 1892. Final meeting return regd. 4 Jan. 1895........ **1893**

VOL. FOR

Bratsberg Smelting & Refining Works Ld. Regd. 1889. Vol. liq. 13 Jan. 1892. Final meeting return regd. 31 Jan. 1893 ... **1892**

Braunston (Malay) Rubber Estates Ld. Regd. 1910. Vol. liq. (members') 23 May 1957. Undertaking and assets acquired by Kapar Para Rubber Estates Co. Ld. in which shareholders were entitled to 8 fully-paid shares of 2s. for every £1 stock held. Capital returned to contributories—2s. per £1 stock. £14 7s. 11d. was paid into Companies' Liquidation Account. Final meeting return regd. 25 Jan. 1961 ... **1962**

Braunton Electric Light & Power Co. Ld. Regd. 1911. Vol. liq. (members') 5 June 1936. Undertaking acquired by Bideford & District Electric Supply Co. Ld. for 11,600 shares of £1. Final meeting return regd. 5 Aug. 1936 ... **1937**

Bravo Mine Syndicate Ld. Regd. 1887. Vol. liq. 25 Nov. 1899. Final meeting return regd. 23 Feb. 1900 ... **1900**

Bray & Enniskerry Railway Co. Inc. by Special Act 1886 as Bray & Enniskerry (Light) Railway Co.; name changed by Act of 1890. Undertaking believed to be abandoned ... **1910**

Brazil Diamond Fields Corporation Ld. Regd. 1902. Removed from Register 1913 ... **1908**

Brazil Great Southern Railway Co. Ld. Regd. 1883. Struck off Register 8 Aug. 1946 ... **1946**

Brazil Great Southern Railway Extensions Ld. Regd. 1909. Struck off Register 25 Mar. 1938 ... **1945**

Brazil Great Southern St. Angelo Extension Railway Co. Ld. Regd. 1890. Struck off Register Nov. 1931 ... **1932**

Brazil Land Cattle & Packing Co. Inc. in Maine, U. S. A. 1911. By decree of 22 July 1940 company's assets were taken over by the Brazilian Government. Capital returned to contributories—6s. 9d. per share of $5. Company was dissolved on 30 Dec. 1952 ... **1954**

Brazil North Eastern Railways Ld. Regd. 1910. Company has been in receivership since 1915. In 1974 the Trustees stated that it was not their intention to appoint a new receiver ... **1974-5**

Brazil Plantations Syndicate Ld. Regd. 1924. Vol. liq. (members') 31 May 1937. Assets were distributed in specie to Parana Plantations Ld., and its subsidiary. Final meeting return regd. 13 Aug. 1937 ... **1938**

Brazilian & Portuguese Bank Ld. See British Bank of South America Ld

Brazilian, Canadian & General Trust Ld. Regd. 1906 as Prudential Deposit Trust Ld.; name changed Jan. 1910. Vol. liq. (members') 31 Dec. 1931. Capital returned to contributories—£8,613 12s 1d. to ordinary shareholders; £1,721 13s. 1d. to preference shareholders; certain assets were distributed in specie. Final meeting return regd. 16 Mar. 1933 ... **1932**

Brazilian Coffee Estates Ld. Regd. 1925. Struck off Register Jan. 1933 ... **1933**

Brazilian Diamond & Exploration Co. Ld. Regd. 1902. Removed from Register 1911 ... **1910**

Brazilian Extract of Meat & Hide Factory Ld. Regd. 1887. The property was sold to a Brazilian company in 1921. In Oct. 1928 it was stated that receipts were insufficient to repay debenture holders in full. Vol. liq. 7 Nov. 1928. Final meeting return regd. 30 Oct. 1929 ... **1929**

Brazilian Gold Exploring Syndicate Ld. Regd. 1894. Struck off Register 10 Apr. 1959 ... **1946**

Brazilian Gold Mines Ld. Regd. 1880. Removed from Register 1904 ... **1888**

Brazilian Golden Hill Ld. Regd. 1909. Receiver appointed in May 1912. Struck off Register 1916 ... **1913**

Brazilian Goldfields Ld. Regd. 1901 as Vista Allegre Gold Mining Estate Ld.; name changed Jan. 1909. Vol. liq. 9 Sept. 1915. Capital returned to contributories—7d. per share of £1; further payments (if any) not known. Final meeting return regd. 16 Nov. 1916 ... **1916**

Brazilian Imperial Central Bahia Railway Co. Ld. See Central Bahia Railway Co. Ld.

Brazilian Land & Mining Co. Ld. Regd. 1857. Vol. liq. 27 Aug. 1885. Final meeting return regd. 21 Aug. 1899 ... *****1886**

Brazilian Mining & General Trust Ld. See United Mining & General Trust Ld.

Brazilian Mining Syndicate Ld. Regd. 1910. Vol. liq. 20 Oct. 1920. Final meeting return regd. 15 Dec. 1920 ... *****1919**

Brazilian Railway Construction Co. Ld. Regd. 1908. Vol. liq. 19 July 1921. Final meeting return regd. 18 Mar. 1925 ... **1922**

Brazilian Rubber Plantations & Estates Ld. Regd. 1906. Court Order to wind up 14 Jan. 1908. Liquidator released 29 May 1913. Struck off Register 10 Oct. 1916 ... **1908**

Brazilian Rubber Trust Ld. Regd. 1901. Vol. liq. July 1910. Undertaking and assets were acquired by Para (Marajo) Islands Rubber Estates Ld. in which company shareholders were entitled to 1 fully-paid

VOL. FOR

share of 5s. for every 5 shares of 5s. held *plus* 2s. 6d. per share in cash. Removed from Register 1912 .. **1911**

Brazilian Street Railway Co. Ld. Regd. 1868. Vol. liq. 14 Apr. 1899 for reconstruction as company of same name. Holders of ordinary shares were entitled to 3 fully-paid ordinary shares of £1 in new company for every 2 ordinary shares of £2 held; holders of preference shares were entitled to 2 fully-paid preference shares of £1 *plus* 1 fully-paid ordinary share in new company for each fully-paid preference share of £2 held or to 2 preference shares of £1 (credited with 13s. 9d. paid) *plus* 1 fully-paid ordinary share of £1 for each preference share of £2 (£1 7s. 6d. paid) held. Holders of debentures were entitled to an equal amount of debenture stock *plus* a certain amount of preference shares. Final meeting return regd. 15 Mar. 1900 ... **1900**

Brazilian Street Railway Co. Ld. Regd. 1899. Vol. liq. 8 Jan. 1918. Undertaking was acquired by Pernambuco Tramways and Power Co. Ld. Final meeting return regd. 18 Oct. 1918 ... **1918**

Brazilian Warrant Co. Ld. Regd. 1909. Vol. liq. Nov. 1911, Reconstructed as company of same name. Shareholders were entitled to 11 shares of 10s. (credited as fully-paid) in new company for each preferred share of £5 held or 1 fully-paid share of 10s. for each fully-paid deferred share of 1s. Removed from Register 1912 ... **1912**

Brazilian Warrant Agency & Finance Co. Ld. See below.

Brazilian Warrant Co. Ld. Regd. 1911 as Brazilian Warrant Co. Ld.; name changed to Brazilian Warrant Agency & Finance Co. Ld. in 1925 and as above in 1942. Struck off Register 27 Apr. 1956 ... **1952**

Brdlik (Fred.) Meat Packing Co. Ld. Regd. 1913. Struck off Register 1927 ... **1916**

Bread Supply Association Ld. Regd. 1890, Court Orders; to wind up 6 Dec. 1890; to dissolve 25 Apr. 1896 *****1891**

Bread Union Ld. Regd. 1889. Vol. liq. 21 Oct. 1890. Final meeting return regd. 29 Dec. 1894 ... **1891**

Brear & Brown Ld. Regd. 1894. Court Order to wind up 15 Feb. 1916. Liquidator released 31 Mar. 1920. Struck off Register 20 Mar. 1925 ... *****1917**

Brechin and Edzell District Railway Co. Inc. by Special Act 1890. In 1923 the undertaking was merged into the London Midland & Scottish Railway Co. Shareholders were entitled to £6 London Midland Ordinary Stock for each £100 of Brechin Ordinary Shares held. The former Company took over the Brechin Company's loans and promissory notes amounting to £27,400 ... **1924**

Brechin Gas Co. Ld. Regd. in Edinburgh 1905 Dissolved 1 May 1949, undertaking being vested in Scottish Area Gas Board under Gas Act 1948. Holders of securities were entitled to receive British Gas 3% guaranteed stock 1990–95 as follows:

	£	s.	d.
Ord. shares (of £1) ...	3	5	0
5% pref. shares (of £10) ...	11	10	0

1952

Breckenridge Cannel Coal Co. Ld. Regd. 1896. Vol. liq. 4 June 1925. Final meeting return regd.4 Feb.1926 **1926**

Breckenridge Co. Ld. Regd. 1885. Removed from Register 1906 ... **1894**

Brecon and Merthyr Tydfil Junction Railway Co. Inc. by Special Act 1859. In 1922 the undertaking was merged into the Great Western Railway Co., in which company stockholders were entitled to stock as follows:

For each £100 held	G. W.
5% Rumney Pref. ...	£125 4% Debenture
4% "A" Deb. ...	£100 4% Debenture
4% "B" Deb. ...	£25 4% Debenture
4% Cons. 1st Pref. ...	£60 5% Cons. Pref.
4% Cons. 1st Pref. ...	£80 5% Cons. Pref.
4% Cons. 2nd Pref. ...	£57 Cons. Ordinary
4% Cons. 3rd Pref. ...	£45 Cons. Ordinary
4% Cons. 4th Pref. ...	£35 Defd. Certs.*
Cons. Ordinary ...	£28 Defd. Certs.*

*Holders are entitled to be registered between 1 Jan. 1929 and 1 Jan. 1932 as the holders of the amounts of Cons. Ord. Stock stated in such Certificates ... **1924**

Brecon Gas Co. Inc. by Special Act 1870. Dissolved 1 May 1949, undertaking being vested in Wales Area Gas Board under Gas Act 1948. Holders of securities were entitled to receive, in respect of each £10 unit held, British Gas 3% guaranteed stock 1990–95 as follows:

	£	s.	d.
Orig. shares (10% stand.) ...	13	0	0
Addit. shares (7% stand.) ...	9	5	0
4% pref. shares ...	10	1	0

1952

Bremang Gold Dredging Co. Ld. Regd. 1936. All capital was owned by Ghana State Mining Corpn. Vol. liq. (members') 30 Oct. 1967. Final meeting return regd. 9 May 1969 ... **1962**

VOL. FOR

Bremnaes Gold Co. Ld. Regd. 1897. Removed from Register 1908 .... **1900**

Brenda Exploration Syndicate Ld. Regd. 1896. Vol. liq. 27 June 1899. Final meeting return regd. 25 July 1900 .... **1900**

Brenner Industries Ld. Regd. 1936 as Hetty (Wholesale Gowns) Ld.; name changed as above 19 Nov. 1946. Vol. liq. (creditors') 23 Dec. 1964. No capital returned to contributories. Final meeting return regd. 12 June 1967 .... **1968**

Brentford & Isleworth Tramways Co. Inc. 1881. In liquidation 1885 .... **1885**

Brentford Electric Supply Co. Ld. Regd. 1904. Dissolved 1 Apr. 1948, undertaking being vested in British (later Central) Electricity Authority and Southern Area Board under Electricity Act 1947 .... **1949**

Brentford Gas Co. Inc. 1821. Re-incorporated by Special Act 1858. Undertaking was acquired by Gas Light and Coke Co. in 1926. Stockholders were entitled to stock in acquiring company as follows: £120 ordinary stock for every £100 A or B ordinary stock held; £125 4% preference stock for every £100 5% preference stock held; £133 6*s*. 8*d*. 3% debenture stock for every £100 4% debenture stock held; £100 6% Brentford redeemable debenture stock for every £100 6% redeemable debenture stock held **1926**

Brentford Town Hall & Market House Co. Inc. by Special Act 1848. The property was sold to Middlesex County Council **1893**

Brentnall Beard (Holdings) Ld. Dissolved 29 July 1986

Brentwood District Electric Co. Ld. Regd. 1920. All shares were acquired from Southern Areas Electric Corpn. Ld. in 1944 by County of London Electric Supply Co. Ld. Dissolved 1 Apr. 1948, undertaking being vested in the British (later Central) Electricity Authority under the Electricity Act 1947 .... **1936**

Brentwood District Electric Installations Ld. Regd. 1928. Vol. liq. (members') 31 Oct 1938. All shares owned by Southern Areas Electric Corporation Ld. Final meeting return regd. 20 Dec. 1939 .... **1939**

Brentwood Gas Co. Established 1836; registered as the Brentwood Gas, Coke and Light Company Limited, in 1898; inc. by Special Act 1905. Under Act of 1931 the undertaking was acquired by the Gas Light & Coke Co., in which company stockholders were entitled to £152 ordinary stock for each £100 original (10% standard) stock held; holders of additional (7% standard) stock were entitled to £106 8*s*. ordinary stock for each £100 held; holders of 5% preference stock were entitled to £125 4% consolidated preference stock for each £100 held; holders of 6% redeemable preference stock were entitled to £100 6% Brentwood redeemable preference stock for each £100 held; holders of 5½% perpetual debenture stock were entitled to £183 6*s*. 8*d*. 3% consolidated debenture stock for each £100 held **1932**

Brereton Collieries Ld. Regd. 1906 as Earl of Shrewsbury's Brereton Collieries Ld.; name changed Sept. 1920. Vol. liq. (members') 24 Nov. 1952. Final meeting return regd. 2 May 1956 .... **1940**

Breslau & District Ice Co. Ld. Regd. 1884. Vol. liq. 21 Feb. 1887. Assets were acquired by United Anglo-Continental Ice Co. Ld., in which company shareholders were entitled to an equal number of shares. Removed from Register 1906 .... **1888**

Brett's Ld. Regd. 1897. Vol. liq. 10 Nov. 1898. Business was transferred to Brett's Stamping Co. Ld. and Brett's Patent Lifter Co. Ld. Final meeting return regd. 25 Oct. 1899 .... **1898**

Brett's Stamping Co. Ld. Regd. 1896. Vol. liq. 1 May 1897. Business was acquired by Brett's Ld. for £87.000 in cash. Final meeting return regd. 2 Feb. 1898 .... **1898**

Breweries Ld. *See* Whitefield Breweries Ld.

Brewers' & Distillers' CO_2, Co. Ld. Regd. 1891. Vol. liq. 31 Mar. 1905. Capital returned to contributories—4% in 1905; further payments (if any) not known. Removed from Register 1906 .... **1906**

Brewers' & General Fire Insurance & Guarantee Corporation Ld. Regd. 1892. Removed from Register 1907 **1899**

Brewers' Investment Corporation Ld. Regd. 1888. Vol. liq. 14 Aug. 1894. Undertaking was acquired by Showells Brewery Co. Ld. [later Ind Coope (South Midlands) Ld.] in which company shareholders were entitled to guaranteed shares of £5 at par for ordinary or preference shares. Final meeting return regd. 12 Jan. 1898 .... **1895**

Brewers' Sugar Co. Ld. Regd. Edinburgh 1896. Vol. liq. Jan. 1927. Shareholders were entitled to 7 ordinary shares of £1 in Manbré & Garton Ld., 7 ordinary shares of £1 in Westburn Sugar Refineries Ld. and approx. £8 10*s*. in cash for each share of £10 held. Final meeting return regd. 27 Jan. 1928 .... **1928**

VOL. FOR

Brewery Assets Corporation Ld. Regd. 1890. Vol. liq. 30 Nov. 1892. Final meeting return regd. 9 Apr. 1895 **1893**

Breyton Collieries Ld. Inc. Transvaal 1909. Vol. liq. Apr. 1922 .... **1923**

Briar Mill (Holdings) Ld. Regd. 1920 as Briar Mill (1920) Ld.; name changed to Briar Mill Ld. in Dec. 1950 and as above on 23 Mar. 1953. A subsidiary of Lancashire Cotton Corpn. Ld. Vol. liq. (members') 30 Apr. 1954. the assets were distributed in specie. £235 8*s*. 11*d*. was paid into Companies' Liquidation Account. Final meeting return regd. 17 Feb. 1955 **1956**

Briar Mill Ld. *See above.*

Briar Mill (1920) Ld. *See above.*

Brice & Co. Ld. Regd. 1892. Removed from Register 1901 .... **1898**

Brich Rubber Estate Ld. Regd. 1909. Vol. liq. 15 Dec. 1931. Undertaking and assets were acquired by Alor Pongsu Amalgamated Estates Ld., in which company shareholders were entitled to 74 shares of 2*s*. (credited as fully-paid) for every 100 shares of 2*s*. held. £176 9*s*. 8*d*. was paid into Companies' Liquidation Account. Final meeting return regd. 1 Dec. 1932 .... **1932**

Bride Steamship Co. Ld. Regd. 1917. Struck off Register 1923 .... **1923**

Bridge Gas, Coke and Coal Co. Ld. Regd. 1858. Vol. liq. (members') 31 Dec. 1932. Undertaking acquired by East Kent Gas Co. Ld. Capital returned to contributories—£2,028 2*s*. Final meeting return regd. 5 Jan. 1934 .... **1933**

Bridge Hotel & Theatre Co., Darlington, Ld. Regd. 1897. Struck off Register 1925 .... ***1922**

Bridge of Allan Hydropathic Co. Ld. Regd. Edinburgh 1865. Vol. liq. Jan. 1914. Final meeting return regd. 13 Nov. 1915 .... **1916**

Bridge of Weir Gas Co. Ld. Regd. in Edinburgh 1846. Dissolved 1 May 1949, undertaking being vested in Scottish Area Gas Board under Gas Act 1948. Holders of ordinary shares (of £1) were entitled to receive £1 6*s*. British Gas 3% guaranteed stock 1990–95 for each share held **1952**

"Bridge" Paper Mills Ld. Regd. 1920. Struck off Register Apr. 1929 .... **1930**

Bridgend Gas Co. Inc. 1869 by Special Act as Bridgend (Glamorganshire) Gas & Water Co.; name changed 1921. Dissolved 1 May 1949, undertaking being vested in Wales Area Gas Board under Gas Act 1948. Holders of securities were entitled to receive British Gas 3% guaranteed stock 1990–95 as follows in respect of each £1 unit, unless otherwise stated, of security held:

	£	s.	d.
Ord. shares (10% max.)	1	12	0
Ord. shares (7% max.)	1	8	0
5% pref. shares	1	2	8
4½% perp. deb. stock (per £100)	112	10	0

Liability in respect of certain mortgage loans assumed by the Board **1952**

Bridges & Co. Ld. Regd. 1914. Vol. liq. (members') 7 July 1933. Capital returned to contributories—9*s*. 0½*d*. per preference share of £1. Final meeting return regd. 22 Dec. 1933 .... **1934**

Bridges & Co. (Proprietors) Ld. Regd. 1923. Vol. liq. (members') 9 July 1932. Noteholders were repaid in cash at 104% in July 1932. Shareholders received 1 ordinary share of 1*s*. and 3 preference shares of 10*s*. in Bridges & Co. Ld. for every 4 preference shares of £1 held or 1 ordinary share of 1*s*. for every 20 ordinary shares of 1*s*. held. Final meeting return regd. 17 Oct. 1933 .... **1933**

Bridgetown & St. Andrews Railway Ld. Regd. 1898. Removed from Register 1906 .... **1904**

Bridgewater (G. & T.) Ld. Regd. 1937. Vol. liq. (members') 26 Mar. 1970. All capital owned by Smiths Food Group Ld. 2nd preference shares (of £1) were repaid at 21*s*. 6*d*. per share in Mar. 1970 **1973-4**

Bridgewater Navigation Co. Ld. Regd. 1872. Vol. liq. 26 Aug. 1887. Undertaking acquired by Manchester Ship Canal Co. Bondholders received £244,279 in cash; shareholders received £16 3*s*. per preference share (£10 paid) or £10 6*s*. 8*d*. per ordinary share (£3 10*s*. paid). Final meeting return regd. 17 Aug. 1892 **1892**

Bridgewater Railway Co. Inc. by Special Act 1882. In 1923 the undertaking was merged into the London & South-Western Railway in which company stockholders were entitled to stock as follows:

For each £100 held		*L. & S. W.*	
4% Debenture	£133⅓	3% Deb. Cons.	
4½% Preference	£112½	4% Cons. Gtd.	
Ordinary	£75	4% Cons. Gtd.	**1924**

Bridgewater, Stowey & Stogursey Light Railway Co. Inc. (under Light Railways Act 1896) 1901 .... **1906**

Bridgnorth Gas Co. Ld. Regd. 1861. Vol. liq. 28 Aug. 1882. Final meeting return regd. 18 June 1883 .... ***1877**

**See Stock Exchange Year-Book.*

VOL. FOR

Bridgwater & District Electric Supply & Traction Co. Ld. Regd. 1902. Dissolved 1 Apr. 1948, undertaking being vested in British (later Central) Electricity Authority and South-Western Area Board under Electricity Act 1947. Holders of securities were entitled to receive British Electricity 3% guaranteed stock (1968–73) as follows in respect of each £1 unit of capital held:

	£ s. d.
7% 1st preference shares	1 14 0
4½% 2nd preference shares	1 2 0
Ordinary shares	4 5 0

1949

Bridgwater Gas Light Co. Inc. by Special Act 1834; reinc. by Special Act 1903. Dissolved 1 May 1949, undertaking being vested in South-Western Area Gas Board under Gas Act 1948. Holders of securities were entitled to receive, in respect of each £100 unit held, British Gas 3% guaranteed stock 1990–95 as follows:

	£ s. d.
Cons ord. stock (5% stand.)	161 0 0
4% red. pref. stock	100 10 0
4% perp. deb. stock	102 10 0
5% perp. deb. stock	125 0 0
4% red. deb. stock	102 0 0

1952

Bridlington & North Frodingham Light Railway Co. Inc. (under Light Railways Act 1896) by order of Light Railway Commissioners, confirmed by Board of Trade 1898 **1902**

Bridlington Gas Co. Inc. by Special Act 1886. Dissolved 1 May 1949, undertaking being vested in North Eastern Area Gas Board under Gas Act 1948. Holders of securities were entitled to receive British Gas 3% guaranteed stock 1990—95 as follows in respect of each £10 unit, unless otherwise stated, of security held:

	£ s. d.
Orig. shares (10% stand.)	26 0 0
Addit. shares (7% stand.)	21 0 0
4½% red. pref. shares	10 6 0
4½% perp. deb. stock (per £100)	113 10 0
3¾% red. deb. stock (1951) (per £100)	100 7 6
3¾% red. deb. 'stock' (1953) (per £100)	100 12 6

1952

Bridport Gas Co. Ld. Regd. 1884; statutory powers 1937. Dissolved 1 May 1949, undertaking being vested in Southern Area Gas Board under Gas Act 1948. Holders of securities were entitled to receive British Gas 3% guaranteed stock 1990–95 as follows:

	£ s. d.
Ord. shares (8% basic) (of £1)	1 11 0
A 5% pref. shares (of £10)	11 4 0
B 6½% pref. shares (of £1)	1 7 0
4% debs. (of £25)	25 2 6
4½% debs. (of £25)	25 1 3

1952

Bridport Railway Co. Inc. by Special Act 1855. Great Western Railway Company under Act of 1901, acquired undertaking. Mortgages (£25,600) were adopted by purchaser; 4% preference shares received £8, 5% preference shares £10, and 6% preference shares £12 of Great Western consolidated preference stock per share respectively; ordinary shares received £6 per share in cash **1902**

Bridport Waterworks Co. Inc. by Special Act 1872. The undertaking vested in the West Dorset Water Board on 1 Oct. 1958 for £55,617 which was distributed to stockholders at the following rates per £100 stock held: 4% perpetual debenture stock, £100; 4½% consolidated preference stock, £75; 5% consolidated stock, £83 5*s*.; 5% maximum ordinary stock, £72; 10% consolidated ordinary stock, £156. Company was dissolved on 8 Oct. 1959 **1960**

Brierley (ABM) & Sons (Holdings) Ld. Regd. 1903 as ABM Brierley & Sons (1904) Ld.; name changed Apr. 1953. Dissolved 15 Mar. 1982 **1957**

Brierley Hill District Gas-Light Co. Inc. by Special Act 1849. Under Order of 1931, the undertaking was acquired by Dudley, Brierley Hill & District Gas Co., in which company shareholders were entitled to £2 5% consolidated ordinary stock for each £1 original stock (10% maximum) held; holders of A, B & C (7% maximum) shares were entitled to £14 5% consolidated ordinary stock for each share held; holders of 4% preference stock were entitled to 16*s*. of 5% consolidated preference stock for each £1 held. The liability in respect of the mortgages was assumed by acquiring company **1932**

Brierley Hill Potteries Ld. Regd. 1897. Vol. liq. 27 Jan. 1898. Final meeting return regd. 17 Jan. 1899 **1899**

Brigg Horse Haulage Appliance Co. Ld. Regd. 1898. Vol. liq. 1900. Removed from Register 1901 **1901**

VOL. FOR

Briggs Collieries Ld. Regd. 1939. Vol. liq. (members') 17 Oct. 1952. Colliery assets vested in National Coal Board. Capital returned to contributories—£2 4*s*. 6·55*d*. per share of 4*s*. £32 3*s*. 10*d*. paid into Companies' Liquidation Account in respect of unclaimed distributions. Final meeting return regd. 16 Oct. 1961 **1963**

Briggs (Henry), Son & Co. Ld. Regd. 1865. Vol. liq. (members') 18 July 1951. Shareholders were entitled to receive 1 share in Briggs Collieries Ld. for each share held. Capital returned to contributories—£2 13*s*. per share of 5*s*. Final meeting return regd. 29 June 1961 **1962**

Briggs Motor Bodies Ld. Regd. 1935. Vol. liq. (members') 31 Oct. 1958. All capital was owned by Ford Motor Co. Ld. Final meeting return regd. 24 Dec. 1958 **1954**

Brightlingsea Gas & Coke Co. Ld. Regd. 1862. Dissolved 1 May 1949, undertaking being vested in Eastern Area Gas Board under Gas Act 1948. Holders of securities were entitled to receive British Gas 3% guaranteed stock 1990–95 as follows:

	£ s. d.
Ord. shares (of £3)	8 10 0
3½% debs. (of £100)	100 0 0

1952

Brighton Alhambra Ld. Regd. 1888. Court Order to wind up 29 July 1893. Removed from Register 1906 **1894**

"Brighton Alhambra" Ld. Regd. 1893. Court Order to wind up 13 Oct 1908; it was anticipated that about 4*s*. in the £ in respect of capital would be made. Struck off Register 1923 **1909**

Brighton and Dyke Railway Co. Inc. by Special Act 1877. In 1923 the undertaking was merged into the Southern Railway Co. in which company stockholders were entitled to stock as follows:

For each £100 *held*		*S. R.*
4% Debenture	£100	4% Debenture
5% B Debenture	£50	Ordinary B

The Ordinary, Preferred and Deferred Shares were cancelled **1924**

Brighton & Hove Co-operative Supply Association Ld. Regd. 1873. Reconstructed 1902 as Brighton and Hove Supply Association Ld. in which company shareholders were entitled to 3 fully-paid ordinary shares of 10*s*. for each share of £2 held. Removed from Register 1904 **1908**

Brighton & Hove Electric Light Co. Ld. Regd. 1885. Removed from Register 1897 **1895**

Brighton & Hove General Gas Co. *See* Brighton, Hove & Worthing Gas Co.

Brighton & Rottingdean Seashore Electric Tramroad Co. Inc. by Special Act 1893. Powers lapsed **1910**

Brighton & South Coast Aerated Bread Co. Ld. Regd. 1889. Struck off Register 1914 **1911**

Brighton & Sussex Union Fire Insurance Co. Ld. Regd. 1881. Business was acquired by Royal Insurance Co. in 1889. Vol. liq. Feb. 1890. Final meeting return regd. 1 Jan. 1891 **1890**

Brighton Aquarium Co. Ld. Regd. 1893. Removed from Register 1902 **1897**

Brighton District Tramways Co. Inc. by Special Act 1882. In liquidation in 1888 **1888**

Brighton Gas Light & Coke Co. Amalgamated 1881 with Brighton and Hove General Gas Co. (later Brighton, Hove & Worthing Gas Co.) in which company shareholders were entitled to 1 original share of £20 *plus* £3 11*s*. 6*d*. for each share held **1883**

Brighton General Omnibus Co. Ld. Regd. 1884, Court Orders: to wind up 21 Mar. 1885: to dissolve 2 June 1891 **1886**

Brighton Hotels Ld. Regd. 1897. Removed from Register 1903 **1904**

Brighton, Hove & Preston United Omnibus Co. Ld. Regd. 1884. Vol. liq. 24 Sept. 1921. Undertaking was acquired by Thomas Tilling Ld. Final meeting return regd. 19 Dec. 1922 **1922**

Brighton, Hove & Worthing Gas Co. Founded by Deed of Settlement 1825 as Brighton & Hove General Gas Co.; inc. by Special Act 1839; name changed 1931. Dissolved 1 May 1949, undertaking being vested in South Eastern Area Gas Board under Gas Act 1948. Holders of securities were entitled to receive, in respect of each £100 unit held, British Gas 3% guaranteed stock 1990–5 as follows:

	£ s. d.
6% stand. cons. stock	151 0 0
5% stand. cons. stock	135 0 0
6% B pref. cons. stock	133 10 0
4% pref. stock	103 0 0
4% red. pref. stock	102 0 0
4% perp. deb. stock	103 0 0
5% perp. deb. stock	125 0 0
3½% red. deb. stock (issued before 1 Jan. 1946)	100 0 0

**See Stock Exchange Year-Book.*

VOL. FOR

3½% red. deb. stock (issued after 31 Dec. 1945).....................................100 0 0   **1952**

Brighton Marine Palace & Pier Co. Inc. by Special Act 1888 ....   **1906**

Brighton Marine Palace & Pier Ld. Regd. 1890. Struck off Register 22 Dec. 1903 ....   **1904**

Brighton, Rottingdean & Newhaven Direct Railway Co. Inc. by Special Act 1886. Undertaking abandoned by Act of 1894 ....   **1895**

Brighton Solvo Laundries Ld. Regd. 1889. Struck off Register 23 July 1901 ....   **1902**

Brighton, Worthing & South Coast Steamboat Co. Ld. Regd. 1891. Removed from Register 1902 ....   **1902**

Bright's Light & Power Ld. Regd. 1898. Struck off Register 1922 ....   **1913**

Brights (Southsea) Ld. Regd. 1908 as Flora Ld.; name changed Nov. 1921. Vol. liq. (members') 28 Nov. 1932. All shares owned by Bright & Colson Ld. Final meeting return regd. 28 June 1938 ....   **1933**

Brights Stores Ld. Regd. 1898. Vol. liq. 7 Aug. 1925. Undertaking and assets were acquired by Bright & Colson Ld., in which company shareholders were entitled to 4 ordinary shares of £1 for every 6 ordinary shares of 10s. held or 1 preference share of £1 for each preference share held. The debentures were repaid at par. Final meeting return regd. 27 Nov. 1926 ....   **1926**

Brightwen & Co. Regd. 1936. In 1939 the assets were sold to Cater Brightwen & Co. Ld. Vol. liq. (members') 29 Dec. 1945. Final meeting return regd. 18 Mar. 1946 ....   **1946**

Brilliant & St. George United Gold Mining Co. Ld. Inc. Queensland 1889. Vol. liq. May 1913. Reconstructed as St. George & Moonstone Gold Mines Ld. Shareholders were entitled in respect of every 100 10s. shares held (a) to 25 fully-paid shares of 5s., (b) to subscribe at par for 50 shares carrying right to a further 25 fully-paid shares as bonus (to be issued as soon as 2s. has been called per contributing share or a dividend had been declared), and (c) to tender for further shares carrying the same bonus rights.......   **1914**

Brilliant Block Gold Mining Co. Ld. Inc. Queensland 1889. In Dec. 1916 shareholders authorised the closing of the mine and selling the plant **1917**

Brilliant Central Gold Mining Co. No Liability. Inc. Queensland 1899. Vol. liq. Feb. 1915 ....   **1916**

Brilliant (Charters Towers) Deep Levels Ld. Inc. Queensland 1896. Reconstructed 1902 as Deep Level Mines of Charters Towers Ld. for 125,000 fully-paid shares of 10s. **1907**

Brilliant Deeps Ld. Inc. Queensland 1907. Vol. liq. Feb. 1918 ....   **1918**

Brilliant Extended Block Gold Mining Co. Ld. Undertaking and property acquired in 1896 by Brilliant (Charters Towers) Deep Levels Ld, for 170,000 fully-paid shares of £1 ....   **1902**

Brilliant Extended Gold Mining Co. Ld. Inc, Queensland 1895. Cable received in 1921 to close London office as company was going into liquidation **1922**

Brilliant Gold Mining Co. Ld. Inc. Queensland 1896. London office closed 26 Apr. 1916, Written off by Registrar of Joint Companies in June 1918 ....   **1916**

Brilliant North Gold Mines Ld. Inc. Queensland 1905. In 1912 company was in liquidation **1912**

Brilliant Stockholm No. 1 South Ld. Inc. Queensland 1906. Vol. liq. June 1910. Property sold to Brilliant Mining Co. Ld. First and final distribution of 7s. 8d. per 100 shares (of 5s.) in Nov. 1910......................   **1911**

Brill's Brighton Baths Co. Ld. Regd. 1865. Vol. liq. 31 Dec. 1919. Final meeting return regd. 17 Apr. 1920   **1920**

Brimsdown Lead Co. Ld. Regd. 1900 as Bischof White Lead Corporation (1900) Ld.; name changed 1903. Vol. liq. 16 June 1905. Court Order to stay proceedings 22 Dec. 1905. Vol. liq. (members') 11 Aug. 1939. Capital returned to contributories—15s. 8·31d. per preference share of 15s., 5s. 8·31d. per ordinary share of 5s. Payments into Companies' Liquidation Account—£354 13s. in respect of unclaimed preference share balances and £847 1s. 2d in respect of unclaimed ordinary share balances. Final meeting return regd. 10 Sep. 1940...............   **1940**

Brinkburn Coal Co. Ld. Regd. 1917. Vol. liq. Feb. 1925. Struck off Register Mar. 1930 ....   **1931**

Brinsmead (John) & Sons Ld. Regd. 1899. Vol. liq. 22 Dec. 1916. Final meeting return regd. 26 July 1917   **1910**

Brinsmead (John) & Sons Ld. Regd. 1916 as Brinsmead (John) & Sons (1916) Ld.; name changed 1917. Court Order to wind up 24 Aug. 1921. Business was acquired by J. B. Cramer & Co. Ld. Holders of 5% debentures were repaid in full in cash. No capital returned to contributories. Struck off Register Apr. 1929 ....   **1930**

VOL. FOR

Brinsmead (Thos. Edw.) & Sons Ld. Regd. 1896. Court Order to wind up 3 Dec. 1896. Struck off Register 1928 ....   **1897**

Brinton (John) & Co. Ld. Regd. 1881. Vol. liq. 19 June 1891. Final meeting return regd. 11 Mar. 1895 .....   ***1886**

Brisbane Electric Tramways Investment Co. Ld. Regd. 1900. The 8% debenture stock was repaid at 102% on 22 Nov. 1924. Vol. liq. 12 Dec. 1924. Final meeting return regd. 5 Oct. 1927 ....   **1925**

Brisbane Tramways Co. Ld. Under Act of 1922 the undertaking was sold to Brisbane Tramways Trust   **1925**

Briseis Tin & General Mining Co. Ld. Regd. 1899 as Briseis Tin Mines Ld.; name changed 1909. Vol. liq. Mar. 1930. Struck off Register Dec. 1932...........   **1933**

Brissam Concession Ld. Regd. 1902. Removed from Register 1907 ....   **1904**

Bristol & Exeter Railway Co. Undertaking acquired by Great Western Railway Company under Act of 1876 ....   **1949**

Bristol & North Somerset Railway Co. Inc. by Special Act 1863. In 1882 the affairs of the company were in Chancery **1883**

Bristol & Portishead Pier & Railway Co. Inc. by Special Act 1863. By Act of 1884 the undertaking was vested in the Great Western Railway Company. The consideration was sufficient to satisfy the debentures, debenture stock and guaranteed stock in full. The preference stock received 6% and the ordinary stock 22% of their nominal values **1888**

Bristol & South Wales Railway Waggon Co. Ld. Regd. 1860 as Bristol & West of England Railway Waggon Co. Ld. Vol. liq. (members') 2 Mar 1934. Capital returned to contributories—£3 16s. 5·85d. per share of £10, £3 paid. £319 5s. 6d. was paid into Companies' Liquidation Account in respect of amount owing to former shareholders out of balance deposited by Yorkshire Railway Waggon Co. Ld. Final meeting return regd. 13 Sept. 1935 ....   **1935**

Bristol & West of England Canadian Land Mortgage & Investment Co. Ld. Regd. 1878. The debentures were repaid between Sept. 1897 and Sept. 1903. Vol. liq. 3 Aug. 1906. Capital returned to contributories—£2 11s. 6d. per share of £25 in Nov. 1906; further payments (if any) not known. Removed from Register 1907 ....   **1907**

Bristol Cab Co. Ld. Regd. 1886. Reconstructed 1887 as Bristol Tramways and Carriage Co, Ld., in which company shareholders were entitled to an equal amount of shares. Final meeting return regd. 7 Aug. 1888 ....   **1888**

Bristol, Cardiff & Swansea Aerated Bread Co. Ld. Regd. 1889. Vol. liq. 6 Apr. 1891. Final meeting return regd, 4 Nov. 1892 ....   **1892**

Bristol Channel Passenger Boats Ld. Regd. 1910. Vol. liq. Dec, 1911. Steamboats were acquired by P. & A. Campbell Ld., in which company shareholders were entitled to 11 ordinary shares of £1 for every 25 shares of £1 held, Removed from Register 1913 ..   **1913**

Bristol Channel Steamers Ld. Regd. 1919. Vol. liq. (creditors') 26 Apr. 1932. Assets realised insufficient to pay creditors in full. Final meeting return regd. 26 Jan. 1933 ....   **1933**

Bristol Commercial Union Bank Ld. Regd. 1882. Removed from Register 1889 ....   ***1886**

Bristol District Super-Aeration Ld. Regd. 1901. Vol. liq. June 1904. Removed from Register 1907 ....   **1905**

Bristol Dock Co. Undertaking purchased by Bristol Corporation in 1881 ....   **1883**

Bristol Empire Ld. Regd. 1920. Receiver appointed 25 July 1931. Court Order to wind up 13 Oct. 1931. All capital held by Theatre Securities Ld. Struck off Register 19 May 1944 ....   **1940**

Bristol Empire Palace of Varieties Ld. Regd. 1891. Removed from Register 1900 ....   ***1895**

Bristol Flour & Bread Concern Ld. Regd. 1899. Vol. liq. (members') 12 Jan. 1933. Capital returned to contributories—£1 2s. 1d. per share of £1. Final meeting return regd. 9 Jan. 1934......................   **1933**

Bristol Garden Suburb Ld. See Bristol Housing Ld.

Bristol Gas Co. Inc. as Bristol United Gas Light Co. by Special Act 1853; name changed 1891. Dissolved 1 May 1949, undertaking being vested in South Western Area Gas Board under Gas Act 1948. Holders of securities were entitled to receive, in respect of each £100 unit held, British Gas 3% guaranteed stock 1990–95 as follows:

	£	s.	d.
Gen. cap stock (5% max.)	118	6	8
4% deb. stock (Acts 1853 & 1873)	102	0	0
4% new deb. stock (Acts 1891, 1899 & 1910)	101	6	8
5% new deb. stock	124	10	0	**1952**

VOL. FOR

Bristol Hippodrome Ld. Regd. 1911 as St. Augustine's Parade Hippodrome, Bristol, Ld. A subsidiary of Stoll Theatres Corpn. Ld. Vol. liq. (members') 20 Oct. 1954. Final meeting return regd. 21 Jan. 1955 **1951**

Bristol Hotel & Palmerston Co. Ld. Regd. 1890 as Manero Ld.; name changed July 1892. Vol. liq. (creditors') 15 July 1932. No capital returned to contributories. Final meeting return regd. 10 May 1933 **1933**

Bristol Housing Ld. Regd. 1909 as Bristol Garden Suburb Ld.; name changed Oct. 1923. Vol. liq. (members') 6 Dec. 1934. Capital returned to contributories—£30,402 15s. 2d. Final meeting return regd. 3 Oct. 1936 **1935**

Bristol Insurance Co. Ld. Regd. 1922. All shares owned by Lancashire & General Assurance Co. Ld. Struck off Register 1929 **1927**

Bristol Joint Stock Bank Ld. Regd. 1884. Court Orders: to wind up 26 Apr. 1890; to dissolve 21 June 1893 ***1891**

"Bristol" Ld. Regd. 1903. Court Order to wind up 23 Jan. 1906. Liquidator released 5 July 1912. Struck off Register 10 Oct. 1916 **1907**

Bristol Pennant Stone Firms Ld. Regd. 1894. Vol. liq. 16 Oct. 1897. Final meeting return regd. 12 Jan. 1899 **1899**

Bristol Port & Channel Dock Co. Inc. by Special Act 1854. Undertaking was purchased by the Corporation of Bristol in 1884 for £390,000 3½% Corporation stock. 5% perpetual debenture stock 6% debenture stock (1877) and Special 6% debenture stock, received Corporation stock at par; 6% A debenture stock received 80% and 6% B debenture stock 60%; further payments (if any) not known **1885**

Bristol Port & Channel Dock Warehouse Co. Ld. Regd. 1875. Undertaking was acquired by Bristol Corporation. Removed from Register 1894 **1885**

Bristol Port Railway & Pier Co. Inc. by Special Act 1862. Under Midland Railway (Additional Powers) Act 1890 the undertaking was vested jointly in the Great Western Railway Co. and the Midland Railway Co. 5% debentures were repaid at par. £50.259 7s. was distributed in discharge of all other capital liabilities **1891**

Bristol Steam Navigation Co. Ld. Regd. 1877. Vol. liq. 19 Dec. 1917. Reconstructed as company of same name; later changed in 1965 to Lovell Shipping and Transport Group Ld. Final meeting return regd. 25 Mar. 1918 **1918**

Bristol Tramways Co. Ld. Regd. 1874. Vol. liq. Sept. 1887. Reconstructed as Bristol Tramways and Carriage Co. Ld., in which company shareholders were entitled to an equal amount of shares. Final meeting return regd. 7 Aug. 1888 **1888**

Bristol United Breweries Ld. Regd. 1889. All capital was owned by Bristol Brewery Georges & Co. Ld. Vol. liq. (members') 28 Sept. 1961. Capital repaid at par 1 Jan. 1962. Final meeting return regd. 11 Sept. 1962 **1964**

Bristol United Gas Light Co. See Bristol Gas Co.

Bristol Wagon & Carriage Works Co. Ld. Regd. 1866 as Bristol Wagon Works Co. Ld.; name changed July 1889. Vol. liq. 24 Oct. 1924. Final meeting return regd. 13 Dec. 1924 **1925**

Brit Holdings Ld. Regd. 1937. Vol. liq. (members') 15 Jan. 1941. All shares were owned by Britannia Electric Lamp Works Ld. Final meeting return regd. 16 Oct. 1943 **1941**

Britannia Batteries Ld. Regd. 1913 as Edison Accumulators Ld.; name changed Jan 1929. Vol. liq. 26 Nov. 1948. Final meeting return regd. 16 Aug. 1949 **1950**

Britannia Gold Mining Co. Ld. Regd. 1897. Vol. liq. 9 Nov. 1904. Removed from Register 1906 **1905**

Britannia (Hauraki) Gold Mining Co. Ld. Regd. 1896. Struck off Register 7 May 1907 **1908**

Britannia Mills Flour & Bread Co., Birmingham (late Mary Bodington & Sons) Ld. Regd. 1862. Vol. liq. 23 Feb. 1887. Final meeting return regd. 25 Feb. 1895 **1888**

Britannia Motor Carriage Co. Ld. Regd. 1896. Vol. liq. 13 Jan. 1899. Undertaking and assets were transferred to London Exploration Co. Ld. Removed from Register 1901 **1899**

Britannia Nitrate Co. Ld. Regd. 1906. Vol. liq. 11 Aug. 1910. Final meeting return regd. 7 Oct. 1921 **1911**

Britannic Merthyr Coal Co. Ld. Regd. 1904. Struck off Register 21 Jan. 1936 **1936**

Britannic Textile Co. Ld. Regd. 1921. Vol. liq. 10 Sept. 1928. Undertaking and assets were acquired by Britannic Textiles (Manchester) Ld. Final meeting return regd. 16 Sept. 1931 **1929**

Britannic Textiles (Manchester) Ld. Regd. 1928. All capital owned by Baerlein Brothers Ld. Vol. liq. 31 Dec. 1954. Final meeting return regd. 28 July 1955 **1938**

British Abrasive Wheel Co. Ld. Regd. 1909. Vol. liq. (members') 19 Nov. 1934. All shares owned by Universal Grinding Wheel Co. Ld. Final meeting return regd. 7 Mar. 1935 **1941**

VOL. FOR

British Acetate Silk Corporation Ld. Regd. 1928. Court Order to wind up 13 Oct. 1931. Struck off Register 17 July 1942 **1945**

British Africa Ld. Regd. 1901. Vol. liq. 15 May 1905. Removed from Register 1907 **1906**

British Aircraft Manufacturing Co. Ld. Regd. 1935. Vol. liq. (members') 30 Nov. 1938. Capital returned to contributories—3·495d. per share of 5s. Final meeting return regd. 10 Aug. 1940 **1939**

British Airways (Atlantic) Ld. Regd. 1937 as Imperial Airways (Atlantic) Ld.; name changed Apr. 1940 to Airways (Atlantic) Ld.; and as above in May 1941. Vol. liq. (members') 8 Oct. 1941. Capital returned to contributories—12s. per share of £1. Final meeting return regd. 22 Jan. 1942 **1940**

British Airways (Bermuda) Ld. Regd. 1936 as Imperial Airways (Bermuda) Ld.; name changed Apr. 1940 to Airways (Bermuda) Ld.; and as above in May 1941. Vol. liq. (members') 8 Oct. 1941. Capital returned to contributories—15s. 2d. per share of £1. Final meeting return regd. 22 Jan. 1942 **1940**

British Airways Ld. Regd. 1935 as Allied British Airways Ld.; name changed Oct. 1935. Liqd. by British Overseas Airways Act 1939. Liq. commenced 1 Apr. 1940. Final meeting return regd. 25 June 1940 **1941**

British Alberta Co. Ld. Regd. 1910. Struck off Register 2 Mar. 1943 **1944**

British Alberta Oil Co. Ld. Regd. 1914. Vol. liq. 20 Nov. 1922. Final meeting return regd. 2 Aug. 1923 **1923**

British Alizarine Co. Ld. Regd. 1882. Vol. liq. (members') 12 Apr. 1939. Capital returned to contributories—8s. 11¾d. per ordinary share of £1. Final meeting return regd. 22 Nov. 1940 **1942**

British Alluvial Tin Syndicate Ld. Regd. 1924. Struck off Register 8 Aug. 1947 **1938**

British Aluminum Co. Ld. Regd. 1894. Vol. liq. 31 Dec. 1909. Reconstructed 1910 as company of same name. Shareholders were entitled to (a) 5 preference shares of £1 (credited with 17s. 6d. paid) for each A preference share of £5 held; (b) 1 preference share of £1 (credited with 16s. 3d. paid) and 3 ordinary shares of £1 (credited with 16s. 3d. paid) for each preference share of £5 held; (c) 3 ordinary shares of £1 (credited with 13s. 4d. paid for each ordinary share of £5 held; and (d) 1 fully-paid ordinary share of £1 for each funding certificate of £1 held. Holders of debenture stock were entitled to an equal amount of debenture stock in new company plus an amount equal to 1½ years' interest. Final meeting return regd. 10 Oct. 1912 **1910**

British America Corporation Ld. Regd. 1897. Court Order to wind up 13 June 1901. Removed from Register 1910 **1902**

British American Continental Bank Ld. Regd 1917 as Hannevig's Bank Ld.; name changed Sept. 1920. Court Order to wind up 25 Jan. 1921. Liquidator released 27 Feb. 1936 **1921**

British American Equities Inc. Liquidated Sept. 1941. Assets were transferred to Chosen Corporation Ld **1943**

British American Goldfields Ld. See British Empire Goldfields Ld.

British American Investment Co. Ld. Regd. 1892. Vol. liq. 16 Jan. 1899. Final meeting return regd. 20 Apr. 1899 **1899**

British American Land Co. Inc. by Royal Charter and Special Act 1834. Charter surrendered to Privy Council Oct. 1947 and company finally dissolved. Capital returned to contributories—27s. 6d. per share of £1 **1949**

British-American Skate Manufacturing Co. Ld. Regd. 1909. Court Order to wind up 22 Feb. 1910. Liquidator released 25 Aug. 1915. Struck off Register 14 Feb. 1919 **1911**

British American Tin Corporation Ld. Regd. 1929. Vol. liq. June 1932. Undertaking and assets were acquired by Tin Holdings Ld. and British Tin Investment Corporation Ld. Shareholders were entitled to 1 fully-paid share of 10s. in British Tin Investment Corporation Ld. and 3 ordinary shares of 1s. in Tin Holdings Ld. for each ordinary share of £1 held or 2 fully-paid shares of 10s. in British Tin Investment Corporation Ld: for each preferred share of £1 held. Final meeting return regd. 17 Dec. 1932 **1933**

British American Tin Mines Ld. Regd. 1934. Vol. liq. (creditors') 12 Sept. 1957. Debenture stockholders received—7s. 1·6d. per £1 6% stock. Final meeting return regd. 5 Oct. 1960 **1962**

British & African Investment Co. Ld. Regd. 1889. Vol. liq. 1 June 1892. Final meeting return regd. 11 Mar. 1895 ***1893**

See Stock Exchange Year-Book.

VOL. FOR

British & African Steam Navigation Co. Ld. Regd. Edinburgh 1883. Vol. liq. Sept. 1900. Final meeting return regd. 4 Sept. 1901 .... **1901**

British & African Steam Navigation Co. Ld. Regd. 1900 as British & African Steam Navigation Co. (1900) Ld.; name changed Dec. 1908. Vol. liq. (members') 18 June 1936. Undertaking was acquired by Elder Dempster Lines Holdings Ld. (later Liner Holdings Ld.). Capital returned to contributories—£73,000. Final meeting return regd. 31 July 1937 .... **1937**

British & Allied Investments Corporation Ld. Regd. 1913 as All Red Route Investments Ld.; name subsequently changed. Vol. liq. 26 Mar. 1925. Undertaking and assets acquired by company of same name in which shareholders were entitled to 1 fully-paid share of £1 for each 4 shares of £1 held. Final meeting return regd. 31 Jan. 1928 .... **1926**

British & Allied Investments Corporation Ld. Regd. 1925. Vol. liq. 28 June 1940. Undertaking and certain assets acquired by Carters (Merchants) Ld. Capital returned to contributories—16s. 4d. per share of £1. Final meeting return regd. 4 Sept.1948 **1949**

British and American Importation Co. Ld. See Mexican National Land Mortgage and Investment Co. Ld.

British & American Mortgage Co. Ld. Regd. 1877. Vol. liq. 18 Feb. 1920. The terminable debentures and debenture stock were repaid on 31 May 1920. Capital returned to contributories—£11 16s. per preference slsare of £10; £7 18s. 7d. per ordinary share of £10 (£2 paid). Final meeting return regd. 9 Sept. 1920 .... **1921**

British & American Trustee & Finance Corporation Ld. Regd. 1890. Vol. liq. 24 Feb. 1899. Final meeting return regd. 27 Oct. 1914 .... **1898**

British & Argentine Corporation Ld. Regd. 1906. Vol. liq. 18 Dec. 1911. Final meeting return regd. 24 Apr. 1915 .... **1912**

British & Argentine Meat Co. Ld. Regd. 1892 as James Nelson and Sons Ld.; name changed May 1914. Vol. liq. 18 May 1923. Final meeting return regd. 1 May 1929 .... **1924**

British & Argentine Steam Navigation Co. Ld. Regd. 1909. Vol. liq. (members') 16 Aug. 1933. The outstanding debentures were redeemed as par. Undertaking was acquired by Furness Withy and Co. Ld. which company owned all shares. Capital returned to contributories—£325,803 9s. 7d. Final meeting return regd. 11 May 1934 .... **1934**

British & Australasian Insurance Co. Ld. Regd. 1918. Vol. liq. Nov. 1919. Undertaking acquired by Greater Britain Insurance Corporation Ld. Shareholders were entitled to 2⅔ shares of £1 (5s. paid) for each share of £1 (10s. paid) held. Final meeting return regd. 27 Mar. 1930 .... **1920**

British & Australasian Trust & Loan Co. Ld. Regd. 1878. Vol. liq. 18 May 1915. Capital returned to contributories—£4 per share of £25 (£2 10s. paid) at Nov. 1915; further payments (if any) not known. Final meeting return regd. 3 Nov. 1916 .... **1916**

British & Beningtons Ld. Regd. 1896 as British & Beningtons Tea Trading Assn. Ld.; name changed Dec. 1911. Vol. liq. 1 Oct. 1937. Capital returned to contributories—15s. per preference share of £1. Final meeting return regd. 12 May 1949 .... **1951**

British & Beningtons Tea Trading Assn. Ld. See above.

British & Brazilian Rubber Planters & Manufacturers Ld. Regd. 1908 as Bahia Rubber & Fibre Plantation Ld.; name changed Dec. 1908. Vol. liq. (creditors') 26 June 1931. No capital returned to contributories. Final meeting return regd. 26 Apr. 1937 .... **1932**

British & Canadian Lead Co. Ld. Regd. 1899. Vol. liq. 21 Jan. 1914. Final meeting return regd. 26 Sept. 1914 **1916**

British and Colonial Agency Ld. See Egyptian Sudan Minerals Ld.

British & Colonial Dermatine Co. Ld. Regd. 1886. Reconstructed 1889 as Dermatine Co. Ld. in which company shareholders were entitled to 1 share of £5 (credited with £4 7s. 6d. paid) for each share of £5 held. Removed from Register 1906 .... **1890**

British & Colonial Estates Ld. Regd. 1895 as Middle Black Reef Gold Mines Ld.; name changed Oct. 1900. Vol. liq. Apr. 1909. Removed from Register 1911 .... **1910**

British & Colonial Investments Ld. Regd. 1909. Undertaking was acquired by Transvaal and Rhodesian Estates Ld., in which company shareholders were entitled to 11 fully-paid shares of 5s. for every 5 shares of 10s. held. Removed from Register 1912 .... **1912**

British & Colonial Securities Ld. Regd. 1884 as British North American Investment Co. Ld. name changed July 1892. Vol. liq. 9 Apr. 1897. Final meeting return regd. 29 Nov. 1898 .... **1898**

British & Colonial Steam Navigation Co. Ld. Regd. 1891. Business was acquired in Nov. 1900 by Bucknall Steamship Lines Ld. (later Ellerman & Bucknall Steamship Co. Ld.) for £265,000 in fully-paid shares of £10 and £385,000 in cash. Removed from Register 1906 .... **1902**

British & Continental Banking Co. Ld.—See Banque de Suez (U. K.) Ld.

British & Continental Plantations Trust Ld. Regd. 1911 as British & Continental Tea Plantations Trust Ld.; name changed Feb. 1921. Vol. liq. (members') 18 Aug. 1933. Undertaking and assets acquired by company of same name in which shareholders were entitled to 1 share of 10s. (with 7s. 6d. credited as paid) for each share of £1 held. Debenture stockholders were entitled to £100 6% income debenture stock and 30 new fully-paid shares of 10s. for every £100 debenture stock. Final meeting return regd. 2 Nov. 1935 .... **1934**

British & Continental Plantations Trust Ld. Regd. 1933. Vol. liq. (members') 1 Mar 1954. The outstanding £13,960 4½% debenture stock was purchased and cancelled between 1 Jan. and 1 Feb. 1954. £4 7s. 8d. was paid into Companies' Liquidation Account. Final meeting return regd. 10 Mar. 1955 .... **1956**

British & Dominions Co-operative Investment Trust Ld. Regd. Industrial & Provident Societies Acts Jan. 1932. Vol. liq. May 1934 .... **1935**

British & Eastern Shipping Co. Ld. Regd. 1863. Vol. liq. 8 Jan. 1906. Removed from Register 1907 .... **1906**

British & European Timber Trust Ld. Regd. 1928. Vol. liq. (members') 20 Sept. 1933. No capital returned to contributories. Final meeting return regd. 5 May 1934 .... **1934**

British & Foreign Banking Corporation Ld. Regd. 1909. Struck off Register 1916 .... **1914**

British & Foreign Bottle Co. Ld. In Mar. 1923 certain assets were acquired by Canning Town Glass Works Ld. (regd. 1923) in exchange for cash, second debentures and shares of £1 ....:...... **1924**

British & Foreign Du Bois Co. Ld. Regd. 1898. Undertaking was acquired in 1901 by Du Bois Co. Ld. Removed from Register 1902 .... **1902**

British & Foreign Electrical Vehicle Co. Ld. See British Electromobile Co. Ld.

British & Foreign Exploration Co. Ld. Regd. 1895. Sturck off Register Jan. 1931 .... **1932**

British & Foreign Films Ld. Regd. 1928. Vol. liq. (creditors') 30 Jan. 1931. Assets realised insufficient to pay creditors in full. Final meeting return regd. 24 Apr. 1936 .... **1931**

British & Foreign Fresh Meat Co. Ld. Regd. 1884. Vol. liq. 16 Mar. 1885. Final meeting return regd. 4 Aug. 1885 .... **1886**

British & Foreign Lee Arms Co. Ld. Regd. 1899. Removed from Register 16 Nov. 1906 .... ***1905**

British & Foreign Mercantile Bank Ld. Regd. 1917. Ceased business at end of 1927. Struck off Register Dec. 1930 .... **1931**

British & Foreign Oxolin Co. Ld. Regd. 1899. Removed from Register 1902 .... **1901**

British & Foreign Steamship Co. Ld. Regd. 1887. Vol. liq. 7 Feb. 1918. Final meeting return regd. 28 Feb. 1918 .... ***1919**

British & Foreign Trading Co. Ld. Regd. 1889. Removed from Register 1910 .... **1907**

British & Foreign Utilities Development Corporation Ld. Regd. 1928. Vol. liq. (creditors') 24 June 1964. No capital returned to contributories. Final meeting return regd. 2 June 1965 .... **1966**

British & Foreign Water & Gas Works Co. Ld. Regd. 1872. Removed from Register 1884 .... ***1880**

British & French Banking & Investment Co. Ld. Regd. 1928. Vol. liq. Nov. 1935. Struck off Register Dec. 1949 .... **1950**

British and General Investment Trust Ld. Regd. 1888. Vol. liq. June 1908. Removed from Register 1912 **1909**

British & International Utilities Ld. See Lincolnshire & Central Electric Supply Co. Ld.

British & Irish Telephone & Electric Works Co. Ld. Regd. 1881. Removed from Register 1888 .... ***1883**

British & Italian Finance Syndicate Ld. Regd. 1896. Struck off Register 17 Nov. 1899 .... **1900**

British & Japanese Finance Corporation Ld. Regd. 1905. Vol. liq. Dec. 1907. Removed from Register 1908 **1908**

British & Korean Corporation Ld. Regd. 1901. Vol. liq. 5 Dec. 1907. Final meeting return regd. 1 Apr. 1914 **1908**

British & Mexican Trust Co. Ld. Regd. 1907. Struck off Register 7 Dec. 1937 .... **1938**

British & New Zealand Mortgage & Agency Co. Ld. Regd. 1881. Vol. liq. 28 Nov. 1889. Court Orders; to wind up under supervision; to dissolve 2 May 1898 **1891**

VOL. FOR

*See Stock Exchange Year-Book.

VOL. FOR

British & North Atlantic Steam Navigation Co. Ld. Regd. 1881. Vol. liq. 21 Dec. 1920. Final meeting return regd. 11 May 1929 1922

British & North European Bank Ld. Regd. 1920. Vol. liq. Nov. 1925. Struck off Register 27 Oct. 1942 1943

British & Overseas Agency Ld. Regd. 1911. Vol. liq. (members') 26 Mar. 1936. Capital returned to contributories—4s. 2½d. per share of £1. Final meeting return regd. 23 Mar. 1937 1937

British & South African Insurance Corporation Ld. Regd. 1917. Vol. liq. 2 Dec. 1919. Shareholders were entitled to 2⅔ shares of £1 (5s. paid) in Greater Britain Insurance Corporation Ld. for each share of £1 (10s. paid) held. Final meeting return regd. 5 Aug. 1931 1920

British & South Pacific Trading Co. Ld. Regd. 1922. Vol. liq. 24 Feb. 1931. Capital returned to contributories—2s. 9d. per share of £1. Final meeting return regd. 30 Nov. 1945 1947

British and Transvaal Financial Co. Ld. See British Transvaal & General Financial Co. Ld.

British Assn. of Glass Bottle Manufacturers Ld. Regd. 1907. Vol. liq. (members') 4 July 1961. Final meeting return regd. 15 June 1962 1947

British Anzani p.l.c. Regd. on 28 June as Branzi Ld., a private company converted into a public company and name changed to British Anzani Engineering Co. Ld. on 28 June 1951; name changed to British Anzani Ld. on 15 Sept. 1972. Compulsorily wound up Aug. 1983 1981–2

British Australian Broken Hill Ld. Inc. South Australia 1922. Vol. liq. Nov. 1923. Undertaking and assets were acquired by North Broken Hill Ld., in which company shareholders were entitled to 4 shares of £1 (credited as fully-paid) plus £5 12s. 6d. in cash for every 15 shares of £1 held 1924

British Australian Cotton Association Ld. Inc. Queensland 1922 as Australian Cotton Growing Association (Queensland) Ld.; name changed Mar. 1923. In liq. London office closed 1931

British Australian Mines Agency Ld. Regd. 1895. Removed from Register 1904 1901

British Australian Oil Co. Ld. Regd Mar. 1910 as Australian Oil Co. Ld.; name changed June 1910. Vol. liq. 3 Sept. 1913 for reconstruction under same name. Shareholders were entitled to 1 share of £1 (credited with 15s. paid) in new company for every share of £1 held. Struck off Register 14 July 1933 1914

British Australian Oil Co. Ld. Regd. 1913. Receiver for debenture holders appointed in Nov. 1914. Struck off Register 1923 1915

British Austrian Oil Investment Co. Ld. Regd. 1910. Vol. liq. Dec. 1924. Struck off Register Jan. 1934 1934

British Automatic Aerators Ld. Regd. 1902. Vol. liq. Sept. 1909 for reconstruction as Consol Automatic Aerators Ld., in which company shareholders were entitled to 1 fully-paid ordinary share of £1 and 5 ordinary shares of £1 (credited with 15s. paid) for every 10 ordinary shares of £1 held or 1 fully-paid ordinary share of £1 and 10 preference shares of £1 (18s. paid) for every 10 preference shares of £1 held. Removed from Register 1912 1910

British Automatic Gramophone Co. Ld. Regd. 1928. Vol. liq. (creditors') 13 July 1931. Assets realised insufficient to pay creditors in full. Final meeting return regd. 29 June 1932 1932

British Automatic Refrigerator Co. Ld. See British Automatic Refrigerators Ld.

British Automatic Refrigerators Ld. Regd. 1935. Vol. liq. (creditors') 21 Oct. 1936. Struck off Register 4 Oct. 1938 1939

British Automobile Development Co. Ld. See Tilling and British Automobile Trust Ld.

British Automobile Traction Co. Ld. See Tilling and British Automobile Trust Ld.

British-Baltic Commercial Corporation Ld. See Baltic & Mediterranean Corporation Ld.

British Banana Margarine Co. Ld. See British Import & Packing Co. Ld.

British Bank of Australia Ld. Inc. Australia 1888 as Victorian Freehold Bank Ld.; name changed Sept. 1889. In liquidation in 1892 1892

British Bank of Central America Ld. In liquidation in 1883 1883

British Bank of South America Ld. Regd. 1863 as Brazilian & Portuguese Bank Ld.; name changed to English Bank of Rio de Janeiro Ld. in 1866 and as above in 1891. Vol. liq. (members') 13 Aug. 1936. Final meeting return regd. 27 Oct. 1961 1937

British Bazaars & Amusements Ld. Regd. 1930. Vol. liq. (members') 2 Apr. 1938. Capital returned to contributories—£2,045 1s. 4d. Final meeting return regd. 17 Dec. 1938 1934

VOL. FOR

British Bechuanaland Co. Ld. Regd. 1889. Vol. liq. 9 July 1891. Final meeting return regd. 21 Nov. 1895 1892

British Beer Breweries Ld. Regd. 1907. Vol. liq. 4 Apr. 1911 for reconstruction under same name. Shareholders were entitled to one ordinary share of 5s. (credited with 2s. paid) in new company for each share of £1 held. Debenture stockholders were entitled to receive income bonds in exchange for their holdings. Final meeting return regd. 17 Sept. 1924 1912

British Beer Breweries Ld. Regd. 1911. Vol. liq. 3 Apr. 1918. Final meeting return regd. 17 Feb. 1920 1918

British Bemberg Ld. Regd. 1928. Vol. liq. (members') 17 June 1953. Capital returned to contributories—1s. 8·51739d. per share of 1s. £5,729 13s. was paid into Companies' Liquidaton Account. Final meeting return regd. 20 Jan. 1956.. 1956

British Berna Motor Lorries Ld. Regd. 1913. Court Order to wind up 14 Mar. 1922. Struck off Register May 1933.. 1934

British Blahnik Arc Light Co. Ld. Regd. 1896. Reconstructed 1900 as New Century Arc Light Co. Ld. Debenture holders were entitled to an equal amount of preference shares in new company. Removed from Register 1909 1901

British Booklet Matches (1928) Ld. Regd. 1928. Vol. liq. (members') 27 June 1932. Capital returned to contributories—0·485d. per share of 1s. The assets were purchased by Bryant & May Ld. Final meeting return regd. 4 Mar. 1933..................................... 1933

British Boot Industry Ld. Regd. 1897. Removed from Register 1905.. *1901

British Borneo & Burma Petroleum Syndicate Ld. Regd. 1908 as British-Borneo Petroleum Syndicate Ld.; name changed May 1910. Vol. liq. 30 Apr. 1912 for reconstruction as British Borneo Petroleum Syndicate Ld., in which company shareholders were entitled to 1 share of 10s. (credited with 7s. paid) for each preference share of 10s. held, or for every 2 deferred shares of 1s. held. Final meeting return regd. 13 July 1915 1913

British Borneo Development Co. Ld. Regd. 1898. Vol. liq. 20 May 1925. Shareholders were entitled to 12 shares in Bangawan Rubber Ld. and 3 shares in Palaw Rubber Co. Ld. for every 2 shares of £1 held; payment (if any) of anticipated cash return not known. Final meeting return regd.1 July 1927 1929

British Borneo Exploration Co. Ld. Regd. 1905. Vol. liq. 11 Aug. 1916. 1 fully-paid share of £1 in British North Borneo (Chartered) Co. (later British North Borneo Co.) was to be distributed for every 60 shares of £1 held in consideration for cancellation of concession. Final meeting return regd. 5 Jan. 1921 1917

British Borneo Gold Mining Co. Ld. Regd. 1886. Removed from Register 1911 1902

British Borneo Para Rubber Co. Ld. Regd. Edinburgh 1905. Vol. liq. (members') 29 Nov. 1960. Capital returned to contributories—15s. 8d. per share of £1. £611 13s. 10d. paid into Companies' Liquidation Account. Final meeting return regd. 5 Mar. 1962 1963

British-Borneo Petroleum Syndicate Ld. See British Borneo & Burma Petroleum Syndicate Ld.

British Borneo Syndicate Ld. Regd. 1902. Certain assets were acquired in 1905 by British Borneo Exploration Co. Ld. for 100,000 fully-paid founders' shares of £1 and 400,000 ordinary shares of £1 (credited with 15s. paid). Removed from Register 1906 1908

British Borneo Trading & Planting Co. Ld. Regd. 1887. Vol. liq. 5 July 1897. Reconstructed as North Borneo Trading Co. Ld., in which company shareholders were entitled to 1 share of 10s. (credited with 8s. paid) for each ordinary or deferred share of £1 held. Final meeting return regd. 22 Feb. 1900 1897

British Bottles Ld. Regd. Edinburgh 1929. Vol. liq. (members') 29 June 1948. Final meeting return regd. 2 Nov. 1948 1940

British Breda Silk Ld. Regd. 1928. Vol. liq. (members') 14 Feb. 1952. Capital returned to contributories— 11s. 6⅝d. per A ordinary share of £1. £17,400 10s. was paid into Companies' Liquidation Account. Final meeting return regd. 5 May 1953 1954

British Briquettes Ld. Regd. 1929. Vol. liq. (members') 27 Feb. 1939. Undertaking acquired by Powell Duffryn Associated Collieries Ld. (later Powell Duffryn Ld.) Capital returned to contributories— £317,710 6s. 1d. Final meeting return regd. 17 Jan. 1940 1940

British Broadcasting Co. Ld. Regd. 1922. Vol. liq. 18 Jan. 1927. Assets were transferred in 1927 to British Broadcasting Corporation (inc. by Royal Charter) and shareholders were repaid at par. Final meeting return regd. 17 Dec. 1929 1927

British Broken Hill Proprietary Ld. Regd. 1887. Vol. liq. 11 Apr. 1923. Undertaking and assets were acquired

VOL. FOR

by British Australian Broken Hill Ld. Shareholders were entitled to either 35s. in cash or 1 fully-paid share of £1 *plus* 15s. in cash for each share of either class held. Final meeting return regd. 4 May 1925 — **1924**

British Brunswick Ld. Regd. 1926. Court Order to wind up 15 Oct. 1929. Struck off Register Dec. 1934..... **1935**

British Bureau Ld. *See* Monomark Ld.

British Burmah Lead Co. Ld. Regd. 1886. Vol. liq. 29 Jan. 1887. Final meeting return regd. 2 Dec. 1890 — ***1887**

British Burmah Petroleum Co. Ld. (The) Regd. 1910. Struck off register 19 Sept. 1983. Dissolved 27 Sept. 1983 .... **1976–7**

British Butte Mining Co. Inc. Montana 1906. London office closed in 1912 .... **1912**

British Californian Oil Co. Ld. Inc. California 1901. London agency was discontinued in May 1910 .... **1910**

British Can Co. Ld. Regd. 1929. Vol. liq. (members') 29 Mar. 1945. Final meeting return regd. 1 July 1948 — **1940**

British-Canadian Asbestos Co. Ld. Inc. Canada 1908. Outstanding 1st mortgage 25-year 5% gold bonds were repaid July 1909 at 105%. Undertaking acquired by Amalgamated Asbestos Corporation Ld **1910**

British Canadian Goldfields of the Klondike Ld. Regd. 1898. Removed from Register 1904 .... **1903**

British Canadian Loan & Investment Co. Ld. Inc. Canada by Special Acts 1877 & 1887. Business acquired by Canada Permanent Mortgage Corporation. Shares of $100 ($20 paid) were repaid June 1906 at par *plus* final distribution of 10% premium — **1908**

British Canadian Lumber Corporation Ld. Inc. Canada 1911. Undertaking was transferred to British Timber Corporation Ld. in 1918. Holders of Securities received securities in new company in exchange for their holdings, but no distribution was made to ordinary shareholders **1919**

British Canadian Lumbering and Timber Co. Ld. Regd. Edinburgh 1880. Vol. liq. Feb. 1886. Final meeting return regd. 19 Jan. 1901 .... **1885**

British Canadian Silver Corporation Ld. Regd. 1920. Vol. liq. 28 Oct. 1936. All shares owned by Selukwe Gold Mining & Finance Co. Ld. Final meeting return regd. 2 Dec. 1937 .... **1937**

British Canadian Timber & Manufacturing Co. Ld. Regd. 1898. Vol. liq. 3 Oct. 1903. Final meeting return regd. 15 Nov. 1904 .... ***1905**

British Canadian Trust Ld. Regd. 1910. Undertaking merged with Dundee & London Investment Trust Ld. in which company ordinary shareholders were entitled to receive 11 ordinary shares of 25p for every 10 shares of 25p. Holders of 5% preference stock. terminal debentures and U.S. debentures received in substitution a similar amount of stock in Dundee & London Investment Trust Ld. Dissolved under Section 208 of the Companies Act, 1948 29 Jan. 1972 .... **1973–4**

British Capital Trust Ld. Regd. 1928. Winding-up Order 2 Nov. 1942. Struck off Register 16 Feb. 1954 .... ***1933**

British Carbide Factories Ld. Regd. 1907. Vol. liq. 23 Nov. 1925. Final meeting return regd. 24 Nov. 1926 — **1926**

British Carbocite Smokeless Fuel Ld. Regd. 1929. Vol. liq. (creditors') 21 July 1930. Debenture holders received £4,546 19s. 5d. Final meeting return regd. 27 Aug. 1931 .... **1913**

British Carbonizing Co. Ld. Regd. 1916. Vol. liq. 16 Nov. 1922. Final meeting return regd. 10 Jan. 1924 — **1923**

British Cattle Foods Ld. Regd. 1888. Removed from Register 1906 .... ***1898**

British Celilynd (Holdings) Ld. Regd. 1935 as British Celilynd Ld.; name changed June 1959. Vol. liq. (members') 26 Nov. 1959. Shareholders entitled to receive 1 fully-paid ordinary share of British Celilynd Ld. for each share held. £246 1s. 11d. was paid into Companies' Liquidation Account. Final meeting return regd. 26 Nov. 1962 .... **1963**

British Celilynd Ld. Regd. as D. Smith & Sons (1924) Ld.; name changed 1934 to D. Smith & Sons Ld. and to above title June 1959. Winding-up Order 11 May 1970. Struck off register 11 Feb. 1982 .... **1981–2**

British Cement Products & Finance Co. Ld. Regd. 1926. Court Order to wind up May 1931. Struck off Register 15 June 1937 .... **1938**

British Central Africa Co. Ld. Regd. 1902. Vol. liq. 30 Jan. 1924. Shareholders were entitled to 1 share of 10s. (credited with 7s. 6d. paid) in a new company for every share of £1 held; shareholders who did not accept received 5d. per share in cash. £891 15s. 5d. was paid into Companies' Liquidation Account. Final meeting return regd. 5 July 1946. Struck off Register 21 Mar. 1947 .... **1947**

British Chain Manufacturing Co. (1913) Ld. Regd. 1913. Vol. liq. 8 July 1915. Final meeting return regd. 21 Oct. 1921 .... **1916**

VOL. FOR

British Chewing Sweets Ld. Regd. 1927. Receiver appointed in Jan. 1934, stated in Nov. 1935 that he had sold the business. Struck off Register 31 Dec. 1940 .... **1941**

British Coal Distillation Ld. Regd. 1928 as Leicestershire (L. & N.) Coal Distillation Ld.; name changed June 1932. Struck off Register 31 July 1953 .... **1952**

British Coalite Co. Ld. Regd. 1907. Vol. liq. 6 Aug. 1919. Undertaking and assets were acquired by Low Temperature Carbonisation Ld. (later Coalite & Chemical Products Ld.) in which company shareholders were entitled to 11 preference shares of £1 (credited as fully-paid) for every 10 ordinary shares of £1 held or 17 preference shares for every 20 deferred shares of £1 held. Final meeting return regd. 6 July 1920 .... **1920**

British Colonial & Foreign Holdings Ld. Regd. 1929 as Trinidad & General Holdings Ld.; name changed Oct. 1933. Struck off register 13 Dec. 1963 .... **1960**

British Colonial & General Investment Trust Ld. Regd. 1883. Court Orders: to wind up 14 Sept. 1897; to dissolve 1 Dec. 1892 .... **1888**

British Colonial Balata & Rubber Co. Ld. Regd. 1911. In Feb. 1934 Secretary stated that company had no assets. Struck off Register 18 Feb. 1936 .... **1936**

British Colonial Mining Corporation Ld. Regd. 1896. Removed from Register 1905 .... **1901**

British Colonial Petroleum Corporation Ld. Regd. 1906. Vol. liq. 20 May 1924. Final meeting return regd. 8 Nov. 1930 .... **1925**

British Columbia Agency Ld. Regd. 1896. Vol. liq. 17 June 1908. Final meeting return regd. 4 May 1918 — **1909**

British Columbia Alluvails Ld. Regd. 1921. Struck off Register 10 Mar. 1936 .... **1937**

British Columbia & New Find Goldfields Corporation Ld. Regd. 1897. Vol. liq. 18 May 1900. Removed from Register 1904 .... **1901**

British Columbia Breweries 1918 Ld. Inc. Canada 1919. The outstanding 6% 1st mortgage gold bonds were redeemed on 1 July 1927 .... **1927**

British Columbia Bullion Extracting Co. Ld. Regd. 1897. Removed from Register 1903 .... ***1901**

British Columbia Canning Co. Ld. Regd. 1889. Vol. liq. 10 Dec. 1895 for reconstruction as company of same name. Shareholders were entitled to 1 share of 15s. for each fully-paid ordinary share of £1 held, to 1 share of 15s. (credited with 10s. paid) for each ordinary share of £1 (15s. paid). Debenture holders were entitled to 66⅔% of holding in 5% debenture stock and 33⅓% in preference shares of £1. Final meeting return regd. 14 Jan. 1898 .... **1908**

British Columbia Canning Co. Ld. Regd. 1895. Vol. liq. 12 Mar. 1924. Capital returned to contributories— 30s. per share of 15s. at July 1924; further payments (if any) not known. Final meeting return regd. 13 July 1925 .... **1925**

British Columbia Corporation Ld. Regd. 1891. Vol. liq. 5 Feb. 1907. Removed from Register 1912 .... **1907**

British Columbia Development Association Ld. Regd. 1895. Reconstructed 1904 as company of same name. Shareholders were entitled to 1 share of £1 in new company for each preference share of £1 held or 66 shares of £1 for each founders' share of £1 held. Removed from Register 1905 .... **1908**

British Columbia Development Association Ld. Regd. 1904. Court Order to wind up July 1912. Struck off Register June 1931 .... **1932**

British Columbia Electric Co. Ld. Inc. British Columbia 1926 as British Columbia Electric Power & Gas Co. Ld.; name changed 1946. Ceased to exist as separate company on amalgamation in 1966 with the British Columbia Hydro & Power Authority which assumed liability for all obligations. **1967**

British Columbia Electric Railway Co. Ld. Regd. 1897. Vol. liq. (members') 12 Dec. 1960. Undertaking and assets acquired by British Columbia Electric Co. Ld. 4½% perpetual consolidated debenture stock and perpetual preference stock repaid at par 13 Jan. 1961 .... **1973–4**

British Columbia Financial Trust & General Corporation Ld. Regd. 1897. Vol. liq. 27 Apr. 1903. Struck off Register 30 Apr. 1946 .... **1947**

British Columbia Fruit Lands Ld. Regd. 1909. Repayments totalling 67·3% were made by the receiver to prior lien debenture stockholders. Struck off Register 22 July 1960 .... **1966**

British Columbia Gold Discovery Co. Ld. Regd. 1896. Vol. liq. Mar. 1914. Struck off Register 1922 .... **1914**

British Columbia Mines, Land & General Finance Co. Ld. Regd. 1910. Vol. liq. 29 Apr. 1914. Struck off Register 18 Jan. 1921 .... ***1915**

British Columbia Phoenix Co. Ld. Regd. 1914. Vol. liq. (members') 13 Dec. 1929. All assets were acquired by Selected Plantations and General Securities

---

*See Stock Exchange Year-Book.

VOL. FOR

Trust Ld. for 18,615 shares of 5s. (credited with 3s. 9d. paid). Final meeting return regd. 19 Feb. 1932 — **1931**

British Columbia Phoenix Syndicate Ld. Regd. 1911. Vol. liq. 21 July 1913. Final meeting return regd. 20 Apr. 1915 — **1931**

British Columbia Power Corp. Ld. Inc. Canada 1928. Vol. liq. 1 Nov. 1963. Capital returned to contributories—$25,5635 per common share of no par value. Dissolved 29 Apr. 1969 — **1970**

British Columbia (Rossland & Slocan) Syndicate Ld. Regd. 1897. Assets were acquired by British Columbia Phoenix Syndicate Ld., in consideration of payment of liabilities. Shareholders had option (since expired) of subscribing for shares at par in new company. Removed from Register 1912 — **1912**

British Columbia Smelting Co. Ld. Regd. 1888. Removed from Register 1906 — **1892**

British Columbia Telephone Co. Ld. Inc. by Special Act in British Columbia 1891 as Vernon & Nelson Telephone Co.; name changed 1904. Undertaking acquired by British Columbia Telephone Co., which company assumed liability for the 1st mortgage debenture stock. Ordinary shareholders were entitled to 3 fully-paid ordinary shares of $100 of purchasing company for every 2 $100 shares and preference shareholders 1 fully-paid preference share of $100 for each $100 share held — **1924**

British Columbia Telephones Ld. Regd. 1898. Vol. liq. 6 Jan. 1905. Preference shares (£10) were repaid 18 Jan. 1905 and ordinary shares (£10, fully and partly paid) plus 10% bonus on 3 Feb. 1905. Final meeting return regd. 2 May 1905 — **1905**

British Columbia Town Properties Syndicate Ld. Regd. 1897. Vol. liq. 15 May 1906. Final meeting return regd. 1 June 1922 — **1907**

British Columbian Enterprise Ld. Regd. 1899. Removed from Register 1907 — **1904**

British Columbian Exploitation & Gold Estates Ld. Regd. 1897. Removed from Register 1909 — **1900**

British Columbian Fisheries Ld. Regd. 1911. Receiver appointed 24 Sept. 1913; ceased to act 17 Nov. 1920. Struck off Register 3 June 1921 — **1915**

British Columbian Mineral Properties Ld. Regd. 1898, Vol. liq. 15 Mar. 1899. Assets were acquired by British Canadian Goldfields of the Klondike Ld., in which company shareholders were entitled to 1 share of £1 (credited with 17s. 6d. paid) for each share of £1 held. Removed from Register 1902 — **1900**

British Combined Investors Trust Ld. Regd. 1927. Vol. liq. (members') 15 Dec. 1964. All capital owned by Romney Trust Ld. £199 18s. 8d. paid into Companies' Liquidation Account in respect of unclaimed dividends. Final meeting return regd. 17 Nov. 1970 — **1971**

British Commercial Bank Ld. See Commercial Bank of London Ld.

British Commercial Corporation Ld. Regd. 1889. Removed from Register 1907 — ***1892**

British Commonwealth Insurance Co. Ld. Regd. 1917. Vol. liq. 10 July 1929. Final meeting return regd. 27 Jan. 1930 — **1930**

British Compressed Air Cleaning Co. Ld. Regd. 1902. Court Orders: to wind up 31 Oct 1905; to dissolve 5 May 1908 — **1907**

British Congo Co. Ld. Regd. 1885. Court Orders; to wind up 10 Dec. 1887: to dissolve 27 Aug. 1891 — **1888**

British Consolidated Oil Corporation Ld. Regd. 1908. Vol. liq. 1 Dec. 1911. Final meeting return regd. 13 June 1918 — **1912**

British Coolgardie Ld. Regd. 1896. Removed from Register 1904 — **1901**

British Coolgardie Prospecting Syndicate Ld. Regd. 1894. Vol. liq. 14 Feb. 1896. Property was acquired by British Coolgardie Ld., in which company shareholders were entitled to 239 fully-paid shares of £1 for each share of £100 held. Final meeting return regd. 4 Jan. 1898 — **1900**

British Copper Manufacturers Ld. Regd. 1924. Vol. liq. (members') 31 Dec. 1942. I.C.I. Metals Ld. held all shares. Final meeting return regd. 29 Sept. 1944 — **1943**

British Cork Asphalt Ld. Regd. 1907. Court Order to wind up 16 Jan. 1912. Liquidator released 13 Aug. 1913. Struck off Register 3 Sept.1918 — **1912**

British Cotton Ginning Co. Ld. Regd. 1907. Vol. liq. 23 June 1916. Final meeting return regd. 12 Dec. 1917 — **1917**

British Cotton-Seed Products Ld. Regd. 1919. Vol. liq. (members') 15 June 1931. Capital returned to contributories—1$\frac{7}{10}$d. per share of 1s. Final meeting return regd. 24 Feb. 1936 — **1932**

British Crown Assurance Corporation Ld. Regd. Edinburgh 1907. Vol. liq. July 1918. Undertaking and assets were acquired by Eagle Star & British Dominions Insurance Co. Ld. (later Eagle Star Insurance Co. Ld.) in which company shareholders were entitled to 1 ordinary share of £3 (credited as

VOL. FOR

fully-paid) for every 3 shares of £5 (£2 paid) held. Final meeting return regd. 27 Oct. 1920 — **1919**

British Cycle Manufacturing Co. Ld. Regd. 1919. Vol. liq. (members') 5 Dec. 1935. Capital returned to contributories—£1,058 6s. 6d. Final meeting return regd. 15 Jan. 1936 — **1936**

British Dairy Produce Co. Ld. Regd. 1899. Vol. liq. 6 Nov. 1906. Undertaking and assets were acquired by British Margarine Co. Ld. Removed from Register 1913 — **1907**

British Danubian Trading Corporation Ld. Regd. 1920. Vol. liq. 16 Dec. 1924. Final meeting return regd. 3 Mar. 1927 — **1925**

British Dardalet Threadlock Ld. Regd. 1929 as British Dardalet Threadlock (D. D. G.) Corpn. Ld.; name changed Sept. 1930. Vol. liq. (members') 8 June 1949. Shareholders were entitled to receive 1 share (of 1s.) in Acton Bolt Ld. for each share (of 3s.) held, if application made by 7 Sept. 1949, plus distribution of 1$\frac{1}{2}$d. cash per share; failing application, liquidator sold the Acton shares on behalf of shareholders at 2s. 3d. per share, payable plus distribution of 1$\frac{1}{2}$d. per share. £8,362 10s. 1d. was paid into Companies' Liquidation Account. Final meeting return regd. 27 Aug. 1954 — **1955**

British Darjeeling Tea Co. Ld. Regd. 1895. Vol. liq. 12 Feb. 1920. Reconstructed as company of same name. Shareholders were entitled to 2 fully-paid shares of £1 in new company for each share of £1 held. Final meeting return regd. 20 May 1921 — **1921**

British Deli & Langkat Tobacco Co. Ld. Regd. 1889 as Deli and Langkat Tobacco Co. Ld.; name changed Aug. 1889. Vol. liq. 28 June 1906. Undertaking was acquired by Rimboen Tabak Mij. Removed from Register 1907 — **1907**

British Deperdussin Aeroplane Co. Ld. Regd. 1912. Vol. liq. July 1913. Struck off Register 1926 — **1914**

British Diatoric Manufacturing Co. Ld. Regd. 1907. Receiver appointed in 1915; ceased to act on 22 Feb 1922. Struck off Register 1923 — **1923**

British Dinner Co. Ld. Regd. 1886. Removed from Register 1906 — **1888**

British Doloment Co. Ld. Regd. 1906. Vol. liq. (members') 31 Mar. 1938. Capital returned to contributories—2s. 2$\frac{1}{4}$d. per share of 7s. 6d. Final meeting return regd. 23 Nov. 1939 — **1940**

British Dominions Exploration Ld. Regd. 1896. Vol. liq. 30 Aug. 1898. Reconstructed as New British Dominions Exploration Ld., in which company shareholders were entitled to 1 share of £1 (credited with 15s. paid) for each share of £1 held. Final meeting return regd. 21 Dec. 1899 — **1899**

British Dominions Insurance Co. Ld. See United Dominions Insurance Co. Ld.

British Dominions Land Settlement Corporation Ld. Regd. 1924. 7% 1st mortgage registered debenture holders received repayments of principal totalling 82.35%. Struck off Register 16 Mar. 1951 — **1952**

British Dominions Steamship Co. Ld. Regd. 1919. Vol. liq. (members') 12 Dec. 1963. Final meeting return regd. 7 Apr. 1974 — **1940**

British Dooars Tea Co. Ld. Regd. 1894. Undertaking was acquired by Imperial Tea Co. Ld. in 1897. Vol. liq. 9 Feb. 1898. Final meeting return regd. 30 Jan. 1900 — **1898**

British Dredging Co. Ld. Regd. 1903. Vol. liq. 19 July 1920. Capital returned to contributories—150% at Sept. 1920; further payments (if any) not known. Final meeting return regd. 18 Dec. 1922 — **1921**

British Drying Co. Ld. Regd. 1897. Court Order to wind up 4 Apr. 1900. Removed from Register 1909 — **1901**

British Du Bois Manufacturing Co. Ld. Regd. 1897. Vol. liq. 26 July 1898. Undertaking was acquired by British and Foreign Du Bois Co. Ld. Final meeting return regd. 30 Mar. 1899 — **1899**

British Dyes Ld. See British Dyestuffs Corporation (Huddersfield) Ld.

British Dyestuffs Corporation (Blackley) Ld. Regd. 1895 as Levinstein Ld.; name changed 1919. Vol. liq. 6 Dec. 1923. Undertaking and assets were acquired by British Dyestuffs Corporation Ld. (later I.C.I. (Dyestuffs) Ld.) Final meeting return regd. 20 Dec. 1928 — **1925**

British Dyestuffs Corporation (Huddersfield) Ld. Regd. 1915 as British Dyes Ld.; name changed Sept. 1919. Vol. liq. 6 Dec. 1923. Undertaking and assets were acquired by British Dyestuffs Corporation Ld. (later I.C.I. (Dyestuffs) Ld.). Final meeting return regd. 20 Dec. 1928 — **1924**

British Dyestuffs Corpn. Ld. See I.C.I. (Dyestuffs) Ld.

British Dyewood & Chemical Co. Ld. Regd. Edinburgh 1898. Vol. liq. Dec. 1910, with a view to the sale of the business to United Dyewood Co. (an American company); it was anticipated that an ultimate return

VOL. FOR

of £9 per preference share of £10 would be made (viz. 12*s.* 8*d.* in 6% preference and £1 18*s.* 2*d.* in common stock of the United Dyewood Co., and £6 9*s.* 2*d.* in cash). A new private company (British Dyewood Co. Ld.) was regd. 1910 to take over business on behalf of United Dyewood Co. Final meeting return regd. 26 Dec. 1935 .... **1911**

British East Africa Co. Ld. *See* Imperial British East Africa Co. Ld.

British East Africa Corpn. Ld. Registered 1906. Vol. liq. (creditors') 30 June 1939. No capital returned to contributories. Struck off Register 24 Sept 1957.... **1958**

British East Africa Rubber & Cotton Estates Ld. Regd. 1909. Vol. liq. Dec. 1913. Receivers were appointed in Jan. 1914. Struck off Register 1923 .... **1914**

British Eastern Investment Trust Ld. Regd. 1910. Vol. liq. 19 May 1921. Capital returned to contributories—1*s.* 1*d.* per share of 1*s.* at 24 Oct. 1921 further payments (if any) not known. Final meeting return regd. 13 May 1931 .... **1922**

British Ecuador Syndicate Ld. Regd. 1908. Struck off Register 24 Oct. 1916 .... **1915**

British Electric Automatic Machines Ld. Regd. 1910. Vol. liq. 3 Sept. 1915. Final meeting return regd. 21 Mar. 1916 .... ***1916**

British Electric Detonator Co. Ld. Regd. 1907. Vol. liq. (members') 30 June 1939. Capital returned to contributories—£1 3*s.* 5*d.* per share of 5*s.* Final meeting return regd. 3 July 1940 .... **1940**

British Electric Glass Ld. Regd. 1932. Vol. liq. (members') 30 Oct. 1936. All shares held by Crompton Parkinson Ld. Final meeting return regd. 20 July 1937 .... **1937**

British Electric Light Co. Ld. Regd. 1878. The debenture holders foreclosed. Removed from Register 1897 .... **1896**

British Electric Plant Co. Ld. Regd. Edinburgh 1900. Vol. liq. (members') 7 Apr. 1938. All assets were acquired by Harland Engineering Co. Ld. Struck off Register 13 Nov. 1945 .... **1939**

British Electric Street Tramways Ld. Regd. 1900. Vol. liq. 2 Dec. 1902. Shareholders were entitled 1 fully-paid share and 9 shares (credited with 15*s.* paid) for each share of £10 held. Removed from Register 1903 **1903**

British Electric Traction (Pioneer) Co. Ld. Regd. 1895. Reconstructed 1896 as British Electric Traction Co. Ld. Capital returned to contributories—£5 per share of £10 (£4 paid). Removed from Register 1905 .... **1896**

British Electric Transformer Manufacturing Co. Ld. Regd. 1898. Business was acquired in 1903 by British Electric Transformer Co. Ld. for £60,000 in fully-paid ordinary shares of £1. Removed from Register 1904 .... **1903**

British Electric Works Co. Ld. Regd. 1899. Assets were acquired by Electric & Ordnance Accessories Co. Ld. Debenture holders were repaid in full. The original allottees were entitled to repayment in full. Removed from Register 1905 .... **1902**

British Electricity Authority *See* Central Electricity Authority

British Electromobile Co. Ld. Regd. 1900 as British & Foreign Electrical Vehicle Co. Ld.; name changed 1902. Undertaking was acquired in 1902 for £5,000 in ordinary shares of £1 and £5,000 in cash. Struck off Register 3 Oct. 1941. .... **1942**

British Embroidery Machine Co. Ld. Regd. July 1897. Vol. liq. 13 Nov. 1897. Final meeting return regd. 29 Jan. 1900 .... **1898**

British Empire Club Ld. Regd. 1906. Vol. liq. (members') 25 July 1938. No capital returned to contributors. Final meeting return regd. 19 Apr. 1939 .... **1939**

British Empire Finance Corporation Ld. Regd. 1896. Removed from Register 1904 .... **1904**

British Empire Goldfields Ld. Regd. 1899 as British American Goldfields Ld.; name changed Apr. 1901. Vol. liq. 26 Nov. 1904. Removed from Register 1907 **1906**

British Empire Investment Trust Ld. Regd. 1956. Holding in Anglo-Scandinavian Investment Corpn. acquired by Hambro Canada Ld. and remaining undertaking and assets by Hambros Investment Trust Ld. on 23 Oct. 1970. Ordinary shareholders received 30 A ordinary and 30 B ordinary shares in Hambros Investment Trust Ld. plus £107 2s. 7½*d.* Guaranteed Unsecured Loan Stock of Hambro Canada Ld. for every 61 shares held; preference stockholders received like amount of preference stock and debenture stockholders like amount of similar stock in Hambros Investment Trust Ld. Company was dissolved in July 1971 under Section 208 of Companies Act 1948 .... **1971**

British Empire Match Co. Ld. Regd. 1886. Court Orders: to wind up Mar. 1887; to dissolve 29 July 1890 .... **1888**

VOL. FOR

British Empire Mutual Life Assurance Co. Est. by deed of settlement 1847. Inc. by Special Act 1852. Regd. under Cos. Act. Amalgamated under title of Pelican and British Empire Life Office in 1903 .... **1903**

British Empire Oilfields Ld. Regd. 1909. Struck off Register 25 Mar. 1938 .... **1939**

British Empire Steel Corporation Ld. Inc. Nova Scotia 1920. Undertaking and assets were acquired in 1930 by Dominion Steel and Coal Corporation Ld., in which company shareholders were entitled to 3½ shares of $25 for each 1st preference share of $100 held or 1 share for every 2 shares of $25 2nd preference stock or 5 shares of common stock held **1931**

British Empire Trust Co. Ld. Regd. 1896. Removed from Register 1909 .... **1901**

British Emulsifiers Ld. *See* Royston Industries Ld.

British Envelope Manufacturing Co. Ld. Regd. 1882. Removed from Register 1890 .... ***1883**

British Equatorial Oil Co. Ld. Regd. 1920. Vol. liq. 10 Oct. 1924. Undertaking was acquired by Lago Petroleum Corporation. Final meeting return regd. 9 Apr. 1929 .... ***1925**

British European Trust Ld. *See* British Printing Trust Ld.

British Ever Ready Co. Ld. Regd. 1913 as New British Ever Ready Co. Ld.; name changed Apr. 1920. Vol. liq. 6 May 1920. Reconstructed as Ever Ready Co. (Great Britain) Ld., in which company shareholders were entitled to 2 ordinary shares of £1 (credited as fully-paid for each ordinary share of £1 held or 6 fully-paid preference shares of £1 for every 5 preference shares of £1 held. Final meeting return regd. 8 Jan. 1921 .... **1921**

British Exhibitors Films Ld. Regd. 1922 as British Exhibitors Films (1922) Ld.; name changed Jan. 1929. Vol. liq. (creditors') 21 Apr. 1938. All shares held by Union Cinemas Ld. Final meeting return regd. 26 Nov. 1942 .... **1939**

British Exploration Co. Ld. Regd. 1895. Court Order to wind up 10 Mar. 1897. Removed from Register 1901 **1898**

British Exploration of Australasia Ld. Regd. 1900. Undertaking was to be sold to Croydon Copper Mines Ld. for £5,000 in debentures. Vol. liq. June 1909. Removed from Register 1912 .... **1910**

British Famous Films Ld. Regd. 1920. Vol. liq. 19 July 1923. Final meeting return regd. 25 Sept. 1923 ..... **1924**

British Farmers' Association Ld. Regd. 1893. Business was acquired by English Farmers' Association Ld. Removed Iron Register 1911 .... **1900**

British Filmcraft Ld. Undertaking and assets were acquired in 1927 by British Filmcraft Productions Ld. for £25,000 in cash and £25,000 in fully-paid shares **1929**

British Filmcraft Productions Ld. Regd. 1927. Vol. liq. (creditors') 11 Aug. 1930. Shareholders were entitled to receive 1 share of 5*s.* (credited with 3*s.* 6*d.* paid) in Audible Filmcraft Ld. for each share held. £21 1*s.* 4*d.* was paid into Companies' Liquidation Account. Final meeting return regd. 5 Oct. 1956 .... **1957**

British Filograph Co. Ld. Regd. 1929. Court Order to wind up 30 Mar. 1931. S1ruck off Register 20 Feb. 1942 .... **1943**

British, Foreign & Colonial Corporation Ld. Regd. 1910. Vol. liq. (members') 4 Apr. 1932. Capital returned to contribuiories—6*d.* per share of 5*s.* *plus* pro rata distribution in £99,530 debenture stock and 1,994,400 shares of 1*d.* in C.F.B. Holdings Ld. Final meeting return regd. 29 Mar. 1934 .... **1933**

British-French Discount Bank Ld. Regd. 1928. Vol. liq. (members') 22 May 1946. A subsidiary of Ottoman Bank. Capital returned to contributories—2*s.* 9·65*d.* per share (of £1, with 15*s.* paid). £14 was paid into Companies' Liquidation Account. Final meeting return regd. 14 Feb. 1957 .... **1958**

British Fuel Economiser & Smoke Preventer Ld. Regd. 1889 as Alves Fuel Economisation Syndicate Ld.; name changed 11 Apr. 1900. Vol. liq. 1903. Removed from Register 1905 .... **1905**

British Gardens Ld. Regd. 1919. Struck off Register Apr. 1929 .... **1930**

British Gas & Fuel Co. Ld. *See* Gas and Fuel Plants Ld.

British Gas Light Co. Ld. Estd. 1824; regd. 1857. Dissolved 1 May 1949, undertaking being vested in North Eastern, Wales, Eastern, South Eastern, Southern & South Western Area Gas Boards under Gas Act 1948. Holders of securities were entitled to receive in respect of each £100 unit held, British Gas 3% guaranteed stock 1990–95 as follows:

	£	s.	d.
Ord. stock	142	10	0
7% pref stock	150	0	0
5½% red pref. stock	116	0	0
Hull 3½% mort debs.	97	10	0

VOL. FOR

Hull 4% mort debs. 102 10 0
Hull 5½% mort debs. 107 10 0
Norwich 3½% mort. debs (Act
1875) 98 0 0
Norwich 3% mort debs. (Act
1896) 90 0 0
Norwich 4% mort. debs. (Act
1896) 100 10 0
Norwich 4% mort. debs. (Act
1903) 100 10 0
Norwich 4% mort. debs. (Act
1918) 101 0 0
Norwich 3½% mort debs. (Act 1918) 99 10 0
Trowbridge 3½% mort debs. 97 10 0
Trowbridge 4½% mort. debs 100 15 0
4% red. deb. stock 97 10 0
5% red. deb. stock 105 0 0
3½% deb stock 1955 .... 99 0 0   1952

British Gas Traction Co. Ld. Regd. 1896. Court Order to wind up 1 Nov. 1899. Liquidator released 29 Aug. 1914. Struck off Register 14 Feb. 1919.................   1900

British General Finance Corpn. Ld. Regd. 1913. Struck off Register 5 June 1953   1947

British General Fixed Trust Ld. Regd. 1934. Vol. liq. (creditors) 10 July 1939. Final meeting return regd. 16 Dec. 1947   1948

British Glass Industries Ld. Regd. 1919. Vol. liq. 15 Nov. 1926. Undertaking and assets were acquired by Canning Town Glass Works Ld in which company shareholders were entitled to 1 share of 9d. (credited as fully-paid) for each share of 5s. held. Final meeting return regd. 13 Feb. 1928   1927

British Gold Coast Co. Ld. Regd. 1900. Vol. liq. Feb. 1909. Undertaking and assets were acquired by Fanti Consolidated Mines Ld., in which company shareholders were entitled to 3 shares of 10s. (credited as fully-paid) for every 2 shares of £1 held and an option (since expired) over further shares. Removed from Register 1909   1909

British Gold Coast Syndicate Ld. Regd. 1899. Reconstructed 1900 as British Gold Coast Co. Ld in which company shareholders were entitled to 1 share of £1 for each ordinary share of £1 held or 7 fully-paid shares of £1 for every 5 deferred shares of 1s. held. Removed from Register 1903   1908

British Gold Fields of West Africa Ld. Regd. 1895. Removed from Register 1908   1899

British Gold Mines of Mexico Ld. Regd. 1896. Vol. liq. 4 Aug. 1909. Property was sold to Carmen Mines of El Oro Ld., in which company shareholders were entitled to 1 fully-paid share of £1 for every 5 shares of £1 held. Final meeting return regd. 7 Apr. 1921   1910

British Griffin Chilled Iron & Steel Co. Ld. Regd. 1899. Vol. liq. 13 Apr. 1923. Final meeting return regd. 24 Mar. 1925   *1924

British Guiana Balata Co. Ld. Regd. 1910. Struck off Register 1927   1926

British Guiana Consolidated Gold Fields Ld. See British Guiana Consolidated Goldfields below.

British Guiana Consolidated Gold Mines Ld. Regd. 1902. Vol. liq. 18 Feb. 1907. Removed from Register 1910   1907

British Guiana Consolidated Goldfields Ld. Regd. 1935 as British Guiana Consolidated Gold Fields Ld.; name changed 1936. Undertaking and assets sold at a price which was not sufficient to provide any funds for unsecured creditors or shareholders. Struck off Register 15 June 1973.................   1971

British Guiana Diamond Syndicate Ld. Regd. 1900. Vol. liq. 28 Sept. 1905. Removed from Register 1912...   1906

British Guiana Gold Dredging Co. Ld. Regd. 1900. Removed from Register 1910   1903

British Guiana Gold Mines Ld. Regd. 1907. Removed from Register 1913   1914

British Guiana Prospecting & General Developing Co. Ld. Regd. 1895. Removed from Register 1901   1900

British Guiana Rubber Corporation Ld. Regd. 1906. Undertaking and assets were sold to Balata and Rubber Corporation Ld. for £60,000 in shares and £9,000 in debentures. Removed from Register 1913   1910

British Heating Industries Ld. Regd. 1931 as Every Heating Need Co. Ld.: name changed 23 Nov. 1932. Vol. liq. (creditors) 1 Mar. 1944. Directly controlled by William Ryder Ld. Final meeting return regd. 7 Jan. 1947   1934

British Hispano Line Ld. See Fairwater Shipping Co. Ld
British Homes Assurance Corporation Ld. See City Life Assurance Co. Ld.

British Honduras Produce Co. Ld. Regd. 1912. Vol. liq. 11 Feb. 1915. Final meeting return regd.17 Jan. 1920   1915

British Honduras Rubber Ld. Regd. 1910. Vol. liq. 11 Aug. 1911. Reconstructed as British Honduras Produce Co. Ld., in which company shareholders were entitled to 2 shares of 10s. (credited with 7s. 6d.

VOL. FOR

paid) for each share of £1 (15s. paid) held. Final meeting return regd 4 Oct. 1913   1914

British Honey Co. Ld. Regd. 1884. Vol. liq. June 1888. Final meeting return regd. 12 July 1889   1889

British Horo-Electric Ld. Regd. 1922. Struck off Register 28 Jan. 1949   1938

British Hosiery Trust Ld. Regd. 1927. Vol. liq. (members') 14 Feb. 1940. Shareholders received 3 shares of 4s. in Aristoc Ld. for every 2 shares of £1 held, plus 2s. 3d. per share in cash. Final meeting return regd. 21 Apr. 1941   1943

British House & Land Assurance Co. Ld. Regd 1906. Removed from Register 1912   1925

British Hydraulic Foundry Co. Ld. Regd. Edinburgh 1891. Vol. liq. Dec. 1923. Final meeting return regd. 14 Jan. 1925   1924

British Hydraulic Jointing Co. Ld. Regd. May 1898. Vol. liq. 22 July 1898. Final meeting return regd. 18 Oct. 1898   1899

British Imperial Assurance Co. Ld. Regd. 1906. Receiver appointed 13 Aug. 1908. Removed from Register 29 Aug. 1911   *1910

British Imperial Insurance Corporation Ld. Regd. 1867 as British Imperial Investment Corporation Ld.; name changed 10 Sept. 1868. Wound up by Court Order 7 Jan. 1876   *1876

British Imperial Investment Corporation Ld. See British Imperial Insurance Corporation Ld.

British Import & Packing Co. Ld. Regd. 1910 as British "Banana" Margarine Co. Ld.; name changed Jan. 1923. Vol. liq. 17 June 1928. Final meeting return regd. 5 July 1929   1929

British Independent Exhibitors (Distribution) Co. Ld. Regd. 1937. Court Order to wind up 6 Feb. 1939. No capital returned to contributories. Liquidator released in Nov. 1949   1950

British Indian Oil Mills Ld. Regd. 1902. Vol. liq. 16 Mar. 1914. Final meeting return regd. 22 Jan. 1918   1915

British Instructional Films (Proprietors) Ld. Regd. 1927. Vol. liq. (members') 11 Jan. 1937. No capital returned to contributories. Final meeting return regd. 22 June 1937   1937

British Insulated & Helsby Cables Ld. See British Insulated Cables Ld.

British Insulated Cables Ld. Regd. 1897 as British Insulated Wire Co. Ld.; name changed to British Insulated & Helsby Cables Ld. in 1902 and as above in Dec. 1925. Vol. liq. (members') 29 June 1945. Undertaking and assets acquired by British Insulated Callender's Cables Ld. in which company stockholders were entitled to receive £1 6%, 1st preference, £1 5%, 2nd preference stock or 3 ordinary shares (of £1) for each £1 of 6% preference, 5½% A preference or ordinary stock held respectively. Final meeting return regd. 28 May 1960   1961

British Insulated Wire Co. Ld. Regd. 1890. Vol. liq. 27 Apr. 1897. Undertaking was acquired by company of same name for £148,125 ordinary shares of £5 and £27,650 preference shares of £5. Final meeting return regd. 14 Jan. 1899   1898

British Insulated Wire Co. Ld. See British Insulated Cables Ld.

British Insulite Co. Ld. Regd. 1882. Vol. liq. 27 Feb. 1885. Final meeting return regd. 1 June 1892   1886

British Internal Combustion Engines Ld. Regd. 1918. Vol. liq. (creditors') 3 Jan. 1930. No capital returned to contributories. Final meeting return regd. 9 Jan. 1936   1930

British International Pictures Ld. Regd. 1928 as United Motion Picture Producers Ld.; name changed July 1933 to B.I.P. (Production) Ld. and as above Oct 1933. Vol. liq. (members') 30 Mar. 1937. All shares held by Film Investments Ld. and Associated British Picture Corporation Ld. Final meeting return regd. 6 Apr. 1939   1938

British International Tarless Fuel Syndicate Ld. Regd. 1909. Struck off Register Jan. 1935   1935

British Investors' Association Ld. Regd. 1919. Vol liq. (members') 1 June 1932. Court Order to wind up 19 July 1932. Liquidator released 15 July 1941. Struck off Register 19 May 1944   *1933

British Isles & General Investment Trust Ld. Regd. 7 Dec. 1936. On 21 July 1975 all capital cancelled holders being entitled to securities of Estates House Investment Trust Ld. as follows:—183 ordinary shares of 25p for every 100 ordinary; 1 3·36% preference share of £1 for every 4% preference; £1 5·1% debenture stock and £1 6% debenture stock for every £1 4½% stock and £1 5% debenture stock respectively. Company to be dissolved without winding up.   1978-9

British Isles Marine & General Insurance Co. Ld. Regd. 1916. Vol. liq. 9 Jan. 1922. Final meeting return regd. 21 May 1929   1922

*See Stock Exchange Year-Book.

VOL. FOR

British Isles Oil Producers Ld. Regd. 1914. Vol. liq. 3 Oct. 1914. Final meeting return regd. 5 Jan. 1921 *1916

British Italian Banking Corporation Ld. Regd. 1916 as British Italian Corporation Ld.; name changed Apr. 1923. Vol. liq. (members') 31 Jan. 1931. Undertaking was acquired by Bank of America National Trust & Savings Association. All shares were held by B. I. Holding Co. Ld. Final meeting return regd. 7 June 1934 1913

British Italian Corporation Ld. See British Italian Banking Corporation Ld.

British Land & Mortgage Co. of America Ld. Regd. 1883. Vol. liq. 15 May 1902. Removed from Register 1903 1903

British Law Fire Insurance Co. Ld. Regd. 1888. Vol. liq. 5 June 1918. Undertaking and assets were acquired by London Assurance Corporation but were sold to British Law Insurance Co. Ld. Shareholders were entitled to 2 ordinary shares of £2 10s. (£1 5s. paid), 5 preference shares of £1, fully-paid, and £13 15s. 10d. in cash for every 5 shares of £10 (£1 paid) held; holders of fully-paid shares of £1 were entitled to 3 preference shares of £1, fully-paid, £3 3s. 2d. in cash. Final meeting return regd. 13 Mar. 1919 1919

British Legal and United Provident Assurance Co. Ld. See British Legal Life Assurance Co. Ld.

British Legal Life Assurance Co. Ld. Regd. Edinburgh 1863 as British Legal Life Assurance & Loan Co. Ld.; name changed to British Legal and United Provident Assurance Co. Ld. in June 1910 and as above in Nov. 1922. Vol. liq. Aug. 1927. Undertaking and assets were acquired by Britannic Assurance Co. Ld. Shareholders were entitled to either 1 fully-paid preference share of £1 in acquiring company plus 15s. in cash or £1 15s. in cash for each fully-paid share of £1 or every 2 shares of £1 (10s. paid) held. Final meeting return regd. 21 Feb. 1929 1928

British Lianosoff White Oil Co. Ld. Regd. 1912. Vol. liq. 24 June 1924. Final meeting return regd. 30 Apr. 1931 1925

British Linen Bank. Inc. by Royal Charter 1746 as British Linen Co.; name changed in June 1906. From 1 Mar. 1971 the undertaking vested in Bank of Scotland under provisions of Bank of Scotland Order 1970 1971

British Lion Film Corpn. Ld. Regd. 1927. Vol. liq. (creditors') 29 June 1955. Undertaking and assets exchanged, under Court Order, by the receiver appointed on behalf of National Film Finance Corpn. for shares in British Lion Films Ld. No capital was returned to contributories. Final meeting return regd. 12 Sept. 1956. 1957

British Lomagunda Development Co. Ld. Regd. 1895. Vol. liq. 24 Aug. 1905. Removed from Register 1907 1906

British Machine Tool Corporation Ld. Regd. Edinburgh 1911. Struck off Register 11 Dec. 1914 1912

British Magnesite Calcining Co. Ld. Regd. 1919. Vol. liq. (creditors') 27 Apr. 1934. Debenture holders received £9,520. No capital returned to contributories. Final meeting return regd. 3 Nov. 1936............ 1935

British Maikop Oil Co Ld. Regd. 1910. Vol. liq. (members') 1920 for reconstruction as Trinidad & British Maikop Oil Ld., in which company shareholders were entitled to 1 share of 2s. (1s. 6d. paid) for every share of 2s. held. Struck off Register 9 Feb. 1954 1947

British Malay Rubber Co. Ld. Regd. 1920. Vol. liq. 30 Dec. 1919 for reconstruction under same name. Shareholders were entitled to 3 shares of £1 fully paid in new company for each share of £1 held. Final meeting return regd. 15 Nov. 1921 1920

British Malay Rubber Co. Ld. Regd. 1919. Vol. liq. (members') 5 Apr. 1954. Undertaking acquired by Oriental Rubber Co. Ld. in which company stockholders were entitled to receive 2 stock units (of 2s.) for every 3 units (of 2s.) held. Final meeting return regd. 21 Sept. 1955 1956

British Malayan Tin Syndicate Ld. Regd. 1924. Vol. liq. (members') 15 Mar. 1954. Holders of outstanding tax-free notes were entitled to receive 1·0064d. per £1 but no capital was returned to contributories. Final meeting return regd. 29 Mar. 1956 1957

British Manifold Co. Ld. Regd. 1902. Vol. liq. 14 Oct. 1904. Final meeting return regd. 7 Sept. 1906 ...... *1905

British Marine Air Navigation Co. Ld. Regd. 1923. Vol. liq. 16 June 1924. Air transport business acquired by Imperial Airways Ld. Final meeting return regd. 7 Feb. 1925 1940

British Marine Navigation Ld. Air Transport business was acquired by Imperial Airways Ld. 1925

British Masterpiece Films Ld. Regd. 1923. Struck off Register 1931 .... *1932

British Match Co. Ld. Regd. 1901. Vol. liq. 5 Aug. 1927. Final meeting return regd. 28 Feb. 1928 1928

VOL. FOR

British Mékarski Improved Air Engine Co. Ld. Regd. 1881. Vol. liq. 12 May 1891. Final meeting return regd. 12 Apr. 1892 1892

British Metal Spray Co. Ld. Regd. 1913. Vol. liq. 27 June 1922. Capital returned to contributories—4s. per share of £1; further payments (if any) not known. Final meeting return regd. 7 Feb. 1923. Court Order declared dissolution void 6 Apr. 1925. Final meeting return regd. 3 Nov. 1925 1923

British Metalising Co. Ld. Regd. 1928. Vol. liq. (creditors') 20 Dec. 1934. Assets realised insufficient to pay creditors in full. Final meeting return regd. 11 Sept. 1935 1935

British Metals Extraction Co. Ld. Regd. 1908. Struck off Register Dec. 1931 1932

British Mexican Development Co. Ld. Regd. 1908. Vol. liq. 15 July 1910. Final meeting return regd. 27 June 1922 1911

British Military Tournament Co. Ld. Regd. 1892. Struck off Register 15 Sept. 1896 1899

British Millerain Co. Ld. Regd. 1894. Vol. liq. 23 Feb. 1921. Final meeting return regd. 8 June 1923 ...... *1922

British Mineral Oil Products Ld. See Tide Water Oil Co. (England) Ld.

British Mines Ld. Regd. 1903. Struck off Register 1915 1910

British Molasses Ld. Regd. 1915. Vol. liq. (members') 30 Apr. 1931. All shares owned by United Molasses Co. Ld. Final meeting return regd. 2 May 1935 .. 1932

British Molybdenite Co. Ld. Regd. 1904. Struck off Register 1916 1914

British Monomarks Ld. See Imperial Monomarks Ld.

British Moss Litter Co. Ld. Regd. 1896. Business was taken over in 1899 by company of same name for £83,906 in fully-paid ordinary shares of £1, £69,900 in fully-paid preference shares of £1, £64,000 in debentures and £7,194 in cash. Removed from Register 1901 1908

British Motor Bus Trust Ld. Regd. 1905. Vol. liq. Jan. 1907. Removed from Register 1911 1908

British Motor Cab Co. Ld. Regd. 1909. Vol. liq. 13 Feb. 1925. Capital returned to contributories—28s. 7d. per preferred ordinary share of £4. Final meeting return regd. 31 Mar. 1947; dissolution deferred by Court Order until 30 Nov. 1947 1948

British Motor Carriage & Cycle Co. Ld. See Universal Motor, Carriage & Cycle Co. Ld.

British Motor Co. Ld. Regd. 1895 as British Motor Syndicate Ld.; name changed Dec. 1897. Reconstructed 1900 as British Motor Traction Co. Ld., in which company shareholders were entitled to 1 preference share of £1 (credited with 17s. paid) for each ordinary or preference share of £1 held. Debenture holders were entitled to 1 fully-paid debenture of 10s. for each debenture of £1 held. Removed from Register 1903 1904

British Motor Finance Co. Ld. Regd. 1919. Vol. liq. (members') 11 Aug. 1930. Capital returned to contributories—£1 4s. 9·2114d. per share of £1. Final meeting return regd. 8 Dec. 1932 1931

British Motor Spirit Co. Ld. Regd. 1913 as British Motor Spirit Synd. Ld.; name changed Jan. 1920. Struck off Register Oct. 1933 1934

British Motor Syndicate Ld. See British Motor Co. Ld.

British Motor Traction Co. Ld. Regd. 1900. Receiver for debenture holders appointed in Feb. 1903. Struck off Register 13 Nov. 1903 1904

British Motor Trading Corporation Ld. Regd. 1919. Vol. liq. 3 July 1924. Final meeting return regd. 21 Feb. 1928 1925

British Motorship Co. Ld. Regd. 1925. Vol. liq. (creditors') 30 Dec. 1935. Assets realised insufficient to pay creditors in full. Final meeting return regd.1 Oct. 1936............ 1936

British Munitions Co. Ld. Regd. 1887 as Lorenz Ammunition & Ordnance Co. Ld.; name changed Nov. 1890. Vol. liq. 14 Nov. 1893. Final meeting return regd. 27 May 1896 1894

British Mutoscope & Biograph Co. Ld. Regd. 1899. Court Order to wind up 19 Nov. 1907. Removed from Register 1911 1908

British Mutual Bank Ld. Regd. 1875 as New British Mutual Investment Co. Ld.; name changed to British Mutual Investment Co. Ld. in 1877; to British Mutual Banking Co. Ld. in 1882 and as above in 1945. Vol. liq. (members') 26 Jan. 1951, the undertaking was acquired by Martins Bank Ld. in which company shareholders were entitled to receive 9 fully-paid shares of £1 for every 5 shares of £5 (£3 paid) and 3 fully-paid shares of £1 for every 5 shares of £1 (fully-paid) held 1959

British Mutual Banking Co. Ld. See above.

British Mutual Investment Co. Ld. See above.

British Mutual Plate Glass Insurance Co. Ld. Regd. 1888. Vol. liq. (members') 1 July 1930. Capital

See Stock Exchange Year-Book.

VOL. FOR

returned to contributories—£461 4s. 3d. Final meeting return regd. 8 Feb. 1932 ... **1931**

British National Opera Co. Ld. Regd. 1921. Struck off Register 1934 ... **1930**

British National Petroleum Refineries Ld. Regd. 1929. Vol. liq. (creditors') 9 July 1931. No capital returned to contributories. Final meeting return regd. 7 Nov. 1939 ... **1932**

British National Trust Ld. Regd. 1913. Struck off Register 24 Jan. 1936 ... **1936**

British Natural-Premium Life Association Ld. See Progressive Assurance Co. Ld.

British Natural-Premium Provident Association Ld. See Progressive Assurance Co. Ld.

British Neopost Ld. Regd. 1927. Vol. liq. (members') 4 June 1931. Capital returned to contributories—£15,715 5s. 5d. Final meeting return regd. 27 July 1931 ... **1932**

British Netherlands Artificial Silk Co. Ld. Regd. 1928. Receiver appointed in Dec. 1930. Vol. liq. Aug. 1931. Struck off Register 17 July 1942 ... **1934**

British New Guinea Development Co. Ld. Regd. 1910. Vol. liq. 22 July 1922 for reconstruction under same name. Shareholders were entitled to 3 shares of 10s. (credited with 7s. 6d. paid) in new company for every 2 ordinary shares held. 3 shares of 10s. (credited with 7s. 6d. paid) for each preference share held; holders of debentures (other than collateral) were entitled to an equal amount of debenture stock in new company. Final meeting return regd. 3 July 1924 ... **1923**

British Nigerian Co. Ld. Regd. 1907. Vol. liq. Aug. 1907. Removed from Register 1912 ... **1908**

British Nigerian Timber Co. Ld. Regd. 1920. Vol. liq. (creditors') 27 July 1931. Dividend of 4d. in £. Final meeting return regd. 21 Feb. 1934 ... **1932**

British (Non-Ferrous) Mining Corpn. Ld. Regd. 1927. Vol. liq. (members') 14 Dec. 1950. Final meeting return 7 Dec. 1951 ... **1952**

British Non-Flammable Wood Co. Ld. Regd. 1897. Reconstructed 1901 as Non-Flammable Wood and Fabrics Co. Ld., in which company shareholders were entitled to 1 fully-paid share of £1 for each share of £1 held. Removed from Register 1901 ... **1901**

British North American Investment Co. Ld. See British & Colonial Securities Co. Ld.

British North American Tobacco Co. Ld. Inc. British Columbia 1912. In hands of Official Receiver in Canada ... **1915**

British North Borneo Co. Ld. Inc. by Royal Charter dated 1 Nov. 1881; Deed of Settlement dated 1882 and supplemental Deeds of Settlement dated 1891, 1909 and 1928; regd. under Companies Act on 23 Apr. 1949. Vol. liq. (members') 11 Aug. 1949. Capital returned to contributories—10s. 6·728d. per £1 stock. £9,617 2s. 10d. was paid into Companies' Liquidation Account. Final meeting return regd. 10 Dec. 1953 ... **1955**

British North Borneo Development Corporation Ld. Regd. 1891. Reconstructed 1898 as British Borneo Development Co. Ld., in which company shareholders were entitled to 1 share of £1 (credited with 15s. paid) for each ordinary share of £1 held or 10 fully-paid shares of £1 for each founders' share of £1 held. Removed from Register 1901 ... **1908**

British North Borneo Gold Concessions Co. Ld. Regd. 1927. Struck off Register Sept. 1933 ... **1934**

British North Rand Mines Ld. Regd. 1895 as North Rand Mines Ld.; name changed 1901. Struck off Register 1916 ... **1908**

British Northern Trust Co. Ld. Regd. 1912. Vol. liq. 15 Dec. 1919. Final meeting return regd. 1 Jan. 1921 ... ***1920**

British Oil & General Securities Corporation Ld. See Union Oil Co. of Roumania Ld.

British Oil and Guano Co. Ld. Regd. Edinburgh 1896. Vol. liq. (members') June 1934. Capital returned to contributories—6s. 10⁷⁄₁₀d. per share of £1. Final meeting return regd. 24 Aug. 1935 ... **1935**

British Oil Engines Ld. Regd. 1925. Struck off Register Jan. 1934 ... **1934**

British Oil Lighting and Heating Ld. Regd. 1928. Vol. liq. (members') 9 July 1935. No capital returned to contributories. £198 was paid into Companies' Liquidation Account. Final meeting return regd. 14 May 1957 ... **1958**

British Oil Securities Ld. Regd. 1922. Struck off Register 1928 ... **1928**

British Oil Shipping Co. Ld. Regd. 1927. All capital was owned by Anglo Norness Shipping Co. Ld. Vol. liq. (members') 17 Mar 1966. Final meeting return regd. 27 Mar. 1969 ... **1964**

British Orchards Ld. Regd. 1921. Vol. liq. 7 June 1924. Controlling interest was held by British Gardens Ld. Final meeting return regd. 16 Nov. 1925 ... **1926**

VOL. FOR

British Ore Concentration Syndicate Ld. Regd. 1900. Vol. liq. 23 Jan. 1920. Final meeting return regd. 20 May 1921 ... **1921**

British Oriental Bank Ld. Regd. 1909. Vol. liq. (creditors') 30 Sept. 1930. No capital returned to contributories. Final meeting return regd. 4 July 1933 ... **1931**

British Orion Oil Co. Ld. Regd. 1922. Vol. liq. 27 Nov. 1923. Final meeting return regd. 2 July 1924 ... **1924**

British "Orto" Tyres Ld. Regd. 1912. Struck off Register 1927 ... **1927**

British Overseas Bank Ld. Regd. 1919. Vol. liq. (members') 8 June 1954. Capital returned to contributories—49s. 4d. per share (of £4). £1,543 was paid into Companies' Liquidation Account. Final meeting return regd. 8 Nov. 1962 ... **1964**

British Para Trust Ld. Regd. 1912. Vol. liq. 15 Nov. 1927. Final meeting return regd. 7 Apr. 1928 ... **1928**

British Patent Fuel, Coal & Coke Co. Ld. Regd. 1889. Vol. liq. 12 May 1891. Final meeting return regd. 24 Apr. 1895 ... **1892**

British Patent Portland Cement Co. Ld. Regd. 1888. Removed from Register 1901 ... **1892**

British "Pattisson" Hygienic Cycle Saddle Co. Ld. Regd. 1896. Court Order to wind up 14 Dec. 1899. Removed from Register 1909 ... **1900**

British Permel Enamelled Wire Ld. Regd. 1932. Vol. liq. (creditors') 9 Dec. 1938. A direct controlling interest was held by Johnson & Phillips Ld. Final meeting return regd. 15 July 1941 ... **1939**

British Petolite & Fuel Co. Ld. Regd. 1899. Vol. liq. 10 May 1900. Undertaking was acquired by Petolite Fuel Syndicate Ld. for 16,000 shares of £1 and £2,000 in cash. Removed from Register 1901 ... **1901**

British Petrol & Motor Equipment Ld. Regd. 1921. Assets realised insufficient to satisfy debenture holders. Struck off Register Apr. 1929 ... **1930**

British Petroleum Co. Ld. Regd. 1906. Distributing business was acquired by Shell-Mex and B.P. Ld. Vol. liq. (members') 12 May 1932. Capital returned to contributories—11s. 5·2d. per share of £10; plus 3,000,000 fully-paid shares of £1 of Shell-Mex and B.P. Ld. which were distributed in specie. Final meeting return regd. 16 May 1933 ... ***1933**

British Photomaton Trading Co. Ld. Regd. 1930. Vol. liq. 10 Apr. 1931. No capital returned to contributories. Final meeting return regd. 9 Nov.1934 ... **1932**

British Phototone Ld. Regd. 1928. Court Order to wind up 14 Apr. 1930. Struck off Register 16 Aug. 1938 ... **1939**

British Pioneers Ld. Regd. 1893. Assets and liabilities were taken over by Pioneer Estates Ld. Struck off Register 1927 ... **1898**

British Plate Glass Co. Ld. Regd. 1871. Removed from Register 1904 ... ***1902**

British Platinum & Gold Corporation Ld. Regd. 1918. Receiver appointed in Feb. 1928. Assets realised only sufficient to discharge arrears of debenture interest to Feb. 1929. Struck off Register 26 Jan. 1940 ... **1940**

British Pluviusin Co. Ld. Regd. 1920 as British Pluviusin Co. (1920) Ld.; name changed July 1923. Vol. liq. (members') 1 June 1931. Capital returned to contributories—£479,600. Final meeting return regd. 25 Apr. 1932 ... **1932**

British Porcupine Development Co. Ld. The assets were acquired in 1923 by Porcupine Goldfields Development & Finance Co. Ld., for £50,000 in cash and 200,000 fully-paid shares of £1 ... **1924**

British Possessions Corporation Ld. Regd. 1896. Stated in 1909 to be moribund. Removed from Register 1910 ... **1909**

British Power & Light Corpn. Ld. Regd. 1929 as British Power & Light Corpn. (1929) Ld.; name changed 17 May 1935. Dissolved 1 Apr. 1948, undertaking being vested in British (later Central) Electricity Authority under Electricity Act 1947. Holders of securities were entitled to receive British Electricity 3% guaranteed stock (1968–73) as follows in respect of each £1 unit of capital held:

	£	s.	d.
6% preference stock	1	9	10
4½% preference stock	1	4	0
Ordinary stock	1	17	10	**1949**

British Power Co. Ld. Regd. 1900 as South Wales Electrical Power Distribution 'Co. Ld.'; name subsequently changed to above. Receiver appointed 17 Dec. 1912; ceased to act 3 Apr. 1923. Vol. liq. 24 June 1914. Final meeting return regd. 11 Apr. 1923 ... ***1913**

British Primary Syndicate Ld. Undertaking and assets were acquired by British Surety Insurance Co. Ld. for £2.750 in cash and £9,750 in shares ... **1928**

See Stock Exchange Year-Book.

British Printing Trust Ld. Regd. 1911 as British European Trust Ld.; name changed Mar. 1923. Struck off Register 4 Aug. 1939 .... **1939**

British Produce Supply Association Ld. Regd. 1896. Vol. liq. 12 Sept. 1900. Final meeting return regd. 20 Dec. 1938. Court Order deferred dissolution until 31 July 1939 .... **1901**

British Property Investment Co. Ld. Regd. 1879. Removed from Register 1888 .... ***1882**

British Prospecting Co. Ld. Regd. 1894. Removed from Register 1904 .... ***1900**

British Provincial Securities Trust Ld. Inc. in Jersey 1963. Vol. liq. (members') 29 June 1971. Shareholders received 17 ordinary shares of £1 of Jersey External Trust Ld. for every 80 shares of 25p held **1977-8**

British Pure Ice Manufacturing Co. Ld. Regd. 1884. Vol. liq. Dec. 1887. Final meeting return regd. 3 Apr. 1890 .... **1888**

British Quarrying Co. Ld. Regd. 1929. Vol. liq. (members') 31 Oct. 1947 for the purpose of completing the merger of this company's group of companies with Amalgamated Roadstone Corporation Ld. (which company formerly owned practically all the A ordinary and all the B ordinary shares). Holders of 4½% debenture stock and 7½% participating preference shares (of £1) were given the option of exchanging all or part of their holdings into 5% 2nd preference shares of Amalgamated Roadstone Corpn. Ld. as follows: (a) debenture stock at the rate 100 of such shares for every £100 stock held, holders being required to make a cash payment at the rate of £3 10s. all stock not thus exchanged was repaid in cash at 101⅜%; and (b) 7½% participating preference shares at the rate of 5 2nd preference shares of the corporation for every 4 shares held, holders being entitled to receive a cash payment of 1s. 9d. per share; 7½% preference shares not thus exchanged were repaid in cash at 28s. 7·515d. per share. 723 A ordinary shares of £1 each held by minority interests have been repaid at par and the balance of the net assets has been distributed in specie by way of return of capital on the ordinary shares. Final meeting return regd.6 July 1963 .... **1964**

British Radiostat Corpn. Ld. Inc. in Canada under Dominion Laws 1929. Vol. liq. Apr. 1948. In Jan. 1949 it was stated that no returns on account of capital or debenture stock had been made and none would be made **1949**

British Radium Corporation Ld. Regd. 1908. Struck off Register 1921 .... **1917**

British Re-Insurance Co. Ld. Regd. 1880. Struck off Register 1916 .... **1887**

British Reserve Trust Co. Ld. Regd. 1914. Struck off Register 1923 .... **1917**

British Rola Ld. Regd. 1938. Vol. liq. (creditors') 5 Oct. 1949. Capital returned to contributories 6s. 9·038d. per preference share (of £1). Final meeting return regd. 29 Jan. 1953 .... **1953**

British Roumanian Oil Co. Ld. Regd. 1910. Vol. liq. Apr. 1912. Undertaking was acquired by Roumanian Consolidated Oilfields Ld., in which company shareholders were entitled to 5 fully-paid shares of £1 for every 8 shares of £1 held. Struck off Register Feb. 1930 .... **1930**

British Rubber & General Trust Ld. Regd. 1925. Court Order to wind up 15 Nov. 1937. Struck off Register 24 Aug. 1943 .... **1938**

British Rubber Estates of Java Ld. Regd. 1910. Vol. liq. (members') 16 Nov. 1932. Undertaking and assets were acquired by British Rubber Estates of Java (1932) Ld. in which company shareholders were entitled to 1 share of 2s. (credited with 1s. 9d. paid) for each share of 2s. held. Debenture stockholders were entitled to £110 debenture stock held. £140 4s. 6d. was paid into Companies' Liquidation Account. Final meeting return regd. 1 Feb. 1938 .... **1933**

British Safeglass Ld. Regd. 1930. Vol. liq. (creditors') 1 Mar. 1932. No capital returned to contributories. Final meeting return regd. 14 Feb. 1938 .... **1933**

British Safety Glass Co. Ld. Regd. 1928. Vol. liq. (creditors') 24 Feb. 1930. Undertaking and assets acquired by British Safeglass Ld in which company shareholders were to receive 1 share of 2s. (credited with 1s. 4d. paid) for each share of 2s. held. Non-claiming shareholders received 0·05d. per share in cash. Final meeting return regd. 9 Aug. 1932 ...... **1931**

British Screen Classics Ld. Undertaking and certain assets were acquired by British Screen Productions Ld. for £41,500 in cash **1929**

British Screen Productions Ld. Regd. 1928, Vol. liq. (members') 2 June 1930. Shareholders were entitled to 1 share of 5s. (credited with 3s. 6d. paid) in Audible Filmcraft Ld. for each share of 5s. held. Final meeting return regd. 3 Jan. 1935 .... **1931**

British Securities & Estates Ld. Regd. 1926. Vol. liq. (members') 2 July 1951. Final meeting return regd.7 Oct. 1952 .... ***1933**

British Settlement of South Africa Ld. Regd. 1903. Vol. liq. (members') 19 Mar. 1930. Capital returned to contributories—2·188d. per preference share of £1. Final meeting return regd. 7 June 1932 .... **1931**

British Shareholders Trust Ld. Regd. 1921 as B.S.T. (South America) Ld.; name changed 21 May 1924. All capital was owned by Philip Hill Investment Trust Ld. Vol. liq. (members') 5 Oct. 1956. Final meeting return regd. 14 May 1957 .... **1956**

British Shares Investment Corporation Ld. Regd. 1893. Assets were acquired by Home & Colonial Stores Ld. (later Allied Suppliers Ld.). Removed from Register 1901 .... **1898**

British Shipowners' Co. Ld. Regd. 1864. Vol. liq. Nov. 1906. Removed from Register 1909 .... **1907**

British-Siberian Mining Co. Ld. Regd. 1906. Vol. liq. June 1908. Removed from Register 1909 .... **1909**

British Sinai Petroleum Co. Ld. Regd. 1920. Vol. liq. 10 Dec. 1925. Final meeting return regd. 16 Dec. 1926 **1926**

British Somaliland Fibre & Development Co. Ld. Regd. 1905. Vol. liq. June 1911. Capital returned to contributories—20s. per preference share of £1; 9d. per ordinary share of £1 at Oct. 1911; further payments (if any) not known. Removed from Register 1912 .... **1912**

British South Africa Co.'s Mines Development Co. Ld. In liquidation. All shares were owned by British South Africa Co. **1933**

British South Africa Tobacco Plantations Ld. See Hunyani Rhodesia Tobacco Plantations Ld.

British South Africa Townships Ld. Regd. 1905. Vol. liq. Mar. 1910. Assets were acquired by Salisbury (Rhodesia) Estates Ld., in which company shareholders were entitled to 1 fully-paid share of 5s. for every share of 10s. (5s. paid) held. Removed from Register 1912 .... **1911**

British South Africa Transport & Trading Co. Ld. Regd. 1892. Vol. liq. Dec. 1908. Removed from Register 1910 .... **1909**

British South African Explosives Co. Ld. Regd. 1902. Vol. liq. (members') 25 July 1930. Capital returned to contributories—£1 13s. 1d. per share of £1. £1,962 3s. 1d. was paid into Companies' Liquidation Account in respect of unclaimed dividends and £8,314 9s. 6d. in respect of unclaimed capital. Final meeting return regd. 24 Jan. 1931 .... **1931**

British South American Syndicate Ld. Regd. 1907. Struck off Register Apr. 1930 .... **1931**

British South West African Land & Mining Co. Ld. Regd. 1893. Vol. liq. 11 Apr. 1906. Undertaking was acquired by Roper River Land & Minerals Co. Ld., for 200,000 shares of 10s. (credited with 7s. 3d. paid). Final meeting return regd. 25 June 1931 .... **1907**

British Spiral Telephone Wire Syndicate Ld. Regd. 1884. Removed from Register 1906 .... **1886**

British Stamp & Ticket Automatic Delivery Co. Ld. Regd. 1907. Vol. liq. 2 Feb. 1927. Undertaking acquired by Hall Telephone Accessories Ld. (later Associated Automation Ld.). Capital returned to contributories at Oct. 1927—14s. 3d. per A share of £1; 8s. 6d. per B share of 14s.; further payments (if any) not known. Final meeting return regd. 11 May 1928 .... **1928**

British Standard Cement Co. Ld. Regd. 1912. Business acquired by Allied Portland Cement Manufacturers Ld. **1930**

British Steam Users' Insurance Society Ld. Regd. 1889. Vol. liq. 5 Aug. 1896. Final meeting return regd. 8 Sept. 1898 .... **1899**

British Steel & Wire Co. Ld. Regd. 1908. Court Order to wind up 5 June 1912. Liquidator released 1 Aug. 1914. Struck off Register 14 Feb. 1919 .... **1913**

British Steel Corporation Ld. Regd. 1918. Vol. liq. 30 Nov. 1929. Direct controlling interest held by Baldwins (Holdings) Ld. Final meeting return regd. 3 Dec. 1929 .... **1929**

British Stock & Share Trust Ld. Regd. 1919. Struck off Register 8 Mar. 1935 .... **1936**

British Stone & Marble Co. Ld. Regd. 1902 as Lithographic Stone & Marble Co. Ld.; name changed Mar. 1908. Vol. liq. 8 Aug. 1912. Final meeting return regd. 16 Nov. 1915 .... **1913**

British Sugar Co. Ld. Regd. 1900. Vol. liq. 29 Dec. 1921. Final meeting return regd. 6 Apr. 1922 .... ***1922**

British Sugar Manufacturers Ld. Regd. 1925. Vol. liq. (members') 15 Sept. 1936. Certain assets were sold to British Sugar Corporation Ld. for 254,498 fully-paid shares of £1. The 6½% 1st mortgage debentures were cancelled prior to liquidation, but holders became creditors for amount at par. Capital

VOL. FOR

returned to contributories—7s. 10½d. per share of £1.
Final meeting return regd. 11 Nov. 1940 .... **1937**

British Sulphides Smelting Co. Ld. Regd. 1899. Receiver
appointed 9 Aug. 1930. Struck off Register Apr.
1933 .... **1934**

British Sulphur Co. Ld. Regd. 1912. Vol. liq. 17 Nov.
1922. Final meeting return regd. 15 Feb. 1923 .... **1923**

British Sun Ray Institute (Belfast) Ld. Regd. 1928. All
shares owned by National Sun Ray & Health
Centres Ld. Struck off Register 1934. .... **1932**

British Sun Ray Institute (Birmingham) Ld. Regd. 1928.
All shares owned by National Sun Ray & Health
Centres Ld. Struck off Register 1934 .... **1932**

British Sun Ray Institutes (Leeds) Ld. Regd. 1928. All
shares owned by National Sun Ray & Health
Centres Ld. Struck off Register 1934 .... **1932**

British Surety Insurance Co. Ld. Regd. 1927. Court
Order to wind up 12 May 1930. Struck off Register
14 Oct. 1938 .... **1939**

British Swiss International Corporation Ld. Regd. 1928.
Struck off Register 17 Dec. 1935 .... **1936**

British Synthetics Ld. Regd. 1923. Vol. liq. (members') 2
Apr. 1938. All shares owned by British Alizarine
Co. Ld. Final meeting return regd. 16 Sept. 1935 **1937**

British Talking Pictures Ld. Regd. 1928. Assets realised
insufficient to meet claims of creditors. Struck off
Register 4 Aug. 1939 .... **1940**

British Taman Oilfields Ld. Regd. 1912. Vol. liq. 14 Oct.
1921. Undertaking and assets were acquired by East
& West African Exploration Co. Ld., in which
company shareholders were entitled to 5 shares of
2s. (credited with 1s. 4d.) paid) for every 2 shares of
5s. held. Final meeting return regd. 10 Apr. 1922 **1922**

British Tanning Co. Ld. Regd. 1889. Vol. liq. 3 May
1893. Removed from Register 1903 .... **1894**

British Tea & Trading Association Ld. Business acquired
by British & Bennington's Ld. Struck off Register 8
Dec. 1931 .... **1937**

British Tea Table Co. (1897) Ld. Regd. 1897. Court
Order to wind up Nov. 1909. Struck off Register
1916 .... **1901**

British Thomson-Houston Ld. Regd. 1889 as Laing
Wharton & Down Construction Syndicate Ld.;
name changed Aug. 1894. Certain assets were
acquired in 1896 by British Thomson-Houston Co.
Ld. Removed from Register 1903 .... **1897**

British Timber Corporation Ld. Inc. Brit. Columbia
1918. Assets were sold 1 Jan. 1926 and Corporation
liquidated; holders of 7% A debenture stock
received approximately 97¼% on account of capital **1927**

British Timber Plantations Ld. Regd. 1919. Struck off
Register 1927 .... ***1923**

British Timken Ld. Regd. 1920. Ordinary capital was
acquired by Timken Roller Bearing Co., U.S.A.
Vol. liq. (members') 13 Oct. 1959. Preference shares
(of £1) redeemed at 22s. 6d. per share in Oct. 1959.
Final meeting return regd. 26 Sept. 1962 .... **1963**

British Tin Corporation Ld. Regd. 1912. Struck off
Register 7 Dec.1937... **1938**

British Tobacco Co. (Australia) Ld. Regd. 1904. Vol. liq.
5 Dec. 1927. Assets acquired by Consolidated
Investment Co. Ld. (later British Tobacco Co.
(Australia) Ld.) in which company ordinary shareholders received 7 ordinary shares of £1 for every 5
shares of £1 held. Preference shareholders were
entitled to be paid off at par, but were given option
of taking up 1 preference share of £1 in new
company for each share held. Final meeting return
regd. 5 Sept. 1928 .... **1928**

British Tobacco Co. of Turkey Ld. Regd. 1910. Vol. liq.
19 Aug. 1914. Final meeting return regd. 29 June
1915 .... **1915**

British Tobacco Plantations (Pullen-Burry System) Ld.
Regd. 1913. Vol. liq. May 1915. Struck off Register
Mar. 1929 .... **1930**

British Trade Corporation Ld. Inc. by Royal Charter
1917. Regd. 1926. Vol. liq. Oct. 1926. Undertaking
and assets were acquired by Anglo International
Bank Ld. Holders of A shares were entitled to cash
at par or 9 fully-paid shares of £1 in new company
for every 10 A shares of £1 held. Holders of ordinary
shares were entitled to 3 fully-paid shares of £1 in
new company for every 2 ordinary shares of £2 10s.
held. Struck off Register 7 July 1939.................... **1940**

British Tramways & General Construction Co. Ld. Regd.
1903. Vol. liq. Nov. 1911. All capital was returned to
contributories either in cash or shares of another
company *plus* surplus representing profits earned.
Removed from Register 1912 .... **1913**

British Transport Commission. Inc. by Transport Act
1947. Dissolved by Transport Act 1962. the property, rights and liabilities were transferred on 1 Jan.
1963 to 4 public authorities, viz. British Railway
Board, London Transport Board, British Transport

VOL. FOR

Docks Board and British Waterways Board, and the
Commission's share holdings to Transport Holding
Co. The existing guaranteed stocks became the
liability of H.M. Treasury. Final dissolution of the
Commission was postponed until 1 Jan. 1964 by The
British Transport Commission (Continuation No.
4) Order 1963.. **1963**

British Transvaal & General Financial Co. Ld. Regd.
1890 as British & Transvaal Financial Co. Ld.;
name changed Jan. 1900. Vol. liq. 25 May 1906.
Final meeting return regd. 27 June 1928 .... **1907**

British Transvaal Gold Exploration Co. Ld. Regd. 1902.
Vol. liq. 14 Mar. 1906. Removed from Register 1908 **1907**

British Transvaal Mines Ld. Regd. 1899. Vol. liq. Sept.
1907. Reconstructed as New British Transvaal
Mines Ld. Removed from Register 1910 .... **1908**

British Trust & Barning Co. Ld. Regd. 1910. Court
Order to wind up 31 Oct. 1932. Liquidator released
13 May 1939. Struck off Register 1 May 1953 ...... **1933**

British Trust Corporation Ld. Regd. 1907. Removed
from Register 1914 .... **1915**

British Trusts & Securities Corporation Ld. Regd. 1926.
Vol. liq. (members') 21 May 1957. Final meeting
return regd. 27 Apr. 1959 .... **1933**

British Tube Co. Ld. Regd. 1895. Removed from
Register 1906... **1905**

British Tulle & Net Co. Ld. Regd. 1923. Vol. liq. 3 Apr.
1926. Final meeting return regd. 7 June 1928 .... ***1926**

British Turpentine Corporation Ld. Regd. 1904. Vol. liq.
Apr. 1909. Undertaking was acquired by private
company of same name. Removed from Register
1910 .... **1910**

British Union & National Insurance Co. Ld. Regd. 1909.
Vol. liq. under Court supervision 2 July 1912. Court
Order to dissolve 4 July 1924 .... **1931**

British Union Insurance Co. Ld. Regd. 1892. Vol. liq. 27
Jan. 1897. Final meeting return regd. 24 July 1899 **1898**

British Union Oil Co. Ld. Regd. 1914. Vol. liq.
(members') 31 Jan. 1957. Final meeting return
regd.5 July 1957.. **1955**

British Uralite Co. Ld. Regd. 1899. Vol. liq. 17 Jan.
1907. Final meeting return regd. 28 Oct. 1908 .... ***1908**

British Vegetable Oil Extraction Corporation Ld. Regd.
1915. Receiver appointed in May 1921; ceased to act
on 6 July 1926. Assets realised insufficient to satisfy
debenture stockholders. Struck off Register Mar.
1929 .... **1930**

British Visada Ld. Regd. 1925. Vol. liq. (members') 28
Dec. 1932. Certain assets which were sold to British
Breda Silk Ld. were transferred to Breda Visada Ld.
Holders of preferred ordinary shares were entitled to
2 fully-paid A shares of £1 for every 5 preferred
shares of £1 held *plus* 11d. per preferred share in
cash. Final meeting return regd. 5 Jan. 1934 .... **1933**

British Wagon Co. Ld. Regd. 1869. Vol. liq. 9 Feb. 1898
for reconstruction under same name. Shareholders
were entitled to 1 share of £20 (credited with £3
paid) in new company for every £3 paid up capital
held. Final meeting return regd. 23 Mar. 1908 ..... **1908**

British Water-Gas Syndicate Ld. Regd. 1889. Vol. liq. 29
Nov. 1893. Reconstructed as Amalgamated Water-
Gas Companies Ld. which company acquired the
assets for 115,000 fully-paid shares of £1. Final
meeting return regd. 10 Aug. 1897...................... **1897**

British West Africa & Ashanti Ld. Regd. 1900. Assets
were acquired by Ashanti & Gold Coast United Ld.
Removed from Register 1904 .... **1904**

British West African Trading Co. Ld. Regd. 1910 as Tin
Areas of Nigeria Ld.; name changed Sept 1920.
Court Order to wind up 22 Feb. 1921. Struck off
Register 1928 .... **1922**

British West Charterland Ld. Regd. 1895. Removed
from Register 1902 .... **1900**

British Westfalite Ld. Regd. 1906. Vol. liq. (members')
31 Dec. 1942. All capital held by I.C.I. (Explosives)
Ld. Final meeting return regd. 25 May 1946 .... **1943**

British Westralia Syndicate Ld. Regd. 1894. Removed
from Register 1902 .... **1902**

British Westralian Mines & Share Corporation Ld.
Regd. 1895. Vol. liq. 22 July 1898. Undertaking was
acquired by London and Westralian Mines and
Finance Agency Ld in which company shareholders
were entitled to 1 ordinary share of £1 (credited with
10s. paid) for each similar share held. Holders of
each founders' share of £1 were entitled to 2 fully-
paid deferred shares of 6s. 8d. in acquiring
company. Final meeting return regd. 24 Feb. 1900 **1896**

British Widows Assurance Co. Ld. Regd. 1902. Vol. liq.
(members') 31 Aug. 1936. Undertaking and assets
were acquired by Prudential Assurance Co. Ld.,
which company purchased all the shares at £1 12s.
6d. per share of 5s. Final meeting return regd. 11
Dec. 1936 .... **1937**

See Stock Exchange Year-Book.

VOL. FOR

British Window Glass Co. Ld. Regd. 1919. Vol. liq. 3 Dec. 1924. Final meeting return regd. 24 May 1930 **1926**

British "Zenith" Adjustable Cycle Co. Ld. Regd. 1897. Removed from Register 1906 .... **1899**

Briton Ferry Chemical & Manure Co. Ld. Regd. 1886. Assets realised insufficient to meet claims of debenture holders. Struck off Register 29 Aug. 1941 **1942**

Briton Life Association Ld. Regd. 1875. Vol. liq. Sept. 1887. Undertaking was transferred to Marine and General Mutual Life Assurance Society Ld. Final meeting return regd. 28 Feb. 1890 .... **1887**

Briton Medical & General Life Association Ld. Established 1854. Regd. 1883. Vol. liq. 22 Apr. 1892. Business was acquired by Sun Life Assurance Society. Final meeting return regd. 12 June 1895.. **1892**

Briton Motor Co. Ld. Regd. 1912 as Briton Motor Co. (1912) Ld.; name changed June 1919. Vol. liq. 13 Jan. 1922. Final meeting return regd. 26 Oct. 1923 **1923**

Britons United Gold Mines Ld. Regd. 1895. Reconstructed 1899 as company of same name in which company shareholders were entitled to 1 share of £1 (credited with 17*s.* paid) for each share of £1 held. Removed from Register 1903 .... **1901**

Britons United Gold Mines Ld. Regd. 1899. Struck off Register 16 Nov. 1906 .... **1907**

Brittany China Clay Co. Ld. Regd. 1908 Vol. liq. (members') 23 May 1933. No capital returned to contributories. Final meeting return regd. 8 Mar. 1934 .... **1934**

Brixham Gas & Electricity Co. Incorporated as Brixham Gas Light Co. by Deed of Settlement in 1838; reincorporated as Brixham Gas Co. by Special Act 1904; name changed to present title in 1930. Dissolved 1 Apr. 1948, undertaking being vested in British (later Central) Electricity Authority and South-Western Area Board under Electricity Act 1947. Holders of securities were entitled to receive British Electricity 3% guaranteed stock (1968–73) as follows in respect of each £1 unit, unless otherwise stated, of capital held:

	£	s.	d.	
5% preference shares	1	3	0	
4½% preference shares (1958)	1	0	3	
4½% preference shares (1959)	1	0	3	
Ordinary shares	1	0	0	
5½% perpetual debenture stock	1	6	8⅖	
5% perpetual debenture stock	1	4	8⅖	
4½% perpetual debenture stock	1	2	6	
5½% mortgage debentures (per £100)..	108	10	0	**1949**

Broad Arrow Gold Co. Ld. Regd. 1900. Vol. liq. 1 Feb. 1905. Removed from Register 1905 .... **1905**

Broadbottom Gas Co. Ld. Regd. 1892. Dissolved 1 May 1949, undertaking being vested in North Western Area Gas Board under Gas Act 1948. Holders of securities were entitled to receive, in respect of each £1 unit held, British Gas 3% guaranteed stock 1990–95 as follows:

	£	s.	d.	
Ord. shares	1	17	6	
5% pref. shares	1	2	0	**1952**

Broadfield Paper Staining Co. Ld. Amalgamated with Wall Paper Manufacturers Ld. between Sept. 1915 and Mar. 1924 .... **1924**

Broadhurst & Co. Ld. Regd. 1907. Vol. liq. (members') 25 Aug. 1933. All shares were owned by Dunlop Rubber Co. Ld. (later Dunlop Co. Ld.). Final meeting return read. 24 Aug. 1934 .... **1934**

Broadmount Investment Trust Ld. Regd. 1927. Vol. liq. (creditors') 28 May 1930. Final meeting return regd. 4 Mar. 1937 .... ***1931**

Broadstairs Gas Co. Inc. by Special Act 1875. Dissolved 1 May 1949. undertaking being vested in South Eastern Area Gas Board under Gas Act 1948. Holders of securities were entitled to receive, in respect of each £100 unit held, British Gas 3% guaranteed stock 1990–95 as follows:

	£	s.	d.	
Cons. stock (7% stand.)	130	0	0	
5% pref. stock	112	0	0	
5% perp. deb. stock	125	0	0	
4% perp. deb. stock	102	0	0	
3½% deb. stock	100	0	0	**1952**

Broadstairs Hotel & Land Co. Ld. Regd. 1884. Vol. liq. 14 Dec. 1886. Final meeting return regd. 22 Oct. 1887 .... **1887**

Broadstairs Waterworks Co. Inc. by Special Act. Undertaking acquired for £42,800 by Broadstairs and St. Peter's Urban District Council, who assumed liability for debenture debt. **1902**

VOL. FOR

Broadstone Mills Ld. Regd. 1920. Vol. liq. (members') 15 Dec. 1965. Final meeting return regd. 17 July 1967 .... **1961**

Broadwater Rubber Estate Co. Ld. Regd. 1910. Vol. liq. 18 June 1924. Final meeting return read. 9 Feb. 1925 **1925**

Broadway Damask Co. Ld. *See* Donegall Fabrics Ld.

Broadway Finance & Investment Co. Ld. Regd. 1901. As Electric & Ordnance Accessories Co. Ld.; name changed 5 Apr. 1928. Vol. liq. (members') 30 Nov. 1935. Capital returned to contributories—20*s.* per share of £1. Final meeting return regd. 21 Jan. 1936 **1927**

Broadway Gold Mining Co. Ld. Regd. 1881. Removed from Register 1888 .... ***1884**

Broadway Spinning Co. (1919) Ld. Regd. 1919. Vol. liq. (members') 28 Apr. 1939. Capital returned to contributories—£39,882 *plus* £2,525 4*s.* 11*d.* repayment of capital paid in advance of calls. Final meeting return regd. 21 Sept. 1939 .... **1940**

Broadway Varieties Ld. Regd. 1927. Vol. liq. 20 Nov. 1928. Properties purchased by Denman Picture Houses Ld. Struck off Register 14 July 1933 .... **1940**

Broadways (Retailers) Ld. Regd. 1934. Winding up order 23 Jan. 1939. Unsecured creditors received 1*s.* 3·765*d.* in the £. Liquidator released 16 Nov. 1950. Struck off Register 2 Feb. 1954 .... **1951**

Brockenhurst Gas Co. Inc. by Special Act 1907. Undertaking was acquired in 1938 by Bournemouth Gas and Water Co. (later Bournemouth & District Water Co.) **1908**

Brockie-Pell Arc Lamp Ld. Regd. 1900. Vol. liq. July 1907. Removed from Register 1911 .... **1909**

Brocklebank & Co. Ld. Regd. as unlimited 1933 and as limited 1936. Vol. liq. (members') 30 Mar. 1943. Capital was returned to contributories, together with surplus assets in cash or specie. Final meeting return regd. 8 Apr. 1944 .... **1945**

Brock's Gold Fields Ld. Regd. 1901. Reconstructed 1902 as Commonwealth Gold Fields Ld in which company shareholders were entitled to 1 share of 10*s.* (credited with 7*s.* 6*d.* paid) for each share of £1 held. Removed from Register 1904 .... **1903**

Brock's Gold Fields Ld. Regd. 1901. Reconstructed 1902 as Commonwealth Gold Fields Ld., in which company shareholders were entitled to 1 share of 10*s.* (credited with 7*s.* 6*d.* paid) for each share of £1 held. Removed from Register 1904 .... **1903**

Brock's Gold Fields of the Northern Territories of Australia Ld. Regd. 1896. Reconstructed 1898 as Brock's Gold Fields of the Northern Territories of South Australia Ld., in which company shareholders were entitled to 1 share of £1 (credited with 17*s.* paid) for each share of £1 held. Debenture holders were entitled to an equal amount of debentures in new company. Removed from Register 1901 .... **1899**

Brock's Gold Fields of the Northern Territories of South Australia Ld. Regd. 1898. Vol. liq. 27 Feb. 1901. Reconstructed as Brock's Gold Fields Ld., in which company shareholders were entitled to 1 share of £1 (credited with 17*s.* paid) for each share of £1 held. Removed from Register 1905 .... **1902**

Brod Brewery Co. Ld. Regd. 1890. Struck off Register 11 June 1895.. **1899**

Broderick (James) & Co. Ld. Regd. 1936 as James Broderick & Co. (1936) Ld.; name changed as above Nov. 1936. All capital was owned by Jays & Campbell's (Holdings) Ld. Vol. liq. 17 May 1963. Final meeting return Regd. 17 Nov. 1964............ **1960**

Brodie (Thomas & James) & Co. Ld. Regd. 1896. Court Order to wind up 14 Mar. 1906. Removed from Register 1911 .... **1907**

Brodsworth & District Gas Co. Regd. as limited 1909; inc. by Special Act 1912. By Act of 1931 the undertaking was amalgamated with those of Royston (Yorks) & District Gas Co. Ld., and the South Elmsall & District Gas Co. under the title of Royston and Brodsworth Gas Company. Holders of original ordinary (10% standard) and additional ordinary (7% standard) shares of £1 were entitled to £1 1*s.* 8*d.* and 15*s.* 2*d.* respectively in Ordinary (6% standard) stock of the new company for each share held; holders of 6% and 7% preference shares of £1 were entitled to £1 and £1 3*s.* 4*d.* respectively in 6% preference stock of the new company for each share held. The liability for the mortgages was assumed by the new company.. **1932**

Brodsworth Main Colliery Co. Ld. Regd. 1905. The undertaking was acquired by Doncaster Amalgamated Collieries Ld., in which company shareholders were entitled to 78·2 fully-paid ordinary shares of £1 and 38·2 fully-paid preference shares of £1 for each share of £100 held. Dissolved under Sec. 154 of Companies Act 1929 on 22 Mar. 1937 .... **1938**

Brogden (Robert), Sons & Co. Ld. Regd. 1897. Undertaking was acquired in 1904 by John J. Hunt Ld.

**See Stock Exchange Year-Book.*

VOL. FOR

Vol. liq. 8 May 1913. Final meeting return Regd. 1 Dec. 1913 .... **1899**

Broken Hill Junction Mining Co., No Liability. Inc. S. Australia 1901; reconstructed as Broken Hill Junction Lead Mining Co., N.L., in which company shareholders were entitled to 1 share of 10s. (credited with 4s. paid) for each share of 10s. (with 9s. 6d. paid) held **1909**

Broken Hill Junction Mining Co. Ld. Inc. Australia 1900. Reconstructed as Broken Hill Junction Mining Co., N.L. in 1901 .... **1908**

Broken Hill Junction North Mining Co, Ld. Inc, Victoria 1896. In liquidation in 1902 .... **1902**

Broken Hill Junction North Silver Mining Co., No Liability. Inc. Victoria 1890. London office closed in July 1907 .... **1908**

Broken Hill Junction Silver Mining Co. Ld. Inc. Victoria 1886. Reconstructed 1900 as Broken Hill Junction Mining Co. Ld., in which company shareholders were entitled to 1 fully-paid share of £1 and 1 share of £1 (credited with 15s. paid) for every share of £1 held **1901**

Broken Hill Proprietary Block 10 Co. Ld. Inc. Victoria 1888. Vol. liq. May 1932. Capital returned to contributories—5½d. per share of £10 (with £9 18s. paid); further payments (if any) not known **1925**

Broken Hill Proprietary Block 14 Co. Ld. Inc. Victoria 1887. Vol. liq. May 1932 .... **1933**

Broken Hill South Blocks Ld. Regd. 1905. Vol. liq. June 1911. Undertaking was acquired by Zinc Corporation Ld., in which company shareholders were entitled to 3 ordinary shares of 10s. and 1 preference share of £1 (credited as fully-paid) for every 3 shares of £1 held. Removed from Register 1913 .... **1912**

Broken Hill South Extended Ld. Regd. 1907. Vol. liq. 3 Nov. 1913. Reconstructed as Barrier South Ld., in which company shareholders were entitled to 1 ordinary share of 2s. (credited fully-paid) for each share of 10s. held. Final meeting return regd. 4 June 1914 .... **1914**

Broken Hill South Silver Mining Co. No Liability. Inc. Victoria 1893. Vol. liq. Sept. 1918. Reconstructed as Broken Hill South Ld. in which company shareholders were entitled to 4 shares of £1 (credited as fully-paid) for each share of £1 held. Holders of fully-paid shares were entitled to 10s. 6d. per share in cash **1919**

Broken Hill Syndicate Ld. Regd. 1905. Vol. liq. 21 Aug. 1906. Capital returned to contributories—15s. 8¾d. per A share of £1 or B share of 1s.; further payments (if any) not known Removed from Register 1907 .... **1907**

Broken Hill Water Supply Ld. Inc. Victoria 1890. Vol. liq. Mar. 1916. Capital returned to contributories—5s. per share of 5s.; further payments (if any) not known **1916**

Broit Ld. Regd. 1920, Vol. liq 19 Feb. 1926. Final meeting return Regd. 6 Dec. 1927 .... **1927**

Bromborough Port Estate Ld. Regd. 1908 as Bromboro Port Estate Ld.; name changed July 1932. Vol. liq. (members') 13 Dec. 1950. Final meeting return regd. 16 Aug. 1951 .... **1940**

Bromley & Crays Gas Co. Established 1854. Inc. by Special Act 1865 as Bromley Gas Consumers Co.; name changed 1908. Under Act of 1912 the undertaking was acquired by South Suburban Gas Co. Debenture stockholders were entitled to an equal amount of debenture stock in acquiring company bearing same rate of interest. Other stockholders were entitled to ordinary 5% standard stock as follows: £111 8s. 8d. for every £100 A stock held; £85 14s. 4d. for every £100 B stock held; £102 17s. 2d. for every £100 C stock held **1913**

Bromley (Kent) Electric Light & Power Co. Ld. Regd. 1897, Vol. liq. 19 Dec. 1927. Undertaking was purchased by Bromley Town Council. The 1st debenture stock was repaid at 105%. Final meeting return Regd. 11 Aug. 1928 .... **1928**

Brompton & Gillingham Consumers' Waterworks Co. Ld. *See* Chatham & District Water Co.

Brompton & Kensington Electricity Supply Co. Ld. Regd. 1888 as House to House Electric Light Supply Co. Ld.; name changed 1899. Undertaking was acquired by Central London Electricity Ld in which company shareholders were entitled to 1 fully-paid ordinary share of £1 for each ordinary share of £1 held. The preference shareholders received 6,242 6% preference and 617 ordinary shares of £1. Dissolved under Sec. 154 of Companies Act 1929 .... **1938**

Brompton & Piccadilly Areas Railway Co. *See* London Electric Railway Co.

Brompton, Chatham, Gillingham & Rochester Waterworks Co. *See* Chatham & District Water Co.

Bromsgrove Gaslight & Coke Co. Estd. 1869; inc. by Special Act 1882. Dissolved 1 May 1949, undertaking being vested in West Midland Area Gas Board

VOL. FOR

under Gas Act 1948. Holders of securities were entitled to receive British Gas 3% guaranteed stock 1990–95 as follows in respect of each £10 unit, unless otherwise stated, of security held:

	£	s.	d.	
Orig. shares (10% stand.)	19	10	0	
B shares (7% stand.)	14	0	0	
4% mort. debs. (per £100)	100	5	0	**1952**

Bromsgrove Light Railway Co. Inc. (under Light Railways Act of 1896) by order of Light Railway Commissioners and confirmed by Board of Trade in 1900 .... **1902**

Bromyard Gas Co. Ld. Regd. 1856. Dissolved 1 May 1949. undertaking being vested in West Midland Area Gas Board under Gas Act 1948. Holders of securities were entitled to receive, in respect of each £10 unit held, British Gas 3% guaranteed stock 1990–95 as follows:

	£	s.	d.	
Ord. shares (10% max.)	12	10	0	
4% pref. shares	10	2	0	
4% addit. pref. shares	10	2	0	**1952**

Brook & Amos Ld. Regd. Edinburgh 1923. Vol. liq. (members') 4 July 1933. Directly controlled by Scottish Motor Traction Co. Ld. Capital returned to contributories—20s. per share of £1. Final meeting return regd. 3 May 1934 .... **1934**

Brooke (Alec.) Ld. Regd. 1926. Vol. liq. (members') 1 Jan. 1942. All capital held by I.C.I. (Rexine) Ld. Final meeting return Regd. 13 Mar. 1943 .... **1942**

Brooke & Prudencio Ld. Regd 1889. Vol. liq. 21 Oct. 1920. Undertaking and assets were acquired by Bristol Industries Ld., in which company shareholders were entitled to 5 ordinary shares of £1 for each ordinary share of £5 held, or 5 preference shares of £1 for every preference share of £5 held, Final meeting return Regd. 25. May 1921 .... **1921**

Brooke (Benjamin) & Co. Ld. Regd. 1895. Vol. liq. 20 Feb. 1899, the undertaking was acquired by Lever Brothers Ld. (later Unilever Ld.). Struck off Register 1904 .... **1900**

Brooke, Simpson & Spiller Ld. Regd. 1886. Vol. liq. 29 Mar. 1905. Final meeting return regd. 3 Dec. 1909 .... **1906**

Brooke's Cycle Co. Ld. Regd. 1896. Removed from Register 1904 .... **1900**

Brookfield Linen Co. Ld. Regd. Dublin 1866; transferred to Belfast under Government of Ireland Act 1920. Vol. liq. June 1933 .... **1934**

Brooklands (Weybridge) Ld. Regd. 1936. Vol. liq. (members') 2 Aug. 1946. Capital returned to contributories—10s. 2.11d. per preference share of 10s.; 9s. 6.3d. per ordinary share of 5s. £173 was paid into Companies' Liquidation Account. Final meeting return regd. 4 Aug. 1948 .... **1949**

Brookman Brothers' Boulder Gold Mining Co. Ld. Regd. 1895. Vol. liq. 16 Aug. 1901. Reconstructed as North Kalgurli Co. Ld., in which company shareholders were entitled to 1 share of 10s. (credited with 7s. 6d. paid) for each share of £1 held. Removed from Register 1904 .... **1902**

Brookman's Gold Exploration & Finance Association of Western Australia Ld. Regd. 1895. Vol. liq. 24 Feb. 1899. Final meeting return regd. 17 Apr. 1900 .... **1900**

Brooks & Doxey Ld. Regd. 1898. In Feb. 1920 shareholders were offered £45 per ordinary share of £10 or £12 10s. per preference share of £10. Vol. liq. 8 June 1920. The undertaking and assets were sold to Brooks & Doxey (1920) Ld. later Lord Brothers (Cottons) Ld. Final meeting return regd. 1 Aug. 1924 .... **1921**

Brooks & Hamilton Ld. *See* Morrisons Economic Stores Ld.

Broomassie Mines Ld. Regd. May 1901. Reconstructed 1904 as company of same name. Shareholders were entitled to 1 share of £1 (credited with 15s. paid) for each share of £1 held. Removed from Register 1904 .... **1908**

Broomassie Mines Ld. Regd. 1904. Vol. liq. 16 Oct. 1909. Reconstructed as company of same name. Shareholders were entitled to 1 fully-paid share of 10s. for each share of £1 held. Final meeting return Regd. 14 Dec. 1910 .... **1910**

Broomassie Mines Ld. Regd. 1909. Vol. liq. 30 Mar. 1917. Final meeting return Regd. 29 Sept. 1924 .. **1917**

Broomassie-Prestea Main Reef Proprietary Syndicate Ld. Regd. 1908. Struck off Register 1924 .... **1923**

Broome (Selangor) Rubber Plantations Ld. Regd. 1912. Vol. liq. (creditors') 3 July 1933. Reconstructed as Broome Rubber Plantations Ld., in which company shareholders were entitled to 2 shares of 2s. (credited as fully-paid) for each share of £1 held. Final meeting return regd. 30 June 1934 .... **1934**

*See Stock Exchange Year-Book.

VOL. FOR

Broomhill Collieries Ld. Regd. 1900. Vol. liq. (members') 6 Feb. 1953. Capital returned to contributories—£4 3s. 10d. per ordinary share of £1. Final meeting return regd. 10 May 1955 1956

Broseley Gas & Coke Co. Ld. Regd. 1872. Vol. liq. (members') 27 July 1936. Undertaking acquired by Iron Bridge & District Gas Co. Ld., in which shareholders received 7 ordinary shares of £1 for each share held. Final meeting return regd. 23 Apr. 1937 1937

Brotex Cellulose Fibres Ld. Regd. 1928. Vol. liq. (creditors') 28 Oct 1931. No capital returned to contributories. Final meeting return regd. 29 Oct. 1935 1932

Brotex Ld. Undertaking and assets were acquired by Brotex Cellulose Fibres Ld. for 600,000 preferred shares of £1 and 3,600,000 ordinary shares of 1s. all credited as fully-paid 1930

Brotherton Ediswan Tubes & Conduits Ld. Regd. 1897 as New Brotherton Tube Co. Ld.; name changed to Brotherton Tubes & Conduits Ld. in 1913 and as above 1919. Vol. liq. July 1922. Struck off Register 1929 1923

Brotherton (John) Ld. Regd. 1886. Vol. liq. 20 Sept. 1922. Final meeting return regd. 17 Aug. 1924 1923

Brotherton Tubes & Conduits Ld. See Brotherton Ediswan Tubes & Conduits Ld.

Brotton Gas Light & Coke Co. Ld. Regd. 1868. Dissolved 1 May 1949, undertaking being vested in Northern Area Gas Board under Gas Act 1948. Holders of securities were entitled to receive British Gas 3% guaranteed stock 1990–95 as follows:

	£	s.	d.
Ord. shares (10% max.) (of £5 fully-paid)		18	0
Ord. shares (10% max.) (of £5 with £2 paid)		4	0

1952

Brough, Nicholson & Hall Ld. Regd. 1907. Vol. liq. (members') Dec. 1930. Undertaking and assets were acquired by Brough, Nicholson & Hall (1930) Ld. for 275,880 fully-paid A ordinary shares of 10s. The preference shareholders were repaid in cash. Final meeting return regd. 13 Jan. 1932 1931

Broughton Collieries Ld. Inc. Nova Scotia 1929. Vol. liq. (members') 30 Sept. 1941 1942

Broughton Copper Co. Ld. Regd. 1897. Vol. liq. 15 May 1928. Undertaking and assets were acquired by Broughton Copper Works (1928) Ld. (later Broughton Copper Co. Ld.). Holders of debenture stock were entitled to £102 in cash *plus* interest; shareholders were entitled to 20s. per preference share of £1 or £3 5s. 6d. per ordinary share of £1. Final meeting return regd. 23 Oct. 1928 1929

Broughton Copper Co. Ld. Regd. 1928 as Broughton Copper Works (1928) Ld. Vol. liq. (members') 31 Dec 1942 I.C.I. Metals Ld. held all shares, but £655 16s. 4d. was paid into Companies' Liquidation Account in respect of dissentient shareholders' account. Final meeting return regd. 29 Sept. 1944 1943

Browett, Lindley & Co. Ld. Regd. 1899 as Browett, Lindley & Co. (1899) Ld.; name changed 1902. Assets were expected to provide for repayment of about 50% of 1st debentures. Struck off Register 1934 1932

Brown (Allen) Ld. Regd. 1875. Vol. liq. 18 Sept. 1962. Final meeting return regd. 19 Apr. 1963 1911

Brown & Barlow Ld. Regd. 1904. Vol. liq. 1 Nov. 1928. All capital acquired by Amal Ld. Final meeting return regd. 3 Aug. 1929 1936

Brown & May Ld. Regd. 1895. Court Order to wind up 6 May 1913. Struck off Register 1921 1914

Brown & Richards Ld. Undertaking and assets were acquired by Richards (Thomas) (Textiles) Ld. for 120,000 fully-paid preference and 80,000 fully-paid ordinary shares of 5s. 1930

Brown & Thomson Ld. Regd. Edinburgh 1920. Vol. liq. (members') 30 June 1932. All shares held by Wiggins. Teape & Alex. Pirie (Merchants) Ld. Certain assets were distributed in specie and undertaking and balance of assets were transferred to Allied Paper Merchants (W.T. & Co.) Ld. Final meeting return regd. 4 Nov.1933 1933

Brown Bayley & Dixon Ld, Regd. 1873. Vol. liq. 18 Jan. 1881. Court Order to wind up 31 Jan. 1881. Final meeting return regd. 7 Aug. 1884 .... *1882

Brown Bayley's Steel Works Ld. Regd. 1888. Removed from Register 1904. Restored to Register 1905. Vol. liq. 30 July 1918. Reconstructed as company of same name. Shareholders were entitled to 4 ordinary shares of £5 for each share of £10 held, or 2 ordinary shares of £5 for each share of £5 held. Final meeting return regd. 15 July 1919 1919

Brown Bayley's Steel Works Ld. Regd. 1918. Vol. liq. (members') 27 Sept. 1957. The undertaking was sold

to Brown Bayley Ld. in which company shareholders were entitled to receive 8 fully-paid shares of £1 for each share of 2s. 6d. held. £11 1s. was paid into Companies' Liquidation Account. Final meeting return regd. 26 July 1958 1959

Brown (Charles) & Co. Ld. Regd. 1922. Vol. liq. (members') 1 Feb. 1958. All capital held by company of same name. Final meeting return regd. 29 Oct. 1958 1940

Brown (Charles) & Co. Ld. Regd. 1933 as Charles Brown Holdings Ld.; name changed 2 Feb. 1959. All capital was owned by Spillers Ld. Vol. liq. (members') 1 Feb. 1962. £1 12s. 6d. in respect of unclaimed dividends was paid into Companies' Liquidation Account. Final meeting return regd. 26 Sept. 1962 1963

Brown (D. M.) Ld. Regd. Edinburgh 1927. Vol. liq. (members') 30 Jan. 1953. Final meeting return regd. 1 May 1962 1940

Brown, Davis & Co. Ld. Regd. 1879. Vol. liq. 5 Mar. 1889. Court Order to continue winding up under supervision 26 Mar. 1889. Final meeting return regd. 3 Aug. 1893 1890

Brown (F.) Ld. Regd. 1920. Vol. liq. (creditors') 12 Jan. 1938. Assets realised insufficient to pay unsecured creditors in full. Final meeting return regd. 15 Nov. 1938 1938

Brown Hill Extended Ld. Regd. 1895. Vol. liq. 31 May 1929. Final meeting return regd. 1 Oct. 1930........ 1930

Brown Hill North (Hannan's) Ld. Regd. 1896. Removed from Register 1905 1903

Brown (James) & Co. Ld. Regd in Edinburgh 1898. Winding-up order 29 Apr. 1968. Interlocutor dissolving company under Sec. 274 of Companies' Act 1948 sent to Registrar 15 May 1974. 1975-6

Brown (James) 1919 (Brentwood) Ld. Regd. 1919. Vol. liq. 12 Apr. 1935. Capital returned to contributories—£9,525 9s. 3d. Final meeting return regd. 20 Feb. 1936 1936

Brown (James) of Chisworth Ld. Regd. 1912. Vol. liq. (members') 24 Aug. 1944. A direct controlling interest was held by Bleachers' Association Ld. (later Whitecroft Industrial Holding Ld.). Final meeting return regd. 27 Oct. 1944 1945

Brown Marshalls & Co. Ld. Regd. 1870. Vol. liq. 16 Nov. 1897. Reconstructed as company of same name. Shareholders were entitled to 4 ordinary and 4 preference shares of £1 in new company for each share of £1 held. Final meeting return regd. 13 Aug. 1898 1902

Brown, Marshalls & Co. Ld. Regd. 1897. Reconstructed 1902 as Metropolitan Amalgamated Railway Carriage & Wagon Co. Ld. (later Metropolitan Cammell Carriage Wagon and Finance Co. Ld.), in which company shareholders were entitled to 1½ ordinary shares of £1 for each ordinary share of £1 held or to 1 preference share of £1 for each preference share of £1 held. Removed from Register 1903 1903

Brown (Thomas) & Co. (Carlisle) Ld. Regd. 1915. Vol. liq. (creditors') 21 Mar. 1938. Assets realised insufficient to pay unsecured creditors in full. Final meeting return regd. 28 Apr. 1939 1939

Brown (William) & Co. of Liverpool Ld. Regd. 1898. Vol. liq. (members') 5 Jan. 1961. Preference shares (of £1) were repaid at par in 1961 plus distribution of 22s. 4¾d. per share on account of arrears of dividend. Amount paid into Companies' Liquidation Account—in respect of unclaimed dividends £147 12s. 10d.; distributions £1,379 19s. 9d. Final meeting return regd. 16 Feb. 1962 1936

Browne (Harris) Ld. Regd. 1930. Vol. liq. (members') 27 July 1939. All shares held by Fremlins Ld. Final meeting return regd. 21 Mar. 1940 1940

Brownhill Central Gold Mines Ld. Regd. 1896. Vol. liq. 7 Jan. 1907. Undertaking was acquired by Australian Share Trust Ld. for £300 in cash and payment of debts and liabilities. Removed from Register 1907 1907

Brownhill Great Southern Ld. Regd. 1896. Reconstructed as Brownhill Great Southern (1900) Ld in which company shareholders were entitled to 1 fully-paid share of £1 for each share of £1 held, on payment of 2s. per share. Struck off Register 18 Nov. 1902 1902

Brownhill Great Southern (1900) Ld. Regd. 1900. Removed from Register 1904 1903

Brownhill Mining Syndicate Ld. Regd. 1895. Vol. liq. 25 May 1899. Leases were sold to Brown Hill North Ld. Final meeting return regd. 17 Dec. 1900 1900

Brownhill Proprietary Gold Mines Ld. Regd. 1895. Removed from Register 1902 1903

Brownlac Ld. Regd. 1929. Vol. liq. (members') 15 July 1932. Capital returned to contributories—£4,000 *plus* a further possible distribution after payment of

See Stock Exchange Year-Book.

VOL. FOR

liquidators' remuneration and certain expenses. Final meeting return regd. 11 July 1934................. **1933**

Brown's Creek Co. Ld. Regd. 1898. Removed from Register 1910 .... **1902**

Brown's Paddock Gold Mines Ld. Regd. 1900. Removed from Register 1907 .... **1904**

Bruas-Perak Rubber Estate Ld. *See* Perthpoint Investment Ld.

Bruce Copper Mines Ld. Regd. 1905. Vol. liq. Dec. 1908. Removed from Register 1913 .... **1909**

Bruce Land & Mining Co. Ld. Regd. 1878. Vol. liq. 29 Nov. 1895. Final meeting return regd. 4 Mar. 1897 **1896**

Brunei (Borneo) Rubber & Land Co. Ld. Regd. 1909. Vol. liq. (members') 6 Aug. 1959. Capital returned to contributories—5s. 5d. per share of £1. £25 2s. 7d. was paid into Companies' Liquidation Account. Final meeting return regd. 17 Feb. 1961................. **1962**

Brunei Estates Ld. Regd. 1910. Vol. liq. 18 Dec. 1923. Amalgamated with Lafayette Rubber Estates Ld., in which company shareholders were entitled to 2 shares of 5s. (credited with 6s. paid) for each ordinary share of £1 held, or 4 fully-paid ordinary shares of 5s. for each preference share of £1 held. Final meeting return regd. 25 Feb. 1924 .... **1924**

Brunner Collieries Ld. Regd. 1912. Vol. liq. 3 Dec. 1915. Final meeting return regd. 4 Apr. 1916 .... **1916**

Brunner Mond & Co. Ld. *See* I.C.I. (Alkali) Ld.

Brunswick Syndicate Ld. Regd. 1897. Struck off Register 1923 .... **1908**

Brunt, Bucknall & Co. Ld. Regd. 1890. Vol. liq. 10 May 1928. Undertaking and assets were acquired by Bass, Ratcliff & Gretton Ld. Final meeting return regd. 2 Oct. 1930 .... **1929**

Brunton (W.) & Co. Ld. Regd. 1919. Vol. liq. 30 Mar. 1927. Direct controlling interest held by Nobel Industries Ld. Final meeting return regd. 5 Sept.1928 .... **1928**

"Brush" Electric Light & Power Co. of Scotland Ld. Regd. 1882. Vol. liq. Oct. 1883. Court Order to continue under supervision Nov. 1883. Final meeting return regd. 9 May 1884 .... **1884**

Brush Midland Electric Light & Power Co. Ld. Regd. 1882. Vol. liq. Jan. 1885. Assets were acquired by Anglo-American Brush Electric Light Corporation Ld., in which company shareholders were entitled to 4 fully-paid shares of £5 for every 27 shares of £2 10s. held. Final meeting return regd. 10 Apr. 1888 ..... **1885**

Brussels Motor Cab Co. Ld. Regd. 1909. Vol. liq. 31 July 1929. Final meeting return regd. 24 Dec. 1931 ..... **1930**

Brussels Palace of Varieties Ld. Regd. 1892. Removed from Register 1907 .... **1895**

Brustad Mines Ld. Inc. Guernsey 1905. Vol. liq. Apr. 1907 .... **1908**

Bruton Gas & Coke Co. Ld. Regd. 1924. Dissolved 1 May 1949, undertaking being vested in South Western Area Gas Board under Gas Act 1948. Holders of securities were entitled to receive, in respect of each £1 held, British Gas 3% guaranteed stock 1990–95 as follows:

	£	s.	d.
Ord. shares	2	6	0
6% pref. shares	1	6	5	**1952**

Brutton & Burney Ld. Regd. 1899. Undertaking and assets were acquired by Burney's New Cross Brewery Ld. Removed from Register 1907 .... **1904**

Bruzac Hydro-Carbon Processes Ld. *See* Improved Hydro Carbon Processes Ld.

Bryan (G. A.) Ld. Regd. 1914. Vol. liq. 7 June 1928. Business acquired by Selecta Gramophones Ld. Final meeting return regd. 15 Jan. 1930 .... **1941**

Bryant & Langford Quarries Ld. Regd. 1925. Vol. liq. July 1934. Business was acquired by Roads Reconstruction (1934) Ld., [later Roads Reconstruction Ld. (Regd. 1960)] in which company shareholders were entitled to 1 preference share of £1 for each preference share of £1 held or 1 ordinary share of 10s. for every 10 ordinary shares of 6d. held. Final meeting return regd. 24 July 1939 .... **1935**

Bryant, Powis & Bryant Ld. Regd. 1885. Vol. liq. 1 Sept. 1891. Final meeting return regd. 17 Jan. 1895 ..... **1894**

Brycourt Investments Ld. Regd. 1972. Vol. liq. 13 Nov. 1978. Capital returned to contributries (per ordinary share of 50p)—131p. Final meeting return regd. 13 July 1979 .... **1981–2**

Brymbo Steel Co. Ld. Regd. 1884. Receiver appointed in June 1931. Assets realised insufficient to meet claims of debenture holders. Struck off Register 19 June 1936 .... **1937**

Bryn Gwiog Mines Ld. Regd. 1906. Mining rights were acquired in 1928 by Halkyn District United Mines Ld., for 3,841 fully-paid shares of £1 which were distributed to shareholders who also were entitled to 2d. per share. £7 19s. 6d. was paid into Companies' Liquidation Account in respect of sale of unclaimed

VOL. FOR

shares and £4 16s. 4d. in respect of unclaimed dividends. Vol. liq. (members') 31 Dec. 1930. Final meeting return regd. 31 Dec. 1938 .... **1911**

Bryn Tivy Private Hotel (Blackpool) Ld. Regd. 1920. Struck off Register 1924 .... ***1924**

Brynamman Collieries Co. (1923) Ld. Regd. 1923. Vol. liq. 12 May 1924. Undertaking acquired by Henderson's Welsh Anthracite Collieries Ld. Struck off Register 3 Oct. 1941 .... **1940**

Bryncethin Colliery Co. Ld. Regd. 1906. Removed from Register 1910 .... **1910**

Brynhenllys Anthracite Colliery Ld. Regd. 1925. Struck off Register 4 Dec. 1964 .... **1940**

Brynmawr & Blaina Gas Co. Inc. by Special Act 1866. Dissolved 1 May 1949, undertaking being vested in Wales Area Gas Board under Gas Act 1948. Holders of securities were entitled to receive British Gas 3% guaranteed stock 1990–95 as follows in respect of each £100 unit of security held:

	£	s.	d.
Ord. stock (10% max.)	165	0	0
5% pref. stock	112	0	0
4% per deb. stock	102	0	0	**1952**

Brynmawr Coal & Iron Co. Ld. Regd. 1873. Removed from Register 1885 .... ***1877**

Brynymor Steamship Co. Ld. Regd. 1920. Vol. liq. (members') 15 Feb. 1946. Capital returned to contributories—ordinary: 8s. 1⅝d. per 2s. stock; preference: £1 0s. 7·2d. per £1 stock. £1,409 6s. 10d. was paid into Companies' Liquidation Account on account of unclaimed distributions. Final meeting return regd. 5 Sept. 1960 .... **1961**

Brysilka Ld. Regd. 1920. Vol. liq. (creditors') 28 May 1931. Assets realised insufficient to pay creditors in full. Final meeting return regd. 11 Feb. 1936 ...... **1932**

Buatuim (Wassau) Gold Mine Ld. Regd. 1901. Vol. liq. 18 Dec. 1902. Undertaking was acquired by Gold Coast United Ld., in which company shareholders were entitled to 4 shares of 10s. (credited with 3s. 9d. paid) for every 3 shares of £1 (10s. paid) held. Removed from Register 1905 .... **1904**

Bucaramanga Gold & General Mining Co, Ld. Regd. 1899. Struck off Register 17 Aug.1951 .... **1903**

Buchanan & French Ld. Regd. 1905. Vol. liq. Apr. 1907. Struck off Register 7 Apr. 1937 .... **1938**

Buchanan Estates Ld. *See* Leicester Square Estates Ld.

Buchholtz & Co. Ld. Regd. 1900. Vol. liq. (members') 15 Mar. 1956. Undertaking and assets were transferred to Buchholtz & Co. Ld. (later Copthall Holdings Ld.) in which company preference shareholders were entitled to receive 4 fully-paid ordinary shares of 4s. plus 8s. cash for each share of £1 held. The ordinary shares, which were vested in the Custodian of Enemy Property, were entitled to the remaining 40,000 ordinary shares and £4,000 cash. Amount paid into Companies' Liquidation Account in respect of (1) unclaimed dividends £89 19s. 8d.; (2) distributions, £254. Final meeting return regd. 22 Aug. 1957 .... **1958**

Buckfastleigh, Totnes & South Devon Railway Co, Inc. by Special Act 1864. Undertaking purchased, under Act of 1897, by Great Western Railway Co. "A" and "B" debenture stocks were exchanged for an amount of G.W. Rly. 4% debenture stock producing a like amount of interest; each preference share of £10 was exchanged for £7 10s. 5% consolidated preference stock; holders of ordinary shares received £3 5s. per share **1898**

Buckie Gas Light Co. Ld. Regd. in Edinburgh 1931. Dissolved 1 May 1949, undertaking being vested in Scottish Area Gas Board under Gas Act 1948. Holders of securities were entitled to receive, in respect of each £1 unit held, British Gas 3% guaranteed stock 1990–95 as follows:

	£	s.	d.
Ord. shares	5	10	0
7½% pref. shares	1	12	0
5% pref shares	1	2	6	**1952**

Buckingham & Adams Cycle & Motor Co. Ld. Regd. 1899. Removed from Register 1907 .... **1902**

Buckingham & Adams Ld. Regd. 1889. Vol. liq. 11 Mar. 1891. Final meeting return regd. 2 Dec. 1893 ...... ***1891**

Buckingham Brick & Tile Co. Ld. Regd. 1928. Court Order to wind up 15 Oct. 1929. Struck off Register 1936 .... **1930**

Bucklands Estate & Diamond Co. Ld. Regd 1912. Vol. liq. (members') 9 Oct. 1945. Undertaking was acquired by Central Underwriters Syndicate Ld., in which company shareholders were entitled to 1 fully-paid share of £1 for every 6 shares of 5s. held. Final meeting return regd. 2 May 1946 .... **1947**

Buckley & Nunn Ld. Regd. 1902. Vol. liq. June 1919. Undertaking and assets were sold to company of same name (inc. Victoria). Final meeting return

VOL. FOR

regd. 4 Dec. 1919. Court Orders deferred dissolution 30 Oct. 1920 **1920**

Buckley Gas Co. Ld. Regd. 1888. Dissolved 1 May 1949, undertaking being vested in Wales Area Gas Board under Gas Act 1948. Holders of securities were entitled to receive British Gas 3% guaranteed stock 1990–95 as follows:

	£	s.	d.	
Ordinary shares (of £10)	17	10	0	
Ordinary shares (of £10—£8 10s. paid)	14	17	6	**1952**

Buckley Railway Co, Inc. by Special Act 1860. Great Central Railway Act of 1904 provided for vesting of undertaking in that company from 1 Jan. 1905, holders of 5% preference stock and ordinary capital were entitled to receive an amount of Great Central 3½% second debenture stock sufficient to produce the same income **1905**

Bucknall's Gold Estate Co. Ld. Regd. 1886. Court Orders: to wind up 29 Oct. 1887; to dissolve 10 June 1891 **1888**

Bucks & Oxon Union Bank Ld. Regd. 1866. Business was acquired by Lloyds Bank Ld., in which company shareholders were entitled to 1 share of £50 (credited with £8 paid) for every 2 shares of £25 (£5 paid) held. Removed from Register 1905 **1903**

Bucks Expresses (Watford) Ld. See London General Omnibus Co. Ld.

Buck's Fleet Motors Ld. Regd. 1920 as Buck's Swift Fleet Motors Ld.; name changed 15 Sept. 1920. Vol. liq. 17 Nov. 1921. Final meeting return regd. 24 Nov. 1925 ***1924**

Bucks Reef Gold Mines Ld. Inc. Rhodesia 1909. Vol. liq. Apr. 1916 **1917**

Buck's Swift Fleet Motors Ld. See Buck's Fleet Motors Ld.

Buckton (Joshua) & Co. Ld. Regd. 1883. Vol. liq. 10 Aug. 1928. Receiver stated that there was no possibility of debentures being repaid in full. Struck off Register 21 May 1954 **1954**

Buda-Pesth Ice Co. Ld. Regd. 1883. Assets were acquired in 1887 by United Anglo-Continental Ice Co. Ld., in which company shareholders were entitled to an equal number of shares. Removed from Register 1906 **1888**

Budden & Biggs Brewery Ld. Regd. 1897 Vol. liq. (members') 26 Jan. 1931. Undertaking and assets were acquired by Ind Coope & Co. Ld. (later Ind Coope Ld.) which company owned all share and debenture capital. Final meeting return regd. 27 Sept. 1932 **1932**

Budderpore Tea Co. Ld. Regd. 1905. Vol. liq. (creditors') Jan 1933. Preference shares of £1 were repaid. Liquidation stayed 4 Apr. 1938. Vol. liq. (members') 15 Sept. 1941. Capital returned to ordinary shareholders—£8,187 10s. Final meeting return regd. 19 Sept. 1942 **1933**

Bude Gas Co. Inc. by Special Act 1907. Dissolved 1 May 1949, undertaking being vested in South Western Area Gas Board under Gas Act 1948. Holders of securities were entitled to receive British Gas 3% guaranteed stock 1990–95 as follows in respect of each £10 unit, unless otherwise stated, of security held:

	£	s.	d.	
Ord. shares (10% stand.)	12	10	0	
Ord. shares (7% stand.)	10	0	0	
6% pref. shares	13	10	0	
6% deb. stock (per £100)	111	0	0	
3½% red. deb. stock (1951) (per £100)	100	0	0	
3½% red. deb. stock (1953) (per £100)	100	0	0	
3½% red. deb. stock (1956) (per £100)	100	0	0	**1952**

Bude Harbour & Canal Co. Inc. by Special Act 1819. Under Act of 1901 the undertaking was sold to the Stratton and Bude Urban District Council for £8,000. Shareholders received £4 per share of £50; further payments (if any) not known **1903**

Budleigh Salterton Electric Light & Power Co. Ld. Regd. 1925. Vol. liq. (members') 26 Mar. 1934. Undertaking acquired by East Devon Electricity Co. Ld. for 22,000 fully-paid shares of £1. Final meeting return regd. 9 Aug. 1934 **1936**

Budleigh Salterton Gas Co. Ld. Regd. 1867. Dissolved 1 May 1949, undertaking being vested in South Western Area Gas Board under Gas Act 1948. Holders of securities were entitled to receive British Gas 3% guaranteed stock 1990–95 as follows in respect of each £5 unit, unless otherwise stated, of security held:

	£	s.	d.
Ordinary shares (10% max.)	10	5	0

VOL. FOR

	£	s.	d.	
Addit. ord. shares (7% max.)	7	5	0	
5% pref. shares	5	12	6	
4⅛% pref. shares	5	9	0	
4½% red. mort. debs. (per £100)	104	5	0	**1952**

Budleigh Salterton Railway Co. Inc. by Special Act 1894. London & South Western Railway's Act of 1911 confirmed an agreement for acquistion as from 1 Jan. 1912 **1912**

Budurua Tin Mines Ld. Regd. 1912. Vol. liq. Jan. 1914. Undertaking was acquired by Ex-Lands Nigeria Ld. Removed from Register 1914 **1914**

Buell Combustion Co. Ld. Regd. 1927. Vol. liq. (creditors') 22 Aug. 1940. With Court consent business sold as going concern to Buell (1952) Ld. Pre-liquidation creditors repaid in full; preference shareholders received distribution of 13s. 11·721d. per share (of £1). Final meeting return regd. 18 Nov. 1959 **1960**

Buell Combustion (Foreign) Ld. Regd. 1927. Vol. liq. (members') 13 Mar. 1934. Shareholders were to receive 2s. 6d. in cash and 2 fully-paid shares of £1 in Buell Combustion Co. Ld. for every 5 fully-paid ordinary shares of £1 held. Final meeting return regd. 20 Sept. 1935 **1935**

Buena Tierra Mining Co. Ld. Regd. 1912. Vol. liq. (creditors') 7 June 1946. Holders of registered notes received 3s. 4.2852d. per £. Final meeting return regd. 5 June 1947 **1947**

Buena Ventura Co. Ld. Regd. 1878. Vol. liq. Mar. 1890. Final meeting return regd. 5 Dec. 1890 **1891**

Buena Ventura Nitrate Co. Ld. Regd. 1913. Vol. liq. 31 Aug. 1920, assets and liabilities acquired by Liverpool Nitrate Co. Ld., in which company shareholders were entitled to receive 1 fully-paid share of 5s. for every 7 shares of £1 held, plus 5s. per share in cash. Final meeting return regd. 23 Sept. 1921 **1921**

Buenos Aires Central Railroad & Terminal Co. Inc. in Argentina 1927. Placed in liquidation July 1945. The undertaking was transferred to City of Buenos Aires Transport Corporation in 1938–9. Holders of preferred shares assenting to an offer made by Lacroze Bros. & Co. received in Aug. 1945 £1 12s. 10d. per share (of $0/s100) as first and final payment; non-assenting preferred shareholders could apply to Lacroze Bros. & Co. in Buenos Aires with reference to their shares **1947**

Buenos Aires City and Suburban Tramways Ld. Regd. 1911. Under Law of 1936 undertaking and assets were acquired by City of Buenos Aires Transport Corporation for $m/n 1,000,000 in shares of that Corporation. Struck off Register 24 Nov. 1944 **1945**

Buenos Aires Lacroze Light & Power Co. Ld. Inc. Argentine 1913. Holders of 6½% sterling redeemable mortgage debenture stock were satisfied by a payment of £87 10s. in cash for every £100 stock held in respect of principal, premium and accrued interest **1940**

Buenos Aires Port & City Tramways Ld. Regd. 1905. Vol. liq. 30 Dec. 1927. Undertaking was acquired by Buenos Aires Town and Docks Tramways Ld. Final meeting return regd. 26 Mar. 1928 **1928**

Buenos Aires & Belgrano Electric Tramway Co. Ld. Regd. 1898. Vol. liq. July 1908. Undertaking was acquired by Anglo-Argentine Tramways Co. Ld. The 1st debenture and 2nd debenture stocks were repaid at 115% and 105% respectively. Capital returned to contributories: £5 per A or B preference share of £5; a return of £4 18s. per ordinary share of £5 was anticipated. Removed from Register 1909 **1909**

Buenos Aires & Campana Railway Co. Ld. See Central Argentine Railway Ld.

Buenos Aires & Ensenada Port Railway Co. Ld. Regd. 1872. Undertaking acquired in 1898 by Buenos Aires Great Southern Railway Co. in which company stockholders were entitled to stock as follows: for each £100 4% debenture stock held—£100 4% debenture stock; for each £100 5% preference stock held—£92 5% preference stock; for each £100 6% preference stock held—£70 ordinary stock; for each £100 ordinary stock held—£50 ordinary stock. Removed from Register 1903 **1899**

Buenos Aires & Pacific Railway Co. Ld. Regd. 1882. Vol. liq. 1 Apr. 1948. Capital returned to contributories (per £100 stock)—5% 1st preference, £55 4s. 1·6d. 5% 2nd preference and 6% preference, £39 8s. 8d.; ordinary, £19 14s. 4d. Final meeting return regd. 5 June 1964 **1965**

Buenos Aires & Pacific Railway Equipment & Goods Depot Co. Ld. Regd. 1890. Vol. liq. 25 Jan. 1894. Assets were acquired by Buenos Aires and Pacific Railway Co. Ld. Final meeting return regd. Aug. 15, 1895 **1894**

Buenos Aires & Rosario Railway Co. Ld. See Central Argentine Railway Ld.

See Stock Exchange Year-Book.

VOL. FOR

Buenos Aires & Valparaiso Transandine Railway Co. Ld. *See* Argentine Transandine Railway Co. Ld.

Buenos Aires Central Railway Co. Ld. *See* Buenos Aires Midland Railway Co., Ld.

Buenos Aires Central Railway Ld. [Ferroearril Central de Buenos Aires Limitada.] Inc. in the Argentine Republic by Notarial Deed 15 June 1906. The Argentine Government (which acquired all shares of company under agreement of Apr. 1949) offered, under an agreement signed in Buenos Aires on 25 Mar. 1949 and subsequently ratified, £950,000 in sterling in London in full satisfaction of all claims for capital and interest in respect of the 4½% 1st and 5% 2nd mortgage debentures and 6½% secured notes; holders of the aforementioned securities were entitled to repayments, at the offices of the respective trustees, of the following amounts in full satisfaction of principal moneys (all unpaid premiums, interest and bonus having been waived) as from 12 Oct. 1949: 4½% mortgage debentures, 65%; 5% 2nd mortgage debentures, 10½%; and 6½% secured notes, 17½% **1951**

Buenos Aires Electric Tramways Co. (1901) Ld. Regd. 1901. Vol. liq. Dec. 1908. All shares were owned by Anglo-Argentine Tramways Co. Ld., which company acquired undertaking and assets. The 5% debenture stock was repaid at par and the 5½% B debenture stock at 105%. Removed from Register 1909 .... **1909**

Buenos Aires, Ensenada & South Coast Railway Co. Ld. Regd. 1888. Vol. liq. (members') 2 Apr. 1948. The undertaking was acquired by Argentine Government as from 1 July 1946. The compensation of £533,115 was paid to Buenos Aires Great Southern Railway Co. Ld. as company's only creditor. Final meeting return regd. 5 Apr. 1954 .... **1955**

Buenos Aires Gas Co. Ld. *See* Buenos Aires (New) Gas Co. Ld.

Buenos Aires Grand National Tramways Co. Ld. Regd. 1889 as Buenos Aires Metropolitan Tramways Co. Ld.; name changed Dec. 1889. Vol. liq. Mar. 1909. Undertaking and assets were acquired by Anglo-Argentine Tramways Co. Ld., in which company shareholders were entitled to 1 3rd preference share of £5 for each preference share of £5 held or 7 3rd preference shares of £5 for every 10 ordinary shares of £5 held. In Jan. 1909. holders of 5½% debenture bonds, 5% debenture stock and 6% debenture bonds were entitled to £116 13*s.* 4*d.* 4% debenture stock for every £100 held; holders of income bonds were entitled to £111 2*s.* 3*d.* 4% debenture stock for every £100 bonds held. Removed from Register 1910 .... **1910**

Buenos Aires Great Southern Railway Co. Ld. Regd. 1862. Vol. liq. (members') 2 Apr. 1948. The undertaking was acquired by Argentine Government as from 1 July 1946. 4%, 5½% redeemable and 4½% special debenture stocks were redeemed at par on 11 May 1948. Capital returned to contributories (per £100 stock): 5% preference, £85 0*s.* 7½*d.*; 6% preference, £56 13*s.* 9*d.*; and ordinary £22 13*s.* 6*d.* Final meeting return regd. 29 Jan. 1959 .... **1960**

Buenos Aires Land & Cattle Co. Ld. Regd. 1882. Conveyance of land to company not executed. Directors liquidated company and capital was returned in full to shareholders. Removed from Register 1889 .... **1884**

Buenos Aires Metropolitan Tramways Co. Ld. *See* Buenos Aires Grand National Tramways Co. Ld.

Buenos Aires Midland Railway Co., Ld. Regd. Feb. 1906 as Buenos Aires Central Railway Co. Ld.; name changed Apr. 1906. Vol. liq. (members') 2 Apr. 1948, the undertaking, together with all other British-owned railways in the Argentine, having been sold to Argentine Government as from 1 July 1946. The 4% debenture stock was repaid at par. Capital returned to contributories—per £100 stock, preference, £100; ordinary £80. £3,248 paid into Companies' Liquidation Account. Final meeting return regd. 28 Mar. 1956 .... **1957**

Buenos Aires National Tramways Co. Ld. Regd. 1871. Vol. liq. 17 May 1878. Merged into Anglo-Argentine Tramways Co. Ld. Final meeting return regd. 25 June 1880 .... ***1879**

Buenos Aires (New) Gas Co. Ld. Regd. 1875 as Buenos Aires Gas Co. Ld.; name changed Nov. 1880. Vol. liq. Dec. 1909. Undertaking and certain assets were acquired by Primitiva Gas and Electric Lighting Co. of Buenos Aires Ld. (later Primitiva Gas Co. of Buenos Aires Ld.). Shareholders were entitled to £2 10*s.* in ordinary and £5 in preference shares of £5 for every £7 share capital held; shareholders were also entitled to distribution in specie of 15,000 shares in South Barracas (Buenos Aires) Gas and Coke Co. Ld. The purchasing company assumed liability for debenture stock. Removed from Register 1911 .... **1910**

Buenos Aires New Tramways Co. Ld. Regd. 1888. Vol. liq. Apr. 1909. Undertaking and assets were acquired by Anglo-Argentine Tramways Co. Ld. The debenture stock was repaid at 105% and the prior lien bonds and 4% debentures at par. Removed from Register 1910 .... **1910**

Buenos Aires Northern Railway Co. Ld. Regd. 1862 as Northern Railway of Buenos Aires Co. Ld.; name changed by Act of 1885. By Act of 1898 undertaking was acquired by Central Argentine Railway Co. Ld. from 1 Jan. 1898. Contributories were entitled to receive such an amount of 3½% debenture stock in Central Argentine Railway Co. as would secure the following income; 12½% p.a. to holders of preference stock and guaranteed preference shares of £10; 10⅔% p.a. to holders of ordinary stock and deferred shares of £10 (the latter after adding 30% to nominal value). Central Argentine Railway Co. agreed to pay interest and provide for repayment of capital for 5% and 4% debenture stocks. Final meeting return regd. 18 Feb. 1904 .... **1899**

Buenos Aires Southern Dock Co. Ld. Regd. 1898. Undertaking sold to the Argentine Government 1 July 1946. Vol. liq. (members') 2 Apr. 1948. Capital returned to contributories—£20 3*s.* 4*d.* per ordinary share of £10. £532 5*s.* 5*d.* was paid into Companies' Liquidation Account. Final meeting return regd. 27 Mar. 1958 .... **1959**

Buenos Aires Water Supply & Drainage Co. Ld. Regd. 1888. Vol. liq. 30 June 1891. Debenture holders were entitled to an equal amount of sterling 5% bonds of Argentine Government *plus* two years' interest in funding loan bonds. Preference shareholders were entitled to an equal amount of sterling 5% bonds of Argentine Government *plus* one year's interest in funding loan bonds. Final meeting return regd. 22 Dec. 1893 .... **1894**

Buenos Aires Western Railway Ld. Regd. 1890. Vol. liq. (members') 2 Apr. 1948. The undertaking was acquired by Argentine Government as from 1 July 1946. The 4% and 5% debenture stocks were redeemed at par and the 5½% collateral debenture stock was redeemed at 102% all on 11 May 1948. Capital returned to contributories (per £100 stock)—5% and 4½% preference, £100; ordinary, £31 6*s.* 8*d.* Final meeting return regd. 28 Nov. 1958 .. **1960**

Buff Book Ld. Regd. 1923. Vol. liq. (members') 24 June 1937. Capital returned to contributories—10*s.* 3½*d.* per ordinary share of £1; no return to deferred shares of 1*s.* Final meeting return regd. 24 June 1939 **1938**

Buffalo Reef Gold Mining Co. Ld. Regd. 1898. Removed from Register 1903 .... **1903**

Buffels Land and Mining Co. Ld. Regd. Edinburgh 1889. Vol. liq. Apr. 1900 for reconstruction as Transvaal Proprietary Ld. Final meeting return regd.16 Jan.1902 .... **1907**

Buffelsdoorn A Gold Mining Co. Ld. Inc. Transvaal 1895. Vol. liq. Mar. 1908 .... **1909**

Buffelsdoorn Consolidated Gold Mining Co. Ld. Inc. Transvaal 1895. Vol. liq. Aug. 1908 .... **1909**

Buffelsdoorn Estate & Gold Mining Co. Ld. Inc. Transvaal 1889. In liquidation by order of the High Court **1908**

Buffington Acetylene Gas Light Co. Ld. Regd 1899. Removed from Register 1902 .... **1901**

Building & Loan Association. Inc. Canada 1870. Reconstructed 1899 as Toronto Mortgage Co. **1901**

Building Construction Co. Ld. Regd. 1906 as Waring & White (1909) Ld.; name changed 1910. Vol. liq. 10 Dec. 1912. Final meeting return regd. 29 Apr. 1914 **1910**

Building Estates & Property Association Ld. Regd. 1902. Vol. liq. 28 May 1912. Final meeting return regd 1 Sept.1920 .... **1913**

Building, Fitting and Furnishing Co. Ld. Regd. 1883. Vol. liq. 5 Mar. 1886. Final meeting return regd. 25 Mar. 1891 .... ***1884**

Building Securities Co. Ld. Regd. 1884. Court Order to wind up 17 Dec. 1892. Removed from Register 1911 **1894**

Building Society and General Fire Insurance Co. Ld. *See* North of England Fire Insurance Co. Ld.

Bujong Rubber Estate Ld. Regd. 1909. Vol. liq. 18 June 1920. The property was acquired by Kepong (Malay) Rubber Estates Ld. in which company shareholders were entitled to 4 fully-paid shares of 2*s.* *plus* 6*s.* in cash for each share of £1 held. Final meeting return regd. 19 July 1921 .... **1921**

Bukit Badang Rubber Co. Ld. Regd. 1912 as Merbau (Selangor) Rubber Co. Ld.; name changed July 1918. All capital was owned by Seafield Amalgamated Rubber Co. Ld. Vol. liq. (members') 3 Nov. 1964. Final meeting return regd. 9 Aug. 1968 ...... **1960**

**See Stock Exchange Year-Book.*

VOL. FOR

Bukit Cloh Rubber Co. Ld. Regd. 1909. All capital was owned by Seafield Amalgamated Rubber Co. Ld. Vol. liq. (members') 13 Jan. 1961. Final meeting return regd. 4 Jan. 1964 .... **1960**

Bukit Ijok (Selangor) Rubber Co. Ld. Regd. 1910 Vol. liq. (members') 29 Dec. 1961. Majority capital was owned by Merliman Pegoh Ld under a capital reduction scheme in Nov. 1961 minority interests received 3 Merliman Pegoh units (of 2s.) for every 2 units (of 2s.) held. Final meeting return regd. 30 Nov. 1962 .... **1964**

Bukit Kajang Rubber Estates Ld. Regd. 1909. All capital acquired by London Asiatic Rubber & Produce Co. Ld. Vol. liq. (members') 29 Dec. 1961. Final meeting return regd. 4 Dec. 1962 .... **1958**

Bukit Lintang Rubber Estates Ld. *See* Lintang Investments Ld.

Bukit Paniong Syndicate Ld. Regd. 1906. Vol. liq. 12 Feb. 1920. Reconstructed as Bukit Panjong Ld in which company shareholders were entitled to 4 shares of 2s. (credited as fully-paid) for each share of 2s. held. Final meeting return regd. 11 Jan. 1921 **1920**

Bukit Rajah Rubber Co. Ld. Regd. 1903. Vol. liq. 22 Mar. 1920. Reconstructed as company of same name. Shareholders were entitled to 5 fully-paid shares of £1 for each share of £1 held. Final return regd. 17 Nov. 1921 .... **1921**

Bukit Rajah Rubber Co. Ld. Regd. 1920 in reconstruction of company of same name (Regd. 1903). All capital was owned by Seafield Amalgamated Rubber Co. Ld. Vol. liq. (members) 3 Nov. 1964. Final meeting return regd. 31 Jan. 1979 .... **1960**

Bukit Selangor Rubber Estates Ld. Regd. 1910. Vol. liq. 23 Apr. 1920 for reconstruction as Bukit Selangor Rubber Estates (1920) Ld., in which company shareholders were entitled to 2¼ fully-paid shares of 2s. *plus* 3d. in cash for each share of 2s. held. Final meeting return regd. 9 May 1921 .... **1921**

Bukit-Sympa Rubber & Cotton Estates Ld. Regd. 1910. Struck off Register 17 Nov. 1916 .... **1913**

Bukit Tambun Coconut Co. Ld. Regd. 1911. Vol. liq. 28 Apr. 1915 for reconstruction as Bukit Tambun Estates Ld. in which company shareholders were entitled to 1 share of £1 (credited with 16s. paid) for each share of £1 held. Final meeting return regd. 3 Feb. 1917 .... **1916**

Bukit Tambun Estates Ld. Regd. 1915. Vol. liq. (members') 2 Apr. 1952. Estates sold for £54,142. Capital returned to contributories—preference shares at par and 3s. 11·375d. per ordinary share of 2s. £1,634 4s. 11d. was paid into Companies' Liquidation Account. Final meeting return regd. 12 Mar. 1956 .... **1957**

Bukit Tupah Rubber Estates Ld. Regd. 1924. Court Order to wind-up 17 Dec. 1962. Struck off Register 28 Sept. 1973 .... **1970**

Bukoba (Tanganyika) Tinfields Ld. Regd. 1927. Vol. liq. (creditors') 30 Dec. 1932. Assets realised insufficient to pay creditors in full. Final meeting return regd. 7 Oct. 1936 .... **1933**

Bulawayo & General Exploration Co. Ld. Regd. 1903. Reconstructed 1906 as Bulawayo and General Exploration Co. (1906) Ld., in which company shareholders were entitled to 1 share of £1 (credited with 16s. paid) for each share of £1 held. Removed from Register 1910 .... **1908**

Bulawayo Commonage Claims Ld. Regd. 1904. Vol. liq. Apr. 1908. Capital returned to contributories—6d. per share of £1 in June 1908; further payments (if any) not known. Removed from Register 1910 .... **1909**

Bulawayo Exploration Co. Ld. Regd. 1897. Vol. liq. 1903. Undertaking was acquired by Bulawayo and General Exploration Co. Ld. in which company shareholders were entitled to 1 fully-paid share of £1 for each share of £1 held. Removed from Register 1910 .... **1904**

Bulawayo Gold Reefs Development Ld. Regd. 1897. Vol. liq. 7 Dec. 1904. Undertaking was acquired by African & General Exploration Co. Ld. Shareholders were entitled to 1 share of £1 (credited with 15s. paid) in S.A. Proprietary Ld. for every 6 shares of 2s. 6d. held. Removed from Register 1911 .... **1906**

Bulawayo Market & Offices Co. Ld. Regd. 1897. Vol. liq. Aug. 1911 for amalgamation with Transvaal & Rhodesian Estates Ltd., in which company shareholders were entitled to 1 fully-paid share of 5s. for each share of 5s. held. Removed from Register 1912 **1912**

Bulawayo Waterworks Co. Ld. Regd. 1895. Vol. liq. 10 Dec. 1924. Undertaking expropriated by Municipality on 1 July 1924. Capital returned to contributories—7s. per share of £1 at Dec. 1924; further payments (if any) not known. Final meeting return regd. 3 Mar. 1926 .... **1925**

VOL. FOR

Bull Ant Proprietary of Western Australia Ld. Regd. 1910. Capital returned to contributories—6s. per share of £1 at Oct. 1911; further payments (if any) not known. Removed from Register 1912 .... **1912**

Bull Creek Mineral Estates Ld. Regd. 1899. Struck off Register 27 Oct. 1936 .... **1937**

Bull (Henry) & Co. Ld. Regd. 1898. Vol. liq. 13 July 1920. Undertaking and assets were acquired by D. & W. Murray Ld., in which company shareholders were entitled to 1¼ fully-paid preference shares of £1 for each ordinary share of £1 held. Preference shareholders were entitled to £1 in cash for each preference share of £1 held. Final meeting return regd. 21 June 1923 .... **1921**

Bull Motors Ld. Regd. 1902 as East Anglian Engineering Co. Ld.; name changed to A.G.E. Electric Motors Ld. 17 Aug. 1920 and as above 23 Nov. 1922. Vol. liq. (members') 25 Aug. 1933. The undertaking (with the exception of certain book debts) was transferred to E. R. & F. Turner Ld. in satisfaction of a debt. Final meeting return regd. 12 Oct. 1933 **1932**

Bullcroft Main Collieries Ld. Regd. 1913. Undertaking was acquired by Doncaster Amalgamated Collieries Ld., in which company shareholders were entitled to 11 fully-paid preference shares of £1 or 5·8 fully-paid preference shares of £1 and 11·7 fully-paid ordinary shares of £1 for every 10 shares (preference or ordinary) of £1 held. Dissolved under Sec. 154 of Companies Act 1929 on 22 Mar. 1937 .... **1938**

Bullen Bros. & Sons (1921) Ld. Regd. 1921. Vol. liq. (members') 2 Dec. 1936. Capital returned to contributories—£458 16s. 2d. Final meeting return regd. 8 May 1937 .... **1937**

Buller & Bassett Tin & Copper Co. Ld. Regd. 1887. Removed from Register 1892 .... **1891**

Bulletin Co. Ld. Regd. 1898. Removed from Register 1910 .... **1901**

Bulletin Proprietary Ld. Regd. 1897. Vol. liq. 5 Dec. 1898. Reconstructed as Bulletin Co. Ld., in which company shareholders were entitled to 1 share of £1 (credited with 16s. 8d. paid) for every 10 shares of £1 held. Final meeting return regd. 7 July 1899 .... **1900**

Bullfinch East Gold Mining Co. Ld. Regd. 1910. Vol. liq. July 1911. Capital returned to contributories—5s. 6d. per share of £1 at Aug. 1911; further payments (if any) not known. Removed from Register 1912 **1912**

Bullfinch Proprietary (W.A.) Ld. Regd. 1910. Vol. liq. 28 July 1919. Reconstructed as Bullfinch Proprietary (1919) Ld., in which company shareholders were entitled to 1 fully-paid share of 5s. for each share of £1 held. Final meeting return regd. 27 Sept. 1921 .... **1920**

Bullfinch Proprietary (1919) Ld. Regd. 1919. Vol. liq. 30 Oct. 1925. Final meeting return regd. 3 May 1927 **1926**

Bullion Corporation Ld. Regd. 1896. Vol. liq. 17 Mar. 1899. Certain investments were distributed to shareholders to the value of 17s. per share of £1. Final meeting return regd. 3 Aug. 1906 .... **1900**

Bullion Mines Ld. Inc. Western Australia 1920. Vol. liq. Jan. 1933 .... **1933**

Bullion Mining Co. Ld. Regd. 1884. Removed from Register 1894 .... ***1885**

Bullivants Aerial Ropeways Co. Ld. Regd. 1910. Vol. liq. 28 Oct. 1926. All shares owned by British Ropes Ld. Final meeting return regd. 15 Apr. 1930 .... **1928**

Bullman Machine Co. Ld. Regd. 1928. Struck off Register Feb. 1933 .... **1933**

Bulloch Brothers & Co. Ld. Regd. 1894. Vol. liq. (creditors') 12 Jan. 1933. Assets realised in sufficient to pay unsecured creditors in full. Final meeting return regd. 22 Nov. 1940 .... **1933**

Bulloch, Lade & Co. Ld. Regd. Edinburgh 1896. Vol. liq. Feb. 1920. Final meeting return regd. 13 Jan. 1922 **1920**

Bullock (B.) Ld. *See* Slade & Bullock Ld.

Bullrush Gold Estates. No Liability. Inc. South Australia 1910. London office closed Nov. 1911 .... **1912**

Bulmer Rayon Co. Ld. Regd. 1925. Vol. liq. Apr. 1932. Undertaking and assets transferred to B.R. Finance Co. Ld. Shareholders were entitled to receive 1 fully-paid preference share of that company for every 3 preference shares of £1 held and 1 fully-paid ordinary share for every deferred ordinary share of 1s. held. Final meeting return regd. 5 Aug. 1947 **1949**

Buloh Akar Rubber Estates Ld. Regd. 1912. Vol. liq. 31 Mar. 1921. Final meeting return regd. 16 Dec. 1921 ***1922**

Buloh River Rubber Estates Ld. Regd. 1925. Vol. liq. 15 Aug. 1928 for reconstruction as company of same name. Shareholders were entitled to 1 share of £1 (credit with 13s. 4d. paid) in new company for each share of £1 held. Debenture stockholders were entitled to an equal amount of 8% debenture stock in new company. Final meeting return regd. 21 June 1932 .... **1929**

VOL. FOR

Buloh River Rubber Estates Ld. Regd. 1928. All shares owned by Kuala Lumpur Rubber Co. Ld. (later Kuala Lumpur-Kepong Amalgamated Ld.). Vol. liq. (members') 25 May 1954. Final meeting return regd. 16 Sept. 1958 1950

Bulong Mining, Tramway & Ore Reduction Co. of Western Australia Ld. Regd. 1896. Vol. liq. 27 Apr. 1898. Final meeting return regd. 27 Jan. 1900 1899

Bultfontein Homestead Co. Ld. Regd. 1880. Vol. liq. 5 Apr. 1887. Property taken over by African Diamond Mining Co. Ld. Final meeting return regd. 2 Sept. 1891 .... *1888

Bultfontein Mining Co. Ld. Regd. 1880. Vol. liq. 28 Apr. 1888. Final meeting return regd. 9 Dec. 1891 1890

Bultfontein Mining Co. Ld. Regd. 1888 as New Bultfontein Mining Co. Ld.; name changed May 1888. Vol. liq. 3 Feb. 1890. Final meeting return regd. 11 Jan. 1893 1890

Bultfontein Star Diamond Mining Co. Ld. Inc. South African Republic in 1896. In liquidation in 1897. Amalgamated with Bultfontein Diamond Mining Co. Ld. 1897

Bultfontein Sun Diamond Mine Ld. Regd. 1895. Removed from Register 1903 1898

Buluwayo Consolidated Gold Fields Ld. Regd. 1899. Vol. liq. 9 Jan. 1906. Final meeting return regd. 31 July 1906 1906

Buluwayo Estate & Trust Co. Ld. Regd. 1896. Removed from Register 1911 1910

Buluwayo Syndicate Ld. Regd. 1893. Vol. liq. 15 Mar. 1916. Reconstructed as New Buluwayo Syndicate Ld. (later Hallmark Securities Ld.) in which company shareholders were entitled to 1 share of 5s. (credited as fully-paid) plus 1s. in cash for each share of 10s. held. Final meeting return regd. 26 Oct. 1916 1916

Buluwayo Town-Stands Syndicate Ld. Regd. 1895. Vol. liq. (members') 30 Aug. 1939. Undertaking and assets were acquired by New Buluwayo Syndicate Ld. (later Hallmark Securities Ld.) in which company shareholders were entitled to 6 shares of 5s. (credited as fully-paid) for every 11 shares of 4s. held. £170 15s. 3d. was paid into Companies' Liquidation Account; £59 3s. 3d. in respect of unclaimed dividends and £111 12s. in respect of sale of shares and fractions. Final meeting return regd. 11 Sept. 1940 1940

Bulwark Land & House Co. Ld. Regd. 1881. Vol. liq. May 1885. Final meeting return regd. 13 Jan. 1886 1886

Bundi Tin Mining Syndicate Ld. Regd. 1899. Vol. liq. 26 Sept. 1902. Final meeting return regd. 30 Dec. 1902 1903

Bungay Gas & Electricity Co. Ld. Regd. 1927 as Electrical Enterprise Ld. name changed in 1929. Dissolved 1 Apr. 1948. undertaking being vested in the British (later Central) Electricity Authority and Eastern Area Board under the Electricity Act 1947. Holders of ordinary and 7% preference shares were entitled to receive British Electricity 3% guaranteed stock. 1968–73; as follows: £2 stock for each ordinary share (of £1) held and £1 12s. 6d. stock for each preference share (of £1) held 1949

Bungay, Harleston & Eye Water Co. Inc. by Special Act 1909 1911

Bunge & Co. Ld. Regd. 1919. Vol. liq. (members') 19 Feb. 1931 for reconstruction as company of same name. Capital returned to contributories—£12,647 2s. 6d. in cash, plus certain investments distributed in specie and 99,998 shares of £10 fully paid in new company. Final meeting return regd. 15 May 1933 1931

Buntar Rubber Estates Ld. Regd. 1925. Vol. liq. (members') 23 May 1933. Reconstructed as company of same name. Shareholders were entitled to 10 shares of 2s. (credited with 1s. 9d. paid) in new company for each share of £1 held. Final meeting return regd. 12 Nov. 1934 1934

Bunting (Charles) Ld. Regd. 1895. Vol. liq. (members') 30 Sept. 1939. All A and B ordinary shares of £1 were owned by Parkers' Burslem Brewery Ld. [later Ind Coope (Parkers) Ld.]. The preference shares were acquired by that company by exchanging 5 fully-paid preference shares of £1 for every 10 5% preference shares of £1 held or 1 fully-paid preference share of £1 for each 6% preference share of £1 held. Final meeting return regd. 11 Mar. 1940 1940

Bunting (Robert) & Sons Ld. Regd. 1897. Removed from Register 1904 1900

Bunyip Gold Mines Ld. Regd. 1896. Removed from Register 1905 1902

Burbank Gold Mining Co. Ld. See South Weld Hercules Gold Mining Co. Ld.

Burbank Southern Goldfields Ld. Regd. 1897. Vol. liq. 9 July 1906. Reconstructed as Jourdie United Gold Mines Ld. in which company shareholders were entitled to 1 share of 5s. (credited with 4s. paid) for each share of 5s. held. Removed from Register 1910 1907

VOL. FOR

Burbank's Birthday Gift Gold Mines Ld. Regd. 1895. Reconstructed 1904 as Burbank's Birthday Gold Mines Ld., in which company shareholders were entitled to 1 share of £1 (credited with 16s. paid) for each share of £1 held. Removed from Register 1907. 1908

Burbanks Birthday Gold Mines Ld. Inc. in Western Australia 6 July 1904. Vol. liquidation for purpose of reconstruction in Apr. 1923. Shareholders were entitled to 3 shares of 5s. credited with 3s. 9d. paid in new company [Burbanks (Pilbarra) Copper Mines Ld.] for each share held 1924

Burbanks Grand Junction Ld. Regd. 1897. Removed from Register 1904 1904

Burbank's Main Lode Ld. Regd. 1896. Reconstructed 1900 as company of same name. Shareholders were entitled to 1 share of £1 (credited with 15s. paid) in new company for each share of £1 held. Removed from Register 1905 1901

Burbank's Main Lode Ld. Regd. 1900. Vol. liq. 6 Aug. 1902 for reconstruction as Burbank's Main Lode (1902) Ld., in which company shareholders were entitled to subscribe for shares of 4s. (credited with 3s. paid); for every 4 shares so subscribed a bonus of 1 fully-paid share was allotted. Final meeting return regd. 10 Nov. 1904 1904

Burbank's Main Lode (1902) Ld. Regd. 1902. Reconstructed 1904 as Burbank's Main Lode (1904) Ld. in which company shareholders were entitled to 1 share of 4s. (credited with 2s. 6d. paid) for each share of 4s. held. Removed from Register 1906 ... 1908

Burbank's Main Lode (1904) Ld. Regd. 1904. Vol. liq. 26 Apr. 1915. Struck off Register 30 Nov. 1917 1916

Burbanks Mining & Investment Trust Ld. Regd. 1923 as Burbanks (Pilbarra) Copper Mines Ld.; name changed Dec. 1927. Vol. liq. (creditors') 31 Oct. 1932. Shareholders were entitled to 1 share of 3d. (credited with 1d. paid) in Houtpoort-Burbank Goldfields Ld. for every share of 5s. held. Final meeting return regd. 10 Oct. 1933 1933

Burbank's North Gold Mine Ld. Regd. 1898. Reconstructed Aug. 1901 as Amalgamated Gold Mines Ld., in which company shareholders were entitled to 2 shares of 10s. (credited with 7s. 9d. paid) for each share of £1 held. Removed from Register 1903 ... 1902

Burbank's No. 1 South Extended Gold Mine Ld. Regd. 1897. Struck off Register 16 Nov. 1906 1907

Burbank's No. 1 West Gold Mines Ld. Regd. 1895. Struck off Register 16 Nov. 1906 1907

Burbanks (Pilbarra) Copper Mines Ld. See Burbanks Mining & Investment Trust Ld.

Burford Electric Light & Power Co. Ld. Regd. 1909. Dissolved 1 Apr. 1948. undertaking being vested in the British (later Central) Electricity Authority and Southern Area Board under the Electricity Act 1947. Holders of ordinary and founders' shares and 5% debentures were entitled to receive British Electricity 3% guaranteed stock, 1968–73; as follows: £1 11s. 6d. and £10 stock for each ordinary and founders' share of £1 held respectively and £50 10s. for every £50 of debentures held 1949

Burford (H. G.) & Co (1926) Ld. Regd. 1926. Vol. liq. 21 Oct. 1929. Final meeting return read 12 Dec. 1932 *1930

Burgess Dairy Ld. Regd. 1924. Vol. liq. (members') 14 Feb. 1961. Final meeting return regd. 30 Mar. 1962 1948

Burgess (H. E.) & Co. Ld. Regd. 1928. Vol. liq. (members') 25 Apr. 1933. Direct controlling interest held by Stevenson & Howell Ld. Final meeting return regd. 21 June 1933 1934

Burgess Hill & St. John's Common Gas Co. Regd. as limited 1867; reinc. by Special Act 1903. Dissolved 1 May 1949, undertaking being vested in South Eastern Area Gas Board under Gas Act 1948. Holders of securities were entitled to receive British Gas 3% guaranteed stock 1990–95 as follows in respect of each £5 unit, unless otherwise stated, of security held:

	£	s.	d.	
Orig. shares (10% max.)	10	5	0	
New ord. shares (7% max.)	7	5	0	
5% red. pref. shares	5	5	0	
3½% red. deb. stock (issued since 31 Dec. 1945—per £100)	105	10	0	
3½% red. deb. stock (issued before 1 Jan. 1946—per £100)	101	15	0	1952

Burgess Hill & St. John's Common Water Co. Ld. (See below).

Burgess Hill Water Co. Regd. 1870 as Burgess Hill & St. John's Common Water Co. Ld.; reincorporated under present title by Special Act 1886. By Order of 15 June 1955 the undertaking vested in the Newhaven, Seaford & Ouse Valley Water Co. [later Mid-Sussex Water Co. Ld.] as from 24 June 1955. Holders of the 3¾% mortgage debentures, the 4½%

VOL. FOR

redeemable debenture stock and the 3½% and 4½% preference shares of this company were allotted a like amount of precisely the same interest or dividend-bearing security, under the same terms, in the Newhaven company, and holders of the original ordinary (10% maximum) and new ordinary (7% maximum) shares of £10 of this company were allotted £10 15s. 9d. and £7 11s. 2d. per share respectively of 7% stock in the Newhaven company. The company was dissolved by resolution of directors dated 28 July 1955 .... **1957**

Burglary Insurance Corporation Ld. Regd. 1890. Vol. liq. 12 Jan. 1893. Final meeting return regd. 11 Apr. 1893 .... *****1894**

Burgon & Co. Ld. Regd. 1896. Vol. liq. 24 Nov. 1904. Removed from Register 1905 .... **1905**

Burgons Founders Ld. Regd. 1917. Vol. liq. 16 July 1929. Shareholders were entitled to 1 fully-paid share of 10s. in Burgons Ld. in exchange for each share of £1 held. Final meeting return regd. 23 Sept. 1929 .... **1930**

Burgoyne, Burbridges & Co. Ld. See Rawson Chemicals Ld.

Burke (Edward & John) Ld. Regd. Dublin 1890. Reconstructed as company of same name (Regd. Dublin 1893) **1894**

Burlington Hotel (London) Ld. Regd. 1935. Vol. liq. (members') 25 July 1935. Capital returned to contributories—20s. 5·5225d. per preference share of £1; 15s. 10d. per ordinary share of £1. Final meeting return regd. 11 July 1936 .... **1936**

Burlington Hotels Co. Ld. Regd. 1896. Vol. liq. (members') 10 Jan. 1935 for reconstruction as Burlington Hotel (London) Ld., in which company shareholders were entitled to 4 fully-paid 6% cumulative preference shares of £1 and 1 fully-paid ordinary share of £1 for every 5 preference shares of £1 and 2 ordinary shares of £1 held respectively. The debenture stock was to be repaid. Final meeting return regd. 6 Mar.1936 .... **1935**

Burma Corporation Ld. Regd. 1913. Vol. liq. 23 Aug. 1920. Shareholders were entitled to 1 share in Burma Mines Ld. and thereby to 14 shares of Rs. 10 in Burma Corporation Ld. (inc. Rangoon). Final meeting return regd. 29 July 1912 .... **1912**

Burma Development Syndicate Ld. Regd. 1903. Vol. liq. 31 Oct. 1911. Reconstructed as company of same name. Shareholders were entitled to 1 ordinary share of £1 (credited with 15s. paid) in new company for each ordinary share of £1 held, or 2 fully-paid deferred shares of 1s. for each deferred share of 1s. held. Debenture holders were entitled to an equal amount of 6% debentures in new company and an option (since expired) over deferred shares. Final meeting return regd. 4 Mar. 1919 .... **1912**

Burma Development Syndicate Ld. Regd. 1911. Vol. liq. Nov. 1912. to reconstruct under same name. Shareholders were entitled to 1 fully-paid share of 10s. in new company for each ordinary share of £1 held or for every ten deferred shares of 1s. held. Struck off Register 12 Mar. 1935 .... **1913**

Burma Development Syndicate Ld. Regd. 1912. Holders of 6% debentures received 12s. 6d. in £ out of sale of rubber estates. Struck off Register Dec. 1931 .... **1932**

Burma Estates Ld. Regd. 1933. Vol. liq. (members') 12 Mar. 1953. From sale of certain assets stockholders received 6 Kyats stock in Panga Plantations Ld. for every 50s. stock held. Capital returned to contributories (per 2s. stock)—1s. 7·9d. £10.626 12s. 3d. paid into Companies' Liquidation Account. Final meeting return regd. 31 July 1962 .... **1963**

Burma Mines Development & Agency Ld. Regd. 1903. Removed from Register 1913 .... **1911**

Burma Mines Ld. Regd. 1906 as Burma Mines Railway and Smelting Co. Ld.; name changed May 1908. Vol. liq. Aug. 1920. Reconstructed as Burma Corporation Ld., in which company shareholders were entitled to 14 shares of Rs.10 (credited as fully-paid) for each share of 4s. held. Final meeting return regd. 6 Aug. 1921 .... **1921**

Burma Mines Railway and Smelting Co. Ld. See Burma Mines Ld.

Burma Queensland Corporation Ld. Regd. 1919. Vol. liq. 22 June 1920. Final meeting return regd. 20 Feb. 1931 .... **1921**

Burma Railways Co. Ld. Regd. 1896. Vol. liq. 31 Dec. 1928. Capital returned to contributories—£118 8s. 9·26d. per £100 ordinary stock. Fina¹ meeting return regd. 19 Mar. 1930. The outstanding 3% debenture stock was acquired under Treasury Order of 15 Jan. 1943 at £88 6s. 10d. per £100 nominal **1944**

Burma Rubber Estates Ld. Regd. 1925. Vol. liq. (members') 4 Apr. 1933. Reconstructed as Burma Estates Ld., in which company shareholders were entitled to 1 share of £1 (credited with 18s. paid) for

VOL. FOR

each share of £1 held. Noteholders were entitled to an equal amount of notes in new company. £37 8s. 2d. was paid into Companies' Liquidation Account. Final meeting return regd. 9 Apr. 1934 .... **1934**

Burma Ruby Mines Ld. Regd. 1889. Vol. liq. 7 Dec. 1925. Final meeting return regd. 27 July 1934 ...... **1926**

Burmah Solid Petroleum Fuel Co. Ld. Regd. 1911. Vol. liq. 18 June 1920. Final meeting return regd. 1 Mar. 1921 .... *****1913**

Burmeister & Wain (Diesel System) Oil Engine Co. Ld. Regd. 1912. Vol. liq. 29 Oct. 1937. All shares owned by Harland & Wolff Ld. Final meeting return regd. 20 Sept. 1938 .... **1934**

Burmeister & Wain, Engineers & Shipbuilders, Ld. Inc. Denmark 1872. Under Law of 1933 company was divided into 2 independent companies. viz. Part I under the original title to continue the company's original activities and Part II as Burmeister & Wain Ld., Liquidation Department to wind up that part of the company not taken over by Part I **1934**

Burmeister & Wain Ld., Liquidation Dept. Inc. in Denmark under Law of 28 Feb. 1933. Proposals to conclude the work of this department were approved by creditors on 10 Apr. 1937 and by shareholders on 24 May 1937. Creditors' claims were satisfied as to ½ths in cash and remaining ½ths by allotment of preference shares of Burmeister & Wain, Engineers & Shipbuilders, Ld. and shareholders of the old A/S Burmeister & Wain were satisfied by allotment of ordinary shares of Burmeister & Wain, Engineers & Shipbuilders, Ld. at the rate of 1 share of 1 Kr.1 for every old share of Kr.100 held **1938**

Burmese Hydraulic Tin Ld. Regd. 1935. Vol. liq. (creditors') 27 Sept. 1937. Capital returned to contributories—½d. per share of 5s. Final meeting return regd. 14 Nov. 1939 .... **1938**

Burmese Minerals Exploration Ld. Regd. 1920. Vol. liq. 19 Dec. 1928. Final meeting return regd. 24 May 1929 .... **1929**

Burnard & Alger Ld. Regd. 1890. Vol. liq. (members') 6 Apr. 1944. Capital returned to contributories—18s. 4·7438d. per preference share of £1; all ordinary shares owned by National Fertilisers Ld. which company acquired the undertaking and assets. Final meeting return regd. 8 Sept.1944 .... **1945**

Burnard's Dairy Equipment Ld. Regd. 1929. Assets realised insufficient to repay debentures. Struck off Register 24 Jan. 1936 .... **1936**

Burnard's (Established 1899) Ld. Undertaking and assets were acquired by Burnard's Dairy Equipment Ld. for £9.000 in cash and 155,000 fully-paid ordinary shares of 2s. **1930**

Burndept Ld. Undertaking and assets were acquired in 1925 by Burndept Wireless Ld. **1926**

Burndept Wireless Ld. Regd. 1925. Vol. liq. 21 Aug. 1928. Undertaking and assets were acquired by Burndept Wireless (1928) Ld. in which company shareholders were entitled to 2 ordinary shares of 5s. (credited with 1s. 9d. paid) for each preferred ordinary share of £1 held or 1 ordinary share of 5s. (credited with 1s. 9d. paid) for every 20 deferred ordinary shares of 1s. held. Final meeting return regd. 16 Feb. 1933 .... **1929**

Burndept Wireless (1928) Ld. Regd. 1928. Vol. liq. (creditors') 23 Oct. 1931. Assets realised insufficient to pay unsecured creditors in full. Final meeting return regd. 2 May 1934 .... **1932**

Burney's New Cross Brewery Ld. Regd. 1898. Court Order to wind up 13 Dec. 1904. Removed from Register 1911 .... **1905**

Burnham, Dorney and Hitcham Waterworks Co. Ld. Regd. 1891. Under provisions of the Middle Thames Water Board Order 1966 undertaking vested in the Middle Thames Water Board on 1 Apr. 1966 for a consideration of £290.388. Vol. liq. (members') 4 Apr. 1966. On 28 Apr. 1966 the 4%, 3½% and 5½% debentures were repaid at par; and shareholders received the following distributions (per £1 share)—original, 26s. 5d.; 7% ordinary and 7% ordinary B, 21s. 11d.; preference 20s. Final meeting return registered 9 Oct. 1970 .... **1970**

Burnham Gas Co. Ld. (Somerset). Regd. 1858. Vol. liq. (members') 22 Dec. 1934. Undertaking was acquired under Special Order 1934 by Weston-super-Mare & District Gas Co. Shareholders were entitled to consolidate ordinary stock in acquiring company or cash as follows: for each £100 10% standard shares held—£225; for each £100 7% standard shares held—£157 10s.; for each £100 6% standard shares held—£135. The acquiring company assumed liability for the mortgages. Final meeting return regd. 4 Feb. 1936 .... **1935**

See Stock Exchange Year-Book.

VOL. FOR

Burnham Gas Co. Ld. Regd. 1862. Dissolved 1 May 1949, undertaking being vested in Eastern Area Gas Board under Gas Act 1948. Holders of securities were entitled to receive British Gas 3% guaranteed stock 1990–95 as follows in respect of each £5 unit, unless otherwise stated, of security held:

	£	s.	d.	
Orig. shares (10% max.)	10	1	0	
Addit. shares (7% max.)	7	2	6	
6½% perp. debs. (per £100)	152	10	0	
4% red. debs. (per £100)	101	5	0	1952

Burnham Shipping Co. Ld. Regd. 1919. Vol. liq. (creditors') 31 Oct. 1931. Assets realised insufficient to pay creditors in full. Final meeting return regd. 19 May 1932 1932

Burnham (Somerset) Pier Co. Inc. by Special Act 1907. Powers lapsed 1912

Burnhope Lead Mining Co. Ld. Regd. 1884. Struck off Register 3 Dec. 1891 1888

Burnie (Tasmania) Timber & Brick Co. Ld. Regd. 1908. Vol. liq. (members') 10 Dec. 1930. Undertaking and certain assets were acquired by Van Diemen's Land Co., in which company shareholders were entitled to 1 fully-paid share of 11*s. plus* 6*s.* 3⅜*d.* in cash for each share of £1 held. The 7½% 1st mortgage debentures were repaid at 105% in Feb. 1930. A return on account of capital was anticipated. Final meeting return regd. 26 Nov. 1934 1931

Burnley & District Tramways Co. Ld. Regd. 1881. Undertaking was acquired by local authorities. Capital returned to contributories—£1 1*s.* 8*d.* per share of £1; further payments (if any) not known. Removed from Register 1902 1902

Burnley, Clitheroe & Sabden Railway Co. Inc. by Special Act 1886. Undertaking abandoned by Act of 1890 1891

Burns Brothers. Inc. New Jersey 1913. Assets transferred in 1936 to Burns Bros. (inc. in New York), stockholders receiving 1 common share of no par value for every $100 share of preferred stock, 10 class A or 50 class B shares held; creditors (including 5% serial gold bondholders) were satisfied by allotment of A or B debentures and common shares of the New York company 1937

Burns Steamship Co. Ld. Regd. Edinburgh 1908. Vol. liq. Jan. 1923. Undertaking was acquired by Burns & Laird Lines Ld. Final meeting return regd. 15 Mar. 1923 1940

Burnside Gold Mines Ld. Regd. 2 Mar. 1914. Vol. liq. Apr. 1920. Amalgamated with Kirkland Lake Proprietary (1919) Ld in which company shareholders were entitled to receive 1 share of £1 for every 2 shares of £1 held. Final meeting return regd. 8 Feb. 1922 1921

Burnside Tea Co. of Ceylon Ld. Regd. 1896. Vol. liq. 5 July 1920. Capital returned to contributories—£15 4*s.* per share of £10. Final meeting return regd. 4 Mar. 1921 1921

Burntisland Oil Co. Ld. Regd. Edinburgh 1893. Vol. liq. July 1896. Final meeting return regd. 24 Feb. 1905 1897

Burrell & Co. Ld. Regd. as private company 19 Feb. 1912; converted to a public company 1 July 1947. Vol. liq. 14 Aug. 1981. Final meeting held 5 Mar. 1987. Dissolved 5 June 1987 1987–8

Burrell (Charles) & Sons Ld. Regd. 1898. Vol. liq. (members') 29 Dec. 1932. Capital returned to contributories—£1 12*s.* 2·71*d.* per share of £10. Final meeting return regd. 19 July 1935 1932

Burrell's Hiring Co. Ld. Regd. 1887. Vol. liq. (creditors') 29 Dec. 1932. Assets realised insufficient to meet claims of creditors in full. Final meeting return regd. 19 July 1935 1932

Burroughs Adding & Registering Machine Co. Ld. Regd. 1898. Vol. liq. 24 June 1909. Business was acquired by Burroughs Adding Machine Ld. [now Burroughs Machines Ld.] Final meeting return regd. 1 Dec. 1909 1910

Burroughs Registering Accountant (British & Colonial) Ld. Regd. 1894. Vol. liq. 25 July 1894. Final meeting return regd. 21 Mar. 1895 1896

Burry Port and Gwendreath Valley Railway Co. Inc. by Special Act 1866. In 1922 the undertaking was merged into the Great Western Railway Co. in which company stockholders were entitled to stock as follows:

For each £100 *held*		*G.W.R.*
4% Debentures	£100	4% Debenture
4% Debenture St.	£100	4% Debenture
5% Pref. Shares	£100	5% Cons. Pref.
Ordinary Shares	£143	Cons. Ord.

This company was also to retain £23,500 out of its funds in hand 1924

Burry Port & North Western Junction Railway Co. Inc. by Special Act 1876. Undertaking abandoned by Act of 1889 1890

VOL. FOR

Burthy China Clays Ld. Regd. 1926. Vol. liq. (members') 28 June 1933. All shares owned by English China Clays Ld. Final meeting return regd. 7 Feb. 1935 1934

Burt (J. L.) & Co. Ld. Regd. 1925. Vol. liq. (members') 22 Mar. 1966. Final meeting return regd. 23 Dec. 1967 1938

Burton & Lincoln Breweries Ld. Regd. 1889. Removed from Register 1904 1899

Burton Brewery Co. Ld. Regd. 1887. Undertaking and assets were acquired in 1927 by Ind Coope & Co. Ld. (later Ind Coope Ld.) The liquidator stated that B debenture holders would be repaid in full and that a return would be made to contributories. Struck off Register 12 Mar. 1935 1936

Burton Brick Co. Ld. Regd. 1926. Vol. liq. 29 Jan. 1929. Final meeting return regd. 18 Feb. 1931 1929

Burton Brine & Read Ld. Regd. 1899. Removed from Register 1905 1903

Burton (James) & Sons Ld. Regd. 1920. Receiver was appointed Apr. 1925. Court Order to wind up July 1925. Struck off Register 14 Oct. 1938 1939

Burton, Son & Sanders Ld. Regd. 1897. Vol. liq. 29 Apr. 1920 for reconstruction as company of same name. Shareholders were entitled to 10 preference shares of £1 for each preference share of £10 held. or 1 preferred ordinary share of £1 for each preferred ordinary share of 5*s.* held, or 1 deferred ordinary share of 10*s.* for each deferred ordinary share of 1*s.* held. Final meeting return regd. 29 Jan. 1921 1921

Burton Union Bank Ld. Regd. 1880 as Burton, Uttoxeter and Ashbourn Union Bank Ld.; name changed Oct. 1893. Business was transferred in 1899 to Lloyds Bank Ld., in which company shareholders were entitled to 7 shares of £50 (credited with £8 paid) *plus* £1 in cash for every 5 shares of £50 (£10 paid) held. Removed from Register 1902 1899

Burton, Uttoxeter and Ashbourn Union Bank Ld. *See* Burton Union Bank Ld.

Bury & District Joint Water Board. *See* Irwell Valley Water Board.

Bury & Heap Commercial Co. Ld. Regd. 1859. Vol. liq. (members') 15 Feb. 1933. Capital returned to contributories—£7 4*s.* per share of £10. fully-paid: £2 4*s.* per share of £10, £5 paid. Final meeting return regd. 17 Apr. 1934 1934

Bury & Tottington District Railway Co. Inc. by Special Act 1877. Under Lancashire and Yorkshire Railway Act 1888 undertaking was merged in that company in consideration of £100,000 debenture stock, which was distributed to holders of debenture stock and preference and ordinary shares 1889

Bury Banking Co. Ld. In 1888 the business and assets were acquired by Lancashire and Yorkshire Bank Ld., in which company shareholders received four shares of £10 for every 9 original shares held 1889

Bury Brothers Ld. Regd. 1923. Vol. liq. (members') 23 Jan. 1934. Undertaking was acquired by Joshua Hoyle and Sons Ld. Final meeting return regd. 8 Dec. 1934 1934

Bury Paper Making Co. Ld. Regd. 1875 as Bury Paper Making & Cotton Spinning & Manufacturing Co. Ld.; name changed Aug. 1904. Struck off Register Jan. 1933 1938

Bury. Rochdale & Oldham Tramway Co. Ld. Regd. 1889. Vol. liq. 28 Oct. 1904. Undertaking was acquired by local authority for £163,025. Removed from Register 1909 1905

Bury St. Edmunds' Gas Co. Inc. by Special Act 1849. Dissolved 1 May 1949, undertaking being vested in Eastern Area Gas Board under Gas Act 1948. Holders of securities were entitled to receive British Gas 3% guaranteed stock 1990–95 as follows in respect of each £50 unit, unless otherwise stated, of security held:

	£	s.	d.	
5% cons. stock (per £100)	123	0	0	
3½% debs	50	0	0	
4% bonds	50	0	0	1952

Burys' & Co. Ld. Regd. 1890. Vol. liq. 19 Aug. 1915. Final meeting return regd. 24 Nov. 1926 .... *1916

Busby & District Gas Co. Ld. Regd. in Edinburgh 1888. Dissolved 1 May 1949, undertaking being vested in Scottish Area Gas Board under Gas Act 1948. Holders of ordinary shares (of £10) were entitled to receive £9 10*s.* British Gas 3% guaranteed stock 1990–95 for each share held 1952

Busby Waterworks Co. Inc. by Special Act 1875. Undertaking transferred to Renfrew County Council May 1908. Purchase price £29,764 1908

Bush House, Ld. Regd. 1923. Vol. liq. (members') 26 Apr. 1955. Final meeting return regd. 15 Dec. 1955 1940

Bushell, Watkins & Smith Ld. Regd. 1894. Vol. liq. (members') 19 July 1961. Final meeting return regd.

**See Stock Exchange Year-Book.*

VOL. FOR

6 Dec. 1961. Dissolution declared void 4 June 1962. Final meeting return regd. 24 Dec. 1963 .... **1951**

Bushman's Gold Mines of Western Australia Ld. Regd. 1895. Vol. liq. 13 Sept. 1897. Undertaking was acquired by East Wealth of Nations Ld. Final meeting return regd. 1 Feb. 1900 .... **1904**

Bushveld Tin Mines Ld. Inc. Transvaal 1904. London office closed June 1911. Liquidated in 1928. A distribution of 1d. per share was made, which may be recovered from the Master of the Supreme Court, Pretoria **1912**

Business Computers Ld. Regd. 1939 as Low's Calculators Ld.; name changed July 1962 to Business Mechanisation Ld.; to Bismec Group Ld. in Dec. 1967 and to above title May 1969. Winding-up Order 3 Nov. 1975. Liquidator Released 30 Oct. 1978 .... **1981–2**

Business Investment Co. Ld. Regd. 1881. Vol. liq. 23 Dec. 1896. Final meeting return regd. 19 July 1898 **1899**

Business Mechanisation Ld. See Business Computers Ld.

Bussey Coal Distillation Co. Ld. Regd. 1928. Court Order to wind up 28 Nov. 1928. Liquidator released 19 July 1943. Struck off Register 28 May 1946 ... **1939**

Bussey (Geo. G.) & Co. Ld. Regd. 1906. Vol. liq. (members') 13 Apr. 1932. Capital returned to contributories—3s. 3½d.per preference share of £1. Final meeting return regd. 28 Dec. 1934 .... **1933**

Bussey International Ld. Regd. 1929. Court Order to wind up 28 Nov. 1938. Liquidator released 19 July 1943. Struck off Register 28 May 1946 .... **1939**

Bussey Low Temperature Process Ld. Regd. 1938. Struck off Register 8 Aug. 1950 .... **1938**

Bussie Asie Concessions Ld. Regd. 1901. Reconstructed 1904 as New Nimrod Co. Ld. in which company shareholders were entitled to 1 fully-paid share of £1 for every 10 shares of £1 held. Removed from Register 1905 .... **1905**

Busum-Wassau Ld. Regd. 1901. Vol. liq. Apr. 1907. Removed from Register 1908 .... **1908**

Butcher (W.) & Sons Ld. Regd. 1907. Vol. liq. Jan. 1927. All capital owned by British Photographic Industries Ld. Final meeting return regd. 16 Apr. 1928 **1927**

Butcher's Hide, Skin & Wool Co. Ld. Regd. 1890. Vol. liq. 2 Aug. 1906. Final meeting return regd. 25 Sept. 1907 .... ***1894**

Bute Docks Co. See Cardiff Railway Co.

Bute Insurance Co. Ld. Regd. Edinburgh 1873. Undertaking acquired by State Fire Insurance Co. Ld. Vol. liq. Sept. 1898. Final meeting return regd. 20 Oct. 1899 .... **1899**

Butler Estates Co., Ld. Regd 1925. Vol. liq. (members') 30 Mar. 1965. Final meeting return regd. 3 Nov. 1971 .... **1952**

Butler (George) & Co., Ld. Regd. 1873. Vol. liq. (members') 9 Sept. 1952. Final meeting return regd. 17 Sept. 1955 .... **1940**

Butler (John) & Co. Ld. Regd. 1906. Vol. liq. 5 Oct. 1931. All shares and debentures owned by Monk Bridge Iron & Steel Ld. Final maeting return regd. 22 Jan. 1932 .... **1932**

Butlin (Thos.) & Co. Ld. Regd. 1889. Vol. liq. 18 Feb. 1921. Direct controlling interest owned by United Steel Companies Ld. Final meeting return regd. 31 Mar. 1921 .... **1927**

Butlin's (Bahamas) Ld. Inc. in Bahamas 1948. Winding up order in London 9 Oct. 1950 and Bahamas 15 Dec. 1953. No capital was returned to contributories. Finally dissolved 16 May 1960 .... **1961**

Butte Electric and Power Co. Inc. New Jersey 1901. Reorganised as Montana Power Co. **1937**

Butterfly Gold Development Co. Ld. Regd. 1898. Vol. liq. 31 Dec. 1906. Certain assets were acquired by Indarama Gold Mining Co. Ld in which company shareholders were entitled to 1 fully-paid ordinary share for every 2 shares of £1 held. Removed from Register 1910 .... **1907**

Butters (Chas.) & Co. Ld. Regd. 1899. Struck off Register 3 Mar. 1944 .... **1944**

Butters Salvador Mines Ld. Regd. 1899. Vol. liq. 12 Dec. 1913 for reconstruction as a Canadian company of same name. Shareholders were entitled to 1 share of $5 in new company tor each share held. Final meeting return regd. 19 Nov. 1915 .... **1915**

Butters Salvador Mines Ld. Inc. Canada 1912. Vol. liq. 1917 .... **1918**

Butterworth & Stringer Ld. Regd. 1877. Vol. liq. 3 Oct. 1894. Final meeting return regd. 31 Oct. 1896 ..... **1895**

Butterworth-Springer Ld. See Pergamon Press Ld.

Butts Mills Ld. Regd. 1920. Vol. liq. (members') 23 Sept. 1960. Capital returned to contributories—3s. 5·371d. per preferred ordinary share of 2s. and 1s. per deferred ordinary share of 1s. Final meeting return regd. 7 Feb. 1962 .... **1962**

VOL. FOR

Buxton Hydropathic Ld. Regd. 1899. Struck off Register 3 Mar. 1944 .... **1944**

Buxton Lime Firms Co. Ld. See I.C.I. (Lime) Ld.

Bwana M'Kubwa Copper Mining Co. Ld. Regd. 1910. Vol. liq. 25 Jan. 1922 for reconstruction under same name. Shareholders were entitled to 1 share of 5s. (credited with 2s. 6d. paid) in new company for each share of 10s. held. Final meeting return regd. 11 Dec. 1922 .... **1922**

Bwana M'Kubwa Copper Mining Co. Ld. Regd. 1922. In Aug. 1934 shareholders were offered 3 shares of 10s. in Rhodesian Anglo American Ld. [later Zambian Anglo American Ld.] for every 10 shares of 5s. held. Vol. liq. (members') 23 Jan. 1935. Final meeting return regd. 24 Dec. 1935 .... **1935**

Bwich Creolan Silver Lead Mine Ld. Regd. 1881. Court Orders; to wind up 14 Mar. 1883; to dissolve 28 Mar 1885 .... **1883**

Bwllfa & Cwmaman Collieries Ld. Regd. 1891 as Bwllfa & Merthyr Dare Steam Collieries (1891) Ld.; name changed Sept. 1928. Vol. liq. (members') 29 Apr. 1938. Undertaking was acquired by Powell Duffryn Associated Collieries Ld. (later Powell Duffryn Ld.) Capital returned to contributories—£198.258 2s. 6d. Final meeting return regd. 18 Nov. 1938 .... **1939**

Bwllfa & Merthyr Dare Steam Collieries Ld. Regd. 1890. Vol. liq. 9 May 1892. Final meeting return regd. 19 Apr. 1894 .... **1938**

Bwllfa & Merthyr Dare Steam Collieries (1891) Ld. See Bwllfa & Cwmaman Collieries Ld.

Byers' Patents Ld. Regd. 1889. Vol. liq. 22 Oct. 1891. Final meeting return regd. 20 Apr. 1892 .... **1892**

Byker Bridge Co. Inc. by Special Act 1874. Undertaking purchased by Corporation of Newcastle-upon-Tyne in 1895 for £112,000. .... **1896**

Bylock Electric Ld. Regd. 1934. Vol. liq. (creditors') 7 May 1965. Final meeting return regd. 20 Feb. 1973 **1974–5**

Bynea Steelworks Ld. Regd. 1912. All capital was owned by Bynea Holdings Ld. Vol. liq. (members') 26 Jan. 1965. Final meeting return regd. 8 June 1965 **1958**

Bynoe Harbour Tin Syndicate Ld. Regd. 1926. Struck off Register 24 Jan. 1936 .... **1936**

Byrom (Joseph) & Sons (Droylesden) Ld. Regd. 1929. Vol. liq. (creditors') 24 July 1933. Assets realised insufficient to pay unsecured creditors in full. Final meeting return regd. 4 Dec. 1934 .... **1934**

Byrom (Joseph) & Sons Ld. Regd. 1920. Vol. liq. 16 Apr. 1929. Undertaking and assets were acquired by Joseph Byrom & Sons (Droylesden) Ld. in which company shareholders were entitled to 8 shares of 5s. (credited with 2s. 6d. paid) for every 7 shares of 10s. held. Final meeting return regd. 30 Dec. 1932 **1930**

Bywater (M.) & Co. Ld. Regd. 1935. Vol. liq. 6 Oct. 1939. Undertaking sold to new company of same name. Shareholders were entitled to receive £1 debenture stock of new company together with 10·44d. cash (being 1 year's preference dividend) for each preference share held and 1 ordinary share of new company for each ordinary share held. Final meeting return regd. 25 Sept. 1948 .... **1949**

C

C.A.S. Punch & Ticket Co. Ld. Regd. 1903. Receiver appointed 5 July 1910. Removed from Register 23 Feb. 1912 .... **1910**

C. & E. M. (1912) Ld. Regd. 1912. Vol. liq. 23 Nov. 1954. Preference shares of £1 were repaid at par and remaining assets distributed in specie to ordinary shareholders. £100 11s. was paid into Companies Liquidation Account in respect of unclaimed dividends and £895 in respect of unclaimed distributions. Final meeting return regd. 3 Feb. 1960 .... **1960**

C. & E. Morton Ld. See Beechport Ld.

C. & H. (Hotels) Ld. Regd. 1920 as Crosses & Winkworth Consolidated Mills Ld.; name changed to Crosses & Heatons Ld. Aug. 1944 and to above title June 1973. Winding-up Order 1 Dec. 1975. Liquidator released 17 July 1978. Struck off Register 13 Feb. 1981 .... **1981–2**

C. & M. Productions Ld. Regd. 1925. All issued shares owned by Gaumont-British Picture Corporation Ld. Struck off Register June 1937 .... **1938**

C. B. & M. Tailors Ld. Regd. 1929 as Curzon Brothers & Maxims Ld.; name changed 1929. Court Order to wind up 1930. Struck off Register 24 Nov. 1944 .. **1945**

C.B.B. Syndicate Ld. In 1929 all the assets were acquired by Sunfruit Products Ld. for 210,000 shares **1930**

C. D. Cinemas Ld. Regd. 1923. Vol. liq. (members') 16 July 1935. All capital owned by Associated British Cinemas Ld. Final meeting return regd. 3 Nov. 1939 **1936**

VOL. FOR

C. D. Mills Ld. In 1928 the flour milling properties and goodwill were acquired by Spillers Ld. for cash ... **1929**

C. E. Exploration Syndicate Ld. Regd. 1895. Removed from Register 1904 ... **1902**

C. F. N. Development Co. Ld. Regd. 1926. Vol. liq. (creditors') 18 July 1934. No capital returned to contributories. Final meeting return regd. 11 Sept. 1935 ... **1935**

C. H. Johnson (Machinery) Ld. *See* J. C. E. G. p.l.c.

C.I.M. Holdings Ld. Regd. 1935. Undertaking and assets were acquired by London & Thames Haven Oil Wharves Ld., in which company shareholders were entitled to 1 4% cumulative redeemable preference share of £1 for each preference share of £1 held. All ordinary shares were held by purchasing company. Dissolved (under Sec. 154 of Companies Act 1929) on 30 July 1940 ... **1941**

C.K.P. Developments Ld. Inc. Canada 1911 as Cockshutt Plow Co. Ld.; name changed 1951 to Cockshutt Farm Equipment Ld. and as above Oct. 1962. All capital acquired by C.K.P. Developments Inc. (later Deltona Corpn.) in Oct. 1962 by exchange of shares—one for one. Charter surrendered Oct. 1962 and company dissolved 13 Nov. 1963 ... **1964**

C. M. L. Properties Ld. *See* Amalgamated London Properties Ld.

C. M. Securities Ld. Regd. 1935 as Crown Flour Mills Ld.; name subsequently changed. Vol. liq. (members') 21 Dec. 1953. Final meeting return regd. 27 Apr. 1954 ... **1949**

C. O. P. Investments Ld. Regd. 1925 as Cotton Plantations Ld.; name changes Nov. 1958. Vol. liq. (members') 26 Oct. 1964. Capital returned to contributories—1*s*. 1½*d*. per share (of 2*s*.). £1,619·66 was pais into Companies' Liquidation Account in respect of unclaimed dividends and £6,698·27 in respect of distributions. Final meeting held 23 Aug. 1979 ... **1980–1**

C. S. & E. (Holdings) Ld. Regd. 1909 as Chatwood Safe Co. Ld.; name changed to Chatwood Safe & Engineering Co. Ld. and subsequently as above. Vol. liq. (members') 23 Sept. 1963. Final meeting return regd. 1 Jan. 1964 ... **1938**

C. S. Options Ld. Regd. 1910. Vol. liq. Aug. 1911. Struck off Register 24 July 1936 ... **1937**

C. T. C. Bazaars (Proprietary) Ld. *See* Ginkap Investments (Proprietary) Ld.

CTD Resources Group Ld. Regd. 1914 as Cheuderiang Tin Dredging Co. Ld.; name changes May 1973. Vol. liq. (members') 30 July 1977. Capital returned to contributories—$US4·58 per share (of 25p). $US2,031·16 was paid into Companies' Liquidation Account in respect of unclaimed distributions. Final meeting return regd. 7 Apr. 1979 ... **1980–1**

C.X.T. Ld Regd. 1920 as Carpet Trades Ld.; name changed Jan. 1936. Vol. liq. (members') 29 Jan. 1936. Undertaking acquired by Carpet Trades Ld. (later John Crossley-Carpet Trades Holdings Ld.) in which company shareholders were entitled to 1 fully-paid ordinary share of 10*s*. for each share of £1. Final meeting return regd. 28 May 1936 ... **1936**

Caamaño Tenguel Estate Ld. Regd. 1910. Struck off Register 4 Oct. 1935 ... **1936**

Cabins Ld. Regd. 1901 as Cabins (1901) Ld.; name changed May 1911. Vol. liq. 15 Oct. 1915. Final meeting return regd. 30 June 1917 ... **1916**

Cabins (1917) Ld. In 1928 the undertaking was acquired by W. Hill & Son Ld. for £75,931 ... **1929**

Cable Trust Ld. Regd. 8 Apr. 1929 as Cables and Wireless Ld.; name changed 1934 to Cable and Wireless (Holding) Ld. and to present title 5 May 1971. On 15 Sept. 1977 the undertaking and assets transferred to Globe Investment Trust Ld., ordinary stockholders received £1·75 ordinary stock for every £1·25 held; 6¼% convertible unsecured loan stock cancelled holders received a similar amount of Globe 6¼% convertible unsecured loan stock. Company to be dissolved without winding up ... **1978-9**

Cachar Co. Ld. Regd. 1888. Vol. liq. 26 Feb. 1896. Estates were acquired by Cachar and Dooars Tea Co. Ld. for £51,000. Final meeting return regd. 17 May 1897 ... **1895**

Cadas Ld. Regd. 1908. Receiver appointed in Sept. 1910. Struck off Register 1922 ... **1911**

Caddy Tyre Syndicate Ld. Regd. 1922. Struck off Register 1926 ... ***1924**

Cadiz Waterworks Ld. Regd. 1881. Vol. liq. Nov. 1883. Capital returned to contributories—£18 per share of £20 at Dec. 1883; further payments (if any) not known. Final meeting return regd. 24 Sept. 1886 **1885**

Cadogan & Hans Place Estate Ld. Regd 1875. Vol. liq. 8 May 1894. Final meeting return regd. 16 Feb. 1898 **1895**

Cadogan Electric Light Co. Ld. Regd. 1887. Vol liq. 2 Mar. 1891. Final meeting return regd. 18 Dec. 1895 **1892**

Cadogan Mansions Ld. Regd. 1878. Vol. liq. 24 Nov. 1881. Final meeting return regd, 12 Feb. 1884...... ***1882**

Cadora Ld. Regd. 1922 as Robinson & Co. (Hull) Ld.; name subsequently changed. Vol. liq. (members') 27 Feb. 1956. Final meeting return regd. 2 Apr. 1957 **1940**

Caerbryn Anthracite Colliery Co. Ld. Regd. 1927. All shares were owned by Amalgamated Anthracite Collieries Ld. Struck off Register 10 Mar. 1939 ... **1939**

Café Verrey Ld. Regd. 1904. Vol. liq. (creditors') 13 Nov. 1929. No capital returned to contributories. Final meeting return regd. 12 Dec. 1930 ... **1930**

Cagliari Gas & Water Co. Ld. Regd. 1866. Vol. liq. Jan. 1909. An agreement provided for sale of undertaking to Municipality on terms which return about £26 per share of £20 to shareholders. Removed from Register 1910 ... **1909**

Caima Timber Estate & Wood Pulp Co. Ld. Regd. 1888. It was estimated that 20*s*. would be returned for each fully-paid ordinary share of £1 and 12*s*. 6*d*. for each ordinary share of £1 (10*s*. paid). Vol. liq. 25 Nov. 1921. Final meeting return regd. 10 Oct. 1922 ..... **1922**

Caird & Co. Ld. Regd. Edinburgh 1888. Vol. liq. (members') 29 Oct. 1937. All creditors were to be paid in full. All shares owned by Harland & Wolff Ld. Final meeting return regd. 3 Oct. 1939 ... **1938**

Cairntable Gas Coal Co. Ld. Regd Edinburgh 1873. Vol. liq. Mar. 1915. Final meeting return regd. 5 May 1927 ... **1916**

Cairnton Investment Trust Ld. Regd. 21 May 1928 as Registry Investment Trust Ld.; name changed to Cairnton Trust & Finance Co. Ld. Nov. 1937 and to present title 16 Jan. 1964. On 21 July 1975 all capital cancelled, holders being entitled to securities of Estates House Investment Trust Ld. as follows—153 ordinary shares of 25p for every 100 ordinary; 1 4·2% preference share of £1 for every 5% preference and £1 6·6% debenture stock for every £1 5½% debenture stock. Company to be dissolved without winding up ... **1978-9**

Cairo, Alexandria & General Land Agency Ld. Regd. 1906. Vol. liq. Apr. 1909. Removed from Register 1912 ... **1910**

Cairo Exchange Ld. Regd. 1907. Vol. liq. 23 Apr. 1924. Struck off Register Apr. 1929 ... **1930**

Cairo Mills (Holdings) Ld. Regd. 1920 as Cairo Mill Co. (1920) Ld.; name changed 1947 to Cairo Mills Ld. and to above title 1953. Vol. liq. (members') 14 Nov. 1960. Capital returned to contributories—7*s*. 10⅝*d*. per 2*s*. stock. Final meeting return regd. 25 Oct. 1962 ... **1963**

Cairo Syndicate Ld. Regd. 1904. Vol. liq. 24 July 1914. Final meeting return regd. 28 June 1915 ... **1915**

Caisse Générale de Reports et de Dépôts. Inc. Belgium 1874. Liquidated 20 Jan. 1940. Business taken over by Banque de Reports et de Dépots ... **1940**

Caistor Gas & Coke Co. Ld. Regd. 1856. Dissolved 1 May 1949, undertaking being vested in East Midland Area Gas Board under Gas Act 1948. Holders of securities were entitled to receive British Gas 3% guaranteed stock 1990–95 as follows:

	£	s.	d.	
Ord. shares (of £10) ...	10	0	0	
Ord. shares (of £4) ...	4	0	0	**1952**

Cakemore Blue Brick Co. Ld. Regd. 1883 as New Cakemore Blue Brickworks Ld.; name changed Dec. 1885. Vol. liq. Mar. 1889. Business was acquired in Jan. 1890 by South Staffordshire Blue Brick Co. Ld. Final meeting return regd. 31 Dec. 1890 ... **1894**

Cakemore Brickworks & Collieries Ld. Regd. 1879 as Cakemore Causeway, Green & Lower Holt Brickworks & Colliery Co. Ld.; name changed Mar. 1882. Court Orders: to wind up 16 Aug. 1882; to dissolve 19 Mar. 1894 ... **1883**

Cakemore Causeway Green & Lower Holt Brickworks & Colliery Co. Ld. *See* Cakemore Brickworks & Collieries Ld.

Calais Tramways Co. Ld. Regd. 1879. Vol. liq. Nov. 1906. Undertaking was acquired by La Compagnie Mutuelle de Tramways of Brussels. Removed from Register 1907 ... **1907**

Calaveras Consolidated Gold Mining Co. Ld. Regd. 1888. Vol. liq. 27 Mar. 1893 for reconstruction as New Calaveras Gold Mining Co. Ld. Final meeting return regd. 11 Aug. 1896 ... **1895**

Calcott Brothers Ld. Regd. 1896. Vol. liq. 22 June 1926. Final meeting return regd. 9 May 1927 ... **1927**

Calder & Hebble Navigation (Co. of Proprietors Of The). Inc. by Special Act 1768. Undertaking vested from 1 Jan. 1948 in British Transport Commission under Transport Act 1947. Holders of ordinary stock were entitled to receive £32 British Transport 3% guaranteed stock 1978–88 for every £100 ordinary stock held... **1949**

**See Stock Exchange Year-Book.*

VOL. FOR

Calder (James) & Co. Ld. Regd. Edinburgh 1894. Vol. liq. Dec. 1921. The Bo'ness and Gartloch distilleries were acquired by Distillers Co. Ld. Final meeting return regd. 18 July 1929 ...... **1923**

Calderbank Steel & Coal Co. Ld. Regd. Edinburgh 1890. Vol. liq. Dec. 1897. Undertaking was acquired by James Dunlop A Co. (1900) Ld. (later James Dunlop & Co. Ld.) Final meeting return regd. 27 Sept. 1900 **1889**

Calders Margarine Co. Ld. Regd. 1917. Vol. liq. 11 May 1922. Final meeting return regd. 28 Nov. 1922 .... ***1923**

Calders Yeast Co. Ld. Regd. 1909. Vol. liq. (members') 14 Mar. 1948. Final meeting return regd. 29 Oct. 1948 ...... **1912**

Caldicott & District Gas Light & Coke Co. Ld. Regd. 1907. Dissolved 1 May 1949. undertaking being vested in Wales Area Gas Board under Gas Act 1948. Holders of ordinary shares (of £1) were entitled to receive £2 6*s*. British Gas 3% guaranteed stock 1990–95 for each share held **1952**

Caledonia and British Columbia Mortgage Co. Ld. Regd. Edinburgh 1912. Vol. liq. Aug. 1927. Final meeting return regd. 11 Feb. 1929 ...... **1928**

Caledonia Copper Co. Ld. Regd. 1899. Vol. liq. Sep. 1909. Removed from Register 1910 ...... **1910**

Caledonia (Cripple Creek) Gold Mine Ld. Regd. 1897. Vol. liq. Dec. 1911. Removed from Register 1913 **1912**

Caledonia Steamship Co. Ld. Regd. 1880. Vol. liq. Jan 1910. Removed from Register 1910. ...... **1910**

Caledonian and Australian Mortgage and Agency Co. Ld. Regd. Edinburgh 1887. Vol. liq. Jan. 1898 for reconstruction under same name. Final meeting return regd. 24 July 1926 ...... **1898**

Caledonian and Australian Mortgage and Agency Co. Ld. Regd. Edinburgh 1898. Vol. liq. July 1920. Assets acquired by a syndicate on terms which entitled shareholders to be repaid at 30*s*. per share of £1. Final meeting return regd. 24 July 1926 ...... **1921**

Caledonian & Dominion Investment Co. Ld. Regd. Edinburgh 1911 as Caledonian Canadian Investment Co. Ld.; name changed Mar. 1912. Vol. liq. June 1921. Final meeting return regd. 29 Dec. 1934 **1922**

Caledonian Assets Trust Ld. Regd. 1903. Vol. liq. Mar. 1905. Undertaking sold to British Assets Trust Ld., in which company shareholders were entitled to 7 ordinary shares of £1 for every 10 shares of £1 held and a bonus of 1½% in cash. Removed from Register 1905 ...... **1906**

Caledonian Banking Co. Ld. Established 1838. Regd. as unlimited 1862. Regd. Edinburgh as limited 1882. Vol. liq. July 1907. Undertaking and assets were acquired by Bank of Scotland, in which company shareholders were entitled to £1 5*s*. stock or £5 in cash for each share of £12 10*s*. (£2 10*s*. paid) held. Removed from Register 1909 ...... **1908**

Caledonian Bleaching & Printing Co. Ld. Regd. 1903. Removed from Register 29 Aug. 1911 ...... ***1910**

Caledonian Canadian Investment Co. Ld. *See* Caledonian & Dominion Investment Co. Ld.

Caledonian Carpet Co. Ld. Regd. Edinburgh 1898. Vol. liq. (members') 30 Nov. 1933. Direct controlling interest held by Stoddard (A. F.) & Co. Ld., to which company business was transferred. Capital returned to contributories—£13 0*s*. $7\frac{1652}{2000}$*d*. per share of £10. Final meeting return regd. 30 May 1934 ...... **1934**

Caledonian (Ceylon) Tea Plantations Ld. Regd. 1892. Vol. liq. 31 July 1897. Properties were acquired by Caledonian (Ceylon) Tea Estates Ld. [later Caledonian (Ceylon) Tea & Rubber Estates Ld.] Final meeting return regd. 14 Dec. 1898 ...... **1898**

Caledonian Gas Corporation Ld. Regd. Edinburgh 1935. Vol. liq. (members') June 1945. Business was transferred to United Kingdom Gas Corporation. Shareholders were entitled to an equal number of ordinary, 4½% preference and 4½% 2nd preference shares in that company in exchange for ordinary, preference and preferred ordinary shares respectively held. Final meeting return regd. 8 Dec. 1945 ... **1946**

Caledonian Gold Mining Co. Ld. Regd. 1895. Vol. liq. 25 Aug. 1899. Final meeting return regd. 21 Mar. 1900 **1900**

Caledonian Mineral Oil Co. Ld. Regd. 1889. Vol. liq. 1 Mar. 1897. Final meeting return regd. 3 Aug. 1899 ***1898**

Caledonian Mineral Oil Co. Ld. Regd. Edinburgh 1898. Vol. liq. Feb. 1903. Court Orders: to continue winding up Feb. 1903; to dissolve Oct. 1905 ...... **1904**

Caledonian Mining Corporation Ld. Regd. 1899. Removed from Register 1904 ...... **1904**

Caledonian Motor Car & Cycle Co. Ld. Regd. 1896. Struck off Register 22 Sept. 1936 ...... **1937**

Caledonian Motor Co. Ld. Regd. Edinburgh 1908. Vol. liq. Nov. 1909. Struck off Register 4 June 1937.... **1938**

Caledonian Railway Co. Inc. by Special Act 1845. In 1923 the undertaking was merged into the London Midland & Scottish Railway Co. in which company stockholders were entitled to stock as follows:

For each £100 *held*		*L.M. & S.*
4% Gtd. Annuities	£100	4% Debenture
4% Debenture	£100	4% Debenture
5% Debenture	£125	4% Debenture
4% Cons. Gtd.	£100	4% Guaranteed
4% Gtd. Annuities No. 2	£100	4% Guaranteed
4% (Lanarks. & Dumbarts.) Guar.	£100	4% Guaranteed
4% Cons. Pref. No. 1	£100	4% Preference
4% Cons. Pref. No. 2	£100	4% Preference
5% Cons. Pref.	£125	4% Preference
4% Pref. (1884)	£100	4% Preference
4% Pref. (1887)	£100	4% Preference
4% Pref. (1902)	£100	4% Preference
4% Conv. Pref. (1904)	£100	4% Preference
4% Conv. Pref. (1906)	£100	4% Preference
Ord. (Uncon.)	£50	4% Pref. (1923)
	£23½	Ordinary
Prefd. Conv. Ord	£50	4% Pref. (1923)
	£13½	Ordinary
Defd. Conv. Ord	£10	Ordinary

Nothing was allocated to the holders of the Deferred Ordinary Stocks Nos. 1 and 2 ...... **1924**

Caledonian Steam Trawling Co. Ld. Regd. 1899. Vol. liq. Mar. 1918. Struck off Register 27 Oct. 1936 ...... **1937**

Caledonian Telephone Co. Ld. Regd. 1891. Business acquired by National Telephone Co. Ld. Dissolved before 1931 ...... **1892**

Caledonian Theatres Ld. Regd. Edinburgh 1935. Vol. liq. (members') 2 Nov. 1973. Capital returned to contributories—£2 per share (of £1) in 1973 and £2.26 in Sept. 1974. Final meeting held 21 June 1976 **1976-7**

Caledonian Trust Co. Ld. Regd. Edinburgh 1910. On 12 Nov. 1959 the undertaking was acquired by Scottish Western Investment Co. Ld. in which company stockholders received 4 fully-paid ordinary shares of 5*s*. for every 25*s*. ordinary stock and 1 fully-paid 4½ preference share of £1. for every £1 preference stock held. Liability for 3½% debenture stock and terminable debentures was assumed by Scottish Western. Company was dissolved on 29 Feb. 1960 ...... **1961**

Caley (A. J.) & Son Ld. Regd. 1898. Vol. liq. (members') 22 June 1939. Undertaking and assets were acquired by John Mackintosh A Sons Ld. who owned all the ordinary shares. Preference shareholders, 4% 1st mortgage debenture stockholders received £1 of 5% debenture stock in purchasing company for each £1 share or stock held. Final meeting return regd. 11 July 1940 ...... **1940**

Calgary & Edmonton Land Co. Ld. Regd. 1902. Vol. liq. Oct. 1928. Certain assets were acquired by Calgary & Edmonton Corporation Ld. (inc. Canada); the remainder were acquired by company of same name (regd. England). Shareholders were entitled to 1 share of 10*s*. in the English company and 10 shares of no par value in the Canadian company for each share of 1*s*. held **1929**

Calgary & Medicine Hat Land Co. Ld. Regd. 1884. Vol. liq. Mar. 1910. Removed from Register 1912 ...... **1911**

Calgary Brewing & Malting Co. Ld. Inc. by Letters Patent in Canada 1892; reincorporated under Canadian Companies Act in 1912. The outstanding gold bonds were redeemed in Nov. 1934 ...... **1936**

Calgary Power Co. Ld. Inc. in Canada under Dominion laws 20 Oct. 1909. Wound-up in Dec. 1947, undertaking having been acquired by Calgary Power Ld. (inc. in Canada 12 May 1947). Common shareholders were entitled to receive 8 common shares (of no par value) of Calgary Power Ld. and 1 share (of no par value) of Calgary Power Investments Ld. for each common share (of $100) held. 5% 1st mortgage gold bonds were redeemed on 31 May 1947 ($8,171,500 due 1960 at 103% and $1,702,000 due 1964 at 104%). $5,900,000 preferred stock was redeemed on 16 June 1947 at 105% **1948**

California Exploration Co. Ld. Regd. 1911. Vol. liq. 29 Mar. 1926. Undertaking and assets were acquired by London, Australasian & General Exploration Co. Ld., in which company shareholders were entitled to 1 share of 2*s*. 6*d*. (credited as fully-paid) for each share of 10*s*. held. Final meeting return regd. 12 Aug. 1926 ...... **1927**

California Exploration Ld. Regd. 1897. Vol. liq. Oct. 1908. Removed from Register 1911 ...... **1909**

California Gold Mine Co. Ld. Formed 1881. Reconstructed Aug. 1886 as New California Ld. **1906**

California-Idaho Co. Inc. Delaware 1910. The 5% 1st mortgage and collateral trust sinking fund bonds were exchanged at par for collateral trust 20-year gold bonds of American Water-Works & Electric Co. Inc. in 1914 ...... **1915**

California (Mexico) Land Co. Ld. Regd. 1888. Debenture holders were satisfied in May 1934 by allotment

VOL. FOR

Camarones Copper Mining & Smelting Co. Ld. Regd. 1888. Vol. liq. 15 Dec. 1892. Final meeting return regd. 6 July 1897 1893

Camberwell Palace of Varieties Ld. Regd. 1898. Court Order to wind up 16 Mar. 1909. Liquidator released 12 Jan. 1917. Struck off Register 1 July 1921 1910

Camberwell Productions Ld. Regd. 1916. Vol. liq. 29 Mar. 1928. Subsidiary of London Theatres of Varieties Ld. Final meeting return regd. 2 June 1932 1929

Camborne Electricity Supply Co. Ld. Regd. 1898. Vol. liq. (members') 24 Jan. 1938. Undertaking transferred to Cornwall Electric Power Co. Capital returned to contributories—£16,831 9*s.* 7*d.* Final meeting return regd. 12 May 1938 1938

Camborne Gas Co. Ld. Regd. 1889. Dissolved 1 May 1949, undertaking being vested in South Western Area Gas Board under Gas Act 1948. Holders of securities were entitled to receive British Gas 3% guaranteed stock 1990–95 as follows in respect of each £100 unit, unless otherwise stated, of security held:

	£	s.	d.
Ord. shares (of £5)	5	0	0
3½% red. debs	100	0	0
3½% red. 1st mort. debs.	100	0	0

1952

Camborne Water Co. Ld. Inc. by Special Act 1867 as Camborne Water Co.; regd. as limited company and name changed 5 July 1966. Vol. liq. (members') 2 Apr. 1968. Undertaking transferred to South Cornwall Water Board 1 Apr. 1968. Holders were entitled to receive stock in the Board as follows: £19 and £13 6*s.* 6% stock respectively for every ordinary A and ordinary B share of £10; £1 4½% stock, £1 4½% stock and £1 5½% stock respectively for every £1 4½% preference share, £1 4½% preference stock and £1 5½% preference stock; and £1 4½% stock and £1 6% stock respectively for every £1 3½% and £1 6% debenture stock. Final meeting return regd. 15 Aug. 1968 1969

Cambria Cycles Ld. Regd. 1897. Struck off Register 2 Aug. 1904 1905

Cambrian Aircraft Constructors Ld. Regd. 1917. Vol. liq. 8 Jan. 1920. Final meeting return regd. 6 June 1921 .... *1920

Cambrian Collieries Ld. Regd. 1895. Vol. liq. Nov. 1928. Struck off Register 21 Jan. 1936 1936

Cambrian Consolidated Mines Ld. Regd. 1900. Removed from Register 1907 1904

Cambrian Electrolytic Zinc Co. Ld. Regd. 1922. Receiver appointed in Sept. 1924, ceased to act 1927. Assets realised insufficient to provide any return for the debenture holders. Struck off Register Apr. 1929 1930

Cambrian Lead & Zinc Mines Ld. Regd. 1912. Court Order to wind up Dec. 1918. Struck off Register 1925 1919

Cambrian Railways Co. Inc. by Special Act 1864. In 1922 the undertaking was merged into the Great Western Railway Co. in which company stockholders were entitled stock as follows:

For each £100 *held*		*G.W.R*
4% "A" Deb.	£100	4% Debenture
4% "B" Deb.	£87 10*s.*	4% Debenture
4% "C" Deb.	£70	5% Cons. Preference
4% "D" Deb.	£60	5% Cons. Preference
No. 1 4% Pref.	£28·57	Cons. Ordinary
No. 2 4% Pref.	£21·454	Cons. O. Def. Certs.*
No. 3 4% Pref.	£9·297	Do.
No. 4 4% Pref.	£7·866	Do.
O. Cap. No. 1	£2·86	Do.
Ct. Cons. O.	£2·86	Do.

* Holders were entitled to be registered between 1 Jan. 1929 and 1 Jan. 1932 as the holders of the amounts of Cons. Ord. Stock stated in such Certificates 1924

Cambridge Electric Supply Co. Ld. Regd. 1892. Dissolved 1 Apr. 1948. undertaking being vested in British (later Central) Electricity Authority and Eastern Area Board under Electricity Act 1947. Holders of ordinary shares and 4½% debentures were entitled to receive British Electricity 3% guaranteed stock (1968–73) as follows: £1 14*s.* stock for each ordinary share (of £1) held and £101 stock for each £100 debenture capital held 1949

Cambridge Gaslight Co. *See* Cambridge University & Town Gaslight Co.

Cambridge Ld. Regd. 1896. Vol. liq. 9 Aug. 1898. Reconstructed as Cambridge Theatre of Varieties Ld., in which company shareholders were entitled to 5 shares of £1 (credited with 15*s.* paid) for each share of £5 held. Final meeting return regd. 1 July 1899 1903

VOL. FOR

Cambridge Street Tramways Co. Inc. by Special Act 1879. Winding-up order made 3 Feb. 1914 1914

Cambridge Theatre of Varieties Ld. Regd. 1898. Reconstructed 1903 as Cambridge Variety Theatre Ld., in which company shareholders were entitled to 1 share of £1 (credited with 17*s.* 6*d.* paid) for each share of £1 held. Removed from Register 1906 ... 1905

Cambridge University & Town Fire Insurance Co. Ld. Regd. 1887. Vol. liq. 24 Aug. 1896. Absorbed by Manchester Fire Assurance Co. Final meeting return regd. 18 Dec. 1897 .... *1897

Cambridge University & Town Gas-Light Co. Inc. as Cambridge Gaslight Co. in 1834; reinc. as above by Special Act 1867. Dissolved 1 May 1949, undertaking being vested in Eastern Area Gas Board under Gas Act 1948. Holders of securities were entitled to receive, in respect of each £100 unit held, British Gas 3% guaranteed stock 1990–95 as follows:

	£	s.	d.
Cons. orig. stock (10% max.)	205	16	8
Cons. B stock (7% max.)	145	10	0
Cons. C stock (5% max.)	106	10	0
5% irred. deb. stock	126	5	0
4% irred. deb. stock	101	0	0

1925

Cambridge Variety Theatre Ld. Regd. 1903. Court Order to wind up 25 July 1905. Removed from Register 1910 1906

Cambuhy Coffee & Cotton Estates Ld. Regd. 1925. Vol. liq. (members') 26 Mar. 1954. Holders of the £420,000 stock were entitled to (*a*) distribution (pro rata) of 350,000 ordinary shares of Cr.$300 in Cia. Agricola Fazendas Paulistas (*now* Cambuhy S/A Agricola e Industrial) which shares S. G. Warburg & Co. Ld. offered to purchase at 82*s.* 6*d.* per share and (*b*) 6*d.* per £1 stock. Final meeting return regd. 12 Apr. 1956 1957

Camden Brewery Co. Ld. Regd 1889. Vol. liq. 31 Mar. 1926. Final meeting return regd. 3 June 1927 1927

Camden Exploration Co. Ld. Regd. 1896. Vol. liq. June 1909. Struck off Register May 1929 1930

Camden Syndicate Ld. Regd. 1895. Vol. liq. 28 May 1896. Certain assets were acquired by Camden Exploration Co. Ld. for £120,000 in fully-paid shares of £1. Final meeting return regd. 26 Mar. 1898 1908

Camelia Mining Co. Ld. Regd. 1899. Vol. liq. 1904. Mine was acquired by Atlas Gold Mines Co. Ld. Capital returned to contributories—1*s.* 3*d.* per share of £1 further payments (if any) not known. Removed from Register 1906 1905

Cameron Block Ld. Regd. Dublin 1895. In liquidation in 1900 1900

Cameron Freehold Land & Investment Co. Ld. Regd. 1884. Removed from Register 1902 1892

Cameron's Surgical Specialities Ld. Regd. 1929. Vol. liq. (members') 6 Feb. 1945. Capital returned to contributories—2.75*d.* per share of 5*s.* £418 12*s.* 7*d.* was paid into Companies' Liquidation Account. Final meeting return regd. 13 Feb. 1946 1947

Camerton Coal & Fire-Brick Co. Ld. Regd. 1918. Vol. liq. 18 Mar. 1931. An interest was held by Millom & Askam Hematite Iron Co. Ld. Final meeting return regd. 15 Dec. 1931 1925

Camina Nitrate Co. Ld. Regd. 1901. Vol. liq. 13 Nov. 1906. All debentures have been redeemed. Struck off Register 1925 1907

Cammell (Charles) & Co. Ld. Regd. 1864. Vol. liq. 29 Dec. 1897. Reconstructed as company of same name (later Cammell Laird & Co. Ld.), in which company shareholders were entitled to 5 preference shares of £5 for each A share of £20 held, to 12 preference and 12 ordinary shares of £5 for each ordinary share of £100 (£80 paid) held, or to 3 preference and 3 ordinary shares of £5 for each B share of £20 held. Final meeting return regd. 29 Dec. 1898 1898

Camp Bird Ld. Regd. 8 Sept. 1900. Winding-up Order 7 Oct. 1963. Dissolved 18 June 1985 1984–5

Campana Consolidated Gold Mines Ld. Regd. 1897. Reconstructed 1903 as Golden Bell Mines Ld., in which company shareholders were entitled to 1 share of £1 (credited with 17*s.* 6*d.* paid) for each share of £1 held. Struck off Register 1926 1906

Campbell (Donald) & Co. Ld. Regd. 1919, Vol. liq. 1 Mar, 1921. Final meeting return regd, 9 Oct. 1931 *1922

Campbell, Gifford & Co. Ld. *See* Electric Furnace Co. Ld.

Campbell Johnstone & Co. Ld. Regd. 1896, Vol. liq. June 1909. Undertaking and assets were acquired by Charrington & Co. Ld., in which company shareholders were entitled to £4 in debenture stock *plus* 5*s.* in cash for each share of £5 held. The ordinary shares were entitled to £15,100 in cash. Holders of debenture stock were entitled to an equal amount of 4½% debenture stock in acquiring company. Removed from Register 1910 1909

**See Stock Exchange Year-Book.*

VOL. FOR

Campbell (R. H.) Gold Mining Co. Ld. Regd. 1892. Struck off Register 5 May 1896 .... **1899**

Campbell (Robert) & Sons Ld. Regd. 1881. A Dividend of 135% for 1916 absorbed the greater part of the funds in hand. Vol. liq. 2 Apr. 1917. Final meeting return regd. 13 Jan. 1920 .... **1917**

Campbells Ld. Regd. Edinburgh 1885. Vol. liq. (members') 14 May 1945. Capital returned to contributories—£2 8s. 9½d. per share of £1 (10s. paid). Final meeting return regd. 2 July 1946 .... **1947**

Campbeltown & Machrihanish Light Railway Co. Inc. (under Light Railways Acts 1896) by Order of Light Railway Commissioners confirmed by Board of Trade 1905 .... **1934**

Camperdown Pressing Co. Ld. Regd. Edinburgh 1868. Vol. liq. 4 July 1876. Company was directly controlled by Jute Industries Ld. [later Jute Industries (Holdings) Ld.] Final meeting returned regd. 27 Dec. 1876 .... **1941**

Camperdown Trust Co. Ld. (The). Regd. 1913. Amalgamated with Northern American Trust Co. Ld. in 1970 shareholders receiving 96 ordinary shares for every 100 ordinary shares held and preference stockholders a like amount of 5% preference stock. Liability for debenture stocks and dollar loans was assured by that company. Company finally dissolved 13 Apr. 1970 .... **1970**

Campling (Gilbert) Ld. Regd. Sept. 1919. Vol. liq. 22 Oct. 1920. Final meeting return regd. 12 Jan. 1927 **1921**

Campos & Carangola Railway. Established 1874. The outstanding 5½% debentures were converted in Jan. 1905, into an equal amount of fully-paid ordinary shares of £10 in Leopoldina Railway Co. Ld. **1905**

Campos Syndicate Ld. Regd. 1885. Vol. liq. 23 Sept. 1913. Capital returned to contributories—45% at 28 Jan. 1914; further payments (if any) not known. Final meeting return regd. 24 Apr. 1914 .... **1914**

Campro Cameras & Films Ld. Regd. 1928. Court Order to wind up 13 May 1929. Struck off Register May 1933 .... **1934**

Canada Atlantic Railway. Inc. Canada by Special Act 1879. Reincorporated 1899 on amalgamation with Ottawa, Amprior and Parry Sound Railway Co. Under Act of 1914 the undertaking was merged with Grand Trunk Railway Co. of Canada. The capital stocks were exchanged at par for consolidated stock of acquiring company. The liability for the 4% 1st consolidated 1st mortgage sterling bonds was assumed by acquiring company and later by Canadian National Railways; these bonds were acquired by H. M. Treasury in Jan. 1942 at £108 6s. 11d. for every £100 bond held **1945**

Canada Cement Co. Ld. Inc. Canada 1909. Vol. liq. Oct. 1927. Undertaking acquired by company of same name. Shareholders were entitled to $125 for each preferred and $250 for each common share of $100 held **1928**

Canada Central Railway Co. Inc. Canada 1868. Undertaking incorporated in the Canadian Pacific Railway system June 1881 .... **1899**

Canada Co. Ld. Inc. by Royal Charter in 1826; further powers in 1828, 1856, 1881 and 1916; regd. as limited 1953. Vol. liq. (members') 12 Aug. 1953. Final meeting return regd. 18 Dec. 1953 .... **1955**

Canada Gold Co. Ld. Regd. 1879. Struck off Register 27 Apr. 1894 .... **1899**

Canada Iron Corporation Ld. Inc. Canada 1908. Winding up order Aug. 1913. Undertaking was acquired by Canada Iron Foundries Ld. Holders of 1st mortgage bonds were entitled to an equal amount of 6% B debenture stock plus 10% of holding in common stock in acquiring company; holders of 2nd bonds were entitled to 80% of holding in preference shares and 40% in ordinary shares; shareholders were entitled to subscribe for A debenture stock (with bonus of common shares) but nothing further **1915**

Canada Land & Irrigation Co. Ld. Regd. 1917. Vol. liq. (members') 1 Apr. 1952. The proceeds of the sale of company's assets were applied in payment of (a) premium and interest up to 23 Jan. 1947 to 7% A prior lien debenture stockholders (the principal of this stock had been repaid in 1948). (b) principal, premium and interest up to 30 June 1948 to 7% B prior lien debenture stockholders, (c) principal to 7% C prior lien debenture stockholders, (d) 7½% on account of principal to 6% debenture stockholders and (e) after payments to directors and staff an amount equal to 80% of premium to 7% C prior lien debenture stockholders, The final distribution was made to 7% C prior lien debenture stockholders of 8½% on the nominal amount of the stock. No capital was returned to contributories. Final meeting return regd. 3 Oct. 1953 .... **1955**

VOL. FOR

Canada Mines Syndicate Ld. Regd. 1922. Vol, liq, 4 June 1931, About 60% of the capital was owned by Anglo-Continental Mines Co. Ld, Final meeting return regd, 16 Apr, 1932 .... **1926**

Canada Mortgage Agency Ld. Formed 1880, Business was transferred to British Canadian Loan A Investment Co. Ld. **1885**

Canada North West Coal & Lumber Syndicate Ld. Regd. 1889. Struck off Register 1928 .... ***1912**

Canada Northern Power Corporation Ld. Inc. in Canada under Dominion laws 9 Dec. 1924. Vol. liq, 25 Oct. 1955, Holders of common shares were entitled to 1 1⁄16 common shares of Northern Quebec Power Co. Ld. for each 2 common shares held. Charter surrendered 2 Oct. 1956 .... **1957**

Canada Permanent Loan & Savings Co. Inc, Canada by Special Act 1855, Reconstructed 1899 as Canada Permanent and Western Canada Mortgage Corporation (later Canada Permanent Mortgage Corporation) **1900**

Canada Petroleum Co. Ld. Regd. 1899. Removed from Register 1905 .... **1902**

Canada Power & Paper Corporation. Inc, Quebec 1928. Undertaking and assets were acquired by Consolidated Paper Corporation Ld,, in which company shareholders were entitled to 1 share of no par value for every 10 shares of no par value held, Debenture stockholders were entitled to $15 1st mortgage bonds and 1½ shares of no par value in acquiring company for every $100 debentures held **1932**

Canada Settlers' Loan & Trust Co. Ld. Regd. 1889. Vol. liq. Apr, 1910. Capital returned to contributories—35s. 9d. per share of £1 at Feb. 1911; further payments (if any) not known. Removed from Register 1912 .... **1911**

Canada Switch & Spring Co. Ld. Inc. Quebec 1897. Assets were taken over by Montreal Steel Works Ld. Shareholders received £10 10s. for each share of £10 held **1904**

Canada Works Engineering & Shipbuilding Co. Ld. Regd. 1886, Vol. liq. 19 Oct. 1888, Final meeting return regd. 21 Mar. 1891 .... **1889**

Canadian Agricultural, Coal & Colonisation Co. Ld. Regd, 1888, Property and assets were acquired in 1895 by Canadian Land & Ranche Co. Ld, for £21,000 in cash. Removed from Register 1906 .... **1904**

Canadian Agricultural Land & General Investment Co. Ld. Regd. 1912. Struck off Register 16 Nov. 1948 **1938**

Canadian & American Mortgage & Trust Co. Regd. 1884. Vol. liq. 30 Dec. 1926. All capital held by Oregon Mortgage Co. Ld. Final meeting return regd. 3 Oct. 1928 .... **1927**

Canadian & Empire Investment Trust Ld. Regd. 1910. Vol. liq. 27 Mar. 1914, Undertaking and assets were sold to Western Canada Trust Ld. (later Equitable Trust of London Ld.) in which company shareholders were entitled to 1 fully-paid preference share of £10 for each £10 preference stock held; the balance of the purchase price was distributable among the ordinary shareholders. Final meeting return regd. 7 Jan. 1920 .... **1915**

Canadian & English Stores Ld. See Northgate & English Stores Ld.

Canadian and Foreign Investment Trust p.l.c. Regd. 23 Mar. 1909.; re-regd. Apr. 1982. Vol. liq. (members') 20 July 1982. Shareholders received (per ordinary share of 25p) 4 units in Canadian and Foreign International Unit Trust and units at offered prices to value of £1 for each preference share. First and final distribution of 0·18p per ordinary share on 14 Dec. 1982. Final meeting held 22 Dec. 1982 and regd. 12 Jan. 1983. .... **1983–4**

Canadian & General Trust Ld. Regd. 1909 as Canadian & General Securities Corporation Ld.; name changed Sept. 1910. Struck off Register 19 June 1936 .... **1937**

Canadian Banking & Trust Ld. Regd. 1919 as Home & Overseas Trading Trust Ld.; name changed to Newfoundland Banking & Trust Corpn. Ld. in June 1920 and as above in Mar. 1928. Struck off Register 22 Nov. 1940 .... **1941**

Canadian Birkbeck Investment & Savings Co. See Canadian Mortgage Investment Co.

Canadian, British Columbian & Dawson City Telegraph Co. Ld. Regd. 1898. Removed from Register 1905 **1904**

Canadian-British Engineering Co. Ld. Regd. 1912. Vol. liq. 12 Jan. 1916. Final meeting return regd. 2 Aug. 1919 .... **1916**

Canadian Canning Co. Ld. Regd. 1899. Vol. liq. 12 May 1914, Final meeting return regd. 1 Feb. 1918 ...... **1915**

Canadian City & Town Properties Ld. Regd. 1910. Under scheme of arrangement in Oct. 1969 the assets and obligations were transferred to Melbourne & General Investment Trust Ld. in which company shareholders received 3 ordinary shares of 5s. and 1 preference share of £1 per ordinary share of £1 held. Company was dissolved by Order of Court on 28 Feb.1970 .... **1970**

Canadian Copper and Sulphur Co. Ld. Regd. Edinburgh 1876. Court Orders: to wind up Jan. 1887; to dissolve 3 July 1912 .... **1888**

Canadian (Direct) Meat Co. Ld. Regd. 1889. Vol. liq. 16 Apr. 1890. Court Order to dissolve 22 Jan. 1914 .. **1891**

Canadian Doloment Co. Ld. See Colonial Doloment Co. Ld.

Canadian Dominion Development Ld. Regd. 1911. Vol. liq. (members') 7 Nov. 1921. Capital returned to contributories—9s. 10¾d. per preferred share of £1. Final meeting return regd. 10 Jan.1947................ **1947**

Canadian Eagle Oil Co. Ld. Inc. in Canada 1928. In July 1959 assets were acquired by Royal Dutch Shell Group. Shareholders received 2 Royal Dutch shares of Fl. 20 each and 3 Shell Transport shares of £1 each for every 12 shares of no par value held. Company surrendered its Charter and was dissolved on 16 June 1961. .... **1962**

Canadian Electric Traction Co. Ld. Regd. 1904. Vol. liq. 11 Aug. 1911. Final meeting return regd. 14 Oct. 1914 .... **1912**

Canadian Finance & Land Co. Ld. Regd. 1912. Struck off Register Oct. 1932 .... **1933**

Canadian General Investment Trust Ld. Inc. Canada 1926. Undertaking and assets were acquired by Canadian General Investments Ld. in which company shareholders were entitled to 4 shares of no par value for each share of $100 held **1932**

Canadian Land & Ranche Co. Ld. Regd. 1895. Undertaking and assets were acquired in 1904 by company of same name for £20.000 in fully-paid shares and £60,000 in cash deposit certificates. Removed from Register 1906 .... **1908**

Canadian Land & Ranche Co. Ld. Regd. 1904. Vol. liq. (members') 25 May 1926. Capital returned to contributories—5s. 10⅝d. per share of 2s. 6d. Struck off Register 14 Aug. 1956 .... **1957**

Canadian Land Corporation Ld. Inc. Canada. Direct controlling interest was held by Investment Corporation of Canada Ld. (later London Midland & Associated Properties) **1942**

Canadian Lorrain Silver Mines Ld. Inc. Canada 1922. Vol. liq. 1931 .... **1932**

Canadian Merchants & General Trust, Ld. Regd. 1909. Struck off Register 23 Aug. 1949 .... **1939**

Canadian Middle West Trust Ld. Regd. 1912. Vol. liq. Nov. 1915. Struck off Register 15 Aug. 1944 .... **1945**

Canadian Mills & Timber Ld. Inc. British Columbia 1910 .... **1912**

Canadian Mineral Rubber Co. Ld. Inc. Canada 1909. The outstanding 5% guaranteed trust stock was redeemed at par 23 Apr. 1932 .... **1933**

Canadian Mines Development Co. Ld. Regd. 1899. Removed from Register 1904 .... **1902**

Canadian Mining Corporation Ld. Regd. 1914. Vol. liq. 14 Feb. 1917. Shareholders were entitled to 1 share in Mining Corporation of Canada Ld. of $5 for each share of £1 held. Final meeting return regd. 7 Aug. 1918 .... **1917**

Canadian Mining Syndicate Ld. Regd. 1897. Vol. liq. 26 June 1903. Final meeting return regd. 18 July 1921 **1904**

Canadian Mortgage Investment Co. Inc. Canada by Special Act 1893 as Canadian Birkbeck Investment & Savings Co.; name changed Mar. 1912. In Oct. 1929 it was stated that the company would probably go into liquidaton shortly **1930**

Canadian National Electric Railways. Inc. Canada 1923. Operations ceased in Aug. 1931, when a receiver was appointed. In July 1934 holders of the Toronto Suburban Railway Co. debenture stock agreed to accept a payment of 25% in full satisfaction **1935**

Canadian National Railway Co. Inc. Canada 1919 by Special Act. Amalgamated with Grand Trunk Railway Co. of Canada to form Canadian National Railways **1924**

Canadian North Pacific Fisheries Ld. Inc. Canada 1910 as Canadian Northern Fisheries Ld.; name changed 1910. Receiver and manager appointed 13 Nov. 1914; property and assets realised by Order of the Court 24 June 1915. Debenture stockholders received 1s. 2·3362d. in the £ **1919**

Canadian North West Irrigation Co. Inc. Canada by Special Act 1893 as Alberta Irrigation Co.; name changed by Act of 1899. amalgamated with Alberta Rly. and Coal Co. and St. Mary's River Rly. Co. under the title of Alberta Rly. and Irrigation Co.. **1908**

Canadian Northern Alberta Railway Co. Inc. Canada by Special Act 1910. Undertaking was acquired by Canadian National Railways. Canadian Northern Railway System owned all capital stock. The 3½%

Dominion guaranteed debenture stock was acquired in Jan. 1942 by H.M. Treasury at £103 18s. for every £100 stock held **1924**

Canadian Northern Fisheries Ld. See Canadian North Pacific Fisheries Ld.

Canadian Northern Ontario Railway Co. Inc. Canada by Special Act 1895 as James Bay Railway Co.; name changed 1906. Undertaking was acquired by Canadian National Railways. Canadian Northern Railway System owned all capital stock. The outstanding 3½% 1st mortgage debenture stocks were redeemed on 10 July 1936 and 30 June 1938. The outstanding 4% perpetual consolidated debenture stock and 3½% Dominion guaranteed debenture stock were acquired in Jan. 1942 by H.M. Treasury at £94 17s. 3d. and £105 8s. 1d. respectively for every £100 stock held **1924**

Canadian Northern Pacific Railway Co. Inc. British Columbia 1910. Undertaking was acquired by Canadian National Railways. Canadian Northern Railway system owned all capital stock. The outstanding 4% 1st guaranteed debenture stock 1950 and 4½% 1st mortgage terminal debenture stock 1950 were acquired in Jan. 1942 by H.M. Treasury at £102 17s. 11d. and £113 0s. 10d. respectively for every £100 stock held **1924**

Canadian Northern Prairie Lands Co. Ld. Inc. Canada 1905. Vol. liq. Nov. 1926. Certain assets were transferred to a new Canadian company in exchange for all its capital stock and 6% debentures, the remaining assets (including the capital stock and debentures of the new Canadian company but excluding certain other securities of an approximate value of $1,350,000) were acquired by Canadian & Foreign Securities Co. Ld.; shareholders received $4·50 in cash and $4 in 6% debenture stock and 1 share of no par value of Canadian & Foreign Securities Co. Ld. for each share of $5 held **1927**

Canadian Northern Quebec Railway Co. Inc. Canada by Special Act 1906. Undertaking was acquired by Canadian National Railways. The 1st mortgage guaranteed 4% gold bonds (Great Northern Railway of Canada) were redeemed on 1 Oct. 1934. The 4% perpetual guaranteed debenture stock was acquired in Jan. 1942 by H.M. Treasury for £94 17s. 3d. for every £100 bonds held **1924**

Canadian Northern Railway Co. Inc. Canada 1899 by Special Act. The undertaking was acquired by Canadian National Railways. All capital stock was owned by Dominion Government. In 1930 the following stocks were redeemed: 4% 30-year (Ontario Division) 1st mortgage debenture bonds, 4% 1st mortgage consolidated debenture bonds, 5% income charge convertible debenture stock and 4% 1st mortgage Manitoba guaranteed debenture stock. In 1934 the following stocks were redeemed: 4% 1st mortgage Alberta guaranteed debenture stock and 4% 1st mortgage Saskatchewan guaranteed debenture stock. In Jan. 1942 the following stocks were acquired by H.M. Treasury—for every £100 4% perpetual consolidated debenture stock held—£95 2s. 4d.; for every £100 3% 1st mortgage debenture stock—£101 7s. 9d.; for every £100 3½% Dominion guaranteed debenture stock held—London issue, £104 8s.; Canadian issue £110 3s. 7d.; for every £100 3½% Dominion guaranteed debenture stock held—£22 12s. 10d. 6½% 25-year sinking fund debenture bonds held by British nationals were acquired by H.M. Treasury in Jan. 1942 at £27 9s. 7d. for every $100 bonds held **1924**

Canadian Northern Railway System. Inc. Canada by Special Act 1914 .... **1924**

Canadian Northern Western Railway Co. Inc. Alberta 1910. Undertaking was acquired by Canadian National Railways. All capital stock was owned by Canadian Northern Railway System. The outstanding 1st mortgage 4½% Alberta guaranteed debenture stock or bonds were redeemed on 16 Feb. 1942 and the outstanding 4½% 1st mortgage guaranteed debenture stock or bonds (Brazean line) were redeemed on 22 Oct. 1943 .... **1924**

Canadian Oil Fields Ld. Regd. 1902. Vol. liq. Jan. 1909. Removed from Register 1910 .... **1909**

Canadian Oil Producing & Refining Co. Ld. Regd. 1910. Vol. liq. 8 Aug. 1923. Final meeting return regd. 15 July 1927 .... **1924**

Canadian Ore Concentration Ld. Regd. 1902. Vol. liq. 2 Jan. 1920. Final meeting return regd. 19 Mar. 1924 **1920**

Canadian Pacific Exploration Ld. Regd. 1897. Vol. liq. 19 Nov. 1902. Final meeting return regd. 8 Dec. 1914 .... **1903**

Canadian Pacific Land & Mortgage Co. Ld. Regd. 1888. Business and property were acquired by British Columbia Land and Investment Agency Ld. for

VOL. FOR

£162,090 in 4% debenture stock, £16,209 in cash and assumption of liability for £45,900 debentures. Vol. liq. 1 Oct. 1896. Final meeting return regd. 19 Nov. 1896 ... **1896**

Canadian Pacific Lumber Co. Ld. Inc. British Columbia 1900. Property was sold for $780,000 on behalf of bondholders, who were expected to receive about 20% return ... **1921**

Canadian Pacific Sulphite Pulp Co. Ld. Regd. 1906. Vol. liq. Oct. 1910. Property was sold to Swanson Bay Forests, Wood Pulp and Timber Mills Ld. The debenture stock was repaid at 105%; the income certificates were exchanged at par for bonds in purchasing company. Removed from Register 1913 ... **1911**

Canadian Pacific Timber Co. Ld. Regd. 1906. Vol. liq. 3 Feb. 1908. Property acquired by Western Canada Timber Co. Ld. Final meeting return regd. 10 Feb. 1909 ... ***1908**

Canadian Phosphate Co. Ld. Regd. 1887. Removed from Register 1898 ... **1899**

Canadian (Queensland) Gold Mining Co. Ld. Undertaking amalgamated with three other companies to form Etheridge United Gold Mining Co. Ld., in which company, shareholders were entitled to an equal number of fully-paid shares of £1 ... **1891**

Canadian Real Properties Ld. Regd. 1902. Vol. liq. July 1909. The assets were acquired by British Columbia Fruit Lands Ld. in which company shareholders were entitled to 3 fully-paid shares of £1 for every 2 shares of £1 held; a further small distribution of shares was anticipated. Removed from Register 1910 ... **1910**

Canadian Resources Development Ld. Regd. 1910. Assets realised insufficient to meet claims of debenture stockholders. Struck off Register Feb. 1933 ... **1933**

Canadian Selection Co. Ld. Inc. Canada 1930. In Dec. 1933 certain assets were sold to Selection Trust Ld. for £3,238,000 in cash and shareholders were entitled to 4 fully-paid shares of 10s. of that company for each share of no par value held ... **1934**

Canadian Share Investment Co. Ld. Regd. 1928. Struck off Register 20 Apr. 1943 ... **1944**

Canadian Steel Corporation Ld. *See* Dominion Steel Corporation Ld.

Canadian Steel Foundries Ld. Inc. Canada 1910. All assets were transferred in 1935 to Canadian Car & Foundry Co. Ld. which company owned all capital ... **1936**

Canadian Timber & Saw Mills Ld. Regd. 1903. Vol. liq. 7 Dec. 1905. Undertaking acquired by Canadian Pacific Timber Co. Ld. Final meeting return regd. 25 Oct. 1909 ... ***1907**

Canadian Timber Investment Co. Ld. Regd. 1911. Vol. liq. Dec. 1914 for reconstruction as Pacific Timber Co. Ld. in which company shareholders were entitled to an equal number of ordinary or preference shares of £1 5s. (credited with 20s. paid). Struck off Register July 1933 ... **1934**

Canadian Vickers Ld. Inc. Canada 1911. The sterling 6% 1st mortgage registered debentures were redeemed on 1 Feb. 1928 as 103% ... **1928**

Canadian Western Natural Gas, Light, Heat & Power Co. Ld. Inc. Alberta 1911. The outstanding 5% 1st mortgage debenture stock was redeemed at 105% in June 1933 ... **1933**

Canadian Wheat Lands Ld. Regd. 1911. Vol. liq. 29 June 1917 for reconstruction as Canada Land & Irrigation Co. Ld., in which company shareholders were entitled to 1 fully-paid share of £1 for each share of £1 held. Final meeting return regd. 15 Jan. 1919 ... **1918**

Canary Islands Co. Ld. Regd. 1888. Vol. liq. 15 Sept. 1919. No capital was returned to contributories. Final meeting return regd. 29 Apr. 1922 ... **1920**

Canas Mines Ld. Regd. 1896. Removed from Register 1910 ... **1909**

Candelaria Land, Mining and Power Co. Ld. Regd. 1911. Vol. liq. 8 July 1915. The debenture holders agreed to accept shares at par in San Dimas Co. No return was made to shareholders. Final meeting return regd. 4 May 1916 ... **1916**

Candelaria Waterworks & Milling Co. Ld. Regd. 1885. Vol. liq. 7 Dec. 1897. Removed from Register 1903 ... **1898**

Candover Estates Ld. Inc. Natal 1920. Wound up by Order of the Court Aug. 1929 ... **1930**

Cankin Bamoo Gold Mines Ld. Regd. 1882. Removed from Register 1889 ... ***1884**

Cannan's Soap Works Ld. Regd. 1906. Court Order to wind up 25 Oct. 1910. Liquidator released 29 Feb. 1912. Struck off Register 16 July 1915 ... **1911**

Canning Jarrah Timber Co. Ld. Regd. 1900. Undertaking was acquired in 1902 by Millar's Karri and Jarrah Co. (1902) Ld. (later Millar's Timber and Trading Co. Ld.) for £82,500 in 4% debenture stock and £50,875 in ordinary shares of £1. Debenture

VOL. FOR

stock holders were entitled to £82 10s. debenture stock for every £100 stock held. The ordinary shares were distributed *pro rota* to ordinary shareholders. Removed from Register 1912 ... **1904**

Canning Jarrah Timber Co. (Western Australia) Ld. Regd. 1897. Reconstructed 1900 as Canning Jarrah Timber Co. Ld., in which company shareholders were entitled to 1 share of 10s. (credited with 7s. 6d. paid) for each share of £1 held. Debenture holders were entitled to an equal amount of debenture stock in new company. Removed from Register 1901 ... **1902**

Canning Town Glass Works Ld. Regd. 1923. Vol. liq. 15 Nov. 1926. Undertaking acquired by company of same name. Final meeting return regd. 9 July 1930 ... **1927**

Cannock & Huntington Colliery Co. Ld. Regd 1873. Removed from Register 1904 ... ***1886**

Cannock & Rugeley Colliery Co. Ld. Regd 1868. Vol. liq. (members') 5 Sept. 1955. Final meeting return regd. 22 Sept. 1956 ... **1940**

Cannock Associated Collieries Ld. Regd. 1936. Vol. liq. (members') 6 Sept. 1948, the collieries &c. having vested in National Coal Board. Capital returned to contributories (per share of £1)—1st preference, 22s.; 2nd preference. 22s.; ordinary, 56s. 8d. £7,219 7s. 11d. paid into Companies' Liquidation Account. Final meeting return regd. 22 Sept. 1956 ... **1957**

Cannock Chase & Wolverhampton Railway Co. Inc. by Special Act 1864. Undertaking vested in National Coal Board ... **1950**

Cannock District Gas Co. Ld. Regd. 1897 as Cannock, Hednesford & District Gas Co. Ld.; name changed 1932. Dissolved 1 May 1949. undertaking. being vested in West Midland Area Gas Board under Gas Act 1948. Holders of securities were entitled to receive British Gas 3% guaranteed stock 1990–95 as follows in respect of each £100 unit, unless otherwise stated, of security held:

	£	s.	d.
Ord. shares (7% stand.) (of £1)	1	10	0
5% pref. shares (of £5)	5	15	0
4½% red. pref. shares (of £1)	1	1	5
4½% red. deb. stock	101	0	0
3½% red. debs. (1956)	100	0	0
4% red. debs. (1963)	102	10	0

... **1952**

Canons Park Estate Co. Ld. Regd. 1896. Vol. liq. Nov. 1912 for reconstruction as private company of same name. Removed from Register 1913 ... **1913**

Cantabrian Copper Mines Ld. Regd. 1890. Vol. liq. 19 Dec. 1892. Final meeting return regd. 23 June 1896 ... **1893**

Cantareira Water Supply & Drainage Co. of the City of Sao Paulo. Founded 1877. The outstanding 5% debentures (second series) were redeemed on 1 Oct. 1920 at par. ... **1921**

Canterbury and District Water Co. Inc. by Special Act 1822 as Canterbury Gas Light & Coke Co.; re-incorporated as Canterbury Gas & Water Co. 1886: name changed 1952.
Under the provisions of the Mid Kent Water (Canterbury) Order, 1968 the undertaking vested in the Mid Kent Water Co. on 1 Jan. 1969 and shareholders received a like holding, both as to amount and type, of Mid Kent Water Co. stock in exchange for their holdings. The outstanding mortgages and debenture stocks of this company became mortgages and debenture stocks of the Mid Kent Water Co. Company was dissolved upon a declaration by the directors on 18 July 1969 ... **1970**

Canterbury & Herne Bay Light Railway Co. Inc. (under Light Railways Act 1896) 1903 ... **1908**

Canterbury & Paragon Ld. Regd. 1887. Vol. liq. 23 May 1912. Final meeting return regd. 19 Jan. 1914 ..... **1913**

Canterbury Gas Light & Coke Co.—later Canterbury Gas & Water Co.—*see* Canterbury & District Water Co.

Cap Martin Hotel Ld. Regd. 1890. Struck off Register 8 Jan. 1965 ... **1959**

Capato (A, H.) & Co. Ld. In liquidation. Direct controlling interest was held by Contomichalos, Darke & Co. (1929) Ld. (later Cotts, Darke & Co. Ld.) ... **1935**

Cape Breton Coal, Iron & Railway Co. Ld. Inc. Nova Scotia 1895. Properties acquired by Broughton Collieries Ld. in 1929 ... **1941**

Cape Coast Exploration Ld. Inc. Transvaal 1928. Undertaking and assets were acquired in 1941 by De Beers Consolidated Mines Ld. Vol. liq. 15 Dec. 1941. Capital returned to contributories—£2 per share of £1 ... **1943**

Cape Colonisation Co. Ld. Regd. 1896. Removed from Register 1908 ... **1898**

Cape Copper Co. Ld. Regd. 1888. Receivers appointed in June 1922. Returns amounting to 7s. in £ were made to debenture holders and a small final return was anticipated. Struck off Register Jan. 1935 ..... **1935**

VOL. FOR

Cape Copper Mining Co. Ld. Regd. 1863. Vol. liq. Apr. 1888. Reconstructed as Cape Copper Co. Ld., in which company shareholders were entitled to 15 fully-paid shares of £2 for each share of £10 (£8 paid) held. Final meeting return regd. 12 Dec. 1889 ..... **1908**

Cape Electric Tramways Ld. Regd. 29 Oct. 1897. Vol. liq. (members') 30 Dec. 1949 for reconstruction as Cape Electric Tramways (1949) Ld. in which company shareholders were entitled to 4 shares of £1 for every 3 held. Debenture holders had the option of exchanging for new 5% debentures at par or repayment at 103%. £75 was paid into Companies' Liquidation Account. Final meeting return regd. 17 Oct. 1950 ...... **1952**

Cape Glass Co. Ld. Regd. 1902. Vol. liq. 15 Dec. 1905. Removed from Register 1907 .... **1906**

Cape Mill Ld. Regd. 1920. Vol. liq. (creditors') 11 Sept. 1939. Assets realised insufficient to pay creditors in full. Final meeting return regd. 10 Oct. 1940 ...... **1940**

Cape of Good Hope Diamond Mining Co. Ld. Regd. 1881. Removed from Register 1888 .... **1888**

Cape Pioneers Ld. Regd. 1897. Vol. liq. 19 May 1920. Final meeting return regd. 13 June 1922 .... **1921**

Cape Stock Farming Co. Ld. Regd. 1880. Vol. liq. 14 Sept. 1891. Court Order to continue winding up under supervision Oct. 1891. Final meeting return regd. 17 Apr. 1894 .... **1892**

Cape Town Consolidated Tramways & Land Co. Ld. Regd. 1901. Reconstructed 1906 as company of same name. Shareholders were entitled to 2 shares of £1 (credited with 17s. 6d. paid) in new company for every 3 shares of £1 held. Holders of debentures were entitled to debentures in new company. Removed from Register 1907 .... **1906**

Cape Town Consolidated Tramways & Land Co. Ld. Regd. 1906. Vol. liq. (members') 14 July 1936. Capital returned to contributories—4s. 7½d. per preference share of 5s.; no return to deferred shares of 1s. Final meeting return regd. 18 Dec. 1936 .... **1937**

Cape Town District Waterworks Co. Ld. Regd. 1889. Vol. liq. 4 Dec. 1900. Undertaking was acquired by local authorities. Capital returned to contributories was expected to exceed £8 per share of £5. Removed from Register 1901 .... **1901**

Capel Court Explorers Ld. Regd. 1896. Vol. liq. 24 June 1898. Final meeting return regd. 18 Nov. 1898..... **1899**

Capillitas Consolidated Mines Ld. Regd. 1909. Vol. liq. June 1922. Struck off Register June 1932 .... **1933**

Capillitas Copper Co. Ld. Regd. 1901. Vol. liq. Jan. 1909 for reconstruction as Capillitas Consolidated Mines Ld. Debenture holders were entitled to 30% of holdings in cash and 70% in fully-paid shares of £1. Preference shareholders were entitled to 1 new share of £1 (credited with 14s. paid) for each preference share of £1 held. Ordinary shareholders were entitled to 1 new share of £1 (credited with 12s. 6d. paid) for each ordinary share of £1 held. Deferred shareholders were entitled to 1 new share of £1 (credited with 14s. paid) for every 5 deferred shares of £1 held. Removed from Register 1911 .... **1909**

Capital & Counties Bank Ld. Regd. 1880. Established 1834 as Hampshire & North Wilts. Banking Co. Vol. liq. Aug. 1918. Business was acquired by Lloyds Bank Ld., in which company shareholders were entitled to 1 share of £50 (credited with £8 paid) *plus* £2 in cash for each share of £50 (£10 paid) held... **1919**

Capital & Counties Industrial Corporation Ld. Regd. 1919. Court Order to wind up 18 Oct. 1921. Liquidator released 6 Mar. 1931. Struck off Register 10 Oct. 1933 .... *****1922**

Capital & Counties Insurance Co. Ld. Regd. 1908. Court Order to wind up 31 Jan. 1922. Struck off Register 20 Mar 1936 .... **1937**

Capital & Provincial News Theatres Ld. Regd. 1935. Vol. liq. (members') 11 June 1964. Capital returned to contributories (per share of 5s.)—£1 9s. 0½d. Final meeting return regd. 6 Oct. 1979. Amount apid into Companies' Liquidation Account in respect of unclaimed distributions £3,279 .... **1081–2**

Capital Fire Insurance Association Ld. Regd. Jan. 1881 as Universe Fire Insurance Association Ld.; name changed July 1881. Court Orders: to wind up 5 Feb. 1883; to dissolve 24 Mar. 1893 .... **1884**

Capital Investment Co. Ld. Regd. 1919. Vol. liq. (creditors) 13 June 1939. No capital returned to contributories. Final meeting return regd. 1 Mar. 1940 .... **1940**

Capital Share and General Guarantee Co. Ld. Regd. 1895. Vol. liq. 17 Sept. 1923. All paid-up capital was returned to contributories. Final meeting return regd. 8 Oct. 1927 .... **1924**

Capital Syndicate Ld. Regd. 1908. Vol. liq. 29 Mar. 1928. Subsidiary of London Theatres of Varieties Ld. Final meeting return regd. 13 June 1931 .... **1929**

VOL. FOR

Capital (Epsom) Ld. Regd. 1929. Undertaking acquired by London and District Cinemas Ld. Struck off Register 3 Mar. 1944 .... **1945**

Capitol Freehold Land & Investment Co. Ld. Regd. 1885. Vol. liq. 8 May 1918. Final meeting return regd. 1 Oct. 1927 .... **1919**

Capitol National Bank & Trust of New York. *See* United Capitol National Bank & Trust of New York.

Capitol National Bank of New York. *See* United Capitol National Bank & Trust of New York.

Caprington & Auchlochlan Collieries Ld. Regd. Edinburgh 1910. Vol. liq. 6 May 1932. In 1934 The Mauchline Colliery assets were acquired by Bairds & Dalmellington Ld. Capital returned to contributories—18s. 1·21d. per preferred share of £1. Final meeting return regd. 20 Dec. 1938 .... **1937**

Caprotti Valve Gears, Ld. Regd. 1923 as Valve Gears Ld.; name changed Oct. 1927. Vol. 1 iq. (members') 26 Jan. 1945, the assets were acquired by Associated Locomotive Equipment Ld. Capital returned to contributories —1s. 9d. per preference share of £1. £303 17s. 9d. was paid into Companies' Liquidation Account. Final meeting return regd. 17 Mar. 1947 **1948**

Caprottis Bank (1929) Ld. *See* Federated European Bank Ld.

Capsuloid Co. Ld. Regd. 1902. Taken over by Capsuloids (1909) Ld. (later Cicfa Co. Ld.). Removed from Register 1913 .... **1940**

Capsuloids (1909) Ld. *See* Cicfa Co.

Captain Cook Brewery Ld. Regd. 1895. Vol. liq. 18 June 1906. Business was acquired by Hancock & Co. (New Zealand) Ld., in which company shareholders were entitled to 5 fully-paid ordinary shares of £1 for each ordinary share of £5 held or to 6 fully-paid preference shares of £1 for each preference share of £5 held. The debentures were to be repaid at 102%. Removed from Register 1910 .... **1907**

Captain Robinson's Gold Reefs Ld. Regd. 1896. Removed from Register 1912 .... **1899**

"Captain" Rim Co. Ld. Regd. 1911. Struck off Register 1934 .... **1913**

Car Illustrated Ld. Regd. 1902. Court Order to wind up 1 Feb. 1916. Liquidator released 18 Jan. 1918. Struck off Register 1 July 1921 .... **1916**

Car Trust Investment Co. Ld. Regd. 1888. Property and assets were acquired by Car Trust Realisation Co. Ld., for £250,000 with which to repay debentures, 100,000 shares of 5s. and £737,500 in income bonds. Removed from Register 1912 .... **1908**

Car Trust Realisation Co. Ld. Regd. 1905. Vol. liq. 29 Mar. 1926. A return of 62½% was made to debenture stockholders in May 1926. Final meeting return regd. 13 Dec. 1930 .... **1927**

Carabaya Mining Syndicate Ld. Regd. 1903. Struck off Register 31 Oct. 1916 .... **1907**

Carabobo Venezuela Gold Mines Ld. Regd. 1910 as Transvaal (North) Gold Mining Co. Ld.; name changed May 1928. Vol. liq. (creditors') 4 Dec. 1929. Assets realised insufficient to pay creditors in full. Final meeting return regd.11 July 1934 .... **1930**

Caramanian Iron Corporation Ld. Regd. 1906. Vol. liq. (creditors') 3 Apr. 1936. No capital returned to contributories. Final meeting return regd. 3 Sept. 1936 .... **1937**

Carandotta Pastoral Co. Ld. Regd. 1883. Vol. liq. 24 Jan. 1895. Final meeting return regd. 2 Feb. 1895 *****1896**

Caraquet Railway Co. Inc. New Brunswick 1882 ...... **1907**

Caratal Gold Mining & Trading Co. Ld. Inc. Guernsey 1902 .... **1909**

Caratal Mining Co. Ld. Regd. 1892. Vol. liq. 16 Oct. 1896. Reconstructed as Caratal (New) Mines Ld., in which company shareholders were entitled to 1 share of 2s. 6d. (credited with wish 2s. paid) for each share of 2s. 6d. held. Final meeting return regd. 27 June 1900 .... **1897**

Caratal (New) Mines Ld. Regd. 1896. Reconstructed under the same name in 1902. Removed from Register 1909 .... **1902**

Carata (New) Mines Ld. Regd. 1902. Court Order to wind up 3 June 1902. Removed from Register 1905 **1903**

Caratinga Gold Mining & Estates Co. Ld. Regd. 1925. Vol. liq. 16 Aug. 1927. Struck off Register 29 Dec. 1942 .... *****1928**

Carballino Gold and Arsenic Mines Ld. Regd. 1905. Vol. liq. 28 Jan 1910. Struck off Register 18 Jan. 1917 **1911**

Carbide & Electro Products Ld. Inc. Victoria 1911 as Hydro Electric Power & Metallurgical Co. Ld. name changed May 1922 .... **1927**

Carbis China Clay & Brick Co. Ld. Regd. 1920. Vol. liq. (members') 28 June 1933. All capital owned by English China Clays Ld. Final meeting return regd. 7 Feb. 1935 .... **1934**

Carbo Plaster Ld. Regd. 1935. Vol. liq. (members') 14 June 1940. Capital returned to contributories—1½d.

VOL. FOR

per share of 10*s.* £236 6*s.* 5*d.* was paid into Companies' Liquidation Account. Final meeting return regd. 14 July 1943 1945

Carbo Plastering Co. Ld. *See* Victoria Plastering Co. Ld.

Carbo Products Ld. Regd. 1933. Vol. liq. (members') 2 Apr. 1935. Reconstructed as Carbo Plaster Ld. Final meeting return regd. 31 Mar. 1936 1940

Carboil Syndicate Ld. Regd. 1913. Vol. liq. June 1922. Struck off Register Feb. 1932 1932

Carbolic Smoke Ball Co. (1893) Ld. Regd. 1893. Vol. liq. 19 June 1895. Final meeting return regd. 20 Aug. 1896 .... *1895

Carbon Cement Co. Ld. Undertaking and assets were acquired in Dec. 1928 by Turner & Newall Ld..... 1929

Carbon Products & Oil Distillation Ld. Regd. 1919. Vol. liq 7 Nov. 1922. Final meeting return regd. 13 June 1924 1923

Carbrook Steel Works Ld. Regd. 1898 as New Carbrook Steel Works Ld.; name changed July 1899. Court Order to wind up 13 Jan. 1903. Liquidator released 13 June 1904. Struck off Register 11 Feb. 1910 1903

Carbrook Steel Works Ld. Regd. 1909. Receiver appointed 12 Mar. 1938; ceased to act 1 Nov. 1930. Struck off Register 19 Mar. 1937 1938

Carburation (Temperature Control) Ld. Regd. 1919. Vol. liq. 10 Feb. 1922. Final meeting return regd. 31 Mar. 1923 1923

Carbutt & Co. Ld. Regd. 1899. Vol. liq. 24 June 1927. Undertaking was acquired by Carbutt & Co. (1928) Ld. Final meeting return regd. 19 Apr. 1929 1926

Cardenden Gas Co. Ld. Regd. in Edinburgh 1909. Dissolved 1 May 1949, undertaking being vested in Scottish Area Gas Board under Gas Act 1948. Holders of ordinary shares (of £1) were entitled to receive £2 6*s.* 8*d.* British Gas 3% guaranteed stock 1990–95 for each share held 1952

Cardiff and Channel Mills Ld. Regd. 1903 Vol. liq. 31 Jan. 1927. Final meeting return regd. 23 Jan. 1928 1927

Cardiff and Newcastle Steam Coal Co. Ld. Regd. 1883. Court Orders: to wind up 22 July 1890; to dissolve 6 May 1897 1891

Cardiff & Newport Insurance Co. Ld. Regd. 1922. All shares owned by Lancashire & General Assurance Co. Ld. Struck off Register 1929 1927

Cardiff & Newport Patent Fuel Co. (Arrow Brand) Ld. Regd. 1884. Vol. liq. 28 Sept. 1920. Final meeting return regd. 3 Feb. 1921 1921

Cardiff & Swansea Smokeless Steam Coal Co. Ld. Regd. 1873. Vol. liq. 11 Apr. 1891. Final meeting return regd. 30 May 1893 1892

Cardiff Castle Gold Mines Ld. Regd. 1895. Vol liq. 10 June 1895. Final meeting return regd. 29 Apr. 1897 1898

Cardiff District & Penarth Harbour Tramway Co. Ld. Regd. 1880. Undertaking was acquired by Cardiff Corporation. Capital returned to contributories—£2 10*s.* per share of £5; further payments (if any) not known. Removed from Register 1903 1904

Cardiff District Collieries Ld. Regd. 1904. Vol. liq. June 1910. Removed from Register 1911 1911

Cardiff Floating Docks & Ship Repairing Co. Ld. Regd. 1890. Vol. liq. 24 Dec. 1892. Final meeting return regd. 12 Oct. 1893 1894

Cardiff Gas-Light & Coke Co. Inc. by Special Act 1837. Dissolved 1 May 1949, undertaking being vested in Wales Area Gas Board Gas Act 1948. Holders of securities were entitled to receive, in respect of each £100 unit held, British Gas 3% guaranteed stock 1990–95 as follows:

	£ s. d.
Cons. ord. stock (5% basic)	125 6 8
4½% pref. stock	107 0 0
5% perp. deb. stock (tax-free)	163 0 0
4% perp. deb. stock	102 3 4
5% red. deb. stock	109 0 0

A distribution on cons. ord. stock of 15·164% out of reserves (plus 1·008% final adjustment of dividend) was made in Oct. 1953 1952

Cardiff Hotel Co. Ld. Regd. 1864. Vol. liq. May 1888. Final meeting return regd. 26 June 1888 1889

Cardiff Junction Dry Dock Engineering Co. Ld. Regd. 1881. Vol. liq. Jan. 1956. Final meeting return regd. 24 Sept. 1956 1940

Cardiff Marine Insurance Co. Ld. Regd. 1880. Vol. liq. Mar. 1885. Final meeting return regd. 4 Mar. 1887 1887

Cardiff Milling Co. Ld. Regd. 1889 as James Tucker Ld. Business was acquired in 1898 by New Cardiff Milling Co. Ld. for £80,000 in cash and £44,511 in deferred ordinary shares. Removed from Register 1909 1908

Cardiff, Newport & Swansea Empire Palaces Ld. Regd. 1895. Vol. liq. 27 Feb. 1900. Reconstructed as Moss Empires Ld. later M. E. Theatres Ld. in which company shareholders were entitled to 12 preference shares of £5 (credited as fully-paid) for every 10 preference shares of £5 held subject to payment of £1. Ordinary shareholders were entitled to 7 fully-paid preference shares 7 fully-paid ordinary shares of £5 and £1 5*s.* in cash for every 10 ordinary shares of £5 held. Final meeting return regd. 7 July 1909 1900

Cardiff, Penarth & Barry Junction Railway Co. Inc. by Special Act 1885. Under Taff Vale Railway Act 1889 undertaking was amalgamated with that company 1 July 1889; shareholders received an equal amount of Taff Vale 4% preference stock.... 1890

Cardiff Railway Co. Inc. by Special Act 1886 as Bute Docks Co.; name changed by Act of 1897. In 1923 the undertaking was merged into the Great Western Railway Co. in which company stockholders were entitled to stock as follows:

For each £100 *held*		*G.W.R.*
3% Debenture	£75	4% Debenture
First 4% Pref.	£80	5% Cons. Pref.
Second 4% Pref.	£80	5% Cons. Pref.
4% Prefd. Ord.	£80	5% Cons. Pref.
3% 2nd Prefd. Ord.	£45	£45 Cons. Ord.

The £445,200 and £547,666 Loans and £2,600,000 Ordinary (£100) shares were exchanged for £100.000 4% Debenture; £420,000 5% Consolidated Preference and £268,000 Consolidated Ordinary 1924

Cardiff Smokeless Fuel Co. Ld. Regd. 1905. Vol. liq. 25 Feb. 1914. Final meeting return regd. 8 Aug. 1914 1915

Cardiff Steam Laundry Dyeing, Carpet & Window Cleaning Co. Ld. Regd. 1891. Vol. liq. 4 Apr. 1918. Final meeting return regd. 24 July 1920 1918

Cardiff Tramways Co. Ld. Regd. 1871. Vol. liq. (members') 8 June 1936. Undertaking acquired by Cardiff Corporation. Final meeting return regd. 31 Dec. 1936 1937

Cardigan Mines Ld. Regd 1906. Vol. liq. 30 Dec. 1908. Final meeting return regd. 31 Mar. 1911 1909

Cardigan Slate Quarries Ld. Regd. 1884. Removed from Register 1894 1887

"Cardigan" Steamship Co. Ld. Regd. 1907. Vol. liq. 31 Mar. 1921. Certain assets were sold to Anglesea Steamship Co. Ld. in which company shareholders received 9 shares for every 25 shares held, *plus* £1 5*s.* per share in cash at 25 Nov. 1921 further payments (if any) not known. Final meeting return regd. 29 May 1922 1922

Cardigan United Mines Ld. Regd. 1886. Removed from Register 1906 1891

Cardinal & Harford Ld. In May 1922 Cardinal & Harford (London & Persia) Ld. acquired the undertaking and assets for £10,000 in cash, £30,000 fully-paid preference shares and £100,000 fully-paid ordinary shares of 5s. At 16 Jan. 1929 42,953 ordinary shares had not been allotted 1929

Cardinal & Hartford (London & Persia) Ld. Regd. 1922. Vol. liq. (creditors') 28 Apr. 1930. Assets realised insufficient to meet claim of debenture holder. Undertaking was acquired by Cardinal & Harford Ld. Final meeting return regd. 13 Mar. 1931 1931

Cardinal Prospecting Syndicate Ld. Regd. 1910. Vol. liq. (members') 2 Feb. 1932. Capital returned to contributories— $\frac{7}{16}$*d.* per share of £1. £12 1*s.* 3*d.* was paid into Companies' Liquidation Account in respect of unclaimed distributions. Final meeting return regd. 24 June 1940 1932

Cardonald Housing Corporation Ld. Regd. 1926. Vol. liq. 9 Dec. 1929. Final meeting return regd. 6 Aug. 1946 .... *1930

Cardwell & Co. Ld. Regd. 1889 as Chester Road Brewery Co. Ld.; name changed July 1889 to Cox's Brewery Ld. and as above in June 1894. Vol. liq. 18 July 1899. Business acquired by Wilson's Brewery Ld. Final meeting return regd. 12 Apr. 1900 1900

Care & Marquand Shipping Co. Ld. Regd. 1919. Struck off Register 8 Mar. 1935 1936

Carenero Railway & Navigation Co. Ld. Regd. 1888. Undertaking taken over by Carenero Spoorweg en Stoomvaart Maatschappij. Vol. liq. 11 July 1895. Final meeting return regd. 28 May 1896 1900

Carey United Rubber Estates Ld. Regd. Edinburgh 1909. Vol. liq. Jan. 1920. Undertaking and assets were acquired by Jugra Land and Carey Ld., in which company shareholders were entitled to 2½ shares of £1 (credited as fully-paid) for each share of £1 held. Final meeting return regd. 11 Sep. 1922 1920

Cargill Steam Trawling Co. Ld. Regd. 1897. Vol. liq. 17 Aug. 1920. Capital returned to contributories—£1 per share; further payments (if any) not known. Final meeting return regd. 29 Aug. 1925 1921

Cariboo Consolidated Ld. Regd. 1897. Vol. liq. 22 Feb. 1905. Reconstructed as company of same name. Shareholders were entitled to apply for ordinary shares of £1 (credited with 17*s.* paid). Final meeting return regd. 22 Mar. 1907 1908

**See Stock Exchange Year-Book.*

VOL. FOR

Cariboo Consolidated Ld. Regd. 1904. Vol. liq. Oct. 1909. Struck off Register 1922 .... **1910**

Cariboo Gold Fields Ld. Regd. 1900. Vol. liq. 2 May 1906. Removed from Register 1907 .... **1907**

Cariboo Mining Syndicate Ld. Regd. 1910. Struck off Register 18 Feb. 1936 .... **1936**

Caridad Copper Mining Co. Ld. Regd. 1899. Struck off the Register 1930 .... **1931**

Cark & District Electricity Co. Ld. Regd. 1924. Dissolved 1 Apr. 1948, undertaking being vested in the British (later Central) Electricity Authority and North-Western Area Board under the Electricity Act 1947. Holders of ordinary shares and 5% debentures were entitled to receive British Electricity 5% guaranteed stock (1968–73) as follows: £4 7s. 6d. stock for each £1 ordinary capital held and £101 10s. stock for each £100 debenture capital held ... **1949**

Carl Rosa Opera Co. Ld. See Royal Carl Rosa Opera Co. Ld.

Carliol Investment Trust Ld. Regd. 1907 as Waste Heat & Gas Electrical Generating Stations Ld.; name changed 1948. Vol. liq. 12 June 1980. Ordinary shareholders received under scheme of arrangement 3·67616 units in Target Energy fund for every share held. Final meeting held 15 Feb. 1982 .... **1982–3**

Carlisle & Border Counties Insurance Co. Ld. Regd. 1908. Vol. liq. (members') 12 Dec 1951. Final meeting return regd. 5 Mar. 1952................ **1940**

Carlisle & Cumberland Banking Co. Ld. Established 1836. Regd 1880, Vol. liq. 20 Mar. 1911. Undertaking and assets were acquired by Bank of Liverpool Ld. (later Martins Bank Ld.) in which company shareholders entitled to 2 shares of £100 (credited with £12 10s. paid) plus £8 15s. in cash for every 5 shares of £20 (£5 paid) held. Struck off Register 14 July 1970 .... **1912**

Carlisle & District Transport Co. Ld. Regd. 1899 as City of Carlisle Electric Tramways Co. Ld. name changed Apr. 1926. Vol. liq. (members') 20 Oct. 1932. Undertaking was acquired by Ribble Motor Services Ld. £4 12s. 8d. was paid into Companies' Liquidation Account in respect of unclaimed dividends. Final meeting return regd. 23 June 1933.... **1933**

Carlisle Bread & Flour Co. Ld. Regd. 1900 as Carr's (Carlisle) Bread & Flour Co. Ld.; name changed 29 Mar. 1905. Vol. liq. 12 Apr. 1920. Final meeting return regd. 9 June 1920...................... **1921**

Carlisle City & District Banking Co. Ld. Established 1837. Regd. 1880. Vol. liq. 26 Aug. 1896. Business was acquired by London and Midland Bank Ld. (later Midland Bank Ld.) **1896**

Carlisle Gold Mining Co. Ld. Regd. 1886. Vol. liq. 29 Nov. 1889. Reconstructed as Golden Leaf Ld., in which company shareholders were entitled to 1 share of £1 (credited with 17s. 6d.) paid) for each share of £1 held. Final meeting return regd. 13 July 1892 .... **1890**

Carlisle New Brewery Co. Ld. Regd. 1899. Vol. liq. 18 June 1918. Company taken over by Central Control Board (Liquor Traffic) in Aug. 1916. Final meeting return regd. 10 Jan. 1919 .... **1919**

Carlisle Plaster & Cement Co. Ld. Regd. 1911. Vol. liq. 6 June 1917. Final meeting return regd. 11 Mar. 1919 **1918**

Carlshamn Spirit Co. Ld. Regd. 1888. Removed from Register 1903 .... **1901**

Carlton Bank Ld. Regd. 1880. Vol. liq. 9 Apr. 1901 Capital returned to contributories—8s. per 1st preference share of £1; further payments (if any) not known. Final meeting return regd. 13 Apr. 1926 **1902**

Carlton (Edinburgh) Hotel Co. Ld. Regd. in Edinburgh 1901. Vol. liq. 31 Oct. 1939. Struck off Register 12 Oct. 1951 .... **1953**

Carlton Hotel Ld. Regd. 1899. Vol. liq. (members') 28 May 1951. Capital returned to contributories—£10 4s 7d. per £10 preference stock and 16s. 5½d. per £1 ordinary stock; ordinary stockholders were also entitled to receive £225 5% debenture stock, £60 preferred ordinary and £80 ordinary stock in Ritz Hotel (London) Ld. and 20 ordinary stock units (of 6s. 8d.) and 5 deferred stock units (of 1d.) in Ritz Hotel Development Co. Ld. per £100 stock, £3,120 8s. 0d. was paid into Companies' Liquidation Account. Final meeting return regd. 17 Aug. 1953 **1954**

Carlton Hotels (South Africa) Ld. Regd. 1902. Vol. liq. 13 Sept. 1921. Final meeting return regd. 20. Apr. 1923 .... **1922**

Carlton Iron Co. Ld. Regd. 1870 as North of England Industrial Iron and Coal Co. name changed May 1877. Vol. liq. 25 June 1914. for reconstruction as company of same name. Holders of shares and debentures were entitled to fully-paid shares and debentures respectively in new company at par. Final meeting return regd. 31 July 1916 .... **1915**

VOL. FOR

Carlton Iron Co. Ld. Regd. 1914 Vol. liq. 2. May 1923. Undertaking and assets were aquired by Dorman Long & Co. Ld. Final meeting return regd. 17 May 1935 .... **1924**

Carlton Main Colliery Co. Ld. Regd. 1872 as Yorkshire & Derbyshire Coal & Iron Co. Ld.; name changed 1900. Vol. liq. (members') 14 May 1952. Returns to contributories, £2 5s. 3·75d cash per 10s. stock and shares in Carlton Hldgs. Ld. at rate of 44·80983 shares of £1 per £50 stock held. £9,273 5s 6d. was paid into Companies' Liquidation Account. Final meeting return regd. 4 Aug. 1962 .... **1963**

Carlton Shoe Co. Ld. Regd. 1928. Vol. liq. (creditors') 10 Dec. 1931. Debenture holders received 3s. 9d. in £. No capital returned to contributories. Final meeting return regd. 4 Jan. 1934 .... **1932**

Carluke Gas Co. Ld. Regd. in Edinburgh 1898. Dissolved 1 May 1949. undertaking being vested in Scottish Area Gas Board under Gas Act 1948. Holders of ordinary shares (of £1) were entitled to receive £3 5s. British Gas 3% 1 guaranteed stock 1990–95 for each share held **1952**

Carlyle Consolidated Gold Mines, Ld. Regd. 1897. Vol. liq. 1 Aug. 1901. for the purpose of amalgamation with El Mundo (Mexico) Gold Mining Co. Ld. and reconstruction as King's Treasury Gold Mines, Ld. Under scheme of reconstruction shares were issued (one new for one old) credited with 7s. 6d. paid. Struck off Register 31 Dec. 1949 .... **1950**

Carlyle Gold Mines Ld. Regd. 1894. Vol. liq. 17 Feb. 1897. Reconstructed as Carlyle Consolidated Gold Mines Ld., in which company shareholders were entitled to 1 share of £1 (credited with 17s. 6d. paid) for each share of £1 held. Final meeting return regd. 22 Aug. 1900 .... **1901**

Carlyle (Thomas) Ld. Regd. 1897. Reconstructed 1907 at Buttons Ld., in which company shareholders were entitled to 5 preference shares of £1 (credited as fully-paid) for each preference share of £5 held or 4 ordinary shares of £1 (credited as fully-paid) for each ordinary share of £5 held. Removed from Register 1909 .... **1908**

Carmarthen & Cardigan Railway Co. Inc. by Special Act 1864. Undertaking sold to Great Western Railway Co. from 1 Sept. 1881 for £245,700. G.W.Rly. assumed liability for rent charges, rent charge stock and debenture stock.................... **1882**

Carmarthen Electric Supply Co. Ld. Regd. 1909. Dissolved 1 Apr. 1948, undertaking being vested in the British (later Central) Electricity Authority and South Wales Area Board under the Electricity Act 1947. Ordinary shareholders were entitled to receive £3 British Electricity 3% guaranteed stock (1968–73) for each share of £1) held **1949**

Carmarthen Gas Co. Inc. by Special Act 1870. Dissolved 1 May 1949. undertaking being vested in Wales Area Gas Board under Gas Act 1948. Holders of securities were entitled to receive British Gas 3% guaranteed stock 1990–95 as follows in respect of each £25 unit, unless otherwise stated, of security held:

	£ s. d.
Orig. ord. shares (7½% max.)	40 0 0
New ord. shares (7% max.)	37 10 0
5% pref. shares................	28 15 0
4% pref. shares................	25 3 0
4% deb. stock (per £100)..................	102 10 0
5% deb. stock (per £100)..................	125 0 0	**1952**

Carmarthenshire Electric Power Co. Inc. by Special Act 1903. Under Act of 1905 the powers were acquired by South Wales Electrical Power Distribution Co. (later South Wales Electric Power Co.) for £1,000 cash and 1,800 fully-paid shares of £10 .... **1908**

Carmelite Trust Ld. Regd. 1928. Vol. liq. 10 July 1931. Court Order to wind up 27 July 1931. Struck off Register 16 Aug. 1938 .... **1939**

Carmen Alto Mining Co. Ld. Regd. 1892. Vol. liq. 23 Mar. 1896. Final meeting return regd. 17 Nov. 1898 **1897**

Carmen Copper Mines Ld. Regd. 1900. Struck off Register 19 Mar. 1907 - **1908**

Carmen Mines of El Oro Ld. Regd. 1909. Vol. liq. 11 Nov. 1911. Property was sold to Consolidated Mines of El Oro Ld. In which company shareholders were entitled to 1 fully-paid share of £1 for every share of £1 held. Final meeting return regd. 16 Feb. 1923 **1912**

Carmichael (James) (Contractors) Ld. Regd. 1921. Vol. liq. (members') 1 July 1935. Capital returned to contributories—£76,939 to sundry preference shares of £1 £2. 9s. 0½d. per ordinary share of £1. Final meeting return regd. 24 Apr. 1937 .... **1936**

Carmichael Soap & Perfumery Co. Ld. Regd. 1908. Struck off Register 23 Aug. 1949 .... **1911**

Carmont Elastic Wheel Ld. Regd. 1891. Struck off Register 14 May 1897 .... **1910**

See Stock Exchange Year-Book.

VOL. FOR

Carn Brea & Tincroft Mines Ld. Regd. 1896. Reconstructed 1900 as company of same name (later Tincroft Mines Ld.) in which company shareholders were entitled to 1 ordinary or priority share of £1 (credited with 15s. paid) for each ordinary or priority share of £1 held. Removed from Register 1908 ..... **1908**

Carn Brea & Tincroft Mines Ld. Regd. 1900. *See* Tincroft Mines Ld.

Carn Brea Mine. Established under cost book system. In 1896 the undertaking was acquired by Carn Brea & Tincroft Mines Ld. in which company shareholders were entitled to 6 shares of £1 (credited with 10s. paid) for each share held - **1897**

Carnarvon Brickworks Ld. Regd. 1908 as New Parkia Brick Co. Ld.; name changed Sept. 1913. Receiver was appointed in Aug. 1930 and sold the works. Struck off Register Oct. 1934 ..... **1935**

Carnarvon Copper Mining Co. Ld. Regd. 1900. Vol. liq. 26 Nov. 1883. Final meeting return regd. 12 Dec. 1884 ..... ***1884**

Carnarvon (Selangor) Rubber Co. Ld. Regd. 1910. Vol. liq. (members') 10 Jan. 1952 for amalgamation with Sungei Buloh Rubber Co. Ld. in which company shareholders were entitled to receive £1 stock plus 2·108832d. cash for each share of £1 held. £1 8s. 11d. was paid into Companies' Liquidation Account. Final meeting return regd. 16 Mar. 1953 ..... **1954**

Carnarvonshire Great Consols Lead Mining Co. Ld. Regd. 1881. Removed from Register 1888 ..... ***1886**

Carnforth Gas Co. Ld. Regd. 1871. Dissolved 1 May 1949, undertaking being vested in North Western Area Gas Board under Gas Act 1948. Holders of ordinary shares (of £10) were entitled to receive £19 British Gas 3% guaranteed stock 1990—95 for each share held **1952**

Carnforth Hæmatite Iron Co. Ld. Regd. 1864. Struck off Register 29 July 1902 ..... **1930**

Carnforth Hematite Iron Co. (1915) Ld. Regd. 1915. Vol. liq. (creditors') 24 Mar. 1931. Capital returned to debenture holders—18·34%; no return of capital to contributories. Final meeting return regd. 18 Aug. 1931 ..... **1923**

Carnon Valley (Cornwall) Ld. Regd. 1913. Vol. liq. 18 Oct. 1918. Final meeting return regd. 28 Jan. 1921 ..... **1919**

Carolina Development Syndicate Ld. Regd. 1906. Vol. liq. 8 Aug. 1919. Final meeting return regd. 21 Apr. 1920 ..... **1920**

Carolina Gold Mines Ld. Regd. 1910. Struck off Register 1914 ..... **1912**

Caroni Sugar Estates (Trinidad) Ld. Regd. 1924. Vol. liq. (members') 30 Nov. 1937. The undertaking was acquired by Caroni Ld. in which company shareholders were entitled to 1 preference share of £1 (credited as fully-paid) for every 4 preference shares of 5s. held or 105 fully-paid ordinary shares of 2s. plus 7s. 9¾d. cash for every 52 ordinary shares of 2s. held. Final meeting return regd. 28 Feb. 1939 ..... **1938**

Carpathanian Mines Ld. Regd. 1907. Vol. liq. 31 Dec. 1909. Struck off Register 16 July 1915 ..... ***1911**

Carpathian Oil Co. Ld. Regd. 1911. Vol. liq. 20 July 1927. Final meeting return regd. 25 Oct. 1927 ..... **1928**

Carpet Trades Ld. *See* C.X.T. Ld.

Carr & Co. Ld. Regd. 1881. Removed from Register 1906 ..... **1888**

Carr & Co. Ld. *See* Cavenham Ld.

Carr (Charles) Ld. *See* Cornwall Property (Holdings) Ld.

Carr Hill Mills Ld. *See* Danesbury Estates Ld.

Carr Mine & Colorado Co. Ld. Regd. 1900. Removed from Register 1907 ..... **1906**

Carr, Wild & Co. Ld. Regd. 1909. Vol. liq. 3 Feb. 1921. Undertaking acquired by Sheffield Steel Products Ld. Final meeting return regd. 9 Aug. 1921 ..... ***1921**

Carreg-y-Llan Quarries Ld. Regd. 1920. Vol. liq. (members') 14 June 1935. Undertaking was acquired by Amalgamated Roadstone Corporation Ld. Final meeting return regd. 14 Aug. 1936 ..... **1936**

Carriage Insurance Co. Ld. Regd. 1891. Vol. liq. 17 Nov. 1897. Absorbed by Imperial Live Stock Insurance Association Ld. Final meeting return regd. 5 Aug. 1904 ..... ***1899**

Carrickfergus & Larne Railway Co. Inc. by Special Act 1860. Under Belfast and Northern Counties Railway Act 1890 undertaking was amalgamated 1 July 1890 with that company in which holders of ordinary shares of £25 received an equal amount of ordinary stock and 4% debenture stockholders an equal amount of debenture stock **1891**

Carrington Gold Mining Co. Ld. Regd. 1892. Reconstructed 1897 as Lady Cascade Gold Mines Ld., in which company shareholders were entitled to 2 shares of 5s. (credited with 3s. 9d. paid) for each share of 12s. 6d. held. Removed from Register 1907 ..... **1899**

Carrington's Lion P. C. Mining Co. Ld. Inc. Queensland 1905. Vol. liq. Nov. 1906 for amalgamation with Carrington's Excess Ground Gold Mining Co. Ld. as Carrington's United Mines Ld. Shareholders were entitled to receive 1 share in new company for each share held **1907**

Carrington's United Mines Ld. Inc. Queensland 1906. In Nov. 1913 it was stated that a deposit had been received and an option granted for sale of all company's assets **1914**

Carrizal & Cerro Blanco Railway Co. Inc. Chile 1866 & 1880. Vol. liq. in Oct. 1925 was legally authorised by Chilian Government in Dec. 1925 ..... **1927**

Carrizal Share Trust Ld. Regd. 1900. Vol. liq. 30 Oct. 1916. Capital returned to contributories—5s. per share of £1 at Nov. 1916; further payments (if any) not known. Final meeting return regd. 28 June 1918 ..... **1917**

Carron Grove Paper Co. Ld. Regd. Edinburgh 1877. Vol. liq. Feb. 1923. Undertaking and assets were acquired by Esparto Paper Mills Ld. [later Carrongrove Paper Co. Ld.]. Capital returned to contributories—£11 per 1st or 2nd preference share of £10; £7 13s. 3d. per ordinary share of £5. Final meeting return regd. 18 Aug. 1923. Restored to Register 15 Nov. 1924. Struck off Register 26 Sept. 1933 ..... **1924**

Carr's (Carlisle) Bread & Flour Co. Ld. *See* Carlisle Bread & Flour Co. Ld.

Carsevène & Developments Anglo-French Gold Mining Co. Ld. Regd. 1900. Reconstructed 1903 as company of same name. Shareholders were entitled to apply for shares of £1 (credited with 17s. paid) in new company. Removed from Register 1904 ..... **1908**

Carsevène & Developments Anglo-French Gold Mining Co. Ld. Inc. Guernsey 1903. Secretary stated on 12 Dec. 1907 that company "is practically dead" **1908**

Carshalton (B.M.L.) Mines No Liability. Inc. Victoria 1934. Vol. liq. 22 Feb. 1940 ..... **1941**

Carson (Tailors) Ld. Undertaking and assets were acquired by Mortimers (London) Ld. **1929**

Carta Para Gold Mining Co. Ld. Regd. 1881. Court Orders: to wind up Sept. 1882; to dissolve Aug. 1889 ..... **1883**

Cartagena (Colombia) Railway Co. Ld. *See* Colombia Railways & Navigation Co. Ld.

Cartagena (Colombia) Waterworks Co. Ld. Regd. 1905. Court Order to wind up 28 July 1940. Liquidator released 3 July 1942. Struck off Register 5 Oct. 1945 ..... **1946**

Cartagena (Spain) District Water Supply Co. Ld. Regd. 1906. Removed from Register 24 Feb. 1911 ..... ***1910**

Cartago Ld. Regd. 1884. Court Orders; to wind up 8 May 1886; to dissolve 27 June 1893 ..... **1888**

"Cartavio" Sugar Co. (Peru) Ld. Regd. 1890. Vol. liq. Apr. 1909. Undertaking and assets were sold to "Cartavio" Sugar Co. of West Virginia. Shareholders received 4,000 new shares for the 9,740 held and debenture stockholders received $90,072 new 1st debenture stock for the £13,500 debenture stock held. Removed from Register 1910 ..... **1910**

Carter (H. W.) & Co. Ld. Regd. 1898. Vol. liq. 25 Oct. 1920. Undertaking and assets were acquired by Bristol Industries Ld. Final meeting return regd. 25 May 1921 ..... **1921**

Carter's Deep Leads Ld. Inc. Guernsey 1906 ..... **1913**

Carthage & Adirondack Railway. Chartered New York 1883. Merged 1913 into New York Central & Hudson River Railroad Co. **1913**

Carthagena Mining & Water Co. Ld. Regd. 1889 as Carthagena Waterworks Co. Ld.; name changed 1907. Vol. liq. (members') 29 Mar. 1946. Capital returned to contributories—1s. 7 ⁹⁄₆₄d. per ordinary share (of £1). £70 8s. was paid into Companies' Liquidation Account. Final meeting return regd. 30 Apr. 1955 ..... **1956**

Carthagena Waterworks Co. Ld. *See* above.

Cartland (James) & Son Ld. Regd. 1899. Winding-up order 17 May 1954. Capital returned to contributories—31s. 7¼d. per share of 5s. Liquidator released 24 Feb. 1958. Struck off Register 28 Feb. 1961 ..... **1959**

Carton (Joseph) & Co. Ld. Regd. 1925. Vol. liq. (members') 18 Aug. 1931. Capital returned to contributories—25s. 3d. per share of £1. Final meeting return regd. 31 Mar. 1932 ..... **1932**

Carver Looms Ld. Regd. 1899. The assets were purchased in 1903 by Textile Appliances Ld. for £12,500 in shares. Removed from Register 1907 ... **1913**

Carway Collieries Ld. Regd. 1927. All shares were owned by Amalgamated Anthracite Collieries Ld. Struck off Register 10 Mar. 1939 ..... **1939**

Casano Copper Mining & Smelting Co. Ld. Inc. Guernsey 1902. Dissolved before 1949 ..... **1905**

Cascade (1906) Power Co. Ld. Regd. 1906. The outstanding 4% 1st mortgage debenture stock was called for redemption 1 Mar. 1910. Vol. liq. Sept. 1910. Capital returned to contributories—1s. per

VOL. FOR

share of £1 in Nov. 1910; further payments (if any) not known. Removed from Register 1911 .... **1911**

Cascade Water, Power & Light Co. Ld. Inc. British Columbia 1897. The 1st mortgage 4½% 33-year sinking fund gold coupon bonds were called for redemption at par on 1 May 1932 .... **1937**

Cascalho Syndicate Ld. Regd. 1914. Struck off Register 18 Feb. 1936 .... **1936**

Casebourne & Co. Ld. Regd. 1882. Vol. liq. 25 May 1926. The assets were transferred to Casebourne & Co. (1926) Ld. 100,000 fully-paid shares of that company were allotted to shareholders of this company. Dissolved before 1931 .... **1927**

Casebourne & Co. (1926) Ld. Regd. 1926. Vol. liq. (members') 31 Dec. 1943. The undertaking was transferred to the controlling company, Imperial Chemical Industries Ld. Final meeting return regd. 31 June 1949 .... **1950**

Casey Cobalt Mining Co. Ld. Regd. 1907. Vol. liq. 8 Nov. 1920. Removed from Register 22 May 1923 **1921**

Casey Developments Co. Ld. Regd. 1913. Struck off Register 1929 .... ***1924**

Cashman s Brilliant Reward Claim Gold Mining Co. Ld. Regd. 1894. Vol. liq. 27 Aug. 1895. Reconstructed as Ethel-Hope Gold Mines Ld. in which company-shareholders were entitled to 4 shares of 5s. (credited with 3s. 6d. paid) for each share of £1 held. Final meeting return regd. 23 Dec. 1897 .... **1897**

Cashwell Lead Mining Co. Ld. Regd. 1865. Vol. liq. 22 Oct. 1891. Final meeting return regd. 15 Sept. 1892 **1892**

Casino Municipal de Cannes Ld. Regd. 1906. Vol. liq. Apr. 1922. Shareholders were entitled to 1 fully-paid bearer share of Frs.100 in Societe d'Exploitation de Casinos et d'Hotels for every 4 shares of £1 held. Struck off Register 1932 .... **1923**

Caslon (H. W.) & Co. Ld. Regd. 1900. Vol. liq. (creditors') 11 Jan. 1937. Assets realised insufficient to pay unsecured creditors in full. Final meeting return regd. 28 May 1940 .... **1937**

Casoid Ld. Regd. 1923. Vol. liq. 25 May 1927. All ordinary shares were owned by Dunlop Rubber Co. Ld. [later Dunlop Co. Ld.]. Final meeting return regd. 6 Oct. 1928 .... **1928**

Cason Gold Mines Ld. Inc. Transvaal 1902. Vol. liq. May 1908. Undertaking was acquired by East Rand Proprietary Mines Ld. in which company share-holders were entitled to 1 share of £1 (credited as fully-paid) for each share of £1 held **1909**

Cassa di Sconto e di Risparmio. Inc. Alexandria 1887 **1934**

Casse (J.) & Fils Ld. Regd. 1895. Vol. liq. Feb. 1907. Capital returned to contributories—1s. 3d. per preference share of £1 in Oct. 1907; further payments (if any) not known. The outstanding 5% 1st mortgage debentures were redeemed on 19 Dec. 1906. Removed from Register 1911 .... **1908**

Cassel Clydesdale (Springs) Gold Mines Ld. Inc. Transvaal 1919. Vl. liq. Apr. 1929 .... ***1930**

Cassel Coal Co. Ld. Inc. Transvaal 1893 as Cassel Colliery Co. Ld.; name changed Aug. 1895. Vol. liq. Feb. 1921. Undertaking and assets sold to South African Coal Estates (Witbank) Ld. in which company shareholders received 2 shares of £1 for each share of £1 held, together with an option (since expired) to subscribe for further shares **1922**

Cassel Cyanide Co. Ld. Regd. 1884 as Cassel Gold Extracting Co. Ld.; name changed 1906. Vol. liq. (members') 30 June 1941. All capital owned by I.C.I. (General Chemicals) Ld. Final meeting return regd. 22 Jan. 1942 .... **1942**

Cassel Tramways Co. Ld. Regd. 1877. Court Orders: to wind up 3 June 1879; to dissolve 18 Nov. 1885 ... ***1880**

Cassidy Hill Coolgardie Gold Mines Ld. Regd. Edinburgh 1894. Vol. liq. July 1898 for reconstruction as Paringa Consolidated Mines Ld. Final meeting return regd. 3 Mar. 1899 .... **1902**

Cassinga Concessions Ld. Regd. 1895. Vol. liq. 18 Oct. 1920. No return was made to shareholders. Final meeting return regd. 24 Nov. 1920 .... **1921**

Cassio Ld. Regd. 1917. Receiver appointed in Mar. 1922. Assets realised insufficient to repay 1st debentures. Struck off Register Dec. 1930 .... **1931**

Casswell Ld. Regd. 1896. Vol. liq. 2 Feb. 1905. Removed from Register 1907 .... **1905**

Castañeda (Havana) Cigar Factories Ld. Regd. 1904. Vol. liq. July 1911. Removed from Register 1913 **1912**

Castara Estates Ld. Regd. 1908. Vol. liq. 20 Nov. 1912. Final meeting return regd. 31 Jan. 1925............. **1913**

Castellana Consolidated Mines Ld. Regd. 1901. Vol. liq. 29 Dec. 1915. Final meeting return regd. 16 June 1920 .... **1916**

Castellon Oil Co. Ld. Regd. 1910. Receiver appointed in Dec. 1914. Struck off Register May 1929 .... **1930**

VOL. FOR

Castilla Rubber Plantations Ld. Regd. 1910. Vol. liq. 27 Nov. 1911. Winding up continued under supervision of Court Apr. 1912. Final meeting return regd. 25 June 1914 .... **1912**

Castillion (Pyrenees) Mining Co. Ld. Regd. Dec. 1886. Vol. liq. 30 June 1893. Final meeting return regd. 21 Aug. 1894 .... **1894**

Castle Arcade Co. Ld. Regd. 1886. Vol. liq. 8 Jan. 1907. Removed from Register 1907 .... **1907**

Castle Cary Gas & Coke Co. Ld. Constituted by Deed of Settlement 1853; regd. as limited 1896. Dissolved 1 May 1949, undertaking being vested in South Western Area Gas Board under Gas Act 1948. Holders of securities were entitled to receive British Gas 3%, guaranteed stock 1990–95 as follows:

	£	s.	d.
Ord. shares (of £5)...............	10	5	0
3¾% debs. (per £100)............	100	0	0	**1952**

Castle Douglas Gas Co. Ld. Regd. in Edinburgh 1935. Dissolved 1 May 1949, undertaking being vested in Scottish Area Gas Board under Gas Act 1948. Holders of shares (of 1s.) were entitled to receive 1s. 4¼d. British Gas 3% guaranteed stock 1990–95 for each share held. **1952**

Castle General Insurance Co. Ld. Regd. 1898. Court Order to wind up 12 Dec. 1905. Liquidator released 14 Aug. 1908. Removed from Register 10 Mar. 1911 ***1907**

Castle Gold Exploration Syndicate Ld. Regd. 1896. Vol. liq. 11 Nov. 1902. Capital returned to contributories—15s. per share of £1 at Feb. 1903; further payments (if any) not known. Removed from Register 1904 .... **1903**

Castle (Henry) & Sons Ld. Regd. 1894, Vol. liq. 14 Dec. 1904. Removed from Register 1909. .... **1905**

Castle Ld. Regd. 1903. Court Order to wind up 1905. Struck off Register 1914 .... **1906**

Castle Steel & Ironworks Co. Ld. Regd. 1882. Court Orders: to wind up 16 Jan. 1883; to dissolve June 1888 .... **1884**

Castleblaney, Keady & Armagh Railway Co. Inc. by Special Act 1900 as Kingscourt, Keady & Armagh Railway Co.; name changed by Act of 1902......... **1912**

Castlecary Fireclay Co. Ld. Regd. Edinburgh 1919. Vol. liq. (members') 3 Jan. 1939 for amalgamation with Glenboig Union Fireclay Co. Ld. in which company shareholders were entitled to 1 share of £1 for each share (ordinary or preference of £1 held) **1940**

Castlecomer Railway. Under terms of Irish Free State Railways Act 1924 the undertaking was acquired by Great Southern Railways Co. from 1 Jan. 1929.... **1941**

Castledale Steamship Co. Ld. Regd. 1882. Vol. liq. 22 Sept. 1894. Final meeting return regd. 10 Feb. 1896 ***1886**

Castlederg & Victoria Bridge Tramway Co. Inc. by Special Act 1883. Court Order to wind up Nov. 1933 **1934**

Castleford & Whitwood Gaslight Coke Co. Inc. by Special Act 1878. Dissolved 1 May 1949, undertaking being vested in North Eastern Area Gas Board under Gas Act 1948. Holders of securities were entitled to receive, in respect of each £100 unit held, British Gas 3% guaranteed stock 1990–95 as follows:

	£	s.	d.
Orig. stock (10% stand.).......................285		0	0
Addit. stock (7% stand.)........................225		0	0
3¾% red. deb. stock 100		10	0
Liability in respect of certain mortgage loans assumed by the Board....................................			**1952**

Castlegate Steamship Co. Ld. Regd. 1882. Vol. liq. 19 June 1893. Final meeting return regd. 25 Sept. 1894 ***1886**

Casualty Insurance Co. Ld. Regd. 1904. Court Order to wind up 9 Aug. 1908. Liquidator released 26 Nov. 1913. Struck off Register 3 Sept.1918 .... ***1909**

Catalana Tinplate Co. Ld. Regd. 1912. Vol. liq. 1 Dec. 1914. Final meeting return regd. 11 Aug. 1917 .... ***1916**

Catalina Gold Mines Ld. Regd. 1893. Struck off Register 18 Nov. 1902 .... **1903**

Catalinas Warehouses & Mole Co. Ld. Regd. 1897. Vol. liq. (members') 28 Feb. 1946. Capital returned to contributories; preference shares (of £5)—£7 19s. 6d.; ordinary shares (of £2), £3 3s. 9¾d. Amounts paid into Companies' Liquidation Account in respect of unclaimed dividends £830 9s. 2d.; unclaimed distributions £2,610 5s. Final meeting return regd. 17 June 1963 .... **1964**

Catalinas Warehouse and Mole Company of Buenos Aires. Established 1875. Undertaking acquired in 1897 by Catalinas Warehouses and Mole Co. Ld. Holders of each £100 debentures were entitled to about £50 debentures and £65 preference shares in the new company, Ordinary shareholders received £2 ordinary shares in new company for each ordinary share of $100 held **1899**

Catalogue Publishing Co. Ld. See Country Gentlemen's Association Ld.

*See Stock Exchange Year-Book.

VOL. FOR

Cataract Barberton Gold Mining Co. Ld. Regd. 1896. Vol. liq. 11 July 1900. Reconstructed as Cataract Gold Mining Co. Ld., in which company shareholders were entitled to 1 share of 10*s.* (credited with 7*s.* 6*d.* paid) for each share of £1 held. Final meeting return regd. 22 Apr. 1921 .... **1907**

Cataract Gold Mining Co. Ld. Regd. 1900. Vol. liq. 19 Mar. 1907. Final meeting return regd. 6 Apr. 1922 **1908**

Caterham & District Gas Co. Inc. by Special Act 1902. In 1905 undertaking was transferred to Croydon Gas Co. Holders of preference or ordinary shares were entitled to an equal amount of D and E stocks respectively in acquiring company, which also assumed liability for debenture stock and other debts **1905**

Caterham and District Gas Light and Coke Co. Ld. Regd. 1869 as Caterham and Kenley Gas Co. Ld.: name changed Oct. 1885. Undertaking and assets were acquired by Caterham & District Gas Co., in which company shareholders were entitled to an equal number of fully-paid shares of same class. Dissolved by Act in 1902 .... **1905**

Caterham and Kenley Gas Co. Ld. *See* Caterham and District Gas Light and Coke Co. Ld.

Caterham Works Ld. *See* Precious Metal Industries Ld.

Cathcart District Railway Co. Inc. by Special Act 1880. In 1923 the undertaking was merged into the London Midland & Scottish Railway Co. in which company stockholders were entitled to stock as follows:

For each £100 held	*L. M. & S.*	
4% Debs. 1880, 1887, & 1890	£100 4% Deb.	
Ordinary Capital	£51 Ordinary	**1924**

Cathedral Consols Mining Co. Estab. 1881. In liquidation in 1889 .... **1889**

Catherine Street Publishing Association Ld. Regd. 1886. Vol. liq. Nov. 1887. Taken over by Macrae, Curtice & Co. Ld. Final meeting return regd. 19 Aug. 1889 **1888**

Catherwood Gold Mines (1898) Ld. Regd. 1898. Reconstructed May 1901 as Amalgamated Gold Mines Ld., in which company shareholders were entitled to 2 shares of 10*s.* (credited with 8*s.* 6*d.* paid) for each share of £1 held. Removed from Register 1902 - **1902**

Catherwood (H. M. S.) Ld. Regd. Belfast 1928. Vol. liq. 27 Feb. 1936. Undertaking acquired in 1935 by Northern Ireland Road Transport Board **1940**

Cathode Corporation Ld. Regd. 1929. Vol. liq. (members') 11 Nov. 1936. No capital returned to contributories. Final meeting return regd. 13 Feb. 1937 .... **1937**

Catholic & General Insurance Association Ld. Regd. Dublin 1913. Vol. liq. Sept 1915. Undertaking and assets sold to Consolidated Assurance Co. Ld., in which company shareholders were to receive 1 fully-paid share of £1 for every 3 partly-paid shares of £1 (10*s.* paid) or 2 fully-paid shares of £1 for every 3 fully-paid shares of £1 held **1916**

Catrine Gas Co. Ld. Regd. in Edinburgh 1898. Dissolved 1 May 1949, undertaking being vested in Scottish Area Gas Board under Gas Act 1948. Holders of ordinary shares (of £1 15*s.*) were entitled to receive £4 15*s.* British Gas 3% guaranteed stock 1990–95 for each share held **1952**

Catseye (Parent) Co. Ld. Regd. 1928. Vol. liq. (members') 16 Sept. 1930. No capital returned to contributories. Final meeting return regd. 10 June 1933 .... **1931**

Cattle Ranche Co. Ld. Regd. 1889. Vol. liq. 28 July 1893. Capital returned to contributories—10*s.* 5½*d.* per share. Final meeting return regd. 1 Nov. 1894 .... **1895**

Cattle Trade Bank Ld. Regd. 1920. Vol. liq. Aug. 1923. Undertaking and assets were acquired by Bank of Liverpool & Martins Ld. (later Martins Bank Ld.). Capital returned to contributories—£1 10*s.* per fully-paid share of £1; 15*s.* per share of £1 (10*s.* paid). Struck off Register 14 July 1970 .... **1924**

Cauca Gold Estates Ld. Regd. Edinburgh 1895. Vol. liq. July 1899. Final meeting return regd. 17 May 1901 **1900**

Caucasian (Tchermoeff) Oilfields Ld. Regd. 1913. Properties in Lands of Soviet Government. Struck off Register 19 Dec. 1947 .... **1948**

Caucasus Asphalte Co. Ld. Regd. 1905. Vol. liq. 27 Dec. 1906. Removed from Register 1914 .... **1907**

Caucasus Copper Co. Ld. Regd. 1900. Vol. liq. (creditors') 18 Dec. 1930. Struck off Register 17 Dec. 1954 **1955**

Caucasus Domains Ld. Regd. 1911. Struck off Register 19 Feb. 1915 .... ***1913**

Caucasus Minerals Syndicate Ld. Regd. 1905. Struck off Register 1916 .... **1910**

Caucasus Silver Lead Mines Ld. Regd. 1906. Removed from Register 1911 .... **1911**

Cauldon (Brown-Westhead, Moore & Co.) Ld. Undertaking and assets acquired by Cauldon Potteries Ld **1924**

VOL. FOR

Cauldon Potteries Ld. Regd. 1920. The freehold and leasehold properties were sold to Mercia Estates Ld. Debenture stockholders were entitled to £5 in shares and £50 in 3% debenture stock in that company for every £100 stock held. No capital returned to contributories. Struck off Register Feb. 1935 ...... **1935**

Caustic Lime & Macadam Co. Ld. *See* Central Portland Cement Co. Ld.

Caustic Soda & Chlorine Syndicate Ld. Regd. 1891. Struck off Register 17 June 1898 .... **1901**

Cavan, Leitrim & Roscommon Light Railway & Tramway Co. Ld. *See* Cavan and Leitrim Railway Co. Ld.

Cavan and Leitrim Railway Co. Ld. Regd. 1883, under the Tramways and Public Companies (Ireland) Act, 1883, as Cavan, Leitrim & Roscommon Light Railway & Tramway Co. Ld.; name changed in 1895. In 1925 the undertaking was merged into the Great Southern Railways Co., stockholders were entitled to £125 Great Southern Railways 4% Preference Stock for every £100 stock held **1925**

Cavehill & Whitewell Tramway Co. Inc. by Order in Council 1881. Undertaking and assets were sold in 1910 to Belfast Corporation for £56,155 .... **1912**

Cavendish Furniture Co. Ld. Regd. 1929. All capital was owned by British & Colonial Furniture Co. Ld. Vol. liq. (members') 27 Aug. 1965. Final meeting return regd. 10 Dec. 1965 .... **1961**

Cavendish Hotel Co. Ld. Regd. 1899. Receiver appointed Mar. 1906. Removed from Register 29 Aug. 1911 **1910**

Cavendish House Co. Ld. Regd. 1888. Vol. liq. 18 Apr. 1929. Undertaking and assets were acquired by Cavendish House (Cheltenham) Ld. All debentures were repaid at par. In June 1928 Standard Industrial Trust Ld. offered shareholders £25 per ordinary share of £10; £12 10s. per preference share of £10. Final meeting return regd. 8 Aug. 1929 .... **1929**

Cavendish Waterproof Asbestos Sole Co. Ld. Regd. 1896. Vol. liq. 10 Aug. 1897. Final meeting return regd. 31 Jan. 1898 .... **1898**

Cavenham Ld. Regd. 1894 as Carr & Co. Ld.; converted into private company 1908 and into public company 1927.; name changed to Cavenham Foods Ld. 1965; to Cavenham Ld. 1971; to Allied Suppliers (Holdings) Ld. 1981 and to present title 1982. Vol. liq. (members') 17 mar. 1986. All ordinary owned by Generale Occidentale S.A. Holders of preference shares (of £1) received as follows per share on 17 Mar. 1986: 4½%, 107·0712p; 6½%, 107·9918p; 7%, 108·2219p; 7½%, 108·4521p; 10%, 115·0558p........ **1986–7**

Cavenham Foods Ld. *See* Cavenham Ld.

Cawdaw Industrial Holdings Ld. Regd. 12 Feb. 1900 as The British Cotton Wool Dyers' Association Ld.; name changed 1 Oct. 1976; winding-up order made 24 Oct. 1983 .... **1984–5**

Cawdery's Patent Switchback Steeplechase Ld. Regd. 1896. Removed from Register 1902 .... **1902**

Cawley & Co. Ld. Regd. 1886. Business was sold to Fuller's Earth Union Ld. Vol. liq. 19 Dec. 1890. Final meeting return regd. 6 Feb. 1892 .... **1891**

Cawnpore Electric Supply Corporation Ld. Regd. 1905 as Indian Electric Supply & Traction Co. Ld., name changed Mar. 1923. Vol. liq. (members') 25 Oct. 1950. Undertaking campulsorily acquired in Sept. 1947 by Government of United Provinces for £2,135,000 (approx.). Capital returned to contributories— £4 15*s.* per £1 unit of stock. £6,236 3*s.* 1*d.* was paid into Companies' Liquidation Account. Final meeting return regd. 3 Jan. 1957 .... **1958**

Cawood, Wistow & Selby Light Railway Co. Inc. by Special Act 1896. Opened 1897 as a Light Railway subject to Regulation of Railways Act 1868. Under North Eastern Railway Co. Act 1900 line was transferred to that company. Holders of preferred and deferred half shares of £25 and 5% debenture stock were repaid at par **1901**

Cawston Ostrich Farm Ld. Inc. California 1906. Vol. liq. Mar. 1912 .... **1914**

Cawthra (J.) & Co. Ld. Regd. 1891. Vol. liq. 19 June 1968. Capital returned to contributories—20*s.* per preference share (of £1) and 4*s.* *plus* 1·6218*p.* per ordinary stock unit (of 5*s.*). £1,100·80 was paid into Companies' Liquidation Account in respect of unclaimed dividends. Final meeting return regd. 20 Dec. 1972 .... **1974-5**

Caxton Insurance Co. Ld. Regd. 1907 as Printing Trades & General Insurance Co. Ld.; name changed Sept. 1916. Vol. liq. 17 July 1922. Final mseting return regd. 21 Feb. 1928 .... **1923**

Caylloma Silver Mining Co. Ld. Regd. 1890. Vol. liq. 7 May 1906. Removed from Register 1907 .... **1907**

Ceara Gas Company Ld. Regd. 1866. Struck off Register Sept. 1951 .... **1948**

Ceara Harbour Corporation Ld. Regd. 1884. Vol. liq. 23 May 1900. Undertaking was acquired by Brazilian

**See Stock Exchange Year-Book.*

VOL. FOR

Government. Capital returned to contributories—5s. per ordinary share of £10; preference debenture holders received 10s. in £; sterling debenture holders 3s. 6d. in the £; further payments (if any) not known. Removed from Register 1902 ...... **1901**

Ceara Rubber Estates Ld. Regd. 1910. Vol. liq. Apr. 1916. Struck off Register 1927 .... **1916**

Cecil Syndicate Ld. Regd. 1897. In 1908 it was stated that bankers had taken over the property. Removed from Register 1910 .... **1909**

Cedar Creek Gold Mines & Water Co. Ld. Regd. 1872. Vol. liq. 11 Feb. 1879. Final meeting return regd. 29 Jan. 1881 .... *****1879**

Cedar Investment Trust p.l.c. Regd. as private company 25 Sept. 1918.; converted into a public company Nov. 1926. Vol. liq. (members') 17 Dec. 1982. Final meeting held 18 May 1987. Company unitised; ordinary holders received units in TR Income Growth Fund; TR Overseas Growth Fund; TR Special Opportunities Fund; and TR General Growth Fund on basis of 5·834747527 units per ordinary share of 25p. Final distribution made of:

Fund	Unit per share held in Cedar
TR Income Growth	0·03574
TR Overseas Growth	0·04738
TR Special Opportunities	0·02639
TR General Growth	0·04080

Preference holders were repaid at par. Debenture stocks redeemed at par on 18 Dec. 1982 **1987–8**

Cedar Island Gold Mining Co. Ld. Regd. 1897. Vol. liq. 17 Jan. 1900. Final meeting return regd. 29 July 1920 .... **1900**

Cedar Syndicate Ld. Regd. 1909. Struck off Register 1929 .... **1928**

Cedar Valley Land Cattle & Co. Ld. Regd. 1885. Vol. liq. 22 Feb. 1909. Final meeting return regd. 20 Mar. 1919 .... **1909**

Cedars Rapids Manufacturing & Power Co. Inc. Canada by Special Act 1904. The 5% 40-year 1st mortgage sinking fund gold bonds were called for redemption at 110%, on 1 July 1939. Undertaking and assets were acquired in 1943 by Montreal Light Heat and Power Consolidated **1940**

Cefn Gyfelach Colliery Co. Ld. See Tirdonkin Collieries Ld.

Cefn Mawr & Rhos-Y-Medre Gas Co. Ld. Regd. 1865. Dissolved 1 May 1949, undertaking being vested in Wales Area Gas Board under Gas Act 1941. Holders of ordinary shares (of £1) were entitled to receive £1 9s. British Gas 3% guaranteed stock 1990–95 for each share held **1952**

Celebration Gold Mines Ld. Regd. 1925. Vol. liq. 11 May 1926. Capital returned to contributories—2d. per share of 5s. in Oct. 1926; further payments (if any) not known. Final meeting return regd. 6 Sept. 1930 .... **1927**

Celebritone Ld. Regd. 1928. Vol. liq. (members') 11 Feb. 1930. Court Order to continue winding up under supervision 14 Apr. 1930. Assets realised insufficient to pay unsecured creditors in full. Final meeting return regd. 24 June 1932 .... **1930**

Celebrity Gramophones Ld. Regd. 1928 Vol. liq. May 1931. Struck off Register 1935 .... **1932**

Celestion Ld. Regd. 1928. Vol. liq. (members') 9 Apr. 1931. Shareholders were entitled to receive 1 preferred ordinary' share of £1 or deferred ordinary-share of 6d. in company of same name for each preferred ordinary share of £1 or deferred ordinary share of 5s. held respectively. Final meeting return regd. 17 May 1935 .... **1932**

Celestion Ld. Regd. 1931. Vol. liq. (members') 28 Apr. 1950. Capital returned to contributories—34s. 5d. per preference or ordinary share (of £1). Final meeting return regd. 7 Apr. 1953 .... **1953**

Celestion Radio Co. The British Empire business and certain inventions were purchased in 1928 by Celestion Ld. for £69,000 in cash, 400,000 deferred ordinary shares of 5s. and an option (since expired) over 30,000 preferred ordinary shares of £1 at par **1930**

Celluloid Corporation. Merged with Celanese Corporation of America in 1941. Capital not owned by that company was exchanged for 5% series prior preferred stock and common shares of that company **1942**

Celluloid Ld. Regd. 1907. Receiver appointed in Feb. 1909. Struck off Register 1914 .... **1911**

Cellulose Co. Ld. Regd. 1905. Vol. liq. Sept. 1908. Capital returned to contributories 7s. 7½d. per share of £1 further payments (if any) not known. Removed from Register 1908 .... **1909**

Cellulose Holdings & Investment Co. Ld. See International Holdings & Investment Co. Ld.

Celtic Collieries Ld. Regd. 1900 as Elder's Navigation Collieries Ld.; name changed to Elder's Navigation Collieries

VOL. FOR

Ld. in 1910 and as above in 1915. Court Order to wind up Mar. 1930. Struck off Register 1 Sept. 1936 **1937**

Celtic Insurance Co. Ld. Inc. Dublin 1907. Vol. liq. (members') 9 Feb. 1961. Struck off Register Apr. 1962 .... **1940**

Cement Industries Ld. See Rodmell Works Ld.

Cement Waterproofing Co. Ld. Regd. 1931 as Sika Dominion Ld.; name changed Oct. 1933. Court Order to wind up June 1934. Struck off Register 14 Oct. 1938 .... **1939**

Ceniza Gold Mines Ld. Regd. 1911. Vol. liq. 21 May 1914. Final meeting return regd. 6 Dec. 1915 ...... **1915**

Centaur Cycle Co. Ld. Regd. 1897 as New Centaur Cycle Co. Ld.; name changed Jan. 1906. Vol. liq. 15 Nov. 1910. Final meeting return regd. 5 Sept.1912 **1911**

Centenillo Silver Lead Mines Co. Ld. Regd. 1886. Reconstructed 1898 as New Centenillo Silver Lead Mines Co. Ld. Removed from Register 1913........ **1908**

Centennial Gold Mine Ld. Regd. 1885. Vol. liq. June 1888. Final meeting return regd. 31 Dec. 1890 ..... **1889**

Central African & Zoutpansberg Exploration Co. Ld. Regd. 1892. Vol. liq. 13 Sept. 1894. Undertaking was acquired by Oceana Co. Ld. Final meeting return regd. 11 Sept. 1895 .... **1895**

Central African Mining Co. Ld. Regd. Edinburgh 1901. Vol. liq. Dec. 1911. Final meeting return regd. 23 Mar. 1912 .... **1912**

Central African Co. Ld. Regd. 1890. Vol. liq. 9 Nov. 1894. Final meeting return regd. 9 July 1895........ *****1895**

Central America Exploration (Consolidated) Ld. Regd. 1926. Struck off register 9 Jan. 1953 .... **1953**

Central American Association Ld. Regd. 1866. Vol. liq. 5 Feb. 1923. Final meeting return regd. 29 Feb. 1924 **1888**

Central American Mines Ld. Regd. 1913. Vol. liq. 28 Dec. 1916. Reconstructed as Leonesa Mines Ld. in which company shareholders were entitled to 1 share of 4s. (credited with 2s. paid) for each share of 5s. held. Final meeting return regd. 30 Jan. 1930 **1917**

Central American Trust Ld. Regd. 1891. Removed from Register 1901 .... *****1902**

Central & West Boulder Gold Mines Ld. Regd. 1901. Vol. liq. May 1911. Reconstructed as company of same name. Shareholders were entitled to 1 share of 10s. (credited with 8s. paid) for each share of 10s. held. Removed from Register 1913 .... **1912**

Central & West Boulder Gold Mines Ld. Regd. 1911. Vol. liq. 1 Nov. 1928. Final meeting return regd. 26 Jan. 1929 .... **1929**

Central & West Boulder Gold Mines (W. A.) Ld. Regd. 1898. Reconstructed 1901 as Central & West Boulder Gold Mines Ld., in which company shareholders were entitled to 1 share of £1 (credited with 17s. paid) for each share of £1 held. Removed from Register 1902 .... **1902**

Central Ankobra Syndicate Ld. Regd. 1900. Removed from Register 1903 .... **1903**

Central Argentine (Carpa Valley) Exploration Co. Ld. Regd. 1888. Removed from Register 1906 .... **1892**

Central Argentine Gold Fields Ld. Regd. 1887. Removed from Register 1906 .... **1892**

Central Argentine Land Co. Ld. Regd. 1870. Reconstructed 1889 as Argentine Land and Investment Co. Ld. [now Tribune Investment Trust Ld.] in which company shareholders were entitled to 1 preference share of £4 (credited as fully-paid) for each share of £1 held. Removed from Register 1906 **1888**

Central Argentine Railway Co. Ld. Regd. 1864. Amalgamated in 1902 with Buenos Aires and Rosario Railway Co. Ld. (later Central Argentine Railway Ld.) in which company ordinary stockholders were entitled to £30 in 7% preference shares of £10 and £115 in ordinary stock in acquiring company. The liability for the debenture stocks and Western Annuity was assumed by the acquiring company. Dissolved 21 Oct. 1908 under Central Argentine & Rosario Railway Act (1902).................... **1902**

Central Argentine Railway Ld. Regd. 1873 as Buenos Aires & Campana Railway Co. Ld.; named changed 1884 to Buenos Aires & Rosario Railway Co. Ld. and in 1908 as above. Vol. liq. 2 Apr. 1948. Capital returned to contributors (per £100 stock)—6% preference, £41 18s. 9d.; 4½% preference, £36 6s. 11d. consolidated ordinary, £23 15s. 3½d. deferred, £16 15s. 6d. Final meeting return regd. 10 Dec. 1963 **1965**

Central Aspen Silver Mining Co. Ld. Regd. 1891. Reconstructed 1897 as New Aspen Silver Mines Ld., in which company shareholders were entitled to 40 shares of £1 (credited as fully-paid) for every 100 shares of £1 held. Removed from Register 1910 .. **1900**

Central Australian Exploration Syndicate Ld. Regd. 1897. Removed from Register 1903 .... **1903**

Central Bahia Railway Co. Ld. Regd. 1875 as Brazilian Imperial Central Bahia Railway Co. Ld.; name changed May 1895. Undertaking sold to Federal

VOL. FOR

Government of Brazil for £1,135,000 in 4% rescission bonds in 1902. Pursuant to Sec. 63 Trustee Act 1925 all unclaimed Rescission Bands, Funding Bands and moneys were paid by Trustees into Court. The Trust was finally wound up and the trustees released and discharged **1946**

Central Bahia Railway Trust. Established by trust deed 1902 by Order of High Court. Wound up by deed poll 26 Apr. 1944. Holders of A certificates were entitled to £625 Brazilian Government Railway Guarantee Rescission 4% bonds for each A certificate of £500 held. Holders of B certificates were entitled to £100 4% rescission bonds *plus* £1 0s. 9d. in cash for each B certificate of £500 held. The trustees were released and discharged **1946**

Central Bank of London Ld. Established 1863 as East London Bank Ld.; name changed 1869. Business was acquired in 1891 by Birmingham and Midland Bank Ld. (later Midland Bank Ld.) in which company shareholders were entitled to 2 shares of £60 (credited with £12 10s. paid) for every 5 shares of £5 held **1891**

Central Bank of the Savings Banks of Bohemia and Moravia. *See* Zemska Banks Pro Cechy.

Central Borneo Co. Ld. Regd. 1887. Vol. liq. 23 Aug. 1892. Reconstructed as New Central Borneo Co. Ld., in which company shareholders were entitled to 1 share of £1 (credited with 15s. paid) for each share of £1 held. Final meeting return regd. 12 Jan. 1893 **1893**

Central Boulder Gold Mines (W.A.) Ld. Regd. 1895. Vol. liq. 4 July 1898. Reconstructed as Central & West Boulder Gold Mines (W.A.) Ld., in which company shareholders were entitled to 1 share of £1 (credited with 17s. paid) for each share of £1 held. Final meeting return regd. 24 Feb. 1899 .... **1899**

Central Carpathian Oil Co. Ld. Regd 1911. Vol. liq. Oct. 1912. The undertaking was sold to Premier Oil and Pipe Line Co. Ld., in which company shareholders were entitled to 3½ fully-paid shares of £1 for every 5 shares of £1 held. Removed from Register 1914 .. **1913**

Central Cheleken Oilfields Ld. Regd. 1912. The properties in Russia were nationalised by the Soviet Government. Struck off Register Apr. 1930 .... **1931**

Central Chili Copper Co. Ld. Regd. 1894. Reconstructed 1898 as company of same name. Shareholders were entitled to 1 share of £1 (credited with 18s. 6d. paid) for each ordinary share of £1 held. Priority shareholders were entitled to 1 share of £1 (credited with 18s. 6d. paid) and an equal nominal amount of debentures for each share of £1 held *plus* 1 share of £1 (credited with 18s. 6d. paid) for each £1 arrears of Interest. Removed from Register 1905 .... **1908**

Central Chili Copper Co. Ld. Regd. 1898. Vol. liq. Aug. 1923. Struck off Register Oct. 1931 .... **1932**

Central Coffee (Nairobi) Estates Ld. Regd. 1923. Vol. liq. (members') 23 Apr. 1958. Majority of the capital was owned by East African Estates Ld. Final meeting return regd. 20 Nov. 1958 .... **1954**

Central Company of Western Australia Ld. Regd. 1900. Struck off Register 1921 .... **1914**

Central Copper Mines of Spain Ld. *See* Huelva Central Copper Mining Co. Ld.

Central Co-operate Stores Ld. Regd. 1890. Vol. liq. 20 May 1891. Final meeting return regd.3 Aug. 1893 **1892**

Central Corporation. 1904, Ld. Regd. 1904. Vol. liq. 29 Sep. 1919. Final meeting return regd. 25 Nov. 1921 **1920**

Central Cyclone Co. Ld. Regd. 1891. Properties were transferred to debenture holders. Removed from Register 10 Feb. 1911 .... *1908

Central de Kaap Gold Mines Ld. Regd. 1895. Reconstructed as Westralian de Kaap Ld. Removed from Register 1908 .... **1900**

Central Development Syndicate Ld. Regd. 1896. Reconstructed 1898 as Westralian de Kaap Ld. (later Consolidated Finance Corporation Ld.) in which company shareholders were entitled to 1 share of 5s. (credited with 3s. 6d. paid) for each share of 5s. held. Removed from Register 1903 .... **1902**

Central Egypt Exploration Co. Ld. Regd. 1903. Vol. liq. Nov. 1908. Removed from Register 1911 .... **1909**

Central Electric Supply Co. Ld. Regd. 1897. Vol. liq. members') 25 Oct. 1932. Certain assets were acquired by London Power Co. Ld. Capital returned to contributories—£5 8s. 8d. per share of £5; part of this amount was satisfied by investments in specie. Final meeting return regd. 15 Feb. 1933 .... **1933**

Central Electricity Authority—Est. under Electricity Act 1947 as British Electricity Authority; name changed 1955. Dissolved as from 1 Jan. 1958 under the Electricity Act 1957, its duties and powers being allocated to the Electricity Council and the Central Electricity Generating Board.............................. **1958**

VOL. FOR

Central Electricity Board. Incorporated by Electricity (Supply) Act 1926. Dissolved 1 Apr. 1948, undertaking being vested in British (later Central) Electricity Authority under Electricity Act 1947. Holders of securities were entitled to receive British Electricity 3% guaranteed stock (1968–73) as follows in respect of each £1 unit, unless otherwise stated, of capital held:

	£	s.	d.
5% Stock (1950–70)	1	1	8¾
5% Stock (1955–75)	1	3	5¼
4⅛% Stock (1951–73)..................	1	1	7¾
4¼% Stock (1957–82)..................	1	3	4¼
4% Stock (1959–89)	1	2	8¾
3⅜% Stock (1963—93)..................	1	2	7¼
3½% Stock (1974–94)..................	1	2	4
3% (Civil Defence) redeemable			
stock (1955–60) (*per* £100)........104	0	0	**1949**

Central European Metal Corporation Ld. Regd. 1923. Vol. liq. 1 Oct. 1928. Final meeting return regd. 20 July 1929 .... **1929**

Central European Mines Ld. Regd. 1921. Vol. liq. (members') 1 Apr. 1958. Final meeting return regd. 14 Nov. 1959 .... **1905**

Central European Oilfields Ld. Regd. 1902. Struck off Register 23 Aug. 1949 .... **1950**

Central Exchange Bank of India Ld. Vol. liq. (members') 28 Nov. 1941. Dissolved before 1949 .... **1939**

Central Exploration and Investment Corporation Ld. Regd. 1895. Vol. liq. 4 Feb. 1898. Reconstructed as New Central Investment Corporation Ld., in which company shareholders were entitled to 1 fully-paid ordinary share of £1 for every 2 ordinary shares of £1 (15s. paid) held or to 1 fully-paid founders' share of 10s. for each founders' share of £1 held. Final meeting return regd. 14 Jan.1899 .... **1903**

Central Exploration Co. of Western Australia Ld. Regd. 1895. Reconstructed 1900 as Central Co. of Western Australia Ld. in which company shareholders were entitled to 1 ordinary or deferred share of £1 (credited with 19s. paid) for each ordinary or deferred share of £1 held. Removed from Register 1901 .... **1908**

Central Finance Corporation Ld. Regd. Edinburgh 1896. Vol. liq. Oct. 1909. Final meeting return regd. 31 Dec. 1913 .... **1910**

Central Geduld Gold Mining Co. Ld. Inc. Transvaal 1902. Vol. liq. Oct. 1906. Undertaking was acquired by Geduld Proprietary Mines Ld., in which company shareholders were entitled to 7 shares of £1 for every 20 shares of £1 held **1907**

Central Graving Dock & Engineering Co. Ld. Regd. 1884. Vol. liq. 21 Mar. 1896. Final meeting return regd. 18 Nov. 1896 .... *1887

Central Halls Co. Ld. Regd. Edinburgh 1878. Vol. liq. Apr. 1918. Struck off Register 27 Sept. 1932 .... **1919**

Central Hotel Co. Ld. Regd. Dublin 1878. Reconstructed under same name. Shareholders were entitled to 1 share of 15s. (credited with 10s. paid) in new company for each share of £1 held. Removed from Register 1908 .... **1903**

Central Insurance Co. Ld. Regd. 1899 as Birmingham Mutual Fire & General Insurance Association Ld.; name changed 1902. Vol liq. 15 Mar. 1907. Undertaking was acquired by Liverpool and London and Globe Insurance Co. Capital returned to contributories—£1 per share of £5 (10s. paid); further payments (if any) not known. Removed from Register 1913 .... **1908**

Central International Trust Ld. Regd. 1928 as New International Trust Ld.; name changed as above 17 Jan. 1929. Vol. liq. (members') 1 Feb. 1961. Final meeting return regd. 18 Jan. 1963 .... **1951**

Central Ireland Railway Co. Undertaking vested in Great Southern & Western Railway Co. Ireland in July 1900. Stockholders became holders of Separate Stock in Great Southern Co. but charged in same manner as Central Ireland stock **1901**

Central Italian (M.S.T.R.) Sulphur Co. Ld. Regd.1899. Vol. liq. 2 Feb. 1900. Subscriptions were returned to debenture holders after deducting formation expenses. Final meeting return regd. 4 July 1900 .... **1900**

Central Jagersfontein Diamond Mining Co. Ld. Regd. 1881. Vol. liq. May 1885. Final meeting return regd. 12 Aug. 1889 .... **1886**

Central Java Rubber Plantations Ld. Regd. 1910. Vol. liq. Aug. 1912 for reconstruction as Java Hevea Rubber and Tobacco Estates Ld. in which company shareholders were entitled to 1 share of 2s. (credited with 1s. paid) for every 2 shares of 2s. held. Removed from Register 1913 .... **1913**

Central Johore Rubber Estates Ld. Regd. 1925. Vol. liq. (members') 29 Dec. 1961. Majority capital was owned by Merlimau Pegoh Ld., under a capital

See Stock Exchange Year-Book.

VOL. FOR

reduction scheme in Nov. 1961, minority interests received 1 Merlimau Pegoh unit (of 2*s.*) for every 2 units (of 2*s.*) held. Final meeting return regd. 30 Nov. 1962 1964

Central Kelantan Rubber Co. Ld. Regd. 1910. Struck off Register 1925 .... *1918

Central Killham Tin Mines Ld. Regd. 1909. Vol. liq. 4 Aug. 1910. Reconstructed as Pensilva Tin Mines Ld., in which company shareholders were entitled to 1 ordinary share of 1*s.* (credited with 9*d.* paid) for every 2 ordinary shares of 1*s.* held, or 1 preference share of 1*s.* (credited with 9*d.* paid) for each preference share of 1*s.* held. Struck off Register 18 Jan. 1921 1911

Central Lafon Tinfields of Nigeria Ld. Regd. 1912. Vol. liq. 14 Apr. 1914. Reconstructed as New Lafon Tinfields Ld., in which company shareholders were entitled to 7 shares of 2*s.* (credited with 1*s.* paid) for every 5 shares of 5*s.* held. Final meeting return regd. 30 July 1915 1915

Central Langlaagte Gold Mining Co. Ld. Inc. Pretoria 1888. Amalgamated 1890 into Paarl Central Gold Mining & Exploration Co. Ld. in which company shareholders received 1 share of £1 for each share of £1 held 1891

Central London Electricity Distribution Committee, 1934, Ld. Regd. 1934. Vol. liq. (members') 4 Feb. 1938. Capital returned to contributories—20*s.* per ordinary share of £1. Final meeting return regd. 12 July 1938 1939

Central London Electricity Ld. Regd. 1889 as Electricity Supply Corpn. Ld.; name changed to Charing Cross & Strand Electricity Supply Corpn. Ld. in 1893; to Charing Cross, West End & City Electricity Supply Co. Ld. in 1905; to Charing Cross Electricity Supply Co. Ld. in 1924; and as above in 1938. Dissolved 1 Apr. 1948, undertaking being vested in British (later Central) Electricity Authority and London Area Board under Electricity Act 1947. Holders of ordinary and 3½% mortgage debenture stock were entitled to receive, in respect of each £1 stock held, £1 14*s.* 5*d.* and £1 0*s.* 3¾*d.* British Electricity 3% guaranteed stock (1968–73) respectively 1949

Central London Railway Co. Inc. by Special Act 1891. The undertaking was transferred on 1 July 1933 to the London Passenger Transport Board in which Board, stockholders were entitled to stock as follows-for every £100 4% debenture stocks held-£88 17*s.* 9*d.* of 4½% A stock; 4½% redeemable debenture stock 1942–72, equal nominal amount of 4½% T. F. A. stock; 5% redeemable debenture stock 1935, equal nominal amount of 5% A stock; 5% redeemable debenture stock 1985–95, equal nominal amount of 5% A stock; for every £100 4½% preference stock held £90 of B stock; for every £100 ordinary stock held-£92 10*s.* of C stock; for every £100 preferred ordinary stock held-£85 of C stock; and deferred ordinary stock, equal nominal amount of C stock. All the Central London guaranteed assented stocks, viz. £1,593,194 ordinary, £580,878 preferred ordinary and £644,167 deferred ordinary were converted into equal nominal amounts of Central London (New) Guaranteed Assented Stock. After distribution of the transport stock and the remaining assets the company was to be dissolved 1934

Central Lydenburg Gold Fields Ld. Inc. Transvaal 1895. In vol. liq 1904

Central Menzies Gold Mine Ld. Regd. 1895. Removed from Register 1908 1902

Central Middlesex Water Co. Ld. Regd. 1885. Vol. liq. 5 Jan. 1900. Removed from Register 1901 1900

Central Mill Co. Ld. Registered 6 Sept. 1869. Vol. liq. (members') 8 Jan. 1953. Capital returned to contributories—£2 5*s.* 1*d.* per 10*s.* stock. £1,358 2*s.* 6*d.* was paid into Companies' Liquidation Account. Final meeting return regd. 22 Nov. 1954 1955

Central Mines Development Co. Ld. Regd. 1906. Vol. liq. Dec. 1909. Removed from Register 1911 1910

Central Mining Co. of Dorstfontein Ld. Regd. 1880. Vol. liq. 18 Mar. 1889. Property was acquired by Gordon Diamond Mining Co. Ld. Final meeting return regd. 16 May 1891 1890

Central Mining Free State Areas Ld. Inc. in Union of South Africa 1949. Vol. liq. (Members') 18 Nov. 1957. Shareholders were entitled to receive 1 fully-paid share of 5*s.* of Harmony Gold Mining Co. Ld., for every 6 shares (of 5*s.*) held plus 9·52852167*d.* per share cash. Removed from Register in 1958 1959

Central Monomotapa Ld. Regd. 1896 as Firm Syndicate Ld., name changed Mar. 1898. Undertaking and assets were acquired by Zambesia Exploring Co. Ld. for 26,528 fully-paid shares of £1. Vol. liq. 6 June 1898. Final meeting return regd. 12 Oct. 1898 1899

VOL. FOR

Central Montrose Estate & Gold Mining Co. Ld. Regd. 1889. Vol. liq. June 1909. Removed from Register 1910 1925

Central National Bank. Inc. Ohio 1890. Reconstructed as Central United National Bank of Cleveland (now Central National Bank of Cleveland) 1930

Central National Bank of the City of New York, Inc. New York 1926. Absorbed by Manhattan Co. Mar. 1930, the business being merged with that of the Bank of Manhattan Trust Co. 1931

Central Nigel Deep Ld. Inc. Transvaal 1895. Vol. liq. Nov. 1907 1908

Central Nigeria Tin Mines Ld. Regd. 1926. Vol. liq. 23 May 1930. Final meeting return regd. 15 Apr. 1931 1931

Central Ontario Railway. Inc. Ontario by Special Act 1873 as Prince Edward County Railway Co.; name changed 1882. Undertaking was acquired by Canadian National Railways. The 5% 1st mortgage bonds were redeemed on 1 Jan. 1934 1924

Central Pacific Coal & Coke Co. Ld. Regd. 1879. Struck off Register 18 Nov. 1902 1903

Central Pacific Railroad Co. Chartered Caliornia 1870. Reorganised 1899 as company of same name (inc. Utah). Holders of common stock were entitled to an equal amount of common stock *plus* 25% of holdings in 4% gold bonds in Southern Pacific Co. Bondholders were entitled to securities in new company and cash as follows-for every $1000 1st mortgage bonds series A held $33⅓ in cash, $1000 new 4% 1st refunding mortgage gold bonds and $50 new 3½% mortgage gold bonds; for every $1000 1st mortgage bonds, series B, C, D, E, F, G, H or I held—$29·17 in cash, $100 new 4% 1st refunding mortgage gold bonds and $50 mortgage gold bonds; for every $1000 land bonds held—$41·67 in cash, $500 in 4% gold bonds and $700 in 3½% gold bonds; for every $1000 California & Oregon division 5% gold bonds Series A or B held—$29·17 in cash, $1000 in 4% gold bonds and $200 in 3½% gold bonds 1899

Central Panhalanga Gold Mining Co. Ld. Regd. 1895. Vol. liq. (members') 29 Sept. 1931. Capital returned to contributories—1*s.* 9·388*d.* per share of £1, fully-paid. £251 4*s.* 4*d.* was paid into Companies' Liquidation Account. Final meeting return regd. 29 Nov. 1932 1932

Central Perak Rubber Co. Ld. Regd. 1925. All capital acquired by Kulim Rubber Plantations Ld. Vol. liq. fmembers') 29 Dec. 1961. Final meeting return regd.4 Jan. 1964 1961

Central Petroleum & General Corporation Ld. Regd. 1922. Vol. liq. Oct. 1927. Undertaking and assets were acquired by Transvaal & Mexican Estates Ld. Holders of 10% 5-year notes were entitled to £7 in certificates in new company for every £5 principal and interest held. Shareholders were entitled to 1 ordinary share of 2*s.* (credited with 1*s.* 6*d.* paid) for each ordinary share of 1*s.* held; preference shareholders were entitled to 1 preference share of 2*s.* (credited with 1*s.* 6*d.* paid) for each preference share of 1*s.* held. Struck off Register June 1932 1933

Central Picture Houses (Sheffield) Ld. Regd. 1919. Vol. liq. (members') 2 Oct. 1950. Capital returned to contributories—preferred ordinary shares (of 1*s.*), 1*s.*; ordinary shares (of £1), 26*s.* 11¼*d.* £258 paid into Companies' Liquidation Account in respect of unclaimed dividends or distributions. Final meeting return regd. 11 May 1954 1955

Central Portland Cement Co. Ld. Regd. 1916 as Caustic Lime & Macadam Co. Ld.; name changed 17 Sept. 1923. Vol. liq. (members') 17 Mar. 1936. Undertaking was transferred to Alpha Cement Ld., in which company shareholders were entitled to 12 ordinary shares of £1 (credited as fully-paid) for every 100 ordinary shares of 4*s.* held, *plus* 3·8*d.* per ordinary share in cash. Preference shareholders were repaid at par. Proceeds of 1,269 shares unclaimed were paid into Companies' Liquidation Account. Final meeting return regd. 13 Nov. 1936 1937

Central Produce Market of Buenos Aires. Established in Argentina 1886. The outstanding 4½% 1st mortgage sterling debentures were redeemed at par 1 May 1918 1918

Central Public Service Corporation. Inc. Maryland 1923 as Southern Gas & Power Corporation; name changed Mar. 1927. On 8 Mar. 1933 the Corporation was adjudicated bankrupt. 1934

Central Public Utility Corporation. Inc. Delaware 1932 1936

Central Queensland Land Corporation Ld. Regd. 1896. Removed from Register 1907 1904

Central Queensland Meat Export Co. Ld. Regd. 1901. Operations transferred to Australia in 1928 1936

Central Railway Co. of Canada. Inc. Canada by Special Act 1903 as Ottawa River Railway Co.; name changed 1905. Holders of the 5% 1st mortgage bonds

*See *Stock Exchange Year-Book.*

VOL. FOR

were entitled to receive a first and final distribution of 14*s.* 7*d.* per £100 bond in Mar. 1928 .... **1928**

Central Railway Co. of Ecuador Ld. Regd. 1910. Court Order to wind up 6 June 1932. Liquidator released 24 Mar. 1939. Struck off Register 28 May 1946.... **1933**

Central Railway of Chubut Co. Ld. Regd. 1886. Vol. liq. (members') 18 Dec. 1936, the line having been sold to the Argentine Government. Capital returned to contributories—15*s.* 4½*d.* per share of £1. £65 15*s.* was paid into Companies' Liquidation Account. Final meeting return regd. 31 July 1947 .... **1948**

Central Rhodesia Ld. Regd. 1911. Vol. liq. 16 Sept. 1920. Final meeting return regd. 9 Jan. 1922 .... **1921**

Central Rhodesian Reefs Ld. Regd. 1899 as Austen (Gwelo) Development Syndicate Ld.; name changed July 1902. Vol. liq. 21 Dec. 1903 for reconstruction as company of same name. Final meeting return regd. 28 Feb. 1906 .... **1904**

Central Rhodesian Reefs Ld. Regd. Mar. 1904. Vol. liq. 6 Oct. 1904. Final meeting return regd. 30 Mar. 1906 **1905**

Central Roumanian Oil Fields Ld. *See* Beciu (Roumania) Oil Fields Ld.

Central Roumanian Petroleum Co. Ld. Regd. 1909. Vol. liq. 1 May 1912. The undertaking was acquired by Roumanian Consolidated Oilfields Ld., in which company shareholders were entitled to 1 fully-paid share of £1 for every 2 shares of £1 held. Final meeting return regd. 7 Jan. 1914 .... **1913**

Central Scotland Motors Ld. Regd. Edinburgh 1925. Vol. liq. (creditors') Feb. 1933. Assets realised insufficient to pay creditors in full. Final meeting return regd. 17 Dec. 1935 .... **1934**

Central Search Association Ld. In 1890 undertaking and assets were acquired by United Concessions Co. Ld. **1895**

Central Shops & Offices Ld. *See* Supersites Ld.

Central Siberia Ld. Regd. 1906. Vol. liq. July 1908 for reconstruction as New Central Siberia Ld., in which company shareholders were entitled to 1 share of £1 for every 4 shares of £1 held. Removed from Register 1909 .... ***1909**

Central Steam Fishing Co. Ld. Regd. 1898. Vol. liq. 25 Feb. 1903. Final meeting return regd. 7 Aug. 1906 ***1900**

Central Sugar Co. Ld. Regd. 1925. Vol. liq. (members') 30 July 1936. Undertaking was transferred to British Sugar Corporation Ld., in which company shareholders were entitled to 15 shares of £1 (credited as fully-paid) for 8 shares of £1 held. Capital returned to contributories—£2 3*s.* 8·85*d.* per share of £1 payable partly in cash and partly in shares of acquiring company. Final meeting return red. 22 Aug. 1940 .... **1937**

Central Sugar Factories of Brazil Ld. Regd. 1881. Court Orders; to wind up 18 Dec. 1886; to dissolve 28 June 1895 .... **1887**

Central Sumatra Rubber Estates Ld. Regd 1910. Vol. liq. 15 July 1915. Reconstructed as company of same name. Shareholders were entitled to 1 share of 10*s.* (credited with 5*s.* paid) in new company for each share of £1 held. Final meeting return regd. 21 Jan. 1918 .... **1916**

Central Sussex Electricity Ld. Regd. 1922 as Haywards Heath & District Electric Supply Co. Ld.; name changed 1929. Dissolved 1 Apr. 1948, undertaking being vested in the British (later Central) Electricity Authority and Southern-Eastern Area Board under the Electricity Act 1947. Ordinary shareholders were entitled to receive £1 5*s.* British Electricity 3, guaranteed stock 1968–73 for each share (of £1) held **1949**

Central Swedish Iron & Steel Co. Ld. Regd. 1872. Vol. liq. 25 Apr. 1876. Final meeting return regd. 25 May 1886 .... ***1876**

Central Tea & Coffee Houses Co. Ld. Regd. 1881. Vol. liq. 27 Apr. 1899. Capital returned to contributories in full. Final meeting return regd. 18 Nov. 1899... **1900**

Central Tea Co. of Ceylon Ld. Regd. 1895. In Dec. 1920 the shareholders were offered 10 fully-paid preference shares of £1 in Ceylon Tea Plantations Co. Ld. (later Ceylon Tea Plantations Holdings Ld.) for every 7 ordinary shares of £1 held or 6 fully-paid preference shares of £1 for every 7 preference shares of £1 held. Vol. liq. 30 June 1921. Final meeting return regd. 17 Oct. 1922.. **1922**

Central Tramways Co. of Monte Video Ld. Regd. 1890. Business was acquired by Oriental Investment Co. Ld. in which company shareholders were entitled to 10 shares of 5*s.* (credited with 4*s.* 6*d.* paid) for each share of £10 held. Holders of each mortgage bond of £50 were entitled to shares of 5*s.* (credited with 4*s.* 6*d.* paid) to nominal value of principal and 90% of interest due; remaining 10% of interest was payable in cash. Holders of each 6% prior lien bond of £50 were entitled to 6% 1st mortgage debentures equal to nominal amount of principal and half interest due; the remaining interest due was payable in cash. Removed from Register 1906 .... **1896**

Central Transvaal Gold Mining Co. Ld. Regd. 1886. Removed from Register 1892 .... **1889**

Central Travancore Rubber Co. Ld. Regd. in Edinburgh 1907. Vol. liq. (members') 1 May 1945. Capital returned to contributories—£3 1*s.* 9·61*d.* per £1 ordinary and preference stock. £422 14*s.* 11*d.* was paid to the Accountant of the Court. Final meeting return regd. 18 Apr. 1949 .... **1950**

Central Uruguay Eastern Extension Railway Ld. Regd. 1889. Under scheme of arrangement the undertaking was transferred in 1937 to Central Uruguay Railway Co. of Monte Video Ltd. in which company shareholders were entitled to 60 fully-paid ordinary shares of £1 for every £100 ordinary shares held or to 100 fully-paid ordinary shares of £1 for every £100 preference shares held. Holders of debenture stock were entitled to £12 10*s.* 4½% 1st debenture stock £60 5% 2nd debenture stock and 40 fully-paid ordinary shares of £1 for every £100 stock held. Dissolved under Sec. 154 of Companies Act 1929 on 5 Aug. 1937 .... **1938**

Central Uruguay Northern Extension Railway Co. Ld. Regd. 1888. Under scheme of arrangement the undertaking was transferred to Central Uruguay Railway Co. of Monte Video Ld., in which company shareholders were entitled to 60 fully-paid ordinary shares of £1 for every £100 shares held. Holders of permanent 5% debenture stock were entitled to £12 10*s.* 4½% 1st debenture stock £40 5% 2nd debenture stock and 40 fully-paid ordinary shares of £1 for every £100 stock held. Dissolved under Section 154 of Companies Act 1929 on 25 Aug. 1937 .... **1938**

Central Uruguay Railway Co. of Montevideo, Ld. Regd. 1876. Vol. liq. (members') 24 Feb. 1949. Undertaking sold to Uruguayan Government under agreement ratified in Dec. 1948. Ordinary stockholders received a distribution of 12½% out of balance of purchase consideration after all prior charges. Final meeting return regd. 27 Nov. 1961 .... **1962**

Central Uruguay Western Extension Railway Ld. Regd. 1899. Under scheme of arrangement the undertaking was transferred in 1937 to Central Uruguay Railway Co. of Monte Video Ld. The shares and debenture stock held by that company were cancelled the holders of the remaining shares were entitled to 60 fully-paid ordinary shares of £1 in acquiring company for every £100 shares held. Dissolved under Sec. 154 of Companies Act 1929 on 25 Aug. 1937 .... **1938**

Central Vermont Railway Co. Chartered Vermont 1898. Undertaking was acquired by Canadian National Railways at a foreclosure auction in July 1929 for $27,000,000 .... **1930**

Central Wales & Carmarthen Junction Railway Co. Inc. by Special Act 1873. Under London and North Western Railway Act 1891 the undertaking was sold to that company for £137,500 in cash.................... **1892**

Central Wales Emporium Ld. Regd. 1908. Vol. liq. June 1927. Struck off Register Mar. 1930 .... **1931**

Central Wealth Consolidated Gold Fields Ld. Regd. 1897. Removed from Register 1912 .... **1900**

Central Wealth of Nations Ld. Regd. 1895. Vol. liq. 29 Jan. 1897. Reconstructed as Central Wealth Consolidated Gold Fields Ld., in which company shareholders were entitled to 1 share of £1 (credited with 16*s.* paid) for each share of £1 held. Final meeting return regd. 10 Aug. 1899 .... **1899**

Central West Gold Mining Co. Ld. Inc. Transvaal 1923. Provisional winding-up order made Oct. 1927....... **1928**

Central Wynaad Gold Mining Co. Ld. Regd. 1881. Court Orders: to wind up 16 Aug. 1882; to dissolve 21 July 1891 .... **1883**

Central Zinc Co. Ld. Regd. 1906. Vol. liq. 3 June 1916. Undertaking and assets were acquired by Sulphide Corporation Ld. in which company shareholders were entitled to 1 fully-paid 10% participating preference share of £1 and 1 fully-paid ordinary share of 15*s.* *plus* 6*s.* in cash for every 3 shares of £1 held. Struck off Register 30 Jan. 1923 .... **1917**

Centralised Estates & Properties Trust Ld. *See* Lombard Property Trust Ld.

Centrifugal Separators Ld. Regd. 1919. Vol. liq. 30 Aug. 1926. Assets were transferred to Cooke. Throughton & Simms Ld. in consideration of payment of all debts and cost of liquidation. Final meeting return regd. 5 Oct. 1928 .... **1927**

Century European Timber Corporation Ld. Regd. 1921. Vol. liq. (members') 31 Dec. 1931. Capital returned to contributories—13*s.* 1·3963*d.* per preference share of £1. Final meeting return regd. 16 June 1939 **1932**

Century Shipping Co. Ld. Regd. 1898. Vol. liq. 7 Apr. 1920. Final meeting return regd. 23 Dec. 1920.

**See Stock Exchange Year-Book.*

VOL. FOR

Court Order declared dissolution void 27 Feb. 1923. Final meeting return regd. 27 Sept. 1929 .... **1921**

Century Theatre Ld. See Adephi Theatre Ld.

Century Trust Ld. Regd. 1923. Vol. liq. 7 Oct. 1929. Final meeting return regd. 5 Nov. 1936 .... **1930**

Cerais Petroleum Co. Ld. See Anglo-Mexican Oil & Shipping Co. Ld.

Cerebos Ld. Regd. 1894 as Cerebos Salt Co. Ld.: name changed Sept. 1895. Undertaking acquired in 1903 by Cerebos (1903) Ld. (later Cerebos Ld.), in which company shareholders were entitled to 3¼ fully-paid shares of £1 for each share of £1 held. Removed from Register 1905 .... **1904**

Cerro de Pasco Ld. Regd. 1890. Vol. liq. 15 June 1892. Final meeting return regd. 11 Aug. 1899.............. **1893**

Cerro de Pasco (Transvaal) Gold Fields Ld. Regd. 1888. Vol. liq. 18 June 1891. Reconstructed as Cerro de Pasco Ld., in which company shareholders were entitled to 1 share of 5s. (credited with 2s. 6d. paid) for each share of £1 held. Final meeting return regd. 11 August 1899 .... **1892**

Cerro Muriano Mines Ltd. Regd. 1903. Vol. liq. June 1908 for reconstruction as Cordoba Copper Co. Ld., in which company shareholders were entitled to 2 fully-paid shares of 5s. for each preference share of 6s. held. Ordinary shareholders were entitled to 1 fully-paid share of 5s. for every 10 ordinary shares of £1 held. Removed from Register 1911................. **1909**

Cesena Sulphur Co. Ld. Regd. 1871. Struck off Register 27 Apr. 1894............ **1901**

Cevreni-Breg Mining Co. Ld. Regd. 1906. Vol. liq. Feb. 1913. Shareholders were to be entitled to 1 share of £4 (credited with £3 paid) in proposed new company for each share of £4 held. Struck off Register 1925 .... **1913**

Ceylon & Oriental Estates Co. Ld. Regd. 1892. Undertaking was acquired in 1897 by Cooper Cooper & Johnson Ld. (later Rajawella Produce Co. Ld.) Vol. liq. 23 Nov. 1898. Holders of shares and debentures were offered cash at par or shares in acquiring company. Final meeting return regd. 27 July 1899................. **1899**

Ceylon & Oriental Investment Corporation Ld. Regd. 1890. Vol. liq. 18 Feb. 1892. Final meeting return regd. 21 Oct. 1892 .... **1892**

Ceylon (Bibile) Rubber Estates Ld. Regd. 1926. Assets realised insufficient to meet claims of prior lien debenture holders. Struck off Register 1937 .... **1938**

Ceylon Café Co. Ld. Regd. 1902. Vol. liq. July 1909. Undertaking was sold to J. Lyons & Co. Ld., for 25,000 ordinary shares of £1. Purchasers assumed liability for debenture stocks. Removed from Register 1910 .... **1910**

Ceylon Cocoa & Rubber Co. Ld. Regd. 1904. Vol. liq. (members') 19 July 1933 for reconstruction as Ceylon Cocoa & Rubber Co. (1933) Ld. (later Airfix Industries Ld.), in which company shareholders were entitled to 2 preference shares of 1s. (credited with 9d. paid) for each preference share of 2s. held and 1 ordinary share of 1s. (credited with 9d. paid) for each ordinary share of 2s. held. Final meeting return regd. 14 Dec. 1934 .... **1934**

Ceylon Co. Ld. Regd. 1862. Vol. liq. under supervision of the Court June 1884. Final meeting return regd. 13 Aug. 1890 .... **1885**

Ceylon Co. of Pearl Fishers Ld. Regd. 1906. Vol. liq. June 1912. Removed from Register 1913 .... **1913**

Ceylon Consolidated Estates Ld. Regd. 1914. Vol. liq. (members') 18 Nov. 1920. Undertaking acquired by Ceylon Consolidated Estates (1920) Ld., in which company shareholders were entitled to receive 3 shares of 2s. (credited with 1s. 6d. paid) for every 2 shares of 2s. held. Final meeting return regd. 14 Jan. 1955 .... **1956**

Ceylon Consolidated Estates Ld. Regd. 1929. Vol. liq. (members') July 1931. Undertaking acquired by Ceylon Consolidated Estates Ld., in which company shareholders were entitled to receive 1 ordinary share (of 1s. (credited with 10½d. paid) for each share of 1s. held. Debenture holders were entitled to exchange their holdings for a similar amount of debentures of the new company ranking in same order as their existing debentures. Final meeting return regd. 14 Jan. 1955. .... **1956**

Ceylon Consolidated Estates (1920) Ld. Regd. 1920. Vol. liq. (members') 11 Apr. 1929. Undertaking acquired by Ceylon Consolidated Estates (regd. 1929), in which company shareholders were entitled to receive 1 share of 1s. or share of 2s. held. Liability for outstanding 8% 1st & 2nd debentures was assumed by new company. Final meeting return regd. 14 Jan. 1955 .... **1956**

Ceylon Consolidated Rubber Estates Ld. Regd. 1910. Vol. liq. 24 Sept. 1914. Reconstructed as Ceylon

VOL. FOR

Consolidates Estates Ld., in which company shareholders were entitled to 1 share of 2s. (credited with 1s. 6d. paid) for each share of 2s. held. Final meeting return regd. 2 Jan. 1917 .... **1915**

Ceylon Estates Investment Association Ld. Regd. 1885. Vol. liq. (members') 5 Apr. 1946. Estates, &c. sold for £63,826. Capital returned to contributories— 44s. 0·2d. per share of 10s. Final meeting return regd. 11 June 1948 .... **1949**

Ceylon Investment Association Ld. Regd. Edinburgh 1878. Vol. liq. 7 May 1885. Undertaking was acquired by Ceylon Estates Investment Association Ld., in which company shareholders were entitled to 1 share of £4 (credited with £2 paid) for each share of £2 held. Final meeting return regd. 27 July 1886 .... **1885**

Ceylon Mines Ld. Regd. 1920. Vol. liq. (creditors') 27 Nov. 1933. No capital returned to contributories. Final meeting return regd. 8 Jan. 1935 .... **1934**

Ceylon Prospecting Syndicate Ld. Regd. 1896. Struck off Register 1915 .... **1902**

Ceylon Rubber, Tea & General Produce Co. Ld. Regd. 1910. Vol. liq. 13 Mar. 1914. Reconstructed as Tea and Rubber Plantations (Ceylon) Ld., in which company shareholders were entitled to 1 share of 4s. (credited with 3s. paid) for each share of 5s. held. Final meeting return regd. 24 July 1918 .... **1915**

Ceylon-Travancore Rubber & Tea Estates Ld. Regd. 1910. Court Order to wind up 5 June 1912. Liquidator released 16 Apr. 1915. Struck off Register 14 Feb. 1919 .... **1913**

Ceymal Ld. Regd. 1922 as Duro Rubber Products Ld.: name changed Sept. 1925. Vol. liq. 26 Oct. 1928. Final meeting return regd. 3 Apr. 1929................. **1929**

Chade. See Compañia Hispano-Americana de Electricidad S. A. [Chade].

Chadwick's Walmersley Brewery Ld. Regd. 1891. Vol. liq. (members') 6 July 1934. Undertaking and assets were acquired by Manchester Brewery Co. Ld. Capital returned to contributories–£7 1s. 9·949d. per share of £5. Final meeting return regd. 2 Oct. 1934 **1935**

Chaffers Extended Ld. Regd. 1897. Undertaking and assets were acquired by New Chaffers Extended Ld., in which company shareholders were entitled to 1 share of 4s. (credited with 3s. paid) for each share of 4s. held. Removed from Register 1904................. **1903**

Chaffers Gold Mining Co. Ld. Regd. 1895. Vol. liq. 17 Jan. 1905. Reconstructed as company of same name. Shareholders were entitled to 1 share of 4s. (credited with 2s. paid) in new company for each share of 4s. held. Removed from Register 1906 ... **1905**

Chaffers Gold Mining Co. Ld. Regd. 1905. Vol. liq. 23 July 1913 for reconstruction as Chaffers Gold Mining Co. (1913) Ld., in which company shareholders were entitled to 1 share of 4s. (credited with 2s. 6d. paid) for each share of 4s. held. Final meeting return regd. 28 Mar. 1914 .... **1914**

Chaffers Gold Mining Co. (1913) Ld. Regd. 1913. Vol. liq. 8 Dec. 1915. The property was sold under order of Court in Australia. Final meeting return regd. 20 Dec. 1916 .... **1916**

Chaffers Gold Mining Co. (1916) Ld. Inc. Western Australia 1916. Vol. liq. 1920 .... **1922**

Chagford & Devon Electric Light Co. Ld. Regd. 1890. Receiver appointed for debenture holders in Aug. 1927, ceased to act in Oct. 1930. Assets realised insufficient to pay debentures. Struck off Register Dec. 1932................. **1932**

Chalet Co. Ld. Regd. 1880. Vol. liq. 21 Oct. 1887. Final meeting return regd. 7 Oct. 1892 .... **1888**

Chalk Fuel, Power Gas & By-Products Corporation Ld. Regd. 1914. Struck off Register May 1929 .... **1930**

Challenge Gold Estates Proprietary Co. (W. A.) Ld. Regd. 1895. Vol. liq. 25 May 1897. Reconstructed as Challenge Mining & Milling Co. Ld., in which company shareholders were entitled to 1 share of 10s. (credited with 8s. paid) for each share of £1 held. Final meeting return regd.4 May 1899 .... **1900**

Challenge Mining & Milling Co. Ld. Regd. 1897. Preferred first mortgage debenture holders foreclosed on property. Removed from Register 1902 **1901**

Challenge Reinforced Tube Co. Ld. See Victor Tyre Co. Ld.

Challiner & Willoughby Carriage Tyre Co. Ld. Amalgamated 1900 with Shrewsbury & Talbot S. T. Cab & Noiseless Tyre Co. Ld. to form Shrewsbury S. T. & Challiner Tyre Co. Ld. (later Shrewsbury & Challiner Tyre Co. Ld.) **1925**

Chalmers & Guthrie (Merchants) Ld. Regd. 1926. Vol. liq. Feb. 1934. Court Order to wind up Oct. 1934. Struck off Register 19 May 1944 .... **1945**

Chalmers Guthrie & Co. Ld. Regd. 1899. Vol. liq. 16 Dec. 1927. Final meeting return regd. 17 Mar. 1937 **1928**

Chalmers Guthrie & Co. Ld. Regd. 1928. Receiver appointed in Oct. 1932, ceased to act Oct. 1933.

VOL. FOR

Debenture holders' claims were satisfied in full. Struck off Register 24 May 1938 .... **1939**

Chamberlins Ld. Reg. 1903. Vol. liq. (members') 3 Apr. 1964. All capital was owned by Debenhams Ld. Final meeting return Regd. 27 Apr. 1967 .... **1963**

Chambers & Co. Ld. Regd. 1898. Vol. liq. Dec. 1910. Removed from Register 1913 .... **1911**

Chambers (Reuben) Ld. Regd. 1897. Struck off Register 18 Nov. 1902 .... **1903**

Chamelicon Gold Mining Co. Ld. Regd. 1889. Removed from Register 1902 .... **1895**

Champagne Frères Ld. Regd. 1897. Receiver appointed in Mar. 1911. Struck off Register 1914 .... **1912**

Champagne Frères (1911) Ld. Regd. 1911. Vol. liq. 28 Apr. 1924. Final meeting return regd. 5 Sept.1924 **1929**

Champdany Jute Co. Ld. Regd. Edinburgh 1873. Vol. liq. Sept 1921. Undertaking and assets sold to company of same name (inc. in India). Shareholders were entitled to about £27 per share in cash, of which £20 could be applied in exercise of an option (since expired). Final meeting return regd. 12 Apr. 1922. Court Order declared dissolution void. Final meeting return regd.9 Apr. 1927 .... **1922**

Champion Channelling Machines Ld. *See* International Channelling Machines Ld.—regd. 1902.

Champion Extended & Home Rule Gold Mines Ld. Regd. 1896. Vol. liq. 28 Nov. 1899. Undertaking acquired by Yagahong Exploration Co. Ld. Removed from Register 10 Oct. 1916 .... ***1901**

Champion Gold & Silver Mines New Zealand Ld. Regd. 1888. Vol. liq. 30 June 1893. Removed from Register 1895 .... **1894**

Champion (J. B.) & Co. Ld. Regd. 1901. Vol. liq. (members') 24 Aug. 1944. A direct controlling interest was held by Bleachers' Association Ld. (later Whitecroft Industrial Holdings Ld.). Final meeting return regd. 1 1 Nov. 1944 .... **1945**

Champion (Nigeria) Tin Fields Ld. Regd. 1909 as Champion Gold Reefs of West Africa Ld.; name changed Mar. 1911. Vol. liq. 29 Dec. 1926. Final meeting return regd. 5 Apr. 1929 .... **1927**

Champion Proprietary Ld. Regd. 1900. Vol. liq. 28 Dec. 1905. Removed from Register 1907 .... **1906**

Champion Reef Gold Mines of India Ld. Regd. 1921. Vol. liq. (members') 4 Mar. 1957. The undertaking of Champion Reef Gold Mines of India (K.G.F.) Ld. (to which the undertaking and assets of this company had been transferred) was vested in the Government of Mysore in Nov. 1956; compensation received Rs.52,81,000. Capital returned to contributories—15s. 5¼d. per 10s. stock. Final meeting return regd. 11 Jan. 1961 .... **1961**

Champion Reef Gold Mining Co. of India Ld. Regd. 1889. Vol. liq. 27 Oct. 1921 for reconstruction as Champion Reef Gold Mines of India Ld., in which company shareholders were entitled to 1 share of 10s. (credited with 4s. paid) and 3 shares of 10s. (credited with 1s. paid) for every 4 shares of 2s. 6d. held. Final meeting return regd. 21 July 1922 ...... **1922**

Champion Reef (Nannine, W. A.) Gold Mining Co. Ld. Regd. 1895. Reconstructed 1898 as Australian Champion Reef Co. Ld., in which company shareholders were entitled to 1 share of £1 (credited with 15s. paid) for each share of £1 held. Removed from Register 1901 .... **1899**

Champion Reef (Wales) Gold Mine Co. Ld. Regd. 1889. Court Order to wind up 27 June 1891. Removed from Register 1906 .... **1892**

Champion Weldless Tubes Ld. Regd. 1897. Removed from Register 1909 .... **1900**

Chance & Hunt Ld. Regd. 1898. Vol. liq. (members') 30 June 1939; all shares held by I.C.I. (General Chemicals) Ld. Final meeting return regd. 12 Sept. 1941 .... **1940**

Chandler's Reward Gold Mines Ld. Regd. 1896. Assets to be acquired by West Australian Minerals & Finance Co. Ld., in which company shareholders were entitled to 1 share of 5s. (credited with 4s. paid) for each share held. Removed from Register 1898 **1902**

Changkat Salak Syndicate Ld. Regd. Edinburgh 1906. Vol. liq. May 1909. Undertaking and assets were acquired by Changkat Salak Rubber and Tin Ld., in which company shareholders were entitled to 1 deferred ordinary share of £1 (credited as fully-paid) for every 2 shares of £1 held. Removed from Register 1910 .... **1910**

Changkat Tin Dredging Ld. Inc. Federated Malay States 1925. Vol. liq. Feb. 1935. Undertaking and assets were acquired by Southern Kinta Consolidated Ld., in which company shareholders were entitled to 4 shares of 5s. for each share of £1 held **1936**

VOL. FOR

Channel Bridge & Railway Co. Ld. Regd. 1884. Undertaking and assets were acquired by International Railway Co. Ld in which company shareholders were entitled to 1 fully-paid share for each share held. Removed from Register 1904 .... **1904**

Channel Collieries Trust Ld. Regd. 1910. Vol. liq. 12 July 1917. Reconstructed as Channel Steel Co. Ld., in which company shareholders were entitled to 4 fully-paid preferred ordinary shares of £1 and 21½ deferred ordinary shares of 1s. (credited as fully-paid) for every 5 shares of £1 held. Final meeting return regd. 25 Feb. 1919 .... **1918**

Channel Ferry (Dover) Co. Inc. by Special Act 1906. In Nov. 1923 it was stated that company was defunct **1924**

Channel Islands Bank Ld. Est. 1858; inc. in Jersey 1887. In 1897 the business was taken over by London & Midland Bank Ld. (later Midland Bank Ld.), for £30 in cash for each share of £10 paid up, with option to purchase, at £45 per share, 2 further shares for every 3 shares held **1898**

Channel Steel Co. Ld. Regd. 1917. Vol. liq. (members') 28 Sept. 1949. Capital returned to contributories— 1s. 4·375d. per preferred ordinary share of £1. Final meeting return regd. 21 Dec. 1955 .... **1957**

Channel Tunnel Co. Ld. Regd. 1872. Placed in liquidation, the undertaking was acquired in 1886 by Submarine Continental Rly., Ld. (later Channel Tunnel Co. Ld.), for 19,815 fully-paid shares of £1. Dissolved before 1931 .... **1887**

Chapel-en-le-Frith, Chinley and District Gas Co. Ld. Undertaking was acquired by Chapel Whaley and District Gas Co **1912**

Chapel House Colliery Co. Ld. Regd. 1873. Wound up by Order of Court 14 Mar. 1884 .... ***1883**

Chapel Whaley & District Gas Co. Inc. by Special Act 1911. Dissolved 1 May 1949, undertaking being vested in North Western Area Gas Board under Gas Act 1948. Holders of securities were entitled to receive British Gas 3% guaranteed stock 1990–95 as follows in respect of each £1 unit, unless otherwise stated, of security held:

	£ s. d.
Orig. ord. shares (6% stand.)................	19 6
Addit. ord. shares (6% stand.)...............	19 6
4% red. deb. stock (per £100)...............100 10 0	**1952**

Chaplin, Milne, Grenfell & Co. Ld. Regd. 1899. Court Order to wind up June 1914. Struck off Register 24 Oct. 1939 .... **1940**

Chapman (Alfred) (1936) Ld. Regd. 1936. Controlling interest held by Wallpapers (Consolidated) Ld. [later Blaskey's (Wallpapers) Ld.] Struck off Register 21 Oct. 1941 .... **1942**

Chapman & Sons, Eastbourne, Ld. Regd. 1921. Vol. liq. (members') 1 Feb. 1933. Undertaking was acquired by Southdown Motor Services Ld. Capital returned to contributories—£23,481 6s. 4d. Final meeting return regd. 1 May 1935 .... **1933**

Chaplin Holdings Ld. Regd. 1898 as W. H. Chaplin & Co. Ld.; name changed May 1936. Vol. liq. 14 Apr. 1975. Remaining assets (other than holding in Emu wine Holdings Ld.) transferred to new unit trust (Mercury International Fund). Preference shares repaid at par. Initial payment to ordinary shareholders (per 100 shares)–400 units in Mercury International Fund *plus* 85·24 ordinary stock units of 25p of Emu Wine Holdings Ld. Further distributions (per 100 shares held) to ordinary shareholders in units of Mercury Unit Fund—80 distribution or accumulation in 1975. 16·67 distribution or 16·29 accumulation in 1976 and7·56 distributions or 6·85 accumulation units in 1980. Final meeting held 15 Feb. 1980. No amounts were paid into Companies' Liquidation Account 1981–2

Chaplin (W. H.) & Co. Ld. *See* Chaplin Holdings Ld.

Charbonnages de Rodez Ld. Regd. 1891. Vol. liq. Apr. 1905. Struck off Register 1922 .... **1906**

Charcoal Iron Co. of America. Inc. Michigan 1915. Property conveyed under foreclosure sale to Newburry Lumber & Chemical Co. **1931**

Chard Gas Co. Regd. as Chard Gas & Coke Co. Ld. in 1870; re-incorporated by Special Act 1902. The undertaking was transferred to Chard Corporation for £35,000 and costs **1905**

Chardonnet Silk Co. Ld. Regd. 1900. Reconstructed 1901 as Commercial Enterprise Ld in which company shareholders were entitled to 1 fully-paid ordinary share of £1 for every 10 ordinary shares of 10s. held or to 1 fully-paid preference share of £1 for every 2 preference shares of 10s, held. Removed from Register 1902 .... **1908**

Chardwar Tea Co. Ld. Regd. 1895. Vol. liq. 29 Jan. 1925. Undertaking and assets were purchased by Belseri-Chardwar Tea Estates Ld., for £65,000 in cash. Final meeting return regd. 3 Dec. 1925 ...... **1925**

*See Stock Exchange Year-Book.

VOL. FOR

Chargeurs Réunis (S. A.) Cie. Francaise de Navigation a Vapeur. *See* French Steam Navigation Co.

Chargola Tea Association Ld. Regd. 1891. Vol. liq. (members') 11 Feb. 1957. Capital returned to contributories—preference: 16s. 4d. per £1 stock; ordinary: 18s. 6½ per £1 stock. £1,559 5s. 4d. was paid into Companies' Liquidation Account. Final meeting return regd. 10 Feb. 1961 .... **1962**

Chargola Tea Co. Ld. Regd. 1877. Vol. liq. 17 June 1891. Reconstructed as Chargola Tea Association Ld. Final meeting return regd. 27 Apr. 1892 .... **1891**

Charing Cross & City Electric Co. Ld. *See* Suppliers Construction Co. Ld.

Charing Cross & Waterloo Electric Railway Co. Inc. by Special Act 1882 .... **1886**

Charing Cross Electricity Supply Co. Ld. Formerly Charing Cross, West End & City Electricity Supply Co. Ld. and Charing Cross & Strand Electricity Supply Corpn. Ld. See Central London Electricity Ld.

Charing Cross, Euston and Hampstead Railway Co. Inc. by Special Act 1893. Amalgamated with Great Northern, Piccadilly and Brompton Railway Co. (later London Electric Railway Co.). Holders of £100 debenture stock received a like amount of debenture stock in the new company and shareholders received £17 12s. 4½d. preference stock or £82 7s. 7½d. ordinary shares for each £100 preference or ordinary shares held respectively **1911**

Charing Cross Gold Mine (W. A.) Ld. Regd. 1897. Struck off Register 16 Nov. 1906 .... **1907**

Charing Cross Hotel Co. Ld. Regd. 1867. Taken over by South Eastern Railway Co. (later Southern Railway Co). Removed from Register 1884 .... *1881

Charlaw and Sacriston Collieries Co. Ld. Regd. 1890. Vol. liq. (members') 12 Sept. 1952. Capital returned to contributories—13s. 7·6d. per share of 16s. Final meeting return regd. 2 Oct. 1961 .... **1963**

Charles Carr Ld. *See* Cornwall Property (Holdings) Ld.

Charles Dickens Mining Co. Ld. Regd. 1886. Vol. liq. Dec. 1887 for reconstruction as Dickens Custer Co. Ld., in which company shareholders were entitled to 2 shares of £1 (credited with 17s.) paid) for each fully-paid share of £1 held. The debentures were repaid in cash. Final meeting return regd. 27 Apr. 1889 ..... **1889**

Charlestown Brick & Tile Co. Ld. Regd. 1873. Vol. liq. Mar. 1909. Removed from Register 1911 .... **1910**

Charlesworth (J. & J.), Ltd. Regd. 1888. Vol. liq. (members') 27 May 1954. Final meeting return regd. 23 June 1960 .... **1950**

Charlotte Plains Consolidated Gold Mines Ld. Regd. 1902. Reconstructed 1907 as company of same name. Shareholders were entitled to 1 share of 10s. (credited with 9s. paid) in new company for each ordinary share of £1 held or each A or B share of 3s. 4d. held. Removed from Register 1909 .... **1908**

Charlotte Plains Consolidated Gold Mines Ld. Regd. 1907. Vol. liq. Oct. 1908. Undertaking acquired by Charlotte Plains Gold Mining Co. Ld. (inc. Melbourne 1908). The fully-paid deferred shares of £1 in the new company were to be issued to shareholders who also had option (since expired) to subscribe at par for ordinary shares. Struck off Register 1916 . **1909**

Charlotte Plains Proprietary Gold Mines Ld. Regd. 1895. Reconstructed 1902 as Charlotte Plains Consolidated Gold Mines Ld., in which company shareholders were entitled to 130,000 shares of £1 (credited with 15s. paid). Removed from Register 1903 .... **1907**

Charlton Iron Co. Ld. Regd. 1872 Court Orders: to wind up 11 Dec. 1875; to dissolve 19 Dec. 1890 .... **1886**

Charnwood Forest Railway Co. Inc. by Special Act 1874. In 1923 the undertaking was merged with the London Midland & Scottish Railway Co., in which company stockholders were entitled to stock as follows:

For each £100 held	L.M. & S.	
5% Debenture	£125	4% Debenture
5% Preference	£125	4% Pref. (1923)
Ordinary	£30	cash

.... **1924**

Charron Ld. Regd. 1906. Vol. liq. 10 Oct. 1913. Reconstructed as company of same name. Shareholders were entitled to 1 fully-paid ordinary share of £1 for every 2 preferred ordinary shares of £1 or 4 deferred shares of 1s. held. Final meeting return regd. 23 Dec. 1914 .... **1914**

Charron Ld. Regd. 1913. Assets realised insufficient to meet claims of debenture holders. Struck off Register 26 Apr. 1940 .... **1943**

Charter Oak Copper Mines Ld. Regd. 1898. Vol. liq. Mar. 1908. Capital returned to contributories—4s. 9d. per share of £1; further payments (if any) not known. Removed from Register 1908 .... **1909**

VOL. FOR

Charter Trust & Agency Ld. Regd. 1902. Undertaking and certain assets were acquired company of same name in 1907. Shareholders were entitled to 3 shares of £1 (credited as fully-paid) in new company and £2 debenture stock in Trust & Agency Assets Ld., for every 5 shares of £1 held. Removed from Register 1911 .... **1908**

Chartered Mercantile Bank of India, London & China. Inc. by Royal Charter 1857. Reconstructed 1892 as Mercantile Bank of India Ld. (later Mercantile Bank Ld.), in which company shareholders were entitled to 1 B share of £25 (credited with £12 10s. paid) for each fully-paid share of £25 held **1892**

Charterhouse Caterers Ld. Regd. 1929. Vol. liq. (creditors') 2 Apr. 1930. No capital returned to contributories. Final meeting return regd. 23 May 1935 **1931**

Charteries, Spence and Co. Ld. Regd. 19 Mar. 1906. Vol. liq. (members') 3 June 1937. Capital returned to contributories—preference shares (of £1), £1; ordinary shares (of £1) 10s. 8·3d. £423 3s. 8d. paid into Companies' Liquidation Account in respect of unclaimed dividends or distributions. Final meeting return regd. 30 Nov. 1954 .... **1955**

Charterland Consolidated Ld. Regd. 1895. Removed from Register 1908 .... **1898**

Charterland Goldfields Ld. Regd. 1895. Vol. liq. Aug. 1909. Reconstructed as Charterland and General Exploration and Finance Co. Ld., (later Charterland & General Ld.), in which company shareholders were entitled to 3 shares of 5s. (credited as fully-paid) for every 2 shares of £1 held and an option (since expired) over further shares. Removed from Register 1911 .... **1910**

Charterland Stores and Trading Co. Ld. Regd. 1897. Removed from Register 1905 .... **1901**

Charters Exploration Ld. Regd. 1895. Struck off Register 20 Nov. 1908 .... **1909**

Charters Towers Consolidated Gold Mines Ld. Regd. 1895. Vol. liq. 27 July 1899. Amalgamated with Union Jack Consolidated Mines Ld., in which company shareholders were entitled to 4 shares of 5s. (credited with 3s. 6d. paid) for each share of £1 held. Removed from Register 1901 .... **1900**

Charters Towers South Gold Mining Co. Ld. Regd. 1886. Vol. liq. 14 Mar. 1889. Final meeting return regd. 21 Feb. 1893 .... **1890**

Chase, Harris, Forbes Ld. *See* Balfour Boardman & Co. Ld.

Chasetown & District Electricity Co. Ld. Regd. 1929. Dissolved 1 Apr. 1948, undertaking being vested in the British (later Central) Electricity Authority and Midlands Area Board under the Electricity Act 1947. Ordinary shareholders were entitled to receive £5 British Electricity 3% guaranteed stock, 1968–73, for each share of (£1) held **1949**

Chasetown Gas Co. Inc. by Special Act 1911. Dissolved 1 May 1949, undertaking being vested in West Midland Area Gas Board under Gas Act 1948. Holders of securities were entitled to receive, in respect of each £5 unit held, British Gas 3% guaranteed stock 1990–95 as follows:

	£	s.	d.
Ord. shares (10% stand.)	10	5	0
5% pref. shares	5	12	0

.... **1952**

Chastan Syndicate Ld. Regd. 1906. Vol. liq. Sept. 1908. Removed from Register 1911 .... **1909**

Chatham & District Water Co. Regd. 1856 as Brompton & Gillingham Consumers' Waterworks Co. Ld.; inc. by Special Act 1860 as Brompton, Chatham, Gillingham & Rochester Waterworks Co.; name changed June 1926. Under provisions of Kent Water Act 1955 the undertaking vested in the Medway Water Board as from 1 Apr. 1956. Holders of 5% (maximum) consolidated stock were entitled to receive £76 13s. 4d. cash per £100 stock held (plus interest thereon at 4% from 1 Apr. 1956 to 19 Nov. 1957); holders of all classes of preference and debenture stock were entitled to receive a like amount of a similar Medway Water Board stock (except that stock issued to holders of the *irredeemable* debenture stocks will be redeemable on 31 Mar. 1996) carrying the same interest rates and redemption terms. Company was dissolved in Jan. 1960 **1960**

Chatham Empire Theatre of Varieties Ld. *See* Stoll Theatres (South) Ld.

Chatham, Rochester & District Electric Lighting Co. Ld. Regd. 1887. Undertaking was acquired in 1905 by Kent Electric Power Co. Vol. liq. 14 June 1907. Removed from Register 1908 .... **1908**

Chatma Oilfield Co. Ld. Regd. 1902. Struck off Register Feb. 1930 .... **1930**

Chatterley Iron Co. Ld. Regd. 1865. Vol. liq. Jan. 1879. Court Orders: to continue winding up under supervision Dec. 1881; to stay proceedings Dec.

VOL. FOR

1881; to continue winding up under supervision 26 Apr. 1884; to dissolve 12 Feb. 1896 .... **1886**

Chatterley-Whitfield Collieries Ld. Regd. 1891. Vol. liq. (members') 28 Apr. 1950. Final meeting return regd. 30 Jan. 1959 .... **1940**

Chatwood Safe Co. Ld. *See* C. S. & E. (Holdings) Ld.

Chatwood's Patent Safe & Lock Co. Ld. Regd. 1864. Vol. liq. Dec. 1909 for reconstruction. Removed from Register 1911 .... **1910**

Cheadle & Churnet Valley Gas Co. Ld. Regd. 1914. Dissolved 1 May 1949, undertaking being vested in West Midland Area Gas Board under Gas Act 1948. Holders of ordinary shares (of £1) were entitle to receive 12*s.* 6*d.* British Gas 3% guaranteed stock 1990–95 for each share held **1952**

Cheadle Railway Co. Inc. 1878. Abandoned by Act of 1882 .... **1883**

Cheadle Railway Co. Inc. by Special Act 1887 as Cheadle Railway Mineral & Land Co. Ld.; name changed by Act of 1896. Undertaking sold to North Staffordshire Railway Co. in Jan. 1907 for £40,000 3% perpetual preference stock. **1908**

Cheap Wood Co. Ld. Regd. 1899. Vol. liq. 16 Apr. 1901. No capital returned to contributories. Removed from Register 1902 .... **1902**

Checkogram Ld. Regd. 1904. Vol. liq. Dec. 1907 for reconstruction as Checkogram (1908) Ld. in which company shareholders were entitled to 1 new share of £1 (credited with 15*s.* paid) for each share of £1 held. Removed from Register 1909 .... **1909**

Checkogram (1908) Ld. Regd. 1908. Vol. liq. Jan. 1913. Struck off Register Apr. 1929 .... **1930**

Cheethams Ld. Regd. 1910. Vol. liq. (members') 18 July 1933. Direct controlling interest owned by Mills & Rockleys Ld. Capital returned to contributories—£1,116 3*s.* 1*d.* Final meeting return regd. 18 Oct. 1933 .... **1934**

Cheleken Oilfields, Ld. Regd. 1910. Struck off Register 14 Apr. 1961 .... **1962**

Chelmsford Brewery (Wells & Perry) Ld. Regd. 1890. Outstanding debenture stock was redeemed at 105% on 1 Mar. 1935. Vol. liq. (members') 5 Apr. 1935. Undertaking was acquired by Taylor Walker & Co. Ld. (later Ind Coope (East Anglia) Ld.), which company owned all shares. Final meeting return regd. 28 Mar. 1936 .... **1936**

Chelmsford Electric Lighting Co. Ld. Regd. 1892. Vol. liq. Oct. 1907. Undertaking and assets were acquired by Electric Supply Corporation Ld. Removed from Register 1908 .... **1908**

Chelmsford Gas Co. Established by Deed of Settlement 1819 as Chelmsford Gas Light and Coke Co. Inc. by Special Act 1874; name changed by Special Act in 1914. Under Act of 1915 the undertaking was transferred to Chelmsford Corporation **1917**

Chelonia Ld. Regd. Edinburgh 1920. Vol. liq. (creditors) 7 June 1935. Certain assets were distributed in specie. Struck off Register 29 Dec. 1967 .... **1968**

Chelsea Brewery Co. Ld. *See* Welch Ale Brewery Co. Ld.

Chelsea Electricity Supply Co. Ld. Regd. 1884. Undertaking was acquired by Central London Electricity Ld. The holder of the ordinary and preference shares received 30.000 6% preference shares and 427,864 ordinary shares of £1 in purchasing company. Dissolved under Sec. 154 of Companies Act 1929 .... **1938**

Chelsea Picture House Ld. Regd. 1921. Struck off Register 27 Oct. 1944 .... **1945**

Chelsea Waterworks Co. Inc. by Royal charter 1723. Undertaking taken over by Metropolitan Water Board June 1904 under the provisions of the Metropolis Water Act 1902 .... **1905**

Cheltenham & District Gas Co. Inc. as Cheltenham Gas Light & Coke Co. by Special Act 1918; name changed 1931. Dissolved 1 May 1949, undertaking being vested in South Western Area Gas Board under Gas Act 1948. Holders of securities were entitled to receive, in respect of each £100 unit held, British Gas 3% guaranteed stock 1990–95 as follows:

	£	s.	d.
5% cons. ord. stock	110	15	0
4% red. pref. stock (issued before 1 Jan.1946)	102	5	0
4% red. pref. stock (issued since 31 Dec. 1945)	100	1	5
4% perp. deb. stock	103	0	0
3½% red. deb. stock	100	0	0

A distribution on cons. ord. stock of 5·821% out of reserves was made in Oct. 1953 .... **1952**

Cheltenham & Swansea Railway Carriage & Wagon Co. Ld. *See* Swansea Wagon Co. Ld.

VOL. FOR

Cheltenham Brewery Holdings Ld. *See* West Country Brewery Holdings Ld.

Chemainus Copper Mine Co. Ld. "Non-Personal Liability." Inc. British Columbia 1906. London office closed in Mar. 1908 .... **1909**

Chembong Malay Rubber Co. Ld. Regd. 1910. Vol. liq. 23 Apr. 1920. Reconstructed as Chembong Malay Rubber Co. (1920) Ld., in which company shareholders were entitled to 2 fully-paid shares of 2*s.* for each share of 2*s.* held; a cash payment of 2⅔*d.* per share was made in Oct. 1920; further payments (if any) not known. Final meeting return regd. 29 June 1923 .... **1921**

Chemical & Metallurgical Corporation Ld. Regd. 1919. Vol. liq. (members') 31 Mar. 1939. All shares held by I.C.I. (General Chemicals) Ld. Final meeting return regd. 3 Sept. 1941 .... **1940**

Chemical & Wood Industries Ld. Regd. 1929. Vol. liq. (members') 27 July 1932. Capital returned to contributories—6*s.* 2⅔*d.* per share of £1. Final meeting return regd. 8 May 1933 .... **1933**

Chemical Refineries Ld. Regd. 1926 as Rayweavers Ld.; name changed Aug. 1937. Struck off Register 7 Mar. 1947 .... **1947**

Chemists, Aerated & Mineral Waters Association Ld. Regd. 1878. Reconstructed 1900 as Camwall Ld., in which company shareholders were entitled to 4 ordinary and 1 preference shares of £1 (credited as fully-paid) for each share of £1 held. Removed from Register 1901 .... **1908**

Chemists' Co-operative Society Ld. Regd. 1895. Vol. liq. 18 Sept. 1897. Final meeting return regd. 7 Oct. 1898 **1898**

Chendai Consolidated Ld. Regd. 1914. Vol. liq. (members') 21 Dec. 1957. Capital returned to contributories—5*s.* 8¾*d.* per share of £1. Final meeting return regd. 15 Sept. 1958 .... **1959**

Chepstow Gas Co. Estd. 1827 as Chepstow Gas & Coke Consumers Co. (Limited); inc. as Chepstow Gas & Coke Consumers Co. by Special Act 1857; name changed 1918. Dissolved 1 May 1949, undertaking being vested in Wales Area Gas Board under Gas Act 1948. Holders of ordinary stock (7½% max.) were entitled to receive in respect of each £100 unit held £175 British Gas 3% guaranteed stock 1990–95 .... **1952**

Chepstow Water Co. Inc. by Special Act 1843. The Newport & South Monmouthshire Water Board Order 1959 provided (inter alia) for the undertaking of this company' to vest in the Newport & South Monmouthshire Water Board from 1 Oct. 1960 for a consideration of £22,050, and for the dissolution of the company. **1922**

Cheque Bank Ld. Regd. 1873. Vol. liq. Dec. 1875. Final meeting return regd. 27 Feb. 1878 .... **1901**

Cheque Bank Ld. Regd. 1876. Vol. liq. 22 Dec. 1893. Final meeting return regd. 13 Feb. 1897 .... **1901**

Cheque Bank Ld. Regd. 1893. Vol. liq. 15 Jan. 1901. Court Order to continue winding up under supervision 16 Jan. 1901. Final meeting return regd. 25 Feb. 1915. Court Order to dissolve 1 May 1915 .... **1901**

Cherakara Tea Estates Ld. Regd. 1912. Vol. liq. 10 Aug. 1920. Capital returned to cootributories—10*s.* per share of £1 at Oct. 1920; further payments (if any) not known. Final meeting return regd. 15 Dec. 1921 **1921**

Cherambadi (Wynaad) District Gold MIning Co. Ld. Regd. 1880. Removed from Register 1888 .... **1883**

Cheras Rubber Estates Ld. Regd. 1912. Vol. liq. (members) 19 Sept. 1973. Capital returned to contributories per £1 share—£18·67. £24·99 paid into Companies' Liquidation Account in respect of unclaimed dividends and £552·70 in respect of unclaimed distributions. Final meeting return regd. 11 Sept. 1975 .... **1976-7**

Cheriaman & Akoko Gold Mines Ld. Regd. 1934. A subsidiary of Amalgamated Banket Areas Ld. Vol. liq. 20 Dec. 1957. Final meeting return regd. 9 Dec. 1958 .... **1957**

Cherokee Goldfields Ld. Regd. 1905. In 1908 the property and assets were sold to Torres Mines Ld., in which company shareholders were entitled to 1 fully-paid A share of 1*s.* for each share of £1 held and an option to apply for further ordinary shares. Struck off Register 1922 .... **1909**

Cherokee (Mexican) Proprietary Ld. Regd. 1902. Reconstructed 1905 as Cherokee Goldfields Ld., in which company shareholders were entitled to 1 share of £1 (credited with 18*s.* paid) for each share of £1 held. Removed from Register 1906 .... **1908**

Cherra Tea Co. Ld. Regd. 1880. Removed from Register 1911 .... **1899**

Chersonese (F. M. S.) Estates Ld. Regd. 1909. Voluntary winding-up 26 Nov. 1985. All capital owned by Barlow Holdings p.l.c. **1980–1**

Chertsey Gas Consumers' Co. Ld. Regd. 1861; statutory powers in 1864. Dissolved 1 May 1949, undertaking

VOL. FOR

being vested in North Thames Area Gas Board under Gas Act 1948. Holders of securities were entitled to receive, in respect of each £100 unit held, British Gas 3% guaranteed stock 1990–95 as follows:

	£	s.	d.
Ord. stock (10% stand.)	250	0	0
Ord. stock (7% stand.)	200	0	0
Ord. stock (5% stand., 7% max.)	140	0	0
6% pref. stock	134	0	0
4% red. pref. stock	100	10	0
3½% red. deb. stock	100	0	0

1952

Cherubang Gold Mining & Exploration Co. Ld. Regd. 1895. Amalgamated with Straits & General Development Co. Ld., in which company shareholders were entitled to 1 share of £1 (credited with 14s. paid) for each share of £1 (18s. 6d. paid) held. Removed from Register 1904 1903

Chesapeake & Ohio Steamship Co. Ld. Regd. 1892. Vol. liq. 31 Oct. 1913. Final meeting return regd. 18 Feb. 1914 1914

Chesham & Brackley Breweries, Ld. Regd. 1895 as Chesham Brewery Ld.; name changed 5 July 1946; all ordinary capital was owned by Taylor Walker & Co. Ld. later Ind Coope (East Anglia) Ld. Vol. liq. (members') 4 June 1953. Final meeting return regd. 24 August, 1963. 1959

Chesham & District Gas Co. Inc. by Special Act 1911. Dissolved 1 May 1949 undertaking being vested in Eastern Area Gas Board under Gas Act 1948. Holders of securities were entitled to receive in respect of each £100 unit held British Gas 3% guaranteed stock 1990–95 as follows:

	£	s.	d.
A ord. stock (5% stand.)	160	0	0
B pref. stock (5% max.)	112	0	0

1952

Chesham Automobile Supply Co. Ld. See Chesham Supply Co. Ld.

Chesham Brewery Ld. See Chesham & Brackley Breweries Ld.

Chesham Electric Light & Power Co. Ld. Regd. 1906. Dissolved 1 Apr. 1948, undertaking being vested in British (later Central) Electricity Authority and Eastern Area Board under Electricity Act 1947 ... 1949

Chesham Finance Co. Ld. Regd. 1926. Vol. liq. (members') 11 Mar. 1943. All shares were owned by Universal Insurance Co. Ld. Assets realised insufficient to meet claims of creditors in full. Final meeting return regd. 1 Feb. 1945 1941

Chesham Supply Co. Ld. Regd. 1908 as Chesham Automobile Supply Co. Ld.; name changed May 1913. Vol liq. Feb. 1920. Shareholders were entitled to 1 fully-paid ordinary share of £1 in Unic Motors Ld. (later United Motors Ld.) for each £1 paid-up ordinary capital held or 1 fully-paid preference share of £1 in that company for each £1 paid-up preference capital held. Final meeting return regd. 1 Dec. 1920 1920

Cheshire Alkali & Salt Co. Ld. Regd. 1895. Vol. liq. 14 May 1897. Undertaking was acquired by Brunner Mond & Co. Ld. [now I.C.I. (Alkali) Ld.] Final meeting return regd. 8 Mar. 1898 1898

Cheshire Alkali Co. Ld. Regd. 1887. Vol. liq. 20 Sept. 1894. Final meeting return regd. 14 July 1896 1895

Cheshire Amalgamated Salt Works Co. Ld. Regd. 1865. Vol. liq. Nov. 1888. Absorbed by Salt Union Ld. [now I.C.I. (Salt) Ld.] Final meeting return regd. 22 Nov. 1889 1889

Cheshire & Broad Green Margarine Ld. See English Margarine Works Ld.

Cheshire Banking Co. Ld. Regd. 1882. Vol. liq. Oct. 1884. Court Order to continue winding up under supervision Nov. 1884. Final meeting return regd. 5 Dec. 1895 1885

Cheshire Creamery Co. Ld. See English Margarine Works Ld.

Cheshire Lines Committee. Inc. by Cheshire Lines Act 1867. Dissolved 2 Apr. 1949; undertaking vested 1 Jan. 1948 in British Transport Commission under Transport Act 1947 1949

Cheshire's Brewery Ld. Regd. 1896. Vol. liq. 14 Jan. 1914. Undertaking and assets were acquired by Mitchells & Butlers Ld. in which company shareholders were entitled to 5 ordinary and 12½ preference shares of £1 for each ordinary share of £10 held, or 8 A preference and 2 B preference shares of £1 for each preference share of £10 held. Final meeting return regd. 5 Jan. 1916 1914

Chesil Court Ld. Regd. 1934. Vol. liq. 27 Jan. 1937. Undertaking acquired by London Associated Electricity (Properties) Ld. Final meeting return regd. 24 July 1937 1938

Chester & Birkenhead Railway Co. See Birkenhead Railway Co.

VOL. FOR

Chester (Edward) & Co. Ld. Regd. 1898. Vol. liq. 20 Nov. 1903. Court Order to continue winding up under supervision 8 Dec. 1903. Final meeting return regd. 22 July 1911 .... *1905

Chester & Birkenhead Railway Co. See Birkenhead Railway Co.

Chester (Edward) & Co. Ld. Regd. 1898. Vol. liq. 20 Nov. 1903. Court order to continue winding up under supervision 8 Dec. 1903. Final meeting return regd. 22 July 1911 .... *1905

Chester Lion Brewery Co. Ld. Regd. 1896. The goodwill and properties were acquired in 1901 by Bent's Brewery Co. Ld., for £81,550 in cash, 2,548 preference shares of £10 and £67,500 in debenture stock. Removed from Register 1904 1903

Chester Race-Course Co. Ld. Regd. 1883. Vol. liq. 25 May 1892. Capital returned to contributories—£200 per share of £75 (£50 paid) at July 1892; further payments (if any) not known. Final meeting return regd. 5 Apr. 1893 1893

Chester Road Brewery Co. Ld. See Cardwell & Co. Ld.

Chester Tramways Co. Inc. 1878. Undertaking taken over by Chester Corporation in Jan. 1902. Shareholders received £6 per share return on account of capital 1903

Chester United Gas Co. Inc. by Special Act 1858. Dissolved 1 May 1949, undertaking being vested in North Western Area Gas Board under Gas Act 1948. Holders of securities were entitled to receive in respect of each £100 unit held British Gas 3% guaranteed stock 1990–95 as follows:

	£	s.	d.
Ord. stock (5% basic)	123	0	0
4% pref. stock (1901)	102	15	6
4% pref. stock (1935)	102	15	6
4% pref. stock (1947)	102	15	6
3½% irred. deb. stock (1901)	99	0	0
3½% irred. deb. stock (1935)	99	0	0
4% red. deb. stock	102	0	0
3% irred. deb. stock	100	8	3

A distribution on ord. stock of 6·04583% out of reserves was made in Feb. 1955 1952

Chesterfield Tube Co. Ld. Regd. 1906. Vol. liq. 9 Apr. 1920. Reconstructed as company of same name. Shareholders were entitled to 1 preference share of £1 for each preference share of £1 held or 3 ordinary shares of 5s. for each ordinary share of 5s. held. The debentures were repaid at 105%'. Final meeting return regd. 8 Jan. 1921 1921

Chesterfield Water Works & Gaslight Co. Inc. by Special Act 1825. Wound up 1896, the undertaking having been transferred to the Chesterfield Gas & Water Board 1897

Chesters Renfrew Engineering Co. Ld. Regd. 1911. Vol. liq. 29 Apr. 1914. Final meeting return regd. 7 Jan. 1916 .... *1913

Chesterton Gaslight Co. Ld. Regd. 1901. By Special Act of 1906 undertaking acquired by Wolstanton United Urban District Council for £2,600. Final meeting return regd. 17 Aug. 1907, on which date company was deemed by Act to be dissolved 1907

Chetwynd Park Estates Ld. Regd. 1924. Vol. liq. (members') 13 Apr. 1953. Final meeting return regd.5 June 1954 .... *1933

Cheudriang Tin Dredging Ld. See C. T. D. Resources Group Ld.

Cheviot Rubber Ld. Regd. 1909. Vol. liq. (members') 22 Dec. 1952. Undertaking amalgamated with Labu (F.M.S.) Rubber Co. Ld. under title of Labu Cheviot Rubber Ld. stock-holders were entitled to receive 1 fully-paid share of 2s. for each 2s. stock unit held. Final meeting return regd. 21 Feb. 1955 1956

Cheviot Trust Ld. Regd. 1939. Vol. liq. (creditors') 2 June 1950. Creditors received a dividend of 1s. 10d. in the £1. Final meeting return regd. 7 Dec. 1964 1966

Chez Taglioni Restaurant Ld. Regd. 1928. Receiver appointed in Nov. 1930 ceased to act in Mar. 1931. Assets realised insufficient to meet claims of debenture holders. Struck off Register Jan. 1933... 1933

Chiapas Mining Co. Ld. Regd. 1889. Vol. liq. 1904. Capital returned to contributories—20s. per preference share of £1; further payments (if any) not known. Removed from Register 1905 1905

Chiapas Zone Exploration Co. Ld. Regd. 1889. Vol. liq. 22 June 1916. Final meeting return regd. 23 Mar. 1917 1917

Chic Clothing Co. Ld. See Salisbury Service Co. Ld.

Chic Ld. Regd. 1902. Court Order to wind up 1905. Removed from Register 1911 1906

Chicago and Grand Trunk Railway Co. Reconstructed in 1900 as Grand Trunk Western Railway Co. which was incorporated in Maine. 1924

Chicago & North-West Granaries Co. Ld. Regd. 1889. Vol. liq. Dec. 1910. Removed from Register 1914 ... 1911

VOL. FOR

Chicago Breweries Ld. Regd. 1889. Vol. liq. in Dec. 1927. No capital returned to contributories. Final meeting return regd. 21 Jan. 1949 1950

Chicago Consolidated Brewing & Malting Co. Ld. Inc. Illinois. All shares were owned by City of Chicago Brewing & Malting Co. Ld. In July 1926 a receiver was in possession of the property and negotiations for its sale were in progress.............................. 1927

Chicago-Gaika Development Co., Ld. Regd. 1897. Vol. liq. (members') 9 Aug. 1965. Final meeting return regd. 11 Nov. 1966 1964

Chicago Great Western Railroad Co. Ld. Inc. Illinois 1909. Reorganised 1935 as Chicago Great Western Railway Co. Holders of 1st mortgage 50-year 4% bonds were to receive in exchange for each $1,000 bond and unpaid interest thereon to 1 Jan. 1938, $285 of 1st mortgage 4% bonds, $172 of general income mor.gage 4½% bonds, $515 of 5% preferred stock and $172 of common stock. The capital stock 1st mortgage and all bonds issued thereunder were cancelled 1941

Chicago, Indianapolis & Louisville Railway Co. Organised Indiana 1897 1910

Chicago Junction Railways & Union Stock Yards Co. Organised New Jersey 1890. Period for which company was organised expired July 1940. Since in liquidation 1942

Chicago, Lake Shore & Eastern Railway. Inc. Illinois and Indiana 1897. Merged into Elgin, Joliet and Eastern Railway Co. in 1938 1943

Chicago, Milwaukee & St. Paul Railway Co. Organised Wisconsin 1863. Reorganised 1927 as Chicago, Milwaukee, St. Paul and Pacific Railroad Co. The following securities (since redeemed) were taken over by new company: Bellingham & Northern Railway 1st mortgage bonds and Milwaukee & Northern Railway 1st mortgage bonds and consolidated bonds. The general mortgage bonds Series A, B and C were also taken over. Holders of the following securities were entitled to 20% of holding in 50-year 5% mortgage gold bonds and 80% of holding in 50-year 5% adjustment mortgage bonds in new company. Interest due being paid in cash: 4% 25-year gold bonds 1909; 4% gold bonds 1925; 4½% convertible gold bonds; 4% Chicago, Milwaukee & Puget Sound Railway 1st mortgage bonds; 4% 15-year bonds 1910 (European issue); 4½% general and refunding mortgage bonds and 5% general and refunding mortgage convertible bonds. After payment of $28, holders of every $100 preferred stock were entitled to $24 50-year 5% mortgage gold bonds and $100 preferred stock in new company; after payment of $32. Holders of every $100 common stock were entitled to $28 50-year 5% mortgage gold bonds plus 1 share of no par value of common stock in new company 1928

Chicago Packing & Provision Co. Ld. Regd. 1890. Removed from Register 1904 1901

Chicago, Rock Island & Pacific Railroad Co. Organised Iowa 1902. In May 1914 company defaulted in payment of interest on 4% bonds. In Dec. 1914 bondholders received $98·50 per bond of $1,000 in cash and were given an option (since expired) to subscribe for stock in the Chicago Rock Island & Pacific *Railway* Co. 1915

Chicago, St. Louis & New Orleans Railroad Co. Consolidated in 1877 in Mississippi, Tennessee, Kentucky and Louisiana. Outstanding bonds were repaid and properties transferred to Illinois Central Railroad Co.; this company was liquidated and dissolved in 1951 1953

Chicago Silver Mining Co. Ld. Regd. 1873. Vol. liq. 11 June 1879. Final meeting return regd. 28 June 1881 *1879

Chicago Terminal Transfer Railroad Co. Organised Illinois 1897. A receiver was appointed on behalf of holders of 1st mortgage 50-year 4% gold bonds in Apr. 1906 1907

Chichiwelli Gold Mines Ld. Regd. 1903. Vol liq. 5 Jan. 1926. Final meeting return regd. 26 Aug. 1926 1926

Chiciura Oilfields of Roumania Ld. Regd. 1913. Vol. liq. (members) 17 Nov. 1932. Capital returned to contributories—14s. 10·808d. per share of £1. Final meeting return regd. 20 Jan. 1933 .... *1933

Chicoutimi Pulp Co. Inc. by Letters Patent in Quebec 1900. Under plan of reorganisation approved in 1925 the undertaking and assets were acquired by Quebec Pulp & Paper Mills Ld. Bondholders were entitled to receive in exchange for their bonds an equal amount of 7% cumulative preferred stock plus 50% in common stock in the new company 1927

Chida (Wassaw) Mines Ld. Regd. 1901. Vol liq. Oct. 1908. Assets were acquired by Gold Coast Amalgamated Mines Ld. (later Amalgamated Mining Trust Ld.). in which company shareholders were entitled

to 2 fully-paid shares of £1 for every 5 shares of £1 held. Removed from Register 1910 1909

Chignecto Marine Transport Railway Co. Ld. Inc. in 1882 by Act of Canadian Parliament. In 1908 the assets were sold for £25,889 and the bonds (of £100) were repaid as follows—11 at £6 10s. per bond; 3,945 bonds at £2 per bond; the remaining 103 bonds received no repayment as no claims were made by holders thereof and the balance of cash and investments (sufficient to pay £6 10s. per bond) was retained by the Trustees and subsequently placed in the hands of the High Court 1952

Chigwell, Loughton & Woodford Gas Co. Established 1863; inc. by Special Act 1873. Under Act of 1911, the undertaking was acquired by Gas Light & Coke Co., in which company shareholders were entitled to £155 7s. ordinary stock for every £100 ordinary stock held. Debenture stockholders were entitled to £133 6s. 8d. debenture stock in acquiring company for every £100 stock held 1912

Chijoles Oil Ld. Regd. 1913. Vol. liq. 30 Jan. 1929. Final meeting return regd. 15 Jan. 1931 1929

Child & Co. Undertaking was acquired in 1924 by Glyn Mills & Co. Ld 1925

Child (J. K.) & Co. Ld. Regd. 1905. Vol. liq. Jan. 1910. Undertaking was acquired by Corocoro United Copper Mines Ld., in which company shareholders were entitled to 11 shares of £1 (credited as fully paid) for every 7 shares of £1 held. Removed from Register 1911 1910

Childe Harold Gold Mining Co. Ld. Regd. 1900. Removed from Register 1905 1905

Chile Gold Mining Co. Ld. Regd. 1881. Undertaking was acquired in 1884 by New Chile Gold Mining Co. Ld., in which company shareholders were entitled to 1 share of £1 (credited with 15s. paid) for each share of £1 held. Removed from Register 1905 1885

Chilean Nitrate & Iodine Sales Corpn. Inc. in Chile 1934. Dissolved as from 30 June 1968 upon expiration of special law under which the Chilean nitrate industry operated 1969

Chilean Nitrate Co. Inc. Chile 1912. Undertaking and assets were sold to Nitrate Corporation of Chile .. 1932

Chilham Consumers' Gas Co. Ld, Regd. 1868. Vol. liq. (members') 31 Dec. 1932. Undertaking was acquired by East Kent Gas Co. Ld. Capital returned to contributories—£1,408 9s. Final meeting return regd. 5 Jan. 1934 .... *1933

Chili Gold Gravels Ld. Regd. 1896. Removed from Register 1905 1900

Chili Telephone Co. Ld. Regd. 1899. Vol. liq. (members') 22 Dec. 1930. Undertaking and assets acquired by Compania de Telefonos de Chile. Capital returned to contributories—£1,448,726. £25 18s. 11d. was paid into Companies' Liquidation Account. Final meeting return regd. 30 Apr. 1932 1930

Chilian Concessions Syndicate Ld. *See* Chilian Mills Co. Ld.

Chilian Eastern Central Railway Co. Ld. Regd. 1910. Receiver appointed in May 1913, ceased to act in Apr. 1923. During 1918 the Court authorised the sale of the Company's property; a first and final distribution of £3 15s. 10d. per £20 1st mortgage bond was declared in Aug. 1923. Struck off Register 1923 1924

Chilian Electric Tramway and Light Co. Ld. Regd. 1898. Vol. liq. 29 Dec. 1921. Undertaking was acquired by Compania Chilena de Electricidad Limitada in which company shareholders were entitled to 1 fully-paid ordinary and 1 preference share of £1 for each preference share of £1 held or 1½ preference and 2 ordinary shares all fully-paid of £1 for each ordinary share of £1 held. Final meeting return regd. 30 July 1932.. 1927

Chilian Exploration & Development Syndicate. *See* Mano Marques (Mexico) Rubber & Tobacco Estates Ld.

Chilian Manganese Mines Ld. Regd. 1899. Vol. liq. 3 Jan. 1905. No capital returned to contributories. £1,577 paid into Companies' Liquidation Account. Final meeting return regd. 4 Jan. 1949 1949

Chilian Mills Co. Ld. Regd. 1900 as Chilian Concession Syndicate Ld.; name changed Dec. 1900. Struck off Register Apr. 1930 1931

Chilian Transandine Railway Co. Ld. Regd. 1888 as Clark's Transandine Railway Co. Ld.; name changed 1905. Vol. liq. (creditors') 31 Mar. 1942. Struck off Register 28 May 1963. Final redemption of 7½% 1st Mortgage Debenture Stock made on 1 June 1971 at par... 1974-5

Chilimayo Gold Mining Co. Ld. Regd. 1906. Vol. liq. Feb. 1909. Removed from Register 1909 1910

VOL. FOR

Chillagoe Co. Ld. Inc. Queensland 1905. Vol. liq. 1913 for reconstruction as Willagoe Ld. in which company shareholders were entitled to receive 1 share of 10s. (credited with 7s. paid up) for each share of 10s. held and to apply for further shares (credited with 7s. paid up)...... **1914**

Chillagoe Ld. Inc. Queensland 1913. Vol. liq. July 1923. Undertaking transferred to Queensland Government...... **1924**

Chillagoe Railway & Mines Ld. Inc. Queensland 1898. Reconstructed as New Chillagoe Railway and Mines Ld. in which company shareholders were entitled to 1 share of £1 (credited with 16s. paid) for every share of £1 held...... **1904**

Chillington Iron Co. Ld. Regd. 1872. Vol. liq. 28 Jan. 1885. Court Order to continue winding up under supervision 6 Feb. 1885. Final meeting return regd. 31 Dec. 1890 ...... ***1886**

Chilnit Ld. *See* Anglo-South American Bank Ld.

Chilworth Gunpowder Co. Ld. Regd. 1885. Vol. liq. 30 June 1920. Final meeting return regd. 30 Oct. 1927 ***1894**

Chimbote (Peru) Coal & Harbour Syndicate Ld. Regd. 1908. Vol. liq. 19 Feb. 1925. Final meeting return regd. 23 Dec. 1927...... **1925**

Chimes Exploration Co. Ld. Inc. Transvaal 1897. Reconstructed under same name in 1899. Shareholders received 1 share in new company for every 3 shares held...... **1903**

Chimes Exploration Co. Ld. Inc. Transvaal 1899. In compulsory liquidation in 1903...... **1903**

"Chimes" Gold Mining Co. Ld. Inc. Natal 1888. Property sold to New Chimes Gold Mining Co. Ld. for 11,955 fully-paid shares...... **1891**

Chimes Mines Ld. Inc. Transvaal 1895. Property sold for 359,925 shares of £1 in Van Ryn Deep Ld. and 114,075 shares of Kleinfontein Deep Ld. **1904**

Chimes West Ld. Inc. Transvaal 1895. Undertaking and assets were sold in Jan. 1909 to Benoni Consolidated Gold Mines Ld. Shareholders were entitled to 1 fully-paid share of £1 for every 6 shares held and options (since expired) to subscribe for further shares **1909**

Chimpul Negri (Sembilan) Rubber Estates Ld. Regd. 1910. Vol. liq. 14 May 1915. Reconstructed as Chimpul M. S.) Rubber Estates Ld. Shareholders were entitled to 1 share of 2s. (credited with 1s. 4d. paid) in new company for each share of 2s. held. Final meeting return regd. 29 Nov. 1923 ...... **1916**

China & Japan Telephone & Electric Co. Ld. Regd. 1883 as China & Japan Telephone Co. Ld.; name changed 1901. All capital owned by Oriental Telephone & Electric Co. Ld. (later Flag Investment Co Ld) Vol. liq. (members') 7 Feb. 1956. Final meeting return regd. 10 Nov. 1956...... **1920**

China & Japan Telephone Co. Ld. *See above.*

China Clay Corporation Ld. Regd. 1910. Vol. liq. 22 June 1923. Final meeting return regd. 23 Apr. 1924 **1924**

China Clay Exploration Syndicate Ld. Regd. 1911. Vol. liq. 5 Dec. 1916. Final meeting return regd. 29 Nov. 1917 ...... **1917**

China Clay Union Ld. Regd. 1890. Struck off Register 11 June 1895...... **1899**

China Shippers' Mutual Steam Navigation Ld. Regd. 1882. Vol. liq. 27 Nov. 1891. Business was acquired by China Mutual Steam Navigation Co. Ld. Final meeting regd. 20 Mar. 1894 ...... **1900**

China Soap & Candle Co. Ld. Regd. 1917. Vol. liq. 11 Nov. 1925. Final meeting return regd. 21 July 1932 **1926**

Chindras Gold Mines Ld. Regd. 1901. Vol. liq. 15 June 1904. Final meeting return regd. 7 Dec.1909 ...... **1906**

Chinese Engineering & Mining Co. Ld. Regd. 1900. Vol. liq. 27 June 1912. Reconstructed as company of same name (later Knitmaster Holdings Ld., later Amalgamated Industries Ld.). Shareholders were entitled to 1 fully paid share of £1 for each share of £1 held. Debenture holders were entitled to repayment at 103% or an equal amount of bonds in new company *plus* a premium of 3% in cash. Final meeting return regd. 3 Sept. 1914 ...... **1913**

Chino Copper Co. Inc. Maine 1909. Dissolved in Feb. 1924. Undertaking and assets transferred to Ray Consolidated Copper Co., in which company shareholders were to receive 1⅗ shares of $10 for each share of $5 held **1925**

Chipande Coffee & Rubber Co. Ld. Regd. 1909. Struck off Register 7 Dec. 1937 ...... **1938**

Chippenham Gas Co. Established by Deed of Settlement 1834; regd. as limited 1876; reincorporated by Special Act 1904. By Special Order of 1932 the undertaking was acquired by Bath Gas Co. in which company holders of original stock A were entitled to £2·3841 consolidated stock for each £1 held; holders of improvement stock B were entitled to £1·19205 consolidated stock for each £1 held; holders of

VOL. FOR

additional ordinary stock were entitled to £1·669 consolidated stock for each £1 held; holders of 6% preference stock were entitled to £1 4s. 5% debenture stock for each £1 held; holders of 4% debenture stock were entitled to £1 4% debenture stock for each £1 held **1933**

Chipperfield and Butler Ld. *See* Marshalls Ld.

Chippindales Ld. *See* Shuters Chippendales and Colyers Ld.

Chipping Norton Gas Light & Coke Co. Ld. Regd. 1911. Dissolved 1 May 1949. undertaking being vested in Southern Area Gas Board under Gas Act 1948. Holders of securities were entitled to receive British Gas 3% guaranteed stock 1990–95 as follows, in respect of each £100 unit, unless otherwise stated, of security held:

	£	s.	d.
Ord. shares (of £5)......	1	0	0
6% 2nd mort. debs. 100	0	0	
6% 3rd mort. debs. 100	0	0	**1952**

Chipping Sodbury Gas & Coke Co. Ld. Regd. 1870. Dissolved 1 May 1949, undertaking being vested in South Western Area Gas Board under Gas Act 1948. Holders of ordinary shares (of £5) were entitled to receive £6 5s. British Gas 3% guaranteed stock 1990–95 for each share held...... **1952**

Chipstead Valley Railway Co. Inc. by Special Act 1893. Under Act of 1899 the undertaking was vested in the South Eastern Railway Co., in which company shareholders received an equal amount of 3% preference stock...... **1900**

Chislehurst Electric Supply Co. Ld. Regd. 1897. All shares were owned by County of London Electric Supply Co. Ld. Dissolved 1 Apr. 1948, undertaking being vested in the British Electricity Authority under the Electricity Act 1947 ...... **1937**

Chislet Colliery Ld. Regd. 1913 as Anglo-Westphalian (Chislet Kent) Colliery Ld.; name changed Nov. 1914. Vol. liq. (members') 12 Sept. 1950. Company's colliery &c. were vested in National Coal Board as from 1 Jan. 1947. Capital returned to contributories—£2 3s. 0·8468d. per preference share of £1 and 6s. 5·05d. per ordinary share of 4s. Final meeting return regd. 14 Dec. 1953 ...... **1955**

Chiswick Electricity Supply Corporation Ld. Regd. 1893 as Bourne & Grant Electricity Supply Co. Ld.; name changed to Aberystwyth & Chiswick Electricity Supply Corporation Ld. May 1898, and as above Feb. 1904. Vol. liq. (members') 18 Feb. 1936. Capital returned to contributories—£1 3s. 9d. per share of 2s. Final meeting return regd. 15 Dec. 1936 **1936**

Chiswick Polish Co. Ld. Regd. 1913. Vol. liq. (members') 30 July 1954. Final meeting return regd. 17 May 1957 ...... **1940**

Chlorination Syndicate Ld. Regd. 1889. Vol. liq. 12 June 1890. Final meeting return regd. 9 Mar. 1891...... ***1891**

Chontales Consolidated Mining Co. Ld. Regd. 1871. Vol. liq. 15 May 1880. Final meeting return regd. 21 Sept. 1882 ...... ***1880**

Chontales Mines Ld. Regd. 1886. Removed from Register 1901 ...... **1891**

Choonsali Tea Co. Ld. Regd. 1888. Vol. liq. 8 Nov. 1906. Removed from Register 1908 ...... **1907**

Chorley & District Tramways Ld. Regd. 1909. Removed from Register 1912 ...... **1911**

Chosen Corporation Ld. Regd. 1923 as Chosen Syndicate Ld.; name changed Aug. 1929. Winding-up order 11 Nov. 1943. Capital returned to contributories—10s. per share of £1. The Official Receiver stated in 1954 that the liquidation was completed. Liquidator released 27 Nov. 1956. Struck off Register 14 July 1959 ...... **1955**

Chosen Gold Mines Ld. Regd. 1912. Vol. liq. 22 Sept. 1919. Final meeting return regd. 1 Oct. 1920...... **1920**

Chosen Syndicate Ld. *See* Chosen Corporation Ld.

Chota Rubber Estates Ld. *See* Corinthian Investments Ld.

Christchurch Gas Co. Inc. by Special Act 1877; further powers in 1912. Undertaking acquired in Dec. 1913 by Bournemouth Gas & Water Co. [later Bournemouth & District Water Co.] subject to the 5% mortgage debentures which remained a charge on the undertaking **1914**

Christie & Co. Ld. Regd. 1903. Vol. liq. 19 Apr. 1928. Undertaking and assets were acquired by Cannon Brewery Co. Ld. [later Ind Coope (London) Ld.] Final meeting return regd. 1 Oct. 1928 ...... **1929**

Christineville Rubber Estates Ld. Regd. 1910. Vol. liq. 31 Dec. 1915. Final meeting return regd. 3 Jan. 1923 **1916**

Christmas Reef (Rhodesia) Development Co. Ld. Regd. 1895. The assets and undertaking were transferred to Goldfields of Victoria Ld. for 97,885 fully-paid shares of 10s. Struck off Register 1923 ...... **1920**

VOL. FOR

Christopher Spence Investment Co. Ld. *See* Anglo-Welsh Investment Trust (Continuation) Ld.

Christy Brothers & Co. Ld. Regd. 1906. Dissolved 1 Apr. 1948. undertaking being vested in the British (later Central) Electricity Authority under the Electricity Act 1947. Ordinary and 6% preference stockholders were entitled to receive in respect of each £1 stock held, £4 4s. 7d. and £1 10s. 6d. British Electricity 3% guaranteed stock (1968–73). respectively. Certain assets were sold to Christy Brothers (Chelmsford) Ld. (now Christy Bros. Ld.) before dissolution **1949**

Chrome Mines Co. Ld. Regd. 1894. court Order to wind up 27 July 1908. Removed from Register 1908 ..... **1899**

Chromographic Enamel Co. Ld. Regd. 1889. Vol. liq. 30 Oct. 1962. Final meeting return regd. 2 June 1967 **1938**

Chronosign Advertising (Parent) Co. Ld. Regd. 1897. Removed from Register 1904 .... **1900**

Chrusos Ld. Regd. 1903. Vol. liq. 22 Apr. 1912. Final meeting return regd. 18 May 1916 .... ***1913**

Chudleigh Electric Light & Power Co. Ld. Regd. 1922. Dissolved 1 Apr. 1948, undertaking being vested in the British (later Central) Electricity Authority and South-Western Area Board under the Electricity Act 1947. Ordinary shareholders were entitled to receive £20 10s. British Electricity 3% guaranteed stock (1968–73), for each share (of £5) held **1949**

Chulsa (Selangor) Rubber Co. Ld. Regd. 1923. Vol. liq. (members') 9 Feb. 1961. Estates purchased by Seafield Amalgamated Rubber Co. Ld. in which Company shareholders were entitled to receive 8 shares of 2s. for each share of £1 held. Capital returned to contributories—£1 8s. 10·85d. per share of £1. Final meeting return regd. 27 Mar. 1962 .... **1963**

Chums Consolidated Ld. Regd. 1899. Removed from Register 1904 .... **1903**

Chungloon Rubber Estates Ld. Regd. 1925 as Chungloon (Kedah) Rubber Estate Ld.; name changed Sept. 1925. Vol. liq. (creditors') 12 Sept. 1931. Undertaking and assets transferred to Chungloon Rubber Estate (1932) Ld. in which company shareholders were entitled to 1 share of 2s. (credited with 1s. 6d. paid) for every 2 shares of 2s. held, and holders of 7½% convertible debentures to 100 fully-paid shares (of 2s.) for each £10 debenture held. Final meeting return regd. 30 May 1934 .... **1933**

Chungloon Rubber Estate (1932) Ld. Regd. 1932. Vol. liq. (members') 18 Dec. 1950. Undertaking and assets acquired by Aberfoyle Plantations Ld., in which company shareholders were entitled to 110·523 fully-paid shares of that company for every 100 shares (of 2s.) held. Final meeting return regd. 26 Mar. 1954 .... **1955**

Chuquitambo Gold Mines Ld. Regd. 1901. Vol. liq. 4 Mar. 1908. Reconstructed as New Chuquitambo Gold Mines Ld., in which company shareholders were entitled to 2 shares of £1 for every 33 shares of £1 held. Final meeting return regd. 16 May 1917 **1908**

Church Colonisation Land Society Ld. Regd. 1884. Vol. liq. 20 Nov. 1893. Struck off Register 18 Jan. 1921 **1899**

Church Fenton, Cawood & Wistow Railway Co. *See* Selby & Mid-Yorkshire Union Railway Co.

Church Ironworks Co. Ld. Regd. 1909. Vol. liq. (members') 24 Jan. 1936. Direct controlling interest owned by Monks, Hall & Co Ld. Final meeting return regd. 24 Mar. 1937 .... **1936**

Church Literature Co. Ld. Regd. 1894. Vol. liq. 16 Aug. 1906. Removed from Register 1908 .... **1907**

Church of England Life & Fire Assurance Trust & Annuity Institution. *See* England Assurance Institution.

Church Pictorial Movement Ld. Regd. 1920. Vol. liq. (members') 29 Apr. 1936. Capital returned to contributories—13s. 5d. per share of £1. Final meeting return regd. 19 July 1937 .... **1937**

Church Stretton Gas Co. Ld. Regd. 1927. Dissolved 1 May 1949, undertaking being vested in West Midland Area Gas Board under Gas Act 1948. Holders of securities were entitled to receive British Gas 3% guaranteed stock 1990—95 as follows:

	£	s.	d.
Ord. shares (of £10)	10	0	0
5% pref. shares (of £1)	1	2	0	**1952**

Church Stretton Hydropathic Hotel Ld. *See* Longmynd Hotel Ld.

Church Stretton Ld. Regd. 1897 as Church Stretton Land Co. Ld. Receiver appointed in Nov. 1909. Struck off Register 1915 .... **1916**

Churiman Exploration Syndicate Ld. Regd. 1901. Struck off Register 1915 .... **1911**

Cicfa Co. Ld. Regd. 1909 as Capsuloids (1909) Ld., name changed Apr. 1934. Vol. liq. (members') 14 Nov. 1952. Final meeting return regd. 29 Apr. 1953 **1940**

VOL. FOR

Cigar-Making Machine Co. Ld. Regd. 1895. Removed from Register 1904 .... **1901**

Cilgwyn Slate Co. Ld. Regd. 1896. Vol. liq. 15 Mar. 1918. Undertaking was acquired by Amalgamated Slate Association Ld. Final meeting return regd. 15 Dec. 1920 .... **1918**

Cincinnati Breweries Ld. Regd. 1889. Vol. liq. 23 Feb. 1925. Distribution of 20% was made to debenture holders in Feb. 1925; further payments (if any) not known. Final meeting return regd. 6 May 1926 ... **1926**

Cincinnati Gas Transportation Co. Inc. West Virginia 1908. Holders of common shares of $100 were offered an equal number of preferred shares series B of $100 in Columbia Gas & Electric Corporation **1936**

Cincinnati, Hamilton & Dayton Railway Co. Inc. Ohio 1895. Holders of guaranteed 1st and refunding mortgage bonds were entitled to an equal amount of Toledo-Cincinnati Division 1st lien and refunding mortgage bonds Series A and the holders of the unguaranteed balance were entitled to 85% of holding in such bonds.......... **1917**

Cinderella Consolidated Gold Mines Ld. Inc. Transvaal 1895 as Cinderella Deep Ld.; name changed May 1910. Vol. liq. Nov. 1926. Undertaking and assets were acquired by East Rand Proprietary Mines Ld., for £165,945 in fully-paid shares of 10s. and £250,000 in cash **1927**

Cinderford Gas Co. Ld. Regd. 1907. Dissolved 1 May 1949, undertaking being vested in South Western Area Gas Board under Gas Act 1948. Holders of ordinary shares (of £1) were entitled to receive £3 6s. British Gas 3% guaranteed stock 1990–95 for each share held **1952**

Cinema Combine Ld. Regd. 1920. Court Order to wind up 22 Nov. 1921. Struck off Register 1928 .... **1922**

Cinema Development Ld. Regd. 1936. Vol. liq. (creditors') 30 Mar. 1938. A direct controlling interest was held by Union Cinemas Ld. Final meeting return regd. 23 Nov. 1940 .... **1939**

Cinema Developments (Warrington) Ld. *See* Warston Pictures Ld.

Cinematograph Finance Corporation Ld. Regd. 1910. Court Order to wind up Jan. 1912. Struck off Register 1923 .... **1912**

Cinescopic Instruments & Services Ld. Regd. 1935. Struck off the Register 25 Nov. 1949 .... **1937**

Cinnamon Bippo Co. Ld. Regd. 1902. Vol. liq. 17 Dec. 1918. Final meeting return regd. 24 Feb. 1920...... **1919**

Cirencester Electric Supply Co. Ld. Regd. 1912. Vol. liq. (members') 15 Feb. 1938. Undertaking transferred to Wessex Electricity Co. Capital returned to contributories—£5 5s. per preference share of £5; £1 9s. 5¼d. per preferred ordinary or ordinary share of £1. Final meeting return regd. 18 July 1938 .... **1939**

Cirencester Gas Co. Regd. as limited 1865. Dissolved 1 Jan. 1937 under Cirencester Gas Act, 1936, the undertaking being acquired by Cirencester Gas Co., in which company shareholders received ordinary stock in exchange for their holdings as follows-For each A (10% standard) share (of £15) £36 of ordinary stock, for each B (5% standard) share (of £6 5s.) £7 10s. of ordinary stock and for each C (7% standard) share (of £15) £25 4s. of ordinary stock.............. **1949**

Cirencester Gas Company. Inc. 1937 by Special Act 1936 to acquire undertaking of limited company of same name. In Mar. 1948 undertaking was acquired by Swindon United Gas Co., which company also assumed all liability in respect of outstanding debentures, and the company was dissolved. Stockholders were entitled to receive £1 14s. 4d. cash for each £1 stock held............... **1949**

Cirencester Water Co. Inc. 1882. Undertaking was sold to Cirencester Urban District Council **1898**

Citizen Assurance Corporation Ld. Regd. 1866 as Planet Assurance Corporation Ld.; name changed 6 Nov. 1872. Court Order to wind up 10 Aug. 1874. Final meeting return regd. 9 July 1875 .... ***1875**

Citizen Gold Mining Co. Ld. Regd. 1893. Vol. liq. 4 Apr. 1895. Final meeting return regd. 3 July 1896.......... **1896**

City Accident Insurance Co. Ld. *See* Accident Insurance Co. Ld.

City Amusements (Newcastle-upon-Tyne) Ld. Regd. 1922. Vol. liq. 21 Dec. 1948. Capital returned to contributories—preference shares of £1: £3 16s. 9·29d.; ordinary shares of £1: £5 14s. 8·25d. Final meeting return regd. 13 June 1949 .... **1951**

City & Brixton Railway Co. Inc. by Special Act 1898. Under City and South London Railway Co.'s Act of 1903 the powers were transferred to that company **1904**

City & Central Dwellings Co. Ld. Regd. 1885. Removed from Register 1895 .... **1893**

City & County Bank Ld. Regd. 1872. Removed from Register 1904 .... ***1876**

See Stock Exchange Year-Book.

VOL. FOR

City & Foreign Investment Trust Ld. Regd. 1928. Undertaking transferred in Feb. 1968 to Union Commercial Investment Co. Ld. in which company shareholders were entitled to receive £5 4% preference stock per £4 preference stock and 9 ordinary shares (of 5s.) per 10 ordinary shares of 5s. held; debenture stockholders received a like amount of 4½% debenture stock 1983. Company is to be dissolved under Section 208 of the Companies Act 1948 1970

City & General Properties Ld. Regd. 1909. Vol. liq. Nov. 1950. Capital returned to contributories—£1 per preference share (of £1); £6 12s. 6·936d. per ordinary share (of £1). Final meeting return regd. 16 Jan. 1958 1959

City & Globe Trust & Finance Corporation Ld. Regd. 1899. Removed from Register 1905 1902

City and Gracechurch Investment Trust Ld. Regd. 1962; converted into public company 1964. On 31 Oct. 1975 undertaking and assets transferred to General Investors & Trustees Ld., ordinary shareholders receiving 350 ordinary shares of 25p for every 1000 and convertible ordinary shareholders 413 ordinary shares for every 1000 held. Struck off Register 30 June 1976 1977-8

City and Provincial Trust Ld. Regd. 1927. Vol. liq. (members') 25 Nov. 1929. Capital returned to contributories—2⅜d. per share on 290,490 shares. Final meeting return regd. 22 June 1933 1930

City & South London Railway Co. Inc. by Special Act 1884, as City of London & Southwark Subway Co.; name changed by Act of 1890. The undertaking was, by the London Passenger Transport Act 1933, transferred to the London Passenger Transport Board in which Board, stockholders were entitled to stock as follows-for every £100 4% perpetual debenture stock held-£88 17s. 9d. 4½% A stock; 4½% redeemable second debenture stock 1942-72, an equal amount of 4½% T.F.A. stock; 5% preference stock 1891, an equal amount of 5% B stock; 5% preference stock 1896, an equal amount of 5% B stock; 5%' preference stock 1901, an equal amount of 5% B stock; 5% preference stock 1903, an equal amount of 5% B stock; and for every £100 consolidated ordinary stock held-£92 10s. of C stock. After distribution of the transport stock the company was to be dissolved 1934

City & Suburban Gold Mining & Estate Co. Ld. Inc. Natal 1895. Vol. liq. June 1924. A distribution of 3s. 6d. per share of £4 was made in Aug. 1924, further payments (if any) not known 1925

City & Suburban Gold Mining Co. Ld. Inc. Natal 1887. Reconstructed 1895 as City and Suburban Gold Mining & Estate Co. Ld., in which company shareholders were entitled to 4 shares of £4 for each share of £1 held 1908

City & Suburban Motor Cab Co. Ld. Regd. 1905. Vol. liq. Mar. 1907. Undertaking was acquired by United Motor Cab Co. Ld., in which company shareholders were entitled to 1 fully-paid preferred ordinary share of £1 for each share of £1 held. Removed from Register 1909 1908

City Arcades, Birmingham, Ld. Regd. 1897. Majority of capital was owned by Raventop Developments Ld. Vol. liq. 1 Apr. 1966. Final meeting return regd. 15 Mar. 1967 1956

City Arms Taverns & Hotel Co. Ld. Regd. 5 Apr. 1881. Vol. liq. 14 Feb. 1919. Final meeting return regd. 8 July 1919. Court Order declared dissolution void. Final meeting return regd. 28 Jan. 1921............... 1919

City Ashanti Gold Mines Syndicate Ld. Regd. 1900. Vol. liq. 8 Sept. 1905. Reconstructed as African Mines Ld., in which company shareholders were entitled to 2 shares of 10s. (credited with 8s. paid) for each share of £1 held. Removed from Register 1906 ... 1906

City Association Ld. Regd. 1907. Vol. liq. (members') 8 Mar. 1932. Capital returned to contributories—1s. 6·45d. per share of £1. Final meeting return regd. 13 July 1935 1933

City Bank Farmers Trustee Co. Ld. Regd. 1911 as Farmers' Loan & Trust Co. Ld.; name changed to City Bank Farmers Trust Co. Ld. on 5 Sept. 1929 and as above 10 June 1938. Vol. liq. (members') 21 Dec. 1943. Capital returned to contributories— 11·2264d. per share of £5 (£2 paid) plus $725,000 U. S. Treasury Notes distributed in specie. Final meeting return regd. 6 Feb. 1946 1947

City Bank Ld. Established 1855. Regd. 1880. Vol. liq. 18 Oct. 1898. Amalgamated with London and Midland Bank Ld. (later Midland Bank Ld.). in which company shareholders were entitled to 2 shares of £60 (credited with £12 10s. paid) for every 5 shares of £40 (£10 paid) held 1899

VOL. FOR

City Bank of Sydney. Established 1863. Inc. by Special Act 1864. It was announced in Nov. 1917 that arrangements were being made to transfer the business to Australian Bank of Commerce Ld. 1918

City Buildings Co. Ld. Regd. 1896. Removed from Register 1902 1902

City Co. of New York Inc. Inc. New York 1911 as National City Co.; name changed June 1933 1935

City Equitable Associated Ld. Regd. 1921. Court Order to wind up 28 Feb. 1922. Struck off Register 1 Sept. 1936 1937

City Equitable Fire Insurance Co. Ld. Regd. 1908. Struck off Register 1 Sept. 1939 1940

City Estates of Canada Ld. Inc. Ontario 1912. In 1914 undertaking and assets were acquired by New City Estates Ld., in which company shareholders were entitled to 1 debenture of $5 and 1 share of $2·50 for each preferred share of $5 held or 1 share of $2·50 for each common share of $5 held 1915

City Exploration Co. of West Australia Ld. Regd. 1895. Removed from Register 1901 1902

City Gate Line Ld. Regd. 1916. Vol. liq. 18 Nov. 1925. Final meeting return regd. 23 Dec. 1932 1926

City Housing Trust Ld. Regd. 1934 under Industrial & Provident Societies Acts (1893 to 1928). Receiver for debenture holders—A. W. Turner (Alfred Savill & Sons) 51A Lincoln's Inn Fields, W.C.2 1938

City Life Assurance Co. Ld. Regd. 1897 as British Homes Assurance Corporation Ld.; name changed Sept. 1909. Court Order to wind up 23 July 1923. Struck off Register 24 Oct. 1939 1940

City National Investment Trust Ld. Regd. as private company 12 Mar. 1909 as City National Investment Co. Ld.; name changed 21 May 1917; converted to public company 20 June 1923. Vol. liq. (members') 26 Feb. 1974. Distributions per share (of £10): £1·67 in Mar. 1974; 40p in Apr. 1975 & final of 3p in 1986. Return of final meeting registered 5 Dec. 1986 1986-7

City of Baltimore United Breweries Ld. Regd. 1889. Vol. liq. 31 May 1899. Undertaking was acquired by Maryland Manufacturing and Trading Co. Ld. Shareholders were entitled to shares in Maryland Brewing Co. as follows—for each preference share of £10 held—£8 in preference shares; for each ordinary share of £10—£5 in ordinary shares. Final meeting return regd. 27 Dec. 1899 1900

City of Birmingham Bank Ld. Regd. 1897. Business was transferred to the London City and Midland Bank Ld. (later Midland Bank Ld.) in 1899. Shareholders received £2 8s. per share of £15, £2 paid 1900

City of Birmingham Tramways Co. Ld. Regd. 1896. Vol. liq. 31 May 1912. All tramway undertaking and properties were acquired by Birmingham and Midland Motor Omnibus Co. Ld. The loans and investments were transferred to Electrical and Industrial Investment Co. Ld. The debentures and preference shares were repaid at par, but holders had right of conversion at par into 4½% debenture stock and 5½% debenture stock respectively. Ordinary shareholders were entitled to 1 preference share of £1 and 3 ordinary shares of £1 in new company for each ordinary share of £5 (£1 paid) held or £4 per share in cash. Final meeting return regd. 9 Aug. 1923 1913

City of Brunswick Tramways Co. Ld. Regd. 1878. Removed from Register 1905 .... *1882

City of Buenos Aires Market Co. Ld. Inc. Buenos Aires 1899. Balance of 6% 1st mortgage debenture bonds redeemed in sterling at par 1 Jan. 1920 1920

City of Buenos Aires Tramways Co. Ld. Regd. 1869. Undertaking was acquired in 1905 by Anglo-Argentine Tramways Co. Ld. Removed from Register 1907 1904

City of Buenos Aires Tramways Co. (1904) Ld. Regd. 1904. Vol. liq. 14 nov. 1967. Capital returned to contributories—11s. 10d. per share of £1 up to 1970 and 117·29p per share thereafter. Final meeting return regd. 14 Jan. 1982 1983-3

City of Calgary Oil Synd. Ld. See Positive Retorts Ld.

City of Carlisle Electric Tramways Co. Ld. See Carlisle & District Transport Co. Ld.

City of Chester Gold Mines Ld. Regd. Edinburgh 1895. Vol. liq. 24 May 1898 for reconstruction as company of same name. Shareholders were entitled to 1 share of 5s. (4s. 6d. paid) for each share of £1 held. Struck off Register 22 Sept. 1936 1902

City of Chester Gold Mines Ld. Regd. 1898. Struck off Register 22 Sept. 1936 1937

City of Chicago Brewing & Malting Co. Ld. Regd. 1890. Court Order to wind up May 1927. Struck off Register Apr. 1934 1935

City of Chichester Gas Co. Inc. by Special Act, 1868. The undertaking was transferred in 1940 to Bognor & District Gas & Electricity Co. Stockholders were

VOL. FOR

entitled to £91 consolidated ordinary stock in purchasing company for every £100 ordinary stock held or £100 of 4½% preference stock in purchasing company for every £100 preference stock held. Holders of 4%, 4½% and 5% debenture stock were entitled to £8 9s., £1 and £1 1s. 9d. respectively of 4½% debenture stock in purchasing company for each £1 stock held **1940**

City of Cork Steam Packet Co. Ld. Regd. Dublin 1871. Vol. liq. (members') 16 Dec. 1936. Business and assets were acquired by British & Irish Steam Packet Co. (1936) Ld. **1940**

City of Dublin Brewery Co. Ld. Regd. Dublin 1865. Company completely wound up 12 Jan. 1886 ...... **1889**

City of Dublin Junction Railway. The undertaking was vested in 1925 in Great Southern Railways Co., in which company stockholders were entitled to an equal amount of similar stock **1925**

City of Dublin Steam Packet Co. Inc. by Special Act 1833. Court Order to wind up 18 Nov. 1924......... **1925**

City of Dunedin Suburban Gas Co. Ld. Regd. 1884. Court Orders: to wind up 2 Nov. 1889; to dissolve 12 Aug. 1891 .... **1890**

City of Durham Gas Co. Inc. by Special Act 1873. Dissolved 1 May 1949, undertaking being vested in Northern Area Gas Board under Gas Act 1948. Holders of securities were entitled to receive, in respect of each £1 unit held, British Gas 3% guaranteed stock 1990—95 as follows:

	£	s.	d.
Orig. shares (10% max.)	1	19	0
Ord. shares (7% max.)	1	8	0
4% pref. shares	1	0	0	**1952**

City of Genoa Waterworks Co. Ld. Regd. 1886. Struck off Register 3 Aug. 1894 .... **1899**

City of Glasgow Life Assurance and Reversionary Co. *See* City of Glasgow Life Assurance Co.

City of Glasgow Life Assurance Co. Est. 1838 by Deed of Co.partnery as City of Glasgow Life Assurance and Reversionary Co.; name changed 1861. Regd. Edinburgh as unlimited 1913. Vol. liq. Nov. 1913. Undertaking and assets were acquired by Scottish Union & National Insurance Co. Capital returned to contributories—£7 10s. per share of £25 (£2 10s. paid); further payments (if any) not known. Final meeting return regd. 29 July 1915 .... **1914**

City of Glasgow Union Railway Co. Inc. by Special Act 1864. Holders of debenture stock received sufficient debenture stocks of the South Western and North British companies to produce 60% and 40% of income respectively; holders of preference and College station stocks received sufficient South Western debenture stock and North British 3% debenture stock to produce 60% and 40% of income respectively. The ordinary shares were cancelled .. **1897**

City of Gloucester Tramways Co. Ld. Regd. 1881. Vol. liq. 12 Nov. 1902. Undertaking was acquired by Gloucester Corporation. A capital return to contributories of £5 per share of £10 was anticipated. Removed from Register 1904 .... **1903**

City of Las Palmas Water & Power Co. Ld. Regd. 1913. Vol. liq. (members') 25 July 1946. Under a scheme approved on 29 Mar. 1946 the undertaking and assets in Las Palmas were sold to the Municipality, the consideration being (a) £120,000 sterling payable in London, (b) a sum estimated at £1,300 in respect of loose plant, tools &c. in Las Palmas, (c) an indemnity in respect of all debts and liabilities (with certain exceptions) in Canary Islands and Spain and (d) the rescission of concession for supply of water and electricity to City of Las Palmas and cancellation of relevant obligations. The proceeds were applied (inter alia) in payment of about 80% of principal amount to holders of prior lien debenture stock and about 10% of principal amount to holders of 1st mortgage debenture stock. Final meeting return registered 26 Mar. 1947 .... **1947**

City of Leeds Central Estates Ld. Regd. 1898. Court Order to wind up 21 Mar. 1905. Liquidator released 19 Sept. 1910. Struck off Register 14 Feb. 1919.... ***1907**

City of Liverpool & District Brewery Ld. *See* United Breweries Co., Liverpool. Ld.

City of London & Southwark Subway Co. *See* City & South London Railway Co.

City of London Brewery Co. Ld. Regd. 1860. Vol. liq. 31 Dec. 1891. Reconstructed as New City of London Brewery Co. Ld. (later City of London Brewery & Investment Trust Ld.), in which company shareholders were entitled to £172 10s. in ordinary shares or £212 in 5% preference shares for every 5 preference shares of £25 (£20 paid); £170 fully-paid ordinary or £209 fully-paid 5% preference shares for every £100 ordinary stock held or every 50 new

VOL. FOR

ordinary shares of £5 (£2 paid) held. Final meeting return regd. 8 Dec. 1894... **1891**

City of London Contract Corporation Ld. Regd. 1882. Vol. liq. 17 Sept. 1923. Final meeting return regd. 8 Oct. 1927 .... **1924**

City of London Discount Corporation Ld. Regd. 1878. Vol. liq. 6 Mar. 1924. Capital returned to contributories—£1 5s. 1½d. per fully-paid ordinary share of £1; 12s. 7½d. per ordinary share of £1 (7s. 6d. paid); £1 1s. 1½d. per founders' share of 16s. Final meeting return regd.3 Nov. 1924 .... **1925**

City of London Electric Lighting Co. Ld. Regd. 1891. Dissolved 1 Apr. 1948, undertaking being vested in British (later Central) Electricity Authority and London Area Board under Electricity Act 1947. Holders of securities were entitled to receive British Electricity 3% guaranteed stock (1968–73) as follows in respect of each £1 unit of capital held:

	£	s.	d.
6% 1st preference stock	1	11	5
8% 2nd preference stock	1	13	2
Ordinary stock	1	14	4
5% consolidated debenture stock	1	4	1¼	**1949**

City of London Exploration Syndicate of Western Australia Ld. Regd. 1895. Vol. liq. 27 July 1898. Final meeting return regd. 26 Jan. 1900 .... **1899**

City of London Fire Insurance Co. Ld. Regd. 1881. Vol. liq. 27 Apr. 1892. Business was acquired by Palatine Insurance Co. Ld., for 26,000 shares. Final meeting return regd. 11 Dec. 1894 .... **1900**

City of London Gas Co. Under Act of 1859 the undertaking was amalgamated with Gas Light & Coke Co. **1888**

City of London Gold Mines Ld. Regd. 1896. Removed from Register 1902 .... **1902**

City of London Insurance Co. Ld. Regd. 1908 as City of London Re-Insurance Co. Ld.; name changed Jan. 1921. Court Order to wind up 21 Feb. 1922. Struck off Register 24 Oct. 1939 .... **1940**

City of London Joint Stock Trust Ld. Regd. 1890. Court Order to wind up 9 Feb. 1898. Removed from Register 1912 .... **1899**

City of London Marine Insurance Corporation Ld. Regd. 1881. Vol. liq. 31 July 1888. Final meeting return regd. 29 Jan. 1892 .... **1888**

City of London Printing & Stationery Co. Ld. Regd. 1879. Removed from Register 1901 .... ***1882**

City of London Re-Insurance Co. Ld. *See* City of London Insurance Co. Ld.

City of Melbourne Bank Ld. Inc. 27 Nov. 1873. Re-incorporated Victoria 1893. In liquidation in 1896 **1896**

City of Monte Video Public Works Corporation Ld. Regd. 1909. Court Order to wind up July 1911. Debenture holders were entitled to 8 fully-paid ordinary shares of 1s. in Rambla Co. of Monte Video Ld., for every £20 debentures. Struck off Register 1926 .... **1912**

City of Monte Video Tramways Co. Ld. Regd. 1892. Reconstructed 1894 as Monte Video Southern Tramways Co. Ld., in which company shareholders were entitled to 1 share of £1 (credited with 17s. 6d. paid) for each share of £1 held. Holders of 6% debentures were entitled to an equal amount of 6% 1st mortgage debentures in new company. Removed from Register 1906 .... **1896**

City of Oxford & District Tramways Co. Ld. Regd. 1880. Vol. liq. (members') 5 Sept. 1950 for reconstruction as City of Oxford Investment Trust Ld. Shareholders entitled to 10 fully-paid shares in new company for each £10 share held plus tax free cash distribution of £10 per £10 share held. Final meeting return regd. 18 Aug. 1951 .... **1952**

City of Potsdam Water Works Co. Ld. Regd. 1885. Vol. liq. 26 June 1890. Works were sold to municipality. Removed from Register 1905 .... **1891**

City of San Paulo Improvements and Feehold Land Co. Ld. Regd. 1911. Vol. liq. 11 Dec. 1970. Shareholders received 1 share in Inversiones Paulistis S. A. (inc. in Panama) for each share held. Final meeting return regd. 2 July 1980 .... **1981–2**

City of St. Petersburg New Waterworks Co. Ld. Regd. 1874. Vol. liq. (members') 24 May 1934. Capital returned to contributories—8s. 6½d. per share of £4 12s. Final meeting return regd. 30 Apr. 1936 ...... **1935**

City of Turin Waterworks Ld. Regd. 1881. Vol. liq. June 1885. Court Order stayed proceedings Jan. 1888. Vol. liq. 12 Oct. 1908. Final meeting return regd. 19 May 1909 .... **1885**

City of Wellington Electric Light & Power Co. Ld. Regd. 1890 as New Zealand Electrical Syndicate Ld.; name changed May 1903. Vol. liq. 16 Sept. 1907; undertaking acquired by City of Wellington for £160,000 payable in City of Wellington 4% Bonds. Final meeting return regd. 25 May 1910 .... **1908**

VOL. FOR

City of Worcester Tramways Co. Ld. Regd. 1889. Vol. liq. 25 Apr. 1892. Undertaking was acquired by Worcester Tramways Ld. Final meeting return regd. 6 Apr. 1894 .... **1902**

City of York Tramways Co. Ld. Regd. 1886. Vol. liq. Mar. 1909. Properties were sold to York Corporation. Removed from Register 1909 .... **1910**

City Oil Synd. Ld. *See* Positive Retorts Ld.

City Rink & Winter Gardens Ld. Regd. 1909. Struck off Register 1914 .... **1911**

City Securities Trust Ld. Regd. 1903. Vol. liq. 3 Apr. 1918. Capital returned to contrsbutories—18*s.* 3*d.* per share of £1 at Jan. 1919; further payments (if any) not known. Final meeting return regd. 14 Aug. 1919 .... **1919**

City Share Trust Ld. Regd. as private company 20 Aug. 1936.; converted into public company 22 Apr. 1960. Vol. liq. (creditors') 14 mar. 1969. Final meeting July 1984. £4,500 in respect of unclaimed creditors' dividends paid into Companies' Liquidation Account **1986–7**

City Steamboat Co. Ld. Regd. 1856. Vol. liq. 1875. Amalgamated with others under the title of London Steam Boat Co. Ld. Final meeting return regd. 27 June 1876 .... ***1876**

City Tailors Ld. Regd. 1902. Vol. liq. (members') 8 Aug. 1930. Undertaking acquired by Lockwood & Bradley Ld. Capital returned to contributories—£1 1*s.* 3*d.* per preference or B preference shares of £1; £7 6*s.* 9*d.* per ordinary share of £1. Final meeting return regd. 21 Apr. 1931 .... **1940**

City Underwriters Ld. Regd. 1917. Vol. liq. (members') 21 June 1934. Capital returned to contributories—14*s.* 2·63034*d.* per share of £1. Final meeting return regd. 1 Aug. 1934 .... **1935**

Civic Investment & Industrial Co. *See* Montreal Light, Heat & Power Consolidated.

Civil, Naval & Military Outfitters Ld. Regd. 1897. Removed from Register 1909 .... **1900**

Civil Service Bank Ld. Regd. 1892. Court Order to wind up 12 Jan. 1915. Struck off Register 1927 .... **1915**

Civil Service. Bread Co. Ld. *See* Golden Grain Bread Co. Ld.

Civil Service Co-operative Society Ld. Regd. 1866. Vol. liq. 10 June 1892. Reconstructed as company of same name. Shareholders were entitled to 1 fully-paid share of £5 in new company for each share of £5 held. Final meeting return regd. 8 Mar. 1893 ...... **1908**

Civil Service Co-operative Society Ld. Regd. 1892. Vol. liq. (members') 1 Aug. 1939. Capital returned to contributories—4*s.* 11½*d.* per £1 preference stock. Final meeting return regd. 19 Apr. 1940 .... **1940**

Claeton Gas & Water Co. Regd. 1875 as Clacton-on-Sea Gas & Water Co. Ld. Inc. 1898. Undertaking acquired by Clacton Urban District Council in Apr. 1898 .... **1899**

Clacton-on-Sea & General Land, Building & Investment Co. Ld. Regd. 1877. Vol. liq. 30 Dec. 1898. Assets were acquired by Coast Developinent Co. Ld., in which company shareholders were entitled to 2 5% preference shares of £5 and 3 ordinary shares of £5 for each share of £25 held. Removed from Register 1913 .... **1899**

Clacton-on-Sea & St. Osyth Light Railway Co. Inc. 1904; further powers 1908 .... **1911**

Clacton-on-Sea Hall & Library Co. Ld. Regd. 1875. Undertaking was acquired in 1898 by Coast Development Co. Ld. Removed from Register 1902 **1905**

Clacton-on-Sea Pier Co. Established 1875. Undertaking acquired by Coast Development Co. Ld., in 1898 **1905**

Clacton Palace of Varieties & Skating Rink Ld. Regd. 1909. Vol. liq. Mar. 1911 for reconstruction as Clacton Palace of Varieties Ld. In which company shareholders were entitled to 1 ordinary share of 10*s.* for each share of 10*s.* held. Removed from Register 1912 .... **1912**

Clacton Palace of Varieties Ld. Regd. 1911. Vol. liq. 9 Dec. 1913. Final meeting return regd. 1 Jan. 1915 **1914**

"Clamond" Incandescent Gaslight Co. Ld. Regd. 1887. Vol. liq. 3 June 1890. Final meeting return regd. 18 Feb. 1893 .... **1891**

Clan Steam Trawling Co. Ld. Regd. Edinburgh 1902. Vol. liq. Jan. 1911. Final meeting return regd. 28 Apr. 1911 .... **1911**

Clapham Steamship Co. Ld. Regd. 1884. Vol. liq. 15 Dec. 1914. Final meeting return regd. 24 Jan. 1929 ***1916**

Clapton Stadium Ld. Regd. 1927 as Clapton Stadium Synd. Ld.; name changed Nov. 1928. Vol. liq. (members') Mar. 1966. Capital returned to holders of units of settlement issued by G. R. A. Property Trust Ld—11·103*p.* per unit. Final meeting return regd. 19 Apr. 1973 .... **1973-4**

Clapton Stadium Synd. Ld. *See above.*

VOL. FOR

Clara & Banagher Railway Co. Inc. as Midland Counties and Shannon Junction by Special Act 1861; re-incorporated by Special Act 1880. Under Great Southern & Western Railway Cos. Act 1895, the Commissioners sold the undertaking to the Great Southern Company for £5,000 .... **1897**

Clare (G.) & Co. Ld. Regd. 1922. Vol. liq. (members') 14 July 1930. Capital returned to contributory—£329 15*s.* Final meeting return regd. 24 Oct. 1930 **1931**

Claremont Cycle Manufacturing Co. Ld. Regd. 1896. Removed from Register 1908 .... **1899**

Claremont Gold Mine Ld. Regd. 1906. Vol. liq. 30 Nov. 1911 for reconstruction as Akoko Gold Mines & Estates Ld., in which company shareholders were entitled to 1 share of 5*s.* (credited with 4*s.* paid) for each share of 5*s.* held. Final meeting return regd. 1 Mar. 1921 .... **1912**

Claremont Trust Ld. Regd. 1906. Vol. liq. Nov. 1908. Undertaking was acquired by Claremont Gold Mine Ld., in which company shareholders were entitled to 4 shares of 5*s.* (credited with 4*s.* 6*d.* paid) for each share of £1 held. Removed from Register 1909 .... **1909**

Clarendon Land Investment & Agency Co. Ld. Regd. 1884. Removed from Register 1908 .... **1892**

Clarendon Manufacturing & Engineering Co. Ld. Regd. 1919. Struck off Register 1928 .... ***1923**

Claridge's Hotel Ld. Regd. 1881 as Claridge's Hotel Co. Ld.; name changed Feb. 1882. Reconstructed as New Claridge's Hotel Ld. Struck off Register 14 May 1897 .... **1895**

Claridge's Patent Asphalte Co. Ld. Regd. 1872. Struck off Register 1927 .... ***1920**

Clark, Burnett & Co. Ld. Regd. 1880. Removed from Register 1909 .... ***1885**

Clark (Robt. Ingham) & Co. Ld. Regd. 1895. Vol. liq. (members') 9 Dec. 1929. Pinchin Johnson & Co. Ld. (later Pinchin Johnson & Associates Ld.), owned all share capital. Final meeting return regd. 27 May 1931 .... **1930**

Clark's Consolidated Ld. Regd. 1895. Vol. liq. Jan. 1908. Removed from Register 1910 .... **1909**

Clark's Transandine Railway Co. Ld. *See* Chilian Transandine Railway Co. Ld.

Clarkson-Stanfield Ore Reduction Co. Ld. Regd. 1896. Vol. liq. 10 Feb. 1899. Final meeting return regd. 21 Jan. 1904 .... ***1900**

Claude's Ashanti Goldfields Ld. Regd. 1900. Vol. liq. 18 Sept. 1905. Removed from Register 1911 .... **1906**

Claus & Co. Ld. Regd. 1906, as Claus & Ree Ld.; name changed Sept. 1917. Vol. liq. 6 Dec. 1923. Undertaking acquired by British Dyestuffs Corporation Ld. [later I.C.I. (Dyestuffs) Ld.] Final meeting return regd. 20 Dec. 1928 .... **1940**

Claus & Ree Ld. *See* Claus & Co. Ld.

Clay Cross Gas Co. Ld. Regd. 1913. Dissolved 1 May 1949, undertaking being vested in East Midland Area Gas Board under Gas Act 1948. Holders of securities were entitled to receive British Gas 3% guaranteed stock 1990–95 as follows in respect of each £1 unit, unless otherwise stated, of security held:

	£	s.	d.	
Ord. shares (10% max.)	2	2	0	
Ord. shares (7% max.)	1	10	0	
4½ red. debs. (per £100)	104	0	0	**1952**

Clay Cross Railway Co. Inc. by Special Act 1903. Construction abandoned by Act of 1905 .... **1906**

Clay (Henry) and Bock & Co. Ld. Regd. 1885. Vol. liq. (members') 26 Feb. 1954. Ordinary and preference shares (of £10) repaid at par 26 Feb. 1954 and remaining assets distributed in specie to sole beneficial owner of capital. £360 14*s.* was paid into Companies' Liquidation Account. Final meeting return regd. 14 Feb. 1955 .... **1956**

Clay (James) & Co. Ld. Regd. 1897. Vol. liq. for reconstruction 1 Oct. 1920. Final meeting return regd. 23 Jan. 1926. Court Order declared dissolution void 2 Apr. 1928. Struck off Register 16 Feb. 1932 **1921**

Clay (James) & Co. Ld. Regd. 1920. Vol. liq. (members') 18 Mar. 1931. Capital returned to contributories—19*s.* 7⅞*d.* per preference share of £1. Final meeting return regd. 6 Dec. 1932 .... **1932**

Clay Lane Iron Co. Ld. Regd. 1882. Vol. liq. 27 Feb. 1900. Absorbed by Bolchow, Vaughan & Co. Ld. Final meeting return regd. 5 Sept. 1900 .... ***1901**

Clayton, Allerton & Thornton Gas Co. Inc. 1864. Undertaking sold to Bradford Corporation 30 June 1902 .... **1903**

Clayton & Shuttleworth Ld. Regd. 1901. Vol. liq. (creditors') Feb. 1930. Undertaking was acquired by Marshall Sons & Co. Ld. Certain assets were acquired by Clayton Dewandre Co. Ld. (later Clayton Dewandre Holdings Ld.). The proceeds

**See Stock Exchange Year-Book.*

VOL. FOR

were insufficient to pay debenture holders in full. Final meeting return regd. 9 Dec. 1936 .... **1931**

Clayton Bros. Ld. Regd. 1911 as F. G. Paterson & Clayton Ld.; name changed Sept. 1913. Vol. liq. 9 Mar. 1914. Final meeting return regd. 24 Sept. 1918 ***1915**

Clayton, Marsdens & Co. Ld. *See* Clayton Murgatroyd & Co. Ld.

Clayton, Marsdens, Holden & Co. Ld. *See* Clayton Murgatroyd & Co. Ld.

Clayton-Murdoch Gas Appliances Ld. *See* Clayton-Murdoch Ld.

Clayton-Murdoch Ld.. Regd. 1923 as Clayton-Murdoch Gas Appliances Ld.; name changed June 1925. Court Order to wind up Apr. 1933. Struck off Register 21 Sept. 1937 .... **1938**

Clayton, Murgatroyd & Co. Ld. Regd. 1874 as Clayton, Marsdens, Holden & Co. Ld.; name changed 1 Apr., 1881 to Clayton, Marsdens & Co. Ld., and as above 5 Dec. 1890. Vol. liq. 5 Jan. 1898. Final meeting return regd. 5 May 1898 .... ***1881**

Clayton Wagons Ld. Regd. 1920. Vol. liq. 28 Oct. 1929. Motor engineering section and certain assets were acquired by Clayton Dewandre Co. Ld. (later Clayton Dewandre Holdings Ld.). Final meeting return regd. 9 Dec. 1936.. **1930**

Cleartron Radio Ld. Regd. 1925. Receiver appointed 28 Dec. 1926. Vol. liq. 10 Jan. 1927. Final meeting return regd. 20 Feb. 1930 .... ***1927**

Cleator and Workington Junction Railway Co. Inc. by Special Act 1876. In 1923 the undertaking was merged into the London Midland & Scottish Railway Co., in which company stockholders were entitled to stock as follows:

For each £100 held		L. M. & S.	
3½% Debenture	£87½	4% Debenture	
4½% Preference	£112½	4% Pref. (1923)	
4% Pref. (1882 & 1883)	£100	4% Pref. (1923)	
Ordinary	£65	Ordinary	**1924**

Cleator Moor Gas Co. Ld. Regd. 1871. By Cleator Moor Local Board (Gas) Act 1892 undertaking was transferred to Local Board for £16,000 and assets distributed among shareholders. Company dissolved 28 Nov. 1892 .... **1893**

Clee Hill Granite Co. Ld. Regd. 1906. Vol. liq. 16 Aug. 1929. Undertaking and assets were acquired by British Quarrying Co. Ld., for £40,365 in cash. The debenture holders were repaid in June 1929 at par. Final meeting return regd. 6 May 1930 .... **1930**

Clee Hill Mining & Development Co. Ld. Regd. 1922. Vol. liq. 15 Sept. 1927. Final meeting return regd. 3 Dec. 1929 .... **1928**

Cleethorpes Gas Co. Estd. 1863; inc. by Special Act 1866. Dissolved 1 May 1949, undertaking being vested in East Midland Area Gas Board under Gas Act 1948. Holders of securities were entitled to receive, in respect of each £100 unit held, British Gas 3% guaranteed stock 1990–95 as follows:

	£	s.	d.
Cons. ord. stock (5% stand.)	127	10	0
New ord. stock (5% stand.)	127	10	0
5% red. pref. stock	101	0	0
5⅜% red. deb. stock	116	0	0	**1952**

Cleeves Western Valleys Anthracite Collieries Ld. Regd. 1927. All shares owned by Amalgamated Anthracite Collieries Ld. Struck off Register 10 Mar. 1939 ... **1939**

Clegg (William) Ld. Regd. 1917. Vol. liq. (members') 28 Jan. 1939. Capital returned to contributories— £2,033 18s. Final meeting return regd. 21 June 1939 **1940**

Cleghorn & Bates Ld. Regd. 1920. Vol. liq. (members') 21 Oct. 1933. Undertaking was acquired by I.C.I. (Alkali) Ld. Capital returned to contributories— £55,850. Final meeting return regd. 4 Oct. 1934 . **1929**

Cleland (William) & Co. Ld. *See* Clelands (Shiprepairers) Ld.

Clelands (Shiprepairers) Ld. Regd. 1872 as William Cleland & Co. Ld. Struck off Register 16 Dec. 1938 **1892**

Clément, Gladiator & Humber (France) Ld. Regd. 1896. Vol. liq. 8 Feb. 1901. Reconstructed as Société Française des Cycles Clément et Gladiator Ld., in which company shareholders were entitled to 2 ordinary shares of £1 for every 7 ordinary shares of £1 held or 1 preference share of £1 for every 2 preference shares of £1 held. Removed from Register 1903 .... **1902**

Clement-Smith & Co. Ld. Regd. 1888. Vol. liq. 24 June 1889. Taken over by Hansard Publishing Union Ld. Final meeting return regd. 2 Sept. 1891 .... **1890**

Cleobury Mortimer and Ditton Priors Light Railway Co. Inc. (under Light Railways Act 1896) by order of Light Railway Commissioners confirmed by Board of Trade 1901. In 1922 the undertaking was merged into the Great Western Railway Co. in which company stockholders were entitled to stock as follows:

VOL. FOR

For each £100 held		G.W.R.	
5% Loans	£100	4% Debenture	
Ordinary Shares	£33 6s. 8d.	Cons. Ord.	**1924**

Clergy Mutual Assurance Society. Est. 1829 under Friendly Societies Acts; inc. 1914 by Special Act. All liabilities and assets as at 30 Oct. 1957 were taken over by The London Life Association Ld. Winding-up order 21 July 1958. Liquidator released 18 June, 1959... **1960**

Clerical, Medical & General Investment Trust Ld. Regd. 1920. Vol. liq. (members') 3 Mar. 1939. Capital returned to contributories—£10,138 15s. 8d. Final meeting return regd. 6 Dec. 1939 .... **1940**

Clevedon & District Electric Supply Co. Ld. *See* North Somerset Electric Supply Co. Ld.

Clevedon & Yatton Gas Co. Inc. as Clevedon Gas Co. by Special Act 1868; name changed 1937. Dissolved 1 May 1949, undertaking being vested in South Western Area Gas Board under Gas Act 1948. Holders of securities were entitled to receive British Gas 3% guaranteed stock 1990–95 as follows in respect of each £100 unit held:

	£	s.	d.
Cons. ord. stock (5% basic)	113	10	0
5% cons. pref. stock	113	10	0
4% irred. deb. stock	102	0	0	**1952**

Clevedon, Portishead & District Electric Supply Co. Ld. *See* North Somerset Electric Supply Co. Ld.

Clevedon Water Co. Regd. 1865 as Clevedon Waterworks Co. Ld.; inc. under present title by Special Act 1909. By Order coming into operation 29 Dec. 1952 the undertaking was transferred to the Bristol Waterworks Co. Terms of acquisition: ordinary shareholders to receive £10 cash per share; preference shareholders £9 Bristol preference stock (5%) for each share; and debenture stockholders £1 Bristol 4% debenture stock for each £1 held. Dissolved by resolution of the directors dated 10 Sept. 1953 declaring completion of the winding up **1955**

Clevedon Waterworks Co. Ld. *See* above.

Cleveland & Durham County Electric Power Co. Inc. by Special Act. 1901. By Act of 1932 the undertaking was transferred to North Eastern Electric Supply Co. Ld., which owned indirectly practically all the share capital and debenture stock. The debenture stock was cancelled and the company was dissolved **1933**

Cleveland & Durham Electric Power Ld. Regd. 1906. By Act of 1932. the assets were transferred to North-Eastern Electric Supply Co Ld., which owned nearly all the shares and preference income stock. Shareholders, other than the North-Eastern Co., were entitled to 3 fully-paid ordinary shares of North Eastern Electric Supply Co. Ld. for every 4 shares held, and 4 fully-paid 5% preference shares of that Co. for every 5 preference shares or each £7 funded preference income stock held. Dissolved by Act on 30 Sept. 1932 .... **1933**

Cleveland & Marietta Railway Co. Organised Ohio 1886. Consolidated with Toledo, Walhonding Valley & Ohio Railroad Co. to form Toledo, Columbus & Ohio River Railroad Co. The liability for the 4½% mortgage bonds was assumed by acquiring company and later was assumed by Pennsylvania Ohio & Detroit Railroad Co.; these bonds were redeemed in 1935 .... **1935**

Cleveland Extension Mineral Railway Co. Inc. by Special Act 1873. The powers having expired, a distribution of the Parliamentary deposit was, under Court Order, made among creditors in 1899 .... **1900**

Cleveland Flour Mills Ld. Regd. 1898. Vol. liq. 27 Dec. 1928. Goodwill and other assets were sold to Joseph Rank Ld. Final meeting return regd. 16 Oct. 1934 **1929**

Cleveland Gas Co. Inc. by Special Act 1875. Dissolved 1 May 1949, undertaking being vested in Northern Area Gas Board under Gas Act 1948. Holders of shares of £10 (with £8 paid) were entitled to receive £4 British Gas 3% guaranteed stock 1990–95 for each share held **1952**

Cleveland, Lorain & Wheeling Railway Co. Organised Ohio 1893. Properties were taken over by Baltimore & Ohio Railroad Co. which company owned practically all capital stock. Liability for the 5% consolidated 1st mortgage bonds, 5% general mortgage bonds and 4½% consolidated refunding mortgage bonds (since redeemed) was assumed by acquiring company **1910**

Cleveland Milling Co. Ld. Regd. Edinburgh 1890. Vol. liq. Feb. 1900. Court Order to dissolve 20 Aug. 1906 **1904**

Cleveland Salt Co. Ld. Regd. 1887. Vol. liq. (members') 2 Apr. 1947. Capital returned to contributories—£2 per preference share of £4 (£2 paid) and 14s. per deferred share of £4. Final meeting return regd. 30 Jan. 1951 .... **1952**

VOL. FOR

Cleveland Shipbuilding Co. Ld. Regd. 1923. Vol. liq. (members') 15 Jan. 1930. All capital owned by Parsons Marine Steam Turbine Co. Ld. (later Parsons Marine Turbine Co. Ld.) **1930**

Cleveland Water Co. Inc. by Special Act in 1869. The undertaking vested in the Tees Valley & Cleveland Water Board on 1 Apr. 1958 for £92,000. Capital returned to contributories—£9 (plus a small amount of interest) per £10 capital held. The company was dissolved on 15 Dec. 1958 .... **1960**

Clews (James) & Sons Ld. Regd. 1899. Vol. liq. (members') 20 Nov. 1936. All shares held by Evered & Co. Ld. Final meeting return regd. 24 Apr. 1937 **1937**

Clifford, Hawes & Co. Ld. Regd. 1884. Vol. liq. 1903 for sale of undertaking to William Brothers' Direct Supply Stores Ld. Shareholders were entitled to 5s. in £ for preference shares or 1s. in £ for ordinary shares. Removed from Register 1903 .... **1903**

Cliffs & Norbreck Hydro Ld. (The) See Norbeck Castle Hotel Ld.

Clifton & Kersley Coal Co. Ld. Regd. 1885. Undertaking was acquired in 1935 by Manchester Collieries Ld., in exchange for shares; the terms were not ascertainable. Struck off Register 1935 .... **1936**

Clifton Arms Hotel Co., Lytham Ld. Regd. 1876. Vol. liq. 22 May 1895. Certain properties were acquired by Duttons' Lancashire and Yorkshire Property Corporation Ld. (later Dutton's Lancashire and Yorkshire Brewery Corporation Ld.). Final meeting return regd. 10 Dec. 1985 .... **1896**

Clifton Colliery Co. Ld. Regd. 1876. Court Order to wind-up 28 Nov. 1938. Assets realised sufficient to repay B debenture holders at the rate of 3d. in the £. No capital returned to contributories. Liquidator released 7 Feb. 1949 .... **1950**

Clifton Consolidated Copper Mines of Arizona Ld. Regd. 1901. Removed from Register 1907 .... **1904**

Clifton Consolidated Gold Mines Ld. Regd. 1901. Vol. liq. Jan. 1912. Removed from Register 1913 .... **1912**

Clifton Grand Spa & Hydro, Ld. Regd. 1896. Struck off Register 1923 .... ***1918**

Clifton Hotel Co. Ld. Regd. 1863. Struck off Register 25 Mar. 1938 .... **1939**

Clifton Rubber Co. Ld. Regd. 1901. Vol. liq. 30 Nov. 1905. Undertaking acquired by Clipper Tyre Co. Ld. Final meeting return regd. 15 Aug. 1906 .... **1940**

Clifton Silver Mining Co. Ld. Regd. 1871. Removed from Register 1884 .... ***1876**

Clifton Suspension Bridge Co. Inc. by Special Act 1861. Undertaking transferred, as from 1 Jan. 1953, to the Clifton Suspension Bridge Trust and company dissolved 19 June 1953 .... **1954**

Cliftophone & Records Ld. Regd. 1928. Court Order to wind up 21 Oct. 1929. Struck off Register 20 Mar. 1936 .... **1937**

Cliftophone Ld. Regd. 1921. Vol. liq. 2 July 1928. In 1927 over 99% of the capital was acquired by British Brunswick Ld., for £8,929 in fully-paid preference shares. Final meeting return regd. 1 Aug. 1931. **1928**

Climax Gold Mines (California) Ld. Regd. 1913. Struck off Register 1916 .... **1916**

Climax Rock Drill & Engineering Ld. Regd. 1913 as Climax Rock Drill & Engineering Works Ld.; name changed as above 1958. Vol. liq. (members') 18 Mar. 1966. Struck off Register 14 July 1970 ... **1965**

Climax Weldless Tubes Ld. Regd. 1896. Acquired by Tubes Ld. Vol. liq. 4 July 1897. Final meeting return regd. 24 Apr. 1901 .... ***1898**

Clinch & Co. Ld. Regd. 1950. All capital was owned by Courage Barclay & Simonds Ld. Vol. liq. (members') 6 Nov. 1966. Final meeting return regd. 15 Feb. 1967 .... **1964**

Clinical and General Industries Ld. Regd. 1911 as Sarawak Rubber Estates Ld.; name changed Feb. 1958. Vol. liq. (members') 31 Jan. 1961. Capital returned to contributories—2·94d. per share of 2s. and £24,000 ordinary stock in Lewis & Burrows Ld. (£1 for every 50 shares held). Final meeting return regd. 20 Apr. 1964 .... **1965**

Clinton's Gold Concessions Ld. Regd. 1901. Undertaking and assets were acquired by United Gold Mines of West Africa Ld., in which company shareholders were entitled to 4 fully-paid shares of 5s. for each fully-paid share of £1 held. Removed from Register 1905 .... **1904**

Clippens Oil Co. Ld. Regd. Edinburgh 1878. Vol. liq. 24 Dec. 1892. Final meeting return regu. 11 Dec. 1894 **1908**

Clippens Oil Co. Ld. Regd. Edinburgh 1893. Vol. liq. May 1908. Removed from Register 1912. Court Order to dissolve 6 Feb. 1912. .... **1909**

Clipper Pneumatic Tyre Co. Ld. Regd. 1897. Reconstructed 1904 as Clipper Tyre Co. Ld. in which company shareholders were entitled to 1 fully-paid

VOL. FOR

share of £1 for each share of £1 held. Removed from Register 1905 .... **1908**

Clipper Tyre Co. Ld. Regd. 1904. Vol. liq. (members') 10 May 1954. Final meeting return regd. 19 July 1956 **1940**

Clissold Laundry Ld. Undertaking and assets were acquired by Advance Laundries Ld. **1929**

Clitheroe Estate Co. Ld. Regd. 1898. Vol. liq. 25 Apr. 1945. Final meeting return regd. 10 Dec. 1949 ..... **1950**

Clitters United Mines Ld. Regd. 1900. Vol. liq. May 1908 for reconstruction as Hingston and Clitters Mines Ld., in which company shareholders were entitled to 1 share of 10s. (credited with 5s. paid) for each share of £1 held. Debenture holders received an equal amount of debentures in new company. Removed from Register 1913 .... **1909**

Clogau Mining Co. Ld. Regd. 1880. Removed from Register 1905 .... **1885**

Clogher Valley Railway Co. Ld. Inc. Dublin 3 Dec. 1883 under Tramways & Public Cos. (Ireland) Act 1883 as Clogher Valley Tramways Co. Ld.; name changed July 1894. Railway was closed 31 Dec. 1941 and assets realised. Capital returned to public shareholders—£10 per share of £10. Dissolved under Clogher Valley Railway Co. (Winding-up) Act (Northern Ireland) 1944 .... **1945**

Clonakilty Extension Railway Co. Inc. by Special Act 1881. In 1924 the undertaking was transferred to the Great Southern Railway Co., in which company stockholders were entitled to stock as follows:

For each £100 held	Gt. Sthn. Rly.
4% Debenture	£100 4% Debenture
5% (Baronial Gtee.)	
Pref.	£125 4% Preference
Ordinary	£70 Ordinary

1925

Cloncurry Copper and Smelting Co. Ld. Regd. Edinburgh 1883. Assets purchased by New Cloncurry Copper and Smelting Co. Ld. Vol. liq. June 1895. Final meeting return regd. 10 May 1897 .... **1907**

Cloncurry Syndicate Ld. Regd. 1906. Vol. liq. 26 Oct. 1917. Final meeting return regd. 26 Feb. 1927 .... **1917**

Clontarf & Hill of Howth Tramroad Co. Inc. by Special Act 1898. Court Order to wind up 1 July 1941. First distribution £4 10s. per share of £10 in Dec. 1941; further payments (if any) not known **1942**

Clough (Alfred) Ld. See Grindley of Stoke (Ceramics) Ld.

Clover Mill (Rochdale) Ld. Regd. 1904. Vol. liq. 13 Jan. 1920. Reconstructed as company of same name. Shareholders were entitled to 15 fully-paid shares of £1 in new company for each share of £5 (£3 paid) held. Final meeting return regd. 8 Oct. 1920 ...... **1921**

Clover Mill (Rochdale) Ld. Regd. 1920. A subsidiary of Clover Croft & State Ld. Vol. liq. (members') 19 Jan. 1956. Final meeting return regd. 9 Mar. 1956 **1940**

Cloverfield Mines Ld. Inc. Transvaal 1903. Assets acquired by Modderfontein East Ld., in which company shareholders were entitled to 1 fully-paid share of £1 for every 3 shares held **1919**

Cloxwiches Ld. Regd. 1911 as Venner Time Switches Ld., name changed to Venner Ld. 1951 and changed as above 29 Mar. 1971. Vol. liq. (members') 31 Mar. 1971. Final meeting return reg'd 19 Feb. 1976. Dissolved 19 May 1976. .... **1971**

Clunes Goldfields (1931) Ld. Regd. 1931. Struck off the Register 11 May 1951 .... **1952**

Cluny Rubber Estates Ld. Regd. 1910. Vol. liq 15 Oct. 1947. Undertaking was acquired by Lanadron Rubber Estates Ld., in which company stockholders were entitled to £70 stock for every £100 old stock held. £20 16s. 2d. was paid into Companies' Liquidation Account. Final meeting return regd. 13 Sept 1948 .... **1949**

Clutha Gold Mines Ld. Regd. 1890. Vol. liq. 18 Apr. 1895. Reconstructed as company of same name. Shareholders were entitled to 1 share of £1 (credited with 17s. paid) in new company for each share of £1 held. Final meeting return regd. 2 Dec. 1895 .... **1898**

Clutha Gold Mines Ld. Regd. 1895. Vol. liq. 6 Dec. 1897. Reconstructed as company of same name. Shareholders were entitled to 1 fully-paid share of £1 in new company for every 3 shares of £1 held. Final meeting return regd. 27 Feb. 1899 .... **1898**

Clutha Gold Mines Ld. Regd. Edinburgh 1897. Vol. liq. July 1908. Struck off Register 27 Oct. 1936 .... **1937**

Clutha River Gold Dredging Ld. Regd. 1934. Vol. liq. (members') 24 July 1963. Capital returned to contributories—1s 3¾d. per share of 1s. 5d. £571 9s 9d. was paid into Companies' Liquidation Account in respect of unclaimed distributions. Final meeting return regd. 14 Oct. 1964 .... **1965**

Clyde & Tyne South African Syndicate Ld. Regd. 1895. Reconstructed 1900 as New Clyde Tyne South African Syndicate Ld., in which company shareholders were entitled to 1 share of £1 (credited with

See Stock Exchange Year-Book.

VOL. FOR

15s. paid) for each share of £1 held. Holders of debenture stock were entitled to an equal amount of 6% debenture stock in new company. Removed from Register 1910 .... **1904**

Clyde, Ardrishaig & Crinan Railway Co. Inc. by Special Act 1887. Undertaking abandoned by Act of 1892 **1893**

Clyde Coal Co. Ld. See Wilsons & Clyde Coal Co. Ld.

Clyde Cold Storage Co. Ld. Regd. in Edinburgh 1918. Vol. liq. 30 Dec. 1974. Capital returned to contributories—£1 per preference share (of £1) and £1·6814 per ordinary share (of 75p). On 10 Aug. 1979 it was stated that the company had been fully wound up and that £216·53 had been paid to the Accountant of the Court in respect of unclaimed dividends and distributions **12981-2**

Clyde Cycle & Motor Car. Co. Ld. Regd. 1897. Vol. liq. 7 Jan. 1905. Final meeting return regd. 4 June 1908 ***1900**

Clyde Engineering Iron & Shipbuilding Co. Ld. See London & Glasgow Engineering & Iron Ship building Co. Ld.

Clyde Gold Mines Ld. Regd. 1895. Debenture holders foreclosed; property was acquired by New Clyde Gold Mines Ld., for £12,500 in shares of £1 and £1,000 in cash. Removed from Register 1899 **1898**

Clyde Locomotive Co. Ld. See Sharp, Stewart & Co. Ld.

Clyde Navigation Trust. Inc. Special Act 1858. Outstanding funded debt was exchanged for irredeemable stock of the Clyde Port Authority on 1 Jan. 1966 as follows (per £100 held)—3% funded debt £100 3% stock; 3½% funded debt £75 3% & £25 4% stock; 3½% funded debt £50 3% & £50 4% stock; 4% funded debt £100 4% stock. Bonds outstanding became bonds of the Clyde Port Authority and the Trust was dissolved 1 Jan. 1966 .... **1967**

Clyde Valley Electrical Power Co. Incorporated by Special Act 1901. Dissolved 1 Apr. 1948, undertaking being vested in British (later Central) Electricity Authority and South West Scotland Area Board under Electricity Act 1947. Holders of securities were entitled to receive British Electricity 3% guaranteed stock (1968–73), as follows in respect of each £1 unit of capital held:

	£	s.	d.
6% 1st preference stock	1	11	10
8% 2nd preference stock	2	1	0
Ordinary stock	2	6	5	**1949**

Clydebank Engineering & Shipbuilding Co. Ld. Regd. Edinburgh 1890 as James and George Thomson Ld.; name changed Feb. 1897. Vol. liq. 3 Oct. 1899. Undertaking and assets were acquired in 1899 by John Brown & Co. Ld. for 66,666 ordinary shares of £1 and £856,589 in cash. Final meeting return regd. 9 Feb. 1907.. **1900**

Clydesdale Distillery Co. Ld. Regd. Edinburgh 1894. Vol. liq. July 1914. Undertaking sold to Scottish Malt Distillers Ld., in which company shareholders were entitled to 6·3 ordinary and 3·3 preference shares of £1 for each ordinary share of £10 held or 10 preference shares of £1 for each preference share of £10 held. Final meeting return regd. 4 Jan. 1915 **1915**

Clydesdale Supply Co. Ld. Regd. Edinburgh 1935. Winding-up Order 23 June 1965. Operating subsidiary [Merchants Facilities (Glasgow) Ld.] was sold 1965. No payment was made to shareholders. Liquidator released 30 Dec. 1966. Struck off Register 5 Apr. 1967 .... **1967**

Clyno Engineering Co. (1922) Ld. Regd. 1922. Vol. liq. 19 Aug. 1929. Undertaking acquired by Alfred Herbert Ld. Final meeting return regd. 1 Sept.1931 ***1930**

Coal & Allied Industries Ld. Regd. 1909 as Motor Fuel Proprietary Ld.; name changed Dec. 1934. Receiver appointed in Nov. 1937. Assets realised insufficient to meet claims of debenture holders. Struck off Register 4 Aug. 1939.. **1940**

Coal & Ore Dressing Appliances Ld. Regd. 1890 as Luhrig's Coal & Ore Dressing Appliances Ld.; name changed 1917. Receiver appointed on 25 Apr. 1928. Vol. liq. Jan. 1929. Struck off Register 1932 **1932**

Coal-Brick Co. of the United Kingdom Ld. Regd. 1893. Vol. liq. 28 Nov. 1894. Undertaking was acquired by New Coal Brick Syndicate Ld. Final meeting return regd. 30 May 1895 .... **1895**

Coal-Brick Syndicate Ld. Regd. 1892. Vol. liq. 18 July 1894. Acquired by New Coal-Brick Syndicate Ld. Final meeting return regd. 30 May 1895 .... ***1895**

Coal Commission. Inc. by Coal Act of 1938. Dissolved by Order of 1947, the outstanding rights, liabilities and interest having been transferred to National Coal Board **1947**

Coal Conversion Ld. Regd. 1928. Vol. liq. (members') 29 June 1943. Capital returned to contributories—3s. 6·15d. per share of 10s. Final meeting return regd. 22 Feb. 1944 .... **1945**

VOL. FOR

Coal Co-operative Society Ld. Regd. 1872 under Industrial & Provident Societies Acts **1893**

Coal Co-operative Society Ld. See W. G. Beaton & Co. Ld.—regd. 1894 ....

Coal Mines Syndicate Ld. Regd. 1887. Vol. liq. 11 Jan. 1895. Final meeting return regd. 14 Jan. 1897 ...... **1896**

Coal, Peat & Oil Ld. Regd. 1919. Vol. liq. 3 Nov. 1922. Final meeting return regd. 6 Mar. 1925 .... **1923**

Coal Saving & Smoke Consuming Co. Ld. Regd. 1920. Vol. liq. 22 Mar. 1922. Final meeting return regd. 12 June 1924 .... **1923**

Coal Synd. Ld. Regd. Edinburgh 1914. Vol. liq. 26 Jan. 1925. Undertaking acquired by North British Investment Trust Ld. Final meeting return regd. 17 Jan. 1933 .... **1934**

Calinga British Oil Co. Ld. Regd. 1910. Vol. liq. May 1911. The undertaking was acquired by British Consolidated Oil Corporation Ld., in which company preferred ordinary shareholders were entitled to 104% (inc. bonus) of their holding in debenture stock. Removed from Register 1912 .... **1912**

Coalite Ld. Regd. 1906. Vol. liq. 6 Aug. 1919. Undertaking and assets were acquired by Low Temperature Carbonisation Ld. [later Coalite Chemical Products Ld.] in which company shareholders were entitled to 1 fully-paid preference share of £1 for each ordinary share of £1 held or 16 preference shares for every 20 deferred shares of 1s. Final meeting return regd. 6 July 1920................. **1920**

Coast Development Co. Ld. Regd. 1898. Reconstructed 1905 as company of same name. Ordinary shareholders were entitled to 2 fully-paid ordinary shares of £1 for every 5 ordinary shares of £1 held. Preference shareholders were entitled to 5 fully-paid second preference shares of £1 for every 5 preference shares of £1 held; in respect of arrears of dividend, preference shareholders were entitled to 3 fully-paid second preference shares of £1 for every 5 preference shares of £1 held. Removed from Register 1913 ... **1909**

Coast Development Corporation Ld. Regd. 1905. Vol. liq. 21 May 1915. Final meeting return regd. 11 May 1928 .... **1916**

Coast Syndicate Ld. Regd. 1901. Struck off Register 13 Oct. 1908 .... **1909**

Coastwise Union Shipping Co. Ld. Regd. 1920. Struck off Register 1923 .... **1922**

Coatbridge & Airdrie Electric Supply Co. Ld. Regd. 1906. Vol. liq. (members') 4 Feb. 1936. Capital returned to contributories—£1 5s. 4·9d. per share of £1. £17 15s. 9d. was paid into Companies' Liquidation Account in respect of unclaimed distributions and £11 17s. 8d. in respect of unclaimed dividends to contributories. Final meeting return regd. 22 Feb. 1937 .... **1936**

Coatbridge Gas Co. Inc. by Special Act 1877. Dissolved 1 May 1949, undertaking being vested in Scottish Area Gas Board under Gas Act 1948. Holders of securities were entitled to receive British Gas 3% guaranteed stock 1990–95 as follows in respect of each £100 unit, unless otherwise stated, of security held:

	£	s.	d.
Orig. stock (10% stand.)	280	0	0
Shares (7% stand.) (of £10)	20	10	0
5% red. pref. stock	107	10	0	**1952**

Cobalt Central Mines Co. Inc. Maine 1906. The London office was closed in May 1909 .... **1910**

Cobalt Hydraulic Power Co. Ld. Inc. Ontario 1908. Company amalgamated with others as Northern Ontario Light & Power Co. Ld. Bond holders were offered an equal amount of 6% bonds of the new company, together with a bonus of 50% in common stock, and holders of common stock were entitled to exchange their holdings for equal amount of common stock of the new company **1912**

Cobalt Lake Silver Mining Co. Ld. Regd. 1913. Vol. liq. 14 July 1914. Shareholders were entitled to 2 shares of £1 in Canadian Mining Corporation Ld. for each share of £1 held. Final meeting return regd. 29 Jan. 1920 .... **1915**

Cobalt Town Site Silver Mining Co. of Canada Ld. Regd. 1906. Vol. liq. 14 July 1914. Assets and properties were acquired by Canadian Mining Corporation Ld., in which company shareholders were entitled to 3 fully-paid shares of £1 plus 1s. 11¾d. in cash for each share of £1 held. Final meeting return regd. 30 Jan. 1920 .... **1915**

Cobar Copper Ld. Regd. 1909. Struck off Register 1923 **1911**

Cobar Gold Mines Ld. Regd. 1896. Vol. liq. 3 May 1898. Reconstructed as company of same name. Shareholders were entitled to 1 share of £1 (credited with 15s. paid) in new company for each share of £1 held. Final meeting return regd. 30 May 1899 .... **1908**

VOL. FOR

Cobar Gold Mines Ld. Regd. 1898. Vol. liq. 4. July 1910. The undertaking was acquired by Great Cobar Ld., in which company shareholders were entitled to 1 share of £5 (credited as fully-paid) for every 9 shares of £1 held. Removed from Register 1912 ... **1911**

Coblentz Mynpacht Syndicate Ld. Regd. 1902. Vol. liq. 3 Sept. 1902. Undertaking was acquired by Murchison Proprietary (Transvaal) Ld. for £17,507 in fully-paid shares of £1 and £7,500 in 30,000 shares of £1 (credited with 5s. paid). Removed from Register 1903 ... **1903**

Cobra Banket Co. Ld. Regd. 1901. Removed from Register 1913 ... **1912**

Cockburn Trust Ld. Regd. 1928. Under provisions of a scheme of arrangement effective 3 May 1967 shareholders were entitled to receive approximately 121 units in London & Wall St. Units and 83 ordinary shares in Minster Assets Ld. for every 100 shares held. Dissolved under Section 208 of the Companies Act, 1948 on 3 Sept. 1967 ... **1968**

Cockermouth, Keswick and Penrith Railway Co. Inc. by Special Act 1861. In 1923 the undertaking was merged into the London Midland & Scottish Railway Co. in which company stockholders were entitled to stock as follows:

For each £100 held	L.M. & S.
4% Debenture £100	4% Debenture
5% Cons. Pref. £125	4% Pref. (1923)
Ordinary £32	Ordinary **1924**

Cocks, Biddulph & Co. Business was acquired by Bank of Liverpool and Martins Ld. (later Martins Bank Ld.) for £136,500 in cash and 6,000 shares of £20 (credited with £2 10s. paid) ... **1920**

Cockshutt Farm Equipment Ld. See C. K. P. Developments Ld.

Cockshutt Plow Co. Ld. See C.K.P. Developments Ld.

Cock's Pioneer Gold & Tin Mines (No Liability). Inc. Victoria 1913 ... **1926**

Cocoa Investments Ld. Regd. 1937. Vol. liq. (members') 16 Sept. 1963. Capital returned to contributories—per share of £1; 4s. 5·4027d. cash and 1·1451 (approx.) ordinary shares in British Cocoa Chocolate Co. Ld. Final meeting regd. 25 Apr. 1964 ..... **1965**

Coconut Plantations at Perak Ld. Regd. 1920. Vol. liq. 14 Feb. 1929. Undertaking and assets were acquired by Straits Plantations Ld. in which company shareholders were entitled to 14 shares of £1 for every 29 shares of £1 held. Final meeting return regd. 23 Oct. 1929 ... **1930**

Coddington & Lamb Ld. Regd. 1924. Vol. liq. (members') 16 Dec. 1959. Final meeting return regd. 14 Dec. 1968 ... **1947**

Coe (Alfred) Ld. Regd. 1923. Vol. liq. (members') 6 Apr. 1944. All capital was owned by Fisons Ld. Final meeting return regd. 25 Sep. 1944 ... **1945**

Coed Mawr Pool & Fridd Lead Mining Co. Ld. Regd. 1881. Removed from Register 1906 ... **1888**

Coetzeestroom Estate & Gold Mining Co. Ld. Regd. 1888. Vol. liq. 14 June 1892. Reconstructed as company of same name. Shareholders entitled to 1 share of 5s. (credited with 3s.paid) in new company for each share of £1 held. Final meeting return regd. 31 Dec. 1892 ... **1897**

Coetzeestroom Estate & Gold Mining Co. Ld. Regd. 1892. Vol. liq. 28 Oct. 1897. Reconstructed as company of same name. Shareholders were entitled to 1 share of 5s. (credited with 3s. 9d. paid) in new company for each share of 5s. held. Final meeting return regd. 26 July 1898 ... **1901**

Coetzeestroom Estate & Gold Mining Co. Ld. Regd. 1897. Reconstructed as company of same name. Shareholders were entitled to 1 share of 5s. (credited with 3s. 9d. paid) in new company for each share of 5s. held. Removed from Register 1902 ... **1905**

Coetzeestroom Estate & Gold Mining Co. Ld. Regd. 1901. Reconstructed 1905 as company of same name. Shareholders were entitled to 5 shares of 5s. (credited with 4s. 3d. paid) in new company for every 4 shares of 5s. held. Removed from Register 1911 ... **1908**

Coetzeestroom Estate & Gold Mining Co. Ld. Regd. 1905. Vol. liq. June 1908. Struck off Register 21 Jan. 1936 ... **1936**

Coetzeestroom Estates Ld. Regd. 1909. Vol. liq. 10 Oct. 1913. Final meeting return regd. 29 Jan. 1915 ..... **1914**

Coey & Co. Ld. Regd. Dublin 1872. Vol. liq. 6 Jan. 1899. Removed from Register 1906 ... **1899**

Coffee & Dining Rooms Co. Ld. Regd. 1890. Vol. liq. Oct. 1911 for reconstruction as Popular Restaurants Ld. in which company shareholders were entitled to 1 share of 5s. (credited with 3s. 6d. paid) for each share of 11s. held. Removed from Register 1912 ... **1912**

Coffir & Stanton Ld. Regd. 1889. Vol. liq. 5 Jan. 1891. Final meeting return 19 June 1891 ... ***1895**

VOL. FOR

Cohen, Weenen & Co. Ld. Regd. 1927. Vol. liq. (members') 31 July 1961. All ordinary capital was owned by Godfrey Phillips Ld. Preference capital was repaid at par in Aug. 1961. Amounts paid into Companies' Liquidation Account—£1,068 in respect of unclaimed distributions and £99 0s. 6d. in respect of unclaimed dividends. Final meeting return regd. 4 Aug. 1964 ... **1965**

Coking Co. Ld. Regd. 1904. Vol. liq. (members') 2 July 1955. Final meeting return regd 31 May 1956 ...... **1940**

Colar Central Gold Co. Ld. Regd. 1886. Removed from Register 1903 ... **1897**

Colar Concessionnaires Co. Ld. Regd. 1881. Vol. liq. 2 Sept. 1890. Final meeting return regd. 17 Dec. 1895 **1891**

Colar Gold Mining Co. Ld. Regd. 1880. Vol. liq. 10 Oct. 1883. Final meeting return regd. 3 June 1885 ...... **1884**

Colar. Mysore Gold Co. Ld. Regd. 1886. Company did not go to allotment ... **1896**

Colbeck Brothers Ld. Regd. 1889. Vol. liq. (members') 4 Apr. 1933. Capital returned to contributories—£2 10s. 9d. per preference share of £10 or ordinary share of £10. Final meeting return regd. 7 Feb. 1936 .... **1934**

Colchester Gas Co. Estd. 1826; inc. by Special Act 1866. Dissolved 1 May 1949 undertaking being vested in Eastern Area Gas Board under Gas Act 1948. Holders of securities were entitled to receive British Gas 3% guaranteed stock 1990–95 as follows in respect of each £20 unit unless otherwise stated, of security held:

	£	s.	d.
Orig. A shares (10% stand.)	42	0	0
New B shares (7% stand.)	30	0	0
6% pref. stock (per £100)	133	0	0
5% perp. deb. stock (per £100)	127	0	0
4% red. deb. stock (per £100)	101	0	0	**1952**

Colchester Native Oyster Fishery Co. Ld. Regd. 1888. Receiver appointed in 1900. Struck off Register 18 Nov. 1902 ... **1903**

Colchester, Stour Valley, Sudbury & Halstead Railway Co. Inc. by Special Act 1846. Under Great Eastern Railway Act 1898 the undertaking was transferred to that company. Holders of 5% preference stock received 4% debenture stock on basis of equal income; holders of £100 consolidated stock received £86 13s 4d. 4% debenture stock ... **1899**

Cold Storage Trust Ld. Regd. 1902. Vol. liq. 19 Mar. 1915. Shareholders were entitled to £100 5% 1st mortgage debentures in Imperial Cold Storage and Supply Co. Ld. for every 85 preference shares of £1 held. Ordinary shareholders were entitled to 1 share of £1 in Imperial Cold Storage for every 4 ordinary shares of £1 held plus £100 5% 1st mortgage debentures in that company for every 618 ordinary shares held plus 7d. per share in cash. Holders of less than 618 ordinary shares were entitled to 2s. 9d. per share. Final meeting return regd. 21 Nov. 1916 ... **1917**

Coldstream Gas Co. Ld. Regd. in Edinburgh 1934. Dissolved 1 May 1949 undertaking being vested in Scottish Area Gas Board under Gas Act 1948. Holders of ordinary shares (of £1) were entitled to receive £1 1s. British Gas 3% guaranteed stock 1990–95 for each share held ... **1952**

Coldstream Investment Trust Ld. Regd. Edinburgh 1928. Undertaking and assets acquired on 29 Mar. 1963 by Pentland Investment Trust Ld. in which company shareholders were entitled to receive 38 ordinary shares of 5s. for every £10 ordinary stock and £1 preference stock for every £1 preference stock held. Pentland Investment Trust Ld. also assumed liability for the 4% redeemable deb. stocks 1970–5 and 1976–81 and terminable debentures of this company. Dissolved under Sec. 208 of Companies Act, 1948 18 July 1963 ... **1964**

Cole (C.) Ld. Amalgamated with Wall Paper Manufacturers Ld. between Sept. 1915 and Mar. 1924 ...... **1924**

Colebrook & Co., Ld. Regd. 1897. Vol. liq. (members') 25 Feb. 1966. Final meeting return regd. 21 July 1971 ... **1964**

Coleford, Monmouth, Usk & Pontypool Railway Co. Inc by Special Act 1853. Under Great Western Railway Act 1881 undertaking was amalgamated with that company for £160,000 consolidated guaranteed 5% stock at par ... **1888**

Coleford Railway Co. Inc. by Special Act 1872. All share capital was owned by Great Western Railway Co **1883**

Coleman & Oldland Ld. Regd. 1907. Vol. liq. (members') 19 Nov. 1938. All shares owned by Grainger & Smith Ld. Final meeting return regd. 23 Dec. 1938 **1939**

Coleman Trading Co. Ld. See Mermac Ld.

Coleman's (William) Ordinary Shares Ld. Regd. 1909. Vol. liq. 10 Jan. 1921. Under scheme of arrangement 1st debenture holders received 24 shares in Coleman & Co. Ld. or £18 in cash for each £50 debentures. Final meeting return regd. 23 May 1921 **1921**

See Stock Exchange Year-Book.

VOL. FOR

Colenbrander's Matabeleland Development Co. Ld. Regd. 1895. Undertaking was acquired by Rhodesia Consolidated Ld. in which company shareholders were entitled to 1 share of 10s. (credited with 7s. paid) for each share of £1 held. Removed from Register 1906 1904

Coleridge Financial Trust Ld. *See* American Canadian & General Investment Trust Ld.

Colfix (London) Ld. Regd. 1927. Vol. liq. 11 Apr. 1929. Undertaking acquired by British Bitumen Emulsions Ld. Struck of Register 8 Apr. 1938 1940

Colinton Tramways Co. Inc. by Provisional Order 1909 1911

Coliseum (Manchester) Ld. Regd. 1920. Vol. liq. (members') 21 May 1947. Capital returned to contributories—10s. 7½d. per share (of £1). Final meeting return regd. 3 June 1949 1950

Coliseum Syndicate Ld. Regd. 1907. Vol. liq. (members') 19 Oct. 1955. Capital returned to contributories—preference and B preference: £1 per share (of £1); ordinary: £3 10s. 8·864d, per share (of £1). Final meeting return regd. 18 Oct. 1956 1957

Collett (J.) Ld. Regd. 30 June 1937. Vol. liq. (creditors') 23 July 1974. Final meeting return regd. 5 Apr. 1988. 1988–9

Collie Boulder Coal Co. Ld. Regd. 1901. Receiver for debenture holders was appointed in May 1904, but property was sold on behalf of mortgagee having poor security. Removed from Register 1909 1903

Collie Proprietary Coal Fields of W.A. Ld. Regd. 1899. Vol. liq. 20 Dec. 1911. Final meeting return regd. 30 Dec. 1913 1912

Collier (S.) & Co. Regd. 20 May 1935. Vol. liq. (creditors') 24 Oct. 1974. Final meeting 18 Sept. 1986. First and final distribution of 0·71p per share paid 25 July 1986. All unsecured creditors paid in full 1988–9

Collier Audible Telephone Syndicate Ld. Regd. 1891. Various assets were acquired by Collier Marr Telephone & Electrical Manufacturing Co. Ld., in 1892 for £51,500, payable £4,000 in cash, £25,000 in fully-paid up shares, and balance in cash or shares. Removed from Register 1907 1895

Collier Marr Telephone & Electrical Manufacturing Co. Ld. Regd. 1892. Removed from Register 1903 1896

Colliery & General Contract Co. Ld. Regd. 1896. Court Order to wind up 27 Feb. 1899. Struck off Register 1 Sept. 1936 1937

Collingbourne & Avon Railway Co. Inc. by Special Act 1888 1895

Collingwood Goldfields Ld. Regd. 1900. Removed from Register 1904 1904

Collins & Son Ld. Regd. 1904. Court Order to wind up 1906. Removed from Register 1911 1907

Collins (Edward) & Sons Ld. Regd. Edinburgh 1915. Vol. liq. Aug. 1926. Struck off Register 25 Jan. 1938 1927

Collins (P.) Ld. Regd. 1899. Vol. liq. 14 Feb. 1906. Removed from Register 1906 1907

Collis Diamond Syndicate Ld. Regd. 1906. Removed from Register 1911 1909

Collooney, Ballina & Belmullet Railways & Piers Co. Inc. by Special Act 1907 1922

Colman (J. & J.) Ld. Regd. 1896. Vol. liq. (members') 14 Oct. 1955. Net assets transferred to Reckitt & Colman Holdings Ld.; which owned all capital of this company. £10 10s. paid into Companies' Liquidation Account. Final meeting return regd. 9 July 1956 1957

Colne & Trawden Light Railways Co. Inc. (under Light Railways Act 1896) by order of Light Railway Commissioners confirmed by Board of Trade 1901. Undertaking purchased by Colne Corporation under Act of 1913. Vol. liq. May 1914. Debenture holders and preference shareholders were paid off in full: it was estimated that ordinary shareholders would receive approximately 4s. in £ 1915

Colne Valley and Halstead Railway Co. Inc. by Special Act 1856. In 1923 the undertaking was merged into the London & North Eastern Railway Co. in which company stockholders were entitled to stock as follows:

For each £100 held	L. & N. E.
5% "A" Deb. £125	4% First Pref.
4% "B" Deb. £10	5% Pref. Ord.
Pref. Shares	£1 10s. cash
Ord. Shares	£1 5s. cash	1924

Colne Valley Electric Supply Co. Ld. Regd. 1912. Dissolved 1 Apr. 1948 undertaking being vested in British (later Central) Electricity Authority and Eastern Area Board under Electricity Act 1947 ... 1949

Colney Hatch Gas Co. *See* Southgate & District Gas Co.

Coloil Syndicate Ld. Regd. 1921. Vol. liq. (creditors') 16 Dec. 1930. No capital returned to contributories. Final meeting return regd. 5 June 1936 1931

Colombia Consolidated Ld. Regd. 1908. Vol. liq. June 1911. Removed from Register 1912 1912

Colombia Development Syndicate Ld. Regd. 1902. Vol. liq. Dec. 1909. Removed from Register 1910 1909

Colombia Gold Mining Co. Inc. Venezuela. In liquidation in 1898 1898

Colombia Navigation Co. Ld. Regd. 1909. Vol. liq. 16 Feb. 1915. Undertaking was acquired by Colombia Railways and Navigation Co. Ld. which company assumed liability for the 6% debentures. Final meeting return regd. 31 Dec. 1925 1915

Colombia Railways & Navigation Co. Ld. Regd. 1906 as Cartagena (Colombia) Railway Co. Ld.; name changed 1913. Vol. liq. (members') 28 Nov. 1949. Holders of 6% mortgage debentures (formerly 6% navigation debentures of Colombia Navigation Co. Ld.) received distributions totaling 32⅛%. No capital returned to contributories. Final meeting return regd. 18 Aug. 1958. 1959

Colombia Smelting & Concessions Co. Ld. Regd. 1908. Struck off Register 1923 1923

Colombian Alluvial Mines Ld. Regd. 1909. Removed from Register 27 Sept. 1912 .... *1911

Colombian Central Railway Co. Ld. Regd. 1905. Vol. liq. 18 Sept. 1916. Final meeting return regd. 3 Sept. 1917 1917

Colombian Corporation Ld. Regd. 1919. Vol. liq. May 1930. No capital returned to contributories. Final meeting return regd. 18 Feb. 1948 1948

Colombian Emerald Co. Ld. Regd. 1908. Vol. liq. 23 June 1914. Capital returned to contributories—£1. 5s. per share of £1. Final meeting return regd. 30 July 1920 1915

Colombian Gold Mines Ld. Regd. 1889. Court order to wind up 5 Nov. 1893. Liquidator released 24 Jan. 1898. Removed from Register 21 June 1900 1895

Colombian Goldfields Ld. Regd. 1911. Vol. liq. 13 Dec. 1915. Undertaking and assets were sold to Consolidated Colombia Platinum Gold Mines Ld. for 30,000 fully-paid shares of £1. Final meeting return regd. 28 June 1916 1916

Colombian Government Silver Concessions Union Ld. Regd. 1890. Vol. liq 9 Nov. 1891. Final meeting return regd. 13 July 1892 1892

Colombian Hydraulic Mining Co. Ld. Regd. 1903. Vol. liq. May 1907. Removed from Register 1912 1908

Colombian India-Rubber Exploration Co. Ld. Regd. 1897. Struck off Register Jan. 1932 1932

Colombian Mining & Exploration Co. Ld. Regd. 1908. Winding-up order 19 Dec. 1938. Liquidator stated that there would be no capital returned to contributories 1954

Colombian Mines Corporation Ld. Regd. 1883. Vol. liq. Jan. 1918. Struck off Register 6 Dec. 1918. 1918

Colombian National Railway Co. Ld. Regd. 1899. Vol. liq. 14 May 1923. Final meeting return regd. 20 Nov. 1923 1924

Colombian Northern Railway Co. Ld. Regd. 1898. Vol. liq. 30 Apr. 1928. Capital returned to contributories—£5 per share of £5 at May 1928; later payments (if any) not known. Final meeting return regd. 26 Oct. 1933 1929

Colombian Oilfields Ld. Regd. 1919. Court Order to wind up 16 July 1928. Struck off Register 13 Dec. 1938 1939

Colombian Proprietary Gold Mines Ld. Regd. 1921. Court Order to wind up 1 Nov. 1927. Struck off Register 20 Feb. 1942 1943

Colombian Robber Co. Ld. Regd. 1900. Struck off Register 1915 1913

Colombian Transport, Trading & Development Co. Ld. Regd. 1905. Struck off Register 1924 1910

Colombo Electric Tramways & Lighting Co. Ld. Regd. 1902. Vol. liq. (members') 1st Aug. 1945. Returned to contributories (per share of £10)—£30 11s. 9d. Final meeting return regd. 28 Oct. 1969 1970

Colon Gold Mines Ld. Regd. 1889. Vol. liq. 31 Dec. 1894. Reconstructed as company of same name. Shareholders were entitled to 1 share of 5s. (credited with 3s. 6d. paid) in new company for each share of £1 held. Final meeting return regd. 2 Oct. 1896 .. 1908

Colon Gold Mines Ld. Regd. 1899. Vol. liq. 30 June 1913. Capital returned to contributories—4d. per share of 5s. in July 1913; further payments (if any) not known. Final meeting return regd. 27 Mar. 1914 1914

Colonia Ld. Regd. 1901. Assets were acquired by Cuadro Consolidated Ld. Removed from Register 1904 1908

Colonia Syndicate Ld. Regd. 1896. Removed from Register 1902 1902

Colonial Ammunition Co. Ld. Regd. 1888. Vol. liq. July 1927. Final meeting return regd. 23 Dec. 1927 1928

Colonial & Foreign Banks Guarantee Corporation. Established 1866. Inc. by Special Act 1899. Under Act of 1920 the business was transferred to Alliance Assurance Co. Ld. 1921

VOL. FOR

Colonial & Foreign Glass Industries Ld. Regd. 1920. Struck off Register 7 Mar. 1939 1940

Colonial & Foreign Salt Co. Ld. Regd. 1913. Vol. liq. (members') 26 May 1931. No capital returned to contributories. Final meeting return regd. 20 Apr. 1932 1932

Colonial & General Agency Ld. Regd. 1900 as South African & General Agency Ld.; name changed Apr. 1906. Vol. liq. Mar. 1907. Removed from Register 1910 1908

Colonial and United States Mortgage Co. Ld. Regd. 1880. Vol. liq. 9 Aug. 1920. The debentures were being repaid. Capital returned to contributories—£2 9s. per ordinary share of £10 (£2 10s. paid) at 1920; further payments (if any) not known. Final meeting return regd. 12 July 1922 1921

Colonial Assurance Co. Ld. Established South Africa 1874. Business was acquired in 1899 by Commercial Union Assurance Co. Ld. 1900

Colonial Bank of Australia Ld. Inc. Victoria 1893. Amalgamated in 1918 with National Bank of Australasia, in which company shareholders were entitled to 1 preference share of £10 (credited as fully paid) for each preference share of £9 15s. held or 7 ordinary shares of £8 for every 20 ordinary shares of £4 5s. (£1 15s. paid) 1919

Colonial Bank of New Zealand. Inc. New Zealand 1874. Business and assets were sold in 1895 to Bank of New Zealand for £461,211 1896

Colonial Bank Ld. Inc. in Transvaal, 26 Jan. 1910 as Colonial Banking & Trust Ld.; name changed 18 Nov. 1967. In Mar. 1968 properties, rights. assets and powers were vested in Western Bank Ld. Shareholders received shares in that company in exchange for their holdings and company was dissolved without a winding-up 1969

Colonial Banking Ld. (see above)

Colonial College & Training Farms Ld. Regd. 1885. Removed from Register 1907 1904

Colonial Co. Ld. Regd. 1865. Business was acquired in 1897 by New Colonial Co. Ld., in which company shareholders were entitled to 6 preference shares of £5 (credited with £2 10s. paid), 3 ordinary shares of £5 (credited with £4 paid) and 3 fully-paid ordinary shares of £5 for every 10 shares of £10 held. Removed from Register 1901 1899

Colonial Consignment & Distributing Co. Ld. Regd. 1895. Vol. liq. (members') 29 Apr. 1932. Capital returned to contributories—£102,972 13s. 2d. Final meeting return regd. 29 Nov. 1932 1933

Colonial Consolidated Finance Coporation Ld. Regd. 1898. Vol. liq. June 1909. Shareholders were entitled to 1 fully-paid share of 7s. in Colonial Property and Rubber Co. Ld. plus 10s. in cash for each fully-paid share of £1 held: holders of shares of £1 (17s. 6d. paid) received 7s. 6d. in cash plus the shares; further payments (if any) not known. Removed from Register 1912 1911

Colonial Copper Corporation Ld. Regd. 1899. Vol. liq. Dec. 1911. Removed from Register 1912 1912

Colonial Debenture Corporation Ld. Regd. 1892. Removed from Register 1907 1895

Colonial Doloment Co. Ld. Regd. 1907 as Canadian Doloment Co. Ld.: name changed June 1907. Vol. liq. Nov. 1912. Removed from Register 1913 1913

Colonial Estates & Investment Co. Ld. Regd. 1897. Struck off Register 1900 1906

Colonial Fibre Planting & Trading Co. Ld. Regd. 1909. Receiver appointed in Apr. 1911. Struck off Register 1915 1914

Colonial Finance Corporation Ld. Regd. 1894. Vol. liq. 14 Dec. 1898. Undertaking was acquired by Colonial Consolidated Finance Corporation Ld. Holders of ordinary shares of £1 (15s. paid) were entitled to an equal number of shares of £1 (credited with 15s. paid) in new company plus 1 fully-paid share for every 4 shares held and 1 fully-paid share in Hannan's Proprietary Development Co. Ld., for every 5 shares held. Holders of founders' shares were entitled to 12 fully-paid shares in new company and $7\frac{7}{16}$ fully-paid shares in Hannan's Proprietary Development Co. Ld. for each founders' share held. Removed from Register 1902 1899

Colonial Goldfields Ld. Regd. 1895. Removed from Register 1910 1908

Colonial Investment and Agency Co. Ld. Regd. Edinburgh 1888. Vol. liq June 1888. Capital returned to contributories—2s. 3d. per share of £4 (£1 paid) on 13 June 1898; further payments (if any) not known. Final meeting return regd. 1 Apr. 1899 1899

Colonial Investment & Agency of New Zealand Ld. Regd. Edinburgh 1878. Vol. liq. May 1889 for reconstruction as Colonial Investment & Agency Co. Ld. Final meeting return regd. 1 Apr. 1899 1898

VOL. FOR

Colonial Mines Development Ld. Regd. 1922. Vol. liq. 4 June 1926. Assets were acquired by Saxon Securities Trust Ld., in which company shareholders were entitled to fully-paid contingent certificates of £1 and 2 ordinary shares of £1 (credited with 10s paid) for every 20 shares of 2s. held. Final meeting return regd. 3 Oct. 1928 1927

Colonial Mining & General Syndicate Ld. Regd. 1896. Vol. liq. 6 June 1899. Assets were acquired by Rhodesia Mines Ld. Removed from Register 1901 1900

Colonial Oil Syndicate Ld. Regd. 1906. Vol. liq. Nov. 1909. Removed from Register 1911 1910

Colonial Property and Rubber Co. Ld. Regd. 1910. Vol. liq. 20 June 1923. Capital returned to contributories—7s. per share of 7s. at Oct. 1923; further payments (if any) not known. Final meeting return regd. 17 Jan. 1924 1924

Colonial Real Property Co. Ld. Regd. Edinburgh 1881. Vol. liq. June 1904. Capital returned to contributories—25s. per share of £3 10s. (£1 10s. paid) at 26 July 1904; further distributions (if any) not known. Court Orders; to continue winding up under supervision July 1904; to dissolve 21 Dec. 1905 1905

Colonial Rubber Estates Ld. See Fanashanti Gold Fields Ld.

Colonial Trusts Corporation Ld. Regd. 1858. Removed from Register 1904 .... *1879

Colonial Wharves Ld. Regd. 1886. Vol. liq. (members) 31 Jan. 1956. Undertaking acquired by Browne & Eagle Ld. (later Colonial & Eagle Wharves Ld.), in which company preference stockholders were entitled to 1 fully-paid preference share of £1 for each £1 stock held and ordinary stockholders, 8 fully-paid ordinary shares of £1 for each £5 stock held. Final meeting return regd. 14 Nov. 1957 1958

Colonies Shipping Co. Ld. Regd. 1908. Vol. liq. 14 Mar. 1916. Final meeting return regd. 5 May 1917 1916

Colonist's Land & Loan Corporation Ld. Regd. 1869 as Emigrant & Colonist's Aid Corporation Ld.; name changed 1888. Vol. liq. 15 Oct. 1907. Capital returned to contributories—£1 per share of £1 at Dec. 1907, further payments (if any) not known. Final meeting return regd. 13 Apr. 1916 1908

Colorado Bay Silver Mines Ld. Regd. 1891. Vol. liq. 30 Dec. 1895. Final meeting return regd. 19 Jan. 1897 1896

Colorado Coal & Iron Co. Inc. Colorado 1880. Reconstructed as Colorado Fuel and Iron Co. $4,000,000 common stock and $3,101,000 bonds were distributed to holders of shares and bonds respectively. The real estate was sold to Colorado Coal and Iron Development Co. for an unspecified amount of stock, which was distributed to shareholders 1908

Colorado Deep Level Mining Co. Ld. Regd. 1897. Removed from Register 1906 1900

Colorado Gold and Silver Extraction Co. Ld. Regd. 1888. Removed from Register 1903 1891

Colorado Gold, Silver & Lead Recovery Syndicate Ld. Regd. 1888. Vol. liq. 23 Aug. 1889. Final meeting return regd. 31 Dec. 1890 1890

Colorado Midland Railway Co. Organised Colorado 1897. Property was sold for $1,425,000 1919

Colorado Mortgage and Investment Co. Ld. Regd. 1893. Vol. liq. 25 May 1920. Capital returned to contributories—£1 per share of £5 at July 1920; further payments (if any) not known. The 4% debenture stock was redeemed on Nov. 1919. Final meeting return regd. 10 Feb. 1927 1921

Colorado Mortgage & Investment Co. of London Ld. Regd. 1877. Vol. liq. 17 Jan. 1893. Reconstructed as Colorado Mortgage and Investment Co. Ld., in which company shareholders were entitled to 2 fully-paid ordinary shares of £5 for every 3 shares of £5 (£3 6s. 8d. paid) held. The debentures were repaid in 1897. Final meeting return regd. 13 Jan. 1898.. 1898

Colorado Nitrate Co. Ld. Regd. 1885. Vol. liq. 18 Dec. 1918. Undertaking was acquired by Liverpool Nitrate Co. Ld., in which company shareholders were entitled to 1 fully-paid share of 5s. plus £1 in cash for each share of £5 held. Final meeting return regd. 29 Apr. 1920 1919

Colorado Properties Ld. Regd. 1903. Struck off Register Feb. 1931 1931

Colorado Ranch Co. Ld. Regd. 1879. Vol. liq. 26 Nov. 1889. Final meeting return regd. 2 Mar. 1894........ 1890

Colorado Silver Mining Co. Ld. Regd. 1887. Vol. liq. 2 Nov. 1892. Reconstructed as New Colorado Silver Mining Co. Ld in which company shareholders were entitled to a share of £1 (credited with 17s. paid) for every 5 shares of £1 held. Final meeting return regd. 4 July 1894 1899

Colorado United Mining Co. Ld. Regd. 1870 as Colorado Terrible Lode Mining Co. Ld.; name changed 2 May 1877. Vol. liq. 28 May 1887. Final meeting return regd. 30 May 1893 .... *1892

*See Stock Exchange Year-Book.

VOL. FOR

Colorado Terrible Lode Mining Co. Ld. *See above.*

Colour Photographs (British & Foreign) Ld. *See below.*

Colour Photographs Ld. Regd. 1928 as Colour Photographs (British & Foreign) Ld.; name changed Mar. 1937 . Vol. liq. (members') 14 Jan 1947. Capital returned to contributories—5·461d. per share (of 1s.). Final meeting return regd. 29 Nov. 1949. .... **1950**

Colour Snapshots (Foreign) Ld. Regd. 1928. Vol. liq. (members') 31 Oct. 1934. Shareholders were entitled to receive 1 share of 5s. (credited 3s. paid) of Lone Hand Gold Mines Ld., for every 8 shares of 2s. held and to subscribe at par for 1 share of 5s. for every 8 shares held. Final meeting return regd. 16 June, 1937 .... **1935**

Colour Snapshots (1928) Ld. Regd. 1928. Court Order to wind up 9 Dec. 1929. Struck off Register 20 Mar. 1936 .... **1937**

Colourware Ld. *See* Maul (F. W.) Ld.

Colt Gun & Carriage Co. Ld. Regd. 1899. Vol. liq. Nov. 1907 for reconstruction. Removed from Register 1911 .... **1908**

Colthurst Syndicate Ld. Regd. 1895. Removed from Register 1904 .... **1899**

Coltness Holdings Ld. Regd. Edinburgh 1839 as Coltness Iron Co. Ld.; name changed Oct. 1951. Vol. liq. (members') 8 Oct. 1951. The continuing and operating assets were sold to Coltness Iron Co. Ld. (later Coltness Industries Ld.) in exchange for shares which were distributed to ordinary shareholders, 2 shares of 6s. 8d. for every share held, in May 1953. Under scheme of arrangement, sanctioned by the Court on 1 May 1952, 5% preference and 2nd preference shares (of £1) were repaid at par, with dividend to date of repayment, and cash payment of 3s. 6d. and 4s. per share respectively, in satisfaction of premium and all rights under section 25 of the Coal Industry Nationalistion Act., 1946. Ordinary shareholders received £7 14s. 4d. per share of 15s. Final meeting return regd. 20 Feb. 1962 .. **1963**

Columbia & Kootenay Railway & Navigation Co. Organised in Canada. The 4% 1st mortgage bonds were exchanged for 4% debenture stock of Canadian Pacific Railway Co., in 1891 .... **1892**

Columbia (Charters Towers) Gold Mine Ld. Regd. 1895. Vol. liq. 5 Sept. 1905 for reconstruction as Brilliant North Gold Mines Ld., in which company shareholders were entitled to 1 fully-paid new share of 5s. for every 2 shares of 10s. held. Removed from Register 1906 .... **1908**

Columbia Corporation. *See* Columbia Gas & Electric Co. (of West Virginia).

Columbia Gas & Electric Co. of West Virginia. Inc. West Virginia Sept. 1906 as Columbia Corporation; name changed Nov. 1906. Amalgamated in 1926 with Ohio Fuel Corporation to form Columbia Gas and Electric Corporation in which company shareholders were entitled to 1 share of common stock for each share of common stock held or 1½ shares of 6% cumulative preferred stock, series A, for each share of preferred stock held **1927**

Columbia (International) Ld. Regd. 1925. Vol. liq. (members') 13 Apr. 1931. Capital returned to contributories—2·43382d. per ordinary share of £1 *plus* certain investments distributed in specie. Final meeting return regd. 22 Dec. 1931 .... **1932**

Colombia Phonograph Co. Inc. New York 1924. It was announced in Dec. 1931 that capital was to be transferred to Grigsby Grunow Co. of Chicago at the rate of 4⅔ shares for each share held and that $10 per share in cash was to be distributed before transfer **1932**

Colombia River Lumber Co. Ld. Inc. Canada 1911. All capital stocks were owned by Canadian Western Lumber Co. Ld. In Oct. 1914 holders of debenture stock were offered £50 5% 1st mortgage debenture stock, £50 5% cumulative income debenture and $225 in ordinary shares in that company for every £100 debenture stock held. The undertaking and assets were acquired in 1943 by Canadian Western Lumber Co. Ld. **1945**

Colombia Steam Navigation Co. Ld. Regd. 1885 as Pinkney & Sons Steamship Co. Ld.; name changed 1893. Undertaking acquired by Neptune Steam Navigation Co. Ld. Removed from Register 1901 ***1901**

Colombia Valley Orchards Ld. Inc. British Columbia 1911. The assets were sold in 1922 by order of the Provincial Government with a view to the recovery of overdue taxes. $13,408 was available for distribution amongst debenture holders who received a return of about 8 cents (4d.) per £1 .... **1923**

Columbia Western Lumber Yards Ld. Inc. Canada 1913. Court Order to wind up in Sept. 1929. The preference share capital was repaid in Oct. 1929

VOL. FOR

together with a premium of 10%. Assets were sold to Columbia River Lumber Co. Ld. **1930**

Colville Co. Ld. Regd. 1887. Removed from Register 1898 .... **1897**

Colville (David) & Sons Ld. Regd. Edinburgh 1895. Vol. liq. (members') 20 Feb. 1936. Iron and steel manufacturing business was acquired by Colvilles Ld. Capital returned to contributories—20s. per preference share of £1; £13 7s. 4·6535d. per ordinary share of £10. Final meeting return regd. 19 Feb. 1938 .... **1937**

Colwall Gas Co. Ld. Regd. 1897. Dissolved 1 May 1949, undertaking being vested in West Midland Area Gas Board under Gas Act 1948. Holders of securities were entitled to receive, in respect of each £1 unit held, British Gas 3% guaranteed stock 1990–95 as follows:

	£	s.	d.
Orig. ord. shares (10% max.)	1	6	0
Addit. ord. shares (7% max.)	1	6	0	**1952**

Colwick Park Racecourse Co. Ld. *See* Nottingham Racecourse Co. Ld.

Colyer (J.) & Co. Ld. Regd. 1919. Vol. liq. (members') 9 Sept. 1936. All shares owned by Fruit & Produce Exchange of Great Britain Ld. Final meeting return regd. 17 Nov. 1936 .... **1937**

Colyton Gas, Coke & Coal Co. Ld. Regd. 1894. Dissolved 1 May 1949, undertaking being vested in South Western Area Gas Board under Gas Act 1948. Holders of securities were entitled to receive British Gas 3% guaranteed stock 1990–95 as follows in respect of each £5 unit, unless otherwise stated, of security held:

	£	s.	d.
Ord. shares	3	0	0
Pref. shares	3	0	0
5% debt. (1st and 2nd series) per £100	100	0	0	**1952**

Combe & Co. Ld. Regd. 1888. Vol. liq. 13 Jan. 1899. Reconstructed as Watney Combe Reid & Co. Ld. (later Watney Mann Ld.), in which company shareholders were entitled to 71 preferred ordinary and 71 deferred ordinary shares of £1 for every £100 ordinary stock held. Preference shareholders were entitled to an equal amount of fully-paid preference shares of £1 in new company. Holders of 4%, debenture stock were entitled to either £108 in debenture stock or £112·479 in cash for every £100 stock held; holders of 3½% debenture stock were entitled to £104 in debenture stock or £107·167 in cash for every £100 stock held. Final meeting return regd. 15 July 1899 .... **1899**

Combined Pulp & Paper Mills Ld. Regd. 1927. Vol. liq. (members') 30 June 1932. No capital returned to shares of 1s. £5,930 10s. 6d (subject to liquidator's remuneration and certain expenses) was distributed to 663,449 ordinary shares of £1; the remaining 36,551 ordinary shares having been surrendered. Final meeting return regd. 27 June 1934 .... **1933**

Combined Rhodesia Synd. Ld. Regd. 1899, Vol. liq. 23 Mar. 1917. Dissolved before 1931 .... **1911**

Combustion Engineering Co. Inc. Inc. in Delaware 1933. Merged with Superheater Co. (Inc. in U.S.A.) as from 31 Dec. 1948 under title of Combustion Engineering-Superheater Inc. **1950**

Commerce Tin Mine Ld. Regd. 1900. Vol. liq. 19 Apr. 1905. Removed from Register 1907 .... **1906**

Commercial Bank Buildings Trust Ld. *See* Gracechurch Buildings Co. Ld.

Commercial Bank of Alexandria Ld. Regd. 1876. Vol. liq. July 1884. Capital returned to contributories— £1 15s. per share of £6 (£3 paid) at Dec. 1884; further payments (if any) not known. Final meeting return regd. 19 June 1886 .... **1885**

Commercial Bank of Australia Ld. Inc. Victoria 1866. Reconstructed 1893 as company of same name. Shareholders received 1 ordinary share of £10 (credited with £4 paid) in new company for each share held; shareholders who took up their proportion of ordinary shares were released from liability in respect of uncalled capital in old company **1896**

Commercial Bank of Bohemia. *See* Böhmische Kommerzialbank.

Commercial Bank of Cornwall Ld. Regd. 1881. Vol. liq. 20 May 1891. Final meeting return regd. 21 May 1892 .... ***1892**

Commercial Bank of India Ld. Established India 1885. In liquidation in 1909 .... **1909**

Commercial Bank of London Ld. Regd. 1906 as Anglo-Japanese Bank Ld.; name changed July 1913. Vol. liq. 3 Mar 1914. Reconstructed as company of same name. Shareholders were entitled to 1 fully-paid share of £3 for each share of £5 held. Final meeting return regd. 16 June 1915 .... **1914**

Commercial Bank of London Ld. Regd. 1913 as Reuter's Bank Ld. name changed to British Commercial Bank Ld. in Jan. 1916 and as above June 1918. Vol. liq. 31 Dec. 1919. Reconstructed as company of same name. Shareholders were entitled to 1 ordinary share of £1 in new company *plus* 2s. 6d. in cash for each preference share of £1 held or 1 ordinary share of £1 *plus* 4s. in cash for each deferred share of 1s. held. Final meeting return regd. 12 Oct. 1920....... **1920**

Commercial Bank of London Ld. *See* London & British Industrial Investment Co. Ld.

Commercial Bank of London Ld. *See* Commercial Corporation of London Ld.

Commercial Bank of Manitoba. Inc. by Special Act Canada 1884. Payment was suspended 3 July 1893. In liquidation in 1894 .... **1894**

Commercial Bank of South Australia. Inc. 1878. In liquidation in 1887 .... **1887**

Commercial Bank of Spanish America Ld. Regd. 1904 as Cortes Commercial and Banking Co. Ld.; name changed Nov. 1911. Vol. liq. (members') Jan. 1934. Capital returned to contributories—£518,190 15s. 9d. £559 4s. 3d. was paid into Companies' Liquidation Account. Final meeting return regd. 21 Dec. 1934 .... **1934**

Commercial Bank of the River Plate Ld. *See* Mercantile Bank of the River Plate Ld.

Commercial Banking Co. of Sydney. Established 1834; inc. Australia 1848. Reconstructed 1893 under same name. Shareholders received 2 A shares (credited with £12 10s. per share paid up) in the new company for every share held, together with such a number of B shares as was in the proportion of 2 B shares to every 3 A shares allotted to them **1894**

Commercial Brewery Co. Ld. Regd. 1887. Vol. liq. (members') 16 July 1937. Certain assets were transferred to Charles Hammerton & Co. Ld., for 60,000 preference shares of £1, 78,140 ordinary shares of 10s., and £231,000 in cash. Holders of preference shares were entitled to either £10 per share in cash or 14 fully-paid redeemable preference shares of £1 for each preference share of £10 held. Holders of ordinary shares were entitled to 26 fully-paid ordinary shares of 10s. in Charles Hammerton & Co. Ld., 10 fully-paid ordinary shares of £1 in Thresler & Co. Ld., *plus* 2s. 5·25d. for each ordinary share of £10 held. Final meeting return regd. 12 May 1938 .... **1938**

Commercial Buildings Co. of Cork. Inc. 1808. Wound up by Order of Court 26 Apr. 1948. .... **1949**

Commercial Buildings Co. of Dublin. Inc. Royal Charter 1798. Court order to wind up 26 July 1938. The undertaking was acquired in 1938 by Commercial Buildings (Dublin) Ld. **1939**

Commercial Cable Co. Organised New York 1883 ..... **1940**

Commercial Cars Ld. Regd. 1905. Vol. liq. July 1919. Reconstructed as company of same name. Shareholders were entitled to 7½ shares of £1 in new company for each ordinary share held, or 5 shares of £1 for every 4 preference shares held. Court Order to wind up 26 May 1925. Struck off Register 1932 .. **1926**

Commercial Cars Ld. Regd. 1919. Receiver appointed Apr. 1923; ceased to act Apr. 1927. Undertaking sold to Centaur Ld. (later Commer Cars Ld.). In Aug. 1927 1st debenture holders received 8s. 9d. in £; further payments (if any) not known. Struck off Register Apr. 1929 .... **1930**

Commercial Colonisation Co. of Manitoba Ld. Regd. 1887. Vol. liq. 4 Feb. 1891. Final meeting return regd. 3 Feb. 1898 .... **1891**

Commercial Corporation Ld. Regd. 1897. Vol. liq. 30 Dec. 1911. Final meeting return regd. 29 Sept. 1913 **1912**

Commercial Corporation of London Ld. Regd. 1920 as Commercial Bank of London Ld.; name changed June 1921. Vol.. liq. 2 Oct. 1923. Capital returned to contributories—1s. per share of £1 on 1,812,376 shares and a further 7·3934d. on 1,780,265 shares. Final meeting return regd. 9 Mar. 1938 .... **1924**

Commercial Development Corporation Ld. Regd. 1897. Certain patents were sold in 1902. Shareholders were entitled to 50% of ordinary shareholding or 335% of deferred shareholding in stock of Algoma Tube Co. Struck off Register 29 Oct. 1935 .... **1936**

Commercial Enterprise Ld. Regd. 1901. Vol. liq. Dec. 1910. Removed from Register 1912 .... **1911**

Commercial Exchange National Bank. In 1928 merged with Bank of America National Association........ **1929**

Commercial Fire Insurance of Scotland Ld. Regd. Edinburgh 1887. Undertaking acquired by Mercantile Fire Insurance Co. Ld. Vol. liq. Apr. 1898. Final meeting return regd. 28 Mar. 1901 .... **1899**

Commercial Gas Co. Estd. 1839; Inc. 1847; reinc. by Special Act 1852. Dissolved 1 May 1949, undertaking being vested in North Thames Area Gas Board

under Gas Act 1948. Holders of securities were entitled to receive, in respect of each £100 unit held, British Gas 3% guaranteed stock 1990–95 as follows:

	£	s.	d.
Ord. stock (5% basic)	108	10	0
4% red. pref. stock	100	15	0
3% perp. deb. stock	77	10	0
5% irred. deb. stock	114	0	0
3½% red. deb. stock	102	0	0	**1952**

Commercial Glass Works Ld. Regd. 1919. Court Order to wind up 26 June 1923. Struck off Register 1929 **1924**

Commercial Guarantee Society Ld. Regd. 1874. Removed from Register 1904 .... ***1877**

Commercial, Industrial & Land Co. of Egypt Ld. Regd. 1906. Vol. liq. 6 Mar. 1908. Final meeting return regd. 1 Nov. 1917 .... **1909**

"Commercial Intelligence" Publishing Co. Ld. Regd. 1902. Struck off Register 1916 .... **1914**

Commercial Mills (Holdings) Ld. Regd. 1919 as Commercial Mills Spinning Co. (1919) Ld.; name changed to Commercial Mills Ld. Oct. 1942, and as above in 1953. All capital was owned by James Dunkerley Ld. Vol. liq. (members') 27 Mar. 1957. Final meeting return regd. 6 Nov. 1958 .... **1956**

Commercial Mills Ld. *formerly* Commercial Mills Spinning Co. (1919) Ld. *See* above.

Commercial Mills Spinning Co. Ld. Regd. 1873. Vol. liq. 11 Nov. 1919. Final meeting return regd. 9 Apr.1920 **1906**

Commercial National Bank & Trust Co. of New York. Inc. in New York 2 Nov. 1928. Ceased business 25 May 1951 having been merged with Bankers Trust Co.. .... **1951**

Commercial Ozone Syndicate Ld. Regd. 1896. Removed from Register 1902 .... **1901**

Commercial Railway *See* London and Blackwell Railway Co.

Commercial Rooms, Bristol. Inc. by Special Act 1810 **1901**

Commercial Salt Co. Ld. Regd. 1913. Court Order to wind up Mar. 1927. Goodwill was acquired by Cheshire United Salt Co. Ld. (later Sifta Salt Ld.). Struck off Register 1932 .... **1933**

Commercial Steam Ship Co. Ld. Regd. 1870 as Mutual Steam Ship Co. Ld.; name changed 1871. Vol. liq. 24 Aug. 1881. Final meeting return regd. 6 Apr. 1882 .... **1899**

Commercial Steam Ship Co. Ld. Regd. 1881. Vol. liq. June 1888. Reconstructed as company of same name. Shareholders were entitled to 1 fully-paid share of £10 in new company for each share of £5 held. Final meeting return regd. 8 Apr. 1889........ **1899**

Commercial Steam Ship Co. Ld. Regd. 1888. Vol. liq. 8 Apr. 1910. Final meeting return regd. 4 Nov. 1912 **1911**

Commercial Timber Co. Ld. Regd. 1918. Vol. liq. Feb. 1928. Struck off Register Jan. 1934 .... **1934**

Commercial Trust Co. *See* Bank of North America and Trust Co.

Commercial Union Bank Ld. Regd. 1877. Removed from Register 1905 .... **1884**

Commercial Union Brewery Investment Corporation Ld. Regd. 1888. Vol. liq. 9 Nov. 1892. Taken over by United Discount & Securities Co Ld., in which company shareholders were entitled to 1 fully-paid ordinary share of £7 for every 4 ordinary shares of £3 held or 1 fully-paid preference share of £10 for each preference share of £10 held. Holders of founders' shares were entitled to £20 per share in cash. Final meeting return regd. 22 July 1893 .... **1893**

Commercial Union Trust Ld.. Regd. 1885 as Railway, Tramway & General Trust Ld.; name changed. Removed from Register 1894 .... **1905**

Commodity & Associated Investments Ld. *See* London Wall Investment Trust Ld.

Commonwealth Contract Co. *See* Philadelphia Co.

Commonwealth Gold Fields Ld. Regd. 1902. Removed from Register 1909 .... **1903**

Commonwealth Gold Mines Ld. Regd. 1904. Vol. liq. 19 Dec. 1906. Removed from Register 1907 .... **1907**

Commonwealth Gold Mining Co. Ld. Regd. 1910. Vol. liq. 29 Sept. 1914. Final meeting return regd. 6 Mar.1915 .... **1915**

Commonwealth Jumbo Mines Development Syndicate Ld. Inc. Rhodesia 1902. Vol. liq. 1906 .... **1907**

Commonwealth Mining & Finance Ld. Regd. 1934. Vol. liq. (members') 5 Sept. 1941. Winding-up Order 18 Mar. 1946. Capital returned to contributories—3d. per share of 2s. 6d. Liquidator released 12 Nov. 1954. Struck off Register 17 Mar. 1961 .... **1955**

Commonwealth Oil Corporation Ld. Regd. 1905. Struck off Register May 1930 .... **1931**

Commonwealth Prospecting Ld. Inc. Australia. In liquidation. All capital was owned by Commonwealth Mining & Finance Ld. **1939**

VOL. FOR

Comodoro Oil & Transport Co. Ld. Regd. 1922. Vol. liq. (creditors') 18 July 1933. Assets realised insufficient to pay creditors in full. Final meeting return regd. 28 July 1936 .... **1934**

Compagnia Fondiaria Napolitana. Undertaking acquired by Compagnia Fondiaria Regionale in 1929 **1936**

Compagnia Fondiaria Regionale. Established Italy 1917. Placed in liquidation 1935 .... **1936**

Compagnie Belge pour l'Etranger S.A. Inc. Belgium 1902 as Banque Sino Belge S.A.; name changed to Banque Belge pour l'Etranger S.A. in 1913 and as above in Dec. 1935. In liquidation on and from 1 Jan. 1936; the undertaking was transferred to Société Générale de Belgique. Shareholders were entitled to 1 part de reserve for every 6 fully-paid or 24 partly paid shares held **1936**

Compagnie d'Assurances Générales contre l'Incendie et les Explosions. Established France 1819 .... **1939**

Compagnie de Pulpe de Chicoutimi. See Chicoutimi Pulp Co.

Compagnie des Chemins de Fer de l'Ouest. See Western of France Railway Co.

Compagnie des Chemins de Fer du Nord de l'Espagne. See Northern of Spain Railways.

Compagnie des Chemins de Fer Piree-Athènes Péloponèse. See Piræus, Athens and Peloponnesus Railway Co.

Compagnie des Chemins de Fer Portugais de la Beira Alta. See Companhia dos Caminhos de Ferro Portugueses da Beira Alta.

Compagnie des Mines d'Or (Brown's Creek) Ld. Regd. 1894. Reconstructed 1898 as Brown's Creek Co. Ld., in which company shareholders were entitled to 1 share of £1 (credited with 17s. 6d. paid) for each share of £1 held. Removed from Register 1903 ... **1901**

Compagnie du Chemin de Fer Mersine-Tarsus-Adana. See Mersina, Tarsus & Adana Railway Co.

Compagnie du Katanga. Established Belgium 1891. The London Office had been closed by 1907 .... **1907**

Compagnie du Télégraphe Sous-Marin entre la France et l'Angleterre. Established 1851. Now dissolved....... **1890**

Compagnie Francaise de Banque et de Mines. Founded in 1895 as Compagnie Française de Mines d'Or et d'Exploration; name changed in 1901 to Compagnie Française de Mines d'Or et de l'Afrique du Sud, and to present title in 1910. Now absorbed by Credit Mobilier Français. **1914**

Compagnie Française des Chemins de Fer de la Province de Santa Fé S.A. See French Railways Co. of the Province of Santa Fé.

Compagnie Française des Mines de Diamants du Cap. Inc. France 1880. Undertaking was acquired by De Beers Mining Co. Ld., in 1887. Capital returned to contributories—£33 11s. (fcs. 850) per ordinary share of fcs.500 and £22 11s. 4¼d. (fcs.571·8) per founders' share of fcs.500 in Nov. 1887; further payments (if any) not known............... **1888**

Compagnie Française des Mines du Sunium. Mines were acquired by Laurium Factory Co. **1941**

Compagnie Française des Tramways Electriques et Omnibus de Bordeaux. (S.A.). Established 1898. 5% obligations were redeemed at par in Jan. 1953 ..... **1954**

Compagnie Française du Télégraphe de Paris à New York. Established 1879; in liquidation 1894 for purpose of amalgamation with Compagnie Française des Cables Telegraphiques **1895**

Compagnie Franco-Belge des Chemins de Fer du Nord de la Republique Sud Africaine. See Northern Railway of the South African Republic.

Compagnie Générale de Traction. Established 1897 .... **1902**

Compagnie Générale des Asphaltes de France. Regd. 1872. Property and undertaking were acquired by Val de Travers Asphalte Paving Co. Ld., in which company preference shareholders were entitled to 135% of holding in 1st debenture stock. Holders of ordinary shares were entitled to 6 ordinary shares of £1 in acquiring company for each ordinary share of £6 held. Removed from Register 1913 .... **1904**

Compagnie Générale des Hansom Cabs à Paris. Inc. 1888; in liquidation **1891**

Compagnie Shannon Belge S.A. In liquidation. A controlling interest was held by The Shannon Ld **1934**

Compagnie Sud-Africaine Ld. Regd. 1889. Undertaking and assets were acquired by company of same name for £28,781 in ordinary shares of £1. Removed from Register 1901 .... **1908**

Compagnie Sud-Africaine Ld. Regd. 1899. Vol. liq. 19 Oct. 1920. Final meeting return regd. 3 July 1923 **1921**

Compagnie Sud-Africaine Ld. Regd. 1921. Vol. liq. 9 July 1923. Final meeting return regd. 4 Mar. 1927 **1925**

Compagnie Universelle du Canal Interocéanique (Panama Canal Co.). **1894**

VOL. FOR

Compagnie Vimbos (France-Belge) Ld. Regd. 1897. Court Order to wind up 13 July 1898. Removed from Register 1909 .... **1899**

Companhia America Fabril-Fisção e Tecelagem. Inc. Brazil 1885 as Chia. Fiação e Tecidos Pau-Grande; name changed to Chia. America Fabril 1891 and as above 1941. The outstanding 6½% 1st mortgage 20-year registered sterling debentures were redeemed on 1 Oct. 1945 at 70%, all arrears of interest from 31 Dec. 1940 being cancelled **1946**

Companhia de Ambaca. Incorporated in Portugal (with limited liability) 6 Feb. 1886 as Royal Trans-African Railway Co. under authority of statutes approved by Portuguese Government; name changed to Trans-African Railway Company (Companhia dos Caminhos de Ferro Attravez d'Africa) Nov. 1910 and to present title in 1929. The company has been wound up and a new company (Cia. de Fomento Colonial) formed. By an Order of the High Court of Justice of 14 July 1939 the 5% 1st mortgage bondholders were entitled to receive for every £100 bond-£10 11s. 3d. cash and 5 A shares of Esc. 22 each in the new company; and for every £20 bond— £2 2s. 3d. cash and 1 A share **1943**

Companhia de Electricidade e Viação Urbana de Minas Geraes. See Minas Geraes Electric Light & Tramways Co.

Companhia de Fomento Colonial. See Companhia de Ambaca.

Companhia de Inversiones del Oro. In liquidation. All issued capital was owned by El Oro Mining & Railway Co. Ld. **1939**

Companhia de Mossamedes. Inc. Portugal 1894 .... **1914**

Companhia do Nyassa. See Nyassa Company.

Companhia dos Caminhos de Ferro Atravez d'Africa. See Companhia de Ambaca.

Companhia dos Caminhos de Ferro Portugueses da Beira Alta. Inc. in Portugal 1879. Placed in liquidation 1948. Holders of obligations were offered redemption in 1946—1st rank obligations, Esc.200 per bond (of Frs.500) plus Esc.43·20 for coupons 65 to 80 and Esc.4·80 for coupon 81; 2nd rank obligations, Esc.66·66 per bond (of Frs.500) plus Esc.1·60 for coupon 19 .... **1947**

Companhia Estrada de Ferro de Araraquara. See Araraquara (San Paulo) Railway Co.

Companhia Ferro Carril do Jardim Botanico. Inc. Brazil 1882. The outstanding 5% 40-year 1st mortgage bonds were redeemed on 1 Jan. 1949 at 102½%..... **1949**

Companhia Fiscao e Tecidos Pau-Grande. See Companhia America Fabril-Flação Tecelagem

Companhia Industrial de Pinheiros. In liquidation. All shares were owned by City of San Paulo Improvements & Freehold Land Co. Ld. **1942**

Companhia Mogyana de Estradas de Ferro. See Mogyana Railways Co.

Companhia Mogyana de Estradas de Ferro e Navegação. See Mogyana Railways Co.

Companhia Nacional de Tecidos de Juta S.A. See National Jute Factory.

Companhia Paulista de Estradas de Ferro. Established in 1869 as Companhia Paulista de Estradas de Ferro do Oeste; name changed to Companhia Paulista de Vias Ferreas e Fluviaes in 1883 and to present title in 1911. The outstanding 5% debenture bonds were redeemed in Sept. 1934............... **1935**

Companhia Paulista de Estradas de Ferro do Oeste. See Companhia Paulista de Estradas de Ferro.

Companhia Paulista de Vias Ferreas e Fluviaes. See Companhia Paulista de Estradas de Ferro.

Companhia Viação Ferrea Sapucahy. Constituted 1891 **1909**

Compañia Argentina de Navegacion Mihanovich Ltda. See Argentine Navigation Co. Mihanovich Ld.

Compañia Azucarera Tucumana. See Tucuman Sugar Co.

Compañia Chilena de Salitres. See Chilean Nitrate Co.

Compañia de Electricidad de la Provincia de Buenos Aires Ld. Regd. 1911. Vol. liq. (members') 10 Oct. 1975. Capital returned to contributories—18·275p per share (of 5p). Final meeting return held 31 Jan. 1980 **1980–1**

Compañia de Gas y Electricidad de la Habana. Inc. by Deed in Cuba 1904. Stockholders were offered $110 preferred stock and $25 common stock in Havana Electric Railway Light & Power for each $100 stock held. **1928**

Compañia de los Caminos de Hierro del Norte de Espana. See Northern of Spain Railways.

Compañia de los Ferro-Carriles de Zaragoza al Mediterráneo. See Saragossa & Mediterranean Railway Co.

Compañia de los Puertos de Cuba. See Cuban Ports Co **1934**

Compañia de Luz y Fuerga de Buenos Aires Limitada. See Buenos Aires Lacroze Light Power Co. Ld.

Compañia de Salitre de Chile. See Nitrate Corporation of Chile.

See Stock Exchange Year-Book.

VOL. FOR

Compañia de Salitres de Antofagasta. Inc. Chile 1872. Vol. liq. 1925. The undertaking and assets were acquired by Lautaro Nitrate Co. Ld., in which company shareholders were entitled to 1 fully-paid share of £5 for every $3\frac{3}{4}$ shares of $50 held, or £1 6*s*. 8*d*. for each share held. Debenture and debenture stock holders were given the option of repayment at 102% or exchanging into Lautaro nitrate debenture stock at par *plus* 2% in cash ... **1926**

Compañia de Salitres y Ferrocarril de Agua Santa. Inc. in Chile 1890 ... **1918**

Compañia de Salitres y Ferroearril de Junin. Inc Chile **1916**

Compañia de Trasportes "Expreso Villalonga." Inc. Argentina 1887 as Compania National de Trasportes (National Transport Co.); name changed May 1934. The outstanding 5% 1st debentures were repaid in 1943 ... **1944**

Compañia del Ferro-Carril i Cucuta. Inc. 1865 as San Buena Ventura Road Co.; name changed 1887. The then outstanding 6% 1st mortgage debentures were redeemed 1 Sept. 1920... **1921**

Compañia del Ferrocarril de Zafra à Huelva. *See* Zafra & Huelva Railway Co.

Compañia del Ferrocarril del Pacifico. Inc. Columbia in 1908. The sterling 5% 5-year bonds were paid off in 1916 ... **1917**

Compañia del Ferro-Carril Nacional del Ecuador Ld. Regd. 1891. Struck off Register 5 May 1896. ... **1896**

Compañia Ferro-Carril de Aguas Blancas. *See* Aguas Blancas Railway.

Compañia Ferro-Carril de Copiapo. Inc. 1849. The undertaking was sold to the Chilian Government for £275,000, payable in bonds. Shareholders were entitled to £30 per share of $500 in Government $4\frac{1}{2}$% bonds of £20 and £100, fractions being paid in cash at $87\frac{5}{8}$. Further payments (if any) unknown ... **1912**

Compañia Hispano-Americana de Electricidad S.A. [Chade.]. Formed by deed 22 June 1920; inc. in Spain with limited liability 5 Aug. 1920. Dissolved 26 Jan. 1949 in accordance with Spanish Decree of 17 July 1947. Shareholders were entitled to receive as from 1 Dec. 1948, the following in Soc. D'Electricité (Sodec)—1 warrant of 5 Sodec shares per Chade share series A. B. or C. or per group of 5 Chade shares series D or E and 1 warrant of 1 Sodec share per Chade share series D or E. The liability in respect of bonds and debentures was assumed by Sodec ... **1950**

Compañia Irrigadorn y de Luz y Fuerza del Estado de Hildago S.A. *See* Panchuca Light & Power Co.

Compañia Luz y Fuerza Electrica Cochabamba. *See* Electric Light & Power Co. of Cochabamba.

Compañia Minéra de México Ld. Regd. 1900. Vol. liq. 1906. The undertaking was acquired by Mexican Agency Ld., in which company shareholders were entitled to 3 fully-paid shares of £1 for each ordinary or founders' share held. Removed from Register 1907 ... **1907**

Compañia National de Trasportes. *See* Compañia de Trasportes "Expreso Villalonga."

Compañia Salitrera Anglo-Chilena. *See* Compañia Salitrera Anglo-Lautaro.

Compañia Salitrera Anglo-Lautaro. Inc. in Chile 1931 as Compania Salitrera Anglo-Chilena; name changed June 1951. Dissolved under plan of reorganisation of 1968, holders of A., B. and C shares (of U.S.$12; U.S.$20·25, and U.S.$1·20 respectively) were entitled to receive, share for share, similar A, B and C shares of Anglo Lautaro Nitrate Co., Ld. (inc. in Bahamas) or cash in lieu thereof if so electing. Final report of liquidators issued 31 Jan. 1969 ... **1969**

Compañia Salitrera de Tarapaca y Antofagasta. Inc. in Chile in 1934. Vol. liq. 30 Apr. 1963. At 30 Sept. 1967, 36·44% of 5% debentures had been repaid; later payments (if any) not known ... **1969**

Compañia Salitrera el Loa. *See* Loa Nitrate Co.

Compañia Salitrera Galicia. *See* Galicia Nitrate Co.

Compañia Salitrera Pampa Alta. Inc. by Presidential Decree in Chile 1904. Undertaking and assets were acquired by Loa Nitrate Co. in 1911 ... **1913**

Compañia Salitrera Pedro-Perfetti. *See* Perfetti Nitrate Co.

Company of Proprietors of the Canal Navigation from Leeds to Liverpool. *See* Leeds & Liverpool Canal Co.

Company of Proprietors of the Leicester Navigation. Inc. by Special Act 1791. Vol. liq. 1932. By Grand Union Canal Co. Act of 1931 the undertaking and assets were acquired by that company... **1932**

Company of Proprietors of the Lewes Water Works. *See* Lewes Water Co.

Company of Proprietors of the Oxford Canal Navigation. *See* Oxford Canal Co.

VOL. FOR

Company of Proprietors of the Staffordshire & Worcestershire Canal Navigation. *See* Staffordshire & Worcestershire Canal Co.

Company of Proprietors of the Warwick and Braunston Canal Navigation. *See* Warwick & Napton Canal Navigation.

Compensation and Guarantee Fund Ld. Regd. 1899. Vol. liq. 27 Mar. 1907. Undertaking was acquired by Northern Assurance Co. Removed from Register 1913 ... **1908**

Compin's Patent Springs Ld. Regd. 1900. Removed from Register 1906 ... **1904**

Components Ld. Regd. 1902. 1st debentures were repaid. Struck off Register 2 Oct. 1953 ... **1938**

Components Tube Co. Ld. Regd. 1897. Vol. liq. 11 June 1900. Final meeting return regd. 25 May 1901... ***1901**

Compound Metals Co. Ld. Regd. 1903. Court Order to wind up 1906. Removed trom Register 1906... **1907**

Comptoir d'Escompte de Genève. Established 1855. Reconstructed 1931 as Basque d'Escompte Suisse **1934**

Comptoir Financier et Commercial d'Egypte. Inc. by Khedival Decree 1905. Placed in liquidaton in Nov. 1922 ... **1912**

Comptoir General Ld. Regd. 1868. Removed from Register 1894 ... ***1877**

Comstock Mines (British Columbia) Ld. Regd. 1897. Removed from Register 1904 ... **1900**

Comstock Mining Co. Ld. Regd. 1888. Struck off Register 3 Aug. 1894 ... **1899**

Concentric Tube Co. Ld. Regd. 1896. Vol. liq. 21 Feb. 1898. Final meeting return regd. 7 Mar. 1900... **1899**

Concessions Trust Ld. Regd. 1889. Vol. liq. 3 Aug. 1891. Final meeting return regd. 4 Mar. 1898 ... **1892**

Concordia Consolidated Mines Co. Ld. Regd. 1899. Struck off Register 19 Mar. 1907 ... **1908**

Concrete Building Commodities (London) Ld. Regd. 1934. Vol. liq. (members') 15 Mar. 1935. Capital returned to contributories—£36,150 *plus* 399,965 deferred shares of 1*s*. in Dunbrik Ld. Final meeting return regd. 30 June 1937... **1942**

Condal Water Co. Ld. Regd. 1888. Removed from Register 1892 ... **1891**

Condal Water Co. (1900) Ld. See Rubinat Condal Co. Ld.

Conde d'Eu Railway Co. Ld. Regd. 1875. Vol. liq. Apr. 1906. Line purchased by Brazilian Government for £600.000 Government 4% Railway Guarantees Rescission Bonds. In Jan. 1902 debenture holders were entitled to repayment in cash at par or to new $5\frac{1}{2}$% debentures. In July 1906 holders of $5\frac{1}{2}$% debentures were entitled to repayment in cash at 105% or to £120 Rescission Bonds for each debenture of £100 held. Shareholders were entitled to £18 Rescission Bonds *plus* 9*s*. 6*d*. in cash for each share of £20 held. Removed from Register 1907 .. **1907**

Condensed Gas Co. Ld. Regd. 1917. Vol. liq. (members') 25. Sept. 1940. Capital returned to contributories—20*s*. per share of £1. Final meeting return regd. 4 Jan. 1941 ... **1940**

Condensed Milk & Dairy Co. Ld. Regd. 1883. Removed from Register 1890 ... **1885**

Condensed Milk Co. of Ireland Ld. Regd. Dublin 1889. Vol. liq. Nov. 1923. Reconstructed as Condensed Milk Co. of Ireland (1924) Ld. ... **1924**

Condensed Peptonised Milk Co. Ld. *See* Thew, Hooker & Gilbey Ld.

Conder Claims Ld. Regd. 1900. Struck off Register 14 Dec. 1917... **1911**

Condes Co. of Chili Ld. Regd. 1881. Removed from Register 1910 ... **1900**

Condual Construction Co. Ld. Regd. 1924. All shares were owned by Monolithic Building Co. Ld. Struck off Register 20 June 1947 ... **1928**

Conduit & Insulation Co. Ld. Regd. 1896. Vol. liq. Sept. 1907. Removed from Register 1909 ... **1908**

Condurrow Mines Ld. Regd. 1910. Receiver appointed in Apr. 1913. Struck off Register 1915 ... **1914**

Condurrow United Mines Ld. Regd. 1906. Vol. liq. Mar. 1910 for reconstruction as Condurrow Mines Ld., in which company shareholders were entitled to 1 fully-paid share of 5*s*. for every 2 ordinary shares of 10*s*. and each priority share of 10*s*. held. They were also entitled to apply for further shares (credited with 1*s*. paid) at par and a bonus of 1 fully-paid share for each share so subscribed. Removed from Register 1911 ... **1911**

Condy's White Lead Co. Ld. Regd. 1887. Vol. liq. 19 May 1892. Final meeting return regd. 18 May 1893 **1893**

Confidence Reef Gold Mining Co. Ld. Regd. 1899. Vol. liq. 29 Nov. 1901. Removed from Register 1907... **1902**

Conglomerate Goldfields of Western Australia Ld. Regd. 1897. Vol. liq. Mar. 1909. Removed from Register 1913 ... **1910**

**See Stock Exchange Year-Book.*

VOL. FOR

Congo & Central African Co. Ld. Regd. 1882. Vol. liq. 29 July 1886. Business was transferred to British Congo Co. Ld. Court Order to continue winding up under supervision Mar. 1889. Final meeting return regd. 7 Nov. 1895 1886
Congo Railway Co. Constituted Brussels 1889 1899
Congreso Copper (Mexico) Ld. Regd. 1906. Vol. liq. 18 Nov. 1908. Final Meeting return regd. 16 Sept. 1909 *1910
Conham Chemical Co. Ld. Regd. 1891. Removed from Register 21 June 1907 .... *1899
Conishead Priory Hydropathic Co. Ld. Regd. 1878. Vol. liq. 24 Jan. 1927. Final meeting return regd. 19 Jan. 1928 1900
Coniston Mining Syndicate Ld. Regd. 1892. Struck off Register 26 Feb. 1909 1909
Connah's Quay Gas Co. Ld. Regd. 1875. Dissolved 1 May 1949, undertaking being vested in Wales Area Gas Board under Gas Act 1948. Holders of securities were entitled to receive British Gas 3% guaranteed stock 1990–95 as follows:

	£	s.	d.	
Ord. shares (5% max.) of £10	10	15	0	
4½% 1st mort. red. debs. (per £100)	100	5	0	1952

Connal & Co. Ld. Regd. Edinburgh 1896. Vol. liq. June 1904 for reconstruction as company of same name. Preference stockholders were entitled to 40% of holding in cash, 12½% in B debenture stock and 47½% in A debenture stock. Ordinary shareholders were entitled to an equal number of fully-paid ordinary shares of £1 after payment of 12*s.* per share call had been paid. Final meeting return regd. 10 Feb. 1906 1909
Connaught Trust Ld. Regd. 1914. Vol. liq. (members') 27 Nov. 1929. Capital returned to contributories—£6,275 6*s.* 10*d.* Certain assets were distributed in specie. Final meeting return regd. 7 Mar. 1930 ... *1930
Connemara Green Marble Quarries Ld. Regd. 1911. Struck off Register 1923 1913
Connemara Mining Co. Ld. Regd. 1912. Vol. liq. 31 Oct. 1922. Final meeting return regd. 24 Mar. 1924..... 1923
Conquista-Xicao Gold Mines Ld. Regd. 1907. Vol. liq. (creditors') 25 Nov. 1931. No capital returned to contributories. Final meeting return regd. 20 Feb. 1937 1932
Conrad Stannite Mines Ld. Regd. 1906. Vol. liq. Dec. 1909. Removed from Register 1913 1910
Conservative News Agency Ld. Regd. 1885. Vol. liq. Mar. 1887. Final meeting return regd. 15 June 1888 1888
Consett Spanish Ore Co. Ld. Regd. 1873. Vol. liq. 19 July 1951. Capital returned to contributories—£4 11*s.* 11·088*d.* per share of 13*s.* 4*d.* £2,717 was paid into Companies' Liquidation Account. Final meeting return regd. 16 June 1952.......... 1953
Consett Water Works Co. Inc. 1859. Undertaking transferred to Weardale & Consett Water Co., for £175,000 10% maximum ordinary stock and £105,615 4% preference stock. The Weardale Co. assumed liability for this company's £54,200 mortgages 1903
Consol Automatic Aerators Ld. Regd. 1909. Vol. liq. 3 Dec. 1914. The business assets and goodwill were sold to Consol Automatic Aerators (1914) Ld. The liabilities were satisfied in full. Final meeting return regd. 17 Mar. 1916 1915
Consol Automatic Aerators (1914) Ld. Regd. 1917. Vol. liq. 28 Apr. 1922. Final meeting return regd. 22 Feb. 1927 .... *1923
Consolidated African Copper Trust Ld. Regd. 1902. Vol. liq. Sept. 1910 for reconstruction as South African Copper Trust Ld., in which company shareholders were entitled to 1 fully-paid share of 5*s.* for each preference or ordinary share of £1 held. Removed from Register 1912.......... 1911
Consolidated Anglo-Japanese Co. Ld. Regd. 1905. Vol. liq. Dec. 1910. Removed from Register 1911........ 1911
Consolidated Assurance Co. Ld. Regd. 1903. Court Order to wind up 13 Oct. 1926. Liquidator released 24 May 1939 1927
Consolidated Bank Ld. Regd. 1859 as Bank of Manchester Ld.: name changed May 1896. Vol. liq. 4 June 1896. Undertaking was amalgamated with Parr's Bank Ld., in which company shareholders were entitled to $\frac{2}{15}$ of a share of £100 (£20 paid) for each share of £10 (£4 paid) held.......... 1897
Consolidated Bellingwe Development Co. Ld. Regd. 1895. Undertaking was acquired by Rhodesia Consolidated Ld., in which company shareholders were entitled to 1 share of 10*s.* (credited with 7*s.* paid) for each share of £1 held. Removed from Register 1906 1904
Consolidated Cambrian Ld. Regd. 1913. Vol. liq. 23 May 1930. Final meeting return regd. 12 July 1932 1931
Consolidated Cities Light, Power & Traction Co. Inc. Delaware 1912. The outstanding 1st lien 5% gold bonds were redeemed at 105% on July 1945. All shares were held by Cities Service Co. Company dissolved and assets liquidated Dec. 1945 1947
Consolidated Coal, Iron & Lead Co. Inc. Virginia 1894 1916
Consolidated Coffee Estates Ld. Regd. Edinburgh 1922. Vol. liq. (members' 11 Mar. 1946, the company's holding of capital in Consolidated Coffee Estates (1943) Ld. and Hunsur Works Ld. having been transferred to Consolidated Coffee Investment Trust Ld., for 140,347 fully-paid £1 shares which have been distributed to shareholders of this company in the proportion of 2 shares for every share held. capital returned to contributories—£1 14s. 8¾d. per share (of £1). Final meeting return regd. 10 Oct. 1949 1951
Consolidated Coffee Investment Trust Ld. Regd. in Edinburgh 1945. Vol. liq. (members') 22 Dec. 1953. Capital returned to contributories—17*s.* 6¼*d.* per share of 1*s.* £268 8*s.* 5*d.* was paid into Companies' Liquidation Account. Final meeting return regd. 27 Apr. 1956 1957
Consolidated Colombia Platinum & Gold Mines Ld. Regd. 1915. Vol. liq. 16 Jan. 1920. Final meeting return regd. 30 Oct. 1920 1920
Consolidated Construction Co. Ld. Regd. 1919. Struck off Register 1938 .... *1952
Consolidated Co-operative Textile Mills Ld. Regd. 1929. Struck off Register 1933 .... *1933
Consolidated Copper Co. Ld. Regd. 1899. Struck off Register 4 Oct. 1907.......... 1908
Consolidated Crown Point Gold Mining Co, Ld. Regd. 1896. Vol. liq. 30 June 1899. Struck off Register 18 Jan. 1921 1900
Consolidated Deep Leads Ld. Regd. 1903 as London and Globe Deep Leads Assets Ld.; name changed Dec. 1903. Vol. liq. 20 Nov. 1907 for reconstruction as Australian Deep Leads Trust Ld., in which company shareholders were entitled to one share of 4*s.* (credited with 3*s.* paid) for each share of 4*s.* held. Final meeting return regd. 16 Dec. 1909 1908
Consolidated Deep Levels Ld. Inc. Transvaal 1892. Vol. liq. Shareholders received 2 shares of £1 in South African Real Estate Trust Ld. for every 5 shares of £1 held *plus* cash distribution of 18*s.* 4*d.* per share 1903
Consolidated Diesel Engine Manufacturers Ld. Regd. 1912. Court Order to wind up June 1914. Struck off Register Apr. 1929 1930
Consolidated Dredging & Exploring Co. Ld. Regd. 1906. Vol. liq. June 1908. Removed from Register 1909 1909
Consolidated Electric Co. Ld. Regd. 1883. Removed from Register 1890 1887
Consolidated Electrical Co. Ld. Regd. 1903. Vol. liq. 8 Apr. 1924. Capital returned to contributories—preference shares in full; ordinary shares, 1*s.* per share of £1; further payments (if any) not known. Final meeting return regd. 12 Dec. 1929 1925
Consolidated Engineering & Agency Co. Ld. See below.
Consolidated Engineering Co. Ld. Regd. 1895 as Consolidated Engineering & Agency Co. Ld.; name changed Sept. 1899. Vol. liq. 16 Oct. 1906. Final meeting return regd. 29 Jan. 1910' *1907
Consolidated Esmeralda Ld. Regd. 23 Oct. 1885. Vol. liq. 17 July 1889. Reconstructed as Esmeralda Ld., in which company shareholders were entitled to 1 preferred or 1 ordinary share of £1 (credited with 17*s.* 6*d.* paid) for each preferred or ordinary share of £1 held, Final meeting return regd. 18 Mar. 1914 1893
Consolidated Estates & Mines of South Africa Ld. Regd. 1901. Removed from Register 1912 1904
Consolidated Exploration & Development (Rhodesia) Co. Ld. Regd. 1898. Vol. liq. Sept. 1909 for reconstruction as company of same name. Shareholders were entitled to 1 fully-paid share of £1 in new company for every 4 shares of £1 held. Removed from Register 1911 1910
Consolidated Exploration & Development (Rhodesia) Co. Ld. Regd. 1909. Vol. liq. Feb. 1911. Undertaking and assets were sold to Gold Fields Rhodesian Development Co. Ld., in which company shareholders were entitled to 1 fully-paid share of £1 for each share of £1 held. Removed from Register 1912 1911
Consolidated Exploration and Finance Co. Ld. Regd. 1893. Removed from Register 1908 1899
Consolidated Finance Corporation Ld. Regd. 1898 as Westralian De Kaap Ld.; name changed Dec. 1900. Vol. liq. Nov. 1907 for reconstruction as Wheal Nut Ld., in which company shareholders were entitled to 1 share of 5*s.* (credited with 3*s.* 6*d.* paid) for each share of 10*s.* held. Removed from Register 1903 1909
Consolidated Finance Corporation Ld. Regd. 1910. Vol. liq. 27 Nov. 1914. Final meeting return regd. 7 Feb.1918 1915

**See Stock Exchange Year-Book.*

VOL. FOR

Consolidated Fur Farms Ld. Regd. 1928. Court Order to wind up 5 May 1930. Struck off Register 20 Mar. 1936 1937

Consolidated Gem Group of Murchison Gold Mines Ld. Regd. 1896. Struck off Register Apr. 1929 1930

Consolidated Gem Mines of Ceylon Ld. Regd. 1910. Vol. liq. 3 Dec. 1912. Final meeting return regd. 8 Oct. 1919 .... *1914

Consolidated Gold Coast Properties Ld. Regd. 1900. Struck off Register 1923 1909

Consolidated Gold Fields of Mexico Ld. Regd. 1896. Removed from Register 1911 1903

Consolidated Gold Fields of Victoria Ld. Regd. 1899. Removed from Register 1901 .... *1902

Consolidated Gold Mines of California Ld. Regd. 1897. Vol. liq. 25 June 1898. Reconstructed as company of same name. Shareholders were entitled to 1 share of £1 (credited with 17s. 6d. paid) in new company for each share of £1 held. Final meeting regd. 5 Dec. 1898. 1899

Consolidated Gold Mines of California Ld. Regd. 1898. Reconstructed 1899 as company of same name. Shareholders were entitled to 1 share of £1 (credited with 18s. paid) in new company for each share of £1 held. Removed from Register 1901 1900

Consolidated Gold Mines of California Ld. Regd. 1899. Vol. liq. 1904. Undertaking sold to Golden Valley Mines of West Australia Ld., in which company shareholders were entitled to 1 share of 10s. (credited with 7s. 6d. paid) for every share of £1 held. Removed from Register 1906 1904

Consolidated Gold Mines of Mulatos Ld. Regd. 1886. Removed from Register 1892 1888

Consolidated Gold Mines of Western Australia Ld. Regd. Edinburgh 1894. Reconstructed 1895 as company of same name. Shareholders received 88,050 fully-paid shares of £1 and 24,450 of £1 (credited with 15s. paid). Removed from Register 1902 1896

Consolidated Gold Mines of Western Australia Ld. Regd. 1895. Vol. liq. 11 Nov. 1897. Reconstructed as company of same name. Shareholders were entitled to 1 share of 5s. (credited with 4s. paid) for each share of £1 held. Final meeting return regd. 30 Oct. 1900 1898

Consolidated Gold Mines of Western Australia Ld. Regd. 1898. Removed from Register 1901 1902

Consolidated Goldfields of Ashanti Ld. Regd. 1900. Vol. liq. 4 Dec. 1905. Removed from Register 1907..... 1906

Consolidated Gold Fields of New Zealand Ld. Regd. 1896. Vol. liq. (creditors') 30 Nov. 1951. Assets realised sufficient to make a distribution of 19s. 8d. in the £1 to creditors. Final meeting return regd. 15 May 1957 1958

Consolidated Goldfields of the Ivory Coast Ld. Regd. 1902. Vol. liq. 24 Mar. 1905 for reconstruction as Anglo French Colonial Syndicate Ld. Removed from Register 1908 1907

Consolidated Investment Corporation of Australasia Ld. Regd. 1895. Vol. liq. 30 Dec. 1911. Final meeting return regd. 23 May 1916 1912

Consolidated Investment Corporation of Canada. Inc. Quebec 1929. Undertaking and assets were acquired by United Corporations Ld. for 64.270 fully-paid A shares and 239,790 fully-paid B shares of no par value and $4,498,900 bonds. Dissolved 26 Aug. 1933 ... 1934

Consolidated Kent Collieries Corporation Ld. Regd. 1899. Vol. liq. 2 Aug. 1905. Reconstructed as Kent Collieries Ld., in which company shareholders were entitled to 1 fully-paid share of 5s. for every 5 preference shares of 5s. held. Final meeting return regd. 29 Jan. 1921 1908

Consolidated Langlaagte Mines Ld. Inc. Transvaal 1902. Vol. liq. May 1923. Undertaking and assets were acquired by Langlaagte Estate & Gold Mining Co. Ld., in which company shareholders were entitled to 2 shares of £1 (credited as fully-paid) for every 3 shares of £1 held...................................... 1924

Consolidated London Properties Ld. Regd. 1898. All capital was owned by Capital & Counties Property Co. Ld. Vol. liq. (members') 22 Mar. 1966. Final meeting return regd. 25 Mar. 1968 1965

Consolidated Mexican Syndicate Ld. Regd. 1904. Vol. liq. Jan. 1908. Removed from Register 1908........ 1909

Consolidated Mines & Minerals Development Corporation Ld. Regd. 1930. Struck off Register Jan. 1935 1935

Consolidated Mines Ld. Regd. 1905. Court Order to wind up 16 Apr. 1907. Liquidator released 30 Aug. 1910. Removed from Register 6 June 1913 .... *1906

Consolidated Mines of Cornwall Ld. Regd. 1919. Vol. liq. (members') 25 Nov. 1938. Final meeting return regd. 15 May 1939 1939

Consolidated Mines of El Oro Ld. Regd. 1911. Vol. liq. 11 Aug. 1920 for reconstruction as Africa Corporation Ld., in which company shareholders were

VOL. FOR

entitled to 1 share of £1 (credited with 17s. paid) for every 2 shares of £1 held. Final meeting return regd. 28 Mar. 1921 1921

Consolidated Mining and Investment Corporation Ld. Regd. 1904. Vol. liq. 11 Jan. 1912. Shareholders were entitled to 4 shares of 10s. (credited with 9s. paid) for every 5 shares of 10s. held; a cash distribution was expected. Final meeting return regd. 24 Aug. 1914 1912

Consolidated Mining Co. Ld. Regd. 1878. Reconstructed as New Consolidated Mining Co. Ld. Removed from Register 1905 .... *1887

Consolidated Motor Cab Co. Ld. Regd. 1908. Vol. liq. Apr. 1910. Removed from Register 1912 1911

Consolidated Murchison Gold Mines Ld. Regd. 1895. Vol. liq. 3 May 1897. Reconstructed as company of same name. Shareholders were entitled to 1 share of 10s. (credited with 6s. 6d. paid) in new company for each share of £1 held. Final meeting return regd. 3 May 1898 1898

Consolidated Murchison Gold Mines Ld. Regd. 1897. Vol. liq. 20 Apr. 1899. Reconstructed as Great Fingall Consolidated Ld. Final meeting return regd. 10 May 1900 1908

Consolidated Nickel Mines Ld. Regd. 1903. Court Order to wind up 18 Oct. 1910. The assets were acquired by Nickel Mines & Smelting Co. Ld. Liquidator released 20 Mar. 1915. Struck off Register 14 Feb. 1919 1911

Consolidated Nitrate Co. Ld. Regd. 1893. Removed from Register 1905 1904

Consolidated Oil Fields of California Ld. Regd. 1910. Court Order to wind up 7 Feb. 1912. Liquidator released 12 Jan. 1917. Struck off Register 1 July 1921 1912

Consolidated Oil Fields of South Africa Ld. Regd. 1912. Vol. liq. 25 June 1915. The assets were sold to Union Oil Co. of South Africa Ld. (later Union Oil Trust Ld.), in which company shareholders were entitled to 5 shares of 5s. (credited with 4s. paid) for each share of £1 held. Final meeting return regd. 22 May 1923 1916

Consolidated Oil Fields of Trinidad Ld. Regd. 1911 Receiver for debenture holders appointed on 7 Mar. 1914. Struck off Register 3 Jan. 1919 1915

Consolidated Oil Trust Ld. Regd. 1910. Struck off Register Jan. 1932 1932

Consolidated Oilfields of India Ld. Regd. 1914. Vol. liq. (creditors') 8 Feb. 1930. No capital returned to contributories. Final meeting return regd. 20 May 1930 1930

Consolidated Produce Corporation Ld. Regd. Feb. 1926. Court Order to wind up Mar. 1926. Struck off Register Mar. 1932 1933

Consolidated Railway Co. of Vancouver. Inc. British Columbia. Property and assets were acquired by British Colombia Electric Railway Co. Ld., for £250,000 1st mortgage debentures, £12,000 income bonds, and £200,000 in ordinary shares of £1 1899

Consolidated Rand Rhodesia Trust & General Exploration Co. Ld. Inc. Rhodesia 1902 under Ordinances of British South Africa Co. Vol. liq. Dec. 1908; assets to be sold to British & Colonial Investments Ld. (regd. 1909). Shareholders were entitled to 1 share of 10s. in that company for every 5 shares of £1 held 1909

Consolidated Rubber & Balata Estates Ld. Regd. 1909. Vol. liq. 1922. Struck off Register 15 Aug. 1944 ... 1945

Consolidated Rubber Trust Ld. Regd. 1910. Struck off Register Apr. 1930 1931

Consolidated Signal Co. Regd. 16 Aug. 1901 as Pneumatic Electric & General Engineering Co. Ld.; name changed in 1903. Dissolved 30 Oct. 1984 ... 1975–6

Consolidated Sisal Estates of East Africa Ld. Regd. 1936. Vol. liq. (members') 2 Nov. 1959. All capital was held by Bird & Co. (Africa) Ld., and capital was returned in full. Final meeting return regd. 17 July 1962 1963

Consolidated South Rand Mines Deep Ld. Regd. 1902. Vol. liq. 7 Jan. 1909. Court Order to wind up 3 Feb. 1909. Liquidator released 12 Mar. 1915. Struck off Register 1 July 1921 1909

Consolidated Supply Co. Ld. Regd. 1905. Receiver appointed May 1908. Struck off Register 1917...... 1919

Consolidated Telephone Construction & Manufacturing Co. Ld. Regd. 1881 as Consolidated Telephone Construction & Maintenance Co. Ld.; name changed 1895. Reconstructed 1903 as Consolidated Electrical Co. Ld., in which company shareholders were entitled to 1 share of £1 (credited with 15s. paid) for every 2 shares of 10s. held. Removed from Register 1907 1908

Consolidated Tin Mines of Burma Ld. Regd. 1921. In 1956 company's assets outside Burma were transferred to Contin Finance & Mining Co. Ld., the

*See Stock Exchange Year-Book.

shares of which were distributed to shareholders of this company. Vol. liq. (members') 4 Aug. 1960. Struck off Register 8 Oct. 1976 .... **1977-8**

Consolidated Tin Smelting Co. Ld. Regd. 1891. Vol. liq. 19 Nov. 1912. Final meeting return regd. 10 Mar. 1913 .... **1912**

Consolidated Trust, Ld. (The). Regd. 1889. On 1 Jan. 1974 undertaking and assets transferred to Second Consolidated Tr. Ld., deferred shareholders receiving 130 ordinary shares for every 100 deferred shares and preferred stockholders 1 2·8% preference share for every £1 4% 1st preference stock and 11 3·5% preference shares for every £10 5½% 2nd preferred stock. Holders of 4½% perpetual debenture stock and 6½% convertible unsecured loan stock 1994 received an equivalent amount of 4½% debenture stock 1983 and 6½% A loan stock 1994 respectively. The company was dissolved 13 July 1976 .... **1977-8**

Consolidated Water Works Co. of Rosario Ld. Regd. 1896. Vol. liq. (members') 28 Oct. 1948, the undertaking was sold to the Argentine Government. Capital returned to contributories—£17 12s. 9d. per £10 ordinary and preference capital. Final meeting return regd. 2 Jan. 1956 .... **1957**

Consolidated Welsh Mines Ld. Regd. 1919. Struck off Register 1925 .... ***1924**

Consolidation Coal Co. Organised Delaware 1935. In Nov. 1945 company was amalgamated with Pittsburgh Coal Co. under the title of Pittsburgh Consolidation Coal Co. Shareholders were entitled to 1 share of common stock (par value $1) and $7·50 3½% debentures in new company for each share of common stock held **1946**

Consort Consolidated Mines Ld. Inc. Transvaal 1895. In liquidation in 1905 .... **1905**

Consort Deep Level Gold Mines Ld. Regd. 1895. Court Order to wind up 27 Oct. 1897. Removed from Register 1908 .... **1898**

Consorzio Commerciale Britannico Italo Ld. Regd. 1919. Struck off Register 1924 .... **1925**

Constance Rhodesia Development Co. Ld. Regd. 1910. Vol. liq. May 1911. The assets and undertaking were acquired by Amalgamated Properties of Rhodesia Ld., in which company shareholders were entitled to 3 shares of 5s. for every 2 shares of £1 held. Removed from Register 1912 .... **1912**

Constantine (Joseph) Steamship Line Ld. Regd. 1920. Vol. liq. 31 Mar. 1966. Final meeting return regd. 11 Aug. 1971 .... **1947**

Constantine Oilfields Ld. Regd. 1912. Vol. liq. 5 July 1923. Reconstructed as company of same name. Shareholders were entitled to 5 preferred ordinary shares of 2s. (credited with 1s. paid) in new company for every 2 preferred ordinary shares of 10s. held, or 5 ordinary shares of 2s. (credited with 1s. paid) for every 2 ordinary shares of 10s. held. Final meeting return regd. 8 Apr. 1927 .... **1924**

Constantine Oilfields Ld. Regd. 1923. Vol. liq. (creditors') 16 May 1931. Struck off Register 7 Aug. 1945 **1946**

Constantine Properties Ld. Regd. 1912. Struck off Register 1916 .... **1915**

Constantinople Land & Building Co. Ld. Regd. 1879. Vol. liq. (members') 24 Nov. 1941. Capital returned to contributories—6s. 6·9d. per share of £1. £108 7s. 5d. was paid into Companies' Liquidation Account. Final meeting return regd. 14 Jan. 1947 .... **1947**

Constantinople Telephone Co. |Société Anonyme Turque des Téléphones d'Istanbul| Inc. in Turkey 28 Nov. 1911 with limited liability as Société Anonyme Ottomane des Téléphones de Constantinople; name changed in Apr. 1925 to Société Anonyme Turque des Téléphones de Constantinople (now known as Société Anonyme Turque des Téléphones d'Istanbul). Liquidated 26 May 1936. Capital returned to contributories—145·7% per £100 obligation; 145·7% per £22 certificate and £3 18s. 4d. per share of £5. Final meeting and dissolution of company 25 Mar. 1954 .... **1955**

Construction & Investment Co. Ld. Regd. 1890 as Aragon & Catalonia Railway Co. Ld.; name changed Nov. 1895. Amalgamated July 1902 with Electric Equipment & Securities Ld. (later Reed, Evans & Co. Ld.), in which company shareholders were entitled to 1 share of £1 (credited with 16s. paid) for every £4 in preference shares held. Removed from Register 1906 .... **1903**

Construction Holdings p.l.c. Regd. as private company 24 Apr. 1958; converted into public company 10 June 1958; re-registered as public limited company Feb. 1983. Vol. liq. 9 May 1984. Distribution per ordinary share—31·37p paid 10 May 1984 and 0·88p paid 23 Nov. 1984. £3·14 paid into Insolvency Services Account. Return of final meeting regd. 8 Jan. 1985 .... **1985-6**

Constructive Finance & Investment Co. Ld. Regd. 1924. Vol. liq. (members') 2 June 1937. Capital returned to contributories—£4,562 14s. 5d. plus certain investments distributed in specie. Final meeting return regd. 14 July 1938 .... **1938**

Constructive Finance Co. Ld. Regd. 1919. Vol. liq. 4 Nov. 1924. Final meeting return regd. 22 July 1926 **1926**

Consuelo Gold Mines Ld. Regd. 1897. Struck off Register 23 July 1901 .... **1902**

Consumers' Direct Fish Supply Association Ld. Regd. 1887. Removed from Register 1906 .... **1889**

Consumers' Economic Water Softening & Purifying Co. Ld. See National Pure Water Engineering Co. Ld.

Containers Ld. Regd. 1919. all capital was owned by Cropper & Co. Ld. Vol. liq. (members') 30 Dec. 1964. Final meeting return regd. 11 Feb. 1965 .... **1940**

Contin Finance & Mining Co. Ld. Regd. 1956 as New Consolidated Tin Mines of Burma Ld.; name changed 30 Aug. 1956. Vol. liq. 4 July 1966. Undertaking and assets sold to London & Associated Investment Trust Ld., shareholders were entitled to receive 1 share of 2s. in that company for each share held. Final meeting return regd. 6 July 1967 **1968**

Continental and Commercial National Bank of Chicago. See Continental National Bank and Trust Co. of Chicago.

Continental & Western Australian Trust Ld. See Continental Gold Trust Ld.

Continental Automatic Supply Co. Ld. See Société Continentale des Distributeurs Automatiques (Systeme Ingrey) Ld.

Continental Cotton Oil Co. Inc. New Jersey 1899. Liquidation in 1914, following internal reorganisation among subsidiaries, of which Southland Cotton Oil Co. was principal. Stock in subsidiaries was to be distributed pro rata to stockholders of Continental Cotton Oil Co. **1915**

Continental Diamond Rock Boring Co. Ld. Regd. 1876. Vol. liq. 26 Nov. 1919. Final meeting return regd. 19 Mar. 1920 .... ***1882**

Continental Gold Trust Ld. Regd. 1895 as Continental & Western Australian Trust Ld.; name changed July 1901. Vol. liq. 7 July 1903. Final meeting return regd. 29 Dec. 1904 .... **1904**

Continental Grape Products Ld. Undertaking and assets were acquired in 1928 by Anglo-Continental Grape Products Ld. **1929**

Continental Guaranty Corporation. Established New York 1915 as Guaranty Securities Corporation; name changed Apr. 1918 .... **1922**

Continental Metropolitan Tramways Co. Ld. Regd. 1887. Vol. liq. 22 Dec. 1896. Certain assets were acquired by Compagnie Française pour l'Exploitation des procédés Thomson-Houston. Final meeting return regd. 16 Feb. 1898 .... **1897**

Continental National Bank and Trust Co. of Chicago. Inc. Chicago 1883 as Continental National Bank of Chicago; name changed 1910 to Continental and Commercial National Bank of Chicago and in Dec. 1927 as above. The undertaking was acquired in 1928 by Continental and Illinois National Bank and Trust Co. [later Continental Illinois National Bank and Trust Co.] **1929**

Continental Oxygen Co. Ld. Regd. 1886. Struck off Register 17 June 1898 .... **1901**

Continental Sparklets Co. Ld. Regd. 1898. Vol. liq. 6 Mar. 1907, the patents, trade-marks and goodwill were acquired by Aerators Ld., in which company preference shareholders were entitled to 1 fully-paid ordinary share for every 2 shares held. £300 1s. 4d. was paid into Companies' Liquidation Account. Struck off Register 4 May 1948 .... **1946**

Continental Waste Food Products Ld. Regd. 1928. Investments were realised and proceeds applied towards repayment of a secured loan. Struck off Register Dec. 1932 .... **1933**

Continuous Coal Carbonisation Ld. Regd. 1927. Vol. liq. (creditors') 27 Aug. 1931. No capital returned to contributories. Final meeting return regd. 9 Apr. 1932 .... **1932**

Continuous Gramophones Ld. Regd. 1928. Court Order to wind up Mar. 1931. Struck off Register 21 Sept. 1937 .... **1938**

Continuous Reaction Co. Ld. Regd. 1913. Vol. liq. 27 Aug. 1925. Direct controlling interest owned by Nobel Industries Ld. Final meeting return regd. 3 Apr. 1929 .... **1928**

Contomichalos, Darke & Co. Ld. Regd. 1912. Vol. liq. 31 Dec. 1928. Undertaking and assets acquired by Cotts Darke & Co. Ld. Final meeting return regd. 5 Jan. 1932 ... **1940**

Contract Construction Co. Ld. Regd. 1886. Removed from Register 1904 .... ***1904**

Contract Loan & Trust Corporation Ld. Regd. 1889. Vol. liq. Mar. 1912 for reconstruction as company of same name. Removed from Register 1912 .... **1913**

Contractors Ld. Regd. 1900. Vol. liq. June 1913. Operations continued by company of same name in which company shareholders were invited to subscribe for shares at par, subject to commission of 50%. Struck off Register Apr. 1929 .... **1930**

Contractors Ld. Regd. 1913. Struck off Register Apr. 1930 .... **1931**

Contraflo Condenser & Kinetic Air Pump Co. Ld. *See* Contraflo Engineering Co. Ld.

Contraflo Engineering Co. Ld. Regd. 1910 as Contraflo Condenser & Kinetic Air Pump Co. Ld. name changed in Jan. 1924. Vol. liq. (members') 19 Nov. 1945. Undertaking was acquired by G. & J. Weir Ld. [now G. & J. Weir (Holdings) Ld.]. Capital returned to contributories—5s. 11·891d. per share of 16s. 6d. Final meeting return regd. 2 Nov. 1946 .. **1947**

Conway Gas Co. Ld. Regd. 1936. Dissolved 1 May 1949, undertaking being vested in Wales Area Gas Board under Gas Act 1948. Holders of ordinary shares (of £1) were entitled to receive £1 6s. British Gas 3% guaranteed stock 1990–95 for each share held **1952**

Cook (James W.) & Co. Ld. Regd. 1897. Vol. liq. (members') 20 Feb. 1964. All capital was owned by Wm. Cory & Son, Ld. Final meeting return regd. 4 Apr. 1964 .... **1965**

Cook (Thomas) & Son (Egypt) Ld. Regd. 1894. Vol. liq. 26 Apr. 1923. The debentures were redeemed. All the shares were held by Messrs. Thomas Cook & Son. Final meeting return regd. 21 Nov. 1923 ..... **1924**

Cook (W. & R.) Ld. Regd. 1898. Vol. liq. 25 June 1963. Capital returned to contributories 16s. 10·0659828d. per ordinary share of £1. Final meeting return regd. 10 Jan. 1966 .... **1966**

Cook (W. H.) & Co. Ld. Regd. 1888. Vol. liq. 15 Dec. 1892. Removed from Register 1906 .... **1896**

Cooke (Wm.) & Co. Ld. Regd. 1873. Vol. liq. 31 Oct. 1898. Business and assets were acquired by company of same name. Final meeting return regd. 26 Oct. 1899 .... **1908**

Cookham & District Electricity Corporation Ld. Regd. 1920 as Bourne End and District Electricity Corporation Ld.; name changed July 1923. Vol. liq. (members') 15 Feb. 1938. Undertaking acquired by Wessex Electricity Co. Capital returned to contributories—£1 15s. 9¾d. per share of £1. Final meeting return regd. 6 Jan. 1939 .... **1939**

Cooks Kitchen Mine. In 1895 the mine was acquired by Tincroft Mines for 600 shares in the purchasing company **1896**

Cookson & Co. Ld. Regd. 1904. Vol. liq. (members') 26 Apr. 1944. Capital returned to contributories—)£65 14s. 3·208d. per ordinary share of £10. Final meeting return regd. 8 Mar. 1956 .... **1957**

Coolgardie Austral Gold Mining Proprietary Ld. Regd. 1896. Vol. liq. 25 Mar. 1897. Struck off Register Apr. 1929 .... **1930**

Coolgardie Centra Ld. Regd. 1895. Court Order to wind up 24 Nov. 1897. Removed from Register 1908.... **1898**

Coolgardie Consolidated Gold Mines Ld. Regd. 1895. Removed from Register 1908 .... **1899**

Coolgardie Gold Fields Ld. Regd. 1897. Court Order to wind up 23 Aug. 1899. Removed from Register 1909 **1900**

Coolgardie Gold Syndicate Ld. Regd. 1894. Vol. liq. 20 Feb. 1914. Reconstructed as Ontario Gold Mines Ld. Final meeting return regd. 4 Jan. 1924.......... **1926**

Coolgardie Mining Co. Ld. Regd. 1894. Reconstructed 1902 as Mysore United Gold Co. Ld. (later New Exploring & Finance Co. Ld.), in which company shareholders were entitled to 2 shares of 5s. for every 3 shares of 2s. held. Removed from Register 1905 **1905**

Coolgardie Mint & Iron King Gold Mines Ld. Regd. 1894. Reconstructed 1897 as Kalgoorlie Mint & Iron King Gold Mines Ld., in which company shareholders were entitled to 1 share of £1 (credited with 16s. 8d. paid) for each share of £1 held. Removed from Register 1908 .... **1898**

Coolgardie Waterworks Ld. Regd. 1895. Undertaking was acquired by Hampton Plains Estate Ld., in which company shareholders were entitled to 1 fully-paid share of 16s., for every 5 shares of £1 held. Removed from Register 1907 .... **1902**

Coomassie Consols Corporation Ld. Regd. 1901. Vol. liq. 1903. Capital returned to contributories—1s. 1¼d. per share of £1; further payments (if any) not known. Removed from Register 1903 .... **1904**

Coombe & Danescombe Arsenic Co. Ld. Regd. 1896. Removed from Register 1904 .... **1903**

Coombe, Wood & Co. Ld. Regd. 1897. Vol. liq. Oct. 1910. Removed from Register 1912 .... **1911**

Cooper, Box & Co. Ld. Regd. 1880. Vol. liq. 4 Dec. 1906. Final meeting return regd. 25 May 1911 .... ***1908**

Cooper, Cooper & Co. Ld. Regd. 1895. Vol. liq. 14 Dec. 1898. Business was acquired by Cooper, Cooper & Johnson Ld. (later Rajawella Produce Co. Ld.). Final meeting return regd. 28 Sept. 1901 .... **1898**

Cooper, Cooper & Co. Ld. Regd. 1908 as Cooper, Cooper & Co. (1908) Ld.; name changed June 1917. Vol. liq. (members') 28 May 1935. Capital returned to contributories—£2 6s. 3d. per share of £1. Final meeting return regd. 28 July 1936 **1934**

Cooper, Cooper & Co. (1901) Ld. Regd. 1901. Court Order to wind up 27 Oct. 1908. Business was sold to Cooper, Cooper & Co. (1908) Ld., later Cooper, Cooper & Co. Ld. Liquidator released 21 Feb. 1913. Struck off Register 10 Oct. 1916 .... **1909**

Cooper (George) & Co. Ld. Regd. 1912. Vol. liq. 20 June 1927. Final meeting return regd. 1 Oct. 1929 .... **1928**

Cooper (John) & Sons (Beehive) Ld. Regd. 1919. Court Order to wind up 8 Feb. 1927. Assets realised insufficient to discharge debenture debt. Struck off Register Mar. 1932 .... **1933**

Cooper (William) & Goode Ld. Regd. 1897. Vol. liq. 4 Mar. 1918. Shareholders were entitled to 1 5% cumulative preference share of £10 in Eliott's Metal Co. Ld., for every 10 preference shares of £1 held or 4 fully-paid ordinary shares of £1 in that company for every 5 ordinary shares of £1 held. Final meeting return regd. 14 Nov. 1918 .... **1918**

Co-operative Cinematograph Co. Ld. *See* Tomler Productions Ld.

Co-operative Cruising Co. Ld. *See* Cruising Co. Ld.

Co-operative Forage Supply Association Ld. Regd. 1881. Removed from Register 1905 .... **1883**

Co-operative Lighterage Association Ld. Regd. 1890. Struck off Register 17 June 1898 .... **1899**

Co-operative Transitbank. Inc. Riga 1923. In liquidation in 1936 .... **1936**

Cooper's Australasian Exploring Co. Ld. Regd. 1895. Removed from Register 1905 .... **1901**

Coosheen Minerals Ld. Regd. 1906. Struck off Register 1914 .... **1913**

Cootacovil Cinchona Co. Ld. Regd. 1881 as Cootacovil Gold Mining Co. Ld.; name changed Dec. 1883. Vol. liq. May 1885. Final meeting return regd. 26 July 1888 .... **1886**

Cootacovil Gold Mining Co. Ld. *See* Cootacovil Cinchoms Ld.

Copan Oilfields Ld. Regd. 1913. Vol. liq. 20 Aug. 1925. Reconstructed as Saxon Securities Trust Ld., in which company shareholders were entitled to 1 ordinary share of £1 (credited with 12s. 6d. paid) and 1 7% security note for every 7 preference shares of 2s. held, or every 3 ordinary shares of 5s. held. Final meeting return regd. 2 Nov. 1926 .... **1926**

Copaquire Copper Sulphate Co. Ld. Regd. 1900. Court Order to wind up 28 Feb. 1911. Liquidator released 21 Feb. 1913. Struck off Register 10 Oct. 1916 ..... **1912**

Co-Partnership Tenants Ld. Regd. 1907 under Industrial and Provident Societies Act (1893). In 1930, society was amalgamated with Hampstead Heath Extension Tenants Ld., Oakwood Tenants Ld., and Fallings Park Garden Suburb Tenants Ld. to form society of same name. **1936**

Co-Partnership Tenants Ld. Regd. 1930 under Industrial & Provident Societies Acts (1893 to 1928). On 31 Dec. 1925 society was amalgamated with Hampstead Tenants Ld. and Second Hampstead Tenants Ld. to form society of same name (later Suburb Leaseholds Ld.). Shareholders received 1 share of £10 in new society for each share of £4 held. Holders of loan and co-partnership stocks were entitled to an equal amount of stock in new society. The company then ceased to exist **1937**

Cope & Timmons Ld. Regd. 1899. Vol. liq. 14 Nov. 1919. Final meeting return regd. 19 Aug. 1920............. ***1920**

Cope Sportswear Ld. Regd. 17 Nov. 1954 and converted into public company 23 Nov. 1964. Winding-up order made 26 July 1983. With effect from 18 Dec. 1980 Inland Revenue accepted that ordinary shares of 5p became of negligible value within the meaning of section 22 (2) of the Capital Gains Tax Act 1979. Dissolved Apr. 1988 .... **1988–9**

Copiapo Gas Co. Ld. Regd. Jan. 1858. Works and undertaking were acquired for £5,400. Removed from Register 1905 .... **1902**

Copiapo Mining Co. Ld. Regd. 1861. Vol. liq. May 1911. Reconstructed as Copper Mines of Copiapo Ld. Removed from Register 1913. .... **1925**

Copiapo Railway Co. Inc. Chile 1849. Undertaking was sold to Chilian Government for £275,000 in bonds. Shareholders received £30 per share of $50 in Chilian Government 4½% bonds of £20 and £100 **1912**

Copland & Berrie (1908) Ld. Regd. Edinburgh 1908. Vol. liq. Aug. 1917. Final meeting return regd. 10 Sept. 1919 .... **1918**

VOL. FOR

Copper Cliff Mines of Montana Ld. Regd. 1903. Vol. liq. Apr. 1907. Removed from Register 1908 .... **1908**

Copper Company Ld. Regd. 1903. Vol. liq. Feb. 1908. Removed from Register 1912 .... **1910**

Copper Corporation of Chile Ld. Regd. 1898. Vol. liq. 12 Dec. 1900. Removed from Register 1902 .... **1901**

Copper Estates of Western Australia Ld. Regd. 1898. Removed from Register 1903 .... **1900**

Copper Fields of Namaqualand Ld. Regd. 1897. Vol. liq. 2 Apr. 1908. Struck off Register 10 Oct 1916........ **1909**

Copper King Ld. Regd. 1899. Removed from Register 1908 .... **1905**

Copper Mines of Copiapo Ld. Regd. 1912. Vol. liq. (creditors') 9 Feb. 1932. No capital returned to contributories. Final meeting return regd. 6 Oct. 1934. Court Order declared dissolution void 15 Dec. 1936. Final meeting return regd. 30 Dec. 1937 .... **1932**

Copper Mines of Mount Lyell West Ld. Regd. 1897. Vol. liq. Nov. 1907. Undertaking acquired by West Mount Lyell Ld., in which company shareholders were entitled to receive 1 share of £1 (15*s*. paid) for each share of £1 held. Removed from Register 1908 **1908**

Copper Mining & Smelting Co. of Ontario Ld. Inc. Ontario 1905 .... **1909**

Copper Selection Syndicate Ld. Regd. 1902. Vol. liq. Nov. 1911. Removed from Register 1912 .... **1912**

Coppull Ring Spinning Co. Ld. Regd. 1920. Vol liq. (members') 7 Aug. 1941. Capital returned to contributories—9*s*. 6*d*. per share of £1. Final meeting return regd. 30 Jan. 1947 .... **1948**

Copster Mill (1920) Ld. Regd. Sept. 1920. Vol. liq. 14 Dec. 1927. Final meeting return regd. 1 Dec. 1934 **1928**

Copthall Stands Syndicate Ld. *See below.*

Copthall Stores Ld. Regd. 1897 as Copthall Stands Syndicate Ld.; name changed in 1899. Vol. liq. 19 Sept. 1929 for reconstruction as Anglo-Rhodesian & General Investment Co. Ld., in which company shareholders were entitled to 1 fully-paid share of 8*s*. for each share of 10*s*. held. Final meeting return regd. 13 Aug. 1947. Struck off Register 7 Sept. 1948 **1948**

Coquimbo Gold Syndicate Ld. Regd. 1895. Vol. liq. Jan. 1909. Struck off Register 9 Mar. 1954 .... **1954**

Coquimbo Railway Co. Formed Chile 1860. After Feb. 1896 the undertaking was worked on account of Chilian Government. The share capital was to be redeemed by the issue of 4½% sterling bonds **1899**

Coral Mill (Holdings) Ld. Regd. 1919 as Coral Mill (1919) Ld.; name subsequently changed. Subsidiary of Smith & Nephew Associated Cos. Ld. Vol. liq. (members') 3 Aug. 1956. Final meeting return regd. 19 Oct. 1956 .... **1954**

Coral Mill (1919) Ld. *See above.*

Córas Iompair Éireann [Irish Transport Organisation]. Inc. 1945 under provision of Transport Act 1944. Company dissolved 1 June 1950, undertaking acquired under provision of Transport Act 1950, by an organisation of the same name. Holders of 3% guaranteed debenture stock 1955–60, 2½% guaranteed debenture stock 1965–75 and 2½% Transport stock 1965–75 were entitled to receive in respect of each £100 stock held £100 3% Transport stock 1955–60, £100, 2½% Transport stock 1965–75 and £80 3% Transport stock 1975–85 respectively **1951**

Corbacorl Goldfields Ld. Regd. 1900. The subscriptions were to be returned in full. Removed from Register 1902 .... **1902**

Corbett, Williams & Son Ld. Regd. 1909. Receiver appointed and vol. liq. 13 Dec. 1923. Struck off Register June 1932 .... **1933**

Corbitt (Wm.) & Co. Ld. Regd. 1873. Vol. liq. 13 Nov. 1891. Final meeting return regd. 9 July 1892........ **1892**

Corbridge Gas Co. Regd. 1864 as Corbridge Gas Co. Ld.; inc. by Special Act 1904. Dissolved 1 May 1949, undertaking being vested in Northern Area Gas Board under Gas Act 1948. Holders of securities were entitled to receive British Gas 3% guaranteed stock 1990–95 as follows in respect of each £100 unit, unless otherwise stated, of security held:

	£	s.	d.	
Ord. stock A	105	0	0	
Ord. stock B	105	0	0	
Addit. B stock	105	0	0	**1952**

Corder & Turley Ld. Regd. 1898 as Corder & Turley (1898) Ld.; name changed June 1899. Vol. liq. 21 Oct. 1902. Undertaking was acquired by Wright Bindley and Gell Ld. Final meeting return regd. 13 Nov. 1923 .... **1903**

Corderoy Mines Ld. Regd. 1924 as Corderoy South Gold Mines Ld.; name changed 1926. Struck off Register 7 July 1964 .... **1960**

Corderoy Syndicate Ld. Regd. 1895. Vol. liq. (members') 17 Jan. 1934 for reconstruction as Maryborough Mining & Finance Co. Ld., in which company (*a*) the liquidator had the right to call for allotment of 400,000 shares of 1*s*. (credited 6*d*. per share paid), (*b*) shareholders had the right (since expired) to subscribe for 1 share (credited with 6*d*. paid) for each share of 5*s*. held and (*c*) 300,000 shares of 1*s*. fully-paid were to be allotted as purchase consideration for the Maryborough properties. Final meeting return regd. 13 Dec. 1938 .... **1934**

VOL. FOR

Cordes (Dos Works), Ld. Regd. 1903. Vol. liq. 16 June 1959. Final meeting return regd. 23 Sept. 1966..... **1958**

Cordeux (John) & Sons Ld. Regd. 1897. Vol. liq. May 1911. Removed from Register 1912 .... **1912**

Cordoba Central Buenos Aires Extension Railway Ld. Regd. 1905. Vol. liq. 15 Nov. 1912. Undertaking was acquired by Cordoba Central Railway Co. Ld. (later Cordoba Central Trust Ld.). Holders of 5% debentures were entitled to an equal amount of 4% 1st debenture stock *plus* 20% of holding in 5% second preference income stock of acquiring company; ordinary shares held by acquiring company were cancelled and holders of the remaining ordinary shares were entitled to 90% of holding in registered ordinary income stock of acquiring company. Final meeting return regd. 15 July 1915 .... **1913**

Cordoba Central Railway Co. Ld. *See* Cordoba Central Trust Ld.

Cordoba Central Trust Ld. Regd. 1887 as Cordoba Central Railway Co. Ld.; name changed Apr. 1939. Vol. liq. (members') 26 Nov. 1959. 99·7% of each holding of B debenture stock had been repaid at time of liquidation and holders received a final distribution of 23*s*. 9*d*. per £1 stock. Final meeting return regd. 31 Aug. 1964...................................... **1959**

Cordoba Copper Co. Ld. Regd. 1908 Vol. liq. 21 July 1924. Undertaking and assets were acquired by Indian Copper Corporation Ld., in which company shareholders were entitled to 1 share of 2*s*. (credited with 1*s*. paid) for each share of 2*s*. held. Final meeting return regd. 18 July 1927 .... **1925**

Cordova & North Western Railway Co. Ld. Regd. 1889. Vol. liq. Apr. 1908. Prior debenture holders were repaid in cash. Income debenture holders were entitled to 30% of their holdings in debentures in Cordova & North Western Railway Co. (1908) Ld., and 60% in claim certificates. Ordinary shareholders were entitled to 10% in debentures and 20% in claim certificates. Removed from Register 1910 .. **1909**

Cordova & North Western Railway Co. (1908) Ld. Regd. 1908. Removed from Register 1910.................. **1910**

Cordova Exploration Co. Ld. Regd. 1897. Vol. liq. 8 Oct. 1908. Final meeting return regd. 16 July 1914 ..... ***1909**

Cordova Union Gold Co. Ld. Regd. 1888. Removed from Register 1906 .... **1891**

Corinth Mines Ld. Regd. 1897. Vol. liq. Aug. 1909. Removed from Register 1911 .... **1910**

Corinthian Investments Ld. Regd. 1909 as Chota Rubber Estates Ld.; name changed as above June 1957. All capital was owned by City of London Real Property Co. Ld. Vol. liq. (members') 11 Jan. 1966. Final meeting return regd. 3 Oct. 1968.......................... **1963**

Corinthian Shipping Co. Ld. Regd. 1872 as Corinthian Steam Ship Co. Ld.; name changed 17 July 1876. Vol. liq. 20 Nov. 1919. Final meeting return regd. 19 Mar. 1920 .... ***1882**

Corinthian Steam Ship Co, Ld. *See* above.

Cork & Fermoy Railway Co. Inc. by Special Act 1890 as Cork and Fermoy and Waterford and Wexford Railway Co.; name changed by Act of 1893......... **1897**

Cork & Kenmare Railway Co. *See* Kenmare Junction Railway Co.

Cork and Macroom Direct Railway Co. Inc. by Special Act 1861. In 1924 the undertaking was transferred to the Great Southern Railway Co., in which company stockholders were entitled to stock as follows:

For each £10 held	*Gt. Sthn. Rly.*	
4% Debenture Stock £10	4% Deb. Stock	
5% Pref. Share .... £12 10*s*.	4% pref. Stock	
Ordinary Share £10	Ordinary Stock	**1925**

Cork and Muskerry Light Railways Co. Ld. Regd. 1883, under the Tramways and Public Companies (Ireland) Act, 1883. In 1925 the undertaking was merged into the Great Southern Railways Co. stockholders were entitled to £125 Great Southern Railways 4% Preference Stock for every £100 shares held **1925**

Cork Bandon and South Coast Railway Co. Inc. by Special Act 1845, as the Cork and Bandon Railway Company; name changed by Act of 1888. In 1924 the undertaking was transferred to the Great Southern Railway Co., in which company shareholders were entitled to stock as follows:

For each £100 held	*Gt. Sthn. Rly.*
4% Debenture £100	4% Debenture

**See Stock Exchange Year-Book.*

VOL. FOR

5½% Gtd. Pref. ...... £137 10s.   4% Gtd. Pref.
4% Gtd. Pref. .... £100   4% Gtd. Pref.
4% West Cork Pref. .... £100   4% Gtd. Pref.
4% Kinsale Pref. .... £100   4% Gtd. Pref.
4% Ilen Valley Pref. .... £100   4% Gtd. Pref.
4% Pref. (1900) .... £100   4% Preference
Ordinary .... £80   Ordinary **1925**

Cork, Blackrock and Passage Railway Co. Inc. by Special Act 1846. In 1924 the undertaking was transferred to the Great Southern Railway Co., in which company stockholders were entitled to stock as follows:

For each £100 held   Gt. Sthn. Rly.
4½% Debenture 1846 £112 10s.   4% Deb
4½% Debenture 1846 £106 5s.   4% Deb
4% Debenture 1846 .... £100   4% Debenture
4% Debenture 1881 .... £100   4% Gtd. Pref.
4% Debenture 1896 .... £100   4% Gtd. Pref.
4% Debenture 1901* .... £20   4% Preference
5% Preference 1868 ....   £10   Ordinary
4% Preference 1881 ....   £10   Ordinary
4% Preference 1896 ....   £10   Ordinary
Ord. (Undivided) ....   £5   Ordinary
Ord. (Preferred) ....   £5   Ordinary
Ord. (Deferred) ....   £5   Ordinary

*Holders were not entitled to arrears of interest accrued to the date of vesting. The liability for the £65,000 4% Loans was to be assumed by the Great Southern Railway Co. under the operation of the Railway Clauses Act (1863) **1925**

Cork Brick Manufacturing Co. Ld. Regd. Dublin 1897. Vol. liq. Mar. 1913 ....   **1914**

Cork City Railways Co. Inc. by Special Act 1906. In 1925 the undertaking was merged into the Great Southern Railways Co. All the stocks of this company were cancelled **1925**

Cork Co. Ld. Regd. 1894. Vol. liq. 5 Dec. 1899. Final meeting return regd. 12 July 1920 ....   **1901**

Cork Electric Supply Co. Ld. Regd. Dublin 1897 as Cork Electric Tramways & Lighting Co. Ld.; name changed Aug. 1927. Vol. liq. June 1931. Electric Light undertaking sold to Electricity Supply Board of the Irish Free State. 4% mortgage debenture holders were repaid at 115%. Capital returned to contributories—£1 9s. per ordinary or preference share of £1 at Nov. 1931; further payments (if any) not known **1932**

Cork Harbour, Dock & Warehouses Co. Regd. Dublin 1872. In liquidation in 1883 ....   **1883**

Cork Mineral Development Syndicate Ld. Regd. 1903. Removed from Register 1911 ....   **1908**

Cork Palace Theatre of Varieties Ld. Regd. Dublin 1896. Court Order to wind up 15 Nov. 1898. Removed from Register 1908 ....   **1899**

Cork Steam Ship Co. Ld. Regd. Dublin 1872. Vol. liq. Dec. 1922 ....   **1923**

Cork Warehousing, Cold Storage & Pure Ice Co. Ld. Regd. Dublin 1897 ....   **1900**

Corn Exchange National Bank. Absorbed in 1924 by Illinois Merchants Trust Co. **1928**

Cornborough Shipping Line Ld. Regd. 1919. Struck off Register 1926 ....   **1926**

Cornelly Quarry Co. Ld. Regd. 1910. Vol. liq. 30 Nov. 1928. Direct controlling interest was held by Baldwins Ld. [later Baldwins (Holdings) Ld.]. Final meeting return regd. 3 Dec. 1929 ....   **1929**

Cornhill Issues Corpn., Ld. Regd. 1928. Struck off Register 1939 ....   **1935**

Cornish Adventurers Ld. See Tarkwa Consols Ld.

Cornish Bank Ld. Regd. 1879. Undertaking was acquired by Capital & Counties Bank Ld., in which company shareholders were entitled to receive 1 share (£10 paid) and £3 cash for every share (£15 paid) held. The £25 paid shares and 940 (£15 paid) shares were repaid in cash **1904**

Cornish China Clay Railway Co. Ld. Regd. 1888. Removed from Register 1906 ....   **1891**

Cornish Consolidated Tin Mines Ld. Regd. 1906. Vol. liq. 3 Feb. 1910. Undertaking acquired by Cornish Consols Ld., in which company shareholders were entitled to 16 fully-paid ordinary shares of 10s. for every 10 ordinary shares of £1 held or 2 fully-paid ordinary shares for every deferred share of £1 held. Final meeting return regd. 18 Nov. 1915 ....   **1910**

Cornish Consols Ld. Regd. 1910. Vol. liq. 14 May 1913. Shareholders were entitled to (inter alia) 1 fully-paid share of £1 in Botallack Ld., for about every 7 ordinary shares of 10s. held. Final meeting return regd. 24 Feb. 1916 ....   **1901**

Cornish Dairy Co. Ld. Regd. 1900. Removed from Register 1903 ....   **1924**

Cornish Development Co. Ld. Regd. 1907. Vol. liq. 3 Feb. 1910. Undertaking acquired by Cornish Consols Ld., in which company shareholders were

VOL. FOR

entitled to 4 fully-paid ordinary shares of 10s. for every 10 fully-paid shares of 10s. held. Final meeting return regd. 18 Nov. 1915 ....   **1910**

Cornish Exploration Co. Ld. Regd. 1912. Vol. liq. 27 May 1915. Final meeting return regd. 15 July 1918   ***1916**

Cornish Hotels Ld. Regd. 1890. Vol. liq. (members') 17 July 1946. Final meeting return regd. 1 Nov. 1947   **1948**

Cornish Kaolin Ld. Regd. 1912. Vol. liq. members') 12 Sept. 1938. The undertaking was acquired by English Clays Lovering Pochin & Co. Ld., for £25,000 cash and 31,111 fully paid 1st preference shares, which became payable to Leonora Corporation Ld. Final meeting return regd. 12 Sept. 1939   **1939**

Cornish Meledor China Clay Co. Ld. Regd. 1919. Receiver appointed 8 July 1925; ceased to act 2 Feb. 1927. Struck off Register Dec. 1929 ....   **1930**

Cornish Proprietary Mines Ld. Regd. 1906. Struck off Register 1928 ....   **1911**

Cornish Salvage Co. (1918) Ld. Regd. 1918. Vol. liq. 5 Apr. 1929. Capital returned to contributories—3s. 4½d. per share of £1 at June 1929; further payments (if any) not known. Final meeting return regd. 10 Aug. 1929 ....   **1930**

Cornish Tin Properties Ld. Regd. 1906. Struck off Register 1916 ....   **1907**

Cornish Tin Sands Ld. Regd. 1912. Struck off Register 1924 ....   **1917**

Cornish Traders Ld. Regd. 1916. Vol. liq. 19 Jan. 1929. Final meeting return regd. 28 July 1932 ....   **1929**

Cornish Trust Ld. Regd. 1907. Vol. liq. 3 Dec. 1910. Undertaking acquired by Cornish Consols Ld., in which company shareholders were entitled to 13 fully-paid ordinary shares of 10s. for every 10 ordinary shares held or 2 fully-paid deferred shares for each fully-paid deferred share of £1 held. Final meeting return regd. 18 Nov. 1915 ....   **1910**

Cornish Valley Slate Quarries Ld. Regd. 1920. Vol. liq. Nov. 1923. Struck off Register Oct. 1931 ....   **1932**

Cornubia Tin Co. Ld. Regd. 1913. Vol. liq. 31 Dec. 1915. Final meeting return regd. 15 July 1918 ....   **1916**

Cornwall Chemical Co. Ld. Regd. 1871 as West of England Fire Clay, Bitumen & Chemical Co. Ld.; name changed 10 Mar. 1876. Court Orders: to wind up 21 Nov. 1876; to dissolve 18 Mar. 1892 ....   ***1876**

Cornwall China Clays Ld. Regd. 1920. Vol. liq. Oct. 1929. Struck off Register Feb. 1932 ....   **1932**

Cornwall (De Lank) Granite Quarries Ld. Regd. 1920. Vol. liq. 5 Nov. 1921. Final meeting return regd. 3 Aug. 1922 ....   **1922**

Cornwall Electric Power Co. Inc. by Special Act 1902. Dissolved 1 Apr. 1948, undertaking being vested in British (later Central) Electricity Authority and South-Western Area Board under Electricity Act 1947. Holders of 5% debenture stock were entitled to receive £1 5s. British Electricity 3% guaranteed stock (1968–73) in respect of each £1 debenture stock held **1949**

Cornwall Minerals Railway Co. Inc. by Special Act 1873. Under Great Western Railway Act 1896. undertaking was purchased by that company. Holders of debenture stock received an amount of 4% debenture stock sufficient to produce equal interest. Holders of preference stock received a first dividend of 37% and holders of ordinary stock 18½%; further distributions (if any) not known **1897**

Cornwall Power Co. Ld. Regd. 1926. Dissolved 1 Apr. 1948, undertaking being vested in British (later Central) Electricity Authority and South Western Area Board under Electricity Act 1947. Holders of 7% preference shares were entitled to receive £1 13s. British Electricity 3% guaranteed stock (1968–73) in respect of each share (of £1) held **1949**

Cornwall Property (Holdings) Ld. Regd. 1898 as Charles Carr Ld.; name changed Jan. 1965. Vol. liq. (members) 4 Mar. 1977. Capital returned to contributories—£1·10 per preference share (of £1) and 52·84073p per ordinary share (of 5p). £2,767·94 was paid into Companies' Liquidation Account. Final meeting return regd. 11 July 1980 ....   **1980–1**

Cornwall Railway Co. Inc. by Special Act 1846. Under Great Western and Cornwall Railways Co.'s Amalgamation Act 1889 the line was transferred to the Great Western Railway Co. Holders of ordinary shares of £20, A shares of £10 or B shares of £10 received £8, £4 or £4 in cash respectively; holders of the 4½% preference stocks received £90 5% guaranteed stock of the G. W. Rly. for every £100 held; holders of 4½% debenture stock received an equal amount of 4½% debenture stock **1890**

Cornwall Slate Quarries Ld. Regd. 1919. Receiver appointed 12 Apr. 1928. Struck off Register Feb. 1935 ....   **1935**

Cornwall Tailings Co. Ld. Regd. 1910. Vol. liq. 19 Jan. 1920. Capital returned to contributories—5s.

*See Stock Exchange Year-Book.

VOL. FOR

11·378d. per share of £1 at Oct. 1920; further payments (if any) not known. Final meeting return regd. 28 Jan. 1921 .... **1921**

Cornwall Tin Mines & Alluvials Ld. Regd. 1920. Vol. liq. (creditors') 7 June 1932. No capital returned to contributories. Final meeting return regd. 21 June 1934 .... **1933**

Coromandel Co. of India Ld. Regd. 1900. Reconstructed 1902 as Coromandel Gold Mines of India Ld. in which company shareholders were entitled to 1 share of £1 (credited with 12s. 6d. paid) for each share of £1 held. Removed from Register 1904 ... **1904**

Coromandel Gold Co. Ld. Regd. 1889. Vol. liq. 17 Aug. 1891. Property was acquired by Kapanga Gold Mining Co. Ld. for 65,000 shares of £1 (credited with 18s. 6d. paid). Final meeting return regd. 19 Nov. 1892 .... **1892**

Coromandel Gold Mines of India Ld. Regd. 1902. Reconstructed 1904 as Coromandel Gold Mining Co. of India Ld. in which company shareholders were entitled to 1 share of £1 (credited with 15s. paid) for each share of £1 held. Removed from Register 1905 .... **1905**

Coromandel Gold Mining Co. of India Ld. Regd. 1892. Reconstructed 1900 as Coromandel Co. of India Ld. in which company shareholders were entitled to 1 share of £1 (credited with 15s. paid) for each share of £1 held. Removed from Register 1910 .... **1902**

Coromandel Gold Mining Co. of India Ld. Regd. 1904. Vol. liq. 19 Feb. 1907. Reconstructed as Hosur Gold Mines of Dharwar Ld., in which company shareholders were entitled to 1 share of £1 (credited with 13s. 4d. paid) for each share of £1 held. Final meeting return regd. 4 Mar.1910 .... **1907**

Corona Cinema (Great Crosby) Ld. Regd. 1919. Vol. liq. 2 Aug. 1928. Properties purchased by Denman Picture Houses Ld. Final meeting return regd. 13 Dec. 1928 .... **1940**

Corona Consolidated Ld. Regd. 1904. Vol. liq. May 1907. Mining leases and plant were acquired by Mount Yagahong Exploration and Finance Co. Ld. (later Finance & Industrial Trust Ld.), for 50,000 shares of 10s. (credited with 7s. 6d. paid). Removed from Register 1910 .... **1908**

Corona Hill Silver Mining Co. Ld. Regd. 1889. Vol. liq. 8 Sept. 1891. Final meeting return regd. 22 Feb. 1897 **1899**

Corona Tin Fields Ld. Regd. 1912. Vol. liq. 29 July 1915. Final meeting return regd. 1 Dec. 1915 .... **1916**

Corona Wines Ld. Regd. 1928. Vol. liq. (members') 13 Oct. 1920. Capital returned to contributories—1s 11¾d. per share of 5s. Final meeting return regd. 17 Oct. 1932 .... **1931**

Coronation Extension Syndicate (Transvaal) Ld. Regd. 1902. Struck off Register 26 Feb. 1909 .... **1909**

Coronation South Strike Ld. Regd. 1904. Vol. liq. May 1909. Capital returned to contributories—0·434d. per share of £1 in Nov. 1909; further payments (if any) not known. Removed from Register 1910 .... **1910**

Corporacion de Ventas de Salitre y Yodo de Chile. See Chilean Nitrate & Iodine Sales.

Corporate Guarantee Ld. See Corporate Guarantee Trust Ld.

Corporate Guarantee Trust Ld. Regd. 1971 as Holdenbrook Ld.; name changed to Corporate Guarantee Ld. 14 Oct. 1971 and to above title 1 June 1972. Vol. liq. (creditors') 11 Sept. 1975. No capital was returnedto contributories. final meeting held 8 june 1979 .... **1980–1**

Corporation & General Securities Ld. Regd. 1926 as Corporation & General Securities (1926) Ld.; name changed Jan. 1927. Court Order to wind up 15 Oct. 1929. Struck off Register 27 Oct. 1942 .... **1943**

Corporation of Shareholders & Bondholders Ld. Regd. 1894. Vol. liq. 25 Feb. 1895. Final meeting return regd. 12 July 1895 .... **1896**

Corporation of South Australian Copper Mines Ld. Regd. 1880. Vol. liq. 1888. Reconstructed as South Australian Mining & Smelting Co. Ld., in which company shareholders were entitled to 1 share of £1 (credited as fully-paid) for every 10 shares of £1 held. Court Orders: to wind up Jan. 1888; to dissolve 16 Feb. 1888 .... **1891**

Corporation of Western Egypt Ld. Regd. 1904. Vol. liq. 11 Aug. 1915. Final meeting return regd. 7 Dec. 1922 .... **1916**

Correcta Light Ld. Regd. 1927. Struck off Register 1934 ***1929**

Corris Railway Co. Inc. by Special Act. 1858 as Corris Machyulleth and River Dovey Tramroad; name changed 1864. Undertaking was acquired by Great Western Railway Co., in June 1920 .... **1930**

Corrwg Rhondda Colliery Co. Ld. Regd. 1894. Vol. liq. May 1912. Removed from Register 1913 .... **1913**

Corsair Consolidated Gold Mines Ld. Regd. 1896. Vol. liq. 23 Mar. 1898. Reconstructed as Gold Finance

VOL. FOR

Co. Ld., in which company shareholders were entitled to 1 fully-paid share of 7s. 6d. for each share of £1 held. Final meeting return regd. 18 Mar. 1899 **1908**

Corsican Copper and Chemical Co. Ld. Regd 1884. Vol. liq. Dec. 1889. Final meeting return regd. 12 May 1890 .... **1895**

Cors-y-Gedol & Marine Hotels, & Freehold Land Co. Ld. Regd. 1889. Vol. liq. (members') 10 May 1954. Final meeting return regd. 12 Mar. 1955 .... **1891**

Cortes Commercial and Banking Co. Ld. See Commercial Bank of Spanish America Ld.

Cortez Mines Ld. Regd. 1888. Vol. liq. 28 May 1896. Undertaking was acquired by Tenabo Mill and Mining Co., in which company shareholders were entitled to fully-paid shares equal in nominal value to old holdings. Final meeting return regd. 27 July 1896 .... **1897**

Corticine Floor Covering Co. Ld. Regd. 1884. Vol. liq. June 1908. Removed from Register 1910 .... **1909**

Corticine Floor Covering Co. Ld. Regd. 1909. Vol. liq. (members') 22 Dec. 1936. Capital returned to contributories—20s. per preference or ordinary share of £1. Final meeting return regd. 5 July 1937 **1937**

Cortonwood Collieries Co. Ld. Regd. 1883. Vol. liq. (members') 24 Apr. 1953. Capital returned to contributories—19s. 9d. per share of 5s. Final meeting return regd. 24 Oct. 1956 .... **1958**

Coruna Copper Co. Ld. Regd. 1901. Vol. liq. 27 June 1906. Removed from Register 1911 .... **1907**

Coruña, Santiago & Peninsular Railway Co. Ld. See West Galicia Railway Co. Ld.

Corwen & Bala Railway Co. Inc. by Special Act 1862. Under Great Western Railway Act 1896 undertaking was amalgamated 1 July 1896 with that company in which holders of 4½% debenture stock received an equal amount of 4⅛% debenture stock; holders of 4% preference stock received 80% of 5% consolidated guaranteed stock; holders of ordinary stock received 72½% of 5% consolidated guaranteed stock **1897**

Corwen Gas Co. Ld. Regd. 1865. Dissolved 1 May 1949, undertaking being vested in Wales Area Gas Board under Gas Act 1948. Holders of ordinary shares (of £5) were entitled to receive £10 British Gas 3% guaranteed stock 1990–95 for each share held **1952**

Cosmelli Packing Co. Ld. Regd. 1913. Controlling interest was held by Crosse & Blackwell Ld. [later Crosse & Blackwell (Holdings) Ld.]. Struck off Register 1929 .... **1926**

Cosmopolitan Gold Mining Co. Ld. Regd. 1893 Vol. liq. 27 July 1899. Final meeting return regd. 25 Apr. 1913 .... **1900**

Cosmopolitan Proprietary Ld. Regd. 1898. Vol. liq. 19 Jan. 1914. Final meeting return regd. 25 Oct. 1917 **1914**

Cosmopolitan Publications Ld. Regd. 1908. Court Order to wind up 19 Apr. 1910. Liquidator released 31 May 1912. Struck off Register 10 Oct. 1916 .... **1911**

Costa Rica Coffee Estates Ld. Regd. 1897. Vol. liq. 26 July 1920. Final meeting return regd. 3 Mar. 1921 **1921**

Costa Rica Electric Light and Traction Co. Ld. Regd. 1898. Assets were transferred to Cia Nacional de Fuerza v Luz S.A. (inc. Costa Rica) for 4,382 shares of colones 500; the acquiring company assumed liability for the 6% prior lien debentures; the outstanding debentures were refunded into long term bonds of acquiring company. Vol. liq. (members') 23 June 1942. £52 17s. was paid into Companies' Liquidation Account in respect of sale of unclaimed shares. Final meeting held 29 Mar. 1943 .... **1945**

Costa Rica Markets & Tramway Co. Ld. See Costa Rica Markets Co. Ld.

Costa Rica Markets Co. Ld. Regd. 1886 as Costa Rica Markets & Tramway Co. Ld.; name changed 1902. Vol. liq. (members) 3 Nov. 1941. Capital returned to contributories—£3,049 14s. Final meeting return regd. 7 Feb. 1942 .... **1942**

Costa Rica "Pacific" Gold Mining Co. Ld. Regd. 1889. Vol. liq. 4 Mar. 1895. Removed from Register 1903 **1896**

Costopulo (J. F.) Amalgamated with Banque de Calamata in 1924 to form Credit Commercial Hellenique S.A. **1926**

Cotching, Cain & Skinner Ld. See below.

Cotchings, Ld. Regd. 1912 as Cotching, Cain & Skinner Ld.; name changed in 1936. Vol. liq. (members') 2 Apr. 1952, Final meeting return regd. Feb. 1955 .. **1938**

Côte d'Ivoire & Adulessa Co. Ld. Regd. 1902. Vol. liq. 21 June 1905. Removed from Register 1906 .... **1906**

Cotehele Co. Ld. Regd. 1881. Vol. liq. Mar. 1883. Absorbed by Okel Tor Co. Ld. Final meeting returned regd. 3 Nov. 1885 .... **1883**

Cothy Mines Ld. Regd. 1909. Vol. liq. Feb. 1912. Struck off Register 1925 .... **1913**

See Stock Exchange Year-Book.

VOL. FOR

Cottle (James) (Manchester) Ld. Regd. 1920. Vol. liq. (members') 23 June 1937. Capital returned to contributories—£10,071 12s. Final meeting return regd. 2 Sept. 1938 .... **1938**

Cotton Cleaners Ld. Regd. 1909. Vol. liq. Jan 1912. Removed from Register 1913 .... **1913**

Cotton (John) Ld. Regd. Edinburgh 1927. Vol. liq. (members') 13 Aug. 1953. Final meeting return regd. 28 July 1954 .... **1947**

Cotton Lands of Egypt Ld. *See* Sidi Salem Estates of Egypt Ld.

Cotton (Lawrence) Ld. Regd. 1948. Vol. liq. (members') 27 Apr. 1960. Capital returned to contributories— 21s. per preference share (of £1); 4s. 10·95d. per ordinary share (of 5s.). Final meeting return regd. 16 Jan. 1962 .... **1962**

Cotton Machinery Trust Ld. Regd. 1899. Vol. liq. 12 Aug. 1919. Capital returned to contributories—14s. 10d. per ordinary share of £1 (10s. paid); £3 13s. 1d. per deferred ordinary share of £1. Final meeting return regd. 14 Nov. 1919 .... **1920**

Cotton Plantations Ld. *See* C. O. P. Investments Ld.

Cotton Powder Co. Ld. Regd. 1875. Vol. liq. 22 Oct. 1890. Reconstructed as company of same name. Shareholders were entitled to an equal number of shares of similar class in new company. Final meeting return regd. 1 Jan. 1892 .... **1904**

Cotton Powder Co. Ld. Regd. 1890. Reconstructed 1904 as company of same name. Shareholders were entitled to 5 preference shares of £1 in new company for each A preference share of £2 10s. held or to 3½ preference shares of £1 for each B preference share of £2 10s. held or to 4 ordinary shares of £1 for each ordinary share of £2 10s. held. Removed from Register 1905 .... **1908**

Cotton Powder Co. Ld. Regd. 1904. Vol. liq. 15 Dec. 1919. Final meeting return regd. 6 Jan. 1927 .... **1920**

Cotton Seed Co. Ld. Regd. 1900. Vol. liq. 30 Dec. 1912. Final meeting return regd. 9 Mar. 1921 .... **1913**

Cotton (Wilfred) Ld. Regd. 1904. Court Order to wind up 21 June 1904. Liquidator released 26 Sept. 1907. Struck off Register 24 May 1910 .... **1905**

Cottonwood River (B.C.) Alluvial Gold Mining Co. Ld. Regd. 1897. Removed from Register 1905 .... **1905**

Cottonwood Water Power & Electric Co. Ld. Regd. 1896. Vol. liq. 24 Sept 1897. Property was acquired by Union Light and Power Co. of Utah. Final meeting return regd. 1 Dec. 1899 .... **1898**

Counties and General Insurance Co. Ld. Regd. 1909. Vol. liq. 16 Aug. 1912. Final meeting return regd. 2 Jan. 1918 .... **1913**

Counties Gas Co. Ld. *See* United District Gas Co.

Country Gentlemen's Association Ld. Regd. 1896 as Catalogue Publishing Co. Ld.; name changed Mar. 1898. Vol. liq. 1 Dec. 1903. Undertaking and assets acquired by Country Gentlemen's Association (1903) Ld. (later Country Gentlemen's Association Ld.). Final meeting return regd. 1 Mar. 1904 ...... **1925**

County & Lane Ends Hotel Ld. *See* County Hotel (Blackpool) Ld.

County Bank Ld. Regd. 1862 as Manchester & County Bank Ld.; name changed Nov. 1934. Vol. liq. (members') 25 Sept. 1935. Undertaking and assets were acquired by District Bank Ld., in which company shareholders were entitled to 2⅔ C shares of £1 (credited as fully-paid) plus 5s. in cash for each share of £20 (£4 paid) held **1936**

County Donegal Railways Joint Committee. The Transport (Miscellaneous Provisions) Bill 1971 provided for the dissolution of the Committee and the transfer of its assets to Coras Iompair Eireann **1971**

County Fire Office Ld. Inc. 1808. Regd. 1905. Vol. liq. Mar. 1906; undertaking sold to Alliance Assurance Co. Ld., for 125,760 shares of £1. Removed from Register 1907 .... **1906**

County Hail-Storm Insurance Co. Inc. 1847. Regd. 1862. Vol. liq. 10 Aug. 1892. Final meeting return regd. 19 Jan. 1893 .... **1893**

County Hotel (Blackpool) Ld. Regd. 1896 as County & Lane Ends Hotel Ld.; name changed June 1927. Struck off Register 28 Sept. 1962 .... **1960**

County Loan Co. Ld. *See* York Investment Co. Ld.

County of Dorset Electric Supply Co. Ld. Regd. 1912. Vol. liq. 9 Jan. 1924. Final meeting return regd. 15 Apr. 1926 .... **1924**

County of Durham Electrical Power Distribution Co. Ld. Regd. 1899. By Act of 1932 the undertaking was transferred to North-Eastern Electric Supply Co. Ld., which owned all the share capital. Dissolved by Act 30 Sept. 1932 .... **1933**

County of Durham Electric Power Supply Co. Inc. by Special Act 1900. By Act of 1932 the undertaking was transferred to North-Eastern Electric Supply

VOL. FOR

Co. Ld. which owned indirectly practically all the shares and the company was dissolved **1933**

County of Gloucester Bank Ld. Established 1836. Regd. 1889. Amalgamated in 1897 with Lloyds Bank Ld., in which company shareholders were entitled to 2¼ shares of £50 (credited with £8 paid) *plus* £2 10s. in cash for each share of £100 (£25 paid) held. Removed from Register 1903 .... **1938**

County of Kent Electrical Power Distribution Co. Ld. *See* Sheerness & District Electric Supply Co. Ld.

County of London Electric Supply Co. Ld. Regd. 1891 as County of London Electric Lighting Co. Ld.; name changed to County of London & Brush Provincial Electric Lighting Co. Ld. in 1893 and as above in 1904. Dissolved 1 Apr. 1948, undertaking being vested in British (later Central) Electricity Authority and London Area Board under Electricity Act 1947. Holders of securities were entitled to receive British Electricity 3% guaranteed stock (1968–73) as follows in respect of each £1 unit of capital held:

	£	s.	d.
6% Preference shares	1	16	4
4% Preference shares	1	3	9
Ordinary shares	2	9	5
5% Debenture stock	1	3	11½
3½% Debenture stock	1	0	6

.... **1949**

County of Sussex Electrical Power Distribution Co. Ld. *See* Lewes & District Electric Supply Co. Ld.

County of Stafford Bank Ld. Est. 1836. Regd. as limited 1882. Vol. liq. 6 Mar. 1899. Business transferred to National Provincial Bank of England Ld. (later National Provincial Bank Ld.), on terms providing £15 10s. cash per share (£5 paid) and £6 4s. (£2 paid). Final meeting return regd. 17 May 1900 .... **1900**

County of Surrey Electrical Power Distribution Co. Ld. *See* South Metropolitan Electric Tramways & Lighting Co. Ld.

County Shipping Co. Ld. Regd. 1918. Vol. liq. 28 Jan. 1924. Final meeting return regd. 3 July 1924 .... ***1925**

Coupar Angus Gas Co. Ld. Regd. in Edinburgh 1937. Dissolved 1 May 1949, undertaking being vested in Scottish Area Gas Board under Gas Act 1948. Holders of ordinary shares (of £1) were entitled to receive 15s. British Gas 3% guaranteed stock 1990– 95 for each share held **1952**

Coupe & Dunlop Brougham Co. Ld. Regd. 1896. Vol. liq. July 1908. Undertaking was acquired by Coupe Co. and Motor Cab Co. of Great Britain Ld. for £30,547 in fully-paid shares of £1. Removed from Register 1909 .... **1909**

Coupon Agency Ld. Regd. 1896. Vol. liq. 31 Dec. 1907. Final meeting return regd. 12 July 1909 .... ***1909**

Court Estates Ld. Regd. 1933. Vol. liq. (members') 10 July 1947. Undertaking acquired by Property Holding & Investment Trust Ld., in which company shareholders were entitled to receive 5 preference shares for every 4 preference shares, 3 preference shares for every 7 preferred ordinary shares, 53 ordinary shares for every 25 preferred ordinary shares, 3 preference shares for every 2 deferred ordinary shares and 37 ordinary shares for every 5 deferred ordinary shares held. Final meeting return regd. 5 Oct. 1951 .... **1953**

Court Holding Co. Ld. Regd. 1913 as St. James' Court Ld.; name changed Mar. 1928. Vol. liq. (members') 29 Dec. 1931. All shares owned by H. E. Proprietary (New) Ld. Final meeting return regd. 26 July 1932 **1932**

Court Line Ld. Regd. 1905. Vol. liq. 1 July 1929. Shareholders were entitled to 15s. in cash, 10s. in 6% debenture stock and 8s. in fully-paid shares of £1 in United British Steamship Co. Ld. (later Court Line Ld.), for each share of £1 held; further cash payments not known. Final meeting return regd. 3 July 1930 .... **1930**

Court Line Ld. Regd. 1921 as United British Steamship Co. Ld.; name changed 1936. Vol. liq. (members') 16 June 1947. Fleet acquired by United British Steamship Co. Ld. (later Court Line Ld.) in which company shareholders were entitled to receive 1 stock unit (of 1s.) and 30s. 6d. cash per share (of 6s. 8d.) held. £3,014 was paid into Companies' Liquidation Account. Final meeting return regd. 16 Apr. 1952 .... **1953**

Courtauld (Samuel) & Co. Ld. Regd. 1891. Removed from Register 1909 .... ***1898**

Courtauld (Samuel) & Co. Ld. Regd. 1904. Vol. liq. 27 Mar. 1913. Reconstructed as Courtaulds Ld. in which company shareholders were entitled to 50 fully-paid shares of £1 for each ordinary share of £5 held. Preference shareholders were entitled to repayment at par or an equal amount of 5¼% 2nd mortgage debenture stock. Debenture stockholders were entitled to repayment at 105% or an equal amount of 4½% 1st mortgage debenture stock in new company. Final meeting return regd. 5 June 1914 — **1914**

Couserans Mines Ld. Regd. 1898 as Mining & Smelting Co. of Nescus (Ariége) Ld.; name changed 1905. Struck off Register 1923 — **1910**

Cove Copper Mines. Regd. 1907. Vol. liq. Nov. 1911. Removed from Register 1913 — **1912**

Covent Garden Estate Co. Ld. *See* Walbrook Trust Ld.

Covent Garden Fortune Theatre Ld. Regd. 1927. Vol. liq. (creditors') 19 May 1930. Assets realised insufficient to pay preferential creditors in full. Final meeting return regd. 24 Aug. 1933 — **1931**

Coventry & District Tramways Co. Inc. by Special Act 1880. Property seized in Feb. 1892 by debenture holders and ultimately sold — **1894**

Coventry & Warwickshire Banking Co. Est. 1835. Absorbed by Lloyds' Banking Co. Ld. (later Lloyds' Bank Ld.). Removed from Register 1883 — ***1879**

Coventry Canal Navigation (Company of Proprietors of The). Inc. by Special Act 1768. Dissolved 3 June 1949; undertaking vested from 1 Jan. 1948 in British Transport Commission under Transport Act 1947. Holders of ordinary shares were entitled to receive £160 British Transport 3% guaranteed stock 1978–88 for every £100 of capital held — **1949**

Coventry Chain Co. Ld. Regd. 1907 as Coventry Chain Co. (1907) Ld.; name changed 1911. Vol. liq. (members') 17 Nov. 1932. Undertaking and assets were acquired by Renold & Coventry Chain Co. Ld. (later Renold Ld.); the beneficial owners of all share capital. Final meeting return regd. 17 May 1935 — **1938**

Coventry Cotton Spinning & Weaving Co. Ld. Regd. 1860. Vol. liq. 5 Aug. 1896. Final meeting return regd. 11 Mar. 1898 — **1897**

Coventry Cross Cycle Co. Ld. Regd. 1896. Vol. liq. 4 May 1899. Court Order to continue winding up under supervision 1899. Reconstructed as New Coventry Cross Cycle Co. Ld. Final meeting return regd. 4 Sept 1900 — **1901**

Coventry Electric Tramways Co. Inc. by Special Act 1897. Undertaking sold to Coventry Corporation in Jan. 1912 for £202,132 — **1912**

Coventry Electric Tramways Ld. Regd. 1893. Vol. liq. 1 Jan. 1898; assets sold to Coventry Electric Tramways Co. for £50,000 cash. Final meeting return regd. 5 July 1899 — **1898**

Coventry Gas Co. Undertaking acquired by Coventry Corporation under local Act of 1884. Terms of purchase: Issue to holder of each of the 1,600 original shares of £25, an annuity of £2 for 15 years from 1 July 1884 and payment on 30 June 1899 of principal sum of £48; to holder of each of the 1,600 new shares of £25 an annuity of £1 17s. 6d. for 15 years from 1 July 1884 and payment on 30 June 1899 of principal sum of £45 — **1899**

Coventry Gear Case & Belting Co. Ld. Regd. 1897. Removed from Register 1909 — **1886**

Coventry General Investment Co. Ld. Vol. liq. (members') 10 Aug. 1977. Capital returned to contributories—3·65p per share. Final meeting return regd. 30 Dec. 1977 — **1978-9**

Coventry Greyhounds Ld. Regd. 1927. Struck off Register 25 Oct. 1932 — ***1933**

Coventry Machnists' Co. Ld. Business was acquired in Sept. 1895 by Swift Cycle Co. Ld. for £375,000 in cash — **1901**

Coventry Ordnance Works Ld. Regd. 1905. Vol. liq. 29 May 1925. Final meeting return regd. 26 Apr. 1929 — **1926**

Coventry Premier Ld. Regd. 1896 as New Premier Cycle Co. Ld.; name changed to Premier Cycle Co. Ld. in Jan. 1903 and as above Nov. 1914. Vol. liq. 11 Oct. 1920. Undertaking and assets were acquired by Singer & Co. Ld. for £90,000 which was distributed among debenture holders. Final meeting return regd. 24 Sept. 1921 — **1921**

Coventry Repetition Co. Ld. Regd. 1909 as Trickett Bailey & Co. Ld. name changed Mar. 1913. Vol. liq. 17 Nov. 1924. All shares owned by Coventry Chain Co. Ld. Final meeting return regd. 4 Sept. 1925 — **1925**

Coventry Stamping Co. Ld. Regd. 1897. The works were carried on by Midland Engineering & Stamping Co. Ld. Struck off Register 4 Oct. 1935 — **1936**

Coventry Tube & Metal Co. Ld. Regd. 1900. Vol. liq. 25 Sept. 1901. Removed from Register 1903 — **1902**

Coventry Union Banking Co. Business was acquired in 1889 by London City and Midland Bank Ld. (later Midland Bank Ld.) — **1890**

Coverden Rubber & Produce Co. Ld. Regd. 1907. Vol. liq. 23 July 1912 for reconstruction as Demerara and Coverden Produce Co. Ld. in which company shareholders were entitled to 1 share of 2s. (credited with 1s. 6d. paid) for every 2 shares of 2s. held. Final meeting return regd. 3 Mar. 1921 — **1913**

Cowan (L.) & Sons Ld. Regd. 1890. Vol. liq. 2 Nov. 1891. Final meeting return regd. 27 Feb. 1894 — ***1892**

Cowan (William) Ld. Regd. Dublin 1893; transferred to Belfast under Government of Ireland Act 1920. Vol. liq. (members') 27 May 1935 — **1936**

Cowbridge & Aberthaw Railway Co. Inc. by Special Act 1889. Under Taff Vale Railway Act 1894 undertaking was amalgamated 1 Jan. 1895 with that company. Holders of share and debenture stock received sufficient 3% debenture stock in purchasing company on basis of equal income — **1895**

Cowbridge Gas Co. (1935) Ld. Regd. 1935. Dissolved 1 May 1949, undertaking being vested in Wales Area Gas Board under Gas Act 1948. Holders of ordinary shares (of £1) were entitled to receive £2 10s. British Gas 3% guaranteed stock 1990–95 for each share held — **1952**

Cowbridge Railway Co. Inc. by Special, Act 1862. Under Taff Vale Railway Amalgamations and Capital Act 1889 undertaking was amalgamated 1 July 1889 with that company in which holders of ordinary shares of £10 received 4% preference stock; holders of 4½% A debenture 3% B debenture and 2½% C debenture stocks received 3% debenture on basis of equal income — **1890**

Cowbrough & Co. Ld. Regd. 1896. Vol. liq. (members') 27 Feb. 1931. Undertaking sold to J. Hey & Co. Ld. Capital returned to contributories—£5 0s. 10¾d. per preference share of £5 or ordinary share of £5. Final meeting return regd. 14 Aug. 1935 — **1932**

Cowdenbeath Coal Co. Ld. Regd. Edinburgh 1892. Vol. liq. Nov. 1896. Undertaking transferred to Fife Coal Co. Ld. Final meeting return regd. 31 July 1897 — **1897**

Cowdenbeath Gas Co. Ld. Regd. in Edinburgh 1891. Dissolved 1 May 1949 undertaking being vested in Scottish Area Gas Board under Gas Act 1948. Holders of ordinary shares (of £1, fully and partly paid) were, entitled to receive £3 2s. 6d. British Gas 3% guaranteed stock 1990–95 for each £1 paid up — **1952**

Cowell, Craft & Co. Ld. Regd. 1896. Removed from Register 1908 — **1899**

Coverings Ld. *See* Selby Manufacturing Co. Ld.

Cowes & Newport Railway Co. Inc. by Special Act 1859. Undertaking merged 1 July 1887 in Isle of Wight Central Railway Co. for £92,000 3% debenture stock A which was distributed among holders of debenture preference and ordinary stocks — **1888**

Cowey Automobile Suspension Co. Ld. Regd. 1909. Vol. liq. 9 July 1915. Struck off Register 3 Sept. 1918.. — **1916**

Cowie Harbour Coal Co. Ld. Regd. 1905. Vol. liq. (members') 28 July 1937. No capital to contributories. Final meeting return regd. 29 Nov. 1937 — **1938**

Cowley's De Kaap Ld. Regd. 1902. Vol. liq. 4 July 1904. Undertaking was acquired by New De Kaap Ld. in which company shareholders were entitled to 4 shares of 5s. (credited with 4s. paid) for each share of £1 held. Final meeting return regd. 20 Mar. 1920 — **1905**

Cowlishaw, Walker & Co. (1920) Ld. Regd. 1920. Receiver appointed 13 May 1924; ceased to act 4 Feb. 1926. Struck off Register in Dec. 1931. Assets were sold to C. W. Engineering Co. Ld. [later Cowlishaw Walker & Co. (1920) Ld.] — **1932**

Cox & Co. Undertaking was acquired by Lloyds Bank Ld. — **1923**

Cox & Co. (France) Ld. Regd. 1915. Vol. liq. 21 Dec. 1923. Banking business acquired by Barclays Bank (France) Ld. Final meeting return regd. 23 Feb. 1934 — **1940**

Cox's Brewery Ld. *See* Cardwell & Co. Ld.

Cox's Horse Repository Ld. *See* London Horse Repository Co. Ld.

Cox Industries Ld. Regd. as private company 10 Nov. 1966;converted nto a public company 27 Aor. 1973. Winding-up order made 28 July 1975. Official receiver released 26 Oct. 1981 — **1987-8**

Coytrahen Park Colliery Co. Ld. Regd. 1910. Vol. liq. 31 Dec. 1928. Controlling interest was held by Baldwins Ld. [later Baldwins (Holdings) Ld.]. Final meeting return regd. 3 July 1930 — **1930**

Cozens & Sutcliffe (Holdings) Ld. Regd. 1941. Vol. liq. (members') 29 Nov. 1967. Capital returned to contributories—10s. 3d. per ordinary share of 4s. £2,285·39 paid into Companies' Liquidation Account. Final meeting return regd. 23 Feb. 1972 — **1972**

Cradley Heath Gas Co. Inc. by Special Act 1871. Dissolved 1 May 1949, undertaking being vested in West Midland Area Gas Board under Gas Act 1948. Holders of 3% tax-free irred. deb. stock were entitled to receive, in respect of each £100 unit held, £112 10s. British Gas 3% guaranteed stock 1990–95 — **1952**

Craggs Steamship Co. Ld. Regd. 1919. Vol. liq. 30 Mar. 1921. Final meeting return regd. 29 Dec. 1924 — **1922**

Craig, Mills & Co. Ld. Regd. 1898. Struck off Register 23 July 1901 — **1902**

VOL. FOR

Craig (R. Hunter) & Co. Ld. Regd. Edinburgh 1899. Vol. liq. (members') 15 Feb. 1956. Final meeting return regd. 11 Nov. 1956 .... **1947**

Craig, Taylor & Co. Ld. Regd. 1905. Vol. liq. (members') 6 Dec. 1935. Capital returned to contributories—20*s*. per preference share of £1; 2*s*. 0$\frac{1}{64}$*d*. per ordinary share of £1. Final meeting return regd. 13 Aug. 1937 .... **1936**

Craigellachie Brewery Co. Ld. Regd. Edinburgh 1895. Vol. liq. May 1907. Final meeting return regd. 31 Jan. 1912 .... **1908**

Craigellachie-Glenlivet Distillery Co. Ld. Regd. Edinburgh 1896. Vol. liq. Dec. 1915. Capital returned to contributories—preference and ordinary shares were repaid at par; further payments (if any) not known. Final meeting return regd. 16 May 1919 **1917**

Craiggiemore Proprietary Ld. Regd. 1899. Vol. liq. Dec. 1908. Removed from Register 1912 .... **1909**

Craigpark Electric Cable Co. Ld. Regd. 1903. Vol. liq. (members') 26 Aug. 1955. Capital returned to contributories—£4 7*s*. 1*d*. per ordinary share of £1 and £1 per preference share of £1. Final meeting return regd. 24 Nov. 1958 .... **1959**

Cramlington Coal Co. Ld. Regd. 1901. Under a scheme confirmed by the Railway and Canal Commission on 9 Apr. 1929 the company was dissolved on 16 May 1929 and the undertaking and assets transferred to Hartley Main Collieries Ld., in which company shareholders received 50 ordinary and 75 preference shares of £1 for each ordinary or preference share of £100 held. Debenture holders received a like amount of debenture in new company **1930**

Cran (John) & Co. Ld. Regd. Edinburgh 1886. Vol. liq. Mar. 1910. Business sold to Highland Agricultural Co. Ld. Court Order to dissolve 18 Dec. 1913..... **1911**

Cranbrook & Paddock Wood Railway Co. Inc. by Special Acts 1877 and 1887. Under South Eastern Railway Co. Act 1900 the Paddock Wood line was amalgamated 1 July 1900 with that company and in which holders of ordinary shares and 3¼% debenture stock received an equal amount of 3¼% debenture stock **1901**

Cranbrook District Water Co. Inc. by Special Act 1895. The undertaking was acquired as from 1 Oct. 1955 by the Mid-Kent Water Co., under provisions of the Kent Water Act 1955. 5% debenture stockholders received £105 for every £100 stock held, and holders of 5% preference, 10% original ordinary and 7% new ordinary shares received £1 2*s*., £1 17*s*. 4*d*. and £1 6*s*. 2*d*. per share of £1 respectively. Company was dissolved on 31 Mar. 1956 .... **1957**

Crandon Shipping Co. Ld. Regd. 1927. Struck off Register Mar. 1934 .... **1935**

Crane (Fredk.) Chemical Co. Ld. Regd. 1916. Vol. liq. (members') 30 Sept. 1940. Direct controlling interest owned by Imperial Chemical Industries Ld. Capital returned to contributories—20*s*. per share of £1. Final meeting return regd. 18 June 1941 .... **1942**

Cranleigh & Chiddingfold Water Co. Ld. Regd. 1885 as Cranleigh Water Co. Ld., name changed 1926. Undertaking transferred to Guildford, Godalming and District Water Board in 1952. Shareholders were entitled to £11 8*s*. 5·7*d*. per 10% ordinary share, £7 19*s*. 11·7*d*. per 7% ordinary share and £5 9*s*. 7*d*. per 5% preference share. Final meeting return regd. 2 Sept. 1953 .... **1954**

Cranley Tea Estates Ld. Regd. Edinburgh 1907. Vol. liq. 14 Nov. 1945. Estates sold to Lunuva (Ceylon) Tea & Rubber Estates Ld., for £72,500. Shareholders were entitled to apply for 38,666 shares in Lunuva Co. at 37*s*. 6*d*. per share. Capital returned to contributories—41*s*. 2·143*d*. (per share of £1). Final meeting return regd.4 Feb. 1948.......................... **1949**

Cranston & Elliot Ld. Regd. Edinburgh. 1897. Vol. liq. May 1908. Court Order to dissolve 28 June 1911.. **1940**

Cranston's Tea Rooms Ld. Regd. Edinburgh 1896. Business acquired by Cranston's Tea Rooms (1905) Ld. (later Cranston's Tea Rooms Ld.), for £70,000 in ordinary shares and £320,000 in cash. Vol. liq. Jan. 1906. Final meeting return regd. 12 Aug. 1907 .... **1906**

Cranston's Tea Rooms Ld. Regd. in Edinburgh 1905 as Cranston's Tea Rooms (1905) Ld.; name changed 1906. Vol. liq. (members') 30 Nov. 1954. Capital returned to contributories—£1 7*s*. 10½*d*. per ordinary share of £1. Final meeting return regd. 9 Oct. 1956 **1957**

Craven Bank Ld. Regd. 1880. Vol. liq. 26 Apr. 1906. Business was acquired by Bank of Liverpool Ld. (later Martins Bank Ld.). Shareholders were entitled to £23 17*s*. per share in cash or 3 shares of £100 (£12 10*s*. paid) in acquiring company *plus* £10 in cash for every share of £30 (£7 paid) held **1907**

VOL. FOR

Craven Hydro-Electric Supply Co. Ld. Regd. 1929. Dissolved 1 Apr. 1948, undertaking being vested in the British (later Central) Electricity Authority and Yorkshire Area Board under the Electricity Act 1947. Holders of ordinary shares and 5% debentures were entitled to receive British Electricity 3% guaranteed stock (1968—73). as follows—£1 16s. stock for each £1 ordinary capital held and £100 stock for each £100 debenture capital held **1949**

"Cravenette" Co. Ld. Regd. 1892. Undertaking was acquired by Bradford Dyers' Association Ld. Removed from Register 1904 .... **1904**

Craven's Caledonia Gold Mining Co., No Liability. Inc. Queensland 1893. Reconstructed 1904 as New Craven's Caledonia Gold Mining Co. Ld., in which company shareholders were entitled to 1 share of 5*s*. (credited with 2*s*. 6*d*. paid) for each share of 6*s*. held **1908**

Crawford Mills Ld. Regd. 1920. Vol. liq. (members') 26 July 1937. Capital returned to contributories—4¾*d*. per share of £1. Final meeting return regd. 26 Apr. 1938 .... **1938**

Crawford Spinning Co. Ld. Regd. 1882. Vol. liq. 23 Feb. 1920. Undertaking was acquired by Crawford Mills Ld. Final meeting return regd. 25 Sept. 1920 ...... **1921**

Crawshaw & Holliday Ld. Regd. 1932. Vol. liq. (members') 5 Mar. 1954. Capital returned to contributories—£1 7*s*. 11½*d*. per share of 10*s*. £643 18*s*. 7*d*. was paid into Companies' Liquidation Account. Final meeting return regd. 3 Oct. 1956.. **1957**

Crawshaw & Warburton Ld. Regd. 1900. Vol. liq. (members') 18 Jan. 1954. Final meeting return regd. 12 Apr. 1956 .... **1957**

Crays Gas Co. Established 1863; inc. by Special Act 1865. Dissolved in Aug. 1908. undertaking and assets sold to Bromley & Crays Gas Co., which took over the debenture stock of this company and agreed to allot £100 5% standard C ordinary stock for every £100 ordinary stock held **1909**

Credit Assurance & Guarantee Corporation Ld. *See* United Dominion Insurance Co. Ld.

Credit Co. Ld. Regd. 1866 as Crédit Foncier of England Ld.; name changed 9 Dec. 1876. Vol. liq. 13 Feb. 1879. Court Order to continue winding up under supervision 14 Mar. 1879. Final meeting return regd. 17 Nov. 1894 .... **1883**

Crédit de la Suisse Française Geneva. Business was absorbed in 1921 by Banque Commerciale de Bâle **1945**

Crédit Foncier D'Algerie et de Tunisie S. A. Inc. France (with limited liability) 1880. Court Order to wind up in respect of the London Office was made 21 Oct. 1940 .... **1941**

Crédit Foncier de Hongrie. *See* Hungarian Land Mortgage Institute.

Crédit Foncier of England Ld. *See* Credit Co. Ld.

Crédit Foncier of Mauritius Ld. Regd. 1864. Vol. liq. 27 May 1920. The outstanding 1st and 2nd debenture stocks were repaid at par in 1920. Capital returned to contributories—100%; further payments (if any) not known. Final meeting return regd. 25 July 1923 **1921**

Crédit Général Ottoman. Established 1869. Concession came to an end 5 Jan. 1899. Vol. liq. 26 Nov. 1898 **1899**

Credito Italiano. Inc. Italy 1870 as Banca di Genova; name changed 1895. Under Trading with Enemy Act 1939 and Defence Regulations the Board of Trade made an order on 25 Sept. 1940 for winding up London branch **1941**

Crediton Gas Co. Inc. by Special Act 1904. Dissolved 1 May 1949, undertaking being vested in South Western Area Gas Board under Gas Act 1948. Holders of securities were entitled to receive British Gas 3% guaranteed stock 1990—95 as follows in respect of each £10 unit, unless otherwise stated, of security held:

	£	s.	d.
Orig. ord shares (10% stand.)	4	0	0
Addit. ord. shares (7% stand.)	2	16	0
Orig. 5% pref. shares	11	0	0
Addit. 5% pref. shares	11	0	0
6% perp. deb. stock (per £100)	135	0	0

1952

Credo Gold Estates Ld. Regd. 1901. Vol. liq. June 1908. Removed from Register 1909 .... **1909**

Credo Gold Mines Ld. Regd. 1896. Reconstructed 1901 as Credo Gold Estates Ld., in which company shareholders were entitled to 4 shares of 5*s*. (credited with 4*s*. paid) for each share of £1 held. Removed from Register 1911 .... **1906**

Creighton (R. & J. R.) Ld. Regd. 1900. Vol. liq. (members') 14 Mar. 1930. Capital returned to contributories—20*s*. per preference share of £1; 17*s*. 2½*d*. in cash *plus* a distribution in specie per ordinary share of £1. Final meeting return regd. 20 Apr. 1932 **1931**

Cremier Ice Cream Co. Ld. Regd. 1915 as Hislop & Williams Ld.; name changed Aug. 1922. Vol. liq. (members') 29 Mar. 1941. Capital returned to

VOL. FOR

contributories—20s. per preference share of £1; £1 11s. 8d. per ordinary share of £1. Final meeting return regd. 16 Mar. 1944 .... **1943**

Crepe Yarns Ld. Regd. 1933. Vol. liq. (members') 26 Apr. 1935. Final meeting return regd. 20 Apr. 1936 **1936**

Crescens (Matabele) Mines & Land Co. Ld. Regd. 1895. Vol. liq. 29 Oct. 1925. Undertaking and assets were transferred to Exploring Land and Minerals Co. Ld., in which company shareholders were entitled to 2 fully-paid shares of 4s. and 1s. in cash for each 10s. share held. Final meeting return regd. 3 Dec. 1926 **1926**

Crescent Gold Mining Co. Ld. Regd. 1895. Vol. liq. 22 July 1898. Amalgamated with New Options Ld. Shareholders were entitled to 2,000 fully-paid shares of £1. Final meeting return regd. 17 July 1899 .... **1899**

Cressington Steamship Co. Ld. Regd. 1907. Vol. liq. 27 May 1925. Capital returned to contributories—£2 16s. 11½d. per share of £1. Final meeting return regd. 23 Dec. 1925 .... **1926**

Crest Ring Mill Ld. Regd. 1906. Vol. liq. 21 Oct. 1919. Reconstructed as Crest Ring Mill (1919) Ld. Final meeting return regd. 16 Sept. 1920 .... **1925**

Crest Ring Mill (1919) Ld. Regd. 1919. Vol. liq. 8 May 1950. Final meeting return regd. 7 Nov. 1950....... **1952**

Creswick Gold Mines Ld. Regd. 1913. Struck off Register 1922 .... **1915**

Crewe's Rhodesia Development Co. Ld. Regd. 1899. Vol. liq. 19 Oct. 1904. Amalgamated with Goldfields of Matabeleland Ld. Removed from Register 1906 .. **1905**

Crewkerne Gas & Coke Co. Ld. Regd. 1935. Dissolved 1 May 1949, undertaking being vested in Southern Area Gas Board under Gas Act 1948. Holders of securities were entitled to receive British Gas 3% guaranteed stock 1990—95 as follows:

	£	s.	d.
Ord.shares (of £10)	11	0	0
6% pref. shares (of £5)	6	13	0
3½% red. debs.(per £100)	100	0	0	**1952**

Crewkerne, South Petherton & Martock Light Railway Co. Inc. (under Light Railways Act 1896) by order of Light Railway Commissioners confirmed by Board of Trade 1909 .... **1913**

Crieff & Comrie Railway Co. Inc. by Special Act 1890. Under Caledonian Railway Co. Act 1898 the undertaking was amalgamated with that company the purchase consideration being £45,000 in cash **1899**

Crieff Gas-Light Co. Ld. Regd. in Edinburgh 1903. Dissolved 1 May 1949, undertaking being vested in Scottish Area Gas Board under Gas Act 1948. Holders of ordinary shares (of £1) were entitled to receive £3 8s. 9d. British Gas 3% guaranteed stock 1990—95 for each share held...................... **1952**

Criggleston Collieries, Ld. Regd. 1906. Vol. liq. 27 Dec. 1920. Final meeting return regd. 6 Oct. 1921 .... ***1921**

Crigglestone Coal Co. Ld. Regd. 1895. Court Order to wind up 1906. Removed from Register 1911......... **1907**

Cripple Creek Bonanza Gold Mines Ld. Regd. 1896. Vol. liq. 21 Jan. 1898. Final meeting return regd.4 July 1899 .... ***1899**

Cripple Creek Exploitation Syndicate Ld. Regd. 1895. Vol. liq. 5 Jan. 1897. Undertaking acquired by Monarch Syndicate Ld., for 50,251 fully-paid shares of £1 and 1,685 shares of £1 (credited with various amounts up to 15s. paid). Final meeting return regd. 21 Feb. 1899 .... **1898**

Cripple Creek Gold & Exploration Ld. Regd. 1896. Removed from Register 1903 .... **1898**

Cripple Creek Gold Fields Ld. Regd. 1895. Reconstructed 1897 as company of same name. Shareholders were entitled to 1 share of £1 credited with 16s. paid for each share of £1 held. Removed from Register 1902 .... **1908**

Cripple Creek Gold Mines Ld. Regd. 1897. Struck off Register 31 July 1953 .... **1911**

Cripple Creek Mines Ld. Regd. 1896. Struck off Register 23 July 1901 .... **1902**

Cripple Creek Ore Reduction Works Ld. Regd. 1898. Removed from Register 25 Feb. 1910.................. ***1902**

Cripple Creek Pioneers Ld. Regd. 1896. Vol. liq. 19 Mar. 1898. Undertaking was acquired by Cripple Creek Proprietary Ld., in which company shareholders were entitled to 3 shares of £1 (credited with 18s. paid) for every 2 shares of £1 held. Removed from Register 1903 .... **1899**

Cripple Creek Proprietary Ld. Regd. 1896. Struck off Register 16 Aug. 1901 .... **1902**

Cripple Creek Shakespear Gold Mines Ld. Regd. 1896. Vol. liq. 6 Mar. 1899. Final meeting return regd. 3 Nov. 1908 .... ***1899**

Cripplegate Bank Ld. *See* London Commercial & Cripplegate Bank Ld.

Crisp & Co. Ld. Regd. 1894. Reconstructed 1905 as company of same name. Shareholders were entitled to 1 ordinary share of 10s. (credited with 5s. 6d.

VOL. FOR

paid) for each preference share of £1 held. Ordinary shareholders were entitled to 3 ordinary shares of 10s. (credited with 4s. paid) for every 5 ordinary shares of £1 held. Founders' shareholders were entitled to 3 ordinary shares of 10s. (credited with 4s. paid) for every 5 founders' shares of £1 held. Removed from Register 1911 .... **1909**

Crisp & Co. Ld. Regd. 1905. Receiver and Manager appointed for debenture stockholders. Vol. liq. June 1909. Removed from Register 1912 .... **1910**

Cristo Gold & Silver Mines Ld. Regd. 1896. Struck off Register 1927 .... **1906**

Criterion Gold Mining Co. Ld. Regd. 1887. Debenture holders foreclosed on the property. Struck off Register 3 Aug. 1894 .... **1899**

Croatian Discount Bank. *See* Hrvatska Eskomptna Banka **1929**

Croatian Syndicate Ld. Regd. 1921. Vol. liq. (members') 28 July 1930. Capital returned to contributories— 5⅞d. per share of £1. Final meeting return regd. 10 Jan. 1931 .... **1931**

Crocker Sons & Co. Ld. See Crockers Ld

Crocker, Sons & Co. Ld. Regd. 1899. Business was acquired by Crocker Sons & Co. (1901) Ld. (later Crockers Ld.) for £28,333 in ordinary shares, £28,333 in preference shares, £100,000 in debenture stock and £113,334 in cash. Removed from Register 1903 .... **1902**

Crockers Ld. Regd. 1901 as Crocker Sons & Co. (1901) Ld.; name changed to Crocker Sons & Co. Ld. in 1904 and as above in Mar. 1919. Vol. liq. (members') 20 Feb. 1939. Undertaking acquired by Hayes, Candy & Crockers Ld. Shareholders received £1 cash and 1 fully-paid B preference share of 10s. in new company for every 5 preference shares of £1 held; and £1 10s. cash, 2 fully-paid B preference shares and 8 fully-paid ordinary shares of 5s. for every 40 ordinary shares of 10s. held. £44 11s. was paid into Companies' Liquidation Account. Final meeting return regd. 4 Aug. 1944............... **1940**

Crœsor & Portmadoc Railway Co. *See* Portmadoc, Crœsor & Beddgelert "Tram" Railway Co.

Crœsus North No. 1 Ld. Regd. 1896. Struck off Register 1921 .... **1913**

Crœsus South Gold Mines Ld. Regd. 1898. Vol. liq. 12 Oct. 1915. Final meeting return regd. 12 Dec. 1916 **1916**

Croft Mill Ld. Regd. 1905. Vol. liq. 13 Jan. 1920. Final meeting return regd. 8 Oct. 1920 .... **1921**

Croft Mill Ld. Regd. 1920. Placed in liquidation. Final meeting return regd. 13 Oct. 1954 .... **1940**

Cromarty & Dingwall Light Railway Co. Inc. (under Light Railway Act 1896) 1902. Vol. liq. Dec. 1925 **1926**

Cromer Gas Co. Regd. 1874; inc. by Special Act 1898. Dissolved 1 May 1949, undertaking being vested in Eastern Area Gas Board under Gas Act 1948. Holders of securities were entitled to receive, in respect of each £100 unit held, British Gas 3% guaranteed stock 1990—95 as follows:

	£	s.	d.
Ord. stock (5% stand.)	140	0	0
4% perp. deb. stock	101	10	0	**1952**

Cromford & High Peak Railway Co. Inc. by Special Act 1862. Under London and North Western Railway Act 1887 undertaking was amalgamated with that company, in which holders received 4% debenture stock at the following rates—4½% 1st preference shares, 112%; A3½% preference shares, 87½%; B1¾% debenture stock, 43¾%; and ordinary stock, £12 3s. 5d.% **1888**

Cromlix Rubber Estates & Produce Syndicate Ld. Regd. 1909. Vol. liq. (members') 22 Feb. 1939. The property was sold in 1939 to Jeram Rubber Estates Ld., in which company shareholders were entitled to 1 share of £1 (credited as fully-paid) for every 30 shares of 2s. held *plus* 3·36d. per share in cash. Final meeting return regd. 22 Feb. 1940 .... **1940**

Crompton & Co. Ld. Regd. 1888. Vol. liq. 19 June 1913. Reconstructed as company of same name (later Crompton Parkinson Ld.). Shareholders were entitled to 5 fully-paid ordinary shares of £1 and 8 preference shares of £1 (credited with 12s. 6d. paid) for every 5 shares of £3 held. Final meeting return regd. 13 June 1917............................ **1914**

Crompton & Evans' Union Bank Ld. Regd. 1877. Vol. liq. Dec. 1913. Undertaking and assets acquired 31st December 1913 by Parr's Bank Ld., in which company shareholders were entitled to 7 shares of £50 (with £10 per share credited as paid) and £2 in cash for every 20 shares of £20 (with £4 paid) held **1914**

Crompton & Shaweross Ld. Regd. 1897. Vol. liq. (members') 27 Jan. 1943. Final meeting return regd. 4 June 1943 .... **1947**

Crompton Electric Supply Co. of Australia Ld. Regd. 1889. Removed from Register 1906 .... **1898**

See Stock Exchange Year-Book.

Cromwell Gold Co. Ld. Regd. 1889. Vol. liq. 20 Aug. 1894. Final meeting return regd. 20 June 1899 1895

Cromwell Gold Mining Co. Ld. Regd. 1887. Vol. liq. 14 Nov. 1889 for reconstruction into a company of same name. Shareholders were entitled to 1 share of £1 with 18s. credited as paid up in new company for each share of £1 held. Final meeting return regd. 3 Mar. 1891 1894

Cromwell Gold Mining Co. Ld. Regd. 1889. Vol. liq. 20 Aug. 1894. Final meeting return regd. 20 June 1899 1895

Cromwell Proprietary Gold Mining Co. Ld. Regd. 1897. Removed from Register 1904 1904

Cromwell Trust Ld. See Dundee Trust Ld.

Crook Burn Mining Co. Ld. Regd. 1879. Vol. liq. 14 Apr. 1887. Final meeting return regd. 10 Sept. 1895 1888

Crook Gas Co. Ld. Regd. 1856. Dissolved 1 May 1949, undertaking being vested in Northern Area Gas Board under Gas Act 1948. Holders of ordinary shares (of £1) were entitled to receive 2s. 6d. British Gas 3% guaranteed stock 1990–95 for each share held 1952

Crooke (F. A.) & Co, Ld. Undertaking and assets were acquired in 1929 by Hodgson's Kingston Brewery Ld., for £151,600 in cash 1930

Crooke's Mining & Smelting Co. Ld. Regd. 1882. Court Orders: to wind up Aug. 1885; to dissolve Jan. 1890 1886

Crosfields Ld. Regd. 1901. Vol. liq. 5 Mar. 1906. Removed from Register 1911 1907

Cross (Alexander) & Sons Ld. Regd. Edinburgh. Vol. liq. (members') 30 June 1943. All shares were owned by Scottish Agricultural Industries Ld. Final meeting return regd. 24 Jan. 1945 1946

Cross & Matthews Ld. Regd. 1897. Vol. liq. 21 Feb. 1898. Dissolved before 1931 1899

Cross Street Buildings (Manchester) Ld. Regd. 1923 as D.I.C. House (Cross Street) Ld.; name changed Feb. 1938. Vol. liq. (members') 9 May 1969. Capital returned to contributories—£1 per preference share of £1; 12s. per ordinary share of 1s. Final meeting return regd. 23 Sept. 1970 1970

Crosse & Blackwell (Holdings) Ld. Regd. 1920 as Crosse & Blackwell Ld.; name changed as above 19 Dec. 1945. Vol. liq. (members') 15 July 1964. All capital was owned by Nestle Alimentana Co. (Ste. An.). Final meeting return regd. 17 Nov. 1967 1961

Cross's Chemical Co. Ld. Regd. Edinburgh. Vol. liq. (members') 30 June 1943. All shares were owned by Scottish Agricultural Industries Ld. Final meeting return regd. 24 Jan. 1945 1946

Crosses & Heatons' Associated Mills Ld. Regd. 1922. Vol. liq. (creditors') Nov. 1931. Undertaking was acquired by Crosses & Winkworth Consolidated Mills Ld. (later Crosses at Heaton Ld.). Final meeting return regd. 27 Sept. 1932 1932

Crosses & Heatons Ld. See C. & H. (Hotels) Ld.

Crosses & Winkworth Consolidated Mills Ld. See C. & H. (Hotels) Ld.

Crosses & Winkworth Ld. Regd. 1875. Vol. liq. 28 Feb. 1920. Undertaking and assets were acquired by Crosses & Winkworth Consolidated Mills Ld. (later Crosses & Heaton Ld.) for £2,856,250 in cash. A return of £46 per share of £10 (£7 paid) was anticipated. Final meeting return regd. 6 Dec. 1929 1921

Crossgates Picture House Ld. Regd. 1919. Vol. liq. (members') 19 Dec. 1938. Capital returned to contributories—7d. per preference share of £1. Final meeting return regd. 18 Dec. 1939 1939

Crossley Brothers Ld. Regd. 1897. Vol. liq. (creditors') 19 Dec. 1966. Struck off Register 21 July 1972 1972

Crowborough District Gas and Electricity Co. See Crowborough District Gas Co.

Crowborough District Gas Co. Inc. by Special Act 1889 as Crowborough District Gas Co.; name changed to Crowborough District Gas and Electricity Co. in 1923 and as above in 1928. The electricity part of the undertaking was acquired by Weald Electricity Supply Co. Ld. The 5% mortgage debentures, 8% (A) preference, 7% debenture and 6% debenture stocks were repaid. Holders of ordinary stock were entitled to 75% of holding in sliding scale stock of Tunbridge Wells Gas Co.; holders of 8% and 7% redeemable preference and 6% debenture stocks were entitled to an equal amount of similar stock in that company 1930

Crowborough District Water Co. Inc. by Special Act 1897. Under provisions of the Newhaven Seaford and Ouse Valley Water (No. 2) Order of 16 Mar. 1960 the undertaking vested in the Mid-Sussex Water Co., from 1 Oct. 1960. Contributories received capital in the Mid-Sussex company in exchange for their holdings at the following rates-£14 5s. 9d. 7% ordinary stock per ordinary share of £10 (10% maximum); £10 7% ordinary stock per ordinary share of £10 (7% maximum); £10 7%

ordinary stock per ordinary share of £10 1953 issue (7% maximum); a like amount of an identical stock for the 5% redeemable preference stock 1978—9; £12 12s. 8d. 4¾% irredeemable preference stock per 6% preference share of £10 and £9 9s. 6d. 4¾% irredeemable preference stock per 4½% preference share of £10. The outstanding £21,900 4% and £22,100 5% perpetual debenture stocks became debenture stocks of the Mid-Sussex Company. Dissolved on 31 May 1961 1962

Crowhurst, Sidley & Bexhill Railway Co. Inc. by Special Act 1897. Undertaking transferred to South Eastern and Chatham Railway Co.'s Managing Committee. Holders of 3% debenture stock and ordinary shares received an equal amount of South Eastern Railway 3% debenture stock. 1907

Crowley, Russell & Co. Ld. Regd. 1920. Vol. liq. (creditors') 16 Feb. 1962. Ordinary creditors received 1s. 10d. in the £. No capital returned to contributories. Final meeting return regd. 18 Feb. 1969 1969

Crown Accident Insurance Co. Ld. Regd. 1887. Vol. liq. 15 Jan. 1897. Amalgamated with Norwich and London Accident Insurance Association. Capital was repaid in full to contributories. Final meeting return regd. 9 Oct. 1897 1898

Crown Collieries Ld. Regd. 1899. Reconstructed 1903 as Crown Collieries (1903) Ld., in which company shareholders were entitled to 1 ordinary share of £1 (credited with 15s. paid) for each share of £1 held or to 1 fully-paid preference share of £1 for each preference share of £1 held. Removed from Register 1905 1908

Crown Collieries (1903) Ld. Regd. 1903. Proceeds of assets realised by Receiver were to be applied in part repayment of claims of debenture holders. Struck off Register 1915 1912

Crown Cork Co. Ld. See Southall Investment Trust Ld.

Crown Cork Syndicate Ld. Regd. 1894. Vol. liq. 4 Jan. 1897. Final meeting return regd. 26 Sept. 1898 1936

Crown Diamond Mining & Exploration. Inc. Orange River Colony 1908 1941

Crown Exploration Co. Ld. Regd. 1896. Vol. liq. 14 Mar. 1905. Removed from Register 1909 1906

Crown Flour Mills Ld. See C. M. Securities Ld.

Crown Gold Mines Ld. Regd. 1903. Reconstructed 1906 as Gullewa Mines Ld., in which company shareholders were entitled to 3 shares of 5s. (credited with 3s. 6d. paid) for every 2 shares of 5s. held 1907

Crown Life Assurance Co. Established 1825. Inc. 1872. Amalgamated 1891 with Law Union Fire and Life Insurance Co. (later Law Union and Crown Fire and Life Insurance Co., later Law Union and Rock Insurance Co. Ld.) in which company shareholders were entitled to 7 shares of £10 (credited with 12s. paid) and £46 Law Union and Crown debenture stock for each share of £50 held. Struck off Register 13 Nov. 1959 1892

Crown Merthyr Steam Navigation Collieries Ld. Regd. 1882 as Garth Merthyr Steam Navigation Collieries Ld. Removed from Register 1906 1885

Crown Point Gold Mines Ld. Regd. 1898. Removed from Register 1902 1901

Crown Preserved Coal Co. Ld. Regd. 1860. Vol. liq. 28 May 1878. Final meeting return regd. 27 Sept. 1878 *1878

Crown Preserved Coal Co. Ld. Regd. 1920. Vol. liq. (members') 31 July 1931. Patent fuel manufacturing works acquired by British Briquettes Ld., for £32,267 in cash and 300,000 ordinary and 300,000 preference shares. Final meeting return regd. 31 May 1932 1939

Crown Reef Gold Mining Co. Ld. Inc. Transvaal 1888. Undertaking and assets were acquired in 1909 by Crown Deep Ld. (later Crown Mines Ld.), for 160,000 shares 1909

Crown Theatre Ld. Regd. 1898. Struck off Register 1914 1912

Crown United Gold Mines Ld. Regd. 1897. Vol. liq. 10 July 1899. Final meeting return regd. 11 June 1900 1900

Crowther & Nicholson Ld. Regd. 1900. Vol. liq. 2 Nov. 1976. Capital returned to contributories (per ordinary share of 5p)—5·8p. Final meeting return regd. 5 nov. 1981 1982–3

Croxon Jones & Co. (Old Bank) Ld. Regd. 1893. Vol. liq. 28 Dec. 1894. Absorbed by Paris Banking Co. & the Alliance Bank Ld. Final meeting return regd. 28 Aug. 1895 *1895

Croydon & Norwood Tramways Co. Inc. 1883, In liquidation in 1888 1888

Croydon Commercial Gas & Coke Co. See Croydon Gas Co.

Croydon Consols Ld. Inc. Queensland 1895. Reconstructed under company of same name inc. 1899 .. 1900

Croydon Consuls Ld. Inc. Queensland 1899. Reconstructed under company of same name inc. 1906 .. 1908

VOL. FOR

Croydon Consols Ld. Inc. Queensland 1906. Vol. liq. 1912. Reconstructed under company of same name inc. 1912. Shareholders were entitled to 3 shares of 2s. credited with 1s. 3d. paid in new Co. for every 2 shares of 2s. 6d. held **1913**

Croydon Consols Mines Trust Ld. Inc. Queensland 1903. Vol. liq. 1908, the assets and liabilities having been acquired by United Properties Ld., in which company shareholders were entitled to 1 share of 2s. credited with 1s. 3d. paid for each share of 2s. 6d. held **1909**

Croydon Gas Co. Inc. as Croydon Commercial Gas & Coke Co. by Special Act 1847; name changed 1904. Dissolved 1 May 1949, undertaking being vested in South Eastern Area Gas Board under Gas Act 1948. Holders of securities were entitled to receive British Gas 3% guaranteed stock 1990–95 as follows sn respect of each £1 unit, unless otherwise stated, of security held:

	£	s.	d.
Sliding scale stock (3½% stand.)	138	0	0
Max. div. stock	115	0	0
4% pref. stock	101	0	0
4% perp.deb.stock (per £100)	102	10	0
5% perp. deb. stock (per £100)	126	6	8
4% deb. stock (per £100)	100	10	0	**1952**

Croydon Goldfields Ld. Inc. Queensland 1897. Amalgamated with two other companies and reconstructed in 1898 under company of same name. Shareholders received 100,000 shares of 5s. (credited with 4s. paid) and 112,000 shares of 5s. (credited with 3s. paid) in the new company **1899**

Croydon Goldfields Ld. Inc. Queensland 1898. Reconstructed in 1904 under company of same name. Shareholders were entitled to 1 share of 5s. (credited with 3s. 6d. paid) for every share of 5s. held and to 2 fully-paid shares in respect of each share subscribed after payment of all calls **1908**

Croydon Goldfields Ld. Inc. Queensland 1904. Voluntary liquidation 1908 .... **1909**

Croydon Hippodrome Ld. Regd. 1909. Vol. liq. 24 May 1928. Final meeting return regd. 20 Dec. 1929 .... **1929**

Croydon Hotels Ld. Regd. 1882. Removed from Register 1897 .... *1887

Croydon Picture House Co. Ld. Regd. 1920. Vol. liq. 3 Feb. 1922. Court Order to stay proceedings 29 Aug. 1923. Vol. liq. (members') 14 Aug. 1931. Capital returned to contributories—4s. 3d. per 5% non-cumulative preference share of £1. Final meeting return regd. 21 Nov. 1931 .... **1932**

Croydon Tramways Co. Inc. 1889. The company was sold to Croydon Corporation for £50,388 14s. Preference and debenture holders were repaid in full; distribution to ordinary shareholders (if any) unknown **1901**

Crude Oil Engines Ld. Regd. 1919. Vol. liq. 10 Mar. 1925. Undertaking acquired by British Oil Engines Ld. Final meeting return regd. 6 Oct. 1928.......... **1934**

Crude Rubber Washing Co. Ld. See Alperton Rubber Co. Ld.

Cruising Co. Ld. Regd. 1900 as Co-operative Cruising Co. Ld.; name changed Jan. 1910. Vol. liq. (creditors') 31 Dec. 1936. Debenture stock was redeemed at par. £490 8s. 11d. was paid into Companies' Liquidation Account in respect of unclaimed debenture stock repayments. No capital returned to contributories. Final meeting return regd. 31 Dec. 1937 .... **1937**

Cruse Syndicate Ld. Regd. 1913. Vol. liq. 29 Dec. 1916. Undertaking was sold to Trinidad Central Oilfields Ld., in which company shareholders were entitled to 1 share of £1 (credited as fully-paid) or 1 fully-paid share of £1 held or 1 share of £1 (credited with 15s. paid) for each share of £1 (15s. paid) held. Final meeting return regd. 24 Sept. 1917 .... **1917**

Crusoe Gold Claims Ld. Regd. 1902. Vol. liq. Nov. 1908. Removed from Register 1910 .... **1909**

Crynant Colliery Co. Ld. Regd. 1900. Vol. liq. (members') 18 Sept 1944. Capital returned to contributories—£1 19s. 10·08d. per share. Final meeting return regd. 4 June 1945 .... **1946**

Crystal Palace Co. Inc. by Royal Charter 1853; re.incorporated by Special Act 1877. Court Order to wind up 1909. Assets realised insufficient to meet claims of 1st debenture stockholders. Liquidation closed in 1914 .... **1910**

Crystal Palace District Electric Supply Co. Ld. Regd. 1883 as Electric Construction and Maintenance Co. Ld.; name changed Dec. 1889 to Electric Installation and Maintenance Co. Ld. and as above Dec. 1891. Undertaking and assets were sold to Blackheath and Greenwich District Electric Light Co. Ld. (later South Metropolitan Electric Light and Power Co. Ld.). Removed from Register 1907 .... **1905**

VOL. FOR

Crystal Palace District Gas Co. *See* South Suburban Gas Co.

Crystal Reef Gold Mining Co. Ld. Regd. 1889. Removed from Register 1904 .... **1893**

Crystalate Gramophone Record Manufacturing Co. Ld. See below.

Crystalate Ld. Regd. 1928 as Crystalate Gramophone Record Manufacturing Co. Ld.; name changed 1938. Vol. liq. (members') 18 Aug. 1958, the undertaking and assets being transferred to Crystalate (Holdings) Ld., in which company holders of ordinary and preference stock were entitled to an equal holding of ordinary and preference shares. Final meeting return regd. 25 Nov. 1959 .... **1961**

Crystalline Gold Mines Ld. Regd. 1899. Struck off Register 27 Oct. 1926 .... **1937**

Crystalline Mining Co. Ld. Regd. Edinburgh 1902. Struck off Register 22 Dec. 1908 .... **1904**

Cuadro Consolidated Ld. Regd. 1903. Vol. liq. Dec. 1908. Removed from Register 1911 .... **1909**

Cuadro Ld. Regd. 1901. Vol. liq. 28 Jan. 1903. Removed from Register 1904 .... **1903**

Cuba-Bartle Sugar Plantations Ld. Regd. 1915. Court Order to wind up 30 Nov. 1926. Struck off Register 20 Mar. 1936 .... **1937**

Cuba Submarine Telegraph Co. Ld. Regd. 1870. Vol. liq. (members') 26 Mar. 1945. All shares were owned by Direct West India Cable Co. Ld. Final meeting return regd. 12 June 1947 .... **1948**

Cuba Telephone Co. Inc. Delaware 1908. The outstanding 5% 1st mortgage convertible bonds were redeemed on 1 Jan. 1946 at 105% **1947**

Cuban Asphalt Co, Ld. Regd. 1915. Vol. liq. 2 Oct. 1929. Final meeting return regd. 24 Feb. 1932 .... **1930**

Cuban Central Railways Ld. Regd. 1899. Undertaking was acquired by United Railways of the Havana and Regla Warehouses Ld., which company assumed liability for the 5% (increased to 5½%) debenture stock and the 4½% debentures. Shareholders were entitled to £110 5% preference shares in acquiring company for every £100 5½% preference shares held or to £71 10s. ordinary shares in acquiring company for every £100 ordinary shares held. Vol. liq. 29 Jan. 1921. Final meeting return regd.1 Apr.1924 .... **1921**

Cuban Exploration Syndicate Ld. Regd. 1901. Vol. liq. 29 Aug. 1902. Shareholders were entitled to a cash payment *plus* fully-paid shares in Cuban Mining & Development Co. Ld. Removed from Register 1903 **1903**

Cuban Land and Development Co. Ld. Regd. 1905. Vol. liq. Nov. 1909. Removed from Register 1912 ...... **1910**

Cuban Land and Development Co. (1911) Ld. Regd. 1911. Vol. liq. 28 Oct. 1920. Final meeting return regd. 14 July 1921 .... **1921**

Cuban Mining & Development Co. Ld. Regd. 1902. Reconstructed 1905 as Cuban Land and Development Co. Ld., in which company shareholders were entitled to 1 share of £1 (credited with 17s. paid) for each share of £1 held. Removed from Register 1907 **1908**

Cuban National Syndicate. Inc. Delaware 1927. In 1932 it was stated that syndicate was out of business .. **1933**

Cuban Oilfields Ld. Regd. 1920. Vol. liq. 16 May 1928. Final meeting return regd. 11 July 1933 .... **1929**

Cuban Petroleum Co. Ld. Regd. 1902. Vol. liq. 5 Oct. 1920. Final meeting return regd. 27 May 1921 .... **1921**

Cuban Ports Co. Inc. Cuba 1911. Dissolved by Presidential Decree 1918; assets sold to Havana Marine Terminals Ld., in which company shareholders were entitled to 20 common shares of $5 (vested in a voting trust) for each common share of $100 held **1934**

Cuban Steamship Co. Ld. Regd. 1893. Vol. liq. 3 Mar. 1916. Final meeting return regd. 8 Mar. 1920 ...... **1916**

Cuban Utilities Co. Consolidated in 1926 into Havana Electric Railway Light & Power Co. (Inc. 1926) . **1927**

Cubitt (John) Gostling & Co. Ld. Regd. 1883. Removed from Register 1902 .... *1885

Cubitts' Engineering Co. Ld. Regd. 1919. Court Order to wind up 23 June 1925. Struck off Register 1933 ... **1926**

Cuckfield Gas Co. Ld. In 1925 the undertaking was acquired by Haywards Heath District Gas Co...... **1927**

Cucuta Railway Co. Inc. 1865 as San Buena Ventura Road Co.; name changed 1887. The outstanding 6% 1st mortgage debentures were redeemed on 1 Sept. 1920 .... **1921**

Cuddingwara Gold Mines Ld.. Regd. 1896. Vol. liq. 14 Apr. 1899. Reconstructed as company of same name. Shareholders were entitled to 1 share of £1 (credited with 17s. paid) in new company for each share of £1 held. Final meeting return regd. 13 July 1899 .... **1901**

Cuddingwara Gold Mines Ld. Regd. 1899. Vol. liq. 31 May 1901 for reconstruction as Fingall Proprietary Ld., in which company shareholders were entitled to

See Stock Exchange Year-Book.

VOL. FOR

2 shares of 10s. (credited with 8s. paid) for each share of £1 held. Final meeting return regd. 26 Feb. 1902 ... **1908**

Cue Consolidated Finance Co. Ld. Regd. 1900. Vol. liq. 6 Sept. 1921. Final meeting return regd. 4 Oct. 1922 **1922**

Cue Consolidated Gold Mines Ld. Regd. 1898. Reconstructed 1900 as Cue Consolidated Finance Co. Ld., in which company shareholders were entitled to 1 fully-paid share of £1 for every 5 shares of 10s. held. Removed from Register 1901 ... **1902**

Cue Gold Mining & Exploration Co. Ld. Regd. 1901. Removed from Register 1904 ... **1905**

Cue 1 Gold Mine Ld. Regd. 1895. Vol. liq. 2 Mar. 1898. Reconstructed as Cue Consolidated Gold Mines Ld., in which company shareholders were entitled to 1 share of 10s. (credited with 7s. 6d. paid) for each share of £1 held. Final meeting return regd. 17 Dec. 1898 ... **1899**

Cue Victory Mines Ld. Regd. 1898. Removed from Register 1902 ... **1901**

Cul & Co. Ld. Regd. 1935. Vol. liq. (members') 25 June 1943. Capital returned to contributories—£250,000 to preference shareholders: £298,523 19s. 2d. plus certain assets distributed in specie to ordinary shareholders. Final meeting return regd. 6 Oct. 1944 **1945**

Cullen District Gas Co. Ld. Regd. in Edinburgh 1924. Dissolved 1 May 1949, undertaking being vested in Scottish Area Gas Board under Gas Act 1948. Holders of ordinary shares (of £1) were entitled to receive £2 4s. British Gas 3% guaranteed stock 1990–95 for each share held ... **1952**

Culley Plowman Ld. Regd. 1907 as Plowman, Barrett & Co. Ld.; name changed as above 1 Oct. 1964. All capital was owned by Bass, Mitchells & Butlers (South East) Ld. Vol. liq. (members') 12 Dec. 1966. Capital returned to contributories—20s. per ordinary share of £1. Final meeting return regd. 6 Mar. 1967 ... **1968**

Culliford (C. J.) & Sons Ld. Regd. 1905. Court Order to wind up 1906. Struck off Register Aug. 1930 ... **1931**

Cullingworth Gas Co. Ld. Regd. 1891. Removed from Register 1902 ... **1903**

Culloden Consolidated Co. Ld. Regd. 1915. Vol. liq. (members') 11 July 1962 for amalgamation with Hevea Investment Co. Ld. Stockholders were entitled to receive 1 fully-paid share of £1 of Culloden Investment Trust Ld. for every 10s. stock held. Final meeting return regd. 2 Apr.1963 ... **1964**

Culloden Tea & Rubber Investment Co. Ld. Regd. 1911. Vol. liq. 15 Apr. 1915. Amalgamated with Rubber Share Trust and Finance Co. Ld. to form Culloden Consolidated Co. Ld., in which company shareholders were entitled to 7 shares of £1 (credited as fully-paid) for every 20 shares of £1 held. Final meeting return regd. 1 Feb. 1918 ... **1916**

Culm Valley Dairy Co. Ld. Regd. 1888. Vol. liq. (members') 22 Dec. 1933. Capital returned to contributories—£1 19s. 10¼d. per share of £5. Final meeting return regd. 20 Dec. 1935 ... **1934**

Cumberland Coal Power and Chemicals Ld. Regd. 1919. Vol. liq. 22 Dec. 1922. Final meeting return regd. 12 Feb. 1927 ... **1923**

Cumberland Gold Mining Co. Ld. Regd. 1894. Removed from Register 1904 ... **1904**

Cumberland Lands Ld. Regd. 1890. Vol. liq. 30 Apr. 1896. Reconstructed as Cumberland River Estates Ld., in which company shareholders were entitled to 1 ordinary share of £1 (credited with 16s. paid) for each ordinary share of £1 held or to 1 fully-paid preference share of £1 for every 4 preference shares of 5s. held. Final meeting return regd. 29 Apr. 1897 **1899**

Cumberland Lead Mines Ld. Regd. 1882. Removed from Register 1895 ... *****1893**

Cumberland Niagara Gold Mines Ld. Regd. 1903. Vol. liq. 23 July 1906. Final meeting return regd. 17 Oct. 1907 ... **1907**

Cumberland River Estates Ld. Regd. 1896. Vol. liq. 21 Sept 1905. Removed from Register 1909 ... **1906**

Cumberland Silica Bricks Ld. Regd. 1934. Vol. liq. (members') 28 Aug. 1939. Capital returned to contributories—¼d. per share of 1s. Final meeting return regd. 29 July 1940 ... **1941**

Cumberland Union Banking Co. Ld. Established 1829, regd. 1865. The business was acquired as from 1 Jan. 1901 by York City and County Banking Co. Ld., in which company shareholders were entitled to 1 share of £10 (£3 credited as paid up) for each share of £30 (£12 10s. paid up) held. Removed from Register 1906 ... **1902**

Cumbre Trust Ld. Regd. 1932. Vol. liq. 28 Oct. 1949. Final meeting return regd. 12 June 1950 ... **1940**

Cumbrian Mining Co. Ld. Regd. 1907. Vol. liq. 11 July 1912. Final meeting return regd. 6 Nov. 1914 ... **1913**

VOL. FOR

Cumnock Gas Co. Ld. Regd. in Edinburgh 1908. Dissolved 1 May 1949, undertaking being vested in Scottish Area Gas Board under Gas Act 1948. Holders of ordinary shares (of £1) were entitled to receive £3 British Gas 3% guaranteed stock 1990–95 for each share held ... **1952**

Cunliffe (Roger), Sons & Co. Established 1819; regd. as unlimited 1939. Vol. liq. (members') 28 Jan. 1944. In 1941 the assets were sold to Cater, Brightwen & Co. Ld. Final meeting return regd. 23 June 1945 ... **1947**

Cunningham & De Fourier Co. Ld. Regd. 1884. Vol. liq. 6 May 1895. Reconstructed as company of same name. Shareholders were entitled to 1 fully-paid share of £20 for each A share of £20 held; or to 127 fully-paid shares of £20 for every 50 A shares of £1 held. Final meeting return regd. 30 Sept. 1895 ... **1905**

Cunningham & De Fourier Co. Ld. Regd. 1895. Vol. liq. June 1907. Removed from Register 1909 ... **1908**

Cunningham (J. & J.) See S.A.I. (Leith) Ld.

Cunningham (R. N.) & Co. Ld. Regd. 1882. Removed from Register 1901 ... **1885**

Cupar Gas Co. Ld. Regd. in Edinburgh 1896. Dissolved 1 May 1949, undertaking being vested in Scottish Area Gas Board under Gas Act 1948. Holders of securities were entitled to receive British Gas 3% guaranteed stock 1990–95 as follows:

	£	s.	d.	
Ord. shares (of £30)	82	10	0	
5% pref. shares (of £1)	1	2	6	**1952**

Curamalan Land Company. Inc. Buenos Aires 1884. In liquidation in 1904 ... **1904**

Curtin Davis Proprietary Co., No Liability. Inc. Victoria 1896. Company has been wound up ... **1909**

Curtis Bros. & Dumbrill Ld. Regd. 1899 as Wraight, Dumbrill & Co. Ld.; name changed June 1917. Vol. liq. (members') 28 Jan. 1931. Capital returned to contributories—£61,151 2s. 8d. £16 19s. 6d. was paid into Companies' Liquidation Account. Final meeting return regd. 25 Jan. 1934 ... **1931**

Curtis's and Harvey Ld. Regd. 1898. Vol. liq. (members') 31 Dec. 1942. The undertaking having been acquired by Imperial Chemical Industries Ld. Final meeting return regd. 25 Oct. 1952 ... **1952**

Curzon Brothers & Maxims Ld. See C. B. & M. Tailors Ld.

Curzon Brothers Ld. Business acquired by C. B. & M. Tailors Ld ... **1930**

Curzon Exhibition Hall Co. Ld. Regd. 1865. Struck off Register 1916 ... **1913**

Curzon Hotel (London) Ld. Regd. 1919. Struck off Register 1936 ... **1934**

Curzon Mill Co. Ld. See Alger Spinning Co. Ld.

Custodian Investment Corporation Ld. Regd. 1924 as London & Foreign Banking Corpn. Ld.; name changed 25 Feb. 1926. Vol. liq. (members') 18 Dec. 1930. Capital returned to contributories—3s. per share of £1. Struck off Register 1 Sept. 1953 ... **1954**

Customs & Bonded Warehouses Co. (Societa Anonima Magazzini Generali) Ld. Regd. 1897 as Customs & Bonded Warehouses Co. Ld.; name changed 1906. Vol. liq. Apr. 1909. Capital returned to contributories—approx. £4 15s. per share of £1 in Oct. 1909; further payments (if any) not known. Struck off Register 1929 ... **1910**

Cutlack & Harlock Ld. Regd. 1907. Vol. liq. (members') 28 May 1931. Undertaking and assets were acquired by Hall, Cutlack and Harlock Ld. in exchange for shares. Final meeting return regd. 14 Aug. 1931 **1932**

Cwm Avon Estate & Works Co. Ld. Regd. 1881. Court Orders: to wind up Aug. 1882; to dissolve June 1887 **1883**

Cwm Dwyfor Mining Co. Ld. Regd. 1877. Removed from Register 1905 ... *****1882**

Cwmaman Coal Co. Ld. Regd. 1882. Vol. liq. 7 May 1928. Undertaking acquired by Bwilfa & Cwmaman Collieries Ld. Struck off Register 23 Oct. 1931 ... **1938**

Cwmbran Chemical Co. Ld. Regd. 1911. Vol. liq. (members') 31 Mar. 1939. Capital returned to contributories—27s. 0·7d. per share of £1. Final meeting return regd. 30 Nov. 1940 ... **1929**

Cwmllynfell Anthracite Collieries Ld. Regd. 1924. Vol. liq. 12 Mar. 1929. Undertaking was acquired by Henderson's Welsh Anthracite Collieries Ld. Final meeting return regd. 12 July 1929 ... **1930**

Cwmystwyth Co. Ld. Regd. 1886. Vol. liq. 18 Nov. 1892. Final meeting return regd. 7 Sept. 1893 ... **1893**

Cwmystwyth Mines New Co. Ld. Regd. 1875. Vol. liq. 19 Nov. 1885. Struck off Register 10 Feb. 1903 ... **1886**

Cwmystwyth Mining Co. Ld. See Kingside Zinc Blende Co. Ld.

Cyanite Fire Prevention Corporation Ld. Regd. 1887. Removed from Register 1895 ... **1892**

Cycle Automatic Manufacturing Co. Ld. Regd. 1896. Struck off Register 28 July 1899 ... **1901**

See Stock Exchange Year-Book.

VOL. FOR

Cycle Components Manufacturing Co. Ld. Regd. 1894. Reconstructed 1902 as Components Ld., in which company shareholders were entitled to 1 share of £1 (credited with 16s. paid) for each share of £1 held. Removed from Register 1904 .... **1908**

Cycle Industries Corporation Ld. Regd. 1896. Business was acquired by Home Industries Ld., in which company shareholders were entitled to 1 share of £1 of each class (preference and ordinary) for each share of £1 held. Removed from Register 1903 ... **1899**

Cycle Manufacturers' Tube Co. Ld. Regd. 1896. Vol. liq. 23 Jan. 1900. Reconstructed as Coventry Tube & Metal Co. Ld., in which company shareholders were entitled to 1 fully-paid share of £1 for every 4 shares of £1 held. Removed from Register 1903 .... **1901**

Cycle Rubber Works Ld. Regd. 1892. Vol. liq. 12 Jan. 1895. Final meeting return regd. 22 May 1900...... ***1897**

Cycledom Ld. Regd. 1896. Vol. liq. Feb. 1908. Court Order to wind up June 1908. Struck off Register 12 Jan. 1937 .... **1937**

Cyclists' Accident Assurance Corporation Ld. Regd. 1883. Court Orders: to wind-up 31 July 1884; to dissolve 17 May 1887 .... ***1885**

Cynon Colliery Co. Ld. Regd. 1906. Vol. liq. (creditors') 23 June 1931. Assets realised insufficient to pay unsecured creditors in full. Final meeting return regd. 14 Sept. 1933 .... **1932**

Cyprus & General Asbestos Co. Ld. Inc. Cyprus 1931. Undertaking and assets were acquired by Tunnel Asbestos Cement Co. Ld. in which company shareholders were entitled to 3 deferred shares of 1s. (credited as fully-paid) for every 2 ordinary shares of £1 held. A return of 10s. per preference share of £1 was anticipated... **1937**

Cyprus Co. Ld. Regd. 1891. Vol. liq. 30 Jan. 1897. Final meeting return regd. 27 Nov. 1899 .... ***1898**

Cyprus Oil Trust Ld. Regd. 1910. Vol. liq. 16 Aug. 1929. Undertaking and assets were transferred to Universal & General Securities Ld. in which company shareholders were entitled to 5 fully-paid ordinary shares of 1s. and 3 fully-paid deferred shares of 1s. for every 10 preference shares of 2s. held or 1 fully-paid deferred share of 1s. for every 25 ordinary shares of 2s. held. Final meeting return regd. 21 Jan. 1931 .... **1930**

Cyprus Silk Filature Ld. Regd. 1925. Vol. liq. 10 June 1943. Dissolved before 1952 .... **1939**

Cyprus Sulphur & Copper Co. Ld. Regd. 1909 as New Lymni Ld.; name changed Nov. 1919. Vol. liq. (members') 2 Sept. 1940. Undertaking sold to company of same name since formed in Cyprus. Final meeting return regd. 4 Mar. 1943 .... **1941**

Cystic Fibrosis Research Investment Trust p.l.c. Regd. 19 Feb. 1981. Vol. liq. (members') 26 June 1986. Final meeting held 12 Aug. 1987. Company unitised and net assets of Company transferred, after liabilities, to Midland Bank Trust Co. Ld. as trustee of 2 authorised unit trusts. Holders could elect to receive units in either or both of these unit trusts on the following basis: for each ordinary share either 3·47584 accumulation units in Fidelity Special Situations Trust or 5·72256 income units in Fidelity Growth and Income Trust. 1·23p per ordinary share distributed on 17 July 1987. Amount paid into Insolvency Services Account in respect of unclaimed dividends was £990·41 .... **1988–9**

D

D.A.W.S. Ld. Regd. 1904 as Direct Supply Aerated Water Co.; name changed Sept. 1963. Court Order to wind up 25 July 1966. Debenture stockholders received £1 plus interest accrued on 8 Aug. 1969 per £1 stock. No distributions to ordinary shareholders. Liquidator released 22 Jan. 1974 and company dissolved 24 June **1974-5**

D. & M. I. Co. Ld. Regd. 1887 as Darwen & Martyn Iron Co. Ld.; name changed 1959. All capital was owned by Barrow Haematite Steel Co., Ld. which later acquired the undertaking and assets. Vol. liq. (members') 1 Apr. 1959. Capital returned to contributories—£117,636 4s. 10d. in cash and £1,254,143 19s. 4d. in specie. Final meeting return regd. 26 May 1965.................................... **1966**

D.C.D. Syndicate Ld. See Trevethoe Co. Ld.

D.C.I. Ld. Regd. Edinburgh 1919. Vol. liq. (members') 10 Sept 1954. Capital returned to contributories—£1 per preference share of £1; 13s. 11·96d. per ordinary share of 13s. 4d. Paid into Companies' Liquidation Account—£13 10s. 11d. in respect of unclaimed dividends, £95 in respect of preference capital and

VOL. FOR

£158 9s. 2d. in respect of ordinary share distributions. Final meeting return regd. 16 Oct. 1958....... **1959**

D. I. C. House (Cross Street) Ld. See Cross Street Buildings (Manchester) Ld.

D. Motors (1932) Ld. See Douglas Motors (1932) Ld.

D. R. Cotton Mills Ld. Regd. 1916. Vol. liq. 1 Sept. 1919. Undertaking and assets were sold to No. 2 D. R. Cotton Mills Ld. (later Dunlop Cotton Mills Ld. (later Dunlop Textiles Ld.). The liquidator was to receive sufficient to repay preference shares at par. Final meeting return regd. 12 June 1920 .... **1920**

D. S. Holdings Ld. Regd. 1932 as Ductile Steels Ld. Undertaking acquired by Ductile Steels Ld., in 1936. Struck off Register 15 Oct. 1943 .... **1945**

D. Smith & Sons (1924) Ld. See British Celilyn Ld.

D.S.R. Syndicate Ld. Regd. 1913. Vol. liq. 29 Nov. 1915. Final meeting return regd. 30 Mar. 1917..... **1916**

Dackawell Tea Co. Ld. Regd. 1898. Vol. liq. 16 June 1904. Final meeting return regd. 4 Jan. 1907........ ***1905**

Daejan (Java) Rubber Estate Ld. Regd. 1910. Vol. liq. 12 Apr. 1922. Assets and liabilities were taken over by Daejan Rubber Co. Ld., in which company shareholders were entitled to 1 ordinary share of 1s. 6d. (credited with 10½d. paid) for each share of 1s. 6d. held. Debenture holders were entitled to 70 fully-paid preference shares of 1s. 6d. Final meeting return regd. 18 Jan. 1927 .... **1923**

Daejan Rubber Co. Ld. Regd. 1922. Vol. liq. (members') 5 Sept. 1935. Undertaking and assets were acquired by Daejan Samoedra Estates Ld. (later Daejan Holdings Ld.) in which company shareholders were entitled to 3 shares of 2s. (credited as fully-paid) for every 4 shares of 1s. 6d. held. Final meeting return regd. 17 Dec. 1936 .... **1936**

Daggafontein Gold Mining Co. Ld. Regd. 1902. Vol. liq. 19 Nov. 1917. Undertaking was acquired by Daggafontein Mines Ld. Final meeting return regd. 15 Oct. 1934 .... **1918**

Daggafontein Mines Ld. Inc. in Transvaal 1916. Struck off Register 17 Dec. 1976 .... **1977-8**

Daggafontein Prospecting Syndicate Ld. Regd. 1899. Vol. liq. 25 June 1917. Shareholders were entitled to 1 fully-paid share of £1 in Daggafontein Gold Mining Co. Ld., plus 11s. 9d in cash for every share of £1 held. Final meeting return regd. 24 Oct. 1917 **1918**

Dagwin Syndicate Ld. Regd. 1900. Vol. liq. 4 Feb. 1907. Removed from Register 1907 .... **1907**

Dahan Rubber Estates Ld. Regd. 1925. Vol. liq. (creditors') 22 Dec. 1932. Undertaking and assets were acquired by Dahan Rubber Estates (1933) Ld., in which company shareholders were entitled to 1 share of 2s. (credited with 1s. 8d. paid) for each share of 2s. held. Debenture stockholders were entitled to an equal amount of similar debenture in new company. Final meeting return regd. 20 Sept. 1933 .... **1933**

Dahan Rubber Estates Ld. Regd. 1946 in reconstruction of Dahan Rubber Estates (1933) Ld. Vol. liq. (creditors') 16 Apr. 1959. Capital returned to contributories—10·15d. per share of 2s. £453 paid into Companies' Liquidation Account in respect of unclaimed distributions. Final meeting return regd. 8 Oct. 1969 .... **1970**

Dahan Rubber Estates (1933). Ld. Regd. 1933. Vol. liq. (members') 3 June 1946 for reconstruction as Dahan Rubber Estates Ld. in which company shareholders were entitled to receive 1 share of 2s. (credited with 1s. 6d. paid) for each share of 2s. held and debenture holders £115 income convertible debentures for each £100 debenture held. A distribution of 1·12d. per share was made to shareholders not exercising their right to take up shares in new company. £162 was paid into Companies' Liquidation Account. Final meeting return regd. 29 Nov. 1947 .... **1948**

Dahlonega Co. Ld. Regd. 1889. Struck off Register 11 June 1895 .... **1899**

Dai Hyaku Ginko. Inc. Tokyo 1878. Amalgamated in Sept. 1927 with Kawasaki Bank as Kawasaki-One Hundredth Bank Ld. **1928**

Daily Chronicle Investment Corporation Ld. Regd. 1927. Vol. liq. (members') 4 May 1938. Capital returned to contributories—£3,333 1s. 8d. A further £58 12s. 10d. was paid into Companies' Liquidation Account. Final meeting return regd. 27 Apr. 1939 ... **1939**

Daily Express Building Co. Ld. Regd. 1929. Vol. liq. (members') 9 Feb. 1933. The outstanding 6% debenture stock was redeemed at 105% on 15 Feb. 1933. Capital returned to contributories—£18,557. Final meeting return regd. 30 July 1934.................... **1933**

Daily Express (1908) Ld. Regd. 1908. Vol. liq. 10 Nov. 1915. Undertaking and assets were acquired by London Express Newspaper Ld. (later Beaverbrook Newspapers Ld.); 1st mortgage debenture holders were entitled to 15% 1st debenture of £25 and 3

VOL. FOR

preference shares of £25 fully-paid, for every £100 bond held. Shareholders were entitled to 1 ordinary share of £1, fully-paid, for every 10 ordinary shares of £1 held or 1 ordinary share of £1 for every 5 preference shares of £1 held. Holders of ordinary and preference shares were entitled to 24,000 non-voting ordinary shares. Final meeting return regd. 3 June 1920 .... **1916**

Daimler Motor Co. Ld. Regd. 1896. Vol. liq. 5 Jan. 1905. Undertaking and assets were acquired by Daimler Motor Co. (1904) Ld. Holders of the 99,630 shares were entitled to 62,269 fully-paid shares of £1 in new company. Final meeting return regd. 2 Nov. 1927 **1908**

Daimler Motor (1904) Ld. Regd. 1904. Vol. liq. 3 Nov. 1910. Undertaking and assets were acquired by Birmingham Small Arms Co. Ld., in which company shareholders were entitled to 5 ordinary shares of £1 (credited as fully-paid) for every 4 ordinary shares of £1 held or £1 5s. in cash per preference share of £1 held. Final meeting return regd. 2 Nov. 1927 .... **1911**

Daira Sanieh Co. Ld. Regd. 1898. Vol. liq. 10 June 1905. Undertaking was acquired by La Société Egyptienne de la Daira Sanieh (inc. Egypt), in which company shareholders were entitled to 1 share for each share held. Removed from Register 1906 .... **1906**

Daira Sanieh Sugar Corporation Ld. Regd. 1902. Vol. liq. 3 Aug. 1906. Capital returned to contributories—£5 6s. 10d. per ordinary share of £5; 20s. per deferred share of £1; further payments (if any) not known. Removed from Register 1908 .... **1907**

Dairymaids Ld. Regd. 1914. Vol. liq. 31 Dec. 1917. Final meeting return regd. 13 May 1918 .... **1932**

Dakota Stock & Grazing Co. Ld. Regd. 1883. Vol. liq. 6 Aug. 1886. Final meeting return regd. 29 Mar. 1899 **1888**

Dalbeattie Gas Light Co. Ld. Regd. in Edinburgh 1858. Dissolved 1 May 1949, undertaking being vested in Scottish Area Gas Board under Gas Act 1948. Holders of ordinary shares (of £5) were entitled to receive £7 British Gas 3% guaranteed stock 1990–95 for each share held **1952**

Dalby. Welch & Co. Ld. Regd. 1901 as Dalby Welch & Co. (1901) Ld.; name changed 13 Sept. 1910. Vol. liq. 23 Dec. 1910. Undertaking acquired by Smith, Dalby-Welch Ld. Final meeting return regd. 29 May 1911 .... **1938**

Dale, Forty & Co. Ld. Regd. 1909. Vol. liq. (members') for purposes of reconstruction. The preference shares (of £1) were repaid at par. Final meeting return regd. 20 Feb. 1956 .... **1956**

Dale Mill (Holdings) Ld. Regd. 1920 as Dale Mill Ld.; name changed 24 Mar. 1953. Vol. liq. (members') 24 Mar. 1953, the undertaking and assets (excluding certain cash) being transferred to a new company (Dale Mill Ld.). Redeemable preference stock was repaid at par on 7 Apr. 1953 and ordinary stockholders received 1 fully-paid share of 5s. in the new company for every 5s. unit of stock held. £60 13s. 9d. paid into Companies' Liquidation Account. Final meeting return regd. 31 Aug. 1956 .... **1957**

Dale Mill Ld. Regd. 1953. A subsidiary of Smith & Nephew & Associated Cos. Ld. Vol. liq. (members') 8 May 1959. Final meeting return regd. 14 Dec. 1961 **1958**

Dale Ring Co. Ld. Regd. 1905. Vol. liq. Feb. 1920. Struck off Register June 1932 .... **1933**

Dalkeith Gas Light Co. Ld. Regd. in Edinburgh 1932. Dissolved 1 May 1949 undertaking being vested in Scottish Area Gas Board under Gas Act 1948. Holders of ordinary shares (of £1) were entitled to receive £2 10s. British Gas 3% guaranteed stock 1990–95 for each share held **1952**

Dallas Dome Wyoming Oilfields Co. Inc. in Delaware U.S.A. 1924. Resolution for dissolution was approved 3 Sept. 1947 and filed 4 Sept. 1947 .... **1953**

Dallas (John E.) & Sons Ld. Regd. as private company 29 Mar. 1947; converted public company 18 June 1947. Vol. liq. (creditors') 27 Feb. 1975. Final meeting held 8 Nov. 1983 .... **1984–5**

Dalmellington Iron Co. Ld. Regd. Edinburgh 1885. Vol. liq. Oct. 1931. Undertaking and assets were acquired by Bairds & Dalmellington Ld., in which company shareholders were entitled to 6 shares of £1 (credited as fully-paid) for every 5 ordinary shares of £1 held plus 7s. per ordinary share in cash. The preference shares were repaid in Oct. 1931. Final meeting return regd. 20 June 1934 .... **1932**

Dalmeny Oil Co. Ld. Regd. Edinburgh 1871. Vol. liq. 24 Nov. 1896 for reconstruction under same name. Final meeting return regd. 10 Aug. 1897 .... **1898**

Dalmeny Oil Co. Ld. Regd. Edinburgh 1896. Vol. liq. (members') 28 June 1933. Preference shareholders received £9,676 1s. 9d. in cash and investments. Final meeting return regd. 6 Dec. 1933 .... **1934**

VOL. FOR

Dairy Gas Light Co. Ld. Regd. in Edinburgh 1929. Dissolved 1 May 1949. undertaking being vested in Scottish Area Gas Board under Gas Act 1948. Holders of ordinary shares (of £10 10s.) were entitled to receive £30 British Gas 3% guaranteed stock 1990–95 for each share held **1952**

Dalrymple (Tasmania) Tin Mining Co. Ld. Regd. 1904. Removed from Register 1912 .... **1908**

Dalton, Barclay & Co. Ld. Regd. 1896. Trustees for debenture holders took possession of the assets in Aug. 1898. Removed from Register 1903 .... **1900**

Dalton Investment Corporation Ld. See Private & Industrial Banking Co. Ld.

Dalton Main Collieries Ld. Regd. 1899. Vol. liq. (members') 31 Mar. 1954. Final meeting return regd. 28 May 1956. Dissolution declared void June 1958. Restored to register 9 June 1958. Final meeting return regd. 30 Nov. 1960 .... **1962**

Daly (John) & Co. Ld. Regd. Dublin 1876. Vol. liq. 4 Mar. 1888 .... **1886**

Dalzell's (Joseph) Parton & Harrington Breweries Ld. Regd. 1892. Vol. liq. 23 Mar. 1927. In 1925 72 licensed houses were acquired by Matthew Brown & Co. Ld. Final meeting return regd. 8 Dec. 1930 .. **1928**

Damansara (Selangor) Rubber Co. Ld. Regd. 1906. Vol. liq. (members') 29 Mar. 1920 for reconstruction under same name. Shareholders were entitled to 3 fully-paid shares of £1 in new company for each share of £1 held. A dividend out of profits was paid by the liquidator. Final meeting return regd. 31 Dec. 1921 .... **1921**

Damansara (Selangor) Rubber Co. Ld. Regd. 1920. All capital acquired by Seafield Amalgamated Rubber Co. Ld. Vol. liq. 13 Jan. 1961. Final meeting return regd. 4 Jan. 1964 .... **1961**

Damo (Nigeria) Tin Co. Ld. Regd. 1912. Struck off Register 9 Dec. 1930 .... **1931**

Dandicolle & Gaudin Ld. Regd. 1889. Vol. liq. Oct. 1905. Undertaking and assets were acquired by Etablissements Dandicolle & Gaudin (inc. France 1905), in which company shareholders were entitled to an equal par value in shares. Removed from Register 1907 .... **1906**

Dane's Discount Co. Ld. Regd. 1895. Business was acquired in 1898 by New London Discount Co. Ld. for £90,021 in fully-paid and partly-paid shares. Removed from Register 1903 .... **1900**

Danesbury Estates Ld. Regd. 1920 as Carr Hill Mills Ld. Vol. liq. 10 June 1981. Final meeting return regd. 15 Dec. 1981 .... **1941**

Dangan Rubber Co. Ld. Regd. 1905 as Rubber Plantations Ld.; name changed Oct. 1909. Vol. liq. 15 Aug. 1913. Reconstructed as company of same name. Shareholders were entitled to 1 share of 2s. (credited with 1s. paid) for each share of 2s. held. Final meeting return regd. 29 Dec. 1919 .... **1941**

Dangan Rubber Co. Ld. Regd. 1913 as Dangan Rubber Co. (1913) Ld.; name changed Oct. 1919. Vol. liq. 26 Oct. 1921 for reconstruction as Dangan Rubber Estates Ld. (later Tanker Investment Trust Ld.) in which company shareholders were entitled to 1 ordinary share of 2s. (credited with 1s. 4d. paid) for each share of 2s. held. Debenture stockholders were entitled to fully-paid preference shares in new company. Final meeting return regd. 27 Dec. 1929 **1922**

Daniel (Thomas) & Co. Ld. Regd. 1886. Vol. liq. 26 Aug. 1892. Court Orders: to continue winding up under supervision 1 Sept. 1892; to dissolve on 27 Jan. 1914 **1893**

Daniell, Cazenove & Co. Established 1913. In Sept. 1943 the assets were acquired by Cater Brightwen & Co. Ld. **1948**

Dansebu Gold Mining Co. Ld. Regd. 1901. Removed from Register 1913 .... **1908**

Dansette Products Ld. Regd. 1943 as J. & A. Mangolin: name changed 1961. Vol. liq. (creditors') 10 Aug. 1970. No capital returned to contributories. Final meeting return registered 28 Jan. 1976 . ... **1977-8**

Danube Collieries & Minerals Co. Ld. Regd. 1889. Removed from Register 1907 .... **1893**

Danube Mining Concession Ld. Regd. 1910. Struck off Register 1922 .... ***1923**

Danube Oil Trading Co. of Roumania Ld. Regd. 1914; receiver appointed 21 Feb. 1940. Certain assets sold and a dividend of 2s. 6d. paid to debenture holders. Capital returns (if any) unknown. Struck off register 17 June 1966 .... **1941**

Danubian Navigation Co. Ld. Regd. 1869. Vol. liq. 21 June 1893. Capital returned to contributories—£3 per share of £10 on 1 July 1893; further payments (if any) not known. Final meeting return regd. 12 Apr. 1894 .... **1894**

Danygraig Omnibus Services Ld. Regd. 1932. Vol. liq. (members') 31 Oct. 1940. Capital returned to

See Stock Exchange Year-Book.

VOL. FOR

contributories—£1 9s. 3d. per share of £1. Final meeting return regd. 19 Mar. 1941 ...... **1941**

Danziger Bank für Hande und Gewerbe, A. G. Inc. in Danzig 1922. Business transferred to Dresdner Bank in Danzig (affiliated to the Dresdner Bank) in 1933 ...... **1934**

Dapoota Tea Co. Ld. Regd. 1894. Vol. liq. 12 Oct. 1896. Properties were sold to Empire of Indian & Ceylon Tea Co. Ld. Final meeting return regd. 20 Dec. 1897 **1897**

D'Arcy Estates Gold Mining Co. Ld. Regd. 1894. Reconstructed 1899 as D'Arcy Wentworth Gold Mines Ld. in which company shareholders were entitled to 3 fully-paid shares of £1 for each share of £1 held. Removed from Register 1903 ...... **1902**

D'Arcy Wentworth Gold Mines Ld. Regd. 1899. Mortgagees took possession of property. Removed from Register 1904 ...... **1903**

Dare Valley Railway Co. Inc. by Special Act 1863. Under Taff Vale Railway Amalgamation and Capital Act 1889 undertaking was acquired by the Taff Vale Railway Co. in which holders of capital stock and shares received 4% preference stock and holders of 3½% debenture stock received 3% debenture stock on basis of equal income. The loans were taken over by the purchaser **1890**

Dareheib & African Syndicate Ld. Regd. 1905. Vol. liq. Mar. 1909. Removed from Register 1911 ...... **1910**

Darien Gold Mining Co. Ld. Regd. 1887. Reconstructed as company of same name. Struck off Register 1921 **1907**

Darien Gold Mining Co. Ld. Regd. 1891. Vol. liq. 7 Sept 1906. Reconstructed as company of same name. Shareholders were entitled to 1 ordinary share of £1 (credited with 10s. paid) for each share of £1 held. Holders of 10% debentures were entitled to an equal amount of fully-paid preference shares in new company. Struck off Register 18 Jan. 1921 ...... **1908**

Darien Gold Mining Co. Ld. Regd. 1907. Vol. liq. 10 Mar. 1913. Struck off Register 18 Jan. 1921 ...... **1914**

Darjeeling Consolidated Tea Co. Ld. (The) Regd. 8 July 1896. Vol. liq. 10 Mar.1987. All capital having been acquired by Eastern Tea Holdings Ld **1969**

Darjeeling Himalayan Railway Co. Ld. Regd. in India 1879 as Darjeeling Steam Tramway Co. Ld.; name changed July 1881. Resolution to wind-up passed 19 Oct. 1948; railway taken over by Government of India on 20 Oct. 1948. Capital returned to contributories.—Rs.122·22 per ordinary share (of Rs. 100) **1970**

Darjeeling Holdings Ld. Regd. as private company 5 Nov. 1973; converted into public company 21 Dec. 1973; winding-up order made 17 Oct. 1977.Dissolved and struck off register 29 Nov. 1983 ...... **1984–5**

Darjeeling Steam Tramway Co. Ld. See above.

Darlaston Coal & Iron Co. Ld. Regd. 1877. Vol. liq. 11 June 1895. Final meeting return regd. 26 Feb. 1896 **1896**

Darlaston Steel & Iron Co. Ld. Regd. 1866. Removed from Register 1902 ...... ***1877**

Darling Downs & Western Land Co. Ld. Inc. Queensland 1881. Company was stated to be defunct at 27 Nov.1902 ...... **1903**

Darlington District Joint Stock Banking Co. Ld. Established 1831. Regd. as limited 1881. Business was transferred to York City & County Banking Co. Ld. The paid-up capital and guarantee fund were to be repaid to shareholders **1884**

Darlington Forge Co. Ld. Regd. 1873. Vol. liq. 6 June 1919 for reconstruction as Darlington Forge Ld. in which company shareholders were entitled to 5 ordinary shares of £1 for each ordinary share of £1 held or 5 preference shares of £1 for each preference share of £1 held. Final meeting return regd. 5 Jan. 1928 ...... **1919**

Darlington Rustless Steel & Iron Co. Ld. Regd. 1930. Receiver appointed in July 1933. Struck off Register 27 Jan. 1942 ...... **1942**

Darlington Steel & Iron Co. Ld. Regd. 1872 as Darlington Iron Co. Ld.; name changed June 1882. Vol. liq. 17 Aug. 1896. Final meeting return regd. 6 Nov. 1899 ...... **1898**

Darlington Wagon and Engineering Co. Ld. Regd. 1884. Vol. liq. 18 Apr. 1905. Removed from Register 1909 **1906**

Darlot Exploration Co. of Western Australia Ld. Regd. 1895. Removed from Register 1903 ...... **1901**

Darmstaedter und Nationalbank. Inc. Berlin 1922. Absorbed by Dresdner Bank. The bank's holding of RM.35,000,000 of its own shares was cancelled and the remaining RM.25.000,000 of shares were exchanged for RM.7,500,000 of the Dresdner Bank held by the Reich **1933**

Darracq (A.) & Co. Ld. Regd. 1903. Removed from Register 1911 ...... **1905**

Darracq (A.) & Co. (1905) Ld. See S.T.D. Motors Ld.

Darracq Serpollet Omnibus Co. Ld. Regd. 1906. Vol. liq. 14 Aug. 1912. Final meeting return regd. 6 Feb. 1923 **1918**

VOL. FOR

Dartford District Light Railways Co. Inc. (under Light Railways Act 1896) 1903. No capital had been raised at 31 Dec. 1909 ...... **1911**

Dartford Gas Co. Inc. by Special Act 1867. Amalgamated in 1919 with South Suburban Gas Co. Holders of consolidated ordinary and 4% debenture stocks were entitled to £105 or £80 respectively in 5% perpetual debenture stock for every £100 stock held **1919**

Dartford Portland Cement Co. Ld. Regd. 1895. Court Order to wind up 1907. Removed from Register 1911 ...... **1908**

Dartmouth Gas, Coke & Coal Co. Ld. Regd. 1858. Dissolved 1 May 1949 undertaking being vested in South Western Area Gas Board under Gas Act 1948. Holders of securities were entitled to receive British Gas 3% guaranteed stock 1990—95 as follows in respect of each £1 unit, unless otherwise stated of security held:

	£	s.	d.
Ord. shares (10 basic)	1	8	0
6% 1st pref. shares	1	5	5
6% 2nd pref. shares	1	5	0
4% 1st mort. debs. (per £100)	101	0	0
4% 2nd mort. debs. (per £100)	100	10	0

A distribution on ordinary shares of 18·3365% out of reserves was made in Nov. 1955 ...... **1952**

Darton Main Colliery Co. Ld. Regd. 1913. Vol. liq. (members') 12 Jan. 1940. All capital held by Maltby Main Colliery Co. Ld. Final meeting return regd. 9 Aug. 1940 ...... **1940**

Darvel Bay (Borneo) Tobacco Plantations Ld. Regd. 1889. Vol. liq. 12 Sept 1892. Reconstructed as New Darvel Bay (Borneo) Tobacco Plantations Ld. in which company shareholders were entitled to 3 shares of £1 (credited with 15s. paid) for each share of £5 held. Final meeting return regd. 16 Nov. 1893 **1908**

Darwen & Martyn Iron Co. Ld. See D. & M. I. Co. Ld.

Darwen (J. S.) & Co. Ld. Regd. 7 Jan. 1924. Winding-up order 1964. Struck off register July 1986. Distributions per ordinary share (of 10p)—1·22p on 31 Mar. 1983 and 0·09352p on 26 Feb. 1985. Distributions per preference share (of £1): 50p on 12 May 1972 and 50p (final) together with arrears of dividend on 14 Apr. 1975 ...... **1986–7**

Darwin Investment Trust Ld. Regd. 1910 as Mount Darwin Gold Mining Syndicate Ld.; name changed 1924. Struck off Register Feb. 1935 ...... **1935**

Darwins Ld. Regd. 1926. Court Order to wind up 19 July 1927. Undertaking acquired by company of same name (later Darwins Group Ld.). Liquidator released 21 May 1931. Struck off Register 13 Apr. 1934 ...... **1928**

Darymusu (West Coast) Development Co. Ld. Regd. 1910. Vol. liq. (members') 15 Dec. 1941. Capital returned to contributories—12⅙d. per share of £1. £541 18s. 7d. was paid into Companies' Liquidation Account. Final meeting return regd. 17 Nov. 1943 **1945**

Date Coffee Co. Ld. Regd. 1879. Court Orders: to wind up 18 Nov. 1882: to dissolve 14 Nov. 1895 ...... **1883**

Davenière & Co. Ld. Regd. 1890. Vol. liq. 16 Mar. 1922. Capital returned to contributories—£5 per preference share of £10; further payments (if any) not known. Final meeting return regd. 17 Aug. 1929 **1923**

Daventry Gas Co. Ld. Regd. 1859 as Daventry Gas & Coke Co. Ld. Dissolved 1 May 1949 undertaking being vested in East Midland Area Gas Board under Gas Act 1948. Holders of ordinary shares (of £10) were entitled to receive £31 16s. British Gas 3% guaranteed stock 1990–95 for each share held **1952**

Davey, Paxman & Co. Ld. Regd. 1898. Business and assets were acquired by Davey Paxman & Co. (Colchester) Ld. (later Davey Paxman and Co. Ld.). Court Order to wind up 27 June 1932. Liquidator released 30 Nov. 1934. Struck off Register 15 June 1937 ...... **1933**

Davidson, Laroche & Partners Ld. Regd. 1923. Struck off Register July 1932 ...... **1933**

Davidson Steamship Co. Ld. See Grampian Steamship Co. Ld.

Davidson (Trafford Park) Ld. Regd. 1920. Vol. liq. (creditors') 3 Feb. 1930. Debenture holders received 1s. 2·965d. in £. No capital returned to contributories. Final meeting return regd. 23 Dec. 1931 ...... **1930**

David S. Smith (Packaging) Ld. See Smith (David S.) (Packaging) Ld.

Davies & Evans Ld. Regd. 1895. Removed from Register 1903 ...... **1903**

Davies Bottled Fruits Ld. Regd. 1934. Vol. liq. (members') 29 Dec. 1942. Assets were acquired by Wm. P. Hartley Ld. Capital returned to contributories—7s 0·32d. per share of 5s. £1,162 13s. 7d. was paid into Companies' Liquidation Account. Final meeting held 6 Mar. 1944 ...... **1945**

VOL. FOR

Davies Bros. (Timber & Joinery) Ld. Undertaking and assets were acquired in 1928 by Davies Bros. (Timber & Joinery) 1928 Ld. for £15,000 cash and 750,000 fully-paid shares **1929**

Davies Bros. (Timber & Joinery) 1928 Ld. Regd. 1928. Vol. liq. (members') 14 Dec. 1932, Capital returned to contributories—1s. 6d. per ordinary share of 3s. Final meeting return regd. 19 Mar. 1934 .... **1933**

Davies Buluwayo Syndicate Ld. Regd. 1895. Removed from Register 1902 .... **1900**

Davies (D.) & Sons Ld. Regd. 1890. Vol. liq. (members') 16 Feb. 1937. All shares were owned by Powell Duffryn Associated Collieries Ld. (later Powell Duffryn Ld.), which company acquired the undertaking. Capital returned to contributories—£892,299 6s. 7d. £330 7s. 1d. was paid into Companies' Liquidation Account. Final meeting return regd. 1 July 1937 .... **1938**

Davies (D. M.) (Holloway) Ld. Undertaking and assets were acquired in 1928 by Davies (D. M.) Woodwork Ld., for £25,000 in cash and 500,000 fully-paid shares of 2s. **1930**

Davies (D. M.) (Slough), Ld. Regd. 1936. Court Order to wind up 18 Mar. 1940. Liquidator released on 15 Sept. 1941. Receiver appointed 6 Apr. 1939 and ceased to act 5 Apr. 1946. No capital returned to contributories. Struck off Register 25 Feb. 1947.... **1946**

Davies (D. M.) Woodwork Ld. Regd. 1929. Court Order to wind up Apr. 1931. Struck off Register 1 Sept. 1936 .... **1937**

Davies' (M. C.) Karri & Jarrah Co. Ld. Regd. 1897. Undertaking and assets were acquired in 1901 by Millars' Karri and Jarrah Co. Ld. (later Millars' Timber and Trading Co. Ld.). Debenture holders were entitled to an equal amount of debentures in new company. Holders of preference or ordinary shares were entitled to 17s. in preference shares or 11s. 2d. in ordinary shares respectively for each share held. Removed from Register 1905 .... **1905**

Davies Selukwe Development Co. Ld. Regd. 1900. Vol. liq. Oct. 1907 for amalgamation with Rhodesia Matabeleland Development Co. Ld., in which company shareholders were entitled to 1 fully-paid share of £1 for every 20 shares of £1 held. Removed from Register 1911 .... **1908**

Davis (H. & C.) & Co. Ld. Regd. as private company 22 Jan. 1987; converted into public company 5 Oct. 1948. Vol. liq. (creditors') 20 Apr.1979. Dissolved 24 Jan. 1985 .... **1984–5**

Davis & Frost Ld. Regd. 1946. Vol. liq. (creditors') 28 Apr. 1958. Final meeting return regd. 18 Oct. 1961 **1962**

Davis Entertainments (Croydon) Ld. Regd. 1927 as Davis Theatre (Croydon) Ld.; name subsequently changed. Vol. liq. (members') 27 July 1951. Final meeting return regd. 25 Feb. 1953...................... **1947**

Davis (S.) Sons & Goodbody Ld. Regd. Dublin 1896. Business was transferred to Henry Pattison & Co. Ld. **1900**

Davis Theatre (Croydon) Ld. *See* Davis Entertainments (Croydon) Ld.

Davis's Wharf Estates Ld. Regd. 1897. Vol. liq. 1903. Undertaking was acquired by Leach & Co. Ld. The debentures were to be repaid; a capital return to contributories of £12 per share of £10 was anticipated. Removed from Register 1903 .... **1903**

Davy Gravure Ld. Regd. 1932. Court Order to wind up 15 Nov. 1937. Business acquired by Thomas De La Rue & Co. Ld. (later De La Rue Co. Ld.). Liquidator released 21 Nov. 1940. Struck off register 19 Mar. 1965 .... **1942**

Dawes (G. R.) Holdings Ld. Regd. as private company 17 June 1952 as Neville Developments Ld.; converted public company Dec. 1957; name changed to The Neville Group Ld. Oct. 1966 and to present title Nov. 1973. Vol. liq. (members') 9 Dec. 1977. Distributions per ordinary share (of 25p)—£1 in Dec. 1977; 35p in Apr. and 25p in July 1978; 5p in Dec. 1979 and Feb. 1982; 11p in Dec. 1984 and final of 5·38p in Apr. 1985. Amounts paid into Companies' Liquidation Account: £36,507 in respect of unclaimed dividends; £2,468 in respect of unclaimed distributions. Final meeting held and return regd. 24 Mar. 1986 .... **1986–7**

Dawley Gas Co. Ld. Regd. 1905. Vol. liq. (members') 27 July 1936. Undertaking acquired by Iron-Bridge & District Gas Co. Ld., in which company shareholders were entitled to 12 fully-paid ordinary shares of £1 for each share of £12 held. Final meeting return regd. 23 Apr. 1937...................... **1937**

Dawlish Gas & Coke Co. Ld. Regd. 1900. Dissolved 1 May 1949, undertaking being vested in South Western Area Gas Board under Gas Act 1948. Holders of securities were entitled to receive, in respect of each £1 unit held, British Gas 3%

VOL. FOR

guaranteed stock 1990–95 as follows:

	£	s.	d.	
Ord. shares (8% basic)	1	18	6	
5% pref. shares (issued before 1 Jan.1946)	1	2	9	
5% pref. shares (issued since 31 Dec. 1945)...........	1	2	9	
4½% red. pref. shares	1	0	3	**1952**

Dawn Mill (1919) Ld. Regd. 1919. Vol. liq. (members') 10 Oct. 1941. Capital returned to contributories—6s. 3⅜d. per share of 5s. Struck off register 17 Dec. 1954 .... **1955**

Dawson City (Klondyke) & Dominion Trading Corporation Ld. Regd. 1897. Removed from Register 1901 **1901**

Dawson (Dan) Brothers, Ld. Regd. 1889. Removed from Register 17 June 1898 .... *1896**

Dawson, Grand Forks and Stewart River Railway Corporation Ld. Regd. 1904. Vol. liq. 15 Mar. 1916. Final meeting return regd. 13 Apr. 1922 .... **1916**

Dawson (Joseph) (Holdings) Ld. Regd. 1950. Undertaking and assets acquired by Dawson International Ld. in June 1974, in which company shareholders received same number and class of shares. All liabilities in respect of loan capital assumed by Dawson International Ld. Company will be dissolved without winding up under Section 108 of Companies Act 1948 .... **1974-5**

Day & Martin Ld. Regd. 1899 as Day & Martin (1899) Ld.; name changed Apr. 1899. Vol. liq. 2 Sept. 1925. Undertaking acquired by Carr & Day & Martin Ld. Final meeting return regd. 20 Dec. 1926 .... **1925**

Day Dawn & Norfolk Mines Ld. Regd. 1904. Reconstructed 1907 as New Day Dawn & Norfolk Mines Ld., in which company shareholders were entitled to 1 share of £1 (credited with 17s. paid) for each share of £1 held. Removed from Register 1908 .... **1908**

Day Dawn Block & Wyndham Gold Mining Co. Ld. Regd. 1886. Vol. liq. June 1909. Capital returned to contributories—2s. 8½d. per share of £1 at Nov. 1910; further payments (if any) not known. Removed from Register 1911 .... **1911**

Day Dawn 8 & 9 Gold Mining Co. Ld. Regd. 1887. Vol. liq. 13 Nov. 1890. Struck off Register 3 Sept 1918 **1891**

Day Dawn P.C. Gold Mines Ld. Regd. 1906. Vol. liq. 13 Nov. 1914. Final meeting return regd. 12 Oct. 1916 **1915**

Day Dawn P.C. Gold Mining Co. Ld. Regd. 1887. Vol. liq. 4 July 1906. Reconstructed as Day Dawn P. C. Gold Mines Ld., in which company shareholders were entitled to 1 share of 10s. (credited with 8s. paid) for every 2 shares of £1 held. Final meeting return regd. 21 Mar. 1907 .... **1908**

Day (T.) & Co. Ld. Regd. 1888. Struck off Register 1929 *1927**

Daylesford Gold Mines Ld. Regd. 1903. Vol. liq. Feb. 1911. Removed from Register 1911 .... **1911**

Dayton Coal & Iron Co. Ld. Regd. 1897. Struck off Register 1927 .... *1925**

De Beers Mining Co. Ld. Inc. Cape of Good Hope 1881. Reconstructed 1888 as De Beers Consolidated Mines Ld., in which company shareholders were entitled to 2 shares of £5 (credited as fully-paid) for each share of £10 held. The 7% 2nd mortgage debentures were redeemed at 104% on 1 Nov. 1888 and the 7% 1st mortgage debentures at 104% on 1 Feb. 1889 .... **1888**

De Berhams, Ld. Regd. 1922 as Deberhams Ld.; name changed June 1928. Vol. liq. (members') 31 Mar. 1958. Final meeting return regd. 17 Nov. 1962..... **1939**

De Bruyn Ld. Regd. 1912. Vol. liq. 24 Sept. 1924. Undertaking acquired by company of same name. Final meeting return regd. 21 Apr. 1925 .... **1925**

De Dion-Bouton Motor Cab Co. Ld. Regd. 1908. Vol. liq. 3 Jan. 1912. Struck off Register 24 July 1923 **1912**

De Dion-Bouton (1907) Ld. Regd. 1907. Vol. liq. 10 Apr. 1919. Assets sold to Langham Steel Co. Ld. for consideration sufficient to provide 15s. in cash and 5s. in shares of purchasing company for each ordinary share of £1 held and one share of £1 for every 20 deferred shares of 1s. held. Final meeting return regd. 1 Feb. 1922. Court Order declared dissolution void 20 Nov. 1922. Final meeting return regd. 6 Nov. 1924 .... **1919**

De Faye (Yvonne) Ld. *See* Kell (Josephine) Ld.

De Ferranti (S. Z.). Regd. 1890. Business was acquired in 1901 by Ferranti Ld. **1905**

De Forrest Phonofilms Ld. Regd. 1923. Court Order to wind up 3 Nov. 1930. Undertaking acquired by British Talking Pictures Ld. Liquidator released 17 Dec. 1932. Struck off Register 15 Oct. 1935........ **1938**

De Jersey & Co. Ld. Regd. 1913. Vol. liq. (creditors') 11 Feb. 1930. Amount paid into Companies' Liquidation Account £254. Struck off Register 30 Aug. 1968 **1956**

De Kaap Gold Mines Ld. Regd. 1889. Court Order to wind up 30 Jan. 1892. Removed from Register 1906 **1893**

See Stock Exchange Year-Book.

VOL. FOR

De Keyser's Royal Hotel Ld. Regd. 1897. Vol. liq. 13 Aug. 1920. Capital returned to contributories—20*s*. per preference share of £1; 2*s*. 6*d*. per ordinary share of £1 at 16 Dec. 1920; further payments (if any) not known. Final meeting return regd. 3 June 1921 ... **1921**

De Lamar Co. Ld. Regd. 1901. Struck off Register Oct. 1934 ... **1935**

De Lamar Mining Co. Ld. Regd. 1891. Reconstructed 1901 as De Lamar Co. Ld., in which company shareholders were entitled to 1 fully-paid share of £1 for every 5 shares of £1 held. Removed from Register 1904 ... **1908**

De Lavaud Free-Wheel Differential Ld. Regd. 1929. Vol. liq. (creditors') 30 Dec. 1932. No capital returned to contributories. Final meeting return regd. 2 Apr. 1938 ... **1933**

De Mare Incandescent Gas Light System Ld. Regd. 1895. Removed from Register 1902 ... **1897**

De Mello Brazilian Rubber Co. Ld. Regd. 1906. Vol. liq. 17 Dec. 1924. Final meeting return regd. 13 Mar. 1925 ... **1925**

De Trey & Co. Ld. Regd. 1911. Vol. liq. 18 Dec. 1924. Undertaking and assets were acquired by Amalgamated Dental Co. Ld., in which company shareholders were entitled to 5 5½% preference shares and 1 preferred ordinary share of £1, all fully-paid for every 5 preference shares of £1 held or 2 5½% preference and 9 preferred ordinary shares of £1 and 7 deferred ordinary shares of 5*s*. for every 11 ordinary shares of £1 held. Final meeting return regd. 27 Nov. 1931 ... **1925**

De Vries (H.) & Boutigny Ld. *See* Union Corporation of Egypt Ld.

De Vries Industrial Diamonds Ld. Regd. 1963. Receiver appointed June 1965. Ceased to act Apr. 1972. Winding-up order 4 Oct. 1965. Dissolved 21 Mar. 1978 ... **1977-8**

Deakin (James) & Sons Ld. Regd. 1897. Struck off the Register 14 Dec. 1951 ... **1940**

Deal & Walmer Coalfield Ld. Regd. 1910. Vol. liq. (members') 1 Dec. 1942. No capital returned to contributories. Final meeting return regd. 23 Feb. 1944 ... **1945**

Deal & Walmer Gas Co. Inc. as Deal & Walmer Gas Co. by Special Act 1864; name changed to Deal & Walmer Gas & Electricity Co. 1914 and as above in 1925. Dissolved 1 May 1949, undertaking being vested in South Eastern Area Gas Board under Gas Act 1948. Holders of securities were entitled to receive British Gas 3% guaranteed stock 1990–95 as follows in respect of each £100 unit of security held:

	£	s.	d.
Ord. stock (5% stand.) ...	120	0	0
4% red. pref. stock ...	100	10	0
5% red. deb.stock ...	107	15	0

1952

Deal Waterworks Co. Inc. by Special Act 1840. In liquidation in 1899, the undertaking having been transferred to the local authorities of Deal and Walmer on 24 Dec. 1897 ... **1899**

Dean (A. R.) Ld. Regd. 1896. Vol. liq. 1903. Removed from Register 1911 ... **1904**

Dean Shipping Co. Ld. Regd. 1919. Vol. liq. 28 July 1925. Final meeting return regd. 17 Mar. 1926 ... **1926**

Deanhead Light Railway Co. Inc. (under Light Railways Act 1896) by Order of Light Railways Commissioners, confirmed by Board of Trade 1902. No capital had been raised at 31 Dec. 1905 ... **1907**

Deansgate Foundry Ld. Regd. 1899. Vol. liq. (members') 1 Oct. 1935. Undertaking and certain assets were acquired by Bennis Combustion Ld., for £15.500 in cash. Capital returned to contributories—£7,889 to preference shareholders; £7,232 to ordinary shareholders. Final meeting return regd. 25 Sept. 1937 **1936**

Dear & Co. Ld. Regd. 1886. Vol. liq. 27 Feb. 1888. Final meeting return regd. 4 Apr. 1892 ... **1889**

Dearne Valley Railway Co. Inc. by Special Act 1897. In 1922 the undertaking was merged into the London & North Western Railway Co. in which company stockholders were entitled to stock as follows:

For each £100 held	*L. & N.W.*
4% Debenture ...	£133 6*s*. 8*d*. 3% Debenture
Ordinary ...	£100 cash

Dearne Valley Stocks held by the North Western Company were cancelled ... **1924**

Deary & Co. Ld. Regd. 1899. Vol. liq. 1903 for sale of undertaking and assets to Rhodesia Cold Storage & Trading Co. Ld. (later Rhodesia Trading Co. Ld.). Removed from Register 1905 ... **1904**

Debenham Securities Ld. Regd. 1926. Undertaking and assets were acquired by Debenhams Ld., in which company shareholders were entitled to 4 ordinary shares of 1*s*. for every 3 preference shares of £1 held or 1 ordinary share of 1*s*. for every 4 ordinary shares of 5*s*. held. Dissolved under Sec. 154 Companies Act 1929 on 29 Apr. 1934 ... **1934**

Debenture and Capital Investment Trust Ld. Regd. 1873. All capital was owned by Anglo-American Securities Corpn. Ld. Vol. liq. (members') 14 June 1963. Final meeting return regd. 22 Jan. 1965 ... **1961**

Debenture Corporation Founders' Share Co. Ld. Regd. 1889. Vol. liq. June 1919. Final meeting return regd. 18 Nov. 1919 ... **1920**

Debenture Guarantee & Investment Co. Ld. Regd. 1887. Removed from Register 1906 ... **1898**

Decatur Mines Syndicate Ld. Regd. 1892. Removed from Register 1901 ... **1897**

Deccan Gold Fields Development Co. Ld. Regd. 1905. Vol. liq. 18 July 1913. Final meeting return regd. 19 June 1914 ... **1914**

Dee Estates Ld. Regd. 1897. Removed from Register 1910 ... **1903**

Dee Mill Ld. Regd. 1906. Vol. liq. (members') 30 Dec. 1948. The undertaking was acquired by Fine Spinners & Doublers Ld., which company owned all shares. Final meeting return regd. 21 Sept. 1949 . **1950**

Dee Oil Co. Ld. Regd. 1888. Reconstructed 1894 as company of same name. Holders of debenture stock were entitled to an equal amount of fully-paid ordinary shares in new company. Removed from Register 1906 ... **1894**

Dee Oil Co. Ld. Regd. 1894. Vol. liq. (members') 17 Mar. 1933. Undertaking and assets transferred to new company of same name. Shareholders received 1 fully-paid share of £1 in new company *plus* 5*s*. in cash for every 2 ordinary shares of £1 held or 1 fully-paid share of £1 for every 12 deferred shares of £1 held. Final meeting return regd. 16 Nov. 1933 .... **1934**

Deebook Dredging, No Liability. Regd. Victoria 1913. London office closed Mar. 1928 ... **1929**

Deep Leads Electric Transmission Co. Ld. Regd. 1898. Vol. liq. Apr. 1907. Removed from Regtster 1910 **1925**

Deep Level Development Co. Ld. Regd. 1891. In liquidation in 1894, having sold its interests to the Consolidated Deep Levels Ld. Removed from Register 1907 ... **1894**

Deep Level Mines of Charters Towers Ld. Inc. Queensland 1902. London office closed in 1907 ... **1907**

Deep Navigation Collieries Ld. Regd. 1888. Vol. liq. (members') 16 Mar. 1945. All shares were owned by Ocean Coal Co. Ld. Final meeting return regd. 28 Jan. 1946 ... **1946**

Deerlodge Consolidated Mines Ld. Regd. 1907. Vol. liq. Nov. 1909. Removed from Register 1911 ... **1910**

Defries Safety Lamp & Oil Co. Ld. Regd. 1886. Court Orders: to wind up 3 Oct. 1889; to dissolve 24 May 1893 ... **1890**

Dehane Plantations Ld. Regd. 1914. Vol. liq. 21 Sept. 1917. Struck off Register 26 Apr. 1929 ... ***1916**

Del Monte Mines (Mexico) Ld. Regd. 1911. Removed from Register 1919 ... **1913**

Del Rey Tea Co. Ld. Regd. 1909. Vol. liq. 17 Nov. 1921. Final meeting return regd. 10 Feb. 1923 ... **1922**

Dela Rubber Co. Ld. Regd. 1926 as Dela Rubber Shoe Co. Ld.; name changed July 1927. Vol. liq. (members') 25 Aug. 1933. All shares owned by Dunlop Rubber Co. Ld. (later Dunlop Co. Ld.). Final meeting return regd. 24 Aug. 1934 ... **1934**

Delacre's Extract of Beef Co. Ld. Regd. 1881. Court Orders: to wind up July 1883; to dissolve 1 Sept. 1887 ... **1884**

Delagoa Bay & African Express Ld. Regd. 1888. Vol. liq. 22 Jan. 1891. Struck off Register 10 Oct. 1916...... **1892**

Delagoa Bay & East African Railway Ld. Regd. Mar. 1887. Line was seized by Portuguese Government. An award of £950,821 as compensatton was made. Holders of 1st debentures were entitled to lOO% return of principal *plus* 11 years' interest at 4%. English holders of 2nd debentures were entitled to 51¾% return of principal; American holders of 2nd debentures were entitled to 16¾%. Struck off Register 22 Dec. 1903... **1906**

Delagoa Bay Development Corporation Ld. Regd. 1903. Vol. liq. 18 Feb. 1948. Capital returned to contributories—17*s*. 2·457*d*. per ordinary share of 10*s*. and £1 13*s*. 5*d*. per preference share of 5*s*. £61 12*s*. paid into Companies' Liquidation Account. Final meeting return regd. 25 Apr. 1950 ... **1951**

Delagoa Bay Syndicate Ld. Regd. 1902. Removed from Register 1905 ... **1903**

Delahaye & Co. Ld. Regd. 1906. Vol. liq. 5 Aug. 1916. Undertaking and assets were sold to Société des Automobiles Delahaye in which company shareholders were entitled to 1 fully-paid preference share (action privilégiée) of Frs.115 for every 4 preferred ordinary shares of £1 held or 1 fully-paid ordinary share of Frs.115 for every 2 ordinary shares of £1

*See Stock Exchange Year-Book.

See Stock Exchange Year-Book.

VOL. FOR

Denver United Breweries Ld. Regd. 1889. Vol. liq. 3 May 1926, subject to Court supervision of 26 July 1927. No capital returned to contributories. Debenture holders received £19 5s.%. Struck off Register 17 Aug. 1956 1954

Dependable Upholstery Ld. Regd. 1928. Court Order to wind up 20 Nov. 1933. Liquidator released 6 Apr. 1944. Struck off Register 28 Jan. 1940 1934

Deptford Dry Docks Co. Ld. Regd. 1895. Vol. liq. 17 Feb. 1925. Capital returned to contributories—£1 15s. per share of £10 at Sept. 1925; further payments (if any) not known. Final meeting return regd. 21 July 1926 1926

Derby & Ashbourne Light Railway Co. Inc. (under Light Railways Act 1896) by order of Light Railway Commissioners, confirmed by Board of Trade 1902 1903

Derby & Derbyshire Building Trades Mutual Insurance Corporation Ld. Regd. 1898. Vol. liq. 26 Nov. 1926. Undertaking was acquired by Royal Insurance Co. Ld. Final meeting return regd. 1 June 1927 1946

Derby and Derbyshire Banking Co. Ld. Est 1833, and regd. as limited in 1880. In 1898 this bank was amalgamated with the Parr's Bank Ld. 1899

Derby Commercial Bank Ld. Regd. 1868: Vol. liq. 22 Jan. 1890. Taken over by Birmingham and Midland Bank (later Midland Bank Ld.), in which company shareholders were entitled either to 1 share of £60 (credited with £12 10s. paid) for every 3 shares of £20 (£5 paid) held or to £12 10s. per share in cash. Final meeting return regd. 10 June 1891 1890

Derby Dome Wyoming Oil Co. Inc. Wyoming 1921. Reconstructed 1924 as Dallas Dome Wyoming Oilfields Co., in which company shareholders were entitled to 9 priority shares of $1 (credited with 75c. paid) and 1 fully-paid deferred share of 11 for each share of $5 held 1925

Derby Gas Light & Coke Co. Estd. 1820; inc. by Special Act 1852. Dissolved 1 May 1949, undertaking being vested in East Midland Area Gas Board under Gas Act 1948. Holders of securities were entitled to receive, in respect of each £100 unit held, British Gas 3% guaranteed stock 1990–95 as follows:

	£	s.	d.
Cons. stock (5% stand.)	140	10	0
5% pref. stock	115	0	0
4% perp. deb. stock	103	0	0
4% red. deb. stock	103	0	0

.... 1952

Derby Lamp Works Ld. Regd. 1914. Struck off Register 1922 1921

Derby Tramways Co. Ld. Regd. 1877. Undertaking acquired 1 Jan. 1899 by Corporation of Derby for £32,000 under Derby Corporation Tramways, &c. Act 1899. Vol. liq. 26 Sept. 1899. Final meeting return regd. 21 Mar. 1902 1900

Derbyshire & Nottinghamshire Electric Power Co. Inc. by Special Act 1901. All share and debentures were owned by Midland Counties Electric Supply Co. Ld. Dissolved 1 Apr. 1948, undertaking being vested in the British (later Central) Electricity Authority and East Midlands Area Board under the Electricity Act 1947. Holders of 4% debentures were entitled to receive British Electricity 3% guaranteed stock (1968—73), as follows—£104 10s. stock for each £100 debenture issued on or before 8 Nov. 1946 and £100 stock for each £100 debenture issued after 8 Nov. 1946 1949

Derbyshire Mining & Exploration Ld. Regd. 1923. Struck off Register Feb. 1931 1931

Dereenalomane Barytes Mines Ld. Regd. 1907. Vol. liq. 9 Apr. 1914 for reconstruction as Dunmanus Bay Barytes Co. Ld. in which company shareholders were entitled to 3 preferred ordinary shares of £1 (credited with 14s. paid) for every 4 preference shares of £1 held, or 3 ordinary shares of £1 (credited with 14s. paid) for every 4 ordinary shares of £1 held. Final meeting return regd. 23 July 1915 1915

Derek's Tin Mines Ld. Regd. 1920. Receiver appointed 16 Feb. 1925. Struck off Register Apr. 1929 1930

D'Eresby & Gwydyr Mines Ld. Regd. 1890. Removed from Register 1904 1892

D'Eresby Mining Co. Ld.. Regd. 1884. Reconstructed 1890 as D'Eresby & Gwydyr Mines Ld. in which company shareholders were entitled to 1 share of £1 (credited with 17s. paid) for each share of £1 held. Removed from Register 1906 1891

Dermatine Co. Ld. Regd. 1889. Reconstructed 1891 as company of same name. Shareholders were entitled to 1 share of £5 (credited with £4 10s. paid) in new company for each share of £5 held. Removed from Register 1906 1906

Dermatine Co. Ld. Regd. 1891. Reconstructed 1906 as company of same name. Shareholders were entitled to 5 preference shares of £1 in new company for every 4 preference shares of £1 held or 1 ordinary

VOL. FOR

share of 10s. for each deferred share of £1 held. Removed from Register 1907 1908

Dermatine Co. Ld. Regd. 1906. Winding-up order 16 Dec. 1957. No capital returned to contributories. Liquidator released 19 Nov. 1966. Struck off Register 13 June 1969 1968

Derry Central Railway Co. Inc. by Special Act 1875. Under Belfast and Northern Counties Railway Co. Act 1901 the undertaking was acquired by that company for £105.000 in cash 1902

Derry City & County Railway Co. Inc. by Special Act 1892. Abandoned by Special Act 1895 1896

Derwen Shipping Co. Ld. Regd. 1925. Vol. liq. (creditors') 15 June 1933. No capital returned to contributories. Final meeting return regd. 6 Mar. 1944 1934

Desang Co. Ld. Regd. 1896. Vol. liq. 8 June 1921. Property and assets were acquired by Jorehaut Tea Co. Ld., in which company shareholders were entitled to 7 shares of £1 (credited as fully-paid) for each share of £10 held. Final meeting return regd. 31 May 1922 1922

Desborough Gas Co. Ld. Regd. 1884. Dissolved 1 May 1949, undertaking being vested in East Midland Area Gas Board under Gas Act 1948. Holders of ordinary shares (of £5) were entitled to receive £8 15s. British Gas 3% guaranteed stock 1990—95 for each share held 1952

Desford Coal Co. Ld. Regd. 1900. Vol. liq. (members') 7 Mar. 1951, the collieries, &c. having vested in National Coal Board. Capital returned to contributories—£3 17s. 6d. per share of 10s. Final meeting return regd. 5 Oct. 1955 1957

Desirable Proprietary Gold Mines (W.A.) Ld. Regd. 1898. Vol. liq. 19 Apr. 1900. Final meeting return regd. 10 June 1901 1910

Dessolle Electro Plating Co. Ld. Regd. 1901. Removed from Register 1906 1904

Detachable Pneumatic Tyre Syndicate Ld. Regd. 1894. Court Order to wind up 11 Jan. 1900. Removed from Register 1908 1900

Detroit Breweries Ld. *See* Goebel Brewing Co. Ld.

Detroit, Grand Haven & Milwaukee Railway Co. Chartered Michigan 1878. The outstanding 6% equipment mortgage bonds and consolidated mortgage bonds were redeemed in Nov. 1920 at 101% 1920

Deucher (James) Ld. Regd. 1898. In Sept. 1959 company was amalgamated with Newcastle Breweries Ld., which already owned all ordinary capital. Debenture stockholders received £50 4% and £55 4½% Newcastle debenture stock for every £100 4% perpetual 1st mortgage debenture stock held and £103 4¾% debenture stock for every £100 4½% redeemable mortgage A debenture stock held, and preference shareholders received equivalent amounts of Newcastle 5½% 2nd preference shares. Company was dissolved on 1 Oct. 1959 1961

Deutsche Grammophon Aktiengesellschaft. Inc. Germany 1895 as Polyphonwerke A.G.; name changed Sept. 1932 1938

Devala-Moyar Gold Mining Co. Ld. Regd. 1880. Vol. liq. 25 Aug. 1890. Reconstructed as New Devala-Moyar Gold Mining Co. Ld., in which company shareholders were entitled to 1 share of 10s. (credited with 8s. paid) for each share of £1 held. Final meeting return regd. 21 May 1891 1892

Devala-Provident Gold Mining Co. Ld. Regd. 1880. In 1886 the properties were acquired by Mysore-Wynaad Consolidated Gold Mining Co. Ld. Shareholders had option of taking up shares of £1 (credited with 15s. paid) in new company on payment of 1s. per share. Removed from Register 1905 1883

Devalah Central Gold Mines Co. Ld. Regd. 1880. Vol. liq. Mar. 1884. Court Order to continue winding up under supervision Mar. 1884. Final meeting return regd. 17 Apr. 1885 1885

Devas, Routledge Holdings Ld. Regd. 1878 as Devas Routledge & Co. Ld.; name changed Feb. 1964. Vol. liq. (members') 29 Jan. 1965. Shareholders received £5 ordinary stock of Spencer, Turner & Boldero Ld., for every 7 shares (of £1) held plus 17s. 6·48d. per share. Amount paid into Companies' Liquidation Account—unclaimed dividends: £104 18s.; distributions: £65 16s. Final meeting return regd. 25 Oct. 1965 1966

Development & Exploration Co. Ld. Regd. 1897 as Industrial and Exploration Co. Ld.; name changed 1901. It was stated in Sept. 1908 that company had no assets. Struck off Register 1918 1909

Development & Finance Co. Ld. Regd. 1895. Vol. liq. May 1907. Removed from Register 1910 1908

Development Co. of Santa Fé Ld. Regd. 1909. Vol. liq. 30 Mar. 1921. Capital returned to contributories—£1 per share of £1 at 30 Mar. 1921; further payments (if

VOL. FOR

any) not known. Final meeting return regd. 24 Nov. 1927 .... **1922**

Development Corporation of East Africa Ld. Regd. 1919. Vol. liq. (members') 26 Feb. 1940. Capital returned to contributories—9·28704*d*. per share of £1. Final meeting return regd. 3 Oct. 1940 .... **1941**

Devitt & Moore Ld. Regd. 1921. Vol. liq. (members') 2 Aug. 1935. Capital returned to contributories—£1 7*s*. 3*d*. per share of £1. Final meeting return regd. 30 Apr. 1936 .... **1936**

Devon & Cornwall Banking Co. Ld. Established 1832. Regd. as unlimited 1875 and as limited 1884. Vol. liq. 16 Feb. 1906. Undertaking was acquired in 1906 by Lloyds Bank Ld., in which company shareholders were entitled to 3 shares of £50 (credited with £8 paid) for each share of £100 (£20 paid) held. Final meeting return regd. 31 Dec. 1908. Removed from Register 1909 .... **1907**

Devon & Cornwall Central Railway Co. Under Act of 1884 company was dissolved and powers were transferred to Plymouth, Devonport and South Western Junction Railway Co. **1885**

Devon & Cornwall Dairy Farm Co. Ld. Regd. 1881. Removed from Register 1906 .... **1884**

Devon & Cornwall Electric Light & Power Co. Ld. Regd. 1882. Court Orders: to wind up 24 Aug. 1883; to dissolve 24 July 1891 .... **1884**

Devon & East Cornwall Mines Development Ld. Regd. 1906 as Devonshire Mines Ld.; name changed. Vol. liq. Mar. 1912. Removed from Register 1913.... **1913**

Devon & Somerset Railway Co. Inc. by Special Act 1864. Undertaking sold to Great Western Railway Co., in 1901 for £12,650 in cash, and the issue of £120, £50 or £2 10*s*. 2½% debenture stock for every £100 "A," "B" or "C" debenture stocks respectively held **1902**

Devon Australasian Syndicate Ld. Regd. 1896. Vol. liq. 28 Mar. 1898. Final meeting return regd. 22 Dec. 1898 .... **1899**

Devon China Clay, Minerals & Railway Ld. Regd. 1911. Struck off Register 1928 .... **1926**

Devon Estates (Malacca) Ld. Regd. 1910. Vol. liq. 15 July 1920 for reconstruction under same name (inc. in Singapore). Shareholders were entitled to $42·50 per share of £1 to be applied in acquiring shares in new company *plus* 2*s*. 6*d*. per share. Final meeting return regd. 8 Oct. 1926 .... **1921**

Devon Estates (Malacca), Ld. Inc. in Straits Settlements 1920. Vol. liq. (members') 10 Apr. 1953. Capital returned to contributories (per share of $4½ Malayan) $3·97375. $18,237·22 paid into Companies' Liquidation Account, $7,086·5 in respect of unclaimed dividends and $11,150·72 in respect of unclaimed distributions. Final meeting return regd. 28 Feb. 1961 .... **1962**

Devon Friendship Mining Co. Ld. Regd. 1880. Vol. liq. 25 Nov. 1885. Final meeting return regd. 9 Mar. 1891 .... ***1885**

Devon Gas Association Ld. Regd. 1906. Dissolved 1 May 1949, undertaking being vested in Southern & South Western Area Gas Boards under Gas Act 1948. Holders of securities were entitled to receive British Gas 3% guaranteed stock 1990—95 as follows in respect of each £10 unit, unless otherwise stated, of security held:

	£	s.	d.
Ord. shares	15	10	0
7½% pref. shares	16	0	0
5% mort. debs. (of £100) (1949)	102	10	0
5% mort. debs. (of £100) (1952)	104	10	0
,, (1953)	105	0	0
,, (1955)	106	10	0

1952

Devon Gawton Co. Ld. Regd. 1894. Removed from Register 1903 .... **1903**

Devon Great Consols Co. Ld. Regd. Truro 1872. Reconstructed 1899 as Devon Great Consols Ld., in which company shareholders were entitled to 4 shares of £1 (credited with 15*s*. paid) for each share of £5 (£2 paid) held. Removed from Register 1903 **1902**

Devon Great Consols Ld. Regd. 1899. Vol. liq. 28 Nov. 1901. Final meeting return regd. 22 Apr. 1903 .... **1902**

Devon Great United Co. Ld. Regd. Truro 1880. Vol. liq. 26 Nov. 1884. Final meeting return regd. 19 Dec. 1885 .... **1885**

Devon Mill Ld. Regd. 1908. Majority of capital was owned by Lily Mills Ld. Vol. liq. (members') 1 Apr. 1966. Struck off Register 21 June 1973 .... **1949**

Devon South Hams Light Railways Co. Inc. (under Light Railways Act 1896) 1905 .... **1910**

Devon United Co. Ld. Regd. Truro 1888. Vol. liq. 5 Aug. 1892. Final meeting return regd. 3 May 1893 .... **1893**

Devon United Mines (1906) Ld. Regd. 1906. Receiver appointed in Apr. 1915. Properties were sold to Cantin Syndicate Ld. Struck off Register 1917 .... **1916**

VOL. FOR

Devonian Gold Mines Ld. *See* Mountain Maid & Iron Prince Gold Mines Ld.

Devonport & District Tramways Co. Inc. by Special Act 1898. Vol. liq. Apr. 1918. Undertaking was acquired by Plymouth Corporation **1919**

Devonport and Tiverton Brewery Co. Ld. Regd. 1876. Vol. liq. 7 June 1923. Capital returned to contributories—20*s*. per preference share of £1; approx. £4 15*s*. per ordinary share of £5 at Oct. 1923; further payments (if any) not known. Final meeting return regd. 2 Jan. 1924 .... **1924**

Devonport Gas & Coke Co. Inc. 1845. Undertaking transferred to local Corporation under Act of 1901 **1902**

Devonport Water Co. Inc. by Act 1793. Undertaking transferred to local Corporation in June 1906. under Act of 1902 .... **1907**

Devonshire House Ld. Regd. 1925. All capital was owned by United City Property Trust Ld. Dissolved under section 208 of Companies Act, 1948 on 28 July 1955 .... **1950**

Dewar (D.), Son & Sons Ld. Regd. 1872. Removed from Register 1904 .... ***1886**

Dewars & Bournes Ld. Regd. 1886. Vol. liq. 18 June 1888. Court Order to continue winding up under supervision Aug. 1888. Final meeting return regd. 10 Apr. 1900 .... **1889**

Dewar's Matabele Reefs Ld. Regd. 1897. Struck off Register 2 Aug. 1904 .... **1906**

Dewhurst (Geo. & R.) Ld. Regd. 1898. Vol. liq. 15 Mar. 1920. Undertaking and assets acquired by Geo. & R. Dewhurst (1920) Ld. (later Geo. & R. Dewhurst Ld.) in which company shareholders were entitled to 14²⁄₇ ordinary shares of £1 for each ordinary share of £10 held or 10 preference shares of £1 for each preference share of £10 held. Final meeting return regd. 17 Nov. 1920 .... **1921**

Dewsbury, Batley & Birstal Tramways Co. Ld. Regd. 1872. Vol. liq. 4 Dec. 1905. Undertaking was acquired by local authorities. Removed from Register 1906.... **1906**

Dewsnap (James) Ld. Regd. 1895. Vol. liq. (members') 5 Nov. 1941. Final meeting return regd. 27 Oct. 1950 **1947**

Dharwar Gold Mines Ld. Regd. 1902. Vol. liq. 3 Jan. 1912. Final meeting return regd. 12 Aug. 1915 .... **1912**

Dharwar Reefs Co. Ld. Regd. 1904. Vol. liq. Apr. 1908 for reconstruction as Dharwar Reefs Gold Mining Co. Ld., in which company shareholders were entitled to 1 share of £1 (credited with 15*s*. paid) for each share of £1 held. Removed from Register 1910 **1909**

Dharwar Reefs Gold Mining Co. Ld. Regd. 1908. Vol. liq. Dec. 1910. The undertaking was sold to Kabulgitti Gold Mines Ld., in which company shareholders were entitled to 1 ordinary share of 5*s*. (credited as fully-paid) for each share of £1 held. Removed from Register 1912. .... **1912**

Dhendai Tea Co. Ld. Regd. 1904. Vol. liq. 25 June 1947. Capital returned to contributories—£3 3*s*. 5$\frac{15}{16}$*d*. per share of £1. Final meeting return regd. 1 Oct. 1952 **1953**

Diamantfontein Development Syndicate Ld. Regd. 1911. Struck off Register Apr. 1929 .... **1930**

Diamantino Rubber Planatations Ld. Regd. 1910. Court Order to wind up 5 June 1912. Liquidator released 12 May 1916. Struck off Register 14 Feb. 1919 ... **1913**

Diamond Cycle Components & Engineering Co. Ld. Regd. 1897. Business was acquired in 1902 by New Hudson Cycle Co. Ld. (later Girling Ld.), in which company shareholders were entitled to 1 B preference share of £1 for each preference share held or 1 ordinary share of £1 for every 3 ordinary shares held. All shares were held by nominees of New Hudson Cycle Co. Ld. Removed from Register 1909 .... **1903**

Diamond Exploration and Finance Syndicate Ld. Regd. 1902. Vol. liq. 4 Jan. 1916. Final meeting return regd. 5 July 1921 .... **1916**

Diamond Fields of Africa (D.F.A.) Exploring Co. Ld. Inc. Orange Free State 1920. Wound up 1927 .... **1928**

Diamond Fuel Co. Ld. Regd. 1873. Wound up by Order of Court 10 June 1879 .... ***1878**

Diamond Hill Gold Mines Ld. Regd. Edinburgh 1896. Court Orders: to wind up Dec. 1897; to dissolve 29 Mar. 1901 .... **1899**

Diamond Hill Gold Mines Ld. Regd. Edinburgh 1898. Vol. liq. Mar. 1908. Final meeting return regd. 28 Mar. 1947 .... **1947**

Diamond Match Co. Ld. Regd. 1897. Undertaking was acquired by Bryant & May Ld., in which company shareholders were entitled to 1 deferred share of £1 for each ordinary share of £1 held. The preference shareholders were entitled to 16,000 preference shares of £5. Removed from Register 1907 .... **1902**

"Diamond" Moss Peat Works Ld. Regd. 1889. Struck off Register 14 May 1897 .... **1899**

Diamond Proprietary Mines Ld. Regd. 1910. Vol. liq. (members') 23 May 1939. Shareholders were entitled

VOL. FOR

to 5 shares of 2s. (credited with 1s. per share paid) in Vaal River Diamond Co. Ld. (regd. May 1939) for every 2 shares of 5s. held. Final meeting return regd. 8 Dec. 1939 .... **1940**

Diamond Rock Boring Co. Ld. Regd. 1872. Vol. liq. Jan. 1879. Reconstructed as Aqueosis Works & Diamond Rock-Boring Co. Ld. Final meeting return regd. 26 Aug. 1879 .... **1890**

Diamond Stone Working Co. Ld. Regd. 1898. Removed from Register 1903 .... **1903**

Diamondfontein Estates Ld. Regd. 1895. Removed from Register 1903 .... **1902**

Diana Mine Ltd. Regd. 1913. Struck off Register 1921 **1921**

Diaz Mines Ld. Regd. 1902. Undertaking was acquired in May 1903 by Parral Mines Ld. in which company shareholders were entitled to 1 fully-paid share for each share held. Removed from Register 1904 .... **1904**

Dick, Kerr & Co. Ld. Regd. 1890. Vol. liq. 24 Aug. 1899. Reconstructed as company of same name. Shareholders were entitled to 2 fully-paid ordinary shares of £1 in new company for each ordinary share of £5 held or to 3 fully-paid preference shares of £5 held. Holders of debentures were entitled either to £103 in cash or in 4% debenture stock in new company. Final meeting return regd. 21 Dec. 1900 .... **1908**

Dick, Kerr & Co. Ld. Regd. 1899. Vol. liq. 21 Oct. 1919. Shareholders who did not accept exchange into equal amount of similar shares in English Electric Co. Ld., were entitled to 20s. per preference share of £1 or 30s. per ordinary share of £1. The debentures were to be repaid. Final meeting return regd. 2 July 1927 .... **1920**

Dickbalata Ld. Regd. Edinburgh 1919. Vol. liq. 15 Jan. 1927. Controlling interest held by R. & J. Dick. Ld. Final meeting return regd. 29 Dec. 1931 .... **1928**

Dickella (Ceylon) Rubber Estate Ld. Regd. 1909. Vol. liq. (members') 17 Dec. 1946 company's estate having been sold to Ceylon Government. Capital returned to contributories—£2 5s. 10·711d. (per share of £1). Final meeting return regd. 5 July 1951 **1952**

Dicken Green Mill (1919). Regd. 1919. Struck off Register 29 June 1946 .... **1941**

Dickens (Charles) Mining Co. Ld. See Charles Dickens Mining Co. Ld.

Dickens Custer Co. Ld. Regd. 1887. Vol. liq. Mar. 1889. Reconstructed as Dickens Custer Mines Ld., in which company shareholders were entitled to 1 share of £1 (credited with 16s. 6d. paid) for each share of £1 held. Final meeting return regd. 17 Jan. 1890 .... **1898**

Dickens Custer Mines Ld. Regd. 1889. Reconstructed 1898 as company of same name. Shareholders were entitled to 1 share of £1 (credited with 19s. paid) in new company for each share of £1 held. Removed from Register 1904 .... **1904**

Dickens Custer Mines Ld. Regd. 1898. Vol. liq. 30 Nov. 1905. Removed from Register 1907 .... **1906**

Dickeson (Richard) & Co. Ld. Regd. 1901. Vol. liq. 30 May 1918. Final meeting return regd. 17 July 1923 **1919**

Dickson and Benson, Ld. Regd. 1900. Vol. liq. (members') 18 Mar. 1963. All capital was owned by Great Universal Stores Ld. Final meeting return regd. 11 Mar. 1964 .... **1960**

Dickson & Mann Ld. Reg'd Edinburgh 1892. Vol. liq. (creditors') 15 Apr. 1969. No capital return. £290.86 paid to Accountant of the Court. Final meeting return regd.20 Feb. 1975 .... **1975-6**

Dickwella Tea Syndicate Ld. Regd. 1911. Vol. liq. 17 Dec. 1920. Undertaking acquired by Dickwella Tea Co. Ld. (later Dickwella Holdings Ld.). Final meeting return regd. 16 Feb. 1921 .... *****1920**

Didcot & Watlington Light Railway Co. Inc. (under Light Railways Act 1896) by order of Light Railway Commissioners confirmed by Board of Trade 1899. No capital had been issued at Nov. 1901 .... **1902**

Didcot, Newbury and Southampton Railway Co. Inc. by Special Act 1873. In 1923 the undertaking was merged into the Great Western Railway Co., in which company stockholders were entitled to stock as follows:

For each £100 held		G.W.R.	
5% Debenture	£100	5% Debenture	
4% Debenture	£100	4% Debenture	
5% Debenture	£100	4% Debenture	
3% Debenture	£50	5% Cons. Pref.	
Cons. Pref.	£15	cash	
Cons. Ord.	£5	cash	**1924**

Diesel Engine Co. Ld. Regd. 1900. Vol. liq. 26 June 1914. Final meeting return regd. 10 Jan. 1925 ..... **1915**

Diesel-Steam Locomotives Ld. Regd. 1920 as Still Engine Co. Ld.; name changed Sept. 1933. Receiver appointed in Aug. 1934. Struck off Register 24 April 1939 .... **1940**

VOL. FOR

Dietz, Davis & Co. Ld. Regd. 1888. Removed from Register 1906 .... **1898**

Dieu-Donné Gold Co. Ld. Regd. 1880. Vol. liq. May 1883. Final meeting return regd. 9 Aug. 1883 ...... **1884**

Digalla Ceylon Tea Estate Co. Ld. Regd. 1896. Vol. liq. Feb. 1911. The undertaking was acquired by Sapumalkande Rubber Co. Ld. for £30,000 in fully-paid shares of £1 and £11,436 in cash; holders of the 600 preference shares were entitled to £10 in cash and 5 fully-paid shares of £1 in purchasing company for each preference share of £10 held; ordinary shareholders were entitled to the balance. Removed from Register 1912 .... **1911**

Digby Colliery Co. Ld. Regd. 1899. Vol. liq. (members') 19 Aug. 1953. Capital returned to contributories—£2 3s. 3·2188d. per A ordinary share of 10d.; 3s. 6·65047d. per B ordinary share of ¼d. Final meeting return regd. 26 Dec. 1955 .... **1957**

Digloy Tea Co. Ld. Regd. 1880. Vol. liq. 20 Dec. 1893. Final meeting return regd. 18 Dec. 1894 .... **1894**

Dillington Cottage Co. Ld. Regd. 1912. Vol. liq. (members') 28 Sept. 1933. A direct controlling interest held by Penrikyber Navigation Colliery Co. Ld. Capital returned to contributories—£4,500. Final meeting return regd. 28 Feb. 1934 .... **1935**

Dillwyn & Co. Ld. Regd. 1902. Vol. liq. 1 Apr. 1926. Final meeting return regd. 24 Jan. 1928 .... **1927**

Dim-Dazzle (Parent) Co. Ld. Regd. 1929. Vol. liq. (creditors') 23 June 1930. Assets realised insufficient to pay creditors in full. Final meeting return regd. 24 Sept. 1932 .... **1931**

Dimplex Industries Ld. Regd. as private company 9 May 1946 as Habin Ld.; name changed to Dimplex Ld. 1950; converted into public company 1959; name changed 1956 .... **1986-7**

Dines, Ld. Regd. 1924. Vol. liq. (creditors') 31 Dec. 1945. No capital returned to contributories. Final meeting return regd. 20 Dec. 1949 .... **1947**

Dingle Picturedome Ld. Regd. 1912. Vol. liq. 2 Aug. 1928. Properties purchased by Denman Picture Houses Ld. Final meeting return regd. 13 Dec. 1928 **1940**

Dingley Dell Estates & Gold Mining Co. Ld. In 1886 the properties were acquired by Mysore-Wynaad Consolidated Gold Mining Co. Ld. Shareholders had option of taking up shares of £1 (credited with 15s. paid) in new company on payment of 1s. per share **1894**

Dinnington Main Coal Co. Ld. Regd. 1900. Vol. liq. (members') 30 Mar. 1949. Final meeting return regd. 28 Dec. 1949 .... **1940**

Dinsdale Smelting Co. Ld. Regd. 1900. Vol. liq. 4 Jan. 1904. Undertaking acquired by Linthorpe Dinsdale Smelting Co. Ld. Final meeting return regd. 28 Apr. 1904 .... *****1904**

Dinsmore Gas Co. Ld. Regd. 1887. Vol. liq. 12 Apr. 1897. Final meeting return regd. 15 Mar. 1898 .... *****1898**

Diorite King Consols Ld. Regd. 1899. Vol. liq. 22 Dec. 1903. Struck off Register 18 Jan. 1921 .... **1903**

Diorite King Gold Mines (W.A.) Ld. Regd. 1896. Reconstructed 1899 as Diorite King Consols Ld., in which company shareholders were entitled to 1 share of £1 (credited with 17s. paid) for each share of £1 held. Removed from Register 1908 .... **1903**

Diphwys Cssson Slate Co. Ld. Regd. 1863. Vol. liq. 22 Jan. 1892. Final meeting return regd. 3 Jan. 1893 **1892**

Direct Fish Supplies Ld. Regd. 1919. Court Order to wind up 28 Mar. 1922. Struck off Register Apr. 1934 **1953**

Direct Home Supply Stores Ld. Regd. 1896. Vol. liq. 3 June 1898. Final meeting return regd. 1 Nov. 1898 **1899**

Direct Produce (London) Ld. Regd. 1929. Vol. liq. (creditors') 11 June 1930. Undertaking and assets were transferred to Direct Stores Ld. Struck off Register 7 Aug. 1945 .... **1946**

Direct Stores Ld. Regd. 1930. Vol. liq. (creditors') 4 Feb. 1931. No capital returned to contributories. Final meeting return regd. 16 May 1931 .... **1931**

Direct Supply Aerated Water Co. See D.A.W.S. Ld.

Direct Tea Supply Association of India & China Ld. Regd. 1882. Vol. liq. 6 Aug. 1890. Final meeting return regd. 9 Feb. 1891 .... *****1885**

Direct United States Cable Co. Ld. Regd. 1877. Vol. liq. 25 May 1923. Capital returned to contributories—£6 18s. 3d. per share of £10 at Oct. 1923; further payments (if any) not known. Final meeting return regd. 19 Oct. 1923 .... **1924**

Direct West India Cable Co. Ld. Regd. 1897. All capital was owned by Cable & Wireless Ld. Vol. liq. (members') 6 Oct. 1966. Final meeting return regd. 7 Dec. 1966 .... **1949**

Direction der Disconto-Gesellschaft. Inc. Berlin 1851. Merged in 1929 with Deutsche Bank (later Deutsche Bank und Disconto-Gesellschaft), in which company shareholders were entitled to 1 share for each share held **1924**

Discount Bank Ld. See London & District Bank Ld.

Discount Banking Co. of England & Wales Ld. Regd. 1891. Vol. liq. 17 June 1895 for reconstruction as Discount Bank Ld. (later London and District Bank Ld.), in which company shareholders were entitled to 1 fully-paid share of £5 for each share of £10 held. Final meeting return regd. 2 Feb. 1897 .... **1901**

Discount Corporation of Ireland Ld. Regd. Dublin 1878. Removed from Register 1904 .... **1895**

Discoverers Finance Corporation Ld. Regd. 1911. Vol. liq. 26 Feb. 1906. Removed from Register 1911 ... **1907**

Disraeli Mine Syndicate Co. Ld. Regd. 1885. Vol. liq. Aug. 1899. Reconstructed as New Disraeli Mines Co. Ld., in which company shareholders were entitled to 1 share of £1 (credited with 18s. paid) for each share of £1 held. Final meeting return regd. 4 Mar. 1890 .... **1890**

Dissolved Acetylene Co. Ld. Regd. 1912. Vol. liq. (members') 16 Oct. 1933. All shares were owned by Allen-Liversidge Ld. No capital returned to contributories. Final meeting return regd. 19 Dec. 1933 **1933**

Distington Hematite Iron Co. Ld. Regd. 1881. Vol. liq. 28 May 1919. Court Order to stay proceedings 13 Dec. 1921. Vol. liq. (members') 9 Dec. 1930. All shares held by United Steel Companies Ld., or nominees. Final meeting return regd. 1 Aug. 1931 **1931**

Distributing Kitchens Ld. Regd. 1900 as Reformed Food (Vegetarian) Co. Ld.; name changed Oct. 1900. Court Order to wind up Jan. 1904. Removed from Register 1910 .... **1904**

District Bank Ld. Constituted as Manchester & Liverpool District Banking Co. by deed of settlement 1 June 1830; regd. as unlimited in 1870 and as limited in 1880; name changed Feb. 1924. From 1 Jan. 1970 the undertaking vested in National Westminster Bank Ld. under provisions of National Westminster Bank Act 1969 which also provided for eventual dissolution of this bank **1971**

District Bank of London Ld. Regd. 1882. Vol. liq. 21 Mar. 1887. Final meeting return regd. 16 May 1889 ***1888**

District Messenger Co. of Paris Ld. Regd. 1893. Vol. liq. 29 Nov. 1894. Final meeting return regd. 1 July 1896 **1895**

District of Chemnitz Tramways Co. Ld. Regd. 1879. Vol. liq. May 1882. Final meeting return regd. 28 Nov. 1882 .... **1883**

Divisadero Gold & Silver Mining Co. Ld. Regd. 1888. Removed from Register 1906 .... **1892**

Dixcove Syndicate Ld. Regd. 1901. Removed from Register 1905 .... **1903**

Dixie Gold Mine Ld. Regd. 1898. Removed from Register 1903 .... **1903**

Dixie Gold Mining Co. Ld. Regd. 1895. Vol. liq. 10 Sept. 1898. Reconstructed as Dixie Gold Mine Ld., in which company shareholders were entitled to subscribe for shares of £1 (credited with 17s. paid). Final meeting return regd. 18 Nov. 1899 .... **1902**

Dixon Investment Co. Ld. Regd. 1885. Vol. liq. (members') 4 Apr. 1949. Final meeting return regd. 9 Oct. 1954 .... **1947**

Dixon (William) Ld. Regd. Edinburgh 1906. Collieries, &c. vested in National Coal Board Jan. 1947. Vol. Liq. (members') 27 May 1952. Capital returned to contributories—£1·34 per stock unit of £0·166. Final meeting return regd. 20 Sept. 1973 .... **1975-6**

Dixon's Iron Works Ld. Regd. Edinburgh 1947. Vol. liq. (members') 3 Mar. 1960. All capital was owned by Colvilles Ld. Final meeting return regd. 1 Feb. 1963 **1956**

Djaboong (Java) Rubber Estates Ld. Regd. 1910. Vol. liq. 12 Oct. 1928. Undertaking and assets were transferred to Java Produce Co. Ld., in which company shareholders were entitled to 1 fully-paid share of £1 for every 2 shares of 5s. held and to subscribe at par for 7% convertible debenture stock. Final meeting return regd. 3 Feb. 1930 .... **1929**

Djambi (Sumatra) Rubber Estates Ld. Regd. 1910. Vol. liq. 10 Apr. 1912. Final meeting return regd. 8 Dec. 1913 .... **1913**

Djapoera Rubber Estates Ld. Regd. 1935. Vol. liq. (members') 17 Dec. 1951. Estates sold for £4,400. Capital returned to contributories—4·6d. per share of 1s. £2,388 12s. 7d. was paid into Companies' Liquidation Account. Final meeting return regd. 4 Nov. 1955 .... **1957**

Djapoera (Sumatra) Rubber Co. Ld. Regd. 1913. Vol. liq. (members') 25 Feb. 1935. Reconstructed as Djapoera Rubber Estates Ld., in which company shareholders were entitled to 1 share of 1s. (credited with 9d. paid) for each share of 2s. held. Final meeting return regd. 8 May 1936 .... **1936**

Djebel Charra Mining Co. Ld. Regd. 1903. Vol. liq. July 1908. Struck off Register 1938 .... **1909**

Djibouti Coal Syndicate Ld. See Société des Charbons de Djibouti Ld.

Dobbin & Cloncurry Mines Ld. Regd. 1914. Under scheme of arrangement sanctioned by the Court on

12 July 1945 the undertaking, property and assets were acquired by Mount Elliott Ld., by an exchange of shares at the rate of 1 fully-paid share of 5s. in Mount Elliott Ld. for every 4 shares of £1 held. The company was dissolved under Sec. 154 of the Companies Act 1929 on 25 July 1945 .... **1946**

Dobbin, Oglivie & Co. Ld. Regd. Dublin 1894. Vol. liq. May 1926 .... **1927**

Dobson & Barlow Ld. Regd. 1907. Vol. liq. 30 June 1923. Reconstructed as Dobson & Barlow Ld. [later Dobson & Barlow (Securities) Ld.]. Shareholders were entitled to 2 fully-paid shares of £1 in new company plus £3 in cash for each ordinary share of £1 held. Preference shareholders received 25s. per preference share of £1. The debenture stock was repaid at 105%. Final meeting return regd. 28 May 1925 .... **1924**

Dobson & Barlow (Securities) Ld. Regd. 1923 as Dobson & Barlow Ld.; name changed 1931 as above. All capital was owned by Capital & Counties Property Co. Ld. Vol. liq. (members') 22 Mar. 1966. Final meeting return regd. 25 Mar. 1959 .... **1968**

Dobson Steam Fishing Co. Ld. Regd. 1920. Vol. liq. May 1931. Struck off Register Jan. 1934 .... **1934**

Docker Brothers Ld. Regd. 1899. Vol. liq. 7 May 1907. Undertaking and assets were acquired by Metropolitan Amalgamated Railway Carriage & Wagon Co. Ld. (later Metropolitan-Cammell Carriage Wagon & Finance Co. Ld.). in which company shareholders were entitled to 11 fully-paid ordinary shares of £1 plus 10s. in cash for each ordinary share of £5 held or 6 fully-paid A preference shares of £1 plus 1s. 3d. in cash for each preference share of £5 held. Removed from Register 1908 .... **1908**

Dockrell (Thomas), Sons and Co. Ld. Regd. Dublin 1890. Reconstructed 1897 as company of same name. Shareholders were entitled to 1 ordinary and 1 preference share of £1 for each ordinary share of £1 held **1897**

Dr. Carl Peters' Estates & Exploration Co. Ld. See South East Africa Ld.

Dr. Tibbles' Vi-Cocoa (1898) Ld. See Watford Manufacturing Co. Ld.

Dodge Brothers Inc. Inc. Maryland 1925. In 1928 the assets were acquired by Chrysler Corporation in which company shareholders were entitled to 1 common share of no par value for every 5 common A shares of no par value held or 10 common B shares of no par value held or 1 preference share of no par value held **1929**

Dodge (Josh. & Robt.) Ld. Regd. 1875. Vol. liq. May 1884. Final meeting return regd. 3 Feb. 1888 ...... **1885**

Dodgson (Henry) Ld. Regd. 1916. Vol. liq. 2 Apr. 1928. Final meeting return regd. 15 Aug. 1928 .... **1934**

Dodgson (Henry) Ld. Regd. 1928 as Henry Dodgson (1928) Ld.; name changed Apr. 1929. Vol. liq. (members') Apr. 1934. Amalgamated with Swears & Wells Ld., in which company shareholders were entitled to 2 preference shares of £1 for every 3 preference shares of 10s. held or 2 ordinary shares of £1 for every 20 ordinary shares of 1s. held. Final meeting return regd. 1 Aug. 1935 .... **1935**

Doeuillet Ld. Regd. 1907. Vol. liq. 17 Sept. 1924. Undertaking and assets were transferred to Maison Doeuillet (inc. France), in which company shareholders were entitled to 1 fully-paid share of Fr. 100 for every 3 ordinary shares of 10s. or 10 deferred shares of 1s. held. Final meeting return regd. 1 July 1926 .... **1925**

Dolcoath Gold Mining Co. Ld. Regd. 1896. Struck off Register 26 Oct. 1900 .... **1901**

Dolcoath Mine. Established 1799. Acquired by company of same name. Shareholders were entitled to 40 shares of £1 for each share of £9 12s.6d. held **1908**

Dolcoath Mine Ld. Regd. 1895. Vol. liq. 27 Apr. 1923. Reconstructed as company of same name. Shareholders were entitled to 1 share of 10s. (credited with 5s. paid) for each ordinary share of £1 held, or 2 fully-paid shares of 10s. for every 20 priority shares of 1s. held. Debenture holders received 2 fully-paid shares of 10s. for each £1 stock held; further shares were allotted in respect of arrears of interest. Final meeting return regd. 16 Feb. 1924 .... **1924**

Dolcoath Mine Ld. Regd. 1923. The assets realised insufficient to meet liability of 1st mortgage debenture. Struck off Register 21 Apr. 1939 .... **1940**

Dolgelly Copper Mines Ld. Regd. 1907. Vol. liq. 23 Dec. 1914. Final meeting return regd. 17 Aug. 1917 .... **1915**

Dolgelly Gas & Coal Co. Ld. Regd. 1895. Dissolved 1 May 1949 undertaking being vested in Wales Area Gas Board under Gas Act 1948. Holders of ordinary shares (of £10) were entitled to receive £10 16s. British Gas 3% guaranteed stock 1990—95 for each share held **1952**

---

*See Stock Exchange Year-Book.

VOL. FOR

Dollar Gas Co. Ld. Regd. in Edinburgh 1924. Dissolved 1 May 1949, undertaking being vested in Scottish Area Gas Board under Gas Act 1948. Holders of shares (of £1) were entitled to receive 15s. British Gas 3% guaranteed stock 1990—95 for each share held 1952

Dollar Gold Mines Ld. Regd. 1895. Vol. liq. 22 May 1900. Final meeting return regd. 7 July 1900 1901

Dolok Rubber Estates Ld. Regd. 1910. Vol. liq. 17 Feb. 1920. Undertaking and assets were acquired by Amalgamated Rubber Estates Ld. (later Amalgamated Rubber & General Estates Ld.), in which company shareholders were entitled to 1 fully-paid share of 2s. for each share of 2s. held. Final meeting return regd. 2 Feb. 1921 1920

Dolores Ld. Regd. 1904. Vol. liq. Feb. 1908. Shareholders were entitled to an equal number of shares of $5 in Dolores Mines Co. of Maine. Removed from Register 1909 1908

Dolphin Hotel and Restaurant Company and Michael Nugent Ld. Inc. 1894. Vol. liq. (members') 22 Feb. 1966 Capital returned to contributories—£5·7085p for every preference and ordinary share of £5. Final meeting return regd. 21 Feb. 1972 1972

Dolphin Square Ld. Regd. 7 Dec. 1936. Vol. liq. (members') 28 Aug. 1963. All capital was owned by Lintang Investments Ld., 3¾% 1st mortgage debenture stock repaid at 96½% May 1963. Final meeting return regd. 13 Apr. 1965 1966

Dolphin's Barn Brick Co. Ld. Regd. Dublin 1896. Vol. liq. July 1912. Undertaking and assets were acquired by Dublin Brick Co. Ld., in which company shareholders were entitled to 5 ordinary shares of £1 for every 4 shares of £1 held. The debentures were redeemed. Removed from Register 1913 1913

Dolter Electric Traction Ld. Regd. 1901. Vol. liq. July 1908. Removed from Register 1913 1909

Domains Co. Ld. Regd. 1903 as Domains Co. of Siberia Ld.; name changed Jan. 1905. Vol. liq. 22 Sept. 1908. Final meeting return regd. 29 Nov. 1911..... 1925

Dome Oil Co. of Wyoming Ld. Regd. 1903. Vol. liq. Apr. 1911. Removed from Register 1912 1911

Dome (Yukon) Gold Mines Ld. Regd. 1901. Vol. liq. 12 Jan. 1905. Capital returned to contributories—2s. 3d. per share of £1 at Feb. 1905; further payments (if any) not known. Removed from Register 1908 1905

Dome (Yukon) Gold Mining Co. Ld. Regd. 1899. Court Order to wind up 5 Dec. 1900. Removed from Register 1910 1901

Domes of Silence Ld. Regd. 1910. Vol. liq. 27 Feb. 1920. Undertaking and assets acquired by Domes of Silence (1920) Ld. in which company shareholders were entitled to one share of 6d. for each share of 5s. held. Final meeting return regd. 26 June 1920...... 1921

Domestic and General Investment Trust, Ld. Regd. 1946. Undertaking and assets were acquired by Scottish Overseas and Commonwealth Investment Trust Ld.; holders received 4 preference shares (of £1) and 15 ordinary shares (of 5s.) for every £8 of stock held. Dissolved on 18 Apr. 1965 under Sect. 208 of Companies Act 1948 1966

Domestic Supplies Ld. Regd. 1930. Vol. liq. (members') 11 Dec. 1936. All capital held by Shaw (John) & Sons, Wolverhampton Ld. Final meeting return regd. 23 June 1937 1937

Domingo Tomba's Estates (Bodegas and Vineyards). Inc. Buenos Aires 1911. The outstanding 6% 1st mortgage debentures were redeemed on 1 Jan. 1938 at 102% 1938

Dominica Forests & Sawmills Ld. Regd. 1911. Vol. liq. 28 Dec. 1923. Final meeting return regd. 25 Aug. 1924 1924

Dominican Gold Mines Ld. Regd. 1895. Removed from Register 29 Aug. 1911 .... *1908

Dominion and General Trust p.l.c. Regd. in Edinburgh 6 Apr. 1910 as Dominion of Canada Investment & Debenture Co. Ld.; name changed Feb.1926; converted public company Oct. 1981. Vol. liq., (members') 23 Aug. 1983. Company unitised, net assets transferred to 4 unit trusts; holders of ordinary shares entitled to elect for units in one or more of Scottish Pacific Fund, Scottish North American Fund Scottish World Growth Fund or Scottish Income Fund; any cash balance remaining on termination of liquidation will be paid to ordinary holders. Ordinary shares of 25p: a first and final distribution of £0·0816p per share paid 30 Apr. 1985. Preference shares repaid at par on 22 Aug. 1983. Debenture stocks repaid at par on 22 Aug. 1983. Amount paid into Accountant of Court: £4,210 in respect of unclaimed dividends; £6,865 in respect of unclaimed distributions. Final meeting held 20 Aug. 1985.................................... 1986—7

VOL. FOR

Dominion Bank. Inc. by Special Act of the Dominion of Canada 1869. In 1955 amalgamated with Bank of Toronto as Toronto-Dominion Bank. Shareholders received 1 share of $10 of the new bank for each share of $10 held 1956

Dominion Brewery Co. Ld. Regd. 1889. Vol. liq. Dec. 1908. Capital returned to bondholders—£55 6s. 7d. per £100 bond. Removed from Register 1910 1909

Dominion Carpet Co. Ld. Regd. 1900. Removed from Register 1905 1904

Dominion Fairview Copper Co. Ld. Regd. 1897 as Dominion Fairview & Golden Klondyke Syndicate Ld.; name changed 1907. Struck off Register 1916 1914

Dominion Gold Mines Ld. Regd. 1912 as Dominion Gold Mines (Rhodesia) Ld.; name changed Apr. 1927. Struck off Register 28 Feb. 1939 1940

Dominion Gold Mining & Reduction Co. Ld. Regd. 1895. Removed from Register 1912 1903

Dominion Gold Mining Association Ld. Regd. 1881. Vol. liq. Nov. 1882. Final meeting return regd. 3 Sept. 1885 1883

Dominion Gramophone Records (Foreign & Colonial) Ld. Regd. 1928. Vol. liq. (creditors') 9 July 1930. No capital returned to contributories. Final meeting return regd. 7 Nov. 1934 1931

Dominion Gramophone Records Ld. Regd. 1928. Court Order to wind up 2 June 1930. Struck off Register 15 June 1937 1938

Dominion Iron & Steel Co. Ld. Inc. Nova Scotia 1899 by Special Act. Undertaking and assets were acquired by Dominion Steel and Coal Corporation Ld., in which company shareholders were entitled to 3 common B shares of $25 for each preferred share of $100 held. Holders of 5% consolidated mortgage bonds were entitled to an equal amount of 6% sterling debenture stock series A plus 10½% in cash 1931

Dominion Mining Development & Agency Co. Ld. Regd. 1896. Vol. liq. 1903. Undertaking was acquired by Dominion Trust Ld., in which company shareholders were entitled to 1 share of £1 (credited with 15s. paid) for each share of £1 held. Debenture holders were entitled to debentures in new company. Removed from Register 1904 1904

Dominion of Canada Freehold Estate & Timber Co. Ld. Regd. 1881. Removed from Register 1906 1887

Dominion of Canada General Insurance. Inc. Canada by Special Act 1887 as Manufacturers' Accident Insurance Co.; name changed to Manufacturers' Guarantee & Accident Insurance Co. in 1893, to Dominion of Canada Guarantee & Accident Insurance Co. in 1898 and as above in 1929. From 30 Apr. 1940 the business carried on in the United Kingdom was transferred to United Kingdom Fire and Accident Insurance Co. 1941

Dominion of Canada Investment & Debenture Co. Ld. See Dominion & General Trust p.l.c.

Dominion of Canada Land & Colonisation Co. Ld. Regd. 1880. Court Orders: to wind up 22 Nov. 1884: to dissolve 27 Nov. 1888 1885

Dominion of Canada Mortgage Co. Ld. Regd. Edinburgh 1886. Vol. liq. (members') 30 June 1938. Capital returned to contributories—£12,018 12s. Final meeting return regd. 1 June 1945 1939

Dominion of Canada Trust Corporation Ld. Regd. Apr. 1910. Vol. liq. Sept. 1914. Court Order to wind up Nov. 1914. Struck off Register 20 Mar. 1925 1915

Dominion Oil Co. Ld. Regd. Feb. 1909. Vol. liq. 1 May 1911. Struck off Register 30 Jan. 1923 1911

Dominion Oilfields Ld. Regd. 1912 as Mediterranean Oilfields Ld.; name changed Aug. 1924. Struck off Register Feb. 1933.. 1933

Dominion Reefs (Klerksdorp) Ld. Regd. 1935. Vol. liq. (members') 25 June 1965. Capital returned to contributories—10s. 5·4d. per share of 5s. Final meeting return regd. 29 Dec. 1966 1968

Dominion Savings & Investment Society. Inc. Canada 1872. Undertaking and assets were acquired by Huron & Erie Mortgage Corporation 1923

Dominion Sawmills & Lumber Ld. Inc. British Columbia 1910. Vol. liq. 1912 for the purpose of reconstruction. Common shareholders were entitled to 6 shares of $1 in Forest Mills of British Columbia Ld. for each share of $100 held; preference shareholders to 4 shares of $1 plus £20 11s. of income debenture stock for each share of $100 held, and debenture holders to £20 in debenture stock plus 3 shares of $1 for each £20 of debentures held 1913

Dominion Steel Corporation Ld. Inc. Nova Scotia 1909 as Canadian Steel Corporation Ld.; name changed Mar. 1910. Undertaking and assets were acquired by Dominion Steel and Coal Corporation Ld., in which company shareholders were entitled to 4 B common shares of $25 for each preference share of $100 held 1931

*See Stock Exchange Year-Book.

VOL. FOR

Co.) in which company debenture stockholders received an equal amount of 5% debenture stock. Stockholders were entitled to 5½% preference A stock in acquiring company as follows—for each A and B (10% maximum) share of £25 held—£50; for each C (7% maximum) share of £25 held—£35; for each D (5% maximum) share of £25 held—£25 ... **1929**

Dorking Water Co. Inc. by Special Act 1869. Under provisions of the East Surrey Water Order 1958 the undertaking vested in the East Surrey Water Co. from 1 Jan. 1959. Shareholders received shares in the East Surrey company in exchange for their holdings at the following rates (per share of £10)—£20 5% preference stock per ordinary share; £14 5% preference stock per class B share; £12 5% preference stock per preference A share and £10 5% preference stock per preference B share. Debenture stockholders were entitled to a like amount of 4% debenture stocks of the East Surrey company in exchange for their holdings. Company was dissolved by a resolution of directors passed on 4 Nov. 1960 .... **1961**

Dornoch Light Railway Co. Inc. (under Light Railways Act 1896) by order of Light Railway Commissioners confirmed by Board of Trade 1898. In 1923 the undertaking was merged into the London Midland & Scottish Railway Co. Holders of each £100 Dornoch 4% Debenture Stock were entitled to £75 in cash and holders of each £100 Dornoch Ordinary Shares were entitled to £15 in cash **1924**

Dorran Construction Ld. Regd. in Edinburgh 1945 as Robert G. Tarran & Son Ld.;name changed 1956. Winding-up Order 21 July 1967. Official liquidator discharged 7 Aug. 1979. £1,057·64 was paid to Accountant of Court in respect of unclaimed dividends **1981–2**

Dortmund Breweries Co. Ld. Regd. 1888. Vol. liq. 1 Sept. 1926. Capital returned to contributories—£1 10*s.* per preference share of £1 10*s.*; £3 15*s.* per ordinary share of £4 5*s.* at Oct. 1926; further payments (if any) not known. Final meeting return regd. 12 Apr. 1927 .... **1927**

Doughty Richardson Fertilizers Ld. Regd. 1923. Vol. liq. (members') 1 July 1939. All capital was owned by Fisons Ld. Final meeting return regd. 29 Sept. 1944 **1945**

Douglas & Laxey Coast Electric Tramway Ld. (later Isle of Man Trams) **1910**

Douglas & Oliver Ld. Regd. 1910. Vol. liq. Jan. 1912. Court Order to wind up May 1912. Struck off Register 1921 .... **1913**

Douglas Colliery Ld. Inc. Transvaal 1895. The London office was closed in 1907 .... **1908**

Douglas Developing Syndicate Ld. Regd. 1888. Vol. liq. 19 Mar. 1902. Capital returned to contributories—£1 3*s.* per share of £1 at 5 Nov. 1902; further payments (if any) not known. Removed from Register 1904 .... **1903**

Douglas Head Marine Drive Ld. Inc. Isle of Man 1889. Vol. liq. for purpose of reconstruction June 1909 **1910**

Douglas Head Suspension Bridge Ld. Inc. 1889. Isle of Man court order to wind up 4 May 1892 .... **1893**

Douglas, Laxey & Ramsey Railway Co. Ld. Inc. 1883. Wound up 1886 .... **1888**

Douglas Motors (1932) Ld. Regd. 1932 as D. Motors (1932) Ld. name changed Aug. 1932. Court Order to wind up July 1934. Struck off Register 17 July 1942 **1943**

Douglas Southern Electric Tramways Ld. Regd. 1895. Vol. liq. 14 May 1926. Final meeting return regd. 16 Apr. 1929 .... **1927**

Douro Gold Mines Ld. Regd. 1886. Vol. liq. 19 June 1889. Final meeting return regd. 6 Apr. 1892 ...... ***1890**

Dover & Newsome Baxter Ld. Regd. 1897. Vol. liq. Nov. 1909. Removed from Register 1912 .... **1910**

Dover Cliffe Land Co. Ld. Regd. 1903. Vol. liq. (creditors') 28 Sept. 1949. No capital was returned to contributories. Final meeting return regd. 12 May 1954 .... **1955**

Dover Electricity Supply Co. Ld. Regd. 1893. Undertaking was acquired by Corporation. Debenture stock was to be repaid at 110%. A return of £6 5*s.* per preference share of £5 or £8 10*s.* per ordinary share of £5 was anticipated. Removed from Register 1904 **1905**

Dover Gas Co. Estd. 1822; reinc. as Dover Gas Light Co. by Special Act 1860; name changed 1901. Dissolved 1 May 1949 undertaking being vested in South Eastern Area Gas Board under Gas Act 1948. Holders of securities were entitled to receive British Gas 3% guaranteed stock 1990–95 as follows in respect of each £100 unit unless otherwise stated, of security held:

	£	s.	d.	
Cons. cap. stock (7½% basic)	170	0	0	
New ord. stock (7½% basic)	170	0	0	
Ord. shares of £10 (7½% basic)	17	0	0	
3½% perp. deb. stock	99	0	0	
4% perp. deb. stock	103	0	0	
5¼% perp. deb. stock	130	0	0	**1952**

Dover Gas Light Co. *See* Dover Gas Co.

Dover Graving Dock Co. Inc. by Special Act 1908. In Nov. 1914 the late Secretary stated that powers had lapsed and the undertaking abandoned **1915**

Dover House Properties Ld. Regd. 1920 as Montagu Higginson (Cardiff) Ld.; name changed 9 Mar. 1925 to Montagu Higginson (Collieries) Ld. and subsequently as above. Vol. liq. (members') 9 Feb. 1962. Final meeting return regd. 16 Mar. 1964 .... **1937**

Dover Reefs Development Syndicate Ld. Regd 1905. Removed from Register 26 July 1912 .... ***1908**

Dover Tivoli Ld. Regd. 1896. Vol. liq. 8 May 1899. Final meeting return regd. 19 Dec. 1899 .... **1900**

Dovercourt Cliff Hotel Co. Ld. Regd. 1883. Vol. liq. July 1888. Final meeting return regd. 13 July 1889 ..... **1889**

Dovey Valley Silica Syndicate Ld. Regd. 1918. A direct controlling interest was held by Port Lincoln Copper Co. Ld. Struck off Register 25 Oct. 1932 .... **1932**

Dowdall's Buttapat Dairies Ld. Regd. 1911. Vol. liq. 22 May 1924. Final meeting return regd. 22 May 1925 **1925**

Dowgate Steamship Co. Ld. Regd. 1894. Vol. liq. 3 Dec. 1915. Final meeting return regd. 10 Feb. 1917 .... **1916**

Dowlais Gas & Coke Co. Regd. as limited 1856; inc. by Special Act 1906. Dissolved 1 May 1949, undertaking being vested in Wales Area Gas Board under Gas Act 1948. Holders of Cons. ord. stock were entitled to receive, in respect of each £100 held, £90 British Gas 3% guaranteed stock 1990–95 .... **1952**

Dowlen's Ashanti Goldfields Ld. Regd. 1902. Vol. liq. Apr. 1910. Removed from Register 1911 .... **1911**

Downham & Stoke Ferry Railway Co. Inc. by Special Act 1879. Under Great Eastern Railway Co. Act 1897 the undertaking was purchased by that company which took over the mortgage debt and the rent charge **1898**

Downing (T. H.) & Co. Ld. Regd. 1918. Vol. liq. (members') 9 Dec. 1938. Capital returned to contributories—preference capital was repaid in full; 1*s.* 0·66*d.* per ordinary share of 5*s.* £850 13*s.* 3*d.* was paid into Companies' Liquidation Account. Final meeting return regd. 4 June 1946 .... **1947**

Dowry Spinning Co. Ld. *See below.*

Dowry Spinning Co. (Holdings) Ld. Regd. 1882 as Dowry Spinning Co. Ld. Vol. liq. 31 Mar. 1959. Final meeting return regd. 5 Oct. 1959 .... **1941**

Drake Properties Ld. Regd. 1897. Vol. liq. Dec. 1909. Removed from Register 1910 .... **1910**

Drake Spinning Co. Ld. Regd. 1905. Vol. liq. 12 Mar. 1912. Court Order to stay proceedings June 1918. Vol. liq. (creditors') 28 Aug. 1936. Assets realised insufficient to pay unsecured creditors in full. Final meeting return regd. 11 Sept. 1940 .... **1937**

Drake Trust Co. Ld. Regd. 1920. Vol. liq. (members') 12 Mar. 1941. Capital returned to contributories—£10,684 13*s.* 7*d.* Final meeting return regd. 30 Oct. 1943 .... **1942**

Drakewalls Ld. Regd. 1900. Vol. liq. 18 Oct 1905. A small return of capital to contributories was anticipated. Removed from Register 1906 .... **1906**

Drakewalls Mining Co. Ld. Regd. 1892. Vol. liq. 8 Oct. 1896. Final meeting return regd. 29 Aug. 1900 .... **1897**

Drammens og Oplands Kreditbank. Taken over in 1922 by Drammens Privatbanker A/S **1926**

Drammens Privatbank (*see* Drammens Privatbanker) **1926**

Drammens Privatbanker A/S. Inc. Norway 1921. Placed under public administration Feb. 1927 .... **1928**

Draperstown Railway Co. Inc. by Special Act 1878 ... **1895**

Drapery & General Investment Trust Ld. *See* Drapery Trust Ld.

Drapery Trust Ld. Regd. 1925 as Drapery & General Investment Trust Ld.; name changed Nov. 1926. Undertaking and assets were acquired by Debenhams Ld., in which company shareholders were entitled to 6 3rd preference shares of 10*s.* and 5 ordinary shares of 1*s.* for every 6 preference shares of £1 held. The ordinary shares were cancelled. Dissolved under Sec. 154 of Companies Act. 1929 on 29 Apr. 1934 .... **1934**

Drapkin (Alfred A.) (Tobacco) Ld. Regd. 1929. Court Order to wind up 27 July 1931. No capital returned to contributories. Liquidator released 13 Aug. 1957. Struck off Register 5 Feb. 1960 .... **1958**

Drawing Room Cars Co. Ld. Regd. 1882 as Pullman Co. Ld.; name changed Oct. 1915. Vol. liq. 29 July 1927. Cars stocks &c. and goodwill were held by Pullman Car Co. Ld. Final meeting return regd. 17 Jan. 1928 **1924**

Draycott Gas Co. Inc. by Special Act 1888. Undertaking was acquired by Long Eaton Gas Co. in which company preference shareholders were entitled to an equal amount of preference capital. A payment

VOL. FOR

was to be made of £17,000 (equivalent to 17s. per £1 consolidated ordinary stock held) **1923**

Dreadnought Investment Trust Ld. Regd. 1928. Vol. liq. (members') 29 June 1956. Final meeting return regd. 6 Feb. 1957 .... ***1933**

Dreamland, Margate, Ld. Regd. 1921. Vol. liq. 4 Dec. 1928. The undertaking and assets were transferred to Margate Estates Ld. in which company shareholders were entitled to 1 fully-paid ordinary share of 2s. and 10 fully-paid preference shares of 2s. for each preference share of £1 held. The holder of the ordinary shares received 232,843 fully-paid ordinary and 18,430 preference shares of 2s. in new company *plus* £7,500 in cash. The debentures were repaid at 105%. Final meeting return regd. 20 Jan. 1930 .... **1929**

Drecoll (Ch.) Ld. Regd. 1908. Vol. liq. May 1925. Undertaking and assets transferred to a new company (regd. in France under title of Ch. Drecoll) in which shareholders received 1 preferred share (of fr. 100) for each participating preferred ordinary share of £4 and 1 B share (of fr. 100) for every 80 deferred shares of 1s. held. Struck off Register 1936 **1926**

Dredging Development Co. Ld. Regd. 1926. Struck off Register 30 Jan. 1934 .... **1934**

Dreghorn Gas Co. Ld. Regd. Edinburgh 1924. Vol. liq. (members') 20 July 1939. Undertaking acquired by Irvine Gas Co. Ld. in which company shareholders were entitled to 1 share for every 2 shares held. Final meeting return regd. 20 Feb. 1940 .... **1940**

Dresden & District Ice Co. Ld. Regd. 1885. Vol. liq. 21 Feb. 1887. Assets were acquired by United Anglo-Continental Ice Co. Ld. in which company shareholders were entitled to an equal number of shares. Removed from Register 1906 .... **1888**

Drew (Alexander) & Sons Ld. Regd. 1906. Vol. liq. 13 Feb. 1929. Undertaking and assets were transferred to company of same name for £180,000 in cash and 210,000 fully-paid ordinary shares of £1. Final meeting return regd. 10 July 1935 .... **1929**

Drey Simpson & Co. Ld. Regd. 1906. All capital was owned by Armitage & Rigby (Holdings) Ld. Vol. liq. (members') 20 Nov. 1967. Final meeting return regd. 28 Nov. 1968 .... **1961**

Dreyfus & Co. Ld. Regd. 1901. Vol. Liq. (creditors') 16 May 1966. No capital returned to contributories. Final meeting return regd. 20 Mar. 1976 .... **1976-7**

Dreyfus Offshore Trust N.V. Inc. in Netherlands Antilles 1969. Vol. liq. 16 July 1974. Substantially all assets transferred to Dreyfus Intercontinental Investment Fund N. V. in which holders of common stock of this company received (per share) approx. 0·740 shares of common stock. Participating debentures redeemed at par 15 July 1974 .... **1975-6**

Driefontein Consolidated Mines Ld. Inc. Transvaal 1895. Vol. liq. May 1908. Undertaking was acquired by East Rand Proprietary Mines Ld., in which company shareholders were entitled to 6 shares of £1 (credited as fully-paid) for every 9 shares of £1 held **1909**

Driefontein Deep Ld. Inc. Transvaal 1899. Vol. liq. May 1908. 129 claims and £97,000 in cash were acquired by East Rand Proprietary Mines Ld.; 125 claims and £40,000 in cash were acquired by Witwatersrand Deep Ld. **1909**

Drighlington & Gildersome Gas-Light Co. *See* Morley Gas Co.

Drogheda Steam Packet Co. Ld. Regd. Dublin 1856. Undertaking acquired by Lancashire and Yorkshire Railway Co. 1 May 1902 under Act of 1902. Capital returned to contributories—£12 7s. 8d. per share of £20. Removed from Register 1903 .... **1904**

Droitwich Canal Navigation Co. Inc. by Special Act 1767. Under Act of 1939 the lease held by Sharpness Docks & Gloucester & Birmingham Navigation Co. was surrendered in consideration of payment of annuities to shareholders and the canal was vested in Droitwich Corporation. The shares were converted into Sharpness Docks Perpetual Annuities. Dissolved on 25 Sept. 1939 .... **1940**

Droitwich Junction Canal Co. Inc. by Special Act 1852. Under Act of 1939 the lease held by Sharpness Docks & Gloucester & Birmingham Navigation Co. was surrendered in consideration of payment of annuities to shareholders and the canal was vested in Droitwich Corporation. The shares were converted into Sharpness Docks 1952 Annuities. Dissolved on 25 Mar. 1940 .... **1940**

Droitwich Salt Co. Ld. Regd. 1868. Vol. liq. 2 Mar. 1920. Final meeting return regd. 22 Mar. 1921 .... **1921**

Dronfield Gas Light & Coke Co. Inc. by Special Act 1879. Vol. liq. Sept. 1924. Undertaking and assets were acquired by Sheffield Gas Co. (later Sheffield & District Gas Co.) in consideration of payment of debentures in full and 80% of paid-up capital **1925**

VOL. FOR

Drouet (R.) & Co. Ld. Regd. 1910. Vol. liq. (members') 9 Sept. 1936. All shares owned by Fruit Produce Exchange of Great Britain Ld. Final meeting return regd. 17 Nov. 1936 .... **1937**

Drug. Inc. Inc. Delaware 1928. Various assets were acquired by 5 new companies. Shareholders were entitled to 2 shares of $5 in Bristol-Myers Co., 1 share of $5 in Life Savers Corporation. 5 shares of $10 in Sterling Products Inc., 4 shares of $5 in United Drug Inc. [later United-Rexall Drug Inc.] and 2 shares of $5 in Vick Chemical Inc. for every 10 shares of no par value held **1934**

Drumcondra & North Dublin Link Railway Co. Inc. by Special Act 1894. Under Great Southern and Western Railway Ireland Act of 1896 the powers (other than capital) were transferred to that company **1897**

Drummond, Messrs. Assets and liabilities acquired by Royal Bank of Scotland 12 Jan. 1924 .... **1924**

Dry Docks Corporation of London Ld. Regd. 1886. Vol. liq. Court Order to continue winding up under supervision 25 June 1888. Property was sold by Receiver for debenture holders. Final meeting return regd. 6 July 1896 .... **1891**

Dryden Paper Co. Ld. Inc. Canada 1920. The outstanding 6% 10-year notes and 6% debenture stock were redeemed at par in Apr. 1929 .... **1930**

Dryden Pulp & Paper Co. Ld. Inc. Ontario 1918. The undertaking and assets were acquired by Dryden Paper Co. Ld **1930**

Dryden Timber & Power Co. Ld. Inc. Ontario 1910. In Nov. 1918 the company was reorganised as Dryden Pulp and Paper Co. Ld. **1919**

Drysdale Manufacturing Co. Ld. Business was acquired in 1928 by Waste Food Products Ld. **1929**

Du Bois Manufacturing Co. Ld. The business carried on in Germany (as C. Herbert Torrey) was acquired in 1898 by British & Foreign Du Bois Co. Ld. **1901**

Dua (Nigeria) Tin Fields Ld. Regd. 1912. Vol. liq. 22 Mar. 1922. Final meeting return regd. 23 June 1925 **1923**

Dual Syndicate Ld. Regd. 1896. Vol. liq. 20 Mar. 1901. Final meeting return regd. 5 Oct. 1901 .... **1902**

Dualvest p.l.c. Regd. 2 Apr. 1965. Converted into public company 4 May 1965. Vol. liq. (members') 23 Feb. 1987. Return of final meeting regd. 22 Sept. 1988. Dissolved 22 Dec. 1988. Company was unitised effective 23 Feb. 1987, net assets transferred to Trustee in consideration of issue of 37 accumulation units of MIM Britannia Assets and Earnings Trust for each capital share held. Income shareholders repaid at par (50p) *plus* a premium of 5p per share on 24 Feb. 1987. Amounts paid into Companies' Liquidation Account in respect of unclaimed dividends £1,721·74, repayment of 50p income shares £14,478·90 and unclaimed distributions of 1·36p per £1 capital share £419·84 .... **1988–9**

Dubarry Perfumery Co. Ld. Regd. 1923. Dissolved 13 Apr. 1983 .... **1964**

Dubby Syke Mining Co. Ld. Regd. 1875. Vol. liq. 18 Apr. 1882. Final meeting return regd. 15 Dec. 1897 **1883**

Dublin & Belfast Aerated Bread Co. Ld. Regd. Dublin 1889. Court Order to wind up 23 Feb. 1891. Removed from Register 1892 .... **1892**

Dublin & Blessington Steam Tramway Co. Inc. by Order of Privy Council in Ireland 1887. The undertaking was transferred as from 1 Jan. 1928 to a Committee of Management appointed by the County Councils of Dublin and Wicklow **1930**

Dublin & Glasgow Sailing & Steam Packet Co. Established 1836; regd. as unlimited 1872. Vol. liq. Apr. 1908 the undertaking having been acquired by Burn's Steamship Co. Ld. **1909**

Dublin and Kingstown Railway Co. Inc. by Special Act 1831. In 1925 the undertaking was merged into the Great Southern Railways Co. in which company stockholders were entitled to stock as follows:

For each £100 held	Gt. Sthn. Rly.
3½ Debenture	£87½ 4% Debenture
General Capital	£100 4% Debenture / £60 4% Gtd. Pref.

The liability for loans for £300 was assumed by the Great Southern Railways Co. **1925**

Dublin & Liverpool Steamship Building Co. Established by deed of agreement 1840. By Act of 1910 the undertaking and assets were acquired by City of Dublin Steam Packet Co. in which company shareholders were entitled to £50 5% preference stock for each share of £50 held **1911**

Dublin & Lucan Electric Railway Co. Inc. by Order in Council as Dublin & Lucan Steam Tramway Co.: name changed 1900. Undertaking was acquired in 1926 by Dublin United Tramways Co. (1896) Ld. (later Dublin United Transport Co. Ld.) **1926**

See Stock Exchange Year-Book.

VOL. FOR

Dublin & Lucan Steam Tramway Co. *See* Dublin & Lucan Electric Railway Co.

Dublin & Meath Railway Co. Inc. by Special Act 1858. Under Midland Great Western, Dublin & Meath & Navan & Kingscourt Railways Purchase Act 1888 line was vested in Midland Great Western Railway of Ireland Co., 4% debenture stock of which was distributed among holders of debenture stock, preference stocks and ordinary shares **1889**

Dublin and South Eastern Railway Co. Inc. by Special Act 1846, as Waterford, Wexford, Wicklow & Dublin Railway Co.; name changed to Dublin & Wicklow Railway Co. by Act of 1851, to Dublin, Wicklow & Wexford Railway Co. by Act of 1860 and as above by Act of 1906. In 1925 the undertaking of this Company (including the City of Dublin Junction Railways and the New Ross & Waterford Extension Railways) was vested in the Great Southern Railways Co., in which company stockholders were entitled to stock as follows:

For each £100 held	*G. Sthn. Rly.*
4% Cons. A Deb. £100	4% Debenture
4% Cons. B Deb. £100	4% Debenture
4% Cons. Pref. £100	4% Preference
Cons. Ord. £47	10s. Ordinary **1925**

Dublin & Wicklow Manure Co. Ld. Regd. Dublin 1877. Reconstructed in 1890 under same name **1891**

Dublin & Wicklow Railway Co. *See* Dublin and South Eastern Railway Co.

Dublin Brick & Tile Co. Ld. Regd. Dublin 1890. Vol. liq. July 1912. Undertaking and assets were acquired by Dublin Brick Co. Ld., in which company shareholders were entitled to 2 ordinary shares of £1 for every 3 ordinary shares of £1 held or 5 preference shares of £1 for each preference share of £5 held. Removed from Register 1913 .... **1913**

Dublin Brick Co. Ld. Inc. in Dublin 1912. Vol. liq. (members') 23 July 1948. Capital returned to contributories—£1 3s. 7d. per share (of 5s.). Final meeting return regd. 30 Mar. 1953 .... **1954**

Dublin Central Tramways Co. Amalgamated with Dublin United Tramways Co. (1896) Ld. (later Dublin United Transport Co. Ld.), in 1881 .... **1883**

Dublin City Distillery (Great Brunswick Street, Dublin) Ld. Regd. Dublin 1890. Court Order to wind up 31 July 1905 .... **1906**

Dublin Distillers Co. Ld. Regd. 1889 in London, registration transferred to Dublin by Special Act of Parliament of 1893. Vol. liq. (members') 21 Oct. 1941. Capital returned to contributories in respect of each £1 of ordinary stock and each 5s. A share 27s. 5 7/10 d. Final meeting return regd. 27 Apr. 1949 ..... **1950**

Dublin Dockyard Co. Ld. Regd. Dublin 1912. Vol. liq. Feb. 1923. Undertaking acquired by Vickers Ld. **1924**

Dublin Drapery Warehouse Ld. Regd. Dublin 1872 as McSwiney & Co. Ld.; name changed 1882. In liquidation in 1885 .... **1885**

Dublin Electric Light Co. Ld. Regd. Dublin 1881. In liquidation in 1884 .... **1884**

Dublin Granaries Ld. Regd. 1875. Vol. liq. (members') 26 Aug. 1963. Struck off register Sept. 1964 .... **1946**

Dublin Southern District Tramways Co. Undertaking acquired by Dublin United Tramways Co. (1896) Ld. (later Dublin United Transport Co. Ld.). Dissolved Aug. 1905 .... **1945**

Dublin Theatre Co. Ld. Regd. Dublin 1897. Vol. liq. 21 Aug. 1924. Dissolved before 1930 .... **1925**

Dublin Theatre Co. Ld. Regd. Dublin 1924. A subsidiary of Irish Cinemas Ld. Dissolved before Dec. 1955 ...... **1940**

Dublin Tramways Co. Amalgamated with Dublin United Tramways Co. (1896) Ld. (later Dublin United Transport Co. Ld., in 1881 .... **1883**

Dublin United Transport Co. Inc. 1881. Undertaking acquired by Dublin United Tramways Co. (1896) Ld. (later Dublin United Transport Co. Ld.) by Act of 1905 and dissolved in Aug. 1905 .... **1945**

Dublin United Transport Co. Ld. Regd. Dublin 1896 as Dublin United Tramways Co. (1896) Ld.; name changed 5 May 1941. Undertaking acquired in 1945 by Córas Iompair Eireann in which company holders of ordinary and preference stocks were entitled to £145 3% debenture stock for every £100 stock held. Dissolved 1 Jan. 1945 .... **1945**

Dublin Whisky Distillery Co. Ld. Regd. Dublin. Undertaking acquired in 1889 by Dublin Distillers Co. Ld. **1941**

Dublin, Wicklow & Wexford Railway Co. *See* Dublin and South Eastern Railway Co.

Dubowski (B.) & Sons Ld. Regd. 1897. Removed from Register 1912 .... **1896**

Duchess Property Co Ld. Regd. 1929 as Duchess Trust Ld.; name changed July 1930. Struck off Register 9 Feb. 1951 .... **1951**

Duchess Trust Ld. *See above.*

VOL. FOR

Duchy Peru Ld. Regd. 1883. Removed from Register 1906 .... **1887**

Ducktown Sulphur, Copper & Iron Co. Ld. Regd. 1891. Vol. liq. 20 May 1926. Capital returned to contributories—1s. per ordinary share of £1 at Nov. 1926; further payments (if any) not known. Final meeting return regd. 13 July 1927 .... **1927**

Ductile Steels Ld. *See* D. S. Holdings Ld.

Dudbridge Iron Works Ld. Regd. 1899. Vol. liq. 2 July 1923. Final meeting return regd. 2 Jan. 1928. ...... *****1924**

Dudley & Oldbury Junction Railway Co. *See* Oldbury Railway Co.

Dudley & Stourbridge Steam Tramways Co. Ld. *See* Dudley Stourbridge & District Electric Traction Co. Ld.

Dudley & Wolverhampton Tramways Ld. Regd. 1893. Vol. liq. 11 Nov. 1898. Undertaking was acquired by British Electric Traction Co. Ld. Final meeting return regd. 11 Feb. 1902 .... **1900**

Dudley, Brierley Hill & District Gas Co. Estd. 1821, inc. as Town of Dudley Gas Light Co. by Special Act 1853; name changed 1931. Dissolved 1 May 1949, undertaking being vested in West Midland Area Gas Board under Gas Act 1948. Holders of securities were entitled to receive, in respect of each £100 unit held, British Gas 3% guaranteed stock 1990–95 as follows:

	£	s.	d.
Cons. ord. stock (5% basic)	121	0	0
5% cons. pref. stock	115	0	0
3½% red. pref. stock	100	10	2
4% perp. deb. stock	102	15	0
4½% perp. deb. stock		do.	
4% red. deb. stock (1950–60)	100	15	0
4% red. deb. stock (1956)	102	10	0
3½% red. deb. stock	101	15	0 **1952**

Dudley Empire Picture House Ld. Regd. 1921. Vol. liq. 8 Oct. 1928. Final meeting return regd. 29 June 1932 **1929**

Dudley, Sedgley & Wolverhampton Tramways Co. Ld. Regd. 1879. Court Orders: to wind up 30 Dec. 1887; to dissolve 14 Aug. 1890 .... **1888**

Dudley, Son & Co. Ld. Regd. 1919. Court Order to wind up 14 Nov. 1922. Struck off Register 1929 .... *****1923**

Dudley, Stourbridge & District Electric Traction Co. Ld. Regd. 1880 as Dudley, Stourbridge & Kingswinford Tramways Co. Ld.; name changed to Dudley & Stourbridge Steam Tramways Co. Ld. in 1882 and as above in 1898. Vol. liq. (creditors') 24 Sept. 1930. Holders of £25,640 6% debenture stock received £2,813 11s. 6d. Final meeting return regd. 29 Jan. 1931 .... **1931**

Dudley Zoological Society Ld. Regd. as private company 16 Jan. 1936; converted public limited company 15 Sept. 1947. All ordinary acquired by Scotia Investments Ld. Dissolved 5 Aug. 1986...... **1975–6**

Dufaycolor Co. Inc. Inc. USA. In liquidation. A substantial interest was held by Dufay-Chromex Ld. (later Dufay Ld.) **1944**

Duff & Stewart Ld. Regd. 1891. Vol. liq. 8 Jan. 1903. Final meeting return regd. 14 Apr. 1913 .... **1902**

Duff Development Co. Ld. Regd. 1903. Vol. liq. (members') 8 Apr. 1932 for reconstruction under same name. Shareholders were entitled to 1 share of 5s. (credited with 4s. paid) in the new company for each share of 10s. held. Final meeting return regd. 11 Apr. 1933 .... **1933**

Duff Development Co. Ld. Regd. 1932. Vol. liq. (member's) August 1973. Undertaking, property and assets in Malaysia acquired by Duff Development Berhad in which company stockholders were entitled to 15 shares of Ma $1 for every 25p stock held. Amount paid into Companies' Liquidation Account £41·11 in respect of unclaimed dividends. Final meeting return registered 19 Jan. 1976 ...... **1976-7**

Duff House Ld. Regd. 1909. Vol. liq. May 1913. Struck off Register 1921 .... **1914**

Duffield Coal Products Ld. Regd. 1928. Struck off Register 24 Apr. 1953 .... **1954**

Duffield Iron Corporation Ld. Regd. 1928. Struck off Register 8 Oct. 1957 .... **1958**

Duffryn Aberdare Colliery Co. Ld. Regd. 1919. Vol. liq. Nov. 1928. Court Order to continue winding up under supervision Jan. 1929. Struck off Register 1935 .... **1929**

Duffryn Rhondda Colliery Co. Ld. Regd. 1903. Receiver appointed 1 Oct. 1913 for holder of £145,000 2nd mortgage debenture. Undertaking sold in Mar. 1914 to Imperial Navigation Coal Co. Ld., for £50,000 in B debentures and shares and £25,000 in cash. Struck off Register 1917 .... **1916**

Duke Anthracite Collieries Ld. Regd. 1924 Struck off Register 10 Mar. 1936 .... **1937**

*See Stock Exchange Year-Book.

VOL. FOR

Dunkwa Mining Syndicate Ld. Regd. 1910. Vol. liq. 2 Nov. 1920. Undertaking was acquired by Winnebah Tinfields Ld., in which company shareholders were entitled to 2 fully-paid shares of 5s. for each share of 10s. held. Final meeting return regd. 23 Mar. 1922 1921

Dunlop Gas Light Co. Ld. Regd. in Edinburgh 1934. Dissolved 1 May 1949, undertaking being vested in Scottish Area Gas Board under Gas Act 1948. Holders of shares (of £1) were entitled to receive 17s. 6d. British Gas 3% guaranteed stock 1990–95 for each share held 1952

Dunlop (J. B.) Cycle Fittings & Engineering Co. Ld. Regd. 1896. Removed from Register 1903 1902

Dunlop (James) & Co. Ld. Regd. Edinburgh 1900 as Dunlop (James) & Co. (1900) Ld.; name changed 1903. Vol. liq. (members') 14 Mar. 1952. All shares owned by Nimmo & Dunlop Ld. Capital returned to contributories—preference: repaid at par; ordinary: 23s. 10¾d. per share of £1. Final meeting return regd. 12 June 1958 1959

Dunlop (James) & Co. (1900) Ld. *See above.*

Dunlop Pneumatic Tyre Co. A/G. Dunlop Rubber Co. Ld. held a controlling interest before company was placed in liquidation on 4 Nov. 1916 by German Government 1917

Dunlop Pneumatic Tyre Co. (France) Ld. Regd. 1896. Vol. liq. 19 Oct. 1900. Reconstructed as Société Française des Pneumatiques Dunlop Ld., in which company shareholders were entitled to 1 fully-paid ordinary and 1 preference share of £1 for every 13 shares of £1 held. Final meeting return regd. 8 Nov. 1901 1901

Dunlop Pneumatic Tyre Co. *See* Parent Trust and Finance Co. Ld.

Dunlop Sports Co. Ld. Regd. 1927. Vol. liq. (members') 25 Aug. 1933. All shares were owned by Dunlop Rubber Co. Ld. (later Dunlop Co. Ld.). Final meeting return regd. 19 Mar. 1934 1934

Dunlop-Truffault Cycle and Tube Manufacturing Co. Ld. *See* Truffault Cycle and Tube Manufacturing Co. Ld.

Dunmanus Bay Barytes Co. Ld. Regd. 1914. Vol. liq. 31 Mar. 1920. Capital returned to contributories—20s. per preference share of £1 : 14s. per ordinary share of £1 at 25 Jan. 1921; further payments (if any) not known. Final meeting return regd. 26 Sept. 1929 1921

Dunmanway & Skibbereen Railway Co. *See* Ilen Valley Railway Co.

Dunmow Light & Heat Co. Ld. Regd. 1934. Dissolved 1 May 1949, undertaking being vested in Eastern Area Gas Board under Gas Act 1948. Holders of ordinary shares (of £1) were entitled to receive £1 9s. British Gas 3% guaranteed stock 1990–95 for each share held 1952

Dunmurry Electric Light & Power Co. Ld. Inc. Dublin 1922. All shares held by Lisburn Electric Supply Co. Ld., were sold to Electricity Board for Northern Ireland 1934

Dunning Gas Co. Ld. Regd. in Edinburgh 1922. Dissolved 1 May 1949, undertaking being vested in Scottish Area Gas Board under Gas Act 1948. Holders of ordinary shares (of £1) were entitled to receive £1 British Gas 3% guaranteed stock 1990–95 for each share held 1952

Dunoon and District Electricity Supply Co. Ld. Regd. 1929. All shares were owned by Johnson & Phillips Ld. Dissolved 1 Apr. 1948, undertaking being vested in the North of Scotland Hydro-Electric Board under the Electricity Act 1947. Ordinary shareholders were entitled to receive £1 12s. 6d. British Electricity 3% guaranteed stock, 1968–73 for each share (of £1) held 1949

Dunraven Gold Mining Co. Ld. Regd. 1897, Vol. liq. May 1908. Removed from Register 1909 1909

Dunrobin Shipping Co. Ld. Regd. 1902. Vol. liq. Oct. 1911. Removed from Register 1912 1912

Duns Gas Co. Ld. Regd. in Edinburgh 1943. Dissolved 1 May 1949, undertaking being vested in Scottish Area Gas Board under Gas Act 1948. Holders of securities were entitled to receive, in respect of each £1 held, British Gas 3% guaranteed stock 1990–95 as follows:

	£ s. d.	
Ord. shares	1 5 0	
5% red. pref. shares	1 1 9	1952

Dunstable Gas & Water Co. Inc. by Special Act 1871. Dissolved 1 May 1949, undertaking being vested in Eastern Area Gas Board under Gas Act 1948. Holders of securities were entitled to receive British Gas 3% guaranteed stock 1990–95 as follows in respect of each £1 unit, unless otherwise stated. of security held:

VOL. FOR

Gas Undertaking	£	s.	d.
A ord. shares (10% max.)...............	2	1	2
B ord. shares (5% max.)................	1	1	4
C ord. shares (7% max.)................	1	9	1
5% pref. stock (per £100)	112	10	0
5% pref. stock (issued since			
31 Dec 1945—per £100)...............	105	13	0
4% perp. deb. stock (per £100).......	102	0	0
Water Undertaking	£	s.	d.
Ord. shares (10% max.)................	2	2	0
Ord. shares (7% max.)..................	1	11	0
5% pref. stock (per £100)	125	0	0
5% pref. stock (issued since			
31 Dec 1945—per £100)...............	123	11	4
5% perp. deb. stock (per £100)........	130	0	0

Liability in respect of certain mortgage loans assumed by the Board 1952

Dunstable Portland Cement Co. Ld. Regd. 1925. Vol. liq. (members') 30 Oct. 1931. Undertaking and assets were acquired by Associated Portland Cement Manufacturers Ld. Capital returned to contributories—20s. per preference share of £1; 11s. 10·9d. per ordinary share of £1. Final meeting return regd. 5 Nov. 1934 1932

Dunville & Co. Ld. Regd. Dublin 1879; transferred to Belfast under Government of Ireland Act 1920. Vol. liq. (members') 31 Dec. 1936. Final meeting regd. 27 Oct. 1952 1937

Dunville (Wm.) & Co. Ld. Inc. Dublin. Vol. liq. (members') June 1941. All shares were owned by Dunville & Co. Ld. All creditors were to be paid in full... 1937

Duophone & Unbreakable Record Co. Ld. Regd. 1926. Court Order to wind up 24 May 1930. Struck off Register 21 Sept. 1937 1938

Duophone (Foreign) Ld. Regd. 1928. Court Order to wind up 14 July 1930. Struck off Register 20 Mar. 1936 1937

Duophone Syndicate Ld. Regd. 1922. In 1926 the undertaking and assets were acquired by Duophone & Unbreakable Record Co. Ld for £87,500 in fully-paid ordinary shares and £7,500 in cash. Court Order to wind up 12 Mar. 1928. Liquidator released 27 Aug. 1931. Struck off Register 13 Apr. 1934.... 1927

"Duplex" Electric Light Power & Storage Co. Ld. Regd. 1882. Court Orders: to wind up July 1883; to dissolve 12 Apr. 1888 1884

Duram Ld. Regd. 1912. Vol. liq. (members') 14 May 1957. Final meeting return regd. 4 Sept. 1958 1938

Duran (Ecuador) Wharves & Warehouses Ld. Regd. Apr. 1906 as Guayaquil & Quito Railway Wharves & Warehouses Ld., name changed July 1906. Removed from Register 29 Aug. 1911 .... *1907

Durand Gold Mines Ld. Regd. 1893. Removed from Register 1900

Durani Syndicate Ld. Regd. 1924. Vol. liq. 26 Oct. 1949. No capital returned to contributories. Final meeting return regd. 13 Oct. 1950 1951

Durban Gold Mines Ld. Regd. 1895. Removed from Register 1907 1904

Durban Mill Co. Ld. *See* below.

Durban Mill (Holdings) Ld. Regd. 1905 as Durban Mill Co. Ld.; name changed 20 Mar. 1953. A subsidiary of Lancashire Cotton Corpn. Ld. Vol. liq. (members') 7 Mar. 1958. Final meeting return regd. 3 July 1958 1956

Durban Navigation Collieries Ld. Regd. 1903. Vol. liq. 22 Nov. 1912. Reconstructed as company of same name. Shareholders were entitled to 1 share of 4s. (credited as fully-paid) in new company for each share of £1 held. Final meeting return regd. 2 June 1915 1913

Durban Oil & Soap Co. Ld. Regd. 1902. Removed from Register 1912 1910

Durban Roodepoort Gold Mining Co. Ld. Regd. 1888. Vol. liq. 31 Oct. 1918. Final meeting return regd. 31 July 1920 1919

Durban-Winni Gold Mines Ld. Regd. 1895. Removed from Register 1910 1909

Durelco Ld. Regd. 1920. Vol. liq. (members') 16 July 1930. Capital returned to contributories—15s. 8·328d. per ordinary share of £1. Final meeting return regd. 20 Oct. 1931 1931

Durham "Allan Reef" Gold Mining Co. Ld. Regd. 1888. Struck off Register 22 Dec. 1904 1904

Durham & Lord Byron Amalgamated Gold Mining Co. Ld. Regd. 1887. Vol. liq. 20 June 1892. Final meeting return regd. 6 Sept. 1894 1893

Durham & North Yorkshire Public House Trust Co. Ld. Regd. 1901. Vol. liq. (members') 18 Aug. 1930. Capital returned to contributories—6s. 7¼d. per ordinary share of £1. Final meeting return regd. 16 Mar. 1932. 1931

See Stock Exchange Year-Book.

Durham & Yorkshire Fire Insurance Co. Ld. Regd. 1894. Vol. liq. 29 Oct. 1906. Undertaking was sold to Royal Insurance Co. Ld. Removed from Register 1907 .... **1946**

Durham Collieries Electric Power Co. Ld. Regd. 1905. Vol. liq. 19 July 1912. Final meeting return regd. 18 July 1914 .... ***1913**

Durham Prospect Gold Mines Ld. Regd. 1905. Struck off Register 1923 .... **1918**

Durham Salt Co. Ld. Regd. 1888. Court Order to wind up 16 Oct. 1889. Struck off Register Mar. 1930 .... **1931**

Durian Sebatang Rubber Estate Ld. Regd. 1925. Vol. liq. (members') 14 Apr. 1931. Undertaking and assets were acquired by Durian Sebatang Rubber Estates (1931) Ld. in which company shareholders were entitled to 1 share of 2s. (credited with 1s. 9d. paid) for each share of 2s. held. Final meeting return regd. 1 Jan. 1934 .... **1932**

Durian Sebatang Rubber Estates (1931) Ld. Regd. 1931. Vol. liq. (members') 5 Dec. 1952. Properties were acquired in 1950 by Aberfoyle Plantations Ld. in which company shareholders were entitled to (inter alia) about 7 shares of 2s. for every 10 shares of 2s. held. Capital returned to contributories—3d. per share of 2s. Amounts paid into Companies' Liquidation Account were—£129 4s. 10d. in respect of unclaimed dividends and £727 12s. 2d. in respect of unclaimed distributions. Final meeting return registered 25 June 1958 .... **1959**

Durie (R. & J.) Ld. Regd. Edinburgh 1896. Vol. liq. Apr. 1907. Undertaking was acquired by Edinburgh Collieries Co. Ld. in which company shareholders were entitled to 1 preference share of £1 for each preference share of £1 held or 1 ordinary share of £1 for each ordinary share of £1 held. Removed from Register 1908 .... **1908**

Duro Rubber Products Ld. See Ceymal Ld.

Durquem Mines Ld. Inc. in Canada 1928 as Mining Corpn.(Quebec) Ld. name changed to Quemont Mining Corpn. Ld. 1929 and to above title in 1968 on sale of undertaking. Shareholders were entitled to receive 2 shares of Kerr Addison Mines Ld. for every 3 shares held and company's charter was surrendered **1969**

Dursley Gas Light & Coke Co. Ld. Regd. 1887. Dissolved 1 May 1949 undertaking being vested in South Western Area Gas Board under Gas Act 1948. Holders of securities were entitled to receive British Gas 3% guaranteed stock 1990–95 as follows in respect of each £10 unit unless otherwise stated of security held:

	£	s.	d.
Ord. shares (10% stand.)	23	0	0
Ord. shares (8% stand.) (of £1)......	1	19	0
Ord. shares (7% stand.)	17	8	0
4½% red. pref. shares (of £1)	1	0	1
4% red. debs (of £100)	102	0	0
3½% debs. (of £100)	100	0	0

.... **1952**

Durward (Kenneth) Ld. Regd. 1919. Vol. liq. (members') 3 May 1934. Capital returned to contributories—1s. 9·42d. per preference share of £1. Final meeting return regd. 6 Apr. 1935 .... **1935**

Dusun Durian Rubber Estate Ld. Regd. 1912. Vol. liq. 27 Oct. 1947. Undertaking was acquired by Lumut Rubber Estates Ld. in which company stockholders were entitled to one fully-paid share of £1 for every £1 old stock held. £20 10s. was paid into Companies' Liquidation Account. Final meeting return regd. 13 Sept. 1948 .... **1949**

Dutch Artificial Silk Industry Ld. See Naamlooze Vennootschap Hollandsche Kunstzijde Industrie.

Dutch Co. for the Exploitation of Margarine Factories. (N. V. Hollandsche Vereeniging tot Exploitatie van Margarine Fabrieken "Hovema.") Inc. Holland by Royal Decree 1902. Vol. liq. 30 Nov. 1938. Undertaking was acquired by subsidiaries of Lever Brothers & Unilever N. V. (later Unilever N. V.) which company owned all ordinary shares. Holders of 6% preference shares were offered a like amount of 6% preference shares in acquiring company or repayment at par. Holders of 5½% preference shares were offered a like amount of 5½% preference capital in Van den Bergh's en Jurgens' Fabrieken N. V. or repayment at par in cash.

Dutch Guiana Balata & Rubber Concessions Ld. Regd. May 1910. Vol. liq. Aug. 1910. Removed from Register 1911 .... **1911**

Dutch Guiana Concessions Ld. Regd. 1897. Vol. liq. Dec. 1909. Removed from Register 1910 .... **1919**

Dutch Guiana Exploration Syndicate Ld. Regd. 1890. Vol. liq. 7 Dec. 1896. Final meeting return regd. 20 July 1897 .... **1870**

Dutch Rayon Industry Ld. See Naamlooze Vennootschap Hollandsche Kunstzijde Industrie.

Dutch Rhenish Railway Co. Established 1845. The concern was acquired by Netherlands Government in Oct. 1890. The two 3½% loans 1887 and 1888 were repaid on 1 Mar. 1892. The 6% bonds 1870 and 5% bonds 1876 were repayable 1 Jan. 1899 .... **1896**

Dutch South Eastern Railway Co. Established 1872. The line was sold to the company for the Exploitation of State Railways for Fl.6,666,000 in Dec. 1894. A first payment of 15% on A and B shares was made; further payments (if any) not known. Holders of 4% bonds 1881 were notified of repayment at par on 23 May 1895. Holders of 2nd mortgage 4% bonds were offered an equal amount of 3% bonds in the Company for Exploitation of State Railways **1896**

Duval Restaurants for London Ld. Regd. 1893. Removed from Register 1908 .... **1897**

Dvinsk and Vitebsk Railway Co. Ld. Regd. 1863 as Dunaburg and Witepsk Railway Co. Ld.; name changed June 1893. Vol. liq. 21 May 1894. Shareholders were entitled to £240 Russian Government 4% bonds for every 10 shares held. Final meeting return regd. 9 July 1895 .... **1896**

Dwarf Gold Mining Co. Ld. Regd. 1909. Vol. liq. 30 Mar. 1914. The properties were sold to Newdwarf Gold Ld. Final meeting return regd. 28 Sept. 1915 .... **1915**

Dynamic Income Investment Trust Ld. See Anglo-Welsh Investment Trust (Continuation) Ld.

Dynevor, Duffryn & Neath Abbey United Collieries Co. Ld. Regd. 1874. Removed from Register 1904 ..... ***1878**

Dysnni Gas Co. Ld. See Towyn & Aberdovery Gas Co. Ld.

E

E.B. Contractors Ld. Regd. Edinburgh 1861 as Edinburgh Co-Operative Building Co. Ld.; name subsequently changed. Vol. liq. 5 Apr. 1956. Struck off Register 16 Oct. 1970 .... **1939**

"E.C." Powder Co. Ld. Regd. 1883. Vol. liq. 10 Sept. 1923. Final meeting return regd. 28 Dec. 1926 .... **1925**

E.D. Investment Co. Ld. Regd. 1914 as Edinburgh. Dundee & Aberdeen Investment Co. Ld.; name changed to Edinburgh & Dundee Investment Co. Ld. in 1924 and to present title in 1969. Undertaking and assets were transferred to Edinburgh & Dundee Investment Co. Ld. on 14 Nov. 1969—ordinary shareholders received 135 ordinary shares for every 100 stock units held, preference and debenture stockholders received like amounts of identical stocks. Company finally dissolved 14 Mar. 1970 .. **1970**

E.D. Realisation Co. Ld. Regd. 1935. Vol. liq. (members') 14 Dec. 1937. Shareholders were entitled to receive £13 ordinary stock of Union Castle Mail Steamship Co. Ld. for every 10 shares (of £1) held and cash distributions of £1 1s. 1·125d. per share (of £1). Final meeting return regd. 21 June 1966 .... **1967**

E.D. Sassoon & Co. Ld. See Sassoon (E.D.) & Co. Ld.

E. Shipton & Co. (Holdings) Ld. See Shipton Automation Ld.

E.G. Syndicate Ld. Regd. 1910. Vol. liq. 22 Feb. 1915. Final meeting return regd. 4 Mar. 1916 .... **1915**

E. M. Y. Trust Ld. See Embassy Wine & Club Co. Ld.

Eadie (Albert) Chain Co. Ld. See Ecco Works Ld.

Eadie (James) Ld. Regd. 1893. Vol. liq. 29 June 1896. Reconstructed as company of same name. Certain assets were acquired by new company for £1,000,000 and premium on preference shares and debenture stock. Final meeting return regd. 15 Mar. 1897 ... **1908**

Eadie Manufacturing Co. Ld. Regd. 1897 as New Eadie Manufacturing Co. Ld.; name changed Nov. 1897. Vol. liq. June 1907. Undertaking and assets were acquired by Birmingham Small Arms Co. Ld., in which company shareholders were entitled to 17 ordinary shares of £5 for every 60 ordinary shares of £1 held or 23s. in cash for each preference share of £1 held. Removed from Register 1912 .... **1908**

Eagle Creek Oil Co. (California) Ld. Regd. 1911. Vol. liq. 18 Mar. 1921. Final meeting return regd. 2 Sept. 1922 .... **1922**

Eagle Edge Tool Co. Ld. Regd. 1866. Struck off Register 2 Aug. 1904. Restored to Register 1905. Removed from Register 1911 .... **1906**

Eagle Electric Light & Power Co. Ld. See Faringdon Electricity Supply Co. Ld.

Eagle Insurance Co. Ld. Established 1807. Inc. by Special Act 1813. Regd. 1897. Vol. liq. 5 Jan. 1917. Amalgamated with British Dominions General Insurance Co. Ld. (later Eagle Star Insurance Co. Ld.), in which company shareholders were entitled to 5 preferred ordinary shares of £3) (credited with 6s. paid) for every 3 shares of £5 (10s. paid) held. Struck off Register 18 Feb. 1955 .... **1917**

VOL. FOR

Eagle Lead Co. Ld. Regd. 1920. Vol. liq. (creditors') 12 June 1931. No capital returned to contributories. Final meeting return regd. 14 July 1932 .... **1932**

Eagle Range & Gas Stove Co. Ld. Regd. 1894 as Eagle Range and Foundry Co. Ld.; name changed May 1899. Vol. liq. 22 Oct. 1900. Acquired by John Wright and Eagle Range Ld., in which company preference shareholders were entitled to an equal amount of shares in new company and ordinary shareholders to 120% of holding in shares in new company. Final meeting return regd. 24 Dec. 1901 **1901**

Eagle Spinning Co. (Holdings) Ld. Regd. 1890 as Eagle Spinning Co. Ld.; name changed 21 Mar. 1953. Vol. liq. 1 Oct. 1957. Final meeting return regd. 3 Feb. 1958 .... **1958**

Eagle Spinning Co. Ld. *See above.*

Eagle Tinplate Co. Ld. Regd. 1890. Vol. liq. 30 Nov. 1928. Final meeting return regd. 3 Dec. 1929 ...... **1929**

Eagle Transfer (Holdings) Ld. Regd. 1920. Undertaking was acquired by Eagle Transfer Ld. Struck off Register 25 Mar. 1938 .... **1945**

Eagle Transfer Ld. Regd. 1936. Vol. liq. (members') 16 Oct. 1940. Capital returned to contributories—2s. 3$\frac{23}{32}$d. per share (of 2s.). £214 was paid into Companies' Liquidation Account. Final meeting return regd. 23 Mar. 1953 .... **1954**

Eagle-Vulture Mines Ld. Regd. 1899. Vol. liq. 13 Dec. 1904. Undertaking was acquired by East Gwanda Mines Ld., in which company shareholders were entitled to 2 shares of £1 (credited with 14s. paid) for every 5 shares of £1 held. Removed from Register 1908 .... **1905**

Eaglehawk Consolidated Gold Mining Co. Ld. Regd. 1887. Vol. liq. 11 Oct. 1892. Reconstructed as company of same name. Shareholders were entitled to 1 share of £1 (credited with 17s. 6d. paid) in new company for each share of £1 held. Final meeting return regd. 29 Nov. 1893 .... **1893**

Eaglehawk Consolidated Gold Mining Co. Ld. Regd. 1892. Vol. liq. 12 July 1895. Reconstructed as company of same name. Shareholders were entitled to 1 share of £1 (credited with 17s. 6d. paid) in new company for each share of £1 held. Final meeting return regd. 24 Nov. 1896 .... **1896**

Eaglehawk Consolidated Gold Mining Co. Ld. Regd. 1895. Vol. liq. 28 Mar. 1898. Reconstructed as company of same name. Shareholders were entitled to 1 share of £1 (credited with 18s. paid) in new company for each share of £1 held. Final meeting return regd. 18 Jan. 1899 .... **1908**

Eaglehawk Consolidated Gold Mining Co. Ld. Regd. 1898. Vol. liq. 12 Nov. 1909. Reconstructed as company of same name. Shareholders were entitled to 1 share of 10s. (credited with 7s. 6d. paid) for each share of £1 (19s. 6d. paid) held. Final meeting return regd. 22 July 1910 .... **1910**

Eaglehawk Consolidated Gold Mining Co. Ld. Regd. 1909. Vol. liq. Feb. 1912. Capital returned to contributories—1$\frac{1}{4}$d. per share of 10s.; further payments (if any) not known. Removed from Register 1912 .... **1913**

Eaglehurst Rubber Estates Ld. Regd. 1925. Vol. liq. (members') 18 Dec. 1950. Undertaking and assets acquired by Aberfoyle Plantations Ld in which company shareholders were entitled to 35·939 fully-paid shares of that company for every 100 shares (of 2s.) held. Final meeting return regd. 26 Mar. 1954 **1955**

Eagle's Nest Gold Mining Co. Ld. Regd. 1895. Vol. liq. 16 Dec. 1898. Removed from Register 1911 .... **1899**

Eagle's Nest (Mount Margaret) Gold Mining Co. Ld. Regd. 1895. Removed from Register 1908 .... **1899**

Ealing & South Harrow Railway Co. Inc. by Special Act 1894. Under Metropolitan District Railway Co. Act 1900 undertaking was purchased by that company. Holders of ordinary shares and 3$\frac{1}{2}$% debenture stock received an equal amount of Metropolitan District (Ealing and Harrow) 3$\frac{1}{2}$% rent-charge stock **1901**

Earby & Thornton Gas & Lighting Co. Ld. Regd. 1893. Dissolved 1 May 1949. undertaking being vested in North Western Area Gas Board under Gas Act 1948. Holders of securities were entitled to receive, in respect of each £10 unit held, British Gas 3% guaranteed stock 1990–95 as follows:

	£	s.	d.
A shares (10% stand.)	13	10	0
B shares (7% stand.)	10	0	0
C shares (7% stand.)	10	0	0	**1952**

Earl of Dudley's Baggeridge Colliery Ld. Regd. 1911. Vol. liq. (members') 29 Dec. 1954. Final Meeting return regd. 3 Oct. 1956 .... **1955**

Earl of Dudley's Round Oak Iron and Steel Works Ld. Regd. 1891. Vol. liq. 26 Nov. 1894. Final meeting return regd. 23 May 1895 .... **1895**

VOL. FOR

Earl of Rosslyn's Collieries Ld. Regd. Edinburgh 1897. Vol. liq. 31 Mar. 1927. Assets and undertaking acquired by Fife Coal Co. Ld. **1928**

Earl of Shrewsbury's Brereton Collieries Ld. *See* Brereton Collieries Ld

Earle (G. & T.) Ld. Regd. 1912. Vol. liq. 25 Sept. 1925. Reconstructed as G. & T. Earle (1925) Ld. Final meeting return regd. 10 May 1929 .... *1926

Earle's Shipbuilding & Engineering Co. Ld. Regd. 1871. Reconstructed 1901 as company of same name. Removed from Register 1905 .... **1925**

Earle's Shipbuilding & Engineering Co. Ld. Regd. 1901. Vol. liq. (members') 24 June 1933. Capital returned to contributories—£2 11s. per share of £10. Final meeting return regd. 15 Oct. 1934 .... **1934**

Earls Colne Gas Light & Coke Co. Ld. Regd. 1864. Dissolved 1 May 1949, undertaking being vested in Eastern Area Gas Board under Gas Act 1948. Holders of securities were entitled to receive British Gas 3% guaranteed stock 1990–95 as follows:

	£	s.	d.
Ord. shares (of £5)	5	0	0
4% red. debs. (of £100)	100	0	0	**1952**

Earl's Court Ld. Regd. 1910. Struck off Register 1923 *1915

Earlesfield Manufacturing Co. Ld. Regd. 1920, as Record Gas Mantle Co. Ld.; name changed to Lighting Trades, Ld. in Nov. 1920 and subsequently as above. Vol. liq. (members') 30 Dec. 1944. The undertaking was transferred to Imperial Chemical Industries Ld. Final meeting return regd. 25 Nov. 1948 .... **1949**

Earlston Gas Co. Ld. Regd. in Edinburgh · 1887. Dissolved 1 May 1949, undertaking being vested in Scottish Area Gas Board under Gas Act 1948. Holders of ordinary shares (of £5) were entitled to receive £5 British Gas 3% guaranteed stock 1990–95 for each share held **1952**

Easdale Slate Quarries Co. Ld. Regd. Edinburgh 1895. Vol. liq. Aug. 1907. Final meeting return regd. 3 Feb. 1910 .... **1908**

Easington Coal Co. Ld. Regd. 1899. Vol. liq. (members') 17 June 1952. Capital returned to contributories— £225 per preference share of £100; £590 16s. 6d. per ordinary share of £100. Final meeting return regd. 1 July 1955 .... **1956**

Easingwold Gas Light & Coke Co. Ld. Regd. 1857. Dissolved 1 May 1949, undertaking being vested in North Eastern Area Gas Board under Gas Act 1948. Holders of shares (of £5) were entitled to receive £8 15s. British Gas 3% guaranteed stock 1990–91 for each share held **1952**

Easingwold Railway Co. Ld. Inc. by Special Act 1887 as Easingwold Railway Co.; Light Railway Order obtained and name changed to Easingwold Light Railway Co. 1928; [regd. as limited under above title 6 Jan. 1958]. Vol. liq. (creditors') 17 Apr. 1958. No capital returned to contributories. Final meeting return regd. 21 Oct. 1959 .... **1961**

East African Cotton Co. Ld. Regd. 1911. Vol. liq. Mar. 1916. Final meeting return regd. 13 Oct. 1916 ...... **1961**

East African Estates Co. Ld. Regd. 1904. Vol. liq. 12 Apr. 1906. Removed from Register 1908 .... **1907**

East African Flax Lands Ld. Regd. 1918. Vol. liq. (members') 30 July 1941. Capital returned to contributories—11·4d. per share of £1. £458 17s. 11d. was paid into Companies' Liquidation Account. Final meeting return regd. 8 Aug. 1942 .... **1942**

East African Goldfields Ld. Inc. Tanganyika 1932. Struck off Register Apr. 1944 .... **1946**

East African Investments Co. Ld. Regd. 1926. Vol. liq. (members') 24 Sep. 1936. Capital returned to contributories—20s. per preference share of £1; 13s. 8$\frac{1}{2}$d. in cash *plus* 0·9442 ordinary share of 5s. in Sisal Estates Ld. for every ordinary share of £1 held. Final meeting return regd. 26 Jan. 1942 .... **1937**

East African Pearl and Sponge Co. Ld. *See* Pearl Trading and Investment Co. Ld.

East African Pearl Co. Ld. *See* Pearl Trading and Investment Co. Ld

East African Rubber Plantation Co. Ld. Regd. 1909. Vol. liq. (members') 23 Apr. 1930. Capital returned to contributories—1s. 4·125d. per share of £1. £1,972 was paid into Companies' Liquidation Account. Final meeting return regd. 24 Feb. 1950 .... **1951**

East African Selection Syndicate Ld. Regd. 1934. Controlling interest was held by Central Oil, Mining & Chemicals Trust Ld. Struck off Register 17 July 1942 .... **1943**

East & West African Exploration Co. Ld. Regd. 1919. Vol. liq. 4 May 1925. Undertaking and assets were transferred to West Coast Mines Ld. in which company shareholders were entitled to 1 share of 2s. (credited with 1s. 4d. paid) or each share of 2s. held. Final meeting return regd. 21 Sept. 1925 .... **1926**

VOL. FOR

East & West India Docks & Birmingham Junction Railway Co. *See* North London Railway Co.

East & West India Dock Co. Inc. by Special Act 1838. On 1 Jan. 1901 the company was amalgamated with London and St. Katherine Docks Co. under title of London and India Docks Co. **1904**

East & West Junction Railway Co. Inc. by Special Act 1864 .... **1909**

East and West Yorkshire Union Railways Co. Inc. by Special Act 1883. In 1923 the undertaking was merged into the London & North Eastern Railway Co. in which company stockholders were entitled to stock as follows:

For each £100 held		*L. & N.E.*
$3\frac{3}{4}$% Debenture	£$93\frac{3}{4}$	4% First Gtd.
$4\frac{1}{4}$% Debenture	£$106\frac{1}{4}$	4% First Gtd.
5% Debenture	£125	4% First Gtd.
4% Preference	£50	4% Second Pref.
	£40	Preferred Ord.
Ordinary	£25	Preferred Ord.
	£75	Deferred Ord.

1924

East Anglesey Gas Co. Inc. by Special Act 1937. Dissolved 1 May 1949. undertaking being vested in Wales Area Gas Board under Gas Act 1948. Holders of securities were entitled to receive in respect of each £100 unit held, British Gas 3% guaranteed stock 1990-95 as follows:

	£	s.	d.
Orig. ord. stock (10% stand.)	50	0	0
5% mort. debts.	101	0	0
$4\frac{1}{2}$% mort. debts.	100	0	0

1952

East Anglian Electric Supply Co. Ld. Regd. 1925. Dissolved 1 Apr. 1948 undertaking being vested in British (later Central) Electricity Authority and Eastern Area Board under Electricity Act 1947. Holders of 7% preference and ordinary shares were entitled to receive, in respect of each share (of £1) held £1 16*s.* and £1 6*s.* British Electricity 3% guaranteed stock (1968-73) respectively **1949**

East Anglian Engineering Co. Ld. *See* Bull Motors Ld.

East Anglian Gold Mining & Trust Co. Ld. Business and assets were acquired in 1895 by Anglian Mining and Finance Co. Ld. for 70,000 fully paid shares of £1 **1908**

East Anglian Light Railway Co. Inc. (under Light Railways Act 1896) **1903**

East Anglian Ploughing Co. Ld. Regd. 1936. Vol. liq. (creditors') 3 Dec. 1940. No capital returned to contributories. Final meeting return regd. 13 Dec. 1941 .... **1941**

East Anglian Rabbit Warren, Game & Poultry Farm Co. Ld. Regd. 1882. Removed from Register 1889 ..... **1883**

East Ardsley Gas Co. Inc. by Special Act 1903. In 1936 United Kingdom Gas Corporation Ld. offered holders of original capital stock £193 6*s.* 8*d.* in cash or in 4% preferred ordinary shares of £1 (at 20*s.* 6*d.* per share) for every £100 stock held. Undertaking was acquired by Morley Gas Co. in 1940 .... **1937**

East Arévalo (Mexican) Mining Co. Ld. Regd. 1886. Vol. liq. 15 Dec. 1891. Final meeting return regd. 14 Feb. 1894 .... **1892**

East Argentine Railway Co. Ld. Regd. 1871. Vol. liq. 21 Jan. 1907. Under scheme of arrangement the undertaking and assets were acquired by Argentine North Eastern Railway Co. Ld. The 4% 1st mortgage debenture stock was repaid at par on 1 Nov. 1907. Stockholders were entitled to £100 5% A debenture stock and £100 in special shares of acquiring company for every £100 ordinary stock held. Removed from Register 1909 .... **1908**

East Bay Land & Development Co. In liquidation. All capital was owned by New York City Freehold Estates Corporation (1905) Ld. **1942**

East Blue Hills Mine.................... **1892**

East Broken Hill Consols Ld. In Sept. 1893 the business was acquired by Australian Broken Hill Consols Ld. in which company shareholders were entitled to 1 fully-paid share of £1 and 2 shares of £1 (credited with 15*s.* paid) for every 2 shares of £1 (15*s.* paid) held **1896**

East Cannock Colliery Co. Ld. Regd. 1870. Vol. liq. Sept. 1880. Court Order to continue winding up under supervision Nov. 1880. Final meeting return regd. 23 May 1882 .... **1893**

East Caradon Mine **1890**

East Champ D'or Gold Mining Co. Ld. Inc. in South Africa 1918. Final capital repayment instalment of R0-$02\frac{1}{2}$ per share of R0-25 made in 1968 making total return of capital of R0-20 per share. Struck off Register in Pretoria 14 Mar. 1969 .... **1970**

East Chillaton & Atway Manganese & Felstone Co. Ld. Regd. Truro 1881. Vol. liq. 27 Aug. 1883. Struck off Register 7 Mar. 1913 .... **1885**

East Coast Drifters Ld. Regd. 1900. Vol. liq. Mar. 1908. Undertaking and assets were acquired by Richard Imin & Sons Ld. Removed from Register 1908 ... **1909**

VOL. FOR

East Coast Mutoscope Ld. Regd. 1899. Removed from Register 1910 .... **1903**

East Coast Steam Trawling Co. Ld. Regd. 1897. Vol. liq. 19 Feb. 1901. Final meeting return regd. 25 Oct. 1901 .... **1902**

East Coast Steel Corporation Ld. Regd. 1917. Vol. liq. (members') 26 Nov. 1930. Final meeting return regd. 1 Sept. 1932 .... **1931**

East Cornwall China Clay Co. Ld. Regd. 1913. Vol. liq. 7 Jan. 1921. Final meeting return regd. 24 May 1922 ***1921**

East Cornwall Electricity Supply Co. Ld. Regd. 1914 as Torpoint Electric Supply Co. Ld.; name changed July 1929. Undertaking transferred to Cornwall Electric Power Co. Capital returned to contributories—£127 6*s.* to preference shareholders; further payments (if any) not known. Final meeting return regd. 12 May 1938 .... **1938**

East Cornwall Gunpowder Co. Ld. Regd. 1892. Vol. liq. 20 Jan. 1899. Undertaking acquired by Curtis's & Harvey Ld. Final meeting return regd. 8 May 1900 **1940**

East Cornwall Mineral Railway Co. Inc. by Special Act 1869. Undertaking purchased, 1887, by Plymouth, Devonport & South Western Junction Railway Co. for £48,250 ordinary shares and £21,500 in cash. Holders of ordinary shares of £10 received nil; preference shareholders received £1 1*s.* 4*d.* in cash and £6 12*s.* 1*d.* in shares of the Plymouth Co. for each share of £10 held; loans were paid in cash and Lloyds Bonds received cash and shares **1894**

East Cowes Gas Co. Inc. as limited 1859; inc. by Special Act 1905. Dissolved 1 May 1949, undertaking being vested in Southern Area Gas Board under Gas Act 1948. Holders of securities were entitled to receive, in respect of each £100 unit held British Gas 3% guaranteed stock 1990-95 as follows:

	£	s.	d.
Orig ord. stock (10% max.)	210	0	0
4% perp. deb. stock	102	0	0

1952

East Darren Mines Co. Ld. Regd. 1858. Vol. liq. 29 Apr. 1884. Final meeting return regd. 30 June 1891 ..... **1885**

East Devon Electricity Co. Ld. Regd. 1929. All capital was owned by West of England Electric Investments Ld. Dissolved 1 Apr. 1948 under Electricity Act of 1947 .... **1936**

East Fife Central Railway Co. Inc. by Special Act 1893. Under North British Railway Act 1895 undertaking was amalgamated with that company **1897**

East Fingall Gold Mines Ld. Regd. 1902. Reconstructed 1904 as company of same name. Shareholders were entitled to 1 share of 5*s.* (credited with 4*s.* paid) in new company for each share of 5*s.* held. Removed from Register 1906 .... **1905**

East Fingall Gold Mines Ld. Regd. 1904. Reconstructed 1907 as company of same name. Shareholders were entitled to 1 share of 5*s.* (credited with 4*s.* paid) in new company for each share of 5*s.* held. Removed from Register 1910 .... **1908**

East Fingall Gold Mines Ld. Regd. 1907. Vol. liq. Dec. 1909 for amalgamation with Murchison Associated Gold Mines Ld. in which company shareholders were entitled to 1 share of 1*s.* (credited with 6*d.* paid) for each share of 5*s.* held. Removed from Register 1911 .... **1910**

East Florida Land & Produce Co. Ld. Regd. 1883. Removed from Register 1901 .... **1901**

East Geduld Mines Ld. Inc. South Africa 1927. Vol. liq. (members') 22 Dec. 1972. Capital returned to contributories: $U.S. 0·0833149627 per stock unit (of R0-20) **1973-4**

East Gloucestershire Railway Co. Inc. by Special Act 1864. Under Great Western Railway Act 1890 undertaking was absorbed by that company. Holders of ordinary stock received £2 7*s.* 6*d.* cash for each £10 held. $4\frac{1}{2}$% 1st mortgage bonds and $4\frac{1}{2}$% rent charges were assumed by purchaser **1891**

East Grassington Mines Ld. Regd. 1887. Removed from Register 1906 .... **1895**

East Grinstead Gas & Water Co. Estd. 1855; inc. by Special Act 1878. Dissolved 1 May 1949, undertaking being vested in South Eastern Area Gas Board under Gas Act 1948. Holders of securities were entitled to receive British Gas 3% guaranteed stock 1990–95 as follows in respect of each £100 unit, unless otherwise stated, of security held—

	£	s.	d.
Cons. ord. stock (6% max.)	140	0	0
6% pref. shares (of £10)	15	0	0
4% perp. deb. stock	106	0	0
$3\frac{1}{2}$% red. deb. stock (issued June 1946)	103	15	8
$3\frac{1}{2}$% red. deb. stock (issued Mar. 1947)	103	0	0

1952

**See Stock Exchange Year-Book.*

VOL. FOR

East Gwanda Mines Ld. Regd. 1905. Court Order to wind up 19 Nov. 1912. Liquidator released 10 July 1915. Struck off Register 14 Feb. 1919 .... **1913**

East Halkyn Mining Co. Ld. Regd. 1890. Vol. liq. 27 May 1930. Shareholders were entitled to 3 fully-paid ordinary shares of £1 in Halkyn District United Mines Ld. for every 4 shares of £1 held, also cash payments amounting to 8*s.* 4*d.* per share. £1,170 11*s.* 6*d.* was paid into Companies' Liquidation Account. Final meeting return regd. in July 1953 .... **1954**

East Ham Palais de Danse Ld. Regd. 1923. Vol. liq. 12 Dec. 1928. Final meeting return regd. 2 Oct. 1930 **1929**

East Hants Gas Co. Ld, *See* Bordon & District Gas Co.

East Hauraki Gold Mines Ld. Regd. 1895. Vol. liq. 2 Nov. 1897. Taken over by Triumph Komata Gold Mine Ld. Final meeting return regd. 30 Aug. 1898 ***1898**

East Hony Mining Co. Ld. Regd. 1882. Reconstructed 1884 as Hony United Mining Co. Ld., in which company shareholders were entitled to 1 share of £1 (credited with 17*s.* 6*d.* paid) for each share held. Removed from Register 1906 .... **1890**

East Hull Gas Co. Estd. by Deed of Settlement 1846; inc. as Sutton Southcoates & Drypool Gas Co. by Special Act 1867; name changed 1906. Dissolved 1 May 1949, undertaking being vested in North Eastern Area Gas Board under Gas Act 1948. Holders of securities were entitled to receive, in respect of each £100 unit held, British Gas 3% guaranteed stock 1990–95 as follows:

	£	s.	d.
Ord. stock (5% basic)	110	0	0
4½% pref. stock	109	0	0
4% perp. deb. stock	101	10	0
5½% perp. deb. stock	134	0	0
7% perp. deb. stock	155	0	0
5½% red. deb. stock	109	0	0

A distribution on ord. stock of 3·1508% out of reserves was made in Aug. 1954 **1952**

East India Association Ld. Regd. 1898. Vol. liq. 8 Feb. 1906. Final meeting return regd. 3 Apr. 1910 ...... ***1907**

East India Co. for Exploration and Mining Ld. Regd. Edinburgh 1881. Vol. liq. June 1889. Court Orders: to continue winding up under Supervision July 1889; to dissolve 29 May 1896 .... **1890**

East India Construction Syndicate Ld. Regd. 1903. Vol. liq. 6 Nov. 1906. Removed from Register 1907 .... **1907**

East India Tramways Co. Ld. Regd. 1884. Reconstructed 1902 as company of same name. Holders of debenture stock were entitled to 1 fully-paid ordinary share of £1 for every £1 of claim. Shareholders were entitled to 4 deferred shares of £1 fully-paid for each share of £10 subject to subscription at par for 2 preference shares of £1 in respect of every 4 deferred shares. Removed from Register 1903 .... **1903**

East India Tramways Co. Ld. Regd 1902 Vol liq (members') 15 Nov. 1950. Capital returned to contributories—£1 6*s.* 5*d.* per share of £1. Final meeting return regd. 18 Dec. 1953 .... **1955**

East Indian Railway Company. Inc. by Special Act 1849. The undertaking was purchased by the Government in 1878 by means of annuities which terminated on 14 Feb. 1953 with the following final distributions per £1 annuity—Class A, 1*s.* 7·69*d.*; Class B, £17 17*s.* 1·4*d.*; Class C, £22 5*s.* 2·58*d.*; and Class D, £22 4*s.* 3·79*d* **1954**

East Indian Tea & Produce Co. Ld. Regd. 1907. Vol. liq. 27 Apr. 1923. The estates and equipment were transferred to Malayalam Plantations Ld. Holders of 1st and 2nd mortgage debenture stocks and loans were entitled to either repayment in cash or fully-paid shares of £1 at a price of 28*s.* per share. Shareholders were entitled to 22 fully-paid shares of £1 for every 100 shares of £1 held. Final meeting return regd. 22 Dec. 1923 .... **1924**

East Indies Finance Syndicate Ld. Regd. 1927. Struck off Register Feb. 1935 .... **1935**

East Java Rubber Co. Ld. Regd. 1910. Vol. liq. (members') 29 Dec. 1933. Reconstructed as East Java Rubber Estates Ld., in which company shareholders were entitled to 1 share of £1 (credited with 16*s.* paid) for each share of £1 held. Final meeting return regd. 10 Jan. 1935 .... **1934**

East Java Rubber Estates Ld. Regd. 1934. Vol. liq. (members') 26 June 1953. Capital returned to contributories—2*s.* 8·36*d.* per share of £1. £309 0*s.* 8*d.* was paid into Companies' Liquidation Account. Final meeting return regd. 1 Sept. 1955 .... **1956**

East Kent Colliery Co. Ld. Regd. 1907. The undertaking and assets were acquired by Tilmanstone (Kent) Collieries Ld. (later Tilmanstone Holdings Ld. and Tilmanstone Investment Trust Ld.). The holders of 1st mortgage debentures received an equal amount of 1st mortgage debentures in the purchasing company. The receiver stated that no funds were available for holders of 2nd mortgage participating debenture stock, income bonds or shares. Struck off Register 8 June 1945 .... **1946**

East Kent Contract and Financial Co. Ld. Regd. 1907. Vol. liq. 9 Sept. 1924. Final meeting return regd. 11 June 1931 .... **1925**

East Kent District Water Co. Inc. by Special Act 1889. By Order made 31 Dec. 1953 the undertaking was acquired by the Mid-Kent Water Co., with effect 1 Apr. 1954. Stockholders of this company were entitled to receive stock (credited as fully-paid) in that company as follows—£10 Mid-Kent ordinary (10% maximum) for every original ordinary share of £10; £8 Mid-Kent ordinary (10% maximum) for every ordinary share (8% maximum) of £10; £10 Mid-Kent ordinary (7% maximum) for every ordinary share (7%. maximum) of £10; £14 Mid-Kent 5% consolidated preference stock for every 7% preference share of £10; £11 Mid-Kent 5% consolidated preference stock for every 5½% preference share of £10 and £10 Mid-Kent 5% consolidated preference stock for every 5½% preference share of £10. Holders of the 5% and 4% perpetual debenture stocks of this company were entitled to receive a like amount of 5 and 4% perpetual debenture stock of the Mid-Kent company respectively. Liability for the redeemable debentures and debenture stock was assumed by the Mid-Kent company. Dissolved 31 Mar. 1954 .... **1955**

East Kent Gas Co, Ld. Regd. 1923. Dissolved 1 May 1949, undertaking being vested in South Eastern Area Gas Board under Gas Act 1948. Holders of ordinary shares (of £1) were entitled to receive £1 1*s.* British Gas 3% guaranteed stock 1990—95 for each share held **1952**

East Kent Light Railways Co. Inc. 19 June 1911 under Light Railways Act 1896. Dissolved 3 June 1949: undertaking vested 1 Jan. 1948 in British Transport Commission under Transport Act 1947. Holders of securities were entitled to receive British Transport 3% guaranteed stock 1978–88 as follows:

	£	s.	d.	
Ordinary shares (of £1)			6	
5% debenture stock (for each £100)	55	0	0	**1949**

East Kent Railway Co. *See* London, Chatham and Dover Railway Co.

East Lincolnshire Railway Co. Inc. by Special Act. 1846. In 1923 the undertaking was merged into the London & North Eastern Railway Co., in which company stockholders were entitled to £150 4%. Debenture Stock for every £100 East Lincolnshire Consolidated Stock held **1924**

East London Bank Ld. *See* Central Bank of London Ld.

East London Cold Storage & Ice Co. Ld. Regd. 1924. Vol. liq. (creditors') 24 Feb. 1930. Assets realised insufficient to pay creditors in full. Final meeting return regd. 25 June 1931 .... **1931**

East London Railway Co. Inc. by Special Act 1865. In 1925 undertaking was vested in the Southern Railway Co., in which company stockholders were entitled to stock as follows:

East London *For each £100 held*	*S.R.*	
2½% Whitechapel Ext. Deb.	£62½ 4% Deb.	
First 3½% Debenture	£87½ 4% Deb.	
2nd Charge 4% Deb., A.	£100 4% Deb.	
2nd Charge 4% Deb., B.	£100 4% Deb.	
3rd Charge 4% Deb.	£30 5% Pref.	
4th Charge 4% Deb.	£12½ 5% Pref.	
Consolidated	£5½ cash	**1929**

East London Railway Joint Committee. Dissolved 2 Apr. 1949; undertaking vested 1 Jan. 1948 in British Transport Commission under Transport Act 1947 **1949**

East London Waterworks Co. Inc. by Special Act 1807. Undertaking was taken over by Metropolitan Water Board from 24 June 1904, under provisions of the Metropolis Water Act 1902 .... **1905**

East Long Rake Lead Mining Co. Ld. Regd. 1880. Removed from Register 1894 .... **1891**

East Magdalena Exploitation Co. Ld. Regd. 1906. Vol. liq. 21 Oct. 1910. Struck off Register 30 Jan. 1923 **1911**

East Malay Coconut Co. Ld. Regd. 1912. Vol. liq. 14 Jan. 1920. Final meeting return regd. 7 Mar. 1922 **1920**

East Metropolitan Brickworks Ld. Regd. 1927. Vol. liq. (creditors') 27 June 1930. No capital returned to contributories. Final meeting return regd. 23 Sept. 1931 **1931**

East Morley & Bradford Deposit Bank Ld. Regd. 1901. Vol. liq. 2 Dec. 1918. Undertaking acquired by Union Bank of Manchester Ld. **1940**

East Mulwarrie Gold Mines Ld. Regd. 1900. Vol. liq. May 1908. Removed from Register 1909 .... **1909**

East Murchison United Ld. Regd. 1895. Vol. liq. 25 May 1905. Removed from Register 1907 .... **1906**

**See Stock Exchange Year-Book.*

*See Stock Exchange Year-Book.

undertaking being vested in Southern Area Gas Board under Gas Act 1948. Holders of securities were entitled to receive, in respect of each £100 unit held, British Gas 3% guaranteed stock 1990–95 as follows:

	£	s.	d.	
Cons. ord. stock (5% stand.)	150	0	0	
5% pref. stock	112	0	0	
4% perp. deb. stock	102	0	0	
4% red. deb. stock	100	10	0	
4% mort. debs. (Sandown Gas & Coke Co.)	100	0	0	1952

Eastbourne & District Motor Cab Co. (1909) Ld. *See* Eastbourne Motors Ld.

Eastbourne Electric Light Co. Ld. Regd. 1882. Undertaking was acquired by Eastbourne Corporation for £83,000. Capital returned to contributories—£20 (approx.) per ordinary or original share of £10; £10 (approx.) per preference share of £10 (£5 paid). Removed from Register 1901 — **1900**

Eastbourne Gas Co. Estd. 1852; inc. by Special Act 1868. Dissolved 1 May 1949, undertaking being vested in South Eastern Area Gas Board under Gas Act 1948. Holders of securities were entitled to receive, in respect of each £100 unit held, British Gas 3% guaranteed stock 1990–95 as follows:

	£	s.	d.	
A stock (5% stand.)	127	10	0	
B stock (3½% stand.)	110	10	0	
5% irred. pref. stock	114	10	0	
4% red. pref. stock	100	15	0	
5% irred. deb. stock	125	0	0	
4% perp. deb. stock	102	0	0	
3½% red deb. stock	102	0	0	
3½% red deb. stock (1970)	100	0	0	
3½% red deb. stock (1962)	99	10	0	1952

Eastbourne Motors Ld. Regd. 1909 as Eastbourne & District Motor Cab Co. (1909) Ld.; name changed Mar. 1916. Vol. liq. 26 Feb. 1919. Final meeting return regd. 26 Mar. 1920 — **1910**

Eastbourne, Seaford & Newhaven Railway Co. Inc. by Special Act 1886. Undertaking abandoned by Act of 1892 — **1893**

Easter Extended Gold Mine Ld. Regd. 1897. Struck off Register 22 Dec. 1903 — **1904**

Easter Gift Proprietary Gold Mines Ld. Regd. 1896. Court Order to wind up 26 Apr. 1899. Removed from Register 1908 — **1900**

Eastern Agency Ld. Regd. 1873. Vol. liq. 8 Dec. 1884. Final meeting return regd. 15 May 1896 — **1885**

Eastern Akkim Ld. Regd. 1910. Vol. liq. 26 June 1919. Undertaking was acquired by Goldfields of Eastern Akkim Ld. Final meeting return regd. 27 Apr. 1920 — **1920**

Eastern & African Cold Storage Supply Co. Ld. Inc. South Australia 1903. Vol. liq. July 1909 — **1910**

Eastern & Australian Trading Association Ld, Regd. 1896. Removed from Register 1901 — **1901**

Eastern & General Trust & Development Co. Ld. Regd. 1912 as Sekampong (Sumatra) Rubber Estates Ld.; name changed Mar. 1922. Vol. liq. (creditors') 4 Oct. 1932. Shareholders received one share in Normont Gold Mines Ld. (inc. in Canada) for every 50 shares held. Final meeting return regd. 4 Jan. 1934 — **1933**

Eastern & Midlands Railway Co. Inc. by Special Act 1883. From 1893 the undertaking was vested in the Midland Railway Co. (later London Midland & Scottish Railway Co.) and Great Northern (later London & North Eastern Rly. Co.); holders of securities being entitled to receive Midland & Great Northern Joint Line Rent Charge Stock in satisfaction of their rights and arrears of interest — **1895**

Eastern & Overseas Products Ld. Regd. 1928. Vol. liq. (members') 8 Oct. 1934. Undertaking and assets were acquired by Eastova Ld., in which company shareholders were entitled to 1 share of 5s. (credited with 3s. paid) for each share of £1 held. Final meeting return regd. 5 Mar. 1941 — **1935**

Eastern Bengal Railway Co. Formed 1857 under East India Co's. guarantee. In 1884 the Secretary of State for India purchased the line, for an annuity of £6 3s. 4·79d. per £100 consolidated stock. The payment of interest on debentures and debenture stock was also taken over. — **1884**

Eastern Canada Co. Ld. Regd. 1911. Vol. liq. 1 Dec. 1913. Final meeting return regd. 30 June 1916 — **1914**

Eastern Carpathian Oil Co. Ld, Regd. 1913. Struck off Register 19 Mar. 1937 — **1938**

Eastern Chemical Company Ld. Regd. 1913. Vol. liq. (members') 11 Jan. 1945. Capital returned to contributories—20s. 4·0005d. per participating ordinary share (of £1) and 48s. 1·29d. per deferred share (of 2s.). £12,433 paid into Companies' Liquidation account. Final meeting return regd. 27 Sept. 1954 — **1955**

Eastern Claims Syndicate Ld. *See* Eastern Gold Mines Ld.

Eastern Co. of Transport and Insurance Ld. Regd. 1918. Court Order to wind up 9 Nov. 1926. Struck off Register 1934 — **1927**

Eastern Counties & British Farmers' Condensed Milk Co. Ld. Regd. 1888. Vol. liq. 17 Apr. 1890. Final meeting return regd. 11 Feb. 1891 — **1891**

Eastern Counties Bacon Factory Ld. Regd. 1890. Removed from Register 1903 — **1896**

Eastern Counties Dairy Farmers Ld. Regd. 1918 as Excelsior Dairies Ld.; name changed July 1920 to Abbot Bros. Dairies Ld. and as above in Dec. 1921. Vol. liq. 19 Mar. 1931. Capital returned to contributories—£26,703 8s. 9d. Final meeting return regd. 20 Mar. 1931 — **1932**

Eastern Counties Insurance Co. Ld. Regd. 1890. Vol. liq. 16 Feb. 1901. Part of fire business was acquired by National Reliance Insurance Co. Ld., and the burglary insurance business by National Burglary Insurance Corporation Ld. (later National Burglary & Fire Office Ld.). Removed from Register 1905 — **1902**

Eastern Counties Navigation & Transport Co. Ld. Regd. 1889. Vol. liq. 16 Sept. 1901. Final meeting return regd. 17 Sept. 1902 — **1902**

Eastern Counties Road Car Co. Ld. Regd. 1919. Vol. liq. (members') 5 Nov. 1931. Undertaking and assets were acquired by Eastern Counties Omnibus Co. Ld., in which company shareholders were entitled to 2 shares of £1 (credited as fully-paid) for each share of £1 held. Final meeting return regd. 4 Aug. 1932 — **1932**

Eastern Development Corporation Ld. Regd. 1912. Receiver appointed on 16 Jan. 1925. Some assets were realised and proceeds applied in repaying debenture holders to the extent of 6s. 5⅞d. per £1. Struck off Register Oct. 1934 — **1935**

Eastern Dry Dock & Engineering Co. Ld. Regd. 1883 as Newport (Mon.) Slipway, Dry Dock & Engineering Co. Ld.; name changed Nov. 1887. Vol. liq. 17 June 1895. Final meeting return regd. 6 Nov. 1895. — ***1898**

Eastern Electric Light and Power Co, Ld. Regd. 1881. Vol. liq. 22 Apr. 1884. Final meeting return regd.3 Mar. 1891 — **1885**

Eastern Europe Development Co. Ld. Regd. 1920. Struck off Register 1925 — ***1924**

Eastern Gold Farms Syndicate Ld. Regd. 1902. Vol. liq. Apr. 1909. Removed from Register 1913 — **1910**

Eastern Gold Mines Ld. Inc. Transvaal 1898 as Eastern Claims Syndicate Ld.; name changed June 1902. Vol. liq. 11 Mar. 1937. The assets were acquired in 1936 by African & European Investment Co. Ld in which company shareholders were entitled to 1 share of £1 (credited as fully-paid) for every 8 shares of 5s. held — **1938**

Eastern Gympie Gold Mines Ld. Regd. Edinburgh 1902. Vol. liq. Jan. 1907. Final meeting return regd. 8 Dec. 1908 — **1907**

Eastern Investment Co. Ld. Regd. 1895. Principal assets were acquired in 1903 by Associated Share and Investment Co. Ld. (later New Eastern Investment Co. Ld.), for £425,000 in fully-paid shares of £1; other assets were sold for £375,000 in cash. Shareholders were entitled to £15 in cash and 17 shares of £1 in acquiring company for every 30 shares of £1 held. Vol. liq. 20 May 1903. Final meeting return regd. 22 Sept. 1904. Court Order deferred dissolution 4 Dec. 1904. Struck off Register 24 Feb. 1922 — **1943**

Eastern Irrigations Ld. Regd. 1924. Vol. liq. 21 Nov. 1928. Final meeting return regd. 2 Dec. 1930 — **1929**

Eastern Kentucky Land Exploration & Development Co. Ld. Regd. 1890. Vol. liq. 15 Dec. 1899. Struck off Register Mar. 1930 — **1931**

Eastern Massachusetts Street Railway Co. Inc. Massachusetts 1919. The outstanding 6% 1st mortgage gold bonds (Lynn & Boston Railroad) were redeemed at par on 1 Dec. 1929 — **1929**

Eastern Minerals Ld. Regd. 1924. Vol. liq. (members') 14 Apr. 1930. Capital returned to contributories—5s. 4d. per share of £1. Final meeting return regd. 16 Mar. 1931 — ***1931**

Eastern Mortgage & Agency Co. Ld. Regd. 1890. Vol. liq. 9 July 1902. Reconstructed as Eastern Mortgage and Agency Co. (1902) Ld. (later London and Overseas Investment Co. Ld.) in which company shareholders were entitled to £2 in preference shares £5 2nd debenture stock and one fully-paid ordinary share of 10s. for each fully-paid ordinary or A share of £10 held or 1 fully-paid ordinary share of 10s. for each ordinary share of £10 (£3 paid) held or 1 founders' share of £1 for each founders' share of £1 held. Holders of 4½% debenture stock were entitled to £105 4½% debenture stock for every £100 stock held. Final meeting return regd. 16 Sept. 1920 — **1903**

Eastern Mysore Gold Co. Ld. Regd. 1886. Vol. liq. 26 July 1889. Property was acquired by Colar Central Gold Co. Ld. Final meeting return regd. 18 Mar. 1891 ... **1890**

Eastern Oil Industries Ld. Regd. 1919 as Palestine Oil Industry "Shemen" Ld.; name changed Oct. 1928. Vol. liq. (members') 17 Dec. 1929. Undertaking and assets sold to Eastern & Overseas Products Ld. in which company shareholders received 3 shares of £1 fully-paid for every 2 shares of £1 held. £111 18s. 5d. was paid into Companies' Liquidation Account in respect of unclaimed balances arising from sale of shares. Final meeting return regd. 23 May 1932 .. **1930**

Eastern Oregon Gold Mining Co. Ld. Regd. 1888. Vol. liq. 28 Dec. 1891. Final meeting return regd. 1 Jan. 1894 ... **1892**

Eastern Petroleum and Finance Co. Ld. Regd. 1921. Court Order to wind up 1940. Struck off Register 1 Sept 1944 ... **1945**

Eastern Petroleum Co. Ld. Regd. 1909. Vol. liq. 25 Aug. 1913 for reconstruction as Eastern Petroleum Co. (1913) Ld. in which company shareholders were entitled to 1 share of £1 (credited with 16s. paid) for each share of £1 fully-paid held. Final meeting return regd. 17 May 1916 ... **1914**

Eastern Petroleum Co. (1913) Ld. Regd. 1913. Vol. liq. 14 Dec. 1915. Reconstructed as Suez Oil Co. (1915) Ld. in which company shareholders were entitled to 1 share of 10s. (credited with 9s. paid) for each share of £1 held. Final meeting return regd. 30 Sept. 1916 **1916**

Eastern Pioneer Co. Ld. Regd. 1899. Vol. liq. Aug. 1921. Undertaking and assets were acquired by Yangtse Corporation Ld. (later J. B. Holdings Ld.) in which company shareholders were entitled to 1 preferred ordinary share of 5s. (credited with 3s. paid) for each share of £1 held. Struck off Register 3 Oct. 1941 . **1942**

Eastern Plantations and General Investment Co. Ld. Regd. 1928 as Eastern Plantations Finance Co. Ld.; name changed 2 Nov. 1950. Vol. liq. (members') 31 Dec. 1963. Investments were distributed in specie in Dec. 1963. Capital returned to contributories— 3·47d. per share of £1. Final meeting return regd. 29 Oct. 1965 ... **1967**

Eastern Plantations Finance Co. Ld. See Eastern Plantations and General Investment Co. Ld.

Eastern Rand Exploration Ld. Inc. Transvaal 1899 ... **1907**

Eastern Rand Syndicate Ld. Regd. 1895. Vol. liq. 14 Aug. 1916. Final meeting return regd. 15 Feb. 1930 **1917**

Eastern Rhodesia Gold Reef Development Co. Ld. Regd. 1896. Vol. liq. 25 Nov. 1898. Final meeting return regd. 21 Nov. 1899 ... ***1899**

Eastern Siam Tin Dredging Ld. Regd. 1925. Receiver appointed on 17 July 1931; ceased to act on 12 Sept. 1933. Struck off Register 1935 ... **1935**

Eastern Steam Fishing Co. Ld. Regd. Edinburgh 1901. Vol. liq. 17 Aug. 1906. Undertaking and assets acquired by North British Steam Fishing Co. Ld. in which company shareholders were entitled to 7 fully-paid shares of £1 and 1s. 3d. in cash for every 10 shares of £1 (15s. paid) held. Final meeting return regd. 26 Jan. 1907 ... **1907**

Eastern Steamship Co. Ld. Regd. 1871. Vol. liq. 1 Feb. 1905. Final meeting return regd. 24 June 1908 ..... ***1906**

Eastern Syndicate Ld. Regd. 1910 as Eastern Syndicate (1910) Ld.; name changed Apr. 1912. Vol. liq. Oct. 1931. Struck off Register 24 July 1936 ... **1937**

Eastern Tin Trust Ld. Regd. 1925. Vol. liq. 30 July 1926. The investments were sold to Tin Selection Trust Ld. in which company shareholders were entitled to 22 shares of £1 for every 25 shares of £1 held. Final meeting return regd. 3 July 1928 ... **1927**

Eastern Transvaal Plantations Ld. Regd. 1905. Vol. liq. 9 Oct. 1913. The property was taken over by debenture holders; no funds were available for contributories. Final meeting return regd. 23 Mar. 1914 ... **1914**

Eastern Van Ryn & Modderfontein Gold Reefs Ld. Regd. 1917. Struck off Register 29 Oct. 1935 ... **1936**

Eastham Ferry Pleasure Gardens & Hotel Co. Ld. Regd. 1897. Struck off Register 1915 ... **1902**

Eastleigh (Block "A") Gold Mines Ld. Inc. Transvaal 1896. In voluntary liquidation in 1904 ... **1904**

Eastleigh Deep Ld. Inc. Transvaal 1895. In voluntary liquidation in 1904 ... **1904**

Eastleigh Mines Ld. Inc. Transvaal 1894. Vol. liq. 25 May 1906 ... **1907**

Eastman Photographic Materials Co. Ld. Regd. 1889. Vol. liq. 21 Feb. 1899. Undertaking was acquired by Kodak Ld. Removed from Register 1901 ... **1900**

Easton & Church Hope Railway Co. Inc. by Special Act 1867. Dissolved 3 June 1949; undertaking vested 1 Jan. 1948 in British Transport Commission under Transport Act 1947. Holders of securities were entitled to receive British Transport 3°₀ guaranteed

stock 1978–88 as follows:

	£	s.	d.
Ordinary shares (of £20)	1	0	
5% preference stock (£100)	5	0	
4½% debenture stock (£100)	5	0	**1949**

Easton, Anderson & Goolden Ld. Regd. 1894. Vol liq. 28 Oct. 1898. Absorbed by United Ordinance & Engineering Co. Ld. Final meeting return regd. 22 Feb. 1916 ... **1899**

Easton, Neston, Mineral & Towcester, Roade & Olney Junction Railway Co. See Stratford-upon-Avon Towcester & Midland Junction Railway Co.

Eastova Holdings Ld. Regd. 1934 as Eastova Ld.; name changed 16 Aug. 1948. Vol. liq. (members') 16 Nov. 1948. Shareholders were entitled to receive for each share (of 5s.)—1 share (of 5s.) of Eastova Ld. and 15s. in cash. £654 was paid into Companies' Liquidation Account. Final meeting return regd. 14 Sept 1951 ... **1952**

Eastova Ld. Regd. 1948. Vol. liq. (members') 16 Sept. 1968. Capital returned to contributories—10s. 2·175d. plus 13·55p. per share of 5s. Final meeting return regd. 13 Nov. 1971 ... **1972**

Eastwood & Co. Ld. Regd. 1902. Receiver was appointed on behalf of debenture holders Feb. 1912. Vol. liq. 12 Mar. 1915. Business was acquired by Eastwoods Ld. Final meeting return regd. 31 Jan. 1922 ... **1916**

Eastwood, Swingler & Co. Ld. Regd. 1886. Vol. liq. Mar. 1925. Struck off Register Mar. 1930 ... **1931**

Eastwoods Cement Ld. Regd. 1925. Vol. liq. (members') 13 Dec. 1945. Undertaking was acquired by Eastwoods Ld. in which company shareholders were entitled to 1 ordinary share of £1 (credited as fully-paid) for every £1 stock held. Final meeting return regd. 23 July 1948 ... **1949**

Eastwoods Fletton Ld. Regd. 1927. Vol. liq. (members') 13 Dec. 1945. Undertaking was acquired by Eastwoods Ld. in which company shareholders were entitled to 7 ordinary shares of £1 (credited as fully-paid) for every £10 preferred stock held and 4 ordinary shares of £1 (credited as fully-paid) for every 15s. deferred stock held. Final meeting return regd. 23 July 1948 ... **1949**

Eastwoods Humber Ld. Regd. 1936. Vol. liq. (members') 13 Dec. 1945. Undertaking was acquired by Eastwoods Ld. in which company ordinary stock- holders were entitled to receive 7 ordinary shares of £1 (credited as fully-paid) for every £10 stock held and debenture holders an equal amount of 4½% debenture stock. Final meeting return regd. 23 July 1948 ... **1949**

Eastwoods Lewes Cement Ld. Regd. 1929. Vol. liq. (members') 13 Dec. 1945. Undertaking was ac- quired by Eastwoods Ld. in which company shareholders were entitled to 3 ordinary shares of £1 (credited as fully-paid) for every £4 ordinary stock held and 1 ordinary share of £1 (credited as fully- paid) for every 12s. founders' stock held. Final meeting return regd. 23 July 1948 ... **1949**

Ebano Oil Co. Ld. Regd. 1929. Vol. liq. (members') 19 June 1936. Undertaking acquired by Anglo-Ameri- can Oil Co. Ld. (later Esso Petroleum Ld.) on 31 Dec. 1935. All shares held by Pan American Foreign Corporation (of New York). Final meeting held 4 Mar. 1937 ... **1937**

Ebbw Vale Steel, Iron and Coal Co. Ld. Regd. 1868. Receiver for 6% mortgage debenture holders ap- pointed and ceased to act in Oct. 1936; receiver for 2nd debenture holders appointed 21 Oct. 1936. Iron and steel assets were sold in 1935 to Richard Thomas & Co. Ld. (later Richard Thomas & Baldwins Ld.). The colliery properties were sold in Oct. 1936 to Partridge, Jones & John Paton Ld. The assets realised insufficient, after meeting liability for capital and interest of 6% mortgage debentures to satisfy claims of 2nd debenture holders. Struck off Register 1 May 1942 ... **1943**

Ebenezer Gold Mining Co. Ld. Regd. 1901, Court Order to wind up 25 Apr. 1906. Removed from Register 1911 ... **1907**

Eberhardt & Aurora Mining Co. Ld. Regd. 1870. Vol. liq. Jan. 1881. Reconstructed as Eberhardt Co. Ld., in which company shareholders were entitled to 3 shares of £1 (credited with 10s. paid) and 3 fully- paid shares of £1 for each share of £10 held. Final meeting return regd. 25 June 1890 ... **1885**

Eberhardt & Monitor Co. Ld. Regd. 1885. Vol. liq. Aug. 1888. Reconstructed as New Eberhardt Co. Ld. (later Thistle Reef Gold Mining Co. Ld.) in which company shareholders were entitled to 1 ordinary share of 5s. (credited with 1s. paid) for each share of £1 held. Debenture holders were entitled to 4 fully-

VOL. FOR

VOL. FOR

paid preference shares of 5s. for each £1 debenture held. Final meeting return regd. 17 July 1890 ...... **1893**

Eberhardt Co. Ld. Regd. 1881. Vol. liq. Oct. 1885. Court Order to wind up Dec. 1885. Reconstructed as Eberhardt & Monitor Co. in which company shareholders were entitled to 1 share of £1 (credited with 15s. paid) for each ordinary share of £1 held or 1 share of £1 (credited with 15s. paid) & 1 fully-paid share of £1 for each preference share of £1 held. The debentures were taken over by new company. Final meeting return regd. 25 June 1890 .... **1888**

Eberle's Hotel & Restaurant Co. Ld. Regd. 1877. Wound up by Order of Court 5 June 1885 .... **1885**

Ebor Investment and Trading Co. Ld. Regd. 1899. Vol. liq. 6 Oct. 1905. Final meeting return regd. 17 Nov. 1924 .... **1934**

Ebor Newspapers Ld. Regd. 1929. Vol. liq. (members') 31 Jan. 1934. Capital returned to contributories— £42,735 15s. 8d. Final meeting return regd. 15 Dec. 1934 .... **1900**

Eburite Corrugated Paper Co. Ld. *See* Bowater Eburite Ld.

Eburite Paper Co. Ld. *See* Bowater-Eburite Ld.

Eccles Bleaching Co. Ld. Regd. 1899. Removed from Register 1901 .... **1901**

Eccles' Glenariff Hotel Co. Ld. Regd. Dublin 1888. Vol. liq. Jan. 1914 for reconstruction. **1914**

Eccles (John) & Son Ld. Regd. 1899. Struck off Register 2 Aug. 1904 .... **1905**

Eccles Rubber & Cycle Co. Ld. Regd. 1897. Removed from Register 1906 .... **1905**

Eccles Spinning & Manufacturing Co. Ld. Regd. 1905. Vol. liq. (members') 1 Apr. 1953. Final meeting return regd. 26 Sept. 1955 .... **1952**

Ecco Works Ld. Regd. 1897 as Albert Eadie Chain Co. Ld.; name changed Nov. 1906. Vol. liq. 8 Oct. 1906. Reconstructed as Abingdon-Ecco Ld. (later Abingdon Works Ld.), in which company shareholders were entitled to 5 fully-paid ordinary shares of £1 for every 8 ordinary shares of £1 held or to 1 preference share of £1 for each preference share of £1 held. Final meeting return regd. 8 Oct. 1907 .... **1907**

Eclipse Automatic Devices Ld. Regd. 1929. Vol. liq. (creditors') 15 May 1930. No capital returned to contributories. Final meeting return regd. 14 July 1932 .... **1931**

Eclipse Boiler Furnace (London & South) Ld. Regd. 1909. Struck off Register 1915 .... **1913**

Eclipse Gold Mining & Quartz Crushing Co. Ld. Regd. 1874. Vol. liq. 9 Jan. 1878. Court Order to continue winding up under supervision 5 Feb. 1878. Final meeting return regd. 13 June 1878 .... **1878**

Eclipse Gold Mining Co. Ld. Regd. 1895. Vol. liq. 3 Dec. 1896. Undertaking and assets were acquired by Golden Link Consolidated Gold Mines Ld., in which company shareholders were entitled to 1 fully-paid share of £1 for each share of £1 held. Final meeting return regd. 17 July 1897 .... **1902**

Eclipse Mill Co. Ld. Regd. 1920. Vol. liq. 10 June 1981. Final meeting return regd. 15 Dec. 1981 .... **1961**

Eclipse Saloon Services Ld. Regd. 1931. Vol. liq. (members') 10 Sept. 1940. Undertaking acquired by United Welsh Services Ld. All capital held by Red & White United Transport Ld. (later United Transport Co. Ld.). Final meeting return regd. 18 Dec. 1940 .... **1941**

Eclipse Shipping & Trading Co. Ld. Regd. 1920. Vol. liq. (members') 1 July 1941. Capital returned to contributories—23s. per share of 10s. Final meeting return regd. 1 Jan. 1942 .... **1942**

Economic & Smokeless Steam Firing Patents Ld. Regd. 1889. Struck off Register 9 May 1893 .... **1901**

Economic Bank Ld. Regd. 1893. Court Order to wind up 21 June 1905. Removed from Register 1911 .... **1906**

Economic Bank of Bihar. Inc. Bihar 1890. Absorbed in 1918 into Savings & Economic Bank of Bihar Ld **1929**

Economic Electric Co. Ld. Regd. 1883. Removed from Register 1891 .... **1885**

Economic Fire Office Ld. Regd. 1886. Removed from Register 1906 .... **1895**

Economic Gold Extraction Co. Ld. Regd. 1889. Vol. liq. 18 Feb. 1899. Final meeting return regd. 10 Aug. 1899 .... **1900**

Economic Life Assurance Society. Established by Deed of Settlement 1823. Regd. 1891. Vol. liq. June 1912. Business was acquired by Alliance Assurance Co. Ld. Removed from Register 1913........................ **1913**

Economic Printing & Publishing Co. Ld. Regd. 1890. Struck off Register 18 Nov. 1902 .... **1903**

Economic Smokeless Fire Co. Ld. Regd. 1894. Vol. liq. 6 Sept. 1895. Final meeting return regd. 17 Mar. 1897 *****1896**

Economin Motor Spirit Co. Ld. Regd. 1913. Vol. liq. 1 May 1914. Capital returned to contributories—8s.

VOL. FOR

per share of £1 (10s. paid); further payments (if any) not known. Final meeting return regd. 10 June 1915 **1915**

Ecton Co. Ld. Regd. 1883. Vol. liq. June 1889. Final meeting return regd. 11 July 1890 .... **1890**

Ecuador Land Co. Ld. Regd. 1859. Struck off Register 15 Feb. 1952 .... **1953**

Ecuador Telephone Co. Ld. Regd. 1889. Vol. liq. 7 Oct. 1914. Final meeting return regd. 30 Oct. 1915 ...... **1915**

Ecuadorian Association Ld. Regd. Edinburgh 1899. Vol. liq. Apr. 1904. Court Orders: to wind up Mar. 1906; to dissolve 19 Oct. 1908 .... **1905**

Ecuadorian Corporation Ld. Regd. 1913. Vol. liq. 6 July 1928. Undertaking was acquired by Canadian company of same name. Debenture holders were entitled to 1 fully-paid share of $100 for every £20 debentures held and 2 ordinary shares of no par value for each share of £1 to issue of which debenture holders were entitled under talons attached to debentures. Ordinary shareholders were entitled to 2 fully-paid shares of no par value for every 10 shares of £1 (1s. paid) held *****1930**

Ecuadorian Corporation Ld. Inc. Canada 1928. Undertaking and assets were acquired in 1937 by Ecuadorian Corporation Ld., in which company shareholders were entitled to 1 fully-paid ordinary share of $5 for each ordinary share of no par value held and $100 income debentures for each preference share of $100 held **1939**

Eddystone Granite Quarries Ld. Regd. 1889 as Marble, Granite & Stone Co. Ld.; name changed 4 Sept. 1889. Vol. liq. 24 Mar. 1899. Final meeting return regd. 15 May 1899 .... *****1893**

Edenbridge & District Gas Co. Inc. 1867. Dissolved 1 May 1949, undertaking being vested in South Eastern Area Gas Board under Gas Act 1948. Holders of securities were entitled to receive, in respect of each £100 unit held, British Gas 3% guaranteed stock 1990–95 as follows:

	£	s.	d.
Ord. stock (7% stand.)................	145	0	0
4% mort. debs.	50	2	6
6% irred. deb. stock	145	0	0
4% irred.deb.stock	102	10	0

1952

Edgbaston Brewery Co. Ld. Regd. 1887. Removed from Register 1898 .... **1894**

Edge Brothers Ld. Regd. 1886. Court Orders: to wind up 15 Jan. 1887; to dissolve 17 Feb. 1891 .... **1888**

Edge (S. F.) Ld. Regd. 1907 as S. F. Edge (1907) Ld.; name changed June 1910. Vol. liq. 2 Jan. 1913. Undertaking and assets were sold to D. Napier & Son Ld. Capital returned to contributories—20s. per share of £1 in Feb. 1913; further payments (if any) not known. Final meeting return regd. 23 Oct. 1929 **1913**

Edge's (S. F.) Pig Farms Ld. Regd. 1922. Receiver appointed in Sept. 1925. Assets were realised and a small distribution to debenture holders was expected. Struck off Register Feb. 1930 .... **1931**

Edgware & Hampstead Railway Co. Inc. by Special Act. 1902. Under Act of 1912 the undertaking was amalgamated with London Electric Railway Co., in which company ordinary shareholders received an equal amount of 4% debenture stock.................... **1913**

Edibell Sound Film Apparatus Ld. Regd. 1929. Vol. liq. (creditors') 25 Sept. 1931. Assets realised insufficient to pay unsecured creditors in full. Final meeting return regd. 12 Oct. 1934 .... **1932**

Edie Development Co. Ld. Inc. New Guinea 1929. Vol. liq. July 1930. Shareholders were entitled to 18¾ fully-paid shares of £1 in New Guinea Goldfields Ld., for every 100 shares of 5s. held **1931**

Edinburgh and Bathgate Railway Co. Inc. by Special Act 1846. In 1923 the undertaking was merged into the London & North Eastern Railway Co., in which company stockholders were entitled to £125 4% Debenture Stock (bearing interest from 1st February, 1923) for each £100 Consolidated Stock of the Edinburgh & Bathgate Co. (which Company or its nominees, was to receive an allotment of similar Debenture Stock for its holding of £2,972 Consols) **1924**

Edinburgh & District Motor Omnibus Co. Ld. Regd. 1906. Vol. liq. 20 Mar. 1907. Removed from Register 1908 .... **1908**

Edinburgh and District Tramways Co. Ld. Regd. Edinburgh 1894. Vol. liq. June 1920. Undertaking was acquired by the Edinburgh Corporation. Final meeting return regd. 12 Aug. 1921 .... **1921**

Edinburgh & District Water Trustees. Under Edinburgh Boundaries Extension and Tramways Act 1920 the trust was dissolved on 4 Aug. 1920. The Edinburgh Corporation became responsible for the bonds and mortgages **1921**

Edinburgh & Dundee Investment Co. Ld. See E. D. Investment Co. Ld.

VOL. FOR

Edinburgh and Dundee Investment Co. Ld. (The) Regd. in Edinburgh 10 Oct. 1924 as The Scottish Central Investment Trust Ld.; name changed 15 Nov. 1969. Vol. liq. (members') 29 July 1978. Preference stock repaid at par in Sept. 1978. First and final distribution of £1·594773 per ordinary share made on 4 June 1979. Amount paid into Companies' Liquidation Account was £1,929·85 in respect of unclaimed preference shareholders distribution and £3909·91 unclaimed dividends. Final meeting held 9 July 1979 .... **1983–4**

Edinburgh & Leith Corporations Gas Commissioners. Under Edinburgh Boundaries Extension and Tramways Act 1920 the trust was dissolved on 4 Aug. 1920. The Edinburgh Corporation became responsible for the bonds and mortgages **1921**

Edinburgh and San Francisco Redwood Co. Ld. Regd. Edinburgh 1885. Vol. liq. Dec. 1902. Final meeting return regd. 22 Nov. 1906 .... **1908**

Edinburgh Autocar Co. Ld. Regd. Edinburgh 1899. Vol. liq. 1901. Final meeting return regd. 26 Dec. 1903 **1902**

Edinburgh, Ballarat, Gold Quartz Mine Ld. Regd. 1890. Vol. liq. 11 Mar. 1892. Final meeting return regd. 16 Apr. 1894 .... **1893**

Edinburgh Cemetery Co. Ld. *See* Edinburgh Industrial Holdings Ld.

Edinburgh Co-Operative Building Co. Ld. *See* E. B. Contractors Ld.

Edinburgh Collieries Co. Ld. Regd. Edinburgh 1900. Collieries, etc. vested in National Coal Board as from 1 Jan. 1947. Vol. liq. (members') 25 June 1954. Capital returned to contributories—21*s*. 7·65*d*. per ordinary share of £1. Amounts paid to Accountant of Court—unclaimed dividends, £22 19*s*. 4*d*.; unclaimed distributions £4.691 6*s*. 10*d*. Final meeting return regd. 21 Jan. 1961 .... **1962**

Edinburgh, Dundee & Aberdeen Investment Co. Ld. See E.D. Investment Co. Ld.

Edinburgh Empire Palace Ld. Regd. Edinburgh 1891. Reconstructed 1899 as Moss Empires Ld. (later M. E. Theatres Ld.). Shareholders were entitled to 13 fully-paid preference and 13 fully-paid ordinary shares of £5 for every 20 shares of £5 held or 6 fully-paid preference and 6 ordinary shares of £5 *plus* £6 5*s*. in cash for every 10 shares of £5 held. Removed from Register 1909 .... **1900**

Edinburgh Evening News Ld. Regd. Edinburgh 1900. Vol. liq. Jan. 1929. Undertaking and assets were acquired by Provincial Newspapers Ld., (later United Newspapers Publications Ld.) in which company shareholders were entitled to 1 fully-paid 1st 6½% preference share of £1 for each 5% preference share of £1 held. Struck off Register 23 June 1931 .... **1930**

Edinburgh Gaslight Co. Inc. by Special Act 1818. Under Edinburgh and Leith Corporations Gas Act 1888, the undertaking was transferred to those Corporations for £27,000 in cash and £20,000 annuities **1888**

Edinburgh Heritable Security Co. Ld. Regd. Edinburgh 1874. Vol. liq. July 1902. Capital returned to contributories—15*s*. per share at Oct. 1902; further payments (if any) not known. Final meeting return regd. 28 Feb. 1903 .... **1903**

Edinburgh House Proprietors Co. Ld. Regd. Edinburgh 1896. Vol. liq. Aug. 1913. Final meeting return regd. 9 Sept. 1936 .... **1914**

Edinburgh Industrial Holdings Ld. Incorporated by Contract of Co-partnery in 1840 as Edinburgh Cemetery Co. Ld.; regd. in Edinburgh 6 Feb. 1903; name changed 8 Mar. 1965 .... **1983–4**

Edinburgh Lombard Investment Co. Ld. See Scottish Pacific Mortgage Co. Ld.

Edinburgh Marine Gardens Ld. Regd. Edinburgh 1908. Vol. liq. July 1921. Final meeting return regd. 5 Apr. 1922 .... **1922**

Edinburgh Mortgage Co. Ld. Regd. Edinburgh 1905. Vol. liq. (members') 5 Mar. 1958. Final meeting return regd. 19 May 1959 .... **1956**

Edinburgh North American Investment Co. Ld. Regd. Edinburgh 1892. Vol. liq. Apr. 1917. Final meeting return regd. 29 Mar. 1921 .... **1918**

Edinburgh Northern Tramways Co. Inc. by Special Act 1884. Undertaking and assets (with certain exceptions) were sold to Edinburgh Corporation on 31 Dec. 1896 for £115,000. Capital returned to contributories—£13 18*s*. per share of £10 at 1898; further payments (if any) not known. Company was dissolved by Edinburgh Corporation Act of 1896 **1899**

Edinburgh Rubber Estate, Selangor Ld. Regd. Edinburgh 1909. Vol. liq. Jan. 1920. Reconstructed as Edinburgh Rubber Estates Ld., in which company shareholders were entitled to 5¼ fully-paid shares of 2*s*. for each share of 2*s*. held. Final meeting return regd. 11 Sept. 1922 .... **1920**

VOL. FOR

Edinburgh Southern Cemetery Co. Inc. by contract of co-partnery 1845 **1911**

Edinburgh Street Tramways Co. Inc. by Special Act 1871. The tramways within the Burgh of Leith were sold to that Corporation for £60,000. Capital returned to contributories—19*s*. 6*d*. per ordinary share of £3 up to 1905; further payments (if any) not known **1906**

Edinburgh Suburban & Southside Junction Railway Co. Inc. by Special Act 1846. Under North British Railway Co. Act 1885 undertaking was amalgamated with that company for £225,000 4% Lien Stock; debentures of company became debenture of North British Railway Co **1886**

Edinburgh Suburban Electric Tramways Co. Inc. by Special Act 1906 .... **1911**

Edinburgh United Breweries Ld. Regd. Edinburgh 1889. Court Orders: to wind up Feb. 1934; to dissolve July 1936; to declare dissolution void July 1938; to dissolve Dec. 1943 .... **1935**

Edison Accumulators Ld. See Britannia Batteries Ld.

Edison-Bell Consolidated Phonograph Co. Ld. Regd. 1898. Vol. liq. 3 Dec. 1901. Reconstructed as company of same name. Shareholders were entitled to 1 ordinary share of £1 in new company for every 4 ordinary shares of £1 held or to 2½ preference shares of £1 for each preference share of £10 held. Final meeting return regd. 12 Mar. 1902. **1908**

Edison-Bell Consolidated Phonograph Co. Ld. Regd. 1901. Vol. liq. Dec. 1909. Removed from Register 1910 .... **1910**

Edison Bell Ld. Regd. 1909 as J. E. Hough Ld. name changed May 1926. Receiver appointed in Apr. 1932. Court Order to wind up Jan. 1933. Struck off Register 24 Oct. 1939 .... **1940**

Edison Bell (International) Ld. Regd. 1928. Receiver appointed by Order of Court 8 Apr. 1936. Struck off Register 17 Jan. 1969 .... **1956**

Edison-Bell Phonograph Corporation Ld. Regd. 1892. Vol. liq. 5 May 1898. Business was acquired by Edison-Bell Consolidated Phonograph Co. Ld. Final meeting return regd. 7 Mar. 1899 .... **1899**

Edison Electric Light Co. Ld. Regd. 1882. Vol. liq. 27 Aug. 1884. Reconstructed as Edison Swan Electric Co. Ld. Final meeting return regd. 31 Mar. 1896 **1940**

Edison Gower-Bell Telephone Co. of Europe Ld. Regd. 1898. Vol. liq. 19 Sept. 1904. Removed from Register 1911 .... **1905**

Edison Ore Milling Syndicate Ld. Regd. 1898. Vol. liq. 19 Aug. 1909. Final meeting return regd. 10 Dec. 1914 .... **1910**

Edison & Swan United Electric Light Co. Ld. *See* Edison Swan Electric Co. (Branches) Ld.

Edison Swan Electric Co. (Branches) Ld. Regd. 1883 as Edison & Swan United Electric Light Co. Ld.; name changed to Edison Swan Electric Co. Ld. in Aug. 1916 and subsequently as above. Vol. liq. (members') 16 July 1957. Final meeting return regd. 29 Mar. 1963 .... **1940**

Edison's Indian and Colonial Electric Co. Ld. Regd. 1882. Vol. liq. June 1886. Amalgamated with Australasian Electric Light, Power & Storage Co. Ld., to which company shareholders were entitled to 1 ordinary and 1 deferred share of £1 for each share held. Final meeting return regd. 14 Oct. 1887 ..... **1887**

Edjudina Consolidated Gold Mines Ld. Regd. 1935. Vol. liq. (creditors') 8 Dec. 1954. No capital returned to contributories. Final meeting return regd. 28 Jan. 1956 .... **1956**

Edjudina Gold Fields Ld. Regd. 1910. Struck off Register Feb. 1931 .... **1931**

Edmonton, Dunvegan & British Columbia Railway Co. Inc. Canada 1907 by Special Act. The undertaking was acquired jointly by Canadian National Railways and Canadian Pacific Railway Co., and transferred to Northern Alberta Railways Co. The liability for the 1st mortgage 4% guaranteed debenture stock and 4½% guaranteed 1st mortgage bonds was assumed by purchasing company **1930**

Edmundian Copper Mining Co. Ld. Regd. 1907. Vol. liq. Oct. 1912. Removed from Register 1913 .... **1913**

Edmunds & Swaithe Collieries Co. Ld. Regd. 1879. Removed from Register 1912 .... ***1883**

Edmundsons Electricity Corpn. Ld. Regd. 1897. Dissolved 1 Apr. 1948, undertaking being vested in British (later Central) Electricity Authority under Electricity Act 1947. Holders of securities were entitled to receive British Electricity 3% guaranteed stock (1968–73) as follows in respect of each £1 unit of capital held:

	£	s.	d.
7% preference stock	1	16	1
6% preference stock	1	11	0
Ordinary stock	1	11	6

**See Stock Exchange Year-Book*.

VOL. FOR

4% debenture stock 1 0 9⅛
3½% debenture stock 1 0 3⅜ **1949**

Eduapriem Exploration Co. Ld. Regd. 1903. Vol. liq. 25 Jan. 1905. Final meeting return regd. 30 Apr. 1917 **1905**

Edubja Syndicate Ld. Regd. 1901. Vol. liq. 9 Nov. 1904. Removed from Register 1906 .... **1905**

Edward Bates & Sons (Holdings) Ld. *See* Bates (Edward) & Sons (Holdings) Ld.

Edwards Air Pump Syndicate Ld. Regd. 1897. Vol. liq. 5 Dec. 1911. Final meeting return regd. 15 Sept. 1915 **1912**

Edwards & Armstrong Ld. Regd. 1913. Vol. liq. 31 Oct. 1930. A direct controlling interest was held by Western Electricity Supply Co. Ld. Final meeting return regd. 17 Feb. 1931 .... **1931**

Edwards & Co. (Bread St.) Ld. Regd. 1910 as Leopold Schwabacher Ld.; name changed June 1915. Vol. liq. Sept. 1927. Struck off Register 12 Mar. 1935 . **1936**

Edwards & James Ld. Regd. 1914. Vol. liq. (members') 28 Jan. 1931. Capital returned to contributories—£57,503 9*s*. 3*d*. Final meeting return regd. 25 Jan. 1934 .... **1931**

Edwards & Sons Ld. Regd. 1904. Vol. liq. (members') 28 Jan. 1931. Capital returned to contributories—£30,622 15*s*. 7*d*. Final meeting return regd. 25 Jan. 1934 .... **1931**

Edwards Creameries Ld. Regd. 1898. Vol. liq. (members') 30 Mar. 1937. Undertaking was acquired by United Dairies Ld. Capital returned to contributories—£5 per preference share of £5, £4 19*s*. 11·7*d*. per ordinary share of £5. £1 5*s*. 3*d*. was paid into Companies' Liquidation Account in respect of dividends. Final meeting return regd. 17 Sept. 1938 **1938**

Edwards' Dental Manufacturing Co. Ld. Regd. 1911. Court Order to wind up 15 Oct. 1928. Struck off Register 1933 .... ***1929**

Edwards (E.) & Co. Ld. Regd. 1897. Vol. liq. 3 May 1909. Final meeting return regd. 20 July 1913 ..... **1910**

Edwards (William) (Swansea) Ld. Regd. 1920. Vol. liq. (members') 5 Dec. 1939. Capital returned to contributories—£87,500. Final meeting return regd. 2 Sept. 1942 .... **1940**

"Edwin Bray" Gold Mining Co. Ld. Regd. 1894. Vol. liq. 1 Oct. 1897. Final meeting return regd. 2 Feb. 1900 **1898**

Eerste Fabrieken Hatherley Distillery Ld. Inc. Transvaal 1892. In voluntary liquidation in 1903 company having agreed to cancellation of its concession on terms which provided (inter alia) for payment by the Government of £296,875 in cash; company retained all its other assets. Capital returned to contributories—15*s*. per share of £1 on 1 Aug. 1903; further payments (if any) not known.............................. **1904**

Eerstegeluk Platinum Mines Ld. Inc. Transvaal 1925. Vol. liq. Oct. 1928. Undertaking and assets were acquired by Potgietersrust Platinums Ld., in which company shareholders were entitled to 1 share of 5*s*. (credited as fully-paid) for each share of 5*s*. held **1929**

Eersteling Exploring Co. Ld. Regd. 1894. Removed from Register 1909 .... **1901**

Effectol Ld. Regd. Feb. 1935. Vol. liq. (creditors') 6 Nov. 1935. No capital returned to contributories. Final meeting return regd. 29 Dec. 1937 .... **1936**

Effuenta Gold Mines Co. Ld. Regd. 1879. Removed from Register 1905 .... **1885**

Effuenta Mines Ld. Regd. 1926. Vol. liq. (members') 31 Jan. 1935. Shareholders received 32⅔ shares of 2*s*. in Gold Coast Banket Areas Ld for every 100 shares of 1*s*. held. £1,230 15*s*. 6*d*. was paid into Companies' Liquidation Account in respect of sale of unclaimed shares and £56 18*s*. 10*d*. in respect of unclaimed proceeds from sale of fractions. Final meeting return regd. 24 Sept. 1938 .... **1935**

Effuenta (Wassaw) Mines Ld. Regd. 1901. Vol. liq. 4 Jan. 1909 for reconstruction under same name. Shareholders were entitled to 1 share of 5*s*. fully-paid in new company for each share of £1 held and an option (since expired). Final meeting return regd. 7 July 1909 .... **1909**

Effuenta (Wassaw) Mines Ld. Regd. 1909. Vol. liq. 31 Dec. 1925. Undertaking and assets transferred to Effuenta Mines Ld., in which company shareholders were entitled to 1 fully-paid share of 1*s*. for every 2 shares of 5*s*. held. Final meeting return regd. 15 Jan. 1927 .... **1926**

Egginton Dairy Co. Ld. Regd. 1887. Vol. liq. (members') 22 Dec. 1933. Capital returned to contributories—£4 19*s*. 11*d*. per share of £5. Final meeting return regd. 28 Dec. 1934 .... **1934**

Eggo Ld. Regd. 1911. Vol. liq. (members') 1 Jan. 1951. Final meeting return regd. 15 Feb. 1951 .... **1938**

Egham & Staines Electricity Co. Ld. Regd. 1908 as Egham & District Electric Light Co. Ld.; name changed 1911. Dissolved 1 Apr. 1948, undertaking being vested in British (later Central) Electricity Authority and Southern Area Board under Electricity Act 1947. Holders of 7½% preference shares (of £1) were entitled to receive £1 13*s*. 9*d*. British Electricity 3% guaranteed stock (1968–73) in respect of each share held **1949**

Eginasie (Wassau) Banket Gold Reefs Ld. Regd. 1901. Court Order to wind up 28 Feb. 1905. Removed from Register 1911 .... **1906**

Egypt & Levant Steamship Co. Ld. Regd. 1906. Vol. liq. 9 June 1924. Ships were acquired by New Egypt & Levant Shipping Co. Ld. Final meeting return regd. 10 Feb. 1931 .... ***1925**

Egypt and Sudan Mining Syndicate Ld. Regd. 1901. Vol. liq. 1909. Properties were sold to Barramia Mining & Exploration Ld., in which company shareholders were entitled to 1·045 ordinary shares of 5*s*. (credited as fully-paid) for each share of £1 held. Removed from Register 1910 .... **1910**

Egypt & Sudan Trust Ld. Regd. 1903. Struck off Register 1928 .... **1909**

Egyptian & Foreign Trust Ld. Regd. 1905 as Egyptian Investment & Agency Ld.; name changed Nov. 1912. Vol. liq. 5 Oct. 1925. Reconstructed as Anglo-Scottish Amalgamated Corporation Ld., in which company shareholders were entitled to 3 ordinary shares of £1 and 1 deferred share of 1*s*. (credited as fully-paid) for every 75 shares of 2*s*. held. The debentures were repaid at 105% on 29 Nov. 1925. Final meeting return regd. 13 July 1937 .... **1926**

Egyptian & General Syndicate Ld. Regd. 1898. Removed from Register 1906 .... **1904**

Egyptian (Assiout) Explorers Ld. Regd. 1905. Vol. liq. 25 July 1922. Undertaking and assets were transferred to Anglo Afric Gold & Tin Mines Ld., in which company shareholders were entitled to 5 shares of 1*s*. (credited with 8*d*. paid) for each share of 5*s*. held. Final meeting return regd. 31 May 1923 **1925**

Egyptian Central Oilfields Ld. Regd. 1921. Vol. liq. 21 Feb. 1928. Final meeting return regd. 5 Nov. 1930 **1928**

Egyptian Consolidated Lands Ld. Regd. 1919. Vol. liq. (members') 1 Apr. 1943. Capital returned to contributories—1*s*. 6*d*. per share of 1*s*.; £9,017·80 was paid into Companies' Liquidation Account. Final meeting return regd. 2 Oct. 1974 .... **1975-6**

Egyptian Cotton Mills Ld. Regd. 1899. Vol. liq. 16 May 1907. Final meeting return regd. 14 May 1925 .... **1908**

Egyptian Development Syndicate Ld. Regd. 1900. Removed from Register 1903 .... **1903**

Egyptian Estates Ld. Regd. 1905. Vol. liq. July 1908 for reconstruction as Egyptian Agricultural Co. Ld., in which company debenture holders were entitled to £102 4*s*. in debentures and £19 1*s*. in shares for every £100 debentures held. Struck off Register 27 Oct. 1942 .... **1944**

Egyptian Gold & Gem Syndicate Ld. Regd. 1903. Vol. liq. 23 Sept. 1907. Final meeting return regd. 29 May 1912 .... **1908**

Egyptian Government Irrigation Trust Certificates. The final instalment of these Certificates was paid on 1 Jan. 1933 and the Trust came to an end **1933**

Egyptian Investment & Agency Ld. *See* Egyptian & Foreign Trust Ld.

Egyptian Irrigation Society. Inc. Egypt 1896. The concession expired in Dec. 1937 and the undertaking was transferred to the Egyptian Government in 1938 for £82.000 in cash. Vol. liq. 22 Jan. 1938 .. **1939**

Egyptian Land & General Trust Ld. Regd. 1905. Court Order to wind up 23 June 1930. Struck off Register 21 Sept. 1937 .... **1938**

Egyptian Mail Steamship Co. Ld. Regd. 1906. Vol. liq. 7 July 1908. Final meeting return regd. 14 Apr. 1919 **1909**

Egyptian Markets Ld. Regd. 1898. In 1961 company was converted into limited company enjoying nationality of U.A.R. Old shares of 2*s*. 6*d*. were converted into new shares of £E1·200. Struck off Register 29 May 1964 .... **1962**

Egyptian Minerals Corporation Ld. Regd. 1890. Removed from Register 1907 .... **1892**

Egyptian Mines Exploration Co. Ld. Regd. 1900. Vol. liq. Dec. 1907 for reconstruction as Egyptian Mines Development Co. Ld., in which company shareholders were entitled to 1 share of 5*s*. (credited with 1*s*. paid) for each share of £1 held. Removed from Register 1913 .... **1908**

Egyptian Oil Trust Ld. Regd. 1907. Vol. liq. 30 Dec. 1913. The assets, mainly shares of Anglo-Egyptian Oilfields Ld. (later Al Nasr Oilfields Co.) were to be distributed. Final meeting return regd. 5 Aug. 1919 **1914**

Egyptian Options Ld. Regd. 1905. Vol. liq. 3 Sept. 1908. Final meeting return regd. 20 Mar. 1920 .... **1909**

Egyptian Petroleum Co. Ld. Regd. 1905. Vol. liq. June 1910. Properties taken over by Red Sea Oilfields Ld., in which company shareholders received 1⅞

**See Stock Exchange Year-Book.*

shares for every share held. Removed from Register 1911 ... **1911**

Egyptian Sudan Minerals Ld. Regd. 1896 as British and Colonial Agency Ld.; name changed Dec. 1900. Vol. liq. 15 July 1904. Final meeting return regd. 13 July 1911 ... **1905**

Egyptian Trading and Finance Co. Ld. Regd. 1907. Vol. liq. 11 Aug. 1908. Undertaking and assets were sold to Credit Local (Société Anonyme Egyptienne). Struck off Register 1921 ... **1909**

Egyptian Trust & Investment Ld. Regd. 1905. Vol. liq. 26 June 1906. Amalgamated with Building Lands of Egypt (inc. Egypt), in which company shareholders were entitled to 3 shares of £4 for every 10 shares of £1 held. Removed from Register 1909 ... **1907**

Einasleigh Freehold Copper Mines Ld. Regd. 1899. Vol. liq. Aug. 1907. Properties were acquired by New Einasleigh Copper Mines Ld., in which company shareholders were entitled to 2 fully-paid shares of £1 for every 5 shares of £1 held. Removed from Register 1911 ... **1908**

Einstein's Electro Chemical Process Ld. See Electro Chemical Processes Ld.

Eirene Steamship Co. Ld. Regd. 1920. Vol. liq. 1 Dec. 1925. Final meeting return regd. 23 Mar. 1926 ... **1926**

Eisenbahn-Gesellschaft Mersina-Tarsus-Adana. See Mersina, Tarsus & Adana Railway Co.

Ejudina Gold Mines Ld. Regd. 1895. Vol. liq. 1895. Absorbed by Triumph Leases Ld. Final meeting return regd. 6 Jan. 1899 ... ***1898**

Ekenberg Milk Products Co. Ld. Regd. 1906. Vol. liq. 19 Apr. 1910. Final meeting return regd. 31 Oct. 1911 **1911**

Ekman Pulp & Paper Co. Ld. See Northfleet Paper Mills Ld.

El Amparo Mine Ld. Regd. 1913. Vol. liq. 24 May 1917. Final meeting return regd. 31 Dec. 1920 ... **1918**

El Callas General Gold Mining Co. Ld. Regd. 1906. Vol. liq. 5 Feb. 1912. Undertaking acquired by New Callao Gold Mining Co. Ld. Final meeting return regd. 30 Dec. 1912 ... ***1906**

El Callao Gold Mining Co. Inc. Venezuela 1870 and 1878. Stated to be in liquidation in Dec. 1896 ..... **1898**

El Deir Lands Ld. Regd. 1907. Vol. liq. June 1909. Capital returned to contributories—20s. per share of £1; further payments (if any) not known. Removed from Register 1910 ... **1910**

El Dorado Gold & Gem Co. of Montana. Inc. Michigan 1896 when the business of Sapphire Ruby Co. of Montana Ld. was acquired for 425,000 ordinary and 400 deferred shares of $2 ... **1898**

El Dorado Rubber, Balata & Gold Mining Co. Ld. Regd. 1907. Struck off Register 1933 ... **1922**

El Mayo Mines of Mexico Ld. Regd. 1902 as Mechaco (Mexico) Mining & Milling Co. Ld.; name changed Jan. 1910. Struck off Register 25 July 1922 .... **1917**

El Mundo (Mexico) Gold Mining Co. Ld. Regd. 1897. Vol. liq. 1 Aug. 1901, for the purpose of amalgamation with Carlyle Consolidated Gold Mines Ld., and reconstruction as King's Treasury Gold Mines Ld. in which company shareholders were entitled to receive 1 share (credited with 7s. 6d. paid) for each share held. Struck off Register 30 Dec. 1949 ...... **1950**

El Oro Mining and Railway Co. Ld. Regd. 1899. Vol liq (members') 12 Nov. 1946 for the purpose of reconstruction under title of E Oro Mining and Exploration Co. Ld.; stockholders were entitled to receive 1 fully-paid share (of 3s. 6d.) in the new company for every 5s. stock held; £2,461 was paid into Companies' Liquidation Account. Final meeting return regd. 19 Nov. 1948 ... **1949**

El Palmar Rubber Estates Ld. Regd. in Edinburgh 10 Mar. 1910. Vol. liq. (members') Mar. 1925. Final meeting return regd. 22 Sep. 1964 ... **1955**

El Progreso Mexican Mines Ld. Regd. 1907. Properties were abandoned. Struck off Register 28 Feb. 1939 **1940**

El Refugio Mining Concessions Ld. Regd. 1891. Struck off Register 5 May 1896 ... **1899**

El Salto Ld. Regd. 1924. Vol. liq. (members') 16 July 1952. Final meeting return regd. 30 Oct. 1953 ..... **1938**

Elaeis Plantations Ld. Regd. 1924. Vol. liq. (members') 31 Oct. 1957. All capital was owned by Oil Palms of Malaya Ld. Final meeting return regd. 2 Dec. 1958 **1956**

Elak (Southern India) Rubber Co. Ld. Regd. 1910. Receiver appointed Jan. 1915. Struck off Register 1924 ... **1916**

Elands Drift Diamond Estates Ld. Inc. Cape of Good Hope 1901. Vol. liq. Aug. 1910 ... **1911**

Elands Laagte Collieries Ld. Inc. Natal 1901. London office was closed in 1915 ... **1917**

Elandsfontein Deep Ld. Regd. 1902. Vol. liq. 29 May 1905. Undertaking was acquired by Consolidated Rand Rhodesia Trust & General Exploration Co. Ld., in which company shareholders were entitled to

1 fully-paid share of £1 for each share of £1 held. Removed from Register 1911 ... **1906**

Elandsfontein Ld. Regd. 1934. Struck off Register 25 Aug. 1961 ... **1953**

Elandsfontein No. 2 Gold Mining Co. Ld. Regd. 1896. Vol. liq. 1903. Undertaking was acquired by Elandsfontein Deep Ld. Removed from Register 1905 ... **1904**

Elastes Co. Ld. Regd. 1906. Vol. liq. 8 Jan. 1909. Final meeting return regd. 12 Feb. 1915 ... **1909**

Elba Tinplate Co. Ld. Regd. 1925. Vol. liq. (members') 30 June 1953, the undertaking being transferred to Richard Thomas & Baldwins Ld. Final meeting return regd. 24 Mar. 1954 ... **1955**

Elbe Colliery Co. Ld. Regd. 1861. Vol. liq. Aug. 1886. Final meeting return regd. 22 July 1878 ... **1887**

Elche Waterworks Co. Ld. Regd. 1900. Vol. liq. 11 Oct. 1917. Final meeting return regd. 23 Jan. 1918 ..... **1918**

Elder Dempster & Co. Ld. Regd. 1910. Assets were acquired in 1935 by E. D. Realisation Co. Ld. The 5% debenture stock was repaid in cash at 103% on 3 Apr. 1935. The 5% A debenture stock was satisfied by issue of £50 1st debenture stock, £50 income debenture stock and 30 fully-paid shares of £1 in acquiring company for every £100 stock held; accrued interest was cancelled. Dissolved 4 May 1937 ... **1937**

Elder-Dempster Shipping Ld. See Elder Line Ld.

Elder Dempster (Teneriffe) Ld. Regd. 1912. Vol. liq. (members') 11 Nov. 1937. Capital returned to contributories—£30,675. Final meeting return regd. 29 Dec. 1942 ... **1938**

Elder Line Ld. Regd. 1899 as Elder-Dempster Shipping Ld.; name changed May 1910. Vol. liq. (members') 12 June 1936. Dissolved before 1952 ... **1937**

Elders Collieries Ld. See Celtic Collieries Ld.

Elders' Navigation Collieries Ld. See Celtic Collieries Ld.

Eldorado Banket Gold Mining Co. Ld. Regd. 1906. Vol. liq. 23 Jan. 1920. Final meeting return regd. 3 Mar. 1921 ... **1920**

Eldorado Mining & Refining Ld. Inc. Ontario by letters patent 1926 as Eldorado Gold Mines Ld. name changed May 1943. Property was taken over in 1944 under War Measures Act by Canadian Government, which purchased all shares ... **1944**

Eldoret Mining Syndicate Ld. Inc. Kenya Colony 1933. Vol. liq. 24 Apr. 1937 ... **1938**

"Electra" Apparatenbau G.m.b.H. Inc. Austria. Direct controlling interest was held by Aron Electricity Meter Ld. (later Aron Meters Ld., later Astaron Electronics Ld., later Stocklake Holdings Ld.) **1939**

Electramonic Co. Ld. Regd. 1928. Vol. liq. June 1930 for reconstruction as Electramonic Co. (1930) Ld., in which company shareholders were entitled to 1 preferred ordinary share of 10s. (credited with 6s. 8d. paid) for each deferred ordinary share of 10s. held or 1 deferred ordinary share of 1s. (credited with 8d. paid) for each deferred ordinary share of 1s. held. Struck off Register Aug. 1934 ... **1935**

Electramonic Co. (1930) Ld. Regd. 1920. Vol. liq. (creditors') 27 Apr. 1931. No capital returned to contributories. Final meeting return regd. 27 Apr. 1932 ... **1932**

Electramonic (Foreign Rights) Ld. Regd. 1928. Vol. liq. members') 31 Oct. 1935. Struck off Register 1 Apr. 1938 ... **1939**

Electric & Gas Industries Ld. Regd. 1931. Struck off Register 18 Sept. 1936 ... **1937**

Electric & General Assurance Ld. Regd. 1903. Vol. liq. Dec. 1911 Removed from Register 1913 ... **1912**

Electric & Ordnance Accessories Co. Ld. See Broadway Finance & Investment Co. Ld.

Electric Carbon Storage & Apparatus Manufacturing Co. of Scotland Ld. Regd. 1882. Vol. liq. 1883. Removed from Register 1906 ... **1884**

Electric Construction and Maintenance Co. Ld. See Crystal Palace District Electric Supply Co. Ld.

Electric Construction Corporation Ld. Regd. 1889. Vol. liq. 20 July 1893. Reconstructed as Electric Construction Co. Ld., in which company shareholders were entitled to 2 fully-paid ordinary shares of £2 for each ordinary share of £10 held; 5 preference shares of £2 for each preference share of £10 held; 2 fully-paid ordinary shares of £2 for each founders' share of £10; 2 fully-paid ordinary shares of £2 for each income bond of £10 held; holders of 1st and 2nd debentures, an equal amount of 1st and 2nd mortgage debs. in new co. Final meeting return regd. 21 Nov. 1904 ... **1894**

Electric Control Ld. Regd. Edinburgh 1908. Vol. liq. (members') 23 Aug. 1937. All ordinary and deferred shares held by Allen West & Co. Ld. Preference

VOL. FOR

shares were repaid in full. Final meeting return regd. 30 Nov. 1938 .... **1938**

Electric Date and Time Stamp Co. Ld. Regd. 1888. Vol. liq. 4 Oct. 1892. Final meeting return regd. 26 Apr. 1899 .... **1893**

Electric Development & Securities Trust Ld. Regd. 1928. Dissolved 1 Apr. 1948, undertaking being vested in British (later Central) Electricity Authority under Electricity Act 1947. Shareholders were entitled to receive £3 14s. British Electricity 3% guaranteed stock (1968–73) in respect of each share (of £1) held **1949**

Electric Equipment & Securities Ld. *See* Reed, Evans & Co. Ld.

Electric Extension Co. Ld. Regd. 1897. Removed from Register 1905 .... **1905**

Electric Fires Ld. *See* Heatrae Ld.

Electric Furnace Co. Ld. Regd. 1921 as Campbell Gifford & Co. Ld.; name changed Apr. 1924. Vol. liq. 9 Aug. 1928. Undertaking acquired by company of same name. Final meeting return regd. 15 Oct. 1928 .... **1930**

Electric Heating and Hardware Ld. Regd. 1919 as National Electric Co. (Birmingham) Ld.; name changed July 1919. Vol. liq. (members') 30 Oct 1936. A direct controlling interest was held by British Electric Transformer Co. Ld. Final meeting return regd. 19 Apr. 1937 .... **1937**

Electric Holdings Ld. Regd. 1917. Vol. liq. (members') 30 Nov. 1935. Vickers Ld. held all shares. Final meeting return regd. 21 Jan. 1936 .... **1936**

Electric Installation and Maintenance Co. Ld. *See* Crystal Palace District Electric Supply Co. Ld.

Electric Installation Co. Ld. Regd. 1898. Removed from Register 1912 .... **1905**

Electric Landaulet Co. Ld. See Landaulet Co. Ld.

Electric Light & Power Co. of Cochabamha. Inc. Bolivia 1908. Outstanding bonds were redeemed at par on 15 June 1929 .... **1929**

Electric Light & Power Generator Co. Ld. *See* Maxim-Weston Electric Co. Ld.

Electric Lighting & Traction Co. of Australia Ld. *See* Melbourne Electric Supply Co. Ld.

Electric Lighting Boards (British Manufacturing Co.) Ld. Regd. 1900. Vol. liq. 18 Aug. 1902. Removed from Register 1904 .... **1903**

Electric Lighting Boards Ld. Regd. 1899. Vol. liq. 29 Dec. 1902. Final meeting return regd. 22 May 1905 .... *****1904**

Electric Lighting Contract & Maintenance Co. Ld. Regd. 1882. Vol. liq. May 1883. Final meeting return regd. 16 Oct. 1883 .... **1884**

Electric Locomotive and Power Co. Ld. Regd. 1885. Business and patents were taken over by Elieson Electric Co. Ld for £180,000 in fully-paid shares of £5. Removed from Register 1906 .... **1888**

Electric Metal Working Syndicate Ld. Regd. 1897. Struck off Register 23 July 1901 .... **1902**

Electric News Telegraph Co. Ld. Regd. 1882. Vol. liq. Oct. 1884. Business was transferred to Exchange Telegraph Co. Ld. [later Exchange Telegraph Co. (Holdings) Ld.]. Final meeting return regd. 27 Oct. 1885 .... **1885**

Electric Organ Co. Ld. Regd. 1895. Vol. liq. 5 May 1899. Business and assets were sold by Receiver and Manager for debenture holders. Removed from Register 1901 .... **1900**

Electric Palaces Ld. Regd. 1909. Vol. liq. Feb. 1916. Struck off Register 19 Mar. 1937 .... **1938**

Electric Picture Palaces (Midlands) Ld. Regd. 1910. Vol. liq. 26 Mar. 1912. Final meeting return regd.4 June 1913 .... *****1913**

Electric Portable Battery & Gas Igniting Co. Ld. Regd. 1882. Removed from Register 1906 .... *****1885**

Electric Power Development Co. Ld. Regd. 1904. Removed from Register 1908 .... **1906**

Electric Railway and Tramway Carriage Works Ld. *See* United Electric Car Co. Ld.

Electric Resistance & Heating Co. Ld. Regd. 1898. Removed from Register 1904 .... **1902**

Electric Sun Lamp and Power Co. Ld. Regd. 1882. Vol. liq. 15 Oct. 1885. Final meeting return regd. 20 May 1892 .... **1886**

Electric Supply Co. of Victoria Ld. Regd. 1900. Vol. liq. (members') Oct 1934. Undertaking was acquired by State Electricity Commission of Victoria (Australia) in 1931. Capital returned to contributories—20s. per preference share of £1; 16s. 11⅜d. per ordinary share of £1. Final meeting return regd. 7 May 1937 ...... **1935**

Electric Supply Co. of Western Australia Ld. Regd. 1898. Vol. liq. 15 Nov. 1920. Final meeting return regd. 26 May 1921 .... **1921**

Electric Supply Corpn. Ld. Regd. 1897. Dissolved 1 Apr. 1948, undertaking being vested in British (later Central) Electricity Authority and South-West Scotland Area Board under Electricity Act 1947.

VOL. FOR

Holders of ordinary and 6% preference stock were entitled to receive, in respect of each £1 stock held, £2 10s. 8d. and £1 10s. 4d. British Electricity 3% guaranteed stock (1968–73) respectively **1949**

Electric Theatres (1908) Ld. Regd. 1908. Vol. liq. (members') 19 Nov. 1926. Capital returned to contributores—3s. 0·24d. per share of 10s. £941 18s. 8d. was paid into Companies' Liquidation Account. Final meeting return regd. 13 Mar. 1937 .... **1937**

Electric Timber-Seasoning & Preservation Co. Ld. Regd. 1899. Court Order to wind up 8 Mar. 1904. Removed from Register 1912 .... **1905**

Electric Totalisators Ld. Regd. 1931. Vol. liq. (members') 6 Sept. 1937. All shares were owned by Ericsson Telephones Ld. Final meeting return regd. 2 Mar. 1938 .... **1938**

Electric Traction Co. Ld. Regd. 1888. Vol. liq. 23 July 1890. Business transferred to General Electric Power & Traction Co. Ld. Final meeting return regd. 24 Oct. 1891 .... *****1891**

Electric Traction Co. Ld. Regd. 1894. Removed from Register 1907 .... **1904**

Electric Traction Co. of Hongkong Ld. *See* Hong Kong Tramway Co. Ld.

Electric Welding Co. Ld. Regd. 1890. Vol. liq. 14 Nov. 1923. Final meeting return regd. 3 July 1924 .... **1924**

Electrical & Radio Products Ld. Regd. 1930. Vol. liq. (creditors') 28 July 1931. Undertaking and assets transferred to Electrical & Radio Products (1931) Ld., in which company shareholders were entitled to 1 fully-paid redeemable preference share of 6d. for every 3 shares of 2s. 6d. held. Final meeting return regd. 2 Feb. 1938 .... **1932**

Electrical & Radio Products (1931) Ld. Regd. 1931. Court Order to wind up Apr. 1934. Struck off Register 16 Aug. 1938 .... **1939**

Electrical Automatic Delivery Box Co. Ld. Regd. 1888. Court Orders: to wind up 3 Aug. 1889; to dissolve 10 Nov. 1892. .... **1890**

Electrical Bleaching Co. (1904) Ld. Regd. 1904. Removed from Register 1910 .... **1907**

Electrical Copper Co. Ld. Regd. 1896. Removed from Register 1904 .... **1903**

Electrical Development and Finance Corporation Ld. Regd. 1896. Vol. liq. 30 Dec. 1921. Struck off Register 9 July 1926 .... **1922**

Electrical Development Co. of Ontario Ld. Inc. 1903 by Letters Patent under Companies Act of Ontario .. **1932**

Electrical Distribution of Yorkshire Ld. Regd. 1905. Dissolved 1 Apr. 1948. undertaking being vested in British (later Central) Electricity Authority and Yorkshire Area Board under Electricity Act 1947. Holders of securities were entitled to receive British Electricity 3% guaranteed stock (1968–73) as follows in respect of each £1 unit of capital held:

	£ s. d.
6% preference stock	1 11 7
Ordinary stock	2 11 0
3¼% redeemable debenture stock	1 0 3½	**1949**

Electrical Engineering Corporation Ld. Regd. 1890. Vol. liq. 23 Apr. 1891. Removed from Register 1907 .. **1892**

Electrical Enterprise Ld. *See* Bungay Gas & Electricity Co. Ld.

Electrical Finance & Securities Co. Ld. Regd. 1914. Dissolved 1 Apr. 1 948, undertaking being vested in British (later Central) Electricity Authority under Electricity Act 1947. Holders of securities were entitled to receive British Electricity 3% guaranteed stock (1968–73) as follows in respect of each £1 unit of capital held:

	£ s. d.
Ordinary stock	3 7 0
7% preference stock	1 12 3
4% debenture stock	1 0 3½	**1949**

Electrical Power Distribution Co. Ld. Regd. 1898. Vol. liq. 8 Dec. 1902. Undertaking was acquired by British Electric Traction Co. Ld., in which company ordinary and preference shareholders were entitled to an equal number of shares of same class. Final meeting return regd. 2 May 1935 .... **1902**

Electrical Power Storage Co. Ld. Regd. 1882. Vol. liq. 1 Nov. 1889. Undertaking was acquired by Electric Construction Corpn. Ld. Final meeting return regd. 2 June 1904 .... **1890**

Electrical Power Storage Co. Ld. Regd. 1889 as Foreign and Colonial Electrical Power Storage Co. Ld.; name changed Sept. 1891. Vol. liq. June 1915. Amalgamated to form Pritchett & Gold and Electrical Power Storage Co. Ltd., in which company shareholders were entitled to 1 10% B ordinary share of £1 and ½ deferred share of 1s. for each ordinary or founders' share or £5 held. Removed from Register 1904 .... **1916**

---

*See Stock Exchange Year-Book.

Electrical Securities Trust Ld. Regd. Edinburgh 1907. Balance of debentures was repaid in 1918 when remaining assets were sold. Vol. liq. Nov. 1919. Final meeting return regd. 29 Jan. 1920............... 1920

Electrical Utilities Corporation. Inc State of Maine 1909. Undertaking and assets acquired in 1924 by Electric Investors Inc., in which company shareholders were entitled to receive 1 preferred share of no par value for each preferred share of $100 held and 5 common shares of no par value for each common share of $100 held 1926

Electricity (Civil Defence) 3% Redeemable Stock 1955–60. *See* under Central Electricity Board.

Electricity Commissioners. Constituted under Sect. 1 of Electricity (Supply) Act 1919. Dissolved by Order of 1948, the property, rights, liabilities and obligations having been transferred to the Minister of Fuel & Power as from 1 Aug. 1948 1947

Electricity Co. of Macclesfield Ld. Regd. 1910 as New Electricity Co. of Macclesfield Ld.; name changed July 1914. Vol. liq. (members') 29 Mar. 1940. Undertaking acquired by Macclesfield Corporation. Capital returned to contributories—£627,801 8s. 10d. Final meeting return regd. 26 June 1940 1940

Electricity Distribution of North Wales & District Ld. Regd. 1925. Dissolved 1 Apr. 1948, undertaking being vested in British (later Central) Electricity Authority and Merseyside & North Wales Area Board under Electricity Act 1947 1949

Electricity Supply Co. for Spain Ld. Regd. 1889. Vol. liq 4 Apr. 1918. Final meeting return regd. 12 June 1919 1919

Electricity Supply Corpn. Ld. *See* Central London Electricity Ld.

Electro-Amalgamator Co. Ld. Regd. 1883. Removed from Register 1891 .... *1886

Electro Bleach & By-Products Ld. Regd. 1914. Vol. liq. members') 30 June 1931. All shares held by I.C.I. (Alkali) Ld., or its nominees. Final meeting return regd. 23 Mar. 1932 1932

Electro Chemical Co. Ld. Regd. 1894. Vol. liq. 14 Feb. 1900. Reconstructed as Electro-Chemical Co. (1900), Ld. Final meeting return regd. 29 Aug. 1900 *1901

Electro-Chemical Co. (1900) Ld. Regd. 1900. Removed from Register 1905 1902

Electro Chemical Processes Ld. Regd. 1928 as Einstein's Electro Chemical Process Ld.: name changed Feb. 1932. Court Order to wind up 1936. Struck off Register 19 May 1944 1945

Electro Magneto Motors Ld. Regd. 1914. Struck off Register 1924 .... *1924

Electro-Peat Coal Co. Ld. Regd. 1904. Vol. iiq. Dec. 1909. Removed from Register 1911 1910

Electrolytic Alkali Co. Ld. Regd. 1899. Vol. liq. 17 Apr. 1913. The undertaking and assets were sold to Electro Bleach and By Products Ld. Debenture holders were repaid in full; no capital returned to contributories. Final meeting return regd. 19 Jan. 1927 1915

Electrolytic Plating Apparatus Co. Ld. Regd. 1896. Vol. liq. (members') 16 Oct. 1935 for reconstruction as Electrolytic Plating Co. Ld. Final meeting return regd. 16 Feb. 1937 1913

Electromobile Co. Ld. Regd. 1902. Vol. liq. 27 Mar. 1914. Business was sold to Hertford Street Hiring Co. Ld. Assets realised insufficient to pay debentures in full. Struck off Register 3 Sept. 1918 1965

Electromotors Ld. Regd. 1899. Vol. liq. 26 Mar. 1929. Undertaking and assets were acquired by Laurence Scott & Electromotors Ld., in which company shareholders were entitled to 3 shares of £1 (credited as fully-paid) for every 5 shares of £1 held. Final meeting return regd. 19 Dec. 1929 1930

Electrophone Ld. Regd. 1903. Vol. liq. 16 July 1925. Final meeting return regd. 1 Oct. 1926 1926

Elektra Oil Syndicate of Mexico Ld. Regd. 1910. Struck off Register 1931... *1915

Elektron Mount (Queensland) Gold Mining Co. Ld. Regd. 1886. Vol. liq. 26 Nov. 1888 for reconstruction as Etheridge United Gold Mining Co. Ld., in which company shareholders were entitled to an equal number of fully-paid shares of £1. Final meeting return regd. 24 Feb. 1891...................... 1891

Elephant & Castle Horse & Carriage Repository Ld. Regd. 1888. Vol. liq. 5 Nov. 1894. Court Order to continue winding up under supervision 14 Nov. 1894. Final meeting return regd. 15 Apr. 1896...... 1895

Elephant & Castle Theatre Ld. Regd. 1928. Vol. liq. (members') 11 Apr. 1938. Capital returned to contributories—£22,140 10s. Final meeting return regd. 21 Mar. 1940 1939

Elephants Kloof Gold Mining Co. Ld. Regd. 1895. Vol. liq. 9 Sept. 1899. Reconstructed as Belfast Gold Mining Co. Ld., in which company shareholders were entitled to 1 share of 5s. (credited with 2s. 6d.

paid) for each share of £1 held. Removed from Register 1910 1900

Elerbar Ld. Regd. 1897 as Barrett & Elers Ld.; name changed 18 Feb. 1959. Vol. liq. (members') 30 Sept. 1963. £634 8s 6d. was paid into Companies' Liquidation Account in respect of unclaimed distributions. Final meeting return regd. 18 Sept. 1964 1965

Elettricita e Gas di Roma. Est. 1852; inc. 1870 with limited liability as a Societa in Accomandita per Azioni; converted into Soc. Anon. Jan. 1910; name changed to Societa Anglo-Romana per l'Illuminazione di Roma Col Gas ed Altri Sistemi S.A. (Anglo Romana Gas Co.) and as above in 1924. Vol. liq. Dec. 1931. Undertaking and assets were acquired by Societa Romana di Elettricita, in which company shareholders were entitled to 3 shares of lire 250 (credited as fully-paid) *plus* lire 220 for each share of lire 750 held... 1933

Eley Brothers Ld. Regd. 1874. Vol. liq. 1 Jan. 1929. Final meeting return regd. 11 Aug. 1931. 1929

Elgin & Havelock Railway Co. Inc. by Act of Canadian Parliament 1894. The line of this company (all the capital of which was held in this country) was sold in 1902 to a Canadian syndicate............................ 1903

Elgin, Joliet & Eastern Railway Co. Inc. Illinois 1888 and Indiana 1889... 1943

Elgin, Joliet & Eastern Railway of Illinois. Reconstructed 1889 as Elgin, Joliet & Eastern Railway 1943

Elgin, Joliet & Eastern Railway of Indiana. Reconstructed 1889 as Elgin, Joliet & Eastern Railway 1943

Elgin, Petitcodiac & Havelock Railway Co. Inc. New Brunswick 1885. Sold under foreclosure in 1892. Depositing bondholders received about 17s. per bond. A new company was formed in 1894 to purchase the railway... 1895

Elham Valley (Light) Railway Co. Inc. 1881. Amalgamated with South Eastern Railway Co. in 1891.... 1892

Elham Valley Water Co. Ld. Regd. 1905. Vol. liq. (members') 19 Dec. 1949. Undertaking acquired by Folkestone Waterworks Co. (later Folkestone & District Water Co.), in which company shareholders were entitled to 1 fully-paid 5% maximum ordinary share of £10 for every 2 £5 shares (10% or 7%) held, and debenture holders to an equal amount of 4% redeemable debenture stock in the Folkestone Co. or to repayment at par, at holders' option. Final meeting return regd. 20 Dec. 1950 1952

Elieson Electric Co. Ld. Regd. 1887. Removed from Register 1892 1892

Elite Picture Palace (Wimbledon) Ld. Regd. 1916. Vol. liq. (members') 26 Feb. 1962. Final meeting return regd. 5 Mar. 1965 1955

Elite Picture Theatre (Kingston-on-Thames), Ld. Regd. 1919. Vol. liq. (members') 29 Jan. 1947. Capital returned to contributories—22s. per preference share of £1 and £2 5s. 11¾d. per ordinary share of 10s. £210 was paid into Companies' Liquidation Account. Final meeting return regd. 4 Nov. 1949 1950

Elk Hill Coffee Estates Ld. Regd. Edinburgh 1914. Vol. liq. (members') 20 Mar. 1953. Final meeting return regd. 21 Mar. 1956 1951

Elkhart Mining Corporation Ld. Regd. 1900. Removed from Register 1904 1903

Elkhorn Mining Co. Ld. Regd. 1890. Vol. liq. 3 Dec. 1895. Reconstructed as New Elkhorn Mining Co. Ld., in which shareholders received 1 share of £1 for every 5 shares of £1 held. Final meeting return regd. 19 May 1897 1896

Ella (Transvaal) Gold Mining Co. Ld. Regd. Dublin 1895. Removed from Register 1901 1901

Elland-cum-Greetland Gas Co. Inc. by Special Act 1861. Dissolved 1 May 1949, undertaking being vested in North Eastern Area Gas Board under Gas Act 1948. Holders of securities were entitled to receive, in respect of each £100 unit held, British Gas 3% guaranteed stock 1990–95 as follows:

	£ s. d.
Conv. ord. stock (5% stand.)...............	140 0 0
New ord. stock (5% max.)...................	111 5 0
4% cons. pref. stock	101 10 0

Liability in respect of certain mortgage loans assumed by the Board................................. 1952

Ellawattee Ceylon Tea Estates Ld. Regd. 1911. Company dissolved 16 Aug. 1980 1955

Ellenroad Mill p.l.c. Regd. 11 Aug. 1958 as Ellenroad Ring Mill Ld.; name changed Aug. 1980. Winding-up Order 18 Feb. 1985 1988–9

Ellenroad Ring Mill Ld. *See* Ellenroad Mill p.l.c.

Ellenroad Ring Mill Ld. Regd. 1919. Vol. liq. (members') 11 Aug. 1958 for the purpose of reconstruction. The undertaking and assets, except £86,173 cash which was distributed to shareholders at the rate of 10s. per share, was sold to Ellenroad Ring Mill Ld., in which company shareholders were

VOL. FOR

entitled to receive 6 fully-paid shares of 5s. for each share (of £1) held. £404 10s. was paid into Companies' Liquidation Account in respect of distributions. Final meeting return regd. 18 Nov. 1959 .... **1960**

Ellesmere & Glyn Valley Railway. See Glyn Valley Tramway Co.

Ellesmere Port Lighterage Co. Ld. Regd. 1919. Vol. liq. (members') 10 Mar. 1930. Capital returned to contributories—20s. per share of £1. Final meeting return regd. 11 Dec. 1930 .... **1931**

Elliott (E.) p.l.c. Regd. as private company 23 May 1936; converted public company 31 Aug. 1950. Winding-up order 3 May 1983. Inland Revenue declared shares of negligible value from 1984–4. Liquidator released 30 Mar. 1984 .... **1987–8**

Elliotts Metal Co. Ld. Regd. 1874. Vol. liq. (members') 31 Dec. 1942. All shares owned by I.C.I. Metals Ld. Final meeting return regd. 29 Sept. 1944 .... **1945**

Ellis, Warde & Co. Ld. Regd. 1897 as Ellis, Warde, Webster & Co. Ld. name changed Sept. 1919. Vol. liq. (members') 30 Sept. 1955 for purpose of transferring undertaking and assets to Peter Walker (Warrington) Ld. holding all ordinary capital. Preference capital repaid at par. Final meeting return regd. 16 Feb. 1959 .... **1960**

Ellis-May Vacuum Steel Syndicate Ld. Regd. 1897. Vol. liq. 18 Mar. 1903. Final meeting return regd. 17 Mar. 1904 .... ***1903**

Ellyou Goldfields Development Corporation Ld. Regd. 1928. Vol. liq. 14 Aug. 1929. Undertaking and assets were acquired by Edie Development Co. Ld., in which company shareholders were entitled to 1 fully-paid share of 5s. for each share of 5s. held, Final meeting return regd. 11 Dec. 1930 .... **1930**

Elmhurst (Ceylon) Tea & Rubber Estates, Ld. Regd. 1910. Vol. liq. (members') 13 Dec. 1955. Capital returned to contributories—£4 1s. 5¼d. per share of £1. Final meeting return regd. 28 Feb. 1958 .... **1959**

Elmina Concessions Ld. Regd. 1901. Vol. liq. 14 Mar. 1906. Shareholders were entitled to 1 share of 4s. in Consolidated Deep Leads Ld, plus 1s. in cash for each share of £1 held. Removed from Register 1908 .... **1907**

Elmira, Cortland & Northern Railroad Co. In 1905 the railroad was absorbed into Lehigh Valley Rail Way Co. **1914**

Elmore Gold Co. Ld. Regd. 1889. Reconstructed 1891 as Elmore Gold Ld., in which company shareholders were entitled to 1 share of 5s. (credited with 4s. paid) for each share of £1 held, Removed from Register 1906 .... **1892**

Elmore Gold Ld. Regd. 1891. Reconstructed 1892 as Ida Gold Co. Ld. Removed from Register 1907.......... **1893**

Elmore's American & Canadian Patent Copper Depository Co. Ld. Regd. 1892. Vol. liq. 17 July 1899. Assets were acquired by Elmore's Trust Ld., in which company shareholders were entitled to 1 fully-paid ordinary share of £1 for each priority share of £2 held. Removed from Register 1911 ... **1900**

Elmore's Austro-Hungarian Patent Copper Depositing Co. Ld. See Rohren Ld.

Elmore's Foreign & Colonial Patent Copper Depositing Co. Ld. Regd. 1889. Vol. liq. 17 July 1899. Assets were acquired by Elmore's Trust Ld., for 45,000 fully-paid ordinary shares of £1. Removed from Register 1911 .... **1900**

Elmore's French Patent Copper Depositing Co. Ld. Regd. 1890. Removed from Register 1907 .... **1900**

Elmore's German & Austro-Hungarian Metal Co. Ld. See Rohren Ld.

Elmore's Metal Co. Ld. See Rohren Ld.

Elmore's Patent Copper Depositing Co. Ld. Regd. 1889. Vol. liq. 17 July 1899. Assets were acquired by Elmore's Trust Ld., in which company shareholders were entitled to 2 fully-paid preference shares of £1 for each preference share of £2 held or 1 fully-paid ordinary share of £1 for each ordinary share of £1 held. Removed from Register 1911 .... **1900**

Elmore's Trust Ld. Regd. 1899. Removed from Register 1911 .... **1910**

Elmore's Wire Manufacturing Co. Ld. Regd. 1890. Vol. liq. 17 July 1899. Assets were acquired by Elmore's Trust Ld., in which company shareholders were entitled to 2 fully-paid preference shares of £1 for each preference share of £2 held or 1 fully-paid ordinary share of £1 for each ordinary share of £2 held. Removed from Register 1911 .... **1900**

Elmslie (Australia) Ld. See Atlas Corporation Ld.

Elmslie Ld. Regd. 1898. Vol. liq. July 1907. Undertaking and assets were acquired by company of same name (later Atlas Corporation Ld.), in which company shareholders were entitled to 1 share for each share held. Removed from Register 1908 .... **1908**

Elmslie Ld. See Atlas Corporation Ld.

VOL. FOR

Elphil Rubber Co. Ld. Regd. 1909. Vol. liq. 31 Jan. 1921. Property and assets were acquired by London Asiatic Rubber & Produce Co. Ld., in which company shareholders were entitled to 5 shares of 2s. (credited as fully-paid) for each share of £1 held. Final meeting return regd. 16 Feb. 1922 .... **1921**

Elstree & Boreham Wood Gas Co. Ld. Established 1872. Regd. 1895. Vol. liq. 16 Mar. 1932. Undertaking was acquired by Watford & St. Albans Gas Co., in which company shareholders were entitled to £18 9s. or £12 18s. 6d. in B consolidated stock for each original ordinary A (10% standard) share of £10 or B (7% standard) share of £10 respectively held; preference shareholders were entitled to £10. £12, and £13 in 5% preference stock for every 5%, 6% or 6½% preference share of £10. Liability for debenture bonds was assumed by acquiring company. Final meeting return regd. 19 May 1932...................... **1931**

Elstree Film Laboratories Ld. Regd. 1921. Vol. liq. (members') 27 Sept. 1937. All shares owned by Associated British Picture Corporation Ld. Final meeting return regd. 22 Mar. 1938...................... **1938**

Elswick Coal Co. Ld. Regd. 1881. Vol. liq. 9 Dec. 1954. Struck off Register 23 Oct. 1956 .... **1947**

Elswick Cycles and Manufacturing Co. Ld. Regd. Edinburgh 1900. Vol. liq. Sept. 1910. Court Order to dissolve 9 June 1914 .... **1911**

Elswick Cycles Co. Ld. Regd. 1896. Vol. liq. 30 Jan. 1900. Business was acquired by Elswick Cycles and Manufacturing Co. Ld. The 1st and 2nd debenture holders were to be repaid in full. Removed from Register 1901 .... **1901**

Elswick Steam Shipping Co. Ld. Regd. 1899. Vol. liq. (members') 26 Oct. 1956. Final meeting return regd. 15 July 1959 .... **1940**

Elterwater Gunpowder Co. Ld. Regd. 1866. Vol. liq. (members') 11 Aug. 1930. Capital returned to contributories—£98 3s. 6d. per share of £100. Final meeting return regd. 10 Aug. 1932...................... **1931**

Eltringham (Jos. T.) & Co. Ld. Regd. 1914. Vol. liq. 20 Oct. 1919. Reconstructed as Eltringhams Ld., in which company shareholders were entitled to 1 fully-paid preference share of £1 for each preference share of 5s. held or 1 fully-paid ordinary share of 10s. for each ordinary share of 1s. held. Final meeting return regd. 16 July 1920 .... **1920**

Eltringhams Ld. Regd. 1919. Vol. liq. (creditors') 13 Jan. 1933. Assets realised insufficient to pay unsecured creditors in full. Final meeting return regd. 24 Nov. 1934 .... **1933**

Elvedon Shipping Co. Ld. Regd. 1919. Struck off Register 1929 .... **1929**

Elworthy Brothers & Co. Ld. Regd. 1866. Receiver appointed Feb. 1934. Struck off Register 25 Mar. 1938 .... **1939**

Ely & Newmarket Railway Co. Inc. by Special Act 1875. Undertaking transferred to Great Eastern Railway Co., in 1898. Holders of 5% capital stock received £125 Great Eastern 4% debenture stock for every £100 stock held and holders of 3½% debenture stock received £87 10s. Great Eastern 4% debenture stock for every £100 stock held.............. **1899**

Ely & St. Ives Railway Co. Inc. by Special Act 1864 as Ely, Haddenham & Sutton Railway Co.; name changed 1878. Undertaking transferred to Great Eastern Railway Co., in 1898. Holders of 4% capital stock received an equal amount of Great Eastern 4% debenture stock; holders of 5% debenture stock received £125 Great Eastern 4% debenture stock for every £100 stock held **1899**

Ely Beet Sugar Factory Ld. Regd. 1924. Vol. liq. (members') 9 July 1936. The factory was transferred to British Sugar Corporation Ld., for 324,500 fully-paid ordinary shares of £1. Shareholders were entitled to 13 such shares for every 18 shares of £1 held plus approximately 13s. per share in cash. Final meeting return regd. 13 July 1937 .... **1937**

Ely Brewery Co. Ld. Regd. 1887. Vol. liq. 3 Apr. 1920. Undertaking and assets were acquired by Rhondda Valley Breweries Co. Ld. (later Ely Brewery Co. Ld.), in which company shareholders were entitled to 2 shares of £10 for each share of £10 held. Final meeting return regd. 4 Jan. 1921................ **1920**

Ely Gas & Electricity Co. Ld. Regd. 1871. Dissolved 1 May 1949, undertaking being vested in Eastern Area Gas Board under Gas Act 1948. Holders of securities were entitled to receive British Gas 3% guaranteed stock 1990–95 in respect of each £100 unit, unless otherwise stated, of security held:

	£	s.	d.
Orig. cap. stock (10% max.)................	202	10	0
Addit. cap. shares of £10	14	4	0
(7% max.)			

*See Stock Exchange Year-Book.

VOL. FOR

5% pref. shares (of £10)........................ 12 10 0
4% debs ....100 0 0 — **1952**

Ely Valley Railway Co. Inc. by Special Act 1857. Line purchased by Great Western Railway Co. in 1903. Holders of consolidated ordinary stock received £120 Great Western 5% consolidated guaranteed stock for every £100 stock held; holders of 4½% and 4% debenture stock received an equal amount of Great Western 4½% and 4% debenture stock respectively. The £35,000 consolidated ordinary stock held by purchasing company was cancelled — **1904**

Ely Tidal Harbour & Railway Co. See Penarth Harbour Dock and Railway Co.

Elysée Palace Hotel Co. Ld. Regd. 1897. Vol. liq. 16 Apr. 1925. Undertaking and assets were sold to Société Immobiliere de l'Elysée Palace for 51,000 shares of Frs.500. The outstanding 4½% debenture stock and 5% debentures were repaid at 95% in cash. Final meeting return regd. 1 May 1926 .... — **1926**

Emba Caspian Oil Co. Ld. Regd. 1912. Struck off Register 10 Oct. 1961 .... — **1960**

Embassy Club Ld. Regd. 1918 as Martans Club Ld.; name changed Dec. 1932. Receiver appointed 9 Feb. 1938; ceased to act 7 July 1938. Struck off Register 23 Oct. 1942 .... — **1935**

Embassy Wine & Club Co. Ld. Regd. 1923 as E.M.Y. Trust Ld.; name changed Nov. 1928. Vol. liq. (members') 7 Mar. 1938. Capital returned to contributories—9s. 6½d. per preference share of £1; an unspecified amount was paid into Companies' Liquidation Account. Final meeting return regd. 20 Sept. 1940 .... — **1939**

Embreeville Iron Co. Ld. Regd. 1894. Vol. liq. 17 May 1900. Properties were acquired by Virginia Coal, Coke and Iron Co. in exchange for bonds and common stock. Removed from Register 1901 ...... — **1901**

Embreeville Town Co. Ld. Regd. 1891. Vol. liq. 16 Sept. 1896. Final meeting return regd. 22 May 1897 ..... — **1896**

Embreville Freehold Land, Iron & Railway Co. Regd. 1889. Vol. liq. 7 Nov. 1893. Final meeting return regd. 30 Nov. 1896 .... — **1894**

Emerald and Phœnix Brewing Co. Ld. Regd. 1889. Vol. liq. 15 May 1912. 67% of outstanding debentures were redeemed by Dec. 1912; further redemptions (if any) not known. Final meeting return regd. 12 May 1914 .... — **1913**

Emerald Land and Mines Trust Co. Ld. Regd. 1888. Removed from Register 1904 .... — **1904**

Emerald Mines of Colombia Ld. Regd. 1888 as Standard Mining Co. Ld.; name changed Sept. 1888. Vol. liq. 22 Dec. 1891. Reconstructed as New Esmeralda Co. Ld. Final meeting return regd. 31 Aug. 1895 ...... — **1908**

Emerald (Reward) Gold Mining Co. Ld. Regd. 1897. Vol. liq. 22 Feb. 1900. Final meeting return regd. 12 Dec. 1902 .... — **1901**

Emigrant & Colonist's Aid Corporation Ld. See Colonist's Land & Loan Corporation Ld.

Emily Copper Mines Ld. Regd. 1882. Removed from Register 1889 .... — *****1887**

Emily Edith Mines Ld. Regd. 1900. In Dec. 1908 it was stated that properties had been sold. Removed from Register 1911 .... — **1909**

Emny Anthracite Co. Ld. Regd. 1904. Vol. liq. 1939. Distributions amounting to 9s. 3d. per share on account of capital were made. Final meeting return regd. 18 Jan. 1950 .... — **1951**

Emma Co. Ld. Regd. 1890. Vol. liq. 9 May 1895. Reconstructed as company of same name. Shareholders were entitled to 1 share of 5s. (credited with 3s. paid) in new company for each share of 5s. held. Debenture holders were entitled either to fully-paid shares to amount of principal and interest or to 5 shares of 5s. (credited with 4s. paid) for each £1 principal and interest. Final meeting return regd. 29 Apr. 1898 .... — **1900**

Emma Co. Ld. Regd. 1895. Vol. liq. 18 Apr. 1900. Reconstructed as Emma Co. (1900) Ld. in which company shareholders were entitled to 1 share of 2s. 6d. (credited with 2s. 3d. paid) for each share of 5s. held. Final meeting return regd. 21 Dec. 1901 ..... — **1902**

Emma Co. (1900) Ld. Regd. 1900. Removed from Register 1909 .... — **1903**

Emma Silver Mining Co. Ld. Regd. 1871. Shareholders received an equal number of shares in New Emma Silver Mining Co. Ld.; debenture holders received 5,282 shares in satisfaction of balance of principal and interest. Removed from Register 1904 .... — **1885**

Emmaburg Natural Table Waters Ld. Regd. 1897. Vol. liq. 31 Mar. 1898. Final meeting return regd. 29 May 1902 .... — **1925**

Emmotts & Wallshaw Ld. Regd. 1899. Vol. liq. (members') 21 June 1935. Capital returned to contributories—£15,250. Final meeting return regd. 29 Oct. 1938 .... — **1936**

Emperor Fire Insurance Society Ld. Established 1854. Regd. as unlimited 1862; regd. as limited 1882. Vol. liq. May 1886. Business taken over by Queen Insurance Co. Final meeting return regd. 20 Nov. 1890 .... — **1887**

Emperor Gold Mines Ld. Regd. 1902. Vol. liq. 3 Apr. 1905. Undertaking was acquired by Field's Reward Gold Mines Ld., in which company shareholders were entitled to 1 fully-paid share of 10s. for every 4 shares of 5s. held. Removed from Register 1907 ... — **1906**

Emperor Life Assurance Society. Inc. by Special Act 1853; regd. as unlimited 1862; regd. as limited 1882. Vol. liq. Oct. 1885. Court Order to continue winding up under supervision Nov. 1885. Final meeting return regd. Sept. 1889 .... — **1886**

Empire Contract Co. See Philadelphia Co.

Empire, Croydon, Co. Ld. Regd. 1897. Removed from Register 1909 .... — **1899**

Empire Economic Steam Produce Ld. Regd. 1895. Vol. liq. 26 Apr. 1900. Removed from Register 11 Aug. 1905 .... — *****1901**

Empire Electric Light & Power Co. Ld. Regd. 1902. Court Order to wind up 1906. Removed from Register 1913 .... — **1907**

Empire Gold Fields Ld. Regd. 1900. Vol. liq. 26 Mar. 1906. Undertaking acquired by Roper River Lands & Minerals Co. Ld., in which company shareholders were entitled to 1 share of 10s. (7s. 3d. paid) for each share of £1 held. Struck off Register 2 Oct 1953 ... — **1954**

Empire Guarantee & Insurance Corporation Ld. Regd. Edinburgh 1900. Court Orders: to wind up 14 July 1911; to dissolve 7 Nov. 1924 .... — **1912**

Empire, Liverpool, Ld. Regd. 1894. Removed from Register 22 May 1908 .... — *****1898**

Empire Mining Co. Ld. Regd. 1886. Vol. liq. 31 Oct. 1889. Reconstructed as Golden Leaf Ld., in which company shareholders were entitled to 1 share of £1 (credited with 13s. paid) for each share of £1 held. Final meeting return regd. 13 July 1892 .... — **1890**

Empire New Mutual Marine Assurance Association Ld. Regd. 1879. Vol. liq. 24 Jan. 1929. Final meeting return regd. 1 Oct. 1929 .... — *****1925**

Empire of India Corporation Ld. Regd. 1890. Vol. liq. 31 Dec. 1894. Final meeting return regd. 8 Feb. 1899 — **1896**

Empire Oil Engine Syndicate Ld. Regd. 1904. Vol. iiq. 27 Feb. 1923. Final meeting return regd.4 July 1923 — **1924**

Empire Palace Ld. Regd. 1887. Vol. liq. 27 Sept. 1926. Final meeting return regd. 6 July 1927................ — **1927**

Empire Palace (Poplar) Ld. Regd. 1907. Vol. liq. 29 Mar. 1928. Subsidiary of London Theatres of Varieties Ld. Final meeting return regd. 21 Dec. 1928 .... — **1929**

Empire Palace (Woolwich) Ld. Regd. 1907. Vol. liq. 29 Mar. 1928. Subsidiary of London Theatres of Varieties Ld. Final meeting return regd. 21 Dec. 1928 .... — **1929**

Empire Seamless Steel Tube Co. Ld. Regd. 1896. Vol. liq. 28 Nov. 1898. Final meeting return regd. 6 Jan. 1900 .... — **1899**

Empire Steam Fishing Co. of Aberdeen Ld. Regd. Edinburgh 1902. Vol. liq. (members') 22 May 1939. Capital returned to contributories—£1 14s. 6d. per share of £1 (10s. paid). £47 4s. was paid to Accountant of the Court. Final meeting return regd. 4 Dec. 1939 .... — **1940**

Empire Steam Trawling & Fishing Co. Ld. Regd. 1891. Removed from Register 1903 .... — **1893**

Empire Steamship Assurance Association Ld. Regd. as limited by guarantee 2 Feb. 1882. Vol. liq. (members') 26 Oct. 1943. No assets have been distributed among members. Final meeting return regd. 6 Jan. 1944 .... — **1945**

Empire Telephone Co. Ld. Regd. 1885 as Mechanical Telephone Co. Ld.; name changed 6 July 1886. Subsequently placed in liquidatton. Final meeting return regd. 1 Mar. 1888 .... — *****1888**

Employers' Indemnity Co. Ld. Regd. 1898. Vol. liq. 12 Mar. 1901. Business was acquired by Ocean Accident & Guarantee Corporation Ld., in which company shareholders were entitled to 1 share of £5 (credited with £1 paid) for every 5 shares of £5 (£1 paid) held plus 1s. 10¾d. per share in cash. Removed from Register 1901 .... — **1902**

Employers' Liability & Work-peoples Provident & Accident Insurance Co. Ld. Regd. 1881. Vol. liq. 21 Dec. 1896. Final meeting return regd. 16 July 1898 — *****1898**

Employers' Mutual Assurance Association Ld. Regd. 1898. Vol. liq. 12 Mar. 1901. Business was acquired by Vulcan Boiler & General Insurance Co. Ld. Capital was repaid with bonus of 7½%. Final meeting return regd. 10 Oct. 1901 .... — **1902**

Empresa de Melhoramentos Urbanos de Paranagua, S.A. Dissolved in Apr. 1944; all shares were owned by Southern Brazil Electric Co. Ld. .... — **1946**

*See Stock Exchange Year-Book.

VOL. FOR

Empress Assurance Corporation Ld. Regd. 1895. Vol. liq. 22 Aug. 1902. Final meeting return regd. 31 July 1908 — **1903**

Empress Base Metals (Rhodesia) Ld. Regd. 1927. Vol. liq. (members') 23 Dec. 1931. Capital returned to contributories—£3,271 10s. Final meeting return regd. 13 Sept. 1939 — **1932**

Empress Brewery Co. Ld. Regd. 1896. Vol. liq. (members') 30 Sept. 1955 for purpose of transferring undertakings and assets to Peter Walker (Warrington) Ld. holding all ordinary capital. Preference capital repaid at par. £100 paid into Companies' Liquidation Account in respect of distributions. Final meeting return regd. 16 Feb. 1959 — **1960**

Empress Club Ld. Regd. 1897 as Hotel & Club Investment Co. Ld.; name changed 31 May 1902. Vol. liq. 10 Nov. 1905. Removed from Register 16 July 1915 — ***1906**

Empress of Coolgardie Gold Mine Ld. Regd. 1894. Vol. liq. 8 May 1896. Reconstructed as Empress of Coolgardie Gold Mine (1896) Ld., in which company shareholders were entitled to 1 share of £1 (credited with 17s. paid) for each share of £1 held. Final meeting return regd. 31 Mar. 1897 — **1898**

Empress of Coolgardie Gold Mine (1896) Ld. Regd. 1896. Undertaking was acquired in 1899 by Phoenix Gold Mines Ld., in which company shareholders were entitled to 2 shares of 10s. (credited with 8s. paid) for each share of £1 held. Struck off Register 1926 — **1903**

Empress of Gwalia Ld. Regd. 1899. Reconstructed 1899 as Gwalia Consolidated Ld., in which company shareholders were entitled to 1 fully-paid share of £1 for each share of £1 held. Removed from Register 1905 — **1901**

Empress (Rhodesia) Mines Ld. Regd. 1899. Vol. liq. 10 Aug. 1911. The undertaking was sold to Rhodesia Ld., in which company shareholders were entitled to 1 fully-paid share of £1 for every 10 shares of £1 held. Final meeting return regd. 13 Feb. 1914 — **1912**

Emu Bay & Mount Bischoff Railway Co. Ld. Regd. 1887. Vol. liq. Feb. 1925. Undertaking and assets were acquired by Emu Bay Railway Co., for £500 in cash, £61,500 in fully-paid preference shares and £39,100 in 5% irredeemable debenture stock. The debenture stockholders were entitled to an equal amount of 4½% irredeemable debenture stock. Shareholders were entitled to 5 fully-paid 7% A preference shares of £1 for each share of £5 held *plus* participation in distribution of 5% irredeemable debenture stock. Final, meeting return regd. 29 June 1926 — **1926**

Enabra Syndicate Ld. Regd. 1910. Struck off Register 1920 — **1914**

Enamelled Metal Products Corporation Ld. Regd. 1907 as International Pfaudler Ld.; name changed Aug. 1919. Vol. liq. (members') 26 Feb. 1934. Capital returned to contributories—£41,277 1s. 3d. Final meeting return regd. 15 May 1934 — **1935**

Encinillas Mines & Smelting Works of Santa Rosalia Ld. Regd. 1907. Mines in Mexico were destroyed by revolutionaries in 1913. Struck off Register Apr. 1930 — **1931**

Encinillas Mines Ld. Regd. 1902. Vol. liq. Jan. 1908. Reconstructed as Encinillas Mines & Smelting Works of Santa Rosa Ld., in which company shareholders were entitled to 1 share of £1 (credited with 10s. paid) for each share of £1 held. Struck off Register Mar. 1929 — **1930**

Endcliffe Estates Co. Ld. Regd. 1895. Vol. liq. 27 Sept. 1920. Final meeting return regd. 15 June 1922 — **1921**

Endell Street Estates Ld. Regd. 1926. Vol. liq. June 1932. In 1932 certain assets were sold to Odhams' Properties Ld. for 209,500 fully-paid ordinary shares which were subsequently transferred to Odhams Press Ld. Holders of 7½% mortgage debenture stock were entitled to 7% 1st mortgage debenture stock of Odhams Properties Ld. at 105%, or repayment in cash at 102½% on 19 July 1932 — **1933**

Endurance Tube & Engineering Co. Ld. Regd. 1896. Vol. liq. 10 Oct. 1898. Final meeting return regd. 10 June 1899 — **1899**

Enelsee Estates Ld. Regd. 1916. Vol. liq. 22 Aug. 1924. Final meeting return regd. 14 July 1925 — ***1925**

Enfield Alldays Motors Ld. Regd. 1908 as Enfield Autocar Co. Ld.; name changed 15 Jan. 1919. Vol. liq. 30 Apr. 1923. Final meeting return regd. 13 Nov. 1924 — ***1909**

Enfield Autocar Co. Ld. Regd. 1906. Receiver for debenture holders appointed in 1907. Vol. liq. Jan. 1908. Removed from Register 1909 — **1908**

Enfield Autocar Co. Ld. See Enfield Alldays Motors Ld.

Enfield Gas Co. Inc. by Special Act, 1867. Under Act of 1913 the undertaking was acquired by Tottenham & Edmonton Gas Light & Coke Co. (later Tottenham and District Gas Co.). in which company stockholders were entitled to £105 B consolidated

VOL. FOR

ordinary stock for every £100 ordinary stock held. Holders of preference stock were entitled to an equal amount of 5% preference stock. Holders of 5% and 4% debenture stocks were entitled to £125 and £100 respectively in 4% debenture stock for each £100 stock held — **1914**

"Engineer" Cycle Works Ld. Regd. 1897. Vol. liq. 27 Sept. 1900. Final meeting return regd. 25 Apr. 1902 — ***1901**

Engineering & General Contract Corporation Ld. Regd. 1892. Vol. liq. 6 Nov. 1899. Reconstructed as General Investment and Finance Co. Ld., in which company shareholders were entitled to 1 fully-paid share of 5s. for every 4 ordinary shares of £1 held or 4 fully-paid shares of 5s. for every 3 preference shares of £1 held. Final meeting return regd. 4 Sept. 1900 — **1901**

Engineering Instruments Ld. Regd. 1900 as Schattner Electricity Meter Co. Ld.; name changed Jan. 1905. Vol. liq. 27 May 1913. Final meeting return regd. 27 Feb. 1914 — **1910**

England Assurance Institution. Inc. by Special Act 1841 as Church of England Life & Fire Assurance Trust & Annuity Institution; name changed 1892. Business acquired by Imperial Life Insurance Co. in 1893 for £74,000 — **1902**

England (Gordon) Ld. Undertaking and assets were acquired in 1929 by England (Gordon) (1929) Ld. for £80,536 in cash and 352,000 fully-paid shares of 5s. — **1930**

England (Gordon) (1929) Ld. Regd. 1929. Vol. liq. (creditors') 14 Jan. 1931. Assets realised insufficient to pay unsecured creditors in full. Final meeting return regd. 7 Mar. 1934 — **1931**

England's Premier Cobalt Mining Co. Ld. Inc. Ontario 1907 — **1909**

Englisch Deutsche Terrain und Industrie A.G. Ld. *See* International Land & Industries Ld.

English & African Corporation Ld. Regd. 1902. Removed from Register 1910 — **1907**

English and American Freehold Land Mortgage Co. Ld. *See* English and American Mortgage Co. Ld.

English & American Mortgage Co. Ld. Regd. 1887 as English and American Freehold Land Mortgage Co. Ld.; name changed Mar. 1888. Vol. liq. 2 May 1895. Final meeting return regd. 11 Apr. 1902 — **1896**

English & American Shipping Co. Ld. Regd. 1888. Vol. liq. 16 Apr. 1919. Final meeting return regd. 25 Nov. 1927 — ***1920**

English and Australian Assets Co. Ld. Regd. 1897. Vol. liq. 2 Nov. 1903. Undertaking was acquired by Melbourne Trust Ld. (later Standard Trust Ld.). Shareholders were entitled to 7 shares of 4s., £2 2s. in debenture stock and 4s. 3d. in cash. Final meeting return regd. 12 Aug. 1926 — **1904**

English & Australian Copper Co. Ld. Established 1851. Regd. 1866. Vol. liq. 17 Feb. 1920. Final meeting return regd. 6 Feb. 1923 — **1921**

English & Australian Mortgage Bank Ld. Inc. Australia 1884. In liquidation in 1895 — **1895**

English & Colonial Syndicate Ld. Regd. 1895. Removed from Register 1905 — **1901**

English & Dutch Meat Co. Ld. Regd. 1923. Vol. liq. (members') 2 Apr. 1935. Capital returned to contributories—3·168d. per share of £1. Final meeting return regd. 3 Jan. 1936 — **1936**

English & European Corporation Ld. Regd. 1927. Vol. liq. (members') 10 Oct. 1930. Capital returned to contributories—£238,863 3s. Final meeting return regd. 29 June 1931 — ***1931**

English & French Bank Ld. Regd. 1880. Removed from Register 1905 — **1883**

English & French Gold Mines Syndicate Ld. Regd. 1895. Struck off Register 23 July 1901 — **1902**

English & Italian Banking Corporation Ld. Regd. 1891. Vol. liq. 31 Dec. 1895. Final meeting return regd. 15 Sept. 1896 — **1897**

English & Scottish American Mortgage & Investment Co. Ld. Regd. 1886. Vol. liq. 2 Nov. 1904. Final meeting return regd. 16 Sept. 1922 — **1905**

English & Scottish Boiler Insurance Co. Ld. Regd. 1897. Vol. liq. 15 May 1888. Business transferred to Scottish Boiler Insurance & Engine Inspection Co. Ld. Final meeting return regd. 9 July 1889 — ***1889**

English and Scottish Finance Corporation Ld. Regd. 1898. Struck off Register 20 Nov. 1908 — **1909**

English & Scottish Investment Co. of Canada Ld. Regd. Edinburgh 1877. Vol. liq. Dec. 1881. Business transferred to a Canadian Company. Struck off Register 27 Sept. 1932 — **1883**

English & Scottish Law Life Assurance Association. Established by Deed of Settlement 1839. Vol. liq. Dec. 1918. Amalgamated with Eagle Star and British Dominions Insurance Co. Ld. (later Eagle Star Insurance Co. Ld.), in which company shareholders were entitled to 1 ordinary share of £3

VOL. FOR

(credited as fully-paid) *plus* £1 in 5% War Stock for each share of £50 (£3 10s. paid) held. Struck off Register 27 Jan. 1956 .... **1919**

English & Scottish Mercantile Investment Trust Ld. Regd. 1886. Court Order to wind up Nov. 1894. Removed from Register 1906 .... **1895**

English & Spanish Produce Co. Ld. Regd. 1901. Court Order to wind up 15 Apr. 1902. Liquidator released 12 Dec. 1904. Removed from Register 10 May 1910 ***1903**

English Antimony Co. Ld. Regd. 1889. Removed from Register 1896 .... **1899**

English Association Sterling Fund Ld. Inc. in Jersey 26 July 1978. Vol. liq. (members') 4 Apr. 1985. Final meeting return regd. 22 Apr. 1985. First distribution of £92·14 per share on 30 Apr. 1985 and 2nd and final distribution of £4·47 per share on 31 July 1985. £1,226 paid into Companies' Liquidation Account **1986-7**

English-Australian Gold Mining Co. Ld. Regd. 1877. Vol. liq. 11 June 1886. Properties acquired by Fryerscreek Gold Mining Co. Ld. Final meeting return regd. 18 July 1888 .... ***1887**

English Bank of Rio de Janeiro Ld. *See* British Bank of South America Ld.

English Bank of the River Plate Ld. Regd. 1881. Reconstructed as New English Bank of the River Plate Ld., in which company shareholders were entitled to apply for shares at par. Removed from Register 1905 .... **1894**

English Beet Sugar Corporation Ld. Regd. 1916. Vol. liq. 27 Mar. 1924. Reconstructed as company of same name. Shareholders were entitled to 7 fully-paid shares of £1 for every 2 ordinary shares of £1 or 2¼ fully-paid preference shares of £1 held. Final meeting return regd, 17 Sept. 1924 .... **1925**

English Beet Sugar Corporation Ld. Regd. 1924. Vol. liq. (members') 9 July 1936. The factory was transferred to British Sugar Corporation Ld.. for 410,774 fully-paid ordinary shares of £1. Shareholders were entitled to approximately 11 such shares for every 10 shares of £1 held *plus* 17s. 6d. per share in cash. Final meeting return regd. 13 July 1937 .... **1937**

English Celluloid Co. Ld. Regd. 1900. Vol liq. 21 Mar. 1906. Undertaking and assets were acquired by Celluloid Ld. No capital returned to contributories. Debenture holders were entitled to a similar amount of debentures in new company. Removed from Register 1908 .... **1908**

English Channel Steamship Co. Ld. Regd. 1872. Removed from Register 1904 .... ***1878**

English Clocks & Gramophones Ld. Regd. 1920. Vol. liq. 25 Jan. 1921. Final meeting return regd. 29 Aug. 1924 .... **1923**

English Company of San Miguel de Colquechana Ld. Regd. 1889. Vol. liq. 13 July 1891. Final meeting return regd. 9 Dec. 1897 .... **1892**

English Crown Spelter Co. Ld. Regd. 1883. Vol. liq. (members') 20 Mar. 1931. Capital returned to contributories—3s. 6¹¹⁄₁₆d. per share of £1. Final meeting return regd. 21 Nov. 1931 .... **1932**

English Electric Manufacturing Co. Ld. Regd. 1899.Vol. liq. 31 Mar. 1903. The capital was acquired by Dick, Kerr & Co. Ld. in which company shareholders were entitled to 1 ordinary share of £5 for every 2 ordinary shares of £5 held or to 1 preference share of £5 for each preference share of £5 held. The debenture stock was exchanged at par for debenture stock in acquiring company *plus* 5% in cash. Final meeting return regd. 5 Mar. 1904 .... **1904**

English Electro-Metallurgical Co. Ld. *See* Leeds Copper Works Ld.

English, European & General Trust Ld. Regd. 1923. Vol. liq. (members') 21 May 1931. Capital returned to contributories—£16,005 4s. 2d. Final meeting return regd. 24 Jan. 1935 .... **1932**

English Exploration Co. Ld. Regd. 1896. Removed from Register 1901 .... **1899**

English Farmers' Association Ld. Regd. 1897. Struck off Register 22 Dec. 1903............................ **1904**

English Feister Printing Co. Ld. Regd. 1891. Court Order to wind up 10 July 1900. Removed from Register 1907 .... **1901**

English Fibre Industries Ld. Regd. 1896. Removed from Register 1901 .... **1901**

English Freeholds Ld. Regd. 1905. Vol. liq. 21 Jan. 1907. Removed from Register 7 Nov. 1911 .... ***1908**

English Fruit & Rose Co. (Cranston's) Ld. Regd. 1889. Receiver for debenture holders appointed. Removed from Register 1901 .... **1892**

English Gelatine & Phosphates Ld. Regd. 1933. Vol. liq. (members') 1 Jan. 1942. All capital held by I.C.I. (General Chemicals) Ld. Final meeting return regd. 20 July 1942 .... **1942**

English Incandescent Gas Share Co. Ld. Vol. liq. 29 Mar. 1898. Acquired by Welsbach

Incandescent Gas Light Co. Ld. for £833,330 in cash, £79,925 preference shares, £79.925 ordinary shares and £256,820 deferred shares. Final meeting return regd. 17 Mar. 1899 .... **1898**

English Lager Beer Brewery Ld. Regd. 1890. Removed from Register 1907 .... **1894**

English Land & Investment Co. Ld. Regd. 1879. Court Order to wind up Nov. 1926. Struck off Register Aug. 1932 .... **1933**

English McKenna Process Co. Ld. Regd. 1903. Receiver appointed 14 July 1911. Court Order to wind up 12 Sept. 1911. Liquidator released 13 Jan. 1915. Struck off Register 14 Feb. 1919............................ ***1912**

English Manufacturers' Export Co. Ld. Regd. 1892. Removed from Register 1908 .... **1903**

English Margarine Works Ld. Regd. 1899 as Cheshire Creamery Co. Ld.; name changed Dec. 1908 to Cheshire & Broad Green Margarine Ld. and as above Feb. 1911. Vol. liq. 23 Dec. 1919. Final meeting return regd. 18 May 1920............................ **1940**

English Mining Syndicate Ld. Regd. 1897. Vol. liq. 29 Mar. 1905. Removed from Register 1906 .... **1906**

English Oilfields Ld. Regd. 1918. Vol. liq. (members') 30 Dec. 1960. Capital returned to contributories—12s. per share of £1. £52,322 15s. 6d. was paid into Companies' Liquidation Account. Final meeting return regd. 3 July 1969 .... **1970**

English Portland Cement Co. Ld. Regd. 1889. Vol. liq. 28 Sept. 1894. Final meeting return regd. 15 Nov. 1895 .... **1896**

English Railway and Tramway Carriage Works Ld. *See* United Electric Car Co. Ld.

English Record Co. Ld. Regd. 1911. Vol. liq. Apr. 1913. Struck off Register 1929 .... **1930**

English San Andres Gold Mines Ld. Regd. 1909. Vol. liq. Nov. 1918. Struck off Register 7 July 1939 .... **1945**

English, Scottish and Australian Chartered Bank. Inc. by Royal Charter 1852. Reconstructed as English, Scottish and Australian Bank Ld., in which company shareholders were entitled to an equal number of shares of £35 (£15 paid) after payment of £5 per share **1897**

English Syndicate Ld. Regd. 1905. Vol. liq. 1 Dec. 1911. Final meeting return regd. 1 July 1914 .... **1913**

English Watch Co. Ld. Regd. 1882. Vol. liq. 11 Feb. 1895. Final meeting return regd. 8 Feb. 1898 .... **1896**

Ennis & West Clare Railway Co. Inc. by Special Act 1880. Abandoned by Act of 1883 .... **1884**

Enniskillen, Bundoran & Sligo Railway Co. Inc. by Special Act 1861 .... **1898**

Eno Proprietaries Ld. Regd. 1934. Vol. liq. (members') 23 Nov. 1954. All ordinary shares were owned by Beecham Group Ld. Preference and A preference shares (of £1) repaid at par 30 Nov. 1954. £2,893 2s. 11d. was paid into Companies' Liquidation Account. Final meeting return regd. 1 Feb. 1957 ..... **1957**

Ensign Shipping Co. Ld. Regd. 1919. Vessel was sold and creditors paid in full. No capital returned to contributories. Struck off Register 10 Mar. 1936... **1937**

Enterprise (British Columbia) Mines Ld. Regd. 1899. Vol. liq. 29 Dec. 1913. Final meeting return regd. 24 June 1930 .... **1914**

Enterprise Gold Mining & Estates Co. Ld. Regd. 1899. Vol. liq. 19 Jan. 1920. Assets were acquired by London and Rhodesian Mining and Land Co. Ld. (later Lonrho Ld.), in which company shareholders were entitled to 1 share of 5s. (credited as fully-paid) for each share of £1 held. Final meeting return regd. 12 Oct. 1920 .... **1920**

Enticknap Concrete Machines Ld. Regd. 1928. Receiver appointed 16 Sept. 1931. Vol. liq. (creditors') 7 July 1932. Assets realised insufficient to meet claims of creditors in full. All capital owned by Knap Concrete Machines Ld. Final meeting return regd. 13 Aug. 1935 .... **1932**

Entre Rios (Argentine) Extract of Meat Co. Ld. Regd. 1889. Vol. liq. 25 Aug. 1895. Final meeting return regd. 22 Dec. 1899 .... **1899**

Entre Rios Railways Co. Ld. Regd. 1891. Vol. liq. (members') 31 Mar. 1948, the undertaking having been sold to the Argentine Government as from 1 July 1946. Capital returned to contributories per £100 stock—6% preference, £30 8s. 7·125d.; 4% 2nd preference, £18 5s. 1·875d.; ordinary £15 4s. 3·5625d. £23,702 was paid into Companies' Liquidation Account. Final meeting return regd. 27 June 1957 .... **1958**

Entwistle & Stevens Ld. Regd. 1899. Vol. liq. 1 July 1929. Final meeting return regd. 17 Feb. 1930...... **1930**

Eow Seng Rubber Co. Ld. Regd. 1909. All capital was owned by Warren Rubber Holdings Ld. Vol. liq. (members') 23 Feb. 1966. Final meeting return regd. 4 July 1967 .... **1962**

VOL. FOR

Epping Gas Co. Ld. Regd. as limited in 1862; re-incorporated by' Special Act 1905. Undertaking amalgamated 1 Jan. 1911, with certain other companies under the title of the Bishop's Stortford, Harlow & Epping Gas & Electricity Co. (later Bishop's Stortford, Epping and District Gas Co.), in which company holders of the £23,500 ordinary share capital received an equivalent amount of B stock **1911**

Epps (James) & Co. Ld. Regd. 1893. Vol. liq. (members') 29 Dec. 1950. Final meeting return regd. 30 Nov. 1951 .... **1947**

Epsom & Ewell Gas Co. Inc. by Special Act 1877. Reconstructed as Wandsworth, Wimbledon and Epsom District Gas Co. (later Wandsworth and District Gas Co.), which company assumed liability for debentures. Ordinary stockholders were entitled to an equal amount of 5% standard "Epsom" stock **1913**

Epsom Downs Extension Railway Co. Inc. by Special Act 1892. Undertaking purchased by South Eastern Railway Co., in 1899, the consideration being paid in 3% preference stock of South Eastern Co. to amount of shares held in Epsom Co **1900**

Epstein Electric Accumulator Co. Ld. Regd. 1891. Court Order to wind-up 18 Aug. 1897. Liquidator released 24 Mar. 1902. Removed from Register 27 Aug. 1907 .... ***1898**

Epworth Gas Co. Ld. Regd. 1864. Dissolved 1 May 1949, undertaking being vested in East Midland Area Gas Board under Gas Act 1948. Holders of shares (of £5) were entitled to receive £6 5s. British Gas 3% guaranteed stock 1990–95 for each share held **1952**

Equi Valley Marble Co. Ld. Regd. 1903. Receiver for 1st debenture holders appointed in 1907. Struck off Register 1917 .... **1912**

Equitable Aberdeen (Drapers) Ld. *See below.*

Equitable Aberdeen (Drapers) Holdings Ld. Regd. Edinburgh 1911 as North of Scotland Equitable Loan Co. Ld.; name changed to Equitable Aberdeen (Drapers) Ld. in Oct. 1925 and subsequently as above. All capital was owned by Morrison's Economic Stores Ld. Vol. liq. (members') 14 Apr. 1958. Final meeting return regd. 30 Nov. 1961 .... **1931**

Equitable Bank Ld. Regd. 1899 as Halifax Equitable Bank Ld.; name changed Oct. 1913. Vol. liq. 13 July 1927. Undertaking and assets were acquired by Bank of Liverpool & Martins Ld. (later Martins Bank Ld.), in which company shareholders were entitled to 1 share of £1 (credited as fully-paid) plus 15s. in cash for each share held **1928**

Equitable Building Co. Ld. Regd. 1900. Vol. liq. (members') 15 Aug. 1956. £100,000 3½% mortgage debenture stock (with £51,373 interest arrears) was repaid at par 5 Mar. 1956. Capital returned to contributories—preference stock at par; ordinary stock: £3 11s. 1½d. per £1 stock. £332 2s. 4d. paid into Companies' Liquidation Account in respect of unclaimed distributions. Final meeting return regd. 4 Mar. 1958 .... **1958**

Equitable Debenture & Assets Corporation Ld. Regd. 1888. Vol. liq. 3 Aug. 1894. Reconstructed as company of same name. The ordinary shares of £10 were divided into equal moieties of deferred and preferred stocks which were convertible into an equal amount of similar stock in new company. Holders of founders' shares of £10 were entitled to an equal number of founders' shares of £10 in new company. Final meeting return regd. 27 May 1898 .... **1894**

Equitable Fire & Accident Office Ld. Regd. 1890. Vol. liq. 11 June 1901. Undertaking and assets were acquired by London and Lancashire Fire Insurance Co. (later London & Lancashire Insurance Co.). Shareholders were entitled to 1 share of £25 (credited with £2 10s. paid) in acquiring company for every 20 shares of £5 (£1 paid) held *plus* 5 ordinary and 5 preference shares of £1, all fully-paid, in Equitable Buildings Co. Ld. for every 16 shares held. A cash payment was anticipated. Final meeting return regd. 6 Feb. 1902 .... **1902**

Equitable Fire Insurance Co. Ld. Regd. 1873. Vol. liq. 10 Dec. 1890. Final meeting return regd. 27 Jan. 1902 .... **1901**

Equitable Guarantee & Accident Co. Ld. Regd. 1884. Vol. liq. 10 Dec. 1890. Reconstructed as Equitable Fire & Accident Office Ld. Final meeting return regd. 27 Jan. 1902 .... **1901**

Equitable Mortgage Co. Established 1884. Reconstructed as Equitable Securities Co. **1899**

Equitable Office Building Corpn. Inc. New York 1913. All capital was owned by Webb & Knapp Inc. Dissolved 19 Apr. 1955 .... **1957**

Equitable Plate Glass Insurance Co. Ld. Regd. 1881. Removed from Register 1906 .... **1888**

VOL. FOR

Equitable Securities Co. Inc. New York 1894. Business taken over by Securities Company in 1899. Debenture holders were entitled to 90% of holdings in either Consols A or B and 10% in capital stock of new company **1900**

Equitable Trust Co. of New York. Inc. New York 1871 as Traders Deposit Co.; name changed May 1895 to American Deposit & Loan Co. and as above in May 1902. Merged with Chase National Bank of the City of New York (later The Chase Manhattan Bank) in which company shareholders were entitled to 4 shares of $20 for every 5 shares of $20 held **1931**

Equitable Trust of London Ld. Regd. 1906 as Western Canada Trust Ld.; name changed Feb. 1914. Vol. liq. Dec. 1928. Final meeting return regd. 14 Oct. 1929 .... **1929**

"Era" Incandescent Oil Lamp Co. Ld. Regd. 1898. Undertaking was acquired by New Incandescent Oil Light Co. Ld. Shareholders were entitled to 1s. 6d. per share of £1 or to 1 fully-paid share of £1 in new company for every 2 shares of £1 held. Removed from Register 1904 .... **1904**

Era Industrial & General Fire Insurance Co. Ld. Regd. 1880. Removed from Register 1905 .... ***1885**

Era Mining Properties Development Syndicate Ld. Regd. 1910. Vol. liq. 31 Mar. 1914. Struck off Register 18 Jan. 1921 .... ***1915**

Era Welsh Slate Quarries Ld. Regd. 1897. Removed from Register 1910 .... **1905**

Ericsson Shipping Co. Ld. Regd. 1909. Vol. liq. 6 Jan. 1920. Capital returned to contributories—£2 per share of £1; further payments (if any) not known. Final meeting return regd. 21 Sept. 1921 .... **1920**

Eridia (Egypt) Exploring Co. Ld. Regd. 1903. Vol. liq. 4 Dec. 1906. Removed from Register 1907 .... **1907**

Eritrea Gold Mines Co. Inc. Italy 1900. Vol. liq. (in Rome) Aug. 1914 .... **1915**

Erlangers Ld. Regd. 1928. Business acquired by Philip Hill, Higginson & Co. Ld. (now Philip Hill, Higginson, Erlangers Ld.), in Sept. 1959. Vol. liq. (members') 16 Oct. 1959. Final meeting return regd. 18 Oct. 1962 .... **1963**

Ernest Scragg & Sons (Holdings) Ld. *See* Scragg (Ernest) & Sons (Holdings) Ld.

Ervedosa Tin Mines Ld. Regd. 1920. Vol. liq. (creditors') 14 Oct. 1930. No capital returned to contributories. Final meeting return regd. 21 July 1939 .... **1931**

Eryldon Steamship Co. Ld. Regd. 1919 as Adelaide Steamship Co. Ld., name changed Jan. 1920. Vol. liq. 9 Nov. 1925. Final meeting return regd. 27 Oct. 1927 .... **1926**

Escot Rubber Estates Ld. Regd. 1909. Vol. liq. 29 Mar. 1920. Reconstructed as company of same name. Shareholders were entitled to 3 fully-paid shares of 2s. in new company for each share of 2s. held. Final meeting return regd. 15 Dec. 1920 .... **1921**

Escurial Copper Mines Ld. Regd. 1901. Vol. liq. Dec. 1911. Removed from Register 1913 .... **1912**

Esher Development Co. Ld. Regd. 1931. Vol. liq. 7 June 1934. Capital returned to contributories—£41,893 2s. 6d. Final meeting return regd. 23 Mar. 1939 .. **1934**

Eskdale Railway Co. Inc. by Special Act 1909. Line closed **1911**

Eskside Steam Shipping Co. Ld. Regd. 1898. Vol liq. 26 Mar. 1918. Final meeting return regd. 17 July 1920 .... **1918**

Esmeralda Consolidated Mines (Mexico) Ld. Regd. 1910. Vol. liq. 22 Oct. 1913. Final meeting return regd. 5 Oct. 1926 .... **1914**

Esmeralda Gold Mines Ld. Regd. 1895. Vol. liq. 19 Mar. 1897. Capital returned to contributories—2s. 2½d. per share of £1 at 11 Oct. 1897; further payments (if any) not known. Final meeting return regd. 30 Nov. 1897 .... **1898**

Esmeralda Ld. Regd. 1889. Vol. liq. Jan. 1893. Properties were acquired by Durand Gold Mines Ld. Removed from Register 1903 .... **1900**

Espana Mining Co. Ld. Regd. 1910. Struck off Register Feb. 1930 .... **1931**

Española Propriety Co. Ld. Regd. 1925. Vol liq. Aug. 1926. Capital returned to contributories—8·071d. per share of 10s. £713 paid into Companies' Liquidation Account. Final meeting return regd. 21 Oct. 1950 .... **1951**

Espartillar Estancia Co. Ld. Regd. 1886. Vol. liq. (members') 14 Aug. 1946. Capital returned to contributories—£24 19s. 1d. per share of £10. Final meeting return regd. 27 Nov. 1953 .... **1954**

Esperance Bay Co. Ld. Regd. 1890. Vol. liq. (members') 21 May 1953. Capital returned to contributories—£2 15s. 8¼d. per share of £5. £560 10s. 4d. paid into Companies' Liquidation Account. Final meeting return regd. 11 Dec. 1959 .... **1961**

Esperance Proprietary Co. Ld. Regd. 1897. Vol. liq. June 1908. Removed from Register 1909 .... **1909**

See Stock Exchange Year-Book.

Esperanza Ld. Regd. 1903. Vol. liq. 12 June 1923. Reconstructed as company of same name. Shareholders were entitled to 5 shares of 10s. (credited with 8s. paid) for every 2 shares of £1 held. Final meeting return regd. 29 July 1924 .... **1924**

Esperanza Ld. Regd. 1923. Vol. liq. (members') 7 Jan. 1932. Capital returned to contributories—£2,563 3s. 7d. Final meeting return regd. 12 July 1933 .... **1932**

Esperanza Gold Mines Ld. See Nueva Esperanza Gold Mines Ld.

Esperanza Nitrate Co. Ld. Regd. 1899. Vol. liq. 4 Feb. 1925. Reconstructed as Andrade Nitrate Co. Ld., in which company shareholders were entitled to 25 fully-paid ordinary shares of £1 for every 100 ordinary shares or 2,000 B shares of 1s. held. Holders of every £100 1st mortgage income debentures were entitled to 65 fully-paid shares of £1; holders of every £100 2nd mortgage income debenture were entitled to 40 fully-paid shares of £1; holders of every £100 B prior lien bonds were entitled to £40 in cash, £60 in 7% debentures and 1½ B shares of 1s. Final meeting return regd. 13 Jan. 1931 .... **1926**

Esperanza Westralia Ld. Regd. 1905. Struck off Register 1914 .... **1911**

Espirito Santo & Caravellas Railway Co. Regd. 1897. Vol. liq. Feb. 1908. The railway and equipment were acquired by Leopoldina Railway Co. Ld., in which company shareholders were entitled to 6 ordinary shares of £10 for every 10 shares of £10 held; shareholders were expected to receive a further return of approximately £2 5s. per share from sale of securities received in respect of expropriation of warehouses. Removed from Register 1909 .... **1908**

Espirito Santo Silva & Co. See Banco Espirito Santo.

Espuela Land and Cattle Co. Ld. Regd. 1884. Vol. liq. 7 Sept. 1908. Capital returned to contributories—£2 per preference share of £5 at Sep. 1908; further payments (if any) not known. Final meeting return regd. 8 Sept. 1911 .... **1909**

Essaman Gold Mining Co. Ld. Regd. 1885. Vol. liq. 10 Apr. 1890. Property and assets were acquired by Gie Appantoo Gold Mining Co. Ld. for £5,000 in cash and 25,000 shares of £1. Final meeting return regd. 27 Jan. 1892 .... **1891**

Essar Ld. Regd. 1921. Receiver appointed Nov. 1931; ceased to act Dec. 1939. Court Order to wind up 8 Feb. 1932. All shares owned by Amalgamated Wallpaper Mills Ld. Struck off Register 14 May 1943 .... **1932**

Essekuma Syndicate Ld. Regd. 1901. Removed from Register 1904 .... **1903**

Essequibo Rubber and Tobacco Estates Ld. Regd. 1910. Court Order to wind up 25 June 1912. Liquidator released 16 July 1920. Struck off Register 24 July 1923 .... **1913**

Esser-Barratt Repeating Arms Co. Ld. Regd. 1906. Removed from Register 1912 .... **1908**

Essex & Suffolk Accident Indemnity Society Ld. Regd. 1907. Vol. liq. Aug. 1909. Undertaking and assets were acquired by Essex and Suffolk Equitable Insurance Society Ld. (later Essex & Suffolk Insurance Society Ld.). in which company shareholders were entitled to 1 share of £10 (credited with £1 paid) for every 5 shares of £1 (5s. paid) held. Removed from Register 1910 .... **1910**

Essex Union Insurance Co. Ld. Regd. 1898. Vol. liq 13 Feb. 1922. Final meeting return regd. 4 Sept. 1937 **1923**

Essington & Ashmore Light Railway Co. Inc. (under Light Railways Act 1896) by order of Light Railway Commissioners confirmed by Board of Trade 1900 **1903**

Esson (John) & Son Ld. Regd. 1905. Vol. liq. 17 Apr. 1907. Assets were anticipated to realise insufficient to pay a dividend to preference shareholders. Final meeting return regd. 7 Sept.1918 .... **1908**

Estate Co. Ld. Regd. 1864. Vol. liq. 2 Jan. 1920. Final meeting return regd. 17 July 1920 .... **1920**

Estate, Finance & Mines Corporation Ld. Regd. 1897. Vol. liq. Dec. 1908. Assets were to be sold to British and Colonial Investments Ld., in which company shareholders were entitled to 1 fully-paid share of 10s. for each share of £1 held. Removed from Register 1911 .... **1909**

Estates' Agency & Loan Co. of Mauritius Ld. Regd. 1884. Vol. liq. 20 July 1891. Final meeting return regd. 18 Mar. 1892 .... **1892**

Estates & Mining Co. of Rhodesia Ld. Regd. 1902. Vol. liq. Oct. 1912. Removed from Register 1913 .... **1913**

Estates Investment and Villa Farm Co. Ld. Regd. 1883. Vol. liq. June 1890. Final meeting return regd. 25 Aug. 1890 .... **1891**

Eston Sheet & Galvanising Co. Ld. Regd. 1912. Vol. liq. (members') 21 Aug. 1936. Dissolved before 1951 .. **1935**

Etablissements Grafton (Francais) Ld. Regd. 1902 as Manufacture D'Impressions de Malaunay Ld.;

name changed Jan. 1905. Vol. liq. 14 Dec. 1926. Final meeting return regd. 3 May 1927 .... ***1927**

Ethel-Hope Gold Mines Ld. Regd. 1895. Vol. liq. 29 Mar. 1897. Final meeting return regd. 28 Nov. 1898 **1898**

Ethel Reef Gold Mining Co. Ld. Regd. 1896. Reconstructed 1902 as Tano Bippo Gold Mines Ld., in which company shareholders were entitled to 1 share of 5s (credited with 4s. paid) for every 2 shares of 5s. held. Removed from Register 1906............. **1903**

Ethelburga Syndicate, Limited. Regd. 1902. Vol. liq. (members') 23 Nov. 1945. Capital returned to contributories—7s. 6d. and 13.98p. Assets distributed in specie—19,988 shares of £1, in Ethelburga Agency Ld. and 16,655 ordinary shares of £1 and 28,534 deferred shares of 1s., in San Paulo Land Co. Ld. Final meeting return regd. 9 Mar. 1976 .... **1976-7**

Etheridge Gold Field (Queensland) Ld. Regd. 1886. Vol. liq. Nov. 1888 for reconstruction at Etheridge United Gold Mining Co. Ld., in which company shareholders were entitled to 3½ shares of £1 for every share of £1 held. Final meeting return regd. 11 Apr. 1890 .... **1889**

Etheridge Gold Mines Ld. Inc. Victoria 1911. Vol. liq. Aug. 1913. Reconstructed under same title. Shareholders were entitled to 1 share of 10s. (credited with 6s. paid) in new company for each fully-paid share of 10s. held **1914**

Etheridge Gold Mines Ld. Inc. Victoria 1913. Vol. liq. July 1919 .... **1920**

Etheridge Gold Mining Co. Ld. Regd. 1891. Vol. liq. 9 Jan. 1894. Final meeting return regd. 7 Jan. 1895 **1894**

Etheridge Reefs (Queensland) Gold Mining Co. Ld. Regd. 1886. Vol. liq. 26 Nov. 1888 for reconstruction as Etheridge United Gold Mining Co. Ld., in which company shareholders were entitled to 2 shares of £1 for every share of £1 held. Final meeting return regd. 24 Feb. 1891 .... **1891**

Etheridge United Gold Mining Co. Ld. Regd. 1888. Vol. liq. 2 July 1891. Reconstructed as Etheridge Gold Mining Co. Ld., in which company shareholders were entitled to 1 share of 5s. (credited with 4s. paid) for each share of £1 held. Final meeting return regd. 19 Mar. 1897 .... **1893**

Ethiopian General Trading Co. Ld. Regd. 1906 as Ethiopian Rainproof Monopoly Co. Ld.; name changed May 1907. Vol. liq. Apr. 1908. Removed from Register 1913 .... **1909**

Ethiopian Gold Mining Co. Ld. Regd. 1889. Vol. liq. 17 Oct. 1890. Final meeting return regd. 30 June 1893 **1891**

Ethiopian Rainproof Monopoly Co. Ld. See Ethiopian General Trading Co. Ld.

Ethniki Trapeza Tis Ellados. [National Bank of Greece]. Inc. in Greece 30 Mar. 1841. Merged by Royal Decree of 26 Feb. 1953 with Bank of Athens as National Bank of Greece and Athens S. A. (later National Bank of Greece S. A.). Shareholders were entitled to receive 1 share of the new bank for every share held **1954**

Eticoal Syndicate Ld. Regd. 1912. Vol. liq. 3 May 1915. Final meeting return regd. 1 Feb. 1917 .... **1916**

Etna Development Co. Ld. Regd. 1903. Vol. liq. Sept. 1910 for sale of undertaking to Rhodesia Exploration and Development Co. Ld., in which company shareholders were entitled to 1 fully-paid share of £1 for every 2 shares of £1 held. Removed from Register 1912 .... **1911**

Eton Gold Mining Co. Ld. Inc. Transvaal 1899. Amalgamated in 1902 with Windsor Gold Mining Co. Ld., as Windsor Gold Mines Ld., in which company shareholders received 1 share of £1 for each share of £1 held **1903**

Etruscan Copper Estates Ld. Regd. 1900. Vol. liq. 16 Nov. 1904. Reconstructed as company of same name. Shareholders were entitled to 1 share of £1 (credited with 16s. paid) in new company for each share of £1 held. Final meeting return regd. 9 Nov. 1905 .... **1908**

Etruscan Copper Estates Ld. Regd. 1904. Vol. liq. 31 Dec. 1908. Final meeting return regd. 3 Jan. 1913 **1909**

Eureka Gold Mines Ld. Regd. 1898. Vol. liq. 1903. Undertaking was acquired by Associated Financial Corporation Ld. in which company shareholders were entitled to 2 fully-paid shares of £1 for every 5 shares of £1 held. Removed from Register 1906 .. **1904**

Eureka (Nevada) Silver Mining Co. Ld. Regd. 1880. Removed from Register 1905 .... **1885**

Eureka Refrigerating Co. Ld. Regd. 1887. Court Orders; to wind up Jan. 1891; to dissolve Dec. 1891.... **1891**

Euroflame Holdings p.l.c. Regd. as a private company 17 Feb. 1976 as Amexway Ld.; name changed to present title 3 Feb. 1981. Winding-up order made 4 Feb. 1985 and concluded 14 Apr. 1987 .... **1988-9**

Euro Gold Mines Ld. Regd. 1899. Removed from Register 1905 .... **1904**

VOL. FOR

European Accident Insurance Co. Ld. See European General Reinsurance Co. Ld.

European & General Corpn. Ld. Regd. 1928 as European & General Finance Corpn. Ld.; name changed Aug. 1931. In 1968 the undertaking was transferred to Union Commercial Investment Co. Ld. in which company share and stockholders were entitled to receive fully-paid capital as follows-£5 4% preference stock per £4 5% preference stock, and 9 ordinary shares of 5s. per 10 ordinary shares held; debenture stockholders received a like amount of 4½% debenture stock 1983. Company is to be dissolved under Section 208 of the Companies Act 1948 .... **1970**

European & General Finance Corpn, Ld. See above.

European & North African Mines Ld. Regd. 1927. Vol. liq. (members') 1 June 1955. Capital returned to contributories—preferred ordinary, 6d. per share (of 10s.); deferred, ¼d. per share (of 1s.) to holders of 480 shares or over; £1,260 14s. 9d. was paid into Companies' Liquidation Account. Final meeting return regd. 27 Aug. 1957 .... **1958**

European Commercial Corpn. Ld. Regd. 1929 as European Meat & Packing Corpn. Ld.; name changed 1931. Struck off Register 8 Jan. 1965 ..... **1961**

European Gas Co. Ld. Est. 1835; regd. as limited 1859. Vol. liq. 10 Apr. 1952. Stockholders received a first and final distribution of one 3% bond of Caisse Nationale De l'Energie of Frs. 10,000 (nominal) and a cash payment of Frs. 1,790 and 8s. sterling for each £20 (nominal) of stock. Final meeting in Paris 28 July 1953 .... **1954**

European General Reinsurance Co. Ld. Regd. 1911 as European Accident Insurance Co. Ld.; name changed Apr. 1920. Vol. liq. (members') 25 Jan. 1951, undertaking and assets having been acquired by North American Casualty & Reinsurance Corpn. Final meeting return regd.9 Aug.1951 .... **1952**

European Meat & Packing Corpn. Ld. See European Commercial Corpn. Ld.

European Merchant Banking Co, Ld. Regd. 1927. Vol. liq. (members') 31 Dec. 1930. Capital returned to contributories—£5,000 plus £750 preferential dividend to management shareholders; £251 13s. 8d. to ordinary shareholders. Final meeting return regd. 31 Dec. 1931 .... **1931**

European Petroleum Co. Ld. Regd. 1896. Undertaking and assets were acquired in 1900 by European Petroleum Co. (1900) Ld. (later European Petroleum Co. Ld.), for £770,000 in cash, £180,000 in preference shares and £550,000 in ordinary shares of £1. Removed from Register 1903 .... **1901**

European Petroleum Co. Ld. Regd. 1900 as European Petroleum Company (1900) Ld.; name changed Sept. 1900. Vol. liq. 3 July 1911 for reconstruction as European Oilfields Corporation Ld. 1st debenture holders were entitled to 30% in cash, 35% in 1st debenture stock and 10% in fully-paid shares of 10s. of the new company; 2nd debenture holders were entitled to 7½% in 1st debenture stock, 5% in fully-paid shares and 5% in profit-sharing notes; preference shareholders were entitled to 8% in fully-paid shares, and ordinary shareholders to 4% in fully-paid shares and 6½% in profit-sharing notes. Final meeting return regd. 2 June 1923 .... **1912**

European Sims-Edison Electrical Torpedo Co. Ld. Regd. 1891. Vol. liq. 11 Feb. 1895. Final meeting return regd. 21 June 1895 .... **1896**

Eustace & Co. Ld. Inc. Dublin 1898. Vol. liq. 22 Aug. 1958. No capital returned to contributories........... **1972**

Euxine Trading Co. Ld. Regd. 1919. Vol. 3 June 1921. Capital returned to contributories—5% at 28 Sept. 1921; further payments (if any) not known. Final meeting return regd. 20 Apr. 1922 .... **1922**

Evancon Gold Mining Co. Ld. Regd. 1901. Vol. liq. 8 Dec. 1909. Final meeting return regd. 28 Aug. 1917 **1910**

Evans & Allen Ld. Regd. 1895. Vol. liq. (members') 28 Nov. 1958. Final meeting return regd. 17 Mar. 1959 **1955**

Evans (Ben) & Co. Ld. Regd. 1895. Vol. liq. (members') 3 Sept. 1965. Final meeting return regd. 10 Dec. 1965 .... **1956**

Evans (D. H.) & Co. Founders' Shares Co. Ld. Regd. 1900. Vol. liq. 17 July 1919. Final meeting return regd. 12 Dec. 1919 .... **1920**

Evans (J. & C. H.) & Co. Ld. Regd. 1897. Vol. liq. (members') 13 Apr. 1970. Capital returned to contributories; £12 10s. per preference share (of £10) and £42 per ordinary share (of £10). Final meeting return regd. 14 Aug. 1973 .... **1974-5**

Evans (Joseph) & Sons Ld. Regd. 1897. Vol. liq. (creditors') 30 July 1930. Assets realised insufficient to pay debenture holders in full. Final meeting return regd. 2 July 1931 .... **1931**

VOL. FOR

Evans (Lavington) & Co. Ld. Regd. 1895. Removed from Register 1908 .... **1901**

Evans (Richd.) & Co. Ld. Regd. 1889. Vol. liq. (members') 1 Aug. 1951. Capital returned to contributories-£12 6s. 7·68247d. per A or B share of £7 10s. £2,595 10s. paid into Companies' Liquidation Account. Final meeting return regd. 31 Oct. 1957 .... **1958**

Evans Sons Leschsr & Webb Ld. Regd. 1902. Vol. liq. 19 Nov. 1925. The 6½% debenture stock was repaid at 102½% in 1926. Reconstructed as company of same name [later Evans Medical Ld.]. Shareholders were entitled to 2 preference shares of 6s. 8d. (credited with 5s. paid) in new company for each preference share of £1 held, or 1 ordinary share of 6s. 8d. (credited with 4s. paid) for each ordinary share of £1 held. Final meeting return regd. 18 Aug. 1926...... **1926**

Evans (T. Fencott) & Co. Ld. Regd. 1898. Vol. liq. A dividend of 2s. in the £ was paid on the preference capital on 2 Oct. 1903; further payments (if any) not known. Removed from Register 1905 .... **1904**

Evelyn Gold Mining Co. Ld. Regd. 1898. Removed from Register 1905 .... **1895**

Evening Echo Printing & Publishing Co. Dublin Ld. Regd. Dublin. Removed from Register 1908 .... **1895**

"Evening News" Ld. Regd. 1896. Vol. liq. 17 Apr. 1905. Undertaking and assets were acquired by Associated Newspapers Ld., in which company shareholders were entitled to 1 fully-paid ordinary share of £1 plus 5s. 6d. in cash for each ordinary share of £1 held; preference shareholders were entitled to £5 10s. per share of £5 in cash. Removed from Register 1906 **1906**

Everard (W.) & Co. Ld. Regd. 1925. Vol. liq. (members') 3 May 1937. Undertaking was acquired by Everard Brewery Ld., in which company shareholders were entitled to 6 5% preference shares for every 5 preference shares of £1 held. Ordinary shareholders were entitled to £1 3s. 5·8d. per ordinary share of £1 plus participation in 499,999 ordinary shares in acquiring company. Final meeting return regd. 6 Nov. 1937.. **1938**

Evered & Co. Ld. Regd. 1884. Vol. liq. 8 June 1922. Undertaking and assets were transferred to company of same name. Holders of A shares were entitled to fully-paid shares in new company as follows-12s. 6d. per fully-paid A share of £1 held; 8s. for each A share of £1 (14s. paid) held. Holders of B shares were entitled to debenture stock in new company as follows—12s. 6d. per fully-paid B share of £1 held, 8s. for each B share of £1 (14s. paid) held. Debenture holders were entitled to repayment at 102% in cash or 80% of holding in new debenture stock. Final meeting return regd. 5 Oct. 1923 ...... **1923**

Everett (R. A.) & Co. Ld. Regd. 1903. Court Order to wind up 1905. Removed from Register 1910......... **1906**

Everitt (Allen) and Sons Ld. Regd. 1890. Vol. liq. (members') 31 Dec. 1942. All capital owned by 1. C.1. Metals Ld. Final meeting return regd. 28 Sept. 1944 .... **1945**

Everitt's Ld. Regd. 1899. Vol. liq. 2 Sept. 1904. Removed from Register 1901 .... **1905**

"Everlasting Blotter" and Advertising Co. Ld. Regd. 1897. Removed from Register 1911.................. **1909**

Everlite Ld. Regd. Oct. 1928. Vol. liq. (creditors') 8 May 1931. Assets realised insufficient to pay creditors in full. Final meeting return regd. 9 Aug. 1933 .... **1932**

Evershed (Sydney) Ld. Regd. 1899. Vol. liq. Jan. 1907. Undertaking and assets were acquired by J. Marston Thompson & Co. Ld. (later Marston Thompson & Evershed Ld.) for £20,000 in ordinary shares, £65,000 in preference shares, £100,000 in Evershed debenture stock and £21,000 in cash. Holders of 4% debenture stock received certificates of 4% "Evershed" debenture stock in purchasing company. Removed from Register 1907 .... **1908**

Every Heating Need Co. Ld. See British Heating Industries Ld.

Everyman's Co-operative Investment Trust (First Series) Ld. Regd. 15 Feb. 1928 under Industrial & Provident Societies Acts as Everyman's Co-operative Investment Trust Ld.; name changed Mar. 1931. Vol. liq. 22 July 1937 for amalgamation with three companies as Confederated Trust Ld. in which company shareholders were entitled to 1 fully-paid share of £5 for every 175 shares of 2s. held but whenever a shareholding is by reason of the amalgamation to exceed £200 such excess is to be satisfied by the allotment of loan stock **1938**

Everyman's Co-operative Investment Trust (Second Series) Ld. Regd. 4 Sept. 1928 under Industrial & Provident Societies Acts as Everyman's Second Co-operative Trust Ld.; name changed Mar. 1931. Vol. liq. 22 July 1937 for amalgamation with three companies as Confederated Trust Ld. in which

VOL. FOR

(later Lonrho Ld.) in which company shareholders were entitled to 3 fully-paid shares of 5s. for every 4 shares of 4s. held. Final meeting return regd. 8 Jan. 1930 .... **1929**

Explosives Co. Ld. Regd. 1881. Vol. liq 28 May 1885. Reconstructed as New Explosives Co. Ld. in which company shareholders were entitled to 1 share of £5 (credited with £4 paid) for each share of £5 held. Final meeting return regd. 8 May 1894............ **1906**

Explosives Trades Ld. See Nobel Industries Ld.

Express Motor Cab Co. Ld. Regd. 1907. Court Order to wind up 9 May 1911. Liquidator released 11 Feb. 1913. Struck off Register 10 Oct. 1916 .... **1912**

Extended Extensions Ld. Regd. 1909. Assets realised insufficient to repay debenture holders in full. Struck off Register 25 Nov. 1958 .... **1960**

Eyemouth Gas Co. Ld. Regd. in Edinburgh 1947. Dissolved 1 May 1949 undertaking being vested in Scottish Area Gas Board under Gas Act 1948. Holders of ordinary shares (of £1) were entitled to receive 15s. British Gas 3% guaranteed stock 1990–95 for each share held **1952**

Eyemouth Railway Co. Inc. under a Board of Trade certificate 1884. Under North British Railway Act 1900 undertaking was purchased by that company in which holders of ordinary and 3% debenture stocks received 3% consolidated lien and 3% debenture (1893) stocks respectively on basis of equal income **1901**

Eyre Arms Hotel Co. Ld. Regd. 1886. Court Orders: to wind up 24 Aug. 1887; to dissolve 15 June 1891 **1888**

Eyre's (Elijah) Brewery Ld. Regd. 1896. Vol. liq. (members') 11 Mar. 1938. The undertaking was acquired in 1938 by Morgan's Brewery Co. Ld. which company owned all share capital. The 4% 1st mortgage debentures were repaid at 110% on 31 Mar. 1938. Final meeting return regd. 7 Sept. 1938 **1939**

F

F. I. A. T. Motor Cab Co. Ld. Regd. 1907. Vol. liq. 24 June 1913. Struck off Register 12 Apr. 1929 .... **1914**

F. J. Parsons Ld. See Parsons (F. J.) Ld.

F. McNeill Holdings Ld. See McNeill (F.) Holdings Ld.

F. M. S. Rubber Planters Estates Ld. Regd. 1913. Court Order to wind up 20 May 1963. Removed from Register 23 Mar. 1971 .... **1970**

(F. M. S.) Securities & General Trust Ld. Regd. 1927. Vol. liq. (creditors') 12 Nov. 1935. No capital returned to contributories. Final meeting return regd. 20 Mar. 1936 .... **1936**

F. M. S. Timah Ld. Regd. 1912. Vol. liq. 30 Apr. 1920. Reconstructed as company of same name. Shareholders were entitled to 6 fully-paid shares of £1 for each share of £1 held. Final meeting return regd. 20 Jan. 1921 .... **1921**

F. M. S. Timah Ld. Regd. 1920. Vol. liq. 8 May 1928. Final meeting return regd. 16 July 1929 .... **1929**

F.P.M. Holdings Ld. Regd. 1927 as Ford Paper Mills Ld.; name subsequently changed. All shares were owned by Wiggins Teape & Co. (1919) Ld. (later Wiggins Teape & Co. Ld.). Vol. liq. (members') 28 May 1954. Final meeting return regd. 18 Dec. 1957 **1940**

F.W.B. Ld. See Hayes Candy & Crockers Ld.

Fabbrica Italiana Automobile-Torino. Founded 1899. Undertaking acquired by Fiat Soc. An. in 1906 .. **1940**

Fabrique de Sucre de Vierzy. Inc. France 1913. Vol. liq. Apr. 1929. Undertaking and assets were acquired by Compagnie Sucrière, in which company shareholders were entitled to 1 share of Frs.500 (credited as fully-paid) for each share of Frs. 100 held after payment of capitalised bonus of 100% **1930**

Facit Mill Co. Ld. Regd. 1904. Vol. liq. Dec. 1919. Reconstructed as company of same name. Final meeting return regd. 19 June 1920 .... **1921**

Facit Mill Co. Ld. Regd. 1920. Vol. liq. 1 Nov. 1967. Final meeting return regd. (members') 12 Dec. 1969 **1941**

Factory Buildings Ld. See Welwyn Commerical Buildings Ld.

Factory Holding Ld. Regd. 1899 as Royce Ld.; name changed Nov. 1932. Vol. liq. (creditors') 17 Dec. 1934. No capital returned to contributories. Final meeting return regd. 20 Dec. 1935 .... **1935**

Fairbairn Engineering Co. Ld. Regd. 1864. Dissolved under Companies Act 1880 restored to Register by Court Order 19 July 1887. Final meeting return regd. 29 Apr. 1899 .... ***1876**

Fairbairn, Naylor, Macpherson & Co. Ld. Regd. 1883. Removed from Register 1901 .... ***1886**

Fairbairn Pastoral Co. of Australia Ld. Regd. 1896. Vol. liq. 2 May 1916. Final meeting return regd. 18 May 1917 .... **1916**

VOL. FOR

Fairbanks Gold Dredging Co. Ld. Regd. 1921. Vol. liq. 6 Jan. 1948. Capital returned to contributories—1s. 2¼d. per share of £1. £631 paid into Companies' Liquidation Account. Final meeting return regd. 12 Dec. 1950 .... **1951**

Fairbank's Rim Manufacturing Co. Ld. Regd. 1896. Vol. liq. 20 Jan. 1899. Final meeting return regd. 31 Mar. 1900 .... **1899**

Fairfax & Co. Ld. Regd. 1931. Vol. liq. (members') 25 Oct. 1944. Final meeting return regd. 14 Sept. 1945 **1946**

Fairfield Exploration Syndicate Ld. Regd. 1897. Removed from Register 1911 .... **1901**

Fairfield Shipbuilding & Engineering Co. Ld. Regd July 1889. Receiver appointed Oct. 1965. Jan. 1966 shipbuilding fixed assets, work in progress, stocks, &c. sold to Government backed consortium. Vol. Liq. (creditors') 17 Mar. 1966. No capital returned. £288·52 paid to Companies' Liquidation Account in respect of unclaimed dividends, £55·03 in respect of distribution. Final meeting return regd. 24 Apr. 1975 .... **1975-6**

Fairfield Steam Ship Co. (1920) Ld. Regd. 1920. Struck off Register 2 Dec. 1924 .... **1925**

Fairliey's Creek Gold Mines Ld. Regd. 1896. Vol. liq. 19 Dec. 1900. Final meeting return regd. 8 Oct. 1901 **1901**

Fairrie & Co. Ld. Business was acquired in Aug. 1929 by Tate & Lyle Ld **1930**

Fairview Gold Mining Co. Ld. Regd. 1897. Removed from Register 1903 .... **1900**

Fairwater Shipping Co. . Ld. Regd. 1919 as British Hispano Line Ld.; name changed 1927. Vol. liq. (members') 19 Nov. 1951. Capital returned to contributories—£2 5s. 4¼d. per share of £1 .... **1977-8**

Faith Gold Mining Co. Ld. Regd. 1895. Vol. liq. 6 Mar. 1899. Reconstructed as Phoenix Gold Mines Ld. in which company shareholders were entitled to 2 shares of 10s. (credited with 8s. paid) for each share of £1 held. Final meeting return regd. 7 June 1900 **1900**

Fakenham Gas & Coke Co. Ld. Regd. 1860. Dissolved 1 May 1949 undertaking being vested in Eastern Area Gas Board under Gas Act 1948. Holders of ordinary shares (of £10) were entitled to receive £8 14s. British Gas 3% guaranteed stock 1990–95 for each share held **1952**

Falcon Cliff Castle Hotel & Grounds Co. Ld. Inc. Douglas 1883. Wound up in 1898. Undertaking and assets were acquired by Palace and Derby Castle Ld **1928**

Falcon Engine and Car Works Ld. Regd. 1882. Vol. liq. 15 Aug. 1889. Undertaking was acquired by Brush Electrical Engineering Co. Ld. (later Hawker-Siddeley Industries Ld.) for 11,100 fully-paid preference shares of £2 each, 11,100 fully-paid ordinary shares of £3 each and £500 in cash. Final meeting return regd. 29 Jan. 1892............ **1889**

Falcon Mill Ld. Regd. 1920 as Falcon Mill Ld.: name changed to Falcon Mill (Holdings) Ld. 1953, and as above 1957. Vol. liq. (members') 24 Mar. 1960. Capital returned to contributories—13s. 6d. per share of 6s. 8d. £2,354 5s. paid into Companies' Liquidation Account in respect of unclaimed distributions. Final meeting return regd. 10 Dec. 1963 **1964**

Falcon (Rhodesia) Development Co. Ld. Regd. 1903. Vol. liq. June 1910. Undertaking and assets were sold to Falcon Mines Ld., for £100,000 in fully-paid shares of £1. Removed from Register 1911 .... **1911**

Falconer (W. A.) & Co. Ld. Regd. 1893. Vol. liq. 23 Aug. 1894. The plant and book debts were acquired by Newcastle Breweries Ld., and the freehold properties by Northern Breweries Corporation Ld. Final meeting return regd. 16 Nov. 1894...................... **1895**

Falk Investment Trust Ld. Regd. 1933 as O. T. Falk Ld., name subsequently changed. Court Order to wind up 8 Oct. 1956. Struck off Register 19 Dec. 1972... **1934**

Falkirk & District Traction Co. Inc. by Special Act 1901 as Falkirk & District Tramways Co.; name changed by Act of 1929. Regd. Sept. 1942. Vol. liq. (members') 17 Nov. 1943. Capital returned to contributories—£30,606 10s. 7d. Final meeting return regd. 28 Sept. 1944 .... **1940**

Falkirk & District Tramways Co. Ld. Regd. Edinburgh 1904 as Falkirk Electric Construction Syndicate Ld.; name changed June 1914. Vol. liq. Dec. 1920. Undertaking and assets acquired by Fife Tramway Light & Power Co. Ld., for 60,000 fully-paid ordinary and 600,000 fully-paid preference shares of £1. Final meeting return regd. 3 Feb. 1923 .... **1921**

Falkirk Electric Construction Syndicate Ld. See Falkirk & District Tramways Co. Ld.

Falkirk Iron Co. Ld. Regd. Edinburgh 1912. Undertaking acquired by company of same name. Vol. liq. June 1920. Struck off Register 15 Oct. 1937 .... **1940**

Falkirk Iron Co. Ld. Regd. in Edinburgh 1920. All capital was owned by Allied Ironfounders Ld. Vol.

liq. (members') 29 Mar. 1963. Final meeting return regd. 21 Nov. 1963 .... **1940**

Falkland Light Railway Co. Inc. (under Light Railways Act 1896) 1906 .... **1921**

Fallings Park Garden Suburb Tenants Ld. *See* Co-Partnership Tenants Ld. (regd. 1907).

Falls Paper Mill Co. Ld. Regd. 1917. Receiver appointed in July 1925; ceased to act July 1933. Undertaking and assets were acquired by Henry Cooke & Co. (1932) Ld. Struck off Register Oct. 1934 .... **1935**

Falmouth Consolidated Mines Ld. Regd. 1907. Assets realised by order of Court were insufficient to permit any return to debenture holders. Struck off Register 31 Oct. 1916 .... **1916**

Falmouth Docks Company. Inc. by Special Act 1859.. **1921**

Falmouth Gas Co. Regd. as Falmouth Gas, Coal & Coke Co. Ld. in 1866; inc. as above by Special Act 1890. Dissolved 1 May 1949. undertaking being vested in South Western Area Gas Board under Gas Act 1948. Holders of securities were entitled to receive, in respect of each £100 unit held, British Gas 3% guaranteed stock 1990–95 as follows:

	£	s.	d.
A stock (10% stand.)	350	0	0
6%, pref. B stock	140	0	0
5%, pref. stock	115	0	0
4% irred. deb. stock	102	10	0

1952

Falmouth Water Works Co. Inc. by Special Act 1847. Under Act of 1930 the undertaking was acquired, as from 1 Jan. 1931, by Falmouth Corporation. Holders of 10% and 6% ordinary stocks received £210 and £120 respectively in Falmouth Corporation 5% stock for each £100 held, and holders of 5% preference and 4% perpetual debenture stocks received £102 10s. and £85 respectively in Falmouth Corporation 5% stock for each £100 held. The liability in respect of the 5% redeemable stock (due 1 July 1949 at 105%) was assumed by the Corporation **1931**

Famatina Co. Ld. Regd. 1912. Struck off Register 1916 **1915**

Famatina Copper & Gold Syndicate Ld. Regd. 1902. Undertaking was acquired by Famatina Development Corporation Ld., for 200,000 fully-paid shares of £1. Removed from Register 1906 .... **1904**

Famatina Development Corporation Ld. Regd. 1903. Vol. liq. 10 June 1912 for reconstruction as Famatina Co. Ld., in which company shareholders were entitled to 2 shares of 10s. (credited with 7s. paid) for each share of £1 held. Debenture holders were entitled to £120 new debentures for every £100 held. Income bondholders were entitled to 40 fully-paid shares of 10s. for principal, *plus* 40 fully-paid shares in respect of bonus for each unconverted £10 bond. Profit sharing bondholders were entitled to 4 fully-paid shares of £1 for every 10 bonds of 2s. held. Final meeting return regd. 10 Nov. 1923 .... **1913**

Famous Films (Midlands) Ld. The producing and distributing organisation was acquired in 1928 by British & Foreign Films Ld. **1929**

Fanashanti Gold Fields Ld. Regd. 1897 as Colonial Rubber Estates Ld.; name changed May 1902. Vol. liq. 22 Jan. 1913. Final meeting return regd. 31 Oct. 1917 .... **1913**

Fanti Consolidated Mines Ld. Regd. 1900. Vol. liq. Dec. 1908. Reconstructed as Fanti Consolidated Mines Ld. (later Fanti Consolidated Investment Co. Ld.). Shareholders were entitled to 1 share of 10s. (credited as fully-paid) in new company for every share of £1 held. Removed from Register 1909..... **1909**

Fanti Corporation Ld. Regd. 1900. Undertaking was acquired in Feb. 1904 by Fanti Consolidated Mines Ld., in which company shareholders were entitled to 1 fully-paid share of £1 for every 2 shares of £1 held. Removed from Register 1904 .... **1904**

Fanti Mines Ld. Regd. 1901. Vol. liq. 12 Apr. 1906. Reconstructed as company of same name. Shareholders were entitled to 1 fully-paid share of 5s. for each ordinary share of £1 held. No provision was made for deferred shareholders. Final meeting return regd. 5 Apr. 1907 .... **1907**

Fanti Mines Ld. Regd. 1906. Vol. liq. (members') 31 Jan. 1935. Shareholders were entitled to 47½ shares of 2s. in Gold Coast Banket Areas Ld., for every 100 shares of 5s. held. £6,240 4s. 4d. was paid into Companies' Liquidation Account in respect of unclaimed proceeds of sale of shares or fractions. Final meeting return regd. 22 Sept. 1938 .... **1935**

Fanti Syndicate Ld. Regd. 1909. Struck off Register Dec. 1931 .... **1932**

Far & Middle East Banking Corporation Ld. Regd. 1924. Vol. liq. 16 Mar. 1926. Final meeting return regd. 26 May 1925 .... ***1927**

Far East Finance Corporation Ld. Regd. 1921. Vol. liq. 14 Mar. 1927. Practically all shares owned by British

& Allied Investments Corporation Ld. Final meeting return regd. 24 Aug. 1928 .... **1928**

Far Eastern Insurance Co. Ld. Inc. Hongkong 20 Aug. 1917. Direct controlling interest held by Union Insurance Society of Canton Ld. **1941**

Far Eastern Photomaton Corporation Ld. Inc. Canada 1928. It was stated in 1934 that company was out of existence **1935**

Faradex-Seraphone Co. Ld. Regd. 1929. Struck off Register 21 Sept. 1932 .... **1938**

Fareham Gas & Coke Co. Undertaking acquired by Gosport District Co., in 1925 .... **1936**

Fargrove Steam Navigation Co. Ld. Regd. 1903. Vol. liq. 5 Apr. 1918. Final meeting return regd. 23 Sept. 1921 .... **1918**

Faria Gold Mining Co. of Brazil Ld. Regd. 1901. Vol. liq. 23 May 1902. Final meeting return regd. 18 July 1905 .... **1903**

Faringdon Electricity Supply Co. Ld. Regd. 1919 as Eagle Electric Light & Power Co. Ld.; name changed in May 1926. Vol. liq. (members') 16 Nov. 1931. All shares were owned by Edmundson's Electricity Corporation Ld. Capital returned to contributories—£7 3s. 10·8d. per share of £10. Final meeting return regd. 26 May 1932 .... **1928**

Faringdon Railway Co. Under Great Western Railway Act 1886 undertaking was vested in that company which assumed the debenture debt and the rent charge; £9,250 was distributed among shareholders **1887**

Farm and Colonization Co. Ld. Regd. 1893. Removed from Register 1904 .... **1904**

Farm Lands of Rhodesia Ld. Regd. 1912. Vol. liq. 31 Dec. 1923. Assets were acquired by London & Rhodesian Mining & Land Co. Ld., in which company shareholders were entitled to 1 share of 4s. (credited as fully-paid) for every 2 shares of 4s. held. Final meeting return regd. 23 Aug. 1924.............. **1924**

Farmers & Cleveland Dairies Co. Ld. Regd. 1891. Vol. liq. (members') 24 Apr. 1931. No capital returned to contributories. Final meeting return regd. 31 Dec. 1935 .... **1932**

Farmers and General Fire and Life Insurance and Loan and Annuity Co. *See* Royal Farmers and General Insurance Co.

Farmers' & Landowners' Insurance Co. Ld. *See* Scottish County & Mercantile Insurance Co. Ld.

Farmers' Glory Ld. Regd. 1934. Receiver appointed 22 Oct. 1938. Struck off Register 21 Oct. 1941 .... **1942**

Farmers' Landowners' & Mercantile Insurance Co. Ld. *See* Scottish County & Mercantile Insurance Co. Ld.

Farmers' Loan & Savings Co. Inc. Canada. In liquidation in Nov. 1897 .... **1899**

Farmers' Loan & Trust Co. Ld. *See* City Bank Farmers Trustee Co. Ld.

Farmland Mortgage & Debenture Co. Inc. Iowa 1888. In 1897 business was acquired by Mortgage & Debenture Co. Ld. Holders of 5% sterling debentures were entitled to an equal amount of (a) preference shares or (b) 4½% debenture stock in the new company; holders not converting were to be repaid at maturity **1908**

Farms Exploitation Ld. Inc. Transvaal 1903 .... **1907**

Farncombe & Co. Ld. Regd. 1899. Vol. liq. 26 June 1928. Undertaking and assets were acquired by Farncombe & Co. (1928) Ld. in which company shareholders were entitled to 3 fully-paid shares of £1 *plus* £2 in cash for each share of £5 held. Final meeting return regd. 31 May 1929 .... **1929**

Farnham Gas & Electricity Co. Estd. 1834; regd. 1898 as Farnham Gas Co. Ld.; inc. by Gas Orders Confirmation Act 1899; reinc. as above 1911. Dissolved 1 May 1949 undertaking being vested in Southern Area Gas Board under Gas Act 1948. Holders of securities were entitled to receive British Gas 3% guaranteed stock 1990–95 as follows in respect of each £100 unit unless otherwise stated of security held:

	£	s.	d.
Ord. shares (7% stand.) (of £10)	14	0	0
5% pref. shares (of £10)	11	8	0
6% pref. shares (of £10)	13	10	0
4% perp. deb. stock	102	10	0
5% perp. deb. stock	125	0	0
3½% red. deb. stock	101	0	0
4½%red. deb. stock	104	0	0

1952

Farnham United Breweries Ld. Regd. 1889. Vol. liq. 27 June 1951. Company was a wholly owned subsidiary of Courage & Co. Ld. Final meeting return regd. 30 Oct. 1951 .... **1953**

Farnham Water Co. Ld. Regd. 1875. Vol. liq. 29 Oct. 1924. Undertaking was acquired by the Farnham U.D.C. Final meeting return regd. 14 Jan. 1926... **1925**

Farnworth & Kearsley Gas Co. *See* Radcliffe, Farnworth & District Gas Co.

VOL. FOR

Farrington's Girls' School Ld. Regd. 1909 as Girls' College Association Ld.; name changed Apr. 1911. Vol. liq. 18 May 1927. Final meeting return regd. 1 May 1929 .... **1911**

Farrow's Bank Ld. Regd. 1907. Court Order to wind up 11 Jan. 1921. Struck off Register Apr. 1929 .... **1930**

Farthing Letter Card Co. Ld. Regd. 1888. Court Orders: to wind up 7 June 1890; to dissolve 26 Nov. 1892 **1891**

Fashion Shoes Ld. Regd. 1926. Vol. liq. (members') 2 Feb. 1937. Goodwill and undertaking acquired by Popular Footwear Ld. Capital returned to contributories—£1 3s. per share of £1. Final meeting return regd. 11 Aug. 1937 .... **1938**

Fassifern Coal Co. Ld. Regd. 1895. Vol. liq. (members') 20 Dec. 1933. Capital returned to contributories—10s. 3d. per share of £1. £569 2s. 3d. was paid into Companies' Liquidation Account. Final meeting return regd. 14 Mar. 1936 .... **1934**

Fatira (Egypt) Exploring Co. Ld. Regd. 1903. Vol. liq. 4 Dec. 1906. Removed from Register 1907 .... **1907**

Faudels Ld. Regd. 1907. Vol. liq. (members') 2 Mar. 1960. All capital was owned by Great Universal Stores Ld. Final meeting return regd. 26 Apr. 1962 **1963**

Fauldhouse Gas Co. Ld. Regd. in Edinburgh 1909. Dissolved 1 May 1949 undertaking being vested in Scottish Area Gas Board under Gas Act 1948. Holders of ordinary shares (of £1) were entitled to receive £1 13s. 4d. British Gas 3% guaranteed stock 1990—95 for each share held **1952**

Faure Electric Accumulator Co. Ld. Regd. 1882. Vol. liq. 7 July 1884. Court Order to continue winding up under supervision July 1884. Final meeting return regd. 18 Apr. 1895 .... **1885**

Fauvel Gold Recovery Co. Ld. Regd. 1895. Struck off Register 18 Nov. 1902 .... **1903**

Faversham Gas Co. Inc. by Special Act 1889. Dissolved 1 May 1949 undertaking being vested in South Eastern Area Gas Board under Gas Act 1948. Holders of securities were entitled to receive British Gas 3% guaranteed stock 1990—95 as follows in respect of each £100 unit held:

	£	s.	d.
Orig. stock (10% stand.)	215	0	0
New stock (7% stand.)	168	0	0
5% pref. stock	112	10	0
4% perp. deb. stock	102	0	0

1952

Faversham Water Co. Regd. 1863. Inc. by Special Act 1901. Undertaking vested in Mid-Kent Water Co. from 1 July 1963 in which company shareholders received capital stock as follows (per share of £10): A ordinary-£20 5% consolidated ordinary stock; B ordinary and ordinary-£14 5% consolidated ordinary stock: A preference—£16 5% consolidated preference stock plus 1s. cash. Outstanding debenture stock became debenture stock of Mid-Kent Water Co. Dissolved 10 Feb. 1964 .... **1965**

Fawcett, Preston & Co. Ld. Regd. 1888. In 1905 undertaking acquired by company of same name. Shareholders were entitled to 2 fully-paid shares of £1 in new company for each share of £10 held. Removed from Register 1906 .... **1908**

Fay (J. G.) & Co. Ld. Regd. 1889. Vol. liq. 31 Dec. 1912. Firsal meeting return regd. 1 Sept. 1915 .... **1913**

Fe-Ni-Ca Accumulators Ld. (see Britannia Batteries Ld.) **1937**

Fearncombe (Henry) & Co. Ld. Regd. 1891. Undertaking acquired in 1902 by Orme Evans & Co. Ld. Struck off Register 10 Feb. 1911 .... **1940**

Feaver (John) Ld. Regd. 8 July 1922. Vol. liq. (creditors') 28 July 1969. No capital returned to contributories. Final meeting return regd. 27 June 1973 .... **1974-5**

Federal Assets Co. Ld. Regd. 1897. Vol. liq. 2 Nov. 1903. Reconstructed as Melbourne Trust Ld. (later Standard Trust Ld.), in which company shareholders were entitled to £4 4s. in fully-paid shares and £6 6s. in 4% debenture stock for each share of £1 held. Final meeting return regd. 12 Aug. 1926............. **1904**

Federal Bank of Australia Ld. Inc. Australia 1881. Bank suspended payment 28 Jan. 1893 and went into liquidation **1894**

Federal Fire Insurance Co. Ld. Regd. 1887. Vol. liq. Jan. 1890. Business was transferred to Patriotic Assurance Co. of Ireland (later Patriotic Assurance Co.). Final meeting return regd. 14 Feb. 1893 .... **1890**

Federal Supply & Cold Storage Co. of South Africa Ld. Regd. 1902. Vol. liq. Mar. 1909. Removed from Register 1912 .... **1910**

Federal Syndicate Ld. Regd. 1895. Vol. liq. 22 Dec. 1897. Final meeting return regd. 9 Feb. 1898 ...... **1898**

Federated British Insurance Co. Ld. Regd. 1906 as National British & Irish Millers' Insurance Co. Ld.; name changed Nov. 1918. Vol. liq. (members') 26 June 1930. Capital returned to contributories—15s.

VOL. FOR

1·96d. per share of £5 and distribution in specie of preference and ordinary shares of £1 in United British Insurance Co. Ld. Final meeting return regd. 23 Dec. 1931 .... **1931**

Federated European Bank Ld. Regd. 1929 as Caprotti's Bank (1929) Ld.; name changed 4 Feb. 1930. Struck off Register 1934 .... ***1932**

Federated Ld. Regd. 1897. Removed from Register 1901 **1900**

Federated Mines of Rhodesia Ld. Regd. 1902. Vol. liq. 1904. Undertaking was acquired by Rhodesia Mines Ld. Removed from Register 1910 .... **1905**

Federated Mines Prospecting & Finance Co. Ld. Regd. 1895. Vol. liq. 6 Jan. 1897. Reconstructed as Federated Ld., in which company shareholders were entitled to 2 shares of £1 (credited with 17s. paid) for each share of £1 held. Final meeting return regd. 6 Jan. 1898 .... **1899**

Federated Rubber Growers & Manufacturers Ld. Regd. 1919. Vol. liq. 1 June 1928. Shareholders received in June 1928 5 ordinary shares of 5s. in George Spencer Moulton & Co. Ld.,or every 4 preferences shares of £1 held. or 7 ordinary shares of 5s. in that company for 20 ordinary shares of £1 held. Final meeting return regd. 24 June 1936 .... **1929**

Federated (Selangor) Rubber Co. Ld. Regd. 1905. Vol. liq. 15 Mar. 1920. Reconstructed as company of same name. Shareholders were entitled to 4 fully-paid shares of £1 in new company, plus 10s. in cash for each share of £1 held. Final meeting return regd. 13 Dec. 1921 .... **1921**

Federated (Selangor) Rubber Co. Ld. Regd. 1920. Vol. liq. (members') 6 Oct. 1932. Undertaking and assets transferred to Federated (Selangor) Rubber Co. (1932) Ld. (later Federated & General Investments Ld.), in which company shareholders received 5 shares of 2s. (credited with 1s. 8d. paid) for each share held; contributories who did not exercise right received 2d. per share of £1; 50,000 fully-paid shares of 2s. were allotted to contributories. Final meeting return regd. 7 Oct. 1933 .... **1933**

Federation Co. Ld. Regd. 1900. Vol. liq. 15 Dec. 1904. Struck off Register 1927 .... **1905**

Federation Syndicate Ld. Inc. Transvaal 1903. Vol. liq. Nov. 1906 .... **1907**

Federation Tin Mining Co. Ld. Regd. 1906. Struck off Register 5 Mar. 1909 .... **1909**

Federation Tin Mines Ld. Regd. 1926. Vol. liq. (members') 28 Aug. 1934. Holders of £22,500 1st debenture stock were satisfied by payment of £9,850 in cash; holders of 2nd debenture stock were entitled to 5 fully-paid shares of 2s. in company of same name for every £1 stock held; the 2nd debenture stock held by Tasmanian Government was repaid at par. Shareholders were entitled to 9 shares of 2s. (credited with 1s. 2d. paid) in new company for every 2 shares of £1 held **1950**

Federation Tin Mines Ld. Regd. 1934, Struck off Register 25 Nov. 1949 .... **1950**

Federation United Gold Mines Ld. Regd. 1899. Vol. liq. 30 Nov. 1899. Final meeting return regd. 30 Oct. 1901 .... **1900**

Federative Insurance Co. Ld. Regd. 1875. Vol. liq. 15 May 1897. Absorbed by State Fire Insurance Co. Ld. Final meeting return regd. 28 Jan. 1899 .... ***1898**

Feldes & Shepherd Ld. Regd. 1929. Direct controlling interest was held by Shepherd (William) & Sons Ld. Struck off Register 1935 .... **1933**

Felicia Syndicate Ld. Regd. 1901. Vol. liq. 7 Dec. 1904. Removed from Register 1907 .... **1905**

Felicidad Gold Co. Ld. Regd. 1908. Vol. liq. Sept. 1910. Removed from Register 1911 .... **1911**

Felix Klondyke Co. Ld. Regd. 1898. Removed from Register 1901 .... **1901**

Felixstowe & Bawdsey Ferry Railway Co. Inc. by Special Act 1887. Undertaking abandoned by Act 1892 .. **1893**

Felixstowe & District Water Co. Regd. as limited 1894; incorporated by Special Act 1895 as Felixstowe & Walton Waterworks Co.; name changed in 1931. Under the provisions of the Ipswich Water (Felixstowe & District) Order 1967 the undertaking was transferred as from 1 Apr. 1967 to the Ipswich Corpn. for a consideration of £289,718 and a winding-up order was made on 31 July 1967. A scheme of distribution was finally approved by High Court on 29 July 1968 and on 4 Sept. 1968 the following first and final distribution was made (per £10 share and £100 debenture stock respectively) plus in each case a further sum expressed as a percentage of each distribution in respect of interest earned since liquidation—7½% original ordinary share £11 plus 5·9355%; 7% new ordinary shares £10 5s. 4d. plus 5·9355%; 6% redeemable preference shares (1980) £9 5s. 6d. plus 5·9355%; 5% redeemable preference shares (1980) £8 5s. plus 5·9355%; 5%

See Stock Exchange Year-Book.

VOL. FOR

redeemable preference shares (1972) £9 10*s.* 4*d.* *plus* 5·9355%; 5% non-cumulative preference shares £7 8*s.* 10*d.* *plus* 5·9355%; 4½% non-cumulative preference shares (other than those entitled on winding up to repayment at a premium) £6 14*s.* 11*d.* *plus* 5·9355%; 4½% non-cumulative preference shares (entitled to repayment at £11 0*s.* 6*d.*), £11 0*s.* 6*d.* *plus* 3·3396%; 3½% perpetual debenture stock £100 *plus* 2·7254%. Amounts paid into Companies' Liquidation Account—£11 1*s.* 9*d.* in respect of unclaimed dividends and 13*s.* 11*d.* in respect of undistributable fraction. Final meeting regd. 30 Apr. 1969 .... **1970**

Felixstowe & Walton Waterworks Co. *See above.*

Felixstowe Gas Light Co. Regd. as limited in 1883; reincorporated by Special Act in 1904. By Special Order of 1929 the undertaking was acquired by Ipswich Gas Light Co. in which company stockholders were entitled to stock as follows—for each £100 A original ordinary stock held—£100 ordinary consolidated (3½% standard) stock and £65 5% redeemable stock; for each £100 B additional ordinary stock held—£70 ordinary consolidated (3½% standard) stock and £45 5% redeemable stock; for each £100 5% preference stock held—£100 5% preference stock; for each £100 7% redeemable preference stock held £100 7% redeemable preference stock of the Ipswich Company. Holders of 5% mortgage debenture bonds were entitled to £100 5% debenture bonds in acquiring company for each £100 held; holders of 4% perpetual debenture stock £80 of 5% debenture stock for each £100 held and holders of 5½% redeemable debenture stock—£100 5½% redeemable debenture stock (1935) for each £100 held **1930**

Fell (William) & Co. (Hexham) Ld. Regd. 1901. Vol. liq. (members') 31 Mar. 1966. Final meeting return regd. 10 July 1972 .... **1939**

Fellows Magneto Co. Ld. Regd. 1916. Vol. liq. June 1927 for reconstruction as Fellows Manufacturing Co. Ld. in which company shareholders were entitled to 1 preferred ordinary share of 10*s.* (credited with 7*s.* paid) for each preferred share of £1 held or 1 deferred share of 2*s.* 6*d.* (credited with 6*d.* paid) for each ordinary share of 10*s.* held. Struck off Register July 1933 .... **1934**

Fellows Manufacturing Co. Ld. Regd. 1927. Court Order to wind up 9 Dec. 1929. Struck off Register 10 May 1935 .... **1936**

Fellows, Morton & Clayton Ld. Regd. 1889. Vol. liq. 22 Apr. 1921 for reconstruction as company of same name. Final meeting return regd. 12 Jan. 1922 .... **1922**

Fellows, Morton & Clayton Ld. Regd. 1921. Vol. liq. (members') 2 Nov. 1948. Final meeting return regd. 12 Dec. 1950 .... **1951**

Fenn & Co. Ld. Regd. 1877. Vol. liq. 8 Jan. 1895. Final meeting return regd. 20 June 1895 .... **1882**

Fenton Collieries Ld. Regd. 1910. Vol. liq. (members') 21 July 1953. Final meeting return regd. 7 Feb. 1956 **1940**

Fenton Textile Association Ld. Regd. 1919. Court Order to wind up 12 June 1923. Undertaking was acquired by John Fenton & David Bradley Mills Ld. Liquidator released 22 Oct. 1925. Struck off Register 7 July 1942 .... **1924**

Ferghana Oil Fields Ld. Regd. 1910. Struck off Register Dec. 1931 .... **1932**

Ferguson (Alex.) & Co. Ld. Regd Edinburgh 1896. Vol. liq. Feb. 1901. Struck off Register 22 Sept. 1936 .. **1937**

Ferguson Randfontein Gold Mining Co. Ld. Inc. Transvaal 1899. Vol. liq. 1909 the assets and undertaking having been sold to Randfontein Central Gold Mining Co. Ld. for 139,584 fully-paid shares of £1 **1910**

Fermans Die Castings Ld. Regd. 1918 as Fermans (1918) Ld.; name changed Jan. 1923. Vol. liq. 16 Nov. 1923. Business and assets were sold to company of same name. Final meeting return regd. 1 Aug. 1924 **1924**

Fermans Die Castings Ld. Regd. 1923. Struck off Register 28 Jan. 1949 .... **1929**

Fermoy & Lismore Railway Co. Inc. by Special Act 1869. Under Fishguard & Rosslare Railways & Harbours Act 1898 undertaking was amalgamated with that company for £80,000 .... **1899**

Fern Cotton Spinning Co. (1920) Ld. Regd. 1920. Vol. liq. (members') 15 Nov. 1939. Capital returned to contributories—1*s.* 11·9424*d.* per share of £1 (12*s.* paid). Final meeting return regd. 17 Apr. 1940 ... **1940**

Fernhill Collieries Ld. Regd. 1910. Vol. liq. 12 Nov. 1956. Final meeting return regd. 5 Mar. 1957 ...... **1955**

Fernhill Gold Mines Ld. Regd. 1896. Reconstructed 1899 as Caledonian Mining Corporation Ld. in which company shareholders were entitled to 1 fully-paid share of £1 for every 2 shares of £1 held. Removed from Register 1901 .... **1903**

Fernhurst Mill Ld. Regd. 1919. Vol. liq. (members') 29 Jan. 1953. Final meeting return regd. 5 Jan. 1956 **1950**

VOL. FOR

Ferns Pure Milk & Cream Co. Ld. Business acquired in May 1929 by British Feeding Meals & Milk Products Co. Ld., for £16,000 in cash **1930**

Ferranti Ld. Regd. 1901. Vol. liq. 29 July 1904. Reconstructed 1905 as company of same name. Shareholders were entitled to 1 fully-paid ordinary share of £1 in new company for every 2 preference shares of £1 held: ordinary shareholders received nothing. Holders of debenture stock or 2nd mortgage debenture were entitled to an equal amount of debenture stock or 2nd mortgage debenture respectively in new company. Final meeting return regd. 26 Sept. 1908 .... **1905**

Ferranti, Thompson & Ince Ld. Regd. 1882. Vol. liq. 2 Jan. 1884. Absorbed by Hammond Electric Light & Power Supply Co. Ld. Final meeting return regd. 7 July 1884 .... ***1884**

Ferreira Deep Ld. Inc. Transvaal 1898. Vol. liq. June 1929. Undertaking and assets were acquired by Ferreira Estate Co. Ld. in which company shareholders were entitled to 1 share of £1 (credited as fully-paid) *plus* 2*s.* 6*d.* in cash for every 5 shares of £1 held **1930**

Ferreira Diamonds Ld. Regd. 1911. Struck off Register 17 Nov. 1916 .... ***1917**

Ferreira Gold Mining Co. Ld. Inc. Transvaal 1888. Vol. liq. 1912 for purpose of sale of undertaking and assets to Ferreira Deep Ld. in which company shareholders were entitled to 1 share of £1 for each share of £1 held *plus* a cash distribution of 10*s.* per share **1913**

Ferro-Carril de Carrizal y Cerro Blanco. *See* Carrizal & Cerro Blanco Railway.

Ferro-Carril Terminal Central de Buenos Aires S. A. *See* Buenos Aires Central Railroad & Terminal Co.

Ferrobamba Ld. Regd. 1909. Court Order to wind up Apr. 1931. Struck off Register 10 May 1935 .... **1936**

Festiniog Slate Co. Ld. Regd. 1877. Vol. liq. 8 Aug. 1890. Final meeting return regd. 28 Jan. 1892 ..... **1891**

Fetish Mines Ld. Regd. 1901. Removed from Register 1906 .... **1906**

Feuerheerd's (Rotors) Consolidated Ld. Regd. 1923. Vol. liq. (creditors') 18 July 1938. Return to debenture holders 4*d.* in £. Final meeting return regd. 19 Jan. 1939 .... **1939**

Ffaldau Colliery Co. Ld. Regd. 1884. Vol. liq. under Court supervision Sept. 1888. Court Orders: to wind up 10 Nov. 1888; to dissolve 16 Feb. 1894. .... **1889**

Fiat Motors Ld. *See* Wembley Motors Ld.

Fibrous Petroleum & Oil Fuel Co. Ld. Regd. 1898. Removed from Register 1908 .... **1901**

Fidelity Accident, Sickness & General Assurance Co. Ld. Regd. Edinburgh 1886. Business taken over by Century Insurance Co. Ld., in 1888. Vol. liq. Feb. 1889. Struck off Register 13 Feb. 1903 .... **1903**

Field & Mackay Ld. Undertaking and assets were acquired by British Quarrying Co. Ld. **1930**

Field Line (Cardiff) Ld. Regd. 1902. Vol. liq. 7 Oct. 1920. Shareholders were entitled to £4 8*s.* in War Loan *plus* 2*s.* in cash for each share held. Final meeting return regd. 24 Aug. 1922 .... **1921**

Field Press Ld. Regd. 1919. Vol. liq. (members') 20 Feb. 1930. Undertaking acquired by Field Press (1930) Ld. Final meeting return regd. 26 Jan. 1931 .... ***1931**

Fielding Brothers Ld. Regd. 1886. Removed from Register 1906 .... **1888**

Field's Find Gold Mines Ld. Regd. 1897. Reconstructed 1903 as Field's Reward Gold Mines Ld., in which company shareholders were entitled to 5 shares of 10*s.* (credited with 8*s.* paid) for every 2 shares of £1 held. Removed from Register **1904**

Field's Reward Gold Mines Ld. Regd. 1903. Vol. liq. 20 Oct. 1904. Reconstructed as company of same name. Shareholders were entitled to 1 share of 10*s.* (credited with 8*s.* paid) in new company for each share of 10*s.* held. Final meeting return regd. 20 July 1907 .... **1906**

Field's Reward Gold Mines Ld. Regd. 1904. Vol. liq. 14 Aug. 1906. Reconstructed as Reward Gold Mines Ld., in which company shareholders were entitled to 1 share of 10*s.* (credited with 8*s.* paid) for each share of 10*s.* held. Final meeting return regd. 7 Aug. 1907 **1908**

Fife & Kinross Coal Co. Ld. Regd. Edinburgh 1897. Vol. liq. Sept. 1901. Final meeting return regd. 5 Mar. 1903 .... **1902**

Fife Coal Co. Ld. Regd. Edinburgh 1872. Vol. liq. Jan. 1895 for reconstruction under same name. Final meeting return regd. 8 Oct. 1895 .... **1908**

Fife Coal Co. Ld. Regd. in Edinburgh 1895. Collieries, &c. vested in National Coal Board as from 1 Jan. 1947. Vol. liq. (members') 5 May 1952. Capital returned to contributories—£5 13*s.* 7⅛*d.* per ordinary share (of 6*d.*). Final meeting return regd. 8 Aug. 1960 .... **1961**

*See Stock Exchange Year-Book.

VOL. FOR

Fife Electric Power Co. Inc. by Special Act 1903. All capital owned by Scottish Power Co. Ld. Dissolved 1 Apr. 1948 under Electricity Act of 1947 .... **1940**

Fife Linoleum and Floor-Cloth Co. Ld. Regd. Edinburgh 1894. Undertaking and assets sold to Fife Linoleum Co. Ld. Vol. liq. May 1904. Court Order to dissolve 31 July 1906 .... **1905**

Fife Linoleum Co. Ld. Regd. Edinburgh 1904. Vol. liq. (members') Oct. 1933. Undertaking and assets acquired by Michael Nairn & Co. Ld. Capital returned to contributories—16s. 2d. per share of £1. Final meeting return regd. 29 June 1934............... **1934**

Fife Tramway Light & Power Co. Ld. Regd. Edinburgh 1909. Vol. liq. (members') 17 Nov. 1943. £263 was paid to Accountant of the Court of which £56 was in respect of a dissenting shareholder. Final meeting return regd. 27 Sept. 1944 .... **1945**

Fifeshire Main Collieries Ld. Regd. 1891. Property was sold by trustees for debenture holders. Removed from Register 1897 .... **1897**

Fifth Avenue Bank of New York. Inc. in New York 1875. As from 30 Apr. 1948 merged with Bank of New York as Bank of New York & Fifth Avenue Bank **1948**

Figaro Gold Mining Co. Ld. Inc. South Africa 1888. In liquidation in 1893 .... **1893**

Filabusi & Insiza Development Co. Ld. Regd. 1900. Removed from Register 1904 .... **1904**

Filabusi (Charterland) Goldfields Ld. Regd. 1898. Vol. liq. 1903. Properties were acquired by Rhodesia Exploration & Development Co. Ld. for 1,000 fully-paid shares of £1. Removed from Register 1906 ... **1904**

Filisola Rubber & Produce Estate Ld. Regd. 1910. Vol. liq. 3 Jan. 1918. Final meeting return regd. 2 Oct. 1919 .... **1918**

Fillers Ld. Regd. 1924. Vol. liq. 10 Oct. 1927. Final meeting return regd. 11 Nov. 1929 .... **1928**

Filmophone Ld. Regd. 1928. Court Order to wind up 18 Feb.1935. Struck off Register 17 July 1942 .... **1943**

Filter Engineers Ld. Regd. 1886 as Maignen's "Filtre Rapide" & "Anti-Calcaire" Co. Ld.; name changed Mar. 1938. Vol. liq. (members') 15 Apr. 1941. Capital returned to contributories—£13,216 4s. 4d. Final meeting return regd. 17 Oct. 1941............... **1942**

Finance & Investment Corporation Ld. Regd. 1898. Removed from Register 1911 .... **1901**

Finance Co. of Great Britain & America Ld. Regd. 1928. Vol. liq. (members') 2 June 1936. Capital returned to contributories—£1,395,735 2s. 10d. plus investments distributed in specie. Final meeting return regd. 12 Aug. 1936 .... **1937**

Finance Corporation of Western Australia Ld. Regd. Edinburgh 1894. Court Order to wind up Dec. 1898. Struck off Register 10 Mar. 1936 .... **1937**

Financial & Commercial Bank Ld. Regd. 1901. Court Order to wind op 1905. Removed from Register 1911........................ **1906**

Financial News Ld. Regd. 1885. Vol. liq. Dec. 1888. Final meeting return regd. 4 Sept. 1889 .... **1893**

Financial News Ld. Regd. 1888. Vol. liq. 15 Mar. 1898. Undertaking and assets were acquired by company of same name for £100,000 in cash, £50,000 in ordinary shares of £1 and £50,000 in preference shares of £1. Final meeting return regd. 14 Dec. 1898 **1898**

Financial Newspaper Proprietors Ld. Regd. 1928. Vol. liq. (members') 7 Jan. 1935. Shareholders were entitled to 1 ordinary share of 2s. in Financial News Ld., for each ordinary share of £1 held. Holders of management shares were entitled to apply for ordinary shares in that company. £4 5s. was paid into Companies' Liquidation Account. Final meeting return regd. 25 Feb. 1936 .... **1935**

Financial Times Ld. Regd. 1888. Vol. liq. 25 Feb. 1928. Undertaking was acquired by Financial Times (1928) Ld. (later Financial Times Ld.). The 1st mortgage debenture stock was repaid at 102% in May 1928. Final meeting return regd. 21 Nov. 1928 **1929**

Financial World Investments Ld. Regd. 1929 as Financial World Ld.; name subsequently changed. Vol. liq. (members') 29 July 1955. Final meeting return regd. 6 June 1956 .... **1935**

Financial World Ld. See obove.

Financier & Bullionist Ld. Regd. 1901. Vol. liq. 7 June 1924. Undertaking and assets were acquired by Financial Times Ld. Final meeting return regd. 20 Nov. 1924 .... **1925**

Findhorn Railway Co. Inc. by Special Act 1859 Board of Trade Returns stated that revenue never paid working expenses and working of line was discontinued in 1869 .... **1893**

Findlay, Richardson & Co. (Japan) Ld. Regd. 1926. All shares owned by Thorne & Co. Ld. Struck off Register 26 Oct. 1940 .... **1941**

Finedon Gas Co. Ld. Regd. 1866. Dissolved 1 May 1949, undertaking being vested in East Midland Area Gas

Board under Gas Act 1948. Holders of securities were entitled to receive. in respect of each £5 unit held, British Gas 3% guaranteed stock 1990–95 as follows:

	£	s.	d.
Orig. shares (10% max.)	9	19	0
Addit. shares (7% max.)	6	19	0

1952

Finegold (Charles) Ld. Regd. 1928. Vol. liq. Dec. 1931. Struck off Register 24 Oct. 1939 .... **1940**

Fingall Proprietary Ld. Regd. 1901. Removed from Register 1910 .... **1908**

Fingall Reefs Extended Ld. Regd. 1895. Reconstructed 1901 as company of same name. Shareholders were entitled to 1 share of £1 (credited with 16s. paid) in new company for each share of £1 held. Removed from Register 1904 .... **1903**

Fingall Reefs Extended Ld. Regd. 1901. Vol. liq. 1903. Property sold to Vivien Gold Mining Co. Ld., in which company shareholders were entitled to 1 fully-paid share of £1 for every 10 shares of £1 held. Removed from Register 1905 .... **1904**

Finland Trading Co. Ld. Regd. 1909. Vol. liq. 18 Dec. 1911. Struck off Register 20 Mar. 1925 .... **1912**

Finn Valley Railway Co. Inc. by Special Act 1860 ..... **1892**

Finsbury Estate Co. Ld. Regd. 1884. Vol. liq. Feb. 1915. Struck off Register 1934 .... **1915**

Fir Spinning Co. Ld. Regd. 1905. Final meeting return regd. 21 Aug. 1963 .... **1941**

Firbank (Joseph T.) Ld. Regd. 1903. Court Order to wind up 17 July 1906. Liquidator released 30 Aug. 1910. Removed from Register 6 June 1913 .... ***1907**

Firbeck Main Collieries Ld. Regd. 1913. Vol. liq. (members') 30 June 1939. Undertaking was acquired by Doncaster Amalgamated Collieries Ld. £1 8s. 10d. was paid into Companies' Liquidation Account in respect of share fractions. Capital returned to contributories—£5,790 14s. 5d. Final meeting return regd. 11 May 1940 .... **1939**

Fire Insurance Association Ld. See Albion Fire Insurance Association Ld.

Fire Reinsurance Co. of London Ld. Regd. 1895. Vol. liq. 6 Dec. 1904. Undertaking was acquired by King Insurance Co. Ld. Removed from Register 1907 .. **1905**

Fire Re-Insurance Corporation Ld. Regd. 1874. Vol. liq. 16 Mar. 1882. Final meeting return regd. 20 Dec. 1892 .... ***1882**

Fire-Resisting Corporation Ld. Regd. 1904. Vol. liq. Jan. 1908. Removed from Register 1912 .... **1908**

Fireproof Wood (Oxylene) Manufacturing Ld. Regd. 1920. Vol. liq. 6 Nov. 1922. Undertaking was acquired by Timber Fireproofing Co. Ld., in which company shareholders were entitled to 1 share of £1 (credited as fully-paid) for every 2 shares of £1 held. Final meeting return regd. 17 Mar. 1924 .... **1923**

Firhill Greyhound Racing Co. Ld. Regd. in Edinburgh 1932. Vol. liq. (creditors') 15 Feb. 1957. Capital returned to contributories—1s. 4d. per 20% non-cumulative preference share of 2s. 6d. £36 13s. 4d. was paid into Companies' Liquidation Account in respect of unclaimed distributions and £98 17s. 7d. in respect of unclaimed dividends. Final meeting return regd. 19 Jan. 1962 .... **1962**

Firm Syndicate Ld. See Central Monomotapa Ld.

Fir View Furniture Holdings Ld. Regd. as private company 12 Mar. 1965; converted into public company 10 June 1966. Winding-up order 21 Dec. 1970. Struck off Register 29 June 1985. Dissolved 16 July 1985. 8% unsecured loan stockholders received 11% of principal on 30 Apr. 1975 and a final distribution of 9·395% on 6 May 1983 .... **1985–6**

First Avenue Hotel Co. Ld. Regd. 1881. Taken over by Gordon Hotels Ld. Removed from Register 1905 **1891**

First Find Consolidated Gold Mines (Bulla Bulling) Ld. Regd. 1896. Vol. liq. 30 Sept. 1897. Final meeting return regd. 22 Dec. 1898 .... **1898**

First Garden City Ld. Regd. 1903. Vol. liq. (members') 17 Mar. 1966. Capital returned to contributories—£2 14s. 6·1d. per ordinary share of 10s. £3,238 was paid into Companies' Liquidation Account in respect of dividends and £7,618 in respect of distributions. Final meeting return regd. 18 June 1968. .... **1969**

First Investors American Trust S.A. Inc. in Luxembourg 1968. Vol. liq. 15 Mar. 1974. Capital returned to contributories—$US4·134 per share (of $US4) **1982–3**

First National Pathé Ld. Regd. 1927. Vol. liq. (members') 31 Oct. 1931. Capital returned to contributories—£15 3s. per share of £1. Final meeting return regd. 28 May 1941 .... **1932**

First National Reinsurance Co. Ld. Regd. 1919. Court Order to wind up June 1923. Struck off Register 27 Jan. 1942 .... **1942**

See Stock Exchange Year-Book.

VOL. FOR

10s. 10·77d. per ordinary share of £5. Final meeting return regd. 26 July 1961 .... **1962**

Flint Gas & Water Co. Ld. Inc. by Gas & Water Orders Confirmation (Chapel-en-le-Frith) Act 1876. Vol. liq. Feb. 1932. Under the Holywell and Flint Gas Order 1931 the gas undertaking was acquired (at 31 July 1931) by British Gas Light Co. Ld. and the water undertaking was purchased (at 17 Aug. 1931) by the Flint Corporation **1932**

Flintshire Oil & Cannel Co. Ld. Regd. 1864. Vol. liq. Sept. 1885. Court Order to dissolve 23 Sept. 1889 **1887**

Flora Ld. See Brights (Southsea) Ld.

Floral Hall (Bridlington) Ld. Regd. 1921. Vol. liq. 26 May 1924. Final meeting return regd. 3 Mar. 1926 ***1925**

Florence Coal & Iron Co. Ld. Regd. 1896. In liquidation. Final meeting return regd. 19 Apr. 1962 .... **1953**

Florence Gold Mine Ld. Regd. 1895. Vol. liq. 20 May 1897. Reconstructed as company of same name. Shareholders were entitled to 1 share of £1 (credited with 15s. paid) in new company for each share of £1 held. Final meeting return regd. 4 Dec. 1899 .... **1908**

Florence Gold Mine Ld. Regd. 1897. Vol. liq. 10 Feb. 1909. Assets were sold to Florence Gold Mines Ld. in which company shareholders were entitled to 1 share of £1 (credited with 17s. paid) for each share of £1 (19s. 6d. paid) held. Final meeting return regd. 20 June 1911 .... **1910**

Florence Gold Mines Ld. Regd. 1909. Vol. liq. Nov. 1911. Property and machinery were sold to Gold Coast Consolidated Lands Ld., in which company shareholders were entitled to 4 shares of 5s (credited with 4s. paid) for each share of £1 held. Removed from Register 1912 .... **1912**

Florencia Nitrate Co. Ld. Regd. 1904. Vol. liq. 7 May 1913. Final meeting return regd. 21 Apr. 1915....... **1914**

Florida Land & Mortgage Co. Ld. Regd. 1883. Land was purchased in 1890 by Land & Trust Co. of Florida Ld. for £16,518 in cash, £109,087 in B debentures and £90,395 in ordinary shares of £1. Struck off Register 1914.. **1891**

Florida Phosphate Co. Ld. Regd. 1890. Receiver appointed Aug. 1895. Removed from Register 1908 **1904**

Florida Syndicate Ld. Regd. 1892. Vol. liq. (members') 21 Jan. 1932. Shareholders received 1 share of £1 fully-paid in Keighley Land Co. Ld. for each share of £10 held. Capital returned to contributories— £18,612 16s 5d. Final meeting return regd. 30 Sept. 1932 .... **1932**

Flotation & General Investment Trust Ld. Regd. 1928. Court Order to wind up 22 July 1929. Struck off Register Dec. 1934 .... **1935**

Flower Motor Ship Co. Ld. Regd. 1912. Vol. liq. 8 Nov. 1917. Final meeting return regd. 2 Mar. 1922......... ***1918**

Flowers (A.) & Co. Ld. Regd. 1910. Vol. liq. (members') 8 Feb. 1944. Certain assets were distributed in specie. Capital returned to contributories—11s. 5d. per share of £1. Final meeting return regd. 30 May 1944 .... **1943**

Focus Head Light Co. Ld. Regd. 1921. Struck off Register 19 Feb. 1937... **1938**

Fodens Ld. Regd. 16 May 1902. Vol. liq. (creditors') 3 Mar. 1981. Return of final meeting registered 12 Dec. 1987. £45,613 paid into Companies' Liquidation Account in respect of unclaimed dividends. Name changed to Denfo (Realisations) Ld. on 3 Mar. 1981 .... **1988–9**

Foel (Clynnog) Slate Quarries Ld. Regd. 1879. Court Order to wind up 3 Nov. 1893. Removed from Register 1905 .... **1894**

Foldal Copper & Sulphur Co. Ld. Regd. 1906. Vol. liq. (creditors') 12 Sept. 1938. No capital returned to contributories. Final meeting return regd. 26 Apr. 1939 .... **1939**

Földhitelbank Részvénytársasàg. Inc. Budapest 1911. In liquidation in 1931... **1931**

Folkestone Amalgamated Cinemas Ld. Regd. 1929. Court Order to wind up 22 Apr. 1940. Direct controlling interest held by Union Cinemas Ld. Liquidator released 26 Mar. 1942. Struck off Register 4 Apr. 1967 .... **1941**

Folkestone Electricity Supply Co. Ld. Regd. 1897. Dissolved 1 Apr. 1948, undertaking being vested in British (later Central) Electricity Authority and South-Eastern Area Board under Electricity Act 1947. Holders of ordinary and 5% preference shares were entitled to receive, in respect of each share (of £1) held, £2 and £1 3s. 2d. British Electricity 3% guaranteed stock (1968–73) respectively **1949**

Folkestone Gas & Coke Co. Inc. by Special Act 1865. Dissolved 1 May 1949, undertaking being vested in South Eastern Gas Board under Gas Act 1948. Holders of securities were entitled to receive, in respect of each £100 unit held, British Gas 3% guaranteed stock 1990-95 as follows:

	£	s.	d.	VOL. FOR
Ord. stock (5% stand.)	140	0	0	
4% perp. deb. stock	103	0	0	
5% perp. deb. stock	125	0	0	**1952**

Folkestone Race Course Co. Ld. Regd. 1896. Undertaking acquired by company of same name. Removed from Register 1904 .... **1899**

Folkestone, Sandgate & Hythe Tramways Co. Inc. by Special Act 1906 .... **1911**

Foncage Syndicate Ld. Regd. 1906. Vol. liq. 20 Apr. 1927. Final meeting return regd. 7 Apr. 1931 ...... **1928**

Fonotipia Ld. Regd. 1906. Court Order to wind up under Trading with the Enemy (Amendment) Act (1916) on 18 Oct. 1916. Liquidator released 1 Apr. 1925. Dissolved under the above Act 1 May 1926 .... **1916**

Food Products Ld. Regd. 1920. Receiver appointed 29 May 1928; ceased to act 3 Jan. 1930. Vol. liq. 8 June 1928. Final meeting return regd. 3 Jan. 1930 ...... ***1929**

Foods Ld. Regd. 1902 as Moseleys Food Ld.; name changed June 1904. Vol. liq. 1 Mar. 1915. Final meeting return regd. 22 Mar. 1916 .... **1915**

Foothills (Malaya) Rubber Estate Ld. Regd. 1912. Vol. liq. (members') 8 Sept. 1932. Undertaking and assets transferred to new company of same name, in which company shareholders were entitled to receive 10 shares of 2s. (credited with 1s. 6d. paid) for each share of £1 held. £15 15s. 2d. was paid into Companies' Liquidation Account in respect of sale of unclaimed shares. Final meeting return regd. 21 Dec. 1933 .... **1933**

Foothills (Malaya) Rubber Estate, Ld. Regd. 1932. Vol. liq. 24 July 1951. Capital returned to contributories—3s 9·29d. per share. £781 4s. 10d. was paid into Companies' Liquidation Account. Final meeting return regd. 28 Nov. 1956 .... **1958**

Forbes, Forbes, Campbell & Co. Ld. Regd. 1904. Vol. liq. 28 Dec. 1928 for reconstruction as company of same name. Final meeting return regd. 11 Dec. 1943 ... **1929**

Forbes, Forbes, Campbell & Co. Ld. Regd. 1928. Vol. liq. Dec. 1934. The Indian business was transferred to company of same name (regd. in India) and the London and Liverpool business to Forbes, Campbell & Co. Ld. Final meeting return regd. 29 Dec 1953 .... **1938**

Forbes Reef Gold Mining Co. Ld. Regd. 1885. Vol. liq. Jan. 1889. Reconstructed as company of same name. Final meeting return regd. 22 May 1889 ... **1889**

Forbes Reed Gold Mining Co. Ld. Regd. 1889. Vol. liq. 11 Dec. 1893. Shareholders were entitled to 1 new share of £1 (with 18s. credited as paid) in company of same name, for every 4 shares of £1 held. Final meeting return regd. 23 Aug. 1894 .... **1894**

Forbes Reef Gold Mining Co. Ld. Regd. 1894. Vol. liq. 19 Apr. 1905. Concessions and properties were acquired by Swaziland Corporation Ld. for £35,000 in cash. A return of 4s. 3d. per share of £1 was anticipated. Final meeting return regd. 4 Dec.1905 **1906**

Forbes Rhodesia Syndicate Ld. Regd. 1895. Vol. liq. 8 May 1906. Removed from Register 1909 .... **1907**

Forbes Rhodesia Syndicate Ld. Inc. Southern Rhodesia 1906. A winding-up order was made in Rhodesia Dec. 1915.. **1916**

Forbes Syndicate Ld. Regd. Edinburgh 1900. Vol. liq. (members') 24 Aug. 1943. Capital returned to contributories—4s. 8d. per share of £1. Final meeting return regd. 13 Apr. 1944 .... **1945**

Forcett Railway Co. Inc. by Special Act 1865. In 1923 the undertaking was merged into the London & North Eastern Railway Co. Holders of each £100 of Forcett Ordinary shares were entitled to £100 in cash **1924**

Ford & Pointon Ld. Undertaking and assets were acquired by Cauldon Potteries Ld. ***1924**

Ford (Henry) & Co. Ld. Regd. 1890. Vol. liq. 5 Jan. 1923. Final meeting return regd. 14 July 1923 ..... **1924**

Ford (Henry) & Son Ld. Inc. Dublin 1917. All shares held by Ford Motor Co. Ld. **1929**

Ford (J. J.) & Sons, Ld. Regd. 1906. Vol. liq. (members') 21 June 1948 the main assets having been sold to Trust Houses Ld. All ordinary shares were owned by Suvretta Ld. The 4½% 1st mortgage debentures and the preference shares were repaid at par. £102 paid into Companies' Liquidation Account on account of unclaimed dividends. Final meeting return regd. 8 Dec. 1948 .... **1950**

Ford Paper Mills Ld. See F.P.M. Holdings Ld.

Ford Paper Works (1923) Ld. Regd. 1923. Land, buildings, plant, machinery and goodwill were acquired by Ford Paper Mills Ld. (later F.P.M. Holdings Ld.). Struck off Register 1932 .... **1940**

Forder & Co. Ld. Regd. 1882. Vol. liq. 17 Apr. 1886. Business was acquired by company of same name, for £66,000 in cash. Final meeting return regd. 26 Mar. 1895 .... **1906**

VOL. FOR

Forder & Co. Ld. Regd. 1886. Removed from Register 1911 .... **1906**

Fordham & Co. Ld. Regd. 1906. All shares held by British Photographic Industries Ld. Struck off Register 22 Nov. 1940 .... **1930**

Fordham (W. B.) & Sons Ld. Regd. 1885. Vol. liq. (creditors') 6 Jan. 1930. Assets realised insufficient to pay unsecured creditors in full. Final meeting return regd. 10 Nov. 1932 .... **1930**

Fordingbridge Gas Co. Ld. Regd. 1866. Dissolved 1 May 1949, undertaking being vested Southern Area Gas Board under Gas Act 1948. Holders of ordinary shares (of £5) were entitled to receive £6 10s. British Gas 3% guaranteed stock 1990–95 for each share held **1952**

Foreign, American and General Investments Trust Co. Ld. (The). Regd. 1883. In Dec. 1959 securities of the company were exchanged for those of Foreign & Colonial Investment Trust Co. Ld. on the basis of £104 ordinary per £100 deferred; £110 preference per £100 preferred; £1 4¼% debenture stock per £1 4% debenture stock and £1 5% debenture stock per £1 5% 2nd debenture stock held. Holders of 2nd debenture stock had the option of repayment in cash at par plus accrued interest. The company was dissolved 23 May 1960 .... **1961**

Foreign and Colonial Debenture Corporation Ld. Regd. 1889. Vol. liq. 9 Feb. 1894. Final meeting return regd. 8 Feb. 1902 .... **1894**

Foreign & Colonial Diamond Co. Ld. Regd. 1922. Vol. liq. 22 Oct. 1925. Final meeting return regd. 3 Feb. 1936 .... **1926**

Foreign & Colonial Electrical Power Storage Co. Ld. See Electrical Power Storage Co. Ld.

Foreign & Colonial Gold Recovery & Trading Co. Ld. Regd. 1897. Vol. liq. 12 July 1904. Final meeting return regd. 13 Sept. 1905 .... *****1905**

Foreign & Colonial Lands Co. Ld. Regd. 1911. The property in Mexico was lost owing to revolution. Struck off Register Mar. 1934 .... **1935**

Foreign & Colonial Tunnelling & Prospecting Co. Ld. Regd. 1874. Vol. liq. 9 Jan. 1888. Final meeting return regd. 31 Dec. 1888 .... **1886**

Foreign Banks Syndicate Ld. Regd. 1923. Struck off Register 1931 .... **1931**

Foreign Mines Development Co. Ld. Regd. 1908. Vol. liq. 22 Apr. 1918. Final meeting return regd. 13 May 1919 .... **1919**

Foreign Pilsen Electric Light & Power Co. Ld. Regd. 1885. Vol. liq. 16 Mar. 1897. Final meeting return regd. 28 June 1897 .... *****1898**

Forest Creek (Victoria) Gold Reefs Co. Ld. Regd. 1899. Vol. liq. 29 Jan. 1907. Removed from Register 1908 **1907**

Forest Hill Brewery Co. Ld. See Whitbread's Properties Ld.

Forest Mills of British Columbia Ld. Inc. British Columbia 1912. In Mar. 1923 the Secretary stated that the assets had been sold by the Receiver and the proceeds would barely cover the amount of the prior lien issue **1924**

Forest of Dean Central Railway Co. Inc. by Special Act 1856. In 1923 the undertaking was merged into the Great Western Railway Co. **1924**

Forester Paper Co. (1917) Ld. Regd. 1917. Vol. liq. 17 Jan. 1923. Business acquired by A. E. Mallandain Investments Ld. Final meeting return regd. 5 Dec. 1923 .... **1937**

Forfar & Brechin Railway Co. Inc. by Special Act 1890. Under Caledonian Railway Co. Act 1894 undertaking was vested in that company for £168,400. The mortgage was repaid and the balance, after paying other debts, was distributed among holders of ordinary capital **1896**

Formby Gas Co. Ld. Regd. 1877. Vol. liq. (members') 22 Jan. 1935. Undertaking was acquired by Liverpool Gas Co. Capital returned to contributories—£10 10s. per preference share of £10, £14 per ordinary share of £10. Final meeting return regd. 26 July 1935 **1935**

Formby's Cement Works Co. Ld. Regd. 1881. Vol. liq. Mar. 1909. Removed from Register 1911 .... **1910**

Formosa Sugar and Development Co. Ld. Regd. 1908. Vol. liq. 14 June 1911. Final meeting return regd. 17 Mar. 1914 .... **1912**

Forres Gas Light Co. Ld. Regd. in Edinburgh 1889. Dissolved 1 May 1949, undertaking being vested in Scottish Area Gas Board under Gas Act 1948. Holders of ordinary shares (of £12) were entitled to receive £23 British Gas 3% guaranteed stock 1990–95 for each share held **1952**

Forrest Australian Corporation Ld. Regd. 1896. Vol. liq. 24 Oct. 1899. Final meeting return regd. 11 Dec. 1901 .... **1900**

Forrest King of Coolgardie Ld. Regd. 1895. Vol. liq. 11 Oct. 1897. Reconstructed as Lady Loch Gold Mines

VOL. FOR

Ld., in which company shareholders were entitled to 2 shares of 10s. (credited with 7s. paid) for each share of £1 held. Final meeting return regd. 24 Apr. 1900 .... **1902**

Forsters' Bishop Middleham Brewery Ld. Regd. 1897. Vol. liq. (members') 5 Oct. 1953. The undertaking and assets were absorbed by Newcastle Breweries Ld. which company owned all capital. Final meeting return regd. 22 July 1954 .... **1955**

Fort Fraser Land Co. Ld. Regd. 1911. Vol. liq. 17 Feb. 1925. Final meeting return regd. 22 Dec. 1926 .... **1926**

Fort Shipping Co. Ld. Regd. 1919. Struck off Register Jan. 1927 .... **1927**

Fort Steele (B.C.) Gold Mines Co. Ld. Regd. 1902. Vol. liq. 31 Oct. 1905. Removed from Register 1907 .... **1909**

Forth & Clyde & Sunnyside Iron Co's Ld. Regd. Edinburgh 1898. All capital was owned by Allied Ironfounders Ld. Vol. liq. (members') 2 Dec. 1963. Final meeting return regd. 30 Sept. 1964 .... **1940**

Forth and Clyde Junction Railway Co. Inc by Special Act 1853. In 1923 the undertaking was merged into the London & North-Eastern Railway Co., in which company stockholders were entitled to stock as follows:

For each £100 *held*	L. & N.E.R.
4% Debenture £100	4% First Gtd.
5% Preference .... { £50 / £9¼	Defd. Ordinary / cash
5% Pref. Shares .... { £20 / £11	Defd. Ordinary / cash
6% Pref. Shares .... { £12½ / £14	Defd. Ordinary / cash
7% Cons. Stock £17	cash **1924**

Forth Bridge Railway Co. Inc. by Special Act 1873. Dissolved 10 June 1949; undertaking vested 1 Jan. 1948 in British Transport Commission under Transport Act 1947. Holders of securities were entitled to receive British Transport 3% guaranteed stock 1978–88 as follows in respect of every £100 of old security held:

	£ s. d.	
4% ordinary stock	104 17 6	
4% debenture stock	109 0 0	**1949**

Forth Building & Investment Co. Ld. Regd. 1903. Vol. liq. (members') 19 May 1960. Final meeting return regd. 15 Dec. 1960 .... **1911**

Forth Collieries (1903) Ld. Regd. Edinburgh 1903. Vol. liq. Apr. 1907. Undertaking was acquired by Edinburgh Collieries Co. Ld. in which company shareholders were entitled to 2½ ordinary shares of £1 (credited as fully-paid) and 1 preference share of £1 for every 5 shares of £1 held. Removed from Register 1908 .... **1908**

Forth Glass Works Ld. Regd. Edinburgh 1920. Vol. liq. May 1924. Final meeting return regd. 14 Apr. 1928 **1925**

Forth Shipbuilding & Engineering Co. (1921) Ld. Regd. 1921. Vol. liq. 28 Dec. 1927. Final meeting return regd. 28 Mar. 1928 .... **1929**

Forth Steam Trawling Co. (1922) Ld. Regd. Edinburgh 1922. During 1925 the 4 steam trawlers were sold and the proceeds applied to reducing bank overdraft; the balance of the overdraft was met by the directors. Struck off Register 28 Apr. 1933 .... **1928**

Fortis Powder & Explosives Co. Ld. Regd. 1890. Vol. liq. 5 Oct. 1897. Removed from Register 21 June 1907 *****1898**

Fortnum & Mason Inc. Inc. New York 1931. On 2 Mar. 1936 the directors filed a voluntary petition in bankruptcy in the Federal Court **1937**

Forton Trust Ld. Regd. 1924. Vol. liq. (members') 24 Mar. 1944. Capital returned to contributories—£1 6s·72d. per share of £1. Final meeting return regd. 22 Mar. 1946 .... **1947**

Fortrose Rubber Ld. Regd. 1925. Vol. liq. 26 Oct. 1927. Undertaking and assets were acquired by Malacca Rubber Plantations Ld., in which company shareholders were entitled to 4 ordinary shares of £1 (credited as fully-paid) for every 15 shares of £1 held. Final meeting return regd. 17 Sept. 1928 .... **1928**

Fortuna Co. Ld. Regd. 1856. Vol. liq. 11 June 1901. Reconstructed as company of same name. Shareholders were entitled to 2 shares of £1 (credited with 12s. 6d. paid) in new company for each share of £2 held. Final meeting return regd. 2 Apr. 1903 .... **1908**

Fortuna Co. Ld. Regd. 1901. Vol. liq. 27 Jan. 1914. Final meeting return regd. 20 Aug. 1917 .... **1914**

Fortuna Nitrate Co. Ld. Regd. 1900. Vol. liq. 13 May 1920. Capital returned to contributories—£2 10s. per share of £1; further payments (if any) not known. Final meeting return regd. 1 Sept. 1921 ... **1921**

Fortune Syndicate Ld. Regd. 1895. Vol. liq. 20 May 1896. Assets were acquired by Buluwayo Estate & Trust Co. Ld. Final meeting return regd. 10 Nov. 1897 .... **1897**

VOL. FOR

Forum River (Nigeria) Tin Co. Ld. Regd. 1912. Vol. liq. 21 Dec. 1920. Assets were acquired by Bisichi Tin Co. (Nigeria) Ld in which company shareholders were entitled to 2 fully-paid shares of 10s. for each share of £1 held. Final meeting return regd. 6 Nov. 1922 ..... **1921**

Forward Components Ld. Regd. as Pneumatic Compensation Cycle Co. Ld.; name changed Dec. 1897. Removed from Register 1901 ..... **1899**

Forward Engineering Co. Ld. Regd. 1898. Undertaking acquired in Apr. 1907 by Kynoch Ld. [later I.C.I. (Metals) Ld.]. Struck off Register 20 Nov. 1908.... **1909**

Foster (C. Orton) Ld. Regd. 1921 as Greenhill & Foster Ld.; name changed Apr. 1927. Vol. liq. (members') 16 Feb. 1935. Final meeting return regd. 24 Apr. 1935 ..... **1931**

Foster (Edward) & Son Ld. Regd. 1897. Vol. liq. (creditors') 21 June 1933. Assets realised insufficient to pay unsecured creditors in full. Final meeting return regd. 16 July 1936 ..... **1934**

Foster (Lancelot) & Co. Ld. Regd. 1923. Vol. liq. (members') 6 Apr. 1944. All capital was owned by Fisons Ld. Final meeting return regd. 29 Sept. 1944 **1945**

Foster (M. B.) & Sons Ld. Regd. 1890. Vol. liq. 20 Jan. 1896. Reconstructed as company of same name. Shareholders were entitled to an equal number of shares in new company. Final meeting return regd. 31 Mar. 1896 ..... **1908**

Foster (M. B.) and Sons Ld. Regd. 1896. Vol. liq. 15 Jan. 1920. Reconstructed as company of same name (later Foster-Probyn Ld.). Shareholders were entitled to 10 shares of £1 (credited as fully-paid) for each ordinary share of £1 5s. held. The 1st and 2nd preference shares were repaid in cash at par. Final meeting return regd. 14 Oct. 1920 ..... **1920**

Foster (M. B.) Holdings Ld. Regd. 1957. A realisation company. The capital was distributed to shareholders of Foster-Probyn Ld. under scheme of reduction of capital of that company. Vol. liq. (members') 12 May 1958. Distributions—in specie: 15s. ordinary stock of Ind, Coope Allsopp Ld. per 2 shares of 10s. held and 45s. ordinary stock of Ind, Coope & Allsopp Ld. per 10 shares of 10s. held; in cash: 25s. 8⅝d. per share of 10s. Final meeting return regd. 26 Mar. 1960 ..... **1960**

Foster (Nevile) & Co. Ld. Regd. 1921. Vol. liq. (members') 17 July 1940. Capital returned to contributories—£2,607 19s. 2d. Final meeting return regd. 28 Aug. 1941 ..... **1941**

Foster Yates & Thom Ld. Regd. 1936. All capital acquired by Hick, Hargreaves & Co. Ld. Dissolved 4 Sept. 1980 ..... **1958**

Foucar & Co. Ld. Regd. 1905. Vol. liq. (members') 30 Jan. 1953. Capital returned to contributories—£1 per preference share (of £1), 22s. 7·125d. per preferred ordinary share (of 10s.) and 4s. 6·225d. per deferred ordinary share (of 2s.). Amounts paid into Companies' Liquidation Account—£3,752 9s. 1d. in respect of unclaimed distributions and £14 4s. 3d. in respect of unclaimed dividends. Final meeting return regd. 2 Feb. 1962 ..... **1962**

Foundation Co. Ld. Regd. 1922. Court Order to wind up 1930. Struck off Register 19 May 1944 ..... **1945**

Founders' Stock & Share Trust Ld. Regd. 1889. Vol. liq. 4 Aug. 1893. Reconstructed as New Investment Co. Ld., in which company shareholders were entitled to 1 ordinary share of £4 (credited as fully-paid) for each ordinary share of £10 held. Deferred shareholders were entitled to subscribe at par for 2 deferred shares of £4 for each deferred share of £10 held. Final meeting return regd. 2 May 1894 ..... **1893**

Founders' Syndicate Ld. Regd. 1900. Removed from Register 1903 ..... **1903**

Founders' Trust & Investment Co. Ld. Regd. 1928. Struck off Register 19 Feb. 1937 ..... **1938**

Foundling Estates Ld. Regd. 1925. Vol. liq. (members') 29 Dec. 1953. Final meeting return regd. 30 Apr. 1954 ..... **1948**

Fountain Free Brewery Co. Ld. Business and licensed properties were acquired by Daniel Thwaites & Co. Ld. **1928**

Fourth Conversion Investment Trust Ld. Regd. 1937. Vol. liq. (members') 20 Dec. 1945 for amalgamation with First Conversion Investment Trust Ld. (later Hambros Investment Trust Ltd.), in which company shareholders were entitled to 7 fully-paid shares of £1 and 8s. 9·376d. cash for every £7 ordinary stock held. Final meeting return regd. 18 Mar. 1947...... **1947**

Fourth Street National Bank of Philadelphia. Inc. Washington 1886. The assets and liabilities were merged with those of the Franklin National Bank 1 Apr. 1926, under the title of Franklin Fourth Street National Bank of Philadelphia **1927**

VOL. FOR

Fourwheel Jacks Ld. Regd. 1929. Vol. liq. (creditors') 21 Dec. 1934. No capital returned to contributories. Final meeting return regd. 17 Sept. 1937 ..... **1935**

Fowey Gas Co. Ld. Regd. 1893. Dissolved 1 May 1949, undertaking being vested in South Western Area Gas Board under Gas Act 1948. Holders of securities were entitled to receive British Gas 3% guaranteed stock 1990–95 as follows in respect of each £100 unit unless otherwise stated:—

	£	s.	d.
Ord. shares (of £5)	3	0	0
4½% debs.	100	0	0
5% debs.	100	0	0	**1952**

Fowler Brothers Ld. Regd. 1890. Vol. liq. 28 July 1902. Final meeting return regd. 22 July 1903 ..... **1903**

Fowler (George), Son & Co. Ld. Regd. 1891. Vol. liq. 28 July 1902. Undertaking was acquired by Swift & Co. of Chicago. A capital return to contributories of £4 per ordinary share of £10 (£7 paid) was anticipated. Removed from Register 1908 ..... **1903**

Fowler (John) & Co. (Leeds) Ld. Regd. 1886. All ordinary capital owned by Marshall Sons & Co. Ld. Outstanding preference shares were redeemed at 22s. per share on 31 dec. 1968. Vol. liq. 21 Aug. 1981. Final meeting return regd. 2 Oct. 1981 ..... **1969**

Fowler-Waring Cables Co. Ld. Regd. 1896. Vol. liq. 25 May 1898. Final meeting return regd. 18 June 1902 **1899**

Fox (Edwin) & Co. Ld. Regd. 1882. Court Orders: to wind up Feb. 1888; to dissolve Mar. 1890. ..... **1889**

Fox Film Corpn. See Twentieth Century Fox Film Corpn.

Foxdale Railway Co. Inc. by Act of Tynwald 1883. Vol. liq. July 1891. Under Isle of Man Railway Act 1904 undertaking acquired by that company for £7,000 **1905**

Foxfield Colliery Ld. Regd. 1918 as Parkhall Colliery Co. Ld.; name changed 30 July 1936. Vol. liq. (members') 28 Nov. 1951, the colliery having vested in National Coal Board. Capital returned to contributories—preference (per share of £1) 24s.; ordinary (per share of 5s.) 12s. 6d. cash and 1 share of 5s. in Trecastell Lead Mines Ld. £23 10s. 4d. paid into Companies' Liquidation Account. Final meeting return regd. 21 July 1956 ..... **1957**

Foxton Cement Co. Ld. Regd. 1903. Vol. liq. 3 Apr. 1907. Removed from Register 1911 ..... **1908**

Foxton Phosphate Mining Co. Ld. Regd. 1889. Removed from Register 1906 ..... ***1894**

Foy, Morgan & Co. Ld. Regd. 1925. Vol. liq. (members') 21 May 1935. Undertaking was acquired by company of same name for 260,000 preference shares and 100,000 2nd redeemable preference shares and 1,000 ordinary shares of £1, all credited as fully-paid. Final meeting return regd. 27 Dec. 1935...... **1936**

Framlingham Gas Light Co. Inc. by Special Act 1849. Dissolved 1 May 1949, undertaking being vested in Eastern Area Gas Board under Gas Act 1948. Holders of shares (of £5) were entitled to receive £13 10s. British Gas 3% guaranteed stock 1990–95 for each share held **1952**

Francevalor Societe D'Investissement En Valeurs Francaises. Inc. in France 1959 as Société Europeene D'Investissement en Valeurs Francaises; name changed 1964. All capital was owned by Société Epargne-Valeur. Dissolved 13 June 1966 ..... **1967**

Francis Canal Company (Hungary). Inc. in Hungary under laws of 1870 & 1873. The concession expired in 1945. No dividend was paid on the ordinary and preference shares and interest on the £500,000 1st preference bonds has been paid only to 1 May 1882 **1952**

Francis (H.A.) Ld. Regd. 1904. Vol. liq. (creditors') 12 May 1932. Capital returned to contributories—4s. 0½d. per preference share of £1. Final meeting return regd. 18 Nov. 1933 ..... **1933**

Francis, Newton Ld. Regd. 1903. Vol. liq. 21 Oct. 1909. Final meeting return regd. 3 Jan. 1914 ..... **1925**

Franck (P.) & Co. Ld. Regd. 1928. Vol. liq. (members') 31 Oct. 1935. No capital returned to contributories. Final meeting return regd. 23 June 1941 ..... **1936**

Franco-African Exploration & Investment Co. Ld. Regd. 1895. Vol. liq. May 1910. Capital returned to contributories—12s. 10d. per share of £1 at Aug. 1910; further payments (if any) not known. Removed from Register 1913 ..... **1911**

Franco-Australian Exploration Co. Ld. Regd. 1895. Removed from Register 1903 ..... **1903**

Franco-British Oil Trust Ld. Regd. 1911. Vol. liq. (creditors') 9 Mar. 1936. No capital returned to contributories. Final meeting return regd. 11 June 1938 ..... **1937**

Franco-British Provision & Packing Co Ld. Regd. 1909. Struck off Register 1915 ..... **1910**

Franco-Egyptian Bank. Inc. France 1870. Shareholders were offered 1 share of Frs. 500 in Banque

VOL. FOR

Internationale de Paris for each share of Frs. 500 held **1901**

Franco-English Tunisian Esparto Fibre Supply Co. Ld. Regd. 1882. Removed from Register 1898 .... **1888**

Frank (William) 1928 Ld. Regd. 1928. All shares were owned by Meurisse Ld. Struck off Register Dec. 1934 .... **1935**

Frankau (Adolph) & Co. Ld. Regd. 1899. Court Order to wind up Dec. 1926. Struck off Register 15 June 1937 **1938**

Frankfort, Hanau & District Ice Co. Ld. Regd. 1884. Vol. liq. 21 Feb. 1887. Assets were acquired by United Anglo-Continental Ice Co. Ld., in which company shareholders were entitled to an equal number of shares. Removed from Register 1906 .. **1888**

Franklin Fourth Street National Bank of Philadelphia. Inc. Washington 1900 as Franklin National Bank; name changed 1926. In Apr. 1928 the undertaking and assets were acquired by Philadelphia National Bank, in which company shareholders were entitled to 1 share of $100 for each share of $100 held *plus* a cash payment of $15. .... **1929**

Franklin National Bank. See Franklin Fourth Street National Bank of Philadelphia.

Franzpoort Exploration Co. Ld. Regd. 1921. Vol. liq. 25 June 1948. Final meeting return regd. 19 Nov. 1948 **1949**

Fraser & Chalmers Ld. Regd. 1890. Vol. liq. 23 Jan. 1919. Certain assets were sold to General Electric Co. Ld. Capital returned to contributories—£1 5s. per ordinary or preference share of £1; further payments (if any) not known. Final meeting return regd. 4 Apr. 1922 .... **1920**

Fraser Gold Reefs Ld. Inc. Guernsey 1905. In 1909 the late Secretary stated "the company has long since ceased to carry on business and has no offices in London" **1909**

Fraser River Consolidated Gold Ld. Regd. 1897. Removed from Register 1903 .... **1902**

Fraser River Gold Dredging Co. (1905) Ld. Regd. 1905. Vol. liq. May 1907. Removed from Register 1910 **1908**

Fraser Ross & Co. Ld. Regd. Edinburgh 1899. Vol. liq. 26 Feb. 1906. Court Orders: to continue winding up under supervision; to dissolve 21 Dec. 1921 .... **1907**

Fraser South Extended Gold Mining Co. Ld. Regd. 1896. Court Order to wind up 13 Dec. 1904. Removed from Register 1911 .... **1905**

Fraserburgh & North of Scotland Steam Trawling Co. Ld. Regd. Edinburgh 1898. Vol. liq. Sept. 1909. Final meeting return regd. 31 May 1911 .... **1910**

Freddies North Lease Area, Ld. Inc. in South Africa 1947. Vol. liq. 1 June 1954. The undertaking and assets were acquired by Freddies Consolidated Mines Ld., in which company shareholders were entitled to receive 1 fully-paid share of £1 for every 3 shares of 10s. of this company held. Holders of the outstanding £148,621 5% regd. unsecured convertible loan stock 1953–60 were given the option of repayment at 102½% or conversion (at the rate of 41 shares for every £50 loan stock) into fully-paid £1 shares of the consolidated company. £110,735 stock was so converted. Company finally dissolved 24 June 1954 .... **1955**

Freddies South Lease Area, Ld. Inc. in South Africa 1947. Vol. liq. 1 June 1954. The undertaking and assets were acquired by Freddies Consolidated Mines Ld., in which company shareholders were entitled to receive 1 fully-paid share of £1 for every 3 shares of 10s. of this company held. Holders of the outstanding £153,784 5% registered unsecured convertible loan stock 1953–60 were given the option of repayment at 102½% or conversion (at the rate of 41 shares for every £50 loan stock) into fully-paid £1 shares of the consolidated company. £108,496 stock was so converted. Company finally dissolved 24 June 1954 .... **1955**

Frederick (Henry) & Co. Ld. Regd. 1898. Vol. liq. 29 May 1912. Final meeting return regd. 2 July 1913 ***1903**

Frederick Hygienic Laundry Ld. Undertaking and assets were acquired in 1928 by Advance Laundries Ld **1929**

Frederick Investment Corporation Ld. Regd. 1928. Court Order to wind up 4 May 1931. Liquidator released 11 Feb. 1938. Struck off Register 20 Feb. 1942 .... ***1932**

Frederick the Great Gold Mining & Recovery Co. Ld. Regd. 1894. Vol. liq. 29 Dec. 1897. Reconstructed as Frederick the Great Gold Mining Co. Ld., in which company shareholders were entitled to 1 share of £1 (credited with 17s. paid) for each share of £1 held. Final meeting return regd. 22 Feb. 1900 .... **1903**

Frederick the Great Gold Mining Co Ld. Regd. 1898. Reconstructed 1903 as Frederick the Great Gold Mining Co. (1903) Ld., in which company share-holders were entitled to 3 shares of 10s. (credited with 7s. 6d. paid) for each share of £1 held. Removed from Register 1906 .... **1904**

VOL. FOR

Frederick the Great Gold Mining Co. (1903) Ld. Regd. 1903. Vol. liq. 13 Oct. 1905. Removed from Register 1906 .... **1906**

Frederick's Matabeleland Syndicate Ld. Regd. 1895. Removed from Register 1909 .... **1903**

Free Rodwell & Co. Ld. Regd. 1893. All capital was owned by Ind Coope & Allsopp Ld. now Allied Breweries Ld. Vol. liq. (members') 29 May 1963. Final meeting return regd. 30 Aug. 1963 .... **1958**

Free State Banket Development Co. Ld. Regd. 1909. Vol. liq. 30 July 1915. Final meeting return regd. 10 Oct. 1916 .... **1916**

Free State Mines Ld. Inc. Orange Free State 1895. In liquidation in 1900 .... **1900**

Free State Mines Selection Ld. Regd. 1911 as Lewis & Marks Ld.; name changed in 1946. Vol. liq. (members') 10 Dec. 1952. Final meeting return regd. 19 Jan. 1955 .... **1946**

Free State Rand Ld. Regd. 1910. Vol. liq. 29 Nov. 1915. Final meeting return regd. 26 May 1937 .... **1916**

Free Wall Paper Co. Ld. Regd. 1900. Vol. liq. 30 Mar. 1908. Struck off Register 10 Oct. 1916 .... **1909**

Freehold & General Housing Society Ld. Regd. 1934 under Industrial & Provident Societies Acts 1893 to 1928. Amalgamated in 1939 with two other societies under the title of Feeehold, Leasehold and Property Developments Ld., in which company shareholders were entitled to 1 A ordinary share of 2s. for each £1 of capital held, and debenture holders to 10s. 5% debenture stock *plus* 2·6% participating preference shares of 1s. for each £1 debenture held **1940**

Freehold Assets Realisation Co. Ld. Inc. Victoria 1895. Reconstructed 1907 as Freehold Assets Co. Ld. Holders of unredeemed "A" deposit receipts were entitled to 20% in interminable debenture stock and 15% in fully-paid shares in new company **1907**

Freehold Cottage Dwellings Co. Ld. See below.

Freehold House Property Co. Ld. Regd. 1876 as Freehold Cottage Dwellings Co. Ld.; name changed Sept. 1883. Vol. liq. 5 May 1892. Final meeting return regd. 26 June 1896 .... **1925**

Freehold Investment & Banking Co. of Australia Ld. Inc. Australia 1882. In liquidation in 1893 .... **1893**

Freeho'd Loan & Savings Co. of Toronto. Established Canada 1859. Reconstructed 1899 as Canada Permanent and Western Canada Mortgage Corporation (later Canada Permanent Mortgage Corporation) **1900**

Freehold Property Society Ld. Regd. 1934 under Industrial and Provident Societies Acts 1893 to 1928. Amalgamated in 1939 with two other societies under the title of Freehold Leasehold & Property Developments Ld. in which company shareholders were entitled to 1 A ordinary share of 2s. for each £1 of capital held and debenture holders to 10s. 5% debenture stock *plus* two 6% participating preference shares of 1s. for each £1 debenture held **1940**

Freehold Trust Co. of Australia Ld. Regd. 1887. The advances were taken over by Australian Mercantile Land and Finance Co. Ld. which company repaid the debentures and debenture stock on 31 Dec. 1898. Shareholders were expected to receive a full return of capital *plus* 7s. 6d. premium. Vol. liq. 11 Nov. 1898. Final meeting return regd. 27 Apr. 1899 .... **1899**

Freeholders Co. Ld. Regd. 1876. Vol. liq. (members') 12 July 1938. Capital returned to contributories—£5,452 15s. 1d. Final meeting return regd. 15 Dec. 1938 .... **1939**

Freeholds Trust Ld. Regd. 1925. Court Order to wind up 1 July 1932. Liquidator released 20 Dec. 1935. Struck off Register 16 Aug. 1938 .... ***1931**

Freeland Reef Gold Mining Co. Ld. Regd. 1901. Removed from Register 1905 .... **1905**

Freeman Cohen's Consolidated Ld. Regd. 1895. Vol. liq. Apr. 1908. Removed from Register 1909 .... **1909**

Freeman, Hardy & Willis (Burlington Works) Ld. Regd. 1920 as Leavesley & North Ld.; name changed July 1926. Vol. liq. (members') 21 Mar. 1935. All shares owned by Freeman Hardy & Willis Ld. (later B.S.C. Ld.). Final meeting return regd. 29 July 1935 ...... **1936**

Freeman Hardy & Willis (Kettering) Ld. Regd. 1879. Vol. liq. (members') 21 Mar. 1935. All shares owned by Freeman Hardy & Willis Ld. (later B.S.C. Ld.). Final meeting return regd. 29 July 1935 .... **1936**

Freeman's Journal Ld. Regd. Dublin 1887. Court Order to wind up 17 Sept. 1919 .... **1920**

Fregor Holdings Ld. Regd. 1903 as Frederick Gorringe Ld.; name changed Mar. 1961. All capital was owned jointly by Gresham Trust Ld. and Charles Neale Investments Ld. Vol. liq. (members') 12 Aug. 1962. Final meeting return regd. 23 Oct. 1968 ...... **1962**

Fréjus Oil Co. Ld. Regd. 1888. Struck off Register 18 Nov. 1902. .... **1903**

*See Stock Exchange Year-Book.

VOL. FOR

Fremantle Smelter Ld. Regd. 1903. Vol. liq. June 1907. Reconstructed as Fremantle Trading Co. Ld. in which company shareholders were entitled to 1 fully-paid ordinary share of £1 for every 10 shares of £1 held. At Sept. 1907 13*s*. per share of £1 had been returned; further payments (if any) not known. Removed from Register 1910 .... **1911**

Fremantle Smelting Works Ld. Regd. 1900. Removed from Register 1904 .... **1902**

Fremantle Trading Co. Ld. Regd. 1909. Receiver appointed in May 1926. Proceeds of sale of practically all assets were insufficient to meet liabilities. Struck off Register 4 Apr. 1930 .... **1929**

Fremont Oil Co. Ld. Regd. 1914. Vol. liq. 14 Jan. 1918. At least a return of 6*s*. per share of £1 was expected from sale of assets. Final meeting return regd. 2 June 1921 .... **1918**

Fremont Syndicate Ld. Regd. 1910. Struck off Register 1928 .... **1918**

French Ayrshire & Lo-Magondi District Development Co. Ld. Regd. 1896. Removed from Register 1912 **1911**

French Bob Extension Gold Mining Co. Ld. Regd. 1888. Vol. liq. 2 Mar. 1896. Final meeting return regd. 3 June 1896 .... **1897**

French Bobs Mines Ld. Regd. 1905 as French Bobs Exploration Syndicate Ld.; name changed June 1909. Vol. liq. 11 Sept. 1912. Struck off Register 3 Sept. 1918 .... **1913**

French, British & Foreign Trust Ld. Regd. 1924. Court Order to wind up 12 Jan. 1931. Struck off Register 1935 .... ***1932**

French Date Coffee Co. Ld. Regd. 1881. Removed from Register 1905 .... **1883**

French Electrical Power Storage Co. Ld. Regd. 1882. Removed from Register 1906 .... ***1885**

French Exploration Co. Ld. Regd. 1895. Vol. liq. 29 Dec. 1898. Reconstructed as Upper Nile Co. Ld. in which company shareholders were entitled to 1 fully-paid deferred share of £1 for every 5 shares of £1 held. Final meeting return regd. 16 Aug. 1922 .... **1900**

French Feister Printing Co. Ld. Regd. 1891. Vol. liq. 14 Apr. 1895. Final meeting return regd. 17 May 1897 ***1896**

French Guinea & Soudan Mining Co. Ld. Regd. 1902 as Ivory Coast Exploring Syndicate Ld.; name changed Mar. 1904. Vol. liq. 21 June 1906. Removed from Register 1906 .... **1907**

French-Hickman Flax Fibre Co. Ld. Regd. 1899. Vol. liq. 28 Nov. 1906. Removed from Register 1908... **1907**

French (J. W.) & Co. Ld. *See* J. W. F. Trust Ld.

French Kier Ld. Regd. as private company 23 Mar. 1931 as W. & C. French Ld.; converted public company 19 Sept. 1949; nbame changed to French Kier Holdings Ld. 9 Nov. 1973 and to present title 1987. Winding-up order 28 May 1987. All capital acquired by C. H. Beazer (Holdings) p.l.c. **1986–7**

French Metropolitan General Electric Co. Ld. Regd. 1882. Removed from Register 1890 .... ***1885**

French Mines Ld. Regd. 1891. Vol. liq. 16 Jan. 1893. Final meeting return regd. 25 Nov. 1896 .... **1893**

French North Rand Estates Gold Mining Co. Ld. Regd. 1895. Struck off Register 23 July 1901 .... **1902**

French Phototone Ld. Regd. 1928. Vol. liq. (members') 21 Mar. 1932. No capital returned to contributories. Final meeting return regd. 14 Nov. 1940 .... **1933**

French Railways Co. of the Province of Santa Fé. Inc. France 1888 as Compagnie Française des Chemins de Fer de la Province de Santa Fé S.A. Name changed 1949 to Santa Fé Compagnie Financiére Française pour la République Argentine et l'Etranger. The outstanding sterling 3% mortgage obligations were redeemed on 1 Jan. 1948 at par.. **1949**

French Rand Gold Mining Co. Ld. Inc. Transvaal 1895. Vol. liq. July 1915 .... **1916**

French Rhodesia & Transvaal Exploration Co. Ld. Regd. 1902. Removed from Register 1909 .... **1907**

French Soudan Goldfields & Exploration Co. Ld. Regd. 1895. Struck off Register 28 July 1899 .... **1901**

French South African Development Co. Ld. Regd. 1895. Vol. liq. 27 Feb. 1907. Removed from Register 1912 **1907**

French Steam Navigation Co. Inc. France by Notarial Act Jan. 1872. The outstanding 6½% sterling bonds were redeemed 1 May 1938 .... **1938**

French Western Nigel Ld. Inc. South African Republic 1895. Undertaking and assets were acquired by Sub-Nigel Ld. for 236,000 shares of £1 .... **1900**

French Zoedone Co. Ld. Regd. 1880. Removed from Register 1903 .... **1883**

Frenchman's Peak Ld. Regd. 1895. Vol. liq. 10 May 1897. Capital returned to contributories—1*s*. 7 $\frac{5}{16}$*d*. per share of £1 at 15 Sept. 1897; further payments (if any) not known. Final meeting return regd. 21 Dec. 1897 .... **1898**

French's Motor Engineering Works Ld. Regd. 1921. Vol. liq. (members') 31 May 1933. All shares owned by United Service Transport Co. Ld. Final meeting return regd. 29 Aug. 1933 .... **1934**

Freshwater Gas Co. Ld. Regd. 1897. Dissolved 1 May 1949 undertaking being vested in Southern Area Gas Board under Gas Act 1948. Holders of securities were entitled to receive British Gas 3% guaranteed stock 1990–95 as follows:

	£	s.	d.
Orig. shares (10% max.) (of £5)	8	15	0
Addit. shares (7% max.) (of £5)	6	5	0
4½% pref. shares (of £1)	1	0	2
4% mort. debs. (of £100)	100	0	0

1952

Freshwater, Yarmouth and Newport Railway Co. Inc. by Special Act 1880. In 1923 the undertaking was merged into the Southern Railway Co. in which company stockholders were entitled to stock as follows:

For each £100 held		*S.R.*
3½% A pre-Deb.	£87½	4% Debenture
5% Perp. Deb.	£80	5% Preference
5% B Perp. Deb.	£40	Prefd. Ordinary
5% Perp. Pref.	£50	Ordinary B

The Preferred Ordinary and Deferred Ordinary Stocks were cancelled **1924**

Fresno Copper Co. Ld. Regd. Edinburgh 1902. Vol. liq. 25 Jan. 1907 for reconstruction under same name. Shareholders were entitled to be allotted 1 share of 4*s*. (credited with 2*s*. paid) in new company for each share of £1 held. Final meeting return regd. 5 Feb. 1937 .... **1907**

Fresno Copper Co. Ld. Regd. Edinburgh 1907. Vol. liq. Apr. 1914. Final meeting return regd. 18 June 1924 **1915**

Friary Holroyd & Healy's Breweries Ld. Regd. 1895. All capital owned by Friary Meux Ld. Vol. liq. 10 Nov. 1961. Final meeting return regd. 13 Mar. 1963 .... **1960**

Frickers Metal Co. Ld. Regd. 1918. Vol. liq. (members') 9 May 1932. Undertaking and assets were acquired by Fricker's Metal & Chemical Co. Ld. in which company shareholders were entitled to 1 fully-paid preference share of £1 for each preference share of £1 held or 3 fully-paid ordinary shares of £1 for every 2 ordinary shares of £1 held. Final meeting return regd. 16 Dec. 1932 .... **1933**

Friendship Gold Mine Ld. Regd. 1896. Vol. liq. 7 May 1900. Struck off Register 12 Apr. 1929 .... **1901**

Frinton-on-Sea and District Electric Light and Power Co. Ld. Regd. 1901. Dissolved 1 Apr. 1948 undertaking being vested in the British (later Central) Electricity Authority and Eastern Area Board under the Electricity Act 1947. Ordinary shareholders were entitled to receive £1 British Electricity 3% guaranteed stock (1968–73) for each share (of £1) held ... **1949**

Frisby, Dyke & Co. Ld. Regd. 1904. Vol. liq. 12 July 1927. Business was acquired by Frisby Dyke & Co. (1927) Ld. (later Frisby Dyke & Co. Ld.). Final meeting return regd. 14 Apr. 1928 .... **1928**

Frisby, Dyke & Co. Ld. Regd. 1927 as Frisby Dyke & Co. (1927) Ld.; name changed Nov. 1927. Vol. liq. (members') 19 Mar. 1936. No capital returned to contributories. Final meeting return regd. 24 Apr. 1939 .... **1937**

Friswell (1906) Ld. Regd. 1906. Vol. liq. Aug. 1912 for reconstruction as Friswells Ld. Removed from Register 1913 .... **1913**

Friswells Ld. Regd. 1912. Vol. liq. 10 Nov. 1915. Final meeting return regd. 28 May 1920 .... ***1916**

Frith (W. G.) & Co. Ld. Regd. 1935. Vol. liq. 12 Mar. 1979. Capital returned to contributories—on ordinary shares (of 1p): 61·85 per share. Final meeting return regd. 2 Nov. 1981 .... **1982–3**

Frodair Iron and Steel Co. Ld. Regd. 1905. Vol. liq. (members') 30 Apr. 1965. Final meeting return regd. 18 Mar.1967 .... **1940**

Frodingham Iron & Steel Co. Ld. Regd. 1904. Vol. liq. (members') 3 Oct. 1934. Reconstructed as Appleby-Frodingham Steel Co. Ld. Final meeting return regd. 9 Sept. 1935 .... **1936**

Frodsham Gas & Water Co. Registered 9 Oct. 1856; incorporated by Special Act 1888. In 1935 United Kingdom Gas Corporation Ld. acquired a controlling interest under an offer to ordinary shareholders in Sept. 1935 as follows—For each 10% A (Gas) ordinary £10 share £24 8*s*. 10*d*. cash; for each 7% B (Gas) ordinary £10 share £17 15*s*. 6*d*. cash; purchase price could be applied (*a*) in 4½%, preferred ordinary shares of £1 of acquiring company taken at par or (*b*) in 4½% cumulative preference shares of £1 taken at 21*s*. 6*d*. per share. In 1938 the undertaking was acquired by Runcorn and District Gas Co. **1936**

Froggatt's Electric Lighting Co. Ld. Regd. 1894. Struck off Register 1927 .... ***1897**

Frome & Lamb Ld. Regd. 1889 as Frome United Breweries Co. Ld.; name changed 6 June 1955. All capital was owned jointly by Stroud Brewery Co. Ld.

**See Stock Exchange Year-Book.*

VOL. FOR

and Ushers Wiltshire Brewery Ld. The 4% A debentures were exchanged for 4½% 2nd debenture stocks of Ushers Wiltshire Brewery Ld. in Apr. 1959. Vol. liq. (members') 1 Apr. 1960. Final meeting return regd. 3 Oct. 1960 1960

Frome United Breweries Ld. *See above.*

Frontenac Consolidated Mines Ld. Regd. 1910. Struck off Register 1916 1916

Frontenac Mining Co. Ld. Regd. 1908. Vol. liq. June 1910. The undertaking and assets were sold to Frontenac Consolidated Mines Ld. in which company shareholders were entitled to 1 fully-paid share of £1 for every 2 shares of £1 held. Removed from Register 1911 1911

Frontenac Syndicate Ld. Regd. 1907. Vol. liq. May 1909. Removed from Register 1910. 1910

Frontier Exploration Syndicate Ld. Regd. 1899. Vol. liq. Jan. 1909. Removed from Register 1909 1909

Frontino & Bolivia (South American) Gold Mining Co. Ld. Regd. 1886. Vol. liq. 17 July 1911. Reconstructed as company of same name (later Frontino Gold Mines Ld.). Shareholders were entitled to 1 ordinary share of £1 (credited with 14s. paid) for each ordinary share of £1 held or 1 fully-paid preference share of £1 for each preference share of £1 held. The debenture stock was exchanged at par for debenture stock in new company. Final meeting return regd. 1 July 1914 1912

Frood (Herbert) Co. Ld. Regd. 1907. Vol. liq. 22 Jan. 1914. Final meeting return regd. 26 Oct. 1916 1940

Frost Brothers Ld. Regd. 1896. Vol. liq. 1 June 1929. Undertaking and assets were acquired by British Ropes Ld. Final meeting return regd. 16 June 1930 ... 1930

Frost (F. A.) & Sons Ld. Regd. 1920. Vol. liq. 31 Jan. 1927. A direct controlling interest was held by Spillers Milling & Associated Industries Ld. (later Spillers Ld.). Final meeting return regd. 23 Jan. 1928 1927

Fruit & Flower Supply Corporation Ld. Regd. 1888. Vol. liq. 5 Mar. 1896. Final meeting return regd. 10 Jan. 1900 1897

Fruit & Flowers Ld. Regd. 1928. All shares were owned by Bournemouth Markets Ice and Cold Stores Ld. Struck off Register 1 Sept. 1942 1943

Fruit and Vegetable Growers' Association Ld. Regd. 1911. Vol. liq. 29 Dec. 1914. Court Order to continue winding up under supervision 23 Feb. 1915. Final meeting return regd. 12 May 1916 1916

Fruit Juice Co. Ld. Regd. 1907. Vol. liq. 3 Feb. 1910. Reconstructed as company of same name. Shareholders were entitled to 1 share of 2s. (credited with 1s. paid) for each ordinary or deferred share held. Final meeting return regd. 17 Dec. 1913 1911

Fruit Juice Co. Ld. Regd. 1910. Vol. liq. 25 July 1918. Final meeting return regd. 13 Dec. 1918 1919

Fry (J. S.) & Sons Ld. Regd. 1896. Vol. liq. (members') 11 Dec. 1935 for amalgamation with J. S. Fry & Sons (Africa) Ld. (later J. S. Fry & Sons Ld.). Capital returned to contributories—25s. 6d. per 1st preference share of £1; 20s. 6d. per 2nd preference share of £1; 21s. 6d. per preferred ordinary share of £1; 22s. 6d. per B preferred ordinary share of £1. £196 17s. 6d. was paid into Companies' Liquidation Account in respect of unclaimed distributions. Final meeting return regd. 2 Dec. 1939 1936

Fryerscreek Gold Mining Co. Ld. Regd. 1888. Vol. liq. 14 Jan. 1891. Final meeting return regd. 28 Aug. 1891 1891

Fulham Pottery & Cheavin Filter Co. Ld. Regd. 1891. Vol. liq. 11 Apr. 1919. Final meeting return regd. 18 Aug. 1921 1911

Fuller Accumulator Co. Ld. Regd. 1913. Vol. liq. 5 Sept. 1919. The undertaking and assets were sold to Fuller's United Electric Works Ld. in which company shareholders were entitled to 6 fully-paid preference shares of £1 for every 5 preference shares of £1 held or 5 fully-paid ordinary shares of £1 for every 3 ordinary shares of £1 held. Final meeting return regd. 14 July 1920 1920

Fuller, Storey & Co. Ld. Regd. 1899. Vol. liq. (members') 3 Feb. 1922. Final meeting return regd. 22 June 1923 .... *1922

Fuller's Carbon & Electric Co. Ld. Regd. 1916. Vol. liq. 5 Sept. 1919. The undertaking and assets were sold to Fuller's United Electric Works Ld. in which company shareholders were entitled to 6 fully-paid preference shares of £1 for every 5 preference shares of £1 held or 5 fully-paid ordinary shares of £1 for every 3 ordinary shares of £1 held. Final meeting return regd. 14 July 1920 1920

Fuller's Reef Gold Mining Co. Ld. Regd. 1873. Removed from Register 1885 .... *1880

VOL. FOR

Fuller's United Electric Works Ld. Regd. 1919. Court Order to wind up June 1926. Struck off Register Aug. 1932 1933

Fulton (John) & Co. Ld. Regd. Dublin 1898; transferred to Belfast under Government of Ireland Act 1920. Vol. liq. Jan. 1930. Court Order to wind up 7 Mar. 1930 1931

Fundicion Templeman Ld. Regd. 1897. Removed from Register 1911 1903

Fura Gold Dredging Co. Ld. Regd. 1908. Struck off Register 1927 1927

Fura Mining Co. Ld. Regd. 1900. Removed from Register 1912 1908

Furnaces Ld. Regd. 1910. Vol. liq. 8 May 1920. Directly controlled by Industrial Appliances & Oil & Coal Corporation Ld. Final meeting return regd.6 Oct. 1920 1934

Furness (Far East) Ld. Regd. 1920. Vol. liq. (creditors') Apr. 1948. Final meeting return regd. 12 Nov.1948 1939

Furness (Hellas) Ld. Regd. 1920. Vol. liq. (members') 10 June 1930. Capital returned to contributories— £2,286 9s. 2d. Final meeting return regd. 16 June 1934 1931

Furness (Sir Christopher), Westgarth & Co. Ld. Regd. 1896. Vol. liq. 8 Dec. 1900. Undertaking was acquired by Richardsons, Westgarth & Co. Ld. Final meeting return regd. 11 Mar. 1903 1901

Furness Railway Co. Inc. by Special Act 1844. In 1923 the undertaking was merged into the London Midland & Scottish Railway Co. in which company stockholders were entitled to stock as follows:

For each £100 held		L. M. & S.	
3% Debenture		£75	4% Debenture
4% Cons. Gtd.		£100	4% Guarant'd
4% Cons. Pref.		£100	4% Preference
4% Pref. A		£100	4% Pref. (1923)
4% Pref. B		£100	4% Pref. (1923)
4% Pref. (1894)		£100	4% Pref. (1923)
4% Pref. (1899)		£100	4% Pref. (1923)
Cons. Ordinary		£30	Ordinary 1924

Furness (Thomas) & Co. Ld. Regd. 1895 as Furness (Thos.) & Co.'s Stores Ld.; name changed 1898. Vol. liq. June 1908. Removed from Register 1910 1909

Furnevall & Co. Ld. Regd. 1897. Removed from Register 1901 1940

Furnishers Ld. Regd. 1936. Vol. liq. 1 Feb. 1943. Capital returned to contributories—£1 plus a sum equivalent to arrears of interest at the rate of 6% p.a. from 1 Nov. 1938 to 10 Oct. 1944 per preference share of £1 and 7·465d. per ordinary share of 2s. Final meeting return regd. 6 Oct. 1948 1949

Furniture Appliances Ld. Regd. 1928 as Anty Sag Parent Co. Ld.; name changed July 1930. Vol. liq. (members') 18 Aug. 1930. Shareholders were entitled to shares in Bed Settees Ld. (later Argyll Furnishing Co. Ld.) *plus* £1,363 3s. 8d. in cash. Final meeting return regd. 4 Nov. 1933 1931

Fustian Cutting Machine Co. Ld. Regd. 1890. Court Order to wind up 23 July 1894. Liquidator released 16 Dec. 1898. Removed from Register 21 June 1907 *1895

Futtickcherrie Tea Co. Ld. Regd. 1897. Vol. liq. (creditors') 8 Dec. 1931. Final meeting return regd. 3 Nov. 1934 1932

Futurist (Liverpool) Ld. Regd. 1920. Vol. liq. (members') 11 Oct. 1960. Capital returned to contributories—£1 5s. 3d. per share of £1. £322 7s. 1d. paid into Companies' Liquidation Account in respect of unclaimed dividends and £866 5s. 6d. in respect of unclaimed distributions. Final meeting return regd. 14 Mar. 1962 1963

Fyffe, Hudson & Co. Ld. Regd. 1897. Vol. liq. 21 June 1901. Fruit and vegetable business acquired by Elders & Fyffes Ld. Final meeting return regd. 2 Dec. 1903 1940

Fylde Waterworks Co. Inc. by Special Act. 1861. Property and undertaking were transferred in Aug. 1899 to Fylde Water Board for £802,455 1900

G

G. & H. Plantations Ld. *See* Anglo Oriental Plantations Ld.

G.C. Vaporiser (Foreign Patents) Ld. Regd. 1912. Vol. liq. 25 Aug. 1914. Final meeting return regd 23 Dec. 1920 1915

G.G. Syndicate Ld. Regd. 1903. Vol. liq. 27 Feb. 1905. Properties were acquired by Messina (Transvaal) Development Co. Ld. for £100,000 in shares. Removed from Register 1909 1906

G. M. Oil Fields Ld. Regd. 1909. Vol. liq. 1 Feb. 1915. Final meeting return regd. 14 Aug. 1915 1915

VOL. FOR

G. W. K. (1919) Ld. Regd. 1919. Vol. liq. 26 Mar. 1923. Final meeting return regd. 19 Jan. 1924 .... **1924**

Gabait Gold Mines Ld. Regd. 1933 as Sudan Gold Mines Ld.; name changed May 1933. Vol. liq. (members') 29 Dec. 1942. Capital returned to contributories—1s. 4½d. per share of 2s. £641 4s. 4d. was paid into Companies' Liquidation Account. Final meeting return regd. 1 Feb. 1946 .... **1946**

Gabait (Sudan) Mining Syndicate Ld. Regd. 1903. Vol. liq. 5 May 1905. Capital returned to contributories—252%. Removed from Register 1906 .... **1906**

Gabait Tributing Syndicate Ld. Regd. 1912. Vol. liq. (creditors') 28 Mar. 1939. No capital returned to contributories. Final meeting return regd. 12 Apr. 1940 .... **1941**

Gabarrot (E.) & Co. Ld. Regd. 1899. Vol. liq. 18 Dec. 1900. Reconstructed as company of same name. Shareholders were entitled to 1 fully-paid share of £1 in new company for every 10 ordinary shares of £1 held or to 1 fully-paid share for each preference share of £1 held. Final meeting return regd. 18 Sept. 1901 .... **1908**

Gabarrot (E.) & Co. Ld. Regd. 1900. Vol. liq. 15 Mar. 1926. Final meeting return regd. 27 Jan. 1934 ..... **1927**

Gadjah Rubber Estates Ld. Regd. 1922. Vol. liq. (members') 7 July 1932. Undertaking and assets were acquired by Gadjah Rubber Estates (1932) Ld. in which company shareholders were entitled to 1 share of 2s. (credited with 1s. 4½d. paid) for each share of 2s. held. Final meeting return regd. 13 June 1936 .... **1933**

Gadjah Rubber Estates (1932) Ld. Regd. 1932. Vol. liq. (creditors') 19 May 1965. E. B. Ridsolel & Co. Ld. was appointed as trustee in respect of compensation monies which may be received in the future from Indonesian assets. 17s. 9d. in the £1 was paid to creditors. £114 19s. 10d. was paid into Companies' Liquidation Account in respect of unclaimed dividends. Final meeting return regd. 29 Dec. 1965 .. **1967**

Gadjinsky Cheleken Oil Co. Ld. Regd. 1912. Properties were in hands of Soviet Governments. Struck off Register 28 Sept. 1939 .... **1940**

Gadong Coconut Estates Ld. Regd. 1920. Vol. liq. 10 Aug. 1922. Reconstructed as Gadong Coconut Plantations Ld. in which company shareholders were entitled to 5 shares of £1 (credited with 16s. paid) for every 4 shares of £1 held. Final meeting return regd. 20 July 1923 .... **1923**

Gaerwen Syndicate Ld. Regd. 1909. Struck off Register 1914 .... **1912**

Gaeta Pioneer Mining Co. Ld. Regd. 1905. Vol. liq. May 1908. Struck off Register 9 Apr. 1937 .... **1909**

Gaiety Cinema (Manchester) Ld. See Gaiety Theatre (Manchester) Ld.

Gaiety Theatre Co. Ld. Regd. 1888. Vol. liq. (members') 28 Dec. 1939. Capital returned to contributories—£68,218 15s. Final meeting regd. 23 June 1944 **1940**

Gaiety Theatre (Manchester), Ld. Regd. 1921 as Gaiety Cinema (Manchester) Ld.; name changed 15 Nov. 1937. Receivers were appointed in 1939 and 1942 on behalf of mortgagees but ceased to act in 1954 and 1955. Struck off Register 30 Jan. 1956 .... **1956**

Gaika Gold Mining Co. Ld. Regd. 1902. Vol. liq. (members') 12 Dec. 1930. Assets sold to Q.Q. Mines Ld. (inc. Rhodesia). Capital returned to contributories—5s. 11½½d. per share of £1. £206 5s. 7d. was paid into Companies' Liquidation Account in respect of unclaimed dividends. Final meeting return regd. 10 Feb. 1932. .... **1931**

Gainsborough (Bootle) Ld. Regd. 1919. Vol. liq. (members') 20 May 1937. Practically all shares were owned by Associated British Cinemas Ld. Final meeting return regd. 4 Sept. 1947 .... **1938**

Gainsborough Pictures Ld. Regd. 1924. Vol. liq. 26 June 1928. Undertaking was acquired by Gainsborough Pictures (1928) Ld. Final meeting return regd. 10 Dec. 1945. .... **1945**

Galang Besar Rubber Plantations Ld. Regd. 1910. Vol. liq. (members') 25 June 1942. Preference shares were repaid at par with arrears of dividend. Ordinary shareholders received 4½d. per share of 2s. £18,180 was paid into Companies' Liquidation Account. Final meeting return regd. 8 Aug. 1952. **1953**

Galapitakande Ceylon Estates Ld. Regd. 1934. Vol. liq. (members') 2 Feb. 1951. Property sold. Preference shares repaid at par in Feb. 1951. Ordinary shareholders received £2 13s. 1d. per share of £1. Final meeting return regd. 17 Apr. 1953. .... **1954**

Galashiels Gas Co. Ld. Regd. in Edinburgh 1943. Dissolved 1 May 1949 undertaking being vested in Scottish Area Gas Board under Gas Act 1948. Holders of ordinary stock were entitled to receive in respect of each £1 unit held, £2 8s. British Gas 3% guaranteed stock 1990–95 .... **1952**

VOL. FOR

Galbraith (A. & A.) Ld. Regd. Edinburgh 1907. Vol. liq. Dec. 1915. Final meeting return regd. 10 May 1916 **1916**

Gale Baiss & Co. Ld. Regd. 1934. Vol. liq. (members') 1 Apr. 1949 for reconstruction under same name. All assets distributed in specie. Final meeting return regd. 6 Apr. 1954 .... **1954**

Gale (John C.) & Co. Ld. Regd. 1898. Vol. liq. 20 Dec. 1921. Court Order to continue winding up under supervision 27 Feb. 1922. Final meeting return regd. 26 Mar. 1929 .... **1922**

Galena Mines Ld. Regd. 1896. Vol. liq. 31 Dec. 1898. Final meeting return regd. 22 Dec. 1899 .... **1899**

Galicia Nitrate Co. Inc. Chile 1917. In vol. liq. in 1932. Undertaking and assets were sold for 12,000 fully-paid series B preferred shares of 100 pesos to Nitrate Corporation of Chile which assumed all liability in respect of debentures **1932**

Galician Oil Trust Ld. Regd. 1912. Vol. liq. 7 July 1914. Final meeting return regd. 17 Dec. 1926 .... **1915**

Galician Petroleum Producers Ld. Regd. 1913. Vol. liq. 15 Apr. 1914. Final meeting return regd. 13 Mar. 1922 .... ***1915**

Galician State Lands Petroleum Co. Ld. Regd. 1910. Struck off Register 11 Feb. 1949. .... **1950**

Galician Victoria Petroleum Co. Ld. Regd. 1914. Vol. liq. 27 Dec. 1922. Final meeting return regd. 12 Apr. 1927 .... ***1915**

Galkandewattee Tea Co. Ld. Regd. 1899. Vol. liq. 20 Oct. 1921. Undertaking was sold for £26,250 and discharge of liabilities. Final meeting return regd. 6 June 1922. .... **1922**

Gallay Radiator Co. Ld. Regd. 1914. Vol. liq.(members') 4 Apr. 1933. Controlling interest held by Harper Bean Ld. in 1924. Final meeting return regd. 8 Oct. 1936 .... **1924**

Galletti's Wireless Telegraph & Telephone Co. Ld. Regd. 1912. Vol. liq. 25 Nov. 1925. Direct controlling interest held by Indo-European Telegraph Co. Ld. Final meeting return regd. 18 July 1929................ **1927**

Galloway (John) & Co. Ld. Regd. in Edinburgh 1935. Winding-up order 10 Dec. 1971. Distributions on loan stock 34p (per £1 stock) Dissolved 5 Oct. 1977 **1979–80**

Galloway Water Power Co. Inc. by Special Act 1929. Dissolved 1 Apr. 1948 undertaking being vested in British (later Central) Electricity Authority and South West Scotland Area Board under Electricity Act 1947. Holders of securities were entitled to receive British Electricity 3% guaranteed stock (1968—73) as follows in respect of each £1 unit of capital held:

	£	s.	d.
Ordinary shares	5	7	6
5% redeemable debenture stock	1	0	7¾
4% redeemable debenture stock	1	0	6¾	**1949**

Galloways Ld. Regd. 1899. Receiver appointed 21 Dec. 1931. Struck off Register 27 July 1937 .... **1938**

Gallymont Gold Fields Ld. Regd. 1896. Vol. liq. 30 Dec. 1902. Removed from Register 1904..................... **1903**

Galphele Tea and Rubber Estate Ld. Regd. 1907. Vol. liq. (members')—15 Aug. 1951. Capital returned to contributories—5s. 1·15d. per 2s. stock. £2,750 16s. 8d. was paid into Companies' Liquidation Account. Final meeting return regd. 31 Jan. 1955. .... **1956**

Galston Gas Co. Ld. Regd. in Edinburgh 1904. Dissolved 1 May 1949 undertaking being vested tn Scottish Area Gas Board under Gas Act 1948. Holders of securities were entitled to receive British Gas 3%, guaranteed stock 1990—95 as follows:

	£	s.	d.
Ord. shares (of £1)	2	0	0
Defd. shares (of 10s)		1	0	**1952**

Harrison & Larner Ld. Final meeting return regd. 22 Oct. 1900 .... **1900**

Galvez Rubber Estates Ld. Regd. 1907. Vol. liq. 2 July 1920. Final meeting return regd. 2 Apr. 1925. ...... **1921**

Galway & Salthill Tramways Co. Inc. by Special Act in 1877. Court Order to wind up Feb. 1918 .... **1918**

Gamage-Bell Motor Cab Co. Ld. Regd. 1909 as Gamage Motor Cab Co. Ld.; name changed Jan. 1910. Vol. liq. 27 Mar. 1916. Final meeting return regd. 3 July 1920. .... **1916**

Gamages (West End) Ld. Regd. 1928. Court Order to wind up May 1931. Struck off Register 14 Oct. 1938 **1939**

Game & Son Ld. Regd. 1899 as Game, Son, Harrison & Larner Ld.; name changed July 1908. Vol. liq. (members') 20 Jan. 1930. Undertaking and assets acquired by Joseph Travers & Sons Ld. Capital returned to contributories—preference shares of £1, repaid in full; 11s. 8d. per ordinary share of £1. Final meeting return regd. 13 Nov. 1930..................... **1930**

Game, Harrison & Larner Ld. Regd. 1891. Vol. liq. 1 July 1899. Undertaking acquired by Game, Son, Harrison & Larner Ld. Final meeting return regd. 22 Oct. 1900 .... ***1900**

See Stock Exchange Year-Book.

VOL. FOR

Gamelsoo Concessions Ld. Regd. 1901. Removed from Register 1909 1909

Gamnes Copper Co. Ld. Regd. 1907. Vol. liq. 3 Aug. 1910. Final meeting return regd. 22 Mar. 1922..... 1911

Ganapalla Estate Co. Ld. Regd. 1891. Vol. liq. (members') 19 Sept. 1950. Capital returned to contributories (per share of £1):—preference £1; ordinary £2 0s. 7d. Final meeting return regd. 16 May 1952 1953

Gangwarily Estates Co. of Ceylon Ld. Regd. 1896. Vol. liq. (members') 19 June 1935. Final meeting return regd. 15 Mar. 1937 1936

Garden City Houses Ld. Undertaking and assets were acquired by Welwyn Garden City Public Utility Society Ld 1929

Garden City Pioneer Co. Ld. Regd. 1902. Vol. liq. 1904. Assets were acquired by First Garden City Ld. Removed from Register 1905 1904

Gardiner Shipbuilding & Engineering Co. Ld. Regd. 1919. Court Order to wind up Apr. 1921. Struck off Register Apr. 1929 1930

Gardner British Typewriter Co. Ld. Regd. 1893. Vol. liq. 11 July 1895. Final meeting return regd. 4 Dec. 1897 *1896

Gardner, Mountain & D'Ambrumenil Ld. See below.

Gardner, Mountain, D'Ambrumenil & Rennie Ld. Regd. 1949 as Gardner, Mountain & D'Ambrumenil Ld.; name changed 30 June 1949. A subsidiary of Staplegreen Insurance Holdings Ld. Vol. liq. (members') 31 Mar. 1967. Final meeting return regd. 24 Mar. 1969 1970

Gardner's Royal Hotel Ld. Inc. Guernsey 1893. Wound up June 1918 1928

Garfield Ld. Regd. 1889. Vol. liq. 4 Mar. 1895. Reconstructed as Hampton Plains Exploration Co. Ld. in which company shareholders were entitled to 1 share of £1 (credited with 17s. 6d. paid) for each share of £1 held. Final meeting return regd. 12 Nov. 1895 - 1905

Garibaldi Gold & Antimony Mining Co. Ld. Regd. 1895. Vol. liq. Feb. 1908. Removed from Register 1911 1908

Garing (Malacca) Rubber Estate Ld. Regd. 1910. Vol. liq. 31 Aug. 1911. Reconstructed as company of same name (later Garing Estates Ld.). Shareholders were entitled to 1 share of £1 (credited with 12s. paid) in new company for each share of £1 held. Final meeting return regd. 30 Mar. 1917 1912

Garland Steamship Corporation. Inc. New York 1916. Vol. liq. Dec. 1927. Capital returned to contributories—$3·10 per common share of $3 at 22 Aug. 1932 1928

Garland Steamship Corporation (of Delaware) Inc. Delaware 1920. Dissolved in Nov. 1920. Shareholders were entitled to 1 share of $3 in Garland Steamship Corporation (of New York) and a cash distribution estimated at $4·50 for each share (of no par value) held 1921

Garnant Anthracite Collieries Ld. Regd. 1909. Receiver appointed Feb. 1913; ceased to act Nov. 1914. Struck off Register 9 Apr. 1921 .... *1914

Garnant Collieries Co. Ld. Regd. 1874. Vol. liq. 1876. Final meeting return regd. 4 Mar. 1879 .... *1878

Garnwilt Anthracite Colliery Co. Ld. Regd. 1925. Vol. liq. 12 Mar. 1929. Undertaking acquired by Henderson's Welsh Anthracite Collieries Ld. Final meeting return regd. 12 July 1929 1940

Garrett (Richard) & Sons Ld. Regd. 1897. Receiver appointed 28 June 1932; ceased to act 13 Dec. 1935. Struck off Register 1937 1932

Garrucha Waterworks Co. Ld. Regd. 1884. Struck off Register 31 Dec. 1895 1901

Garstang & Knott End Railway Co. Inc. by Special Act 1864. Under Knott End Railway Co. Act 1908 undertaking was purchased by that company for £50,000 in cash and £5,000 in fully-paid ordinary shares... 1909

Garstang Gas Co. Ld. Regd. 1879. Dissolved 1 May 1949 undertaking being vested in North Western Area Gas Board under Gas Act 1948. Holders of securities were entitled to receive in respect of each £5 unit held British Gas 3% guaranteed stock 1990–95 as follows:

	£	s.	d.
Orig. shares (10% max.)	5	5	0
Addit. shares (7% max.)	4	0	0
5% pref. shares	5	12	0

Garswood Coal & Iron Co. Ld. Regd. 1873. Vol. liq. 29 May 1929. Amalgamated with Garswood Hall Collieries Co. Ld. Final meeting return regd. 13 Nov. 1929 1940

Garswood Hall Collieries Co. Ld. Regd. 1883. Removed from Register 1906 1940

Garswood Hall Collieries Co. Ld. Regd. 1905. Vol. liq. (creditors') 18 Dec. 1951. No capital returned to contributories. Final meeting return regd. 23 Aug. 1956 1957

VOL. FOR

Garth Gell Exploration Syndicate Ld. Regd. 1924. Struck off Register Jan. 1931 1931

Garth Merthyr Steam Navigation Collieries Ld. See Crown Merthyr Steam Navigation Collieries Ld.

Gartheniog Slate Co. Ld. Regd. 1881. Removed from Register 1882 1883

Gartmore Ceylon Tea Co. Ld. Regd. 1896. Vol. liq. 17 Mar. 1950. Preference shares repaid in Apr. 1950 together with arrears of dividend since 1946. Ordinary shareholders received a total of £4 15s. 2·783d. per share of £10. Final meeting return regd. 25 Nov. 1952 1954

Gartside & Co. of Manchester Ld. Regd. 1894. Undertaking was acquired by Calico Printers Association Ld. Removed from Register 1905 1900

Garve & Ullapool Railway Co. Inc. by Special Act 1890. Undertaking was abandoned by Act 1893 1894

Garvin (Theo) Ld. Regd. 25 Sept. 1955. Winding up order 3 May 1965. Liquidation closed in Nov. 1973. Co. dissolved 1 Dec. 1977 1977-8

Garw & Braichycymer Collieries Ld. Regd. 1903. Receiver for 1st mortgage debenture holders appointed in Aug. 1909. Removed from Register 1911 1911

Garw & Ogmore Gas Co. Inc. by Special Act 1891. Dissolved 1 May 1949 undertaking being vested in Wales Area Gas Board under Gas Act 1948. Holders of securities were entitled to receive British Gas 3% guaranteed stock 1990–95 as follows in respect of each £10 unit unless otherwise stated, of security held:

	£	s.	d.
Ord. shares (10% max.)	19	10	0
Ord. shares (7% max.)	14	0	0
5% pref. shares	11	4	0
4% perp. deb. stock (per £100)	102	12	6
6% red. deb. stock (per £100)	101	0	0

...... 1952

Gas & Fuel Plants Ld. Regd. 1918 as Low Temperature Construction Ld.; name changed to British Gas and Fuel Co. Ld. in Aug. 1922 and as above in Feb. 1924. Vol. liq. 15 Oct. 1926. Undertaking (except Tully gas plant rights) was acquired by Low Temperature Carbonisation Ld. (later Coalite & Chemical Products Ld.). Final meeting return regd. 7 Nov. 1927 1928

Gas & Light Co. of Portugal Ld. Regd. 1886. Vol. liq. 29 Oct. 1891. Final meeting return regd. 8 Oct. 1895 1892

Gas Appliances Co. Ld. Regd. 1883. Struck off Register 17 June 1898.. 1899

Gas Chambers & Coke Ovens Ld. Regd. 1929. Vol. liq. (members') 23 Jan. 1959. Final meeting return regd. 23 Apr. 1960 1938

Gas Consolidation Ld. Regd. 1934. Dissolved 1 May 1949, undertaking being vested in the Gas Council under Gas Act 1948. Holders of securities were entitled to receive British Gas 3% guaranteed stock 1990—95 as follows in respect of each £1 unit, unless otherwise stated, of security held:

	£	s.	d.
A ord. stock	1	2	10
B ord. stock..	1	2	9
4% red. pref. stock	1	0	0
4½% pref. stock	1	3	0
3½% red. deb. stock (per £100)	100	15	0

...... 1952

Gas Light & Coke Co. Inc. by Royal Charter 1812. Dissolved 1 May 1949, undertaking being vested in North Thames Area Gas Board under Gas Act 1948. Holders of securities were entitled to receive British Gas 3% guaranteed stock 1990–95 as follows in respect of each £100 unit, unless otherwise stated, of security held:

	£	s.	d.
Ord. stock (5% basic) (per £1)...............	1	6	6
3½% max. stock	95	0	0
4% cons. pref. stock	105	10	0
3⅛% red. pref stock..............................	104	5	0
3% cons. deb. stock	90	6	8
3½% red. deb. stock	100	0	0
4½% red. deb. stock	108	11	8
5% red. deb. stock................................	108	11	8

...... 1952

Gas Lighting Improvement Co. Ld. See Glico Petroleum Ld.

Gas, Water & General Investment Trust Ld, Regd. 1889. Receiver appointed in Apr. 1930. Struck off Register 31 Dec. 1940 1941

Gascon Trust Ld. Regd. 1935. Vol. liq. (members') 22 Aug. 1949. Capital returned to contributories—£1 9s. 8·4d. (including 8s. 8·4d. on account of arrears of dividend) per preference share of £1; £1 1s. 7·8624d. per ordinary share of 10s.; 2s. 1·98614d. per deferred share of 1s. Final meeting return regd. 27 July 1950 1951

Gascoyne (Murchison) Gold Fields Exploring Co. Ld. Regd. 1895. Vol. liq. 22 June 1898. Final meeting return regd. 16 Feb. 1900 1899

Gaspé Syndicate Ld. Regd. 1904. Vol. liq. 29 Apr. 1907. Capital returned to contributories—3s. 7½d. per

VOL. FOR

share of £1; further payments (if any) not known. Removed from Register 1908 .... **1908**

Gaston Ld. Regd. 1919. Struck off Register 19 Feb. 1937 **1938**

Gateshead Breweries Corporation Ld. Regd. 1900. Vol. liq. 20 Nov. 1919. Undertaking was acquired by John Rowell & Son Ld. for £45,920 in cash and £26,240 in 6% debentures. Final meeting return regd. 18 June 1921 .... **1920**

Gatling Arms & Ammunition Co. Ld. Regd. 1888 as Gatling Gun Ld.; name changed Jan. 1890. Court Orders: to wind up Oct. 1890; to dissolve 29 June 1895 .... **1891**

Gatling Gun Ld. See Gatling Arms & Ammunition Co. Ld.

Gatling Hill Gold Mining Co. Ld. Regd. 1899. Property was acquired by Etna Development Co. Ld. for 15,000 fully-paid shares of £1. Removed from Register 1905 .... **1904**

Gatooma Syndicate Ld. Regd. 1910. Vol. liq. (members') 2 July 1931. All capital held by Salisbury Trust Ld. Final meeting return regd. 16 Jan. 1932.............. **1931**

Gaumont Construction Co. Ld. Regd. Feb. 1928 as Denman Allied Cinematograph Theatres Ld.; name changed in Apr. 1928 to Denman Construction Co. Ld.; and as above in Apr. 1932. Vol. liq. (members') 26 Feb. 1940. Properties were conveyed to Gaumont British Picture Corporation Ld., which company owned direct controlling interest. Capital returned to contributories—£253,125. Final meeting return regd. 25 Feb. 1941 .... **1941**

Gaumonts Trust Corporation Ld. Regd. 1922. Vol. liq. 9 Sept. 1929. Final meeting return regd. 14 Apr. 1930 **1930**

Gauntietts (1913) Ld. See Kingswinford Forge Ld.

Gavilan Gold Syndicate Ld. Regd. 1895. Removed from Register 1901 .... **1901**

Gavin's House-to-House Cycle Cleaning & Insurance Co. Ld. Regd. 1896. Struck off Register 23 July 1901.. **1902**

Gawton Co. Ld. Regd. 1883. Removed from Register 1906 .... **1893**

Gaze (Henry) & Sons Ld. Regd. 1897. Vol. liq. 13 July 1903. Court Order to wind up 6 Aug. 1903. Liquidator released 16 Nov. 1906. Struck off Register 27 Aug. 1909 .... **1904**

Gazi (British East Africa) Rubber & Fibre Estate Ld. Regd. 1910. Vol. liq. 22 Nov. 1917 for amalgamation with East African Estates Ld. Final meeting return regd. 16 Jan. 1919 .... **1918**

Gearless Motor Omnibus Co. Ld. Regd. 1906. Vol. liq. Mar. 1922. Omnibuses were acquired by London General Omnibus Co. Ld. Capital returned to contributories—11s. 11d. per ordinary share of £1; 7·15d. per deferred share of 1s. Struck off Register May 1929 .... **1930**

Geashill Extension Railway Co. See Great Southern and Western Railway Co. Ireland.

Gedaref Railway & Development Co. (Sudan) Ld. Regd. 1926. Vol. liq. 3 July 1962. Final meeting return regd. 4 Oct. 1963... **1965**

Gedong Investments Ld. Regd. 1910 as Gedong (Perak) Rubber Estate Ld. Vol. liq. 16 July 1979. Fianl meeting return regd. 4 Oct. 1979 ....**1979–80**

Gedong (Perak) Rubber Estate Ld. See Gedong Investments Ld.

Geduld Deep Ld. Inc. Transvaal 1902. Vol. liq. Aug. 1908 for purpose of reconstruction. Shareholders were entitled to 1 fully-paid share of 2s. in New Geduld Deep Ld. for each share of £1 held. Capital returned to contributories—8s. 6d. per £1 share in Oct. 1908; further payments (if any) not known ... **1909**

Gee Floor Scrubbing Machine Co. Ld. Regd. 1897. Vol. liq. 8 Aug. 1898. Court Order to continue winding up under supervision 26 Oct. 1898. Final meeting return regd. 12 June 1902 .... **1899**

Geelong Gold Mining Co. Ld. Regd. 1897. Vol. liq. 13 Dec. 1904. Undertaking was acquired by East Gwanda Mines Ld., in which company shareholders were entitled to 2 shares of £1 (credited with 14s. paid) for every 5 shares of £1 held. Removed from Register 1908 .... **1905**

Gel Tin Lode & Alluvial Co. Ld. Regd. 1910. Vol. liq. 30 Oct. 1929. Final meeting return regd. 23 Apr. 1931 **1930**

Geldenhuis Estate & Gold Mining Co. (Elandsfontein No. 1) Ld. Inc. Transvaal 1887. Vol. liq. Nov. 1909. Undertaking and assets were acquired by Geldenhuis Deep Ld., in which company shareholders were entitled to 1 fully-paid share of £1 for every 4 shares of £1 held **1910**

Geldenhuis Main Reef Gold Mining Co. Ld. Inc. Transvaal 1889. Vol. liq. 1907 .... **1908**

Geldfontein Estates & Gold Mining Co. Ld. Regd. 1895. Vol. liq. 30 Apr. 1897. Reconstructed as Golden State Mines Ld. Final meeting return regd. 27 May 1898 .... **1908**

VOL. FOR

Gell Telegraphic Appliances Syndicate Ld. Regd. 1903. Vol. liq. 13 May 1919. Final meeting return regd. 20 Feb. 1920 .... **1919**

Gellings Iron Foundry Co. Ld. Inc. Isle of Man 1877. Vol. liq. Mar. 1919 for reconstruction **1919**

Gellyceidrim Collieries Co. Ld. Regd. 1927. All shares owned by Amalgamated Anthracite Collieries Ld. Struck off Register 10 Mar. 1939 .... **1939**

Gellydeg Colliery Co. Ld. Regd. 1874. Removed from Register 1885... ***1876**

Geluk Syndicate Ld. Regd. 1905. Struck off Register 22 Nov. 1940.. **1941**

Gem of Cue Ld. Regd. 1898. Struck off Register 22 Dec. 1903.. **1904**

Gem of Murchison Gold Mine Ld. Regd. 1895. Removed from Register 1906 .... **1899**

Gem (Rhodesia) Gold Fields Ld. Regd. 1911. Vol. liq. 2 Apr. 1928. Undertaking and assets acquired by Rhodesian Corporation Ld., in which company shareholders were entitled to 1 fully-paid share of 5s. for every 2 shares of 5s. held. Final meeting return regd. 7 July 1937 .... **1929**

Gemming and Mining Co. of Ceylon Ld. Regd. 1889. Removed from Register 1905 .... **1895**

Gemsah Oil Reefs Ld. Regd. 1914. Vol. liq. 7 Jan. 1926. Final meeting return regd. 20 Apr. 1926 .... **1926**

General Accident & Employers Liability Assurance Association Ld. Regd. Edinburgh 1885. Vol. liq. Feb. 1891. Business was amalgamated with General Accident Fire & Life Assurance Corporation Ld, Final meeting return regd. 21 June 1892.............. **1892**

General Aircraft Ld. See Hanworth Securities Ld.

General Amusements Corporation Ld. Regd. 1929 as Auto-Rides Ld.; name changed Oct. 1930. Vol. liq. (creditors') 14 Feb. 1934. No capital returned to contributories. Final meeting return regd. 9 Sept. 1935 .... **1935**

General & Industrial Securities Co. Ld. See Industrial Securities Co. Ld.

General Asbestos Co. Ld. See Rhomines Ld.

General Assets Purchase Co. Ld. Regd. 1885. Vol. liq. 26 Feb. 1896. Reconstructed as General Assets Purchase Co. Ld. in which company shareholders were entitled to £10 1st income debenture *plus* one 1st bonus certificate for £2 for each 1st preference share of £10 held; holders of each B preference share of £10 were entitled to £10 2nd income debenture *plus* one 2nd bonus certificate for £2 10s.; holders of each ordinary share of £2 10s. (£1 paid) to 1 ordinary share of £2 (£1 paid); holders of each founders' share of £2 10s. to 1 fully-paid deferred share of £2 10s. Final meeting return regd. 1 Mar. 1897 .... **1898**

General Assets Trust Ld. Regd. 1896. Vol. liq. 27 Oct. 1898 for reconstruction as Atlas Trust Ld. Holders of securities were entitled to securities in new company as follows:—for each £100 1st income debentures held—£100 debenture stock; for each £100 2nd income debentures—£60 preference shares; for each £100 ordinary capital—£40 ordinary shares; for each £100 1st income debenture bonus certificate—£50 ordinary shares; for each £100 2nd income debenture bonus certificate—£40 ordinary shares. Final meeting return regd. 16 Feb. 1900 .... **1899**

General Association Ld. Regd. 1896. Vol. liq. 4 Jan. 1899. Final meeting return regd. 6 June 1900 ...... **1899**

General Automatic Co. Ld. Regd. 1928. The undertaking was assigned to Automatic Chewing Sweet Sales Ld. Struck off Register 19 Jan. 1934 .... **1934**

General Cinema Finance Corpn. Ld. Regd. 1936 as G. C. F. Corpn. Ld.; name changed 1936. Vol. liq. 26 June 1962. Final meeting return regd. 20 Oct. 1970 ...... **1957**

General County Omnibus Co. Ld. Regd. 1927. Vol. liq. 19 May 1936. Undertaking acquired by Northern General Transport Co. Ld. Capital returned to contributories—£18,618 3s. 10d. Final meeting return regd. 21 Dec. 1936 .... **1938**

General Credit & Discount Co. Ld. Regd. 1866. Reconstructed 1885 as Union Discount Co. of London Ld. in which company shareholders were entitled to 3 shares of £10 (credited with £5 paid) for every 10 shares of £6 (£3 10s. paid) *plus* £2 per share in cash at Dec. 1885; further payments (if any) not known. Final meeting return regd. 16 Dec. 1892 ..... **1885**

General Credit Co. Ld. Regd. 1856. Re-regd. 1891. Vol. liq. 3 Aug. 1893. Court Order to continue winding up under supervision 26 Oct. 1893. Final meeting return regd. 21 Dec. 1897 .... **1894**

General Electric Power & Traction Co. Ld. Regd. 1890. Vol. liq. 11 Dec. 1894. Electric launch department was acquired by Immisch Electric Launch Co. Ld. for £8,965 in fully-paid preference shares of £1; remainder of undertaking was reconstructed as

*See Stock Exchange Year-Book.

VOL. FOR

Acme and Immisch Electric Works Ld. Removed from Register 1907 .... **1895**

General Electrolytic Parent Co. Ld. Regd. 1893. Vol. liq. 30 Dec. 1914. Final meeting return regd. 10 July 1916 .... **1915**

General Engineering Development Trust Ld. Regd. 1924. Struck off Register 24 Sept. 1943 .... **1944**

General Enterprise Co. Ld. Regd. 1895. Vol. liq. 14 Jan 1899. Undertaking acquired by New Eastern Investment Co. Ld. Final meeting return regd. 15 Jan. 1900 .... **1943**

General Explorers Ld. Regd. 1910. Struck off Register 1923 .... *****1923**

General Fibre Co. Ld. Regd. 1884. Vol. liq. 1886. Final meeting return regd. 16 Mar. 1889 .... **1887**

General Film Renting (1920) Co. Ld. Regd. 1920. Court Order to wind up Feb. 1923. Struck off Register Apr. 1929 .... **1930**

General Financial Bank Ld. Regd. 1880. Court Orders: to wind up 21 Feb. 1882; to dissolve 1 Dec. 1893 .... **1883**

General Fire Assurance Co. *See* Compagnie d'Assurances Générales contre l'Incendie et les Explosions.

General Founders' Share Co. Ld. Regd. 1887. Vol. liq. 29 Apr. 1896. Final meeting return regd. 27 Nov. 1896 *****1897**

General Gold Extracting Co. Ld. Regd. 1898. Vol. liq. 19 July 1904. Final meeting return regd. 30 July 1906 **1905**

General Goldfields Ld. Regd. 1900. Vol. liq. 9 Mar. 1905. Absorbed by Victorian Consolidated Goldfields Ld. in which company shareholders were entitled to 1 fully-paid share of 5s. for each share of £1 held. Removed from Register 1907 .... **1906**

General Gordon Gold Mining Co., No Liability. Inc. Western Australia 1896. In liquidation **1899**

General Hail-storm Insurance Society. Established by deed of settlement 1843. Taken over by Norwich and London Accident Insurance Association **1899**

General Ice Factory Co. Ld. Regd. 1877. Vol. liq. Sept. 1887. Court Order to continue winding up under supervision 21 Sept. 1887. Final meeting return regd. 12 Sept. 1893 .... **1888**

General Industrials Development Syndicate Ld. Regd. 1899. Vol. liq. 7 Feb. 1911. Final meeting return regd. 14 June 1911 .... *****1912**

General International Wireless Telegraph & Telephone Co. Ld. Regd. 1902. Vol. liq. Feb. 1907. Removed from Register 1910 .... **1907**

General Investment and Finance Co. Ld. Regd. 1899. Vol. liq. 19 June 1901. Capital returned to contributories—2s. 10d. per share of 5s. at 19 Nov. 1901; further payments (if any) not known. Final meeting return regd. 15 Sept. 1902 .... **1902**

General Land Drainage & Improvement Co. Inc. by Special Act 1849. Business transferred to the Lands Improvement Co. Court Order to wind up 18 Apr. 1916 in Mar. 1911 .... **1912**

General Mines Investment Ld. Regd. 1908. Vol. liq. (members') 14 Feb. 1936 for reconstruction under same name. Shareholders were entitled to 1 share of 2s. (credited with 1s. paid) in new company for each ordinary or founders' share of 2s. held and an option (since expired) over further shares. Final meeting return regd. 11 Jan. 1937 .... **1936**

General Mines Investment Ld. Regd. 1936. Vol. liq. (members') 17 Mar. 1939. Undertaking and assets were acquired by National Mining Corporation Ld. (later N. M. C. Investments Ld.) in which company shareholders were entitled to 1 share of 2s. 6d. (credited as fully-paid) for every 4 shares of £1 held. Option certificate holders were entitled to an option (since expired) over further shares. Final meeting return regd. 1 Oct. 1940 .... **1940**

General Mining Association Ld. Established 1825 regd. 1869. Vol. liq. in 1901 the undertaking was sold to Nova Scotia Steel Co. Ld. for cash. Capital returned to contributories—£10 per share of £5 10s.; further payments (if any) not known. Removed from Register 1901 .... **1901**

General Mortgage and Investment Co. Ld. Regd. 1880. Vol. liq. 30 May 1892. Final meeting return regd. 31 May 1893 .... **1893**

General Motor Cab Co., Ld. Regd. 1906. Vol. liq. 22 Aug. 1913 the undertaking and assets having been acquired by British Motor Cab Co. Ld. by exchange of shares at the rate of 2 fully-paid preferred ordinary shares of £4 and 1 deferred share of 1s. of that company for every 11 preferred ordinary and 20 deferred ordinary shares respectively. Struck off Register 4 May 1948 .... **1949**

General Motors Ld. Regd. 1909 as Bedford Motors Ld.; name changed Feb. 1912 to General Motors (Europe) Ld.; name changed Aug. 1919. Vol. liq. (members') 8 Feb. 1933. Capital returned to contributories—£155,615 5s. *plus* 109,480 shares of

VOL. FOR

£1 in General Motors Ld. (regd. 1933). Final meeting return regd. 21 Feb. 1934 .... **1933**

General Oil & Finance Corporation Ld. Regd. 1910. Vol. liq. May 1912. Undertaking and assets were acquired by Oilfields Finance Corporation Ld. in which company shareholders were entitled to 3 shares of £1 (credited with 13s. 4d. paid) for every 4 shares of £1 (15s. paid) held. Removed from Register 1913 .... **1913**

General Oilfields Ld. Regd. 1912. Court Orders: to wind up 11 Feb. 1913; to stay proceedings 8 Apr. 1913. Vol. liq. 22 Feb. 1922 for reconstruction as Newfoundland & General Oilfields Ld. in which company shareholders were entitled to 3 ordinary shares of 2s. (credited with 1s. 6d. paid) for each ordinary share of 5s. held or 5 deferred shares of 1s. (credited with 9d. paid) for every 4 deferred shares of 1s. held or 1 fully-paid preference share of 5s. for each preference share of 5s. held. Final meeting return regd. 22 Aug. 1924 .... **1923**

General Oilfields of Galicia Ld. Regd. 1912. Struck off Register 1924 .... **1924**

General Omnibus Supply (Manufacturing Co.) Ld. Regd. 1914. Court Order to wind up 18 Apr. 1916. Struck off Register 1925 .... **1916**

General Petroleum Co. Ld. Regd. 1914. Vol. liq. (creditors') 8 Dec. 1938. No capital returned to contributories. Final meeting return regd. 28 Feb. 1939 .... **1939**

General Petroleum Company of Trinidad Ld. Regd. 1919. Vol. liq. 5 Jan. 1925. Reconstructed as Oropuche (Trinidad) Oilfields Ld., in which company shareholders were entitled to 1 share of 4s. (credited with 2s. paid) for each A or every 2 B shares of 4s. held. Final meeting return regd. 1 Jan. 1929 .... **1925**

General Petroleum Properties of Trinidad Ld. Regd. 1910. Vol. liq. 20 Feb. 1914. Properties were sold to Trinidad Leaseholds Ld. (later Trinidad Oil Co. Ld.) in which company shareholders were entitled to 1 share of £1 (credited as fully-paid) for every 2 shares of £1 held. Final meeting return regd. 28 Apr. 1914 .... **1914**

General Phosphate Co. Ld. Regd. 1907. Vol. liq. 19 Aug. 1921. Final meeting return regd. 13 Dec. 1921 ..... *****1911**

General Phosphate Corporation Ld. Regd. 1890. Removed from Register 1907 .... **1894**

General Property Development Ld. Regd. 1896 as West Australian Gold Properties Development Ld.; name changed Nov. 1905. Vol. liq. May 1909. Removed from Register 1911 .... **1910**

General Real Estates Investment and Trust, Ld. Regd. 1918. Vol. liq. (members') 31 Mar. 1953. Howard de Walden Estates Ld. acquired certain assets of company and assumed liability for outstanding 4½% 1st Mortgage Debenture Stock. Preference shares repaid at par in Mar. 1953. Distributions in specie were made to ordinary shareholders in Mar. & Apr. 1953 and Sept. 1961. Capital returned to contributories—4s. 10·562d. per share of £1. Final meeting return regd. 18 Dec. 1961 .... **1963**

General Reinsurance Co. Ld. Regd. 1919. Vol. liq. 14 Jan. 1926. Final meeting return regd. 24 June 1931 **1926**

General Rubber Co. Ld. Regd. 1906 as Wm. Symington & Co. Ld.; name changed Dec. 1919. All shares held by General Rubber Co. of New York. Vol. liq. (members') 26 Apr. 1938. Final meeting return regd. 30 June 1938 .... **1940**

General Scottish Trust Ld. Regd. Edinburgh 1914. Vol. liq. (members') 18 Nov. 1936. Undertaking acquired by Scottish & Canadian General Investment Co. Ld. (later General Scottish Trust Ld.), in which company shareholders received 1 preference share of £1 for every preference share of £1 held, or 1 ordinary share of £1 for every 2 ordinary shares of £1 held. Terminable debentures were exchanged for new debentures. Final meeting return regd. 8 Apr. 1937 .... **1937**

General Seating Co. Ld. Regd. 1905. Vol. liq. 18 Apr. 1921. Final meeting return regd 23 Sept. 1926 ...... **1922**

General Securities Investment Trust Co. Ld. Regd. 1908. By scheme of arrangement 21 July 1975 the 4% debenture stock cancelled holders receiving like amount of 4·8% debenture stock of Estate House Investment Trust Ld. Dissolved 31 Dec. 1977 .... **1977-8**

General Securities Trust & Agency Ld. Regd. 1890. Vol. liq. 8 Aug. 1896. Final meeting return regd. 18 June 1897 .... *****1897**

General Service Co-operative Stores Ld. Regd. 1890. Removed from Register 1907 .... **1892**

General Sewage & Manure Co. Ld. Regd. 1872. Court Orders: to wind up 24 Aug. 1876: to dissolve 10 Apr. 1884 .... *****1876**

VOL. FOR

Gibbs Fertilisers Ld. Regd. 1906 as Gibbs Fertilizers Ld.; name changed 1906. Vol. liq. (members') 6 Apr. 1944. All shares owned by National Fertilizers Ld. Final meeting return regd. 8 Sept. 1944 .... **1945**

Gibbs (James) & Co. Ld. Regd. 1886. Vol. liq. 8 May 1906. Undertaking acquired by Gibbs Fertilizers Ld. Final meeting return regd. 3 Oct. 1906 .... **1940**

Gibraltar Consolidated Gold Mines Ld. Regd. 1895. Reconstructed 1900 as company of same name. Shareholders were entitled to 1 share of 10s. (credited with 7s. 6d. paid) in new company for each share of £1 held. Removed from Register 1901 ... **1901**

Gibraltar Consolidated Gold Mines Ld. Regd. 1900. Vol. liq. 15 July 1918. Final meeting return regd. 11 Apr. 1919 .... **1919**

Gibson (S.) & Sons Ld. Regd. 1931. Vol. liq. (members') 26 Oct. 1964. Capital returned to contributories—4s. 11½d. per 2s. 6d. ordinary stock. £9,395 12s. was paid into Companies Liquidation Account in respect of unclaimed distributions. Final meeting held 23 Aug. 1979 .... **1980–1**

Gie Appantoo Gold Mining Co. Ld. Regd. 1886. Vol. liq. 4 Aug. 1893. Reconstructed as Appantoo Gold Mining Co. Ld. in which company shareholders were entitled to 1 share of £1 (credited with 15s. paid) for each share of £1 held. Final meeting return regd. 20 Dec. 1897 .... **1897**

Gieves Realisations Ld. Regd. 1904 as Gieve, Matthews & Seagrove Ld.; converted private company 1908; name changed Gieves ld. 1916; reconverted private company 1920; name changed The Gieves Group Ld. 1971 and to present title 1980. Vol. liq. (members') 31 Mar. 1980. Holders received 120p cash for each 5% preference share or 5% B preference share and 60p cash and 1 ordinary share of 20p of The Gieves Group (1980) Ld. (now The Gieves Group Ld.) for each ordinary share held, under a scheme of reconstruction pursuant to Section 287 of Companies Act 1948. Return of final meeting registered 19 July 1985 .... **1986–7**

Giffard Gun & Ordnance Co. Ld. Regd. 1890. Vol. liq. 5 Sept. 1893. Final meeting return regd. 29 Dec. 1924 **1894**

Gifford and Garvald Railway Co. Inc. by Special Act 1891. In 1923 the undertaking was merged into the London & North Eastern Railway Co. in which company shareholders were entitled to £90 4% Second Guaranteed Stock for each £100 Gifford Ordinary Shares held **1924**

Giffre Electro-Chemical & Power Co. Ld. Regd. 1899. Vol. liq. 3 Dec. 1900. Undertaking was acquired by Société Electro-Chimique du Giffre. Removed from Register 1904 .... **1902**

Gigantic Wheel and Recreation Towers Co. Ld. Regd. 1894. Vol. liq. 5 Jan. 1899. Reconstructed as London Gigantic Wheel Co. Ld. in which company share-holders were entitled to 1 fully-paid share of 10s. for each share of £1 held. Final meeting return regd. 27 Apr. 1899 .... **1906**

Gilbart Ld. See Whiteside (H. S.) & Co. Ld.

Gilbert (D. M.) & Co. Ld. Regd. 1937. Vol. liq. (members') 20 June 1956. Capital returned to contributories—4s. 1¼d. per share of 4s. £74 17s. 7d. was paid into Companies' Liquidation Account on account of unclaimed dividends. Final meeting return regd. 20 Mar. 1957 .... **1958**

Gilbert (F. W.) Ld. Regd. 1907. Vol. liq. (members') 28 Jan. 1931. Capital returned to contributories—£49,321 19s. 3d. Final meeting return regd. 19 Jan. 1934 .... **1931**

Gilbert Gold Mine Ld. Regd. 1901. Vol. liq. 6 Nov. 1912. Final meeting return regd. 12 Nov. 1913 .... **1913**

Gilbert, Hoare & Co. Ld. Regd. 1897. Struck off Register 9 Dec. 1902 .... **1902**

Gilbert River Goldfields Ld. Regd. 1900. Removed from Register 1906 .... **1903**

Gilberton (Queensland) Gold Mining Co. Ld. Regd. 1888. Vol. liq. 31 Dec. 1895. A payment of 6¾d. in £ was made to debenture holders; further payments (if any) not known. Final meeting return regd. 6 Mar. 1897 .... **1898**

Gilbertson (W.) & Co. Ld. Regd. 1885. Vol. liq. (members') 30 Mar. 1946. Undertaking acquired by Richard Thomas & Baldwins Ld. Final meeting return regd. 1 June 1948 .... **1941**

Gilford Motor Co. Ld. Regd. 1926. Vol. liq. (creditors') 31 Dec. 1935. Assets realised insufficient to pay unsecured creditors in full. Final meeting return regd. 23 Mar. 1937 .... **1936**

Gill & Bibbey Ld. Regd. 1909. Vol. liq. 30 June 1939. Undertaking acquired by I. C. I. Salt Ld. Capital returned to contributories—20s. per preference share of £1; 17s 3·49d. per ordinary share of £1. Final meeting return regd. 26 June 1940.............. **1943**

VOL. FOR

Gill & Reigate Ld. Regd. 1899. Vol. liq. (members') 30 Dec. 1935. Capital returned to contributories—£100 to ordinary, deferred and special shareholders. Final meeting return regd. 30 June 1937 .... **1936**

Gill McDowell Jarrah Co. Ld. Regd. 1900. Undertaking was acquired in 1902 by Millars' Karri and Jarrah Co. (1902) Ld. (later Millars' Timber and Trading Co. Ld.) for £134,375 in ordinary and preference shares. Vol. liq. 29 June 1903. Final meeting return regd. 18 July 1905 .... **1904**

Gillespie, Sons & Co. Ld. Regd. Edinburgh 1895. Vol. liq. 29 Oct. 1908. Struck off Register 22 Feb. 1924 **1910**

Gillett's Stores Ld. Regd. 1895. Vol. liq. 30 Dec. 1898. Final meeting return regd. 16 July 1902 .... **1899**

Gillingham Gas & Coke Co. Ld. Regd. 1860. Vol. liq. (members') 6 Apr. 1936. All shares held by Shaftesbury, Gillingham & District Gas Co. Ld. Final meeting return regd. 5 Sept. 1930 .... **1937**

Gillis Concession Syndicate Ld. Regd. 1905. Vol. liq. 26 June 1908. Final meeting return regd. 11 Dec. 1909 **1909**

Gillman & Spencer Ld. Regd. 1886. Undertaking was acquired by Messrs. R. S. & S. W. Paul of Ipswich. Capital returned to contributories—2s. in £; further payments (if any) not known. Removed from Register 1904 .... **1903**

Gilpin Gold Ld. Regd. 1895. Removed from Register 1909 .... **1898**

Gilroy, Sons & Co. Ld. Regd. Edinburgh 1890. Vol. liq. (members') 30 Dec. 1932. Undertaking was ac-quired by Jute Industries Ld. (later Jute Industries (Holdings) Ld.). Final meeting return regd. 1 Apr. 1933 .... **1932**

Gilwen Shipping Co. Ld. Regd. 1920. Struck off Register 1928 .... **1928**

Gimson Shoe Machinery Co. Ld. Regd. 1919. Vol. liq. (members') 9 May 1930. Undertaking way acquired by British United Shoe Machinery Co. Ld. Capital returned to contributories—20s. per preference share of £1; £1 6s. 1d. per ordinary share of £1. Final meeting return regd. 25 Mar. 1933 .... **1931**

Ginkap Investments (Proprietary) Ld. Inc. as C. T. C. Bazaars (Proprietary) Ld.; name subsequently changed. Undertaking acquired by C. T. C. Bazaars (Proprietary) Ld. **1937**

Ginsberg Gold Mining Co. Ld. Inc. Transvaal 1893. Vol. liq. Oct. 1920 .... **1921**

Giona Sulphur Co. Ld. Regd. 1886. Struck off Register 14 May 1897 .... **1901**

Gippsland Proprietary Co. Ld. Regd. 1890. Vol. liq. 12 Dec. 1892. Final meeting return regd. 28 July 1893 **1893**

Gipsy Queen Gold Mining Co. Ld. Regd. Edinburgh 1889. Vol. liq. Jan. 1893. Final meeting return regd. 19 Aug. 1896 .... **1893**

Girls' College Association Ld. See Farrington's Girls' School Ld.

Girvan & Portpatrick Junction Railway Co. Inc. by Special Act 1865. Under Act of 1886 line was sold to Ayrshire & Wigtownshire Railway Co. Holders of debenture stocks received A £53,635; B £42,910 and C (with creditors) £21,473. Ordinary and preference shareholders received no portion of purchase money **1890**

Girvan Gas Co. Ld. Regd. in Edinburgh 1907. Dissolved 1 May, 1949, undertaking being vested in Scottish Area Gas Board under Gas Act 1948. Holders of ordinary shares (of £1) were entitled to receive £2 British Gas 3% guaranteed stock 1990–95 for each share held **1952**

Glade Mining Co. Ld. Regd. 1899. Vol. liq. 18 Feb. 1904. Final meeting return regd. 5 Dec. 1905.............. **1905**

Gladiators Ld. Regd. 1898. Removed from Register 1904 .... **1902**

Gladstone Spinning Co. Ld. Regd. 1875. Vol. liq. (members') 28 Jan. 1946. Capital returned to contributories—11s. 6d. per 10s. stock. £51 15s. was paid into Companies' Liquidation Account. Final meeting return regd. 22 June 1946 .... **1947**

Gladwin (S.) Holdings Ld. Regd. 1922. Vol. liq. (members') 7 Nov. 1957. Undertaking and assets were acquired by Gladwin Ld. Capital returned to contributories—1st and 2nd preference shares of £1 were repaid at par; ordinary shares of £1, £1 19s. 2d. Amounts paid into Companies' Liquidation Ac-count—£590 15s. 4d. in respect of unclaimed distributions and £68 6s. in respect of unclaimed dividends. Final meeting return regd. 14 Aug. 1959 **1960**

Gladys Proprietary Gold Mines Ld. Regd. 1900. Re-moved from Register 1913 .... **1911**

Glamorgan Coal Co. Ld. Regd. 1892. Vol. liq. Nov. 1928. Struck off Register 24 July 1936 .... **1937**

Glamorgan Public House Trust Co. Ld. See South Wales Public House Trust Co. Ld.

Glamorgan Wagon Co. Ld. Regd. 1913. Vol. liq. (members') 28 June 1948. Capital returned to contributories—£20 16s. 11d. per share (of £10 with

VOL. FOR

£3 called up). Final meeting return regd. 22 Dec. 1955 .... **1956**

Glamorganshire Banking Co. Ld. Regd. 1884. Amalgamated in 1898 with Capital and Counties Bank Ld ... **1899**

Glanamman Anthracite Collieries Ld. Regd. 1907. Struck off Register 1915 .... **1910**

Glanrhyd Tinplate Co. Ld. Regd. 1883. Vol. liq. (members') 24 July 1933. All capital owned by Gilbertson (W.) & Co. Ld. Final meeting return regd. 13 Apr. 1934 .... **1934**

Glare-Visor Parent Co. Ld. Regd. 1928. Vol. liq. (creditors') 10 Feb. 1930 for amalgamation with Sphinx Electric Ld., in which company shareholders were entitled to 2 ordinary shares of 1s. (credited with 6d. paid) for every share of 2s. held. Assets realised insufficient to pay unsecured creditors in full. Final meeting return regd. 24 Sept. 1936 ...... **1930**

Glasbrook Brothers Ld. Regd. 1898. Vol. liq. (members') 9 Apr. 1952. Capital returned to contributories—13s. 3·114016d. per A ordinary share of 1s. and 4s. 5·289649d. per ordinary share of £1. £14 13s. 8d. paid into Companies' Liquidation Account. Final meeting return regd. 7 Mar.1957 .... **1958**

Glasgow African Trust Ld. Regd. Edinburgh 1895. Vol. liq. Sept. 1911. Final meeting return regd. 21 Oct. 1912 .... **1912**

Glasgow Albion Racing Company Ld. Regd. Edinburgh 1934. Vol. liq. (members') 8 Oct. 1959. Capital returned to contributories—5s. per ordinary share of 5s.; 9d. per deferred ordinary share of £220 8s. 8d. was paid to Accountant of the Court. Final meeting return regd. 30 Oct. 1962 .... **1963**

Glasgow Alhambra Ld. Regd. Edinburgh 1909. Vol. liq. Dec. 1919 for reconstruction under same name. Ordinary shareholders were entitled to 2 preference and 3 ordinary shares all of £1 in new company for every 2 shares of £1 held and deferred shareholders to the remaining 52,940 ordinary shares. Final meeting return regd. 12 Jan. 1921 .... **1920**

Glasgow Alhambra Ld. in Edinburgh 1919. Vol. liq. (members') 30 Mar. 1954. Undertaking acquired by Howard & Wyndham Ld. (all capital previously held by that company). £330 18s. 9d. deposited with the Accountant of the Court. Final meeting return regd. 6 Apr. 1955 .... **1956**

Glasgow American Trust Co. Ld. Regd. Edinburgh 1914. Vol. liq. (creditors') 16 Jan. 1946. Final meeting return regd. 5 Mar. 1948 .... **1949**

Glasgow and General Mutual Investment Trust Ld. Regd. 1928 under Industrial & Provident Societies' Acts; converted into company registered under Companies' Act in 1940. Vol. liq. (members') 27 Mar. 1945. Capital returned to contributories—2s. 1·9d. per share of 2s. Final meeting return regd. 7 Feb. 1946 .... **1947**

Glasgow & Ibrox Tramway Co. Inc. 1877. Line was sold to Govan commissioners **1892**

Glasgow & Montreal Asbestos Co. Ld. Regd. Edinburgh 1891. Vol. liq. Jan. 1908. Final meeting return regd. 14 Mar. 1910 .... **1908**

Glasgow & Renfrew District Railway Co. Inc. by Special Act 1897. Under Glasgow & South Western Railway Order Confirmation Act 1906 undertaking was transferred to Caledonian Railway Co. and Glasgow & South Western Railway Co................... **1907**

Glasgow & South African Co. Ld. Regd. Edinburgh 1865. Vol. liq. Sept. 1920. Capital returned to contributories—10s. per share of 10s. in Nov. 1920; further payments (if any) not known. Final meeting return regd. 4 Sept. 1923 .... **1921**

Glasgow and South Western Railway Co. Inc. by Special Act 1837 as Glasgow, Paisley, Kilmarnock & Ayr Railway Co.; name changed by Act of 1847 on amalgamation with the Glasgow, Dumfries & Carlisle Railway Co. In 1923 the undertaking was merged into the London Midland & Scottish Railway Co. in which company stockholders were entitled to stock as follows:

For each £100 held		L. M. & S.	
4% Debenture	£100	4% Debenture	
St. Enoch Sn. 4% Rent Charge	£100	4% Debenture	
4% Guaranteed	£100	4% Guarant'd	
4% Preference	£100	4% Preference	
4% Pref. No.2	£100	4% Preference	
4% Pref.(1888)	£100	4% Preference	
4% Pref. (1891)	£100	4% Preference	
4% Pref. (1894)	£100	4% Preference	
3% Preference	£75	4% Preference	
2⅞% Prefd. Ord.	£62½	4% Pref. (1923)	
Deferred Ord.	£34	Ordinary	
Deferred Stock	£3	Ordinary	**1924**

Glasgow and Western Exploration Co. Ld. Regd. Edinburgh 1896. Vol. liq. Mar. 1913. Final meeting return regd. 21 Apr. 1921 .... **1914**

Glasgow Assurance Corporation Ld. Regd. Edinburgh 1908. Vol. liq. 27 Feb. 1912. Court Order to continue winding up under supervision 20 Mar. 1912. Struck off Register 4 June 1937 .... **1938**

Glasgow Bag Wash and Laundry Services Ld. Regd. Edinburgh 1928. Vol. liq. (members') 19 Apr. 1944. Capital returned to contributories—9s. 3·788d. per deferred ordinary share of 6d.; 4s. 5·8188d. per preferred ordinary share of 2s. 8d. £141 6s. 1d. was paid into Companies' Liquidation Account. Final meeting return regd. 28 July 1945 .... **1946**

Glasgow Bonding Co. Ld. Regd. 1925. Vol. liq. (creditors') 30 Dec. 1929. Capital returned to contributories—3s. 3·72d. per preference share of £1. Final meeting return regd. 21 Mar. 1938 .... **1930**

Glasgow Caradon Consolidated Copper Mining Co. Ld. Regd. Edinburgh 1860. Vol. liq. 5 Mar. 1888. Final meeting return regd. 28 June 1889 .... **1889**

Glasgow Central Railway Co. Inc. by Special Act 1888. Under Caledonian Railway Co. Act undertaking was acquired by that company by repayment of capital at par **1890**

Glasgow Central Stores Ld. Regd. 1900. Vol. liq. Jan. 1909. Struck off Register 27 Oct. 1936 .... **1937**

Glasgow City & District Railway Co. Inc. by Special Act 1882. Under North British Railway Act 1887 undertaking was amalgamated with that company in which holders of ordinary stock received an equal amount of 5% perpetual lien stock; mortgages were exchanged for mortgages of purchasing company **1888**

Glasgow Coal Exchange Co. Ld. Regd. Edinburgh 1876. Vol. liq. 18 Dec. 1888. Final meeting return regd. 19 June 1896 .... **1890**

Glasgow Corn Exchange Co. Ld. Regd. Edinburgh 1897. Vol. liq. (members') 14 Dec. 1939. Capital returned to contributories—£8 10s. 5d. per share of £10. Final meeting return regd. 18 Apr. 1940 .... **1940**

Glasgow Cotton Spinning Co. Ld. Regd. Edinburgh 1883. Vol. liq. 22 Sept. 1928. Court Orders: to continue winding up under supervision 23 Oct. 1928: to dissolve 29 Nov. 1932 .... **1929**

Glasgow District Subway Co. See Glasgow Subway Railway Co.

Glasgow, Dublin & Londonderry Steam Packet Co. Ld. See Laird Line Ld.

Glasgow Empire Palace Ld. Regd. Edinburgh 1895. Reconstructed 1899 as Moss Empires Ld. in which company shareholders were entitled to 8 fully-paid preference shares of £5 plus £2 10s. in cash for every 10 shares of £5 held. Debenture holders were entitled to £105 debenture stock in new company for every £100 bonds held. Removed from Register 1909 .... **1900**

Glasgow Greyhound Racecourse Ld. Regd. Edinburgh 1927 Vol. liq. (members') 4 Dec.1936. The undertaking was acquired by White City (Glasgow) Ld., in which company shareholders were entitled to 3 shares of 1s. (credited as fully-paid) plus 4d. in cash for each preference share of 5s. held or 1 share of 1s. (credited as fully-paid) plus 1d. in cash for every 2 deferred shares of 1s. held. Final meeting return regd. 11 Nov. 1937 .... **1937**

Glasgow Harbour Tunnel Co. Inc. 1889 by Special Act. Vol. liq. May 1926. Undertaking sold to Glasgow Corporation for £100,000. Capital returned to contributories—(a) £5 4s. 6d. per share of £10 to 3 preference shareholders who did not agree to waive their preferences (b) £2 6s. 4d. per share of £10 to all other holders. **1927**

Glasgow Heritable Securities Co. Ld. Regd. Edinburgh 1873. Vol. liq. Aug. 1898. Final meeting return regd. 16 Aug. 1899 .... **1899**

Glasgow Merino Spinning Co. Ld. Regd. Edinburgh 1889. Vol. liq. Nov. 1899. Final meeting return regd. 27 Jan. 1902 .... **1900**

Glasgow Murchison Gold Mines Development Co. Ld. Regd. Edinburgh 1895. Undertaking acquired by United Australian Exploration Ld. Vol. liq. July 1896. Final meeting return regd. 30 Mar. 1900 .... **1879**

Glasgow Olympia Theatre of Varieties Ld. Regd. Edinburgh 1910. Vol. liq. (members') 30 Dec. 1937. Undertaking sold for £15,000 in cash. Capital returned to contributories—10s. 3¾d per share of £1. £109 6s. 5d. was paid to Accountant of the Court in respect of capital. Final meeting return regd. 6 Jan. 1939 .... **1938**

Glasgow, Paisley, Kilmarnock & Ayr Railway Co. See Glasgow & South Western Railway Co.

Glasgow Port Washington Iron and Coal Co. Ld. Regd. Edinburgh 1872. Vol. liq. Oct. 1881. Final meeting return regd. 19 Mar. 1888 .... **1883**

*See Stock Exchange Year-Book.

VOL. FOR

Glasgow Public Halls Co. Ld. Regd. Edinburgh 1873. Property sold to Glasgow Corporation for £37,500. Vol. liq. Feb. 1890. Final meeting return regd. 16 Dec. 1890 1891

Glasgow Rhodesian & Transvaal Mining Syndicate Ld. *See* Benzies Consolidated Gold Mines of South Africa Ld.

Glasgow Subway Railway Co. Inc. by Special Act as Glasgow District Subway Co.; name changed by Act of 1914. Undertaking sold to Glasgow Corporation in 1923. Capital returned to contributories—16s. 1d. per preference share; 10s. 8d. per ordinary share 1924

Glasgow Super-Aeration Ld. Regd. Edinburgh 1901. Vol. liq. Dec. 1902. Business transferred to London Super-Aeration Ld. in which company shareholders were entitled to 3 fully-paid shares of £1 for every 5 shares of £1 held. Final meeting return regd. 17 Aug. 1904 1903

Glasgow Tramway and Omnibus Co, Ld. Regd. 1871. Removed from Register 1908 .... 190?

Glasgow Union Banking Co. *See* Union Bank of Scotland Ld.

Glasgow Westralian Gold Mines Ld. Regd. Edinburgh. 1895. Vol. liq. Apr. 1898. Final meeting return regd. 11 Dec. 1901 1898

Glasgow Workmen's Dwellings Co. Ld. Regd. Edinburgh 1890. Vol. liq. (members') 25 Apr. 1950. Capital returned to contributories—£5 10s. per share (of £10). Return of final meeting regd. 28 May 1952 1954

Glasgow, Yoker & Clydebank Railway Co. Inc. by Special Act 1878. Under North British Railway Act 1897 undertaking was amalgamated with that company in which holders of 4% and 3½% debenture stocks received 3% debenture on basis of equal income; ordinary shareholders received £200 3% consolidated lien stock for every £100 held 1898

Glass Houghton & Castleford Collieries Ld. Regd. 1902. Vol. liq. 6 Aug. 1924. Undertaking was acquired by company of same name. Final meeting return regd. 18 Dec. 1925 1906

Glass Houghton and Castleford Collieries Ld. Regd. 1924 as Glass Houghton & Castleford Collieries (1924) Ld.; name changed Dec. 1926. Vol. liq. (members') 4 Apr. 1955 the undertakings having vested in National Coal Board. Capital returned to contributories—8s. 2·6d. per share of 4s. Final meeting return regd. 3 Sept. 1956 1957

Glass Houghton & Castleford Collieries (1924) Ld. *See above.*

Glass-Lined Syphon Co. Ld. Regd. 1891. Removed from Register 1900 1906

Glastonbury & District Gas Co. Ld. Regd. 1938. Dissolved 1 May 1949 undertaking being vested in South Western Area Gas Board under Gas Act 1948. Holders of securities were entitled to receive British Gas 3% guaranteed stock 1990-95 as follows;

	£ s. d.	
Ord.shares (5% stand.) (of £1)	1 2 0	
4% red. debs (of £100)	101 10 0	1952

Glave (Henry) Ld. Regd. 1922. Struck off Register 24 Jan. 1936 1936

Glazebrooks (Holdings) Ld. *See* Permoglaze Holdings Ld.

Gleboff Grosny Petroleum Co. Ld. Regd. 1910. Vol. liq. (creditors') 1 July 1930. No capital returned to contributories. Final meeting return regd. 29 July 1931 1931

Gleeson's Success Gold Mines Ld. Regd. Edinburgh 1897. Vol. liq. Apr. 1902. Final meeting return regd. 7 May 1903 1903

Glen Bervie Rubber Co. Ld. Regd. 1908. Vol. liq. (members') 6 Jan. 1933. Undertaking and assets were acquired by company of same name. Shareholders were entitled to 10 shares of 2s. (credited with 1s. 8d. paid) in new company for each share of £1 held and option (since expired) over further shares. Final meeting return regd. 3 Nov. 1934 ... 1933

Glen Bervie Rubber Co. Ld. Regd. 1933. Acquired undertaking and assets of company of same name. Vol. liq. (members') 27 Oct. 1955. Capital returned to contributories—1d. per share of 2s. Final meeting return regd. 3 Nov. 1962 1964

Glen Deep Ld. Inc. Transvaal 1895. Vol. liq. Nov. 1909. Undertaking and assets were acquired by Rose Deep Ld. in which company shareholders were entitled to 45 fully-paid shares of £1 for every 100 shares of £1 held. 1910

Glen Elgin Gold Mines Ld. Regd. 1891. Struck off Register 13 Oct. 1908 1909

Glen Lorna Tea Co. Ld. Regd. 1914. Vol. liq. 14 Nov. 1928. Final meeting return regd. 13 Mar. 1930 1929

VOL. FOR

Glen May (Rhodesia) Mines Ld. Regd. 1914. Court order to wind up Dec. 1915. Struck off Register 1923 1916

Glen Mill Ld. Regd. 1902. Vol. liq. (members') 10 Oct. 1938. Capital returned to contributories—8s. 10d. per preference share of £1. Final meeting return regd. 6 Dec. 1939 1939

Glen Muar Rubber Estates Ld. Regd. 1925. Vol. liq. 27 June 1928. Reconstructed as Glen Muar Estates Ld. in which company shareholders were entitled to 4 shares of 1s. (credited with 1s. 3d. paid) for every 5 shares of 2s. held. Final meeting return regd. 22 Mar. 1929. Court Order deferred dissolution until 19 Sept. 1929 1926

Glen Rubber & Tea Co. Ld. *See below.*

Glen Rubber Co. Ld. Regd. 1910 as Glen Rubber & Tea Co. Ld.; name changed Dec. 1929. Vol. liq. (members') 23 July 1951. Capital returned to contributories—4s. 6½d. per share (of 2s.). £34 4s. 2d. was lodged with the Accountant of the Court. Final meeting return regd. 14 Oct. 1955 1956

Glenariff Railway & Pier Co. Inc. by Special Act 1865 1890

Glenburn Hydropathic Co. Ld. Regd. Edinburgh 1897. Vol. liq. (creditors') 28 Jan. 1936. Final meeting return regd. 15 June 1938 1936

Glencairn Main Reef Gold Mining Co. Ld. Inc. Transvaal 1889. Vol. liq. Oct. 1920 1921

Glencoe (Natal) Collieries Ld. Inc. Natal 1901. Vol. liq. June 1921. Undertaking and certain assets were acquired by Natal Navigation Collieries & Estate Co. Ld., in which company shareholders were entitled to 1 share of £1 (credited as fully-paid) for every 3 shares held; a first cash distribution of 2s. 6d. per share was made; further payments (if any) not known 1922

Glendower Hotel Ld. Regd. 1887. Vol. liq. 7 Oct. 1890. Final meeting return regd. 23 Oct. 1893 1891

Gleneagles Shoe Co. Ld. Regd. Edinburgh 1927. Vol. liq. (members') 18 June 1942. Direct controlling interest was held by Saxone Shoe Co. Ld. [later Saxone Lilley & Skinner (Holdings) Ld.] £887 2s. 8d. was returned to contributories. Final meeting return regd. 28 Nov. 1942 1943

Glengarnock Iron & Steel Co. Ld. Regd. Edinburgh 1892. Vol. liq. July 1917. Undertaking was acquired by David Colville & Sons Ld. Final meeting return regd. 24 May 1918 1918

Glenhafod Collieries Ld. Regd. 1920. Vol. liq. (members') 9 Apr. 1952. Capital returned to contributories—12s. per share of 5s. Final meeting return regd. 9 Oct. 1956 1958

Glenlossie-Glenlivet Distillery Co. Ld. Regd. Edinburgh 1897. Vol. liq. (members') 30 June 1930. Capital returned to contributories—£167,506 7s. 3d. Final meeting return regd. 4 Sept. 1931 1931

Glenluce Gold Mining Co. Ld. Inc. South African Republic 1895. Amalgamated 1896 with Glencairn Main Reef Gold Mining Co. Ld. 1909

Glenmore (Nigeria) Tea Co. Ld. Regd. 1912. Vol. liq. 16 Aug. 1920. Final meeting return regd. 5 July 1921 *1921

Glenmurray Investment Trust Ld. *See* Murray Minor Investment Trust Ld.

Glenny's Brewery Ld. Undertaking and assets were acquired by Taylor Walker & Co. Ld. (later Ind Coope (East Anglia) Ld.) 1930

Glenrock Co. Ld. Regd. 1884. Vol. liq. 3 May 1890. Reconstructed 1895 as Glenrock Consolidated Ld., in which company shareholders were entitled to 2 shares of 10s. (credited with 8s. paid) for each share of £1 held. Final meeting return regd. 25 Mar. 1901 1899

Glenrock Consolidated Ld. Regd. 1895. Reconstructed 1899 as company of same name. Shareholders were entitled to 1 share of 10s. (credited with 9s. paid) in new company for each share of 10s. held. Removed from Register 1905 1901

Glenrock Consolidated Ld. Regd. 1899. Reconstructed 1901 as Indian Glenrock (Wynaad) Co. Ld. in which company shareholders were entitled to 1 share of 10s. (credited with 8s. 6d. paid) for each share of 10s. held. Removed from Register 1905 1902

Glenshiel Rubber Estates Co. Ld. Regd. 1908. Vol. liq. 19 Dec. 1919. Reconstructed as company of same name. Shareholders were entitled to 5 shares of £1 (credited as fully-paid) in new company for each share of £1 held. Final meeting return regd. 10 Feb. 1922 1920

Glenshiel Rubber Estates Company Ld. Regd. 1919. Vol. liq. 31 Dec. 1946. Undertaking was acquired by Bagan Serai Rubber Estates Ld. in which company shareholders were entitled to 3 fully-paid shares of £1 for every 2 shares of £1 held. £30 19s. 9d. was paid into Companies' Liquidation Account. Final meeting return regd. 1 June 1948 1949

Glentaffe Tea Estates, Ld. Regd. 1925. Vol. liq. (members') 8 Dec. 1955. Capital returned to

See Stock Exchange Year-Book.

VOL. FOR

contributories—10s. 9d. per share of 2s. 6d. £94 9s. 4d. was paid into Companies' Liquidaton Account. Final meeting return regd. 3 May 1957.............. **1958**

Glico Petroleum Ld. Regd. 1888 as Gas Lighting Improvement Co. Ld.; name changed May 1924. Vol. liq. (members') 5 Oct. 1931. Undertaking and assets absorbed by Redline Motor Spirit Co. Ld. (later Redline-Glico Ld.) in which company shareholders were entitled to 1½ fully-paid shares for every preference or ordinary share of £1 held. £45 10s. was paid into Companies' Liquidation Account in respect of undistributed balance and £85 13s. 1d. in respect of unclaimed dividend. Final meeting return regd. 4 June 1936 .... **1932**

Globe Accident Insurance Co. Ld. Regd. 1890. Vol. liq. 18 May 1901. Final meeting return regd. 7 Aug. 1902 **1902**

Globe Blocks Gold Mining Co. Ld. Regd. 1895. Vol. liq. 30 June 1896. Liquidator released 2 June 1898. Removed from Register 10 July 1908 .... ***1897**

Globe Cashier (British and Foreign) Ld. Regd. 1897. Vol. liq. 23 July 1901. Final meeting return regd. 11 Sept. 1902 .... **1902**

Globe Collieries Ld. Regd. 1914. All capital was owned by Town Line (London) Ld. Receiver appointed Jan. 1925; ceased to act Sept. 1928. Struck off Register 9 Dec. 1930 .... **1926**

Globe Cotton Spinning and Manufacturing Co. Ld. Regd. 1865. Vol. liq. (members') 15 Mar. 1934. Capital returned to contributories—9¾d. per share of £7, £6 paid. Final meeting return regd. 30 Apr. 1935 **1935**

Globe Industrial & General Trust Corporation Ld. Regd. Nov. 1889. Vol. liq. 17 Jan. 1896. Final meeting return regd. 24 Oct. 1899 .... **1896**

Globe Marine Insurance Co. Ld. Regd. 1870. Vol. liq. 22 Feb. 1899. Goodwill (subject to certain qualifications) was taken over by United Dutch Marine Insurance Companies. FInal meeting return regd. 1 Aug. 1911 .... **1899**

Globe Minerals Exploration Co. Ld. Regd. 1898. Vol. liq. 14 Feb. 1902. Removed from Register 1903 .. **1902**

Globe Oilfields Ld. Regd. 1919. Vol. liq. (members') 15 Dec. 1930. Undertaking and assets acquired by Premier Globe Ld. in which company shareholders received 2 fully-paid shares of 5s. for every 5 fully-paid 1st preference shares of 2s. held. Final meeting return regd. 20 Jan. 1938 .... **1931**

Globe Plate Glass Insurance Co. Ld. Regd. 1882. Removed from Register 1889 .... ***1885**

Globe Rubber Corporation Ld. Regd. 1910. Removed from Register 29 Aug. 1913 .... ***1913**

Globe Shipping Co. Ld. Regd. 1915. Vol. liq. (members') 28 Aug. 1940. Capital returned to contributories— £250. Final meeting return regd. 12 Dec. 1945 ..... **1946**

Globe Trading Co. Ld. Regd. 1898. Removed from Register 26 July 1912 .... ***1908**

Globe Venture Syndicate Ld. Regd. 1896. Court Order to wind up 26 June 1900. Removed from Register 1909 **1901**

Globe-Wernicke Co. Ld. Regd. 1906. Vol. liq. 26 May 1947. Final meeting return regd. 27 May 1948 ... **1938**

Globe Wine Co. Ld. Regd. 1882. Removed from Register 1906 .... ***1884**

Globe Worsted Co. Ld. Regd. 1887. Vol. liq. 5 Mar. 1953. Final meeting return regd. 28 Oct. 1953 ..... **1948**

Glossop Gas Co. Inc. by Special Act 1845. Dissolved 1 May 1949 undertaking being vested in North Western Area Gas Board under Gas Act 1948. Holders of securities were entitled to receive British Gas 3% guaranteed stock 1990-95 as follows in respect of each £10 unit unless otherwise stated of security held:

	£	s.	d.
Orig. shares (10% max.)	19	10	0
Orig. ½ shares (10% max.) (of £5)...	9	15	0
New shares (7½% max.)	14	12	0
B shares (7½% max.)	14	12	0
C shares (7% max.)	13	12	0

1952

Gloucester (City Of) Tramways Co. Ld. Regd. 1881. Undertaking sold to Corporation of Gloucester. Struck off Register 1904 .... **1903**

Gloucester Gas Light Co. Inc. by Special Act 1820. Dissolved 1 May 1949 undertaking being vested in South Western Area Gas Board under Gas Act 1948. Holders of securities were entitled to receive in respect of each £100 unit held British Gas 3% guaranteed stock 1990-95 as follows:

	£	s.	d.
Cons. ord. stock (5% basic)	122	10	0
4% red. pref. stock	102	5	0
4% perp. deb. stock	103	0	0
3½% red. deb. stock (1963)	99	10	0
3½% red. deb. stock (1961)	100	0	0

A distribution on cons. ord. stock of 7·577% out of reserves was made in Oct. 1953 .... **1952**

Gloucester & Berkeley Canal Co. See Sharpness Docks & Gloucester & Birmingham Navigation Co.

Gloucester Gold Mining Co. Ld. Regd. 1896. Vol. liq. 12 Jan. 1900. Properties were acquired by Amalgamated Gold Mines Ld. for 5,000 fully-paid shares of 10s. Final meeting return regd. 18 Mar. 1902 .... **1901**

Gloucester Paper Mills Ld. Regd. 1915. Vol. liq. 18 June 1917. Final meeting return regd. 24 Dec. 1917 ..... **1918**

Gloucester Wagon Co. Ld. Regd. 1860. Vol. liq. Sept. 1888. Reconstructed as Gloucester Railway Carriage and Wagon Co. Ld. in which company shareholders were entitled to 1 A share of £7 (credited as fully-paid) for each fully-paid share of £10 held or 1 B share of £7 (credited with £3 10s. paid) for each share of £10 (£5 paid) held. Final meeting return regd. 28 Aug. 1889 .... **1889**

Gloucestershire Banking Co. Ld. Est. 1831; regd. 1882. Amalgamated in Aug. 1885 with the Capital and Counties Bank Ld in which company shareholders received 27,500 shares of £50 .... **1886**

Gloucestershire Cinemas (1920) Ld. See Plough Hotel Cheltenham Ld.

Gloucestershire County Ground Co. Ld. Regd. 1888. Vol. liq. 6 Feb. 1917. Final meeting return regd. 13 May 1918 .... **1917**

Gloucestershire Electric Power Co. Inc. by Special Act 1902 .... **1909**

Glover & Sons Ld. Regd. 1898. Vol. liq. 10 June 1920. Brewery and certain licensed properties were acquired by J. W. Green Ld. (later Flowers Breweries Ld.). Final meeting return regd. 25 Nov. 1921...... **1921**

Glover (William) & Sons Ld. Regd. 1891. Vol. liq. 30 Dec. 1907. Removed from Register 1911 .... **1908**

Glyn Quarries Ld. Regd. 1910. Vol. liq. 12 Sept. 1947. Final meeting return regd. 16 Sept. 1952 .... **1938**

Glyn Slate Co. Ld. Regd. 1892. Vol. liq. 16 July 1910. Undertaking acquired by Glyn Quarries Ld. Final meeting return regd. 14 Dec. 1911 .... ***1911**

Glyn Valley Tramway. Inc. by Special Act 1866 as Ellesmere & Glyn Valley Railway; name changed by Act of 1870. Vol. liq. (creditors') 7 Oct. 1935 .. **1936**

Glyncorrwg Colliery Co. Ld. Regd. 1890. Struck off Register Feb. 1930 .... **1931**

Glyndwr Mining Co. Ld. Regd. 1889. Vol. liq. 19 Mar. 1891. Final meeting return regd. 22 June 1894 ..... **1892**

Glynhir Tin Plate Co. Ld. Regd. 1910. All capital was owned by Bynea Steel Works Ld. Vol. liq. 12 Jan. 1965. Final meeting return regd. 22 June 1965 ..... **1958**

Glynn Shipping Co. Ld. Regd. 1919. Vol. liq. 10 Apr. 1922. Struck off Register 1929 .... ***1923**

Glynn's Extension (Lydenburg) Ld. Regd. 1909. Vol. liq. June 1910 for reconstruction as Glynn's Extension (1910) Ld. in which company shareholders were entitled to 4 shares of 5s. (credited with 4s. paid) for each share of £1 held. Removed from Register 1912 **1911**

Glynn's Extension (1910) Ld. Regd. 1910. Vol. liq. Feb. 1912. Removed from Register 1914................... **1913**

Glynn's Lydenburg Ld. Inc. in Transvaal 1895. Vol. liq. (members') 13 Dec. 1950. Undertaking and assets acquired by Transvaal Gold Mining Estates Ld. in which company shareholders were entitled to receive 1 fully-paid share of £1 plus 1s. accrued dividend for every 2 shares of £1 held. Dissolved 16 Aug. 1951. Outstanding monies handed to Master of Supreme Court and Custodian of Enemy Property 30 Jan. 1952 .... **1952**

Goch (George) Amalgamated Gold Mining Co. Ld. Inc. Pretoria 1889. Reconstructed 1892 as company of same name. Shareholders were entitled to 2 shares of £1 in new company for every 5 shares of £1 held **1893**

Goch (George) Amalgamated Gold Mining Co. Ld. Inc South African Republic 1892. Reconstructed 1899 as New Goch Gold Mines Ld. in which company shareholders were entitled to 1 fully-paid share of £1 for every 3 shares of £1 held **1908**

Godalming Gas & Coke Co. Ld. Inc. by Deed of Co-partnership 1836; registered as limited 1874; parliamentary powers 1878. Dissolved 1 May 1949 undertaking being vested in South Eastern Area Gas Board under Gas Act 1948. Holders of securities were entitled to receive British Gas 3% guaranteed stock 1990-95 as follows:

	£	s.	d.
Orig. ord. shares (10% stand.) (of £5).................................	10	5	0
New ord. shares (7% stand.) (of £10)...............................	14	10	0
5% pref. shares (of £5)	5	12	0
4% mort. debs. (red.) (of £100)	100	5	0
4% red. debs. (1962) (of £100)	101	10	0

1952

Godavari Estates Ld. Regd. 1898. Removed from Register 29 Aug. 1911 .... ***1910**

Goddard, Massey & Warner Ld. Regd. 1898. Receiver appointed on 1 Apr. 1914. Struck off Register 1921 **1915**

Godsell & Sons Ld. Regd. 1905. Vol. liq. 26 July 1928. Undertaking and assets were acquired by Stroud Brewery Co. Ld. Final meeting return regd. 11 July 1929 1929

Godstone District Gas Co. Ld. Regd. 1890. Undertaking was acquired by East Surrey Gas Co. in 1924 1911

Godwin & Son Ld. Regd. 1905. Court Order to wind up 1906. Removed from Register 1911 1907

Goebel Brewing Co. Ld. Regd. 1889 as Detroit Breweries Ld.; name changed Mar. 1891. Vol. liq. 27 Mar. 1919. Final meeting return regd. 27 Mar. 1922 1919

Gokak Cotton Mills Ld. Regd. 1919. Vol. liq. 2 Dec. 1920. Final meeting return regd. 10 Aug. 1921 1921

Golborne Gas Co. Inc. by Special Act 1901. Dissolved 1 May 1949 undertaking being vested in North Western Area Gas Board under Gas Act 1948. Holders of ordinary shares and ¼ shares were entitled to receive in respect of each £10 unit held £13 10s. British Gas 3% guaranteed stock 1990-95 1952

Golconda Gold Mines Ld. Regd. 1894. Vol. liq. 20 Jan. 1896. Reconstructed as company of same name. Shareholders were entitled to 1 share of £1 (credited with 15s. paid) in new company for each share of £1 held. Final meeting return regd. 7 Nov. 1896 1902

Golconda Malay Rubber Co. Ld. Regd. 1907. Vol. liq. (members') 9 Jan. 1959. Undertaking and assets acquired by Anglo Oriental Plantations Ld. in which shareholders were entitled to 9 fully-paid shares of 2s. plus 5s. cash for each share of £1 held. £62 10s. paid into Companies' Liquidation Account. Final meeting return regd. 7 Dec. 1960 1962

Golconda Gold Mines Ld. Regd. 1896. Vol. liq. 13 May 1902. Reconstructed as Golconda Mines Ld. Shareholders were entitled to 1 share of £1 (credited with 17s. paid) in new company for each share of £1 held. Final meeting return regd. 23 July 1903 1908

Golconda Mines Ld. Regd. 1902. Struck off Register 9 Mar. 1928 1928

Gold & General Investment Trust Ld. Regd. 1933. Vol. liq. (members') 27 May 1946. Capital returned to contributories—£1 5s. per share of £1. Final meeting return regd. 21 Feb. 1947 1947

Gold and Silver Extraction Co. of America Ld. Regd. Edinburgh 1893. Vol. liq. April 1907. Final meeting return regd. 1 July 1907 1908

Gold Coast Agency Ld. Regd. 1900. Vol. liq. 10 Aug. 1901. Reconstructed as New Gold Coast Agency Ld. in which company shareholders were entitled to 10 fully-paid shares of £1 for each share of £1 held. Final meeting return regd. 2 May 1902 1908

Gold Coast Amalgamated Mines Ld. See Amalgamated Mining Trust Ld.

Gold Coast & Ashanti Corporation Ld. Regd. 1903. Removed from Register 1911 1909

Gold Coast & Ashanti Explorers Ld. Regd. 1899. Vol. liq. July 1908. Assets were acquired by Ashanti Rivers and Concessions Ld. for 20,000 ordinary and 20,000 deferred shares of 10s. (credited as fully-paid) and 19,993 shares of 6d. in Ashanti Properties Ld. Removed from Register 1909 1909

Gold Coast & Ashanti Stool Concessions Ld. Regd. 1934. Vol. liq. 25 Nov. 1938. All shares owned by General Mines Investment Ld. Final meeting return regd. 24 Jan. 1941 1939

Gold Coast and General Syndicate, Limited. Regd. 1925. Vol. liq. (members') 6 July 1942. Capital returned to contributories—4¾d. per share of 5s. Final meeting return regd. 17 Mar. 1948 1948

Gold Coast Associated Companies Ld. Regd. 1934. Vol. liq. (members') 22 June 1938. Undertaking and assets were acquired by London & African Mining Trust Ld. (later London & Associated Investment Trust Ld.) in which company shareholders were entitled to 7 shares of 1s. (credited as fully-paid) for every 2 shares of 5s. held. Final meeting return regd. 3 May 1941............................... 1939

Gold Coast Banket Areas Ld. Regd. 1933. Vol. liq. (members') 28 Feb. 1950. Undertaking and assets (excluding certain shares in South Banket Areas Ld. were acquired by Amalgamated Banket Areas Ld. in which company shareholders were entitled to receive 1 share (or stock unit) of 3s. for every 2 shares of 2s. held. Final meeting return regd. 28 Sept. 1962 1963

Gold Coast Cold Storage Co. Ld. Regd. 1912. Vol. liq. 8 July 1920. Direct controlling interest owned by United Africa Co. Ld. Final meeting return regd. 13 Mar. 1934 1930

Gold Coast Concessions Ld. Regd. 1902. Vol. liq. (members') 1 Apr. 1935 for amalgamation with Associated Ashanti Gold Mine Areas Ld. Final meeting return regd. 12 July 1937 1936

Gold Coast Consolidated Lands Ld. Regd. 1909. Vol. liq. 24 Feb. 1921. Reconstructed as company of same

name. Shareholders were entitled to 5 shares of 2s. (credited with 1s. 4d. paid) in new company for every 2 shares of 5s. held. Final meeting return regd. 5 Sept. 1921 1922

Gold Coast Consolidated Lands Ld. Regd. 1921. Vol. liq. 23 Jan. 1929 for reconstruction as company of same name. Shareholders were entitled to 1 fully-paid share of 2s. for each preferred ordinary share of 2s. or every 4 ordinary shares of 2s. held. Final meeting return regd 27 June 1930 1929

Gold Coast Consolidated Lands, Ld. Regd. 1929. Vol. liq. (members') 11 Mar. 1931. Undertaking and assets were acquired by company of same name. Shareholders were entitled to 1 fully-paid share and 1 share of 2s. 6d. (credited with 2s. 2d. paid) for each ordinary share of 2s. held or 1 share of 2s. 6d. (credited with 2s. 2d. paid) for each deferred share of 2s. held. Final meeting return regd. 24 Mar. 1932 ... 1932

Gold Coast Development Syndicate Ld. Regd. 1895. Winding-up Order 24 July 1961. Struck off Register 19 Jan. 1968 1959

Gold Coast Estates Ld. Regd. 1900. Reconstructed 1903 as company of same name. Shareholders were entitled to 1 share of £1 (credited with 16s. 6d. paid) in new company for each share of £1 held. Removed from Register 1904 1908

Gold Coast Estates Ld. Regd. 1903. Struck off Register 1915 1914

Gold Coast Exploration and Trading Co. Ld. Regd. 1895. Court Order to wind up 17 July 1906. Liquidator released 29 Aug. 1912. Struck off Register 10 Oct. 1916 1907

Gold Coast Exploration Co. Ld. Regd. 1933. Vol. liq. (members') 11 Oct. 1934 for amalgamation with Anglo-Egyptian Land Co. Ld. Final meeting return regd. 6 Mar. 1935 1935

Gold Coast Explorers Ld. Regd. 1909. Vol. liq. 15 June 1927. Reconstructed as Ariston Gold Mines Ld. in which company shareholders were entitled to 1 share of 1s. (credited with 4d. paid) for each share of 1s. held. Final meeting return regd. 5 Apr. 1930 ... 1928

Gold Coast Founders' Syndicate Ld. Regd. 1901. Struck off Register 20 Nov. 1908 1909

Gold Coast Investment Co. Ld. Regd. 1901. Removed from Register 1909 1942

Gold Coast Machinery & Trading Co. Ld. Regd. 1901. Vol. liq. (members') 20 Feb. 1931. All shares owned by United Africa Co. Ld. Final meeting return regd. 4 Apr. 1942 1931

Gold Coast Mining Co. Ld. Regd. 1880. Removed from Register 1905 1886

Gold Coast Oil & Bitumen Corporation Ld. Regd. 1906. Vol. liq. Sept. 1909. Undertaking and assets were sold to Société Francaise de Pétrole Ld. in which company shareholders were entitled to 5 fully-paid shares of £1 for every 4 shares of £1 held. Removed from Register 1910 1910

Gold Coast Petroleum Ld. Regd. 1926. Vol. liq. (members') 18 Feb. 1949. Capital returned to contributories—5¾d. per share of 2s. £2,366 6s. 4d. was paid into Companies' Liquidation Account. Final meeting return regd. 10 July 1952............. 1953

Gold Coast Pioneer Syndicate Ld. Regd. 1900. Vol. liq. 25 July 1906. Removed from Register 1907 1907

Gold Coast Proprietary Mines Ld. See Gold Proprietary Mines Ld.

Gold Coast Prospectors' Syndicate Ld. Regd. 1900. Vol. liq. 18 Dec. 1902. Undertaking was acquired by Gold Coast United Ld. in which company shareholders were entitled to 9 fully-paid shares of 10s. for every 5 shares of £1 held. Removed from Register 1904 1904

Gold Coast Rubber and Mahogany Estates Ld. Regd. 1910. Court Order to wind up 26 Feb. 1912. Liquidator released 7 Oct. 1920. Struck off Register 20 Mar. 1923 1913

Gold Coast United Ld. Regd. 1902. Vol. liq. May 1910. Removed from Register 1913 1911

Gold Coast (Wassaw) Deep Levels Syndicate Ld. Regd. 1901. Vol. liq. Feb. 1909. Undertaking and assets were acquired by Fanti Consolidated Mines Ld., in which company shareholders were entitled to 1 share of 10s. (credited as fully-paid) for each ordinary share of £1 held or 3 shares of 10s. (credited as fully-paid) for each deferred share of £1 held. Removed from Register 1909 1909

Gold Consols Ld. Regd. 1895. Removed from Register 1914 1900

Gold Corporation Ld. Regd. 1933. Vol. liq. (members') 5 Aug. 1937. Undertaking and certain assets were acquired by Nigel Van Ryn Reefs Ld. [later Nigel Finance and Investment Ld.), in which company shareholders were entitled to 2 shares of 1s. (credited

VOL. FOR

as fully-paid) for each share of 2s. 6d. held. Final meeting return regd. 3 Aug. 1940 .... **1938**

Gold Creek Placer Mines, Montana Ld. Regd. 1906. Vol. liq. 4 Jan. 1922. Final meeting return regd. 19 Dec. 1922 .... **1922**

Gold Discovery Co. Ld. Regd. Edinburgh 1895. Vol. liq. June 1896. Final meeting return regd. 12 Apr. 1910 **1897**

Gold Estates of Australia Ld. Regd. 1894. Undertaking and assets were acquired by Gold Estates of Australia (1903) Ld. for £50,000 in shares of 2s. Removed from Register 1905 .... **1902**

Gold Estates of Colombia Ld. Regd. 1898. Vol. liq. 31 May 1905. Property was acquired by Anglo-Colombian Investment Co. Ld in which company shareholders were entitled to 95 shares of £1 for every 100 shares of £1 held. Removed from Register 1906 .... **1905**

Gold Estates Transvaal Co. Ld. Regd. 1888. Vol. liq. 17 Mar. 1896. Reconstructed as company of same name. Shareholders were entitled to 1 share of £1 for every 2 shares of £1 held. Final meeting return regd. 14 June 1898 .... **1897**

Gold Estates Transvaal Co. Ld. Regd. 1896. Vol. liq. 2 Jan. 1902. Assets were acquired by Henderson's Transvaal Estates Ld. for 34,790 fully-paid shares of £1. Final meeting return regd. 15 Dec. 1903 .... **1902**

Gold Exploration & Finance Co. of Australia Ld. Regd. 1934. Vol. liq. (members') 30 Nov. 1949 undertaking having been acquired by Western Mining Corpn. Ld. Stockholders received 15s. stock of Western Mining Corpn. Ld. per £1 stock held. £365 3s. 4d. was paid into Companies' Liquidation Account. Final meeting return regd. 6 Mar. 1951 .... **1952**

Gold Exploration of Western Australia Ld. Regd. 1894. Vol. liq. 13 Dec. 1897. Reconstructed as West Australian Gold Concessions Ld. in which company shareholders were entitled to 1 share of £1 (credited with 17s. 6d. paid) for each share of £1 held. Final meeting return regd. 20 July 1899 .... **1903**

Gold Explorers Ld. Regd. 1895. Vol. liq. 3 June 1898. Assets were acquired by Emperor Gold Mines Ld. in which company shareholders were entitled to 1 share of 10s. (credited with 7s. 6d. paid) for every 2 shares of 5s. held. Removed from Register 1901 . **1899**

Gold Explorers of Canada Ld. Regd. 1896. Vol. liq. 30 Dec. 1908. Struck off Register 10 Oct. 1916.......... **1909**

Gold Extraction & Bromine Recovery Co. Ld. Regd. 1897. Vol. liq. 20 May 1904. Removed from Register 1905 .... **1905**

Gold Field of Appolonia Mining Co. Ld. Regd. 1887. Court Orders: to wind up Feb. 1890; to dissolve 11 Jan. 1892 .... **1891**

Gold Fields Australian Development Co. Ld. Regd. 1932. Vol. liq. (members') 28 Dec. 1967. Capital returned to contributors—2s. 0·7d. per share of 1s. Final meeting return regd. 24 Mar. 1969 .... **1970**

Gold Fields Deep Ld. Inc. South African Republic 1893. Assets were acquired by Consolidated Gold Fields of South Africa Ld. in which company shareholders were entitled to 2 shares of £1 (credited as fully-paid) plus 4s. in cash for each share of £1 held. The debentures were repaid at 105% **1899**

Gold Fields Hydraulic Mining & Exploration Co. Ld. Inc. Transvaal 1925. Vol. liq. Sept. 1927 .... **1928**

Gold Fields of British Columbia Ld. Regd. 1897. Vol. liq. 19 Jan. 1897. Assets were acquired by Empire Gold Fields Ld. In which company shareholders were entitled to 1 share of £1 (credited with 19s. paid) for every 5 shares of £1 held. Struck off Register 19 Oct. 1906 .... **1901**

Gold Fields of Dharwar (India) Ld. Regd. 1904. Vol. liq. 17 June 1910. Capital returned to contributories—6d. per share of £1 in July 1910; further payments (if any) not known. Final meeting return regd. 31 May 1934 .... **1911**

Gold Fields of Eastern Akim Ld. Regd. 1898. Vol. liq. June 1908. Removed from Register 1912 .... **1909**

Gold Fields of India Ld. Regd. 1896. Vol. liq. 27 Dec. 1899. Removed from Register 1903 .... **1900**

Gold Fields of Lydenburg Ld. Inc. South African Republic 1895. Undertaking and property acquired by Alice Proprietary Mines (Rhodesia) Ld., in which company shareholders were entitled to 1 fully-paid share of £1 for every 6 shares of £1 held. Final meeting return regd. 1 June 1901................. **1908**

Gold Fields of Mazoe Ld. Regd. 1895. Vol. liq. 28 Mar. 1899. Taken over by Alice Proprietary Mines (Rhodesia) Ld. Final meeting return regd.6 Dec. 1901 .... **1908**

Gold Fields of Mexico Ld. Regd. 1896. Undertaking was transferred to Palmarejo and Mexican Gold Fields Ld. for £60,000 in fully-paid shares, £25,000 in debentures and £13,000 in cash. Removed from Register 1906 .... **1899**

VOL. FOR

Gold Fields of Mozambique Ld. Regd. 1893. Removed from Register 1908 .... **1904**

Gold Fields of Mysore Ld. Regd. 1886. Vol. liq. 2 Feb. 1898. Reconstructed as company of same name. Shareholders were entitled to 1 share of £1 (credited with 15s. paid) in new company for each share of £1 held. Final meeting return regd. 17 June 1899 ..... **1902**

Gold Fields of Mysore Ld. Regd. 1898. Vol. liq. 27 Mar. 1902. Reconstructed as Gold Fields of Mysore & General Exploration Co. Ld., In which company shareholders were entitled to 1 share of £1 (credited with 12s. 6d. paid) for each share of £1 held. Final meeting return regd. 27 Mar. 1903..................... **1907**

Gold Fields of New Zealand Ld. Regd. 1895. Vol. liq. 30 Aug. 1899. Final meeting return regd.8 Nov. 1901 **1900**

Gold Fields of North Queensland Ld. Regd. 1888. Vol. liq. 3 Sept. 1891. Final meeting return regd. 8 Apr. 1893 .... **1892**

Gold Fields of Siam Ld. Regd. 1888. Struck off Register 18 Nov. 1902 .... **1903**

Gold Fields of South Africa Ld. Regd. 1887. Vol. liq. 21 Nov. 1892. Reconstructed as Consolidated Gold Fields of South Africa Ld., (later Consolidated Gold Fields Ld.) in which company shareholders were entitled to 1 share of £1 (credited as fully-paid) for each ordinary share of £1 held. Final meeting return regd. 18 Dec. 1894..................... **1892**

Gold Fields of Tierra del Fuego Ld. Regd. 1888. Struck off Register 26 Oct. 1900 .... **1901**

Gold Fields of Uruguay Ld. Regd. 1888. Removed from Register 1906 .... **1898**

Gold Fields of Venezuela Ld. Regd. 1896. Vol. liq. 12 June 1902. Final meeting return regd. 7 Dec. 1927 **1903**

Gold Fields Prospecting Co. Ld. Regd. 1887. Vol. liq. 2 Mar. 1896. Final meeting return regd. 3 June 1896 **1894**

Gold Fields Rhodesian Development Co. Ld. Regd. 1911. Vol. liq. Jan. 1912. Reconstructed as company of same name. Shareholders were entitled to 1 share of £1 (credited as fully-paid) in new company for every 2 shares of £1 held. Removed from Register 1913 **1912**

Gold Finance Co. Ld. Regd. 1898. Vol. liq. 30 Nov. 1914. Final meeting return regd. 11 July 1917................. **1915**

Gold Hill Mines Ld. Regd. 1881. Reconstructed 1885 as Gold Hill Mining Co. Ld., in which company shareholders were entitled to 1 share of £1 (credited with 17s. paid) for each ordinary share of £1 held or 1 fully-paid share of £1 for each preference share of £1 held. Removed from Register 1905 .... **1889**

Gold Hill Mining Co. Ld. Regd. 1885. Vol. liq. 26 Apr. 1889. Reconstructed as New Gold Hill Co. Ld., in which company shareholders were entitled to 1 share of £1 (credited with 17s. 6d. paid) for each share of £1 held. Final meeting return regd. 13 June 1891 .... **1895**

Gold Key Syndicate Ld. Regd. 1898. Removed from Register 1907 .... **1901**

Gold King Ld. Regd. 1888. Struck off Register 16 Aug. 1892 .... **1899**

Gold Lands Corporation Ld. Regd. 1895. Vol. liq. 25 Jan. 1905. Undertaking was acquired by Cariboo Consolidated Ld. for 100,000 shares of £1 (credited with 17s. paid). Removed from Register 1907 ..... **1905**

Gold Mines Investment Co. Ld. Regd. 1905. Vol. liq. 10 June 1921. Reconstructed as company of same name. Shareholders were entitled to 1 fully-paid share of 10s. in new company for each share of £1 held. Final meeting return regd. 4 July 1929........ **1922**

Gold Mines Investment Co. Ld. Regd. 1921. Vol. liq. 28 Feb. 1927. Undertaking and assets were acquired by Gold Coast Amalgamated Mines Ld. (later Amalgamated Mining Trust Ld.), in which company shareholders were entitled to 1 fully-paid share of £1 for every 2 shares of 10s. held. Final meeting return regd. 4 July 1929 .... **1927**

Gold Mines of Kalgoorlie Ld. Regd. 1934. Vol. liq. (members') 9 Oct. 1951, the undertaking and assets having been transferred to Gold Mines of Kalgoorlie (Aust.) Ld. in which company stockholders were entitled to receive 5 stock units of 10s. (Aust.) for each 4 stock units of 10s. (stg.) held. Final meeting return regd. 28 Jan. 1953..................... **1953**

Gold Mines Trust and Finance Co. Ld. Regd. 1899. Struck off Register 3 June 1921 .... **1915**

Gold Mining Association of Canada Ld. Regd. 1881. Court Orders: to wind up Nov. 1884; to dissolve June 1890 .... **1881**

Gold Options Syndicate Ld. Regd. 1933. Vol. liq. (members') 5 Aug. 1937. Undertaking and certain assets were acquired by Nigel Van Ryn Reefs Ld., [later Nigel Finance and Investment Ld.] in which company shareholders were entitled to 4 shares of 1s. (credited as fully-paid) for each share of 5s. held. Final meeting return regd. 3 Aug. 1940 .... **1938**

*See Stock Exchange Year-Book.

VOL. FOR

Gold Ore Treatment Co. Ld. Regd. 1894. Vol. liq. 7 Apr. 1905. Assets were acquired by Gold Ore Treatment Co. of Western Australia Ld. Removed from Register 1906 1906

Gold Ore Treatment Co. of Western Australia Ld. Regd 1895. Vol. liq. 16 Mar. 1906. Capital returned to contributories—1s. 3d. per share of £1 at 1 May 1906; further payments (if any) not known. Final meeting return regd. 4 Nov. 1908. Court Orders deferred dissolution until 6 Dec.1919 1907

Gold Ores' Reduction Co. Ld. Regd. 1889. Removed from Register 1906 1893

Gold Producers Fixed Trust Ld. Regd. 1933. A subsidiary of British Industrial Corpn. Ld. Vol. liq. (members') 8 May 1957. Final meeting return regd. 25 Apr. 1958 1940

Gold Peoprietary Mines Ld. Regd. 1899 as Gold Coast Proprietary Mines Ld.; name changed Dec. 1904. Reconstructed 1907 as New Gold Proprietary Mines Ld., in which company shareholders were entitled to 2 shares of 5s. (credited with 4s. 6d. paid) for each share of £1 held. Removed from Register 1911 ... 1908

Gold Reefs Exploration Co. Ld. Inc. Queensland 1905 1912

Gold Reefs of Barima Ld. Regd. 1910. Vol. liq. 3 Aug. 1915. Final meeting return regd. 28 June 1919 1916

Gold Reefs of Georgia Ld. Regd. 1897. Struck off Register 1922 ..... *1909

Gold Reefs of Georgia Ld. Regd. 1902. Vol. liq. Dec. 1907. Struck off Register 1922 1908

Gold Reefs of West Africa Ld. Regd. 1900. Vol. liq. 7 Aug. 1901. Undertaking was acquired by Broomassie Mines Ld. for £120,000 In fully-paid shares. Final meeting return regd. 6 Jan. 1903 1902

Gold Reefs of Western Australia Ld. Regd. 1896. Vol. liq. 9 Sept. 1896. Final meeting return regd. 8 Apr. 1899 1897

Gold Run Gravels Ld. Regd. 1897. Removed from Register 1907 1905

Gold Run Hydraulic Mining Co. Ld. Regd. 1872. Vol. liq. Apr. 1880. Property acquired by New Gold Run Co. Ld. for 20,963 fully-paid preference shares of £1 and 29,199 ordinary shares of £1 (credited with 18s. paid). Final meeting return regd. 15 Dec. 1881 ... 1883

Gold Run (Klondike) Mining Co. Ld. Regd. 1902. Struck off Register 1914 1911

Gold Schists of Rhodesia Ld. Regd. 1910. Vol. liq. Sept. 1910. Undertaking and assets were sold to Rhodesia Exploration & Development Co. Ld., In which company shareholders were entitled to 1 fully-paid share of £1 for every 2 shares of £1 held. Removed from Register 1912 1911

Gold Trust & Investment Co. Ld. Regd. 1889. Vol. liq. 13 June 1892. Undertaking acquired by South African General Syndicate Ld. Final meeting return regd. 9 July 1895 ..... *1893

Goldareas Proprietary Ld. Regd. 1896. Removed from Register 1911 1908

Golden Age Consolidated Ld. Regd. 1900. Removed from Register 1906 1905

Golden Age, Lake Way Ld. Regd. 1897. Vol. liq. 16 Jan. 1901. Undertaking was acquired by Golden Age Consolidated Ld. for 230,000 fully-paid shares of £1. Removed from Register 1904 1902

Golden Alexandra Mining Co. Ld. Inc. Queensland 1902. The London office was closed in Jan. 1909 1910

Golden Arrow Mine Ld. Regd. 1904. Vol. liq. 13 Jan. 1906. Undertaking was acquired by Claremont Gold Mine Ld. in which company shareholders were entitled to apply for shares. Final meeting return regd. 22 June 1907 1906

Golden Australia Ld. Regd. 1895. Vol. liq. 22 Oct. 1900. Assets were acquired by West Australian Mining Co. Ld., in which company shareholders were entitled to 10 shares of 2s. (credited with 1s. 6d. paid) for each share of £1 held. Final meeting return regd. 24 Feb. 1902 1901

Golden Bardoc Mines Ld. Regd. 1896. Vol. liq. 12 Apr. 1900. Reconstructed as Premier Gold Mines Ld., in which company shareholders were entitled to 3 shares of 10s. (credited with 1s. paid) for each share of £1 held. Final meeting return regd. 19 Oct. 1901 1901

Golden Bell Mines Ld. Inc. Guernsey 1903 1906

Golden Blocks (Taitapu) Ld. Regd. 1898. Vol. liq. 26 June 1916. Final meeting return regd. 7 May 1920 1917

Golden Bullfinch Mine Ld. Regd. 1910. Vol. liq. May 1912. Shareholders were entitled to 1 fully-paid share of 1s. in Murchison Associated Ld. plus 2¼d. in cash for each share of 5s. (4s. paid) held; further cash payments (if any) not known. Removed from Register 1914 1913

Golden Cement Claims Ld. Regd. 1895. Vol. liq. 15 Mar. 1899. Leases were sold to White Feather Reward Claim Ld. for 12,500 fully-paid shares. Shareholders were entitled to 1 share of £1 (credited with 16s.

VOL. FOR

paid) in Delano Milling & MIning Co. Ld. for every 2 shares held. Removed from Register 1901 1900

Golden Cliffs Ld. Regd. 1896. Vol. liq. 12 July 1898. Final meeting return regd. 29 Jan. 1900 1899

Golden Contact Mines Ld. Regd. 1904. Vol. liq. 16 Nov. 1911. Final meeting return regd. 27 June 1913 1912

Golden Crest Mines Ld. Regd. 1896. Removed from Register 17 Nov. 1880 ..... *1898

Golden Cross Hotel & Simpson's Restaurant Ld. Regd. Mar. 1897. Allotment of shares was cancelled and Golden Cross Ld. formed to take over the hotel. Struck off Register 22 Oct. 1897 1899

Golden Cross Ld. Regd. Apr. 1897. Vol. liq. 2 Oct. 1897. Removed from Register 1909 1899

Golden Crown Ld. Regd. 1895. Vol. liq. 20 Apr. 1898. Taken over by Standard Exploration Co. Ld. Final meeting return regd. 27 May 1903 1899

Golden Dove Mining Co. Ld. Regd. 1894. Removed from Register 1903 1900

Golden Dundee Ld. Regd. 1895. Vol. liq. 15 Jan. 1897. Final meeting return regd. 26 Jan. 1898 1898

Golden Eagle Syndicate Ld. Regd. 1898. Vol. liq. 13 Apr. 1908. Capital returned to contributories—2s. 6¾d. per share of £1; further payments (if any) not known. Final meeting return regd. 1 July 1908 1909

Golden Feather Channel Ld. Regd. 1890. Vol. liq. 8 Jan. 1895. Reconstructed as Golden Feather Ld., in which company shareholders were entitled to 1 share of £1 (credited with 18s. paid) for each share of £1 held. Final meeting return regd. 26 June 1895 1897

Golden Feather Ld. Regd. 1895. Vol. liq. 5 Feb. 1897. Reconstructed as company of same name. Shareholders were entitled to 1 ordinary or priority share of £1 (credited with 19s. paid) for each ordinary or priority share of £1 respectively held. Final meeting return regd. 16 July 1897 1898

Golden Feather Ld. Regd. 1897. Vol. liq. 9 Mar. 1898. Reconstructed as Magalia Consolidated Gold Mines Ld., in which company shareholders were entitled to 1 share of £1 (credited with 18s. paid) for each share of £1 held. Final meeting return regd. 3 July 1900 1900

Golden Gate Alluvial Syndicate Ld. Regd. 1888. Vol. liq. 8 Dec. 1893. Reconstructed as Golden Gate of California Ld., in which company shareholders were entitled to 1 share of £1 (credited with 17s. 6d. paid) for each share of £1 held. Final meeting return regd. 8 Nov.1894 1894

Golden Gate Corporation Ld. Inc. Queensland 3 Sept. 1901. Vol. liq. June 1908 for amalgamation with the Croydon Consols Mines Trust Ld. and Queensland Mining Ld. Shareholders were entitled to 1 share of 2s. (credited with 1s. 3d. paid), in the United Properties Ld. for each share of 5s. held 1909

Golden Gate Gold Mining Co. Ld. Regd. 1892. Vol. liq. 31 July 1899. Reconstructed as Union Jack Consolidated Mines Ld., in which company shareholders were entitled to 2 shares of 5s. (credited with 3s. 6d. paid) for each share of 10s. held. Removed from Register 1901 1900

Golden Gate of California Ld. Regd. 1898. Vol. liq. 13 July 1900. Reconstructed as Mines Development Co. of Victoria Ld in which company shareholders were entitled to 1 share of 10s. (credited with 1s. 6d. paid) for each share of £1 held. Final meeting return regd. 26 Mar. 1901 1901

Golden Gate (Victoria) Gold Mining Co. Ld. Regd. 1897. Vol. liq. Jan. 1900. Removed from Register 1901 1900

Golden Grain Bread Co. Ld. Regd. 1886 as Civil Service Bread Co. Ld.; name changed Jan. 1889. Vol. liq. 15 Oct. 1906. Removed from Register 1910 1907

Golden Gully Gold Mines Ld. Regd. 1895. Vol. liq. 1903. Removed from Register 1904 1904

Golden Horse Shoe Estates Co. Ld. Regd. 1899. Vol. liq. Sept. 1929. Certain assets were sold to Lake View & Star Ld., the undertaking and remaining assets were acquired by Golden Horse-Shoe (New) Ld. Shareholders were entitled to 1 fully-paid share of 4s. in new company and 1 fully-paid share of 4s. in Lake View & Star Ld. for each preferred ordinary share of 5s. held or 3 fully-paid shares of 4s. in new company and 1 fully-paid share of 4s. in Lake View & Star Ld. for every 3 ordinary shares of £5 held. Final meeting return regd. 20 Jan. 1932 1930

"Golden Horse Shoe" Gold Mining Co. Ld. Regd. 1894. Vol. liq. 5 June 1899. Reconstructed as Golden Horse Shoe Estates Co. Ld., in which company shareholders were entitled to 3 fully-paid shares of £5 for each share of £1 held. Final meeting return regd. 7 Mar. 1900 1899

Golden Horse Shoe (New) Ld. Regd. 1929. Vol. liq. (members') 18 Mar. 1957. Capital returned to contributories—2s. 1½d. per share (of 2s. 6d.). £1,173 3s. 7d. was paid into Companies' Liquidation

See Stock Exchange Year-Book.

VOL. FOR

Account in respect of unclaimed dividends and £876 17s. 5d. in respect of distributions. Final meeting return regd. 8 Apr. 1959 .... **1960**

Golden Kopje Proprietary Mines Ld. Regd. 1912. Vol. liq. 15 May 1917. Final meeting return regd. 21 Mar. 1919 .... **1917**

Golden Leaf Ld. Regd. 1889. Removed from Register 1906 .... **1905**

Golden Leases Mining Co. Ld. Regd. 1896. Removed from Register 1909 .... **1902**

Golden Link Consolidated Gold Mines Ld. Regd. 1896. Reconstructed 1902 as Golden Links Ld. in which company shareholders were entitled to 1 share of £1 (credited with 15s. paid) for each share of £1 held. Removed from Register 1903 .... **1907**

"Golden Link" Gold Mining Co. Ld. Regd. 1894. Vol. liq. 4 Dec. 1896. Undertaking and assets were acquired by Golden Link Consolidated Gold Mines Ld. in which company shareholders were entitled to 5 fully-paid shares of £1 for every 4 shares of £1 held. Final meeting return regd. 1 Mar. 1897 .... **1902**

Golden Links Ld. Regd. 1902. Removed from Register 1913 .... **1908**

Golden Links Ld. Regd. 1907. See Oroya Links Ld.

Golden Mint Mines Ld. Regd. 1900. Vol. liq. 7 Oct. 1903. Reconstructed 1905 as Brustad Mines Ld. in which company shareholders were entitled to 1 share of £1 (credited with 15s. paid) for every 2 shares of £1 held. Debenture stock was to be issued in part settlement of claims of debenture stockholders. Final meeting return regd. 18 July 1906 .... **1907**

Golden Pah (Hauraki) Ld. Registered 1896. Reconstructed 1902 as Tano Bippo Gold Mines Ld. in which company shareholders were entitled to 1 share of 5s. (credited with 4s. paid) for every 4 shares of 2s. 6d. held. Removed from Register 1904 ...... **1903**

Golden Pike & Lake View East Mines Ld. Regd. 1899. Vol. liq. May 1912. Removed from Register 1913 **1913**

Golden Plum Consolidated Gold Mines Ld. Regd. 1895. Court Order to wind up 8 Feb. 1897. A small return to shareholders was anticipated. Removed from Register 1908 .... **1898**

Golden Pole Gold Mines Ld. Inc. Western Australia 1903. London office was closed in 1911 .... **1912**

Golden Province Mines of British Columbia Ld. Regd. 1897. Vol. liq. Feb. 1908. Removed from Register 1908 .... **1908**

Golden Quarry Deep Level Mining Co. Ld. Reconstructed as Oriental and Sheba Valley United Gold Mining Co. Ld. in 1889 .... **1893**

Golden Reefs Ld. See Wassau Gold Reefs Ld.

Golden Rhine Gold Mines (W. A.) Ld. Regd. 1899. Removed from Register 1909 .... **1904**

Golden Rhodesia Ld. Regd. 1896. Vol. liq. Oct. 1910 for reconstruction as Hartley (Rhodesia) Consolidated Mines Ld. in which company shareholders were entitled to 1 share of 10s. (credited with 7s. paid) for each share of £1 held. Struck off Register Mar. 1929 **1930**

Golden Ridge Syndicate Ld. Regd. 1895. Removed from Register 1901 .... **1900**

Golden Ridge (West Australia) Proprietary Co. Ld. Regd. 1896. Vol. liq. 27 Mar. 1899. Final meeting return regd. 29 June 1900 .... **1900**

Golden Ring Gold Mines Ld. Regd. 1896. Struck off Register 29 Nov. 1907 .... **1908**

Golden River Quesnelle Ld. Regd. 1896. Removed from Register 1908 .... **1901**

Golden Spur Gold Mines Ld. Regd. 1894. Vol. liq. 6 Dec. 1897. Property was acquired by Tasmanian New Golden Gate Extended Mines Ld. Final meeting return regd. 26 Feb. 1900 .... **1902**

Golden State Mines Ld. Regd. 1897. Vol. liq. Dec. 1908. Removed from Register 1911 .... **1909**

Golden Steam Syndicate Ld. Regd. 1903. Removed from Register 1911 .... **1907**

Golden Valley Citrus Estates Ld. Inc. in Natal 1917. Vol. liq. (members') Apr. 1944. Finally dissolved 1 Oct. 1946 .... **1947**

Golden Valley Ld. Regd. 1908. Vol. liq. 17 Jan. 1921. Final meeting return regd. 26 Oct. 1926 .... **1922**

Golden Valley (Mashonaland) Mines Ld. Regd. 1902. Vol. liq. Sept. 1907. Reconstructed 1908 as Golden Valley Ld. in which company shareholders were entitled to 1 fully-paid B share of 2s. for every 5 shares of £1 held. Removed from Register 1908 .. **1909**

Golden Valley Mines Ld. Regd. 1890. Removed from Register 5 May 1896 .... *****1896**

Golden Valley Mines of West Australia Ld. Regd. 1896. Removed from Register 1906 .... **1905**

Golden Valley Railway Co. Inc. by Special Act 1876. Under Great Western Railway Act 1899 line was sold to that company. Holders of 1st debenture stock received 1s. in £ and holders of 2nd debenture stock

VOL. FOR

received 6d. in £ in Dec. 1899; further payments (if any) not known **1900**

Golden Wealth Ld. Regd. 1895. Vol. liq. Dec. 1908. Removed from Register 1911 .... **1910**

Golden Zelma Ld.. Regd. 1897. Vol. liq. 3 Dec. 1900. Final meeting return regd. 29 Nov. 1901 .... **1902**

Goldfields of Eastern Akkim Ld. Regd. 1919. Vol. liq. 5 Jan. 1922 for reconstruction as Akim Ld., in which company shareholders were entitled to 5 ordinary shares of £1 (credited as fully-paid) for every 4 shares of 5s. held. Final meeting return regd. 13 Nov. 1931 .... **1922**

Goldfields of Manica Ld. Regd. 1891. Vol. liq. 18 Jan. 1893. Final meeting return regd. 24 Apr. 1894...... *****1893**

Goldfields of Matabeleland Ld. Regd. 1895. Vol. liq. 30 Aug. 1906. Reconstructed as company of same name. Shareholders were entitled to 1 share of 10s. (credited with 7s. 6d. paid) for each share of £1 held. Final meeting return regd. 22 Sept. 1910. Court Orders deferred dissolution until 21 Jan. 1911 .... **1908**

Goldfields of Matabeleland Ld. Inc. Rhodesia 1906. Vol. liq. July 1909. Assets sold to the Amalgamated Properties of Rhodesia Ld. in which company shareholders were entitled to 5 fully-paid shares of 5s. for every 12 shares of 10s. held **1910**

Goldfields of Surinam Ld. Regd. 1897. Vol. liq. 23 Nov. 1899. Final meeting return regd. 30 Sept. 1938 .... **1908**

Goldfields of Victoria Ld. Regd 1899. Vol. liq. 12 Mar. 1902. Reconstructed as Victoria Proprietary Ld. in which company shareholders were entitled to 1 share of 5s. (credited with 4s. paid) for each share of 10s. held. Final meeting return regd. 28 Sept. 1914 **1903**

Goldfields of Zambesia Ld. Regd. 1894. Vol. liq. Apr. 1909. Removed from Register 1909 .... **1910**

Goldring Ld. Regd. as private company 27 July 1916 as Vernon Lockwood Manufacturing Co. Ld.; name changed to The Goldring Manufacturing Co. (Great Britain) Ld. 12 Nov. 1953 and to present title 17 Nov. 1972.; converted into a public company 11 Jan. 1973. Winding-up order 18 Jan.1982 .... **1982–3**

Goldring Manufacturing Co. (Great Britain) Ld. (The) See Goldring Ld.

Goldsbrough, Mort and Co. Ld. Inc. Melbourne 1881. Reconstructed 1893 as company of same name. Holders of debentures, debenture stock and deposit certificates received 5% debentures in new company to full amount of their debts. Each shareholder who applied for 2 shares of £4 15s. (5s. paid) in respect of each share of £10 (£1 paid) held was released from paying the unpaid £9 .... **1894**

Goldsmiths & General Burglary Insurance Association Ld. Regd. 1891. Vol. liq. 19 Dec. 1901. Business was acquired by Guardian Fire and Life Assurance Co. Ld. (later Guardian Assurance Co. Ld.) for cash. Final meeting return regd.7 Aug.1902 .... **1902**

Gomei Kaisha Mitsui. Established 1683. Business acquired by Mitsui Bank Ld. in 1909 .... **1941**

Gomersal Gas Co. Inc. by Special Act 1865. The works and plant were purchased by Spenborough Urban District Council as from 31 Mar. 1921......... **1922**

Gondar Tin Mines Ld. Regd. 1926. Vol. liq. 29 Feb. 1928. Final meeting return regd. 10 Nov. 1928..... **1928**

Gongo Soco and Rossa Grande Land and Gold Co. Ld. Regd. 1894. Vol. liq. 24 Sept. 1897. Amalgamated with Brazilian Gold Exploring Syndicate Ld. in which company shareholders were entitled to 1 fully-paid share of £1 for every 7 shares of 2s. 6d. held. Final meeting return regd. 1 Apr. 1899 .... **1898**

Gonnessa Mining Co. Ld. Regd. 1864. Vol. liq. 13 Sept. 1893. Final meeting return regd. 22 Jan. 1902...... **1894**

Gooch's Ld. Regd. 1910. Vol. liq. 23 Aug. 1928. Undertaking and assets acquired by Gooch's (1928) Ld. for £1,197 in cash and £158,000 in fully-paid shares of 10s. Final meeting return regd.17 Jan. 1935 **1929**

Gooch's (1928) Ld. Regd. 1928. Vol. liq. (members') 16 Apr. 1934. Undertaking and assets were acquired by Swears & Wells Ld., in which company shareholders were entitled to 1 share of £1 (credited as fully-paid) for every 3 shares of 10s. held. Final meeting return regd. 1 Aug. 1935 .... **1935**

Gooch's Stores Ld. Regd. 1898. Vol. liq. Feb. 1910 for reconstruction as Gooch's Ld. in which company shareholders were entitled to 1 fully-paid 2nd preference share of £1 for every 20 ordinary or 8 preference shares held. Holders of debentures received 50% of holding in new 2nd mortgage debentures. Removed from Register 1912............ **1911**

Good Hope Gold Mining Co. Ld. Inc. Queensland 1895. Company has been wound up **1899**

Goodall & Hatton Ld. Regd. 1910. Vol. liq. 14 Sept. 1925. Final meeting return regd. 11 July 1927 ..... **1926**

Goodall (E.) & Co. Ld. See Goodall, Lamb & Heighway Ld.

VOL. FOR

Goodall, Lamb & Heighway Ld. Regd. 1888 as E. Goodall & Co. Ld. name changed Jan. 1899. Receiver appointed 31 Mar. 1933. Vol. liq. (members') Apr. 1933. Final meeting return regd. 13 Nov. 1953 .... **1954**

Goodfare Dining Rooms Ld.. Regd. 1895 as Lockharts Ld.; name changed Aug. 1923. Vol. liq. 12 July 1928. The properties were sold to J. P. Restaurants Ld. Final meeting return regd.8 Feb. 1929 .... **1929**

Goodlass, Wall & Co. Ld. Regd. Feb. 1920 as Goodlass, Wall & Co. (1920) Ld.; name changed Oct. 1920. Court sanctioned Scheme of Arrangement 31 Oct. 1930 to transfer assets to Goodlass, Wall & Lead Industries Ld., in which company shareholders were entitled to 15 7% cumulative preference shares of £1 for every 14 preference shares of £1 held; ordinary shareholders were entitled to 3 7% preferred ordinary shares of 10s. and 2 ordinary shares of 10s. for every ordinary share of £1 held; a payment of 2s. 4½d. in cash was to be paid in respect of each ordinary share held. Dissolved under Sec. 154 of Companies Act 1929 on 7 Apr. 1931 .... **1931**

Goodson Gramophone Record Co. Ld. Regd. 1928. Vol. liq. Dec. 1930. Struck off Register 24 Oct. 1939 ... **1940**

Goodson's Ld. Regd. 1895. Vol. liq. (members') 4 Jan. 1939. Capital returned to contributories—£6 5s. 7¾d. per share of £1. Final meeting return regd. 5 Oct. 1939 .... **1938**

Goodson's Mantle & Costume Co. (1920) Ld. Regd. 1920. Vol. liq. (members') 30 Dec. 1938. Undertaking and assets (except book debts and cash) acquired by J. V. Hutton. Capital returned to contributories—9s. per preference share of £1; 1s. per preferred participating share of 3d.; and 1d. per ordinary share of 3d. Final meeting return regd. 5 Oct. 1939 .... **1939**

Goodwin Brothers Ld. Regd. 1891. Vol. liq. 5 Oct. 1897. Final meeting return regd. 8 Mar. 1899 .... **1925**

Goodwins, Jardine & Co. Ld. Regd. 1889. Removed from Register 1913 .... **1892**

Goole & Marshland Light Railway Co. Inc. (under Light Railways Act 1896) by order of Light Railway Commissioners confirmed by Board of Trade 1898. Under North-Eastern Railway Act 1902 line was sold to that company and Lancashire & Yorkshire Railway Co. for £73,500. 4% debenture stock was paid off at 102% **1903**

Goole Moss Litter Co. Ld. Regd. 1894. Vol. liq. 5 June 1899. Absorbed by British Moss Litter Co. Ld. Final meeting return regd. 4 Sept. 1900 .... ***1900**

Goole Steam Shipping Co. Ld. Regd. 1864. Undertaking was acquired by Lancashire & Yorkshire Railway Co. Removed from Register 1908 .... **1905**

Goole Tillage Co. Ld. Regd. 1870. Vol. liq. (members') 1 July 1939. All capital was owned by Fisons Ld. Final meeting return regd. 29 Sept. 1944 .... **1945**

Goomera (Ceylon) Tea Estates Co. Ld. Regd. 1894. Vol. liq. 17 Oct. 1919. Property was acquired by General Ceylon Rubber and Tea Estates Ld. Final meeting return regd. 8 Dec. 1920. .... **1920**

Goongarrie Gold Fields Ld. Regd. 1895. Vol. liq. 19 May 1898. Property was acquired by Mimosa Gold Mines Ld. in which company shareholders were entitled to 1 fully-paid share of £1 for every 4 shares of £1 held. Removed from Register 1904 .... **1899**

Goongarrie United Gold Mines Ld. Regd. 1898. Reconstructed 1903 as New Goongarrie Gold Mines Ld., in which company shareholders were entitled to 1 share of 2s. 6d. (credited with 2s. paid) for each share of 5s. held. Removed from Register 1905 ... **1905**

Gooninnis Mining Co. Established 1899. Vol. liq. 18 Dec. 1902. .... **1903**

Gopeng Consolidated Ld. Regd. 24 Sept. 1912. Re-regd. as public limited company 1982 and as private company 29 June 1984. Vol. liq. (members') 9 Oct. 1984. Dissolved 4 Apr. 1989. All assets transferred to Gopeng Berhad following acquisition in which shareholders received 2 ordinary shares of 50 sen plus 31p cash for each share held. Unclaimed dividends between 1974 and 1983 amounting to £3,126 paid into Companies' Liquidation Account **1988-9**

Gopeng (Perak) Rubber Estates Ld. Regd. 1925. All capital acquired by Kuli Rubber Plantations Ld. Vol. liq. (members') 29 Dec. 1961. Final meeting return. regd. 4 Jan. 1964 .... **1961**

Gopeng Tin Mining Co. Ld. Regd. 1892. Vol. liq. 25 July 1901. Reconstructed as company of same name. Shareholders were entitled to 100 fully-paid shares of £1 in new company for each share of £25 held. Final meeting return regd. 18 Nov. 1901 .... **1908**

Gopeng Tin Mining Co. Ld. Regd. 1901. Vol. liq. 20 Sept. 1912. Reconstructed as Gopeng Consolidated Ld., in which company shareholders were entitled to 3 shares of £1 (credited as fully-paid) plus 1s. 6d. in

VOL. FOR

cash for each share of £1 held. Final meeting return regd. 24 Dec. 1912. .... **1913**

Gordon (Alexander) & Co. Ld. Regd. 1882. Vol. liq. Aug. 1887. Business was acquired by London Restaurants Ld. for £123,890 in cash and £31,110 in fully-paid shares of £1. Final meeting return regd. 9 Aug. 1888 .... **1888**

Gordon & Blair Ld. Regd. Edinburgh 1898. Vol. liq. Mar. 1923. Struck off Register 22 Sept. 1936 .... **1937**

Gordon Diamond Co. Ld. Regd. 1888. Vol. liq. 11 Dec. 1890. Court Orders: to continue winding up under supervision 20 Dec. 1890; to dissolve 6 Aug. 1894 **1891**

Gordon Drills Ld. Inc. Transvaal 1906. London office was closed in 1910 .... **1910**

Gordon (J. E. H.) & Co. Ld. Regd. 1890. Vol. liq. 30 Jan. 1893. Final meeting return regd 30 June 1897 .... ***1894**

Gordon Mining Co. Ld. Regd. 1881. Removed from Register 1905 .... ***1885**

Gordon (William) & Co. Ld. Regd. 1902. Court Order to wind up 1906. Removed from Register 1910 .... **1907**

Gorebridge Gas Light Co. Ld. Regd. in Edinburgh 1861. Dissolved 1 May 1949, undertaking being vested In Scottish Area Gas Board under Gas Act 1948. Holders of ordinary shares (of £1) were entitled to receive 16 British Gas 3% guaranteed stock 1990-95 for each share held. **1952**

Gorehill Coal Co. Ld. Business and assets were acquired in 1928 by Scottish Coal Products Ld. **1929**

Gorgona Island Coconut Estate Co. Ld. Regd. 1914. Struck off Register 1920 .... **1916**

Goriach Coal Mining & Gypsum Works Ld. Regd. 1900. Removed from Register 1904 .... **1904**

Goring & Streatley District Gas & Water Co. Ld. See South Oxfordshire Water Co.

Gorleston & Southtown Gas Co. Inc. by Special Act 1876. Dissolved 1 May 1949, undertaking being vested in Eastern Area Gas Board under Gas Act 1948. Holders of securities were entitled to receive, in respect of each £10 unit held, British Gas 3% guaranteed stock 1990-95 as follows:

	£	s.	d.
Old ord. shares (10% max.)	20	0	0
New ord. shares (7% max.)	14	4	0	**1952**

Gorringe (Frederick) Ld. See Fregor Holdings Ld.

Gorse Galvanizing Co. Ld. Regd. 1911. All capital was owned by Bynea Steel Works Ld. Vol. liq. 12 Jan. 1965. Final meeting return regd. 8 June 1965 .... **1958**

Gorsedda Junction & Portmadoc Railway Co. Inc. by Special Act 1872. .... **1899**

Gorsllan Colliery Co. Ld. Regd. 1926. Vol. liq. 4 May 1928. Undertaking acquired by New Gorsllan Colliery Co. Ld. Struck off Register 23 Oct. 1931 . **1938**

Gorton Rubber Co. Ld. Regd. 1899. Vol. liq. 1913. Struck off Register 1922 .... **1914**

Goschens & Cunliffe. Inc. under Limited Partnership Act 1920. The business was acquired in 1941 by Guinness, Mahon & Co. (later Guinness, Mahon Holdings Ld.) **1941**

Gosport & Alverstoke Electric Lighting Co. Ld. Regd. 1904. Vol. liq. (members') 8 June 1936. Undertaking acquired by Gosport Corporation for £181,801. Capital returned to contributories—£45 19s. 10d. per share of £10. Final meeting return regd. 31 Dec. 1936 .... **1937**

Gosport District Gas Co. Established by Deed of Association 1835 as Gosport Gas & Coke Co.; Inc. by Special Act 1865; name changed Jan. 1925. Undertaking was acquired by Portsmouth & Gosport Gas Co., in which company shareholders were entitled to £100 consolidated stock plus £10 in cash for every £100 consolidated stock held; preference stockholders were entitled to an equal amount of 5% preference stock. The liability for debenture stocks and mortgage debentures was assumed by acquiring company **1936**

Gosport Waterworks Co. Inc. by Special Act 1858. Under provisions of The Portsmouth & Gosport Water Order 1955 this company was amalgamated with the Portsmouth Water Co. under the title of Portsmouth & Gosport Water Co. on the following terms:—(1) The whole of the undertaking and assets of this company were transferred to the Portsmouth company, this company was dissolved by resolution of the directors on 23 Aug. 1955, and (2) Holders of securities of this company were entitled to receive securities of the Portsmouth company (per £10 stock in each case) as follows:—10% ordinary, £21 Portsmouth 5% ordinary; 7% ordinary £14 8s. Portsmouth 5% ordinary; 5% ordinary, £10 5% Portsmouth ordinary; 5% cumulative preference, £12 10s. Portsmouth 4% debenture stock; 4½% preference, £15 Portsmouth 3% preference; 5% preference stock redeemable 1 July 1955, £10 Portsmouth 5% preference stock redeemable on

VOL. FOR

same date, and 5% preference stock redeemable on 31 Dec. 1972, £10 Portsmouth 5% preference stock redeemable on same date. Liability for the perpetual debenture stocks and the 4½% debenture stock was assumed by the Portsmouth company **1956**

Goss Moor Ld. Regd. 1909. Vol. liq. Apr. 1911 for reconstruction as Goss Moor Tin Alluvials Ld., in which company shareholders were entitled to 4 shares of 5s. (credited with 4s. paid) for each share of £1 held. Removed from Register 1912 .... **1912**

Goss Moor Tin Alluvials Ld. Regd. 1911. Vol. liq. Sept. 1914. Struck off Register 1922 .... **1915**

Gothenburg Commercial Co. Ld. Regd. 1872. Court Orders: to wind up 3 July 1884; to dissolve 26 May 1887 .... **1880**

Gothenburg Tramways Co. Ld. Regd. 1879. Vol. liq. 18 Apr. 1900. Undertaking was acquired by Municipality. Capital returned to contributories—£6 per share of £5 on 19 Apr. 1900; further payments (if any) not known. Removed from Register 1901 .... **1901**

Gotlieb (J. L.) & Co. Ld. Business acquired in 1928 by Aeonic Radio Ld.. **1929**

Goudey Gum Co. of Canada Ld. In liquidation. Direct controlling interest was owned by British Chewing Sweets Ld **1936**

Goudey Gum Co. of Canada Ld. (*See* British Chewing Sweets)

Gould Steamships & Industrials Ld. Regd. 1920. Vol. liq. 19 May 1925. Final meeting return regd. 20 Nov. 1933 .... **1926**

Goulding (W. and H. M.) Ld. Regd. Dublin 1872. Reconstructed as company of same name. Holders of 2 fully-paid shares of £8 were entitled to £10 debenture stock, 2 preference shares and 1 ordinary share of £5 in new company............................. **1895**

Gouria Petroleum Corporation Ld. Regd. 1913. Struck off Register Feb. 1933 .... **1933**

Gouria Syndicate Ld. Regd. 1912. Properties were sold to Gouria Petroleum Corporation Ld. in 1913. Struck off Register Feb. 1933 .... **1933**

Gourlay's Rhodesia Development Co. Ld. Regd. 1895. Vol. liq. 29 Dec. 1896. Undertaking sold to Rhodesian Mining & Finance Co. Ld. for 29,000 shares. Final meeting return regd. 17 Feb. 1898 ... **1897**

Gouverneux & Oswegatchie Railroad. Inc. New York 1892 .... **1913**

Govan Forge & Steel Co. Ld. Regd. Edinburgh 1880. Vol. liq. Mar. 1884. Final meeting return regd. 30 July 1890 .... **1885**

Govan Shafting & Engineering Co. Ld. Regd. Edinburgh 1916. Vol. liq. 5 Jan. 1925. Property and plant acquired by Steel Co. of Scotland Ld. Final meeting return regd. 6 May 1926 .... **1940**

Govanhill Cinema Ld. Regd. Edinburgh 1926. Vol. liq. (members') 28 Mar. 1930. Undertaking acquired by Scottish Cinema & Variety Theatres Ld. £9,862 was returned to contributories. Final meeting return regd. 15 Feb. 1932 .... **1940**

Gover Consols. Regd. Truro 1880. Vol. liq. 16 Nov. 1882. Final meeting return regd. 23 Feb. 1883 ...... **1883**

Government & General Investment Co., Ld. Regd. 1880. In 1968 the undertaking was transferred to Union Commercial Investment Co. Ld. in which company shareholders were entitled to receive 13 ordinary shares of 5s. for every 9 deferred shares of 5s. and £1 4% preference stock per £1 preferred ordinary stock held, and debenture stockholders received a like amount of 3% debenture stock 1983 in exchange for their holdings. Company is to be dissolved under Section 208 of the Companies Act 1948 .... **1970**

Government Savings Bank of New South Wales. In Dec. 1931 the bank was acquired by Commonwealth Bank of Australia **1932**

Governments Stock and other Securities Invest. Co. Ld. Regd. 1871 as Government Stock Invest. Co. Ld.; name changed 1892. On 1 Jan. 1974 undertaking and assets transferred to Premier Invest. Co. Ld., deferred ordinary shareholders received 87 ordinary shares for every 100 shares and preference stockholders 1 3·5% preference share for every £1 stock. Holders of 4% perpetual debenture stock, 3¾% 2nd debenture stock and 7½% convertible unsecured loan stock 1993 received an equivalent nominal amount of 4½% perpetual debenture stock, 4% debenture stock and 7½%. A convertible unsecured loan stock 1993 respectively. The company was dissolved 13 July 1976 .... **1977-8**

Governor & Company of the Island of Anticosti Ld. Regd. 1886. Vol. liq. 16 Apr. 1889. Final meeting return regd. 10 May 1897 .... **1890**

Govett European Trust Ld. Regd. 1972 as John Govett (Investments) Ld.;name changed Mar. 1972. Vol. liq. 4 Sept. 1980. Under scheme of unitisation ordinary shareholders received 1 income unit of

VOL. FOR

Stockholders European Trust per share held. Final meeting return regd. 11 May 1981. £1,957 was paid into Companies' Liquidation Account **1981–2**

Govett (John) (Investments) Ld. *See* Govett European Trust Ld.

Gow (Nigeria) Tin Co. Ld. Regd. 1912. Vol. liq. 23 Apr. 1914. Undertaking and assets were to be sold to Minna (Nigeria) Tin Co. (1914) Ld., in which company shareholders were entitled to 1 fully-paid share of 5s. for every 2 shares of 5s. held. Final meeting return regd. 20 Jan. 1916...................... **1915**

Gower Light Railway Co. Inc. (under Light Railways Act 1896) by order of Light Rly. Commissioners confirmed by Board of Trade 1898 .... **1903**

Gower Vanguard Motors (1920) Ld. Regd. 1920. Vol. liq. (members') 10 Sept. 1940. All shares held by Red & White United Transport Ld. (later United Transport Co. Ld.). Undertaking acquired by United Welsh Services Ld. Final meeting return regd. 18 Dec. 1940 .... **1941**

Gowerton Gas Co. Regd. 1907; Inc. by Special Act 1910. Dissolved 1 May 1949, undertaking being vested in Wales Area Gas Board under Gas Act 1948. Holders of securities were entitled to receive, in respect of each £5 unit held, British Gas 3% guaranteed stock 1990—95 as follows:

	£	s.	d.
Ord. shares (10%max.)	11	0	0
5% pref. shares.................................	5	12	0

Liability in respect of certain mortgage loans assumed by the Board **1952**

Gowrie & Blockhouse Collieries Ld. Regd. 1898. Vol. liq. 4 Dec. 1907. Final meeting return regd. 13 Mar. 1913 .... *****1909**

Goy & Co. Ld. Regd. 1899. Court Order to wind up 1905. Removed from Register 1910 .... **1907**

Goy Ld. Regd. 1886. Court Order to wind up 23 Sept. 1891. Removed from Register 1906 .... **1892**

Goyt Spinning Co. (Holdings) Ld. Regd. 1905 as Goyt Spinning Co. Ld.; name changed 23 Oct. 1953. Vol. liq. (members') 29 Apr. 1960. Capital returned to contributories—4s. 0·8d. per 2s. 6d. stock. Paid into Companies' Liquidation Account—in respect of unclaimed dividends £1,131 0s. 10d., distributions £1,245 18s. 10d. Final meeting return regd. 8 Aug. 1962 .... **1963**

Grabham & Co. Ld. Regd. 1887. Struck off Register 16 Aug. 1892 .... **1889**

Grace Bros. & Co. Ld. Regd. 1899. Vol. liq. (members') 31 May 1937. Capital returned to contributories— 20s. 7d. per share of £1. Final meeting return regd. 23 May 1938 .... **1938**

Gracechurch Buildings Co. Ld. Regd. 1920 as Commercial Bank Buildings Trust Ld.; name changed June 1921. Vol. liq. (members') 25 June 1936. The assets were acquired by Legal & General Assurance Society Ld. Final meeting return regd. 31 Dec. 1936 **1937**

Gradidge (H.) & Sons Ld. Regd. 1928. Vol. liq. (members') 3 July 1933. All shares held by Slazengers Ld. Final meeting return regd. 28 Sept. 1934 **1934**

Grafton (Management) Ld. Regd. 1928 as Stoneware (1928) Ld.; name changed to Stoneware Ld. 1947; to Newcrest Ld. 1955 and as *above* 1956. Vol. liq. (members') 30 July 1965. Final meeting return regd. 24 Apr. 1973 .... **1956**

Grafton Trust Ld. Regd. 1928. Struck off Register 1931 *****1930**

Graham Island (British Columbia) Oilfields Ld. Regd. 1919. Struck off Register 4 Feb. 1930. Restored 15 June 1934. Vol. liq. (members') 28 Dec. 1934. Capital returned to contributories—¼d. share of 5s. £68 16s. 9d. was paid into Companies' Liquidation Account. Final meeting return regd. 27 Aug. 1945 **1946**

Graham (J. H.) Ld. Regd. 1900. Vol. liq. 21 Sept. 1920. Final meeting return regd. 2 Nov. 1921 .... **1921**

Graham, Morton Ld. Regd. 1905. Vol. liq. 27 Dec. 1905. Final meeting return regd. 19 Mar. 1909 .... *****1907**

Grahame-White Co., Ld. Regd. Mar. 1911 as Grahame-White, Bleriot & Maxim, Ld.; name changed to Grahame-White Aviation Co., Ld. Aug. 1911 and as above 1918. Vol. liq. 14 Oct. 1965. Final meeting return regd. 24 Mar. 1966 .... **1932**

Graham's Navigation (Merthyr) Collieries Ld. Regd. 1905. Vol. liq. 24 Nov. 1924. Final meeting return regd. 9 Mar. 1927 .... *****1925**

Grahamstown & Port Alfred Railway Co. Ld. Regd. 1880. Compulsory winding-up order made in Mar. 1886. Removed from Register 1905 .... **1887**

Graigola Merthyr Co. Ld. Regd. 1885. Vol. liq. (members') 30 Dec. 1937. Shareholders were entitled to 4 ordinary shares of £1 in company of same name (regd. 1937) for every 5 ordinary or preference shares of £1 held. Final meeting return regd. 16 Aug. 1941 .... **1938**

See Stock Exchange Year-Book.

VOL. FOR

Gramophone Cabinet Manufacturers Ld. Undertaking and business were acquired in 1928 by Gramophone Cabinets Ld. for £40,500 in cash 1929

Gramophone Cabinets Ld. Regd. 1928. Court Order to wind up and Receiver appointed on 2 June 1930. Struck off Register 21 Sept. 1937 1938

Gramophone Records Ld. Regd. 1928. Vol. liq. 9 Mar. 1928. Undertaking and assets were acquired by British Homophone Co. Ld., in which company shareholders were entitled to 18 ordinary shares of 5s. (credited as fully-paid) for every 10 ordinary shares of 1s. held or 1 deferred share of 1s. for each deferred share of 1s. held. Final meeting return regd. 27 July 1928 1929

Grampian Electricity Supply Co. Inc. by Special Act 1922. All capital owned by Scottish Power Co. Ld. Dissolved 1 Apr. 1948 under Electricity Act 1947 1940

Grampian Fishing Co. Ld. Regd. Edinburgh 1901. Vol. liq. Jan. 1928. Capital returned to contributories—£1 3s. 1d. per share of £1 (10s. paid) at Oct. 1928; further payments (if any) not known. Final meeting return regd. 19 Dec. 1928 1929

Grampian Freehold Estates Ld. Regd. 1909. Vol. liq. 19 Nov. 1927. Struck off Register 12 July 1935 ...... *1915

Grampian Steamship Co. Ld. Regd. Edinburgh 1884 as Davidson Steamship Co. Ld.; name changed Mar. 1886. The company's steamers were purchased by Adam Steamship Co. Ld. for £26,750, paid in 10,700 shares of £3 15s. each credited with £2 10s. paid. Vol. liq. Sept. 1896. Final meeting return regd. 2 Nov. 1897 1897

Granada Railway Co. Ld. Regd. 1894. Vol. liq. 6 Aug. 1918. Final meeting return regd. 13 Mar. 1919 1919

Grand Canal Co. Inc. by Special Act 1772; reconstructed 1848. Undertaking acquired on 1 June 1950 by Coras Iompair Eireann. Holders of ordinary and preference shares and the 3% irredeemable debenture stock were entitled to receive £100 3% guaranteed Transport Stock, 1975–85 (of Coras Iompair Eireann) for each £100 capital or debenture stock held. Company dissolved 1 June 1950 1951

Grand Canary, Teneriffe & Atlantic Coaling Co. Ld. See A. C. C. Holdings Ld.

Grand Central Mining Co. Ld. Regd. 1896. Vol. liq. 14 Apr. 1905. Capital returned to contributories—2s. 6d. per share of £1; further payments (if any) not known. Removed from Register 1909 1906

Grand Central Silver Mines Ld. Regd 1891. Vol. liq. 24 Nov. 1893. Final meeting return regd. 10 Sept. 1894 1894

Grand Champion (Manicaland) Ld. Regd. 1901. Vol. liq. July 1907. Absorbed by Rhodesia Matabeleland Development Co. Ld., in which company shareholders were entitled to 1 fully paid share of £1 for every 4 shares of £1 held. Removed from Register 1911 1908

Grand Hotel Co. Ld. Regd. 1879. Removed from Register 1905 1891

Grand Hotel Co., Scarborough Ld. Regd. 1865. Vol. liq. 3 Sept. 1920. Final meeting return regd. 18 July 1928 1921

Grand Hôtel des Alpes. Murren Ld. See Palace Hotel & Grand Hotel des Alpes, Mürren Ld.

Grand Hotel (Jersey), Ld. Regd. 1889. Vol. liq. (members') 8 Mar. 1950. Shares were privately held. Final meeting return regd. 16 Oct. 1954 1955

Grand Hotel (Leicester) Ld. Regd. 1902. All ordinary capital was owned by Ind Coope Ld. Vol. liq. (members') 28 Nov. 1960. Final meeting return regd. 28 Nov. 1960 1956

Grand Hotel (Llandudno) Ld. Regd. 1900. Receiver appointed 26 Apr. 1913; ceased to act 22 Sept. 1919. Struck off Register 3 July 1921 .... *1920

Grand Hotel, Monte Carlo Ld. Regd. 1897. Vol. liq. 15 Jan. 1928. Struck off Register 12 Apr. 1929 1917

Grand Hotel, Prague, Ld. Regd. 1889. Vol. liq. 10 Mar. 1893. Final meeting return regd. 16 May 1901...... *1892

Grand Junction Railways Ld. Inc. Cape of Good Hope 1894. In vol. liq. in 1904 1904

Grand Junction Water Works Co. Inc. by Special Act 1811. Undertaking taken over by Metropolitan Water Board on and from 24 June 1904 under provisions of Metropolis Water Act 1902 1905

Grand Manica Development Co. Ld. Regd. 1899. Vol. liq. 18 Dec. 1906. Removed from Register 1907 .. 1907

Grand Opera Syndicate Ld. Regd. 1896. Vol. liq. 22 Jan. 1929. Final meeting return regd. 1 Jan. 1930 1930

Grand Picture Houses (Sheffield)Ld. Regd. 1920. Vol. liq. (members') 10 Mar. 1938. Capital returned to contributories—£11,096 5s. 2d. Final meeting return regd. 26 Sept. 1938 1939

Grand Rapids & Indiana Railways. Inc. Michigan and Indiana 1896. All capital stock was owned by Pennsylvania Railroad Co., which company leased the lines 1942

VOL. FOR

Grand Reef Ld. Regd. 1897. Vol. liq. 23 Apr. 1903. Assets were acquired by Grand Champion (Manicaland) Ld. Final meeting return regd. 2 May 1906 1904

Grand Theatre & Opera House, Glasgow Ld. Regd. Edinburgh 1903. Vol. liq. May 1908. Final meeting return regd. 25 Aug. 1910 1904

Grand Theatre (Clapham) Ld. Regd. 1931. Vol. liq. (members') 16 Dec. 1937. All shares owned by London & District Cinemas Ld. Final meeting return regd. 9 Feb. 1938 1938

Grand Theatre, Croydon Ld. Regd. 1901. Removed from Register 1903 1903

Grand Theatre (Hanley) Ld. Regd. 1920. Vol. liq. (members') 8 Nov. 1932. Capital returned to contributories—7s. 8½d. per ordinary share of £1. Final meeting return regd. 8 Mar. 1935 1933

Grand Theatre (Islington) Ld. Regd. 1896. Removed from Register 1905 1903

Grand Trunk Junction Railway Co. Organised Illinois 1880. All capital was held by Canadian National Railway Co. Undertaking was acquired by Canadian National Railways. The 5% 1st mortgage bonds were redeemed on 1 Jan. 1934 1924

Grand Trunk Junior Stocks. Regd. 1923 as Grand Trunk Junior Stockholders' Protection Committee; name changed July 1927. Struck off Register 29 Aug. 1941 1942

Grand Trunk Pacific Branch Lines Co. Inc. Canada by Special Act 1906. All capital was acquired by Grand Trunk Pacific Railway Co. The undertaking was acquired by Canadian National Railways. The 4% 1st mortgage sterling bonds 1939 Saskatchewan Lines and Alberta Lines, and 4% 1st mortgage sterling bonds 1942. Alberta Lines, were redeemed at maturity.......... 1924

Grand Trunk Pacific Railway Co. Inc. Canada by Special Act 1904. All capital was held by Grand Trunk Railway Co. of Canada. The undertaking was acquired by Canadian National Railways. The 4% debenture stock was redeemed on 1 Sept. 1936. The following bonds were acquired for cash in Jan. 1942. by H. M. Treasury:—for every £100 3% 1st mortgage sterling bonds held—£107 5s. 8d.; for every £100 4% mortgage sterling bonds, series A or B, held—£109 8s. 5d.; for every £100 4% Lake Superior Branch 1st mortgage sterling bonds held—£109 8s. 5d.......... 1924

Grand Trunk Railway Co. of Canada. Inc. Canada by Special Act 1852. In 1921 the 1st, 2nd and 3rd preference and consolidated stocks were vested in H. M. the King. The 5% perpetual debenture stock was acquired in Jan. 1942 by H. M. Treasury at £126 9s. 8d. for every £100 stock held; the 4% perpetual consolidated debenture stock was acquired at £104 4s. 5d. for every £100 stock held 1924

Grand Trunk Senior Stocks Co. Ld. Regd. 1932. Struck off Register Jan. 1949 .... *1933

Grand Trunk Western Railway Co. Inc. Michigan 1900. All capital held by Canadian National Railway Co. The undertaking was acquired by Canadian National Railways. The outstanding 1st mortgage 4% 50-year gold bonds were acquired in Jan. 1942 by H. M. Treasury at £21 13s. 8d. for every £100 bonds held 1924

Grand Union Canal Co. Inc. by Special Act 1882 as Regent's Canal City & Docks Railway Co.; name changed to North Metropolitan Railway & Canal Co. in 1892, to Regent's Canal & Dock Co. in 1900 and to above title in 1929. Undertaking vested from 1 Jan. 1948 in British Transport Commission under Transport Act 1947. Dissolved 11 Dec. 1950; holders of securities were entitled to receive British Transport 3% guaranteed stock 1978–88 as follows in respect of every £100 of old security held:

	£	s.	d.
Capital (ordinary) stock	21	5	0
6% non-cum. pref. stock..........	89	0	0
3% perp. deb. stock..........	87	10	0
5⅛% perp. deb. stock..........111	17	6	
Development loan No. 1 4% red. deb. stock..........102	10	0	
4% red. deb. stock (red. 1956 at 102%)..........103	10	0	
3½% perp. deb. stock..........	95	0	0

1949

Grande Union Belge de Transports S. A. (See Grand Union Canal)

Grange & Cartmel District Gas Co. Inc. by Special Act 1866. Dissolved 1 May 1949, undertaking being vested in North Western Area Gas Board under Gas Act 1948. Holders of ordinary shares (of £1) were entitled to receive £1 4s. 6d. British Gas 3% guaranteed stock 1990–95 for each share held....... 1952

Grange Oil Co. Ld. Regd. 1911. Vol. liq. 29 Dec. 1917. Final meeting return regd. 27 May 1918 1918

VOL. FOR

Granite City Steam Fishing Co. Ld. Regd. Edinburgh 1901. Vol. liq. Nov. 1909. Final meeting return regd. 4 Mar. 1910 .... **1910**

Granite City Steam Ship Co. Ld. Regd. Edinburgh 1883. Vol. liq. (members') 26 Sept. 1940. Capital returned to contributories—£1 8*s.* 7½*d* per share of £1. Final meeting return regd. 26 Sept. 1941 .... **1941**

Granite Corporation Ld. Regd. 1901. Vol. liq. 10 June 1903. Struck off Register 20 Mar. 1925 .... **1904**

Granite Gold Exploration Syndicate Ld. Regd. 1895. Struck off Register 16 Nov. 1902 .... **1904**

Granite Gold Mines Ld. Regd. 1899. Vol. liq. 6 May 1901. Final meeting return regd. 11 July 1902 .... **1902**

Granite Mount Associated Gold Mines (Victoria) Ld. Regd. 1899. Removed from Register 1907 .... **1903**

Granitese (Great Britain) Ld. Regd. 1934. Vol. liq. (members') 25 June 1942. Direct controlling interest owned by C[illegible]entation Co. Ld. Final meeting return regd. [illegible] Aug. 1944 .... **1943**

Grant (A. C.) Ld. Regd. Edinburgh 1908. Vol. liq. Mar. 1924. Final meeting return regd. 17 Dec. 1924 .... **1925**

Grant & Maddison's Union Banking Co. Ld. Regd. 1888. Acquired by Lloyds Bank Ld. in which company shareholders were entitled to 1 share of £50 (credited with £8 paid) for each share of £50 (£16 paid) held. Removed from Register 1905 .... **1904**

Grant Envelope Machine Co. Ld. Regd. 1887. Vol. liq. 12 Oct. 1891. Final meeting return regd. 1 Mar. 1894 **1892**

Grantham & District Billposting & Advertising Co. Ld. Regd. 1897. Vol. liq. 16 Mar. 1899. Business acquired by Rockley's Ld. Final meeting return regd. 16 Dec. 1899 .... **1940**

Grantham Gas Co. Inc. by Special Act 1874. Dissolved 1 May 1949, undertaking being vested in East Midland Area Gas Board under Gas Act 1948. Holders of securities were entitled to receive, in respect of each £100 unit held, British Gas 3% guaranteed stock 1990—95 as follows:

	£	s.	d.
Cons. ord. stock (5% basic)	160	0	0
3¾% red. cons. pref. stock	100	10	5
4% red. deb. stock	102	0	0

1952

Grantham Waterworks Co. Inc. by Special Act 1873. Undertaking vested in Kesteven Water Board from 1 Apr. 1962. Holders of 5½% redeemable preference stock and 5% consolidated ordinary stock received respectively (per £100 stock) £86 19*s.* 9*d.* and £74 7*s.* 5*d.* plus £9 1*s.* 9*d.* and £7 19*s.* 4*d.* accumulated deposit interest. Dissolved 14 Apr. 1965 .... **1966**

Grantown-on-Spey Electricity Supply Co. Ld. Regd. Edinburgh 1930. Vol. liq. (members') 15 July 1937. Capital returned to contributories—26*s.* 11·0246*d.* per share of £1. Final meeting return regd. 13 Dec. 1937 .... **1938**

Granville (A.) Ld. Regd. 1927. Receiver appointed Mar. 1933; ceased to act July 1935. Vol. liq. (creditors') 11 Aug. 1933. All capital owned by S. D. H. Pianos Ld. Assets realised insufficient to meet claims of unsecured creditors in full. Final meeting return regd. 25 July 1935 .... **1933**

Granville Colliery Co. Ld. Regd. 1872. Vol. liq. (members') 15 Feb. 1951. Final meeting return regd. 9 Nov. 1957 .... **1894**

Granville Hotel Co. Ld. Regd. 1888. Vol. liq. 17 Oct. 1895. Final meeting return regd. 14 Nov. 1899..... ***1896**

Granville Mining Co. Ld. Regd. 1911. Vol. liq. 11 May 1928. Ordinary shares of $1 in Yukon Consolidated Gold Corporation Ld. were distributed as follows—for every 100 shares of £1 held—1 share; for every £10 receivers notes—45 shares; for every £100 7% prior lien debentures—375 shares: for every £100 6% 1st mortgage debenture stock—25 shares; for every £100 provisional certificates for income notes and 6% debenture stock—25 shares; for every £100 provisional certificates for income notes only—2 shares. Final meeting return regd. 12 Sept. 1929 . **1929**

Granville Theatre of Varieties (Walham Green) Ld. Regd. 1897. Receiver appointed 8 May 1941. Vol. liq. (members') 1 Feb. 1946. Capital returned to contributories—2*s.* 3*d.* per share of £1. £261 9*s.* was paid into Companies' Liquidation Account. Final meeting return regd. 5 July 1946 .... **1947**

Grape Mill Ld. Regd. 1925. Dissolved under Sect. 208 of Companies Act 1948 on 25 Nov. 1949 the undertaking and assets having been acquired by Royton Textile Corpn. Ld. as from 30 June 1949; stockholders received 10·44 fully-paid shares of 5*s.* of Royton Textile Corpn. Ld. for every £1 stock held **1950**

Grape Produce Ld. Regd. 1928. Vol. liq. (members') 4 Sept. 1931. Undertaking and assets were acquired by Vine Products Ld. Capital returned to contributories—2*s.* 8*d.* per preferred ordinary share of 5*s.* Final meeting return regd. 3 June 1932 .... **1932**

Graphic & Bystander Ld. *See* A I P Trust Ld.

VOL. FOR

Graphic Publications Ld. Regd. 1869 as H. R. Baines & Co. Ld.; name changed 10 Aug. 1920. Vol. liq. (members') 26 Mar. 1947. Final meeting return regd. 20 Dec. 1948 .... **1938**

Grappler Pneumatic Tyre & Cycle Co. Ld. Regd. Dublin 1893. Vol. liq. for reconstruction as New Grappler Pneumatic Tyre Co. Ld. Removed from Register 1908 .... **1903**

Graskop Exploring Co. Ld. Regd. 1896. Reconstructed 1903 as New Graskop Exploring Co. Ld. in which company shareholders were entitled to 2 shares of 2*s.* 6*d.* (credited with 2*s.* paid) for each share of 5*s.* held. Removed from Register 1912 .... **1908**

Graskop Gold and Stores Co. Ld. Regd. 1885. Vol. liq. 3 Dec. 1888. Property was acquired by Graskop Mill & Mining Co. Ld., in which company shareholders were entitled to 4 shares of 5*s.* (credited with 4*s.* 3*d.* paid) for each share of £1 held. Final meeting return regd. 30 Apr. 1891 .... **1889**

Graskop Ld. Regd. 1893. Vol. liq. 23 Mar. 1897. Reconstructed as company of same name. Shareholders were entitled to 1 share of 5*s.* (credited with 4*s.* 3*d.* paid) in new company for each share of 5*s.* held. Final meeting return regd. 25 Jan. 1899....... **1899**

Graskop Ld. Regd. 1897. Vol. liq. 13 July 1899. Reconstructed as company of same name. Shareholders were entitled to 1 share of 5*s.* (credited with 3*s.* 6*d.* paid) in new company for each share of 5*s.* held. Final meeting return regd. 28 Mar. 1900...... **1905**

Graskop Ld. Regd. 1899. Certain assets were acquired in 1905 by United Reefs (Sheba) Ld. for 42,000 fully-paid shares of 10*s.* and 48,000 shares of 10*s.* (credited with 7*s.* 6*d.* paid). Removed from Register 1910 .... **1908**

Graskop Mill & Mining Co. Ld. Regd. 1888. Vol. liq. 29 Mar. 1893. Reconstructed as Graskop Ld., in which company shareholders were entitled to 1 share of 5*s.* (credited with 3*s.* 6*d.* paid) for each share of 5*s.* held. Final meeting return regd. 11 July 1894 .... **1897**

Grassmoor Co. Ld. Regd. 1928. Vol. liq. (members') 8 Aug. 1952. Capital returned to contributories—17*s.* 2*d.* per share of 8*s.* £324 12*s.* 8*d.* paid into Companies' Liquidation Account. Final meeting return regd. 30 June 1956 .... **1957**

Gravel Gold Mines of Colombia Ld. Regd. 1893. Vol. liq. 28 July 1898. Final meeting return regd. 22 Dec. 1898 .... **1899**

Graves (Henry) & Co. Ld. Regd. 1896 as Henry Graves and Co. Ld.: name changed Oct. 1920 to Henry Graves, Gooden and Fox Ld.; and to original title in Jan. 1922. Vol. liq. 17 Nov. 1922. Reconstructed as company of same name. Final meeting return regd. 8 June 1923 .... **1923**

Graves (J. G.) Ld. Regd. 1906. Vol. liq. (members') 14 Sept. 1967. Capital returned to contributories—10*s.* per preference share of £1; 3*s.* 9·25*d.* per preferred ordinary share of 5*s.* £1,927 4*s.* 10*d.* was paid into Companies' Liquidation Account in respect of distributions and £523 1*s.* 1*d.* in respect of unclaimed dividends. Final meeting return regd. 12 Oct. 1970 .... **1971**

Gravesend & Milton Gas Light Co. Inc. by Special Act 1863. Dissolved 1 May 1949, undertaking being vested in South Eastern Area Gas Board under Gas Act 1948. Holders of securities were entitled to receive, in respect of each £100 unit held, British Gas 3% guaranteed stock 1990-95 as follows:

	£	s.	d.
Ord. cons. stock (5% stand.)	150	0	0
5% pref. stock	115	0	0
5% irred. deb. stock	125	0	0
3½% red. deb. stock 1955	100	0	0

1952

Gravesend and Milton Waterworks Co. Inc. by Special Act 1846. Under provisions of the Kent Water Act 1955 the undertaking vested in the Medway Water Board from 1 Apr. 1956. Holders of the 4% irredeemable debenture stock received an equivalent amount of Water Board stock carrying the same rights (except that it is redeemable on 31 Mar. 1996) as the stock surrendered, with interest from 1 Apr. 1956, and shareholders received cash with interest at 4% thereon since 1 Apr. 1956 at the following rates—£21 12*s.* per 6% preference share of £20; £16 4*s.* per 4½% preference share of £20; £30 13*s.* 4*d.* per 10% maximum ordinary share of £20, and £1 1*s.* 5*d.* per 7% maximum ordinary share of £1. Company was dissolved by resolution of directors passed on 6 Feb. 1960 .... **1961**

Gravesend & Northfleet Electric Tramways Ld. Regd. 1901. Vol. liq. (members') 18 Feb. 1930 Omnibus business was acquired by Maidstone & District Motor Services Ld. Capital returned to contributories—9*s.* per ordinary or preference share of £1. Final meeting return regd. 5 Jan. 1931 .... **1930**

**See Stock Exchange Year-Book.*

Gravesend Railway Co. Inc. 1881. Dissolved under Act of 1883 .... **1884**

Gray & Paulette Ld. Regd. 1928. Vol. liq. (members') 1 Jan. 1946. Capital returned to contributories—10s. per preference share of 10s. and 9s. 11d. per ordinary share of 5s. £270 was paid into · Companies' Liquidation Account. Final meeting return regd. 7 Nov. 1947 .... .1948

Gray (John) & Co. Ld. Regd. Edinburgh 1894. Vol. liq. (creditors') 18 Nov. 1937. No capital was returned to contributories. Final meeting return regd. 1 Aug. 1952 .... **1953**

Gray (William) & Co. Ld. Regd. 1888. Vol. liq. 3 Feb. 1919. Reconstructed as William Gray and Co. (1918) Ld. (later William Gray and Co. Ld.), in which company shareholders were entitled to 250 shares of £1 (credited as fully-paid) for each share of £100 held. Final meeting return regd. 10 Dec. 1919 **1919**

Gray (William) & Co. Ld. Regd. 1918 as William Gray & Co. (1918) Ld.; name changed 1922. Vol. liq. (members') 22 Oct 1962. Capital returned to contributories—25s. 9½d. per share of £1. Final meeting return regd. 16 Aug. 1968 .... **1969**

Grays & Tilbury Gas Co. Established as Grays Thurrock Gas and Coke Company by Deed of Settlement in 1853; registered as Grays Gas Company, Limited, in 1884; incorporated as above by Special Act in 1907. By Act of 1929 the undertaking was acquired by the Gas Light & Coke Co., in which company holders of A shares were entitled to £18 10s. per share in ordinary stock; holders of B shares £13 per share in ordinary stock; holders of 6% preference shares £15 per share in 4% consolidated preference stock and holders of 5% and 4% perpetual debenture stocks £166 13s. 4d. and £133 6s. 8d. per £100 respectively in 3% consolidated debenture stock. Holders of 6% redeemable debenture stock an amount of 6% Grays redeemable debenture stock **1930**

Grays Chalk Quarries Co., Ld. Regd. 1862. Vol. liq. (members') 12 May 1954. Final meeting return regd. 22 Mar. 1957 .... **1938**

Grays Gas Co. Ld. *See* Grays & Tilbury Gas Co.

Gray's Golden Crown Ld. Regd. 1895. Vol. liq. 28 Dec. 1900. Removed from Register 1908 .... **1901**

Grays Thurrock Gas and Coke Co. *See* Grays & Tilbury Gas Co.

Grayson & Vaughan Ld. Regd. 1919 as Grayson, Rising & Barbour Ld.; name changed to Grayson. Rawlinson & Vaughan Ld. in June 1922 and as above in Apr. 1923. Vol. liq. 30 Nov. 1927. Final meeting return regd. 12 July 1928 .... **1929**

Grayson (H. & C.) Ld. Regd. 1890. Vol. liq. June 1920. Reconstructed as company of same name (later Grayson Rollo & Clover Docks Ld.). Shareholders were entitled to 1 fully-paid preference share of £1 in new company for each preference share of 5s. held or 4 fully-paid deferred share of £1 for each deferred share of 1s. held. Struck off Register July 1933 .... **1934**

Grayson Ld. Regd. 1904. Vol. liq. (creditors') 10 Oct. 1932. Assets realised sufficient to pay creditors 8s. 9d. in £. Final meeting return regd. 23 June 1934 **1933**

Grayson, Rawlinson & Vaughan Ld. *See* Grayson & Vaughan Ld.

Grayson, Rising & Barbour Ld. *See* Grayson & Vaughan Ld.

Grayson's Slipways Ld. Regd. 1907. Vol. liq. (members') 14 Nov. 1930. Capital returned to contributories—£13 4s. 6d. per share of £10. Final meeting return regd. 26 Nov. 1931 .... **1931**

Great B Syndicate Ld. Regd. 1894. Vol. liq. 24 Jan. 1905. Removed from Register 1910 .... **1905**

Great Berkhampstead Water Works Co. Regd. as limited 1864; inc. by Special Act 1900. Undertaking was acquired by Rickmansworth & Uxbridge Valley Water Co., as from 1 July 1953. Stockholders were entitled to receive £10 4% preference stock of that company for every £10 stock (ordinary or preference) held. Debentures and other liabilities were assumed by acquiring company and this company was dissolved by resolution of directors on 8 Nov. 1954 .... **1956**

Great Bonanza Gold Mining Co, Ld. Regd. 1891. Removed from Register 1914 .... **1912**

Great Boulder East Extended Gold Mine Ld. Regd. 1895. Vol. liq. 22 Feb. 1897. Undertaking was acquired by Golden Link Consolidated Gold Mines Ld., in which company shareholders were entitled to 1 fully-paid share of £1 for every 3 shares of £1 held. Final meeting return regd. 24 Sept. 1897 ...... **1902**

Great Boulder Junction Reefs Ld. Regd. 1895. Vol. liq. 18 July 1896. Property was acquired by company of same name for £135,000 in fully-paid shares of £1. Final meeting return regd. 6 Jan. 1899 .... **1897**

Great Boulder Junction Reefs Ld. Regd. 1896. Vol. liq. 24 Sept. 1900. Reconstructed as Mertons Boulder Ld., in which company shareholders were entitled to 1 share of £1 (credited with 16s. 6d. paid) for each share of £1 held. Final meeting return regd. 15 Feb. 1902 .... **1906**

Great Boulder Main Reef Ld. Regd. 1895. Vol. liq. 8 Feb. 1905. Reconstructed as company of same name. Shareholders were entitled to 1 share of 5s. (credited with 3s. paid) in new company for each share of 10s. held. Removed from Register 1906 **1905**

Great Boulder Main Reef Ld. Regd. 1905. Reconstructed 1907 as company of same name. Shareholders were entitled to 1 share of 5s. (credited with 3s. paid) in new company for each share of 5s. held. Removed from Register 1908 .... **1908**

Great Boulder Main Reef Ld. Regd. 1907. Vol. liq. Jan. 1910 for amalgamation with Chaffers Gold Mining Co. Ld., in which company shareholders were entitled to 1 fully-paid share of 4s. for each share of 5s. held; the company received £7,250 in cash. Removed from Register 1912 .... **1910**

Great Boulder Mining & Finance Ld. Regd. 1935. Vol. liq. (members') 4 Sept. 1941. Winding-up Order 18 Mar. 1946. Capital returned to contributories—1¼d. per share of 5s. Liquidator released 12 Nov. 1954. Struck off Register 17 Mar. 1961 .... **1955**

Great Boulder No. 1 Ld. Regd. 1901. Vol. liq. (creditors') 3 June 1941. No capital returned to contributories. £87 11s. 8d. was paid into Companies' Liquidation Account. Final meeting return regd. 12 July 1943 .... **1945**

Great Boulder Perseverance Gold Mining Co. Ld. Regd. 1903. Vol. liq. 20 Nov. 1917. Reconstructed 1923 as Boulder Perseverance Ld. in which company shareholders were entitled to 1 ordinary share of 1s. (credited as fully-paid) for each share of 2s. held. Final meeting return regd 26 May 1925 .... **1918**

Great Boulder Proprietary Gold Mines Ld. Regd. 1894. Vol. liq. (members') 12 June 1957. Reconstructed as Great Boulder Gold Mines Ld., in which company shareholders were entitled to 1 fully-paid share of 2s. 6d. for each 2s. unit of stock held. Final meeting return regd. 22 July 1958 .... **1959**

Great Boulder South Gold Mining Co. Ld. Regd. 1895. Vol. liq. 1903. Reconstructed as Boulder Deep Levels Ld., in which company shareholders were entitled to 1 share of £1 (credited with 17s. paid) for each share of £1 held. Removed from Register 1904 **1904**

Great Britain & Canada Investment Corp. Inc. in Quebec 1929. In 1968 assets and liabilities were sold to Great Britain & Canada Investments (1968) Ld., in which company shareholders received 1 5¼% 1st redeemable preferred share for each preferred share held; and 1 1% 2nd redeemable preferred share plus 1 common share for each common share held. Income debenture holders received a like amount of identical stock in the new company. Company was wound-up and its charter surrendered **1970**

Great Britain Gold Mining & Estate Co. of Witwatersrand Ld. Inc. Transvaal 1888. Vol. liq. Feb. 1927. Capital returned to contributories—5s. per share of £1 .... **1928**

Great Britain Smoke Consuming & Fuel Saving Co. Ld. Regd. 1881. Court Orders: to wind up 31 July 1883; to dissolve 22 July 1886 .... ***1884**

Great Buninyong Estate Gold Mining Co. Ld. Regd. 1895. Reconstructed 1898 as Great Buninyong Ld., in which company shareholders were entitled to 1 share of £1 (credited with 17s. paid) for each share of £1 held. Removed from Register 1901 .... **1901**

Great Buninyong Ld. Regd. 1898. Removed from Register 1903 .... **1902**

Great Cement Proprietary Ld. Regd. 1896. Struck off Register 1921 .... **1912**

Great Central & Midland Joint Committee. Inc. by Special Act 1872 as Sheffield & Midland Railway Companies Committee; reconstituted under above title by Special Act 1904. Dissolved 2 Apr. 1949; undertaking vested 1 Jan. 1948 in British Transport Commission under Transport Act 1947. Holders of Great Central & Midland 3½% guaranteed stock were entitled to receive, in respect of every £100 stock held, £101 10s. British Transport 3% guaranteed stock 1978—88 .... **1949**

Great Central & North Staffordshire Railways Committee. Dissolved 2 Apr. 1949; undertaking vested 1 Jan. 1948 in British Transport Commission under Transport Act **1949**

Great Central & North Western Railways Joint Committee. Dissolved 2 Apr. 1949; undertaking vested 1 Jan. 1948 in British Transport Commission under Transport Act 1947 .... **1949**

VOL. FOR

Great Central Freehold Mines Ld. Inc. Victoria 1900. In liq. in 1904 1904

Great Central Gas Consumers' Co. Undertaking acquired by Gas Light and Coke Co. under Act of 1851 1888

Great Central, Hull & Barnsley & Midland Committee. Dissolved 2 Apr. 1949; undertaking vested 1 Jan. 1948 in British Transport Commission under Transport Act 1947 1949

Great Central Railway Co. Inc. by Special Act 1894 as Manchester, Sheffield & Lincolnshire Railway Co.; name changed 1897. In 1923 the undertaking was merged into the London North Eastern Railway Co., in which company stockholders were entitled to stock as follows:

For each £100 *held*	*L. & N. E. R.*	
4% Debenture	£100	4% Debenture
4½% Debenture	£112½	4% Debenture
5% Debenture	£125	4% Debenture
3½% 2nd Debenture	£58½	3% Debenture
	£43¾	4% 1st Gtd.
3½% 2nd Deb.(Red)*	£125	4% 1st Gtd.
4½% 1st Pref.	£112½	4% 2nd Gtd.
3¼% Preference	£81¼	4% 2nd Gtd.
6% Preference	£150	4% 2nd Gtd.
5% Guaranteed	£125	4% 2nd Gtd.
4% Gtd. S. Yorks. Rentcharge	£100	4% 2nd Gtd.
5% Perp. Pref.	£125	4% 1st Pref.
5% S. Yorks. Rentcharge	£125	4% 1st Pref.
4¼% S. Yorks. Rentcharge	£106¼	4% 1st Pref.
4% Preference	£100	4% 1st Pref.
5% Conv. Pref. 1872	£125	4% 1st Pref.
5% Conv. Pref. 1874	£125	4% 2nd Pref.
5% Conv. Pref. 1876	£125	4% 2nd Pref.
5% Conv. Pref. 1879	£125	4% 2nd Pref.
5% Conv. Pref. 1881	£125	4% 2nd Pref.
4% Preference 1889	£100	4% 2nd Pref.
4% Preference 1891	£50	4% 2nd Pref.
	£40	5% Prefd. Ord.
5% Preference 1894	£100	5% Prefd. Ord.
Preferred Ordinary	£20	5% Prefd. Ord.
	£35	Deferred Ord.
Deferred Ordinary	£30	Defd Ord.

*Holders had an option until 31 Jan. 1923 of retaining their rights of redemption by requiring the new Company to assume the obligations of the Great Central Railway Co. in respect of their holdings 1924

Great Chaffinch Gold Mining Co. No Liability. Inc. South Australia 1910 1911

Great Challinor Mines Ld. Regd. 1914. Vol. liq. 19 Oct. 1920. Final meeting return regd. 2 Sept. 1922 1921

Great City Steamship Co. Ld. Regd. 1913. Vol. liq. 1 May 1917 for amalgamation with St. Just Steamship Co. Ld. (later Reardon Smith Line Ld.). Final meeting return regd. 7 Dec. 1917 1918

Great Cobar Ld. Regd. 1906. Receiver was discharged May 1926 after realising all assets. Debenture holders received 6*s.* 6⅔*d.* in £. Struck off Register Apr. 1929 1930

Great Cobar North Ld. Regd. 1906. Vol. liq. 4 Mar. 1913 for reconstruction as North Cobar Ld.; in which company shareholders were entitled to 3 shares of 5*s.* (credited with 4*s.* 3*d.* paid) for each share of £1 held. Final meeting return regd. 5 Oct. 1914 1913

Great Consolidated Electric Power Co. Ld. (Daido Denryoku Kabushiki Kaisha). Inc. Japan 1921. In Apr. 1939 the assets were transferred to Japan Electric Generation & Transmission Co. Ld., which company assumed liability in respect of issued bonds. Company dissolved 2 Apr. 1939 1940

Great Coolgardie Gold Mine Ld. Regd. 1897. Court Order to wind up 17 Jan. 1905. Liquidator released 21 Feb. 1907. Final meeting return regd. 27 Aug. 1909 1905

Great De Kaap (Moodies') Gold Field Ld. Regd. 1895. Vol. liq. 4 July 1904. Undertaking was acquired by New De Kaap Ld. in which company shareholders were entitled to 1 share of 5*s.* (credited with 4*s.* paid) for each ordinary share of 5*s.* held or 1 fully-paid share of 5*s.* for each preference share of 5*s.* held. Final meeting return regd. 20 Mar. 1920 1905

Great Dowgas Tin Mines Ld. Regd. 1905. Vol. liq. Nov. 1911. Removed from Register 1912 1912

Great Dundas Gold Mining Co. Ld. Regd. 1894. Vol. liq. 8 June 1896. Taken over by Menzies Niagara Proprietary Ld. Final meeting return regd. 5 Nov. 1897 1898

Great Dyliffe Lead Mining Co. Ld. Regd. 1876. Court Orders: to wind up 11 May 1878; to dissolve 13 Feb 1880 .... *1878

Great Eastern Collieries Ld. Inc. Transvaal 1894. Vol. liq. Nov. 1911 1912

VOL. FOR

Great Eastern Lode Ld. Regd. 1892. Removed from Register 1899 1895

Great Eastern London Motor Omnibus Co. Ld. Regd. 1906. Vol. liq. June 1911. All shares were acquired by London General Omnibus Co. Ld. Removed from Register 1912 1912

Great Eastern London Suburban Tramways & Omnibus Co. Ld. Regd. 1897. Vol. liq. May 1911. Removed from Register 1912 1912

Great Eastern Railway Co. Inc. by Special Act 1862. In 1923 the undertaking was merged into the London & North Eastern Railway Co., in which company stockholders were entitled to stock as follows:—

For each £100 *held*	*L. & N. E. R.*	
4% Debenture	£100	4% Debenture
4% Deb. E. Anglian	£100	4% Debenture
4¼% Debenture	£106¼	4% Debenture
4½% Debenture	£112½	4% Debenture
5% Irred. Deb. A.	£125	4% Debenture
5% Red. Deb. B*	£125	4% 1st Gtd.
5% Metropolitan	£125	4% 1st Gtd.
4% Rentcharge	£100	4% 1st Gtd.
4% Cons. Irred. Gtd.	£100	4% 2nd Gtd.
4% Cons. Pref	£101	4% 1st Pref.
3½% Preference 1890	£87½	4% 2nd Pref.
3½% Preference 1893	£87½	4% 2nd Pref.
Ordinary	£35	5% Prefd. Ord.
	£45	Deferred Ord.

Certs. A for Contingent Rights...7*s.* 6*d.* cash
Certs. B for Contingent Rights...2*s.* 0*d.* cash

*Holders had option until 31 Jan., 1923, of retaining their rights of redemption by requiring the new Company to assume the obligations of tbe Great Eastern Railway Co. in respect of their holdings 1924

Great Eastern Steamship Co. Ld. Regd. 1864. Court Orders: to wind up May 1885; to dissolve 23 Sept. 1889 1868

Great Eastern Train Ferries Ld. Regd. 1923. Vol. liq. (members') 27 July 1933. Principal assets were acquired by London & North Eastern Railway Co., for £150,000. Capital returned to contributories—15*s.* 2·3*d.* per share of 16*s.* 8*d.* at Jan. 1934. Final meeting return regd. 29 May 1936 1934

Great Eukaby Silver Field (South Australia) Ld. Regd. 1889. Court Order to wind-up 2 Apr. 1892. Removed from Register 1907 1893

Great Fingall Consolidated Ld. Regd. 1899. Vol. liq. 1 1 July 1923. Undertaking and assets were acquired by London Australian & General Exploration Co. Ld., in which company shareholders were entitled to 1 share of 2*s.* 6*d.* (credited as fully-paid) for each share of 10*s.* held. Final meeting return regd. 28 Jan. 1924 1924

Great Fingall Reefs Ld. Regd. 1895. Vol. liq. 20 Apr. 1899. Reconstructed as Great Fingall Consolidated Ld. Final meeting return regd. 10 May 1900 1908

Great Fingall Southern Blocks Ld. Inc. Guernsey 1904. Wound up in 1904 1928

Great Fitzroy Gold & Copper Mines Ld. Inc. Victoria 1907. Vol. liq. July 1908 for reconstruction. Shareholders were entitled to 1 £1 share (credited 18*s.* paid) in new company (Great Fitzroy Mines Ld.), for each share (of £1) held 1909

Great Fitzroy Mines Ld. Inc. Victoria 1908. Vol. liq. Apr. 1912 for reconstruction under same name. Shareholders were entitled to 1 share of 5*s.* (credited 2*s.* paid) in new company for each share (of £1) held, and received an option (until 31 May 1913) to subscribe pro rata for shares. Debenture holders were entitled to exchange their holdings at par for debentures in new company 1913

Great Fitzroy Mines Ld. Inc. Victoria 1912. Vol. liq. Dec. 1920 1921

Great Gold Zone Mining, Exploration & Estate Co. Ld. Regd. 1889. Vol. liq. 28 Dec. 1900. Final meeting return regd. 15 Aug. 1902 1901

Great Grimsby Fish & Steam Trawling Co. Ld. Regd. 1884. Vol. liq. July 1888. Final meeting return regd. 27 Nov. 1889 1889

Great Grimsby Gas Co. Inc. by Special Act 1846. Dissolved 1 May 1949, undertaking being vested in East Midland Area Gas Board under Gas Act 1948. Holders of securities were entitled to receive British Gas 3% guaranteed stock 1990-95 as follows in respect of each £100 unit, unless otherwise stated, of security held:

	£ s. d.
A stock (10% max.)	200 0 0
B stock (10% max.)	200 0 0
C stock (7% stand.)	195 0 0
New ord. shares (7% stand.) (of £10)	17 0 0
4% pref. stock	100 0 0
4% red. deb. stock	100 0 0

Great Grimsby Street Tramways Co. Wound up in 1937. Lines in Grimsby were transferred to Grimsby

3% Debenture................£100	3% Debenture	
6% Leeds Bradford & Halifax.....................£150	4% 1st Gtd.	
4% Perp. Gtd. £100	4% 1st Gtd.	
4% Cons. Perp. Pref { £50	4% 2nd Gtd.	
£50	4% 1st Pref.	
3% Pref. 1896 ....£75	4% 1st Pref.	
3% Pref. 1898 ....£75	4% 1st Pref.	
3% Pref. 1899 ....£75	4% 1st Pref.	
3% Pref. 1901 ....£75	4% 1st Pref.	
6% Cons. B ....{ £110	4% 2nd Pref.	
£32	5% Prefd. Ord.	
4% Prefd. Conv. Ord.{ £66⅔	4% 2nd. Pref.	
£26⅓	5% Prefd. Ord.	
Consolidated A. .... { £35	5% Prefd. Ord.	
£65	Deferred Ord.	
Defd. Conv. Ord...... { £35	5% Prefd. Ord.	
£65	Deferred Ord.	1924

Great Northern Railway Co. (Ireland) Inc. 1876. Confirmed by Special Act 1877. Undertaking acquired by Governments of Republic of Ireland and of Northern Ireland in Sept. 1953. Holders of 4% debenture stock received £89 2s. 6d. per £100 stock. Holders of capital stocks received compensation at the following rates per £100 stock:—consolidated 4% guaranteed stock £66; 4% preference stock £35; ordinary stock £28 10s. The company was dissolved 27 Feb. 1958 1959

Great Northern Railway Co. of Canada. Inc. Canada 1883. Amalgamated with 2 other companies in 1906 to form Canada Northern Quebec Railway Co. The liability for the 1st guaranteed 4% gold bonds was assumed by the new company; they were acquired by H. M. Treasury in 1942 at £94 17s. 3d. for every £100 bonds held 1924

Great Oriental Gold Mines Ld. Regd. 1908. Vol. liq. 8 Mar. 1917. Final meeting return regd. 9 Oct. 1917 *1918

Great Polgooth United Tin Mines Co. Ld. Regd. 1881. Vol. liq. Apr. 1883. Taken over by Tregontrees and Old Polgooth Consols Mining Co. Ld. Final meeting return regd. 7 June 1883 1885

Great Reef Ld. Regd. 1895. Removed from Register 1901 1899

Great San Anton Gold Mining Co. Ld. See Tweefontein Gold Mining Co. Ld.

Great Sandstone United Gold Mines Syndicate Ld. In 1895 the properties were acquired by Black Horse and Sandstone Gold Reefs Ld., for 45,742 fully-paid shares of £1 1897

Great She Gold Mining Co. Ld. Regd. 1887. Reconstructed 1890 as East Sheba Reef Mining Co. Ld., in which company shareholders were entitled to 1 share of 5s. (credited with 4s. paid) for each share of £1 held or 1 fully-paid share of 5s. for every 5 shares of £1 held. The debentures were to be repaid. Removed from Register 1906 1891

Great Sheba Gold Mine Ld. Regd. 1888. Vol. liq. 23 Dec. 1890. Final meeting return regd. 10 July 1893 1891

Great Southern and Western Railway Co., Ireland. Inc. by Special Act 1844. In 1924 the undertaking was transferred to the Great Southern Railway Co., in which company stockholders were entitled to stock as follows:

For each £100 held	Gt. Sthn. Rly.
4% Debenture £100	4% Debenture
7% Red. (1925) Deb..........£100	7% Red. (1925) Deb.
4% Gtd. Pref............................£100	4% Gtd. Pref.
4% Baronial Gtd. Share, Co. Sligo......................................£100	4% Preference
4% Baronial Gtd. Share, Co. Mayo......................................£100	4% Preference
4% Preference £100	4% Preference
Geashill Extension ....£ 43 15s.	4% Pref.
Ordinary £100	Ordinary

Holders of North Wall Extension Lines 1 & 2 shares were entitled to an equal amount of similar shares in the new company 1925

Great Southern Extended Ld. Regd. 1899. Removed from Register 1904 1904

Great Southern Mysore Gold Mining Co. Ld. Regd. 1880. Court Orders: to wind up 3 Apr. 1882; to dissolve Jan. 1891 1883

Great Southern of Spain Railway Co. Ld. Regd. 1885. Following expropriation of company's assets in Spain distributions amounting to 60·43% were made to 6% 1st. mtg. deb. stockholders. No distributions were made to income deb. or ordinary stockholders. Struck off Register 4 Feb. 1955 1956

Great Southern Railway Co. Inc. 1924 under Irish Free State Railways Act 1924. In 1925 the undertaking of this company were vested in the Great Southern Railways Co., on terms which provided that holders

of stock in this company should receive stock of the like class, denomination, and amount in that company 1925

Great Southern Railways Co. Inc. 1 Jan. 1925. Dissolved 1 Jan. 1945 under the Transport Act 1944. Undertaking acquired by Coras Iompair Eireann. Stockholders were entitled to £100 common stock for every £100 ordinary or preference stock held; £50 common and £50 3% redeemable debenture stock for every £100 4% guaranteed preference stock held, and £100 3% redeemable debenture stock for every £100 4% debenture stock held 1946

Great Southern Tin & Gold Fields Ld. Regd. 1893. Removed from Register 1908 1903

Great Talunga Gold Mine Ld. Regd. 1895. Removed from Register 1903 1899

Great Tower Hill Gold Mines Ld. Inc. Western Australia 1904. Vol. liq. June 1908 for reconstruction as Gwalia Proprietary Ld in which company shareholders were entitled to 6 ordinary shares of 5s. (credited with 4s. paid) for every 5 ordinary shares of 5s. held and 1 preference share of 5s. for every 2 preference shares of 1s. held. Debenture holders were entitled to a like amount of debentures in new company 1909

Great Tower Hill Gold Mines (1908) Ld. See Gwalia Proprietary Ld.

Great Victoria Gold Mining Co. Ld. Regd. 1896. Removed from Register 1911 1900

Great West Permanent Loan & Savings Co. See Great Western Permanent Loan Co.

Great West Permanent Loan Co. Inc. Manitoba 1902 as Great West Permanent Loan & Savings Co.; Special Act of Canadian Parliament obtained 1909 when name was changed. Winding-up order made in Oct. 1927 1928

Great West Shepherds Ld. Regd. 1884. Vol. liq. July 1886. Final meeting return regd. 5 June 1889 1887

Great Western & Great Central Railways Joint Committee. Inc. by Special Act 1899. Dissolved 2 Apr. 1949; undertaking vested 1 Jan. 1948 in British Transport Commission under Transport Act 1947. Holders of Great Western & Great Central 3½% guaranteed stock were entitled to receive in respect of every £100 stock held. £102 10s. British Transport 3% guaranteed stock 1978—88 1949

Great Western & Great Northern Junction Railway Co. Inc. by Special Act 1888. Undertaking abandoned by Act of 1891 1892

Great Western Colliery Co. Ld. Regd. 1878. Vol. liq. 31 Dec. 1889. Reconstructed 1890 as company of same name. Holders of A shares were entitled to 1 fully-paid A share of £5 and 1 B share of £5 (credited with £3 paid) for each A share of £5 held. Holders of B shares were entitled to 1 fully-paid B share of £5 and 1 B share of £5 (credited with £3 paid) for each B share of £5 held. Final meeting return regd. 9 Mar. 1891 1908

Great Western Colliery Co. Ld. Regd. 1890. Vol. liq. (members') 11 Dec. 1934. Undertaking and assets acquired by Powell Duffryn Steam Coal Co. Ld. Capital returned to contributories—£477,289 16s. 8d. £33 16s. 9d. was paid into Companies' Liquidation Account in respect of unclaimed dividends. Final meeting return regd. 21 Dec. 1935 1935

Great Western Consolidated No Liability. Inc. Victoria. Vol. liq. (members') Oct. 1970. No capital returned to contributories. The co. was to be dissolved 6 Apr. 1972 1975-6

Great Western Cotton Co. Ld. Regd. 1885. Vol. liq. 29 Dec. 1925. Certain assets were sold to Western Viscose Silk Mills Ld., for £30,000 in cash £58,334 in preference shares and £11,666 in deferred shares. Final meeting return regd. 26 Sept. 1930 1926

Great Western Electric Light and Power Co. Ld. Regd. 1882. Vol. liq. Dec. 1884. Taken over by Anglo-American Brush Electric Light Corporation Ld. Shareholders were entitled to 10s. per share in cash and 3 fully-paid shares of £3 in acquiring company for every 20 shares of £2 10s. held. Final meeting return regd. 10 Apr. 1888 1885

Great Western Farm Dairies Co. Ld. Regd. 1881. Business was acquired by Great Western & Metropolitan Dairies Ld. for £66,381 in cash. Removed from Register 1901 1908

Great Western Ochre & Colour Works Ld. Regd. 1887. Vol. liq. 27 July 1891. Final meeting return regd. 10 Apr. 1893 1893

Great Western of Brazil Railway Co. Ld. Regd. 1872. Vol. liq. (members') 1 Nov. 1950; undertaking acquired by Brazilian Govt. for £3,798,750. The outstanding permanent 6% debenture stock and 5½% (formerly 4%) debentures were redeemed at par on 15 Nov. 1950 with interest from 1 Jan. 1947 to

See Stock Exchange Year-Book.

redemption date. Capital returned to contributories—£9 4s. (per £10 unit of stock) to preferred and ordinary stockholders. Paid into Companies' Liquidation Account—(1) unclaimed dividends £707; (2) distributions £1,910. Final meeting return regd. 9 Dec. 1959. Struck off Register 10 Mar. 1960 .... **1961**

Great Western Railway Co. Inc. by Special Act 1835 constituted as an amalgamated company from 1 July 1923 under provisions of Railways Act 1921. Dissolved 23 Dec. 1949; undertaking vested 1 Jan. 1948 in British Transport Commission under Transport Act 1947. Holders of securities (including Ross & Monmouth Railway Co. 3½% debentures) were entitled to receive British Transport 3% guaranteed stock 1978—88 as follows in respect of each £100 of capital held:

	£	s.	d.
Consolidated ordinary stock	59	1	3
5% rent charge stock	139	13	9
5% con. guaranteed stock	137	0	0
5% con. pref. stock	125	3	9
5% red pref. stock 1950	106	10	0
2½% deb. stock	95	10	0
4% deb. stock	128	3	9
4½% deb. stock	128	13	9
4½% deb. stock	130	7	6
5% deb.stock	142	7	6
Ross & Monmouth Railway Co.			
3½% red. debs.	102	0	0

1949

Great Western Railway of Canada. Inc. Canada 1849. Amalgamated 1882 with Grand Trunk Railway Co. of Canada. The securities were taken over by the amalgamating company. The 5% perpetual debenture stock was acquired in Jan. 1942 by H. M. Treasury at £126 9s. 8d. for every £100 stock held **1882**

Great Western Steam Laundry Co. Ld. Regd. Edinburgh 1883. Vol. liq. Mar. 1920. Final meeting return regd. 31 Mar. 1921 .... **1921**

Great Western Steamship Co. Ld. Regd. 1881. Vol. liq. 28 June 1895. Capital returned to contributories—£8 15s. per preference share of £15; £7 per ordinary share of £12 in July 1895; further payments (if any) not known. Final meeting return regd. 12 June 1896 **1896**

Great Wigston Gas Co. Inc. by Special Act 1889. Dissolved 1 May, 1949, undertaking being vested in East Midland Area Gas Board under Gas Act 1948. Holders of securities were entitled to receive, in respect of each £100 unit held, British Gas 3% guaranteed stock 1990-95 as follows:

	£	s.	d.
Orig. stock (10% stand.)	210	0	0
New ord.stock (7% stand.)	150	0	0
Ord. 1934 stock (6% stand.)	132	0	0

1952

Great Work Tin Mines Ld. Regd. 1934. Vol. liq. (creditors') 13 May 1938. No capital was returned to contributories. Final meeting return regd. 12 Oct. 1949 .... **1950**

Great Wyrley Colliery Co, Ld. Regd. 1875. Receiver appointed 21 Apr. 1925; ceased to act 21 Oct. 1927. Vol. liq. 21 Apr. 1925. Final meeting return regd. 27 June 1935 .... *1926*

Great Yarmouth Fish Selling & Curing Co. Ld. Regd. 1922. Vol. liq. Oct. 1924. Struck off Register Aug. 1929 .... **1930**

Great Yarmouth Gas Co. Estd. 1824; inc. by Special Act 1863. Dissolved 1 May 1949, undertaking being vested in Eastern Area Gas Board under Gas Act 1948. Holders of securities were entitled to receive British Gas 3% guaranteed stock 1990—95 as follows:

	£	s.	d.
Shares(8½%max.)(of£30)	51	0	0
New shares (7½% max.)(of £30)	45	0	0
Ord. shares (7% max.)(of £10)	14	0	0
5½%perp.deb.stock(per £100)	134	0	0
4% perp. deb. stock (per £100)	101	15	0

1952

Great Yarmouth Waterworks Co. Inc. by Special Act 1853. Dissolved 17 Dec. 1964, undertaking being vested in East Anglian Water Co. under East Anglian Water Order 1961. Stockholders received stock in East Anglican Water Co. in exchange as follows:-£20 5% consolidated ordinary stock per £10 ordinary (10% maximum) held, £14 5% consolidated ordinary stock per £10 new ordinary stock held, £3 4% consolidated preference stock per £2 6% preference A stock held, £5 4% consolidated preference stock per £4 5% preference B stock held £1 5½% redeemable preference stock 1980-1 per £1 5½% redeemable preference stock held, £1 6% redeemable preference stock 1978—80 per £1 6% redeemable preference stock held. The outstanding debenture stocks became stocks of East Anglian Water Co. **1916**

Great Zaruma Gold Mining Co. Ld. Regd. 1881. Reconstructed 1887 as Zaruma Gold Mining Co. Ld. Removed from Register 1905 .... **1894**

Greater Britain Insurance Corporation Ld. Regd. 1918. Court Order to wind up 21 Feb. 1922. Struck off Register 24 Oct. 1939 .... **1940**

Greater London and Counties Trust Ld. Regd. 1925 as Greater London Trust Ld.; name changed July 1926. Vol. liq. (members') 28 Aug. 1936. Capital returned to contributories—£3,300,000 to ordinary shareholders; £88,067 14s. 4d. to B shareholders and 2,747,025 ordinary shares of £1 fully-paid in Edmundson's Electricity Corporation Ld. to A shareholders. Final meeting return regd. 8 Mar. 1937 .... **1937**

Greater Omnibus Services Ld. Regd. 1913. Vol. liq. 26 May 1916. Final meeting return regd. 12 Apr. 1923 **1917**

Greatrex (C.) & Son Ld. Regd. 1901. Vol. liq. 19 Apr. 1906. Final meeting return regd. 14 Jan 1910 ...... *1907*

Greaves Bull & Lakin (Harbury Works) Ld. Regd. 1927. Vol. liq. (members') 30 Oct. 1931. Undertaking and assets were acquired by Associated Portland Cement Manufacturers Ld. In Nov. 1931 the debenture stockholders were repaid in full. Capital returned to contributories—1s. 10·275d. per share of 5s. Final meeting return regd. 5 Nov. 1934 .... **1930**

Greek Iron Ore Corporation Ld. Regd. 1907. Struck off Register 4 Aug. 1939 .... **1942**

Green (A. H.) & Co. Ld. Regd. 1922. Vol. liq. 19 Jan. 1926. Controlled by Bowater (W. V.) & Sons Ld. (later Bowaters Sales Co. Ld.). Final meeting return regd. 14 Apr. 1927 .... **1926**

Green Engine Co. Ld. Regd. 1912. Vol. liq. 18 Oct. 1929. All shares owned by British Internal Combustion Engines Ld. Final meeting return regd. 24 May 1930 **1930**

Green (Forster) and Co. Ld. Regd. 1891. Vol. liq. (members') 31 May 1943. Capital returned to contributories—£2 debenture stock and 1 share of £1 in Green Estates (Belfast) Ld. *plus* £2 in cash for every share of £2 10s. held. Final meeting return regd. 31 Mar. 1944 .... **1944**

Green (Harry) Ld. Regd. 1922. Vol. liq. (members') 27 June 1956. Liquidator stated that assets would realise insufficient to meet the unsecured creditors' claims in full. Final meeting return regd. 17 Feb. 1958 .... **1958**

Green (Herbert) & Co. Ld. Regd. 1934. No capital returned to contributories. Assets reaiised sufficient to make a payment of £30% to 1st mortgage debenture stockholders. Struck off Register 1 May 1942 .... **1943**

Green Hurth Lead Mining Co. Ld. Regd. 1887. Vol. liq. 5 July 1902. Final meeting return regd. 22 Sept. 1904 **1903**

Green Line Coaches Ld. *See* London General Omnibus Co. Ld.

Green Valley Synd. (Pty.) Ld. In liquidation. All capital was owned by Eastern Transvaal Consolidated Mines Ld. **1939**

Greenacres Cotton Spinning Co. Ld. Regd. 1871. Vol. liq. 30 Jan. 1920. The undertaking and assets were sold to Greenacres Spinning Co. (1919) Ld. Final meeting return regd. 10 Feb. 1921 .... **1921**

Greenbushes Tin Fields Ld. Regd. 1901. Vol. liq. May 1908. Removed from Register 1908 .... **1909**

Greene Stabell Mines Ld. (No Personal Liability). Inc. Quebec by Letters Patent 1928 as Stabell Gold Mines N.P.L.; name changed Mar. 1928. Co. surrendered its charter and transferred its property to Jacola Mines Ld. in Feb. 1937 .... **1938**

Greenfriar Investment Co. Ld. Regd. 1935. Vol. liq. (members') 10 Apr. 1963. The undertaking and assets were transferred to Witan Investment Co. Ld.; the 3½% and 4½% preference stocks were repaid 11 Apr. 1963. Final meeting return regd. 20 Oct. 1966 .... **1967**

Greenhill Bleaching Co. Ld. Regd. 1921. Vol. liq. (members') 17 Aug. 1944. A direct controlling interest was held by Bleachers' Association Ld. (later Whitecroft Industrial Holdings Ld.). Final meeting return regd. 18 Nov. 1944 .... **1945**

Greenhill & Foster Ld. *See* C. Orton Foster Ld.

Greenhill & Sons Ld. Part of the business was sold in 1928 to Acetate Products Corporation Ld. for £205,000 in cash and £25,000 in fully-paid deferred shares of 1s. **1929**

Greenmount & Boyne Ld. Inc. in Dublin 1919 as Boyne Weaving & Finishing Co. Ld.; name changed to Greenmount & Boyne Linen Co. Ld. 1923 and to present title 1972 .... **1986-7**

Greenmount Gold Mines Ld. Regd. 1903. Vol. liq. 16 Aug. 1904. Removed from Register 1910 .... **1905**

Greenock & Wemyss Bay Railway Co. Inc. by Special Act 1862. Under Caledonian Railway Act 1893 undertaking was amalgamated with that company.

VOL. FOR

Holders of ordinary and preference shares received fully-paid ordinary stock of same nominal amount in Caledonian Railway Co.; holders of debenture stock received an equal nominal amount of debenture stock **1894**

Greenock Port & Harbour Trustees. Inc. by Special Act 1866. Debenture stocks were exchanged for Clyde Port Authority stocks on 1 Jan. 1966 as follows (per £100 stock held)—A debenture, £70 4% & £80 3% stock; B preferred debenture, £100 4% stock; B deferred debenture, £83 15s. 4% & £16 5s. 3% stock. Dissolved 1 Jan. 1966 .... **1967**

Greenock Railway Guaranteed Co. Inc. by Special Act 1851. Dissolved Aug. 1883 .... **1883**

Greenwich Dock & Railway Co. Inc. by Special Act 1881. Line acquired by South Eastern Railway Co.in 1882 .... **1884**

Greenwich Ferry Co. Ld. Regd. 1890. Receiver for debenture holders was appointed 16 Jan. 1893. Struck off Register 5 May 1896 .... **1896**

Greenwich Inlaid Linoleum Co. Ld. Regd. 1895 as Greenwich Inlaid Linoleum (Frederick Walton's New Patents) Co. Ld.; name changed June 1932. Vol. liq. (members') 31 Mar. 1934. Final meeting return regd. 31 Dec. 1934 .... **1935**

Greenwich Pier Co. Inc. by Act. Vol. liq. 4 Dec. 1905. Undertaking acquired by London County Council **1906**

Greenwood (John) Millers (1934) Ld. Regd. 1934. Vol. liq. (members') 19 Nov. 1940. Preference shares were repaid; further returns of capital to contributories (if any) not known. £22 19s. 5d. was paid into Companies' Liquidation Account. Final meeting return regd. 12 Mar. 1946 .... **1947**

Greenwood Proprietary Ld. Regd. 1958. Vol. liq. (members') 15 Oct. 1964. The undertaking and assets having been transferred to Assam & African Investments Ld. Final meeting return regd. 17 Apr. 1965 .... **1966**

Greer (H. & W.) Ld. Regd. 1904. Vol. liq. 31 Mar. 1922. Final meeting return regd. 8 July 1932 .... **1923**

Grein (J. T.) Financial Agency Ld. Regd. 1910. Vol. liq. 25 Aug. 1920. Final meeting return regd. 24 Oct.1922 .... ***1921**

Grenville United Mines Ld. Regd. 1906. Vol. liq. 22 Sept. 1919. Reconstructed as company of same name. Shareholders were entitled to 2 shares of 5s. (credited with 3s. 6d. paid) for each share of 10s. held. Final meeting return regd. 31 Dec. 1923 ..... **1920**

Grenville United Mines Ld. Regd. 1919. Vol. liq. 25 Jan. 1921. Final meeting return regd. 26 Dec. 1923 .... **1921**

Gresham Gold Exploring Syndicate Ld. Regd. 1894. Removed from Register 1903 .... **1900**

Gresham Real Estates Ld. Undertaking acquired in Dec. 1927 by British Foreign & Colonial Corporation Ld. **1928**

Gresham Syndicate Proprietary Ld. Inc. Victoria. In liquidation. All capital was owned by New Broken Hill Consolidated Ld **1940**

Gresham Trust Ld. see Petrotim Securities, Ld. ....

Greta Collieries Ld. Regd. 1890. Vol. liq. 28 June 1894. Removed from Register 1905 .... **1895**

Greville (H. M.) & Sons Ld. Regd. 1897. Vol. liq. 19 May 1900. Removed from Register 1901 .... **1901**

Greyfriars Ld. Regd. 1923 as Greyfriars Press Ld.; name changed Mar. 1926. Vol. liq. (members') 23 May 1930. Capital returned to contributories— £289,186 4s. 7d. Final meeting return regd. 7 Apr. 1931 .... **1931**

Greyfriars Press Ld. (The). Regd. 1929. Vol. liq. (members') 29 June 1960. £612 14s. was paid into Companies' Liquidation Account in respect of unclaimed dividends. Final meeting return regd. 7 Dec. 1961 .... **1962**

Greyhound Motors Ld. Regd. 1921. Vol. liq. (members') 1 Jan. 1936. Undertaking acquired by Bristol Tramway & Carriage Co. Ld. Capital returned to contributories—20s. per preference share of £1; £1 19s. 5d. per ordinary share of £1. Final meeting return regd. 13 Nov. 1936 .... **1937**

Greyhound Training & Breeding Kennels Ld. Regd. 1927. Vol. liq. 1 Jan. 1929. Final meeting return regd. 12 July 1929 .... **1929**

Greylingstadt Gold Mining & Exploration Co. Ld. Regd. 1896. Removed from Register 1903 .... **1899**

Greymouth-Point Elizabeth Railway & Coal Co. Ld. Regd. 1893. Properties were sold. Holders of 6% 1st mortgage debentures received at Feb. 1912, 15s. 6d. in the £; further payments (if any) not known. Struck off Register 1914 .... **1912**

Greys Brewery Ld. Regd. 1879. Court Orders: to wind up 14 Oct. 1884; to dissolve 31 Aug. 1888 .... ***1882**

Grey's Mynpacht Gold Mining Co. Ld. Inc. in Transvaal. Liquidated by order of Witwatersrand High Court in Dec. 1905 .... **1906**

VOL. FOR

Greystone Wood Manganese Syndicate Ld. Regd. 1907. Struck off Register 1918 .... **1910**

Grice, Grice & Son Ld. Regd. 1904. Vol. liq. 25 Mar. 1929. All shares owned by British Copper Manufacturers Ld. Final meeting return regd. 4 Jan. 1930 **1930**

Griendtsveen Moss Litter Co. Ld. Regd. 1893. Removed from Register 1909 .... **1905**

Griendtsveen Moss Litter Co. Ld. Regd. 1905 as Griendtsveen Moss Litter Co. (1905) Ld.; name changed to above Dec. 1909. Vol. liq. (members') 30 Nov. 1966. Final meeting return regd. 8 Dec. 1967 **1938**

Grierson's Gold Mines Ld. Regd. 1896. Vol. liq. Dec. 1908. Removed from Register 1910 .... **1909**

Griffin Foundry Co. Ld. Regd. 1897. Vol. liq. 19 Sept. 1904. Removed from Register 1908 .... **1905**

Griffin Silver Lead Mining Co. Ld. Regd. 1878. Removed from Register 1887 .... ***1884**

Griffiths & Browett Ld. Regd. 1890. Vol. liq. 11 Oct. 1901. Reconstructed as Griffiths & Browett (1901) Ld. Final meeting return regd. 24 Mar. 1902........ **1907**

Griffiths & Browett Ld. Regd. 1901 as Griffiths & Browett (1901) Co. Ld.; name changed Nov. 1903. Vol. liq. 28 July 1921. Final meeting return regd. 8 Dec. 1922.. **1907**

Griffiths & Co., Port Elizabeth Ld. Regd. 1910. Vol. liq. 10 Oct. 1928. Final meeting return regd. 8 May 1929 **1929**

Griffiths (Eli) & Sons Ld. Regd. 1925. Vol. liq. 7 Jan. 1963. Final meeting return regd. 8 Jan. 1964 .... **1939**

Griffiths Lewis Steam Navigation Co. Ld. Regd. 1906 as Manoravon Steamship Co. Ld.; name changed Dec. 1913. Vol. liq. Feb. 1920. Ordinary shareholders were entitled to 4½ fully-paid shares of £1 of Gould Steamships & Industrials, Ld., for each ordinary share of £1 held. Preference shareholders were entitled to repayment at £1 3s. per preference share of £1. Struck off Register 31 Aug. 1937.................. **1938**

Griffiths' Pyrodene Fire-Proofing Co. Ld. Regd. 1887. Struck off Register 31 Dec. 1895 .... **1899**

Griffiths (William) & Co. Ld. Regd. 1900. Reconstructed 1909 as company of same name. Shareholders were entitled to 5 shares of 10s. for each ordinary share of £5 held or £2 10s. in debenture stock and 5 shares of 10s. for each preference share of £5 held. Removed from Register 1912 .... **1910**

Grigg & Griffiths Ld. Regd. 1924 as Grigg (1924) Ld.; name changed Aug. 1926. Vol. liq. 2 Sept. 1927. Final meeting return regd. 15 Mar. 1928 .... **1928**

Grimaldi (Adam) & Co. Ld. All shares were acquired by Gwynnes Engineering Co. Ld. Court Order to wind up Jan. 1924 .... **1926**

Grimsby & Saltfleetby Light Railway Co. Inc. (under Light Railways Act 1896) by order of Light Railway Commissioners confirmed by Board of Trade 1899 **1903**

Grimshaw (J.) Ld. Regd. 1897. Vol. liq. 27 June 1928. Undertaking and certain assets were acquired by Massey's Burnley Brewery Ld. for £216,875 in cash, £400,000 5½% debenture stock, 25,000 fully-paid preference and 25,000 fully-paid ordinary shares of £1. Final meeting return regd. 18 Dec. 1936 .... **1929**

Grindell-Matthews Wireless Telephone Syndicate Ld. Regd. 1910. Court Order to wind up 13 Jan. 1914. Liquidator released 11 Dec. 1914. Struck off Register 14 Feb. 1919 .... **1914**

Grindleford, Baslow & Bakewell Railway Company by Special Act 1903 .... **1924**

Grindlay & Co. Ld. *See below.*

Grindlays Bank Ld. Regd. 1924 as Grindlay & Co. Ld., name changed 1947. Dissolved under Sections 206 and 208 of the Companies Act, 1948 on amalgamation with National Bank of India Ld. as from 31 Dec. 1947 under the title of National Overseas & Grindlays Bank Ld. (later National & Grindlays Bank Ld.) **1958**

Grindley Hotel Ware Co. Ld. Undertaking and assets were acquired by Cauldon Potteries Ld. **1908**

Grindley of Stoke (Ceramics) Ld. Regd. 1935 as Alfred Clough Ld.; name changed 1978. Vol. liq. 13 Mar. 1986 .... **1982–3**

Grinton Mining & Smelting Co. Ld. Regd. 1888. Struck off Register 31 Dec. 1895 .... **1901**

Groeswen & Caradog Collieries Ld. Regd. 1900. Removed from Register 1904 .... **1904**

Grogwinion Lead Mining Co. Ld. Regd. 1872. Vol. liq. Apr. 1884. Final meeting return regd. 16 Nov. 1885 **1885**

Grootfontein Exploration Co. Ld. Regd. 1895. Vol. liq. July 1907. Removed from Register 1908 .... **1908**

Grootvlei Plantation Syndicate Ld. Inc. South Africa 1922. All assets were sold and it was intended to strike company off Register at end of Feb.1936.... **1936**

Grootvlei Prospecting Syndicate Ld. Regd. 1901. Vol. liq. 13 Oct. 1905. Removed from Register 1906 ... **1906**

Gropi Oil Co. Ld. *See* Nordic Oil Co. Ld.

Grosvenor & West End Railway Terminus Hotel Co. Ld. Regd. 1858. Under Act of 1899 undertaking and

VOL. FOR

assets were acquired by London, Brighton and South Coast Railway for £230,000. A return of £15 per share of £10 after repayment of mortgages and debentures was anticipated. Vol. liq. 7 Feb. 1900. Final meeting return regd. 20 Dec. 1900 .... **1900**

Grosvenor Battery Co. Ld. Regd. 1926. Vol. liq. (members') 28 July 1930. Undertaking acquired by Grosvenor Electric Batteries Ld. Final meeting return regd. 26 May 1932 .... **1943**

Grosvenor Dairies Ld. Regd. 1897. Struck off Register Jan. 1931 .... **1931**

Grosvenor Dairy Co. Ld. Regd. 1884. Court Orders: to wind up 17 Nov. 1888; to dissolve 13 Mar. 1891.. **1889**

Grosvenor Electric Batteries Ld. Regd 1930. Vol. liq. (members') 1 Dec. 1948. Subsidiary of Ever Ready Co. (Great Britain) Ld. Final meeting return regd. 1 Mar. 1949 .... **1948**

Grosvenor Gallery Library Ld. Regd. 1879 as Grosvenor Library Ld.; name changed 24 Mar. 1880. Vol. liq. May 1883. Court Order to continue winding up under supervision May 1883. Final meeting return regd. 11 May 1888 .... **1885**

Grosvenor Gardens Estates Ld. Regd. 1927 as Grosvenor Gardens Syndicate Ld.; name changed Nov. 1932. Vol. liq. (creditors') 30 Aug. 1938. Capital returned to contributories—£39,042 18s. 9d. Final meeting return regd. 6 Dec. 1938 .... **1939**

Grosvenor Hotel Dublin Ld. Inc. in Dublin 1899 as Metropole Hotels Co. (Ireland) Ld.; name changed Apr. 1943. Vol. liq. (members') 22 July 1959. Capital returned to contributories—12s. per share of £1. Final meeting return regd. 20 Feb. 1961 .... **1962**

Grosvenor Hotel (Westcliff) (1911) Ld. Regd 1911. Receiver appointed 23 May 1912. Struck off Register 17 Nov. 1916...................................... ***1913**

Grosvenor Library Ld. *See* Grosvenor Gallery Library Ld.

Grosvenor Mansions Co. Ld. Regd. 1898. Removed from Register 1903 .... **1900**

Grosvenor Property & Commercial Trust Ld. *See* Victoria (London) Property & Commercial Trust Ld.

Ground Rent Securities Association Ld. Regd. 1876. Removed from Register 1905 .... ***1880**

Group Units Investment Trust Ld. Regd. 1934. A subsidiary of British Industrial Corpn. Ld. Vol. liq. (members') 8 May 1957. Final meeting return regd. 25 Apr. 1958 .... **1940**

Grove (Edward) Ld. Business was acquired by C. B. & M. Tailors Ld **1930**

Grove Mills Ld. Regd. 1904. Vol. liq. 5 May 1920. Final meeting return regd. 24 Jan. 1921. Court Order declared dissolution void Apr. 1923. Final meeting return regd. 23 Sept. 1927 .... **1921**

Grove Mills (1920) Ld. Regd. 1920. Vol. liq. (members') 5 June 1930. Undertaking acquired by Lancashire Cotton Corporation Ld., in which Corporation shareholders were entitled to £1·069 income debenture stock, 21·453 ordinary shares of £1 fully-paid, and 21·453 deferred shares of 1s. fully-paid, for every £100 paid up and in addition one deferred share, fully-paid, for every 2s. 6d. of the one-half of capital called but not paid on such shares acquired of the Corporation as and when such capital is received by Corporation. Final meeting return regd. 9 Jan. 1939 .... **1931**

Groveland Gold Mining Co. Ld. Regd. 1888 as Mount Jefferson Gold Mining Co. Ld.; name changed May 1893. Court Order to wind up 31 Oct. 1894. Liquidator released 22 Aug. 1898. Struck off Register 19 Oct. 1906 .... **1893**

Grover (J. T.) & Co. Ld. Regd. 1895. Vol. liq. 13 Aug. 1900. Final meeting return regd. 8 Aug. 1902 ...... **1901**

Groves (John) & Sons Ld. *See* Groveson (Weymouth) Ld.

Grovesend Steel and Tinplate Co. Ld. Regd. 1904. Vol. liq. (members') 30 Mar. 1946 for the purpose of merging the assets and liabilities (other than the debenture stock) with those of Richard Thomas & Baldwins Ld. 4½% debenture stockholders were repaid at 102% and preference shareholders at 25s. per share and remaining assets were transferred to Richard Thomas & Baldwins Ld. as owners of all ordinary shares. £1,108 (amounts unclaimed by preference shareholders and debenture stockholders) was paid into Companies' Liquidation Account. Final meeting return regd. 26 May 1948 **1949**

Groveson (Weymouth) Ld. Regd. 1895 as John Groves & Sons Ld.; name changed Aug. 1936. Vol. liq. (members') 21 Sept. 1936. Undertaking was transferred to John Groves & Sons Ld. The 4½% and 5% debenture stocks were repaid at 110% and 105% respectively. Capital returned to contributories—£1 2s. 6d. per preference share of £1; £3 12s. 10½d. per

VOL. FOR

ordinary share of £1. Final meeting return regd. 13 Aug. 1938 .... **1937**

Growth Stocks Investment Co. Ld. Regd. 1961 as Investing in Foreign Growth Stocks Ld.; name changed 1966. Vol. liq. (members') 17 May 1967. Capital returned to contributories—5s. 8½d. per ordinary share (of 5s.) plus 1 ordinary share of 5s. of Anglo Nippon Trust Ld. for every 4 shares. Final meeting return regd. 3 Sept. 1969 .... **1970**

Grozny Oil Co. Ld. Regd. 1910. Struck off Register 1916 **1915**

Guadalajara Gold & Silver Mining Co. of Spain Ld. Regd. 1878. Removed from Register 1905 .... ***1884**

Guadaleazar Quicksilver Mines Ld. Regd. 1890. Vol. liq. 6 Aug. 1895. Reconstructed as New Guadaleazar Quicksilver Mines Ld., in which company shareholders were entitled to 2 shares of 10s. (credited with 8s. paid) for each ordinary or preference share of £1 held. Debenture stockholders were entitled to 2 fully-paid shares of 10s. in new company for each £1 principal or interest due. Final meeting return regd. 12 Aug. 1896 .... **1903**

Guadalupe (Honduras) Gold & Silver Mining Co. Ld. Regd. 1880. Vol. liq. 6 Nov. 1894. Reconstructed as company of same name. Shareholders were entitled to 1 share of 10s. (credited with 8s. paid) for each ordinary share of £1 held; preference shareholders were entitled to an equal number of preference shares in new company. Final meeting return regd. 31 Aug. 1897 .... **1898**

Guanacevi Co. Ld. Regd. 1906. Vol. liq. 5 Nov. 1917. Final meeting return regd. 10 Oct. 1918 .... **1918**

Guanta Co. Ld. Regd. 1893. Vol. liq. 18 Jan. 1897. Final meeting return regd. 23 Jan. 1899 .... **1897**

Guanta Railways, Harbour & Coal Trust Co. Ld. Regd. 1890. Vol. liq. 13 Apr. 1893. Final meeting return regd. 23 Jan. 1899 .... **1894**

Guapo (Trinidad) Oil Co. Ld. Regd. 1919. Vol. liq. 31 Oct. 1912. Final meeting return regd. 19 Nov. 1918 **1913**

Guarantee and General Trading Corporation Ld. Regd. 1896. Vol. liq. 10 July 1900. Final meeting return regd. 13 Aug. 1902 .... **1901**

Guarantee Association of Scotland Ld. Regd. Edinburgh 1873. Business disposed of to London Guarantee and Accident Co. Ld. Vol. liq. Sept. 1884. Final meeting return regd. 31 Mar. 1887 .... **1885**

Guaranty Securities Corporation. *See* Continental Guaranty Corporation.

Guardax Safety Glass Ld. Regd. 1928. Vol. liq. (members') 17 Jan. 1930. Capital returned to contributories—1s. 1·66d. per share of 2s. Final meeting return regd. 6 Aug. 1930 .... **1930**

Guardian Horse, Vehicle & General Insurance Co, Ld. Regd. 1880. Court Orders: to wind up 16 Oct. 1909; to dissolve 6 June 1895 .... **1891**

Guardian Plate Glass Insurance Co. Ld. Regd. 1863. Vol. liq. (members') 2 Jan. 1952. Final meeting return regd. 15 May 1953 .... **1940**

Guardian Trust Co. Inc. Missouri 1889 as Missouri, Kansas & Texas Trust Co.; name changed July 1899. On 16 Dec. 1901 it was stated that the company was being liquidated **1902**

Guarino Hydraulic Gold Mines Ld. Regd. 1896. Vol. liq. 27 Mar. 1902. Undertaking was acquired by Pavas Gold Mines Ld. for £1,500 in cash and £35,346 in fully-paid shares of £1. Final meeting return regd. 24 Mar. 1904 .... **1908**

Guatemala Plantations Ld. Regd. 1926. Vol. liq. (members') 18 Dec. 1931. Capital returned to contributories—£182,278 9s. 8d. plus certain assets distributed in specie. Final meeting return regd. 28 June 1933 .... ***1932**

Guatrache Land Co. Ld. *See* Tokengate Investment Co. Ld.

Guayaquil Quito Railway Wharves & Warehouse Ld. *See* Duran (Ecuador) Wharves & Warehouses Ld. ......

Guayule Rubber Co. Ld. Regd. 1910. Vol. liq. (members') July 1927. Capital returned to contributories—8⅝d. per share (of 2s.). Final meeting return regd. 1 Aug. 1950 .... **1951**

Gubbins & Co. Ld. Regd. 1920. Struck off Register 1 July, 1960 .... ***1933**

Gudalur (Nilgiri) Tea & Coffee Estates Ld. Regd. 1927. Vol. liq. (members') 19 Apr. 1945. Capital returned to contributories—£1 13s. 8·137d. per share (of £1). Final meeting return regd. 22 Mar. 1950 .... **1951**

Guelph (Coolgardie) Gold Mine Ld. Regd. 1895. Court Order to wind up 12 Jan. 1898. Removed from Register 1908 .... **1898**

Gueret (L.) & Co. Ld. *See* below.

Gueret, Llewellyn & Merrett Ld. Regd. 1920 as L. Gueret & Co. Ld.; name changed Jan. 1927. All capital was owned by Powell Duffryn Ld. Vol. liq. (members') 31 Dec. 1951. Final meeting return regd. 12 Oct. 1961 .... **1940**

*See Stock Exchange Year-Book.

Guernica Silver & Copper Mines (Bolivia) Ld. Regd. 1908. Vol. liq. 10 Nov. 1913. Final meeting return regd. 27 Jan. 1923 .... **1914**

Guernsey Banking Co. Ld. Established 1827. Inc. Guernsey 1898. Vol. liq. Feb. 1924. Undertaking and assets were acquired by National Provincial Bank Ld., in which company shareholders were entitled to 2 shares of £5 (credited as fully-paid) and £18 nominal 5% War Loan 1929–47 for each share of £50 (£10 paid) held **1925**

Guernsey Commercial Banking Co. Ld. Established 1835. Inc. Guernsey 1912. Vol liq. May 1924. Undertaking and assets were acquired by Westminster Bank Ld., in which company shareholders were entitled to 6 shares of £1 (credited as fully-paid) and £20 nominal value 5% War Loan 1929–47 for each share of £25 (£5 paid) held **1925**

Guernsey Flower and Fruit Co. Ld. Regd. 1887. Vol. liq. 21 June 1895. Final meeting return regd. 18 Dec. 1895 .... **1896**

Guernsey Steam Tramways Co. Ld. Regd. 1878. Vol. liq. Nov. 1888. Final meeting return regd. 2 Oct. 1889 **1889**

Guernsey Water Co, Ld. Regd. 1906. Vol. liq. 10 Mar. 1921. The undertaking was purchased by State of Guernsey for £65,000. Final meeting return regd. 28 Dec. 1921 .... **1922**

Guernsey Waterworks Co. Ld. Regd. 1888. Vol. liq. 27 July 1893. Certain assets were acquired by company of same name for £15,000 in ordinary shares, £15,000 in 1st debentures and £15,000 in 2nd debentures. Final meeting return regd. 20 June 1895 **1897**

Guernsey Waterworks Co. Ld. Regd. 1894. Vol. liq. 25 Apr. 1906. Reconstructed 1906 as Guernsey Water Co. Ld., in which company shareholders were entitled to 3 shares of £1 for each share of £10 held. Final meeting return regd. 6 Oct. 1921 .... **1909**

Guest, Keen & Piggotts Ld. Regd. 1925. Vol. liq. (members') 23 May 1934. Final meeting return regd. 16 Apr. 1935 .... **1935**

Guests Gold Mine Ld. Regd. 1899. Vol. liq. 31 Dec. 1902 for reconstruction as New Guest's Gold Mine Ld. Removed from Register 1903 .... **1902**

Guests Trust Ld. Regd. 1920. Vol. liq. (members') 25 July 1935. Capital returned to contributories—£11,415 3s. *plus* certain assets which were distributed in specie. Final meeting return regd. 3 June 1936 **1936**

Guiana Gold Co. Ld. Regd. 1905. Court Order to wind up 26 June 1923. Liquidator released 24 Jan. 1929. Struck off Register 11 Mar. 1932 .... **1924**

Guiana Gold Fields Ld. Regd. 1889. Removed from Register 9 May 1893 .... ***1892**

Guild Finance Ld. Regd. 1929. Vol. liq. (members') 22 Nov. 1932. Capital returned to contributories—£1,470. Final meeting return regd. 22 Mar. 1933 **1934**

Guildford & District Motor Services Ld. Regd. 1914. Vol. liq. 26 Oct. 1926. All shares held by Aldershot & District Traction Co. Ld. Final meeting return regd. 16 Feb. 1927 .... **1927**

Guildford Electricity Supply Co. Ld. Regd. 1892 as Holloway Electricity Supply Co. Ld.; name changed Nov. 1894. Vol. liq. 25 Oct. 1921. The undertaking was acquired by Guildford Corporation. The debentures were to be repaid at par and shares of both classes were to rank *pari passu* for surplus assets. Final meeting return regd. 23 Oct. 1923 .... **1922**

Guildford Gas Light & Coke Co. Estd. 1824; inc. by Special Act 1857. Dissolved 1 May 1949. The electricity undertaking was vested on 1 Apr. 1948 in the British (later Central) Electricity Authority and South Eastern Area Electricity Board. Remaining undertaking being vested in South Eastern Area Gas Board under Gas Act 1948. Holders of securities were entitled to receive in respect of each £100 unit held British Gas 3% guaranteed stock 1990—95 as follows:—

	£ s. d.
Cons. ord. stock (5% stand.)	170 0 0
Elec. ord. stock	220 0 0
5% pref. stock	120 0 0
6% pref. stock	145 0 0
6% elec. pref. stock	145 0 0
4% red. pref. stock	101 0 0
4% perp. (Gas) deb. stock	102 10 0
5% perp. (Gas) deb. stock	121 0 0
5% red. (Gas) deb. stock	105 0 0
4½% red. (Gas) deb. stock 1959	105 0 0

1952

Guildford (Loddon) Deep Leads Ld. Regd. 1906. Vol. liq. Mar. 1910. No capital returned to contributories. Removed from Register 1910 .... **1911**

Guildford Stores Ld. Regd. 1918. Vol. liq. (members') 1 Feb. 1963. Redeemable preference shares repaid Sept. 1964 at 22s. per share; 2nd preference shares repaid at par June 1965 (partly in specie). Ordinary shareholders were entitled to receive 3s. 6·96d. per share (of 5s.). Final meeting return regd. 7 Jan. 1966 **1967**

Guildhall Development Co. Ld. Regd. 1934. Vol. liq. (members') 4 Mar. 1964. All capital was owned by Guildhall Property Co. Ld. Final meeting return regd. 11 Nov. 1965 .... **1967**

Guildhall Investment Property and Advance Co. Ld. Regd. Apr. 1884. Vol liq. 13 June 1923. Capital returned to contributories—1s. 4d.per share of £5, £1 paid. £784 19s 8d. was paid into Companies' Liquidation Account. Final meeting return registered 21 Jan. 1957 .... **1958**

Guildhall Trust Ld. Regd. 1926. Vol. liq. (members') 8 Apr. 1942. Capital returned to contributories—6s 8d (approx) per share *plus* certain investments distributed in specie. Final meeting return regd. 17 Apr. 1943 .... **1945**

Guinea Coast Exploration Syndicate Ld. Regd 1900. Removed from Register 1908 .... **1905**

Guinea Coast Gold Mining Co. Ld. Regd. 1881. Vol. liq. 31 July 1885. Final meeting return regd. 25 Feb. 1887. Court Orders deffered dissolution until 1 Apr. 1892. .... **1886**

Guinea Fowl Mines Ld. Inc. Rhodesia 1905. Vol. liq. Dec 1913 .... **1914**

Guinea Portable Gramophone Co. Ld. Regd. 1929. Vol. liq. Nov. 1931. Undertaking and assets were acquired by Valophone Ld. in which company shareholders were entitled to 1 share of 5s. (credited with 4s. paid) for every 5 shares of 1s. held. Struck off Register 31 Aug. 1937 .... **1938**

Guion Steamship Co. Ld. Regd. 1888. Vol. liq. 20 Feb. 1900. Final meeting return regd. 21 Aug. 1900 .... ***1901**

Guisborough Gas Co. Ld. Regd. 1885. Dissolved 1 May 1949 undertaking being vested in Northern Area Gas Board under Gas Act 1948. Holders of ordinary shares (of £10) were entitled to receive £19 5s British Gas 3% guaranteed stock 1990–95 for each share held **1952**

Guiseley, Yeadon & Headingley Railway Co. Inc. by Special Act 1885 as Guisely, Yeadon & Rawdon Railway Co. name changed by Act of 1891. Under Midland Railway Act 1892 undertaking was acquired by that company for £36,250 4% perpetual preference stock **1895**

Guiterman (S.) & Co. Ld. Regd. 29 June 1899. Vol. liq. (creditors') 8 June 1966. No capital returned to contributories. Final meeting held 28 Mar. 1974 . **1975-6**

Gula Investments Ld. Regd. 1910 as Gula Kalumpong Rubber Estates Ld.; name changed Nov. 1959. Vol. liq. (members') 20 Mar. 1967. Capital returned to contributories—11s. 3d. and 3·507969p per share of 25p. £15,280·83 was paid into Companies' Liquidation Account. Final meeting return regd. 4 Oct. 1974 **1975-6**

Gülcher Electric Light and Power Co. Ld. Regd. 1882. Vol. liq. 27 May 1887. Court Order to continue under supervision 13 Sept. 1887. Final meeting return regd. 3 July 1933 .... **1883**

Gülcher (New Electric Light & Power Co. Ld.). Regd. 1888. Vol. liq. 19 June 1894. Final meeting return regd. 29 July 1896 .... **1895**

Gulf Creek Ld. Regd. 1899. Vol. liq. 10 Oct. 1904. Removed from Register 1906 .... **1905**

Gulf Line Ld. Regd. Edinburgh 1899. Vol. liq. Feb, 1929. Capital returned to contributories—12s. 6d. per share of £1 in Feb. 1929; further payments (if any) not known. Final meeting return regd. 24 Dec. 1931 .... **1929**

Gulf States Steel Co. Inc. Delaware 1913. Undertaking was acquired by Republic Steel Corporation 1n Apr. 1937 .... **1921**

Gulf Syndicate Ld. Regd. 1905. Vol. liq. 15 Nov. 1906. Final meeting return regd. 3 Jan. 1907 .... ***1908**

Gulgong Alluvial Gold Fields Ld. Regd. 1889. Struck off Register 11 June 1895 .... **1901**

Gullewa Gold Mines Ld. Regd. 1896. Undertaking was acquired in 1899 by Phoenix Gold Mines Ld. in which company shareholders were entitled to 2 shares of 10s. (credited with 8s. paid) for each share of £1 held. Removed from Register 1904 .... **1903**

Gullewa Mines Ld. Regd. 1906. Vol. liq. July 1907. Removed from Register 1909 .... **1908**

Gunning & Campbells Ld. Regd. Dublin 1865. Vol. liq. May 1932 .... **1933**

Gunpowder Co. Ld. *See* Ballin Collig Royal Gunpowder Mills Co. Ld.

Gurlyn Consolidated Tin Mines (Cornwall) Ld. Regd. 1906. Struck off Register 1920 .... **1912**

Gurnos Anthracite Collieries Co. Ld. Regd. 1927. All shares owned by Amalgamated Anthracite Collieries Ld. Struck off Register 10 Mar. 1939 .... **1939**

Gurum River (Nigeria) Tin Mines Ld. Regd. 1911. Vol. liq. 26 July 1927. Final meeting return regd. 30 Sept. 1927 .... **1928**

Guston Silver Mine Co. Ld. Regd. 1886. Vol. liq. 26 Aug. 1887. Reconstructed as New Guston Co. Ld. in

VOL. FOR

which company shareholders were entitled to 1 share of £1 (credited with 17s. 6d. paid) for each share of £1 held. Final meeting return regd. 11 Feb. 1891 .... **1898**

Gutta-Percha Corporation Ld. Regd. 1897. Court Order to wind up 11 July 1900. Removed from Register 1910 .... **1901**

Guy Fawkes Reef Ld. Regd. 1894. Vol. liq. 14 Jan. 1898. Reconstructed as Mozambique Consolidated Mines Ld. in which company shareholders were entitled to 2 shares of 10s. (credited with 9s. paid) for each share of 10s. held. Final meeting return regd. 27 Sept. 1898 .... **1900**

Guy Motors Ld. Regd. 1914. Court order to wind up 6 Nov. 1961 No capital returned to contributories. Liquidator released 26 June 1964 .... **1965**

Guzzwell Steam Fishing Co. Ld. See Monarch Steam Fishing Co. Ld.

Gwalia Central Gold Mines Ld. Inc Western Australia 1911. Vol. liq. May 1920. Undertaking and assets acquired by Hampton Consolidated Ld. in which company shareholders were entitled to 5 fully-paid preference shares of 2s. for every 2 preference shares of 5s. held and 1 fully-paid preference share of 2s. and 2 ordinary shares of 2s. (credited 1s. per share paid) for every 2 ordinary palaces of 5s. held **1921**

Gwalia Consolidated Ld. Regd. 1898 as Star of Gwalia Ld.; name changed July 1900. Vol. liq. 19 Dec. 1912. Reconstructed as company of same name. Shareholders were entitled to 1 share of 2s. 6d. (credited with 1s. 6d. paid) for each share of 2s. 6d. held. Final meeting return regd. 19 Feb. 1914 .... **1913**

Gwalia Consolidated Ld. Regd. 1912. Vol. liq. 14 Oct. 1913. Final meeting return regd. 16 June 1914 .... **1914**

Gwalia Proprietary Ld. Inc. Western Australia 1908 as Great Tower Hill Gold Mines (1908) Ld.; name changed Nov. 1908. Vol. liq. Oct. 1911 for reconstruction. Scheme was not carried out and in Mar. 1912 ordinary and preference shareholders were offered 6 shares of 5s. (credited 4s. paid) in Gwalia Central Gold Mines Ld. for every 5 shares of 5s. held **1913**

Gwanda Mines Ld. Regd. 1899. Vol. liq. 31 Dec. 1912. Final meeting return regd. 4 May 1915 .... **1913**

Gwanda Railway Syndicate Ld. Regd. 1898. Vol. liq. 25 Feb. 1910. Capital returned to contributories—100% further payments (if any) not known. Final meeting return regd. 10 Aug. 1914 .... **1911**

Gwanda (Rhodesia) Consolidated Developing Co. Ld. Regd. 1895. Vol. liq. Oct. 1910. Removed from Register 1911 .... **1911**

Gwaun-Cae-Gurwen Colliery Co, Ld. Regd. 1874. Vol. liq. (members') 5 Dec. 1929. Guest, Keen & Nettlefolds Ld. owned all issued shares. Final meeting return regd. 3 Apr. 1934 .... **1934**

Gwelo (Matabeleland) Exploration & Development Co. Ld. Regd. Dublin 1895. Winding-up order made 14 Dec. 1897 .... **1899**

Gwelo Trust & Finance Co. Ld. Regd. 1900. Removed from Register 1904 .... **1904**

Gwendraeth Valley Anthracite Collieries Co. Ld. Regd. 1927. All shares owned by Amalgamated Anthracite Collieries Ld. Struck off Register 10 Mar. 1939 ... **1939**

Gwendraeth Valleys Railway Co. Inc. by Special Act 1864. In 1923 the undertaking was merged into the Great Western Railway Co. for payment of £17,000 in cash **1924**

Gwern-y-Mynyd Lead Co, Ld. Regd. 1885. Removed from Register 1891 .... **1898**

Gwinear Tin Mines Ld. Regd. 1919. Struck off Register Jan. 1933 .... **1933**

Gwydyn Amalgamated Mines Co, Ld. Regd. 1881. Vol. liq. 3 Feb. 1883. Final meeting return regd. 28 Aug. 1885 .... ***1884**

Gwyn Mines (Merioneth) Ld. Regd. 1901. Reeeivers were appointed in Jan. 1913. Struck off Register 1916 .... **1914**

Gwynnes Engineering Co. Ld. Regd. 1920. Court Order to wind up Oct. 1926. Struck off Register Aug. 1934 **1935**

Gwynnes Ld. Regd. 1897 as J. & H. Gwynne Ld.; name changed 1903. Vol. liq. July 1925. Court Order to wind up Oct. 1926. Undertaking was acquired by Gwynnes Engineering Co. Ld. Struck off Register Mar. 1932 .... **1933**

Gympie Copper Mines Ld. Regd. 1900. Removed from Register 1906 .... **1905**

Gympie Gold Mines Ld. See Scottish Gympie Gold Mines Ld.

Gympie Golden Crown Mining Co. Ld. Regd. 1887. Vol. liq. 18 May 1892. Final meeting return regd. 27 July 1895 .... **1893**

Gympie Great Eastern Gold Mining Co. Ld. See Australasian Mining Co. Ld.

H

VOL. FOR

H. & C. Davis & Co. Ld. See Dasvis (H. & C.) & Co. Ld.

H. & U. Rubber & Coffee Estates Ld. Regd. 1910. Vol. liq. and Court Order to wind up Oct. 1912. Struck off Register 1927 .... **1913**

H. D. Syndicate Ld. See Piccadilly Hotel Ld.

H. E. H. Company Ld. Regd. 1925. Vol. liq. (members') 22 Sept. 1952. 170,000 ordinary shares of 10s. of Hunt Edmunds & Co. Ld. were distributed share for share to holders of the A and B shares (of 1s.) of this company. Final meeting return regd. 5 Apr. 1955 **1956**

H. E. Proprietary Ld. Regd. 1901. Vol. liq. 24 Mar. 1914. Undertaking sold to New Districts Development Co. Ld. [later H. E. Proprietary (New) Ld.], in which company shareholders were entitled to 3 fully-paid shares of 10s. for every 4 shares of £1 held. Final meeting return regd. 26 Nov. 1924 .... **1915**

H. E. Proprietary (New) Ld. Regd. 1912 as New Districts Development Co. Ld.; name changed Apr. 1914. Vol. liq. (members') 22 Dec. 1931. Undertaking and assets were acquired by H. E. Proprietary Ld., in which company shareholders were entitled to 1 share of 10s. (credited as fully-paid) for each share of 10s. held. Final meeting return regd. 28 July 1932 **1932**

H. F. Co. Ld. Inc. Transvaal 1898. Vol. liq. May 1908. Undertaking and assets were acquired by East Rand Proprietary Mines Ld., in which company shareholders were entitled to 1½ shares of £1 (credited as fully-paid) for each share of £1 held **1909**

H. Goldman Group p.l.c. See Goldman (H.) Group p.l.c.

H. L. (Clothiers) Ld Regd. 1916 as H. Lotery & Co. Ld.; name changed Dec. 1935. Vol. liq. (members') 20 Jan. 1936. Capital returned to contributories—£250,700. Final meeting return regd. 31 Mar. 1936. Court Orders deferred dissolution to 1 Jan. 1937 **1936**

H. M. R. Syndicate Ld. Regd. 1905. Vol. liq. (members') 1 Dec. 1942. Shareholders were entitled to 134·461 shares of £1 in Heidelberg Estates & Exploration Co. Ld. (later Town Centre Properties Ld.) for every 100 shares of £1 held plus £2 0s. 6d. per share in cash. £71 2s. 2d. was paid into Companies' Liquidation Account. Final meeting return regd. 10 May 1943 **1945**

H. 0. Siberian Exploration Ld. Regd. 1905. Vol. liq. 14 May 1908. Final meeting return regd. 3 Apr. 1909 ***1909**

H. P. Syndicate Ld. Regd. 1906. Vol. liq. July 1908. Removed from Register 1909 .... **1909**

H. T. Investments Ld. Regd. 1913 as Herbert Terry & Sons Ld.; name changed 1971. All capital acquired by Trafford Park Estates Ld. Company dissolved 24 Dec. 1980 ....**1979–80**

H. W. Phillips & Co. Ld. See Phillips (H. W.) & Co. Ld.

Habilis Patent Self-Opening Umbrella Co. Ld. Regd. 1895. Vol. liq. 19 Aug. 1896. Final meeting return regd. 1 Mar. 1899 .... **1897**

Habin Ld. See Dimplex Industries Ld.

Haboneh (Anglo-Palestine) Building Co. Ld. Regd. 1899 as Haboneh Society for Promoting Building Operations (in Palestine) Ld.; name changed Apr. 1920. Vol. liq. May 1924. Struck off Reigister 12 Mar. 1935 .... **1936**

Hackney & Shepherd's Bush Empire Palaces Ld. See below.

Hackney & Shepherd's Bush Empire Palaces Ld. See below.

Hackney Empire Ld. Regd. 1900 as Hackney Empire Palace Ld.; name changed to Hackney & Shepherd's Bush Empire Palaces Ld. in Aug. 1902, to Hackney & Shepherd's Bush Empires Ld. in Nov. 1942 and as above in Dec. 1953. Vol. liq. (members') 30 Oct. 1957. The lst mortgage debenture stock was repaid at 105%. Capital returned to contributories—20s. per preference share of £1 and 25s. 4·8d. per ordinary share of £1. Final meeting return regd. 13 Oct. 1958 .... **1959**

Hackney Empire Palace Ld. See above.

Hackney Furnishing Co. Ld. Regd. 1928 as Hackney Furnishing Co. (1928) Ld.; name changed Feb. 1930. Vol. liq. (creditors') 25 Jan. 1933. Struck off Register 29 Dec **1945**

Hackney Furnishing Co. Ld. (Regd. 1942. See Mare Street Furnishing Co. Ld. 1901).

Haddington Brewery Co. Ld. Regd. Edinburgh 1896. Vol. liq. Nov. 1899. Court Order to dissolve 28 Mar. 1901. .... **1900**

Haddington Gas Co. Ld. Regd. in Edinburgh 1934. Dissolved 1 May 1949, undertaking being vested in Scottish Area Gas Board under Gas Act 1948. Holders of ordinary stock were entitled to receive, per £1 unit held, British Gas 3% guaranteed stock 1990–95, £2 4s. **1952**

Hadleigh Castle Gold Mining Co. Ld. Regd 1896. Vol. liq. 31 Jan. 1900. Removed from Register 1904.... **1901**

VOL. FOR

Hadleigh Gas Consumers Co. Ld. Regd 1862. Dissolved 1 May 1949, undertaking being vested in Eastern Area Gas Board under Gas Act 1948. Holders of securities were entitled to receive British Gas 3% guaranteed stock 1990–95 as follows:

	£ s. d.
Ord. shares (of £5)	11 5 0
5% debs. (of £100)	100 10 0

1952

Hadley & Shorthouse Ld. Regd. 1898. Vol. liq. 16 July 1901. Undertaking was acquired by Kynoch Ld. [later I. C. I. (Metals) Ld.] in which company shareholders were entitled to 1 preference share of £10 for every 2 shares of £5 held. Final meeting return regd. 12 Mar. 1902 ... **1902**

Hadley (Felix) & Co. Ld. Regd. 1888. Vol. liq. 24 Dec. 1898. Reconstructed as Hadley & Shorthouse Ld., in which company shareholders were entitled to 1 ordinary and 1 preference share of £5 (credited as fully-paid) for each share of £10 held. Final meeting return regd. 15 June 1900 ... **1901**

Hadley's Stores Ld. Regd. 1897. Vol liq. 28 Dec. 1879. Final meeting return regd. 14 Oct. 1902 ... ***1901**

Hadlow Light Railway Co. Inc. (under Light Railways Act 1896) by order of Light Railway Commissioners confirmed by Board of Trade 1897 ... **1903**

Hadwen (John) & Sons Ld. Regd. 1902. Court Order to wind up 20 Oct. 1936. Struck off Register 17 July 1942 ... **1943**

Hænertsberg Gold Mines Ld. Regd. Dublin 1895. Removed from Register 1908 ... **1899**

Hafna Mining & Smelting Co. Ld. Regd. 1885. Removed from Register 1895 ... ***1896**

Hagemann & Co. Ld. Regd. 1896. Vol. liq. 30 June 1906. Removed from Register 1909 ... **1907**

Hagemann's Creameries Ld. Regd. 1903. Vol. liq. 30 Aug. 1929. Undertaking and assets were acquired by Van den Berghs & Jurgens Ld. Capital returned to contributories—8*s.* per preference share of £1. Final meeting return regd. 3 Sept. 1930 ... **1930**

Hagerup Doughty & Co. Ld. Regd. 1896. Vol. liq. 19 Jan. 1906. Absorbed by Consolidated Steam Fishing & Ice Co. (Grimsby) Ld. Final meeting return regd. 7 May 1907 ... ***1907**

Haggie (Peter) & Co. Ld. Undertaking was acquired in 1928 by British Ropes Ld ... **1929**

Hahnite (1907) Ld. Regd. 1907. Vol. liq. Apr. 1911. Removed from Register 1912 ... **1912**

Haig & Haig Ld. Regd. 1906 as Haig & Haig (1906) Ld.; name changed Feb. 1907. Vol. liq. 16 Mar. 1923. Final meeting return regd. 2 Dec. 1925 ... **1907**

Haig Shipping Co. Ld. Regd. 1919. Vol. liq. (members') 16 July 1930. Capital returned to contributories—£1,692 15*s.* 7*d.* £14 1*s.* 10*d.* was paid into Companies' Liquidation Account in respect of unclaimed returns and dividends. Final meeting return regd. 31 July 1934 ... **1931**

Haig's Cooperage, Ld. *See* Holdup (M. H.) Ld.

Hailes Estate & Quarry Co. Ld. Regd. Edinburgh 1898. Vol. liq. (members') 15 Aug. 1945. Final meeting return regd. 18 Jan. 1949 ... **1939**

Hailsham Water Co. Inc. by Special Act 1885. Undertaking amalgamated with Eastbourne Waterworks Co. as from 1 Jan. 1949. Ordinary shareholders were entitled to receive £10 10*s.* per £10 share and preference shareholders 22*s.* per £1 share. The outstanding debenture stock was repaid at 108% ... **1951**

Hainault Gold Mine Ld. Regd. Edinburgh 1895. Vol. liq. Feb. 1913. Undertaking was acquired by South Kalgurli Consolidated Ld. in 1913. Final meeting return regd. 19 June 1919 ... **1913**

Halcomb & Co. (Sack Contractors) Ld. Regd. 1864. Vol. liq. 27 Mar. 1894. Business was acquired by West of England Sack Hiring Co. Ld. Final meeting return regd. 12 Feb. 1895 ... **1895**

Hales, Dancy & Co. Ld. Regd. 1897, Vol. liq. (members') 7 Sept. 1938. All shares owned by Fruit & Produce Exchange of Great Britain Ld. Final meeting return regd. 17 Nov. 1936 ... **1937**

Hales Tours of the World (United Kingdom) Ld. Regd. 1906. Court Order to wind up 10 Nov. 1908. Removed from Register 1914 ... **1909**

Halesowen and Bromsgrove Branch Railways Co. *See* Halesowen Railway.

Halesowen Gas Co. Inc. by Special Act 1883. Dissolved 1 May 1949 undertaking being vested in West Midland Area Gas Board under Gas Act 1948. Liability in respect of certain mortgage loans assumed by the Board ... **1949**

Halesowen Lighting & Traction Co. Ld. *See* S. W. & S. Development Co. Ld.

Halesowen Railway. Inc by Special Act 1865 as Halesowen and Bromsgrove Branch Railways Co.: name changed 1876. Under Act of 1906 the line was vested in Midland Railway Co. and Great Western Railway Co. jointly. Shareholders were entitled as follows:

	For each £100 held
1st deb.	£56 5*s.* G.W. 5% cons. pref.
	£75 G.W. or Mid. deb.
2nd deb.	£133 6*s.* 8*d.* 2½% Mid. pref.
3rd deb.	£80 2½% Mid. perp. pref.
1st pref. shares	£12 10*s.* 2½% Mid. perp. pref.
2nd pref. shares	£6 5*s.* 2½% Mid. perp. pref.

1907

Halesworth Gas Co. Ld. Regd 1913. Dissolved 1 May 1949, undertaking being vested in Eastern Area Gas Board under Gas Act 1948. Holders of securities were entitled to receive British Gas 3% guaranteed stock as follows:

	£ s. d.
Ord.shares(of 10*s.*)	0 6 0
8% ptpg. prefd. ord. shares (of £1)	1 14 0

1952

Haleybridge Investment Trust Ld. Regd. 1947 as Haleybridge Investment Trust (1947) Ld.; name changed Dec. 1957. All capital owned by British Land Co. Ld. Dissolved 17 Oct. 1980 ... **1972**

Haleybridge Investment Trust Ld. Regd. 1932. Vol. liq. (members') 14 May 1947. Undertaking acquired by Haleybridge Investment Trust (1947) Ld. [later Haleybridge Investment Trust Ld.] in which company shareholders were entitled to receive 4 preference and 1 ordinary share for each ordinary share held. Final meeting return regd. 2 Oct. 1951 ... **1953**

Half-Mile Reef Ld. Regd. 1896. Reconstructed as Half-Mile Reef Mines Ld., in which company shareholders were entitled to 2 shares of 10*s.* (credited with 8*s.* 6*d.* paid) for each share of £1 held. Removed from Register 1908 ... **1902**

Half-Mile Reef Mines Ld. Regd. 1899. Reconstructed 1902 as company of same name. Removed from Register 1903 ... **1903**

Half-Mile Reef Mines Ld. Regd. 1902. Removed from Register 1906 ... **1906**

Halfpenny Letter Co. Ld. Regd. 1888 as Halfpenny Letter Post Co. Ld.; name changed Aug. 1888. Vol. liq. Oct. 1889. Final meeting return regd. 30 May 1890 ... **1890**

Halfpenny Letter Post Co. Ld. See Halfpenny Letter Co. Ld.

Halifax and Bermuda Cable Co., Ld. Regd. 1889. All capital was owned by Direct West India Cable Co. Ld. Winding-up order 6 Oct. 1966. Liquidator released 7 Dec. 1966 ... **1949**

Halifax and District Coal Supply Association Ld. Regd. 1899. Vol. liq. 15 May 1923. Final meeting return regd. 2 Aug.1924 ... **1924**

Halifax & District Mineral Water Manufacturers Association Ld. Regd. 1898. Vol. liq. 4 Sept. 1900. Removed from Register 11 Aug. 1905 ... ***1901**

Halifax & District Permanent Banking Co. Ld. Regd. 1909. Vol. liq. 9 May 1917. Struck off Register 27 Jan. 1956 ... **1917**

Halifax & Huddersfield Union Banking Co. Ld. Established 1836. Inc. 1874. Regd. as limited 1882. Vol. liq. June 1910. Undertaking and assets sold to the Halifax Joint Stock Banking Co. Ld. (later West Yorkshire Bank Ld.) in which company shareholders were entitled to receive 1 share of £25 (£10 paid) for every 3 shares of £40 (£10 paid) and £5 6*s.* 8*d.* per share in cash ... **1911**

Halifax & Ovenden Joint Committee. Dissolved 2 Apr. 1949; undertaking vested 1 Jan. 1948 in British Transport Commission under Transport Act 1947 **1940**

Halifax Breweries Ld. Regd. 1895. Vol. liq. 15 Mar. 1923. Undertaking and assets were sold to Durbar Trust Ld. Debenture holders were repaid at par in cash. Shareholders were entitled to £50 in cash and 50 fully-paid preferred shares of £1 in purchasing company for every 2,000 preference shares of 2*s.* held or £25 in cash and 25 fully-paid preferred shares of £1 for every 2,000 ordinary shares of 2*s.* held. Final meeting return regd. 16 Apr. 1924 ... **1924**

Halifax Cocoa House & Refreshment Co. Ld. Regd. 1878. Vol. liq. 21 Oct. 1904. Removed from Register 1906 ... **1905**

Halifax Commercial Banking Co. Ld. Established 1810. Inc. 1836. Regd. 1864. Vol. liq. 16 Jan. 1920. Undertaking was acquired by Bank of Liverpool and Martins Ld. (later Martins Bank Ld.), in which company shareholders were entitled to 4 shares of £20 (credited with £2 10*s.* paid) for each share of £20 (£10 paid) held. Struck off Register 14 July 1970 . **1921**

Halifax Doubling Co. Ld. Regd. 1920 as Thomas Reynolds (1920) Ld.; name changed to Stockport Doubling Co. Ld. in June 1925, and as above in July 1928. The Stockport Group of mills were acquired by Fine Cotton Spinners' & Doublers' Association Ld. now Fine Spinners & Doublers Ld. Struck off Register 26 Sept. 1933 ... **1934**

**See Stock Exchange Year-Book.*

VOL. FOR

Halifax Equitable Bank Ld. *See* Equitable Bank Ld.

Halifax Graving Dock Co. Ld. Regd. 1885. Vol. liq. 17 Sept. 1920. Final meeting return regd. 21 June 1922 **1921**

Halifax High Level Joint Committee. Dissolved 2 Apr. 1949; undertaking vested 1 Jan. 1948 in British Transport Commission under Transport Act 1947 **1949**

Halifax High Level Railway Co. Inc. by Special Act 1884 as Halifax High Level & North & South Junction Railway Co.; name changed by Act of 1892 **1895**

Halifax Joint Stock Banking Co. Ld. *See* West Yorkshire Bank Ld

Halifax Skating Rink Co. Ld. Regd. 1876. Vol. liq. May 1889. Final meeting return regd. 15 Oct. 1889 **1890**

Halifax Sugar Refinery Ld. Regd. Edinburgh 1890. Business taken over by Acadia Sugar Refining Co. Ld. Vol. liq. July 1893. Final meeting return regd. 26 Nov. 1895 **1894**

Halkyn Mining Co, Ld. Regd. 1883. Vol. liq. (members') 21 Dec. 1934. Mining rights were acquired by Halkyn District United Mines Ld. Capital returned to contributories—£2,000. Final meeting return regd. 23 Mar. 1935 **1935**

Hall & Bartholomew Ld. Regd. 1920. Vol. liq. (members') 24 Feb. 1930. Capital returned to contributories—6*s*. 6⅓*d*. per preference share of £1. Final meeting return regd. 14 Aug. 1930 **1931**

Hall (Ben) & Son Ld. *See* B. H. & S. Ld.

Hall, Cutlack & Harlock Ld. Regd. 1930. Vol. liq. (members') 14 July 1950. Undertaking acquired by East Anglian Breweries Ld. Final meeting return regd. 17 Dec. 1952 **1954**

Hall (J. & E.) Ld. Regd. 1888. Business was acquired in 1900 by company of same name, for £100,000 in ordinary shares of £1 and £150,000 in cash. Removed from Register 1902 **1900**

Hall (John) & Son Ld. Regd. 1896. Vol. liq. 2 Mar. 1899. Undertaking acquired by Curtis's & Harvey Ld. Final meeting return regd. 6 Sept. 1900 **1940**

Hall, Lewis & Co. Ld. Regd. 1925. Vol. liq. (members') 26 June 1929. Struck off Register 30 Apr. 1954 ... **1954**

Hall Mines Ld. Regd. 1893. Vol. liq. May 1900. Reconstructed as Hall Mining & Smelting Co. Ld., in which company shareholders were entitled to 1 share of £1 (credited with 15*s*. paid) for each ordinary share of £1 held or to 1 fully-paid share of £1 for each preference share of £1 held. Final meeting return regd. 2 Oct. 1901 **1908**

Hall Mining & Smelting Co. Ld. Regd. 1900. Receiver appointed in 1907. Removed from Register 1913 **1911**

Hall Motor Fuel Ld. Regd. 1914. Vol. liq. 11 Nov. 1920. Final meeting return regd. 7 Jan. 1930 ***1921**

Hall (R. F.) Ld. Regd. 1897. Electrical engineering business was acquired in 1899 by British Electric Works Co. Ld. for £40,000 in ordinary shares of £1 and £102,000 in cash. Removed from Register 1901 **1901**

Hall (Robert) Ld. Regd. 1912. Vol. liq. (members') 7 Apr. 1937. Capital returned to contributories—20*s*. per preference share of £1; £1 1*s*. 1½*d*. per ordinary share of £1. Final meeting return regd. 10 June 1937 **1938**

Hall (Thomas) & Son Ld. Regd. 1914. Vol. liq. (members') 3 Dec. 1929. Business acquired by British Automatic Refrigerators Ld. Capital returned to contributories—18*s*. per preference share of 18*s*.; 13*s*. 1½*d*. per ordinary share of £1. Final meeting return regd. 15 Aug. 1935 **1935**

Hallamshire Cinemas Ld. Regd. 1921. Vol. liq. (members') 29 June 1960. Capital returned to contributors—10s. 0·2*d*. per share (of £1). £26 11*s*. paid into Companies' Liquidation Account in respect of unclaimed distributions. Final meeting return regd. 20 Oct. 1960 **1961**

Hallett, Dixon & Co. Ld. *See* Harrison (G. A.) & Hallett Dixon, Ld.

Halley Motors Ld. Regd. Edinburgh 1927. Vol. liq. (creditors') 11 Sept. 1935. No capital returned to contributories. Final meeting return regd. 27 Oct. 1936 **1936**

Halley's Industrial Motors Ld. Regd. Edinburgh 1906. Vol. liq. Jan. 1927. Assets acquired by Halley Motors Ld., in which company noteholders agreed to accept fully-paid preference shares of £1 at par; shareholders were entitled to 1 ordinary share of 6*s*. 8*d*. (credited with 4*s*. 2*d*. paid) for each share of £1 held and an option (since expired). Final meeting return regd. 28 Mar.1929 **1928**

Hallidie Patent Cable Tramways Corporation Ld. *See* Patent Cable Tramways Corporation Ld.

Hallivet China Clay Co. Ld. Regd. 1913. Vol. liq. (members') 28 June 1933. All shares owned by English China Clays Ld. Final meeting return regd. 7 Feb. 1935 **1934**

Hall's Collieries Ld. Regd. 1899. Vol. liq. (members') 17 Nov. 1950. Capital returned to contributories—£4 10*s*. 4*d*. per share of 10*s*. Final meeting return regd. 9 Aug. 1957 **1958**

Hall's Glue & Bone Works Ld. Regd. 1900. Vol. liq. 24 Mar. 1924. Final meeting return regd. 18 May 1925 **1925**

Halstead Gas Co. Ld. Regd. 1880. Dissolved 1 May 1949. undertaking being vested in Eastern Area Gas Board under Gas Act 1948. Holders of securities were entitled to receive British Gas 3% guaranteed stock 1990–95 as follows in respect of each £10 unit, unless otherwise stated, of security held:

	£	s.	d.	
A ord. shares (10% stand.)	11	10	0	
6% pref. shares	13	6	0	
4% red. deb. bonds (of £100)	100	0	0	
5% red. deb. bonds (of £100)	100	5	0	**1952**

Haltwhistle Gas Light Co. Ld. Regd. 1856. Dissolved 1 May 1949 undertaking being vested in Northern Area Gas Board under Gas Act 1948. Holders of ordinary shares (of £5) were entitled to receive—£6 10s. British Gas 3% guaranteed stock 1990–95 for each share held **1952**

Hambleden Estates Ld. Regd. 1929. Vol. liq. (members') 6 Feb. 1954. The preference shares (of £1) were exchanged in Feb. 1954 for an equal number of 7% preference shares (of £1) in W. H. Smith & Son (Holdings) Ld. The 4¾ 1st Mortgage A and 4½% 1st Mortgage B debenture stocks were redeemed at 112% on 1 Apr. 1954 but stockholders were given the right to convert their holdings into 4½% redeemable debenture stock in W. H. Smith & Son (Holdings) Ld. at either £100 stock and £12 10*s*. cash or £112 stock and 11*s*. 3*d*. cash per £100 held. Capital returned to contributories—£1 0*s*. 5·0736*d*. per preference share (of £1) and 3*s*. 9·524*d*. per ordinary share (of £1). Final meeting return regd. 8 Feb. 1955 **1956**

Hamblet's Blue Brick Co. Ld. Regd. 1898. Vol. liq. 1 July 1918. Final meeting return regd. 4 May 1920 **1919**

Hambley Freehold Gold Mine Ld. Regd. 1889. Vol. liq. 15 Dec. 1891. Final meeting return regd. 21 Aug. 1895 ***1893**

Hambro (C. J.) & Son. Amalgamated with British Bank of Northern Commerce Ld. (later Hambros Bank Ld.) **1921**

Hamburg, Altona & North Western Tramways Co. Ld. Regd. 1883. Vol. liq. 26 May 1892. Final meeting return regd. 10 June 1893 **1893**

Hamburg-Heligoland Telegraph Co. Established 1873. Company was wound up **1890**

Hamby Mountain Gold Mines Ld. Regd. 1886. Struck off Register 31 Dec. 1895 **1899**

Hamer (John C.) Ld. Regd. 1896. Vol. liq. (creditors') 2 July 1931. Final meeting return regd. 12 Dec. 1933 **1932**

Hamilton & North Western Railway. Inc. Canada 1872. Acquired in 1888 by Grand Trunk Railway Co. of Canada **1910**

Hamilton (Claud) Ld. Regd. Edinburgh 1898. Vol. liq. (members') 25 Feb. 1965. Capital returned to contributories—preference (of £1), £1 per share; ordinary (of £1), £2 10*s*. per share. Struck off Register 26 Dec. 1968 **1969**

Hamilton, Motherwell & Wishaw Tramways Co. *See* Lanarkshire Traction Co. Ld.

Hamilton Provident & Loan Corporation. Inc. Canada 1871 as Hamilton Provident and Loan Society, name changed 1920. Assets sold to Huron & Erie Mortgage Corporation 1 Jan. 1926. Shareholders received $100 in cash and $117 in debentures of the purchasing company for every fully-paid share of $100 held; holders of each share of $100 ($20 paid) received one-fifth of those amounts **1927**

Hamilton's Oil Concessions (Roumania) Ld. Regd. 1920. Vol. liq. (creditors') 31 Dec. 1935. Assets realised insufficient to pay creditors in full. Final meeting return regd. 20 Aug. 1936 **1936**

Hammersmith & City Railway Co. Inc. by Special Act 1861. Dissolved 2 Apr. 1949; undertaking vested 1 Jan. 1948 in British Transport Commission under Transport Act 1947. Holders of securities were entitled to receive British Transport 3% guaranteed stock 1978—88 as follows:

	£	s.	d.	
Cons. ord. stock (£100)	140	0	0	
5% irred. pref. shares 1864 (£10)	13	0	0	
5% irred. pref. shares 1865 (£2 paid)	2	12	0	
5% irred. pref. shares 1865 (£10 fully-paid)	13	0	0	**1949**

Hammersmith Baths & Washhouses Co. Ld. Regd. 1868. Vol. liq. 31 Mar. 1913. Capital returned to contributories—5*s*. 8*d*. per share of £1; further payments (if any) not known. Final meeting return regd. 16 Oct. 1913 **1914**

Hammersmith Distillery Co. Ld. Regd. 1899. Vol. liq. (members') 31 Mar. 1930. Undertaking was aquired

**See Stock Exchange Year-Book.*

VOL. FOR

by Distillers Co. Ld. Final meeting return regd. 17 Dec. 1930 .... **1931**

Hammersmith Palace of Varieties Ld. Regd. 1908. Vol. liq. 29 Mar. 1928. Subsidiary of London Theatres Varieties Ld. Final meeting return regd. 21 Dec. 1928 .... **1929**

Hammersmith Palais Ld. Regd. 1946. Vol. liq. 8 Apr. 1982. Final meeting return regd, 23 Sept. 1982 .... **1961**

Hammond Electric Light & Power Supply Co. Ld. Regd. 1882. Vol. liq. June 1885. Court Order to continue winding up under supervision July 1885. Capital returned to contributories—3s. per share of £5 in Nov. 1887; further payments (if any) not known. Final meeting return regd. 11 Apr. 1889 .... **1888**

Hammond (G. H.) Co. Ld. Regd. 1890. Goodwill and certain assets were acquired by an American company (G. H. Hammond Co.). Stockholders were entitled to cash or to subscribe for shares in new company. Removed from Register 1903 .... **1902**

Hammond (John) & Co. (1918) Ld. Regd. 1918. Vol liq. 31 Oct. 1922. Certain assets acquired by Enderley Mills Ld. Final meeting return regd. 26 Mar. 1923 **1940**

Hammond Manufacturing Co. Ld. Regd. 1914. Vol. liq. 27 Aug. 1919. Final meeting return regd. 6 Jan. 1921 **1920**

Hammond Turner & Sons Ld. Regd. 1903. Receiver appointed on 10 Dec. 1930. Assets were acquired by Lion Works Ld. Struck off Register 19 Feb. 1937. **1938**

Hammond (W. G.) & Co. Ld. Regd. 1913. Vol. liq. (members') 3 July 1939. All capital was owned by Fisons Ld. Final meeting return regd. 29 Sept. 1944 **1945**

Hammond's Matabele Gold Mines Development Ld. Regd. 1895. Removed from Register 1908 .... **1900**

Hamonite Ld. Regd. 1924. Struck off Register 5 Dec. 1933. Restored to Register 6 Feb. 1939. Court Order to wind up 20 Mar. 1939. Liquidator released 29 May 1943. Struck off Register 5 Oct. 1945............ **1946**

Hampden Cloncurry Copper Mines Ld. Inc. Victoria 1906. Vol. liq. July 1909. Reconstructed under same name. Shareholders were entitled to 1 share of £1 (credited with 15s. paid) in new company for each share of £1 held **1910**

Hampden Cloncurry Copper Mines Ld. Inc. Victoria 1909. Vol. liq. Sept. 1928. Capital returned to contributories—19s. per share of £1 at Feb. 1929; further payments (if any) not known **1929**

Hampshire & North Wilts Banking Co. See Capital & Counties Bank Ld.

Hampshire Light Railways (Electric) Co. Ld. Regd. 1897. Vol. liq. (members') 8 June 1936. All issued capital owned by Provincial Traction Co. Ld, Final meeting return regd. 31 Dec. 1936 .... **1937**

Hampstead Electric Supply Co., Ld. Regd. 1898. Undertaking and assets were acquired by North West London Electric Supply Co. Ld. for £55,000 in ordinary shares, £15,150 in 5% debentures and £14,850 in cash. Removed from Register 1910......... **1906**

Hampstead Garden Suburb Trust, Ld. Regd. 1906. Vol. liq. 26 Sept. 1968. Capital returned to contributories: 22·60s. per ordinary share (of £1) and 1s. per deferred share (of 1s.). £443·78 was paid into Companies' Liquidation Account in respect of unclaimed distributions. Final meeting return regd. 15 Dec. 1972.. **1973–4**

Hampstead Heath Extension Tenants Ld. See Co-Partnership Tenants Ld. (regd. 1907).

Hampstead Tenants Ld. See Co-Partnership Tenants Ld. (regd. 1930).

Hampstead West Heath Land Co. Ld. Regd. 1895. Vol. liq. 18 July 1912. Final meeting return regd. 17 Apr. 1913 .... ***1913**

Hampton Celebration (W. A.) Ld. Regd. 1919. Vol. liq. 5 Jan. 1925 for reconstruction as Celebration Gold Mines Ld., in which company shareholders were entitled to 1 share of 5s. (credited with 4d. paid) for each ordinary share of £1 held or 1 fully-paid share of 5s. for each preference share of 1s. held. Debenture holders were entitled to cash payment for arrears of interest and 50% of principal in cash and 50% in fully-paid shares. Final meeting return regd. 19 May 1926 .... **1925**

Hampton Consolidated Ld. Inc. Western Australia 1920. Vol. liq. Oct. 1924. Reconstructed as Bullion Mines Ld. in which company shareholders were entitled to 1 ordinary share of 2s. (credited with 1s. 6d. paid) for each ordinary share of 2s. held and to 1 preference share of 2s. (credited with 1s. 6d. paid) for each preference share of 2s. held.................................. **1925**

Hampton Court Gas Co. Estd. 1851; inc. by Special Act 1867. Dissolved 1 May 1949, undertaking being vested in South Eastern Area Gas Board under Gas Act 1948. Holders of securities were entitled to receive, in respect of each £100 unit held, British Gas 3% guaranteed stock 1990–95 as follows:

VOL. FOR
£ s. d.

Cons. ord. stock (5% stand.) 102 10 0
4% pref. stock 101 10 0
4% perp.debs 101 10 0
5% red. deb. stock 103 0 0 **1952**

Hampton Cycle & Foundry Co. Ld. Regd. 1896. Removed from Register 1908 .... **1898**

Hampton Gold Fields Ld. Regd. 1898. Vol. liq. 11 Nov. 1902. Final meeting return regd. 16 Aug. 1904 .... **1903**

Hampton Gold Hill Mines Ld. Regd. 1895. Vol. liq. Mar. 1905. Undertaking was acquired by Victorian Consolidated Goldfields Ld., in which company shareholders were entitled to 1 share of 5s. (credited with 4s. paid) for each share of 10s. held. Removed from Register 1906 .... **1906**

Hampton Lands & Railway Syndicate Ld. Regd. 1889. Vol. liq. 30 Oct. 1895. Final meeting return regd. 16 Oct. 1903 .... ***1896**

Hampton Lands & Railway Syndicate Ld. Regd. 1895. Vol. liq. Dec. 1904. Struck off Register Apr. 1929 **1930**

Hampton Plains Estate Ld. Regd. 1894. Reconstructed 1906 as Hampton Plains Estate (1906) Ld., in which company shareholders were entitled to 1 share of 10s. (credited with 7s. 6d. paid) for each share of 16s. held. Debenture stockholders agreed to accept a similar amount of debenture stock. Removed from Register 1909 .... **1908**

Hampton Plains Estate (1906) Ld. Regd. 1906. Vol. liq. Aug. 1909 for reconstruction as Hampton Uruguay Ld., in which company shareholders were entitled to 1 share of 10s. (credited with 6s. 6d. paid) for each share of 10s. held. Debenture stockholders were entitled to an equal amount of new debenture stock. Removed from Register 1912 .... **1910**

Hampton Plains Exploration Co, Ld. Regd. Mar. 1895. Vol. liq. 25 Mar. 1905. Reconstructed as Victorian Consolidated Goldfields Ld., in which company shareholders were entitled to 1 share of 5s. (credited with 4s. paid) for each share of £1 held. Final meeting return regd. 19 June 1906 .... **1906**

Hampton Properties Ld. Regd. 1898. Vol. liq. 12 May 1924. Reconstructed as company of same name. Shareholders were entitled to 1 share of 4s. (credited as fully-paid) in new company for each share of £1 held. Final meeting return regd. 30 July 1925....... **1925**

Hampton Timber Co. Ld. Regd. 1928. Vol. liq. (members') 15 July 1958. No capital returned to contributories. Final meeting return regd. 29 Apr. 1960 .... **1961**

Hampton Trust Ld. Regd. 1895. Removed from Register 1905.. **1899**

Hampton Uruguay Ld. Regd. 1909. Vol. liq. 31 Jan. 1916. Property and assets were acquired by Hampton Gold Mining Areas Ld. Holders of 4% 1st mortgage debenture or 10% debenture stocks were entitled to 50% of holding in cash and 50% in fully-paid shares of new company. Shareholders were entitled to 1 share of £1 (credited as fully-paid) for every 2 shares held. Final meeting return regd. 4 Jan. 1921 .... **1921**

Hamstead Building Co. Ld. Regd. 1882. Vol. liq. 29 Feb. 1892. Property was acquired by Hamstead Colliery Co. Ld. Final meeting return regd. 3 May 1893..... **1893**

Hamstead Colliery Co. Ld. Regd. 1875. Vol. liq. (members') 12 Nov. 1930. The assets were acquired by Handsworth Wood Estates Ld. and Hamstead Colliery (1930) Ld. Shareholders were entitled to 1 fully-paid ordinary share of 5s. and 10s. in debenture stock in each of these companies for every preferred or ordinary share of £1 held. Shares not claimed within specified time were sold. £445 18s. 4d. of proceeds was paid into Companies' Liquidation Account. Final meeting return regd. 20 July 1932 **1931**

Hamstead Colliery (1930) Ld. Regd. 1930. Vol. liq. (members') 7 Apr. 1954, company's interests having vested in National Coal Board. Capital returned to contributories—7s. 9½d. per ordinary share of 5s. and 1s. 6·65d. per B share of 1s. £16 4s. 8d. paid into Companies' Liquidation Account. Final meeting return regd. 14 Dec. 1955 .... **1957**

Hancock & Co. (New Zealand) Ld. Regd. 1906. Vol. liq. 19 Sept. 1923. The assets (except Captain Cook Hotel) were sold to New Zealand Breweries Ld. for £250,000. The debenture stock was redeemed at 110% on 1 Jan. 1924. Final meeting return regd. 12 Aug. 1925 .... **1924**

Hancock (Wm.) & Sons (Wiveliscombe) Ld. Regd. 1896. Vol. liq. (members') 21 Sept. 1934. Undertaking and assets were acquired by Arnold & Hancock Ld. (the beneficial owner of all share capital). Holders of 4% 1st mortgage debenture stock were entitled to an equal amount of similar stock in acquiring company; holders of 5% B mortgage debenture stock were entitled to an equal amount of 4% 1st mortgage

debenture stock *plus* £5% in cash. Final meeting return regd. 7 Feb. 1935 .... **1935**

Hand in Hand Fire & Life Insurance Co. Established 1896. Under Act of 1905 the business was acquired by Commercial Union Assurance Co. Ld. **1906**

Handforth Bleaching Co. Ld. Regd. 1901. Vol. liq. 31 Aug. 1944. A direct controlling interest was held by Bleachers' Association Ld. (later Whitecroft Industrial Holdings Ld.). Final meeting return regd. 25 Nov. 1944 .... **1945**

Handicraft Instruments Ld. Regd. 1934. Vol. liq. 28 Jan. 1937. Undertaking acquired by Henri Selmer & Co. Ld. Final meeting return regd. 13 Oct. 1942 .... **1940**

Handicrafts Ld. Regd. 1910. Vol. liq. (members') 26 July 1935. Capital returned to contributories—£26,075. Final meeting return regd. 3 May 1938 .. **1936**

"Hands Across the Sea" Gold Mining Co. Ld. Regd. 1895. Vol. liq. 13 May 1901. Struck off Register 10 Oct. 1916 .... **1902**

Handsworth Wood Estates Ld. Regd. 1930. Vol. liq. (members') 30 Nov. 1950. Capital returned to contributories—16s. 5·52292d. per ordinary share of 5s. and 6s. 3·6646d. per B share of 1s. £389 6s. 1d. was paid into Companies' Liquidation Account in respect of unclaimed distributions and £33 9s. 2d. in respect of unclaimed dividends. Final meeting return regd. 19 Mar. 1955 .... **1956**

Handsworth Woodhouse Gas Co. Ld. Regd. 1865. In 1924 the undertaking was acquired by Sheffield Gas Co. [later Sheffield & District Gas Co.]. Struck off Register 1929 .... **1925**

Handyside (Andrew) & Co. Ld. Regd 1873. Vol. liq. 28 Sept. 1910. Final meeting return regd. 27 Jan. 1920 **1911**

Handyside (Andrew) & Co. Ld. Regd. 1915. Vol. liq. 24 Aug. 1923. Final meeting return regd. 26 Mar. 1925 **1924**

Handyside (Andrew) & Co. Ld. Regd. 1924. Vol. liq. (creditors) 13 Apr. 1931. No capital returned to contributories. Final meeting return regd. 10 Feb. 1933 .... **1932**

Hankow Light & Power Co. Ld. Regd. 1906. struck off register 18 June 1965 .... **1966**

Hanley & Co. Ld. Regd. 1890. Vol. liq. 30 Mar. 1898. Undertaking was acquired by Halls Oxford Brewery Ld. for £150,000 in 4% debenture stock, £80,000 fully-paid preference shares of £5 and £25,000 in fully-paid ordinary shares of £5. Final meeting return regd. 24 Nov. 1898 .... **1899**

Hanley Theatres & Circus Ld. Regd. 1899. Vol. liq. May 1921. Undertaking was acquired by Grand Theatre (Hanley) Ld. Struck off Register 1929 .... **1922**

Hanman Cycle & Needle Co. Ld. Regd. 1897. Removed from Register 1905 .... **1906**

Hanman Cycle Co. Ld. Regd. 1896. Vol. liq. 27 July 1897. Final meeting return regd. 30 Dec. 1898 .... ***1898**

Hannan's Amalgamated Gold Mines Ld. Regd. 1900. Removed from Register 1909 .... **1904**

Hannan's Associated Mines Ld. Regd. 1897. Struck off Register 16 Nov. 1906 .... **1907**

Hannan's Belle Vue Gold Mining Co. Ld. Regd. 1896. Vol. liq. 22 Oct. 1900. Struck off Register Apr. 1929 **1930**

Hannan's Block 45 Ld. Regd. 1896. Vol. liq. July 1902. Undertaking was acquired by Kalgoorlie Amalgamated Ld., in which company shareholders were entitled to 5 fully-paid shares of £1 for every 12 shares of £1 held. Removed from Register 1903 .. **1903**

Hannan's Britannia Gold Mines Ld. Regd. 1896. Vol. liq. 20 Nov. 1900. Reconstructed as Hannan's Amalgamated Gold Mines Ld. in which company shareholders were entitled to 2 shares of 10s. (credited with 8s.) paid) for each share of £1 held. Struck off Register 30 Jan. 1923 .... **1903**

Hannan's Brownhill Gold Mining Co. Ld. See Oroya Brownhill Co. Ld.

Hannan's Central Ld. Regd. 1895. Vol. liq. 5 Dec. 1902. Undertaking was acquired by Kalgoorlie Amalgamated Ld., in which company shareholders were entitled to 1 fully-paid share of £1 for every 3 shares of 10s. held. Struck off Register 10 Oct. 1916 ...... **1903**

Hannan's Consolidated Gold Mines Ld. Regd 1895. Vol. liq. 16 May 1898. Final meeting return regd. 13 Mar. 1899 .... **1899**

Hannan's Consols Ld. Regd. 1895. Vol. liq. Dec. 1906. Removed from Register 1908 .... **1907**

Hannan's "Crœsus" Gold Mining Co. Ld. Regd. 1896. Vol. liq. 25 Sept. 1900. Reconstructed as Hannan's Crœsus Ld., in which company shareholders were entitled to 2 shares of 10s. (credited with 8s. 6d. paid) for each ordinary share of £1 held or to 3 fully-paid shares of 10s. for each preference share of £1 held. Final meeting return regd. 17 Sept. 1902 .... **1902**

Hannan's Crœsus Ld. Regd. 1900. Vol. liq. 21 Dec. 1902. Undertaking was acquired by Kalgoorlie Amalgamated Ld., in which company shareholders were

entitled to 1 fully-paid share of £1 for every 6 shares of ,10s. held. Struck off Register 10 Oct. 1916 ...... **1903**

Hannan's Development and Finance Corporation Ld. Regd. Edinburgh 1896. Vol. liq. 7 Nov. 1898. Court Order to wind up under supervision 7 July 1900. Struck off Register 23 June 1931 .... **1901**

Hannan's "Empress" Gold Mining & Development Co. Ld. Regd. 1896. Vol. liq. 20 Jan. 1899. Amalgamated with Phoenix Gold Mines Ld., in which company shareholders were entitled to 2 shares of 10s. (credited with 8s. paid) for each share of £1 held. Final meeting return regd. 7 June 1900 .... **1900**

Hannan's Excelsior Gold Mines Ld. Regd. 1895. Vol. liq. 28 July 1899. Reconstructed as New Hannan's Excelsior & Crœsus Ld., in which company shareholders were entitled to 5 shares of £1 (credited with 16s. paid) for every 8 shares of £1 held. Final meeting return regd. 19 July 1900 .... **1902**

Hannan's Find Gold Reefs Ld. Regd. 1895. Removed from Register 1905 .... **1903**

Hannan's Gold Estates Ld. Regd. 1900. Removed from Register 1905 .... **1905**

Hannan's Golden Dream Ld. Regd. 1896. Vol. liq. 16 Mar. 1900. Property was acquired by Standard Exploration Co. Ld., in which company shareholders were entitled to 2 shares for every 5 shares held. Removed from Register 1903 .... **1901**

Hannan's Golden Dyke Mines Ld. Regd. 1896. Struck off Register 18 Nov. 1902 .... **1903**

Hannan's Golden Group Ld. Regd. 1895. Taken over by Standard Exploration Co. Ld. Removed from Register 1903 .... **1899**

Hannan's Golden Pebbles Ld. Regd. 1896. Vol. liq. 3 Dec. 1897. Final meeting return regd. 19 Apr. 1900 **1898**

Hannan's Golden Treasure Ld. Regd. 1895. Taken over by Standard Exploration Co. Ld. Removed from Register 1903 .... **1899**

Hannan's 100 Acres Corporation Ld. Regd. 1897. Removed from Register 1904 .... **1902**

Hannan's Kalgoorlie Proprietary Ld. Regd. 1896. Removed from Register 1908 .... **1905**

Hannan's Kapai Ld. Regd. 1900. Removed from Register 1904 .... **1904**

Hannan's King (Brownhill) Gold Mining Co. Ld. Regd. 1896. Reconstructed as Hannan's Amalgamated Gold Mines Ld., in which company shareholders were entitled to 2 shares of 10s. (credited with 8s. paid) for each share of £1 held. Struck off Register Oct. 1931 .... **1932**

Hannan's Lake View Central Ld. Regd. 1896. Vol. liq. 24 July 1905. Removed from Register 1906 .... **1902**

Hannan's Lode Ld. Regd. 1895. Vol. liq. 11 Jan. 1898. Final meeting return regd. 16 July 1900. Court Order deferred dissolution until 16 Oct. 1900 .... **1900**

Hannan's Main Reef Gold Mining Co. Ld. Regd. 1895. Vol. liq. 15 Nov. 1897. Reconstructed as company of same name. Shareholders were entitled to 1 share of 10s. (credited with 7s. 6d. paid) for each share of 10s. held. Final meeting return regd. 11 Dec. 1899 .... **1900**

Hannan's Main Reef Gold Mining Co. Ld. Regd. 1897. Vol. liq. 17 Oct. 1900. Reconstructed as company of same name. Shareholders were entitled to 1 share of 10s. (credited with 7s. 6d. paid) in new company for each share of 10s. held. Final meeting return regd. 2 Jan. 1903 .... **1903**

Hannan's Main Reef Gold Mining Co. Ld. Regd. 1900. Vol. liq. 7 Sept. 1903. Reconstructed as company of same name (later Orion Mines Ld.). Shareholders were entitled to 1 fully-paid share of 2s. for each share of 10s. held. Final meeting return regd. 6 Apr. 1909 .... **1904**

Hannan's Main Reef Gold Mining Co. Ld. Regd. 1903. See Orion Mines Ld.

Hannan's Mount Charlotte West Ld. Regd. 1895. Removed from Register 1905 .... **1898**

Hannan's Mount Ferrum Gold Mines Ld. Regd. 1896. Removed from Register 1904 .... **1902**

Hannan's Napier Gold Co. Ld. Regd. 1895. Vol. liq. 29 Jan. 1898. Final meeting return regd. 20 Jan. 1900 **1899**

Hannan's North Crœsus Gold Mining Co. Ld. Regd. 1896. Vol. liq. 8 Dec. 1897 for reconstruction as company of same name. Final meeting return regd. 7 June 1898 .... **1898**

Hannan's North Gold Mines Ld. Regd. 1902. Vol. liq. Jan. 1907. Reconstructed 1907 as Mara Mines Ld., in which company shareholders were entitled to 1 share of 2s. (credited with 6d. paid) for every 2 shares of 4s. held. Removed from Register 1912... **1909**

Hannan's North Gold Mining Co. Ld. Regd. 1900. Vol. liq. 11 Apr. 1902. Shareholders were entitled to 1 share of 4s. (credited with 3s. paid) in Hannan's North Gold Mines Ld for each share of 10s. held. Final meeting return regd. 5 June 1903 .... **1907**

VOL. FOR

Hannan's Oroya Gold Mining Co., Western Australia, Ld. Regd. 1895. Undertaking and assets were acquired by Hannan's Brownhill Gold Mining Co. Ld. (later Oroya Brownhill Co. Ld.), in which company shareholders were entitled to an equal number of shares. Removed from Register 1904 ..   1903

Hannan's Paringa Gold Mine Ld. Regd. 1895. Vol. liq. 16 July 1898. Reconstructed as Paringa Consolidated Mines Ld., in which company shareholders were entitled to 2 shares of 10s. (credited with 8s. paid) for each share of £1 held. Final meeting return regd. 28 Feb. 1899   1902

Hannan's Premier Gold Mines Ld. Regd. 1896. Vol. liq. 18 Oct. 1899. Final meeting return regd. 21 Aug. 1900   1900

Hannan's Proprietary Development Co. Ld. Regd. 1895. Reconstructed 1904 as Hannan's Proprietary Ld., in which company shareholders were entitled to 1 share of £1 (credited with 16s. paid) for each share of £1 held. Removed from Register 1913   1908

Hannan's Proprietary Ld. Inc. Western Australia 1904. Vol. liq. Apr. 1914   1915

Hannan's Public Crushing, Condensing & Saw Mills Co. Ld. Regd. 1896. Vol. liq. Jan. 1909. Removed from Register 1909   1909

Hannan's Queen Gold Mines Ld. Regd. 1896. Vol. liq. 16 May 1898. Final meeting return regd. 15 Feb. 1899   1899

Hannan's Reward & Mount Charlotte Ld. Regd. 1902. Reconstructed 1907 as Hannan's Reward Ld in which company shareholders were entitled to fully-paid share of 2s. 6d. for each share of £1 held. Removed from Register 1908   1925

Hannan's Reward Gold Mining Co. Ld. Regd. 1894. Vol. liq. 15 July 1898. Reconstructed as Hannan's Reward Ld., in which company shareholders were entitled to 1 share of £1 (credited with 17s. paid) for each share of £1 held. Final meeting return regd. 15 July 1899   1902

Hannan's Reward Ld. Regd. 1898. Reconstructed 1902 as Hannan's Reward & Mount Charlotte Ld., in which company shareholders were entitled to 1 share of £1 (credited with 18s. paid) for each share, of £1 held. Removed from Register 1903   1902

Hannan's Reward Ld. Regd. 1907. Struck off Register 1925   1925

Hannan's "Sir John Forrest" Gold Mines Ld. Regd. 1895. Vol. liq. 25 Apr. 1898. Reconstructed as Paringa Consolidated Mines Ld., in which company shareholders were entitled to 3 shares of 10s. (credited with 8s. paid) for each share of £1 held. Final meeting return regd. 28 Feb. 1899   1902

Hannan's South Brownhill Gold Mine Ld. Regd. 1895. Amalgamated with Phoenix Gold Mines Ld., in which company shareholders were entitled to 2 shares of 10s. (credited with 8s. paid) for each share of £1 held. Removed from Register 1901   1900

Hannan's Star Consolidated Ld. Regd. 1909. Vol. liq. Nov. 1910. Gold-mining properties were acquired by Lake View and Star Ld., certain other assets were acquired by Star Explorations Ld. Removed from Register 1911   1911

Hannan's Star Gold Mines Ld. Regd. 1895. Reconstructed 1905 as Hannan's Star Ld., in which company shareholders were entitled to 1 share of £1 (credited with 16s. paid) for each share of £1 held. Removed from Register 1906   1908

Hannan's Star Ld. Regd. 1905. Vol. liq. Oct. 1909 for reconstruction as Hannan's Star Consolidated Ld., in which company shareholders were entitled to 1 share of 4s. (credited with 1s. paid) for each share of £1 held. Removed from Register 1910   1910

Hannan's Treasure Trove Ld Regd. 1896. Removed from Register 1909   1903

Hannan's Trust Ld. Regd. 1897. Court Order to wind up 6 June 1905. Liquidator released 30 July 1913. Struck off Register 3 Sept. 1918   1906

Hannan's Virginia Gold Mining & Developing Co. Ld. Regd. 1896. Undertaking was acquired by Premier Gold Mines Ld. Removed from Register 1908   1900

Hannan's West Ld. *See* Lady Bess Gold Mines Ld.

Hannefords Ld. Regd. 1912. Vol. liq. 8 Apr. 1915. Final meeting return regd. 17 June 1938   1916

Hannevig Shipping & Trading Co. Ld. Regd. 22 Dec. 1892. Dissolved on 18 Nov. 1902   1903

Hannevig's Bank Ld. *See* British American Continental Bank Ld.

Hanover National Bank of City of New York. Inc. New York 1851. The assets & liabilities were merged into those of Central Union Trust Co. of New York (later Central Hanover Bank & Trust Co., later The Hanover Bank, later Manufacturers Hanover Trust) in which company shareholders were entitled to 3 shares of $20 for each share of $100 held   1930

VOL. FOR

Hans Crescent Hotel Co. Ld. Regd. 1896. Receiver appointed by Order of Court 6 Oct. 1939. Properties were sold and the £140,000 perpetual 1st mortgage debenture stock was repaid at par (final payment being in Dec. 1950 with 1½ years' interest, leaving 10 years' arrears unpaid). Receiver ceased to act 28 May 1954. Struck off Register 15 May 1959   1956

Hansard Publishing Union Ld. Regd. 1889. Removed from Register 1904   1892

Hanseatic Syndicate Ld. Regd. 1904. Vol. liq. 6 July 1905. Undertaking was acquired by International Metal Co. Ld., in which company shareholders were entitled to 1½ shares of £1 for each share of 2s. 6d. held. Removed from Register 1906   1906

Hansen Bros, Ld. Regd. 1914. Struck off Register Apr. 1929   1930

Hansen Shipbuilding & Ship Repairing Co. Ld. Regd. 1919. Struck off Register 1929   *1925

Hansford Land & Cattle Co. Ld. Regd Edinburgh 1882. Vol. liq. Mar. 1912. Final meeting return regd. 9 May 1914   1913

Hanson (H. T.) & Co. Ld. Regd. 1923. Vol. liq. Nov. 1927. Struck off Register May 1930   1931

Hanwella Rubber Estates, Ld. Regd. 1920. Vol. liq. (members') 9 Sept. 1943. Capital returned to contributories—13s. 9·45d. per share of 2s. Final meeting return regd. 31 Dec. 1946   1947

Hanworth Securities Ld. Regd. 1934 as General Aircraft Ld.; name changed 29 Dec. 1948. Vol. liq. (members') 4 Apr. 1951, the assets having been sold. Capital returned to contributories—13s. 4·22d. per share of 5s. £7,354 17s. 10d. was paid into Companies' Liquidation Account in respect of unclaimed dividends and distributions. Final meeting return regd. 1 Oct. 1953   1953

Hapo (Peruvian) Exploration Ld. Regd. 1927. Struck off Register 24 Jan. 1936   1936

Haputale Co. Ld. Regd. Edinburgh 1888. Vol. liq. Dec. 1925. Estates and certain assets were acquired by Scottish Trust & Loan Co. of Ceylon Ld. (later Scottish Tea & Lands Co. of Ceylon Ld.). Anticipated return to shareholders—6·52 fully-paid shares of £1 in acquiring company *plus* £2 5s. 4d. in cash per preference share of £16 10s. held; 4·53 fully-paid shares of £1 *plus* £1 12s. 5d. in cash per ordinary share of £2 (£1 paid) held. Final meeting return regd. 20 July 1926   1926

Harbinger (Gippsland) Gold Mine Ld. Regd 1896. Struck off Register 2 Aug. 1904   1905

Harborne Railway Co. Inc. by Special Act 1866. In 1923 the undertaking was merged into the London Midland & Scottish Railway Co., in which company stockholders were entitled to stock follows:

For each £100 held	L. M. & S.
5% Prefd. Deb.	£125 4% Debenture
5% Defd. Deb.	£125 4% Debenture
Ordinary Capital	£55 cash	1924

Hardebeck & Bornhardt Ld. Regd. 1898. Vol. liq. (members') 6 July 1932. Capital returned to contributories—2s. 4d. per preferred share of 5s. Final meeting return regd. 18 Apr. 1934   1933

Harden Star & Sinclair Fire Appliance Co. Ld. *See* Harden Star, Lewis and Sinclair Co. Ld.

Harden Star, Lewis & Sinclair Co. Ld. Regd. 1888 to amalgamate Harden Star and Sinclair Fire Appliance Co. Ld. and Lewis Hand Fire Extinguisher Co. Ld. Removed from Register 1906   1891

Hardie Cinnabar Mines Ld. Regd. 1902. Vol. liq. 15 Jan. 1920. Final meeting return regd. 23 June 1920 ...   1921

Hardy (C. J.) & Co. Ld. Regd. 1902. Vol. liq. (members') 15 Sept. 1936. Preference shares were repaid at par. Payments to ordinary shareholders not known. Final meeting return regd. 31 Mar. 1943   1937

Hare Spinning Co. Ld. Regd. 1897. Struck off Register 1928   *1915

Harefield Grove & Springwell Water Co. Ld. Regd. 1894. Vol. liq. 30 June 1897. Struck off Register 3 Sept. 1918   1898

Harehope Gill Mine Ld. Regd. 1875. Vol. liq. Apr. 1885. Final meeting return regd. 22 June 1886   1886

Harewood Rubber Estates Ld. Regd. 1910. Vol. liq. 27 Sept. 1922. Final meeting return regd. 20 Nov. 1923   1923

Harewood Rubber Estates Ld. Regd. 1925. Vol. liq. (members') 18 Dec. 1950. Undertaking and assets acquired by Aberfoyle Plantations Ld., in which company shareholders were entitled to 18·019 fully-paid shares of that company for every 100 shares (of 2s.) held. Final meeting return regd. 26 Mar. 1954   1955

Hargreaves Bros. & Co. Ld. Regd. 1906. Vol. liq. 4 July 1923; assets were acquired by Reckitt & Sons Ld. Capital returned to contributories—15% to preference shareholders; further payments (if any) not known. Final meeting return regd. 15 Apr. 1926   1924

See Stock Exchange Year-Book.

VOL. FOR

Carpet Trades Holdings, Ld.). Final meeting return regd. 15 June 1921 .... **1936**

Harrison (Charles) Kempson & Co. Ld. *See* Harrison (Charles) & Son Ld.

Harrison (G. A.) & Hallett Dixon, Ld. Regd. 1919 as Hallett Dixon & Co. Ld.; name changed Mar. 1925. Receiver appointed May 1930; ceased to act Sept. 1931. Vol. liq. (creditors') 2 June 1930. Final meeting return regd. 20 Jan. 1932 .... **1926**

Harrison (J. & C.) Ld. Regd. 1898. Vol. liq. 29 Mar. 1920. Final meeting return regd. 22 Dec. 1920 ..... **1921**

Harrison (John) & Co. Ld. Regd. 1872. Vol. liq. 10 July 1889. Final meeting return regd. 9 Jan. 1892 .... **1890**

Harrison, Sons & Co. Ld. Regd. 1916. Vol. liq. 29 Dec. 1925. All capital owned by Town Line (London) Ld. Struck off Register 1930 .... **1926**

Harrissmith Stc:m Shipping Co. Ld. Regd. 1919. Vol. liq. 8 Apr. 1920. Final meeting return regd. 4 May 1921 .... ***1921**

Harrod's Stores Founders' Shares Co. Ld. Regd. 1895. Vol. liq. 1 Aug. 1918. Shareholders were entitled to 5 fully-paid ordinary shares of £1 in Harrods Ld., for every 2 shares of £1 held. Final meeting return regd. 16 May 1919 .... **1919**

Harrogate Gas Co. Inc. 1846; reinc. by Special Act 1863. Dissolved 1 May 1949, undertaking being vested in North Eastern Area Gas Board under Gas Act 1948. Holders of securities were entitled to receive, in respect of each £100 unit held, British Gas 3% guaranteed stock 1990-95 as follows:

	£	s.	d.
New cons. stock (6% max.).............	130	0	0
4% pref. stock	102	0	0
6% irred. pref. stock......................	134	0	0
4% red. pref. stock	101	10	1
4½% perp. deb. stock	113	10	0
5% perp. deb. stock........................	127	0	0
5% red. deb. stock..........................	110	0	0

Liability in respect of certain mortgage loans assumed by the Board **1952**

Harrogate Red Brick Co. Ld. Regd. 1898. Vol. liq. (members') 18 Apr. 1934. Final meeting return regd. 21 Sept. 1936. Struck off Register 9 Feb. 1951...... **1935**

Harrow & Stanmore Gas Co. Inc. by Special Act 1873 as Harrow District Gas Co.: name changed 1895. Undertaking acquired by Brentford Gas Co., in which company stockholders were entitled to stock as follows:

For each £100 stock held	Brentford Gas.
Ordinary........................£112 10s.	"B" Cons.
5% Preference...................£100	5% Preference
4% Debenture..............:......£100	4% Debenture
5% Debenture £125	4% Debenture **1925**

Harrow & Stanmore Railway Co. Inc. by Special Act 1886. Under London & North Western Railway Act 1899 undertaking was vested in that company for £34,000, which was distributed among shareholders after repaying loans **1900**

Harrow & Uxbridge Railway Co. Inc. by Special Act 1897. Metropolitan Railway Co., acquired the undertaking under Act of 1905. Holders of share capital (not held by purchasing company) received 3½% A debenture on basis of equal income **1906**

Harrow District Gas Co. *See* Harrow & Stanmore Gas Co.

Harrow Electric Light & Power Co. Ld. Regd. 1895. Vol. liq. (members') 1 Dec. 1937. Undertaking was vested in North Metropolitan Electric Power Supply Co. Ld. (later Northmet Power Co.). Capital returned to contributories—£5 per preference share of £5 held; £19 2s. 8d. per ordinary share of £5. Final meeting return regd. 19 Mar. 1938 .... **1938**

Harrow Road & Paddington Tramways Co. Inc. by Special Act 1886. Wound up. Undertaking purchdase by Metropolitan Electric Tramways Ld. Outstanding 5% mortgage bonds were repaid. A first distribution of £3 15s. per share was made in Aug. 1906 .... **1907**

Harrow Waterworks Co. Under Act of 1885 the undertaking was acquired by Colne Valley Water Co. **1910**

Harrowing Steamship Co. Ld. Regd. 1899. Vol. liq. (members') 10 June 1938. Capital returned to contributories—£643,832 17s. 11d. Final meeting return regd. 29 Nov. 1939 .... **1939**

Hart Accumulator Co. Ld. Regd. 1898. Vol. liq. (members') 30 Nov. 1951. Final meeting return regd. 16 Apr. 1952 .... **1940**

Hart & Grindell Ld. Regd. 1889. Vol. liq. 11 Jan. 1896. Final meeting return regd. 6 Sept. 1898 .... ***1897**

Hart & Levy Ld. and **Hart, Levy & John Barran Ld.** *See* Town and Central Holdings (Leeds) Ld.

VOL. FOR

Hart Bros. & Co. Ld. Regd. 1902. Vol. liq. (members') 3 July 1939. All capital was owned by Fisons Ld. Final meeting return regd. 29 Sept. 1944 .... **1945**

Hart (W. H.) & Sons Ld. Regd. 1896. Vol. liq. (members') 6 Nov. 1953. Preference shares were repaid at par. All ordinary shares were privately owned. Final meeting return regd. 26 Feb. 1955 . **1940**

Hartelust (B.) Ld. Regd. 1911. Vol. liq. Sept. 1913. Undertaking and assets were sold to De Nederlandsche Ijzerhandel for Fl.450,000 in fully-paid shares. Removed from Register 1914 .... **1914**

Hartlepool Electric Tramways Co. Ld. Regd. 1896. Vol. liq. Nov. 1912. Tramways were sold to local authority for £32,500. Removed from Register 1913 **1913**

Hartlepools Paper Mill Co. Ld. Regd. 1920. In 1926 undertaking and assets were acquired by Durham Paper Mills Ld. Holders of 1st mortgage debenture stock were entitled to 38% of holding in fully-paid preference shares of £1 in acquiring company and about 14% in cash in June 1927. Struck off Register Mar. 1929 .... **1930**

Hartlepools Pulp & Paper Co. Ld. Regd. 1891. Vol. liq. 16 Nov. 1920. The undertaking and assets were sold to Hartlepools Paper Mill Co. Ld., for £300,000 in cash. Final meeting return regd. 2 June 1932....... **1921**

Hartlepools Steam Tramways Co. Ld, Regd. 1883. Removed from Register 1891 .... **1890**

Hartley Crosland Group Ld. Regd. 1946 as James Austin & Sons Ld.; name changed 2 Feb. 1960 to James Austin & Sons (Holdings) Ld. and 12 July 1967 to above title. Vol. liq. (creditors') 27 Mar. 1973. Company was dissolved under Section 208 of the Companies Act 1948 on 18 Aug. 1979 .... **1980-1**

Hartley & Moore Ld. Regd. 1918. Struck off Register 1923 .... **1924**

Hartley & Sebakwe Development Co. Ld. Regd. 1902. Vol. liq. Feb. 1909. Removed from Register 1910 **1909**

Hartley, Cooper & Co. Ld. *See below.*

Hartley, Cooper & Co. (1922) Ld. Regd. 1922 as Hartley, Cooper & Co. Ld; name subsequently changed. Vol. liq. (members') 1 Jan. 1951. Final meeting regd. 6 Nov. 1954 .... **1938**

Hartley Main Collieries Ld. Regd. 1929. Collieries &c. vested in National Coal Board as from 1 Jan. 1947. Vol. liq. (members') 17 Dec. 1952. Capital returned to contributories—£1 16s. 2·28571d. per ordinary share of £1. Final meeting return regd. 4 Aug. 1961 **1962**

Hartley (Rhodesia) Consolidated Mines Ld. Regd. 1910. Struck off Register 1916 .... **1916**

Harton Coal Co. Ld. Regd. 1885; converted into private company 1908. Collieries &c. vested in National Coal Board as from 1 Jan. 1947. Vol. liq. (members') 19 July 1952. Final meeting return regd. 2 Aug. 1963 **1964**

Harvey & Williams Ld. Regd. 1899. Removed from Register 1910 .... **1900**

Harvey Continental Steel Co. Ld. Regd. 1894. Vol. liq. 22 Aug. 1901. Undertaking and assets were acquired by Harvey United Steel Co. Ld., in which company shareholders were entitled to 8·602 shares of £1 (credited as fully-paid) for each fully-paid share of £10 held or to 6·451 fully-paid shares of £1 for each share of £10 (£7 10s. paid). Final meeting return regd. 8 May 1902 .... **1902**

Harvey (James) & Co. Ld. Regd. Edinburgh 1895. Vol. liq. June 1915. Final meeting return regd. 21 Sept. 1922. Court Order declared dissolution void July 1923. Final meeting return regd. 24 Sept.1923 ...... **1916**

Harvey Steel Co. of Great Britain Ld. Regd. 1893. Vol. liq. 22 Aug. 1901. Final meeting return regd. 8 May 1902.. **1902**

Harvey United Steel Co. Ld. Regd. 1901. Vol. liq. 31 July 1912. Capital returned to contributories—5s. per share of 5s. in Oct. 1912; further payments (if any) not known. Final meeting return regd. 7 Nov. 1913.. **1913**

Harvey's Yoker Distillery Ld. Regd. Edinburgh 1898. Vol. liq. Jan. 1906. Final meeting return regd. 29 June 1909... **1906**

Harwich Gas & Coke Co. Ld. Estd. by Deed of Settlement 1854; regd. as limited 1922. Dissolved 1 May 1949, undertaking being vested in Eastern Area Gas Board under Gas Act 1948. Holders of securities were entitled to receive British Gas 3% guaranteed stock 1990-95 as follows, in respect of each £5 unit, unless otherwise stated, of security held:

	£	s.	d.
Orig. shares (10% max.)	5	0	0
Addit. shares (7% max.)................	3	10	0
6% pref. shares	5	9	6
4½% perm. deb. stock (per £100)	103	15	0 **1952**

Harwood Mining Co. Ld. Regd. 1857. Removed from Register 1891 .... **1883**

See Stock Exchange Year-Book.

VOL. FOR

Harwood Self-Winding Watch Co. Ld. Regd. 1928. Vol. liq. (creditors') 23 Sept. 1932. Assets realised insufficient to pay unsecured creditors in full. Final meeting return regd. 9 Mar. 1935 .... **1933**

Haslam & Great Lever Co. Ld. Regd. 1901. Certain assets were acquired by Great Lever Spinning Co. Ld. and Haslam Spinning Co. Ld. The debenture stock was repaid at 105%. Capital returned to contributories—20s. per preference share of £1; £1 10s. 0½d. per ordinary share of £1; further payments (if any) not known. Removed from Register 1905 **1905**

Haslam Foundry & Engineering Co. (1927) Ld. Regd 1927. Vol. liq. 15 Jan. 1929. Undertaking and assets were acquired by Haslam & Newton Ld. [later Newton Brothers (Derby) Ld.]. Final meeting return regd. 18 July 1939 .... **1929**

Haslam (John) & Co. Ld. Regd. 1882. All assets (subject to liabilities) were transferred to Amalgamated Cotton Mills Trust Ld., in which company shareholders were entitled to £10 5% A debenture stock for each preference share of £10 held. All ordinary shares were held by acquiring company. Dissolved under Sec. 154 of Companies Act 1929 on 8 Nov. 1937 .... **1938**

Haslemere & District Gas Co. Regd. as Haslemere Gas Co. Ld. 1868; reinc. by Special Act 1917 under above title. Dissolved 1 May 1949, undertaking being vested in Southern Area Gas Board under Gas Act 1948. Holders of securities were entitled to receive, in respect of each £100 unit held, British Gas 3% guaranteed stock 1990-95 as follows:

	£	s.	d.
A ord. stock (10% max.)	205	0	0
B ord. stock (7% max.)	145	0	0
4% red. pref. stock	101	0	0
4% irred. deb. stock	102	10	0
5% irred. deb. stock	125	10	0
5½% irred. deb. stock	134	0	0

1952

Haslingden Union Gas Co. Inc. by Special Act 1861. Dissolved 1 May 1949, undertaking being vested in North Western Area Gas Board under Gas Act 1948. Holders of securities were entitled to receive, in respect of each £10 unit held, British Gas 3% guaranteed stock 1990-95 as follows:

	£	s.	d.
A shares (10% max.)	12	10	0
B shares (7½% max.)	12	10	0

1952

Hassocks & District Gas Co. Ld. Regd. 1929. Dissolved 1 May 1949, undertaking being vested in South Eastern Area Gas Board under Gas Act 1948. Holders of ordinary shares (of £1) were entitled to receive £1 6s. British Gas 3% guaranteed stock 1990-95 for each share held **1952**

Haste Pump Co. Ld. Regd. 1904. Vol. liq. 22 June 1908. Receiver appointed 6 July 1908; ceased to act 29 Nov. 1912. Removed from Register 21 Oct. 1913 ***1909**

Hastings & District Electric Tramways Co. Ld. Regd. 1904. Vol. liq. (members') 16 Dec. 1935. Shareholders were entitled to 1 fully-paid ordinary share of £1 in Maidstone & District Motor Services Ld., for every 14 ordinary shares of 10s. held and an option (since expired) over further shares. The income stock was to be redeemed at par. £69 12s. 7d. was paid into Companies' Liquidation Account. Final meeting return regd. 25 Jan. 1938 .... **1936**

Hastings & St. Leonards Gas Co. Inc. by Special Act 1854. Dissolved 1 May 1949, undertaking being vested in South Eastern Area Gas Board under Gas Act 1948. Holders of securities were entitled to receive, in respect of each £100 unit held, British Gas 3% guaranteed stock 1990-95 as follows:

	£	s.	d.
Conv. stock (5% stand.)	140	0	0
Conv. stock (3⅛% stand.)	115	0	0
Addit. stock (5% stand.)	126	0	0
3½% perp. deb. stock	99	0	0
4% perp. deb. stock	103	0	0

1952

Hastings & St. Leonards Medical Baths & Kurhaus Ld. Regd. 1911. Vol. liq. Jan. 1913. Removed from Register 1921 .... **1913**

Hastings & St. Leonards Omnibus Co. Ld. Regd. 1883. Vol. liq. 2 July 1906. Capital returned to contributories—£1 10s. per share of £5 at July 1906; further payments (if any) not known. Final meeting return regd. 14 Nov. 1911 .... **1907**

Hastings & St. Leonards-on-Sea Alexandra Hotel Co. Ld. Regd. 1876. Receiver was appointed. Removed from Register 1909 .... **1907**

Hastings & St. Leonards-on-Sea Electric Light Co Ld. Regd. 1882. Vol. liq. 28 Jan. 1899. Company was to be taken over by Corporation and debentures repaid at par. Final meeting return regd.4 Jan.1900 .... **1899**

Hastings & St. Leonards-on-Sea Ladies' College Ld. Regd. 1883. Struck off Register 1925 .... **1911**

VOL. FOR

Hastings & St. Leonards-on-Sea Public Baths & Aquarian Co. Ld. Regd. 1875. Property was sold in June 1911 by the mortgagee. No capital returned to contributories. Removed from Register 1913 .... **1912**

Hastings & St. Leonards Sports Depot Ld. Regd 1927. Vol. liq. (creditors') 8 Jan. 1935. Assets realised insufficient to meet claims of creditors in full. Final meeting return regd. 17 Feb. 1936 .... **1932**

Hastings (B. C.) Exploration Syndicate Ld. Regd. 1897. Vol. liq. 1 Apr. 1915. Final meeting return regd. 20 Dec. 1938 .... **1916**

Hastings Harbour District Railway Co. Inc. by Special Act 1897. Construction abandoned by Act of 1905 **1906**

Hatchett's Hotel Co. Ld. Regd. 1882. Court Orders: to wind up 16 Feb. 1888; to dissolve 11 Jan. 1889 .. ***1886**

Hateley's Ld. Regd. 1897. Vol. liq. 19 Nov. 1906. Removed from Register 1908 .... **1907**

Hatfield & Harpenden Breweries Ld. Regd. 1902. Vol. liq. 10 June 1920. Capital returned to contributories—20s. per share of £1 at June 1920; further payments (if any) not known. Final meeting return regd. 25 Nov. 1921 .... **1921**

Hatfield & St. Albans Railway Co, Inc. by Special Act 1862. Under Great Northern Railway Co. Act 1883 undertaking was transferred to that company for £51,500. Ordinary shareholders received 23% of paid-up value of shares **1884**

Hatfield Gas Co. Ld. Regd. 1860. Inc. by Special Act 1888. Undertaking transferred to Welwyn, Knebworth & District Gas Co. Ld. (later Welwyn & Hatfield Gas Co. Ld.). Holders of ordinary shares and preference stock received equivalent amount of securities in Welwyn Co **1926**

Hatfield Main Colliery Co. Ld. Regd. 1910. Vol. liq. (members') 14 May 1952. Final meeting return regd. 2 Feb. 1956 .... **1940**

Hathersage & District Gas Co. Ld. Regd. 1906. Dissolved 1 May 1949, undertaking being vested in East Midland Area Gas Board under Gas Act 1948. Holders of ordinary shares (of £1) were entitled to receive £2 British Gas 3% guaranteed stock 1990-95 for each share held **1952**

Hathersaw Spinning Co. Ld. Regd. 1875. Removed from Register 1908 .... **1892**

Hattangalla Tea & Rubber Co. Ld. Regd. 1911. Vol. liq. (members') 1 Aug. 1956. Capital returned to contributories—£4 9s. 11½d. per share of £1. Final meeting return regd. 28 July 1960 .... **1961**

Hattersley (Jonathan) and Son, Ld. Regd. 1890. Vol. liq. (members') 22 July 1958. Capital returned to contributories—30s. 5d. plus 52·604p per A share of £1 and 24s. 2d. plus 21·04p per B share of £1. Final meeting return regd. 13 Feb. 1973 .... **1975-6**

Hauraki Gold Mining Co. Ld. *See* North Lachlan Gold Mining Co. Ld.

Hauraki Golden Age Mines Ld. Regd. 1895 as Whitehead & Sultan Gold Mines Ld.; name changed Dec. 1896. Removed from Register 1901 .... **1900**

Hauraki Golden Bay Mines Ld. Regd. 1896. Struck off Register 2 Aug. 1904 .... **1905**

Hauraki Main Lodes Ld. Regd. 1896. Vol. liq. 19 Nov. 1900. Final meeting return regd. 18 June 1902 .... **1901**

Hauraki Mines Ld. Regd. 1900. Removed from Register 1904 .... **1904**

Hauraki (N. Z.) Associated Gold Mines Ld. Regd. 1897. Vol. liq. 31 Oct. 1900. Reconstructed as Hauraki Mines Ld., in which company shareholders were entitled to 1 fully-paid share of 2s. 6d. and 14 shares of 2s. 6d. (credited with 2s. paid) for every 15 shares of 4s. held. Final meeting return regd. 14 Jan. 1903 **1903**

Hauraki (N. Z.) Associated Gold Reefs Ld. Regd. 1896. Vol. liq. 7 May 1897. Reconstructed as Hauraki (N. Z.) Associated Gold Mines Ld., in which company shareholders were entitled to 6 shares of 4s. (credited with 3s. 3d. paid) for every 5 shares of 4s. held. Final meeting return regd. 11 May 1898 .... **1900**

Hauraki South Gold Mining Co. Ld. Regd. 1896. Vol. liq. 15 Feb. 1900. Final meeting return regd. 18 Mar. 1901 .... **1901**

Hausa (Nigeria) Ld. Regd. 1912. Vol. liq. (members') 19 June 1930. Undertaking transferred to company of same name. Shareholders were entitled to 5 shares of 4s. (credited with 2s. 6d. paid) in new company, for every 4 shares of 5s. held. Final meeting return regd. 23 Aug. 1933 .... **1931**

Hausa (Nigeria) Ld. Regd. 1930. Vol. liq. (members') 30 June 1933 for amalgamation with Tano Consolidated Mines Ld., in which company shareholders were entitled to 1 fully-paid share of 2s. 6d. and 2 shares of 2s. 6d. (credited with 1s. 9d. paid) for every 2 shares of 5s. held. Final meeting return regd. 2 July 1934 **1934**

Havana Cigar & Tobacco Factories Ld. Regd. 1898. Vol. liq. (members') 26 Feb. 1954. Company was a subsidiary of American Cigarette & Cigar Co.

See Stock Exchange Year-Book.

VOL. FOR

(through Henry Clay & Bock & Co. Ld.). Final meeting return regd. 14 Feb. 1955 .... **1954**

Havana Docks & Warehouse Co. *See* Port of Havana Docks Co.

Havana Electric Railway Co. Inc. Maine 1926. The outstanding consolidated mortgage 5% 50-year bonds of 1952 (Havana Electric Railway Co. of 1899) were redeemed at $426·31 per $1,000 in Nov. 1950 .... **1952**

Havana Electric Railway, Light & Power Co. Inc. New Jersey 1912. Reconstructed 1926 as company of same name **1927**

Havana Electric Railway, Light & Power Co. Inc. New Jersey 1926. The Compañia de Gas y Electricidad de la Habana 5% 37-year sinking fund mortgage bonds were redeemed at 105% on 1 Sept. 1927. The street railways were acquired in 1926 by Havana Electric Railway Co. **1928**

Havana Electricity Co. Ld. Regd. 1903. Vol. liq. May 1906. Undertaking and assets were acquired by Compañia de Gas y Electricidad de la Habana, in which company shareholders were entitled to 1 bond of £100 for every 10 shares of £10 held. The debentures were to be repaid at par. Removed from Register 1907 .... **1907**

Havana Exploration Co. Ld. Regd. 1909. Vol. liq. and Receiver appointed June 1913. Court Order to wind up July 1914. Struck off Register 1927 .... **1915**

Havana Investment Syndicate Ld. Regd. 1908. Vol. liq. 23 Aug. 1908. Final meeting return regd. 27 May 1915 .... ***1911**

Havana Marine Terminals Ld. Inc. Canada 1919. In 1932 mortgagees instituted foreclosure proceedings over certain lands and it seemed probable that unencumbered lands would also be seized **1935**

Havana Oil Co. Ld. Regd. 1910. Vol. liq. (members') 31 Dec. 1935. Capital returned to contributories—4·2375d. per share of 2s. Final meeting return regd.2 Dec.1943 .... **1936**

Havana Railways Co. Inc. 1842. Amalgamated June 1889 with Bank of Commerce & Regla Warehouses and Railway of the Bay of Havana, in which company shareholders received 1 share of $200 and $150 cash for each share of £100 held **1899**

Havant Gas Co. Inc. by Special Act 1910. Undertaking acquired by Portsmouth Gas Co. (later Portsmouth & Gosport Gas Co.), as from 1 July 1926 .... **1911**

Havelock Gold Mining & Exploration Co. Ld. Regd. 1888. Vol. liq. 9 Feb. 1893. Final meeting return regd. 30 June 1896 .... ***1894**

Hawaiian Commercial & Sugar Co. Inc. California 1882. The outstanding 5½% sterling debentures were redeemed on 1 Apr. 1907 .... **1908**

Hawaiian Investment & Agency Co. Ld. Regd. Edinburgh 1880. Vol. liq. 12 Nov. 1883. Business was acquired by Western and Hawaiian Investment Co. Ld. (later Second Alliance Trust Co. Ld.), in which company shareholders were entitled to 1 share of £5 (credited with £1 paid) for each share of £5 (£1 paid) held. Final meeting return regd. 10 Nov. 1896 .... **1883**

Hawaiian Tramways Co. Ld. Regd. 1888. Undertaking was acquired by Honolulu Rapid Transit and Land Co. of Hawaii. Removed from Register 1906 ...... **1904**

Hawarden Gas & Coke Co. Ld. Regd. 1864. Dissolved May 1949, undertaking being vested in Wales Area Gas Board under Gas Act 1948. Holders of ordinary shares (partly and fully-paid) were entitled to receive, in respect of each £5 held £7 10s. British Gas 3% guaranteed stock 1990—95 .... **1952**

Hawd & Spicer Ld. Regd. 1907. Vol. liq. Dec. 1908. Removed from Register 1911 .... **1909**

Hawes Electric Lighting Co. Ld. Regd. 1920. Dissolved 1 Apr. 1948, undertaking being vested in the British (later Central) Electricity Authority and North-Eastern Area Board under the Electricity Act 1947. Ordinary shareholders were entitled to receive £1 16s. British Electricity 3% guaranteed stock (1968—73), for each share (of £1) held **1949**

Hawick Gas Co. Ld. Regd. in Edinburgh 1930. Dissolved 1 May 1949, undertaking being vested in Scottish Area Gas Board under Gas Act 1948. Holders of securities were entitled to receive British Gas 3% guaranteed stock 1990—95 as follows:

	£	s.	d.	
Ord. shares (of £1)	1	17	0	
4% red. debs. of (£100)	100	10	0	**1952**

Hawker (H. G.) Engineering Co. Ld. Regd. 1920. Vol. liq. (members') 26 Oct. 1933. Undertaking acquired by Hawker Aircraft Ld. Capital returned to contributories—£828,482 17s. 5d. *plus* certain shares in specie. Final meeting return regd. 16 Sept. 1935 . **1940**

Hawkers' Ld. Regd. 1897. Vol. liq. (members') 16 June 1933. Capital returned to contributories—1s. 6d. per share of £1. Final meeting return regd. 21 July 1934 **1911**

VOL. FOR

Hawkes (O. C.) Ld. Regd. 1896. Vol. liq. (members') 21 Dec. 1932. Capital returned to contributories—1s. 6d. per preference share of £1. Final meeting return regd. 11 Feb. 1934 .... **1933**

Hawkhurst Gas Co. Ld. Regd. 1868. Dissolved 1 May 1949, undertaking being vested in South Eastern Area Gas Board under Gas Act 1948. Holders of securities were entitled to receive British Gas 3% guaranteed stock 1990—95 as follows in respect of each £1 unit, unless otherwise stated, of security held:

	£	s.	d.	
Orig. ord. shares (5% max.)	1	2	0	
Addit. ord. shares (5% max.)	1	2	0	
4½% red. mort. debs. (1st & 2nd) of £50	51	15	0	**1952**

Hawkins & Parfitt South Berks Brewery Co. Ld. *See* South Berks Brewery Co. Ld.

Hawkins Gold Hill Mines Ld. Regd. 1893. Vol. liq. 15 Mar. 1897. Final meeting return regd. 8 Nov. 1898 **1898**

Hawkins Hill Consolidated Gold Mining Co. Ld. Regd. 1882. Removed from Register 10 Feb. 1903 .... ***1886**

Hawk's View Gold Mining Co. Ld. Regd. 1958. Reconstructed 1900 as Hannan's Kapai Ld., in which company shareholders were entitled to 1 share of £1 (credited with 17s. paid) for each share of £1 held. Removed from Register 1901 .... **1902**

Hawthorns & Co. Ld. Regd. Edinburgh 1896. Vol. liq. May 1928. Final meeting return regd. 16 July 1932 **1929**

Hawthorn's Hotel (Bournemouth) Ld. Regd 1911. Vol. liq. 6 Feb. 1963. Final meeting return regd. 6 May 1965 .... **1957**

Hay Gas & Coke Co. Ld. Regd. 1862. Dissolved 1 May 1949, undertaking being vested in Wales Area Gas Board under Gas Act 1948. Holders of securities were entitled to receive British Gas guaranteed stock 1990–95 as follows:

	£	s.	d.	
Ord. shares (of £5)	2	10	0	
4½% 2nd mort. debs. (of £100)	100	0	0	**1952**

Hay Gold Mining Co. Ld. Regd. 1910. Vol. liq. 16 June 1919. Undertaking was acquired by London and Rhodesian Mining and Land Co. Ld. (later Lonrho Ld.). Final meeting return regd. 24 Feb. 1920 ...... **1920**

Hay (J. & J.) Ld. Regd. Edinburgh 1896. Vol. liq. May 1921. Undertaking and assets were acquired by J. Hay & Sons Ld. Capital returned to contributories—£10 per preference share of £10; £20 per ordinary share of £10. Final meeting return regd. 22 Aug. 1924 .... **1922**

Hay Merricks & Co. Ld. Regd. Edinburgh 1876. Vol. liq. 27 Jan. 1899. Undertaking acquired by Curtis's & Harvey Ld. Final meeting return regd. 10 July 1899 .... **1940**

Haycroft Gold Reduction & Mining Co. Ld. Reed. 1896. Vol. liq. 27 Dec. 1899. Removed from Register 1909 **1900**

Haydella Tea and Rubber Estates Ld. Regd. 1907. Vol. liq. (members') July 1943. Capital returned to contributories—4s. 4·416d. per share of 2s. Final meeting return regd. 10 Oct. 1947 .... **1948**

Hayes Candy & Co. Ld. Regd. 1900. Vol. liq. (members') 20 Feb. 1939. Undertaking and assets were acquired by Hayes Candy & Crockers Ld. Ordinary shareholders were entitled to 15s. cash, 3 fully-paid B preference shares of 10s. and 2 fully-paid ordinary shares of 5s. in new company for every 15 ordinary shares of 15s. held. A preference shareholders were entitled to £1 in cash and 1 fully-paid A preference share of £1 in new company for each A preference share of £2 held. B preference shareholders were entitled to 10s. in cash and 1 fully-paid A preference share of £1 in new company for every 4 B preference shares of 8s. held. £10 15s. was unclaimed in respect of payments under Sec. 155 of the Companies Act 1929. Final meeting return regd. 4 Aug. 1944 ...... **1940**

Hayes Candy & Crockers Ld. Regd. 1938 as F.W.B. Ld., name changed 1939. All capital was owned by Hickson, Lloyd & King Ld. Vol. liq. (members') 7 Feb. 1964. Final meeting return regd. 4 May 1964 **1959**

Hayes Cocoa Co. Ld. See J. F. S. Ld.

Hayes Homesteads Ld. Regd. 1936. Vol. liq. (members') 10 May 1938. Capital returned to contributories—£19 6s. 9d. per share of £1. Final meeting return regd. 20 Sept. 1941 .... **1939**

Hayfield Gas Co. Ld. Regd. 1858. Dissolved 1 May 1949, undertaking being vested in North Western Area Gas Board under Gas Act 1948. Holders of securities were entitled to receive, in respect of each £5 unit held, British Gas 3% guaranteed stock 1990—95 as follows:

	£	s.	d.	
Orig. shares (10% max.)	6	10	0	
Addit. shares (7% max.)	5	5	0	**1952**

Hayle Gas Co. Ld. Regd. 1889. Dissolved 1 May 1949. undertaking being vested in South Western Area Gas Board under Gas Act 1948. Holders of ordinary shares (of £5) were entitled. to receive £6 15s. British Gas 3% guaranteed stock 1990—95 for each share held 1952

Hayling Railways Co. Inc. by Special Act 1860. In 1923 the undertaking was merged into the London, Brighton & South Coast Railway Co. in which company stockholders were entitled to stock as follows:

For each £100 held	L.B. & S,C.R.	
Deb. Stock	£106 5s. 7d.	4% Deb.
Preference Shares	£125 0s. 0d.	4% Deb.
Ordinary Shares	£15 4s. 10d.	4% Deb.	1924

Haymarket Estates Ld. Regd. 1924. Vol. liq. (members') 2 Dec. 1948. Final meeting return regd. 13 May 1963 1940

Hayoep (Dutch Borneo) Rubber Estates Ld. Regd. 1910. Vol. liq. 13 July 1921. Undertaking and assets were acquired by New Hayoep Rubber Estates Ld., in which company shareholders were entitled to 10 shares of 2s. (credited with 1s. 3d. paid) for each share of £1 held. Final meeting return regd. 4 Mar 1924 1922

Hayward (W. G. C.) & Co. Ld. Regd. 1916. Vol. liq. 2 Nov. 1921. Final meeting return regd. 29 Aug. 1923 1922

Haywards Heath & District Electric Supply Co. Ld. See Central Sussex Electricity Ld.

Haywards Heath District Gas Co. Regd. 1865 as Haywards Heath Gas Light & Coke Co. Ld.; inc. by Special Act 1895 as above. Dissolved 1 May 1949. undertaking being vested in South Eastern Area Gas Board under Gas Act 1948. Holders of securities were entitled to receive, in respect of each £100 unit held, British Gas 3% guaranteed stock 1990—95 as follows:

	£	s.	d.
Cons. stock (5% stand)	174	0	0
5¼% irred. pref. stock	128	10	0
4½% irred. pref. stock	110	0	0
5% perp. deb. stock	125	0	0
3¾ red. deb. stock	102	0	0	1952

Hazelwood Shipping Co. Ld. Regd. 1910. Vol. liq. (members') 12 June 1940. Capital returned to contributories—½d. per share of £1. Final meeting return regd. 12 Apr. 1945 1946

Hazleton, Connor & Co. Ld. See Roches Stores Dublin Ld.

Head (Henry) & Co. Ld. See below.

Head (Henry) (1897) Ld. Regd. 1897 as Henry Head & Co. Ld.; name subsequently changed. Vol. liq. (members') 3 Apr. 1956. Final meeting return regd. 24 May 1960 1947

Head, Wrightson & Co. (South Africa) Ld. Regd. 1908. Vol. liq. (members') 14 Aug. 1937. All shares held by Head, Wrightson & Co. Ld. Final meeting return regd. 28 Nov. 1938 1938

Headlands Ld. Regd. 1899. Vol. liq. Mar. 1910. Removed from Register 1910 1911

Healeyfield Mining Co, Ld. Regd. 1889. Vol. liq. 21 Jan. 1891 for reconstruction as company of same name. Shareholders were entitled to apply for shares in new company. Final meeting return regd. 18 Apr. 1895 1891

Health Insurance Corporation Ld. Regd. 1888. Court Order to wind up 27 Oct. 1903. Struck off Register 21 June 1912 1904

Heaps (E. H.) & Co. Ld. Inc. British Columbia 1907. Receiver appointed Jan. 1919 and assets were realised 1943

Hearl & Tonks (1897) Ld. Regd. 1897. Vol. liq. 17 Feb. 1899. Assets were not expected to realise sufficient to repay debenture holders. Removed from Register 1908 1900

Hearts of Oak Assurance Co. Ld. Regd. 1903 as Hearts of Oak Life & General Assurance Co. Ld.: name changed Apr. 1920. Court Order to wind up Dec. 1932. No distribution was made 1945

Heath & Co. Ld. Regd. 1882. Court Order to wind up May 1925. Struck off Register May 1933 1934

Heath (Robert) & Low Moor Ld. Regd. 1888 as Low Moor Co. Ld.; name changed Jan. 1920. Colliery undertaking was acquired by Norton & Biddulph Collieries Ld. Vol. liq. Oct. 1929. Struck off Register Oct. 1934 1935

Heathfield & District Water Co. Inc. by Special Act 1913. Under the Eastbourne Water Order, 1959 the undertaking vested in the Eastbourne Waterworks Co., from 1 Nov. 1959. Shareholders received shares in the Eastbourne company in exchange for their holdings at the following rates—7½ ordinary shares of £1 (7% maximum) per A ordinary share of £5 (10% maximum); 5 ordinary shares of £1 (7%

maximum) per B ordinary share of £5 (7% maximum) 1 4% preference share of £5 per 4% preference share of £5 and 1 5¾% preference share of £10 per 5¾% preference share of £10 held. The 4% irredeemable debenture stock, 5% mortgage bonds and 4¾% redeemable debenture stock became securities of the Eastbourne company as from 1 Nov. 1959. Company was dissolved by a resolution of the directors passed on 19 Sept. 1960 1961

Heaton (William) & Sons Ld. Regd. 1914. Vol. liq. 2 Oct. 1922. Undertaking and assets were acquired by Crosses & Heaton's Associated Mills Ld. Final meeting return regd. 8 Feb. 1923 1923

Heatrae Ld. Regd. 1920 as Electric Fires Ld.; name changed Apr. 1935. Vol. liq. (members') 17 Apr. 1936. All shares privately held. Undertaking acquired by company of same name. Final meeting return regd. 1 Aug. 1936 1937

Hebburn Transport Co. Ld. Regd. 1920. Controlling interest was held by Palmers Shipbuilding & Iron Co. Ld. Struck off Register 8 Mar. 1935 1936

Heberlein Co. Ld. Regd. 1904. Vol. liq. Apr. 1908. Removed from Register 1909 1909

Heberlein Self-Acting Railway Break Co. Ld. Regd. 1872. Undertaking was acquired by Heberlein Co. Ld., for 9,498 shares of £1. Removed from Register 1904 1908

Heckington Gas Co. Ld. Regd. 1860. Dissolved 1 May 1949, undertaking being vested in East Midland Area Gas Board under Gas Act 1948. Holders of securities were entitled to receive British Gas 3% guaranteed stock 1990—95 as follows:

	£	s.	d.
Ord. shares (of £10)	24	0	0
4½% red. mort. debs. (of £100) ...	101	0	0	1952

Heckmondwike & Liversedge Gas Co. Inc. by Special Act 1862 as Heckmondwike Gas Co.; name changed in 1909. The undertaking has ceased to exist, having been purchased on 19 Sept. 1921 by the Spenborough Urban District Council 1922

Hedderwick (James) & Sons Ld. Regd. Edinburgh 1905. Vol. liq. (members') 29 Sept. 1939. Direct controlling interest held by Outram (George) & Co. Ld. Capital returned to contributors—£195,520 16s. 8d. Final meeting return regd. 27 Sept. 1940 1940

Hedley (Thomas) & Brothers Ld. Regd. 1922. Vol. liq. 12 Dec. 1924. The property and assets were sold to South Moor Colliery Co. Ld. [later Holmside & South Moor Collieries Ld.]. Final meeting return regd. 13 Aug. 1925 1925

Hedley (Thomas) & Co. Ld. Regd. 1898. Removed from Register 1906 1903

Hedley Trust Ld. Regd. 1920. Vol. liq. 26 Sept. 1924. Final meeting return regd. 17 Oct. 1929 1925

Heeley (Charles) Ld. Regd. 1898. Vol. liq. (members') 17 Dec. 1937. Assets were acquired by Holt Brewery Co. Ld. Capital returned to contributories—5s. 1½d. per share of 5s. Final meeting return regd. 5 Oct. 1938 1938

Heenan Beddow Ld. Regd. 1937 as Heenan Beddow & Sturmey Ld.; name changed 1970. Compulsorily wound-up 6 Oct. 1975 1986-7

Heenan Spark Ld. Regd. as private company 1946 as Spark Alloys Ld.; name changed Spark Holdings Ld. 1957 and to present title 1973. Winding-up order made 12 Jan. 1976 1986-7

Heidelberg Gold Mines Ld. Regd. 1895 as Rothschild's Gold Mines Ld.; name changed June 1895. Removed from Register 1908 1898

Heidelberg Proprietary Mining Co. Ld. Regd. 1895. Vol. liq. 29 Dec. 1898. Final meeting return regd. 22 Dec. 1899 1899

Heidelberg Union Land Co. Ld. Regd. 1895. Vol. liq. 2 Mar. 1900. Properties were acquired in 1896 by South Rand Gold Corporation Ld., for £700,000 in fully-paid shares of £1. Final meeting return regd. 21 Dec. 1901 1898

Heidelburg Estates and Exploration Co. Ld. Regd. 1895. Vol. liq. Jan. 1900. Reconstructed as company of same name [later Town Centre Properties Ld.]. Removed from Register 1906 1900

Heilbut Symons & Co. Ld. Regd. 1920. Struck off Register 8 Apr. 1938 1939

Helbert, Wagg & Co. Ld. Regd. 1919. Undertaking vested in J. Henry Schroder Wagg & Co., Ld. in 1962. Dissolved 4 Mar. 1964 1965

Helicorid Locknut Patents (Parent) Co. Ld. Regd. 1898. Vol. liq. 7 Apr. 1902. Removed from Register 4 Mar. 1910 .... *1903

Hellifield & District Gas Co. Ld. Regd. 1903. Dissolved 1 May 1949, undertaking being vested in North Eastern Area Gas Board under Gas Act 1948. Holders of securities were entitled to receive British Gas 3% guaranteed stock 1990—95 as follows:

	VOL. FOR

Ord. shares (of £1) .... £ s. d. 1 4 6

5% 1st mort. debs. (of £100) 51 15 0 **1952**

Hellyer's Steam Fishing Co. Ld. Regd. 1897. Vol. liq. 4 Nov. 1919. Final meeting return regd. 20 May 1927 ***1920**

Helmsley Lighting Co. Ld. Regd 1912. Dissolved 1 May 1949, undertaking being vested in North Eastern Area Gas Board under Gas Act 1948. Holders of shares (of £1) were entitled to receive £1 British Gas 3% guaranteed stock 1990–95 for each share held **1952**

Helouan Petroleum Co. Ld. Regd. 1909. Vol. liq. 20 Jan. 1916. Final meeting return regd. 23 July 1923 ..... **1916**

Helston & District Gas Co. Ld. Regd. 1934. Dissolved 1 May 1949, undertaking being vested in South Western Area Gas Board under Gas Act 1948. Holders of securities were entitled to receive, in respect of each £1 unit held, British Gas 3% guaranteed stock 1990—95 as follows:

£ s. d.

Ord. shares (10% max.) 0 5 0

6% red. pref. shares 0 10 0 **1952**

Helston Railway Co. Inc. by Special Act 1880. Under Great Western Railway Act 1898 the undertaking was amalgamated with that company. Holders of 5% debenture stock received £2 2½% debenture stock in Great Western Railway Co. for each £1 held; purchasing company adopted the Lloyds Bonds and paid liquidator £45,500 in cash **1899**

Hemel Hempstead District Gas Co. Inc. by Special Act 1878. Under Special Order of 1931 the undertaking was acquired by the Watford & St. Albans Gas Co., in which company, holders of A & B ordinary stock were entitled to £167 ordinary stock for each £100 held; holders of C ordinary stock were entitled to £116 18s. ordinary stock for each £100 held; holders of C 6% preference stock were entitled to £120 5% preference stock for each £100 held; holders of 6% redeemable debenture stock were entitled to £100 6% redeemable debenture stock for each £100 held. The liability in respect of the 4% and 5% permanent mortgage bonds was taken over by the Watford & St. Albans Co **1932**

Hemingways Ld. Regd. 1900. Vol. liq. 25 Mar. 1904. Final meeting return regd. 20 Feb. 1907 .... ***1905**

Hemlock (B.C.) Mines Ld. Regd. 1909. Vol. liq. Sept. 1915. Struck off Register 1922 .... **1916**

Hemmings (A.B.) Ld. Regd. as private company 1930; converted into public company 1947. All capital was owned by Associated British Foods Ld. Vol. liq. (members') 30 July 1962. Final meeting return regd. 8 June 1966 .... **1967**

Hemoco Ld. Regd. 1930 as Hesselman Motor Corpn. Ld.; name changed in Dec. 1938. Vol. liq. (members') 21 Dec. 1938, the undertaking and assets (other than shares owned in Hesselman Motor Corpn. A/B.) were acquired by Patent Oil Engines Ld. (later Hesselman Motor Corpn. Ld.). Shareholders (except Patent Oil Engines Ld.) received 1 share of Kr. 60 in Hesselman Motor Corpn. A/B. in respect of every £5 capital paid up of either class. Final meeting return regd. 1 Sept 1952 .... **1954**

Hemp, Yarn & Cordage Ld. Regd. 1892. Vol. liq. 21 May 1894. Court Order to continue winding up under supervision 14 June 1894. Final meeting return regd. 12 Oct. 1899 .... **1896**

Hemsworth, Grimethorpe & District Gas Co. Ld. Regd. 1883. Dissolved 1 May 1949, undertaking being vested in North Eastern Area Gas Board under Gas Act 1948. Holders of ordinary shares (of £1) were entitled to receive £2 1s. British Gas 3% guaranteed stock 1990–95 for each share held. Liability in respect of certain mortgage loans assumed by the Board **1952**

Henderson & Forbes Gold Mining Co. Ld. Regd. 1889. Vol. liq. 1 Feb. 1915. Final meeting return regd. 1 Nov. 1922 .... **1915**

Henderson (David & William) & Co. Ld. Regd. Edinburgh 1900. Vol. liq. (creditors') 29 Mar. 1935. Assets realised insufficient to pay creditors in full. Final meeting return regd. 19 Aug. 1938 .... **1936**

Henderson (Laurence), Sons & Co. Ld. Regd. Edinburgh 1896. Vol. liq. Feb. 1901. Final meeting return regd. 16 May 1905 .... **1901**

Henderson's Nigel Ld. Regd. 1895. Vol. liq. Jan. 1910. Removed from Register 1911 .... **1910**

Henderson's Transvaal Estates Ld. Regd. 1894. Vol. liq. Feb. 1908 for reconstruction as company of same name. Shareholders were entitled to 1 share of £1 (credited with 17s. 6d. paid) for each share of £1 held. Removed from Register 1910 .... **1909**

Henderson's Transvaal Estates Ld, Inc. Rhodesia 1908. Vol. liq. Dec. 1912. Reconstructed as company of same name. Shareholders were entitled to 5 shares of 5s. (credited as fully-paid) in new company for every

	VOL. FOR

4 shares of £1 held and an option (since expired) over further shares **1913**

Hendies Gold Mines Ld. Regd. 1925 as Hendies Lydenburg Platinum Ld.; name changed 1934. Vol. liq. (members') 25 Aug. 1950. Capital returned to contributories—1s. 2½d. per share of 5s. Final meeting return regd. 21 Sept. 1951 .... **1952**

Hendies Lydenburg Platinum Ld. See above.

Hendon Electric Supply Co. Ld. Regd. 1907. Vol. liq. (members') 6 Dec. 1939. Undertaking was transferred to Northmet Power Co. The 4% debenture stock was redeemed at 102% on 1 Jan. 1940. Capital returned to contributories—20s. per preference share of £1; £1 8s. 5d. per ordinary share of £1. Final meeting return regd. 20 Mar. 1940 .... **1940**

Henery Diamond Syndicate Ld. Regd. 1902. In liquidation in 1905. Removed from Register 1905 .... **1905**

Heneward China Clay Co. Ld. Regd. 1913. The mine was closed and the company was without funds. Struck off Register 14 Apr. 1939 .... **1940**

Hengrave Estates Ld. Regd. 1922. Vol. liq. (members') 1 Apr. 1954. Final meeting return regd. 29 Mar. 1956 **1947**

Henley & Sons Cyder Co. Ld. Regd. 1921. Vol. liq. (members') 24 Apr. 1933. Capital returned to contributories—£516 19s. 1d. Final meeting return regd. 30 June 1938 .... **1934**

Henley-in-Arden and Great Western Junction Railway Co. Inc. by Special Act. 1873. Powers were revived by Birmingham and Henley-in-Arden Railway Co. in 1884 .... **1901**

Henley-in-Arden Gas, Coal & Coke Co. Ld. Regd. 1862. Dissolved 1 May 1949, undertaking being vested in West Midland Area Gas Board under Gas Act 1948. Holders of ordinary shares (of £5) were entitled to receive £1 5s. British Gas 3% guaranteed stock 1990—95 for each share held **1952**

Henley-in-Arden Railway Co. Inc. by Special Act 1861. Powers were revived by Henley-in Arden & Great Western Junction Railway Co. in 1873 .... **1894**

Henley-on-Thames Gas Co. Inc. by Special Act 1888. By special Order of 1930 the undertaking was acquired by Yorktown (Camberley) & District Gas and Electricity Co., in which company stockholders were entitled to consolidated ordinary (5% standard) stock as follows:—for every £100 10% standard stock held—£200; for every £100 5% standard stock held—£120; for every £100 7% standard stock held—£152 .... **1931**

Henley-on-Thames Water Co. Ld. Regd. 1880. Undertaking and assets transferred to Thames Valley Water Board from 1 Apr. 1960. Vol. liq. (members') 28 July 1960. 4% and 3½% mortgage debenture bonds and 5% preference shares were repaid at par; holders of original A and additional B shares received £171·07 and £119·75 per £100 respectively. Final meeting return regd. 20 Dec. 1960 .... **1963**

Henley's (W. T.) Electric Light & Power Co. Ld. Regd. 1882. Undertaking was acquired in 1885 by W. J. Henley's Telegraph Works Co. Ld. Vol. liq. 7 Apr. 1892. Final meeting return regd. 31 Jan. 1893 ..... **1908**

Henriett Mining & Smelting Co. Ld. Regd. 1882. Vol. liq. Feb. 1883. Final meeting return regd. 22 Feb. 1884 .... **1884**

Henriques Estates Ld. Regd. 1908. Reconstructed as Panama Rubber & Timber Estates Ld. in which company shareholders were entitled to 1 share of 5s. (credited with 4s. paid) for every 2 shares of 2s. held. Removed from Register 1912 .... **1912**

Henriquez South Rubber Estates Ld. Regd. 1910. Reconstructed as Panama Rubber & Timber Estates Ld., in which company shareholders were entitled to 1 share of 5s. (credited with 4s. paid) for every 2 shares of 2s. held. Removed from Register 1913 .... **1912**

Henrite Explosives Ld. Regd. 1906. Vol. liq. 26 Jan. 1909. Final meeting return regd. 15 July 1909 ..... **1909**

Henry (C. S.) & Co. Ld. Regd. 1902. Vol. liq. 14 Jan. 1920. Final meeting return regd. 24 Sept. 1920 .... ***1920**

Henry Rifled Barrel Engineering & Small Arms Co. Ld. Regd. 1895. Vol. liq. 7 Mar. 1900. Business was acquired by Blenheim Engineering Co. Ld. Removed from Register 1901 .... **1901**

Henry Street Warehouse Co. Ld. See Roches Stores Dublin Ld.

Hentschel (Carl) Ld. Regd. 1899. Undertaking and assets were acquired by Carl Hentschel (1906) Ld. (later Knight's Manufacturing Co. Ld.) for £20,500 in ordinary shares, £39,500 in preference shares of £1 and £4,966 in cash. Removed from Register 1912 **1907**

Hentschel (Carl) (1908) Ld. See Knight's Manufacturing Co. Ld.

Hentschel Colourtype (1901) Ld. Regd. 1901. Undertaking and assets were acquired by Carl Hentschel (1906) Ld. (later Knight's Manufacturing Co. Ld.), for £16,060 in ordinary shares, £5,000 in preference shares of £1 and £3,974 in cash. Removed from Register 1912 1907

Henty & Constable (Brewers) Ld. Regd. 1893 as George Henty & Sons Ld.; name changed July 1921. Vol. liq. (members') 6 May 1955. All capital was owned by Tamplins Brewery Ld. Majority of remaining assets distributed in specie. Final meeting return regd. 9 Jan. 1964 1965

Hepburn Alluvial Mining Co, Ld. Regd. 1903. Undertaking was acquired by New Deep Leads Syndicate Ld., in which company shareholders were entitled to apply for shares. Removed from Register 1909 1907

Hepburn Deep Leads Ld. Regd. 1900. Reconstructed 1903 as Hepburn Alluvial Mining Co. Ld., in which company shareholders were entitled to 7 fully-paid shares of 2s. for every 50 shares of 10s. held. Removed from Register 1907 1905

Heppells Ld. Regd. 1924. Court Order to wind up Mar. 1931. Struck off Register 9 June 1936 1937

Hepworth Picture Plays (1922) Ld. Regd. 1922. Receiver appointed in June 1924. No return to shareholders was anticipated. Struck off Register Jan. 1932 ... 1932

Herbert (George) Ld. Regd. in Edinburgh 1896. Vol. liq. (members') 31 Oct. 1929. Struck off the Register 8 June 1948 1949

Herbert Terry & Sons Ld. *See* H. T. Investments Ld.

Herbertsons Ld. Regd. Edinburgh 1899. Vol. liq. Nov. 1917. Final meeting return regd. 16 Sept. 1919 1918

Hercules Co. Ld. Inc. South African Republic 1895 as Hercules Syndicate Ld.; name changed 1902. Vol. liq. May 1908. Undertaking and assets were sold to East Rand Proprietary Mines Ld. for 160,000 shares of £1 1909

Hercules Patent Soap Co. Ld. Regd. 1899. Struck off Register 9 Dec. 1902 1903

Hercules Syndicate Ld. *See* Hercules Co. Ld.

Hercynia Copper Co. Ld. Regd. 1891. Court Order to wind up 21 Jan. 1893. Removed from Register 1907 1893

Herd (Walter) & Son Ld. Regd. Edinburgh 1898. Vol. liq. Apr. 1908. Property and undertaking acquired by Bowhill Coal Co. (Fife) Ld. Capital returned to contributories—preference shares were repaid in full; ordinary shareholders received a return of capital. Final meeting return regd. 19 Apr. 1910 1909

Heredia Lead Mines Ld. Regd. 1902. Struck off Register Feb. 1930 1930

Hereford and Tredegar Brewery Ld. Regd. 1899 as Tredegar & Hereford Brewery Co. Ld.; name changed Dec. 1902. Vol. liq. (members') 30 Sept. 1947. Final meeting return regd. 2 Oct. 1948 1949

Hereford (Travancore) Tea Estates Ld. Regd. 1924. Vol. liq. (creditors') 2 Dec. 1931. Prior lien debenture stockholders received 1s. 7d. in £. Final meeting return regd. 2 Dec. 1932 1932

Herefordshire & Gloucestershire Canal Navigation (Co. Of Proprietors Of The). Inc. by Special Act 1792. Dissolved 3 June 1949; undertaking vested from 1 Jan. 1948. in British Transport Commission under Transport Act 1947. Holders of ordinary shares (of £140) and 7½% preference shares (of £20) were entitled to receive 7s. and £48 17s. 9d. British Transport 3% guaranteed stock 1978—88 respectively 1949

Heriot Gold Mining Co. Ld. Inc. Natal 1887. Reconstructed as New Heriot Gold Mining Co. Ld., in 1892 1909

Heritable Property Co. of Glasgow, Ld. Regd. Edinburgh 1894. Vol. liq. Mar. 1914. Capital returned to contributories—16s. 8d. per share of £10. Final meeting return regd. 24 Feb. 1947 1947

Heritages Association of Scotland Ld. Regd. Edinburgh 1877. Vol. liq. Feb. 1895. Capital returned to contributories—9s. per share of £5 (£1 paid) at 30 Sept. 1895; further payments (if any) not known. Final meeting return regd. 27 Jan. 1898 1896

Hermand Oil Co. Ld. Regd. Edinburgh 1890. Vol. liq. Mar. 1899 for reconstruction as New Hermand Oil Co. Ld. in which company shareholders were entitled to 1 share of £1 (credited with 16s. 8d. paid) for every 5 shares of £1 held. Final meeting return regd. 2 Feb. 1901 1902

Hermeton Ld. Regd. 1930. Vol. liq. (creditors') 29 Nov. 1933. Assets realised insufficient to pay unsecured creditors in full. Final meeting return regd. 15 Mar. 1943 1934

Herne Bay & District Electricity Supply Co. Ld. Regd. 1927. Dissolved 1 Apr. 1948, undertaking being vested in the British (later Central) Electricity Authority and South Eastern Area Board under the Electricity Act 1947. Holders of ordinary shares were entitled to receive £1 15s. British Electricity 3% guaranteed stock (1968—73), for each £1 ordinary capital held 1949

Herne Bay Gas Co. Ld. Estd. 1853; regd. 1882 as Herne Bay Gas & Coke Co. Ld.; name changed to Herne Bay Gas & Electricity Co. Ld. 1913 and as above 1921. Dissolved 1 May 1949, undertaking being vested in South Eastern Area Gas Board under Gas Act 1948. Holders of securities were entitled to receive British Gas 3% guaranteed stock 1990—95 as follows in respect of each £5 unit, unless otherwise stated of security held:

	£	s.	d.	
Orig. shares (10% stand.)	10	10	0	
Addit. shares (7% stand.)	7	8	0	
6½% pref. shares	7	0	0	
4½% irred. deb. stock (per £100) ..	114	0	0	
5% red. debs. (1950) (per £100)	104	0	0	1952

Herne Bay Pier Co. Ld. Regd. 1883. Receiver appointed in Feb. 1905. Struck off Register 1915 1907

Herne Bay Waterworks Co. Inc. by Special Act 1867. Dissolved under the Kent Water Act 1955 on 24 Aug. 1957. The undertaking vested in the Canterbury & District Water Co., as from 1 Apr. 1956. Stockholders were entitled to receive securities in that company as follows (per £100 stock held):— 10% ordinary—£200 5% ordinary stock; 7% ordinary—£140 5% ordinary stock; 6% preference—£120 5% preference stock; 5% preference—£100 5% preference stock. Holders of the 4% and 5% debenture stock received like amounts of the 4% and 5% debenture stock of the Canterbury company respectively 1958

Heron Mill (1919) Ld. Regd. 1919, Vol. liq. (members') 26 Nov. 1937. Capital returned to contributories—£69,779 13s. Final meeting return regd. 12 Mar. 1940 1938

Herring Drifter Insurance Co. Ld. Regd. Edinburgh 1903. Vol. liq. Feb. 1912. Reconstructed as United Scottish Herring Drifter Insurance Co. Ld. [later United Scottish Insurance Co. Ld.], in which company shareholders were entitled to 1 share of £1 (credited with 5s. paid) for each share of £1 (2s. paid) held. Struck off Register 5 Feb. 1937 1938

Hertford & District Gas Co. Inc. by Special Act 1864 as the Hertford Gaslight Company; name changed in 1929. By Special Order of 1932 the undertaking was acquired by the Tottenham and District Gas Co. in which company holders of consolidated stock were entitled to £12 5½% preference stock for every £10 held, and holders of preference stock were entitled to £10 5½% preference stock for every £10 held. Liability for the debentures was assumed by acquiring company 1933

Herts & Essex Water Co. Regd. as limited company 21 July 1879 as Herts & Essex Waterworks Co. Ld.; reincorporated as a statutory company and name changed by Act of 6 May 1953. Undertaking vested in Lee Valley Water Co. from 1 Apr. 1960. Stockholders received capital stock in new company (per £1 stock held) as follows:
Ordinary (10% maximum): £1 12s. 6d. 5% ordinary.
Ordinary (7% maximum): £1 8s. 5% ordinary.
Ordinary (5% maximum): £1 5% ordinary.
5½% redeemable preference 1972: £1 5½% redeemable preference.
4½% redeemable preference 1978: £1 4½% redeemable preference.
4½% redeemable preference 1974–5: £1 4½% redeemable preference.
5% preference: £1 5s. 4% preference.
Outstanding debenture capital of this company became debenture capital of new company. Dissolved 28 Oct. 1964 1966

Hesperus Gold Mining Co. Ld. Regd. 1896. Vol. liq. 3 Dec. 1896. Absorbed into Golden Link Consolidated Gold Mines Ld. Final meeting regd.1 Mar.1897 *1897

Hesselman Motor Corpn. Ld. *See* Hemoco Ld.

Hessle Gas Co. Regd. 1861 as Hessle Gas Light & Coke Co. Ld.; inc. by Special Act 1905; name changed 1922. Dissolved 1 May 1949 undertaking being vested in North Eastern Area Gas Board under Gas Act 1948. Holders of securities were entitled to receive in respect of each £100 unit held British Gas 3% guaranteed stock 1990–95 as follows:

	£	s.	d.	
Orig. cap. stock (10% stand.)	205	0	0	
Addit. ord. stock (8% stand.)	167	0	0	
Ord. stock (7% stand.)	147	0	0	
6% pref. stock	132	0	0	
6% perp. deb. stock	145	0	0	
4% red. deb. stock	102	0	0	
5% red. deb. stock	103	0	0	1952

Hester & Co. Ld. Regd. 1873. Removed from Register 1904 1876

Hetty Gold Mine Ld. Regd. 1895. Vol. liq. 15 Feb. 1898. Capital returned to contributories—1s. per share of

VOL. FOR

Hill (H. & J.) Group Ld. Regd. as private company 22 Sept. 1923 as H. & J. Hill (Willenhall) Ld.; converted into public company 20 Aug. 1946; name changed 31 Dec. 1970. Vol. liq. (creditors') 6 May 1981. Final meeting return regd. 15 Nov. 1982 .... **1984-5**

Hill (Philip) Higginson (Registrars) Ld. Regd. 1927 as Quadrant Trust Ld.; name subsequently changed. Vol. liq. (members') 2 Feb. 1955 Final meeting return regd. 14 May 1959 .... **1940**

Hill (R. & J.) Ld. See Shoreditch Property Disposals Ld.

Hill Steamship Co. Ld. Regd. 1902. Vol. liq. 25 Apr. 1913. Final meeting return regd. 11 Oct. 1913 ..... ***1914**

Hill (W.) & Son Ld. Regd. 1901. Vol. liq. (members') 21 May 1934. Undertaking and assets were acquired by Aerated Bread Co. Ld., in which company shareholders were entitled to 1 6¼% preference share of £1 (credited as fully-paid) for each preference share of £1 held or 1 fully-paid ordinary share of £1 for every 4 ordinary shares of 5s. held. £4,800 was paid to preference shareholders in accordance with agreement with acquiring Co. Final meeting return regd. 21 May 1935 .... **1935**

Hillbrigg Textiles Ld. Regd. 1888 as B. Vickerman & Sons Ld.; name changed Nov. 1938. Vol. liq. (members') 21 Nov. 1938. Capital returned to contributories—19s. 0½d. per share of £1. Final meeting return regd. 11 Dec. 1939 .... **1939**

"Hille" Indiarubber Co. Ld. Regd. 1893. In liquidation in 1898. Removed from Register 1907 .... **1898**

Hillgrove Proprietary Mines Ld. Regd. 1897. Reconstructed 1902 as New Hillgrove Proprietary Mines Ld., in which company shareholders were entitled to 1 share of £1 (credited with 17s. 6d. paid) for each share of £1 held. Removed from Register 1903 ... **1908**

Hillman's Airways Ld. Regd. 1934. Vol. liq. (members'). 2 May 1940. Capital returned to contributories—2s. 0·54d. per share of 5s. Final meeting return regd. 13 Jan. 1941 .... **1941**

Hills' Dry Docks & Engineering Co. Ld. Regd. 1882. Vol. liq. (creditors') 6 May 1930. Assets realised insufficient to pay creditors in full. Final meeting return regd. 29 Dec. 1930 .... **1931**

Hill's Gas Plants Ld. Regd. 1912. Vol. liq. 8 Aug. 1912. Final meeting return regd. 16 Feb. 1915 .... ***1913**

Hill's Ld. See Shoreditch Property Disposals Ld.

Hills Patent Glazing Co. Ld. See Hills (West Bromwich) Ld.

Hill's Union Brewery Co. Ld. Regd. 1888. Trustees for debenture holders foreclosed. Removed from Register 1901 .... **1901**

Hill's Waterfall Estate and Gold Mining Co. Ld. Regd. 1889. Vol. liq. 21 Aug. 1891. Court Order to wind up under supervision 2 Sept. 1891. Undertaking and assets were acquired in 1895 by Waterfall Estate & Gold Mines Ld. Final meeting return regd. 29 Jan. 1898 .... **1900**

Hills (West Bromwich) Ld. Regd. 1932 as Hills Patent Glazing Co. Ld., name changed 5 Feb. 1949. Vol. liq. (creditors') 3 Aug. 1962. No capital returns to contributories made. Unsecured creditors, and holders of 5% unsecured notes received 17s. 3d. in the £; holders of 6% debenture stock were repaid at £106 1s. 5d.%£181 9s. 6d. was paid into Companies' Liquidation Account in respect of unclaimed dividends. Final meeting return regd. 5 Mar. 1966 .... **1966**

Hilton Main & Holly Bank Collieries Ld. Regd. 1935. Vol. liq. 19 Mar. 1951. Capital returned to contributories—£3 7s. 1¾d. per share of £1. £5,575 19s. 5d. paid into Companies' Liquidation Account. Final meeting return regd. 31 Aug. 1955 .... **1956**

Himan Central Gold Mines Ld. Regd. 1903. Struck off Register 16 Feb. 1951 .... **1910**

Himan Concessions Ld. Regd. 1900. Vol. liq. 31 Mar. 1922. Final meeting return regd. 10 Nov. 1926 .... **1923**

Hinco Ld. Regd. 1928. Vol. liq. (creditors') 14 Oct. 1938. Assets realised insufficient to pay creditors in full. Final meeting return regd. 16 Aug. 1940 .... **1939**

Hindell's Dairy Farmers Ld. Regd. 1920. All capital was owned by Associated Dairies & Farm Stores Ld., (later Association Dairies Ld.). Vol. liq. 30 Oct. 1954. Final meeting return regd. 29 July 1955 .... **1949**

Hindhead & District Electric Light Co, Ld. Regd. 1902. Vol. liq. 12 Mar. 1929. Undertaking was acquired by Aldershot Gas, Water District Lighting Co. (later Mid Southern Utility). Capital returned to contributories—£2 per share of £1; further payments (if any) not known. Struck off Register 7 June 1932 .... **1930**

Hinemoa Mines Ld. Regd. 1898. Removed from Register 1903 .... **1903**

Hingrakadua Rubber Estates Ld. Regd. 1910 as Uva Ceylon Rubber Estates Ld.; name changed Feb. 1911. Vol. liq. 26 May 1913. Final meeting return regd. 26 Feb. 1917 .... **1914**

VOL. FOR

Hingston & Clitters Mines Ld. Regd. 1908. Receiver for debenture holders appointed in Nov. 1911. Struck off Register 1914 .... **1912**

Hingston Down Consols Mining Co. Ld. Regd. Truro 1864. Vol. liq. 10 June 1884. Final meeting return regd. 12 May 1886 .... **1885**

Hingurugama Tea & Rubber Estates Ld. Regd. 1913. Vol. liq. 12 Mar. 1920. Reconstructed as company of same name. Shareholders were entitled to 2 fully-paid shares of £1 in new company for each share of £1 held. Final meeting return regd. 12 Mar. 1925 **1921**

Hingurugama Tea & Rubber Estates Ld. Regd. 1920. Vol. liq. 14 June 1926. Certain assets were acquired by Lunuva (Ceylon) Tea & Rubber Estates Ld. Shareholders were expected to receive 1 fully-paid share of £1 in the purchasing company and 3d. in cash for each share of £1 held; an option to purchase further shares has since expired. Final meeting return regd. 2 Aug. 1927 .... **1927**

Hinks (James) & Son Ld. Regd. 1888. Vol. liq 7 Sept. 1896. Reconstructed as company of same name. Final meeting return regd. 22 Jan. 1897 .... **1908**

Hinks (James) & Son Ld. Regd. 1896. Vol. liq. 10 Sept. 1923. Final meeting return regd. 20 Mar. 1925 .... **1924**

Hinterland Exploration Syndicate Ld. Regd. 1901. Vol. liq. 7 May 1912. Final meeting return regd. 30 Apr. 1914 .... **1913**

Hirsch Syndicate Ld. Regd. 1908. Vol. liq. 20 Dec. 1911. Final meeting return regd. 15 Apr. 1915 .... ***1913**

Hirsch's Copenhagen Oil Mills Co. Ld. Regd. 1896. Vol. liq. 13 Aug. 1896. Final meeting return regd.9 Feb. 1898 .... **1897**

Hirst, Brooke & Southon Ld. Regd. 1949. Vol. liq. (members') 22 Aug. 1950. Capital returned to contributories—3s. 9·017d. per share of 4s. Final meeting return regd. 12 Mar. 1952 .... **1952**

His Exalted Highness the Nizam's Guaranteed State Railways Co. Ld. Regd. 1883 as H. H. the Nizam's Guaranteed State Railways Co. Ld. name changed Dec. 1918. Vol. liq. (members') 31 Mar. 1930. Capital returned to contributories—£111 15s. 7d.% in cash and 200% in Nizam's Government 5½% debenture stock. Final meeting return regd. 15 Dec. 1930 .... **1931**

Hislop & Williams Ld. See Cremier Ice Cream Co. Ld.

Hispano-Suiza Motors Ld. Regd. 1927. Vol. liq. 3 Aug. 1929. Final meeting return regd. 18 Mar. 1930. Struck off Register 17 June. 1949 .... **1930**

Hit or Miss Proprietary Gold Mines Ld. Regd. 1897. Vol. liq. 16 Jan. 1899. Undertaking and assets were acquired by Phoenix Gold Mines Ld., in which company shareholders were entitled to 2 shares of 10s. (credited with 8s. paid) for each share of £1 held. Final meeting return regd. 25 July 1900 ...... **1903**

Hitchin & District Gas Co. Established by Deed of Settlement 1834 as Hitchin Gas Co. Regd. 1873. Inc. by Special Act 1905. Undertaking was acquired by Tottenham & District Gas Co. Preference stockholders were entitled to an equal amount of 6% redeemable preference stock in acquiring company. The liability for debentures and debenture stock was assumed by acquiring company **1936**

Hitchin Gas Co. See Hitchin & District Gas Co.

Hitchings Ld. Regd. 1897. Undertaking was acquired in 1936 by Stanhope General Investment Co. Ld in which company shareholders were entitled to 1 fully-paid ordinary or 1 preference share of £1 for each ordinary or preference share of £1 respectively held. Dissolved 22 June 1936 under Sec. 154 of Companies' Act 1929 .... **1937**

Hitchins' Fire Proof Plastering Co. Ld. Regd. 1883. Vol. liq. 26 Aug. 1887. Reconstructed as company of same name. Shareholders were entitled to 1 fully-paid share of £1 for 3 vendors' shares of £1 held or each other share of £1 held. Struck off Register 20 Mar. 1906 .... **1891**

Hitchins Laminated Wood Products Ld. See Laminated Wood Products Ld.

Hoare & Co. Ld. Regd. 1894. Vol. liq. (members') 1 Apr. 1938. Undertaking and assets were acquired by Charrington & Co. Ld., which company owned all shares and debentures. Final meeting return regd. 6 Dec. 1938 .... **1939**

Hobart Electric Tramway Co. Ld. Regd. 1892 as Hobart Tramway Co. Ld.; name changed June 1894. Vol. liq. 1 Sept. 1913. The undertaking was sold to Hobart Municipal Council. Capital returned to contributories—£2 2s. per share of £1 at Mar. 1914; further payments (if any) not known. The 5% 1st and 2nd mortgage debentures were redeemed on 1 Aug. 1913 at 105%. Final meeting return regd. 4 Aug. 1916 .... **1914**

Hobbs Hill Tin Mines Ld. Regd. 1913. Vol. liq. 2 June 1915 for reconstruction as Hobbs Hill Tin Mines

VOL. FOR

(1916) Ld. in which company shareholders were entitled so 1 share of 10s. (credited with 8s. paid) for each share of £1 held. Final meeting return regd. 3 Jan. 1917 .... **1916**

Hobbs (J. W.) & Co. Ld. Regd. 1885. Removed from Register 1911 .... *1893

Hocking Valley Coal Co. Ld. Regd. 1892. Vol. liq. 16 Nov. 1893. Company never did business and money was returned to subscribers. Final meeting return regd. 22 Feb. 1894 .... **1894**

Hockley Hall & Whateley Collieries & Brickfields Ld. See Kingsbury Collieries Ld.

Hodbarrow Mining Co. Ld. Regd. 1888. Vol. liq. (members') 11 Aug. 1959. Capital returned to contributories—£9 18s. 9¼d. per ordinary share of £8. Final meeting return regd. 25 Aug. 1961 ...... **1962**

Hoddesdon Gas Coke Co. Ld. Regd. 1856. By Special Order of 1932 the undertaking was acquired by Tottenham and District Gas Co. in which company holders of original (10% standard) shares of £5 were entitled to £11 7s. 3d. 5½% preference stock for each share held, and holders of additional (7% standard) shares of £5 were entitled to £8 12s. 9d. 5½% preference stock for each share held. The Tottenham Co. assumed liability for the mortgages **1933**

Hodgson (George) Ld. Regd. 1898. Vol. liq. (members') 26 June 1930. Capital returned to contributories—£37,312 10s. Undertaking was acquired by George Hattersley & Co. Ld. Final meeting return regd. 19 Oct. 1934 .... **1931**

Hodgson Road Contractors Ld. Regd. 1923. Receiver appointed 27 Aug. 1928. Assets realised insufficient to meet claims of debenture holders in full. Struck off Register 30 Jan. 1934 .... **1932**

Hodgson (Walter) Gold Mines Ld. Regd. 1895. Vol. liq. 17 Nov. 1899. Final meeting return regd. 17 Jan. 1901 .... *1900

Hodsman (George) & Sons (1928) Ld. Regd. 1928. All capital was owned by Hargreaves Group Ld. Vol. liq. (members') 16 Feb. 1967. Final meeting return regd. 19 Feb. 1968 .... **1964**

Hohler & Co. Established 1820. In Sept. 1942 the business was acquired by Gillett Brothers Discount Co. Ld. **1943**

Hohonu Gold Sluicing Co. Ld. Regd. 1921. Vol. liq. (members') 12 Jan. 1932. Assets realised insufficient to pay unsecured creditors in full. Final meeting return regd. 17 Apr. 1940 .... **1932**

Hokkaido Colliery & Steamship Co. Ld. Organised Japan 1889 as Hokkaido Colliery & Railway Co. Ld.; name changed 1906 .... **1921**

Hokkaido Takushoku Ginko (Hokkaido Colonisation Bank Ld.) Established by Special Law of Japanese Government 1900. The outstanding 5% mortgage debentures, 8th series, mark H, were redeemed in 1933 .... **1933**

Holborn & Frascati Ld. Regd. 1895. All capital was owned by Land Securities Investment Trust Ld. Dissolved under section 208 of Companies Act, 1948 on 28 July 1955 .... **1954**

Holborn Empire Ld. Regd. 1905. Vol. liq. (members') 29 Mar. 1928. Subsidiary of London Theatre of Varieties Ld. Final meeting return regd. 16 June 1931 .... **1929**

Holborough Cement Co. Ld. Regd. 1925. Vol. liq. (members') 30 Oct. 1931. Undertaking and assets were acquired by Associated Portland Cement Manufacturers Ld. Capital returned to contributories—15s. 4·16d. per share of £1. Final meeting return regd. 5 Nov.1934 .... **1932**

Holbourne Ld. Regd. 1928. Vol. liq. (creditors') 6 Dec. 1929. Assets realised insufficient to pay creditors in full. Final meeting return regd. 20 Sept. 1932....... **1930**

Holbrooks Ld. See Sauce Holdings Ld.

Holbrook's Worcestershire Sauce Ld. Regd. 1898. Removed from Register 1904 .... **1899**

Holbrook's Worcestershire Sauce Ld. Regd. 1901. Removed from Register 1909 .... **1902**

Holcomb Valley Co. Ld. Regd. 1892. Vol. liq. 8 Mar. 1897. Reconstructed as company of same name. Shareholders were entitled to 1 ordinary share of 1s. (credited with 6d. paid) and 1 preference share of 1s. (credited with 6d. paid) in new company for each ordinary share of 5s. held. Struck off Register 11 Aug. 1905 .... **1901**

Holcomb Valley Co. Ld. Regd. 1897. Struck off Register 18 Nov. 1902 .... **1903**

Holden, Burnley & Co. Ld. Regd. 1922. Vol. liq. (members') 27 Apr. 1939. Capital returned to contributories—20s. per preference share of £1; £25,781 5s. (including £8,973 19s. 4d. distributed in specie) to ordinary shareholders. Final meeting return regd. 23 Oct. 1940 .... **1940**

VOL. FOR

Holden (Samuel) of Barrowford Ld. Regd. 1951. All capital was owned by Hindley Brothers (Holdings) Ld. Vol. liq. (members') 16 Apr. 1962. Final meeting return regd. 13 Nov. 1967 .... **1961**

Holdenbrook Ld. See Corporate Guarantee Trust Ld.

Holderness Gas Co. Ld. Regd. 1903. Dissolved 1 May 1949, undertaking being vested in North Eastern Area Gas Board under Gas Act 1948. Holders of securities were entitled to receive British Gas 3% guaranteed stock 1990–95 as follows in respect of each £1 unit, unless otherwise stated, of security held:—

	£	s.	d.
Ord. shares		5	0
6% pref. shares	1	0	0
4½% mort. debs. (of £100)	100	0	0	**1952**

Holdup (M.H.) Ld. Regd. 1896 as Haig's Cooperage, Ld. name subsequently changed. Vol. liq. (members') 13 Apr. 1960. Final meeting return regd. 19 Apr. 1961 .... **1911**

Hole's and Davignor Hygienic Dairies, Ld. Regd. 1930. The A shares were owned by South of England Dairies Ld. Vol. liq. (members') 22 Mar. 1966. Final meeting return regd. 18 Mar. 1967 .... **1951**

Holfontein (T.C.L.) Gold Mining Co. Ld. Inc. in Union of S.A. 1936. Vol. liq. (members') 7 Feb. 1951. Capital returned to contributories—2s. 4·65d. per share of 10s. Final accounts lodged with and approved by Master of Supreme Court 29 Oct. 1951 **1952**

Holgatfontein Gold Farm Ld. Regd. 1903. Struck off Register 1915 .... **1913**

Holland & Holland (Northwood) Ld. Regd. 1898 as Holland & Holland Ld.; name changed 1960. All capital was owned by Holland, Farlow & Lyell Ld. Vol. liq. (members') 25 July 1960. Final meeting return regd. 16 June. 1964 .... **1960**

Hollando-Belge (Société Anonyme) Chaleur et Lumière. Inc. Belgium in 1902. The business was leased to société Anonyme Belge "Bec Auer" **1913**

Hollinger Gold Mines Ld. Inc. Ontario 1910. Reconstructed as Hollinger Consolidated Gold Mines Ld. in which company shareholders were entitled to 4 shares of $5 (credited as fully-paid) for each share of $5 held **1917**

Hollingworth Gas Co. Ld. Regd. 1875; statutory powers 1890. Dissolved 1 May 1949, undertaking being vested in North Western Area Gas Board under Gas Act 1948. Holders of securities were entitled to receive, in respect of each £1 unit held, British Gas 3% guaranteed. stock 1990—95 as follows:

	£	s.	d.
Ord. shares (10% stand.)		2	6
Addit. ord. shares (7% stand.)		2	6	**1952**

Hollinwood Spinning Co. (1919) Ld. Regd. 1919. Vol. liq. (creditors') 14 Nov. 1930. Certain assets were acquired by Lancashire Cotton Corporation Ld., in which corporation debenture holders received £31,901 income debenture stock and 8,848 ordinary shares of £1; shareholders received 63,607 deferred shares of 1s. Final meeting return regd. 13 Feb. 1934 **1931**

Hollis Cycle-Brake & Fittings Co. Ld. Regd. 1897. Removed from Register 26 Oct. 1900 .... *1898

Holloway Electricity Supply Co. Ld. See Guildford Electricity Supply Co. Ld.

Holly Bank Trust Co. Ld. Regd. 1895. Vol. liq. 1 July 1910. Final meeting return regd. 9 June 1911 ...... *1910

Holly Mill Ld. Regd. 1920. Dissolved under Section 208 of Companies Act 1948 on 25 Nov. 1949 undertaking having been acquired by Royton Textile Corpn. Ld. (later Royton Textile Corpn. Ld.) in which company stockholders were entitled to receive 3·6 fully-paid shares (of 5s.) for every £1 stock held .. **1950**

Hollybush Trust Ld. Regd. 1932 as British Greyhound Investment Ld. Vol. liq. (members') 19 Dec. 1951. Final meeting return regd. 3 May 1956 .... **1947**

Holman (John) & Sons Ld. Regd. 1900. Vol. liq. 31 Dec. 1917. Final meeting return regd. 22 Mar. 1918 .... **1918**

Holman's Gold Mine Ld. Regd. 1899. Removed from Register 1901 .... **1901**

Holman's Lucky Hill Gold Mine Ld. Regd. 1896. Vol. liq. 10 Dec. 1897. Reconstructed as company of same name. Shareholders were entitled to 2 shares of 10s. (credited with 8s. 6d. paid) in new company for each share of £1 held. Final meeting return regd. 24 Aug. 1898 .... **1899**

Holman's Lucky Hill Gold Mine Ld. Regd. 1897. Vol. liq. 24 July 1899. Reconstructed as Holman's Gold Mine Ld., in which company shareholders were entitled to 1 share of 5s. (credited with 4s. 3d. paid) for each share of 10s. held. Final meeting return regd. 9 Jan. 1900 .... **1901**

Holme & Ramsey Railway Co. Inc. by Special Act. 1861. Undertaking was acquired by Great Eastern Railway Co. by Act in 1875, but it was worked under lease by Great Northern Railway 1903

Holme (George) Ld. Regd. 1894. Court Order to wind up 10 Nov. 1903. Liquidator released 17 Oct. 1907. Struck off Register 10 Mar. 1911 1905

Holmes Chapel Wall Paper Co. Ld. Amalgamated with Wall Paper Manufacturers Ld., between Sept. 1915 and Mar. 1924 1924

Holmes, Goldrich & Co. Ld. Regd. 1937. Majority of capital was owned by Mahuma Fabrics Ld. Vol. liq. (members') 31 Aug. 1966. Final meeting return regd. 22 Nov. 1967 1961

Holmes Oil Co. Ld. Regd. Edinburgh 1884. Court Orders: to wind up Oct. 1900; to dissolve 25 Feb. 1904 1901

Holmfield & Southowram Light Railway Co. Inc. (under Light Railways Act 1896) by order of Light Railway Commissioners, confirmed by Board of Trade 1902 1910

Holmholmen Copper Co. Ld. Regd. 1910. Struck off Register Apr. 1929 1930

Holmside and South Moor Collieries Ld. Regd. 1889 as South Moor Colliery Co. Ld.; name changed 3 Jan. 1925. Vol. liq. (members') 13 July 1955. Final meeting return regd. 29 June 1957 1955

"Holophane" Ld. Regd. 1896. Vol. liq. 5 May 1905. Removed from Register 1908 1906

Holophone Ld. Regd. 1910. Vol. liq. 28 Dec. 1925. Reconstructed as company of same name. Shareholders were entitled to 1 share of £1 (credited as fully-paid) in new company for each ordinary share of 1s. held; preference shareholders were repaid at par. Final meeting return regd. 31 Dec. 1926 1927

Holsworthy & Bude Railway Co. Inc. by Special Act 1883. Undertaking abandoned by Act of 1892 1893

Holt & Co. Undertaking was acquired in 1923 by Glyn Mills & Co. 1923

Holt Brewery Co. Ld. Regd. 1887. Vol. liq. 18 Mar. 1896. Reconstructed as company of same name. The 4½% debentures were redeemed at 110%. Capital returned to contributories—£15 per 1st and 2nd preference share of £10. Ordinary shareholders were entitled to 3 preference and 2 ordinary shares of £10 for each ordinary share of £10 held. Final meeting return regd. 10 Oct. 1896 1895

Holt Brewery Co. Ld. Regd. 1896. All capital was owned by Ansells Brewery Ld. Vol. liq. (members') 29 Mar. 1966. Final meeting return regd. 30 Dec. 1966 1963

Holt (Thomas) Holdings (Rochdale) Ld. Regd. 1953. Vol. liq. (members') 29 Sept. 1959. Capital returned to contributories—2s. 3·94d. per ordinary share (of 1s.). Final meeting return regd. 5 Oct. 1960 1961

Holton Consolidated Co. Ld. Regd. 1899. Vol. liq. 1903. Reconstructed as Rhodesia Consolidated Ld., in which company shareholders were entitled to 1 share of 10s. (credited with 7s. paid) for each share of £1 held. Removed from Register 1906 1904

Holton Land & Mining Co. Ld. Regd. 1895. Undertaking and assets were acquired by Holton Consolidated Co. Ld., in which company shareholders were entitled to 1 fully-paid share of £1 for each share of £1 held. Removed from Register 1901 1900

Holway United Mines Ld. Regd. 1886. Receiver for debenture holders appointed. Struck off Register 14 May 1897 1899

Holyhead & North Wales Gas & Water Corpn. Ld. Regd. 1896. Dissolved 1 May 1949 undertaking being vested in Wales Area Gas Board under Gas Act 1948. Holders of ordinary shares (of £1) were entitled to receive £1 7s. 6d. British Gas 3% guaranteed stock 1990—95 for each share held 1952

Holyhead Water Works Co. Inc. by Special Act 1866. On 1 Jan. 1945 the undertaking was transferred to Anglesey County Council and the company was dissolved. For each original ordinary and additional ordinary share (all of £10) holders were entitled to £18 and £12 10s. respectively in Anglesey County Council stock. The outstanding 4% debenture stock and mortgages became a charge of the County Council 1945

Holyrood Mill Co. (1920) Ld. Regd. 1920. Vol. liq. (members') 19 Oct. 1953. Capital returned to contributories—3s. 11¾d. per share of 2s. Final meeting return regd. 18 Oct. 1956 1957

Holzer Steel Process Syndicate (United Kingdom) Ld. Regd. 1902. Struck off Register 24 Feb. 1922 1913

Homan Syndicate Ld. Regd. 1910. Vol. liq. 21 July 1914. Final meeting return regd. 4 Nov. 1916 .... *1915

Home & Colonial Assets & Debenture Corporation Ld. Regd. 1888. Removed from Register 1912 1910

Home & Colonial Assurance Co. Ld. See Home & Colonial Marine Insurance Co. Ld.

Home & Colonial Marine Insurance Co. Ld. Regd. 1864 as Home & Colonial Assurance Co. Ld.; name changed Apr. 1867. Vol. liq. 25 Feb. 1890. Assets were acquired by Royal Exchange Assurance Corporation. Shareholders were entitled to 15s. per share of £50 (£5 paid). Final meeting return regd. 1 Mar. 1892 1891

Home & Colonial Steam Fishing Co. Ld. Regd. 1919. Vol. liq. May 1922 for reconstruction as Great Yarmouth Fish Selling & Curing Co. Ld., in which company shareholders were entitled to 10 shares of 2s. (credited with 1s. 6d. paid) for each preference share of £1 held or 1 share of 2s. (credited with 1s. 6d. paid) for each founders' share of 1s. held. Struck off Register Aug. 1929 1930

Home & Foreign Investment & Agency Co. Ld. Regd. 1872. Vol. liq. 17 Nov. 1908. Final meeting return regd. 28 Oct. 1913 1909

Home and Foreign Investment Trust Ld. Regd. in Edinburgh 1926. Undertaking transferred to Great Northern Investment Trust Ld. in July 1969; ordinary shareholders received 106 ordinary stock units of 5s. for every 100 shares. preference shareholders £1 4⅗% preference stock for each share, and debenture stockholders a like amount of similar stock. Company was dissolved on 14 Oct. 1969 under Section 208 of Companies Act 1948 1970

Home & Foreign Reinsurance Co. Ld. Regd. Edinburgh 1914. Vol. liq. 8 Apr. 1938. Undertaking acquired by Commercial Union Assurance Co. Ld. Final meeting return regd. 25 Feb. 1939 1939

Home and Foreign Securities Corporation Ld. Regd. 1925. Vol. liq. (creditors') 2 Nov. 1933. No capital returned to contributories. Final meeting return regd. 1 Aug. 1934 1934

Home & Foreign Trust Ld. Regd. 1911. Vol. liq. 27 July 1922. Capital returned to contributories—100%; further payments (if any) not known. Final meeting return regd. 7 Sept. 1923 1923

Home & Overseas Trading Trust Ld. See Canadian Banking & Trust Ld.

Home Coal Estates Ld. Inc. Transvaal 1895. London transfer office closed Apr. 1907 1903

Home Counties Land and Investment Co. Ld. Regd. 1879. Vol. liq. 22 Apr. 1895. Capital returned to contributories—£1 10s. per share of £25; further payments (if any) not known. Final meeting return regd. 28 May 1902 1896

Home Counties Newspapers p.l.c. Regd. as private company 1934.; converted into public company 1969; re-registered 1981. Vol. liq. Oct. 1984. All capital acquired by Home Counties Newspapers Holdings p.l.c. 1985–6

Home Grown Sugar Ld. Regd. 1920. Vol. liq. (members') 9 Sept. 1936. The factory was transferred to British Sugar Corporation Ld. for 132,782 fully-paid shares of £1. Shareholders were entitled to approximately 2 shares of £1 for every 9 shares of 5s. held plus approximately 1s. 7d. per share in cash. £10 14s. 3d. was paid into Companies' Liquidation Account in respect of unclaimed dividends. Final meeting return regd. 6 Oct. 1938 1937

Home Industries Ld. Regd. 1897. Removed from Register 1909 1900

Home Investment and Savings Association. Inc. Canada 1892. The outstanding sterling debentures were repaid in 1942 at par. 1944

Home Mines Trust Ld. Regd. 1881. Vol. liq. Nov. 1886. Final meeting return regd. 23 July 1887 1887

Home Petroleum Co. Ld. Regd. 1920. Struck off Register Dec. 1931 1923

Home Railway Rolling Stock Co. Ld. Regd. 1878. Vol. liq. Aug. 1886. Final meeting return regd. 11 Sept. 1890 1887

Homebush Gold Mining Co. Ld. Inc. in Victoria in 1934. Vol. liq. (members') 31 Jan. 1950. Capital returned to contributories: 1s. 7·326d. (U.K. 1s. 3·461d.) per 5s. share. £A987 was paid into Companies' Liquidation Account (Melbourne). Final meeting return registered 27 Oct. 1952 1953

Homelight Oil Co. Ld. Regd. 1902. Vol. liq. (members') 29 Jan. 1945. All shares were owned by Anglo Iranian Oil Co. Ld. (later British Petroleum Co. Ld.). Final meeting return regd. 26 Apr. 1945 1946

Homer (Alfred) Ld. Regd. 1898. Vol. liq. 13 Nov. 1899. Business was acquired by Henry Mitchell & Co. Ld. (later Mitchells and Butlers Ld.). in which company shareholders were entitled to 24 ordinary shares of £5 for every 25 ordinary shares of £10 held or 1 ordinary share of £5 plus £2 in cash for every 2 preference shares of £10 held. Final meeting return regd. 14 Feb. 1900 1900

VOL. FOR

Homer-District Consolidated Gold Mines Ld. Regd. 1884. In liquidation in 1891. Struck off Register 1906 .... **1891**

Homes Ld. Regd. 1902. Placed in liquidation. Final meeting return regd. 10 Sept. 1955 .... **1939**

Homestead (Konati) Gold Fields of South Africa Ld. Regd. 1887. Struck off Register 17 Jan. 1893 ...... **1899**

Homeward Bound Mine Ld. Regd. 1899. Reconstructed 1906 as Rocky Point Gold Mines Ld. in which company shareholders were entitled to 1 fully-paid share of 1s. for every 5 shares of 10s. held. Removed from Register 1907 .... **1907**

Homocea Ld. Regd. 1897. Vol. liq. (creditors') 27 Mar. 1931. No capital returned to contributories. Final meeting return regd. 9 July 1931 .... **1932**

Homtini Gold Mines Ld. Regd. 1895. Removed from Register 4 Oct. 1898 .... ***1897**

Honduras Co. Ld. Regd. 1888. Vol. liq. 28 May 1894. Final meeting return regd. 1895 .... ***1895**

Honduras Gold Placer Mining Co. Ld. Regd. 1888. Struck off Register 3 Aug. 1894 .... **1899**

Honduras Government Banking & Trading Co. Ld. Regd. 1893. Removed from Register 1911 .... **1904**

Honduras Inter-Oceanic Railway Co. Ld. Regd. 1873. Wound up by Court Order 28 May 1883 .... ***1882**

Honeywell Cotton Spinning Co. Ld. Regd. 1874. Vol. liq. (members') 13 May 1946. Capital returned to contributories—£8 15s. 7d. per share of £5. Final meeting return regd. 15 Mar. 1947 .... **1948**

Hongkong Tramway Co. Ld. Regd. 1902 as Electric Traction Co. of Hongkong Ld.; name changed Aug. 1910. Vol. liq. 31 Oct. 1923. Undertaking and assets were acquired by Hongkong Tramways Ld. Shareholders were entitled to 1 share of $5 for each share of 5s held. Final meeting return regd. 31 July 1924 **1924**

Honiton Gas & Coke Co. Ld. Regd. 1890. Dissolved 1 May 1949, undertaking being vested in South Western Area Gas Board under Gas Act 1948. Holders of securities were entitled to receive British Gas 3% guaranteed stock 1990—95 as follows in respect of each £10 unit, unless otherwise stated, of security held :

	£	s.	d.
Ord. shares	15	10	0
4% pref. shares	10	2	0
4% deb. bonds (1947 & 1948 issues) (of £100)	100	0	0
4% deb. bonds (issued before 1 Jan. 1946) (of £100)	100	0	0

1952

Hony United Mining Co. Ld. Regd. 1884. Removed from Register 1891 .... **1891**

Honywood Hotels Ld. Regd. 1924. Vol. liq. (members') 26 Oct. 1964. Capital returned to contributories—15s. 9½d. per 5s. ordinary share of Moore Ld., in which company preference shareholders were entitled to 1 fully-paid share of 8s. plus 1s. 8½d. in cash for each preference stock. Final meeting return regd. 12 Apr. 1966 .... **1967**

Hood & Moore's Stores Ld. Regd. 1895. Business was acquired in 1905 by New Hood and share of £1 held. No return was made to ordinary shareholders. Removed from Register 1907 .... **1908**

Hook Pneumatic Tyre Co. Ld. Regd. 1893. Vol. liq. 19 July 1894. Removed from Register 21 June 1907 ***1895**

Hooker (Peter) Ld. Regd. 1900. Vol. liq. 6 July 1920. Final meeting return regd. 21 Dec. 1928 .... **1921**

Hooley (T.) Ld. Regd. 1887. Vol. liq. 13 Sept. 1920. Final meeting return regd. 25 Feb. 1921 .... **1921**

Hooper (George) & Co., London Ld. Regd. 1898. Vol. liq. 19 July 1928. Capital returned to contributories—£2 per preference share of £5 at Aug. 1928; further payments (if any) not known. Final meeting return regd. 27 Mar. 1930 .... **1929**

Hooper's Telegraph Works Ld. Regd. 1870. Court Orders; to wind up 1 Mar. 1877; to dissolve 17 Dec. 1884 .... ***1878**

Hoover Hill Gold Mining Co. Ld. Regd. 1881. Reconstructed as New Hoover Hill Gold Mining Co. Ld. Removed from Register 1905 .... ***1885**

Hop Bitters Co. Ld. Regd. 1889. Vol. liq. 19 Oct. 1900. Final meeting return regd. 30 Dec. 1901 .... **1891**

Hop Tea Foreign & Colonial Syndicate Ld. Regd. 1891. Struck off Register 5 May 1896 .... **1910**

Hopcraft & Norris, Ld. Regd. 1895. Vol. liq. (members') 4 May 1948. the undertaking having been amalgamated with Chesham & Brackley Breweries Ld. £17,409 distributed to contributories. Final meeting return regd. 12 July 1957 .... **1958**

Hopcraft Furnace Co. Ld. Regd. 1889. Removed from Register 1907 .... **1894**

Hope, Bradwell & Castleton Light Railway Co. Inc. (under Light Railways Act 1896) 1905 .... **1908**

Hope Cotton Spinning Co. Ld. Regd. 1874. Vol. liq. 21 Oct. 1919. The undertaking was acquired by Hope

Cotton Spinning Co. (1919) Ld. for £156,000 in cash. Final meeting return regd. 8 Mar. 1920 .... **1920**

Hope Cotton Spinning Co. (1919) Ld. Regd. 1919. Vol. liq. (creditors') 18 Oct. 1934. Assets realised insufficient to pay unsecured creditors in full. Final meeting return regd. 1 Aug. 1936 .... **1935**

Hope (John Vernon) & Co. Ld. Regd. 1881. Court Orders: to wind up June 1885; to dissolve Mar. 1887 **1886**

Hope Tea Holdings, Ld. Regd 1961. Vol. liq. (members') 16 Nov. 1965. Undertaking and assets were acquired by Assam-Dooars Holdings Ld. Capital returned to contributories—£1 per share of £1. Final meeting return regd. 21 Dec. 1965 .... **1967**

Hope's Hill Co. Ld. Regd. 1901. Shareholders were entitled to 4 shares of 5s. in Zoroastrian Ld., for each £1 capital subscribed and to 2 shares of 5s. (credited with 4s. paid) for each share of £1 held. Removed from Register 1903 .... **1903**

Hope's Hill Gold Mines Ld. Regd. 1896. Vol. liq. 11 Oct. 1898. Reconstructed as Hope's Hill Gold Mining Co. Ld., in which company shareholders were entitled to 1 share of £1 (credited with 17s. paid) for each share of £1 held. Final meeting return regd. 19 Sept. 1900 .... **1901**

Hope's Hill Gold Mining Co. Ld. Regd. 1898. Vol. liq. 15 Apr. 1901. Reconstructed as Hope's Hill Co. Ld., in which company shareholders were entitled to 1 share of 10s. (credited with 7s. 6d. paid) for each share of £1 held. Final meeting return regd. 24 Dec. 1901 .... **1902**

Hopewell Tea Co. Ld. Regd. Edinburgh 1897. Vol. liq. June 1907. Final meeting return regd. 28 June 1910 **1908**

Hopkins (J. H.) & Sons Ld. Regd. 1890. Removed from Register 1901 .... **1899**

Hopper (F.) & Co. Ld. Regd. 1907. Undertaking was acquired by Elswick-Hopper Cycle & Motor Co. Ld. Struck off Register 17 Dec. 1915 .... **1945**

Hopwood & Crew Ld. Regd. 1898. Vol. liq. Dec. 1906. Undertaking and assets were acquired by Ascherberg Hopwood & Crew Ld., in which company shareholders were entitled to 1 preferred ordinary share of 10s. for each share of £1 held. Removed from Register 1907 .... **1907**

Horbury Junction Iron Co. Ld. Regd. 1873. Vol. liq. 10 Sept. 1923. Capital returned to contributories—20% in Nov. 1923; further payments (if any) not known. Final meeting return regd. 10 June 1924 .... **1924**

Horden Collieries Ld. Regd. 1900. Vol. liq. (members') 22 July 1952 the collieries &c. being vested in National Coal Board. Capital returned to contributories—£1 17s. 9d. per 2s. ordinary stock. Final meeting return regd. 9 Oct. 1956 .... **1957**

Horley & District Electricity Supply Co. Ld. Regd. 1924. Dissolved 1 Apr. 1948, undertaking being vested in the British (later Central) Electricity Authority and South-Eastern Area Board under the Electricity Act 1947. Holders of fully-paid ordinary shares (of £1) were entitled to receive £2 British Electricity 3% guaranteed stock (1968—73),for each share held .. **1949**

Horley District Gas Co. Inc. by Special Act 1901. Dissolved 1 May 1949, undertaking being vested in South Eastern Area Gas Board under Gas Act 1948. Holders of securities were entitled to receive, in respect of each £100 unit held, British Gas 3% guaranteed stock 1990—95 as follows:

	£	s.	d.
A cap. stock (10% stand.)	210	0	0
Addit. B stock (7% stand.)	150	0	0
5% pref. stock	114	0	0
4⅛% red. pref. stock	103	0	0
4% 1st mort. deb. bonds (of £50) ..	50	10	0
4% irred. deb. stock (issued before 1 Jan. 1946)	103	0	0
4% irred. deb. stock (issued since 31 Dec. 1945)	106	5	0

1952

Hornachos Silver Lead Mining Co. Ld. Regd. 1885. Vol. liq. 17 May 1888. Final meeting return regd. 19 Jan. 1897 .... **1889**

Hornby & West Ld. Regd. 1910. Vol. liq. (members') 21 Sept. 1933. Capital returned to contributories—£1 4s. 1½d. per share of £1. Final meeting return regd. 31 May 1934 .... **1934**

Hornby's Dairies Ld. Regd. 1935. Vol. liq. (members') 29 Sept. 1955. A subsidiary of Home Counties Dairies (Holdings) Ld. Final meeting return regd. 8 Oct. 1956 .... **1952**

Horncastle Railway Co. Inc. by Special Act 1854. In 1923 the undertaking was merged into the London & North Eastern Railway Co., in which company shareholders were entitled to £80 4% Second Preference, £60 5% Preferred Ordinary, and £52 Deferred Ordinary Stock for each £100 of Horncastle Ordinary Shares held; the London & North Eastern Company assumed all liability in respect of

See Stock Exchange Year-Book.

VOL. FOR

the Horncastle Company's £15,400 6% Debenture Bonds and the annual rent-charge of £64 16s. **1924**

Hornillo Co. Ld. Regd. 1899. Vol. liq. 3 July 1913. All shares were acquired by Great Southern of Spain Railway Co., in which company shareholders were entitled to £5 in 6% 1st mortgage debenture stock for each share of £1 held. Final meeting return regd. 25 Nov. 1914 .... **1914**

Hornsby (Richard) & Sons Ld. Regd. 1879. Vol. liq. 9 Aug. 1918. Undertaking was amalgamated with Ruston Proctor & Co. Ld. (later Ruston & Hornsby Ld.), in which company shareholders were entitled to 17 ordinary shares of £1 (credited as fully-paid) for every 2 ordinary shares of £10 held and 1 B preference share of £1 (credited as fully-paid) for each £1 preference stock held. Debenture stockholders were entitled to an equal amount of similar debenture stock in new company. Final meeting return regd. 31 July 1919 .... **1919**

Hornsea Gas Light & Coke Co, Ld. Regd. 1864. Dissolved 1 May 1949, undertaking being vested in North Eastern Gas Board under Gas Act 1948. Holders of ordinary shares (of £2 10s.) were entitled to receive £4 2s. 6d. British Gas 3% guaranteed stock 1990–95 for each share held **1952**

Hornsey Gas Co. Inc. by Special Act 1866. Dissolved 1 May 1949, undertaking being vested in North Thames Area Gas Board under Gas Act 1948. Holders of securities were entitled to receive, in respect of each £100 unit held, British Gas 3% guaranteed stock 1990–95 as follows:

	£	s.	d.
5% stand. stock	149	0	0
3½% stand. stock	115	10	0
5% pref. stock	115	0	0
4% perp. deb. stock	103	0	0
3½% red. deb. stock	101	15	0

1952

Hornung & Co. Ld. Regd. 1920 as Hornung & Co. (1920) Ld.; name changed 1921. Vol. liq. (members') 18 Feb. 1932; undertaking being acquired by company of same name. Capital returned to contributories—£91,122 2s. 5d. Final meeting return regd. 30 Nov. 1934 .... ***1933**

Horo Concession Exploration Co. of Swaziland Ld. Inc. South Africa 1886. Reconstructed as New Horo Concession Exploration Co. of Swaziland Ld. Shareholders were entitled to subscribe for 6,400 shares in new company at par **1893**

Horse Shoe Manufacturing Co. Ld. Regd. 1881. Vol. liq. Aug. 1883. Court Order to continue winding up under supervision Sept. 1883. Reconstructed as United Horse Shoe and Nail Co. Ld., in exchange for 126,980 fully-paid ordinary shares of 5s. Final meeting return regd. 5 Mar. 1885 .... **1909**

Horsebro Tin Co. Ld. Regd. 1907. Struck off Register 1914 .... **1911**

Horseshoe (Peak Hill) Goldfield Ld. Regd. 1899. Removed from Register 1907 .... **1905**

Horseshoe Wiluna Gold Mines Ld. Inc. Western Australia. In liquidation in 1944. All capital was held by Gold Fields Australian Development Ld. Co. **1944**

Horsey's Patent Broom & Brush Manufacturing Co. Ld, Regd. 1882. Removed from Register 1906 .... ***1885**

Horsfall Destructor Co. Ld. Regd. 1899. Receiver appointed in May 1913. Struck off Register 1915 **1914**

Horsham Gas Co. Ld. Estd. 1835; regd. 1876. Dissolved 1 May 1949, undertaking being vested in South Eastern Area Gas Board under Gas Act 1948. Holders of securities were entitled to receive British Gas 3% guaranteed stock as follows in respect of each £10 unit, unless otherwise stated, of security held:

	£	s.	d.
Orig. ord. A shares (10% max.)	20	10	0
Addit. ord. B shares (7% max.)	14	10	0
4½% pref. shares	10	15	0
4% irred. deb. stock (per £100)	101	10	0

1952

Horton Kirby Paper Mills Ld. Regd. 1922. Vol. liq. 28 Dec. 1927. Final meeting return regd. 28 Apr. 1928 **1928**

Hoscote (Malaya) Rubber Estates Ld. Regd. 1925. Vol. liq. (members') 17 May 1932. Undertaking and assets were acquired by Hoscote Rubber Estates Ld., in which company shareholders were entitled to 1 share of £1 (credited with 15s. paid) for every 2 shares of £1 held. Debenture stockholders were entitled to £125 7% 1st mortgage debenture stock for every £100 stock held. Final meeting return regd. 1 Mar. 1933 .... **1933**

Hosegood Industries Ld. Regd. 1936. All capital was owned by Spillers Ld. Vol. liq. (members') 7 Feb. 1966. Final meeting return regd. 3 Jan. 1967 .... **1962**

Hosur Gold Mines Ld. Regd. 1909. Vol. liq. 6 May 1910. Capital returned to contributories—6d. per share of

10s. in July 1910; further payments (if any) not known. Final meeting return regd. 27 Nov. 1914 **1911**

Hosur Gold Mines of Dharwar Ld. Regd. 1907. Vol. liq. Apr. 1909 for reconstruction as Hosur Gold Mines Ld., in which company shareholders were entitled to 1 share of 10s. (credited with 6s. paid) for each share of £1 held. Removed from Register 1910 .... **1910**

Hotchkiss Ordnance Co. Ld. Regd. 1887. Vol. liq. Apr. 1912 for fusion with Société Hotchkiss et Cie,. in which company shareholders were entitled to 1 fully-paid share of Fr.100 for every 10 preference shares of £1 or 20 ordinary shares of £1 held. 1st mortgage debenture stockholders received an equal amount of 5% obligations; 2nd debenture stockholders received 90% of holding in 5% obligations and 10% in shares; rate of exchange of Fr.25 to £. Removed from Register 1913 .... **1913**

Hotel & Club Investment Co. Ld. See Empress Club Ld.

Hotel Belgravia Ld. Regd. 1921. Receiver appointed 2 May 1936. Assets realised insufficient to repay debenture holders; no capital returned to contributories. Struck off Register 21 Apr. 1939 .... **1940**

Hotel Cecil Ld. Regd. 1896. Vol. liq. (members') 8 Aug. 1930. Land, buildings and fixtures were sold to Shell-Mex Ld. Capital returned to contributories—£5 per preference share of £5; 17s. 6½d. per ordinary share of £1. £182 17s. 2d. was paid into Companies' Liquidation Account in respect of unclaimed dividends and £356 14s. 10d. in respect of unclaimed repayments. Final meeting return regd. 10 Dec. 1931 .... **1931**

Hotel Chatham Ld. Regd. 1909. Receiver appointed 7 Feb. 1910; ceased to act 15 Dec. 1910. Vol. liq. 7 Feb. 1910. Removed from Register 6 June 1913 ... ***1911**

Hotel Continental Ld. Regd. 1883. Vol. liq. Oct. 1909. Removed from Register 1912 .... **1910**

Hotel d l'Europe (Hamburg) Ld. Regd. 1894. Struck off Register 18 Nov. 1902 .... **1902**

Hotel du Nord (Cologne) Ld. Regd. 1886. Vol. liq. 31 Dec. 1904. Removed from Register 1906 .... **1905**

Hotel Métropole, Bournemouth Ld. Regd. 1898. Vol. liq. (members') 21 May 1930. Undertaking and assets acquired by Levy & Franks Ld. Capital returned to contributories—£3,000 in cash. Final meeting return regd. 13 Aug. 1930 .... **1931**

Hotel Métropole Ld. Regd. 1882. Taken over by Gordon Hotels Ld. Removed from Register 1906 ***1891**

Hotel Métropole (Scarborough) Ld. Regd. 1895. Removed from Register 1908 .... **1897**

Hotel St. Petersbourg, Paris Ld. Regd. 1899. Vol. liq. 1 Jan. 1926. Final meeting return regd. 23 Dec. 1932 **1926**

Hotel Victoria Ld. Regd. 1887. Vol. liq. 27 Dec. 1893. Undertaking sold to Gordon Hotels Ld. Final meeting return regd. 4 May 1895 .... ***1895**

Hotel Victoria (Newquay) Ld. Regd. 1897. Vol. liq. (members') 23 July 1946. The outstanding £10,000 4% debentures were redeemed at par. Capital returned to contributories—£5 per preference share of £5 and £8 per ordinary share of £5. £288 10s. 11d. was paid into Companies' Liquidation Account. Final meeting return regd. 3 May 1948 .... **1949**

Hotel Windsor (Paris) Ld. Regd. 1899. Vol. liq. 24 Apr. 1902. Struck off Register 3 Sept. 1918 .... **1903**

Hotels & City Properties Share Trust Ld. Regd. 1882. Vol. liq. 11 Nov. 1895. Final meeting return regd. 16 July 1897 .... ***1886**

Hough (J. E.). See Edison Bell Ld.

Houghton-le-Spring & District Electric Lighting Co. Ld. Regd. 1905. Under the North Eastern Electric Supply Act 1932 the undertaking was transferred to that company which owned all the share capital. Dissolved under Act on 30 Sept. 1932................. **1933**

Houghton-le-Spring District Gas Co. Inc. by Special Act 1879. Dissolved 1 May 1949. undertaking being vested in Northern Area Gas Board under Gas Act 1948. Holders of securities were entitled to receive British Gas 3% guaranteed stock 1990—95 as follows in respect of each £10 unit, unless otherwise stated, of security held:-

	£	s.	d.
Ord. shares (10% max.)	15	0	0
6% pref. shares	13	6	0
5% perp. deb. stock (per £100).......	125	0	0
4½% red. deb. stock (per £100)	105	10	0

1952

Houghton Main Colliery Co., Ld. Regd. 1900. Vol. liq. (members') 30 June 1953. Capital returned to contributories—18s 2½d. per share of 15s. £1,358 17s. 1d. was paid into Companies' Liquidation Account. Final meeting return regd. 4 Mar. 1958 .... **1959**

Hounslow & Metropolitan Railway Co. Inc. by Special Act 1880. Under Metropolitan District Railway Co. Act 1903 line was purchased by that company. Holders of stock received £165,714 3½% rent charge stock **1904**

VOL. FOR

House & Land Investment Trust Ld. Regd. 1875. Court Order to wind up 25 Oct. 1892. Liquidator released 18 Oct. 1910. Struck off Register 1 July 1921........ **1893**

House & Mill Co. Ld. Regd. 1888. Vol. liq. (members') 9 June 1953. Capital returned to contributories—£17 3s. 2d. per share of £10; £511 12s. 2d. was paid into Companies' Liquidation Account. Final meeting return regd. 7 May 1954........................ **1955**

House Property & Investment Co. Ld. Regd. 1876. Vol. liq. (members') 19 July 1951. Capital returned to contributories—£107 per £100 5% preference stock, 25s. per 6% B preference or 6% redeemable preference share of £1 and £8 7s. 6·68d. per ordinary share of £1. Final meeting return regd. 10 Sept. 1954 **1956**

House Property Trust Ld. Regd. 1881. Removed from Register 1888.......................... ***1886**

House to House Electric Light Supply Co. Ld. See Brompton & Kensington Electricity Supply Co. Ld.

Household Stores Association Ld. Regd. 1872. Vol. liq. 22 Dec. 1922. Final meeting return regd.4 Apr.1924 **1924**

Householders' Tea Association Ld. See Northern Guarantee & Finance Corpn. Ld.

Houtpoort-Burbank Goldfields Ld. Regd. 1932. Vol. liq. (members') 5 Apr. 1938. Shareholders were entitled to receive 1 share (of 2s.) of Southern Van Ryn Reef Gold Mining Co. Ld., for every 4 shares (of 3d.) held. Liquidator stated that liquidation was completed early in 1955 .... **1956**

Houtpoort Ld. Regd. 1902. Vol. liq. 11 Apr. 1924 for reconstruction as Houtpoort Proprietary Ld., in which company shareholders were entitled to 1 share of 1s. (credited with 8d. paid) for each share of 2s. held. Debenture holders were entitled to an equal amount of debentures in new company. Final meeting return regd. 21 Mar. 1930 .... **1925**

Houtpoort Proprietary Ld. Regd. 1924. Vol. liq. (creditors') 31 Oct. 1932. Subject to rights of debenture holders certain assets were transferred to Houtpoort-Burbank Goldfields Ld., in which company shareholders were entitled to 1 share of 3d. (credited with 1d. paid) for every 3 shares of 1s. held. Final meeting return regd. 10 Oct. 1933 .... **1933**

Hove Banking Co. Ld. Regd. 1876. Vol. liq. 29 Apr. 1891. Final meeting return regd. 16 June 1893 .... **1891**

Hove Electric Lighting Co. Ld. Regd. 1892. Vol. liq. 7 May 1914. The undertaking was acquired by Hove Corporation. Capital returned to contributories—£5 per preference share of £5; £10 per ordinary share of £5 at Aug. 1914; further payments (if any) not known. Final meeting return regd. 3 June 1915.... **1915**

Hovenden (R.) & Sons Ld. Regd. 1899. Vol. liq. (members') 2 Jan. 1956. Preference shares were repaid at par. Certain premises were transferred to holders of A preference shares (Timothy Whites & Taylors Ld.), and the remainder of surplus assets, after satisfying the balance due on the A preference shares, was distributed to holders of ordinary shares (Taylors (Cash Chemists) Trust Ld.). Final meeting return regd. 19 Dec. 1956 .... **1957**

Howard Ford & Co. Ld. See Bear Brand Ld.

Howard (James & Fredk.). Regd. 1916. All capital owned by Agricultural & General Engineers Ld. Receiver appointed Mar. 1932; ceased to act Dec. 1935. Struck off Register 22 June 1937 .... **1932**

Howardsgate Trust Ld. Regd. 1932 under Industrial & Provident Societies Act 1893; converted into company registered under Companies Act in 1939. Vol. liq. (members') 17 Dec. 1954. Capital returned to contributories—34s. 10·242d. per ordinary share of £1. Final meeting return regd. 5 Oct. 1957 .... **1958**

Howden Buell Combustion Co. Ld. Regd. 1929. Vol. liq. (members') 1 Mar. 1933. Capital returned to contributories—£1 per share of £1. Final meeting return regd. 14 Dec. 1933 .... **1934**

Howden Gas Co. Ld. Regd. 1859. Dissolved 1 May 1949, undertaking being vested in North Eastern Area Gas Board under Gas Act 1948. Holders of ordinary shares (of £10 with £7 paid) were entitled to receive £19 British Gas 3% guaranteed stock 1990–95 for each share held. **1952**

Howe Bridge Cotton Co. (1920) Ld. Regd. 1920. Vol. liq. (members') 2 Sept. 1929. Undertaking and assets acquired by Combined Egyptian Mills Ld. (later Combined English Mills (Spinners) Ld.) in which company shareholders were entitled to receive fully-paid shares as follows: 15% preference share of £1 for each preference share of £1 held and 3 ordinary shares of £1 for every 20 ordinary shares of £1 held. Struck off Register 1 Sept. 1953 .... **1954**

Howe Cycle & Sewing Machine Co. Ld. Regd. 1896. Vol. liq. 11 Feb. 1897. Final meeting return regd. 28 Jan. 1898 .... **1898**

VOL. FOR

Howe Machine Co. Ld. Regd. 1873. Vol. liq. 16 Sept. 1887. Court Orders: to wind up 28 Sept. 1887; to dissolve 19 May 1892 **1888**

Howell & James Ld. Regd. 1884. Vol. liq. 21 Sept. 1911. Final meeting return regd. 11 Apr. 1929 .... **1912**

Howell (John) & Co. Ld. Regd. 1871. Vol. liq. (members') 6 Jan. 1930. Capital returned to contributories—10s. 1d. per share of £1. Final meeting return regd. 22 Feb. 1935 ...... **1930**

Howell's Consolidated Gold Mines Ld. Regd. 1896. Removed from Register 1904 .... **1930**

Howes & Burley Ld. Regd. 1900. Receiver appointed in Mar. 1927. The prior 1st mortgage debentures were repaid at par in July 1927; the remaining assets were insufficient to meet the claims of 1st mortgage debenture holders. Struck off Register. Dec. 1929. **1930**

Howie Gold Mines Ld. Regd. 1896. Vol. liq. (creditors') 14 Feb. 1938. No capital returned to contributories. Final meeting return regd. 4 Sept. 1941 .... **1939**

Howley Gold Mines Ld. Regd. 1897. Reconstructed 1901 as Northern Territories Gold Fields of Australia Ld., in which company shareholders were entitled to 1 share of £1 (credited with 18s. 6d. paid) for each share of £1 held. Removed from Register 1903 .... **1902**

Howroyd McArthur & Co. Ld. See Liverpool Chemical Products Ld.

Hoyal Body Corporation Ld. Business and undertaking was acquired in 1928 by Hoyal Body Corporation (1928) Ld for £125,998 in cash **1929**

Hoyal Body Corporation (1928) Ld. Regd. 1928. Vol. liq. (creditors') 28 Aug. 1931. Assets realised insufficient to pay unsecured creditors in full. Final meeting return regd. 23 Dec. 1933 .... **1932**

Hoylake & Birkenhead Rail & Tramway Co. (See Seacombe, Hoylake & Deeside) **1891**

Hoylake & West Kirby Gas & Water Co. Inc. by Special Act in 1923. Undertaking transferred to Urban District Council in 1926. Capital returned to contributories—£123 15s. in respect of each £100 stock (preferred or ordinary); further payments (if any) not known **1926**

Hoylake Railway Co. See Seacombe, Hoylake and Deeside Railway Co **1891**

Hoyland Silkstone Colliery Co. Ld. Regd. 1874 as Wells, Birch Ryde & Co. Ld.; name changed 20 Mar. 1882. Vol. liq. 22 Jan. 1884. Court Order to continue winding up under supervision 14 Jan. 1884. Final meeting return regd. 2 Apr.1891 .... ***1881**

Hoyle (James) Ld. Regd. 1919. Vol. liq. (members') 11 Feb. 1935. All shares owned by Dunlop Rubber Co. Ld. (later Dunlop Co. Ld.). Final meeting return regd. 17 Dec. 1935 .... **1936**

Hrvatska Eskomptna Banks. Inc. Zagreb 1868. In Mar. 1928 assets and liabilities were merged with those of Hrvatska-Slavonska Zemaliska Hipotekarna Banka. Shareholders received 4 fully-paid shares of din. 200 in that bank for every 5 shares of din. 100 held **1929**

Hubert & Fast Colour Eyelet Co. Ld. Regd. 1901. Vol. liq. (members') 12 June 1939. Capital returned to contributories—19s. 2½d. per share of £1. Final meeting return regd. 3 June 1940 .... **1941**

Huddersfield Banking Co. Ld. Established 1827. Regd. 1882. Vol. liq. 8 July 1897. Amalgamated with London and Midland Bank Ld. (later Midland Bank Ld.), in which company shareholders were entitled to 1⅔ shares of £60 (credited with £12 10s. paid) for each share of £100 (£25 paid) held **1898**

Hudson & Co. Ld. Regd. 1892. Vol. liq. 7 May 1894. Final meeting return regd. 12 Sept. 1894 .... ***1895**

Hudson (Bradford) Ld. Regd. 1929. Direct controlling interest was held by Richards (Thomas) (Textiles) Ld. Struck off Register 1932 .... **1932**

Hudson Brothers Ld. Regd. 1897. Vol. liq. 23 Aug. 1905. Removed from Register 1907 .... **1906**

Hudson Companies. Inc. New York 1905. The outstanding $10,000,000 6% secured convertible gold coupon notes were redeemed 1 Feb. 1913 .... **1912**

Hudson Hotels Ld. Regd. 1898. Vol. liq. 3 Mar. 1914. Final meeting return regd. 1 May 1914 .... **1915**

Hudson Scott & Sons Ld. Regd. 1898. Vol. liq. (members') 31 Oct. 1945. Undertaking acquired by Metal Box Co. Ld. Final meeting return regd. 30 June 1948 .... **1940**

Hudson Shipping Co. Ld. Regd. 1884. Vol. liq 20 May 1896. Final meeting return regd 13 Apr. 1899....... ***1897**

Hudson, Sykes & Bousfield Ld. Regd. 1899. Struck off Register 26 Apr. 1940 .... **1941**

Hudson's Bay Co. Overseas Settlement Ld. Regd. 1925. Vol. liq. (members') 5 Nov. 1953. Final meeting regd. 23 Apr. 1954 .... **1952**

Hudson's Cambridge and Pampisford Breweries Ld. Regd. 1892. Vol. liq. (members') 2 Feb. 1949

VOL. FOR

undertaking having been acquired by Wells & Winch Ld. [later Greene King (Biggleswade) Ld.] Final meeting return regd. 3 June 1949 .... **1950**

Hudsons' Consolidated Ld. Regd. 1905. Removed from Register 1910 .... **1910**

Hudsons' Consolidated Ld. Regd. 1910. Vol. liq. 13 Nov. 1922. Business was taken over by a new Canadian company of the same name. Preference shareholders were entitled to 1 fully-paid preference share of $5 in new company for each share of £1 held, and a distribution (in satisfaction of arrears of dividend from 1 July 1919) of 30% in fully-paid ordinary shares (or common stock). Ordinary shareholders were entitled to 1 ordinary share—or common stock—of $5 in the new company for each share of £1 held on payment of 1s. per share. Final meeting return regd. 6 May 1925. Court Orders deferred dissolution to 21 Dec. 1925.......................... **1923**

Hudsons' Consolidated Ld. Inc. Canada 1923. The assets of the old company had not been handed over at 13 Feb. 1931. No accounts were issued or business done at that date **1932**

Hudswell, Clarke & Co. Ld. Regd. 1899. Vol. liq. 17 Oct. 1923 for reconstruction as private company of same name. Final meeting return regd. 5 Feb. 1924 ...... **1924**

Huelva Central Copper Mining Co. Ld. Regd. 1896 as Central Copper Mines of Spain Ld.; name changed Oct. 1899. Vol. liq. 24 Sept. 1902. Removed from Register 1911 .... **1903**

Huelva Gas & Electricity Co. Ld. Regd. Edinburgh 1878 as Huelva Gas Co. Ld.; name changed May 1897. Vol. liq. June 1919. Final meeting return regd. 21 Sept. 1922 .... **1920**

Huggins & Co. Ld. Regd. 1894. Vol. liq. 26 Mar. 1898. Business was acquired by company of same name for £116,500 in ordinary shares of £10, £250,000 in preference shares of £10. £413,600 in debenture stock and £319,900 in cash. Holders of every £100 4½% 1st mortgage debenture stock or 4½% B debenture stock were entitled to £116 and £114 3½% 1st mortgage irredeemable debenture stock respectively. Final meeting return regd. 28 Nov. 1898 .. **1898**

Huggins' Soap Works Ld. Regd. 1896. Vol. liq. 13 Apr. 1898. Final meeting return regd. 23 Aug. 1900 ..... **1899**

Hughes (Daniel), Evans & Co. Ld. Regd. 1899. Vol. liq. 16 Oct. 1899. Subscriptions were returned in full. Removed from Register 1902 ....

Hughes (Edwin) & Co. Ld. See Pluckley Brick & Tile Co. Ld.

Hughes's Locomotive & Tramway Engine Works Ld. Regd. 1877. Business was acquired in 1882 by Falcon Engine and Car Works Ld. Removed from Register 1903 .... **1883**

Hughes Stubbs Metal Co. Ld. Regd. 1906. Undertaking acquired in 1918 by Elliott's Metal Co. Ld. Vol. liq. 25 Mar. 1929. Final meeting return regd.4 Jan. 1930 **1940**

Huinac Consolidated Copper Ld. Regd. 1912. Struck off Register 1927 .... **1926**

Huinac Copper Mines Ld. Regd. 1904. Court Order to wind up 14 Feb. 1911. Struck off Register 16 Oct. 1916 .... **1912**

Hull & Barnsley Railway Co. Inc. by Special Act as Hull, Barnsley & West Riding Junction Railway & Dock Co.; name changed by Act of 1905. In 1922 the undertaking was merged into the North Eastern Railway Co., in which company stockholders were entitled to stock as follows:

For each £100 held	N. E.	
1st Debenture 3%.........£100	3%	Debenture
3½% Preference £87½	4%	Preference
4% Preference £100	4%	Preference
Cons. Ordinary.............£55		Consols

For each £100 2nd debenture (3% + 1% contingent on earnings) held—£100 3% debenture and £25 4% preference. The £1,581,617 capital advanced by the North Eastern Company under the Hull Joint Dock Act, 1899, was cancelled **1924**

Hull & North Western Junction Railway Co. Inc. by Special Act 1887. Undertaking abandoned by Act of 1894 .... **1895**

Hull & South Yorkshire Railway Co. Inc. by Special Act 1897. By Act of 1898 powers were acquired by Hull, Barnsley & West Riding Junction Railway & Dock Co. **1899**

Hull Banking Co. Ld. Regd. 1880. Taken over by York City & County Banking Co. Ld., in which company shareholders were entitled to 1 share of £10 (credited with £3 paid) for each share of £20 (£4 paid) held. Removed from Register 1901 .... **1895**

Hull Central Dry Dock & Engineering Works Ld. Regd. 1886. Vol. liq. (members') 1 Jan. 1935. Capital returned to contributories—£13 6s. 8d. per preference, ordinary or deferred share of £10. Final meeting return regd. 1 Oct. 1937. .... **1935**

VOL. FOR

Hull District Bank Ld. Regd. 1879. Struck off Register 1929 .... *****1881**

Hull Dock Railway Co. Inc. by Special Act 1774. By North Eastern Railway (Hull Docks) Act 1893 undertaking was amalgamated with North Eastern Railway, in which holders of ordinary consolidated stock received 30% of their holding in consolidated ordinary stock; 4½% convertible preference stock (1881) received 75% of 4% preference stock; holders of 4% and 4½% debenture stock received 87½% and 93¾% of 4% debenture stock respectively; the rent charge, terminable bonds and temporary loans were assumed by purchasing company **1894**

Hull Insurance Co. Ld. Regd. 1922. All shares were owned by Lancashire & General Assurance Co. Ld. Struck off Register 1929 .... **1927**

Hull Joint Dock Committee. Inc. by Special Act 1899. Dissolved in accordance with North Eastern Railway Co., and Hull & Barnsley Railway Co. Amalgamated Scheme 1922 .... **1924**

Hull Steam Fishing & Ice Co. Ld. Regd. 1897. Vol. liq. (creditors') 6 Mar. 1936. Assets realised insufficient to pay unsecured creditors in full. Final meeting return regd. 24 Nov. 1936 .... **1937**

Hull Steam Shipping Co. Ld, Regd. 1889. Vol. liq. 3 Jan. 1910. Final meeting return regd. 2 Aug. 1911 ...... *****1911**

Hull Street Tramways Co. Inc. 1875. In liquidation in 1890 .... **1890**

Hulme Estate Co. Ld. Regd. 1922 as Hulme Trust Ld.; name changed 1927. Vol. liq. (members') 25 Aug. 1943. Final meeting return regd. 17 June, 1952 ... **1953**

Hultafall Mining Co. Ld. Regd. 1877. Vol. liq. 10 June 1885. Final meeting return regd. 5 Mar. 1891 .... **1886**

Hulton Colliery Co. Ld. Regd 1886. Vol. liq. (members') 11 Apr. 1949. Capital returned to contributories— 43s. 9¾d. per £1 stock. Final meeting return regd. 8 Apr. 1958 .... **1959**

Humber & Co. (America) Ld. Regd. 1894. The property was in the hands of a Receiver in 1902. Struck off Register 18 Nov. 1902 .... **1903**

Humber & Co. (Extension) Ld. Regd. 1896. Reconstructed 1900 as Humber Ld., in which company shareholders were entitled to 10 ordinary shares of £1 (credited with 18s. paid) and 10 fully-paid preference shares of £1 for every 21 shares of £1 held. Removed from Register 1907 .... **1901**

Humber & Co. Ld. Regd. 1887. Vol. liq. 22 Nov. 1895. Reconstructed as company of same name. Shareholders were entitled to 10 fully-paid ordinary shares, 8 fully-paid preference shares of £1 and 2 preference shares of £1 (credited with 10s. paid) for each share of £5 held. Final meeting return regd. 12 Nov. 1906 .... **1900**

Humber & Co. Ld. Regd. 1895. Vol. liq. 23 Mar. 1900. Reconstructed as Humber Ld in which company shareholders were entitled to 2 ordinary shares of £1 (credited with 18s. paid) for every 3 ordinary shares of £1 held and 2 fully-paid preference shares of £1 for every 3 preference shares of £1 held. Final meeting return regd. 12 Nov. 1906 .... **1901**

Humber & Co. (Portugal) Ld. Regd. 1899. Removed from Register 1905 .... **1902**

Humber & Co. (Russia) Ld. Regd. 1895. Removed from Register 1905 .... **1902**

Humber & Goddard Ld. Regd. 1896. Removed from Register 1905 .... **1900**

Humber Commercial Railway and Dock Company. Inc. by Special Act 1901. In 1923 the undertaking was merged into the London & North Eastern Railway Co., in which company stockholders were entitled to stock as follows:

For each £100 held	L. N. E. R.	
Ord.	£100	4% First Gtd.
Special Gtd.	£150	4% First Gtd.

The London & North Eastern Railway Company assumed all liability for the £719,000 7% Debentures and other obligations of the Humber Company ... **1924**

Humber Graving Dock and Engineering Co. Ld. Regd. 1909. Winding-up order 3 Mar. 1986. All capital owned by Richardson Westgarth & Co. Ld. **1970**

Humber Ld. Regd. 1900. Vol. liq. 17 Feb. 1909 for reconstruction as company of same name. Shareholders were entitled to 4 preference shares of £1 (credited with 16s. 6d. paid) in new company for every 3 preference shares of £1 held or 1 ordinary share of £1 (credited with 15s. 4d. paid) for each ordinary share of £1 held. Struck off Register 7 Dec. 1926 .... **1909**

Humber Portland Cement Co. Ld. Regd. 1919. Vol. liq. 29 July 1924. Undertaking and assets were transferred to G. & T. Earle Ld. Final meeting return regd. 8 Apr. 1926 .... **1925**

See Stock Exchange Year-Book.

VOL. FOR

Humber Steam Shipping Co. Ld. Regd. 1877. Vol. liq. 15 Jan. 1895. Absorbed by Goole Steam Shipping Co. Ld. Final meeting return regd. 18 Oct. 1895 .... ***1896**

Humboldt Electric Power and Mining Co. Ld. Regd. 1888. Removed from Register 1906 .... **1891**

Hummums Hotel & "Rockleys" Ld. Regd. 1888. Court Order to wind up 26 Aug. 1891. Removed from Register 1906 .... **1892**

Humphrey Pump Co. Ld. Regd. 1913. Vol. liq. Dec. 1922. Struck off Register 1927 .... **1923**

Humphrey's Gully United Gold Mining Co. Ld. Inc. New Zealand. In 1898 the business was acquired by Humphrey's Sluicing Co. Ld...................... **1903**

Humphrey's Hydraulic Sluicing Co. Ld. Regd. 1898. Vol. liq. 1903. Amalgamated with Consolidated Gold Fields of New Zealand Ld., in which company shareholders were entitled to 1 fully-paid share of £1 for every 4 shares of £1 held. Removed from Register 1905 .... **1904**

Humphries (James) & Sons Ld. Regd. 1891. Vol. liq. 16 Sept. 1920. Undertaking acquired by Carpet Trades Ld. (later John Crossley—Carpet Trades Holdings Ld.). Final meeting return regd. 15 June 1921 ..... **1930**

Hunasgeria Coffee Co. Ld. Regd. 1865. Vol. liq. 9 July 1884. Properties acquired by Hunasgeria Tea Co. Ld. (later Consolidated Commercial Co. Ld.). Final meeting return regd. 29 Sept. 1885 .... ***1885**

Huncoat Plastic Brick & Terra Cotta Co. Ld. Regd. 1897 as Huncoat Brick & Terra Cotta Co. Ld.; name changed Feb. 1902. Vol. liq. 8 Aug. 1917. Final meeting return regd. 21 Mar. 1922 .... **1918**

Hundred of Manhood & Selsey Tramways Co. Ld. Regd. 1896. Struck off Register 23 Sept. 1938 .... **1939**

Hungarian-Bulgarian Bank. *See* Ungarisch Bulgarische Bank.

Hungarian Copper Co. Ld. Regd. 1882. Vol. liq. Apr. 1883. Capital returned to contributories—11½d. per share of £1. Final meeting return regd. 14 Nov. 1884 **1884**

Hungarian General Savings Bank Ld. Inc. Hungary 1881. Merged with Hungarian General Creditbank, in which company shareholders were entitled to 1 share of P.50 for every 5 shares of P.50 held. The liability of the bonds was assumed by that bank **1936**

Hungarian Gold & Silver Reduction Works Ld. Regd. 1883. Vol. liq. 16 Jan. 1886. Final meeting return regd. 29 Oct. 1891 .... ***1887**

Hungarian Land Mortgage Bank. Established 1895. The outstanding 4½% mortgage bonds, series A, were repaid, and it was stated in Jan. 1927 that this bank had amalgamated with the Banca Ungaro-Italiana Societa Anomima, Budapest...................... **1927**

Hungarian Land Mortgage Institute. Inc. Hungary by Royal Charter 1863. Undertaking and assets were acquired in 1936 by National Land Mortgage Institute which also assumed liabilities (including 7½% sterling land mortgage bonds) **1937**

Hungarian National Petroleum Co. Ld. Regd. 1912. Struck off Register Dec. 1931 .... **1932**

Hungarian Oil Syndicate Ld. Regd. 1921. Vol. liq. (members') 28 July 1930. Capital returned to contributories—7¹¹⁄₁₆d. per share of £1. Final meeting return regd. 10 Jan. 1931 .... ***1931**

Hungerford Gas Co. Ld. Regd. 1901. Vol. liq. 19 Apr. 1948, when the undertaking was acquired by Swindon United Gas Co. Final meeting return regd. 18 June 1948 .... **1909**

Hunslet Railway Co. Inc. by Special Act 1893. Under Great Northern Railway Co. Act 1894 powers were transferred to that company **1895**

Hunstanton & West Norfolk Railway Co. Inc. by Special Act 1874. Under Great Eastern, Hunstanton & Norfolk Railway Cos. Act 1890 undertaking was purchased by Great Eastern Railway Co. Holders of ordinary stocks received cash:—A, £200 for every £100 held; B, £53 6s. 8d. for every £100 held. Holders of preference stocks received 4% preference stock 1888:—4%, £100 for every £100 held; 4½%, £112 10s. for every £100 held. Holders of debenture stocks received 4% irredeemable debenture stock:—4½%, £112 10s. for every £100 held; 5%, £125 for every £100 held **1891**

Hunt Partners Ld. Regd. 1920. A subsidiary of Bowater Paper Corpn. Ld. Vol. liq. (members') 1 Jan. 1960. Final meeting return regd. 12 Feb. 1963 .... **1958**

Hunter-Penrose-Littlejohn Ld. Regd. 13 Feb. 1902 as Hunters Ld.; converted private company 20 May 1908; name changed to Hunter-Penrose Ld. 15 Oct. 1927; reconverted into public company 7 June 1935;name changed 15 Oct. 1962. All capital acquired by Johnsons-H.P.L. Ld. in Aug. 1965 ..... **1966**

Hunters Ld. and **Hunter Penrose Ld.** *See* Hunter-Penrose-Littlejohn Ld.

Hunters The Teamen Ld. Regd. 1897. All capital was held by Castlewood Finance Co. Ld. Vol. liq.

VOL. FOR

(members') 7 Apr. 1960. Final meeting return regd. 24 Feb. 1961 .... **1956**

Hunter's Road Syndicate Ld. Regd. 1911. Struck off Register Feb. 1931 .... **1931**

Huntingdon & Godmanchester Gas & Coke Co. Ld. Regd. 1856. Dissolved 1 May 1949, undertaking being vested in Eastern Area Gas Board under Gas Act 1948. Holders of ordinary shares (of £10) were entitled to receive £19 British Gas 3% guaranteed stock 1990–95 for each share held **1952**

Huntingdon Copper and Sulphur Co. Ld. Regd. Edinburgh 1872. Vol. liq. 15 Jan. 1883. Court Order to continue winding up under supervision 13 Mar. 1883. Final meeting return regd. 27 Feb. 1890...... **1884**

Huntly Gas Co. Ld. Regd. in Edinburgh 1905. Dissolved 1 May 1949, undertaking being vested in Scottish Area Gas Board under Gas Act 1948. Holders of ordinary shares (of £1) were entitled to receive £2 12s. 0d. British Gas 3% guaranteed stock 1990–95 for each share held...................... **1952**

Hunyani Rhodesia Tobacco Plantations Ld. Regd. 1904 as British South Africa Tobacco Plantations Ld.; name changed May 1909. Vol. liq. 22 Oct. 1913. Final meeting return regd. 4 Mar. 1914 .... **1914**

Huon Timber Co. Ld. Regd. Edinburgh 1902. Struck off Register 9 May 1930 .... **1930**

Hupfield Brothers Ld. Regd. 1937. At 25 July 1975 it was stated that there would be no funds available for shareholders. **1975–6**

Huron & Erie Loan & Savings Co. Inc. 1864 .... **1908**

Huronian Belt Co. Ld. Regd. 1914. Vol. liq. 12 Dec. 1929. Undertaking and assets were acquired by Huronian Mining & Finance Co. Ld in which company shareholders were entitled to 3½ fully-paid shares of no par value and option (since expired) over further shares for each share of £1 held. Final meeting return regd.10 July 1931...................... **1930**

Huronian Mining & Finance Co. Ld. Inc. Canada 1929. Vol. liq. Nov. 1933. Reconstructed as Anglo-Huronian Ld. in which company shareholders were entitled to 1 share of no par value for every 5 shares of $1 held and an option (since expired) over further shares **1934**

Hurst, Nelson & Co. Ld. Regd. Edinburgh 1909. All capital was acquired by Charles Roberts & Co. Ld. in 1958. Vol. liq. (members') 28 Mar. 1960. Final meeting return regd. 8 May, 1962 .... **1959**

Hutchings & Crowsley Ld. Regd. 1881. Vol. liq. 27 July 1888. Final meeting return regd. 24 Feb. 1894 .... ***1884**

Hutchings & Crowsley Ld. Regd. 1888. Vol. liq. 21 Apr. 1892. Final meeting return regd. 8 Dec.1898 ...... **1893**

Hutchinson (W. H.) & Sons Ld. Regd. 1898. Vol. liq. 29 Dec. 1914. Undertaking and assets were acquired by Home Brewery Co. Ld., in which company shareholders were entitled to 1 preference share of £100 for every 10 preference shares of £10 held. Debenture stockholders were entitled to an equal amount of debenture stock in new company. Ordinary shareholders were entitled to £30,000. Final meeting return regd. 10 Feb. 1916 .... **1915**

Hutchison's Ld. In 1919 the business was acquired by Hutchisons (1919) Ld...................... **1921**

Hutchisons (1919) Ld. Regd. 1919. Vol. liq. 17 Sept. 1920. Final meeting return regd. 20 Oct. 1922 ..... **1921**

Hutchison's No. 2 Ld. In 1919 the business was acquired by Hutchison's (1919) Ld. **1921**

Huth (Fredk.) & Co. Established 1809. The banking business was acquired by British Overseas Bank Ld and the fur business by C. M. Lampson & Co. Ld. Dissolved Mar. 1936 .... **1937**

Hutti (Nizams) Gold MInes Ld. Regd. 1901. Vol. liq. 18 Mar. 1920. Capital returned to contributories—20s. per share of £1; further payments (if any) not known. Final meeting return regd. 5 Apr. 1921 ... **1921**

Hutton Henry Coal Co. Ld. Regd. 1873. All preference shares and 90% of ordinary shares were acquired by North Brancepeth Coal Co. Ld., for £26,080 in fully-paid shares. Removed from Register 1906 .... **1902**

Hutton (John V.) Ld. Regd. 1928. Vol. liq. (members') 30 Dec. 1938. Undertaking and assets' [except shares held in Goodson's Mantle & Costume Co. (1920) Ld., book debts and cash] acquired by J. V. Hutton. Ordinary shareholders received 5s. 9d. per share of 5s. and deferred shareholders 1s. per share of 1s. Final meeting return regd. 5 Oct. 1939 ...... **1939**

Hutton's (Bechuanaland) Gold Reefs Development Co. Ld. Regd. 1896. Struck off Register 17 Nov. 1899 **1900**

Hutton's Brewery Ld. Regd. 1890. Removed from Register 1907...................... **1892**

Huyton & Robey Gas Co. Regd. 1856. inc. by special Act 1867. By Special Order of 1932 the undertaking was acquired by Liverpool Gas Co. Holders of original (10% maximum) shares of £10 were entitled to £11 13s. 4d. ordinary stock of acquiring company for each share held, and holders of new (7% maximum) shares of £10 were entitled to £10 ordinary stock for each share held. The liability for the mortgage debentures was assumed by acquiring company **1933**

Hyam & Co. Ld. Regd.1900 as Hyam & Co. (1900) Ld.; name changed Mar. 1905. Vol. liq. 19 June 1928. Final meeting return regd. 21 Nov. 1928 ...... **1929**

Hyatt Ld. Undertaking and assets were acquired in 1924 by Delco-Remy & Hyatt Ld. **1925**

Hyatt's Ld. Regd. 1904. Court Order to wind up 17 Feb. 1914. Struck off Register 14 Feb. 1919 ...... **1915**

Hyde Gas Co. *See* North Cheshire & District Gas Co.

Hyde Imperial Rubber Co. Ld. Business acquired in 1902 by Hyde Rubber Works Ld., for £16,451 11s. in cash **1905**

Hyde Park Cab Co. Ld. Regd. 1882. Removed from Register 1907 ...... ***1884**

Hyde Rubber Works Ld. Regd. 1902. Vol. liq. 1 Feb. 1905. Works were acquired by Unity Rubber Co. Ld. Removed from Register 1907 ...... **1906**

Hyderabad (Deccan) Co. Ld. Regd. 1886. Vol. liq. (members') 31 Oct. 1944. Certain assets were sold to Government of H. E. H. the Nizam of Hyderabad. Capital returned to contributories—£3 11s. 1d. per share of £3. £934 14s. 11d. was paid into Companies' Liquidation Account. FInal meeting return regd. 28 Aug. 1945 ...... **1946**

Hydes & Wigfull Ld. Regd. 1873. Vol. liq. July 1883. Final meeting return regd. 11 Dec. 1888 ...... **1884**

Hydra Combined Mineral Water Bottling and Syphon Filling Machines Ld. Regd. 1902. Court Order to wind up 21 June 1905. Liquidator released 15 Dec. 1909. Struck off Register 10 Oct. 1916. ...... **1906**

Hydraulic Power & Smelting Co. Ld. Regd. 1911. Vol. liq. 29 Dec. 1924. Final meeting return regd. 19 June 1925 ...... **1925**

Hydraulic Power Co. of Scandinavia Ld. Regd. 1913. Vol. liq. 14 Aug. 1914. Absorbed by Aktieselskabet Tyssefaldene (inc. Norway), in which company shareholders were entitled to Kr. 3·135 in ordinary shares for each share of 10s. held. Debenture holders were entitled to an equal amount in 6% preference shares in new company. Final meeting return regd. 8 July 1915 ...... **1915**

Hydrautomat Ld. Regd. 1924. Vol. liq. (members') 9 Jan. 1931. Undertaking sold to Hydroautomat (1931) Ld., in which company shareholders were entitled to 1 fully-paid ordinary share of 5s. for every 20 shares of £1 held. Final meeting return regd. 4 June 1931 ...... **1931**

Hydrautomat (1931) Ld. Regd. 1931. Majority of capital was owned by Glenfield & Kennedy Ld. Vol. liq. (members') 11 Aug. 1967. Final meeting return regd. 18 Dec. 1967 ...... **1939**

Hydro-Carbon Syndicate Ld. Regd. 1883. Removed from Register 1896 ...... ***1886**

Hydro-Electric Power & Metallurgical Co. Ld. *See* Carbide & Electro Products Ld.

Hydro-Electric Securities Corpn. Inc. in Quebec 1926. Undertaking and assets sold to International Holdings Corpn. and company liquidated in Jan. 1959. 440,638 preferred and 321,410 common shares owned by International Holdings Ld. were cancelled, the remaining preferred shares were repaid at par on 1 Feb. 1959 and holders of the remaining common shares received 1 share of $1 in International Holdings Corpn. for every 2 shares held plus a cash distribution of 20 cents per share; shares of International Holdings Corpn. remaining unclaimed at 22 July 1961 were sold by the liquidator, the proceeds (U.S.$41·75 net per share) being available for distribution to holders entitled thereto **1969**

Hydro-Incandescent Gas Light Co. Ld. Regd. 1898. Removed from Register 1906 ...... **1901**

Hydro-Thermal Power Ld. Regd. 1929. A receiver was appointed Oct. 1931. Most of the assets were sold, the proceeds being insufficient to provide any return to debenture-holders. Receiver ceased to act 9 Dec. 1940. Struck off Register 19 Dec. 1947 ...... **1969**

Hydroleine Co. Ld. Regd. 1887. Struck off Register 31 Dec. 1895 ...... **1901**

Hygienic Soap Granulator Co. Ld. Regd. 1903. Vol. liq. 30 Aug. 1905. Removed from Register 6 June 1913 ...... ***1906**

Hygienic Food Supply Co. Ld. Regd. 1905. Court Order to wind up 1906. Removed from Register 1911 ... **1907**

Hylton, Southwick & Monkwearmouth Railway Co. Inc. by Special Act 1871. Under North Eastern Railway Act 1883 undertaking was amalgamated with that company for £130,000 ...... **1884**

Hythe & Sandgate Gas Co. Inc. by Special Act 1868. Undertaking was acquired in 1916 by Folkestone Gas and Coke Co. **1913**

I

I.C.I. (Alkali) Ld. Regd. 1881 as Brunner Mond & Co. Ld.; name changed Dec. 1931. Vol. liq. (members') 30 Dec. 1944. the undertaking was transferred to controlling company—Imperial Chemical Industries Ld. £1,144 was paid into Companies' Liquidation Account. Final meeting return regd. 22 Feb. 1951 ...... **1951**

I.C.I. (Dyestuffs) Ld. Regd. 1919 as British Dye-stuffs Corpn. Ld.; name changed 1940. Vol. liq. (members') 31 Dec. 1943, undertaking having been acquired by controlling company (Imperial Chemical Industries Ld.). Final meeting return regd. 30 Nov. 1953 ...... **1952**

I.C.I. (Explosives) Ld. Regd. 1932. Vol. liq. (members') 31 Dec. 1945. undertaking having been acquired by Imperial Chemical Industries Ld. Final meeting return regd. 5 Nov. 1965 ...... **1952**

I.C.I. (Fertilizers & Synthetic Products) Ltd. Regd. 1920 as Synthetic Ammonia & Nitrates Ld.; name changed 1931. Vol. liq. (members') 31 Dec. 1943, undertaking was transferred to controlling company—Imperial Chemical Industries Ld. Final meeting return regd. 25 June 1949 ...... **1950**

I.C.I. (General Chemicals) Ld. Regd. 1890 as United Alkali Co. Ld., name changed 1931. Vol. liq. (members') 31 Dec. 1945; the undertaking was transferred to controlling company—Imperial Chemical Industries Ld. £3,880 was paid into Companies' Liquidation Account. Final ineeting return regd. 4 June 1951 ...... **1952**

I.C.I. (Lime) Ld. Regd. 1891 as Buxton Lime Firms Co. Ld.; name changed Oct. 1931. Vol. liq. (members') 31 Dec. 1943. The undertaking was transferred to controlling company—Imperial Chemical Industries Ld. Final meeting return regd. 3 Oct. 1947... **1948**

I.C.I. Metals Ld. Regd. 1897 as Kynoch Ld.; name changed 1929. Vol. liq. (members') 31 Dec. 1945, undertaking having been acquired by controlling company (Imperial Chemical Industries Ld.). Final meeting return regd. 6 Oct. 1953 ...... **1952**

I.C.I. (Salt) Ld. Regd. 1888 as Salt Union Ld.; name changed 28 Mar. 1940. Vol. liq. (members') 31 Dec. 1942, the undertaking was transferred to controlling company—Imperial Chemical Industries Ld. £5,336 13s. 9d. was paid into Companies' Liquidation Account. Final meeting return regd. 12 Nov. 1948 ...... **1949**

I. E. S. Accumulator Co. Ld. Regd. 1895. Removed from Register 10 Feb. 1903 ...... ***1898**

I. M. (Oldham) Ld. Regd. 1907 as Iris Mill Ld.; name subsequently changed. Final meeting return regd. 21 July 1964 ...... **1959**

I. R. Process Ld. Regd. 1908. Struck off Register 1920 **1918**

I. R. T. Group Ld. *See* London Bridge Securities Ld.

I. T. S. Properties Development Co. Ld. Regd. 1932. Vol. liq. (members') 23 Mar. 1942. All shares owned by International Tea Co.'s Stores Ld. Final meeting return regd. 4 Nov. 1942 ...... **1943**

I. X. L. Gold & Silver Mining Co. Ld. Regd. 1871. Struck off Register 27 Apr. 1894 ...... **1899**

Ibex Development Co. Ld. Regd. 1896. Struck off Register 17 Nov. 1899 ...... **1900**

Ibo & Nyassa Corporation Ld. Regd. 1899. Court Order to wind up 11 Jan. 1910. Struck off Register 1927 **1910**

Ibo Investment Trust Ld. Regd. 1897. Vol. liq. 30 Sept. 1902. Final meeting return regd. 13 Nov. 1923 .... **1903**

Ibo Syndicate Ld. Regd. 1895. Vol. liq. 31 May 1897. Final meeting return regd. 2 Mar. 1905 ...... ***1897**

Ibstock Colliery Co. Ld. Regd. 1873. Wound up by Order of Court 12 Sept. 1884 ...... ***1876**

Ice Skating & Supply Co. Ld. Regd. 1894. Vol. liq. 26 Mar. 1897. Final meeting return regd. 27 June 1898 **1898**

Iceland Sulphur & Copper Co. Ld. Regd. 1882. Court Orders: to wind up Mar. 1885; to dissolve Dec. 1888 **1886**

Ichthemic Guano Co. Ld. Regd. 1929. Vol. liq. (members') 6 Apr. 1944. All capital was owned by Fisons Ld. Final meeting return regd. 29 Sept. 1944 ...... **1945**

Icke & Sharpe Ld. Regd. 1897. Vol. liq. 23 July 1907. FInal meeting return regd. 4 June 1918 ...... **1908**

Icofund (International Commodity Share Fund). Inc. in Luxembourg 28 Mar. 1968. As from 20 Apr. 1979 all assets were transferred to Energy International NV, shareholders receiving as consideration 0·4885 of a share in that company for every 0·share held. Company liquidated in Mar. 1980 ...... **1983–4**

Ida Gold Co. Ld. Regd. 1892. Vol. liq. 22 Feb. 1893. Struck off Register May 1929 ...... **1930**

Ida H. Gold Mining Co. Ld. Regd. 1900. Vol. liq. 15 Apr. 1920 for reconstruction as Ida H. Mining Co. Ld in which company shareholders were entitled to 1 share of 5s. (credited with 3s. paid) for each share of 5s. held. Final meeting return regd. 14 Oct. 1922 **1921**

VOL. FOR

Ida H. Mining Co. Ld. Regd. 1920. Vol. liq. 20 Sept. 1926. Final meeting return regd. 2 Oct. 1928 .... **1927**

Idaho-Alamo Consolidated Mines Ld. Regd. 1903. Vol. liq. Nov. 1911. Removed from Register 1912 ...... **1912**

Idaho Exploring Co. Ld. Regd 1893. Vol. liq. 4 Feb. 1897 for reconstruction as company of same name. Shareholders were entitled to 3 fully-paid ordinary shares and 1 fully-paid preferred share of 5s. for every 4 shares of 5s. (4s. 8d. paid). Final meeting return regd. 16 Nov. 1897 .... **1906**

Idaho Exploring Co. Ld. Regd 1897. Vol. liq. 17 Nov. 1905. Capital returned to contributories—6d. per share of 5s. further payments (if any) not known. Final meeting return regd. 12 Sept. 1907 .... **1906**

Idaho Gold & Silver Mines Ld. Regd. 1887. Vol. liq. 6 Aug. 1889. Final meeting return regd. 22 Feb. 1894 ***1890**

Idaho Mining Co. Ld. Regd. 1889. Vol. liq. 25 Oct. 1893. Reconstructed as Idaho Exploring Co. Ld., in which company shareholders were entitled to 1 share of 5s. (credited with 4s. 6d. paid) for each share of £1 held. Final meeting return regd. 7 Dec. 1894 .... **1897**

Ideal Films Ld. Regd. 1920. Vol. liq. (members') 9 Feb. 1943. All capital was owned by Gaumont British Picture Corporation Ld. Final meeting return regd. 1 May 1943 .... **1943**

Ideal Restaurants Ld. Undertaking and assets were acquired in 1928 by J. P. Restaurants Ld. **1929**

Ideal Sewing Machine Co. Ld. Regd. 1919. Vol. liq. 7 Jan. 1926. Undertaking and assets transferred to Simplex Ld in which company shareholders were entitled to receive, in respect of every 10 shares of 1s. held, 1 deferred share of 1s. (credited as fully-paid) and 10 ordinary shares of 1s. (credited with 8d. per share paid); shareholders taking up their full proportion of ordinary shares were entitled, in respect of every 10 shares held, to a further allotment of 1 fully-paid deferred share. Final meeting return regd. 8 Aug. 1941 .... **1926**

Idiens (John) & Sons Ld. Regd. 1899. Receiver appointed 8 Apr. 1909; ceased to act 15 Mar. 1911. Struck off Register 31 Oct. 1916 .... ***1911**

Ifton Rhyn Collieries Ld. Regd. 1873. Removed from Register 1904 .... ***1876**

Ilaro Rubber and Produce Estates Ld. Regd. 1910. Vol. liq. 22 May 1917. Final meeting return regd. 9 Oct. 1917 .... **1925**

Ildokani Oil Syndicate Ld. Regd. 1912. Vol. liq. 5 Dec. 1919. Shareholders received 100 fully-paid shares of £1 in Petroleum Co. of Ildokani Ld., for each ordinary share of £100 held or 3 fully-paid shares in that company for every 10 deferred shares of 1s. held. Final meeting return regd. 4 Jan 1920 .... **1902**

Ilen Valley Railway Co. Inc. by Special Act as Dunmanway & Skibbereen Railway Co.; name changed by Act of 1874. Under Cork, Bandon & South Coast Railway Co. Act 1909 undertaking was acquired by that company in which holders of 5% baronial guarantee and ordinary stocks received 4% preference stock; debentures were exchanged for debentures of purchasing company **1910**

Ilex Gold Mining Co. Ld. Regd. 1887. Vol. liq. 16 Nov. 1892. Final meeting return regd. 24 Sept. 1897 ..... **1893**

Ilford Gas Co. Inc. by Special Act 1899. Undertaking was acquired in 1922 by Gas Light & Coke Co., in which company stockholders were entitled to ordinary stock as follows—for every £100 ordinary A or C held—£155; for every £100 ordinary B held—£123. Holders of 7½% redeemable debenture stock were entitled to similar debenture stock in acquiring company. Holders of 4% debenture stock were entitled to £133 6s. 8d. 3% debenture stock for every £100 stock held **1923**

Ilford Gas Light and Coke Co. Ld. Regd. 1881. Dissolved by Act 1899 when undertaking was acquired by Ilford Gas Co **1899**

Ilfracombe Electric Light & Power Co. Ld. Regd. 1901. Company which was directly controlled by Edmundsons Electricity Corpn. Ld., was dissolved 1 Apr. 1948 under Electricity Act 1947 .... **1937**

Ilfracombe Gas Co. Estd. 1837; inc. by Special Act 1872. Dissolved 1 May 1949, undertaking being vested in South Western Area Gas Board under Gas Act 1948. Holders of securities were entitled to receive, in respect of each £100 unit held, British Gas 3% guaranteed stock 1990—95 as follows:

	£	s.	d.
Cons. ord. stock (5% stand.)	145	0	0
5% pref. stock	112	0	0
4% red. pref. stock	101	0	0
3½% red. deb. stock	102	0	0

.... **1952**

Ilfracombe Hotel Co. Ld. Regd. 1863. Vol. liq. (members') 27 Aug. 1946. Capital returned to contributories—£10 1s. 6d. per share of £8. Final meeting return regd. 11 May 1948 .... **1949**

VOL. FOR

Iliffe & Sons Ld. Regd. 1898 as Iliffe Sons & Sturmey Ld.; name changed July 1901. Vol. liq. 2 Nov. 1923. Final meeting return regd. 28 Oct. 1924............... **1940**

Ilirian-Palembang Petroleum Liquid Fuel Co. Ld. Regd. 1898. Vol. liq. Jan. 1907. Removed from Register 1908 .... **1907**

Ilkley Brewery and Aerated Water Co. Ld. Regd. 1873. Vol. liq. (members') 16 July 1951. Undertaking acquired by Hammonds United Breweries Ld. £506 13s. 3d. was paid into Companies' Liquidation Account. Final meeting return registered 1 Aug. 1952 .... **1953**

Ilkley Gas Co. Purchased by Ilkley Local Board **1894**

Ilkley Wells Hydropathic Co. Ld. Regd. 1884. Receiver appointed 9 Apr. 1938; ceased to act 31 Oct. 1939. All assets were sold and proceeds applied in part satisfaction of debenture. Nothing remained for unsecured creditors. Struck off Register 21 Apr. 1944 .... **1945**

Illawarra Harbour & Railway Corporation Ld. Regd. 1895. Removed from Register 1910 .... **1910**

Illingworth Carbonization Co. Ld. Regd. 1928. Receiver appointed 30 Sept. 1937. No return to debenture holders was anticipated. Struck off Register 26 Apr. 1940 .... **1941**

Illingworth (James) Ld. Regd. 1916. Vol. liq. 7 July 1931. Final meeting return regd. 1 Jan. 1932 .... **1932**

Illinois Car & Equipment Co. Inc. New Jersey 1897. Placed "in dissolution" Aug. 1931. £1 1s. 9¼d. (per share of $5) was distributed under dissolution by way of reduction of capital; it was stated that a very small surplus may eventually be available for distribution **1949**

Illinois Merchants Trust Co. Inc. Illinois 1857 as Merchants' Loan and Trust Co.; name changed Apr. 1923. Undertaking acquired in 1928 by Continental Illinois Bank and Trust Co. [later Continental Illinois National Bank and Trust Co.] **1930**

Illinois Terminal Railroad Co. See Liquidating Railway Corporation.

Illinois Traction Inc. Inc. Illinois 1923. Amalgamated in 1937 with Illinois Terminal Railroad Co. to form new company [Illinois Terminal Railroad Co.— later Liquidating Railway Corporation]. The liability for the 5% St. Louis Springfield & Peorie Railroad 1st and refunding mortgage gold bonds (later redeemed 1 Dec. 1939) and the 5% Bloomington Decatur & Champaign Railroad 1st and refunding mortgage gold bonds (later redeemed 1 Nov. 1940) was assumed by new company **1938**

Illinois Trust & Savings Bank. Absorbed in 1923 by Illinois Merchants' Trust Co. **1928**

Ilo Valley Rubber & Cocoa Plantations Ld. Regd 1910. Vol. liq. Jan. 1913. Struck off Register 1926 .... **1913**

Imani Gold Mining Co. Ld. Regd. 1902. Vol. liq. Feb. 1905. Undertaking was acquired by V. V. (Gwanda) Syndicate Ld in which company shareholders were entitled to 1 share of £1 for every 3 shares of £1 held. Removed from Register 1906 .... **1906**

Imco Participating Co. Ld. Regd. 1936. Vol. liq. 3 Oct. 1938. Final meeting return regd. 11 Jan. 1939 ..... **1939**

Imperial Accident Insurance Co. Ld. See Imperial Live Stock & General Insurance Co. Ld.

Imperial Accident Live Stock & General Insurance Co. Ld. See Imperial Live Stock & General Insurance Co. Ld.

Imperial Airways (Africa) Ld. See Airways (Africa) Ld.

Imperial Airways (Atlantic) Ld. See British Airways (Atlantic)Ld.

Imperial Airways (Bermuda) Ld. See British Airways (Bermuda) Ld.

Imperial Airways (Far East) Ld. Regd. 1935. Vol. liq. (members') 1 Nov. 1940. Capital returned to contributories—£1 5s. 2d. per share of £1. Final meeting return regd. 21 July 1941 .... **1940**

Imperial Airways Ld. Regd. 1924. Liquidated under Act of 1939. Undertaking acquired by British Overseas Airways Corporation. Capital returned to contributories—£1 14s. 6·615d. per ordinary share of £1. Final meeting return regd. 13 Oct. 1941 .... **1941**

Imperial Airways (Nigeria & Gold Coast) Ld. Regd. 1935. Vol. liq. (members') 1 May 1940. Capital returned to contributories—£1 3s. 6d. per share of £1. Final meeting return regd. 18 Sept. 1940 .... **1940**

Imperial Airways (Repair Works) Ld. Regd. 1937. Vol. liq. (members') 1 May 1940. Capital returned to contributories—£3 3s. 5d. per ordinary share of £1. Final meeting return regd. 18 Sept. 1940 .... **1940**

Imperial Airways (South Africa) Ld. See Airways (Africa) Ld.

Imperial & Foreign Corpn. Ld. Regd. 1911. Vol. liq. (members') 4 Dec. 1953. Capital returned to contributories—3½d. per preference share of 8s.

VOL. FOR

Final meeting return regd. 4 Feb. 1955; £2,299 12s. 6d. was paid into Companies' Liquidation Account — **1956**

Imperial and Foreign Investment and Agency Corporation Ld. Regd. 1889. Vol. liq. 25 May 1892. Reconstructed as New Imperial Investment Co. Ld., in which company stockholders were entitled to £25 deferred stock for every £100 deferred stock held or to £35 deferred stock for each founders' share held or to £100 preferred stock for every £100 preferred stock held. Final meeting return regd. 27 July 1893 — **1899**

Imperial & Foreign Investments Corporation Ld. Regd. 1900. Vol. liq. 11 Aug. 1903. Struck off Register 18 Jan. 1921 — **1904**

Imperial & General Securities Ld. Regd. 1906. Struck off Register 27 Mar. 1953 — **1942**

Imperial Bank Ld. Regd. 1862. Vol. liq. 5 Jan. 1893. Business was acquired by London Joint Stock Bank Ld. Capital returned to contributories—£23 per share. Final meeting return regd. 27 July 1894 .... — **1895**

Imperial Bank of India. Inc. in 1920 by Special Act of Government of India. On 1 July 1955 the shares were transferred to Reserve Bank of India. Shareholders receiving compensation at rate of Rs. 1,765 10 annas per fully-paid share and Rs. 431 12 annas 4 pies per partly-paid share, and the undertaking was acquired by State Bank of India. The Bank ceased to carry on business in Great Britain on 31 Dec. 1963 — **1965**

Imperial Banking Co. Ld. (of Melbourne). In liquidation in 1892 — **1892**

Imperial Brazilian Collieries Ld. Regd. 1871. Vol. liq. 4 July 1876. Final meeting return regd. 27 Dec. 1877 — ***1876**

Imperial Brazilian, Natal & Nova Cruz Railway Co. Ld. See Natal & Nova Cruz (Brazilian) Railway Ld.

Imperial British East Africa Co. Ld. Inc. by Royal Charter 1888. The charter, concession and property in East Africa were surrendered to the British Government for £250,000 in cash — **1896**

Imperial Chemical Co. Ld. Regd. 1872. Removed from Register 1884 — ***1878**

Imperial Chest & General Agency, Ld. Regd. 1906 as Imperial Tea Chests Agency Ld.; name changed Jan. 1932. Vol. liq. 24 July 1957. Final meeting return regd. 28 Nov. 1957 — **1939**

Imperial College Ld. Regd. 1887. Vol. liq. Dec. 1890. Removed from Register 1906 — **1891**

Imperial Continental Water Corporation Ld. Regd. 1879. Court Orders: to wind up 6 Dec. 1884; to dissolve 16 Dec. 1898 — **1886**

Imperial Continental Waterworks Ld. Regd. 1897. Removed from Register 1910 — **1910**

Imperial Contract Corporation Ld. Regd. 1897. Removed from Register 26 July 1912 — ***1903**

Imperial Co-operative Stores Ld. Regd. 1897. Vol. liq. 23 Sept. 1897. Final meeting return regd. 21 June 1898 — **1898**

Imperial Credit Co. Ld. Regd. 1871. Vol. liq. Mar. 1881. Final meeting return regd. 14 June 1889 — **1884**

Imperial Credit Co. Ld. Regd. 1881. Vol. liq. May 1883. All shares were surrendered and paid off. Final meeting return regd. 14 June 1889 — **1884**

Imperial Direct Line Ld. Regd. 1901 as Imperial Direct West Indian Mail Service Co. Ld.; name changed June 1911. Vol. liq. 18 June 1936. Dissolved before 1951 — **1937**

Imperial Direct West Indian Mail Service Co. Ld. See above.

Imperial Discount Co. Ld. Regd. 1875. Vol. liq. 22 Aug. 1883. Final meeting return regd. 28 Mar. 1884 .... — ***1884**

Imperial Ethiopian Rubber Co. Ld. Regd. 1907. Vol. liq. 8 Nov. 1915. Final meeting return regd. 23 Mar. 1916 — **1916**

Imperial Federation Insurance Corporation Ld Regd. 1902. Removed from Register 29 May 1906......... — ***1904**

Imperial Fire Insurance Co. See Imperial Insurance Co. Ld.

Imperial Food Supplies Ld. Regd. 1902. Vol. liq. July 1908. Undertaking and assets were acquired by London Central Markets Cold Storage Co. Ld., in which company shareholders were entitled to about 2 shares of £1 for every 3 shares held. Removed from Register 1912 — **1909**

Imperial Gas Co. Under Act of 1869 the undertaking was acquired by Gas Light and Coke Co. .... — **1888**

Imperial Gold Co. Ld. Regd. 1897. Vol. liq. 1903. Shareholders were entitled to participate in distribution of 27,333 shares in Golden Age Consolidated Ld. Removed from Register 1905 — **1904**

Imperial Gold Mines Ld. Regd. 1935. Vol. liq. (members') Aug. 1956. No capital was returned to contributories. Final meeting return regd. 9 Jan. 1957 — **1958**

Imperial Goonbarrow Clays Ld. Regd. 1924. Vol. liq. (members') 28 June 1933. All shares owned by English China Clays Ld. Final meeting return regd. 7 Feb. 1935 — **1934**

VOL. FOR

Imperial Hotel, Cork, Ld. Inc. Dublin 1889. Vol. liq. (members') 28 Mar. 1946. Capital returned to contributories—£5 per preference share and £2 per ordinary share (both of £5). Final meeting held 30 Dec. 1947 — **1950**

Imperial Hydropathic Hotel Co., Blackpool Ld. Regd. 1877. Vol. liq. 28 July 1897. Reconstructed as company of same name (later Imperial Hotel Blackpool Ld.). Final meeting return regd.4 July 1898 — **1908**

Imperial Insurance Co. See Imperial Insurance Co. Ld.

Imperial Insurance Co. Ld. Est. 1803 as Imperial Insurance Co.; name changed in 1869 to Imperial Fire Insurance Co.; regd. as limited and name changed as above 1891. Vol. liq. 26 May 1902. Undertaking was acquired by Alliance Assurance Co. Ld., in which company shareholders were entitled to 25 fully-paid shares of £1 for every 8 shares of £20 (£5 paid) held. Final meeting return regd. 3 Dec. 1909 — **1903**

Imperial Jarrah Wood Corporation Ld. Regd. 1898. The undertaking was acquired in 1902 by Millars' Karri and Jarrah Co. (1902) Ld. (later Millars' Timber and Trading Co. Ld.), in which company shareholders were entitled to 1 share of £1 for every share of £1 held. Removed from Register 1905 — **1904**

Imperial Life Insurance Co. Established 1820. Undertaking was acquired in 1902 by Alliance Assurance Co. Ld., in which company shareholders were entitled to 3 shares of £1 (credited as fully-paid) for every 4 shares of £20 (£4 paid) held — **1903**

Imperial Light Ld. Regd. 1905 as Imperial Automatic Light Ld.; name changed Aug. 1909. Vol. liq. (members') 16 Oct. 1933. No capital returned to contributories. Final meeting return regd. 19 Dec. 1933 — **1933**

Imperial Live Stock & General Insurance Co. Ld. Regd. 1878 as Imperial Live Stock Insurance Association Ld.; name changed 1897 to Imperial Accident Live Stock & General Insurance Co. Ld. and in 1922 as above. Vol. liq. (members') 30 May 1947. Undertaking acquired by Commercial Union Assurance Co. Ld. Final meeting return regd. 2 Mar. 1948 .... — **1939**

Imperial Marine Insurance Co. Ld. Regd. 1871. Vol. liq. 12 Jan. 1882. Final meeting return regd. 17 Nov. 1892 — **1882**

Imperial Mexican Railway Co. Ld. See Mexican Railway Co. Ld.

Imperial Monomark Ld. Regd. 5 July 1924 as British Bureau Ld.; name changed to British Monomarks Ld. on 7 July 1925, to B. M. Group Ld. on 1 Nov. 1960 and to above title 20 Sept. 1965. Winding-up order 29 Apr. 1974 — **1984–5**

Imperial Mortgage and Debenture Co. Ld. Regd. 1892. Vol. liq. 1 Mar. 1927. Final meeting return regd. 1 Mar. 1928 — **1928**

Imperial Navigation Coal Co. Ld. Regd. 1900. Vol. liq. 23 Jan. 1928. Final meeting return regd. 9 Nov. 1932 — **1928**

Imperial Ottoman Ice Co. Ld. Regd. 1886. Assets were sold in 1891 by Receiver for debenture holders. Removed from Register 1894 — **1893**

Imperial Paper Mills of Canada Ld. Inc. Ontario 1903. Property sold by order of the Ontario Court. Prior lien bonds were repaid to the extent of 65¼% ...... — **1919**

Imperial Press Ld. Regd. 1873. Removed from Register 1903 — **1900**

Imperial Property Investment Co. Ld. Regd. 1875. Vol. liq. 17 July 1894. Reconstructed as company of same name. Shareholders were entitled to 1 preference and 1 ordinary share of £5 (each credited with £2 10s. paid) in new company for each share of £10 (£5 paid) held. Debenture holders were entitled to an equal amount of debentures in new company. Final meeting return regd. 28 Nov. 1900 — **1899**

Imperial Property Investment Co. Ld. Regd. 1894. Vol. liq. (members') 12 Nov. 1931. Amalgamated London Properties Ld., was sole shareholder. Final meeting return regd. 30 June 1934 — **1932**

Imperial Russian Cotton & Jute Factory Ld. Regd. 1886. Vol. liq. 25 May 1910. Final meeting return regd. 23 Mar. 1921 — **1911**

Imperial S. C. Acetylene Gas Co. Ld. Regd. 1898. Vol. liq. 7 Oct. 1904. Final meeting return regd. 17 Mar. 1906 — ***1905**

Imperial Standard Timber Ld. Regd. 1904. Removed from Register 1911 — **1909**

Imperial Steamship Co. Ld. Regd. 1903. Vol. liq. 16 July 1917. Final meeting return regd. 24 Feb. 1919 .... — ***1918**

Imperial Tea Chests Agency Ld. See Imperial Chest & General Agency Ld.

Imperial Tobacco Corporation of Persia Ld. Regd. 1890. Vol. liq. 9 May 1892. Final meeting return regd. 4 July 1893 — **1893**

VOL. FOR

Imperial Tramways Co. Ld. Regd. 1878. Reconstructed 1898 as company of same name. Shareholders were entitled to 1 fully-paid ordinary share of £10 for each ordinary share of £6 held or 1 fully-paid preference share of £10 for each preference share of £10. Removed from Register 1904 .... **1899**

Imperial Tramways Co. Ld. 1898. Vol. liq. (members') 12 May 1930. Capital returned to contributories—£15 14s. 9½d. per preference or ordinary share of £10. Final meeting return regd. 6 May 1931 .... **1931**

Imperial Union Accident Assurance Co. Ld. Regd. 1875. Vol. liq. 5 Sept. 1894. Business was acquired by Ocean Accident & Guarantee Corporation Ld. Final meeting return regd. 30 Oct. 1896............... **1908**

Imperial Water & Gas Corporation Ld. Regd. 1878. Removed from Register 1905 .... ***1882**

Imperial Western Australian Corporation Ld. Regd. 1894. Vol. liq. 23 Aug. 1898. Final meeting return regd. 12 July 1902 .... **1899**

Imported Meat Co. Ld. Regd. 16 Jan. 1885. Court Orders: to wind up 10 Dec. 1885; to dissolve 31 Jan. 1889 .... ***1887**

Importers & Exporters Marine Insurance Co. Ld. Regd. 1918. Court Order to wind up 27 Oct. 1930. Struck off Register 24 Oct. 1939 .... **1940**

Importers & Traders Bank of New York. In 1923 this company was amalgamated with Equitable Trust Co., of New York **1924**

Improved Britannia Motors Ld. Regd. 1899. Vol. liq. 10 July 1903. Final meeting return regd. 7 Mar. 1905 ***1904**

Improved Chilling & Transport Ld. Regd. 1919. Vol. liq. 26 Sept. 1921. Final meeting return regd. 16 May 1923 .... **1922**

Improved Chilling Co. Ld. Regd. 1906. Vol. liq. 26 June 1919. The undertaking was sold to Improved Chilling & Transport Co. Ld in which company shareholders were entitled to 1 fully-paid share of £1 plus £1 in cash for every 2 shares of 2s. held; a further cash payment was expected but is not known. Final meeting return regd. 1 June 1921 .... **1920**

Improved Cork Pavement Co. Ld. Regd. 1898. Removed from Register 1910 .... **1900**

Improved Electric Glow Lamp Co. Ld. Regd. 1896 as International Improved Electric Co. Ld.; name changed 28 July 1896. Vol. liq. 21 June 1900. Final meeting return regd. 2 Nov. 1909 .... ***1906**

Improved Electric Supplies Ld. Regd. 1905. Vol. liq. 6 Mar. 1907. Court Order to wind up 16 Apr. 1907. Liquidator released 29 Aug. 1910. Removed from Register 6 June 1913 .... ***1908**

Improved Hydro-Carbon Processes Ld. Regd. 1930 as Bruzac Hydro-Carbon Processes Ld.; name changed Apr. 1931. Directly controlled by Anglo-Foreign Oil & General Trust Ld. Struck off Register 25 Apr. 1939 .... **1936**

Improved Steel Co. Ld. Regd. 1920. Vol. liq. (members') 23 Oct. 1935. All shares were owned by Dunlop Rubber Co. Ld. (later Dunlop Co. Ld) Final meeting return regd. 19 Dec. 1935 .... **1936**

Improved Twisted Steel Bar Co. (1919) Ld. See Twisted Steel Bar Co. Ld.

Improved Whaling Ld. Regd. 1920. Vol. liq. 17 Sept. 1925. Controlled by Lever Brothers Ld. (later Unilever Ld.). Final meeting return regd. 23 Apr. 1926 .... **1926**

Improving Securities Trust Ld. Regd. 1936. Vol. liq. (creditors') 11 July 1939. Assets realised insufficient to pay creditors in full. Final meeting return regd. 8 Jan. 1942 .... **1940**

Imuris Mines Ld. Regd. 1889. Reconstructed 1892 as New Imuris Mines Ld., in which company shareholders were entitled to 1 share of £1 (credited with 15s. paid) for each share of £1 held. Removed from Register 1907 .... **1893**

Inambari Gold Dredging Concessions Ld. Regd. 1908. Receiver appointed in Apr. 1912. Struck off Register 1918 .... **1914**

Inambari Para-Rubber Estates Ld. Regd. 1907. Vol. liq. 4 Dec. 1922. Final meeting return regd. 7 Feb. 1924 **1923**

Inca Gold Development Corporation of Peru Ld. Regd. 1903. Vol. liq. 9 Dec. 1908. Property and assets were sold to Inambari Gold Dredging Concessions Ld., in which company shareholders were entitled to 1 ordinary share of £1 for every 9 ordinary shares of £1 held or 1 preference share of £1 for every 2 preference shares of £1 held. Struck off Register 18 Jan. 1921 .... **1909**

Inca (Matabeleland) Development Co. Ld. Regd. 1895. Vol. liq. Mar. 1908. Removed from Register 1908 **1909**

Incahuara Dredging Co. Ld. Regd. 1907. Vol. liq. Jan 1910 for reconstruction as Incahuara Gold Dredging Co. Ld in which company shareholders were entitled to 1 fully-paid share of £1 for each ordinary

VOL. FOR

A share of £1 held or 1 share of £1 (credited with 15s. paid) for each ordinary share of £1 held. Removed from Register 1912 .... **1910**

Incahuara Gold Dredging Co. Ld. Regd. 1910. Vol. liq. 3 Jan. 1912. Vol. liq. for reconstruction as Incahuara Ld., in which company shareholders were entitled to 1 share of £1 (credited with 16s. paid) for each share of £1 held. Final meeting return regd. 8 Dec. 1913 **1912**

Incahuara Ld. Regd. 1912. Vol. liq. 8 Oct. 1912. Final meeting return regd. 3 June 1915 .... **1913**

Incandescent Fire-Mantel & Stove Co. Ld. Regd. 1897. Vol. liq. 1 Dec. 1900. Final meeting return regd. 3 Feb. 1902 .... **1901**

Incandescent Gas Light Co. Ld. Regd. 1887. Vol. liq. 29 Mar. 1898. Reconstructed as Welsbach Incandescent Gas Light Co. Ld. Final meeting return regd. 17 Mar. 1889 .... **1898**

Inch Kenneth Rubber Estates Ld. Regd. Edinburgh 1904. Vol. liq. July 1933. Undertaking and assets were acquired by Inch Kenneth Kajang Rubber Ld., in which company shareholders were entitled to 5 shares of £1 (credited with 15s. paid) for every 3 shares of £1 held. Final meeting return regd. 16 May 1934 .... **1934**

Inchinnan Tyre & Rubber Co. Ld. Regd. Edinburgh 1927 as India Tyre & Rubber Co. (Great Britain) Ld.; name changed to India Tyre & Rubber Co. Ld. in Nov. 1933 and as above in Oct. 1936. Vol. liq. (members') 9 Nov. 1936. Undertaking acquired by India Tyre & Rubber Co. Ld. for 850,000 fully-paid shares of £1. which were subsequently acquired by Dunlop Rubber Co. Ld. (later Dunlop Co: Ld.) at a price sufficient to pay 27s. 6d. per preference share of £1 or 3s. 3d. per ordinary share of 1s.; shareholders were given an option (since expired) to purchase ordinary shares of Dunlop Rubber Co. Ld., £881 6s. 1d. was paid to Accountant of the Court (see preface). Final meeting return regd. 10 Aug. 1937 .... **1937**

Inchterff Sand Quarry Co. Ld. Regd. Edinburgh 1915. Vol. liq. (members') 28 Aug. 1933. Final meeting return regd. 21 Sept. 1934 .... **1934**

Incomati Co. Ld. See below.

Incomati Estates, Ld. Regd. 1914 as Incomati Co. Ld.; name changed in May 1915. Vol. liq. (members') 20 Aug. 1953. Preference and preferred ordinary shares were repaid at 22s. and 26s. per share (of £1) respectively in Sept. 1953. Capital returned to contributories: £2 19s. 11·3d. per ordinary share (of £1). Final meeting return regd. 18 Feb. 1958 .... **1958**

Incorporated Anglo-Roumanian Industries Ld. Regd. 1923. Struck off Register 1927 .... ***1928**

Incorporated Exploration Co. of British Columbia Ld. Regd. 1897. Reconstructed 1900 as Slough Creek Ld in which company shareholders were entitled to 1 share of £1 (credited with 18s. paid) for each share of £1 held. Removed from Register 1908 .... **1901**

Ind Coope & Co. Ld. Regd. 1886. Certain assets were acquired from 1 Oct. 1910 by Ind Coope & Co. (1912) Ld., (later Ind Coope Ld.), for £700,000 in 4% mortgage debenture stock, £415,520 in income debenture stock and £276,737 in fully-paid shares of £1. These securities were distributed among the holders of A mortgage debenture, B mortgage debenture and irredeemable debenture stocks. Struck off Register 24 Feb. 1922 .... **1914**

Ind Coope (North East) Ld. Regd. 1890 as Lichfield Brewery Co. Ld.; name subsequently changed. All ordinary capital was owned by Ind Coope & Allsopp Ld. (later Ind Coope Ld.) Vol. liq. 14 Apr. 1966. Final meeting return regd. 30 Aug. 1966 .... **1959**

Ind Coope (South Midlands) Ld. Regd. 1887 as Walter Showell & Sons Ld.; name changed to Showells Brewery Co., Ld. 1894 and as above Sept. 1959. All capital was owned by Ind Coope Ld. Vol. liq. 28 Jan. 1966. Final meeting return regd. 22 Sept. 1966 .... **1960**

Ind Coope (South Wales) Ld. Regd. 1886 as Norfolk & Suffolk Brewery Co. Ld.; name changed to Colchester Brewing Co. Ld. 1887 and as above 1960. All capital was owned by Ind Coope Ld. Vol. liq. 4 Apr. 1966. Final meeting return regd. 19 July 1966 ...... **1960**

Indemnity Association Ld. Regd. 1903. Vol. liq. 19 Dec. 1911. Final meeting return regd. 4 June 1914 ...... **1912**

Independent Gaslight & Coke Co. Under Act of 1864 the undertaking was acquired by Gas Light and Coke Co........... **1888**

Indestructible Rolled Steel Axle Box Ld. Regd. 1899. Reconstructed 1902 as Rolled Steel Axle Box & Forge Co. Ld in which company shareholders were entitled to 1 share of £1 (credited with 16s. paid) for each share of £1 held. Removed from Register 1904 **1904**

India Corporation Ld. Regd. 1899. Removed from Register 1906 .... **1903**

See Stock Exchange Year-Book.

VOL. FOR

India Development Ld. Regd. 1901. Vol. liq. 14 May 1908. Final meeting return regd. 21 Nov. 1918..... **1909**

India Rubber Estates Co. Ld. Regd. 1890. Removed from Register 1907 ... **1892**

India Rubber (Mexico) Ld. Regd. 1897. Removed from Register 1906 ... **1902**

India Tyre & Rubber Co. (Great Britain) Ld. *See* Inchinnan Tyre & Rubber Co. Ld.

Indian & Ceylon Tea Trust Co. Ld. Regd. 1897. Removed from Register 1909 ... **1900**

Indian & Colonial Goldfields Ld. Regd. 1896. Vol. liq. Mar. 1912. Capital returned to contributories—6*d*. per share of £1 in Oct. 1912; further payments (if any) not known. Removed from Register 1913 .... **1913**

Indian & Eastern Druggists (1922) Ld. Regd. 1922. Vol. liq. (members') 8 Nov. 1935. Capital returned to contributories—17*s*. 9*d*. per preference share of £1. Final meeting return regd. 17 Feb. 1936 .... **1936**

Indian & Oriental Electrical Storage & Works Co. Ld. Regd. 1882. Vol. liq. May 1885. Final meeting return regd. 2 July 1887 .... **1886**

Indian Branch Railway Co. Ld. *See* Oude & Rohikund Railway Co.

Indian Collieries Syndicate Ld. Regd. 1902. Vol. liq. 29 Dec. 1916. Final meeting return regd. 17 July 1918 **1917**

Indian Consolidated Gold Co. Ld. Regd. 1881. Vol. liq. 30 Apr. 1890. Reconstructed as Indian Consolidated Gold Mining Co. Ld., in which company shareholders were entitled to 1 share of £1 (credited with 17*s*. paid) for each share of £1 held. Final meeting return regd. 14 Jan.1893.... **1893**

Indian Consolidated Gold Mining Co. Ld. Regd. 1890. Reconstructed 1893 as Kempinkote Gold Field Ld., in which company shareholders were entitled to 1 share of 5*s*. (credited with 2*s*. paid) for each share of 10*s*. held. Removed from Register 1904 ... **1900**

Indian Electric Supply & Traction Co. Ld. *See* Cawnpore Electric Supply Corpn. Ld.

Indian Glenrock Gold Mining Co. Ld. Regd. 1880. Vol. liq. 12 Feb. 1884. Property was acquired by Glenrock Co. Ld., for 182,428 shares of £1. Final meeting return regd. 28 June 1892 .... **1885**

Indian Glenrock (Wynaad) Co. Ld. Regd. 1901. Vol. liq. Dec. 1908 for reconstruction as Nilambur Rubber Estates Ld in which company shareholders were entitled to 1 share of 3*s*. (credited with 1*s*. paid) for every share of 10*s*. held. Removed from Register 1910 ... **1909**

Indian Gold Estates Purchasing Co. Ld. Regd. 1881. Removed from Register 1905 ... *****1885**

Indian Gold Mines Co. Ld. Regd. Edinburgh 1890. Vol. liq. Oct. 1893. A return of about 3*d*. per share was expected. Final meeting return regd. 11 Feb. 1898 **1894**

Indian Hardwoods Ld. Regd. 1913. Vol. liq. 17 Aug. 1923. Practically all capital held by Eastern Development Corporation Ld. Final meeting return regd. 27 Nov. 1923 ... **1923**

Indian, Kingston & Sandhurst Gold Mining Co. Ld. Regd. 1881. Court Orders: to wind up 1 Dec. 1882; to dissolve 7Aug. 1893 ... **1883**

Indian Manganese Co. Ld. Regd. 1904. Vol. liq. (members') 24 Sept. 1936. Capital returned to contributories—17*s*. 11·409*d*. per share of £1. £533 12*s*. 5*d*. was paid into Companies' Liquidation Account. Final meeting return regd. 22 Sept. 1941 **1937**

Indian Mica Co. Ld. Regd. 1898. Removed from Register 1907 ... **1905**

Indian Midland Railway Co. Ld. Regd. 1885. Vol. liq. Dec. 1910. Stock was repaid at par on 31 Dec. 1910. Secretary of State assumed liabilities in respect of debentures. Removed from Register 1911 .... **1911**

Indian Mines Development Syndicate Ld. Regd. 1903. Reconstructed 1907 as Indian Mines Syndicate Ld in which company shareholders were entitled to 1 share of 4*s*. (credited with 3*s*. paid) for each share of 4*s*. held. Removed from Register 1909.................. **1908**

Indian Mines Syndicate Ld. Regd. 1907. Vol. liq. Nov. 1908. Removed from Register 1911 .... **1909**

Indian Motor Taxi-Cab Co. Ld. Regd. 1909. Vol. liq. 2 Dec. 1919. Final meeting return regd. 20 Jan. 1922 **1920**

Indian Peninsula Rubber & Tea Estates, Ld. Regd. 1909. Vol. liq. 20 May 1919. Reconstructed as company of same name. Shareholders were entitled to 1 share of £1 (credited with 12*s*. 6*d*. paid) in new company for each share of £1 held. Debenture holders were entitled to an equal amount of similar debentures in new company. Final meeting return regd. 22 Jan. 1921 ... **1919**

Indian Peninsula Rubber & Tea Estates Ld. Regd. 1919. Vol. liq. (members') 29 Aug. 1950. Capital returned to contributories—6·65*d*. per share of 6*d*. Final meeting return regd. 28 Aug. 1951 ... **1952**

Indian Phenix Gold Mining Co. Ld. Regd. 1880. Vol. liq. July 1883. Amalgamated with Indian Consolidated

VOL. FOR

Gold Co. Ld., in which company shareholders were entitled to an equal number of shares. Final meeting return regd. 10 Feb. 1885 ... **1884**

Indian Queen's Consols Ld. Regd. Truro 1880. Vol. liq. 2 Nov. 1882. Final meeting return regd. 23 Feb. 1883 **1883**

Indian Tea Co. of Cachar Ld. Regd. 1863. Vol. liq. (members) 16 July 1952. Capital returned to contributories—£6 19*s*. 10*d*. per share of £10. £220 2*s*. 9*d*. was paid into Companies' Liquidation Account in respect of unclaimed dividends £752 3*s*. 4*d*. in respect of unclaimed distributions. Final meeting returned regd. 11 Jan. 1956 ... **1957**

Indian Transcontinental Airways Ld. Direct controlling interest was held by Imperial Airways Ld. **1940**

Indian Trevelyan Gold Mining Co. Ld. Regd. 1880. Vol. liq. July 1883. Undertaking and assets were acquired by Indian Glenrock Gold Mining Co. Ld., in which company shareholders were entitled to an equal number of fully-paid shares of £1. Final meeting return regd. 13 Nov. 1883 ... **1884**

Indian Zoedone Co. Ld. Regd. 1881. Vol. liq. Oct. 1883. Court Order to continue winding up under supervision 15 Oct. 1883. Final meeting return regd. 9 Oct. 1891 ... **1884**

Indianapolis Breweries Ld. Regd 1889. Vol. liq. (creditors') 19 Dec. 1929. Debentures were not repaid in full. Final meeting return regd. 4 Dec. 1934 .... **1930**

Indicators Ld. Regd. 1919. Court Order to wind up 27 Nov. 1923. Struck off Register Dec. 1934 .... **1935**

Indigo Co. Ld. Regd. 1886. Struck off Register 31 Dec. 1895 ... **1899**

Indimba Tin Alluvials Ld. Regd. 1912. Struck off Register 20 Mar. 1923 ... **1916**

Indo Burma Oilfields (1920) Ld. Regd. 1920. Receiver appointed in July 1926. Struck off Register 7 Dec. 1937 ... **1938**

Indo-China Tea Association Ld. Regd. 1881. Vol. liq. Nov. 1886. Final meeting return regd. 18 Jan. 1888 **1887**

Indo-Chinese Hevea Rubber Estates Ld. Regd. 1918. Vol. liq. 28 June 1920. Final meeting return regd. 3 Aug. 1922 ... **1921**

Indo-European Telegraph Co. Ld. Regd. 1868. Vol. liq. (members') 8 Nov. 1932. Capital returned to contributories—£20,871 16*s*. 3*d*. *plus* certain assets in specie. £2,342 was paid into Companies' Liquidation Account in respect of dividends and £3,930 5*s*. 5*d*. in respect of purchase consideration of shares. Final meeting return regd. 16 Sept. 1936 .... **1933**

Industrial & Exploration Co. Ld. *See* Development & Exploration Co. Ld.

Industrial & Life Assurance Amalgamation Co. Ld. Inc. in Dublin 1938. Company's business was merged. from 1 Jan. 1947, with that of the Irish Assurance Co. Ld and the company was placed in vol. liq. Shares held in Irish Assurance Co. Ld. were distributed to shareholders of this company. Final meeting return regd 9 May 1949 ... **1950**

Industrial Appliances Ld. Regd. 1915. Vol. liq. 18 Sept. 1924. Directly controlled by Industrial Appliances & Oil & Coal Corporation Ld. Final meeting return regd. 11 Apr. 1925 ... **1934**

Industrial Appliances & Oil & Coal Corporation Ld. Regd. 1920 as United Oil & Coal Corporation Ld.; name changed Dec. 1924. Vol. liq. (members') 8 May 1934. Capital returned to contributories—4*s*. 7*d*. per preference share of £1. Final meeting return regd. 25 Jan. 1936 ... **1935**

Industrial Assurance Co. of Great Britain Ld. Regd. 1886. Vol. liq. 2 May 1890. Court Order to continue winding up under supervision 29 May 1890. Final meeting return regd. 11 Aug. 1899 ... *****1891**

Industrial Bank Ld. Regd. 1899. Vol. liq. 6 Dec. 1905. Final meeting return regd. 5 Sept. 1907 ... *****1907**

Industrial Bank of Scotland Ld. Regd. in Edinburgh 1921. Court Order to wind up 6 Sept. 1945. The right to company's name was sold and a new company was registered with that title on 13 Apr. 1946. Return of final meeting regd. 24 June 1948 .... **1949**

Industrial Contract Corporation Ld. Regd. 1897 as Auxiliary Stores Ld.; name changed Aug. 1898. Vol. liq. 6 Sept. 1899. Court Order to wind up 28 Nov. 1899. Final meeting return regd. 17 June 1901 .... **1900**

Industrial Credit Co. Ld. Regd. 1905. Court Order to wind up Apr. 1909. Removed from Register 1914 **1910**

Industrial Finance Corporation Ld. Regd. 1897. Removed from Register 1911 ... **1905**

Industrial Glass Works Ld. Regd. 1920. Vol. liq. 8 Feb. 1921. Final meeting return regd. 13 Apr. 1923 .... **1922**

Industrial Housing Association Ld. Regd. 1922. Vol. liq. 5 Apr. 1948. The shares were repaid in full in July 1948. Final meeting return regd. 30 July 1948 ...... **1949**

Industrial Housing Association (No. 2) Ld. Regd. 1924. Vol. liq. 1 Apr. 1960. Capital repaid 2 Aug. 1960 (*a*) 12 shares of £1 each, fully-paid, at 20*s*. per share and

VOL. FOR

(b) 431,725 shares of £1, 4s. per share paid, at 4s. per share. Final meeting return regd. 5 Sept. 1960...... **1961**

Industrial Insurance Corporation Ld. Regd. 1896. Removed from Register 1901 **1900**

Industrial Mutual Trust Ld. Regd. 1919. Struck off Register 30 Mar. 1951 **1952**

Industrial Rubber Manufacturers Ld. Regd. 1928. Court Order to wind up 4 June 1930. Struck off Register 21 Sept. 1937 **1938**

Industrial Securities Co. Ld. Regd. 1908 as General & Industrial Securities Co. Ld.; name changed as above 1909. Winding up Order 4 Oct. 1965. Struck off Register 11 Dec. 1970 **1947**

Industrial Securities Investment Co. Ld. Regd. 1891. Removed from Register 1907 **1897**

Industrial Silica Ld. Regd. 1923. Debenture holders took over all the assets. Struck off Register Apr. 1929 **1930**

Industrial Steels Ld. Regd. 1922. Vol. liq. (members') 26 Oct. 1934. English Steel Corporation Ld., was sole beneficial owner of issued share capital. Debenture holders were satisfied in full. Final meeting return regd. 6 Dec. 1934 **1935**

Industrial Storage Battery Syndicate Ld. Regd. 1903. Vol. liq. 28 Dec. 1904. Removed from Register 1908 **1905**

Industrial Syndicate Ld. Regd. 1897. Removed from Register 1906 **1909**

Industrial Tea and Rubber Trust Ld. Regd. 1924. Vol. liq. (members') Dec. 1930 for reconstruction under same name. Shareholders were entitled to 1 fully-paid share of 2s. in new company for every 5 shares of 2s. held. Struck off Register 20 Feb.1945 .... **1948**

Industrial Tea & Rubber Trust Ld. Regd. 1931. Vol. liq. (creditors') 23 Apr. 1935. No capital returned to contributories. Final meeting return regd. 30 Mar. 1936 **1936**

Industrial Traders Co. Ld. Inc. Guernsey 1904. Dissolved before 1948 **1910**

Industrial Trust Co. of Ireland Ld. Regd. Dublin 1925. Vol. liq. Aug. 1933 **1934**

Industries Development Co. Ld. Regd. 1899. Struck off Register 20 Nov. 1908 **1908**

Inez Gold Mining Co. Ld. Regd. 1903. Vol. liq. 12 Feb. 1918. Final meeting return regd. 22 May 1919 .... **1918**

Ingall, Parsons, Clive & Co. Ld. Regd. 1888. Vol. liq. 12 July 1894. Reconstructed as company of same name. Holders of shares of £5 were entitled to an equal number of shares of £2 of the same class, credited as fully-paid. Final meeting return regd. 11 Dec. 1896 **1894**

Ingamasonga Reef Ld. Regd. 1895. Vol. liq. 14 Jan. 1898. Undertaking acquired by Mozambique Consolidated Mines Ld in which company shareholders received 1 share of 10s. (credited with 9s. paid) for each fully-paid 10s. share. Final meeting return regd. 22 Sept. 1898 **1898**

Ingatestone & Fryerning Gas Light & Coke Co. Ld. Undertaking was acquired in 1926 for £1,700 in cash by Brentwood Gas Co **1927**

Ingersoll-Sergeant Drill Co. Ld. Regd. 1897. Undertaking and assets were acquired in 1905 by Ingersoll-Rand Co. for $2,000,000 in common stock and $3,125,000 in preferred stock. Shareholders were entitled to $7·50 preferred stock for each ordinary share of £1 held or $10 preferred stock and $10 common stock for each ordinary share of £1 held. Debenture stockholders were entitled to either repayment in cash at 105% or £105 bonds of new company for every £100 held (exchange at $4·86 to £). Removed from Register 1906 **1906**

Ingham's Thornhill Collieries Ld. Regd. 1898. Vol. liq. (members') 22 Mar. 1951. Final meeting return regd.28 Feb. 1958 **1948**

Ingleton Collieries Ld. Regd. 1903. Vol. liq. Jan. 1910. Removed from Register 1911 **1910**

Ingliston Extended Gold Mines Ld. Regd. 1904. Struck off Register Oct.1928 **1930**

Ingram Houses Ld. Regd. 1900. Vol. liq. 29 Nov. 1920. Final meeting return regd. 30 Mar. 1922 **1921**

Inkermann Combined Gold Mines Ld. Regd. 1896. Vol. liq. 28 Apr. 1898. Reconstructed as New Inkerman Mines Ld in which company shareholders were entitled to 1 share of £1 (credited with 16s. paid) for each share of £1 held. Final meeting return regd. 1 May 1899 **1904**

Inkran Cotton Estates Ld. Regd. 1911. Struck off Register 19 June 1936 **1937**

Inlaid Linoleum (Thomson's Patent) Co. Ld. Regd. 1898. Vol. liq. 26 June 1900. Court Order to continue winding up under supervision 12 Mar. 1901. Final meeting return regd. 24 Oct. 1903 ***1901**

Inman & International Steamship Co. Ld. Regd. 1886. Vol. liq. 25 June 1894. Assets and liabilities were acquired by International Navigation Co. Ld. Final meeting return regd. 7 Sept. 1894 **1907**

Inman Steamship Co. Ld. Regd. 1875; subsequently placed in liquidation. Final meeting return regd. 24 Dec. 1890 ***1877**

Innerleithen Gas-Light Co. Ld. Regd. in Edinburgh 1902. Dissolved 1 May 1949, undertaking being vested in Scottish Area Gas Board under Gas Act 1948. Holders of ordinary shares (of £1) were entitled to receive £3 6s. 8d. British Gas 3% guaranteed stock 1990—95 for each share held **1952**

Innocuous White Lead Manufacturing Co. Ld. Regd. 1881. Vol. liq. Mar. 1883. Final meeting return regd. 12 Apr. 1887 **1884**

Innox Tannery Co. Ld. Regd. 1896. Reconstructed 1897 as company of same name. Struck off Register 13 Nov. 1903 **1904**

Innox Tannery Co. Ld. Regd. 1897. Removed from Register 1907 **1900**

Inns Of Court Hotel Co. Ld. Regd. 1873. Court Order to wind up 4 July 1911. Liquidator released 7 Nov. 1914. Struck off Register 14 Feb. 1919 ***1912**

Inshaw Seamless Iron & Steel Tubes Ld. Regd. 1905. Court Order to wind up 13 Oct. 1909. Liquidator released 4 Dec. 1917. Struck off Register 1 July 1921 ***1910**

Insiza Mines Ld. Inc. Rhodesia 1910. Vol. liq. Nov. 1917 **1918**

Insoles Ld. Regd. 1897. Vol. liq. (members') 13 Apr. 1939. Assets realised insufficient to pay unsecured creditors in full. Final meeting return regd. 4 Nov. 1941 **1940**

Instituto di Credito Fondiario D'Ungheria. See Hungarian Land Mortgage Institute.

Instone Air Line Ld. Regd. 1921. Vol. liq. 21 July 1924. Air transport business acquired by Imperial Airways Ld. Final meeting return regd. 9 June 1925 **1940**

Instone Transport and Trading Co. Ld. Regd. 1917. Vol. liq. 16 Sept. 1921. Final meeting return regd. 10 Mar. 1923 **1922**

Instow Steamship Co. Ld. Regd. 1905. Vol. liq. 10 Aug. 1915. Final meeting return regd. 17 Jan. 1917 .... **1916**

Insulators Ld. Regd. 1919. court Order to wind up Dec. 1922. Removed from Register 1930 **1923**

Insulite Co. Ld. Regd. 1882. Vol. liq. 17 Nov. 1884. Final meeting return regd. 14 Oct. 1891 ***1885**

Insurances Corporation Ld. Regd. 1896. Vol. liq. 28 July 1898. Taken over by Metropolitan Fire Insurance Co. Ld. Removed from Register 1911 **1899**

Insurances Trust & Agency Ld. Regd. Edinburgh 1889. Vol. liq. Jan. 1894. Court Order to stay proceedings Apr. 1894. Vol. liq. June 1896. Court Orders: to wind up July 1896; to dissolve Oct. 1912 **1897**

Inter-City Investment Co. Ld. See Anglo-Welsh Investment Trust (Continuation) Ld.

Inter-Northern Corporation Ld. Regd. 1920. Vol. liq. 23 May 1923. Final meeting return regd. 26 Oct. 1938 ***1924**

Inter-Transport Co. Ld. Regd. 1912. Vol. liq. 11 Nov. 1915. Final meeting return regd. 27 Feb. 1917 .... **1916**

Interallied Trade and Banking Corporation Ld. Regd. 1918. Vol. liq. 31 Dec. 1920. Shareholders were entitled to 1 preference share of £1, fully-paid. in H. & W. Greer Ld., for each 2 shares of £1 held. Final meeting return regd. 23 Mar. 1923 **1921**

Interborough Rapid Transit Co. Inc. New York 1902. Resolution to dissolve passed 18 Dec. 1940. Assenting 1st & refunding 5% mortgage gold bondholders received $825 per $1,000 bond ($821·91 in 3% corporate stock of City of New York and $3·09 in cash), plus in lieu of interest $23·73 less expenses **1941**

Intercontinent Petroleum Corporation. Inc. Delaware 1916 as Mexican Panuco Oil Co.; name changed 1927. Charter forfeited in 1934 for non-payment of franchise taxes **1936**

Intercontinental Railway Co. Ld. Regd. 1903. Struck off Register Feb. 1933 **1933**

Intermediate Equipments Ld. Regd. 1910. Receiver on behalf of the 10% 1st mortgage debenture holders was appointed on 17 Feb. 1943 and discharged on 25 Feb. 1944. All funds that came into hands of Receiver were paid into Court by whom a distribution to debenture holders was made. Struck off Register 19 Mar. 1948 **1949**

Intermediates & Explosives Ld. Regd. 1919. Vol. liq. 31 July 1929. All shares owned by Bolckow, Vaughan & Co. Ld. Final meeting return regd. 18 Mar. 1930 **1925**

International A. B. C. Ld. Regd. 1908. Vol. liq. Aug. 1912. Removed from Register 1913 **1913**

International Acceptance Bank Inc. Inc. New York 1921. Merged with Bank of the Manhattan Co. later Chase Manhattan Bank in 1932 **1933**

International Acoustic Films Ld. Regd. 1928. Vol. liq. (members') 27 June 1935. Distributions made in form of specie. Final meeting return regd. 30 Mar. 1955 **1956**

International Aluminium Co. Ld. Regd. as private Co. 1908 as Bauxite Refining Co. Ld.; converted into

VOL. FOR

public Co. and name changed 1926. Vol. liq. 15 Jan. 1948. Capital returned to contributories—20*s.* per preference share (of £1) and 15*s.* 8·21*d.* per ordinary share (of £1). Final meeting return regd. 7 Sept. 1951 **1952**

International & Mortgage Bank of Mexico. *See* Banco Internacional e Hipotecario de Mexico.

International Artificial Silk Co. Ld. Regd. 1927. Receivers appointed: for 1st debenture holders in Feb. 1931; for 2nd debenture holders in Nov. 1931. Returns amounting to 10*s.* 7*d.* in £ were made to 7½% 1st mortgage convertible debentures. Struck off Register 21 Oct. 1941 **1942**

International Assets Co. Ld. Regd. 1899. Vol. liq. 20 Sept. 1907. Assets were acquired by National Union Society Ld., in which company shareholders were entitled to 1 share of £5 for every 16⅔ shares of £1 held or to 5*s.* per share in cash. Final meeting return regd. 20 Feb. 1933 **1904**

International Bank of London Ld. Regd. 1879. Vol. liq. 26 June 1905. Court Order to continue winding up subject to supervision 1 July 1905. Final meeting return regd. 14 Jan. 1914 **1906**

International Brick Co. Ld. Regd. 1928. Struck off Register Mar. 1934 **1935**

International Cable Co. Ld. Regd. 1885. Court Orders: to wind up 8 Aug. 1890; to dissolve 25 Mar. 1896 **1891**

International Carbonizing Co. Ld. Regd. 1907. Struck off Register 9 Aug. 1946 **1939**

International Channelling Machines Ld. *See* Siskol Machines Ld.

International Coal Co. Ld. Regd. 1889. Vol. liq. 22 Oct. 1928. Final meeting return regd. 29 Jan. 1931 **1929**

International Colfix Ld. Regd. 1927. Vol. liq. 11 Sept. 1928. Undertaking and assets were acquired by International Bitumen Emulsions Ld. (later I. B. E. Ld.), in which company shareholders were entitled to 3 shares of 5*s.* for every 4 preferred ordinary shares of 5*s.* held or 1 share of 5*s.* for every 2 deferred shares of 1*s.* held. Final meeting return regd. 25 July 1939 **1929**

International Combustion Ld. *See* Taylor, Usher & Young Ld.

International Company of Mexico. Business and property acquired by Mexican Land & Colonization Co. Ld., in 1899 **1942**

International Concessions Ld. *See* Atlas Banking Corporation Ld.

International Conversion Trust Ld. Regd. 1889. Vol. liq. Mar. 1906. Removed from Register 1909 **1907**

International Copper Co. Ld. Regd. 1905. Vol. liq. 31 July 1913. Final meeting return regd. 27 May 1915 **1914**

International Copper Corporation Ld. Regd 1896. Reconstructed 1899 as Caledonian Mining Corporation Ld., in which company shareholders were entitled to 1 fully-paid share of £1 for every 2 shares of £1 held. Removed from Register 1901 **1903**

International Corporation Ld. Regd. 1897. Reconstructed 1899 as Caledonian Mining Corporation Ld., in which company shareholders were entitled to 1 fully-paid share of £1 for every 2 shares of £1 held. Removed from Register 1901 **1903**

International Diatomite Co. Ld. Regd. 1935. Vol. liq. (members') 31 Oct. 1952. Shareholders received 2 shares of 4*s.* (credited as fully-paid) in Moler Products Ld., for each share of 5*s.* held. Final meeting return regd. 20 Oct. 1953 **1954**

International Electric Co. Ld. Regd. 1882 as Anglo Austrian Brush Electrical Co. Ld.; name changed May 1883. Vol. liq. Jan. 1886. Court Order to continue winding up under supervision Feb. 1886. Final meeting return regd. 29 July 1889 **1887**

International Electric Storage Ld. Regd. 1894. Removed from Register 1903 **1896**

International Ethiopian Railway Trust & Construction Co. Ld. Regd. 1901. Vol. liq. Nov. 1929. Struck off Register 3 Oct. 1941 **1942**

International Finance & Development Corporation Ld. Regd. 1907. Court Order to wind up 1 Nov. 1910. Struck off Register 1927 **1911**

International Financial Society, Ld. Regd. 1863. In July 1969 the undertaking was transferred to Second Consolidated Trust Ld. in which company stockholders were entitled to receive fully-paid capital as follows—1 5% preference share of £1 per preference share; 110 ordinary shares of 5*s.* per 100 ordinary shares; and a like amount of 4½% debenture stock 1969–80 in exchange for debenture stock held. Struck off Register 27 Apr. 1973 **1970**

International (Giffard) Gun & Ordnance Co. Ld. Regd. 1890. Vol. liq. 25 July 1894. Final meeting return regd. 1 Jan. 1925 **1895**

International Granite Co. Ld. Regd. 1910. Struck off Register 1919 **1917**

International Harvester Co. of New Jersey. Inc. New Jersey 1902 as International Harvester Co.; name changed Feb. 1913. Undertaking and assets were acquired by International Harvester Co. (inc. New Jersey 1918), in which company shareholders were entitled to 1 share of preferred stock or 1⅓ share of common stock for each share of common stock held **1920**

International Harvester Corporation. Inc. New Jersey 1913. Undertaking and assets were acquired by International Harvester Co. (inc. New Jersey 1918), in which company shareholders were entitled to 1 share of preferred stock for each share of preferred stock held or ⅔ of share of common stock for every share of common stock held **1920**

International Holding & Investment Co. Ld. Inc. Quebec 1927. Undertaking and assets were acquired in 1937 by International Holdings Ld in which company shareholders were entitled to 1 common share of no par value for every 5 shares of no par value held *plus* 10 cents Canadian per share in cash **1939**

International Holdings & Investment Co. Ld. Regd. 1922 as Cellulose Holdings & Investment Co. Ld., name changed Oct. 1926. Vol. liq. 13 Dec. 1927. Undertaking was acquired by International Holding & Investment Co. Ld. Final meeting return regd. 13 Sept. 1928 **1938**

International Holdings Ld. Inc. in Canada under Dominion Laws 1937. Resolutions 6 Jan. 1959 provided for sale of undertaking and assets (other than shares owned in Hydro Electric Securities Corpn.) to International Holdings Corpn. and liquidation of company. Shareholders were entitled to receive 1 share in International Holdings Corpn. plus a cash distribution of 43·76 cents per share held; shares of International Holdings Corpn. remaining unclaimed at 22 July 1961 were sold by the liquidator, the proceeds (U.S. $41·75 net per share) being available for distribution to holders entitled thereto. Company finally wound up 18 Dec. 1964. Claims concerning outstanding shares should be addressed to Montreal Trust Co Transfer Dept., P.O. Box 1900. Station B, Montreal 2, Canada ... **1967**

International Improved Electric Co, Ld. *See* Improved Electric Glow Lamp Co. Ld.

International Industrial Syndicate Ld. Regd. 1898. Removed from Register 1907 **1901**

International Insurance Co. Ld. Regd. 1918 as International Marine Insurance Co. Ld.; name changed Apr. 1921. Vol. liq. 22 May 1922. Final meeting return regd. 5 Mar. 1935 **1923**

International Inventions Corporation Ld. Regd. 1891. Struck off Register 26 Oct. 1900 **1901**

International Investments & Trading Ld. Regd. 1930. Struck off Register 31 Jan. 1939 **1939**

International Land & Industries Ld. Regd. 1910 as Englisch Deutsche Terrain und Industrie A.G. Ld.; name changed 1910. Struck off Register 1915 ...... **1913**

International Line Steamship Co. Ld. Regd. 1884. Vol. liq. 31 Dec. 1917. Final meeting return regd. 25 Feb. 1919 **1918**

International Linotype Ld. Regd. 1909. Vol. liq. (members') 9 Dec. 1957. Shareholders were entitled to receive 10·33 shares of Mergenthaler Linotype Co. (holders of up to £100 stock being given option to receive cash in lieu of shares) and £5 17*s.* 3*d.* cash per £100 stock held. £1,902 paid into Companies' Liquidation Account in respect of unclaimed distributions. Final meeting return regd. 16 Dec. 1959 **1960**

International Lighting Association Ld. Regd. Edinburgh 1898. Vol. liq. (members') 31 Mar. 1949. Capital returned to contributories: £1 per preference share of £1; and 1*s.* 1·84*d.* per ordinary share of 5*s.* Final meeting return regd. 30 Nov. 1962. £29 13*s.* 6*d.* was paid to Accountant to the Court **1964**

International Maikop Ld. Regd. 1910. Vol. liq. 20 Jan. 1913. Reconstructed as International Russian Oilfields Ld in which company shareholders were entitled to 1 share of 5*s.* (credited with 4*s.* paid) for each ordinary share of 5*s.* or deferred share of 1*s.* held. Struck off Register 18 Jan. 1921 **1931**

International Marine Insurance Co. Ld. Regd. 1879. Vol. liq. 10 July 1893. Business acquired by Union Marine Insurance Co. Ld. (later Union Marine & General Insurance Co. Ld.) for 24,760 shares of £20 (credited with £2 10*s.* paid). Final meeting return regd. 29 July 1902 **1909**

International Marine Insurance Co. Ld. Regd. 1918. See International Insurance Co. Ld.

International Metal Co. Ld. Regd. 1905. Court Order to wind up 18 Dec. 1917. Struck off Register 18 Feb. 1938 **1939**

International Mexican Oil Syndicate Ld. Regd. 1914. Vol. liq. 19 Oct. 1925. Final meeting return regd. 6 Feb. 1926 **1926**

**See Stock Exchange Year-Book.*

VOL. FOR

International Mexico Syndicate Ld. Regd. 1911. Struck off Register 10 Mar. 1936 .... **1937**

International Mining Corporation Ld. Regd. 1895. Vol. liq. 4 Mar. 1897. Removed from Register 1905 ... **1898**

International Navigation Co. Ld. Regd. 1893. Vol. liq. 26 May 1927. Final meeting return regd. 29 Dec. 1930. Court Order declared dissolution void 5 Oct. 1932. Final meeting return regd. 10 Apr. 1935 .... **1932**

International Newspaper Co. Ld. Regd. 1889. Vol. liq. 9 Mar. 1891. Court Order to wind up under supervision 14 Mar. 1891. Final meeting return regd. 16 July 1894 .... **1892**

International Nickel Co. Inc. New Jersey 1902. Undertaking acquired by company of same name (inc. 1912). Preferred stockholders received $100 preferred stock in the new company for each $100 stock and common stockholders received $250 common stock for each $100 stock. The 5% 1st mortgage gold bonds were repaid on 1 Apr. 1913 at 110% **1913**

International Nickel Corporation Ld. Regd. 1896. Properties were acquired by Nickel Corporation Ld. for £95,000 in cash and £535,000 in shares or cash. Removed from Register 1905 .... **1900**

International Nitrogen and Power Co. Ld. Regd. 1913. Struck off Register 2 Feb. 1932 .... *****1922**

International Oil-Briquette Co. Ld. Regd. 1911. Vol. liq. Sept. 1913. Removed from Register 1914 .... **1914**

International Oil Lamp & Stove Ld. Regd. 17 Mar. 1931. Assets insufficient to meet claims of debenture holders. Struck off Register 28 Oct. 1955 .... **1956**

International Oil Lands Ld. Regd. 1914. Vol. liq. 15 Oct. 1924. Undertaking and assets were sold to Oilfields Ld in which company shareholders were entitled to 1 share of 2s. (credited with 1s. 6d. paid) for each preference share of 2s. or 3 shares of 2s. (credited with 1s. 6d. paid) for every 5 ordinary shares of 1s. held. Final meeting return regd. 28 June 1928 ..... **1925**

International Okonite Co. Ld. See Okonite Co. Ld.

International Packing & Provision Co. Ld. Regd. 1892. Vol. liq. 10 Feb. 1896. Taken over by International Packing Co. of Chicago (inc Illinois). Final meeting return regd. 26 Oct. 1896 .... **1897**

International Petroleum Co. Ld. Inc. Ontario 1914. Undertaking and assets were acquired by company of same name. Shareholders were entitled to 2 common shares of no par value for each common share of £1 held or 1 fully-paid preference share of $5 and 1 common share of no par value for each preference share of £1 held **1921**

International Pfaudler Ld. See Enamelled Metal Products Corporation Ld.

International Plasmon Ld. See Plasmon Ld.

International Pneumatic Tyre Co. Ld. Regd. 1894. Vol. liq. 8 July 1895. Court Order to continue winding up under supervision 7 Aug. 1895. Liquidator released 16 Nov. 1897. Removed from Register 22 May 1908 *****1896**

International Portland Cement Co. Ld. Inc. Ontario 1902. Vol. liq. Dec. 1909. Undertaking acquired by Canada Cement Co. Ld **1910**

International Proprietaries Ld. Inc. Canada 1928. In Sept. 1934 the undertaking and assets were acquired by London & Yorkshire Trust Ld for £2,559,414 and subsequently sold to Eno Proprietaries Ld **1935**

International Pulp & Chemical Co. Ld. Regd. 1926. In June 1927 Inveresk Paper Co. Ld. (holders of practically all ordinary shares) offered 1 fully-paid ordinary and 5 fully-paid B preference shares of £1 and 5s. cash for every 5 preference shares of £1 held. Vol. liq. Nov. 1927. Final meeting regd. 29 Aug. 1939 .... **1928**

International Pulverizing & Grinding Machines (Parent) Corporation Ld. Regd. 1929. Vol. liq. (creditors') 7 Dec. 1932. Final meeting return regd. 25 June 1945 **1946**

International Rice Co. Ld. Regd. 1934. Vol. liq. (members') 16 Mar. 1954. Final meeting return regd. 13 Dec. 1958 .... **1938**

International Rubber Manufacturing Co Ld. Regd. 1919. Receiver appointed in Dec. 1927. Struck off Register Jan. 1932 .... **1932**

International Russian Corpn. Ld. Regd. 1911. Vol. liq. (members') 14 Mar. 1941. Final meeting return regd. 15 July 1950 .... **1951**

International Russian Oilfields Ld. Regd. 1913. Vol. liq. (members') 27 Feb. 1941. No capital returned to contributories. Final meeting return regd. 19 May 1941 .... **1942**

International Salt Co. Ld. Regd. 1908. Court Order to wind up 29 June 1915. Liquidator released 26 Apr. 1930. Struck off Register 31 Jan. 1933 .... **1916**

International Selection Trust Ld. Regd. 1929. Vol. liq. (members') 1 Feb. 1934. Capital returned to contributories—6·144d. per share of 5s. £100 was paid into Companies' Liquidation Account. Final meeting return regd. 11 Mar. 1939 .... **1934**

VOL. FOR

International Sleeping Car Share Trust Ld. Regd. 1927. Vol. liq. (members') 26 Mar. 1956. Contributories received a first and final distribution of 0·01885714 part of one ordinary share (of Frs.500) and 0·0114286 part of one preference share (of Frs.500) of International Sleeping Car & European Express Trains Co. and cash payment of 2·832d. per share of £1 held. Amount paid into Companies' Liquidation Account £2,436 13s. 8d. Final meeting return regd. 24 Feb. 1958 .... **1958**

International Steam Trawling Co. Ld. Regd. 1891. Vol. liq. 22 Mar. 1898. Final meeting return regd. 23 Feb. 1899 .... *****1899**

International Syndicate Ld. Regd. 1902. Vol. liq. 23 May 1923. Shareholders were entitled to 1 share of £1 in Mayo (Rhodesia) Development Co. (1908) Ld., for every 3 shares held plus 4s. per share in cash. Final meeting return regd. 8 July 1924 .... **1924**

International Talking Screen Productions Ld. Regd. 1929. Vol. liq. (creditors') 2 June 1930 for amalgamation under title of Audible Filmcraft Ld., in which company shareholders were entitled to 2 shares of 5s. (credited with 3s. 6d. paid) for every share held. Interest of dissentient shareholders was purchased for £12 14s. 10d. Final meeting return regd. 3 Jan.1935 .... **1931**

International Tower Construction Co. Ld. See Metropolitan Tower Construction Co. Ld.

International Trust and Finance Corporation Ld. Regd. 1895. Vol. liq. 31 Dec. 1909. Final meeting return regd. 1 Mar. 1933 .... **1910**

International Trustee, Assets & Debenture Corporation Ld. Regd. 1889. Reconstructed 1899 as International Assets Co. Ld., in which company shareholders were entitled to 1 fully-paid share of £1 for each ordinary share of £1 held or 2 fully-paid shares for each founders' share of £2 held. Removed from Register 1901 .... **1903**

International Vacuum Power Ld. Regd. 1928. Vol. liq. Mar. 1931 for reconstruction as International Oil Lamp and Stove Ld., in which company shareholders were entitled to 1 share of 1s. (credited as fully-paid) for every 8 shares of 1s. held and an option (since expired) over further shares. Struck off Register 7 July 1939 .... **1940**

International Water & Sewage Purification Co. Ld. Regd. 1887. Removed from Register 1900 .... *****1897**

Internationale Bank te Amsterdam N.V. Inc. Netherlands 1924. Merged with N.V. Hollandsche Koopmansbank from 1 July 1937 .... **1938**

Interoceanic Railway of Mexico (Acapulco to Vera Cruz), Ld. Regd. 1888. Vol. liq. (members') 20 Dec. 1945. the undertaking having been sold to the Mexican Government. Holders of debenture stock received the following amounts—4% debenture stock £295,974 (26% of holdings); 2nd debenture stock £78,000 (6% of holdings); B debenture stock £18,778 (4% of holdings). Capital returned to contributories—1·2578% on 1st preference, 0·619% on 2nd preference and 0·3139% on ordinary stock; and 1·758% on series 38 & 39 and 1·824% on series 25 & 26 deferred interest warrants. £18,712 6s. 4d. was to be paid into Companies' Liquidation Account. Final meeting return regd. 26 Nov. 1946 .... **1947**

Intractable Ore Treatment Co. Ld. Regd. 1900. Removed from Register 1904 .... **1904**

Inventions (Manchester) Ld. Regd. 1917. Vol. liq. (members') 6 Mar. 1942. Directly controlled by Ward & Goldstone Ld. Capital returned to contributories—£36 15s. 2d. Final meeting return regd. 27 Aug. 1942 .... **1942**

Inverell Diamond Fields Ld. Regd. 1903. Vol. liq. 4 Dec. 1907. Certain assets were acquired by Plumbago Trust Ld., in which company shareholders were entitled to 1 fully-paid share of 2s. 6d. for each share of £1 held. Final meeting return regd. 15 Apr. 1908 **1908**

Inveresk Real Property Co. Ld. Regd 1927. Vol. liq. (members') 10 Dec. 1936. Final meeting return regd. 23 July 1937 .... **1937**

Invergarry & Fort Augustus Railway Co. Inc. by Special Act 1896. Line purchased by North British Railway Co. for £27,500 .... **1915**

Inverkeithing Gas Light Co. Ld. Regd. in Edinburgh 1868. Dissolved 1 May 1949, undertaking being vested in Scottish Area Gas Board under Gas Act 1948. Holders of securities were entitled to receive, in respect of each £1 unit held, British Gas 3% guaranteed stock 1990–95 as follows:

	£	s.	d.
Ord shares	2	8	0
6% red. pref. shares	1	1	0	**1952**

Inverness Railway & Coal Co. Inc. Nova Scotia 1887 as Inverness & Richmond Railway Co.; name changed 1902. Receiver appointed in 1915. In 1929 the railway was acquired by Canadian National Railways 1930

Inverurie Gas Co. Ld. Regd. in Edinburgh 1911. Dissolved 1 May 1949, undertaking being vested in Scottish Area Gas Board under Gas Act 1948. Holders of securities were entitled to receive in respect of each £1 held, British Gas 3% guaranteed stock 1990–95 as follows:

	£	s.	d.
Ord. shares (issued in 1947)	1	0	0
Ord. shares (issued before 1 Jan. 1946)	1	5	0	1952

Investing in Foreign Growth Stocks Ld. See Growth Stocks Investment Co. Ld.

Investment & Agency Co. Ld. Regd. 1902. Court Order to wind up 1906. Struck off Register Apr. 1929 ... 1930

Investment & Property Trust Ld. Regd. 1914 as Thornton-Smith Ld.; name changed 1937. By scheme of arrangement 21 July 1975 capital cancelled holders receiving 55 ordinary shares of Estates House Investment Trust Ld. for every 100 ordinary. Company dissolved 31 Dec. 1976 1977-8

Investment Corporation of India Ld. Regd. 1899. Vol. liq. 9 Nov. 1905. Final meeting return regd. 10 Feb. 1906 .... *1906

Investment Guarantee Trust Co. Ld. Regd. 1885. Removed from Register 1906 .... *1906

Investment Registry & Stock Exchange Ld. Regd. 1880. Vol. liq. 14 Sept. 1903. Undertaking acquired by Investment Registry Ld. Final meeting return regd. 26 July 1905 .... *1886

Investments & Land Owners Ld. Regd. 1922. Vol. liq. (members') 6 May 1963. Capital returned to contributories: £3 3s. 10d. plus 3·38p. (per ordinary and preference share of 2s. 6d.). Ordinary and preference shareholders also received 47,000 ordinary shares (of £1) in Estates Development (Torquay) Ld. in Oct. 1963. Applications in respect of unclaimed distributions etc. should be made to the Department of Trade & Industry. Final meeting return regd. 9 May 1973 1973-4

Investments (Yeovil) Ld. Regd. 1911 as St. Ivel Ld.; name subsequently changed. All capital was owned by Aplin & Barrett Ld. Vol. liq. (members') 14 Sept. 1960. Final meeting return regd. 26 Sept. 1961 1954

Investors' Rubber Trust Ld. Regd. 1925. Vol. liq. (creditors') 2 June 1932. No capital returned to contributories. Final meeting return regd. 10 Mar. 1933 1933

Investors Trust Association Ld. Regd. 1928. In Aug. 1970 the undertaking was transferred to London Trust Co. Ld. in which company shareholders were entitled to receive 4 deferred shares of 5s. for every 5 held and preferred stockholders 51 deferred shares for every £50 stock held. The 4½% debenture stock was repaid at 71%. Company is to be dissolved under Section 208 of the Companies Act 1948 1970

Invicta Gold Mines Ld. Regd. 1895. Vol. liq. 16 July 1908. Final meeting return regd. 3 Jan. 1919 1909

Inyoka (Rhodesia) Tobacco Co. Ld. Regd. 1906. Vol. liq. 31 Dec. 1924. Final meeting return regd. 2 Dec. 1926 1925

Iora Oilfields Ld. Regd. 1911. Struck off Register 1928 ... 1928

Ipoh Rubber Estates Ld. Regd. Edinburgh 1925. Vol. liq. Sept. 1932. Undertaking and assets were acquired by Ipoh Rubber Estates (1932) Ld. (later Ipoh Rubber Estates Ld.). in which company shareholders were entitled to 5 shares of 2s. (credited with 1s. 6d. paid) for each share of £1 held. Final meeting return regd. 15 June 1933 1933

Ipoh Tin Dredging Ld. See Jipoh Investments Ld.

Ipswich Beet Sugar Factory Ld. Regd. 1924. Vol. liq. (members') 9 July 1936. The factory was transferred to British Sugar Corporation Ld., for 230,000 fully-paid shares of £1. Shareholders were entitled to approximately 11 such shares for every 20 shares of £1 held plus 8s. per share in cash. Final meeting return regd. 13 July 1927 1937

Ipswich Gas Light Co. Inc. 1821; reinc. by Special Act 1847. Dissolved 1 May 1949, undertaking being vested in Eastern Area Gas Board under Gas Act 1948. Holders of securities were entitled to receive, in respect of each £100 unit held, British Gas 3% guaranteed stock 1990–95 as follows:

	£	s.	d.
Ord. cons. stock (3½% stand.)	131	0	0
5% pref. stock	114	16	8
5% perp. deb. stock	125	0	0
5% red. deb. stock	106	0	0
4% red. deb. stock	101	0	0
Liability in respect of certain mortgage loans assumed by the Board				1952

Ipswich Tramways Co. Inc. by Special Act 1881. Lines purchased by Ipswich Corporation in 1901 1902

Iquique Silver Co. Ld. Regd. 1888. Vol. liq. 10 May 1895. Final meeting return regd. 24 Feb. 1897 1897

Iquitos Harbour Ld. Regd. 1912. Directly controlled by Booth Steamship Co. Ld. Struck off Register 18 Feb. 1936 1937

Irene (Hauraki) Gold Mine Ld. Regd. 1896. Reconstructed 1902 as Tano Bipps Gold Mines Ld., in which company shareholders were entitled to 1 share of 5s. (credited with 4s. paid) for every 2 shares of 5s. held. Removed from Register 1904 1903

Iris Investment Co. Ld. Business was acquired in 1925 by London County Freehold and Leasehold Properties Ld 1935

Iris Mill Ld. See I. M. (Oldham) Ld.

Irish & Overseas Investment Trust Ld. Inc. in Dublin 1963. Vol. liq. (members') 6 June 1967. Capital returned to contributories—10s. 0·288d. per 10s. stock. There were unclaimed dividends and distributions amounting to £88 and £6,215 respectively. Struck off Register Oct. 1968 1969

Irish American Colonization Co. Ld. Regd. Dublin 1880. Vol. liq. Dec. 1909. Removed from Register 1910 1910

Irish Barytes & Umber Co. Ld. Regd. 1902. Court Order to wind up 26 Aug. 1906. Liquidator released 5 July 1912. Struck off Register 10 Oct. 1916 1907

Irish Distillery Ld. Regd. Dublin 1889. Vol. liq. Mar. 1930. Preference shares were repaid at par. Undertaking was transferred to United Distilleries Ld. 1931

Irish Fresh Meat Ld. Regd. Dubin 1927. Vol. liq. Mar. 1929 1930

Irish Incandescent Gas Light Co. Ld. Regd. 1895. Vol. liq. 29 Mar. 1898. Undertaking was acquired by Welsbach Incandescent Gas Light Co. Ld., for £15,000 preference shares, £15,000 ordinary shares and £15,000 in deferred shares. Final meeting return regd. 17 Mar. 1899 1898

Irish Land Purchase and Settlement Co. Ld. Regd. Dublin 1884. Removed from Register 1894 1894

Irish Life & General Assurance Co. Ld. Regd. Dublin 1923. Business was transferred to Insurance Corporation of Ireland Ld., and Industrial & Life Assurance Amalgamation Co. Ld., in 1939 1940

Irish Meat Co. Ld. Inc. Dublin. Removed from Register 1892 1892

Irish National Refineries Ld. Inc. Dublin 1936. Vol. liq. 4 June 1949. Dissolved before 1956 1946

Irish Omnibus Co. Ld. Inc. Dublin 1926. Vol. liq. Nov. 1933. Undertaking was acquired by Great Southern Railways Co 1934

Irish Packing Co. Ld. Regd. 1918. Vol. liq. 31 Aug. 1921. Final meeting return regd. 1 July 1927 1922

Irish Paper Mills Co. Ld. Regd. 1914. Receiver appointed in Nov. 1923. Struck off Register Dec. 1930 1931

Irish Proprietary Oilfields of Gaspe, Canada, Ld. See Bonaventure Mines Trust Ld.

Irish Salt Co. Ld. Inc. Dublin 1931. In liquidation. Undertaking acquired in 1939 by I. C. I. Salt Ld. 1943

Irish Shipowners' Co. Ld. Regd. Dublin 1883. Vol. liq. Dec. 1917 1918

Irish Shoe Supplies (1946), Ld. Inc. in Dublin 1946. Vol. liq. (members') 23 June 1959. Undertaking transferred to Irish Shoe Supplies Ld. (inc. June 1959). Capital repaid Apr. 1960 at 26s. 8d. per share of £1. Final meeting return regd. 10 May 1960 1961

Irish Steel Ld. Inc. in Dublin 5 Apr. 1938. Receiver appointed 8 Jan. 1947, but ceased to act 9 Sept. 1949, having realised the assets which produced sufficient to make distributions amounting to 7·383s. in the £ to holders of A 1st mortgage debenture stock and trade loan debentures 1950

Irish Sugar Manufacturing Co. Ld. Inc. Dublin 1925. Vol. liq. Nov. 1933. The Carlow factory was acquired by Comlucht Siuicre Eireann Teoranta 1934

Irish Transport Organisation. See Coras Iompair Eireann.

Irkdale Bleachworks Ld. Regd. 1901. Vol. liq. (members') 7 Sept. 1944. A direct controlling interest was held by Bleachers' Association Ld. (later Whitecroft Industrial Holdings Ld.). Final meeting return regd. 2 Dec. 1944 1945

Iron & Land Co. of Minnesota Ld. Regd. 1888. Removed from Register 1894 .... *1892

Iron & Steel Corporation of Great Britain. Established under Iron & Steel Act, 1949. Dissolved as from 13 Aug. 1953 by Iron & Steel Act, 1953. all property, obligations, &c. transferred to Iron & Steel Holding & Realisation Agency. Liability in respect of the then outstanding British Iron & Steel 3½% guarantee stock 1979–81 was assumed by the Treasury and the stock renamed 3½% Treasury Stock 1979–81 1954

Iron & Steel Holding & Realisation Agency. Established 1953. Dissolved by a Statutory Order, made under the Iron and Steel Act, 1967, as from 1 Oct. 1967 1968

Iron Bridge & District Gas Co. Ld. Regd. 1892. Dissolved 1 May 1949, undertaking being vested in

VOL. FOR

West Midland Area Gas Board under Gas Act 1948. Holders of ordinary shares (of £1) were entitled to receive £1 9s. British Gas 3% guaranteed stock 1990–95 for each share held **1952**

Iron Ore Co. Ld. *See* Ore & Shipping Co. (Wm. H. Muller & Co.) Ld.

Ironclad (Australia) Gold Mining Co. Ld. Regd. 1889. Vol. liq. 17 Nov. 1891. Final meeting return regd. 26 Mar. 1895 .... **1893**

Ironmonger & Co. Established 1867. A receiving order was made on 22 Nov. 1929 .... **1930**

Irrawaddy Flotilla Co. Ld. Regd. Edinburgh 1 Dec. 1875. Vol. liq. (members') 26 June 1950. The business was taken over by Burmese Government on 1 June 1948. Capital returned to contributories— £1 18s. 5·545d. per £1 stock. £848 1s. 6d. was paid to Accountant of the Court. Final meeting return regd. 24 Apr. 1957 .... **1958**

Irrigation Investment Corporation Ld. Regd. 1898. Removed from Register 1903 .... **1903**

Irthlingborough Gas & Coke Co. Ld. Regd. 1893. In 1936 the undertaking was acquired by Wellingborough Gas Light Co. Ld., in which company shareholders were entitled to 10⅝ or 7⅞ additional 7% standard shares of £1 for each original ordinary 10% standard or additional ordinary 7% standard share of £10 respectively held. Vol. liq. (members') 5 Aug. 1936. Final meeting return regd. 11 Nov. 1936 .... **1937**

Irtysh Corporation Ld. Regd. 1914. Vol. liq. 30 Dec. 1919. Undertaking and assets were sold to Russo Asiatic Corporation Ld in which company share-holders were entitled to 2 fully-paid shares of £1 for each share of £1 held. The new company were to satisfy the debentures. Final meeting return regd. 23 Jan. 1922 .... **1920**

Irvine & District Gas Co. Ld. Regd. in Edinburgh 1908 as Irvine Gas Co. Ld.; name changed 1940. Dissolved 1 May 1949, undertaking being vested in Scottish Area Gas Board under Gas Act 1948. Holders of ordinary shares (of £1) were entitled to receive £3 British Gas 3% guaranteed stock 1990–95 for each share held **1952**

Irvine's Ship Building & Dry-Docks Co. Ld. Regd. 1920. Vol. liq. (creditors') 30 Jan. 1930. Mortgage deben-ture stock was repaid in full. Assets realised insufficient to pay unsecured creditors in full. Final meeting return regd. 1 May 1931 .... **1930**

Irvine's Shipbuilding & Dry Docks Co. Ld. Regd. 1897. Vol. liq. 30 June 1920 for reconstruction as Irvine's Ship Building & Dry Docks Co., in which company shareholders were entitled to 1 fully-paid preference share of £1 for each preference share of £1 held or 1 fully-paid ordinary share of £1 for each ordinary share of 1s. held. Final meeting return regd. 31 Mar. 1921 .... **1921**

Irving's Sea Vitoids Ld. Regd. 1929. Court Order to wind up Oct. 1931. Struck off Register 24 Aug. 1943 **1944**

Irwell Bank Spinning Co. Ld. Regd. 1933. Vol. liq. (members') 29 Feb. 1960. Capital returned to contributories—10s. per preference share of 10s.; 21s. 0·6459d. per ordinary share of 10s. Final meeting return regd. 23 Jan. 1963 .... **1963**

Irwell Valley Water Board. Inc. by Special Act 1900 as Bury & District Joint Water Board; name changed 1935. Dissolved and undertaking vested in the Bolton Corporation on 1 Apr. 1963 .... **1964**

Irwin River (W. A.) Coal Syndicate Ld. Regd. 1911. Vol. liq. 30 June 1926. Final meeting return regd. 6 Oct. 1926 .... ***1927**

Isaac & Samuel Ld. Regd. 1923. Vol. liq. June 1927. Reconstructed as Isaac & Samuel (1927) Ld. (later Isaac & Samuel Ld.). Struck off Register Feb. 1932 **1932**

Isaac & Samuel Ld. Regd. 1927 as Isaac & Samuel (1927) Ld.; name changed Sept. 1931. Court Order to wind up Mar. 1933. Struck off Register 19 May 1944 .... **1945**

Isabelle Gold & Silver Mining Co. Ld. Regd. 1876. Struck off Register 27 Apr. 1894 .... **1899**

Isamungu Gold Mine Ld. Regd. 1931. Struck off Register 7 Dec. 1937 .... **1938**

Isherwood, Foster & Stacey Ld. Regd. 1891. Vol. liq. (members') 24 July 1970. Final meeting return regd. 11 Dec. 1970 .... **1972**

Isis Investment Co. of Queensland Ld. Regd. 1887. Removed from Register 1908 .... **1900**

Island Block Gold Mining Co. Ld. Regd. 1888. The mortgagees foreclosed. Struck off Register 18 Nov. 1902 .... **1901**

Island (Para) Rubber Estates Ld. Regd. 1910. Vol. liq. 3 Apr. 1914. Final meeting return regd. 7 Oct. 1915 **1915**

Island Steam Shipping Co. Ld. Regd. 1883. Removed from Register 1891 .... **1886**

Island Trading Co. Ld. Regd. 1911. Vol. liq. (members') 26 Apr. 1957. £121 0s. 2d. was paid into Companies'

VOL. FOR

Liquidation Account in respect of unclaimed divi-dends. Final meeting return regd. 2 Mar. 1961 ..... **1962**

Islas del Guadalquivir S. A. Inc. Spain 1926. Assets were transferred in 1934 to Islas Mayor del Guadalquivir. Debenture holders were to be satisfied by allotment of 1 share in new company for every Ptas. 1,500 debentures held; no compensation to shareholders **1935**

Isle of Axholme Light Railway Co. Inc. (under Light Railways Act 1896) by order of Light Railway Commissioners by Board of Trade 1899. Under North Eastern Railway Act 1902 line was sold to North Eastern Railway Co. and Lancashire & Yorkshire Railway Co. jointly for £27,500. The 4% debenture stock was repaid at 102% **1903**

Isle of Axholme Railway Co. Inc. by Special Act 1885. Undertaking abandoned by Act of 1888 .... **1889**

Isle of Man Breweries Ld. Inc. Isle of Man 1899. Vol. liq. 1902 .... **1903**

Isle of Man Insurance Co. Ld. Inc. Isle of Man. Business was acquired in 1891 by Palatine Insurance Co. Ld. **1928**

Isle of Man, Liverpool and Manchester Steamship Co. Ld. Regd. 1886. Vol. liq. Nov. 1888. Final meeting return regd. 27 Nov. 1889 .... **1889**

Isle of Man Mining Co. Ld. Regd. 1856. Vol. liq. 24 Apr. 1911. Final meeting return regd. 4 June 1917 .... **1912**

Isle of Man Railway Co. Inc. by Act of Tynwald in 1872. Vol. liq. commenced 4 May 1978. Capital returned to contributories—£28·27 per £5 ordinary or prefer-ence share. Final meeting held 4 Nov. 1981 .... **1982–3**

Isle of Man Tramways & Electric Power Co. Ld. Inc. Isle of Man 1893. Court Order to wind up 11 July 1900 **1901**

Isle of Thanet Electric Supply Co. Ld. Regd. 1896 as Isle of Thanet Light Railways (Electric) Co. Ld. name changed to Isle of Thanet Electric Tramways and Lighting Co. Ld. in July 1899 and as above in June 1924. Vol. liq. (members') 16 July 1948. Undertak-ing transferred to the Margate, Broadstairs & District Electricity Board [dissolved 1 Apr. 1948, undertaking vested in British (later Central) Elec-tricity Authority]. Preference stock was repaid at par ordinary stockholders received 19s. 11¾d. per £1 stock. Final meeting return regd. 1 Aug. 1952 ..... **1953**

Isle of Thanet Gas Light & Coke Co. Inc. by Special Act 1824. Dissolved 1 May 1949, undertaking being vested in South Eastern Area Gas Board under Gas Act 1948. Holders of securities were entitled to receive, in respect of each £100 unit held, British Gas 3% guaranteed stock 1990–95 as follows:

	£	s.	d.
Cons. ord. stock (3½% stand.)	180	0	0
Addit. ord. stock (3½% stand.)	180	0	0
5% perp. deb. stock	126	6	8	**1952**

Isle of Thanet Light Railways (Electric) Co. Ld. *See* Isle of Thanet Electric Supply Co. Ld.

Isle of Walney Estates Co. Ld. Regd. 1899. Vol. liq. (members') 4 June 1951. Final meeting return regd. 27 Dec. 1951 .... **1947**

Isle of Wight Central Railway Co. Inc. by Special Act 1887. In 1923 the undertaking was merged into the London & South Western Railway, in which company stockholders were entitled to stock as follows:

For each £100 held		L.& S. W.
Debenture A £100		3% Deb. Cons.
Debenture B .... { £100		3% Deb. Cons.
	{ £43	3½% Preference
Debenture C .... { £100		3% Deb. Cons.
	{ £ 22	3½% Preference
First Pref....................£100		3½% Preference
Second Pref.................. £15		cash
Ordinary...................... £3		cash	**1924**

Isle of Wight Eastern Section Railway Co. *See* Isle of Wight Railway Co.

Isle of Wight Electric Light & Power Co. Ld. Regd. 1897 as Ventnor Electric Light & Power Co. Ld.; name changed in 1900. Dissolved 1 Apr. 1948, undertak-ing being vested in British (later Central) Electricity Authority and Southern Area Board under Electric-ity Act 1947. Holders of ordinary and 5 preference shares were entitled to receive, in respect of each share (of £5) held, £10 and £6 7s. 6d. British Electricity 3% guaranteed stock (1968–73) respec-tively **1949**

Isle of Wight (Newport Junction) Railway Co. Inc. by Special Act 1868. Consolidated 1887 into Isle of Wight Central Railway Co., in which holders of ordinary stock received an equal amount of 5% 2nd preference stock; holders of 6% preferred stock received an equal amount of 5% 1st preference stock; holders of debenture stock received deben-ture stocks in the purchasing company **1888**

Isle of Wight Railway Co. Inc. by Special Act 1860 as Isle of Wight Eastern Section Railway Co.; reincor-porated and name changed by Act of 1863. In 1923

See Stock Exchange Year-Book.

VOL. FOR

the undertaking was merged into the Southern Railway Co., in which company stockholders were entitled to stock as follows:

For each £100 held	S. R.
4% Debenture £100	4% Debenture
4% Preference £80	5% Preference
Pref. Conv. Ord. ..., £80	Preferred Ord.
Defd. Conv. Ord. { £5 16s. 6d. Prefd. Ord.	
{ £101 9s. Defd. Ord.	1924

Isle of Wight Sanatorium Co. Ld. *See* Isle of Wight Spa Ld.

Isle of Wight Spa Ld. Regd. 1884 as Isle of Wight Sanatorium Ld.; name changed Sept. 1885. Struck off Register 20 Mar. 1906 1887

Isle Royale Land Corporation Ld. Regd. 1889. Undertaking was acquired in 1901 by Wendigo Copper Co. Ld. (later Isle Royale Land Corporation Ld.) for £8,600 in debentures, £8,060 in fully-paid ordinary shares of £5. £5,445 in fully-paid preference shares of £5 and £6,388 in cash. Removed from Register 1906 1908

Isle Royale Land Corporation Ld. Regd. 1890 as Wendigo Copper Co. Ld.; name changed Nov. 1901. Vol. liq. 31 Mar. 1909. Capital returned to contributories—£2 13s. 6d. per 1st preference share of £5; further payments (if any) not known. Final meeting return regd. 3 Sept. 1914 1910

Isles Steam Shipping Co. Ld. *See* Sutherland Steamship Co. Ld.

Isleworth Brewery Ld. Regd. 1886. Vol. liq. 9 Nov. 1923. Undertaking was acquired by Watney Combe Reid & Co. Ld. (later Watney Mann Ld.). Final meeting return regd. 1 July 1924 1924

Isleworth Rubber Co. Ld. Regd. 1916. Vol. liq. 21 Dec. 1927. Final meeting return regd. 29 Aug. 1928 1928

Ismay Cables Ld. *See* Midland Holdings Ld.

Issuing & Underwriting Corporation Ld. Regd. 1920. Struck off Register 1928 1928

Istituto Italiano di Credito Marittimo. Inc. Rome 1916. Liquidated July 1935 1936

Itabira Iron Ore Co. Ld. Regd. 1911. Winding-up order 22 Jan. 1945. Capital returned to contributories—7s. 9¾d. per 1st preference share of £1. Liquidator released 7 Sept. 1959 1906

Italian & General Exploring Co. Ld. Regd. 1890. Vol. liq. 12 Jan. 1894. Final meeting return regd. 21 Aug. 1899 1895

Italian Gold Mining Co. Ld. *See* Belcher Consolidated Gold Mining Co. Ld.

Italian Land & Investment Co. Ld. Regd. 1872. Vol. liq. 11 Aug. 1879. Final meeting return regd. 13 July 1892 1883

Italian Spare Motor Wheel Ld. Regd. 1908. Struck off Register Jan. 1932 1932

Italo-Britannica Royal Italian Mail Steam Navigation Co. Ld. Regd. 1890. Vol. liq. 10 Jan. 1895. Final meeting return regd. 19 Apr. 1895 1896

Ito Syndicate Ld. Regd. 1902. Vol. liq. Apr. 1904. Removed from Register 1905 1906

Itonia Gramophones Ld. *See* Itonia Ld.

Itonia Ld. Regd. 1928 as Itonia Gramophones Ld.; name changed Sept. 1931. Vol. liq. (creditors') 22 July 1936. Assets realised insufficient to pay unsecured creditors in full. Final meeting return regd. 18 Apr. 1941 1937

Itsin Wassau Gold Syndicate Ld. Regd. 1901. Removed from Register 1906 1905

Itter's Brick Co. Ld. Regd. 1926. Vol. liq. (members') 30 Oct. 1936. Undertaking was acquired by London Brick Co. Ld., which company owned all shares. All assets were distributed in specie. Final meeting return regd. 26 Sept. 1946 1947

Ituana Railway Co. Established Sao Paulo 1870. In 1892 the company was amalgamated with Sorocabana Railway Co. to form Uniao Sorocabana e Ytuana. In 1904 the Brazilian Government paid £128 10s. for each £100 6% 1st mortgage debentures in respect of principal and arrears of interest 1905

Ivanhoe Consols Proprietary Co. Ld. Regd. 1896. Removed from Register 1907 1899

Ivanhoe Gold Corporation Ld. Regd. 1897. Vol. liq. 17 July 1924. The mine and mining assets were sold to Lake View and Star Ld., in which company shareholders were entitled to 5 shares of 4s. (credited as fully-paid) for every 2 shares of £5 held. A cash payment of 10s. per share of £5 was made in Oct. 1924; further payments (if any) not known. Final meeting return regd. 30 Jan. 1939 1925

Ivanhoe Gold Mining Co., No Liability. Inc. Victoria 1895. Undertaking acquired by Ivanhoe Gold Corporation Ld. Shareholders received 1 share of £5 for each share of £1 held and about £10 10s. in cash 1898

Ivanhoe Junction Gold Mining Co., No Liability. Inc. South Australia 1895. Reconstructed 1906 under

similar title. Shareholders were entitled to 1 share of £1 (credited 10s. paid) in new company for each share of £1 held 1908

Ivanhoe Junction Gold Mining Co., No Liability Inc. South Australia 1906. In liquidation in 1909 1909

Ivanhoe South Extended Gold Mining Estates Co. Ld. Regd. 1899. Vol. liq. Jan. 1908. Property and machinery were acquired by Golden Horse Shoe Estate Co. Ld. Distributions per share of £1: 5s. in Feb. 1908 and 1d. in Mar. 1908. Removed from Register 1908 1908

Ivory Coast Corporation Ld. Regd. 1910. Vol. liq. 15 Feb. 1915. Final meeting return regd. 16 Jan. 1918 1915

Ivory Coast Development Co. Ld. Regd. 1903. Struck off Register 5 Jan. 1943 1945

Ivory Coast Exploring Syndicate Ld. *See* French Guinea and Soudan Mining Co. Ld.

Ivory Coast Finance Syndicate (1902) Ld. Regd. 1902. Struck off Register 13 Oct. 1908 1909

Ivory Coast Goldfields Ld. Regd. 1901. Removed from Register 1913 1906

Ivory Coast Mining Corporation Ld. Regd. 1902. Court Order to wind up 19 Apr. 1904. Struck off Register 10 Oct. 1916 1905

Ivory Coast Rubber Estates Ld. Regd. 1909. Vol. liq. 1911. Struck off Register 1 Feb. 1944 1944

Ivory Coast Trading Co. Ld. Regd. 1902. Vol. liq. 13 July 1904. Final meeting return regd. 24 Feb. 1913 1905

Izmir-Kasaba ve Temdidi Demir Yolu Türk Sirketi. *See* Ottoman Smyrna & Cassaba & Extension Railway Co.

J

J. & A. Margolin Ld. *See* under Dansette Products Ld

J. & C. Manufacturing Co. Ld. Undertaking and assets were acquired in 1928 by Auto-Electric Devices Ld. for £6,000 in fully-paid shares of 1s. 1929

J. C. E. G. p.l.c. Regd. as private company 1945 as C. H. Johnson (Machinery) Ld.; name changed to Johnson Construction Equipment Group Ld. in 1965; and to present title 1976; re-registered in 1983. Vol. liq. 1 Feb. 1983. Final meeting held 1 Feb. 1985. Distributions per ordinary share (of 25p): 5p on 29 Apr. 1983 and final of 6·87p on 19 Dec. 1984 1986–7

J. C. E. Investments Ld. Regd. 1926. Vol. liq. 19 May 1928. Final meeting return regd. 14 Sept 1928 ..... *1929

"J.D." Insulating & Refrigerating Co. Ld. Regd. 1916. Court Order to wind up 7 Apr. 1924. Struck off Register Mar. 1929 1930

J.F.S. Ld. Regd. 1916 as Hayes Cocoa Co. Ld.; name subsequently changed. Majority of capital was owned by Nestlés Milk Products Ld. Vol. liq. (members') 30 Sept. 1964. Final meeting return regd. 3 Mar. 1966 1940

J. F. Willis (Cinderella Shoes) Ld. *See* Willia (J. F.) (Cinderella Shoes) Ld.

J. G. Development Syndicate (Rhodesia) Ld. Regd 1900. Vol. liq. June 1909. Removed from Register 1913 1910

J. G. White & Co. Ld. See White Drummond & Co. Ld.

J. J. Minor Ld. *See* Pedder Japan Investment Co. Ld.

J. L. Manufacturing Co. Ld. Regd. 1908. Vol. liq. 11 Nov. 1911. Undertaking acquired by Submersible Motors Ld. Final meeting return regd. 19 Nov. 1912 *1913

"J.M." Motor Fenders Ld. Regd. 1929. Court Order to wind up Oct. 1929. Struck off Register 21 Sept. 1937 1938

J. P. Restaurants Ld. Regd. 1905. Vol. liq. (members') 7 Feb. 1933. Undertaking was acquired by Aerated Bread Co. Ld. Capital returned to preference shareholders £9,986 11s. 8d. £163 8s. 4d. was paid into Companies' Liquidation Account. Final meeting return regd. 1 June 1934 1933

J.P. Trust Ld. Regd. 1901. Vol. liq. 29 Mar. 1910. Final meeting return regd. 27 May 1910 .... *1905

J. R. Exploration Syndicate Ld. Regd. 1897. Vol. liq. 30 June 1904. Final meeting return regd. 14 June 1909 1905

J. R. Holdings Ld. Regd. 1920 as John Reddihough Ld.; name changed 1948. Vol. liq. (members') 28 Feb. 1948. Undertaking and assets acquired by John Reddihough Ld. Final meeting return regd. 4 Mar. 1949 1951

J. R. Syndicate Ld. Regd. 1904. Vol. liq. 22 Mar. 1910. Final meeting return regd. 15 Dec. 1911 .... *1911

J. S. Darwen & Co. Ld. *See* Darwen (J. S.) & Co. Ld.

J. W. F. Trust Ld. Regd. 1888 as J. W. French and Co. Ld.; name changed Oct. 1934. Vol. liq. (members') 19 Nov. 1934. Undertaking acquired by J. W. French and Co. Ld. Capital returned to contributories—£17 16s. 1d. per ordinary or pref. share of £10 *plus* participation in distribution of 209,993 ordinary shares of 5s. fully-paid in J. W. French and Co. Ld. Final meeting return regd. 25 July 1936 1936

VOL. FOR

Jabi Rubber Plantations Ld. Regd. 1925. Vol. liq. (creditors') 29 Sept. 1932. Undertaking and assets were acquired by Jabi Rubber Plantations (1932) Ld. in which company shareholders were entitled to 1 share of 2s. (credited with 1s. 9d. paid) for each share of 2s. held. Final meeting return regd. 30 Jan. 1934 .... **1933**

Jabi Rubber Plantations (1932) Ld. Regd. 1932. Vol. liq. (members') 18 Dec. 1950. Undertaking and assets acquired by Aberfoyle Plantations Ld. in which company shareholders were entitled to 36·359 fully-paid shares of that company for every 100 shares (of 2s.) held. Final meeting return regd. 26 Mar. 1954 **1955**

Jablochkoff Electric Light and Power Co. Ld. Regd. 1882. Vol. liq. 20 Feb. 1884. Court Orders: to continue winding up under supervision July 1884; to dissolve 26 Jan. 1899 .... **1885**

Jack (R. & T.) & Co. Ld. Regd. Edinburgh 1916. Vol. liq. (members') 1 Jan. 1942. Direct controlling interest held by Nobel's Explosives Ld. to which company all assets were assigned. Final meeting return regd. 15 Mar. 1943 .... **1942**

Jack (Ronald) & Co. Ld. Regd. Edinburgh 1909. Undertaking and assets acquired by A. F. Stoddard & Co. Ld. Vol. liq. 31 Oct. 1933. Capital returned to contributories—£1 5s.5\frac{1781}{10000}d. per share of £1. Final meeting return regd. 30 May 1934 .... **1934**

Jackson Exploration & Development Co. Ld. Regd. 1896. Reconstructed Feb. 1899 as company of same name. Shareholders were entitled to 1 share of 5s. (credited with 4s. 10d. paid) in new company for each share of 5s. held. Final meeting returned regd. 15 June 1900 .... **1901**

Jackson Exploration & Development Co. Ld. Regd. Feb. 1899. Vol. liq. 25 Oct. 1899. Reconstructed as company of same name. Shareholders were entitled to apply for shares of 4d. at par. Final meeting return regd. 18 July 1901.................................. **1901**

Jackson Exploration & Development Co. Ld. Regd. Oct. 1899. Vol. liq. 17 Oct. 1900. Final meeting return regd. 13 Nov. 1905 .... **1901**

Jackson Gold Fields Ld. Regd. 1893. Vol. liq. Sept. 1896. Reconstructed as Jackson Exploration & Development Co. Ld., in which company shareholders were entitled to 1 share of 5s. (credited with 4s. 6d. paid) for each share of 5s. held. Final meeting return regd. 15 June 1900 .... **1899**

Jackson (J. C.) & Co. Ld. Regd. 1937. Struck off Register 11 Apr. 1939 .... **1940**

Jackson (John) & Son Ld. Regd. 1912. Vol. liq. 31 Jan. 1927. Direct controlling interest held by Spillers Milling & Associated Industries Ld. (later Spillers Ld.). Final meeting return regd. 23 Jan. 1928 ...... **1927**

Jackson (P. R.) & Co. Ld. Regd. 1891. Vol. liq. (members') 1 July 1930. Undertaking and assets were acquired by David Brown & Sons (Huddersfield) Ld. for £62,000 in cash and £73,474 in 300,000 ordinary shares. Final meeting return regd. 26 Sept. 1930 .... **1931**

Jackson (R. R.) & Co. Ld. Regd. 1878. Vol. liq. 24 Dec. 1884. Final meeting return regd. 21 Apr. 1885 .... ***1885**

Jackson Rae Phosphate Co. Ld. Regd. 1889. Removed from Register 1893 .... **1891**

Jackson's Stores Ld. Regd. 1895. All capital acquired by Great Universal Stores Ld. Vol. liq. (members') 17 May 1961. Final meeting return regd. 19 Feb. 1964 **1960**

Jackson's Theatrical Enterprises Ld. Regd. 1919. Vol. liq. (members') 10 Feb. 1937. All shares held by Proprietary Theatres Ld. Final meeting return regd.4 June 1937.. **1938**

Jacobus-Marler Estates Ld. Regd. 1905. Vol. liq. 9 Aug. 1916. Final meeting return regd. 19 Dec. 1917 .... ***1917**

Jacoletti Gold Mines Ld. Regd. 1904. Struck off Register 1915 .... **1914**

"Jadoo" Ld. Regd. 1895. Removed from Register 1904 **1903**

Jaffa Oilfields Ld. See New Suvoroff Oilfields Ld.

Jagersfontein & South African Diamond Mining Association Ld. Regd. 1888. Vol. liq. Sept. 1889. Property was acquired by New Jagersfontein Mining and Exploration Co. Ld. Final meeting return regd. 24 Oct. 1890 .... **1890**

Jagersfontein United Mining Co. Ld. Inc. Kimberley 1888. Assets and liabilities were transferred in 1891 to New Jagersfontein Mining and Exploration Co. in which company shareholders were entitled to 1 fully-paid share of £10 for every 17 shares of £1 held **1892**

Jahncke Ld. Regd. 1893. Majority of capital was owned by Bryant & May Ld. Final meeting return regd. 13 Mar. 1962 .... **1940**

Jaipur Tea Co. Ld. Regd. 1898. Vol. liq. 5 Nov. 1926. Undertaking and assets were acquired by Jhanzse Tea Association Ld. in which company shareholders were entitled to 4 shares of £1 (credited as fully-

VOL. FOR

paid) for each share of £5 held. Final meeting return regd. 8 Mar. 1927 .... **1927**

Jalisco (Mexican) Mining Syndicate Ld. Regd. 1906. Struck off Register 1921 .... **1911**

Jamaica Copra & Estates Co. Ld. Regd. 1913. Vol. liq. Aug. 1921. Struck off Register 1926 .... **1922**

Jamaica Estates & Rubber Plantations Ld. Regd. 1909. Removed from Register 1914 .... ***1914**

Jamaica Railway Co. Inc. 1889. Line taken over by Government in 1900. Each 1st mortgage bond of £100 was exchanged for £100 Jamaican Government 3½% inscribed stock and received interest arrears for 2 years from 24 Jan. 1897 at 3½% p.a., less £1 paid 1 July 1897. One year's interest on Jamaican stock (to 24 Jan. 1900) was paid at same time, making total cash distribution £9 10s. per bond on bonds Nos. 1–14500. Bonds Nos. 14501–14550 were entitled to cash payment of £10 10s. and bonds Nos. 14801–14820 to £8 15s. per bond **1901**

Jamaican & General Mortgages Investment & Trust Co. Ld. Regd. 1922 as Mortgage Co. of Jamaica Ld.; name changed July 1929. Vol. liq. (members') 28 June 1949. Capital returned to contributories—£11 3s. 5d. per share of £10 plus 166 shares of 10s. of Kilifi Plantations Ld. for every 100 shares held. Final meeting return regd. 30 July 1964............... **1965**

Jamangalum Syndicate Ld. Regd. 1897. Vol. liq. 3 Feb. 1911. Final meeting return regd. 8 May 1916 ...... **1911**

James & Shakespeare Ld. Regd. 1917. Court Order to wind up 25 Feb. 1935. Liquidator released 21 May 1943. Struck off Register 5 Oct. 1945 .... **1946**

James Austin & Sons (Holdings) Ld. See Hartley Crosland Group Ld.

James Bay Railway Co. See Canadian Northern Ontario Railway Co.

Jameson (William) Ld. Regd. 1905. Vol. liq. 21 July 1914. Final meeting return regd. 28 Apr. 1920...... ***1915**

Jameson's Patent Coking Co. Ld. Regd. 1883. Vol. liq. 5 Apr. 1893. Final meeting return regd. 8 July 1896 **1888**

Jandus Arc Lamp & Electric Co. Ld. See Arc & General Equipment Ld.

Janjevo Mines Ld. Regd. 1929. Vol.liq. (members') 24 June 1930. Undertaking acquired by Novo Brdo Mines Ld. Final meeting return regd. 1 Apr. 1939 **1938**

Jantar (Cornwall) Ld. Regd. 1927. Receiver appointed in June 1932; ceased to act 23 Jan. 1934. Struck off Register 17 Dec.1935 .... **1936**

Japan Electric Generation & Transmission Co. Ld. (Nippon Hatusoden Kabusiki Kaisyal. Inc. in Japan in 1939. Succeeded by Kanto Electric Supply Co. Ld., in Sept. 1943 .... **1948**

Japanese & Eastern Corporation Ld. Regd. 1905. Vol. liq. 8 Mar. 1909. Assets were realised by receiver for debenture stockholders. Struck off Register 10 Oct. 1916 .... **1910**

Jappa Gold Mines Ld. Regd. 1901. Undertaking was acquired by Ebenezer Gold Mining Co. Ld., in which company shareholders were entitled to 25 shares of £1 (credited with 17s. 6d. paid) for every 100 shares of 5s. held. Removed from Register 1904 **1904**

Jarawa Tin Dredging Ld. Regd. 1926. Vol. liq. 14 May 1928. Undertaking acquired by Associated Tin Mines of Nigeria Ld. Final meeting return regd. 21 July 1930 .... **1939**

Jardine Japan Investments Trust Ld. Regd. as private company on 6 Sept. 1971; converted into public company 2 Feb. 1972. Vol. liq. (members') 10 Dec. 1980. By Scheme of Unitisation holders received 0·3300189 units of Jardine Japan Fund for each ordinary share and cash in respect of any fractions. Final distribution of 2·0602899p per ordinary share. Final meeting held in Nov. 1983. Dissolved 6 Oct. 1984 .... **1984–5**

Jardim Botanico Tramway Co. See Companhia Ferro Carril do Jardim Botanico.

Jared Terret Hunt & Son, Ld. Regd. 1873. Vol. liq. 22 Mar. 1928. Final meeting return regd. 3 Dec. 1931 ***1885**

Jarrah Timber & Wood Paving Corporation Ld. Regd. 1898. Undertaking was acquired in 1902 by Millars' Karri and Jarrah Co. (1902) Ld. (later Millars' Timber and Trading Co. Ld.), in which company shareholders were entitled to 10 ordinary shares of £1 for every 100 ordinary shares of £1 held or 20 preference shares of £1 for every 100 preference shares of £1 held. The debenture holders were entitled to an equal amount of debentures in new company. Removed from Register 1905 .... **1905**

Jarrah Wood & Saw Mills Co. Ld. Regd. 1898. Undertaking was acquired in 1902 by Millars' Karri & Jarrah Co. (1902) Ld. (later Millars' Timber and Trading Co. Ld.), in which company shareholders were entitled to 4 shares of £1 for every 25 shares of £1 held. Removed from Register 1904 .... **1904**

See Stock Exchange Year-Book.

VOL. FOR

Jarradale Jarrah Forests & Railways Ld. Regd. 1897. Undertaking was acquired in 1902 by Millars' Karri and Jarrah Co. (1902) Ld. (later Millars' Timber and Trading Co. Ld.). in which company shareholders were entitled to 20 preference shares of £1 for every 3 preference shares of £10 held. Ordinary shareholders were entitled to £2 12s. 6d. in ordinary shares of £1 for each ordinary share of £10 held. Holders of 1st debentures and B debenture stock were entitled to £111 10s. or £100 respectively in 4½% debenture stock for every £100 held. Removed from Register 1905 1904

Jarrow & District Electric Traction Co. Ld. Regd. 1903. Railways were abandoned under Act of 1929. Vol. liq. (members') 24 Nov. 1948. Capital returned to contributories—1s. 4·45d. per share of £1. Final meeting return regd. 22 Nov. 1949 1951

Java Amalgamated Rubber Estates Ld. See Amalgamated Transport Services Ld.

Jarvis-Conklin Mortgage Trust Co. Inc. Missouri 1886. Under scheme of reorganisation in 1897, the company was wound up. Holders of debentures, municipal bonds, guaranteed mortgages and deposit receipts were entitled to fully-paid shares of $100 in North American Trust Co. 1898

Jarvis Island Silver Co. Ld. Regd. 1871. Reconstructed 1886 as Jarvis Silver Mining Co. Ld., in which company shareholders were entitled to 10 fully-paid shares of £1 for each share of £10 held. Removed from Register 1904 1889

Jarvis Silver Mining Co. Ld. Regd. 1886. Removed from Register 1905 1890

Jasin (Malacca) Rubber Estates Ld. Regd. 1910. All capital owned by Merlimau Pegoh, Ld. Vol. liq. (members') 31 Aug. 1961. Final meeting return regd. 30 Nov.1962 1961

Jasper Town & Lands Ld. Regd. 1890. Removed from Register 1903 1902

Java & Borneo Co. Ld. Regd. 1909. Vol. liq. 7 Nov. 1918. Final meeting return regd. 10 May 1920 1919

Java Hevea Rubber & Tobacco Estates Ld. Regd. 1912. Vol. liq. 7 Apr. 1920. Final meeting return regd.1 July 1924 1921

Java Oil Exploration Co. Ld. Regd. 1925. Struck off Register 7 Dec. 1937 1938

Java Produce Co. Ld. Regd. 1928. Vol. liq. (members') 16 Mar. 1932. Undertaking and assets were acquired by Java Produce Co. (1932) Ld. (later Java Produce Co. Ld.), in which company shareholders were entitled to 10 shares of 2s. (credited with 1s. 6d. paid) for each share of £1 held. Debenture stockholders were entitled to an equal amount of similar debenture stock in new company. Final meeting return regd. 19 Dec. 1933 1933

Java Produce Co. Ld. Regd. 1932 as Java Produce Co. (1932) Ld.; name changed Dec. 1942. Struck off Register 15 Sept. 1961 1962

Java Rubber & Produce Co. Ld. Regd. 1906. Vol. liq. 12 Oct. 1928. The undertaking and assets were transferred to Java Produce Co. Ld. in which company shareholders were entitled to 2 fully-paid shares of £1 for each share of £1 held and an option (since expired) to subscribe at par for 7% convertible debenture stock. Final meeting return regd. 3 Feb.1930 1929

Java Syndicate Ld. See Sumatra Syndicate Ld.

Javali Co. Ld. Regd. 1867. Property was acquired in 1899 by Javali Gold Mine & Trading Co. Ld. Vol. liq. 19 July 1901. Final meeting return regd. 2 Dec.1901 1902

Javali Gold Mine & Trading Co. Ld. Regd. 1899. Vol. liq. Dec. 1908. Removed from Register 1910 1909

Jax Stores Ld. Regd. 1936. Vol. liq. (members') 20 Mar. 1964. All capital was owned by Great Universal Stores Ld. Final meeting return regd. 15 Apr. 1970 1951

Jay (E. & S.) Ld. Regd. 1897. Capital returned to contributors–10s. per preference share of £1 at Jan. 1903; further payments (if any) not known. Removed from Register 1903 1903

Jay Hawk & Lone Pine Consolidated Mining Co. Ld. Regd. 1891. Vol. liq. 30 Jan. 1895. Reconstructed as company of same name. Shareholders were entitled to 1 share of £1 (credited with 18s. 9d. paid) in new company for each share of £1 held. Final meeting return regd. 24 May 1907 1896

Jay Hawk & Lone Pine Consolidated Mining Co. Ld. Regd. 1895. Vol. liq. 16 Aug. 1896. Reconstructed as Ethel Reef Gold Mining Co. Ld., in which company shareholders were entitled to 1 share of 5s. (credited with 3s. paid) for each share of £1 held. Final meeting return regd. 30 Sept. 1907 1902

Jay Hawk Mining Co. Ld. Regd. 1888. Vol. liq. 10 May 1889. Reconstructed as company of same name. Shareholders were entitled to 1 share of £1 (credited

VOL. FOR

with 18s. 6d. paid) for each share of £1 held. Struck off Register 19 Oct. 1906 1890

Jay Hawk Mining Co. Ld. Regd. 1889. Vol. liq. 30 Aug. 1890. Reconstructed as company of same name, in which company shareholders were entitled to 1 share of £1 (credited with 18s. paid) for each fully-paid share of £1 held. Final meeting return regd. 18 Jan. 1892 1892

Jay Hawk Mining Co. Ld. Regd. 1890. Vol. liq. 20 Aug. 1891. Reconstructed as Jay Hawk & Lone Pine Consolidated Mining Co. Ld., in which company shareholders received 165,000 shares of £1 (credited with 16s. paid). Debenture holders were entitled to an equal amount of debenture in new company. Final meeting return regd. 23 Nov. 1892 1894

Jazpampa Bajo Nitrate Co. Ld. Regd. 1902. Vol. liq. 5 Nov. 1917. Final meeting return regd. 22 Nov. 1918 1918

Jedburgh Gas Co. Ld. Regd. in Edinburgh 1937. Dissolved 1 May 1949, undertaking being vested in Scottish Area Gas Board under Gas Act 1948. Holders of ordinary shares (of £1) were entitled to receive £1 8s. 6d. British Gas 3% guaranteed stock 1990–95 for each share held 1952

Jeetwarpore Indigo Planting Co. Ld. Regd. 1880. Removed from Register 1890 1890

Jeffree Line Ld. Regd. 1919. Court Order to wind up 17 Oct. 1922. Struck off Register June 1931 1932

Jeher Hydraulic Tin Mining Co. Ld. Regd. Edinburgh 1905. Vol. liq. Oct. 1913. Final meeting return regd. 30 Dec. 1914 1914

Jelapang Tin Dredging Ld. Inc. in Federated Malay States in 1925. Control was transferred to London in 1944 and returned to Kuala Lumpur in 1947. Vol. liq. (members') 1 Feb. 1960. Capital returned to contributories—13s. 1d. per share of 1s. £157 9s. 7d. was paid to Official Receiver. Federation of Malaya in respect of unclaimed dividends. Final meeting return regd. 27 Feb. 1961 1962

Jemaa Exploration Co. Ld. Regd. 1912. Vol. liq. 11 Nov. 1920. Undertaking was acquired by Keffi Consolidated Tin Co. Ld in which company shareholders were entitled to 9 fully-paid shares of 5s. for every 5 shares of 5s. held. Final meeting return regd. 9 Aug.1921 1921

Jenderak Planting Syndicate Ld. Regd. 1925. Vol. liq. (members') 22 Apr. 1930. Undertaking and assets were acquired by Amherst Estates (Selangor) Rubber Co. Ld. in which company shareholders were entitled to 2·97 shares of 2s. (credited as fully-paid) for each share of £1 held. Final meeting return regd. 20 Nov. 1930 1931

Jenkin & Purser (Holdings) p.l.c. Regd. 20 Nov. 1957. Winding-up order 26 Jan. 1987 1973–4

Jenkins (John) & Sons Ld. Regd. 16 Mar. 1899. Liquidated under supervision of Court. Removed from Register 1906 1905

Jensen (J.) & Co. Ld. Regd. 1886. Removed from Register 1908 1893

Jepson's Mercantile Directory & Manufacturers' Guide Ld. Regd. 1887. Vol. liq. 18 Dec. 1894. Final meeting return regd. 17 Jan. 1896 1895

Jequié Rubber Syndicate Ld. Regd. 1908. Court Order to wind-up 16 Oct. 1917. Struck off Register 1928 .. 1918

Jerantut Rubber Co. Ld. Regd. 1924. Vol. liq. 13 Aug. 1926. Property was sold in 1925 to Djember Rubber Estates Ld. (later Djember Holdings Ld.), in which company shareholders were entitled to 3 fully-paid shares of £1 for every 100 shares of 2s. held. Final meeting return regd. 2 June 1927 1927

Jerantut Syndicate Ld. Regd. 1920. Vol. liq. 31 Dec. 1923 for reconstruction as Jerantut Rubber Co. Ld in which company shareholders were entitled to 8 shares of 2s. (credited with 1s. paid) for each share of £1 held. Debentures were exchanged for an equal amount of 6% debenture stock in new company. Final meeting return regd. 2 June 1927.................. 1925

Jerez to Algeciras Gibraltar Direct Railway Co. Established Madrid 1880. Reconstructed in 1888 as Algeciras (Gibraltar) Railway Co. Ld. 1908

Jersey Eastern Railway Co. Ld. Inc. Jersey 1872. Vol. liq. June 1929 1930

Jersey Electric Lighting & Power Co. Ld. Regd. 1914. Vol. liq. (members') 24 Apr. 1934. Capital returned to contributories—£89,273 13s. 5d. Ordinary shareholders received 84 shares of £1 in Electric Supply Corporation Ld for every 100 ordinary shares of £1 held. Final meeting return regd. 30 Sept. 1936. Court Orders deferred dissolution until 15 Oct. 1937 1935

Jersey Lily Gold Mines Ld. Regd. 1895. Court Order to wind up 15 Mar. 1899. Removed from Register 1908 1898

Jersey Railways & Tramways Ld. Inc. Jersey 1896. Vol. liq. 1937; real estate and concessions acquired by State of Jersey. Outstanding 4½% debentures and 5% notes were repaid at par. Company's holding of

VOL. FOR

shares of Jersey Motor Transport Co. Ld. was transferred to Jersey Road Transport Ld. in exchange for ordinary and preference shares of that company. Shareholders received 1 ordinary and 1 preference share for each ordinary and preference share of £10 respectively held.............................. **1938**

Jersey Railways Co. Ld. Regd. 1883. Vol. liq. 29 Oct. 1895. Final meeting return regd. 13 Feb. 1897 .... **1896**

Jersey Shipping Investment Co. Ld. Inc. Jersey 1933. Vol. liq. Nov. 1937. Shareholders received £2 11s. 10·2d. per share of £1 .... **1939**

Jersey United Shipping Co. Ld. Inc. Jersey 1938. Vol. liq. (members') 23 Oct. 1953. Shareholders were entitled to receive one 2s. share in United Transport Ld for each £1 share held also cash payments of £1 7s. 1¼d. per share. Company dissolved since Oct. 1953 .... **1962**

"Jerusalem" Ld. Regd. 1880. Vol. liq. 26 Oct. 1892. Final meeting return regd. 5 Apr. 1899 .... **1893**

Jesshope (Holdings) Ld. Regd. 1953. Vol. liq. (creditors') 7 Mar. 1963. Creditors received 18s. in the £1. No capital returned to contributories. Final meeting return regd. 22 Dec. 1971 .... **1971**

Jessie Gold Mining Co. Ld. Regd. 1899. Reconstructed as East Gwanda Mines Ld in which company shareholders were entitled to 3 shares of £1 (credited with 14s. paid) for every 5 shares of £1 held. Removed from Register 1908 .... **1905**

Jevons Cooper Ld. Regd. 1970. Vol. liq. 31 July 1981. Final meeting return regd. 1 Sept. 1982 .... **1978–9**

Jewel-Denero Mines Ld. Regd. Edinburgh 1912. Vol. liq. Jan. 1924. Final meeting return regd. 15 Apr. 1924 .... **1924**

Jewel Pneumatic Tyre Co. Ld. Regd. 1897. Struck off Register 18 Nov. 1902 .... **1903**

Jewel Syndicate Ld. Regd. Edinburgh 1907. Vol. liq. Nov. 1912. Undertaking sold to Jewel-Denero Mines Ld in which shareholders were entitled to 4 fully-paid shares of 5s. for each share of £1 held. Final meeting return regd. 30 Jan. 1914.............. **1913**

Jhoori Valley Tea Co. Ld. Regd. 1885. Receiver appointed in Dec. 1892. Vol. liq. 5 Feb. 1894. Final meeting return regd. 20 Mar. 1894 .... **1895**

Jibutil (Anantapur) Gold Mines Ld. Regd. 1913. Vol. liq. 8 Apr. 1925. Final meeting return regd. 11 Mar. 1927 .... **1926**

Jibutil Gold Mines of Anantapur Ld. Regd. 1911. Vol. liq. 28 Nov. 1913. Reconstructed as Jibutil (Anantapur) Gold Mines Ld., in which company shareholders were entitled to 1 fully-paid ordinary share of 10s. for every 5 ordinary shares of 10s. held; preference shareholders were entitled to an equal number of preference shares of 10s. in new company. Final meeting return regd. 15 Mar. 1917 **1914**

Jicaro Gold Estates Ld. Regd. 1910. Vol. liq. 23 Mar. 1914. Final meeting return regd. 24 Nov. 1914 .... **1915**

Jinman Steam Shipping Co. Ld. *See* Neptune Steam Shipping Co. Ld.

Jipoh Investments Ld. Regd. 1913 as Ipoh Tin Dredging Ld.; name changed 1962. Vol. liq. (members') 21 Nov. 1962. Capital returned to contributories—15s. 6d. per share (of 8s.). Final meeting return regd. 3 Mar. 1967 .... **1968**

Jirnkee Gold Mining Co. Ld. Regd. 1903. Receiver sold all assets, the proceeds were insufficient to pay claims of debenture holders. Struck off Register 1909 .... **1909**

Jirnkee Hydraulic Sluicing Gold Mining Co. Ld. Regd. 1898. Reconstructed 1903 as Jirnkee Gold Mining Co. Ld., in which company shareholders were entitled to 1 fully-paid share of 5s. for each share of 5s. held. Removed from Register 1910 .... **1908**

Jitra Rubber Plantations Ld. Regd. 1920. Vol. liq. (members') 5 Sept. 1933. Reconstructed as company of same name. Shareholders were entitled to 1 share of 2s. (credited as fully-paid) in new company for every 2 shares of 2s. held. Preference shares were repaid in cash at par. Final meeting return regd. 26 July 1934 .... **1934**

Joe's Luck & Bon Accord (Sheba) Gold Mining Co. Ld. Regd. 1887. Vol. liq. 16 Sept. 1890. Reconstructed as company of same name. Shareholders were entitled to 1 share of £1 (credited with 15s. paid) for each fully-paid share of £1 held. Final meeting return regd. 11 July 1893 .... **1900**

Joe's Luck & Bon Accord (Sheba) Gold Mining Co, Ld. Regd. 1890. Vol. liq. 25 Apr. 1894. Reconstructed as Joe's Reefs United (Sheba) Ld., in which company shareholders were entitled to 1 share of £1 (credited with 17s. paid) for each share of £1 held. Final meeting return regd. 17 Apr. 1896 .... **1895**

Joe's Reefs United (Sheba) Ld. Regd. 1894. Vol. liq. 15 July 1895. Reconstructed as company of same name. Shareholders were entitled to 3 shares of £1 (credited

with 15s. paid), in new company for every 2 shares of £1 held. Final meeting return regd. 17 Apr. 1896 **1897**

Joe's Reefs United (Sheba) Ld. Regd 1895. Vol. liq. 12 Jan. 1897. Reconstructed as United Reefs (Sheba) Ld., in which company shareholders were entitled to 1 fully-paid share of £1 for every 4 shares of £1 held. Final meeting return regd. 13 July 1898.............. **1898**

Johannesburg & Auckland Park Estate Ld. Regd. 1893. Removed from Register 1899; restored to Register 1900. Reconstructed 1902 as Auckland Park Real Estate Ld., in which company shareholders were entitled to 1 fully-paid share of £1 for each share of £1 held. Removed from Register 1904.................... **1903**

Johannesburg Building Estate Syndicate Ld. Regd. 1889. Vol. liq. 28 Dec. 1896. Final meeting return regd. 11 Aug. 1898 .... **1899**

Johannesburg City & Suburban Tramway Co. Ld. Inc. Transvaal 1889. Vol. liq.; undertaking and assets sold to Municipality of Johannesburg. Capital returned to contributories—15s. 6d. per share of £1 at Feb. 1905; further payments (if any) not known **1905**

Johannesburg Coal Co. Ld. Regd. 1889. Vol. liq. 5 Nov. 1895. Final meeting return regd. 28 Dec. 1899 ..... **1896**

Johannesburg Commercial Buildings Ld. Regd. 1909. Vol. liq. 19 June 1914. Final meeting return regd. 27 July 1916 .... **1915**

Johannesburg Gold Fields Ld. Regd. 1889. Vol. liq. June 1910. Reconstructed as company of same name. Shareholders were entitled to 1 fully-paid share of 10s. in new company for each share of £1 held or 50 fully-paid shares of 10s. for each founders' share of £1 held. Removed from Register 1912 .... **1911**

Johannesburg Gold Fields Ld. Regd. 1910. Vol. liq. (members') 20 Dec. 1929. Capital returned to contributories—6s. 1·9d per share of 10s. £2,351 9s. 5d. was paid into Companies' Liquidation Account. Final meeting return regd. 22 Dec. 1930.............. **1930**

Johannesburg Land, Building & Investment Co. Ld. Regd. 1903. Vol. liq. Nov. 1909 for reconstruction as Johannesburg Commercial Buildings Ld., in which company shareholders were entitled to 1 fully-paid share of 5s. for each share of £1 held. Removed from Register 1911 .... **1910**

Johannesburg Lighting Co. Ld. Regd. 1891. Vol. liq. 31 May 1895. Undertaking was acquired by Johannesburg Sanitary Board. Final meeting return regd. 17 June 1897 .... **1896**

Johannesburg Office & Safe Deposit Co. Ld. Regd. 1893. Struck off Register 1927 .... **1926**

Johannesburg Waterworks, Estate & Exploration Co. Ld. Inc. Cape Colony 1888 and Transvaal 1889. Vol. liq. undertaking transferred to Rand Water Board. Capital returned to contributories—£2 0s. 6d per share of £1 at Feb. 1906; further payments (if any) not known. Debentures repaid by Rand Water Board in Dec. 1905 at £109 2s. 5d.% (inclusive of interest) **1907**

Johannessen (L. P.) Ld. Regd. Edinburgh 1900. Vol. liq. Mar. 1918. Final meeting return regd. 7 Dec. 1920 **1918**

Johannis Ld. Regd. 1895. Vol. liq. 24 Mar. 1897. Business and assets were acquired by Apollinaris and Johannis Ld. (later Mineral Water Holdings Ld.), in which company shareholders were entitled to £1 2s. 6d. in ordinary shares and £1 2s. 6d. in preference shares for each ordinary share of £1 held or to 5 preference shares of £10 and 5 ordinary shares of £10 for every 2 deferred shares of £1 held. Final meeting return regd. 24 Feb.1900 .... **1908**

Johannis Natural Mineral Water Co. Ld. Regd. 1887. Vol. liq. 10 Dec. 1888. Final meeting return regd. 10 Sept. 1889 .... ***1889**

John Barran Ld. *See* Town and Central Holdings (Leeds) Ld.

John Brothers' Abergarw Brewery Co. Ld. Regd. 1895. Court Order to wind up 27 Oct. 1930. Struck off Register 17 July 1942 .... **1943**

John Bull Gold Mine Ld. Regd. 1898. Vol. liq. 14 Apr. 1898. Reconstructed 1899 as Union Jack Consolidated Mines Ld in which company shareholders were entitled to 2 shares of 5s. (credited with 3s. 6d. paid) for each share of 10s. held. Removed from Register 1901 .... **1900**

John Bull Insurance Co. Ld. *See* Protector Fire Insurance Co. Ld.

John Bull Ld. Regd. 1908. Vol. liq. 22 Mar. 1920. Reconstructed as Odhams Press Ld., in which company shareholders were entitled to 3 preference shares of £1 (credited as fully-paid) for every £2 preference capital held or 5 fully-paid ordinary shares of £1 for every £2 ordinary capital held. Final meeting return regd. 9 Oct. 1924 .... **1921**

John Bull Stores Ld. Regd. 1928. Over 90% of shares held by Sunbeam Presswork & Conveyors Ld. Struck off Register 29 Nov. 1932 .... **1933**

See Stock Exchange Year-Book.

VOL. FOR

John E. Dallas & Sons Ld. *See* Dallas (John E.) & Sons Ld.

John Galloway & Co. Ld. *See* Galloway (John) & Co. Ld.

John Govett (Investments) Ld. *See* Govett European Trust Ld.

John's Bottling & Stopper Co. Ld. Regd. 1888. Vol. liq. 7 Jan. 1889. Final meeting return regd. 22 Sept. 1892 .... **1890**

Johns, Son & Watts Ld. Regd. 1895. Vol. liq. 8 Mar. 1898. Undertaking and assets were acquired by Company of same name for £30,000 in ordinary shares of £1, £30,000 in preference shares of £1, £35,000 in debentures and £5,000 in cash. Final meeting return regd. 21 Dec. 1898 .... **1898**

Johnson (C. H.) (Machinery) Ld. *See* J. C. E. G. p.l.c.

Johnson & Barnes Ld. Regd. as private company 22 Jan. 1912; convertedinto a public company 24 Nov. 1928. Vol. liq. (creditors') 8 Aug. 1983. Return of final meeting regd. 5 Jan. 1987 .... **1988–9**

Johnson & Co. Ld. Regd. 1878. Court Orders: to wind up 29 Mar. 1890; to dissolve 22 Jan. 1894 .... **1891**

Johnson Construction Equipment Group Ld. *See* J. C. E. G. p.l.c.

Johnson & Darlings Ld. Regd. 1892. Vol. liq. (members') 25 Mar. 1946. Undertaking acquired by Fisons Ld. Final meeting return regd. 21 May 1947 **1938**

Johnson Brothers (Dyers) Ld. Regd. 1898. Vol. liq. (members') 4 Sept. 1953. Reconstructed as (*a*) Johnson Brothers (Dyers) Ld. [later Johnson Group Cleaners Ld.] and (*b*) Johnson Brothers (Dyers) Properties Ld. [later Johnson Group Cleaners Properties Ld.] Shareholders were entitled to-preference: one 9% preference share (of £1) of (*a*) for each share (of £1) held; employees' preference: one employees' preference share (of £1) of (*a*) plus 5*s*. nominal value of 4¾% debenture stock of (*b*) for each share (of £1) held; A and B ordinary: one A or B ordinary share (of £1) of (*a*) plus £1 nominal value of 4¾% debenture stock of (*b*) and cash distributions totalling 13*s*. 4½*d*. for each A or B ordinary share (of £1) held. £43 15*s*. 3*d*. was paid into Companies' Liquidation Account. Final meeting return regd. 10 Dec. 1956 .... **1957**

Johnson (Edmond) Ld. Inc. Dublin. Vol. liq. 15 Feb. 1927. All creditors were to be paid in full. Practically all shares held by Switzer & Co. Ld. **1928**

Johnson (Henry) (Birmingham) Ld. Regd. 1912. Vol. liq. (members') 30 June 1939. Undertaking acquired by I. C. I. (Salt) Ld. Capital returned to contributories—7*s*. per preference share of 7*s*.; 13*s*. 10*d*. per ordinary share of £1. Final meeting return regd. 26 June 1940 .... **1943**

Johnson (Jabez), Hodgkinson and Pearson Ld. Regd. 1892. Vol. liq. 29 July 1929. Reconstructed as Quilt Manufacturers Ld. (later Vantona Textiles Ld.). Shareholders were entitled to 15 preference shares of £1 in new company for every 14 preference shares of £1 held or 1 preference share of £1 *plus* 13*s*. in cash for every 2 preference shares held; 1 ordinary share of £1 in new company *plus* 6*s*. in cash or 2 ordinary shares of £1 *plus* £1 18*s*. in cash for every 3 preferred ordinary or deferred ordinary shares of £1 held. Final meeting return regd. 27 Aug. 1930 .... **1930**

Johnson-Lundell Electric Traction Co. Ld. Regd. 1900. Vol. liq. Dec. 1911. Removed from Register 1913 .... **1912**

Johnson, Tyler & Co. Ld. Regd. 1911. Receiver for debenture holders appointed in Oct. 1912. Struck off Register 1915 .... **1913**

Johnson's Saccharin Co. Ld. Regd. 1876. Business was acquired by Sugar & Malt Products Ld. for £11,000 in cash, £5,000 in ordinary shares and £5,000 in deferred shares of £1. Removed from Register 1907 **1908**

Johnston Die Press Co. Ld. Regd. 1898. Court Order to wind up 29 Apr. 1902. Removed from Register 1910 **1903**

Johnston Foreign Patents Co. Ld. Regd. 1899. Court Order to wind up 28 May 1902. Removed from Register 1910 .... **1903**

Johnston Line Ld. Regd. 1914. Vol. liq. (members') 15 Nov. 1934. Undertaking acquired by Johnston Warren Lines Ld. Capital returned to contributories—£497,953. Final meeting return regd. 20 Mar. 1936 .... **1940**

Johnston Mill Ld. Regd. 1922. Struck off Register 1934 **1935**

Johnstone Randfontein Gold Mining Co. Ld. Inc. Transvaal 1899. Vol. liq. Apr. 1909; undertaking sold to Randfontein Central Gold Mining Co. Ld. for 139,583 fully-paid shares of £1 .... **1910**

Johore Fibre & Planting Co. Ld. *See* Batu Pahat Coffee Co. Ld.

Johore River Rubber Plantations Ld. Regd. 1925. Vol. liq. (members') 31 Aug. 1961. Undertaking and assets acquired by Craigielea Rubber Plantations. Final meeting return regd. 30 Nov. 1962 .... **1964**

VOL. FOR

Johore Rubber Lands (Malaya) Ld. Regd. 1909 as Jonore Rubber Lands (Malay States) Ld.; name changed July 1909. Vol. liq. 6 Nov. 1913. Reconstructed as Johore Rubber Lands (1913) Ld. Shareholders were entitled to 4 shares of £1 (credited with 14*s*. paid) for every 3 shares of £1 held. Final meeting return regd. 3 Dec. 1914 .... **1914**

Johore Rubber Lands (1913) Ld. Regd. 1913. Vol. liq. 30 July 1920. Capital returned to contributories—£2 8*s*. per share of £1; further payments (if any) not known. Final meeting return regd. 27 Apr. 1921 **1921**

Johore Rubber Lands Ld. Regd. 1925. Vol. liq. 18 Dec. 1950. Undertaking and assets acquired by Aberfoyle Plantations Ld., in which company shareholders were entitled to 23·354 fully-paid shares of that company for every 100 shares (of 2*s*.) held. Final meeting return regd. 26 Mar. 1954 .... **1955**

Johore Tea Co. Ld. *See* Batu Pahat Coffee Co. Ld.

Joint Industries Ld. Regd. 1919 as Belgian Corporation Ld.; name changed Mar. 1923. Vol. liq. (members') 31 Mar. 1930. Capital returned to contributories—13*s*. 7·1598*d*. per preference share of £1. Final meeting return regd. 30 Nov. 1944 .... **1931**

Joint-Stock Association Ld. Regd. 1882. Removed from Register 1907 .... ***1891**

Joint Stock Company for Trading in Tobacco ("Tabacus"), formerly M. L. Herzog & Co., Cavalla. See "Tabacus" N. V.

Joint Stock Conversion & Investment Trust Ld. Regd. 1897. Removed from Register 1905 .... **1901**

Joint Stock Development Trust Ld. Regd. 1926. Vol. liq. (creditors') 26 Nov. 1934. No capital returned to contributories. Final meeting return regd. 9 Sept. 1936 .... **1935**

Joint Stock Discount Co. Ld. Regd. 1863. Court Order to wind up 17 Mar. 1866. Removed from Register 29 July 1902 .... ***1875**

Joint Stock Investment Co. Ld. Regd. 1899. Struck off Register 16 Nov. 1906 .... **1907**

Joint Stock Trust & Finance Corporation Ld. Regd. 1904. Court Order to wind up 8 May 1906. Struck off Register Aug. 1934 .... **1935**

Jointless Rim Ld. Regd. 1897 as New Jointless Rim Ld.; name changed Mar. 1898. Vol. liq. 19 May 1905. Receiver appointed for 1st debenture holders realised assets which produced sufficient only to pay 10*s*. in £; no return was made to 2nd debenture holders. Final meeting return regd. 27 Jan. 1906 **1906**

"Joker" Proprietary Gold Mines Ld. Regd. 1896. Vol. liq. 27 Apr. 1899. Shareholders were entitled to 1 fully-paid share of £1 in Norwegian Copper Mines Ld. for each share of £1 held. Removed from Register 1901 .... **1900**

Joker (Yalgoo) Gold Mines Ld. Regd. 1896. Vol. liq. 3 Jan. 1898. Shareholders were entitled to 1 share of £1 (credited with 16*s*. paid) in Field's Find Gold Mines Ld. for each share of £1 held. Final meeting return regd. 3 July 1899 .... **1898**

Joliet & Blue-Island Railway Co. Merged in 1938 with Elgin. Joliet & Eastern Railway **1943**

Jolly & Son (Holdings) Ld. Regd. 1968. Vol. liq. (members') 16 Nov. 1972. All ordinary capital owned by E. Dingle & Co. Ld. 7¾% Unsecured Loan Stock was repaid at par in Oct. 1972 .... **1973-4**

Jonas & Colver Ld. Regd. 1907 as Jonas & Colver Ld.; name changed to Sir Joseph Jonas, Colver & Co. Ld. in Nov. 1914 and as above Jan. 1919. Assets were sold in 1929 to Neepsend Steel & Tool Corporation Ld.; proceeds were insufficient to satisfy debenture holders. Struck off Register Oct. 1933 .... **1935**

Jonas (Sir Joseph), Colver & Co. Ld. *See* Jonas & Colver Ld.

Jones and Higgins Ld. Regd. 1896. Voluntary winding-up order 20 Feb. 1986. All capital owned by Great Universal Stores p.l.c. **1960**

Jones (A. I.) and Co. Ld. Regd. 1898. Vol. liq. (members') 28 Feb. 1955. A subsidiary of Imperial Tobacco Co. (of Great Britain and Ireland) Ld. Capital returned to contributories—£1 per guaranteed share (of £1) and £1·4448 per deferred share (of £1). Final meeting return regd. 15 Aug. 1955 .... **1956**

Jones (B. Owen) & Co. Ld. Regd.1898 Vol. liq. 16 Dec. 1904. Removed from Register 1906 .... **1905**

Jones (Buckley) Ld. Regd. 1927. Vol. liq. (members') 13 Mar. 1946. Capital returned to contributories—10*s*. (plus accrued dividend) per preference share of 10*s*.; 1*s*. 1½*d*. per deferred share of 1*s*. Final meeting return regd. 6 Feb. 1947 .... **1947**

Jones, Evans & Co. Ld. Regd. 1888. Vol. liq. (creditors') 8 July 1935. Assets realised insufficient to pay debenture holders in full. Final meeting return regd. 30 Dec. 1937 .... **1936**

Jones (Frank) Brewing Co. Ld. Regd. 1889. Court Order to wind up Oct. 1926. Struck off Register May 1933 **1934**

**See Stock Exchange Year-Book*.

VOL. FOR

Jones (Peter) Ld. Regd. 1900. Vol. liq. (members') Nov. 1933. Undertaking and assets were acquired by John Lewis & Co. Ld., in which company shareholders were entitled to 1 5% 1st cumulative preference share of £1 (credited as fully-paid) for each preference share or every 5 ordinary shares of £1 held, 1,036 preference shares were not exchanged at date of final meeting. The debenture stockholders were repaid at 101%. Final meeting return regd. 14 Nov. 1934 .... **1934**

Jones, Pope & Co. Ld. Regd. 1927. Vol. liq. (members') 29 Apr. 1936. Capital returned to contributories—3½d. per share of £1. Final meeting return regd. 14 July 1939 .... **1937**

Jones (Pryce) (Canada) Ld. Regd. 1910. Vol. liq. 5 Oct. 1915. Final meeting return regd. 4 Oct. 1920....... **1916**

Jones (R. E.) Ld. Regd. 1895. Vol. liq. (members') 30 Nov. 1962. Capital returned to contributories—20s. 7¼d. per share of 10s.). Final meeting return regd. 5 Nov. 1964 .... **1965**

Jones Rock Drill (Africa) Co. Ld. Regd. 1897. Struck off Register 8 Aug. 1905 .... **1906**

Jones (W. & C. T.) Steamship Co. Ld. Regd. 1902. Vol. liq. 23 Oct. 1918. Final meeting return regd. 27 Sept. 1924 .... **1919**

Jones (Walter) & Sons Ld. Regd. 1923. Vol. liq. 5 Dec. 1929. Final meeting return regd. 30 May 1934...... **1930**

Joseph (Leopold) Investment Trust Ld. Regd. 1972. Vol. liq. (members') 4 Oct. 1977. Capital returned to contributories—£1 per preference share (of 50p) and 93·126p per ordinary share (of 25p) £584·21 was paid into Companies' Liquidation Account in respect of unclaimed distributions. Dissolved 3 Nov. 1978 **.1979–80**

Josephine Mining Co. Ld. Regd. 1887. Vol. liq. 6 June 1890. Final meeting return regd. 3 June 1891 ...... **1891**

Josz Métallochrome Printing Co. Ld. Regd. 1889. Removed from Register 1907 .... **1893**

Jourdie Hills Gold Mining Co. Ld. Regd. 1901. Vol. liq. July 1906. Undertaking was acquired by Jourdie United Gold Mines Ld., in which company shareholders were entitled to 2 shares of 5s. (credited with 4s. paid) for each share of 10s. held. Removed from Register 1910 .... **1907**

Jourdie United Gold Mines Ld. Regd. 1906. Vol. liq. 27 July 1910. Final meeting return regd. 1 May 1911 **1911**

Joviel Properties Ld. Regd. as private company 20 Feb. 1957; converted public company 30 June 1972. Vol. liq. (creditors') 17 Mar. 1976. Return of final meeting regd. Sept. 1987. Amount paid into Companies' Liquidation Account in respect of unclaimed dividends £19,619·91 .... **1988–9**

Joyce (F.) & Co. Ld. Regd. 1888. Vol. liq. Nov. 1909. Removed from Register 1910 .... **1910**

Joy's Ld. Regd. 1924. Vol. liq. (creditors') 23 Aug. 1935. No capital returned to contributories. Final meeting return regd. 6 Dec. 1941 .... **1936**

Juanita Mines of Rhodesia Ld. Regd. 1910. Vol. liq. 29 Mar. 1923. Shareholders were entitled to 2 fully-paid shares of 2s. and 3 shares of 2s. (credited with 1s. 4d. paid) in East & West African Exploration Co. Ld. for every 2 shares of 5s. held. Final meeting return regd. 8 Apr. 1925 .... **1924**

Jubal Webb Ld. See Webb (Jubal) Ld.

Jubilee Consols Ld. Inc. Queensland 1895. Reconstructed 1898 as company of same name. Shareholders were entitled to 1 share of 5s. (credited with 4s. paid) in new company for each share of 5s. held **1901**

Jubilee Consols Ld. Inc. Queensland 1898. Acquired in 1901 by Golden Gate Corporation Ld., in which company shareholders were entitled to 1 share of 5s. (credited with 3s. 6d. paid) for each share of 5s. held **1908**

Jubilee Diamond Mining Syndicate Ld. Regd. 1911. Vol. liq. 21 Nov. 1912. Final meeting return regd. 3 Aug. 1913 .... *1914

Jubilee Gold Co. Ld. Inc. Natal 1886. Vol. liq. Aug. 1913 **1914**

Jude Hanbury & Co. Ld. Regd. 1919. Vol. liq. (members') 14 Mar. 1961. Final meeting return regd. 21 Nov. 1961 .... **1940**

Judson (Daniel) & Son Ld. Regd. 1889. Vol. liq. 14 Nov. 1902. Final meeting return regd. 3 Mar. 1903...... **1903**

Juga (Nigeria) Tin & Power Co. Ld. Regd. 1910. Vol. liq. 10 Dec. 1914. Final meeting return regd. 15 Sept. 1915 .... **1915**

Juga Valley Tin Areas Ld. Regd. 1927. Vol. liq. (creditors') 18 Jan., 1939., Assets realised insufficient to pay creditors in full. Final meeting return regd. 21 Sept. 1939 .... **1940**

Jugra Estate, Ld. Regd. 1900. All capital was owned by Anglo Oriental Plantations Ld. Vol. liq. 31 Dec. 1962. Final meeting return regd. 9 Nov. 1964 ..... **1960**

Jugra Land and Rubber Estates Ld. Regd. Edinburgh 1906. Vol. liq. Jan. 1920. Undertaking and assets were acquired by Jugra Land and Carey Ld., in which company shareholders were entitled to 3½

VOL. FOR

shares of £1 (credited as fully-paid) for each share of £1 held. Final meeting return regd. 11 Sept. 1922 **1920**

Jules Rolez Ld. Regd. 1895. Vol. liq July 1908. Removed from Register 1912 .... **1909**

Julia Nitrate Co. Ld. Regd. 1889. Reconstructed 1894 as Julia Taltal Nitrate Co. Ld. in which company shareholders were entitled to 7 shares of £1 (credited with 16s. paid) for each share of £5 held. Removed from Register 1901 .... **1896**

Julia Taltal Nitrate Co. Ld. Regd. 1894. Reconstructed as New Julia Nitrate Co. Ld. in which company shareholders were entitled to 2 shares of 10s. (credited with 7s. 6d. paid) for each share of £1 held. Removed from Register 1901 .... **1898**

Jumbil (Nigeria) Tin Areas Ld. Regd. 1912. Struck off Register Mar. 1934............... **1935**

Jumbo Gold Mining Co. Ld. Regd. 1903. Vol. liq. 2 Nov. 1927. Final meeting return regd. 1 July 1929....... **1928**

Jumper Gold Syndicate, California Ld. Regd. Edinburgh 1895. Vol. liq. Jan. 1907 for reconstruction under same name. Shareholders were entitled to 1 share of 10s. (credited with 8s. paid) in new company for each share of £1 held. Final meeting return regd. 1 Feb. 1917 .... **1908**

Jumper Gold Syndicate. California Ld. Regd. Edinburgh 1907. Vol. liq. May 1911. Capital returned to contributories—2s. 6d. per share of 10s.; further payments (if any) not known. Final meeting return regd. 1 Feb. 1917 .... **1912**

Jumpers Deep Ld. Inc. Transvaal 1894. Vol. liq. Nov. 1909. Undertaking and assets were acquired by Geldenhuis Deep Ld in which company shareholders were entitled to 45 shares of £1 (credited as fully-paid) for every 100 shares of £1 held **1910**

Jumpers Extended Ld. Regd. 1895. Removed from Register 1901 .... **1898**

"Jumpers (The)" Gold Mining Co. Ld. Inc. Transvaal 1887 as Jumpers Gold Mining Co. Ld.; name changed 1911. Vol. liq. Sept. 1914. Capital returned to contributories—1s. 3d. per share of £1 in Oct. 1914; further payments (if any) not known **1915**

Junction Deep Leads of Victoria Ld. Regd. 1898. Vol. liq. Oct. 1906. Undertaking was acquired by New Junction Deep Leads Ld., in which company shareholders were entitled to apply for shares. Removed from Register 1909 .... **1907**

Junction Tin Mine (Nigeria) Ld. Regd. 1923. Vol. liq. (creditors') 28 July 1933. No capital returned to contributories. Final meeting return regd. 8 Mar. 1935 .... **1934**

Jungle Syndicate Ld. Regd 1901. Removed from Register 1907............... **1903**

Junin Nitrate & Railway Co. Inc. in Chile. The 5% first mortgage debentures known here were repaid at 103% on 1 Jan. 1916............... **1916**

Junun Rubber Estates Ld. Regd. 1925. Vol. liq. (members') 28 July 1955. Undertaking and assets were acquired by Bukit Tupah Rubber Estates Ld. Shareholders were entitled to one 2s. share in purchasing company for each 2s. share held. Amount paid into Companies' Liquidation Account in respect of unclaimed dividends was £163 16s. 0d. Final meeting return registered 24 Dec. 1957........ **1959**

Jupiter Gold Mining Co. Ld. Inc. Transvaal 1896. Vol. liq. Dec. 1920. Capital returned to contributories— 2s. 9d. per share of £1 in May 1921; further payments (if any) not known **1922**

Jurgens' (Anton) United (Margarine) Works. [Anton Jurgens' Vereenigde Fabrieken N. V.] Inc. Netherlands 1906. Undertaking and assets were absorbed by the Lever Bros. & Unilever group. Holders of ordinary and preference shares (all classes) were offered an equal nominal amount of ordinary or 6% preference shares in Lever Bros. & Unilever N. V. (later Unilever N. V.); preference shares not so exchanged were repaid at par on 1 Aug. 1938. Payments (if any) to ordinary and priority shareholders not known. Dissolved 18 May 1938 .... **1940**

Just in Time Gold Mines Ld. Regd. 1895. Vol. liq. 11 June 1897. Reconstructed as Majestic Gold Mines Ld in which company shareholders were entitled to 1 share of £1 (credited with 10s. paid) for each share of £1 (10s. paid) held or 1 share of £1 (credited with 16s. 6d. paid) for each vendors' share held. Final meeting return regd. 21 July 1902 .... **1898**

Jutland Amalgamated Trawlers Ld. Regd. 1920. Vol. liq. (members') 9 Jan. 1951. Capital returned to contributories—£1 7s. 8d. per share of 5s. £1,606 2s. 3d. was paid into Companies' Liquidation Account in respect of unclaimed distributions. Final meeting return regd. 10 July 1952 .... **1953**

*See Stock Exchange Year-Book.

K

VOL. FOR

Kalgurli West Ld. Regd. 1899. Vol. liq. July 1905. Removed from Register 1905 .... **1906**

Kalidjeroek Rubber Co. Ld. Regd, 2 Apr. 1910. Vol. liq. (members') 9 June 1959. Preference stockholders received (per 2s. stock)—1s. 3d. in Aug. 1960 and 5d. in Aug. 1962. £73 15s. in respect of unclaimed distributions paid into Companies' Liquidation Account. Dissolved and struck off Register 15 nov. 1983 .... **1984–5**

Kali Glagah Rubber Co. Ld. Regd. 17 Oct. 1933. Winding-up order 1 Apr. 1963. Capital returned to contributories—12·3p per share (of 10p) in Mar. 1978; further distributions (if any) not known. Struck off Register 3 Sept. 1982 .... **1983–4**

Kali Glagah (Java) Rubber & Produce Co. Ld.. Regd. 1910. Vol. liq. (members') 18 Sept 1933. Reconstructed as Kali Glagah Rubber Co. Ld., in which company shareholders were entitled to 1 share of 2s. (credited with 1s. 8d. paid) for each share of 2s. held. Debenture stockholders were entitled to £70 convertible debenture stock and 400 fully-paid shares of 2s. in new company for every £100 debenture stock held. Final meeting return regd. 15 Oct. 1935 ..... **1934**

Kali Selogiri Syndicate Ld. Regd. 1907. Vol liq. May 1911. Property and assets were sold to New Kali Selogiri (Java) Plantations Ld. for £36,000. Removed from Register 1912 .... **1912**

Kalomo Syndicate Ld. Regd. 1902. Vol liq. 30 Jan. 1905. Undertaking was acquired by Northern Copper (B. S. A.) Co. Ld. Removed from Register 1905 .... **1906**

Kalulu Syndicate Ld. Regd 1901. Reconstructed 1904 as New Nimrod Co. Ld., in which company shareholders were entitled to 1 fully-paid share of £1 for every 10 shares of £1 held. Removed from Register 1905 **1905**

Kama Volga Steam Navigation Co. Established Russia 1855. The first mortgage bonds were redeemed by drawings between 1876 and 1888 .... **1889**

Kameelfontein Diamond Development Syndicate Ld. Regd 1920. Vol. liq. (creditors') 6 May 1931. No capital returned to contributories. Final meeting return regd. 4 Nov. 1938 .... **1932**

Kamsfersdam Mines Ld. Regd. 1896. Vol. liq. 6 Oct. 1926. Final meeting return regd. 29 June 1927 .... **1927**

Kaministiquia Power Co. Ld. Inc. Ontario 1905. Undertaking and assets acquired in Nov. 1925 by company of same name. Thirty-year 5% gold bonds were redeemed at 105% on 1 Jan. 1926. Shareholders were entitled to receive $95 in cash and $50 in 7 cumulative redeemable preference shares of new company for each share of $100 held **1926**

Kaministiquia Power Ld. Inc. Canada 1925. The outstanding 1st mortgage bonds and debenture stock were redeemed at 104% on 1 Nov. 1928 ..... **1929**

Kamloops Mines Ld. Regd 1904. Vol. liq. Jan. 1905. Reconstructed as company of same name. Shareholders were entitled to 1 share of £1 (credited with 16s. paid) in new company for each share of £1 held. Debenture holders were entitled to debentures in new company. Removed from Register 1906 .... **1905**

Kamloops Mines Ld. Regd. 1905. Vol. liq. 1 Aug. 1919. Assets realised insufficient to meet claims of debenture holders in full. Final meeting return regd. 16 July 1920 .... **1920**

Kamounghia Tavoy Tin Ld. Regd 1927. Vol. liq. Mar. 1934. Shareholders were entitled to 3 shares of 4s. in Tavoy Tin Dredging Corporation Ld., for every 10 shares of 5s held plus 1¼d. per share in cash. Final meeting return regd. 18 July 1938 .... **1935**

Kampar Malaya Tin Dredging Ld, Regd. 1927. Vol. liq. (members') 9 Aug. 1934. Undertaking and assets were acquired by Southern Kinta Consolidated Ld., in which company shareholders were entitled to 4 shares of 5s. (credited as fully-paid) for every 3 shares of 10s. held. Final meeting return regd. 1 Sept. 1936 .... **1935**

Kanbauk (Burma) Wolfram Mines Ld. Inc. in India 24 Mar. 1917. Vol. liq. 10 Jan. 1949. No capital was returned to contributories **1951**

Kandahena Estate Ld. Regd. 1909. Vol. liq. 7 May 1926. All shares held by Anglo-Ceylon & General Estates Co. Ld. Final meeting return regd. 19 Oct. 1927 **1928**

Kandapolla Tea Co. Ld. Regd. 1897. Vol. liq. (members') 14 Feb. 1947. Estates sold in 1946 for £138,500 (£45,500 cash and £93,000 in 31,000 fully-paid ordinary £1 shares in Nuwara Eliya Tea Estates Co. Ld. Capital returned to contributories—£1 per share to ordinary and preference shareholders, and the shares mentioned above (1 share for every 3 held of either class). £5 15s. 2d paid into Companies' Liquidation Account. Final meeting return regd. 21 Apr. 1953 .... **1954**

Kandula Ld. Regd. 1963. Vol. liq. (members') 11 Mar. 1966. All capital owned by Consolidated Commercial Co. Ld. Distributions per share of £1—20s 11⁹⁄₁₆. Final meeting return regd. 4 Mar. 1968 .... **1969**

Kandyan Tea Estates Ld. Regd. 1927. Receiver appointed in Oct. 1932. Holders of 1st mortgage convertible debenture stock were entitled to 46·7% of holding. Struck off Register 8 Dec. 1936 .... **1937**

Kaneika United Goldfields Ld. Regd. 1906. Vol. liq. Feb. 1908. Undertaking was acquired by West Altai Gold Claims Ld., in which company shareholders were entitled to 4 fully-paid shares of 5s. for every 5 shares of £1 held. Removed from Register 1909 .. **1908**

Kangarilla Proprietary Silver Mines (South Australia) Ld. Regd. 1888, Vol. liq. 29 June 1892. Reconstructed as Kangarilla Silver Mines Ld., in which company shareholders were entitled to 1 share of £1 (credited with 17s. paid) for each share of £1 held. Final meeting return regd. 15 Feb. 1894 .... **1897**

Kangarilla Silver Mines Ld. Regd 1892. Removed from Register 1901 .... **1898**

Kangol Ld. Regd. as private company 28 June 1952; converted into public company 1 July 1952. All capital acquired by American Safety Equipment Corpn. in Nov. 1972. Dissolved 24 July 1986 ...... **1973–4**

Kangundi Syndicate Ld. Regd. 1886. Vol. liq. 15 Mar. 1900. Final meeting return regd 20 Jan. 1902 ..... **1901**

Kannenbeer Supply (London) Ld. Regd 1903. Vol. liq. 10 July 1906. Final meeting return regd. 14 Aug. 1907 ***1904**

Kano (Nigeria) Tin Areas Ld. Regd. 1911. Receiver appointed in Apr. 1921; ceased to act July 1926. Properties were acquired by Limoro-Kano Tin (Nigeria) Ld. Struck off Register May 1929 .... **1930**

Kanowna Consolidated Gold Mines Ld. Regd. 1899. Reconstructed as company of same name. Shareholders were entitled to 1 share of 10s. (credited with 9s paid) in new company for each share of 10s held. Removed from Register 1904 .... **1903**

Kanowna Consolidated Gold Mines Ld. Regd. 1902. Removed from Register 1911 .... **1904**

Kanowna Gold Mining Co. Ld. Regd 1894. Removed from Register 1898 .... **1898**

Kansai Electric Co. Ld., formerly Kansai Water Power Co. Ld. See Toho Electric Power Co. Ld.

Kansas City, Mexico & Orient Railway Co. Inc. Kansas 1900. The line, which was sold under foreclosure to Kansas City, Mexico & Orient Railroad Co., was again sold under foreclosure to a new company, Kansas City, Mexico & Orient Railway Co. and holders of 4% 1st mortgage 50-year gold bonds ceased to have any interest............................. **1942**

Kansas Irrigation Co. Ld. Regd. 1894. Removed from Register 1910 .... **1903**

Kansas-Oklahoma Oil & Refinery Co. Ld. Regd 1912. Vol. liq. 14 Feb. 1927. Final meeting return regd. 8 June 1928... **1927**

Kantamantu (Wassau) Gold Mine Ld. Regd. 1901. Vol. liq. 18 Dec. 1902. Undertaking was acquired by Gold Coast United Ld., in which company shareholders were entitled to 1 fully-paid share of 10s. for every 2 shares of £1 held. Struck off Register 10 Oct. 1961 .... **1904**

Kanturk & Newmarket Railway Co. Inc. by Special Act 1887. Purchased by Great Southern & Western Railway Co., Ireland, in 1892 for £60,000 in cash, which was paid to Accountant-General of Supreme Court of Ireland and distributed as Court ordered **1893**

Kanya Exploration Co. Ld. Regd. 1889. Vol. liq. 9 July 1897. Reconstructed as Kanya Ld., in which company shareholders were entitled to 1 share of 10s (credited with 8s. 6d. paid) for each share of £1 held. Final meeting return regd 4 Apr. 1899 .... **1905**

Kanya Ld. Regd. 1897. Undertaking was acquired by South Rhodesia Land and Mining Co. Ld., in which company shareholders were entitled to 2 fully-paid shares of 2s. 6d. for every 3 shares of 10s. held. Removed from Register 1908 .... **1906**

Kapai-Vermont Gold Mining Co. Ld. Regd. 1896. Properties were acquired in 1900 by Kuaotunu Syndicate Ld., for 5,000 shares of £1 (credited with 16s. 6d. paid). Removed from Register 1909 .... **1903**

Kapala Rubber Estates of Malaya Ld. Regd. 1934. All capital acquired by Kulim Rubber Plantations Ld. Vol. liq. (members') 29 Dec. 1961. Final meeting return regd 4 Jan. 1964 .... **1961**

Kapanga Gold Mining Co. Ld. Regd. 1893. Vol. liq. 20 May 1901. Reconstructed as Tarkwa Proprietary Ld., in which company shareholders were entitled to 1 share of 10s. (credited with 8s. paid) for each share of £1 held. Final meeting return regd. 19 July 1904 **1902**

Kapanga Gold Mining Co. of New Zealand Ld. Regd. 1880. Vol. liq. Jan. 1885, Final meeting return regd. 23 Jan. 1888 .... **1886**

See Stock Exchange Year-Book.

VOL. FOR

Kapar Para Rubber Estates Co. Ld. Regd. 1905. Vol. liq. (members') 7 Aug. 1958. Undertaking and assets acquired by Seafield Amalgamated Rubber Co. Ld., shareholders receiving 5 fully-paid shares (of 2s.) in that company plus 2s. cash for every 4 shares (of 2s.) held. £582 13s 7d. paid into Companies' Liquidation Account. Final meeting return regd. 31 Oct. 1961   1963

Kara Gold Mining Co. Ld. Regd 1903. Receiver appointed 13 Nov. 1907; ceased to act 31 Dec 1914. Struck off Register 31 Oct. 1916   1908

Karabournou Mercury Syndicate Ld. Regd. 1905. Vol. liq. June 1912. Capital returned to contributories— 1·91d. per share of £1; further payments (if any) not known. Removed from Register 1913   1913

Karaka Mines Ld. Regd. 1910. Vol. liq. 5 Dec. 1913. Final meeting return regd. 10 June 1915   1914

Kalgurli Reefs Ld. Regd. 1897. Removed from Register 1911   1909

Karre Tin Co. Ld. Regd. 1925. Vol. liq. 11 Apr. 1928. The undertaking and assets were acquired by Associated Tin Mines of Nigeria Ld., in which company shareholders were entitled to 1 fully-paid share of 5s. for every 7 shares of 2s. held. Final meeting return regd. 5 Feb. 1929   1929

Karrier Motors Ld. Regd. 1920. Vol. liq. (creditors') Dec. 1934. Goodwill and certain assets acquired by Karrier Motors (Successors) Ld. (later Karrier Motors Ld.). Struck off Register 30 Dec. 1949   1952

Kasbek Syndicate Ld. Regd. 1900. Vol. liq. June 1911. Removed from Register 1912   1913

Kasempa Concessions Ld. Regd. 1926. Vol. liq. 23 Feb. 1928. Undertaking and assets were acquired by Loangura Concessions (Northern Rhodesia) Ld., in which company shareholders were entitled to 3 fully-paid shares of 5s. for each share of £1 held. Final meeting return regd. 12 Sept. 1928   1928

Kasintoe Rubber Estates Ld. Regd. 1910. Vol. liq. 9 Dec. 1913. Reconstructed as company of same name. Shareholders were entitled to 1 share of £1 (credited with 10s. paid) in new company for each share of £1 held. Final meeting return regd. 24 Jan. 1916.......   1914

Kasintoe Rubber Estates Ld. Regd. 1913. Vol. liq. (members') 14 July 1954. Capital returned to contributories—4s. 0½d. per £1 stock. £99 was paid into Companies' Liquidation Account. Final meeting return regd. 27 Feb. 1958   1959

Kaslo-Slocan Mining & Financial Corpn. Ld. Regd. 1902. Properties were transferred to West Kootenay Milling Corporation Ld. Struck off Register 1923   *1913

Kassa Mining Co. Ld. Regd. 1919. Vol. liq. (members') 20 July 1936. Undertaking and assets were acquired by Gold & Base Metal Mines of Nigeria Ld., in which company shareholders were entitled to 7 shares of 2s. 6d. (credited as fully-paid) and 2s. in cash for every 4 shares of 5s. held. Final meeting return regd. 22 Mar. 1938   1937

Kassala Cotton Co. Ld. Regd. 1922. Vol. liq. (members') 4 Apr. 1951. Concession expired 30 June 1950. Capital returned to contributories—4s. 4·687d. per share of 1s. Final meeting return regd. 12 May 1952   1953

Kassala Railway Co. Ld. Regd. 1922. Vol. liq. (members') 6 Apr. 1955. Under terms of concession railway and works became property of Sudan Government on 31 Dec. 1953 without payment. The outstanding 4½% debenture stock was redeemed at par on 1 Jan. 1953. Final meeting return regd. 6 Jan. 1956   1954

Kassa-Ropp Tin Co. Ld. Regd. 1917. Vol. liq. 6 Apr. 1923. Final meeting return regd. 18 Sept. 1923   1924

Kasuto Gold Mining Co. Ld. Regd. 1910. Vol. liq. July 1912. Court Order to continue winding up under supervision Oct. 1912. Struck off Register 1929 ...   1913

Katanga Co. See Compagnie du Katanga.

Katary (Nilgiri) Tea Estates Ld. Regd. 1925. Vol. liq. (members') 8 June 1944. Capital returned to contributories—£212 10s. per share of £100. Final meeting return regd. 2 Sept. 1950   1950

Kathleen Crown Ld. Regd. 1896. Reconstructed 1900 as company of same name. Shareholders were entitled to 1 share of 2s. 6d. (credited with 2s. paid) for each share of 2s. 6d. held. Removed from Register 1910   1908

Kathleen Crown Ld. Regd. 1900. Vol. liq. Dec. 1908. Removed from Register 1911   1909

Kathleen Gold Mine Ld. Regd. 1898. Vol. liq. 20 May 1901. Reconstructed as Tarkwa Proprietary Ld., in which company shareholders were entitled to 1 share of 10s. (credited with 8s. paid) for every 8 shares of 2s. 6d. held. Final meeting return regd. 5 July 1905   1902

Kathlekhan Estates Ld. Regd. 1926 as Kathlekhan Tea Estates Ld. Vol. liq. (members') 16 Mar. 1945. Capital returned to contributories:—15s. 9·90d. per share of £1. Final meeting return regd. 18 Oct. 1952   1953

Kathlekhan Tea Estates Ld. See above.

VOL. FOR

Kaufmann (H.) Ld. Regd. 1950. All ordinary capital was owned by Qualcast Ld. Vol. liq. (members') 25 Mar. 1960. Final meeting return regd. 6 Apr. 1961   1959

Kauri Freehold Gold Estates Ld. Regd. 1896. Reconstructed 1898 as company of same name. Shareholders were entitled to 1 share of £1 (credited with 15s. paid) for each share of £1 held. Removed from Register 1901   1900

Kauri Freehold Gold Estates Ld. Regd. 1898. Reconstructed 1900 as company of same name. The debentures were to be repaid at par. Shareholders were entitled to 1 share of £1 (credited with 15s. paid) for each share of £1 held. Removed from Register 1906   1905

Kauri Freehold Gold Estates Ld. Regd. 1900. Vol. liq. Jan. 1905. Reconstructed 1905 as company of same name. Shareholders were entitled to 9d. in cash and 1 fully-paid share of 3d. in new company for each share of £1 held. Removed from Register 1910 ...   1908

Kauri Freehold Gold Estates Ld. Regd. 1905. Vol. liq. 10 Dec. 1908. Capital returned to contributories—1s. 5d. per share of 3d. at Dec. 1908; further payments (if any) not known. Final meeting return regd. 17 Jan. 1910   1909

Kavirondo Gold Mines Ld. Regd. 1936. Vol. liq. (members') 29 Sept. 1950. Capital returned to contributories: 1s. 8·85d. per share of 10s. Final meeting return regd. 1 Jan. 1952   1952

Kawasaki Savings Bank. Absorbed by One Hundredth Bank Ld. in 1936.   1942

Kawie (Java) Rubber Estates Ld. Regd. 1910. Vol. liq. (members') 30 Dec. 1953. Capital returned to contributories—0·35d. per 2s. stock. Final meeting return regd. 29 Oct. 1955   1957

Kay & Co. (Engineers) Ld. Regd. 1937. Vol. liq. (members') 30 June 1950. Reconstructed as company of same name (later Alenco Ld.). Shareholders were entitled to receive 3 shares of 2s. 6d. (credited as fully-paid) in new company plus 15s. 1d. in cash per share of 5s. held. £93 2s. 2d. was paid into Companies' Liquidation Account in respect of unclaimed distributions. Final meeting return regd. 15 May 1952   1953

Kay (P. E.) Ld. Regd. 1889. Vol. liq. (members') 8 Sept. 1949. Final meeting return regd. 13 Mar. 1952   1928

Kay Yew (Kinta Valley) Tin Mines Ld. Regd. 1927. Vol. liq. (members') 26 Sept. 1932. Undertaking and assets were acquired by Kay Tin Mines (Kinta) Ld. (later Kay Kinta Ld., later Charterhall Finance Holdings Ld.) in which company shareholders were entitled to 2 shares of 1s. (credited with 10½d. paid) for each share of 5s. held. £16 6s. 11d. was paid into Companies' Liquidation Account in respect of sale of unclaimed shares. Final meeting return regd. 20 Sept.1934   1933

Kayan (F. M. S.) Coconut Co. Ld. Regd. Edinburgh 1913. Vol. liq. (members') 8 Oct. 1937. The coconut estate was sold to Straits Plantations Ld., in which company shareholders were entitled to 7 shares of £1 (credited as fully-paid) for every 8 shares of £1 held. Final meeting return regd. 2 July 1938   1938

Kaye's Rubber Latex Process Ld. Regd. 1922. Vol. liq. (members') 16 Dec. 1929. Capital returned to contributories—19s. 6d. per ordinary share of £1. Final meeting return regd. 6 Aug. 1931   1930

Kayiankor Block 1 Ld. Regd. 1919. Struck off Register 17 Aug. 1951   1952

Kayu Rubber Estates Ld. Regd. 1917. Undertaking acquired by Batang Consolidated Rubber Estates Ld. [later Batang Properties Ld.]. Struck off Register 30 Apr. 1946; reinstated by Order of Court and finally struck off Register 3 July 1953   1946

Kazan Oil Syndicate Ld. Regd. 1912. Struck off Register Feb. 1933   1933

Kazan Oilfields Ld. Regd. 1913. Struck off Register Feb. 1933   1933

Keane & Turnbull Ld. Regd. Dublin 1895. Vol. liq. Mar. 1922 for reconstruction under same name   1923

Keane & Turnbull Ld. Inc. Dublin 1922. Vol. liq. (members') 7 Mar. 1938. Capital returned to contributories—10s. per preference share of £1; further payments (if any) not known   1939

Kearney High Speed Railway Co. Ld. Regd. 1907. Court Order to wind up Oct. 1924. Struck off Register June 1931   1932

Kearney Vineyard Co. The shares were privately held and all outstanding debentures were redeemed on 1 July 1909   1909

Kearton (Malcolm) & Co. Ld. Regd. 1896. Removed from Register 1909   1904

Keat's Feather-Weight Spool Co. Ld. Regd. 1893. Vol. liq. 16 Nov. 1896. Final meeting return regd. 21 June 1898   1897

See Stock Exchange Year-Book.

VOL. FOR

Keay (F.) & Co. Ld. Regd. 1903. Vol. liq. (members') 30 June 1932. All shares held by Wiggins, Teape & Alex. Pirie (Merchants) Ld. Undertaking and assets transferred to Allied Paper Merchants (W. T. & Co.) Ld. Final meeting return regd. 30 Oct. 1933 .... **1933**

Kebonso Rubber Estates Ld. Regd. 1910. Vol. liq. 10 Dec. 1922. Final meeting return regd. 26 Jan. 1927 **1923**

Kedamakal Rubber Syndicate, Ld. Regd. Edinburgh 1909. Vol. liq. Feb. 1931. Undertaking and assets were acquired by company of same name. Shareholders were entitled to 1 share of 2s. (credited with 1s. 6d. paid) in new company for each share of 2s. held. Final meeting return regd. 6 July 1932 .... **1932**

Kedamakal Rubber Syndicate Ld. Regd. Edinburgh 1931. Vol. liq. (members') 14 Feb. 1945. Capital returned to contributories—4s. 5d. per share of 1s. £154 11s. 8d. was paid into Companies' Liquidation Account. Final meeting return regd. 16 July 1946 **1947**

Keegan (Peter) & Co. Ld. Regd. Dublin 1898. Vol. liq. Mar. 1926 **1927**

Keeley Silver Mines Ld. Regd. 1920. Vol. liq. 31 July 1922. The business was transferred to Keeley Silver Mines Ld., in which company shareholders were entitled to 5 fully-paid shares of $1 for each share of 10s. held. Final meeting return regd. 28 July 1923 **1923**

Keeley Silver Mines Ld. Inc. Ontario 1922. Vol. liq. Nov. 1933. Reconstructed as Anglo-Huronian Ld. in which company shareholders were entitled to 1 share of no par value for every 5 shares of $1 held and an option (since expired) over further shares **1934**

Keeling's Oxides (1921) Ld. Regd. 1921. Receiver appointed in Feb. 1926; ceased to act June 1929. Struck off Register Dec. 1930 .... **1931**

Keep (Alfred H.) Ld. Regd. 1904. Struck off Register 1922 .... ***1911**

Keffi & General Finance Co. Ld. Regd 1927. Vol. liq. 12 Nov. 1928. Final meeting return regd. 9 July 1929 **1929**

Keffi Consolidated Tin Co. Ld. Regd. 1920. Vol. liq. 28 Mar. 1928. The undertaking and assets were aquired by Associated Tin Mines of Nigeria Ld., in which company shareholders were entitled to 3 fully-paid shares of 5s. for every 11 shares of 5s. held. Final meeting return regd. 5 July 1929 .... **1929**

Keffi Tin Co. Ld. Regd. 1912. Vol. liq. 11 Nov. 1920. Property and assets were acquired by Keffi Consolidated Tin Co. Ld., in which company shareholders were entitled to 2 fully-paid shares of 5s. for each share of 5s. held. Final meeting return regd. 9 Aug. 1921 **1921**

Kehoe, Donelly & Pakenham Ld. Regd. Dublin 1891. Vol. liq. 19 June 1905 for reconstruction **1926**

Kehoe Donelly Ld. *See* Donnelly Ld.

Keighley & Worth Valley Railway Co. Vested in Midland Railway under Special Act of 1881 .... **1886**

Keighley Brothers (Omnibuses) Ld. Regd. 1928. Vol. liq. (members') 16 Dec. 1929. Capital returned to contributories—20s. per share of £1. Final meeting return regd. 10 Feb. 1930 .... **1930**

Keighley Green Mill Co. Ld. Regd. 1874. Vol. liq. 10 June 1914. Final meeting return regd. 2 May 1916 ***1882**

Keighley Tramways Co. Ld. Regd. 1887. Vol. liq. 14 Nov. 1901. Undertaking was acquired by Keighley Corporation. Capital returned to contributories—11s. 8d. per share of £1 in Dec. 1901; further payments (if any) not known. Final meeting return regd. 29 Aug. 1902 .... **1902**

Keiller (James) & Son (Germany) Ld. Regd. 1906. Vol. liq. 1 Feb. 1922. Capital returned to contributories—5s. per preference or ordinary share of £1; further payments (if any) not known. Final meeting return regd. 23 Nov. 1928 .... **1923**

Keith Gas Co. Ld. Regd. in Edinburgh 1924. Dissolved 1 May 1949 undertaking being vested in Scottish Area Gas Board under Gas Act 1948. Holders of ordinary shares (of £1) were entitled to receive £1 13s. British Gas 3% guaranteed stock 1990–95 for each share held **1952**

Kek Ld. Regd. 1925. Struck off Register 1931 .... **1928**

Kelantan Coconut Estates Ld. Regd. 1913. Vol. liq. (creditors') 5 Aug. 1931. Assets realised insufficient to meet claims of creditors in full. Final meeting return regd. 12 Jan. 1934 .... **1929**

Kelantan Copra Co. Ld. Regd. 1912. Vol. liq. 29 Sept. 1926. Final meeting return regd. 6 June 1928 ..... **1927**

Kelantan Exploration Syndicate Ld. Regd. 1907. Vol. liq. Aug. 1909. Removed from register 1910 .... **1910**

Kelantan Gold Dredging Co. (No. 1) Ld. Regd. 1904. Vol. liq. Nov. 1906. Undertaking was acquired by Duff Development Co. Ld. in which company shareholders were entitled to 4 fully-paid shares of £1 and £1 debenture stock for every 5 shares of £1 held. Removed from Register 1909 .... **1907**

VOL. FOR

Kelantan Produce and Development Co. Ld. Regd. 1912. Vol. liq. 18 Jan. 1916. Final meeting return regd. 5 Oct. 1926 .... **1916**

Kelantan Rubber Estates Ld. Regd. Edinburgh 1909. Vol. liq Apr. 1933. Reconstructed as company of same name. Shareholders were entitled to 10 shares of 2s. (credited with 1s. 6d. paid) in new company for each share of £1 held. Final meeting return regd. 12 Apr. 1934 .... **1934**

Kelham Rolling Mills Co. Ld. Regd. 1873. Vol. liq. June 1910. Removed from Register 1913 .... **1911**

Kell (Josephine) Ld. Regd. 1914 as Lawson & Co. (Bristol) Ld.; name changed to Yvonne de Faye Ld. in Jan. 1936; and as above in Apr. 1936. Vol. liq. 1 Aug. 1941. Capital returned to contributories—20s. per share of £1. Final meeting return regd. 30 Oct. 1941 .... **1926**

Kellas Ld. Regd 1906. Vol. liq. 7 May 1913. Undertaking and assets were sold to Mount Yagahong Exploration & Finance Co. Ld. (later Finance & Industrial Trust Ld.) in which company shareholders were entitled to 11 ordinary shares of 2s. (credited as fully-paid) for each ordinary share of £1 held; preference shareholders were entitled to 1 preference share of £1, and 11 ordinary shares of 2s. in new company *plus* £1 in cash for each preference share of £1 held. Final meeting return regd. 6 Jan 1917 .... **1914**

Kelsall & Kemp Ld. Regd. 1890. Vol. liq. 9 Sept. 1919. Reconstructed as company of same name. Final meeting return regd. 15 Sept. 1920 .... **1920**

Kelsey-Hayes Wheel Co. Ld. Regd. 1930. Vol. liq. (members') 9 Apr. 1953. Final meeting return regd. 7 Dec. 1953 .... **1951**

Kelso Gas Co. Ld. Regd. in Edinburgh 1909. Dissolved 1 May 1949, undertaking being vested in Scottish Area Gas Board under Gas Act 1948. Holders of ordinary shares (of £1) were entitled to receive £2 3s. 6d. British Gas 3% guaranteed stock 1990–95 for each share held **1952**

Kelty Gas Co. Ld. Regd. in Edinburgh 1905. Dissolved 1 May 1949, undertaking being vested in Scottish Area Gas Board under Gas Act 1948. Holders of securities were entitled to receive British Gas 3% guaranteed stock 1990–95 as follows in respect of each £100 unit, unless otherwise stated, of security held:

	£	s.	d.	
Ord. shares (of £1)	1	6	0	
4% red. debs.	101	10	0	
3% debs. (1948 issue)	100	0	0	
3% debs. (1947 issue)	100	0	0	**1952**

Kelvin Investment Trust Ld. (The) Regd. 1928. On 3 May 1967 the greater part of investments were transferred to London & Wall Street Units and the remainder of assets to Minster Assets Ld. Shareholders were entitled to receive approx. 135 units of London & Wall Street Units and approx. 95 fully-paid ordinary shares of 5s. of Minster Assets Ld. for every 100 shares held. Company was dissolved on 3 Sept. 1967 under Section 208 of the Companies Act, 1948 .... **1968**

Kelvin Valley Railway Co. Inc. by Special Act 1873. Under North British Railway Act 1885 undertaking was amalgamated with that company, in which holders of stock were entitled to £125 4% consolidated lien stock for every £100 stock held **1886**

Kelvinside Electricity Co. Ld. Regd. Edinburgh 1889. Undertaking and Order sold to Glasgow Corporation. Vol. liq. Sept. 1899. Final meeting return regd. 23 Nov. 1900 .... **1900**

Kemball Bishop & Co. Ld. Regd. 1919. Vol. liq. (members') 30 Nov. 1963. Final meeting return regd. 18 Aug.1964 .... **1947**

Kempinkote Gold Field Ld. Regd. 1893. Vol. liq. 10 Dec. 1900. Reconstructed as New Kempinkote Gold Field Ld., in which company shareholders were entitled to 1 share of 5s. (credited with 3s. 3d. paid) for each share of 5s. held. Final meeting return regd. 14 June 1906 .... **1908**

Kempshall Tyre Co. Ld. Business was acquired in 1924 by Chas. Macintosh & Co. Ld. **1928**

Kenilworth Gas Co. Inc. by Special Act 1856 as Kenilworth Gas Light & Coke Co.; reincorporated and name changed by Special Act 1917. Undertaking acquired by Coventry Corporation in 1926 for £38,500. Ordinary and preference stockholders received £1 8s. per £1 stock held **1928**

Kenilworth Sugar Estates Ld. Regd. 1898. Business and assets were acquired by United Railway & Trading Co. Ld. Debenture stockholders were entitled to an equal amount of 5% debentures in new company *plus* 10% bonus; preference shareholders to an equal amount of preference shares *plus* 20% bonus;

See Stock Exchange Year-Book.

VOL. FOR

ordinary shareholders to an equal amount of ordinary shares *plus* 15% bonus and 25% of holding in preference shares. Struck off Register 31 Oct. 1916 .... **1902**

Kenilworth Tea Co. Ld. Regd. 1919. Vol. liq. (members') 6 Mar. 1936. Undertaking was acquired by Tea Corporation Ld., in which company shareholders were entitled to 4 shares of £1 (credited as fully-paid) for every 9 shares of £1 held. Holders of 5% debentures were entitled either to repayment in cash at par or an equal amount of 4½% debenture stock in purchasing company. Final meeting return regd. 23 June 1939 .... **1937**

Kenilworth Water Co. Ld. Regd. 1882. Vol. liq 18 Aug. 1922. Final meeting return regd. 30 Dec. 1922 ..... **1923**

Kenkast Ld. Regd. 1959 as Kenkast (Holdings) Ld.; name changed 1968. Vol. liq. 19 Jan. 1978. Final meeting held Apr. 1982 .... **1986–7**

Kenley Waterworks Co. Ld. Regd. 1869. In 1900 the undertaking was transferred to East Surrey Water Co. for £35,000 pre-preference stock. Removed from Register 1901 .... **1901**

Kenmare Junction Railway Co. Inc. by Special Act 1881 as Cork and Kenmare Railway Co.; name changed by Act of 1884. Undertaking abandoned by Act of 1890 .... **1891**

Kennan's Hotel (Cheapside) Ld. Regd. 1886. Removed from Register 1912 .... **1904**

Kennedy Leigh Properties Ld. Regd. 1960. Vol. liq. (members') 9 Sept. 1965. Capital returned to contributories: 13s. 4d. *plus* 2·1p. per ordinary share (of 5s.). £3,577·50 was paid into Companies' Liquidation Account in respect of unclaimed distributions and £94·69 in respect of unclaimed dividends. Final meeting return regd. 31 Oct. 1972 ... **1973–4**

Kennoway & Largo Gas Co. Ld. Regd. in Edinburgh 1919. Dissolved 1 May 1949, undertaking being vested in Scottish Area Gas Board under Gas Act 1948. Holders of securities were entitled to receive, in respect of each £1 unit held, British Gas 3% guaranteed stock 1990–95 as follows:

	£	s.	d.
Ord. shares	2	0	0
5½% pref. shares	1	5	0	**1952**

Kenny (Selangor) Rubber Co. Ld. Regd. Edinburgh 1912. Vol. liq. Mar. 1920 for reconstruction under same name. Shareholders were entitled to 4 fully-paid shares of £1 in new company for each share held. Struck off Register 15 Oct. 1937 .... **1921**

Kenny (Selangor) Rubber Co. Ld. Regd. Edinburgh 1920. Vol. liq. (members') July 1935. Undertaking and assets were acquired by Scottish Malayan Estates Ld., in which company shareholders were entitled to 1 fully-paid share of £1 for every 2 shares of £1 held. Struck off Register 15 Oct. 1937 .... **1938**

Kensington & Knightsbridge Electric Lighting Co. Ld. Regd. 1888. Undertaking was acquired by Central London Electricity Ld. in which company shareholders were entitled to 55 4½% preference, 5 6% preference and 1 ordinary fully-paid shares of £1 for every 10 1st preference, one 2nd preference share of £5 and one ordinary share of £1 respectively held. Dissolved under Sec. 154 of Companies Act 1929 **1938**

Kensington Hotel Syndicate Ld. Regd. 1893. Properties transferred to Palace Hotel Ld. Removed from Register 1899 .... ***1897**

Kent (F. M. S.) Tin Dredging Ld. Regd. 1926. Dissolved 8 Nov. 1981 .... **1970**

Kent & East Sussex Light Railway Co. Inc. by Special Act 1896 as Rother Valley (Light) Railway Co.; name changed Apr. 1904. Dissolved 23 Dec, 1949; undertaking vested 1 Jan. 1948 in British Transport Commission under Transport Act 1947. Holders of securities were entitled to receive British Transport 3% guaranteed stock 1978–88 as follows:

	£	s.	d.
Ord. shares (of £10)			6
4% deb. stock	10	0	0	**1949**

Kent Brick, Tile & Pottery Co. Ld. *See* Pluckley Brick & Tile Co. Ld.

Kent Central Coal Estates Ld. Regd. 1912. Struck off Register 1921 .... **1915**

Kent Coal Concessions Ld. Regd. 1904. Vol. liq. (members') 24 Mar. 1954. Capital returned to contributories—1s. 2·65d. per A share (of 2s.). and 4·05d. per B share (of 2s.). £5,351 11s. 10d. was paid into Companies' Liquidation Account. Final meeting return regd. 31 Oct. 1955 .... **1956**

Kent Coal Exploration Co. Ld. Regd. 1897. Vol. liq. 28 Oct. 1899. Undertaking was acquired by Consolidated Kent Collieries Corporation Ld. for shares of £1 (credited with 17s. 7d. paid). Removed from Register 1905 .... **1900**

Kent Coal Finance and Development Co. Ld. Regd. 1891. Undertaking was acquired by Consolidated Kent Collieries Corporation Ld. for shares of £1 (credited with 17s. 7d. paid). Removed from Register 1906 **1900**

Kent Coalfields Syndicate Ld. Regd. 1896. Vol. liq. 24 Nov. 1897. Undertaking and assets were acquired by Kent Collieries Corporation Ld. in which company shareholders were entitled to 2 fully-paid shares of £1 *plus* £4 in cash for each ordinary share of £1 held or 3 fully-paid shares of £1 *plus* £3 10s. in cash for each preference share of £1 held. Removed from Register 1901 .... **1898**

Kent Collieries Corporation Ld. Regd. 1897. Vol. liq. 11 Oct. 1899. Undertaking was acquired by Consolidated Kent Collieries Corporation Ld. for shares of £1 (credited with 17s. 7d. paid). Removed from Register 1907 .... **1900**

Kent Collieries Ld. Regd. 1905. Vol. liq. 16 July 1917. Reconstructed as Channel Steel Co. Ld. in which company shareholders were entitled to 15% in deferred ordinary shares of 1s. for each ordinary share of 5s. held or 33⅓% in preferred ordinary shares of £1 and 66⅔% in deferred ordinary shares of 1s. for each preference share of £1 held. Holders of 5% debentures were entitled to 1 preferred ordinary share of £1 for each £1 debenture held. Holders of deposited debentures were entitled to 294,440 preferred ordinary shares of £1. Final meeting return regd. 12 Oct. 1928 .... **1918**

Kent County Gas Light and Coke Co. Ld. Regd. 1906. Court Order to wind up 20 Feb. 1907. Liquidation released 28 May 1915. Struck off Register 14 Feb. 1919 .... **1907**

Kent County Gold Mine Co. Ld. Regd. 1883. Court Orders: to wind up 19 July 1890; to dissolve 19 Mar. 1892 .... **1891**

Kent Electric Power Co. Inc. by Special Act 1902. Dissolved 1 Apr. 1948 undertaking being vested in British (later Central) Electricity Authority and South-Eastern Area Board under Electricity Act 1947. Holders of securities were entitled to receive British Electricity 3% guaranteed stock (1968–73) as follows in respect of each £1 unit of capital held:

	£	s.	d.
Ordinary shares	2	4	9
4½% irred. deb. stock	1	1	1¼
3½% red. deb. stock	1	0	8⅞	**1949**

Kent Fire Insurance Co. Established under deed of Settlement 1802. The undertaking was acquired by Royal Insurance Co. **1901**

Kent (Francis) & Co. Ld. Regd. 1900. Removed from Register 1908 .... **1902**

Kent Freehold and Minerals Ld. Regd. 1912. Vol. liq. 15 Jan. 1924. Final meeting return regd. 31 May 1924 ***1925**

Kent Mill (1920) Ld. Regd. 1920. Vol. liq. (members') 1 May 1939. Undertaking sold to Lancashire Cotton Corporation Ld. Capital returned to contributories—1⅜d. per preference share of 1s. Final meeting return regd. 29 July 1940 .... **1940**

Kent-Mitchell Ld. Regd. 1911. Vol. liq. 5 Aug. 1930. Final meeting return regd. 21 July 1932 .... **1931**

Kent Portland Cement Co. Ld. Regd. 1920. Vol. liq. 19 Apr. 1922. Undertaking was sold to Associated Portland Cement Manufacturers Ld. in which company shareholders were entitled to 1 ordinary share of £1 (credited as fully-paid) for every 10 shares of £1 held. 1st debenture holders were entitled to an equal amount of 6½% debenture stock in acquiring company. 2nd debenture holders were entitled to 85% of holding in cash. Final meeting return regd. 25 Apr. 1923 .... **1923**

Kent Super-Aeration Ld. Regd. 1900 as Thanet Super-Aeration Ld.; name changed July 1902. Removed from Register 1905 .... **1904**

Kent Water Works (Company of Proprietors of). Inc. 1809. Undertaking taken over by Metropolitan Water Board from 24 June 1904 .... **1905**

Kentucky Securities Corporation. Inc. Virginia 1911 .. **1920**

Kentucky Traction & Terminal Co. Inc. Kentucky 1911. Common stock sold to Lexington Utilities Co. **1936**

Kenya & African Trust Ld. Regd. 1926. Struck off Register 18 Feb. 1936 .... **1936**

Kenya Consolidated Goldfields Ld. Inc. in Kenya Colony 1933. Vol. liq. (creditors') 25 Mar. 1952. Liquidator stated that no capital will be returned to contributories as assets will not realise an amount sufficient to meet claims of creditors **1956**

Kenya Gold Mining Syndicate Ld. Regd. 1928. Vol. liq. (members') 7 Nov. 1945. Capital returned to contributories—3s. 2¼d. per share of 5s. £574 5s. 2d. was paid into Companies' Liquidation Account. Final meeting return regd. 5 Mar. 1947 .... **1947**

Kenyon (John) Ld. Regd. 1896. Vol. liq. (members') Apr. 1930. Undertaking was acquired by Massey's

VOL. FOR

Burnley Brewery Ld., which company was beneficial owner of all share capital. Final meeting return regd. 31 July 1931 .... **1931**

Keokuk & Hamilton Water Power Co. Undertaking acquired under Act of Congress of 1905 by Mississippi River Power Co. **1946**

Kepong Dredging Co. Ld. Regd. 1923. Vol. liq. (members') 19 Jan. 1965. Capital returned to contributories—6s. 10d. per share of 3s. £4,091 16s. 4d. was paid into Companies' Liquidation Account. Final meeting return regd. 28 Feb. 1968 .... **1969**

Keraia Rubber Estates Ld. Regd. 1910. Vol. liq. 27 Nov. 1914. Final meeting return regd. 7 Mar. 1916...... **1915**

Kerala Calicut Estates Ld. Regd. 1920. Vol. liq. (members') 18 Nov. 1932. Undertaking and assets were acquired by company of same name. Shareholders were entitled to 6 shares of 2s. (credited with 1s. 8d. paid) in new company for each share of £1 held. £30 10s. 4d. was paid into Companies' Liquidation Account in respect of sale of unclaimed shares. Final meeting return regd. 16 Feb. 1935 .. **1933**

Kerala Calicut Estates Ld. Regd. 1932. Vol. liq. (members') 13 Dec. 1956. Capital returned to contributories—4s. 5·128d. per 2s. stock. Final meeting return regd. 4 Jan. 1967 .... **1968**

Kerala Rubber Co. Ld. Regd. 1909. Vol. liq. 19 July 1920. Undertaking acquired by Kerala Calicut Estates Ld. (regd. 1920). Final meeting return regd. 6 July 1923 .... ***1921**

Kerala Tea Co. Ld. Regd. 1923. Vol. liq (members') 23 Nov. 1944. Capital returned to contributories—5s. 0½d. per share of 2s. Struck off register 30 Dec. 1949 **1950**

Kern Burner Co. Ld. Regd. 1899. Removed from Register 1903 .... **1904**

Kern County Consolidated Gold Mines Ld. Regd. 1906. Vol. liq. 12 July 1909. Properties transferred to California General Mining Co. Ld. Final meeting return regd. 18 Oct. 1910 .... ***1910**

Kern Romana Ld. Regd. 1920. Vol. liq. (creditors') 30 May 1935. Direct controlling interest held by Kern River Oilfields of California Ld. (later Kern Oil Co. Ld.). Final meeting return regd. 30 Apr. 1936 ...... **1936**

Kerosene Co. Ld. Regd. 1888. Removed from Register 1903 .... ***1903**

Kerr (John L.) Ld. Regd. Edinburgh 1898. Court Orders: to wind up Apr. 1901; to dissolve 25 June 1903 .... **1901**

Kerr Lake Mining Co. Inc. New York 1905. Assets were sold to Kerr Lake Mines Ld., in which company shareholders were entitled to 1 share of $5 for each share of $5 held. Company was dissolved **1918**

Kerr, Stuart & Co. Ld. Regd. 1910. Court Order to wind up 14 Oct. 1930. Liquidator released 4 May 1932. Struck off Register 20 Mar. 1936 .... **1931**

Kershaw (James) & Co. Ld. Regd. 1897. Vol. liq. (members') 29 Mar. 1956, Final meeting return regd. 8 June 1957 .... **1938**

Kertch-Taman Oilfields Ld.. Regd. 1913. A subsidiary of Oilfields Finance Corpn. Ld. Struck off Register 22 June 1956 .... **1955**

Kestell Steamship Co. Ld. Regd. 1915. Vol. liq. 11 May 1923. Final meeting return regd. 24 Mar. 1924 .... **1924**

Kesterton (E.) & Co. Ld. Regd. 1890. Vol. liq. 6 Nov. 1905. Removed from Register 1909 .... **1906**

Keswick Electric Light Co. Ld. Regd. 1889. All shares were owned by Windermere and District Electricity Supply Co. Ld. Dissolved 1 Apr. 1948 under Electricity Act 1947 .... **1936**

Keswick Gas Co. Inc. by Special Act 1888. Dissolved 1 May 1949 undertaking being vested in Northern Area Gas Board under Gas Act 1948. Holders of securities were entitled to receive, in respect of each £10 unit held unless otherwise stated, British Gas 3% guaranteed stock 1990–95 as follows:

	£	s.	d.	
Orig. shares (10% stand.)	20	10	0	
Orig. shares (10% stand.) of £5	10	5	0	
Addit. shares (7% stand.)	14	10	0	**1952**

Ketchau (Pahang) Corporation Ld. Regd. 1889. Vol. liq. 3 Aug. 1893. Final meeting return regd.9 June 1896 **1894**

Kettering & District Billposting & Advertising Co. Ld. Regd. 1895. Vol. liq. 16 Mar. 1899. Business acquired by Rockley's Ld. Final meeting return regd. 16 Dec. 1899 .... **1940**

Kettering Gas Co. Inc. by Special Act 1891. Dissolved 1 May 1949, undertaking being vested in East Midland Area Gas Board under Gas Act 1948. Holders of securities were entitled to receive, in respect of each £100 unit held, British Gas 3% guaranteed stock 1990–95 as follows:

	£	s.	d.	
Cons. ord. stock (5% stand.)	156	0	0	
4% perp. deb. stock	102	0	0	
4% perp. deb. stock (tax free)	145	0	0	**1952**

VOL. FOR

Kettering, Thrapston & Huntingdon Railway Co. Inc. by Special Act 1862 as Kettering & Thrapston Railway Co. Undertaking amalgamated with Midland Railway Co. in which holders of debenture and A and B stocks received 3% debenture and 4% guaranteed stocks respectively on basis of equal income; holders of ordinary stock received 4% preference stock ... **1898**

Kettle & District Gas Co. Ld. Regd. in Edinburgh 1926. Dissolved 1 May 1949, undertaking being vested in Scottish Area Gas Board under Gas Act 1948. Holders of ordinary shares (of £1 10s.) were entitled to receive £1 17s. 6d. British Gas 3% guaranteed stock 1990–95 for each share held **1952**

Kettle River Power Co. Ld. Regd. 1900. Reconstructed 1906 as Cascade (1906) Power Co. Ld. Debenture holders received £49,755 in shares and £49,755 debentures in new company in exchange for their holdings. Removed from Register 1907 .... **1909**

Key and Season Ticket Insurance Registry Ld. Regd. 1896. Vol. liq. 20 May 1912. Undertaking was absorbed by Scottish National Key Registry & Assurance Association Ld. Final meeting return regd. 25 July 1912 .... ***1913**

Key Lens Optical Co. Ld. Regd. 1891 as Automatic Sight Testing & Optical Supply Co. Ld.; name changed 1905. Vol. liq. (creditors') 28 Oct. 1950. No capital returned to contributories. Final meeting return regd. 17 Apr. 1951 .... **1952**

Key of Komata Ld. Regd. 1896. Vol. liq. 18 May 1899. Final meeting return regd. 11 June 1900 .... **1900**

Keyes-Baker Cigar Rolling Machine Co. Ld. Regd. 1897. Struck off Register 9 Dec. 1902 .... **1901**

Keystone Knitting Mills (1928) Ld. Regd. 1928. Vol. liq. (creditors') 5 Jan. 1960. No capital returned to contributories or holders of funding certificates. Final meeting return regd. 29 June 1965.............. **1966**

Kharas Exploration Co. Ld. Regd. 1909. Vol. liq. Nov. 1910. Removed from Register 1911 .... **1911**

Kharijan Tea Co. Ld. Regd. 1900. Vol. liq. Aug. 1907. Undertaking and asset were aquired by Budla Beta Tea Co. Ld., in which company shareholders were entitled to 1 7/10 shares of £10 for each share of £10 held. Removed from Register 1908 .... **1908**

Khedivial Mail Steamship & Graving Dock Co. Ld. Regd. 1898. Vol. liq. (members') 7 Oct. 1938, the undertaking was transferred to an Egyptian company, The Pharaonic Mail Line, S. A. in which shareholders were entitled to receive 3 fully-paid shares of £10 for every 5 preference shares of £5 or 50 ordinary shares of £1 held. £837 (due to holders of bearer shares) was paid into Companies' Liquidation Account. Final meeting return regd. 12 Oct. 1949 .... **1950**

Khota Tampan Rubber Co. Ld. Regd. Edinbiirgh 1910. Vol. liq. (members') 18 Feb. 1953. Estates sold for £46,667. Capital returned to contributories—2s. 5·7257d. per share (of 2s.). £464 19s. 7d. was paid into Companies' Liquidation Account. Final meeting return regd. 29 Jan. 1954 .... **1955**

Kibwezi Rubber Lands Ld. Regd. 1910. Vol. liq. 15 Jan. 1918. Final meeting return regd. 15 Jan. 1925...... **1918**

Kibworth Gas Co. Ld. Regd. 1912. Dissolved 1 May 1949, undertaking being vested in East Midland Area Gas Board under Gas Act 1948. Holders of ordinary shares (of £1) were entitled to receive £2 British Gas 3% guaranteed stock 1990–95 for each share held **1952**

Kidd & Hotblack Ld. Regd. 1906. Vol. liq. 10 Dec. 1926. Undertaking and assets were acquired by Tamplin and Son's Brewery Brighton Ld. (later Tamplins Brewery Ld.) for £203,145 in cash and £100,000 in fully-paid B preference shares of £1. Final meeting return regd. 18 Jan. 1928...................................... **1927**

Kidder Mercantile Printing Machine Co. Ld. Regd, 1881. Removed from Register 1889 .... ***1884**

Kidderminster & District Electric Lighting & Traction Co Ld. See Kidderminster & District Electric Supply Co. Ld.

Kidderminster & District Electric Supply Co. Ld. Regd. 1898 as Kidderminster & District Electric Lighting & Traction Co. Ld.; name changed Oct. 1930. Vol. liq. (members') 19 May 1939. Undertaking and assets were acquired in 1938 by Shropshire, Worcestershire & Staffordshire Electric Power Co. Capital returned to contributories—£10 2s. 3d. per preference or ordinary share of £10. £32 0s. 10d. was paid into Companies' Liquidation Account, £20 4s. 6d. preference return and £11 16s. 4d. for unclaimed dividends. Final meeting return regd. 16 Feb. 1940 **1940**

Kidderminster & Stourport Electric Tramway Co. Inc. by Special Act 1896. In liquidation in 1930 .... **1930**

Kidderminster Cycle Co. Ld. Regd. 1897. Vol. liq. 14 Feb. 1900. Final meeting return regd. 20 Feb. 1901 **1901**

VOL. FOR

King & Mortimer Ld. Regd. 1902. Vol. liq. July 1906. Removed from Register 1911 .... **1907**

King & Shaxson. Established 1933. Business was acquired in 1936 by King & Shaxson Ld. **1936**

King Arthur's Castle Hotel Co. Ld. Regd. 1896. Removed from Register 1904 .... **1904**

King Asbestos (Rhodesia) Ld. Regd. 1914. Vol. liq. 18 Jan. 1921. Undertaking was acquired by Rhodesian King Asbestos Co. Ld. Final meeting return regd. 20 Oct. 1923 .... **1921**

King Conrad Silver & Lead Mining Co., No Liability. Inc. Victoria 1900. Liquidated 1903 .... **1904**

King [George] (Coventry) Ld. Regd. 1917. Vol. liq. (members') 11 Jan. 1933. A direct controlling interest was held by Civil Service Supply Association Ld. Capital returned to contributories—£4,250. Final meeting return regd. 5 Aug. 1941 ... **1933**

King (Henry S.) & Co. In 1922 the business was acquired by Cox & Co **1923**

King, Howmann & Co. Ld. Regd. 1897. Vol. liq. 9 Mar. 1908, Final meeting return regd. 22 Sept. 1911..... **1909**

King Insurance Co. Ld. Regd. 1901. Vol. liq. 12 Apr. 1915. Court Order to wind up 17 Oct. 1916. Struck off Register Apr. 1929 .... **1930**

King Mill Ld. Regd. 1920. Vol. liq. (members') 3 Mar. 1960. Final meeting return regd. 14 Dec. 1962 .... **1941**

King of the Hills Gold Mining Co. Ld. Regd. 1899. Reconstructed 1900 as company of same name (*see below*). Shareholders were entitled to 1 share of 5s. (credited with 4s. paid) in new company for each share of 5s. held. Removed from Register 1904.... **1903**

King of the Hills Gold Mining Co. Ld. Regd. 1900. Vol. liq. 16 June 1903. Final meeting return regd. 14 Dec. 1904 .... **1904**

King of the West Gold Mining Co. Ld. Regd. 1896. Removed from Register 1901 .... **1899**

King Prempeh Treasure Mines Ld. Regd. 1901. Properties were acquired by London Ashanti Gold Mining Co. Ld. in which company shareholders were entitled to 1 share of £1 (credited with 15s. paid) for every 4 shares of £1 held. Removed from Register 1905 .... **1904**

King Solomon's Gold Mines Ld. Regd. 1894. Receiver for debenture holders appointed in Sept. 1904. Removed from Register 1909 .... **1908**

King, Sons & Co. Ld. Regd. 1904. Vol. liq. 1 Jan. 1923. Controlling interest held by Hargreaves Bros. & Co. Ld. Final meeting return regd. 10 May 1924 .... **1923**

Kingan & Co. Ld. Regd. Dublin 1875. Vol. liq. Nov. 1920 .... **1921**

Kinghorn Gas-Light Co. Ld. Regd. in Edinburgh 1891. Dissolved 1 May 1949, undertaking being vested in Scottish Area Gas Board under Gas Act 1948. Holders of securities were entitled to receive British Gas 3% guaranteed stock as follows:

	£	s.	d.
Ord. shares (of £1)	2	4	0
4% red. debs. (per £100)	100	0	0	**1952**

King's Hall (Penge) Ld. Regd. 1920. Vol. liq. 9 July 1929. Properties purchased by Denman Picture Houses Ld. Final meeting return regd. 12 Mar. 1930 **1940**

King's Lynn Beet Sugar Factory Ld. Regd. 1927. Vol. liq. (member's) 9 July 1936. The factory was transferred to British Sugar Corporation Ld. for 303,750 fully-paid ordinary shares of £1. Shareholders were entitled to 2 such shares for every 3 shares of £1 held *plus* 4s. 5d. *per* share in cash. Final meeting return regd. 13 July 1937 .... **1937**

King's Lynn Docks & Railway Co. Inc. by Special Act 1865. Undertaking vested from 1 Jan. 1948 in British Transport Commission under Transport Act 1947. Holders of securities were entitled to receive British Transport 3% guaranteed stock 1978–88 in respect of every £100 of old security held:

	£	s.	d.
4% pref. stock (1869)	50	0	0
4% con. pref. stock	15	0	0
5% pref. stock (1884)	3	0	0
Capital stock	2	0	0
Extension capital stock	1	0	0
4¼% deb. stock	90	0	0	**1949**

King's Lynn Gas Co. Inc. by Special Act 1870. Dissolved 1 May 1949, undertaking being vested in Eastern Area Gas Board under Gas Act 1948. Holders of securities were entitled to receive, in respect of each £100 unit held, British Gas 3% guaranteed stock 1990–95 as follows:

	£	s.	d.
A cap. stock (5% stand.).	112	10	0
4% pref. stock	101	0	0	**1952**

King's Motors (Oxford) Ld. *See* Williams Hudson Group

King's Norton Metal Co. Ld. Regd. 1890. Vol. liq. 1 Jan. 1929. Final meeting return regd. 4 Jan. 1930. ...... **1929**

VOL. FOR

King's Theatre & Hippodrome (Dundee) Ld. Regd. Edinburgh 1908. Vol.liq. May 1912. Court Order to continue winding up under supervision June 1912. Court Order to dissolve 23 Apr. 1915 .... **1913**

King's Treasury Gold Mines Ld. Regd. 1901 Vol. liq. 11 Mar. 1914. Struck off Register 18 Jan 1921 ...... **1915**

Kingsbridge & Salcombe Railway Co. Inc. by Special Act 1862. Undertaking purchased by Great Western Railway Co. **1888**

Kingsbury Collieries Ld. Regd. 1878 as Hockley Hall & Whateley Collieries & Brickfields Ld.; name changed 27 Feb. 1905. Vol. liq. (members') 24 Jan. 1955. All capital owned by Debenture Corpn. Ld. Final meeting return regd. 26 Sept. 1956 .... **1954**

Kingsbury Engineering Co. Ld. Regd. 1919. Vol. liq. 2 May 1921. Final meeting return regd. 16 Sept. 1922 **1922**

Kingsbury (St Albans) Brewery Co. Ld. Regd. 1894. Vol. liq. 20 Apr. 1898. Undertaking and assets were aquired by Benskins Watford Brewery Ld. (regd. 1898). Final meeting return regd. 15 June 1899 ... **1898**

Kingsclere Gas Co. Ld. Regd. 1919. Vol. liq. (members') 3 Apr. 1941. Capital returned to contributories—£1,317 9s. Final meeting return regd. 14 July 1941 **1941**

Kingscourt, Keady & Armagh Railway Co. *See* Castleblaney, Keady & Armagh Railway Co.

Kingsdown & Tincroft Mines Ld. Regd. 1919 as Kingsdown (Hewas Water) Tin Mines Ld.; name changed Mar. 1925. Struck off Register June 1934 **1935**

Kingside Mining Co. Ld. Regd. 1886. Vol. liq. 9 Sept. 1892. Final meeting return regd. 7 Sept. 1893 ...... **1893**

Kingside Zinc-Blende Co. Ld. Regd. 1898 as Cwmystwyth Mining Co. Ld.; name changed Mar. 1905. Vol. liq. Sept. 1909. Removed from Register 1910 .... **1910**

Kingston & London Railway Co. Undertaking transferred to London & South Western Railway and Metropolitan District Railway Co **1883**

Kingston Cotton Mill Co. Ld. Regd. 1879. Court Order to wind up 18 Apr. 1894. A first dividend of 1s. was payable in Dec. 1894. Removed from Register 1905 **1895**

Kingston (Kalgurli) Gold Mines Ld. Regd. 1897. Removed from Register 1910 .... **1909**

Kingston Mill, Stockport Ld. Regd. 1900. Vol. liq. 29 Sept. 1930. Shareholders received 4,151 fully-paid preference shares of £1, 24,792 fully-paid ordinary shares of £1, and 26,465 fully-paid deferred shares of 1s. in Lancashire Cotton Corporation Ld. Final meeting return regd. 3 Oct. 1931 .... **1931**

Kingston-upon Thames Gas Co. Inc. by Special Act 1854. Under Special Order of 1930 the undertaking was acquired by the Wandsworth Wimbledon and Epsom District Gas Co. (later Wandsworth & District Gas Co.). Holders of consolidated ordinary stock were entitled to £50 consolidated stock and £80 5% preference stock of the acquiring company for every £100 held; debenture stockholders were entitled to £80 of 5% debenture stock in acquiring company for every £100 stock held. The liability in respect of the mortgage bonds was assumed by the acquiring company **1931**

Kingstown & Kingsbridge Junction Railway Co. Inc. by Special Act 1887. Undertaking abandoned **1898**

Kingsway Chemists Ld. Regd. 1928. Vol. liq. (members') 20 Feb. 1931. Capital returned to contributories—£4,524. Final meeting return regd. 8 Sept. 1933 ... **1931**

Kingsway Super Cinema Ld. Regd. 1928. Vol. liq. (members') 3 Feb. 1936. Capital returned to contributories—20s. per preference share of £1; 7s. 6d. per ordinary share of 7s. 6d. Final meeting return regd. 17 Oct. 1936 .... **1936**

Kingswinford Forge Ld. Regd. 1913 as Gauntletts (1913) Ld.; name changed Jan. 1916. Struck off Register Dec. 1931 .... **1932**

Kington & Eardisley Railway Co. Inc. by Special Act 1862. Under Great Western Railway Act 1897 undertaking amalgamated with that company. Holders of A1 debenture stock received cash payment of 62¼% of nominal value; A2 debenture stock, 25%; A3 debenture stock, 20%; A4 debenture stock, 15%; B debenture stock, 13%; 1st preference stock, 8%; 2nd preference stock, 3%, and ordinary stock, 2% **1898**

Kinross & Milnathort Gas Light Co. Ld. Regd. in Edinburgh 1918. Dissolved 1 May 1949, undertaking being vested in Scottish Area Gas Board under Gas Act 1948. Holders of ordinary shares (of £1) were entitled to receive £1 17s. 6d. British Gas 3% guaranteed stock 1990–95 for each share held **1952**

Kinsella Gold Mines Ld. Regd. 1896. Vol. liq. 5 Apr. 1897. Undertaking was acquired by Agamemnon Ld., in which company shareholders were entitled to 2 shares of £1 for every 5 shares of £1 held. Final meeting return regd. 16 May 1898 .... **1899**

See Stock Exchange Year-Book.

Kinta Tin Dredging Co. Ld. Undertaking and assets were acquired by Southern Kinta Consolidated Ld.   1935

Kinta Tin Mines, Ld. Regd. 1900. Voluntary winding-up order 30 Jan. 1986. All capital owned by Gopeng Consolidated Ld.   1961

Kintore Gold Mines Ld. Regd. 1895. Vol. liq. 21 Dec. 1896. Final meeting return regd. 18 June 1900   1897

Kippax & District Gas Co. Ld. Regd. 1907. Dissolved 1 May 1949. undertaking being vested in North Eastern Area Gas Board under Gas Act 1948. Holders of ordinary shares (of £1) were entitled to receive £2 British Gas 3% guaranteed stock 1990–95 for each share held   1952

Kipushi Syndicate Ld. Regd. 1929. Vol. liq. 5 Jan. 1932. Capital returned to contributories—2s. 0½d. per fully-paid share of 5s. Final meeting return regd. 23 Dec. 1932   1932

Kirby Banks Screw Co. Ld. Regd. 1897. Vol. liq. (creditors') 13 Sept. 1932. No capital returned to contributories. Final meeting return regd. 10 June 1933   1933

Kirbymoorside Lighting Co. Ld. Regd. 1909, Dissolved 1 May 1949, undertaking being vested in North Eastern Area Gas Board under Gas Act 1948. Holders of ordinary shares (of £1) were entitled to receive £1 British Gas 3% guaranteed stock 1990–95 for each share held   1952

Kirk & Randall Ld. Regd. 1912. Vol. liq. 18 Mar. 1926. Court Order to wind up 13 July 1926. Liquidator released 9 May 1929. Struck off Register 19 May 1933 ....   *1927

Kirk Michael Mining Co. Ld. Regd. 1880. Removed from Register 1905 ....   *1885

Kirk Shipping Co. Ld. Regd. 1919. Struck off Register 1926 ....   *1923

Kirkaldy (John) Ld. Regd. 1887. Vol. liq. (creditors') 24 June 1932. Direct controlling interest held by Mumford (A. G.) Ld. Final meeting return regd. 12 Mar. 1935   1932

Kirkburton Gas Light Co. Ld. Regd. 1856. Vol. liq. 31 Dec. 1936. Undertaking acquired by Kikburton, Shelley & Shepley Gas Co. Ld. in which company shareholders were entitled to 2 ordinary shares of £1 (credited as fully-paid) for each A share of £1 held or to 7 fully-paid ordinary shares of £1 for every 5 B shares of £1 held. Final meeting return regd. 5 Apr. 1938   1940

Kirkburton, Shelley & Shepley Gas Co. Ld. Regd. 1935. Dissolved 1 May 1949, undertaking being vested in North Eastern Area Gas Board under Gas Act 1948. Holders of ordinary shares (of £1) were entitled to receive £1 4s. British Gas 3% guaranteed stock 1990–95 for each share held   1952

Kirkby Lonsdale Gas Co.Ld. Inc. by Special Act 1850; regd. as unlimited 1856. Dissolved 1 May 1949, undertaking being vested in North Western Area Gas Board under Gas Act 1948. Holders of securities were entitled to receive British Gas 3% guaranteed stock 1990–95 as follows:

	£	s.	d.
Ord. shares (of £5 fully-paid)	4	10	0
Ord. shares (of £5 with £2 12s. 6d. paid)	2	7	3
3% debs. (of £50)	50	0	0	1952

Kirkby Stephen Gas Co. Ld. Regd. 1863. Dissolved 1 May 1949, undertaking being vested in Northern Area Gas Board under Gas Act 1948. Holders of ordinary shares (of £5) were entitled to receive £6 15s. British Gas 3% guaranteed stock 1990–95 for each share held   1952

Kirkcaldy & District Railway Co. Inc. by Special Act 1883 as Seafield Dock & Railway Co.; name changed by Act of 1888. Under North British Railway Co. Act undertaking was acquired by that company. Holders of ordinary shares were repaid at par in cash   1896

Kirkcaldy Gas Light Co. Ld. Established 1830. Regd. Edinburgh as limited 1883. Vol. liq. May 1911. Undertaking purchased by Corporation. Final meeting return regd. 18 Sept. 1913   1912

Kirkconnel Gas Co. Ld. Regd. in Edinburgh 1911. Dissolved 1 May 1949, undertaking being vested in Scottish Area Gas Board under Gas Act 1948. Holders of ordinary shares (of 5s.) were entitled to receive £1 5s. British Gas 3% guaranteed stock 1990–95 for each share held   1952

Kirkham Gas Co. Ld. Regd. 1880. Dissolved 1 May 1949, undertaking being vested in North Western Area Gas Board under Gas Act 1948. Holders of original A stock were entitled to receive in respect of each £100 held, £160 British Gas 3% guaranteed stock 1990–95. Liability in respect of certain mortgage loans assumed by the Board.   1952

Kirkland Goldfields Ld. Regd. 1914. Vol. liq. 22 Mar. 1916. Final meeting return regd. 19 Oct. 1918   1916

Kirkham, Hulett & Chandler Ld. Regd. 1879. Vol. liq. (members') 12 Nov. 1964. Capital returned to contributories—3s. 8d. per share of £20. Paid into Companies' Liquidation Account-unclaimed dividends: £42 16s. 10d.; distributions: £23 13s. Final meeting return regd. 18 Feb. 1965   1965

Kirkland Lake Exploration Ld. Regd. 1914. Vol. liq. 26 Feb. 1929. Final meeting return regd.8 June 1929   1930

Kirkland Lake Proprietary Ld. Regd. 1913 Vol.liq. 5 Sept. 1919. Reconstructed as company of same name. Shareholders were entitled to 2 shares of £1 for each share of £1 held. Final meeting return regd. 9 Mar. 1923   1920

Kirkland Lake Proprietary (1919) Ld. Regd. 1919. Vol. liq. (creditors') 17 Aug. 1932. Capital returned to contributories—9d. per share of 10s. Final meeting return regd. 14 Dec. 1938   1933

Kirklands Ld. Regd. 1920. Vol. liq. (creditors') 30 May 1933. Assets realised insufficient to pay unsecured creditors in full. Final meeting return regd. 16 Oct. 1933   1934

Kirklees Artificial Silk Manufacturing Co. Ld. Regd. 1925. Vol. liq. 24 Aug. 1928. Undertaking and assets were acquired by Kirklees Ld. for £130,000 in cash. Final meeting return regd. 16 Aug. 1929   1929

Kirkstall Brewery Co. Ld. Regd. 1871. Vol. liq. 1 Dec. 1898. Reconstructed as company of same name. Shareholders were entitled to 2 preference and 2 ordinary shares of £5 for every share of £4 held. Final meeting return regd. 22 July 1899   1899

Kirkstall Brewery Co. Ld. Regd. 1899. Vol. liq. (members') 22 Mar. 1954 in accordance with a scheme of arrangement of Dutton's Blackburn Brewery Ld. (later Duttons Brewery Ld.) owning all ordinary capital. Preference capital repaid at par. 4% mortgage debentures and 4% (Albion) debenture stock redeemed at 102% 31 Mar. 1954. Amounts paid into Companies' Liquidation Account (a) unclaimed dividends £186 3s. 7d., and (b) distributions—£140. Final meeting return regd. 4 May 1959   1960

Kirriemuir Gas Co. Ld. Regd. in Edinburgh 1914. Dissolved 1 May 1949, undertaking being vested in Scottish Area Gas Board under Gas Act 1948. Holders of ordinary shares (of £5) were entitled to receive £8 British Gas 3% guaranteed stock 1990–95 for each share held   1952

Kirton Gas Co. Ld. Regd. 1913. Dissolved 1 May 1949, undertaking being vested in East Midland Area Gas Board under Gas Act 1948. Holders of securities were entitled to receive British Gas 3% guaranteed stock 1990—95 as follows:

	£	s.	d.
Ord. shares (of £1)	1	8	0
5% red. debs. (of £100)	100	0	0	1952

Kis-Banya Mining Co. Ld. Regd. 1906. Vol. liq. 23 Feb. 1914. The undertaking was sold to a French company for shares. Final meeting return regd. 29 Jan. 1915   1915

Kisumu Rubber Estates Ld. Regd. 1910. Vol. liq. 2 Dec. 1912. Final meeting return regd. 25 Feb. 1916......   1913

Kit-Cat Restaurants Ld. Regd. 1928. Court Order to wind up Mar, 1931. Struck off Register 15 June 1937   1938

Kit Hill Great Consols Co. Ld. Regd. Truro 1881. Vol. liq. 8 June 1885. Final meeting return regd. 21 May 1891   1886

Kit Tin Mines Ld. Regd. 1900. Vol. liq. June 1911. Struck off Register 7 July 1939   1940

Kitson Incandescent Lighting Co. of South Africa Ld. Regd. 1903. Vol. liq. 24 May 1905. Removed from Register 1909   1906

Kitson Lighting Co of Great Britain Ld. Regd. 1901. Undertaking and assets were acquired by United Kingdom Lighting Trust Ld. for 14,715 4% preference shares of £1 and £9,000 by release of debt due to the Trust. Removed from Register 1909   1905

Kitty's Own Alluvial Gold Fields Ld. Regd. Edinburgh 1908. Vol. liq. June 1911. Struck off Register 4 June 1937   1938

Kivuvu (Uganda) Rubber Co. Ld. Regd. in Dublin 1910. Vol. liq. (members') 22 Nov. 1948. Capital returned to contributories—15s. 2¼d. share (of £1). £1,104 16s. 4d. was paid into Companies' Liquidation Account. Final meeting return regd. 14 Dec. 1953..............   1955

Kjoli Mines Ld. Regd. 1903. Removed from Register 31 Oct. 1916   1910

Klabang Rubber Co. Ld. Regd. 1909. Vol. liq. 24 Mar. 1920. Reconstructed as company of same name. Shareholders were entitled to 2 fully-paid shares of £1 in new company for each share of £1 held. Final meeting return regd. 22 Apr. 1922   1921

See Stock Exchange Year-Book.

VOL. FOR

Klanang Produce Co. Ld. Regd. 1899. Vol. liq. (members') 18 Mar. 1960. Capital returned to contributories—£4 19s. 2d. per £1 stock. Final meeting return regd. 15 Sept. 1961 1962

Kledang Tin Mining Co. Ld. Regd. 1906. Vol. liq. Jan. 1910. Reconstructed as company of same name. Shareholders were entitled to 1 share of 10s. (credited with 7s. 6d. paid) for each share of £1 held. Removed from Register 1912 1911

Kledang Tin Mining Co. Ld. Regd. 1910. Receiver appointed in Dec. 1931; ceased to act July 1932. Assets realised insufficient to meet claims of debenture holders. Struck off Register Oct. 1934 . 1953

Kleenglas Ld. Undertaking and assets were acquired in 1929 by Kleenglas (1929) Ld. for £20,000 in cash and £55,000 in fully-paid shares of 5s 1930

Kleenglas (1929) Ld. Regd. 1929. Vol. liq. (creditors') 28 Dec. 1934. No capital returned to contributories. Final meeting return regd. 27 Feb. 1936 1935

Kleinfontein Central Gold Mines Ld. Inc. South African Republic 1895. Property and undertaking were acquired in 1902 by New Kleinfontein Co. Ld., in which company shareholders were entitled to 1 share of £1 (credited as fully-paid) for each share of £1 held 1903

Kleinfontein Deep Ld. Inc. Transvaal 1902. Vol. liq. Nov. 1908. Assets were sold to Van Ryn Deep Ld., in which company shareholders were entitled to 1 share of £1 (credited as fully-paid) for each share of £1 held 1909

Kleinfontein Estate and Gold Mining Co. Ld. Regd. 1890. Vol. liq. 16 Jan. 1894. Reconstructed 1893 as New Kleinfontein Co. Ld., in which company shareholders were entitled to 1 share of £1 (credited as fully-paid) for every 3 shares of £1 held. Final meeting return regd. 9 Mar. 1896 1893

Kleinworts Ld. Regd. 1947 as Kleinwort, Sons & Co. Ld.: name changed 30 June 1955. Vol. liq. (members') 15 Dec. 1961. Final meeting return regd. 4 Feb.1963... 1964

Klerksdorp Estates Ld. Regd. 1891. Vol. liq. 27 Sept. 1894. Reconstructed as Klerksdorp Gold & Diamond Co. Ld., in which company shareholders were entitled to 8 shares of 10s. (credited with 7s. paid) for every 3 shares of £1 held. Final meeting return regd. 13 Mar. 1897 1898

Klerksdorp Exploration Land & Estate Co. Ld. Inc. Transvaal 1896. London office closed Dec. 1911 .. 1913

Klerksdorp Extended Ld. Regd. 1906. Vol. liq. 30 Sept. 1907. Undertaking was acquired by Vaal River Gold Fields Ld., in which company shareholders were entitled to 1 share of 5s. (credited with 4s. 6d. paid) for each share of 5s. held. Final meeting return regd. 5 Mar. 1908 1908

Klerksdorp-Fourteen Steams Railway Co. Ld. Inc. Cape of Good Hope. Line expropriated by Government Apr. 1911 1911

Klerksdorp Gold & Diamond Co. Ld. Regd. 1894. Reconstructed 1898 as Klerksdorp Gold Mining & Diamond Co. Ld., in which company shareholders were entitled to 1 share of 10s. (credited with 8s. 6d. paid) for each share of 10s. held. Removed from Register 1904 1901

Klerksdorp Gold & Diamond Co. Ld. Regd. 1901. Undertaking and assets were acquired by Klerksdorp Gold & Diamond Co. (1904) Ld. Removed from Register 1906 1906

Klerksdorp Gold & Diamond Co. (1904) Ld. Regd. 1904. Vol. liq. 10 Aug. 1906. Undertaking and assets were acquired by Klerksdorp Gold Mines Ld. for £30,000 in cash. Final meeting return regd. 31 July 1907 ... 1907

Klerksdorp Gold Estates Ld. Regd. 1888. Vol. liq. 7 May 1891. Reconstructed as Klerksdorp Estates Ld., in which company shareholders were entitled to 1 share of £1 (credited with 18s. paid) for each share of £1 held. Final meeting return regd. 7 Oct. 1896 .. 1894

Klerksdorp Gold Mines Ld. Regd. 1906. Vol. liq. Sept. 1907. Undertaking was acquired by Vaal River Gold Fields Ld., in which company shareholders were entitled to 1 share of 5s. (credited with 4s. 6d. paid) for each share of 5s. held. Removed from Register 1910 1908

Klerksdorp Gold Mining & Diamond Co. Ld. Regd. 1898. Vol. liq. 2 July 1901. Reconstructed as Klerksdorp Gold & Diamond Co. Ld. Shareholders were entitled to subscribe for shares of 5s. (credited with 3s. 9d. paid) in new company. Final meeting return regd. 9 Oct. 1903 1902

Klerksdorp Proprietary Mines Ld. Inc. Transvaal 1895. Vol. liq. Feb. 1921. First distribution of 2s. 6d. per share of 2s. 6d. in May 1921; further payments (if any) not known 1922

Klerksdorp Reefs Ld. Regd. 1895. Removed from Register 1908.. 1897

VOL. FOR

Klian-Kellas Ld. Regd. 1912. Vol. liq. (creditors') Sept. 1931. Assets (excluding cash) were acquired in 1934 by Aberfoyle Plantations Ld. the proceeds were distributed to debenture holders. Final meeting return regd. 30 Nov. 1935 1932

Klian-Kellas Tin & Rubber Co. Ld. Regd. 1910. Vol. liq. 5 Dec. 1912 for reconstruction as Klian-Kellas Ld., in which company shareholders were entitled to 5 shares of 2s. (credited with 1s. 6d. paid) for every 4 shares of 2s. held. Final meeting return regd. 15 Dec. 1914 1913

Klip Colliery (Elandslaagte) Ld. Regd. 1902. Removed from Register 1906 1906

Klip Deep Ld. Inc. Transvaal 1899. Vol. liq. Oct. 1906. Undertaking was acquired by South Wolhuter Ld., in which company shareholders were entitled to receive 5 fully-paid £1 shares for every 6 £1 shares held 1907

Klip River Estate & Gold Mines Ld. Regd. 1902. Vol. liq. Sept. 1906. Removed from Register 1911.............. 1907

Klipfontein Estate & Gold Mining Co. Ld. See Rand Klip Ld.

Klondike & N.W. Territories Exploration Co. Ld. Regd. 1897. Vol. liq. 15 Mar. 1899. Undertaking and assets were acquired by British Canadian Goldfields of the Klondyke Ld., in which company shareholders were entitled to 1 share of £1 (credited with 17s. 6d. paid) for every 2 shares of 10s. held. Removed from Register 1902.. 1900

Klondike Gold Reefs Exploration Co. Ld. Regd. 1897. Struck off Register 23 July 1901 1902

Klondike Hydraulic Ld. Regd. 1898. Vol. liq. 28 Dec. 1898. Final meeting return regd. 14 July 1900 1899

Klondyke & Kootenay Venture Syndicate Ld. Regd. 1898. Removed from Register 1904 1903

Klondyke Bonanza Ld. Regd. 1897. Vol. liq 15 Mar. 1906. Struck off Register 18 Jan. 1921 1906

Klondyke Consolidated Gold Fields Ld. Regd. 1901. Removed from Register 1911 1907

Klondyke Consols Ld. Regd. 1899. Removed from Register 1906 1905

Klondyke Corporation Ld. Regd. 1900. Removed from Register 1905 1905

Klondyke Dome Mining Co. Ld. Regd. 1899. Vol. liq. 16 Dec. 1921. Final meeting return regd. 1 Feb.1924 ... 1923

Klondyke Estates Corporation Ld. Regd. 1900. Vol. liq. Dec. 1908. Removed from Register 1911 1909

Klondyke Government Concession Ld. Regd. 1898. Vol. liq. 30 Aug. 1923. Capital returned to contributories—6s. 4d. per priority share of £1. Final meeting return regd. 10 Nov. 1925 1924

Klondyke Parent Pioneer Corporation Ld. Regd. 1898. Removed from Register 1910 .... *1899

Klondyke Pioneer Syndicate Ld. Regd. 1897. Removed from Register 1904 1901

Klondyke, Yukon & Stewart Pioneers Ld. Regd. 1897. Removed from Register 1909 1901

Kluchi Gold Mines Ld. Regd. 1906. Vol. liq. Jan. 1912. Removed from Register 1913 1912

Knap Concrete Machines Ld. Regd. 1928. Vol. liq. (creditors') 7 July 1932. Assets realised insufficient to pay unsecured creditors in full. Final meeting return regd. 13 Aug. 1935 1933

Knaresborough & Claro Bank Co. Ld. Regd. 1881. Acquired in Nov. 1902 by National Provincial Bank of England Ld. (later National Provincial Bank Ld.). Capital returned to contributories—£22 10s. per share of £25 (£5 paid). Removed from Register 1911 1904

Knight & Crowther Ld. Regd. 1890. Vol. liq. 1 Aug. 1901. Business was acquired by E. P. & W. Baldwin Ld. Final meeting return regd. 11 Apr. 1902 1902

Knight Central Ld. Inc. Transvaal 1895. Vol. liq. May 1923. Capital returned to contributories—4s. 9d. per share of £1 at Dec. 1923; further payments (if any) not known 1924

Knight (Fred) & Co. Ld. Regd. 1898. Removed from Register 1903 1904

Knight Steamships Co. Ld. Regd. 1886. Vol. liq. 20 July 1917. Final meeting return regd 22 May 1918....... *1918

Knights Deep Ld. Inc. Transvaal 1895. Vol. liq. Mar. 1921. Capital returned to contributories—16s. per share of £1 at Oct. 1921; further payment (if any) not known 1922

Knight's Manufacturing Co. Ld. Regd. 1906 as Carl Hentschel (1906) Ld.; name changed to Carl Hentschel Ld. in Oct. 1908 and as above In Oct. 1914. Vol. liq. 6 July 1916. Final meeting return regd. 13 Apr. 1922 1917

Knight's Pietersburg Gold Mines Ld. Inc. Transvaal 1903. Vol. liq. Nov. 1910 1911

Knightsbridge Mansions Ld. Regd. 1906 as Knightsbridge & Bradford Estate Co. Ld.; name changed Aug. 1930. Vol. liq. (members') 14 Mar. 1934.

*See Stock Exchange Year-Book.

VOL. FOR

Undertaking and assets acquired by London County Freehold & Leasehold Properties Ld. (which owned all shares). Final meeting return regd. 24 Nov. 1934 **1935**

Knott End Railway Co. Inc. by Special Act 1898. In 1923 the undertaking was merged into the London Midland & Scottish Railway Co., in which company stockholders were entitled to stock as follows:

For each £100 held	L. M. & S.	
4% Debenture	£100	4% Preference
Ordinary	£6¼	Ordinary

1924

Knottingley Gas Co. Inc. by Special Act 1856. Dissolved 1 May 1949, undertaking being vested in North Eastern Area Gas Board under Gas Act 1948. Holders of securities were entitled to receive British Gas 3% guaranteed stock 1990-95 as follows in respect of each £1 unit, unless otherwise stated, of security held:

	£	s.	d.
Cons. ord. shares (7% stand.)	2	0	0
Ord. stock (7% max.) (per £100)	150	0	0
5% pref. shares	1	2	3

Liability in respect of certain mortgage loans assumed by the Board **1952**

Knowles & Foster. Established 1828; inc. as unlimited liability company 1949. Winding-up order made 11 Jan. 1956. Creditors received 52.85p in £1. Liquidator released 23 Sept. 1977. Struck off Register 24 June 1980 **1978-9**

Knowles (Andrew) & Sons Ld. Regd. 1873. Undertaking and assets were acquired by Manchester Collieries Ld. Shareholders were entitled to 0·7564 ordinary and 0·199 preference shares of £1 in acquiring company *plus* 3s. in cash for each share of £1 held. Final meeting return regd. 21 Jan. 1931 **1930**

Knowles, Conke & Co. Ld. Regd. 1920. Vol. liq. (members') 8 Mar. 1933. Capital returned to contributories—£1 1s. 4·19d. per ordinary share of £1. Final meeting return regd. 22 Nov. 1933 **1934**

Knowles Ld. *See* Roundhill Textiles Ld.

Knysna Concession Gold Mining Co. Ld. Regd. 1888. Removed from Register 1901 **1892**

Knysna Consolidated Gold Mining Co. Ld. Regd. 1889. Removed from Register 1895 **1892**

Kobolondo Development Syndicate Ld. Regd. 1892. Vol. liq. (creditors') 20 Dec. 1929. Assets realised insufficient to pay creditors in full. Final meeting return regd. 21 June 1935 **1930**

Kobonella Estates Co. of Ceylon Ld. Regd. 1901. Vol. liq. (members') 10 Aug. 1945. Capital returned to contributories—22s. 3d. per ordinary share of £1. Final meeting return regd. 18 Nov. 1946 **1947**

Koffyfontein Estates Ld. Inc. Kimberley 1881 as London & Orange Free State Exploration Co. Ld.; name changed 1902. Undertaking was acquired in 1935 by De Beers Consolidated Mines Ld. **1936**

Koffyfontein Mines Ld. Regd. 1893. Vol. liq. 16 Mar. 1927. Reconstructed as company of same name. Shareholders were entitled to 1 ordinary share of £1 for each ordinary share of £1 or 1 life governor's share of £100 for each life governor's share of £100 held. Final meeting return regd. 8 June 1928 **1928**

Koffyfontein Mines Ld. Inc. Union of South Africa 1927. Vol. liq. (members') 3 Sept. 1935. Undertaking and assets were acquired by De Beers Consolidated Mines Ld. Capital returned to contributories—£2 0s. 1¼d. per ordinary share of £1 further payments (if any) not known **1936**

Kofi-Mansi Gold Mines Ld. Regd. 1900. Vol. liq. Sept. 1905. Undertaking was acquired by African Mines Ld. in which company shareholders were entitled to 2 shares of 10s. (credited with 8s. paid) for each share of £1 held. Removed from Register 1906 **1906**

Kohinoor & Donaldson Consolidated Mining Co. Ld. Regd. 1880 as Kohinoor Silver Mining Co. Ld.; name changed Oct. 1882. Removed from Register 1903 **1900**

Kohinoor Silver Mining Co. Ld. *See* Kohinoor & Donaldson Consolidated Mining Co. Ld.

Kokumbo (Ivory Coast) Co. Ld. Regd. 1902. Vol. liq. (creditors') 26 Nov. 1931. No capital returned to contributories. Final meeting return regd. 23 Jan. 1958 **1958**

Kolar Mines Power Station Ld. Regd. 1903. Vol. liq. (members') 30 June 1952. Final meeting return regd. 2 Mar. 1954 **1920**

Koley Mines & Exploration Ld. Regd. 1900. Struck off Register 1914 **1907**

Koliabar & Seconée Tea Co. Ld. Regd. 1923. Vol. liq. (members') 27 Jan. 1964. Capital returned to contributories—70s. 11¼d. per share (of £1). Amount paid into Companies' Liquidation Account-unclaimed dividends £59 19s. 1d.;—distributions £2,362 12s. 2d. Final meeting return regd. 23 June 1970 **1970**

VOL. FOR

Kolster-Brandes Ld. Regd. 1929. Vol. liq. (members') 2 May 1938. Capital returned to contributories (other than International Telephone & Telegraph Corporation)—3s. 9d. per share of 5s. £569 5s. was paid into Companies' Liquidation Account. Final meeting return regd. 7 Oct. 1943 **1939**

Komata Queen Ld. Regd. 1896. Vol. liq. 8 Oct. 1897. Absorbed by Komata Reefs Gold Mining Co. Ld. Final meeting return regd. 30 Jan. 1899 ***1898**

Komata Reefs Gold Mining Co. Ld. Regd. 1895. Vol. liq. 26 Sept. 1900. Reconstructed as company of same name (later Komata Investments Ld.). Shareholders were entitled to 1 share of 5s. (credited with 4s 3d. paid) for each share of 5s. held. Final meeting return regd. 11 Aug. 1902 **1900**

Komati (Transvaal) Goldfields Ld. Regd. 1909. Vol. liq. Dec. 1910. Removed from Register 1912 **1911**

Komatie Reefs Ld. Regd. 1903 as D. M. Wilsons' Komatie Reefs Ld.; name changed 1908. Removed from Register 1913 **1911**

Komatsu Ld. Inc. in Japan 13 May 1921 as Komatsu Manufacturing Co. Ld.; dissolved 6 May 1976 **1975-6**

Kombok (F. M. S.) Rubber Co. Ld. Regd. 1911. Vol. liq. (members') 1 Nov. 1956. Undertaking and certain assets were acquired by Linggi Plantations Ld. in which company stockholders were entitled to 4s. stock for every 6s. stock held. Stockholders also received 4s. 3d. cash per 2s. stock held. £958 15s. 10d. was paid into Companies' Liquidation Account in respect of unclaimed dividends and £1,373 3s. 4d. in respect of unclaimed distributions. Final meeting return regd. 1 July 1959 **1960**

Komposill Universal Ld. Regd. 1928. Vol. liq. (creditors') 17 July 1935. Assets realised insufficient to pay unsecured creditors in full. Final meeting return regd. 20 July 1936 **1936**

Kong Haakon Gold Mines Ld. Regd. 1905. Removed from Register 1913 **1911**

Kong Lee (Perak) Plantations Ld. Regd. Edinburgh 1910. A subsidiary of Chersonese (F. M. S.) Estates, Ld. Vol. liq. 7 Nov. 1962. Final meeting return regd. 9 Aug. 1963 **1953**

Kong Sang Rubber Co. Ld. Inc. Federated Malay States in 1920. In liquidation in 1933 **1933**

Koniah Mercury Syndicate Ld. Regd. 1905. Vol. liq. June 1912. Removed from Register 1913 **1913**

Konongo Gold Mines Ld. Regd. 1933. Vol. liq. (members') 3 May 1966. Capital returned to contributories—10½d. per share of 5d. Amount paid into Companies' Liquidation Account £5,666 1s. 9d. Final meeting return regd. 22 Nov. 1968 **1970**

Koomsong Holdings Ld. Regd. 1962. All capital was owned by Williamson Tea Holdings Ld. Vol. liq. (members') 16 Nov. 1966. Final meeting return regd. 24 Mar. 1972 **1966**

Kootenay British Columbia Mining Syndicate Ld. Regd. 1897. Struck off Register Aug. 1929 **1930**

Kootenay Development Syndicate Ld. Regd. 1908. Struck off Register 1921 **1911**

Kootenay Exploration Co. Ld. Inc. West Virginia **1902**

Kootenay Goldfields Syndicate Ld. Regd. 1896. Struck off Register 26 Feb. 1909 **1909**

Kootenay Mining Co. Ld. Regd. 1900. Reconstructed 1902 as Rossland-Kootenay Mining Co. Ld., in which company shareholders were entitled to 3 fully-paid shares of £1 for every 5 shares of £5 held. Removed from Register 1904 **1905**

Kootenay Ore Co. Ld. Regd. 1896. Vol. liq. 17 June 1927. Final meeting return regd. 1 Aug. 1928 **1928**

Kootenay (Perry Creek) Gold Mines Ld. Regd. 1899. Reconstructed 1902 as Fort Steele (B. C.) Gold Mines Ld., in which company shareholders were entitled to 2 shares of £1 (credited with 19s. paid) for each share of £1 held. Removed from Register 1903 **1903**

Kootenay Railway and Navigation Co. Ld. Regd. 1898. Removed from Register 1911 **1912**

Kootenay Valleys Co. Ld. Regd. 1887. Vol. liq. 20 Apr. 1894. Reconstructed as company of same name. Shareholders were entitled to 1 share of £5 (credited with £4 paid) for each share of £5 held. Final meeting return regd. 8 May 1896 **1908**

Kootenay Valleys Co. Ld. Regd. 1895. Vol. liq. (members') 12 Feb. 1920. Capital returned to contributories—£1,539 1s. 4d. £78 0s. 4d. was paid into Companies' Liquidation Account. Final meeting return regd. 3 Mar. 1931 **1930**

Kopaonik Mines Ld. Regd. 1930. Vol. liq. (members') 16 Aug. 1938. The undertaking and assets were acquired by Trepca Mines Ld., in which company shareholders were entitled to 1 fully-paid share of 5s. for every 4 shares of 5s. held. Final meeting return regd. 25 July 1947 **1948**

Kopermyn Ld. Regd. 1923. Vol. liq. Apr. 1926. Struck off Register 27 Oct. 1942 **1943**

*See Stock Exchange Year-Book.

VOL. FOR

Kopf's Extract of Meat Co. Ld. Regd. 1879. Vol. liq. 18 May 1883. Removed from Register 11 Aug. 1905 .... **1883**

Korale Tea Estates Ld. Regd. 27 May 1896 as Serendib Tea Estates Co. Ld. (Ceylon); name changed July 1896. Vol. liq. (members') 21 Nov. 1952. Capital returned to contributories—£3 14*s*. 1*d*. per share (of 10*s*.). Final meeting return regd. 12 Mar. 1954 .... **1955**

Kordofan Trading Co. Ld. Regd. 1904. Vol. liq. 27 Aug. 1917. Final meeting return regd. 1 Dec. 1919 ...... **1918**

Korean Syndicate Ld. Regd. 1905. Vol. liq. 10 Mar. 1927. Capital returned to contributories—£2 6*s*. 2½*d*. per ordinary share of 14*s*.; £3 13*s*. 6*d*. per deferred share of 1*s*.; further payments (if any) not known. Final meeting return regd. 13 Mar. 1928 .... **1928**

Korean Waterworks Ld. Regd. 1906. Vol. liq. Feb. 1911. The prior lien debenture stock was repaid at 102½%; the debenture at 85%. Capital returned to contributories—3*s*. 6*d*. per share of £1; further payments (if any) not known. Removed from Register 1911 .... **1911**

Koshe Tin Co. Ld. Regd. 1926. Vol. liq. 10 Apr. 1928. Undertaking and assets were acquired by Associated Tin Mines of Nigeria Ld., in which company shareholders were entitled to 2 fully-paid shares of 5*s*. for every 11 shares of 2*s*. held. Final meeting return regd. 5 Feb. 1929 .... **1929**

Koshea Rubber & Produce Co. Ld. Regd. 1910. Vol. liq. Oct. 1911. Removed from Register 1913 .... **1912**

Kota Tinggi (Johore) Rubber Co. Ld. Regd. 1910. Winding-up order 5 Apr. 1965. Liquidator realeased. Dissolved 1 Dec. 1977 .... **1960**

Kotin Gear Co. Ld. Regd. 1896. Struck off Register 17 June 1898.... **1901**

Kotter (Otto) Ld. Regd. 1902. Vol. liq. 5 July 1904. Final meeting return regd. 5 Jan. 1905 .... ***1905**

Kotuku Oilfields Syndicate Ld. Regd. 1910. Vol. liq. 29 Jan. 1917. Final meeting return regd. 13 Jan.1923 **1917**

Kremer (Norman) Ld. Regd. 1921. Struck off Register May 1929 .... **1930**

Kreuger & Toll Co. Inc. Sweden 1917. Placed in bankruptcy in Sweden and U.S.A. in 1932. Distributions on 5% secured sinking fund gold debentures (per $1,000)—on debentures deposited with protective committees, U.S. $330·66 and Kr.1,314·32; on debentures not deposited U.S. $326·06 and Kr.1,500·45 .... **1955**

Krian Rubber Plantations Co. Ld. Regd. as Kuala Lumpur Rubber Co. Ld.; name changed 1960. Vol. liq. 1 Oct. 1973, the undertaking and assets having been acquired by Kuala Lumpur Kepong Bhd. in which company shareholders received 4 shares of $Ma1 for every share of 10p held. Final meeting return regd. 4 Sept. 1981 .... **1982–3**

Kriel's Oriental Sheba Reef Syndicate Ld. Inc. Transvaal. Reconstructed as Oriental and Sheba Valley United Gold Mining Co. Ld **1889**

Krinjabo Gold Mines Ld. Regd. 1903. Vol. liq. July 1907. Removed from Register 1908 .... **1908**

Krishnarajpur Gold Mining Co. of India Ld. Regd. 1898. Removed from Register 1903 .... **1904**

Kroatische Escomptebank. *See* Hrvataska Eskomptna Banka.

Kromfontein Coal & Coke Co. Ld. Regd. 1898. Vol. liq. 1 Oct. 1903. Removed from Register 21 June 1907.. ***1899**

Kronand Metal Co. Ld. Regd. 1897. Vol. liq. 3 Aug. 1899. Capital returned to contributories—2*s*. per ordinary share of £1; further payments (if any) not known. Final meeting return regd. 10 July 1900 .. **1900**

Krubong (Malacca) Rubber Plantations Ld. Regd. 1909. Vol. liq. (members') 30 Jan. 1952. Capital returned to contributories—4*s*. 5¾*d*. per 2*s*. stock. £1,470 12*s*. 11*d*. was paid into Companies' Liquidation Account. Final meeting return regd. 20 Mar. 1956 .. **1957**

Krüger & Co. Ld. Regd. 1896. Wound up in 1916 under Trading with the Enemy Amendment Act 1916. The assets in Burma were sold ***1918**

Kruger Syndicate Ld. Regd. 1895. Court Order to wind up 27 May 1897. Removed from Register 1908 ... **1898**

Krugersdorp Proprietary & Gold Mining Co. Ld. Regd. 1896. Reconstructed 1902 as Krugersdorp Proprietary Ld., in which company shareholders were entitled to 1 share of £1 (credited with 15*s*. paid) for every 3 shares of £1 held. Removed from Register 1904 .... **1904**

Krugersdorp Proprietary Ld. Regd. 1902. Vol. liq. Sept 1904. Removed from Register 1909 .... **1905**

Kruisrivier (Whitehead's), Roodepoort & Bloemkof (Transvaal) Estates Co. Ld. Regd. 1899. Vol. liq. 2 Oct. 1889. Final meeting return regd. 8 Apr.1890 ***1890**

Kuala Dingin Rubber Estate Ld. Regd. 1923. Vol. liq. 28 Aug. 1928. Undertaking and assets were acquired by North Malay Rubber Estates Ld., in which company shareholders were entitled to 1 fully-paid share of 2*s*. for each share of 2*s*. held. Final meeting return regd. 19 Oct. 1929.... **1929**

VOL. FOR

Kuala Geh Estates Ld. Regd. 1934. Vol. liq. (members') 28 July 1947. Shareholders were entitled to receive 1 share of 1*s*. (6*d*. paid) in Kuala Geh Plantations Ld. (later Crown House Investments Ld.) for each share of 1*s*. held. Holders of 7½% convertible income debenture stock received equal amount of 7½% stock in the new company. Final meeting return regd. 16 Dec. 1953 .... **1955**

Kuala Geh Rubber Co. Ld. Regd. 1919. Vol. liq. (members') 20 Dec. 1933. Reconstructed as Kuala Geh Estates Ld., in which company shareholders were entitled to 1 share of 2*s*. (credited with 1*s*. 9*d*. paid) for each share of 2*s*. held. Debenture stockholders were entitled to £11 convertible debenture stock for every £10 stock held. Final meeting return regd. 13 Sept. 1934 .... **1934**

Kuala Hidong Rubber Estate Ld. Regd. 1919. Vol. liq. Dec. 1928. Struck off Register July 1933 .... **1934**

Kuala Klang Rubber Estate Ld. Regd. 1908. Vol. liq. 7 June 1920. Undertaking was acquired by Golconda Malay Rubber Co. Ld., in which company shareholders were entitled to 1 share of £1 (credited as fully-paid) for each share of £1 held. Final meting return regd. 14 Sept. 1920 .... **1921**

Kuala Krau Rubber Co. Ld. Regd. 1917. Vol. liq. (members') 14 Jan. 1935. Undertaking and assets were acquired by Hoscote Rubber Estates Ld., in which company shareholders were entitled to 1 share of £1 (credited as fully-paid) for every 10 preference or 80 ordinary shares of 2*s*. held. Final meeting return regd. 13 June 1935 .... **1935**

Kuala Lumpur Rubber Co. Ld. *See* Kuala-Kepong Amalgamated Ld.

Kuala Muda Rubber Estates Ld. Regd. 1925. Vol. liq. (members') 16 Nov. 1960. Capital returned to contributories—52*s* 11*d*. per share of £1. Final meeting return regd. 24 Sept. 1963 .... **1964**

Kuala-Nal Kelantan Rubber Co. Ld. Regd. 1909. Majority of capital was owned by Java Para Rubber Estates Ld. Struck off Register 30 Oct. 1970.... **1960**

Kuala Pahi Rubber Estate Ld. Regd.' 1910. Vol. liq. 16 Oct. 1922. Reconstructed as Pahi Plantations Ld., (later Kenwell Property Holdings Ld.) in which company shareholders were entitled to 1 share of 2*s*. (credited with 1*s*. 4½*d*. paid) for each share of 2*s*. held. Final meeting return regd. 26 May 1923 .... **1923**

Kuala Pergau Rubber Plantations Ld. Regd. 1911. Vol. liq. (members') 5 Feb. 1934. Reconstructed as company of same name. Shareholders were entitled to 1 share of 2*s*. (credited with 1*s*. 6*d*. paid) in new company for each share of 2*s*. held. Final meeting return regd. 4 Sept. 1935 .... **1934**

Kuala Pilah Rubber Estates Ld. Regd 1919. Vol. liq. (members') 15 June 1966. Capital returned to contributories—4*s*. 2*d*. per ordinary share of 2*s*. Final meeting return regd. 9 Apr. 1968 .... **1969**

Kuala Tigra (Sumatra) Rubber Plantations Ld. Regd. 1920. Vol. liq. 18 Oct. 1923. Undertaking and assets were sold to Insulinde (Sumatra) Rubber Estates Ld., in which company shareholders were entitled to 1 fully-paid share of 2*s*. for every 5*s*. paid-up capital held. Final meeting return regd. 20 Mar. 1924 .... **1924**

Kuang (Selangor) Rubber Co. Ld. Regd. 1907. Vol. liq. May 1910. Removed from Register 1911 .... **1911**

Kuaotunu Syndicate Ld. Regd. 1900. Removed from Register 1904 .... **1904**

Kuban Black Sea Oilfields Ld. Regd. 1911. Struck off Register 17 Jan. 1950 .... **1951**

Kuban Refining Co. Ld. Regd. 1913. Struck off Register 17 Jan. 1950 .... **1950**

Kubula Stores Nyasaland Ld. Regd. 1914. All capital held by British Central Africa Co. Ld. Struck off Register 6 Aug. 1943 .... **1943**

Kuils River Tin Mines Ld. Regd. 1906. Vol. liq. July 1912. Removed from Register 1913 .... **1913**

Kukicherra Tea Co. Ld. Regd. 1 July 1914. Vol. liq. (members') 1 July 1974. Distributions: £1 per preference share *plus* arrears of dividend on 3 Dec. 1974 and 1st and final distribution of 177p per ordinary share on 16 Dec. 1983. £1,610·70 paid into Companies' Liquidation Account in respect of unclaimed dividends. Fianl meeting held 26 Jan. 1984 .... **1984–5**

Kuma Tin Co. Ld. Regd. 1927. Vol. liq. 11 Apr. 1928. Undertaking and assets were acquired by Associated Tin Mines of Nigeria Ld., in which company shareholders were entitled to 1 fully-paid share of 5*s*. for every 9 shares of 2*s*. held. Final meeting return regd. 5 Feb. 1929 .... **1929**

Kumassi Syndicate Ld. Regd. 1900. Vol. liq. Mar. 1908. Removed from Register 1909 .... **1909**

Kundang Tin Dredging Ld. Inc. in Federated Malay States 1924. Vol. liq. (members') 16 Feb. 1960.

**See Stock Exchange Year-Book.*

VOL. FOR

Capital returned to contributories—18s. 8d. per share of 1s. Final meeting return regd. 18 Nov. 1963 **1965**

Kuranti Syndicate Ld. Regd. 1910. Vol. liq. (members') 23 Dec. 1943. No capital returned to contributories. Final meeting return regd. 4 Oct.1945. **1946**

Kuranui Caledonian Gold Mining Co. Ld. Regd. 1896. Reconstructed 1905 as Kuranui Caledonian Ld in which company shareholders were entitled to 1 share of 2s. (credited with 1s. paid) for each share of £1 held. Removed from Register 1906 **1908**

Kuranui Caledonian Ld. Regd. 1905. Vol. liq. 23 Oct. 1913. Reconstructed as company of same name. Shareholders were entitled to 1 share of 2s. (credited with 6d. paid) for each share of 2s. held. Final meeting return regd. 19 Nov. 1914 **1914**

Kuranui Caledonian Ld. Regd. 1913. Vol. liq. 22 Oct. 1918. Final meeting return regd. 2 Dec. 1919 **1919**

Kurau Rubber Estate Ld. Regd. 1909. Vol. liq. 29 Dec. 1919. Reconstructed as company of same name. Shareholders were entitled to 3 fully-paid shares of £1 for every 10 shares of 2s. held. Final meeting return regd. 24 Sept. 1921 **1920**

Kurau Rubber Estate Ld. Regd. 1919. Vol. liq. (members') 15 Aug. 1935. Reconstructed as Bagan Serai Rubber Estates Ld. in which company shareholders were entitled to 1 share of £1 (credited as fully-paid) plus 5s. in cash for every 2 shares of £1 held. Final meeting return regd. 13 Aug. 1936 **1936**

Kurnalpi Gold Exploration & Development Co. (W. A.) Ld. Regd. 1896. Removed from Register 1903 **1901**

Kurnalpi Gold Mining Co. Ld. Regd. 1897. Vol. liq. 27 Jan. 1899. Final meeting return regd. 11 July 1900 **1900**

Kuru South Ld. Regd. 1919. Vol. liq. 16 Nov. 1922. In Jan. 1923 shareholders received 3 shares of 5s. in Jantar Nigeria Co. Ld. for every 2 shares of 5s. held. Final meeting return regd. 13 Apr. 1923 **1923**

Kuru Syndicate Ld. Regd. 1918. Vol. liq. 9 Dec. 1920. Undertaking was acquired by Jantar Nigeria Co. Ld., in which company shareholders were entitled to 1 share of 5s. (credited as fully-paid) for each share of 5s. held. Final meeting return regd. 9 June 1921 **1921**

Kurugama Tea Estate Ld. Regd. 1912. Vol. liq. (members') 10 July 1950. Capital returned to contributories—£2 5s. 10½d. per share of £1. Final meeting return regd. 12 Oct. 1955 **1956**

Kurungela Rubber Co (1929) Ld. Regd. 1929. Vol. liq. 28 jan. 1981. Final meeting return regd. 17 June 1981 **1970**

Kurunegala Rubber Co. Ld. Regd. 1906. Vol. liq. 3 Jan. 1929. Reconstructed at Kurunegala Rubber Co. (1929) Ltd., in which company shareholders were entitled to 1 share of 2s. (credited with 1s. 6d. paid) for each share of 2s. held. Final meeting return regd. 9 Dec. 1933 **1929**

Kuskie (Nigeria) Tin Fields Ld. Regd. 1912. Vol. liq. 9 Jan. 1922. Assets were acquired by East & West African Exploration Co. Ld. in which company shareholders were entitled to 5 shares of 2s. (credited with 1s. 4d. paid) for every 2 shares of 5s. held. Final meeting return regd. 8 Apr. 1925 **1922**

Kutais Mining & Timber Concessions Ld. Regd. 1906. Struck off Register 1919 **1933**

Kwaben Mines Ld. Regd. 1900. Vol. liq. May 1908. Removed from Register 1912 **1909**

Kwahu Mining Co. Ld. Regd. 1920 as West African Diamonds Ld.; name changed Nov. 1921. Vol. liq. 21 Dec. 1925. Reconstructed as Kwahu Mining Co. (1925) Ld. (later Kwahu Co.) in which company shareholders were entitled to 1 share of 2s. (credited with 1s. paid) for each share of 5s. held. Final meeting return regd.3 Apr. 1928 **1926**

Kwall Tin Fields of Nigeria Ld. Regd. 1912. Vol. liq. 4 Aug. 1920. Assets and liabilities were acquired by Nigerian Base Metals Corporation Ld in which company shareholders were entitled to 1 fully-paid share of 5s. for each share of 5s. held. Final meeting return regd. 26 May 1923 **1921**

Kwaloe Rubber Estates Ld. Regd. 1910. Vol. liq. (members') 2 Dec. 1931. Undertaking and assets transferred to Kwaloe Rubber Estates (1931) Ld., in which company shareholders were entitled to 1 share of 2s. (credited with 1s. 8d. paid) for every 2 shares of 2s. held. Final meeting return regd. 14 Mar. 1934 **1932**

Kwaloe Rubber Estates Ld. Regd. 1934 in reconstruction of Kwaloe Rubber Estates (1931) Ld. Removed from Register 30 Jan. 1970 **1970**

Kwaloe Rubber Estates (1931) Ld. Regd. 1931. Vol. liq. (members') 22 Mar. 1934. Reconstructed as Kwaloe Rubber Estates Ld., in which company shareholders were entitled to 1 share of 2s. (credited with 1s. 8d. paid) for each share of 2s. held. Final meeting return regd. 3 Apr. 1935. **1935**

VOL. FOR

Kwapa Tin Mines Ld. Regd. 1925. Vol. liq. 11 Apr. 1928. Undertaking and assets were acquired by Associated Tin Mines of Nigeria Ld., in which company shareholders were entitled to 1 fully-paid share of 5s. for every 9 shares of 2s. held. Final meeting return regd. 5 Feb. 1929 **1929**

Kyebi Lands Corporation Ld. Regd. 1901. Vol. liq. 30 Oct. 1908. Final meeting return regd. 26 Oct. 1916 **1909**

Kynoch Arklow Ld. Regd. 1912. Vol. liq. 28 Feb. 1921. Final meeting return regd. 15 Nov. 1927 **1922**

Kynoch Estate Co. Ld. Regd. 1899. Vol. liq. 11 Dec. 1901. Amalgamated with Kynoch Ld. [later I.C.I. (Metals) Ld.]. Final meeting return regd. 25 Apr. 1902 **1902**

Kynoch (G.) & Co. Ld. Regd. 1884. Vol. liq. 1 Mar. 1897. Reconstructed as Kynoch Ld. [later I.C.I. (Metals) Ld.] in which company shareholders were entitled to an equal number of fully-paid ordinary shares of £10 and an equal number of preference shares of £10 (credited with £5 paid). Final meeting return regd. 19 June 1900 **1898**

Kynoch Ld. See I.C.I. (Metals) Ld.

Kyshtim Corporation Ld. Regd. 1908. Vol. liq. 30 Dec. 1919. The undertaking and assets were sold to Russo-Asiatic Consolidated Ld., in which company shareholders were entitled to 2 fully-paid shares of £1 for each share of £1 held. Final meeting return regd. 23 Jan. 1922 **1920**

L

"L. & N." Brown Coal Ld. Regd. 1927. Vol. liq. (creditors') 29 Dec. 1933. No capital returned to contributories. Final meeting return regd. 27 May 1953 **1954**

"L. & N." Coal Distillation Ld. Regd. 1927. Vol. liq. (creditors') 4 Nov. 1932. No capital returned to contributories. Final meeting return regd. 5 June 1953 **1954**

L. & N. W. (Realisation) Ld. Regd. 1891 as Liverpool & North Wales Steamship Co. Ld.; name changed 1954. Vol. liq. (members') 17 Nov. 1954. Capital returned to contributories—24s. 8·155d. per share of 10s. Final meeting return regd. 15 Sept. 1955 **1956**

L. B. (Clundel) Ld. Regd. 1906 as Lindsay Blee and Co. Ld.; name subsequently changed. Final meeting return regd. 1 Jan. 1966 **1938**

L. C. & P. Co. Ld. See Leicestershire Colliery & Pipe Co. Ld.

L. D. C. Founders Shares Co. Ld. Regd. 1937. Vol. liq. (members') 5 July 1946. Capital returned to contributories—0·2d. per share of 5s. £60,000 ordinary stock of Law Debenture Corporation Ld. was distributed in specie. Final meeting return regd. 30 Nov. 1946 **1947**

L. G. Automatic Services Ld. Regd. 1929. Court Order to wind up 14 Apr. 1930. Struck off Register 14 Oct. 1938 **1939**

"L" Hotel Co. Ld. See Langham Hotel Co. Ld.

L. V. T. Syndicate Ld. Regd. 1937. Vol. liq. (members') 15 Feb. 1938. Capital returned to contributories—1¾d. per share of 1d. plus a proportion of 669,544 deferred ordinary shares of 2s. 6d. in Baird Television Ld. £153 12s. was paid into Companies' Liquidation Account. Final meeting return regd. 5 Nov. 1938 **1939**

La Banque Russe pour le Commerce Etranger. See Russian Bank for Foreign Trade.

La Bufa Mexican Gold Mines Ld. Regd. 1895. Court Order to wind up 28 Oct. 1896. Liquidator released 1 Mar. 1898. Removed from Register 10 July 1908 ***1897**

La Capital (Extensions) Tramways Co. Ld. Regd. 1898. Vol. liq. Sept. 1909. Undertaking and assets were acquired by Anglo-Argentine Tramways Co. Ld. The debentures were repaid at par. Removed from Register 1910 **1910**

La Capital Traction & Electric Co., Buenos Aires Ld. Regd. 1899. Vol. liq. Apr. 1909. Undertaking and assets were acquired by Anglo-Argentine Tramways Co. Ld. The debentures were repaid at 105%. Removed from Register 1910 **1910**

La Capital Tramways Co. Ld. Regd. 1896. Vol. liq. Apr. 1909. Undertaking and assets were acquired by Anglo-Argentine Tramways Co. Ld. The 1st debentures were repaid at 105% and the 2nd debentures at par. Removed from Register 1910 **1910**

La Compañia Molinera Anglo-Argentina Ld. Regd. 1898. Vol. liq. 24 May 1910. Final meeting return regd. 31 Dec. 1910 ***1911**

La Compañía Primitiva de Gas de Buenos Aires. Inc. Buenos Aires 1855. Undertaking was acquired in 1901 by Primitiva Gas and Electric Lighting Co. of

*See Stock Exchange Year-Book.

VOL. FOR

Buenos Aires Ld. (later Primitiva Gas Co. of Buenos Aires Ld.) in which company shareholders were entitled to 1 ordinary and 2 preference shares of £5 for each share of $50 held. The 5% debentures were replaced by 4% debentures in new company **1901**

La Concorde & City & Suburban (Matabeleland) Gold Development Co. Ld. Regd. 1895. Vol. liq. 13 Apr. 1898. Final meeting return regd. 8 Dec. 1899 ...... **1899**

La Concordia Estancia Co. Ld. Regd. 1867 as Pranges Estancia Co. Ld.; name changed Oct. 1916. Vol. liq. (members') 10 Mar. 1930. Capital returned to contributories—£13 7s. per share of £3. Final meeting return regd. 17 Nov. 1936.................... **1931**

La Estrella Copper Mines Ld. Regd. 1906. Vol. liq. June 1908. Removed from Register 1909 .... **1909**

La Fe Mining Co. Ld. Regd. 1911. Vol. liq. 29 July 1925. Final meeting return regd. 24 Sept. 1925 .... **1926**

La Gran Compaña Gold & Silver Mining Co. Ld. Regd. 1881. Vol. liq. 17 Feb. 1888. Final meeting return regd. 1 June 1891 .... **1889**

La Guaira & Caracas Railway Co. Ld. Regd. 1882. Vol. liq. (members') 11 Oct. 1951, company's properties having been sold to Venezuelan Government. 5% debenture stock repaid at par. Capital returned to contributories—120$\frac{1}{10}$% on ordinary stock. £1,194 was paid into Companies' Liquidation Account, being unclaimed dividends prior to liquidation. Final meeting return regd. 1 July 1952 .... **1953**

La Guaira Harbour Corporation Ld. Regd. 1885. Vol. liq. (members') 9 Aug. 1937. Debenture holders were repaid (a) £95 per £100 1st mortgage debenture stock, (b) £85 per £100 2nd mortgage stock (series B) and (c) £70 per £100 2nd mortgage stock (series A) in full satisfaction. Capital returned to contributories—8s. 9d. per share of £1. £4,870 10s. was paid into Companies' Liquidation Account. Final meeting return regd. 5 Oct. 1938 .... **1938**

La Libertad Rubber & Cocoa Estate Co. Ld. Regd. 1910. Vol. liq. (members') 17 Oct. 1930. Final meeting return regd. 11 Dec. 1930 .... **1931**

La Luz Mines of Mexico Ld. Regd. 1887. Vol. liq. 29 May 1890. Reconstructed as Silver Mines of La Luz Ld., in which company sharcholders were entitled to 1 share of £1 held (credited with 17s. paid) for each share of £1 held. Final meeting return regd. 13 Nov. 1897 **1892**

La Marguerite Co. Ld. Regd. 1894. Vol. liq. 7 Dec. 1898. Final meeting return regd. 17 July 1899 .... **1899**

La Martona Rubber Estates Ld. Regd. 1910. Vol. liq. June 1911. Removed from Register 1913 .... **1912**

La Nouvelle Fleur de Lys (Cardiff District) Colliery Co. Ld. Regd. 1906. Removed from Register 1910...... **1908**

La Plata & Ensenada Tramways Co. Ld. Regd. 1890. Reconstructed 1909 as La Plata Electric Tramways Co. Ld. Debenture holders agreed to accept 10% of nominal value of debentures in fully-paid ordinary shares in new company in full satisfaction of claims. Shareholders of both classes agreed to accept 2$\frac{1}{2}$% of their holding in fully-paid ordinary shares of new company. Removed from Register 1912 .... **1909**

La Plata Mines Ld. Regd. 1890. Vol. liq. 4 Oct. 1892. Reconstructed as company of same name, in which company shareholders were entitled to 1 ordinary or preference share of 5s. (credited with 3s. paid) for each ordinary or preference share of 5s. respectively held. Final meeting return regd. 18 Sept. 1896 .... **1893**

La Plata Mines Ld. Regd. 1892. Vol. liq. 12 Nov. 1897. Reconstructed as Imperial Gold Co. Ld., in which company shareholders were entitled to 1·29 ordinary shares of 5s. (credited with 4s. paid) for each ordinary or preference share of 5s. held. Final meeting return regd. 4 Oct. 1898 .... **1903**

La Plata Mining & Smelting Co. Ld. Regd. 1883. Vol. liq. 18 Aug. 1886. Reconstructed as New La Plata Mining & Smelting Co. Ld., in which company shareholders were entitled to 1 share of £1 (credited with 17s. 6d. paid) for each share of £1 held. Holders of debentures were entitled to an equal amount of debentures in new company. Final meeting return regd. 18 Sept. 1896 .... **1887**

La Reforma Mines of Mexico Ld. Regd. 1912. Vol. liq. 27 Dec. 1923. Struck off Register 30 Apr. 1946 .... ***1924**

La Reina de Plata Ld. Regd. 1905. Vol. liq. 22 Dec. 1913. Final meeting return regd. 19 June 1918 ...... **1914**

La Reine d'Or Gold Mining Co. Ld. Inc. Queensland 1895. Property sold to Queensland Mining Ld., in which company shareholders were entitled to 4 shares of 5s., credited 3s. 9d. paid, for each share of £1 held **1920**

La Reunion Française. *See* Reunion Française et Compagnie d'Assurances Universelles Reunies.

La Rose Consolidated Mines Co. Inc. Maine 1908. It was resolved in Dec. 1917 to dissolve the company. Shareholders were entitled to 1 share of $1 in La Rose Mines Ld. for each share of $5 held.............. **1918**

VOL. FOR

La Trinidad Ld. Regd. 1884. Court Orders: to wind up 22 June 1889; to dissolve 12 Aug. 1891................ **1890**

La Velera Ld. Regd. 1886. Reconstructed 1891 as New La Velera Ld., in which company shareholders were entitled to 1 share of £1 (credited with 18s. paid) for each share of £1 held. Removed from Register 1904 **1893**

La Yesca Gold & Silver Mines Ld. Regd. 1893. Removed from Register 1905 .... **1900**

Labour Newspapers Ld. Regd. 1912. Converted into society under Industrial & Provident Societies Act (1893) in Apr. 1915 .... **1916**

Labu (F.M.S.) Rubber Co. Ld. Regd. 1907. Vol. liq. (members') 22 Dec. 1953. Undertaking and assets were acquired by Labu Cheviot Rubber Ld. in which company stockholders were entitled to 50 shares of 2s. for every £4 stock held. Final meeting return regd. 21 Feb. 1955 .... **1956**

Labuan & Borneo Ld. Regd. 1897. A receiver was appointed by the Court on behalf of debenture stockholders. Removed from Register 1903.......... **1904**

Labuan Coalfields Co. Ld. Regd. 1902. Vol. liq. 2 Nov. 1916. Final meeting return regd. 7 Sept.1922........ **1917**

Labugama (Kelani Valley, Ceylon) Rubber & Tea Co. Ld. Regd. Edinburgh 1907. Vol. liq. Mar. 1926. Capital returned to contributories—£2 14s. 6$\frac{1}{4}$d. per share of £1; further payments (if any) not known. Final meeting return regd. 8 Dec. 1926 .... **1927**

Laburnum Spinning Co. (1920) Ld. Regd. 1920. Vol. liq. 30 July 1929. Undertaking and assets were acquired by Combined Egyptian Mills Ld. (later Combined English Mills (Spinners) Ld.) in which company shareholders were entitled to 1 fully-paid ordinary share of £1 for every 8 shares of £1 held. Debenture holders were entitled to an equal amount of income debenture stock. Struck off Register 4 Oct. 1938... **1939**

Lace Diamond Mining Co. Ld. Inc. Transvaal 1899. Assets were taken over by Crown Diamond Mining and Exploration Co. Ld. **1939**

Lace Proprietary Mines Ld. Inc. Transvaal 1904. Vol. liq. 11 Feb. 1949. Capital returned to contributories—5s. 0·6d. cash plus $\frac{7}{8}$ths of one share (of 10s.) of Vlakfontein Gold Mining Co. Ld. for every share of 5s. held. Company's records were closed 31 Dec. 1950 and all unclaimed dividends and liquidation distributions have been paid to the Master of the Supreme Court, Pretoria........................ **1951**

Lachian Gold Fields Ld. Regd. 1907. Vol. liq. Dec. 1907. Removed from Register 1909 .... **1908**

Ladas & Foston United Gold Mines Ld. Regd. 1895. Vol. liq. 5 Jan. 1897. Final meeting return regd. 6 Aug. 1897 .... **1939**

Ladies' Dress Association Ld. Regd. 1877. Vol. liq. 16 Dec. 1896. Final meeting return regd. 19 Nov. 1901 **1897**

Ladies Dwellings Co. Ld. *See* Sloane Securities Ld.

Lady Bess Gold Mines Ld. Regd. 1895 as Hannan's West Ld.; name changed 1896. Struck off Register 17 Nov. 1899 .... **1897**

Lady Bountiful Extended Gold Mining Co. Ld. Regd. 1896. Struck off Register 26 Oct. 1900 .... **1897**

Lady Carrington Gold Mines Ld. Regd. 1897. Reconstructed 1899· as Union Jack Consolidated Mines Ld., in which company shareholders were entitled to 1 share of 5s. (credited with 3s. 6d. paid) for each share of 5s. held. Removed from Register 1901 ... **1900**

Lady Charlotte Gold Mines Ld. Regd. 1897. Removed from Register 1904 .... **1904**

Lady Emily Gold Mining Co. Ld. Regd. 1896. Removed from Register 1904 .... **1903**

Lady Evelyn Gold Mines Ld. Regd. 1896. Vol. liq. 31 May 1901. Property was acquired by Fingall Proprietary Ld in which company shareholders were entitled to 1 share of 10s. (credited with 8s. paid) for each share of £1 held. Final meeting return regd. 22 Oct. 1901 .... **1908**

Lady Forrest (Murchison) Gold Mine Ld. Regd. 1895. Removed from Register 1909 .... **1899**

Lady Franklin Mining Co. Ld. Regd. 1886. Removed from Register 1904 .... **1892**

Lady Hampton Consolidated Gold Mines Ld. Regd. 1896. Removed from Register 1904 .... **1901**

Lady Helen Gold Mining Syndicate Ld. Regd. 1895. Vol. liq. 21 Feb. 1896. Final meeting return regd. 28 July 1897 .... **1897**

Lady Isabelle Ld. Inc. Queensland 1895. Reconstructed 1898 as Croydon Goldfields Ld., in which company shareholders were entitled to 1 share of 5s. (credited with 3s. paid) for each share of 5s. held **1904**

Lady Loch Gold Mine Ld. Regd. 1894. Vol. liq. 11 Oct. 1897. Reconstructed as Lady Loch Gold Mines Ld., in which company shareholders were entitled to 2 shares of 10s. (credited with 7s. paid) for each share of £1 held. Final return meeting regd. 24 Apr. 1899 **1902**

VOL. FOR

Lake Valley of Switzerland Railway Co. Ld. Regd. 1881. Property was acquired by a Swiss company. In Aug. 1894 debenture holders were entitled to £11 5*s.* per £50 bond held; further payments (if any) not known. Removed from Register 1897 .... **1896**

Lake View and Oroya Exploration Ld. Regd. 1911 as Lake View Consols Ld.; name changed Dec. 1911. Vol. liq. 22 Dec. 1919. Investments and assets acquired by Lake View Investment Trust Ld., in which company shareholders were entitled to 1 share of 10*s.* for each share of 10*s.* held. Struck off Register 1 Sept. 1953 .... **1954**

Lake View & Boulder Junction Gold Mines Ld. Regd. 1901. Removed from Register 1906 .... **1905**

Lake View Consols Ld. Regd. 1896. Vol. liq 6 June 1911. Reconstructed as company of same name [later Lake View and Oroya Exploration Ld.], in which company shareholders were entitled to 1 share of 10*s.* (credited as fully-paid) for each share of £1 held Final meeting return regd. 2 Dec. 1916................ **1912**

Lake View Consols Ld. (regd. 1911). *See* Lake View & Oroya Exploration Ld.

Lake View Extended Gold Mine (W. A.) Ld. Regd 1899. Removed from Register 1911 .... **1902**

Lake View South (G. M. K.). Inc. Australia. In liquidation. Direct controlling interest was owned by Gold Mines of Kalgoorlie Ld. **1940**

Lake View South Gold Mine (W. A.) Ld. Regd. 1895. Vol. liq. 2 Sept. 1901. Reconstructed as company of same name. Shareholders were entitled to 1 ordinary share of £1 (credited with 16*s.* 6*d.* paid) for each share of £1 held. Final meeting return regd. 25 Sept. 1902 .... **1906**

Lake View South Gold Mine (W.A.) Ld. Regd. 1901. Vol. liq. 4 Apr. 1906. Reconstructed as Lake View South Ld., in which company shareholders were entitled to 1 share of 4*s.* (credited with 2*s.* paid) for each ordinary share of £1 held, and an option (since expired) over further shares at par. The holders of 12,000 preference shares of £1 agreed to extinguish shares for payment of £1,000 in cash. Final meeting return regd. 24 May 1918 .... **1908**

Lake View South Ld. Regd. 1906. Vol. liq. 16 Apr. 1917. Final meeting return regd. 30 Jan. 1930...............

Lake Way Gold Mine Ld. Regd. 1897. Assets were sold to Golden Age Consolidated Ld. for 60,000 fully-paid shares of £1. Removed from Register 1905 .. **1901**

Lake Way Goldfield, 1899, Ld. Regd. 1899. Reconstructed 1903 as Lake Way Goldfield Ld. Shareholders were entitled to 2 shares of 10*s.* (credited with 5*s.* paid) in new company for each share of £1 held. Removed from Register 1909 .... **1905**

Lake Way Goldfield Ld. Regd. 1903. Struck off Register 1914........................ **1905**

Lakeman & Tucker Ld. Regd. 1910 as Lakeman, Tucker & Gemmell Ld.; name changed Jan. 1915. Vol. liq. (members') 5 Jan. 1942. All shares owned by Hazell, Watson & Viney Ld. (later Hazell Sun Ld.). Final meeting return regd. 9 Apr. 1942 .... **1942**

Lamag Rubber Estates Ld. Regd. 1910. Vol. liq. 17 Mar. 1913. Reconstructed as Lamag Rubber Estates (1913) Ld. Shareholders were entitled to 1 share of 1*s.*) credited with 7½*d.* paid) for each share of 2*s.* held. Final meeting return regd. 21 Mar. 1923 .... **1913**

Lamag Rubber Estates (1913) Ld. Regd. 1918. Vol. liq. 17 Oct. 1923. Final meeting return regd. 28 Aug. 1924 .... **1924**

Lamb Brewery Ld. Regd. 1893. All capital was acquired by Frome & Lamb Ld. Vol. liq. (members') 1 Apr. 1960. Final meeting return regd. 3 Oct.1960 .... **1957**

Lambe (J.B.) & Co. Ld. Regd. 1880. Court Orders: to wind up 22 Mar. 1883; to dissolve 11 Mar. 1886.. ***1884**

Lambert & Norris Ld. Regd. 1897. Vol. liq. (members') 25 Mar. 1935. The undertaking was merged with Friary, Holroyd Healy's Breweries Ld., which company held all share capital. The 4% irredeemable 1st mortgage debenture stock was repaid at par on 30 Apr. 1935. Final meeting return regd. 5 Mar. 1936 .... **1936**

Lambeth Waterworks (Company of Proprietors of). Inc. 1785, reincorporated 1848. Undertaking was taken over by Metropolitan Water Board in 1904 .... **1905**

Lamborn & Co. Ld. Regd. 1922. Vol. liq. (members') 22 Dec. 1932. Private company. Final meeting return regd. 13 Feb. 1934 .... **1933**

Lambourn Valley Railway Co. Inc. by Special Act 1883. Under Great Western Railway Co. Act 1905 undertaking was acquired by that company for £40,000 .... **1906**

Lambton & Hetton Collieries Ld. *See below.*

Lambton Collieries Ld. *See below.*

Lambton, Hetton & Joicey Collieries Ld. Regd. 1896 as Lambton Collieries Ld.; name changed Aug. 1911 to Lambton & Hetton Collieries Ld. and to above title Dec. 1924. Vol. liq. (members') 8 Oct. 1952. Capital returned to contributories—preference: at par; ordinary; £1 13*s.* 10·9723*d.* per share of 5*s.* Final meeting return regd. 13 Mar. 1956 .... **1957**

Lami River Rubber, Cocoa & Banana Plantations Ld. Regd. 1910. Court Order to wind up 11 Feb. 1913. Liquidator released 23 June 1915. Struck off Register 14 Feb. 1919 .... **1913**

Lamina Ld. Regd. 1923. Vol. liq. (members') 15 June 1932. All shares held by British Feeding-meals & Milk Products Co. Ld. Final meeting return regd. 27 Oct. 1933 .... **1933**

Laminated Coal Ld. Regd. 1919. Court Order to wind up May 1923. Struck off Register 1929 .... **1924**

Laminated Wood Products Ld. Regd. 1929 as Hitchins Laminated Wood Products Ld.; name changed in Sept. 1930. Vol. liq. (members') 18 Aug. 1938. Undertaking and assets were acquired by Saro Laminated Wood Products Co. Ld. for £540 15*s.* in cash and £12,155 5*s.* in shares of 5*s.* of acquiring company. 10,985 shares were distributed among ordinary shareholders and 37,636 shares among preferred ordinary shareholders. Final meeting return regd. 22 Apr. 1939 .... **1939**

Lamlah Rubber Estate Ld. Regd. 1926. Struck off Register Sept. 1934........................ **1935**

Lamp Manufacturing Co. Ld. Regd. 1890. Vol. liq. 25 Apr. 1895. Final meeting return regd. 15 June 1897 ***1895**

Lampa Mining Co. Ld. *see* Lampa Securities Ld.

Lampa Securities Ld. Regd. 30 June 1906 as Lampa Mining Co. Ld.; name changed 16 Apr. 1974. Vol. liq. (members') 17 Dec. 1976. Return of final meeting regd. 23 Jan. 1985. Distributions per share (of 50p)—90p in Feb., 12p in May, 8p in July and Nov. 1977; 4p in Mar. & 8p in Nov. 1978; 7p in Sept. 1979; 7p in July 1980 and 4½p in Sept. 1982.£26,008 paid into Companies' Liquidation Account in respect of unclaimed distributions **1985–6**

Lampeter, Aberayron and New Quay Light Railway Company. Inc. (under Light Railways Act 1896) by order of Light Railway Commissioners confirmed by Board of Trade 1906. In 1922 the undertaking was merged into the Great Western Railway Co., in which company debenture holders were entitled to £33 6*s.* 8*d.* 2½% Debenture Stock for each £100 Debentures held (other than those held by the Great Western Company and the National Provincial Bank Ld.), the Great Western Company to pay £8,840 in cash in discharge of all liability in respect of the loan to the Lampeter Company by the said Bank. The Debenture held by the Great Western Company and the said Bank, and the Preference and Ordinary Shares were to be cancelled **1924**

Lampeter, Llandyssul, Tregaron & Aberayron Gas Co. Inc. by Special Act 1867. Dissolved 1 May 1949, undertaking being vested in Wales Area Gas Board under Gas Act 1948. Holders of ordinary shares (of £10) were entitled to receive £13 10*s.* British Gas 3% guaranteed stock 1990-95 for each share held **1952**

Lamplough Gold Mining Co. Ld. Regd. 1934. Vol. liq. (creditors') 16 Dec. 1937. Noteholders received 2*s.* 10·44*d.* per note of £1. Final meeting return regd. 27 June 1941 .... **1938**

Lamplough (Henry) Ld. Regd. 1886. Vol. liq. 28 Dec. 1923. Capital returned to contributories—3*s.* per share of 5*s.* at Feb. 1924; further payments (if any) not known. Final meeting return regd. 25 Mar. 1925 **1924**

Lamport & Holt Ld. Regd. 1911. Receiver appointed 27 Aug. 1930; ceased to act 15 Jan. 1940. Debenture holders were entitled to 50 shares of 6*s.* 8*d.* in Lamport & Holt Line Ld., £20 5% debenture stock in Coast Lines Ld. and £48 in cash for each £100 debenture held. Struck off Register 17 July 1942 . **1943**

Lanark Oil Co. Ld. Regd. Edinburgh 1883. Court Orders: to wind up Nov. 1886; to dissolve 25 Apr. 1890........................ **1888**

Lanark Picture House Ld. Regd. Edinburgh 1914. Vol. liq (members') 7 May 1931. Capital returned to contributories—£5,137 1*s.* 7*d.* Final meeting return regd. 7 Nov. 1931 .... **1932**

Lanarkshire and Ayrshire Railway Co. Inc. by Special Act 1883 as the Barrmill & Kilwinning Railway Co., name changed by Act of 1884. In 1923 the undertaking was merged into the London Midland & Scottish Railway Co., in which company stockholders were entitled to stock as follows:

For each £100 held		*L.M. & S.*	
4% A Debenture	£100	4% Debenture	
4% B Debenture	£100	4% Debenture	
4% C Debenture	£100	4% Debenture	
Ordinary	£41½	Ordinary	**1924**

Lanarkshire & Dumbartonshire Railway Co. Inc. 1891. Under Caledonian Railway Act 1909 undertaking was transferred to that company. Holders of

VOL. FOR

ordinary shares received an equal amount of Caledonian Railway 4% (Lanarkshire & Dumbartonshire Railway) guaranteed stock. Holders of debenture stock received an equal amount of 4% debenture stock in purchasing company **1910**

Lanarkshire Hydro-Electric Power Co. Inc. by Special Act 1924. All capital was owned by Clyde Valley Electrical Power Co. Dissolved 1 Apr. 1948 under Electricity Act 1947 .... **1938**

Lanarkshire Traction Co. Ld. Inc. by Special Act 1900 as Hamilton, Motherwell & Wishaw Tramways Co.; name changed to Lanarkshire Tramways Co. in 1903 and to Lanarkshire Traction Co. in 1929; regd. in Edinburgh as limited Sept. 1933. Vol. liq. (members') 28 Nov. 1949 undertaking having been acquired by Central S. M. T. Co. Ld. Final meeting return regd. 2 Dec. 1950. £40 was paid to Accountant of Court in respect of unclaimed dividends &c **1952**

Lanarkshire Tramways Co. *See above.*

Lancarrow Tin Alluvials Ld. *See* Treskillard Minerals Ld.

Lancashire & Central Counties Vacuum Cleaner Co. Ld. Regd. 1903. Vol. liq. 11 Nov. 1915. Final meeting return regd. 14 Mar. 1917 .... **1916**

Lancashire & Cheshire Insurance Corporation Ld. Regd. 1904. Vol. liq. 25 Aug. 1925. Final meeting return regd. 18 July 1929 .... **1926**

Lancashire & Cheshire Telephonic Exchange Co. Ld. Regd. 1881. Vol. liq. 4 July 1889. Taken over by National Telephone Co. Ld. Final meeting return regd. 4 Mar. 1892 .... **1890**

Lancashire & General Assurance Co. Ld. Regd. 1907. Court Order to wind up 14 June 1927. Struck off Register 9 June 1936 .... **1937**

Lancashire & Yorkshire Bank Ld. Regd. 1872. Vol. liq. 3 Jan. 1928. Undertaking and assets were acquired by Bank of Liverpool & Martins Ld. (later Martins Bank Ld.), in which company shareholders were entitled to 17 shares of £1 (credited as fully-paid) *plus* £1 in cash for each share of £20 (£12 paid) held **1928**

Lancashire & Yorkshire Counties Shipping Co. Ld. Regd. 1919. Vol. liq. (creditors') 30 Dec. 1930. No capital returned to contributories. Final meeting return regd. 11 Mar. 1936 .... **1931**

Lancashire and Yorkshire Discount Co. Ld. Regd. 1885. Vol. liq. 27 Nov. 1888. Final meeting return regd. 19 Nov. 1894 .... **1889**

Lancashire & Yorkshire Insurance Co. Ld. Regd. 1877 as Lancashire & Yorkshire Accident Insurance Co. Ld.; name changed Aug. 1906. Undertaking and assets were acquired by Scottish Union and National Insurance Co. Shareholders were entitled to £55 in cash for every 10 shares of £5 (£1 10*s.* paid) held; fractions were paid off at £5 12*s.* 9*d.* per share. Removed from Register 1908 .... **1907**

Lancashire & Yorkshire Railway Co. Inc. by Special Act, 1836 as Manchester & Leeds Railway Co., name changed by Act of 1847. In 1922 the undertaking was merged into the London & North Western Railway Co., in which company stockholders were entitled to stock as follows:

For each £100 held		*L. & N.W.*
3% Debenture	£100	3% Debenture
6% Min. Pref.	£156¼	4% Gtd. (a)
4½% Min. Pref.	£125	4% Gtd. (b)
4% Guaranteed	£100	4% Guarant'd
3% Preference	£75	4% Preference
4% Preference (1903)....	£100	4% Pref. (1902)
4% Preference (1908)....	£100	4% Pref. (1902)
5% Red. Pref. (1916)....	£100	5% Red. Pref.
Ordinary......................	£73	Ordinary

(a) Including £6¼ for surrender of contingent rights.
(b) Including £12½ for surrender of contingent rights **1924**

Lancashire & Yorkshire Waggon Co. Ld. Regd. 1862. Vol. liq. (members') 15 Mar. 1951. Undertaking and assets (excluding £197,388 cash) acquired by Foundry Equipment & L. & Y. Holdings Ld. (later Foundry Holdings Ld.). in which company shareholders were entitled to receive (per share of £2 10*s.*) 14 preference shares of £1 and 10½ ordinary shares of 10*s.* plus £10 cash. Further capital returned to contributories—£8 6*s.* 8*d.* per share. Final meeting return regd. 29 Oct. 1962 .... **1964**

Lancashire Automatic Glass Manufacturing Co. Ld. Regd. 1920. Reconstructed as Automatic Bottle Makers Ld. Struck off Register 1926. .... **1926**

Lancashire Cinematograph Theatres Ld. Regd. 1910. Vol. liq. Apr. 1911. The property was acquired by United Electric Theatres Ld. Removed from Register 1913 .... **1913**

Lancashire Cotton Spinners & Weavers Ld. Regd. 1913. Struck off Register 3 Jan. 1919 .... ***1914**

Lancashire Cotton Spinning Co. Ld. Regd. 1874. Court Orders: to wind up 14 Nov. 1885; to dissolve 31 Oct. 1890 .... **1887**

Lancashire, Derbyshire & East Coast Railway Co. Inc. by Special Act 1891. Amalgamated in 1907 with Great Central Railway Co. Holders of debenture stock and shares received £1,854,368 3½% 2nd debenture, £557,500 preferred ordinary and £557,500 deferred ordinary stocks **1907**

Lancashire Electric Light & Power Co. Ld. Regd. 1903 as Lancashire Power Construction Co. Ld.; name changed 1921. Dissolved 1 Apr. 1948, undertaking being vested in British (later Central) Electricity Authority under Electricity Act 1947. Holders of securities were entitled to receive British Electricity 3% guaranteed stock (1968-73). as follows in respect of each £1 unit of capital held:

6% 1st preference stock	1	18	4
7% ptpg. preference stock	1	18	3
3¾% preference stock	1	3	2
Ordinary stock............................	1	17	7
5% redeemable debenture stock ...	1	2	1⅓

1949

Lancashire Electric Power Co. Inc. by Special Act 1900. Dissolved 1 Apr. 1948; undertaking being vested in British (later Central Electricity Authority and North-Western Area Board under Electricity Act 1947 .... **1949**

Lancashire Entertainments, Ld. Regd. 1920. Vol. liq. (members') 3 Sept. 1963. Final meeting return regd. 17 Feb. 1965 .... **1957**

Lancashire Explosives Co. Ld. Regd. 1892. Vol. liq. (members') 30 June 1939. Capital returned to contributories—£1 12*s.* 3⅝*d.* per ordinary share of £1; 20*s.* per preference share of £1. Final meeting return regd. 3 July 1940 .... **1940**

Lancashire Houseowners' Investment Co. Ld. Regd. 1881. Wound up by Order of Court 13 Apr. 1887 ***1887**

Lancashire Insurance Co. Established by Deed of Settlement 1852. Business was acquired in 1901 by Royal Insurance Co. Shareholders were entitled to 1 share of £20 (£3 paid) in acquiring company *plus* £25 in cash for every 20 shares of £20 (£2 paid) held **1902**

Lancashire Maxim-Weston Electric Co. Ld. Regd. 1882. Vol. liq. Mar. 1884. Final meeting return regd. 22 Jan. 1886 .... **1885**

Lancashire Ordinance Accessories Co. Ld. Regd. 1919. Receiver appointed 12 Oct. 1923. Court Order to wind up 6 Aug. 1924 .... ***1925**

Lancashire Power Construction Co. Ld. *See* Lancashire Electric Light & Power Co. Ld.

Lancashire Public House Trust Co. Ld. Regd. 1902. Vol. liq. (members') 31 May 1937. Capital returned to contributories—15*s.* per ordinary share of £1 (15*s.* paid). £3 14*s.* 10*d.* was paid into Companies' Liquidation Account in respect of unclaimed dividends and £52 10*s.* in respect of capital. Final meeting return regd. 4 Apr. 1938 .... **1938**

Lancashire Supply Association Ld. Regd. 1880. Vol. liq. 11 Nov. 1889. Final meeting return regd. 26 Mar. 1891 .... **1890**

Lancashire Trust & Mortgage Insurance Corporation Ld. Regd. 1890. Vol. liq. Feb. 1908. Removed from Register 1910 .... **1909**

Lancashire Union Railway Co. Inc. by Special Act 1864. Under London & North Western Railway Act 1883 undertaking amalgamated with that company **1884**

Lancashire Waggon Co. Ld. Regd. 1903. Vol. liq. (members') 27 Oct. 1932. Capital returned to contributories—20*s.* per preference share of £1; 14*s.* 2·4*d.* per ordinary share of £1 (2*s.* 6*d.* paid). Final meeting return regd. 13 Sept. 1935 .... **1933**

Lancashire Watch Co. Ld. Regd. 1888. Business was acquired by company of same name. Removed from Register 1906 .... **1907**

Lancashire Watch Co. Ld. Regd. 1897. Receiver appointed in 1906. Struck off Register 1914 .... **1911**

Lancaster & District Tramways Co. Ld. Regd. 1888. Receiver appointed 7 Oct. 1925; ceased to act 16 June 1926. Struck off Register 1928 .... **1927**

Lancaster Banking Co. Ld. Established 1826. Regd. as unlimited 1874 and as limited 1896. Vol. liq. 20 Nov. 1907. Undertaking was acquired by Manchester and Liverpool District Banking Co. Ld. (later District Bank Ld.). in which company shareholders were entitled to 3 shares of £60 (credited with £12 paid) for every 5 shares of £35 (£5 10*s.* paid) held, *plus* £1 1*s.* per share in cash **1908**

Lancaster Canal Navigation Co. Inc. by Special Act 1792. By London & North Western Railway Act 1885 canal was sold to that company. Shareholders received £43 15*s.* 4% debenture stock for each share held. Company ceased to exist on 1 Jan. 1886...... **1886**

Lancaster Gold Mining Co. Ld. Inc. Transvaal 1895. Wound up 1909. Assets and undertaking were sold to Lancaster West Gold Mining Co. Ld., in which company shareholders were entitled to 3 fully-paid £1 shares for every 10 shares of £1 held **1910**

Lancaster Railway Carriage & Wagon Co. Ld. Regd. 1863 as Lancaster Wagon Co. Ld.; name changed 1892. Reconstructed 1902 as Metropolitan Amalgamated Railway Carriage and Wagon Co. Ld. (later Metropolitan-Cammell Carriage Wagon & Finance Co. Ld.), in which company shareholders were entitled to 7¼ ordinary shares of £1 (credited as fully-paid) for each share of £5 held. Struck off Register 1903 .... **1903**

Lancaster Shipowners' Co. Ld. Regd. 1865. Undertaking was acquired in 1896 by Lancashire Shipping Co. Ld. Vol. liq. 1 Mar. 1897. Final meeting return regd. 6 Nov. 1897 .... **1898**

Lancaster Syndicate Ld. Regd. 1904. Vol. liq. Aug. 1909. Removed from Register 1910 .... **1910**

Lancaster Wagon Co. Ld. *See* Lancaster Railway Carriage & Wagon Co. Ld.

Lancaster West Gold Mining Co. Ld. Inc. Transvaal 1897. Wound up 1915 .... **1915**

Lancefield Gold Mining Co. Ld. Regd. 1904. Vol. liq. Apr. 1908 for reconstruction as company of same name. Shareholders were entitled to 1 share of 10s. (credited with 8s. paid) for each share held. Removed from Register 1909 .... **1909**

Lancefield Gold Mining Co. Ld. Inc. Western Australia 1908 .... **1914**

Lancefield (W.A.) Gold Mine, No Liability. Inc. Victoria 1933. Vol. liq. 1940. Returns: per share of 4s.—1s. 3d. in 1940, and 1s. 3⁷⁄₁₀d. in 1941. Books finally closed Nov. 1941 .... **1942**

Lancegaye Safety Glass Ld. Regd. 1928. Vol. liq. (members') 7 Mar. 1934. Reconstructed as Lancegaye Safety Glass (1934) Ld., in which company shareholders were entitled to 1 fully-paid share and 2 shares of 1s. (credited with 6d. paid) for every 3 shares of 1s. held. Final meeting return regd. 25 May 1935 .... **1935**

Lancegaye Safety Glass (1934) Ld. Regd. 1934. Vol. liq. (members') 24 Sept. 1952. Final meeting return regd. 7 May 1953 .... **1951**

Lancelot Freehold Tin & Copper Mines Ld. Regd. 1903. Vol. liq. Dec. 1908. Removed from Register 1910 .... **1909**

Lancelot Tin Mines Ld. Regd. 1909. Vol. liq. 30 Nov. 1911. Final meeting return regd. 22 Jan. 1913 ..... ***1913**

Lanchester Engine Co. Ld. Regd. 1899. Removed from Register 1906 .... **1907**

Land & Banking Agency Ld. Regd. 1909 as Argentine Farmers' Bank Ld.; name changed July 1911. Struck off Register July 1923 .... ***1913**

Land & Loan Co. of New Zealand Ld. Regd. 1884. Vol. liq. Dec. 1906. Removed from Register 1907 .... **1907**

Land & Mortgage Co. of Egypt Ld. Regd. 1880. Vol. liq. 29 Oct. 1926. Final meeting return regd.5 Aug. 1931 **1927**

Land & Trust Co. of Florida Ld. Regd. 1890. The debentures were redeemed. Capital returned to contributories—10s. per share of £1; further payments (if any) not known. Removed from Register 1910 .... **1906**

Land Co. of Australasia Ld. Inc. Sydney 1885. Wound up 1893 .... **1894**

Land Co. of Chiapas, Mexico, Ld. Regd. 1905. Vol. liq. (members') 20 Jan. 1943. Capital returned to contributories—1s. 10·2d. per share of 18s. £472 11s. 8d. was paid into Companies' Liquidation Account (*see preface*). Final meeting return regd. 11 Jan. 1944 **1947**

Land Corporation of Canada Ld. Regd. 1881. Vol. liq. (members') 14 Dec. 1926, the undertaking having been acquired by South British Investment Trust Ld., in which company shareholders were entitled to 1 fully-paid 10s. share for each share of £1 held. Final meeting return registered 22 Jan. 1953. Struck off Register 9 Feb. 1954 .... **1954**

Land Corporation of Ireland Guarantee Co. Ld. Regd. 1883. Removed from Register 1903 .... **1903**

Land Corporation of Ireland Ld. Regd. 1883. Vol. liq. 22 Jan. 1901. Final meeting return regd. 20 Jan. 1902 **1901**

Land Corporation of West Australia Ld. Regd. 1885. Vol. liq. 30 Jan. 1896. Capital returned to contributories—£4 per share of £5 at July 1896; further payments (if any) not known. Removed from Register 1901 .... **1897**

Land Creditbank Co. Ld. *See* Foldhitelbank Reszventyarsasag.

Land Development and Property Co. Ld. Regd. 1903. Court Order to wind up 14 Apr. 1908. Removed from Register 1914 .... **1909**

Land Development Association Ld. Regd. 1880, Court Orders: to wind up 20 Apr. 1886; to dissolve 15 May 1895 .... **1837**

Land Loan & Enfranchisement Co. Inc. 1860. Vol. liq. 1897 .... **1898**

Land Mortgage and Agency of Fiji Ld. *See* Mortgage & Agency Co. of Australasia Ld.

Land Mortgage & Credit Co. of England Ld. Regd. 1883. Court Order to wind up 1905. Removed from Register 1911 .... **1906**

Land Mortgage Bank of Florida Ld. Regd. 1889. Vol. liq. 20 Dec. 1895. In 1955 12s. 6d. per £100 was paid in respect of arrears of interest on debentures which were finally repaid in 1929. No capital returned to contributories. £402 9s. was paid into Companies' Liquidation Account. Final meeting return regd. 22 Nov. 1955. Struck off Register 14 Aug. 1956 .... **1957**

Land Mortgage Bank of India (Crédit Foncier Indien) Ld. Regd. 1863. Vol. liq. 26 Nov. 1896. Estates and properties were sold for £360,994. The £1,620 5% debentures 1866 were to be repaid in Jan. 1897 and the 4½% terminable debentures in Dec. 1896. Final meeting return regd. 3 Sept. 1897 .... **1897**

Land Mortgage Bank of North Western America Ld. Regd. 1892. Capital returned to contributories—7s. 8d. in £; further payments (if any) not known. Removed from Register 1905 .... **1905**

Land Mortgage Bank of Texas Ld. Regd. 1886. Vol. liq. 17 July 1922. Final meeting return regd. 16 Dec. 1922 .... **1923**

Land Mortgage Investment and Agency Co. of America Ld. Regd. 1881. Vol. liq. 23 July 1919. Capital returned to contributories—1s. 0¼d. per share in Nov. 1919; further payments (if any) not known. Final meeting return regd. 20 Feb. 1920 .... **1920**

Land Securities Assets Co. Ld. Regd. 1905. Vol. liq. (members') 1 Jan. 1932. All shares owned by Land Securities Investment Trust Ld. Final meeting return regd. 23 Aug. 1932 .... **1942**

Land Securities Co. Ld. Regd. Dec. 1863. Vol. liq. 10 Apr. 1894. Court Order to continue winding up under supervision 3 May 1894. Properties taken over by Land Securities Assets Co. Ld. Debenture holders received 75% approx. of their holdings. Struck off Register 21 Feb. 1911 .... **1905**

Land Securities Investment Trust Ld. (The). Regd. 1931. Undertaking and assets transferred to a new company (Land Securities Investment Trust Ld.), shareholders were entitled to receive one preference share of £1 and 4 ordinary shares of 10s. in the new company for each share (of 10s.) held. Dissolved under section 208 of Companies Act, 1948 on 28 July 1955 .... **1956**

Landaulet Co. Ld. Regd. 1902 as Electric Landaulet Co. Ld.; name changed Jan. 1911. Vol. liq. Aug. 1918. Struck off Register 12 Mar. 1935 .... **1936**

Landaulette Motor Cab Co. Ld. Regd. 1906. Vol. liq. 4 May 1908. Removed from Register 1909 .... **1909**

Landore Siemens Steel Co. Ld. Regd. 1870. Vol. liq. 2 Oct. 1888. Dissolved by Order of Court 16 July 1896 ***1889**

Lands Allotment Co. Ld. Regd. 1867. Court Order to wind up 16 Jan. 1893. Liquidator released 18 Oct. 1910. Struck off Register 1 July 1921 .... **1893**

Lands Development Syndicate Ld. Regd. 1899. Removed from Register 1902 .... **1903**

Land's Puncture-Proof Tyre & Automatic Valve Co. Ld. Regd. 1895. Struck off Register 23 July 1901 .... **1902**

Lands Trading Co. Ld. Regd. 1882. Struck off Register 8 Mar. 1935 .... **1936**

Lands Trust Co. Ld. Regd. 1888. Vol. liq. 24 Apr. 1895. Court Order to stay proceedings 22 May 1895. Vol. liq. 20 Nov. 1903. The Debentures were repaid. A dividend on account of capital of 12s. 6d. was payable 15 Jan. 1904. Final meeting return regd. 7 Feb. 1916 .... **1904**

Landscape Rubber Estates Co. Ld. Regd. Edinburgh 1907. Vol. liq. May 1925. Estate sold for £17,038 in cash. Final meeting return regd.14 Jan. 1927 .... **1926**

Lane Ends Estate Co. Ld. Regd. 1875. Vol. liq. 12 July 1897. Property was acquired by Alhambra (Blackpool) Ld. Capital returned to contributories—£26 per share of £10. Final meeting return regd. 30 Sept. 1897 .... **1898**

Lane Fox & Co. Ld. Regd. 2 Sept. 1936. Vol. liq. (creditors') 10 Sept. 1975. return of final meeting regd. 19 dec. 1986 .... **1988–9**

Lane (John) The Bodley Head Ld. Regd. 1921. Vol. liq. (creditors') 23 Jan. 1937. Assets realised insufficient to pay creditors in full. Final meeting return regd. 12 Nov. 1938 .... **1937**

"Lane" Rubber & Finance Ld. Regd. 1910. Vol. liq. (members') 28 June 1939. No capital returned to contributories. Final meeting return regd. 11 July 1940 .... **1940**

Lang & Stevenson Ld. Regd. Edinburgh 1927. Vol. liq. (members') 30 Mar. 1936. Capital returned to contributories—4s. 0¼d. per preference share of £1. Final meeting return regd. 14 Apr. 1937 .... **1937**

VOL. FOR

Lang Propellers Ld. Regd. 1936. Vol. liq. (members') 15 May 1936. Assets were acquired by Aeronautical Corporation of Great Britain Ld. for 60,000 shares. Final meeting return regd. 8 July 1936 .... **1937**

Langbourn Investment Trust Ld. See Sheet Anchor Investment Co. Ld.

Langdale's Chemical Manure Co. Ld. Regd. 1871. Vol. liq. (members') 12 June 1934. Capital returned to contributories—£3 18s. 7·418d. per share of £5. Final meeting return regd. 27 Dec. 1934 .... **1935**

Langdon & Co. Ld. Regd. 1920. Vol. liq. (members') 10 Dec. 1935. Final meeting return regd. 3 Dec. 1936 **1937**

Langdon-Davies Motor Co. Ld. Regd. 1898 as Langdon-Davies Electric Motor Co. Ld.; name changed Sept. 1902. Vol. liq. 16 Jan. 1903 for sale of undertaking and assets to company of same name. £1,000 debentures were redeemed and the remaining £5,000 transferred to new company. Final meeting return regd. 28 June 1905 .... **1905**

Langen (Java) Rubber Estates Co. Ld. Regd. 1909. Vol. liq. (members') 27 Apr. 1951. Capital returned to contributories—9s. 6d. per £1 stock. £691 was paid into Companies' Liquidation Account. Final meeting return regd. 18 Jan. 1952................ **1953**

Langham Hotel Co. Ld. Regd. 1868. Vol. liq. (members') 13 Sept. 1945 for reconstruction as company of same name, in which company shareholders were entitled to receive for each fully-paid share of £10, 8 "A" and 2 "B" shares of £1; for each share of £10 (£6 paid up, and including 46 shares upon which a further £4 per share had been paid in advance), 4 "A" and "B" shares; and for each share of £10 (£2 paid up), 2 "B" shares. The 4% perpetual debenture stock and the 4½% 2nd debenture stock were repaid with accrued interest by the new company on 19 Aug. 1946. Final meeting return regd. 5 Dec. 1947 **1948**

Langham Hotel Co. Ld. Regd. 8 Sept. 1945 as "L" Hotel Co. Ld.; name changed 17 Dec. 1945. All capital was owned by Land Securities Investment Trust Ld. Dissolved under section 208 of Companies Act, 1948 on 28 July 1955 .... **1954**

Langham Steel Co. Ld. Regd. 1915. Receiver appointed 22 June 1921; ceased to act 12 June 1924. Court Order to wind up 12 July 1921. Liquidator released 2 Mar. 1926. Struck off Register 2 Apr. 1929 .... ***1922**

Langham Gas & Electricity Supply Co. Ld. Regd. in Edinburgh 1924. Dissolved 1 May 1949, undertaking being vested in Scottish Area Gas Board under Gas Act 1948. Holders of ordinary shares (of £1) were entitled to receive 15s. British Gas 3% guaranteed stock 1990–95 for each share held........ **1952**

Langlaagte Deep Ld. Inc. Transvaal 1895. Vol. liq. June 1909. Undertaking and assets were acquired by Crown Deep Ld. (later Crown Mines Ld.), in which company shareholders were entitled to 7 shares of 10s. for every 20 shares of 10s. held **1910**

Langlaagte Estate & Gold Mining Co. Ld. Inc. in Transvaal 1888. Vol. liq. (members') 15 Dec. 1945. Capital returned to contributories—18s. 7·056d. per share of £1. Struck off the Register 15 Feb. 1962 . **1963**

Langlaagte Exploration & Building Co. Ld. Inc. Transvaal 1895. Vol. liq. Sept. 1909. Undertaking and assets were acquired by Langlaagte Estate and Gold Mining Co. Ld., in which company shareholders were entitled to 40 shares of £1 (credited as fully-paid) for every 100 shares of £1 held **1910**

Langlaagte Proprietary Co. Ld. Regd. 1897. Struck off Register 2 Aug. 1904. Restored to Register 9 July 1912. Court Order to wind up 8 Aug. 1912. Struck off Register 10 Aug. 1928 .... **1913**

Langlaagte Royal Gold Mining Co. Ld. Inc. Transvaal 1889. Vol. liq. Apr. 1909. Undertaking and assets were acquired by Crown Deep Ld. (later Crown Mines Ld.), for 60,000 shares of 10s. and £10,000 in cash. The purchase consideration was allotted to Johannesburg Consolidated Investment Co. in satisfaction of a loan due. The shares were later offered for cash to shareholders of this company .. **1910**

Langlaagte Star Gold Mining Co. Ld. Inc. Transvaal 1894. Property was sold to Consolidated Langlaagte Mines Ld in which company shareholders were entitled to 1 share of £1 (credited as fully-paid) for each share of £1 held **1903**

Langley Mill & Heanor Gas Light & Coke Co. Ld. Regd. 1868. Vol. liq. (members') 30 Aug. 1935. By Special Order of 1935 the undertaking was acquired by Derby Gas Light & Coke Co., in which company shareholders were entitled to 5% preference stock as follows: for each ordinary (10% standard) share of £5 held—£12; for each ordinary (7% standard) share of £5 held—£9; for each 5% preference share of £5 held—£5; for each 6% preference share of £5 held— £6. Liability in respect of mortgages was assumed by

VOL. FOR

acquiring company. Final meeting return regd. 2 July 1936 .... **1936**

Langport, Huish & Curry Rivel Gas Co. Ld. Regd. 1902. Dissolved 1 May 1949, undertaking being vested in South Western Area Gas Board under Gas Act 1948. Holders of 5% pref. shares (of £1) were entitled to receive £1 3s. British Gas 3% guaranteed stock 1990–95 for each share held **1952**

Langsuan Tin Mining Co, Ld. Regd. Edinburgh 1905. Vol. liq. Sept. 1908. Final meeting return regd. 29 Sept. 1922 .... **1909**

"Lankat Maatschappy" Ld. Regd. 1889. Removed from Register 1907 .... **1894**

Lanner Syndicate Ld. Regd. Edinburgh 1914. Operations at company's mine ceased; plant sold to pay off loans guaranteed by Government. Vol. liq. July 1932. Final meeting return regd. 31 Jan. 1933. .... **1930**

Lansdowne Estate Co. Ld. Regd 1875. Removed from Register 1895 .... ***1892**

Lansdowne House (Berkeley Square) Ld. Regd. 1936. Vol. liq. (members') 5 Dec. 1952. Capital returned to contributories (per £1 share)—preference not owned by Land Securities Investment Trust Ld., 20s. 6d.; other preference, £1; ordinary, £7 7s. 0·8d. £72 7s. 4d. was paid into Companies' Liquidation Account. Final meeting return regd. 2 Jan. 1958 .... **1959**

Lanston Monotype Corporation Ld. Regd. 1897. Vol. liq. 17 June 1908 for reconstruction as Lanston Monotype Corporation Ld. (later Monotype Corporation Ld.), in which corporation shareholders were entitled to 2 fully-paid shares of £1 for every 3 preference shares of £1, and 9 fully-paid shares of £1 for every 20 ordinary shares of £1 and 1 fully-paid share of £1 for every 40 deferred shares of 5s. held. Debenture stockholders received a like amount of debenture stock in new company. Final meeting return regd. 1 May 1924 .... **1909**

Lanzi Exploration Ld. Regd. 1897. Removed from Register 23 July 1901 .... ***1901**

La Plata Electric Tramways Co. Ld. Regd. 4 Feb. 1909. Winding-up order made 10 May 1943 .... **1987–8**

Laras (Sumatra) Rubber Estates Ld. Regd. 1910. Holders of 5% mortgage debenture bonds received repayment of £77 10s. and £7·7375 per bond. Struck off Register 22 Aug. 1975 .... **1975-6**

Larkfold Holdings Ld. Regd. as private company 3 Aug. 1971; converted public company 14 Oct. 1971. Winding-up order 19 jan. 1976. Stay of proceedings 21 Nov. 1980. Inland Revenue declared ordinary shares of negligible value from 1978–9 .... **1987–8**

Larkhall Collieries Ld. Regd. Edinburgh 1900. Business was acquired by United Collieries Ld. Removed from Register 1909 .... **1902**

Larue "Air-Tight" Inner Tube Ld. Regd. 1896. Vol. liq. 24 Aug. 1898. Final meeting return regd. 14 Feb. 1900 .... **1899**

Las Animas Copper Mining & Smelting Co. Ld. Regd. 1902. Vol. liq. Dec. 1910. Removed from Register 1911 .... **1911**

Las Barrancas Estancia Co. Ld. Regd. 1894. Vol. liq. 19 July 1910. Final meeting return regd. 9 Dec.1910 ***1911**

Las Brujas (Colombia) Hydraulic Gold Mines Ld. Regd. 1889. Vol. liq. 20 June 1892. Final meeting return regd. 7 Dec. 1893 .... **1893**

Las Cabesses Manganese Mines Ld. Regd. 1894. Vol. liq. June 1908. Removed from Register 1909 .... **1909**

Las Cabezas Estancia Co. Ld. Regd. 1876. Reconstructed 1906 as company of same name. Removed from Register 1908 .... **1906**

Las Encinas Gold Mines Ld. Regd. 1901. Removed from Register 1909 .... **1902**

Lascelles, Tickner & Co. Ld. Regd. 1889. Vol. liq. (members') Nov. 1933. Assets and business were merged with those of Friary Holroyd & Healy's Breweries Ld., which company held all share capital. Final meeting return regd. 14 Jan. 1937 . **1934**

Last Chance Consolidated Silver Mining Co. Ld. Regd 1880. Vol. liq. Oct. 1884. Final meeting return regd. 30 Dec. 1886 .... **1885**

Last Chance Silver Mining Co. of Utah Ld. Regd. 1872. Taken over by last Chance Consolidated Silver Mining Co. Ld. Removed from Register 1904 ..... **1938**

Lastingham & Rosedale Light Railway Co. Inc. (under Light Railways Act 1896) 1900 .... **1907**

Latex Developments Ld. Regd. 1923. Vol. liq. 11 Aug. 1926. Final meeting return regd. 23 Feb. 1929 .... **1927**

Latimer Road & Acton Railway Co. Inc. by Special Act 1882. Construction authorised to be abandoned by Act of 1909 .... **1901**

Lauder Light Railway Co. Inc. (under Light Railways Act 1896) by order of Light Railway Commissioners confirmed by Board of Trade 1898. In 1923 the undertaking was merged into the London & North

See Stock Exchange Year-Book.

VOL. FOR

Eastern Railway Co. in which company shareholders were entitled to £31 17s. 1d. 5% preferred ordinary stock for each £100 ordinary shares held (but holders of 25 shares or less to be paid in cash at the rate of £3 2s. 6d. per share of £10). The liability for the mortgage loans was transferred to the North Eastern Company ... **1924**

Launceston & District Electric Supply Co. Ld. Regd. 1911. Vol. liq. (members') 24 Jan. 1938. Undertaking transferred to Cornwall Electric Power Co. Capital returned to contributories—20s. per preference share of £1; £1 3s. 11¼d. per ordinary share of £1. Final meeting return regd. 12 May 1938 ... **1938**

Launceston Gas Co. Ld. Regd. 1874. Dissolved 1 May 1949, undertaking being vested in South Western Area Gas Board under Gas Act 1948. Holders of securities were entitled to receive British Gas 3% guaranteed stock 1990–95 as follows in respect of each £5 unit, of security held:

	£	s.	d.
Orig. shares (8% stand.)	7	5	0
Addit. shares (7% stand.)	6	7	6	**1952**

Laundry Services Ld. Regd. 1933. Vol. liq. 25 Oct. 1968. Capital returned to contributories (per shares of £1)—£1 per ordinary and £1 per preference share. Final meeting return regd. ... **1969**

Laurencekirk Lighting Society Ld. Regd. in Edinburgh 1908 under the Industrial & Provident Societies Act. Dissolved 1 May 1949, undertaking being vested in Scottish Area Gas Board under Gas Act 1948. Holders of securities were entitled to receive British Gas 3% guaranteed stock 1990–95 as follows:

	£	s.	d.
A shares (of £1 with 15s. paid)	1	0	0
B shares (of £1 with 10s. paid)	1	0	0	**1952**

Laurentide Co. Ld. Inc. Canada 1911. Undertaking acquired by company of same name. Shareholders were entitled to 3 shares of $100 in new company for each share of $100 held ... **1921**

Laurentide Co. Ld. Inc. Canada 1920. Undertaking was acquired by Consolidated Paper Corporation Ld., in which company stockholders were entitled to $100 5½% 30-year sinking fund debenture and 1 ordinary share of no par value for each share of $100 stock held ... **1932**

Laurie & Marner Ld. Regd. 1873. Vol. liq. 6 Nov. 1896. Final meeting return regd. 4 July 1898 ... *****1896**

Lavant Rubber Co. Ld. Regd. 1910 as Lavant Rubber & Tea Co. Ld.; name changed Aug. 1923. Vol. liq. (members') 4 May 1938. Undertaking and assets acquired by Kepitigalla Rubber Estates Ld., in which company shareholders were entitled to 7 fully-paid shares of 2s. for every 10 shares of 2s. held. £23 10s. 9d. was paid into Companies' Liquidation Account. Final meeting return regd. 12 Aug. 1939 **1939**

Lavertons Ld. Regd. 1896. Removed from Register 1903 **1902**

Lavy (Charles) & Co. Ld. Regd. 1907. Vol. liq. (members') 29 Nov. 1945. Capital returned to contributories—14s. 4½d. per preference share of £1. Final meeting return regd. 30 Mar. 1960 ... **1956**

Law Car & General Insurance Corporation Ld. Regd. 1906. Court Order to wind up 20 Dec. 1910. Struck off Register 1927 ... **1911**

Law Debenture Investment Trust Ld. Regd. 1958. All capital owned by Law Debenture Corpn p.l.c. Vol. liq. 1 Dec. 1975 when the 5% debenture stock and both of the 4% debenture stocks were cancelled, holders receiving a like amount of stock in Law Debenture Corpn. p.l.c. Dissolved 27 Apr. 1979 .**1979–80**

Law Fidelity & General Insurance Corporation Ld. Regd. 1891 as London & Provincial Law Investment Corporation Ld.; name changed to Law Investment & Reinsurance Corporation Ld. in Jan. 1893, to Law Investment & Insurance Corporation Ld. in Sept. 1897, and as above in June 1903. Vol. liq. 19 Oct 1920. Final meeting return regd. 26 Jan. 1921 ... **1921**

Law Fire Insurance Society. Established 1845. Regd. as unlimited 1862. Vol. liq. Mar. 1907. Undertaking was acquired by Law Fire Insurance Society Ld., in which company shareholders were entitled to 1 share of £1 (credited as fully-paid) plus £14 in cash for each share of £100 (£2 10s. paid) held. Removed from Register 1908 ... **1908**

Law Guarantee and Trust Society Ld. See Law Guarantee Trust & Accident Society Ld.

Law Guarantee Trust & Accident Society Ld. Regd. 1888 as Law Guarantee and Trust Society Ld.; name changed July 1907. Vol. liq. 13 Dec. 1909. Court Order to continue winding up under supervision 14 Dec. 1909. Part of the business was acquired by Guardian Assurance Co. Ld. Court Order to continue winding up under supervision 11 Mar. 1910. Final meeting return regd. 19 Dec. 1922 .... **1910**

VOL. FOR

Law Integrity Insurance Co. Ld. Regd. 1906. Vol. liq. 19 Dec. 1918. Undertaking acquired by City Life Assurance Co. Ld. Final meeting return regd. 1 Oct.1921 ... *****1919**

Law Life Assurance Society. Established 1823. Regd. 1894. Vol. liq. Mar. 1910. Undertaking and assets were acquired by Phoenix Assurance Co. Ld., in which company shareholders were entitled to £120 debenture stock and 1 ordinary share of £5 (credited as fully-paid) for every 6 shares of £20 held. Removed from Register 1911 ... **1911**

Lawdon (Builders) Ld. See Lawdon Ld.

Lawdon Ld. Regd. 21 Mar. 1961 as Lawdon (Builders) Ld.; name changed 25 June 1965. Winding-up order 20 Oct. 1980 ... **1986–7**

Lawes Chemical Co. Ld. Regd. 1872 as Lawes' Chemical Manure Co. Ld.; name changed Sept. 1935. Vol. liq. (creditors') 8 Aug. 1969. No capital returned to contributories. Final meetings convened 7 Nov. 1978 and company dissolved 15 Feb. 1979 ... **1978-9**

Lawler's Gold Mines Ld. Regd. 1895. Vol. liq. 27 Dec. 1899. Final meeting return regd. 12 Sept. 1902 .... **1900**

Lawrence Automatic Gas Co. Ld. Regd. 1887. Vol. liq. 10 Dec. 1890. Final meeting return regd. 6 Oct. 1892 **1891**

Lawrence Gas Co. of Lancashire & Cheshire Ld. Regd. 1888. Vol. liq. 25 July 1890. Final meeting return regd. 23 Jan. 1891 ... **1891**

Lawrence Stores Ld. Regd. 1903. Vol. liq. (creditors') 21 Apr. 1932. Assets realised insufficient to pay creditors in full. Final meeting return regd. 5 Mar. 1937 ... **1933**

Lawson & Co. (Bristol) Ld. See Kell (Josephine) Ld.

Lawther, Latta & Co. Ld. Regd. 1921. Vol. liq. (members') 3 Aug. 1943. Capital returned to contributories—£20 8s. 3·3d. per share (of £5). Final meeting return regd. 20 Jan. 1955 ... **1956**

Layang Rubber Plantations Ld. Regd. 1925. All capital was owned by Craigielea Rubber Plantations Ld. Vol. liq. (members') 31 Aug. 1961. Final meeting return regd. 8 Feb. 1966 ... **1967**

Laycock Engineering Co. Ld. Regd. 1925. Receiver appointed. Assets realised insufficient to meet claims of debenture holders in full. Business was carried on by Thos. W. Ward Ld. Struck off Register 1933 ... *****1932**

Laycock Engineering Co. Ld. See below.

Laycock Holdings Ld. Regd. 1935 as Laycock Engineering Co. Ld.; name changed 13 Jan. 1939. Vol. liq. (members') 10 Oct. 1944. Stockholders were entitled to receive £1 6% "L" redeemable cumulative preference stock in Birfield Industries Ld. (later Birfield Ld.) for each 15s. stock held and £3 "L" ordinary stock in Birfield Industries Ld. for each £20 stock held, plus 5·832d. per 5s. stock held. Final meeting return regd. 5 Apr. 1949 ... **1950**

Laycock (W. S.) Ld. Regd. 1900. Court Order to wind up: 15 Apr. 1924; proceedings stayed 21 Apr. 1925. Vol. liq. 9 Nov. 1925. Final meeting return regd. 22 July 1926 ... **1926**

Lazard Investment Co. Ld. Regd. 1862 as Rio de Janeiro City Improvements Co. Ld. name subsequently changed. Vol. liq. (members') 30 June 1966. Final meeting return regd. 20 Dec. 1969 ... **1949**

Le Bon Jenie S,A. In liquidation. Direct controlling interest was held by Aux Classes Laborleuses Ld **1940**

Le Champ d'Or French Gold Mining Co. Ld. Regd. 1890 as Le Champ d'Or French Misgund Gold Mining Co. Ld.; name changed Feb. 1891. Court Order to wind up 18 Mar. 1936. Struck off Register 20 Feb. 1942 ... **1943**

Le Nouveau Monde Compagnie Franco-Anglaise pour l'Exploration des Mines d'Or. Established by Notarial Act in Paris 1850. Reconstructed in 1889 as Nouveau Monde Gold Mining Co. Ld. (later Tarryall Creek Gold Co. Ld.). Shareholders were entitled to 1 share of £1 in new company for every two shares of £1 held subject to cash payment of 2s. 6d. for every old share held ... **1893**

Le Roi Mining Co. Ld. Regd. 1898. Vol. liq. 2 Sept. 1910. Final meeting return regd. 20 Dec. 1922 .... **1911**

Le Roi No. 2 Ld. Regd. 1900. Vol. liq. 12 Mar. 1923. Final meeting return regd. 30 July 1925 ... **1924**

Lea Bridge District Gas Co. Estd. 1868; inc. by Special Act 1878. Dissolved 1 May 1949, undertaking being vested in North Thames Area Gas Board under Gas Act 1948. Holders of securities were entitled to receive, in respect of each £100 unit held, British Gas 3% guaranteed stock 1990–95 as follows:

	£	s.	d.
Cons. ord. stock (5% standard)	160	0	0
4% pref. stock	103	0	0
5% pref. stock	115	0	0
6% pref. stock	134	0	0
4% irred. deb. stock	103	0	0

*See Stock Exchange Year-Book.

VOL. FOR

5% perp. deb. stock	125	0	0	
5½% red. deb. stock	114	10	0	
4% red. deb. stock	101	10	0	1952

Lea Bridge, Leyton & Walthamstow Tramways Co. Inc. Special Act 1889. Undertaking sold to Leyton Urban District Council. Shareholders received £10 10*s*. per share on 1 Aug. 1905 ... **1906**

Lea-Francis Cars Ld. Regd. 1937 as Lea-Francis Engineering (1937) Ld., name changed 1945. Receiver appointed Aug. 1962; discharged Feb. 1967. Funds insufficient to meet liability to debenture holders. Struck off Register 29 May 1970 ... **1969**

Lea Ld. Regd. 1914 as Lea (1914) Ld.; name changed June 1917. Undertaking acquired by Carpet Trades Ld. (later John Crossley—Carpet Trades Holdings Ld.). Final meeting return regd. 15 June 1921 ... **1936**

Lea (R. J.) Ld. Regd. 1919. Vol. liq. (members') 4 Oct. 1937. Capital returned to contributories—8*s*. 4½*d*. per A preference share of £1: no return to B preference or ordinary shares. Final meeting return regd. 22 Sept. 1938 ... **1938**

Lea Shipbuilding and Repairing Co. Ld. Regd. 1918. Vol. liq. 23 Jan. 1923. Capital returned to contributories—2*s*. 6*d*. per share of £1 at Nov. 1923; further payments (if any) not known. Final meeting return regd. 24 Oct. 1929 ... **1924**

Lead Warrant Co. Ld. Regd. 1883. Vol. liq. 15 July 1897. Final meeting return regd. 4 Nov. 1897 ... **1888**

Leader Box Machine Syndicate Ld. Regd. 1895. Struck off Register 26 Oct. 1900 ... **1901**

Leadhills Co. Ld. Regd. 1903. Vol. liq. 18 Oct. 1929. Final meeting return regd. 8 Aug. 1930 ... **1930**

Leadhills Silver-Lead Mining & Smelting Co. Ld. Regd. 1876. Reconstructed 1903 as Leadhills Co. Ld., in which company shareholders were entitled to 1 share of £1 (credited with 10*s*. paid) for each share of £6 held. Removed from Register 1904 ... **1908**

Leading Investment Trust Ld. Regd. 1935. Winding up Order 9 Oct. 1939. Debentures repaid at par in July 1947. No capital returned to contributories. Liquidator released 25 Sept. 1964. Struck off Register 3 May 1968 ... **1966**

Leadville Mines Ld. Regd. 1888. Vol. liq. 18 Oct. 1889. Removed from Register 1901 ... **1890**

Leamington Cycle Co. Ld. Regd. 1896. Removed from Register ... **1898**

Leamington Priors & Warwickshire Banking Co. Ld. Regd. 1880. Vol. liq. May 1889. Business acquired by Birmingham & Midland Bank Ld. (later Midland Bank Ld.). Final meeting return regd. 17 May 1890 **1908**

Leamington Priors Gas Co. Inc. by Special Act 1865. Dissolved 1 May 1949, undertaking being vested in West Midland Area Gas Board under Gas Act 1948. Holders of securities were entitled to receive British Gas 3% guaranteed stock 1990–95 as follows in respect of each £20 unit, unless otherwise stated, of security held:

	£	s.	d.	
A shares (10% max.)	41	0	0	
B shares (7% max.)	30	10	0	
C shares (7% max.)	30	10	0	
4% deb. stock (per £100)	100	5	0	1952

Leasehold Investment Co. Ld. Regd. 1863. Court Order to wind up 7 Nov. 1894. Liquidator released 15 Aug. 1899. Struck off Register 29 July 1902 ... **1895**

Leaseholders' Fund Corporation Ld. Regd. 1886. Vol. liq. 21 Jan. 1892. Business was transferred to Rock Life Assurance Co. Final meeting return regd. 3 Nov. 1897 ... **1893**

Leather Shod Wheel Co. Ld. Regd. 1897. Removed from Register 1903 ... **1900**

Leather Trades & General Insurance Co. Ld. *See* North-Western Insurance Co. Ld.

Leatherhead & District Waterworks Co. Inc. by Special Act 1883. By Act of 1927 the undertaking was acquired by East Surrey Water Co. Shareholders were entitled to 7% ordinary B shares of £10 in acquiring company and cash as follows—for each original share (1883) of £10 held—2 shares; for each new share of £10 held—1 share *plus* 5*s*. in cash; for each new share of £10 (issued under Order of 1890)—1 share *plus* £1 9*s*. in cash for shares Nos. 1–100; 17*s*. for shares 101–600; 8*s*. for shares 601–900 and 5*s*. for shares 901–1250. Holders of 5% and 4% debenture stocks were entitled to £125 and £100 respectively in 4% consolidated debenture stock for every £100 stock held ... **1928**

Leatherhead Gas and Lighting Co. Formed by Deed of Settlement in 1850; regd. as unlimited in 1896 and as limited in 1897; inc. by Special Act 1901. Under Special Order of 1936 the undertaking was acquired by Wandsworth and District Gas Co. Holders of ordinary shares were entitled to £14 of 5% preference stock of the acquiring company for each ordinary share of £10 held; holders of 6% preference stock were entitled to £120 of 5% preference stock of the acquiring company for every £100 preference stock held. Holders of 6½% redeemable preference, 4% debenture or 5½% redeemable debenture stocks were entitled to an equal amount of 6½% Leatherhead redeemable preference, 4% debenture or 5½% Leatherhead redeemable debenture stocks respectively of the acquiring company ... **1937**

Leaventhorpe Wool Scouring & Carbonizing Co. Ld. Regd. 1916. Vol. liq. (members') 25 Apr. 1930. Capital returned to contributories—1s. 4¼*d*. per share of £1 *plus* certain assets in specie. Final meeting return regd. 5 Mar. 1931 ... **1931**

Leavesley & North Ld. *See* Freeman, Hardy Willis (Burlington Works) Ld.

Lebong Tea Co. Ld. Regd. 5 Dec. 1862. All capital owned by Assam Dooars Holdings Ld. Vol. winding-up order 21 Oct. 1986 ... **1978–9**

Leckhampton Quarries Co. Ld. Regd. 1899. Receiver apppointed Oct. 1925. Assets realised insufficient to meet indebtedness to 1st and 2nd mortgage debenture holders. Struck off Register Feb. 1930 ... **1930**

Ledang Rubber Plantations Ld. Regd. 1925. Vol. liq. (members') 26 June 1931. Undertaking and assets were acquired by Ledang Bahru Ld., in which company shareholders were entitled to share of £1 (credited with 16*s*. paid) for each share of £1 held. £4 5*s*. 3*d*. was paid into Companies' Liquidation Account. Final meeting return regd. 11 Aug. 1932 **1932**

Ledbury Gas, Coal & Coke Co. Ld. Regd. 1877. Dissolved 1 May 1949, undertaking being vested in West Midland Area Gas Board under Gas Act 1948. Holders of original ordinary shares (of £10) were entitled to receive £29 5*s*. British Gas 3% guaranteed stock 1990–95 for each share held ... **1952**

Lebus (Harris) Ld. Regd. 11 June 1947. All capital acquired by P. M. A. Holdings Ld. ... **1980–1**

Ledbury Rubber Estates Ld. Regd. 1908. Vol. liq. (members') 15 Oct. 1947. Undertaking and assets acquired by Lanadron Rubber Estates Ld. Stockholders were entitled to 103 £1 stock units in that company for every 100 units (of £1) held. £18 was paid into Companies' Liquidation Account. Final meeting return regd. 13 Sept. 1948 ... **1949**

Lee (Arthur) & Sons Ld. Regd. 1894. Vol. liq. (members') 28 Mar. 1958 for purpose of reconstruction. Shareholders were entitled to receive 1 A or 1 B preference share of £1 of Arthur Lee & Sons Ld. for each A or B preference share of £1 held and 1 ordinary share of 2*s*. 6*d*. of Arthur Lee & Sons Ld. and 1 ordinary share of 4*d*. of Arthur Lee (Investment) Ld. for every 2*s*. 6*d*. ordinary stock held. Final meeting return regd. 17 Feb. 1959 ... **1960**

Lee Conservancy Board. Inc. by Special Act 1868. Undertaking vested from 1 Jan. 1948 in British Transport Commission under Transport Act 1947. Dissolved 11 Dec. 1950; holders of following securities received under-mentioned amounts of British Transport 3% guaranteed stock 1978–88 in respect of each £100 of old security held:

	£	s.	d.
4% perp. deb. stock	117	10	0
3½% deb. stock	101	10	0
3% advances from development fund:			
Stout Navigation		5	0
Remainder	99	0	0
3⅛% Mort. loan	102	0	0

Holders of 3⅛% mortgage loan received £42,372 of the above-mentioned British Transport stock and holders of £95,200 3½% mortgage loan received an equal amount of British Transport 3½% guaranteed stock 1952 ... **1949**

Lee (Sydney) & Co. Ld. *See* National Inventions Trust Ld.

Lee (Thomas & David) Ld. Regd. 1922. Vol. liq. (members') 26 Nov. 1947. Final meeting return regd. 5 June 1950 ... **1938**

Lee (William), Son & Co. Ld. Regd. 1900. Vol. liq. 14 Feb. 1912. Final meeting return regd. 23 Oct. 1913 **1913**

Lee-on-the-Solent Railway Co. Inc. by Board of Trade Certificate 1890. In 1923 the undertaking was merged into the Southern Railway Company. The shares were cancelled ... **1924**

Leech, Neal & Co. Ld. Regd. 1889. Vol. liq. (members') 31 Dec. 1940. All shares owned by I.C.I. (Dyestuffs) Ld. Final meeting return regd. 26 Sept. 1941 ... **1941**

Leechdale Rhodesia Development Co. Ld. Regd. 1895. Removed from Register 1901 ... **1900**

Leechman Prospecting Co. Ld. Regd. Edinburgh 1890. Vol. liq. July 1904. Struck off Register 2 Apr. 1935 **1905**

Leeds & Batley Breweries Ld. *See below.*

**See Stock Exchange Year-Book.*

VOL. FOR

Leeds & Batley Properties Ld. Regd. 1898 as Leeds & Batley Breweries Ld., name subsequently changed. Vol. liq. (members') 13 Mar. 1946. Final meeting return regd. 21 May 1947 .... **1919**

Leeds & County Bank Ld. Regd. 1862. Vol. liq. 2 June 1890. Taken over by Birmingham and Midland Bank Ld. (later Midland Bank Ld.), in which company shareholders were entitled to 1 share of £60 (credited with £12 10s. paid) for every 5 shares of £25 (£5 paid) held or to 1 share of £60 (credited with £12 10s. paid) *plus* £1 10s. in cash for every 3 shares of £85 (£10 paid) held. Final meeting return regd. 2 June 1892 .... **1891**

Leeds & County Conservative Club-house Co. Ld. Regd. 1883. Vol. liq. (members') 27 June 1977. Capital returned to contributories—£51·54 per share (of £5). £3,247 was pais into Companies' Liquidation Account in respect of unclaimed distributions. Final meeting return regd. 29 Oct. 1979 .... **1980-1**

Leeds & Hanley Theatres of Varieties Ld. Regd. 1897. Removed from Register 1909 .... **1899**

Leeds & Liverpool Canal Co. Inc. by Special Act 1770 as Co. of Proprietors of the Canal Navigation from Leeds to Liverpool; name changed 1891. Dissolved 3 June 1949; undertaking vested from 1 Jan. 1948 in British Transport Commission under Transport Act 1947. Holders of sercurities were entitled to receive British Transport 3% guaranteed stock 1978–88 as follows in respect of every £100 of old security held:—

	£	s.	d.	
Cons. ord. stock	13	8	9	
3¼% pref. stock	65	0	0	
3½% deb. stock	79	10	0	**1949**

Leeds & North of England Boiler & Accident Insurance Co. Regd. 1886. Vol. liq. 26 Feb. 1895. Business aquired by Vulcan Boiler and General Insurance Co. Ld. Final meeting return regd. 30 Oct. 1895 .... **1909**

Leeds & Wakefield Breweries Ld. *See* Melbourne Brewery (Leeds) Ld.

Leeds & Yorkshire Co-operative Coal Mining Co. Ld. *See* Lofthouse Colliery Ld.

Leeds Assets Ld. Regd. 1968. Vol. liq. 29 July 1980. Final meeting return regd. 8 May 1981 .... **1973-4**

Leeds City Brewery, Ld. Regd. 1897. All capital owned by Ind. Coope & Allsopp Ld. [later Ind Coope Ld.]. Vol. liq. (members') 5 Sept. 1955. Final meeting return regd. 3 Apr. 1956. .... **1949**

Leeds Copper Co. Ld. Regd. 1891. Vol. liq. 16 Jan. 1893. Final meeting return regd. 30 Sept. 1896 .... **1894**

Leeds Copper Works Ld. Regd. 1899 as English Electro-Metallurgical Co. Ld.; name changed June 1902. Vol. liq. 31 Mar. 1908. Removed from Register 1911 .... **1909**

Leeds Daily News Ld. Regd. 1890. Vol. liq. 26 Apr. 1897. The business was aquired by the company of same name. The debentures were repaid at 110%. Capital returned to contributories—£8 per ordinary share of £5 and £120 per founders' share of £5. Final meeting return regd. 10 June 1898 .... **1905**

Leeds Daily News Ld. Regd. 1897. Vol. liq. 24 Mar. 1905. Undertaking and assets were aquired by Yorkshire Liberal Newspaper and Publishing Co. Ld. Capital returned to contributories—£3 15s. per preference share of £5; £2 7s. 6d. per ordinary share of £5; further payments (if any) not known. Removed from Register 1906 .... **1906**

Leeds Forge Co. Ld. Regd. 1889 as New Leeds Forge Co. Ld.; name changed May 1889. Vol. liq. (members') 4 May 1932. Undertaking and assets were aquired by Metropolitan-Cammell Carriage, Wagon & Finance Co. Ld. 5% 1st mortgage debenture stock was redeemed at par. Final meeting return regd. 9 Mar. 1933 .... **1933**

Leeds Industrial Dwellings Co. Ld. Regd. 1866. Vol. liq. (members') 14 Oct. 1937. Capital returned to contributories—£70,605 16s. 8d. £6 10s. 6d. was paid into Companies' Liquidation Account in respect of unclaimed dividends. Final meeting return regd. 11 Dec. 1939 .... **1938**

Leeds Insurance Co. Ld. Regd. 1922. All shares were owned by Lancashire & General Assurance Co. Ld. Struck off Register 1927 .... **1927**

Leeds Joint Stock Bank Ld. Regd. 1891. Business acquired by London and Northern Bank Ld., at a price equal to £9 10s. per share of £20 (£5 paid). Removed from Register 1909 .... **1899**

Leeds Phosphate Works Ld. Regd. 1921. Vol. liq. (members') 23 Nov. 1934. Certain assets were distributed in specie. Capital returned to contributories—1·5236d. per share of £1. Final meeting return regd. 10 Jan. 1936 .... **1935**

Leeds Picture Playhouse Ld. Regd. 1920. A subsidiary of Provincial Cinematograph Theatres Ld. Vol. liq.

VOL. FOR

(members') 21 June 1956. Final meeting return regd. 23 May 1967 .... **1951**

Leeds South Market. Established 1825 .... **1892**

Leeds Steel Works Ld. Regd. 1888. Vol. liq. 11 Jan. 1901. Final meeting return regd. 13 Feb. 1902 .... **1936**

Leeds Tramways Co. Inc. Special Act 1872. Vol. liq. 1896. Capital returned to contributories—£5 1s. per share of £10 at 7 Oct. 1895; further payments (if any) not known **1896**

Leek and Manifold Valley Light Railway Co. Inc. (under Light Railways Act 1896) by order of Light Railway Commissioners confirmed by Board of Trade 1899. In 1923 the undertaking was merged into the London Midland & Scottish Railway Co., Staffordshire County Council and H. M. Treasury were to receive certain agreed sums in satisfaction of their claims. Holders of 4% debenture stock were entitled to £83 6s. 8d. cash for every £100 stock held. The ordinary shares to be cancelled **1925**

Leender's Syndicate Ld. Regd. 1902. Vol. liq. Aug. 1904. Removed from Register 1907 .... **1905**

Lees Brook Spinning Co. (1920) Ld. Regd. 1920. All capital was owned by Newroyd Mill Ld. Vol. liq. (members') 4 Sept. 1964. Final meeting return regd. 16 May 1967 .... **1947**

Lees Brothers Ld. Regd. 1920. Vol. liq. (creditors') 28 Nov. 1935. Assets realised insufficient to pay unsecured creditors in fuil. Final meeting return regd. 25 Jan. 1938 .... **1936**

Lees (John Henry) Ld. Regd. 1897. Receiver appointed 23 Jan. 1913. Struck off Register 1917 .... **1915**

Leesh River Tea Co. Ld. Regd. 1877. Vol. liq. Jan. 1911. Reconstructed as company of same name. Shareholders and debenture holders were repaid in cash. Removed from Register 1911 .... **1911**

Leeson Sponge & Rubber Co. Ld. Assets were acquired by Sorbo Rubber-Sponge Products Ld. **1930**

Leeston Shipping Co. Ld. Regd. 1916. Vol. liq. (creditors') 14 Dec. 1931. No capital returned to contributories. Final meeting return regd. 2 Aug. 1932 .... **1932**

Leetham (Henry) & Sons Ld. Regd. 1899. Vol. liq. 27 Dec. 1928. Milling properties and goodwill were acquired by Spillers Ld. Final meeting return regd. 28 Jan. 1938 .... **1929**

Leeuwpoort Tin Mines Ld. Inc. Transvaal 1912 as Leeuwpoort (African Farms) Tin Mines Ld.; name changed June 1925. Vol. liq. (members') 9 June 1936 **1937**

Lefevre (H. S.) & Co. Est. prior to 1790. Discontinued business 31 May 1949 .... **1950**

Lefroy Gold Mines (W. A.) Ld. Regd. 1896. Removed from Register 1904 .... **1899**

Legal & Commercial Insurance Co. Ld. Regd. 1907. Vol. liq. 9 Mar. 1911 for amalgamation with North Western Insurance Co. Ld. by means of an exchange of shares. Final meeting return regd. 6 May 1922 ... **1911**

Legal & General Fire Office Ld. *See* London Caledonian Reinsurance Co. Ld.

Legeh Concessions Syndicate Ld. Regd. 1906. Vol. liq. 24 Feb. 1913. Final meeting return regd. 27 May 1914 .... **1914**

Leh Chin Mining Co. Ld. Regd. Dublin 1891. In liquidation in 1905 .... **1905**

Lehigh and Wilkes-Barre Coal Co. Inc. New York 1864. The outstanding 1st mortgage 6% sterling bonds were redeemed in 1898 .... **1898**

Lehigh Valley Terminal Railway Co. Inc. New Jersey 1891. Consolidated with 5 other companies to form Lehigh Valley Railroad Co. of New Jersey. The 1st mortgage 5% gold bonds were taken over by the new company **1903**

"Lehner" Artificial Silk Co. Ld. Regd. 1894. Vol. liq. 1 May 1902. Capital returned to contributories—£2 7s. 4d. per ordinary share of £10; further payments (if any) not known. Final meeting return regd. 6 Sept. 1902 .... **1904**

Leicester & District Light Railway Co. Inc. (under Light Railways Act 1896) by order of Light Railway Commissioners confirmed by Board of Trade 1904 **1911**

Leicester Billposting & Advertising Co Ld. Regd. 1888. Vol. liq. 16 Mar. 1899. Business acquired by Rockley's Ld. Final meeting return regd. 16 Dec. 1899 .... **1940**

Leicester Consolidated Diamond Mines Ld. Inc. Cape of Good Hope 1896. In liquidation in 1900 .... **1900**

Leicester Insurance Co. Ld. Regd. 1922. All shares were owned by Lancashire & General Assurance Co. Ld. Struck off Register 1929 .... **1927**

Leicester Manufacturing Co. Ld. Regd. 1890. Vol. liq. 29 Jan. 1892. Court Order to continue winding up under supervision Feb. 1892. Final meeting return regd. 18 Oct. 1893 .... **1893**

Leicester Mortgage Co. Ld. Regd. 1866. Removed from Register 1904 .... **1903**

See Stock Exchange Year-Book.

VOL. FOR

Leicester Navigation. Inc. by Special Act 1791. By Act of 1931 undertaking and assets were acquired by Grand Union Canal Co. **1932**

Leicester Palace Theatre, Ld. Regd. 1900. A subsidiary of Stoll Theatres Corpn. Ld. Vol. liq. (members') 23 Dec. 1959. Final meeting return regd. 29 Dec. 1960 **1952**

Leicester Patent Brick & Tile Co. Ld. Regd. 1873. Removed from Register 1903 .... ***1882**

Leicester Square Estates Ld. Regd. 1929 as Buchanan Estates Ld.; name changed in Dec. 1930. Vol. liq. (members') 3 Dec. 1947. Capital returned to contributories—9s. 6¼d. per share of 5s. Certain assets distributed in specie. £2,343 paid into Companies' Liquidation Account. Final meeting return regd. 1 Dec. 1949 .... **1950**

Leicester Tramways Co. Inc. Special Act 1877. Vol. liq. Undertaking acquired by the corporation for £110,210. At 3 Nov. 1902 shareholders had been paid £10 per share in cash and interest at 5% up to 31 Dec. 1901 .... **1903**

Leicestershire and Warwickshire Electric Power Co. Inc. by Special Act 1902. Dissolved 1 Apr. 1948, undertaking being vested in the British (later Central) Electricity Authority and East Midlands Area Board under the Electricity Act 1947. Holders of 4% debentures were entitled to receive £100 British Electricity 3% guaranteed stock (1968–73), for every £100 debentures held **1949**

Leicestershire Banking Co. Ld. Established 1829. Regd. 1880. Vol. liq. 13 Aug. 1900. Business was acquired by London City and Midland Bank Ld. (later Midland Bank Ld.), in which company shareholders were entitled to 7 shares of £60 (credited with £12 10s. paid) for every 12 shares of £25 (£10 paid) held **1901**

Leicestershire Colliery & Pipe Co. Ld. Regd. 1913. Under Scheme of Arrangement undertaking transferred to L. C. & P. Co. Ld. (later Leicestershire Colliery & Pipe Co. Ld.). in which company shareholders received 5 fully-paid redeemable preference shares of £1 for every 4 preference shares of £1 held or 5 fully-paid ordinary shares of £1 for each ordinary share of £1 held **1940**

Leicestershire Colliery & Pipe Co. Ld. Regd. 1939 as L. C. & P. Co. Ld.; name changed Nov. 1939. Vol. liq. (members') 17 Jan. 1951; the collieries, &c. having been vested in National Coal Board. Capital returned to contributories—21s. per preference share of £1 and £2 19s. 4·73d. per ordinary share of £1. Final meeting return regd. 13 July 1964 ...... **1965**

Leicestershire (L. & N.) Coal Distillation Ld. See British Coal Distillation Ld.

Leicestershire Super-Aeration Ld. Regd. 1900. Undertaking and assets were acquired by London Super Aeration Ld., in which company shareholders were entitled to 1 share of £1 (credited as fully-paid) for every 4 fully-paid shares of £1 held, or 3 shares of £1 (credited with 5s, paid) for every 5 shares of £1 (5s. paid) held. Removed from Register 1911. .... **1903**

Leigh Smokeless Fuels Ld. Regd. 1924. Vol. liq. (members') 20 Dec. 1930. Final meeting return regd. 17 Aug. 1932. .... **1931**

Leigh Waste Co., Oldham (1920) Ld. Regd. 1920. Court Order to wind up 28 May 1925. Liquidator released 15 Jan. 1934. Struck off Register 9 June 1936 ..... **1926**

Leigh Woods Land Co. Ld. Regd. 1865. Vol. liq. (members') 28 May 1953. Capital returned to contributories—£7 7s. 7d. per share of £4. £37 paid into Companies' Liquidation Account in respect of unclaimed dividends or distributions. Final meeting return regd. 2 Mar. 1954 .... **1955**

Leighton Buzzard & Hitchin Light Railway Co. Inc. (under Light Railways Act 1896) by order of Light Railway Commissioners confirmed by Board of Trade 1903 .... **1908**

Leighton Buzzard Gas Co. Estd. 1835; regd. 1857; inc. by Special Act 1891 as Leighton Buzzard Gas Co.; name changed 1926. Dissolved 1 May 1949, undertaking being vested in Southern Area Gas Board under Gas Act 1948. Holders of securities were entitled to receive, in respect of each £100 unit held, British Gas 3% guaranteed stock 1990–95 as follows:

	£	s.	d.	
Cons. ord. stock (5% stand.)	115	0	0	
5% red. pref. stock	104	0	0	
4% perm. deb. stock	101	10	0	**1952**

Leipzig, Halle & District Ice Co. Ld. Regd. 1885. Removed from Register 1906 .... **1888**

Leipzig Tramways Co. Ld. Regd. 1871. Vol. liq. 19 Dec. 1895. Undertaking was sold to a German company. Notice of repayment of second and third series of debentures was given 14 Jan. 1896; similar repayment of first and fourth series was expected. A return of 300 marks per ordinary share of £10 and

VOL. FOR

350 marks per preference share of £10 was anticipated. Final meeting return regd. 23 Mar. 1897 .... **1896**

Leiston Gas Co. Ld. Regd. 1910. Dissolved 1 May 1949, undertaking being vested in Eastern Area Gas Board under Gas Act 1948. Holders of securities were entitled to receive British Gas 3% guaranteed stock 1990–95 as follows in respect of each £1 unit, unless otherwise stated, of security held:—

	£	s.	d.	
Ord. shares	1	0	0	
7% B pref. shares	1	8	0	
5% mort. debs. (of £100)	100	0	0	**1952**

Leith (Gordon) & Co. Dissolved 1 Apr. 1927 .... **1928**

Leith Harbour and Docks (Commissioners for). Inc. by Special Act 1875. On 1 Jan. 1968 the undertaking was transferred to the Forth Ports Authority and the Commission dissolved **1969**

Lejeau (Paris) Ld. Regd. 1909. Vol. liq. 20 Jan. 1913. No capital was expected to be returned to ordinary shareholders; payments (if any) to preference shareholders not known. Final meeting return regd. 17 Feb. 1915 .... **1913**

Leland Stanford Gold Mining Co. Ld. Regd. 1895. Vol. liq. 18 Apr. 1898. Final meeting return regd. 4 Oct.1899 .... **1899**

Lemberg-Czernowitz-Jassy Railway Co, Inc. in Vienna in 1864; regd. in Czernowitz and domicile transferred to Roumania 4 May 1920. It is understood company was placed in liquidation in 1940 .... **1952**

Lemercier-Iohnston Co. Ld. Regd. 1901. Removed from Register 1907 .... **1904**

Lena Goldfields Ld. See Scottish, Overseas & Commonwealth Investment Trust Ld.

Lena Investment Trust Ld. See Scottish, Overseas & Commonwealth Investment Trust Ld.

Leney (Alfred) & Sons, Ld. Regd. 1896. Vol. liq. (members') 31 Dec. 1959. Final meeting return regd. 18 Oct. 1962 .... **1952**

Lennard's Carrying Co. Ld. Regd. 1901. Vol. liq. (members') 6 Nov. 1961. Capital returned to contributories—£1 per share of £1. £726 4s. 3d. was paid into Companies' Liquidation Account. Final meeting return regd. 28 Mar. 1962 .... **1963**

Lennard's Petroleum Carrying Co. Ld. Regd. 1892. Vol. liq. 15 Jan. 1901. Carrying business was acquired by Lennard's Carrying Co. Ld. Final meeting return regd. 25 Oct. 1902 .... **1940**

Leominster & Bromyard Railway Co. Inc. by Special Act 1874. Under Great Western Railway Act 1888 undertaking vested in that company. Shareholders received 10s. per share held **1889**

Leominster & Kington Railway Co. Inc. by Special Act 1854. Under Great Western Railway Act 1898 undertaking was amalgamated with that company. Holders of shares received £9 5% consolidated guaranteed stock for each share held. The 3½% debentures were assumed by purchasing company **1899**

Leominster Gas & Coke Co. Ld. Regd. 1859. Dissolved 1 May 1949, undertaking being vested in West Midland Area Gas Board under Gas Act 1948. Holders of securities were entitled to receive British Gas 3% guaranteed stock 1990–95 as follows in respect of each £10 unit held:

	£	s.	d.	
Ord. shares (10% max.)	19	10	0	
Addit. shares (7% max.)	13	16	6	
3½% red. debs.	10	3	0	**1952**

Leon Cobalt & Copper Mining Co. Ld. Regd. 1890. Court Order to wind up 21 Nov. 1894. Liquidator released 7 May. 1897. Removed from Register 21 June 1907. .... ***1895**

Leon Syndicate Ld. Regd. 1905. Vol. liq. Oct. 1911. Removed from Register 1912 .... **1912**

Leonesa Mines Ld. Regd. 1917. Vol. liq. Dec. 1920. Capital returned to contributories—4¼d. per share. Final meeting return regd. 30 Sept. 1952 .... **1953**

Leonor Nitrate Co. Ld. Regd. 1906. Vol. liq. 28 Dec. 1916. Final meeting return regd. 20 Apr. 1917 .... **1917**

Leopold Joseph Investment Trust Ld. See Joseph (Leopold) Investment Trust Ld.

Leopold Ld. Regd. 1907. Vol. liq. 28 Oct. 1908. Removed from Register 1910 .... **1910**

Leopoldina Railway Co. Established Rio de Janeiro 1872. Undertaking and assets were acquired by Leopoldina Railway Co. Ld. Bondholders were entitled to fully-paid shares in new company as follows:

For every £100 held

6% bonds (1884)	£100 shares
5% bonds (1888)	£70 shares
5% bonds (1890)	£50 shares	**1897**

Leopoldina Railway Co. Ld. Regd. 1897. Vol. liq. (members') 27 Dec. 1951. Holders of 4% debenture stock and 6½% terminal debentures were entitled to

VOL. FOR

Leyland Gas Co. Inc. by Special Act 1863 as Leyland & Farington Gas Co.; name changed 1909. Dissolved 1 May 1949, undertaking being vested in North Western Area Gas Board under Gas Act 1948. Holders of securities were entitled to receive in respect of each £100 unit held, British Gas 3% guaranteed stock 1990–95 as follows:

	£	s.	d.
Ord. stock (5% stand.)	122	10	0
5% pref. stock	112	0	0
4½% red. pref. stock	104	0	0
4% red. pref. stock	101	10	2
3½% red. deb. stock	100	10	0

Liability in respect of certain mortgage loans assumed by the Board **1952**

Leyland Motors (1914) Ld. Regd. 1914. Vol. liq. 22 Sept. 1919. Reconstructed as Leyland Motors Ld. (later Leyland Motor Corpn. Ld.). in which company shareholders were entitled to 3 ordinary shares of £1 (credited as fully-paid) for each ordinary share of £1 held, or 1 6% preference share of £1 (credited as fully-paid) for each preference share of £1 held. Final meeting return regd. 17 June 1920 .... **1920**

Leyland Rubber Co. Ld. Regd. 1873 as James Quin & Co. Ld.; name changed 25 Apr. 1883. Vol. liq. 16 May 1898. Undertaking was acquired by Leyland and Birmingham Rubber Co. Ld. Final meeting return regd. 20 Dec. 1901 .... **1898**

Leyland Shipping Co. Ld. Regd. 1896. Vol. liq. 16 Jan. 1922. Final meeting return regd. 17 Mar. 1924 .... **1922**

Liang Tin Lands Ld. Regd. 1899. Vol. liq. Nov. 1905. Receiver appointed June 1907 on behalf of debenture holders. Removed from Register 1911 .... **1910**

Liberia Coffee Co. Ld. Regd. 1879. Court Orders: to wind up 10 Aug. 1880; to dissolve 22 Apr. 1886 . *__1881__

Liberian Development Co., Chartered & Ld. Regd. 1900 as West African Gold Concessions Ld.: name changed Mar. 1904. Controlled by African International Corporation Ld. Struck off Register 1925 .. **1925**

Liberian Diamond & Gold Trust Ld. Regd. 1911. Vol. liq. Aug. 1922. Priority shareholders were entitled to 89,250 fully-paid ordinary shares in African International Corporation Ld.; holders of ordinary shares were entitled to 1 fully-paid ordinary share in that company for every 5 ordinary shares of 4s. held. Struck off Register Mar. 1930 .... **1931**

Liberian Government Concessions & Exploration Co. Ld. Regd. 1890. Removed from Register 1907 .... **1895**

Liberian International Corporation Ld. See African International Corporation Ld.

Liberian Rubber Corporation Ld. Regd. 1905. Vol. liq. 22 Mar. 1921. Final meeting return regd. 1 Nov. 1938 .... **1922**

Liberty Consolidated Gold Mines Ld. Regd. 1895. Removed from Register 1908 .... **1900**

Libiola Copper Mining Co. Ld. Regd. 1888. Vol. liq. (members') 7 Feb. 1935. Final meeting return regd. 20 Feb. 1937 .... **1935**

Lichfield Brewery Co. Ld. See Ind Coope (North East) Ld.

Lichfield Gas Co. Inc. by Special Act 1878. Dissolved 1 May 1949, undertaking being vested in West Midland Area Gas Board under Gas Act 1948. Holders of securities were entitled to receive British Gas 3% guaranteed stock 1990–95 as follows:

	£	s.	d.
A cap. stock (10% stand.) per £100	215	0	0
6% B cap. pref. shares of £10	13	8	0

.... **1952**

Life and Health Assurance Association Ld. Regd. Edinburgh 1898. Vol. liq. May 1909. Court Orders: to continue winding up under supervision June 1909; to dissolve 12 June 1913 .... **1910**

Life-Belt Coffee Co. Ld. Regd. 1909. Receiver sppointed in Apr. 1923; ceased to act Jan. 1926. Struck off Register 1928 .... **1927**

Light Aircraft Ld. Regd. 1935. Vol. liq. (members') 15 May 1936. Assets were acquired by Aeronautical Corporation of Great Britain Ld. Final meeting return regd. 8 July 1936 .... **1937**

Light Castings Ld. Regd. 1921. Vol. liq. (members') 15 Oct. 1936. The assets were distributed in kind to contributories. Final meeting return regd. 11 Jan. 1937. Struck off Register 19 Dec. 1947 .... **1937**

Light Controlled Installations Ld. Regd. 1932. Vol. liq. (members') 3 Aug. 1934 for reconstruction as Automatic Electrical & Mechanical Controls Ld., in which company shareholders were entitled to 1 share of 2s. (credited with 1s. paid) for every share of 5s. held. Final meeting return regd. 10 Oct. 1935 .... **1935**

Light of Asia Amalgamated Gold Mines Ld. Regd. 1895. Vol. liq. 2 Mar. 1898. Reconstructed as Cue Consolidated Gold Mines Ld., in which company shareholders were entitled to 1½ shares of 10s.

VOL. FOR

(credited with 7s. 6d. paid) for each share of £1 held. Final meeting return regd. 23 Nov. 1898 .... **1899**

Lightalloys Ld. Regd. 1926. All capital was owned by Manganese Bronze & Brass Co. Ld. (later Manganese Bronze Holdings Ld.). Vol. liq. (members') 2 Jan. 1961. Final meeting return regd. 13 Dec. 1962 **1957**

Lighterage Co. of Monte Video Ld. Regd. 1901. Vol. liq. 7 Jan. 1918. Final meeting return regd. 6 Feb. 1919 **1918**

Lighting Corporation Ld. Regd. 1895. Struck off Register 16 Nov. 1906 .... **1907**

Lighting Trades Ld. See Earlsfield Manufacturing Co. Ld.

Lightning Creek (British Columbia) Hydraulic Mining Co. Ld. Regd. 1910. Struck off Register 26 Jan. 1951 **1951**

Lightwood Concrete & Aggregates Ld. Regd. 1926. All assets sold and proceeds applied towards meeting claims of debenture holders. Struck off Register 24 Nov. 1944 .... **1945**

Lilita Nitrate Co. Ld. Regd. 1907. Vol. liq. 15 May 1918. Capital returned to contributories—4s. 10d. per share of £1; further payments (if any) not known. Final meeting return regd. 17 Jan. 1919 .... **1919**

Lilley & Skinner Ld. Regd 1894. Vol. liq. (members') 8 Jan. 1952. Undertaking and assets acquired by Lilley & Skinner (Holdings) Ld. Preference shares were repaid at par and ordinary shareholders received £8 13s. 6·4509d. per share (of £1) **1973–4**

Lillie (Cripple Creek) Gold Mining Co. Ld. Regd. 1898. Vol. liq. Nov. 1904. Property was to be sold to Vindicator Consolidated Gold Mining Co. Ld. It was estimated that £13,529 would be distributed among shareholders. Removed from Register 1906 **1905**

Lillooet (British Columbia) Mining Ld. Regd. 1914. Undertaking was acquired by British Columbia Alluvials Ld. Struck off Register 10 Mar. 1936 .... **1937**

Lillooet, Fraser River & Cariboo Gold Fields Ld. Regd. 1895. Removed from Register 1904 .... **1903**

Lily Australis Gold Mines Ld. Regd. 1895. Vol. liq. 20 Feb. 1899. Amalgamated with Phoenix Gold Mines Ld., in which company shareholders were entitled to 2 shares of 10s. (credited with 8s. paid) for each share of £1 held. Final meeting return regd. 15 July 1900 .... **1900**

Lilybank Soap Co. Ld. Regd. Edinburgh 1884. Vol. liq. Nov. 1890. Final meeting return regd. 18 Aug. 1891 **1891**

Lima Railways Co. Ld. Regd. 1865. Vol. liq. (members') 20 Mar. 1961. Capital returned to contributories— 9s. 10d. Per share of £10. Final meeting return regd. 28 Sept. 1962 .... **1963**

Limavady & Dungiven Railway Co. Inc. by Special Act 1878. Undertaking transferred to Midland Railway Co. by Act of 1907 for £2,000 cash **1908**

Limbuguri Tea Co. Ld. Regd. 1906. Vol. liq. 20 Dec. 1950. Undertaking and assets acquired by Eastern Assam Tea Co. Ld. in which company shareholders were entitled to receive 1 share of £1 for every 3 shares of £1 held. Final meeting return regd. 22 Dec. 1951 .... **1953**

Limerick & Kerry Railway Co. Inc. by Special Act 1873. Under Great Southern and Western Railway Act 1901 line was purchased by that company for £280,000 .... **1906**

Limerick Brewery Co. Ld. Regd. 1895. Court Order to wind up 29 June 1896. Removed from Register 1908 **1897**

Limerick Gold Mines Ld. Regd. 1895. Removed from Register 1904 .... **1904**

Limoro-Kano Tin (Nigeria) Ld. Regd. 1914 as Timoro Tin (Nigeria) Ld.; name changed Oct. 1924. Vol. liq. 3 Dec. 1926. Reconstructed as Baba River Tin Fields (Nigeria) Ld., in which company shareholders were entitled to 1 share of 5s. (credited with 2s. 6d. paid) for every 5 shares of 1s. held. Final meeting return regd. 5 Aug. 1933 .... **1927**

Limoro Tin (Nigeria) Ld. Regd. 1913. Vol. liq. 15 Mar. 1924 for reconstruction under same name (later Limoro-Kano Tin (Nigeria) Ld.) Shareholders were entitled to 2 fully-paid shares of 1s. and 2 shares of 1s. (credited with 9d. paid) for each preferred ordinary share of 2s. held, or 2 shares of 1s. (credited with 9d. paid) for each ordinary share of 2s. held. Final meeting return regd. 9 Feb. 1927 .... **1925**

Limoro Tin (Nigeria) Ld. See Limoro-Kano Tin (Nigeria) Ld.

Limpopo Ranching Co. Ld. Regd. 1910. Vol. liq. (creditors') 20 Nov. 1929. No capital returned to contributories. Final meeting return regd. 22 Aug. 1941 .... **1930**

Limpsfield & Oxted Water Co. Regd. 1886. Inc. by Special Act 1888. Under Act of 1930 the under taking was acquired by East Surrey Water Co. Holders of 4% and 5% debenture stock were entitled to £100 and £125 respectively in 4% consolidated debenture stock in acquiring company. Shareholders were entitled to 10 ordinary (B) shares (7%

---

*See Stock Exchange Year-Book.

VOL. FOR

maximum) for every 7 10% maximum shares or every 10 7% maximum shares held **1931**

Linares Lead Mining Co. Ld. Est. 1852. Regd. 1856 and 1863. Reconstructed 1906 as company of same name. Shareholders were entitled to 3 shares of £1 (credited as fully-paid) in new company for each share of £3 held *plus* 8*s*. per share in cash in lieu of half-yearly dividend due Sept. 1906. Removed from Register 1907 .... **1908**

Linares Lead Mining Co. Ld. Regd. 1906. Vol. liq. 7 Mar. 1917. Final meeting return regd. 20 Aug. 1917 **1917**

Linchwe Concession Co. Ld. Regd. 1899. Vol. liq. (members') 8 Feb. 1952. Capital returned to contributories: 1·6*d*. per fully-paid share of £1 and 0·8475*d*. per share with 10*s*. 7*d*. paid. Final meeting return regd. 24 Oct. 1952 .... **1954**

Lincoln & East Coast Dock Railway & Co. Inc. by Special Act 1897. Undertaking abandoned by Act of 1902 .... **1903**

Lincoln & Lindsay Banking Co. Ld. Established 1833. Regd. 1880. Vol. liq. 17 July 1913. Undertaking and assets were acquired by London City and Midland Bank Ld. (later Midland Bank Ld.), in which company shareholders were entitled to 16 shares of £60 (credited with £12 10*s*. paid) for every 3 shares of £200 (£70 paid) held or 4 shares of £60 (credited with £12 10*s*. paid) for every 3 shares of £50 (£17 10*s*. paid) held **1914**

Lincoln Gas Light & Coke Co. Inc. by Special Act 1828. The properties were acquired by the Corporation **1885**

Lincoln, Horncastle, Spilsby & Skegness Railway Co. Inc. by Special Act 1887. Undertaking abandoned by Act of 1891 .... **1892**

Lincoln Hotels Ld. Regd. 1926. Vol. liq. (members') 14 June 1947 the undertaking having been acquired by company of same name. Ordinary shareholders were entitled to receive £5 ordinary stock in the new company for every 3 shares (of £1) held, and preference shareholders were entitled to receive £1 preference stock for every share (of £1) held. Final meeting return regd. 6 Aug. 1948 .... **1949**

Lincoln Tramways Co. Ld. Regd. 1880. The undertaking was acquired by Lincoln Corporation. Capital returned to contributories—£3 per share of £5 (£4 paid); further payments (if any) not known. Removed from Register 1906 .... **1905**

Lincoln Wagon & Engine Co. Ld. Regd. 1873. Vol. liq. (members') 6 Jan. 1941. Certain assets were distributed in specie. Capital returned to contributories—preference capital and debentures were repaid at par; 1*s*. 9·698350*d*. per ordinary share of £1 (3*s*. paid). Final meeting return regd. 24 June 1946 ... **1947**

Lincolnshire & Central Electric Supply Co, Ld. Regd. 1930 as British & International Utilities Ld.; name changed 1935. Dissolved 1 Apr. 1948, undertaking being vested in British (later Central) Electricity Authority under Electricity Act 1947. Holders of securities were entitled to receive British Electricity 3% guaranteed stock (1968–73) as follows in respect of each £1 unit of capital held:

	£	s.	d.
4½% preference shares	1	4	6
Ordinary shares (fully-paid)	3	7	0
Ordinary shares (11*s*. paid)	1	16	10
4% debenture stock	1	0	8⅖

1949

Lincolnshire Beet Sugar Co. Ld. *See* Lincolnshire Sugar Co. Ld.

Lincolnshire Iron Smelting Co. Ld. Regd. 1872. Removed from Register 1904 .... **1883**

Lincolnshire Sugar Co. Ld. Regd. 1927 as Lincolnshire Beet Sugar Co. Ld.; name changed Dec. 1929. Vol. liq. (members') 15 Sept. 1936. Undertaking was transferred to British Sugar Corporation Ld. for 319,275 fully-paid ordinary shares of £1. Capital returned to contributories—£1 11*s*. 7*d*. per preference share of £1; 9*s*. 6·3*d*. per ordinary share; shareholders of both classes were entitled to participate in distribution of shares of acquiring company. Final meeting return regd. 17 Jan. 1940 .... **1937**

Lindall's Cycle Fittings Co. Ld. Regd. 1897. Removed from Register 1901 .... **1900**

Lindrea & Co. Ld. Regd. 1897. Vol. liq. 29 Apr. 1927. Final meeting return regd. 10 Oct. 1929 .... **1928**

Lindsay & Low, Ld. Regd. Edinburgh 1898. Vol. liq. (members') 26 Jan. 1938. Capital returned to contributories—preference shares were repaid at par; £10 18*s*. 1¼*d*. per ordinary share of £10. £3 15*s*. 2*d*. was paid into Companies' Liquidation Account. Final meeting return regd. 16 Apr. 1947 .... **1948**

Lindsays' Consolidated Ld. Regd. 1901. Vol. liq. Nov. 1904. Removed from Register 1906 .... **1905**

Lindsays' Consolidated Mines Ld. Regd. 1896. Vol. liq. 19 Sept. 1901. Reconstructed as Lindsays' Consolidated Ld., in which company shareholders were entitled to 1 share of 5*s*. (credited with 3*s*. 9*d*. paid) for each share of £1 held. Final meeting return regd. 18 July 1902 .... **1904**

Lindsay's Extended (East) Gold Mines Ld. Regd. 1895. Vol. liq. 28 July 1896. Reconstructed 1896 as Lindsay's Consolidated Mines Ld., in which company shareholders were entitled to 1 share of £1 (credited with 17*s*. paid) for each share of £1 held. Final meeting return regd. 16 Nov. 1898 .... **1900**

Lindsay's Find Proprietary Ld. Regd. 1896. Removed from Register 1904 .... **1901**

Lindsay's Gold Mines Ld. Regd. 1895. Vol. liq. 28 July 1896. Reconstructed in 1896 as Lindsay's Consolidated Mines Ld. which company shareholders were entitled to 1 share of £1 (credited with 17*s*. paid) for each share of £1 held. Final meeting return regd. 16 Nov. 1898 .... **1900**

Lindum Gold Mines Ld. Inc. Transvaal 1896. In liquidation in 1903. The undertaking was acquired by Randfontein Deep Ld., in which company shareholders received 1 share of £1 for each 2 shares of £1 held **1903**

Linen & Artsilk Ld. Regd. 1928. Court Order to wind up Mar. 1930. Struck off Register 24 Oct. 1939 .... **1940**

Lines Bros. Ld. Regd as private company 1 May 1919; converted into public company 7 June 1933. Vol. liq. (creditors') 28 Sept. 1971. Final meeting held 13 Nov. 1984 and registered 20 Mar. 1985 .... **1986–7**

Lingham Timber & Trading Co. Ld. Regd. 1902. Vol. liq. 13 June 1905. Reconstructed as African Timber & Trading Co. Ld. Shareholders were entitled to 3 shares of £1 (credited with 13*s*. 4*d*. paid) in new company for every 4 shares of £1 held. Final meeting return regd. 10 Feb. 1909. Court Order deferred dissolution until 5 May 1911 .... **1908**

Lingham Timber & Trading Co. Ld. Regd. 1905 as African Timber & Trading Co. Ld.; name changed July 1905. Vol. liq. 4 Aug. 1908. Final meeting return regd. 7 Mar. 1919 .... **1905**

Lingholm Trust Ld. Regd. 1923. Vol. liq. 29 Mar. 1966. Final meeting return regd. 13 Apr. 1971 .... **1947**

Linkwood-Glenlivet Distillery Ld. Regd. Edinburgh 1897. Vol. liq. (members') 18 Sept. 1933. All preference shares were repaid at par in 1924. Capital returned to contributories—£37 15*s*. 10½*d*. per share of £10. Final meeting return regd. 12 Dec. 1934 .... **1934**

Linlithgow Gas Co. Ld. Regd. in Edinburgh 1925. Dissolved 1 May 1949, undertaking being vested in Scottish Area Gas Board under Gas Act 1948. Holders of ordinary shares (of £10) were entitled to receive £10 British Gas 3% guaranteed stock 1990–95 for each share held **1952**

Linlithgow Oil Co. Ld. Regd. Edinburgh 1884. Vol. liq. 13 Feb. 1902. Court Order to dissolve 17 Dec. 1904 **1902**

Linotype Co. Ld. Regd. 1896. Reconstructed 1903 as Linotype and Machinery Ld. Holders of 1st mortgage 4% debenture stock were entitled to an equal amount of "B" 4½% debenture stock. Holders of preference shares were entitled to an equal amount of preference shares; holders of preferred ordinary shares were entitled to 2 preference shares of £1, 1 ordinary share of £1 *plus* 2*s*. in cash for each preferred ordinary share of £5 held; holders of deferred ordinary shares were entitled to 1½ ordinary shares of £1 *plus* 1*s*. in cash for each deferred ordinary share of £5 held. Removed from Register 1912 .... **1904**

Lintang Investments Ld. Regd. in Edinburgh 1907 as Bulit Lintang Rubber Estates Ld., name changed 21 May 1958. Vol. liq. (members') 2 Oct. 1964. Capital returned to contributors—20*s*. 4*d*. per share of 5*s*. £25 2*s*, was paid into Companies' Liquidations Account in respect of unclaimed dividends and £11,292 6*s*. 8*d*. in respect of unclaimed distributions. Final meeting return regd. 21 Apr. 1967 .... **1967**

Linthorpe-Dinsdale Smelting Co. Ld. Regd. 1920. Vol. liq. (members') 20 Aug. 1946. Capital returned to contributories—6*s*. 1·94*d*. per share of 5*s*. Final meeting return regd. 18 Jan. 1952 .... **1953**

Linton's Angarpatra Colliery Ld. Regd. 1924. Struck off Register 1934 .... ***1930**

Lion Brewery Co. Ld. Regd. 1865. Vol. liq. 31 Jan. 1924. Undertaking was acquired by Hoare & Co. Ld. Capital returned to contributories—20*s*. per preference or preferred ordinary share of £1; £1 2*s*. 4*d*. per ordinary share of £1. The 6% debentures were repaid at par and the 4% B mortgage debenture at 108%. Final meeting return regd. 8 June 1926 .... **1925**

Lion Fire Insurance Co. Ld. Regd. 1879 as Anglo French Fire Insurance Co. Ld.; name changed Jan. 1880. Vol. liq. 24 Mar. 1902. Undertaking and assets were acquired by Yorkshire Fire and Life Insurance Co. (later Yorkshire Insurance Co. Ld.), in which

**See Stock Exchange Year-Book.*

company shareholders were entitled to 10 shares of £10 (credited with £1 paid) for every 128 shares of £8 5s. (£1 5s. paid) held: fractions were paid at 17s. 2d. per share. Final meeting return regd. 24 Apr. 1915 ... **1903**

Lion Life Insurance Co. Ld. Regd. 1880. Vol. liq. 15 Apr. 1884. Capital returned to contributories—13s. per share of £10 (£2 paid); further payments (if any) not known. Struck off Register 24 July 1923 .... **1885**

Lion (Mozambique) Gold Co. Ld. Regd. 1894. Removed from Register 1908 .... **1903**

Lion Spinning Co. Ld. (The). Regd. 1889. Vol. liq. 15 Mar. 1968. Amount returned to contributories—8s. 9·06d. per share (of 2s.). Final meeting return regd. 24 July 1969 .... **1970**

Lionsdale Estates & Gold Mining Co. Ld. Regd. 1897. Vol. liq. 22 July 1901. Undertaking and assets were acquired by Transvaal Exploring Land and Minerals Co. Ld., in which company shareholders were entitled to 1 share of 5s. (credited as fully-paid) for each share of £1 held. Final meeting return regd. 17 Apr. 1926 .... **1902**

Lionsdale Estates Ld. Regd. 1894. Vol. liq. 19 July 1897. Reconstructed as Lionsdale Estates & Gold Mining Co. Ld. Final meeting return regd. 6 June 1898 .. ***1898**

Liphook Gas Co. Ld. Regd. 1909. Vol. liq. 11 Oct. 1911. Undertaking was acquired by Bordon & District Gas Co. Final meeting return regd. 17 Jan. 1912 . **1936**

Liquidating Railway Corporation. Inc. Illinois 1937 as Illinois Terminal Railroad Co.; name subsequently changed. An amalgamation of Illinois Terminal Railroad Co. (inc. as Illinois Terminal Co. in 1937) and Illinois Traction, Inc. In Dec. 1945 practically all property and assets were purchased by Purchaser Railway Corporation (later Illinois Terminal Railroad Co.—Inc. 1945) **1946**

Lisboa Gold Mining and Development Co. Ld. Regd. 1901. Vol. liq. 26 Feb. 1917. Final meeting return regd. 13 Dec. 1918 .... **1909**

Lisbon-Berlyn Co. Ld. Regd. 1889. Vol. liq. 14 Nov. 1892. Reconstructed as company of same name. Shareholders were entitled to 1 share of 2s. 6d. (credited with 1s. 6d. paid) for each share of £1 held. Final meeting return regd. 20 Apr. 1894 .... **1893**

Lisbon-Berlyn Co. Ld. Regd. 1892. Vol. liq. 3 July 1902. Reconstructed as Lisbon-Berlyn Ld. Shareholders were entitled to 1 share of 2s. 6d. (credited with 1s. 9d. paid) for each share of 2s. 6d. held. Final meeting return regd. 6 July 1905 .... **1930**

Lisbon-Berlyn Gold Fields Ld. Regd. 1888. Vol. liq. Jan. 1890. Reconstructed as Lisbon-Berlyn Co. Ld in which company shareholders were entitled to 1 share of 2s. 6d. (credited with 1s. 6d. paid) for each share of £1 held. Final meeting return regd. 14 Aug. 1891 .... **1892**

Lisbon-Berlyn Ld. Regd. 1902. Vol. liq. 21 Mar. 1906. Reconstructed as New Lisbon-Berlyn Ld., in which company shareholders were entitled to 1 share of 2s. 6d. (credited with 1s. 6d. paid) for each share of 2s. 6d, held. Final meeting return regd. 11 Aug. 1932 **1906**

Lisbon-Berlyn Quicksilver Exploration Co. Ld. Regd. 1899. Reconstructed 1903 as company of same name. Shareholders were entitled to 2 fully-paid shares of 2s. 6d. and 1 share of 2s. 6d. (credited with 1s. 6d. paid) in new company for each share of 5s. held. Removed from Register 1904 .... **1903**

Lisbon-Berlyn Quicksilver Exploration Co. Ld. Regd. 1903. Removed from Register 1909 .... **1906**

Lisbon-Berlyn (Transvaal) Gold Fields Ld. Regd. 1883. Vol. liq. 27 Aug. 1885. Court Order to continue winding-up under supervision 31 Oct. 1885. Reconstructed as New Lisbon-Berlyn (Transvaal) Gold Fields Ld. Final meeting return regd. 25 Apr. 1888 **1886**

Lisbon Steam Tramways Co. Ld. Regd. 1871. Court Orders: to wind up 29 Aug. 1878; to dissolve 29 Feb. 1884 .... ***1876**

Lisburn Electric Supply Co. Ld. Regd. Belfast 1927. Vol. liq. June 1933. Undertaking sold to Electricity Board for Northern Ireland. Capital returned to contributories—35s. per share of £1 at Oct. 1933; further payments (if any) not known **1934**

Lisburne Development Syndicate Ld. Regd. 1907. Vol. liq. 7 Mar. 1922. Reconstructed as Cambrian Electrolytic Zinc Co. Ld., in which company shareholders were entitled to 5 preference shares of 5s. (credited with 3s. paid) for each preference share of £1 held, or 4 preference shares of 5s. (credited with 3s. paid) for each ordinary share of £1 held. Final meeting return regd. 17 Mar. 1923 .... **1923**

Lisburne Mines Co. Ld. Regd. 1864. Vol. liq. 30 June 1893. Final meeting return regd. 23 Feb. 1894...... **1894**

Liskeard & Caradon Railway Co. Inc. by Special Act 1843. Under Great Western Railway Act 1909 undertaking was acquired by that company. Holders of debentures were repaid in full *plus* 5% of

amount of arrears of interest. Purchasing company paid the liquidator £2,350 in cash **1910**

Liskeard & Looe Union Canal Co. *See* Liskeard & Looe Railway Co.

Liskeard & Looe Railway Co. Inc. by Special Act 1825 as Liskeard & Looe Union Canal Co., name changed by Act of 1895. In 1923 the undertaking was merged into the Great Western Railway Co. Holders of every £100 loans were entitled to £87 10s. Great Western 4% debenture stock. Holders of every £100 Liskeard preference stock were entitled to £34 4s. 1d. in cash **1924**

Liskeard Gas Co. Ld. Regd. 1925. Dissolved 1 May 1949, undertaking being vested in South Western Area Gas Board under Gas Act 1948. Holders of securities were entitled to receive, in respect of each £1 unit held, British Gas 3% guaranteed stock 1990–95 as follows:

	£	s.	d.	
Ord. shares	1	0	0	
7% pref. shares	1	10	0	**1952**

Liss Gas Co. Ld. Regd. 1910. Vol. liq. 11 Oct. 1911. Undertaking was acquired by Bordon & District Gas Co. Final meeting return regd. 17 Jan. 1912 **1936**

Lissen Ld. Regd. 1923. Vol. liq. (members') 31 Dec. 1930. Undertaking acquired by company of same name for 500,000 8% preference shares of £1 fully-paid and 400,000 ordinary shares of £1 fully-paid. Final meeting return regd. 12 Aug. 1932 .... **1940**

Lissen Ld. Regd. 1931. Vol. liq. (members') 17 Dec. 1948. Subsidiary of Ever Ready Co. (Great Britain) Ld. Final meeting return regd. 11 May 1949 .... **1940**

Lister (R. A.) & Cie, G.m.b.H. In liquidation. Direct controlling interest was held by Lister (R. A.) & Co. Ld **1935**

Listowel & Ballybunion Railway Co. Inc. by Special Act 1886 .... **1903**

Little Lever Paper Staining Co. Ld. Amalgamated with Wall Paper Manufacturers Ld. between Sept. 1915 and Mar. 1924 .... **1924**

Littleborough Gas Co. Inc. by Special Act 1865. Dissolved 1 May 1949, undertaking being vested in North Western Area Gas Board under Gas Act 1948. Holders of ordinary shares (of £10) were entitled to receive £20 12s. 6d. British Gas 3% guaranteed stock 1990—95 for each share held. Liability in respect of certain mortgage loans assumed by the Board **1952**

Littleburn & Adelaide Collieries Ld. Regd. 1920. Vol. liq. 8 Feb. 1934. Final meeting return regd. 30 Oct. 1936 **1935**

Littlehampton Gas Co. Inc. by Special Act 1909. Under Special Order of 1934 the undertaking was acquired by Brighton, Hove & Worthing Gas Co. Contributories were entitled to stock in acquiring company as follows:—for each A ordinary (10% standard) share of £5 held—£7 17s. 5% standard consolidated stock; for each B ordinary (7% standard) share of £5 held— £5 14s. 2d. 5% standard consolidated stock; for each C ordinary (5% standard) share of £5 held-£3 18s. 7d. 5% standard consolidated stock; holders of 6% preference stock were entitled to an equal amount of 6% B preference consolidated stock. The acquiring company assumed the liability for the 5% redeemable debenture stock **1935**

Littlestone-on-Sea & District Water Co. Inc. by Special Act 1904. Undertaking was acquired by the Folkestone Waterworks Co. (later Folkestone & District Water Co.) in Apr. 1953. Ordinary shareholders were entitled to 6 Folkestone Co. 7% ordinary shares for every 7 held and preference shareholders to £10 Folkestone Co. 4% redeemable preference stock 1965–75 per share. Dissolved 11 Sept. 1953 under terms of order made 17 Mar. 1953 .... **1954**

Littleton Collieries Ld. Regd. 1899. All capital was owned by Cannock Associated Collieries Ld. Vol. liq. (members') 5 Sept. 1955. Final meeting return regd. 22 Sept. 1956 .... **1940**

Littlewood's Ariel Wheel Works Ld. *See* Ariel Pram Wheel Works Ld.

Live Stock Insurance Co. of Great Britain Ld. Regd. 1874. Vol. liq. 25 Jan. 1878. Court Order to continue winding up under supervision 5 Feb. 1878. Final meeting return regd. 1 Dec. 1880 .... ***1878**

Liver Ice & Cold Storage Co. Ld. Regd. 1913. Court Order to wind up 15 Sept. 1914. Liquidator released 14 Mar. 1918. Struck off Register 1 July 1921 ..... ***1914**

Liverpool Adelphi Hotel Co. Ld. Regd. 1864. Hotel was acquired in Dec. 1890 by Midland Railway Co. Removed from Register 1895 .... **1892**

Liverpool & Axim Syndicate Ld. Regd. 1897. Vol. liq. July 1904. Removed from Register 1908 .... **1905**

Liverpool & Edinburgh Investment Trust Ld. Regd. 1957 as Wm. & Jno. Lockett Ld.; name changed Mar. 1963. Vol. liq. 29 Oct. 1971. Under a scheme of

VOL. FOR

arrangement 5 Nov. 1971 ordinary shareholders received 224·9540938 units of Target Thistle Fund for every 100 ordinary shares held and a terminal dividend of 0·6425p per share. Final meeting return regd. 9 Oct. 1979 .... **1981–2**

Liverpool & Great Western Steamship Co. Ld. Regd. 1886. Vol. liq. 28 Sept. 1893. Final meeting return regd. 25 Sept. 1894 .... ***1894**

Liverpool & Manchester Aerated Bread & Café Co. Ld. Regd. 1888. Vol. liq. 2 Feb. 1894. Final meeting return regd. 31 Jan. 1895 .... **1895**

Liverpool Ashanti Gold Concessions Ld. Regd. 1899. Undertaking and assets were acquired in 1903 by Axim Mines Ld., in which company shareholders were entitled to 1 share of £1 (credited with 9s. paid) for each share of £1 (9s. paid) held, or 1 fully-paid share for every 5 fully-paid shares held. Removed from Register 1905 .... **1904**

Liverpool Carriage Co. Ld. Regd. 1907. Vol. liq. 6 Apr. 1923. Capital returned to contributories—9s. 3 13/32d. per share of £1; further payments (if any) not known. Final meeting return regd. 4 Aug. 1923 .. **1924**

Liverpool Chemical Products Ld. Regd. 1925 as Howroyd McArthur & Co. Ld. name changed 20 Apr. 1937. Struck off Register 14 Apr. 1961 .... **1938**

Liverpool Clerks' Café Co. Ld. Regd. 1884. Court Order to wind up 8 July 1909. Liquidator released 15 Feb. 1917. Struck off Register 1 July 1921 .... **1913**

Liverpool Cold Storage & Ice Co. Ld. Regd. 1890. Vol. liq. 19 Dec. 1907. Removed from Register 1909 ... **1908**

Liverpool Commercial Banking Co. Ld. Established 1833. Regd. 1860. Vol. liq. 3 Jan. 1889. Business was transferred to Bank of Liverpool Ld. (later Martins Bank Ld.), in which company shareholders were entitled to 4 shares of £100 (credited with £12 10s. paid) for every 7 shares of £20 (£10 paid) held, *plus* 7s. 6d. per share in cash. Removed from Register 1911 .... **1889**

Liverpool Commercial Investment Co. Ld. Regd. 1872. Vol. liq. 6 Nov. 1908. Final meeting return regd. 3 Apr. 1914 .... **1909**

Liverpool Corn Exchange Co. Ld. Established 1810. Regd. 1881. Vol. liq. 14 Apr. 1897. The business was transferred to Liverpool Corn Trade Association Ld. for £43,000 in cash, and £162,000 in A, B or C debentures. Final meeting return regd. 21 Dec. 1897 **1897**

Liverpool Corn Trade Association Ld. Regd. 1886. Vol. liq. 7 Apr. 1897. Reconstructed as company of same name. Shareholders were entitled to 1 share of £150 (credited with £75 paid) in new company. Final meeting return regd. 23 July 1898 .... **1897**

Liverpool Cotton Exchange Ld. Constituted by deed of settlement 1810; inc. 1881 .... **1883**

Liverpool District Lighting Co. Ld. Regd. 1895. Vol. liq. 26 Jan. 1923. Final meeting return regd. 3 Aug. 1923 **1924**

Liverpool Electric Supply Co. Ld. Regd. 1883. Undertaking transferred to Liverpool Corporation by Act of 1896. Capital returned to contributories—£8 5s. per share of £5. Dissolved by Act 2 Mar. 1898 ..... **1897**

Liverpool Exchange Banking Co. Ld. Regd. 1884. Court Orders: to wind up 16 Aug. 1887; to dissolve 30 Jan. 1893 .... **1888**

Liverpool Exchange Co. Ld. Inc. by Special Act 1859; registered as limited in 1936. Vol. liq. (members') 5 Apr. 1943. Undertaking acquired by Liverpool Syndicate Ld. (later Liverpool Exchange Co. Ld.) which company held majority of the shares. Final meeting return regd. 31 Jan. 1947 .... **1948**

Liverpool Gas Co. Estd. 1816; inc. by Special Act 1848 as Liverpool United Gas Light Co.; name changed 1914. Dissolved 1 May. 1949 undertaking being vested in North Western Area Gas Board under Gas Act 1948. Holders of securities were entitled to receive, in respect of each £100 unit held, British Gas 3% guaranteed stock 1990—95 as follows:

	£	s.	d.	
Ord. stock (5% stand.)	127	6	8	
4% perp. deb. stock	103	0	0	
5% red. deb. stock	106	10	0	
3½% red. deb. stock	99	10	0	
4% red. deb. stock 1952–67	102	2	8	**1952**

Liverpool Gas Fittings Co. Ld. Regd. 1876. Vol. liq. May 1911. Capital returned to contributories—30s. per share of £1; further payments (if any) not known. Removed from Register 1912 .... **1912**

Liverpool Grain Contract Insurance Co., Ld. Regd. 1902. Vol. liq. (members') 25 Feb. 1964. Nearly all capital was owned by Liverpool Corn Trade Assn. Ld. Final meeting return regd. 4 Sept. 1965 .... **1960**

Liverpool Greyhound Club Ld. Regd. 1926. Vol. liq. (members') 15 Apr. 1952. Final meeting return regd. 21 Mar. 1961 .... **1950**

VOL. FOR

Liverpool Household Stores Association Ld. Regd. 1887. Court Orders: to wind up 4 Aug. 1888; to dissolve 12 Nov. 1891 .... **1890**

Liverpool Land Co. Ld. Regd. 1863. Vol. liq. (members') 9 June 1944. Capital returned to contributories—£1 12s. 4½d. per share of £1. £154 10s. paid into Companies' Liquidation Account in respect of unclaimed dividends or distributions. Final meeting return regd. 21 Apr. 1954 .... **1955**

Liverpool Law Association Ld. Regd. 1898. Vol. liq. 10 Nov. 1920. Capital returned to contributories—10s. per share of £1 (8s. 7d. paid) in Nov. 1920; further payments (if any) not known. Final meeting return regd. 16 June 1921 .... **1921**

Liverpool, Leeds & Hull Empire Palaces Ld. Regd. Edinburgh 1897. Reconstructed 1899 as Moss Empires Ld. (later M. E. Theatres Ld.). Shareholders were entitled to 7 preference and 7 ordinary shares of £5 (all fully-paid) *plus* £6 5s. in cash for every 10 shares of £5 held or 15 preference and 15 ordinary (all fully-paid) for every 20 shares of £5 held. Removed from Register 1909 .... **1900**

Liverpool Magazines Co. Ld. Regd. 1885. Vol. liq (members') 1 Jan. 1942. All capital held by Nobel's Explosives Co. Ld. Final meeting return regd. 13 Mar. 1943 .... **1942**

Liverpool Mortgage Insurance Co. Ld. Regd. 1887. Vol. liq. 4 Jan. 1923. Capital returned to contributories—£4 per share of £10 (£4 paid); further payments (if any) not known. Final meeting return regd. 13 Feb. 1929 .... **1923**

Liverpool Nitrate Co. Ld. Regd. 1883. Vol. liq. 3 June 1931. Undertaking and assets sold to Nitrate Corporation of Chile, in which corporation shareholders received 28 series B shares of 100 pesos for every 100 shares of £1 held. £3 8s. 7d. was paid into Companies' Liquidation Account in respect of sale of unclaimed shares. Final meeting return regd. 10 Mar. 1932 .... **1932**

Liverpool Overhead Railway Inc. by Special Act 1888. Vol. liq. Sept. 1957. Capital returned to contributories (per share of £10)—£3 6s. per 6½% preference and preference share (1900) and £3 13s. 1d. per ordinary share. £1,361 2s. 6d. on account of unclaimed dividends and £3,031 16s. on account of unclaimed distributions was paid into Companies' Liquidation Account. Final meeting return regd. 31 Oct. 1960 **1962**

Liverpool Palace of Varieties Ld. Regd. 1896. Vol. liq. 3 Jan. 1898. Taken over by New Liverpool Palace of Varieties Ld. Final meeting return regd. 5 July 1898 **1898**

Liverpool Palais de Luxe, Ld. Regd. 1913. Vol. liq. (members') 9 Dec. 1959. Final meeting return regd. 6 Apr. 1961 .... **1957**

Liverpool Road & Railway Omnibus Co. Ld. *See* Liverpool United Tramways & Omnibus Ld.

Liverpool Rubber Co. Ld. Regd. 1861. Vol. liq. 15 June 1894. Reconstructed as company of same name. Shareholders were entitled to 1 ordinary share of £5 (credited as fully-paid) for each ordinary share of £5 (£4 15s. paid) or 1 preference share of £3 10s. (credited as fully-paid) for each preference share of £5 (£3 10s. paid) held. Final meeting return regd. 25 Feb. 1896. .... **1908**

Liverpool Rubber Co. Ld. Regd. 1894. Vol. liq. 23 May 1910. The undertaking and assets were acquired by New Liverpool Rubber Co. Ld. (later Liverpool Rubber Co. Ld.), in which company shareholders were entitled to 2 fully-paid preference shares of £1, £1 in debenture stock and £1 in cash for each ordinary share of £5 held; preference shareholders were entitled to £3 10s. in cash for each preference share of £3 10s. held. Final meeting return regd. 4 Apr. 1911 .... **1911**

Liverpool Rubber Co. Ld. Regd. 1910 as New Liverpool Rubber Co. Ld.; name changed July 1926. Vol. liq. (members') 25 Aug. 1933. Capital returned to contributories—20s. per preference share of £1; £60,028 8s. 8d. was paid to ordinary shareholders. Final meeting return regd. 24 Aug. 1934 .... **1934**

Liverpool Safe Deposit Co. Ld. Regd. 1879. Vol. liq. Dec. 1888. Final meeting return regd. 25 June 1889 **1889**

Liverpool, St. Helens & South Lancashire Railway Co. Inc. by Special Act 1885 as St. Helens & Wigan Railway Co. Ld.; name changed by Act of 1889. Under Great Central Railway Co. Act 1905 undertaking was acquired by that company. Holders of 4% 1st and 2nd debenture stocks received 3½% 2nd debenture stock on basis of equal income; holders of preference shares received £35 preferred ordinary stock for every £100 held; holders of ordinary shares received £20 deferred ordinary stock for every £100 held **1906**

Liverpool (South African) Exploring Syndicate Ld. Regd. 1895. Vol. liq. (members') 19 June 1934.

VOL. FOR

Capital returned to contributories—3s. 8d. per share of £1. £569 5s. was paid into Companies' Liquidation Account. Final meeting return regd. 16 Mar. 1935 .... **1935**

Liverpool, Southport & Preston Junction Railway. Inc. by Special Act 1884. The shares have been exchanged for Lancashire and Yorkshire Railway Co. 3% debenture stock (the ordinary shares at £8 7s. 9½d. per share in July 1917); the undertaking has ceased to exist **1918**

Liverpool Spice Co. Ld. Regd. 1885. Vol. liq. 4 Nov. 1889. Final meeting return regd. 11 Nov. 1891 .... **1890**

Liverpool Stables & Motors Ld. Regd. 1912. Vol. liq. 2 Feb. 1950. Final meeting return regd. 19 Oct. 1950 **1919**

Liverpool Steam Tug Co. Ld. Regd. 1859. Vol. liq. Jan. 1910. Removed from Register 1911 .... **1910**

Liverpool Sugar & Produce Clearing House Ld. Regd. 1913. Vol. liq. 7 June 1922. Capital returned to contributories—£1 1s. 0½d. per share of £5 (£1 paid) in Oct. 1922; further payments (if any) not known. Final meeting return regd. 26 Oct. 1922 .... **1923**

Liverpool Tin Canister Co. Ld. See Taylor (Earnest) Ld.

Liverpool Union Bank Ld. Established 1835. Regd. as unlimited 1874, as limited 1882. Amalgamated in 1900 with Lloyds Bank Ld., in which company shareholders were entitled to 11 shares of £50 (credited with £8 paid) for every 6 shares of £100 (£20 paid) held. Removed from Register 1905 ..... **1901**

Liverpool United Gas Light Co. See Liverpool Gas Co.

Liverpool United Tramways & Omnibus Co. Founded 1860 as Liverpool Road & Railway Omnibus Co. Ld.; name changed 1876. Inc. by Special Act 1879. Taken over by Liverpool Corporation **1898**

Liverpool Victoria Insurance Corporation Ld. Regd. Dec. 1907. Vol. liq. 29 May 1914. Goodwill and certain insurance business was acquired by Commercial Union Assurance Co. Ld. The life fund was to be operated as a closed fund of the absorbing company. Final meeting return regd. 12 Aug. 1921 **1915**

Liverpool Vienna Bakery Co. Ld. Regd. 1896. Vol. liq. 25 June 1920. Reconstructed as Kirklands Ld., in which company shareholders were entitled to 3 preference shares of £1 for every 10 preference shares of £1 held, or 1 preference share of £1 for every 10 ordinary shares of £1 held. Debenture holders were entitled to an equal amount of preference shares in new company. Final meeting return regd. 3 Feb. 1922 .... **1921**

Liverpool Warehouse Construction Co. Ld. Regd. 1895. Vol. liq. 1 Oct. 1920. Final meeting return regd. 23 Nov. 1922 .... **1921**

Liverpool Western Canada Land Co. Ld. Regd. 1911. Vol. liq. (creditors'), 5 Apr. 1939. No capital returned to contributories. Final meeting return regd. 30 Nov. 1945 .... **1946**

Liverpool Zoological Gardens Co. Ld. Regd. 1882. Removed from Register 1890 .... **1887**

Livingstone African Exploration Co. Ld. Regd. 1895. Vol. liq. 6 Jan. 1896. Final meeting return regd. 7 Oct. 1896 .... **1896**

Livingstone Gold Mining Co. Ld. Regd. 1886. Vol. liq. Mar. 1889. Reconstructed as New Livingstone Gold Mining Co. Ld., in which company shareholders were entitled to 1 share of £1 (credited with 17s. paid) for each share of £1 held or to 1 share of £1 (credited with 16s. 10d.) for each share of £1 (19s. 10d. paid) held. Final meeting return regd. 19 Mar, 1890 .... **1892**

Liwadzi Ld. Regd. 1912. Vol. liq. 18 Feb. 1915. Final meeting return regd. 9 Mar. 1916 .... **1915**

Lixa Mining Co. Ld. Regd. 1887. Vol. liq. 31 July 1925. Final meeting return regd. 23 Apr. 1926 .... **1926**

Lizard Light Railway Co. Inc. (under Light Railways Act 1896) by order of Light Railway Commissioners confirmed by order of Board of Trade 1898 .... **1906**

Llanarmon District Mining Co. Ld. Regd. 1891. Vol. liq. 30 July 1929. Final meeting return regd. 23 Aug. 1930 .... **1930**

Llandilo & Lampeter Light Railway Co. Inc. (under Light Railways Act 1896) by order of Light Railway Commissioners confirmed by Board of Trade 1908 **1913**

Llandilo Gas Light Co. Ld. Regd. 1914. Dissolved 1 May 1949, undertaking being vested in Wales Area Gas Board under Gas Act 1948. Holders of 5% red. mort. debs. were entitled to receive, in respect of each £100 unit held, £100 10s. British Gas 3% guaranteed stock 1990—95 .... **1952**

Llandovery Gas Co. Ld. Regd. 1861. Dissolved 1 May 1949, undertaking being vested in Wales Area Gas Board under Gas Act 1948. Holders of securities were entitled to receive British Gas 3% guaranteed stock 1990—95 as follows:

	£	s.	d.

VOL. FOR

Ord. shares (of £5)	8	6	8	
4% red. debs.(of £100)	100	0	0	**1952**

Llandrindod Wells Gas Co. Inc. by Special Act 1907. Dissolved 1 May 1949, undertaking being vested in Wales Area Gas Board under Gas Act 1948. Holders of securities were entitled to receive British Gas 3% guaranteed stock 1990–95 as follows in respect of each £100 unit, unless otherwise stated, of security held:

	£	s.	d.	
Ord. shares (10% max.) (of £10) ...	10	10	0	
4½% irred. deb. stock	104	0	0	
6% red. deb. stock	108	0	0	**1952**

Llandudno & Colwyn Bay Electric Railway, Ld. Regd. 1906 as Llandudno & District Electric Tramway Construction Co. Ld.; name changed May 1909. Vol. liq. (members') 14 Nov. 1961. Capital returned to contributories—10s. per preferred share of 10s. and ¼d. per deferred share of 1s. £964 7d. was paid into Companies' Liquidation Account in respect of unclaimed distributions. Final meeting return regd. 17 Dec. 1966 .... **1968**

Llandudno & District Electric Tramway Construction Co. Ld. See above.

Llandudno Coaching and Carriage Co. Ld. Regd. 1897. Vol. liq. (members') 5 Feb. 1931. Undertaking and assets transferred to Crosville Motor Services Ld., in which company shareholders were entitled to 5 shares of £1 for every 4 shares of £1 held. Final meeting return regd. 27 July 1931 .... **1931**

Llanelly & District Electric Supply Co. Ld. Regd. 1899 as Llanelly & District Electric Lighting & Traction Co. Ld.; name changed 1924. Dissolved 1 Apr. 1948, undertaking being vested in British (later Central) Electricity Authority and South Wales Area Board under Electricity Act 1947. Holders of ordinary and 6% preference shares were entitled to receive, in respect of each share (of £1) held, £1 9s. 1d. and £1 8s. 2d. British Electricity 3% guaranteed stock (1968–73) respectively **1949**

Llanelly and Mynydd Mawr Railway Co. Inc. by Special Act 1875. In 1923 the undertaking was merged into the Great Western Railway Co., in which company shareholders were entitled to stock as follows:

For each £100 held   G. W.

5% Perp. A Deb. ....£100   5% Debenture

5% Debenture .... { £100   5% Debenture
                    { £70½ cash for unpaid
                          interest

Ordinary share .... £80   Cons. Ordinary A debt of £25,918 owing by the Company was to be satisfied by £25,918 5% Consolidated Preference Stock of the Great Western Co. **1924**

Llanelly Associated Tinplate Cos. Ld. Regd. 1939. Vol. liq. (members') 6 July 1951. Capital returned to contributories—preference: £1 cash per share (of £1); ordinary: £2 3½% guaranteed stock 1979–81 per share (of £1) plus 9s. 11·2398d. per share cash. £1,420 15s. 8d. was paid into Companies' Liquidation Account. Final meeting return regd. 6 Dec. 1956 .... **1958**

Llanelly Gaslight Co. Inc. in 1835; reinc. by Special Acts 1874 & 1908. Dissolved 1 May 1949, undertaking being vested in Wales Area Gas Board under Gas Act 1948. Holders of securities were entitled to receive British Gas 3% guaranteed stock 1990–95 as follows in respect of each £20 unit, unless otherwise stated, of security held:

	£	s.	d.	
Orig. shares (10% stand.)	44	0	0	
New A shares (5% stand.)	24	0	0	
New B shares (7% stand.)	32	0	0	
New ord. shares (7% stand.)	32	0	0	
New ord. stock (7% stand.) (per)				
£100	160	0	0	
4½% red. pref. stock (per £100)	104	0	0	
4% red. pref. stock (per £100)	101	10	0	
3⅜% red. deb. stock (per £100)	100	10	0	
4½% deb. stock (per £100)	106	10	0	
Liability in respect of certain mortgage loans assumed by the Board				**1952**

Llanelly Iron Shipping Co. Ld. Regd. 1863. Vol. liq. 11 Sept. 1894. Struck off Register 29 July 1902 .... **1895**

Llanelly Railway & Dock Co. Inc. by Special Act 1828; consolidated 1853. Under Great Western Railway Act 1889 undertaking was acquired by that company in which holders of consolidated stock received £120 5% consolidated guaranteed stock for every £100 held; holders of A preference or B 6% preference stock received £120 5% guaranteed stock for every £100 held. Holders of 5% and 4% debenture stocks received 5% and 4% debenture stocks respectively at par **1890**

See Stock Exchange Year-Book.

VOL. FOR

Llanfyllin Gas Co. Ld. Regd. 1860. Dissolved 1 May 1949, undertaking being vested in Wales Area Gas Board under Gas Act 1948. Holders of ordinary shares (of £1) were entitled to receive £1 10s. British Gas 3% guaranteed stock 1990–95 for each share held **1952**

Llangammarch & Neath & Brecon Junction Railway Co. Inc. by Special Act 1882. Undertaking abandoned by Act of 1890 .... **1891**

Llangollen & Corwen Railway Co. Inc. by Special Act 1860. Under Great Western Railway Act 1896 undertaking was amalgamated with that company. Holders of 4¼% debenture stock received 4¼% debenture stock at par; holders of 4% preference stock received £80 5% consolidated guaranteed stock for every £100 held; holders of ordinary stock received £72 10s. 5% consolidated guaranteed stock for every £100 held **1897**

Llangollen Gas Co. Ld. Regd. 1871. Dissolved 1 May 1949, undertaking being vested in Wales Area Gas Board under Gas Act 1948. Holders of securities were entitled to receive, in respect of each £5 unit held, British Gas 3% guaranteed stock 1990—95 as follows:

	£	s.	d.
Ord. shares	5	0	0
5% pref. shares	5	12	0
5% pref. shares (£3 10s. paid)	3	18	5	**1952**

Llanidloes Gas, Coal & Coke Co. Ld. Regd. 1859. Dissolved 1 May 1949, undertaking being vested in Wales Area Gas Board under Gas Act 1948. Holders of ordinary shares (of £5) were entitled to receive £5 British Gas 3% guaranteed stock 1990–95 for each share held **1952**

Llannon Coal Boring Syndicate Ld. Regd. 1901. Vol. liq. Mar. 1906. Removed from Register 1907 .... **1907**

Llantrisant & District Gas Co. Inc. by Special Act 1913. Dissolved 1 May 1949, undertaking being vested in Wales Area Gas Board under Gas Act 1948. Holders of securities were entitled to receive British Gas 3% guaranteed stock 1990–95 as follows in respect of each £100 unit, unless otherwise stated, of security held:

	£	s.	d.
Ord. shares (7% stand.) (of £5)	4	2	6
5% pref. shares (of £5)	5	12	0
4½% mort. debs.	104	5	0
4% mort. debs. (1957)	101	0	0
4% mort. debs. (1953)	100	0	0	**1952**

Llantrissant & Taff Vale Junction Railway Co. Inc. by Special Act 1861. Under Taff Vale Railway Co. Amalgamations & Capital Act 1889 undertaking was amalgamated with that company. Holders of £100 ordinary stock received £125 4% preference stock; holders of £100 3½% debenture stock received £116 13s. 4d. 3% debenture stock **1890**

Llay Hall Coal & Clay Works Co. Ld. Regd. 1881. Court Orders: to wind up Mar. 1885; to dissolve Aug. 1887 **1886**

Llewellyn Shipping Co. Ld. Regd. 1919. Struck off Register 1934 .... **1935**

Lloyd & Lloyd Ld. Regd. 1898. Business was acquired in 1903 by A. & J. Stewart and Menzies Ld. (later Stewarts & Lloyds Ld.), for £350,000 in ordinary shares, £200,000 in preference shares and £145,500 in debentures. Preference shareholders were entitled to an equal number of preference shares of £10; debenture holders were entitled to an equal number of debentures of amalgamated company or repayment at 105% in cash. Removed from Register 1906 **1903**

"Lloyd" Copper Co. Ld. Regd. 1899. Vol. liq. 9 Jan. 1912. Reconstructed as company of same name. Shareholders were entitled to 1 share of £1 (credited with 17s. 6d. paid) in new company for each share of £1 held. Final meeting return regd. 3 Nov. 1913 **1912**

"Lloyd" Copper Co. Ld. Regd. 1912. Struck off Register 1921 .... **1915**

Lloyd (Edward) Investment Co. Ld. Regd. 1927. Vol. liq. (members') 3 July 1947 the assets being transferred to Bowater Paper Corpn. Ld., which owned all ordinary capital of company. The £2,000,000 5% redeemable preference stock was redeemed at 105% (plus additional premium of 22½% in lieu of arrears of dividend) on 30 June 1947. £765 was paid into Companies' Liquidation Account on account of amounts unclaimed for redemption of preference stock. Final meeting return regd. 27 Aug. 1949 .... **1950**

Lloyd (Edward) Ld. See Bowater's Lloyd Pulp & Paper Mills Ld.

Lloyd Royal Belge (Great Britain) Ld. Regd. 1917. Vol. liq. (members') 7 Apr. 1932. No capital returned to contributories. Final meeting return regd. 1 May 1933 .... **1933**

Lloyd (T.) & Co. Ld. Regd. 1905. Vol. liq. 5 Nov. 1920. All capital held by Selfridge & Co. Ld. [later

VOL. FOR

Selfridge (Holdings) Ld.—later Selfridges Ld.] Final meeting return regd. 1 Sept.1927 .... **1927**

Lloyd's Avenue Estate Co. Ld. Regd 1900. Vol. liq. (members') 24 June 1952; assets acquired by Capital & Counties Property Co. Ld. Capital returned to contributories—25s. 7·645412d. per 5s. stock. Final meeting return regd. 30 Oct. 1953 .... **1955**

Lloyd's Cambrian Chain & Anchor Public Testing Co. Ld. Regd. 1865. Undertaking was acquired in 1900 by Lloyds' British Testing Co. Ld. Capital returned to contributories—£9 per share of £10; further payments (if any) not known. Removed from Register 1901 .... **1901**

Lloyd's (W. A.) Cycle Fittings Ld. Regd. 1896. Vol. liq. Dec. 1906. Assets were in hands of Receiver for debenture holders. Removed from Register 1910 **1907**

Llynvi & Ogmore Railway Co. Inc. by Special Act 1866. Under provisions of Great Western Railway Co. and Llynvi & Ogmore Railway Co. Amalgamation Act 1883 undertaking was amalgamated. Holders of 5% guaranteed perpetual (1855), 5% preference (1862) and 5% preference perpetual stock (1872) received an equal amount of 5% consolidated guaranteed stock. Holders of 4½% shares received 90% of holding in 5% consolidated guaranteed stock and holders of Llynvi ordinary, Ogmore ordinary or Cardiff ordinary stocks received 120% of holding in 5% consolidated guaranteed stock **1884**

Llynvi & Tondu Co. Ld. Regd. 1880. Court Orders: to wind up 15 Jan. 1887; to dissolve 26 Apr. 1890 ... **1887**

Llynvi Valley Gas Co. Inc. by Special Act 1868. Dissolved 1 May 1949, undertaking being vested in Wales Area Gas Board under Gas Act 1948. Holders of securities were entitled to receive, in respect of each £10 unit held, British Gas 3% guaranteed stock 1990–95 as follows:

	£	s.	d.
Ord. shares (10% max.)	6	10	0
Ord. A shares (7% max.)	4	11	0
5% pref. shares	10	0	0	**1952**

Lo Magundi Central Ld. See Axim & Tarkwa Goldfields Ld.

Loa Nitrate Co. Inc. in Chile 1905. Undertaking and assets were sold for 239,774 fully-paid series B preference shares of 100 pesos to Nitrate Corporation of Chile, which company assumed all liability in respect of the debentures **1932**

Loan & Finance Corporation Ld. Regd. 1889. Vol. liq. 1 Feb. 1898. Final meeting return regd. 21 Apr. 1898 **1899**

Loanda Gas Co. Ld. Regd. 1894. Removed from Register 1906 .... **1900**

Loangwa Concessions (Northern Rhodesia) Ld. Regd. 1925. Vol. liq. (members') 5 Jan. 1938. All shares were owned by Rhodesian Anglo-American Ld., (later Zambian Anglo-American, Ld.) which company absorbed the business and assets. Capital returned to contributories—£625,387 11s. 5d. plus certain investments in specie. Final meeting return regd. 3 Aug. 1939 .... **1938**

Loanhead Gas Co. Ld. Regd. in Edinburgh 1896. Dissolved 1 May 1949, undertaking being vested in Scottish Area Gas Board under Gas Act 1948. Holders of ordinary shares (of £1) were entitled to receive £1 8s. British Gas 3% guaranteed stock 1990–95 for each share held **1952**

Lobito, Benguella & Catumbella Electric Light & Power Co. Ld. Regd. 1910. Receiver appointed in 1919; ceased to Act Oct. 1922. The undertaking and assets were sold for benefit of debenture stockholders. The proceeds were paid into Court and distributed to stockholders. Struck off Register 1925 .... **1923**

Locarno (The) Ld. Regd. Edinburgh 1926. Vol. liq. (creditors') May 1930. Assets realised insufficient to pay creditors in full. Final meeting return regd. 3 Apr. 1936 .... **1931**

Loch Leven Electricity Supply Co. Ld. Regd. 1910. Dissolved 1 Apr. 1948, undertaking being vested in the North of Scotland Hydro-Electric Board under the Electricity Act 1947. Ordinary shareholders were entitled to receive £21 British Gas 3% guaranteed stock (1968–73), for each share (of £10) held **1949**

Loch Leven Trust Ld. Regd. 1938. Vol. liq. 16 Apr. 1953. Final meeting return regd. 21 Feb. 1956 .... **1953**

Loch Leven Water & Electric Power Co. Inc. by Special Act 1901. Under Act of 1910 the undertaking was transferred to British Aluminium Co. Ld, Loch Leven Electricity Supply Co. Ld., and Loch Leven Pier Co. Ld. **1911**

Loch Line Steam Trawling & Fishing Co. Ld. Regd. Edinburgh 1902. Vol. liq. (members') 22 May 1939. Capital returned to contributories—£2 16s. per share of £1. Final meeting return regd. 4 Dec. 1939 **1940**

*See Stock Exchange Year-Book.

Loch Mines Ld. Regd. 1905. Vol. liq. 28 Aug. 1907. Shareholders were entitled to 1 share of 2s. in Jacoletti Gold Mines Ld., for each share of 2s. held. Struck off Register 10 Oct. 1916.................... **1908**

Lochearnhead, St. Fillans & Comrie Railway Co. Inc. by Special Act 1897. Under Caledonian Railway Act 1902 undertaking was vested in that company. Shareholders were repaid at par in cash................ **1903**

Lochgelly Gas Co. Ld. Regd. in Edinburgh 1886. Dissolved 1 May 1949, undertaking being vested in Scottish Area Gas Board under Gas Act 1948. Holders of securities were entitled to receive British Gas 3% guaranteed stock 1990–95 as follows:

	£	s.	d.
Ord. shares (of £1)	1	7	3
3% term. debs. (of £100)	100	0	0	**1952**

Lochgelly Iron & Coal Co. Ld. Regd. Edinburgh 1896. Vol. liq. (members') 5 Sept. 1951. Capital returned to contributories—£2 0s. 2·668d. per ordinary share of 3d. Final meeting return regd. 3 June 1958 ..... **1959**

Lochinvar Gold Mines Ld. Inc. Western Australia. In liquidation. All shares were owned by Great Boulder Mining & Finance Ld. **1942**

Lochnagar (Ceylon) Produce Co. Ld. Regd. 1909. Vol. liq. (members') 14 Feb. 1933 for reconstruction under same name. Shareholders were entitled to 1 share of £1 (credited with 15s. paid) in new company for each share of £1 held. £91 14s. 1d. was paid into Companies' Liquidation Account. Final meeting return regd. 23 Jan. 1935 .... **1933**

Lochnagar (Ceylon) Produce Co. Ld. Regd. Feb. 1933. Vol. liq. (members') 28 Nov. 1933. Undertaking and assets were acquired by Dangan Rubber Estates Ld. (later Harvard Investment Trust Ld., now Tanker Investment Trust Ld.). in which company shareholders were entitled to 22½ ordinary shares of 2s. (credited as fully-paid) for each fully-paid share of £1 held or 22½ ordinary shares of 2s. (credited with 1s. 10d. paid) for each share of £1 (16s. 3d. paid) held. Final meeting return regd. 23 Nov. 1935 ..... **1934**

Lochner's Navigation Coal & Coke Co. Ld. Regd. 1903. Court Order to wind up 2 Aug. 1904. Liquidator released 29 Nov. 1906. Removed from Register 24 May 1910 .... ***1905**

Lochore and Capledrae Cannel Coal Co. Ld. Regd. Edinburgh 1872. Court Orders: to wind up Jan. 1880; to stay proceedings Mar. 1880; to wind up Mar. 1889; to stay proceedings June 1892. Vol. liq. Nov. 1900. Final meeting return regd. 22 Dec. 1902 **1890**

Lochwinnoch Gas Light Co. Ld. Regd. in Edinburgh 1938. Dissolved 1 May 1949, undertaking being vested in Scottish Area Gas Board under Gas Act 1948. Holders of ordinary shares (of £5) were entitled to receive £13 British Gas 3% guaranteed stock 1990–95 for each share held **1952**

Locke & Co. (Newland) Ld. Regd. 1896. Vol. liq. (members') 7 May 1954. Final meeting return regd.6 June 1956... **1946**

Locke & Smith Ld. Regd. 1897. Receiver appointed 30 June 1911. The property and assets were sold in 1913 to Benskin's Watford Brewery Ld., for £37,600 in cash. Struck off Register 1915 .... **1914**

Locke, Lancaster & W. W. & R. Johnson & Sons Ld. Regd. 1892, Vol. liq. (members') 8 Nov. 1949. Final meeting return regd. 6 Apr. 1951 .... **1925**

Locke Steel Chain Co. Ld. Regd. 1901. Reconstructed 1905 as Locke Steel Chain Co. (1905) Ld., in which company shareholders were entitled to 1 share of 10s. (credited with 8s. paid) for each share of £1 held. Removed from Register 1906 .... **1908**

Locke Steel Chain Co. (1905) Ld. Regd. 1905. Vol. liq. June 1910. Removed from Register 1913 .... **1911**

Locket's Merthyr Collieries (1894) Ld. Regd. 1894. Receiver appointed in Oct. 1931. Assets realised insufficient to meet claims of debenture holders. Struck off Register 14 Jan. 1936.......................... **1936**

Lockett (Wm. & Jno) Ld. See Liverpool & Edinburgh Investment Trust Ld.

Lockharts Ld. See Goodfare Dining Rooms Ld.

Locks Ld. Regd. 1893 as Ward, Lock & Bowden Ld.; name changed to Ward Lock & Co. Ld. in Aug. 1896 and as above in Oct. 1924. Vol. liq. (members') 10 Mar. 1937. Capital returned to contributories—£435,493 11s. 6d. Final meeting return regd. 26 Apr. 1937 .... **1938**

Lockwood & Bradley Ld. Regd. 1915. Receiver appointed 19 Jan. 1939. Assets realised insufficient to meet claims of debenture holders. Struck off Register 24 Sept. 1943 .... **1944**

Lockwood & Keighley Ld. Regd. 1900. Vol. liq. 17 Nov. 1915. The assets and liabilities were acquired by private company of same name. Final meeting return regd. 5 Apr. 1916 .... **1916**

Lockwood's Clean Coal Process Ld. Regd. 1928. Vol. liq. (members') 27 Mar. 1934. Capital returned to contributories—2⅝d. per share. Final meeting return regd. 23 Sept. 1937 .... **1935**

Lockwood (Vernon) Manufacturing Co. Ld. See Goldring Ld.

Lockyer (T. H.) Ld. Regd. 1917. Vol. liq. (members') 28 Jan. 1931. Capital returned to contributories—£7,592 10s. 5d. Final meeting return regd. 25 Jan. 1934 .... **1931**

Loddon Deep Leads (Caralulup) Ld. Regd. 1912. Vol. liq. 26 Jan. 1914. Reconstructed as Talbot Alluvials Ld., in which company shareholders were entitled to 1 share of 4s. (credited with 1s. paid) for every 3 shares of 1s. held. Final meeting return regd. 27 Feb. 1916 .... **1914**

Loddon Deep Leads (Victoria) Ld. Regd. 1903. Reconstructed 1904 as company of same name. Shareholders were entitled to 1 share of 3s. (credited with 3s. 6d. paid) in new company for each share of £1 held. Removed from Register 1908 .... **1908**

Loddon Deep Leads (Victoria) Ld. Regd. 1904. Vol. liq. 3 July 1912 for reconstruction as Loddon Deep Leads (Caralulup) Ld., in which company shareholders were entitled to 1 share of 1s. (credited with 8d. paid) for each preferred share of 1s. for each ordinary share of 5s. held; preferred shareholders were entitled to a bonus of 1 fully-paid share for every 5 shares subscribed. Debenture holders were entitled to £11 fully-paid shares for each £10 bond held. Final meeting return regd. 23 July 1915 ..... **1913**

Loddon Valley Goldfields Ld. Regd. 1900. Reconstructed 1903 as company of same name. Shareholders were entitled to 1 share of £1 (credited with 15s. paid) in new company for each share of £5 held. Removed from Register 1908 .... **1907**

Loddon Valley Goldfields Ld. Inc. New South Wales 1903 .... **1908**

Loddon Valley Goldfields (1907) Ld. Inc. New South Wales 1907. Vol. liq. Dec. 1908 .... **1909**

Loder (Giles) Ld. Regd. 1889. Removed from Register 1904 .... **1900**

Lodynia Petroleum Syndicate Ld. Regd. 1887. Vol. liq. 5 Aug. 1893. Final meeting return regd. 4 May 1898 ***1893**

Loengoer (Java) Rubber Ld. Regd. 1925. Vol. liq. 2 Sept. 1931. Final meeting return regd. 13 July 1934 ..... **1932**

Loewenthal, Herger & Co. Ld. Regd. 1897. Struck off Register 1923 .... ***1916**

Lofthouse Colliery Ld. Regd. 1872 as Leeds & Yorkshire Co-operative Coal Mining Co. Ld.; name changed 1880. Vol. liq. (members') 13 Jan. 1953. Capital returned to contributories—£9 14s. 10d. per share of 5s. £1,883 5s. 4d. was paid into Companies' Liquidation Account. Final meeting return regd. 27 Aug. 1956 .... **1957**

Logan (David) & Son Ld. Regd. Edinburgh 1898. Vol. liq. Sept. 1901. Court Orders: to continue winding up under supervision Oct. 1901; to dissolve 1 July 1914.. **1902**

Loma Gold Mines Ld. Regd. 1890. Vol. liq. 1 July 1896. Reconstructed as Nueva Esperanza Gold Mines Ld., in which company shareholders were entitled to 1 share of 5s. (credited with 4s. 6d. paid) for each share of £1 held. Final meeting return regd. 21 Apr. 1898 .... **1898**

Lomagunda Development Co. Ld. Regd. 1894. Vol. liq. July 1909 for amalgamation with Amalgamated Properties of Rhodesia Ld., in which company shareholders were entitled to 3 shares of 5s. for every 2 shares of £1 held. Removed from Register 1912 **1910**

Lomagunda Reefs Ld. Regd. 1895. Undertaking was acquired by Lomagunda Development Co. Ld., in which company shareholders were entitled to 1 share of £1 for every 6 shares of £1 held. Removed from Register 1903 .... **1902**

Lomagundi (Rhodesia) Chrome Mines Ld. Regd. Edinburgh 1925. Vol. liq. (members') 28 June 1933. Capital returned to contributories—4s. 1½d. per share of £1. Final meeting return regd. 18 July 1934 **1934**

Lomah Banket Proprietary Ld. Regd. 1910. Struck off Register Dec. 1931 .... **1932**

Lomah (Rhodesia) Exploration Co. Ld. Regd. 1909 as Lomah Stoessel (Banket) Rhodesia Ld.; name changed Aug. 1912. Vol. liq. 14 Feb. 1913. Reconstructed as Lomah (Rhodesia) Exploration Ld. Shareholders were entitled to 3 shares of 5s. (credited with 3s. 6d. paid) in new company for each share of 10s. held. Final meeting return regd. 13 Jan. 1915 .... **1913**

Lomah (Rhodesia) Exploration Ld. Regd. 1913. Vol. liq. 30 May 1924. Reconstructed as Lomah (Rhodesia) Mining Co. Ld., in which company shareholders were entitled to 5 shares of 5s. (credited with 3s.

VOL. FOR

paid) for every 3 shares of 5s. held. Final meeting return regd. 23 Dec. 1929 .... **1925**

Lomah (Rhodesia) Mining Co. Ld. Regd. 1924. Vol. liq. (members') 15 Feb. 1932. Undertaking and assets were acquired by Lomah (Rhodesia) Gold Mines Ld., (later Mount Charlotte Investments Ld.) in which company shareholders were entitled to 1 share of 5s. (credited with 4s. paid) for each share of 5s. held. Final meeting return regd. 30 Oct. 1944 **1932**

Lomah Stoessel (Banket) Rhodesia Ld. See Lomah (Rhodesia) Exploration Co. Ld.

Lomas (Robert) Ld. [See Lomas (Robert) (Proprietors)]

Lomas (Robert) (Proprietors) Ld. Regd. 1923. Vol. liq. (members') 15 Jan. 1936. Capital returned to contributories—8·3d. per preference share of 10s. £41 3s. 1d. was paid into Companies' Liquidation Account. Final meeting return regd. 7 Nov. 1936 **1936**

Lomatie (Lydenburg) Exploration Co. Ld. In 1900 the assets were acquired by Development & Finance Co. Ld., for 74,294 fully-paid shares of £1 .... **1907**

Lombard Gold Mine (W. A.) Ld. Regd. 1897. Struck off Register 16 Nov. 1906 .... **1907**

Lombard Unit Investment Ld. Regd. 1938. Vol. liq. (members') 3 Oct. 1950. Final meeting return regd. 23 July 1954 .... **1940**

Lombard Investment Co. (of Missouri). Founded 1854. Inc. Kansas 1882. Re-inc. Missouri 1890. Receivers appointed 1893 and discharged 1895. Share capital was stated to be valueless. Assets were realised, but distributions to bondholders (if any) not known .. **1899**

Lombard Property Trust Ld. Regd. 27 Mar. 1931 as Centralised Estates & Properties Trust Ld.; name changed 5 May 1931. Vol. liq. (members') 20 Feb. 1935. Undertaking was acquired by Monument Property Trust Ld. Capital returned to contributories—£1,760; all assets (excepting cash at bank) were distributed in specie. Final meeting return regd. 19 Oct. 1935 .... **1946**

Lombardo-Venetian Railway. The main line of this company from Milan to Venice formed the basis on which the South Austrian Railway Co. was built either by construction or purchase of further lines **1918**

Lombardy Gold Mine Ld. Regd. 1898. Vol. liq. Jan. 1909. Removed from Register 1912 .... **1909**

Lombardy Road Railways Co. Ld. Regd. 1881. Vol. liq. 15 Jan. 1920. Final meeting return regd. 11 Dec. 1922 .... **1920**

London & African Trading Co. Ld. Regd. 1901. Removed from Register 1903 .... ***1902**

London & Amsterdam Borneo Tobacco Co. Ld. Regd. 1889. Vol. liq. 12 Dec. 1892. Reconstructed as New London & Amsterdam Borneo Tobacco Co. Ld., in which company shareholders were entitled to 1 share of £10 (credited with £7 10s. paid) for each share of £10 held or 10 shares of £10 (credited with £7 10s. paid) for each founders' share held. Final meeting return regd. 14 Dec. 1893 .... **1893**

London & Amsterdam General Investment Co. Ld. Regd. 1889. Vol. liq. 19 Feb. 1892. Final meeting return regd. 9 Aug. 1894 .... **1893**

London & Argentine Bank Ld. See Anglo-Argentine Bank Ld.

London & Australasian Debenture Corporation Ld. Regd. 1889. Majority of securities were sold to London and Provincial Trust Ld. Struck off Register Mar. 1930 .... **1931**

London & Australian Investment Co. Ld. Inc. Western Australia 1907. Wound up Oct. 1928. Capital returned to contributories—3s. 10¼d. per share of 10s. in Nov. 1928; further payments (if any) not known **1929**

London & B. C. Alliance Syndicate Ld. Regd. 1896. Vol. liq. 17 Nov. 1902. Struck off Register Mar. 1930 **1931**

London & Birmingham Assurance Co. Ld. Regd. 1865 as Birmingham Alliance Life Assurance Co. Ld.; name changed 16 Mar. 1870. Vol. liq. 4 Apr. 1876. Final meeting return regd. 10 Mar. 1877 .... ***1875**

London & Birmingham Brass Foundry Co. Ld. Regd. 1897 as Nunan & Stove Ld. Wound up under supervision of Court. Removed from Register 1909 **1901**

London and Blackwall Railway Co. Inc. by Special Act 1836 as Commercial Railway; name changed by Act of 1839. In 1923 the undertaking was merged into the London & North Eastern Railway Co., in which company stockholders were entitled to stock as follows:

For each £100 held	L. N. E.	
Cons. Ordinary	£112½ 4% Debenture	
4½% Preference	£112½ 4% Debenture	
4½% Debenture	£106½ 4% Debenture	**1924**

London & Boston Scientific Trust Ld. Regd. 1963. Vol. liq. (members') 19 Oct. 1965. Capital returned to contributories: 21s. 0·4d. per share of £1. Final meeting return regd. 1 Feb. 1967 .... **1968**

VOL. FOR

London & Brazilian Bank Ld. Regd. 1862 as London & Brazilian Bank Ld.; name changed to New London and Brazilian Bank Ld. in 1871; resumed original title in 1886. Vol. liq. Nov. 1923. Undertaking and assets were acquired by London & River Plate Bank Ld. (later Bank of London & South America Ld.) in which company shareholders were entitled to 1 shares of £5 (credited as fully-paid) for each share of £20 (£10 paid) held. Final meeting return regd. 20 Aug. 1945 .... **1924**

London & Brighton Dairy Co. Ld. Regd. 1887. Removed from Register 1906 .... **1893**

London and Brighton Mansions Ld. Regd. 1892. Vol. liq. Dec. 1908. Removed from Register 1910 .... **1909**

London & British Columbia Goldfields Ld. Regd. 1896. Vol. liq. 28 Feb. 1899. Final meeting return regd. 30 Nov. 1899 .... **1899**

London & British Columbia Goldfields Ld. Regd. 1899. Vol. liq. 4 June 1903. Reconstructed as company of same name. Shareholders were entitled to 1 share of £1 (credited with 16s. paid) in new company for each share of £1 held. Final meeting return regd. 17 Nov. 1908 .... **1908**

London & British Columbia Goldfields Ld. Regd. 1903. Vol. liq. 31 Dec. 1912. Final meeting return regd. 20 Sept. 1919 .... **1913**

London & British Industrial Investment Co. Ld. Regd. 1914 as Commercial Bank of London Ld.; name changed June 1918. Vol. liq. 21 Jan. 1926. Final meeting return regd. 20 Jan. 1927 .... **1926**

London & British North America Co. Ld. Regd. 1911. Vol. liq. (members') 12 June 1929 and ratified 7 Jan. 1930. Capital returned to contributories—preference stock was redeemed at par in cash; £17l 14s. 3d. per £100 ordinary stock. Final meeting return regd. 25 Oct. 1930 .... **1930**

London & Buda-Pest Oil Syndicate Ld. Regd. 1911. Vol. liq. 23 Jan. 1928. Final meeting return regd. 5 Apr. 1929 .... **1928**

London & Caledonian Trust Ld. Regd. 1900. Removed from Register 1903 .... **1904**

London & California Mining Co. Ld. Regd. 1872. Vol. liq. Dec. 1882. Court Order to continue winding up under supervision Mar. 1883. Final meeting return regd. 20 Feb. 1886 .... **1883**

London & Canada Syndicate Ld. Regd. 1898. Struck off Register 9 Dec. 1902. Restored to Register 13 May 1904. Struck off Register 26 Mar. 1915 .... **1903**

London and Canadian Explorers Co. Ld. Regd. 1899. Vol. liq. June 1908. Removed from Register 1909 .... **1909**

London & Canadian Loan & Agency Co. Ld. Inc. Canada by Special Act 1863. Undertaking and assets were acquired by Canada Permanent Mortgage Corporation, in which company shareholders were entitled to 4 shares of $10 (credited as fully-paid) for each share of $50 held **1922**

London & Chicago Contract Corporation Ld. Regd. 1890. Vol. liq. 17 Sept. 1923. Final meeting return regd. 13 Oct. 1927 .... **1924**

London & China Syndicate Ld. Regd. 1900. Vol. liq. Dec. 1910. Removed from Register 1912 .... **1911**

London and Colonial Finance Corporation Ld. Regd. 1888. Vol. liq. 31 July 1894. Removed from Register 1903 .... **1895**

London & Colonial General Agency Ld. Regd. 1890. Vol. liq. 14 June 1893. Final meeting return regd. 10 Feb. 1897 .... **1894**

London & Continental Bank & Exchange Ld. Regd. 1888. Removed from Register 1906 .... ***1896**

London & Continental Investment Corporation Ld. Regd. 1897. Vol. liq. Oct. 1909. Removed from Register 1913 .... **1910**

London & Continental Investment Corporation of Western Australia Ld. Regd. 1895. Vol. liq. 31 May 1897. Reconstructed as London and Continental Investment Corporation Ld., in which company shareholders were entitled to 4 shares of 10s. (credited with 6s. 3d. paid) for every 5 ordinary shares of £1 (5s. paid) held or 1 share of 10s. (credited with 5s. paid) for each deferred share of £1 (5s. paid) held. Final meeting return regd. 2 June 1898 .... **1908**

London & Coolgardie Explorers Ld. Regd. 1896. Removed from Register 1907 .... **1905**

London & County Banking Co. See Westminster Bank Ld.

London & County Bread Co. Ld. Regd. 1889. Taken over by Bread Union Ld. Removed from Register 1902 ***1890**

London & County Land & Building Co. Ld. Regd. 1860. Vol. liq. (members') 12 Dec. 1949. Capital returned to contributories—15s. 6d. per share (of £1). £970 was paid into Companies' Liquidation Account. Final meeting return regd. 10 Dec. 1952 .... **1954**

London & County Stockholders Investment Trust Ld. See London Stockholders Investment Trust Ld.

See Stock Exchange Year-Book.

VOL. FOR

London & Coventry Cycle Co. Ld. Regd. 1896. Struck off Register 4 Oct. 1898 .... **1899**

London & Cripple Creek Reduction Corporation Ld. Regd. 1895. Vol. liq. 11 Feb. 1898. Reconstructed as Cripple Creek Ore Reduction Works Ld. Removed from Register 11 Feb. 1910 .... ***1899**

London & Denver Mining Corporation Ld. Regd. 1896. Vol. liq. Feb. 1908. Removed from Register 1908 **1908**

London & District Bank Ld. Regd. 1895 as Discount Bank Ld.; name changed Oct. 1897. Vol. liq. 16 Oct. 1901. Final meeting return regd. 29 June 1903 .... **1902**

London & District Land & Building Co Ld. Regd. 1893 as London & District House-owner's Investment Co., Ld.; name changed Apr. 1900. Vol. liq. 13 Feb. 1918. Final meeting return regd. 17 Apr. 1919 .... **1918**

London & District Motor Bus Co. Ld. Regd. 1905. Vol. liq. 24 June 1907. Undertaking and assets were acquired by Vanguard Motorbus Co. Ld., in which company shareholders were entitled to 1 preference share of £1 and $\frac{1}{4}$ ordinary share of £1 for each ordinary share of £1 held, or $\frac{21}{100}$ ordinary share of £1 for each deferred share of 1*s*. held. Removed from Register 1912 .... **1908**

London & District Mutoscope Co. Ld. Regd. 1898. Removed from Register 1903 .... **1902**

London and District Omnibus Co. Ld. *See* London Road-Car Co. Ld.

London & District Westrumite Co. Ld. Regd. 1903. Vol. liq. 22 May 1905 for transfer of undertaking to Westrumite Ld. Removed from Register 1907 ..... **1906**

London & Eastern Trade Bank Ld. Regd. 1920. Winding up order made 12 Dec. 1949 .... **1976-7**

London & Foreign Banking Corpn. Ld. *See* Custodian Investment Corpn. Ld.

London & Foreign Contract Corporation Ld. Regd. 1895. Vol. liq. 8 June 1898. Reconstructed as company of same name. Shareholders were entitled to 10,000 fully-paid shares of £10. Final meeting return regd. 24 Jan. 1900 .... **1908**

London & Foreign Contract Corporation Ld. Regd. 1898. Vol. liq. 24 June 1909. Struck off Register 27 Nov. 1959 .... **1958**

London & Foreign Hotel Syndicate Ld. Regd. 1893. All capital held by Savoy Hotel Ld. The Grand Hotel, Rome was sold in 1919. Struck off Register 1931 **1920**

London & General Bank Ld. Regd. 1882. Court Order to wind up 14 Sept. 1892. Liquidator released 12 Sept. 1906. Removed from Register 21 Feb. 1911. Court Order declaring dissolution void 2 July 1912. Struck off Register 3 Sept. 1918. Restored to Register Feb. 1931. Struck off Register 2 Oct. 1953 .... ***1893**

London and General Exploration Co. Ld. Regd. 1896. Vol. liq. 15 Jan. 1907. Final meeting return regd. 1 May 1908 .... ***1909**

London & General Trade Bank Ld. *See* Rubber & Mercantile Corporation Ld.

London & Glasgow Engineering & Iron Shipbuilding Co. Ld. Regd. 22 Apr. 1864 as Clyde Engineering & Iron Ship Building Co. Ld.; name changed June 1864. Vol. liq. Dec. 1925. Undertaking was acquired by Harland & Wolff Ld. Final meeting return regd. 11 Feb. 1926 .... **1926**

London and Globe Deep Leads Assets Ld. *See* Consolidated Deep Leads Ld.

London & Globe Finance Corporation Ld. Regd. 1895. Vol. liq. 25 Feb. 1897. Reconstructed as company of same name, in which company shareholders were entitled to 2½ fully-paid shares of £1 *plus* 9½*d*. in cash for each ordinary share of £1 held or 3 fully-paid shares of £1 *plus* 1*s*. in cash for each deferred share of 1*s*. held. Final meeting return regd. 21 Dec. 1905 **1897**

London & Globe Finance Corporation Ld. Regd. 1897. Court Order to wind up Oct. 1901. Removed from Register 1909 .... **1902**

London & Globe Telephone & Maintenance Co. Ld. Regd. 1882. Vol. liq. Oct. 1885. Final meeting return regd. 5 Dec. 1887 .... **1886**

London and Greenwich Railway Co. Inc. by Special Act 1833. In 1923 the undertaking was merged into the Southern Railway Co., in which company stockholders were entitled to stock as follows:—

For each £100 held	*S. R.*		
4% Loans..........	£100	4% Debenture	
3½% Debenture..........	£87½	4% Debenture	
4% Debenture..........	£100	4% Debenture	
5% Preference..........	£125	4% Debenture	
Ordinary..........	£71⅕	4% Debenture	**1924**

London & Hamburg Gold Recovery Co. Ld. Regd. 1896. Vol. liq. 7 June 1905. Reconstructed London & Hamburg Gold Recovery Co. (1905) Ld. Ordinary shareholders were entitled to 1 share of 5*s*. in new company for each share of £1 held. Preference shareholders were repaid as to 75% in cash and 25% in debenture stock (later repaid). Final meeting return regd. 4 Nov. 1901. Court Orders deferred dissolution until 6 Dec. 1919 .... **1909**

London & Hamburg Gold Recovery Co. (1905) Ld. Regd. 1905. Vol. liq. 28 Nov. 1921. Final meeting return regd. 29 Mar. 1924 .... **1922**

London & Hampshire Canal & Water Co. Ld. Regd. 1883. Vol. liq. Mar. 1887. Final meeting return regd. 17 Dec. 1890 .... **1888**

London and Home Counties Electricity Authority. Inc. by the London & Home Counties Electricity District Order 1925, and (Amendment) Orders 1931 & 1932, made under Sect. 7 of the Electricity (Supply) Act 1919. Dissolved 1 Apr. 1948, undertaking being vested in British (later Central) Electricity Authority and South-Eastern Area Board under Electricity Act 1947. Holders of securities were entitled to receive British Electricity 3% guaranteed stock (1968–73), as follows in respect of each £1 unit of capital held:

	£	s.	d.	
5% redeemable stock	1	3	8⅖	
4½% redeemable stock	1	3	0	
3¼% redeemable stock	1	1	0	**1949**

London & Hull Soap Works Ld. Regd. 1906. Vol. liq. 22 Oct. 1907. Struck off Register 3 Sept. 1918 .... ***1908**

London & India Docks Co. Inc. by Special Act 1864 as London & St. Katherines Docks Co.; name changed Jan. 1901. Under Port of London Act 1908 the undertaking was transferred to Port of London Authority. Stockholders were entitled to Port of London stock as follows—A, B and C debenture stocks—100% A Port stock; A and B preference and preferred ordinary stocks—100% B Port stock; deferred ordinary stock—75% B Port stock. Holders of mortgage bonds continued to hold their bonds **1909**

London & Jagersfontein Diamond Mining Co. Ld. Regd. 1881. Vol. liq. 26 Jan. 1883. Final meeting return regd. 30 Dec. 1896 .... **1884**

London & Johannesburg Syndicate Ld. Regd. 1895 as Anglo-French Gold Mining Syndicate Ld. Assets acquired by Westralian, London and Johannesburg Co. Ld., for £15,000 in cash and £25,000 in fully-paid shares. Removed from Register 1908 .... **1891**

London & Johannesburg Trust Co. Ld. Regd. 1905. Vol. liq. 30 Sept. 1910. Final meeting return regd. 16 Apr. 1921 .... **1919**

London & Lancashire Paper Mills Co. Ld. Regd. 1886. Court Orders: to wind up 12 Feb. 1887; to dissolve 28 July 1894.......... ***1888**

London & Leicester Hosiery Co. Ld. Regd. 1881. Vol. liq. Mar. 1887. Final meeting return regd.7 Nov.1889 .... **1888**

London & Lisbon Cork Wood Co. Ld. Regd. 1863. Removed from Register 1908 .... **1903**

London & Liverpool Ashanti Ld. *See* West African Securities Co. Ld.

London & Liverpool Bank of Commerce Ld. Regd. 1879 as German Bank of London Ld.; name changed Feb. 1913. In Mar. 1923 all the shares were purchased by British Overseas Bank Ld at £10 5*s*. per share of £10. Vol. liq. and undertaking transferred 14 May 1923. Struck off Register 3 Oct. 1941 **1942**

London & Liverpool Trust p.l.c. Regd as private company 22 Mar. 1973; converted into a public company 4 Apr. 1973; winding-up order 26 Nov. 1984. Official Receiver released 7 Aug. 1986 .... **1987–8**

London & Maikop Oil Corporation Ld. Regd. 1910. Vol. liq. 14 Aug. 1919. Final meeting return regd. 11 Oct.1922.......... **1920**

London and Manchester Plate Glass Co. Ld. Regd. 1863. Vol. liq. 30 Aug. 1894. Final meeting return regd. 20 Mar. 1897 .... **1895**

London & Manchester Warehouse Co Ld. Regd. 1898. Removed from Register 1901 .... ***1902**

London & Middlesex Freehold Estates Co Ld. Regd. 1896. Vol. liq. 17 June 1920. Final meeting return regd. 18 Apr. 1928 .... **1921**

London & Middlesex Land Co. Ld. Regd. 1884. Removed from Register 1889 .... ***1885**

London & Midland Insurance Co. Ld. Regd. 1908 as Midland Insurance Co. Ld.; name changed to Midland & Textile Insurance Co. Ld. in Nov. 1910 and as above in May 1913. Court order to wind up 13 Mar. 1917. Part of business was acquired by British General Insurance Co. Ld. Struck off Register 15 Oct. 1935 .... **1936**

London & Midland Oil Co. Ld. Regd 1920. Vol. liq. 23 Jan. 1936. Final meeting return regd. 6 Nov.1936 **1936**

London & Midland Transport Co. Ld. *See* Allied Road Transports (Southern) Ld.

London & Montrose Shipbuilding & Repairing Co. Ld. Vol. liq. 12 Mar. 1923. Final meeting return regd. 15 Apr. 1932 .... ***1924**

**See Stock Exchange Year-Book.*

VOL. FOR

London & New Zealand Exploration Co. Ld. Regd. 1896. Removed from Register 1906 .... **1904**

London & North British Plate Glass Insurance Co. Ld. Regd. 1911. Vol. liq. 21 Aug. 1916. Undertaking acquired by Liverpool & London & Globe Insurance Co. Ld. Final meeting return regd. 30 Oct. 1917 ***1917**

London & North Eastern Railway Co. Inc. 1 Jan. 1923 as an amalgamated company under provisions of Railways Act 1921. Dissolved 23 Dec. 1949: undertaking vested 1 Jan. 1948 in British Transport Commission under Transport Act 1947. Holders of securities were entitled to receive British Transport 3% guaranteed stock 1978—88 as follows in respect of each £100 of capital stock held:

	£	s.	d.
Def. ord. stock	3	12	6
5% pref. ord. stock	7	6	3
4% 1st guaranteed stock	106	17	6
4% 2nd guaranteed stock	100	15	0
4% 1st preference stock	58	5	0
5% red. pref. stock (1955)	103	13	9
4% 2nd pref. stock	29	5	0
3% debenture stock	103	5	0
4% deb.stock	118	7	6
4½% sinking fund deb. stock	107	10	0
West Hartlepool "primary charges", Hartlepool & Clarence C pref. shares	86	0	0

London & North-West American Mortgage Co. Ld. Regd. 1886. Debenture holders received £64 14*s*. 6*d*. per £100 debenture at July 1915; further payments (if any) not known. Vol. liq. 12 Nov. 1915. Final meeting return regd. 17 Feb. 1916 .... **1916**

London and North Western District Bank Co. Ld. Regd. 1893. Vol. liq. 26 Feb. 1894. Final meeting return regd. 28 Dec. 1906 .... **1895**

London & North Western Fire Insurance Co. Ld. Regd. 1879 as North Western Fire Insurance Co. Ld.; name changed Apr. 1881. Vol. liq. 18 Nov. 1884. Final meeting return regd. 21 Dec. 1892 .... **1885**

London and North Western Railway Co. Inc. by Special Act 1846. In 1922 the undertaking was merged into the London & North Western Railway Co. (inc. 1922). Stockholders were entitled to stock of the like class, denomination and amount in the new company **1924**

London and North Western Railway Co. Inc. by Special Act 1922. In 1923 the undertaking was merged into the London Midland & Scottish Railway Co. (inc. 1923), in which company stockholders were entitled to stock as follows:

For each £100 *held*		*L. M. & S.*
3% Debenture	£75	4% Debenture
Cons. 4% Guaranteed	£100	4% Guarant'd
Cons. 4% Preference	£100	4% Preference
4% Pref. (1902).	£100	4% Preference
4½% Red. Pref.*	£100	4½% Red. Pref*
5% Red. Pref (1916)§	£100	5% Red. Pref.§
Consolidated	£100	Ordinary

*Red. 30 June 1925. §Red. 30 June 1926. **1924**

London & Northern Assets Corporation Ld. Regd. 18 Vol. liq. 22 Dec. 1898. Amalgamated with London and Northern Debenture Corporation Ld., for 59,736 fully-paid shares of £2 and £1,255 in shares or cash. Struck off Register 20 Nov. 1928 .... **1899**

London & Northern Bank Ld. Regd. 1898. In liquidation under supervision of Court in 1899. Removed from Register 1909 .... **1900**

London & Northern Debenture Corporation Ld. Regd. 1889. Assets were acquired in 1900 by London and Provincial Trust Ld. Struck off Register 1927 ...... **1945**

London & Northern Steamship Co. Ld. Regd. 1890. Vol. liq. 30 Nov. 1916. The assets were sold in Feb. 1917 to private company of same name, which went into liquidation in Dec. 1917. Final meeting return regd. 21 Mar. 1917 .... **1918**

London & Ontario Investment Co. Inc. Canada 1876. Reconstructed 1899 as Canada Permanent and Western Canada Mortgage Corporation (later Canada Permanent Mortgage Corporation) **1900**

London & Orange Free State Exploration Co. Ld. *See* Koffyfontein Estates Ld.

London & Overseas Investment Co. Ld. Regd. 1902 as Eastern Mortgage & Agency Co. (1902) Ld.; name changed Dec. 1928. In Apr. 1968 the undertaking was transferred to Union Commercial Investment Co. Ld. in which company shareholders were entitled to receive 21 ordinary shares of 5*s*. per 20 ordinary shares held and £9 preference stock per £8 preference stock held; the 4½% debenture stock was repaid at par in May 1968. Company is to be dissolved under Section 208 of the Companies Act 1948 .... **1970**

London & Pacific Petroleum Co. Ld. Regd. 1889. Vol. liq. 27 Apr. 1916. Final meeting return regd. 19 Sept. 1928 .... ***1917**

London & Paris Banking Corporation Ld. Regd. 1874. Removed from Register 1903 .... ***1876**

London & Paris Investments Ld. Regd. 1965. In Apr. 1970 the undertaking was transferred to Capital & National Trust Ld. in which company shareholders were entitled to receive 20 ordinary and 4 "B" ordinary shares of 5*s*. for every 83 ordinary shares of 5*s*. held. Company is to be dissolved under Section 208 of tbe Companies Act 1948 .... **1970**

London & Pretoria Financial Co. Ld. Regd. 1890. Capital returned to contributories—£6 per share of £5 at Oct. 1902; further payments (if any) not known. Removed from Register 1904 .... **1903**

London & Provincial Assurance Co. Ld. *See* London General Insurance Co. Ld.

London & Provincial Automatic Machine Co. Ld. Regd. 1893. Vol. liq. Oct. 1908. Removed from Register 1910 .... **1909**

London and Provincial Bank Ld. *See* London Provincial & South Western Bank Ld.

London & Provincial Dairy Co. Ld. Regd. 1897. Vol. liq. 9 Feb. 1914. Final meeting return regd. 23 June 1916 **1915**

London & Provincial Dance Halls Ld. Regd. 1924. Struck off Register 1933 .... **1938**

London and Provincial Drapery Exchange Ld. Regd. 1888. Vol. liq. 7 Oct. 1889. Final meeting return regd. 22 Mar. 1893 .... **1890**

London & Provincial Electric Lighting & Power Generating Co. Ld. Regd. 1882. Court Orders: to wind up 3 Nov. 1883; to dissolve 16 Nov. 1893 .... **1884**

London & Provincial Electric Theatres Ld. Regd. 1909. Court Order to wind up under Trading with Enemy (Amendment) Act (1916) 2 Oct. 1918. Dissolved under that Act on 19 Sept. 1919 .... **1916**

London & Provincial Fire Insurance Co. Ld. Regd. 1881. Vol. liq. 2 Mar. 1891. Business was acquired by London and Lancashire Fire Insurance Co. (later London & Lancashire Insurance Co.), in which company shareholders were entitled to 1 share of £25 (credited with £2 10*s*. paid) for every 30 shares of £9 (10*s*. paid) held. Final meeting return regd. 4 May 1896 .... **1892**

London & Provincial House, Land, Mortgage & Investment Co. Ld. Regd. 1882. Removed from Register 1889 .... ***1883**

London & Provincial Law Investment Corporation Ld. *See* Law Fidelity & General Insurance Corporation Ld.

London & Provincial Motor Bus & Traction Co. Ld. Regd. 1906 as Provincial Motor Bus and Traction Co. Ld.; name changed May 1906. Vol. liq. 24 June 1907. Undertaking and assets were acquired by Vanguard Motorbus Co. Ld., in which company shareholders were entitled to 1 preference share of £1 and ¼ ordinary share of £1 for each ordinary share of £1 held, or $\frac{3}{10}$ ordinary share of £1 for each deferred share of 1*s*. held. Removed from Register 1912 .... **1908**

London & Provincial Rubber Co. Ld. *See* Warne (William) (Holdings) Ld.

London & Provincial Trust p.l.c. (The). Regd. 31 Jan. 1900; re-registered1981. Vol. liq. 8 Nov. 1982. Company unitised. Ordinary holders received units in Save & Prosper United States Growth Fund; Save & Prosper Japan Growth Fund; Save & Prosper South East Asia Growth Fund on basis of 234·41157p net asset value per ordinary share of 25p. Preference holders received units in Save & Prosper Special Situations Fund at 46·7p per unit. First and final distribution of 3·142p per share made 11 Mar. 1985. Final meeting held 17 June 1985. Amounts paid into Companies' Liquidation Account; £4,866 in respect of unclaimed dividends (pre liquidation); L13,207 in respect of distributions (post liquidation) **1986–7**

London & St. Katherines Docks Co. *See* London & India Docks Co.

London & San Francisco Bank Ld. Regd. 1880. Vol. liq. 23 Feb. 1905. Assets and liabilities were acquired by Bank of California, San Francisco. A return of £16 12*s*. 6*d*. per share of £10 was anticipated. Final meeting return regd. 22 Nov. 1905 .... **1906**

London and Scottish Banking and Discount Corporation Ld. Regd. Edinburgh 1892. Court Orders: to wind up 16 Jan. 1895; to dissolve 1 Aug. 1900.............. **1896**

London & Silverton Mining Co. Ld. Regd. 1882. Vol. liq. 10 Mar. 1887 for reconstruction as Silverton Mines Ld. Final meeting return regd. 23 Jan. 1894 .... **1892**

London & South African Agency Ld. Regd. 1901. Vol. liq. 17 Dec. 1908. Final meeting return regd. 27 July 1928 .... ***1910**

**See Stock Exchange Year-Book.*

VOL. FOR

London & South African Development & Finance Co. Ld.
Regd. 1896. Vol. liq. Mar. 1907. Removed from Register 1911 1908

London & South African Exploration Co. Ld. Regd. 1870. Undertaking was acquired in 1899 by De Beers Consolidated Mines Ld., for £1,625,000. Capital returned to contributories—£16 per share of 10s. Removed from Register 1905 1900

London & South African Land Finance & Trust Agency Ld. Regd. 1886. Struck off Register 31 Dec. 1895 1899

London & South Coast Hotels Ld. Regd. 1902. Removed from Register 1910 1905

London & South Coast Land Co. Ld. Regd. 1888. Vol. liq. 29 Apr. 1922. Final meeting return regd. 15 Dec. 1922 1923

London & South Coast Motor Service Ld. Regd. 1905. Vol. liq. 18 Mar. 1914. Final meeting return regd. 24 Sept. 1917 1915

London and South Western Railway. Inc. by Special Act 1834 as London & Southampton Railway Co.; name changed by Act of 1839. In 1923 the undertaking was merged into the Southern Railway Co., in which company stockholders were entitled to stock as follows:

For each £100 held	S. R.
3% Loans (Deb. Bonds)	£100 Term. Loans
3% Debenture (A)	£75 4% Debenture
3% Debenture (Cons.) .	£75 4% Debenture
4% Cons. Guaranteed .	£80 5% Gtd. Pref.
4% Cons. Preference ...	£80 5% Preference
4% Perp. Preference (1884)	£80 5% Preference
3½% Preference	£70 5% Preference
5% Red. Pref. (1914) ...£100 5% Red. Pref. (1924)
Undivided Ordinary. {	£80 Pref. Ordinary £94 11s. 3d. Def. Ord.
Prefd. Conv. Ord	£80 Prefd. Ordinary
Defd. Conv. Ord.	£94 11s. 3d. Defd. Ord. 1924

London and Southampton Railway Co. See London and South Western Railway

London & Southern Counties Investment Advance and Discount Co. Ld. Regd. 1886. Court Order to wind up 7 Aug. 1906. Liquidator released 3 Apr. 1913. Struck off Register 10 Oct. 1916 1907

London & Southern Garages Ld. Regd. 1927. Vol. liq. 28 Nov. 1929. Final meeting return regd. 30 June 1930 *1930

London & Southern Super Cinemas Ld. Regd. 1929. Vol. liq. (members') 17 June 1943. Undertaking acquired by Odeon Theatres Ld. (later Rank Organisation Ld.). Capital returned to contributories—2s. 6d. per share of 1s. to shareholders other than Odeon Theatres Ld.; any remaining assets were to be distributed to that company. £520 8s. 6d. was paid into Companies' Liquidation Account. Final meeting return regd. 26 Sept. 1946 1947

London and Staffordshire Fire Insurance Co. Ld. Regd. 1870 as Staffordshire Fire Insurance Co. Ld.; name changed 10 July 1880. Vol. liq. June 1883. Undertaking was absorbed by Lancashire Insurance Co. Final meeting return regd. Mar. 1884 1884

London & Suburban Co-operative Stores Ld. Regd. 1890. Removed from Register 1907 1896

London & Sudan Mining Syndicate Ld. Regd. 1903. Vol. liq. 2 Feb. 1926. Final meeting return regd. 20 Apr. 1926 1922

London & Tilbury Lighterage Co. Ld. See Tilbury Contracting & Dredging Co. Ld.

London & Tilbury Lighterage, Contracting & Dredging Co. Ld. See Tilbury Contracting & Dredging Co. Ld.

London and Tilbury Steam Laundry Co. Ld. Regd. 1885. Vol. liq. Mar. 1889. Final meeting return regd. Mar. 1890 1890

London & Universal Bank Ld. Regd. 1889. Court Order to wind up 6 May 1896. Liquidator released 9 May 1902. Struck off Register 21 Feb. 1911 1897

London & Vancouver Finance & Development Co. Ld. Regd. 1897. Removed from Register 1907 1903

London & Wales Steel Construction Co. Ld. Regd. 1926. Vol. liq. (members') 2 June 1939. Capital returned to contributories—£18,449 18s. 1d. Final meeting return regd. 9 Apr. 1942 1940

London & West African Gold Syndicate Ld. Regd. 1900. Reconstructed 1904 as New Nimrod Co. Ld., in which company shareholders were entitled to 1 share of £1 (credited as fully-paid) for each share of £1 held. Removed from Register 1905 1905

London and West Australian Syndicate Ld. Regd. 1894. Reconstructed as company of same name. Shareholders were entitled to 160 fully-paid shares of £1 for each ordinary share of £50 held after subscribing for 40 shares, or 24 fully-paid shares of £1 for each deferred share of £1 held after subscribing for 6 shares 1905

VOL. FOR

London & West Australian Syndicate Ld. Regd. 1896. Removed from Register 1912 1906

London & West of England Trust & Investment Corporation Ld. Regd. 1890. Court Order to wind up 9 Feb. 1896. Removed from Register 21 June 1907 *1893

London & Western Australian Exploration Co. Ld. Regd. 1894. Vol. liq. 25 Nov. 1895. Reconstructed as company of same name. Shareholders received 2 shares of £1 and £1 in cash for each ordinary share of £1 held or £1 in cash and 90 shares of £1 for each deferred share of £1 held. Final meeting return regd. 30 Apr. 1896 1909

London & Western Australian Exploration Co. Ld. Regd. 1895. Vol. liq. July 1909. Reconstructed as London Australian and General Exploration Co. Ld., in which company shareholders were entitled to 1 share of 5s. (credited as fully-paid) for each share of £1 held and an option (since expired) over further shares. Removed from Register 1910 1910

London & Western Australian Investment Co. Ld. Regd. 1899. Vol. liq. 9 Aug. 1907. Undertaking and assets were acquired by London and Australian Investment Co. Ld. in which company shareholders were entitled to 1 share of 10s. (credited with 8s. paid) for each share of £1 held. Final meeting return regd. 23 Jan. 1909 1908

London & Westminster Bank Ld. Established 1834. Regd. 1880. Vol. liq. 24 Aug. 1909. Undertaking was amalgamated with London and County Banking Co. Ld. (later Westminster Bank Ld.), in which company shareholders were entitled to 2½ shares of £20 (credited with £5 paid) for each share of £100 (£20 paid) held 1910

London & Westminster Bread Co. Ld. Regd. 1889. Taken over by Bread Union Ld. Removed from Register 1906 *1890

London & Westminster Contract Corporation Ld. Regd. 1896. Court Order to wind up 2 Aug. 1897. Struck off Register June 1931 1932

London & Westminster Game Supply Association Ld. See West London & Provincial Electric General Investment Co. Ld.

London & Westminster Investment Trust Ld. Regd. 1899 as West London & Provincial Electric Supply Co. Ld.; name changed 1926 to West London & Provincial Electric & General Trust Ld. and to present title 1956. Undertaking and assets were acquired on 1 Feb. 1971 by Cardinal Investment Trust Ld. in which company ordinary shareholders received 1 deferred share for each share held and preference stockholders like amount of similar preference stock; 3½% debenture holders received like amount of 3½% A debenture stock and 4½% debenture holders like amount of 4½% Second debenture stock. Company will be dissolved under Section 208 of Companies Act 1948 1971

London & Westminster Stores Ld. See West London & Provincial Electric & General Investment Co. Ld.

London and Westralian Mines and Finance Agency Ld. Regd. 1895. Vol. liq. Dec. 1899 for reconstruction as company of same name. Shareholders were entitled to 3⅓ shares of £1 for each ordinary share of £1 held, or 41⅔ shares of £1 for each deferred share of 6s. 8d. held. Removed from Register 1901 1905

London & Westralian Mines & Finance Agency Ld. Regd. 1900. Shareholders were entitled to 1 share in Sons of Gwalia Ld., for every 20 shares of £1 held; a small cash distribution was anticipated. Removed from Register 1906 1905

London & Yorkshire Accident Insurance Co. Ld. See Lancashire & Yorkshire Insurance Co. Ld.

London & Yorkshire Bank Ld. Regd. 1872. Re-regd. 1880. Vol. liq. 4 June 1903. Undertaking acquired by Union of London & Smiths Bank Ld., in which company shareholders were entitled to one share of £100 (credited with £15 10s. paid) for every 6 shares of £9 10s. (£2 10s. paid) held plus 10s. in cash for every share held 1904

London & Yorkshire Steam Trawling & Fish Carrying Co. Ld. Regd. 1898. Vol. liq. 1902. Removed from Register 4 Oct. 1907 *1904

London & Yorkshire Trust Holdings Ld. Formerly Anglo Allied Traders Ld., Anglo Allied Ld., London & Yorkshire Trust Ld. Vol. winding-up order 2 Aug. 1986

London Artizans & Labourers' Dwellings Co. Ld. Regd. 1880. Removed from Register 5 July 1889 .... *1884

London Ashanti Gold Mining Co Ld. Regd. 1900. Vol. liq. 25 Oct. 1906. Four concessions were purchased by Ashanti Quartzite Gold Mining Co. Ld in which company shareholders were entitled to 1 share of 4s. (credited as fully-paid) for every 2 shares of £1 held and 2 shares of 4s. (credited with 2s. paid) for every 3 shares held. Final meeting return regd.7 Apr.1915 1907

VOL. FOR

London Ashanti Syndicate Ld. Regd. 1900: Undertaking was acquired by London Ashanti Gold Mining Co. Ld., in which company shareholders were entitled to 1 share of £1 (credited with 15*s.* paid) and 1 fully-paid share for each share of £1 held. Removed from Register 1905 1906

London Associated Electricity Undertakings Ld. Regd. 1935. Dissolved 1 Apr. 1948, undertaking being vested in British (later Central) Electricity Authority under Electricity Act 1947. Holders of securities were entitled to receive British Electricity 3% guaranteed stock (1968–73) as follows in respect of each £1 unit of capital held:

	£	s.	d.
6% preference stock	1	8	7
4½% preference stock	1	5	11
Ordinary stock	1	9	6

1949

London Associated Reinsurance Corporation Ld. Regd. 1919. Vol. liq. Oct. 1932. Undertaking was acquired by London Assurance. Capital returned to contributories—£64,300 in cash, and £290,197 in investments. £230 8*s.* 1*d.* was paid into Companies' Liquidation Account. Final meeting return regd. 18 Dec. 1934 1933

London Bank of Australia Ld. Regd. 1893. Vol. liq. 23 June 1921. Undertaking was acquired by English, Scottish and Australian Bank Ld. Holders of ordinary shares of £22 10*s.* (£10 paid) were entitled to 5 shares of £25 (£12 10*s.* paid) in purchasing company for every 9 ordinary shares held; a cash payment of £1 per partly-paid ordinary share was made. Holders of fully-paid ordinary shares of £22 10*s.* were entitled to £24 10*s.* per share in cash. Holders of preference shares of £10 were entitled either to £13 per share in cash or 5 shares of £25 (credited with £12 10*s.* paid) for every 9 preference shares held; a cash distribution of £2 per preference share was made. 1922

London Bank of Central America Ld. Regd. 1893 as Bank of Nicaragua Ld.; name changed Dec. 1894. Vol. liq. 18 Jan. 1918. Capital returned to contributories—£1 1*s.* per share of £1 at Feb. 1918; further payments (if any) not known. Final meeting return regd. 16 Feb. 1921 1918

London Bank of Commerce Ld. Regd. 1872. Vol. liq. 3 June 1876. Final meeting return regd. 30 May 1877 *1877

London Bank of Mexico & South America Ld. Regd. 1877 as Pacific Bank Ld.; name changed July 1877. Vol. liq. 25 Oct. 1912. The undertaking and assets were acquired by Anglo-South American Bank Ld., in which company shareholders were entitled to 1 share of £10 (credited with £5 paid) *plus* £8 in cash for each share of £10 (£6 paid) held. Final meeting return regd. 24 July 1914 1913

London Bank of Utah Ld. Regd. 1877. Court Orders: to wind up June 1884; to dissolve Feb. 1889 1885

London Banking Association Ld. Regd. 1872. Vol. liq. July 1884. Final meeting return regd. 13 Sept. 1886 1885

London Banking Corporation Ld. Regd. 1890 as London Banking and Assets Corporation Ld.; name changed July 1892. Vol. liq. 4 Nov. 1896. Final meeting return regd. 23 Dec. 1897 1897

London Banking Corporation Ld. Regd. 1896. Court Order to wind up 19 Dec. 1911. Liquidator released 30 July 1942 1912

London Barge Owning Co. Ld. Regd. 1878. Business taken over by Thames Barge Co. Ld. Removed from Register 1887 .... *1887

London, Birmingham & Manchester Insurance Co. Ld. Regd. 1899. Removed from Register 1911 1903

London Border & General Trust Ld.. Regd. 1928. On 21 Oct. 1963 undertaking was acquired by Border & Southern Stockholders Trust Ld., in which company preference stockholders received 105 5% preference shares per £100 preference stock; ordinary stockholders received 8 ordinary shares per 9 held; and the 3½% debenture stock was exchanged for a like amount of 3½% stock of that company. Dissolved on 21 Feb. 1964 under Sec. 208 of Companies Act 1948 1965

London Borneo Tobacco Co. Ld. Regd. 1888. Reconstructed 1892 as New London Borneo Tobacco Co. Ld in which company shareholders were entitled to 10 shares of £1 (credited with 15*s.* paid) for each share of £10 held. Removed from Register 1903 .. 1908

London Brick Co. Ld. Regd. 1900. Undertaking acquired by London Brick Co. & Forders Ld. (later London Brick Co. Ld.). Struck off Register 1923 . 1945

London Bridge Securities Ld. Regd. as private company 22 Oct. 1970 as I. R. T. Group Ld.; converted into public comapny 6 Dec. 1970; name changed 22 Jan. 1973; winding-up order made 3 May 1976; dissolved and struck off Register 6 Oct. 1983 1984–5

London, Brighton and South Coast Railway. Inc. by Special Act 1846. In 1923 the undertaking was merged into the Southern Railway Co., in which company stockholders were entitled to stock as follows:

For each £100 held		*S. R.*
4% Debenture	£100	4% Debenture
4½% Debenture	£112 10*s.*	4% Deb.
5% Cons. Guaranteed .	£100	5% Gtd. Pref.
Certs of Contingent Rights in respect of late 6% Stock No. 1	£20	Ordinary B
5% Cons. Preference	£100	5% Preference
5% 2nd Cons. Pref.	£100	5% Preference
Undivided Ordinary.	£60	Prefd. Ordinary
	£88 10*s.* 9*d.*	Defd. Ord.
Preferred Ordinary	£120	Prefd. Ordinary
Deferred Ordinary	£177 1*s.* 6*d.*	Defd. Ord.

1924

London Caledonian Re-insurance Co. Ld. Regd. 1907 as Legal and General Fire Office Ld.; name changed Nov. 1920 to Anglo American Assurance Co. Ld. and as above in Feb. 1922. Vol. liq. 22 Oct. 1926. All issued capital held by London-Caledonian Trust Ld. Final meeting return regd. 23 Jan. 1933 1927

London-Caledonian Trust Ld. Regd. 1912. as Middlesex Trust Ld.; name changed Jan. 1913. Vol. liq. 6 July 1927. Final meeting return regd. 14 Dec. 1932. Court Order declared dissolution void 11 May 1933. Final meeting return regd. 12 July 1933 1928

London, Camberwell & Dulwich Tramways Co. Inc. by Special Act 1882. Undertaking purchased by London County Council in 1904. 1905

London Canadian Investment Corporation. Inc. in Quebec 1928. In Aug. 1959 United Corporations Ld. offered to purchase the net assets of this corporation for $7,985,483, to be satisfied by the issue of 80,290 5% cumulative redeemable preferred shares 1959 series of $30 and 178,131 class B shares of no par value. The merger was completed on 23 Dec. 1959. This corporation was placed in liquidation and the said shares distributed to shareholders in the following proportions:—for each preferred share: two 5% preferred shares plus, in respect of the common share issuable under outstanding warrants attached to certificates, one-half B share; for each class A share: one and one-half 5% preferred shares plus, in respect of the common share issuable under outstanding warrants attached to certificates, one-half B share; for each common share (including the 46,151 common shares held by Montreal Trust Co. in respect of warrants attached to certificates for outstanding preferred and class A shares); one-half class B share; in addition holders of common shares received a liquidation payment of $1·26 per share. The outstanding $371,060 3% notes were repaid at par on 25 Jan. 1960 1962

London Canning Co (1901) Ld. Regd. 1901. Vol. liq. 16 Sept. 1904. Removed from Register 1905.......... 1905

London Central Markets Cold Storage Co. Ld. Regd. 1898 as Smithfield Market Cold Storage Co. Ld.; name changed Mar. 1889. Vol. liq. (members') Jan. 1930. Capital returned to contributories—£265,447 3*s.* 9*d.* Final meeting return regd. 21 Nov. 1930 .. 1930

London Central Motor Omnibus Co. Ld. Regd. 1906. The undertaking and assets were acquired by New Central Omnibus Co. Ld., in which company shareholders were entitled to 5 shares of £1 (credited as fully-paid) for every 4 shares of £1 held; a cash distribution was anticipated. Removed from Register 1913 1912

London Chartered Bank of Australia. Inc. by Royal Charter 1852. Reconstructed 1893 as London Bank of Australia Ld., in which company shareholders were entitled to 1 ordinary share of £22 10*s.* (credited with £15 paid) for every share of £20 held 1908

London, Chatham and Dover Railway Co. Inc. by Special Act 1853 as East Kent Railway Co.; name changed by Act of 1859. In 1923 the undertaking was merged into the Southern Railway Co., in which company stockholders were entitled to stock as follows:—

For each £100 held		*S.R.*
Terminable Deb.	£100	Term. Loans
4½% Sheerness Rent . Charge	£56¼	4% Debenture
	£9	5% Gtd. Pref.
	£36	5% Preference
For each £100 *held*		*S.R.*
4½% Arbitration Deb.	£56¼	4% Debenture
	£9	5% Gtd. Pref.
	£36	5% Preference
4½% B Debenture	£56¼	4% Debenture
	£9	5% Gtd. Pref.
	£26	5% Preference
4% Debenture (1879)	£50	4% Debenture
	£8	5% Gtd. Pref.
	£32	5% Preference

**See Stock Exchange Year-Book.*

VOL. FOR

4% Debenture (1883)
{ £50 4% Debenture
{ £8 5% Gtd. Pref.
{ £32 5% Preference

3% Debenture (1890)
{ £37½ 4% Debenture
{ £6 5% Gtd. Pref.
{ £24 5% Preference

3% Debenture (1899)
{ £37½ 4% Debenture
{ £6 5% Gtd. Pref.
{ £24 5% Preference

3½% Debenture........
{ £43¾ 4% Debenture
{ £7 5% Gtd. Pref.
{ £28 5% Preference

4% Debenture (1909)
{ £50 4% Debenture
{ £8 5% Gtd. Pref.
{ £32 5% Preference

3½% Shortlands Gtd. ....
{ £70 5% Preference
{ £27 5% Preference

4½% Arbitration Pref.
{ £43½ Prefd. Ord.
{ £31¼ Ordinary A

4½% 2nd Preference..
{ £60 Prefd. Ordinary
{ £43¾ Ordinary A

Arbitration Ordinary £52½ Ordinary B   **1924**

London Cinematograph (1909) Ld. Regd. 1909. Vol. liq. Nov. 1910. Removed from Register 1913 ....   **1911**

London Clinic & Nursing Home Ld. Regd. 1929. Court Order to wind up 22 June 1936. Struck off Register 27 Jan. 1942 ....   **1942**

London Coliseum Ld. Regd. 1902. Vol. liq. May 1906. Properties were acquired by Coliseum Syndicate Ld., for £114,975 in 1st debenture stock, £47,259 in 2nd debenture stock and £31,000 in cash. Removed from Register 1909 ....   **1907**

London Commercial & Cripplegate Bank Ld. Established 1819. Regd. 1879 as Cripplegate Bank Ld.; name changed 1 Jan. 1900. Business acquired by Union Bank of London Ld. later Union of London & Smiths Bank Ld.—Removed from Register 1907   **1901**

London Commercial Sale Rooms, Ld. Formed under Deed of Settlement 4 Feb. 1811; regd. as limited 1890. Vol. liq. (members') 30 May 1947. £1 16s. 10½d. per share (of £1) was returned to contributories. Final meeting return regd. 17 Mar. 1953. £151 was paid into Companies' Liquidation Account ..   **1954**

London Consumers' Pure Sanitary Milk Co. Ld. Regd. 1886. Court Orders: to wind up Mar. 1890; to dissolve 1 Aug. 1893 ....   **1890**

London Co-operative Supply Stores Ld. Regd. 1890. Court Order to wind up Jan. 1893. Removed from Register 1907 ....   **1893**

London Cordage, Sack & Wagon Cover Co. Ld. Regd. 1883. Removed from Register 1906 ....   ***1885**

London Corn Exchange Co. Inc. by Special Act 1826. Under Special Act of 1929 the undertaking and assets were acquired by Corn Exchange Co. **1930**

London County & Westminster Bank Ld. See Westminster Bank Ld.

London County Commercial Re-insurance Office Ld. Regd. 1910 as London County Commercial Fire & Accident Office Ld.; name changed Feb. 1911. Vol. liq. 28 Feb. 1919. Final meeting return regd. 2 Apr. 1929 ....   **1919**

London County Westminster & Parr's Bank Ld. See Westminster Bank Ld.

London, Deptford & Greenwich Tramways Ld. Inc. by Special Act 1879 as Southwark & Deptford Tramways Co.; name changed 1891. Regd. as limited 1905; resolution to wind up Apr. 1905, the undertaking having been sold to London County Council in 1905. Capital returned to contributories—£1 10s. per half share (preferred or deferred) of £5; further payments (if any) unknown **1906**

London Direct Transit Service Ld. Regd. 1912 as Home Counties Transport Co. Ld.; name changed 21 Apr. 1913. Vol. liq. 11 Oct. 1916. Final meeting return regd. 6 July 1917 ....   ***1914**

London Distilling & Yeast Co. Ld. Regd. 1895. Vol. liq. May 1900. Removed from Register 1901 ....   **1901**

London Distributing Kitchens Ld. Regd. 1901. Removed from Register 1904 ....   **1904**

London District Empire Palaces Ld. Regd. Edinburgh 1898. Reconstructed 1899 as Moss Empires Ld. (later M. E. Theatres, Ld.) in which company debenture stockholders were entitled to £105 debenture stock for every £100 stock held. Shareholders were entitled to (a) 6 preference and 6 ordinary shares of £5 (all fully-paid) subject to payment of £5 for every 10 ordinary shares of £5 held, (b) 11 preference and 11 ordinary shares of £5 (all fully-paid) plus £2 10s. in cash for every 20 ordinary shares of £5 held or (c) 11 fully-paid preference shares of £5 (subject to payment of 10s.) for every 10 preference shares of £5 held. Removed from Register 1909 ..   **1900**

London Drapery Stores Ld. Regd. 1896. Removed from Register 1908 ....   **1899**

London, Dublin & Paris Gold Coast Syndicate Ld. See London, Dublin Gold Coast Syndicate Ld.

London, Dublin Gold Coast Syndicate Ld. Regd. 1901 as London, Dublin & Paris Gold Coast Syndicate Ld.; name changed Dec. 1910. Vol. liq. 2 Nov. 1920. Undertaking and assets were acquired by Winnebah Tinfields Ld., in which company shareholders were entitled to 2 fully-paid shares of 5s. for each share of 10s. held. Final meeting return regd. 23 Mar. 1922 ....   **1921**

London, East India & Colonial Life Assurance Co. Ld. Regd. 1870. Placed in liquidation in 1883. Final meeting return regd. 25 Mar. 1884 ....   ***1884**

London, Edinburgh & Glasgow Assurance Co. Ld. Regd. 1881. Vol. liq. Aug. 1910. Undertaking and assets were acquired by Pearl Life Assurance Co. Ld. (later Pearl Assurance Co. Ld.), in which company shareholders were entitled to 1 preference share of £1 (credited as fully-paid) for each ordinary or preference share of £1 held; a cash bonus was anticipated. Removed from Register 1911 ....   **1911**

London Electric Omnibus Co. Ld. Regd. 1896. Vol. liq. 30 Jan. 1901. Final meeting return regd. 26 Mar. 1902 ....   **1901**

London Electric Railway Company. Inc. by Special Act 1897 as Brompton & Piccadilly Circus Railway Co.; name changed to Great Northern Piccadilly & Brompton Railway Co. by Act of 1902 and as above by Act of 1910. Undertaking (including all lands, works and other property, assets powers, rights &c.) was transferred under Act of 1933 to London Passenger Transport Board. Stockholders were entitled to stock in the Board as follows:

For every £100 Stock	L.P.T.B.
4% debenture	£88 17s. 9d. 4½% A
5% red. deb.1985–95	£100 5% A
4½% red. 2nd deb. 1942–72	£100 4½% T. F. A.
4% preference	£80 5% B
Cons. ordinary	£92 10s. C

After distribution of stock the company was to be dissolved **1934**

London Electric Supply Corpn. Ld. Regd. 1887. Dissolved 1 Apr. 1948, undertaking being vested in British (later Central) Electricity Authority and London Area Board under Electricity Act 1947. Holders of ordinary shares (of £1) and 6% preference shares (of £5) were entitled to receive, in respect of each share held, £1 11s. 4d. £6 10s. British Electricity 3% guaranteed stock (1968–73) respectively **1949**

London Electric Transport Finance Corporation Ld. Regd. 1935. Vol. liq. (members') 22 Dec. 1955. Capital returned to contributories—20s. per share (of £1). Royal Exchange Assurance (trustees for debenture holders) took over £359 6s. 4d. unclaimed redemption monies in Dec. 1955. Final meeting return regd. 29 Nov. 1956 ....   **1958**

London Electrical Cab Co. Ld. Regd. 1896. Removed from Register 1903 ....   **1901**

London Electricity Joint Committee (1920) Ld. See London Power Co. Ld.

London Electrobus Co. Ld. Regd. 1906. Vol. liq. 17 Jan. 1910. Final meeting return regd. 12 Mar. 1923 ....   **1910**

London Exchange Steamship Co. Ld. Regd. 1898. Vol. liq. May 1913. Capital returned to contributories—£7 8s. 3d. per share of £10; further payments (if any) not known. Removed from Register 1913 ....   **1914**

London Exhibitions Ld. Regd. 1894. Undertaking and assets were sold to Earl's Court Ltd. [later E. C. (Holdings) Ld.] for £35,000 in fully-paid shares of £1. Court Order to wind up 13 Dec. 1910. Liquidator released 15 Aug. 1914. Struck off Register 14 Feb. 1919 ....   **1911**

London Exploration Co. Ld. Regd. 1896. Removed from Register 1911 ....   **1908**

London Film Co. Ld. Regd. 1913. Vol. liq. (members') 25 Nov. 1931. 6% 1st mortgage debentures were repaid with accrued interest. Capital returned to contributories—£39,021 9s. 8d. plus 36,000 shares of 5s. in Williamson Film Printing Co. Ld. (in vol. liq.). Final meeting return regd. 2 Jan. 1934 ....   **1932**

London Financial Association Ld. Regd. 1863. Vol. liq. 3 Jan. 1896. Assets and liabilities were acquired by London & Middlesex Freehold Estates Co. Ld., in which company shareholders were entitled to 1 share of £10 (credited with £1 paid) or 15s. in cash for each share of £10 held. Final meeting return regd. 7 May 1896..   **1896**

London Financial Trust Ld. Regd. 1907. Vol. liq. 9 Jan. 1911. Final meeting return regd. 11 Mar. 1911 ....   ***1912**

See Stock Exchange Year-Book.

VOL. FOR

London Fish Co. Ld. Regd. 1902 as Fish Supper Co. Ld.: name changed June 1902. Vol. liq. July 1906. Removed from Register 1907 .... **1907**

London Fish Market & National Fishery Co. Ld. Name changed June 1902. Vol. liq. July 1906. Removed from Register 1907 .... **1907**

London, Foreign & Colonial Securities Ld. (Private Company) Regd. 1914. Vol. liq. (members') 2 Nov. 1977 .... **1978-9**

London Founders' Association Ld. Regd. 1883. Vol. liq. 3 June 1889. Final meeting return regd. 17 June 1898 **1890**

London Foundry Co. Ld. Regd 1915. Vol. liq. 2 Apr. 1924. Final meeting regd. 20 June 1925 .... **1925**

London Freehold & Leasehold Property Co. Ld. Regd. 1883. Vol. liq. (members') 2 Mar. 1936. Undertaking was acquired by House Property and Investment Co. Ld. Capital returned to contributories—£250 per share of £100 held. Final meeting return regd. 4 Mar. 1938 .... **1937**

London Fur & General Trust Ld. Regd. 1928. Vol. liq. (members') Apr. 1934. Undertaking and assets were acquired by Swears & Wells Ld., in which company shareholders were entitled to 1 preference share of £1 for every 2 preference shares of 10*s.* held or 1 ordinary share of £1 for every 4 ordinary shares of 10*s.* held. Final meeting return regd. 27 June 1935 **1935**

London Gaslight Co. Amalgamated with Gas Light & Coke Co., in 1883 .... **1884**

London Gate Steamship Co. Ld. Regd. 1898. Vol. liq. 16 May 1902. Absorbed by Dowgate Steamship Co. Ld. Final meeting return regd. 25 Mar. 1903 .... ***1902**

London General Assets Corporation Ld. Regd. 1892. Removed from Register 1904 .... **1899**

London General Cab Co. Ld. Regd. 1875. Vol. liq. Aug. 1887. Final meeting return regd. 21 Apr. 1890 .... **1888**

London General County Services Ld. *See* London General Omnibus Co. Ld. (regd. 1912)

London General Insurance Co. Ld. Regd. 1906 as London & Provincial Assurance Co. Ld.; name changed Feb. 1918. Winding-up order made 7 May 1935. No capital returned to contributories. Fund distributions (per £)—life 2*s.* bond investment 1*s.* 4*d.* Dividends (per £) 7*s.* Liquidator released 15 Sept. 1967. Struck off Register 1 Sept. 1972 .... **1969**

London General Investment Trust, Ld. Regd. 1889. Vol. liq. (members') 14 June 1974. Holders of deferred stock received on 14 June 1974 88·848 income units of New Count Income Fund for every 100 units of £1 and on 7 Jan. 1977 a final distribution of 1·546 income units for every 100 units of £1; preferred stockholders repaid at par 18 July 1974. Return of final meeting regd. 23 Feb. 1977. £59·80 paid into Companies' Liquidation Account in respect of unpaid dividends **1977-8**

London General Omnibus Co. Ld. Regd. 1858. Vol. liq. 18 July 1912 for reconstruction. The 4% debentures, C debenture stock and preference shares were redeemed at par; the B debenture stock was redeemed at 110% and the ordinary stock was redeemed at 275%. Final meeting return regd. 22 May 1922 .... **1913**

London General Omnibus Co. Ld. Regd. 1912. Undertaking (including land, works and other property, assets, powers, &c.) was transferred by Act of 1933 to London Passenger Transport Board. The following undertakings were included in the transfer—Acme Pullman Services Ld., Bucks Expresses (Watford) Ld., General Country Services Ld., Green Line Coaches Ld., Morden Station Garage Ld., Skylark Motor Coach Co. Ld. and Overground Ld. Holders of 4½% 1st debenture or 5% cumulative income debenture stocks were entitled to an equal amount of 4½% A or 5% B respectively. Holders of ordinary shares were entitled to £18 10*s.* C stock per share held. Final meeting return regd. 18 Dec. 1934 **1934**

London Gigantic Wheel Co. Ld. Regd. 1899. Vol. liq. 31 Jan. 1907. Final meeting return regd. 19 Oct. 1918 **1909**

London, Gloucestershire & North Hants Dairy Co. Ld. *See* Higgs (R.) & Son's Dairies Ld.

London Grain Elevator Co. Ld. Regd. 1898. Vol. liq. Dec. 1910. Undertaking was acquired by Port of London Authority for £95,000 in cash. Removed from Register 1911 .... **1911**

London Gull Lake Mines Ld. Regd. 1923. Vol. liq. (members') 2 Dec. 1936. Capital returned to contributories—4*s.* 4½*d.* per share of £1. Final meeting return regd. 31 Dec. 1937 .... **1937**

London, Hendon & Harrow Railway Co. Inc. by Special Act 1883. Line abandoned by Act of 1887 .... **1888**

London Hippodrome Ld. Regd. Edinburgh 1898. Reconstructed 1899 as Moss Empires Ld. (later M. E. Theatres Ld.). Shareholders were entitled either to 7 preference and 7 ordinary shares of £5 (all fully-paid) in new company (subject to payment of £5) for every 10 shares of £5 held or to 13 preference and 13 ordinary shares of £5 (all fully-paid) *plus* £2 10*s.* in cash for every 20 shares of £5 held. Debenture stockholders were entitled to £105 debenture stock in new company for every £100 stock held. Removed from Register 1909 .... **1900**

London Holeproof Hosiery Co. Ld. Regd. 1928. Vol. liq. (creditors') 30 Mar. 1939. Assets realised insufficient to pay unsecured creditors in full. Final meeting return regd. 11 Apr. 1941 .... **1941**

London Horse Repository Co. Ld. Regd. 1887 as Cox's Horse Repository Ld.; name changed May 1889. Vol. liq. 31 Mar. 1890. Final meeting return regd. 23 July 1891 .... **1891**

London House Trust Ld. Regd. 1898. Vol. liq. (members') 25 May 1936. Berkeley Property & Investment Co. Ld., were beneficial owners of all shares. Final meeting return regd. 11 Nov. 1938 .... **1937**

London Improved Cab Co. Ld. Regd. 1887. Receiver appointed in Aug. 1932; ceased to act May 1934. Assets realised insufficient to provide any return to debenture holders. Struck off Register 29 Oct. 1935 **1936**

London Industrial Finance Trust Ld. Regd. 1928. Vol. liq. (members') 22 Aug. 1933. Undertaking and assets were acquired by Mutual Finance Indemnity & Guarantee Corporation Ld. (later Mutual Finance Ld.). Capital returned to contributories—£69,291 18*s.* 2*d.* Final meeting return regd. 27 Oct. 1933 .... **1934**

London Industrial Finance Trust Ld. Regd. 1933. Winding-up order made 25 Nov. 1940. All shares owned by Charter Trust & Agency Ld. Struck off Register 13 Aug. 1965 .... **1941**

London Joint Stock Bank Ld. Established 1836. Regd. as unlimited 1873 and as limited 1882. Vol. liq. 30 Sept. 1918. Business was united with London City and Midland Bank Ld. (later Midland Bank Ld.), in which company shareholders were entitled to 4 shares of £12 (credited with £2 10*s.* paid) for each share of £100 (£15 paid) held **1919**

London Jute Works (1871) Ld. Regd. 1871. Vol. liq. 13 Apr. 1882. Final meeting return regd. 3 Dec. 1884 ***1882**

London Land Association Ld. Regd. 1896. Vol. liq. Dec. 1906. Removed from Register 1912 .... **1907**

London Land Co. Ld. Regd. 1880. Vol. liq. May 1887. Final meeting return regd. 11 May 1889 .... **1888**

London Langkat Syndicate Ld. Regd. 1909. Vol. liq. 29 Dec. 1921. Final meeting return regd. 15 Jan. 1924 **1922**

London Loan & Savings Co. of Canada. Inc. Canada 1877 as London Loan Co. of Canada; name changed 1906. In 1909 the undertaking was acquired by Huron & Erie Mortgage Corporation, which company assumed liability for the debentures. Shareholders were entitled to $35 in cash and 1 share in London Loan Assets Ld. for each share of$50 held **1930**

London Mail Ld. Regd. 1913. Vol. liq. 5 Sept. 1917. Final meeting return regd. 6 June 1918 .... **1918**

London Malayan Tin Trust Ld. Regd. 1928. Vol. liq. 14 Jan. 1930. Undertaking and assets were acquired by London Tin Syndicate Ld. (later London Tin Corporation Ld.), in which company shareholders were entitled to 3 shares of £1 (credited as fully-paid) for every 8 shares of £1 held. Final meeting return regd. 18 July 1931 .... **1930**

London Marine Steamship Co. Ld. Regd. 1901. Struck off Register 1922 .... **1914**

London Metal Banking Co. Ld. Regd. 1907. Vol. liq. 7 Dec. 1917. Final meeting return regd. 23 June 1923 **1918**

London Midland & Scottish & Great Western Railways Joint Committee. Dissolved 2 Apr. 1949; undertaking vested 1 Jan. 1948 in British Transport Commission under Transport Act 1947 .... **1949**

London Midland and Scottish Railway Co. Inc. 1 Jan. 1923 by North Western, Midland and West Scottish Group Amalgamation Scheme 1922. The undertaking was merged into the London Midland & Scottish Railway Company (inc. 1 July 1923). Holders of stock were entitled to stock of the like class, denomination and amount in the new Company . **1924**

London Midland & Scottish Railway Co. Inc. 1 July 1923 as an amalgamated company under provisions of the Railways Act 1921. Dissolved 23 Dec. 1949. undertaking vested 1 Jan. 1948 in British Transport Commission under Transport Act 1947. Holders of securities were entitled to receive British Transport 3% guaranteed stock 1978–88 as follows in respect of each £100 of capital stock held:

	£	s.	d.
Ord. stock	29	10	0
4% guaranteed stock	107	18	9
4% pref. stock	85	8	9
5% red. pref. stock (1955)	105	10	0
4% pref. stock (1923)	62	15	0

**See Stock Exchange Year-Book.*

VOL. FOR

	£	s.	d.	
4% deb. stock	118	13	9	
5% red. deb. stock (1952)	108	17	6	1949

London Midland and Scottish Stock Conversion Trust—constituted by trust deed in 1924—Wound-up by court order dated 19 July 1949. Holders of securities were entitled to receive British Transport 3% guaranteed stock 1978–88 in respect of each £100 stock held:

	£	s.	d.	
4% non-cum. preference stock	24	16	3·3517	
5% non-cum. preferred stock	5	19	1·2844	
deferred stock	1	9	9·3211	1952

London Mineral Waters Co. Ld. Regd. 1904. Vol. liq. Mar. 1906. Removed from Register 1911 .... **1907**

London Mortgage & Guarantee Society Ld. Regd. 1864. Removed from Register 1901 .... ***1889**

London Motor Co. Ld. Regd. 1900. Vol. liq. 15 July 1901. Final meeting return regd. 13. Jan. 1902 ..... **1902**

London Motor Omnibus Co. Ld. Regd. 1905. Vol. liq. 10 July 1907. Undertaking and assets were acquired by Vanguard Motorbus Co. Ld., in which company shareholders were entitled to 1·5 ordinary shares of £1 for each deferred share of 1*s.* held, or 1·45 preference shares of £1 and ·595 ordinary share of £1 in that company for each ordinary share of £1 held or £5 debenture stock in that company for each preference share of £5 held. Final meeting return regd. 2 Aug. 1912 .... **1908**

London Music Hall Ld. Regd. 1893. Struck off Register 24 Oct. 1916 .... ***1917**

London Nigerian Power Co. Ld. Regd. 1930. Vol. liq. (creditors') 29 Jan. 1936. No capital returned to contributories. Final meeting return regd. 6 Oct. 1936 .... **1936**

London Nigerian Tin Mines Ld. Regd. 1928 as London Nigerian Tin Trust Ld.; name changed 12 Jan. 1931. Vol. liq. (members) 31 Mar. 1939. Undertaking and assets were acquired by Amalgamated Tin Mines of Nigeria Ld., in which company shareholders were entitled to 1 share of 5*s.* (credited as fully-paid) for each share of 5*s.* held. Final meeting return regd. 3 Feb. 1941 .... **1940**

London Nigerian Tin Trust Ld. *See* London Nigerian Tin Mines Ld.

London Nitrate Co. Ld. Regd. 1887. Vol. liq. 21 Sept. 1926. The undertaking and assets were acquired by New Tamarugal Nitrate Co. Ld., in which company shareholders were entitled to $2\frac{1}{4}$ fully-paid shares of £1 for each share of £1 held. Final meeting return regd. 15 Oct. 1927 .... **1927**

London Non-Flammable Wood Co. Ld. Regd. 1899. Business acquired 1901 by Non-Flammable Wood and Fabrics Ld., for 97,500 fully-paid shares of £1 of which 63,460 were allotted to British Non-Flammable Wood Co. Ld. Removed from Register 1901 **1901**

London Offices Co. Ld. Regd. 1911. Vol. liq. (members') 1946. Final meeting return regd. 12 Oct. 1949 ..... **1920**

London Oil Development Co. (1902) Ld. Regd. 1902. Vol. liq. 12 July 1905. A return of 5*s.* in £ was made; further payments (if any) not known. Removed from Register 1907 .... **1906**

London Oil Syndicate Ld. Regd. 1910. Vol. liq. 31 Dec. 1915. Final meeting return regd. 25 Nov. 1916 .... **1916**

London Omnibus-Carriage Co. Ld. Regd. 1886. Vol. liq. 7 June 1906. Removed from Register 1908 .... **1907**

London Oxygen Consumers Ld. Regd. 1922. Vol. liq. (members') 16 Apr. 1931. Final meeting return regd. 29 July 1931 .... **1933**

London Panorama Co. Ld. Regd. 1889. Vol. liq. 28 Jan. 1891. Court Order to continue winding up under supervision 7 Feb. 1891. Final meeting return regd. 18 Jan. 1892 .... **1892**

London Parcels Delivery Co. Ld. Regd. 1863. Vol. liq. (members') 21 Feb. 1934. Capital returned to contributories—£10 2*s.* per share of £3. Final meeting return regd. 30 Aug. 1934 .... **1934**

London, Paris & American Bank Ld. Regd. 1884. Vol. liq. June 1908. Business was acquired by London, Paris National Bank of San Francisco (inc. under American Laws) in which company shareholders were entitled to 1 share of $100 for each share of £20 (£16 paid) held. Removed from Register 1909 ..... **1909**

London-Paris Oil & Rubber Trust Ld. Regd. 1910. Vol. liq. 22 Jan. 1914. Final meeting return regd. 29 July 1921 .... **1914**

London Paris Securities Corporation Ld. Regd. 1895. Vol. liq. June 1905. Undertaking and assets were acquired by Trust Union Ld. Stockholders were entitled to £5 in cash and £30 in ordinary shares and £60 in preference shares of £10 (or £5 in cash and £45 in ordinary shares and £45 in preference shares) for every £100 ordinary stock held or £65 in ordinary shares for each £100 deferred ordinary stock held. Removed from Register 1907 .... **1906**

London Passenger Transport Board. Inc. by London Passenger Transport Act 1933. Dissolved 23 Dec. 1949: undertaking vested from 1 Jan. 1948 in British Transport Commission under Transport Act 1947. Holders of securities were entitled to receive British Transport 3% guaranteed stock 1978–88 as follows in respect of each £100 of capital held:

	£	s.	d.	
$4\frac{1}{2}$% A stock (1985–2023)	133	3	9	
5% A stock (1985–2023)	142	3	9	
5% B stock (1965–2023)	128	3	9	
C stock (1956 or thereafter)	67	3	9	
$4\frac{1}{2}$% L.A. stock (1975–2023)	128	10	0	1949

London Plate Glass Insurance Co. Ld. Regd. 1885. All shares owned by Yorkshire Insurance Co. Ld. Struck off Register 9 Aug. 1946 .... **1945**

London Platino-Brazilian Telegraph Co. Ld. Regd. 1878. Vol. liq. (members') 1 Nov. 1932. Capital returned to contributories—£5,963 6*s.* 7*d.* in cash *plus* investments and assets in specie. £290 15*s.* 10*d.* was paid into Companies' Liquidation Account in respect of unclaimed dividends and £560 6*s.* 10*d.* in respect of unclaimed assets. Final meeting return regd. 1 May 1933 .... **1933**

London Portland Cement Co. Ld. Regd. 1876. Undertaking acquired by Associated Portland Cement Co. Ld. Removed from Register 1901 .... ***1885**

London Power Co. Ld. Regd. 1920 as London Electricity Joint Committee (1920) Ld.; name changed 1925. Dissolved 1 Apr. 1948, undertaking being vested in British (later Central) Electricity Authority and London Area Board under Electricity Act 1947. Holders of securities were entitled to receive British Electricity 3% guaranteed stock (1968–73), as follows in respect of each £1 unit of capital held:—

	£	s.	d.	
5% redeemable debenture stock	1	0	$10\frac{2}{5}$	
4% redeemable debenture stock	1	0	$8\frac{4}{5}$	
$3\frac{1}{2}$% redeemable debenture stock	1	0	$7\frac{1}{5}$	
$3\frac{1}{4}$% redeemable debenture stock	1	0	$7\frac{1}{5}$	1949

London Power Omnibus Co. Ld. Regd. 1905. Vol. liq. 22 July 1907. Removed from Register 1912 .... **1908**

London Premier Omnibus Co. Ld. Regd. 1912 as Premier Omnibus Co. Ld.; name changed May 1914. Amalgamated with Greater Omnibus Services Ld., in 1914. Struck off Register 17 Sept. 1920 .... **1915**

London Printing and Publishing Alliance Ld. Regd. 1889. Vol. liq. 11 Dec. 1891. Court Order to continue winding up under supervision 8 Jan. 1892. Final meeting return regd. 31 Mar. 1897 .... **1893**

London Property Co. Ld. Regd 1894. Vol. liq. 20 May 1913. Final meeting return regd. 11 Apr. 1916 .... **1914**

London Property Investment Tr. Ld. Regd. 30 Sept. 1893. Vol. liq. 21 Mar. 1978 .... **1962**

London Prospecting Co. Ld. Regd. 1896. Undertaking and assets were acquired by Development and Finance Co. Ld., in which company shareholders were entitled to 5 shares of £1 (credited as fully-paid) for every 6 shares of £1 held. Removed from Register 1909 .... **1900**

London Provincial & South Western Bank Ld. Established 1864 as Provincial Banking Corporation. Regd. 1871 as London and Provincial Bank Ld.; name changed Jan. 1918. Vol. liq. 2 Oct. 1918. Business was acquired by Barclays Bank Ld., in which company shareholders were entitled to $6\frac{1}{4}$ shares of £2 (credited with £1 paid) for each share of £10 (£5 paid) held **1919**

London Public Omnibus Co. Ld. Regd. 1927. Vol. liq. 23 Dec. 1929. Undertaking was acquired by London General Omnibus Co. Ld. Final meeting return regd. 29 Dec. 1930 .... ***1930**

London Pure Milk Association Ld. Regd. 1908. Vol. liq. 30 Dec. 1910. Court Order to wind up 21 Feb. 1911. Liquidator released 14 Aug. 1913. Struck off Register 3 Sept. 1918 .... **1911**

London Restaurants Ld. Regd. 1887. The property was sold under foreclosure. 1st debenture-holders received about 12*s.* 6*d.* in £. Removed from Register 1901 .... **1901**

London Restaurants Ld. Regd. 1923. Vol. liq. (creditors') 23 Dec. 1940. Capital returned to contributories—$9\frac{3}{4}$*d.* per preference share of 6*s.* £1,420 was paid into Companies' Liquidation Account in respect of unclaimed distributions. Final meeting return regd. 3 May 1962 .... **1964**

London Rice Mill Co. Ld. Regd. 1865. Vol. liq. Feb. 1889. Final meeting return regd. 29 Aug. 1890 ..... **1901**

London (Riverside) Cold Storage Co. Ld. Regd. 1901. Removed from Register 1911 .... **1906**

London Riverside Fish Market Co. Inc. 1882 and 1885. Company was acquired by Corporation of London **1904**

London Road-Car Co. Ld. Regd. 1880 as London and District Omnibus Co. Ld.; name changed April

VOL. FOR

1881. Vol. liq. Dec. 1882. Final meeting return regd. 31 Jan. 1887 ...... **1883**

London Road-Car Co. Ld. Regd. 1883. Vol. liq. 29 June 1909. The undertaking and assets were sold to London General Omnibus Co. Ld. in which company preference shareholders were entitled to an equal amount of preference shares; debenture stockholders were entitled to an equal amount of B debenture stock. Holders of ordinary shares were entitled to £3 10s. in ordinary shares of new company for every £6 ordinary share held. Final meeting return regd. 25 July 1912 ...... **1910**

London Scottish American Trust Ld. Regd. 1889. By scheme of arrangement 17 Aug. 1977 undertaking and assets transferred to United States Debenture Corporation Ld. holders received 147 ordinary stock units for every 100 ordinary stock units and £1 3·85% preference for every £1 5% preference. Holders of 4% perpetual debenture stock and 4% debenture stock 1979–84 received a like amount of 4½% irredeemable 2nd debenture stock and 4½% 3rd debenture stock 1979–84 respectively. Dissolved without winding up 21 Jan. 1978 ...... **1978-9**

London Scottish Exploration Syndicate Ld. Regd. 1900. Vol. liq. 13 Jan. 1913. Final meeting return regd. 14 July 1915 ...... **1913**

London Scottish Investment Trust Ld. Regd. in Edinburgh 1909. Undertaking and assets were acquired on 31 Dec. 1970 by Pentland Investment Trust Ld. in which company 5% preferred and 4½% preferred stockholders received respectively £102 5% preference and £102 4½% preference stock for each £100 held and deferred shareholders received 185 ordinary shares for every 100 shares held. 4½%, 4% and 3½% debenture stockholders received like amounts of identical stock. Company dissolved by Order of the Court on 26 July 1971 ...... **1971**

London Share & Debenture Co. Ld. Regd. 1888. Vol. liq. Aug. 1907. Removed from Register 1909 ...... **1908**

London Sherardizing Co. Ld. Regd. 1906. Vol. liq. 14 Jan. 1911. Struck off Register 30 Jan. 1923 ...... **1911**

London Shipping Exchange Ld. Regd. 1892. Vol. liq. 10 May 1900. Absorbed by Baltic Mercantile and Shipping Exchange Ld. Shareholders were repaid in cash. Final meeting return regd. 10 Aug. 1900 .... **1901**

London Ship's Stores Co. Ld. Regd. 1880. Court Orders: to wind up 26 Jan. 1884; to dissolve 16 Apr. 1887 **1885**

London Shoe Co. Ld. Regd. 1899. Vol. liq. (members') 6 Feb. 1936. Undertaking transferred to company of same name. Preference shareholders were entitled to 1 fully-paid preference share of 10s. in new company, plus 6d. in cash for every preference share of £1 held; ordinary shareholders were given option (since expired) to subscribe for ordinary shares at par. £17 3s. was paid into Companies' Liquidation Account. Final meeting return regd. 29 Dec. 1936 **1936**

London Singapore & Java Bank Ld. See Rubber & Mercantile Corporation Ld.

London Small Property Trust Ld. Regd. 1874. Reconstructed 1902 as London Small Property Trust (1902) Ld. Removed from Register 1903 ...... **1902**

London Smelting Co. Ld. Regd. 1921. All preferred and deferred capital owned by Amalgamated Smelters Ld. Receiver appointed July 1927; ceased to act July 1932. Struck off Register 19 Oct. 1934 ...... **1927**

London Southern Tramways Co. Inc. by Special Act 1882. Undertaking transferred to London County Council in 1906 ...... **1908**

London Standard Motor Omnibus Co. Ld. Regd. 1906. Vol. liq. June 1908. Removed from Register 1909 **1909**

London Steam Collier & Coal Co. Ld. See Original Hartlepool Collieries Co. Ld.

London Steam Omnibus Co. Ld. See Motor Traction Co. Ld.

London Steam Boat Co. Ld. Regd. 1875. Vol. liq. Mar. 1884. Reconstructed as River Thames Steamboat Co. Ld. Final meeting return regd. 22 Sept. 1886 **1885**

London Stereoscopic & Photographic Co. Ld. Regd. 1885. Shareholders were entitled to 1 share of 10s. (credited as fully-paid) in London Stereoscopic Co. Ld., for each share held; the whole of the debentures and one third of debenture stock were redeemed, the remaining two thirds debenture stock was entitled to an equal amount of debenture stock in new company. Removed from Register 1913 ...... **1913**

London Stereoscopic Co. Ld. Regd. 1912. Vol. liq. 2 Oct. 1922. Final meeting return regd. 24 Dec. 1929 .... **1923**

London Stockholders Investment Trust Ld. Regd. 1928 as London & County Stockholders Investment Trust Ld.; name changed Feb. 1929. Vol. liq. (members') 22 Sept. 1949. 4½% and 4% debenture stocks were repaid at 105% and 102½% respectively. Capital returned to contributories (per share of £1)—

VOL. FOR

preference, £1 5s.; ordinary, £2 0s. 11·84d. Final meeting return regd. 30 Oct. 1951 ...... **1953**

London Street Railway Co. Inc. Ontario 1873. The outstanding 5% 1st mortgage gold debentures were redeemed in 1951 ...... **1952**

London Street Tramways Co. Inc. by Special Act 1870. Undertaking sold and all assets realised in 1911... **1911**

London Suburban House Property Co. Ld. Regd. 1880. Removed from Register 1905 ...... *****1883**

London Sumatra Rubber & Produce Estates Ld. Regd. 1909. Vol. liq. 31 May 1916. Final meeting return regd. 28 Sept. 1917 ...... **1916**

London Super-Aeration Ld. Regd. 1901. Reconstructed in 1904 as London Mineral Waters Co. Ld. in which company shareholders were entitled to 1 share of 10s. (credited with 9s. paid) for each share of £1 held. Removed from Register 1906 ...... **1906**

London Taverns Co. Ld. Regd. 1863 as London Tavern Co. Ld.; name changed 1876. Vol. liq. Feb. 1908. Removed from Register 1909 ...... **1909**

London Theatre of Varieties Ld. Regd. 1908. Vol. liq. 18 Apr. 1928. Shareholders were entitled to £1 in cash and £1 7s. 6d. in Notes of Argyll Trust Ld. for each share of £1 held. Final meeting return regd. 11 Mar. 1932 ...... **1930**

London, Tilbury & Southend Railway Co. Authorised by Special Act 1852. Inc. by Special Act 1862 ...... **1913**

London Tin Corporation Ld. Regd. as private company 1925 as London Tin Syndicate Ld.; converted public company 1927; name changed Jan. 1930. By scheme of arrangement 30 July 1976 all capital acquired by London Tin (Malaysia) Sdn. Bhd. for shares. Wound-up 4 July 1978 ...... **1977-8**

London Traction Haulage Co. Ld. Regd. 1899. Vol. liq. (members') 17 Mar. 1937. Capital returned to contributories—£1 0s. 11d. per share of £1. Final meeting return regd. 10 June 1937 ...... **1893**

London Traders Ld. Regd. 1885. Vol. liq. 14 June 1887. Final meeting return regd. 31 Aug. 1892 ...... *****1888**

London Trading Bank Ld. Regd. 1878 (under Industrial & Provident Societies Act 1876); regd. under the Companies Acts 1905. Court Order to wind up Dec. 1910. Struck off Register Dec. 1934 ...... **1935**

London Tramways Co. Ld. Regd. 1870. Vol. liq. 1899. Undertaking was sold to London County Council in 1899. Removed from Register 1901 ...... **1899**

London Tramways' Omnibus Co. Ld. Regd. 1882. Properties taken over by South London Tramways Co. Removed from Register 1906 ...... **1886**

London United House Property Investment Association Ld. Regd. 1881. Vol. liq. 1886. Removed from Register 1905 ...... **1887**

London United Investment Co. Ld. Regd. 1895 as United Goldfields Exploration & Investment Co. Ld.; name changed Feb. 1900. Vol. liq. May 1907. Removed from Register 1908 ...... **1908**

London United Tramways Ld. Regd. 1894. Undertaking acquired by London United Tramways (1901) Ld. for £600,000 ordinary shares, £450,000 debenture stock and £240,000 in cash. Removed from Register 1908 ...... **1908**

London United Tramways Ld. Regd. 1901 as London United Tramways (1901) Ld.; name changed Apr. 1907. Undertaking (including all lands, works and other property, assets, powers, &c.) was transferred by Act of 1933 to London Passenger Transport Board. Holders of securities were entitled to stock in Board and cash as follows:

For every £100 held		L.P.T.B.
4% 1st mort. deb.		£50 5% B
		£25 C
		15s. in cash
For each share held		L.P.T.B.
preference of £1		6s. C
ordinary of 5s.		7¼d. C

Final meeting return regd. 18 Dec. 1934 ...... **1934**

London United Trust Ld. Regd. 1929. Vol. liq. (members') 25 July 1938. Capital returned to contributories—£3,725 3s. 7d. plus certain investments distributed in specie. Final meeting return regd. 6 July 1939 **1939**

London Varnish & Enamel Co. Ld. Regd. 1907 as Conrad Wm. Schmidt (F. A. Glaeser) Ld.; name changed Jan. 1917. Vol. liq. 23 Mar. 1928. Undertaking acquired by Jenson & Nicholson Ld. (later Jenson & Nicholson Group Ld.). Capital returned to contributories—£1 per share of £1 in Apr. 1928; further payments (if any) not known. Final meeting return regd. 20 May 1931 ...... **1929**

London Venture Corporation Ld. Regd. 1908. Vol. liq. 20 Dec. 1912. Shareholders were entitled to 1 share of 4s. (credited with 2s. 9d. paid) in a new company for each share of 4s. held. Final meeting return regd. 1 July 1915 ...... **1913**

See Stock Exchange Year-Book.

London Wall Investment Trust Ld. Regd. 1918 as Pusing Rubber & Tin Ld.; name changed 27 Sept. 1961 to Commodity & Associated Investments Ld. and as above 11 Aug. 1964. Vol. liq. (members') 21 June 1966. Capital returned to contributories—4s. 4·2984648d. per ordinary or deferred ordinary share of 2s. Final meeting return regd. 6 Nov. 1967 ..... **1969**

London Wall Trust Ld. Regd. 1909. Vol. liq. 21 Mar. 1919. Final meeting return regd. 5 Mar. 1921 ..... **1919**

London, Walthamstow & Epping Forest Railway Co. Inc. by Special Act 1894. Construction authorised to be abandoned by Act of 1900. ..... **1901**

London Warehouse Co. Ld. Regd. 1874. Removed from Register 1904 ..... ***1878**

London White Lead Manufacturing Co. Ld. Regd. 1889. Removed from Register 1906 ..... **1893**

London Woollen Co. Ld. Regd. 1896. Reconstructed 1912 as company of same name. Shareholders were entitled to 2 shares of 5s. (credited with 3s. 9d. paid) for each ordinary or preference share of £1 held. Removed from Register 1912 ..... **1913**

London Woollen Co. Ld. Regd. 1912. Court Order to wind up 29 July 1924. Liquidator released 16 June 1930. Struck off Register 31 Jan. 1933 ..... **1933**

London Woollen Co. Ld. Regd. 1924. Receivers appointed in Mar. 1930. Assets realised insufficient to meet claims of debenture holders. Struck off Register 30 Jan. 1934 ..... **1934**

London, Woolwich & Clacton-on-Sea Steamboat. See Belle Steamers Ld.

Londonderry & Enniskillen Railway Co. Inc. by Special Act 1852. Under Special Act 1883 undertaking was amalgamated with Great Northern Railway Co. (Ireland). Holders of £100 A, B, C or original stocks received £100, £100 19s. 4d., £100 19s. 4d., or £137 11s. 5d. Great Northern (Ireland) Londonderry guaranteed stock **1884**

Londonderry Collieries Ld. Regd. 1899. Vol. liq. (members') 2 Oct. 1953. The collieries, &c. having been vested in National Coal Board. Capital returned to contributories—£100 for preference share (of £100) and £214 10s. per ordinary share (of £100); certain assets were distributed in specie. Final meeting return regd.15 Jan.1965 ..... **1966**

Londonderry Consols Ld. Regd. 1895. Struck off Register 8 Dec. 1899 ..... **1902**

Londonderry Extended Gold Mining & Exploration Co. Ld. See Kalgoorlie Prince Gold Mining Co. Ld.

Londonderry Gold Mine Ld. Regd. 1894. Vol. liq. 30 Mar. 1899. Reconstructed as company of same name. Shareholders were entitled to 1 share of 10s. (credited with 7s. 6d. paid) for every 5 shares of £1 held. Final meeting return regd. 29 Mar. 1900 ..... **1905**

Londonderry Gold Mine Ld. Regd. 1899. Vol. liq. 29 Sept. 1905. Reconstructed as Field's Reward Gold Mines Ld. in which company shareholders were entitled to 1 share of 10s. (credited with 8s. paid) for each share of 10s. held. Final meeting return regd. 7 Dec. 1906 ..... **1906**

Londonderry (Seaham to Sunderland) Railway. Inc. by Special Act 1863. Purchased by North Eastern Railway Co. for £400,000 ..... **1901**

Lone Hand Gold Mines Ld. Regd. 1895. Vol. liq. 23 Jan. 1899. Reconstructed 1899 as Phoenix Gold Mines Ld. in which company shareholders were entitled to 2 shares of 10s. (credited with 8s. paid) for each share of £1 held. Final meeting return regd. 25 July 1903 ..... **1903**

Lone Hand Gold Mines Ld. Regd. 1934. Assets were sold by Receiver. Struck off Register 28 Feb. 1939 ..... **1940**

Lone Pine Mining and Milling Co. of Montana. Reconstructed in 1891 as Jay Hawk and Lone Pine Consolidated Mining Co. Ld. Shareholders received 120,000 fully-paid shares of £1. $125,000 in cash and £1,600 in debentures **1894**

Lone Ridge Gold Mine Ld. Regd. 1896. Removed from Register 1909 ..... **1902**

Lonely Reef Gold Mining Co. Ld. Inc. in Southern Rhodesia 1910. Vol. liq. (members') 11 July 1944. Capital returned to contributories—5s. 4d. per share of £1 ..... **1948**

Long Acre Press Ld. Regd. 1925. Vol. liq. 10 June 1932. The goodwill and licence to print "The People" were acquired by Odhams Properties Ld., in which company shareholders were entitled to 5 ordinary shares of £1 for each A ordinary share of £1 held or 1 ordinary share of £1 for every 2 B ordinary shares of £1 held or 1 8°/₀ participating preference share of £10 for each preference share of £10 held. Final meeting return regd. 23 Aug. 1933 ..... **1933**

Long & Co. (Southsea) Ld. Regd. 1924. Vol. liq. (members') 1 Dec. 1941. All ordinary and majority of preference shares owned by Brickwood & Co. Ld.

(later Brickwoods Ld.). Final meeting return regd. 1 July 1943 ..... **1945**

Long & Pocock Ld. Regd. 1916. Vol. liq. (members') 6 Jan. 1931. Capital returned to contributories— £22,177 19s. 3d. Final meeting return regd. 25 Jan. 1934 ...·..... **1931**

Long Eaton Gas Co. Regd. as limited 1864; reinc. by Special Act 1901. Dissolved 1 May 1949, undertaking being vested in East Midland Area Gas Board under Gas Act 1948. Holders of securities were entitled to receive British Gas 3% guaranteed stock 1990–95 as follows in respect of each £100 unit, unless otherwise stated, of security held:—

	£	s.	d.
A stock (7% stand)	188	0	0
B stock (5% stand)	157	0	0
5% pref. shares (of £10)	11	10	0
5⅛% red. deb. stock	104	10	0
5% perp. deb. stock	126	10	0 **1952**

Long Island Railroad, North Shore Branch. Inc. New York 1892. Acquired in 1921 by Long Island Railroad Co. The 1st consolidated mortgage 5% bonds were taken over by acquiring company **1921**

Long John Syndicate Ld. Regd 1906. Vol. liq. May 1909. Removed from Register 1909 ..... **1910**

Long Meadow Mills Ld. Regd. 1917. Vol. liq. 16 Sept. 1920. Undertaking acquired by Carpet Trades Ld. (later John Crossley—Carpet Trades Holdings Ld.). Final meeting return regd. 15 June 1921 ..... **1936**

Long Melford & Hadleigh Light Railway Co. Inc. (under Light Railways Act 1896) by order of Light Railway Commissioners confirmed by Board of Trade 1901. Powers expired 1906 ..... **1903**

Long Range (Newfoundland) Slate Quarries Ld. Regd. 1906. Receiver for A debenture holders appointed in Sept. 1909. Struck off Register 19 Feb. 1937 ..... **1938**

Long Reef Gold Mining Co. Ld. Regd. 1895 at Kinambia (Wealth of Nations) Ld.; name changed Mar. 1899. The property sold by auction realised only sufficient to pay mortgage and expenses. Removed from Register 1905 ..... **1905**

Long Sutton & Sutton Bridge Gas Co. Ld. Regd. 1856 as Long Sutton Gas & Coke Co. Ld. Dissolved 1 May 1949, undertaking being vested in East Midland Area Gas Board under Gas Act 1948. Holders of securities were entitled to receive British Gas 3% guaranteed stock 1990–95 as follows in respect of each £100 unit, unless otherwise stated, of security held:

	£	s.	d.
Ord. shares (of £10)	9	0	0
6% 1st mort. debs. A	105	0	0
4% 1st Mort. debs. B	100	10	0
6% 2nd mort. debs. £39 2s. 3d. repaid)	65	0	0
5% 3rd mort. debs.	100	0	0 **1952**

Long (W. & E.) (Dairy Farmers) Ld. Regd. 1885 as Alliance Dairy Co. Ld.; name changed May 1920. Vol. liq. (members') 28 Jan. 1931. £20 17s. 10d. was paid into Companies' Liquidation Account. Final meeting return regd. 25 Jan. 1934 ..... **1931**

Longfellow Gold Syndicate Ld. Regd. Edinburgh 1898. Vol. liq. Mar. 1902. Final meeting return regd. 14 Nov. 1902 ..... **1903**

Longmore (William) & Co. Ld. Regd. Edinburgh 1880. Winding-up order 10 June 1949. Liquidator released 12 Feb. 1959. Struck off Register 17 Feb. 1959 ... **1960**

Longmynd Hotel Ld. Regd. 1901 as Church Stretton Hydropathic Hotel Ld.; name changed Jan. 1919. Vol. liq. 17 Dec. 1928. Final meeting return regd. 9 Dec. 1929 ..... **1910**

Longridge Gas Co. Ld. Regd. 1866. Dissolved 1 May 1949, undertaking being vested in North Western Area Gas Board under Gas Act 1948. Holders of ordinary shares (of £5) were entitled to receive £9 10s. British Gas 3% guaranteed stock 1990–95 for each share held **1952**

Long's Hotel Ld. Regd. 1888. Vol. liq. 2 Mar. 1899. Final meeting return regd. 8 Dec. 1899 ..... **1900**

Longton, Adderley Green & Bucknall Railway Co. Inc. by Special Act 1866. By Special Act 1894 undertaking was transferred to North Staffordshire Railway Co. for £22,500 ..... **1895**

Longton Hall Co. Ld. Regd. 1889. Struck off Register 14 May 1897 ..... **1899**

Longwood and Slaithwaite Gas Co. Inc. by Special Act 1875 as Longwood Gas Co.; name changed 1914. Under Huddersfield Gas Act 1919 the undertaking was transferred to the Corporation. Preference shareholders were entitled to 95% of their holding in cash; ordinary shareholders were entitled to cash at par. The liabilities and loan debts were assumed by the Corporation **1920**

VOL. FOR

Lonsdale Investment Trust Ld. Regd. 1898 as J. & J. Lonsdale & Co. Ld.; name changed May 1931. Vol. liq. (members') 8 July 1947; undertaking acquired by Lonsdale Investment Trust Ld. (regd. 1947—later Kleinwort Benson Investment Trust Ld.) in which company shareholders were entitled to 27 ordinary shares of £1 for every 10 ordinary shares; 5 preference shares of £1 for each 5% preference share and 15 preference shares of £1 for every 4 6% preference shares; further distributions made of 1 ordinary share of £1 of the new Lonsdale Investment Trust Ld. for 5 old ordinary shares; 1 ordinary stock unit of 5s. of the new Lonsdale Investment Trust Ld. for 5 old ordinary shares; 18·111 ordinary shares of 25p of Kleinwort, Benson, Lonsdale Ld. for every 160 old ordinary shares; cash distributions made of 1s. 6d. and 0·65p per share. Final meeting return regd. 23 Dec. 1974. .... **1975-6**

Looe Electricity Co. Ld. Regd. 1926. Vol. liq. (members') 14 Feb. 1935. Capital returned to contributories—8s. 1·7d. per share of £1. Final meeting return regd. 18 Nov. 1935 .... **1936**

Looe Gas & Coke Consumers Co. Ld. Regd. 1865. Dissolved 1 May 1949, undertaking being vested in South Western Area Gas Board under Gas Act 1948. Holders of securities were entitled to receive, British Gas 3% guaranteed stock 1900–95 as follows in respect of each £1 unit, unless otherwise stated, of security held:

	£	s.	d.
Ord shares	1	10	6
6% ptpg. pref. shares (of £10)	16	10	0
4½% pref. shares	1	1	8
4% deb. stock (per £100)	102	10	0
4½% deb. stock (per £100)	112	10	0	**1952**

Lord (Cyril) Ld. Regd. in Belfast 23 June 1945 and converted into public company 10 May 1954. Winding-up order 13 Jan. 1969. Dissolved 19 June 1989. Ordinary and preference shares accepted by the Inland Revenue to be of negligible value from 26 Nov. 1968. Outstanding £1,500,000 7¼% debenture stock repaid at par with accrued interest 27 May 1969. Total distribution to unsecured creditors amounted to £532,946 on admitted claims of £1,260,017 .... **1988-9**

Lord Ross & Co. (Broadheath) Ld. See Radium Polishes Ld

Lorenz Ammunition & Ordnance Co. Ld. See British Munitions Co. Ld.

Lorna's Luck Ld. Regd. 1902. Vol. liq. June 1907. Removed from Register 1911 .... **1908**

Lorrain Trout Lake Mines Ld. (No Personal Liability). Inc. in Ontario 20 Mar. 1923. Resolutions passed on 19 June 1943 authorised sale of property for $5,000 and a winding up of company. No return was made to shareholders and the company was dissolved 8 Nov. 1943 .... **1944**

Lorraine Glass Co. Ld. Regd. 1881. Vol. liq. Jan. 1885. Final meeting return regd. 22 Apr. 1886 .... **1886**

Lost Property Insurance Co. Ld. See Property Insurance Co. Ld.

Lostwithiel & Fowey Railway Co. Inc. by Special Act 1862. Under Lostwithiel & Fowey Railway Act 1892 the Cornwall Mineral Railway Co. purchased undertaking for £40,000 4% preference stock, £45,000 ordinary stock, and £974 in cash **1893**

Lostwithiel Gas Light & Coke Co. Ld. Regd. 1858. Dissolved 1 May 1949, undertaking being vested in South Western Area Gas Board under Gas Act 1948. Holders of securities were entitled to receive British Gas 3% guaranteed stock 1990–95 as follows:

	£	s.	d.
Ord. shares (of £5)	7	10	0
Pref. B shares (of £1)	1	10	0
Ord. C shares (of £1)	1	10	0	**1952**

Lotery (H.) & Co. Ld. See H. L. (Clothiers) Ld.

Lothammer Gas Manufacturing Co. Ld. Regd. 1889. Court Orders: to wind up Mar. 1890; to dissolve 11 Aug. 1893 .... **1891**

Lothian Coal Co. Ld. Regd. Edinburgh 1890. Vol. liq. (members') 27 Feb. 1953. Capital returned to contributories—£4 18s. 6·725d. per ordinary share of 5s. Final meeting return regd. 13 Feb. 1956 .... **1957**

Lothians Electric Power Co. Inc. by Special Act 1904. Dissolved 1 Apr. 1948, undertaking being vested in British (later Central) Electricity Authority and South-East Scotland Area Board under Electricity Act 1947. Holders of ordinary shares (of £10) were entitled to receive £18 15s. British Electricity 3% guaranteed stock (1968–73), in respect of each share held **1949**

Lots Road Power House Joint Committee. Inc. by Act of 1911. Undertaking (including all lands, works and

VOL. FOR

other property. assets, powers. &c.), was transferred by Act of 1933 to London Passenger Transport Board. Holders of Metropolitan District and London Electric Railways Joint power house rent charge stock were entitled to £88 17s. 9d. 4½% A stock in Board for every £100 stock held. After distribution of stock the committee was to be dissolved **1934**

Loughborough & District Light Railway Co. Inc. (under Light Railways Act 1896) by order of Light Railway Commissioners confirmed by Board of Trade 1901 **1903**

Loughborough & Sheepshed Railway Co. Inc. by Special Act 1899. Powers expired 1904 .... **1909**

Loughborough Gas Co. Established 1836. Inc. 1868. Undertaking acquired by Corporation **1900**

Loughrea and Attymon Light Railway Co. Ld. Regd. 1885 under the Tramways and Public Companies (Ireland) Act 1883. In 1925 the undertaking was merged into the Great Southern Railways Co., in which company shareholders were entitled to £125 4% Preference Stock for every £100 held **1925**

Louis d'Or (Main Reef) Gold Mining Co. Ld. Regd. 1890. Reconstructed 1893 as New Louis d'Or (Main Reef) Gold Mining Co. Ld., in which company shareholders were entitled to 1 share of £1 (credited with 18s. paid) for each share of £1 held. Removed from Register 1912 .... **1895**

Louis Moore Proprietary Mines Ld. Inc. Transvaal 1909. The London office was closed in June 1911 **1912**

Louise & Co. Ld. Regd. 1895. Vol. liq. 27 July 1927. Final meeting return regd. 11 Dec. 1934 .... **1928**

Louth & East Coast Railway Co. Inc. by Special Act 1872. Undertaking was transferred to Great Northern Railway Co. for £87,000 .... **1909**

Louth & Lincoln Railway Co. Inc. by Special Act 1866. Under Great Northern Railway Co. Act 1882 undertaking was transferred to that company. Holders of preference shares received £6; second preference shares £5 and ordinary shares £2 per share **1884**

Louth Gaslight Co. Inc. by Special Act 1825. Dissolved 1 May 1949, undertaking being vested in East Midland Area Gas Board under Gas Act 1948. Holders of securities were entitled to receive British Gas 3% guaranteed stock 1990–95 as follows:

	£	s.	d.
Ord, shares (10% stand.) (of £25) ..	62	10	0
Imp. A stock (5% max.) (per £100) ..	110	0	0
Imp. B stock (5% max.) (per £100) ..	110	0	0
New ord. shares (7% stand.) (of £200 with £45 paid)	90	0	0	**1952**

Loveden Mine Ld. Regd. 1900. Reconstructed 1903 as Loveden Mining Co. (1903) Ld. in which company shareholders were entitled to 4 shares of 5s. (credited with 3s. 9d. paid) for each share held. Removed from Register 1908 .... **1908**

Loveden Mining Co. (1903) Ld. Regd. 1903. The debenture holders took possession of the property under Court Order. Removed from Register 1910 **1908**

Lovering China Clays Ld. Regd. 1929. Vol. liq. (members') 15 Apr. 1953. Final meeting return regd. 15 Dec. 1953 .... **1952**

Lovibond (Henry) & Son (1900) Ld. Regd. 1900. Court Order to wind up 6 Feb. 1901. Undertaking was acquired in 1902 by John Lovibond and Sons Ld. Removed from Register 1910. .... **1901**

Low Beechburn Coal Co. Ld. Regd. 1889. Vol. liq. 9 Jan. 1925. Final meeting return regd. 31 Oct. 1925 ..... **1925**

Low Engineering Co. Ld. Regd. 1920. Court Order to wind up Jan. 1935. Struck off Register 14 Oct. 1938 **1945**

Low Moor Co. Ld. See Heath (Robert) & Low Moor Ld.

Low Moor Iron Co. Ld. Regd. 1929. Vol. liq. (members') 11 Mar. 1938. Final meeting return regd. 2 Oct. 1939 **1939**

Low Point, Barrasois & Lingan Mining Co. Inc. Nova Scotia 1883. The property of the company was purchased by Dominion Coal Co. of Boston **1895**

Low, Sons & Bedford Ld. Regd. 1899. Removed from Register 1910 .... **1902**

Low's Calculators Ld. See Business Computers Ld.

Low Temperature Construction Ld. See Gas and Fuel Plants Ld.

Low (W. S.), Ld. Regd. 1908. Vol. liq. (members') 30 Apr. 1943. Preference and employees' shares were repaid in full, the remaining assets having been distributed in specie to ordinary shareholders. Final meeting return regd. 18 Dec. 1947 .... **1949**

Lowe, Sons & Co. Ld. Regd. 1922. Vol. liq. (members') 3 June 1935. Capital returned to contributories—£64,997 11s. 3d. plus certain assets in specie. Final meeting return regd. 19 Feb. 1937 .... **1936**

Lower Ancobra (Gold Coast) Areas Ld. Regd. 1934. Court Order to wind up 20 July 1936. Liquidator

VOL. FOR

released 11 Feb. 1944. Struck off Register 26 July 1946 .... **1947**

Lower Assam Co. Ld. Regd. 1861. Removed from Register 1903 .... **1902**

Lower California Development Co. Ld. Regd. 1890. Vol. liq. (members') 26 Apr. 1940. Assets acquired by Mexican Land & Colonization Co. Ld. Capital returned to contributories—1s. per share of £5. Final meeting return regd. 18 Jan. 1941 .... **1942**

Lower Langlaate Gold Mines Ld. Regd. 1889. Removed from Register 16 Nov. 1906 .... ***1892**

Lower Roodeport Ld. Regd. Dublin 1895. Court Order to wind up 1 Dec. 1897. Removed from Register 1898 .... **1898**

Lower Segama Rubber Estates Ld. Regd. 1920. Vol. liq. (creditors') 25 Mar. 1931. Assets realised insufficient to pay the debenture holder in full. Final meeting return regd. 1 Nov. 1932 .... **1932**

Loweswater Lead Co. Ld. Regd. 1887. Vol. liq. 27 July 1891. Final meeting return regd. 16 Sept. 1892 .... **1892**

Lowlands Rubber Estates (Ceylon) Ld. Regd. 1911. Vol. liq. 19 May 1914. Assets were sold to Trincomalee Estates Ld. in which company shareholders were entitled to 1 fully-paid share of 2s. for each share of 5s. held. Final meeting return regd. 21 July 1910 .... **1915**

Lowmont Estates Co. Ld. Regd. 1911. Vol. liq. (members') 2 Aug. 1939. Estate sold to St. George Rubber Estates Ld. in which company shareholders received 5 fully-paid shares of £1 for every 7 shares of 2s. held *plus* 2·1285d. per share in cash. Final meeting return regd. 19 July 1940 .... **1940**

Lowood (J. Grayson) & Co. Ld. Regd. 1890. Vol. liq. (members') 31 Mar. 1939. All shares were owned by General Refractories Ld. (later General Refractories Group Ld.) for nominees. Final meeting return regd. 25 July 1942 .... **1940**

Lowrie (W. P.) & Co. Ld. Regd. in Edinburgh 1906. Vol. liq. (members') 31 Mar. 1949. The undertaking was acquired by James Buchanan & Co. Ld. which company owned all shares. Final meeting return regd. 3 Nov. 1949 .... **1951**

Lowther Hematite Iron & Steel Co. Ld. Regd. 1897. Vol. liq. 7 May 1903. Final meeting return regd. 6 July 1905 .... ***1904**

Loyal British Assurance Co. Ld. Regd. 1902. Court Order to wind up 28 Apr. 1903. Liquidator released 27 Mar. 1907. Removed from Register 24 May ... ***1904**

Loyal Line Ld. Regd. 1919. Vol. liq. (creditors') 18 July 1932. No capital returned to contributories. Final meeting return regd. 8 Feb. 1933. Court Order deferred dissolution until 14 July 1933 .... **1933**

Lubricants Producers Ld. *See* Anglo-Mexican Oil & Shipping Co. Ld.

Lucas & Co. Ld. Regd. 1897. All capital was owned by Ansells Brewery Ld. Vol. liq. (members') 29 Mar. 1966. Final meeting return regd. 30 Dec. 1966 .... **1963**

Lucia Silver Mines Ld. Regd. 1896. Vol. liq. 24 Aug. 1904. Final meeting return regd. 30 Nov. 1929 ... **1905**

Luckimpore Tea Co. of Assam Ld. Regd. 1865. Vol. liq. 9 Aug. 1889. Shareholders received 4,000 fully-paid shares of £10 in Majuli Tea Co. Ld. Final meeting return regd. 24 May 1894 .... **1894**

Luck's Explosives Ld. Regd. 1898. Vol. liq. June 1906. Removed from Register 1910 .... **1907**

Lucky Chance Mines Ld. Regd. 1905. Vol. liq. 1 June 1926. Final meeting return regd. 25 Apr. 1928 .... **1927**

Lucky Guss Gold Mine Ld. Regd. 1896. Vol. liq. 2 May 1898. Reconstructed as Lucky Guss Ld. in which company shareholders were entitled to 1 share of £1 (credited with 17s. 6d. paid) for every 2 shares of £1 held. Final meeting return regd. 25 Oct. 1899 ..... **1901**

Lucky Guss Ld. Regd. 1898. In liquidation in 1901. Capital returned to contributories—7s. per share of £1; further payments (if any) not known. Removed from Register 1901 .... **1901**

Lucky Hit Gold Mining Co. Ld. Regd. 1900. Removed from Register 1904 .... **1902**

Lucky Tiger-Combination Gold Mining Co. Inc. Arizona 1903. The London office was closed in 1913 .... **1913**

Ludlow & Clee Hill Railway Co. Inc. by Special Act 1861. Under Great Western Railway Act of 1892 undertaking was vested under control of Shrewsbury and Hereford Joint Committee **1893**

Ludlow Electric Light Co. Ld. Regd. 1906. Vol. liq. (members') 19 May 1939. Capital returned to contributories—20s. per preference share of £1; £2 7s. 1d. per ordinary share of £1. Final meeting return regd. 16 Feb. 1940 .... **1940**

Ludlow Gold Mines Ld. Regd. 1897. Removed from Register 1904 .... **1904**

Ludlow Union Gas Co. Ld. Regd 1874. Dissolved 1 May 1949, undertaking being vested in West Midland Area Gas Board under Gas Act 1948. Holders of securities were entitled to receive British Gas 3%

VOL. FOR

guaranteed stock 1990–95 as follows in respect of each £5 unit, unless otherwise stated, of security held:—

	£	s.	d.	
Ord. A shares (10% stand.)	7	15	0	
Ord. C shares (5% stand.)	4	4	0	
4½% pref. shares	5	8	0	
5% pref. shares	5	14	0	
6% pref. shares	6	12	0	
4% red. debs. (per £100)	101	10	0	**1952**

Luebecker Privatbank. Absorbed in 1926 by Deutsche Bank **1928**

Lugo Goldfields Ld. Regd 1901. In 1907 all assets were transferred to Cabrera Mines Ld. for 3,000 fully-paid ordinary shares of £1. Removed from Register 1911 .... **1909**

Luhrig Coal & Ore Dressing Appliances Ld. *See* Coal & Ore Dressing Appliances Ld.

Luipaards Vlei Estate and Gold Mining Co. Ld. Regd. 1888. Reconstructed 1896 as company of same name. Shareholders were entitled to 2 fully-paid shares of £1 for every 5 shares of £1 held. Removed from Register 1901 .... **1896**

Luiri Gold Areas Ld. Regd. 1937. Vol. liq. (members') 23 June 1941. No capital returned to contributories. Final meeting return regd. 3 Nov. 1943 .... **1945**

Luker (Henry) & Co. Ld. Regd. 1895. Vol. liq. 2 Apr. 1929. The licensed houses were acquired by Mann Crossman & Paulin Ld. Capital returned to contributories—£90 per ordinary share of £10 at Dec. 1929; further payments (if any) not known. Final meeting return regd. 12 Apr. 1930 .... **1930**

Lumber & Development Co. of Michoacan Ld. Regd. 1905. Removed from Register 26 July 1912 .... ***1912**

Lumbys Ld. Regd. 1886. Vol. liq. (members') 30 June 1960. All capital and assets acquired by Crane Ld. Final meeting return regd. 13 Dec. 1960 .... **1961**

Lumex Ld. Inc. Dublin 1920. Dissolved before 1956 . **1938**

Lumiére North American Co. Ld. Regd. 1901. Vol. liq. July 1906. Undertaking was sold to Société Anonyme des Plaques et Papiers Photographiques A. Lumiere et ses Fils, in which company shareholders were entitled to 1 share (credited as fully-paid) for every 3 shares held. Removed from Register 1909 .... **1907**

Lu-Mi-Num Manufacturing Co. Ld. Regd. 1896. Vol. liq. 1 June 1898. Final meeting return regd. 30 Nov. 1898 .... **1899**

Lumut Rubber Estates, Ld. Regd. 1909. Vol. liq. (members') 27 Oct. 1952. Estates, undertaking and assets were transferred to Golden Hope Rubber Estate Ld. in which company stockholders were entitled to receive 1 share of £1 for each £2 stock held. Final meeting return regd. 19 Sept. 1953 .... **1954**

Lunderston Rubber Co. Ld. Regd. 1916. Vol. liq. 10 June 1925. Undertaking and assets were acquired by New Crocodile River (Selangor) Rubber Co. Ld. in which company shareholders were entitled to 7 shares of 2s. (credited as fully-paid) for every 10 shares of 2s. held. Final meeting return regd. 30 May 1927 .... **1926**

Lundy Cable Co. Ld. Regd. 1884. Vol. liq. 3 Apr. 1890. Final meeting return regd. 19 Sept. 1895 .... **1891**

Lunt (John H.) & Co. Ld. *See* Thomas Scott & Sons (Bakers) Ld.

Luotto-Pankki-Oy. Undertaking acquired by Kansallis-Osaki-Pankki in 1933 .... **1942**

Lupa Exploration Syndicate Ld. Regd. 1933. Vol. liq. (creditors') 16 Oct. 1952. No capital was returned to contributories. Final meeting return regd.2 Apr.1953 .... **1953**

Lusitanian Mining Co. Ld. Regd 1856. Removed from Register 1905 .... ***1881**

Lustrous Steamship Co. Ld. Regd. 1927. Vol. liq. (members') 28 Feb. 1951. Final meeting return regd. 14 Aug. 1952 .... **1950**

Luton Gas Co. Inc. by Special Act 1858. Dissolved 1 May 1949, undertaking being vested in Eastern Area Gas Board under Gas Act 1948. Holders of securities were entitled to receive British Gas 3% guaranteed stock 1990–95 as follows in respect of each £100 unit, unless otherwise stated, of security held:—

	£	s.	d.	
Cons. ord. stock A (5% stand.)	165	0	0	
Cons. ord. stock B (3½% stand.)	135	0	0	
4% pref. B shares (of £5)	5	0	0	
5% pref. C shares (of £5)	5	12	0	
5% red. pref. stock	104	5	0	
4% perp. deb. stock	102	0	0	
5% perp. deb. stock	124	0	0	
4½% red. deb. stock	103	5	0	**1952**

Luton Mutual Plate Glass Insurance Association Ld. Regd. 1898. All capital was owned by London &

VOL. FOR

County Insurance Co. Ld. Vol. liq. (members') 26 May 1964. Final meeting return regd. 15 Dec. 1964 — **1940**

Luton Water Co. Inc. by Special Act, 1865. The undertaking was vested in the Lee Valley Water Co. 1 Jan. 1973 in which company stockholders received equivalent amounts of similar stocks. The outstanding debenture stocks became stocks of the Lee Valley Water Co. Company was dissolved 23 Mar. 1973 — **1973-4**

Lutterworth Gas Light & Coke Co. Ld. Constd. by Deed of Settlement 1850; regd. 1907. Dissolved 1 May 1949, undertaking being vested in East Midland Area Gas Board under Gas Act 1948. Holders of ordinary shares (of all denominations) were entitled to receive, in respect of each £1 unit held, £1 17s. British Gas 3% guaranteed stock 1990-95 — **1952**

Luxor (Eastbourne) Ld. Regd. 1932. Vol. liq. (members') 31 Mar. 1938. A direct controlling interest was held by Union Cinemas Ld. Final meeting return regd. 6 July 1944 — **1939**

Lyall (P.) & Sons Construction Co. Ld. Inc. Canada 1911. Wound up Sept. 1929 — **1930**

Lyceum (1903) Ld. Regd. 1903. Struck off Register 29 Nov. 1907 — **1908**

Lyceum Theatre Ld. Regd. 1899. Reconstructed 1903 as Lyceum (1903) Ld. in which company shareholders were entitled to 1 share of £1 (credited with 15s. paid) for each ordinary share of £1 held. Removed from Register 1904 — **1904**

Lydbrook Cables Ld. Regd. 1925. Vol. liq. 31 May 1926. Undertaking was acquired by Edison Swan Cables Ld. Final meeting return regd. 26 Mar. 1929 — **1940**

Lydd Gas Co. Ld. Regd. 1867. Vol. liq. (members') 16 Dec. 1937. Directly controlled by South Eastern Gas Corporation Ld. Final meeting return regd. 16 Dec. 1938 — **1938**

Lydd Railway Co. Inc. by Special Act 1881. Under South-Eastern Railway Act 1895 undertaking was absorbed by that company. Proprietors received an equal amount of 4% debenture stock in absorbing company — **1896**

Lydenburg Central Platinum Co. Ld. Inc. Transvaal 1925. In Nov. 1929 it was stated that company had ceased to exist owing to lack of funds and lapsed options on all properties — **1930**

Lydenburg Consolidated Mines Ld. Regd. 1895. Court Order to wind up 19 May 1897. Removed from Register 1908 — **1898**

Lydenburg Estates Ld. Regd. 1895. Vol. liq. 18 Jan. 1899. Reconstructed as company of same name. Shareholders were entitled to 1 share of £1 (credited with 16s. 6d. paid) in new company for each share of £1 held. Final meeting return regd. 26 July 1902 — **1899**

Lydenburg Estates Ld. Regd. 1899. Vol. liq. (members') 17 June 1938. Reconstructed as company of same name. Shareholders were entitled to 1 share of 5s. (credited as fully-paid) in new company for every 4 shares of 1s. held. The outstanding debenture stock was repaid at par on 31 Oct. 1938. Final meeting return regd. 31 May 1945 — **1939**

Lydenburg Gold Farms Co. Ld. Inc. Transvaal 1890. Under scheme of amalgamation in Nov. 1969 undertaking, assets and liabilities were transferred to New Witwatersrand Gold Exploration Co. Ld. in which company shareholders received 50 shares of R0·50 per 100 shares — **1973-4**

Lydenburg Land and Exploration Co. Ld. Inc. Transvaal 1895. Vol. liq. 30 Dec. 1931. Capital returned to contributories—1s. 1·2d. per share of £1. Company has been finally wound up — **1944**

Lydenburg Minerais Exploring Co. Ld. Regd. 1895. Vol. liq. 28 Mar. 1900. Reconstructed as New Lydenburg Minerals Exploring Co. Ld. in which company shareholders were entitled to 1 share of 10s. (credited with 7s. 6d. paid) for each share of £1 held. Final meeting return regd. 15 Aug. 1919 — **1908**

Lydenburg Platinum Areas Ld. Regd. 1925. Vol. liq. (members') 2 Apr. 1942. Capital returned to contributories—6·71d. per share of 4s. Final meeting return regd. 3 Oct. 1946 — **1947**

Lydenburg Proprietary Mines Ld. Regd. 1925. Vol. liq. (creditors') 17 Aug. 1932. No capital returned to contributories. Final meeting return regd. 25 May 1935 — **1933**

Lydney & Lydbrook Steel & Tin Plate Co. Ld. Regd. 1881. Vol. liq. Feb. 1883. Final meeting return regd. 2 Nov. 1883 — **1883**

Lydney & Wigpool Iron Ore Co. Ld. Regd. 1871. Court Orders: to wind up Feb. 1886; to dissolve Dec. 1888 — **1887**

Lydney Gas Light & Coke Co. Ld. Regd. 1860. Dissolved 1 May 1949, undertaking being vested in South Western Area Gas Board under Gas Act 1948. Holders of ordinary shares (of £1) were

VOL. FOR

entitled to receive £1 15s. 6d. British Gas 3% guaranteed stock 1990-95 for each share held — **1952**

Lyeesi Ld. Regd. 1928. Vol. liq. (members') 4 Oct. 1937. Dissolved before 1952 — **1938**

Lyell Comstock Consolidated Copper Co. Ld. Regd. 1898 as Mount Lyell Comstock Copper Co. Ld.; name changed Apr. 1903. Reconstructed 1907 as Mount Lyell Comstock Copper Co. Ld. in which company shareholders were entitled to 1 share of 4s. (credited with 2s. paid) for each share of £1 held. The debentures were repaid. Removed from Register 1909 — **1908**

Lyell Tharsis Mining Co. No Liability. Inc. Victoria 1897. Property was sold in 1905 to Mount Lyell Mining and Railway Co. Ld. Capital returned to contributories—3·895d. per share of £1 in Aug. 1905; further payments (if any) not known — **1906**

Lyme Regis Cement Co. (1902) Ld. Regd. 1902. Vol. liq. 22 Feb. 1905. Removed from Register 1909 — **1906**

Lyme Regis District Water Co. Regd. as limited 1932; inc. by Special Act. 1933. The undertaking vested in the East Devon Water Board as from 1 Dec. 1958 Holders of the original and further original ordinary stock received 28s. cash per £1 stock held; holders of the 4½% redeemable preference stock 1967 received a like amount of 4½% mortgages of the Board subject to the same terms of redemption; holders of the 4% debenture stock received a like amount of 4% mortgages of the Board redeemable at the expiration of 30 years from 1 Dec. 1958 or on any previous date on 3 months' notice from the Board or from the holders. The company was dissolved on 26 Jan. 1959 — **1960**

Lymni Copper Mining Syndicate Ld. Regd. 1897. Vol. liq. Oct. 1910. Removed from Register 1911 — **1911**

Lyndhurst Deep-Level (Gold & Silver) Ld. Regd. 1896. Vol. liq. (members') 24 Jan. 1956. Fixed assets in the Gold Coast were sold to Konongo Gold Mines Ld., in which company stockholders were entitled to receive 2 shares (of 1s.) per 5s. of stock held, in addition stockholders received 11·2d. in cash per stock unit (of 1s.) held. Final meeting return regd. 20 May 1957 — **1958**

Lyndhurst Gold Field Ld. *See* Lyndhurst Railway & Mines Ld.

Lyndhurst Railway & Mines Ld. Regd. 1895 as Lyndhurst Gold Field Ld. Arrangements have been made for transfer of undertaking to local company in Australia. Struck off Register Dec. 1920 — **1931**

Lyndhurst (South Australia) Copper Co. Ld. Regd. 1907. Vol. liq. 2 Dec. 1912. The undertaking and assets were transferred to Union Consolidated Copper Mines (1911) Ld., in which company shareholders were entitled to 1 share of 5s. (credited with 3s. 6d. paid) for each share of £1 held. Final meeting return regd. 27 Oct.1916 — **1913**

Lyndon Shipping Co. Ld. Regd. 1919. Struck off Register 1926 — **1925**

Lynedoek Investments Ld. Regd. 1950. Vol. liq. (members') 15 Aug. 1961. Capital returned to contributories—£2 15s. 9·89d. per £1 stock. Final meeting return regd. 8 May 1962 — **1963**

Lynn & Boston Railroad Co. *See* Eastern Massachusetts Street Railway.

Lynton and Barnstaple Railway Co. Inc. by Special Act 1895. In 1923 the undertaking was merged into the Southern Railway Co. Holders of the 483 shares not held by the Southern Railway Co. were entitled to 12s. in cash per share — **1924**

Lynton & Lynmouth Electric Light Co. Ld. Regd. 1894. Dissolved 1 Apr. 1948. undertaking being vested in the British (later Central) Electricity Authority and South-Western Area Board under the Electricity Act 1947. Holders of ordinary and preference shares were entitled to receive British Electricity 3% guaranteed stock (1968–73), as follows—£1 13s. 4d. stock for each ordinary share (of £1) held and £1 3s. 6d. stock for each preference share (of £1) held — **1949**

Lynton & Lynmouth Hotel & Property Co. Ld. Regd. 1888. Vol. liq. 15 June 1894. Final meeting return regd. 24 Apr. 1896 — **1895**

Lyon & Tucker, Established 1866. Dissolved 1933 — **1935**

Lyon Bros. Ld. Regd. 1886. Vol. liq. 24 Oct. 1890. Struck off Register May 1929 — **1930**

Lyonnaise Mexican Concessions Ld. Regd. 1894. Struck off Register 18 Nov. 1902 — **1903**

Lyons Brewery & Malting Co. Ld. Regd. 1896. A receiver was appointed. Removed from Register 1901 — **1899**

Lyons Ink Ld. Regd. 1896. Vol. liq. 1 Mar. 1928. Reconstructed as company of same name. Final meeting return regd. 1 Dec. 1928 — **1929**

See Stock Exchange Year-Book.

M

M. & G. Finance Ld. Regd. 1932. Vol. liq. (members') 2 July 1941. Capital returned to contributories—9s. 6·8d. per share of £1. Final meeting return regd. 12 Mar. 1942 .... **1942**

M.C. Mining Co. of British Columbia Ld. Regd. 1923. Vol. liq. (creditors') 8 Apr. 1931. No capital returned to contributories. Final meeting return regd. 1 June 1932 .... **1932**

M.D.E. Co. Ld. Regd. 1928 as Midhurst & District Electricity Ld. Undertaking was acquired in 1931 by Mid Southern Utility Co. Ld. Struck off Register 14 Oct. 1938 .... **1939**

M.E.C. Holdings Ld. Regd. 1944 as The Rothermel Corpn. Ld.; name changed to Motor & Electronics Corpn. Ld. in 1954 and as above in 1958. A former subsidiary of Simms Motor & Electronics Corpn. Ld. Vol. liq. (members') 31 Dec. 1959. Final meeting return regd. 19 Dec. 1961 .... **1959**

M.F. Exploration Co. Ld. Regd 1912. Vol. liq. Nov. 1921. Capital returned to contributories—5s. per share of 10s. in Dec. 1921; further payments (if any) not known. Struck off Register June 1932 .... **1933**

M.F. (Rhodesia) Proprietary Ld. Inc. Transvaal 1909 as M. F. (Rhodesia) Proprietary Syndicate Ld.; name changed 1911. The assets were sold to M. F. Exploration Co. Ld. in Jan. 1913 .... **1913**

M.H. (Methane Hydrogen) Gas Plant Ld. Regd. 1908. Vol. liq. 5 Dec. 1913. Final meeting return regd. 10 Mar. 1914 .... **1914**

MIM Sterling Reserves Fund Ld. Inc. in Jersey 24 Jan. 1980 as 117 Sterling Reserves Fund Ld.; name changed to Montagu Sterling Reserves Fund Ld. on 31 May 1983 and to present title on 25 Sept. 1985. Vol. liq. (members') in Nov. 1986. Liquidation completed 1987. By Scheme of Amalgamation effective 25 Nov. 1986 holders received 0·889429 of a Participating Redeemable Preference share in MIM Britannia Capital Deposit Fund for each share held **1988–9**

M.M.T. Holdings Ld. Regd. 1928 as Modern Machine Tools Ld.; name changed Jan. 1935. Vol. liq. (members') 12 Apr. 1937. Undertaking acquired by Modern Machine Tools Ld. (later Modern Engineering Developments Ld.) for £30,000 fully-paid shares of £1 and £10,000 in cash. Final meeting return regd. 15 July 1939 .... **1936**

M.P.A. Wireless Ld. Regd. 1928. Vol. liq. Apr. 1930. Struck off Register 8 Apr. 1938 .... **1939**

M.P. Concrete Construction Ld. Regd. 1919. Vol. liq. Jan. 1924 for reconstruction as "M. P." Construction & Cleaning Co. Ld., in which company shareholders were entitled to 10 shares of 2s. (credited with 1s. 6d. paid) for each ordinary share of £1 held or 1 share of 2s. (credited with 1s. 6d. paid) for each deferred share of 1s. held. Struck off Register Apr. 1929 .... **1930**

M.P. Construction & Cleaning Co. Ld. Regd. 1924. Struck off Register May 1929 .... **1930**

M.R.S. Ld. Regd. 1926 as A. C. Marston & Co. (Northern) Ld.; name changed Aug. 1927 to Marston's Road Services Ld. and as above Oct. 1929. Vol. liq. (creditors') 26 Sept. 1935. No capital returned to contributories. Final meeting return regd. 15 July 1937 .... **1936**

M. W. Ld. Regd. 1924 as Matthews, Wrightson & Co. Ld.; name changed Jan. 1935. Vol. liq. (members') 12 June 1935. Reconstructed as Matthews, Wrightson & Co. Ld. Final meeting return regd. 31 Dec. 1935 .... **1936**

M. X. H. Ld. Regd. 1932 as Madame Hetty Ld.; name changed 16 Apr. 1936. Vol. liq. (members') 19 Apr. 1938. Undertaking acquired by Hetty (Wholesale Gowns) Ld. (later Brenner Industries Ld.). Final meeting return regd. 28 May 1940 .... **1938**

Maakuntain Pankki Oy. Undertaking was acquired in 1933 by Kansallis-Osaki-Pankki **1942**

Mablethorpe & Sutton Gas Co. Ld. Regd. 1899. Dissolved 1 May 1949, undertaking being vested in East Midland Area Gas Board under Gas Act 1948. Holders of securities were entitled to receive British Gas 3% guaranteed stock 1990–95 as follows in respect of each £1 unit, unless otherwise stated, of security held:

	£	s.	d.
Orig. ord. shares (10% stand.) (of £10)	10	10	0
B ord. shares (7% stand.)		15	0
Addit. ord. shares (7% stand.)		15	0
5% pref. shares	1	1	0
4% red. debs. (of £100) (all red. dates)	100	0	0	**1952**

Macabé & Campos Railway Co. Inc. Brazil 1869. Undertaking and assets were acquired in 1897 by Leopoldina Railway Co. Ld. Bondholders were entitled to fully-paid shares of £10 in new company as follows:

For every £100 held	
5% 1st mtg. deb. 1888	£70 shares
5% debentures 1889	£70 shares	**1898**

McArthur, Atkins & Co. Ld. Regd. 1905. Vol. liq. Feb. 1909. Removed from Register 1913 .... **1909**

McArthur (Harold M.) & Co. Ld. Regd. 1919. Vol. liq. 16 Oct. 1929. Business was acquired by Liverpool Chemical Products Co. Ld. Final meeting return regd. 7 May 1930 .... **1938**

McArthur (W. & A.) Ld. Regd. 1898. Vol. liq. 12 Dec. 1907 for reconstruction as company of same name. Holders of 1st mortgage debenture stock were entitled to 4½% debenture stock in new company plus a bonus of 5%; holders of 2nd mortgage debenture stock were entitled to similar stock in new company. Preference shareholders were entitled to 5 shares of £1 (credited with 12s. 6d. paid) in new company for each preference share of £10 held. Removed from Register 1913 .... **1908**

McArthur (W. & A.) Ld. Regd. 1908. Vol. liq. 12 Oct. 1926. Final meeting return regd. 15 Nov. 1932 .... **1927**

Macassar Plantations Ld. Regd 1926. Vol. liq. (members') 25 Sept. 1933. Undertaking and assets were acquired by Bajoe Kidoel Rubber & Produce Co. Ld., in which company shareholders were entitled to 1 share of £1 (credited as fully-paid) for every 4 shares of £1 held. Debenture holders were repaid at 105% in Apr. 1932. Final meeting return regd. 6 Mar. 1934 .... **1934**

Macate Mining Co. Ld. Regd. 1896. Vol. liq. 22 Dec. 1902. Final meeting return regd. 1 Jan. 1910 .... **1903**

McCabe (James) & Co. Ld. Business acquired by Cave, Austin and Co. Ld **1909**

McClelland (T. & A.) Ld. Regd. Edinburgh 1911. Vol. liq. (members') 31 Mar. 1937. Capital returned to contributories—£5,227 9s. 6d. Final meeting return regd. 7 Apr. 1942 .... **1937**

McClory (John) & Sons Ld. Regd. 1898. Court Order to wind up 12 Nov. 1938. Liquidator released 16 Nov. 1943. Struck off Register 26 July 1946 .... **1939**

McConnell's Distillery Ld. Regd. Dublin 1898. Vol. liq. Nov. 1928 .... **1929**

McCracken's City Brewery Ld. Inc. Victoria 1888. Vol. liq. Dec. 1907. Certain assets were acquired by Carlton and United Breweries Proprietary Ld. (later Carlton and United Breweries Ld.), in which company preference shareholders were entitled to 19,000 shares and ordinary shareholders to 22,625. Certain assets were acquired by Melbourne City Properties Trust Ld., in which company debenture holders were entitled to 30 shares of £1 and £40 debenture stock for every £100 bond held **1900**

McCulloch Coolgardie Gold Mines Ld. Regd. 1896. Vol. liq. 11 Mar. 1898. Final meeting return regd. 16 Nov. 1899 .... **1899**

Macdonald (Alex.) & Co. Ld. Regd. Edinburgh 1885. Vol. liq. Apr. 1911. Final meeting return regd. 18 Dec. 1913 .... **1912**

MacDonald Gold Mines Ld. Regd. 1900. Vol. liq. 3 July 1905. Final meeting return regd. 22 Aug. 1905 .... **1906**

Macdonald, Greenlees & Williams (Distillers) Ld. Regd. Edinburgh 1899 as William & Williams & Sons Ld.; name changed Sept. 1919. Vol. liq. Jan. 1926. Capital returned to contributories—21s. per preference share of £1; ordinary shares were privately held. Final meeting return regd. 15 Dec. 1926. Court Orders deferred dissolution till 15 Mar. 1928 .... **1927**

McDonald's Bonanza (Klondike) Ld. Regd. 1899. Capital returned to contributories—2s. 6d. per share. Further payments (if any) not known. Removed from Register 1904 .... **1904**

McDonald's Puncture-proof Pneumatic Tyre Co. Ld. Regd. 1893. Vol. liq. 31 Dec. 1894. Final meeting return regd. 27 June 1898 .... **1899**

Macedonian Tobacco Co. Ld. Regd. 1911. Vol. liq. 1920. A distribution of Dr. 100 per share (of £4) was made in Nov. 1920. Struck off Register 4 May 1948 ..... **1948**

McEvoy (P.), Sons & Pinnington Ld. Regd. 1898. Vol. liq. (members') 30 Mar. 1937. Capital returned to contributories—£75,750. Final meeting return regd. 1 Nov. 1943 .... **1938**

McEwan (James) & Co. Ld. Regd. 1887. The assets were sold by the Receiver for £79,250 which was applied to principal and interest of 1st mortgage debentures. Removed from Register 1912 .... **1911**

Macey Co. Ld. Regd. Edinburgh 1915. Vol. liq. Dec. 1925. Final meeting return regd. 19 July 1926 ..... **1927**

VOL. FOR

Macfarlane & Robinson Ld. Regd. Edinburgh 1909. Vol. liq. Nov. 1927. Final meeting return regd. 6 Apr. 1929 .... **1928**

MacGeorge & Jardine Ld. Regd. 1930. Vol. liq. (members') 13 Mar. 1942. Capital returned to contributories—£12,133 6s. 8d. Final meeting return regd. 22 Oct. 1942 .... **1943**

Macgregor Cloncurry Copper Mines Ld. Inc. Victoria 1906. Wound up Sept. 1910 for reconstruction under same name. Shareholders were entitled to 1 share of 10s. (credited with 7s. paid) in new company for each share of 10s. held and right to apply for a further 25,000 shares credited with 7s. paid **1911**

Macgregor Cloncurry Copper Mines Ld. Inc. Victoria 1910. Wound up Jan. 1913. Assets sold to Hampden Cloncurry Copper Mines Ld. for £108,500 cash. Shareholders were entitled to receive about 6s. 9d. per share of 10s. (8s. paid) **1913**

Macgregor Ld. Regd. Edinburgh 1897. Vol. liq. 5 Nov. 1909. Court Orders: to continue winding up under supervision 11 Dec. 1909; to dissolve 1 June 1912 **1910**

Machine Cooperage Co. Ld. See Nightingale's Cooperage Co. Ld.

Machine-Made Sales Ld. Regd. 1927. Vol. liq. (members') 26 Nov. 1930, the undertaking and assets having been acquired by Direct Automatic Sales, Ld. (Struck off Register 28 June 1957). Winding-up order 8 June 1931. Shareholders were entitled to receive 4 fully-paid shares of Direct Automatic Sales Ld. for every 5 shares held. Liquidator released Mar. 1955. Struck off Register 28 June 1957 .... **1955**

Machinery Insurance Co. Ld. Regd. 1895. Vol. liq. 21 Dec. 1898. Final meeting return regd. 26 Jan. 1900 **1899**

Machinery (Smith's Patents) Ld. Regd. 1934. Vol. liq. (members') 29 Oct. 1947. Capital returned to contributories—preference shares were repaid in full; 3s. 10·45d. per ordinary share (of 1s.). Final meeting return regd. 2 Dec. 1948 .... **1949**

Machinery Trust Ld. Regd. 1893. Vol. liq. 31 July 1903. Reconstructed as Linotype and Machinery Ld. Holders of 1st mortgage 4% debenture stock were entitled to an equal amount of B 4½% debenture stock. Holders of preference shares were entitled to an equal amount of preference shares; holders of preferred ordinary shares were entitled to 2 preference shares and 1 ordinary share of £1 for each preferred ordinary share of £5; holders of deferred ordinary shares were entitled to 1½ ordinary shares of £1 for each deferred ordinary share of £5 held. Final meeting return regd. 1 Dec. 1908 .... **1904**

McHugh & Co. Ld. Regd. Dublin 1899. Vol. liq. July 1906. Removed from Register 1912 .... **1907**

Machynlleth Electric Supply Co. Ld. Regd. 1932. Dissolved 1 Apr. 1948, undertaking being vested in the British (later Central) Electricity Authority and Merseyside & North Wales Area Board under the Electricity Act 1947. Ordinary shareholders were entitled to receive £10 British Electricity 3% guaranteed stock (1968–73), for each share (of £5) held **1949**

Machynlleth Gas Co. Ld. Regd. 1863. Dissolved 1 May 1949, undertaking being vested in Wales Area Gas Board under Gas Act 1948. Holders of shares (of £5) were entitled to receive £5 British Gas 3% guaranteed stock 1990–95 for each share held **1952**

McIlwraith. McEachuarn & Co., Proprietary Ld. Inc. Victoria 1891. The 5% 1st debenture stock was repaid 15 May 1918 .... **1920**

McIlroy (William) Ld. Regd. 1900. Vol. liq. (members') 17 Aug. 1955. Stockholders were entitled to receive (1) at their option either (a) £1 10s. cash per 5s. stock held or (b) £1 4s. 8d. cash per 5s. stock held plus 16 ordinary shares of 5s. in William McIlroy Swindon Ld., per £3 15s. stock held, and additional ordinary shares in that company could be taken in specie in lieu of cash at 5s. per share; and (2) a further 15s. per 5s. stock held. Final meeting return regd. 28 June 1957 .... **1958**

McIlroys Stores (Hanley) Ld. Regd.1928. Vol. liq. (members') 1 Jan. 1936. Assets were acquired by Lewis's Ld., for £255,000 in cash. Capital returned to contributories—6s. 6d. per share of 5s. Final meeting return regd. 23 June 1936 .... **1936**

McIlwraith, McEacharn's Line Proprietary Ld. Inc. Sydney 1913. Vol. liq. Nov. 1926 for reconstruction as McIlwraith McEacharn Ld. **1927**

Macinlop Ld. Regd. 1928. Vol. liq. (members') 25 Aug. 1933. All shares were owned by Dunlop Rubber Co. Ld. (later Dunlop Co. Ld.). Final meeting return regd. 27 Jan. 1934 .... **1934**

MacIver (David) & Co. Ld. Regd. 1894 as MacIver (David), Sons, & Co. Ld.; name changed 1919. Vol. liq. (members') 28 Apr. 1933. The fleet was transferred to Royal Mail Lines Ld., for 160,000

VOL. FOR

fully-paid shares. Capital returned to contributories—£282,427 10s. plus certain investments distributed in specie. Final meeting return regd. 16 Mar. 1942 .... **1934**

MacIvor's Patents Ld. See Northfleet White Lead Co. Ld.

Mack Syndicate Ld. Regd. 1895. Vol. liq. 26 Nov. 1895. Final meeting return regd. 15 July 1897 .... **1898**

Mackay & Revolution Silver Mining Co. Ld. Regd. 1883. Vol. liq. 17 Aug. 1888. Final meeting return regd. 3 Feb. 1891 .... **1889**

Mackay Companies. See Associated Companies.

Mackenzie & Mackenzie Ld. Regd. Edinburgh 1898. Vol. liq. May 1911. Court Order to continue winding up under supervision June 1911. Business sold to William Crawford & Son Ld. Court Order to dissolve 23 Jan. 1925 .... **1912**

Mackenzie Brick & Tile Co. Ld. Undertaking and assets were acquired by Vimax Machinery Co. Ld., for £5.000 in cash and £30,000 in fully-paid shares of 10s. **1930**

McKenzie Gold Mines Ld. Regd. 1895. Court Order to wind up 9 Mar. 1898. Struck off Register Aug. 1930 **1931**

Mackenzie (P.) & Co. Distillers Ld. Regd. Edinburgh 1897. Vol. liq. (members') 10 Nov. 1933. Capital returned to contributories—£45,625. Final meeting return regd. 18 July 1935 .... **1934**

Mackie Brazier & Co. Ld. Regd. 1916. Vol. liq. (members') 21 Jan. 1944. Capital returned to contributories—2s. 1d. per share of £1. Final meeting return regd. 10 May 1944 .... **1943**

McIntyre & Sons Ld. Regd. as private company 1953 as McIntyre & Sons (Holdings) Ld.; name changed 1954 .... **1984–5**

McKinley-Darragh-Savage Mines of Cobalt Ld. Undertaking was acquired by McKinley Mines Securities Co. Ld **1938**

McKinley Mines Securities Co. Ld. Inc. Ontario 1928. Vol. liq. Oct. 1938. Argus Interests Ld. offered shareholders one of its shares of no par value plus $0·40 cash for each share of $1 held; shareholders who did not accept offer received $1·42¼ per share in cash **1939**

Mackintosh (John) Ld. Regd. 1899. Vol. liq. 13 Aug. 1921. Undertaking was acquired by John Mackintosh & Sons Ld., for 299,216 fully-paid ordinary shares of £1 and £289,746 in cash. Final meeting return regd. 7 Apr. 1923 .... **1922**

McLaren Bros. (Manchester) Ld. Regd. 1920. Vol. liq. 4 Apr. 1929. All shares held by United Africa Co. Ld. Struck off Register 1943 .... **1930**

M'Laren (William) Sons & Co. Ld. Regd. Edinburgh 1899. Vol. liq. (members') 27 Mar. 1956. Preference capital was repaid at par in Apr. 1956. Capital returned to ordinary shareholders—£5 15s. 4½d. per share of £1. Amounts paid into Companies' Liquidation Account—£288 8s. 10d. in respect of unclaimed distributions and £356 5s. 2d. in respect of unclaimed dividends. Final meeting return regd. 12 Apr. 1957 .... **1958**

MacLaurin Phosphate Mining Syndicate Ld. Regd. 1889. Winding-up Order made 8 July 1893. Removed from Register 1907 .... **1894**

McLean Bros. & Rigg. Ld. Inc. Victoria 1887. In liquidation in 1907 .... **1907**

McLintock (W. & J.) Ld. Regd. Edinburgh 1924. All capital was owned by Carrick's (Caterers) Ld. Vol. liq. (members') 25 Mar. 1960. Final meeting return regd. 6 Feb. 1962 .... **1957**

McMichael (L.) (Holdings) Ld. Regd. 1922 as L. McMichael Ld.; name changed Nov. 1932. Vol. liq. (members') 30 Jan. 1933. Undertaking acquired by McMichael Radio Ld. Final meeting returned regd. 14 May 1936 .... **1936**

McMichael (L.) Ld. See above.

McMillan (Archibald) & Son Ld. Regd. Edinburgh 1890. Vol. liq. (creditors') 7 Dec. 1932. All capital held by Lamport & Holt Ld. Final meeting return regd. 3 Sept. 1936 .... **1933**

McMullans (Calor Gas), 1937, Ld. Inc. Dublin 1937. Vol. liq. (members') 8 July 1954. Preference shares (of 10s.) repaid Oct. 1954. Capital returned to contributories—17·959p per ordinary share of 25p. Winding up order 8 Aug. 1975. Final meeting return regd. 9 Oct. 1975. Liquidator released 9 Jan. 1976 **1976-7**

McMurray's Royal Paper Mills Ld. Regd. 1891. Receiver appointed in 1906. Court Order to wind up June 1906. Struck off Register Aug. 1930 .... **1931**

McNab (John) & Co. Ld. Regd. 1901. Vol. liq. (members') 12 Nov. 1931. Direct controlling interest held by Bleachers' Association Ld. (later Whitecroft Industrial Holdings Ld.) Final meeting return regd. 17 Jan. 1933 .... **1932**

*See Stock Exchange Year-Book.

VOL. FOR

McNamara & Co. Ld. Regd. 1877. Vol. liq. 30 May 1921. Reconstructed as McNamara & Co. (1921) Ld. (later McNamara & Co. Ld.) in which company shareholders were enlitled to 20 Shares of £1 (credited with 17s. 6d. paid) for each share of £10 held. Holders of 5% debentures and 8% debentures received 8s. 6d. and 7s. in £ respectively; further payments (if any) not known. Final meeting return regd 27 Oct. 1923 .... **1922**

McNamara & Co. Ld. Regd. 1921 as McNamara & Co. (1921) Ld.; name changed 16 May 1938. Vol. liq. (members') 17 Dec. 1948. Undertaking taken over by British Transport Commission. Capital returned to contributories—£1 14s. 9·9d. per 12s. stock. £433 17s. 2d. was paid into Companies' Liquidation Account. Final meeting return regd. 9 Mar. 1956 **1956**

McNamara & Co. (1921) Ld. See above.

McNeill (F.) Holdings Ld. Regd. 18 May 1925 as F. McNeill & Co. (1925) Ld.; name changed to F. McNeill & Co. Ld. 27 Aug. 1925 and to present title 2 Oct. 1967. All capital acquired by British Insulated Callenders' Cables Ld. in Sept. 1968. Dissolved 2 May 1986 .... **1969**

Mace Rainbow & Stone Ld. Regd. 1939. Winding-up order 16 Sept. 1976. Final meeting return regd. 9 Sept. 1980 .... **1981–2**

Maco Spinning Co. Ld. Regd. 1905. Struck off Register Dec. 1930 .... **1931**

Maconochie's Solderless Tinning Syndicate Ld. See Solderless Tin Co. Ld.

McPhail & Simpson Ld. Regd. 1907. Vol. liq. 15 Jan. 1918. Final meeting return regd. 19 May 1921 .... ***1919**

McPhail & Simpsons' Dry Steam Patents Co. Ld. Regd. 1895. Court Order to wind up 26 Feb. 1907. Capital returned to contributories—3s. 4d. per share; further payments (if any) not known. Removed from Register 1912 .... **1908**

Macrae, Curtice & Co. Ld. Regd. 1887. Vol. liq. 30 July 1889. Taken over by Hansard Publishing Union Ld. Final meeting return regd. 19 May 1890 .... ***1890**

McSwiney Co Ld. See Dublin Drapery Warehouse Ld.

Madagascar Forests Co. Ld. Regd. 1889. Struck off Register 23 July 1901 .... **1902**

Madagascar Mercantile & Development Syndicate Ld. Regd. 1889. Vol. liq. 8 Jan. 1891. Final meeting return regd. 23 Jan. 1893 .... **1891**

Madagascar Oil Development Co. Ld. Regd. 1909. Struck off Register 1918 .... **1917**

Madagascar Rubber Co. Ld. Regd. 1910. Vol. liq. 1913. Struck off Register 1 Feb. 1944 .... **1944**

Madagascar Shipping Co. Ld. Regd. 1889. Struck off Register 11 June 1895 .... **1899**

Madagascar (Sumbava & Antalaha) Forests Syndicate Ld. Regd. 1890. Removed from Register 1908 ..... **1896**

Madagascar Syndicate Ld. Regd. 1888. Vol. liq. Feb. 1908. Removed from Register 1908 .... **1909**

Madam Hopkins Gold Mining Co. Ld. Inc. Victoria 1934. Vol. liq. (members') 21 Sept. 1936. Undertaking and assets were acquired by Talbot Alluvials Ld., in which company shareholders were entitled to 4 shares of 5s. (credited as fully-paid) for every 5 shares of 5s. held **1937**

Madame Ernest Ld. Regd. 1908 as Madame Ernest (1908) Ld., name changed May 1910. Vol. liq. (members') 17 Mar. 1932. Capital returned to contributories—£5,421 6s. 8d. Final meeting return regd. 4 May 1933 .... **1933**

Madame Hetty Ld. See M. X. H. Ld.

Madame Tussaud & Sons Ld. Regd. 1889. Vol. liq. 30 Aug. 1926. Reconstructed as Madame Tussaud's (1926) Ld. (later Madame Tussaud's Ld.). Final meeting return regd. 22 Nov. 1929 .... **1927**

Madame Val Smith Ld. Regd. 1897. Vol. liq. 28 Jan. 1927. Final meeting return regd. 12 Apr. 1928 .... **1927**

Madeira-Mamord Railway Co. Inc. in Maine in 1907. Company is now dormant, having ceased to operate and handed over the railway to the Brazilian Government as from 30 June 1931; in Apr. 1948 it was stated that there were no other assets remaining to be realised. Holders of 6% & 5½% 1st mortgage cumulative income bonds received a total of £14 6s.% **1952**

Madeira Mamoré Trading Co. Ld. Regd. 1919. Vol. liq. (creditors') 6 Nov. 1935. All shares were held by Madeira Mamoré Railway Co. and were deposited with trustees for bondholders. Final meeting return regd. 2 Jan. 1936 .... **1946**

Madeley Collieries Ld. Regd. 1924. Vol. liq. (members') 25 Feb. 1953. Capital returned to contributories—preference: 23s. 4d. per share of £1; ordinary: nil. £1,070 1s. 7d. was paid into Companies' Liquidation Account. Final meeting return regd. 12 Apr. 1956 **1957**

VOL. FOR

Madeline Witwatersrandt Gold Mining Co. Ld. Regd. 1889. Vol. liq. 7 Jan. 1895. Final meeting return regd. 2 June 1896 .... **1895**

Madras & Southern Mahratta Railway Co. Ld. Regd. 1882 as Southern Mahratta Railway Co. Ld., name changed Jan. 1908. Vol. liq. (members') 31 Mar. 1944. Capital returned to contributories—£112 6s. per £100 stock. £481 2s. 7d. was paid into Companies' Liquidation Account. Final meeting return regd. 13 Mar. 1950 .... **1951**

Madras Diamond Mining Co. Ld. Regd. 1899. Vol. liq. 17 May 1904. Final meeting return regd. 23 June 1914 .... **1905**

Madras Electric Supply Corporation Ld. Regd. 1906. Vol. liq. (members') 29 Sept. 1950. Undertaking acquired by Government of Madras. Capital returned to contributories (per £1 stock)—preference: £1; ordinary 27s. 9·1d. Final meeting return regd. 31 Dec. 1960 .... **1961**

Madras Electric Tramways Co. Ld. Regd. 1892. Court Order to wind up 15 Nov. 1899. Removed from Register 1904 .... **1900**

Madras Electric Tramways (1904) Ld. Regd. 1904. All ordinary capital was owned by Madras Electric Supply Corpn. Ld. Wound-up by order of Madras High Court in Jan. 1954. Holders of 5½% Registered Debentures received 8s. 2d. per £1 of the £63,400 outstanding principal amount. Struck off register 29 July 1966 .... **1965**

Madras Gold Mining Co. Ld. Regd. 1881. Vol. liq. Jan. 1883. Court Order to continue winding up under supervision Feb. 1883. Final meeting return regd. 25 Apr. 1884 .... **1884**

Madras Ice Manufacturing Co. Ld. Regd. 1879. Removed from Register 1903 .... **1902**

Madras Irrigation & Canal Co. Inc. by Special Act 1858. Vol. liq. 23 Mar. 1881, when negotiations were proceeding for sale of undertaking to Indian Government **1882**

Madras Presidency Diamond Fields Ld. Regd. 1888. Vol. liq. 24 July 1890. Final meeting return regd. 28 Sept. 1900 .... **1891**

Madras Railway Annuities. The A and B annuities terminated on 1 Apr. 1956. B annuities being entitled to a final distribution of £26 18s. 9d. per £1 annuity on 6 Apr. 1956 .... **1957**

Madras Railway Co. Inc. by Special Act 1853. Line purchased on 31 Dec. 1907 by Secretary of State for India by means of annuity. Liability for debentures was assumed by Secretary of State. Final distribution of realised value of surplus profits and property at rate of 3s. 6d. per £100 of old stock, free of income tax, was made in Mar. 1909. Dissolved 30 June 1909 **1910**

Madras Telephone Co. Ld. A substantial interest was acquired by the Government of India **1941**

Madras Tramways Co. Ld. Regd. 1873. Vol. liq. 1 Jan. 1877. Final meeting return regd. 6 Jan. 1883 .... ***1877**

Madrid & Portugal Direct Railway (Avila & Salamanca) Ld. Regd. 1887. Vol. liq. 20 Oct. 1927. Final meeting return regd. 22 Dec. 1927 .... **1928**

Madrid Markets Co. Ld. Regd. 1872. Court Orders: to wind up 14 Apr. 1877; to dissolve 28 Feb. 1888 .. ***1876**

Madsen's Patent Food Co. Ld. Regd. 1894. Struck off Register 22 Oct. 1897 .... **1899**

Madubi Tin Co. Ld. Regd. 1925. Vol. liq. 9 May 1929. Final meeting return regd. 16 May 1931 .... **1930**

Madulseema Coffee & Cinochona Co. Ld. Regd. 1880. Vol. liq. 29 Dec. 1925. The estates and certain assets were acquired by Scottish Trust & Loan Co. of Ceylon Ld. (later Scottish Tea & Lands Co. of Ceylon Ld.). Anticipated return to shareholders— 4·71 fully-paid shares of £1 in acquiring company plus £1 13s. 4d. in cash per preference share of £5 held; 9·42 fully-paid shares of £1 plus £3 6s. 8d. in cash per ordinary share of £10 held. Final meeting return regd. 14 July 1926 .... **1926**

Magadi Soda Co. Ld. Regd. 1911. Vol. liq. 13 Feb. 1924. Court Order to wind up 8 Apr. 1924. Undertaking and assets were acquired by company of same name. Shareholders were entitled to 1 2nd preference share of 5s. (credited as fully-paid) in new company for each ordinary share of £1 or 20 deferred shares of 1s. held. Holders of 1st debentures were entitled to an equal amount of 6%, 1st mortgage debentures. Holders of 2nd debentures were entitled to 75% of holding in 1st preference shares of £1. Court Order to dissolve 22 Mar. 1928 .... **1925**

Magalia Consolidated Gold Mines Ld. Regd. 1898. Reconstructed 1900 as Mines Development Co. of Victoria Ld., in which company shareholders were entitled to 1 share of 10s. (credited with 8s. 6d. paid) for each share of £1 held. Removed from Register 1901 .... **1901**

VOL. FOR

Magasins du Louvre (Paris & London), Ld. Regd. 1922. Vol. liq. (members') 13 May 1963. Nearly all capital was owned by Société du Louvre. Final meeting return regd. 30 Sept. 1963 .... **1938**

Magdeburg Tramways Co. Ld. Regd. 1884. Vol. liq. 3 Mar. 1897. Undertaking and assets were acquired by a German company. Capital returned to contributories—£4 5s. per share of £10 at Mar. 1897; further payments (if any) not known. Final meeting return regd. 11 May 1899 .... **1898**

Magnet Cinema (Wavertree) Ld. Regd. 1914. Vol. liq. 12 July 1928. Properties purchased by Denman Picture Houses Ld. Final meeting return regd. 13 Dec. 1928 **1940**

Magnetic Transmission Co. Ld. Regd. 1920. All available assets were distributed among debenture holders by Receiver. Struck off Register Apr. 1929 **1930**

Magor Ld. Regd. 1897. Undertaking and assets were acquired by Needhams Ld. Removed from Register 1903 .... **1904**

Magpie Mining Co. In liquidation in 1884 .... **1884**

Maguire & Gatchell Ld. Inc. in Dublin 1896. Vol. liq. 29 June 1962. Preference shares (of £5) repaid at par Aug. 1963. Distributions (if any) to ordinary shareholders not known. Amount paid into Companies' Liquidation Account; unclaimed dividends £81 5s 10d.; distributions £100. Final meeting return regd. 5 Jan. 1970 .... **1970**

Maguire, Paterson & Palmer Ld. Regd. 1919. Vol. liq. 12 Feb. 1923. Undertaking and assets were acquired by Bryant & May Ld. Final meeting return regd. 2 Sept. 1924 .... **1924**

Magyar Agrár-és Járadékbank R. T. See Hungarian Land Mortgage Bank.

Magyar Altalanos Takarék pénztar Részvénytarsasag. See Hungarian General Savings Bank.

Magyar Foldhitelintezet (see Hungarian Land Mortgage Institute) **1937**

Magyar Gold Mining Co. Ld. Regd. 1886. Struck off Register 26 Oct. 1900 .... **1901**

Mahara Royal Ld. Regd. 1896. Vol. liq. 8 Jan. 1903. Removed from Register 1908 .... **1903**

Mahawale Rubber & Tea Co. Ld. Regd. 1897 as Mahawale Tea Estate Co. Ld.; name changed Feb. 1907. Vol. liq. 12 Mar. 1920. Reconstructed as company of same name. Shareholders were entitled to 4 fully-paid shares of £1 for each share of £1 held. Final meeting return regd. 1 Aug. 1922 .... **1921**

Maiangwa Tin Mines Ld. Regd. 1927. Vol. liq. (creditors') 13 Nov. 1935. Assets realised insufficient to pay unsecured creditors in full. Final meeting return regd. 16 June 1937 .... **1936**

"Maid of Erin" Silver Mines Ld. Regd. 1891. Vol. liq. 25 Jan. 1893. Business was to be transferred to Maid of Erin Silver Mines Co. Ld. (inc. Colorado). Final meeting return regd. 31 Aug. 1894 .... **1893**

Maidenhead Gas Co. Established 1850. Inc. by Special Act 1876. Undertaking was acquired in 1924 by Uxbridge. Wycombe and District Gas Co. (later Uxbridge, Maidenhead, Wycombe & District Gas Co.), in which company holders of 5% standard consolidated stock were entitled to an equal amount of stock (5% standard) **1925**

Maidenhead Rubber Plantations Ld. Regd. 1919. Vol. liq. 31 Aug. 1923. Undertaking was acquired by Sungel Reyla (F. M. S.) Rubber Estate Ld. Final meeting return regd. 20 Nov. 1924 .... **1936**

Maidenhead Waterworks Co. Inc. by Special Act 1875. Under provisions of the Mid-Wessex Water Order 1956 the undertaking vested in the Mid-Wessex Water Co as from 1 Jan. 1957. Holders of the £153,224 5% consolidated ordinary stock received £10 5% additional ordinary stock of the Mid-Wessex Co. for every £10 stock held, and liability for the outstanding debenture stocks was assumed by that company. Company was dissolved by resolution of directors on 2 Sept. 1957 .... **1958**

Maidstone & Ashford Railway Co. Inc. by Special Act 1880 .... **1884**

Maidstone & Faversham Junction Light Railway Co. Inc. 1901 .... **1903**

Maidstone Gas Co. Inc. by Special Act 1858. Dissolved 1 May 1949, undertaking being vested in South Eastern Area Gas Board under Gas Act 1948. Holders of securities were entitled to receive, in respect of each £100 unit held, British Gas 3% guaranteed stock 1990—95 as follows:

	£	s.	d.	
Cap. stock (5% stand.)	175	0	0	
3% perp. deb. stock	85	0	0	**1952**

Maidstone Pavilion Ld. Regd. 1920. Vol. liq. (members') 31 July 1930. Capital returned to contributories—£1 2s. 8¾d. per preference share of £1. Final meeting return regd. 23 Dec. 1930 .... **1931**

VOL. FOR

Maidstone Waterworks Co. Inc. by Special Act 1860. Undertaking vested in Mid-Kent Water Co. on 1 Jan. 1971, stockholders received a like amount of a similar stock of that company in exchange for their holdings; the outstanding debenture stocks became debenture stocks of the Mid-Kent Water Co. Company was dissolved by declaration of directors on 16 Apr. 1971. .... **1971**

Maignen's "Filtre Rapide" & "Anti-Calcaire" Co. Ld. See Filter Engineers Ld.

Maikop Alliance Syndicate Ld. Regd. 1910. Vol. liq. 19 Jan. 1915. Final meeting return regd. 2 Mar.1918 **1915**

Maikop & Eastern Oil Co. Ld. Regd 1910. Vol. liq. Sept. 1912. Removed from Register 1913 .... **1913**

Maikop & General Petroleum Trust Ld. Regd. 1910. Vol. liq. 14 Oct. 1912. Reconstructed as Maikop Combine Ld., in which company shareholders were entitled to 1 share of 10s. (credited with 5s. paid) for each ordinary share of £1 held or each deferred share of 1s. held. Final meeting return regd. 21 June 1913 **1913**

Maikop Apsheron Oil Co. Ld. Regd. 1910. Vol. liq. 14 Oct. 1912. Undertaking was acquired by Maikop Combine Ld., in which company shareholders were entitled to 1 share of 10s. (credited with 7s. 6d. paid) for each share of £1 held. Final meeting return regd. 2 Dec. 1913 .... **1913**

Maikop Areas Ld. Regd. 1910. Vol. liq. 14 Oct. 1912. Undertaking was acquired by Maikop Combine Ld., in which company shareholders were entitled to 1 share of 10s. (credited with 7s. 6d. paid) for each share of £1 held. Final meeting return regd. 29 July 1913 .... **1913**

Maikop Central Co. Ld. Regd. 1910. Properties were abandoned. Struck off Register 20 July 1937 .... **1938**

Maikop Combine Ld. Regd. 1912. Struck off Register 17 Jan. 1950 .... **1951**

Maikop Co-operative Petroleum Co. Ld. Regd. 1910. Vol. liq. Feb. 1913. Struck off Register May 1929 **1930**

Maikop Deep Drilling Co. Ld. Regd. 1912. Vol. liq. 27 Jan. 1920. Shareholders were entitled to 2 fully-paid preference shares of 5s. in International Russian Oilfields Ld., for each share of £1 held. Final meeting return regd. 1 July 1920 .... **1920**

Maikop District Oil Co. Ld. Regd. 1910. Struck off Register 1922 .... **1922**

Maikop, European & General Oil Trust Ld. Regd. 1910. Court Order to wind up 21 Nov. 1911. Liquidator released 10 Dec. 1915. Struck off Register 14 Feb. 1919 .... **1913**

Maikop Hadijensky Syndicate Ld. Regd. 1910. Vol. liq. 14 Oct. 1912. Undertaking was acquired by Maikop Combine Ld., in which company shareholders were entitled to 1 share of 10s. (credited as fully-paid) for each share of £1 held. Final meeting return regd. 23 Apr. 1913 .... **1913**

Maikop Midland Oilfields Ld. Regd. 1910. Struck off Register 17 Jan. 1950 .... **1951**

Maikop Moscow Oil Co. Ld. Regd. 1910. Vol. liq. 31 July 1914. Final meeting return regd. 29 Sept. 1914 **1915**

Maikop Mutual Oil Transport Co. Ld. Regd. 1910. Vol. liq. 19 Dec. 1912. Undertaking and assets were acquired by Maikop Pipeline and Transport Co. Ld. in which company shareholders were entitled to 1 ordinary share of £1 (credited as fully-paid) for every 2 preference shares of £1 held or 1 deferred share of 1s. (credited as fully-paid) for every 5 deferred shares of 1s. held. Debenture holders were entitled to £105 debenture stock for every £100 debentures held. Final meeting return regd. 14 Dec. 1915 ...... **1913**

Maikop New Producers Ld. Regd. 1912. Vol. liq. 17 Mar. 1915 for purpose of amalgamation with Black Sea Oil Fields Ld. and Maikop Victory Oil Co. Ld., under title of Black Sea Amalgamated Oilfields Ld. Shareholders were entitled to receive 2 fully-paid shares of 10s. in the new company for every 5 shares of 10s. held **1955**

Maikop Oil and Petroleum Producers Ld. Regd. 1910. Vol. liq. 20 Dec. 1912. The undertaking was acquired by Maikop New Producers Ld., in which company shareholders were entitled to 1 fully-paid share of 10s. for every 5 shares of £1 held. Final meeting return regd. 21 Dec. 1913 .... **1913**

Maikop Oil Proprietary Co. Ld. Regd 1910. Vol. liq. 22 Jan. 1913. The undertaking was sold to International Russian Oilfields Ld., in which company shareholders were entitled to 2 shares of 5s. (credited as fully-paid) for each ordinary share of £1 held or 1 fully-paid share of 5s. for every 2 deferred B shares of 1s. held. Final meeting return regd. 23 July 1917 **1913**

Maikop Orient Oil Co. Ld. Regd. 1911. Struck off Register 13 Apr. 1951 .... **1952**

Maikop Pipeline & Transport Co. Ld. Regd. 1910. Struck off Register 17 Jan. 1950 .... **1950**

*See Stock Exchange Year-Book.

VOL. FOR

Maikop Premier Oil Syndicate Ld. Regd. 1910. Vol. liq. Jan. 1917. Struck off Register 31 Aug. 1937 1938

Maikop Refineries Ld. Regd. 1910. Struck off Register 17 Jan. 1950 1912

Maikop Russian Oil Co. Ld. Regd. 1910. Vol. liq. 21 Jan. 1913. The undertaking was sold to International Russian Oilfields Ld in which company shareholders were entitled to 2 shares of 5*s*. (credited as fully-paid) for each share of £1 (17*s*. 6*d*. paid) held. Final meeting return regd. 27 Oct. 1917 1913

Maikop Shirvansky Oil Co. Ld. Regd. 1910. Vol. liq. 20 Nov. 1911. The undertaking was acquired by Maikop Apsheron Oil Co. Ld., in which company shareholders were entitled to 112 fully-paid shares of £1 for every 100 shares of £1 held. Final meeting return regd. 14 Jan. 1915 1912

Maikop Spies Co. Ld. Regd. 1910. Struck off Register 28 Feb. 1939 1940

Maikop Standard Oilfields Ld. Regd. 1910. Vol. liq. 21 Jan. 1913. The undertaking was sold to International Russian Oilfields Ld., in which company shareholders were entitled to 1 share of 5*s*. (credited with 4*s*. paid) for each share of 5*s*. held. Final meeting return regd. 25 Sept. 1918 1913

Maikop Taman Oil Co. Ld. Regd. 1910. Struck off Register 23 Oct. 1942 1943

Maikop Touapse Oil Co. Ld. Regd. 1910. Vol. liq. 5 Mar. 1913. The undertaking was sold to International Russian Oilfields Ld., in which company shareholders were entitled to 1 share of 5*s*. (credited with 4*s*. paid) for each preferred share of £1 or every 2 deferred shares of 1*s*. held. Final meeting return regd. 22 Oct. 1913 1913

Maikop Valley Oil Co. Ld. Regd. 1910. Struck off Register 17 Jan. 1950 1951

Maikop Victory Oil Co. Ld. Regd. 1911. Vol. liq. 17 Mar. 1915 for purpose of amalgamation with Black Sea Oil Fields Ld. and Malkop New Producers Ld. under title of Black Sea Amalgamated Oilfields Ld. Shareholders were entitled to receive 1 fully-paid share of 10*s*. in the new company for each ordinary share of £1 held or 3 fully-paid shares of 10*s*. for every 20 deferred shares of 1*s*. held 1955

Maikop Water Works Ld. Regd. 1910. Struck off the Register 14 Dec. 1951 1917

Mailele Mining Co. Ld. Regd. 1935. Vol. liq. (members') 6 Sept. 1938. All capital owned by Gold & Base Metal Mines of Nigeria Ld. Final meeting return regd. 5 June 1939 1939

Main (A. & J.) & Co. Ld. Regd. in Edinburgh 1 Jan. 1896 as A. & J. Main & Co. Ld.; name changed to Armstrongs & Main Ld. in Sept. 1919 and to present title in Sept 1923. Vol. liq. (creditor') 11 July 1968. Return of final meeting regd. 30 June 1987. Distributions per preference share (of £1)—20p in Apr. & June and 10 p in Oct. 1971; 25p in June 1972; 12½p in June 1974 and final payment of 1·5p in Dec. 1985. Unclaimed distributions consigned with Accountant of the Court amounted to £666·92 1988–9

Main Colliery Co. Ld. Regd. 1889. Vol. liq. (creditors') 7 June 1934. Assets realised insufficient to pay creditors in full. Final meeting return regd. 6 Sept. 1935 1930

Main Mother Lode Syndicate Ld. Regd. 1905. Struck off Register 1919 1911

Main Reef Deep Ld. Inc. Transvaal 1899. Vol. liq. June 1909. Undertaking and assets were acquired by Consolidated Main Reef Mines and Estate Ld., in which company shareholders were entitled to 9 fully-paid shares of £1 for every 10 shares of £1 held 1910

Main Reef East Ld. Inc. Transvaal 1899. Vol. liq. June 1909. Undertaking and assets were acquired by Consolidated Main Reef Mines and Estate Ld., in which company shareholders were entitled to 9 fully-paid shares of £1 for every 10 shares of £1 held 1910

Main-Reef Extension Ld. Regd. 1896. Vol. liq. Apr. 1914. Capital returned to contributories—½*d*. per share of £1. Struck off Register Mar. 1930 1931

Main Reef Extension Ld. Regd. 1902. Vol. liq. Apr. 1914. Capital returned to contributories—½*d*. per share of £1; further payments (if any) not known. Struck off Register 1928 1915

Main Reef Gold Mining Co. Ld. Inc. Cape of Good Hope 1888. Assets and liabilities were taken over by Consolidated Main Reef Gold Mines and Estate Ld., in 1896 for 135,000 shares 1897

Main Reef West Ld. Inc. Transvaal 1899. Vol. liq. Jan. 1918. Undertaking and assets were acquired by Consolidated Main Reef Mines and Estate Ld., in which company shareholders were entitled to 1 fully-paid share of £1 for every 5 shares of £1 held or 9 fully-pald shares of £1 for every £10 debentures 1919

Main Ropeways Ld. Regd. 1922. Vol. liq. (creditors') 1 Dec. 1930. Assets realised insufficient to pay creditors in full. Final meeting return regd. 8 Apr. 1936 1931

Maindy Shipping Co. Ld. Regd. 1915. Vol. liq. 2 Dec. 1921. Final meeting return regd. 11 July 1928 1922

Mainland Consols Ld. Regd. 1895. Undertaking was acquired by Standard Exploration Co. Ld. Removed from Register 1903 1899

Mainland East Ld. Regd. 1897. Vol. liq. 20 Dec. 1898. Removed from Register 1901 1899

Main's Manufacturing Co., Carlisle Ld. Regd. 1877. Vol. liq. (creditors') 2 Sept. 1930. Assets realised insufficient to pay unsecured creditors in full. Final meeting return regd. 23 Dec. 1931 1931

Maisels Petroleum Trust Ld. Regd. 1911. Receiver appointed in 28 May 1938. Struck off Register 26 Jan. 1940 1940

Maison Doeuillet (Soc. Anon.). Inc. France 1924. Amalgamated with La Société Doucet as Doeuillet-Doucet S. A. Holders of *Actions* de *Jouissance* were entitled to receive 1 share in new company for each *Action* de *Jouissance* held 1929

Maison Virot Ld. Regd. 1897. Vol. liq. (creditors') 14 May 1930. No capital returned to contributories. Final meeting return regd. 29 July 1930 1931

Majestic Cinema (Stoke-on-Trent) Ld. Regd. 1920. Vol. liq. (members') 16 July 1935. All shares owned by Associated British Cinemas Ld. Final meeting return regd. 28 Dec. 1936 1936

Majestic Gold Mines Ld. Regd. 1897. Vol. liq. 9 Feb. 1903. Removed from Register 1905 1903

Majestic Mill Co. Ld. Regd. 1903. Vol. liq. 18 Nov. 1941. Redeemable preference and 10% tax-free preference shares repaid in full; ordinary shareholders received £2 8*s*. 11⅓*d* per share of £5—£4 10*s*. paid. £76 18*s*. 9*d*. was paid into Companies' Liquidation Account. Final meeting regd. 24 Nov. 1950 1951

Majunga Oilfields of Madagascar Ld. Regd. 1919. Struck off Register Feb. 1927 1927

Makaha Gold Fields Ld. Regd. 1899. Removed from Register 1906 1904

Makua Trading Corporation Ld. Regd. 1910. Vol. liq. 18 Nov. 1912. Final meeting return regd. 2 Sept. 1913 1913

Makwana, Transvaal, Tin Ld. Regd. 1909. Vol. liq. Sept. 1911. Removed from Register 1912 1912

Malabar Estates & Planting Co. Ld. Regd. 1913. Vol. liq. 14 Mar. 1916. Final meeting return regd. 5 Mar. 1926 1919

Malabar Oil Extraction Co. Ld. Regd. 1914. Vol. liq. 17 Jan. 1924. Practically all capital held by Eastern Development Corporation Ld. Final meeting return regd. 19 Sept. 1924 1924

Malacate Mining & Smelting Co. Ld. Regd. 1895. Court Order to wind up 10 Nov. 1897. Removed from Register 1908 1898

Malaga Electricity Co. Ld. Regd. 1896. Vol. liq. 26 Aug. 1921. Capital returned to contributories—£2 15*s*. per ordinary share of £5 in Sept. 1921; further payments (if any) not known. Final meeting return regd. 27 July 1923 1922

Malang Rubber Estates Ld. Regd. 1910. Vol. liq. 17 Feb. 1920. Undertaking and assets were acquired by Amalgamated Rubber Estates Ld. (later Amalgamated Rubber & General Estates Ld.), in which company shareholders were entitled to 1 fully-paid share of 2*s*. for each share of 2*s*. held. Final meeting return regd. 2 Feb. 1921 1920

Malay & Foreign Contract Syndicate Ld. *See* Tin & Trading Co. of Nigeria Ld.

Malay & General Finance Corporation Ld. Regd. 1926. Vol. liq. (members') 8 Feb. 1932. Capital returned to contributories—4*s*. 3$\frac{11}{32}$*d*. per share of 5*s*. Final meeting return regd. 24 June 1932 1932

Malay Coconut Estates (21st Mile) Syndicate Ld. Regd. 1920. Vol. liq. (members') 4 Nov. 1935. Undertaking was acquired by Malay Coconut Estates Ld., in which company shareholders were entitled to 2 shares of £1 (credited as fully-paid) for every 3 shares of £1 held. Final meeting return regd. 18 Sept. 1936 1936

Malay Peninsula Coffee Co. Ld. Regd. 1896. Vol. liq. 12 July 1901. Final meeting return regd. 6 Nov.1901 1902

Malay States Tin Mines Ld. Regd. 1896. Vol. liq. 2 Dec. 1904. Final meeting return regd. 29 Aug. 1907 1905

Malaya and Siam Corporation Regd. 1907. Vol. liq. 9 Aug. 1929. Final meeting return regd. 10 Dec. 1931 1929

Malaya Consolidated Tin Dredging Co. Ld. Inc. Straits Settlements 1926. Vol. liq. (members') 29 Mar. 1935. Shareholders received 7 shares of 5*s*. in Southern Kinta Consolidated Ld., for every 100 shares of $1 held and 1·16 cents cash for every share held 1936

Malaya Rubber Investment Corporation Ld. Regd. 1925. Assets were pledged to bankers for sums in excess of their value. Struck off Register 19 Feb. 1937 1938

VOL. FOR

Malayalam Rubber & Produce Co. Ld. Regd. 1909. Vol. liq. 8 July 1921. Reconstructed as Malayalam Plantations Ld., in which company shareholders were entitled to 3 shares of £1 (credited with 13s. 4d. paid) for every 2 shares of £1 held. Final meeting return regd. 30 Dec. 1922 .... **1921**

Malayan & General Trust Ld. Regd. 1926 as Malayan & General Tin Trust Ld.; name changed June 1928. Vol. liq. (members') 15 May 1933. Debenture stockholders received 5 fully-paid shares of 5s. in Kamra Tin Dredging Ld. (later Kamra Investments Ld.), for each £1 stock held. Undertaking and assets acquired by Malayan & General Trust (1933) Ld., in which company shareholders received 1 share of 4s. (credited with 2s. 10d. paid) for each share held. Final meeting return regd. 10 Sept. 1941 .... **1939**

Malayan & General Trust (1933) Ld. Regd. 1933. Vol. liq. (members') 15 Dec. 1938. Capital returned to contributories—3·85d. per share of 2s. £900 6s. 10d. was paid into Companies' Liquidation Account. Final meeting return regd. 2 Sept. 1941 .... **1945**

Malayan (Pahang) Concession Co. Ld. Regd. 1888. Reconstructed 1895 as Malayan (Pahang) Exploration Co. Ld., in which company shareholders were entitled to 1 share of £1 (credited as fully-paid) for each share of £1 held; debenture holders were entitled to 1 fully-paid share of £1 for every £1 debenture held. Removed from Register 1903 ...... **1902**

Malayan (Pahang) Exploration Co. Ld. Regd. 1895. Removed from Register 1903 .... **1903**

Malayan Tinfields Ld. Regd. 1925. Vol. liq. (members') 19 Apr. 1937. Shareholders were entitled to receive either (a) pro rata portion of investments held, or (b) £1 11s. 2½d. per share of £1 in cash. Final meeting return regd. 28 Dec. 1937 .... **1938**

Malcolm Mines Ld. Regd. 1902. Vol. liq. Dec. 1908. Removed from Register 1909 .... **1909**

Maldon Gas Light Co. Ld. Regd. 1869. Dissolved 1 May 1949, undertaking being vested in Eastern Area Gas Board under Gas Act 1948. Holders of securities were entitled to receive, in respect of each £1 unit held, British Gas 3% guaranteed stock 1990–95 as follows:

	£	s.	d.
Ord. shares (8½% max)	14	0	
5% pref. shares	1	2	5

1952

Maldon Goldfields Ld. Regd. 1901. Vol. liq. 11 Dec. 1905. Final meeting return regd. 9 June 1906 ...... **1906**

Maliboda Tea Estate Ld. Regd. 1913. Vol. liq. 28 Feb. 1921. Final meeting return regd. 27 Nov. 1922 .... **1922**

Malim Nawar Tin Ld. Inc. Federated Malay States 1923. Vol. liq. (members') 14 July 1939. Undertaking and assets were acquired by Kuala Kampar Tin Fields Ld., in which company shareholders were entitled to 3 shares of 10s. (credited as fully-paid) for every 5 shares of £1 held **1940**

Maliwan Rubber Co. Ld. Regd. 1926. The estate was acquired in 1936 by Hevea (Burma) Co. Ld., for £7,500 in fully-paid shares of 2s. Vol. liq. (members') 4 Aug. 1937. Final meeting return regd. 18 May 1938 **1938**

Mallandain (A. E.) Investments Ld. Regd. 1923 as Albert E. Mallandain Ld.& name changed Jan. 1937. Vol. liq. (members') 23 Apr. 1937. Holders of A preference and employees shares were repaid in full. Holders of B preference and ordinary shares received £6,715 and £5,407 12s. respectively in cash and a proportion of shares in Albert E. Mallandain Ld. (regd. 1937). Final meeting return regd. 5 Nov. 1940 .... **1938**

Mallina Consols Ld. Regd. 1895. Vol. liq. 11 Feb. 1897. Final meeting return regd. 28 July 1898 .... **1898**

Mallina Gold Mine Ld. Regd. Edinburgh 1896. Vol. liq. July 1903. Undertaking sold to Melvin & Oriental Mines Ld in which company shareholders received 4 fully-paid preference shares of 5s. for every preferred ordinary share of £1 held or 2 ordinary shares of 5s. (credited with 3s. paid) for every 1 ordinary share of £1 held. Final meeting return regd. 6 Mar. 1905 .... **1904**

Malloch (G. S.) & Co. Ld. Regd. 1928. Vol. liq. (members') 30 June 1932. Undertaking and assets were transferred to Allied Paper Merchants (W. T. & Co.) Ld. All shares held by Wiggins, Teape & Alex. Pirie (Merchants) Ld. Final meeting return regd. 30 Oct. 1933 .... **1933**

Malmani Gold Syndicate Ld. Regd. 1894. Receiver for debenture holders appointed in July 1911. Struck off Register 1915. Court Order to restore Oct. 1918. Struck off Register 19 Mar. 1948 .... **1912**

Malmesbury Electric Supply Co. Ld. Regd. 1923. Vol. liq. (members') 3 Oct. 1933. Electric supply undertaking acquired by Wessex Electricity Co. Final meeting return regd. 22 Feb. 1934 .... **1934**

Malmesbury Gas & Coke Co. Ld. Regd. 1887. Dissolved 1 May 1949, undertaking being vested in South

Western Area Gas Board under Gas Act 1948. Holders of securities were entitled to receive British Gas 3% guaranteed stock 1990–95 as follows in respect of each £10 unit, unless otherwise stated, of security held:

	£	s.	d.	
A ord. shares	23	0	0	
B ord. shares	23	0	0	
C ord. shares (of £1)	2	6	0	
3½% debs. (of £100)	100	0	0	**1952**

Malta and Mediterranean Gas Co. Ld. Regd. 1861. Vol. liq. (members') 27 Mar. 1953. Undertaking reverted to the local authority Nov. 1952. Capital returned to contributories amounted to £293 5s. per £100 ordinary and 1st and 2nd preference stocks. Final meeting return regd. 22 May 1959 .... **1960**

Malta Mill Co. Ld. Regd. 1920. Vol. liq. (members') 27 Aug. 1941. Capital returned to contributories (per share of 6s. 8d.) 7s. 4·45d. £52 was paid into Companies' Liquidation Account. Final meeting return regd. 24 Apr. 1952 .... **1953**

Malta Railway Co. Ld. Regd. 1879. Court Order to wind up 2 May 1891. Liquidator released 15 June 1894. Struck off Register 11 Aug. 1905 .... **1892**

Malta Tramways Ld. Regd. 1908. Vol. liq. 17 May 1918. Final meeting return regd. 17 Jan. 1920 .... **1919**

Maltby Main Colliery Co. Ld. Regd. 1907. Vol. liq. (members') 30 Mar. 1949. Final meeting return regd. 28 Dec. 1949 .... **1940**

Maltby's Motor Works & Garage Ld. Regd. 1906. Undertaking acquired by Caffyn's Ld. (which company owned all capital). Vol. liq. 15 Dec. 1954. Final meeting return regd. 16 Dec. 1955 .... **1938**

Malton Gas Co. Inc. by Special Act 1880. Dissolved 1 May 1949, undertaking being vested in North Eastern Area Gas Board under Gas Act 1948. Holders of original shares (of £10) were entitled to receive £26 British Gas 3% guaranteed stock 1990–95 for each share held. Liability in respect of certain mortgage loans assumed by the Board. **1952**

Malton Investment Trust Ld. Regd. 1933. Vol. liq. (members') 7 Dec. 1977. Capital returned to contributories—524·77p (per £1 ordinary share). Amount apaid into Companies' Liquidation Account £268·45 in respect of unclaimed dividends and £1,039·56 in respect of unclaimed distributions. Final meeting return regd. 4 Oct. 1978 ....**1979–80**

Mambau (F. M. S.) Rubber Co. Ld. Regd. 1909. Winding-up order 17 Apr. 1962. 100p in £1 paid to all creditors and 100p in £1 paid per preference share of £1 and £1·75 paid per ordinary share of £1. £1,242·50 paid into Companies' Liquidation Account **1977-8**

Mamia River Rubber Estates Ld. Regd. 1910. Vol. liq. Oct. 1911. Removed from Register 1913 .... **1912**

Mammoth Collins Gold Mines Ld. Regd. 1895. Removed from Register 1906 .... **1903**

Mammoth Copper Mine Ld. Regd. Edinburgh 1907. Vol. liq. Dec. 1925. Final meeting return regd. 8 Jan. 1927 .... **1926**

Mananu Gold Mining Co. Ld. Regd. 1899. Reconstructed 1902 as company of same name. Removed from Register 1904 .... **1903**

Mananu Gold Mining Co. Ld. Regd. 1902. Removed from Register 1906 .... **1940**

Manáos Improvements Ld. Regd. 1906. Receiver appointed Apr. 1923. 6% prior lien bonds were repaid in full plus accrued interest. Struck off Register 9 Jan. 1948 .... **1948**

Manaos Tramways & Light Co. Ld. Regd. 1909. Final meeting regd. 4 Jan. 1977 .... **1970**

Manbré Saccharine Co. Ld. Regd. 1897. Vol. liq. 19 Aug. 1919. Reconstructed as Manbré Sugar and Malt Ld. (later Manbré & Garton Ld.). Final meeting return regd. 3 Aug. 1920 .... **1920**

Manchester & County Bank Ld. See County Bank Ld.

Manchester & County Property Co. Ld. Regd. 1874. Removed from Register 1904 .... **1891**

Manchester & District Billiard Halls Ld. See Temperance Billiard Halls Ld.

Manchester & District Edison Electric Light Co. Ld. See Manchester Edison Swan Co. Ld.

Manchester & District Picture House Co. Ld. Regd. 1920. Court Order to wind up 1 Dec. 1925. Struck off Register Aug. 1930 .... **1931**

Manchester & Leeds Railway Co. See Lancashire and Yorkshire Railway Co.

Manchester & Liverpool Electric Express Railway Co. Inc. 1901. In July 1903 the share capital was offered for public subscription, but no allotment was made **1904**

Manchester & Liverpool Electric Railway Syndicate Ld. Regd. 1899. Removed from Register 1910 .... **1907**

Manchester & Liverpool Transport Co. Ld. Regd. 1898. Removed from Register 1910 .... **1904**

VOL. FOR

Manchester & London Fire Insurance Co. Ld. Regd. 1878. Vol. liq. Dec. 1883. Business was taken over by Manchester Fire Assurance Co. Final meeting return regd. 9 Mar. 1885 1885

Manchester & Milford Railway Co. Inc. by Special Act 1860. Undertaking sold to Great Western Railway Co., in July 1911 on following terms; priority debentures to receive £200 and the 5% and 4½% debentures £92 of Great Western 2½% debenture stock for each £100 held. Holders of ordinary and preference capital received nothing 1912

Manchester & Oldham Bank Ld. Regd. 1880 as Bank of Oldham Ld.; name changed Sept. 1881. Vol. liq. 29 Apr. 1884. Court Order to continue winding up under supervision May 1884. Final meeting return regd. 25 Mar. 1895 1885

Manchester & Salford Steamship Co. Ld. Regd. 1898. Struck off Register 18 July 1919 .... *1919

Manchester Assurance Co. Established 1824 and regd. as unlimited 1846. Vol. liq. 24 June 1904. The assets and liabilities were acquired by Atlas Assurance Co. Ld., in which company shareholders were entitled to 1 share of £10 (credited with £1 4s. paid) for each share of £20 (£2 paid) held 1905

Manchester Balata Belting Co. Ld. Regd. 1909. Vol. liq. 8 Feb. 1927. All shares owned by Dunlop Rubber Co. Ld. (later Dunlop Co. Ld.). Final meeting return regd. 30 July 1928 1928

Manchester Brewery Co. Ld. Regd. 1888. A subsidiary of Wilson & Walker Breweries Ld. Vol. liq. (members') 6 Nov. 1956. Final meeting return regd. 14 Mar. 1957 1955

Manchester, Bury, Rochdale & Oldham Steam Tramways Co. Inc. 1884. In liq. in 1888 1888

Manchester Canadian Investments Ld. See Manchester Trust Ld.

Manchester Carriage & Tramways Co. Ld. Inc. 1880; regd. as limited 1901. Undertaking acquired by Corporation of Manchester and other local authorities. Capital returned to contributories—10s. in the £ in Oct. 1903; further payments (if any) not known. Removed from Register 1907 1904

Manchester Collieries Ld. Regd. 1929. Vol. liq. (members') 19 Nov. 1954. Capital returned to contributories—9s. 1·6836d. per ordinary share of 5s. £2,892 11s. 1d. was paid into Companies' Liquidation Account. Final meeting return regd. 24 July 1956 ... 1957

Manchester District Motor Omnibus Co. Ld. Regd. 1906. Vol. liq. 4 Dec. 1906. Removed from Register 1909 1907

Manchester Dry Docks Co. Ld. Regd. 1891 as Manchester Ship Canal Pontoons & Dry Docks Co. Ld.; name changed Feb. 1906. Vol. liq. 7 Aug. 1924. Business acquired by company of same name. Final meeting return regd. 21 Aug. 1926 1925

Manchester Edison-Swan Co. Ld. Regd. 1882 as Manchester and District Edison Electric Light Co. Ld.; name changed Oct. 1887. Vol. liq. 21 Dec. 1896. Final meeting return regd. 20 June 1898 1896

Manchester Freeholds Ld. Regd. 1897. Vol. liq. 27 Mar. 1924. Final meeting return regd. 15 Jan. 1926 ..... *1925

Manchester Gold Coast Corporation Ld. Regd. 1901. Vol. liq. July 1905. Removed from Register 1907 1906

Manchester Hippodrome & Ardwick Empire Ld. See below.

Manchester Hippodrome Ld. Regd. Edinburgh 1903 as Manchester Hippodrome & Ardwick Empire Ld.; name changed 1942. A subsidiary of Stoll Theatres Corpn. Ld. Vol. liq. (members') 20 Oct. 1954. Final meeting return regd. 10 May 1955 1951

Manchester Hotel Co. Ld. Regd. 1879. Vol. liq. 13 June 1907. Struck off Register 10 Oct. 1916. 1908

Manchester Investors Ld. Regd. 1900. Vol. liq. 29 Oct. 1920. Final meeting return regd. 29 June 1922 1921

Manchester Joint Stock Bank Ld. Regd. 1873. Vol. liq. 1892. Business taken over by London and Midland Bank Ld. (later Midland Bank Ld.), in which company shareholders were entitled to receive 1 share (credited with £12 10s. paid) together with cash payment of £2 15s. 0d. for every 3 shares (with £6 paid) held; shareholders who preferred cash received £13 5s. per share 1893

Manchester Motor Transport Co. Ld. Regd. 1902. Vol. liq. 8 Nov. 1906. Removed from Register 1907 ... 1907

Manchester Palace of Varieties, Ld. Regd. 1889. All capital was owned by Moss Empires Ld. (later M. E. Theatres Ld.). Vol. liq. (members') 8 Nov. 1960. Final meeting return regd. 9 Feb. 1962 1960

Manchester Patent Fuel Works Ld. Regd. 1897. Removed from Register 1909 1905

Manchester Public Hall Co. Ld. Regd. as unlimited 1857; re-regd. as limited 1896. Vol. liq. 31 Mar. 1921. Capital returned to contributories—£24 5s. 9d. per share of £10 at Sept. 1921; further payments (if

VOL. FOR

any) not known. Final meeting return regd. 19 Jan. 1922 1922

Manchester Real Ice Skating & Supply Co. Ld. Regd. 1896. Removed from Register 1908 1900

Manchester, Salford & District Public House Trust Co. Ld. Regd. 1902. Vol. liq.. 7 July 1914. Final meeting return regd. 18 Nov. 1915 .... *1914

Manchester, Sheffield & Lincolnshire Railway Co. See Great Central Railway Co.

Manchester Ship Canal Pontoons & Dry Docks Co. Ld. See Manchester Dry Docks Co. Ld.

Manchester Ship Canal Warehousing Co. Ld. Regd. 1895. Vol. liq. 21 Jan. 1949. Capital returned to contributories—21s. per £1 preference stock; £1 6s. 8½d. per £1 ordinary stock. Final meeting return registered 22 Apr. 1950 1951

Manchester South Junction & Altrincham Railway Co. Dissolved 2 Apr. 1949; undertaking vested 1 Jan. 1948 in British Transport Commission under Transport Act 1947 1949

Manchester Temperance Hotels Co. Ld. Regd. 1892. Vol. liq. 6 Jan. 1964. Final meeting return regd. 19 June 1981 1947

Manchester Timber Importers Ld. Regd. 1899. Removed from Register 1904 1904

Manchester Traction Co. Ld. Regd. 1897. Removed from Register 1904 1904

Manchester Trust Ld. Regd. 1889. Vol. liq. 23 Nov. 1921. Capital returned to contributories—£50 per founders' share; £1 per ordinary share in Dec. 1921; further payments (If any) not known. Final meeting return regd. 4 July 1923 1922

Manchester Trust Ld. Regd. 1912 as Manchester Canadian Investments Ld.; name changed Oct. 1924. Vol. liq. (members') 18 Dec. 1952. Final meeting return regd. 15 Sept. 1953 1950

Manchester Underwriters' Association Ld. Regd. 1882. Vol. liq. 19 Mar. 1891. Business was acquired by International Marine Insurance Co. Ld. Final meeting return regd. 13 July 1893 1892

Manchester Victoria Hotel Co. Ld. Regd. 1888. Vol. liq. 19 Mar. 1891. Court Order to continue winding up under supervision 21 Mar. 1891. Final meeting return regd. 28 Apr. 1892 .... *1892

Manchester Warehouse Property Co. Ld. Regd. 1874. Vol. liq. (members') 25 Oct. 1948. Capital returned to contributories—£17 0s. 4d. per share of £20. Final meeting return regd. 17 Oct. 1949 1950

Manchu Syndicate Ld. Regd. 1905. Vol. liq. June 1913. Removed from Register 1913 1914

Mancora Oilfields Ld. Regd. 1920. Removed from Register 1 May 1942 1943

Mandalay Gold Dredging Co. Ld. Regd. 1902 as Mazoe Alluvial Gold Co. Ld.; name changed Dec. 1904. Vol. liq. Aug. 1906. Removed from Register 1908 1907

Manero Ld. See Bristol Hotel & Palmerston Co. Ld.

Mangana Gold Reefs Ld. Regd. 1906. Removed from Register 1911 1910

Mangana (Tasmania) Gold Reefs Ld. Regd. 1896. Reconstructed 1906 as Mangana Gold Reefs Ld., in which company shareholders were entitled to 12 shares of 10s. (credited as fully-paid) for each preference share of £1 held or 1 fully-paid share of 10s. for each ordinary share of £1 held. Removed from Register 1909 1908

Manganese Bronze & Brass Co. Ld. Regd. 1882. Vol. liq. 8 Mar. 1899. Reconstructed as company of same name (later Manganese Bronze Holdings Ld.). Shareholders were entitled to 10 preference and 10 ordinary shares of £1, all fully-paid, for each share of £10 (£6 paid) held or 14 preference and 10 ordinary shares of £1, all fully-paid, for each fully-paid share of £10 held. Final meeting return regd. 17 Feb. 1900 1899

Mangara Exploration Ld. Regd. 1897. Vol. liq. June 1913. Removed from Register 1913 1914

Mangara Exploration (1909) Ld. Regd. 1909. Vol. liq. 20 Oct. 1913. Final meeting return regd. 25 Mar. 1918 *1914

Mangles Bros. Coorg Coffee Estates Ld. Regd. 1922. Vol. liq. (members') 14 Aug. 1956. Capital returned to contributories—18s. 9d. per share of 5s. £2,526 9s. 6d. paid into Companies' Liquidation Account. Final meeting return regd. 16 Jan. 1962 1963

Manhattan Railway Co. Organised in New York 1875. Resolution to dissolve passed 16 Dec. 1940. 4% consolidated mortgage gold bondholders received $825 per $1,000 bond in 3% corporate stock of City of New York *plus* a sum in cash 1941

Manica & Mashonaland Exploring Co. Ld. Regd. 1891. Vol. liq. 20 Mar. 1905. Final meeting return regd. 23 July 1918 1906

Manica Copper Development Co. Ld. Regd. 1902. Vol. liq. Aug. 1909. The property was sold on behalf of 1st debenture holders. No capital returned to contributories. Removed from Register 1911 1910

See Stock Exchange Year-Book.

	VOL. FOR
Manica Development Syndicate Ld. Regd. 1903. Vol. liq. Jan. 1908. Removed from Register 1911	1908
Manica Explorers Ld. Regd. 1896 as Western Explorers Ld.: name changed Jan. 1903. Removed from Register 1908	1904
Manica Explorers Ld. Inc. Guernsey 1904. Vol. liq. Jan. 1909	1910
Manica Gold Dredging & Mining Syndicate (East Africa) Ld. Regd. 1901. Removed from Register 1906	1904
Manica Ophir Mining Co. Ld. Regd. 1889. Vol. liq. 4 July 1892. Final meeting return regd. 11 Sept. 1893	1893
Manihot Rubber Plantations Ld. Regd. 1910. Court Order to wind up 3 Feb. 1926. Debenture holders received 6s. 3¾d. in £. £78 18s. 1d. was paid to Official Receiver in respect of unclaimed dividends. Liquidator released 10 Oct. 1940. Struck off Register 19 May 1944	1926
Manila & General Investment Trust Ld. See Abchurch & General Investment Trust Ld.	
Manila Electric Company. Inc. Philippine Is. 1919. All outstanding bonds were paid off in Sept. 1945	1946
Manila Exploration Co. Ld. Regd. 1900. Vol. liq. 12 May 1901. Final meeting return regd. 23 Dec. 1901	1902
Manila Railroad Co. (of New Jersey), Inc. New Jersey 1906. Assets and liabilities were transferred to Manila Railroad Co. of Alabama, which company was merged into Manila Railroad Co. (Inc. Philippine Islands). All capital held by Philippine Government. The (Southern Lines) 1st mortgage 4% gold bonds were taken over by the Manila Railroad Co. of Philippine Islands	1922

Manila Railway Co. Ld. Regd. 1888. Vol. liq. 3 Jan. 1806. Court Order to stay proceedings 5 May 1900. Vol. liq. 7 June 1907. Reconstructed as Manila Railway Co. (1906) Ld. Holders of securities were entitled to securities in new company as follows:

For every £100 held
5% 1st mort. regd. stk.
....£112 4% A deb. bonds
6%p. lien mort. bds. A
....£120 4% A deb. bonds
6%p. lien mort. bds. B ...£115 4% A deb. bonds
6% Secured notes ....£112 4% A deb. bonds
⎰£100 4% B deb. bonds
6% debentures ....⎨£100 pref. shares
⎱£6 cash
7% cum. pref. shares ......£150 pref. shares
Ordinary shares ....£300 ord. shares
Deferred shares ....£300 ord. shares
Final meeting return regd. 24 June 1919 .... **1907**

	VOL. FOR
Manila Railway Co. (1906) Ld. Regd. 1906. Vol. liq. (members') 16 June 1954. Capital returned to contributories—£1 per £1 preference stock and 10s. 3¾d. per 1s. ordinary stock. FInal meeting return regd. 26 Sept. 1956	1958
Manitoba Land Co Ld. Regd. 1882. Removed from Register 1906	1887
Manitoba Land Co. Ld. Regd. 1888. Removed from Register 1910	1898
Manitoba Land Co. Ld. Regd. 1898. Vol. liq. Mar. 1909. Removed from Register 1910	1910
Manitoba Mortgage & Investment Co. Ld. Regd 1880. Vol. liq. 18 July 1906. Struck off Register 30 Jan. 1923	1908
Manitoba Mortgage & Investment Co. Ld. Regd. 1806. Vol. liq. (creditors') 6 July 1912. Holders of B income bonds received 9d. in £. Final meeting return regd. 2 Aug. 1933	1933
Manitoba Real Estate Co. Ld. Regd. 1888. Assets were acquired by Manitoba Mortgage & Investment Co. Ld. Removed from Register 1910	1896
Manitoulin & North Shore Railway Co. See Algoma Eastern Railway Co.	
Mann, & Cook (West Africa) Ld. Regd. 1920. Vol. liq. 6 Jan. 1922. Final meeting return regd. 26 May 1926	1922
Mann, Byars & Co. Ld. Regd. 1920 as Mann, Byars & Co. (1920) Ld.; name changed Aug. 1921. Vol. liq. (members') 24 Apr. 1939. Capital returned to contributories—15s. 6·81d. per preference share of £1. Final meeting return regd 12 Aug. 1941	1943
Mann, Little & Co. Ld. Regd. 1920 as Thompson Alpine & Co. Ld.; name changed 8 Feb. 1921. Vol. liq. 17 Dec. 1926. Final meeting return regd. 29 July 1927	*1927
Mannesmann Tube Co. Ld. Regd. 1888. Vol. liq. 1 Dec. 1898. Court Order to continue winding up under supervision 11 Mar. 1899. Undertaking was acquired by Newport & South Wales Tube Co. Ld. Struck off Register 19 Oct. 1906	1940
Mannheim Exploring Co. Ld. Regd 1895. Removed from Register 1904	1901
Manning Wardle & Co. Ld. Regd. 1905. Receiver for debenture stockholders appointed in Sept 1927. All the assets were realised and the goodwill was taken over by Kitson & Co. Ld. The proceeds were	

	VOL. FOR
insufficient to satisfy claims of prior lien debenture holders. Struck off Register 8 Dec. 1931	1930
Manningtree & Mistley Gas Co. Ld. Regd. 1899. Dissolved 1 May 1949, undertaking being vested in Eastern Area Gas Board under Gas Act 1948. Holders of securities were entitled to receive in respect of each £5 unit held, British Gas 3% guaranteed stock 1990–95 as follows:	

	£	s.	d.	
Ord. shares	7	10	0	
5% pref. shares	5	14	0	1952

	VOL. FOR
Mano Marques (Mexico) Rubber & Tobacco Estates Ld. Regd. 1903 as Chilian Exploration and Development Syndicate Ld.; name changed Mar. 1910. Struck off Register Feb. 1933	1933
Manor Farm Dairy Ld. Regd. 1894. Vol. liq. (members') 19 Mar. 1931. Capital returned to contributories—£117,565 6s. 10d. Final meeting return regd. 20 Mar. 1934	1932
Manor Powis Coal Co. Ld. Regd. Edinburgh 1910. Vol. liq. (creditors') 28 Dec. 1954. £14 8s was paid to Accountant of the Court. Final meeting return regd. 11 Mar. 1960	1961
Manor Trust Ld. Regd 1922. Vol. liq. Feb. 1928. Struck off Register 2 Feb. 1937	1937
Manoravon Steamship Co. Ld. See Griffiths Lewis Steam Navigation Co. Ld.	
Manchester & District Tramways Ld. See below.	
Mansfield District Omnibus Co. Ld. Regd. 1906 as Mansfield & District Tramways Ld.; name changed May 1933. Vol. liq. (members') 24 Nov. 1937. DIssolved before 1951	1938
Mansfield Engineering Co. Ld. Regd. 1923 as Mansfield Engineering Co. (1923) Ld.; name changed Oct. 1924. Vol. liq. (members') 29 June 1932. Capital returned to contributories—1s. 10½d. per share of 12s. 6d. Final meeting return regd. 18 Oct. 1939	1933

Mansfield Railway Co. Inc. by Special Act 1910. In 1923 the undertaking was merged into tbe London & North Eastern Railway Co., in which company stockholders were entitled to stock as follows:

For every £100 held — L. N. E. R.
5% Preference ....£125 4% 2nd Pref.
⎰£112½ 5% Prefd. Ord.
Ordinary ....⎨£25 Defd. Ordinary
The liability for £120,000 5% Terminable Debenture Stock was transferred to the London & North Eastern Railway Company **1924**

	VOL. FOR
Mansions Proprietory Ld. Regd. 1896. Court Order to wind up Feb. 1902. Reconstructed 1903 as St. Ermin's Hotel Ld., in which company shareholders were entitled to 1 ordinary share of £1, fully-paid, for every 10 shares of £1 held. Removed from Register 1909	1908
Mansu (Wassau) Gold Mines Ld. Regd 1900. Vol. liq. Sept. 1905. Removed from Register 1906	1906
Manta Mining Co. Ld. Regd. 1909. Vol. liq. (creditors') 30 Mar. 1939. Assets realised insufficient to pay unsecured creditors in full. Final meeting return regd. 16 Mar. 1940	1941
Mantle (John) & Sons Ld. Regd. 1898. Vol. liq. 31 Jan. 1925. Final meeting return regd. 23 Oct. 1925	1926
Mantraim (Wassau) Ld. Regd 1901. Removed from Register 1906	1906
Manufacture D'Impressions de Malannay Ld. See Etablissements Grafton (Français) Ld.	
Manufacturers' Accident Insurance Co. See Dominion of Canada General Insurance Co.	
Manufacturers' Guarantee & Accident Insurance. See Dominion of Canada General Insurance Co.	
Manufacturers' Trust & Finance Co. Ld. Regd. 1899. Vol. liq. 4 Jan. 1910. Final meeting return regd. 17 Jan. 1922	1910
Manvers Main Collieries Ld. Regd. 1889. Vol. liq. (members') 25 Sept. 1952. Capital returned to contributories—£2 9s. 0·9d. per share of 5s. £1,401 4s. 8d. was paid into Companies' Liquidation Account. Final meeting return regd 16 Oct. 1956	1957
Manx Bank Ld. Inc. under Act of Tynwald 1882. Undertaking was acquired by Mercantile Bank of Lancashire Ld	1901
Manx Electric Railway Co. Ld. See Atholl Investments Ld.	
Manx Northern Railway Co. Inc. by Act of Tynwald 1878. Under Isle of Man Railway Act 1904, undertaking was sold to that company for £60,000	1906
Manxland Bus Services Ld. In liquidation. Direct controlling interest was held by Isle of Man Railway Co.	1931
Maori Dream Gold Mines Ld. Regd 1896. Removed from Register 1906	1900
Maori Gold Mine Ld. Regd. 1895. Vol. liq. 17 June 1897. Final meeting return regd. 7 June 1899	1898

VOL. FOR

Maoriland Gold Mines Ld. In 1897 the business was amalgamated with Ethel Reef Gold Mining Co. Ld. Shareholders received 267,692 fully-paid shares of 5s. **1902**

Mapalagama Rubber Estates Ld. Regd. 1910. Vol. liq. (members') 1 May 1933. Undertaking and assets were acquired by Mapalagama Rubber Co. Ld., in which company shareholders were entitled to 1 share of 2s (credited with 1s. 9d. paid) for each share of 2s. held. Final meeting return regd 18 Apr. 1935 **1934**

Mapeke Asbestos Mines Ld. Regd. 1910 as Mapeke Mines Ld.; name changed Aug. 1928. Vol. liq. (members') 16 Dec. 1931. Undertaking and assets transferred to Mapeke Mines Ld., in which company shareholders were entitled to 1 share of 5s. (credited with 4s. paid) for every share of 5s. held. Final meeting return regd. 18 May 1934 .... **1932**

Mapeke Mines Ld. Regd. 1910. See Mapeke Asbestos Mines Ld.

Mapeke Mines Ld. Regd. 1932. Vol liq. (creditors') 2 Oct. 1933. No capital returned to contributories. Final meeting return regd. 30 Oct. 1935. .... **1934**

Maple Cross Properties Ld. Regd. 1952 as Maple Cross Storage Co. Ld.; name changed Sept. 1960. Vol. liq. 24 July 1981. Final meeting return regd. 19 Sept. 1981 .... **1974–5**

Maple Cross Storage Co. Ld. See Maple Cross Properties Ld.

Mapleton's Nut Foods Co. Ld. See below.

Mapleton's Proprietaries Ld. Regd. 1907 as Mapleton's Nut Foods Co. Ld.; name subsequently changed. Vol liq. (members') 1 Nov. 1954. Final meeting return regd. 16 Feb. 1956 .... **1911**

Maponite Ld. Regd. 1898. Removed from Register 1904 **1904**

Mappin & Webb Ld. Regd. 1898. Vol. liq. 25 Jan. 1909. Business was acquired by Mappin & Webb (1908) Ld. (later Mappin & Webb Ld.), for £66,666 in ordinary shares, £66,666 in preference shares of £1 £83,333 in debenture stock and £393,335 in cash. Final meeting return regd. 28 June 1917 .... **1909**

Mappins Stores (Brazil) Ld. See Anglo-Brazilian Stores Ld.

Mara Mines Ld. Regd. 1907. Vol. liq. Dec. 1911. Removed from Register 1913 .... **1913**

Maraben (Transvaal) Land Co. Ld. Regd. 1890. Vol. liq. 29 May 1894. Undertaking was acquired by Balkis Land Co. Ld. for 225,000 fully-paid shares of 10s. Final meeting return regd. 13 Aug. 1896 .... **1895**

Marangu Coffee Estates Ld. Regd. 1909 as Marangu Rubber & Coffee Estates Ld. Vol. liq. 14 Dec. 1927. Final meeting return regd. 28 Dec. 1929 .... **1928**

Marangu Rubber & Coffee Estates Ld. See Marangu Coffee Estates Ld.

Maranhao Obras Publicas Co. Ld. Regd. 1909. Vol liq. 10 Dec. 1913. Final meeting return regd. 26 Apr. 1917 .... **1914**

Maratonga Development Co. Ld. Regd. 1896. Vol. liq. Sept. 1905. Removed from Register 1906 .... **1906**

Marbella Iron Ore Co. Ld. Regd. 1871. Vol liq (members') 20 July 1933. Capital returned to contributories—2$\frac{7}{32}$d. per share of 5s. £126 15s. 4d was paid into Companies' Liquidation Account. Final meeting return regd. 20 May 1936 .... **1934**

Marble, Granite & Stone Co. Ld. See Eddystone Granite Quarries Ld.

March Gas & Coke Co. Ld. Regd. 1859. Dissolved 1 May 1949, undertaking being vested in Eastern Area Gas Board under Gas Act 1948. Holders of securities were entitled to receive British Gas 3% guaranteed stock 1990—95 as follows in respect of each £6 unit, unless otherwise stated, of security held:

	£	s.	d.
Ord. shares (8% stand.) issued before 1 Jan. 1946	12	0	11
Ord. shares (8% stand.) issued since 31 Dec. 1945	12	0	11
3½%mort. deb. stock (per £100) ...	100	0	0

1952

Marconi Steamship Co. Ld. Regd. 1937. Vol. liq. (members') 13 Aug. 1942. Direct controlling interest owned by Royal Mail Lines Ld. Final meeting return regd. 21 Dec. 1944 .... **1944**

Marconi Wireless Telegraph Co. of America. Inc. New Jersey 1899. Property and certain assets were transferred to Radio Corporation of America, in which company shareholders were entitled to 1 common share of no par value and 1 preferred share of $5 for each share of $5 held. Shareholders received a scrip certificate with right to proportion of moneys received from assets not sold to Radio Corporation of America **1921**

Mardon, Son & Hall Ld. Regd. 1897. The undertaking and assets were acquired in 1902 by Imperial Tobacco Co. (of Great Britain and Ireland) Ld. Removed from Register 1904 .... **1904**

Mare Street Furnishing Co. Ld. Regd. 1901 as Hackney Furnishing Co. Ld.; name changed Feb. 1929. Receiver appointed July 1934; ceased to act Mar. 1936. Struck off Register 19 Mar. 1937 .... **1933**

Margate & Southend Kursaals Ld. Regd. 1897 as Southend-on-Sea Tower & Marine Park Co. Ld.; name changed. Receiver appointed 1899 by Court on behalf of debenture stockholders. Struck off Register 9 Dec. 1902 .... **1903**

Margate Estates Ld. Regd. 1928. Vol. liq. (members') 5 Dec. 1933. Reconstructed as Margate Estates Co. Ld., in which company shareholders were entitled to 2 fully-paid preference shares of £1 and 3 fully-paid ordinary shares of 2s. for every 20 preference shares of 2s. held or 9 fully-paid ordinary shares of 2s. for every 8 ordinary shares of 2s. held. Debenture holders were entitled either to repayment at 102% or to £102 debenture stock for every £100 debentures held. Final meeting return regd. 2 Aug. 1934 ...... **1940**

Margate Hotel Co. Ld. Regd. 1884. Vol. liq. 31 Oct. 1892. Final meeting return regd. 26 Nov. 1895 .... **1893**

Margate Palace Ld. Regd. 1909. Vol. liq. 17 May 1911. Removed from Register 17 July 1914. .... ***1913**

Margate Super Cinema Ld. Regd. 1929. Court Order to wind up Mar. 1930. Struck off Register 9 June 1936 **1937**

Margetts British Sectional Tyre Co. Ld. Regd. 1910. Court Order to wind up 13 July 1915. Struck off Register 1921 .... **1916**

Margolin (J. & A.) Ld. See under Dansette Products Ld.

Marie Elsie Steamship Co. Ld. Regd. 1895. Vol. liq. Dec. 1911. Removed from Register 1912 .... **1912**

Marie Rose Gold Mining Co. Ld. Regd. 1895. Struck off Register 26 Oct. 1900 .... **1901**

Marievale Nigel Gold Mines & Estates Ld. Inc. Transvaal 1895. Certain assets were acquired by Marievale Consolidated Mines Ld., in which company shareholders were entitled to 5 shares of 10s. (credited as fully-paid) for every 4 shares of 5s. held **1936**

Marine & Industrial Trust Ld. Regd. 1919. Vol. liq. 29 Dec. 1922. Final meeting return regd. 22 Dec. 1923 ***1923**

Marine & Locomotive Superheaters Ld. Regd. 1910 as Schmidt's Superheating (1910) Ld.; name changed to Marine & Locomotive Superheaters Ld., in Mar. 1920, to Superheater Co. Ld., in Dec. 1924 and as above in Oct. 1938. Capital returned to contributories—£105,276 10s. plus 240,150 ordinary shares of 5s. in Superheater Co. Ld. Final meeting return regd. 21 Apr. 1941 .... **1941**

Marine Fibres & Yarns Ld. Regd. 1910. Court Order to wind up 22 July 1913. Liquidator released 10 Dec. 1915. Struck off Register 14 Feb. 1919 .... **1914**

Marine Hotel, Gullane, Ld. Regd. 1923. Vol. liq. (members') 28 Mar. 1947. Final meeting return regd. 7 Mar.1950 .... **1939**

Marine Securities Corporation Ld. Regd. 1890. Vol. liq. 2 Mar. 1896. Final meeting return regd. 20 Jan. 1898 **1897**

Marine Transport Co. Ld. Regd. 1919. Struck off Register 1929 .... ***1924**

Mariposa Gold Mining Co. Ld. Regd. 1897. Vol. liq. 7 Feb. 1901. Property was sold to Kauotonu Syndicate Ld. for 5,000 fully-paid shares of £1. Final meeting return regd. 7 Mar. 1902 .... **1901**

Maritime Coal Co. Ld. Regd. 1885. Removed from Register 1906 .... **1935**

Maritime Oilfields Ld. Regd. 1908. Vol. liq. (members') 31 July 1947. Capital returned to contributories—£1 9s. 11·9d. per ordinary share (of £1) and £1 19s. 6·849d. per deferred share (of 1s.). £286 was paid into Companies' Liquidation Account. Final meeting return regd. 9 Oct. 1950 .... **1952**

Maritime Salvors Ld. Regd. 1918. Vol. liq. 8 Apr. 1927. Capital returned to contributories—1s. per share of £1 at May 1927; further payments (if any) not known. Final meeting return regd. 30 Nov. 1928 **1928**

Mark (John) & Co. Ld. Regd. 1894. Vol. liq. 29 Apr. 1968. Ordinary capital was owned by John Lupton & Son (Bradford) Ld. Amount distributed per preference share (of £1), 21s. 5⅜d. Amount paid into Companies' Liquidation Account in respect of unclaimed distributions-£346 8s. 4d. Final meeting return regd. 4 June 1970 .... **1970**

Marke Valley Mine. Established 1839. Committee of shareholders appointed to wind up the company 1890 .... **1891**

Market Deeping Gas-Light & Coke Co. Ld. Regd. 1868. Dissolved 1 May 1949, undertaking being vested in East Midland Area Gas Board under Gas Act 1948. Holders of ordinary shares (of £10) were entitled to receive £23 British Gas 4% guaranteed stock 1990–95 for each share held **1952**

Market Deeping Railway Co. Inc. by Special Act In 1878. Undertaking abandoned by Act of 1883 ..... **1884**

Market Drayton Electric Light & Power Co. Ld. Regd. 1902. Dissolved 1 Apr. 1948. undertaking being vested in the British (later Central) Electricity Authority and Midlands Area Board under the Electricity Act 1947. Ordinary shareholders were entitled to receive £2 5s. British Electricity 3% guaranteed stock (1968–73), for every £1 of capital held **1949**

Market Drayton Gas Co. Inc. 1861; reinc. by Special Act 1903. Dissolved 1 May 1949. undertaking being vested in West Midland Area Gas Board under Gas Act 1948. Holders of securities were entitled to receive, in respect of each £10 unit held, British Gas 3% guaranteed stock 1990–95 as follows:

	£	s.	d.
Orig. ord. shares	21	0	0
Addit. ord. shares	15	0	0

1952

Market Rasen New Lighting Co. Ld. Regd. 1888. Dissolved 1 May 1949, undertaking being vested in East Midland Area Gas Board under Gas Act 1948. Holders of securities were entitled to receive, in respect of each £10 unit held, British Gas 3% guaranteed stock 1990–95 as follows:

	£	s.	d.
Ord. shares (10% stand.)	17	15	0
Addit. shares (7% stand.)	12	10	0

1952

Market Rasen Water Co. Inc. by Special Act 1875. Winding-up Order made 15 June 1953 .... **1910**

Market Weighton Gas Light & Coke Co. Ld. Regd. 1871. Dissolved 1 May 1949. undertaking being vested in North Eastern Area Gas Board under Gas Act 1948. Holders of shares (of £1) were entitled to receive £1 British Gas 3% guaranteed stock 1990–95 for each share held **1952**

Markinch Gas Co. Ld. Regd. in Edinburgh 1919. Dissolved 1 May 1949, undertaking being vested in Scottish Area Gas Board under Gas Act 1948. Holders of ordinary shares (of £1) were entitled to receive £2 2s. British Gas 3% guaranteed stock 1990–95 for each share held **1952**

Marks (Henry) & Sons Ld. Regd. 1899. Undertaking and assets were acquired in 1905 by International Sponge Importers Ld. (later World Natural Sponge Suppliers Ld) for £30,125 in preference shares of £1 and £45,821 in ordinary shares of £1. Removed from Register 1905 .... **1905**

Marlborough & Grafton Railway Co. Inc. by Special Act 1896. Undertaking vested in Midland & South-Western Junction Railway Co. Holders of ordinary and debenture stocks received rent charge stock. **1900**

Marlborough Railway Co. Inc. by Special Act 1861. Under Great Western Railway Act 1896 undertaking was amalgamated with that company. Holders of 3½% debenture stock received 4% debenture stock on basis of equal income; holders of £100 6% preference stock received £120 5% consolidated preference stock; holders of £100 ordinary stock received £120 in cash **1897**

Marlborough Steamship Co. Ld. Regd. 1919. Struck off Register 1923 .... ***1922**

Marle. See Société Sucrière Anonyme de Marle.

Marley Hill Chemical Co. Ld. Regd. 1920. Vol. liq. (members') 27 Oct. 1936. Capital returned to contributories—3s. 11·3142d. per share of £1. Final meeting return regd. 12 Jan. 1938 .... **1937**

Marloid Manufacturing (Parent) Co. Ld. Regd. 1896. Vol. liq. 12 Oct. 1899. Removed from Register 13 Nov. 1903 .... ***1900**

Marlow Water Co. Inc. by Special Act 1935. Undertaking vested in Bucks Water Board from 1 Apr. 1960. Consideration distributed as follows (per £100 stock); 5% ordinary, £85 5s.; 5% redeemable preference, £98; 4¼% debenture, 4% perpetual debenture, 5% debenture bonds and 4% debenture bonds, all £100. Dissolved 19 July 1963 .... **1964**

Marlu Gold Mining Areas Ld. Regd. 1926. Vol. liq. (members') 26 May 1955. Capital returned to contributories—1s. 3d. per 5s. stock. £629 9s. 4d. in respect to unclaimed dividends and £3,103 7s. 7d in respect to distributions paid into Companies' Liquidation Account. Final meeting return regd. 18 Nov. 1960 .... **1963**

Marmajito Mines Ld. Regd. 1916. Vol. liq. (members') 13 May 1931. Undertaking and assets were transferred to Frontino Gold Mines Ld, in which company shareholders were entitled to 7 fully-paid ordinary shares of £1 for every 4 ordinary shares of £1 held or 2 fully-paid preference shares of £1 for every 2 preference shares of £1 held. FInal meeting return regd. 20 June 1932 .... **1932**

Marodian Gold Mining Co. Ld. Regd. 1901. Vol. liq. Sept. 1907. Struck off Register 5 Feb. 1937 .... **1937**

Marovoay Rice Lands Ld. Regd 1911. Vol. liq. (creditors') 14 Jan. 1931. Holders of 1st debentures

received £1,489 10s. on account of capital. Final meeting return regd. 1 Mar. 1932 .... **1931**

Marquis, Clayton & Co. Ld. Regd. 1917. Vol. liq. (creditors') 2 Nov. 1931. Assets realised insufficient to pay unsecured creditors in full. Final meeting return regd. 22 May 1935 .... **1932**

Marriages Flour Mills Ld. Regd. 1935. Vol. liq. (members') 13 Dec. 1956. Assets and liabilities were transferred to E. Marriage & Son Ld. in which company shareholders were entitled to receive 11 fully-paid preference shares of £1 for every 10 preference shares of £1 held, and 1 fully-paid preference share of £1 and 14 fully-paid ordinary shares of 5s. for every 10 ordinary shares of 5s. held. Final meeting return regd. 12 Mar. 1958 .... **1959**

Marriott & Williams Ld. Regd. 1892. Removed from Register 1907 .... **1895**

Marsden (Charles) & Sons Ld. Regd. 1903. Receiver appointed in Oct. 1923. Court Order to wind up Dec. 1923. Struck off Register 15 June 1937 .... **1938**

Marsh & Baxter Ld. Regd. 1912. Vol liq (members') 3 Nov. 1947. Final meeting return regd. 15 May 1950 **1947**

Marsh Jones & Cribb Ld. See Boar Lane Properties Ld.

Marsh Mills Trading Co. Ld. Regd. 1925. Direct controlling interest owned by Dartmoor China Clay Co. Ld. Struck off Register 26 Sept. 1939 .... **1940**

Marshall & Marshall Ld. Regd. 1898 as Marshall & Elvey Ld.; name changed Jan. 1907. Vol. liq. (members') 22 Feb. 1939. Undertaking acquired by Stansfeld and Co. Ld. Capital returned to contributories—preference £37,285 9s. 2d. ordinary, £36,587 4s. plus certain assets distributed in specie. Final meeting return regd. 17 Apr. 1940 .... **1940**

Marshall & Snelgrove Ld. Regd. 1898. Vol. liq. Mar. 1919. The undertaking was acquired by Debenhams Ld. Debenture holders were entitled to debenture stock in purchasing company. Struck off Register 2 Apr. 1943 .... **1944**

Marshall, Ashby & Co. Ld. Regd. 1896. Removed from Register 1901 .... **1899**

Marshall (M.) & Son. See below.

Marshall (M. W.) & Co. Fst. 1860 as M. Marshall & Son; name changed 1922. Ceased business 30 Sept. 1955; business was transferred to M. W. Marshall & Co. Ld (regd. 1952) **1957**

Marshall (Sir Herbert) & Sons Ld. Regd. 1911. Vol. liq. (creditors') 13 Oct. 1931. Assets realised insufficient to pay unsecured creditors in full. Final meeting return regd. 23 Mar. 1933 .... **1932**

Marshall, Sons & Co. Ld. Regd. 1862. Receiver was appointed May 1934; ceased to act 13 Nov. 1935. The undertaking was acquired from Thos. W. Ward Ld. in 1935 by Marshall Sons & Co. (Successors) Ld. (later Marshall Sons & Co. Ld.) A return of 3s. 9d. in the £ to the 1st mortgage debenture holders was anticipated. Struck off Register 20 Apr. 1943 .... **1944**

Marshalls Ld. Regd. 1903 as Chipperfield and Butler Ld.; name changed Feb. 1918. Vol. liq. 6 July 1920. Reconstructed as company of same name. Shareholders were entitled to 1 share of £1 (credited as fully-paid) for each share of 4s. held. Final meeting return regd. 4 Apr. 1921 .... **1921**

Marston (A. C.) & Co. (Northern) Ld. See M. R. S. Ld.

Marston-Ridgmont Properties Ld. Regd. 1936. Vol. liq. (members') 11 Aug. 1954. Ordinary shareholders agreed to repayment of preference shares at 22s. 6d. per share of £1; 29s. 10½d per share of £1 was repaid to ordinary shareholders. Final meeting return regd. 4 Jan. 1956 .... **1957**

Marston's Dolphin Brewery Ld. Regd 1897. Vol. liq. 6 Dec. 1928. Undertaking was acquired by Strong & Co., of Romsey Ld. Final meeting return regd. 30 July 1936 .... **1929**

Marstons Road Services Ld. See M. R. S. Ld.

Martans Club Ld. See Embassy Club Ld.

Martha Gold Mining Company (Waihi) Ld. Regd. 1935. Vol. liq. (members') 27 Mar. 1956. Capital returned to contributories—2s. 7·25d. per share (of 6d.). FInal meeting return regd. 15 May 1957 .... **1958**

Martin (A.) & Son Ld. Regd 1934. Vol. liq. (members') 2 Apr. 1935. Reconstructed as Carbo Plaster Ld. Final meeting return regd. 31 Mar. 1936 .... **1940**

Martin, Hall & Co. Ld. Regd. 1866. Receiver appointed in Aug. 1929. Assets realised sufficient to repay lst debenture holders but insufficient to repay 2nd debenture holders. Struck off Register 16 Oct. 1936 **1937**

Martin Patent Davit Co. Ld. Regd. 1912. Vol. liq. July 1925. Struck off Register 7 July 1939 .... **1940**

Martin (T. & C.) Ld. Inc. in Dublin 1886. Vol. liq. (members') 29 Mar. 1968. Preference stock was repaid at par 30 Sept. 1968. Amount returned to ordinary stockholders (per £1 stock) £4 18s. Final meeting return regd. 27 Apr. 1971) **1971**

VOL. FOR

Martineau (David) & Sons Ld. Regd. 1889. Vol. liq. 28 Jan. 1895. Assets were being realised on behalf of debenture holders. Final meeting return regd. 12 Oct. 1898 .... **1897**

Martinet Slate & Sheet Co. Ld. Regd 1918. Vol. liq. (members') 17 Apr. 1931. All shares owned by United Africa Co. Ld. Final meeting return regd. 2 Mar. 1933 .... **1932**

Martinez Alluvial Gold Co. Ld. Regd. Edinburgh 1897. Vol. liq. Sept. 1899. Final meeting return regd. 20 Nov. 1901 .... **1900**

Martini Automobile Co. Ld. Regd. 1905, Vol. liq. 3 Apr. 1908. Final meeting return regd. 6 Jan 1909 .... ***1909**

Martino Steel & Metal Co. Ld. Regd 1905. Vol. liq. (members') 31 Dec. 1930. Capital returned to contributories—20*s*. per preference share of £1; all ordinary shares held by United Steel Companies Ld. Final meeting return regd. 10 Sept. 1931 .... **1931**

Martin's Bank Ld. Regd. 1891. Vol. liq. Dec 1918. Business acquired 1 July 1918 by the Bank of Liverpool Ld. (later Martins Bank Ld.), in which company shareholders received 2½ shares of £20 (credited with £2 10*s*. paid) and £4 12*s*. in cash .. **1919**

Martins Bank Ld. Regd. 1882 as Bank of Liverpool; name changed to Bank of Liverpool & Martins Ld. in Dec. 1918 and to present title In Jan. 1928. Undertaking was vested in Barclays Bank Ld. under the provisions of Barclays Bank Act 1969 which also provided for dissolution of this bank **1973-4**

Martin's Oilfields of Madagascar (Parent) Co. Ld. Regd. 1919. Struck off Register Feb. 1927 .... **1927**

Martinstown (Dorchester) Brewery Ld. Regd. 1888. Removed from Register 1892 .... **1890**

Martinsyde Ld. Regd. 1915. Receiver appointed in May 1921. Struck off Register 1936 .... **1923**

Martock & District Gas Consumers' Co. Ld. Regd. 1898. Dissolved 1 May 1949 undertaking being vested in South Western Area Gas Board under Gas Act 1948. Holders of securities were entitled to receive British Gas 3% guaranteed stock 1990–95 as follows in respect of each £1 unit, unless otherwise stated, of security held:

	£	s.	d.	
Ord. shares (7% stand.)	1	6	0	
4½% pref. shares (of £5)	5	7	6	
4½% deb. bonds (of £10)	10	5	0	**1952**

Marudu Consolidated Estates Ld. Regd. 1927. Vol. liq. (members') 28 Feb. 1952. Capital returned to contributories—6*s*. 10·9*d*. per 2*s*. stock of both classes. Final meeting return regd. 12 June 1953 **1954**

Marudu Rubber Ld. Regd 1917. Vol. liq. (members') 10 Jan. 1952. Capital returned to contributories—£2 8*s*. 5½*d*. per share of 5*s*. £1,224 11*s*. 8*d* was paid into Companies' Liquidation Account. Final meeting return regd. 1 June 1954 .... **1955**

Marvin & Co. (Brazil) Ld. Regd. 1928. Vol. liq. (members') 27 Oct. 1941. Capital returned to contributories—10*s*. 7½*d*. per preferred ordinary share of £1. Final meeting return regd. 16 May 1942 **1943**

Mary Murphy Gold Mining Co. Ld. Inc. Colorado in 1909. In Nov. 1931 receiver stated that company had "no funds to redeem the bonds or for any other purpose" but distributions of $14·87, $10 and $14 per $1,000 bond were made in Dec. 1935, Jan. and Dec. 1937 respectively; further distributions (if any) not known **1932**

Maryborough Leviathan Gold Mines Ld. Regd. 1899. Vol. liq. Oct. 1907. Removed from Register 1910 **1908**

Maryborough Mining & Finance Co. Regd. 1934. Vol. liq. (members') 12 July 1938. No capital returned to contributories. Final meeting return regd. 13 Dec. 1938 .... **1939**

Maryland Securities Co. In 1927 the properties and assets were transferred to Consolidated Gas Electric Light and Power Co. of Baltimore (later Baltimore Gas & Electric Co.) **1928**

Maryport and Carlisle Railway Co. Inc. by Special Act 1837. In 1923 the undertaking was merged into the London Midland & Scottish Railway Co., in which company stockholders were entitled to stock as follows:

For every £100 held	*L. M. & S.*	
4% Debenture	£100 4% Debenture	
Ordinary	£50 4% Pref.(1923) £60 Ordinary	
4% Minimum	£50 4% Pref.(1923) £60 Ordinary	**1924**

Maryport Brewery Ld. Regd. 1890. Vol. liq. 25 Mar. 1919. Absorbed by Central Control Board (Liquor Traffic) in Nov. 1916. Final meeting return regd. 19 Nov. 1921 .... **1919**

Mashonaland Agency Ld. Regd. 1890. Vol. liq. 22 Aug. 1894. Reconstructed as company of same name. Shareholders were entitled to 1 fully-paid share of £1 in new company for every 2 shares of £1 (10*s*. paid) held. Final meeting return regd. 18 Jan. 1895 ..... **1919**

Mashonaland Agency Ld. Regd. 1894. Vol. liq. 28 Feb. 1916. Reconstructed as company of same name: Shareholders were entitled to 1 share of 7*s*. 6*d*. (credited as fully-paid) in new company *plus* 1*s*. in cash for each share of £1 held; shareholders were also entitled to 1 fully-paid share of 10*s*. in Wankie Colliery Co. Ld., for every 3 shares held. Final meeting return regd. 29 Dec. 1917 .... **1916**

Mashonaland Agency Ld. Regd. 1916. Vol. liq. 8 Oct. 1924. Final meeting return regd. 5 Aug. 1926 ...... **1925**

Mashonaland (Central) Gold Mining Co. Ld. Regd. 1893. Vol. liq. Dec. 1899. Removed from Register 1903 .... **1900**

Mashonaland Consolidated Development Co. Ld. Regd. 1898. Reconstructed 1902 as Mashonaland Consolidated Ld., in which company shareholders were entitled to 1 share of £1 (credited with 16*s*. paid) for each share of £1 held. Removed from Register 1910 **1908**

Mashonaland Consolidated Ld. Regd. 1902. Vol. liq. Sept. 1909. Reconstructed as Mashonaland Consolidated (1909) Ld., in which company shareholders were entitled to 3 shares of 5*s*. (credited with 4*s*. paid) for every 2 shares of £1 held. Removed from Register 1911 .... **1910**

Mashonaland Consolidated (1909) Ld. Regd. 1909. Vol. liq. 4 Nov. 1912 for amalgamation with Rhodesian Mining & Finance Co. Ld. under title of Mashonaland Consolidated (1912) Ld., in which company shareholders were entitled to 1 share of 5*s*. (credited with 4*s*. paid) for each share of 5*s*. held. Struck off Register 1 Oct. 1946 .... **1947**

Mashonaland Consolidated (1912) Ld. Regd. 1912. Vol. liq. 29 July 1926. Undertaking and assets were acquired by New Albion Transvaal Gold Mines Ld., in which company shareholders were entitled to 2 shares of 5*s*. (credited with 3*s*. 6*d*. paid) for every 7 ordinary of 1*s*. or 5 deferred shares of 4*s*. held. Final meeting return regd. 12 May 1932 .... **1927**

Mashonaland Development Co. (Willoughby's) Ld. Regd. 1893. Vol. liq. 28 Dec. 1894. Assets and properties were acquired by Willoughby's Consolidated Co. Ld., in which company shareholders were entitled to 2 shares of £1 (credited as fully-paid) for each fully-paid share of £1 held. Final meeting return regd. 17 Jan. 1900 .... **1894**

Mashonaland Gold & Land Syndicate Ld. Regd. 1894. Struck off Register 26 Oct. 1900 .... **1901**

Mashonaland Railway Co. Ld. Regd. 1897. Vol. liq. (members') 31 Mar. 1937. Undertaking and assets were acquired by Rhodesia Railways Ld. for 150.000 fully-paid shares of £1 and discharge of all debts. Holders of 1st mortgage 5% debentures and 5% guaranteed mortgage debentures (1905) were offered either conversion into an equal amount of 4½ debenture stock *plus* 7% bonus in cash or repayment at 105% on 31 Mar. 1937. Final meeting return regd. 15 June 1944 .... **1938**

Maskelyne British Typewriter Ld. Regd. 1896. Vol. liq. 4 Oct. 1897. Removed from Register 1914 .... **1898**

Maskelyne's Checking Apparatus Co. Ld. Regd. 1881. Court Orders: to wind up Sept. 1883; to dissolve June 1888 .... **1848**

Mason and Barry Ld. Regd. 2 June 1892. Winding-up order made 30 July 1968 .... **1984–5**

Mason & Barry Ld. Regd. 1878. Vol. liq. 25 May 1892. Reconstructed as company of same name. Shareholders were entitled to 1 fully-paid share of £5 in new company *plus* £1 in cash for each share of £10 held. Final meeting return regd. 29 Mar. 1893 .... **1892**

Mason & Mason Ld. Regd. 1889. Vol. liq. 26 Aug. 1920. Capital returned to contributories—15*s*. per preference or ordinary share of £5; further payments (if any) not known. Final meeting return regd. 14 May 1923 .... **1921**

Mason Brothers Ld. Regd. 1883. Removed from Register 1906 .... **1892**

Mason (Samuel) Ld. Regd. 1896. Vol. liq. 26 Jan 1910. The bar-fitting business was acquired by Gaskell and Chambers Ld. Final meeting return regd. 26 July 1912 .... **1911**

Masonic and General Fire and Life Assurance Co. Ld. *See* Masonic and General Life Assurance Co. Ld.

Masonic and General Life Assurance Co. Ld. Regd. 1868 as Masonic and General Fire and Life Assurance Co. Ld. name changed 21 Jan. 1874. Court Orders: to wind up June 1886; to dissolve 28 Apr. 1898 .. **1887**

Masonic Hall & Club Co. Ld. Regd. 1864. Vol. liq. 21 Oct. 1920. Final meeting return regd. 28 Nov. 1921 **1921**

Massi Kessi Reefs Ld. Regd. 1894. Vol. liq. 14 Jan. 1898. Reconstructed as Mozambique Consolidated Mines Ld., in which company shareholders were entitled to 1 share of 10*s*. (credited with 9*s*. paid) for

**See Stock Exchange Year-Book*.

VOL. FOR

each share of 10s. held. Final meeting return regd.
27 Sept. 1898 .... **1898**

Masters & Sons Ld. The undertaking and assets were
acquired in 1928 by Hackney Furnishing Co. (1928)
Ld **1929**

Matabele Ancient Gold Reefs Ld. Regd. 1895. Reconstructed 1897 as Associated Rhodesian Gold Estates
Ld., in which company shareholders were entitled to
1 share of 10s. for every 2 shares of £1 held.
Removed from Register 1909 .... **1900**

Matabele Central Estates Co. Ld. Regd. 1895. Vol. liq.
Jan. 1910. Undertaking and assets were acquired by
Willoughby's Consolidated Co. Ld., in which
company shareholders were entitled to 3 shares of
10s. (credited as fully-paid) for every 5 shares of £1
held. Removed from Register 1911 .... **1910**

Matabele Consols Ld. Regd. 1899. Removed from
Register 1909 .... **1907**

Matabele Gold Properties Ld. Regd. 1895. Struck off
Register 28 July 1899 .... **1901**

Matabele Gold Reefs and Estates Co. Ld. Regd. 1894.
Vol. liq. 3 Mar. 1899. Reconstructed as company of
same name. Shareholders were entitled to 3 fully-
paid shares of £1 in new company for every share of
£1 held. Final meeting return regd. 2 July 1900 ... **1905**

Matabele Gold Reefs & Estates Co. Ld. Regd. 1899. Vol.
liq. 2 Mar. 1905. Reconstructed as Matabele Reefs
and Estate Co. Ld., in which company shareholders
were entitled to 1 share of £1 (credited with 14s.
paid) for every 2 shares of £1 held. Debenture
holders were entitled to an equal amount of 5%
debentures of new company. Final meeting return
regd. 2 Mar. 1909 .... **1905**

Matabele Mines Ld. Regd. 1895. Reconstructed as
Matabele Reefs and Estates Co. Ld. in which
company shareholders were entitled to 1 share of £1
(credited with 14s. paid) for every 4 shares of £1
held. Debenture holders were entitled to an equal
amount of 5% debentures in new company. Re-
moved from Register 1909 .... **1905**

Matabele Proprietary Assets Realisation Co. Ld. Regd.
1910. Vol. liq. Dec. 1912. Property and assets were
to be sold to Bechuanaland Exploration Co. Ld.
Shareholders were entitled to 1 share in Matabeleland Ranching Co. Ld. for every 3 shares of 1s. held
plus 3s. per share in cash. Removed from Register
1914 .... **1913**

Matabele Proprietary Mines Ld. Regd. 1900. Vol. liq.
Dec. 1909 for reconstruction as Matabele Proprietary Realisation Co. Ld in which company shareholders were entitled to 1 fully-paid share of 1s. and
1 share of 5s. in Wanderer (Selukwe) Gold Mines
Ld. for each share of £1 held. Removed from
Register 1911 .... **1911**

Matabele Queen's Co. Ld. Regd. 1910. Vol. liq. 15 Dec.
1919. Final meeting return regd. 3 June 1921 ...... **1920**

Matabele Reefs & Estates Co. Ld. Regd. 1905. Vol. liq.
12 May 1911. Undertaking and assets were acquired
by Willoughby's Consolidated Co. Ld. Debenture
holders were entitled to an equal amount of 5%
debentures in purchasing company or 15s in the £ in
cash. No return was made to shareholders. Struck
off Register 3 Sept. 1918 .... **1912**

Matabele Sheba Gold Mining Co. Ld. Regd. 1896. Vol.
liq. Apr. 1909. Removed from Register 1911 ...... **1910**

Matabeleland Adventurers Ld. Regd. 1894. In liquidation in 1901. Capital returned to contributories—
16s. 6d per share of £1; further payments (if any) not
known. Removed from Register 1903 .... **1901**

Matabeleland and Mashonaland Syndicate Ld. Regd.
1893. Vol. liq. 4 Mar. 1895. Final meeting return
regd. 16 Nov. 1895 .... **1896**

Matabeleland Co. Ld. Regd. 1889. Vol. liq. 11 Feb.
1896. Shareholders were entitled to 2 fully-paid
shares of £1 in Suffolk Trust Co. Ld. for every 5
shares of 10s. held. Final meeting return regd. 21
Sept. 1896 .... **1897**

Matabeleland Development Co. Ld. Regd. 1895. Vol, liq.
7 July 1903. Undertaking and assets were acquired
by the Exploring Land and Minerals Co. Ld., for
92,000 fully-paid shares of £1. Final meeting return
reg. 3 Sept. 1906 .... **1904**

Matabeland Exploring Syndicate Ld. Regd. 1895. Vol.
liq. 28 Apr. 1899. Undertaking and assets were
acquired by Crescens (Matabele) Mines and Land
Co. Ld., in which company shareholders were
entitled to 2 shares of £1 for every 3 shares of £1 held.
Final meeting return regd. 28 Apr. 1902 .... **1900**

Matabeleland Ranching Co. Regd. 1895 as Moonie
Creek Development Co. Ld.; name changed June
1910. Vol. liq. 15 Jan. 1915. the undertaking was
acquired by Bechuanaland Exploration Co. Ld.
Final meeting return regd. 2 May 1916 .... **1915**

VOL. FOR

Matacong & North West African Co. Ld. Regd. 1881.
Wound up by Order of Court 24 Mar. 1885 .... ***1884**

Matador Land & Cattle Co. Ld. Regd. in Edinburgh
1882. Vol. liq. 24 Aug. 1951. Final meeting return
regd. 8 July 1957 .... **1954**

Matale Ceylon Rubber Co. Ld. Regd. 1906. Vol liq.
(members') 3 Aug. 1944. Estate was sold for £31,875.
Capital returned to contributories—2s 10-181d. per
share of 2s. £692 2s. 1d. was paid into Companies'
Liquidation Account in respect of unclaimed capital
and £61 8s. 10d. in respect of unclaimed dividends.
FInal meeting return regd. 27 Nov. 1945 .... **1946**

Matale Valley Cacao & Rubber Co. Ld. See Warriapolla
Estates Co. Ld.

Matang (Perak) Rubber Syndicate Ld. Regd. 1907. Vol
liq. 21 Nov. 1910. Final meeting return regd. 13
June 1912 .... ***1911**

Matanzas & Sabanilla (Cuba) Railroad Co. Inc. by
Spanish Royal Charter 1843. In 1906 all capital was
acquired by United Railways of the Havana and
Regla Warehouses Ld, 5% £912,750 ordinary shares
and £608,500 for unredeemable debenture stock
1906 .... **1908**

Matchless Motor Cycles (Colliers) Ld. See Associated
Motor Cycles Ld.

Mather Lane Spinning Co. (1920) Ld. Regd. 1920. Vol.
liq. 29 July 1929. Shareholders were entitled to 1
ordinary share of £1 in Combined Egyptian Mills
Ld. (later Combined English Mills (Spinners) Ld.)
for every 6 shares of £1 (11s. paid) held. Struck off
Register 20 Feb. 1945 .... **1930**

Mathews (F. H) & Sons Ld. Regd. 1897. Removed from
Register 1910 .... **1903**

Mathinna Union Ld. Regd 1896. Removed from
Register 1912 .... **1902**

Matlock & District Gas Co. Regd. 1887. Inc. by Special
Act 1904. Undertaking was acquired in June 1935
by Sheffield Gas Co. (later Sheffield & District Gas
Co.), in which company shareholders were entitled
to £12 18s. ordinary consolidated (5% basic) stock
for each share of £10 held. The outstanding 4%
debentures were redeemed **1936**

Matoko Gold Fields Ld. Regd 1899. Vol. liq. Dec.
1903. Final meeting return regd. 13 Mar. 1906 ..... **1904**

Matthew (J.) & Son Ld. Regd. 1921. Vol. liq. (creditors')
1 Mar. 1933. Final meeting return regd. 7 Mar. 1934 **1928**

Matthews & Co. Ld. Regd. 1898. Vol. liq (creditors') 6
June 1935. Capital returned to contributories—2d.
per preference share of £1. Final meeting return
regd. 22 Sept. 1937 .... **1936**

Matthews, Wrightson & Co. Ld. Regd. 1911. Vol. liq. 4
Jan. 1924. Final meeting return regd. 4 Oct. 1924 **1934**

Matthews, Wrightson & Co. Ld. Regd. 1924. See M.W
Ld.

Maturata Tea and Rubber Co. Ld. Regd. 1897 as
Maturata Tea Co. Ld.; name changed 1910. Vol. liq.
(members') 29 Mar. 1951; estates sold as from 1 July
1950. Preference shares were repaid at par on 12
Apr. 1951. Capital returned to ordinary shareholders—£2 19s. 5¼d per share of £1. Final meeting
return regd. 29 Nov. 1952. .... **1954**

Maturata Tea Co. Ld. See above.

Matwapa Rubber Estates Ld. Regd. 1910. Court Order
to wind up 24 Jan. 1911. Liquidator released 14 June
1913. Struck off Register 10 Oct. 1916 .... ***1912**

Maudesley, Sons & Field Ld. Regd. 1889. Receivers for
debenture holders appointed In 1899; ceased to act
1909. Assets remaining after repaying 1st mortgage
debenture stock were applied in partly repaying
temporary debentures. No return was made to 2nd
debentures, special debenture holders or sharehold-
ers. Struck off Register 1915 .... **1910**

Maul (F. W.) Ld. Regd. 1928 as Colourware Ld.; name
changed July 1934. Direct controlling interest was
held by Metduro Ld. Struck off Register 29 Apr.
1938 .... **1931**

Mauritius Estates & Assets Co. Ld. Regd. 1889. Vol. liq.
1 Apr. 1920. Capital returned to ordinary stockholders—150% in May 1920; further payments (If
any) not known. Final meeting return regd. 16 Jan.
1922 .... **1921**

Mauritius Land Credit & Agency Co. Ld. Regd. Dec.
1863. Vol. liq. 14 July 1898. A return of 3s. per share
of £10 (£4 10s paid) was anticipated. Final meeting
return regd. 1 Feb. 1899 .... **1899**

Mavis Mills Ld. Regd. 1925. Receiver appointed in May
1934. Assets realised insufficient to meet claims of
debenture holders. Struck off Register 8 Dec. 1936 **1937**

Mavis Spinning Co. Ld. Regd 1907. Vol. liq. 25 Feb.
1925. Undertaking acquired by Mavis Mills Ld.
Final meeting return regd. 26 Oct. 1925 .... **1934**

Mawchi Tin & Wolfram Mines Ld. Regd 1911. Vol. liq.
27 Oct. 1914. Reconstructed as Mawchi Mines Ld.
(later Mawchi Holdings Ld., in which company

VOL. FOR

shareholders were entitled to 1 share of £1 (credited with 16s. paid) for each share of £1 held. Holders of debentures were entitled to an equal amount of debentures In new company. Final meeting return regd. 28 June 1918 1915

Mawddwy Railway Co. Inc. by Special Act 1865. In 1923 the undertaking was merged into the Great Western Railway Co. Holders of every £100 debenture stock were entitled to £100 in cash; holders of every £100 ordinary share capital were entitled to £105 16s. 8d. cash 1924

Mawman & Anfield Ld. See Anfield & Co. Ld.

Mawson's "Reward" Claim Ld. Regd. 1894. Amalgamated with Majestic Gold Mines Ld. in which company shareholders were entitled to 1 share of £1 (credited with 17s. 6d. paid) for each share of £1 held. Removed from Register 1901 1900

Max Greger Ld. Regd 1881. Removed from Register 1901 .... *1898

Maxim Electrical and Engineering Export Co. Ld. See Sir Hiram Max Electrical and Engineering Co. Ld.

Maxim Electrical Co. Ld. Regd 1905. Receiver for debenture holders appointed in 1908. The business was sold to Maxim Lamp Works Ld. Struck off Register 1925 1911

Maxim Gun Co. Ld. Regd. 1884. Vol. liq. 1 Aug. 1888. The business was acquired by Maxim Nordenfelt Guns and Ammunition Co. Ld. for 120,000 fully-paid shares of £5 and £150,000 5% debenture stock in purchasing company. Final meeting return regd. 17 May 1892 1897

Maxim (Hiram S.) Electrical Corporation Ld. Regd. 1898. Business was acquired by Sir Hiram Maxim Electrical and Engineering Co. Ld. Removed from Register 1901 1902

Maxim (Sir Hiram) Electrical & Engineering Co. Ld. Regd. 1899 as Maxim Electrical and Engineering Export Co. Ld.; name changed Jan. 1901. Vol liq. 31 Oct. 1904. Court Order to wind up 29 Nov. 1904. Removed from Register 1911 1906

Maxim (Sir Hiram S.) Captive Flying Machine Co. Ld. Regd. 1904. Vol liq. Feb. 1908. Removed from Register 1909 1909

Maxim-Weston Electric Co. Regd. 1881 as Electric Light & Power Generator Co. Ld.; name changed 26 July 1882. Vol. liq. 21 Dec. 1888. Reconstructed as company of same name, In which company shareholders were entitled to 1 share of 3s. (credited with 2s. paid) for each share of 5s. held. Final meeting return regd. 13 Apr. 1892 1890

Maxim-Weston Electric Co. Ld. Regd. 1889. Vol. liq 7 Sept. 1890. Final meeting return regd. 13 Apr. 1892 1891

Maxims (Tailors) Ld. Business acquired by C. B. & M. Tailors Ld. 1930

Maxlim Fashions Ld. Regd. 1966 as Maxlim Maternity Fashions Ld.; name changed 16 Aug. 1973. Vol. liq. (creditors') 13 Mar. 1978. Struck off Register 1981 1981–2

Maxlim Maternity Fashions Ld. See Maxlim Fashions Ld.

Maxsons Ld. See S. & M. Ld.

Maxwell Cattle Co. Inc. America. Debentures were exchanged for debentures of an Amsterdam company 1890

May & Glencairn Deep Level Syndicate. In voluntary liquidation in 1894 1894

May Consolidated Gold Mining Co. Ld. Inc. Transvaal 1889. Vol. liq. Apr. 1917 1917

May Diamonds Ld. Inc. Transvaal 1904 1907

May Mill Spinning Co. (1920) Ld. Regd. 1920. Receiver appointed in Mar. 1931. Proceeds of sale of assets were passed to debenture holders. Struck off Register 20 July 1937 1938

May Morn Estates (New Zealand) Ld. Regd. 1912. In Jan. 1954 it was stated that all assets had been sold and realised insufficient to meet claims and prior charges in full. Struck off Register 9 Nov. 1958 .. 1959

May Morn Gold Mining Co. Ld. In July 1927 the assets were acquired by Sable (Transvaal) Gold Mining Co. Ld 1928

May-Oatway Fire Appliances Ld. Regd. 1901. Reconstructed 1907 as company of same name. Shareholders were entitled to 1 share in new company for every 4 ordinary shares of £1 held or 1 share for every 2 founders' shares of 1s. held. Removed from Register 1908 1908

May-Oatway Fire Appliances Ld. Regd. 1907. Vol. liq. Apr. 1911. Reconstructed as Associated Fire Alarms Ld., in which company shareholders were entitled to 6 ordinary shares of 5s. (credited with 4s. paid) for each share of £1 held. Debenture holders were entitled to fully-paid preference shares of £1. Removed from Register 1912 1912

May Queen, Hauraki Ld. Regd. 1896. Removed from Register 1904 1903

VOL. FOR

May Queen Reward Ld. Regd. 1911. Removed from Register 1914 1913

Mayall & Co. Ld. Regd. 1888. Vol. liq. Feb. 1906. Struck off Register 1915 1907

Mayblossom Mining Co. Ld. Regd. 1899. Struck off Register 28 Feb. 1939 1940

Maybole Gas Light Co. Ld. Regd. in Edinburgh 1884. Dissolved 1 May 1949, undertaking being vested in Scottish Area Gas Board under Gas Act 1948. Holders of ordinary shares (of £5) were entitled to receive £12 10s. British Gas 3% guaranteed stock 1990–95 for each share held 1952

Mayer (Max) Ld. Regd. 1925. Vol. liq. (members') 11 Dec. 1933. Reconstructed as Max Mayer (1933) Ld. [later Max Mayer Ld.] Final meeting return regd. 24 July 1936 1934

Mayer (Max) Ld. Regd. 1933 as Max Mayer (1933) Ld.; name changed June 1938. Struck off Register 25 Nov. 1949 1947

Mayer (Max) (1933) Ld. See above.

Mayfair & General Property Trust Ld. Regd. 1915 as Regency General Service Co. Ld.; name changed in 1916 to Mayfair Trust Ld.; and as above in 1930. All properties sold or abandoned, proceeds insufficient to meet claims of holders of 5% 1st mortgage debenture stock. Struck off Register 9 Feb. 1951 .. 1951

Mayfair Decorating Co. Ld. See Maygen Ld.

Mayfair Development Co. Ld. Regd. 1900. Vol. liq. July 1907. Absorbed by Rhodesia Matabeland Development Co. Ld., in which company shareholders were entitled to 1 fully-paid share of £1 for every 20 shares of £1 held. Removed from Register 1911 1908

Mayfair Electric Gramophones Ld. Regd. 1928. Court Order to wind up June 1930. Struck off Register 20 Mar. 1936 1937

Mayfair Gold Mining Co. Ld. Inc. Southern Rhodesia 1928. Vol. liq. Sept. 1931 1932

Mayfair Trust Ld. See Mayfair & General Property Trust Ld.

Mayflower Gold Mines Ld. Regd. Edinburgh 1896. Struck off Register 22 Sept. 1936 1937

Maygen Decorating Co. Ld. See Maygen Ld.

Maygen Ld. Regd. 1931 as Mayfair Decorating Co. Ld.; name changed Jan. 1932 to Maygen Decorating Co. Ld. and as above July 1935. Vol. liq. (members') 2 Jan. 1936. Direct controlling interest was held by Mayfair & General Property Trust Ld. Capital returned to contributories—£1 2s. 3d. per share of £1. FInal meeting return regd. 18 Jan. 1939 1938

Mayhew Compo-Board Co. Ld. Regd. 1904. Court Order to wind up 30 Apr. 1907. Liquidator released 9 Dec. 1911. Struck off Register 10 Oct. 1916 1908

Mayhew Compo-Board Ld. Regd. 1908. Receiver appointed Dec. 1908. Struck off Register 18 Dec. 1917 .... *1912

Mayo (Rhodesia) Development Co. Ld. Regd. 1900. Vol. liq. July 1908 for reconstruction as Mayo (Rhodesia) Development Co. (1908) Ld., in which company shareholders were entitled to 1 share of £1 (credited with 15s. paid) for each share of £1 held. Removed from Register 1909 1909

Mayo (Rhodesia) Development Co. (1908) Ld. Regd. 1908. Vol. liq. (members') 17 Dec. 1930. Undertaking and assets were acquired by Mining, Ranching Cotton & Tobacco Lands of Rhodesia Ld. (later Union and Rhodesian Mining & Finance Co. Ld.), in which company shareholders were entitled to 5 shares of 5. for every 8 shares of £1 held. Final meeting return regd. 20 June 1932 1931

Maypole Co. (1899) Ld. Regd. 1899. Struck off Register 4 Feb. 1930 1930

Maypole Co. Ld. Regd. 1896. Undertaking was acquired by Maypole Co. (1899) Ld. Removed from Register 1903 1899

Mazapil Copper Co. Ld. Regd. 1896. Struck off Register 5 June 1981 1970

Mazarron Electric Light Co. Ld. Regd. 1893. The assets were sold on behalf of debenture holders. Struck off Register 16 Nov. 1906 1970

Mazaruni (British Guiana) Diamond Mines Ld. Regd. 1902. Vol. liq. Jan. 1908. Removed from Register 1908 1908

Mazoe Alluvia Gold Co. Ld. See Mandalay Gold Dredging Co. Ld.

Mazoe Development Co. Ld. Regd. 1895. Vol. liq. 26 Feb. 1897. Undertaking and assets were acquired by Exploring Land and Minerals Co. Ld., for 64,155 shares of £1. Final meeting return regd. 16 Mar. 1898 1906

Mazoe Mines Ld. Regd. 1910. Vol. liq. 31 Dec. 1924. Final meeting return regd. 2 Dec. 1926 1925

Mazoe Vesuvius Gold Mining Co. Ld. Assets were acquired in 1895 by Gold Fields of Mazoe Ld. for 62,500 fully-paid shares of £1 and £1,000 in cash 1899

VOL. FOR

Mead Cycle Co. Inc. Business acquired in 1928 by Mead Ld., for 80,000 fully-paid shares of 5*s*. and £60,000 in cash ... 1929

Mead Ld. Regd. 1928. Vol. liq. (creditors') 17 Dec. 1930. No capital returned to contributories. Final meeting return regd. 4 Jan. 1932 ... 1931

Meade Brothers Ld. Regd. 1899 as Francis Meade & Co. Ld.; name changed 1911. Vol. liq. 25 Sept. 1929 for reconstruction under same name; shareholders received 1 fully-paid ordinary share of £1 in new company for each ordinary share of £1 held or 1 ordinary and 2 preference shares of £1 for every 2 preference shares of £1 held. Final meeting return regd. 10 Jan. 1930 ... 1930

Meade Brothers Ld. Regd. 1929. Vol. liq. (creditors') 3 Oct. 1934. No capital returned to contributories. Final meeting return regd. 19 Feb. 1936 ... 1935

Meadow Dairy Co. Ld. Regd. 1906. Vol. liq. 8 June 1981. Final meeting return regd. 18 Aug. 1981 ... 1959

Meadow Hall Steel Co. Ld. Regd. 1920 as Henry Rossell & Co. Ld.; name changed Dec. 1935. Receiver appointed in June 1931. Struck off Register 3 Mar. 1944 ... 1944

Meadow Mills Ld. Regd. 1932. Vol. liq. (members') 1 Apr. 1938. Undertaking and assets were acquired by Ruberoid Co. Ld. Capital returned to contributories—£10,160 8*s*. 1*d*. Final meeting return regd. 21 July 1938 ... 1939

Meakers Ld. Regd. as private company 27 Aug. 1919; converted public company in June 1927. Vol. liq. (members') 19 Apr. 1978 ... 1988–9

Mears (Joseph) Theatres Ld. Regd. 1921. Vol. liq. (members') 5 June 1945. Capital returned to contibutories—£64,485 16*s*. 7*d*. Final meeting return regd. 23 Aug. 1946 ... 1944

Measham Gas Works Ld. Regd. 1947. Dissolved 1 May 1949, undertaking being vested in East Midland Area Gas Board under Gas Act 1948. Holders of ordinary shares (of £1) were entitled to receive £1 British Gas 3% guaranteed stock 1990–95 for each share held ... 1952

Measures Brothers Ld. Regd. 1899 as Measures Brothers (1899) Ld.; name changed Oct. 1899. Court Order to wind up 13 Oct. 1909. Liquidator released 8 May 1914. Struck off Register 3 Sept. 1918 ... 1910

Meccano Tri-Ang Realisations Ld. Regd. 1908 as Meccano Ld.; name changed 15 Jan. 1970 to Meccano Tri-Ang Ld. and as above on 8 Dec 1971. Vol. liq. (creditors') 29 Sept. 1971. Distribution: £1 per 7% preference share and 5½% 2nd. preference share respectively on 23 Jan. 1975. Amount paid into Companies' Liquidation Account; unclaimed creditors £5,116, members £992. Final meeting return regd. 6 Apr. 1978. Dissolved 6 July 1978. .. 1978-9

Mechaco (Mexico) Mining & Milling Co. Ld. *See* El Mayo Mines of Mexico Ld.

Mechanical Telephone Co. Ld. *See* Empire Telephone Co. Ld.

Mechanics & Metal National Bank. Inc. New York 1810. Assets and liabilities were merged with Chase National Bank of the City of New York (later The Chase Manhattan Bank) ... 1927

Meckla Nuddee Saw Mills Co. Ld. Regd. 1904. Vol. liq. 18 Dec. 1918. Final meeting return regd. 8 Mar. 1920 ... 1919

Medan Rubber Estates Ld. Regd. 1923. Vol. liq. 18 June 1924. Final meeting return regd. 9 Feb. 1925 ... 1925

Medapola Ld. Regd. 1906. Vol. liq. (creditors') 30 Apr. 1930. No capital returned to contributories. Final meeting return regd. 8 Jan. 1935 ... 1931

Medina Gold Mines Ld. Regd. 1903. Vol. liq. 29 July 1911. Final meeting return regd. 30 Apr. 1914 ... 1913

Médinger Cycle Co. Ld. Regd. Edinburgh 1896. Court Order to supervise winding up 21 Dec. 1898. Struck off Register 13 Feb. 1903 ... 1899

Medini Rubber Co. Ld. Regd. 1917. Vol. liq. (members') 29 July 1959. Capital returned to contributories—9*s*. 3½*d*. per share of £1; £1,015 7*s*. 6*d*. was paid into Companies' Liquidation Account. Final meeting return regd. 29 July 1959 ... 1960

Mediterranean Asbestos Quarries Ld. Regd. 1922. Vol. liq. 26 Nov. 1927. Final meeting return regd. 6 Feb. 1937 ... 1928

Mediterranean Co. for General Trade Ld. Regd. 1919. Vol. liq. (creditors') 8 Jan. 1930. No capital was returned to contributories. Final meeting return regd. 10 Oct. 1930 ... 1930

Mediterranean Extensions Telegraph Co. Ld. Regd. 1857. Vol. liq. Oct. 1883. Cables and other property were acquired by Eastern Telegraph Co. for £35,000 in 4% mortgage debenture stock. Final meeting return regd. 22 July 1887 ... 1884

Mediterranean Hotel Co. Ld. Regd 1863. Vol. liq. 25 May 1912. Final meeting return regd. 27 May 1924 1913

VOL. FOR

Mediterranean Oilfields Ld. *See* Dominion Oilfields Ld.

Medway & Thames Canal Co. Inc. by Special Act 1902 1910

Medway Insurance Co. Ld. Undertaking and assets were transferred to Northern Assurance Co. Ld., in 1925 1927

Medway Paper Mills Co. Ld. Regd. 1882. Vol. liq. 22 Nov. 1899. Final meeting return regd. 12 June 1900 1900

Medway Portland Cement Co. Ld. Regd. 1885. Removed from Register 3 Aug. 1894 ... 1901

Medway Trust Ld. Regd. 1927. Vol. liq. (members') 31 May 1934. Capital returned to contributories—20*s*. per preference share of £1; £1 5*s*. 5·65*d*. per ordinary share of £1; 3*s*. 8·825*d*. per deferred share of 1*s*. Final meeting return regd. 1 Oct. 1935 ... 1935

Medway's Safety Lift Co. Ld. Regd. 1920. Vol. liq. (members') 4 Oct. 1932. Direct controlling Interest held by Hall (J & E.) Ld. Final meeting return regd. 25 July 1933 ... 1933

Meekatharra Gold Mines Ld. Regd. 1935. Vol. liq. (members') 5 Sept. 1941. Winding-up Order 18 Mar. 1946. Capital returned to contributories—½*d*. per share of 2*s*. Liquidator released 27 Apr. 1955. Struck off Register 17 Mar. 1961. ... 1956

Meekes Ld. Regd. 1912. Court Order to wind up 16 Oct. 1923. Liquidator released Jan. 1926. Struck off Register 9 Apr. 1929 ... 1924

Meenglas Tea Holdings Ld. Regd. 1961. All capital was owned by Western Dooars Tea Holdings Ld. Vol liq. (members') 30 Apr. 1965. Final meeting return regd. 24 Dec. 1965 ... 1965

Meggitt (Samuel) & Sons Ld. Regd. 1893. Receiver appointed by Court on behalf of debenture holders. Removed from Register 1905 ... 1903

Meggitt (Samuel) & Sons Ld. Regd. 1903. Court Order to wind up 16 July 1918. Liquidator released 21 June 1920. Struck off Register 2 Apr. 1929 ... 1930

Mein & Co. Ld. Regd. 1907. Vol. liq. June 1908 for reconstruction as Mein & Co. (1908) Ld., in which company shareholders were entitled to 1 share of 10s. (credited with 5*s*. paid) for each share of £1 held. Removed from Register 1910 ... 1909

Mein & Co. (1908) Ld. Regd 1908. Vol. liq. Sept. 1909. Removed from Register 1910 ... 1910

Melbourne and General Investment Trust Ld. Regd. 1938. On 21 July 1975 all capital was cancelled, holders being entitled to securities of Estates House Investment Trust Ld as follows:— 149 ordinary shares of 25p for every 200 shares; 1 5·46% preference share of £1 for every 6½% preference; £1 7·5% debenture stock and £1 6·6% debenture stock for every £1 6¼% and £1 5½% stock respectively. Company dissolved without winding up on 31 Dec. 1976. ... 1977-8

Melbourne Assets Co. Ld. Regd. 1897. Vol. liq. 2 Nov. 1903. Reconstructed as Melbourne Trust Ld. (later Standard Trust Ld.), in which company shareholders were entitled to £6 in fully-paid shares, £9 in 4% debenture stock and 11*d*. In cash. Final meeting return regd. 12 Aug. 1926 ... 1904

Melbourne Brewery & Distillery Ld. Regd. 1894. Court Order to wind up 10 Apr. 1902. Removed from Register 1911 ... 1903

Melbourne Brewery (Leeds) Ld. Regd. 1889 as Leeds and Wakefield Breweries Ld.; name changed as above Dec. 1957. All capital was owned by Joshua Tetley & Son Ld. Vol. liq. 23 Aug. 1965. Final meeting return regd. 26 Oct. 1967 ... 1963

Melbourne City Properties Trust Ld. Regd. 1907. All shares were acquired by Melbourne & General Investment Trust Ld., in exchange for its own shares. Vol. liq. (members') 4 Oct. 1938. Final meeting return regd. 17 Apr. 1939 ... 1939

Melbourne Democrat Gold Mines Ld. Regd. 1896. Struck off Register 18 Nov. 1902 ... 1903

Melbourne Electric Supply Co. Ld. Regd. 1899 as Electric Lighting & Traction Co. of Australia Ld; name changed July 1908. Vol. liq. (members') 17 Nov. 1937. Undertaking was acquired by State Electricity Commission of Victoria (Australia). Shareholders were entitled to 1 fully-paid share of £1 in Melbourne Investment Trust Ld., *plus* 1·8*d*. in cash for every £1 stock held. £121 0*s*. 5*d*. was paid into Companies' Liquidation Account in respect of unclaimed balances. Final meeting return regd. 13 Aug. 1941 ... 1938

Melbourne Gas Light & Coke Co. Ld. Regd. 1946. Dissolved 1 May 1949, undertaking being vested in East Midland Area Gas Board under Gas Act 1948. Holders of ordinary shares (of £10) were entitled to receive £18 10*s*. British Gas 3% guaranteed stock 1990—95 for each share held ... 1952

Melbourne Investment Trust Ld. Inc. Victoria 1925 as Melbourne Investment Trust Proprietary Ld.; name changed Oct. 1937. Vol. liq. 7 June 1939. Capital

**See Stock Exchange Year-Book.*

VOL. FOR

returned to contributories—11s. 9¼d. per share of 10s. **1942**

Melbourne Mills (Holdings) Ld. *See below.*

Melbourne Mills Ld. Regd. 1920 as Melbourne Mills Ld.; name changed to Melbourne Mills (Holdings) Ld. 30 Mar. 1953 and as above 22 Jan. 1959. Vol. liq. (members') 16 Mar. 1960. Capital returned to contributories—6s. 6⁴³⁄₆₄d. per share of 2s. 6d. £4 7s. 8d. was paid into Companies' Liquidation Account on account of unclaimed dividends. Final meeting return regd. 28 Nov. 1963 .... **1964**

Melbourne Real Estate Co. Ld. Regd. 1903. Vol. liq. July 1918. Final meeting return regd. 8 Sept.1921 **1920**

Melbourne Tramway & Omnibus Co. Ld. Inc. Melbourne 1877. Vol liq June 1919. Capital returned to contributories—10s. per share (being amount of paid-up capital) and a final payment of about 7d. per share was to be made. Properties were acquired by the Municipality of Melbourne **1920**

Meldreth & Melbourn District Gas & Water Co. Ld. Regd. 1903. Vol. liq. 29 July 1910. Removed from Register 6 June 1913 .... ***1907**

Meldrum Brothers Ld. Regd. 1900. Vol. liq. 18 May 1908. Court Order to wind up 28 July 1908. LIquidator released 25 Aug. 1915. Struck off Register 14 Feb. 1919 .... **1911**

Melford Industrial Corporation Ld. Regd. 1922. Vol. liq. (creditors') 11 Nov. 1932. Capital returned to contributories—1s. 3d. (approx.) per share of £1. Final meeting return regd. 28 Dec. 1944 .... **1945**

Melkedalen Copper Mines Ld. Regd. 1899. Reconstructed 1902 as company of same name. Shareholders were entitled to 1 share of £1 (credited with 18s. paid) for each share of £1 held. Removed from Register 1904 .... **1902**

Melkedalen Copper Mines Ld. Regd. 1902. Removed from Register 1910 .... **1905**

Melkedalen Ld. Regd. 1904. Struck off Register 1920 **1912**

Melksham Gas Light & Coke Co. Ld. Regd. 1885. Vol. liq. (members') 30 June 1936. Undertaking was acquired by Bath Gas Co. Holders of original ordinary (10% standard) or additional ordinary (7% standard) shares of £20 were entitled to £37 10s. or £26 5s. respectively in consolidated ordinary stock of acquiring company. The 5% and 5½% mortgage debentures were repaid. Final meeting return regd. 1 Jan. 1937 .... **1937**

Mellanear Copper Mine Co. Ld. Regd. Truro 1876. Vol. liq. 11 July 1889. Final meeting return regd. 14 June 1890 .... **1890**

Mellersh & Neale Ld. Regd. 1899. Vol. liq. 8 June 1962. Final meeting return regd. 7 Nov. 1962 .... **1949**

Mellin's Food Co. for Australia & New Zealand Ld. Regd 1898. Vol. liq Mar. 1912. The business and certain assets were acquired by Mellin's Food Ld., in which company shareholders were entitled to 1 preference share of £1 (credited as fully-paid) *plus* 1s. 11d. In cash for each share of £1 held. All ordinary shares were held by Mellin's Food Ld. Removed from Register 1913 .... **1913**

Mellin's Food Co. for India Ld. Regd. 1887. Vol. liq. 11 Mar. 1913. Undertaking and assets were acquired by Mellin's Food Ld. Capital returned to contributories—£8 per share; further payments (if any) not known. Final meeting return regd. 19 Dec. 1913 .. **1914**

Mellis & Eye Railway Co. Inc. by Special Act 1865. Under Great Eastern Railway Act 1898, undertaking was sold to that company for £15,000 ordinary stock **1899**

Mellor (J. & J. J.) (Bury 1920) Ld. Regd. 1920. Vol. liq. 8 Oct. 1925. The assets were acquired by Warth Mills (1924) Ld. Struck off Register 13 July 1934. Restored to Register 25 Mar. 1935. Struck off Register 31 Aug. 1937 .... **1926**

Melody Mills p.l.c. Regd. as private company 17 Sept. 1934 as Leicester Paper Staining Co. Ld.; name changed 9 Mar. 1948; converted into public company 5 Jan. 1968. Winding-up order 12 May 1984. Final meeting held 5 Apr. 1988 .... **1988–9**

Melrose Gas Co. Ld. Regd. in Edinburgh 1894. Dissolved 1 May 1949, undertaking being vested in Scottish Area Gas Board under Gas Act 1948. Holders of ordinary shares (of £1) were entitled to receive 15 15s British Gas 3% guaranteed stock 1990–95 for each share held **1952**

Meltham Spinning Co. (1920) Ld. Regd. 1920. Vol. liq. (members') 6 Apr. 1934. Capital returned to contributories—3·69d. per share of £1 (10s. paid). £12 6s. was paid into Companies' Liquidation Account. Final meeting return regd. 16 Oct. 1934 **1935**

Melton Court Ld. Regd. 1934. Vol. liq. (members') Feb. 1936. All capital owned by London County Freehold & Leasehold Properties Ld. Final meeting return regd. 14 Apr. 1936. .... **1937**

Melton Mowbray Electric Light Co. Ld. Regd. 1897. Dissolved 1 Apr. 1948, undertaking being vested in British Electricity Authority and East Midlands Area Board under Electricity Act 1947. Holders of ordinary shares (of £5) were entitled to receive £12 7s. 6d. British Electricity 3% guaranteed stock (1968–73) for each share held **1949**

Melton Mowbray Gas Light & Coke Co. Ld. Inc. by Special Act 1834; regd. as limited 1870. Dissolved 1 May 1949, undertaking being vested in East Midland Area Gas Board under Gas Act 1948. Holders of securities were entitled to receive British Gas 3% guaranteed stock 1990–95 as follows in respect of each £1 unit, unless otherwise stated, of security held:

	£	s.	d.
Ord. shares (of £20)	47	0	0
5% pref. shares	1	3	0
4% red. pref. shares		19	9¾
4% red. debs. (of £100)	101	10	0

1952

Meltzer (A. & H.) (Holdings) Ld. Regd.as a private company 21 Dec. 1960; converted into public company 8 Mar. 1961. Dissolved and struck off Register 14 Feb. 1984 .... **1984–5**

Melville Coal Co. Ld. Regd. 1904. Vol. liq. Feb. 1906. Court Order to continue winding up under supervision. Struck off Register 22 Sept. 1936 .... **1937**

Melville, Fickus & Co. Ld. Regd. 1890. Business was acquired in 1902 by Fredk. Huth & Co. Removed from Register 1904 .... **1909**

Melville (Johore) Rubber Estates Ld. Inc. Straits Settlements. Property acquired by United Sua Betong Rubber Estates Ld. in 1929 .... **1943**

Melville Trust Ld. Regd. Edinburgh 1929. On 28 Feb. 1961, undertaking acquired by Securities Trust of Scotland Ld. Ordinary stockholders received £240 ordinary and 5% preference stockholders £112 4½% preference capital of that company per £100 held. The 4% debenture stock was amalgamated with a similar security of Securities Trust and the 5% debenture stock and terminable debentures became the liability of that company. Company was dissolved under Section 208 of the Companies Act 1948 on 31 Oct. 1961 .... **1963**

Melville Water Park Estate Ld. Regd. 1896. Vol. liq. 20 Mar. 1899. The undertaking was acquired in 1899 by London and Western Australian Investment Co. Ld., in which company shareholders were entitled to 1 share of £1 (credited as fully-paid) for each share of £1 held. Final meeting return regd. 21 Mar. 1900 **1900**

Melville's New Zealand Corporation Ld. Regd. 1896. Vol. liq. 19 Jan. 1900. Final meeting return regd. 1 Aug. 1902 .... **1900**

Melvin & Oriental Mines Ld. Regd. 1903. Vol. liq. Jan. 1905. Removed from Register 1907 .... **1907**

Melvin Mines Syndicate Ld. Regd. Edinburgh 1899. Property acquired by Melville & Oriental Mines Ld. Vol. liq. Jan. 1904. Final meeting return regd. 6 Mar. 1905 .... **1905**

Memba Minerals Ld. Regd. 1909. Vol. liq. 21 Jan. 1913. Final meeting return regd. 21 Sept. 1914 .... **1913**

Memphis Cotton Hull Fibre Inc. Inc. Tennessee 1922. In liq. 1933. Capital returned to contributories—5s. and 35 cents per share of no par value at Sept. 1933; further payments (if any) not known **1934**

Menantic Steamship Co. Ld. *See* North Atlantic Steamship Co. Ld.

Mendi Concessions (West & East Africa) Syndicate Ld. Regd. 1900. Removed from Register 1906 .... **1905**

Mendip Investment Co. Ld. Regd. as St James (Bristol) Trust Ld.; name changed Oct. 1961. Vol. liq. (members') 19 Apr. 1977. Shareholders received (per ordinary share of 25p) 1·08533 units in Cabot Unit Trust and a cash distribution of 11·34 per share. Final meeting return regd. 19 Apr. 1980 .. **1980–1**

Menuphone Publicity Ld. Regd. 1929. Court Order to wind up May 1930. Struck off Register 9 June 1936 **1937**

Menzies Alpha Leases Ld. Regd. 1896. Vol. liq. July 1907. Removed from Register 1908 .... **1908**

Menzies Consolidated Gold Mines Ld. Regd. 1895. Vol. liq. 29 July 1898. Reconstructed as company of same name. Shareholders were entitled to 1 share of £1 (credited with 18s. paid) in new company for each share of £1 held. Final meeting return regd. 10 Aug. 1900 .... **1908**

Menzies Consolidated Gold Mines Ld. Regd. 1898. Vol. liq. 30 June 1926. Final meeting return regd. 8 Mar. 1927 .... **1927**

Menzies "Crusoe" Gold Claims Ld. Regd. 1895. Reconstructed 1902 as Crusoe Gold Claims Ld. in which company shareholders were entitled to 1 share of 5s. (credited with 3s. 6d. paid) for each share of £1 held. Removed from Register 1904 .... **1908**

VOL. FOR

Menzies Gold Development Co. Ld. Regd. 1896. Vol. liq. 30 June 1897. Reconstructed as Menzies Ld. Final meeting return regd. 26 Feb. 1900 .... **1904**

Menzies Gold Estates Ld. Regd 1898. Removed from Register 1904 .... **1901**

Menzies Gold Reefs Proprietary Ld. Regd. 1895. Reconstructed 1900 as Mines Proprietary Ld. in which company shareholders were entitled to 1 share of 5s. (credited as fully-paid) for each share of £1 held. Removed from Register 1905 .... **1908**

Menzies Golden Age Mine Ld. Regd. 1895. Vol liq. 16 June 1900. Final meeting return regd. 15 Apr. 1901 **1901**

Menzies Golden Rhine Gold Mines (W.A.) Ld. Regd. 1896. Vol. liq. 29 Aug. 1899. Reconstructed 1899 as Golden Rhine Gold Mines (W. A.) Ld., in which company shareholders were entitled to 1 share of £1 (credited with 16s. paid) for each share held. Final meeting return regd. 9 May 1900 .... **1903**

Menzies Ld. Regd 1898. Vol. liq. 14 Jan. 1901. Reconstructed as East Mulwarrie Gold Mines Ld., in which company shareholders were entitled to 2 shares of 10s. (credited with 8s 6d. paid) for each share of £1 held. Final meeting return regd 23 July 1901 .... **1908**

Menzies Mining & Exploration Corporation Ld. Regd. 1895. Struck off Register 1923 .... **1914**

Menzies Niagara Proprietary Ld. Regd. 1895. Vol. liq. 1 Nov. 1898. Final meeting return regd. 7 June 1900 **1899**

Menzies Pioneers Ld. Regd. 1895. Removed from Register 1905 .... **1899**

Menzies United Mines Ld. Regd. 1895. Vol. liq. Mar. 1906. Shareholders were entitled to 1 share in Lancefield Gold Mining Co. Ld. for every 15 shares held *plus* 1/10ths of one penny per share in cash; further payments (if any) not known. Removed from Register 1909 .... **1907**

Menzies Waterworks Ld. Regd. 1895. Vol. liq. Jan. 1909. Removed from Register 1910 .... **1909**

Meppadi Wynaad Tea Co. Ld. Regd. 1910. Vol liq. 27 Apr. 1923. The estates and equipment were transferred to Malayalam Plantations Ld., in which company shareholders were entitled to 50 shares of £1 (credited as fully-paid) for every 100 shares of £1 held. Final meeting return regd. 22 Dec. 1923 ..... **1924**

Merah Rubber Estates Ld. Regd. 1925. Vol. liq. (members') 22 Dec. 1930. Undertaking and assets were acquired by Merah Rubber Estates (1931) Ld., in which company shareholders were entitled to 1 share of 2s. (credited with 1s. 9d. paid) for each share of 2s. held. Final meeting return regd. 12 May 1932 .... **1931**

Merah Rubber Estates (1931), Ld. Regd. 1931. Vol. liq. (members') 18 Dec. 1950. Shareholders were entitled to receive 31·227 fully-paid shares of Aberfoyle Plantations Ld., for every 100 shares held. Final meeting return regd 26 Mar. 1954 .... **1955**

Merbau Rubber Estate Ld. Regd. 1910. Vol liq (members') 15 Dec. 1931. Undertaking and assets were acquired by Alor Pongsu Amalgamated Estates Ld., in which company shareholders were entitled to 84 shares of 2s. (credited as fully-paid) for every 100 shares of 2s. held. £98 was paid into Companies' Liquidation Account. Final meeting return regd. 1 Dec. 1932 .... **1932**

Mercantile & General Trust Ld. See Amalgamated Investment & Financial Trust Ld.

Mercantile & Mining Corporation of British West Africa Ld. Regd. 1902. Vol. liq. June 1903, later a Court Order to wind up was made. Removed from Register 1910 .... **1904**

Mercantile Bank Assets Co. Ld. Regd. 1897. Vol. liq. 10 Aug. 1910. Undertaking and assets were acquired by Melbourne Trust Ld. (later Standard Trust Ld.), in which company shareholders were entitled to 9 shares of 4s. (credited as fully-paid) for each share of £1 held. Final meeting return regd. 12 Aug. 1926 **1911**

Mercantile Bank of Australia Ld Established Melbourne 1877. In liquidation in 1893 .... **1893**

Mercantile Bank of Lancashire Ld. Regd. 1890. Undertaking and assets were acquired by Lancashire & Yorkshire Bank Ld., in which company shareholders were entitled to 3 shares of £20 (credited with £10 paid) *plus* £20 in cash for each share of £20 held or 1 share for every £30 paid-up ordinary capital. Removed from Register 1910 .... **1905**

Mercantile Bank of London Ld. Regd. 1891. Vol. liq. 26 Nov. 1913. Final meeting return regd. 10 July 1916 **1914**

Mercantile Bank of Peru Ld. See Mercantile International Bank Ld.

Mercantile Bank of Scotland Ld. Regd Edinburgh 1889 as Peoples Bank of Scotland Ld.; name changed Jan. 1895. Court Orders: to wind up May 1923; to dissolve 12 Feb. 1934 .... **1924**

VOL. FOR

Mercantile Bank of the River Plate Ld. Regd. 1872 as Commercial Bank of the River Plate Ld.; name changed 27 May 1873. Vol. liq. Feb. 1881. Principal assets were bought by River Plate Trust, Loan and Agency Co. Ld. (later River & Mercantile Trust Ld.). Final meeting return regd. 24 May 1888 ..... **1887**

Mercantile Estate & Property Co. Ld. Regd. 1937. Vol. liq. (members') 13 Nov. 1946. Undertaking and assets acquired by Metropolitan Estate & Property Corpn. Ld. Ordinary shareholders were entitled to 7 fully-paid ordinary shares of £1 for every 10 ordinary shares of £1 held. Final meeting return regd. 5 Sept. 1950 .... **1952**

Mercantile Finance Trustees & Agency Co. of Australia Ld. Established 1885. Vol. liq. under supervision of Victorian Court. Compulsory winding-up order made in England Nov. 1893. A first capital return of 1s. per share of £5 (with £2 15s. paid) was payable in England in Dec. 1894; further payments (if any) not known **1895**

Mercantile International Bank Ld. Regd. 1877 as Mercantile Bank of Peru Ld.; name changed May 1880. Vol. liq. Aug. 1884. Final meeting return regd. 21 June 1889 .... **1885**

Mercantile Marine Finance Corporation Ld. Regd. 1920. Vol. liq. (members') 8 July 1932. Capital returned to contributories—10s. 3·354d. per share of 10s. £62 7s was paid into Companies' Liquidation Account. Final meeting return regd. 5 July 1939 .... **1940**

Mercantile Pontoon Co. Ld. Regd. 1895. Vol. liq 18 Jan. 1929. Final meeting return regd. 4 Oct. 1930 .... **1930**

Mercantile Steamship Co. Ld. Regd. 1871. Vol. liq. 10 July 1923. Undertaking was absorbed by Hain Steamship Co. Ld. Final meeting return regd. 9 Jan. 1924 .... **1924**

Merchant Banking Co. Ld. Regd. 1888. Vol. liq. 29 June 1906. Capital returned to contributories—£1 10s per share of £9 (£4 paid) in Dec. 1906. Removed from Register 1910 .... **1907**

Merchant Banking Co. of London Ld. Regd. 1863. Vol. liq. 11 Apr. 1888. Reconstructed as Merchant Banking Co. Ld. Shareholders were entitled to participate in distribution of 75,000 shares of £10 (credited with £4 paid) *plus* £1 per share in cash. Final meeting return regd. 27 Apr. 1893 .... **1897**

Merchant Shipping Co. Ld. Regd. 1864. Vol. liq. Dec. 1886. Final meeting return regd. 27 Apr. 1887...... **1887**

Merchants Bank of Canada. Inc. Canada 1864. Undertaking and assets were acquired by Bank of Montreal, in which company shareholders were entitled to 1 share of $100 *plus* $20 in cash for every 2 shares of $100 held **1923**

Merchants Credit Corpn. Ld. See Merchants' Industrial Corpn. Ld.

Merchants' Exchange & Offices Co. Ld. Regd. 1884. Vol. liq. 13 Nov. 1907. Removed from Register 1908 **1908**

Merchants' Fire Office Ld. Regd. 1888. Removed from Register 1904 .... **1898**

Merchants' Industrial Corporation Ld. Inc. in South Africa 23 Jan. 1925 as Merchants Credit Corpn. Ld.; converted into public company 4 Mar. 1927; name changed 17 Feb. 1944. Vol. liq. 31 Dec. 1959. Distributions to ordinary shareholders per 500 ordinary shares (of 5s.) held—in specie: on 2 Apr. 1960–75 ordinary shares of 5s in Leon Motors Ld., 39 ordinary shares of £1 in Consolidated Goldfields of South Africa Ld. and 40 ordinary shares of 5s in Hendlers' Metal Industries Ld. Capital returned to contributories—in cash: 2s. 7·66844d. The company was deemed to be dissolved on or about 23 Sept. 1963 .... **1964**

Merchant's Loan and Trust Co. See Illinois Merchants Trust Co.

Merchant's Warehousing Co. Ld. Regd. Dublin 1877. Reconstructed as company of same name (regd. Dublin 1889) **1889**

Merchiston Rubber Estate Ld. Regd. 1912 Vol. liq. (members') 31 Dec. 1946. Undertaking and assets acquired by Bagan Serai Rubber Estates Ld, in which company shareholders were entitled to receive 1 fully-paid share of £1 for each £1 share held. £63 11s. 10d. was paid into Companies' Liquidation Account. Final meeting return regd. 1 June 1948 .... **1949**

Mercia Estates Ld. Regd. 1933. Vol. liq. (members') 10 Mar. 1952. Final meeting return regd. 11 May 1955 **1948**

Mercury (Booth Grainge) Film Service Ld. Producing and distributing organisation acquired in 1928 by British & Foreign Films Ld. **1929**

Mercury Cars (Production) Ld. Regd. 1920. Vol. liq. May 1921. Struck off Register May 1930 .... **1931**

Mere Gas, Coal & Coke Co. Ld. Regd. 1866. Dissolved 1 May 1949, undertaking being vested in Southern Area Gas Board under Gas Act 1948. Holders of

VOL. FOR

securities were entitled to receive, in respect of each £1 unit held, British Gas 3% guaranteed stock 1990–95 as follows:

	£	s.	d.
Ord. shares	.2	1	0
4% pref. shares	1	2	8	1952

Meredith-Jones (J.) & Sons Ld. Regd. 1902. Struck off Register 27 June 1958 .... **1940**

Mergui Crown Estates Ld. Regd. 1931. Vol. liq. (members') 1 Dec. 1960. Capital returned to contributories-4s. 9½d. per share of 1s. £8,109 12s. 1d. paid into Companies' Liquidation Account. Final meeting return regd. 22 Dec. 1962.............. **1964**

Mergui Crown Rubber Estates Ld. Regd. 1914. Vol. liq. (creditors') 23 Mar. 1931. Undertaking and assets were acquired by Mergui Crown Estates Ld., in which company shareholders were entitled to 1 share of 2s. (credited with 1s. 6d. paid) for each share of 2s. held. Debenture stockholders were entitled to an equal amount of 6% debenture stock in new company. Final meeting return regd. 30 Mar. 1932 .... **1932**

Mergui Rubber Co. Ld. See Shwegyin (Burma) Rubber Estate Co. Ld.

Merionethshire Railway Co. Inc. by Special Act 1871. Undertaking abandoned by Act of 1887 .... **1888**

Meritini Rubber Estates Ld. Regd. 1910. Vol. liq. 11 Dec. 1925. Final meeting return regd. 30 Sept. 1926 **1926**

Mermac Ld. Regd. 1925 as Coleman Trading Co. Ld.; name changed Feb. 1926. Vol. liq. 27 Aug. 1928. Final meeting return regd. 13 Mar. 1931 .... **1929**

Mermac Ld. See Salisbury Service Co. Ld.

Merrall and Son Ld. Regd. 1891. Vol. liq. 31 Mar 1966. Final meeting return regd. 23 Sept. 1971 .... **1947**

Merrivale Light Railway Co. Inc. 1909. No capital had been raised at 31 Dec. 1909 .... **1911**

Merry & Cuninghame Ld. Regd. Edinburgh 1891. Court Orders: to wind up Mar. 1931; to dissolve 21 Sept. 1937 .... **1932**

Merrybent & Darlington Railway Co. Inc. by Special Act 1866. Under North Eastern Railway Act 1900 undertaking was transferred to that company **1901**

Mersey Forge Land Co. Ld. Regd. 1882 as Mersey Forge Ld: name changed May 1914. Vol. liq. 25 Feb. 1920. Capital returned to contributories—£1 6s. 6½d. per share of £2 (£1 paid) at Oct. 1920; further payments (if any) not known. Final meeting return regd 25 Nov. 1920 .... **1921**

Mersey Forge Ld. See Mersey Forge Land Co. Ld.

Mersey Investment Trust Ld. Regd. 1918. Vol. liq. 14 Nov. 1927. Undertaking was acquired by British Shareholders Trust Ld. Final meeting return regd. 15 May 1928 .... **1928**

Mersey Marine Insurance Co. Ld. Regd. 1876. Vol. liq. 23 Feb. 1881. Final meeting return regd. 5 June 1884 ***1882**

Mersey Mill (1919) Ld. Regd. 1919. Vol. liq. (creditors') 13 July 1971. Capital returned to contributories— 19·12p (per 50p. stock). Final meeting return regd. 14 Oct. 1974 .... **1974-5**

Mersey Pneumatic Railway Co. See Mersey Railway Co.

Mersey Power Co. Ld. Regd. 1911. Dissolved 1 Apr. 1948. undertaking being vested in British (later Central) Electricity Authority and Merseyside & North Wales Area Board under Electricity Act 1947. Holders of 6% preference shares and 3½% debenture stock were entitled to receive, in respect of each £1 capital held, £1 10s 4d. and £1 0s. 5⅞d. British Electricity 3% guaranteed stock (1968–73), respectively **1946**

Mersey Railway Co. Inc. by Special Act 1866 as Mersey Pneumatic Railway Co.; name changed by Special Act 1868. DIssolved 3 June 1949; undertaking vested 1 Jan. 1948 in British Transport Commission under Transport Act 1947. Holders of securities were entitled to receive British Transport 3% guaranteed stock 1978–88 as follows in respect of each £100 of capital held:

	£	s.	d.
Cons. ord. stock	36	7	6
3% perp. pref. stock	76	0	0
4% new 1st perp. deb. stock	116	15	0
4% perp. deb. stock (Acts 1866)	116	12	6
3% perp. deb. stock (Act 1871)	97	0	0
3% perp. deb. stock (Acts 1882 3–5)	97	0	0
3% perp. B deb. stock	97	0	0	1949

Mersey Salt & Brine Co. Ld. Regd. 1881. Vol. liq. Dec. 1888. Final meeting return regd. 27 Nov. 1890 .... **1891**

Mersey Steamship Co. Ld. Regd. 1872. Vol. liq. 24 July 1908. Undertaking was acquired by Royal Mail Steam Packet Co. Final meeting return regd. 7 Dec. 1910 .... ***1909**

Mersey Steel & Iron Co. Ld. Regd. 1864. Business was acquired by Mersey Forge Ld. (later Mersey Forge

VOL. FOR

Land Co. Ld.). Court Orders: to wind up 15 Feb. 1881; to dissolve 24 Aug. 1886 .... **1910**

Merseyside Touring Co. Ld. Regd. 1929. Vol. liq. (members') 4 Feb. 1932. Direct controlling interest held by Ribble Motor Services Ld. Final meeting return regd. 10 May 1934 .... **1932**

Mersina Adana Construction Co. Ld. Regd. 1884. Court Orders: to wind up 21 Jan. 1888; to dissolve 30 Apr. 1892 .... **1891**

Mersina, Tarsus and Adana Railway Co. Established under Ottoman Statutes 1884. In liq.; instalments on arrears certificates not claimed within 5 years from 1 Feb. 1958 were prescribed **1974-5**

Mersing Rubber Estates Ld. Regd. 1918. Vol. liq. 18 Mar. 1920. Reconstructed as Anglo-Mersing Rubber Estates Ld. Final meeting return regd. 21 July 1923 .... ***1921**

Merthyr Electric Traction & Lighting Co. Ld. Regd. 1898. Dissolved 1 Apr. 1948. undertaking being vested in British (later Central) Electricity Authority and South Wales Area Board under Electricity Act 1947. Holders of ordinary and 5% preference share were entitled to receive, in respect of each share (of £5) held, £12 10s. and £7 5s. British Electricity 3% guaranteed stock (1968–73), respectively **1949**

Merthyr Tydfil Gas Co. Estd. 1836; inc. by Special Act 1868. Dissolved 1 May 1949, undertaking being vested in Wales Area Gas Board under Gas Act 1948. Holders of securities were entitled to receive, in respect of each £100 unit held, British Gas 3% guaranteed stock 1990–95 as follows:

	£	s.	d.
Cons. ord. stock (5% stand.)	200	0	0
5% pref. stock	112	0	0
5% perp. deb. stock	125	0	0	1952

Merton Board Mill Ld. Regd. 1922. Court Order to wind up 3 Mar. 1925. Struck off Register 1931 .... **1926**

Merton Metallurgical Co. Ld. Regd. 1907. Vol. liq. 1 Nov. 1918. Final meeting return regd. 19 Mar. 1928 **1919**

Merton's Boulder Ld. Regd. 1900. Vol. liq. Oct. 1906. Removed from Register 1910 .... **1907**

Merton's Reward Gold Mining Co. Ld. Regd. 1902. Vol. liq. Oct. 1910. Removed from Register 1911 .... **1911**

Mertzy's Reward Gold Mines Ld. Regd. 1897. Vol. liq. 28 Nov. 1898. Final meeting return regd.5 Dec.1899 **1899**

Mesopotamia Exploration (Parent) Syndicate Ld. Regd. 1911. Struck off Register 1926 .... ***1914**

Mesquital del Oro Mining Co. Ld. Regd. 1885. Assets were acquired by Mesquital Mines Ld. Purchase money £15,000 in fully-paid shares of 2s. Struck off Register 17 June 1904 .... **1905**

Mesquital Gold Mines Ld. Regd. 1904. Reconstructed 1906 as San Carlos Gold Mine Ld. Shareholders were entitled to 1 share of 5s. (credited as 3s. 6d. paid) for each share of 5s. held. Removed from Register 1910 .... **1908**

Mesquital Mines Ld. Regd. 1899. Reconstructed 1904 as Mesquital Gold Mines Ld. in which company shareholders were entitled to 1 share of 5s. (credited with 3s. 6d. paid) for every share of 2s. held. Removed from Register 1906 .... **1906**

Messina Primrose Copper Corporation Ld. Regd. 1911. Struck off Register 1915 .... **1913**

Messina (Transvaal) Development Co. Ld. Regd. 1905. Vol. liq. (members') 31 Jan. 1950. Undertaking acquired by a company of same name in which company stockholders were entitled to receive 1 fully-paid share of 5s. for every 5s. stock held. Final meeting return regd. 8 Dec. 1954 .... **1955**

Messrs. Cross & Matthews Ld. Regd. 1897. Removed from Register 1905 .... **1899**

Metafilters Ld. Undertaking and assets were acquired by Metafilters (1929) Ld., for £5,000 in cash and 116,000 fully-paid shares of 5s. **1930**

Metafilters (1929) Ld. Regd. 1929. Receiver appointed in Oct. 1931. Struck off Register 18 Feb. 1938 .... **1930**

Metal Products Company (Willenhall) Ld. Regd. as a private company 19 Aug. 1929; converted into public company 16 June 1953; winding-up order made 9 Feb. 1976; dissolved and struck off Register 25 Aug. 1983 .... **1984-5**

Metal Products Ld. Inc. Dublin 1933. Vol. liq. (members') 15 June 1948. Undertaking and assets were acquired by Metal Products (Cork) Ld., in which company ordinary shareholders were entitled to receive 5 ordinary shares of 5s. and preference shareholders (both classes) to 1 preference share of £1 in respect of each share held. Dissolved Nov. 1956 .... **1957**

Metal Recovery Co. Ld. Regd. 1889. Court Order to wind up under supervision 3 May 1890. Removed from Register 1907 .... **1891**

*See Stock Exchange Year-Book.

VOL. FOR

Metal Traders Ld. Regd. as private company 15 May 1920; converted into public company July 1932. Winding-up order made 24 Apr. 1972. Dissolved and struck off Register in Mar. 1984 .... **1984–5**

Metal Tube Jointing Co. Ld. Regd. 1897. Struck off Register 23 July 1901 .... **1899**

Metalite Ld. Regd. 1910. Vol. liq. 30 Oct. 1913. Shareholders were entitled to 1 ordinary share of 5*s.* (credited with 3*s.* 6*d.* paid) in Derby Lamp Works Ld., for each share of £1 held; the mortgage holders received preference shares at par and the preference shareholders received ordinary shares at par. Final meeting return regd. 17 Dec. 1915 .... **1915**

Metallgesellschaft A.G. Inc. Germany 1906 as Berg & Metallbank; name changed to Metallbank & Metallurgische Gesellschaft A.G. in 1910; name changed as above 1928 .... **1940**

Metallbank & Metallurgische Gessellschaft A.G. *See* Metallgesellschaft A.G.

Metallic Ore Reduction Co. Ld. Regd. 1929. Vol. liq. (members') 30 Nov. 1936. Undertaking acquired by Amalgamated Oxides Ld. for 2,028 fully-paid preference shares of £1 and 102,096 fully-paid ordinary shares of 10*s.* Final meeting return regd. 4 Dec. 1936. .... **1939**

Metallic Sulphides Reduction Co. Ld. Regd. 1879. Struck off Register 16 Aug. 1892 .... **1899**

Metallic Tube & Flask Co. Ld. Regd. 1892. Vol. liq. 31 July 1896. (Undertaking was acquired in 1896 by Metallic Seamless Tube Co. Ld.) Final meeting return regd. 13 Nov. 1896 .... **1940**

Metallisation (Sales) Ld. Regd. 1929. All shares were acquired by Metals Coating Co. Ld. Struck off Register 1935 .... **1934**

Metallurgical & Mining Syndicate Ld. Regd. 1895. Vol. liq. Mar. 1925 for reconstruction as British Oil Engines Ld., in which company shareholders were entitled to 1 share of 2*s.* (credited with 3*d.* paid) for every 3 shares held. Struck off Register 3 Oct. 1941 **1942**

Metallurgical Co. Ld. Regd. 1913. Vol. liq. Aug. 1923. Struck off Register Mar. 1929 .... **1930**

Metallurgical Trust Ld. Regd. 1903. Vol. liq. Mar. 1911. Removed from Register 1911 .... **1912**

Metals Coating Co. Ld. Regd. 1929. Struck off Register Jan. 1935 .... **1935**

Metals Extraction Corporation Ld. Inc. Guernsey 1905. Vol. liq. Aug. 1933 .... **1934**

Metals Production Ld. Regd. 1921. Vol. liq. (members') 13 Dec. 1929. All issued capital owned by Minerals Separation Ld. Final meeting return regd. 13 Oct. 1930 .... **1930**

Metduro Ld. Regd. 1928. Struck off Register 27 Jan. 1942 .... **1942**

Meteor (Black Flag) Ld. Regd. 1896. Struck off Register 18 Nov. 1902 .... **1903**

Meteor Diamond Mining Co. Ld. Regd. 1881. Removed from Register 1905 .... ***1884**

Methil Harbour & Dock Co. Inc. by Special Act 1883 **1890**

Methley Railway Joint Committee. Dissolved 2 Apr. 1949: undertaking vested 1 Jan. 1948 in British Transport Commission under Transport Act 1947 **1949**

Metropole Developments Ld. Regd. 1928. Direct controlling interest was held by Metropole Industries Ld. Struck off Register 1935 .... **1933**

Metropole Hotels Co. (Ireland) Ld. Regd. Dublin 1893. Reconstructed 1899 as company of same name (later Grosvenor Hotel, Dublin Ld.) in which company shareholders were entitled to 3 shares of £1 (credited as fully-paid) for each ordinary share of £5 held or 5 preference shares of £1 (credited as fully-paid) for each preference share of £5 held. Removed from Register 1901 .... **1899**

Metropole Palace Co. Ld. Regd. 1912. Struck off Register 23 Dec. 1919 .... ***1917**

Metropolitan Amalgamated Railway Carriage & Wagon Co. Ld. *See* Metropolitan-Cammell Carriage, Wagon & Finance Co. Ld.

Metropolitan and Birmingham Bank Ld. *See* Metropolitan Bank (of England & Wales) Ld.

Metropolitan & General Investment Co. Ld. Regd. 1914. Vol. liq. (creditors') 16 Sept. 1932. Direct controlling interest held by Rock Investment Co. Ld. Final meeting return regd. 27 Aug. 1934 .... **1933**

Metropolitan & Great Central Joint Committee. Dissolved 2 Apr. 1949; undertaking vested 1 Jan. 1948 in British Transport Commission under Transport Act 1947 .... **1949**

Metropolitan & London & North Eastern Railway Companies—Watford Joint Railway Committee. Dissolved 2 Apr. 1949; undertaking vested 1 Jan. 1948 in British Transport Commission under Transport Act 1947.................. **1949**

Metropolitan & Metropolitan District Railways (City Lines & Extensions) Joint Committee. Inc. by Special Act 1879. Ceased to exist upon passing of London Passenger Transport Act 1933 .... **1934**

Metropolitan & Provincial Direct Fish Supply Association Ld. Regd. 1894. Vol. liq. 16 Nov. 1895. Final meeting return regd. 11 Aug. 1896 .... **1896**

Metropolitan and Provincial Stores Ld. Regd. 1896. Vol. liq. 6 Apr. 1898. Final meeting return regd. 25 July 1900 .... **1899**

Metropolitan & St. John's Wood Railway Co. Inc. by Special Act 1864 .... **1882**

Metropolitan & Suburban Milk Supply Association Ld. Regd. 1880. Undertaking and assets were acquired in 1899 by Great Western and Metropolitan Dairies Ld. for £39,550 in cash. Removed from Register 1901 .... **1900**

Metropolitan Auto-Cab Co. Ld. Regd. 1908. Court Order to wind up 5 July 1911. Liquidator released 21 Feb. 1913. Struck off Register 10 Oct. 1916 .... **1912**

Metropolitan Bank (of England & Wales) Ld. Established 1866 as Birmingham Banking Co. Ld.; name changed to Metropolitan and Birmingham Bank Ld. in Aug. 1889, and to Metropolitan Birmingham and South Wales Bank Ld. in Apr. 1892 and as above in June 1893. Vol. liq. 14 July 1914. Amalgamated with London City & Midland Bank Ld. (later Midland Bank Ld.), in which company shareholders were entitled to 11 shares of £12 (credited with £2 10*s.* paid) for every 7 shares of £50 (£5 paid) held....... **1915**

Metropolitan, Birmingham and South Wales Bank Ld. *See* Metropolitan Bank (of England & Wales) Ld.

Metropolitan "Brush" Electric Light & Power Co. Ld. Regd. 1882. Vol. liq. Apr. 1884. Court Order to continue winding up under supervision. Final meeting return regd. 20 July 1887 .... **1885**

Metropolitan-Cammell Carriage Wagon & Finance Co. Ld. Regd. 1902 as Metropolitan Amalgamated Railway Carriage & Wagon Co. Ld.; name changed to Metropolitan Carriage Wagon & Finance Co. Ld. in June 1912 and as above Jan. 1929. Vol. liq. (members') 31 Oct. 1934. Reconstructed as Metropolitan-Cammell Carriage & Wagon Co. Ld. Holders of preference shares were entitled to 110,000 preference shares and 1,312,492 ordinary shares in Electric Holdings Ld., *plus* £89,604 in cash. Holders of ordinary shares were entitled to 1,000,000 ordinary shares in acquiring company. Final meeting return regd. 20 Nov. 1935 .... **1935**

Metropolitan Canadian Corporation Ld. Regd. 1937. Vol. liq. (members') 16 May 1939. Capital returned to contributories—1·846*d.* per preferred ordinary share of £1 *plus* certain investments in specie. Final meeting return regd. 31 Jan. 1942 .... **1940**

Metropolitan Carriage, Wagon & Finance Co. Ld. *See* Metropolitan-Cammell Carriage Wagon & Finance Co. Ld.

Metropolitan Cinema Investment Comoration Ld. Regd. 1928. Vol. liq. (members') 7 June 1946. All shares were held by Odeon Theatres Ld., (later The Rank Organisation Ld.); £871 was paid into Companies' Liquidation Account. Final meeting return regd. 27 Oct. 1947 .... **1948**

Metropolitan Coal Co. of Sydney Ld. Regd. 1886. Vol. liq. 29 June 1921. Capital returned to contributories—22*s.* 9*d.* per 1st preference share of £1: 23*s.* per 2nd preference share of £1; 2*s.* 6*d.* per ordinary share of £1. Shares in Metropolitan Coal were reserved for allotment to 10% preference shareholders. Final meeting return regd. 23 Feb. 1923 .... **1922**

Metropolitan Coal Consumers' Association Ld. Regd. 1889. Court Orders: to wind up Jan. 1890; to dissolve 24 Aug. 1899 .... **1890**

Metropolitan Common Lodging House Association Ld. Regd. 1889. Vol. liq. 11 July 1894. Final meeting return regd. 30 Nov. 1894 .... **1895**

Metropolitan District Bread Co. Ld. Regd. 1889. Taken over by Bread Union Ld. Removed from Register 1907 .... ***1890**

Metropolitan District Electric Traction Co. Ld. Regd. 1901. Undertaking acquired by Underground Electric Railways Co. of London Ld. in which company shareholders were entitled to 1 share of £10 (£5 paid) *plus* £5 in cash for each share of £20 (£15 paid) held. Removed from Register 1905 .... **1904**

Metropolitan District Railway Co. Inc. by Special Act 1864. The undertaking (including all lands, works and other property, assets, powers, &c.) was transferred by Act of 1933 to London Passenger Transport Board. Stockholders were entitled to stock in Board as follows:

For every £100 held	*L.P.T.B.*
4% prior lien deb.	£88 17*s.* 9*d.* 4½% A
6% perp. deb	£120 5% A
4% perp. deb.	£88 17*s.* 9*d.* 4½% A
4% perp. deb. 1903–5	£88 17*s.* 9*d.* 4½% A

**See Stock Exchange Year-Book.*

VOL. FOR

5% red. deb. 1933–43 .... £100 5% A
5% red. deb. 1985–95 .... £100 5% A
3% cons. rent charge ....£66 13s. 4d. 4½% A
4% Mid. rent charge ....£88 17s. 9d. 4½% A
4% guaranteed ....£80 5% B
4½% 1st pref. ....£90 5% B
5% 2nd pref. ....£100 5% B
Ordinary ....£92 10s. C
Holders of assented 1st preference stock on which
Underground Electric Railways Co. of London Ltd.
had guaranteed dividends of 3½% p.a. were entitled
to £75 5% B stock per £100 assented stock held.
After distribution of the stock, the company was to
be dissolved **1934**

Metropolitan Electric Supply Co Ld. Regd 1887 as South
Metropolitan Electric Supply Co. Ld.; name
changed 1888. Dissolved 1 Apr. 1948, undertaking
being vested in British (later Central) Electricity
Authority and Southern Area Board under Electricity Act 1947. Holders of securities were entitled to
receive British Electricity 3% guaranteed stock
(1968–73), as follows in respect of each £1 unit of
capital held:

	£	s.	d.
4½% preference stock	1	4	6
Ordinary stock	2	8	0
3% debenture stock	1	0	0	**1949**

Metropolitan Electric Tramways Ld, Registered 1894 as
Metropolitan Tramways & Omnibus Co. Ld.; name
changed Jan. 1902. The undertaking (including all
lands, works and other property, assets, powers,
&c.) was, by Act of 1933, transferred on 1 July 1933
to the London Passenger Transport Board. Holders
of stocks were entitled to stock in the Board as
follows—holders of 4½% debenture stock-an equal
amount of 4½% A stock; holders of 5% debenture
stock-an equal amount of 5% B stock; holders of 5%
cumulative preference shares of £1—15s. of C stock
per share; and holders of ordinary shares of £1—6s.
of C stock per share. £559 10s. C stock was not
distributed at date of final meeting. Final meeting
return regd. 18 Dec. 1934 .... **1934**

Metropolitan Fare Register Co. (India) Ld. In liquidation. A direct controlling interest was held by
Metropolitan Fare Register Co. Ld. **1932**

Metropolitan Fare Register Co. Ld. Regd. 1905. Vol. liq.
10 July 1912. Final meeting return regd. 3 Apr. 1914 *****1913**

Metropolitan Fare Register Co. Ld. Regd. 1912. Vol. liq.
(members') 25 Feb. 1955. Final meeting return
regd.3 July 1957 .... **1939**

Metropolitan Fire Insurance Co. Ld. Regd. 1897. Vol.
liq. 10 Jan. 1900. Court Order to wind up 11 Jan.
1900. Liquidator released 31 July 1907. Removed
from Register 10 Mar. 1911 .... *****1901**

Metropolitan Freehold Land Co. Ld. Regd. 1883.
Removed from Register 1888 .... **1889**

Metropolitan Gas Company (of Melbourne). Inc. in
Victoria by Special Act 1878. Dissolved under Gas
& Fuel Corporation Act 1950 on 1 July 1951 and
succeeded by Gas & Fuel Corporation of Victoria.
Holders of capital stock exchanged each £1 unit of
stock for two 4% preference shares of £1 of the
corporation and the liability in respect of the
company's debentures was assumed by that corpora-
tion on 1 July 1951.. **1952**

Metropolitan Gold Mining Co. Ld. In 1895 the undertaking was taken over by George Goch Amalgamated
Gold Mining Co. Ld., in which company shareholders were entitled to be issued with 132,000 shares of
£1 .... **1895**

Metropolitan Guarantee and Accident Insurance Co. Ld.
Regd. 1884. Removed from Register 1894 .... **1887**

Metropolitan House Investment & Agency Co. Ld. Regd.
1890. Vol. liq. (members') 6 Mar. 1934. Final
meeting return regd. 15 Nov. 1934 .... **1935**

Metropolitan Housing Corporation Ld. Regd. 1929. Vol.
liq. (members') 13 Nov. 1946; undertaking and
assets acquired by Metropolitan Estate & Property
Corpn. Ld., in which company shareholders were
entitled to receive (a) 1 fully-paid ordinary share of
£1 for each £1 of ordinary stock and (b) 14 fully-paid
preference shares of £1 for each £9 of preference
stock held. Final meeting return regd. 17 Dec. 1955 **1957**

Metropolitan Life Insurance Co. of New York. Inc. New
York 1868. London office was closed in 1933 and
business transferred to Legal & General Assurance
Society Ld. **1934**

Metropolitan Machinists Ld. Regd. 1883. Vol. liq.
(members') 11 Jan. 1933. Capital returned to
contributories—£12,645. Final meeting return regd.
5 Aug. 1941 .... **1933**

Metropolitan Markets Cold Storage Ld. Regd. 1901 as
Smithfield Markets Cold Storage Ld.; name
changed Dec. 1901. Vol. liq. (members') 27 Dec.

VOL. FOR

1929. Capital returned to contributories—4s. 2d. per
share of 17s. 6d. Final meeting return regd. 24 Feb.
1930 .... **1930**

Metropolitan Mills Ld. Regd. 1882. Court Orders: to
wind up 18 July 1885; to dissolve 3 Mar. 1891 .... **1886**

Metropolitan Mineral Water Co. Ld. Regd. 1887.
Removed from Register 1906 .... **1901**

Metropolitan Motor Cab & Carriage Co. Ld. Regd.
1905. Vol. liq. 13 Aug. 1907. Removed from
Register 1910 .... **1908**

Metropolitan Music Hall Co. Ld. Regd. 1887. Vol. liq.
July 1888. Final meeting return regd. 30 Sept. 1890: **1889**

Metropolitan Outer Circle Railway Co. Inc. 1882.
Undertaking abandoned in 1885 .... **1886**

Metropolitan Outer Circle Railway Co. Inc. by Special
Act 1888. Undertaking abandoned by Act of 1895 **1896**

Metropolitan Pipe & Pole Co. Ld. Regd. 1936. Court
Order to wind up 11 Nov. 1940. Liquidator released
21 Mar. 1942. Struck off Register 24 Nov. 1944 .. **1942**

Metropolitan Railway Carriage & Wagon Co. Ld. Regd.
1862. Vol. liq. 19 Feb. 1896. Reconstructed as
company of same name. Shareholders were entitled
to 1 share of £5 (credited as fully-paid) in new
company for each share of £10 (£5 paid) held. Final
meeting return regd. 23 June 1896 .... **1902**

Metropolitan Railway Carriage & Wagon Co. Ld. Regd.
1896. Vol. liq. 23 Apr. 1902. Reconstructed 1902 as
Metropolitan Amalgamated Railway Carriage and
Wagon Co. Ld. (later Metropolitan-Cammell Carriage Wagon & Finance Co. Ld.), in which company
shareholders were entitled to 7½ ordinary shares of
£1 (credited as fully-paid) for each share of £5 held.
Final meeting return regd. 19 May 1903 .... **1903**

Metropolitan Railway Co. Inc. by Special Act 1853 as
North Metropolitan Railway Co.; named changed by
Special Act 1854. Undertaking (including all lands,
works and other property, assets, powers, &c.), but
excluding the undertaking of Surplus Lands Committee (transferred to Metropolitan Railway Surplus
Lands Co. Ld.), was transferred under Act of 1933 to
London Passenger Transport Board Stockholders
were entitled to stock in Board as follows:

For every £100 held		L.P.T.B.
5% red. deb. 1957–62	£100	5% A
3½% debenture	£77 15s. 6d.	4½% A
3½% A debenture	£77 15s. 6d.	4½% A
3½% preference	£70	5% B
3½% A preference	£70	5% B
3½% conv. pref.*	£70	5% B
5% preference	£100	5% B
Consolidated	£67	10s. C

*Holders of 3½% convertible preference stock had
option (since expired) to convert their holdings into
equal nominal amounts of consolidated stock and
holders of all consolidated had option (since
expired) to convert their holdings into equal
nominal amounts of Metropolitan assented stock.
The 4% terminable debenture stock was repaid in
June 1933. After distribution of stock and undistributed earnings the company was to be dissolved **1934**

**Metropolitan Railway of Constantinople, from Galata to
Pera Ld.** Regd. 1872. Removed from Register 1912 **1912**

Metropolitan Real & General Property Trust Ld. Regd.
1890. Vol. liq. (members') 5 July 1967. Preference
shares repaid at par in Aug. 1967. Capital returned
to contributories (per ordinary share of £1)—£3 11s.
4d. Final meeting return regd. 29 Oct. 1968 .... **1969**

Metropolitan Rifle Range Co. Ld. Regd. 1890. The
Middlesex County Council obtained power by Act
of 1906 to acquire the properties by agreement.
Struck off Register 1923 .... **1915**

Metropolitan Steam Omnibus Co. Ld. Regd. 1907.
Undertaking and assets were acquired by London
General Omnibus Co. Ld., in June 1914. Vol. liq.
Dec. 1914. Struck off Register May 1929 .... **1930**

Metropolitan Telephone & Telegraph Co. See New York
Telephone Co.

Metropolitan Tower Construction Co. Ld. Regd. 1891 as
International Tower Construction Co. Ld.; name
changed 13 Oct. 1891. Vol. liq. 19 Jan. 1898. Final
meeting return regd. 18 Dec. 1899 .... *****1899**

Metropolitan Trading Association Ld. See American
Produce Importers Co. Ld.

Metropolitan Tramways & Omnibus Co. Ld. See
Metropolitan Electric Tramways Ld.

Metropolitan United Estates Ld. Regd. 1926. Vol. liq.
(members') 29 Mar. 1935. Undertaking was acquired by Metropolitan Housing Corporation Ld.
which company was beneficial owner of all share
capital. Final meeting return regd. 19 July 1943 .. **1936**

Metzler & Co. (1920) Ld. Regd. 1920. Vol. liq.
(creditors') 20 Oct. 1932. Holders of prior lien
debentures and prior lien A debentures were paid in
full. Holders of 7% mortgage debentures received

See Stock Exchange Year-Book.

VOL. FOR

£38 4s. 2d. per £100 debenture. Final meeting return regd. 18 Sept. 1934 .... **1933**

Meurisse Ld. Regd. 1927. Vol. liq. (members') 16 Nov. 1967. Undertaking and assets transferred to Société Financiere pour le Développement du Commerce S.A., which company acquired all capital in May 1967. Final meeting return regd. 3 July 1968 .... **1970**

Meux's Brewery Co. Ld. Regd. 1888. All capital owned by Friary Meux Ld. Vol. liq. 10 Nov. 1961. Final meeting return regd. 7 Nov. 1962 .... **1960**

Mewossoo (Taquah) Gold Mines Ld. Regd. 1901. Undertaking and assets were acquired by Himan Central Gold Mines Ld. Removed from Register 1906 .... **1904**

Mexborough & Rawmarsh Construction Syndicate Ld. Regd. 1905. Vol. liq. 10 Feb. 1920. Shareholders were entitled to 1 fully-paid share of £5 in Mexborough and Swinton Tramways Co. (later Mexborough and Swinton Traction Co.) for every 5 shares of £1 held, *plus* 3s. 3d. per share in cash. Final meeting return regd. 3 Jan.1921 .... **1921**

Mexican and General Concession Co. Ld. Regd. 1889. Court Order to wind up 9 Nov. 1892. Liquidator released 5 Oct. 1896. Struck off Register 21 June 1907 .... **1893**

Mexican Agency Ld. Regd. 1906. Struck off Register 1916 .... **1915**

Mexican Assets Co. Ld. Regd. 1897. The debenture stock was redeemed on 8 June 1899. In liquidation in 1900. Capital returned to contributories—4s. 2d. per share of 2s. 6d.; further payments (if any) not known. Removed from Register 1901 .... **1901**

Mexican Association Ld. Regd. 1890. Vol. liq. 19 Jan. 1894. Capital returned to contributories—6d. per share of £1; further payments (if any) not known. Removed from Register 1907 .... **1869**

Mexican Central Railway Co. Ld. Inc. Massachusetts 1880. Properties were transferred to National Railways of Mexico in Feb. 1909. Holders of capital stock 1st consolidated income bonds, 2nd consolidated income bonds and registered income bonds were entitled to $1,000, $1,100, $1,000 and $1,100 respectively in 2nd preference stock in new company for each $1,000 securities held. Holders of 7% 1st mortgage bonds received an equal amount of prior lien bonds in new company. Holders of 5% priority bonds received $700 prior lien bonds and $475 general mortgage bonds in new company for every $1,000 bonds held. Holders of 4% consolidated mortgage bonds received $600 prior lien bonds, $325 general mortgage bonds and $75 2nd preference stock for every $1,000 bonds held **1909**

Mexican Central Railway Securities Co. Ld. Regd. 1899. Vol. liq. (members') 11 Mar. 1964. The Mexican Government purchased the remaining 4½% prior lien bonds 1957 and 4% Guaranteed General Mortgage Bonds 1977 in National Railways of Mexico which bonds formed the security for the A Debentures and A Debenture stock. Debenture stockholders were entitled to receive capital repayments amounting to £80 per £100 prior to liquidation and a further £20 in Mar. 1964 plus liquidation distribution of £21 19s. 1d. per £100 stock. Claims in respect of payments should be made to Law Debenture Corpn. Ld. Final meeting return regd. 27 Apr. 1966 .... **1967**

Mexican Central Syndicate Ld. Regd. 1911. Struck off Register 1921 .... **1914**

Mexican Chemical & Metallurgical Corpn. Ld. Regd. 1920. Struck off Register 1933 .... *****1933**

Mexican Company of Loadon Ld. Regd. 1888. Vol. liq. 3 Apr. 1895. Final meeting return regd. 8 May 1917 **1897**

Mexican Copper Co. Ld. Regd 1887. Removed from Register 1892 .... **1890**

Mexican Corporation Ld. Regd 1919. Vol. liq. (members') 6 Mar. 1946. Company's holding of shares of Fresnillo Co. were distributed to shareholders in specie at the rate of 1 share of no par value for every 2 shares of 10s. held. Final meeting return regd. 6 Oct. 1947 .... **1948**

Mexican Cotton Estates of Tiahualilo, Ld. Regd. 1903. Vol. liq. (creditors') 21 Jan. 1970. No capital returned to contributories. Final meeting return regd. 7 Dec. 1971 .... **1972**

Mexican Eagle Oil Co. Ld. (Compania i Mexicana de Petroleo, "El Aguila, S. A."). Inc. Mexico 1908 as Cie de Petroleo El Aguila S. A.; name changed 1909. Vol. liq. 24 May 1963. Amount returned to contributories—U.S. $0·642 per ordinary or participating preference share of no par value. Final meeting 11 Oct. 1969 .... **1970**

Mexican Eastern Railway Co. Ld. Regd. 1901. Vol. liq. (members') 20 Dec. 1945. Undertaking was sold to Mexican Government. Holders of debenture stock

received £72,000 (18% of holdings) and holders of certificates of indebtedness received 8·45% of holdings in Dec. 1945. £4,470 13s. 8d. was paid into Companies' Liquidation Account. Final meeting return regd. 30 Sept. 1946 .... **1947**

Mexican Electric Works Ld. Regd. 1897. Vol. liq. 20 Dec. 1905. Undertaking and assets were acquired in 1903 by Mexican Light and Power Co. Ld. Removed from Register 1906 .... **1906**

Mexican Explorations Ld. Regd. 1889. Vol. liq. 9 Mar. 1909. Final meeting return regd. 6 Aug.1920 .... **1909**

Mexican Fuel & Power Co. Ld. Regd. 1911. Vol. liq. July 1913. Removed from Register 1914 .... **1914**

Mexican General Land Mortgage & Investment Co. Ld. Regd. 1887. Removed from Register 1898 .... **1892**

Mexican Gold & Silver Recovery Co. Ld. Regd. 1893. Vol. liq. 24 Sept. 1895. Reconstructed as company of same name. Shareholders were entitled to 1 share of £1 (credited with 17s. paid) in new company for each share of £1 held. Final meeting return regd. 1 Mar. 1897 .... **1899**

Mexican Gold & Silver Recovery Co. Ld. Regd. 1895. Vol. liq. 5 Dec. 1899. Reconstructed as company of same name. Shareholders were entitled to 1 share of 5s. (credited as fully-paid) in new company for each share of £1 held. Final meeting return regd. 13 Oct. 1900 .... **1908**

Mexican Gold & Silver Recovery Co. Ld. Regd. 1899. Vol. liq. 3 Nov. 1919. Final meeting return regd. 21 Sept. 1921 .... **1920**

Mexican (Inguaran) Copper Co. Ld. Regd. 1889. Struck off Register 11 June 1895 .... **1899**

Mexican International Railroad Co. Organised Connecticut 1882. Properties were acquired by National Railways of Mexico Ld., which company assumed liability for the 4½% prior lien sterling bonds and 1st consolidated mortgage 4% gold bonds.................. **1910**

Mexican Investment Corporation Ld. Regd. 1890. Capital returned to contributories—18s. 9d. per share; further payments (if any) not known. Removed from Register 1904 .... **1903**

Mexican Land and Colonization Co. Ld. Regd. 1889. Vol. liq. (members') 6 Nov. 1942. Capital returned to contributories—13s. 5·9d. per preference share of £10. £7,653 2s. 9d. was paid into Companies' Liquidation Account. Final meeting return regd. 1 Feb. 1945 .... **1945**

Mexican Mineral Railway Co. Ld. Regd. 1888. Vol. liq. 27 Dec. 1894. Final meeting return regd. 12 May 1896 .... **1896**

Mexican Mining & Industrial Corporation Ld. Regd. 1907. Vol. liq. 19 Dec. 1916. Final meeting return regd. 25 Apr. 1921 .... **1918**

Mexican National Land Mortgage & Investment Co. Ld. Regd. 1886 as Anglo-American Fresh Meat Supply Co. Ld.; name changed to British and American Importation Co. Ld. in May 1887 and as above in Apr. 1889. Vol. liq. 29 May 1891. Final meeting return regd. 7 Oct. 1892 .... **1892**

Mexican National Packing Co. Inc. New Jersey 1902 as United States Packing Co.; name changed Oct. 1906. In 1911 company was reorganised as Mexican National Packing Co. Ld. in which company 6% gold bondholders were entitled to $100 preferred stock for every $100 held and 6% Rastro debenture holders to $300 2nd mortgage gold bonds and $200 preferred stock for each $100 bond held; arrears of interest to 30 June 1911 was to be paid as to one-fourth in cash and three-fourths in preferred stock. Preferred and common stockholders were entitled to Trustees' Certificates representing $12·50 fully-paid common stock for each $100 stock held **1913**

Mexican National Packing Co. Ld. Inc. Maine 1911. Control of business was taken over by Mexican Government in 1914 .... **1936**

Mexican National Railway Co. Ld. Regd. 1896. Removed from Register 1903 .... **1903**

Mexican Northern Oilfields Ld. Inc. Canada 1920. In 1926 it was stated that the company was moribund **1927**

Mexican Oil Corporation Ld. Regd. 1904. Vol. liq. 15 Mar. 1910. Final meeting return regd. 5 Aug. 1920 **1911**

Mexican Pacific Gold Mines Ld. Regd. 1910. Vol. liq. 19 Feb. 1915. Final meeting return regd. 19 Feb. 1916 **1915**

Mexican Panuco Oil Co. *See* Intercontinent Petroleum Corporation.

Mexican Petroleum & Liquid Fuel Co. Ld. Regd. 1899. Removed from Register 1902 .... *****1902**

Mexican Proprietary Exploration Co. Ld. Regd. 1907. Vol. liq. 11 Dec. 1918. Final meeting return regd. 27 May 1919 .... **1919**

Mexican Railway Co. Ld. Regd. 1864 as Imperial Mexican Railway Co. Ld.; name changed 1867. Vol. liq. (members') 13 Dec. 1950, the undertaking having been sold to Mexican Government as from 1

June 1946 for Mex. $41,500,000. Capital returned to contributories (%)—6% perpetual debenture stock, 100·9; registered stock issue A (4½%), 165·44; 4½% 2nd debenture, 41·35; registered stock issue B (3½%), 39·37; 1st preference stock, 3·3; 2nd preference stock, 1·98; ordinary 1·32. £17,149 19s. 9d. paid into Companies' Liquidation Account. Final meeting return regd. 8 Dec. 1954 .... **1956**

Mexican Rosario Mining Co. Ld. Regd. 1900. Struck off Register 1922 .... **1937**

Mexican Santa Barbara Mining Co. Ld. Regd. 1887. Removed from Register 1906 .... **1892**

Mexican Smelting Corporation Ld. Regd. 1906. Vol. liq. 20 June 1913. Struck off Register 24 July 1923 ..... **1914**

Mexican Southern Mining Syndicate Ld. Regd. 1905. Vol. liq. Mar. 1908. Capital returned to contributories—6s. 7 ⁷⁄₂₄d. per share; further payments (if any) not known. Removed from Register 1908 .... **1909**

Mexican Southern Railway, Ld. Regd. 1889. Vol. liq. (members') 20 Dec. 1945. Undertaking was sold to Mexican Government. Holders of debenture stock received £139,964 (16½% of holdings) and holders of deferred interest warrants and of ordinary stock received 5·46% and 2·695% respectively of holdings in Dec. 1945. £11,777 8s. 6d. was paid into Companies' Liquidation Account. Final meeting return regd. 30 Sept. 1946 .... **1947**

Mexican Tobacco Plantations Ld. Regd. 1892. Vol. liq. 9 Aug. 1897. Struck off Register 10 Oct. 1916 .... **1898**

Mexican Transportation Co. Ld. See Mexico North Western Railway Co.

Mexican Union Railway Ld. Regd. 1910. Struck off Register Feb. 1931 .... **1932**

Mexico City Banking Corporation. Undertaking was acquired in 1926 by Bank of Montreal **1934**

Mexico City Property Syndicate Ld. Regd. 1890. Vol. liq. 8 Jan. 1904. Final meeting return regd. 1 July 1937 .... **1905**

Mexico Electric Tramways Ld. Regd. 1898. Vol. liq. 30 Sept. 1963. Final meeting return regd. 13 Dec. 1963 **1940**

Mexico Mines of El Oro Ld. Regd. 1904. Vol. liq. (members') 4 Aug. 1930. Shareholders received 8 fully-paid shares of milreis 25 in a Brazilian company for every 5 shares of £1 held. Final meeting return regd. 21 Feb. 1935 .... **1940**

Mexico National Rlys. Co. See Philadelphia Co.

Mexico North-Western Railway Co. Inc. Canada Feb. 1909 as Mexican Transportation Co. Ld.; name changed to Mexico Transportation Co. Ld., in Mar. 1909 and as above May 1909. Undertaking was acquired by a Mexican group under agreement of 21 Jan. 1946 and all proceeds paid over to Mexnorwest Holding Co. Ld. **1949**

Mexico Transportation Co. Ld. See above.

Mexico Venture Syndicate Ld. Regd. 1896. Vol. liq. 6 Mar. 1905. Undertaking and assets were acquired by Mexico Mines of El Oro Ld. in which company shareholders were entitled to 1 fully-paid share of £1 for each share of £1 held. Final meeting return regd. 9 Oct. 1913 .... **1906**

Mexnorwest Holding Co. Ld. Inc. in Canada 1930. Holders of 7½% cumulative 1st income debenture stock received their principal *plus* premium of 300% and accrued interest (from 30 Sept. 1930 to 30 June 1946) and holders of 7% non-cumulative participating 2nd income debenture stock received 13·476% on account of principal. The Charter has been surrendered and the company dissolved as from 31 Dec. 1948 .... **1950**

Meyer & Charlton Gold Mining Co. Ld. Inc. Transvaal 1888. Vol. liq. 31 Oct. 1932. A first distribution of 15s. per share of £1 was declared in Dec. 1932; payment in London [at the rate of £109·89 (sterling) per £100 (S. A. currency)] was made in Jan. 1933 further distributions of 8s. and 7s. 4½d. were subsequently paid and the company was finally wound up on 12 Feb. 1935, all unclaimed monies were handed over to the Master of the Supreme Court, Transvaal Provincial Division, Pretoria, S. A. **1933**

Mica Boiler Covering Co. Ld. Regd. 1899. Court Order to wind up 7 July 1908. Removed from Register 1914 .... **1909**

Mica Manufacturing Co. Ld. Regd. 1897. Vol. liq. 5 Dec. 1910. Struck off Register 10 Oct. 1916 .... **1911**

Michaelsen, Wright & Co. Ld. Regd. 1907. Vol. liq. 15 Mar. 1917. Final meeting return regd. 26 Sept. 1918 ***1918**

Michalinos and General Investment Co. Ld. (The). Regd. 1955 as St. James's Investment Trust Ld.; converted into public company 1955; name changed Apr. 1970. Vol. liq. (members') 17 Sept. 1974. Capital returned to contributories—16p in Oct. 1974 and 2·26p (final) in Mar. 1975. £43·45 in respect of unclaimed distributions and £70·91 in respect of

unclaimed dividends was paid into Companies' Liquidation Account. Final meeting return regd. 23 June 1975 .... **1976-7**

Michell & Aldous Ld. Regd. 1894. Vol. liq. 11 Mar. 1920. Shareholders were repaid in full. Undertaking was acquired by Truman, Hanbury Buxton & Co. Ld. Final meeting return regd. 17 Nov. 1920 ...... **1921**

Michigan Electric Railway Co. Undertaking was acquired by Michigan Electric Shares Corporation **1934**

Michigan Electric Shares Corporation. Inc. Michigan 1929. Dissolved in June 1933 .... **1935**

Michigan United Railways Co. Inc. Michigan 1906. Undertaking and assets were acquired by Michigan Electric Railway Co. Holders of common stock received an equal amount of common shares in the new company. Holders of 6% debentures or preferred stock were entitled to 1 share of Class C preferred stock for each $100 debentures or every 2 shares of preferred stock held. The plan provided for the exchange of 50% 1st and refunding mortgage bonds and 50% Class A preferred stock in new company for an equal amount of 1st and refunding mortgage bond held; arrears of interest were satisfied by Class A preferred stock **1930**

Michipicoten Copper Co. Ld. Regd. 1883. Vol. liq. June 1885. Final meeting return regd. 15 Mar. 1887 .... **1885**

Michipicoten Native Copper Co. Ld. Regd. 1881. Vol. liq. Mar. 1883. Business was acquired by Michipicoten Copper Co. Ld., for £58,683 in fully-paid shares of £1. Final meeting return regd. 28 July 1885 .... **1884**

Michoacan & Pacific Railway Co. Ld. Regd. 1896. Vol. liq. (creditors') 19 Aug. 1963. Debenture holders received 7s. 3½d. £1. £ per 692 14s. 2d. paid to Supreme Court Paymaster in respect of unclaimed distributions. Final meeting return regd. 27 May 1964 .... **1965**

Michoacan Railway & Mining Co. Ld. (The). Regd. 1889. Vol. liq. (members') 22 Feb. 1956. The mining property was acquired by Mexican Government in 1954. Capital returned to contributories—10s. 9½d. per A or B preference share or ordinary share of 10s. Final meeting return regd. 26 Nov. 1958 .... **1960**

Mid-African & Overseas Properties Ld. Regd. 1899 as Anglo-Belgian (Sierra Leone) Corporation Ld.; name changed Jan. 1920. Vol. liq. 13 Nov. 1923 for amalgamation with Rubber & Mercantile Corporation Ld., in which company shareholders were entitled to 1 A share of £1 (credited with 12s. paid) for every 8 shares of £1 held, or 1 fully-paid A share for every 10 preference shares of 2s. held. Final meeting return regd. 7 Jan. 1924 .... **1924**

Mid-Cheshire Electricity Supply Co. Ld. Regd. 1896 as Northwich Electric Supply Co. Ld.; name changed 1925. Dissolved 1 Apr. 1948, undertaking being vested in British (later Central) Electricity Authority and Merseyside & North Wales Area Board under Electricity Act 1947. Holders of securities were entitled to receive British Electricity 3% guaranteed stock (1968–73), as follows in respect of each £1 unit of capital held:

	£	s.	d.
7% preference shares	1	12	6
5% preference shares	1	7	6
4% preference shares	1	2	4
Ordinary shares	2	2	8	**1949**

Mid-Devon Copper Mining Co. Ld. Regd. 1878. Removed from Register 1891 .... **1891**

Mid-Durham Carbonization Co. Ld. Regd. 1928. Vol. liq. (members') 26 Aug. 1952. Final meeting return regd. 20 Dec. 1961 .... **1940**

Mid-East Rubber Investments Ld. Regd. 1910. Vol. liq. Nov. 1911. Capital returned to contributories—6s. 3d. per 10s. paid-up capital in Nov. 1911; further payments (if any) not known. Removed from Register 1912 .... **1912**

Mid-European Oil Co. Ld. Regd. 1910. Struck off Register 1915 .... **1914**

Mid-Hants Railway Co. Inc. by Act of 1861. Acquired by South Western Railway in 1884 .... **1885**

Mid-Kent Coal Syndicate Ld. Regd. 1897. Undertaking and assets were acquired in 1899 by Consolidated Kent Collieries Corporation Ld., for the allotment of shares of £1 (credited with 17s. 7d. paid). Removed from Register 1905 .... **1900**

Mid-Kent Gas-Light & Coke Co. Inc. by Special Act 1889. Dissolved 1 May 1949, undertaking being vested in South Eastern Area Gas Board under Gas Act 1948. Holders of securities were entitled to receive British Gas 3% guaranteed stock 1990–95 as follows in respect of each £10 unit, unless otherwise stated, of security held:

	£	s.	d.
Ord. shares (10% stand.)	9	4	0
6% pref. shares	13	8	0

VOL. FOR

4% red. deb. stock (per £100)......... 101 0 0
Liability in respect of certain mortgage loans
assumed by the Board **1952**
Mid-Kent Railway (Bromley to St. Mary Cray) Co. Inc.
by Special Act 1856. In 1923 the undertaking was
merged into the Southern Railway Co., in which
company stockholders were entitled to £102 4%
debenture stock for every £100 capital stock held.
The £23,000 4½% terminable loans were cancelled **1924**
Mid-Lincolnshire Electric Supply Co. Ld. Regd. 1931.
Dissolved 1 Apr. 1948, undertaking being vested in
British (later Central) Electricity Authority and
East Midlands Area Board under Electricity Act
1947. Holders of ordinary shares (of £1) were
entitled to receive £2 2s. British Electricity 3%
guaranteed stock (1968–73), for each share held .. **1949**
Mid-Lincolnshire Iron Co. Ld. Regd. 1885. Vol. liq.
(members') 4 May 1944. All shares were owned by
John Lysaght Ld. Final meeting return regd. 28 Oct.
1944 .... **1946**
Mid-Lincolnshire Light Railway Co. Inc. (under Light
Railways Act 1896) 1908 .... **1916**
Mid-Moonta Copper Mines Ld. Regd. 1898. Recon-
structed 1901 as Moonta Central Copper Co. Mines
Ld., in which company shareholders were entitled to
1 new share of £1 (credited with 17s. 6d. paid) for
each share of the same class held. The debentures
were repaid. Removed from Register 1911 .... **1906**
Mid-Oxfordshire Gas Light & Coke Co. Ld. Regd. 1905.
Vol. liq. 19 May 1910. Court Order to wind up 28
June 1910. Liquidator released 31 July 1913. Struck
off Register 3 Sept: 1918 .... **1911**
Mid-Southern Utility Co. Inc. by Special Act 1866 as
Aldershot Gas & Water Co.; name changed to
Aldershot Gas, Water & District Lighting Co. in
1909, to Mid-Southern District Utility Co. in 1931
and as above in 1932. Electricity undertaking was
vested in British (later Central) Electricity Authority and Southern Area Board in 1 Apr. 1948; gas
undertaking was vested in Southern Area Gas
Board on 1 May 1949; and water undertaking was
acquired by Mid-Wessex Water Co., from 3 Jan.
1950. Dissolved on 17 Jan. 1952. Holders of
preference and consolidated stocks were entitled to
receive the following—Preference Stock—£22 16s.
4d. British Gas 3% guaranteed stock 1990—5 and
£81 12s. 9d. British Electricity 3% guaranteed stock
1968–73 for every £100 held. A, B and C Consolidated Stocks—(a) in extinction of 66·39% of holdings,
£114 7s 6d. British Electricity 3% guaranteed stock
1968–73 for each £100 A stock extinguished, £81
10s. of such stock for each £100 B stock extinguished
and £109 of such stock for every £100 C stock
extinguished; (b) in extinction of further 21·22% of
holdings, £108 16s. 8d. British Gas 3% guaranteed
stock 1990–5 for each £100 A stock extinguished,
£81 10s. of such stock for each £100 B stock
extinguished and £109 14s. of such stock for each
£100 C stock extinguished; and (c) £4 British Gas
3% guaranteed stock 1990–5 and £1 14s 5d. cash for
every £1 of stock remaining **1953**
Mid-Suffolk Light Railway Co. Inc. (under Light
Railways Act 1896) by order of Light Railway
Commissioners confirmed by Board of Trade 1900.
In 1923 the undertaking was merged into the
London & North Eastern Railway Co. The scheme
provided for the cancellation of the debenture stock
and all the shares **1924**
Mid-Sussex Water Co. Inc. by Special Act 1890. In
voluntary liquidation in 1899, the undertaking
having been sold to the Rural District Council of
Cuckfield **1899**
Mid-Wales Electric Power Co. Ld. Regd. 1935. Dis-
solved 1 Apr. 1948, undertaking being vested in
British (later Central) Electricity Authority and
Merseyside & North Wales Area Board under
Electricity Act 1947. Holders of ordinary shares (of
2s.) and 4½% mortgage debenture stock were entitled
to receive, in respect of each £1 capital held, 15s. and
£1 0s. 9¼d. British Electricity 3% guaranteed stock
(1968–73), respectively **1949**
Mid Wales Railway Co. Inc. by Special Act 1859.
Amalgamated with Cambrian Railways Co., in
1904 .... **1905**
Midas Deep Ld. Inc. Transvaal 1895. In liquidation in
1913 .... **1913**
Midas East Estate & Gold Mining Co. Ld. Inc.
Transvaal 1896. Vol. liq. May 1907. A first and final
distribution of 2s. 6d. per share of £1 was made in
Nov. 1908 .... **1909**
Midas Gold Field Co. Ld. Regd. 1888. Vol. liq. 10 Sept.
1897. Final meeting return regd. 27 Apr. 1900...... **1898**
Midas Polishes Ld. Regd. 1914 as Midas Polishes (1914)
Ld.: name changed Aug. 1919. Vol. liq. 1 Jan. 1923.

VOL. FOR

Controlling interest held by Hargreaves Bros. & Co.
Ld. Final meeting return regd. 10 May 1924 .... **1923**
Middel Vlei Deep Level Gold Mining Co. Ld. Inc.
Transvaal 1895. London office was closed during
1908.. **1909**
Middelburg Steam Coal & Coke Co. Ld. Inc. Cape of
Good Hope 1901. Assets acquired in 1906 by
company of same name for 65,000 ordinary and
65,000 preference shares of £1 and £17,650 in cash **1908**
Middelburg Steam Coal & Coke Co. Ld. Regd. 1906.
Vol. liq. 25 Mar. 1924. Undertaking and assets were
taken over by company of same name (inc.
Transvaal 1924). Ordinary and preference shareholders were respectively entitled to 1 ordinary and
1 preference share in new company for each share
held. Final meeting return regd. 30 Sept. 1925 .... **1925**
Middelburg Steam Coal & Coke Co. Ld. Inc. in
Transvaal 1924. Vol. liq. 12 Dec. 1946. Capital
returned to contributories: preference 21s. 6d. per
share; ordinary £7 11s. 3·248d. per share (of £1).
£3,911 was paid into Companies' Liquidation
Account. Final meeting return regd. 9 Dec. 1952 . **1953**
Middelburg Tranavaal Exploration Co. Ld. Regd. 1895.
Struck off Register 4 Oct. 1898 .... **1901**
Middle Black Reef Gold Mines Ld. See British &
Colonial Estates Ld.
Middle Class Dwellings Co. Ld. See Western Mansions
Ld.
Middle East Development Corporation Ld. Regd. 1919
as Anglo-French Middle East Development Corporation Ld.; name changed Oct. 1922. Court Order to
wind up Mar. 1931. Struck off Register 2 Oct.·1953 **1932**
Middle West Utilities Co. Inc. Delaware 1912. In 1936
undertaking was transferred to Middle West Corporation (inc. Delaware 1935). Holders of serial
convertible gold notes and preferred and common
shares ware entitled to receive securities in new
company as follows: per $1,000 gold note—32
common shares of $5 and scrip for $\frac{7}{80}$ths of a share;
per 4 preferred or 100 common shares of no par
value-1 common share of $5 and warrant (since
expired) entitling holder to purchase 1 further share **1937**
Middlemass (R.) & Son Ld. Regd. Edinburgh 1896. Vol.
liq. (creditors') 26 Aug. 1938. The undertaking was
acquired by company of same name. Assets realised
insufficient to pay creditors in full. Final meeting
return regd. 14 July 1939 .... **1939**
Middlemore & Lamplugh Ld. Regd. 1896. Vol. liq. 30
Sept. 1919. Capital returned to contributories—£2
per preference or ordinary share of £1: further
payments (if any) not known. Final meeting return
regd. 26 June 1920 .... **1925**
Middlesborough Electric Light, Heat & Power Co. Inc.
Kentucky 1890. .... **1905**
Middlesborough Engineering Co. Ld. Regd. 1896. Vol.
liq. 15 Mar. 1898. Final meeting return regd. 12
Sept. 1898.. **1899**
Middlesborough Town & Lands Co. Ld. Regd. 1893.
Receiver for debenture stockholders appointed in
Oct. 1904. Struck off Register May 1929 .... **1930**
Middlesborough Town Co. Organised Kentucky 1888.
Reorganised as Middlesborough Town Lands Co.,
Kentucky, U.S.A., in which company shareholders
received 2 shares of £1 for each share of £5 held... **1908**
Middlesborough Town Lands Co., Kentucky, U.S.A.
Organised Kentucky 1891. In 1893 shareholders
received 1 share of £1 (credited with 17s. paid) for
each share of £1 held **1908**
Middlesborough Water Works Ld. Regd. 1894. The
property was sold under foreclosure to Middlesborough Town & Lands Co. Ld. in July 1901. Struck off
Register 18 Nov. 1902 .... **1902**
Middlesex Aërated Bread & Restaurant Co. Ld. Regd.
1889. Vol. liq. 30 July 1890. Final meeting return
regd. 11 Mar. 1891 .... **1891**
Middlesex Banking Co. Ld. Regd. 1885. Court Order to
wind up 30 Jan. 1939. Liquidator released 29 May
1943. Struck off Register 3 July 1953 .... **1939**
Middlesex Brick Co. Ld. Regd. 1935. Court Order to
wind up 27 July 1942. No capital returned to
contributories. Liquidator released 19 Aug. 1944.
Struck off Register 16 Feb. 1954 .... **1945**
Middlesex Fire Office Ld. Regd. 1874. Wound up by
Order of Court 6 Sept. 1878 .... ***1877**
Middlesex Gold Mines (W.A.) Ld. Regd. 1897. Vol. liq.
19 Jan. 1899. Reconstructed 1899 as Diorite King
Consols Ld., in which company shareholders were
entitled to 1 share of £1 (credited with 17s. paid) for
each share of £1 held. Final meeting return regd. 7
June 1902 .... **1903**
Middlesex Theatre of Varieties Ld. Regd. 1910. Vol. liq.
6 July 1920. Capital returned to contributories—20s.
per ordinary share of £1 in Sept. 1920; further

See Stock Exchange Year-Book.

VOL. FOR

payments (if any) not known. Final meeting return regd. 6 Jan. 1922 ... **1921**

Middlesex Trust Ld. *See* London Caledonian Trust Ld.

Middleton & Payne Ld. Regd. 1924 as Velocium Ld.; name changed Feb. 1926. Struck off Register 2 Feb. 1937 ... **1930**

Middleton (C. A.) Ld. Regd. 1928. Receiver appointed 30 Oct. 1930. Vol. liq. (creditors') 3 Nov. 1930. Debenture holder was paid in full. Receiver ceased to act 18 Jan. 1932. Final meeting return regd. 23 Dec. 1932 ... **1932**

Middleton Electric Traction Co. Ld. Regd. 1900. Vol. liq. 14 Oct. 1925. Undertaking was purchased by local authorities. Final meeting return regd. 15 July 1926 ... **1926**

Middleton's Bedstead Co. Ld. Regd. 1896. Shareholders were entitled to 35% of holding in debentures in company of same name *plus* 65% in cash. Removed from Register 1903 ... **1903**

Middlewich Gas Light & Coke Co. Ld. Regd. 1875. Dissolved 1 May 1949, undertaking being vested in North Western Area Gas Board under Gas Act 1948. Holders of ordinary shares (of £5) were entitled to receive £10 British Gas 3% guaranteed stock 1990–95 for each share held ... **1952**

Midget Motor Ride Ld. Regd. 1927. All shares were owned by General Amusements Corporation Ld. Struck off Register 1936 ... **1934**

Midhurst & District Electricity Co. Ld. *See* M.D.E. Co. Ld.

Midhurst Gas Co. Ld. Regd. 1860. Dissolved 1 May 1949 under Gas Act 1948 and undertaking vested in South Eastern Gas Board ... **1949**

Midland and Central Wales Junction Railway Co. Inc. by Special Act 1883. Undertaking abandoned by Act 1886 ... **1888**

Midland & Eastern Railway Co. Inc. by Special Act 1866. Dissolved 1 July 1883 on amalgamation into Eastern & Midlands Railway Co. ... **1884**

Midland & Great Northern Railways Joint Committee. Inc. by Special Act 1893. Dissolved 2 Apr. 1949; undertaking vested 1 Jan. 1948 in British Transport Commission under Transport Act 1947. Holders of Midland & Great Northern Joint Line rent-charge stock (3%) were entitled to receive, in respect of every £100 stock held, £88 British Transport 3% guaranteed stock 1978–88 ... **1949**

Midland & North Eastern Railway Companies' Committee (Swinton and Knottingley Railway). Dissolved 2 Apr. 1949; undertaking vested in Jan. 1948 in British Transport Commission under Transport Act 1947 ... **1949**

Midland and South Western Junction Railway Co. Inc. by Special Act 1884. In 1923 the undertaking was merged into the Great Western Railway Co., in which company stockholders were entitled to stock as follows:

For each £100 held		*G.W.R.*
3% Rent Charge	£75	4% Debenture
3% A Debenture	£60	5% Cons. Pref.
3% B Debenture	£17	5% Cons. Pref.
3% C Debenture	£6	
5% Swin. Marl. & And. Pref.	£4	Cons.
5% Swin. Marl. & And. Perp. Pref.	£4	Ord.
5% Swin. & Chelt. Pref.	£4	Stock
5% Mid. & S.W. Jc. Pref.	£4	Defd.
5% Mid. & S.W. Jc. Perp. Pref.	£4	Certs.
Mid. & S. W. June. Ord.	£2	

The loan of £244,000 owing to the Midland Railway Co. was satisfied by the issue of £85,000 5% Consolidated Preference Stock of the Great Western Co ... **1924**

Midland & Textile Insurance Co. Ld. *See* London & Midland Insurance Co. Ld.

Midland Arcade, Birmingham, Ld. Regd. 1899. All capital owned by Birmingham Co-Operative Society Ld. Vol. liq. (members') 14 May 1956. Final meeting return regd. 28 Mar. 1957 ... **1946**

Midland Banking Co. Ld. Regd. 1863. Business transferred to Birmingham, Dudley & District Bank Ld. [later United Counties Bank Ld.] Vol. liq. 8 June 1881. Final meeting return regd.26 May 1882 ... ***1882**

Midland Bus Services Ld. Regd. Edinburgh 1929. Vol. liq. (members') Mar. 1934. Undertaking acquired by Western S.M.T. Co. Ld. Final meeting return regd. 9 June 1934 ... **1940**

Midland (Ceylon) Tea Plantations Co. Ld. Regd. 1896. Receiver for debenture holders appointed in Feb. 1907. Struck off Register 1923 ... **1911**

Midland Coal, Coke & Iron Co. Ld. Regd. 1890. Vol. liq. 26 May 1893. Reconstructed as company of same name. Shareholders were entitled to 1 share of £5 (credited with £4 paid) for each share of £10 held. Final meeting return regd.3 Nov.1896 ... **1908**

Midland Coal, Coke & Iron Co. Ld. Regd. 1893. Receiver appointed in Nov. 1929. Assets realised insufficient to meet claims of prior lien debenture holders. Struck off Register 1934 ... **1939**

Midland Counties Aerated Bread Co. Ld. Regd. 1889. Vol. liq. 26 Sept. 1890. Final meeting return regd. 20 Nov. 1894 ... **1891**

Midland Counties & Shannon Junction Railway. *See* Clara and Banagher Railway Co.

Midland Counties & South Wales Railway Co. *See* Northampton & Banbury Junction Railway Co.

Midland Counties District Bank Ld. Regd. 1889 as Nottingham & District Bank Ld.; name changed 1899. Vol. liq. in 1905. Undertaking acquired by the Birmingham District and Counties Banking Co. Ld. (later United Counties Bank Ld.), in which company shareholders were entitled to receive one share of £20 (£4 paid). together with 25s. in cash, for every two shares of £30 (£5 paid) held ... **1905**

Midland Counties Electric Supply Co. Ld. Regd. 1912 as Tramways Light & Power Co. Ld.; name changed 1921. Dissolved 1 Apr. 1948. undertaking being vested in British (later Central) Electricity Authority under Electricity Act 1947. Holders of securities were entitled to receive British Electricity 3% guaranteed stock (1968–73) as follows in respect of each £1 unit of capital held:

	£	s.	d.
6% preference stock	1	11	6
4½% preference stock	1	3	9
Ordinary stock	2	11	5
3½% debenture stock	1	0	6¼	**1949**

Midland Counties Insurance Co. Established 1851. Regd. as unlimited 1862. Vol. liq 10 May 1892. Business was acquired by Royal Insurance Co., in which company shareholders were entitled to 3 shares of £20 (credited with £3 paid) for every 20 shares of £12 10s. (£1 15s. paid) held. Final meeting return regd. 20 Apr. 1893 ... **1892**

Midland Counties Junction Railways Securities Co. Ld. Regd. 1907. Vol. liq. Dec. 1908. Shareholders were entitled to over £3 stock in Stratford-upon-Avon and Midland Junction Railway Co. Removed from Register 1909 ... **1909**

Midland Debenture Trust and Finance Corporation Ld. Regd. 1898. Capital returned to contributories—104%; further payments (if any) not known. Removed from Register 1904 ... **1904**

Midland Electric Corpn. for Power Distribution Ld. Regd. 1897. Dissolved 1 Apr. 1948. undertaking being vested in British (later Central) Electricity Authority and Midlands Area Board under Electricity Act 1947. Holders of securities were entitled to receive British Electricity 3% guaranteed stock (1968–73) as follows in respect of each £1 unit of capital held:

	£	s.	d.
7% preference shares	1	14	6
Ordinary shares	2	7	0
3½% 1st mortgage debenture stock..	1	0	7⅛	**1949**

Midland Electric Light & Power Co. Ld. Regd. 1881. All capital was owned by Midland Counties Electric Supply Co. Ld. Dissolved 1 Apr. 1948 under Electricity Act 1947 ... **1940**

Midland Great Western Railway of Ireland Co. Inc. by Special Act 1845. In 1924 the undertaking was transferred to the Great Southern Railway Co., in which company stockholders were entitled to stock as follows:

For each £100 held		*G. Sthn. Ry.*
4% Debenture	£100	4% Debenture
4½% Debenture	£106 5s.	4% Deb.
4½% Debenture	£112 10s.	4% Deb.
4% Rent-charge	£100	4% Gtd. Pref.
5% Preference	£125	4% Preference
4% Preference	£100	4% Preference
Ordinary	£70	Ordinary	**1925**

Midland Holdings Ld. Regd. as private company as Ismay Cables Ld. 15 Feb. 1936; name changed to S. I. Holdings Ld. 30 Jan. 1939 and to above title 15 July 1946; converted into public company 7 Nov. 1946. Winding-up order made 8 Nov. 1948; no return of capital was made and the liquidator was released on 25 Aug. 1953 ... **1954**

Midland Housing Corporation Ld. Regd. 1934. Vol. liq. (members') 14 May 1935. Holders of debentures were paid in full. Capital returned to contributories—10s. per preference share of 10s. Final meeting return regd. 9 Dec. 1936 ... **1936**

Midland Insurance Co. Ld. *See* London & Midland Insurance Co. Ld.

Midland Iron Co. Ld. Regd. 1865. Vol. liq. 4 Aug. 1899. Reconstructed as company of same name (later Midland & Low Moor Iron & Steel Co. Ld.).

*See Stock Exchange Year-Book.

VOL. FOR

Shareholders were entitled to 4 ordinary and 4 preference shares of £1 in new company for each share of £10 (£8 paid) held or 6 ordinary and 6 preference shares of £1 for each share of £15 (£12 paid) held. Final meeting return regd. 31 Mar. 1900 **1899**

Midland Land & Investment Corporation Ld. Regd. 1870. Vol. liq. 9 July 1881. Court Order to continue winding up under supervision. Final meeting return regd. 3 Dec. 1890 .... *1881

Midland Railway-Carriage & Wagon Co. Ld. Est. by deed of settlement 1853, regd. 1881. Vol. liq. (members') 19 Mar. 1948. Final meeting return regd. 22 Jan. 1949 .... **1940**

Midland Railway Co. Inc. by Special Act 1844. In 1923 the undertaking was merged into the London Midland & Scottish Railway Co., in which company stockholders were entitled to stock as follows:

For each £100 held   L.M. & S.
2½% Debenture ....£62½ 4% Debenture
2½% Cons. Perp. Gtd.
  Preferential ....£62½ 4% Gtd.
2½% Cons. Perp. Pref. .....£62½ 4% Preference
Prefd. Conv. Ord. ....£62½ 4% Pref. (1923)
Defd. Conv. Ord. ....£68   Ordinary **1924**

Midland Railway Co. of Western Australia Ld. Regd. 1890. Vol. liq. (members') 30 July 1964. All capital was owned by Rural & Industries Bank of Western Australia. Total distributions to contributories—£Stg. 2,391,740. Final meeting return regd. 2 June 1967 .... **1968**

Midland Railway of Canada. Inc. 1846 as Port Hope Lindsay & Beaverton Railway; name changed 1869. Taken over on and from 1. Jan. 1884 by Grand Trunk Railway Co. of Canada **1893**

Midland Rubber Co. Ld. Regd. 1896 as "Non-Collapsible" Tyre Co. Ld. Reconstructed as company of same name. Removed from Register 1903 .... **1908**

Midland Rubber Co. Ld. Regd 1900. Vol. liq. Feb. 1911 for reconstruction as company of same name. Shareholders were entitled to 1 preference share of £1 in new company for every 4 preference shares of 5s. held, or 1 preference share of £1 and 1 A ordinary share of £1 for every 4 ordinary shares of 5s. held or 5 B ordinary shares of £1 for every 4 deferred shares of 5s. held. Removed from Register 1913 .... **1912**

Midland Rubber Co. Ld. Regd. 1911. Vol. liq. Nov. 1923. Court Order to wind up Dec. 1923. Struck off Register May 1929 .... **1930**

Midland Rubber Co. (1923) Ld. Regd. 1923 as Midland Rubber Goods Manufacturing Co. Ld.; name changed Aug. 1924. Struck off Register 30 Jan. 1934 **1934**

Midland Rubber Goods Manufacturing Co. Ld. See Midland Rubber Co. (1923) Ld.

Midland Steam Boiler Inspection & Assurance Co. Regd. 1862. Vol. liq. 25 July 1888. Business transferred to Scottish Boiler Insurance & Engine Inspection Co. Ld. *1889

Midland Tramways Co. Ld. Regd. 1888. Vol. liq. 25 Apr. 1892. Court Order to continue winding up under supervision 30 Apr. 1892. Final meeting return regd. 6 Apr. 1894 .... **1893**

Midland Trust Ld. Regd. 1890. Vol. liq. 19 Dec. 1896. Reconstructed as company of same name. Holders of preferred and deferred stocks were entitled to an equal amount of preferred and ordinary shares of £10 respectively. Holders of founders' shares were entitled to 12 ordinary shares of £10 for each founders' share of £10 held. Final meeting return regd. 4 June 1898 .... **1908**

Midland Uruguay Extension Railway Co. Ld. Regd. 1911. Vol. liq. (members') 24 Feb. 1949, undertaking having been sold to Uruguayan Govt. 5% debenture stockholders received distribution amounting to 64·365%. No distribution to ordinary shareholders. £260 was paid into Companies' Liquidation Account. Final meeting return regd. 8 Aug. 1951 .... **1953**

Midland Uruguay Railway Co. Ld. Regd. 1887. Vol. liq. (members') 24 Feb. 1949, undertaking having been sold to Uruguayan Govt. 5% prior lien debenture stock was redeemed at par, plus interest to 31 July 1948. 5% debenture stock was redeemed at 48½%, no interest payment being made. Ordinary stockholders received a distribution of 10·835%. £1,883 was paid into Companies' Liquidation Account. Final meeting return regd. 8 Aug. 1951 .... **1953**

Midlands Entertainments Ld. Regd. 1920. Receiver appointed in Nov. 1924; ceased to act June 1927. Assets realised insufficient to satisfy claims of debenture holders. Struck off Register Apr. 1929 . **1930**

Midlothian Gunpowder Co. Ld. Regd. Edinburgh 1889. Vol. liq. 23 Feb. 1889. Undertaking acquired by Curtis's & Harvey Ld. Final meeting return regd. 14 July 1889 .... **1940**

VOL. FOR

Midlothian Oil Co. Ld. Regd. Edinburgh 1882. Taken over by Clippens Oil Co. Ld. Vol. liq. June 1885. Final meeting return regd. 7 Apr. 1887 .... **1885**

Midsomer Norton Gas & Coke Co. Ld. Regd. 1872; statutory powers 1873. Dissolved 1 May 1949, undertaking being vested in South Western Area Gas Board under Gas Act 1948. Holders of securities were entitled to receive British Gas 3% guaranteed stock 1990–95 as follows in respect of each £100 unit, unless otherwise stated, of security held:

	£	s.	d.
Orig. ord. shares (10% max.) (of £10)	20	0	0
B ord. shares (7% max.) (of £10)....	14	6	0
4½% red. pref. shares (of £1)...........	1	0	8
4% red. mort. debs.	100	10	0
5½% red. mort. debs. (Oct. & Dec. 1951)...................................	103	0	0
5½% red. mort. debs. (1952)..........	104	0	0
3½% red. debs.	100	0	0

1952

Midwinter's Engineering & Cycle Stamping Co. Ld. Regd. 1897. Removed from Register 1905 .... **1905**

Mikado Gold Mining Co. Ld. Regd. 1896. Vol. liq. 24 Apr. 1903 for reconstruction as Mikado Gold Mining Co. (1903) Ld., in which company shareholders were entitled to 1 share of £1 (credited with 15s. paid) for each share of £1 held. Final meeting return regd. 10 Apr. 1926 .... **1909**

Mikado Gold Mining Co. (1903) Ld. Regd. 1903. Vol. liq. 16 July 1915. Final meeting return regd. 10 Apr. 1926 .... **1912**

Mikhalitch Lithographic Stone Co. Ld. Regd. 1898. Vol. liq. 2 Mar 1904. Final meeting return regd. 3 Sept. 1914 .... **1905**

Milborne Port Gas Co. Ld. Regd. 1865. Dissolved 1 May 1949, undertaking being vested in Southern Area Gas Board under Gas Act 1948. Holders of ordinary shares (of £5) and 5% red. mort. debs. (of £100) were entitled to receive £7 5s. and £101 British Gas 3% guaranteed stock 1990–95 for each holding respectively **1952**

Mildred, Goyeneche & Co. Suspended payment on 11 Mar. 1921 .... **1922**

Miles (Eustace) Foods Ld. Regd. 1921 as Eustace Miles Foods (1921) Ld.; name changed Oct. 1924. Receiver appointed 28 Feb. 1936. Assets realised insufficient to pay 1st debenture holders in full. Struck off Register 21 Apr. 1939 .... **1940**

Milford Haven Railway & Estate Co. Ld. Regd. 1882. Removed from Register 1901 .... **1900**

Milford Railway Co. Inc. by Special Act 1856. Under Great Western Railway Act of 1896 undertaking was amalgamated with that company. Holders of 4% debenture stock received 4% debenture stock at par; holders of £100 con. stock received £50 10s. in cash. **1897**

Milford Steam Trawling Co. Ld. Regd. 1936. Vol. liq. (members') 14 Dec. 1961. No capital was returned to contributories. £67 11s. 3d. was paid into Companies' Liquidation Account in respect of unclaimed dividends. Final meeting return regd. 16 Jan. 1965 **1966**

Military Equipment Co. Ld. Regd. 1899. Removed from Register 1906 .... **1903**

Military Equipment Stores & "Tortoise" Tents Co. Ld. Regd. 1890. The assets and liabilities were taken over in 1899 by Military Equipment Co. Ld., in which company shareholders were entitled to 2 ordinary shares of £5 (credited as fully-paid) for every 5 shares of £5 held. Removed from Register 1905 .... **1902**

Mill Close Mines, Ld. Regd. 1920. Vol. liq. (members') 11 July 1945. Capital returned to contributories—£0·2035817 per share of 10s. and £0·122148 per share of 6s. Final meeting return regd. 11 Jan. 1947 ..... **1947**

Mill-Dam Mining Co. Mine worked on cost-book system. In liquidation in 1895 .... **1895**

Millar Loom Co. Ld. Regd. 1897. Removed from Register 1903 .... **1904**

Millar's Karri & Jarrah Forests Ld. Regd. 1897. Reconstructed 1902 as Millar's Karri and Jarrah Co. (1902) Ld. (later Millar's Timber and Trading Co. Ld.), in which company shareholders were entitled to 23 or 22 preference shares of £1 for every 20 1st or 2nd preference shares of £1 respectively held or 20 ordinary shares of £1 for every 30 ordinary shares of £1 held. Removed from Register 1903 .... **1903**

Miller (E. J.) & Co. Ld. Undertaking and assets were acquired in 1927 by Bass Ratcliff & Gretton Ld.... **1929**

Miller (James) & Co. Ld. Regd. Edinburgh 1895. Undertaking was aquired in 1900 by Rivet Bolt and Nut Co. Ld. Removed from Register 1902 .... **1901**

Miller (Lewis) & Co. Ld. Regd. Edinburgh 1900. Vol. liq. May 1929. Final meeting return regd. 20 Nov. 1930 .... **1930**

VOL. FOR

Millers' & General Fire Insurance Co. Ld. Regd. 1875 as Millers' Fire Insurance Co. Ld.; name changed May 1879. Vol. liq. 13 June 1884. Court Order to continue winding up under supervision 14 June 1884. Final meeting return regd. 26 Aug. 1887 .... **1885**

Millers' Mutual Fire Insurance Co. Ld. Regd. 1876. Removed from Register 1905 .... ***1890**

Miller's Tanning Extract Co. Ld. Regd. 1886. Vol. liq. and Receiver for debenture holders appointed in June 1910. Struck off Register 1926 .... **1911**

Millington & Sons Ld. Regd. 1908 as Millington & Sons (1908) Ld.; name changed Oct. 1915. Vol. liq. (members') 18 Oct. 1932. All capital held by John Dickinson & Co. Ld. Final meeting return regd. 11 Dec. 1933 .... **1933**

Millington (Fred. W.) Ld. Regd. 1903. Vol. liq. 17 Jan. 1921. Undertaking and assets were acquired by Fred. W. Millington (1920) Ld. (later Fred. W. Millington Ld.). Shareholders were entitled to £5 in cash or 5 fully-paid ordinary shares of £1 for each ordinary share of £1 held or £1 in cash or 1 fully-paid preference share of £1 for each preference share of £1 held. Final meeting return regd. 15 Oct. 1921 **1922**

Millionaire Ld. Regd. 1900. Vol. liq. 16 Dec. 1912. Final meeting return regd. 17 July 1914 .... **1913**

Millom & Askam Hematite Iron Co. Ld. Regd. 1890. Vol. liq. 25 July 1919. Reconstructed as company of same name. Shareholders were entitled to 5 ordinary shares of £1 (credited as fully-paid) in new company for each ordinary share of £1 held and 1 preference share of £1 for each preference share of £1 held. Debenture holders were entitled to an equal amount of debenture stock. Final meeting return regd. 6 Oct. 1920 .... **1920**

Millom & Askam Hematite Iron Co. Ld. Regd. 1919. Vol. liq. (members') 11 Aug. 1959. Final meeting return regd. 25 Aug. 1961 .... **1959**

Mills' Brewery (Wisbech) Ld. Regd. 1923. Vol. liq. (members') 1 June 1938. The undertaking was acquired by Hall, Cutlack & Harlock Ld. Capital returned to contributories—20*s.* per ordinary share of £1. Final meeting return regd. 10 Aug. 1939 ... **1939**

Mills (C. D.) Ld. In 1928 the flour milling properties and goodwill were acquired by Spillers Ld. for cash **1929**

Mills Day Dawn United Gold Mines Co. Ld. Inc. Queensland 1889. Vol. liq. Apr. 1916 .... **1916**

Mills (J. Lewis) & Co. Ld. Regd. 1886. Court Orders: to wind up 22 June 1889; to dissolve 3 July 1893 ..... ***1890**

Mills Ld. Regd. 1890. Removed from Register 14 May 1897 .... ***1891**

Mill's Machine Cooperage Ld. Regd. 1893. Removed from Register 1908 .... **1898**

Mill's Patent Sectional Boiler Co. Ld. Regd. 1890. Vol. liq. 29 Dec. 1896. Final meeting return regd. 24 Feb. 1898 .... **1897**

Millwall Canal Co. *See* Millwall Dock Co.

Millwall Dock Co. Inc. by Special Act 1864 as Millwall Canal Co. Under Port of London Act 1908 the undertaking was transferred to Port of London Authority. Stockholders were entitled to Port of London stock as follows—for 5% debenture stock—133½% A Port stock and 25% B Port stock; for 5% preference stock—94% B Port stock; for 4½% preference stock—45% B Port stock; for new 5% preference stock (1887)—35% B Port stock; ordinary stock—24½% B Port stock **1909**

Millwall Dock Equipment Co. Ld. Regd. 1901. Vol. liq. Mar. 1910. Undertaking was acquired by Port of London Authority. The debenture stock was repaid at 105%. Capital returned to contributories—110% of paid-up capital. Removed from Register 1910 **1911**

Milne (James) & Son Ld. Regd. Edinburgh 1899. Vol. liq. June 1927. Final meeting return regd. 19 Jan. 1935 .... **1928**

Milners' Safety Cycle Co. Ld. Regd. 1896. Property and business was taken over by Milners' Safe Co. Ld. (later Chatwood Milner Ld.; later Hall Engineering Ld.) for £1,000 in cash and £10,000 in shares. Removed from Register 1900 .... **1899**

Mines (George F.) & Co. Ld. Regd. 1898. Removed from Register 1906 .... **1905**

Milnrow Gas Co. Inc. by Special Act 1869. Undertaking acquired on 18 Feb. 1929 by Rochdale Corporation for £36,325 .... **1930**

Milnthorpe Gas, Coal, Coke & Lime Co. Ld. Regd. 1860. Dissolved 1 May 1949, undertaking being vested in North Western Area Gas Board under Gas Act 1948. Holders of securities were entitled to receive British Gas 3% guaranteed stock 1990—95 as follows:

	£	s.	d.	
Ord. shares (of £5)	3	15	0	
4½% debs. (of £100)	101	0	0	**1952**

Milthorp (G. & F.) Ld. Regd. 1896. Vol. liq. 11 Feb. 1901. Final meeting return regd. 6 Apr. 1903 .... ***1898**

Milton Antiseptic Ld. Regd 1923 as Milton Proprietary Ld.; name changed May 1942. Vol. liq. (members') 5 June 1959. Holders of preference shares were entitled to 26*s.* 2*d.* per share (of £1) and remaining assets were distributed to Vick International Ld. (holders of all ordinary shares). Final meeting return regd. 17 June 1960 .... **1961**

Milton Manufacturing Co. Ld. Regd. 1916. Vol. liq. 29 Jan. 1922. Undertaking was acquired by Milton Proprietary Ld. (later Milton Antiseptic Ld.). Final meeting return regd. 23 Dec. 1926 .... **1926**

Milton Proprietary Ld. *See* Milton Antiseptic Ld.

Milton Sales Ld. Regd. 1928. Vol. liq. (members') 27 Dec. 1933. Amalgamated with Milton Proprietary Ld. [later Milton Antiseptic Ld.] in which company shareholders were entitled to 1 ordinary share of 10*s.* (credited as fully-paid) for every 4 preference or 20 ordinary shares of £1 or 500 deferred shares of 1*s.* held. Final meeting return regd. 2 Jan. 1936 .... **1934**

Milwaukee & Chicago Breweries Ld. Regd. 1890. Vol. liq. 23 Apr. 1920. Capital returned to contributories—100% in Apr. 1920; further payments (if any) not known. Final meeting return regd. 20 Apr. 1921 **1921**

Mimosa Gold Mines Ld. Regd. 1897. Struck off Register 8 Aug. 1905 .... **1906**

Mina Grande (Queretaro) Mining Co. Ld. Regd. 1888. Removed from Register 1909 .... **1901**

"Minah" Consolidated Mining Co. Ld. Regd. 1889. Removed from Register 1909 .... **1892**

Minas & Goyas Finance Co. (1899) Ld. Regd. 1899. Vol. liq. 17 Nov. 1913. Struck off Register 24 July 1923 **1914**

Minas & Goyas Ld. Regd. 1895. Vol. liq. 5 Nov. 1913. Struck off Register 24 July 1923 .... **1914**

Minas & Rio Railway Co. Ld. Regd. 1880. Vol. liq. 15 Jan. 1902. Line was purchased by Brazilian Government. 6% debentures were repaid at par in cash or had option of taking £300 rescission bonds for every £200 debentures held. Shareholders were entitled to £24 in rescission bonds *plus* 23*s.* in cash for each share of £20 held; further cash payments (if any) not known. Removed from Register 1903 .... **1903**

Minas Central Railway of Brazil Ld. Regd. 1883. Removed from Register 1895 .... **1894**

Minas Geraes & Espirito Santo Exploration Co. Ld. Regd. 1912. Struck off Register 4 Apr. 1930 .... **1916**

Minas Geraes Electric Light and Tramways Co. Inc. Brazil 1912. Liability for the outstanding 1st mortgage bonds was assumed by the State of Minas Geraes, which took over the undertaking from 26 July 1926 .... **1936**

Mincing Lane Underwriters Ld. Regd. 1919. Vol. liq. (members') 14 Dec. 1950. Capital returned to contributories—16*s.* 3·4*d.* per share of £1, £203 10*s.* was paid into Companies' Liquidation Account. Final meeting return regd. 3 Apr. 1951 .... **1952**

Minehead Electric Supply Co. Ld. Regd. 1902. Dissolved 1 Apr. 1948, undertaking being vested in the British (later Central) Electricity Authority and South-Western Area Board under the Electricity Act 1947. Preference shareholders were entitled to receive £1 10*s.* British Electricity 3% guaranteed stock (1968–73), for every share (of £1) held **1949**

Minehead Gas-Light & Coke Co. Ld. Regd. 1868. Dissolved 1 May 1949. undertaking being vested in South Western Area Gas Board under Gas Act 1948. Holders of securities were entitled to receive British Gas 3% guaranteed stock 1990–95 as follows in respect of each £1 unit, unless otherwise stated, of security held:

	£	s.	d.	
Orig. ord. shares (10% max.)	1	13	0	
5% red. pref. shares	1	1	2	
4½% red. debs. (of £100)	104	0	0	**1952**

Minehead Railway Co. Inc. by Special Act 1871. Under Great Western Railway Act 1897 undertaking was amalgamated with that company. All shares were held by purchasing company **1898**

Minera Mining Co. Ld. Established 1850. In liquidation in 1895 .... **1895**

Mineral Salts Productions & Moorlands Reclamation Co. Ld. Regd. 1877. Vol. liq. Jan. 1883. Final meeting return regd. 23 Aug. 1883 .... **1884**

Minerals Assets Co. Ld. Regd. 1898. Reconstructed 1903 as Barberton Exploring and Development Co. Ld., in which company shareholders were entitled to 1 share of 10*s.* (credited with 8*s.* 6*d.* paid) for each share held. Removed from Register 1909 .... **1906**

Minerals Exploration Co. Ld. Regd. 1913 as Anglo-German Exploration Co. Ld.; name changed May 1916. Struck off Register Dec. 1931 .... **1932**

**See Stock Exchange Year-Book.*

VOL. FOR

Minerals Separation American Syndicate Ld. Regd. 1910. Vol. liq. 18 Dec. 1922. Final meeting return regd. 6 Mar. 1924 1923

Miner's Dream Extension Ld. Regd. 1896. Vol. liq. 5 Feb. 1900. Final meeting return regd. 14 June 1901 ... 1900

Miner's Dream Gold Mines Ld. Regd. 1895. Reconstructed 1900 as Premier Gold Mines Ld. in which company shareholders were entitled to 2 shares of 10s. (credited with 8s. paid) for each share of £1 held. Removed from Register 1901 1909

Miner's Right Gold Mining Co. Ld. Regd. 1896. Removed from Register 17 Nov. 1899 .... *1898

Minerva Gold Mining Co. Ld. Inc. South Africa 1894. In liquidation in 1899 1899

Minerva Motors (England) Ld. Regd. 1927. Vol. liq. (members') 18 Jan. 1932. Capital returned to preferred ordinary shareholders—£10,312 10s. Final meeting return regd. 26 Aug. 1933 1933

Minerva (Roumania) Oil Co. Ld. Regd. 1923. Vol. liq. Feb. 1932. Struck off Register 2 Apr. 1943 1945

Mines Acquisition & Development Co. Ld. Regd. 1895. Reconstructed 1899 as Industries Development Co. Ld., in which company shareholders were entitled to 1 share of £1 (credited with 15s. paid) for every 4 fully-paid shares of 5s. held. Removed from Register 1901 1905

Mines & Banking Corporation Ld. Regd. 1895. Vol. liq. 5 Aug. 1911. Court Order to wind up 23 Aug. 1911. Struck off Register 7 June 1932; restored to the Register 20 Mar. 1950 to discharge an old mortgage on property in Australia. Struck off Register 9 Feb. 1954 1912

Mines & General Trust Ld. Regd. 1905. Reconstructed 1907 as company of same name. Shareholders were entitled to 15s. in debentures, 1 share of 1s. (credited as fully-paid) in new company plus 5s. in cash for each ordinary share of £1 held, or 14 fully-paid shares of 1s. for each founders' share of 1s. held. Removed from Register 1908 1908

Mines & General Trust Ld. Regd. 1907. Vol. liq. 30 Dec. 1925. Capital returned to contributories—1s. 3¾d. per share of 1s. Final meeting return regd. 12 Nov. 1935 1926

Mines & Land Search Co. Ld. Regd. 1895. Removed from Register 1901 1899

Mines & Lands of Rhodesia Development Co. Ld. Regd. 1899. Vol. liq. July 1907. Absorbed by Rhodesia Matabeleland Development Co. Ld., in which company shareholders ware entitled to 1 share of £1 (credited as fully-paid) for every 17½ shares of £1 held. Removed from Register 1911 1908

Mines & Minerals Exploration Co. (1906) Ld. Regd. 1906. Vol. liq. 11 Sept. 1912. Final meeting return regd. 21 Nov. 1918 1913

Mines & Minerals Exploration Syndicate Ld. Regd. 1901. Vol. liq. June 1906. Reconstructed as Mines and Minerals Exploration Co. (1906) Ld. in which company shareholders were entitled to 1 share of £1 (credited with 15s. paid) for each ordinary share of £1 or moiety share of 1s. held. Removed from Register 1908 1907

Mines Co. Ld. Regd. 1886. Vol. liq. 22 Dec. 1897. Final meeting return regd. 31 July 1902 1898

Mines Co. of America. Inc. Maine 1902. In Nov. 1921 Dolores Esperanza Corpn. stated that it had purchased all the assets and that company had been dissolved 1922

Mines Contract Co. Ld. Regd. 1888. Struck off Register 28 Feb. 1939 1940

Mines Corporation of New Zealand Ld. Regd. 1896. Vol. liq. 27 May 1897. Reconstructed as company of same name. Shareholders were entitled to 3 shares of 2s. 6d. (credited with 1s. 8d. paid) for each ordinary share or deferred share of £1 (5s. paid) held. Final meeting return regd. 25 Apr. 1901 1908

Mines Corporation of New Zealand Ld. Regd. 1897. Vol. liq. 27 Oct. 1909. Final meeting return regd. 17 July 1913 1910

Mines de Pierrefitte Ld. Regd. 1900. Vol. liq. 19 Feb. 1914. Final meeting return regd. 21 Oct. 1918 1914

Mines Development Co. of Victoria Ld. Regd. 1900. Vol. liq. May 1906. Removed from Register 1906 1907

Mines Investment Corporation Ld. Regd. Apr. 1896. Removed from Register 1907 1903

Mines Investment Trust Ld. Regd. 1907. Vol. liq. Apr. 1911. Ordinary shareholders ware entitled to 9½ fully-paid shares of 4s. or 12½ shares of 4s. (credited with 2s. paid) for every 100 shares held. Removed from Register 1913 1912

Mines Issuing Syndicate Ld. Regd. 1895. Vol. liq. 16 Dec. 1897. Final meeting return regd. 27 Oct. 1898 .. *1898

Mines Possession Co. Ld. Regd. 1895. Removed from Register 1907 1898

VOL. FOR

Mines Proprietary Ld. Regd. 1900. Vol. liq. 11 Nov. 1912. Final meeting return regd. 3 Sept. 1920....... 1913

Mines Selection Co. Ld. Regd. 1895. Vol. liq. 25 June 1897. Reconstructed as Consolidated Mines Selection Co. Ld. Final meeting return regd. 2 May 1898 1897

Mines Selection Syndicate Ld. Regd. 1892. Vol. liq. 21 May 1895. Undertaking was acquired by Mines Selection Co. Ld. Final meeting return regd. 12 Nov. 1895 1897

Mines Trust & Guarantee Corporation Ld. Regd. 1899. Vol. liq. 27 Apr. 1908. Final meeting return regd. 19 Aug. 1908 .... *1906

Mines Trust Ld. Regd. 1889. Vol. liq. 1 Mar. 1892. Reconstructed as company of same name. Shareholders were entitled to 5 fully-paid ordinary shares of £1 for each share of £5 (£2 10s. paid) held or 1 founders' share of £5 for each founders' share of £5 held. Final meeting return regd. 16 Feb. 1893 1893

Mines Trust Ld. Regd. 1892. Vol. liq. 21 June 1894. Taken over by South African Gold Trust Ld., in which company shareholders were entitled to 1 fully-paid share of £1 for every 2 shares held. Final meeting return regd. 13 Oct. 1897 1895

Mini Mini Estate Holdings Ld. Regd. 1962. Vol. liq. (members') 9 Dec. 1969. Capital returned to contributories—4s. 10d. and 18·1875p per share of 5s. Final meeting return regd. 25 Sept. 1972 1973-4

Minimax Consolidated Ld. Regd. 1906. Vol. liq. 4 Aug. 1916. Final meeting return regd. 20 Apr. 1931...... 1917

Mining Adventurers Ld. Regd. 1899. Removed from Register 1904 1903

Mining & Financial Trust Syndicate Ld. Regd. 1889. Removed from Register 1906 1905

Mining & General Electric Lamp Co. Ld. Regd. 1888. Removed from Register 1906 .... *1898

Mining & General Exploration Syndicate Ld. Regd. 1903. Reconstructed 1904 as Amalgamated Mining and Exploration Co. Ld., in which company shareholders were entitled to 4 shares of £1 (credited as fully-paid) for each share held. Removed from Register 1905 1905

Mining & General Investment Ld. Regd. 1908. Vol. liq. 31 Dec. 1928. Final meeting return regd. 11 Feb. 1933 1929

Mining and General Trust of Canada Ld. Regd. 1914. Vol. liq. (creditors') 13 June 1930. No capital returned to contributories. Final meeting return regd. 18 Sept. 1935 1931

Mining & Smelting Co. of Nescus (Ariège) Ld. See Couserans Mines Ld.

Mining Co. of Ireland Ld. Established 1824. In liquidation in 1892 1892

Mining Corporation Ld. Regd. 1888. Vol. liq. 31 Oct. 1889. Final meeting return regd. 1 May 1895 1896

Mining Corpn. (Quebec) Ld. See Durquem Mines Ld.

Mining Exploration & General Trust Ld. Regd. 1927. Vol. liq. (members') 13 Apr. 1943. Capital returned to contributories—6s. 11d. per share of £1 plus distribution of investment in specie. Final meeting return regd. 15 Dec. 1943 1945

Mining Exploration Co. Ld. Regd. 1900. Court Order to wind up 16 Jan. 1912. Liquidator released 21 Feb. 1913. Struck off Register 14 Feb. 1919 1912

Mining Finance Syndicate Ld. Regd. 1896. Struck off Register 7 May 1907 1908

Mining Investment Co. of Glasgow Ld. Regd. Edinburgh 1892. Vol. liq. Dec. 1928. Final meeting return regd. 22 Oct. 1929 1929

Mining Machinery Improvements Co. Ld. Regd. 1898. Removed from Register 1903 1903

Mining Properties Syndicate of West Africa Ld. Regd. 1901. Struck off Register 7 May 1907 1908

Mining-Securities Ld. Regd. 1934. Struck off Register 20 June 1947 1939

Mining Shares Investment Co. Ld. Regd. July 1864. Vol. liq. 8 July 1927. Capital returned to contributories— 12s. 6d. per share of £3 10s.; further payments (if any) not known. Final meeting return regd. 4 Apr. 1928 1928

Mining, Transport & General Finance Co. Ld. Regd. 1896. Vol. liq. 19 Sept. 1898. Final meeting return regd. 15 May 1915 1899

Mining Trust Ld. Regd. 1929. Vol. liq. (members') 24 Feb. 1948 for reconstruction as company of same name. Shareholders were entitled to receive (for every 2 shares held) £1 capital stock of Mount Isa Mines Ld. and 2 fully-paid shares of 5s. of the new company. Final meeting regd. 16 Feb. 1949 1949

Mining Trust Ld. Regd. 1948. A subsidiary of Mount Isa Mines Ld. Vol. liq. (members') 7 Apr. 1959. Final meeting return regd. 27 May 1959...................... 1952

Minna (Nigeria) Tin Co. Ld. Regd. 1912. Vol. liq. 19 Feb. 1914. Reconstructed as Minna (Nigeria) Tin Co. (1914) Ld. Shareholders were entitled to 1 share

VOL. FOR

of 5s. (credited with 3s. 6d. paid) in new company for each share of 5s. held. Final meeting return regd. 20 Jan. 1916 .... **1914**

Minna (Nigeria) Tin Co. (1914) Ld. Regd. 1914. Vol. liq. 17 Nov. 1925. Reconstructed as Madubi Tin Co. Ld., in which company shareholders were entitled to 1 share of 2s. (credited with 1s. 6d. paid) for each share of 5s. held. Final meeting return regd. 2 May 1927 .... **1926**

Minneapolis and Pacific Railway. Amalgamated with 3 other companies in 1888 to form the Minneapolis, St. Paul and Sault Ste. Marie Railway Co. **1893**

Minneapolis and St. Croix Railway. Amalgamated with 3 other companies to form the Minneapolis. St. Paul and Sault Ste. Marie Railway Co. **1893**

Minneapolis and St. Louis Railroad Co. Organised Minnesota and Iowa 1894. Reconstructed 1916 as company of same name. The 6% 1st Mortgage Pacific Extension bonds and 5% 1st consolidated mortgage gold bonds were taken over by new company. Holders of every $100 preferred stock were entitled to $70 stock in new company without payment and $80 stock after payment of $20; holders of every $100 ordinary stock were entitled to $22 stock in new company without payment and $78 stock after payment of $20 .... **1916**

Minneapolis and St. Louis Railroad Co. Organised Iowa 1916. Properties were acquired by Minneapolis & St. Louis *Railroad Corporation* and Minneapolis & St. Louis *Railway Company*. Holders of 6% (formerly 5%) 1st consolidated mortgage bonds were entitled to 7·8024 shares in Minneapolis & St. Louis Railway Co. for every $1,000 held. No provision was made for capital stock **1945**

Minneapolis, Sault Ste. Marie & Atlantic Railway Co. Constituted 1883. Amalgamated in 1888 with 3 other companies to form the Minneapolis St. Paul and Sault Ste. Marie Railway Co. **1927**

Minneapolis, St. Paul and Sault Ste. Marie Railway Co. Organised Michigan, Wisconsin, Minnesota and Dakota 1888. Properties were acquired in 1943 by Minneapolis, St. Paul & Sault Ste. Marie *Railroad Co.* Holders of each $1,000 1st consolidated mortgage 50-year bonds (interest guaranteed) were entitled to $40·51 cash. $112·50 1st mortgage bonds, $281·25 general mortgage bonds and 8·15 voting certificates for shares of no par common stock; holders of each $1,000 1st consolidated mortgage 50-year bonds (interest not guaranteed) were entitled to $42·31 cash *plus* cash payment of interest, $117·50 1st mortgage bonds, $293·75 general mortgage bonds and 8·51 voting trust certificates for shares of no par common stock. Holders of 2nd mortgage 4% 50-year gold bonds were entitled to 11·68 voting trust certificates for shares of no par common stock. Holders of leased line stock certificates were entitled to 106,007 shares of Wisconsin Central Railway Co. No provision was made for common and preferred stockholders **1945**

Minneri Mines (Gold Coasi) Syndicate Ld. Regd. 1901. Vol. liq. 18 Mar. 1902. Final meeting return regd. 27 May 1902 .... **1903**

Minton Hollins Ld. Regd. 1936. Vol. liq. (members') 7 Dec. 1962. The preference shares (of £1) were repaid at par in Dec. 1962 and the remaining assets were distributed, in specie, to the ordinary shareholder (Campbell Tile Co. Ld.). Final meeting return regd. 14 Feb. 1963 .... **1963**

Miowera Gold Mining Co. Ld. Regd. 1895. Vol. liq. Nov. 1895. Property transferred to North Kalgurli Gold Mines Ld. Final meeting return regd. 6 May 1896 .... **1899**

"Miraculum" Ld. Regd. 1907. Vol. liq. 30 Sept. 1908. Removed from Register 1910 .... **1909**

Miranda Estancia Co. Ld. Regd. 1912. Struck off Register 21 Jan. 1955 .... **1951**

Miranda (1928) Ld. Regd. 1928. Undertaking and assets were acquired by Alfred A. Drapkin (Tobacco) Ld. for £91,325 in cash and 115,900 fully-paid shares of 5s. Struck off Register 18 Dec. 1934. .... **1930**

Mirfield Gas Co. Inc. by Special Act 1860. Dissolved 1 May 1949, undertaking being vested in North Eastern Area Gas Board under Gas Act 1948. Holders of ordinary stock were entitled to receive, in respect of each £100 unit held, £105 British Gas 3% guaranteed stock 1990–95. Liability in respect of certain mortgage loans assumed by the Board....... **1952**

Mirrlees Watson & Co. Ld. Regd. Edinburgh 1889 as Mirrlees Watson and Yaryan Co. Ld. Vol. liq. May 1926. Undertaking and certain assets were acquired by Mirrlees Bickerton and Day Ld. (later Mirrlees Watson Co. Ld.) for 216,000 fully-paid ordinary shares of £1. Shareholders were entitled to 7 such ordinary shares for every 5 shares of £1 held *plus* 5s.

VOL. FOR

per share in cash. Final meeting return regd. 13 Dec. 1928 .... **1927**

Mirrlees Watson and Yaryan Co. Ld. *See* Mirrlees Watson & Co. Ld.

Mississippi & Dominion Steam Ship Co. Ld. Regd. 1872. Removed from Register 1913 .... **1896**

Mississippi River Power Co. Inc. Maine 1910. Merged May 1945 into Union Electric Co. of Missouri in which company preferred stockholders were entitled to (a) 1 share of preferred stock $4·50 series *plus* $2 per share in cash for each preferred share of $100 held or (b) repayment in cash at $115 per share. Holders of common shares of $70 not held by controlling company were entitled to 3 shares of preferred stock $4.50 series for every 4 shares of common stock held **1946**

Missouri, Kansas & Texas Railway Co. Organised Kansas Missouri & Texas 1870. Reorganised 1922 as Missouri Kansas & Texas *Railroad Co.* Holders of securities were entitled to securities in new company as follows:

For each $1,000 *held*

1st mort. gold bds $\begin{cases} \$500 \ 5\% \text{ P. L. mort. bds. A.} \\ \$500 \ 4\% \text{ P. L. mort. bds. B.} \\ \$23\cdot33 \text{ cash} \end{cases}$

2nd mort. gold bds. $\begin{cases} \$1,192\cdot50 \ 5\% \text{ Adj. mort. bds. A} \\ \$64\cdot16 \text{ preferred stock A} \end{cases}$

4½% S.F. gold bonds $\begin{cases} \$250\cdot5\% \text{ P. L. mort. bds. A} \\ \$250 \ 4\% \text{ P. L. mort. bds. B} \\ \$73\cdot13 \ 5\% \text{ Adj. mort. bds. A} \\ \$719\cdot37 \text{ preferred stk. A} \end{cases}$

*Preferred stock $\begin{cases} \$140 \ 6\% \text{ P. L. mort. bds. C} \\ \$60 \ 5\% \text{ Adj. mort. bds. A} \\ 10 \text{ shares of common stk.} \end{cases}$

§Common stock $\begin{cases} \$175 \ 6\% \text{ P. L. mort. bds. C} \\ \$75 \ 5\% \text{ Adj. mort. bds. A} \\ 10 \text{ shares of common stk.} \end{cases}$

*After payment of $20 per share of $100
After payment of $25 per share of $100.............. **1922**

Missouri Kansas & Texas Trust Co. *See* Guardian Trust Co.

Missouri Land and Live Stock Co. Ld. Regd. Edinburgh 1882. Vol. liq. June 1908. Court Orders: to continue winding up under supervision of Court Aug. 1908 :to dissolve 22 Mar. 1912 .... **1909**

Missouri Land Co. of Scotland Ld. Regd. 1880. Vol. liq. Aug. 1920. Struck off Register 8 June 1948 .... **1921**

Missouri Lead Mining and Smelting Co. Ld. Regd. 1879. Vol. liq. 11 Aug. 1893. Final meeting return regd. 7 Mar. 1896 .... **1894**

Missouri Mining & Land Co. Ld. Regd. 1895. Property was acquired by Bull Creek Mineral Estates Ld. Struck off Register Apr. 1929 .... **1930**

Missouri Pacific Railway Co. Properties were acquired by Missouri Pacific Railroad Co. **1934**

Mrs. Bull Ld. *See* under Mrs.

Misterton & West Stockwith Gas Co. Ld. Regd. 1881. Dissolved 1 May 1949, undertaking being vested in East Midland Area Gas Board under Gas Act 1948. Holders of ordinary shares (of £5) were entitled to receive £10 British Gas 3% guaranteed stock 1990–95 for each share held **1952**

Mitcham & Cheam Brewery Co. Ld. Regd. 1898. Vol. liq. (members') 10 Jan. 1938. All shares held by Hoare & Co. Ld. Final meeting return regd. 29 Apr. 1938 .... **1939**

Mitcham and Wimbledon District Gas Light Co. Inc. by Special Act 1867. Reconstructed as Wandsworth, Wimbledon and Epsom District Gas Co. (later Wandsworth and District Gas Co.), which company assumed liability for debenture bonds. Ordinary stockholders were entitled to an equal amount of 5% standard Wimbledon stock in new company **1913**

Mitcham Brothers of Waterfoot Ld. Regd. 1893. Undertaking and assets were acquired in 1904 by Mitchells, Ashworth, Stansfield & Co. Ld. Removed from Register 1910 .... **1905**

Mitcham Linoleum & Floorcloth Co. Ld. Regd. 1887. Removed from Register 1901 .... ***1900**

Mitchell & Co. of Belfast Ld. Regd. Dublin 1883; transferred to Belfast under Government of Ireland Act 1920. Vol. liq. (members') 14 Nov. 1949. The assets and liabilities were taken over by Distillers Co. (Northern Ireland) Ld., which company owned all shares. Final meeting return regd. 26 July 1951 **1953**

Mitchell Brothers (Bradford) Ld. Regd. 1909. Vol. liq. 25 Oct. 1929. Final meeting return regd. 3 May 1934 **1930**

Mitchell Brothers (London) Ld. Regd. 1909. Court Order to wind up 25 Nov. 1913. Liquidator released 9 Aug. 1917. Struck off Register 1 July 1921 .... ***1915**

Mitchell (J.) Ld. Regd. 1905. Vol. liq. 12 Aug. 1907. Removed from Register 1910 .... **1908**

See Stock Exchange Year-Book.

VOL. FOR

Mitchell Main Colliery Co. Ld. Regd. 1882. All capital privately held. Vol. liq. (members') 30 July 1952. Final meeting return regd. 29 Sept. 1956 .... **1957**

Mitchell's Creek Gold Mines Ld. Regd. 1903. The property was taken over by the debenture holders. Struck off Register 1916 .... **1910**

Mitchell's Library Ld. Regd. 1890. Vol. liq. 2 Mar. 1905. Reconstructed as J. Mitchell Ld., in which company shareholders were entitled to 1 share of £1 for every 4 fully-paid shares of £1 held or every 8 shares of £1 (10s. paid) held. Final meeting return regd. 25 July 1905 .... **1907**

Mitchelson Partners Ld. Regd. 1922. Vol. liq. (members') 8 Nov. 1946. Final meeting return regd. 23 Sept. 1949 .... **1934**

Mitchelstown & Fermoy Light Railway Co. Ld. Inc. under Tramways & Public Companies (Ireland) Act 1883 and an Order in Council 1884. Under Great Southern & Western Railway Co. (Ireland) Act 1900 undertaking was vested in that company. Holders of baronial guaranteed shares received £125 4% preference stock for every £100 held **1901**

Mitford (Calgary) Colliery Co. Ld. Inc. Alberta 1912. Co. defaulted in payment of interest due Oct. 1913. Properties placed in hands of receiver in July 1914 **1915**

Mitre Polish Co. Ld. Regd. 1911. Vol. liq. 1 Jan. 1923. Controlling interest held by Hargreaves Bros. & Co. Ld. Final meeting return regd. 17 June 1924 .... **1923**

Mitre Shipping Co. Ld. Regd. 1899. Vol. liq. 8 Dec. 1919. Final meeting return regd. 21 Aug. 1930 .... ***1920**

Mitre Trust Ld. Regd. June 1932 as South Perak Rubber Syndicate Ld.; name changed Mar. 1961. Wound-up 16 Dec. 1968. Dissolved 21 July 1978. **1976-7**

Mitsubishi Goshi Kaisha. Established 1885. Banking business acquired by Mitsubishi Bank Ld. in 1919 **1941**

Mitterberg Copper Co. Ld. Regd. 1905. Vol. liq. 29 June 1908. Final meeting return regd. 22 Dec. 1913 ..... **1909**

Mkumbi Rubber Plantations Ld. Regd. 1910. Vol. liq. Nov. 1912 for sale of undertaking to Manihot Rubber Plantations Ld., in which company shareholders were entitled to 2½ shares of 2s. (credited as fully-paid) for each share of 5s. held. Removed from Register 1913 .... **1913**

Mnemos Ld. Inc. in Bermuda 14 Apr. 1982; name changed 4 Apr. 1983. Vol. liq. (members') 11 Sept. 1986 and dissolved on 6 Feb. 1987. Assets transferred to new company, Image Storage/Retrieval Systems, Inc.; in compensation holders received a first and final distribution of 0·038504166 common shares for each ordinary share held **1988-9**

Moabund Tea Co. Ld. Regd. 1884. Vol. liq. 17 Dec. 1896. Reconstructed as company of same name. Shareholders were entitled to 2 fully-paid shares of £1 for each ordinary or preference shares of £1 for each ordinary or preference share of £1 respectively held. Final meeting return regd. 20 Dec. 1897 .... **1897**

Moanatairi Gold Mining Co. Ld. Regd. 1895. Vol. liq. 14 Aug. 1899. Reconstructed 1899 as New Moanatairi Gold Mining Co. Ld., in which company shareholders were entitled to 1 share of £1 (credited with 16s. paid) for each share of £1 held. Final meeting return regd. 4 Apr.1900 .... **1903**

Moat-Wood Houses Ld. Undertaking and assets were acquired by Welwyn Public Utility Society Ld. ... **1929**

Moccasin Shoemakers Ld. Regd. as private company 8 June 1950; converted into public company 9 June 1950. Winding-up orser made 7 Dec. 1964. Struck off register 26 Mar. 1982. Distributions: 100p in £1 paid to unsecured creditors on 10 Oct. 1974 and a first and final return of 78·3p per £1 preference share on 24 June 1976 .... **1983-4**

Mocimboa (Mazimbwa) Sisal Development Syndicate Ld. Regd. 1923. In 1931 all shares and debentures were held by Mocimboa Sisal (Holdings) Ld. Court Order to wind up 2 Nov. 1931. Struck off Register 21 Aug. 1945 .... **1931**

Mocimboa Sisal (Holdings) Ld. Regd. 1929. Court Order to wind up Nov. 1931. Struck off Register 14 Oct. 1938 .... **1939**

Moctezuma Oilfields Ld. Regd. 1913. Struck off Register Feb. 1935 .... **1935**

Modderfontein B Gold Mines Ld. Inc. South Africa 1908. Vol. liq. (members') 18 Aug. 1967. Capital returned to contributories—R0·04075 per share (of R0·02½) **1973-4**

Modderfontein Deep Levels Ld. Inc. in Transvaal 26 Apr. 1899. Vol. liq. (members') 13 Nov. 1936. Capital returned to contributories—13s. 3·014d. per share of 5s. Dissolved 13 June 1953 .... **1954**

Modderfontein East Ld. Inc. in the Transvaal 1917. During 1962 to 1967 the nominal value of the shares was reduced from R2 to R0·2198 by repaying, in instalments, R1·7802 per share. Removed from Register June 1967 .... **1969**

Modderfontein Extension Ld. Inc. Transvaal 1895. Vol. liq. Jan. 1909. The property and certain assets were transferred to Modderfontein B Gold Mines Ld., in which company shareholders were entitled to 1 share of £1 (credited as fully-paid) for every 2 shares of £1 held; fractions were paid at £2 7s. 6d. per share **1909**

Modderfontein Gold Mining Co. Ld. Inc. Cape of Good Hope 1888. Reconstructed 1895 as New Modderfontein Gold Mining Co. Ld., in which company shareholders were entitled to 1 share of £4 (credited as fully-paid) for each share of £1 held **1895**

Modderfontein Proprietary Mines Ld. Inc. Transvaal 1903. Vol. liq. Apr. 1914 .... **1915**

Model Fibre Factory Co. Ld. Regd. 1890. Removed from Register 1895 .... **1892**

Modern Electric Homes Ld. Regd 1912 as Modern Kitchens Ld.; name changed Jan. 1928. Vol. liq. (members') 4 Aug. 1936. Capital returned to contributories—5s. 1½d. per preference share of £1. Final meeting return regd. 15 Apr. 1937 .... **1937**

Modern Kitchens Ld. See Modern Electric Homes Ld.

Modern Machine Tools Ld. See M. M. T. Holdings Ld.

Moffat Gas Light Co. Ld. Regd. in Edinburgh 1884. Dissolved 1 May 1949, undertaking being vested in Scottish Area Gas Board under Gas Act 1948. Holders of securities were entitled to receive British Gas 3% guaranteed stock 1990-95 as follows:

	£	s.	d.	
5% gtd. shares (of £2 10s.)	2	16	0	
Ord. shares (of £10)......................	15	0	0	**1952**

Moffat Railway Co. Inc. by Special Act 1881. Under Caledonian Railway (No. 1) Act 1884 undertaking taken over by that company. Holders of £100 ordinary shares received £75 4% convertible preference 1887 stock **1899**

Moffat Steamship Co. Ld. Regd. 1902. Struck off Register 1929 .... ***1925**

Mogul Steamship Co. Ld. Regd 1883. Vol. liq. 4 Dec. 1922. Final meeting return regd. 13 Dec. 1923 ..... ***1923**

Mogyana Railways Co. Inc. San Paulo 1872 as Mogyana Railways & Navigation Co.; name changed Sept. 1923. In Oct. 1941 holders of 1st mortgage 5% sterling bonds Sul Mineira Extensions 1911, 1st mortgage 5% sterling bonds 1914 and 1st mortgage 6% sterling bonds 1927 agreed to accept £34 10s. in satisfaction of principal and arrears of interest **1942**

Moir (John) & Son Ld. Regd. 1880. Vol. liq. (members') 26 Oct. 1950. Capital returned to contributories—10s. 4½d. per share of 2s. Final meeting return regd. 31 Mar. 1951 .... **1952**

Mold and Denbigh Junction Railway Co. Inc. by Special Act 1861. In 1923 the undertaking was merged into the London Midland & Scottish Railway Co., in which company stockholders were entitled to stock as follows:

For each £100 held	L. M.& S.		
	£	s.	d.
5% Perp. Deb. A................£125	4%	Debenture	
5% Perp. Deb. B £112½	4%	Debenture	
5% Perp. Deb. C...............£43¾	4%	Pref.(1923)	
Preference £12½	4%	Pref.(1923)	
Ordinary..........................£6¼	4%	Pref.(1923)	
Preferred Half...................£6¼	4%	Pref.(1923)	
Deferred Half....................£6¼	4%	Pref.(1923)	

The Rent Charges were assumed by the London Midland & Scottish Railway Co. Arrears of interest on the B and C Debenture Stock were cancelled .. **1924**

Mold Collieries Ld. See Bettisfield Colliery Ld.

Mold Gas & Water Co. Inc. by Special Act 1847. Dissolved 1 May 1949, undertaking being vested in Wales Area Gas Board under Gas Act 1948. Holders of securities were entitled to receive in respect of each £10 unit held, British Gas 3% guaranteed stock 1990-95 as follows:

	£	s.	d.	
Ord. A shares	21	12	0	
Ord. B shares	15	0	0	**1952**

Moldacot (Colonial & Foreign) Pocket Sewing Machine Co. Ld. See United Sewing Machine Co. Ld.

Moldacot Pocket Sewing Machine Co. Ld. Regd. 1886. Taken over by Moldacot (Colonial & Foreign) Pocket Sewing Machine Co. Ld. (later United Sewing Machine Co. Ld.) for 25,000 preference and 15,000 ordinary shares of £1. Removed from Register 1906 .... **1888**

Moldacot Royalties Trust Ld. Regd. 1886. Court Orders: to wind up 14 Nov. 1889; to dissolve 12 May 1896 .... **1890**

Molesworth Brothers Rubber Estates Ld. Regd. 1909. Vol. liq. Nov. 1911. Reconstructed as Molesworth Rubber Estates Ld., in which company shareholders were entitled to 1 share of 2s. (credited with 1s. 6d. paid) for each share of 2s. held. Removed from Register 1913...................... **1912**

VOL. FOR

Molesworth Rubber Estates Ld. Regd. 1911. Vol. liq. 19 May 1914. The assets were sold to Trincomalee Estates Ld. Struck off Register 30 Jan. 1923 1915

Moline Plow Co. Inc. Inc. Virginia 1922. Dissolved by order of Court 2 Nov. 1925 1926

Molsons Bank. Established 1853. Inc. Canada by Special Act 1855. Undertaking and assets were acquired by Bank of Montreal Ld., in which company shareholders were entitled to 3 shares of $100 plus $30 in cash for every 3 shares of $100 held 1925

Molyneux Mines Consolidated Ld. Inc. South Africa 1895. In liquidation in 1899 1899

Mombo Rubber Plantation Ld. Regd. 1910. Vol. liq. 23 July 1914. Final meeting return regd. 23 May 1919 1915

Mona & Parys Mines Ld. Regd. 1899. Receiver appointed in Dec. 1921; ceased to act 24 June 1927. Assets realised sufficient to pay £6 9s. 4d. for each £100 1st debenture held. Struck off Register Apr 1929 1930

Mona Consols Copper Mining Co. Ld. Regd. 1881. Removed from Register 1905 .... *1884

Mona Gold Mine Ld. Regd. 1896. Vol. liq. Sept. 1904. Removed from Register 1906 1905

Mona Mills (Holdings) Ld. Regd. 1920 as Mona Mills (1920) Ld.; name subsequently changed. Vol. liq. (members') 24 Feb. 1960. Final meeting return regd. 13 Aug. 1964 1941

Mona Mines Ld. Regd. 1880. Vol. liq. May 1885. Final meeting return regd. 12 Nov. 1885 1885

Monaco Hotel and Restaurant Syndicate Ld. Regd. 1898. Vol. liq. 16 May 1911. Final meeting return regd. 16 Nov. 1915 1912

Monarch Gold Mining Co. Ld. Formed in Pietermaritzburg 1889. In liquidation in 1892. The property was sold to Palmiet Estate & Gold Mining Co. Ld 1892

Monarch Ld. Regd. 1919 as Monarch Mill (1919) Ld.; name subsequently changed. Vol. liq. (members') 22 Feb. 1954. Final meeting return regd. 3 Aug. 1954 1950

Monarch Steam Fishing Co. Ld. Regd. Apr. 1897 as Guzzwell Steam Fishing Co. Ld.; name changed Dec. 1897. Vol. liq. 19 Jan. 1906. Final meeting return regd. 7 May 1907 1898

Monarch Syndicate Ld. Regd. 1895. Removed from Register 1903 1901

Monastery Diamond Mines & Estate Co. Ld. Inc. Transvaal 1895. Wound up in 1904 for purpose of reconstruction as company of the same name. Shareholders were entitled to receive 1 ordinary share of £1 (credited with 17s. 6d. paid up) in new company for every ordinary share of £1 held, and 1 preference share of 5s. for each preference share of 5s. held 1904

Monastery Diamond Mines & Estate Co. Ld. Regd. 1904. Vol. liq. Dec. 1909. Removed from Register 1913 1910

Mond Nickel Co. Ld. Regd. 1900. Vol. liq. 22 July 1914. Reconstructed as company of same name [later International Nickel Co. (Mond) Ld.] Shareholders were entitled to 5 preference shares of £1 (credited as fully-paid) for each preference share of £5 held or 1 preference and 1½ ordinary shares of £1 (credited as fully-paid) for each ordinary share of £1 held or 9 fully-paid ordinary shares of £1 for each deferred share of £1 held. Debenture stockholders were entitled to an equal amount of debenture stock in new company. Final meeting return regd. 11 Oct. 1916 1915

Mondego Tin Dredging Co. Ld. Regd. 1924. Receiver appointed in Sept. 1929; ceased to act Oct. 1931. Struck off Register 19 Jan. 1934 1932

Mondego Valley Tin Syndicate Ld. Regd. 1923. Receiver appointed in Sept. 1929; ceased to act Oct. 1931. Struck off Register Dec. 1933 1934

Monerakelle Rubber Estates Ld. Regd. 1905. Vol. liq. (members') 12 July 1950. Capital returned to contributories—13s. 2d. per share of £1. £235 was paid into Companies' Liquidation Account. Final meeting return regd. 6 Dec. 1951 1953

Money Order Bank Ld. Regd. Edinburgh 1881. Vol. liq. Feb. 1883. Final meeting return regd. 9 May 1889 1884

Money Wigram & Sons Ld. Regd. 1881. Vol. liq. 19 May 1893. Final meeting return regd. 29 Dec. 1893 1894

Monger's West Australian Stores Ld. Regd. 1897. Capital returned to contributories—distributions per preference share of £1—5s., 5s., 4s. and 1s. 6d. in Dec. 1904. Apr. 1905, July 1905 and Dec. 1905 respectively; further payments (if any) not known. Removed from Register 1908 1905

Mongu (Nigeria) Tin Mines Ld. Regd. 1914. Vol. liq. (members') 15 Jan. 1930. Undertaking and assets were acquired by London Tin Corporation Ld., in which company shareholders were entitled to 1 share of £1 (credited as fully-paid) for every 6 shares

of 10s. held. £27 18s. was paid into Companies' Liquidation Account. Final meeting return regd. 18 July 1931 1930

Mongura Tin Mines Ld. Regd. 1922. Vol. liq. 29 Jan. 1926. Undertaking and assets were acquired by North Ropp River Tin Co. Ld., in which company shareholders were entitled to 13 fully-paid shares of 2s. and right to subscribe for 2 shares at 2s. 6d. each for every 13 shares of 2s. held. Final meeting return regd. 26 Oct. 1926 1929

Monitor & Ajax Fraction Ld. Regd. 1899 as Ajax Fraction Development Syndicate Ld.; name changed 30 Apr. 1900. In Jan. 1907 a manager was appointed on behalf of the debenture holders. Struck off Register 1914 1906

Monk Bridge Iron & Steel Co. Ld. Regd. 1886. Vol. liq. 11 Dec. 1911. Undertaking and assets were acquired by company of same name for 250,000 fully-paid ordinary shares of £1 and £250,000 in cash. Final meeting return regd. 3 Dec. 1913 1912

Monk Bridge Iron & Steel Co. Ld. Regd. 1911. Vol. liq. (members') 15 Sept. 1942. Capital returned to contributories—2s. 7½d. per ordinary share of 5s. and 15s. per redeemable preference share of £1. Final meeting return regd. 1 Oct. 1943 1945

Monkland Iron Co. Ld. Regd. Edinburgh 1881. Vol. liq. 23 Nov. 1886. Court Orders: to continue winding up under supervision Dec. 1886; to dissolve 5 June 1891 1887

Monmouth Gas & Water Works Co. Ld. Regd. 1872. Dissolved 1 May 1949, undertaking being vested in Wales Area Gas Board under Gas Act 1948. Holders of securities were entitled to receive, in respect of each £1 unit held, British Gas 3% guaranteed stock 1990-95 as follows:

	£	s.	d.
A ord. shares (10% max.)	2	4	0
B ord. shares (4% max.)	1	0	0
C ord. shares (7% max.)	1	11	0	1952

Monmouth Shipbuilding Co. Ld. Regd. 1920. Vol. liq. 2 Mar. 1925. Direct controlling interest held by Northumberland Shipbuilding Co. Ld. Final meeting return regd. 2 July 1926 1926

Monmouthshire Railway & Canal Co. Inc. by Special Act 1846. Under Great Western and Monmouthshire Act 1880 the undertaking was absorbed by Great Western Railway Co. Holders of every £100 preference stock or ordinary stock received respectively £100 or £130 guaranteed stock in absorbing company. Holders of debenture stocks received an equal amount of similar debenture stocks 1882

Mono Lake Gold Fields of California Ld. Regd. 1888. Removed from Register 1898 .... *1891

Mono Service Containers Ld. Regd. 1907 as Mono Service Vessels Ld.; name changed Mar. 1919. Vol. liq. (members') 15 Apr. 1932. Undertaking and assets were acquired by Mono Containers Ld., in which company shareholders were entitled to 3 shares of £1 (credited as fully-paid) for every 2 A shares of £1 held or 2 fully-paid shares of £1 for each B share of 1s. held. Final meeting return regd. 3 Apr. 1934 1933

Mono Service Vessels Ld. See Mono Service Containers Ld.

Monolithic Building Co. Ld. Regd. 1926. Vol. liq. 31 Aug. 1928. Final meeting return regd. 25 Nov. 1931 1929

Monolithic Concrete Houses Ld. Business and goodwill were acquired by Monolithic Building Co. Ld 1927

Monomotapa Concessions Ld. Inc. Transvaal 1908. Wound up 1913 1914

Monomotapa Development Co. Ld. Regd. Aug. 1897. Vol. liq. 8 Oct. 1908. Shareholders were entitled to 64,000 fully-paid shares of £1 in Monomotapa Concessions Ld. Final meeting return regd. 21 July 1909 1909

Monomotapa Gold Dredging Co. Ld. Regd. 1902. Vol. liq. June 1906. Removed from Register 1907 1907

Monopole Cycle and Carriage Co. Ld. Regd. 1896. Vol. liq. 30 Sept. 1913. Final meeting return regd. 16 Apr. 1915 1914

Monowai Gold Mines Ld. Regd. Edinburgh 1896. Vol. liq. Mar. 1904. Final meeting return regd. 26 Feb. 1913 1904

Mons Mill (1919) Ld. Regd. 1919. Vol. liq. 1929. Struck off Register 1 Feb. 1944 1941

Mons Cupri (Whim Well) Ld. Regd. 1910. Vol. liq. 6 Jan. 1922. Reconstructed as United Copper Mines (Pilbarra) Ld., in which company shareholders were entitled to 2 shares of 5s. (credited with 3s. 9d. paid) for each share of £1 held, or 1 fully-paid share of 5s. for each preferred ordinary share of 5s. held. Debenture holders were entitled to 4 fully-paid shares for every £1 debenture held. Final meeting return regd. 5 July 1924 1922

VOL. FOR

Monsted (Otto) Ld. Regd. 1898. Removed from Register 1907 .... **1906**

Mont Dore of Bournemouth Ld. Regd. 1880. Court Orders: to wind up 8 May 1886; to dissolve 9 Apr. 1894 .... **1887**

Montagu Sterling Reserves Fund Ld. See MIM Sterling Reserves Fund Ld.

Montana Central Railway Co. Organised Montana 1886. All capital was owned by Great Northern Railway Co. The 1st mortgage 50-year gold bonds were taken over by acquiring company; these bonds were redeemed on 1 July 1937 .... **1908**

Montana Co. Ld. Regd. 1883. Vol. liq. 14 Dec. 1892. Reconstructed as Montana Mining Co. Ld., in which company shareholders were entitled to 1 share of £1 (credited with 17s. 6d. paid) for each share of £1 held. Final meeting return regd. 17 Jan. 1895 .... **1908**

Montana Mines & Smelters Corporation, See Nevada-Utah Mines & Smelters Corporation.

Montana Mining Co. Ld. Regd. 1892. Vol. liq. 24 June 1914. Final meeting return regd. 29 Feb. 1916 ..... **1915**

Monte Carlo Club Ld. Regd. 1928. Struck off Register 10 Mar. 1939 .... **1940**

Monte Christo Gold Mines Ld. Regd. 1888. Court Orders: to wind up 9 Nov. 1889; to dissolve 7 Jan. 1893 .... **1890**

Monte del Oro Mining Co. Ld. Regd. 1886. Vol. liq. 24 Nov. 1891. Final meeting return regd. 17 Dec. 1892 **1892**

Monte Mayor Gold & Silver Mining Co. Ld. Regd. 1911. Vol. liq. 4 Jan. 1917. Final meeting return regd. 25 May 1918 .... ***1918**

Monte Rosa Gold Mining Co. Ld. Regd. 1894. Struck off Register 4 Aug. 1939 .... ***1905**

Montebras Ld. Regd. 1907. Vol. liq. 12 Dec. 1912. Final meeting return regd. 12 Jan. 1926 .... **1913**

Monteith, Hamilton & Monteith Ld. Regd. 1902. Vol. liq. 18 May 1928. Final meeting return regd. 8 May 1929 .... **1929**

Montevidean & Brazilian Telegraph Co. Ld. Regd. 1872. Vol. liq. 10 Dec. 1890. Final meeting return regd. 1 Sept. 1891 .... **1891**

Montevideo Assets Co. Ld. Regd. 1893. In liquidation in 1900. Capital returned to contributories—£1 5s. per fully-paid share of £10; further payments (if any) not known. Removed from Register 1903 .... **1901**

Montevideo New Tramway Co. Ld. Regd. 1896. Removed from Register 1907 .... **1907**

Montevideo Southern Tramways Co. Ld. Regd. 1894. Removed from Register 1903 .... **1897**

Montevideo Telephone Co. Ld. Regd. 31 July 1888. Vol. liq. (members') 25 Sept. 1952 (in Montevideo). Distributions per share: £2 5s. 6·3356d. (represented by marketable securities) and 2s. 0·3289d, both in June 1953. Final meeting return regd. 28 July 1953 **1954**

Montevideo Tramways Co. Ld. Regd. 1890. Vol. liq. 4 Mar. 1892. Undertaking acquired by City of Montevideo Tramways Co. Ld. Removed from Register 13 Nov. 1903 .... ***1893**

Montevideo Waterworks Co. Ld. Regd. 1879. Vol. liq. (members') 26 Apr. 1950, undertaking and various assets having been transferred to Uruguayan Government on 31 Jan. 1950. Debenture stocks were repaid at 105% and ordinary stockholders received £170 0s. 9d. per £100 stock. Final meeting return regd. 26 May 1953. £10,250 was paid into the Companies' Liquidation Account **1954**

Montezuma Gold Mining Co. Ld. Regd. 1897. Vol. liq. 7 Mar. 1899. Final meeting return regd. 2 May 1900 **1900**

Montezuma Silver Lead Mines (Colorado) Ld. Regd. 1917. Struck off Register 1931 .... **1931**

Montgomerie & Co. Ld. Regd. Edinburgh 1892. Vol. liq. 22 Apr. 1899. Reconstructed as company of same name. Shareholders were entitled to 2 fully-paid ordinary shares of £1 in new company for each ordinary share of £1 held or 1 preference share of £1 for each preference share of £1 held. Final meeting return regd. 29 Aug. 1900 .... **1899**

Montgomery (W.) & Co. Ld. Regd. 1905. Vol. liq. 21 Mar. 1922. Final meeting return regd. 26 Apr. 1926 ***1923**

Montgomeryshire Brewery Co. Ld. Regd. 1890. Court Order to wind up 26 Oct. 1893. Removed from Register 1907 .... **1894**

Montgomeryshire Flannel Co. Ld. Regd. 1883. Vol. liq. 14 May 1892. Final meeting return regd. 25 Apr. 1892 .... **1892**

Montreal & Champlain Junction Railway. Inc. 1881. Line was consolidated with Grand Trunk system in 1893 .... **1893**

Montreal Light, Heat and Power Consolidated. Inc. by Special Act of the Province of Quebec 16 Mar. 1916 as Civic Investment & Industrial Co.; name changed Feb. 1918. In Apr. 1947 the Quebec Hydro-

VOL. FOR

Electric Commission acquired majority of company's shares under an offer of either (a) $25 per share (plus interest at 2% p.a., from date of deposit of shares to date of payment by paying agents) or (b) $100 10-year 2% sinking fund debenture of the Commission for every 4 shares held. Under Provincial Act of May 1947 provision was made (inter alia) for acquisition of company's remaining shares at $25 per share and for dissolution of company by Order in Council **1948**

Montreal Telegraph Company. Inc. by Special Act of Province of Canada Legislature in 1847. All assets (except cash and securities) sold to Canadian National Railway Co. for $3,000,000 on 20 Apr. 1954 and company dissolved. Dissolution payment (free of income tax)—$60·88 per share of $40 ...... **1956**

Montreal Tramways & Power Co. Ld. Regd. 1910. Vol. liq. 4 Apr. 1927. The undertaking, property and assets were acquired by Consolidated Securities Ld. Final meeting return regd. 9 Dec. 1927 .... **1928**

Montreal Tramways Company. Inc. by Special Act of Quebec Legislature 24 Mar. 1911. The outstanding $2,811,700 series A 5%, $223,100 series A 4½%, $20,318,900 series B 5% and $1,581,600 series B 4½% bonds were redeemed at 100½% on 28 June 1954 **1955**

Montreal Water & Power Co. The outstanding 4½% 1st mortgage prior lien bonds were redeemed on 30 June 1932 at 105%; the outstanding 5% 1st mortgage sterling bonds were redeemed on 30 June 1932 at par **1932**

Montrose & Bervie Railway Co. Inc. by Special Act 1860. Under North British & Montrose Railway Cos. Amalgamation Act 1881 undertaking was vested in North British Railway Co. Shareholders received £6 in cash for every £10 share capital held **1883**

Montrose Diamond Mining Co. Ld. Regd. 1898 as Transvaal Diamond Mines Ld.; name changed 1903. Vol. liq. Jan. 1924 for reconstruction as Pretoria Diamond Mines Ld., in which company shareholders were entitled to 4 shares of 5s. (credited with 4s. paid) for each preference or ordinary share of £1 held; preference shareholders were entitled to fully-paid shares for arrears of dividend. Holders of debentures were entitled to an equal amount of 7% convertible 1st mortgage debentures in new company. Struck off Register 7 July 1939 .... **1940**

Montrose Fishing Co. Ld. Regd. Edinburgh 1917. Vol. liq. May 1922. Final meeting return regd. 21 July 1926 .... **1923**

Montrose Gas Co. Ld. Regd. in Edinburgh 1920. Dissolved 1 May 1949, undertaking being vested in Scottish Area Gas Board under Gas Act 1948. Holders of ordinary shares (of £1) were entitled to receive £2 18s. British Gas 3% guaranteed stock 1990-95 for each share held **1952**

Montrose Matabele Co. Ld. Regd. 1895. Vol. liq. 5 Feb. 1915. Final meeting return regd. 27 July 1920 ..... ***1916**

Montserrat Co. Ld. Regd. 1875. Vol. liq. (members') 2 Sept. 1964. Final meeting return regd. 21 May 1965 **1938**

Monument Property Trust Ld. Regd. 1926. Vol. liq. (members') 13 Nov. 1946. Undertaking and assets acquired by Metropolitan Estate and Property Corpn. Ld. in which company shareholders were entitled to receive (a) 29 fully-paid ordinary shares of £1 for every 25 ordinary shares and (b) 13 fully-paid preference shares of £1 for every 9 preference shares held. Final meeting return regd. 17 Dec. 1955 **1957**

Monument Securities Ld. Regd. as private company 14 Mar. 1962 as Tissus Michels Holdings Ld.; converted into public company 16 Mar. 1962; name changed 1 Jan. 1982. Vol. liq. (creditors') 13 May 1981. Final meeting held 31 Aug. 1982 and regd. 7 Jan. 1983 .... **1983–4**

Moodie's Gold Mining and Exploration Co. Ld. Inc. Natal 1884. Wound up 1932. The undertaking and assets were transferred to Transvaal Exploring Land and Minerals Co. Ld. Shareholders received 2 fully-paid shares of 1s. in new company for every share of 4s. held **1933**

Moodie's Golden Hill Gold Mining Co. Ld. Regd. 1888. Vol. liq. 30 Dec. 1890. Final meeting return regd. 30 Apr. 1895 .... **1891**

Mookhanicherra Tea Co. Ld. Regd. 1881. Taken over by East India & Ceylon Tea Co. Ld. Removed from Register 1903 .... ***1896**

Moon-Anchor Consolidated Gold Mines Ld. Regd. 1898. Removed from Register 1904 .... **1905**

Mooney Biscuit & Candy Co. Ld. Inc. in Ontario 1902. Winding-up Order granted 1916 .... **1917**

Moonie Creek Development Co. Ld. See Matabeleland Ranching Co. Ld.

Moonstone United Gold Mining Co. Ld. Regd. 1892. Vol. liq. 1 Aug. 1895. Absorbed by Jubilee Consols Ld. Final meeting return regd. 13 Feb. 1897......... **1896**

*See Stock Exchange Year-Book.

VOL. FOR

Moonta Central Copper Co. Mines Ld. Regd. 1901. Struck off Register 13 Oct. 1908 .... **1909**

Mooply Valley Rubber Co. Ld. Regd. 1911. Vol. liq. 27 July 1928. Undertaking and certain assets were acquired by Malayalam Plantations Ld., in which company shareholders were entitled to 3 shares of £1 (credited as fully-paid) for every 4 shares of £1 held; a cash payment was anticipated. Final meeting return regd. 19 Oct. 1932 .... **1929**

Moor Line Ld. Regd. 1889 as South Shields Steam Shipping Co. Ld.; name changed Apr. 1897. Vol. liq. 20 Sept. 1920. Final meeting return regd. 29 Dec. 1936 .... **1921**

Moor Park Country Club Co. Ld. Regd. 1923. Vol. liq. (members') Sept. 1937. Practically all shares owned by Moor Park Ld. Final meeting return regd. 3 Dec. 1937 .... **1938**

Moor Park, Ld. Regd. 1922. Vol. liq. (members') 3 Apr. 1957. Final meeting return regd. 6 May 1959 .... **1947**

Moore & Burgess Ld. Regd. 1892. Reconstructed 1894 as company of same name. Shareholders were entitled to 10 shares of £1 (credited with 18s. paid) in new company for each share of £10 held. Removed from Register 1907 .... **1901**

Moore & Burgess Ld. Regd. 1894. In 1900 receivers for the debenture holders were appointed. Removed from Register 1902 .... **1901**

Moore & Burgess Provincial Co. Ld. Regd. 1893. Vol. liq. 29 Aug. 1894. Reconstructed 1894 as Moore & Burgess Ld., in which company shareholders were entitled to 10 shares of £1 (credited with 18s. paid) for each share of £10 held. Final meeting return regd. 9 Nov. 1899 .... **1901**

Moore & Robinson's Nottinghamshire Banking Co. Ld. Established 1836 and regd. as limited 1866. Business acquired by Capital and Counties Bank Ld., in which company shareholders were entitled, in respect of every 23 shares held, to 5 shares (credited with £10 paid up) and 10s. in cash **1902**

Moore (Hugh) & Alexanders Ld. Regd. Dublin 1898. Vol. liq. (members') 4 Oct. 1963. Capital returned to contributories—£1 per preference share of £1; 22s. 11d. per ordinary share of 4s. Final meeting return regd. 27 Mar. 1969 .... **1969**

Moore Steam Turbine Corporation. Inc. New York. All capital was owned by Worthington Pump & Machinery Corporation. Dissolved Dec. 1939 .... **1940**

Moore's Rhodesia Concession Ld. Regd. 1895. Vol. liq. 30 Aug. 1899. Undertaking and assets were acquired in Aug. 1898 by Mashonaland Consolidated Development Co. Ld., in which company shareholders were entitled to 7 shares of £1 (credited as fully-paid) for every 8 shares of £1 held. Final meeting return regd. 14 July 1915 .... **1900**

Moorgate Estates Ld. Regd. 1930. Vol. liq. (members') 31 Dec. 1951. Capital returned to contributories (per £1 share)—preference: £1; ordinary: £4 13s. 3d. Final meeting return regd. 2 July 1953 .... **1955**

Moorgate North American Investment Trust Ld. Regd. 1963. Vol. liq. (members') 8 Sept. 1966 the assets were transferred to British Shareholders Dollar Fund for 7,386,000 units which were distributed to shareholders in Sept. 1966 on basis of 1 unit per share held. Final meeting return regd. 12 Mar. 1968 **1969**

Moorgate Street & Broad Street Buildings Ld. Regd. 1882. Vol. liq. 13 Oct. 1921. Capital returned to contributories—£6 10s. per share of £10 in Nov. 1921; further payments (if any) not known. Final meeting return regd. 20 Feb. 1923 .... **1922**

Moorina Tin Mine Ld. Regd. 1900. Vol. liq. Aug. 1911. Removed from Register 1912 .... **1912**

Moorlort Goldfields Ld. Regd. 1900. Reconstructed 1903 as company of same name. Shareholders were entitled to 1 share of £1 (credited with 15s. paid) in new company for each share of £5 held. Removed from Register 1908 .... **1906**

Moorlort Goldfields Ld. Inc. New South Wales 1903. Reconstructed into Moorlort Goldfields (1906) Ld., in which company shareholders were entitled to 5 fully-paid shares of £1 for every 8 shares of £1 held, and to subscribe at par for a pro rata proportion of a further 100,000 shares of £1 .... **1908**

Moorlort Goldfields (1906) Ld. Inc. New South Wales 1906. Vol. liq. May 1911. Undertaking and assets were acquired by Maikop Orient Oil Co. Ld. in which company shareholders were entitled to 2 shares of 2s. (credited as fully-paid) for each share of £1 held and an option (since expired) over further shares **1912**

Moraleja Gold Bearing Alluvial Concession Ld. Regd. Edinburgh 1901. Struck off Register 12 Nov. 1912. **1907**

Morayshire Railway Co. Under Act of 1881 the railway was amalgamated with Great Northern of Scotland Railway. Ordinary shareholders received ordinary stock at par. Preference shareholders received 5% preference stock (Morayshire Line)—£11,740 at 50% premium and £23,080 at par. The debentures remained a first charge on the undertaking **1883**

Morbeck Gravure Ld. Regd. 1934. Vol. liq. (members') 7 Apr. 1943. Final meeting return regd. 26 July 1943 **1945**

Mordan (S.) & Co. Ld. Regd. 1908. Vol. liq. (members') 30 Dec. 1952. Capital returned to contributories: 11s. 3d. per preference share of £1. £1,099 was paid into Companies' Liquidation Account. Final meeting return regd. 19 Oct. 1953 .... **1954**

Morden Station Garage Ld. See London General Omnibus Co. Ld.

Mordey, Carney & Co. Ld. Regd. 1881. Removed from Register 1911 .... **1911**

Mordey, Carney & Co. Ld. Regd. 1910. Vol. liq. 15 May 1922. Assets were acquired by Mountstuart Dry Docks & Shearmans Ld. (later Mountstuart Dry Docks Ld.) for fully-paid deferred ordinary shares. Final meeting return regd. 8 Mar. 1923 .... **1923**

Morecambe Estate & Gardens Ld. Regd. 1890. Receiver appointed 11 Jan. 1892. Removed from Register 1895 .... **1894**

Morecambe Gas & Light Co. Inc. by Special Act 1879. Under Act of 1900 Morecambe District Council were empowered to purchase the undertaking for £141,000 .... **1901**

Morecambe Pavilion and Summer Gardens Ld. Regd. 1889. Removed from Register 1906 .... **1891**

Morecambe Pier & Pavilion Co. Ld. Regd. 1897. Removed from Register 1912 .... **1912**

Morecambe (Regent Rd., West End) Pier Co. Ld. Regd. 1892. Vol. liq. 10 June 1932. Struck off Register 13 July 1934 .... **1933**

Morecambe Tower Co. Ld. Regd. 1898. Removed from Register 1905 .... ***1902**

Morecambe Winter Gardens Co. Ld. Regd. 1896. Removed from Register 1911 .... **1910**

Morel Bros., Cobbett & Son Ld. Regd. 1887. Vol. liq. 18 May 1920. Final meeting return regd. 27 July 1921 **1921**

Morel Ld. Regd. 1888. Vol. liq. (members') Oct. 1948. Final meeting return regd. 12 Sept. 1950 .... **1940**

Morenci Copper Mines Ld. Regd. 1899. Vol. liq. 24 June 1901. Property was sold to Clifton Consolidated Copper Mines of Arizona Ld. in which company shareholders were entitled to 3 shares of £1 (credited as fully-paid) for every 5 shares of 5s. held. Final meeting return regd. 14 May 1902 .... **1902**

Moreni Pipeline & Transport Co. Ld. Regd. 1911. Vol. liq. Apr. 1913. The property, assets and undertaking were sold to Roumanian Consolidated Oilfields Ld., in which company shareholders were entitled to 9 ordinary shares of £1 (credited as fully-paid) for every 8 preferred ordinary shares of £1 held or 1 fully-paid ordinary share of £1 for every 4 ordinary shares of 1s. held. Removed from Register 1914 . **1914**

Moreni (Roumania) Oilfields Ld. Regd. 1911. Vol. liq. July 1912. Undertaking was acquired by Roumanian Consolidated Oilfields Ld. Shareholders were entitled to 5 fully-paid shares of £1 for every 4 ordinary shares of £1 held or to 1 fully-paid share of £1 for every 2 deferred shares of 1s. held. Struck off Register Feb. 1930 .... **1931**

Morenilla Linares Ld. Regd. 1901. Vol. liq. Apr. 1908. The property was sold to a Spanish company for 30,000 ordinary shares of 50 pesetas. Removed from Register 1912 .... **1909**

Moresby Coal Co. Ld. Regd. 1877. Vol. liq. (members') 6 Aug. 1954. All capital was owned by United Steel Cos. Ld. Final meeting return regd. 3 Oct. 1955... **1940**

Morewood (E.) & Co. Ld. Regd. 1897. Vol. liq. 26 Feb. 1898. Court Order to continue winding up under supervision 23 Mar. 1898. Final meeting return regd. 20 July 1899 .... ***1899**

Morfa Du Mining Co. Ld. Regd. 1877. Vol. liq. 23 Jan. 1885. Final meeting return regd. 8 Aug. 1892 .... **1886**

Morgan & Cadogan Ld. Regd. 1912. Receiver appointed in May 1926; ceased to act 22 Apr. 1936. Struck off Register 19 Mar. 1937 .... **1938**

Morgan & Co. Ld. Regd. 1885. Vol. liq. Nov. 1920. Undertaking and assets were acquired by R. E. Jones Ld., in which company shareholders were entitled to 4 fully-paid preference shares of £1 for each share of £1 held. Struck off Register Dec. 1932 **1933**

Morgan Crucible Co. Ld. Regd. 1890. Court Order sanctioned Scheme of Arrangement. Undertaking and assets acquired by company of same name, in which company shareholders received 10 1st preference, 10 2nd preference, 10 preferred ordinary or 10 deferred ordinary shares of £1 for each 1st preference, 2nd preference, preferred ordinary or deferred ordinary share of £10 held. Dissolved under Section 154 of Companies Act (1929) on 9 Aug. 1930 ...... **1931**

VOL. FOR

contributories—£699,670. Final meeting return regd. 1 July 1937 .... **1937**

Mortgage Company of England Ld. Regd. 1881. Vol. liq. Feb. 1884. The whole of the paid-up capital was returned and £1 per share was paid on 25,000 ordinary shares. Final meeting return regd. 1 July 1887 .... **1885**

Mortgage Co. of Jamaica Ld. *See* Jamaican & General Mortgages Investment & Trust Co., Ld.

Mortgage Company of Mexico Ld. Regd. 1891. Vol. liq. 20 Dec. 1897. Final meeting return regd. 7 Mar. 1899 .... **1898**

Mortgage Co. of South Australia Ld. Regd. Edinburgh 1880. Vol. liq. Nov. 1905. Final meeting return regd. 8 Aug. 1912 .... **1906**

Mortgage Insurance Corporation Ld. Regd. 1886. No capital returned to contributories. Removed from Register 1913 .... **1914**

Mortimer Court (Abbey Road) Ld. Regd. 1933. Receiver appointed 17 Dec. 1937. Struck off Register 21 Apr. 1944 .... **1945**

Mortimer (Edward) London. Ld. Undertaking and assets were acquired by Mortimers (London) Ld. **1929**

Mortimers (London) Ld. Regd. 1928. Vol. liq. Mar. 1933. Court Order to wind up Jan. 1934. Struck off Register 20 Feb. 1942 .... **1945**

Morton (C. & G.) Ld. *See* Beechport Ld.

Morton (Francis) & Co. Ld. Regd. 1898. Vol. liq. (members') 28 Mar. 1960. Capital returned to contributories—11s. $8\frac{7}{16}d$. on each preference and ordinary share (of 5s.). £12 8s. 5d. was paid into Companies' Liquidation Account in respect of unclaimed distributions. Final meeting return regd. 17 Feb. 1967 .... **1967**

Morton (G. & W.) Ld. Regd. 1923. Vol. liq. (members') 26 Mar. 1962. Final meeting return regd. 18 Jan. 1965 .... **1947**

Morton Rose Estate Co. Ld. Regd. 1897. Vol. liq. 31 Oct. 1899. The outstanding $4\frac{1}{2}\%$ debentures were repaid on 1 Nov. 1899. Struck off Register 15 Aug. 1944 .... **1945**

Mortons Ld. Regd. 1903. Receivers appointed in Mar. 1935; ceased to act July 1937. Proceeds of realised assets were applied to repayment of $70\frac{1}{2}\%$ of principal of 1st debentures. Struck off Register 25 Mar. 1938 .... **1939**

Morums Oriental Stores Ld. Regd. 1919. Vol. liq. 24 Oct. 1928. Final meeting return regd. 10 July 1930 **1929**

Moruya Gold & Silver Mining Co. Ld. Regd 1888. Receiver appointed in Jan. 1896. Struck off Register 28 July 1899 .... **1901**

Morven (Rhodesia) Co. Ld. Regd. 1899. Vol. liq. 2 May 1912. Final meeting return regd. 30 Oct. 1913 ...... **1913**

Moseley (William) Ld. Regd. 1919. Vol. liq. (members') 21 Sept. 1944. A direct controlling interest was held by Bleachers' Association Ld. (later Whitecroft Industrial Holdings Ld.). Final meeting return regd. 6 Jan. 1945 .... **1946**

Moseleys Food Ld. *See* Foods Ld.

Moser Machine Co. Ld. Regd. 1894. Removed from Register 1905 .... **1905**

Mosman Gold Mines Ld. Regd. 1894. Vol. liq. 20 Aug. 1897. Reconstructed 1897 as Rainbow and Peabody Gold Mines Ld., in which company shareholders were entitled to 1 share of £1 (credited with 18s. paid) for each share of £1 (19s. paid) held. Final meeting return regd. 6 July 1898 .... **1900**

Mosman Gold Mining Co. Ld. Regd. 1886. Vol. liq. 20 Sept. 1894. Reconstructed as Mosman Gold Mines Ld., in which company shareholders were entitled to 1 share of £1 (credited with 18s. 6d. paid) for each share of £1 held. Final meeting return regd. 28 June 1895 .... **1897**

Moss Bay Hematite Iron & Steel Co. Ld. Regd. 1881. Reconstructed 1891 as company of same name. Shareholders were entitled to 1 fully-paid preference share of £8 and 1 ordinary share of £10 (credited with £6 paid) for each ordinary share of £20 held. Holders of debentures were entitled to debentures in new company. Court Orders: to wind up 19 Apr. 1890; to dissolve 2 Aug. 1893 .... **1893**

Moss Bay Hematite Iron & Steel Co. Ld. Regd. 1891. Vol. liq. 30 July 1909 for reconstruction as Workington Iron & Steel Co. Ld. Ordinary and preference shareholders were entitled to similar shares in new company at par. Debenture holders were entitled to (a) repayment at 105% in cash or (b) 110% of holding in preference shares in new company. Final meeting return regd. 3 Sept. 1915 .... **1910**

Moss' Empires & Howard & Wyndham Tours Ld. Regd. Edinburgh 1934. Vol. liq. (members') 27 Aug. 1936. Capital returned to contributories—£933 6s. 8d. Final meeting return regd. 16 Nov. 1946 .... **1937**

VOL. FOR

Moss Hall Coal Co. Ld. Regd. 1867. Vol. liq. (members') 21 July 1932. Coal and colliery business was acquired by Wigan Coal Corporation Ld. Final meeting return regd. 20 July 1933 .... **1933**

Moss (James) & Co. (Moss Line) Ld. Regd. 1916. Vol. liq. (members') 5 Apr. 1934. Undertaking and assets acquired by Moss Hutchinson Line Ld. Capital returned to contributories—£113 7s. 1½d. (including investments distributed in specie) per share of £100. Final meeting return regd. 24 Aug. 1937 .... **1935**

Moss Litter & Peat Industries Ld. Regd. 1895. Vol. liq. 19 Aug. 1896. Final meeting return regd. 18 Apr. 1898 .... **1897**

Moss Litter Charcoal and Manure Co. Ld. Regd. 1885. Vol. liq. 17 Mar. 1897. Final meeting return regd. 10 Feb. 1898 .... **1898**

Moss Steamship Co. Ld. Regd. 1873. Vol. liq. 31 Dec. 1929. All capital was owned by Moss (James) & Co. Ld. Final meeting return regd. 3 Jan. 1935 .... **1930**

Mosses (Alex.) Radiator Co. Ld. Regd. 1919. Vol. liq. 17 Nov. 1922. Receiver appointed 25 Nov. 1922; ceased to act 10 July 1925. Controlling interest held by Harper Bean Ld. Final meeting return regd. 12 Mar. 1926 .... **1924**

Mossley & Saddleworth Gas Co. Ld. Regd. 1934. Dissolved 1 May 1949, undertaking being vested in North Western Area Gas Board under Gas Act 1948. Holders of securities were entitled to receive British Gas 3% guaranteed stock 1990-95 as follows in respect of each £1 unit, unless otherwise stated, of security held:

	£	s.	d.	
$4\frac{1}{2}\%$ pref. shares	1	2	6	
4% red. pref. shares.................	1	0	0	
3% red. mort. debs. (of £100)........	100	0	0	**1952**

Mossley Victoria Spinning Mills Co. (1920) Ld. Regd. 1920. Vol. liq. (members') 5 Aug. 1941. Capital returned to contributories—11s. 0·92d. per share of 9s. £36 was paid into Companies' Liquidation Account. Final meeting return regd. 2 May 1947.. **1948**

Moston Mill Co. Ld. Regd. 1908. Direct controlling interest was held by Fine Cotton Spinners' & Doublers' Association Ld. now Fine Spinners' & Doublers' Ld. Vol. liq. (members') 30 Mar. 1944. Final meeting return regd. 4 Apr. 1945 .... **1946**

Mosul Oil Fields Ld. Regd. 1932. Vol. liq. (members') 10 Dec. 1942. All shares privately held. Final meeting return regd. 16 Feb. 1944 .... **1945**

Motapa Gold Mining Co. Ld. Inc. Southern Rhodesia 1946. Vol. liq. (members') 14 Dec. 1959. Capital returned to contributories—10·166d. per share of 5s. Company dissolved 1962 .... **1964**

Mother Lode Consolidated Gold Mines Ld. Regd. 1898. Struck off Register 26 Feb. 1909 .... **1909**

Mother-o'-Gold Consolidated Mines Ld. Regd. 1899. Assets realised by receiver were insufficient to meet costs of debenture holders action. Removed from Register 1905 .... **1908**

Motherwell & Bellshill Railway Co. Inc. by Special Act 1900. Undertaking abandoned by Act 1900 .... **1905**

Motherwell Iron and Steel Co. Ld. Regd. Edinburgh 1903. Vol. liq. (creditors') 27 Nov. 1934. Assets realised insufficient to pay creditors in full. Final meeting return regd. 24 Dec. 1935 .... **1935**

Motor Bus Co. Ld. Regd. 1905. Removed from Register 1906 .... **1906**

Motor Cinemas Ld. Regd. 1919. Vol. liq. May 1922. Struck off Register 3 Oct. 1941 .... **1942**

Motor Coaches Ld. Regd. 1920. Vol. liq. (members') 8 Dec. 1942. Capital returned to contributories—9s. per share of £1 plus certain assets which were distributed in specie. Final meeting return regd. 20 Dec. 1943 .... **1945**

Motor Enterprises Ld. Regd. 1906. Court Order to wind up 1906. Removed from Register 1911 .... **1908**

Motor Finance Corpn. of S. Africa (Proprietary) Ld. In liquidation. Direct controlling interest was held by Mutual Finance Ld. **1935**

Motor Fuel Proprietary Ld. *See* Coal & Allied Industries Ld.

Motor Horse Ld. Regd. 1903. Struck off Register 13 Oct. 1908 .... **1909**

Motor Manufacturing Co. Ld. Regd. 1898. Reconstructed 1900 as company of same name. Shareholders were entitled to 1 share of £1 (credited with 17s. paid) for each share of £1 held. Removed from Register 1905 .... **1903**

Motor Manufacturing Co. Ld. Regd. 1900. Reconstructed 1902 as company of same name. Shareholders were entitled to 1 share of 5s. (credited with 3s. paid) in new company for each share of £1 held. **1903**

Motor Manufacturing Co. Ld. Regd. 1902. Removed from Register 1910 .... **1905**

VOL. FOR

Motor Manufacturing Co. (1907) Ld. Regd. 1907. Vol. liq. 28 Dec. 1908. Final meeting return regd. 15 Mar. 1930 .... **1909**

Motor Petrol Association Ld. Inc. (under Industrial and Provident Societies Act) in 1913. Court Order to wind up May 1925 .... **1926**

Motor Pneumatic Tyre Co. Ld. Regd. 1905. Removed from Register 24 Feb. 1911 .... ***1906**

Motor Ricksha Co. Ld. Regd. 1906. Vol. liq. 11 Dec. 1907. Removed from Register 10 Mar. 1911 .... ***1909**

Motor Syndicate (Boscombe) Ld. Undertaking and assets were acquired in Jan. 1927 by Westover Garage Ld. for 12,600 fully-paid shares of £1 .... **1929**

Motor Traction Co. Ld. Regd. 1898 as London Steam Omnibus Co. Ld.; name changed Sept. 1899. Removed from Register 1910 .... **1906**

Motor Traction Co., 1905, Ld. Regd. 1905. Removed from Register 1913 .... **1908**

Motor Vehicles Ld. Regd. 1905. Removed from Register 1910 .... **1909**

Motorailer Transport Co. Ld. Regd. 1922. Struck off Register 8 Nov. 1932 .... **1928**

Mount Albion Silver Mining & Smelting Co. Ld. Regd. 1887. Vol. liq. 16 Oct. 1891. Reconstructed as New Mount Albion Silver Mining & Smelting Co. Ld., in which company shareholders were entitled to 1 share of £1 (credited with 16s. 6d. paid) for each share of £1 held. Final meeting return regd. 3 Apr. 1894 .... **1892**

Mount Arthur Properties Ld. Regd. 1908. Vol. liq. 4 Dec. 1914. Final meeting return regd. 19 Mar.1915 **1915**

Mount Austin (Johore) Rubber Estates Ld. Regd. 1910. Vol. liq. (members') 22 Oct 1968. Amount returned to contributories per share (of £1) 22s. 7¾d. Amount paid into Companies' Liquidation Account £737 12s. 8d. in respect of unclaimed dividends and £1,076 13s. 4d. in respect of unclaimed distributions. Final meeting return regd. 26 Sept. 1969 .... **1970**

Mount Boppy Gold Mining Co. Ld. Regd. 1899. Vol. liq. 8 July 1919. Reconstructed as Mount Boppy Ld., in which company shareholders were entitled to 3 ordinary shares of 10s. (credited with 7s. 6d. paid) for every 2 ordinary shares of £1 held, or 1 fully-paid preference share of 10s. for each preference share of £1 held. Final meeting return regd. 20 Apr. 1920 **1920**

Mount Boppy Ld. Regd. 1919. Vol. liq. 31 Oct. 1924. Final meeting return regd. 10 July 1928 .... **1925**

Mount Britten (Queensland) Gold Mines Ld. Regd. 1886. Court Orders: to wind up 6 Dec. 1890; to dissolve 20 Nov. 1896 .... **1891**

Mount Burgess Gold Mining Co. Ld. Regd. Edinburgh 1896. Vol. liq. Mar. 1901. Final meeting return regd. 6 Dec. 1902 .... **1902**

Mount Carbon Co. Ld. Regd. 1884. Vol. liq. 7 Nov. 1917. Capital returned to contributories—£1 18s. per share of £1; further payments (if any) not known. The debentures were repaid at 102½% in Nov. 1917. Final meeting return regd. 23 Dec. 1918 **1918**

Mount Carrington Mining Co. Ld. Regd. 1887. Vol. liq. 13 Oct. 1892. Final meeting return regd. 17 July 1893 .... **1893**

Mount Catherine Gold Mining Co. Ld. Regd. 1897. Reconstructed as Talunga Consolidated Ld. Removed from Register 1901 .... **1901**

Mount Cattlin Copper Mining Co. Ld. Regd. 1906. Vol. liq. Feb. 1909. Undertaking acquired by Phillips River Gold and Copper Co. Ld., in which company shareholders were entitled to 1 fully-paid share of £1 for every 2 shares of £1 held. Removed from Register 1910 .... **1909**

Mount Chalmers Copper Mines Ld. Regd. 1899. Removed from Register 1904 .... **1902**

Mount Charlotte Gold Mining Co. Ld. Regd. Edinburgh 1894. Vol. liq. Apr. 1899 for reconstruction under same name. Final meeting return regd. 11 Oct. 1900 **1902**

Mount Charlotte Gold Mining Co. Ld. Regd. Edinburgh 1899. Vol. liq. Dec. 1901 for amalgamation under title of Hannan's Reward & Mount Charlotte Ld., in which company shareholders were entitled to 1 share of £1 (credited with 18s. paid) for each share of £1 held. Final meeting return regd. 21 Aug. 1903 **1902**

Mount Coolon Gold Mines N.L. Inc. in Victoria 1931. Vol. liq. (members') 15 Sept. 1958. Shareholders were entitled to receive 1s. 1d. cash per share of 10s. and 1 share of Morning Star Mines N.L. for every 6 shares held. Company dissolved and struck off the Register 2 Oct. 1963 .... **1964**

Mount Cuthbert, No Liability. Inc. Victoria 1907. Wound up Nov. 1909 for reconstruction under same name. Shareholders were entitled to 1 share of £1 (credited with 16s. paid) in new company for each share of £1 held **1910**

Mount Cuthbert, No Liability. Inc. Victoria 1909. Reconstructed 1916 as company of same name.

Shareholders were entitled to 1 share of £1 (credited with 15s. paid) for each share of £1 held *plus* 1 fully-paid share for every 4 shares so subscribed **1917**

Mount Cuthbert, No Liability. Inc. Victoria 1916. Properties were acquired in 1925 by Mount Elliott Ld. **1926**

Mount Darwin Gold Mining Syndicate Ld. *See* Darwin Investment Trust Ld.

Mount Darwin Syndicate Ld. Regd. 1895. Amalgamated 1899 with Holton Consolidated Co. Ld., in which company shareholders were entitled to 2 shares of £1 (credited as fully-paid) for each share held. Removed from Register 1901 .... **1900**

Mount Donaldson Copper Co. Ld. Regd. 1899. Removed from Register 1909 .... **1907**

Mount Dzyshra (Caucasus) Exploration Co. Ld. Regd. 1909. Struck off Register 1931 .... ***1919**

Mount Elliott Ld. Regd. 1907. Vol. liq. (members') 18 May 1953, the undertaking and assets were acquired by Kwahu Mining Co. (1925) Ld. (later Kwahu Co. Ld.), in which company stockholders, other than that company, received one 2s. stock unit for each 5s. unit held. Final meeting return regd. 3 Dec. 1957 **1959**

Mount Garnet Freehold Copper & Silver Mining Co. Ld. Inc. Victoria 1898. In liquidation in 1904. The property was in the hands of the debenture holders. **1904**

Mount Greenock Gold Estates Ld. Regd. 1895. Removed from Register 1907 .... **1900**

Mount Head Ranche Co. Ld. Regd. 1883. Vol. liq. 8 Dec. 1886. Final meeting return regd. 10 Aug. 1891 **1887**

Mount Hepburn Gold Mine Ld. Regd. 1898. Vol. liq. 10 July 1901. Final meeting return regd. 17 Dec. 1901 **1902**

Mount Ida Consols Ld. Regd. 1898. Vol. liq. 20 Nov. 1901. Reconstructed 1901 as company of same name. Shareholders were entitled to 1 share of £1 (credited with 17s. paid) for each share of £1 held. Struck off Register 21 June 1907 .... **1908**

Mount Ida Consols Ld. Regd. 1901. Vol. liq. 11 June 1906. Struck off Register 19 Mar. 1909 .... **1908**

Mount Isa Mines Ld. Inc. Sydney 1924. Vol. liq. Sept. 1933. Undertaking and assets were acquired by company of same name. Shareholders were entitled to 1 share of £1 in new company for each share of £1 held. Holders of 1st debenture stock were entitled to an equal amount of A or B 1st debenture stock in new company; holders of 2nd debenture stock to an equal amount of A or B 2nd debenture stock **1934**

Mount Jackson Gold Mines Ld. Regd. 1895. Reconstructed as company of same name in which shareholders were entitled to receive 1 share of £1 (credited with 15s. paid) for each share held. Struck off Register 1905 .... **1897**

Mount Jackson Gold Mines, Ld. Regd. 1897. Reconstructed as company of same name in which shareholders were entitled to receive 1 share of £1 (credited with 17s. paid) for each share held. Struck off Register 1909 .... **1902**

Mount Jackson Gold Mines Ld. Regd. 1902. Vol. liq. 12 Feb. 1906. Reconstructed as company of same name (incorporated in Western Australia). Final meeting return regd. 6 Apr. 1909 .... **1906**

Mount Jefferson Gold Mining Co. Ld. *See* Groveland Gold Mining Co. Ld.

Mount Kembla Coal & Oil Co. Ld. Regd. 1878. Vol. liq. 8 July 1913. Undertaking and assets were acquired by Mount Kembla Collieries Ld., in which company shareholders were entitled to 35 shares of £1 (credited as fully-paid) for each share of £10 (of either class) held. Final meeting return regd. 16 May 1917 .... **1914**

Mount Kembla Collieries Ld. Regd. 1913. Vol. liq. (members') 3 Oct. 1946. Colliery assets sold to Australian Iron & Steel Ld. [later Australian Iron & Steel (Pty.) Ld.] for £A155,485. Capital returned to contributories—8s. 8¼d. per share of £1. £784 paid into Companies' Liquidation Account. Final meeting return regd. 23 Apr. 1948 .... **1949**

Mount Kimo Gold Mines Ld. Regd. 1897. Vol. liq. 21 Feb. 1900. Reconstructed as Camden Exploration Co. Ld., in which company shareholders were entitled to 1 share of £1 (credited as fully-paid) for each share held. Final meeting return regd. 8 Sept. 1902 .... **1901**

Mount Leyshon Ld. Regd. 1892. Removed from Register 1903 .... **1900**

Mount Leyshon (Queensland) Ld. Regd. 1887. Reconstructed 1892 as Mount Leyshon Ld., in which company shareholders were entitled to 1 share of £1 (credited with 19s. paid) for each share of £1 held. Removed from Register 1903 .... **1900**

Mount Lyell Blocks Copper Corporation Ld. Regd. 1899. Reconstructed 1903 as Mount Lyell Blocks Mining Co., No Liability in which company shareholders were entitled to 1 share of £1 (credited with 17s. 6d.

VOL. FOR

paid) for each share of £1 held. Removed from Register 1904 .... **1908**

Mount Lyell Blocks Copper Mines, No Liability. Inc. Victoria 1910. Vol. liq. Jan. 1920. Property acquired by Mount Lyell Mining and Railway Co. Ld. Capital returned to contributories—8¼d. per share of £1 5s. **1921**

Mount Lyell Blocks Mining Co., No Liability. Inc. Victoria 1910. Wound up May 1910 for reconstruction as Mount Lyell Blocks Copper Mines, No Liability. Shareholders were entitled to 1 share of £1 (credited with 17s. paid) in new company for each share of £1 held **1911**

Mount Lyell Comstock Co., No Liability, Inc. Victoria 1898. Property sold to Mount Lyell Comstock Copper Co. Ld. (later Lyell Comstock Consolidated Copper Co. Ld.), in which company shareholders were entitled to 2 shares of £1 for each share of £1 held **1900**

Mount Lyell Comstock Copper Co. Ld. Regd. 1898. *See* Lyell Comstock Consolidated Copper Co. Ld.

Mount Lyell Comstock Copper Co. Ld. Regd. 1907. Vol. liq. 25 June 1912. Capital returned to contributories—3⁷⁄₁₆d. per share of 4s. in Nov. 1912; further payments (if any) not known. Final meeting return regd. 11 June 1913 .... **1913**

Mount Lyell Comstock Ld. Regd. 1897. Removed from Register 1913 .... **1899**

Mount Lyell Consols Copper Mines, No Liability. Inc. Victoria 1908. Wound up Nov. 1911 for reconstruction as Mount Lyell Consols Wallaroo Copper Mines, No Liability, in which company shareholders were entitled to 1 share of 10s. (credited with 8s. paid) for each share of 7s. 6d. held **1912**

Mount Lyell Consols Mining Corporation, No Liability. Inc. Victoria 1906. Wound up 5 Oct. 1908 for reconstruction as Mount Lyell Consols Copper Mines, No Liability, in which company shareholders were entitled to 1 share of 7s. 6d. (credited with 5s. paid) for each share of 7s. 6d. held. Holders of vendors' shares were entitled to 1 fully-paid share for every 2 held **1909**

Mount Lyell Consols Wallaroo Copper Mines, No Liability. Inc. Victoria 1911. Wound up July 1913 for reconstruction as New Lyell Consols Copper Mine, No Liability, in which company shareholders were entitled to 2 shares of 10s. (credited with 8s. paid) for each share of 10s. held. Holders of vendors' shares were entitled to 1 fully-paid share for each share held **1914**

Mount Lyell Copper Estates Ld. Regd. 1899. Removed from Register 1910 .... **1906**

Mount Lyell Mining & Railway Co. Ld. Inc. Victoria 1893. Reconstructed 1903 as company of same name. Company received 60,000 fully-paid shares of £1 and £15,000 in cash **1903**

Mount Lyell Proprietary Mines Ld. Regd. 1898. Removed from Register 1903 .... **1902**

Mount McClellan Mining Co. Ld. Regd. 1890. Removed from Register 1901 .... **1901**

Mount Magnet Gold Mining Co. Ld. Regd. 1895. Vol. liq. 30 Sept. 1897. Reconstructed as company of same name. Shareholders were entitled to 1 share of 5s. (credited with 3s. 6d. paid) in new company for each share of 5s. held. Final meeting return regd. 24 Oct. 1899 .... **1898**

Mount Magnet Gold Mining Co. Ld. Regd. 1897. Vol. liq. 1 Oct. 1898. Reconstructed as company of same name. Shareholders were entitled to 1 share of 5s. (credited with 4s. 3d. paid) for each share of 5s. held. Final meeting return regd. 13 June 1900 .... **1898**

Mount Magnet Gold Mining Co. Ld. Regd. 1898. Vol. liq. 2 Feb. 1900. The machinery was sold for £3,000 in shares of Windsor Consolidated (W.A.) Gold Mines Ld. Final meeting return regd. 13 June 1900 **1900**

Mount Magnet Golden Crown Ld. Regd. 1896. Struck off Register 26 Oct. 1900 .... **1901**

Mount Malcolm Mines Ld. Regd. 1900. Reconstructed 1902 as Malcolm Mines Ld., in which company shareholders were entitled to 1 share of 10s. (credited with 8s. paid) for each share of 10s. held. Removed from Register 1904 .... **1908**

Mount Malcolm Proprietary Gold Mines Ld. Regd. 1896. Removed 1900 as Mount Malcolm Mines Ld., in which company shareholders were entitled to 3 shares of 10s. (credited with 7s. 6d. paid) for every 2 shares of £1 held. Removed from Register 1901 **1903**

Mount Margaret "Reward" Claim Ld. Regd. 1895. Vol. liq. 30 Apr. 1897. Reconstructed as company of same name. Shareholders were entitled to 1 share of £1 (credited with 15s. paid) for each share of £1 held. Final meeting return regd. 17 Jan. 1900 .... **1902**

VOL. FOR

Mount Margaret "Reward" Claim Ld. Regd. 1897. Vol. liq. 19 Mar. 1902. Reconstructed as Potosi Consolidated Ld., in which company shareholders were entitled to 3 shares of £1 (credited with 17s. paid) for every 5 shares of £1 held. Final meeting return regd. 31 Aug. 1905 .... **1905**

Mount Margaret "Reward" Ld. *See* Potosi Consolidated Ld.

Mount Molloy Ld. Inc. Queensland 1905. Wound up Sept. 1912 for reconstruction but scheme was not carried out **1914**

Mount Morgan Consolidated Gold Mines of Queensland, No Liability. Inc. Victoria 1901. According to information supplied by former London office, company has ceased to exist **1904**

Mount Morgan Extended Gold Mining Co. Ld. Regd. 1893. Vol. liq. 25 May 1893. Final meeting return regd. 30 Nov. 1894 .... **1894**

Mount Morgan Gold Mining Co. Ld. Inc. Queensland 1886. Vol. liq. July 1927. Capital returned to contributories—5s. per share of £1 in Mar. 1928; further payments (if any) not known. Assets in Queensland were acquired in 1929 by Mount Morgan Ld **1928**

Mount Orient Gold Mining Co. Ld. Regd. 1896. The property was acquired in Oct. 1900 by Wild-Hercules Gold Mines Ld. for 48,000 fully-paid shares of £1 and £2,000 in cash. Removed from Register 1903 .... **1902**

Mount Oxide Mines Ld. Inc. 1912 in New South Wales. In liquidation in 1913. Property sold to English company of same name for £490,545 (£470,545 in fully-paid shares and £20,000 in cash) **1915**

Mount Oxide Mines Ld. Regd. Aug. 1913. Vol. liq. 9 June 1920. Property and assets were acquired by Mount Elliott Ld., in which company shareholders were entitled to 41 shares of £5 for every 250 shares of £1 held. Final meeting return regd. 10 Sept. 1940 **1921**

Mount Perry Copper & Reid's Creek Gold Mines and Smelting Co. Ld. Regd. 1887. Vol. liq. 5 Mar. 1901. Capital returned to contributories—1s. 5½d. per share at May 1901; further payments (if any) not known. Final meeting return regd. 21 July 1902... **1902**

Mount Prophecy & Perseverance Gold Mines Ld. Regd. 1895. Vol. liq. 22 Feb. 1900. Reconstructed as Amalgamated Gold Mines Ld., in which company shareholders were entitled to subscribe for 2 shares at par for every 5 shares held; shareholders were entitled to 4 fully-paid shares of 10s. in new company for each contributing share taken up by them. Final meeting return regd. 18 Mar. 1902 ... **1901**

Mount Rea Gold Mining Co. Ld. Regd. 1895. No capital was expected to be returned to contributories. Removed from Register 1912 .... **1903**

Mount Read & Rosebery Mines Ld. Inc. Victoria 1916. Wound up Dec. 1920 .... **1922**

Mount Read Mining Co. Ld. Regd. 1901. Vol. liq. 17 Sept. 1919. Capital returned to contributories—2s. per share of £1 (19s. 3d. paid); further payments (if any) not known. Final meeting return regd. 24 June 1920 .... **1920**

Mount Reid Mining Co. Ld. Regd. 1896. Reconstructed 1901 as Mount Read Mining Co. Ld., in which company shareholders were entitled to 1 share of £1 (credited with 16s. paid) for each share of £1 held. Removed from Register 1908 .... **1908**

Mount Renmark Gold Mining Co. Ld. Regd. 1895 as Mount Torrens Gold Mining Co. Ld.; name changed 1896. Removed from Register 1911 .... **1910**

Mount Roudny Gold Mines Ld. Regd. 1903. Vol. liq. May 1909. Removed from Register 1909 .... **1910**

Mount Rowe Consolidated Mining Co. Ld. Regd. 1895. Vol. liq. 7 Sept. 1898. Final meeting return regd. 30 Nov. 1901 .... **1900**

Mount Shamrock Gold Co. Ld. Regd. 1887. Mortgagee took possession of the property. Removed from Register 1898 .... **1897**

Mount Steamship Co. Ld. Regd. 1923. Vol. liq. 12 July 1929. Final meeting return regd. 24 Oct. 1929 ...... **1930**

Mount Torlesse Collieries (Broken River, N.Z.) Ld. Regd. 1915. Receiver appointed in Dec. 1927. Struck off Register Dec. 1931 .... **1932**

Mount Torrens Gold Mining Co. Ld. *See* Mount Renmark Gold Mining Co. Ld.

Mount Usher Gold Mines Ld. Regd. 1902. Vol. liq. Sept. 1906. Removed from Register 1907 .... **1907**

Mount Waratah Copper Mines Ld. Regd. 1907. Removed from Register 1913 .... **1911**

Mount Wellington Ld. Regd. 1934. Vol. liq. (members') 20 May 1941. No capital returned to contributories. Debenture holders received £6 5s. per £25 debenture. Final meeting return regd.3 Nov.1948 .... **1949**

Mount Yagahong Exploration Co. Ld. Regd. 1898. Reconstructed as Mount Yagahong Exploration and

VOL. FOR

Finance Co. Ld. (later Finance & Industrial Trust Ld.), in which company shareholders were entitled to 1 share of 10s. (credited with 8s. paid) for each share of 10s. held. Removed from Register 1907 — **1903**

Mount Yagahong Gold Mining & Exploration Co. Ld. Regd. 1896. Vol. liq. 13 July 1898. Reconstructed as Mount Yagahong Exploration Co. Ld., in which company shareholders were entitled to 5 shares of 10s. (credited with 8s. 6d. paid) for every 2 shares of £1 held. Final meeting return regd.2 Aug.1899 ..... **1903**

Mount Zeehan (Tasmania) Silver-Lead Mines Ld. Regd. 1889. Vol. liq. 29 June 1922. Final meeting return regd. 30 Sept. 1925 .... **1923**

Mountain Copper Co. Ld. Regd. 1896. Reconstructed 1902 as company of same name. Shareholders were entitled to £4 debenture stock in new company *plus* £1 in cash for each share of £5 held. Removed from Register 1903 .... **1908**

Mountain Ledge Gold Mining Co. Ld. Regd. 1889. Vol. liq. 14 Mar. 1892. Final meeting return regd. 21 July 1892 .... ***1893**

Mountain Maid & Iron Prince Gold Mines Ld. Regd. 1896 as Devonian Gold Mines Ld.; name changed July 1897. Struck off Register 18 Nov. 1902 .... **1903**

Mountain Queen Ld. Regd. 1910. Vol. liq. 15 July 1915. Final meeting return regd. 22 Nov. 1921 .... **1916**

Mountain's Wire Manufacturing Co. Ld. Regd. 1892. Court Order to wind up 11 Mar. 1893. Liquidator released 18 Dec. 1896. Removed from Register 27 Aug. 1907 .... ***1894**

Mountford Phillips & Co. Ld. Regd. 1903. Vol. liq. 5 May 1920. Final meeting return regd. 10 Dec. 1920 **1920**

Mountford, Phillips & Co. (1920) Ld. Regd. 1920. Receiver appointed in April 1926. Assets realised insufficient to satisfy claims of 1st debenture holders. Struck off Register 18 Sept. 1936 .... **1937**

Mount's Bay Consols Ld. Regd. Truro 1881. Vol. liq. 5 Aug. 1885 for reconstruction as Shepherds United Ld., in which company shareholders were entitled to 1 fully-paid share of £1 for each share of £1 held. Final meeting return regd.4 June 1886 .... **1886**

Mountstuart Shipbuilding, Graving Docks & Engineering Co. Ld. Regd. 1882. Reconstructed 1902 as Mountstuart Dry Docks Ld., in which company shareholders were entitled to 5 preferred ordinary and 5 deferred ordinary shares of £10 (credited as fully-paid) for each A or B share of £50 held. Removed from Register 1903 .... **1908**

Mouramba Copper Mines Ld. Regd. 1910. Receiver appointed in July 1926; ceased to act July 1929. All assets were sold. First and final distribution of ¼d. in £ was made to debenture holders in Aug. 1929. Struck off Register 18 Feb. 1936 .... **1930**

Moviecolor Ld. Regd. 1929. Struck off Register 3 Nov.1939 .... **1940**

Moyar Coffee Co. Ld. Regd. 1880. Vol. liq. June 1884. Final meeting return regd. 30 Mar. 1887 .... **1885**

Mozambique Consolidated Mines Ld. Regd. 1898. Vol. liq. 28 Nov. 1900. Reconstructed as Mozambique Macequece Ld., in which company shareholders were entitled to 1 share of 10s. (credited with 8s. paid) for each share of 10s. held. Final meeting return regd. 25 July 1907 .... **1903**

Mozambique Gold Mines Ld. Regd. 1895. Vol. liq. 29 May 1897. Final meeting return regd. 5 May 1898 **1898**

Mozambique Industrial & Commercial Co. Ld. Regd. 1918. Vol. liq. (creditors') 28 Nov. 1940. No capital returned to contributories. Final meeting return regd. 10 Apr. 1946 .... **1947**

Mozambique Macequece Ld. Regd. 1900. Reconstructed 1903 as company of same name. Shareholders were entitled to 1 share of 10s. (credited with 8s. paid) in new company for each share of 10s. held. Removed from Register 1909 .... **1908**

Mozambique Macequece Ld. Regd. 1903. Vol. liq. 19 Nov. 1925. Final meeting return regd. 29 July 1927 **1926**

Mozambique Mines Ld. Regd. 1904. Vol. liq. 19 June 1912. The properties were sold to Andrada Mines, in which company shareholders were entitled to 1 ordinary share of £1 (credited as fully-paid) for each preference share of £1 held, or 1 fully-paid deferred share of 2s. for each ordinary share of £1 held. Final meeting return regd. 2 Jan. 1914 .... **1913**

Mozambique Oil & Minerals Concessions Ld. Regd. 1920. Vol. liq. Mar. 1925. Shareholders were entitled to 1 share of 10s. in Angola Oilfields Ld. for every 8 shares of 5s. held. Struck off Register 20 Feb. 1945 .... **1945**

Mozambique Portland Cement Co. Ld. Inc. in Union of South Africa 1919. Company's property was sold by order of the Court and in Jan. 1938 the Secretary of the London Advisory Committee stated that the company was in liquidation **1938**

VOL. FOR

Mozambique Produce Co. Ld. Regd. 1887. Vol. liq. 17 July 1889. Final meeting return regd. 4 Mar. 1899 **1890**

Mrs. Bull Ld. Regd. 1910. Vol. liq. 18 Feb. 1919. Struck off Register 30 Jan. 1923 .... **1919**

Muar Itam Estates Ld. Regd. 1923. Vol. liq. (members') 25 July 1951. Capital returned to contributories—2s. 3¾d. per share of 2s. £1,807 2s. 9d. was paid into Companies' Liquidation Account. Final meeting return regd. 6 Jan. 1956 .... **1957**

Muar River Rubber Co. Ld. Regd. as private company; converted public company 1929. Voluntary winding-up 26 Nov. 1985. All capital owned by Barlow Holdings p.l.c. **1980–1**

Mucambo Cocoa Estates Ld. Regd. 1920. Vol. liq. (members') 17 Aug. 1943. No capital returned to contributories. Final meeting return regd. 10 Dec. 1946 .... **1947**

Much Wenlock & Severn Junction Railway Co. Inc. by Special Act 1859. Under Great Western Railway Act 1896 undertaking was amalgamated with that company. The debenture debt and annual rent charge were adopted by purchasing company. Holders of Coalbrookdale extension preference share received £15 5% consolidated preference stock for each share held. Holders of 5% preference shares received £11 per share; holders of ordinary shares received £2 11s. 10d per share **1897**

Mudie's Library Ld. Regd. 1864 as Mudie's Select Library Ld.; name changed Mar. 1930. Receiver appointed 17 July 1936; ceased to act 23 Dec. 1937. Assets realised insufficient to meet claims of debenture holders. Struck off Register 4 Aug. 1939 **1940**

Mudsill Mining Co. Ld. Regd. 1888. Vol. liq. 5 June 1896. Final meeting return regd. 8 Mar. 1898 ..... **1897**

Muhesa Rubber Estates Ld. Regd. 1920. Receiver appointed 13 July 1923. Estates were sold and distribution of 14·875% was made to debenture stockholders. Struck off Register Dec. 1930 .... **1931**

Muhesa Rubber Plantations Ld. Regd. 1910. Vol. liq. 7 May 1920. Reconstructed as Muhesa Rubber Estates Ld., in which company shareholders were entitled to 5 shares of 2s. (credited with 1s. 3d. paid) for each share of £1 held. The debenture stockholders were entitled to an equal amount of debenture stock in new company. Final meeting return regd. 17 Dec. 1927 .... **1921**

Muirhead's Trawlers Ld. Regd. Edinburgh 1897. Vol. liq. 21 Nov. 1904. Court Order to dissolve 16 June 1908 .... **1905**

Muirkirk Gas Light Co. Ld. Regd. in Edinburgh 1859. Dissolved 1 May 1949, undertaking being vested in Scottish Area Gas Board under Gas Act 1948. Holders of ordinary shares (of £1) were entitled to receive £2 British Gas 3% guaranteed stock 1990–95 for each share held. **1952**

Muirkirk, Mauchline & Dalmellington Railway Co. Inc. by Special Act 1896. Undertaking abandoned by Act of 1900. .... **1901**

Muller and Co. Ld. Regd. 1900. Vol. liq. 22 Sept. 1908. Undertaking and assets were acquired by Wahnschaffe & Co's Hollandsche Vereeniging tot Exploitatie van Margarinefabrieken (later Wahnschaffe, Muller & Co's Hollandsche Vereeniging tot Exploitatie van Margarinefabrieken). Shareholders were entitled to 1 ordinary or preference share in purchasing company for each such share held **1909**

Muller & Co.'s Margarine Ld. Regd. 1897. Vol. liq. 31 Oct. 1900. Reconstructed as Muller and Co. Ld., in which company shareholders were entitled to 1 preference share of £1 for every 2 preference shares of £1 held, or 3 preference shares of £1 for every 20 ordinary shares of £1 held. Final meeting return regd. 25 Jan. 1902 .... **1908**

Mulliner-Wigley Co. Ld. Regd. 1895 as Mulliners Ld.; name changed 26 Feb. 1902. Vol. liq. 18 Mar. 1903. Absorbed by Charles Camnell & Co. Ld. Removed from Register 22 May 1908 .... ***1904**

Mulliners Ld. Regd. 1919. Vol. liq. 15 May 1924. Final meeting return regd. 7 July 1925 .... **1925**

Mullingar, Kells & Drogheda Railway Co. Inc. by Special Act 1903. Undertaking abandoned **1909**

Multi-Colour Printing Co. Ld. Regd. 1899. Reconstructed 1904 as Multi-Colour Printing Co. (1904) Ld. Removed from Register 1912 .... **1908**

Multi-Colour Printing Co. (1904) Ld. Regd. 1904. Vol. liq. Apr. 1908. Court Order to continue winding up under supervision May 1908. Property was sold by Receiver but realised insufficient to pay unsecured creditors or contributories. Removed from Register 1913 .... **1911**

Multidoor Ld. Regd. 1929. Court Order to wind up Dec. 1929. Struck off Register 14 Oct. 1938 .... **1939**

Multiplex Schaats & Manufacturing Co. Ld. Regd. 1897. Removed from Register 1903 .... **1902**

VOL. FOR

Mulwarrie Exploration Co. Ld. Regd. 1910. Struck off Register May 1929............ 1930

Mumbles Railway & Pier Co. Inc. by Special Act 1889. Under provisions of the South Wales Transport Act 1959 the company was dissolved and the undertaking vested in The South Wales Transport Co. Ld. (which company owned nearly all capital) on 31 Dec. 1959 1959

Mumford (A. G.) Ld. Regd. 1905. Vol. liq. (creditors') 24 June 1932. Capital returned to contributories—2s. 1½d. per share of £1. Final meeting return regd. 28 July 1934 1933

Mummery & Sons Ld. Regd. 1888. Vol. liq. 29 Aug. 1893. Court Order to continue winding up under supervision 20 Sept. 1893. Final meeting return regd. 27 Dec. 1895. Court Order to dissolve 16 Jan. 1896 1894

Mundakayam Valley Rubber Co. Ld. Regd. 1905. Vol. liq. (members') 25 May 1961. Contributories received in exchange for their holdings £2 13s. 10d. per share of £1 held. Final meeting return regd. 28 Mar. 1962 1963

Munderi Rubber Syndicate Ld. Regd. 1908. Vol. liq. 13 Oct. 1910. Final meeting return regd. 17 Aug. 1914 1911

Mundleyes & Holt Gas Co. Ld. Regd 1911. Dissolved 1 May 1949. undertaking being vested in Eastern Area Gas Board under Gas Act 1948. Holders of 7½% preference shares (of £1) were entitled to receive £1 10s. British Gas 3% guaranteed stock 1990–95 for each share held. 1952

Munga Tobacco Plantation Ld. Regd. 1912. Vol. liq. 8 Apr. 1918. Final meeting return regd. 25 Oct. 1922 1918

Mungana (Chillagoe) Mining Co. Ld. Inc. Queensland 1901. Wound up Apr. 1912. for reconstruction as Mungana Mining Co. Ld., in which company shareholders were entitled to 1 share of 6s. (credited with 5s. paid) for each share of 5s. held 1913

Mungledye Tea Co. Ld. Regd. 1874. Removed from Register 1901 1901

Munich Ice Co. Ld. Regd. 1884. Vol. liq. 21 Feb. 1887. Assets were acquired by United Anglo-Continental Ice Co. Ld., in which company shareholders were entitled to an equal number of shares. Removed from Register 1906 1888

Municipal Freehold Land Co. Ld. Regd. 1881. Under provisions of a Scheme of Arrangement effective 1 Oct. 1969, undertaking and assets acquired by Municipal Properties Ld., in which company shareholders received 2 ordinary shares (of 10s.) for each share (of £1) held. Company was dissolved under Section 208 of Companies Act 1948 on 22 Mar. 1970 1970

Municipal House Property Trust Ld. Regd. 1882. Under provisions of a Scheme of Arrangement effective 1 Oct. 1969 undertaking and assets acquired by Municipal Properties Ld., in which company shareholders received 5 ordinary shares (of 10s.) for every 2 shares (of £1) held. Company was dissolved under Section 208 of Companies Act 1948 on 22 Mar. 1970 1970

Municipal Trust Co. Ld. Regd. 1879. On 1 Jan. 1974 undertaking and assets transferred to Second Consolidated Trust Ld. (now Drayton Consolidated Tr. Ld.). Ordinary shareholders received 141 shares for every 100 ordinary; 1 3·5% preference share for every £1 preference stock. Holders of 4½% debenture stock and 6½% convertible unsecured loan stock received a like amount of 4¾% debenture stock 1983 and 6½% B loan stock 1996 respectively. Company dissolved under Section 208 of Companies Act 1948 on 13 July 1976 1977-8

Municipality of Para Improvements Ld. Regd. 1907 as Para Improvements Ld.; name changed Nov. 1909. Vol. liq. 28 July 1916. Final meeting return regd. 1 Feb. 1921 1917

Munnik Myburgh Asbestos (K.H.) Ld. In liquidaton. Direct controlling interest was held by Cape Asbestos Co. Ld. 1941

Munro (James) & Son Ld. Regd. Edinburgh 1904. Vol. liq. 21 Jan. 1926. All creditors were to be paid in full. Controlling interest was held by Macdonald, Greenlees, Williams (Distillers) Ld. Final meeting return regd. 15 Dec. 1926 1926

Munster Bank Ld. Undertaking was acquired by Munster and Leinster Bank Ld. in 1885 1887

Muntz's Metal Co. Ld. Regd. 1863. Vol. liq. 11 June 1890. Reconstructed as company of same name. Holders of every £25 paid-up capital were entitled to 2 fully-paid preference and 3 fully-paid ordinary shares of £5. Final meeting return regd. 4 May 1891 1908

Muntz's Metal Co. Ld. Regd. 1890. Vol. liq. 25 Mar. 1929. Undertaking was acquired by Elliott's Metal Co. Ld. Final meeting return regd.4 Jan.1930 1930

Murchison Associated (Ceylon) Ld. Regd. 1913. Vol. liq. 17 Jan. 1916. The property was sold to Ceylon

VOL. FOR

Consolidated Estates Ld. for 100,000 fully-paid shares of 2s. Final meeting return regd. 2 Jan. 1917 1916

Murchison Associated Gold Mines Ld. Regd. 1900. Reconstructed 1901 as company of same name. Shareholders were entitled to 2 fully-paid shares of 5s. for each share of 10s. held, and an option (since expired) over further shares at par. Removed from Register 1910 1907

Murchison Associated Gold Mines Ld. Regd. 1901. Reconstructed 1907 as company of same name. Shareholders were entitled to 1 share of 5s. (credited with 4s. paid) for each share of 5s. held. Removed from Register 1911 1908

Murchison Associated Gold Mines Ld. Regd. 1907. Vol. liq. 24 Dec. 1909. Reconstructed as Murchison Associated Ld., in which company shareholders were entitled to 1 share of 1s. (credited with 6d. paid) for each share of 5s. held. Final meeting return regd. 4 July 1911. Court Order declared dissolution void 25 June 1912. Final meeting return regd. 4 Mar. 1914 1910

Murchison Associated Ld. Regd. 1909. Vol. liq. 11 Apr. 1913. Reconstructed as Murchison Associated (Ceylon) Ld., in which company shareholders were entitled to 1 share of 1s. (credited with 6d. paid) for each share of 1s. held. Final meeting return regd. 2 Jan. 1917 1914

Murchison Crown Exploration & Mining Co. Ld. Regd. 1889. Vol. liq. 15 July 1892. Properties were acquired by Central African & Zoutpansberg Exploration Co. Ld. for 220,000 fully-paid shares of 5s. and an option (since expired) over further shares. Final meeting return regd. 19 Feb. 1895 1893

Murchison Diamond & Gold Mines Ld. Regd. 1895. Court Order to wind up 17 May 1899. Removed from Register 1908 1900

Murchison Gift Gold Mining Co. Ld. Regd. 1895. Vol. liq. 25 Mar. 1897. Reconstructed as Polar Star Proprietary Ld. in which company shareholders were entitled to 1 share of 10s. (credited with 9s. paid) for each share of 10s. held. Final meeting return regd. 24 Mar. 1898 1898

Murchison Gold Development Ld. Regd. 1934. Vol. liq. (members') 5 Sept. 1941. Winding-up Order 18 Mar. 1946. No capital returned to contributories. Liquidator released 26 Jan. 1956. Struck off Register 17 Mar. 1961 1956

Murchison Goldfields Ld. Regd. 1895. Vol. liq. 29 Jan. 1897. Reconstructed 1897 as Ontario Ld., in which company shareholders were entitled to 1 share of 5s. (credited with 3s. 6d. paid) for each share of 5s. held. Final meeting return regd. 21 Apr. 1898 1904

Murchison New Chum Gold Mines Ld. Regd. 1895. Vol. liq. 7 Apr. 1899. Reconstructed as Chums Consolidated Ld., in which company shareholders were entitled to 1 share of 10s. (credited with 7s. 6d. paid) for each share of £1 held. Final meeting return regd. 11 Aug. 1900 1902

Murchison Proprietary (Transvaal) Ld. Regd. 1902. Vol. liq. Sept. 1906. Removed from Register 1912 1907

Murchison Prospecting Syndicate Ld. Regd. 1895. Vol. liq. 3 May 1898. Final meeting return regd. 31 May 1900 1899

Murchison United Gold Mines Ld. Regd. 1895. Removed from Register 1905 1899

Murchison (Western Australia) Gold Syndicate Ld. Regd. 1895. Removed from Register 1906 1899

Murex Co. Ld. Regd. 1913. Vol. liq. 7 June 1920. Reconstructed as Murex Ld., in which company shareholders were entitled to 1 share of 2s. 6d. for each share of 5s. held. Final meeting return regd. 25 Apr. 1924 1921

Murex Magnetic Co. Ld. Regd. 1909. Vol. liq. June 1913 for reconstruction as Murex Co. Ld., in which company shareholders were entitled to 1 fully-paid share of 5s. for each share of £1 held and the option of subscribing pro rata at par for 38,698 new shares. Struck off Register 1922 1914

Murman Coast Co. Ld. Regd. 1902. Court Order to wind up 1905. Removed from Register 1914 1906

Murphy (Michael) Ld. Regd. Dublin. In liquidation. Undertaking acquired by British & Irish Steam Packet Co. Ld. 1940

Murray Hill Trust Co. Absorbed in Feb. 1930 by Bank of America National Association 1931

Murray Minor Investment Trust Ld. Regd. in Edinburgh as private company 2 Feb. 1962 as Murray Minor Ld.; converted into public company and name changed to Glenmurray Investment Trust Ld. on 20 July 1966 and to present title 4 Dec. 1979. Vol. liq. (members') 11 Feb. 1981. Shareholders received 2 units Murray Smaller Companies Fund for each ordinary or B ordinary share of 25p. Undistributable

See Stock Exchange Year-Book.

balance of £385·27 paid into Companies' Liquidation Account. Final meeting return regd. 12 Apr. 1983 .... **1983–4**

Murray Minor Ld. See Murray Minor Investment Trust Ld.

Murrayfield Ice Rink and Sports Stadium Ld. Regd. in Edinburgh 1938. Vol. liq. (creditors') 29 June 1956. Assets realised insufficient to pay creditors in full. Final meeting return regd. 24 Sept. 1958 .... **1959**

Murrell's Wharf Ld. Regd. 1925. Vol. liq. (creditors') 12 Nov. 1934. Direct controlling interest held by Wiggins & Co. (Hammersmith) Ld. Final meeting return regd. 16 Oct. 1935 .... **1935**

Murrieta & Co. Ld. Regd. 1915. Vol. liq. (members') 12 Dec. 1952. Final meeting return regd. 27 Nov. 1954 **1934**

Murrieta (C. de) & Co. Ld. Regd. 1891. Receivers for debenture holders appointed 16 Mar. 1892. Struck off Register 1926 .... **1895**

Murrin Copper Mines Ld. Regd. 1902. Vol. liq. 22 Mar. 1905. Final meeting return regd. 26 May 1905 ... ***1905**

Murtega Minerals Co. Ld. Regd. 1900. Struck off Register 1915 .... **1913**

Murton (George) & Co. Ld. Regd. 1901. Vol. liq. (members') 28 Sept. 1944. A direct controlling interest was held by Bleachers' Association Ld. (later Whitecroft Industrial Holdings Ld.). Final meeting return regd. 13 Jan. 1945 .... **1946**

Mushets Ld. Regd. Edinburgh 1891. Vol. liq. Aug. 1898. Final meeting return regd. 30 July 1900 .... **1899**

Muskegon & Grand Rapids & Indiana Railroad Co. Inc. Michigan 1886. Undertaking was acquired in 1917 by Grand Rapids & Indiana Railway Co., which company held all capital stock. The Grand Rapids and Indiana Railroad 5% 1st mortgage bonds (Muskegon Division) taken over by acquiring company, were redeemed in July 1926 .... **1918**

Musker (C. & A.) (1901) Ld. Regd. 1901. Receiver appointed June 1910. Struck off Register 1921 .... ***1912**

Musselburgh & District Electric Light & Traction Co. Ld. Regd. 1905. Dissolved 1 Apr. 1948, undertaking being vested in British (later Central) Electricity Authority and South-East Scotland Area Board under Electricity Act 1947. Ordinary stockholders were entitled to receive an equal amount of British Electricity 3% guaranteed stock (1968–73) **1949**

Musselburgh Gas Co. Constd. as Musselburgh & Portobello Gas Light Co. 1831; regd. as Musselburgh Gas Light Co. (unlimited) 1886; reinc. as above by Special Act 1909. Dissolved 1 May 1949, undertaking being vested in Scottish Area Gas Board under Gas Act 1948. Holders of securities were entitled to receive British Gas 3% guaranteed stock 1990–95 as follows:

	£	s.	d.
Ord. shares (5% stand.) (of £1)	2	0	0
5% pref. shares (of £10)	11	10	0	**1952**

Muswell Hill & Palace Railway Co. Inc. by Special Act 1886. Purchased by Great Northern Railway Co. under Act of 1911. Holders of debenture stock and bonds were repaid in full, ordinary stockholders received £8 for every £100 held **1912**

Mutamba Estates Ld, Regd. 1922. Vol. liq. 16 June 1924. Undertaking acquired by Mutamba Sugar Factory Ld. Holders of A certificates of indebtedness were entitled to an equal amount of 7% debentures of Mutamba Sugar Factory Ld., holders of B certificates of indebtedness to an equal amount of fully-paid shares of that company and holders of shares to 1 fully-paid share (of 2s.) of that company for every 2 shares (of 1s.) held. Final meeting return regd. 30 Apr. 1951 .... **1952**

Mutamba Sugar Estates Ld. Regd. 1912. Vol. liq. Mar. 1922. The assets and undertaking were acquired by Mutamba Sugar Factory Ld. and Mutamba Estates Ld. Holders of prior lien debenture stock or debentures were entitled to an equal amount of A or B certificates in Mutamba Estates Ld. respectively and an option (since expired) over shares at par. Shareholders were entitled to 2 shares of 2s. (credited with 1s. paid) in Mutamba Sugar Factory Ld. for every 3 shares of 2s. held plus option over shares in Mutamba Estates Ld. at par. Struck off Register Feb. 1932 .... **1932**

Mutamba Sugar Factory Ld. Regd. 1922. Struck off Register 20 June 1947 .... **1947**

Mutual Accident Association Ld. Regd. 1881. Business acquired in 1890 by Palatine Insurance Co. Ld. Removed from Register 1907 .... **1900**

Mutual Cycle Manufacturing & Supply Co. Ld. Regd. 1895. Removed from Register 1901 .... **1899**

Mutual Exploration, Finance & Underwriting Corporation Ld. Regd. 1896. Struck off Register 23 July 1901 **1902**

Mutual Fire Insurance Corporation Ld. Regd. 1870 as unlimited; re-regd. as limited 1880. Vol. liq. 30 May 1890. Final meeting return regd. 19 July 1893 ...... **1900**

Mutual Life Association of Australasia. Inc. New South Wales by Special Act 1869. Undertaking was acquired in 1907 by Citizen's Life Assurance Co. Ld. (later Mutual Life and Citizen's Assurance Co. Ld.) **1906**

Mutual Life Assurance Society. Founded 1834. Regd. 1871. Reconstructed 1896 as National Mutual Life Assurance Society. Dissolved by Special Act 7 July 1896 .... **1896**

Mutual Life Insurance Co. of New York. Inc. by Special Charter in New York 1842. The undertaking was acquired by Sun Life Assurance Co. of Canada in 1924 .... **1933**

Mutual Reserve Life Insurance Co. (of New York). Formed 1880. Established 1881 as Mutual Reserve Fund Life Association; name changed Apr. 1902, when company was incorporated under legal reserve statute of New York State. The British offices were closed in 1906 .... **1907**

Mutual Steam Ship Co. Ld. See Commercial Steam Ship Co. Ld.

Mutual Telephone Co. Ld. Regd. 1898. Vol. liq. Dec. 1907. Removed from Register 1909 .... **1908**

Mutual Tontine Westminster Chambers Assn. Ld. See Westminster Chambers Association Ld.

Mutual Trust Ld. Regd. 1889. Vol. liq. 11 Dec. 1893. Final meeting return regd. 28 May 1894 .... **1894**

Mwyndy Iron Ore Co. Ld. Regd. 1861. Court Order to continue winding up under supervision 11 July 1884. Final meeting return regd. 15 Feb. 1890 .... **1885**

Myalls & Peak Hill Gold Mines Ld. Regd. 1904. Vol. liq. 28 Nov. 1913. Final meeting return regd. 16 Mar. 1915 .... **1914**

Myalls & Peak Hill Gold Mines (1914) Ld. Regd. 1914. Vol. liq. 14 May 1914. Final meeting return regd.8 Oct. 1914 .... **1915**

Myalls United Gold Mining Co. Ld. Regd. 1895. Reconstructed 1904 as Myalls and Peak Hill Gold Mines Ld. in which company shareholders were entitled to 1 share of 10s. (credited with 8s. 6d. paid) for each share of £1 held. Removed from Register 1905 .... **1908**

Myatt (Frank), Ld. Regd. 1920. All capital was owned by Holt Brewery Co. Ld. Vol. liq. (members') 29 Mar. 1966. Final meeting return regd. 30 Dec. 1966 **1963**

Myers, Gilson & Rose Ld. See Myers, Rose & Co. Ld.

Myers Patent Box & Barrel Machinery Co. Ld. Regd. 1887. Vol. liq. 25 Feb. 1892. Final meeting return regd. 19 Dec. 1893 .... **1893**

Myers, Rose & Co. Ld. Regd. 1900 as Myers, Gilson & Rose Ld.; name changed 1903. Vol. liq. 6 May 1918. Undertaking was acquired by Rose, Smith & Co. Ld. Final meeting return regd. 11 Mar. 1924 .... **1919**

Myers (Walter & George) Ld. Regd. 1901. Vol. liq. Apr. 1910. Removed from Register 1913 .... **1911**

Mynpacnt (Luipaard's Vlei) Gold Mining Co. Ld. Regd. 1889. Vol. liq. 30 July 1891. Absorbed by Luipaard's Vlei Estate and Gold Mining Co. Ld. Final meeting return regd. 5 July 1893 .... **1892**

Mynpacht Randfontein Gold Mining Co. Ld. Inc. Transvaal 1895. Vol. liq. 1907 for amalgamation with two other companies under the title of Randfontein Central Gold Mining Co. Ld. in which company shareholders were entitled to receive 1 share of £1 for every 2 shares of £1 held............. **1908**

Mynyddislwyn Collieries Ld. Regd. 1900. Removed from Register 1905 .... **1903**

Mysore Coffee Co. Ld. Regd. 1866. Vol. liq. 22 Apr. 1881. Taken over by Mysore Estates Co. Ld. Final meeting return regd. 7 Jan. 1891 .... ***1882**

Mysore Estates Co. Ld. Regd. 1881. Court Orders: to wind up 23 Apr. 1887; to dissolve 9 Feb. 1892 ... **1888**

Mysore Estates Co. Ld. Regd. 1889. Vol. liq. 20 Aug. 1897. Final meeting return regd. 21 Jan. 1903 ...... **1898**

Mysore Gold Mining Co., Ld. Regd. 1880. Vol. liq. (members') 18 Apr. 1955. Stockholders were entitled to receive 4 units of stock (of Rs.5) of Mysore Gold Mining Co. (KGF) Ld. for every 3 units (of 10s. held) plus 2s. 7½d. in cash for every 10s. stock held. £6,987 10s. was paid into Companies' Liquidation Account. Final meeting return regd. 13 Jan. 1959 **1960**

Mysore Gold Mining Co. (KGF), Ld. Inc. in India 1950. Under the Kolar Gold Mining Undertakings (Acquisition) Act 1956 the undertaking and assets were acquired by the Mysore Government for £339,241 (Rs. 45,31,080). Vol. liq. (members') 31 Jan. 1957. Capital restored to contributories—Rs. 2·905 per stock unit (of Rs. 5). Rs 647·17 was paid into Companies' Liquidation Account in respect of unclaimed dividends, Rs. 31877·03 in respect of unclaimed distributions and Rs. 8974·00 in respect of undistributed surplus. Final meeting return regd. 17 June 1961 .... **1962**

Mysore Harnhalli Gold Mining Co. Ld. Regd. 1894. Vol. liq. 25 Feb. 1902. Reconstructed as Mysore United Gold Co. Ld. (later New Exploring & Finance Co. Ld.), in which company shareholders were entitled to 3 shares of 5s. for every 2 shares of £1 held. Final meeting return regd. 13 Apr. 1905 .... **1905**

Mysore Nagar Gold Mines Ld. Regd. 1891. Removed from Register 1906 .... **1906**

Mysore Reefs & General Exploration Co. Ld. Regd. 1902. Reconstructed 1905 as Mysore Reefs (1905) and Explorers Ld., In which company shareholders were entitled to 1 ordinary or preference share of 5s. (credited as fully-paid) for each share of £1 of same class held. Removed from Register 1908 .... **1906**

Mysore Reefs Co. Ld. Regd. 1888. Vol. liq. 10 July 1891. Reconstructed as Mysore Reefs Gold Mining Co. Ld., in which company shareholders were entitled to 1 share of £1 (credited with 15s. paid) for each share of £1 held. Final meeting return regd. 10 July 1894 **1892**

Mysore Reefs Gold Mining Co. Ld. Regd. 1880. Reconstructed 1885 as Mysore Reefs Gold Mining Co. (1885) Ld., in which company shareholders were entitled to 1 share of £1 (credited with 15s. paid) for each share held. Court Orders; to wind up Apr. 1883: to dissolve 22 Feb. 1889 .... **1888**

Mysore Reefs Gold Mining Co. Ld. Regd. 1891. Vol. liq. 7 Jan. 1895. Final meeting return regd. 27 Sept. 1897 **1897**

Mysore Reefs Gold Mining Co. (1885) Ld. Regd. 1885. Vol. liq. Mar. 1888. Reconstructed as Mysore Reefs Co. Ld in which company shareholders were entitled to 1 share of £1 (credited with 15s. paid) for each share of £1 held. Final meeting return regd. 25 Mar. 1889 .... **1889**

Mysore Reefs (Kangundy) Co. Ld. Regd. 1895. Reconstructed 1897 as company of same name. Shareholders were entitled to 1 share of £1 (credited with 15s. paid) in new company for each share of £1 held. Removed from Register 1905 .... **1899**

Mysore Reefs (Kangundy) Ld. Regd. 1897. Vol. liq. 30 June 1899. Reconstructed 1899 as Mysore Reefs (Kangundy) Mining Co. Ld. in which company shareholders were entitled to 1 ordinary share of £1 (credited with 15s. paid) for each share of £1 held; preference shareholders were entitled to an equal number of fully-paid preference shares of £1. Final meeting return regd. 6 Nov. 1899 .... **1902**

Mysore Reefs (Kangundy) Mining Co. Ld. Regd. 1899. Vol. liq. 4 Sept. 1902. Reconstructed 1902 as Mysore Reefs and General Exploration Co. Ld., in which company shareholders were entitled to 1 share of £1 (credited as fully-paid) for each fully-paid share of £1 held. Final meeting return regd. 8 Dec. 1904 .. **1905**

Mysore Reefs (1905) & Explorers Ld. Regd. 1905. Vol. liq. 10 July 1912 for reconstruction as Olga Exploration Ld. in which company shareholders were entitled to 1 share of 5s. (credited with 2s. 6d. paid) for each ordinary share of 5s. held, or 2 fully-paid shares of 5s. for each preference share of 5s. held. Final meeting return regd. 31 Mar. 1914 .... **1913**

Mysore Rubber & Coffee Plantations Ld. Regd. 1920. Vol. liq. 4 Feb. 1929. Undertaking and assets were acquired by Bajau Rubber & Produce Estates Ld. in which company shareholders were entitled to 1 fully-paid share of 2s. for every 4 shares of 2s. held. Final meeting return regd. 25 Oct. 1929 .... **1929**

Mysore United Gold Co. Ld. *See* New Exploring & Finance Co. Ld.

Mysore West Gold Co. Ld. Regd. 1888. Vol. liq. 9 May 1894. Reconstructed as company of same name. Shareholders were entitled to 1 share of £1 (credited with 17s. 6d. paid) in new company for each share of £1 held. Final meeting return regd. 12 Oct. 1895 **1898**

Mysore West Gold Co. Ld. Regd. 1894. Vol. liq. 27 July 1898. Reconstructed as company of same name. Shareholders were entitled to 1 share of £1 (credited with 15s. paid) in new company for each share of £1 held. Final meeting return regd. 20 Jan. 1899 ..... **1908**

Mysore West Gold Co. Ld. Regd. 1898. Vol. liq. 11 Aug. 1911. Capital returned to contributories—2s. 4d. per share of £1 at Feb. 1912; further payments (if any) not known. Final meeting return regd. 23 Oct. 1912 **1912**

Mysore West Gold Mining Co. Ld. Regd. 1886. Vol. liq. 23 Nov. 1888. Reconstructed as Mysore West Gold Co. Ld., In which company shareholders were entitled to 3 shares of £1 (credited with 15s. paid) for every 2 shares of £1 held. Final meeting return regd. 8 Mar. 1890 .... **1894**

Mysore-Wynaad Consolidated Gold Mining Co. Ld. Regd. 1886. Vol. liq. 9 May 1894. Reconstructed as company of same name. Shareholders were entitled to 1 share of £1 (credited with 17s. 6d. paid) in new

company for every 2 shares of £1 held. Final meeting return regd. 12 Oct. 1895 .... **1898**

Mysore-Wynaad Consolidated Gold Mining Co. Ld. Regd. 1894. Vol. liq. 27 July 1898. Reconstructed as Mysore-Wynaad Gold Co. Ld., in which company shareholders were entitled to 1 share of £1 (credited with 15s. paid) for each share of £1 held. Final meeting return regd. 20 Jan. 1899 .... **1908**

Mysore-Wynaad Gold Co. Ld. Regd. 1898. Vol. liq. 11 Aug. 1911. Capital returned to contributories—2s. 3d. per share of £1 at Feb. 1912; further payments (if any) not known. Final meeting return regd. 23 Oct. 1912 .... **1912**

N

N. A. P. Bread Co. Ld. Regd. 1897. Removed from Register 1901 .... **1900**

N.B.H.C. Holdings Ld. Inc. 1971. Vol. liq. (members') 29 Nov. 1973. Return to contributories—6 ord. shares in Bourgainville Copper Ld. and 5 ord. shares in Australian, Mining & Smelting Ld. for every 5 ord. shares held. Dissolved 4 Sept. 1974 .... **1976-7**

N.C. Metal Co. Ld. Regd. 1926. Vol. liq. (memhers') 17 June 1935. Undertaking acquired by Amalgamated Oxides Ld., in which company shareholders were entitled to 4 (approx.) fully-paid ordinary of 10s. for every 5 shares of £1 held. Final meeting return regd. 4 Dec. 1936 .... **1936**

N.C. Zinc Oxide Co. Ld. Regd. 1927. Vol. liq. (members') 28 June 1935. Shareholders received 17,252 fully-paid shares of 10s. in Amalgamated Oxides Ld. Final meeting return regd. 18 June 1936 **1936**

N. F. X. Ld. Regd. 1934 at Yuca Films Ld.; name changed Apr. 1935 to Nuro Ld. and as above in Apr. 1936. Vol. liq. (members') 22 June 1936. Undertaking acquired by Nuro (Biggleswade) Ld. for 338,393 ordinary shares of 5s. Final meeting return regd. 7 Sept. 1936 .... **1938**

N. H. & B. Collieries Ld. Regd. 1944. Vol. liq. (members') 23 July 1952. Capital returned to contributories—2s. 6·58608d. per 1d. stock. £17,011 9s. 8d. was paid into Companies' Liquidation Account. Final meeting return regd. 26 Oct. 1956 **1958**

N. P. M. Co. Ld. Regd. 1888 as St. Neots Paper Mill Co. Ld.; name subsequently changed. All capital was owned by Wiggins, Teape & Co. Ld. Vol. liq. (members') 28 May 1954. Final meeting return regd. 18 Dec. 1957 .... **1940**

N.T. Artificial Wool Co. Ld. Regd. 1929. Vol. liq. (members') 30 Nov. 1936. Capital returned to contributories—11s. 4¼d. per preference share of £1. £45 8s. 3d. was paid into Companies' Liquidation Account. Final meeting return regd. 15 Sept. 1937 **1937**

N.V. Gemeenschappelijk Bezit van Andeelen Handel-Mij. H. Albert de Bary & Co. N.V. All capital was acquired by Bary (H. Albert de) & Co. in 1939 in exchange for Fl. 5,000,000 in shares.................. **1941**

N. V. Hollandsche Vereeniging tot Exploitatie van Margarine Fabrieken. *See* Dutch Co. for the Exploitation of Margarine Fabrieken.

Naamlooze Vennootschap Hollandscbe Kunstzijde Industrie. Inc. Holland 1919. The outstanding 6% convertible sterling bonds were redeemed at 140% on 1 Feb. 1929 .... **1953**

Naamlooze Vennootschap Maatscbappij voor Tabakhandel "Tabacus." Inc. Amsterdam 1923. Vol. liq. 1928 **1929**

Nacupai Gold Mining Co. Ld. Regd. 1885. Vol. liq. 6 May 1886. Property acquired by Venezuelan Austin Gold Mining Co. Ld. Struck off Register 20 Mar. 1906 .... **1887**

Nadar Copper Mines Ld. Regd. 1907. Vol. liq. Aug. 1910. Removed from Register 1912 .... **1911**

Naga Ali Tea Co. Ld. Regd. 1902. Vol. liq. 12 Feb. 1926. Capital returned to contributories—£14 per share of £5 at Oct. 1926; further payments (if any) not known. Final meeting return regd. 23 Dec. 1929 **1927**

Nagamally Tea Co. Ld. Regd. 1889. Vol. liq. 11 Mar. 1897. Final meeting return regd. 8 Mar. 1898....... **1898**

Nagrom Syndicate Ld. Regd. 1913. Vol. liq. 6 Oct. 1920. Capital returned to contributories—7½d. per share of 1s. 3d. in Dec. 1920; further payments (if any) not known. Final meeting return regd. 6 Apr. 1926 ... **1921**

Nahor Rani Tea Co. Ld. Regd. 1894. Vol. liq. 15 Nov. 1898. Capital returned to contributories—£2 per share of £1 at Nov. 1898; further payments (if any) not known. Final meeting return regd. 16 Mar. 1899 **1899**

Nailsworth Brewery Co. Ld. Regd. 1889. Vol. liq. May 1908. Undertaking and assets were acquired by Cheltenham Original Brewery Co. Ld. (later Cheltenham & Hereford Breweries Ld.) in which company shareholders were entitled to 2 ordinary shares of £5 for each ordinary share of £10 held or 2 preference shares of £5 for each preference share of £10 held. Holders of debentures were entitled to an equal amount of debentures in new company. Removed from Register 1909 .... **1909**

Nairn Gas Light Co. Ld. Regd. in Edinburgh 1875. Dissolved 1 May 1949, undertaking being vested in Scottish Area Gas Board under Gas Act 1948. Holders of ordinary shares (of £5) were entitled to receive £8 5s. British Gas 3% guaranteed stock 1990–95 for each share held. **1952**

Nairobi Electric Power and Lighting Co. Ld. Regd. 1906. Vol. liq. 29 Mar. 1922. Undertaking and assets were acquired by East African Power & Lighting Co. Debenture holders were repaid in cash at par. Capital returned to contributories—£1 6s. per share of £1 at Oct. 1922; further payments (if any) not known. Final meeting return regd. 19 Sept. 1923.. **1923**

Nakusp & Slocan Railway Co. Inc. 1893 in British Columbia. All issued capital held by Canadian Pacific Railway Co. Bonds repaid July 1918 .... **1918**

Nalder & Collyer's Brewery Co. Ld. *See below.*

Nalder's Brewery & Investment Trust Ld. Regd. 1888 as Nalder & Collyer's Brewery Co. Ld.; name changed Apr. 1941. Nearly all capital was acquired by City of London Brewery & Investment Trust Ld. Vol. liq. (members') 29 July 1960. Final meeting return regd. 23 Jan. 1962 .... **1953**

Namaqua Copper Co. Ld. Regd. 1888. Vol. liq. (members') 7 Dec. 1934. Capital returned to contributories—£2,161 15s. Final meeting return regd. 29 May 1937 .... **1935**

Namaqua Diamonds Ld. Inc. Cape Province 1922. Vol. liq. 1931 .... **1932**

Namaqua River Lands, Ld. Regd. 1920 as South African Agricultural & Ostrich Farms Ld.; name changed in July 1920. Vol. liq. (creditors') 25 Mar. 1935. A compulsory winding-up order was subsequently made in South Africa. A first distribution was made to debenture holders by liquidator in South Africa and a final distribution was made in Apr. 1946. There were no surplus assets available for contributories **1948**

Namaqua United Copper Co. Ld. Regd. 1887. Vol. liq. 15 May 1888 for reconstruction as Namaqua Copper Co. Ld., in which company shareholders were entitled to 3 shares of £2 for each share of £7 (£6 paid) held. Final meeting return regd. 22 May 1889 **1909**

Namma Gold Dredging Co. Ld. Regd. 1905. Vol. liq. Dec. 1906. Removed from Register 1908 .... **1907**

Namoi Pastoral Co. Ld. Inc. New South Wales 1880. Entire debenture issue repaid in 1904. .... **1905**

Namur & Liège Railway Co. Inc. Belgium 1845. Placed in liquidation 30 Sept. 1938. Liquidation was completed 20 July 1946 .... **1948**

Nanette Rubber Plantations Ld. Regd. 1926. Vol. liq. (members') 12 June 1934. Undertaking and assets were acquired by Johore River Rubber Plantations Ld. in which company shareholders were entitled to 1 share of 2s. (credited as fully-paid) for every 4 shares of 2s. held. The debenture stockholders received 165,000 fully-paid shares of 2s. in respect of the £15,000 stock held. Final meeting return regd. 1 Sept. 1936 .... **1935**

Nannine Consolidated Gold Mines Ld. Regd. 1899. Removed from Register 1904 .... **1902**

Nannine Goldfields Ld. Regd. 1899. Undertaking and assets were acquired by Star of the East (1903) Ld. for 127,431 shares of 10s. (credited with 7s. 6d. paid). Removed from Register 1907 .... **1903**

Nantes Butter & Refrigerating Co. Ld. *See* United Butter Cos. of France Ld.

Nantille Vale Gas Co. Ld. Regd. 1921. Dissolved 1 May 1949, undertaking being vested in Wales Area Gas Board under Gas Act 1948. Holders of ordinary shares (of £1) were entitled to receive British Gas 3% guaranteed stock 1990–95 for each share held (amount not yet fixed) **1952**

Nantwich & Market Drayton Railway Co. Inc. by Special Act 1861. Under Great Western Railway Act of 1897 the undertaking was amalgamated with that company. Ordinary shareholders received £18 5% consolidated guaranteed stock per share of £20 **1898**

Nantwich Gas Co. Ld. Regd. 1869. Vol. liq. 3 Oct. 1904. The undertaking was acquired by Urban District Council of Nantwich. Removed from Register 1905 **1905**

Nantwich Gas Co. Ld. Regd. 1937; statutory powers 1938. Dissolved 1 May 1949. undertaking being vested in North Western Area Gas Board under Gas Act 1948. Holders of 4% red. pref. shares (1949—of £1) were entitled to receive £1 0s. 1d. British Gas 3% guaranteed stock 1990–95 for each share held **1952**

Nanwa Gold Mines Ld. Regd. 1902. The sum of £35,500 was paid into the High Court following the discharge of an appointed receiver in 1957. A first

and final distribution of £37 17s. 9d. per £100 of 5% 10-year secured registered convertible notes was made in 1959 after allowance for preferential creditors and costs had been met. Struck off Register 24 Nov. 1966. .... **1960**

Naparima Oilfields of Trinidad Ld. Regd. 1920. Vol. liq. 30 Mar. 1927. Final meeting return regd. 4 Apr. 1928 .... **1928**

Napier & Weir Ld. Regd. 1896. Capital returned to contributories—£4,500 at 5 Nov. 1903; further payments (if any) not known. Removed from Register 1911 .... **1904**

Napoleon (B.M.L.) Mines. Inc. Victoria 1934. Vol. liq. 1940 .... **1941**

Naraguta Acquisitions Ld. Regd. 1926 as Nigerian & General Prospectors Ld.; name changed Sept. 1926. Court Order to wind up July 1930. Struck off Register 9 June 1936 .... **1937**

Naraguta Durumi Areas Ld. Regd. 1929. Vol. liq. (members') 8 Mar. 1934. Undertaking and assets were acquired by Naraguta Tin Mines Ld. in which company shareholders were entitled to 1 share of 10s. (credited as fully-paid) for every 5 shares of 5s. held. £89 6s. 6d. was paid into Companies' Liquidation Account in respect of unclaimed proceeds of fractional shares. Final meeting return regd. 29 Nov. 1935 .... **1935**

Naraguta Extended (Nigeria) Tin Mines Ld. Regd. 1911. Vol. liq. 12 Aug 1930. Reconstructed as Naraguta Extended Areas Ld. (later Forum Extended Ld.), in which company shareholders were entitled to 3 shares of 2s. (credited as fully-paid) for every 2 shares of 5s. held. Final meeting return regd. 24 June 1930 .... **1930**

Naraguta Korot Areas Ld. Regd. 1925. Vol liq. (members') 8 Mar. 1934. Undertaking and assets were acquired by Naraguta Tin Mines Ld. in which company shareholders were entitled to 1 share of 10s. (credited as fully-paid) for every 5 shares of 10s. held. £42 3s. was paid into Companies' Liquidation Account. Final meeting return regd. 29 Nov. 1935 **1935**

Naraguta (Nigeria) Tin Mines Ld. Regd. 1910. Vol. liq. (members') 8 Mar. 1934. Undertaking and assets were acquired by Naraguta Tin Mines Ld. in which company shareholders were entitled to 1 share of 10s. (credited as fully-paid) for each £1 paid-up capital held. Final meeting return regd. 29 Nov. 1935 .... **1935**

Naraguta Tin Mines Ld. Regd. 1934. Vol. liq. 20 Aug. 1957. Capital returned to contributories—5s. 2·4d. per share (of 10s.) £7,395 was paid into Companies' Liquidation Account. Final meeting return regd. 21 Sept.1962 .... **1964**

Narquah Syndicate Ld. Regd. 1901. Vol. liq. 17 Dec. 1917. Final meeting return regd. 13 Feb. 1920 .... **1918**

Nashville, Chattanooga & St. Louis Railway. Chartered in 1845 as Nashville & Chattanooga Railroad Co.; name changed 1873. Nearly all issued capital held by Louisville & Nashville Railroad Co. All bonds redeemed Apr. 1928 .... **1927**

Nashville, Florence & Sheffield Railway. Organised Tennessee and Alabama 1887. Purchased under foreclosure in 1900 by Louisville & Nashville Railroad Co. 93% of capital was held by acquiring company. The 5% 1st mortgage 50-year gold bonds were endorsed by acquiring company, these bonds were redeemed in Aug. 1937 .... **1900**

Nasmyth, Wilson & Co. Ld. Regd. 1882. Vol. liq. (members') 7 Nov. 1940. Capital returned to contributories—£1 13s. 4·4d. per preference share of £1 (this included 13s. 4·4d. arrears of dividend) and 11s. 2·94d. per ordinary share of £1. Final meeting return regd. 8 Apr. 1964 .... **1965**

Nässjö-Oskarshamn New Railway Co. Inc. Sweden 1898. Shares almost entirely held in Sweden. 4% 1st mortgage bonds were repaid at 110% on 1 Aug. 1935 **1935**

Nässjö-Oskarshamn Railway Co. Inc. Sweden 1869. Undertaking taken over by Nässjö-Oskarshamn New Railway Co., in which company shareholders were entitled to receive shares of Kr.100 on payment of Kr.50 in cash and the balance in shares (the 1st class or A shares being taken at Kr.20 and the 2nd class or B shares at Kr.5 per share). The 4% 1st mortgage bonds were taken over by the new company **1908**

Natal Ammonium Ld. Regd. 1913. Vol. liq. 30 Dec. 1924. Final meeting return regd. 29 Sept. 1927 .... **1925**

Natal & Nova Cruz (Brazilian) Railway Ld. Regd. 1878 as Imperial Brazilian Natal & Nova Cruz Railway Co. Ld.; name changed Jan. 1891. Vol. liq. 1 Jan. 1902. The line was purchased by the Brazilian Government. Debenture holders were offered £150 in rescission bonds for each £100 debenture bond held or repayment in cash at par. Preferred

VOL. FOR

shareholders received £10 in rescission bonds; a cash payment of £2 per share was anticipated. Final meeting return regd. 5 Sept. 1903 .... **1903**

Natal Bank Ld. Established 1854. Inc. 1859. Business and goodwill purchased by National Bank of South Africa Ld. In 1914 .... **1915**

Natal Coal Trust Ld. Regd. 1903. Removed from Register 1913 .... **1913**

Natal Collieries & Durban Coaling Station Ld. Regd. 1896. Removed from Register 1903 .... **1900**

Natal Estates Ld. Regd. 1895. Vol. liq. 6 Dec. 1920. Undertaking was acquired by company of same name (inc. Union of South Africa). Final meeting return regd. 8 Mar. 1923 .... **1921**

Natal Graphite & Mineral Mine Ld. Regd. 1906. Vol. liq. 21 Jan. 1914. Struck off Register 3 July 1953 . **1954**

Natal Land and Colonization Co. Ld. Regd. 1860. Control transferred to South Africa in Mar. 1948 and wound up by Order of Supreme Court of South Africa on 25 May 1948 .... **1949**

Natal Motor Industries Ld. In liquidation. All capital was owned by Saker, Bartle (South Africa) Ld. (later Saker's Motor Corpn. Ld.) **1938**

Natal Navigation Collieries Ld. Inc. Transvaal 1897. Reconstructed 1902 as Natal Navigation Collieries and Estate Co. Ld. in which company shareholders were entitled to 5 shares of £1 for every 2 shares of £1 held and an option (since expired) over further shares **1903**

Natal Plantations Co. Ld. Regd. 1869. Struck off Register 31 Dec. 1895. .... **1886**

Natal Prospecting Co. Ld. Regd. 1887. Removed from Register 1910 .... **1903**

Natal Rhondda Collieries Ld. Regd. 1901. Vol. liq. July 1906. Removed from Register 1913 .... **1907**

Natal Steam Coal Co. Ld. Regd. 1897. Vol. liq. 17 Nov. 1916. Undertaking and assets were acquired by company of same name. Shareholders were entitled to 1 share of £1 (credited as fully-paid) in new company for every 2 shares of £1 held. Final meeting return regd. 16 Oct. 1917 .... **1917**

Natal (Victoria) Navigation Collieries Ld. Regd. 1902. Vol. liq. May 1906. Removed from Register 1910 **1907**

Natal-Zululand Railway Ld. Regd. 1896. Vol. liq. (members') 7 Oct. 1947. Capital returned to contributories—22s. 8d. per share of £10. £52 2s. 8d. was paid into Companies' Liquidation Account. Final meeting return regd. 8 Oct. 1948 .... **1949**

Nathan (Joseph) & Co. Ld. Regd. 1899. Vol. liq. (members') 30 Jan. 1947, the undertaking having been acquired by Glaxo Laboratories Ld. (later Glaxo Group Ld.) in which company holders of all classes of stock were entitled to equivalent amounts of similar stocks. £156 was paid into Companies' Liquidation Account. Final meeting return regd. 4 June 1951 .... **1952**

National Accident Compensation Co. Ld. Regd. 1906. Vol. liq. (members') 8 Oct. 1941. Capital returned to contributories—£1 12s. 10½d. per share of 10s. Final meeting return regd. 18 Feb. 1943............ **1942**

National Accident Insurance Co. Ld. Regd. 1894. Business was acquired in 1898 by Credit Assurance and Guarantee Corporation Ld. (later United Dominions Insurance Co. Ld.), in which company shareholders were entitled to 2 shares of £10 (credited with £5 paid) plus £1 in cash for every 10 shares held. Removed from Register 1908 .... **1900**

National Accumulator Co. Ld. Regd. 1928. Vol. liq. (members') 30 Nov. 1951. Final meeting regd. 16 Apr. 1952............ **1940**

National Agricultural Hall Co. Ld. Regd. 1884. Court Orders: to wind up 12 Jan. 1889; to dissolve 14 Mar. 1894 .... **1890**

National Amalgamated Druggists Ld. Regd. 1931. Struck off Register 29 June 1943 .... **1944**

National Arms and Ammunition Co. Ld. Regd. 1872. Vol. liq. Jan. 1883. Final meeting return regd. 22 Dec. 1896 .... **1883**

National Assurance Co. of Ireland. Established 1822. Inc. by Royal Charter 1828. Vol. liq. 1927. The fire, accident, annuity and life business was acquired by Yorkshire Fire & Life Insurance Co. (Later Yorkshire Insurance Co. Ld.)............ **1908**

National Bank of China Ld. Regd. 1891. Vol. liq. 15 July 1911. Final meeting return regd. 21 Feb. 1918 ...... **1912**

National Bank of Commerce in New York. See Bank of Commerce in New York.

National Bank of Greece. See Ethniki Trepeza tis Ellados.

National Bank of Liverpool Ld. Regd. 1863. Business acquired in 1883 by Parr's Banking Co. Ld. (later Parr's Bank Ld.). Capital returned to contributories—£17 6s. per share of £20 (£10 paid). In

VOL. FOR

liquidation in 1884. Final meeting return regd. 1 Aug. 1884 .... **1885**

National Bank of Scotland Ld. Established 1825. Inc. by Royal Charter 1831. In Sept. 1959 undertaking and assets were transferred to Commercial Bank of Scotland Ld. (later National Commercial Bank of Scotland Ld.). Stockholders were entitled to receive 5 fully-paid ordinary shares (of 10s.) for every 6 units of £1 (8s. paid) of consolidated capital stock and 1 fully-paid 5% preference share (of £1) for each £1 A stock held. Dissolved 2 May 1967 .... **1968**

National Bank of South Africa Ld. Inc. Transvaal 1890 as National Bank of South African Republic Ld.; name changed 1902. Vol. liq. Nov. 1925. Undertaking and assets were acquired by Barclays Bank D.C.O. in which company shareholders were entitled to 2 preference and 5 A shares of £1 (credited as fully-paid) for each share of £7 held **1926**

National Bank of South African Republic Ld. See National Bank of South Africa Ld.

National Bank of Turkey (Banque Nationale de Turquie). Inc. Constantinople 1909. Wound up Dec. 1931 ... **1932**

National Bank of Uruguay (Banco Nacional de la Republica Oriental del Uruguay). Established 1887. In liquidation in 1892 .... **1892**

National Bank of Wales Ld. In 1893 the business was acquired by Metropolitan Bank (of England and Wales) Ld. for cash **1894**

National Banking Co. Ld. See National Mercantile Bank Ld.

National Benefit Assurance Co. Ld. Regd. 1890 as National Benefit Trust Ld.; name changed Jan. 1912 to National Benefit Life & Property Assurance Co. Ld. and as above Feb. 1918. Court Order to wind up 25 July 1922. Struck off Register 24 Oct. 1939 .... **1940**

National Bituminous Coal & Coke Co. Inc. District of Columbia 1905. In 1914 Committee of Bondholders reported that certain titles were defective and debts existed on other properties **1916**

National British & Irish Millers' Insurance Co. Ld. Regd. 1896. Reconstructed 1906 as company of same name (later Federated British Insurance Co. Ld.). Shareholders were entitled to 5 shares of £5 (credited with £1 paid) in new company for each share of £10 (£1 paid) held. Removed from Register 1906 .... **1908**

National British & Irish Millers' Insurance Co. Ld. Regd. 1906. See Federated British Insurance Co. Ld

National Building & Land Investment Co. of Ireland Ld. Regd. Dublin 1865. Removed from Register 1908 **1889**

National Burglary & Fire Office Ld. Regd. 1892 as National Burglary Insurance Corporation Ld.; name changed June 1906. Vol. liq. 29 Oct. 1907. Undertaking was acquired by National General Insurance Co. Ld. Shareholders were entitled to £5 per share of £10 (£1 paid) held. Final meeting return regd. 28 July 1908 .... **1908**

National Burglary Insurance Corporation Ld. See National Burglary & Fire Office Ld.

National Cinematograph Theatres Ld. Regd. 1910. Vol. liq. 14 July 1911. Undertaking acquired by United Electric Theatres Ld. Final meeting return regd. 9 June 1913 .... ***1912**

National City Co. See City Co. of New York Inc.

National City Co. Ld. Inc. Canada. All capital was held by City Co. of New York **1934**

National Coke & Oil Co. Ld. Regd. 1933. Vol. liq. 23 Sept. 1953. Final meeting return regd. Jan. 1954.. **1950**

National Commercial Insurance Co. Ld. Regd. 1909. Vol. liq. 14 Feb. 1913. Final meeting return regd. 5 Jan. 1929 .... **1913**

National Co. for the Distribution of Electricity by Secondary Generators Ld. Regd. 1883. Removed from Register 1906 .... **1900**

National Conservative Industrial Dwellings Association Ld. See Alliance Land & Dwellings Co. Ld.

National Cycle & Motor-Car Insurance Co. Ld. Regd. 1896. Removed from Register 1901 .... **1899**

National Diamond Factories (Bernard Oppenheimer) Ld. Regd. 1919 as Bernard Oppenheimer Diamond Works Ld.; name changed Nov. 1920. Vol. liq. 15 Feb. 1923. Final meeting return regd. 6 Sept. 1927 **1924**

National Discount Co. of Ireland Ld. Regd. Dublin 1872. In liquidation in 1884 .... **1884**

National Distributors Ld. Regd. 1930. Vol. liq. (creditors') 13 July 1931. Assets realised insufficient to pay unsecured creditors in full. Final meeting return regd. 2 Dec. 1932 .... **1932**

National Dominion & General Investment Corporation Ld. Regd. 1925. Dissolved under Section 154 of Companies' Act 1929. Undertaking was acquired by European & General Corporation Ld. in which company stockholders were entitled to £60 ordinary

See Stock Exchange Year-Book.

VOL. FOR

or £100 preference stock respectively for every £100 ordinary or preference stock held ... **1947**

National Drug Industries Ld. Regd. 1931. Receiver appointed in Sept. 1935. Undertaking and assets were acquired by C. R. Harker. Stagg & Morgan Ld. (regd. 1937 as N.D.I. Ld.). Struck off Register 16 Dec. 1938 ... **1939**

National Dwellings Society Ld. Regd. 1875. Vol. liq. (members') 26 Sept. 1952. The 4% mortgage debentures were repaid at par and 14*s*. 9¾*d*. per share (of £1) was returned to contributories. Final meeting return regd. 13 Oct. 1953 ... **1954**

National Electric Co. (Birmingham) Ld. *See* Electric Heating & Hardware Ld.

National Electric Supply Co. Ld. Regd. 1889. Vol. liq. 10 Apr. 1922. The undertaking was sold to Preston Corporation. Final meeting return regd. 3 Jan. 1923 **1923**

National Electric Theatres Ld. Regd. 1910. A subsidiary of Denman Picture Houses Ld. Vol. liq. (members') 2 May 1956. Final meeting return 1 Aug.1970 ... **1951**

National Employers' Accident & General Assurance Association Ld. Regd. 1882. Vol. liq. Sept. 1884. Business transferred to Employers' Liability Corporation. Final meeting return regd. 20 Apr. 1886 .. **1885**

National Estates Corporation Ld. Regd. 1899. Removed from Register 20 Feb. 1906 ... ***1901**

National Explosives Co. Ld. Regd. 1888. Vol. liq. 13 Dec. 1892. Reconstructed as company of same name. Shareholders who subscribed for 1 preference share of 10*s*. in new company for each ordinary share of £1 held were allotted 1 ordinary share of £1 (credited as fully-paid); holders of founders' shares of £1 were allotted 1 fully-paid deferred share of £1 for each founders' share held, on the same conditions. Final meeting return regd. 4 Oct. 1893 ... **1908**

National Explosives Co. Ld. Regd. 1893. Vol. liq. 22 July 1907. Reconstructed as company of same name. Debenture stockholders were entitled to 14% of their holdings in prior lien 6% debenture stock in new company 71% in 5% debenture stock and 15% in ordinary shares of £1. Shareholders received no interest in the new company. Final meeting return regd. 1 Feb.1909 ... **1909**

National Explosives Co. Ld. Regd. 1908. Vol. liq. 15 Mar. 1920. Final meeting return regd. 29 Sept. 1925 **1921**

National Fertilizers Ld. Regd. 1934. Vol. liq. (members') 20 June 1947; the undertaking was acquired by Fisons Ld. Final meeting return regd. 21 Apr. 1948 ... **1949**

National Fire Insurance Corporation Ld. Regd. 1878. Vol. liq. 16 Jan. 1889. Business was acquired by Royal Insurance Co. Final meeting return regd. 28 Dec. 1891 ... **1889**

National Flying Services Ld. Regd. 1929. Receiver appointed in June 1933. Assets realised insufficient to meet claims of debenture holders in full. Struck off Register 27 July 1937 ... **1938**

National Fuel Oil Co. (1921) Ld. Regd. 1921. Vol. liq. (creditors') 22 Jan. 1931. No capital returned to contributories. Final meeting return regd. 11 Apr. 1932 ... **1931**

National Funds Assurance Co. Ld. Regd. 1870. Removed from Register 1884 ... ***1876**

National Gas Engine Co. Ld. Regd. 1900 as National Gas Engine Co. (1900) Ld.; name changed July 1900. Vol. liq. June 1911. Reconstructed as National Gas Engine Co. Ld. (later National Gas & Oil Engine Co. Ld.) shareholders were entitled to 3 ordinary shares of £1 (credited as fully-paid) for each ordinary share of £1 held or 6 preference shares of £1 (credited as fully-paid) for every 5 preference shares of £1 held. Removed from Register 1912 ... **1912**

National General Insurance Co. Ld. Regd. 1907. Vol. liq. Jan. 1914. Court Order to continue winding up under supervision. Struck off Register 7 July 1939 **1940**

National Gramopbone Co. Ld. Regd. 1911. Struck off Register 1917 ... ***1915**

National Gramophone Co. (1913) Ld. Regd. 1913. Receiver appointed in Mar. 1915. The assets were realised on behalf of 1st mortgage debenture holders. Struck off Register 1917 ... **1916**

National Guardian Assurance Co. Ld. Regd. 1865. Removed from Register 1911 ... ***1904**

National Ice & Cold Storage Co. of California. Inc. California 1912. The outstanding 1st mortgage 6% gold bonds were redeemed at 105% on 1 June 1946 **1946**

National Ice Producing Co. Ld. Regd. 1895. Removed from Register 1898 ... ***1898**

National Improved Housing Co. Ld. Regd. 1919. Court Order to wind up 20 Apr. 1920. Struck off Register 1927 ... **1921**

National Insurance & Guarantee Corporation Ld. Regd. 1891. Reconstructed 1894 as company of same name. Shareholders were entitled to 1 share of £3 (credited as fully-paid) in new company for each founders' share of £1 held or 1 share of £3 (credited with £2 10*s*. paid) for each ordinary share of £5 (£2 paid) held. Removed from Register 1907 ... **1893**

National Inventions Trust Ld. Regd. 1896 as Sydney Lee & Co. Ld.; name changed Dec. 1927. Struck off Register 11 Oct. 1938 ... **1907**

National Investment Trust Corporation of England Ld. Regd. 1887. Court order to wind up 19 Oct. 1915. Struck off Register 1928 ... **1916**

National Jute Factory (Companhia Nacional de Tecidos de Juta, Sociedade Anonyma). Inc. Brazil 1908. Bankruptcy petition presented in 1934. 7½% 1st mortgage registered debenture holders received distributions on account of principal of 20¼% at June 1939; further payments (if any) not known ... **1938**

National Land Corporation Ld. Regd. 1880 as National Liberal Land Co. Ld.; name changed Mar. 1890. Vol. liq. Dec. 1907. Struck off Register Mar. 1930 **1931**

National Land Fruit & Packing Co. Ld. Inc. Ontario 1910. In liquidation in 1914 ... **1914**

National Liberal Club Buildings Co. Ld. Regd. 1884. Vol. liq. (members') 28 June 1935. Capital returned to contributories other than Marquess of Crewe and Or—£5 1*s*. 5*d*. per fully-paid share of £5 or £3 16*s*. 5*d*. per share of £5 (£3 10*s*. paid). Final meeting return regd. 26 Nov. 1935 ... **1936**

National Liberal Land Co. Ld. *See* National Land Corporation Ld.

National Life Assurance Society. Established 1830. Regd. 1835. Reconstructed 1896 as National Mutual Life Assurance Society. Dissolved by Special Act 7 July 1896 ... **1896**

National Live Stock Insurance Co Ld. Regd 1907. Vol. liq. 23 Jan. 1914. Final meeting return regd. 26 Oct. 1925 ... ***1915**

National Marine Insurance Association Ld. Regd. 1882. Vol. liq. 13 Apr. 1897. Business was acquired by Ocean Marine Insurance Co. Ld. Final meeting return regd. 28 Oct. 1898 ... **1898**

National Match Factory of Bolivia Ld. Regd. 1907. Vol. liq. (creditors) May 1930. No capital return to contributories. Final meeting return regd. 18 Apr. 1951 ... **1955**

National Match Factory of Venezuela Ld. Regd. 1905 as Venezuela Match Monopoly Ld.; name changed 1909; vol. liq. (members') 25 Nov. 1929. Capital returned to contributories—3*s*. 7*d*. per share. Final meeting return regd. 10 Nov. 1950 ... **1951**

National Mercantile Bank Ld. Regd. 1878 as National Banking Co. Ld.; name changed July 1878. Vol. liq. 8 June 1881. Final meeting return regd. 5 June 1882 ***1882**

National Mercantile Trust Ld. Regd. 1928. Vol. liq. (members') 21 Mar. 1951. Capital returned to contributories—ordinary shares (of 5*s*.): 14*s*. 5¼*d*. per share (including 11*s*. 3*d*. per share represented by investments distributed in specie); preference shares (of £1): 29*s*. 5¼*d*. per share. Final meeting return regd. 29 Apr. 1952 ... **1953**

National Minerals Corporation Ld. Regd. 1907. Receiver appointed in Mar. 1915. Struck off Register 1924 **1917**

National Model Dwellings Co. Ld. Regd. 1881. Vol. liq. (members') 26 Oct. 1964. Capital returned to contributories—4*s*. per ordinary share (of 2*s*.). £651 2*s*. 8*d*. was paid into Companies' Liquidation Account in respect of unclaimed dividends and £16,547 13*s*. 4*d*. in respect of unclaimed distributions. Final meeting return regd. 14 Oct. 1966 ..... **1968**

National Motor Cab Co. Ld. Regd. 1908. Vol. liq. 20 Apr. 1917. Final meeting return regd. 23 Oct.1936 **1917**

National Motor Mail-Coach Co. Ld. Regd. 1906. Vol. liq. 25 Sept. 1907. Court Order to continue winding up subject to supervision Oct. 1907. Removed from Register 1910 ... **1908**

Nationsl Omnibus & Transport Co. Ld. Regd. 1911 as National Steam Car Co. (1911) Ld.; name change to National Steam Car Co. Ld. in Aug. 1912 and as above in Jan. 1920. Vol. liq. (members') 31 Dec. 1949. All ordinary and 84% of preference capital was owned by British Transport Commission. Preference shares were repaid at par and the undertaking was transferred to the Commission. Amounts paid into Companies' Liquidation Account: £365 2*s*. 1*d*. on account of unclaimed dividends and £137 on account of unclaimed distributions. Final meeting return regd. 21 Sept. 1950 ... **1951**

National Steam Car (1911) Ld., later **National Steam Car Co. Ld.** *See above.*

National Paper & Pulp Co. (1920) Ld. *See* National Paper Mills Ld.

National Paper Mills Ld. Regd. 1920 as National Paper & Pulp Co. (1920) Ld.; name changed June 1928. Receiver appointed 6 Oct. 1933. The undertaking

**See Stock Exchange Year-Book.*

and assets were acquired by Wycombe Marsh Paper Mills Ld. in 1936. Holders of debentures received 150 fully-paid shares of 5s. in purchasing company for each £50 bond held. Struck off Register 7 Mar. 1939 .... **1940**

National Park Bank of New York. Inc. New York 1856. Assets and liabilities were merged in Aug. 1929 with those of Chase National Bank of City of New York (later The Chase Manhattan Bank) in which company shareholders were entitled to 1 share of $20 for each share of $100 held **1930**

National Penny Bank Ld. Regd. 1875. Vol. liq. 24 Aug. 1914. Court Order to wind up 1 Oct. 1914. Liquidator released 17 June 1921. Struck off Register 3 July 1953 .... **1915**

National Petrol Stations Ld. Regd. 1929. Direct controlling interest was held by National Flying Services Ld. Struck off Register 1937 .... **1934**

National Property Investment Co. Ld. Regd. Edinburgh 1874. Vol. liq. Mar. 1902. Final meeting return regd. 20 Dec. 1907 .... **1903**

National Property Trust Ld. Regd. 1927. Vol. liq. Aug. 1929. Undertaking and assets were acquired by Associated London Properties Ld. in Jan. 1929, in which company shareholders were entitled to 1 fully-paid ordinary share of £1 for each preference share of £1. or every 20 deferred shares of 1s. held. Struck off Register July 1934 .... **1935**

National Provincial Bank Ld. Constituted by Deed of Settlement 1833 as National Provincial Bank of England; regd. as unlimited Dec. 1874 and as limited July 1880; name changed to National Provincial Bank & Union Bank of England Ld. in 1918 and as above Feb. 1924. From 1 Jan. 1970 the undertaking vested in National Westminster Bank. Ld. under provisions of National Westminster Bank Act 1969 which also provided for eventual dissolution of this bank **1971**

National Provincial Cinemas Ld. Regd. 1935. Vol. liq. (members') 16 Dec. 1936 for amalgamation with Union Cinemas Co. Ld. and Oxford & Berkshire Cinemas Ld. to form Union Cinemas Ld. Shareholders, other than Union Cinema Co. Ld. and Oxford & Berkshire Cinema Ld., received 2 A ordinary shares and 1 ordinary share of 5s. of new company for each ordinary share of 5s. held and 17 1st preference and 17 2nd preference shares of £1 of new company for every 24 preference shares of £1 held. Final meeting return regd. 16 Oct. 1942 .... **1936**

National Provincial Insurance Corporation Ld. Regd. 1904. Court Order to wind up 9 Aug. 1911. Liquidator released 28 Feb. 1917. Struck off Register 1 July 1921 .... **1911**

National Provincial Trustees & Assets Corporation Ld. Regd. 1889. Vol. liq. 24 Nov. 1896. Final meeting return regd. 24 May 1900 .... **1897**

National Pure Drinking Water Automatic Supply Association Ld. Regd. 1888. Struck off Register 31 Dec. 1895 .... **1899**

National Pure Water Engineering Co. Ld. Regd. 1886 as Consumers Economic Water Softening & Purifying Co. Ld.; name changed Sept. 1887. Court Orders: to wind up 22 June 1889; to dissolve 1 Aug. 1896 ... **1890**

National Refractory Minerals Process (Martin's Patent) Ld. Regd. 1910. Vol. liq. 2 July 1915. Final meeting return regd. 2 May 1917 .... **1917**

National Reliance Insurance Co. Ld. Regd. 1898. Vol. liq. 6 Nov. 1903. Business was acquired by National Union Society Ld. Final meeting return regd. 10 Mar. 1906 .... **1904**

National Reversionary Investment Co. Ld. Established by Deed of Settlement 1838. Regd. 1895. Vol. liq. Mar. 1910. Undertaking and assets were acquired by Equity and Law Life Assurance Society for £290,108 in cash. Capital returned to contributories—£102 6s. 1d. per £100 paid up capital; further payments (if any) not known. Removed from Register 1910 .... **1911**

National Salt Co. of Venezuela Ld. Regd. 1906 as Venezuelan Salt Monopoly Ld.; name changed July 1909. Vol. liq. Dec. 1910. Removed from Register 1912 .... **1911**

National Salvage Association Ld. Regd. 1910. Struck off Register Jan. 1931 .... **1931**

National Securities Corpn. Ld. Regd. 1920. Vol. liq. 12 Sept. 1961. Final meeting return regd. 10 Nov. 1967 **1933**

National Shipbuilders Security, Ld. Regd. 1930. Vol. liq. (members') 6 Aug. 1958. Final meeting return regd. 13 Nov. 1958 .... **1955**

National Skating Palace Ld. Regd. 1894. A receiver was appointed on behalf of debenture holders. Removed from Register 1899 .... **1899**

National Spanish Silver Lead Mines & Mining Co. Ld. Regd. 1911. Struck off Register 1919 .... **1915**

National Standard Land, Mortgage & Investment Co. Ld. Regd. 1881. Vol. liq. 24 Feb. 1888. Court Order to continue winding up under supervision Apr. 1888. Final meeting return regd. 9 Jan. 1894 ...... **1889**

National Standard Life Assurance Corporation Ld. Regd. 1906. Court Order to wind up 6 June 1916. Liquidator released 21 Nov. 1921. Struck off Register 20 Mar. 1925 .... **1917**

National Steam Ship Co. Ld. Regd. 1867 as Steamship Co. Ld.; name changed Aug. 1867. Vol. liq. 20 Nov. 1914. Final meeting return regd. 8 Nov. 1915....... **1915**

National Stores Ld. Regd. 1897. Removed from Register 1909 .... **1899**

National Stores Ld. Regd. 1930. Court Order to wind up 30 Mar. 1931. Liquidator released 12 Oct. 1938. Struck off Register 20 Feb. 1942 .... **1943**

National Sun Ray & Health Centres Ld. Regd. 1928. Receiver appointed in Feb. 1929; ceased to act Apr. 1932. Assets realised insufficient to meet claims of debenture holders. Struck off Register 2 July 1935 **1933**

National Tea Union (1906) Ld. Regd. 1906. Vol. liq. 7 Dec. 1915. Final meeting return regd. 24 May 1917 ***1917**

National Telephone Co. Ld. Regd. 1881. Vol. liq. 25 Jan. 1912. The debenture stocks, 1st, 2nd and 3rd preference shares were repaid at par; the preferred stock at 105% and the deferred stock at 105·48%. Final meeting return regd. 30 June 1914 .... **1914**

National Telewriter Co. Ld. Regd. 1909. Vol. liq. (members') 22 June 1954. Capital returned to contributories—8d. per £1 preferred ordinary stock. £704 19s. 4d. was paid into Companies' Liquidation Account. Final meeting return regd. 1 Feb. 1957 **1958**

National Temperance Land & Building Co. Ld. Regd. 1864. Vol. liq. Aug. 1910. Shareholders were entitled to (a) 7s. in cash per share of £1 or (b) 9s. 6d. in shares in Present Century Mortgage & Investment Society Ld. Removed from Register 1913 .... **1911**

National Theatres de Luxe Ld. Regd. 1909. Struck off Register 1914 .... **1911**

National Trading Corporation Ld. Regd. 1897. Court Order to wind up 13 June 1900. Removed from Register 1910 .... **1901**

National Transport Co. See Compania de Trasportes "Expreso Villalonga."

National Tunnel & Mines Company. Inc. in Maine 1902 as Utah Apex Mining Co.; name changed Mar. 1937. Court approval for reorganisation in bankruptcy and W. J. Lowe (Salt Lake City, Utah U.S.A.) appointed trustee in Sept. 1947. Company no longer in existence, assets having been sold at public auction yielding insufficient to pay prior claims **1949**

National Union Society Ld. Regd. 1894. Vol. liq. 19 July 1907. The colonial and foreign fire business was sold to Phoenix Assurance Co. Ld.; other business was sold to London & Lancashire Fire Insurance Co. (later London & Lancashire Insurance Co.). Struck off Register May 1929 .... **1930**

National United Laundries Finance & Development Co. Ld. Regd. 1928. Vol. liq. (members') 3 Sept. 1947. Final meeting return regd. 30 June 1948 .... **1940**

National United Laundries (Greater London) Ld. Regd. 1927. Vol. liq. 19 Dec. 1928. Undertaking and assets were acquired by National United Laundries Corporation Ld., in which company shareholders were entitled to 1 A preference share of 5s. (credited as fully-paid) for each preferred ordinary share of 5s. held or 1 B preference share of 5s. and 5 deferred shares of 1s. for every 5 preferred shares of 1s. held. Final meeting return regd. 6 Sept. 1929 .... **1929**

National United Laundries Ld. Regd. 1927. Vol. liq. 19 Dec. 1928. Undertaking and assets were acquired by National United Laundries Corporation Ld in which company shareholders were entitled to 1 A preference share of 5s. (credited as fully-paid) for each preferred ordinary share of 5s. held or 1 B preference share of 5s. and 10 deferred shares of 1s. for every 5 deferred shares of 1s. held. Final meeting return regd. 6 Sept. 1929 .... **1929**

National United (Southern) Laundries Ld. Regd. June 1928. Vol. liq. 19 Dec. 1928. Undertaking and assets were acquired by National United Laundries Corporation Ld., in which company shareholders were entitled to 1 A preference share of 5s. (credited as fully-paid) for each preferred ordinary share of 5s. held or 1 B preference share of 5s. and 5 deferred shares of 1s. for every 5 deferred shares of 1s. held. Final meeting return regd. 6 Sept. 1929 .... **1929**

National Welsh Slate Quarries Ld. Regd. 1920. Vol. liq. 20 Oct. 1921. Final meeting return regd. 8 Nov. 1928 **1922**

National White Oil Co. Ld. Regd. 1904. Struck off Register Jan. 1931 .... **1931**

National Whole Meal Bread & Biscuit Co. Ld. Regd. 1890. Removed from Register 1907 .... **1892**

*See Stock Exchange Year-Book.

VOL. FOR

Nationalbank fur Deutschland. Amalgamated in 1922 with Bank fur Handel und Industrie Darmstädter Bank to form Darmstädter und Nationalbank K.A.A. 1926

Nations' Treasure, Coolgardie Ld. Regd. 1896. Vol. liq. 5 Aug. 1897. Final meeting return regd. 27 June 1898 1898

Native Brands Tea Packing Co. Ld. Regd. 1889. Vol. liq. 4 Sept. 1897. Final meeting return regd. 6 Jan. 1902 1898

Native Guano Co. Ld. Regd. 1869. Vol. liq. 14 July 1926. Capital returned to contributories—2s. 6d. per share of 5s. at Aug. 1926; further payments (if any) not known. Final meeting return regd. 16 Apr. 1927 1927

Natomas Co. of California. Inc. California 1914. Property was sold to Natomas Co. Holders of 6% 20-year general and refunding gold bonds were entitled to 1 share of no par value in acquiring company for every $100 bonds held 1930

Natomas Consolidated of California. Inc. California 1908. Reorganised 1914 as Natomas Co. of California. 1st mortgage bondholders were entitled to $60 bonds and $40 preference shares in new company for every $100 bond held. 2nd mortgage bondholders were entitled to $50 preference shares in new company and 5 fully-paid shares of £1 in Natomas Syndicate Ld. Stockholders were entitled to 1 fully-paid share of £1 in Natomas Syndicate Ld. for every $100 share held 1925

Natomas Land & Dredging Trust Ld. Regd. 1915. Vol. liq. 25 Mar. 1929. Final meeting return regd. 18 Dec. 1929 1930

Natural Bread & Tea Co. Ld. Regd. 1899. Vol. liq. 29 June 1901. Final meeting return regd. 1 Aug. 1902 1902

Natural Gas Fields of England Ld. Regd. 1902. Removed from Register 1908 1950

Natural Portland Cement Co. Ld. See Standard Portland Cement Co. Ld.

"Nautilus" Insurance Co. See New York Life Insurance Co.

Nautilus Steam Shipping Co. Ld. Regd. 1881. Court Order to wind up Oct. 1931. Struck off Register 20 Feb. 1942 1943

Naval & Military Co-operative Hotel Co. Ld. Regd. 1909. Vol. liq. 11 Jan. 1918. Final meeting return regd. 31 Dec. 1919 1919

Naval Colliery Co. (1897) Ld. Regd. 1897. Vol. liq. Nov. 1928. Struck off Register 24 July 1936 1937

Naval Construction & Armaments Co. Ld. Regd. 1888. Vol. liq. 12 July 1897. Undertaking was acquired in 1897 by Vickers Sons & Co. (later Vickers Ld.) for £300,000 in cash. Capital returned to contributories—£5 per share of £5; further payment (if any) not known. Final meeting return regd. 15 Mar. 1898 1898

Naval, Military & Civil Service Co-operative Society of South Africa Ld. Regd. 1902 as Army, Naval & Civil Service Co-operative Society of South Africa Ld.; name changed Aug. 1902. Vol. liq. Sept. 1906. Removed from Register 1911 1907

Navan & Kingscourt Railway Co. Inc. by Special Act 1865. Under Midland Great Western, Dublin and Meath and Navan and Kingscourt Railway (Purchase) Act 1888, the undertaking was vested in Midland Great Western Railway of Ireland Co. for £50,000 in cash 1889

Navarino Recovery Ld. Regd. 1923. Struck off Register Jan. 1931 1931

Navarro Wellesley Aviation Ld. Regd. 1918 as Wellesley-Brown Aircraft Ld.; name changed July 1919. Vol. liq. 18 June 1924. Final meeting return regd. 12 Aug. 1924 1925

Näversberg Falun Copper Mines & Works Ld. See Swedish Metals Extraction Co. Ld.

Navine Manufacturing Co. Ld. Regd. 1905. Removed from Register 1911 1911

Naylor Brothers (London) Ld. Regd. 1907. Vol. liq. 29 Mar. 1934. Capital returned to contributories—20s. 0·0112d. per share of £1. Final meeting return regd. 4 Mar. 1935 1935

Naylor (T. & A.) Ld. Regd. 1910. Vol. liq. (creditors') 28 Sept. 1976. Final meeting return regd. 1 Feb. 1979 1979-80

Naylor (T. & A.) Ld. Regd. as private company 30 Nov. 1910; converted public company 20 Mar. 1953. Vol. liq. (creditors') 29 Sept. 1976. Final meeting return regd. 1 Feb. 1979 1979-80

Nchanga Consolidated Copper Mines (1937) Ld. Regd. 1937 as Nchanga Consolidated Copper Mines Ld.; registration transferred to Northern Rhodesia (now Zambia) 1954; name changed 1970. Assets and liabilities were vested in Bancroft Mines Ld. (now Nchanga Consolidated Copper Mines Ld.) on 26 June 1970; ordinary shareholders received 200 shares in Zambia Copper Investments Ld. for every 100 shares held. Dissolved on 31 Mar. 1971 1971

VOL. FOR

N'Changa Copper Mines Ld. Regd. 1926. Vol. liq. (members') 31 July 1931. Undertaking was acquired by Rhokana Corporation Ld in which company shareholders were entitled to 1 share of £1 for every 4 shares of £1 held. £4 15s. 3d. was paid into Companies' Liquidation Account. Final meeting return regd. 15 Feb. 1933 1932

Neal (George) & Co. Ld. Regd. 1887. Court Orders; to wind up 9 Nov. 1889: to dissolve 4 May 1894 1890

Neal (R. H.) & Co. Ld. Regd. 1925. Vol. liq. (members') 4 Jan. 1965. Preference shares (of £1) repaid Jan. 1965 at 21s. per share. Final meeting return regd. 1 July 1969 1970

Near East Petroleum Co. Ld. Regd. 1926. Vol. liq. (members') 11 Feb. 1931. Undertaking and assets acquired by Zante Oilfields Ld in which company shareholders were entitled to 1 ordinary share of 2s. (credited with 1s. 6d. paid) for each ordinary share of 2s. paid or 1 fully-paid preferred share of 2s. for each preference share of 2s. held. Final meeting return regd. 5 Aug. 1932 1931

Neath and Brecon Railway Co. Inc. by Special Act 1862 as Dulas Valley Mineral Railway Co.; name changed by Act of 1863. In 1922 the undertaking was merged into the Great Western Railway Co., in which company stockholders were entitled to stock as follows:

For each £100 held		G.W.	
4% 1st Debenture	£100	4% Debenture	
4% A1 Debenture	£100	4% Debenture	
4% A2 Debenture	£80	5% Cons. Pref.	
4% B Debenture	£80	5% Cons. Pref.	
4% Preference	£57	Cons. Ordinary	
Ordinary	£15	Cons. Ordinary	1924

Neath Harbour Smelting & Rolling Works Ld. Regd. 1884. Court Orders: to wind up 16 Feb. 1886; to dissolve 29 June 1894 1887

Neath Omnibus Co. Ld. Regd. 1928 as All Blue Transport Ld.; name changed Dec. 1930. Vol. liq. (members') 15 Nov. 1938. Undertaking acquired by United Welsh Services Ld. Capital returned to contributories—£39,774 4s. 4d. Final meeting return regd. 22 Dec. 1939 1941

Neath Water Co. Waterworks sold to Neath Corporation from 1 June 1894 1895

Nechi Mines (Colombia) Ld. Regd. 1914. Vol. liq. 4 Sept. 1925. Capital returned to contributories—4·88d. per preference share (of 10s.) and 1s. 2·64d. per ordinary shares (of 10s.). Final meeting return regd. 25 June 1948 1949

Nedas (L.) (London) Ld. Regd. 1937. Vol. liq. (members') 18 May 1942. Capital returned to contributories—17s. 1·909d. per share of £1. Final meeting return regd. 6 Apr. 1945 1942

Neepsend Rolling Mills Co. Ld. Regd. 1873. Removed from Register, 1904 1892

Negit Ld. Inc. in Burma 1970. Vol. liq. (members') 29 Feb. 1980. Distribution—43·0851 shares of $US1 of Negit S.A. plus £10·8607 cash for every 100 shares hekd. Final meeting return regd. 19 Dec. 1980 1981-2

Negombo Ceylon Coco-nut Estates Ld. Regd. 1913. Vol. liq. 20 Apr. 1928. Capital returned to contributories—19s. 10½d. per preference share of £1; further payments (if any) not known. Final meeting return regd. 4 Sept. 1928 1929

Neilgherry & Southern India Lands Investment Co. Ld. Regd. 1878. Vol. liq. 1 July 1886. Final meeting return regd. 8 Nov. 1892 1887

Neilston Gas Light Co. Ld. Regd. in Edinburgh 1907. Dissolved 1 May 1949. undertaking being vested in Scottish Area Gas Board under Gas Act 1948. Holders of ordinary shares (of £1) were entitled to receive £2 15s. British Gas 3% guaranteed stock 1990–95 for each share held 1952

Nell Gwynne (B.M.L.) Mines, No Liability. Inc. Victoria 1934. Vol. liq. 22 Feb. 1940 1941

Nell (William W.) Ld. Regd. 1890. Vol. liq. 12 Oct. 1927. Undertaking and assets were acquired by Crosswells Cardiff Brewery Ld. A return of £8 per share of £10 was anticipated. Final meeting return regd. 14 June 1928 1928

Nelly & Pioneer Reefs Gold Mining Co. Ld. Regd. 1895. Reconstructed 1903 as Rhodesia Consolidated Ld. in which company shareholders were entitled to 1 share of 10s. (credited with 7s. 6d. paid) for each share of £1 held. Removed from Register 1906..... 1904

Nelson & Co. Ld. Regd. 1901. Court Order to wind up 7 Feb. 1905. Liquidator released 20 Apr. 1911. Removed from Register 17 Feb. 1914 .... *1906

Nelson Bros. Ld. See Nelson Financial Trust Ld.

Nelson Copper Fields Ld. Regd. 1898. Struck off Register Apr. 1930 1931

*See Stock Exchange Year-Book.

VOL. FOR

Nelson Dock Co. Ld. Regd. 1875. Vol. liq. 17 Aug. 1886. Properties taken over by Dry Docks Corporation of London Ld. Final meeting return regd. 23 Mar. 1888 ... ***1887**

Nelson Financial Trust Ld. Regd 1883 as Nelson Bros. Ld.; name changed Sept. 1927. On 21 July 1975 all capital was cancelled, holders being entitled to securities of Estates House Investment Trust Ld. as follows:—210 ordinary shares of 25p for every 100 shares; 1 5·04% preference share of £1 for every 6% preference; £1 7·2% debenture stock for each £1 6% debenture stock and £1 8·5% convertible debenture stock for every £1 8% convertible 2nd debenture stock. Company was dissolved under S.208 without winding up on 31 Dec. 1976 ... **1977-8**

Nelson (H. & W.) Ld. Regd. 1901. Vol. liq. 22 Mar. 1935. Undertaking acquired by Nelson Steam Navigation Co. Ld. Final meeting return regd. 8 June 1940 ... **1937**

Nelson (James) & Sons Ld. *See* British & Argentine Meat Co. Ld.

Nelson Line (Liverpool) Ld. Regd. 1898. Vol. liq. 23 Nov. 1925. In Feb. 1926 the liquidator stated that capital had been returned in full. Final meeting return regd. 30 Nov. 1926 ... **1926**

Nelson Share Syndicate Ld. Regd. 1901. Removed from Register 1911 ... **1907**

Nelson Steam Navigation Co. Ld. Regd. 1910. Vessels were transferred in 1932 to Royal Mail Lines Ld. for 1,760,000 fully-paid shares. Vol. liq. (members') 30 Apr. 1937. The 3½% guaranteed debenture stock was repaid at par on 1 July 1937. At 13 Dec. 1937, distributions aggregating £240,000 were made to R. M. Realisation Co. Ld. which company owned all share capital. Final meeting return regd. 6 Feb. 1943 **1938**

Nelson's Battle-ship "Foudroyant" Ld. Regd. 1894. Removed from Register 1908 ... **1896**

Nelson's (New) River Plate Meat Co. Ld. Regd. 1889. Vol. liq. Jan. 1892. Reconstructed as James Nelson and Sons Ld. (later British & Argentine Meat Co. Ld.). Final meeting return regd. 9 Mar. 1893 ... **1892**

Nenthead & Tyndale Lead & Zinc Co. Ld. Regd. 1882. Vol. liq. 4 Aug. 1896. Final meeting return regd. 16 Nov. 1928 ... ***1897**

Neptune Steam Navigation Co. Ld. Regd. 1891. Vol. liq. (members') 15 Nov. 1934. Undertaking and assets acquired by Johnston Warreb Lines Ld. Capital returned to contributories—£232,442. Final meeting return regd. 20 Mar. 1936 ... **1940**

Neptune Steam Shipping Co. Ld. Regd. 1880 as Jinman Steam Shipping Co. Ld.; name changed in 1880. Vol. liq. 12 Apr. 1888. Final meeting return regd. 5 July 1888 ... ***1881**

Nerbudda Coal & Iron Co. Ld. Regd. 1860. Capital returned to contributories—13*s*. 5*d*. per ordinary share of £3; preference shares repaid at par. Removed from Register 1905 ... **1906**

Nerchinsk Gold Co. Ld. Regd. 1901. Vol. liq. 1 Dec. 1911. Final meeting return regd. 1 Jan. 1914 ... **1912**

Nerchinsk Options Ld. Regd. 1907. Vol. liq. June 1910. Removed from Register 1911 ... **1911**

Nernst Electric Light Ld. Regd. 1899. Vol. liq. 24 July 1905 for sale of undertaking to Allgemeine Electricitäts Gesellschaft for £24,000 in cash. Removed from Register 1906 ... **1906**

Ner-Sag Ld. Regd. 1925. Vol. liq. (members') 7 July 1930. Undertaking and assets transferred to Ner-Sag (1930) Ld., in which company shareholders were entitled to 1 fully-paid ordinary share of 4*s*. *plus* £2 4*s*. 8⅝*d*. in cash for each share of £1 held. Final meeting return regd. 7 Dec. 1931 ... **1931**

Ner-Sag (1930) Ld. Regd. 1930. Vol. liq. (members') 15 Jan. 1934. Capital returned to contributories—2*s*. 1·768*d*. per share of 4*s*. Final meeting return regd. 10 Aug. 1934 ... **1934**

Ner-Sag (Overseas) Ld. Regd. 1928. Vol. liq. (members') 16 June 1930. Capital returned to contributories—1*s*. 10$\frac{1}{20}$*d*. per share of 5*s*. Final meeting return regd. 13 Dec. 1930 ... **1931**

Nero Engine Co. Ld. Regd. 1914. Vol. liq. 4 Jan. 1919. Undertaking was acquired by Riley (Coventry) Ld. Final meeting return regd. 5 Oct. 1921 ... **1938**

Nestle's Milk Products Ld. Regd. 1935. Vol. liq. (members') 26 Sept. 1949. Final meeting return regd. 25 Apr. 1955 ... **1940**

Netherlands Incandescent Gas Light Co. Ld. Regd. 1895. Vol. liq. 2 May 1905. Removed from Register 1906 **1906**

Netherlands India Steam Navigation Co. Ld. Regd. 1864. Vol. liq. 10 Dec. 1890. Final meeting return regd. 25 July 1892 ... ***1892**

Netherlands India Sumatra Tobacco Co. Ld. Regd. 1889. Vol. liq. 2 Oct. 1894. Property acquired by Serdang Tabak Maatschappij, in which company shareholders were entitled to Fl. 12 A shares for each preference share of £1 held or Fl. 9 B shares for each ordinary founders' share of £1 held. Final meeting return regd. 28 June 1895 ... **1908**

Netherlands Land Enclosure Co. Inc. Netherlands 1852. In liquidation Apr. 1906 ... **1907**

Netherlands South African Railway. In 1903 H.M. Government offered to purchase the bonds and shares at following rates: 1892 5% debentures at £115%; 1894 & 1899 4% debentures at £112%; 1890 & 1891 4% debentures at Fl. 1.125 per Fl. 1,000; 1889 4% debentures at Fl. 1,124 per Fl. 1.000; 6% shares at £135 per 1.000 guilders; 4½% shares at £112 10*s*. per 1.000 guilders; 1897 4% debentures at Fl. 1,128 or Mks. 1.906·32 per Fl. 1,000 or Mks. 1,690 **1904**

Nettlefolds Ld. Regd. 1880. Amalgamated in 1902 with Guest Keen & Co. Ld. (later Guest Keen & Nettlefolds Ld.). Shareholders were entitled to £12 10*s*. debenture stock in new company for each preference share of £10 *plus* 5*s*. in cash for each ordinary share of £10 held. Removed from Register 1907 ... **1902**

Neu-Flame (Canada) Ld. Inc. Canada 1929. In liquidation in 1930 ... **1930**

Neu Flame (Parent) Ld. Regd. 1928. Vol. liq. Mar. 1931. Undertaking and assets were acquired by International Oil Lamp and Stove Ld. in which company shareholders were entitled to 1 share of 1*s*. (credited as fully-paid) for every 6 shares of 1*s*. held and an option (since expired) over further shares. Struck off Register 7 July 1939 ... **1940**

Neva Mills (Holdings) Ld. Regd. 1914 as Neva Mills Ld.; name changed 1953. Vol. liq. 16 Dec. 1980. Final meeting return regd. 15 Dec. 1981 ... **1957**

Nevada-Douglas Consolidated Copper Co. Inc. Maine 1904. All property was acquired by Kennecott Copper Corporation, in which company shareholders were entitled to 1 share of no par value for every 2 shares of no par value held ... **1934**

Nevada-Douglas Copper Co. Inc. Utah 1906. In 1915 amalgamated with Moore Mining Co. as Nevada-Douglas Consolidated Copper Co., in which company shareholders received 1 share for each share held ... **1916**

Nevada Land & Cattle Co. Ld. Regd. 1883. Removed from Register 1898 ... **1898**

Nevada Star Mining Co. Ld. Regd. 1913. Vol. liq. 23 Nov. 1914. Reconstructed as company of same name. Shareholders were entitled to 1 share of £! (credited with 15*s*. paid) in new company for each share of £1 held. Final meeting return regd. 18 Nov. 1919 ... **1915**

Nevada Star Mining Co. Ld. Regd. 1914. Receiver appointed 27 Nov. 1922. Struck off Register 1927 **1923**

Nevada-Utah Mines & Smelters Corporation. Inc. Maine 1904 as Montana Mines & Smelters Corporation; name changed Nov. 1904 ... **1912**

Neverest Automatic Supply Ld. Regd. 1929. Court Order to wind up Oct. 1929. Struck off Register 20 Mar. 1936 ... **1937**

Neville Developments Ld. *See* Dawes (G. R.) Holdings Ld.

Neville Group Ld. (The) *See* Dawes (G. R.) Holdings Ld.

Neville Shipping Co. Ld. Regd. 1919. Assets realised insufficient to satisfy claims of mortgagees. Struck off Register 19 Oct. 1934 ... **1934**

Neville (Shoes) Ld. Regd. 1932. Vol. liq. (members') 20 Oct. 1941. Capital returned to contributories—£2,020. Final meeting return regd. 13 Jan. 1943 ... **1942**

Nevin United Granite Quarries (Carnarvonshire) Ld. Regd. 1886. Removed from Register 1903 ... **1889**

New Adansi Goldfields Ld. Regd. 1901. Undertaking and assets were acquired by Gold Coast United Ld., in which company shareholders were entitled to 4 shares of 10*s*. (credited as fully-paid) for every 10 shares of £1 held. Removed from Register 1905 .. **1904**

New Aerated Beverage & Buffet Co. Ld. Regd. 1895. Removed from Register 1904 ... **1901**

New African Co. Ld. Regd. 1894. Struck off Register 14 Apr. 1939 ... **1940**

New African Concessions Syndicate Ld. Regd. 1910. Vol. liq. 14 Apr. 1920. Reconstructed as African Concession Syndicate (1920) Ld. Final meeting return regd. 18 Feb. 1921 ... **1921**

New Afrikander Gold Mining Co. Ld. Regd, 1898. Reconstructed as Afrikander Gold Mining Co. (1902) Ld. Removed from Register 1904 ... **1909**

New Akankoo (Gold Coast) Mining Co. Ld. Regd. 1888. Reconstructed in 1890 as Akankoo Gold Mining Co. Ld in which company preference shareholders were entitled to 2 ordinary shares of 10*s*. fully-paid for each preference share of £1 held; ordinary shareholders were entitled to 1 ordinary share of 10*s*. (credited with 7*s*. 6*d*. paid) for each ordinary share of £1 held. Removed from Register 1906 ... **1891**

**See Stock Exchange Year-Book*.

VOL. FOR

New Akoko Ld. Regd. 1927. Vol. liq. (creditors') 15 May 1935. Struck off Register 8 Apr. 1938 1939

New Albion Transvaal Gold Mines Ld. Regd. 1908. Vol. liq. (members') 21 Apr. 1933. Undertaking and assets were acquired by Ocean Development Co. Ld. in which company shareholders were entitled to 1 share of 5s. (credited as fully-paid) for every 17 ordinary shares of 1s. held. £832 3s. 8d. was paid into Companies' Liquidation Account (see preface). Final meeting return regd. 30 Nov. 1934 1934

New Alburnia Gold Mining Co. Ld. Regd. 1896. Removed from Register 1903 1903

New Amalgamated Tyre Co. Ld. Regd. 1900. Receiver appointed for debenture holders, ceased to act Nov. 1906. The assets had been sold and the proceeds paid into Court. Removed from Register 1906 1907

New Ambrosa Syndicate Ld. Regd. 1909. Vol. liq. (creditors') 10 Mar. 1930. No capital returned to contributories. Final meeting return regd. 21 Apr. 1931 1931

New Anglo-French General Finance Co. Ld. Regd. 1908. Vol. liq. Jan. 1910. Removed from Register 1911 1910

New Anglo Mexican Co. Ld. Regd. 1906. Vol. liq. 1909. Struck off Register 15 Aug. 1944 1945

New Ariston Gold Mining Co. Ld. Inc. in South African Republic in 1893 as Ariston Gold Mining Syndicate Ld.; name changed 1894. Wound up 1906 1923

New Arrow Proprietary Gold Mines (W.A.) Ld. Regd. 1897. In liquidation in 1900. Capital returned to contributories—2d. per share of £1 at Nov. 1900; further payments (if any) not known. Removed from Register 1911 1901

New Artificial Silk Co. Ld. Regd. 1899. Vol. liq. 29 Oct. 1900. Reconstructed as Chardonnet Silk Co. Ld. Final meeting return regd. 27 Mar. 1902 1900

New Asbestos Co. Ld. Regd. 1890. Removed from Register 1904 1892

New Aspen Silver Mines Ld. Regd. 1897. Removed from Register 1910 1901

New Aurora West Gold Mining Co. Ld. Formed 1891. Reconstructed 1895 as Aurora West United Gold Mining Co. Ld. Shareholders were entitled to 1 share of £1 for every 2 shares held 1908

New Austin Gold Mines Ld. Regd. 1895. Vol. liq. 21 Apr. 1897. Final meeting return regd. 27 Nov. 1901 1898

New Austral Co. Ld. Regd. 1894. Vol. liq. Nov. 1906. Removed from Register 1907 1907

New Australasian Gold Mines Ld. Regd. 1896. Vol. liq. 31 Jan. 1899. Capital returned to contributories—3s. 9d. per share; further payments (if any) not known. Final meeting return regd. 16 Sept. 1902 1900

New Australian Broken Hill Consols Ld. Regd. 1896. Reconstructed 1907 as Broken Hill South Extended Ld., in which company shareholders were entitled to 1 share of 10s. (credited as fully-paid) for every 2 preference shares of 1s. held or 1 share of 10s. (credited as 8s. 6d. paid) for each ordinary share of £1 held. Removed from Register 1908 1908

New Australian Electric Co. Ld. Undertaking acquired by Melbourne Electric Supply Co. Ld. in 1889 1937

New Australian Gold Fields Ld. Regd. 1894. Vol. liq. 21 Jan. 1898. Final meeting return regd. 27 May 1898 1899

New Avenue Co. Ld. Regd. 1922. Vol. liq. (members') 20 Feb. 1933. Capital returned to contributories— £431,720. Final meeting return regd. 15 Nov. 1933 1934

New Axim Co. Ld. Regd. 1908. Vol. liq. Oct. 1909 for reconstruction as New Axim Mines Ld in which company shareholders were entitled to 1 share of 5s. for each ordinary share of 5s. held or 2 shares of 5s. for each deferred share of 1s. held. Removed from Register 1911 1910

New Axim Mines Ld. Regd. 1909. Vol. liq. 5 Sept. 1912. Final meeting return regd. 6 July 1916 1913

New Balkis Eersteling Ld. Regd. 1896. Vol. liq. 29 Jan. 1902. Undertaking and assets were acquired by Transvaal Exploring Land and Minerals Co. Ld., in which company shareholders were entitled to 1 share of 5s. (credited as fully-paid) for each share of 10s. held and to subscribe for certain shares in purchasing company. Final meeting return regd. 7 Mar. 1925 1902

New Balla Balla Copper Mines Ld. Regd. 1901. Vol. liq. 2 Mar. 1908. Final meeting return regd. 17 May 1919 1909

New Bayley's Mines Ld. Regd. 1907. Vol. liq. 8 Apr. 1920. Final meeting return regd. 12 June 1920 1921

New Bedford Brewery (Plymouth) Ld. Regd. 1919. Vol. liq. 16 Jan. 1920. Business acquired by New Victoria Brewery Ld. Final meeting return regd. 6 May 1921 *1920

New Beeston Cycle Co. Ld. Regd. 1896. Vol. liq. 2 Nov. 1897. The Northern works and cycle department were acquired by Beeston Cycle Co. Ld., the Southern works and motor department were acquired by Beeston Motor Co. Ld. Shareholders were

VOL. FOR

entitled to either 3 ordinary shares of £1 (credited with 17s. paid) and 2 preference shares of £1 (credited with 17s. paid) in both new companies for each share of £10 held or 20% of holding in debentures in new companies. Final meeting return regd. 12 Aug. 1898 1898

New Beeston Rim & Components Co. Ld. Regd. 1895 as Barton & Loudon Ld.; name changed to Beeston Tyre Rim Co. Ld. May 1896 and as above Dec. 1897. Removed from Register 1901 1901

New Belgium (Transvaal) Land & Development Co. Ld. Regd. 1889. Vol. liq. 14 Jan. 1914. Final meeting return regd. 3 Dec. 1917 1914

New Bentong Co. Ld. Regd. 1891. Vol. liq. 3 Jan. 1894. Final meeting return regd. 29 Sept. 1894 1894

New Berca Petroleum Co. Ld. Regd. 1901. Vol. liq. 16 Nov. 1905. Struck off Register 30 Jan. 1923 1906

New Black Reef Gold Mining Co. Ld. Inc. South African Republic 1893. Stated to be in liquidation in 1895 1895

New Boksburg Gold Mines Ld. Inc. Transvaal 1895 as East Rand Extension Mines Ld.; name changed 1896 to Boksburg Gold Mines Ld. and as above in 1909. Vol. liq. June 1920 1921

New Branston Two-Reel Sewing Machine Co. Ld. Regd. 1892. Vol. liq. 3 Apr. 1903. Final meeting return regd. 31 July 1905 .... *1904

New Brewery (Carlisle) Ld. Regd. 1879. Vol. liq. 29 May 1899 for reconstruction as Carlisle New Brewery Co. Ld. Final meeting return regd. 12 Sept. 1900 ... 1910

New Brighton Mines Ld. Inc. Transvaal 1896. Wound up Oct. 1908 1909

New Brighton Tower & Recreation Co. Ld. Regd. 1896. Vol. liq. 5 Feb. 1917. Final meeting return regd. 9 May 1919 1917

New Brilliant Freeholds Gold Mining Co. Ld. Inc. Queensland 1903. Wound up Mar. 1918 1918

New British Dominions Exploration Ld. Regd. 1898. Vol. liq. 15 Nov. 1899. Final meeting return regd. 25 July 1900 1900

New British Ever Ready Co. Ld. See British Ever Ready Co. Ld.

New British Iron Co. Ld. Constituted by deed of settlement 1843; regd. as limited 1883. Vol. liq. 9 June 1892. Court Order to continue winding up under supervision 25 June 1892. Final meeting return regd. 18 May 1906 .... *1893

New British Mutual Investment Co. Ld. See British Mutual Bank Ld.

New British Rubber & "Wear-well" Hose Pipe Co. Ld. Regd. 1897. Receiver appointed in Nov. 1931; ceased to act Dec. 1932. Struck off Register 4 Oct. 1935 1936

New British Transvaal Mines Ld. Regd. 1908. Vol. liq. 19 Sept. 1922. The assets and undertaking were acquired by Orion Development Co. Ld., in which company shareholders were entitled to 2 shares of 2s. (credited with 1s. 6d. paid) for each share of 5s. held. Final meeting return regd. 11 May 1937 1923

New Brotherton Tube Co. Ld. See Brotherton Ediswan Tubes & Conduits Ld.

New Brunswick Gas and Oilfields Ld. Regd. Edinburgh 1915. Vol. liq. (members') 31 July 1947. Capital returned to contributories—20s. per preference share (of £1) and £2 19s. 6·0465d. per ordinary share (of £1). Final meeting return regd. 6 Oct. 1950...... 1952

New Brunswick Trading Co. of London Ld. Regd. 1885. Court Orders: to wind up 23 Apr. 1890; to dissolve 14 July 1896 1891

New Buckingham & Adams Cycle Co. Ld. Regd. 1897. Removed from Register 1909 1902

New Buffels Land & Mining Co. Ld. See Transvaal Proprietary Ld.

New Bultfontein Mining Co. Ld. Inc. Cape of Good Hope 1895. Property was acquired in 1900 by De Beers Consolidated Mines Ld. for £192,862. The debentures were repaid on 1 Mar. 1901 at 105%. Shareholders were expected to receive 12s. 6d. per share of £1 1901

New Bultfontein Mining Co. Ld. See Bultfontein Mining Co. Ld.

New Cakemore Blue Brickworks Ld. See Cakemore Blue-Brick Co. Ld.

New Calaveras Gold Mining Co. Ld. Regd. 1893. Vol. liq. 18 Mar. 1895. Final meeting return regd. 11 Aug. 1896 1896

New California Ld. Regd. 1886. Vol. liq. 1 Feb. 1893. for reconstruction as California Milling and Mining Co. Ld., in which company shareholders were entitled to 1 share of 10s. (credited with 8s. paid) for each fully-paid share of £1 held. Final meeting return regd. 19 Nov. 1895 1908

New Callao Ld. Regd. 1881. Removed from Register 1903 1886

See Stock Exchange Year-Book.

VOL. FOR

received units of the rate of 0·71007 units per share (of 25p). Final meeting return regd. 22 Feb. 1979 **1979–80**

New Court European Trust Ld. Regd. 1972. Vol. liq. (members') 15 July 1977. Net assets to be transferred to New Court International Fund, an existing authorised unit trust. Shareholders received 0·71007 units per share of 25p. £374 was paid into Companies' Liquidation Account for unclaimed dividends. Final meeting return regd 22 Feb. 1979 **1979–80**

New Coventry Cross Cycle Co. Ld. Regd. 1899. Removed from Register 1910 .... **1902**

New Cransley Iron & Steel Co. Ld. Regd. 1918. All capital was owned by Stewarts & Lloyds Ld. Vol. liq. (members') 11 Dec. 1959. Final meeting return regd. 5 Aug. 1960 .... **1958**

New Craven's Caledonia Gold Mining Co. Ld. Inc. Queensland 1904. Wound up June 1912 .... **1913**

New Credenda Tube Co. Ld. Regd. 1896. Vol. liq. 14 July 1897. Business was acquired by Tubes Ld. Capital returned to contributories—£2 per share of £1. Removed from Register 1901 .... **1898**

New Croesus Gold Mining Co. Ld. Inc. Transvaal 1891. Reconstructed 1898 as company of same name. Shareholders were entitled to 2 shares of £1 in new company for every 5 shares held **1906**

New Croesus Gold Mining Co. Ld. Inc. Transvaal 1898. Reconstructed 1902 as Consolidated Langaagte Mines Ld., in which company shareholders were entitled to 1 fully-paid share of £1 for each share of £1 held **1903**

New Cross Brewery Co. Ld. Regd. 1905. Vol. liq. 17 Apr. 1925. Undertaking was acquired by Hoare & Co. Ld. Final meeting return regd. 22 Mar. 1927 .... **1923**

New Cross Kinema Ld. Regd. 1920. Vol. liq. 17 July 1928. Undertaking was acquired by Denman Picture Houses Ld. Final meeting return regd. 2 Aug. 1929 .... **1940**

New Cumnock Gas Co. Ld. Regd. in Edinburgh 1929. Dissolved 1 May 1949, undertaking being vested in Scottish Area Gas Board under Gas Act 1948. Holders of securities were entitled to receive, in respect of each £1 unit held, British Gas 3% guaranteed stock 1990–95 as follows:

	£	s.	d.
Ord. shares	2	2	6
5% cum. shares	1	2	0

1952

New Cycle Co. Ld. Regd. 1896. Vol. liq. 4 Feb. 1898. Capital returned to contributories 1s. 7¾d. per share of £1 at Dec. 1898; further payments (if any) not known. Final meeting return regd. 2 Mar. 1899 .. **1899**

New Darvel Bay (Borneo) Tobacco Plantations Ld. Regd. 1892. Vol. liq. (creditors') 24 Nov. 1933. Capital returned to contributories—£73 15s. Final meeting return regd. 20 Nov. 1934 .... **1934**

New Day Dawn & Norfolk Mines Ld. Regd. 1907. Vol. liq. 10 Dec. 1912. Final meeting return regd. 13 Mar. 1914 .... **1913**

New De Kaap Ld. Regd. 1904. Vol. liq. 22 June 1906. Reconstructed as New De Kaap (1906) Ld., in which company shareholders were entitled to 6 shares of 5s. (credited with 4s. 6d. paid) for every 5 shares of 5s. held. Final meeting return regd. 20 Mar. 1920 .... **1907**

New De Kaap (1906) Ld. Regd. 1906. Court Order to wind up 4 June 1907. Liquidator released 29 Oct. 1913. Struck off Register 3 Sept. 1918 .... **1908**

New Deep Leads Syndicate Ld. Regd. 1905. Vol. liq. 29 Dec. 1908. Final meeting return regd. 28 Apr. 1915 **1909**

New Devala-Moyar Gold Mining Co. Ld. Regd. 1890. Vol. liq. 16 Jan. 1893. Final meeting return regd.9 July 1894 .... **1893**

New Disraeli Mine Co. Ld. Regd. 1890. Vol. liq. 18 Apr. 1890. Final meeting return regd. 16 Apr. 1891 .... **1891**

New District Development Co. Ld. See H. E. Proprietary (New) Ld.

New Districts Development Co. Ld. Inc. Transvaal 1904. Wound up Feb. 1912 for reconstruction as New Districts Development Co. Ld. [later H. E. Proprietary (New) Ld.]. Shareholders were entitled to 2 fully-paid shares of 10s. in new company for each share of £1 held **1912**

New Dominion Syndicate Ld. Regd. 1899. Vol. liq. 11 Jan. 1926. Final meeting return regd. 23 Mar. 1926 **1926**

New Druce-Portland Co. Ld. Regd. 1907. Court Order to wind up 14 Jan. 1908. Removed from Register 1911 **1908**

New Dunderland Co. Ld. Regd 1913. Vol. liq. 15 Jan. 1919. Final meeting return regd. 31 Oct. 1923 .... **1919**

New Durham Salt Co. Ld. Regd. 1889. Court Orders: to wind up Sept. 1889; to dissolve 18 Nov. 1893 ..... **1890**

New Dynant Anthracite Colliery Ld. Regd. 1907. Receiver appointed in Dec. 1913. Undertaking and assets were sold to New Dynant Anthracite Colliery (1914) Ld. Debenture holders received 14,000 fully-paid shares of £1 and 12,000 shares of £1 (credited

with 10s. paid) in new company in discharge. The purchase consideration also included a further 5,000 fully-paid shares and £4,539 in cash. Struck off Register 17 Dec. 1915 .... **1915**

New Dynant Antbracite Colliery (1914) Ld. Regd. 1914. Vol. liq. Nov. 1923. Undertaking was acquired by Great Mountain Collieries Co. Ld. Capital returned to contributories—15s. per share of £1 in Jan. 1924; further payments (if any) not known. Struck off Register 21 Jan. 1936 .... **1936**

New Eadie Manufacturing Co. Ld. See Eadie Manufacturing Co. Ld.

New Eastern Investment Co. Ld. Regd. 1899 as Associated Share & Investment Co. Ld.; name changed 1903. Vol. liq. (members') 15 July 1943. Capital returned to contributories—1s. 2¼d. per share (of 3s. 9d.). £2,964 16s. 4d. was paid into Companies' Liquidation Account. Final meeting return regd. 22 Feb. 1952 .... **1953**

New Eberhardt Co. Ld. See Thistle Reef Gold Mining Co. Ld.

New Egypt & Levant Shipping Co. Ld. Regd. 1924. Vol. liq. (members') 15 Feb. 1950. Capital returned to contributories—£2 17s. 10d. per share of £1. Amounts paid into Companies' Liquidation Account—£157 13s. in respect of unclaimed dividends and £5,101 1s. 6d. in respect of unclaimed distributions. Final meeting return regd. 4 June 1959 ...... **1960**

New Einasleigh Copper Mines Ld. Regd. 1907. Vol. liq. Dec. 1911 for sale of property to Chillagoe Co. Ld. 118,688 shares of 10s. (credited with 9s. paid) in that company were to be distributed among debenture holders and shareholders were to receive approximately 1 share for every 3 held. Removed from Register 1913 .... **1912**

New Electricity Co. of Macclesfield Ld. See Electricity Co. of Macclesfield Ld.

New Elkhorn Mining Co. Ld. Regd. 1895. Vol. liq. July 1912. Removed from Register 1913 .... **1913**

New Emeralds Co. Ld. Regd. 1892. Vol. liq. 20 Dec. 1916. Final meeting return regd. 4 Mar. 1926 ...... **1917**

New Emma Silver Mining Co. Ld. Regd. 1882. Vol. liq. 19 Apr. 1886. Reconstructed as New Emma Silver Mining Co. (1886) Ld., in which company shareholders were entitled to 4 shares of £1 (credited with 15s. paid) for each share of £10 held. Holders of debentures were entitled to debentures in new company. Final meeting return regd. 16 Dec. 1896 **1887**

New Emma Silver Mining Co. (1886) Ld. Regd. 1886. Vol. liq. 25 Apr. 1890. Reconstructed as Emma Co. Ld., in which company shareholders were entitled to 1 fully-paid share of 5s. for each fully-paid share of £1 held. Holders of debentures were entitled to debentures in new company. Final meeting return regd. 16 Dec. 1896 .... **1891**

New English Bank of the River Plate Ld. Regd. 1892. Court Order to wind up 4 Apr. 1894. Removed from Register 1911 .... **1895**

New Era Assurance Corporation Ld. Regd. 1897. Vol. liq. 17 Nov. 1909. Undertaking was acquired by National Standard Life Assurance Corporation Ld. Final meeting return regd. 26 Apr. 1911 .... ***1910**

New Era Co. Ld. Inc. South African Republic 1895. Reconstructed 1902 as New Era Consolidated Ld. in which company shareholders were entitled to 3 shares of £1 (credited as fully-paid) for each share of £1 held **1902**

New Era National Pictures Ld. Regd. 26 Jan. 1928. Vol. liq. (creditors') 31 Dec. 1935 .... **1976-7**

New European & General Investment Trust Ld. Regd. 1959. Vol. liq. (members') 31 Mar. 1970. Reconstructed as Negit S.A. in which company shareholders were entitled to 1 share of $U.S.1 for every 2 ordinary shares. £12·27 was paid into Companies' Liquidation Account in respect of unclaimed dividends. Final meeting return regd. 1 Feb. 1974 .... **1974-5**

New Explorers Syndicate Ld. Regd. 1896. Struck off Register 8 Aug. 1905 .... **1906**

New Exploring & Finance Co. Ld. Regd. 1902 as Mysore United Gold Co. Ld.; name changed Dec. 1904. Vol. liq. Jan. 1906. Removed from Register 1907 **1906**

New Explosives Co. Ld. Regd. 1885. Reconstructed 1906 as New Explosives Co. (1906) Ld., in which company shareholders were entitled to 3 shares of £1 (credited with 16s. paid) for each share of £3 held. Removed from Register 1907 .... **1908**

New Flag Gold Mining Co. Ld. Regd. 1897. Vol. liq. 11 Aug. 1898. Final meeting return regd. 16 May 1899 **1899**

New Florence Mining Co. Ld. Regd. 1880. Vol. liq. 14 Sept. 1886. Final meeting return regd. 11 Aug. 1892 ***1884**

New Found Out Mines Ld. Regd. 1909. Vol. liq. 12 Nov. 1924. Final meeting return regd. 8 Aug.1925 .... **1925**

New Founders Association Ld. Regd. 1902. Vol. liq. Apr. 1912. Removed from Register 1913 .... **1913**

VOL. FOR

New Fraser River Gold Mines Ld. Regd. 1897. Removed from Register 1903 .... **1903**

New French Flagstaff Gold Mining Co. Ld. Regd. 1898. Vol. liq. July 1906. Removed from Register 1907 **1907**

New G. & S. Processes Syndicate Ld. Regd. 1928. Vol. liq. (creditors') 12 Jan. 1933. Reconstructed as company of same name (later Talbex Ld.). Shareholders were entitled to 1 share of 1s. (credited with 9s. paid) in new company for each share of 1s. held. Final meeting return regd. 19 Mar. 1934 .... **1938**

New Gaiety Restaurant & Hotel Co. Ld. Regd. 1901. Vol. liq. Apr. 1906. Removed from Register 1908 **1907**

New Gas Co. Ld. Regd. 1873. Vol. liq. 22 July 1882. Final meeting return regd. 27 May 1891 .... **1883**

New Geduld Deep Ld. Inc. Transvaal 1908. The London office was closed on 31 Dec. 1923 .... **1923**

New Gellivara Co. Ld. Regd. 1868. Vol. liq. Feb. 1882. Final meeting return regd. 17 July 1883 .... **1883**

New Girling Commercial Cars Ld. Regd. 1913. Vol. liq. 3 May 1915. Final meeting return regd. 12 Oct. 1915 **1916**

New Goch Gold Mines Ld. Inc. Transvaal 1899. Wound up June 1924. Capital returned to contributories— 2s. per share of £1 on 25 Aug. 1924; further distributions (if any) not known **1925**

New Gold Coast Agency Ld. Regd. 1901. Vol. liq. July 1909. Undertaking was sold to Gold Coast Amalgamated Mines Ld. (later Amalgamated Mining Trust Ld.), in which company shareholders were entitled to 2 fully-paid shares of £1 for every 9 shares of £1 held. Removed from Register 1910 .... **1910**

New Gold Fields Syndicate Ld. Regd. 1895. Struck off Register 1929 .... ***1901**

New Gold Hill Company Ld. Regd. 1888. Vol. liq. 24 June 1895. Reconstructed as Hampton Gold Hill Mines Ld., in which company shareholders were entitled to 1 share of 10s. (credited with 8s. paid) for each share of £1 held. Final meeting return regd. 5 Dec. 1895 .... **1905**

New Gold Proprietary Mines Ld. Regd. 1907. Vol. liq. 30 July 1914. Final meeting return regd. 27 Mar. 1919 .... **1915**

New Gold Run Co. Ld. Regd. 1880. Vol. liq. Jan. 1883. Final meeting return regd. 29 Apr. 1884 .... **1884**

New Gold Trust Ld. Regd. 1920. Vol. liq. 13 June 1930. All shares owned by South African Gold Trust Ld., which was acquired by Consolidated Gold Fields of South Africa Ld. Final meeting return regd. 27 June 1931 .... **1931**

New Golden Kopje Ld. Regd. 1895. Vol. liq. 7 Oct. 1896. Final meeting return regd. 3 Apr. 1897 .... **1897**

New Golden Twins (Ontario) Ld. Regd. 1897. Vol. liq. 17 Sept. 1900. Final meeting return regd. 4 Apr. 1901 **1901**

New Goldfields of British Columbia Ld. Regd. 1896. Vol. liq. 11 Feb. 1913. Final meeting return regd. 6 Nov. 1913 .... **1913**

New Goldfields of Venezuela Ld. Regd. 1926. Vol. liq. (members') Oct. 1950. Capital returned to contributories: $\frac{7}{16}d$. per share of 5s. Final meeting return regd. 4 Oct. 1951. £4,211 was paid into Companies' Liquidation Account **1952**

New Goongarrie Gold Mines Ld. Regd. 1903. Struck off Register 7 May 1907 .... **1908**

New Gopeng Ld. Regd. 1903. Vol. liq. 20 Sept. 1912. Reconstructed as Gopeng Consolidated Ld., in which company shareholders were entitled to 155 shares of £1 (credited as fully-paid) for every 100 shares of £1 held; a cash distribution of 1s. 3d. per share was made in Oct. 1912. Final meeting return regd. 24 Dec. 1913 .... **1913**

New Gordon Diamond Co. Ld. Regd. 1891. Vol. liq. 10 Sept. 1896. Debenture holders were repaid. Final meeting return regd. 5 May 1898 .... **1897**

New Gorsllan Colliery Co. Ld. Regd. 1928. Receiver appointed 14 Feb. 1935. Assets realised insufficient to contribute anything towards claims of debenture holders. Struck off Register 11 Apr. 1939 .... **1940**

New Grahamstown Gold Mining Co. Ld. Inc. Kimberley 1889. Property sold to Jubilee Gold Co. Ld. for £15,000 in fully-paid shares of £1, shareholders being entitled to 1 share for every 10 shares of £1 held **1896**

New Grand Hotel, Birmingham, Ld. Regd. 1896. Vol. liq. (members') 17 Dec. 1969. Capital returned to contributories—£5 per preference share of £5 and £2·21 per ordinary share of £5. £569·98 was paid into Companies' Liquidation Account in respect of unclaimed distributions. Final meeting return regd. 3 Dec. 1971 .... **1972**

New Grappler Pneumatic Tyre Co. Ld. Regd. Dublin 1899. Removed from Register 1904. .... **1904**

New Graskop Exploring Co. Ld. Regd. 1903. Vol. liq. 29 Dec. 1908. Final meeting return regd.6 Mar.1914 **1909**

New Great Wheal Fortune Syndicate Ld. Regd. 1908. Vol. liq. Oct. 1910. Removed from Register 1911 **1911**

VOL. FOR

New Grosny Oilfields Ld. Regd. 1916. Struck off Register Feb. 1933 .... **1933**

New Guadalcazar Quicksilver Mines Ld. Regd. 1895. Removed from Register 1904 .... **1904**

New Guayaquil Land Co. Ld. Regd. 1905. Vol. liq. 18 July 1913. The undertaking and assets were sold to Equadorian Corporation Ld in which company shareholders were entitled to 1 share of £1 (credited as fully-paid) for each share of £1 held. Final meeting return regd. 26 Aug. 1914 .... **1914**

New Guinea Copper Mines Ld. Inc. Victoria 1920. Receiver for debenture holders appointed in 1926 stated on 9 Dec. 1929 that company was practically defunct **1930**

New Guston Co. Ld. Regd. 1887. Vol. liq. 10 Feb. 1898. Final meeting return regd. 10 Apr. 1902 .... **1898**

New Halfpenny Letter Co. Ld. Regd. 1889. Vol. liq. 12 Nov. 1890. Final meeting return regd. 20 May 1891 **1891**

New Halwyn China Clay Co. Ld. Regd. 1912. Vol. liq. (members') 28 June 1933. All shares owned by English China Clays Ld. Final meeting return regd. 7 Feb. 1935 .... **1934**

New Hannan's Excelsior & Crœsus Ld. Regd. 1899. Reconstructed 1901 as Kalgoorlie Amalgamated Ld., in which company shareholders were entitled to 1 share of £1 (credited as fully-paid) for every 4 shares of £1 held. Removed from Register 1905 .. **1903**

New Hauraki Gold Properties Ld. Regd. 1895. Removed from Register 1903 .... **1902**

New Havillah Gold Mining Co. Ld. Regd. 1898. Vol. liq. 8 Aug. 1901. Reconstructed as Charlotte Plains Consolidated Gold Mines Ld., in which company 15,000 shares of £1 (credited with 15s. paid) were taken over. Final meeting return regd. 22 Aug. 1902 **1907**

New Heidelberg Roodepoort Gold Mining Co. Ld. Inc. Transvaal 1892. Wound up Feb. 1913 .... **1913**

New Heriot Gold Mining Co. Ld. Inc. Natal & Transvaal 1892. Wound up Mar. 1921. Capital returned to contributories—10s. per share of £1 at Nov. 1921; further distributions (if any) not known **1922**

New Hermand Oil Co. Ld. Regd. Edinburgh 1899. Vol. liq. July 1902. Court Orders: to wind up June 1903; to dissolve June 1905 .... **1904**

New Hibernia Investment Trust Ld. Inc. in Dublin 1963. Vol. liq. (members') 20 Oct. 1977. Capital returned to contributories—106·81p per preference share (of £1) and 52·74p per ordinary share (of 50p). £4,200·37 was paid into Companies' Liquidation Account in respect of unclaimed distributions. Final meeting return regd. 4 Apr. 1979 .... **1980–1**

New Hillgrove Proprietary Mines Ld. Regd. 1902. Vol. liq. Oct. 1909. Removed from Register 1911 .... **1910**

New Hillsborough Gold Mining Co. Ld. Regd. 1895. Vol. liq. 3 Nov. 1898. Final meeting return regd. 5 Nov. 1901 .... **1899**

New Hollingbourne Paper Mills Co. Ld. Regd. 1884. Vol. liq. 13 Apr. 1887. Court Orders: to wind up 28 Sept. 1887; to dissolve 26 Feb. 1896 .... **1888**

New Holmbush Mining Co. Ld. Regd. 1880. Court Order to wind up 7 May 1886. Struck off Register 11 Aug. 1905 .... **1887**

New Hood & Moore Ld. Regd. 1905. Vol. liq. 7 Dec. 1908. Removed from Register 1910 .... **1909**

New Hoover Hill Gold Mining Co. Ld. Regd. 1884. Reconstructed as Grierson's Gold Mines Ld. Removed from Register 1910 .... **1908**

New Hornachos Silver Mines Ld. Regd. 1889. Vol. liq. 19 Sept. 1892. Final meeting return regd. 19 Jan. 1897 .... **1893**

New Horo Concession Exploration Co. of Swazieland Ld. Inc. Cape of Good Hope 1892. Undertaking and assets acquired in 1898 by Swazieland Corporation Ld. for fully-paid shares **1899**

New Hucknall Colliery Co. Ld. Regd. 1879. Undertaking acquired in 1900 by company of same name. Removed from Register 1901 .... **1945**

New Hucknall Colliery Co. Ld. Regd. 1900. Reconstructed 1945 as N. H. and B. Collieries Ld in which company shareholders were entitled to an equal amount of live stock. Dissolved 1 Jan. 1945 .... **1946**

New Hudson Cycle Extension Ld. Regd. 1897. Business was acquired in 1899 by New Hudson Cycle Co. Ld. (later Girling Ld.). Removed from Register 1909 **1900**

New Ice & Cold Storage Co. Ld. Regd. 1921. Receiver appointed in Feb. 1932; ceased to act 9 Feb. 1935. Struck off Register 16 Oct. 1936 .... **1937**

New Imperial Investment Co. Ld. Regd. 1892. Vol. liq. 9 Aug. 1899. Reconstructed as Metropolitan Trust Co. Ld. Stockholders were offered either £70 in cash for every £100 preferred stock held and £12 in cash for every £100 deferred stock held or an equal number of fully-paid paid shares of £1 in new company. Final meeting return regd. 18 Dec. 1899 **1900**

*See Stock Exchange Year-Book.

VOL. FOR

New Mount Albion Silver Mining & Smelting Co. Ld. Regd. 1891. Removed from Register 1907 .... **1894**

New Municipal Trust Co. Ld. Regd. 1890. Vol. liq. 27 July 1894. Undertaking was acquired by Municipal Trust Co. Ld. Final meeting return regd. 9 Nov. 1895 .... **1895**

New Mysore Manganese Co. Ld. Regd. 1907. Undertaking was sold in 1908 to Workington Iron Co. Ld., in which company shareholders were entitled to 1 fully-paid ordinary share of £1 for each share of £1 held. Removed from Register 1911 .... **1909**

New Nigel Asbestos Co. Ld. Regd. 1930. Struck off Register 14 Apr. 1939 .... **1940**

New Nimrod Co. Ld. Regd. 1904. Vol. liq. Dec. 1926 for reconstruction as New Nimrod (1927) Ld., in which company shareholders were entitled to 1 share of 5s. (credited with 3s. 9d. paid) for each share of £1 held. Struck off Register July 1933 .... **1934**

New Nimrod (1927) Ld. Regd. 1927. Struck off Register 17 Jan. 1933 .... **1933**

New North Halkyn Mines Ld. Regd. 1904. Vol. liq. (members') 27 May 1930. Capital returned to contributories—2s. 9d. per preference share of £1 (16s. 6d. paid). Final meeting return regd. 25 June 1953 .... **1954**

New North West Corporation Ld. Inc. Canada 1921. Court Order to wind up 8 Oct. 1935. Undertaking was acquired by Yukon Consolidated Gold Corporation Ld. **1936**

New Oceana Transvaal Coal Co. Ld. Regd. 1899. Vol. liq. 12 Jan. 1903. Properties acquired by Balkis Land Co. Ld. Final meeting return regd. 17 July 1914 .... ***1905**

New Oil Properties Ld. Regd. 1910. Vol. liq. 7 Aug. 1914. Final meeting return regd. 11 Nov. 1919 .... **1915**

New Oil Refining Process Ld. Regd. 1907. Vol. liq. 22 Dec. 1914. Final meeting return regd. 6 Jan. 1917 **1915**

New Options Co. Ld. Regd. 1896. Vol. liq. 22 July 1898. Properties were acquired by New Options Ld., in which company shareholders were entitled to 2½ fully-paid shares for each share of £1 subscribed for by them. Final meeting return regd. 17 July 1899 **1905**

New Options Exploration Ld. Regd. 1905. Vol. liq. 18 Oct. 1911. Final meeting return regd. 12 Dec. 1911 **1913**

New Options Ld. Regd. 1898. Reconstructed 1905 as New Options Exploration Ld., in which company shareholders were entitled to 1 share of 1s. (credited as fully-paid) for each share of £1 held. Removed from Register 1912 .... **1908**

New Organos Gold Mining Co. Ld. Regd. 1888. Removed from Register 1906 .... **1892**

New Oriental Bank Corporation Ld. Regd. 1884. Vol. liq. 23 June 1892. Struck off Register 1922 .... **1893**

New Oscar Gold Co. Ld. Regd. 1886. Vol. liq. 4 July 1888. Reconstructed as Oscar Gold Co. Ld., in which company shareholders were entitled to apply for shares. Final meeting return regd. 29 Mar. 1892 **1891**

New Oscilloscope Co. Ld. Regd. 1925. Court Order to wind up May 1933. Struck off Register 21 Sept. 1937 **1938**

New Oxley (Canada) Ranche Co. Ld. Regd. 1886. A capital return of 110% to contributories was anticipated. Removed from Register 1904 .... **1904**

New Paccha & Jazpampa Nitrate Co. Ld. Regd. 1898. Vol. liq. (members') 23 Apr. 1931. Undertaking and assets acquired by Nitrate Corporation of Chile, in which corporation shareholders were entitled to 1 fully-paid series B share of 100 pesos (either ordinary or 7% cumulative preferred) for every 12 shares of £1 held. £490 11s. 3d. was paid into Companies' Liquidation Account in respect of unclaimed dividends and £6 6s. 5d. in respect of sale of unclaimed shares. Final meeting return regd. 18 Dec. 1934 .... **1932**

New Pachuca Silver Mining Co. Ld. Regd. 1891. Struck off Register 23 July 1901 .... **1902**

New Palladium (Stockwell) Ld. Regd. 1920. Vol. liq. Dec. 1927. Struck off Register 12 Mar. 1935........ **1936**

New Parkia Brick Co. Ld. See Carnarvon Brickworks Ld.

New Pegamoid Ld. Regd. 1901. Vol. liq. 7 June 1926. Final meeting return regd. 20 Apr. 1928 .... **1927**

New Pensacola Trading Co. Ld. Regd. 1921. Vol. liq. 7 Dec. 1923. Final meeting return regd. 6 Feb. 1925 ***1924**

New Peterborough Brick Co. Ld. Regd. 1897. Vol. liq. (members') 4 Jan. 1924. Undertaking acquired by London Brick Co. Ld. Assets were distributed in specie. Final meeting return regd. 27 Sept. 1946 . **1947**

New Pictorial Publishing Co. Ld. Regd. 1891. Vol. liq. 29 Apr. 1892. Final meeting return regd. 3 Feb. 1893 **1893**

New Pierrefitte Mining Co. Ld. Regd 1887. Vol. liq. 6 Jan. 1892. Final meeting return regd. 19 Sept. 1893 **1894**

New Pinos Altos Co. Ld. Regd. 1893. Property seized by bankers in Mexico. Struck off Register 26 Oct. 1900 **1901**

VOL. FOR

New Pittsburg (Grass Valley) Gold Mines Ld. Regd. 1890. Vol. liq. 17 Dec. 1895. Final meeting return regd. 2 Nov. 1897 .... **1896**

New Polbreen Mining Co. Established 1898. In liquidation in 1905 .... **1905**

New Potosi Co. Ld. Regd. 1884 to acquire properties of Potosi Gold Mining Co. Ld. Vol. liq. 16 June 1887. Reconstructed as Potosi Ld., in which company shareholders were entitled to 1 share of £1 (credited with 16s. paid) for each share of £1 held or 1 fully-paid share of £1 for each preference share of £1 held. Final meeting return regd. 4 Oct. 1887 .... **1892**

New Premier Cycle Co. Ld. See Coventry Premier Ld.

New Premier Gold Mines Ld. Regd. 1904. Undertaking was acquired by Union Consolidated Trust Ld in which company shareholders were entitled to 1 share of 5s. (credited with 3s. 9d. paid) for each share of 5s. held. Removed from Register 1910 ... **1908**

New Primrose Gold Mining Co. Ld. Inc. Transvaal 1890. Vol. liq. Nov. 1928 .... **1929**

New Princes (1924) Ld. Regd. 1924. Vol. liq. Apr. 1929. Struck off Register Mar. 1933 .... **1934**

New Purisima Smelting & Mining Co. Ld. Regd. 1893. Vol. liq. Oct. 1925. Struck off Register Mar. 1929 **1930**

New Quebec Graphite Co. Ld. Regd. 1915. Vol. liq. 7 July 1919. Reconstructed as Quebec Graphite Co. Ld. Final meeting return regd. 17 Sept. 1924 ...... ***1920**

New Quebrada Co, Ld. Regd. 1866. Vol. liq. 28 June 1883. Reconstructed as Quebrada Railway Land & Copper Co. Ld., in which company shareholders were entitled to 1 fully-paid shares of £5 for each share of £10 held. Final meeting return regd. 13 Feb. 1892 .... **1884**

New Queen Cross Gold Mines Ld. Inc. Queensland 1908. Vol. liq. Apr. 1918 .... **1919**

New Queen Gold Mining Co. Ld. Regd. 1889. Vol. liq. 20 Aug. 1897. Reconstructed as company of same name. Shareholders were entitled to 1 share of £1 (credited with 17s. 6d. paid) for each share of £1 held. Final meeting return regd. 12 Oct. 1898 ..... **1907**

New Queen Gold Mining Co. Ld. Regd. 1897. Vol. liq. 31 Dec. 1907. Reconstructed as Queen Gold Mining Co. Ld., in which company shareholders were entitled to 1 share of 1s. (credited with 1s. paid) for each share of £1 held and an option (since expired) over further shares. Final meeting return regd. 31 Dec. 1908 .... **1908**

New Queensland Copper Co. Ld. Regd. 1910. Vol. liq. Mar. 1914. Removed from Register 1918 .... **1915**

New Rand Consolidated Ld. Regd. 1919. Vol. liq. (creditors') 24 Mar. 1930. Assets realised insufficient to pay creditors in full. Final meeting return regd. 17 Nov. 1931 .... **1931**

New Rand Gold Mines Ld. Regd. 1894. Amalgamated 1897 with Niekerk (Klerksdorp) Gold Mining Co. Ld. (later Niekerk Ld.). in which company shareholders were entitled to 10 fully-paid shares of £1 for every 7 shares held. Removed from Register 1905 **1900**

New Rand. Inc. Transvaal 1905. Vol. liq. May 1920. Boring operations were continued by New Rand Consolidated Ld. **1920**

New Rand Proprietary Ld. Regd. 1914. Vol. liq. 23 July 1919. Final meeting return regd. 21 Apr. 1920 ... ***1920**

New Rand Southern Gold Mining Co Ld. Regd. 1901. Vol. liq. July 1907. Struck off Register May 1929. **1930**

New Rand Syndicate Ld. Regd. 1905. Vol. liq. Feb. 1907. Removed from Register 1908 .... **1908**

New Randt Reefs Gold Mining Co. Ld. Regd. 1908. Vol. liq. 18 June 1915. Final meeting return regd. 19 Nov. 1915 .... **1916**

New Rapid Cycle Co. Ld. Regd. 1897. Vol. liq. 8 Feb. 1901. Final meeting return regd. 26 May 1906...... **1902**

New Ravenswood Ld. Regd. 1899. Vol. liq. 19 Dec. 1918. Final meeting return regd. 8 Mar. 1920 .... **1919**

New Redmoor Mining Co. Ld. Regd. 1881. Removed from Register 1905 .... **1887**

New Rhodesia District Development Co. Ld. Regd. 1900. Vol. liq. 16 Jan. 1918. Capital returned to contributories—2s. per ordinary share of £1; 1½d. per founders' share of 1s. at Mar. 1918; further payments (if any) not known. Final meeting return regd. 14 Jan. 1920 .... **1918**

New Rhodesia Mines and Investment Co. Ld. Regd. 1922. Vol. liq. 10 Apr. 1928. Canadian assets were transferred to Canadian Share Investment Co. Ld., in which company shareholders were entitled to 1 share of 2s. (credited with 1s. 3d. paid) for each share of 2s. 6d held. South African assets were transferred to Orion Development Co. Ld., in which company shareholders were entitled to 1 fully-paid share of 2s. and 4 shares of 2s. (credited with 1s. paid) for every 10 shares of 1s. 6d. held. Final meeting return regd. 25 Mar. 1936 .... **1929**

See Stock Exchange Year-Book.

VOL. FOR

New Rhodesia Mines Ld. Inc. Rhodesia 1905. Vol. liq. May 1909 for reconstruction under same name. Shareholders were entitled to 3 fully-paid shares in new company for every 2 shares held **1910**

New Rhodesia Mines Ld. Regd. 1909. Vol. liq. 29 May 1922. Reconstructed as New Rhodesia Mines & Investment Co. Ld. in which company shareholders were entitled to 1 share of 2s. 6d. (credited with 1s. 6d. paid) for each share of 2s. 6d. held. Final meeting return regd. 26 Mar. 1931 .... **1923**

New Rhos Anthracite Collieries Ld. Regd. 1927. All shares owned by Amalgamated Anthracite Collieries Ld. Struck off Register 10 Mar. 1939 .... **1929**

New Rhyl Ld. Regd. 1889. Vol. liq. June 1890. Struck off Register Apr. 1929 .... **1930**

New Rietfontein Estate Gold Mines Ld. Inc. Transvaal 1892. Vol. liq. Feb. 1918. Capital returned to contributories—2s. per share of £1 at 20 Apr. 1918; further payments (if any) not known. **1919**

New Rio Manso Estate Co. Ld. Regd. Edinburgh 1900. Vol. liq. Oct. 1910. Capital returned to contributories—6s. 8d. per share of £1 at 19 Nov. 1912; further payment (if any) not known. Final meeting return regd. 6 Mar. 1924 .... **1913**

New Rio Tinto Copper Co. Ld. Regd. 1895. Vol. liq. 14 May 1901. Final meeting return regd. 12 Aug. 1904 ***1902**

New Rip Gold Mining Co. Ld. Regd 1902. Vol. liq. 30 Oct. 1924. Final meeting return regd. 20 Jan. 1926 **1925**

New Romney Gas Light & Coke Co. Ld. Regd. 1856. Dissolved 1 May 1949. undertaking being vested in South Eastern Area Gas Board under Gas Act 1948. Holders of securities were entitled to receive, in respect of each £5 unit held, British Gas 3% guaranteed stock 1990–95 as follows:

	£	s.	d.
Orig. ord. shares...........................	5	2	6
Addit. ord. shares...........................	5	2	6	**1952**

New Ross and Waterford Railways. In 1925 the undertaking was vested in Great Southern Railways Co. in which company stockholders were entitled to an equal amount of similar stock **1925**

New Royalty Kinema (Brixton) Ld. Regd. 1920. Court Order to wind up 14 Mar. 1922. Struck off Register Apr. 1929 .... **1930**

New Rubber Co. Ld. Regd. 1895. Removed from Register 1903 .... **1901**

New Russell Gold and Exploration Ld. Regd. 1897. Vol. liq. 11 Jan. 1899. Final meeting return regd. 4 Aug. 1899 .... **1899**

New Russell Gold Mining Co. Ld. Regd. 1890. Struck off Register 15 Aug. 1893 .... **1899**

New Russia Co. Ld. Regd. 3 July 1869. The properties were nationalised by the Soviet Government. Struck off Register 12 June 1970 .... **1964**

New Rutland Square Cinema Co. Ld. Regd. 1928. Vol. liq. (members') 9 Aug. 1937. Direct controlling interest held by General Theatre Corporation Ld. Final meeting return regd. 7 Feb. 1938 .... **1938**

New St. Augustine Diamond Mining Co. Ld. Regd. 1902. Removed from Register 1909 .... **1904**

New St. Augustine Ld. Regd. 1894. Vol. liq. 20 Nov. 1896. Reconstructed as St. Augustine Diamond Mining Co. Ld., in which company shareholders were entitled to 1 share of £1 (credited with 18s. paid) for each share of £1 held. Struck off Register 22 May 1908 .... **1899**

New St. Augustine Mine Ld. Regd. 1894. Removed from Register 1908 .... **1896**

New St. Helens & District Tramways Co. Ld. Regd. 1898. Vol. liq. 31 Dec. 1919. Undertaking taken over by the Corporation. Final meeting return regd. 25 Sept. 1920 .... **1920**

New Schultze Gunpowder Co. Ld. See Schultze Gunpowder Co. Ld.

New Scotland Land Co. Ld. Regd. Edinburgh 1890. Vol. liq. Oct. 1920. Capital returned to contributories—15s. per share of £1 in Nov. 1920; further payments (if any) not known. Final meeting return regd. 4 Sept. 1923 .... **1921**

New Securities Ld. Regd. 1919. Vol. liq. (members') 27 Dec. 1933. Final meeting return regd. 29 May 1934 **1935**

New Seddon Pneumatic Tyre & Self-closing Tube Co. Ld. Regd. 1896. Vol. liq. 30 June 1899. Reconstructed as Gorton Rubber Co. Ld. Purchase money £12,500 in ordinary shares of £1. Final meeting return regd. 2 July 1900 .... **1908**

New Selukwe Gold Mine Ld. See Selukwe Columbia Gold Mine Ld.

New Share Loan Co. Ld. Regd. 1896. Vol. liq. 22 June 1898. Amalgamated with another under title of New London Discount Co. Ld. Removed from Register 13 Nov. 1903 .... ***1899**

VOL. FOR

New Sharlston Collieries Co., Ld. Regd. 1873. Vol. liq. (members') 3 Aug. 1956. Final meeting return regd.6 July 1957 .... **1921**

New Shimoga Gold Fields Ld. Regd. 1909. Vol. liq. 30 Jan. 1914. The properties were sold to Eastern Development Corporation Ld. for 5.500 shares. Final meeting return regd. 25 June 1915 .... **1914**

New Slug Hill Gold Mining Co. Ld. Regd. 1904. Vol. liq. Mar. 1908. Removed from Register 1908 .... **1909**

New Sombrero Phosphate Co. Ld. Regd. 1871. Vol. liq. 24 Feb. 1879. Final meeting return regd. 31 May 1880 .... ***1880**

New Sonora Mining Co. Ld. Regd. 1889. Removed from Register 1905 .... **1897**

New South-East Wynaad Estates Co. Ld. Regd. 1884. Vol. liq. 25 May 1893. Undertaking was acquired by Wynaad Syndicate Ld. Removed from Register 1906 .... **1894**

New South London Ld. Regd. 1896. Undertaking and assets were acquired in 1904 by Variety Theatres Consolidated Ld. in which company shareholders were entitled to 4 shares of £1 (credited as fully-paid) for each share of £5 held. Holders of 5% 1st mortgage debentures were entitled to an equal amount of 6% debentures in new company. Removed from Register 1907 .... **1905**

New South Rand Ld. Inc. Transvaal 1904. Vol. liq. 1906 **1907**

New South Wales Exploration Ld. Regd. 1896. Removed from Register 1903 .... **1901**

New South Wales Gold Fields Ld. Regd. 1899. Vol. liq. 22 May 1900. Final meeting return regd. 18 Apr. 1902 .... **1901**

New South Wales Land and Agency Co. Ld. Regd. 1897 as New South Wales Mortgage. Loan & Agency Co. Ld.; name changed June 1911. All capital was owned by Scottish Australian Co. Ld. Vol. liq. (members') 12 Aug. 1964. Final meeting return regd. 16 Dec. 1964 .... **1955**

New South Wales Mortgage Loan & Agency Co. Ld. Regd. 1879. Reconstructed 1897 as New South Wales Mortgage Loan & Agency Co. Ld. (later New South Wales Land & Agency Ld.). Shareholders were entitled to 1 share of £5, fully-paid for each share of £10 (£6 10s. paid) held. Removed from Register 1913 .... **1897**

New Southern Van Ryn Gold Mining Co. Ld. Inc. South Africa 1921. London office was closed Mar. 1926 **1929**

New Spa & Gardens Ld. Regd. 1896. Struck off Register 1925 .... ***1920**

New Spes Bona Gold Mining Co. Ld. Regd. 1891. Vol. liq. 27 Sept. 1894. Reconstructed as company of same name (inc. Transvaal). Final meeting return regd. 5 Dec. 1895 .... **1908**

New Spitzkop Ld. Regd. 1887. Reconstructed as Spitzkop Ld in which company shareholders were entitled to 1 share of £1 (credited with 16s. 6d. paid) for each share of £1 held. Removed from Register 1906 .... **1890**

New Standard Exploration Co. Ld. Regd. 1902. Reconstructed 1904 as Great Tower Hill Gold Mines Ld in which company shareholders were entitled to 1 fully-paid ordinary share of 5s. for every 9 shares of 10s. held. Removed from Register 1906 .... **1908**

New Steyn Estate Gold Mines Ld. Inc. Transvaal 1893. Vol. liq. May 1934. Undertaking and assets were acquired by Durban Roodepoort Deep Ld., in which company shareholders were entitled to 4 shares of 10s. for every 3 shares of £1 held and an option (since expired) over further shares **1936**

New Sunlight Incandescent Co. Ld. Regd. 1899. Undertaking and assets were acquired by Welsbach Incandescent Gas Light Co. Ld. Removed from Register 1903 .... **1901**

New Superheater Co. Ld. Regd. 1910. Vol. liq. 3 Jan. 1913. Final meeting return regd. 17 Apr. 1914. Court Order declared dissolution void July 1914. Final meeting return regd. 9 Mar.1917 .... **1930**

New Suvoroff Oilfields Ld. Regd. 1913 as Jaffa Oilfields Ld.; name changed May 1923. Struck off Register 14 Feb. 1939 .... **1940**

New Swindon Gas Co. See Swindon United Gas Co.

New Tamarugal Nitrate Co. Ld. Regd. 1890. Vol. liq. (members') 2 June 1931. Undertaking and assets sold to Nitrate Corporation of Chile for 500,000 fully-paid series B shares of 100 pesos (either ordinary or 7% cumulative preferred). £395 3s. 3d. was paid into Companies' Liquidation Account in respect of unclaimed dividends and £94 16s. 10d. in respect of unclaimed shares proceeds. Final meeting return regd. 21 Mar. 1938 .... **1932**

New Tasmanian Silver Mining Co. Ld. Regd. 1892. Removed from Register 1907 .... **1894**

New Teign Valley Mining Co. Ld. Regd. 1901. Struck off Register 20 Nov. 1908 .... **1909**

See Stock Exchange Year-Book.

New Telephone Co. Ld. Regd. 1884. Vol. liq. May 1889. Court Orders: to continue winding up under supervision 27 May 1889; to stay liquidation July 1891. Vol. liq. 3 Jan. 1895. Final meeting return regd. 23 Aug. 1898 .... **1895**

New Throgmorton Trust p.l.c. (The). Regd. 11 feb. 1966 as private company, converted to public 4 Mar. 1966; re-registered as p.l.c. 30 Nov. 1981. Vol. liq. (members') 21 Apr. 1983. Dissolved 6 Oct. 1984. All assets transferred to The New Throgmorton Trust (1983) p.l.c. by Scheme of Arrangement **1985–6**

New Timbiqui Gold Mines Ld. Regd. 1905. Struck off Register 28 Aug. 1955 .... **1941**

New Tivoli Ld. Regd. 1891. Vol. liq. 13 Nov. 1919. The mortgage was repaid. The debentures (with premium of 5%) were payable on presentation. A return of £4 10s. per share of £5 was anticipated. Final meeting return regd. 4 Jan. 1921 .... **1920**

(New) Toddington & District Gas Light Coke Co. Ld. Regd. 1904. Receiver appointed in Dec. 1912 and works sold May 1914. Struck off Register 1917 ... **1915**

New Tokatea Gold Mines Ld. Regd. 1905. Undertaking was acquired by West Mount Lyell Ld., in which company shareholders were entitled to 1 share of £1 (credited with 15s. paid) for every 2 shares of £1 held. Removed from Register 1908 .... **1908**

New Town Trust Ld. Regd. 1918 under the Industrial & Provident Societies Act as Pioneer Trust Ld.; name changed Feb. 1921. Undertaking and assets were acquired by Welwyn Garden City Ld. in which company shareholders were entitled to 1 share of £1 (credited as fully-paid) for every 20 shares of £1 held. Holders of 6% income stock were entitled to 20 fully-paid shares in acquiring company for every £100 held **1935**

New Townend Brothers Ld. Regd. 1896. Removed from Register 1904 .... **1903**

New Transport Co. Ld. Regd. 1908. Struck off Register 1926 .... **1914**

New Trinidad Lake Asphalte Co. Ld. Regd. 1897. Vol. liq. 13 Oct. 1925. Final meeting return regd. 26 Mar. 1928 .... **1926**

New Triumph Cycle Co. Ld. See Triumph Co. Ld.

New Turner & Wadley Cycle Co. Ld. Regd. 1897. Removed from Register 1909 .... **1900**

New Unified Main Reef Gold Mining Co. Ld. Inc. Transvaal 1893. Vol. liq. Sept. 1926 .... **1927**

New Union Mill Co. Est. 1811. Inc. 1856. Vol. liq. 24 Mar. 1899. Capital returned to contributories—4s. 9d. per share of £1; further payments (if any) not known. Final meeting return regd. 27 Oct. 1899 .. **1900**

New United Reefs (Sheba) Ld. Regd. 1908. Vol. liq. (members') 14 Apr. 1955. Final meeting return regd. 12 Aug. 1955 .... **1956**

New United States Cattle Ranche Co. Ld. Regd. 1883. Struck off Register 17 June 1898 .... **1901**

New Utah Bingham Mining Co. Inc. Maine 1912. Undertaking acquired by New Bingham Mining Co., in which company shareholders were offered share of $2·5 (credited $2·3 paid) for each share of $2·50 .... **1918**

New Van Consols & Glyn Mining Co. Ld. Regd. 1882. Vol. liq. May 1884. Final meeting return regd. 10 Mar. 1893 .... **1885**

New Vancouver Coal Mining & Land Co. Ld. Regd. 1889. Vol. liq. Feb. 1903. Property was to be sold to Western Fuel Co. A return of 22s. per share of £1 was anticipated. Removed from Register 1904 .... **1903**

New Vanguard Cycle Co. Ld. See Vanguard Cycle Co. Ld.

New Velvet Portland Mine Ld. Regd. 1905. Vol. liq. 23 Dec. 1910. Final meeting return regd. 20 Nov. 1929 **1911**

New Ventanas Mining & Exploration Co. Ld. Regd. 1911. Vol. liq. 5 Oct. 1920. Final meeting return regd. 19 May 1926 .... **1921**

New Venture Witwatersrandt Gold Mining Co. Ld. Regd. 1890. Vol. liq. Mar. 1892. Removed from Register 1907 .... **1893**

New Victoria Cycle Manufacturing Co. of Scotland Ld. Regd. Edinburgh 1896. Vol. liq. Apr. 1899 for reconstruction as Victoria Cycle Co. Ld. Struck off Register 22 Sept. 1936 .... **1939**

New Victorian Consolidated Goldfields Ld. Regd. 1907. Vol. liq. Dec. 1909. Removed from Register 1910 **1910**

New Viola Co. Ld. Regd. 1889. Vol. liq. 18 July 1893. Final meeting return regd. 27 Nov. 1897 .... **1896**

New Virginia Transvaal Gold Mines Ld. Regd. 1894. Vol. liq. 12 June 1895. Assets and liabilities were acquired by Hannan's Virginia Gold Mining & Developing Co. Ld in which company shareholders were entitled to 2 shares of 5s. (credited with 2s. 6d. paid) for each share of 10s. held. Final meeting return regd. 26 Aug. 1897 .... **1897**

New Viso Tin Ld. Regd. 1889. Vol. liq. 8 Nov. 1893. Final meeting return regd. 6 July 1895 .... **1894**

(New) Waitekauri Extended Mines Ld. Regd. Feb. 1901. Undertaking and assets were acquired by Waitekauri Gold Mining Co. Ld., in which company shareholders were entitled to 1 share of £1 (credited as fully-paid) for every 5 fully-paid shares of 5s. held. Removed from Register 1904 .... **1903**

New Weld-Hercules Gold Mines Ld. Regd. 1902. Removed from Register 1905 .... **1904**

New Welsh Slate Co. Ld. Regd. 1889. Removed from Register 1903 .... **1903**

New West African Properties Ld. Regd. 1910. Vol. liq. 26 Mar. 1913. Final meeting return regd. 19 Aug. 1915 .... **1914**

New Westminster Brewery Co. Ld. Regd. 1873. Vol. liq. 24 Dec. 1914. Holders of every 2 ordinary shares of £4 were entitled to 3 preferred ordinary shares and 2 ordinary shares of £1 in Lion Brewery Co. Ld. plus £2 in cash. Holders of each preference share of £4 were entitled to 3 6% cumulative preference shares of £1 in Lion Brewery Co. Ld., plus £1 in cash. Final meeting return regd. 23 July 1915 .... **1915**

New Wheal Peevor. Mine worked on cost book principle. Wound up in 1895 .... **1895**

New Wire Wove Roofing Co. Ld. Regd. 1889. Vol. liq. 22 May 1907. Removed from Register 1908 ...... **1908**

New Witpoortje Gold Mining Co. Ld. Regd. 1889. Removed from Register 14 May 1897 .... ***1894**

New World & General Investments Ld. Regd. 1883 as New Zealand Land Mortgage Co. Ld.; name changed to New Zealand and River Plate Land Mortgage Co. Ld. in 1888 and to above 1 Nov. 1968. On 21 July 1975 capital was cancelled, holders being entitled to 111 ordinary shares of 25p of Estates House Investment Trust Ld. for every 200 ordinary shares. Company was dissolved without winding up on 31 Dec. 1976 .... **1977-8**

New Wye Valley Lead Mining Co. Ld. Regd. 1880. Vol. liq. Mar. 1882. Final meeting return regd. 3 Sept. 1883 .... **1883**

New Yelta Copper Mining & Smelting Co. Ld. Regd. 1898. Removed from Register 1904 .... **1904**

New York & Gartmore Investment Trust Ld. Regd. 1972. Winding-up Order 25 Feb. 1980. Final meeting return regd. 25 Feb. 1981 .... **1979–80**

New York & General Trust Ld. Regd. 1896 as New York, Pennsylvania & Ohio First Mortgage Trust Ld.; name changed Mar. 1925. In July 1969 the undertaking was transferred to Second Consolidated Trust Ld., in which company share- and stockholders were entitled to receive fully-paid capital as follows—1 5% preference share of £1 per £1 preference stock. 118 ordinary shares of 5s. per 100 ordinary shares, and a like amount of 5% debenture stock 1983–88 for debenture stock held. Company is to be dissolved under Section 208 of the Companies Act 1948 .... **1970**

New York & Jersey Railroad Co. Inc. New York 1902. Consolidated with 2 other companies to form Hudson & Manhattan Railroad Co. later Hudson Manhattan Corpn. The 1st mortgage 5% 30-year gold bonds were to be redeemed out of proceeds of issue of bonds by acquiring company **1907**

New York & Ontario Land Co. Organised Pennsylvania 1889. Undertaking sold in 1901 to Elk Hill Coal & Iron Co., the bonds being repaid at par, and the stock purchased at 10% ($5 per share) **1902**

New York & Pacific Steamship Co. Ld. Regd. 1892. Vol. liq. 9 Feb. 1922. Final meeting return regd. 5 Mar. 1925 .... ***1922**

New York & Putnam Railroad. Organised New York 1894. Lines acquired by New York Central & Hudson River Railroad Co. in 1913 .... **1913**

New York & Rockaway Beach Railway Co. Organised New York 1887. In 1922 the undertaking was acquired by Long Island Railroad Co. **1927**

New York Belting & Packing Co. Ld. Regd. 1890. Vol. liq. 30 Sept. 1912. The outstanding debentures were repaid at 110% on 1 July 1912. Final meeting return regd. 29 Jan. 1914 .... **1913**

New York Breweries Co. Ld. Regd. 1888. Vol. liq. 22 July 1926. Capital returned to contributories—26 99/64 %, at Aug. 1926; further paymenls (if any) not known. Final meeting return regd. 17 Feb. 1927 .... **1927**

New York, Brooklyn & Manhattan Beach Railway Co. Organised New York 1885. Acquired by Long Island Railroad Co. in 1895. Liability for 1st consolidated mortgage 50-year 5% gold bonds was assumed by acquiring company; these bonds were redeemed in Oct. 1935 .... **1925**

New York Central & Hudson River Railway Co. Organised New York 1869. Consolidated with 10 other companies in 1914 to form New York Central

VOL. FOR

Railroad Co. Holders of capital stock were entitled to an equal amount of capital stock in new company. The funded debt was taken over by the new company 1915

New York City Freehold Estates Corporation (1905) Ld. Regd. 1905. Struck off Register 17 July 1942 1943

New York, Lake Erie & Western Railroad Co. Organised New York 1878. Succeeded in 1895 by Erie Railroad Co. (later Erie-Lackawanna Railroad Co.). Liability for the following securities was assumed by that company—$4\frac{1}{2}\%$ 3rd mortgage currency bonds, 5% 4th mortgage gold bonds 4% 5th mortgage currency bonds, 4% Buffalo branch mortgage bonds, 7% 1st consolidated mortgage bonds and funded coupon bonds. The 7% 1st mortgage currency bonds were to be renewed at maturity (1897) at 4%; the 6% 1st lien reorganisation gold bonds and 6% collateral trust bonds were paid off. Holders of other securities were to receive securities in new company as follows:

For every £100 held   R.R.

6% 2nd cons. mtg. bds.....$\left\{\begin{array}{l}\text{\$75 gen. lien bds.}\\\text{\$55 1st prefd. stk.}\end{array}\right.$

Funded coupon bds.........$\left\{\begin{array}{l}\text{\$75 gen. lien bds.}\\\text{55\% 1st prefd. stk.}\end{array}\right.$

5% fd. coupon bds. 1885.$\left\{\begin{array}{l}\text{\$100 gen lien. bds.}\\\text{\$10 1st prefd. stk.}\\\text{\$10 2nd prefd. stk.}\end{array}\right.$

Income bonds..................$\left\{\begin{array}{l}\text{\$40 gen. lien bds.}\\\text{\$60 1st prefd. stk.}\end{array}\right.$

Preferred stock ,.................$100 prefd. stock*
Common stock.................$100 com. stocks§
* After payment of $12 per share assessment.
§ After payment of $12 per share assessment. 1896

New York Life Insurance Co. Inc. 1841 as "Nautilus" Insurance Co.; name changed by Act of 1849. Business in Great Britain and Ireland was acquired by Sun Life Assurance Co. of Canada 1927

New York, London & China Steamship Co. Ld. Regd. 1872. Vol. liq. 7 May 1883. Final meeting return regd. 16 Dec. 1884 .... *1876

New York Motor Cab Co. Ld. Regd. 1907. See New York Taxicab Co. Ld.

New York, Newfoundland & Halifax Steamship Co. Ld. Regd. 1884. Vol. liq. (members') 25 Nov. 1930. Capital returned to contributories—£48 1s. 3·9d. per share of £100. Final meeting return regd. 22 Nov. 1934 1931

New York, Pennsylvania & Ohio First Mortgage Trust Ld. See New York & General Trust Ld.

New York, Pennsylvania & Ohio Railroad Co. Organised New York, Pennsylvania and Ohio 1880. Reorganised 1896 as Nypano Railroad Co. Prior lien and equipment bonds were assumed by new company. Holders of stocks and other bonds were entitled to securities in new company as follows:

For every $100 held

1st mortgage bonds ....$\left\{\begin{array}{l}\text{\$20 prior lien bds.}\\\text{\$10 1st preferred}\\\text{\$15 common}\end{array}\right.$

2nd mortgage bonds .... $20 common§
3rd mortgage bonds .... $10 common§
Preferred stock .... $2 common§
Common stock................... $1 common§
§After payment of assessment of $12 per share of $100 1943

New York Taxicab Co. Ld. Regd. 1907 as New York Motor Cab Co. Ld.; name changed June 1908. Vol. liq. 26 May 1910. Reconstructed as company of same name. Shareholders were entitled to 10 fully-paid preferred shares and 1 fully-paid deferred share for every 30 preferred shares held or 1 fully-paid deferred share for each deferred share held. Of the £280,940 debentures, £57,920 were surrendered and cancelled, £39,680 were exchanged for 41,664 fully-paid preferred ordinary shares and the balance were entitled to an equal amount of debentures in new company. Final meeting return regd. 28 Dec. 1915 ... 1911

New York Taxicab Co. Ld. Regd. 1910. Vol. liq. 2 June 1920. £4 14s. per debenture of £20 was paid on 5 June 1920; further payments (if any) not known. Final meeting return regd. 8 July 1926................. 1921

New York Telephone Co. Inc. New York 1880 as Metropolitan Telephone & Telegraph Co.; name changed 1896. The outstanding sterling $4\frac{1}{2}\%$ 1st & general mortgage bonds were redeemed on 1 Nov. 1939 at par 1940

New Zealand Agricultural Co. Ld. Regd. 1879. Reconstructed 1899 as company of same name. Holders of each £100 debenture were entitled to 21 shares of £1 (later reduced to 1s. by returning 19s.) and £12 debentures (later redeemed). Removed from Register 1909 1908

VOL. FOR

New Zealand Agricultural Co. Ld. Regd. 1899. Vol. liq. 16 Nov. 1908. Final meeting return regd. 27 Apr. 1909 1909

New Zealand Alford Estate Co. Ld. Regd. 1882. Removed from Register 1906 .... *1905

New Zealand and General Mining Syndicate Ld. Regd. 1895. Vol. liq. Aug. 1908. Removed from Register 1909 1909

New Zealand and River Plate Land Mortgage Co. Ld See New World & General Investments Ld.

New Zealand Antimony Co. Ld. Regd. 1887. Removed from Register 1894 1894

New Zealand Assets Realisation Board. Inc. under Act of 1895. By Order in Council the Board was dissolved on 17 Dec. 1906 and the outstanding debentures which were all held by Bank of New Zealand redeemed 1908

New Zealand Broken Hills Gold Mining Co. Ld. Regd. 1896. Removed from Register 1903 1899

New Zealand Coal & Oil Co. Ld. Regd. 1900. Receiver appointed Dec. 1926. 1st debenture holders received a payment of £4,500 (5%) in Oct. 1930 and £5,890 in 1950. Struck off Register 8 June 1951 1937

New Zealand Collieries Railway & Oil Syndicate Ld. Regd. 1898. Undertaking was acquired in 1900 by New Zealand Coal & Oil Co. Ld. Removed from Register 1903 1937

New Zealand Consolidated Ld. Regd. 1900. Vol. liq. 9 Feb. 1900. Final meeting return regd. 29 Dec. 1905 ... 1900

New Zealand Crown Mines Co. Ld. Regd. Edinburgh 1888. Vol. liq. Apr. 1891 for reconstruction as company of same name. Final meeting return regd. 10 Jan. 1893 1894

New Zealand Crown Mines Co. Ld. Regd. Edinburgh 1891. Vol. liq. Dec. 1894 for reconstruction as company of same name. Final meeting return regd. 26 July 1900 1894

New Zealand Crown Mines Co. Ld. Regd. Edinburgh 1895. Vol. liq. June 1896 for reconstruction as company of same name. Final meeting return regd. 26 July 1900 1908

New Zealand Crown Mines Co. Ld. Regd. 1896. Vol. liq. May 1910. Reconstructed as company of same name. Shareholders were entitled to 1 share of 4s. (credited as fully-paid) for each share of £1 held. Removed from Register 1911. 1911

New Zealand Crown Mines Co. Ld. Regd. 1910. Vol. liq. 5 Jan. 1914. Reconstructed as company of same name (later Development Securities Ld.). Shareholders were entitled to 1 share of 4s. (credited with 2s. paid) in new company for each share of 4s. held. Final meeting return regd. 11 Jan. 1915 1914

New Zealand Electrical Syndicate Ld. See City of Wellington Electric Light & Power Co. Ld.

New Zealand Exploration Co. Ld. Regd. 1896. Removed from Register 1905 1902

New Zealand Forests Ld. Regd. 1926. Vol. liq. (members') 6 Aug. 1947. Shareholders were entitled to 3 fully-paid ordinary shares (of £1) in N. Z. Forest Products Ld. for every 40 shares (of 5s.) held. £806 5s. paid into Companies' Liquidation Account. Final meeting return regd. 6 July 1949 1950

New Zealand Gold Development Syndicate Ld. Regd. 1896. Vol. liq. 14 June 1898. Final meeting return regd. 7 Apr. 1900 1899

New Zealand Gold Extraction Co. (Newbery Vautin Process) Ld. Undertaking acquired in 1892 by Ore Dressing & Gold Extraction Co. Ld. for £47.500 fully-paid shares of £1 1898

New Zealand Gold Share and Finance Co. Ld. Regd. Edinburgh 1896. Struck off Register 8 Dec.1899... 1900

New Zealand Grain Agency & Mercantile Co. Ld. Regd. 1882. Vol. liq. July 1885. Final meeting return regd. 29 July 1887 1886

New Zealand Joint Stock Corporation Ld. Regd. 1900. Removed from Register 1910 1906

New Zealand Jubilee Gold Mine Ld. Regd. 1895. Vol. liq. 14 Sept. 1896. Reconstructed 1896 as company of same name. Shareholders were entitled to 1 share of £1 (credited as fully-paid) in new company for every 2 shares of £1 held. Final meeting return regd. 10 May 1901 1900

New Zealand Jubilee Gold Mine Ld. Regd. 1896. Vol. liq. 16 Nov. 1900. Reconstructed as company of same name. Shareholders were entitled to 1 share of 5s. (credited with 4s. 6d. paid) in new company for each share of £1 held. Final meeting return regd. 11 May 1901 1908

New Zealand Jubilee Gold Mine Ld. Regd. 1900. Vol. liq. 26 Sept. 1912. Final meeting return regd.14 Jan.1914.. 1913

New Zealand Kapanga Gold Mining Co. Ld. Regd. 1872. Vol. liq. 12 Feb. 1880. Final meeting return regd. 25 May 1880 .... *1880

VOL. FOR

New Zealand Land Association Ld. Regd. 1879 as Waikato Land Association Ld.; name changed Aug. 1891. Assets were taken over in 1896 by New Zealand Loan & Mercantile Agency Co. Ld. The debentures were either repaid at par in 1896 or exchanged for an equal amount of prior lien debenture stock. Vol. liq. 26 June 1913. Final meeting return regd. 22 Aug. 1916 .... **1913**

New Zealand Land Corporation Ld. Regd. 1880. Vol. liq. July 1882. Court Order to continue winding up under supervision July 1882. Final meeting return regd. 27 Feb. 1886 .... **1883**

New Zealand Land Mortgage Co. Ld. *See* New World & General Investments Ld.

New Zealand Loan & Mercantile Agency Co. Ld. Regd. 1865. Reconstructed as company of same name. Holders of consolidated 4% debenture stock were entitled to an equal amount of prior lien debenture stock. Holders of 1888 4% debenture stock, 4% perpetual debentures and terminable debentures were entitled to 50% of holding in A and 50% in B debenture stock. Holders of 6th issue shares were entitled to 1 fully-paid preference share of £3 10*s*. and 2 ordinary shares of £10 (credited as fully-paid) for each share held. Holders of remaining shares were entitled to 2 ordinary shares of £10 (credited with 10*s*. paid) for every share held. Struck off Register May 1929 .... **1930**

New Zealand Loan and Mercantile Agency Co., Ld. Regd. 1894. All capital was owned by Dalgety & New Zealand Loan Ld. Vol. liq. (members') 24 Mar. 1964. Final meeting return regd. 16 Dec. 1964 .... **1963**

New Zealand Manganese Mines Ld. Regd. 1874. Vol. liq. 1 Apr. 1880. Court Order to continue winding up under supervision 25 May 1880. Final meeting return regd. 29 June 1881 .... ***1880**

New Zealand Midland Railway Co. Ld. Regd. 1886. Receiver appointed 3 Feb. 1897. Line was confiscated July 1900. Struck off Register 26 Oct. 1900. Restored to Register 16 Mar. 1903. Debenture holders received £11 5*s*. per £100 debenture in cash; further payments (if any) not known. Struck off Register 30 Nov. 1917 .... **1908**

New Zealand Minerals Co. Ld. Regd. 1896. Vol. liq. 6 Feb. 1902. Removed from Register 1905 .... **1902**

New Zealand Mines Trust Ld. Regd. 1895. Vol. liq. Mar. 1905. Reconstructed as New Zealand Mines Trust (1905) Ld., in which company shareholders were entitled to 3 founders' shares of 1*s*. (credited as fully-paid) for every 50 shares of £1 held. Removed from Register 1906 .... **1906**

New Zealand Mortgage & Investment Association Ld. Regd. 1880. Vol. liq. Feb. 1900. Capital returned to contributories—18*s*. 6*d*. per share of £2 10*s*. at 9 Nov. 1900; further payments (if any) not known. Removed from Register 1903 .... **1901**

New Zealand Oilfields Ld. Regd. 1910. Court Order to wind up 29 July 1913. Liquidator released 8 Oct. 1920. Struck off Register 20 Mar. 1925 .... **1914**

New Zealand Petroleum & Iron Syndicate Ld. Regd. 1889. Struck off Register 5 May 1896. .... **1899**

New Zealand Pioneers Ld. Regd. 1898. Vol. liq. 6 Aug. 1901. Final meeting return regd. 24 Nov. 1902 .... **1902**

New Zealand Red Hill Gold Mining Co. Ld. Regd. 1886. Vol. liq. 5 Dec. 1892. Final meeting return regd. 6 Nov. 1894 .... **1893**

New Zealand Talisman Gold Mining Co. Ld. Regd. 1896. Undertaking and assets were acquired in 1898 by Talisman Consolidated Ld., in which company shareholders were entitled to 1 share of £1 (credited as fully-paid) for each share of £1 held. Removed from Register 1901 .... **1901**

New Zealand Thames Valley Land Co. Ld. Regd. 1882. Removed from Register 1907 .... **1904**

New Zealand Trust & Loan Co. Ld. Regd. 1862. Vol. liq. Dec. 1910. Capital returned to contributories—£1 per share of £1 in Mar. 1911; further payments (if any) not known. Removed from Register 1912 ..... **1911**

Newalls Acoustic Products Ld. Regd. 1932. Vol. liq. (members') 7 Apr. 1943. All capital was owned by Turner & Newall Ld. Capital returned to contributories—£106 4*s*. 10*d*. Final meeting return regd. 23 Sept. 1943 .... **1941**

Newark & Ollerton Railway Co. Inc. by Special Act 1887. Under Lancashire, Derbyshire and East Coast Railway Act 1891 the bulk of the lines were taken over by that company **1906**

Newark Gas Co. Inc. Special Act 1839. Undertaking acquired by Newark Corporation 31 Dec. 1923 .... **1927**

Newark-upon-Trent Waterworks Co. Established 1854. Undertaking sold to Newark Corporation 1891 for £38,000 .... **1892**

Newbery-Vautin (Patents) Gold Extraction Co. Ld. *See* Ore Dressing and Gold Extraction Co. Ld.

VOL. FOR

Newbiggin-by-the-Sea Gas Co. Ld. Regd. 1865. Dissolved 1 May 1949, undertaking being vested in Northern Area Gas Board under Gas Act 1948. Holders of securities were entitled to receive British Gas 3% guaranteed stock 1990–95 as follows:

	£	s.	d.	
Shares (of £5)	4	2	6	
4% red. debs. (of £100)	100	0	0	**1952**

Newbould (Samuel) & Co. Ld. Regd. 1867. Vol. liq. 13 Aug. 1901. Business was acquired by Sanderson Brothers and Newbould Ld. (later Sanderson Kayser Ld.) Final meeting return regd. 7 Oct. 1902 **1902**

Newburgh and North Fife Railway Co. Inc. by Special Act 1897. In 1923 the undertaking (except certain assets amounting to £9,897) was merged into the London & North Eastern Railway Co., in which company stockholders were entitled to stock as follows:

For each £100 *held*		*L. & N. E.*	
4% Debenture Stock	£100	4% 1st Gtd.	
5% Pref. Shares	£83⅓	5% Prefd.	
Ordinary Shares	£16⅔	5% Prefd. Ord.	
	£36⅔	Defd. Ordinary	**1924**

Newburgh Gas Co. Ld. Regd. in Edinburgh 1931. Dissolved 1 May 1949, undertaking being vested in Scottish Area Gas Board under Gas Act 1948. Holders of ordinary shares (of £1) were entitled to receive £1 13*s*. British Gas 3% guaranteed stock 1990–95 for each share held **1952**

Newburn Bridge Co. Ld. Regd. 1890. Vol. liq. (members') 22 Dec. 1947. Final meeting return regd. 3 Sept. 1948 .... **1915**

Newbury's Ld. Regd. 1895. Vol. liq. 24 Oct. 1907. Lewis's Ld. owned all the shares. Final meeting return regd. 25 Apr. 1928 .... **1928**

Newcastle & District Electric Lighting Co. Ld. Regd. 1889. Dissolved 1 Apr. 1948, undertaking being vested in British (later Central) Electricity Authority and North-Eastern Area Board under Electricity Act 1947. Holders of securities were entitled to receive British Electricity 3% guaranteed stock (1968–73) as follows in respect of each £1 unit, unless otherwise stated, of capital held:

	£	s.	d.	
Ordinary shares	1	12	7	
4½% mortgage debenture stock	1	1	0	
3% debenture (per £100)	100	0	0	**1949**

Newcastle & Gateshead Theatres Ld. Regd. 1897. Vol. liq. 1 Dec. 1919. Final meeting return regd. 31 Dec. 1920 .... **1920**

Newcastle and Gosforth Tramways and Carriage Co. Ld. Regd. 1888. Vol. liq. 9 May 1901. Final meeting return regd. 6 Dec. 1901 .... **1902**

Newcastle Chemical Works Co. Ld. Regd. 1871. Vol. liq. June 1883. Business was sold to United Alkali Co. Ld. [later I.C.I. (General Chemicals) Ld.]. Final meeting return regd. 10 Oct. 1883 .... **1891**

Newcastle Chronicle Ld. Regd. 1920. Vol. liq. 29 May 1925 for reconstruction under same name. Final meeting return regd. 1 May 1926 .... **1926**

Newcastle Commercial Marine Insurance Co. Ld. Regd. 1864. Vol. liq. 23 June 1887. Business was acquired by Northern Maritime Insurance Co. Ld. Final meeting return regd. 13 Dec. 1887 .... **1888**

Newcastle Empire Palace Ld. Regd. 1894. Vol. liq. 27 Feb. 1900. Reconstructed as Moss Empires Ld. (later M. E. Theatres Ld.), Shareholders were entitled to 6 fully-paid preference shares and 6 fully-paid ordinary shares of £5 and £5 12*s*. 6*d*. in cash or every 10 shares of £5 held or to 13 fully-paid preference and 13 fully-paid ordinary shares of £5 (subject to payment of £1 5*s*.) for every 20 shares of £5 held. Final meeting return regd. 17 July 1909 **1900**

Newcastle Grain & General Warehousing Co. Ld. Regd. 1874. Vol. liq. 15 Nov. 1912. Final meeting return regd. 11 May 1921 .... **1913**

Newcastle Insurance Co. Ld. Regd. 1922. All shares were owned by Lancashire & General Assurance Co. Ld. Struck off Register 1929 .... **1927**

Newcastle (Natal) Steam-Coal Collieries Ld. Regd. 1903. Vol. liq. Jan. 1906. Removed from Register 1913 .... **1907**

Newcastle Purchasing Co. Ld. Regd. 1912. Vol. liq. (members') 9 Aug. 1937. Capital returned to contributories—£1 2*s*. 4*d*. per share of £1. Final meeting return regd. 7 Feb. 1938 .... **1938**

Newcastle-upon-Tyne & Gateshead Gas Co. Inc. by Special Act 1864. Dissolved 1 May 1949. undertaking being vested in Northern Area Gas Board under Gas Act 1948. Holders of securities were entitled to receive British Gas 3% guaranteed stock 1990–95 as follows in respect of each £100 unit. unless otherwise stated, of security held:

£ s. d.

**See Stock Exchange Year-Book.*

VOL. FOR

Ord. stock (5% basic) (per £1)........ 1 6 2
4% pref. stock 103 0 0
3½% perp. deb. stock 99 3 4
5% perp. deb. stock.................... 128 13 4
3½%red. deb. stock..................... 99 5 0
4% red. deb. stock..................... 102 10 0 **1952**

Newcastle-upon-Tyne Electric Supply Co. Ld. See North-Eastern Electric Supply Co. Ld.

Newcrest Ld. *See* Grafton (Management) Ld.

Newdigate Colliery Ld. Regd. 1904. Struck off Register 1922 .... ***1913**

Newdwarf Gold Ld. Regd. 1913. Vol. liq. 28 Oct. 1929. Final meeting return regd. 1 Oct. 1930 .... **1930**

Newent Railway Co. Inc. by Special Act 1873. Under Great Western Railway Act 1892 the undertaking was vested in that company. All issued capital was held by or on behalf of purchasing company **1893**

Newfoundland & Canadian Exploration Trust Ld. Regd. 1891. Struck off Register 28 July 1899. Restored to Register 1903. Removed from Register 1910 .... **1901**

Newfoundland & General Oilfields Ld. Regd. 1922. Vol. liq. 17 Apr. 1925 for reconstruction as Newfoundland Oilfields Ld., in which company shareholders were entitled to 5 shares of 1*s*. (credited with 1*s*. 4*d*. paid) for every 2 preference shares of 5*s*., 3 shares of 2*s*. (credited with 1*s*. 4*d*. paid) for every 2 ordinary shares of 2*s*. held, or 2 shares of 2*s*. (credited with 1*s*. 4*d*. paid) for every 6 deferred shares of 1*s*. held. Final meeting return regd. 8 Mar. 1927 .... **1926**

Newfoundland Banking & Trust Corporation Ld. *See* Canadian Banking & Trust Ld.

Newfoundland Copper Co. Ld. Regd. 1898. Undertaking and assets were acquired by Carmen Copper Mines Ld., in which company shareholders were entitled to 1 fully-paid share of £1 (subject to payment of 10*d*. per share commission) for each share of £1 held. Removed from Register 1906 .... **1902**

Newfoundland Fish Industries Ld. Regd. 1898. Removed from Register 1905 .... **1902**

Newfoundland Fish Products Ld. Regd. 1920. Vol. liq. 12 Dec. 1928. Final meeting return regd. 10 Dec. 1929 **1929**

Newfoundland Iron Ore Co. Ld. Regd. 1898. Vol. liq. 21 Apr. 1900. Final meeting return regd.13 Dec.1901 **1901**

Newfoundland Oil (Parent) Development Syndicate Ld. Regd. 1910. Vol. liq. 21 Sept. 1911. Court Orders; to continue winding up under supervision Mar. 1912; to dissolve 23 Mar. 1916 .... **1912**

Newfoundland Oilfields Ld. Regd. 1910. Vol. liq. 27 Mar. 1914 for reconstruction as Parsons Pond Oil Co. Ld., in which company shareholders were entitled to 1 share of 1*s*. (credited as fully-paid) and 2¾*d*. in cash for each share of £1 held. Final meeting return regd. 17 Jan. 1919 .... **1915**

Newfoundland Oilfields Ld. Regd. 1925. Vol. liq. (creditors') 4 Oct. 1932. Shareholders received 1 share of Normont Gold Mines Ld. (inc. in Canada) for every 50 shares of 2*s*. held. Final meeting return regd. 4 Jan. 1934 .... **1933**

Newfoundland Power & Paper Co. Ld. Inc. Newfoundland 1915 as Newfoundland Products Corporation Ld.; name changed Nov. 1922. Property and assets were acquired in Dec. 1927 by International Power & Paper Co. of Newfoundland Ld. (later Bowaters Newfoundland Ld.). Liability for 4½% A mortgage debenture stock and 5½% B mortgage debenture stock was assumed by acquiring company. The 1st mortgage debenture stock was to be redeemed out of proceeds of issue of 1st mortgage bonds........ **1928**

Newfoundland Products Corporation Ld. *See* Newfoundland Power & Paper Co. Ld.

Newfoundland Railway Co. Inc. Newfoundland 1881. Railway sold in 1897 to Newfoundland Government for £325,000 Government bonds. Bondholders were entitled to £80 of Government bonds for every £100 held **1898**

Newgass (B.) & Co. Ld. Regd. 1891. Removed from Register 20 Nov. 1908 .... ***1894**

Newgass (B.) & Co. Ld. Regd. 1911. Vol. liq. 1 Jan. 1924. Final meeting return regd. 13 Dec. 1937 ..... **1924**

Newhaven Gas & Coke Co. Ld. Estd. by Deed of Settlement 1855; regd. as limited 1897; statutory powers 1927. Dissolved 1 May 1949, undertaking being vested in South Eastern Area Gas Board under Gas Act 1948. Holders of securities were entitled to receive British Gas 3% guaranteed stock 1990–95 as follows in respect of each £100 unit, unless otherwise stated, of security held:

	£	s.	d.	
Ord. (orig. & adds.) shares (8% stand.) (of £1)	1	12	6	
4% red. debs. (1950)	100	10	0	
4% red. debs (June 1951)	101	0	0	
4% red. debs. (Aug. 1951)	101	0	0	
4% red. debs. (Dec. 1951)	101	5	0	
4% red. debs. (1952)	101	10	0	
4½% red. debs.	101	0	0	**1952**

Newhaven Harbour Co. Inc. by Special Act 1878. By Act of 1926 the undertaking was acquired by Southern Railway Co. Stockholders were entitled to £80 5% guaranteed preference stock for every £100 general capital stock held or £112 10*s*. 4% debenture stock for every £100 perpetual 4½% debenture stock held **1927**

Newhey Rings Ld. Regd. 1934. Vol. liq. (members') 5 July 1954. Final meeting return regd. 13 Apr. 1956 **1940**

Newhouse Mines & Smelters. Inc. New York 1903. Reorganised as South Utah Mines & Smelters. Common stockholders were entitled to subscribe for 1 share in new company on payment of $1 per share for each share (of $10) held; bondholders were entitled to 1 fully-paid income bond for each bond (of $1,000) held........ **1910**

Newhouse Tunnel Co. Ld. Regd. 1893. Vol. liq. 21 Feb. 1899. Reconstructed as Argo Tunnel & Mining Co. Ld. Final meeting return regd. 27 June 1906 .... ***1900**

Newland & Nash Ld. Regd. 1897. Vol. liq. (members') 12 Jan. 1938. All shares were owned by Wells & Winch Ld., which company acquired the undertaking. Final meeting return regd. 9 Jan. 1939 .... **1938**

Newlands Syndicate Ld. Regd. 1905. Vol. liq. Nov. 1911. The property was sold to Jubilee Diamond Mining Syndicate Ld. Removed from Register 1912 .... **1912**

Newlands (West Griqualand) Diamond Mines Ld. Regd. 1893. Vol. liq. 19 Aug. 1903. Final meeting return regd. 7 Feb. 1917 .... **1904**

Newlay Wheel Co. Ld. Regd. 1906 as Schoen Steel Wheel Co. Ld.; name changed Jan. 1919. Vol: liq. 3 Feb. 1932. Property sold to Leeds Forge Co. Ld. for £20,000. Final meeting return regd. 22 July 1932 **1932**

Newman & Dale Steamship Co. Ld. Regd. 1899. Vol. liq. Feb. 1906. Removed from Register 1907 .... **1907**

Newman, Smith & Newman Ld. Regd. 1907. Vol. liq. 17 Dec. 1926. Final meeting return regd. 16 Aug. 1928 **1927**

Newman's Exploration Co. Ld. Regd. 1896. Removed from Register 1904 .... **1902**

Newman's Investment Syndicate Ld. Regd. 1901. Vol. liq. May 1907. Removed from Register 1910 .... **1908**

Newmarket Breweries & White Hart Hotel Co. Ld. Regd. 1896. Struck off Register 1922 .... **1898**

Newmarket Electric Light Co. Ld. Regd. 1895. Dissolved 1 Apr. 1948, undertaking being vested in British (later Central) Electricity Authority and Eastern Area Board under Electricity Act 1947. Ordinary shareholders were entitled to receive £20 British Electricity 3% guaranteed stock (1968–73) for each share (of £10) held........ **1949**

Newmarket Gas Co. Estd. 1840; regd. 1865 as Victoria Newmarket Gas Light & Coke Co. Ld inc. by Special Act 1895 as above. Dissolved 1 May 1949, undertaking being vested in Eastern Area Gas Board under Gas Act 1948. Holders of securities were entitled to receive, in respect of each £100 unit held, British Gas 3% guaranteed stock 1990–95 as follows:

	£	s.	d.	
Cons. ord. stock (5% stand.)	160	0	0	
3¼% perp. deb. stock	93	0	0	**1952**

Newnes & Pearson Printing Co. Ld. Regd. 1920. All capital owned by George Newnes Ld. and C. Arthur Pearson Ld. Vol. liq. (members') 1 Mar. 1962. Final meeting return regd. 28 Feb. 1963 .... **1940**

Newnes (George) Ld. Regd. 1891. Vol. liq. 5 Aug. 1897. Reconstructed as company of same name. Shareholders were entitled to 1 fully-paid ordinary share of £1 *plus* £1 in cash for each share of £1 held. Final meeting return regd. 29 Oct. 1898 .... **1897**

Newnham Gas-Light & Coke Co. Ld. Regd. 1856. Dissolved 1 May 1949 undertaking being vested in South Western Area Gas Board under Gas Act 1948. Holders of securities were entitled to receive British Gas 3% guaranteed stock 1990–95 as follows:

	£	s.	d.	
Ord. shares (of £20)	25	4	0	
4% perp. mort. debs. (of £100)	102	0	0	**1952**

Newport, Abercarn Black Vein Steam Coal Co. Ld. Regd. 1873. All assets were sold in 1936 to Partridge Jones & John Paton Ld. for sum sufficient to repay 1st mortgage debentures in full. Struck off Register 1 May 1942 .... **1943**

Newport (Alexandra) Dock Co. Ld. Regd. 1873. Undertaking was acquired in Jan. 1898 by Alexandra (Newport & South Wales) Docks & Railway Co. Dissolved by Special Act 1897 .... **1898**

Newport & South Monmouthshire Water Board. Inc. 1960. Undertaking transferred to Gwent Water Board by Gwent Water Board Order 1969, which provided for dissolution of this Board; liability for

**See Stock Exchange Year-Book.*

VOL. FOR

the 5¾% redeemable stock 1977–9 was assumed by the new Board from 1 Apr. 1970 .... **1970**

Newport, Godshill & St. Lawrence Railway Co. Inc. by Special Act 1885 as Shanklin & Chale Railway Co.; name changed by Act of 1889 .... **1914**

Newport (Isle of Wight) Gas Co. Inc. by Special Act 1870. As from 1 July 1946 undertaking was acquired by Newport (Isle of Wight) Corporation. Ordinary and new ordinary stockholders received £200 4% gas stock of the corporation for every £100 stock held and preference stockholders received £100 4% gas stock for every £100 held. The outstanding £7,500 mortgage was assumed by the corporation **1947**

Newport (Mon.) Cold Storage & Ice Co. Ld. Regd. 1922. Vol. liq. (creditors') 23 Dec. 1930. Assets realised insufficient to pay unsecured creditors in full. Final meeting return regd. 10 July 1931 .... **1931**

Newport (Monmouthshire) Gas Co. Inc. by Special Act 1843. Dissolved 1 May 1949. undertaking being vested in Wales Area Gas Board under Gas Act 1948. Holders of securities were entitled to receive, in respect of each £100 unit held, British Gas 3% guaranteed stock 1990–95 as follows:

	£	s.	d.
Cons. stock (5% basic)	195	0	0
5% perp. deb. stock........................	122	10	0

A distribution on cons. stock of 6·146% out of reserves was made in Sept. 1953 .... **1952**

Newport (Mon.) Shipyard Ld. *See* Rennie, Ritchie & Newport Shipbuilding Co. Ld.

Newport (Mon.) Slipway, Dry Dock & Engineering Co. Ld. *See* Eastern Dry Dock & Engineering Co. Ld.

Newport (Monmouthshire) Tramways. Regd. 1873. Vol. liq. 3 Dec. 1894. Undertaking purchased by local authority in July 1894. Final meeting return regd. 6 Mar. 1895 .... **1895**

Newport Railway Co. Inc. by Special Act 1866. Under North British Railway Act 1900 the undertaking was purchased by that company, in which holders of debenture stock and ordinary stock received 3% debenture stock 1893 and 3% consolidated lien stock respectively on basis of equal income **1910**

Newport Rolling Mills Ld. Regd. 1909. Vol. liq. 12 May 1914. Final meeting return regd. 23 Sept. 1915..... **1915**

Newport Water Works Co. Inc. 1846. Undertaking acquired in 1888 by Newport (Mon.) Corporation in consideration of £10,000 cash for distribution pro rata to holders of A stock and share of an annuity of £8 in respect of every £100 A or B stock, of £6 in respect of £100 preference stock and of 14s. in respect of every C share of £10 fully-paid. 4% debenture stock for £23,000 was assumed by the Corporation **1892**

Newquay & Cornwall Junction Railway Co. Inc. by Special Act 1864. Line was absorbed by Cornwall Minerals Railway Co.............................. **1886**

Newquay & District Water Co. Inc. by Special Act 1882. Undertaking was vested in the North & Mid-Cornwall Water Board. Holders of ordinary capital were entitled to receive £16 2s. 6d. per 10% maximum ordinary share of £10; £10 18s. per 7% maximum ordinary share of £10; and £109 per £100 ordinary stock. Holders of preference and debenture stocks were entitled to receive respectively equivalent amounts of redeemable stock and mortgages of the Board at equivalent rates of interest. Dissolved 5 Oct. 1966 .... **1968**

Newquay (Cornwall) Gas Co. Ld. Regd. 1893 as New Quay Gas Co. Ld.; name changed 1895; statutory powers 1894. Dissolved 1 May 1949, undertaking being vested in South Western Area Gas Board under Gas Act 1948. Holders of securities were entitled to receive British Gas 3% guaranteed stock 1990–95 as follows, in respect of each £1 unit, unless otherwise stated, of security held:

	£	s.	d.
Orig. shares (10% max.)	2	0	0
Addit. shares (7% max.).................	1	8	0
6% pref. shares	1	6	8
5% mort. debs. (of £100)	125	0	0
6% irred. deb. stock (per £100)......	146	0	0
5¾% irred. deb. stock (per £100).....	142	0	0
4½% irred. deb. stock (per £100).....	112	10	0

1952

Newquay Electric Light & Power Co. Ld. Regd. 1905. Vol. liq. (members') 24 Jan. 1938. Capital returned to contributories—£1 4s. 4d. per share of £1. £6 16s. 6d. was paid into Companies' Liquidation Account in respect of unclaimed dividends and £24 6s. 7d. in respect of unclaimed capital. Final meeting return regd.9 Sept.1938 .... **1938**

Newquay Mining Co. Ld. Regd. Truro 1881. Struck off Register 7 Mar. 1913 .... **1885**

Newry, Keady & Tynan Light Railway Co. *See* Newry, Keady & Tynan Railway Co.

VOL. FOR

Newry, Heady & Tynan Railway Co. Inc. by Special Act as Newry, Keady & Tynan Light Railway Co.; name changed to Ulster & Connaught Light Railways Co. by Act of 1900; reverted to original title by Act of 1905 and as above by Act of 1909 **1919**

Newry Navigation Co. Inc. by Special Act 1829. Undertaking sold to Newry Port & Harbour Trustees (inc. 1901) for £20 per share of £50. Outstanding debenture bonds were assumed by new company **1902**

Newry, Warrenpoint & Rostrevor Railway Co. Inc. by Special Act 1846. Undertaking sold to Great Northern Railway Co. (Ireland) in 1886 for £54,000 in cash **1887**

News of the World Ld. Regd. 1891. Reconstructed 1904 as company of same name. Shareholders were entitled to 4½ fully-paid shares of £10 for each share of £10 held. Removed from Register 1905 .... **1904**

Newsome West and Co. Ld. Regd. 1876. Removed from Register 1904 .... **1937**

Newsome, West and Co. Ld. Regd. 1904. Vol. liq. (members') 27 Jan. 1937. Capital returned to contributories—4s. 10½d. per ordinary or preference share of £1. Final meeting return registered 3 Apr. 1942. Dissolution declared void by Order of Court of 1 Nov. 1943. Final meeting return registered 14 Apr. 1945 .... **1945**

Newsum (H.), Sons & Co., Ld. Regd. 1894 as Henry Newsum, Sons & Co. Ld.; name changed 1894. Vol. liq. (creditors') 1 Nov. 1962. Final meeting return regd. 4 Feb. 1969 .... **1970**

Newsum (Henry) Sons & Co. Ld. *See* above.

Newtex Safety Glass Co. Ld. Regd. 1928. Vol. liq. (members') 7 June 1932. No return of capital was made. £8 was paid into Companies' Liquidation Account. Final meeting return regd. 15 Oct. 1952 **1953**

Newthorpe Collieries Ld. Regd 1913. Vol. liq. 2 Mar. 1917. Final meeting return regd. 6 May 1920 ...... **1917**

Newton Abbot & District Gas & Coke Co. Ld. Regd. 1869. Dissolved 1 May 1949, undertaking being vested in South Western Area Gas Board under Gas Act 1948. Holders of securities were entitled to receive, in respect of each £1 unit held. British Gas 3% guaranteed stock 1990–95 as follows:

	£	s.	d.
A ord. shares (7½% basic)...............	1	12	0
B ord. shares (5% basic).................	1	1	6
6½% pref. shares	1	6	6

1952

Newton (A. E.) Ld. Regd. 1921. Vol. liq. (members') 10 Feb. 1932. All shares held by Glico Petroleum Ld. Final meeting return regd. 16 Nov. 1932 .... **1932**

Newton Electrical Works Ld. *See* Rotax Ld.

Newton (J. M.) Vitreo-Colloid (1928) Ld. Regd. 1928. Court Order to wind up 1 Dec. 1930. Struck off Register 17 July 1942 .... **1943**

Newton (J. M.) Wharfingers Co. Ld. Regd. 1928. Vol. liq. (creditors') 4 Aug. 1932. Assets realised insufficient to pay unsecured creditors in full. Final meeting return regd. 24 Aug. 1933 .... **1933**

Newton-on-Ayr Gas Co. Ld. Regd. in Edinburgh 1908. Dissolved 1 May 1949, undertaking being vested in Scottish Area Gas Board under Gas Act 1948. Holders of securities were entitled to receive, in respect of each £1 unit held, British Gas 3% guaranteed stock 1990–95 as follows:

	£	s.	d.
Ord. shares	1	13	6
4% (tax free) pref. shares	1	8	0

1952

Newton Shipbuilding Co. Ld. Regd. 1920. Vol. liq. 6 Oct. 1922. Final meeting return regd. 28 June 1932 .... ***1923**

Newton Stewart Gas Co. Ld. Regd. in Edinburgh 1911. Dissolved 1 May 1949 undertaking being vested in Scottish Area Gas Board under Gas Act 1948. Holders of ordinary shares (of £2) were entitled to receive £2 10s. British Gas 3% guaranteed stock 1990–95 for each share held. **1951**

Newtonbarry & Scarawalsh (Light) Railway Co. Line, as authorised, was abandoned **1896**

Newtonia Wallpapers Ld. Regd. 1928. Receiver appointed Mar. 1933. In Feb. 1934 receiver stated that practically whole of assets and undertaking had been sold. Receiver ceased to act 21 May 1941. Struck off Register 23 Apr. 1954......................... **1934**

Newtons Ld. *See* Rotax Ld.

Neyland Steam Trawling & Fishing Co. Ld. Regd. 1907. Vol. liq. 20 Mar. 1919. Final meeting return regd. 29 July 1920 .... **1919**

Ngerengere Estates Ld. Regd. 1923. Vol. liq. 4 Dec. 1928. Capital returned to contributories—10s. per share of £1 at Dec. 1928; further payments (if any) not known. Undertaking was acquired by East African Sisal Plantations Ld. Final meeting return regd. 7 Dec. 1929 .... **1929**

VOL. FOR

Niagara Ld. Regd. 1889. Court Orders: to wind up 14 Dec. 1889; to dissolve 17 May 1897 .... **1891**

Niagara Proprietary Gold Mines, Western Australia Ld. Regd. 1895. Vol. liq. 17 Mar. 1899. Properties were acquired by Challenge Mining & Milling Co. Ld. for 75,000 shares of 10s. (credited with 8s. paid) plus royalty of 15% in respect of all gold raised from properties transferred. Final meeting return regd. 14 Aug. 1903 .... ***1900**

Nicaragua Co. Ld. Regd. 1890. Removed from Register 1907 .... **1901**

Nicaragua Development Syndicate Ld. Regd. 1900. Vol. liq. 26 Feb. 1924. Assets rested insufficient to allow any distribution to shareholders. Final meeting return regd. 8 May 1924 .... **1925**

Nicholl (Charrington) & Co. Ld. Regd. 1904. Vol. liq. 25 May 1925. All capital held by Colchester Brewing Co. Ld. [later Ind Coope (South Wales) Ld.]. Final meeting return regd. 14 Dec. 1925 .... **1926**

Nicholls, Nagle & Co Ld. Regd. 1911 as Annexe Ld.; name changed Aug. 1912. Vol. liq. 1 Dec. 1924. The undertaking was acquired by Corn Products Co. Ld. Final meeting return regd. 1 June 1928 .... **1925**

Nicholson (W. N.) & Sons Ld. Regd. 1889. Struck off Register 7 Dec. 1973 .... **1973-4**

Nicholson (William) & Sons Ld. Regd. 1898. Vol. liq. 4 Aug. 1921. Final meeting return regd. 6 Mar.1925 **1922**

Nicholson's Discount Co. Ld. Regd. 1875. Court Order to wind up under supervision 26 July 1882. Final meeting return regd. 28 Dec. 1885 .... ***1882**

Nicholson's Patent Ld. Regd. 1889. Struck off Register 11 June 1895 .... **1899**

Nicholson's Wharves Ld. Regd. 1896. Vol. liq. (members) 14 Feb. 1940. Capital returned to contributories—£1 0s. 6d. per ordinary share of £1; £2 6s. 3d. per preference share of £1. Final meeting return regd. 23 Aug. 1944 .... **1941**

Nickel Corporation Ld. Regd. 1899. Vol. liq. 26 Nov. 1926. Capital returned to contributories—2s. 8d. per share of 10s. in Jan. 1927. Final meeting return regd. 22 Mar. 1927 .... **1927**

Nicol Gold Mines of Western Australia Ld. In 1895 the undertaking was acquired by Consolidated Gold Mines of Western Australia Ld. for 61,007 fully-paid shares of £1 and 13,993 shares of £1 (credited with 10s. paid) **1897**

Nicola Mining Co. Ld. Regd. 1887. Vol. liq. 30 Jan. 1925. Capital returned to contributories—9d. per share at Feb. 1925; further payments (if any) not known. Final meeting return regd. 13 Feb. 1937 **1926**

Nictheroy (Brazil) Gas Co. Ld. Regd. 1867. Vol. liq. May 1888. Property was acquired by Provincial Government. Capital returned to contributories—£9 17s. per share of £10; further payments (if any) not known. Final meeting return regd. 18 Dec. 1889 **1890**

Nidd Valley Light Railway Co. Powers conferred by Order of 1901 were transferred by Order of 1904 to Bradford Corporation **1905**

Niddrie & Benhar Coal Co. Ld. Regd. in Edinburgh 1882. Vol. liq. 12 June 1953. Capital returned to contributories—£3 16s. 8d. per 2s. stock. £56 12s. 8d. paid to Accountant of Court in respect of unclaimed dividends &c. and £86 3s. 4d. in respect of unclaimed distributions. Final meeting return regd. 8 Sept. 1960 .... **1961**

Niederosterreichische Escompte-Gesellschaft, See Oesterreichische Industriekredit A.G.

Niekirk Consolidated Ld. Regd. 1896. Vol. liq. July 1908. Removed from Register 1909 .... **1909**

Niekerk (Klerksdorp) Gold Mining Co. Ld. See Niekerk Ld.

Niekerk Ld. Regd. 1895 as Niekerk (Klerksdorp) Gold Mining Co. Ld.; name changed Apr. 1897. Reconstructed under same name in 1906. Shareholders were entitled to 1 share of 10s. (credited 7s. 6d. paid) in new company for each £1 share held. Vol. liq. 15 Jan. 1906. Final meeting return regd. 16 Sept. 1907 **1906**

Niekerk Ld. Regd. 1906. Vol. liq. 25 Feb. 1907. Southern Klerksdorp Gold Mines Ld. took over the properties and satisfied the debenture holder. Shareholders were invited to apply for 2 shares of £1 (credited with 15s. paid) for every 4 shares of 10s. held, applicants receiving a bonus of 1 share credited as fully-paid for every 2 shares applied for. Final meeting return regd. 29 Aug. 1907 .... **1907**

Nieuport & General Aircraft Ld. Regd. 1916. Struck off Register 18 May 1950 .... **1940**

Nigel Deep Ld. Inc. Transvaal 1894. Vol. liq. Dec. 1909. Undertaking and assets were acquired by Sub-Nigel Ld., in which company shareholders were entitled to 1 share of £1 (credited as fully-paid) for every 10 shares of £1 held **1910**

Nigel Extension Ld. See Transvaal United Trust & Finance Co. Ld.

Nigel Finance & Investment Ld. Regd. 1918 as Nigel Van Ryn Reefs Ld., name changed as above 1958. Majority of capital was owned by S. G. Warburg & Co. Ld. Vol. liq. (members) 30 Mar. 1965. Capital returned to contributories—3s. 10½d. per share of 3s. £2,692 10s. was paid into Companies' Liquidation Account in respect of unclaimed distributions. Final meeting return regd. 23 Nov. 1966 .... **1968**

Nigel Main Reef Ld. Regd. 1895. Vol. liq. 8 Aug 1899. Undertaking sold to company of same name for 63,698 fully-paid shares of 5s. and 136,302 shares of 5s. (credited with 4s. paid). Final meeting return regd. 13 June 1902 .... **1908**

Nigel Main Reef Ld. Regd. 1899. Vol. liq. June 1908. Struck off Register 5 Mar. 1909 .... **1909**

Nigel (Transvaal) Goldfield Ld. Regd. 1909. Vol. liq. (members) 14 May 1930 for reconstruction as New Nigel Asbestos Co. Ld., in which company shareholders received 1 fully-paid share of 2s. for each share of 2s. held. Final meeting return regd. 6 Jan. 1931 .... **1931**

Nigel Van Ryn Reefs Ld. See Nigel Finance & Investment Ld.

Nigeria & Tarkwa Mines Ld. Regd. 1912. Struck off Register 1927 .... ***1921**

Nigeria and West African Development Syndicate Ld. Regd. 1902. Vol. liq. 2 Apr. 1906. The rights were sold to Nigeria Bitumen Corporation Ld. for 62,500 fully-paid shares of £1. Final meeting return regd. 8 Feb. 1917 .... **1907**

Nigeria Bitumen Corporation Ld. Regd. 1905. Vol. liq. 6 Feb. 1914. All assets in West Africa were taken in satisfaction of debentures issued to Colonial Government. Final meeting return regd. 19 June 1914 **1915**

Nigeria Investment Co. Ld. Regd. 1906. Vol. liq. 15 Dec. 1913. Final meeting return regd. 7 Dec. 1916 ...... **1914**

Nigeria Properties Ld. Regd. 1902. Vol. liq. Mar. 1906. The rights were sold to Nigeria Bitumen Corporation Ld. in which company shareholders were entitled to 110 shares of £1 (credited as fully-paid) for every 100 shares of £1 held. Removed from Register 1907 .... **1907**

Nigeria Proprietary Co. Ld. Regd. 1911. Struck off Register 9 Jan. 1931 .... **1931**

Nigeria Syndicate Ld. Regd. 1902. Struck off Register 19 Mar. 1907 .... **1908**

Nigerian & Colonial Corporation Ld. Regd. 1910 as West African Rubber & Produce Association Ld.; name changed May 1912. Vol. liq. 17 Apr. 1914. Undertaking and assets were acquired by South Orofu Ld. Final meeting return regd. 13 May 1915 **1915**

Nigerian & General Prospectors Ld. See Naraguta Acquisitions Ld.

Nigerian & Waterberg Tin Fields Trust Ld. Regd. 1912. Vol. liq. 19 Nov. 1913. Final meeting return regd. 7 May 1921 .... **1914**

Nigerian Base Metals Corporation Ld. Regd. 1920. Vol. liq. (members) 12 Dec. 1929 for amalgamation with other companies as Anglo-Nigerian Corporation Ld., in which company shareholders received 1 fully-paid share of 5s. for each share of 5s. held. Final meeting return regd. 13 Dec. 1934 .... **1930**

Nigerian Consolidated Mines Ld. Regd. 1920. Vol. liq. (members) 16 Jan. 1956. Undertaking and assets (except capital stock of Rhodesian Corpn. Ld.) were sold to Rhodesian Corpn. Ld. for 618,550 fully-paid shares of 3s. 4d. Shareholders received 1 share of Rhodesian Corpn. Ld. for each share held. £446 11s. 1d. was paid into Companies' Liquidation Account. Final meeting return regd. 30 Oct. 1958 .... **1960**

Nigerian Consolidated Tinfields Ld. Regd. 1912. Vol. liq. 16 Oct. 1913 for amalgamation with Toro Tin Ld., in which company shareholders were entitled to 1 share of 5s. for each share of £1 held. Final meeting return regd. 17 Apr. 1915 .... **1914**

Nigerian Gold Mines Ld. Regd. 1933. Vol. liq. (members) 17 Mar. 1939. Undertaking and assets were acquired by National Mining Corporation Ld. (later N.M.C. Investments Ld.), in which company shareholders were entitled to 3 shares of 2s. 6d. (credited as fully-paid) for every 2 shares of 2s. held and an option (since expired) over further shares. Final meeting return regd. 24 May 1941 .... **1940**

Nigerian Motors Ld. Regd. 1919. Vol. liq. (members) 20 Feb. 1931. Capital returned to contributories—£16,518 11s. 3d. Final meeting return regd. 23 June 1939 .... **1931**

Nigerian Petroleum Lands Ld. Regd. 1910. Vol. liq. 11 Feb. 1915. Final meeting return regd. 8 Apr.1915 **1915**

Nigerian Power & Tin Fields Ld. Regd. 1927. Vol. liq. (members) 12 Dec. 1929. Reconstructed as Anglo-Nigerian Corporation Ld., in which company shareholders were entitled to 5 fully-paid shares of

VOL. FOR

5s. for every 8 shares of 5s. held *plus* 1s. per share in cash. Final meeting return regd. 19 Dec. 1934 .... **1930**

Nigerian Tin Corporation Ld. Regd. 1909. Receiver sold the property and assets to Entesee Trust Ld. and ceased to act in July 1926. Struck off Register 1928 **1928**

Nigerian Tin Trust & Exploration (1912) Ld. Regd. 1912. Vol. liq. 10 Mar. 1922. Final meeting return regd. 17 June 1922 **1928**

Nightingale's Cooperage Ld. Regd. 1887 as Machine Cooperage Co. Ld.; name changed May 1889. Vol. liq. 26 Aug. 1890. Taken over by Surrey Cooperage Ld. Struck off Register 19 Oct. 1906. .... **1892**

Nil Desperandum Gold Mines Ld. Regd. 1896. Court Order to wind up 29 June 1898. Removed from Register 1908 **1899**

Nilambur Rubber Estates Ld. Regd. 1909. Vol. liq. 11 Nov. 1914. Final meeting return regd. 19 May 1917 **1915**

Nile Cold Storage Co. Ld. Regd. 1904. Vol. liq. 20 May 1911. The undertaking and assets were acquired by Nile Cold Storage Co. Société Anonyme, in which company shareholders were entitled to 1 share of £5 for every 10 ordinary shares of £1 held or 4 shares of £5 for every 125 deferred shares of 1s. held. Final meeting return regd. 20 Jan. 1915 **1912**

Nile Development Syndicate Ld. Regd. 1903. Vol. liq. Nov. 1907. Removed from Register 1908 **1908**

Nile Goldfields Ld. Regd. 1903. Vol. liq. Dec 1905. Removed from Register 1906 **1906**

Nile River Syndicate Ld. Regd. 1903. Vol. liq. Mar. 1908. Removed from Register 1909 **1909**

Nile Valley Block E Ld. Regd. 1903. Removed from Register 1909 **1908**

Nile Valley Co. Ld. Regd. 1901. Undertaking and assets were acquired by Nile Valley (New) Co. Ld. (later Nile Valley Co. Ld.), in which company shareholders were entitled to 4 shares of £1 (credited as fully-paid) for each ordinary share of £1 held or 18 shares of £1 (credited as fully-paid) for each deferred share of 1s. held. Removed from Register 1904. .... **1904**

Nile Valley Co. Ld. Regd. 1903 as Nile Valley (New) Co. Ld.; name changed May 1904. Removed from Register 1907 **1906**

Nile Valley Gold Mining Co. Ld. Inc. Transvaal 1908. Vol. liq. Nov. 1914, undertaking was acquired by Star of Egypt Mines Ld. **1915**

Nile Valley (New) Co. Ld. Regd. 1903. *See* Nile Valley Co. Ld.

Nile Valley (New) Co. Ld. Regd. 1906. Vol. liq. 9 June 1908. Shareholders were entitled to 1 share of £1 (credited with 17s. 6d. paid) in Nile Valley Gold Mining Co. Ld. for each share held. Final meeting return regd. 22 June 1910 **1909**

Nilgiri Plantations Co. Ld. Regd. 1897. Vol. liq. (members') 7 Feb. 1944. Capital returned to contributories—£5 15s. 5d. per share of £1. Final meeting return regd. 4 Sept. 1948 **1949**

Nilgiri Railway Co. Ld. Regd. 1896. Vol. liq. Dec. 1902. Debenture stockholders were repaid at 101%; prior lien debenture holders were repaid at par. Capital returned to contributories—6s. per fully-paid share of £1; further payments (if any) not known. Removed from Register 1904 **1904**

Nimmo & Dunlop Ld. Regd. Edinburgh 1938. Vol. liq. (members') 14 Mar. 1952. Capital returned to contributories—29s. 7·85d per 13s. 4d. stock. £832 17s. paid to the Accountant of Court. Final meeting return regd. 19 June 1958 **1959**

Nimmo (James) & Co. Ld. Regd. Edinburgh 1897. Vol. liq. (members') 14 Mar. 1952. Capital returned to contributories—preference shares (of £1) were re-paid at par and remaining assets were paid to Nimmo & Dunlop Ld. which owned all ordinary capital. £733 16s. 2d. paid to the Accountant of Court. Final meeting return regd. 19 June 1958 .. **1959**

Nimmo (John) & Son Ld. Regd. Edinburgh 1897. The greater part of the business was sold to United Collieries Ld. Vol. liq. Feb. 1903 for reconstruction as company of same name. Removed from Register 1908 **1903**

Nimrod Cycle Co. Ld. Regd. 1895. Removed from Register 4 Oct. 1898 .... ***1896**

Nimrod Syndicate Ld. Regd. 1899. Reconstructed 1904 as New Nimrod Co. Ld., in which company shareholders were entitled to 1 share of £1 (credited as fully-paid) for each share of £1 held. Removed from Register 1905 **1905**

Nine Reefs Co. Ld. Regd. 1895. Reconstructed 1901 as company of same name. Shareholders were entitled to 1 ordinary share of 5s. (credited with 3s. paid) for each ordinary share of 5s. held or 1 fully-paid preference share of 5s. for each preference share of 5s. held. Removed from Register 1907 .... **1906**

Nine Reefs Co. Ld. Regd. 1901. Vol. liq. 21 Mar. 1906. The assets, sold to Balaghât Gold Mining Co. Ld.,

VOL. FOR

realised insufficient to pay the debenture debt. Final meeting return regd. 22 May 1907 .... **1907**

Nine Reefs Gold Mining Co. Ld. Regd. 1881. Vol. liq. 31 Oct. 1889. Reconstructed as Nine Reefs Ld., in which company shareholders were entitled to 1 share of £1 (credited with 15s. paid) for each share of £1 held. Debenture holders were entitled to debentures in new company. Final meeting return regd. 18 Nov. 1898 **1892**

Nine Reefs Gold Mining Co. Ld. Regd. 1892. Vol. liq. 11 Mar. 1895. Reconstructed as Nine Reefs Co. Ld., in which company shareholders were entitled to 1 share of 5s. (credited with 2s. 6d. paid) for each share of 10s. held. Final meeting return regd. 25 Apr. 1896 **1901**

Nine Reefs Ld. Regd. 1889. Reconstructed 1892 as Nine Reefs Gold Mining Co. Ld. Removed from Register 1901 **1895**

1902 Syndicate Ld. Regd. 1902. Vol. liq. 12 Sept. 1910. Final meeting return regd. 5 Aug. 1915 .... ***1911**

Nineteen Twenty-Nine Investment Trust Ld. Regd. 1929. Under scheme of amalgamation effective from 29 June 1960 the ordinary and preference stocks were exchanged for like amounts of ordinary and preference stocks respectively of The Nineteen Twenty-Eight Investment Trust Ld. and company was dissolved on 29 Oct. 1960 under Section 208 of the Companies Act, 1948 .... **1961**

90 Mile (Goongarrie) Consolidated Gold Mines Ld. Regd. 1896. Removed from Register 1901 .... **1900**

"90-Mile" Proprietary Gold Mines Ld. Regd. 1896. Removed from Register 1904 .... **1903**

Ninghi (Nigeria) Tin Co. Ld. Regd. 1912. Vol. liq. 21 Dec. 1920. All assets were acquired by Bisichi Tin Co. (Nigeria) Ld., in which company shareholders were entitled to 2 shares of 10s. for each share of £1 held. Final meeting return regd. 6 Nov. 1922 ..... **1921**

Ninkada Tin Fields of Nigeria Ld. Regd. 1912. Vol. liq. 18 July 1914. Final meeting return regd. 26 Feb. 1915 **1915**

Nipah Distilleries of Malaya Ld. Regd. 1928. Vol. liq. (members') 10 Aug. 1931. Reconstructed as company of same name. Shareholders were entitled to 1 share of 5s. (credited with 4s. paid), in new company for each share of 5s. held. £30 6s. 1d. was paid into Companies' Liquidation Account. Final meeting return regd. 23 June 1933 **1932**

Nipah Distilleries of Malaya Ld. Regd. 1931. Vol. liq. (creditors') 7 Dec. 1948. No capital was returned to contributories. £2 9s. was paid into Companies' Liquidation Account. Final meeting return regd. 10 Jan. 1951 **1952**

Nipissing Mines Co. Inc. Maine 1906. The company was dissolved. The assets (consisting of all capital stock of Nipissing Mining Co. Ld.) was sold to Nipissing Mines Co. Ld. of Ontario, Canada for 1,200,000 shares of $5 **1918**

Nippon Hatusoden Kabusiki Kaisya. *See* Japan Electric Generation & Transmission Co. Ld.

Nippon Syndicate Ld. Regd. 1905. Vol. liq. 26 July 1910. Final meeting return regd. 1 Mar. 1911 .... ***1911**

Nirmala (Java) Plantations and Lands Co. Ld. Regd. 1909. Dissolved 24 May 1961. Assets in Indonesia were sold to repay creditors; no return to contributories or debenture holders. Struck off Register 27 June 1961 **1962**

Nirpuzha Rubber Estates Ld. Regd. 1913. Court Order to wind up 8 July 1924. Struck off Register Apr. 1929 **1930**

Nissum Fiord Co. Ld. Regd. 1867. Removed from Register 1905 **1885**

Nith Dyeing & Finishing Co. Ld. Regd. 1930. Vol. liq. (members') 6 Feb. 1939. Capital returned to contributories—£11,467 18s. 4d. Final meeting return regd. 2 June 1939 **1940**

Nitram Ld. Regd. 1926. Vol. liq. (members') 31 Dec. 1929. Direct controlling interest held by Imperial Chemical Industries Ld. Final meeting return regd. 12 July 1930 **1931**

Nitrate Corporation of Chile. Organised 1931 under special laws of Chilean Congress. Liquidation was ordered by Decree of 1933. The Cia. Salitrera de Tarapaca y Antofagasta took over the nitrate grounds and certain assets; 4,097,904 B preferred and 87,052 B ordinary shares were exchanged for 4,184,956 shares of this company (the A shares held by the Chilean Government and 10,500,000 B ordinary shares being cancelled). The secured sinking fund 7% gold bonds held by the Chilean Government were cancelled, $16,964,995 held by Guggenheim Bros. were converted into certificates of indebtedness of Cia. Salitrera Anglo-Chilena, and $10,510,005 were converted at par into income bonds (series B, D, F, G & H) of Cia. Salitrera de Tarapaca y Antofagasta. The outstanding prior

VOL. FOR

secured 7% sterling bonds were converted at par into 5% sterling income debentures of Chilean Nitrate & Iodine Sales Corpn. all arrears of interest being cancelled up to 31 Dec. 1933. The outstanding prior secured sinking fund 7% gold bonds were converted at par into sinking fund 5% income debentures of Chilean Nitrate & Iodine Sales Corpn. all arrears of interest being cancelled up to 31 Dec. 1933. The following securities *plus* arrears of interest to 30 June 1934 were converted at par into income bonds of Cia Salitrera de Tarapaca y Antofagasta as follows—6% debentures (Aguas Blancas Nitrate Co. (1928) Ld.), 7% 1st mortgage registered debentures (Chilean Nitrate Co.), 7% 1st mortgage registered debentures (Galicia Nitrate Co.), 6% debentures (Lagunas Nitrate Co. Ld.) and 6½% debentures (Cia. Salitrera el Penon)—Series M; 6½% 1st mortgage registered debentures (Loa Nitrate Co.)—Series K; 6½% debentures (Tarapaca & Tocopilla Nitrate Co. Ld.)—Series F. The outstanding 4% income bonds (New Tamarugal Nitrate Co. Ld.) were converted at par into income bonds (Series A) of Cia. Salitrera de Tarapaca y Antofagasta **1935**

Nitrate Producers' Steamship Co. Ld. Regd. 1918. Vol. liq. (members') 27 Nov. 1942. Capital returned to contributories—£41 12*s*. per share of £5. Final meeting return regd. 17 Feb. 1948 .... **1948**

Nitrate Railways Co. Ld. Regd. 1882. Vol. liq. (members') 30 Dec. 1955. The undertaking was transferred to Chilian Government as from 1 Sept. 1951. Capital returned to contributories—£1 2*s*. 9*d*. per ordinary or preferred converted ordinary share of £7. £27,482 was paid into Companies' Liquidation Account. Final meeting return regd. 23 Dec. 1958 **1960**

Nitrates Provision Supply Co. Ld. Regd. 1889. Vol. liq. 6 Feb. 1905. Capital returned to contributories—£1 4*s*. per share of £2 10*s*. at Dec. 1905; further payments (if any) not known. Removed from Register 1907 .... **1906**

Nitrogen Fertilizers Ld. Regd. 1912. Vol. liq. 29 Mar. 1923. Controlling interest held by Alby United Carbide Factories Ld. Final meeting return regd. 9 Nov. 1928 .... **1922**

Nitrogen Produets & Carbide Co. Ld. Regd. 1913. Vol. liq. 27 Nov. 1919 for amalgamation with Alby United Carbide Factories Ld., in which company shareholders were entitled to 1 ordinary share of £1 (credited as fully-paid) for each share of £1 held. Final meeting return regd. 28 Apr. 1924 .... **1920**

Nitro-Phosphate & Odam's Chemical Manure Co. Ld. *See* Odams' Nitro-Phosphate & Chemical Co. Ld.

Nixey Coleclough & Baxter Ld. Regd. 1890. Business was acquired in 1894 by J. W. Cameron & Co. Ld. for £37,500 in ordinary shares of £10, £107,100 in cash, and £28,765 to discharge liabilities. Vol. liq. 27 Feb. 1895. Final meeting return regd. 11 Dec. 1897 **1896**

Nixey (W. G.) Ld. Regd. 1911. Vol. liq. 19 Jan. 1924. Controlling interest held by Hargreaves Bros. & Co. Ld. Final meeting return regd. 16 Mar. 1925 .... **1923**

Nixon's Navigation Co. Ld. Regd. 1882. Vol. liq. Nov. 1928. Struck off Register 12 Mar. 1935 .... **1936**

Noakacharee Tea Co. Ld. Regd. 1866. Vol. liq. 14 June 1897. Final meeting return regd. 1 Sept.1899 .... **1898**

Noakhali (Bengal) Railway Co. Ld. Regd. 1901. Vol. liq. Feb. 1906. The line was acquired by Secretary of State and carried on as Assam-Bengal Railway Co. Ld. Capital returned to contributories—£8 6*s*. 7*d*. per share of £10. Removed from Register 1906 ... **1907**

Nobel-Dynamite Trust Co. Ld. Regd. 1886. Vol. liq. 9 Sept. 1915. Shareholders received 12 ordinary shares of £1 in Nobel's Explosives Co. Ld. for every £10 ordinary capital held or 10 preference shares of £1 in that company for every £10 preference capital held. Final meeting return regd. 12 Mar. 1929 .... **1916**

Nobel Industries Ld. Regd. 1918 as Explosives Trades Ld. Name changed Dec. 1920. Vol. liq. 28 Aug. 1928. Debenture stockholders were entitled to 80 fully-paid preference shares of £1 in Imperial Chemical Industries Ld., or £103 in cash for every £100 stock held. Final meeting return regd. 2 June 1931 .... **1929**

Nobel's Explosives Co. Ld. Regd. in Edinburgh 1900. Vol. liq. (members') 31 Dec. 1942; Undertaking acquired by Imperial Chemical Industries Ld. and liabilities by I.C.I. (Explosives) Ld. Final meeting return regd. 28 Feb. 1966 .... **1952**

Noltzykop Gold Mines Ld. Regd. 1895. Vol. liq. 12 Mar. 1897. Final meeting return regd. 17 Aug. 1899 .... **1898**

"Non-Collapsible" Tyre Co. Ld. Regd. 1896. *See* Midland Rubber Co. Ld.

Non-Explosive Gas Co. Ld. Regd. 1907. Vol. liq. 20 May 1912. Final meeting return regd. 24 Feb. 1914...... **1913**

Non-Ferrous Metal Products. *See* Western Stockholders Investment Trust, Ld.

VOL. FOR

Non-Flammable Wood and Fabrics Co. Ld. Regd. 1901. Reconstructed 1904 as Fire Resisting Corporation Ld., in which company shareholders were entitled to 1 share of £1 (credited as fully-paid for every 2 shares of £1 held. Removed from Register 1905 .... **1908**

Non-Inflammable Films Co. Ld. Regd. 1927. Certain assets were acquired by Cellulose Acetate Silk Co. Ld. (later Lansil Ld.) in 1928. Vol. liq. (members') 30 Apr. 1931. Capital returned to contributories—8·334*d*. in the £. Final meeting return regd. 20 Nov. 1933 .... **1932**

Non-Poisonous "Strike Anywhere" Match Syndicate Ld. Regd. 1898. Removed from Register 1908 .... **1905**

Non-Tariff Mutual Fire Insurance Co. Ld. Regd. 1897. Removed from Register 1909 .... **1899**

"Nonn" Ld. Regd. 1926. Vol. liq. 25 May 1928. Undertaking was acquired by Proprietors of "Nonn" Ld. Final meeting return regd. 30 May 1929 **1934**

Nonoi Tea Co. Ld. Regd. 1881. Vol. liq. 13 Nov. 1893. Undertaking was acquired by Chubwa Tea Co. Ld., in which company shareholders were entitled to 1 preference and 1 ordinary share of £5 for each share of £10 held. Final meeting return regd. 29 June 1895 **1894**

Nooitgedacht Estate & Gold Mining Co. Ld. Regd. 1889. Vol. liq. 3 Mar. 1892. Reconstructed as company of same name. Shareholders were entitled to 1 share of £1 (credited with 17*s*. 6*d*. paid) in new company for each share of £1 held. Final meeting return regd. 22 Aug. 1893 .... **1892**

Nooitgedacht Estate & Gold Mining Co. Ld. Regd. 1892. Vol. liq. 21 Mar. 1894. Final meeting return regd. 6 Mar. 1895 .... **1894**

Noon (Charles) & Co. Ld. Regd. 1865. Vol. liq. Apr. 1883. Final meeting return regd. 17 Sept. 1883..... **1884**

Nor-Rust Liquid Lead Co. Ld. Regd. 1929. Receiver appointed in Oct. 1934. Assets realised insufficient to meet claims of debenture holders. Struck off Register 29 Apr. 1938 .... **1939**

Nora Steamship Co. Ld. *See* Universal Steam Navigation Co. Ld.

Norbreck Castle Hotel Ld. Regd. 1912 as The Cliffs & Norbreck Hydro Ld.; name changed to Norbreck Hydro Ld. in 1935 and to above title in 1971. Winding-up Order 3 June 1975. Struck off Register 26 Mar. 1982 .... **1982–3**

Norbreck Hydro Ld. *See* Norbreck Castle Hotel Ld.

Norbreck Estate & Building Co. Ld. Regd. 1896. Vol. liq. (members') 8 Aug. 1934. Capital returned to contributories—£1 15*s*. per share of 10*s*. £288 was paid into Companies' Liquidation Account in respect of capital. Final meeting return regd. 7 Sept. 1935 .... **1935**

Norchard Syndicate Ld. *See* West Gloucestershire Power Co. Ld.

Nordanal (Johore) Rubber Estates Ld. Regd. 1911. Vol. liq. (members') 9 Feb. 1953. Capital returned to contributories—14*s*. 4⅔*d*. per £1 stock. £668 17*s*. 11*d*. was paid into Companies' Liquidation Account. Final meeting return regd. 17 Apr. 1957 .... **1958**

Norddeutsche Kreditbank A-G. Inc. Germany 1920 as Bankhaus J. F. Shröder K.a.A.; name changed to J. F. Shröder Bank K.a.A. in 1921 and as above in 1931 .... **1934**

Nordenfelt Guns & Ammunition Co. Ld. Regd. 1886. In 1888 the business was acquired by Maxim Nordenfelt Guns and Ammunition Co. Ld. for 120,000 fully-paid shares of £5 and £150,000 5% debenture stock in purchasing company. Removed from Register 1903 .... **1897**

Nordenfelt (Maxim) Guns & Ammunition Co. Ld. Regd. 1888. Undertaking was acquired in 1896 by Vickers, Sons & Co. Ld. (later Vickers Ld.), in which company shareholders were entitled to £2 10*s*. in preference shares and 16*s*. 8*d*. in ordinary shares *plus* 6*s*. 3*d*. in cash for each share of £5 held. The debenture stock was repaid at 105%. Removed from Register 1911 .... **1899**

Nordenham Dock & Warehouse Co. Ld. Regd. 1888. Vol. liq. Nov. 1889. Final meeting return regd. 20 May 1890 .... **1890**

Nordic Oil Co. Ld. Regd. 1914 as Gropi Oil Co. Ld.; name changed June 1932. Vol. liq. (members') 28 Dec. 1934. Capital returned to contributories—£4,481 19*s*. 4*d*. Final meeting return regd. 20 July 1935 .... **1931**

Nordrach-on-Dee Sanatorium Ld. Regd. Edinburgh 1902. Vol. liq. (creditors') Mar. 1931. No capital returned to contributories. Final meeting return regd. 15 Feb. 1936 .... **1932**

Nordur Newspaper Ld. Regd. 1928. Vol. liq. (members') 8 Dec. 1933. Certain assets were distributed in specie. Capital returned to contributories—£53,293 **1933**

Norfolk & Suffolk Brick Co. Ld. Regd. 1921. Struck off Register 5 Nov. 1943 .... **1944**

See Stock Exchange Year-Book.

Norfolk & Suffolk Joint Railways Committee. Dissolved 2 Apr. 1949; undertaking vested 1 Jan. 1948 in British Transport Commission under Transport Act 1947 .... **1949**

Norfolk & Western Railroad Co. Organised Virginia 1881. Reorganised 1896 as Norfolk and Western Railway Co. The following securities were taken over by the new company—divisional lien bonds, general mortgage 6% bonds, New River division 1st mortgage 6% bonds, improvement and extension mortgage 6% bonds, Scioto Valley and New England R.R. 1st mortgage 4% bonds and Columbus Connecting and Terminal R.R. 5% bonds. Holders of securities were entitled to securities in new company as follows :

For every $100 held

Common stock ....$75 common§	
Preferred stock ....$112½ stand§	

7% Adj. Mort. Bds ⎱ $130 1st. cons. mort. bds. / $20 preferred stock / $7 cash

100-yr. mort. bds. ⎱ $62½ cons. mort. bds. / $75 preferred stock

M'land & W'ton ⎱ $70 cons. mort. bonds
Div. bds. ⎰ $67½ preferred stock

Clinch V. Div. bds. ⎱ $50 cons. mort. bds. / $70 preferred stock

Equip. mort. bds. ⎱ $100 cons. mort. bds.
1888 ⎰ $48 preferred stock

5% debs. 1892 .....$100 preferred stock
§ After payment of $12½ per share assessment **1897**

Norfolk Estuary (Company of Proprietors of the Norfolk Estuary). Inc. by Special Act 1846. Norfolk Estuary Act 1964, provided, inter alia, for winding-up and dissolution of company as if it were a company within the meaning of Companies Act 1948. Capital returned to contributories—£63 18s. per share of £50. Final meeting return regd. 8 Mar. 1967 .... **1967**

Norfolk (T.) & Sons Ld. Regd. 1894. In 1904 the undertaking was acquired by Dartford Brewery Co. Ld. Capital returned to contributories—£30 per ordinary share; £10 per preference share. Debenture stockholders were entitled to an equal amount of 4½% and 5% debenture stock in exchange for A and B debenture stocks respectively held; a cash payment of 3% was also made. Removed from Register 1909 .... **1906**

Normal Powder & Ammunition Co. Ld. Regd. 1897. The business was sold by Receiver for debenture holders to New Normal Ammunition Co. Ld. Struck off Register 1914 .... **1912**

Normal Powder Syndicate Ld. Regd. 1895. Vol. liq. 10 Mar. 1897. Taken over by Normal Powder & Ammunition Co. Ld. Final meeting return regd. 9 Dec. 1898 .... ***1898**

Norman & Stacey Ld. Regd. 1888. Vol. liq. 28 Dec. 1904. Removed from Register 1911 .... **1906**

Norman Portland Cement Co. Ld. Regd. 1903. Vol. liq. 19 Jan. 1912. Amalgamated with British Portland Cement Manufacturers Ld., in which company shareholders were entitled to 1 preference share of £10 for every 10 preference shares of £1 held or to 17s. 6d. in preference or ordinary shares (at option of holder) for each ordinary share of £1 held. Ordinary shareholders were entitled to proceeds of certain liquid assets. Struck off Register 16 July 1915 ..... **1921**

Norman Proprietary Gold Mines Ld. Regd. 1896. Removed from Register 1906 .... **1905**

Normanby Coal Syndicate Ld. Regd. 1906. Vol. liq. 8 Oct. 1912. Final meeting return regd. 26 Jan. 1915 **1913**

Normanby Iron Works Co. Ld. Regd. 1900. Vol. liq. 2 July 1923. The undertaking was sold to Pease & Partners Ld. (Later Pease Realisation Ld.). Capital returned to contributories—£1 0s. 2d. per ordinary share of £1; £1 0s. 1d. per preference share of £1; further payments (if any) not known. Final meeting return regd. 4 Mar. 1924 .... **1924**

Normanby Iron Works Co. Ld. Regd. 1947 as Pease & Partners Normanby Iron Works Co. Ld.; name changed Oct. 1953. Vol. liq. (members') 26 Aug. 1959. A subsidiary of Iron & Steel Holding & Realisation Agency. £492,679 returned to the Agency in respect of share and loan capital. Final meeting return regd. 27 mar. 1963. .... **1964**

Normanton Gas Co. Inc. by Special Act 1878. Dissolved 1 May 1949, undertaking being vested in North Eastern Area Gas Board under Gas Act 1948. Holders of securities were entitled to receive, in respect of each £100 unit held, British Gas 3% guaranteed stock 1990–95 as follows:

£   s.   d.

Orig. stock (10% stand.) 310 0 0
Addit. stock (7% stand.) 260 0 0   **1952**

Normetal Mining Corpn. Ld. Inc. Canada 1931. Undertaking and assets acquired by Kerr Addison Mines Ld. in which company shareholders received 3 shares for every 10 shares held **1973-4**

Norrington (Charles) & Co. Ld. Regd. 1895. Vol. liq. (members') 6 Apr. 1944. All shares owned by National Fertilizers Ld. Final meeting return regd. 8 Sept. 1944 .... **1945**

Norris (C. W.) Ld. Regd. 1935. Receivers and Managers were appointed in 1958 and in Jan. 1961 stated that the cash resulting from sale of assets was insufficient to make payments to contributories. Struck off Register 27 Oct. 1964 .... **1962**

Norseman Gold Mines Ld. Regd. 1896. Removed from Register 1908 .... **1902**

Norsk Hoved-Jernbane. *See* Norwegian Trunk Railway **1927**

Norske Lloyd Insurance Co. Ld. Inc. Norway 1913. Winding-up Order in England 17 Jan. 1922 .... **1922**

North Alabama Assets Co. Ld. Regd. 1895, Vol. liq. 1 Dec. 1927. Final meeting return regd. 8 June 1928 **1928**

North Alabama Development Co. Ld. Regd. 1890. Vol. liq. 14 Nov. 1894. Final meeting return regd. 15 June 1897 .... **1895**

North Albion Property Investment Co. Ld. Regd. Edinburgh 1877. Vol. liq. 4 Aug. 1885. Business was acquired by Scottish Deposit and Investment Co. Ld. Final meeting return regd. 9 Apr.1897 .... **1896**

North Alfred Consols Copper Mining Co. Ld. Regd. Truro 1881. Struck off Register 3 Dec. 1884 .... **1883**

North American Exploration Co. Ld. Regd. 1895. Struck off Register 21 Apr. 1939 .... **1940**

North American Land and Timber Co. Ld. Regd. 1882. Vol. liq. 25 Mar. 1920. Capital returned to contributories—£2 3s. 7½d. per share of £1 at June 1920; further payments (if any) not known. Final meeting return regd. 28 July 1920 .... **1921**

North American Land Association Ld. Regd. 1881. Removed from Register 1911 .... **1898**

North American Loan & Trust Co. Inc. 1887 Dakota, U.S.A., as Dakota Farm Mortgage Co.; reconstituted 1891 under present title **1901**

North American Trust Co. Inc. New York 1885. Reconstructed 1905 as Trust Co. of America. Stockholders received 37½% of their holdings in stock in the new Co. *plus* 50% in cash **1908**

North Amman Collieries Ld. Regd. 1913. Vol. liq. (members') 20 Jan. 1930. Final meeting return regd. 17 Nov. 1931 .... **1930**

North Anantapur Gold Mines Ld. Regd. 1908. Vol. liq. 22 Jan. 1929. Preference shareholders received 8 fully-paid shares of 2s. of Indian Copper Corporation Ld. for each share of £1 held. Remaining assets were distributed among ordinary shareholders. Final meeting return regd. 17 Dec. 1930 .... **1929**

North & South Insurance Corporation Ld. Regd. 1909. Court Order to wind up 18 Dec. 1933. Struck off Register 20 Feb. 1942 .... **1945**

North & South Investment Trust Ld. Regd. 1960. Vol. liq. (members') 20 Sept. 1965. Capital returned to contributories—5s. 6·325d. per share of 5s. £73 19s. 7d. was paid into Companies' Liquidation Account in respect of unclaimed distributions. Final meeting return regd.6 Dec. 1967 .... **1969**

North & South Wales Bank Ld. Established 1836. Regd. 1880. Vol. liq. 11 Dec. 1908. Business was acquired by London City and Midland Bank Ld. (later Midland Bank Ld.), in which company shareholders were entitled to 7 shares of £60 (credited with £12 10s. paid) *plus* £3 10s. in cash for every 10 shares of £40 (£10 paid) held **1909**

North and South Western Junction Railway Co. Inc. by Special Act 1851. In 1923 the undertaking was merged into the London Midland & Scottish Railway Co., in which company stockholders were entitled to £178½ 4% debenture stock for every £100 consolidated stock held **1924**

North & South Woolwich Subway Co. Inc. by Special Act 1877. Compulsorily wound up **1885**

North Atlantic Steamship Co, Ld. Regd. 1893 as Menantic Steamship Co. Ld.; name changed 19 Mar. 1901. Vol. liq. 3 Jan. 1913. Final meeting return regd. 6 Aug. 1913 .... ***1914**

North Australian Mining Co. Ld. Regd. 1888. Vol. liq. 19 Feb. 1892. Final meeting return regd. 15 Feb. 1893 **1893**

North Australian Territory Co. Ld. Regd. 1887. Vol. liq. 9 Aug. 1889. Final meeting return regd. 23 June 1896 .... **1890**

North Bitchburn Coal Co. Ld. Regd. 1903. Receiver appointed for 5% mortgage debenture holders in Oct. 1932. Struck off Register 23 Sept. 1938 .... **1939**

North Blue Hills Mine. Wound up **1889**

VOL. FOR

North Bonsor Gold Mining Co. Ld. Regd. 1899. Vol. liq. Jan. 1909. Assets were sold to Willoughby's Consolidated Co. Ld., in which company shareholders were entitled to 1 share of £1 (credited as fully-paid) for every 5 shares of £1 held. Removed from Register 1910 .... **1909**

North Borneo Prospecting & Cultivation Syndicate Ld. Regd. 1895. Removed from Register 1904 .... **1902**

North Borneo State Rubber, Ld. Regd. 2 Nov. 1908. Vol. liq. (members') 28 Dec. 1951. Capital returned to contributories—4s. 8·951d. per preference share of 2s. (including 2s. 8·951d. on account of arrears of dividend); 1⅛d. per ordinary share of 2s. Final meeting return regd. 21 July 1953 .... **1954**

North Borneo Trading Co. Ld. Regd. 1897. Vol. liq. 28 Aug. 1963. Capital returned to contributories—12s. 1·4d. per share of 10s. £945 2s. 3d. was paid into Companies' Liquidation Account Final meeting return regd. 27 May 1965 .... **1967**

North Boulder East Block (1898) Ld. Regd. 1898. Vol. liq. 23 Jan. 1901. The property was acquired by North Boulder Gold Mining Co. Ld., in which company shareholders were entitled to 1 share of 10s. (credited with 7s. 6d. paid) for every 3 shares of 10s. held. Final meeting return regd. 18 Feb. 1902 **1901**

North Boulder, East Block Ld. Regd. 1896. Vol. liq. 16 May 1898. Property acquired by North Boulder East Block (1898) Ld. Final meeting return regd. 27 July 1899 .... ***1899**

North Boulder Gold Mines Ld. Regd. 1902. Vol. liq. Apr. 1907. Removed from Register 1909 .... **1908**

North Boulder Gold Mining Co. Ld. Regd. 1895. Reconstructed 1902 as North Boulder Gold Mines Ld., in which company shareholders were entitled to 1 share of 10s. (credited with 7s. 6d. paid) for each share of 10s. held. Removed from Register 1905 **1907**

North Brancepeth Coal Co. Ld. Regd. 1870. Vol. liq. (members') 27 May 1931. All shares owned by Littleburn and Adelaide Collieries Ld. Final meeting return regd. 30 Oct. 1936 .... **1932**

North Brazilian Sugar Factories Ld. Regd. 1882. Vol. liq. 17 June 1887. Court Order to continue winding up under supervision July 1887. Struck off Register 20 Mar. 1906 .... **1887**

North Brazilian Sugar Factories Ld. Regd. 1887. Vol. liq. 1 Dec. 1919. Final meeting return regd. 20 Feb. 1920 .... **1926**

North British Aluminium Co. Ld. Regd. 1924. All capital owned by British Aluminium Co. Ld. Vol. liq. (members') Nov. 1960. Final meeting return regd. 9 June 1961 .... **1960**

North British and New Zealand Investment Co. Ld. Regd. Edinburgh 1886. Vol. liq. May 1901. Final meeting return regd. 21 May 1903 .... **1902**

North British Artificial Silk Ld. See North British Rayon Ld.

North British Australasian Co. Ld. Established 1839. Regd. 1857. Vol. liq. 7 Apr. 1924. Capital returned to contributories—25% at May 1924; further payments (if any) not known. Final meeting return regd. 31 Dec. 1924 .... **1925**

North British Canadian Investment Co. Ld. Regd. Edinburgh 1876. Reconstructed 1906 as company of same name. Shareholders were entitled to 1 share of £5 (credited with £2 paid) in new company for each share of £10 (£2 paid) held. Struck off Register 27 Sept. 1932 .... **1908**

North British Commercial Ld. Regd. 1926. All capital was owned by Palatine Industrial Finance Co. Ld. Struck off Register 1933 .... **1932**

North British Diesel Engine Works (1922) Ld. Regd. Edinburgh 1922. Vol. liq. 9 Dec. 1925. Undertaking was acquired by Barclay, Curle & Co. Ld. Final meeting return regd. 28 Oct. 1935 .... **1926**

North British Fishing Boat Insurance Co. Ld. Regd. 1886. Vol. liq. Oct. 1900 for reconstruction as company of same name. Shareholders were entitled to 1 fully-paid share of £1 in new company for every 4 shares of 10s. (5s. paid) held. Struck off Register 23 June 1931 .... **1908**

North British Fishing Boat Insurance Co. Ld. Regd. Edinburgh 1900. Vol. liq. June 1905. Struck off Register 23 June 1931 .... **1908**

North British Fishing Boat Insurance Co. Ld. Regd. Edinburgh 1905. Vol. liq. 3 Feb. 1908. Capital returned to contributories—£1 10s. per fully-paid share of £1 or 15s. per share of £1 (10s. paid) in Feb. 1909; further payments (if any) not known. Final meeting return regd 24 Nov. 1909 .... **1909**

North British Fishing Boat Insurance Co. Ld. Regd. Edinburgh 1908. Vol. liq. Apr. 1928. Undertaking and assets acquired by United Scottish Insurance Co. Ld. Capital returned to contributories—24s. per

VOL. FOR

share of £1; further payments (if any) not known. Final meeting return regd. 22 Dec. 1928 .... **1929**

North British Fresh Fish Supply Co. Ld. Regd. Edinburgh 1886. Vol. liq. May 1889. Final meeting return regd. 27 Dec. 1894 .... **1890**

North British Investment Trust Ld. Regd. in Edinburgh 21 Jan. 1914. Vol. liq. (creditors') 27 Aug. 1934. Final meeting return regd. 6 Oct. 19809 .... **1981–2**

North British Locomotive Co. Ld. Regd. in Edinburgh 1903. Vol. liq. (creditors') 19 Apr. 1962. Preferential creditors repaid in full; ordinary creditors received 18s. 0¾d. per £1. Struck off Register 25 July 1969 **1970**

North British Properties Ld. See Bellway Holdings Ld.

North British Property Investment Co. Ld. Regd. Edinburgh 1872. Vol. liq. Apr. 1904. Court Orders: to wind up 23 Aug. 1905; to dissolve 30 Oct. 1905 **1905**

North British Railway Co. Inc. by Special Acts 1844 and 1862. In 1923 the undertaking was merged into the London & North Eastern Railway Co., in which company stockholders were entitled to stock as follows:

For each £100 held		L. & N. E.	
3% Debenture	£100	3% Debenture	
3% Cons. Lien	£75	4% 1st Gtd.	
4% Cons. Pref. No. 1	£100	2nd Gtd.	
4% Cons. Pref. No. 2	£100	4% 1st Pref.	
6% Monkland Pref. (Ordinary)	£150	4% 1st Pref.	
4½% Edin. & Glasgow Preference	£112½	4% 1st Pref.	
5% Preference 1865	£125	4% 1st Pref.	
1% Nor'land Cent. Pref. No. 2	£25	4% 1st Pref.	
5% Conv. Pref. 1874	£125	4% 1st Pref.	
4½% Preference 1875	£112½	4% 2nd Pref.	
4½% Conv. Pref. 1875	£112½	4% 2nd Pref.	
5% Conv. Pref. 1879	£125	4% 2nd Pref.	
4% Conv. Pref. 1884	£100	4% 2nd Pref.	
4% Conv. Pref. 1888	£100	4% 2nd Pref.	
4% Conv. Pref. 1890	£100	4% 2nd Pref.	
4½% Preference 1891	£112½	4% 2nd Pref.	
4% Conv. Pref. 1892	£100	4% 2nd Pref.	
4% Conv. Pref. 1897	£100	4% 2nd Pref.	
4% Conv. Pref. 1901	£100	4% 2nd Pref.	
4% Conv. Pref. 1904	£100	4% 2nd Pref.	
4% Preference 1908	£100	4% 2nd Pref.	
3% Prefd. Ordinary	£60	5% Prefd. Ord.	
Deferred Ordinary {	£10	5% Prefd. Ord.	
	£40	Defd. Ordinary	**1924**

North British Rayon Ld. Regd. 1928 as North British Artificial Silk Ld.; name changed Mar. 1932. Vol. liq. (creditors') 17 June 1959. 92½% of principal of 3½% 1st mortgage debenture stock repaid. Final meeting return regd. 3 Oct. 1969 .... **1970**

North British Water-Gas Syndicate Ld. Regd. 1889. Vol. liq. 19 Dec. 1893. Reconstructed as Amalgamated Water-Gas Companies Ld., which company acquired the assets for 60,000 fully-paid shares of £1. Final meeting return regd. 2 Mar.1899.................. **1897**

North Broken Hill Mining Co. No Liability. Inc. Victoria 1905. Vol liq. Dec. 1912. Reconstructed as North Broken Hill Ld., in which company shareholders were entitled to 3 shares of £1 (credited as fully-paid) for each share of £1 held........................ **1913**

North Brunner Coal Co. Ld. Regd. 1908. Vol. liq. 12 Nov. 1911. Reconstructed as Brunner Collieries Ld in which company shareholders were entitled to 20 ordinary shares of 2s. (credited as fully-paid) for every 5 preference shares of £1 held or 10 ordinary shares of 2s. for every 5 ordinary shares of £1 held. Holders of each £50 debenture were entitled to 500 preference shares of 2s. Final meeting return regd.8 Jan. 1915 .... **1913**

North Burgess Gold Mining Co. Ld. Regd. 1895. Removed from Register 1905 .... **1904**

North Cachar Tea Co. Ld. Regd. 1899. Removed from Register 1903 .... **1903**

North Carolina Estate Co. Ld. Regd. 1886. Removed from Register 1895 .... **1889**

North Caspian Oil Corporation Ld. Regd. 1914. Struck off Register Dec. 1931 .... **1932**

North Central Wagon Co. Rotherham Ld. Est. 1861. Regd. as limited 1894. Dissolved before 1931 ...... **1908**

North Cerro Muriano Copper Mines Ld. Regd. 1906. Vol. liq. June 1908. Shareholders were entitled to 2 fully-paid shares of 5s. in Cordoba Copper Co. Ld. for each share of £1 (19s. paid) held or 10 fully-paid shares of 5s. for every 7 fully-paid shares held. Removed from Register 1912 .... **1909**

North Charterland Exploration Co. Ld. Regd. 1895. Vol. liq. May 1910 for reconstruction as North Chatterland Exploration Co. (1910) Ld. Shareholders were entitled to 1 fully-paid share of 10s. in new company

VOL. FOR

for every 2 shares of £1 held. Struck off Register Mar. 1929 .... **1930**

North Charterland Exploration Co. (1910) Ld. Regd. 1910. Vol. liq. (members') 14 Dec. 1936 for reconstruction as North Charterland Exploration Co. (1937) Ld., in which company shareholders were entitled to 1 share of 1*s.* (credited as fully-paid) for each share of 5*s.* held and option (since expired) over further shares at par. The secured notes were repaid at par on 8 Feb. 1937. Final meeting return regd. 13 Sept. 1937 .... **1937**

North Cheshire & District Gas Co. Inc. by Special Act 1855 as Hyde Gas Co.; name changed 1938. Dissolved 1 May 1949, undertaking being vested in North Western Area Gas Board under Gas Act 1948. Holders of securities were entitled to receive in respect of each £100 unit held, British Gas 3% guaranteed stock 1990–95 as follows:

	£	s.	d.
Cons. ord. stock (5% basic)	120	0	0
4% red. pref. stock	101	0	0
$4\frac{1}{2}$% red. pref. stock	104	15	0
5% red. pref. stock	105	15	0
$3\frac{3}{4}$% red. deb. stock	100	10	0
$4\frac{1}{2}$% deb. stock	104	5	0

Liability in respect of certain mortgage loans assumed by the Board. A distribution on cons. ord. stock of 4·26543% out of reserves was made in Apr. 1951 .... **1952**

North Cheshire & Manchester Brewery Co. Ld. *See below.*

North Cheshire Brewery Co., Ld. Regd. 1897 as North Cheshire & Manchester Brewery Co. Ld.; name changed 1898. Vol. liq. (members') 28 Nov. 1960. Final meeting return regd. 21 Feb. 1961 .... **1951**

North Cheshire Water Co. Inc. by Special Act 1864. Undertaking transferred to Manchester Corporation in Dec. 1919, the Corporation assuming liability for £7,000 3% irredeemable debenture stock **1921**

North China Gold Territories Development Co. Ld. Regd. 1897. Struck off Register 9 Dec. 1902 .... **1903**

North China Insurance Co. Ld. Regd. 1883. Vol. liq. 30 Dec. 1892. Reconstructed as company of same name. Shareholders were entitled to 1 share of £100 (credited with £25 paid) in new company *plus* £25 in cash for each share of £200 (£50 paid) held. Final meeting return regd. 30 Dec. 1893 .... **1903**

North China Insurance Co. Ld. Regd. 1892. Reconstructed 1903 as company of same name. Shareholders were entitled to 2 shares of £15 (credited with £5 paid) in new company *plus* £10 in cash for each share of £100 (£25 paid) held. Removed from Register 1905 .... **1908**

North China Insurance Co. Ld. Regd. 1903. Vol. liq. 30 Mar. 1928. Reconstructed as company of same name. Shareholders were entitled to 1 fully-paid share of £15 in new company for each share of £15 (£5 paid) held. Final meeting return regd. 13 Sept. 1935 .... **1929**

North China Insurance Co. Ld. Inc. in China under Hong Kong Ordinances 30 Mar. 1928. Vol. liq. 10 Dec. 1953. Controlling interest was held by Union Insurance Society of Canton Ld. **1954**

North Coast Land Co. Ld. Inc. British Columbia 1908. Vol. liq. June 1911 for reconstruction under similar title. Ordinary and preference shareholders were respectively entitled to $\frac{3}{5}$ and $1\frac{3}{10}$ share of $5 in new company for each ordinary share of $0·25 and preference share of $5 held **1912**

North Coast Land Co. Ld. Inc. British Columbia 1911 in reconstruction of company of similar title regd. 1908. In Oct. 1919 the Court in British Columbia ordered company to be wound up **1925**

North Cobar Ld. Regd. 1913. Vol. liq. 7 May 1926. Final meeting return regd. 13 June 1932 .... **1927**

North Coolgardie Co. Ld. *See* Winchester Gold Mining Co. Ld.

North Copper Co., Ld. Regd. 1906. Struck off Register 26 Sept. 1952 .... **1911**

North Cornwall China Clay Co. Ld. Regd. 1908 as North Cornwall China Clay Co. (1908) Ld.; name changed June 1913. Vol. liq. 8 Apr. 1919. Reconstructed as English China Clays Ld., in which company shareholders were entitled to $1\frac{1}{2}$ ordinary shares of £1 (credited as fully-paid) for each A or B preferred or ordinary share of £1 held; A and B preferred shareholders were entitled to a bonus of 20% and 10% respectively in ordinary shares. Debentures were discharged by allotment of preference shares. Final meeting return regd. 27 Apr. 1922 .... **1919**

North Cornwall Railway Co. Inc. by Special Act 1882. In 1923 the undertaking was merged into the London & South Western Railway Co. in which company holders of North Cornwall Stock or Deferred Scrip Certificates were entitled to an equal amount of 3% debenture stock **1924**

North Crœsus Gold Mine Ld. Regd. 1894. Vol. liq. 28 July 1899. Reconstructed as New Hannan's Excelsior and Crœsus Ld., in which company shareholders were entitled to 4 shares of £1 (credited with 16*s.* paid) for every 5 shares of £1 held. Final meeting return regd. 9 July 1900 .... **1900**

North Croydon Consols Ld. Inc. Queensland 1895, Reconstructed 1898 as Croydon Goldfields Ld., in which company shareholders were entitled to 1 share of 5*s.* (credited with 3*s.* paid) for each share of 5*s.* held **1904**

North Devon & Cornwall Junction Light Railway Co. Dissolved 3 June 1949; undertaking vested 1 Jan. 1948 in British Transport Commission under Transport Act 1947. Holders of securities were entitled to receive British Transport 3% guaranteed stock 1978–88 as follows:

	£	s.	d.
Ord. share (of £10)	0	0	6
5% debenture stock (£100)	129	0	0

1949

North-East African Exploration Co. Regd. 1899. Vol. liq. 2 Feb. 1926. Direct controlling interest held by London & Sudan Mining Syndicate Ld. Final meeting return regd. 20 Apr. 1926 .... **1926**

North East Lincolnshire Water Co. Inc. by Special Act 1906. Winding-up Order 10 Dec. 1951, the undertaking having been sold. In 1955 the Court ruled that the 3 classes of contributories should participate pari passu in the liquidation, and in Apr. 1956 authorised a return of £8 12*s.* $4\frac{4}{5}$*d.* per £10 capital held. Liquidator released 31 Jan. 1957 .... **1958**

North-East London Railway Co. Inc. by Special Act 1905. Powers expired 1910 .... **1910**

North-Eastern Bultfontein Ld. Regd. 1889. Vol. liq. 25 Sept. 1893. Property was sold for debenture holders. Final meeting return regd.8 Nov.1899 .... **1896**

North-Eastern Electric Supply Co Ld. Regd. 1889 as Newcastle-upon-Tyne Electric Supply Co. Ld.; name changed 1932. Dissolved 1 Apr. 1948, undertaking being vested in British (later Central) Electricity Authority and North Eastern Area Board under Electricity Act 1947. Holders of securities were entitled to receive British Electricity 3% guaranteed stock (1968-73), as follows in respect of each £1 unit of capital held:

	£	s.	d.
7% preference stock	1	16	4
5% preference stock	1	6	7
Ordinary stock	1	16	6
$3\frac{3}{4}$% consolidated debenture stock ...	1	0	$6\frac{4}{5}$
$3\frac{1}{2}$% consolidated debenture stock ...	1	0	6
$3\frac{1}{4}$% consolidated debenture stock ...	1	0	$3\frac{3}{5}$

1949

North Eastern Ice Co. Ld. Regd. Edinburgh 1890. Vol. liq. 29 Aug. 1903. Reconstructed as company of same name. Shareholders were entitled to 1 share of £1 (credited with 12*s.* 6*d.* paid) in new company *plus* 11*s.* 6*d.* in cash for each share of 15*s.* held. Struck off Register 2 Apr. 1935 .... **1908**

Nosth Eastern Ice Co. Ld. Regd. Edinburgh 1903. Vol. liq. (members') 31 Dec. 1958; all capital was acquired by Aberdeen Ice Co. Ld. in 1958. £10 15*s.* 10*d.* paid to Accountant of the Court in respect of unclaimed dividends. Final meeting return regd. 1 July 1960 .... **1960**

North Eastern Insurance Co. Ld. Regd. 1907. Court Order to wind up 10 Mar. 1914. Struck off Register 1927 .... **1915**

North Eastern of Uruguay Railway Co Ld. Regd. 1886. Under scheme of arrangement the undertaking was transferred in 1937 to Central Uruguay Railway Co. of Monte Video Ld. Shareholders were entitled to securities in acquiring company as follows-for every £100 preference shares held—£30 $4\frac{1}{2}$% 1st debenture stock, £80 5% 2nd debenture stock and 50 fully-paid ordinary shares of £1; for every £100 shares held-£10 $4\frac{1}{2}$% 1st debenture stock £80 5% 2nd debenture stock and 50 fully-paid ordinary shares of £1. Dissolved under Sec. 154 of Companies Act 1929 on 25 Aug. 1937 .... **1938**

North Eastern Railway Co Inc. by Special Act 1922. In 1923 the undertaking was merged into the London & North Eastern Railway Co., in which company stockholders were entitled to stock as follows:

For each £100 held	*L. & N.E.*
3% Debenture..........	£100 3% Debenture
4% Gt. Nth. of Eng. Purchase..........	£100 4% 1st Gtd.
4% Guaranteed..........	£100 4% 1st Gtd.
$4\frac{1}{2}$% Red. Pref.	£125 4% 1st Gtd.
4% Preference..........	£50 4% 2nd Gtd. £50 4% 1st Pref.

**See Stock Exchange Year-Book.*

	VOL. FOR

Consols .... { £100 4% 2nd Pref.
£50 5% Prefd. Ord.
£40 Defd. Ordinary

§ Holders had an option until 31 Jan. 1923, of retaining their rights of redemption by requiring the new Company to assume the obligations of the North Eastern Railway Co. in respect of their holdings **1924**

North Eastern Railway Co. Inc. by Special Act 1854. In 1922 the undertaking was merged in the North Eastern Railway Co. (inc. 1922). Holders of the 56 Great North of England Purchase Shares of £17 (£8 13s. 4d. paid), were entitled to 56 fully-paid shares in the new company of £8 13s. 4d. each but otherwise of the like class and denomination. Holders of the other securities were entitled to stocks of the like class, denomination and amount in the new company **1924**

North Eastern Shipping Co. Ld. Regd. Edinburgh 1898. Vol. liq. Oct. 1917. Final meeting return regd. 30 Mar. 1918 .... **1918**

North Eastern Steam Fishing Co. Ld. Regd. 1898. Vol. liq. 26 Nov. 1919. Final meeting return regd. 26 Sept. 1930 .... **1920**

North Eastern Steel Co. Ld. Regd. 1881. Vol. liq. 2 May 1923. Undertaking and assets were acquired by Dorman Long & Co. Ld., which company held all shares. Debenture stockholders were entitled either to cash at 110% or to £100 5½% debenture stock in acquiring company *plus* £15 in cash for every £100 stock held. Debenture holders were entitled either to cash at 105% or to £100 5½% debenture stock *plus* £10 in cash for every £100 stock held. Final meeting return regd. 18 Mar. 1935 .... **1924**

North-Eastern Stevens Mining Co. Ld. Regd. 1878. Vol. liq 17 Feb. 1890. Final meeting return regd. 8 Aug. 1900 .... **1891**

North Egypt Land Co. Ld. Regd. 1905. Vol. liq. 8 Aug. 1907. Final meeting return regd. 17 Jan. 1920 ..... **1908**

North End Spinning Co. Ld. Regd. 1889. Vol. liq. 25 Oct. 1922. The undertaking was acquired by Crosses & Heatons' Associated Mills Ld. Final meeting return regd. 19 Nov. 1930 .... **1923**

North European Cycle Export Co. Ld. Regd 1897. Removed from Register 1909 .... **1899**

North Euston Hotel & Hydro Ld. Regd. 1920. Vol. liq. (members') 19 Apr. 1960. Final meeting return regd. 6 Oct. 1960 .... **1940**

North Fingall Reefs Ld. Regd. 1895. Reconstructed 1910 as Mulwarrie Exploration Co. Ld., in which company shareholders received 1 fully-paid share of 10s. for each share of £1 held. Removed from Register 1903 .... **1908**

North Geduld Gold Mining Co. Ld. Inc. Trsnsvaal 1902. Vol. liq. Oct. 1906. Undertaking was acquired by Geduld Proprietary Mines Ld., in which company shareholders were entitled to 7 shares of £1 for every 20 shares of £1 held **1907**

North Glamorgan Wagon Co. Ld. Regd. 1914. Vol. liq. 28 June 1948. Capital returned to contributories—£23 4s. 3d. per ordinary share of £10 (with £3 paid). Final meeting return regd. 22 Dec. 1955 .... **1956**

North Golden Crown Ld. Regd 1896. Removed from Register 1913 .... **1912**

North Goonbarrow China Clay Ld. Regd. 1923. Vol. liq. 28 Jan. 1933. All shares owned by English China Clays Ld. Final meeting return regd. 7 Feb. 1935 **1934**

North Green Hurth Lead Mining Co Ld. Regd. 1880. Vol. liq. 4 May 1893. Final meeting return regd.4 May 1895 .... **1894**

North Hendre Lead Mining Co. Ld. Regd. 1870. Vol. liq. (members') 27 Feb. 1960. £2,078 3s. 1d. paid into Companies' Liquidation Account. Final meeting return regd. 24 Oct. 1961 .... **1963**

North Holderness Light Railway Co. Inc. (under Light Railways Act 1896) by order of Light Railway Commissioners confirmed by Board of Trade 1898. Under North Eastern Railway Act 1899 that company took over the powers and liabilities **1900**

North Hummock (Selangor) Rubber Co. Ld. Regd. 1907. Vol. liq. 15 Apr. 1920. Reconstructed as company of same name. Shareholders were entitled to 3 fully-paid shares of £1 in new company *plus* 5s. in cash for each share of £1 held. Final meeting return regd. 18 Jan. 1922 .... **1921**

North Hummock (Selangor) Rubber Co. Ld. Regd. 1920 in reconstruction of company of same name (regd. 1907). Vol. liq. (members') 11 Dec. 1963. Final meeting return regd. 21 June 1965. .... **1961**

North Island (N. Z.) Prospecting Syndicate Ld. Regd. 1897. Vol. liq. 29 July 1898. Final meeting return regd. 16 Nov. 1899 .... **1899**

North Kalgurli Co. Ld. Regd. 1901. Vol. liq. 20 Feb. 1913. Reconstructed as North Kalgurli (1912) Ld. in which company shareholders were entitled to 1

	VOL. FOR

share of 2s. (credited as fully-paid) for each share of 10s. held. Final meeting return regd. 20 Feb. 1914 **1913**

North Kalgurli Gold Mines Ld. Regd. 1895. Reconstructed 1901 as North Kalgurli Co. Ld., in which company shareholders were entitled to 1 share of 10s. (credited with 7s. 6d. paid) for each share of £1 held. Removed from Register 1903 .... **1908**

North Kalgurli (1912) Ld. Regd. 1912. Vol. liq. (members') 22 June 1971. Undertaking sold to North Kalgurli Mines Ld. in which company shareholders were entitled to receive 1 share for each share held. £22,909·94 paid into Companies' Liquidation Account in respect of sale of unclaimed entitlements. Final meeting return regd. Dec. 1974 . **1975-6**

North Kalgurli United Gold Development Ld. Regd. 1934. Vol. liq. (members') 4 Sept. 1941. Winding-up Order 18 Mar. 1941. No capital returned to contributories. Liquidator released 23 Jan. 1956. Struck off Register 17 Mar. 1961 .... **1956**

North Kapanga Gold Mining Co. Ld. Regd. 1895. Removed from Register 1899 .... **1898**

North Kennedy Co. Ld. Regd. 1886. Vol. liq. 31 May 1892. Property was acquired by Mount Leyshon Ld., in which company shareholders were entitled to 3 shares for each share held. Final meeting return regd. 29 Dec. 1893 .... **1893**

North Kent Coalfield Ld. Regd. 1911 as Anglo-Westphalian Kent Coal Syndicate Ld.; name changed Apr. 1913 to Anglo-Westphalian Kent Coalfield Ld. and as above Dec. 1914. Vol. liq. (members') 29 Sept. 1942. Capital returned to contributories—7s. 2¼d. per ordinary share of £1 or 4·3125d. per deferred share of 1s. £620 10s. 5d. was paid into Companies' Liquidation Account. Dissolved before 1951 .... **1945**

North Kimberley Diamond Mines Ld. Regd. 1910. Vol. liq. 19 Nov. 1925. Final meeting return regd. 1 Apr. 1926 .... **1926**

North Labis (Johore) Rubber & Produce Co. Ld. Regd. 1910. Vol. liq. (members') 28 Dec. 1933. Undertaking and assets were acquired by Bikam Rubber Estate Ld., in which company shareholders were entitled to 11 shares of 2s. (credited as fully-paid) for each share of £1 held. Final meeting 2 July 1934 **1934**

North Lachlan Gold Mining Co. Ld. Regd. 1894 as Hauraki Gold Mining Co. Ld.; name changed Aug. 1904. Vol. liq. 23 Nov. 1906. Reconstructed as company of same name. Shareholders were entitled to 1 share of 2s. 6d. (credited with 2s. paid) for each share of 2s. 6d. held. Final meeting return regd. 27 Aug. 1909 .... **1908**

North Lachlan Gold Mining Co. Ld. Regd. 1906. Vol. liq. 29 Dec. 1911. Final meeting return regd. 31 Dec. 1914 .... **1912**

North Lake George Syndicate Ld. Regd. 1899. Removed from Register 1910 .... **1901**

North Laxey & Glencherry Consols Silver-Lead Mining Co. Ld. Inc. Isle of Man 1889. In liquidation in 1898 **1898**

North Levant & Geevor Ld. Regd. 1906. Vol. liq. May 1911. Undertaking and assets were acquired by Geevor Tin Mines Ld., in which company shareholders were entitled to 1 share of 10s. (credited as fully-paid) for every 2 A shares of 2s. or 4 ordinary shares of 10s. held. Removed from Register 1912 **1912**

North Lincolnshire Light Railway Co. Inc. by Special Act 1900. Powers expired 1905 .... **1902**

North Lindsey Light Railways Co. Inc. (under Light Railways Act 1896) by order of Light Railway Commissioners confirmed by Board of Trade 1900. In 1923 the undertaking was merged into the London & North Eastern Railway Co. Holders of securities were entitled to cash as follows:

For each £100 held
4½% Term. Deb. Stock .... £102 cash
4% Pref. Shares .... £83 cash
Ordinary Shares .... £86 cash **1924**

North London Cycling & Athetic Ground Co. Ld. Regd. 1895. Reconstructed 1899 as North London Grounds Co. Ld., in which company shareholders were entitled to 1 share of £1 (credited with 15s. paid) for each share of £1 held. Removed from Register 1901 .... **1904**

North London Freehold Land & House Co. Ld. Regd. 1882. Court Orders: to wind up 31 July 1883; to dissolve 7 Dec. 1889 .... ***1884**

North London Grounds Co. Ld. Regd. 1899. Capital returned to contributories—1s. 4½d. per share of £1; further payments (if any) not known. Removed from Register 1907 .... **1905**

North London Railway Co. Inc. by Special Act 1846 as East & West Indian Docks & Birmingham Junction Railway Co.; name changed by Act of 1853. In 1922 the undertaking was merged into the London & North Western Railway Co., in which company

VOL. FOR

for £13,350. The 5% terminable debentures were repaid at par on 1 Oct. 1937 .... **1938**

North Penstruthal Mining Co. Established 1879. In liquidation in 1885.... **1885**

North Perak Rubber Estates Ld. Regd. 1910. Vol. liq. (creditors') 31 July 1931. No capital returned to contributories. Final meeting return regd. 2 Dec. 1932.... **1932**

North Provident and Guarantee Society Ld. Regd. Edinburgh 1895. Amalgamated with Sickness, Accident & Life Association Ld. [later Century Insurance Co. Ld.]. Vol. liq. Jan 1899. Struck off Register 13 Feb. 1903 .... **1900**

North Queensland Mines Agency Ld. Inc. Australia 1892. Reconstructed 1896 as Australian Mines Agency Ld. (inc. Australia 1896), shareholders were entitled to 1 share of £1 for each share of £1 held **1899**

North Queensland Syndicate Ld. Regd. 1904. Vol. liq. Sept. 1906. Removed from Register 1907 .... **1907**

North Rand Mines Ld. *See* British North Rand Mines Ld.

North Randfontein Gold Mining Co. Ld. Inc. Transvaal 1894. Resolutions to wind up were passed in July 1909 for sale of undertaking and assets to Randfontein South Gold Mining Co. Ld., in which company shareholders were entitled to 110 new shares of £1 for each 100 shares of £1 held.... **1910**

North Randt Mines Ld. Inc. Transvaal 1895. The company was liquidated in Johannesburg **1907**

North Ropp River Tin Co. Ld. Regd. 1924. Vol. liq. 10 Apr. 1928. Undertaking and assets were transferred to Associated Tin Mines of Nigeria Ld., in which company shareholders were entitled to 1 fully-paid share of 5*s.* for every 9 shares of 2*s.* held. Final meeting return regd.5 Feb.1929 .... **1929**

North Saskatchewan Land Co. Ld. Inc. under Dominion laws 1911. The receivership (commenced Aug. 1914) was closed by Order of Court on 30 Apr. 1947. The assets rcalised sufficient to repay the £475,000 6% 30-year sterling bonds at the rate of 45⅛%, final payment of 4⅝ having been made in May 1947 .... **1947**

North Sea Steam Co. Ld. Regd. Edinburgh 1902. Vol. liq. Apr. 1911. Final meeting return regd.6 Nov. 1911.... **1913**

North Sea Steam Shipping Co. Ld. Regd. Edinburgh 1882. Vol. liq. Apr. 1894. Final meeting return regd. 31 Jan. 1895 .... **1895**

North Sheba Gold & Exploration Ld. Regd. 1895. Vol. liq. 9 June 1898. Reconstructed as company of same name. Shareholders were entitled to 1 share of £1 (credited with 19*s.* paid) for each share of £1 held. Final meeting return regd. 30 Mar. 1900 .... **1903**

North Sheba Gold & Exploration Ld. Regd. 1898. Vol. liq. 13 May 1903. Reconstructed as company of same name. Shareholders were entitled to 120 shares of £1 (credited with 17*s.* paid) for every 100 shares of £1 held. Final meeting return regd. 15 Mar. 1909 **1907**

North Sheba Gold & Exploration Ld. Regd. 1903. Vol. liq. Feb. 1908. Removed from Register 1909 .... **1908**

North Shields Waterworks Co. Inc. by Special Act 1786. Properties sold to North Shields Corporation **1899**

North Somerset Electric Supply Co. Ld. Regd. 1911 as Clevedon & District Electric Supply Co. Ld.; name changed to Clevedon, Portishead & District Electric Supply Co. Ld. in 1911 and as above in 1918. Dissolved 1 Apr. 1948, undertaking being vested in British (later Central) Electricity Authority and South Western Area Board under Electricity Act 1947. Holders of ordinary and 5½% preference stock were entitled to receive, in respect of each £1 stock held, £1 16*s.* and £1 7*s.* 5*d.* British Electricity 3% guaranteed stock (1968–73) respectively **1949**

North Spanish Silver Mines Ld. Regd. 1889 as North Spanish Copper & Silver Mines Ld.; name changed Apr. 1889, Court Orders: to wind up Feb. 1890; to dissolve 26 Apr. 1894 .... **1891**

North Staffordshire Railway Co. Inc. by Special Act 1847. In 1923 the undertaking was merged into the London Midland & Scottish Railway Co., in which company stockholders were entitled to stock as follows:

For each £100 *held*	*L.M. & S.*	
3% Debenture....	£75	4% Debenture
5% Gtd. (Canal Purchase).	£127¾	4% Guart'd.*
3% Cons. Pref.	£75	4% Preference
Ordinary....	£74	Ordinary

* Including £2 15*s.* for surrender of contingent rights **1924**

North Staffordshire Tramways Co, Ld. Regd. 1878. Vol. liq. (members') 4 Mar. 1932. Capital returned to contributories—£10 per preference share of £10; £6 per ordinary share of £6. £16 was paid into Companies' Liquidation Account in respect of unclaimed capital and £281 15*s.* 6*d.* in respect of unclaimed debenture interest and dividends. Final meeting return regd. 23 Dec. 1932 .... **1933**

North Star Gold Mines Ld. Regd. 1896. Removed from Register 1905 .... **1904**

North Stockton Coal Co. Ld. Regd. 1888. Removed from Register 1906 .... **1893**

North Sunderland Railway Co. Ld. Inc. by Special Act 1892; Light Railway Order obtained in 1898; regd. as limited 25 Apr. 1952. Winding-up order 16 June 1952. No return of capital to contributories. Liquidator released 15 July 1960. Struck off Register 25 July 1969 .... **1962**

North Sussex Gas & Water Co. Inc. by Special Act 1905 as North Sussex Gas Co.; name changed in 1906. Court Order to wind up 17 June 1913 .... **1914**

North Swazieland Syndicate Ld. Regd. 1894. Struck off Register 1927 .... **1924**

North Sydney Investment & Tramway Co. Ld. Formed under Colonial Law 1888. In liquidation in 1897.. **1897**

North Tarkwa Syndicate Ld. Regd. 1901. Vol. liq. 29 July 1921. The undertaking and assets were acquired by East and West African Exploration Co. Ld., in which company shareholders were entitled to 5 shares of 2*s.* (credited with 1*s.* 4*d.* paid) for every 2 shares of 5*s.* held. Final meeting return regd. 7 Mar. 1922 .... **1922**

North Tolima Silver Mines Ld. Regd. 1891. Vol. liq. 2 Mar. 1905. Final meeting return regd. 31 Aug. 1905 **1906**

North Treskerby Tin & Copper Mines Ld. Regd. Truro 1884. Court Order to wind up 1 May 1886. Struck off Register 7 Mar. 1913 .... **1887**

North Union Railway Co. Inc. by Special Act 1834 ... **1889**

North Utah Mining Co. of Bingham. Inc. Maine 1906. In liquidation in 1912 .... **1912**

North Venezuelan Petroleum Co. Ld. Regd. 1920. Vol. liq. (members') 15 Mar. 1950, company's concession and assets in Venezuela having been sold to Creole Petroleum Corpn. Capital returned to contributories—18s. 9·325*d.* per share of 13s. 4*d.* £12,474 on account of unclaimed dividends and reduction of capital account and £14,686 unclaimed distributions were paid into Companies' Liquidation Account. Final meeting return regd. 4 Oct. 1955 .... **1957**

North Wales & Liverpool Railway Committee. Inc. by Special Act 1896. By Great Central Railway Act 1904 the powers were vested in that company and the committee dissolved **1905**

North Wales Development Co. Ld. Regd. 1919. Court Order to wind up Oct. 1921. Struck off Register Apr. 1929 .... **1930**

North Wales Freehold Copper Mines & Smelting Co. Ld. Regd. 1881. Struck off Register Feb. 1921 .... **1931**

North Wales Iron & Manganese Co. Ld. Regd. 1903. Vol. liq. 27 Aug. 1925. No capital returned to contributories. Struck off Register 29 Apr. 1952 ... **1952**

North Wales Narrow Gauge Railway Co. Inc. by Special Act 1872. Undertaking was acquired by Welsh Highland Railway (Light Railway) Co. for £10,000 debentures and £40,000 fully-paid ordinary shares of £1 .... **1923**

North Wales Power Co. Ld. Regd. 1903 as North Wales Power & Traction Co. Ld.; name changed 1922. Dissolved 1 Apr. 1948, undertaking being vested in British (later Central) Electricity Authority and Merseyside & North Wales Area Board under Electricity Act 1947, Holders of ordinary shares were entitled to receive 15*s.* 6*d.* British Electricity 3% guaranteed stock (1968–73) in respect of each share (of 10*s.*) held. Holders of 5% guaranteed 1st debenture stock (1930–53), and 3% guaranteed debenture stock (1946–53) were entitled to receive equal amounts of British Electricity 5% guaranteed stock (1953) and 3% guaranteed stock (1948–53) respectively **1949**

North Wales Shipping Co. Ld. Regd. 1905. Vol. liq 18 Nov. 1921. Final meeting return regd, 25 Oct. 1922 **1922**

North Warwickshire Motor Omnibus & Traction Co, Ld. Regd. 1913. Vol. liq. 30 Sept. 1946. Final meeting return regd. 7 Oct. 1947 .... **1940**

North Warwickshire Water Co. Inc. by Special Act 1898. The undertaking was transferred to Coventry Corporation as from 17 Sept. 1921, for £46,300 cash, with interest at 4% p.a. from 24 June 1920.... **1922**

North West Argentine Railway Co. Ld. Regd. 1886. Undertaking acquired in 1899 by Cordoba Central Railway Co. [later Cordoba Central Trust Ld.]. £334,418 income debenture stock of acquiring company was issued in exchange for preferred and deferred share capital. Holders of new 2nd debenture stock were entitled to an equal amount of income debenture stock. Holders of remaining debenture stocks were entitled to 4% North West Argentine Extension debenture stock in acquiring company as follows-for every £100 prior lien

VOL. FOR

debenture stock held—£116 13s. 4d.; for every £100 6% 1st debenture stock held—£125; for every £100 new 1st debenture stock or 2nd debenture stock held—£100. Removed from Register 1909. .... **1901**

North-West Australian Goldfields Ld. Regd. 1895. Reconstructed as Nullagine Gold Diamond & Exploration Co. Ld. Removed from Register 1901 **1900**

North West Central Railway Co. Inc. by Special Act 1890. Undertaking abandoned by Act of 1893 ..... **1894**

North West Corporation Ld. Regd. 1913. Vol. liq. Feb. 1922. The undertaking and assets were acquired by New North West Corporation Ld. (inc. Canada) for $346,123 income notes. $320,000 preferred A stock, $608,000 preferred B stock, $3,467,430 common stock. Struck off Register 13 Feb. 1931 .... **1922**

North West London Electric Supply Co. Ld. Regd. 1902. In 1906 the undertaking was transferred to Hampstead Borough Council, after being in hands of receiver for debenture holders, who received about 5s. in the £. Removed from Register 1908 .... **1907**

North West London Railway Co. Inc. by Special Act 1899. No capital was in issue at 1 Nov. 1909 ...... **1910**

North West Midlands Joint Electricity Authority. Inc. by the North West Midlands Electricity District Order 1928. Dissolved 1 Apr. 1948, undertaking being vested in British (later Central) Electricity Authority and Midlands Area Board under Electricity Act 1947. Holders of 3% stock (1957) and 5% stock (1950–70) were entitled to receive, in respect of every £100 stock held, £104 and £109 10s. British Electricity 3% guaranteed stock (1968–73) respectively **1949**

North-West Mining Syndicate Ld. Regd. 1897. Removed from Register 1911 .... **1910**

North-West Provinces and Oude Ice Co. Ld. Regd. 1880. Vol. liq. Aug. 1886. Final meeting returned regd. 2 Dec. 1890 .... **1887**

North-West Timber Co. of Canada Ld. Regd. 1883. Court Orders: to wind up 14 Mar 1885; to dissolve 28 Apr. 1891 .... **1886**

North-Western Associated Gold Mines (W. A.) Ld. Regd. 1903. Court Order to wind up 1 Aug. 1905. Liquidator released 23 Feb. 1912. Struck off Register 16 July 1915 .... **1906**

North-Western Bank Ld. Regd. 1864. Amalgamated with the London and Midland Bank Ld. (later Midland Bank Ld.) 30 June 1897, in which company shareholders received 1 share of £60 (£12 10s. paid), together with £3 15s. cash for every 5 shares of £20 (£7 10s. paid) held **1898**

North-Western Coal and Navigation Co. Ld. Regd. 1882. Vol. liq. 9 Mar. 1891. Taken over by Alberta Railway & Coal Co. for $1,000,000 in preference shares and $217,500 in ordinary shares. Final meeting return regd. 12 Apr. 1892 .... **1892**

North Western Cold Storage Co. Ld. Regd. 1897 as North Western Co-operative Cold Storage Co. Ld.; name changed May 1928. Vol. liq. (members') 14 July 1931. Capital returned to contributories—£2 3s. 2⅝d. per preference or ordinary share of £1. Final meeting return regd. 16 Mar. 1932..................... **1932**

North Western Co-operative Cold Storage Co. Ld. *See* North Western Cold Storage Co. Ld.

North-Western Cyanamide Co. Ld. Regd. 1906. Vol. liq. 2 Apr. 1924. Final meeting return regd. 17 May 1932 **1925**

North Western Exploration Co. Ld. Regd. 1898. Court Order to wind up July 1908. Removed from Register 1908.. **1909**

North-Western Fire Insurance Co. Ld. *See* London & North Western Fire Insurance Co. Ld.

North Western Gas Corpn, Ld. Regd. 1934. Dissolved 1 May 1949, undertaking being vested in Gas Council under Gas Act 1948. Holders of ordinary shares (of £1) were entitled to receive £1 10s. British Gas 3% guaranteed stock 1990–95 for each share held. **1952**

North-Western Insurance Co. Ld, Regd. 1899 as Tanners & Leather Trades Insurance Co. Ld.; name changed to Leather Trades & General Insurance Co, Ld., in Mar. 1902 and as above in July 1909. Vol. liq. 30 Mar. 1915, Business was acquired by British Dominions General Insurance Co. Ld. (later Eagle Star Insurance Co. Ld.) for 60,000 ordinary shares of £3 (credited with 15s. paid). Struck off Register 18 Jan. 1921 .... **1916**

North-Western Investment Trust Ld. Regd. Edinburgh 1913. Vol. liq. (members') 25 Feb. 1935. Direct controlling interest held by Great Northern Investment Trust Ld. Final meeting return regd. 7 Aug. 1936 .... **1936**

North Western of Uruguay Railway Co. Ld. Regd. 1882. Vol. liq. (members') 24 Feb. 1949, undertaking having been sold to Uruguayan Govt. 6% 2nd debenture stock was redeemed at 110%, with interest to 31 July 1948 (57¾%) 1st preference, 2nd preference and ordinary stockholders received distributions of 36·2924%, 12·4755% and 5·6706% respectively. £3,764 was paid into Companies' Liquidation Account. Final meeting return regd. 9 Aug. 1951 .... **1953**

North Western Railway Co. of Peru Ld. Regd. 1908. Vol. liq. Jan. 1929. No return of capital was made. Final meeting return regd. 9 Nov. 1949 .... **1951**

North Western Railway of Montevideo Co. Ld. Property acquired by North Western of Uruguay Railway Co. Ld. Removed from Register 1904................. ***1884**

North-Western Volcanic-Aëration Co. Ld. Regd. 1890. Removed from Register 1905 .... **1893**

North White Feather Consolidated Gold Mines Ld. Regd. 1895 as North White Feather Gold Mining Co. Ld.; name changed July 1895. Reconstructed 1900 as North White Feather Gold Mines Ld., in which company shareholders were entitled to 2 shares of 10s. (credited with 8s. paid) for each share of £1 held. Removed from Register 1901 .... **1908**

North White Feather Gold Mines Ld. Regd. 1900. Vol. liq. 17 June 1920. Reconstructed as company of same name. Shareholders were entitled to 1 share of 5s. (credited with 3s. 6d. paid for each share of 10s. held. Final meeting return regd. 17 Sept. 1927 .... **1921**

North White Feather Gold Mines Ld. Regd. 1920. Vol. liq. 22 May 1928. Final meeting return regd. 22 May 1929 .... **1929**

North Witwatersrand Gold Mines Ld. Regd. 1904. Vol. liq. June 1908. Removed from Register 1912....... **1909**

North Worcestershire Breweries Ld. Regd. 1896. Vol. liq. May 1909. Undertaking and assets were acquired by Wolverhampton and Dudley Breweries Ld. for £245,000 4% irredeemable B mortgage debenture stock, 1909 distributed as follows—1st mortgage debenture and B debenture stock—70% of holding; pre-preference shares—40% of holding; preference shares—10% of holding; ordinary shares— 1% of holding. Removed from Register 1910 .... **1910**

North Zambesi Coal Syndicate, Ld. Regd. 1905. Control transferred to S. Rhodesia from 31 Mar. 1952. Struck off Register 23 Oct. 1959 .... **1956**

North Zambesia Concessions Ld. Regd. 1900. Vol. liq. Dec. 1912. Removed from Register 1913 .... **1913**

Northallerton Consumers Gas Co. Ld. Regd. 1870. Dissolved 1 May 1949. undertaking being vested in Northern Area Gas Board under Gas Act 1948. Holders of ordinary shares (of £5) were entitled to receive £8 2s. 6d. British Gas 3% guaranteed stock 1990–95 for each share held **1952**

Northam Milling & Mining Co. Ld. Regd. 1897. Property and assets, were sold to Golden Age Consolidated Ld., in which company shareholders were entitled to; 1 share of £1 (credited as fully-paid) for every 5 shares of £1 held. Removed from Register 1903 .... **1902**

Northampton & Banbury Junction Railway Co. Inc. by Special Act 1863; name changed by Act of 1866 to Midland Counties & South Wales Railway Co.; original name resumed by Act of 1870. Under Act of 1910 the line became part of Stratford-upon-Avon and Midland Junction Railway Co. Stockholders received £27 10s., £6. £2 and £1 for every £100 A debenture, B debenture, preference or ordinary stocks respectively held **1911**

Northampton Electric Light & Power Co. Ld. Regd. 1889. Dissolved 1 Apr. 1948. undertaking being vested in British (later Central) Electricity Authority and East Midlands Area Board under Electricity Act 1947. Holders of securities were entitled to receive British Electricity 3% guaranteed stock (1968–73), as follows in respect of each £1 unit of capital held:

	£	s.	d.
5% preference stock	1	7	6
Ordinary stock..................................	2	10	11
3½% debenture stock..........................	1	0	6

1949

Northampton Electric Power & Traction Co. Ld. See Wellingborough Electric Supply Co. Ld.

Northampton Gaslight Co. Inc. by Special Act 1823. Dissolved 1 May 1949. undertaking being vested in East Midland Area Gas Board under Gas Act 1948. Holders of securities were entitled to receive, in respect of each £100 held, British Gas 3% guaranteed stock 1990–95 as follows:

	£	s.	d.
Cons. stock (5% max.)...................	112	0	0
4% irred. deb. stock	102	10	0
5% red. deb. stock..........................	105	0	0
4% red. deb. stock..........................	101	5	0
3½% red. deb. stock	100	0	0

1952

See Stock Exchange Year-Book.

VOL. FOR

Northampton Street Tramways Co. Inc. by Special Act 1880. In liquidation in 1903, the undertaking having been sold to the Town Council for £37,500 .... **1903**

Northamptonshire Banking Co. Ld. Business acquired by Capital and Counties Bank Ld. Shareholders were offered either £12 per share in cash or 3 shares of £50 (credited with £10 per share paid) in acquiring company for every 10 shares held **1891**

Northamptonshire Union Bank Ld. Established 1836. Regd. 1880. Vol. liq. 2 Dec. 1920. Undertaking and assets were acquired by National Provincial and Union Bank of England Ld. (later National Provincial Bank Ld.), in which company shareholders were entitled to 7 shares of £20 (credited with £4 paid) for every 2 shares of £30 (£11 paid) held *plus* £1 10s. per share in cash **1921**

Northcliffe Newspapers Ld. Regd. 1928. Vol. liq. (members) 22 Dec. 1932. Final meeting return regd. 17 Mar. 1937 **1933**

Northcote (Stafford) & Co. Ld. Regd. 1899. Vol. liq. July 1925. Capital returned to contributories—30s. per preference share of £5; 2s. 3¾d. per ordinary share of £1 at Dec. 1925; further payments (if any) not known. Struck off Register Aug. 1929............ **1930**

Northern Accident Insurance Co. Ld. Regd. Edinburgh 1882., Vol. liq. May 1907. Undertaking was acquired by Royal Insurance Co. Ld. Capital returned to contributories—£7 per share of £5 (£1 paid); further payments (if any) not known. Struck off Register 26 Sept. 1933 **1908**

Northern Agricultural Co. Ld. Regd. Edinburgh 1878 as unlimited and in 1902 as limited. The undertaking was acquired in 1935 by Aberdeen Lime Co. Ld. (later Northern Agricultural & Lime Co. Ld.). Vol. liq. (members) 9 Jan. 1941. Capital returned to contributories—£3 per share of £5. Final meeting return regd. 4 Sept.1941 **1941**

Northern Airways Ld. Regd. 1934 as Northern & Scottish Airways Ld.; name changed Sept. 1937. Vol. liq. (members) 22 Nov. 1939. Company's shareholding in Scottish Airways Ld. (25,515 fully-paid A ordinary shares of £1) was distributed in specie. Capital returned to contributories—£369 11s. 10d. Final meeting return regd. 29 May 1940 **1940**

Northern and Dominions Mortgage Co. Ld. Regd. Edinburgh 1913. Vol. liq. May 1920. Final meeting return regd. 28 May 1921 **1921**

Northern & Eastern European Trading Co. Ld. *See* Northern & Eastern Mining Co. Ld.

Northern & Eastern Mining Co. Ld. Regd. 1919 as Northern & Eastern European Trading Co. Ld name changed Oct. 1928. Struck off Register 25 Mar. 1938 **1939**

Northern & Eastern Railway Co. Inc. by Special Act 1836. Under Great Eastern Railway Act 1902 undertaking was sold to that company. Each 5% £50 original and Newport share received £62 10s. Great Eastern 4% debenture stock and 1 certificate "A" of £50 of contingent rights; each 6% £50 original and Newport share received £75 Great Eastern 4% debenture stock and 1 certificate "B" of £50 of contingent rights **1903**

Northern & Eastern Suburban Industrial Dwellings Co. Ld. Regd. 1874. In liquidation in 1903. A return of £4 17s. per share of £5 was anticipated. Removed from Register 1904 **1903**

Northern & Employers Assurance Co. Ld. Regd. 1960. Vol. liq. (members) 23 Dec. 1968. Formerly a subsidiary of Commercial Union Assurance Co. Ld. Amount returned to contributories (per share of £1)—£1. £306 10s. 9d. paid into Companies' Liquidation Account in respect of unclaimed distributions. Final meeting return regd. 14 Sept. 1970 **1971**

Northern & Scottish Airways Ld. *See* Northern Airways Ld.

Northern & Southern Investment Corporation Ld. Regd. 1922. Court Order to wind up 26 Aug. 1940. Liquidator released 9 Oct. 1942. Struck off Register 21 Aug. 1945 **1946**

Northern & Western American Association Ld. Regd. 1890. Vol. liq. 28 Mar. 1893. Final meeting return regd. 19 June 1893 **1894**

Northern Blocks Syndicate Ld. Regd. 1903. Vol. liq. Oct. 1907. Removed from Register 1908 **1908**

Northern Canada Mining Corporation Ld. Inc. Ontario 1907 as Beaver Consolidated Mines Ld.;name changed July 1928 **1938**

Northern Colonies Extensions Railway of Santa Fé. The outstanding 5% mortgage bonds issued in 1884 were repaid in Jan. 1889 **1896**

Northern Copper (B.S.A.) Co. Ld. Regd. 1895 as Northern Territories (B.S.A.) Exploring Co. Ld.; name changed 1899. Vol. liq. 4 Aug. 1914. Amalgamated with Bechuanaland Exploration Co. Ld., in

VOL. FOR

which company shareholders were entitled to 9 shares of 10s. (credited as fully-paid) for every 10 shares of £1 held. Final meeting return regd. 13 July 1916 **1915**

Northern Corporation Ld. Regd. 1891. Vol. liq. 5 Oct. 1953. Final meeting return regd. 8 Sept. 1954....... **1955**

Northern Counties Bank Ld. Regd. 1871. Vol. liq. 8 Nov. 1881. Court Order to continue winding up under supervision 8 Nov. 1881. Final meeting return regd. 7 Aug. 1895 ***1882**

Northern Counties Electricity Supply Co. Ld. Regd. 1900. The 1st and 2nd mortgage debenture stocks were redeemed on 1 July 1931. Under Act of 1932 the undertaking was acquired by North-Eastern Electric Supply Co. Ld., in which company shareholders were entitled to 1 fully-paid ordinary share of £1 for every 3 shares of £1 held. Dissolved under Act on 30 Sept. 1932 **1933**

Northern Counties Fire Insurance Co. Ld. *See* Northern Counties of England Fire Insurance Co. Ld.

Northern Counties Investment Trust Ld. Regd. 1889. The debentures were repaid on 31 Dec. 1924. Vol. liq. July 1925. Capital returned to contributories—10s. per share in Dec. 1925; further payments (if any) not known. Struck off Register Dec. 1933..... **1934**

Northern Counties Motor & Engineering Co. Ld. Regd. 1919. Vol. liq. (creditors') 23 Oct. 1935. Assets realised insufficient to meet debentures in full. Struck off Register 8 Apr. 1938 **1939**

Northern Counties of England Fire Insurance Co. Ld. Regd. 1876 as Northern Counties Fire Insurance Co. Ld.; name changed 15 Mar. 1876. Court Orders: to wind up 19 Dec. 1879; to dissolve 6 Aug. 1895 ***1880**

Northern Counties Railway of Santa Fé. The outstanding 5% mortgage bonds issued in 1885 were repaid in Jan. 1889 **1896**

Northern Counties Transport Ld. Regd. 1912. Struck off Register 1918 ***1914**

Northern Distilleries Ld. Regd. Edinburgh 1897. Vol. liq. Dec. 1900. Court Order to dissolve 26 Sept. 1905 **1901**

Northern District Telephone Co. Ld. Regd. 1881. Undertaking was acquired by National Telephone Co. Ld. Removed from Register 1891 **1891**

Northern Equitable Insurance Co. Ld. Regd. Edinburgh 1907. Vol. liq. Jan. 1914. Court Order to continue under supervision and to dissove 19 Mar. 1924. Business was acquired by British General Insurance Co. Ld. **1914**

Northern Exploration Co. Ld. Regd. 1910. Assets, sold to Norwegian Government, realised sufficient to repay the 10% debentures but not the 6% debentures. Struck off Register June 1934 **1935**

Northern Exploring Syndicate Ld. Regd. 1898. Vol. liq. June 1908. Removed from Register 1909 **1909**

Northern Greyhound Racers (Hanley) Ld. Regd. 1927. Vol. liq. (members') 14 May 1964. Final meeting return regd. 2 Sept. 1965 **1939**

Northern Guarantee & Finance Corpn. Ld. Regd. 1914 as Primrose Tea Co. Ld.; name changed to Householders' Tea Association Ld. in 1922 and as above in 1926. Vol. liq. (members') 17 July 1934. No capital was returned to contributories. Final meeting return regd. 6 Feb. 1952. Struck off Register 23 Feb. 1954 **1953**

Northern Industries Development Ld. Regd. 1933. Vol. liq. (members') 15 Dec. 1936. Capital returned to contributories—5s. 10d. per share of £1 (15s. paid). Final meeting return regd. 13 May 1937 **1937**

Northern Investment Co. of New Zealand Ld. Regd. Edinburgh 1880. Vol. liq. Oct. 1903. Debenture stock was repaid in Nov. 1903. Capital returned to contributories—£1 per share of £5 (with £1 paid); further payments (if any) not known. Final meeting return regd. 17 Apr. 1905 **1904**

Northern Ireland Road Transport Board. Estd. by Road & Railway Transport Act (Northern Ireland) 1935. Dissolved 1 Oct. 1948 and the undertaking vested in the Ulster Transport Authority under the Transport Act (Northern Ireland) 1948 **1948**

Northern Irish & Scottish Investment Trust Ld. Regd. in Belfast 1963. Vol. liq. (members') 5 Sept. 1977. Capital returned to contributories—36·437p per share (of 25p). £2,143·59 was paid into Companies' Liquidation Account in respect of unclaimed distributions. Fianl meeting return regd. 2 Aug. 1978 **1979-80**

Northern Irish & Scottish Investment Trust Ld. Regd. 5 July 1963. Vol. liq. (members') 5 Sept. 1977. Capital returned to contributories—3·767p per ordinary share of 25p. Final meeting return regd. 2 Aug. 1978 **1979-80**

Northern Light, Power & Coal Co. Ld. Inc. Canada 1909. In 1943 the company was stated to be in a moribund condition **1943**

VOL. FOR

Northern London Estates Co. Ld. Regd. 1875. Vol. liq. 1 Mar. 1887. Court Order to wind up under supervision 19 Feb. 1887. Final meeting return regd. 24 Oct. 1891 .... *1888

Northern Marine Insurance Co. Ld. In 1892 the business was acquired by Marine Insurance Co. Ld 1893

Northern Metals Mining Corporation Ld. Regd. 1911. Vol. liq. Aug. 1912 for reconstruction as Baltic Lead Mines Ld., in which company shareholders were entitled to 1 share of 10s. (credited with 8s. paid) for each share of £1 held. Removed from Register 1914 1913

Northern Mines Ld. Inc. Western Australia 1907. Vol. liq. Dec. 1912. Capital returned to contributories—3s. 9¾d. per share of £1 in Apr. 1913; further payments (if any) not known. 1914

Northern Motor Utilities (B.T.C.) Ld. Regd. 1919 as Northern Motor Utilities Ld.; name changed 1949. All issued capital acquired by British Transport Commission in Apr. 1949; company ceased trading on transfer of all activities to Road Haulage Executive as from Oct. 1949. Outstanding debenture stocks repaid in full in Nov. 1949 1950

Northern Nigeria (Bauchi) Tin Mines Ld. Regd. 1910. Vol. liq. 31 Oct. 1929. Amalgamated with London Tin Syndicate Ld. (later London Tin Corporation Ld.), in which company shareholders were entitled to 1 share of £1 (credited as fully-paid) for every 2 preference or ordinary shares of 10s. held plus 1s. 6d. in cash. Preference shareholders were entitled to 5s. per share in 7½% 1st mortgage debenture stock of London Nigerian Power Co. Ld. Final meeting return regd. 17 Dec. 1932 1930

Northern Nigeria Exploration Syndicate Ld. Regd. 1901. Vol. liq. 21 Jan. 1907. The undertaking was acquired by Nigeria Bitumen Corporation Ld., in which company shareholders were entitled to 68 shares of £1 (credited as fully-paid) for every 100 shares of £1 held, together with right to 25 further shares of £1 (credited with 12s. paid) the balance of 8s. being paid by this Syndicate. Struck off Register 12 Apr. 1929 1907

Northern Nigeria Mining & Exploration Co. Ld. Regd. 1910. Vol. liq. 25 Mar. 1925. Capital returned to contributories—2s. 4¾d. per share of 5s. at 1 Nov. 1925; further payments (if any) not known. Final meeting return regd. 24 Nov. 1925 1926

Northern Nigeria Trust Ld. Regd. 1911. Vol. liq. 21 Dec. 1920. The assets were acquired by Bisichi Tin Co. (Nigeria) Ld., in which company shareholders were entitled to 1 share of 10s. for each share of 10s. held. Final meeting return regd. 6 Nov. 1922 1921

Northern of Europe Rly. Co. Ld. (later Swedish & Norwegian).. 1894

Northern of Spain Railways. Inc. in Spain by Royal Decree of 29 Dec. 1858 & 14 Jan. 1859. Undertaking has been embodied in the Red Nacional de los Ferrocarriles Españoles, share and loan capital being exchanged under Law of 27 Feb. 1943 for 3½ amortisable bonds of the State at the rate of Ptas.329 bonds per share of Ptas.475 and Ptas.388·24 bonds per bond of Ptas.500 (including accrued interest) 1948

Northern Ontario Exploration Co. Ld. Regd. 1911. Vol. liq. 14 Jan. 1914. Undertaking and assets were sold to California Exploration Co. Ld., in which company shareholders were entitled to 3 shares of 10s. (credited as fully-paid) for every 2 shares of £1 held. Final meeting return regd. 23 Mar. 1915 1914

Northern Ontario Light and Power Co. Ld. Inc. Ontario 1911. Amalgamated with Northern Canada Power Ld. in 1928 as Northern Ontario Power Co. Ld. 1929

Northern Ontario Power Co. Ld. Fixed properties were acquired from Dec. 1944 by Hydro Electric Power Commission of Ontario. The 6% debentures were redeemed 1 May 1945 at par and the 6% preferred stock was redeemed on 31 Mar. 1945 at 110%. All common shares were owned by Canada Northern Power Corporation Ld 1946

Northern Pacific Railway Co. Chartered by Special Act of the Wisconsin State Legislature, approved 1870 and amended 1871 and 1895. Merged with Chicago, Burlington & Quincey Railroad Co., Great Northern Pacific Railway Co. and Pacific Coast R.R. Co. in Mar. 1970 to form Burlington Northern Inc., which assumed liability for all debts and obligations of merging companies. Outstanding common shares (of $5) of this company were converted, share for share, into common shares (of no par value) of Burlington Northern Inc. 1973-4

Northern Patent Brick & Tile Co. Ld. Regd. Edinburgh 1882. Amalgamated with Seaton Brick & Tile Co. Ld. Vol. liq. Aug. 1889. Final meeting return eegd. 5 June 1890 1890

VOL. FOR

Northern Plate Glass Insurance Co. Ld. Regd. Edinburgh 1888. Vol. liq. Mar. 1924. Final meeting return regd. 8 May 1924 1925

Northern Platinum Exploration Ld. Inc. Transvaal 1925. Vol. liq. 1 Sept. 1932. Taken over by Potgeistersrust Platinums Ld., in which company shareholders were entitled to receive 1 share for every 10 shares held plus 2·45d. per share cash 1933

Northern Railway Co. of Canada. Inc. Canada 1859. In 1882 the undertaking was acquired by Grand Trunk Railway Co. of Canada. The 4% debenture stock was acquired in Jan. 1942 by H.M. Treasury at £103 7s. 11d. for every £100 stock held; the 6% 3rd preference irredeemable bonds were acquired at £115 8s. 10d. for every £100 bonds held 1888

Northern Railway of Buenos Aires Co. Ld. See Buenos Aires Northern Railway Co. Ld.

Northern Railway of the South African Republic. Established under Belgian Law 1892. The final meeting in the liquidation was held in Brussels on 3 July 1906. The 4% sterling guaranteed bonds were redeemed at 96% between 1906 and 1908 1909

Northern Rowton Houses Ld. Regd. 1904. Vol. liq. 12 Sept. 1919. Final meeting return regd. 1 Dec. 1920 1920

Northern Rubber Co. A/S. Inc. Denmark. Direct controlling interest was owned by Abang Rubber Co. Ld. In Nov. 1933 it was stated that the estate had been sold to the mortgagees and that liquidation was inevitable 1934

Northern Sabulite Explosives Co. Ld. Regd. 1923. Vol. liq. (members') 31 Dec. 1942. Undertaking acquired by I.C.I. (Explosives) Ld. Final meeting return regd. 25 May 1946 1947

Northern Securities Co. Inc. New Jersey 1901. Dissolution of company was approved by stockholders on 11 Aug. 1937 1938

Northern Stockholders Investment Trust Ld. Regd. 1937 as Basic Investment Trust Ld.; name changed Nov. 1953. Vol. liq. (members') 10 Feb. 1960, all assets being distributed to Lake View Investment Trust Ld which acquired all capital in 1959. Final meeting return regd. 30 Apr. 1960 1961

Northern Sulphite Mills of Canada Ld. Inc. Ontario 1905. In Dec. 1911 the property was sold by order of the Ontario Court. 6% mortgage bondholders received £14 10s. per £100 bond held at Dec. 1918; further payments (if any) not known. It was stated that no distribution would be made to shareholders 1920

Northern Tavoy Tin Dredging Ld., Regd. 1926. Vol. liq. (creditors') 26 Aug. 1930. Undertaking and assets were acquired by Tavoy Tin Dredging Corporation Ld., in which company shareholders were entitled to 1 share of 4s. (credited as fully-paid) for each share of 10s. held. Final meeting return regd. 18 July 1931 1931

Northern Territories (B.S.A.) Exploring Co. Ld. See Northern Copper (B.S.A.) Co. Ld.

Northern Territories Gold Fields of Australia Ld. Regd. 1896. Reconstructed 1899 as company of same name. Shareholders were entitled to 1 share of £1 (credited with 16s. paid) in new company for each share of £1 (18s. 6d. paid) held. Removed from Register 1903 1901

Northern Territories Gold Fields of Australia Ld. Regd. 1899. Removed from Register 1904 1902

Northern Territories Gold Fields of Australia Ld. Regd. 1901. Property was acquired in 1902 by Northern Territories Mining and Smelting Co. Ld. for 303,370 shares of 10s. (credited with 6s. paid) 1904

Northern Territories Minerals Prospecting & Development Corporation of South Australia Ld. Regd. 1900. Removed from Register 1906 1905

Northern Territories Mines of Australia Ld. Regd. 1905. Vol. liq. Nov. 1909. Removed from Register 1910 1910

Northern Territories Mining & Smelting Co. Ld. Regd. 1902. Vol. liq. 30 Jan. 1905. Reconstructed as Northern Territories Mines of Australia Ld., in which company shareholders were entitled to 1 share of 10s. (credited with 6s. paid) for each share of 10s. held. Final meeting return regd. 28 Sept. 1905 1905

Northern Territory Exploration Co. Ld. Regd. 1886 as Port Darwin Gold Mining Co. Ld.; name changed 17 Jan. 1890. Removed from Register 17 Oct. 1890 *1891

Northern Tjiliwoeng Plantations Ld. Regd. 1910. Vol. liq. 11 July 1924. Undertaking was acquired by Tjiliwoeng Java Plantations Ld. (later Tjiliwoeng Investments Ld.) in which company shareholders were entitled to 1 6% preference and 1 ordinary share of £1 (credited as fully-paid) for every 4 shares of £1 held. Final meeting return regd. 12 Mar. 1926 1925

Northern Transvaal Gold Mining Co. Ld. Regd. 1886. Court Order to wind up 1 Feb. 1893. Removed from Register 1906 1894

Northern Transvaal Goldfields Ld. Regd. 1934. Vol. liq. (members') 12 June 1939. Undertaking and assets

VOL. FOR

were transferred to Anglo-Transvaal Mining Corporation Ld., in which company shareholders were entitled to 1 fully-paid share of 2*s.* and 9 shares of 2*s.* (credited with 1*s.* 6*d.* paid) for every 4 shares of 5*s.* held. Debenture holders received debentures in new company in exchange for their holdings. Struck off Register 7 Aug. 1945 .... **1946**

Northern Transvaal Lands Co. Ld. Regd. 1889. Reconstructed 1901 as company of same name. Shareholders were entitled to 1 share of 5*s.* (credited with 2*s.* 6*d.* paid) for each fully-paid share of £1 held. Removed from Register 1903 .... **1901**

Northern Transvaal (Messina) Copper Exploration Ld. Inc. in Transvaal 1923. Creditors' liquidation 28 June 1960. Dissolved by Order of the Supreme Court 28 May 1962 .... **1963**

Northern Trust Ld. Regd. 1889. Vol. liq. (members') 19 May 1943. Capital returned to contributories—£9 15*s.* 5*d.* per preference share of £10; 17*s.* 8½*d.* per ordinary share of £5 (£1 paid). £250 6*s.* 3*d.* was paid into Companies' Liquidation Account. Final meeting return eegd. 14 Nov. 1944 .... **1945**

Northern Union Mining Co. Ld. Regd. 1913. Struck off Register 1928 .... ***1918**

Northern Wealth of Nations Ld. Regd. 1897. Vol. liq. 20 Nov. 1899. Struck off Register 12 Apr. 1929 .... **1900**

"Northern Whig" Ld. Regd. Dublin 1875. In Oct. 1902 company ceased to exist, having been acquired by a new private company of same name **1903**

Northfleet & Greenhithe Gas Co. Ld. Regd. 1867 as Greenhithe Gas Co. Ld.; name changed May 1881. By Act of 1929 the undertaking was acquired by South Suburban Gas Co. The liability for the 6% redeemable mortgage debentures was taken over by acquiring company. The preference stock was repaid at par. The 10% and 7% ordinary stockholders were entitled to £18 and £12 respectively in cash for each £10 stock held. The Act also provided that any assets remaining after meeting all obligations and liabilities should be divided amongst the 10% and 7% ordinary stockholders in the proportions shown *above*. Final meeting return regd. 26 June 1930 .... **1930**

Northfleet Paper Mills Ld. Regd. 1883 as Ekman Pulp & Paper Co. Ld.; name changed Mar. 1904. Undertaking and assets were acquired by New Northfleet Paper Mills Ld. Holders of 1st debentures were entitled to £15,825 in fully-paid preference shares of £1 and £89,675 in cash. Holders of 2nd debentures were entitled to fully-paid preference shares in new company. Struck off Register May 1929 .... **1930**

Northfleet White Lead Co. Ld. Regd. 1890 as Mac Ivor's Patents Ld.; name changed Mar. 1892. Vol. liq. 10 Mar. 1893. Final meeting return regd. 26 July 1895 **1894**

Northgate & English Stores Ld. Regd. 1951 as Canadian & English Stores Ld.; name changed 1962. Vol. liq. (members') 22 Aug. 1966. Ordinary shareholders were entitled to 1 fully-paid ordinary share of Northgate Group Ld. and 1 fully-paid ordinary share of Combined English Stores Group Ld. for every 2 shares of 2*s.* 6*d.* held; preference shareholders received 1 fully-paid 7¾% preference share for every preference share of 10*s.* held and loan stockholders £1 7% convertible unsecured loan stock for every £1 stock held. Final meeting regd. 15 July 1971 .... **1971**

Northmet Power Co. Inc. hy Special Act 1900 as North Metropolitan Electric Power Supply Co.; name changed 1939. Dissolved 1 Apr. 1948, undertaking being acquired by British (later Central) Electricity Authority and London Area Board under Electricity Act 1947. Holders of securities were entitled to receive British Electricity 3% guaranteed stock (1968–73), as follows in respect of each £1 unit, unless otherwise stated, of capital held:

	£	s.	d.
6% preference stock	1	11	7
4% preference stock	1	2	5
Ordinary stock..............................	2	8	2
5% mortgage loan (per £100)..........	107	3	4
4% debenture stock	1	0	6
3¼% debenture stock	1	0	1⅕

1949

Northolt Brick Co. Ld. Regd. 1934. Vol. liq. (members') 18 Nov. 1935. All capital acquired by Middlesex Brick Co. Ld. Final meeting return regd. 10 Apr. 1941 .... **1942**

Northolt Park Ld. Regd. 1930. Vol. liq. (creditors') 22 Apr. 1936. No capital returned to contributories. £150.000 5½% debentures and interest arrears repaid 24 June 1948. Final meeting return regd. 2 Feb. 1956 **1956**

Northolt Park Racecourse Ld. Regd. 1927. Vol. liq. (creditors') 30 Jan. 1930. Final meeting return regd. 5 June 1940 .... ***1930**

VOL. FOR

North's Navigation Collieries Syndicate Ld. Regd. 1888. Vol liq. 25 1889. Undertaking acquired by North's Navigation Collieries (1889) Ld. for £350,000 of which £120,000 was payable in shares.................. **1889**

Northumberland Avenue Hotel Co. Ld. Regd. 1882. Vol. liq. Oct. 1884. Final meeting return regd. 16 Mar. 1889 .... **1885**

Northumberland (Ceylon) Rubber & Tea Estates, Ld. Regd. 1910. Vol. liq. (members') 30 Dec. 1932. Undertaking and assets were acquired by company of same name. Shareholders were entitled to 1 share of 1*s.* (credited with 10½*d.* paid) for each share of 1*s.* held. £248 7*s.* 5*d.* was paid into Companies' Liquidation Account in respect of unclaimed dividends. Final meeting return regd. 27 Jan. 1934 ... **1933**

Northumberland (Ceylon) Rubber & Tea Estates Ld. Regd. 1933. Vol. liq. (members') 8 Sept. 1953. Capital returned to contributories—11⅝*d.* per 8*d.* stock. £144 7*s.* 9*d.* was paid into Companies' Liquidation Account in respect of unclaimed dividends and £1,704 12*s.* 4*d.* in respect of unclaimed distributions. Final meeting regd. 1 July 1955 ..... **1956**

Northumberland Land & Coal Co. Ld. Regd. 1886. Vol. liq. 25 May 1891. Reconstructed as Fassifern Coal Co. Ld., in which company shareholders were entitled to 2 shares of £1 (credited as fully-paid) for every 15 shares of £1 held; debenture holders were entitled to 80% of holding in fully-paid shares of £1 *plus* up to 20% of holding in cash. Final meeting return regd. 14 Jan. 1897.................................. **1908**

Northumberland Public House Trust Co. Ld. Regd. 1901. Vol. liq. 28 Feb. 1923. Final meeting return regd. 21 Nov. 1930 .... **1911**

Northumberland Shipbuilding Co. Ld. Regd. 1898. Vol. liq. 3 June 1927. Undertaking and assets were sold to Shipbuilders' Investment Co. Ld. for £320,000 in cash. Final meeting return regd. 3 Mar. 1928 .... **1928**

Northumberland Shipbuilding Co. (1927) Ld. Regd. 1927. Vol. liq. (members') 4 July 1932. All capital owned by Shipbuilders' Investment Co. Ld. Final meeting return regd. 1 Dec. 1932 .... **1933**

Northumberland Steam Shipping Co. Ld. Regd. 1866. Vol. liq. 10 Mar. 1887. Final meeting return regd. 27 Oct. 1883 .... ***1881**

Northwestern Brewery Investments Ld. Regd. 1931. All capital owned by Peter Walker (Warrington) Ld. Vol. liq. (members') 30 Sept. 1955. Final meeting return regd. 18 Feb. 1959 .... **1953**

Northwich Electric Supply Co. Ld. *See* Mid Cheshire Electricity Supply Co. Ld.

Northwich Gas Co. Estd. 1839; inc. by Special Act 1882. Dissolved 1 May 1949, undertaking being vested in North Western Area Gas Board under Gas Act 1948. Holders of securities were entitled to receive British Gas 3% guaranteed stock 1990–95 as follows in respect of each £100 unit, unless otherwise stated, of security held:

	£	s.	d.
Ord. stock (6% max.) issued before 1 Jan. 1946	125	0	0
Ord. stock (6% max.) issued since 31 Dec. 1945....................	101	7	11
6% pref. shares (of £10)..................	13	4	0
5% pref. stock	112	0	0
5% red. pref. stock	105	15	0

Liability in respect of certain mortgage loans assumed by the Board **1952**

Northwich Salt Co. Ld. Regd. 1889. Removed from Register 1906 .... **1892**

Northwood Electric Light & Power Co. Ld. Regd. 1900. Dissolved 1 Apr. 1948, undertaking being vested in British (later Central) Electricity Authority and Eastern Area Board under Electricity Act 1947. Holders of ordinary and 5% preference shares were entitled to receive in respect of each share (of £1) held, £2 6*s.* and £1 9*s.* British Electricity 3% guaranteed stock (1968–73) respectively **1949**

Norton & Biddulph Collieries, Ld. Regd. 1929. Vol. liq. (members') 2 Dec. 1952. Capital returned to contributories—£5 2*s.* 8·2*d.* per share of 2*s.* Final meeting return regd. 21 Oct. 1960.......................... **1962**

Norton & Co. Ld. Regd. 1896. Vol. liq. 16 Nov. 1900. Ccurt Order to wind up 20 Feb. 1901. Liquidator released 10 Apr. 1913. Struck off Register 10 Oct. 1916 .... **1901**

Norton Brothers & Co. Ld. Regd. 1874. Vol. liq. 17 Jan. 1895. Final meeting return regd. 23 Aug. 1895 .... **1896**

Norton St. Philip Central Dairy Co. Ld. Regd. 1906. Vol. liq. (members') 22 Dec. 1933. Capital returned to contributories—£1 10*s.* 5½*d.* per share of £1. Final meeting return regd. 28 Dec. 1934 .... **1934**

Norton (Tom) Ld. *See* Nortons (Cardiff) Ld.

Norton Ventilator Co. Ld. Regd. 1883. Vol. liq. 23 July 1884. Court Order to continue winding up under

**See Stock Exchange Year-Book.*

supervision 23 Dec. 1884. Final meeting return regd. 3 June 1892 .... *1884

Nortons (Cardiff) Ld. Regd. 1908 as Tom Norton Ld.; name changed 1936. Struck off Register 6 Apr. 1982 ... 1969

Nortons Cinemas & Theatres Ld. Regd. 1920. Struck off Register Dec. 1929 1930

Norvic Securities Ld. Regd. 17 May 1907 as Barker Bros. Silversmiths Ld.; name changed to Barker Ellis Silver Co. Ld. 20 Nov. 1967 and to present title 12 June 1972. Winding-up order 9 Oct. 1981 1978–9

Norway Copper Mines Co. Ld. Regd. 1881. Court Orders; to wind up Apr. 1883; to dissolve 10 Apr. 1886 1884

Norwegian & General Exploration Co. Ld. Inc. Guernsey 1899 as Norwegian Exploration Co. Ld.; name changed 1900. The company was wound up in 1907 1928

Norwegian Copper Mines Ld. Regd. 1898. The property was sold under foreclosure by public auction. Removed from Register 1905 1904

Norwegian Exploration Co. Ld. See Norwegian & General Exploration Co. Ld.

Norwegian Trunk Railway. Inc. 1851. By Act of 1926 the company was taken over by the Norwegian Government 1927

Norwegian Zinc Co. Ld. Regd. 1888. Vol. liq. 10 Jan. 1894. Final meeting return regd. 27 June 1894 1894

Norwich & London Accident Insurance Association. Established under deed of settlement 1856. Business was taken over by Norwich Union Fire Insurance Society Ld. in Jan. 1908. Shareholders were entitled to £34 for each share of £10 (with £5 paid) held, viz. £5 in cash and £29 4% 1st debenture stock of the Norwich Union Society 1910

Norwich Electric Tramways Co. See Norwich Omnibus Co.

Norwich Electricity Co, Ld. Regd. 1890. Undertaking and assets were acquired in 1902 by Norwich Town Council for £178,000 in cash and transfer of debentures to Corporation. Removed from Register 1903 1904

Norwich Omnibus Co. Inc. by Special Act 1897 as Norwich Electric Tramways Co.; name changed June 1935. Property and assets vested in British Transport Commission and company dissolved under British Transport Commission Act 1954 1953

Norwood (Middlesex) Waterworks Co. Regd. 1877. Reconstructed 1883 as South West Suburban Water Co., in which company shareholders were entitled to 1 share of £10 for every 2 shares of £5 held. Dissolved by Act Feb. 1886 1884

Notre Dame des Victoires (Transvaal) Gold Mining Co. Ld. Regd. 1888. Vol. liq. 27 Apr. 1893. Reconstructed as Wolverand Gold Mines Ld., in which company shareholders were entitled to 1 share of £1 (credited with 13s. paid) for every 3 shares of £1 held. Final meeting return regd. 21 Oct. 1895...... 1896

Notting Hill Brewery Co. Ld. Regd. 1905. Vol. liq. 8 Feb. 1921. Final meeting return regd. 6 Dec. 1927. Court Order declaring dissolution void 14 Dec. 1928. Final meeting return regd. 26 Mar. 1929 ..... *1921

Notting Hill Electric Lighting Co. Ld. Regd. 1888. Dissolved 1 Apr. 1948, undertaking being acquired by British (later Central) Electricity Authority and London Area Board under Electricity Act 1947. Holders of 6% preference shares and 5% redeemable debenture stock were entitled to receive British Electricity 3% guaranteed stock (1968–73), as follows: £13 5s. per preference share (of £10) held and £1 0s. 9¾d. per £1 redeemable debenture stock held 1949

Nottingham & Derby Water Gas Co, Ld. Regd. 1889. Vol. liq. 30 Nov. 1889. Court Orders: to continue winding up under supervision Dec. 1889; to dissolve 3 Feb. 1897 1890

Nottingham & District Bank Ld. See Midland Counties District Bank Ld.

Nottingham & District Billposting Co. Ld. Regd. 1887. Vol. liq. 16 Mar. 1899. Undertaking acquired by Rockley's Ld. Final meeting return regd. 16 Dec. 1899 1940

Nottingham and District Tramways Co. Ld. Regd. 1877. Vol. liq. 10 Sept. 1897. Undertaking was acquired by Corporation. Debentures were repaid and the par value of the shares was paid in Oct. 1897; further payments (if any) not known. Final meeting return regd. 2 Feb. 1898 1898

Nottingham and Grantham Railway and Canal Co. Inc. by Special Act 1846 as Ambergate. Nottingham. Boston & Eastern Junction Railway; name changed by Act of 1860. In 1923 the undertaking was merged into the London & North Eastern Railway Co., in which company stockholders were entitled to £103½ 4% debenture stock (bearing interest as from 1st Feb. 1923) for each £100 consolidated stock held . 1924

Nottingham & Nottinghamshire Banking Co. Ld. Established 1834. Regd. 1884. Vol. liq. 18 Feb. 1919. Amalgamated with London County Westminster and Parrs Bank Ld. (later Westminster Bank Ld.). in which company shareholders were entitled to 2 shares of £20 (credited with £5 paid) plus £2 in cash for every 3 shares of £20 (£5 paid) held 1919

Nottingham & Retford Railway Co. Inc. by Special Act 1902. Powers expired in 1910 1911

Nottingham Brewery Ld. Regd. 1887. Vol. liq. (members') 1 Apr. 1953. All capital owned by Tennant Brothers Ld. Final meeting return regd. 4 July 1956 1951

Nottingham Builders' Brick Co. Ld. Regd. 1871. Vol. liq. (members') 21 Feb. 1950. Capital returned to contributories—30s. 3½d. per share of £1. Final meeting return regd. 9 Apr. 1956 1957

Nottingham Church Cemetery Co. Ld. See Supersites Ld.

Nottingham Empire Palace Ld. Regd. Edinburgh 1897. Reconstructed 1899 as Moss Empires Ld. (later M. E. Theatres Ld.), in which company shareholders were entitled to 7 fully-paid preference shares and 7 fully-paid ordinary shares of £5 (subject to payment of 10s.) for every share of £5 held. Debenture holders were entitled to £105 debenture stock in new company for every £100 bonds held. Removed from Register 1909.................. 1900

Nottingham Grand Theatre and Estates Ld. Regd. 1897. Vol. liq. 9 Aug. 1926. Final meeting return regd. 3 Sept. 1927 1927

Nottingham Insurance Co. Ld. Regd. 1922. All shares were owned by Lancashire & General Assurance Co. Ld. Struck off Register 1929 1927

Nottingham Joint Station Committee. Inc. by Special Act 1897. In 1923 the undertaking was merged into the London & North Eastern Railway Co., in which company stockholders were entitled to £100 3% debenture stock for each £100 3% stock held 1924

Nottingham Joint Stock Bank Ld. Regd. 1865. Vol. liq. 15 Dec. 1905. Business acquired by London City and Midland Bank Ld. (later Midland Bank Ld.), in which company shareholders were entitled to 1½ shares of £60 (£12 10s. paid) plus £2 in cash for every two shares of £50 (£10 paid) held. Liquidator released 5 Apr. 1939 1906

Nottingham Manufacturing Co. Ld. Regd. July 1864. Vol. liq. 27 May 1903. Reconstructed as company of same name. Shareholders were entitled to 17 fully-paid shares of £1 for each fully-paid share of £20 held or 5 fully-paid shares and 2 shares of £1 (credited with 5s. paid) for each share of £20 (£8 paid) held. Final meeting return regd. 29 May 1905 1904

Nottingham Mining Property (Barberton) Ld. Regd. 1889. Removed from Register 1906 1896

Nottingham Patent Brick Co. Ld. Regd. 1867. Vol. liq. (members') 14 Dec. 1934. Reconstructed as company of same name. Shareholders were entitled to 1 fully-paid preference share of £1 and 2 fully-paid ordinary shares of 10s. plus £1 6s. 5½d. in cash for each share of 10s. beld. Final meeting return regd. 7 Sept. 1935 1935

Nottingham Plate Glass & Boiler Insurance Co. Ld. Regd. 1886. Vol. liq. 27 Apr. 1894. Undertaking transferred to Provident Plate Glass Insurance Co. Ld. Final meeting return regd. 11 May 1895 .... *1895

Nottingham Racecourse Co. Ld. Regd. 1891 as Colwick Park Racecourse & Sports Co. Ld.; name changed 1961. Vol. liq. (members') 28 Feb. 1966. Capital returned to contributories—£8 3s. 1d. per share of £1. £1,391 10s. 2d. was paid into Companies' Liquidation Account. Final meeting return regd. 22 June 1967 1968

Nottingham Suburban Railway Co. Inc. by Special Act 1886. In 1923 the undertaking was merged into the London & North Eastern Railway Co. in which company stockholders were entitled to £87½ 4% first guaranteed stock for each £100 Nottingham ordinary (3½% guaranteed) stock held 1924

Nourse Deep Ld. See Nourse Mines Ld.

Nourse (Henry) Gold Mining Co. Ld. Inc. Transvaal 1887. Vol. liq. Dec. 1905. Undertaking and assets were acquired by Nourse Deep Ld. (later Nourse Mines Ld.), in which company shareholders were entitled to 9 shares of £1 (credited as fully-paid) for every 5 shares of £1 held 1906

Nourse Mines, Ld. Inc. in Transvaal 1894 as Nourse Deep Ld., name changed 1906. Vol. liq. (members') 24 Mar. 1949. Company's only asset, viz 391,832 shares of City Deep Ld. were distributed to shareholders in July 1949 at the rate of 1 share for every 2 shares held. All outstanding monies handed to Master of Supreme Court 2 Oct. 1951 1952

Nouveau Monde and General Mining Co. Ld. Regd. 1893. Removed from Register 1904....................... 1904

VOL. FOR

Nouveau Monde Gold Mining Co. Ld. *See* Tarryall Creek Gold Co. Ld.

Nova Scotia Collieries Ld. Regd. 1903. Vol. liq. 4 Nov. 1907. Struck off Register 18 Jan. 1921 .... **1908**

Nova Scotia Gold Mines Ld. Regd. 1894. Vol. liq. 13 Mar. 1896. Final meeting return regd. 11 June 1897 **1897**

Nova Scotia Land & Manufacturing Co. Ld. Regd. 1873. Removed from Register 1904 .... ***1876**

Novo Brdo Mines Ld. Regd. 1928. Vol. liq. (members') 16 Aug. 1938. The undertaking and assets were acquired by Trepca Mines Ld. in which company shareholders were entitled to receive 1 fully-paid share (of 5*s*.) for every 25 shares (of 5*s*.) held. £3 18*s*. 1*d*. paid into Companies Liquidation Account. Final meeting return regd. 25 July 1947 .... **1948**

Novocrete & Cement Products Co. Ld. Regd. 1925. Vol. liq. 8 Mar. 1929. Final meeting return regd. 28 Apr. 1933 .... **1930**

Nowthanna Gold Mine Ld. Regd. 1899. Vol. liq. 12 Oct. 1900. Final meeting return regd. 21 Oct. 1901 ..... **1901**

Nox Electric Lamp Co. Ld. Regd. 1923. Vol. liq. (members') 9 Nov. 1933. Direct controlling interest held by Crompton Parkinson Ld. Final meeting return regd. 11 Mar. 1937 .... **1934**

Nubia (Sudan) Development Co. Ld. Regd. 1903. Vol. liq. June 1907. Removed from Register 1909 .... **1908**

Nuera Art-Silk Co. Ld. Regd. 1925. Vol. liq. (creditors') 18 July 1930. Assets realised insufficient to pay unsecured creditors in full. Final meeting return regd. 28 Mar. 1934 .... **1931**

Nueva Esperanza Gold Mines Ld. Regd. 1896 as Esperanza Gold Mines Ld.; name changed Aug 1896. Vol. liq. 12 Aug. 1898. Reconstructed as company of same name. Shareholders were entitled to 1 share of 5*s*. (credited with 4*s*. paid) in new company for each share of £1 held. Final meeting return regd. 2 Apr. 1902 .... **1908**

Nueva Esperanza Gold Mines Ld. Regd. 1898. Vol. liq. 26 May 1911. Final meeting return regd. 21 May 1912 .... **1912**

Nugget Exploring Co. Ld. Regd. 1895. Removed from Register 1901 .... **1900**

Nullagine Gold, Diamond & Exploration Co. Ld. Regd. 1899. Undertaking and assets were acquired by Amalgamated Gold Mines Ld., in which company shareholders were entitled to subscribe for 1 share at par for every 10 shares held and to receive 4 fully-paid shares of 10*s*. in purchasing company for each share so subscribed. Removed from Register 1903 **1901**

No. 1 Gold Mines Ld. Inc. Queensland 1906. Vol. liq. 1909 .... **1910**

No. 2 Queen Gold Mining Co. Ld. Regd. 1886. Vol. liq. 24 June 1889. Reconstructed as New Queen Gold Mining Co. Ld., in which company shareholders were entitled to 1 share of £1 (credited with 18*s*. 6*d*. paid) for each share of £1 held. Final meeting return regd. 10 Mar. 1893 .... **1897**

No. 2 South Great Eastern Gold Mining Co. Ld. Inc. Queensland 1896. Decision to wind up 1917 .... **1917**

Nunan & Stove Ld. *See* London & Birmingham Brass Foundry Co. Ld.

Nundydroog Co. Ld. Regd. 1893. Vol. liq. 19 Nov. 1920. Reconstructed as Nundydroog Mines Ld in which company shareholders were entitled to 1 share of 10*s*. (credited with 4*s*. paid) for each share of 10*s*. held. Final meeting return regd. 7 May 1923 .... **1921**

Nundydroog Gold Mining Co. Ld. Regd. 1880. Vol. liq. 20 Apr. 1893. Reconstructed as Nundydroog Co. Ld., in which company shareholders were entitled to 1 share of £1 (credited as fully-paid) for each share of £1 held. Final meeting return regd. 8 Jan. 1895 .. **1908**

Nundydroog Mines, Ld. Regd. 1920. Undertaking vested in Government of Mysore 1956; compensation received Rs. 63,48,000 (£476,100). Vol. liq. (members') 4 Mar. 1957. Capital returned to contributories: 21*s*. 8¾*d*. per share of 10*s*. Final meeting return regd. 14 Jan. 1961 .... **1962**

Nuneaton Gas Co. Inc. by Special Act 1886. Dissolved 1 May 1949. undertaking being vested in West Midland Area Gas Board under Gas Act 1948. Holders of securities were entitled to receive British Gas 3% guaranteed stock 1990–95 as follows in respect of each £100 unit held:

	£	s.	d.	
Orig. Stock	150	0	0	
New Stock	91	5	0	
4% red. deb. stock	103	0	0	
4% (tax-free) red. deb. stock	101	5	0	
5½% irred. deb. stock	135	10	0	**1952**

Nuneaton Theatre & Entertainments Co. Ld. Regd. 1900. Vol. liq. (members') 16 July 1935. All shares owned by Associated British Cinemas Ld. Final meeting return regd. 3 Nov. 1939 .... **1936**

VOL. FOR

Nuneaton Wool & Leather Co. Ld. Regd. 1919. Vol. liq. (members') 29 May 1931. Capital returned to contributories—10*s*. 6½*d*. per share of 15*s*.; 5*s*. was returned prior to liquidation. Final meeting return regd. 25 May 1932 .... **1932**

Nunneley (J.) & Co. Ld. Regd. 1888. Vol. liq. 19 Dec. 1891. Final meeting return regd. 8 Sept. 1897....... **1892**

Nunnery Colliery Co. Ld. Regd. 1929. Vol. liq. (members') 22 Dec. 1955. Capital returned to contributories—30*s*. 8½*d*. per 5*s*. ordinary stock. Final meeting return regd. 1 Oct. 1957 .... **1958**

Nuro (Biggleswade) Ld. Regd. 1936. Vol. liq. (creditors') 5 Aug. 1938. No capital returned to contributories. Final meeting return regd. 18 Oct. 1941.............. **1939**

Nuro Ld. *See* N.F.X. Ld.

Nus River Gold Mines Ld. Regd. 1924. Vol. liq. (creditors') 6 Aug. 1931. No capital returned to contributories. Final meeting return regd. 9 Nov. 1938 .... **1932**

Nuthall (C. H.) & Co. (1920) Ld. Regd. 1920. Vol. liq. (creditors') Aug. 1930. Undertaking and assets sold to Lancashire Cotton Corporation Ld., in which company 1st and 2nd debenture holders received like amounts of income debenture stock; shareholders received 38·408 deferred shares of 1*s*. for every 100 shares held. Final meeting return regd. 3 Apr. 1933 .... **1931**

Nuthall (G. & C. & E.) & Sons Ld. Regd. 1898. Receiver appointed 23 Dec. 1915. Court Order to wind up 8 Mar. 1916. Struck off Register 1927 .... **1916**

Nuttall & Co. (Blackburn) Ld. Regd. 1897. Vol. liq. 30 Sept. 1927. Undertaking and assets were acquired by Nuttall's Breweries Ld. The 1st debenture stock and 2nd debentures were repaid at 108% on 26 July 1927. Final meeting return regd. 30 Dec. 1927 ..... **1928**

Nuttall, Mowlem, Brand & Abboud (Near East) Ld. Regd. 1932. Vol. liq. (members') 26 Nov. 1934. Capital returned to contributories—3½*d*. per share of £1. Final meeting return regd. 29 July 1935 .... **1935**

Nyasaland Minerals Ld. Regd. 1928. Vol. liq. (creditors') 31 Dec. 1930. No capital returned to contributories. Final meeting return regd. 26 Sept. 1938.... **1931**

Nyassa Company. Inc. by Charter of Portuguese Government 1893. Resolutions to wind up 1931 .. **1932**

Nyassa Consolidated Ld. Regd. 1908. Vol. liq. (members') 30 Nov. 1931. Capital returned to contributories—0·4012 preference share of 1*s*., 1·6268 ordinary shares of 1*s*. in Nyassa Plantations Ld. (later London & St. Lawrence Investment Co. Ld.) *plus* 8*s*. 2·57*d*. per share of £1 held. Final meeting return regd. 4 Mar. 1936 .... **1932**

Nyassa Prospectors Ld. Regd. 1919. Vol. liq. (members') 25 Feb. 1930. Capital returned to contributories—1*s*. per share of £1. Final meeting return regd. 16 June 1930 .... **1931**

Nymagee Copper Ld. Regd. 1906. Removed from Register 1911 .... **1910**

Nyong Rubber Plantations Ld. Regd. 1910. Struck off Register 1928 .... **1915**

O

O. F. Syndicate Ld. Regd. 1905. Vol. liq. July 1906. Removed from Register 1907 .... **1907**

O.K. Copper Co., No Liability. Inc. Queensland 1909. Wound up for purpose of reconstruction into company of same name **1912**

O.K. Copper Mines Development Syndicate, No Liability. Inc. Queensland 1902. Wound up for purpose of reconstruction as O. K. Copper Co. No Liability in 1909 .... **1910**

O.P.Q. (Waipori) Gold Mines Ld. Regd. 1897. Vol. liq. June 1908. Removed from Register 1910 .... **1909**

O. S. N. Realisation Co. Ld. Regd. 1939. Vol. liq. (members') 25 Aug. 1947. Capital returned to contributories per share (of £1)—£5 12*s*. 5*d*. per B share and £5 0*s*. 0·5656*d*. per C share. £14 17*s*. 3*d*. was paid into Companies' Liquidation Account. Final meeting return regd. 15 Nov. 1948 .... **1949**

Oak Deposits (1914) Ld. Regd. 1914. Struck off Register Apr. 1929. .... **1930**

Oak Investment Corporation Ld. Regd. 1927. Court Order to wind up 15 Oct. 1929. Struck off Register 27 Oct. 1942 .... **1943**

Oak Spinning Co. Ld. Regd 1874. Vol. liq. 3 May 1920. The undertaking and assets were sold to Oak Spirining Co. (1920) Ld. Final meeting return regd. 20 Jan. 1921 .... **1922**

Oak Spinning Co. (1920) Ld. Regd. 1920. Court Order to wind up Aug. 1930. Struck off Register 24 Oct. 1939. **1940**

Oak Valley Oil Co. Ld. Regd. 1913. Vol. liq. 20 Oct. 1928. Final meeting return regd. 11 Mar. 1929 .... **1929**

**See Stock Exchange Year-Book.*

Oakbank Oil Co. Ld. Regd. 1869. Dissolved before 1931   **1886**

Oakdale Navigation Collieries Ld. Regd. 1906. Vol. liq. (members') 25 June 1953. Final meeting return regd. 28 May 1956 ...... **1940**

Oakes (James) & Co. (Riddings) Ld. See Riddings Collieries Ld.

Oakham Gas & Electricity Co. Ld. Regd. 1874 as Oakham Gas Co. Ld.; name changed 1923. Dissolved 1 Apr. 1948, undertaking being vested in British (later Central) Electricity Authority and East Midlands Area Board under Electricity Act 1947. Holders of securities were entitled to receive British Electricity 3% guaranteed stock (1968–73) as follows:

	£	s.	d.
5% preference shares (of £10)..........	11	10	0
6% preference shares (of £10)..........	13	10	0
10% standard ordinary shares (of £10)	7	10	0
8% standard ordinary shares (of £10)	6	0	0
7% standard ordinary shares (of £10)	5	5	0
10% standard ordinary stock (per £5)	3	15	0
4½% debentures (per £50).................	50	0	0	**1949**

Oakhill Brewery Co. Ld. Regd. 1 Mar. 1889. Vol. liq. 30 Oct. 1963 (members'). Final meeting return regd. 19 Dec. 1963 ...... **1962**

Oakley Collieries Ld. Regd. Edinburgh 1900. Vol. liq. (members') 3 July 1930. Capital returned to contributories—£28,875 to preference shareholders £3,208 6s. 8d. to ordinary shareholders. Dissolved before 1938 ...... **1931**

Oakley Gold Mining Co. Ld. Regd. 1887. Vol. liq. 9 May 1889. Property was acquired by First Netherlands Transvaal Gold Mining Co. Ld. Final meeting return regd. 1 Aug. 1891 ...... **1898**

Oakwell Red & Blue Brick Co. Ld. Regd. 1913. Vol. liq. 30 Sept. 1929. All capital owned by Stanton Ironworks Co. Ld. Final meeting return regd. 12 Feb. 1930 ...... **1930**

Oakwood Tenants Ld. See Co. Partnership Tenants Ld. (regd. 1907)

Oastler, Palmer & Co. Ld. Regd. 1890. Vol. liq. 16 Apr. 1925. The debenture holders were repaid in full (50% in July 1925 and 50% in Sept. 1925). Final meeting return regd. 23 June 1926 ...... **1926**

Oatlands Park Hotel Co. Ld. Regd. 1877. Court Order to wind up 31 May 1921. Liquidator released 31 Aug. 1925. Struck off Register 2 Apr. 1929 .... **1922**

Oaxaca Mines Development Co. Ld. Regd. 1909. Struck off Register 3 June 1921 ...... ***1920**

Oaxaca Petroleum Estates Ld. Regd. 1916. Struck off Register 31 July 1953 ...... **1940**

Oban and Aultmore-Glenlivet Distilleries Ld. Regd. Edinburgh 1898. Vol. liq. June 1923. Undertaking and assets were sold. Final meeting return regd. 29 Nov. 1926 ...... **1924**

Oban & District Gas Co. Ld. Regd. in Edinburgh 1914. Dissolved 1 May 1949, undertaking being vested in Scottish Area Gas Board under Gas Act 1948. Holders of ordinary shares (of £1) were entitled to receive £1 15s. British Gas 3% guaranteed stock 1990–95 for each share held **1952**

Oban Palace Hotel & Hydropathic Co. Ld. Regd. 1896. Removed from Register 1899 ...... **1898**

Obbuassi Mines Ld. Regd. 1900. Vol. liq. (members') 20 June 1930. Undertaking and assets were acquired by Lyndhurst Deep Level (Gold & Silver) Ld in which company shareholders were entitled to 1 share of 1s. (credited with 9d. paid) for each share of 1s. held. Final meeting return regd. 11 Apr. 1935 ...... **1931**

Obbuassi Syndicate Ld. Regd. 1896. Struck off Register Nov. 1931 ...... **1932**

Obenemasi Goldfields Ld. Regd. 1902 as Obenemasi Syndicate Ld.; name changed Apr. 1904. Vol. liq. 19 Apr. 1907. Capital returned to contributories—3d. per share of £1 in Oct. 1907; further payments (if any) not known. Removed from Register 1908 .... **1908**

Obenemasi Syndicate. See Obenemasi Goldfields Ld.

Oberlin Tin Mining Co. Ld. Regd. 1888. Vol. liq. 21 Dec. 1892. Final meeting return regd. 13 Aug. 1900 .... **1893**

Ober-Rosbach Mining Co. Ld. Regd. 1906. Vol. liq. 19 Nov. 1913. Final meeting return regd. 8 Sept. 1928 **1914**

Obrekuku Gold Mining Co. Ld. Regd. 1903. Removed from Register 1909 ...... **1907**

Obuom Gold Mines Ld. Regd. 1934. Vol. liq. (members') 23 June 1938. Undertaking and assets were acquired by London & African Mining Trust Ld. (later London & Associated Investment Trust Ld.) in which company shareholders were entitled to 1 share of 1s. (credited as fully-paid) for every 2 shares of 5s. held. Final meeting return regd. 1 May 1941 **1939**

Occidental Syndicate Ld. Regd. 1896. Struck off Register Jan. 1931 ...... **1931**

Ocean Cotton Spinning Co. Ld. Regd. 1903 as Ocean Spinning Co. Ld.; name changed 2 Mar. 1953 to

Ocean Spinning (Holdings) Ld. and as above on 17 July 1957. Vol. liq. (members') 18 Nov. 1959. Capital returned to contributories—5s. 2·875d. per 10s. stock. Final meeting return regd. 10 Aug. 1960   **1961**

Ocean Dry Docks Co. Ld. Regd. 1895. Vol. liq. 3 Mar. 1937. Undertaking taken over by Swansea Central Dry Docks Ld. Capital returned to contributories—1s. 1·366d. per share. Final meeting return regd. 13 Dec. 1940 ...... ***1904**

Ocean Falls Co. Ld. Inc. British Columbia 1909. In Sept. 1913 receiver for bondholders was appointed. In Aug. 1915 undertaking and assets were acquired by Pacific Mills Ld. (later Crown Zellerbach Canada Ld.). Bondholders were entitled, for every £100 6% 1st mortgage bonds held, to $250 bonds, $150 preference shares and $125 ordinary shares in new company **1916**

Ocean Spinning Co. Ld. See Ocean Cotton Spinning Co. Ld.

Ocean Spinning (Holdings) Ld. See Ocean Cotton Spinning Co. Ld.

Ocean Trawling Co. Ld. Regd. 1899. Vol. liq. Feb. 1908. Removed from Register 1908 ...... **1909**

Ocean Trust Co. Ld. Regd. 1928. Vol. liq. (members') 30 Aug. 1946. Certain assets were distributed in specie. Capital returned to contributories—20s. 10·655d. per share (of £1). Final meeting return regd. 5 Sept. 1950 ...... **1951**

Oceana Coal Co. Ld. See Oceana Transvaal Coal Co. Ld.

Oceana Co. Ld. Regd. 1886 as Oceana Transvaal lend Co. Ld.; name changed June 1894. Vol. liq. 8 Sept. 1896. Reconstructed as Oceana Consolidated Co. Ld., in which company shareholders were entitled to 1 share of £1 (credited as fully-paid) for each share of £1 held. Final meeting return regd. 28 Nov. 1896   **1896**

Oceana Minerals Co. Ld. Regd. 1895. Vol. liq. May 1905. Undertaking and assets were acquired by Oceana Consolidated Co. Ld., in which company shareholders were entitled to 1 share of £1 (credited as fully-paid) for every 3 fully-paid shares of £1 held or 12 shares of £1 (5s. paid) held. Removed from Register 1911 ...... **1906**

Oceana Transvaal Coal Co. Ld. Regd. 1893 as Oceana Coal Co. Ld.; name changed Aug. 1893. Vol. liq. 3 Jan. 1900. Reconstructed as New Oceana Transvaal Coal Co. Ld., in which company shareholders were entitled to 1 share of £1 (credited with 17s. paid) for each share of £1 held. Debenture holders were repaid in cash. Final meeting return regd. 17 July 1914 ...... **1902**

Oceana Transvaal Land Co. Ld. See Oceana Co. Ld.

Oceanic Steam Navigation Co. Ld. Regd. 1869. In July 1934 the North Atlantic fleet and various other assets were transferred to Cunard White Star Ld. for 3,800,000 fully-paid shares credited with £1 per share premium in that company. Under scheme of arrangement sanctioned in Mar. 1939 a new company—O.S.N. Realisation Co. Ld.—was formed to acquire and realise certain assets. Shareholders were entitled to all the 100,000 C shares of £1 in the new company. Dissolved under Sec. 154 of Companies Act 1929 on 21 Aug. 1939 ...... **1940**

Océ-van Der Grinten Finance Ld. Regd. 1977 as Sharegrant Ld.; name changed 2 Mar. 1977. Vol. liq. 14 July 1980. Final meeting return regd. 12 Sept. 1980 ...... **1981–2**

Octagon Brewery, Ld. Regd. 1899. All capital privately held. Vol. liq. (members') 30 June 1955. Final meeting return regd. 21 May 1958 ...... **1950**

Octagon Explorers Ld. Regd. 1896, Vol. liq. Nov. 1906. Removed from Register 1909 ...... **1907**

Odams' Manure & Chemical Co. Ld. See Odams Nitro-Phosphate & Chemical Co. Ld.

Odams' Nitro-Phosphate & Chemical Co. Ld. Constituted by Deeds of Settlement dated Mar. 1855. Jan. 1856 & Mar. 1863 as Patent Nitro-Phosphate or Blood Manure Co. Ld.; name changed to Nitro-Phosphate & Odams' Chemical Manure Co. Ld. in Nov. 1872, to Odams' Manure & Chemical Co. Ld. in Aug. 1893 and as above in 1915, when Memorandum and Articles of Association were adopted. Vol. liq. 23 July 1920. Undertaking acquired by company of same name. Capital returned to contributories—£2 5s. per share of £1 at Jan. 1921 further payments (if any) not known. Final meeting return regd. 13 July 1921 ...... **1921**

Odams Nitro-Phosphate & Chemical Co. Ld. Regd. 1920. Vol. liq. (members') 20 June 1947. All shares were owned by Anglo-Continental Guano Works Ld. Final meeting return regd. 24 Apr. 1948 ...... **1940**

Odessa Water Works Co. Ld. Regd. 1872. Vol. liq. 30 Sept. 1895. Municipality was to purchase undertaking. Final meeting return regd. 11 Feb. 1899 .... **1896**

VOL. FOR

Odhams Ld. Regd. 1898. Vol. liq. 15 Apr. 1920. Reconstructed as Odhams Press Ld., in which company shareholders were entitled to 11 preference shares of £1 for every 10 preference shares of £1 held or 2 ordinary shares of £1 for each ordinary share of £1 held. Final meeting return regd. 29 July 1921 .... **1921**

Oertz International Streamline Rudder Co. Ld. Regd. 1929. Vol. liq. (creditors') 9 Jan. 1941. Assets insufficient to satisfy 8% debenture stockholders. Final meeting return regd. 27 May 1953 .... **1954**

Oesterreichische Central-Boden-Credit Bank. Inc. Vienna. 1871. Resolution to wind up 1926 .... **1927**

Oesterreiehische Industriekredit A.G. Inc. Austria 1853 as Niederosterreichische Escompte-Gesellschaft; name changed June 1934. Banking business ceded to Oesterreichische Creditanstalt-Wiener Bankverein (later Creditanstalt Bankverein) in 1938.......... **1939**

Oesterreichische Nationalbank. Inc. Austria 1922. The business was taken over by Deutsche Reichsbank in 1938 on behalf of the Reich. Shareholders received RM.500 4½% Treasury bonds in exchange for every 4 shares of Kr. (Gold) 100 held **1939**

Oesterreichische Ungarische Bank. Certain assets and liabilities were acquired by Oesterreichische Nationalbank.......... **1926**

Ofenheim & Co. Ld. Regd. 1924. Vol. liq. (members') 31 Mar. 1932. Private company. Final meeting return regd. 26 May 1932 .... **1933**

Offin Rubber Plantations Ld. Regd. 1910. Vol. liq. (members') 3 Apr. 1935. Undertaking and assets were acquired by Offin River Gold Estates Ld. (later Offin River Estates Ld.), in which company shareholders were entitled to 1 share of 5*s*. (credited as fully-paid) for every 12 shares of 5*s*. held; debenture holders waived right to arrears of interest and were entitled to 2 fully-paid shares of 5*s*. for every £1 of principal. Final meeting resurn regd. 16 Oct. 1936 .... **1936**

Offin Syndicate Ld. Regd. 1899. Vol. liq. 13 July 1903. Final meeting return regd. 6 Apr. 1905 .... ***1904**

Offord Hygienic Appliances (1912) Ld. Regd. 1912. Struck off Register 1915 .... **1915**

Oficina Gold Syndicate Ld. Regd. 1896. Vol. liq. 23 Mar. 1914. Final meeting return regd. 24 Nov. 1914.......... **1911**

Ofverum Estates Co. Ld. Regd. 1878. Vol. liq. 21 June 1918. Final meeting return regd. 21 June 1919 .... **1919**

Ogden (Thomas) Ld. Regd. 1890. Vol. liq. 17 Nov. 1897. Undertaking acquired by Ogden's Ld. Final meeting return regd. 4 Oct. 1898 .... **1898**

Ogdens Ld. Regd. 1897. In 1902 the business (other than export trade) was sold to Imperial Tobacco Co. (of Great Britain and Ireland) Ld. for debentures and ordinary and preference shares and cash; the export trade was sold to British American Tobacco Co. Ld. for cash and ordinary shares. Removed from Register 1910 .... **1904**

Ogilvie Flour Mills Co. Ld. Inc. Canada 1902. Undertaking was acquired in 1924 by company of same name. Shareholders were entitled to 1 preferred share of $100 (credited as fully-paid) for each preferred share of $100 held or 3 new common shares of no par value for each common share of $100 held **1925**

Ogleby (Charles) & Co Ld. Regd. 1889. Court Order to wind up 8 July 1893. Removed from Register 1907 **1894**

Ogmore Dock & Railway Co. Inc. by Special Act 1883. Undertaking abandoned by Act of 1891 .... **1892**

Ogmore Valley Electric Light & Power Supply Co. Ld. Regd. 1891. Vol. liq. (members') 29 Oct. 1943. Capital returned to contributories—£21,887 10*s*. 1*d*. Final meeting return regd. 26 Apr. 1944 .... **1911**

Ogston Motor Co. (1918) Ld. Regd. 1918. Receiver appointed in Dec. 1920; ceased to act Feb. 1927. Assets realised insufficient to discharge claims of debenture holders. Struck off Register Apr. 1929 . **1930**

Ohinemuri Syndicate Ld. Regd. 1895. Removed from Register 1906 .... **1903**

Ohio Fuel Corporation. Amalgamated in 1926 with Columbia Gas and Electric Corporation of West Virginia to form Columbia Gas and Electric Corporation of Delaware **1936**

Oil & Asphaltum Co. Ld. Regd. 1903. Vol. liq. 17 May 1905. Removed from Register 1910 .... **1902**

Oil & Carbon Products Ld. Regd. 1912. Vol. liq. 27 May 1919. Final meeting return regd. 18 May 1922.......... **1919**

Oil & Drilling Trust of Roumania Ld. Regd. 1912. Receiver appointed for debenture holders. Struck off Register 1922.......... **1915**

Oil & Ozokerite Co. Ld. Regd. 1910. Court Order to wind up 30 Apr. 1912. Liquidator released 21 Mar. 1919. Struck off Register 20 Mar. 1925 .... **1913**

Oil Concessions of Mayaro (Trinidad) Ld. Regd. 1912. Vol. liq. 29 Dec. 1916. Undertaking was acquired by Trinidad Central Oilfields Ld., in which company shareholders were entitled to 1 share of £1 (credited as fully-paid) for every 2 shares of £1 held. Final meeting return regd. 14 Sept. 1918 .... **1917**

Oil Development Trust Ld. Regd. 1910. Receiver appointed 2 Mar. 1923. Struck off Register Feb. 1935 .... **1935**

Oil Fields of Mexico Co. Inc. Delaware 1903. Properties were sold to company of same name (inc. West Virginia) in 1922 .... **1928**

Oil Fields of Mexico Ld. Regd. 1910. Vol. liq. 30 Oct. 1913. Final meeting return regd. 5 Nov. 1917.......... **1913**

Oil Gas Enrichment Co. Ld. Regd. Edinburgh 1893. Vol. liq. 15 Oct. 1907. Capital returned to contributories—4*s*. 9¼*d*. per preference share of £1 (5*s*. paid); further payments (if any) not known. Final meeting return regd. 8 Feb. 1908 .... **1908**

Oil-Nut Development & Trading Co. Ld. Regd. 1913. Vol. liq. Dec. 1914. Struck off Register Mar. 1929 **1930**

Oil Options Ld. Regd. 1910. Vol. liq. 17 May 1918. Final meeting return regd. 9 Aug. 1919 .... ***1913**

Oil Recovery Syndicate Ld. Regd. 1910. Vol. liq. 14 Dec. 1925. All capital was owned by Tarless Fuel Syndicate Ld. Final meeting return regd. 3 Dec. 1926 .... **1927**

Oil Refiners & Margarine Manufacturers Ld. Regd. 1910. Vol. liq. 11 June 1912 for reconstruction as Oil Refiners Ld. Final meeting return regd. 18 June 1914 .... **1913**

Oil Refiners Ld. Regd. 1912. Vol.liq. 29 July 1921. Final meeting return regd. 18 Mar. 1922.......... **1922**

Oil Royalties Trust Ld. (1912) Ld. Regd. 1912. Struck off Register 1922.......... **1928**

Oil-Seed Crushing Co. Ld. Regd. 1863. Vol. liq. 26 Sept. 1890. Struck off Register 29 July 1902 .... **1891**

Oil Shale Development Co. Ld. Regd. 1910. Vol. liq. 19 Nov. 1917. The assets were sold to South African Cotton and Tobacco Estates Ld., in which company shareholders were entitled to 1 share of 5*s*. (credited as fully-paid) for each share held. Final meeting return regd. 5 Jan. 1922 .... **1918**

Oil Trust Ld. Regd. 1910. Vol. liq. 18 Jan. 1927. Shareholders were entitled to 2 shares of 2*s*. 6*d*. (credited with 1*s*. 6*d*. paid) in Oil Trust (1927) Ld. (later Anglo-Cuban Asphalt & Bitumen Ld.) for every 5 shares of 2*s*. held. Final meeting return regd. 24 Dec. 1929 .... **1927**

Oil Trust (1927) Ld. *See* Anglo-Cuban Asphalt & Bitumen Ld.

Oil Trust of Galicia Ld. Regd. 1911. Vol. liq. May 1912 for reconstruction as Galician Oil Trust Ld., in which company shareholders were entitled to 1 share of 10*s*. (credited with 7*s*. paid) for each share of £1 held. Removed from Register 1914 .... **1913**

Oil Trust of Russia Ld. Regd. 1911. Struck off Register 19 June 1936 .... ***1913**

Oil Ventures Ld. Regd. 1910. Vol. liq. Dec 1911. Removed from Register 1912 .... **1912**

Oil Wharves Ld. Regd. 1933. Vol. liq. (members') 30 Dec. 1937. Reconstructed as company of same name. Shareholders were entitled to 1 share of 2*s*. 6*d*. (credited as fully-paid) in new company *plus* 1*s*. 10*d*. in cash for each share of 5*s*. held. Final meeting return regd. 16 Nov. 1939 .... **1938**

Oil Wharves Ld. Regd. 1937 in reconstruction of company of same name. Vol. liq. (members') 3 Aug. 1949. Capital returned to contributories—3*s*. 7·141*d*. per share of 2*s*. 6*d*. £435 6*s*. 9*d*. was paid into Companies' Liquidation Account. Final meeting return regd. 9 Aug. 1950 .... **1951**

Oilfields Finance Corporation Ld. Regd. 1912. Vol. liq. (members') 25 Sept. 1952. Capital returned to contributories—$\frac{5}{64}$*d*. per share of 4*s*. £950 was paid into Companies' Liquidation Account. Final meeting return regd. 16 Jan. 1956.......... **1957**

Oilfields Ld. Regd. 1924. Vol. liq. Dec. 1930 for reconstruction as Isamungu Gold Mine Ld., in which company shareholders were entitled to 1 share of 1*s*. (credited with 9*d*. paid) for each share of 2*s*. held. Struck off Register 4 Oct. 1938 .... **1939**

Oilfields of Bonaventure Ld. *See* Bonaventure Mines Trust Ld.

Oilfields of Egypt Ld. Regd. 1920. Vol. liq. (members') 17 Mar. 1936. Capital returned to contributories—½*d*. per share of £1. £135 16*s*. 11*d*. was paid into Companies' Liquidation Account in respect of unclaimed dividends. Final meeting return regd. 17 Apr. 1937 .... **1937**

Oilfields of Emilia Ld. Regd. 1913. Struck off Register 1927 .... **1925**

Oilfields of England Ld. Regd. 1918. Struck off Register Jan. 1931 .... **1931**

Oilfields of Gaspe, Canada, Ld. *See* Bonaventure Mines Trust Ld.

**See Stock Exchange Year-Book.*

VOL. FOR

Oilfields of West Indies (Cuba) Ld. Regd. 1920. Vol. liq. 21 Oct. 1929. Final meeting return regd. 22 Oct. 1931 ... **1930**

Oilwells Selection Corporation (Drillers & Contractors) Ld. Regd. 1924. Vol. liq. (creditors') 26 July 1937. No capital returned to contributories. Final meeting return regd. 10 Dec. 1937 ... **1938**

Okehampton Gas Co. Ld. Regd. 1858. Dissolved 1 May 1949, undertaking being vested in South Western Area Gas Board under Gas Act 1948. Holders of securities weee entitled to receive British Gas 3% guaranteed stock 1990–95 as follows in respect of each £5 unit, unless otherwise stated, of security held:

	£	s.	d.
Ord. shares	8	10	0
7% pref. shares	7	10	0
3½% red. debs. 1951 (of £100)	100	0	0	**1952**

Okel Tor Co. Ld. Regd. 1881. Removed from Register 1903 ... **1886**

Oklahoma Copper Co. Inc. Oklahoma 1906. In 1908 London office was closed and late London secretary stated that the mine had been closed down ... **1909**

Oklahoma Oil Co. Ld. Regd. 1910. Vol. liq. 24 Sept. 1917, Final meeting return regd. 23 Feb. 1920 .... **1918**

Okonite Company. Inc. New Jersey 1908. London office closed in 1912 ... **1913**

Okonite Co. Ld. Regd. 1890 as International Okonite Co. Ld.: name changed 1893. Vol. liq. 30 Jan. 1901. Reconstructed as company of same name. Shareholders were entitled to 15,900 ordinary and 31,890 preference shares of £2 10s. Final meeting return regd. 4 Jan. 1902 ... **1908**

Okonite Co. Ld. Regd. 1901. Vol. liq. 16 Apr. 1909. The assets and undertang were sold to Okonite Co., in which company shareholders were entitled to 1 share of $100 for every 8 preference or ordinary shares of £2 10s. held. Final meeting return regd. 15 Mar. 1910 ... **1910**

Oktaha Oilfields Ld. Regd. 1912. Vol. liq. 18 Oct. 1920. Final meeting return regd. 28 Dec. 1920 ... ***1919**

Olathe Silver Mining Co. Ld. Regd. 1881. Absorbed by Fryer Hill Silver Mining Co. Ld. Removed from Register 1905 ... **1885**

Olca Sulphur Co. Ld. Regd. 1910. Struck off Register 29 Aug. 1941 ... **1942**

Old Broad Street Syndicate Ld. Regd. 1896. Vol. liq. 10 June 1897. Final meeting return regd. 13 Jan. 1899 **1898**

"Old Bushmills" Distillery Co. Ld. Regd. 1896. Vol. liq. 5 Aug. 1920. Final meeting return regd. 7 Jan. 1929 **1921**

"Old Calabar" Biscuit Co. Ld. Regd. 1886. Vol. liq. 15 June 1908. Removed from Register 1909 ... **1909**

Old Colony Trust Co. Inc. Massachusetts 1890. The trust business of First National Bank of Boston Ld. was acquired in 1929 and that Bank acquired the commercial business of this company. Shareholders were entitled to 4 shares of $100 in First National Bank of Boston Ld. for each share of $100 held .. **1930**

Old Court Sterling Fund Ld. Regd. in Guernsey 1979. Under a scheme of arrangement the assets were transferred to Old Court International Reserves Ld. in which company holders were to receive 1,224·429 sterling shares per 1,000 shares held. This company was to be placed in liquidation ... **1982–3**

Old Ebenezer Native Mines Ld. Regd. 1901. Removed from Register 1905 ... **1904**

Old Guard Mining Co. Ld. Regd. 1887. Court Orders: to wind up 3 Nov. 1888; to dissolve 17 Feb. 1896 ... **1889**

Old Lout Mining Co. Ld. Regd. 1888. Vol. liq. 18 Dec. 1894. Final meeting return regd. 24 July 1895 ..... **1895**

Old Shepherds Mines Ld. Regd. Truro 1881. Vol. liq. 15 Aug. 1885 for reconstruction as Shepherds United Ld. ... **1886**

Old Silkstone & Dodworth Coal & Iron Co. Ld. Regd. 1882. Removed from Register 1904 ... ***1894**

Old Silkstone Collieries Ld. Regd. 1899. Vol. liq. (members') 2 June 1954. Capital returned to contributories (per 5s. stock)—1st preference: 7s.; 2nd preference; 8s. 6d.; ordinary: 8s. 6·15d. £6,649 3s. 6d. was paid into Companies' Liquidation Account. Final meeting return regd. 13 Apr. 1956 **1957**

Old Union Mill Flour & Bread Co. Regd. 1856. Vol. liq. 20 Aug. 1883. Final meeting return regd. 22 May 1891 ... **1884**

Old Wolverhampton Breweries Ld. Regd. 1910. Vol. liq. Apr. 1920. Undertaking and assets were acquired by Frank Myatt & Co. Ld. The B debenture stock was redeemed at par. Capital returned to contributories—£5 per share of £1; a further £1 5s. per share was anticipated. Final meeting return regd. 10 May 1930 **1921**

Old York Trust Co. Ld. Regd. 1911. Struck off Register 6 July 1920 ... ***1919**

VOL. FOR

Oldbury Railway Carriage and Wagon Co. Ld. Regd. 1886. Reconstructed 1902 as Metropolitan Amalgamated Railway Carriage and Wagon Co. Ld. (later Metropolitan. Cammell Carriage Wagon & Finance Co. Ld.), in which company shareholders were entitled to 7½ ordinary shares of £1 (credited as fully-paid) for each ordinary share of £4 held or 1 preference share of £1 (credited as fully-paid) for each preference share of £4 held. Removed from Register 1903 ... **1903**

Oldbury Railway Co. Inc. by Special Act 1873 as Dudley & Oldbury Junction Railway Co.; reconstituted 1881. Under Great Western Railway Act of 1894 undertaking was merged into that company in which 4% debenture holders received an equal amount of 4% debenture stock. Holders of ordinary shares were repaid at par ... **1895**

Oldbury S. C. Syndicate Ld. Regd. 1912. Vol. liq. 13 June 1927. All shares held by British Cyanides Co. Ld. (later British Industrial Plastics Ld.). Final meeting return regd. 30 Dec. 1927 ... **1928**

Oldfield Brewery Ld. Regd. 1895. All capital owned by Northwestern Brewery Investments Ld. Vol. liq. (members') 30 Sept. 1955. Final meeting return regd. 18 Feb. 1959 ... **1941**

Oldfields Ld. Regd. 1902. Vol. liq. (creditors') 4 Nov. 1935. Assets realised insufficient to pay unsecured creditors in full. Final meeting return regd. 11 Dec. 1936 ... **1936**

Oldfield's Multi-Colour Apparatus Co. Ld. Regd. 1891. Removed from Register 1907 ... **1894**

Oldham & Lees Spinning Co. Ld. Regd. 1881. Vol. liq. 4 Mar. 1920. Final meeting return regd. 15 Sept.1920 **1921**

Oldham Ashton & Hyde Electric Tramway Ld. Regd. 1897. Vol. liq. 8 Aug. 1921. The undertaking was acquired by the local authorities. Capital returned to contributories—£1 6s. 7¾d. per ordinary or preference share of £1. Final meeting return regd. 14 July 1922 ... **1922**

Oldham, Ashton-under-Lyne & Guide Bridge Junction Railway Co. Inc. by Special Act 1857. Dissolved 2 Apr. 1949; undertaking vested 1 Jan. 1948 in British Transport Commission under Transport Act 1947. Holders of ordinary shares were entitled to receive, in respect of every share (of 10) held, £12 19s. British Transport 3% guaranteed stock 1978–88 ... **1949**

Oldham Building & Manufacturing Co. Ld. See Sun Mill Co. Ld.

Oldham Empire Theatre of Varieties Co. Ld. Regd. 1896. Vol. liq. (members') 23 June 1938. Capital returned to contributories—£133,203 0s. 7d. Final meeting return regd. 28 June 1939 ... **1939**

Oldham Fire Insurance Co. Ld. Regd. 1862. Vol. liq. (members') 14 Jan. 1947. Final meeting return regd. 30 Aug. 1947 ... **1948**

Oldham Insurance Co. Ld. Regd. 1922. All shares were owned by Lancashire & General Assurance Co. Ld. Struck off Register 1929 ... **1927**

Oldham Joint Stock Bank Ld. Regd. 1880. Vol. liq. 3 Mar. 1898. Taken over by London and, Midland Bank Ld. (later Midland Bank Ld.), in which company shareholders were entitled to 3 shares of £60 (credited with £12 10s. paid) for every 13 shares of £20 (£4 paid) held ... **1899**

Oldham, Middleton & Rochdale Coal Co. Ld. Regd. 1865. Removed from Register 1904 ... ***1886**

Oldham Rope and Twine Co., Ld. Regd. 1921. Vol. liq. (members') 2 Feb. 1965. Final meeting return regd. 6 Apr. 1965 ... **1937**

Oldham Twist Co. Ld. (The) Regd. 1920 as Oldham Twist Co. Ld., name changed Mar. 1953 to Oldham Twist Co. (Holdings) Ld. and as above in Jan. 1959. Vol. liq. (members') 25 Feb. 1970. Capital returned to contributories—3s. 8d. & 0·766p (per share of 2s.). Final meeting return regd. 9 Mar. 1972 ... **1972**

Oldroyd (M.) & Sons Ld. Regd. 1874. Vol. liq. 26 May 1897. Reconstructed as company of same name. Shareholders were entitled to 1 share of £8 (credited as fully-paid) in new company plus £2 in cash for each share of £10 (£8 paid) held. Final meeting return regd. 3 Dec. 1897 ... **1908**

Oldroyd (M.) & Sons Ld. Regd. 1897. Vol. liq. 10 May 1920. The property and assets were sold to private company of same name (later Oldroyd (Mark) & Sons Ld. Shareholders received £21 per share of £6. Final meeting return regd. 16 Oct. 1920... **1921**

Oldroyd (Mark) Ld. Regd. 1920 as M. Oldroyd & Sons Ld.; name changed 15 July 1949. Vol. liq. (members') 30 Dec. 1959. Capital returned to contributories—per £1 preference stock 22s. 6d.; per £1 ordinary stock 32s. 7½d. Final meeting return regd. 12 Sept. 1961 ... **1963**

Olga Exploration Ld. Regd. 1912. Vol. liq. 14 July 1924. Final meeting return regd. 3 Jan. 1925 ... **1925**

VOL. FOR

Olive Mill Ld. Regd. 1920. Vol. liq. (members') 12 Dec. 1957. Capital returned to contributories—2*s.* 11·015*d.* per ordinary and preference share (of 1*s.*). Final meeting return regd. 14 Jan. 1964 .... **1964**

Olive and Partington Ld. Regd. 1901. All capital was owned by Inveresk Paper Co. Ld. Vol. liq. (members') 16 Dec. 1964. Final meeting return regd. 11 Feb. 1965 .... **1963**

Oliver Industries Ld. Regd. 1928 as Oliver Typewriter Manufacturing Co. Ld.; name changed 1958. Vol. liq. (creditors') 9 Dec. 1960. No return of capital to contributories. Final meeting return regd. 31 May 1967 .... **1969**

Oliver Typewriter (Italy) Ld. Regd. 1930. Vol. liq. 12 Apr. 1932. All capital owned by Oliver Typewriter Manufacturing Co. Ld. (later Oliver Industries Ld.) Final meeting return regd. 18 Dec. 1933 .... **1933**

Oliver Typewriter Manufacturing Co. Ld. See Oliver Industries Ld.

Olivers Ld. Regd. 1892. Removed from Register 1913 **1902**

Olla de Oro (Bolivia) Gold Mine Ld. Regd. 1909. Struck off Register 1932 .... ***1927**

Olot & Gerona Railway Co. Ld. Regd. 1891. Undertaking sold to Cia. de Ferro-Carril de Olot á Gerona, in which company, share and debenture holders were entitled to receive one share of 500 pesetas for each 10 shares of £10 or 10 debentures of £10. Struck off Register 10 Feb. 1911. Restored to Register 27 May 1913. Court Order to wind up 30 June 1914. Liquidator released 19 June 1931. Struck off Register 13 Apr. 1934. Restored to Register 11 Mar. 1935. Court Order to wind up 30 May 1935. Liquidator released 16 Sept. 1949. Struck off Register 2 Oct. 1953 .... **1951**

Olympia Ld. Regd. 1893. Court Order to wind up 1 July 1895. Capital returned to contributories—2*s.* 5*d.* per share. Liquidator released 6 Sept. 1901. Struck off Register 24 Dec. 1907 .... **1901**

Olympia Ld. Regd. 1895. Court Order to wind up 8 July 1896. Liquidator stated that shares were of no value. Liquidator released 6 Sept. 1901. Struck off Register 10 July 1908 .... **1901**

Olympic Fire & General Reinsurance Co. Ld. Regd. 1919. Vol. liq. 26 Mar. 1924. Undertaking and assets were acquired by Tariff Reinsurances Ld. in which company shareholders were entitled to 3 shares of £1 (credited with 15*s.* paid) for every 5 shares of £1 (15*s.* paid) held. Final meeting return regd. 27 Jan. 1926 **1925**

Olympic Portland Cement Co. Ld. Regd. 1911. A subsidiary of Permanente Cement Co. (inc. in U.S.A.). Vol. liq. (members') 7 Apr. 1959. Final meeting return regd. 3 Nov. 1959 .... **1959**

Omai Gold Mining Co. Ld. Regd. 1898. Vol. liq. Feb. 1906. Removed from Register 1907 .... **1906**

Omeo Gold Mines of Victoria Ld. Regd. 1895. Struck off Register 8 Aug. 1905 .... **1906**

Omnibus & Tramcar Cigarette Automatic Supply Co. Ld. Regd. 1898. Removed from Register 1910 .... **1899**

Omnium Gold Mining Assciation Ld. Regd. 1895. The business was transferred in 1898 to Anglo-Continental Gold Syndicate Ld., in which company shareholders were entitled to 1 share of £1 (credited as fully-paid) for every 2 shares of £1 held. Removed from Register 1901 .... **1899**

Omnium Insurance Corporation Ld. Regd. 1909. Vol. liq. 14 May 1912. Life Assurance business was acquired by London & Lancashire Life Assurance Association Ld. (later London & Scottish Assurance Corporation Ld.). The remainder of the assets were acquired by United London & Scottish Insurance Co. Ld., in which company shareholders were entitled to 1 fully-paid share of 1*s.* 6*d.* for each 10s. paid-up capital held. Final meeting return regd. 27 June 1922 .... **1913**

Omnium Investment Co. Ld. Regd. 1887. On 1 Jan. 1974 undertaking and assets transferred to The Premier Investment Co. Ld. preferred stockholders receiving £1 3½% preference stock for every £1 stock and deferred shareholders 87 ordinary shares of 25p for 100 shares. Holders of 4% debenture stock and 7½% convertible unsecured loan stock 1993 received like amounts of 4¼% debenture stock and 7½% A convertible unsecured loan stock respectively. Company was dissolved under Sec. 208 of Companies Act 1948 on 13 July 1976 .... **1977-8**

Omnium Oil Development Co. Ld. Inc. Canada 1920 as Omnium Oil Ld.; name changed 26 Apr. 1922. It was stated in Apr. 1934 that no funds were available for payment of taxes in Venezuela and company had ceased to carry on business **1935**

Omnium Securities Co. Ld. Regd. 1879. In 1887 the business was acquired by Omnium Investment Co. Ld in which company shareholders were entitled to 1 share of £10 (credited as fully-paid) for each A share of £10, for every 10 A shares of £10 (£1 paid) or 5 B shares held. Removed from Register 1905 .... **1887**

Omoa & Cleland Iron & Coal Co. Ld. Regd. Edinburgh 1872. Vol. liq. July 1885. Struck off Register 27 Sept. 1932 .... **1886**

Oncken Patent Staveless Barrel Co. Ld. Regd. 1892. Removed from Register 1907 .... **1901**

1 South Oriental & Glanmire Gold Mining Co. Ld. Inc. Queensland 1902. In liquidation in 1919 .... **1919**

117 Sterling Reserves Fund Ld. *See* MIM Sterling Reserves Fund Ld.

Onions & Sons (Levellers) Ld. Regd. 1940. All capital owned by Vickers Ld. Vol. liq. 19 Nov. 1957. Final meeting return regd. 24 Dec. 1957 .... **1953**

Ontario Breweries Ld. Regd. 1891. Removed from Register 1906 .... **1902**

Ontario Gold Concessions Ld. Regd. 1897 as Ontario Government Gold Concessions Ld.; name changed Feb. 1898. Vol. liq. 2 Aug. 1900. Final meeting return regd. Mar. 1933 .... **1901**

Ontario Gold Mines Ld. Regd. 1914. Struck off Register Jan. 1931 .... **1931**

Ontario Land and Debenture Co. Inc. Canada 1870 as Ontario Savings & Investment Society; name changed 1879. The outstanding sterling debentures were repaid in Feb. 1945 .... **1945**

Ontario Lands & Oil Co. Ld. Regd. 1892. Vol. liq. (members') 19 Dec. 1960. Preference shareholders received £4 4*s.*6*d.* per preference share of £10. Final meeting return regd. 11 Dec. 1961 .... **1963**

Ontario Ld. Regd. 1897. Removed from Register 1904 **1904**

Ontario Porcupine Goldfields Development Co. Ld. Regd. 1911. Vol. liq. 24 Nov. 1920. Final meeting return regd. 11 Oct. 1922 .... **1921**

Ontario Pulp & Paper Co. Ld. The 6% 1st mortgage sinking fund gold bonds were repaid at 110% on 1 Oct. 1928 .... **1929**

Ontario Savings & Investment Society. *See* Ontario Land and Debenture Co.

Onverwacht Platinum Ld. Inc. in Transvaal 1926. Wound up Nov. 1933 .... **1934**

Oodmarie Tea Co. (Assam) Ld. Regd. 1896. Vol. liq. 30 Jan. 1900. Final meeting return regd. 11 Feb. 1902 **1901**

Oonah Mines Ld. Regd. 1908. Vol. liq May 1911. Removed from Register 1912 .... **1912**

Ooregum Gold Mining Company of India, Ld. Regd. 1880. Vol. liq. (members') 11 Nov. 1954. Capital returned to contributories: 5*s.* 4½*d.* per preference share of 10s. (fully-paid); 1*s.* 4·0625*d.* per preference share of 10*s.* (2*s.* 6*d.* paid); 5*s.* 4½*d.* per 10*s.* ordinary stock. Final meeting return regd. 11 Jan. 1961 .... **1962**

Oosten Rand Gold Ld. Regd. 1900. Vol. liq. Mar. 1908. Capital returned to contributories—10·856*d.* per ordinary share of £1; further payments (if any) not known. Removed from Register 1908 .... **1909**

Opal Mines of Queensland Ld. Regd. 1887. Vol. liq. 14 July 1892. Final meeting return regd. 1 Apr. 1893 **1893**

Opera House Syndicate Ld. Regd. 1916. Vol. liq. 30 Nov. 1920. Undertaking acquired by Stoll Picture Theatre (Kingsway) Ld. [later Stoll Theatre (Kingsway) Ld.] Final meeting return regd. 1 May 1922 ***1920**

Operators' Trust Ld. Regd. 1910. Vol. liq. April 1912. Reconstructed as company of same name. Shareholders were entitled to 6 fully-paid shares of 2*s.* in new company for each share of £1 held. Removed from Register 1912 .... **1913**

Operators' Trust Ld. Regd. 1912. Vol. liq. (members') 14 July 1933. Reconstructed as Operators' Trust (1933) Ld. (later Holders Investment Trust Ld.) in which company shareholders were entitled to 1 share of 2*s.* (credited with 1*s.* 8*d.* paid) for each share of 2*s.* held. Holders of 7½% convertible 10-year notes were entitled to an equal amount of 7½% notes in new company. £12 7*s.* 2*d.* was paid into Companies' Liquidation Account. Final meeting return regd. 21 Nov. 1934 .... **1934**

Ophir Concessions and Exploration Co. Ld. Regd. 1892. Reconstructed 1897 as Ophir Exploration Ld., in which company shareholders were entitled to 2 shares of 10*s.* (credited with 8*s.* paid) for each share of £1 held. Removed from Register 1901 .... **1902**

Ophir Concessions Ld. Regd. 1889. Removed from Register 1901 .... **1902**

Ophir Exploration Ld. Regd. 1897. Removed from Register 1909 .... **1906**

Opinto Syndicate Ld. Regd. 1900. Vol. liq. 29 Jan. 1903. Removed from Register 1903 .... **1903**

Oppenheimer (Bernard) Diamond Works Ld. *See* National Diamond Factories (Bernard Oppenheimer) Ld.

Opus Holdings Ld. Regd. as private company 15 Apr. 1964; converted into public company 29 May 1964. Winding-up order made 24 July 1967. Struck off Register 5 Apr. 1983 .... **1983–4**

**See Stock Exchange Year-Book.*

VOL. FOR

Ora Banda United Mines Ld. Regd. 1934. Vol. liq. (creditors') 9 Apr. 1953. No capital was returned to contributories. Final meeting return regd. 4 Aug. 1954 .... **1955**

Oran Oil Co. Ld. Regd. 1910. Vol. liq. Mar. 1914. The undertaking and assets were sold to Ain Zeft Oil Co. Ld., in which company shareholders were entitled to 1 fully-paid share or £1 for every 20 shares of £1 held. Struck off Register Aug. 1929 .... **1930**

Oran Syndicate Ld. Regd. 1913. Direct controlling interest was held by London & Rhodesian Mining & Land Co. Ld. (later Lonrho Ld.) Struck off Register 28 Feb. 1939 .... **1929**

Orange Free State & Transvaal Diamond Mines Ld. Inc. Transvaal 1894 as Robinson Diamond Mining Co. Ld. name changed 14 Oct. 1898. Regd. Pretoria 20 Oct. 1898. Wound up Dec. 1915 .... **1916**

Orange River Estates Co. Ld. Regd. 1891. Struck off Register Mar. 1934 .... **1935**

Orange River Irrigation Ld. Inc. Cape of Good Hope 1901. Wound up 18 July 1905 .... **1906**

Orange Witwatersrand Areas Ld. Regd. 1936. Vol. liq. (members') 2 Nov. 1959. Final meeting return regd. 8 Mar. 1963 .... **1949**

Orchard Sugar Co. Ld. Regd. Edinburgh 1925. Vol. liq. Mar. 1928. Final meeting return regd. 29 Apr. 1938 .... **1929**

Orchestrelle Co., Ld. See Aeolian Co., Ld.

Orchorsol Gramophones Ld. Regd. 1928. Vol. liq. (members') 15 Apr. 1930 for reconstruction as Orchorsol Sound Reproduction Ld., in which company shareholders were entitled to 1 share of 1s. (credited with 8d.) for each share of 1s. held. Final meeting return regd. 15 Apr. 1936 .... **1931**

Orchorsol Sound Reproduction Ld. Regd. 1930. Vol. liq. (creditors') 14 July 1931. Assets realised insufficient to pay unsecured creditors in full. Final meeting return regd. 14 Nov. 1935 .... **1932**

Ordem Coal Mines Ld. Regd. 1925. Vol. liq. (creditors') 29 Dec. 1933. Assets realised insufficient to pay unsecured creditors in full. Final meeting return regd. 4 Dec. 1934 .... **1934**

Ore & Shipping (Wm. H. Muller & Co.) Ld. Regd. 1907 as Iron Ore Co. Ld.; name changed July 1926. Struck off Register 25 Mar. 1938 .... **1939**

Ore Concentration Co. (1905) Ld. Regd. 1905. Vol. liq. (members') 12 Nov. 1931. Capital returned to contributories—£4 6s. 7·64d. per preference share of £1; 5·24d. per ordinary share of £1. £620 12s. 10d. was paid into Companies' Liquidation Account. Final meeting return regd. 27 June 1934 .... **1932**

Ore Dressing & Gold Extraction Co. Ld. Regd. 1887 as Newbery-Vautin (Patents) Gold Extraction Co. Ld.; name changed Feb. 1892. Removed from Register 1901 .... **1899**

Oregon & California Railroad Co. Organised in Oregon 1870. All capital stock owned by Southern Pacific Co. 5% 1st mortgage bonds redeemed 1 July 1927 .... **1927**

Oregon and Washington Mortgage Savings Bank Ld. Regd. Edinburgh 1876. Vol. liq. Aug. 1882. Absorbed by Dundee Mortgage & Trust Investment Co. Ld. Final meeting return regd. 30 Aug. 1912 .... **1883**

Oregon Hydrantic Gold Mines Ld. Regd. 1875. Vol. liq. Jan. 1886. Final meeting return regd. 8 Apr. 1886 .... **1886**

Oregon Mortgage Co. Ld. Regd. Edinburgh 1883. On 28 Feb. 1961 the undertaking was acquired by Securities Trust of Scotland Ld. Ordinary stockholders received £150 ordinary and 44% preference stockholders £100 4½% preference capital of that company per £100 held. The 3% and 5% debenture stocks became the liability of Securities Trust. Company was dissolved under Section 208 of the Companies Act 1948 on 31 Oct. 1961 .... **1963**

Oregon-Washington Railroad & Navigation Co. Inc. Oregon 1910. The outstanding 1st & refunding mortgage 4% series B sterling bonds were redeemed at 105% on 1 Jan. 1945 .... **1945**

Orenburg Proprietary Ld. Regd. 1906. Vol. liq. Dec. 1909. Removed from Register 1911 .... **1910**

Organic Fertilizers Ld. Regd. 1921. Vol. liq. Dec 1929. Struck off Register 2 Feb. 1937 .... **1937**

Oriental Telephone & Electric Co. Ld. See Flag Investment Co. Ld.

Orient Co. Ld. Regd. 1890 as Orient Produce Co. Ld. Vol liq. 29 June 1923. Reconstructed as company of same name. Shareholders were entitled to 1 share of 6s. (credited as fully-paid) in new company for each share of £1 held. No return was made to deferred shareholders Final meeting return regd. 18 Aug. 1923 .... **1924**

Orient Co. Ld. Regd 1923. Vol. liq (members') 12 Dec. 1929. Capital returned to contributories—1s. 9d. per share of £1. Final meeting return regd. 8 June 1934 .... **1930**

Orient Gold Mines Ld. Regd. 1895. Removed from Register 1901 .... **1899**

Orient Oil & Finance Co. Ld. Regd. 1910 as Pacific & Orient Oil Co. Ld.; name changed Sept. 1920. Struck off Register 28 Feb. 1939 .... **1940**

Orient Produce Co. Ld. See Orient Co. Ld.

Orient Steam Navigation Co. Ld. Regd. 1878. Reconstructed 1900 as company of same name. Shareholders were offered 60% of holdings in new preferred shares of £10 or 100% of holdings in deferred shares of £10. Debenture holders were entitled to either an equal amount of 4% debenture stock in new company or repayment in cash. Removed from Register 1901 .... **1901**

Orient Underwriting Co. Ld. Regd. 1935. Vol. liq. (members') 30 Mar. 1960. Capital returned to contributories—21·216785496s. per share (of £1). Final meeting return regd. 19 Oct. 1963 .... **1968**

Orient Underwriting Fund Ld. Regd. 1912. Vol. liq. (members') 29 July 1935. Reconstructed as Orient Underwriting Co. Ld. Certain investments were distributed in specie; other investments were sold and proceeds distributed. Final meeting return regd. 11 Apr. 1942 .... **1936**

Oriental & Sheba Valley United Gold Mining Co. Ld. Regd. 1889. Vol. liq. 30 Aug. 1893. Property was acquired by Sheba Gold Mining Co. Ld. for £150,000 in fully-paid shares of £1. Final meeting return regd. 21 Oct. 1895 .... **1948**

Oriental Bank Corporation. Inc. by Royal Charter 1851. In liquidation **1885**

Oriental Coffee Co. Ld. Regd. 1876. Removed from Register 1903 .... **1903**

Oriental Consolidated Mining Co. Inc. Virginia 1897. In July 1939 the properties were sold to a Japanese company. In Dec. 1939 the shareholders approved a plan of liquidation. Capital returned to contributories—$15·96 per share of $10. The company was subsequently dissolved **1945**

Oriental Consols Gold Mining Co. Ld. Inc. Queensland 1898. Wound up 1908 for reconstruction under same name. Shareholders were entitled to 1 share of 5s. (credited 2s. 6d. paid) in new company for each share of 5s. held **1909**

Oriental Consols Gold Mining Co. Ld. Inc. Queensland 1908. In liquidation in 1916 .... **1916**

Oriental Gold Mining Co. of India Ld. Regd. 1895. Vol. liq. 3 Feb. 1899. Reconstructed as company of same name. Shareholders were entitled to 1 share of £1 (credited with 15s. paid) in new company for each share of £1 held. Final meeting return regd. 3 Jan. 1900 .... **1901**

Oriental Gold Mining Co. of India Ld. Regd 1899. Vol. liq. 19 Feb. 1901. Reconstructed as company of same name. Shareholders were entitled to 1 share of £1 (credited with 10s. paid) in new company for each share of £1 held. Final meeting return regd. 14 Mar. 1902 .... **1904**

Oriental Gold Mining Co. of India Ld. Regd. 1901. Vol. liq. 17 Feb. 1905. Undertaking was sold to Nunnydroog Co. Ld in which company shareholders were entitled to 1 share of 10s. for every 10 shares of £1 held. Final meeting return regd. 3 May 1907 .... **1905**

Oriental Investment Co. Ld. Regd 1895. Struck off Register 20 Nov. 1908 .... **1909**

Oriental Leather & Leatherette Co. Ld. Regd. 1876. Vol. liq. 1 June 1908. Final meeting return regd. 24 Mar. 1909 .... ***1885**

Oriental Palace of Varieties Ld. Regd. 1896. Vol. liq. 18 Dec. 1897. Court Order to continue winding up under supervision 26 Oct. 1898. Final meeting return regd. 29 Sept. 1899 .... **1898**

Oriental Pearl Fisheries & Trading Co. Ld. Regd. 1906. Vol. liq. 19 Mar. 1924. Final meeting return regd. 7 Dec. 1925 .... **1925**

Oriental Rubber Co. Ld. Regd 1906. Vol. liq. 30 Dec. 1919. Reconstructed as company of same name. Shareholders were entitled to 4 shares of £1 (credited as fully-paid) in new company for each share of £1 held. Final meeting return regd. 16 Nov. 1921 .... **1920**

Oriental Steamship Co. Ld. Regd. 1886. Vol. liq. 23 May 1894. Final meeting return regd. 25 May 1899 .... ***1895**

Oriental Syndicate Ld. Regd 1899. Removed from Register 1903 .... **1903**

Oriental Telephone and Electric Co. Ld. Regd. 1881 as Oriental Telephone Co. Ld.; name changed May 1892. Vol liq. 12 Mar. 1894. Reconstructed as company of same name (later Flag Investment Co. Ld.). Holders of fully-paid ordinary shares were entitled to 9 fully-paid shares of £1 for every 10 shares held; holders of ordinary shares (11s. paid) were entitled to 1 share of £1 for every 2 shares held. Final meeting return regd. 9 June 1897 .... **1895**

Oriental Telephone Co Ld. See Oriental Telephone and Electric Co. Ld.

VOL. FOR

Oriental (Transvaal) Land & Exploration Co. Ld. Undertaking acquired by United Africa Lands Ld., in which company shareholders were entitled to 1 share of £1 (credited with 17s. 6d paid) for each share held ... **1900**

Original Hartlepool Collieries Co. Ld. Regd. 1865 as London Steam Collier & Coal Co. Ld.; name changed 17 July 1868. Vol. liq. 18 Jan. 1877. Removed from Register 29 July 1902 ... ***1877**

Original Pittsburg (Grass Valley) Gold Mines Ld. Regd. 1888. Vol. liq. 14 Oct. 1890. Reconstructed as New Pittsburg (Grass Valley) Gold Mining Ld., in which company shareholders were entitled to 1 share of £1 2s. 6d. (credited with £1 paid) for each share of £1 held. Final meeting return regd. 2 Nov. 1897 ... **1895**

Orinoco Oilfields Ld. Regd. 1933. Vol. liq. (members') 30 Apr. 1935. Certain assets were distributed in specie among contributories. Final meeting return regd. 22 Feb. 1936 ... **1936**

Orion Belt Ld. Regd. 1895. Vol. liq. 30 Dec. 1897. Final meeting return regd. 22 June 1898 ... **1898**

Orion Development Co. Ld. Regd. 1914. Vol. liq. (members') 5 Sept. 1935. Undertaking and assets (except certain investments) were acquired by Afric Gold Corporation Ld., in which company share-holders received 1 share of £1 (credited with 13s. 4d. paid) for every 10 shares of 2s. held. Final meeting return regd. 5 Mar. 1937 ... **1936**

Orion Diamond Mining Co. Ld. Regd. 1881. Vol. liq. 16 Jan. 1888. The claims were acquired by Griqualand West Diamond Mining Co. Dutoitspan Mine Ld. for 24,000 fully-paid shares of £10 and £158,000 in 6% 1st mortgage debentures. Final meeting return regd. 1 July 1892 ... **1888**

Orion Gold Mining Co. Ld. Inc. South African Republic 1891. Wound up ... **1899**

Orion Mines Ld. Regd 1903 as Hannan's Main Reef Gold Mining Co. Ld.; name changed May 1907. Vol. liq. 21 Dec. 1911. Shareholders were entitled to 1 share of 2s (credited with 1s. paid) in company of same name for each share of 2s. held. Final meeting return regd. 26 Sept. 1911 ... **1912**

Orion Mines Ld. Regd 1911. Struck off Register Jan. 1931 ... **1931**

"Orion" Societate Anonima de Petrol. In liquidation. Controlling interest was owned by Phoenix Oil & Transport Co. Ld. ... **1936**

Orita Gold Mines Ld. Regd. 1882. Struck off Register 18 Nov. 1902 ... **1903**

Orkaden River (Travancore) Rubber Co. Ld. Regd. Edinburgh 1909. Vol. liq. June 1914. Undertaking and assets sold to Travancore Rubber Co. Ld., in which company shareholders were entitled to 1 fully-paid share of £1 for each share of £1 held. Final meeting return regd. 7 Jan. 1916 ... **1915**

Orlando Jones & Co. Ld. Regd. 1886. Removed from Register 1903 ... ***1903**

Orleans Bar Mining Co Ld. Regd. 1887. Removed from Register 1903 ... **1903**

Orme Ring Mill (1920) Ld. Regd. 1920. Vol liq. 16 Apr. 1930. Undertaking and assets acquired by Lanca-shire Cotton Corporation Ld., in which company shareholders were entitled to deferred shares. Final meeting return regd. 29 Dec. 1944 ... **1931**

Ormond Investment Co. Ld. Regd. 1922. Vol. liq. (members') 16 June 1939. Capital returned to contributories—£109 3s. per £100 stock. Final meeting return regd. 24 Apr. 1941 ... **1940**

Ormonde Cycle Co. Ld. Regd. 1897. Vol liq. 7 Oct 1899. Final meeting return regd. 25 May 1917 ... **1900**

Ormskirk District Gas Co. Inc. by Special Act 1853 as Ormskirk Gas Light Co.; name changed to Orms-kirk & District Gas & Electricity Co. 1915 and as above 1925. Dissolved 1 May 1949, undertaking being vested in North Western Ares Gas Board under Gas Act 1948. Holders of securities were entitled to receive British Gas 3% guaranteed stock 1990–95 as follows in respect of each £10 unit, unless otherwise stated, of security held:

	£	s.	d.
Ord. A shares (10% max.) ...	20	10	0
Ord. B shares (7% max.) ...	14	10	0
4½% red. pref. shares ...	10	8	0
4% red. pref. stock (per £100) ...	100	0	0
5% red. pref. stock (per £100) ...	105	10	0

Liability in respect of certain mortgage loans assumed by the Board ... **1952**

Ormul Products Ld. Regd 1927. Vol. liq. (members') 29 Nov. 1939. Capital returned to contributories—14·57448d. per share of 5s. Final meeting return regd. 19 May 1941 ... **1938**

Ormuz Extended Gold Mines Ld. Regd 1896. Struck off Register 17 Nov. 1899 ... **1900**

Ormuz Gold Mining Co. Ld. Inc. Victoria 1895. In liquidation in 1898 ... **1898**

Oro Grande Co. Ld. Regd. 1889. Vol liq. 1 Apr. 1891. Capital returned to contributories—10s. per share of £1; further payments (if any) not known. Final meeting return regd. 27 Sept 1892 ... **1892**

Oropuche (Trinidad) Oilfields Ld. Regd 1924. Vol liq 7 Jan. 1927. The property in Trinidad was sold for £30,000 in cash. Final meeting return regd. 8 Dec. 1928 ... **1927**

Oroville Dredging Co. Ld. Regd. 1909. Control of company transferred to United States in May 1954. Vol. liq. (members') 10 Dec. 1954. A distribution of U.S. $2,102,411 was paid to shareholders. Final meeting return regd. 11 Oct. 1957 ... **1958**

Oroya Black Range Ld, Regd. 1906. Vol. liq. 13 Dec. 1911. Property and assets were sold to Yuanimi Gold Mines Ld., in which company shareholders were entitled to 1 fully-paid share of £1 for each share of £1 held. Final meeting return regd. 9 Dec. 1913 ... **1912**

Oroya Brownhill Co. Ld. Regd. 1894 as Hannan's Brownhill Gold Mining Co. Ld.; name changed 1902. Vol. liq. Apr. 1910. Shareholders were entitled to 1s. 6d per share of £1 plus 2 fully-paid shares in Oroya Exploration Co. Ld. for every 3 shares held, 1 fully-paid share in Oroya Links Ld. and 4 fully-paid shares in Oroya Leonesa Ld. for every 5 shares held. Removed from Register 1911 ... **1911**

Oroya East (Hannan's) Gold Mine Ld. Regd. 1899. Vol. liq. Jan. 1908. Removed from Register 1913 ... **1908**

Oroya Exploration Co. Ld. Regd. 1910. Vol. liq. 4 Dec. 1911. Undertaking and assets were sold to Lake View Consols Ld. (later Lake View and Oroya Exploration Ld.), in which company shareholders were entitled to 1 share of 10s. (credited as fully-paid) for each share of 10s held. Final meeting return regd. 8 Aug. 1918 ... **1912**

Oroya Leonesa Ld. Regd. 1910. Vol. liq. 26 Nov. 1913. Shareholders were entitled to 1 share of 5s. (credited with 3s. paid) in Central American Mines Ld. for each share of 10s. held. Debenture holders were entitled to a similar amount of debentures in that company. Final meeting return regd. 27 May 1915 ... **1914**

Oroya Links Ld. Inc. Western Australia 1907 as Golden Links Ld.; name changed 1909. Wound up Apr. 1928. Mine, property and certain investments sold to North Kalgurli (1912) Ld. for 383,333 fully-paid shares of 2s. Shareholders were entitled to 2 fully-paid shares of 5s. in Malayan & General Trust Ld. for every 5 shares of 5s. held and 1 share of North Kalgurli (1912) Ld. for every 3 shares held, together with 2d. per share in cash ... **1929**

Orpington, Cudham & Tatsfield Light Railway Co. Inc. (under Light Railways Act 1896) 1902. Powers expired 1906 ... **1905**

Orsett House Ld. Regd. 1934. Court Order to wind up 11 May 1942. All capital was owned by Capital & Counties Freehold Equity Trust Ld. Struck off Register 7 Mar. 1961 ... **1941**

Orsk Goldfields Ld. Regd. 1906. Struck off Register 12 Apr.1949 ... **1950**

Orthodox Unit Trusts Ld. Regd. 1939. Winding Up Order 9 June 1958. Struck off Register 19 Jan. 1968 ... **1940**

Oscar Gold Co. Ld. Regd 1888. Removed from Register 1906 ... **1897**

Oscar Gold Ld Regd. 1891. Vol. liq. 7 Sept 1894. Reconstructed as Bremnaes Gold Co. Ld. Removed from Register 21 June 1907 ... ***1894**

Oscar Gold Mining Co. Ld. Regd. 1883. Vol. liq. 17 Apr. 1886. Properties were acquired by New Oscar Gold Co. Ld. Final meeting return regd. 20 Apr. 1891.. ***1887**

Oslo Gas & Electricity Works. See Oslo Lighting Works.

Oslo Gas og Elektricitets-Verker. See Oslo Lighting Works.

Oslo Lighting Works. Organised 1920 as Oslo Gas og Elektricitets-Verker; name changed 1924. The 6% loan of 1924 was redeemed at par on 1 Dec. 1935. Holders were given option of exchanging their bonds for bonds of a new Oslo City 4½% loan of 1935 at the rate of 95% plus ¼% allowance for conversion ... **1936**

Oslo Lysverker. See Oslo Lighting Works.

Osmonds Ld. Regd 1897. Removed from Register 1904 ... **1904**

Ossett Gas Co. Inc. 1855. Undertaking transferred to Ossett Corporation on 1 July 1901 for £99,800 cash ... **1902**

Ostler (Ernest) Ld. Regd. 1947. All capital was owned by United Bakeries Ld Vol. liq. (members') 30 June 1967. Final meeting return regd. 19 Nov. 1969 .... **1966**

Oswaldtwistle Collieries Ld. Regd. 1899. Vol. liq. 25 Jan. 1926. Final meeting return regd 30 Sept. 1926 ... ***1925**

Oswestry & Llangynog Railway Co. Inc. by Special Act 1882. Undertaking abandoned by Act of 1889 ... **1890**

VOL. FOR

Oswestry Gas Light & Coke Co. Ld. Regd. 1860. Dissolved 1 May 1949, undertaking being vested in West Midland Area Gas Board under Gas Act 1948. Holders of securities were entitled to receive British Gas 3% guaranteed stock 1990–95 as follows:

	£	s.	d.
Ord. shares (of £10)	23	0	0
4% red. pref. shares (of £1)	1	0	0
4½% debs. (of £100)	101	10	0

1952

Otago & Southland Investment Co. Ld. Inc. New Zealand 1864. Wound up July 1906 ... 1907

Otago Syndicate Ld. Regd 1896. Removed from Register 1904 ... 1910

Otavi Exploring Syndicate Ld. Regd. 1909. Vol. liq. (members') 25 May 1936. Capital returned to contributories—£12,248 7s. Final meeting return regd. 24 May 1938 ... 1937

Otis Steel Co. Inc. Ohio 1912. Dissolved 1 July 1942. Property and assets were sold to Jones & Laughlin Steel Corporation, in which company shareholders were entitled to receive: for each common share of no par value, ¼ share of common stock of no par value and $1 cash; for each 1s. preferred share of no par value, of ¼ share of 5% preferred stock ($100 par value) Series A, ¼ share of 5% preferred stock ($100 par value) Series B convertible, 1 share of common stock of no par value and $5·73 cash (representing accrued and unpaid dividends to 1 July 1942). The outstanding $13,063,000 1st mortgage sinking fund 4½% bonds, series A were assumed by Jones & Laughlin Steel Corporation ... 1943

Otis Steel Co. Ld. Regd. 1889. Reconstructed 1895 as company of same name. Shareholders were entitled to 1 ordinary share of £4 (credited as fully-paid) in new company for each ordinary share of £10 held or 1 1⁄10 preference shares of £10 (credited as fully paid) for each preference share of £10 held. Debenture holders were entitled to 50% of holding and interest in A debenture stock of new company and 50% in B debenture stock. Removed from Register 1903 ... 1908

Otis Steel Co. Ld. Regd 1895. Vol. liq. July 1912. Undertaking and assets were sold to Otis Steel Co. (of Ohio) providing for allotment of $10 common and $100 preferred stock for every £20 debenture stock held or $1,175 common and $500 preferred stock for every £100 consolidated stock held. Removed from Register 1913 ... 1913

Otley & Ilkley Joint Line Committee. Dissolved 2 Apr. 1949; undertaking vested 1 Jan. 1948 in British Transport Commission under Transport Act 1947 ... 1949

Otley Gas Co. Regd. as unlimited 1866; inc. by Special Act 1901. Dissolved 1 May 1949, undertaking being vested in North Eastern Area Gas Board under Gas Act 1948. Holders of securities were entitled to receive, in respect of each £100 unit held, British Gas 3% guaranteed stock 1990–95 as follows:

	£	s.	d.
Ord. stock (5% stand.)	122	10	0
4½% red. pref. stock	104	0	0
4% deb. stock	100	0	0
3¾% deb. stock	100	10	0

Liability in respect of certain mortgage loans assumed by the Board ... 1952

Ottawa Light, Heat & Power Co. Ld. Inc. in Canada 1906. By-law to wind up 10 Mar. 1950. Preferred stock redeemed at 103% on 31 Dec. 1949 and bonds at par on 30 Jan. 1950. Distributions per common share of no par value amounted to $24·262, plus shares of Interprovincial Utilities Ld. ... 1955

Ottawa River Railway Co. See Central Railway Co. of Canada.

Ottawa Traction Co. Ld. Inc. Canada 1913. In Dec. 1937 company surrendered its charter and distributed its principal asset of 35,047 shares of Ottawa Electric Railway Co. to shareholders pro rata. The outstanding $2,301,000 5½% 1st mortgage and collateral trust sinking fund gold bonds were redeemed at 103% on 1 July 1937 ... 1938

Otto Coke Oven Co. Ld. Regd. 1900 as Otto Hilgenstock Bye-Product and Non-Bye-Product Coke-ovens and Coal Washing Co. Ld.; name changed Apr. 1901 to Otto Hilgenstock Coke-oven Co. Ld. and as above in Apr. 1912. Vol. liq. 31 Oct. 1917. Final meeting return regd. 15 Mar. 1918 ... 1940

Otto Hilgenstock Bye-Product and Non-Bye-Product Coke-ovens and Coal Washing Co. Ld. See Otto Coke Oven Co. Ld.

Otto Hilgenstock Coke-oven Co. Ld. See Otto Coke Oven Co. Ld.

Ottoman Gas Co. Ld. Regd. 1862. Struck off Register 18 Sept. 1936 ... 1937

Ottoman Paper Manufacturing Co. Ld. Regd 1890. Receiver appointed 1892 ceased to act Dec. 1904. Struck off Register 17 June 1898 ... 1906

VOL. FOR

Ottoman Railway from Smyrna to Aidin. Established 1856 under Turkish Law. Railway and certain properties were sold to Turkish Government. The remaining assets were sold to Ottoman Railway Holding Co Ld. Holders of 1st and 2nd debenture stocks and preference and ordinary shares were entitled to income stock and shares in the holding company and cash as follows: (i) For every £100 1st debenture stock held—£11 12s. in cash and £50 7½% Turkish bonds 1935 plus £10 A income stock, £10 B income stock and 4 fully-paid shares of 1s. (ii) For every £100 2nd debenture stock held—£1 6s. in cash plus £70 B income stock and 14 fully-paid shares of 1s. (iii) For every £100 preference shares held—£15 B income stock and 3 fully-paid shares of 1s. (iv) For every £100 ordinary shares held—£7 10s. B income stock and 1½ fully-paid shares of 1s. ... 1936

Ottoman Railway Holding Co. Ld. Regd. 1935. Vol. liq. (members') 14 July 1949. Capital returned to contributories—9d. per share of 1s. Of outstanding A and B income debenture stocks £141,956 held or purchased by company was cancelled and holders of remainder received £62 10s. per £100 stock. Remaining assets in hands of liquidator at 13 July 1950. viz. £7,795 unclaimed distributions and £33,783 surplus for benefit of debenture stockholders, were paid to trustees under trust deed of 13 July 1950, participating certificates being issued to debenture stockholders entitling them to an interest in one part in the fund for every £1 of stock. Final meeting return regd. 16 Oct. 1950 ... 1951

Ottoman Smyrna & Cassaba & Extension Railway Co. Established in Turkey in 1894. Vol. liq. (members') Aug. 1956. 4½% and 4% bonds were redeemed 15 Nov. 1956 at par. Capital returned to contributories—Frs. 9,300 per action de jouissance. Company dissolved 5 Sept. 1960 ... 1962

Ottos Kopje Diamond Mines Ld. Regd. 1891. Vol. liq. 17 Sept. 1896. Reconstructed as company of same name. Shareholders were entitled to 1 share of £1 (credited with 17s. paid) in new company for each share of £1 held. Debenture holders were entitled to an equal amount of debentures in new company. Final meeting return regd. 14 Dec. 1897 ... 1898

Ottos Kopje Diamond Mines Ld. Regd. 1896. Vol. liq. 5 Aug. 1898. Reconstructed as company of same name. Shareholders were entitled to 1 ordinary share of £1 (credited with 17s. paid) in new company for each ordinary share of £1 held; preference shares were exchanged at par for preference shares in new company. Final meeting return regd. 14 Aug. 1900 ... 1900

Ottos Kopje Diamond Mines Ld. Regd. 1898. Reconstructed 1900 as company of same name. Shareholders were entitled to 2 ordinary shares of 10s. (credited with 8s. paid) in new company for each ordinary share of £1 held or 1 preference share of £1 (credited as fully-paid) for each preference share of £1 held. Removed from Register 1905 ... 1903

Ottos Kopje Diamond Mines Ld. Regd 1900. Vol. liq. 14 Mar. 1904. Reconstructed as Ottos Kopje Diamond Mines (1903) Ld., in which company shareholders were entitled to 1 preference share of £1 (credited as fully-paid) for each preference share of £1 held. Final meeting return regd. 17 Oct. 1904 ... 1907

Ottos Kopje Diamond Mines (1903) Ld. Regd. 1903. Vol. liq. Jan. 1908. Removed from Register 1913 ... 1908

Ottos Kopje Diamond Mining Syndicate, Kimberley Ld. Wound up 12 Dec. 1890 for reconstruction as an English company, Ottos Kopje Diamond Mines Ld., in which company shareholders were entitled to 500,000 shares of £1 (credited with 18s. paid) pro rata ... 1896

Otway Engine Co. Ld. Regd. 1885. Removed from Register 1894 ... *1886

Oude & Rohilkund Railway Co. Regd. 1862 as Indian Branch Railway Co. Ld.; name changed Sept. 1867. Vol. liq. 26 Nov. 1888. Undertaking was acquired by Secretary of State. Capital returned to contributories—£125 7s. 6d. per £100 stock held. The debenture stock was repaid at par on 6 May 1898. Final meeting return regd. 31 July 1889 ... 1898

Oundle Gas Light & Coke Co. (1910) Ld. Regd. 1910. Dissolved 1 May 1949, undertaking being vested in East Midland Area Gas Board under Gas Act 1948. Holders of ordinary shares (of £5) were entitled to receive £10 British Gas 3% guaranteed stock 1990–95 for each share held ... 1952

Ouray Gold Mining Co. Ld. Regd. 1887. Removed from Register 1894 ... 1894

Ouro Preto Gold Mines of Brazil Ld. Regd. 1884. Vol. liq. 28 Dec. 1892. Reconstructed as company of same name. Shareholders were entitled to 1 share of £1 (credited with 15s. paid) for each share of £5 held. Final meeting return regd. 8 Nov. 1893 ... 1908

*See Stock Exchange Year-Book.

VOL. FOR

Ouro Preto Gold Mines of Brazil Ld. Regd. 1893. Vol. liq. 3 July 1914. Reconstructed as company of same name. Shareholders were entitled to fully-paid shares in new company. Final meeting return regd. 9 Feb. 1923 .... **1915**

Ouro Preto Gold Mines of Brazil Ld. Regd 1914. Vol liq. 10 Aug. 1927. Capital returned to contributories—20s. per preference share of £1 at Aug. 1927; further payments (if any) not known. Final meeting return regd. 17 Dec. 1928 .... **1928**

Outram Estates Ld. Regd. 1924. Direct controlling interest held by Richings Park Estate (1928) Ld. Struck off Register 1933 .... **1932**

Ouvah Coffee Co. Ld. Regd. 1864. Vol. liq. 31 July 1896. Reconstructed as Ouvah Coffee Co. Ld. (later Ouvah Ceylon Estates Ld.). Shareholders were entitled to an equal number of fully-paid shares of £10 in new company. Final meeting return regd. 24 July 1897 .... **1896**

Overend, Gurney & Co. Ld. Regd. 1865. Court Order to wind up under supervision 22 June 1866. Final meeting return regd. 17 Nov. 1893 .... ***1875**

Overground Ld. See London General Omnibus Co. Ld.

Overseas Estates Ld. Regd. 1918. Court Order to wind up 14 Dec. 1926. Struck off Register 20 Mar. 1936 **1933**

Overseas Exporters (1919) Ld. Regd. 1919. Vol liq. 7 Sept. 1921. Final meeting return regd. 11 Nov. 1925 ***1922**

Overseas Marine Insurance Co. Ld. Regd. 1916. Vol. liq. 20 Oct. 1912. Final meeting return regd. 3 Dec. 1936 **1923**

Overseas Minerals & General Finance Co. Ld. See Alliance Mining Corpn. Ld.

Overseas Trading Corporation Ld. Inc. Jersey 1920. Vol. liq. 1939. Undertaking and assets were acquired by Overseas Trading Corporation (1939) Ld. **1940**

Oviedo Mercury Mines Ld. Regd 1907 as Provenir Mercury Mines Ld.; name changed May 1907. Vol. liq. Nov. 1911. Struck off Register 1926 .... **1912**

Oviedo Mines Development Syndicate Ld. Regd. 1901. Removed from Register 1908 .... **1905**

Ovoca Copper Syndicate Ld. Regd 1901. Struck off Register Sept 1933 .... **1934**

Owen (Joseph) & Sons Ld. Regd. 1898. Vol liq. 16 Apr 1923. The debenture stockholders were repaid at par on 31 Oct 1923. Final meeting return regd. 14 Apr. 1927 .... **1924**

Owen Owen Ld. Regd. 1899. Vol. liq. 5 May 1920. Reconstructed as company of same name. Shareholders were entitled to 1 A preference, 1 B preference or 1 ordinary share of £1 (credited as fully-paid) in new company for each A preference, B preference or ordinary share respectively held. Final meeting return regd 4 Apr 1923 .... **1921**

Owen Vean & Tregurtha Downs Mines Ld. Regd 1882. Vol. liq. May 1885. Court Order to continue winding up under supervision June 1885. Final meeting return regd 21 Dec. 1889 .... **1886**

Owen (William) Ld. Regd. 1903. Receiver appointed in Aug. 1928. Assets realised insufficient to meet claims of debenture holders. Struck off Register 16 Dec. 1938 .... **1945**

Owners of South Medomsley Colliery Ld. Regd 1898. Vol. liq. 10 Mar. 1931. Undertaking acquired by South Medomsley Colliery Co. Ld., in which company shareholders were entitled to 1 share of £10 (credited with £7 10s. paid) for each share of £10 held. Capital returned to contributories—£10 per share of £10. Final meeting return regd. 17 Nov. 1932 .... ***1932**

Owners of South Pelaw Colliery Ld. Regd. 1909. Controlling interest was held by Palmers Shipbuilding & Iron Co. Ld. Struck off Register 24 Jan 1936 **1936**

Owtram (Robert) & Co. Ld. Regd. 1886. Vol. liq. (creditors') 24 Jan. 1933. Assets realised insufficient to pay creditors in full. Final meeting return regd 21 Aug. 1941 .... **1933**

Oxford & Aylesbury Tramroad Co. Inc by Special Act 1883 as Oxford, Aylesbury & Metropolitan Junction Railway; name changed by Act of 1888 .... **1938**

Oxford & Berkshire Cinemas Ld. Regd 1934. Vol. liq. (members') 16 Dec. 1936 for amalgamation with Union Cinema Co. Ld. and National Provincial Cinemas Ld. Shareholders, other than Union Cinema Co. Ld., received 2 A ordinary shares and 1 ordinary share of 5s. of Union Cinemas Ld. for each ordinary share of 5s. held, and 1 1st preference and 1 2nd preference share of £1 of that company for each preference share of £1 held. Final meeting return regd. 16 Oct. 1942 .... **1937**

Oxford & Cambridge Insurance Co. Ld. Regd. 1922. All shares were owned by Lancashire & General Assurance Co. Ld. Struck off Register 1929 .... **1927**

Oxford & District Gas Co. Inc. by Special Act 1818 as Oxford Gaslight & Coke Co.; name changed 1930. Dissolved 1 May 1949, undertaking being vested in

VOL. FOR

Southern Area Gas Board under Gas Act 1948. Holders of securities were entitled to receive, in respect of each £100 unit held, British Gas 3% guaranteed stock 1990–95 as follows:

	£	s.	d.
Cons. ord. stock (5% stand.)	222	0	0
4½% pref. stock	107	0	0
5% pref. stock	113	0	0
6% red. pref. stock	104	0	0
4% red. pref. stock (1970)	103	10	9
4% red. pref. stock (1962)	100	3	8
4% perp. deb. stock	102	10	0
5% perp. deb. stock	127	0	0
4% red. deb. stock	101	5	0
3½% red. deb. stock (1970)	101	9	6
3½% red. deb. stock (1960)	99	10	0	**1952**

Oxford Canal Co. Inc. by Special Act 1769 as Co of Proprietors of the Oxford Canal Navigation; re-incorporated by Act 1829; name changed 1935. Dissolved 23 Dec. 1949; undertaking vested from 1 Jan. 1948 in British Transport Commission under Transport Act 1947. Holders of ordinary stock were entitled to receive £16 British Transport 3% guaranteed stock 1978–88 in respect of every £100 ordinary stock held **1949**

Oxford Electric Co. Ld. Regd 1891. In 1938 Edmundsons Electricity Corpn. Ld. offered to acquire all preference shares by exchanging 5 6% preference shares of £1 of that company for every 6 shares of this company held, and to purchase all ordinary shares in hands of public for cash at 44s. 9d. per share. Vol. liq. (members') 28 July 1938. Capital returned to contributories—preference—£1 per share of £1; ordinary—38s. 11¾d. per share of £1. Final meeting return regd 3 Mar. 1939 .... **1939**

Oxford Gaslight & Coke Co. See Oxford & District Gas Co.

Oxford Ld. Regd. 1892. Vol liq. 25 June 1926. Capital returned to contributories—£7 5s. 6d. per share of £5. Final meeting return regd. 11 Jan. 1927........... **1927**

Oxford Mill Co. Ld. Regd. 1874. Vol. liq. 16 Mar. 1920. Final meeting return regd 13 Jan. 1922 .... ***1878**

Oxford Mill Co. (Rochdale) Ld. Regd 1890. Vol. liq 28 Jan. 1930. All shares owned by John Bright & Brothers Ld. Final meeting return regd. 9 May 1930 **1931**

Oxine Ld. Regd. 1895. Vol. liq. 29 June 1899. Final meeting return regd. 29 July 1901 .... ***1900**

Oxnam Prospecting Co. (No. 1) Ld. Regd. 1903. Vol. liq. Feb. 1911. Nearly all shares were exchanged for shares in Palmarejo and Mexican Gold Fields Ld. Struck off Register 1914 .... **1911**

Oxted & Groombridge Railway Co. Inc. by Special Act 1881. Absorbed by London, Brighton and South Coast Railway in 1884 .... **1885**

Oxychlorides Ld. Regd 1901. Reconstructed 1907 as Oxychlorides (1907) Ld., in which company shareholders were entitled to 1 share of £1 (credited with 17s. paid) for each share of £1 held. Removed from Register 1908 .... **1908**

Oxychlorides (1907) Ld. Regd 1907. Vol. liq. 12 Feb. 1914. Final meeting return regd. 6 Oct. 1915 ...... **1914**

Oxygen Contracts Ld. Regd. 1924 as Southampton Oxygen Co. Ld.; name changed Jan. 1928. Vol. liq. (members') 16 Apr. 1931. Capital returned to contributories—£629 19s. 4d. Final meeting return regd. 29 July 1931 .... **1932**

P

P. & O. Banking Corporation Ld. Regd. 1920. Vol. liq. (members') 6 Feb. 1939. Undertaking and assets were acquired by Chartered Bank of India, Australia and China (later The Chartered Bank). Capital returned to contributories—£10 per share of £10 . **1940**

P. & R. Syndicate Ld. Regd. 1902. Reconstructed as P. & R. Syndicate (1904) Ld., in which company shareholders were entitled to 125 shares of £1 (credited with 16s. paid) for every 100 fully-paid shares of £1 held. Removed from Register 1905 .. **1905**

P. & R. Syndicate (1904) Ld. Regd. 1904. Vol. liq. 23 Mar. 1905. Removed from Register 1907 .... **1906**

P.R.H.E. Exploration Ld. Regd. 1930. Vol. liq. (members') 11 Dec. 1934. Direct controlling interest held by North Ashanti Mining Co. Ld. Final meeting return regd. 26 Mar. 1935 .... **1935**

P.R.T. Copper Works Ld. Regd. 1917. Vol. liq. 26 Apr. 1920. Final meeting return regd. 2 Nov. 1920 ..... ***1921**

Paardekraal Estates Ld. Inc. Transvaal 1909. Vol. liq. Aug. 1913 .... **1914**

Paarl Central Gold Mining Exploration Co. Ld. Inc. Transvaal 1891. Vol. liq. Apr. 1909. Properties were

VOL. FOR

sold to Crown Deep Ld. (later Crown Mines Ld.), in which company shareholders were entitled to 6 shares of 10s. (credited as fully-paid) for every 100 shares of £1 held. **1910**

Pacasmayo & Guadalupe Railway (Peru) Ld. Regd. 1890. Vol. liq. 19 Mar. 1929. 99% of capital held by Peruvian Corporation Ld. Final meeting return regd. 29 Apr. 1930 .... **1930**

Pacaya Rubber & Produce Co. Ld. Regd. 1910. Court Order to wind up 7 Feb. 1912. Liquidator released 30 June 1920. Struck off Register 20 Mar. 1925 .. **1912**

Paccha & Jazpampa Nitrate Co. Ld. Regd. 1889. Reconstructed as New Paccha & Jazpampa Nitrate Co. Ld. Removed from Register 1901 .... **1908**

Pachuca Light & Power Co. Inc. Mexico 1910 as Cia. Irrigadora y de Luz y Fuerza del Estado de Hildago S. A.; name changed 1910. The outstanding sterling 5% 1st mortgage 50-year bonds were exchanged in 1950 for bonds of Mexican Light & Power Co. Ld. **1951**

Pachuca Silver Mining Co Ld. Regd. 1888. Vol. liq. 20 Nov. 1891. Reconstructed 1891 as New Pachuca Silver Mining Co. Ld., in which company shareholders were entitled to 1 fully-paid share and 4 shares of £1 (credited with 17s. paid) for each share of £1 held. Final meeting return regd. 6 Jan. 1893 **1899**

Pacific & European Telegraph Co. Ld. Regd. 1892. Vol. liq. (members') 29 Sept. 1936. All shares held by Western Telegraph Co. Ld. Final meeting return regd. 19 Feb. 1937 .... **1937**

Pacific & Orient Oil Co. Ld. *See* Orient Oil & Finance Co. Ld.

Pacific & Papua Produce Ld. Regd. 1911. Vol. liq. 12 Dec. 1912. Reconstructed as company of same name. Shareholders were entitled to 1 preference share of £1 (credited with 10s. paid) in new company for each preference share of £1 held or 1 ordinary share of £1 (credited with 10s. paid) for each ordinary share of £1 held. Debenture holders were entitled to bonds in new company. Final meeting return regd. 25 Sept. 1915 .... **1913**

Pacific & Papua Produce Ld. Regd. 1912. Receiver appointed 24 Jan. 1935. Assets realised insufficient to satisfy claims of prior lien debenture holders. Struck off Register 19 Mar. 1937 .... **1936**

Pacific Borax & Redwood's Chemical Works Ld. Regd. 1896. Business was acquired by Borax Consolidated Ld. [later Borax (Holdings) Ld.]. Removed from Register 1906 .... **1900**

Pacific Contract Co. Ld. Regd. 1898. Removed from Register 1904 .... **1902**

Pacific Great Eastern Railway Co. Inc. by Special Act of Province of British Columbia 1912. Outstanding debentures and bonds were redeemed in 1942 ..... **1942**

Pacific Islands Co. (1902) Ld. Regd. 1902. Vol. liq. June 1905. Removed from Register 1907 .... **1906**

Pacific Loan & Investment Co. Ld. Regd. 1878. Vol. liq. June 1886. Final meeting return regd. 8 Nov. 1886 **1924**

Pacific Loan & Investment Co. Ld. Regd. 1886. Vol. liq. 15 May 1923. Capital returned to contributories—£4 per share of £10 (with £2 10s. paid); further payments (if any) not known. Final meeting return regd. 28 May 1943 .... **1924**

Pacific Mining Co. Ld. Regd. 1888. Struck off Register 28 July 1898 .... **1900**

Pacific Nitrate Co. Ld. Regd. 1905. Vol. liq. 31 Dec. 1912. Property was sold to Fortuna Nitrate Co. Ld. for £55,000 in cash. Final meeting return regd. 10 Feb. 1914 .... **1913**

Pacific Northwest Mining Corporation Ld. Regd. 1898. Removed from Register 1908 .... **1904**

Pacific Northwest Public Service Co. Inc. Oregon 1906 as Portland Railway Light & Power Co.; name changed to Portland Electric-Power Co. in 1924 and as above in 1930. The outstanding Portland Railway Light & Power Co. 5% 1st & refunding mortgage 30-year sinking fund gold bonds were redeemed at 105% on 1 Feb. 1931 .... **1931**

Pacific Oil Co. Inc. Delaware 1920. In Jan. 1926 properties were transferred to Standard Oil Co. of California (inc. Delaware). Shareholders received 1 share in new company for each share (of no par value) held. In Dec. 1927 it was stated the company would be finally liquidated and assets distributed **1928**

Pacific Oilfields Ld. Regd. 1907. Vol. liq. (members') 2 Sept. 1930. Capital returned to contributories—4s. 0½d. per share of £1. £1,518 17s. 8d. was paid into Companies' Liquidation Account. Final meeting return regd. 30 May 1931 .... **1931**

Pacific Petroleum Ld. Regd. 1911. Struck off Register 11 May 1951 .... **1952**

Pacific Phosphate Co. Ld. Regd. 1902. Vol. liq. 8 Oct. 1920. The properties were sold for £3,500,000. The ordinary shareholders were entitled to (inter alia) to 750,000 fully-paid shares of 5s. in Anglo-French

VOL. FOR

Phosphate Co Ld. (later Reliable Properties Ld.). Final meeting return regd. 7 Aug.1925 .... **1922**

Pacific Power & Light Co. Inc. Maine 1910. The outstanding bonds were redeemable on 1 Aug. 1930 **1930**

Pacific Railway of Colombia. Inc. Colombia 1908. The sterling 5% 5-year bonds were repaid in 1916 ...... **1917**

Pacific Salt Co. Ld. Regd. 1908. Vol liq. (members') 25 Jan. 1945. Capital returned to contributories—3s. 5·425d. per share of £1. £3,241 was paid into Companies' Liquidation Account. Final meeting return regd. 2 Sept. 1945 .... **1946**

Pacific Smelting Co Ld. Regd. 1902. Vol. liq. 6 Dec 1906. Final meeting return regd. 28 Feb. 1919 .... **1907**

Pacific Timber Co. Ld. Regd. 1915. Struck off Register 19 Jan. 1934 .... **1933**

Pacific Trust Association Ld. Regd. 1889. Vol. liq. 1 Sept. 1922. Final meeting return regd. 8 May 1924 **1923**

Pactol Carbon Co. Ld. In 1923 the goodwill and assets were acquired by British Printing Trust Ld. for 4,900 ordinary shares **1924**

Paddington Consols Ld. Regd. 1895. Absorbed by Standard Exploration Co. Ld. Removed from Register 1903 .... **1899**

Paddington South Ld. Regd. 1896. Vol. liq. 5 Mar. 1900. Assets were sold in 1900 to Standard Exploration Co. Ld., in which company shareholders were entitled to 2 shares for every 5 shares held. Final meeting return regd. 14 July 1900 .... **1901**

Padstow & St. Columb Gas Co. Ld. Regd. 1914 as Padstow Gas Co. Ld.; name changed as above 1930. Dissolved 1 May 1949, undertaking being vested in South Western Area Gas Board under Gas Act 1948. Holders of securities were entitled to receive British Gas 3% guaranteed stock 1990–95 as follows:

	£	s.	d.
Ord. shares (of £1)	1	0	0	
4½% red. debs. (of £100)	103	0	0	**1952**

Padstow, Bedruthan, &c., Light Railway Co. Inc. 1903 under Light Railways Act 1896. No capital had been issued at 11 Nov. 1910 .... **1911**

Padstow Gas Co. Ld. *See* Padstow & St. Columb Gas Co. Ld.

Padstow Granite Quarry Co. Ld. Regd. 1932. Vol. liq. (members') 9 July 1935. Capital returned to contributories—£3,269 17s. 6d. Final meeting return regd. 22 Aug. 1936 .... **1936**

Pafu Concessions Ld. Regd. 1911 as Sefwi (Gold Coast) Concessions Ld.; name changed to Pafu (Gold Coast) Concessions Ld. and as above June 1926. Struck off Register 28 Feb. 1939 .... **1940**

Pafu (Gold Coast) Concessions Ld. *See* Pafu Concessions Ld.

Page & Overton's Brewery Co. Ld. Regd. 1892. Undertaking and assets were acquired by Page & Overton's Brewery Ld. for £90,000 in ordinary shares of £10, £120,000 in preference shares of £10 and £80,000 in debenture stock. Removed from Register 1904 .... **1903**

Page & Pratt Ld. Regd. 1889. Receiver was appointed for debenture holders. Part of the business was sold to Page & Pratt (1907) Ld. Removed from Register 1913 .... **1908**

Page, Arnold & Co. Ld. Regd 1905. Vol. liq. 19 July 1909. Final meeting return regd. 3 Feb 1910 .... ***1907**

Page (Henry) & Co. Ld. *See* Ware Properties Ld

Page, Son & East Ld. Regd. 1905 Vol. liq. 10 Nov. 1927. Undertaking acquired by Thames Steam Tug & Lighterage Co. Ld. Final meeting return regd. 31 May 1928 .... **1940**

Page's Ld. Regd. 1936. Receiver appointed in Sept. 1941; ceased to act Mar. 1945. Struck off Register 24 Jan. 1947 .... **1947**

"Pagoda" Refreshment Co. Ld. Regd. 1903. Vol. liq. 14 Jan. 1905. Removed from Register 1910 .... **1905**

Pahang Central Tin and Exploration Co. Ld. Regd. 1889. Vol. liq. 11 Feb. 1892. Final meeting return regd. 15 June 1894 .... **1893**

Pahang Corporation Ld. Regd. 1887. Vol. liq. Oct. 1906. Reconstructed as Pahang Consolidated Co. Ld., in which company shareholders were entitled to 1 preference share of £1 for each preference share of £1 held. No return was made to ordinary shareholders. Removed from Register 1907 .... **1907**

Pahang Exploration & Development Co. Ld. Regd. 1889. Vol. liq. Dec. 1893. Reconstructed as Straits Development Co. Ld. in which company shareholders were entitled to 1 share of £1 (credited with 17s. paid) for each share of £1 held. Final meeting return regd. 12 Feb. 1897 .... **1894**

Pahang-Kabang Ld. Regd. 1889. Reconstructed 1899 as company of same name. Shareholders were entitled to 1 ordinary share of £1 (credited with 18s. paid) in new company for each ordinary share of £1 held or

VOL. FOR

fully-paid preference share of £1 for each preference share held. Removed from Register 1907 .... **1900**

Pahang Kabang Ld. Regd. 1899. Vol. liq. 8 Nov. 1906. Reconstructed as Pahang Consolidated Co. Ld., in which company shareholders were entitled to 1 preference share of £1 for each £1 arrears of dividend; no return was made to ordinary shareholders. Final meeting return regd. 24 July 1907 .. **1907**

Pahang-Semiliang Ld. Regd. 1890. Vol. liq. 6 Apr. 1891. In 1891 the undertaking was acquired by Pahang-Kabang Ld. for 25,610 shares of £1 (credited with 2*s*. 6*d*. paid) and 169,150 fully-paid shares of £1. Final meeting return regd. 20 Nov. 1891 .... **1900**

Paignton Electric Light & Power Co. Ld. Regd. 1908. Dissolved 1 Apr. 1948, undertaking being vested in British (later Central) Electricity Authority (q.v.) and South-Western Area Board under Electricity Act 1947. Holders of ordinary shares were entitled to receive £2 5*s*. British Electricity 3% guaranteed stock (1968–73) in respect of each share (of £1) held **1949**

Painswick Railway Co. Inc. by Special Act 1889. No capital had been issued at 1896. The Act expired in Aug. 1894 .... **1896**

Paisley & Barrhead District Railway Co. Inc. by Special Act 1897. Under Caledonian Railway Co.'s Provisional Order Confirmation Act 1902 the undertaking was absorbed into that company. Holders of ordinary shares of £10 received cash at par **1903**

Paisley District Tramways Co. Inc. by Provisional Order 1901. By Act of 1923 company was placed in vol. liq. in Aug. 1923 and undertaking sold to Glasgow Corporation. The outstanding debentures and preference shares were repaid at par in Sept 1923. Ordinary shareholders received £10 per share of £10 in Sept. 1923; further payments (if any) not known **1924**

Paiva Tin Development Syndicate Ld. Regd. 1928. Vol liq. (members') 27 Feb. 1933. Capital returned to contributories—6½*d*. per share of 10*s*., fully-paid; 5½*d*. per share of 10s. (8*s*. 6*d*. paid). £93 19*s*. 2*d*. was paid into Companies' Liquidation Account. Final meeting return regd. 8 Oct. 1934 .... **1934**

Pakan Baroe Rubber Estates Ld. Regd. 1910. Vol. liq. 4 Nov. 1913. Assets and liabilities were transferred to Siak (Sumatra) Rubber Estates Ld., in which company shareholders were entitled to 1 share of £1 (credited as fully-paid) for each share of £1 held. Debenture stockholders were entitled to an equal amount of stock in purchasing company. Final meeting return regd. 30 Dec. 1914 .... **1914**

Palace and Burlington Hotels Co. Ld. Regd. 1864, re-registered 1886. Vol. liq. Feb. 1886. Undertaking was acquired by Burlington Hotels Co. Ld. Final meeting return regd. 23 Dec. 1886 .... **1898**

Palace Hotel & Grand Hotel Des Alpes, Mürren Ld. Regd 1910 as Grand Hotel des Alpes, Mürren Ld.; name changed June 1911. Struck off Register Feb. 1933 .... **1933**

Palace Hotel Co, Birkdale Ld. *See* Palace Hotel Hydropathic and Spa Co. Ld.

Palace Hotel Hydropathic and Spa Co. Ld. Regd. 1880 to acquire business of Palace Hotel Co. Birkdale, Ld. Court Orders: to wind up 31 Oct 1887; to dissolve 4 July 1890 .... **1888**

Palace Hotel, Montana (Switzerland) Ld. Regd. 1906. Struck off Register Feb. 1933 .... **1933**

Palace of Varieties Ld. Regd 1888. Vol. liq. 25 May 1898. Final meeting return regd. 13 Sept. 1898 .... **1899**

Palace Shipping Co. Ld. Regd. 1900. The debenture stock was redeemed in 1916. Vol. liq. 3 Aug. 1920. Final meeting return regd. 8 Jan. 1926 .... **1916**

Palace Steamers Ld. Regd. 1893. Removed from Register 1898 .... **1895**

Palace Theatre, Halifax, Ld. Regd. 1902. Vol. liq. (members') 28 Oct. 1958. Capital returned to contributories—47*s*. 1·8336*d*. per share of £1. Paid into Companies' Liquidation Account—£23 13*s*. on account of unclaimed dividends and £84 17*s*. on account of unclaimed distributions. Final meeting return regd. 1 Mar. 1960 .... **1961**

Palace Theatre Ld. Regd. 1892. Vol. liq. 19 June 1893. Reconstructed as company of same name. Shareholders were entitled to 1 share of £1 (credited with 15s. paid) for each ordinary or preference share of £1 held. Final meeting return regd. 6 Oct. 1894 .... **1908**

Palace Theatre Ld. Regd. 1892. Vol. liq. 29 Apr. 1921. Capital returned to contributories—£1 10*s*. per share of 10*s*. (9*s*. paid) in Aug. 1921 further payments (if any) not known. Undertaking was acquired by London Palace (1921) Ld. (later London Entertainments Ld.). Final meeting return regd. 9 Mar. 1922 .... **1922**

Palais Indien Tea Houses Ld. Regd. 1891. Vol. liq. 5 Mar. 1895. Final meeting return regd. 12 Dec. 1895 **1896**

VOL. FOR

Palatine Bank Ld. Regd. 1899. Vol. liq. 30 Dec. 1919. Undertaking was acquired by Bank of Liverpool and Martins Ld. (later Martins Bank Ld.), in which company shareholders were entitled to 1⅖ shares of £20 (credited with £2 10*s*. paid) for each share of £20 (£5 paid) held **1921**

Palatine Guarantee Corporation Ld. Regd. 1924. All capital was owned by Palatine Industrial Finance Co. Ld. Struck off Register 1933 .... **1932**

Palatine Industrial Finance Co. Ld. Regd. 1928. Receiver appointed June 1931. In Oct. 1932 it was stated that proceeds of sale of assets would be insufficient to meet claims of debenture holders. Struck off Register 8 Oct. 1957 .... **1933**

Palatine Wine & Champagne Co. Ld. Undertaking and assets were acquired in June 1928 by Corona Wines Ld., for 160,000 fully-paid shares of 5*s*. **1929**

Palaw (Burma) Rubber Co. Ld. Regd. 1919. Vol. liq. 6 Feb. 1929. The undertaking and assets were transferred to Palace Rubber Estates Ld. in which company shareholders were entitled to 1 share of 2*s*. (credited with 1*s*. 6*d*. paid) for each share of 2*s*. held. Final meeting return regd. 7 Mar. 1930 .... **1929**

Palaw Rubber Estates Ld. Regd. 1929. Vol. liq. (creditors') 25 June 1931. Undertaking was acquired by Mergui Crown Estates Ld. in 1932 for 100,000 shares of 2*s*. £8 2*s*. 7*d*. was paid into Companies' Liquidation Account in respect of unclaimed dividends. Final meeting return regd. 5 Dec. 1932 .... **1932**

Palenque Gold Mining Syndicate Ld. Regd. 1898. Struck off Register 1928 .... **1928**

Palermo, Marsala & Trapani Railway Co. Inc. in Italy 1878. Line expropriated by the State as from 1 Jan. 1905 .... **1952**

Palestine Oil Industries "Shemen," Ld. *See* Eastern Oil Industries Ld.

Palmarejo Mining Co. Ld. Regd. 1886. Reconstructed 1898 as Palmarejo and Mexican Gold Fields Ld., in which company shareholders were entitled to 1 share of £1 (credited with 16*s*. 6*d*. paid) for each share of £1 held. The prior lien debentures were paid. Holders of 1st debentures were entitled to 5 fully-paid shares of £1 for every £4 debentures held. Holders of consolidated debentures were entitled to 1 fully-paid share of £1 for every £2 debentures held. Removed from Register 1903 .... **1898**

Palmarejo Oil Concessions Ld. Regd. 1920. Struck off Register Jan. 1931 .... **1931**

Palmer & Co. Ld. Regd. 1891. Vol. liq. 25 July 1898. Final meeting return regd. 17 Feb. 1900 .... **1898**

Palmer & Co. Ld. Regd. 1898. Vol. liq. (creditors') 15 Dec. 1939. Assets realised insufficient to pay unsecured creditors in full. Final meeting return regd. 20 Dec. 1940 .... **1940**

Palmers Shipbuilding & Iron Co. Ld. Regd. 1865. Receiver appointed 30 June 1933; ceased to act 5 May 1937. Assets realised sufficient to repay 5*s*. 8*d*. in £ to 1st mortgage debenture stockholders. Struck off Register 23 Sept. 1938 .... **1939**

Palmers Stores Ld. Regd. 1897. Reconstructed 1903 as Palmer's Stores (1903) Ld., in which company shareholders were entitled to 2 fully-paid preference shares of £1 *plus* 8⅔*d*. in cash for every 3 preference shares of £1 held or 1 fully-paid ordinary share of £1 for every 3 ordinary shares of £1 held. Removed from Register 1905 .... **1903**

Palmer's Stores (1903) Ld. Regd 1903. A subsidiary of Littlewoods Mail Order Stores Ld. Vol. liq (members') 9 Sept. 1957. Final meeting return regd. 10 Mar. 1960 .... **1956**

Palmerston Ld. Regd 1902. Vol. liq. (members') 30 Sept 1931. Capital returned to contributories—6¾*d* per share of £1. Final meeting return regd. 10 May 1932 **1933**

Palmerston Mining Co. Ld. Regd. 1888 as Palmerston Copper Mining Co. Ld.; name changed Oct. 1889. Removed from Register 1903 .... **1892**

Palmerston Trust Ld. Regd. 1927. Vol. liq. 12 June 1928. Undertaking and assets were acquired by Palmerston Investment Trust Ld., in which company shareholders were entitled to 1 share of £1 (credited as fully-paid) for each ordinary share of £1 held or 3 fully-paid shares of £1 for every 40 deferred shares of 1*s*. held. Final meeting return regd. 8 May 1929 . **1929**

Palmietkuil Gold Mining Co. Ld. Inc. Union of South Africa 1934. Vol. liq. (members') 21 May 1941. Properties were acquired by Grootvlei Proprietary Mines Ld., in which company shareholders received 1 share of £1 for every 25 shares of 10*s*. held. Liquidator released 24 June 1944 .... **1945**

Palsh Plantations Ld. Regd. 1920 as Baling Road Rubber Co. Ld.; name changed as above July 1926. Vol. liq. (members') 30 June 1961. Final meeting return regd. 29 Sept. 1962 .... **1953**

**See Stock Exchange Year-Book.*

Paloor (Travancore) Rubber Co. Ld. Regd. Edinburgh 1910. Vol. liq. July 1914. Undertaking and assets sold to Travancore Rubber Co. Ld., in which company shareholders were entitled to 1 fully-paid share of £1 for every 2 shares of £1 held. Final meeting return regd. 7 Jan. 1916 .... **1944**

Pambula Gold Mines Ld. Regd. 1895. Reconstructed as Pambula Mines Ld., in which company shareholders were entitled to 1 share of £1 (with 17s. 6d. paid) for each share of £1 held. Vol. liq. 31 Dec. 1896. Final meeting return regd. 19 Oct. 1899............ **1899**

Pambula Mines Ld. Regd. 1897. Reconstructed 1899 as company of same name. Shareholders were entitled to 2 shares of 5s. (credited with 4s. paid) in new company for each share of £1 held. Removed from Register 1901 .... **1903**

Pambula Mines Ld. Regd. 1899. Removed from Register 1908 .... **1908**

Pampa Alta Nitrate Co. Inc. Chile 1904. In Dec. 1911 the undertaking and assets were acquired by Loa Nitrate Co. **1913**

Pampa Estancia Co. Ld. Regd. 1884. The estancia and implements were sold to Las Barrancas Estancia Co. Ld. Removed from Register 1910 .... **1906**

Pan-African Syndicate Ld. Regd. 1901. Struck off Register 7 May 1907............. **1908**

Pan American Foreign Corporation. Inc. Delaware 1932. Dissolved 18 Dec. 1936 .... **1937**

Pan de Azucar Nitrate Co. Ld. Regd. 1901. Vol. liq. (members') 3 June 1931. Undertaking and assets were acquired by Nitrate Corporation of Chile, in which company shareholders were entitled to 1 fully-paid series B share of 100 pesos (either ordinary or 7% cumulative preferred) for every $4\frac{1}{3}$ shares of £1 held. Final meeting return regd. 10 Mar. 1932 .... **1932**

Panama Canal Co. Constituted 1881. Winding-up Order made by Civil Tribunal Feb. 1889 .... **1894**

Panama Corporation (Canada) Ld. Inc. in Canada by Letters Patent 9 Mar. 1932. Wound up on 5 June 1948. There were no assets available for distribution to debenture stockholders, debenture holders and shareholders **1949**

Panama Corporation Ld. Regd. 1926. Vol liq. (members') 25 Feb. 1932. Reconstructed as Panama Corporation (Canada) Ld., in which company shareholders were entitled to 1 share of no par value for each share of £1 held. Debenture stockholders were entitled to $50 in 8% convertible debenture stock for every £10 stock held. Final meeting return regd. 24 Feb. 1933 .... **1933**

Panama No. 1 Ld. Regd 1927. Vol liq. (members') 4 July 1935. Preferred shareholders received 1 share of no par value in Panama Corporation (Canada) Ld. for each share of £1 held and deferred shareholders received 1 share of no par value for every 20 shares of 1s. held (holdings of less than 10 shares being ignored and holdings of 10 to 19 shares being treated as 20 shares). Final meeting return regd. 4 Jan. 1938 **1936**

Panama Rubber & Timber Estates Ld. Regd. 1911. Vol. liq. 26 Mar. 1913. Court Order to continue winding up under supervision July 1913. Final meeting return regd. 8 Dec. 1917 .... **1914**

Panama Timber Co. Ld. Regd. 1911. Vol. liq. June 1914. Struck off Register Mar 1929 .... **1930**

Pandan (Johore) Rubber Estates Ld. Regd. 1910. Vol. liq. Oct. 1911. Undertaking and assets were sold to Mount Austin (Johore) Rubber Estates Ld., in which company shareholders were entitled to 1 share of £1 (credited as fully-paid) for each share of £1 held. Removed from Register 1912 .... **1912**

Pandan Tea Co. Ld. Regd. 1923. Vol. liq. (members') 1 Mar. 1933. Undertaking and assets were acquired by Pandan Tea Co. (1933) Ld., in which company shareholders were entitled to 1 ordinary and 1 redeemable preference share of £1 (each credited with 16s. 6d. paid) for every 2 shares of £1 held plus 1s. 6d. per share in cash. £116 14s. was paid into Companies' Liquidation Account. Final meeting return regd. 14 June 1934 .... **1934**

Pandora Folding Box Co. Ld. Regd. 1894. Vol. liq. 5 Sept. 1895. Struck off Register 22 May 1908 .... **1896**

Panga & Silindi United Ld. Regd. 1895 as Panga Co. Ld.; name changed 1898. Reconstructed 1899 as Umtali Exploration Co. Ld., in which company shareholders were entitled to 2 shares of £1 (credited with 17s. 6d. paid) for each share of £1 held. Removed from Register 1911 .... **1900**

Panga Co. Ld. *See* Panga & Silindi United Ld.

Pangnga River Tin Concessions Ld. Regd. 1927. Vol. liq. (members') 12 Apr. 1949. Shareholders were entitled to 5 fully-paid shares of 5s. of Kamunting Tin Dredging Ld. for every 6 shares (of 5s.) held and a

cash distribution of 0·195d. per share. Final meeting return regd. 18 Aug. 1950 .... **1950**

Panni Lands & Rubber Estates Ld. Regd. 1910. Vol. liq. 6 Jan. 1911. Final meeting return regd. 19 Aug. 1913 ***1912**

Panora Tea & Produce Co. Ld. Regd. 1911. Vol. liq. (creditors') 13 Dec. 1932. Estates sold to new company (regd. in India), in which company debenture stockholders received 1 share of Rs. 2 and 10s. in new debenture stock for each £1 debenture stock held. Final meeting return regd. 6 July 1933 **1933**

Pant Glas Slate & Slab Quarry Co, Ld. Regd. 1883. Vol. liq 15 Jan. 1892. Final meeting return regd. 29 Aug. 1892 .... **1892**

Pantone Processes Ld. Regd. 1926. Court Order to wind up Nov. 1929. Struck off Register 10 May 1935 .. **1936**

Pantymwyn Mining Co Ld. Regd. 29 Sept. 1900. Debenture holders received 2s. $4\frac{1}{2}d$ per £1 debenture in 1948. Struck off the Register 8 Aug. 1953 ...... **1953**

Panuco Copper Co. Ld. Regd. 1899. Court Order to wind up 4 Apr. 1900. Capital returned to contributories—4s. per share of £1 in Dec. 1900; further payments (if any) not known. Removed from Register 1910 .... **1901**

Panulcillo Copper Co. Ld. Regd. 1864. Vol. liq. 12 Dec. 1893. Reconstructed as Central Chili Copper Co: Ld., in which company shareholders were entitled to subscribe for shares at par. Final meeting return regd. 14 Mar. 1899 .... **1898**

Paper Bottle Co. Ld. Regd. 1887. Court Orders: to wind up 9 Feb. 1889; to dissolve Jan. 1891 .... **1890**

Paper Tube Makers Association Ld. Regd. 1920. Vol. liq. 29 Feb. 1924. Final meeting return regd. 15 May 1929 .... ***1925**

Papua Co. Ld. Regd. 1914. Vol. liq. 29 Nov. 1920. Final meeting return regd. 2 July 1927 .... **1921**

Papuan Industries Ld. Regd. 1904. Receiver appointed in Jan. 1937; ceased to act 27 July 1940. Proceeds from assets were applied in repaying debentures as far as possible. Struck off Register 29 Aug. 1941 . **1942**

Papuan Minerals Exploration Ld. Regd. 1909. Vol. liq. (creditors') 30 June 1930. No capital returned to contributories. Final meeting return regd. 20 Nov. 1930 .... **1931**

Para Gas Co. Ld. Regd. 1896. Vol. liq. 25 Oct. 1897. Property was acquired by Colonial Lighting Syndicate Ld. Final meeting return regd. 19 Jan. 1899 **1898**

Para Improvements Ld. *See* Municipality of Para Improvements Ld.

Para Industrial & Commercial Co. Ld. Regd. 1926 as Para Plantations Ld.; name changed Aug. 1928. Court Order to wind up Feb. 1932. Struck off Register 15 June 1937 .... **1938**

Para (Marajo) Islands Rubber Estates Ld. Regd. 1910. Struck off the Register 26 Jan. 1940 but restored on 14 Dec. 1948 and vol. liq. (creditors') 12 June 1953. No capital returned to contributories—£30 8s. 10d. was paid into Companies' Liquidation Account. Final meeting return regd. 15 June 1956 .... **1957**

Para Plantations Ld. *See* Para Industrial & Commercial Co. Ld.

Paragon International Ld. Regd. 1916. Vol. liq. 8 Dec. 1926. Final meeting return regd. 2 Nov. 1927 ..... **1927**

Paraguay Land Co. Ld. *See* Anglo-Paraguayan Land Co. Ld.

Paramaribo Rubber & Timber Estates Ld. Regd. Edinburgh 1909. Struck off Register 4 Dec. 1923 **1911**

Paramatta Copper Mines Ld. Regd. 1899. Vol. liq. Aug. 1908. Removed from Register 1913 .... **1909**

Parana Plantations Ld. Regd 1925. Vol. liq. (members') 31 Mar 1944. Capital returned to contributories— 5s. 1·41d. per share of 5s. Final meeting return regd. 13 Nov. 1951 .... **1953**

Parcocha Iron Ore & Railway Co. Ld. Regd. 1890. In Oct. 1909 the Court ordered sale of property; £53 10s. per debenture of £100 had been paid at Jan. 1911; further payments (if any) not known. Removed from Register 1913 .... **1911**

Pardy's Mozambique Syndicate Ld. Regd. 1893. Removed from Register 1908 .... **1907**

Pardy's Range Ld. Regd. 1895. Vol. liq. 14 Jan. 1895. Reconstructed as Mozambique Consolidated Mines Ld., in which company shareholders were entitled to 1 share of 10s. (credited with 9s. paid) for each share of 10s. held. Final meeting return regd. 27 Sept 1898 **1898**

Parent Coal Carbonisation Trust Ld. Regd. 1929. Court Order to wind up June 1932. Receiver appointed in July 1932. Struck off Register 18 Feb. 1938 .... **1939**

Parent Trust and Finance Co. Ld. Regd. 1896 as Dunlop Pneumatic Tyre Co. Ld.; name changed Feb. 1913 to Parent Tyre Co. Ld., and as above Jan. 1925. Court Order to wind up July 1932. Assets realised insufficient to pay unsecured creditors in full. Liquidator released 15 June 1945. Struck off Register 5 Mar 1948 .... **1946**

VOL. FOR

Pares's Leicestershire Banking Co. Ld. Established 1836. Regd as limited Oct. 1880 Vol. liq. 12 June 1902. Business acquired by Parr's Bank Ld., in which company shareholders were entitled to 7 shares of £100 (£20 paid) for every 16 shares of £25 (£12 10s paid) or 40 shares of £25 (£5 paid) **1903**

Parfield Trust Ld. Regd 1939. Vol. liq (members') 9 Oct. 1963. Final meeting return regd 17 Jan. 1964 .... **1947**

Pari Tin Ld. Regd. 1922. Vol. liq. members') 11 Sept 1953. Capital returned to contributories—1*s.* 9½*d.* per share of 2*s.* £361 paid into Companies' Liquidation Account. Final meeting return regd. 3 Jan. 1955 **1955**

Paringa Calebration Mining Syndicate Ld. Regd 1920. Vol. liq. (creditors') 9 Apr. 1930. No capital was returned to contributories. Final meeting return regd. 20 July 1933 .... ***1931**

Paringa Consolidated Mines Ld. Regd. 1898. Reconstructed 1902 as Paringa Mines Ld. in which company shareholders were entitled to 1 share of 5*s.* (credited with 3*s.* paid) for each share of 10*s.* held. Removed from Register 1903 .... **1908**

Paringa Copper Mines Ld. Inc. South Australia 1900. Vol. liq. Apr. 1906. No surplus was available for division amongst shareholders **1907**

Paringa Mines Ld. Regd. 1902. Vol. liq. Aug. 1909. Reconstructed as Paringa Mines (1909) Ld. (later Paringa Mining and Exploration Co. Ld), in which company shareholders were entitled to 1 share of 5*s.* (credited with 4*s.* paid) for each share of 5*s* held. Removed from Register 1913 .... **1910**

Paris Beeston Tyre Co. Ld. Regd 1895. Vol. liq. 30 Apr. 1896. Final meeting return regd 11 Jun 1897 .... **1897**

Paris Carlton Hotel Ld. Regd. 1906. Vol. liq. 23 Apr. 1919. Final meeting return regd 21 Nov. 1921 .... **1919**

Paris Food Supply Association Ld. Regd. 1907. Vol. liq. May 1909. Capital returned to contributories—3*s.* per preferred ordinary share of £1 in June 1909; further payments (if any) not known. Removed from Register 1914 .... **1910**

Paris Gift Gold Mining Co. Ld. Regd. 1895. Vol. liq. 6 May 1897. Final meeting return regd. 24 Jan. 1898 **1898**

Paris Gigantic Wheel & Varieties Co. Ld. Regd 1899. Struck off Register 22 Dec. 1903 .... **1904**

Paris Hippodrome Ld. Regd. 1897. Vol. liq. 19 Aug 1898. Final meeting return regd. 20 Sept 1899 .... **1899**

Paris Investment Co. Ld. Regd. 1902. Removed from Register 1906 .... **1906**

Paris Railway Guide Syndicate Ld. Regd 1897. Removed from Register 1910 .... **1902**

Paris (Transvaal) Gold Mines Ld. Regd. 1895 as Witpoortje Gold Mines Ld.; name changed Aug. 1912. Vol. liq. 25 Mar. 1920. Shareholders were entitled to 1 fully-paid share of £1 in British Platinum & Gold Corporation Ld. for every 8 shares of 2*s.* held, or 5 fully-paid shares in that company for every £4 share warrants to bearer in Witpoortje Gold Mines Ld. later Paris (Transvaal) Gold Mines Ld.—Final meeting return regd. 23 Dec. 1921 .... **1921**

Parit-Bruas (Malay) Rubber Co. Ld. Regd 1911. Vol. liq. (members) 9 Oct. 1969 Capital returned to contributories—2*s* 2*d* plus 1·34*p.* per share (of 2*s.*). £3,706·06 was paid into Companies' Liquidation Account in respect of unclaimed distributions and £185·66 in respect of unclaimed dividends. Final meeting return regd. 22 Aug. 1973 .... **1974-5**

Park & Croesor Slate Quarries Co. Ld. Regd. 1895. Struck off Register Dec. 1931 .... **1932**

Park & Sandy Lane Mills Co. Ld. Regd. 1875. Dissolved under Section 208 of Companies Act 1948 on 25 Nov. 1949, the undertaking and assets having been acquired by Royton Textile Corpn. Ld. Stockholders received ⅘ths fully-paid shares (of 5*s.*) of Royton Textile Corpn. Ld. for every £1 stock held **1950**

Park Foundry Co. Ld. Regd 1900. Receiver appointed 2 Mar. 1903; ceased to act 14 Aug. 1930. Vol. liq. 20 Dec. 1929. Capital returned to contributories—£2,583 6*s.* 8*d.* 15*s.* 10*d* was paid into Companies' Liquidation Account. Final meeting return regd. 7 Feb. 1931 .... ***1910**

Park Gate Iron & Steel Co. Ld. Regd. 1864 as Parkgate Iron Co. Ld.; name changed Oct. 1888. Vol. liq. 12 June 1919. Reconstructed as company of same name. Shareholders were entitled to 3 shares of £1 in new company for each share of £1 held. Final meeting return regd 26 Sept. 1919 .... **1919**

Park Hall Collieries Ld. Regd. 1889. Receiver for debenture holders appointed in 1907. Struck off Register 25 Feb. 1910 .... **1910**

Park Hotel (Pontypridd) Co. Ld. Regd 1899. Vol. liq. 20 Sept 1905 for sale of undertaking. Removed from Register 1907 .... **1906**

Park Mill (Royton) Ld. Regd. 1904. Vol. liq. (members') 31 Mar. 1953. Undertaking and assets sold to Shiloh Spinners Ld., in which company shareholders were entitled to receive, in respect of every £25 nominal stock held, 16 preference shares of £1 and 149 ordinary shares of 5*s.* £92 was paid into Companies' Liquidation Account. Final meeting return regd. 23 Dec. 1953 .... **1954**

Park Road Spinning Co. Ld. Regd. 1891. Vol. liq. (members') 24 Mar. 1964. Final meeting return regd. 6 June 1966 .... **1941**

Park Steel Co. Inc. New Jersey 1899. All common stock and greater part of preferred stock acquired by Crucible Steel Co. of America **1901**

Parka Mines Consols. In liquidation in 1883 .... **1883**

Parka Tin Mines Ld. Regd. 1911. Vol. liq. 10 Dec 1915. Struck off Register 20 Mar. 1925 .... **1916**

Parkanchy Tin Ld. Regd. 1926. Vol liq (creditors') 18 Dec. 1935. Assets realised insufficient to pay unsecured creditors in full. Final meeting return regd 19 Jan. 1939 .... **1936**

Parker Gold Mines Ld. Regd 1890. Vol. liq. 14 Dec. 1892. Reconstructed as New London Estates Co. Ld. Final meeting return regd. 9 Oct. 1896 .... ***1895**

Parker's Joinery & Cabinet Co. Ld. Regd. 1897. Removed from Register 1903 .... **1903**

Parkes Chemists, Ld. Regd. 1894 as Parke's Drug Stores Ld.; name changed May 1924. Vol. liq. (members') 12 Aug. 1948, the undertaking and assets being acquired by Taylors (Cash Chemists) London Ld. Capital returned to contributories—£1 per preference share (of £1) and £1 8*s.* 10*d.* per ordinary share (of £1). £60 12*s.* 6*d.* was paid into Companies' Liquidation Account. Final meeting return regd 18 Mar. 1949 .... **1950**

Parkes Drug Stores Ld. *See above.*

Parkgate Iron Co. Ld. *See* Park Gate Iron & Steel Co. Ld.

Parkgate Wagon Works Co. Ld. Regd 1872. Removed from Register 1904 .... ***1877**

Parkhall and Barlborough Collieries Ld. Regd. Edinburgh 1906. Vol. liq. Mar 1908. Final meeting return regd. 6 Apr. 1909 .... **1909**

Parkhall Colliery Co. Ld. *See* Foxfield Colliery Ld.

Parkhead Cinema Ld. Regd. Edinburgh 1927. Vol. liq. (members') 20 Mar. 1936. Undertaking acquired by Associated British Cinemas Ld. Capital returned to contributories—8*s.* 9½*d* per share of £1. Final meeting return regd. 9 Mar. 1937 .... **1940**

Parkhurst Theatre Ld. Regd 1897. Removed from Register 1899 .... **1899**

Parkside & Birks Mining Co. Ld. Regd. 1920. Vol. liq. (creditors') 20 Apr. 1934. All shares were held by North Lonsdale Iron & Steel Co. Ld. and Whitehaven Hematite Iron & Steel Co. Ld. Final meeting return regd. 13 Apr. 1935 .... **1935**

Parkside Spinning Co. Ld. Regd 1873. Vol. liq. 11 Mar. 1920. Final meeting return regd. 8 Oct. 1920 .... **1921**

Parnall & Evans Ld. Regd 1891. Vol. liq. 19 Aug. 1896. Final meeting return regd 13 Aug. 1897 .... **1897**

Parnall (Robert & Henry) & Co. Ld. Regd. 1897. Capital returned to contributories—7*s* 6*d* per preference share of £1 in Aug. 1904; further payments (if any) not known. Removed from Register 1906 .... **1905**

Parnell Electric Industries Ld. Regd. 13 Apr. 1964 as Val Parnell Investments Ld.; name changed May 1964. Vol. liq. 8 Sept. 1980. Final meeting return regd. 29 May 1981 .... **1971**

Parral Consolidated Gold & Silver Mines Ld. Regd 1892. Vol. liq. 1 Feb. 1900. Final meeting return regd 15 Dec. 1920 .... **1901**

Panal Mines Ld. Regd 1901. Removed from Register 1909 .... **1904**

Parr's Bank Ld. Regd. 1865 as Parr's Banking Co. Ld.; name changed to Parr's Banking and the Alliance Bank Ld. in July 1892 and as above June 1896. Vol. liq. 26 Mar. 1918 for amalgamation with London County and Westminster Bank Ld. (later Westminster Bank Ld.), in which company shareholders were entitled to 2⅓ shares of £20 (credited with £5 paid) for each share of £50 (£10 paid) held **1918**

Parr's Banking and the Alliance Bank Ld. *See* Parr's Bank Ld.

Parr's Banking Co. Ld. *See* Parr's Bank Ld.

Parsonage (Septimus) & Co. Ld. Regd. 1899. Court Order to wind up 24 Apr. 1901 Removed from Register 1910 .... **1902**

Parsons (F. J.) Ld. Regd. 1897. Dissolved 24 June 1981 **1972**

Parsons & Co. Ld. Regd. 1890 as Parsons & Bourgaize Ld.: name changed Mar. 1893. Vol. liq. (members') 16 Aug. 1932. Capital returned to contributories—15*s.* 10¾*d.* per share of £1. £7 3*s.* 11*d.* was paid into Companies' Liquidation Account. Final meeting return regd. 12 July 1934 .... **1933**

Parsons Brothers Ld. Regd. 1900. Vol. liq. 11 Feb. 1913. Final meeting return regd. 13 Oct. 1920 .... ***1914**

**See Stock Exchange Year-Book.*

VOL. FOR

Parsons' Foreign Patents Co. Ld. Regd. 1899. Vol. liq. (members') 15 June 1950. Final meeting return regd. 15 Feb. 1952 1947

Parsons' Pond Oil Syndicate Ld. Regd. 1914. Vol. liq. 6 Mar. 1916. Final meeting return regd. 17 Jan. 1919 *1917

Parsonstown & Portumna Bridge Railway Co. Inc. by Special Act 1861. Line taken possession of by a creditor on 6 Jan 1879, and closed for traffic on that date 1896

Partagas & Co. Ld. Regd. 1888. Removed from Register 1901 1896

Partick, Hillhead and Maryhill Gas Co Ld. Regd. Edinburgh 1871. Under Act of 1891 undertaking transferred to Glasgow Corporation for £202,500. Dissolved before 1931 1892

Partington Pneumatic Wheel Co. Ld. Regd. 1907. Vol. liq. 5 Nov. 1909. Removed from Register 1910 ... 1910

Partington Steel & Iron Co. Ld. Regd. 1910. Vol. liq. (members') 29 Jan. 1942. Capital returned to contributories—20s. per 2nd preference share of £1; 6s. 8d.; per 3rd preference share of 6s. 8d.; the 1st preference and ordinary shares were privately held. £5,897 was paid into Companies' Liquidation Account in respect of unclaimed distributions. Final meeting return regd. 13 June 1945 1946

Parys Copper Corporation Ld. Regd. 1879. Vol. liq. 23 Jan. 1885. Final meeting return regd. 8 Aug. 1892 1885

Pascoe Grenfell & Sons Ld. Regd. 1890. Vol. liq. 12 Oct. 1892. Final meeting return regd. 8 May 1897 ...... *1893

Pass & Joyce Ld. Regd 1929 as Pass & Joyce (1929) Ld.; name changed Aug. 1929. By Vesting Order of '9 Dec. 1938 undertaking and assets were transferred to Pass & Joyce (Successors) Ld., in which company shareholders were entitled to 1 fully-paid ordinary share of 1s. in respect of every 2 preference shares of 10s. or 40 ordinary shares of 1s. held; preference shareholders were also entitled to subscribe at par for 1 ordinary share in respect of each ordinary share allotted under the scheme. Dissolved under Sec. 154 of Companies Act 1929 on 19 Mar. 1939 1939

Pass & Joyce (Successors) Ld. Regd. 1938. Vol. liq. (creditors') 29 Dec. 1939. Assets realised insufficient to pay debenture holders in full. Final meeting return regd. 13 Sept. 1944 1940

Passburg Grains Syndicate Ld. Regd. 1889. Vol. liq. 8 Jan 1892. Reconstructed as Vacuum Drying Co. Ld. Final meeting return regd. 23 Apr. 1896 1894

Pataling Rubber Estates Syndicate Ld. Regd. 1903. Vol. liq. 7 Apr. 1920. Reconstructed as Pataling Rubber Estates Ld., in which company shareholders were entitled to 1 fully-pald share of £1 for each share of 2s. held. Final meeting return regd. 13 Feb. 1922. 1921

Patani Para Plantations Ld. Regd. 1923. All capital acquired by Consolidated Plantations Ld. Dissolved 17 May 1981 1978–9

Pataz & Parcoy Syndicate Ld. See Peruvian Consolidated Gold Trust Ld.

Pateley Bridge Co. Ld. Regd. 1879. Removed from Register 1905 1883

Patent Automatic Sash-Motor Co. Ld. Regd 1883. Vol. liq. 14 Aug. 1888. Final meeting return regd. 4 July 1892 1889

Patent Ball-Castor Co. Ld. Regd. 1881. Vol. liq. 4 May 1891. Final meeting return regd. 19 Jan. 1892 1892

Patent Block Tar, Gaseous Fuel & Asphalte Co. Ld. See Patent Block Tar Motor Oil & Asphalte Co. Ld.

Patent Block Tar Motor Oil & Asphalte Co. Ld. Regd. 1907 as Tar Patents Solidifying & Distilling Co. Ld.; name changed to Patent Solidifying and Distilling Co. Ld.; to Patent Block Tar, Gaseous Fuel & Asphalte Co Ld in Sept. 1908, and as above July 1909. Struck off Register 6 July 1920 1909

Patent Cable Tramways Coporation Ld. Regd. 1882 as Hallidie Patent Cable Tramways Corporation Ld.; name changed Mar. 1884. Court Orders: to wind up Apr. 1888; to dissolve 28 June 1892 1889

Patent Double Pick Loom Co. Ld. Regd 1898. Struck off Register 13 Oct. 1908 1909

Patent Fibre & Extract Co. Ld. Regd. 1881. Court Orders: to wind up Dec. 1882; to dissolve Aug. 1885 1883

Patent Gunpowder Co. Ld. Regd. 1872. Removed from Register 1884 .... *1877

Patent Interchangeable Stopper Co. Ld. Regd. 1913. Vol. liq. (creditors') 9 July 1930. Practically all shares owned by Canning Town Glass Works Ld. Final meeting return regd. 15 Oct. 1930 1926

Patent Invert Sugar and Distillery Co. Ld. Regd. 1883 as Patent Invert Sugar Co. Ld.; name changed Nov 1885. Vol. liq. 1 Dec. 1886. Struck off Register 20 Mar. 1906 1888

Patent Invert Sugar Co. Ld. See Patent Invert Sugar and Distillery Co. Ld.

Patent Nitro-Phosphate or Blood Manure Co. Ld. See Odams' Nitro-Phosphate & Chemical Co. Ld.

VOL. FOR

Patent Nut & Bolt Co. Ld. Regd. 1864. Business was acquired in 1900 by Guest Keen & Co. Ld. (later Guest Keen and Nettlefolds Ld.). Removed from Register 1901 1908

Patent Paper Packing (Foreign) Ld. Regd. 1934. Struck off Register 26 Sept. 1939 1940

Patent Solidifying and Distilling Co. Ld. See Patent Block Tar Motor Oil & Asphalte Co. Ld.

Patent Shaft & Axletree Co. Ld. Regd. 1889. Vol. liq. 28 Nov. 1902. Amalgamated 1902 with Metropolitan Amalgamated Railway Carriage and Wagon Co. Ld. (later Metropolitan-Cammell Carriage Wagon & Finance Co. Ld.), in which company shareholders were entitled to 3½ ordinary shares of £1 (credited as fully-paid) for each ordinary share of £7 (£4 paid) held, or 5 6% cumulative preference shares of £1 (credited as fully-paid) for each 5% non-cumulative preference share of £6 10s. held; ordinary shares of £7 (£3 paid) were repaid in cash at £3 per share. A cash distribution was made of 2s. 5¼d. per ordinary share and 3s. 3d. per preference share. Final meeting return regd. 4 Feb. 1904 1903

Patent Sterilised Cask Co. Ld. Regd. 1899. Amalgamated 1902 with Sterax Co. Ld., in which company shareholders were entitled to 1½ shares of £1 (credited as fully-paid) for each share of £1 held. Removed from Register 1904 1904

Patent Tunnelling & Mining Machine Co. Ld. Regd. 1861. Wound up by Order of Court 4 June 1883 *1884

Patent Ventilating Granary Co. Ld. Regd. 1863. Court Order to continue winding up under supervision 31 Aug. 1887. Final meeting return regd. 21 June 1902. 1889

Patent Waterproof Paper & Canvas Co. Ld. Regd 1881. Vol. liq. 28 Apr 1898. Final meeting return regd. 21 Feb 1899 .... *1893

Patent Wear-Proof Motor Tyres Ld. Regd. 1919. Struck off Register 1924 1923

Patent Weldless Steel Chain & Cable Co. Ld. Regd. 1894. Removed from Register 23 July 1901 .... *1899

Patents Mining & Financial Trust Ld. Regd. 1890. Removed from Register 1907 1894

Patents Securities & Development Association Ld. Regd. 1889. Struck off Register 5 May 1896 1899

Patentwood Keg Syndicate Ld. Regd. 1903. Vol. liq. 17 Dec. 1908. Removed from Register 1909 1909

Paterson (F.G.) Clayton & Ld. See Clayton Bros. Ld.

Paterson, Laing and Bruce Ld. Regd. 1897. Business was acquired by Paterson, Laing and Bruce (1901) Ld. (later Paterson, Laing and Bruce Ld.), for £250,000 in ordinary shares of £1, £200,000 in preference shares of £5, £75,000 in debenture stock and £225,000 in cash. Debenture holders were entitled to an equal amount of debenture stock in new company. Removed from Register 1903 1902

Pather Iron & Steel Co. Ld. Regd. Edinburgh 1880. Vol. liq. (members') 10 Sept. 1953. Capital returned to contributories—3s 8¼d. per share of £1. Final meeting return regd. 26 June 1937 1936

Pathescope Ld. Regd. 1912. Vol. liq. (members') 14 Nov. 1963. Final meeting return regd. 9 Dec. 1971 1961

Pathini Tea Co. Ld. Regd. 1901. Vol. liq. (members') 1 June 1966. Capital returned to contributories (shares of £1)—preference £1; ordinary £1 16s. 6d. Final meeting return regd. 14 Nov. 1969 1970

Patons & Baldwins (Australasia) Ld. Regd. Edinburgh 1907 as John Paton, Son & Co. (Australasia) Ld.; name changed July 1920. Vol. liq. (members') 2 Mar. 1934. Capital returned to contributories— £154,159 10s. 5d. Final meeting return regd. 30 Dec. 1935. All shares owned by Patons & Baldwins Ld. 1935

Patriotic Assurance Co. Established by Deed of Settlement 1824 as Patriotic Assurance Co. of Ireland. Regd. Dublin 1878 and name changed by Act of 1890. Vol. liq. Jan. 1906. All business (except life) was acquired by Sun Insurance Office; the life business was acquired by Sun Life Assurance Society. Capital returned to contributories—£3 12s. 6d. per share of £20 (£2 5s. paid); further payments (if any) not known. Shareholders had option of receiving 1 share of £10 (credited with 10s. paid) plus £23 10s. in cash in respect of every 10 shares held in lieu of cash 1906

Patriotic Assurance Co. of Ireland. See Patriotic Assurance Co.

Pattani Consolidated Alluvial Tin Ld. Regd. 1926. Vol. liq. (creditors') 2 Sept 1930. Undertaking and assets were acquired by Pattani Tin Ld. (later Arcolectric (Holdings) Ld.) in which company shareholders were entitled to 1 share of 5s. (credited with 3s. 1¼d. paid) for each share of 5s. held. Final meeting return regd. 21 July 1939 1931

Pattersyke and Clargill Lead Mining Co. Ld. Regd. 1881. Vol. liq. 19 Oct. 1891. Final meeting return regd. 4 May 1895 1890

*See Stock Exchange Year-Book.

VOL. FOR

Pattison (William & John) Ld. Regd. 1920. Vol. liq. (members') 2 July 1951. Final meeting return regd. 9 June 1952...... **1938**

Pattison's Ld. Regd. Edinburgh 1896. Vol. liq. Jan. 1899. Court Order to dissolve 3 Nov. 1902 .... **1900**

Paul (Gavin) & Sons Ld. Regd. Edinburgh 1898. Vol. liq. June 1922. Reconstructed as company of same name. Final meeting return regd. 12 July 1924 .... **1923**

Paul (Kegan), Trench, Trubner and Co. Ld. Regd. 1889. Vol. liq. (members') 11 Dec. 1947. Undertaking acquired by George Routledge & Sons Ld. (name since changed to Routledge & Kegan Paul Ld.). Capital returned to contributories (other than the aforementioned company) 10s. per preference or ordinary share of £1. Holders of debentures were given the right to exchange, all or part of their holdings for an equal amount of 4% debentures of Routledge & Kegan Paul Ld., any debentures not thus exchanged being repaid in cash at par on 31 Dec. 1947. £1,034 10s. was paid into Companies' Liquidation Account. Final meeting return regd. 31 Mar. 1949 ...... **1950**

Paulista Railway Co. *See* Companhia Paulista de Estrados de Ferro.

Pavas Gold Mines Ld. Regd. 1902. Vol. liq. Sept. 1909 for reconstruction as Columbian Alluvial Mines Ld., in which company shareholders were entitled to 1 deferred share for each share of £1 held. Removed from Register 1911 ...... **1910**

Pavilion (Aylesbury) Ld. Regd. 1927. Undertaking acquired by London and District Cinemas Ld. Struck off Register 24 Dec. 1943 ...... **1945**

Pavilion, Newcastle-upon-Tyne Ld. Regd. 1903. Receiver for debenture holders appointed in May 1913; theatre sold on behalf of mortgagees. Struck off Register 31 Oct. 1916 ...... **1914**

Pavilion Theatre Ld. Regd 1894. Trustees for debenture holders took possession of property. Removed from Register 1913 ...... **1913**

Pay Rock Silver Mines Ld. Regd. 1890. Removed from Register 1897 ...... **1898**

Payette Alluvial Gold Co. Ld. Regd. 1897. Removed from Register 1901 ...... **1901**

Payta to Piura Railway (Peru) Ld. Regd. 1893. Vol. liq. 25 Mar. 1929. 99% of capital held by Peruvian Corporation Ld. Final meeting return regd 29 Apr. 1930 ...... **1930**

Peabody & Berkshire Gold Mines Ld. Regd 1896. Removed from Register 1910 ...... **1909**

Peacehaven Electric Light & Power Co. Ld. Regd. 1922. Dissolved 1 Apr. 1948, the undertaking being vested in the British (later Central) Electricity Authority and South-Eastern Area Board under the Electricity Act 1947. Holders of ordinary and 10% preference shares and 7% debentures were entitled to receive British Electricity 3% guaranteed stock (1968–73). as follows: 1d. stock for each ordinary share (of 1s.) held, £2 stock for each 10% preference share (of 12s.) held and £125 stock for every £100 of 7% debentures held **1949**

Peacehaven Estates Ld. Regd. 1924. Receiver appointed 13 Mar. 1931; ceased to act 11 Mar. 1938. Vol liq. (creditors') 23 Mar. 1931. Final meeting return regd 1 June 1938 ...... ***1932**

Peacehaven Water Co. Ld. Regd. 1922. Undertaking was transferred to Brighton Corporation and Newhaven & Seaford Water Co. (later Mid-Sussex Water Co. Ld.) jointly as from 25 Mar. 1950. A resolution was passed on 9 Sept. 1952 approving the arbitration award of £21.789 and placing the company in voluntary liquidation (creditors'). Capital returned to contributories—16s. 7½d. per preference share of £1. £1,348 1s. 2d. was paid into Companies' Liquidation Account. Final meeting return regd. 2 Feb. 1954 ...... **1955**

Peach & Co. Ld. Regd. 1884. Vol. liq. 14 Dec. 1884. Final meeting return regd. 16 Nov. 1898 ...... ***1897**

Peachey Leather Products Ld. *See* Rhinos Ld

Peachey Process Co. Ld. Regd. 1920. Vol. liq. (members') 20 May 1938. No capital returned to contributories. Final meeting return regd. 4 June 1956 ..... **1957**

Peacock Gold Syndicate Ld. Regd. Edinburgh 1895. Vol. liq. 16 Dec. 1897. Final meeting return regd. 23 Dec. 1898...... **1898**

Peacock's Stores Ld. *See* Swans Departmental Stores Ld.

Peak (George) & Co. Ld. Regd. 1886. In Jan. 1935 Hickson Lloyd & King Ld. offered to acquire shares as follows—£1 1s. per preference share of £1; £2 per fully-paid ordinary share of £10; 10s. per ordinary share of £10 (£6 paid). Vol. liq (members') 1 Apr. 1935. Final meeting return regd. 12 Feb. 1938...... **1936**

Peak Hill Goldfield Ld. Regd. 1897. Receiver appointed in June 1911. Struck off Register 1920 ...... **1912**

VOL. FOR

Pear New Mill (1919) Ld. Regd. 1919. Vol. liq. (members') Aug. 1929, the undertaking and assets were acquired by Combined Egyptian Mills Ld. (later Combined English Mills (Spinners) Ld.) in which company shareholders were entitled to receive 1 fully-paid ordinary share of £1 for every 2 shares of £1 (15s. paid) held. Struck off Register 7 Sept. 1948...... **1949**

Pearce, Reynolds, Withers & Co. Ld. Regd. 1904. Receiver for debenture holders appointed 14 June 1910. Struck off Register 1915 ...... **1911**

Pearks Dairies Ld. Regd. 1914. Vol. liq. 9 Mar. 1981. Final meeting return regd. 10 July 1981 ...... **1940**

Pearks, Gunston & Tee Ld. *See* Pearks Ld.

Pearks Ld. Regd. 1896 as Pearks, Gunston & Tee Ld.; name changed July 1904. Vol. liq. 1 June 1915. Undertaking and assets acquired by Pearks Dairies Ld. in which company preference shareholders received 1 fully-paid preference share of 10s. for each preference share of £1 held; no return was made to ordinary shareholders. Final meeting return regd. 10 Jan. 1916 ...... **1916**

Pearks' Stores (Africa) Ld. Regd. 1902. Vol. liq. June 1910. The undertaking and assets were acquired by United Africa Trading Co. Ld., in which company shareholders were entitled to 1 preferred ordinary share of 5s. and 1 deferred share of 1s. for each share of £1 held. Removed from Register 1911 ...... **1911**

Pearl Automatic Machines Ld. Regd. 1928. Vol. liq. (creditors') 2 Dec. 1930. No capital returned to contributories. Final meeting return regd. 30 Jan. 1933...... **1931**

Pearl Trading and Investment Co. Ld. Regd. 1905 as East African Pearl & Sponge Co. Ld.; name changed Jan. 1909 to East African Pearl Co. Ld. and as above in Feb. 1922. Vol. liq. 1 Apr. 1927. Final meeting return regd. 26 Sept. 1929 ...... **1912**

Pearling & Trading Co. Ld. Regd. 1889. Vol. liq. 25 Nov. 1895. Final meeting return regd. 31 July 1896 **1896**

Pearson and Foster (Bradford) Ld. Regd. as private company 21 Apr. 1922; converted into public company 3 Feb. 1948. Winding-up order made 22 Mar. 1971; dissolved and struck off Register 3 Sept. 1982. First and fianl dividend of 15·69p in £ declared on 10 May 1979 on 241 unsecured claims totalling £752,432·51 ...... **1984–5**

Pearson & Knowles Coal & Iron Co. Ld. Regd. 1874. Vol. liq. (members') 16 Apr. 1953. Capital returned to contributories—7s. 6·195d. per ordinary share of 1s. £6,531 9s. was paid into Companies' Liquidation Account. Final meeting return regd. 17 July 1956 **1957**

Pearson Automatic Fire Indicator Co. Ld. Regd. 1895. Vol. liq. 9 Dec. 1898. Amalgamated with Pearson Fire Alarm Systems Ld. Final meeting return regd. 19 Jan. 1900 ...... **1900**

Pearson Fire Alarm Ld. Regd. 1903. Vol. liq. Apr. 1911. Reconstructed as Associated Fire Alarms Ld., in which company shareholders were entitled to 1 ordinary share of 5s. (credited with 4s. paid) for each share of £1 held. Debenture stockholders were entitled to fully-paid preference shares of £1. Struck off Register 1914 ...... **1912**

Pearson Fire Alarm Syndicate (Railways, Docks & Shipping) Ld. Regd. 1901. Removed from Register 1911 ...... **1906**

Pearson Fire Alarm System Ld. Regd 1898. Vol. liq. Feb. 1903. Reconstructed as Pearson Fire Alarm Ld., in which company shareholders were entitled to 1 share of £1 (credited with 7s. 6d. paid) for each share of £1 held. Removed from Register 1905 ... **1903**

Pearson, Huggins & Co. (1911) Ld. Regd. 1911. Court Order to wind up 13 Jan. 1914. Struck off Register 1919...... **1914**

Pearson (S.) & Son (Contracting Department) Ld. Regd. 1919. Vol liq. (members') 28 Feb. 1941. Capital returned to contributories—£1,003,110 13s. 11d. Final meeting return regd. 18 July 1941 ...... **1942**

Pease and Partners Ld. Regd. 1955. Vol. liq. (members') 20 Aug. 1959. Capital returned to contributories—10·295d. per share (of 1s.) £801 18s 4d. paid into Companies' Liquidation Account. Final meeting return regd. 4 July 1962 ...... **1963**

Pease & Partners Ld. *See below.*

Pease & Partners Normanby Iron Works Co. Ld. *See* Normanby Iron Works Co. Ld.

Pease Realisation Co. Ld. Regd. 1898 as Pease & Partners Ld.; name changed Sept. 1955. Vol. liq. (members') 21 Dec. 1955. Capital returned to contributories—3s. 0·2726d. per share of 1s. £2,702 16s. 9d was paid into Companies' Liquidation Account. Final meeting return regd. 2 Mar 1957 **1958**

Peat-Coke & Oil Syndicate Ld. Regd 1912. Vol. liq. 23 Dec. 1918 for reconstruction as Coal Peat & Oil Ld. Final meeting return regd. 5 Dec. 1921...... ***1919**

*See Stock Exchange Year-Book.

VOL. FOR

entitled to 1 share of 1s. (credited as fully-paid) for each share of 5s. held **1935**

Pencisely Steamship Co. Ld. Regd. 1919. Mortgagees took possession of the vessels. Struck off Register Feb. 1935 .... **1935**

Pencoed Motors Co. Ld. Regd. 1933. Vol. liq. (members') 31 Dec. 1940. Capital returned to contributories—10s. 9¾d. per share of £1. Final meeting return regd. 10 Sept. 1941 .... **1941**

Pendinnie Gold Mines Ld. Regd. 1900. Removed from Register 1904 .... **1904**

Penegarreg Silver Lead Mining Co. Ld. Regd. 1881. Removed from Register 1906 .... **1895**

Peneiro Rubber Estates Ld. Regd. 1910. Vol. liq. 15 Jan. 1919. Final meeting return regd. 21 July 1919 ..... **1919**

Penge Empire Theatre Ld. Regd. 1913. Vol. liq. 29 Mar. 1928. Subsidiary of London Theatres of Varieties Ld. Final meeting return regd. 21 Dec. 1928 ...... **1929**

Penggoong Java Syndicate Ld. Regd. 1909. Vol. liq. 2 Feb. 1920. Final meeting return regd. 9 Nov. 1920 ***1921**

Penhale & Barton United Mines Ld. Regd. Truro 1881. Court Orders; to wind up 19 Jan. 1882; to dissolve 14 Feb. 1883 .... **1883**

Penhalonga Gold Mining Co. Ld. Regd. 1893. Property sold to Penhalonga Proprietary Mines Ld., in which company shareholders were entitled to 1 share of £1 (credited as fully-paid) for each share held. Removed from Register 1901 .... **1900**

Penhalonga Mines Ld. Regd. 1910. Vol. liq. Apr. 1912. Property and assets were sold to Rezende Mines Ld., in which company shareholders were entitled to 1 share of £1 (credited as fully-paid) for every 6 shares of £1 held plus 5s. 6d. per share in cash. Struck off Register 1914 .... **1913**

Penhalonga Proprietary Mines Ld. Regd. 1898. Vol. liq. 14 Oct. 1910. Reconstructed as Penhalonga Mines Ld., in which company shareholders were entitled to 1 share of £1 (credited as fully-paid) for every 20 shares of £1 held; debenture certificate holders were entitled to 1 fully-paid share of £1 for every £3 held. Final meeting return regd. 12 Dec. 1911 .... **1911**

Penhalonga West (Rhodesia) Ld. Regd. 1809. Vol. liq. (members') 30 Sept. 1932. Undertaking and assets acquired by Tano Consolidated Mines Ld in which company shareholders were entitled to 10 shares of 2s. 6d. (credited with 2s. paid) for each share of £1 held. Final meeting return regd. 25 June 1934 ..... **1933**

Penicuik & District Gas Co. Ld. Regd. in Edinburgh 1877. Dissolved 1 May 1949, undertaking being vested in Scottish Area Gas Board under Gas Act 1948. Holders of ordinary shares (of 10s.) wer entitled to receive £1 13s. 4d. British Gas 3% guaranteed stock 1990–95 for each share held **1952**

Peninsular Co. Ld. Regd. 1863. Vol. liq. July 1908. Removed from Register 1909 .... **1909**

Peninsular Copper Co. Ld. Regd. 1882. Vol. liq. 10 Nov. 1888. Removed from Register 1906 .... **1889**

Peninsular Investment Co. Ld. Regd. 1925 as Peninsular Rubber Estates Ld.; name changed 4 Feb. 1955. In Apr. 1968 the undertaking was transferred to Union Commercial Investment Co. Ld. in which company share and stockholders were entitled to receive fully-paid capital as follows—6% ordinary shares of 5s. for every 7 shares of 5s. and a like amount of 3% debenture stock 1983 in exchange for 5% debenture stock 1985–88. Company is to be dissolved under Section 208 of the Companies Act 1948 .... **1970**

Peninsular Rubber Estates Ld. See above.

Penistone & District Gas Co. Inc. by Special Act 1858. Dissolved 1 May 1949, undertaking being vested in East Midland Area Gas Board under Gas Act 1948. Holders of securities were entitled to receive British Gas 3% guaranteed stock 1990–95 as follows:

	£	s.	d.	
Orig. shares (10% max.) (of £20).....	41	10	0	
4¾% red. pref. shares (of £1)..........	1	0	2	**1952**

Penjom Pahang Gold Co. Ld. Regd. 1890. Vol. liq. 30 Dec. 1892. Final meeting return regd. 13 May 1898 **1893**

Penketh Tanning Co. Ld. Regd. 1899. Vol. liq. (members') 25 June 1958. Capital returned to contributories—per preference share of £1: £1; per ordinary share of 5s.: 12s. 10¼d. Final meeting return regd. 16 Feb. 1962 .... **1963**

Penllwyn Railway Co. Inc. by Special Act 1906. Act of 1920 provided for the winding up and dissolution of the company **1921**

Penmark Shipping Co. Ld. Regd. 1919. Vol. liq. 12 Sept. 1922. Final meeting return regd. 9 July 1924 .... ***1923**

Penmon Quarries Ld. Regd. 1886. Vol. liq. 25 June 1890. Final meeting return regd. 15 May 1891 .... **1901**

Penn-Wyoming Copper Co. Inc. Wyoming 1904. Circular issued in Feb. 1909 stated properties had been sold to United Smelters, Railway & Copper Co. Shareholders were entitled to exchange their shares

---

VOL. FOR

($1) at par for common stock, subject to their subscribing for $1·20 of 6% bonds in United Co. in respect of every 10 shares held **1910**

Pennant Shipping Co. Ld. Regd. 9 July 1919. Vol. liq. (creditors') 1 Sept. 1924. No capital returned to contributories. Final meeting return regd. 4 Mar. 1957. Struck off Register 24 Sept. 1957 .... **1958**

Penny-in-the-Slot Electric Supply Synd. Ld. See Bastian Meter Co. Ld.

Penryn Gas Co. Ld. Regd. 1892. Dissolved 1 May 1949, undertaking being vested in South Western Area Gas Board under Gas Act 1948. Holders of securities were entitled to receive British Gas 3% guaranteed stock 1990–95 as follows:

	£	s.	d.	
Ord. shares (10% max.) (of £5).......	2	10	0	
6% debs. (of £100)..........	100	0	0	**1952**

Penshaw Collieries Ld. Inc. Cape of Good Hope 1896 **1907**

Pensilva Tin Mines Ld. Regd. 1910. Struck off Register 1921 .... **1911**

Pentalta Exploration Co. Ld. Regd. 1895. Court Order to wind up 30 Nov. 1898. Removed from Register 1908 .... **1899**

Pentremawr Colliery Co. Ld. Regd. 1927. All shares owned by Amalgamated Anthracite Collieries Ld. Struck off Register 10 Mar. 1939 .... **1939**

Pentwyn Black Vein Collieries Co. Ld. Regd. 1912. Receiver for debenture holders appointed in June 1914. Struck off Register 1923 .... **1916**

Pentwyn Isha Land & Building Co. Ld. Regd. 1902. Vol. liq. (members') 28 Sept. 1933. Capital returned to contributories—£750. Final meeting return regd. 28 Feb. 1934 .... **1935**

Pen-y-bryn Halkyn Lead Mine Ld. Regd. 1895. Struck off Register 16 Nov. 1906 .... **1907**

Penzance & District Electric Supply Co. Ld. Regd. 1903. Vol. liq. (members') 24 Jan. 1938. Capital returned to contributories—£49,797 1s. 4d. Final meeting return regd. 12 May 1938 .... **1938**

Penzance Gas Co. Ld. Estd. 1830; regd. 1896; statutory powers 1937. Dissolved 1 May 1949. undertaking being vested in South Western Area Gas Board under Gas Act 1948. Holders of ordinary shares (5% basic—of £1) were entitled to receive £1 4s. British Gas 3% guaranteed stock 1990–95 for each share held **1952**

Penzance, Newlyn & West Cornwall Light Railway Co. Inc. (under Light Railway Act 1896) by order of Light Railway Commissioners and confirmed by Board of Trade 1899 .... **1902**

Peoples' Bank of Scotland Ld. See Mercantile Bank of Scotland.

People's Bread Co. Ld. Regd. 1888. Removed from Register 1903 .... **1890**

People's Café Co. Ld. Regd. 1874. Removed from Register 1904 .... **1897**

People's Gas Light & Coke Co. of Chicago. Est. Chicago 1855. The outstanding sterling 1st & 2nd mortgage 6% gold bonds were redeemed at par on 1 Nov. & 1 Dec. 1904 .... **1904**

Peoples's Land, Building & Dwellings Co. Ld. Regd. 1887. Vol. liq. (members') 10 Nov. 1949. Capital returned to contributories—£2 10s. 1·843d. per share of £1. £98 4s. 9d. was paid into Companies' Liquidation Account. Final meeting return regd. 31 Aug. 1951 .... **1952**

People's Loan & Deposit Co. Inc. under Consolidated Statutes of Upper Canada 1875. Company's debenture business in this country ceased in 1898.......... **1899**

People's Publishing Co. Ld. Regd. 1922. Court Order to wind up Mar. 1926. Assets sold to Long Acre Press Ld. Struck off Register Mar. 1932 .... **1933**

People's Refreshment House Association, Ld. Regd. 1896. All capital was owned by Charrington & Co. Ld. Vol. liq. (members') 4 Aug. 1965. Final meeting return regd. 18 Nov. 1965 .... **1962**

People's Trust Co. Ld. Regd. 1914. Vol. liq 3 Apr. 1924. Shareholders and debenture holders were repaid in full plus 8½% on their holdings. Final meeting return regd. 22 Jan. 1925 .... **1925**

Pepper (John) & Co. Ld. Regd. 1882. Vol. liq. 26 Mar. 1891. Final meeting return regd. 3 Dec. 1891 ...... ***1885**

Peppercorn Brothers (1913) Ld. Regd. 1913. Court Order to wind up 13 Oct. 1914. Liquidator released 20 Feb. 1920. Struck off Register 20 Mar. 1925 ... **1915**

Peradin Ld. Regd. 1932 as Peradin Rubber & Finance Ld.; name changed Oct. 1953. Vol. liq. (members') 22 May 1951. No capital returned to contributories. Final meeting return regd. 13 Nov. 1954 .... **1956**

Peradin Rubber & Finance Ld. See above.

Perambulata Ld. See Birmingham & Manufacturing Co. Ld.

Perdio Electronics Ld. Regd. 20 Jan. 1956 as Perdio Ld.; name changed 15 June 1962. Winding up order 25

VOL. FOR

Oct. 1965. No capital returned to contributories. Liquidator released 13 Apr. 1971. Struck off Register 4 May 1973 1971

Perfect Automatic Hot Appliance Co. Ld. Regd. 1899. Removed from Register 1910 1908

Perfecta Seamless Steel Tube Co. Ld. Regd. 1896. Vol. liq. 23 Mar. 1905. Removed from Register 1907 . 1906

Perfetti Nitrate Co. Inc. Chile 1916. 7% 1st mortgage debentures known here were purchased at 98% by British Bank for Foreign Trade Ld. which surrendered debentures to company on payment of an agreed sum 1929

Perfumers' Prichard & Constance Ld. See Prichard & Constance, Ld.

Pergamon Press Ld. Regd. 21 Apr. 1949 as Butterworth-Springer Ld.; name changed 17 July 1951. All acquired by Microforms International Marketing Corpn. 1974; winding-up order 24 Mar. 1986 1974–5

Perham Investment Trust Ld. Regd. 1937. Under scheme of amalgamation effective from 29 June 1960 the capital was increased to £700,000 (by a capitalised distribution of 1 fully-paid share for every 6 held) and all shares were exchanged for a like amount of ordinary stock of The Nineteen Twenty-Eight Investment Trust Ld. Company was dissolved on 29 Oct. 1960 under section 208 of the Companies Act, 1948 1961

Perivale Fur Dyeing Co. Ld. Regd. 1930. Receiver appointed 19 May 1937; ceased to act 12 Jan. 1939. Struck off Register 26 Sept. 1939 1940

Perkins (Joshua) & Sons (1909) Ld. Regd. 1909. Vol. liq. (members') 17 Oct. 1933. Capital returned to contributories—20s. per preference share of £1; £1 3s. 7¾d. per ordinary share of £1. Final meeting return regd. 21 Aug. 1934 1934

Perm Corporation Ld. Regd. 1907. Vol. liq. Jan. 1911. Removed from Register 1911 1911

Permanent Hard Tennis Court Co. Ld. Regd. 1922. Vol. liq. (members') 12 Oct. 1932. All shares owned by En-Tout-Cas Co. (Syston) Ld. (later En-Tout-Cas Co. Ld.). Final meeting return regd. 5 Jan. 1933.. 1933

Permanent Reproductions Ld. Regd. 1928. Court Order to wind up 14 Oct. 1930. Struck off Register 15 Oct. 1935 1936

Permas Rubber Co. Ld. Regd. 1910. Undertaking and assets acquired by Bradwall (F.M.S.) Rubber Estate Ld., in which company shareholders were entitled to receive 5 fully-paid shares of 2s. each plus 6d. cash for each share of £1 held. £21 10s. was paid into Companies' Liquidation Account. Final meeting return regd. 8 Feb. 1956 1957

Permatang (Malaya) Rubber Estates Ld. Regd. 1925. Assets were sold for shares and debenture stock in Merlimau Pegoh Ld., which were distributed among debenture stockholders. Struck off Register Jan. 1934 1934

Permoglaze Holdings Ld. Regd. 1950 as Glazebrooks (Holdings) Ld., name changed 3 Nov. 1953. All capital was owned by Blundell Spence & Co. Ld. (later Blundell-Permoglaze Holdings Ld.). Vol. liq. (members') 29 Mar. 1961. Final meeting return regd. 21 Sept. 1961 1961

Pernambang Rubber Estates Ld. Regd. 1920. Vol. liq. (members') 29 Dec. 1932. Undertaking and assets were acquired by Pataling Rubber Estates Ld., in which company shareholders were entitled to 2 shares of £1 (credited as fully-paid) for every 5 shares of £1 held. Final meeting return regd. 31 Aug. 1933 1933

Pemambuco Water Co. By public deed of 11 Oct. 1912 Government of State of Pernambuco took over the undertaking and assumed the 1st and 2nd debenture sterling bonds 1922

Peirrin (E. H.) & Co. Ld. Regd. 1920. Vol. liq. (members') 2 May 1931. Capital returned to contributories—£33,822 10s. 10d. Final meeting return regd. 25 June 1934 1932

Perrins Ld. Regd. 1900. Vol. liq. 2 Oct. 1908. Final meeting return regd. 21 Oct. 1916 1909

Perry & Co. Ld. Regd. 1876. Vol. liq. 13 May 1897. Reconstructed as company of same name, [later Perry & Co. (Holdings) Ld., later Perry Engineering Ld.] Shareholders were entitled to 12 fully-paid A preference shares of £1 for each preference share of £10 held; 25 fully-paid ordinary and 15 fully-paid B preference shares of £1 for each ordinary share of £10 held. Final meeting return regd. 25 Feb. 1904 1897

Perry Engineering Ld. Regd. as Perry & Co. Ld., name changed to Perry & Co. (Holdings) Ld. 1945 and to *above* 1959. Vol. liq. (members') 5 Feb. 1965. Final meeting return regd. 2 Apr. 1965 1960

Perseverance Gold Co. Ld. Regd. 1891. Removed from Register 1907 1894

VOL. FOR

Perseverance Gold Mines Ld. Regd. 1902. Reconstructed 1905 as Esperanza Westralia Ld., in which company shareholders were entitled to 1 share of 1s. 6d. (credited with 1d. paid) for each share of 10s. held. Removed from Register 1910 1908

Perseverance Gold Mining Co. Ld. Regd. 1888. Reconstructed 1891 as Perseverance Gold Co. Ld., in which company shareholders were entitled to 1 share of £1 (credited with 18s. paid) for each share of £1 held. Removed from Register 1903 1893

Perseverance Home Assurance Co. Ld. Regd. 1898. Court Order to wind up 9 May 1904. Struck off Register 14 Feb. 1919 .... *1905

Perseverance Rewarded Gold Mine (N.S.W.) Ld. Regd. 1896. Removed from Register 1909 1899

Persian Bank Mining Rights Corporation Ld. Regd. 1890. Removed from Register 1901 1894

Persian Investment Corporation Ld. Regd. 1889. Vol. liq. 20 Oct. 1890. Court Order to wind up under supervision Nov. 1890. Final meeting return regd. 11 Oct. 1893 1891

Persil Flexible Wheel Tyre Syndicate Ld. Regd. 1892. Vol. liq. 15 May 1894. Struck off Register 7 Aug. 1945 1895

Perspectus Glare Screen Co. Ld. Undertaking and certain assets were acquired by Anti-Dazzle Screens Ld. for 300,000 fully-paid shares of 1s. 1929

Persse (H. S.) Ld. Regd. Dublin 1896. Court Order to wind up 21 Nov. 1906. Removed from Register 1913 1907

Perth & District Tramways Co. Ld. Regd. Edinburgh 1891. Undertaking sold to Perth Corporation. Capital returned to contributories—21s. in the £; further payments (if any) not known. Vol. liq. Mar. 1904. Final meeting return regd. 19 Aug. 1904 1905

Perth & London Explorers Ld. Regd. 1896. Removed from Register 1901 1899

Perth Electric Tramways Ld. Regd. 1898 as Perth Tramways Ld. name changed July 1890. Vol. liq. 1 Aug. 1913. The undertaking was sold to Western Australian Government. The debenture stock was repaid on 30 June 1913 at 107¼% and the debentures at 102½%. Capital returned to contributories—£1 7s. 6d. per preference or ordinary share of £1 at Jan. 1914; further payments (if any) not known. Final meeting return regd. 28 Oct. 1914 1914

Perth Mining & Trading Syndicate of Western Australia Ld. Regd. 1896. In vol. liq. in 1899. Removed from Register 1903 1899

Perth Tramways Ld. See Perth Electric Tramways Ld.

Perthpoint Investments Ld. Regd. in Edinburgh 1911 as Bruas-Perak Rubber Estate Ld.; name changed 1959. Vol. liq. (members') 23 July 1968. Capital returned to contributories—2s. 9·947d. per share of 1s. plus income distribution of 1·2629d. per share gross. £230·38 was paid to Companies' Liquidation Account in respect of unclaimed dividends and £896·33 in respect of unclaimed distributions. Final meeting return regd. 13 Sept. 1971 1972

Peru Mines & Estates Ld. Regd. 1909. Vol. liq. 28 Apr. 1916. Final meeting return regd. 17 Mar. 1917 1916

Peru Syndicate Ld. Regd. 1919. Struck off Register 1 May 1943 1943

Peruvian Amazon Co. Ld. Regd. 1907 as Peruvian Amazon Rubber Co. Ld.; name changed 1908. Court Order to wind up 19 Mar. 1913. Struck off Register 1927 1914

Peruvian Consolidated Gold Trust Ld. Regd. 1911 as Patag & Parcoy Syndicate Ld.; name changed Dec. 1912. Struck off Register Apr. 1930 1931

Peruvian Cotton Manufacturing Co. Ld. Regd. 1890. Vol. liq. 31 Mar. 1897. Reconstructed as company of same name. Shareholders were entitled to 5 shares of £1 (credited as fully-paid) in new company for each preference share of £5 held, or 16 fully-paid shares of £1 for each ordinary share of £1 held. Final meeting return regd. 27 Jan. 1899.............................. 1908

Peruvian Cotton Manufacturing Co. Ld. Regd. 1897. Vol. liq. 15 Mar. 1917. A return of £1 10s. per share of £1 was anticipated. Final meeting return regd. 22 Oct. 1917 1917

Peruvian Guano Co. Ld. Regd. 1876. Vol. liq. 21 May 1883. Final meeting return regd. 18 Jan. 1895 1884

Peruvian Investment & Finance Ld. Inc. Canada 1955 as Peruvian Transport Corpn. Ld.; name changed June 1958. During 1972–4 all assets in Peru and Bolivia were sold by auction to the respective governments. The proceeds were insufficient to provide any repayments.. 1974-5

Peruvian Mining Trust Ld. Regd. 1912. Vol. liq. 16 June 1915. Undertaking and assets were acquired by Anglo-French Ticapampa Silver Mining Co. Ld., in which company shareholders were entitled to 1 share of £1 (credited as fully-paid) for every 5 shares of £1 held. Final meeting return regd. 1 Feb. 1918   1916

*See Stock Exchange Year-Book.

VOL. FOR

Peruvian Railway Construction Co. Ld. Regd. 1906. Vol. liq. 15 July 1914. No capital returned contributories. Final meeting return regd. 10 Sept. 1924 .... **1915**

Peruvian Transport Corpn. Ld. *See* Peruvian Investment & Finance Ld.

Pestarena Mining Co. Ld. Regd. 1899. Removed from Register 1904 .... **1902**

Pestarena United Gold Mining Co. Ld. Regd. 1867. Removed from Register 1904 .... **1901**

Peterborough Electric Traction Co. Ld. Regd. 1902. Vol. liq. (members') 5 Nov. 1931. Undertaking and assets were acquired by Eastern Counties Omnibus Co. Ld in which company shareholders were entitled to 1 share of £1 (credited as fully-paid) for each ordinary or preference share of £1 held. The outstanding 4½% 1st mortgage debenture stock was redeemed at 105% in Mar. 1931. Final meeting return regd. 4 Aug. 1932 .... **1932**

Peterborough Gas Co. Inc. by Special Act 1868. Dissolved 1 May 1949. undertaking being vested in Eastern Area Gas Board under Gas Act 1948. Holders of securities were entitled to receive British Gas 3% guaranteed stock 1990–95 as follows in respect of each £100 unit, unless otherwise stated, of security held:

	£	s.	d.
Cons. ord. stock (7% stand.)	156	0	0
New A 5% pref. shares (of £10)...	11	9	8
3¾% red. pref. stock....................	100	1	8
4% irred. deb. stock (issued before 1 Jan. 1946)...........................	101	0	0
4% irred. deb. stock (issued since 31 Dec. 1945)..........................	100	17	7
3½% red. deb. stock	100	0	0
to	101	0	0†

†More than 1 value applies by reference to Sect. 25 (8) of the Act. **1952**

Peterhead Trawling Co. Ld. Regd. Edinburgh 1898. Vol. liq. July 1927. Capital returned to contributories—4*s*. per share of 10*s*. in Oct. 1927; further payments (if any) not known. Final meeting return regd. 5 July 1928 .... **1928**

Peters' (Dr. Carl) Estates & Exploration Co. Ld. *See* South East Africa Ld.

Petersburg & Viborg Gas Co. Ld. Regd. 1871. Vol. liq. 5 Oct. 1875. Final meeting return regd. 4 May 1877 ***1876**

Petersburgh Syndicate Ld. Regd, 1907. Vol. liq. May 1912. Removed from Register 1912 .... **1913**

Petersen's Water-Tube Boiler Co. Ld. Regd. 1896. Removed from Register 1906 .... **1901**

Petersfield & Selsey Gas Co. Inc. by Special Act 1901. Dissolved 1 May 1949, undertaking being vested in Southern Area Gas Board under Gas Act 1948. Holders of securities were entitled to receive British Gas 3% guaranteed stock 1990–95 as follows in respect of each £5 unit, unless otherwise stated, of security held:

	£	s.	d.
Ord. shares (7% stand.)..................		10	0
5% pref. shares............................	2	0	0
6½% red. pref. shares	2	10	0
5½% red. deb. stock (per £100)	104	0	0
5% irred. deb. stock (per £100)	123	10	0
4% irred. deb. stock (per £100)	100	0	0

1952

Petersfield Electric Light & Power Co. Ld. Regd. 1923. Dissolved 1 Apr. 1948, undertaking being vested in the British (later Central) Electricity Authority and Southern Area Board under the Electricity Act 1947. Holders of ordinary and preference shares were entitled to receive British Electricity 3% guaranteed stock (1968–73). as follows—£2 10*s*. stock for every ordinary share (of £1) held and £1 10*s*. for every preference share (of £1) held **1949**

Petolite & Other Patent Fuel Co. Ld. Regd. 1902. Removed from Register 1905 .... **1903**

Petoong Java Rubber Estates, Ld. Regd. 1910. Vol. liq. (members') 31 Dec. 1951. Capital returned to contributories—1*s*. 11*d*. per 1*s*. 6*d*. stock. £1,908 4*s*. 5*d*. paid into Companies' Liquidation Account. Final meeting return regd. 6 Oct. 1954 .... **1955**

Petrifite Ld. Regd. 1897. Properties, works and business were acquired in 1902 by Anglo-Greek Magnesite Co. Ld. for £49,000 in shares; £40,000 were to be used in repayment of 6% debentures and the remainder in satisfaction of moneys advanced. Removed from Register 7 May 1907 .... **1904**

Petrol Users Society Ld. Undertaking and assets were acquired in 1921 by British Petrol and Motor Equipment Co. Ld. for 80,599 fully-paid shares of £1 and discharge of liabilities **1929**

Petroleum Co. of Ildokani Ld. Regd. 1914. Vol. liq. 28 Apr. 1920. Final meeting return regd. 12 May 1933 **1921**

Petroleum Co. of Roumania Ld. Regd. 1904. Struck off Register 1916 .... **1915**

VOL. FOR

Petroleum Conversion Corpn. Inc. in Delaware in 1926. In Aug. 1950 the trustee in bankruptcy stated that the corporation's "affairs will probably be terminated by the end of 1950." All assets realised; no moneys available for distribution to shareholders **1915**

Petroleum Development Co, Ld. Regd. 1907. Struck off Register 1916 .... **1915**

Petroleum Engine Co. Ld. Regd. 1888. Vol. liq. 26 Feb. 1907. Final meeting return regd. 9 Dec. 1907 ...... **1908**

Petroleum Oil Trust Ld. Regd. 1891. Vol. liq 21 Oct. 1904. Struck off Register 3 Sept. 1918 .... **1905**

Petroleum Options Ld. Regd. 1908. Vol. liq. 15 May 1925. Reconstructed as Petroleum Options (1925) Ld. in which company shareholders were entitled to 2 fully-paid shares of 1*s*. and 4 shares of 1*s*. (credited with 9*d*. paid) for each preference share of 5*s*. held or 4 shares of 1*s*. (credited with 9*d*. paid) for every 3 ordinary shares of 1*s*. held. Final meeting return regd. 11 Dec. 1928............ **1926**

Petroleum Power Investment Corpn., Ld. *See* Power Investment Corporation Ld.

Petroleum Refineries Ld. Regd. 1929. Court Order to wind up Oct. 1931. Struck off Register 20 Mar. 1936 **1937**

Petroleum Securities & General Trust Ld. Regd 1914. Vol. liq. Jan. 1916. Struck off Register 1922 .... **1916**

Petroleum Solid Fuel (Parent) Co. Ld. Regd. 1911. Receiver for debenture holders appointed in Sept. 1917. Struck off Register 1922 .... **1922**

Petrolite (1908) Ld. Regd. 1908. It was stated in 1915 that company had never carried on business. Struck off Register 31 Oct. 1916 .... ***1909**

Petrotim Securities, Ld. Regd. 1925 as Gresham Trust Ld.; name changed Mar. 1959 and undertaking and assets were transferred to Gresham Ld. for £221,504. All capital was indirectly owned by Ridge Securities Ld. Vol. liq. 5 Apr. 1966. Dissolved 10 Feb. 1978 .... **1960**

Petters (Ipswich) Ld. Regd. 1919 as Vickers-Petters Ld.; name changed 7 Feb. 1927. Vol. liq. (creditors') 26 Jan. 1933. All shares and debentures owned by Petters Ld. (later Associated British Engineering Ld.). Final meeting return regd. 7 June 1938 .... **1938**

Pettigrew & Merriman (Continental) Ld. Regd. 1924. Vol. liq. (members') 16 July 1932. All capital was owned by Pettigrew & Merriman (1925) Ld. Capital returned to contributories—£5,775. Final meeting return regd. 2 Sept. 1933 .... **1932**

Pettigrew & Merriman Ld. Undertaking and assets were acquired in 1925 by Pettigrew & Merriman (1925) Ld. **1926**

Pettigrew & Merriman (1925) Ld. Regd. 1925. Vol. liq. (members') 18 Dec. 1931. Capital returned to preference shareholders—£43,422 6*s*. 10*d*. £183 4*s*. 4*d*. was paid into Companies' Liquidation Account. Final meeting return regd.6 Oct. 1934............ **1932**

Pettigrew & Stephens Ld. Regd. in Edinburgh 1904. Vol. liq. (members') 1 June 1955. All ordinary capital was owned by House of Fraser Ld, Capital returned to contributories—20*s*. per preference share of £1 and 20*s*. plus ex gratia payment of 4*s*. per A preference share of £1; all remaining assets were transferred to House of Fraser Ld. £67 17*s*. 3*d*. paid into Companies' Liquidation Account in respect of unclaimed dividends and £89 18*s*. 9*d*. in respect of distributions. Final meeting return regd. 15 Mar. 1965 .... **1966**

Petzold and Co., Engineers, Ld. Regd. 1890 as Petzold and Co. Ld.; name changed Apr. 1891. Vol. liq. 20 July 1897. Final meeting return regd. 31 Jan. 1898 **1898**

Petzold and Co. Ld. *See* Petzold and Co., Engineers, Ld.

Peureula (Sumatra) Rubber Estates Ld. Regd. 1925. Vol. liq. (members') July 1932. Undertaking and assets acquired by company of same name (later Peureula Investments Ld.). Shareholders were entitled to receive 1 share of 2*s*. (credited with 1*s*. 10½*d* paid) for each 2*s*. share held. Struck off Register 11 Feb. 1949 .... **1950**

Peveril Gold Mines Ld. Regd. 1895. Court Order to wind up 19 Jan. 1898. Removed from Register 1908 .... **1898**

Peveril Hotel Co. Ld. Inc. Isle of Man 1876. Vol. liq. 29 Mar. 1967. Creditors received 2*s*. 1½*d*. in the £1. No capital returned to contributories. Final meeting return regd. 28 Nov. 1967 .... **1969**

Pewsey & Salisbury Railway Co. Inc. by Special Act 1883. Undertaking abandoned by Act of 1891 ...... **1892**

Pfeiffer's Day Dawn Gold Mines Ld. Inc. Queensland 1906. Wound up in 1912 for purpose of reconstruction into Pfeiffer's Gold Mines Ld., in which company preference shareholders were entitled to 1 preference share of £1 for each preference share of £1 held, and ordinary and preference shareholders to a pro rata distribution of 50,000 ordinary shares of £1. A further 100,000 ordinary shares of £1 (credited with 10*s*. paid up) were offered to ordinary

**See Stock Exchange Year-Book.*

VOL. FOR

shareholders (1 for every 4 held) *plus* the right to a further pro rata distribution of 50,000 ordinary shares 1913

Pfleumatic (1910) Ld. Regd. 1910. Vol. liq. Nov. 1912 for reconstruction as Pfleumatic (1912) Ld., in which company shareholders were entitled to 1 share of 5s. (credited with 4s. paid) for each share of £1 held. Removed from Register 1913 1913

Pfleumatic (1912) Ld. Regd. 1912. Vol. liq. 30 Sept. 1918. Final meeting return regd. 4 Dec. 1918 1919

Phantestra (Renn's Gramophone & Wireless) Ld. Regd. 1928. Court Order to wind up May 1930. Struck off Register 18 Feb. 1938 1939

Phantom Orchestras Ld. Undertaking and assets were acquired in 1928 by Phantestra (Renn's Gramophone & Wireless) Ld. 1929

Pharmaceutical Products Ld. Regd. 1933. Vol. liq. (members') 1 Apr. 1946. Undertaking was acquired by Savory & Moore Ld. Capital returned to contributories—approximately £1 2s. per share of £1. £135 was paid into Companies' Liquidation Account. Final meeting return regd. 18 Dec. 1946 1947

Philadelphia & Eire Railroad. The line was acquired in 1907 by Pennsylvania Railroad Co. 1920

Philadelphia & Reading Railway Co. Organised Pennsylvania 1896. All capital stock was held by Reading Co., which company acquired undertaking in 1924. The 5% prior mortgage loan, 4% improvement mortgage loan, 4% consolidated 1st mortgage loan and 5% debenture loan of Philadelphia & Reading *Railroad* were taken over by acquiring company . 1924

Philadelphia, Baltimore & Washington Railroad Co. Inc. Pennsylvania. Delaware & Maryland 1902. The outstanding gold 6% 1st mortgage tunnel and main line bonds of Baltimore & Potomac Railroad were redeemed at par on 1 July & 1 Apr. 1911 1911

Philadelphia Co. Inc. in Pennsylvania 1871 as Empire Contract Co.; name changed in 1873 to Mexico National Railway Co., in 1875 to Commonwealth Contract Co. and in 1879 to Rio Grande Extension Co.; organised under above title 1884. In liquidation. Under provisions of plan for liquidation holders of publicly owned stock were entitled to receive stock of Duquesne Light Co. in exchange for their holdings at the following rates—1 share of 4% preferred stock of Duquesne and $13 cash for each share of 6% cumulative preferred stock; 3·6 shares of common stock of Duquesne for each share of 5% cumulative preference stock and dividends accrued thereon and $\frac{7}{200}$ part of a share of common stock of Duquesne for each share of common stock held .. 1954

Philadelphia Securities Co. Inc. in U.S.A. The outstanding sterling debentures were redeemed at 75% on 15 July 1903 1904

Philippines Minerals Syndicate Ld. Regd. 1892. Vol. liq. 20 May 1914. Struck off Register 30 Jan. 1923 1915

Phillimore (Charles) & Co. Ld. Regd. 1899. Court Order to wind up 29 June 1909. Liquidator released 14 Aug. 1913. Struck off Register 3 Sept. 1918 1910

Phillips (Albert) (Ireland) Ld. Inc. in Dublin 1925. Vol. liq. (members') 30 Dec. 1957. Capital returned to contributories—11s. 8d. per share of 5s. Final meeting return regd. 30 Apr. 1959 1960

Phillips & Marriott, Ld. Regd. 1900. Vol. liq. (members') 2 Dec. 1947. Certain assets have been distributed in specie. Final meeting return regd. 31 Aug. 1948 1949

Phillips and Sons, Ld. Regd. 1892. Vol. liq. (members') 31 May 1954, the undertaking being acquired by H. & G. Simonds Ld. Final meeting return regd. 22 Feb. 1955 1956

Phillips (H. W.) & Co. Ld. Regd. 1935. Winding-up Order 21 June 1965. In July 1977 the liquidator stated that the company was in process of dissolution 1982–3

Phillips, Hoskins & Co. Ld. Regd. 1897. Struck off Register 10 Feb. 1903 1903

Phillips (J. A.) & Co. Ld. Regd. 1913. In Nov. 1915 the preference shares of 1 were repaid. Vol. liq. 18 Jan. 1916. Final meeting return regd. 31 Aug. 1920 1916

Phillips River Gold & Copper Co. Ld. Regd. 1906. Vol. liq. 24 June 1912. Shareholders were entitled to 1 fully-paid preference share in Westralian Copper Mines Ld. for every 8 shares of £1 held; debenture holders were entitled to 75,000 fully-paid preference shares for principal and interest. Final meeting return regd. 16 Oct. 1914 1913

Phillips Rubbers Ld. Regd. 1919. Vol. liq. 25 Oct. 1926. The business and net assets were acquired by Phillips Rubber Soles Ld. for £600,000 in cash. Final meeting return regd. 30 June 1927 1927

Phillips (Thomas) & Co. Ld. Regd. 1898. Court Order to wind up 10 Dec. 1907. Liquidator released 31 Dec. 1908. Struck off Register 1 July 1921 1908

VOL. FOR

Phillips (W. G.) & Sons Ld. Regd. 1898. Vol. liq. Dec. 1910. Undertaking was sold to Hall's Oxford Brewery Ld. for £42,580 in cash. Debenture holders were entitled to £80 either in cash or in debenture stock in acquiring company. Capital returned to contributories—£2 per preference share of £10; no return to ordinary shareholders. Removed from Register 1911 1911

Phœbe Gold Mining Co. Ld. Regd. 1887. Vol. liq. 14 Aug. 1913. Final meeting return regd. 13 Aug. 1915 1914

Phenix & West Phenix United Mines. Regd. 1894. Removed from Register 1901 1901

Phenix Bolt & Nut Co. Ld. Regd. 1922. Vol. liq. 28 Jan. 1936. Direct controlling interest held by Monks, Hall & Co. Ld. Final meeting return regd. 15 July 1936 1936

Phenix Brewery Co. Ld. Regd. 1874. Vol. liq. (members') 8 Aug. 1939. Part of undertaking acquired by company of same name. Capital returned to contributories—£5 per preference share of £5; ordinary shareholders received £4,673 6s. 7d. *plus* 19,998 shares of £1 in purchasing company. Final meeting return regd. 27 July 1942 1904

Phenix Brewery (Dublin) Ld. Regd. Dublin 1897. In liquidation in 1906 1909

Phœnix Chemical Co, Ld. Regd. 1919 as Phoenix Chemical Co. (1919) Ld.; name changed Mar. 1922. Receiver appointed 16 July 1924. Struck off Register 26 Apr. 1929 1926

Phoenix Diamond Mining Co. Ld. Regd. 1882. Vol. liq. 8 Aug. 1887. Undertaking absorbed by Anglo African Diamond Mining Co. Ld. Final meeting return regd. 30 Jan. 1888 ...... *1888

Phenix Electric Light & Power Co. Ld. Regd. 1882. Removed from Register 1889 1883

Phoenix Finance Co. Ld. Regd. 1928 as Belgian Finance Co. Ld. Vol. liq. (members') 19 Jan. 1939. Capital returned to contributories—1s. 8d. per share of £1. £601 4s. was paid into Companies' Liquidation Account. Final meeting return regd. 10 Aug. 1950 1951

Phenix Flour Mills & Bread Factory Ld. Regd. 1891. Court Order to wind up 30 Nov. 1893. Removed from Register 1907 1894

Phoenix Gold Mines Ld. Regd. 1899. Reconstructed 1903 as Crown Gold Mines Ld., in which company shareholders were entitled to 1 share of 5s. (credited with 3s. 6d. paid) for every 3 shares of 10s. held. Removed from Register 1909 1903

Phenix Ld. Regd. 1895. Removed from Register 1908 1904

Phenix Mines (Cornwall) Ld. Regd. 1909. Vol. liq. 15 Jan. 1915. Final meeting return regd. 27 Feb. 1917 1915

Phenix Motors Ld. Regd. 1919. Vol. liq. 8 Apr. 1924. Final meeting return regd. 10 Nov. 1928 1925

Phoenix Telephone & Electric Works Ld. Regd. 1950. All capital acquired by Combined Telephone Holdings Ld. Vol. liq. (members') 28 Feb. 1962. Final meeting return regd. 6 Aug. 1964 1961

Phonopore Co. Ld. Regd. 1887 as Phonopore Syndicate Ld.; name changed 12 Aug. 1892. Vol. liq. 5 Nov. 1896. Final meeting return regd. 19 Aug. 1897 ...... *1899

Phonos Ld. Regd. 1926. Direct controlling interest held by Pettigrew & Merriman (1925) Ld. Struck off Register 1933 1932

Phormium Cavity Blocks Ld. Regd. 1928. Vol. liq. (creditors') 21 Aug. 1933. Assets realised insufficient to pay unsecured creditors. Final meeting return regd. 28 June 1935 1934

Phormium Co. Ld. Undertaking and assets were acquired by Richings Park Estate (1928) Ld. 1929

Phosphate Co. of Sombrero Ld. Regd. 1879. Vol. liq. 16 Nov. 1894. Final meeting return regd. 26 Sept. 1899 1895

Phosphate Sewage Co. Ld. Regd. 1871. Court Orders: to wind up 31 Dec. 1877; to dissolve 1 Jan. 1895 ...... *1877

Phospherine (Ashton & Parsons) Ld. Regd. 1928. Vol. liq. (members') 8 Oct. 1935. Undertaking was acquired by Veno Drug Co. Ld. for £480,000. Capital returned to contributories—£1 2s. per ordinary share of £1; 2s. 5·115d. per deferred share of 5s. £1,080 6s. was paid into Companies' Liquidation Account in respect of capital unclaimed, £7. 6s. 10d. in respect of unclaimed dividends. Final meeting return regd. 23 Oct. 1937 1936

Phospho Guano Co. Ld. Regd. 1870. Vol. liq. Apr. 1876. Final meeting return regd. 7 June 1876 1897

Phospho Guano Co. Ld. Regd. 1876 as Seacombe Phospho Guano Co. Ld.; name changed June 1876. Vol. liq. 4 Dec. 1896. Final meeting return regd. 10 Apr. 1897 1897

Phosphor Bronze Co. Ld. Regd. 1874. Court Order to wind up 14 Dec. 1909. Liquidator released 3 Aug. 1911, Struck off Register 17 Feb. 1914 1910

Photographic Co. Ld. Regd. 1887. Court Orders: to wind up 26 Feb. 1889; to dissolve 16 May 1892. 1890

See Stock Exchange Year-Book.

VOL. FOR

Photographic Industries Ld. Regd. 1904. Vol. liq. 2 Oct. 1905. Final meeting return regd. 22 June 1906 ..... ***1906**

Photo-Matik Foreign Corporation Ld. Regd. 1928. Vol. liq. 23 July 1929. Final meeting return regd. 12 June 1930 .... **1930**

Photo-Matik Portraits Ld. Regd. 1928. Court order to wind up 3 Sept. 1930. Struck off Register 20 Mar. 1936 .... **1937**

Photomaton Inc. The receiver of Photomaton Parent Corporation Ld. stated in Dec. 1934 that he believed this company to be out of existence **1935**

Photomaton (International) Ld. Regd. 1927. Vol. liq. 25 Apr. 1928. Struck off Register 14 July 1933 .... **1934**

Photomaton (Lancashire & Midland) Ld. Regd. 1928. Undertaking and assets were acquired in 1930 by British Photomaton Trading Co. Ld. for £165,000 in fully-paid A ordinary and preference shares of 2s. Struck off Register Mar. 1933 .... **1934**

Photomaton Ld. Regd. 1927. Vol. liq. 25 Apr. 1928. Struck off Register 14 July 1933 .... **1934**

Photomaton Parent Corporation Ld. Regd. 1928. Receiver appointed in July 1934. Assets realised insufficient to discharge debentures ranking in priority to income debentures. Struck off Register 8 Apr. 1938 .... **1939**

Photomaton (South Africa) Ld. The receiver of Photomaton Parent Corporation Ld. stated in Dec. 1934 that he believed this company to be out of existence **1935**

Piacenza, Bettola & Cremona Tramways Co. Ld. Regd. 1880. Vol. liq. 27 Mar. 1906. Removed from Register 1906 .... **1907**

Piano & Gramophone Co. Ld. *See* Bell Piano Co. Ld.

Piastowe Petroleum Co. Ld. Regd. 1914. Vol. liq. 5 Feb. 1926. Final meeting return regd. 10 Mar. 1927 ..... **1927**

Piccadilly Art Galleries Co. Ld. Regd. 1881. Vol. liq. (members') 10 Feb. 1920. Final meeting return regd. 19 Aug. 1930 .... ***1931**

Piccadilly Hotel Ld. Regd. 1904. Court Order to wind up 25 May 1909. Liquidator released 6 Mar. 1912. Struck off Register 10 Oct. 1916 .... **1910**

Piccadilly Hotel Ld. Regd. 1909 as H.D. Syndicate Ld. Vol. liq. 1962. Final meeting return regd. 26 June 1964 .... **1949**

Piccadilly Picture Theatre (Manchester) Ld. Regd. 1919. Vol. liq. (members') 22 Mar. 1937. Capital returned to contributories—8s. per preferred share of 10s.; 2$\frac{9}{10}$d. per deferred share of 6d. Final meeting return regd. 8 May 1939 .... **1938**

Piccadilly Studios Ld. Regd. 1926. Vol. liq. 20 Dec. 1928. Undertaking was acquired by Gainsborough Pictures (1928) Ld. Final meeting return regd. 9 Aug. 1930 .... **1945**

Piccadilly Theatre (1928) Ld. Regd. 1928. Receiver appointed in July 1930; ceased to act 6 Mar. 1939. Assets realised sufficient to repay 5s. 5$\frac{1}{4}$d. in £ to holders of 6$\frac{1}{4}$% 1st mortgage debenture stock. Struck off Register 2 Apr. 1940 .... **1941**

Pickering Gas & Water Co. Ld. Regd. 1876. Dissolved 1 May 1949, undertaking being vested in North Eastern Area Gas Board under Gas Act 1948. Holders of ordinary shares (of £10) were entitled to receive £2 British Gas 8% guaranteed stock 1990–95 for each share held. Liability in respect of certain mortgage loans assumed by the Board **1952**

Pickering (J. & T.) Ld. Regd. 1920. Vol. liq. (members') 1 Mar. 1943. Capital returned to contributories— £1,835 0s. 5d.; certain assets were assigned to C. Vaux & Sons Ld. with consent of contributories. Final meeting return regd. 31 Sept. 1943 .... **1944**

Pickles (Robert) Ld. Regd. 1892 as The Robert Pickles Co. Ld.; name changed 1903. Vol. liq. (creditors') 12 Jan. 1970. No capital returned to contributories. Final meeting return regd. 2 Sept. 1974 .... **1975-6**

Pictorial Newspapers Co. (1910) Ld. Regd. 1910. Vol. liq. 25 June 1920. Reconstructed as Daily Mirror Newspapers Ld., in which company shareholders were entitled to 1 8% preference share of £1 (credited as fully-paid) for each preference share of £1 held or 1 fully-paid 8% preference share of £1 *plus* 2s. 6d. in cash for each ordinary share of £1 held, or 7 fully-paid ordinary shares of £1 *plus* a dividend of 25% for each deferred share of £1 held. Final meeting return regd. 7 June 1921 .... **1921**

Picture Gramophone Records Ld. Regd. 1928, Vol. liq, 31 May 1929. Capital returned to contributories— 14s. 7d. per preference share of £1 in Aug. 1929; 1 further payments (if any) not known. Final meeting return regd. 20 May 1930 .... **1930**

Picture Palace (West Bromwich) Ld. Regd. 1920. Struck off Register 4 Aug. 1939 .... **1940**

Picture Theatre (Walthamstow) Ld. Regd. 1930. Vol. liq. (members') 16 July 1935. All shares owned by Associated British Cinemas Ld. Final meeting return regd. 28 Dec. 1936 .... **1936**

VOL. FOR

Picture Theatres Ld. Regd. 1909. Vol. liq. 15 Mar. 1915. Struck off Register 14 Feb. 1922 .... **1916**

Pierrefitte Mining Co. Ld. Regd. 1880. Vol. liq. June 1886. Final meeting return regd. 2 June 1887 ..... **1887**

Piggott (Thomas) & Co. Ld. Regd. 1892. Vol. liq. (members') 10 Mar. 1933. Undertaking and assets were acquired by Horseley Bridge & Engineering Co. Ld. (later Horseley Bridge and Thomas Piggott Ld.), which company held all capital. Final meeting return regd. 12 May 1938 .... **1934**

Pigg's Peak Development Co. Ld. Regd. 1894. Vol. liq. 11 May 1898. Reconstructed as company of same name. Shareholders were entitled to 1 share of £1 (credited as fully-paid) in new company for every 8 shares of £1 held. Final meeting return regd. 22 Mar. 1901 .... **1899**

Pigg's Peak Development Co. Ld. Regd. 1898. Vol. liq. (creditors') 7 Nov. 1933. Property and assets were realised and a distribution of 53% was made to holders of 6% mortgage debentures; no capital returned to contributories. Final meeting return regd. 10 Apr. 1934 .... **1934**

Pigg's Peak Estate & Gold Mining Co. Ld. Regd. 1889. Vol. liq. 25 Jan. 1894. Reconstructed as Pigg's Peak Development Co. Ld., in which company shareholders were entitled to 2 shares of £1 (credited with 18s. paid) for each preference share of £1 held or to 1 share of £1 (credited with 16s. paid) for each ordinary share of £1 held. Final meeting return regd. 20 Jan. 1896 .... **1895**

Pigou, Wilks & Lawrence Ld. Regd. 1872 as Pigou and Wilks Ld. Vol. liq. 1 July 1897. Removed from Register 1905 .... **1898**

Pike, Spicer & Co. Ld. Regd. 1889. Vol. liq. 23 June 1926. Preference shareholders were allotted £100 B debenture stock in Brickwood & Co. Ld. (later Brickwoods Ld.) for each preference share of £100 held. Ordinary shareholders were entitled to 15 ordinary shares of £10 in that company *plus* £1 11s. 4$\frac{1}{2}$d. for each ordinary share of £100 held. Final meeting return regd. 12 Nov, 1926 .... **1927**

Pilaya Gold Syndicate Ld. Regd. Edinburgh 1899. Vol. liq. Oct. 1908. Dissolved before 1931 .... **1909**

Pilbarra Asbestos Co. Ld. Regd. 1907. Vol. liq. 22 May 1912. Final meeting return regd. 17 July 1914 ...... **1913**

Pilbarra Copper Fields Ld. Regd. 1917. Assets realised insufficient to provide any return to debenture holders. Struck off Register 19 Jan. 1934 .... **1933**

Pilbarra Goldfields Ld. Regd. 1895. Vol. liq. 1 Feb. 1899. Removed from Register 1904 .... **1900**

Pilbarra United Gold Mines Ld. Regd. 1895. Vol. liq. 23 May 1898. Final meeting return regd. 15 Feb. 1899 **1899**

Pile Ld. Regd. Dublin 1896. Business acquired by Irish Sterilized Iced Milk and Cold Storage Co. Ld **1902**

Pilgrim's Rest Ld. Regd. 1886. Removed from Register 1892 .... ***1891**

Pilkington (Peter) Ld. Regd. 1921. Receiver appointed 19 Jan. 1925. Vol. liq. (creditors') 5 Feb. 1930. Goodwill and patterns were acquired by Alldays & Onions Ld. Receiver ceased to act 9 Oct. 1920. Final meeting return regd. 18 Jan. 1934 .... **1940**

Pillsbury Flour Mills Inc. Inc. Delaware 1923. Merged in 1935 with Pilsbury Flour Mills Co. (inc. Delaware 1935), in which company shareholders were entitled to 1 share of $25 (credited as fully-paid) for each common share of no par value held. Liability for 6% 1st mortgage 20-year gold bonds was assumed by new company **1936**

Pilmoor Rubber Co. Ld. Regd. 1914. Vol. liq. 27 May 1920. Reconstructed as Pilmoor Rubber Co. (1920) Ld. (later Pilmoor Rubber Co. Ld.) in which company shareholders were entitled to 2 fully-paid shares of £1 for each share of £1 held. Final meeting return regd. 30 June 1922 .... **1921**

Pilmoor Rubber Co. Ld. Regd. 1920 as Pilmoor Rubber Co. (1920) Ld.; name changed June 1923. All capital owned by Seafield Amalgamated Rubber Co. Ld. Vol. liq. (members') 13 Jan. 1961. Final meeting return regd. 4 Jan. 1964 .... **1960**

Pilot Insurance Corporation Ld. Regd 1907. Vol. liq. 18 Dec. 1913. Undertaking was acquired by Essex and Suffolk Equitable Insurance Society Ld. (later Essex & Suffolk Insurance Society Ld.). Final meeting return regd. 10 Nov. 1914 .... **1914**

Pilot Mill (1929) Ld. Regd. 1929. Struck off Register 29 Aug. 1941 .... **1942**

Pilot Spinning Co. Ld. Regd. 1905. Vol. liq. 23 July 1920. Final meeting return regd. 11 Feb. 1921 .... ***1914**

"Pilsen," "Joel" & General Electric Light Co. Ld. Regd. 1882. Vol. liq. Jan. 1889. Final meeting return regd. 5 Sept. 1890 .... **1889**

Pine Mill (1919) Ld. Regd. 1919. Vol. liq. (members') 16 Mar. 1939. Capital returned to contributories— £25,950. Final meeting return regd. 2 Jan. 1940 ... **1940**

VOL. FOR

Pine Vale Copper Syndicate Ld. Regd. 1906. Removed froml Register 1911 .... **1910**

Pinewood Studios Ld. Regd. 1935. Vol. liq. (members') 18 Aug. 1944. Certain assets were distributed in specie. Capital returned to contributories—1s. 2·2688d. per share of £1. Final meeting return regd. 6 Mar. 1945 .... **1944**

Pinhel Wolfram Mines Ld. Regd. 1905. Vol. liq. 27 June 1922. Final meeting return regd. 15 June 1927 .... **1923**

Pink (E. & T.) & Plaistowe (Proprietary) Ld. Regd. 1920. Receiver appointed 30 June 1926. Court Order to wind up July 1926. Debenture stockholders were entitled to £50 6% debenture stock. £33 6s. 8d. in 7% preference shares and £6 13s. 4d. in ordinary shares of 1s. in Plaistowe & Co. Ld. for each £100 debenture stock held. Struck off Register May 1935 **1934**

Pink (E. & T.) Ld. Regd. 1912. Vol. liq. 14 Aug. 1923. Final meeting return regd. 8 Dec. 1924 .... **1934**

Pinkney & Sons Steamship Co. Ld. See Columbia Steam Navigation Co. Ld.

Pinnacles Gold Mine Ld. Regd. 1898. Vol. liq. 16 May 1900. Liquidator stated that no return would be made to shareholders. Final meeting return regd. 8 May 1901 .... **1901**

Pinner Gas Ld. Regd. 1897. Under Gas Light & Coke Company's Act of 1929 the undertaking was acquired by that company. Contributories were entitled to stock in new company as follows—for each A 10% ordinary share of £5 held—£12 10s. ordinary stock; for each B 7% ordinary share of £5 held—£8 15s. ordinary stock; for each 6% preference share of £5 held—£7 10s. 4% consolidated preference stock. Acquiring company assumed liability for debentures. Dissolved under Act on 31 Dec. 1929 .... **1930**

Pinner's Financiers Ld. Regd. 1910. Struck off Register 1921 .... **1913**

Pinos Altos Bullion Co. Ld. Regd. 1886. Vol. liq. 22 Nov. 1893. Reconstructed as New Pinos Altos Co. Ld. Final meeting return regd. 20 June 1895 .... **1898**

Pinos Altos (Mexico) Mining Co. Ld. In 1886 property was acquired by Pinos Altos Bullion Co. Ld. **1893**

Pinto (L. & H.) Ld. Regd. 1897. Struck off Register 1 Aug. 1951 .... **1952**

Pintsch's Patent Lighting Co. Ld. Regd. 1878. Vol. liq. 26 June 1895 for reconstruction as Pintsch's Patent Lighting Co. Ld. (later Patent Lighting Co. Ld.). Final meeting return regd. 13 Jan. 1897 .... **1908**

Pinxton Collieries Ld. Regd 1899 as Pinxton Coal Co. Ld.; name changed 1906. Vol. liq. (members') 27 Feb. 1952. Capital returned to contributories—£3 17s. 9d. per share of 1s. Final meeting return regd. 31 May 1961 .... **1958**

Pinyalling Consols Ld. Regd. 1897. Vol. liq. 20 Jan. 1899. Final meeting return regd. 5 July 1900 ...... **1900**

Pioneer Co. of Siberia Ld. Regd. 1911. Vol. liq. (members') 28 Sept. 1934. Final meeting return regd. 9 Jan. 1935 .... **1935**

Pioneer Development & Exploration Co. of British Columbia Ld. Regd. 1896. Removed from Register 1905 .... **1901**

Pioneer Estates Ld. Regd. 1896. Court Order to wind up 3 Dec. 1897. Removed from Register 1912 .... **1898**

Pioneer Mining Co. Ld. Regd. 1880. Removed from Register 1905 .... **1883**

Pioneer Mining Corporation Ld. Inc. Canada 1926 as Pioneer Mines Ld.; name changed Apr. 1926. In Dec. 1929 shareholders agreed to transfer undertaking and assets to Huronian Mining and Finance Co. Ld., in which company shareholders were entitled to 2 fully-paid shares of no par value for every 10 shares held and an option (since expired) over further shares **1931**

Pioneer Stores Ld. Regd. 1918. Direct controlling interest was held by Waring & Gillow Ld. Struck off Register 28 Apr. 1944 .... **1932**

Pioneer Stores (H.P.) Ld. Regd. 1930. Direct controlling interest was held by Waring & Gillow Ld. Struck off Register 7 Sept. 1945. .... **1932**

Pioneer Trust Ld. See New Town Trust Ld.

Pioneers of Mashonaland Syndicate Ld. Regd. 1891 Vol liq. 21 June 1894. Final meeting return regd. 6 Aug. 1895 .... **1895**

Pioneerville Gravel Gold Co. Ld. Regd. 1894. Removed from Register 1908 .... **1899**

Piræus, Athens & Peloponnesus Railway Co. (Compagnie des Chemins de Fer Piree-Athenes-Péloponese.) Under Greek Emergency Law No. 2378 of 1940 company was declared insolvent and placed in liquidation, the General Council of the Company was appointed liquidator and the assets credited to the State Operation Account **1951**

Pirie, Wyatt & Co. Ld. See St. Cuthbert's Paper Works Ld.

VOL. FOR

Pirraca Trust Ld. Regd. 1926. Vol. liq. (members') 18 Nov. 1936. Capital returned to contributories—5s. 1·357d. per share of £1. £23 18s. 11d. was paid into Companies' Liquidation Account. Final meeting return regd. 13 July 1940 .... **1937**

Pita Fibre & Rubber Estates Ld, See Soengei Parit Rubber Co. Ld.

Pitangui Gold Mining Co. Ld. Regd. 1876. Removed from Register 1912 .... **1899**

Pitchblende, Uranium & Radium Mines Syndicate Ld. Regd. 1909. Struck off Register 8 Mar. 1935 .... **1936**

Pitchikawa Rubber Estate Ld. Regd. Edinburgh 1914. Vol. liq. Jan. 1916. Property sold to Linggi Plantations Ld., in which company shareholders received approximately ⁷⁄₁₀ths of a fully-paid ordinary share of 2s. for each share of 15s. held. Final meeting return regd. 4 Jan.1917 .... **1916**

Pitlochry New Gas Light Co. Ld. Regd. in Edinburgh 1897. Dissolved 1 May 1949, undertaking being vested in Scottish Area Gas Board under Gas Act 1948. Holders of ordinary shares (of £1) were entitled to receive £1 4s. British Gas 3% guaranteed stock 1990–95 for each share held **1952**

Pitt (William) & Co. Ld. Regd. 1924. Vol. liq. 30 June 1932. All shares held by Wiggins, Teape, & Alex. Pirie (Merchants) Ld. Undertaking and assets acquired by Allied Paper Merchants (W.T. & Co.) Ld. Final meeting return regd. 30 Oct. 1933 .... **1933**

Pitts, Son & King Ld. Regd. 1895. Vol. liq. 12 Feb. 1900. Final meeting return regd. 22 June 1905 .... *1901

Pittsburgh, Cincinnati, Chicago & St. Louis Railway Co. Organised Pennsylvania, West Virginia, Ohio, Indiana and Illinois 1890. Reorganised 1916 as Pittsburgh, Cincinnati, Chicago & St. Louis Railroad. Stockholders were entitled to $100 stock in new company for every $100 common stock held or to $10 stock for every $100 preferred stock held. The consolidated mortgage bonds, Chicago, St. Louis & Pittsburgh Railroad Co. consolidated mortgage bonds and 3½% Chartier's Railway Co. 1st mortgage bonds were taken over by new company **1917**

Pittsburgh Consolidated Gold Mines Ld. Regd. 1890. Vol. liq. 4 Mar. 1895. Reconstructed as Hampton Plains Exploration Co. Ld., in which company shareholders were entitled to 1 share of £1 (credited with 17s. 6d. paid) for each share of £1 held. Final meeting return regd. 20 June 1895 .... **1905**

Plancecia de las Armas Co. Ld. Regd. 1887. Vol. liq. (members') 6 Nov. 1945. Vickers Ld. held a direct controlling interest. Final meeting return regd. 14 Dec. 1945.. **1946**

Placerville Gold Quartz Co. Ld. Regd. 1878. Vol. liq. Nov. 1883. Final meeting return regd. 22 May 1889 **1885**

Planet-Arcturus Gold Mines Ld. Regd. 1911. Vol. liq. 24 Nov. 1924. Final meeting return regd. 11 Feb. 1927 **1925**

Planet Assurance Corporation Ld. See Citizen Assurance Corporation Ld.

Plant Brothers Ld. Regd. 1875. Removed from Register 1905 .... *1877

Plant, Green & Manton Ld. Regd. 1900. Vol. liq. Dec. 1907. Undertaking was acquired by Buttons Ld., in which company shareholders were entitled to 5 preference and 1 ordinary share of £1 for each preference share of £5 held or £1 12s. 10d. in ordinary shares of £1 for each ordinary share of £1 held. Removed from Register 1909 .... **1908**

Plantation and General Developments Ld. Regd. 1914. Vol. liq. 21 Feb. 1917. Reconstructed as Batavia and General Plantations Trust Ld., in which company shareholders were entitled to 6 shares of £1 (credited as fully-paid) for every 5 shares of £1 held. Final meeting return regd. 6 Mar. 1919........................ **1918**

Plantation Holdings Ld. Regd. as private company 15 Sept. 1965; converted into public company 29 Oct. 1965. Vol. liq. (members') 29 June 1979. Under scheme of reconstruction effective 29 June 1979, holders received 5 ordinary shares of $Ma. 1 in Malaysian Plantations Bhd. for every 4 ordinary held amd 4 ordinary shares of 10p in Phicom Ld., for every 4 ordianry held **1988–9**

Plantation Securities, Ld. Regd. 1925. Vol. liq. (members') 20 Dec. 1945. Capital returned to contributories—3s. 2¼d. per share of £1 (11s. paid). £1 10s. 8d. was paid into Companies' Liquidation Account. Final meeting return regd. 10 Mar. 1947 .... **1948**

Plantations & General Trust Ld. Regd. 1925. Vol. liq. (members') 22 Mar. 1937. Undertaking acquired by Plantations & General Investment Trust Ld. Shareholders received 2 fully-paid shares (of 2s. each) and 10s. 5% redeemable convertible income debenture stock in respect of each share (of £1) held. Final meeting return regd. 10 Aug. 1950 .... **1951**

Plantations Trust Ld. Regd. 1910 as Vine & General Rubber Trust Ld.; name changed Jan. 1916. Vol.

*See Stock Exchange Year-Book.

VOL. FOR

liq. 21 Feb. 1917. Reconstructed as Batavia and General Plantations Trust Ld. in which company shareholders were entitled to 1 share of £1 (credited as fully-paid) for every 2 A preference or 20 B preference shares of 10s. held. Final meeting return regd. 31 May 1920. Court Order declared dissolution void 27 June 1922. Final meeting return regd. 7 Apr. 1925 .... **1918**

Planters (F.M.S.) Rubber Estates Ld. Regd. 1911. Vol. liq. June 1913. The estate was sold to F.M.S. Rubber Planters Estates Ld. in which company shareholders were entitled to 1 share of £1 (credited as fully-paid) for each share of £1 held. Removed from Register 1914 .... **1914**

Plant's Day Dawn Gold Mines Ld. Inc. Queensland 1903. Vol. liq. Apr. 1912. Capital returned to contributories—1·43d. per share of 10s. at May 1912; further payments (if any) not known **1919**

Plasmon Bread Co. Ld. Regd. 1907. Vol. liq. 30 Nov. 1908. Removed from Register 1910 .... **1903**

Plasmon, Ld. Regd. 1900 as International Plasmon Ld.; name changed Nov. 1918. Vol. liq. (members') 1 Sept. 1954, Capital returned to contributories— preference shares were repaid at par; 2s. 2d. per ordinary share of 4s. Final meeting return regd. 31 May 1955 .... **1956**

Plaster Brick & Stone Co. Ld. Regd. 1902. Vol. liq. Dec. 1906. Removed from Register 1908 .... **1907**

Plate Investment Trust Ld. Regd. 1937 as River Plate Electricity & Other Securities Corpn. Ld.; name changed July 1957. All capital was owned by New Investment Co. Ld. Vol. liq. (members') 29 Sept. 1960. Capital returned to contributories—£275,580. Final meeting return regd. 2 June 1962 .... **1963**

"Plate" Steamship Co. Ld. Regd. 1885. Vol. liq. 14 Jan. 1913. Final meeting return regd. 3 July 1913 .... ***1911**

Platinum & Gold Concessions of Colombia Ld. Regd. 1911. Struck off Register 1942 .... ***1923**

Platinum Areas Ld. Regd. 1925. Vol. liq. Dec. 1930 for reconstruction as Isamungu Gold Mine Ld., in which company shareholders were entitled to 1 share of 1s. (credited with 9d. paid) for each ordinary share of 2s. held or 1 fully-paid share of 1s. for each preference share of 2s. held. Struck off Register 4 Oct. 1938 .... **1939**

Platinum Corporation Ld. Regd. 1907. Court Order to wind up 6 July 1909. Liquidator released 11 Feb. 1913. Struck off Register 10 Oct. 1916 .... **1910**

Platinum Lands of Lydenburg Ld. Regd. 1925. Vol. liq. (members') 15 Mar. 1934. Capital returned to contributories—¹⁄₁₀d. per share of 5s. Final meeting return regd. 3 Nov. 1936 .... **1935**

Platinum Plating Co. Ld. Regd. 1887. Vol. liq. 23 Feb. 1894. Final meeting return regd. 9 Jan. 1895 .... **1895**

Platinum Proprietary (S.A.) Ld. Regd. 1925. Vol. liq. 12 July 1926. Final meeting return regd. 25 Oct. 1926 **1927**

Platte Land Co. Ld.. Regd. 1879. Vol. liq. 7 Oct. 1918. Final meeting return regd. 16 Dec. 1919 .... **1919**

Playa de Oro Co. Ld. Regd. 1903. Vol. liq. 7 May 1907. Removed from Register 1911 .... **1908**

Plaza (New Malden) Ld. Regd. 1928. Undertaking was acquired by London and District Cinemas Ld. Struck off Register 24 Dec. 1943 .... **1945**

Pleiades Gold Mining Co. Ld. Inc. Transvaal 1895. In liquidation in 1904. Final distribution of 6s. 6½d... **1904**

Plenes Investment Co. Ld. Regd. 1920. Vol. liq. 16 Aug. 1926. Final meeting return regd. 24 Dec. 1936 ..... **1927**

Plenty-Still Oil Engines Ld. Regd. 1928. Receiver appointed 5 Jan. 1932. Vol. liq. (creditors') 28 June 1932. Receiver ceased to act 3 Oct. 1933. 61% of A shares held by Still Engine Co. Ld. (later Diesel-Steam Locomotives Ld.). Final meeting return regd. 8 Nov.1933 .... **1933**

Plews & Sons Ld. Regd. 1905. Vol. liq. 11 Aug. 1925. Undertaking and assets were acquired by J. W. Cameron & Co. Ld. Final meeting return regd. 19 Jan. 1926 .... **1925**

Plough Hotel Cheltenham Ld. Regd. 1920 as Gloucestershire Cinemas (1920) Ld.; name changed May 1926. Vol. liq. 4 Oct. 1929. Capital returned to contributories—20s. per preference share of £1 plus 9s. 9d. in respect of arrears of dividend; ordinary distributories (if any) not known. Final meeting return regd. 22 May 1931 .... **1930**

Plowmans Brickfields Ld. Regd. 1919. Vol. liq. (members') May 1928. Undertaking acquired by London Brick Co. Ld. Assets were distributed in specie. Final meeting return regd. 27 Sept. 1946 .... **1947**

Pluckley Brick & Tile Co. Ld. Regd. 1877 as Kent Brick, Tile & Pottery Co. Ld.; name changed 9 Jan. 1884. to Edwin Hughes & Co. Ld. and 28 Dec. 1887 as above. Vol. liq. 17 Oct. 1910. Struck off Register 16 July 1915 .... ***1882**

VOL. FOR

Plum Mill (Holdings) Ld. Regd. 1920 as Plum Mill Ld.; name changed 1953. Vol. liq. 16 Dec. 1980. Final meeting return regd. 15 Dec. 1981 .... **1960**

Plum Mill Ld. See Plum Mill (Holdings) Ld.

Plum Mill Ld. Regd. 1905. Vol. liq. 23 Apr. 1920. Reconstructed as company of same name (later Plum Mill (Holdings) Ld.). Shareholders were entitled to 15 shares of £1 (credited as fully-paid) in new company for each share of £5 held. Final meeting return regd. 17 Jan. 1921 .... **1921**

Plumbago Trust Ld. Regd. 1907. Struck off Register 26 Sept. 1939 .... **1940**

Plumstead Properties Ld. Regd. 1936. Vol. liq. (members') 13 Dec. 1937. Capital returned to contributories—£6 11s. 5d. per share of £1. Final meeting return regd. 20 Sept. 1941 .... **1938**

Plushey's Mining Co. Ld. Regd. 1883. Vol. liq. 4 Apr. 1889. Final meeting return regd. 9 May 1895 .... **1890**

Pluto Hot Water Syndicate Ld. Regd. 1897. Vol. liq. Dec. 1900 for reconstruction as Pluto Engineering Co. Ld in which company shareholders were entitled to 1 share of 2s. 6d. (credited with 1s. paid) for every share of £1 held. Removed from Register 1904 .... **1901**

Plymouth Alpine Mining Co. Ld. Regd. 1887. Removed from Register 1911 .... **1890**

Plymouth and Dartmoor Railway Co. Inc. by Special Acts, 1819 & 1865. In 1923 the undertaking was merged into the London & South Western Railway, in which company stockholders were entitled to stock as follows:

For each £100 held	L. & S.W.
4% Debenture........	£133¼ 3% Deb. Stock Cons.
5% Cattewater Ex.	£130 Undiv. Ordinary

For each £100 held	L. & S.W.
5% Preference........	£10 Undiv. Ordinary

The ordinary shares were cancelled **1924**

Plymouth & North Devon Direct Railway Co. Inc. by Special Act 1895 as Torrington & Okehampton Railway Co.; name changed by Act of 1901. Abandoned by Act of 1907 .... **1908**

Plymouth & Stonehouse Gas Light & Coke Co. Inc. by Special Act 1855. Dissolved 1 May 1949, undertaking being vested in South Western Area Gas Board under Gas Act 1948. Holders of securities were entitled to receive British Gas 3% guaranteed stock 1990–95 as follows in respect of each £100 unit, unless otherwise stated, of security held:

	£	s.	d.
Ord. stock (5% stand.)..................	162	10	0
Addit. shares (7½% stand) (of £10) .	25	14	0
New shares (7% stand.) (of £10)	24	15	0
3% perp. deb. stock	90	0	0
3½% perp. deb. stock	98	15	0
4% perp. deb. stock	103	0	0
5% perp. deb. stock.......................	127	10	0

.... **1952**

Plymouth Consolidated Gold Mines Ld. Regd. 1914. Vol. liq. 2 Mar. 1925. Final meeting return regd. 22 Dec. 1925 .... **1926**

Plymouth, Devonport & District Tramways Co. Inc. by Special Act 1882. In liquidation in 1886 .... **1886**

Plymouth, Devonport and South Western Junction Railway Co. Inc. by Special Act 1883. In 1923 the undertaking was merged into the London & South Western Railway, in which company stockholders were entitled to stock as follows:

For each £100 held	L. & S.W.
4% Debenture....................£133¼	3% Deb. Cons.
4½% Preference £129	3½% Preference
Ordinary....................................£85	3½% Preference

The £187,000 3% Guaranteed Stock held by the London & South Western Railway was cancelled . **1924**

Plymouth Pier Co. Ld. Regd. 1877. Removed from Register 27 Apr. 1894 .... ***1886**

Plymouth Piers, Pavilion, & Saltash, Three Towns Steamship Co. Ld. Regd. 1889 as Plymouth Promenade Pier & Pavilion Co. Ld.; name changed 1912. Vol. liq. (members') 18 Feb. 1953. Capital returned to contributories—18·01s. per preference share of £1. £1,247 1s. 10d. paid into Companies' Liquidation Account. Final meeting return regd. 13 Feb. 1956 .... **1957**

Plymouth Promenade Pier Pavilion Co. Ld. See above.

Plymouth, Stonehouse & Devonport Tramways Co. Vol. liq. 1937. All capital was owned by Provincial Tramways Co. Ld. **1937**

Pneumatic Compensation Cycle Co. Ld. See Forward Components Ld.

Pneumatic Electric & General Engineering Co. Ld. See Consolidated Signal Co.

Pneumatic Road Skate Co. Ld. Regd. 1895. Removed from Register 1903 .... **1898**

Pneumatic Typewriter Ld. Regd. 1894. Vol. liq. 18 July 1895. Final meeting return regd. 23 Dec. 1895 .... **1896**

See Stock Exchange Year-Book.

VOL. FOR

Pneumatic Tyre & Booths Cycle Agency Ld. *See* Pneumatic Tyre Co. Ld.

Pneumatic Tyre Co. Ld. Regd. Dublin 1889 as Pneumatic Tyre & Booth's Cycle Agency Ld. Reconstructed as company of same name regd. 1894 1896

Pneumatic Tyre Co. Ld. Regd. Dublin 1894. In liquidation in 1897. Taken over by Dunlop Pneumatic Tyre Co. Ld. 1897

Pneumatic Wheel Co. Ld. Regd. 1893. Removed from Register 23 July 1901 .... *1899

Pniel Diamond Mining Co. Ld. Inc. Cape of Good Hope 1906. Reconstructed Aug. 1913 as Pniels Ld., in which company shareholders received 1 share of £1 for every 5 shares of £1 held 1914

Pniels Ld. Inc. Cape of Good Hope 1913. Vol. liq. Mar. 1927. Undertaking and assets were acquired by New Vaal River Diamond & Exploration Co. Ld. (now New Vaal Farms Ld.). Capital returned to contributories—2s. 1½d. per share of £1; further payments (if any) not known 1928

Pobjoy Airmotors & Aircraft Ld. Regd. 1935. Vol. liq. (members') 15 Jan. 1947. Capital returned to contributories—6s. 7·815d. per share of (5s.). £214 3s. 1d. was paid into Companies' Liquidation Account. Final meeting return regd. 28 Apr. 1948 ... 1949

Pocklington New Gas Co. Ld. Regd. 1886. Dissolved 1 May 1949, undertaking being vested in North Eastern Area Gas Board under Gas Act 1948. Holders of securities were entitled to receive British Gas 3% guaranteed stock 1990–95 as follows:

	£	s.	d.	
Ord. shares (of £10)......................	13	4	0	
5% red. debs. (per £100)...............	103	0	0	1952

Pocock Estates Trust Ld. Regd. 1908. Struck off Register 1927 .... *1913

Poderosa Mining Co. Ld. Regd 1908. Vol. liq. (creditors') 13 Oct. 1950. Assets sold to Compania Minera Chilena de Collahuasi, in which company holders received 1 fully-paid share of no par value for each share held. Struck off Register 28 May 1963 1964

Polar Star Gold Mines Ld. Regd. 1897. Reconstructed 1899 as Associated Murchison Gold Mines Ld., in which company shareholders were entitled to 1 share of 10s. (credited with 8s. paid) for each share of 10s. held. Removed from Register 1901 1900

Polar Star Proprietary Ld. Regd. 1897. Vol. liq. 17 Dec. 1897. Reconstructed as Polar Star Gold Mines Ld., in which company shareholders were entitled to 1 share of 10s. (credited with 8s. 6d. paid) for each share of 10s. held. Final meeting return regd. 29 Mar. 1899 1899

Polberro Mine. Regd. 1899. Removed from Register 1903 1903

Polberro Tin Ld. Regd. 1937. Vol. liq. 25 Mar. 1941. No capital returned to contributories. Final meeting return regd. 25 June 1945 1946

Polhigey Tin Ld. Regd. 1926. Vol. liq. (creditors') 9 June 1936. Assets realised insufficient to pay unsecured creditors. Final meeting return regd. 25 June 1937 1937

Polikoff (Alfred) (Boots) Ld. Regd. 1915. Undertaking was acquired by Polikoff Ld. Struck off Register 27 Oct. 1942 1943

Polikoff (Alfred) Ld. Regd. 1922. Undertaking was acquired by Polikoff Ld. Struck off Register 27 Oct. 1942 1943

"Political World" Ld. Regd. 1888. Vol. liq. 17 Apr. 1890. Struck off Register 19 Oct. 1906 1891

Pollok Patents Gold Extracting Co. Ld. Regd. Edinburgh 1889. Vol. liq. Nov 1894. Final meeting return regd. 21 Mar. 1901 1895

Pollokshields Baths Co. Ld. Regd. 1883. Vol. liq. 8 Feb. 1937. Dissolved before 1951 1938

Polmont District Gas Co. Ld. Regd. in Edinburgh 1928. Dissolved 1 May 1949, undertaking being vested in Scottish Area Gas Board under Gas Act 1948. Holders of ordinary shares (of £1) were entitled to receive £2 British Gas 3% guaranteed stock 1990–95 for each share held 1952

Polongeni Tin Mines Ld. Regd. 1909. Struck off Register 1921 1920

Polson (Wm.) & Co. Ld. Regd. Edinburgh 1899. Vol. liq. June 1904. Capital returned to contributories— 15s. per share of £1. Final meeting return regd. 8 Mar. 1905 1905

Polychromatic Simultaneous Printing Co. Ld. Regd. 1881. Court Orders: to wind up June 1887; to dissolve Mar. 1890 1888

Polyphonwerke A.G. *See* Deutsche Grammophon A.G.

Pondicheri Railway Co. Ld. Regd. 1869. Vol. liq. (members') 5 June 1961. Capital returned to contributories—£3 10s. per share of £5 with £3 10s. paid). Final meeting return regd. 5 Sept. 1963 1964

Pongola Rubber Estates Ld. Regd. 1910. Vol. liq. 31 Dec. 1914. Final meeting return regd. 2 May 1918 1915

VOL. FOR

Pontardulais Gas Co. (1930) Ld. Regd 1930. Dissolved 1 May 1949, undertaking being vested in Wales Area Gas Board under Gas Act 1948. Holders of ordinary shares (of £1) were entitled to receive 14s. British Gas 3% guaranteed stock 1990–95 for each share held 1952

Pontefract & District Billposting & Advertising Co. Ld. *See* Pontefract Poster Service Ld.

Pontefract Electricity Ld. Regd. 1947. Dissolved 1 Apr. 1948, undertaking being vested in the British (later Central) Electricity Authority and Yorkshire Area Board under the Electricity Act 1947. Ordinary shareholders were entitled to receive £1 British Electricity 3% guaranteed stock (1968–73), for every £1 of ordinary capital held 1949

Pontefract Gas Co. Inc. by Special Act 1873. Pontefract Corporation gave notice in 1906 of intention to acquire undertaking. Removed from Register 1912 1907

Pontefract Poster Service Ld. Regd. 1896 as Pontefract & District Billposting & Advertising Co. Ld.; name changed 4 June 1936. Vol. liq. (members') 1 Nov. 1940. Capital returned to contributories—£2,163 6s. 11d. Final meeting return regd. 18 Sept. 1941 1937

Pontevedra Tin Mines Ld. Regd. Edinburgh 1901. Struck off Register 12 Nov. 1912 1907

Pontgibaud Silver-Lead Mining & Smelting Co. [Société Anonyme des Mines et Fonderies de Pontgibaud.] Est. in France 1853. In 1955 merged with Compagnie Francaise des Metaux, in which company shareholders were entitled to receive 1 share of Frs.5,000 for every 4 shares of Frs.2,500 held. Company was liquidated on 7 July 1955 1956

Pontian (Malay) Rubber Co. Ld. Regd. 1911. Vol. liq. (members') 10 July 1935. Amalgamated with Sedenak Rubber Estates Ld., in which company shareholders were entitled to 1 fully-paid share of £1 plus 1s. 3d. in cash for every 10 shares of 2s. held. Final meeting return regd. 5 June 1936 1936

Pontianak Rubber Estate Ld. Regd. 1910. Receiver appointed 19 July 1918. Struck off Register 1920.. 1920

Ponting Brothers Ld. Regd. 1898. Vol. liq. Dec. 1906. Business was acquired by John Barker & Co. Ld. for £100,000 in cash. Removed from Register 1910 ... 1908

Pontons (Spain) Zinc & Lead Mines Ld. Regd. 1911. Vol. liq. 8 Dec. 1915. Final meeting return regd. 1 Mar. 1918 .... *1917

Pontybodkin Cannel Colliery Co. Ld. Regd. 1895. Undertaking and assets were acquired by Pontybodkin Colliery Co. Ld. Removed from Register 1909 1904

Pontypool and District Water Co. Inc. by Special Act 1873. Undertaking vested in Gwent Water Board from 1 Apr. 1970. Vol. liq. (members') 20 Aug. 1970. By scheme of arrangement effective 25 Jan. 1971 the following first and final distributions were made (per £1 stock held)—redeemable preference £1·036274; consolidated ordinary £0·831475. Amounts paid into Companies' Liquidation Account—£389·97 in respect of unclaimed distributions and £231·07 in respect of unclaimed dividends. Final meeting return regd. 15 Oct. 1971 1972

Pontypool Electric Light & Power Co. Ld. Regd. 1892. Dissolved 1 Apr. 1948, undertaking being vested in the British (later Central) Electricity Authority and South Wales Area Board under the Electricity Act 1947. Ordinary shareholders were entitled to receive 155 British Electricity 3% guaranteed stock (1968– 73), for every share (of £5) held 1949

Pontypridd & Rhondda Joint-Water Board. Inc. by Special Act 1910. The undertaking and liability for the debenture stock was taken over by the Taf Fechan Water Board on 1 Apr. 1966 1967

Pontypridd, Caerphilly & Newport Railway Co. Inc. by Special Act 1878. Under Act of 1897 Alexandra (Newport and South Wales) Docks and Railway Co. absorbed the undertaking by discharging the mortgage debt and other debts and liabilities 1898

Pontypridd Water Works Co. Inc. by Special Act 1864. By Act of 1910 undertaking was transferred in 1911 to Pontypridd and Rhondda Joint Water Board for £282,400 in cash plus value of certain assets. The liability for the debenture stocks was assumed by Water Board 1911

Poole & District Electric Traction Co. Ld. Regd. 1899. Vol. liq. 18 July 1905. The undertaking was sold to Bournemouth Corporation for £117,850. Capital returned to contributories—£10 per share of £10; further payments (if any) not known. Removed from Register 1910 1906

Poole Waterworks Co. Inc. by Special Act 1859. Borough of Poole Corporation acquired undertaking in 1907 for £133,937 exclusive of the debenture issue. liability for which was assumed by Corporation 1908

VOL. FOR

Pooley (Henry) & Son Ld. Regd. Mar. 1900 as Henry Pooley & Son (1900) Ld.; name changed Nov. 1900. Vol. liq. Mar. 1914. Business and assets were acquired by W. & T. Avery Ld., in which company shareholders were entitled to 1 fully-paid ordinary share of £1 for every 2 ordinary shares of £1 held or 5 fully-paid 5½% cumulative B preference shares of £1 for each preference share of £5 held. Holders of debentures were entitled to an equal amount of 4½% debenture stock in acquiring company. Struck off Register June 1932 .... **1933**

Poonagalla Valley Ceylon Co. Ld. Regd. 1895. Vol. liq. 17 Sept. 1923. Final meeting return regd.17 June 1924 .... **1924**

Poonmudi Tea Co. Ld. Regd. 1900. Vol. liq. Apr. 1910. Undertaking was acquired by Poonmudi Tea & Rubber Co. Ld. in which company shareholders were entitled to 15 shares of 2s. (credited as fully-paid) for each share of £1 held. Removed from Register 1911 .... **1911**

Poorman Consolidated Mines Ld. Inc. New Jersey 1893. Reconstructed in 1895 as Poorman Gold Mines Ld. in which company shareholders were entitled to 1 share of 5s. (credited 4s. paid) for each share of $1·25 held **1896**

Poorman Gold Mines Ld. Regd. 1895. Vol. liq. 17 Aug. 1896. Reconstructed as company of same name. Shareholders were entitled to 1 share of 2s. (credited with 1s. 6d. paid) in new company for each share of 5s. held. Struck off Register 17 June 1904............. **1900**

Poorman Gold Mines Ld. Regd. 1896. Vol. liq. 12 Dec. 1899. Reconstructed as company of same name. Shareholders were entitled to 1 share of 2s. (credited with 1s. 6d. paid) in new company for each share of 2s. held. Final meeting return regd. 27 Nov. 1901 **1908**

Poorman Gold Mines Ld. Regd. 1900. Vol. liq. 11 Feb. 1909. Final meeting return regd. 16 Dec. 1914 ..... **1910**

Poorman Mines Ld. Regd. 1890. Vol. liq. 20 July 1893. Reconstructed as Poorman Consolidated Mines Ld. in which company shareholders were entitled to 4 fully-paid shares of 5s. for every 3 shares of 5s. held. Final meeting return regd. 5 Sept. 1893 .... **1895**

Popular Cinemas Ld. Regd. 1919. Vol. liq. (members') 28 Jan. 1930. Properties purchased by Denman Picture Houses Ld. Capital returned to contributories—£141,192 16s. 2d. Final meeting return regd. 20 Aug. 1931 .... **1940**

Popular Footwear Ld. Regd. 1936. Court Order to wind up 25 July 1938. Struck off Register 27 Oct. 1942. **1943**

Popular Life Assurance Co. Ld. Regd. 1904. Vol. liq. Dec. 1906. Assets and liabilities were acquired by United Provident Assurance Co. Ld. for £150,000 in ordinary shares of £1. Removed from Register 1908 **1907**

Porcherine Ld. Regd. 1900. Vol. liq. 28 Apr. 1916. Capital returned to contributories—3s. per fully-paid share of £5; further payments (if any) not known. Final meeting return regd. 20 July 1917... **1917**

Porchester Trust Ld. Regd. 1926. Court Order to wind up 15 Oct. 1929. Struck off Register 24 Aug. 1943 **1944**

Porco Tin Mines Ld. Regd. 1912. Vol. liq. 19 Dec. 1921. Final meeting return regd. 1 Oct. 1924 .... **1922**

Porcupine-Davidson Gold Mines Ld. Inc. in Ontario 18 Aug. 1921. Winding-up order made 21 Mar. 1961. First and final distribution of 4½p per share made on 15 June 1981. £31,663·86 and £3,623·56 remitted to Public Trustee, Ontario, Canada in respect of unclaimed dividends and distributions **1984–5**

Porcupine Goldfields Development & Finance Co. Ld. Regd. 1923. Vol. liq. (creditors') 2 Dec. 1929. Noteholders received £14,500 on realisation of assets; no capital returned to contributories. Final meeting return regd. 10 May 1933 .... **1930**

Porcupine V.N.T. Gold Mines Ld. Reconstructed 1922 as Vipond Consolidated Mines Ld. **1925**

Porges Randfontein Gold Mining Co. Ld. Inc. Transvaal 1895. Vol. liq. July 1909; undertaking and assets sold to Randfontein South Gold Mining Co. Ld., in which company shareholders received 1 share of £1 for each share of £1 held... **1910**

Porhydrometer Ld. Regd. 1909. Vol. liq. 14 Nov. 1913. Final meeting return regd. 8 June 1916 .... **1914**

Porous Carbon Co. Ld. Regd. 1886. Vol. liq. 21 Nov. 1889. Final meeting return regd. 16 June 1893 ..... **1890**

Porous Plastics Ld. See Porvair p.l.c.

Port Argentine Great Central Railways Co. Ld. Regd. 1908. Struck off Register 1929 .... ***1914**

Port Argentine Land and Development Co. Ld. Regd. 1909. Vol. liq. 7 Jan. 1921. Final meeting return regd. 8 June 1921 .... **1922**

Port Arthur (Current River) Estates Ld. Regd. 1911. Vol. liq. 6 May 1915. Final meeting return regd. 25 Jan. 1916 .... ***1916**

Port Arthur Lands Ld. Regd. 1911. Vol. liq. 23 Oct. 1924. Final meeting return regd. 15 Oct. 1927 ..... **1925**

VOL. FOR

Port Arthur (Ontario) Buildings Ld. Regd. 1914. Vol. liq. 11 Dec. 1919. Reconstructed as Port Arthur (Ontario) Developments Ld. Final meeting return regd. 19 June 1923 .... **1921**

Port Arthur (Ontario) Developments Ld. Regd. 1919. Vol. liq. (members') 30 Apr. 1951. Capital returned to contributories—10d. per preference share of £1. Final meeting return regd. 30 Apr. 1952 .... **1953**

Port Beira Pier, Tramway & Telegraph Co. Ld. Regd. 1894. Removed from Register 14 Mar. 1897 .... ***1895**

Port Darwin Gold Mining Co. Ld. See Northern Territory Exploration Co. Ld.

Port Dickson Coffee Co. Ld. Regd. 1895. Vol. liq. 21 Aug. 1899. Final meeting return regd. 4 Apr.1900 **1900**

Port Glasgow Motor Co. Ld. Regd. Edinburgh 1925. Vol. liq. 7 June 1932. All shares held by Greenock Motor Services Co. Capital returned to contributories—£10,346 4s. 8d. Final meeting return regd. 28 Feb. 1933 .... **1933**

Port Hope Lindsay & Beaverton Railway. See Midland Railway of Canada.

Port Lincoln Copper Co. Ld. Regd. 1906. Vol. liq. (creditors') 24 Aug. 1932. £100 was paid into Companies' Liquidation Account. Final meeting return regd. 1 Aug. 1934 .... **1933**

Port Madryn (Argentina) Co. Ld. Regd. 1906. Vol. liq. (members') Aug. 1934. Capital returned to contributories—13s. 3d. per share (of 10s.). £50 was paid into Companies' Liquidation Account in respect of unclaimed dividends or distributions. Final meeting return regd. 23 Apr. 1954 .... **1955**

Port Nigel Lead Co. Ld. Regd. 1874. Vol. liq. Jan. 1882. Final meeting return regd. 4 May 1886 .... **1883**

Port of Beira Development Ld. Regd. 1922. Vol. liq. (members') 31 May 1951. Capital returned to contributories—22s. 9·68d. per share of 1s. Final meeting return regd. 5 Nov. 1956 .... **1957**

Port of Blyth Steam Fishing & Ice Co. Ld. Regd. 1910. Vol. liq. 22 Nov. 1916. Final meeting return regd. 11 Mar. 1921 .... **1917**

Port of Havana Docks Co. Inc. Maine 1910 as Havana Dock & Warehouse Co.; name changed Dec. 1910. The outstanding 5% 1st mortgage 30-year gold bonds were redeemed at par on 1 Feb. 1941......... **1941**

Port of Manchester Insurance Co. Ld. Regd. 1919 as Port of Manchester Marine Insurance (1919) Ld.; name changed Feb. 1921 to Port of Manchester Marine Insurance Co. Ld. and as above June 1923. Court Order to wind up 29 May 1933. Liquidator released 6 May 1943 .... **1934**

Port of Manchester Road Service Ld. Regd. 1921. Vol. liq. 1 May 1929. Final meeting return regd. 25 June 1930 .... ***1930**

Port of Para. Inc. in Maine 1906. Charter terminated 31 Dec. 1968. Corporate existence ceased 31 Dec. 1971. Repayments of funded debt—5½% 1st mortgate 50 year gold bonds ("1st division bonds"). $246·50 per £100 bond or $49·30 per £20 bond; 5% 1st mortgage 60 year bonds ("2nd division bonds"), $22·75 per bond of Frs. 500; 5½% cumulative income bonds: $364·40 per £1,000 bond. **1972**

Port of Queenborough Development Co. Ld. Regd. 1911 as Queenborough Syndicate Ld.; name changed 15 Sept. 1920. Court Order to wind up 24 July 1923. Liquidator released 25 Oct. 1933. Struck off Register 20 Mar. 1936 .... ***1924**

Port Phillip & Colonial Gold Mining Co. Ld. Regd. 1868. Vol. liq. 29 Apr. 1889. Reconstructed as Port Phillip Gold Co. Ld. in which company shareholders were entitled to 2 shares of 5s. (credited with 2s. paid) for each share of £1 4s. held. Final meeting return regd. 27 Jan. 1891 .... **1895**

Port Phillip Gold Co. Ld. Regd. 1889. Vol. liq. 3 July 1895. Reconstructed as company of same name. Shareholders were entitled to 1 share of 5s. (credited with 3s. paid) for each share of 5s. held. Final meeting return regd. 29 July 1898 .... **1896**

Port Phillip Gold Co. Ld. Regd. 1895. Vol. liq. 20 Jan. 1905. Final meeting return regd. 21 Mar. 1905..... **1905**

Port-Said Salt Association Ld. Regd. 1899. Vol. liq. 16 May 1955. Capital repayments of 2s. 6d. per share were sanctioned from 1 Mar. 1961 and 18 Dec. 1961. A 1st distribution (free of Egyptian taxes) of P.T. 16·5 (approx. 2s. 8½d.) per share was made in Feb. 1965. Payments to shareholders were suspended in 1968 pending settlement of a lawsuit.................. **1975–6**

Port St. Mary Fishing & Curing Co. Ld. Regd. 1915. Vol. liq. 14 May 1925. Final meeting return regd. 29 Oct. 1930 .... **1926**

Port Talbot Graving Dock & Shipbuilding Co. Ld. Regd. 1897. Reconstructed 1903 as company of same name. Removed from Register 1905 .... **1909**

Port Talbot Railway and Docks Co. Inc. by Special Act 1894. In 1922 the undertaking was merged into the

Great Western Railway Co. in which company stockholders were entitled to stock as follows:

For each £100 held	G.W.	
4% Debenture	£100 4% Debenture	
4% Preference	£80 5% Cons. Pref.	
Ordinary	£180 5% Cons. Guar.	1924

Port Talbot Steel Co. Ld. Regd. 1906. Vol. liq. 30 Nov. 1928. The outstanding 1st mortgage debenture stock was repaid at 101% on 30 Nov. 1928. Final meeting return regd. 29 Apr. 1930 .... **1929**

Portable Gas Fountain Syndicate Ld. Regd. 1899. Vol. liq. 30 July 1910. Struck off Register 20 Mar. 1925 **1925**

Porterfield Estates Ld. Inc. South Africa 1938 as Porterfield Estates (Proprietary) Ld.; name changed 13 Dec. 1941. Winding-up order 11 Nov. 1958. Assets realised insufficient to meet claims of creditors in full. No capital returned to contributories. In Aug. 1964 it was stated that for all practical purposes liquidation was complete **1965**

Porter's Shipping Co. Ld. Regd. 1880. Removed from Register 1905 .... ***1886**

Portfield Steamship Co. Ld. Regd. 1919. Mortgagees took possession of the vessels and the receiver held the building. Struck off Register 23 June 1944...... **1945**

Porthcawl Steamship Co. Ld. Regd. 1923. Vol. liq. (creditors) 15 Jan. 1932. Assets realised insufficient to pay unsecured creditors in full. Final meeting return regd. 18 Oct. 1932 .... **1932**

Porthdinllyn Railway Co. Inc. by Special Act 1884. Undertaking abandoned by Act of 1892 .... **1893**

Porthgain Harbour Ld. Regd. 1897. Struck off Register 8 Aug. 1905 .... **1906**

Portishead District Water Co. Regd. as Portishead Water Works Co. Ld. in 1872; reincorporated by Special Act 1875. Undertaking was transferred from 1 Jan. 1952 to Bristol Waterworks Co. preference stockholders were entitled to an equal amount of Bristol Water 5% consolidated preference stock plus cash bonus of 2½% the ordinary stock was repaid at 120% and the outstanding debenture stock was repaid at par. Dissolved 7 Oct. **1954**

Portishead Gas Co. Ld, Regd. 1866. Dissolved 1 May 1949 undertaking being vested in South Western Area Gas Board under Gas Act 1948. Holders of securities were entitled to receive in respect of each £10 unit held British Gas 3% guaranteed stock 1990–95 as follows:

	£ s. d.	
Orig. ord. shares (10% stand.)	19 10 0	
Addit. ord. shares (7% stand.)	13 13 0	
6% irred. pref. shares	13 6 0	1952

Portishead Water Works Co. Ld. See Portishead District Water Co.

Portland Buildings Ld. Regd. 1915. Vol. liq. (members') 13 Sept. 1944. Capital returned to ordinary shareholders—£11·84 per share of £1. Final meeting return regd. 6 Mar. 1945 .... **1945**

Portland Cement & Limestone Products Ld. Regd. 1927. Court Order to wind up Nov. 1929. Struck off Register 15 June 1937 .... **1938**

Portland Cement Co. "Nesher" Ld. Regd. 1922. Vol. liq. (members') 4 Dec. 1946. Capital returned to contributories—£3 14s. 6·03406d. and £Isr.1·035 per share of £1. £10,850 paid into Companies' Liquidation Account. Final meeting return regd. 20 Feb. 1954 .... **1954**

Portland Cement Co. of Utah Ld. Regd. 1900. Vol. liq. Dec. 1909. Removed from Register 1911 .... **1910**

Portland Cement Selling & Distributing Co. Ld. Regd. 1927. Vol. liq. (members') 18 Nov. 1931. Assets realised sufficient to meet claims of creditors in full. Final meeting return regd. 23 Aug. 1932............. **1932**

Portland Electric Power Co. See Pacific Northwest Public Service Co.

Portland Railway, Light & Power Co. See Pacific Northwest Public Service Co.

Portland (Rossland) Mine Ld. Regd. 1899. Reconstructed 1904 as Velvet Portland Mine Ld. in which company shareholders were entitled to 4 shares of 10s. (credited as fully-paid) for every 9 shares of £1 held. Removed from Register 1904 .... **1905**

Portland Rubber Co. Ld. Regd. 1909. Vol. liq. (members') 31 Dec. 1935. No capital returned to contributories. Final meeting return regd. 26 May 1936.. **1936**

Portland Town Estate Co. Ld. Regd. 1921. Vol. liq. 6 Oct. 1926. The A debentures were redeemed in accordance with terms of issue. Final meeting return regd. 30 July 1927.. **1927**

Portland Water Co. (Maine, U.S.A.). Inc. by Special Act Maine 1866. Property acquired in 1908 by Portland (Maine) Water District who assumed liability for outstanding consolidated mortgage 4% gold bonds class B. **1927**

Portmadoc, Beddgelert & South Snowdon Railway Co. Inc. by Special Act 1901. Undertaking acquired by Welsh Highland Railway (Light Railway) Co. for 50,000 fully-paid ordinary shares of £1 **1923**

Portmadoc, Crœsor & Beddgelert "Tram" Railway Co. Inc. by Special Act 1865 as Croesor & Portmadoc Railway Co.; name changed by Act of 1879 .... **1901**

Portman Estate Mansions Ld. Regd. 1899. Vol. liq. (members') Mar. 1934. Undertaking and assets were acquired by London County Freehold and Leasehold Properties Ld. Holders of 5% 1st mortgage debenture stock were entitled either to repayment in cash at 107% or to £100 in 4% 1st mortgage debenture stock in acquiring company plus £4 in cash for every £100 either stock held; holders of 6% income bonds were entitled to repayment in cash at par or to £98 4% 1st mortgage debenture stock for each' £100 bonds held. Final meeting return regd. 8 Dec. 1934 .... **1935**

Portman Rooms Ld. Regd. 1887. Vol. liq. 24 Jan. 1923. Final meeting return regd. 12 Apr. 1923 .... **1924**

Portmore Tea Co. of Ceylon Ld. Regd. 1896. Vol. liq. (members') 8 Nov. 1939. Final meeting return regd. 21 Dec. 1940 .... **1940**

Porto Alegre & New Hamburg (Brazilian) Railway Co. Ld. Regd. 1870. Vol. liq. 18 Aug. 1910. Struck off Register 12 July 1935 .... **1912**

Porto Rico Power Co. Ld. Inc. Canada 1906 as Porto Rico Railways Co. Ld.; name changed Nov. 1930. Court Order to wind up 26 Jan. 1944. Preference shares were repaid in full plus arrears of dividend; a 1st distribution of $150 per common share of $100 was made on 2 Feb. 1944 and a further sum of $500,000 was set aside for further distribution when the respective rights of the preference and common shareholders had been determined **1946**

Porto Rico Railways Co. Ld. See Porto Rico Power Co. Ld.

Portpatrick and Wigtownshire Joint Committee. Inc. by Special Act 1885. In 1923 the undertaking was merged into the London Midland & Scottish Railway Co. in which company stockholders were entitled to £87½ 4% Guaranteed Stock (carrying dividend from 1st Feb. 1923) for each £100 Portpatrick 3½% Guaranteed Stock held................ **1924**

Portsea Island Gas Light Co. See Portmouth & Gosport Gas Co.

Portsmouth & Gosport Gas Co. Inc. by Special Act 1821 as Portsea Island Gas Light Co.; name changed to Portsmouth Gas Co. 1926 and as above 1936. Dissolved 1 May 1949 undertaking being vested in Southern Area Gas Board under Gas Act 1948. Holders of securities were entitled to receive in respect of £100 unit held British Gas 3% guaranteed stock 1990–95 as follows:

	£ s. d.	
4% stand. cons. stock	157 0 0	
5% max. stock	111 10 0	
5% pref. stock	114 10 0	
4% pref. stock	101 0 0	
4% perp. deb. stock (1861 issue)	102 10 0	
4% perp. deb. stock (1872 issue)	102 5 0	
5% red. deb.stock	104 10 0	
3½% red.deb.stock	101 0 0	
3½% red. deb. stock (issued before 1 Jan.1946)	100 0 0	
3½% red. deb. stock (issued since 31 Dec. 1945)	101 0 0	1952

Portsmouth & Hayling Light Railway Co. Inc. (under Light Railways Act 1896) by order of Light Railway Commissioners confirmed by Board of Trade 1905 **1911**

Portsmouth & Hayling Railway Co. Inc. by Special Act 1886. Undertaking abandoned **1894**

Portsmouth & Southsea Army & Navy Stores Ld. Regd. 1891. Vol. liq. 17 Jan. 1893. Court Order to continue winding up under supervision 6 Sept. 1893. Struck off Register 21 June 1907 .... **1895**

Portsmouth Empire Palace Ld. Regd. 1890. Vol. liq. (members') 15 Sept. 1958. Final meeting return regd. 27 Jan. 1960 .... **1940**

Portsmouth Gas Co. See Portsmouth & Gosport Gas Co.

Portsmouth New Harbour Co. Ld. Regd. 1913. Court Order to wind up 27 July 1915. Liquidator released 14 Feb. 1921. Struck off Register 20 Mar. 1925 ... **1916**

Portuguese Consolidated Copper Mines Ld. Regd. 1888. Court Orders: to wind up 15 Feb. 1890; to dissolve 31 Dec. 1894 .... **1891**

Portuguese Mining & Exploration Syndicate Ld. Regd. 1903. Removed from Register 1905 .... **1905**

Portuguese Trade Corporation Ld. Regd. 1918. Vol. liq. 13 Sept. 1927. Final meeting return regd. 9 May 1928 .... **1928**

Portvale Steamship Co. Ld. Regd. 1923. Struck off Register Mar. 1934.. **1935**

VOL. FOR

†**Porvair p.l.c.** Regd. as private company 20 Aug. 1919 as Alton Battery Co. Ld.; name changed Porous Plastics Ld. 14 Sept. 1959 and to Porvair Ld. 20 Dec. 1968; converted public company 15 Jan. 1969 & re-registered p.l.c. in 1982. Vol. liq. (members') 6 June 1983
† Name changed Alnery No. 152 p.l.c. 4 Dec. 1982 **1983–4**

Porvenis Mercury Mines Ld. *See* Oviedo Mercury Mines Ld.

Positive Adhesion Railway Accessories Ld. *See* Positive Retorts Ld.

Positive Government Security Life Assurance Co. Ld. Regd. 1870. Vol. liq. 11 Mar. 1896. Taken over by British Empire Mutual Life Assurance Co. Capital returned to contributories—£1 15*s*. per share of £1 7*s*. 6*d*.; further payments (if any) not known. Final meeting return regd. 18 Jan. 1900 .... **1896**

Positive Retorts Ld. Regd. 1911 as City Oil Synd. Ld.; name changed to City of Calgary Oil Synd. Ld. in 1914; to Positive Adhesion Railway Accessories Ld. in 1924 and as above in 1926. Struck off Register 28 May 1948 .... **1949**

Poso-Graph (Great Britain) Distributing Co. Ld. Regd. 1928. Vol. liq. 5 July 1929. Final meeting return regd. 21 Jan. 1932 .... **1930**

Poso-Graph (Parent) Corporation, Ld. Regd. 1928. Winding-up order 9 Dec. 1929. No capital returned to contributories. Liquidator released 29 Jan. 1957. Struck off register 14 Apr. 1959 .... **1957**

Posoltega Rubber Estates Ld. Regd. 1907. Vol. liq. May 1912. Removed from Register 1913 .... **1913**

Postal Telegraph Inc. Inc. Delaware 1939. In dissolution; assets transferred to Western Union Telegraph Co. **1941**

Postal Telegraph & Cable Corporation. Inc. Maryland 1928. Reorganised 1939 when land line system was acquired by Postal Telegraph Inc. No provision was made for holders of preferred or common stocks. Holders of every $1,000 bonds or debenture stock were entitled to 20 shares common and 5 shares preferred stock of Postal Telegraph Inc., $160 income debentures and $20 income debentures series B of All-American Cable & Radio Corporation, 20 shares common stock of American Cable & Radio Corporation and $35 in cash **1943**

Potchefstroom Exploration, Gold Mining & Estate Co. Ld. Inc. Transvaal 1889. Vol. liq. May 1926. Distribution of 1*s*. per share of £1 on 12 July 1926; further payments (if any) not known **1927**

Potchefstroom Gold Fields Co. Ld. Regd. 1887. Vol. liq. 29 May 1895. Taken over by African Mineral Estates Ld. Final meeting return regd. 23 June 1896 **1896**

Potosi Consolidated Ld. Regd. 1902 as Mount Margaret Reward Ld.; name changed Apr. 1903. Reconstructed 1905 as Potosi Consolidated (1905) Ld., in which company shareholders were entitled to 1 share of 10*s*. (credited with 8*s*. paid) for each share of £1 held. Removed from Register 1909 .... **1908**

Potosi Consolidated (1905) Ld. Regd.' 1905. Vol. liq. July 1908. Removed from Register 1909 .... **1909**

Potosi Consols Ld. Regd. 1891. Vol. liq. 13 Apr. 1892. Mortgagee entered into possession of property. Final meeting return regd. 11 Oct. 1892...................... **1893**

Potosi Gold Mining Co. Ld. *See* New Potosi Co. Ld.

Potosi Ld. Regd. 1887. Vol. liq. 31 Mar. 1891. Reconstructed as Potosi Consols Ld., in which company shareholders were entitled to 1 share of £1 (credited with 17*s*. 6*d*. paid) for each ordinary share of £1 held or 1 fully-paid share of £1 for each preference share of £1 held. Final meeting return regd. 30 May 1892 .... **1892**

Potsdam (City of) Waterworks Co. Ld. Regd. 1875. Removed from Register 1905 .... **1891**

Potsdam Reefs Ld. Regd. 1889. Vol. liq. 29 July 1891. Final meeting return regd. 15 Nov. 1895 .... **1892**

Potsdam (Transvaal) Mynpacht Ld. Regd. 1902. Vol. liq. Jan. 1910. Removed from Register 1913 .... **1910**

Potteries, Shrewsbury & North Wales Railway Co. Inc. by Special Act 1866. Undertaking was sold in 1888 to Shropshire Railways Co. for sufficient Shrewsbury separate capital stock to give A debenture stock, 60%; B debenture stock, 40%; C debenture stock, 25%; creditors 20% and shareholders 7% ... **1899**

Poulton-le-Fylde Gas. Coal. Lime & Coke Co. Ld. Undertaking transferred by Act of 1901 to Poulton-le-Fylde Urban District Council. Dissolved before 1931 .... **1902**

Pound (Henry), Son & Hutchins Ld. Regd. 1886. Removed from Register 1904 .... **1891**

Powder River Cattle Co. Ld. Regd. 1882. Vol. liq. 7 Sept. 1886. Final meeting return regd. 3 Mar. 1893 ...... **1888**

Powell & Mooney Ld. Regd. Dublin 1896. Vol. liq. Mar. 1919 .... **1919**

VOL. FOR

Powell & Ricketts Ld. Regd. 1919. Vol. liq. 13 July 1923. Final meeting return regd. 12 Dec. 1923 .... **1924**

Powell & Sing Ld. Regd. 1900. Vol. liq. 24 Jan. 1905. Final meeting return regd. 15 Aug. 1906 .... **1905**

Powell Duffryn Steam Coal Co. Ld. Regd. 1864. Vol. liq. (members') 1 Mar. 1944. Holders of (*a*) 6% non-cumulative preference and 2nd preference shares received repayment of capital in cash at par on 31 Mar. 1944 or at holder's option, a like nominal amount of ordinary shares of £1 in Powell Duffryn Ld., (*b*) preferred ordinary stock received repayment of capital in cash at par on 31 Mar. 1944 or at holder's option, 9 ordinary shares of £1 in Powell Duffryn Ld. for each £10 of stock held, and (*c*) ordinary stock received 1 ordinary share in Powell Duffryn Ld. for each £1 of ordinary stock held. £2,126 10*s*. 3*d*. was paid into Companies' Liquidation Account (*see preface*). Final meeting return regd. 3 Mar. 1945 .... **1946**

Powell (Thomas) Ld. Regd. 1903. Vol. liq. Jan. 1932. Struck off Register June 1932 .... **1933**

Powell's Tillery Steam Coal Co. Ld. Regd. 1904. Assets were sold to Partridge, Jones & John Paton Ld. and realised insufficient to repay debenture holders. Struck off Register 1 May 1942 .... **1943**

Power & Traction Finance Co. (Poland) Ld. Regd. 1923. Vol. liq. (members') 30 Sept. 1964. Final meeting return regd. 3 June 1965 .... **1957**

Power and Traction Ld. Regd. 1897. Struck off Register 30 May 1919 .... ***1918**

Power Investment Corporation Ld. Regd. 1919 as Petroleum Power Investment Corpn., Ld.; name changed Sept. 1926. Undertaking acquired by The Mid-European Corpn., Ld. (later Bishopsgate Trust Ld.) from 31 Jan. 1961. Ordinary and 5% preference stockholders received an equivalent amount of ordinary and 5% preference capital of that company respectively; debenture stockholders received debenture stock in exchange for their holdings at the rate of £102 3½% stock and £100 5½% stock for every £100 3½% stock and 5½% stock held respectively. Dissolved on 31 May 1961 under Section 208 of the Companies Act, 1948 .... **1962**

Power Spirits Ld. Regd. 1920. Vol. liq. (creditors') 13 Jan. 1937. Capital returned to contributories—5*s*. 11¾*d*. per ordinary or B ordinary share of £5. Final meeting return regd. 29 Nov. 1937 .... **1937**

Powolny's (Hull) Ld. Regd. 1902. Receiver appointed 7 July 1908; ceased to act 27 Sept. 1927. Vol. liq. 15 July 1907. Final meeting return regd. 31 Dec. 1927 ***1908**

Powolny's Ld. Regd. 1897. Vol. liq. 24 June 1920. Final meeting return regd. 31 Dec. 1926 .... **1921**

Pradena Silver Mines Ld. Regd. 1888. Vol. liq. Feb. 1890. Final meeting return regd. 18 Apr. 1890 .... **1891**

Prague & Brünn Ice Co. Ld. Regd. 1883. Vol. liq. 21 Feb. 1887. Assets were acquired by United Anglo-Continental Ice Co. Ld., in which company shareholders were entitled to an equal number of shares. Removed from Register 1906 .... **1888**

Prah Gold Mines Ld. Regd. 1901. Undertaking and assets were acquired by South African Goldfields Ld., in which company shareholders were entitled to 5 shares of 10*s*. (credited with 8*s*. paid) for every 2 shares of £1 held. Removed from Register 1907 .. **1905**

Prah Syndicate Ld. Regd. 1900. Removed from Register 1903 .... **1903**

Prah Trading & Development Co. Ld. Regd. 1919. Vol. liq. 5 June 1923. Reconstructed as West African Mahogany Co. Ld., in which company shareholders were entitled to 1 share of 5*s*. (credited as fully-paid) for each share of 5*s*. held. Final meeting return regd. 16 July 1926 .... **1924**

Prairie Cattle Co. Ld. Regd. Edinburgh 1880. Vol. liq. Feb. 1915. Final meeting return regd. 22 Jan. 1921 **1915**

Pranges Estancia Co. Ld. *See* La Concordia Estancia Co. Ld.

Pratt (F. & R.) & Co. Ld. Undertaking and assets were acquired by Cauldon Potteries Ld. **1924**

Precious Metal Industries Ld. Regd. 1923 as Caterham Works Ld.; name changed Mar. 1925. Vol. liq. 13 Apr. 1928. Final meeting return regd. 13 June 1929 **1934**

Precious Minerals Ld. Regd. 1912. Struck off Register 28 Feb. 1939 .... **1940**

Preece (J. A.) & Sons Ld. Regd. 1899. Receiver appointed in Apr. 1914. The business was sold to Preece's Riding School & Motor Carriage Co. Ld. in Oct. 1914; the purchase money was distributed among the debenture stockholders. Struck off Register 1916 .... **1915**

Preece's Point Proprietary (Hauraki) Ld. Regd. 1895. Removed from Register 1909 .... **1901**

Preference Securities Trust Ld. Regd. 1888. Vol. liq. 29 Dec. 1893. Reconstructed as Aegis Investment Co.

**See Stock Exchange Year-Book.*

VOL. FOR

Ld. Preferred shareholders were entitled to debentures in new company and deferred shareholders to 50% of holding in fully-paid shares. Final meeting return regd. 4 Mar. 1895 .... **1894**

Preferential Investment Trust Ld. Regd. 6 Oct. 1959 as private company; converted to public company 9 Nov 1959. On 21 July 1975 the loan capital was cancelled, holders being entitled to £1 8.4% debenture stock of Estates House Investment Trust Ld., for every £1 7% 1st mortgage debenture stock. Company dissolved without winding up on 31 Dec. 1976 .... **1977-8**

Premier Automatic Machine Co. Ld. Regd. 1928. Vol. liq. (creditors') 12 June 1930. No money was available to meet claims of creditors. Final meeting return regd. 20 Jan. 1933 .... **1930**

Premier Briquette Co. Ld. Regd. 1919. Court Order to wind up 24 Oct. 1922. Struck off Register June 1931 **1932**

Premier Coal Estates Ld. Inc. Transvaal 1905. London agency discontinued in 1908 .... **1908**

Premier Concessions of Mozambique Ld. Regd. 1892. Removed from Register 1904 .... **1900**

Premier Consolidated Gold Co. Ld. Regd. 1890. Vol. liq. 8 May 1895. Removed from Register 20 Mar. 1906 ***1896**

Premier Cycle Co. Ld. See Coventry Premier Ld.

Premier Development Corporation of Mexico Ld. Regd. 1905. Vol. liq. 26 May 1908. Properties were being sold to West Mexican Assets Ld. Final meeting return regd. 25 Aug. 1921 .... **1909**

Premier Electric Theatres, Ld. Regd. 1909. Court Order to wind up 23 Jan. 1912. Liquidator released 23 Jan. 1915. Struck off Register 14 Feb. 1919 .... **1912**

Premier Electric Welding Co. Ld. Regd. 1919. Vol. liq. (members') 15 Dec. 1932. All shares owned by Murex Ld. Final meeting return regd. 1 Aug. 1933 **1933**

Premier Exploration Co. Ld. Regd. 1909 as Rhodesian Gold Explorers Ld.; name changed Jan. 1913. Vol. liq. 31 Dec. 1915. Capital returned to contributories—15% at 21 Mar. 1916; further payments (if any) not known. Final meeting return regd. 28 Jan. 1918 **1916**

Premier Globe Ld. Regd. 1931. Vol. liq. (members') 31 Dec. 1935. Capital returned to contributories—1s. 5d. per share. Final meeting return regd. 4 June 1940 **1936**

Premier Glynrhonwy Slate Quarry Ld. Regd. 1919. Vol. liq. (members') 6 May 1931. Capital returned to contributories—1s. 2·9d. per preference share of 10s. £73 4s. 10d. was paid into Companies' Liquidation Account in respect of unclaimed capital and a further £23 19s. 3d. was paid in respect of unclaimed dividends. Final meeting return regd. 20 Dec. 1932 .... **1932**

Premier Gold Mines Ld. Regd. 1900. Reconstructed as New Premier Gold Mines Ld., in which company shareholders were entitled to 2 shares of 5s. (credited with 3s. 6d. paid) for each share of 10s. held. Removed from Register 1908 .... **1907**

Premier Gold Mining Co., No liability. Inc. South Australia 1894. London office closed 30 June 1902 **1903**

Premier Hydraulic Tin Mines of Nigeria Ld. Regd. 1920. Vol. liq. 5 Aug. 1925. Undertaking and assets were sold to Nigerian Base Metals Corporation Ld., in which company shareholders were entitled to 4 fully-paid shares of 5s. for every 5 shares of £1 held; certain debenture holders agreed to accept an equal amount of fully-paid shares in new company, the remainder were to be paid in cash. Final meeting return regd. 4 Feb. 1930 .... **1926**

Premier Insurance Co. Ld. Regd. 1903. Struck off Register Feb. 1930 .... **1931**

Premier Kuban (Maikop) Oil Co. Ld. Regd. 1911. Struck off Register 1925 .... **1925**

Premier New Zealand Gold Mining Co. Ld. Regd. 1898. Vol. liq. Mar. 1912. Removed from Register 1913 **1913**

Premier Oil & Finance Co. Ld. Regd. 1924. Vol. liq. (members') 15 Dec. 1930. Undertaking and assets acquired by Premier Globe Ld in which company shareholders received 1 fully paid share of 5s. for every 6 shares of 5s. held. Final meeting return regd. 24 Dec. 1935 .... **1931**

Premier Oil & Pipe Line Co. Ld. Regd. 1910. Vol. liq. 27 Aug. 1919. Reconstructed as Premier Oil Co. Ld., in which company shareholders were entitled to 1 share of 15s. (credited with 14s. paid) for every ordinary share of £1 held, or 3 shares of 15s. (credited with 14s. paid) for every 2 preference shares of £1 held. Final meeting return regd. 16 June 1920 .... **1920**

Premier Oil Co. Ld. Regd. 1919. Vol. liq. 25 June 1924. Undertaking and assets were acquired by Premier Oil & Finance Co. Ld., in which company shareholders were entitled to 1 share of 5s. and 1s. in cash for every 5 shares of 4s. held. Final meeting return regd. 5 Nov. 1925 .... **1925**

VOL. FOR

Premier Omnibus Co. Ld. See London Premier Omnibus Co. Ld.

Premier Petroleum Co. Ld. Regd. 1908. Vol. liq. 29 June 1911. Final meeting return regd. 22 Oct. 1912 ...... ***1912**

Premier Petroleum Co. Inc. Maine 1910. Assets were realised and distributed **1917**

Premier Re-forming Co. Ld. Regd. 1909. Vol. liq. 24 Oct. 1913. Final meeting return regd. 26 June 1914 **1914**

Premier Rinks Ld. Regd. 1909. Receiver appointed in Apr. 1911. Assets realised insufficient to pay debenture holder in full. Struck off Register 1914 **1912**

Premier Sunrise (New Zealand) Gold Mining Co. Ld. Regd. 1902. Vol. liq. May 1906. Removed from Register 1907 .... **1907**

Premier Tanneries Ld. Regd. Edinburgh 1909. Vol. liq. Apr. 1911. Final meeting return regd. 2 July 1912 **1912**

Premier Tarless Fuels Ld. Regd. 1911. Struck off Register 1918 .... **1916**

Premier Tati Monarch Reef Co. Ld. Regd. 1895. Vol. liq. 24 July 1918. Final meeting return regd. 14 May 1919 .... **1919**

Premier Transport Co. (Keighley) Ld. Regd. 1919. Vol. liq. 9 Jan. 1928. Undertaking was acquired by West Yorkshire Road Car Co. Ld. Final meeting return regd. 1 Sept. 1928 .... **1935**

Premix Gas Plants Ld. Regd. 1928. Vol. liq. (creditors') 17 May 1932. Assets realised insufficient to pay unsecured creditors in full. Final meeting return regd. 21 Oct. 1935 .... **1933**

Prentice & Southern Deep Leads (1907) Ld. Inc. Victoria 1907. Victorian Government foreclosed on the property and London office was closed.................... **1911**

Prentice Brothers Ld. Regd. 1891. Vol. liq. 30 July 1929. Undertaking and assets were acquired by Fison, Packard & Prentice Ld. (later Fisons Ld.) in which company shareholders were entitled to 5 ordinary shares of £1 (credited as fully-paid) for each ordinary share of £10 held or 9 fully-paid preference shares of £1 for each preference share of £10 held. Final meeting return regd. 9 May 1930 .... **1930**

Prepayment Gas Meter Co. Ld. Regd. 1895. Removed from Register 4 Oct. 1898 .... ***1896**

Prescot & District Gas Co. Inc. by Special Act 1867 as Prescot Gas Co.; name changed 1929. Dissolved 1 May 1949, undertaking being vested in North Western Area Gas Board under Gas Act 1948. Holders of securities were entitled to receive British Gas 3% guaranteed stock 1990–95 as follows in respect of each £100 unit, unless otherwise stated, of security held:

	£	s.	d.
Cons. ord. shares (5% max.) (of £1)..	1	2	3
5% cons. ord. stock	111	5	0
6% pref. shares (of £1)	1	6	8
4% C pref. stock	101	0	0
4½% C pref. stock	109	0	0
5% C pref. stock	112	0	0
4% red. pref. stock	101	10	0

Liability in respect of certain mortgage loans assumed by the Board **1952**

Prescott's Bank Ld. Regd. 1890 as Prescott, Dimsdale, Cave, Tugwell & Co. Ld.; name changed Jan. 1903. Vol. liq. 1903. Business acquired by the Union of London and Smiths Bank Ld., which company allotted 34,924 shares (credited with £5 10s. paid up) to the shareholders **1904**

Prescott, Dimsdale, Cave, Tugwell & Co. Ld. See Prescott's Bank Ld.

Preserve Manufacturers Ld. Regd. 1919. Vol. liq. 9 July 1924. Final meeting return regd. 23 Dec. 1926 ..... **1925**

President Land and Exploration Co. Ld. Regd. 1889. Vol. liq. 23 Apr. 1895. Undertaking was acquired by Transvaal Estates & Development Co. Ld. for £64,300 in fully-paid shares. Final meeting return regd. 3 Feb. 1898 .... **1896**

Press Caps Ld. Regd. 1922. Vol. liq. (members') 30 July 1949. Undertaking acquired by Metal Box Co. Ld. £60 was paid into Companies' Liquidation Account. Final meeting return regd. 5 May 1952 .... **1953**

Prestea Block A Ld. Regd. 1903. Receiver appointed in July 1925 for debenture holders. Assets in West Africa were sold to Gold Coast Explorers Ld., in 1925 for £20,000 in cash. Vol. liq. 30 Oct. 1929. Final meeting return regd. 20 Jan. 1930 .... **1930**

Prestea Mines Ld. Regd. 1900. Vol. liq. Apr. 1909. Reconstructed as company of same name. Shareholders were entitled to 1 fully-paid share of 7s. 6d. in new company for each share of £1 held. Removed from Register 1909 .... **1910**

Prestea Mines Ld. Regd. 1909. Vol. liq. May 1911. The assets were transferred to Prestea Block A Ld., in which company shareholders were entitled to 1 fully-paid share of £1 plus 3s. in cash for every 4 shares of 7s. 6d. held; shares in Anfargah Gold

VOL. FOR

Mines Ld. (later Anfargah Gold Mines & Finance Co. Ld.) were to be distributed in specie. Removed from Register 1911 1912

Prested Miners' Gas Indicating Electric Lamp Co. Ld. Regd. 1903. Court Order to wind up 22 July 1913. Liquidator released 31 July 1915. Struck off Register 14 Feb. 1919 1914

Presteigne Gas Co. Ld. Regd. 1933. Dissolved 1 May 1949, undertaking being vested in Wales Area Gas Board under Gas Act 1948. Holders of ordinary shares (of £1) were entitled to receive 2s. British Gas 3% guaranteed stock 1990–95 for each share held 1952

Presto Gear-Case & Components Co. Ld. Regd. 1896. Vol. liq. 20 May 1914. Capital returned to contributories—2s. per share of £1 at Dec. 1914; further payments (if any) not known. Struck off Register 14 Feb. 1922 1915

Presto Stereotyping Machine & Matrix Co. Ld. Regd. 1896. Struck off Register 4 Oct. 1898 1899

Preston & Wyre Railway, Harbour & Dock Co. Inc. by Special Act 1835. Under Act of 1846 amalgamated with Lancashire & Yorkshire Railway Co. and London & North Western Railway Co. Joint Committee, under which shares of £25 were guaranteed £7 1s. 6d. % p.a. or 35s. 4½d. (less tax) for first 8 years from 1847, thereafter £7 17s. 2d. % or 39s. 3½d. per share of £25 in perpetuity 1889

Preston Banking Co. Ld. Established 1844. Regd. as limited 1883. Vol. liq. 17 Dec. 1894. Undertaking acquired by London and Midland Bank Ld. (later Midland Bank Ld.), in which company shareholders received 1 share of £60 (credited with £12 10s. paid) plus £20 8s. in cash for every ordinary share of £100 (£25 paid) held; or 1 share of £60 (credited with £12 10s. paid) plus £12 12s. in cash for each "A" share of £100 (£25 paid) held 1896

Preston Brewery Co. Ld. Regd. 1896. Struck off Register 4 Oct. 1898 1892

Preston Brewery Ld. Regd. 1889. Removed from Register 1893 .... *1892

Preston Coal Co. Ld. Regd. 1899. Vol. liq. 1 Apr. 1905. Final meeting return regd. 26 July 1905 .... *1905

Preston Davies Tyre & Valve Co. Ld. Regd. 1893. Vol. liq. 8 Feb. 1895. Struck off Register 20 Feb. 1945 1945

Preston Gas Co. Estd. 1815; inc. by Special Act 1839; reinc. by Special Act 1865. Dissolved 1 May 1949. undertaking being vested in North Western Area Gas Board under Gas Act 1948. Holders of securities were entitled to receive, in respect of each £100 unit held, British Gas 3% guaranteed stock 1990–95 as follows:

	£	s.	d.
A stock (10% stand.)	194	0	0
B stock (7% stand.)	142	10	0
5% pref. stock	112	0	0
4% perm. deb. stock (issued before 1 Jan. 1946)	101	0	0
4% perm deb. stock (issued since 31 Dec. 1945)	100	0	0
3½% perm. deb. stock	100	0	0
3¼% perm. deb. stock	100	0	0

Liability in respect of certain mortgage loans assumed by the Board 1952

Preston Tramways Co. Inc. 1878. Undertaking was purchased on 1 May 1887 by Preston Corporation for £5,000 1888

Preston Union Bank Ld. Business acquired in 1894 by Lancashire & Yorkshire Bank Ld., in which company shareholders were entitled to 1 share of £20 (credited with £10 paid) for every three shares held 1895

Prestonpans & District Gas Co. Ld. Regd. in Edinburgh 1914. Dissolved 1 May 1949, undertaking being vested in Scottish Area Gas Board under Gas Act 1948. Holders of ordinary shares (of £1) were entitled to receive £2 17s. British Gas 3% guaranteed stock 1990–95 for each share held 1952

Preston's Liverpool Distillery Co. Ld. Regd. 1888. Vol. liq. (members') 31 Mar. 1930. Undertaking was acquired by Distillers Co. Ld. The mortgage debentures were redeemed at 110%. Capital returned to contributories—£9 4s. 10·4835d. per ordinary or preference share of £5. Final meeting return regd. 24 Mar. 1931 1931

Pretoria Diamond Mines Ld. Regd. 1924. Assets were realised but no return to debenture holders was anticipated. Struck off Register 29 Oct. 1935 1936

Pretoria Estates Ld. Regd. 1903. Vol. liq. 18 June 1929. Final meeting return regd. 5 Sept. 1930 1930

Pretoria Lighting Co. Ld. Inc. Transvaal 1890. Reconstructed Nov. 1894. Undertaking was purchased by Municipality of Pretoria in 1904 for £115,000 1905

VOL. FOR

Pretoria-Pietersburg Railway Co. Ld. Inc. in London 1896; inc. South Africa 1896. Railway was expropriated by British Government on 14 Nov. 1903. The Government repaid the debentures in Dec. 1903. Capital returned to contributories—£10 10s. per share of £10 at June 1905; further payments (if any) not known 1906

Pretoria Townships Ld. Inc. Transvaal 1909. Undertaking was acquired in 1918 by Witwatersrand Township Estate & Finance Corporation Ld. (later South African Townships Mining & Finance Corporation Ld.) 1913

Pretsia Mines Ld. Regd. 1927. Insufficient capital was subscribed and subscriptions were returned. Struck off Register 25 Aug. 1939 1940

Pretsia Plantations Ld. Regd. 1913. Vol. liq. (members') 24 Feb. 1955. Preference capital was repaid at par. Capital returned to contributories—11s. 8d. per share (of 10s.). Final meeting return regd. 19 Oct. 1957 1958

Prices, Tailors (Ireland) Ld. Inc. Dublin 1935. Vol. liq. 22 Dec. 1959. Capital returned to contributories—7s. 10d. per preference share of £1. Final meeting return regd. 23 Nov. 1960 1961

Prichard & Constance (Manufacturing), Ld. Regd. 1926 as Perfumers, Prichard & Constance Ld.; name changed 28 Dec. 1926. Vol. liq. (members') 17 May 1954. Capital returned to contributories—preference and preferred ordinary shares were repaid at par; on deferred ordinary shares of 1s.—9½d. cash per share, in addition the freehold and leasehold properties, formulae, trade marks and goodwill, and investments in subsidiaries were distributed in specie to holders of deferred ordinary shares. £1,319 paid into Companies' Liquidation Account. Final meeting return regd. 12 Dec. 1955 1956

Pride of Gwalia Ld. Regd. 1899. Reconstructed 1900 as Gwalia Consolidated Ld., in which company shareholders were entitled to 1 share of £1 (credited as fully-paid) for each fully-paid share of £1 held. Removed from Register 1905 1901

Pride of Mount Margaret Ld. Regd. 1897. Vol. liq. 20 Sept. 1899. Amalgamated 1899 with Mount Margaret "Reward" Claim Ld., in which company shareholders were entitled to 1 share of £1 (credited as fully-paid) for every 2 shares of 10s. held. Final meeting return regd. 2 Apr. 1902 1900

Primary Producers Bank of Australia Ld. Inc. Brisbane 1923. Suspended payment Aug. 1931. Vol. liq. Sept. 1931 1932

Primitiva Gas Co. of Buenos Aires. See La Compania Primitiva de Gas de Buenos Aires

Primitiva Gas Co. of Buenos Aires Ld. Regd. 1901 as Primitiva Gas & Electric Lighting Co. of Buenos Aires Ld. name changed 1910. Vol. liq. (members') 27 Aug. 1959. Capital returned to contributories—13s. 3·2d. per share of 9s. 6d. Final meeting return regd. 15 Jan. 1964 1965

Primitiva Holdings Ld. Regd. 1929. Vol. liq. (members') 15 Oct. 1959. Capital returned to contributories—12s. 8·65d. per share of 7s. 6d. Final meeting return regd. 15 Jan. 1964 1965

Primitiva Nitrate Co. Ld. Regd. 1895. Vol. liq. 15 Dec. 1899. Final meeting return regd. 8 Aug. 1901 1900

Primrose Tea Co. Ld. See Northern Guarantee & Finance Corpn. Ld.

Prince Edward County Rly. Co. (see Central Ontario Rly.) 1924

Prince Fishing Co. Ld. Regd. 1904. Vol. liq. 12 Apr. 1915. The undertaking was acquired by Richard Irvin & Sons Ld., in which company shareholders were entitled to 1 ordinary share of £1 (credited as fully-paid) for each ordinary share of £1 held, or 1 preference share of £1 (credited as fully-paid) for each preference share of £1 held. Struck off Register 14 Feb. 1922 1916

Prince John Mining Co. Ld. Inc. South Dakota 1922 as Bear River Mountain Co. Ld.; name changed Feb. 1923. In May 1942 it was stated that company was moribund 1945

Prince of Gwalia Ld. Regd. 1898. Reconstructed 1900 as Gwalia Consolidated Ld., in which company shareholders were entitled to 1 share of £1 (credited as fully-paid) for each fully-paid share of £1 held. Removed from Register 1903 1901

Prince of Wales Mine Ld. Regd. 1893. Vol. liq. 28 Aug. 1894. Removed from Register 1903 1896

Prince of Wales Slate Co. Ld. Regd. 1885, Vol. liq. 6 Dec. 1895. Struck off Register 10 July 1906 1899

Prince Patrick Lead Mining Co. Ld. Regd. 1872. Vol. liq. 24 Aug. 1886. Final meeting return regd. 6 June 1887 .... *1881

*See Stock Exchange Year-Book.

VOL. FOR

Prince Royal Mine. Mine worked on cost book principle. Work suspended on 30 Sept. 1889 and company ordered to be wound up **1890**

Prince Steam Shipping Co. Ld. Regd. 1884. Vol. liq. 25 May 1898. Final meeting return regd. 21 Aug. 1899 **1896**

Prince's Dock Branch Joint Railway. Dissolved 8 Apr. 1949; undertaking vested 1 Jan. 1948 in British Transport Commission under Transport Act 1947 **1949**

Prince's Gold Mines Ld. Regd. 1895. Vol. liq. 29 Oct. 1897. Final meeting return regd. 7 Mar. 1899 ...... **1898**

Princes' Hall Restaurant Ld. Regd. 1896. Reconstructed 1908 as company of same name. Shareholders were entitled to 3 shares of £1 (credited with 16s. 8d. paid) for each share of £5 held. Removed from Register 1909 ...... **1908**

Princes' Hall Restaurant Ld. Regd. 1908. Vol. liq. 9 May 1924. Business sold to New Princes (1924) Ld. Final meeting return regd. 8 Sept. 1926 ...... **1952**

Prince's Mansions Co. Ld. Regd. 1887. Vol. liq. 10 Aug. 1899. Final meeting return regd. 14 Mar. 1900 ...... **1900**

Princes Risborough Gas Light & Coke Co. Ld. Regd. 1864. Dissolved 1 May 1949, undertaking being vested in Southern Area Gas Board under Gas Act 1948. Holders of ordinary shares (of £5) were entitled to receive £6 5s. British Gas 3% guaranteed stock 1990–95 for each share held **1952**

Princes River Gold Mines Ld. Regd. 1897. Struck off Register 26 Oct. 1900 ...... **1901**

Princesa Gold Mining Co. Ld. Regd. 1890. Vol. liq. 24 July 1894. Capital returned to contributories—2s. 9d. per share of £1; further payments (if any) not known. Final meeting return regd. 3 Jan. 1896...... **1896**

Princess Alix Gold Mine Ld. Regd. 1896. Removed from Register 1903 ...... **1901**

Princes Estate & Gold Mining Co. Ld. Inc. Transvaal 1889. Vol. liq. Feb. 1922. Capital returned to contributories—1s. 2d. per share of 2s. at May 1922 **1923**

Princess (Murchison) Consolidated Ld. Regd. 1896. Court Order to wind up 26 Jan. 1904. Removed from Register 1910 ...... **1904**

Princess Royal (Cue) Ld. Regd. 1895. The Property and undertaking were acquired in 1899 by Princess (Murchison) Consolidated Ld. in which company shareholders were entitled to 1 fully-paid share of 10s. for every 5 shares of 10s. held, or 1 share of 10s. (credited with 8s. paid) for each share of 10s. held. Struck off Register 18 Nov. 1902 ...... **1900**

Princess's Hotel Ld. Regd. 1912. Vol. liq. 1 Dec. 1914. Final meeting return regd. 18 Aug. 1917 ...... **1915**

Princeton B. C. Colliery Co. Ld. Regd. 1924. Receiver appointed in Mar. 1926; ceased to act Mar. 1930. Assets realised insufficient to repay debentures in full. Struck off Register Dec. 1931...... **1932**

Princeton Coal & Land Co. Ld. Regd. 1910. Undertaking was sold in 1934. Holders of prior lien debentures were repaid in cash; holders of 1st mortgage debenture stock were satisfied as regards principal and interest. Struck off Register 5 Nov. 1943 ...... **1944**

Princetown Railway Co. Inc. by Special Act 1878. In 1922 the undertaking was merged into the Great Western Railway Co., in which company stockholders were entitled to stock as follows:

For each £100 held   G.W.
4½% Loans ....£112 10s. 4% Debenture
B Stock .... £7 10s. in cash
C Stock .... £7 in cash
The Lloyd's Bonds and A Stock were held by the Great Western Railway Company and were cancelled...... **1924**

Pring & Thompson Process Ld. Regd. 1911. Vol. liq. 16 Dec. 1918. Struck off Register 24 July 1923 .... **1916**

Printing & Publishing Co. Ld. See Thom (Alexander) & Co. Ld.

Printing Machinery Co. Ld. Regd. 1898. Vol. liq. (members') 17 June 1948. Final meeting return regd. 31 Jan. 1949...... **1939**

Printing Telegraph & Construction Co. of the Agence Havas Ld. Regd. 1893. Vol. liq. 4 Feb. 1893. Struck off Register 5 Nov. 1907 ...... **1896**

Printing Trades & General Insurance Co. Ld. See Caxton Insurance Co. Ld.

Pritchard (D. F.) Ld. Regd. 1904. Receiver, appointed 16 Dec. 1929, stated that assets realised insufficient to repay debenture holders. Bulk of the brewery business was acquired in 1931 by Andrew Buchan's Breweries Ld. (later Rhymney Breweries Ld.). Struck off Register 25 Mar. 1938...... **1939**

Pritchard Flax, Fibre & Pulp Co. Ld. Regd. Edinburgh 1927. Court Orders: to wind up July 1930; to dissolve 21 June 1933 ...... **1931**

Pritchards Restaurants Ld. Regd. 1927. Vol. liq. (members') 26 Nov. 1934. Undertaking and assets were acquired by Aerated Bread Co. Ld., in which

VOL. FOR

company shareholders were entitled to 2 preference shares of £1 (credited as fully-paid) for every 5 preference shares of £1 held. Final meeting return regd. 23 Oct. 1935 ...... **1935**

Private Motor Car Underwriters Ld. Business was acquired by London & Edinburgh Insurance Co. Ld for £5,160 in cash and £2,000 in fullypaid ordinary shares...... **1933**

Privileged Co. to Protect Production & Trade in Currants. Inc. Greece 1905. Rights and privileges of company taken over by Greek Government Aug. 1924 ...... **1925**

Private & Industrial Banking Co. Ld. Regd. 1922 as Dalton Investment Co. Ld.; name changed Jan. 1928. Court Order to wind up 2 July 1928. Liquidator released 17 Dec. 1932. Struck off Register 15 Oct. 1935 ...... **1926**

Pro Patria Films Ld. Regd. 1927. Vol. liq. (members') 3 Feb. 1931 for amalgamation with British Instructional Films (Proprietors) Ld., in which company shareholders were entitled to 1 fully-paid ordinary share of 10s. for every 4 shares of 5s. held. Final meeting return regd. 21 Oct. 1932 ...... **1937**

Probst, Hanbury & Co. Ld. Regd. 1920. Vol. liq. (members') 27 June 1930. Capital returned to contributories—7s. 11d. per preference share of 16s. £1 3s. 5d. was paid into Companies' Liquidation Account. Final meeting return regd. 19 July 1938 **1931**

Produce & General Investments Ld. Regd. 1925. Vol. liq. (members') 30 Mar. 1960. Final meeting return regd. 15 Jan. 1963 ...... **1939**

Produce & General Trust Ld. Regd. 1911. Vol. liq. 15 Feb. 1924. Final meeting return regd. 5 Jan.1925 **1925**

Produce Brokers Co. Ld. Regd 1891. Vol. liq. 20 Mar. 1899 for reconstruction under same name. Preference shareholders received 1 preference and 1 ordinary share (both of £10) in new company for every 3 shares of £10 held. Ordinary shares (£10, £4 paid) were cancelled and liability of £6 per share extinguished. Final meeting return regd. 27 July 1899 ...... **1908**

Produce Brokers Co. Ld. Regd. 1899. Vol. liq. 9 Feb. 1925. All pending contracts were acquired by Produce Brokers New Co. (1924) Ld. Final Meeting return regd. 13 Feb. 1926 ...... **1926**

Produce Trading Co. Ld. Regd. 1913. Struck off Register 30 May 1919 ...... **1917**

Producer Gas Plants Ld. Regd 1917. Vol. liq. 30 Jan. 1922. Final meeting return regd. 24 Sept. 1926...... **1923**

Productions (Richmond) Ld. Regd. 1913. Vol. liq. 29 Mar. 1928. Subsidiary of London Theatres of Varieties Ld. Final meeting return regd. 21 Dec. 1928 ...... **1929**

Professional and Civil Service Supply Association Ld. Regd. under Industrial & Provident Societies Act 1867; regd. Edinburgh as limited 1912. Vol. liq. Sept. 1925. Final meeting return regd. 9 Apr. 1930 **1926**

Profits & Income Insurance Co. Ld. Regd. 1901. Court Order to wind up June 1925. The life business was acquired by British General Insurance Co. Ld.; the profits branch was acquired by Legal Insurance Co. Ld. Struck off Register 18 Feb. 1938 ...... **1939**

Progress Cycle Co. Ld. Regd. 1897. Removed from Register 1908 ...... **1904**

Progress Mines of New Zealand Ld. Regd. 1896. Vol. liq. (creditors') 30 Nov. 1932. No capital was returned to contributories. Final meeting return regd. 10 Mar. 1933 ...... **1933**

Progressive Assurance Co. Ld. Regd. 1891 as British Natural-Premium Provident Association Ld.; name changed 1898 to British Natural-Premium Life Association Ld., and as above Oct. 1908. Court Order to wind up 20 Oct. 1909. Struck off Register 1923 ...... **1910**

Projectile Co. Ld. Regd. 1898. Vol. liq. 26 Mar. 1902. Undertaking was acquired by Projectile Co. (1902) Ld. (later Projectile & Engineering Co. Ld.), for £365,000 in cash. Final meeting return regd. 11 June 1902 ...... **1900**

Promoting & Construction Co. Ld. Regd. 1912. Struck off Register Feb. 1931 ...... **1931**

Properties Investment Trust Ld. Regd. 1896. Vol. liq. 2 June 1969. Capital returned to contributories: 42s. 6d. plus 12·35p. per share (of 6s.). £156·68 was paid into Companies' Liquidation Account in respect of unclaimed dividends and £2,294·23 in respect of unclaimed distributions. Final meeting return regd. 8 May 1974...... **1974-5**

Properties Selection & Investment Trust Ld. Regd. 1928. Vol. liq. (members') 10 July 1947; undertaking acquired by Property Holding & Investment Trust Ld., in which company shareholders were entitled to 49 fully-paid ordinary shares of 10s. for every 10 ordinary shares of £1 and 19 fully-paid preference

VOL. FOR

shares of £1 for every 20 ordinary shares of £1 held. Final meeting return regd. 24 Nov. 1948 .... **1949**

Property Alliance Ld. Regd. 3 May 1899. Struck off Register 16 Nov. 1948 .... **1949**

Property & General Finance Corporation Ld. Regd. 1928. Court Order to wind up 10 Nov. 1930. Struck off Register 21 Sept. 1937 .... **1938**

Property Insurance Co. Ld. Regd. 1898 as Lost Property Insurance Co. Ld.; name changed July 1901. Vol. liq. 17 Nov. 1913. Court Order to continue winding up under supervision 16 Dec. 1913. Final meeting return regd. 21 Dec. 1917 .... **1914**

Property Investment Co. of Scotland Ld. Est. 1857. Regd. Edinburgh 1875. Court Orders; to wind up Aug. 1890; to dissolve 13 July 1912 .... **1891**

Property Marketing Co. Ld. Regd. 1927. Struck off Register 1933 .... ***1931**

Property Units Ld. Regd. 1936 as Unit Trusts Ld.; name changed June 1938. Vol. liq. (members') 30 Jan. 1939. All shares owned by Investment Managers & Secretaries Ld. Final meeting return regd. 15 Sept. 1939 .... **1939**

Proprietary Articles Ld. Regd. 1924. All capital was held by Heppells Ld. Struck off Register 24 Oct. 1933 .... **1926**

Proprietary House & Land Corporation Ld. Removed from Register 1903 .... ***1885**

Proprietary Syndicate Ld. Regd. 1896. Vol. liq. Jan. 1902. Removed from Register 1903 .... **1902**

Proprietors of "Nonn" Ld. Regd. 1928. Receiver appointed in Aug. 1931; ceased to act Aug. 1933. Assets realised sufficient for part repayment of debenture holders. Struck off Register Dec. 1935 . **1936**

Prospecting & General Developing Co. of West Australia Ld. Regd. 1894. Wound up under supervision of Court. Removed from Register 1906 .... **1901**

Prospectors' Association Ld. Regd. 1895. Vol. liq. 5 May 1898. Undertaking and assets were acquired by Key of Komata Ld., in which company shareholders were entitled to 1 share of £1 (credited with 15s. paid) for each share of £1 held and 1 fully-paid share in respect of each partly paid share taken up. Final meeting return regd. 30 Dec. 1898 .... **1899**

Prospectors of Matabeleland Ld. Regd. 1895. Reconstructed 1900 as company of same name. Shareholders were entitled to 1 share of £1 (credited with 17s. paid) in new company for each share of £1 held. Removed from Register 1903 .... **1908**

Prospectors of Matabeleland Ld. Regd. 1900. Vol. liq. July 1908. Shareholders were entitled to 7½ fully-paid shares of £1 in Kaffirs Consolidated Investment & Land Co. Ld. for every 100 shares of £1 held. Removed from Register 1911 .... **1909**

Protected Fixed Trusts Ld. Regd. 1935. Vol. liq. (members') 27 May 1941. Capital returned to contributories—7s. 3¾d. per share of £1. Final meeting return regd. 6 July 1942 .... **1942**

Protector Carriage & Horse Insurance Co. Ld. Regd. 1884 as Union Carriage & Horse Insurance Co. Ld.; name changed 5 Nov. 1884. Dissolved by Order of Court 21 Nov. 1889 .... ***1888**

Protector Endowment Loan & Annuity Co. Est. 1853. In 1886 it was stated that company had ceased to exist **1886**

Protector Fire Insurance Co. Ld. Regd. 1883 as John Bull Insurance Co. Ld.; name changed 4 Oct. 1886. Removed from Register 17 Nov. 1891 .... ***1886**

Protene Co. Ld. Regd. 1896. Struck off Register 1925 **1911**

Provenir Mercury Mines Ld. See Oviedo Mines Development Syndicate Ld.

Providence Tin Mines Ld. Regd. 1907. Receiver appointed in Oct. 1911. Struck off Register 1915 . **1913**

Providencia Mines Co. Inc. in Arizona 1908 .... **1917**

Provident Assurance Co. Ld. See Provident Free Home Assurance Co. Ld.

Provident Clerks' & General Accident Insurance Co. Ld. Regd. 1876. Vol. liq. Apr. 1907. Assets were acquired by Provident Clerks' & General Guarantee Association Ld. (later White Cross Insurance Co. Ld.). in which company shareholders were entitled to 1½ shares of £10 (credited with £4 paid) for each share of £10 held. Removed from Register 1908 . **1908**

Provident Fire Insurance Co. Ld. Regd. 1873. Removed from Register 1904 .... ***1876**

Provident Free Home Assurance Co. Ld. Regd. 1889 as Provident Assurance Co. Ld.; name changed Nov. 1891. Undertaking and assets were acquired by Provident Association of London. (later Provident Life Association of London). Dissolved by Act 30 Dec. 1912 .... **1911**

Provident Institution for Life Assurance and Annuities. See Provident Life Office.

Provident Life Office. Established 1806 as Provident Institution for Life Assurance and Annuities; name changed Aug. 1889. Undertaking was acquired in

VOL. FOR

1906 by Alliance Assurance Co. Ld. for 10,338 fully-paid new shares of £1.. **1906**

Provident Plate-Glass Insurance Co. Ld. Regd. 1886. Vol. liq. Nov. 1910. Removed from Register 1912 **1925**

Provident Stores Ld. Business acquired 1925 by Thrift & Provident Stores Ld. (later Thrift Stores Ld.) **1926**

Province of Buenos Aires Waterworks Co. Ld. Regd. 1908 as Province of Buenos Aires Waterworks (Construction) Synd. Ld.; name changed 13 Mar. 1911. Undertaking transferred to Argentine National Sanitary Works Dept. in May 1944 for £860,552 sterling. Vol. liq. (members') 4 Apr. 1945. Capital returned to contributories—preference shares at par plus arrears of dividend; £1 5s. 5·95d. per ordinary share of £1. £21 11s. 9d. was paid into Companies' Liquidation Account. Final meeting return regd. 26 Nov. 1955 .... **1956**

Province of Buenos Aires Waterworks (Construction) Synd. Ld. See above.

Province of Vicenza Steam Tramway Co. Ld. Regd. 1879. All shares were acquired by an Italian syndicate in 1907. Removed from Register 1910... **1908**

Provincial Banking Corporation. See London Provincial & South Western Bank Ld.

Provincial "Brush" Electric Light & Power Co. Ld. Regd. 1882. Vol. liq. July 1885. Final meeting return regd. 31 July 1888 .... **1886**

Provincial Discount & Credit Co. Ld. See York Investment Co. Ld.

Provincial Discount Co. Ld. See York Investment Co. Ld.

Provincial Homes Investment Co. Ld. See Southern Union Marine & General Insurance Co. Ld.

Provincial Insurance Co. Established 1852. Business was acquired by Alliance Assurance Co. in 1890 .... **1890**

Provincial Motor Bus & Traction Co. Ld. See London & Provincial Motor Bus & Traction Co. Ld.

Provincial Motor Cab Co. Ld. Regd. 1908. Court Order to wind up 7 Feb. 1914. Liquidator released 23 June 1915. Struck off Register 14 Feb. 1919 .... **1915**

Provincial Tramways Co. Ld. Regd. 1872. Vol. liq. (members') 20 Aug 1936. Certain assets were transferred to Provincial Traction Co. Ld. The 5½% 1st mortgage debenture stock was repaid at par on 20 June 1936. Capital returned to contributories—25s. (inc. 5s. premium) per preference share of £1; 4s. in cash and 2 shares of 4s. in acquiring company for each ordinary share of £1 held. £400 was paid into Companies' Liquidation Account in respect of preference share capital, £349 in respect of ordinary share capital and £724 0s. 4d. in respect of unclaimed dividends. Final meeting return regd. 25 Aug. 1937 .... **1937**

Prudential Deposit Trust Ld. See Brazilian, Canadian & General Trust Ld.

Prudential Investment Co. Ld. Regd. 1887. Vol. liq. 9 Jan. 1896. Court Order to continue winding up under supervision Jan. 1896. Removed from Register 1895 .... **1897**

Prudential Loan & Discount Co. Ld. Regd. 1882. Court Orders: to wind up 17 Aug. 1883; to dissolve 16 May 1888 .... ***1884**

Prudential Trust Co. Ld. Inc. by Special Act under laws of Canada in Nov. 1909. Liquidated in Dec. 1963 all assets and liabilities were assumed by Guaranty Trust Co. of Canada in accordance with Treasury Board approval of the Government of Canada, and the company ceased to exist on that date **1965**

Pryce Jones (Canada) Ld. See Jones (Pryce) (Canada) Ld.

Prye Rubber and Coconut Plantations Ld. Regd. 1909. Vol. liq. (members') 24 Feb. 1955; undertaking and assets were acquired by Batu Kawan Rubber and Coconut Plantations Ld. for £99,247 in fully-paid shares of 2s. Shareholders received 10 stock units (of 2s.) in Batu Kawan for every share (of £1) held. Final meeting return regd. 2 May 1957 .... **1958**

Pryor Reid & Co. Ld. Regd. 1896. Vol. liq. 10 June 1920. Brewery and licensed houses were acquired by Benskin's Watford Brewery Ld. Final meeting return regd. 25 Nov. 1921 .... **1921**

Public Companies Share Trust Ld. Regd. 1884. Court Orders: to wind up 15 Dec. 1888; to dissolve 18 June 1896 .... ***1886**

Public Works & Contract Co. Ld. Regd. 1883. Court Orders; to wind up 1 Apr. 1890; to dissolve 3 June 1896 .... **1891**

Public Works Co. of Egypt (Société Générale de Travaux en Egypte). Inc. by Khedival decree 1881. In liquidation in 1886. Return of £5 share of £20 (£5 paid) in Oct. 1885 .... **1886**

Puce River Oilfields Ld. Regd. Edinburgh 1912. Vol. liq. Dec. 1919. Final meeting return regd. IS Sept. 1920 **1920**

*See Stock Exchange Year-Book.

Puchong Tin Dredging Ld. Inc. Federated Malay States 1925. Vol. liq. 11 Feb. 1939. Undertaking was acquired by Austral Amalgamated Tin Ld., in which company shareholders were entitled to 380 shares of 5s. (credited as fully-paid) for every 100 shares of £1 held...... **1940**

Pudsey Coal Gas Co. Inc. by Special Act 1855. Dissolved 1 May 1949, undertaking being vested in North Eastern Area Gas Board under Gas Act 1948. Holders of new cons. 7% stock were entitled to receive, in respect of each £100 unit held, £220 British Gas 3% guaranteed stock 1990–95. Liability in respect of certain mortgage loans assumed by the Board **1952**

Puebla Light & Power Co. Ld.-See below.

Puebla Tramway, Light & Power Co. Inc. in Canada 1903 as Puebla Light & Power Co. Ld.; name changed 1906. Vol. liq. June 1967. Capital returned to contributories—$20·67 per share. Charter surrendered 11 June 1968 ...... **1969**

Puerto Cabello & Valencia Railway Co. Ld. Regd. 1885. Vol. liq. (members') 14 Dec. 1944. Undertaking was acquired by Bolivar Railway Co. Ld. The 5% 1st charge coupon bonds were exchanged for 5% A debenture stock of that company at par. Capital returned to contributories—12s. 6d. per share of £10. £53 15s. was paid into Companies' Liquidation Account. Final meeting return regd. 20 Feb. 1946 ...... **1947**

Pugsley & Wakelin Ld. Regd. 1916. All capital was owned by Hosegood Industries Ld. Vol. liq. (members') 1 Feb. 1954. Final meeting return regd. 5 Feb. 1955...... **1950**

Pulido Mining Co. Ld. Regd. 1895. Vol. liq. Apr. 1908. Removed from Register 1908 ...... **1909**

Pullangode Rubber Co. Ld. Regd. 1934. Vol. liq. (members') 18 Aug. 1943, the estates. &c., having been sold. Capital returned to contributories—4s. 2·6d. per share of 2s. £6 14s. 5d. was paid into Companies' Liquidation Account. Final meeting return regd. 10 Apr. 1946 ...... **1947**

Pullin Thomas and Slade (late James Dole and Co.) Ld. Regd. 1897. Vol. liq. 10 Aug. 1920. Reconstructed as Harris (Calne) & General Produce Co. Ld. (later Allied Produce Co. Ld.) Final meeting return regd. 22 Nov. 1924 ...... **1921**

Pullinger Engineering Co. Ld. Regd. 1919. Court Order to wind up 18 Jan. 1921. Liquidator released 6 Nov. 1923. Struck off Register 13 May 1927...... ***1921**

Pullman Co. Organised Illinois 1867 as Pullman's Palace Car Co.; name changed 1899. Property assets and business of manufacturing department were sold; out of proceeds shareholders were entitled to 1 share of Pullman Inc. for every 2 shares of $100 held; that company also offered 2 shares of no par value for each share of $100 held **1928**

Pullman Co. Ld. See Drawing Room Cars Co. Ld.

Pump House Hotel (Llandrindod) Ld. Regd. 1903. Receiver appointed in Oct. 1929. Assets were realised, the mortgage of £30,000 repaid and debenture stockholders received 15s. 4½d. in £; further payments (if any) not known. Struck off Register 4 Oct. 1935 ...... **1936**

Puncture Proof Pneumatic Tyre Co. Ld. Regd. Dublin 1893. Vol. liq. Dec. 1895. Reconstructed as company of same name. Shareholders were entitled to 1 share of £1 (credited with 16s. paid) in new company for each share of £1 held **1898**

Puncture Proof Pneumatic Tyre Co. Ld. Regd. 1895. Vol. liq. 24 Jan. 1898. Business acquired by Detachable Pneumatic Tyre Syndicate Ld. Final meeting return regd. 11 Dec. 1902 ...... **1898**

Punjab & Cashmere Carpet Co. Ld. Regd. 1884. Court Orders: to wind up 14 Mar. 1887; to dissolve 10 Aug. 1891 ...... **1888**

Punjab Ice Co. Ld. Regd. 1881. Removed from Register 1903 ...... **1902**

Pure Beverage Co. Ld. Regd. 1881. Court Orders: to wind up Oct. 1882; to dissolve Sept. 1889 ...... **1883**

Pure Cane Molasses Co. Ld. Regd. 1921. Vol. liq. (members') 30 Apr. 1931. All shares owned by United Molasses Co. Ld. Final meeting return regd. 4 Dec. 1940 ...... **1932**

Pure Extracts Ld. Regd. 1928. Court Order to wind up 6 July 1931. Struck off Register 27 Jan. 1942........ **1942**

Pure Jamaica Ld. Regd. 1907. Court Order to wind up 17 Jan. 1911. Liquidator released 22 May 1917. Struck off Register 1 July 1921 ...... **1911**

Pure Metal Manufacturing Co. Ld. Regd. 1924. Vol. liq. (members') 3 June 1943. All shares owned by Murex Ld. Final meeting return regd. 6 Nov. 1943 .... **1945**

Pure Spirit Co. Ld. Regd. 1888. Vol. liq. 29 May 1890. Final meeting return regd. 14 Sept. 1895 ...... **1891**

Puriri Gold Estates Ld. Regd. 1897. Removed from Register 1911 ...... **1908**

Purisima Mining & Exploration Co. Ld. Regd. 1889. Reconstructed 1893 as New Purisima Smelting & Mining Co. Ld. Debenture holders were entitled to 1 fully-paid preference share of £1 for every £2 debenture held. Ordinary shareholders received an option (since expired). Removed from Register 1903 **1908**

Purity Bottling Stores Ld. Regd. 1920. Receiver appointed in Mar. 1927. Assets were insufficient to meet debenture debt. Struck off Register Feb. 1935 **1935**

Pusing Bharu Tin Mines Ld. Regd. 1907. Vol. liq. 14 July 1919. Undertaking and assets were acquired by Pusing Rubber & Tin Ld. (later London Wall Investment Trust Ld.) in which company shareholders were entitled to 3 shares of 2s. (credited as fully-paid) for each share of £1 held. Final meeting return regd. 25 May 1921 ...... **1920**

Pusing Lama Tin Mines Ld. Regd. 1904. Vol. liq. 14 July 1919. Undertaking & assets were acquired by Pusing Rubber and Tin Ld. (later London Wall Investment Trust Ld.) in which company shareholders were entitled to 93 shares of 2s. (credited as fully-paid) for every 100 shares of £1 held. Final meeting return regd. 25 May 1921 ...... **1920**

Pusing Rubber & Tin Ld. See London Wall Investment Trust Ld.

Putna Forests and Sawmills Co. Ld. Regd. 1903. Struck off Register 23 Dec. 1919 ...... ***1920**

Pwilbach Colliery Co. Ld. Regd. 1905. Vol. liq. 12 May 1924. Undertaking acquired by Henderson's Welsh Anthracite Collieries Ld. Struck off Register 7 July 1939 ...... **1940**

Pyle & Blaina Works Ld. Regd. 1889. Receiver appointed in Sept. 1909. Struck off Register 1918 **1911**

Pyle Works Ld. Regd. 1880. Court Orders: to wind up 16 Feb. 1889; to dissolve 13 Aug. 1893 ...... ***1886**

Pyman Steamship Co. Ld. Regd. 1894. Vol. liq. 12 Mar. 1918. Final meeting return regd. 14 July 1920 ...... **1918**

Pyne Bros. Ld. Regd. 1923. Vol. liq. (members') 24 Dec. 1958. All capital owned by Great Universal Stores Ld. Final meeting return regd. 17 Mar. 1959........ **1956**

Pyrah & Son Ld. Regd. 1910. Vol. liq. 18 Sept. 1920. Undertaking acquired by Carpet Trades Ld. (later John Crossley-Carpet Trades Holdings Ld.). Final meeting return regd. 15 June 1921 ...... **1936**

Pyramidical Railway Co. Ld. Regd. 1895. Removed from Register 1903 ...... **1900**

Pyramidical Syndicate Ld. Regd 1895. Removed from Register 1908 ...... **1900**

Pyrenees Metals Ld. Inc. Guernsey 1902 ...... **1907**

Pyrenees Minerals Ld. Regd. 1902. Struck off Register 1921 ...... **1907**

Pyrochrom Syndicate Ld. Regd. 1902. Removed from Register 1909 ...... **1904**

Pyrotan Leather Co. Ld. Regd. 1917. Vol. liq. 26 May 1921. Final meeting return regd. 27 Feb. 1926...... **1922**

Q

Quadrant Cycle Co. Ld. Regd. 1895. Removed from Register 1909 ...... **1907**

Quadrant Trust Ld. See Hill (Philip) Higginson (Registrars) Ld.

Quakers Yard Gas & Water Co. Ld. Regd. 1878. Dissolved 1 May 1949, undertaking being vested in Wales Area Gas Board under Gas Act 1948. Holders of 4½% red. debs. were entitled to receive, in respect of each £100 unit held, £100 British Gas 3% guaranteed stock 1990–95 ...... **1952**

Qu'Appelle, Long Lake & Saskatchewan Railroad & Steamboat Co. Inc. Canada 1883 by Special Act. The capital stock was vested in Canadian Northern Railway Co. The undertaking was acquired by Canadian National Railways. The guaranteed 4% mortgage debenture stock was redeemed on 1 July 1936 ...... **1924**

Quarahim International Bridge Co. Ld. Regd. 1911. Vol. liq. (members') 24 Feb. 1949, undertaking having been sold to Uruguayan Govt. 5% 1st debenture stock was redeemed at 70% (partly out of payment received from North Western of Uruguay Railway Co. Ld.). Final meeting return regd. 8 Nov. 1951 **1953**

Quartz Creek (Yukon) Syndicate Ld. Regd. 1900. Vol. liq. 21 Mar. 1904. Final meeting return regd. 2 May 1906........ ***1905**

Quartz Hill Consolidated Gold Mining Co. Ld. Regd. 1881. Vol. liq. Aug. 1882. Reconstructed as Denver Gold Mining Co. Ld., in which company shareholders were entitled to 1 fully-paid share of 5s. for every 2 shares of £1 held. Final meeting return regd. 26 Aug. 1885 ...... **1883**

Quartz Hill Reward Claim Ld. Regd. 1896. Vol. liq. 2 July 1900. Final meeting return regd. 8 Oct. 1901 **1901**

VOL. FOR

Quasie Gold Mining Co. Ld. Regd. 1902. Struck off Register 1927 .... *1916

Quaw Badoo Mines Ld. Regd. 1901. Vol. liq. May 1908. Removed from Register 1909 1909

Quebec & Lake St. John Railway Co. Inc. Quebec 1883. In 1911 the 4% prior lien bonds, 1st mortgage 5% bonds and income 25-year 6% bonds were exchangeable for 4% 1st mortgage debenture stock; the latter stock was acquired by H. M. Treasury in Jan. 1942, for £95 7s. 4d. for every £100 stock held 1924

Quebec Graphite Co. Ld. Regd. 1912. Vol. liq. 4 Feb. 1915. Final meeting return regd. 1 Dec. 1915 1915

Quebec Pulp and Paper Mills Ld. Inc. Quebec 1925. Undertaking and assets were acquired by Quebec Pulp & Paper Corporation. Holders of each preferred share of $100 plus bonus of $50 common share were entitled to either $40 cash and $70 preferred stock or $21 cash and $100 preferred stock; holders of each preferred share of $100 without bonus were entitled to either $100 preferred stock or $20 in cash and $70 preferred shares. Holders of each common share (not surrendered with preferred shares) were entitled to either $5·60 in cash and $51·20 preferred stock or $36·64 in cash and $2·20 preferred stock 1928

Quebec Timber Co. Ld. Regd. Edinburgh 1881. Vol. liq. Aug. 1890. Court Order to dissolve 8 Feb. 1898 .. 1891

"Quebrachales Fusionados" (Sociedad Anonima). Inc. Argentine 1906. 5% 1st mortgage sterling debentures to bearer were repaid in July 1916 1916

Quedrada Railway Land & Copper Co. Ld. Regd. 1883. Vol. liq. 10 Nov. 1894. Reconstructed as Bolivar Railway Co. Ld. Holders of 6% debenture stock were entitled to fully-paid ordinary shares of £10 in respect of capital and arrears of interest. Holders of 6% prior lien mortgage bonds were entitled to £100 6% perpetual debenture stock in new company for every £90 stock held. Final meeting return regd. 19 Oct. 1897 1896

Queen Anne's Chambers Ld. Regd. 1902. Vol. liq. 16 Nov. 1906. Court Order to wind up 16 Nov. 1906. Liquidator released 31 Aug. 1909. Struck off Register 16 July 1915 1908

Queen Anne's Mansions Lighting & Heating Co. Ld. Regd. 1891. Vol. liq. 27 July 1896. Property was sold to Queen Anne Residential Mansions and Hotel Co. Ld. (later Queen Anne's Mansions & Hotel Ld.; later Queen Anne's Hotels & Properties Ld.). Final meeting return regd. 28 Apr. 1897 1897

Queen Bess Proprietary Co. Ld. Regd. 1897. Property passed to bankers under foreclosure in respect of mortgage. Struck off Register 8 Aug. 1905 1906

Queen Cross Reef Gold Mining Co. Ld. Inc. Queensland 1892. Vol. liq. 1908 for reconstruction into New Queen Cross Gold Mines Ld., in which company shareholders were entitled to receive 1 share of 2s. 6d. for each share of 10s. held 1909

Queen Gold Dredging Co. Ld. Regd. 1908. Vol. liq. 30 July 1909. Final meeting return regd. 4 Aug. 1915 1910

Queen Gold Mining Co. Ld. Regd. 1908. Vol. liq. Sept. 1912. Removed from Register 1913 1913

Queen Hotel, Harrogate Ld. Regd. 1881. Vol. liq. (members') 18 July 1947. Capital returned to contributories—£6 11s. per share of £5. £146 was paid into Companies' Liquidation Account. Final meeting return regd. 4 Apr. 1951 1952

Queen Insurance Co. Established 1858. Business was transferred in 1891 to Royal Insurance Co., in which company shareholders were entitled to 1 share of £20 (credited with £3 paid) for every 7 shares of £10 (£1 paid) held. Removed from Register 1893 1892

Queen Line Ld. Regd. Edinburgh 1924. Vol. liq. (members') 30 June 1955. Capital returned to contributories—£11 11s. 5½d. per share (of 15s.). Final meeting return regd. 30 Sept. 1958 1959

Queen Mill, Dukinfield, Ld. Regd. 1900. Vol. liq. (members') 18 Apr. 1962. Final meeting return regd. 20 Apr. 1963 1941

Queenborough Glass Bottle Works Ld. In Mar. 1923 certain assets were acquired by Canning Town Glass Works Ld. in exchange for cash, second debentures and shares. 1924

Queenborough Syndicate Ld. See Port of Queenborough Development Co. Ld

Queen's & High Cliff Hotel Co. Ld. Regd. 1902 as Queen's & High Cliffe Hotels Ld.; name changed Mar. 1908. Vol. liq. 28 Feb. 1920. Final meeting return regd. 18 Aug. 1925 1921

Queen's Birthday United Gold Mines Ld. Regd. 1892. Court Order to wind up 4 Dec. 1895. Removed from Register 1907 1896

Queen's Club Garden Estates Ld. Regd. 1898. Vol. liq. (members') 29 Mar. 1934. Undertaking and assets were acquired by London County Freehold &

VOL. FOR

Leasehold Properties Ld. Holders of 4% 1st mortgage debenture stock were entitled to an equal amount of similar stock in acquiring company. Final meeting return regd. 24 Nov. 1934 1935

Queen's Hotel, Cheltenham, Ld. Regd. 1883. Majority of capital was owned by Honywood Hotels Ld. Vol. liq. (members') 4 Apr. 1963. Final meeting return regd. 1 Oct. 1963 1952

Queen's Hotel Co., Abingdon Ld. Regd. 1864. Vol. liq. July 1889. Final meeting return regd. 7 Dec. 1889 1890

Queen's Hotel Co. (Upper Norwood) Ld. Regd 1860. Vol. liq. Aug. 1909. Removed from Register 1910 1910

Queensland Black Snake Freehold Gold Mining Co. Ld. Regd. 1895. Vol. liq. Dec. 1904. Removed from Register 1905 1905

Queensland Copper Co. Ld. Regd. 1898. Vol. liq. July 1910 for reconstruction as New Queensland Copper Co. Ld., in which company shareholders were entitled to 1 share of 10s. (credited with 5s. paid) for each preference or ordinary share of £1 held. Struck off Register 1918 1911

Queensland Copper Freeholds Ld. Regd. 1907. Vol. liq. 9 Aug. 1915. The properties were acquired by Dobbin & Cloncurry Mines Ld. Final meeting return regd. 30 June 1917 1916

Queensland Exploration Co. Ld. Inc. Queensland 1906. Resolutions to wind up in Dec. 1911 1912

Queensland Investment and Land Mortgage Co. Ld. Regd. 1878. Vol. liq. 14 Jan. 1921. Final meeting return regd. 12 Dec. 1922 1921

Queensland Land & Coal Co. Ld. Regd. 1881. Removed from Register 1888 1885

Queensland Menzies Gold Mining Co., No Liability. Inc. Queensland 1895. Vol. liq. Oct. 1907 for reconstruction. London agents ceased to act June 1907 1908

Queensland Mines Agency Ld. Inc. Queensland 1899. London office was closed in 1910 1910

Queensland Mining Ld. Inc. Queensland 1899. Vol. liq. June 1908 for reconstruction as United Properties Ld., in which company shareholders were entitled to 1 share of 2s. (credited with 1s. 3d. paid) for each share of 5s. held 1909

Queensland National Bank Ld. Inc. in Queensland 1872. Vol. liq. (members') 30 Oct. 1947. Shareholders were entitled to 5 shares of £1 in National Bank of Australasia Ld. for each share of £5 held. The company's licence was cancelled on 20 July 1967 . 1968

Queensland Quicksilver Estates Ld. Regd. 1886. Court Orders: to wind up 24 Mar. 1890; to dissolve 19 June 1894 1891

Queensland Smelting Co. Ld. Regd. 1888. Reconstructed 1899 as company of same name. Shareholders were entitled to 1 share of £1 in new company for every 2 shares held. Removed from Register 1901 1908

Queensland Smelting Co. Ld. Regd. 1899. Vol. liq. 16 June 1908. Final meeting return regd. 6 Apr. 1914 1909

Queensport Brick & Tile Co. Ld. Regd 1887. Vol. liq. 26 Jan. 1892. Final meeting return regd. 22 Mar. 1893 *1893

Queenstown Dry Docks, Shipbuilding & Engineering Co. Ld. Regd. Dublin 1906. Irish Court Order to wind up June 1909. Removed from Register 1913 1910

Queenstown Dry Docks, Shipbuilding & Engineering Co. Ld. Regd. 1917. Vol. liq. 29 Dec. 1930. Final meeting return regd. 12 Apr. 1934 .... *1931

Quemont Mining Corpn. Ld. See Durquem Mines Ld.

Querette (Northern Counties) Ld. Regd. 1903. Vol. liq. Mar. 1906. Removed from Register 1906 1907

Querette (Parent) Co. Ld. Regd. 1903. Struck off Register 13 Oct. 1908 1909

Quibell Brothers Ld. Regd. 1920. Vol. liq. (members') 8 June 1944. All capital was owned by Fisons Ld. Final meeting return regd. 29 Sept. 1944 1945

Quicktho (France) Ld. Regd. 1928. All capital was owned by Quicktho (1928) Ld. Struck off Register 1943 1941

Quin & Axtens Ld. Regd. 1905. Vol. liq. 30 Dec. 1921. The undertaking was acquired by Bon Marché Ld. Capital returned to contributories—20s. per preference share of £1; £3 9s. per ordinary share of £1. Final meeting return regd. 21 June 1922 1923

Quin (James) & Co, Ld. See Leyland Rubber Co. Ld.

Quinine Bitters Manufacturing Co. Ld. Regd. 1888. Vol. liq. Sept. 1906. Removed from Register 1908 1907

Quintera Mining Co. Ld. Regd. 1888. Vol. liq. 7 Jan. 1925. Final meeting return regd. 8 July 1925 1925

Quinton Cycle Co. Ld. Regd. 1891. Vol. liq. 4 Aug. 1896. Business was acquired by New Beeston Cycle Co. Ld. Final meeting return regd. 6 Nov. 1896 1897

Quinton (James) Ld. Regd. 1899. Vol. liq. (members') 1 Jan. 1945. Certain assets were distributed to contributories in specie plus 2s. 1·578d. per share of £1 in cash. Final meeting return regd. 25 Jan. 1946 1946

Quorn Specialities (Holdings) Ld. Regd. 1950. All capital was owned by F. W. Hampshire & Co. Ld.

See Stock Exchange Year-Book.

VOL. FOR

Vol. liq. (members') 29 Oct. 1964. Final meeting return regd. 23 Feb. 1965 .... **1963**

Quorndon & Mountsorrel Gas Co. Inc. by deed 1853 **1909**

R

R. A. G. Ld. Regd. 1929. Winding-up order 13 Jan. 1936. Liquidator released 4 Aug. 1937. Struck off Register 16 Feb. 1954 .... **1950**

R. M. C. (Silks) Ld. Regd. 1929. Court Order to wind up June 1932. Struck off Register 14 Oct. 1938 .... **1939**

R. M. C. Textiles (1928) Ld. Regd. 1928. Court Order to wind up Apr. 1932. Struck off Register 24 Aug. 1943 **1944**

R. M. C. Textiles (Scottish) Ld. Regd. 1929. Vol. liq. (creditors') 7 Mar. 1932. All capital was owned by R. M. C. Textiles (1928) Ld. Assets realised insufficient to meet claims of unsecured creditors in full. £42 5s. 8d. was paid into Companies' Liquidation Account. Final meeting return regd. 11 May 1935 .... **1932**

R. M. Realisation Co. Ld. Regd. 1935. Vol. liq. (members') 14 Dec. 1937. Shareholders were entitled to receive £13 ordinary stock of Union Castle Mail Steamship Co. Ld., for every 10 shares of £1 held. Capital returned to contributories—23s. 6d. per share. Final meeting return regd. 17 Oct. 1956 **1957**

R. M. S. P. Meat Transports Ld. 1914. Vessels were transferred in 1932 to Royal Mail Lines Ld., for 1,200,000 fully-paid shares of £1. Vol. liq. (creditors') 17 Nov. 1937. Assets realised insufficient to pay creditors in full. Final meeting return regd. 21 Jan. 1942 .... **1938**

R. R. Realisations Ld. Regd. 15 Mar. 1906 as Rolls-Royce Ld.; name changed 30 Dec. 1976. Vol. liq. (creditors') 4 Oct. 1971. All principal and accrued interest on debenture stocks paid by 15 May 1972 and on 7¾% Uns. Ln. Stk. 1987–92 paid by 20 Sept. 1973. Distributions per ordinary capital (of £1)— 25p in Feb. and 10p in July 1974, 15p in Feb. 1975, 5p in Feb. 1976 and final payment of 9½p in July 1982. Final meeting held 7 Dec. 1982 .... **1983–4**

Radam's (Wm.) Microbe Killer Co. Ld. Regd. 1890. Struck off Register 17 Jan. 1942 .... **1942**

Radcliffe & Little Lever Joint Gas Board. Inc. by Special Act 1921. Under Radcliffe, Farnworth & District Gas Act 1938 the undertaking was transferred to the Farnworth & Kearsley Gas Co. (later Radcliffe, Farnworth & District Gas Co.), for £316,000 ...... **1939**

Radcliffe & Pilkington Gas Co. Inc. by Special Act 1846. Undertaking was acquired by Radcliffe & Little Lever Joint Gas Board. Capital returned to contributories—£21 per 10% share of £10; £14 14s. per 7% share of £10 .... **1922**

Radcliffe, Farnworth & District Gas Co. Inc. by Special Act 1854 as Farnworth & Kearsley Gas Co.; name changed 1938. Dissolved 1 May 1949, undertaking being vested in North Western Area Gas Board under Gas Act 1948. Holders of securities were entitled to receive. in respect of each £100 unit held, British Gas 3% guaranteed stock 1990–95 as follows:

	£	s.	d.
Ord. stock (5% basic)	115	0	0
4½%red. pref. stock	104	0	0
5%red. pref. stock	105	5	0
4½% deb. stock	104	5	0

Liability in respect of certain mortgage loans assumed by the Board. A distribution on ord. stock of 1·69163% out of reserves was made in Apr. 1951 **1952**

Radcliffe's Edible Products Ld. Regd. 1929. Vol. liq. (members') 20 Nov. 1935 for reconstruction under same name. Shareholders were entitled to 1 fully-paid ordinary share of 1s. or 4 fully-paid preference shares of 1s. in new company for every 4 ordinary shares of £1 or 5 preference shares of 10s. held respectively. Final meeting return regd. 13 Nov. 1937 .... **1934**

Radi-Arc Electrical Co. (1927) Ld. Regd. 1927. Undertaking acquired in 1928 by Mayfair Electric Gramophones Ld. for 550,000 fully-paid shares of 2s. Struck off Register 17 July 1931 .... **1929**

Radio Accessories Ld. Regd. 1925. Vol. liq. 25 July 1927. All share capital owned by Burndept Wireless Ld. Final meeting return regd. 13 June 1928 .... **1928**

Radio Central Exchanges Ld. Regd. 1931. Vol. liq. (members') 27 Mar. 1941. Share capital was repaid in full in cash. Final meeting return regd. 3 Sept. 1942 .... **1945**

Radiovisor Foreign & Colonial Ld. Regd. 1928. Vol. liq. (members') 24 May 1934. Assets realised insufficient to pay unsecured creditors in full. Final meeting return regd. 10 Aug. 1935 .... **1935**

VOL. FOR

Radium Ore Mines Ld. Regd. 1911. Receiver appointed 7 May 1929. Struck off Register 4 Aug. 1939 ...... **1940**

Radium Polishes Ld. Regd. 1906 as Lord Ross & Co. (Broadheath) Ld.; name changed Jan. 1919. Vol. liq. 5 Jan. 1923. Controlling interest held by Hargreaves Bros. & Co. Ld. Final meeting return regd. 28 Sept. 1925 .... **1923**

Radium Springs Ld. Regd. 1928. Struck off Register 20 Feb. 1942 .... **1943**

Radofone (1928) Ld. Regd. 1928. Vol. liq. 3 Jan. 1929. Assets were acquired in 1928 by Universal Gramophone & Radio Co. Ld. for £20,250 in cash and 340,000 fully-paid shares of 5s. Final meeting return regd. 22 Mar. 1932 .... **1929**

Radstock, Wrington & Congresbury Junction Railway Co. Inc. by Special Act 1882. Abandoned by Act of 1886 .... **1888**

Rae (Transvaal) Gold Mining Co. Ld. Regd. 1887. Vol. liq. 7 June 1888. Court Orders: to wind up under supervision 22 Aug. 1888; to dissolve Aug. 1892 **1889**

Raeburn Trust Ld. Regd. 1928. Vol. liq. (members') 30 July 1959. All capital acquired by Romney Trust Ld. in 1959. Final meeting return regd. 18 Dec. 1963 **1965**

Raffety, Thornton & Co. Ld. Regd. 1886. Vol. liq. Aug. 1908. Capital returned to contributories—20s. per share of £1 at 1 Feb. 1909; further payments (if any) not known. Removed from Register 1909 .... **1909**

Raff's Great Western Gold Mining Co., No Liability. Inc. Queensland 1896. In liquidation in 1900 .... **1900**

Rafinpa (Nigeria) Tin Co. Ld. Regd. 1912. Struck off Register Jan. 1931 .... **1931**

Ragalla Tea Estates Ld. Regd. 28 Sept. 1893. Dissolved 2 July 1984 .... **1960**

Raglan Collieries Ld. Regd. 1915. Vol. liq. 12 Apr. 1935. All shares owned by Richard Thomas & Baldwins Ld. Final meeting return regd. 27 Apr. 1936 .... **1936**

Raglan Cycle & Anti-Friction Ball Co. Ld. Regd. 1896. Vol. liq. 30 Sept. 1909. Struck off Register 18 Jan. 1921 .... **1910**

Ragusa Ld. Regd. 1935 as Ragusa Asphalte Paving Ld.; name changed Dec. 1955. Vol. liq. (members') 15 Mar. 1965. Shareholders were entitled to receive 2 ordinary shares (of 5s.) in Derbyshire Stone Ld. for every 5 shares (of 2s. 6d.). Capital returned to contributories—¾d. per share (of 2s. 6d.). Amounts paid into Companies' Liquidation Account £436 4s. 7d. in respect of unclaimed distributions and £142 13s. 3d. in respect of unclaimed dividends. Final meeting return regd. 25 Nov. 1966 .... **1967**

Rahman Rubber Estate Ld. Regd.1926. Vol. liq. 30 Nov. 1932. Undertaking was acquired by company of same name. Final meeting return regd. 10 Nov. 1934 ***1933**

Rahman Rubber Estate Ld. Regd. 1933. Vol. liq. (members') 7 Mar. 1952. Capital returned to contributories—2s. per share of 2s. 10s. 10d. was paid into Companies' Liquidation Account in respect of unclaimed dividends. Final meeting return regd. 17 Sept. 1955 .... **1956**

Raikes Hall Park, Gardens & Aquarium Co. Ld. Regd. 1871. Vol. liq. 11 Jan. 1897. Final meeting return regd. 18 Aug. 1897 .... ***1896**

Railway and Electric Appliances Co. Ld. Regd. 1882. Vol. liq. Nov. 1887. Final meeting return regd. 21 Nov. 1890 .... **1888**

Railway & General Automatic Library Ld. Regd. 1891. Court Order to wind up 3 Dec. 1892. Removed from Register 1907 .... **1893**

Railway & General Light Improvement Co. Ld. Regd. 1872. Court Orders: to wind up 5 Aug. 1876; to dissolve 24 June 1885 .... ***1876**

Railway Audible Signal Co. Ld. Regd. 1908. Struck off Register 1923 .... **1917**

Railway Carriage Co. Ld. Regd. 1862. Vol. liq. Oct. 1886. Undertaking and assets were acquired by Oldbury Railway Carriage and Wagon Co. Ld., in which company shareholders were entitled to 1 share of £4 plus 15s. in cash for each share of £5 held. Final meeting return regd. 1 May 1889 .... **1902**

Railway Concessions and Contract Co. Ld. Regd. 1903. Vol. liq. 16 Nov. 1909. Final meeting return regd. 21 Jan. 1914 .... **1910**

Railway Finance & Construction Co. Ld. See Reed, Evans & Co. Ld.

Railway Finance Corpn. Ld. Regd. 1935. Vol. liq. (members') 30 Oct. 1951. The outstanding 2½% guaranteed debenture stock was redeemed at par on 1 Aug. 1951. Capital returned to contributories—£1 per share of £1. Final meeting return regd. 21 Feb. 1952 .... **1953**

Railway of the Bay of Havana. Formed in 1857 as Bay of Havana & Matanzas Railroad. Amalgamated with Havana Railways and the Regla Warehouses Co. and Bank of Commerce as Bank of Commerce,

VOL. FOR

United Railways of the Havana and Regla Warehouses Co. Holders of Scrip Certificates were repaid at par in Apr. 1890, but had the right to exchange at par for bonds of the United Railways at 95% **1891**

Railway Public Works & Mines Development Co. Ld. Regd. 1893. Court Order to wind up 30 July 1907. Removed from Register 1911 .... **1908**

Railway Rolling-Stock Co. Regd. 1856. Vol. liq. 12 Feb. 1891. Business was acquired by British Wagon Co. Ld. for £110,244. Final meeting return regd. 21 Jan. 1892 .... **1892**

Railway Rolling Stock Trust Ld. Regd. 1896. Vol. liq. Dec. 1907. Capital returned to contributories—£2 0s. 9d. per share of £10 (£2 paid) at Jan. 1908; further payments (if any) not known. Removed from Register 1909 .... **1908**

Railway Share Trust Co. Ld. Regd. 1873. Vol. liq. 27 Nov. 1888. Reconstructed as Railway Share Trust & Agency Co. Ld. (later Share & General Investment Trust Ld.), in which company shareholders were entitled to the same interest. Final meeting return regd. 31 Dec. 1891 .... **1890**

Railway Sleeper Supply Co. Ld. Regd. 1883. Vol. liq. Oct. 1885. Final meeting return regd. 28 Aug. 1886   **1886**

Railway Station Indicator Co. Ld. Regd. 1896. Struck off Register 18 Nov. 1902 .... **1903**

Railway, Tramway & General Trust Ld. See Commercial Union Trust Co. Ld.

Railways and Metropolitan Omnibus Co. Ld. Regd. 1881. Vol. liq. 14 Oct. 1915. Final meeting return regd. 29 Nov. 1916 .... **1911**

Railways Electric Supply Syndicate Ld. Regd. 1897. Removed from Register 1904 .... **1900**

Rainbow & Peabody Gold Mines Ld. Regd. 1897. Vol. liq. 13 Dec. 1900. Final meeting return regd. 27 Dec.1901 .... **1901**

Rainbow Mine (Canada) Ld. Regd. 1910. Struck off Register 1920 .... **1913**

Raine and Co. Ld. See Sinjal (Holdings) Ld.

Rainham Waterworks Company, Limited. Est. 1881; regd. 27 Sept. 1899; statutory powers 1904 and subsequently. Vol. liq. (members') 28 June 1946 the undertaking having been acquired by Chatham & District Water Co. Holders of the 4% redeemable debenture stock received the same amount of a similar stock of the Chatham company. Original ordinary shareholders (10% max.) received 28s. 6d. consolidated ordinary of the Chatham Co. for every share held, additional ordinary shareholders received £1 consolidated ordinary, 4% preference shareholders received £1 4% perpetual debenture stock and 6% preference shareholders received 30s. 4% perpetual debenture stock; dissentient holders were entitled to require liquidators to purchase their interest for cash at the above rates. Final meeting return regd.8 Apr. 1947 .... **1947**

Rainy Lake Lumber Co. Ld. Established in Canada 1882. Company has been dissolved and property sold to a private firm.. **1888**

Rainy River & Ontario Exploration Co. Ld. Regd. 1897. Removed from Register 1901 .... **1901**

Rainy River Development Co. Ld. Regd. 1899. Removed from Register 1910 .... **1908**

Raithwaite Steamship Co. Ld. Regd. 1904. Vol. liq. 8 Apr. 1918. Final meeting return regd. 8 Apr. 1919   **1918**

Rajawelle Coffee Estate Co. Ld. Regd. 1864. Vol. liq. 27 Nov. 1889. Final meeting return regd. 15 June 1892   **1890**

Raleigh Cycle Co. Ld. Regd. 1891. Vol. liq. 18 Feb. 1896. Business acquired by company of same name, for £113,334 cash, £33,333 ordinary shares of £1 and £33,333 preference shares of £1. Final meeting return regd. 5 May 1897 .... **1899**

Raleigh Cycle Co. Ld. Regd. 1896. Vol. liq. 19 Jan. 1899. Reconstructed as company of same name. Shareholders were entitled to 1 ordinary share of 2s. 6d. for each ordinary share of £1 held on payment of 2s. 6d. per ordinary share and 1 deferred ordinary share of £1 for every five ordinary shares of £1 held. Preference shareholders were entitled on payment of 2s. 6d. per share to 1 ordinary share of 2s. 6d. and 2 deferred ordinary shares of £1 for every 5 preference shares of £1 held. Final meeting return regd. 31 Mar. 1900 .... **1908**

Raleigh Cycle Co. Ld. Regd. 1899. Vol. liq. 18 Aug. 1908. Undertaking and assets were sold at price sufficient to return 2s. 6d. per ordinary share of 2s. 6d. and 6s. per deferred share of £1. Struck off Register 12 Mar. 1935 .... **1909**

Ralston Divide Gold Mining Co. Ld. Regd. 1895. Removed from Register 1901 .... **1901**

Ramage Syndicate Ld. Regd. 1894. Vol. liq. 29 Mar. 1897. Final meeting return regd. 25 Jan. 1898 ...... **1898**

Rambla Co. of Montevideo Ld. Regd. 1911. Vol. liq. (creditors') 19 Oct. 1933. No capital returned to

VOL. FOR

contributories. Final meeting return regd. 12 Dec. 1933 .... **1934**

Rambutan Rubber Estates Ld. Regd. 1928. Vol. liq. (members') 14 Oct. 1930. Undertaking and assets were acquired by Rambutan Rubber Estates (1930) Ld. (later Rambutan Rubber Estates Ld.), in which company shareholders were entitled to 1 share of 2s. (credited with 1s. 9d. paid) for each share of 2s. held. Final meeting return regd. 24 Sept. 1931. Court Order declared dissolution void 18 Apr. 1932. Final meeting return regd. 24 Sept. 1932 .... **1908**

Ramie Co. Ld. Regd. 1903. Vol. liq. 21 Sept 1920. Goodwill and assets acquired by Lightning Trades Ld. (later Earlsfield Manufacturing Co. Ld.). Final meeting return regd. 13 Feb. 1923 .... **1940**

Rampah Cocoanut Estates Ld. Regd. 1910. Struck off Register 29 Oct. 1935.. **1936**

Ramsbottom Gas Co. Inc. by Special Act 1854. Dissolved 1 May 1949, undertaking being vested in North Western Area Gas Board under Gas Act 1948. Holders of securities were entitled to receive British Gas 3% guaranteed stock 1990–95 as follows in respect of each £10 unit, unless otherwise stated, of security held:

	£	s.	d.
Orig. shares (10% max.)	20	10	0
Red. scrip shares (7% max.)	14	10	0
3¾% red. deb. stock (per £100)	100	10	0

.... **1952**

Ramsbottom Paper Mill Co. Ld. Regd. 1872. Vol. liq. 13 Feb. 1896. Reconstructed as company of same name. Shareholders were entitled to 2 ordinary shares of £5 (credited with £3 paid) and 6 fully-paid preference shares of £1 in new company for every share of £10 (£5 paid) held. Final meeting return regd. 27 Jan. 1897 .... **1896**

Ramsbottom Paper Mill Co. Ld. (The). Regd. 1896. Business and fixed assets were transferred to North West Lancashire Paper Products Ld. for £90,000 in fully-paid capital of that company which was sold to Liverpool Daily Post & Echo Ld. for £90,000 cash. Vol. liq. (members') 29 Dec. 1964. Capital returned to contributories—17s. 10·2d. per preference share (of 15s.) and 2s. 2·64d. per ordinary share (of 5s.). Final meeting return regd. 14 July 1966 .... **1967**

Ramsden (Archibald) Ld. Regd. 1891. Vol. liq. (members') 4 Mar. 1946. Final meeting return regd.8 July 1946 .... **1938**

Ramsey & Somersham Junction Railway Co. Inc. by Special Act 1875. Under Great Northern Railway Act 1896 undertaking was transferred to Great Northern and Great Eastern Joint Committee for £30,340 .... **1897**

Ramsey Gas Co. Ld. Regd. 1858. Dissolved 1 May 1949, undertaking being vested in Eastern Area Gas Board under Gas Act 1948. Holders of ordinary shares (of £10) were entitled to receive £13 15s. British Gas 3% guaranteed stock 1990–95 for each share held **1952**

Ramsgate & District Electric Supply Co. Ld. Regd. 1903. All capital was owned by County of London Electric Supply Co. Ld. Dissolved 1 Apr. 1948 under Electricity Act 1947 .... **1937**

Ramsgate & Margate Tramways Co. Inc. by Special Act 1881. In liquidation in 1885 .... **1885**

Ramsgate Marina Pier & Lift Co. Ld. Regd. 1895. A liquidation dividend of 5s. 3d. was paid in Apr. 1906. Liquidator released 11 July 1906. Removed from Register 1911 .... **1907**

Ramsley Exploration Syndicate Ld. Regd. 1900. Vol. liq. Dec. 1909. Removed from Register 1912 .... **1910**

Ranald Steamship Co. Ld. Regd. Edinburgh 1899. Vol. liq. Oct. 1902. Final meeting return regd. 23 Dec. 1903 .... **1904**

Rand Central Electric Works Ld. Regd. 1895. The undertaking was sold to Victoria Falls Power Co. Ld. (later Victoria Falls & Transvaal Power Co. Ld.) for £175,000 in preference shares and £175,000 in debentures in that company. The cash assets amounting to £130,000, were not included in the sale. Removed from Register 1908. .... **1908**

Rand Central Gold Mines Ld. Inc. Transvaal 1895. Wound up for purpose of sale of property and assets to Cinderella Consolidated Gold Mines Ld., in which company shareholders were entitled to 4 shares of £1 for every 5 shares of £1 held **1911**

Rand Central Ore Reduction Co. Ld. Inc. Transvaal 1892. In liquidation in 1904 .... **1904**

Rand Collieries Ld. See Witpoort Gold Areas Ld.

Rand Consols Ld. Regd. 1895. Vol. liq. 19 Feb. 1897. Final meeting return regd. 6 Aug. 1898 .... **1898**

Rand d'Or Mines Ld. Regd. 1895. Vol. liq. 24 May 1897. Final meeting return regd. 8 Sept. 1897 .... **1898**

Rand Exploration & Investment Co. Ld. Formed South Africa 1895. In liquidation in 1899 .... **1899**

410   RAND EXPLORATIONS LD.

VOL. FOR

Rand Explorations Ld. Formed South Africa 1895. In liquidation in 1899 .... **1899**

Rand Fixed Trust Ld. Regd. 1934. Vol. liq. (members') 7 Feb. 1951. Final meeting return regd. 29 Mar.1951 **1940**

Rand Gold Estates Ld. Regd. 1902. Vol. liq. Jan. 1906. Removed from Register 1907 **1906**

Rand Goldfields Syndicate Ld. Regd. 1895. Removed from Register 1905 **1905**

Rand Investment Corporation Ld. Regd. 1895. Struck off Register 6 Dec. 1918 ***1919**

Rand Junction Reefs Ld. Regd. 1895. Capital returned to contributories—15s. per fully-paid share. Removed from Register 1905 **1905**

Rand Klip Ld. Inc. Transvaal 1895 as Klipfontein Estate & Gold Mining Co. Ld.; name changed 1909. Vol. liq. Oct. 1918. Assets were acquired by Modderfontein East Ld in which company shareholders were entitled to 3 shares of £1 (credited as fully-paid) for every 8 shares of £1 held **1919**

Rand Klipfontein Co. Ld. Inc. Transvaal 1895. Wound up 1909 for purpose of sale of undertaking and assets to Rand Klip Ld in which company shareholders were entitled to 2 shares of £1 for each share of £1 held, and to subscribe for further shares **1910**

Rand Mines Deep Ld. Inc. Transvsal 1899. Vol. liq. Nov. 1909. Certain assets were acquired by Rand Mines Ld., in which company shareholders were entitled to 9 shares of 5s. (credited as fully-paid) for every 100 shares of £1 held **1910**

Rand Nucleus Gold Mining Co. Ld. Inc. Transvaal in 1902. Resolution to wind up 1929. A distribution of 1s. 8d. per share of £1 was made in June 1929; further payments (if any) not known **1930**

Rand-Rhodesia Exploring Co. Ld. Regd. 1894. Vol. liq. 28 Apr. 1898. Undertaking and assets were acquired by Africa Trust Consolidated & General Exploration Co. Ld., in which company shareholders were entitled to 65 shares of £1 (credited as fully-paid) for every 100 shares of £1 held. Final meeting return regd. 14 Nov. 1899 **1899**

Rand Roodepoort Gold Mining Co. Ld. Regd. 1895. Removed from Register 1910 **1903**

Rand Safe Deposit Co. Ld. In liquidation. Capital was owned by Johannesburg Estate Co. Ld. **1940**

Rand Southern Gold Mining Co. Ld. Regd. 1895. Reconstructed 1901 as New Rand Southern Gold Mining Co. Ld in which company shareholders were entitled to 2 shares of 10s. (credited with 7s. 6d. paid) for each share of £1 held. The £8,000 debentures were paid off for £5,000 in cash and 40,000 shares of 10s. (credited with 7s. 6d. paid). Removed from Register 1906 **1907**

Rand Victoria East Ld. Inc. Transvaal 1899. Wound up for purpose of amalgamation into Simmer Deep Ld in which company shareholders were entitled to receive 3 shares of £1 for every 5 shares of £1 held **1907**

Rand Victoria Mines Ld. Regd. 1895. Reconstructed as Simmer Deep Ld., in which company shareholders were entitled to 7 shares of £1 for every 6 shares of £1 held. Removed from Register 1908 **1907**

Rand Western Syndicate Ld. Regd. 1895. Vol. liq. 11 Feb. 1898. Final meeting return regd. 6 Oct. 1898 **1899**

Randall (C. W.) & Co. Ld. Regd. 1926. Vol. liq. 22 July 1963. Final meeting return regd. 6 Jan. 1965 **1956**

Randfontein Central Gold Mining Co. Ld. Inc. Transvaal 1907. Vol. liq. June 1924. Amalgamated with Randfontein Estates Gold Mining Co. (Witwatersrand) Ld., in which company shareholders were entitled to 3 shares of £1 for every 5 shares of £1 held **1925**

Randfontein Estates Trust Ld. Inc. Transvaal 1907. Resolutions to wind up passed 1909. A return of £1 per share of £1 was made in June 1909; further payments (if any) not known **1910**

Randfontein Extensions Ld. Regd. 1895. Vol. liq. (creditors') 31 Dec. 1931. No capital returned to contributories. Final meeting return regd. 19 Jan. 1934 **1932**

Randfontein South Gold Mining Co. Ld. Inc. Transvaal 1895 as Robinson Randfontein Gold Mining Co. Ld.; name changed 1909. Vol. liq. Mar. 1911. Undertaking and assets acquired by Randfontein Central Gold Mining Co. Ld., in which company shareholders were entitled to receive 1 share of £1 for each share of £1 held **1911**

Randt Coal Mining & Land Co. Ld. Regd. 1889. Vol. liq. 20 May 1895. Final meeting return regd. 2 Dec. 1895 **1896**

Randt Gold Mining Co. Ld. Regd. Dublin 1895. Court Order to wind up 15 May 1901. Removed from Register 1908 **1902**

Randt Reefs Gold Mining Co. Ld. Regd. Dublin 1895. Vol. liq. Feb. 1909. Property sold to New Randt Reefs Gold Mining Co. Ld. **1909**

Ranelagh Club Ld. Regd. 1898. Vol. liq. (members') 25 Jan. 1962. Preference shares repaid plus £1 14s. 5½d.

per share arrears of dividend. Capital returned to contributories—21s. 10d. per share (of £1). £1,495 13s. 1d. was paid into Companies' Liquidation Account. Final meeting return regd. 27 Nov. 1964 **1965**

Ranen Copper Co. Ld. Regd. 1913. Struck off Register 9 Aug. 1921 ***1920**

Ranga Tin Syndicates Ld. Regd 1925. Vol. liq. (creditors') 31 Aug. 1931. No capital returned to contributories. Final meeting return regd. 9 July 1932....... **1932**

Rangalla Tea Co. of Ceylon Ld. Regd. 1891. Vol. liq. 6 June 1923. Estates were acquired by Rangalla Consolidated Ld., in which company shareholders were entitled to 1 share of £1 (credited as fully-paid) plus 18s. 6d. in cash for each share of £1 held; further cash payments (if any) not known. Final meeting return regd. 8 Feb. 1924 **1924**

Rangoon Electric Tramway & Supply Co. Ld. Regd. 1905. Vol. liq. (members') 1 Feb. 1960. Undertaking taken over by Government of Burma as from 1 Oct. 1953. Capital returned to contributories (per share of 15s.)—9s. 9·711d. final meeting return regd. 17 Oct. 1980 **1981–2**

Rangoon Para Rubber Estates Ld. Regd. 14 June 1910. Vol. liq. (members') 27 July 1951. Capital returned to contributories—1s. 1·8d. per 2s. stock; £3,429 17s. 2d. was paid into Companies' Liquidation Account. Final meeting return regd. 7 Aug. 1953 **1954**

Rani Travancore Rubber Co. Ld. Regd. 1910. Vol. liq. Mar. 1945. Capital returned to contributories—£1 17s. 3·7d. per £1 stock. Final meeting return regd. 12 June 1951 **1952**

Rankin Dairy Farms Ld. Regd. 1928. Vol. liq. (creditors') 29 Jan. 1930. Assets realised insufficient to pay creditors in full. Final meeting return regd. 19 Apr.1938 **1931**

Ransome (A.) & Co. Ld. Regd. 1892. Receiver appointed in Sept. 1931. Principal of debentures was repaid in full and the interest thereon was expected to be paid in full. Struck off Register 29 Oct. 1935 .... **1926**

Ranson's Sugar Process Ld. Regd. 1898. Receiver appointed in 1900. Removed from Register 22 Dec. 1903 .... ***1902**

Rantan Tin Dredging Co. Ld. Inc. in Straits Settlements 1925. Vol. liq. (members') 10 Dec. 1965. Capital returned to contributories—$2·735 per $1 stock. Final meeting return regd. in Oct. 1967 **1968**

Rapid Rims Ld. Regd. 1919. Receiver appointed 18 Dec. 1922. Vol. liq. 28 Dec. 1922. Struck off Register 1927 **1928**

Rapid Submersible Ship Cleaner Co. Ld. Regd. 1918. Vol. liq. 22 Sept. 1922. Final meeting return regd. 16 Dec. 1924. **1923**

Rapson Automobile Patents Ld. Regd. 1919. Receiver appointed 12 May 1922; ceased to act 12 Sept. 1933. The assets were sold under a Court Order in a debenture holders' action. Struck off Register 1925 **1924**

Rara Fortuna Silver Mining Co. Ld. Regd. 1881. Vol. liq. June 1884. Final meeting return regd. 16 Oct. 1885 **1885**

Rasa (Selangor) Rubber Estates Ld. Regd. 1923. Vol. liq. 28 Aug. 1928. The undertaking and assets were transferred to Rambutan Rubber Estates Ld., in which company shareholders were entitled to 1 fully-paid share of 2s. for every share of 2s. held. Final meeting return regd. 19 Oct. 1929 **1929**

Rassak (F.M.S.) Rubber Estate Ld. Regd. 1910. Vol. liq. (members') 19 Oct. 1951. Capital returned to contributories—1s. 11·3d. per share of 2s. Final meeting return regd. 13 Oct. 1955 **1956**

Ratanui Rubber Estate Ld. Regd. 1909. Vol. liq. (members') 4 July 1934. Reconstructed as Ratanui Rubber Ld., in which company shareholders were entitled to 6 shares of 2s. (credited with 1s. 8d. paid) for each share of £1 held. £144 13s. 5d. was paid into Companies' Liquidation Account in respect of unclaimed shares and £41 12s. 9d. in respect of unclaimed dividends. Final meeting return regd. 8 Oct. 1935 **1935**

Ratanui Rubber Ld. Regd. July 1934. Winding-up order 5 May 1961. Liquidator released 26 Jan. 1976. Dissolved 21 July 1978 **1976-7**

Rathbone's South African Syndicate Ld. Regd. 1902. Vol. liq. June 1906. Reconstructed as Mines & Minerals Exploration Co. (1906) Ld., in which company shareholders were entitled to 1 share of £1 (credited with 15s. paid) for each ordinary share of £1 or each deferred share of 1s. held. Removed from Register 1909 **1907**

Rathkeale & Newcastle Junction Railway Co. Inc. by Special Act 1861. Under Act of 1901 the undertaking was purchased by Great Southern & Western Railway Co. Ireland for £133,333 **1905**

Ratoczyn Extended Oilfields Ld. Regd. 1914. Vol. liq. (members') in Apr. 1926. Capital returned to

See Stock Exchange Year-Book.

VOL. FOR

contributories—5s. 11·37d. per preference share (of 2s.) and 2s. 3·47d. per ordinary share (of 2d.). £105 was paid into Companies' Liquidation Account. Final meeting return regd. 13 Apr. 1948 .... **1948**

Ratoczyn (Galicia) Oil Co. Ld. Regd. 1911. Vol. liq. 22 July 1920. The capital and arrears of dividend on the preferred and deferred ordinary shares were repaid; further payments (if any) not known. Final meeting return regd. 3 July 1928 .... **1921**

Raub Australian Gold Mining Co. Ld. Inc. In Queensland 1892. Vol. liq. 19 Dec. 1961. The disposal of assets by the Receiver for the secured creditor in Malaya did not realise sufficient to satisfy the secured creditor's claim; there was no payment made to ordinary creditors and no capital returned to shareholders. Final meeting dissolving the company was held on 25 Mar. 1966 and company has since been dissolved **1967**

Raub Rubber Estates Ld. Regd. 1915. Vol. liq. (members') 27 Mar. 1933 for reconstruction under same name. Shareholders were entitled to 7 shares of 2s. (credited with 1s. 6d. paid) in new company for each share of £1 held. Capital returned to contributories—£162 8s. 1d.; £6 4s. 2d was paid into Companies' Liquidation Account. Final meeting return regd. 17 May 1934 .... **1934**

Raub Rubber Estates Ld. Regd. 1933. Vol. liq. (members') 8 Feb. 1939. Shareholders were entitled to 1 share of £1 fully-paid in Hoscote Rubber Estates Ld. for every 31½ shares of 2s. held *plus* ¾d. per share in cash. Final meeting return regd. 22 Sept. 1939 .... **1939**

Raven Anthracite Collieries Ld. See Blama & Raven Anthracite Collieries Ld.

Raven Tinplate Co. Ld. Regd. 1895. Vol. liq. (members') 12 June 1939. Undertaking acquired by Grovesend Steel & Tinplate Co. Ld., which company discharged all debts. Final meeting return regd. 27 June 1942 .... **1946**

Ravenglass & Eskdale Railway Co. Inc. by Special Act 1873. Undertaking transferred to Eskdale Railway Co. by Special Act 1909 .... **1910**

Ravenscliff Mining Co. Ld. Regd. 1890. Vol. liq. 7 Oct. 1898. Final meeting return regd. 8 Apr. 1903 ...... **1899**

Ravenswood Deep Mines Ld. Regd. 1902. Vol. liq. 9 Mar. 1920. Final meeting return regd. 6 July 1922 **1921**

Ravenswood Gold Co. Ld. Regd. 1887. Property was acquired by New Ravenswood Ld. Struck off Register 18 Nov. 1902 .... **1903**

Raw Film Co. Ld. Regd. 1914. Vol. liq. 30 Jan. 1919. The assets were sold to British Film Stock Co. Ld., in which company shareholders were entitled to 1 preference share for each ordinary or preference share of £1 held. Final meeting return regd. 14 Nov. 1930 .... **1919**

Rawang Concessions Ld. Inc. in F.M.S. 1927. Vol. liq. (members') 28 Feb. 1957, the undertaking and assets (except cash) having been acquired by Berjuntai Tin Dredging Ld. for 500,000 fully-paid shares of 5s. Shareholders were entitled to receive 10s. cash and 5 of the *above* fully-paid shares (of 5s.) for every 2 shares of £1 held. Final meeting return regd. 8 July 1959 .... **1962**

Rawang Tin Fields Ld. Inc. F.M.S. 1929. Vol. liq. (members') 28 Feb. 1957. Undertaking and assets (excluding £274,700 and 63,800 ordinary shares (of £1) of Rawang Concessions Ld.) were sold to Berjuntai Tin Dredging Ld. for 716,500 fully-paid shares (of 5s.) of that company. Shareholders were entitled to receive 1 share of Berjuntai Tin Dredging Ld. for every 2 shares of 10s. held. Capital returned to contributories—3s. 6d. for every 2 shares of 10s. held. $14,609·73 (Malayan) was deposited with Official Receiver in Malaysia. Final meeting return regd. 25 June 1964 .... **1967**

Rawang Tin Ld. Inc. F.M.S. 1920. Vol. liq. Aug. 1929. Undertaking and assets were acquired by Rawang Tin Fields Ld in which company shareholders were entitled to 4 shares of 10s. (credited as fully-paid) for each share of £1 held **1931**

Rawcliffe Moss Litter Co. Ld. Regd. 1885 as Peat Moss Litter Co. Ld.; name changed Aug. 1889. Vol. liq. 24 Dec. 1892. Final meeting return regd. 20 June 1893 **1893**

Rawire Ld. Regd. 1936. Receiver appointed Feb. 1938; ceased to act Jan. 1942. Vol. liq. (creditors') 12 May 1938. All shares were owned by Warner's Radio & Electric Ld. Final meeting return regd. 23 Mar. 1942 **1938**

Rawson Chemicals Ld. Regd. 1916 as Burgoyne, Burbridges & Co. Ld.; name subsequently changed. Vol. liq. (members') 24 Jan. 1957. Final meeting return regd. 19 Apr. 1958 .... **1947**

Rawson (John) & Sons (Ireland) Ld. Inc. in Dublin 1932. Vol. liq. (members') 16 Oct. 1967. Capital returned to contributories—Preference stock repaid at par and 9s. 4·25d. paid per 5s. ordinary stock. £4,123·54

VOL. FOR

paid into Companies' Liquidation Account in respect of unclaimed dividends and distributions. Final meeting return regd. 1 Apr. 1971 .... **1971**

Rawson (Thomas) & Co. Ld. Regd. 1896. All capital was owned by Duncan Gilmour & Co. Ld. Vol. liq. (members') 26 Sept. 1966. Final meeting return regd. 6 Sept. 1967 .... **1963**

Rautenstall Cotton Mills Ld. Regd. 1920. Vol. liq. (creditors') 19 July 1934. Assets realised insufficient to pay unsecured creditors in full. Final meeting return regd. 16 Jan. 1936 .... **1935**

Ray Consolidated Copper Co. Inc. Maine 1907. Undertaking and assets sold to Nevada Consolidated Copper Co., in 1926. Stockholders were entitled to receive $15 15-year 5% debentures and 7 cents in cash in respect of each share of $10 held **1927**

Ray Copper Mines Ld. Regd. 1899. Receivers and managers were appointed 11 Jan. 1901. Removed from Register 1911 .... **1903**

Raycol British Corporation Ld. Regd. 1929. Vol. liq. (creditors') 2 Mar. 1937. Struck off Register 3 Oct. 1941 .... **1942**

Rayfield (Cornwall) Tin Syndicate Ld. Regd. 1912. Vol. liq. 30 Dec. 1925. Final meeting return regd. 10 Jan. 1928 .... **1926**

Rayfield (Nigeria) Tin Fields Ld. Regd. 1912. Vol. liq. 28 Mar. 1928. Undertaking acquired by Associated Tin Mines of Nigeria Ld. Final meeting return regd. 5 Feb.1929 .... **1939**

Rayfield Syndicate Ld. Regd. 1910. Vol. liq. 8 May 1912. Reconstructed as Rayfield (Nigeria) Tin Fields Ld., in which company shareholders were entitled to 5 fully-paid shares of £1 for each share of 5s. held. Final meeting return regd. 15 Feb. 1915 .... **1913**

Raylock Fabrics Ld. Regd. 1928. Receiver appointed 21 Jan. 1937. Assets realised insufficient to meet principal due to debenture holders. Struck off Register 16 Dec. 1938 .... **1939**

Raymond (Rhodesia) Development Co. Ld. Regd. 1897. Vol. liq. 18 Nov. 1901. Properties were sold to Sebakwe & District Mines Ld., in which company shareholders were entitled to 1 share for every 5 shares of £1 held. Final meeting return regd. 8 July 1902 .... **1902**

Raynes & Co. Ld. Regd. 1920. Vol. liq. (members') 25 Nov. 1931. I. C. I. (Lime) Ld. was beneficial owner of all issued share capital. Final meeting return regd. 4 Oct. 1933 .... **1932**

Rayon Manufacturing Co. Ld. Regd. 1925. Vol. liq. Apr. 1921. Reconstructed as Rayon Manufacturing Co. (1927) Ld., in which company shareholders were entitled to 1 share of £1 (credited with 10s. paid) for each preference share of £1. or 20 deferred shares of 1s. held. Struck off Register Jan. 1934 .... **1934**

Rayon Manufacturing Co. (1927) Ld. Regd. 1927. Court Order to wind up 7 Nov. 1932. Liquidator released 12 Feb. 1934. Struck off Register 1 Sept. 1936...... **1937**

Raysheen Ld. See Sunsheen Ld.

Rayweavers Ld. See Chemical Refineries Ld.

Rea (Thomas) & Sons Ld. Regd. 1896 as Thomas Rea Sons & Fisher Ld.; name changed Aug. 1906. Vol. liq. 28 Dec. 1915. Final meeting return regd. 17 Apr. 1917 .... **1916**

Rea (Thomas) Sons & Fisher Ld. See Rea (Thomas) & Sons Ld.

Read Brothers Ld. Regd. 1898. Vol. liq. (members') 26 Apr. 1954. All shares were owned by S. G. Warburg & Co. Ld. The debenture stock was repaid at par on 15 May 1954. Final meeting return regd. 12 Dec. 1960 .... **1957**

Read Holliday & Sons Ld. Regd. 1890. Vol. liq. 26 Aug. 1915. The undertaking and assets were acquired by British Dyes Ld. (later British Dyestuffs Corporation (Huddersfield) Ld.). Final meeting return regd. 16 Mar. 1926 .... **1916**

Reading Electric Supply Co. Ld. Regd. 1892. Vol. liq. (members') 17 July 1934. Capital returned to contributories—£2 2s. 2¼d. per share of £1. Final meeting return regd. 13 July 1935 .... **1935**

Reading Gas Co. Inc. by Special Act 1862. Dissolved 1 May 1949, undertaking being vested in Southern Area Gas Board under Gas Act 1948. Holders of securities were entitled to receive British Gas 3% guaranteed stock 1990–95 as follows in respect of each £100 unit, unless otherwise stated, of security held:

	£	s.	d.
Ord. stock (5% max.)	110	0	0
Ord. stock (5½% max.)	121	0	0
5% red. pref stock (1950)	102	0	0
5% red. pref. stock (1960)	105	10	0
4% red. pref. stock	100	0	0
3⅜% red. pref. stock	101	14	8
5% pref. shares (of £10)	11	4	0

*See Stock Exchange Year-Book.

VOL. FOR

5% perp. deb. stock............125 0 0
4% perp. deb. stock............99 14 0
3½% perp. deb. stock............97 10 0
5% red. deb. stock............104 0 0
3½% red. deb. stock (1966–71)............100 0 0
3½% red. deb. stock (1963)............100 0 0 **1952**

Reading Tramways Co. Ld. Regd. 1877. The undertaking was sold to the Reading Corporation. Removed from Register 1911 ***1930**

Real Estate & Mortgage Deposit Bank Ld. Established Victoria 1887. In liquidation in 1907. Holders of 5% debentures were entitled to £30 in income debenture stock and £10 in shares in Melbourne Real Estate Co. Ld. for each £100 debenture held. Holders of 4½% 1st mortgage debentures were entitled to £11,032 second and £8,274 third debenture stocks in New Zealand Loan & Mercantile Agency Co. Ld. in addition to pro rata interest in property in Collins Street, Melbourne **1907**

Real Estate Corpn. of South Africa Ld. Regd. 1889. Vol. liq. (members') 31 Mar. 1955 for reconstruction in South Africa under the same title. Shareholders received 4 shares of 5s. in the new corporation for each share of £1 held. Final meeting return regd. 27 June 1956 **1957**

Real Estate Debenture Corporation Ld. Regd. 1934. Vol. liq. (members') 10 July 1950. Capital returned to contributories—10s. 9¾d. per stock unit (of 5s.). Final meeting return regd. 19 Dec. 1958 **1960**

Real Estate Loan Co. of Canada, Ld. Inc. in Canada 1879. Company dissolved and undertaking acquired by Canada Permanent Mortgage Corporation on 15 Feb. 1945 **1946**

Real Estate Security Co. Ld. Regd. Edinburgh 1876. Vol. liq. Mar. 1893. Final meeting return regd. 17 June 1893 **1894**

Real Property Trust Ld. Regd. 1875. Reconstructed 1902 as company of same name. Shareholders were entitled to 2 shares of £1 for every £5 nominal value of shares held. Removed from Register 1904 **1902**

Real Property Trust Ld. Regd. 1902 in reconstruction of company of same name. Vol. liq. (members') Jan. 1947. Capital returned to contributories—£2 5s. 10d. per share of £1. £136 was paid into Companies' Liquidation Account. Final meeting return regd. 28 June 1949 **1950**

Realisation & Debenture Corporation of Scotland Ld. Regd. Edinburgh 1888. Company was amalgamated with British Investment Trust Ld. from 1 July 1960. Preference stockholders received £100 preference stock of that company for every £100 preference stock held and deferred stockholders received 5 fully-paid ordinary shares of 5s. plus 1s. 4d. cash for every £1 deferred stock held. 3½% redeemable debenture stock 1970–80 and 4% redeemable debenture stock 1973–78 became stocks of British Investment Trust Ld. and the 4% redeemable debenture stock 1976–84 was amalgamated with a similar stock of that company. Company was dissolved on 31 Oct. 1960 **1962**

Realm Fire Insurance Co. Ld. Regd. 1880. Removed from Register 1905 **1884**

Recenia R. Shaerf Ld. See Shaerf (Recenia R.).

Recess Screws Ld. Regd. 1913. Vol. liq. 3 Mar. 1926. Final meeting return regd. 29 June 1929 **1927**

Recess Screws (1926) Ld. Regd. 1926. Vol. liq. 9 May 1927. Undertaking acquired by Recess Screws (1927) Ld. Final meeting return regd. 6 Nov. 1928 ***1928**

Recife & San Francisco (Pernambuco) Railway Co. Ld. Regd. 1856. Vol. liq. 28 Aug. 1901. The debentures were redeemed at par in cash. Stockholders received £125 in 4% sterling bonds plus £2 8s. 9d. in cash for every £100 stock held. Removed from Register 1903 **1903**

Recife Drainage Co. Ld. Regd. 1868. Vol. liq. Dec. 1908. Removed from Register 1910 **1909**

Reckitt & Sons Ld. Regd. 1888. Vol. liq. 22 June 1899. Reconstructed as Reckitts Ld. (later Reckitt & Sons Ld.). Shareholders were entitled to 4 ordinary shares of £10 for each ordinary share of £10 held or 4 4½% preference shares of £10 for every 3 6% preference shares of £10 held. Holders of 4½% debenture stock were entitled to £112 10s. 4% debenture stock in new company for every £100 stock held. Struck off Register 14 Feb.1922 **1900**

Reckitt & Sons Ld. Regd. May 1899 as Reckitts Ld.; name changed June 1899. Vol. liq. (members') 19 Sept. 1955. Debenture stock was repaid at par. All capital stock owned by Reckitt & Colman Hldgs. Ld. Final meeting return regd. 7 Jan. 1957 **1957**

Reckitts Ld. See above.

Record Gas Mantle Co. Ld. See Earlsfield Manufacturing Co. Ld.

Record Reign Procession Syndicate Ld. Regd. 1897. Removed from Register 1907 **1898**

VOL. FOR

Recordaphones Ld. Regd. 1928. Court Order to wind up May 1930. Struck off Register 16 Aug. 1938 **1939**

Recorders Ld. Regd. 1903. Vol. liq. Nov. 1907. Capital returned to contributories—13s. per preference share of £1 (15s. paid) at Jan. 1908; further payments (if any) not known. Removed from Register 1908 **1908**

Recordia (British Columbia) Exploration Co. Ld. Regd. 1897. Vol. liq. 28 Feb. 1900. Struck off Register 16 July 1915 **1901**

Recordia Syndicate Ld. Regd. 1897. Removed from Register 1911 **1901**

Red & White Rose Gold Mining Co. Ld. Regd. 1899. Vol. liq. 13 June 1906. Final meeting return regd. 1 Sept. 1915 **1907**

Red Hill (W.A.) Gold Syndicate Ld. Regd. 1897. Reconstructed 1902 as Red Hill Westralia Gold Mines Ld., in which company shareholders were entitled to 1 share of £1 (credited with 17s. 6d. paid) for each share of £1 held. Removed from Register 1905 **1908**

Red Hill, Westralia, Gold Mines Ld. Regd. 1902. Vol. liq. May 1909. Removed from Register 1910 **1910**

Red Moor Ld. Regd. 1909. Vol. liq. 25 Sept. 1913. Final meeting return regd. 29 Mar. 1917 **1914**

Red Mountain Silver Mines Ld. Regd. 1890. Vol. liq. 30 Dec. 1895. Final meeting return regd. 18 Sept. 1896 **1897**

Red "R." Steamship Co. Ld. Regd. 1887. Vol. liq. 31 Aug. 1917. Final meeting return regd. 7 Mar. 1923 ***1918**

Red Reef Gold Mining Co. Ld. Regd. 1888. Vol. liq. 10 Aug. 1891. Final meeting return regd. 10 Nov. 1892 **1892**

Red Rock Gold Mining Co. Ld. Regd. 1888. Court Order to dissolve 23 Dec. 1890 **1890**

Red Sea Oilfields Ld. Regd. 1910. Vol. liq. 30 Dec. 1913. Assets, mainly B shares of Anglo-Egyptian Oilfields, Ld. (later Al Nasr Oilfields Co.) were to be distributed. Final meeting return regd. 5 Aug. 1919 **1914**

Red, White & Blue Gold Mining Co. Ld. Regd. 1895. It was stated that assets would not realise sufficient to repay debentures. Removed from Register 1899 **1900**

Redcar, Coatham, Marske & Saltburn Gas Co. Inc. by Special Act 1876 as Redcar & Coatham Gas Co.; name changed 1878. In July 1919 the undertaking was acquired by the Redcar Urban District Council for £115,000 **1921**

Redcar Services Ld, Regd. 1923. Vol. liq. (members') 2 Apr. 1935. Undertaking was acquired by Maidstone & District Motor Services Ld. Capital returned to contributories—£1 8s. 4·8d. per preference share of £1 (including arrears of dividend); £1 9s. 3·6d. per preferred share of £1 (including arrears of dividend); £2 15s. 7½d. per ordinary share of £1. Final meeting return regd. 18 Feb. 1936 **1936**

Redcastle Reward Proprietary Gold Mines Ld. Regd. 1896. Struck off Register 16 Nov. 1906 **1901**

Redcroft Steam Navigation Co. Ld. Regd. 1911. Vol. liq. 23 Feb. 1920. Final meeting return regd. 6 May 1922 **1921**

Redcroft Steam Navigation Co. Ld. Regd. 1921 as Redcroft Steam Navigation Co. (1921) Ld.; name changed July 1926. Struck off Register 8 Dec. 1939 **1940**

Reddihough (John) Ld. See J. R. Holdings Ld.

Reddihough (John) Ld. Regd. 1948. Vol. liq. (members') 7 May 1971. £36 was paid into Companies' Liquidation Account in respect of unclaimed dividends. Final meeting return regd. 23 Dec. 1971.... **1972**

Redditch & District Light Railway Co. Inc. (under Light Railways Act 1896) by an order of the Light Railways Commissioners, confirmed by the Board of Trade on 30 Jan. 1900. In Nov. 1902 no capital had been issued and construction had not been commenced **1903**

Redditch Gas Co. Regd. 1872 as Redditch Town & District Gas Co. Ld.; reinc. by Special Act 1899 under above title. Dissolved 1 May 1949, undertaking being vested in West Midland Area Gas Board under Gas Act 1948. Holders of securities were entitled to receive, in respect of each £100 unit held, British Gas 3% guaranteed stock 1990–95 as follows:

	£	s.	d.
Ord. stock (5% stand)	135	0	0
5% pref. stock	112	0	0
5% red. pref. stock	101	15	0
4% red. pref. stock	100	8	11
3½% red. deb. stock	102	0	0
4% red. deb. stock (1955)	101	5	0
5½% red. deb. stock	104	0	0
4% red. deb. stock (1963)	101	5	0
4½% red. deb. stock	101	10	0
3½% red. mort. debs.	99	0	0	**1952**

Redfern Ld. Regd. 1892. Vol. liq. 25 Jan. 1924. Final meeting return regd. 18 Feb. 1926 **1926**

Redheugh Bridge Co. Ld. Inc. by Special Act 1886; regd. as limited 1937. Vol. liq. (members') 29 Sept. 1937,

VOL. FOR

the bridge undertaking having been sold in May 1937 to Newcastle-upon-Tyne and Gateshead Corporations for £110,000 cash. Capital returned to contributories—£11 15s. 4·85557d. per preference or ordinary share of £10. Final meeting return regd. 29 June 1938 1938

Redhill Gas Co. *See* East Surrey Gas Co.

Redhills Tin Mining Co. Ld. Regd. 1905. Vol. liq. 30 Dec. 1914. Property was acquired by Chendai Consolidated Ld. Final meeting return regd. 4 Mar. 1915 1915

Redline Glico Ld. Regd. 1914 as Union Petroleum Products Ld.; name changed 1924 to Redline Motor Spirit Co. Ld. and in 1931 to above. Vol. liq. 1 Nov. 1961. Final meeting return regd. 19 Jan. 1962 1940

Redline Motor Spirit Co. Ld. See above.

Redmayne (E. B.) & Sons Ld. Regd. 1922. Vol. liq. (members') 20 July 1932. Private company. Final meeting return regd. 30 July 1935 1933

Redruth & Chasewater Railway Co. Inc. by Special Act 1824. Court Order to wind up Nov. 1918 1920

Reducto Nitrate Co. Ld. Regd. 1903. Vol. liq. Oct. 1908. Removed from Register 1909 1909

Redwing Safety Services Ld. Regd. 1929. Vol. liq. (members') 30 Nov. 1932. Capital returned to contributories—£27,908 6s. 4d. Final meeting return regd. 21 June 1933 1933

Reed (Albert E.) & Co. (Newfoundland) Ld. Regd. 1907. Vol. liq. 22 Nov. 1928. Final meeting return regd. 25 Apr. 1929 1929

Reed, Evans & Co. Ld. Regd. 1901 as Electric Equipment & Securities Ld.; name changed to Railway Finance & Construction Co. Ld. in Aug. 1909 and as above in Dec. 1923. Court Order to wind up 1947. Struck off Register 19 May 1944.......... 1945

Rees Electric Press Ld. Regd. 1914. Vol. liq. (members') 26 June 1930. All shares held by Spillers Ld. Final meeting return regd. 16 Dec. 1931 1931

Rees Roturbo Manufacturing Co. Ld. Regd. 1908. Receiver appointed in Sept. 1933, ceased to act Aug. 1943. Assets realised insufficient to pay debenture holders in full. Struck off Register 18 Aug. 1944 . 1945

Reeves, Whitburn & Co. Ld. Regd. 1925. Vol. liq. (members') 23 Aug. 1938. Undertaking was acquired by National Discount Co. Ld. Capital returned to contributories—20s per preference share of £1; 17s. 11·432d. per ordinary share of £1 (10s. paid). Final meeting return regd. 20 Mar. 1940 ... 1939

Referee Cycle Co. Ld. Regd. 1892. Removed from Register 22 Dec. 1903................................ *1903

Refineria Argentina S. A. *See* Argentine Refinery Co.

Reformed Food (Vegetarian) Co. Ld. *See* Distributing Kitchens Ld.

Refugio Mining Co. Ld. Regd. Edinburgh 1895. Vol. liq. July 1898. Final meeting return regd. 9 July 1902 1899

Refugio Syndicate Ld. Regd. 1905. Vol. liq. Nov. 1910. Removed from Register 1911 1911

Regal Fire & Accident Co. Ld. Regd. 1900. Court Order to wind up 18 Oct. 1921. Struck off Register 10 May 1935 1936

Regency General Service Co. Ld. *See* Mayfair & General Property Trust Ld.

Regent Carriage Co. Ld. Regd. 1902. Court Order to wind up 1 Dec. 1925. Struck off Register Jan. 1933 1933

Regent Fire Insurance Co. Ld. Regd. Edinburgh 1902. Vol. liq. Aug. 1906. Undertaking and assets sold to General Accident Fire & Life Assurance Corporation Ld. Shareholders were entitled to receive, in cash, the amount of paid-up capital *plus* 5%. Final meeting return regd. 24 Apr. 1908 1907

Regent Piano Co. Ld. Regd. 1926. Vol. liq. 20 June 1932. All capital held by Sir Herbert Marshall & Sons Ld. Final meeting return regd. 6 Feb. 1933 1931

Regent Shears (1918) Ld. Regd. 1918. Vol. liq. 26 Oct. 1922. Final meeting return regd. 20 Dec. 1923 1923

Regent's Canal & Dock Co. *See* Grand Union Canal Co.

Regent's Canal City & Docks Railway Co. *See* Grand Union Canal Co.

Regent's Canal Co. Inc. by Special Act 1812. Merged in the Regent's Canal City and Docks Railway Co. (later Grand Union Canal Co.) in Apr. 1883. Stockholders received £130 cash for every £100 stock held 1884

Regents Park Development Co. Ld. Vol. liq. (members') 25 Aug. 1950. Final meeting return regd. 12 Mar. 1954 1947

Regina (Canada) Gold Mine Ld. Regd. 1896. Vol. liq. 7 Nov. 1901. The property was sold under foreclosure to Black Eagle Gold Mining Co. Ld. Struck off Register 19 Oct. 1906 1902

Regina Diamond Syndicate Ld. Inc. Transvaal 1906. Vol. liq. Feb. 1912. Capital returned to contributories—1s. 9d. per share of £1; further payments (if any) not known 1913

Regina Machine Co. Ld. Regd. 1910. Vol. liq. 20 Dec. 1916. Final meeting return regd. 9 May 1924 1917

Regional Real Estate Co. *See* Compagnia Fondiaria Regionale.

Regis Shipping Co. Ld. Regd. 1916. Struck off Register 1928 1927

Registry Investment Trust Ld. *See* Cairnton Investment Trust Ld.

Reid Estancias Ld. Regd. 1910. Vol. liq. 19 Dec. 1923. Final meeting return regd. 24 Oct. 1928 .... *1924

Reid (Henry) & Sons Ld. Regd. Edinburgh 1921. Vol. liq. 28 Aug. 1931. Direct controlling interest held by Millington (Fred. W.) (1920) Ld. Capital returned to contributories—£2,367 17s. 9d. Final meeting return regd. 6 Dec. 1932 1932

Reid Macfarlane & Co. (Belfast) Ld. Undertaking and assets were acquired in Dec. 1928 by Turner & Newall Ld. 1929

Reid Macfarlane & Co. Ld. Undertaking and assets were acquired in Dec. 1928 by Turner & Newall Ld. 1929

Reid Macfarlane & Co. (London) Ld. Undertaking and assets were acquired in Dec. 1928 by Turner & Newall Ld. 1929

Reid (Peter) & Sons Ld. Regd. 1896. Vol. liq. 26 Feb. 1903. Final meeting return regd. 12 Oct. 1904 1904

Reid (Robert) & Co. Ld. Regd. 1898. Vol. liq. 26 Aug. 1919. Business acquired by company of same name. Preference and ordinary shares were repaid in cash. The debenture stock was repaid at 110%. Final meeting return regd. 4 Dec. 1919. Court Order deferred dissolution until Apr. 1921 1920

Reid (Robert) & Co. Ld. Inc. in Victoria 1919. All capital was owned by Reid Murray Holdings Ld. Vol. liq. (members') 15 July 1966. Final meeting return regd. 1 Nov. 1966 1960

Reid's Brewery Co. Ld. Regd. 1888. Vol. liq. 13 Jan. 1899. Reconstructed as Watney Combe Reid & Co. Ld. (later Watney Mann Ld.), in which company shareholders were entitled to £878 8s. fully-paid ordinary shares for each ordinary share of £700 held. Preference stockholders were entitled to an equal amount of preference shares of £1 in new company. Holders of 4% debenture stock entitled to either £110 debenture stock or £112·833 in cash for every £100 stock held; holders of 3½% debenture stock were entitled to £100 debenture stock or £105 in cash for every £100 debenture stock held. Final meeting return regd. 15 June 1900 1899

Reid's Palace Hotel (Madeira) Ld. Regd. 1927. Properties at Funchal were acquired by Island Hotel (Madeira) Ld. for 55,740 fully-paid shares of 5s. and £48,772 10s. 5% 1st mortgage debenture stock; this consideration *plus* £6,967 10s. in cash was paid to debenture holders. Struck off Register 4 Aug. 1939 1940

Rein River (Nigeria) Tin Mining Co. Ld. Regd. 1910. Vol. liq. 30 June 1916. Final meeting return regd. 30 Aug. 1917 1917

Reinforced Rubber Co. Ld. Regd. 1910. Vol. liq. 12 Nov. 1914. Final meeting return regd. 28 Apr. 1926 1915

Reinsurance & Guarantee Corporation Ld. Regd. 1908. Court Order to wind up 28 Mar. 1911. Liquidator released 30 Mar. 1918. Struck off Register 14 Feb. 1919 1911

Reiss Bros (1923) Ld. *See* below.

Reiss Brothers Ld. *See* below.

Reiss, Shaw & Holmes Ld. Regd. 1923 as Reiss Bros. (1923) Ld.; name changed to Reiss Brothers Ld. in 1929 and as above 21 Oct. 1935. Struck off Register 11 Jan. 1957 1940

Rejang Estate Ld. Regd. 21 Oct. 1936. Vol. liq. (members') 17 June 1949. Capital returned to contributories—10¼d. per share of 2s. £24 7s. 1d. was paid into Companies' Liquidation Account. Final meeting return regd. 30 May 1953 1954

Rejang (Sarawak) Plantations Ld. Regd. 1926. Vol. liq. (creditors') 30 June 1930. No capital returned to contributories. Undertaking was acquired by Tanah Estates Ld. Final meeting return regd. 9 July 1931 1931

Reliance Fuel Co. Ld. Regd. 1919. Vol. liq. 25 June 1924. Final meeting return regd. 1 Sept. 1927 1925

Reliance Mutual Life Assurance Society. Founded 1840. All assets and liabilities were acquired in 1893 by Norwich Union Life Insurance Society 1894

Reliance Portland Cement Works Ld. Regd. 1890. court Order to wind up 3 Mar. 1895; liquidator released 25 Sept. 1896. Removed from Register 21 June 1907 *1895

Reliance Rubber Co. Ld. Undertaking and assets were acquired by Reliance Rubberware Ld. for £23,500 in preferred ordinary shares of 5s. and £21,700 in deferred ordinary shares of 1s. 1929

Reliance Rubberware Ld. Regd. 1928. Vol. liq. (creditors') 9 Apr. 1930. Assets realised insufficient to pay unsecured creditors in full. Final meeting return regd. 8 Oct. 1931 1931

See Stock Exchange Year-Book.

VOL. FOR

Reliance Taxi-Cab Co. Ld. Regd. 1908. Court Order to wind up 2 Nov. 1909. Liquidator released 24 Oct. 1914. Struck off Register 24 July 1923 1910

Reliance Trading Co. (Manchester) Ld. Regd. 1925. Receiver appointed 10 Mar. 1930. All capital held by Palatine Industrial Finance Co. Ld. Court Order to wind up Apr. 1931. Liquidator released 28 Sept. 1939. Struck off Register 17 July 1942 1932

Reliance Tube Co. Ld. Regd. 1896. Removed from Register 1905 1900

Rembia Rubber Estates Ld. Regd. 1909. Vol. liq. (members') 14 Dec. 1933. Undertaking and assets were acquired by Rembia Rubber Co. Ld., in which company shareholders were entitled to 8 shares of 2s. (credited with 1s. 3d. paid) for each ordinary or preference share of £1 held. Debenture holders were entitled to 50% of holding in cash and 50% in 7% convertible debenture stock; arrears of interest were payable in fully-paid shares of new company. £33 7s. 6d. was paid into Companies' Liquidation Account. Final meeting return regd. 10 May 1935 1934

Remedios Columbia United Gold Mines Ld. Regd. 1886. Removed from Register 1898 1901

Remer & Co. Ld. Regd. 1893 as Remer Nowell & Co. Ld.; name changed 1896. Receiver appointed 31 Jan. 1911. Court Order to wind up 6 Mar. 1911. Liquidator released 23 Feb. 1912. Receiver ceased to act 18 Feb. 1914. Struck off Register 16 July 1915 *1911

Remer (John) & Co. Ld. Regd. 1917. Court Order to wind up July 1921. Struck off Register June 1931 1932

Remer Nowell & Co. Ld. See Remer & Co. Ld.

Renard Commercial Motor Co. Ld. Regd. 1912. Vol. liq. 23 July 1914. Final meeting return regd. 14 July 1916 1915

Renard (India) Transport Corporation Ld. Regd. 1907. Struck off Register 24 Oct. 1916 1911

Renard Road & Rail Transport Corporation Ld. Regd. 1907. Vol. liq. June 1912. The undertaking and assets were acquired by Renard Commercial Motor Co. Ld., in which company shareholders were entitled to 2 participating preference shares of 5s. (credited with 4s. paid) for each preferred share of £1 held, or 1 ordinary share of 5s. (credited with 4s. paid) for each ordinary share of £1 held. Removed from Register 1913 1913

Render (Henry) Ld. Regd. 1875. Removed from Register 1903 1884

Renewable Electric Lamp Co. Ld. Regd. 1899. Receiver appointed by Court on behalf of deb. holders. Removed from Register 1905 1904

Renfrew Crusher Co. Ld. Regd. 1901. Vol. liq. June 1905. Removed from Register 1911 1906

Renmark Gold Mines Ld. Regd. 1896. Court Order to wind up 8 Dec. 1897. Removed from Register 1912 1898

Renn, Hounam & Co. Ld. Undertaking and assets were acquired in 1928 by Phantestra (Renn's Gramophone & Wireless) Ld 1929

Rennes Artificial Silk Co. Ld. Regd. 1928. Vol. liq. (creditors') 3 Mar. 1931. No capital returned to contributories. Final meeting return regd. 11 May 1932 1931

Rennie & Prosser Ld. Regd. Edinburgh 1899. Vol. liq. (members') 30 May 1930. All shares were owned by Hamilton (Claud) Ld. Final meeting return regd. 17 Dec. 1930 1930

Rennie, Ritchie & Newport Shipbuilding Co. Ld. Regd. 1918 as Newport (Mon.) Shipyard Ld.; name changed Sept. 1919. Vol. liq. 16 Aug. 1922. Court Order to continue winding up under supervision 16 Aug. 1922. Final meeting return regd. 11 Nov. 1925 1923

Renny, Forbes & Co. Ld. Regd. 1895. Vol. liq. (members') 6 Apr. 1944. All capital was owned by Fisons Ld. Final meeting return regd. 29 Sept. 1944 1945

Renong Dredging Co. Ld. Regd. 1908. Vol. liq. 7 July 1913. Reconstructed as Renong Tin Dredging Co. Ld in which company shareholders were entitled to 1 preference and 1 ordinary share of £1 (both credited as fully-paid) for each preference share of £1 held or 1 fully-paid ordinary share of £1 for each A or B deferred shares of 5s. held. Final meeting return regd. 25 Feb. 1914 1914

Renovators (Cleaners & Dyers) Ld. Regd. 1924. Direct controlling interest was owned by Achille Serre Ld. Struck off Register 1939 1933

Renshaw (W. R.) & Co. Ld. Regd. 1900. Vol. liq. 22 Mar. 1905. Final meeting return regd. 15 July 1913 *1906

Rent and General Collecting and Estate Management Society Ld. Regd. 1874 as Rent Guarantee Society Ld.; name changed Apr. 1887. Vol. liq. 13 Dec. 1894. Court Order to continue winding up under supervision 19 Dec. 1894. Final meeting return regd. 25 May 1899 1895

Rent Guarantee Society Ld. See Rent and General Collecting and Estate Management Society Ld.

VOL. FOR

Repeating Gramophones Ld. Regd. 1920. Struck off Register Feb. 1931 1931

Republican Mountain Silver Mines Ld. Regd. 1880. Removed from Register 1911 1892

Research & Development Co. Ld. Inc. South African Republic 1895. In liquidation in 1900 1900

Reserved Assets Co. Ld. Regd. 1924. All shares held by Grahams Trading Co. Ld. Struck off Register 1938 1937

Reserves Securities Trust Ld. Regd. 1928. Under provisions of a scheme of arrangement and amalgamation effective 3 May 1967 ordinary shareholders were entitled to receive (per 100 shares approx. 105 ordinary shares in Minster Assets Ld.) and approx. 110 units in London & Wall Street Units; and preference shareholders 1 5% preference share of Minster Assets Ld. per preference share. Dissolved 3 Sept. 1967 1968

Reservoir Hub & Components Co. Ld. Regd. 1896. Vol. liq. 31 May 1898. Final meeting return regd. 14 Jan. 1902 1899

Residential & Commercial Properties Ld. Amalgamated in 1939 with two other societies under the title Freehold Leasehold & Property Developments Ld., in which company shareholders were entitled to 1 A ordinary share of 2s. for each £1 of capital held, and debenture holders to 10s. 5% debenture stock *plus* 2 6% participating preference shares of 1s. for each £1 debenture held 1940

Residential Properties Improvement Co. Ld. Regd. 1920. Proceeds from assets were insufficient to satisfy all claims of creditors. £2,495 was repaid to debenture holders. Struck off Register 29 Sept. 1964 1958

Retail Trade Securities Ld. Regd. 1927. Court Order to wind up 15 Oct. 1929. Struck off Register 27 Oct. 1942 1943

Retford, Rotherham & Barnsley Railway Co. Inc. by Special Act 1891 as Rotherham, Blyth & Sutton Railway Co.; name changed by Acts of 1892 and 1893. In 1901 it was stated that this line had been abandoned 1901

Retiro (Honduras) Gold Mining Co. Ld. Regd. 1889. Vol. liq. 22 Dec. 1892. Final meeting return regd 30 Dec. 1895 1894

Réunion Française et Compagnie d'Assurances Universelles Réunies. Established France 1899 as La Réunion Française; name changed Dec. 1929. In 1932 it was stated that the company was no longer doing business in London 1931

Reuter's Bank Ld. See Commercial Bank of London Ld.

Reuter's International Agency Ld. Regd. 1894. Removed from Register 1901 1898

Reuter's Telegram Co. Ld. Regd. 1865. Vol. liq. 17 Jan. 1917. Undertaking acquired by Reuters Ld. Final meeting return regd. 2 Mar. 1920 .... *1918

Reversion Investment Corporation Ld. Regd. 1895. Vol. liq. July 1906. Removed from Register 1909 1907

Reversion Purchase Co. Ld. Regd. 1878. Vol. liq. 17 July 1916. Assets were acquired by Property and Estates Ld. (later Property, Estates & Reversion Co. Ld.). Final meeting return regd. 22 Apr. 1918 1917

Reversionary & General Securities Co. Ld. Regd. 1888. Vol. liq. (members') 14 Aug. 1942. Capital returned to contributories—ordinary shares (of £10): £13 0s. 6d.; founders' shares (of £1): £69 7s. 11d. £65 was paid into Companies' Liquidation Account. Final meeting return regd. 26 Nov. 1952 1955

Reville Ld. Regd. 1926 as Reville (1926) Ld.; name changed Jan. 1930. Vol. liq. 12 Sept. 1946. Capital returned to contributories—£1 1s. 6½d. per preference share of £1. Final meeting return regd. 29 Mar. 1954 1955

Revolution Cycle Co. Ld. Regd. Dublin 1896. Removed from Register 1901 1901

Revolver Gold Mining Co. Ld. Inc. South African Republic 1888 1890

Revue (Manicaland) Gold Mining Co. Ld. Regd. 1901. Vol. liq. Jan. 1908. Absorbed by Rhodesia Matabeleland Development Co. Ld. in which company shareholders were entitled to 1 share of £1 (credited as fully-paid) for every 100 shares of £1 held. Removed from Register 1911 1908

Reward Gold Mines Ld. Regd. 1906. Vol. liq. Oct. 1908. Properties were sold to Claremont Gold Mine Ld. for £2,000 and a right (since expired) to apply for shares in purchasing company. Removed from Register 1909 1909

Rex Consolidated Ld. Regd. 1913. Vol. liq. 14 June 1916. Final meeting return regd. 28 Dec. 1916 1917

Rex Gold Mines Ld. Regd. 1909. Struck off Register 1916 1913

Rex Hotel Co. Ld. Regd. 1920 as Waverley Hotel (Whitley Bay) Co. Ld.; name changed Apr. 1936. Undertaking and property were sold in 1946. Outstanding 5% 1st mortgage debentures and 5%

See Stock Exchange Year-Book.

VOL. FOR

prior lien debentures redeemed in 1946. Vol. liq. (members') 29 Jan. 1947. Capital returned to contributories—4*s.* 6*d.* per share of £1. £52 was paid into Companies' Liquidation Account. Final meeting return regd. 2 Feb. 1948 1949

Rexer Arms Co. Ld. Regd. 1905. Vol. liq. June 1907. Removed from Register 1909 1908

Rexine Ld. Regd. 1915. Vol. liq. (members') 31 Mar. 1932. Capital returned to contributories—£100. Final meeting return regd. 1 June 1933 1933

Reynolds Brothers Ld. Regd. 1891. Vol. liq. 30 Nov. 1907. Reconstructed as company of same name. Shareholders were entitled to 15 fully-paid shares of £1 in new company for each fully-paid ordinary or preference share of £10 held, or 7½ fully-paid shares of £1 for each ordinary share of £10 (£5 paid) held. Final meeting return regd. 30 June 1915 1908

Reynolds Brothers Ld. Inc. Natal 1907. Reconstructed 1913 as company of same name 1912

Reynolds Gold Mining Co. Ld. Regd. 1889. Removed from Register 1904 1892

Reynolds (Thomas) (1920) Ld. *See* Halifax Doubling Co. Ld.

Reyrol Motor Car Co. Ld. Regd. 1900. Removed from Register 1904 .... *1902

Rezende Ld. Regd. 1898. Reconstructed 1905 as company of same name. Shareholders were entitled to 2 fully-paid shares of £1 in new company for every 5 shares of £1 held. Removed from Register 1907 1908

Rezende Ld. Regd. 1905. Vol. liq. Dec. 1908 for reconstruction as Rezende Mines Ld. in which company shareholders were entitled to 1 share of £1 (credited as fully-paid) for every 5 shares of £1 held. Removed from Register 1910 1909

Rezende Mines, Ld. Regd. 1908. Vol. liq. (members') 15 Apr. 1955. Capital returned to contributories—1*s.* 7½*d.* per share of 1*s.* £1,767 5*s.* 1*d.* paid into Companies' Liquidation Account: £464 5*s.* 3*d.* in respect of unclaimed dividends and £1,302 19*s.* 10*d.* in respect of unclaimed distributions. Final meeting return regd. 21 Aug. 1962.......... 1963

Rhayader Gas Light Co. Ld. Regd. 1903. Dissolved 1 May 1949. undertaking being vested in Wales Area Gas Board under Gas Act 1948. Holders of ordinary shares (of £5) were entitled to receive £5 British Gas 3% guaranteed stock 1990–95 for each share held 1952

Rhea Manufacturing Co. Ld. Regd. 1886. Vol. liq. 5 Nov. 1887. Final meeting return regd. 14 July 1892 1888

Rheinbach Copper Mines Ld. Regd. 1907. Struck off Register 1912 1910

Rhind (D. A.) & Co. Ld. Regd. Edinburgh 1897. Vol. liq. Apr. 1922. Capital returned to contributories—£1 10*s.* per preference share; further payments (if any) not known. Final meeting return regd. 28 Dec. 1923 1923

Rhine Valley Oil Concessions Syndicate Ld. Regd. 1913. Struck off Register 1917 1915

Rhinos Ld. Regd. 1923 as Peachey Leather Products Ld.; name changed May 1925. Receiver appointed in Jan. 1930. Assets realised sufficient to pay 3*s.* 10*d.* in £ to 1st mortgage debenture holders. Struck off Register 30 Jan. 1934 1933

Rhins of Galloway Railway Co. Inc. 1878. Undertaking abandoned by Act of 1883 1884

Rhodes Electrical Manufacturing Co. Ld. *See* Rhodes Motors Ld.

Rhodes (J. & H.) Ld. Regd. 1925. Vol. liq. 21 Dec. 1952. Final meeting return regd. 20 Feb. 1954 1938

Rhodes Motors Ld. Regd. 1904 as Rhodes Electrical Manufacturing Co. Ld.: name changed Feb. 1907. Vol. liq. (creditors') 27 July 1934. Capital returned to contributories—£7,677 19*s.* Final meeting return regd. 19 Dec. 1935 1935

Rhodes, Rawling & Shaw, Ld. Regd. 1919. Vol. liq. (members') 31 May 1956. Final meeting return regd. 30 Aug. 1957 1938

Rhodes Reef Gold Mining Co. Ld. Regd. 1880. Vol. liq. June 1884. Assets and property were acquired by Devala-Moyar Gold Mining Co. Ld. for an equivalent of 3*s.* 4½*d.* per share of £1. Final meeting return regd. 11 May 1885 1885

Rhodes (Thomas) Ld. Regd. 1889. Vol. liq. (members') 2 Sept. 1930. Undertaking and assets acquired by Lancashire Cotton Corporation Ld. Preference shareholders received £18,566 5½% non-cumulative income debenture stock, 17,673 ordinary shares of £1, 17,672 deferred shares of 1*s.* and £2,142 12*s.* 2*d.* in cash. Holders of ordinary shares, fully-paid and those with 12*s.* paid, received £55,669 5½% non-cumulative income debenture stock, 53,018 ordinary shares of £1,253,013 deferrred shares of 1*s.* and £12,798 5*s.* 3*d.* in cash. Final meeting return regd. 2 Sept. 1931 1931

Rhodesia Agency Ld. Regd. 1895. Undertaking and assets were acquired by Rhodesia Goldfields Ld. in which company shareholders were entitled to £1 debenture stock and 1 share of £1 (credited as fully-paid) for every 2 shares of £1 held. Removed from Register 1901 1900

Rhodesia & Ashanti Ld. Regd. 1910 as Rhodesia South Ld.; name changed July 1910. Vol. liq. 14 Nov. 1921. The undertaking and assets were acquired by East & West African Exploration Co. Ld. in which company shareholders were entitled to 5 shares of 2*s.* (credited with 1*s.* 4*d.* paid) for every 2 shares of 10*s.* held and an option (since expired) over further shares at par. Final meeting return regd. 20 Apr. 1922 1922

Rhodesia Asbestos & Chrome Syndicate Ld. Inc. Southern Rhodesia 1925. Vol. liq. Dec. 1927. Undertaking and assets were sold to Rhodesia Chrome & Asbestos Co. Ld. for 50,000 shares of £1 1929

Rhodesia Asbestos Co. Ld. Regd. 1908 as T.H.S. Syndicate Ld.; name changed Mar. 1910. Vol. liq. 9 Jan. 1917. It was proposed to distribute certain investments in specie. Final meeting return regd. 8 Oct. 1917 1917

Rhodesia Breweries Ld. Regd. 1895. Vol. liq. 19 Sept. 1905. Struck off Register 26 Mar. 1929 1930

Rhodesia Broken Hill Development Co. Ld. Regd. 1904. Vol. liq. Aug. 1910. Reconstructed as company of same name (later Zambia Broken Hill Development Co. Ld.). Shareholders were entitled to 1 share of 5*s.* (credited as fully-paid) in new company for each share of £1 held and an option (since expired) over further shares. Removed from Register 1911 1911

Rhodesia Chrome & Asbestos Co. Ld. Inc. Southern Rhodesia 1927. Vol. liq. 26 July 1937 1938

Rhodesia Cold Storage & Trading Co. Ld. *See* Rhodesia Trading Co. Ld.

Rhodesia Concessions Ld. Regd. 1895. Vol. liq. Dec. 1909. The assets were sold for £40,887 in cash. Removed from Register 1911 1910

Rhodesia Consolidated Ld. Inc. Rhodesia 1903. Vol. liq. for reconstruction under same name June 1909. Shareholders were entitled to 1 new share of 10*s.* (credited with 7*s.* 6*d.* paid) in new company for each share of 10*s.* held. Debenture holders received 40% in cash and 60% in new shares 1910

Rhodesia Consolidated Ld. Inc. Rhodesia 1909. Vol. liq. Dec. 1924. Undertaking and assets were acquired by Rhodesian Corporation Ld. in which company shareholders were entitled to 3 fully-paid shares of 5*s.* for every 10 ordinary shares of 4*s.* held 1925

Rhodesia Copper and General Exploration and Finance Co. Ld. Regd. 1909 as Rhodesia Copper Co. Ld.; name changed 1911. Vol. liq. (members') 17 Sept. 1945. Assets acquired by Charterland & General Exploration & Finance Co. Ld. (now Charterland & General Ld.) in which company shareholders were entitled to 1 share of 5*s.* (since converted into stock) for every 2 shares (or stock units) of 3*s.* held. Dissolved 5 Nov. 1978 1978-9

Rhodesia Copper & General Exploration & Finance Co. Ld. Regd. 1909 as Rhodesia Copper Co. Ld.; name changed 1911. Vol. liq. 17 Sept. 1945. Net assets acquired by Charterland & General Exploration & Finance Co. Ld., in which company shareholders received 1 ordinary share of 5*s.* foe every 2 shares of 3*s.* held 1982–3

Rhodesia Copper Co. Ld. Regd. 1902. Vol. liq. Feb. 1909 for reconstruction as Rhodesia Copper Co. Ld. (later Rhodesia Copper & General Exploration & Finance Co. Ld.). Shareholders were entitled to 1 fully-paid share of 7*s.* 6*d.* in new company for each share of £1 held and an option (since expired) over further shares. Removed from Register 1910 1909

Rhodesia Copper Ld. *See* Rhodesia Copper & General Exploration & Finance Co. Ld.

Rhodesia Cotton Co. Ld. Regd 1906. Vol. liq. (members') 21 Jan. 1927. Final meeting return regd. 28 Jan. 1949 1950

Rhodesia Esperanza Ld. Regd. 1910. Vol. liq. Apr. 1912. Capital returned to contributories—2*s.* per share of £1 at July 1912; further payments (if any) not known. Removed from Register 1913 1913

Rhodesia Estates & Town Lands Ld. Regd. 1895. Vol. liq. 24 July 1903. Struck off Register 20 Mar. 1925 1904

Rhodesia Exploration & Development Co. Ld. Regd. 1895. Vol. liq. 26 Jan. 1912. Reconstructed as Gold Fields Rhodesian Development Co. Ld. in which company shareholders were entitled to 11¼ shares of £1 (credited as fully-paid) for every 10 shares of £1 held. Final meeting return regd. 7 May 1915 1912

Rhodesia Exploration Co. Ld. Regd. 1917. Vol. liq. 9 Aug. 1929. Undertaking and assets were acquired by Rhodesian Corporation Ld. in which company shareholders were entitled to 1 share of 5*s.* (credited

VOL. FOR

as fully-paid) for every 2 shares of 2s. held. Final meeting return regd. 19 Feb. 1937...................... **1930**

Rhodesia Gold Mines and Exploring Co. Ld. Regd. 1895. Removed from Register 1911 .... **1903**

Rhodesia Gold Mining & Investment Co. Ld. Inc. Rhodesia 1910. Vol. liq. Mar. 1923. Undertaking and assets were acquired by African & European Investment Co. Ld. in which company shareholders were entitled to 2 shares of £1 (credited as fully-paid) for every 3 shares of 10s. held **1924**

Rhodesia Gold Reefs (Purdon's) Ld. Regd. 1895. Vol. liq. 26 Apr. 1907. Removed from Register 1908 ... **1908**

Rhodesia Goldfields Ld. Regd. 1895. Court Order to wind up 26 Mar. 1907. Liquidator released 29 Nov. 1913. Struck off Register 3 Sept. 1918 .... **1908**

Rhodesia Investment Co. Ld. Regd. 1899. All share capital had been returned at 24 Oct. 1902; further payments (if any) not known. Removed from Register 1908 .... **1903**

Rhodesia-Katanga Junction Railway & Mineral Co. Ld. Regd. 1909. The debentures were repaid out of proceeds of sale of railway. Vol. liq. 31 May 1929. Reconstructed as Rhodesia-Katanga Co. Ld. in which company shareholders were entitled to 1 share of £1 (credited as fully-paid) for each ordinary or B share held. Final meeting return regd. 7 Jan. 1935 .... **1930**

Rhodesia Land Bank Ld. Inc. Southern Rhodesia 1911. Vol. liq. (members') 31 Dec. 1943. Capital returned to contributories—20s. 5·65388d. per share of £1. Final meeting return regd. 7 Oct. 1947 .... **1948**

Rhodesia Lands Ld. Regd. 1899. Vol. liq. 24 Feb. 1927. Final meeting return regd. 15 Jan. 1932 .... ***1905**

Rhodesia Ld. Regd. 1895. Reconstructed 1905 as company of same name. Shareholders were entitled to 1 fully-paid share of £1 in new company for every 3 shares of £1 held. Removed from Register 1908 **1908**

Rhodesia Ld. Inc. Rhodesia 1905. Vol. liq. Oct. 1912 for reconstruction as company of same name. Shareholders were entitled to 4 shares of 5s. (credited with 3s. 6d. paid) in new company for each share of £1 held. Holders of debenture stock were entitled to 128,500 shares of 5s. in new company, £24,000 in cash and £33,000 debentures of Town Properties of Bulawayo Ld. **1913**

Rhodesia Ld. Regd. 1912. Vol. liq. 7 Nov. 1921. Undertaking and assets were acquired by London & Rhodesian Mining & Land Co. Ld. (later Lonrho Ld.) in which company shareholders were entitled to 2 shares of 5s. (credited as fully-paid) for every 5 shares of 2s. held. Final meeting return regd. 13 Nov. 1922 .... **1922**

Rhodesia Matabeleland Development Co. Ld. Regd. 1899. Vol. liq. July 1909 for sale of undertaking and assets to Amalgamated Properties of Rhodesia Ld. in which company shareholders were entitled to 4 shares of 5s. for every 3 shares of £1 held. Removed from Register 1910 .... **1910**

Rhodesia Minerals Concession Ld. Regd. 1929. Vol. liq. (creditors') 12 Oct. 1943. No capital returned to contributories. Final meeting return regd. 5 July 1944 .... **1945**

Rhodesia Mines Ld. Regd. 1898. Vol. liq. 4 May 1905. Reconstructed as New Rhodesia Mines Ld. in which company shareholders were entitled to 3 shares of £1 (credited as fully-paid) for every 5 shares of £1 held. Final meeting return regd. 13 Dec. 1906 .... **1906**

Rhodesia Mines Trust Ld. Inc. Rhodesia 1905. Vol. liq. June 1909 for reconstruction under same name (inc. in Rhodesia). Shareholders were entitled to 1 share of 10s. (credited with 5s. paid) in new company for each share of 10s. held **1910**

Rhodesia Mines Trust Ld. Inc. Rhodesia 1909. Wound up 1914 .... **1915**

Rhodesia Mines Trust Ld. Regd. 1905. Vol. liq. (members') 21 Dec. 1950. Undertaking was amalgamated with London Finance & Investment Corpn. Ld. Shareholders received 43,095 shares (of £1) in that company. Final meeting return regd. 15 Apr. 1952 .... **1955**

Rhodesia Options Ld. Regd. 1909. Vol. liq. Mar. 1911. Shareholders were entitled to 13 shares of 4s. in Takinta Oil Co. Ld. for every 8 shares of 5s. held *plus* 5s. 2¼d. per share in cash. Removed from Register 1912 .... **1912**

Rhodesia-Sebawkwe Development Syndicate Ld. Regd. 1896. Vol. liq. Jan. 1907. Removed from Register 1910 .... **1907**

Rhodesia South Ld. *See* Rhodesia & Ashanti Ld.

Rhodesia Trading Co. Ld. Regd. 1895. Removed from Register 1904 .... **1900**

Rhodesia Trading Co. Ld. Regd. 1903 as Rhodesia Cold Storage & Trading Co. Ld.; name changed Oct.

VOL. FOR

1908. Vol. liq. 20 Aug. 1926. Final meeting return regd. 21 Feb. 1935 .... **1927**

Rhodesian Abercorn Shamva Trust Co. Ld. Regd. 1909. Vol. liq. Sept. 1910. Undertaking and assets were sold to Rhodesia Exploration & Development Co. Ld. in which company shareholders were entitled to 4 shares of £1 (credited as fully-paid) for every 5 shares of £1 held. Removed from Register 1912 .. **1911**

Rhodesian & General Corporation Ld. Regd. 1895. Struck off Register 26 Apr. 1940 .... **1941**

Rhodesian & South African Syndicate Ld. Regd. 1911. Struck off Register 1920 .... **1916**

Rhodesian Banket Co. Ld. Regd. 1904. Vol. liq. Sept. 1910 for sale of undertaking and assets to Rhodesia Exploration & Development Co. Ld. in which company shareholders were entitled to 7 fully-paid shares of £1 for every 10 shares of £1 held. Removed from Register 1912 .... **1911**

Rhodesia Broken Hill Development Co. Ld. See Zambia Broken Hill Development Co. Ld.

Rhodesian Cattle & Land Co. Ld. *See* Rhodesian Mining & Land Co. Ld.

Rhodesian Claims Ld. Regd. 1895. Vol. liq. 29 July 1896. Reconstructed 1898 as Rhodesian Gold Trust Ld. in which company shareholders were entitled to 1 share of £1 (credited with 15s. paid) for each share of £1 (15s. paid) held. Final meeting return regd. 26 Mar. 1900 .... **1900**

Rhodesian Corpn. Ld. *See* Afex Corporation Ld.

Rhodesian Corporation Ld. Regd. 1910. Vol. liq. 30 Jan. 1912. Shareholders were entitled to 1 share of 5s. (credited with 4s. paid) in Rhodesian Corporation (1912) Ld. for each share of 5s. held. Final meeting return regd. 30 Dec. 1913 .... **1912**

Rhodesian Corporation (1912) Ld. Regd. 1912. Vol. liq. 28 Dec. 1914. Capital returned to contributories— 2½d. per share of 5s. at Feb. 1915; further payments (if any) not known. Final meeting return regd. 3 Oct. 1916 .... **1915**

Rhodesian Gold Explorers Ld. *See* Premier Exploration Co. Ld.

Rhodesian Gold Trust Ld. Regd. 1896. Reconstructed 1900 as company of same name. Shareholders were entitled to 1 share of £1 (credited with 16s. paid) in new company for each share of £1 held. **1903**

Rhodesian Gold Trust Ld. Regd. 1900. Vol. liq. 31 July 1903. Undertaking & assets were acquired by Bulawayo and General Exploration Co. Ld. in which company shareholders were entitled to 1 share of £1 (credited as fully-paid) for every 5 shares of £1 held. Final meeting return regd. 3 Aug.1906 **1904**

Rhodesian King Asbestos Ld. Regd. 1921. Vol. liq. 4 Nov. 1924. Undertaking acquired by Rhodesian & General Asbestos Corporation Ld. for 79,516 fully-paid shares of £1. Final meeting return regd. 22 Feb. 1928 .... **1940**

Rhodesian Land, Cattle & Ranching Corporation Ld. Inc. Southern Rhodesia 1926. Vol. liq. 1938 the ranch having been sold to Imperial Cold Storage & Supply Co. Ld. Capital returned to contributories— 1s. 7⅜d. in 1939. Further returns (if any) not known **1894**

Rhodesian Mineral Properties Ld. Regd. 1895. Vol. liq. 31 July 1896. Reconstructed as Rhodesian Gold Trust Ld., in which company shareholders were entitled to 1 share of £1 (credited with 12s. 6d. paid) for each share of £1 (12s. 6d. paid) held. Final meeting return regd. 26 Mar. 1900 .... **1900**

Rhodesian Mining Corpn. Ld. *See* Afex Corporation Ld.

Rhodesian Mining & Development Ld. Regd. 1899. Removed from Register 1910 .... **1904**

Rhodesian Mining & Finance Co. Ld. Regd. 1895. Reconstructed 1905 as company of same name. Shareholders were entitled to 4 shares of £1 (credited with 16s. paid) in new company for every 5 shares of £1 held. Removed from Register 1911 .... **1908**

Rhodesian Mining & Finance Co. Ld. Inc. Rhodesia 1905. Vol. liq. for amalgamation under title of Mashonaland Consolidated (1912) Ld. in which company shareholders were entitled to 4 shares of 5s. (credited 4s. paid) for each share of £1 held ... **1913**

Rhodesian Mining & Land Co. Ld. Regd. 1912 as Rhodesian Cattle & Land Co. Ld.; name changed Nov. 1923. Vol. liq. (members') 17 Dec. 1929. Undertaking and assets were acquired by Rhodesian Corporation Ld. in which company shareholders were entitled to 1 share of 5s. (credited as fully-paid) for each share of 10s. held. Final meeting return regd. 11 Oct. 1932 .... **1930**

Rhodesian Pioneers Ld. Regd. 1896. Removed from Register 1909 .... **1907**

Rhodesian Properties Ld. Regd. 1899. Vol. liq. July 1922. Struck off Register Mar. 1929 .... **1930**

Rhodesian Prospectors Ld. Regd. 1895. Vol. liq. Feb. 1908. Removed from Register 1908 .... **1909**

*See Stock Exchange Year-Book.

VOL. FOR

Rhodesian Refractory Minerals Process Ld. Regd. 1910. Struck off Register Dec. 1931 1932

Rhodesian Tobacco Estates Ld. Regd. 1927 as Anglo-Rhodesian Tobacco Co. Ld.; name changed in Aug. 1931. Vol. liq. (members') 12 Aug. 1941. Capital returned to contributories—11*s*. 3*d*. per share of 10*s*. Final meeting return regd. 18 Mar. 1946 1947

Rhokana Copper Refineries Ld. Regd. 1947 as Rhodesia Copper Refineries Ld.; name changed 1965. On 26 June 1970 the mining assets and liabilities vested in Bancroft-Mines Ld. (later Nchanga Consolidated Copper Mines Ld.). Preference shareholders received an equivalent amount of preference shares in that company. Provision was made for dissolution of company without winding up within 3 months from 15 June 1970 1970

Rhokana Corporation Ld. Regd. 1923 as Rhodesian Congo Border Concession Ld.; name changed 1931. On 26 June 1970 the mining and certain other assets and liabilities vested in Bancroft-Mines Ld. (later Nchanga Consolidated Copper Mines Ld.). Ordinary and A ordinary shareholders received (per 100 shares held) 240·7875914 shares of $B.O.24 and 406·31921 units of loan stock 1982 of Zambian Copper Investments Ld. plus, by virtue of this company's interest in Roan Selection Trust Ld. a further 45·5701515 ordinary shares and 81·0883831 units of Zambia Copper Investments Ld. loan stock 1978. Preference shareholders received an equal amount of preference capital of Bancroft-Mines Ld. Provision was made for dissolution of company without winding up within 3 months from 15 June 1970 1970

Rhomines Ld. Inc. in Southern Rhodesia 1 Sept. 1932 as General Asbestos Co. Ld.; name changed 11 Oct. 1933. Company has ceased operations and all assets have been realised for purpose of settling debenture holders' claims and in Jan. 1948 the company was stated to have ceased to exist 1948

Rhondda and Swansea Bay Railway Co. Inc. by Special Act 1882. In 1922 the undertaking was merged into the Great Western Railway Co. in which company stockholders were entitled to stock as follows:

For each £100 held	*G.W.*
4% Debenture	£100 4% Debenture
5 % Preference	£100 5 % Cons. Pref.
Ordinary	£140 5% Cons. Gtd.

..... 1924

Rhondda Merthyr Shipping Co. Ld. Regd. June 1919. Vol. liq. 22 Aug. 1924. Final meeting return regd. 18 July 1925 ..... *1925

Rhondda Shipping & Coal Exporting Co. Ld. Regd. 1919. Vol. liq. 30 Apr. 1929. Capital returned to contributories—4*s*. 2*d*. per share of £1 at Aug. 1929; further payments (if any) not known. Final meeting return regd. 30 Apr. 1930 1930

Rhondda Tramways Construction Syndicate Ld. Regd. 1906. Vol. liq. 18 Apr. 1911. Final meeting return regd.1 Dec. 1922 1911

Rhondda Tramways Electric Supply Co. Ld. Regd. 1907. Vol. liq. (members') 27 Apr. 1939. Capital returned to contributories—£73 10*s*. Final meeting return regd. 26 July 1939 1940

Rhondda Valley & Hirwain Junction Railway Co. Inc. by Special Act 1867. Under Taff Vale Railway Act 1889 the undertaking was absorbed into that company in which holders of ordinary shares of £10 received £5 16*s*. 8*d*. in preference stock or cash; holders of 4% debenture stock received £133⅓ 3% debenture stock for every £100 stock held 1890

Rhos Gas Co. Ld. Regd. 1865. Dissolved 1 May 1949 undertaking being vested in Wales Area Gas Board under Gas Act 1948. Holders of securities were entitled to receive in respect of each £5 unit held British Gas 3% guaranteed stock 1990–95 as follows:

	£	s.	d.
Ord. shares	9	0	0
Ord. shares (£3 10*s*. paid)	6	6	0

..... 1952

Rhosemor Mine Ld. Regd. 1889. The property and plant was sold to East Halkyn Mining Co. Ld. for £5,000. A return of about 5*s*. 6*d*. per share of £1 was anticipated. Removed from Register 1901 1901

Rhosemor Mining Co. Ld. Regd. 1869. Vol. liq. Feb. 1888. Final meeting return regd. 12 Feb. 1890 1889

Rhozambia Mines Ld. *See* Southern Rhodesian Goldfields Ld.

Rhydalun Mining Co. Ld. Regd. 1879. Removed from Register 1905 1888

Rhyl & Prestatyn Light Railway Co. Inc. (under Light Railways Act 1896) by order of Light Railway Commissioners confirmed by Board of Trade 1900. Vol. liq. Nov. 1904 1906

Rhymney & Aber Gas Co. Inc. by Special Act 1898 as Rhymney & Aber Valley Gas & Water Co.; name changed 1922. Dissolved 1 May 1949, undertaking being vested in Wales Area Gas Board under Gas Act 1948. Holders of securities were entitled to receive British Gas 3% guaranteed stock 1990–95 as follows in respect of each £100 unit, unless otherwise stated, of security held:

	£	s.	d.
Cons. ord. stock (7% stand.)	145	10	0
5%pref.shares (of £5)	5	12	0
4% irred. deb. stock	101	10	0
5½%red.deb.stock	108	0	0

Liability in respect of certain mortgage loans assumed by the Board 1952

Rhymney Iron Co. Ltd. Established by Deed of Settlement 1837. Regd. 1871. Vol. liq. (members') 24 Mar. 1936. The 5% mortgage debentures were repaid at par and 5% 1st mortgage New Pits debenture stock at 105% on 15 Apr. 1936. All shares were held by Powell Duffryn Associated Collieries Ld. (later Powell Duffryn Ld.). which company acquired the undertaking. £120 was paid into Companies' Liquidation Account (see preface) for unclaimed mortgage debentures and £101 16*s*. 1*d*. for unclaimed mortgage debenture interest. Final meeting return regd. 13 Dec. 1937 1937

Rhymney Railway Co. Inc. by Special Act 1854. In 1922 the undertaking was merged into the Great Western Railway Co., in which company stockholders were entitled to stock as follows:

For each £100 held	*G. W.*
4% Debenture	£100 4% Debenture
4% Preference	£80 5% Cons. Pref.
Undivided Ordinary	£80 5% Cons. Pref. £80 Cons. Ordinary
Preferred Ordinary	£80 5% Cons. Pref.
Deffered Ordinary	£80 Cons. Ordinary

..... 1924

Rialto (Liverpool) Ld. Regd. 1925. Vol. liq. 10 Apr. 1928. Undertaking was acquired by General Theatre Corporation Ld. Final meeting return regd. 2 May 1929 ..... *1929

Riam Estate Ld. Regd. 1925. Struck off Register Feb. 1933 1933

Ribble Brewery Co. Ld. Regd. 1936. In 1943 the receiver and manager stated that he had sold the brewery and licensed and unlicensed properties to Matthew Brown & Co. Ld. The assets did not realise sufficient to meet the claim of the 1st debenture holders in full. Struck off Register 25 Jan. 1947 1947

Ribble Navigation Co. Established 1838. Acquired by Preston Corporation under Acts 1883, 1888, 1889 and 1890 1891

Ribbon Metals Syndicate Ld. Regd. 1909. Struck off Register 27 July 1937 1938

Ribon Valley (Nigeria) Tinfields Ld. Regd. 1910. Vol. liq. (members') 24 Sept. 1959. Undertaking and assets acquired by United Tin Areas of Nigeria Ld. in which company shareholders were entitled to 1 fully-paid share of 2*s*. 6*d*. for every 6*s*. stock held. Final meeting return regd. 14 Mar. 1962 1963

Rica Gold Mines Ld. Regd. 1902. Vol. liq. 25 May 1912. Final meeting return regd. 8 Apr. 1921 1913

Rice-Hamilton Exploration Syndicate Ld. Regd. 1894. Vol. liq. 10 July 1908. In 1912 the assets were acquired by Rhodesia Ld., in which company shareholders were entitled to 4 shares of 5*s*. (credited with 3*s*. 6*d*. paid) for each share of £1 held. Final meeting return regd. 20 Aug. 1915 1913

Rich (E) & Co. Ld. Regd. 1898. Vol. liq. (members') 9 Mar. 1950. Capital returned to contributories—12s. 10½*d*. (plus 1⅛*d*. on account of profits for period from 1 July 1949) per share of 13*s*. 4*d*. £114 8*s*. 11*d*. was paid into Companies' Liquidation Account. Final meeting return regd. 28 June 1951 1952

Richards & Wallington Industries Ld. regd. as private company 12 Aug. 1959 as Richards & Wallington (Plant Hire) Ld.; converted public company 5 Mar. 1965; name changed 3 May 1971. Winding-up order 18 Nov. 1985 1988–9

Richards & Wallington (Plant Hire) Ld. *See* Richards & Wallington Industries Ld.

Richard's Beau Ideal Cycle Co. Ld. Regd. 1896. Vol. liq. Mar. 1909. Removed from Register 1914 1910

Richards (Thomas) (Textiles) Ld. Regd. 1929. Vol. liq. (creditors') 3 June 1932. Assets realised insufficient to pay unsecured creditors in full. Final meeting return regd. 2 Feb. 1934 1933

Richards (W. Alban) & Co. Ld. Regd. 1918. Court Order to wind up 29 Jan. 1924. Liquidator released 20 June 1932. Struck off Register 18 Dec. 1934 1924

Richards (Westley) & Co. Ld. Regd. 1899. Vol. liq. (members') 24 July 1947. Capital returned to contributories—18*s*. 9*d*. per preference share of £1. £202 10*s*. was paid into Companies' Liquidation Account. Final meeting return regd. 29 Nov. 1951 1952

**See Stock Exchange Year-Book.*

VOL. FOR

Richardson, Duck & Co. Ld. Regd. 1919. Assets realised sufficient to pay debenture holders approx. 4s. in £. Struck off Register Oct. 1933 .... **1934**

Richdale (John) & Co. Ld. Regd. 1898. Vol. liq. (members') Feb. 1960. Practically all capital was owned by Hammonds United Breweries Ld. Final meeting return regd. 1 July 1961 .... **1958**

Richelieu & Ontario Navigation Co. Ld. The property, undertaking and assets were acquired by Canada Steamship Lines Ld. **1914**

Richings Park Estate (1928) Ld. Regd. 1928. A receiver, who ceased to act in 1961, made distributions totalling 9s. (per £1) to holders of the £263,970 1st Mortgage Debenture Stock. Balance of money remaining in Court represents unclaimed distributions **1965**

Richmond & Chandler Ld. Regd. 1896. Vol. liq. (members') 6 Aug. 1958. Capital returned to contributories—£7 5s. 11d. per preference share (of £5). Amount paid into Companies' Liquidation Account, £57 16s. 2d. in respect of unclaimed dividends and £316 8s. 6d. in respect of unclaimed distributions. Final meeting return regd. 29 Feb. 1960 .... **1961**

Richmond Cavendish Co. Ld. Regd. 1901. Vol. liq. 21 May 1902. Undertaking and assets were acquired by Imperial Tobacco Co. (of Great Britain and Ireland) Ld., in which company ordinary shareholders were entitled to preferred and deferred ordinary shares, preference shares and debenture stock *plus* cash estimated to exceed a total of £10 in value for each ordinary share of £5 held. Preference shareholders were entitled to preference shares in purchasing company or cash at par. The debentures were repaid at par. Final meeting return regd. 26 Jan. 1922 ... **1903**

Richmond Consolidated Mining Co. Ld. Regd. 1871. Vol. liq. 31 Dec. 1901. Removed from Register 1906 .. **1902**

Richmond (David) & Co. Ld. Regd. Edinburgh 1900. Vol. liq. May 1912. Undertaking and assets were acquired by Scottish Tube Co. Ld., in which company shareholders were entitled to 24 ordinary and 38 preference shares of £1 (credited as fully-paid) *plus* £4 in cash for every 5 ordinary shares of £10 held. Preference shareholders were entitled to repayment at par or 20% of holding in preference shares in new company and 80% in cash. Final meeting return regd. 25 May 1914 .... **1940**

Richmond Gas Co. Inc. by Special Act 1867. The undertaking was acquired by Brentford Gas Co. from 1 Jan. 1924. Holders of consolidated ordinary stock were entitled to £100 6% redeemable debenture stock in acquiring company for each £100 held and holders of 5% debenture stock for each £100 held **1925**

Richmond (Joseph) & Co. Ld. Regd. 1891. Court Order to wind up 1907. Removed from Register 1914 ... **1908**

Richmond (Surrey) Electric Light & Power Co. Ld. Regd. 1892. Dissolved 1 Apr. 1948, undertaking being vested in British (later Central) Electricity Authority and South-Eastern Area Board under Electricity Act 1947. Holders of ordinary shares were entitled to receive £1 9s. British Electricity 3% guaranteed stock (1968—73) in respect of each share (of £1) held **1949**

Rickmansworth Gas Co. Inc. 1852 as Rickmansworth Gas Light & Coke Co. Ld., but reincorporated by Special Act and name changed in 1902. Wound up 8 Dec. 1904, the undertaking having been transferred to Rickmansworth Urban District Council **1906**

Rico Optical Co. Ld. Regd. 1925. Struck off Register Feb. 1931.. **1931**

Riddings Collieries Ld. Regd. 1925 as James Oakes & Co. (Riddings Collieries) Ld.; name changed 4 Jan. 1949 to James Oakes & Co. (Riddings) Ld. and subsequently as above. Vol. liq. (members') 29 Mar. 1956. Final meeting return, regd. 12 Dec. 1964 ... **1955**

Riddings District Gas Co. Inc. by Special Act 1888. Dissolved 1 May 1949, undertaking being vested in East Midland Area Gas Board under Gas Act 1948. Holders of securities were entitled to receive, in respect of each £100 unit held, British Gas 3% guaranteed stock 1990—95 as follows:

	£	s.	d.
Ord. stock (10% stand.)	180	0	0
5% pref. stock	112	10	0
4% cons. perp. deb. stock	102	0	0

1952

Ridgeford Trust Ld. Regd. 1932. Vol. liq. (members') 5 Mar. 1956. Final meeting return regd. 2 Jan. 1959 **1960**

Ridgmont Fletton Brick Co. Ld. Regd. 1935. Vol. liq. (members') 6 Aug. 1936. Undertaking was acquired by Marston Valley Brick Co. Ld. in which company shareholders were entitled to £1 ordinary stock for every 5 shares of 5s. held. Final meeting return regd. 7 Apr. 1937 .... **1937**

Ridgway (Henry) & Sons (Provision Merchants) Ld. Regd. 1901 as Baines & Sons (Croydon) Ld.; name changed June 1925. Vol. liq. (members') 28 Jan. 1931. Capital returned to contributories—£14,512 7s. 3d. Final meeting return regd. 25 Jan. 1934 ... **1931**

Ridler's & Lowestoft Hotels Ld. Regd. 1897. Struck off Register 17 Nov. 1899 .... **1900**

Ridley Cutler & Firth, Ld. Regd. 1898. All capital owned by Vaux & Associated Breweries Ld. Vol. liq. (members') 4 May 1954. Final meeting return regd. 23 Mar. 1955 .... **1940**

Ridley, Whitley & Co. Ld. Regd. 1900. Receiver for debenture stockholders appointed in July 1915. Struck off Register 1924 .... **1916**

Ridsdale's Railway Lamp and Lighting Co. Ld. Regd. 1886. Court Orders: to wind up Mar. 1889; to dissolve Dec. 1890 .... **1890**

Riebeeck Gold Mining Co. Ld. Inc. Union of South Africa 21 Mar. 1956. In Nov. 1958 undertaking acquired by Loraine Gold Mines Ld. and the company dissolved by an Order of the Court **1961**

Rietfontein "A" Ld. Inc. Transvaal 1896. Wound up 30 Mar. 1905, the undertaking being amalgamated with New Rietfontein Estate Gold Mines Ld., in which company shareholders were entitled to 5 shares of £1 for every 6 shares of £1 held **1906**

Rietfontein "B" Ld. Inc. Transvaal 1902. Wound up 1905. The undertaking was amalgamated with New Rietfontein Estate Gold Mines Ld. **1906**

Rietfontein Central Ld. Regd. 1911. Struck off Register 30 Mar. 1951 .... **1951**

Rietfontein Consolidated Mines Ld. Inc. in South Africa 1934. Vol. liq. (members') 30 Nov. 1967. Capital returned to contributors—R0·56½s. (per share of R0·02½) **1971**

Rietfontein Deep Ld. Regd. 1895. Removed from Register 1912...................................... **1912**

Rietfontein (No. 11) Gold Mines Ld. Inc. Union of South Africa 1934. Vol. liq. 10 May 1940. Property and assets were acquired by East Daggafontein Mines Ld., in which company shareholders were entitled to 1 share of 10s. (credited as fully-paid) for every 16·923 shares of 10s. held **1941**

Rietkuil Gold Mine Ld. Inc. Transvaal 1895. Resolutions to wind up passed May 1919 .... **1919**

Rietpoort Petroleum Syndicate Ld. Regd. 1903. Vol. liq. June 1919. Final meeting return regd. 8 May 1920 **1920**

Riga Commercial Bank. *See* Rigas Komercbanka.

Rigas Komercbanka. Inc. Riga 1871. In liquidation in 1936 .... **1936**

Rights & Exploring of Rhodesia Ld. Regd. 1895. Vol. liq. 30 Dec. 1896. Undertaking and assets were acquired in 1897 by Rhodesian Mining & Finance Co. Ld. for 53,533 shares. Final meeting return regd. 10 Mar. 1899 .... **1905**

Rigi Group Gold Mining Co. Ld. Regd. 1897. Struck off Register Nov. 1931 .... **1932**

Riley (Coventry) Ld. Regd. 1896 as Riley Cycle Co. Ld.; name changed Mar. 1912. Receiver appointed 24 Feb. 1938. Vol. liq. (creditors') 30 Sept. 1938. Undertaking acquired by Riley (Coventry) Successors Ld. (later Riley Motors Ld.). No distribution was made to creditors or shareholders. Final meeting return regd. 1 Aug. 1939 .... **1946**

Rim (Malacca) Rubber Estates Ld. Regd. 1910. Vol. liq. (members') 14 Dec. 1966. Amount returned to contributories—6s. 11¾d. per 2s. stock. £1,021 6d. paid into Companies' Liquidation Account in respect of unclaimed dividends and £4,092 14s. 5d. in respect of unclaimed distributions. Final meeting return regd. 26 Aug. 1970 .... **1970**

Rimmel (Eugene) Ld. Regd. 1889. Vol. liq. (creditors') 1 June 1948. Final meeting return regd. 4 Apr. 1955 **1956**

Richings Park Estate (1928) Ld. Regd. 1928. A receiver appointed on behalf of holders of £263,970 1st mortgage debenture stock; released Nov. 1961. Distributions: 9s. (per £1). Struck off Register 4 Dec.1973 .... **1965**

Rincon Silver-Lead Mine Ld. Regd. 1898. Vol. liq. 20 Sept. 1907. Final meeting return regd. 16 July 1914 **1908**

Rinconada Exploration Syndicate Ld. Regd. 1903. Vol. liq. Feb. 1909. Removed from Register 1912 ...... **1909**

Ring Valley Mining Co. Ld. Regd. 1900. Vol. liq. June 1908. Removed from Register 1910 .... **1909**

Ringarooma Tin (Alluvial) Ld. Regd. 1928. Vol. liq. (creditors') 15 Jan. 1931. No capital returned to contributories. Final meeting return regd. 12 Jan. 1932...................................... **1931**

Ringarooma Tin Mine Ld. Regd. Edinburgh 1900. Vol. liq. July 1904. Final meeting return regd. 28 Mar. 1908 .... **1905**

Ringmer & District Electricity Company Limited. Regd. 1931. Dissolved 1 Apr. 1948, undertaking being vested in the British (later Central) Electricity

See Stock Exchange Year-Book.

VOL. FOR

Authority and South-Eastern Area Board under the Electricity Act 1947. Ordinary shareholders were entitled to receve £1 British Electricity 3% guaranteed stock (1968—73), for every £1 ordinary capital held **1949**

Rinkeries (1909) Ld. Regd. 1909. Receiver appointed 9 Jan. 1911. Struck off Register 1916 .... **1914**

Rio Arriba Land & Cattle Co. Ld. Regd. 1887. Struck off Register 26 Oct. 1900 .... **1901**

Rio Bravo Plantations & Timber Co. Ld. Regd. 1912. Vol. liq. 16 Oct. 1916. Final meeting return regd. 1 Nov. 1924 .... ***1917**

Rio Cape Line Ld. Regd. 1917. A subsidiary of Furness, Withy & Co. Ld. Vol. liq. (members') 10 Aug. 1954. Final meeting return regd. 2 July 1960 .... **1953**

Rio Caris Jet Mines Ld. Regd. 1886. Removed from Register 1892 .... **1888**

Rio Claro Sao Paulo Railway Co Ld. Regd 1889. Vol. liq. Jan. 1912. Reconstructed as Rio Claro Railway & Investment Co. Ld. (later Rio Claro Investment Trust Ld.), in which company shareholders were entitled to 27 ordinary shares of £1 (credited as fully-paid) for each share of £10 held. Debenture stockholders were entitled to an equal amount of debenture stock in new company. Removed from Register 1913 .... **1931**

Rio De Janeiro & Northern Railway Co. Ld. Regd. 1887. Undertaking and assets were acquired in 1897 by Leopoldina Railway Co. Ld. Bondholders were entitled to fully-paid shares of £1 in new company as follows:

For every £100 held
6% debentures .... £50 shares
5% 1st mort.debs. .... £50 shares
Removed from Register 1901 .... **1898**

Rio de Janeiro Central Sugar Factories Ld. Regd. 1882. Removed from Register 1906 .... **1887**

Rio de Janeiro City Improvements Co. Ld. *See* Lazard Investment Co. Ld.

Rio de Janeiro Gas Co. Ld. Regd. 1865. Vol. liq. Nov. 1886. Capital returned to contributories—£25 9s. 6d. per share of £20. Final meeting return regd. 21 July 1888 .... **1888**

Rio de Janeiro Suburban Tramways Ld. Regd 1910. Struck off Register 1934 .... **1940**

Rio del Oro Co. Ld. Regd. 1908. Vol. liq. 6 Jan. 1914. Final meeting return regd. 1 Jan. 1915 .... **1914**

Rio del Oro Gold Mines Ld. Regd. 1886. Court Orders: to wind up 7 Dec. 1889; to dissolve 31 Aug. 1898 **1890**

Rio Flour (Holdings) Ld. Regd. 1960. Vol. liq. (members') 17 Feb. 1967. Capital returned to contributories—16s. 4·4735d. per share of £1. Paid into Companies' Liquidation Account £397 8s. 10d. on account of unclaimed dividends and £1,863 9s. 4d. on account of unclaimed distributions. Final meeting return regd. 1 Nov. 1967 .... **1968**

Rio Grande & Dolores Silver Mining Co. Ld. Regd. 1877. Vol. liq. Aug. 1919. Struck off Register 4 Oct. 1938 **1939**

Rio Grande do Sul (Brazil) Gold Mining Co. Ld. Regd. 1879. Struck off Register 1926 .... **1883**

Rio Grande do Sul Steamship Co. Ld. Regd. 1874. Court Orders: to wind up 29 Apr. 1876; to dissolve 1 July 1878 .... ***1876**

Rio Grande Extension Co. *See* Philadelphia Co.

Rio Grande Irrigation & Land Co. Ld. Regd. 1895. Vol. liq. 1901. Struck off Register 11 Feb. 1949 .... **1901**

Rio Grande Rubber Estates Ld. Regd. Edinburgh 1910. Court Orders: to wind up Aug. 1913; to dissolve Oct. 1918 .... **1914**

Rio Grande Western Railway Co. Organised Colorado and Utah 1889. Consolidated with Denver & Rio Grande Railroad Co. The 1st trust mortgage 50-year bonds and 4% 1st consolidated mortgage bonds were included in the funded debt of Denver & Rio Grande Western Railroad Co. **1902**

Rio Malagon (Sulphur-Copper & Silver) Mines Ld. Regd. 1881. Vol. liq. Aug. 1882. Final meeting return regd. 1 Aug. 1883 .... **1883**

Rio Manso Estate Co. Ld. Regd. Edinburgh 1895. Vol. liq. Feb. 1901. Struck off Register 22 Sept. 1936 . **1937**

Rio Negro (Argentina) Land Co. Ld. Regd. 1907. Vol. liq. (members') 31 Dec. 1947. Capital returned to contributories—£1 6s. 8½d. per share (of £1). £567 paid into Companies' Liquidation Account. Final meeting return regd. 11 Nov. 1954 .... **1956**

Rio Rimal Copper Co. Ld. Regd. 1900 as Afortunada Copper Mines Ld. Struck off Register 1911 .... **1926**

Rio Tambo Development Syndicate Ld. Regd. 1905. Vol. liq. Feb. 1908. Undertaking and assets were sold to Rio Tambo Ld., in which company shareholders were entitled to 3 fully-paid ordinary shares of £1 for each ordinary share of £1 held or 60 fully-paid ordinary shares of £1 for each founders' share of 1s. held. Removed from Register 1910 .... **1909**

VOL. FOR

Rio Tambo Ld. Regd 1908. Vol. liq. June 1911. Removed from Register 1913 .... **1912**

Riordon Co. Ld. Inc. in Canada 1920. In liquidation in 1925 .... **1925**

Riordon Pulp & Paper Co. Ld. Inc. Canada 1912 by Letters Patent. The properties and assets were sold to Riordon Co. Ld. in 1920 for $1,500,000 1st preferred stock, $9,000,000 2nd preferred stock and $112,000,000 common stock of that company **1924**

Rip Gold Mining Co. Ld. Regd. 1895. Reconstructed 1902 as New Rip Gold Mining Co. Ld. Shareholders were entitled to 1 share of £1 (credited as fully-paid) for each share of £1 held. Removed from Register 1904 .... **1908**

Ripanji Mining Co. Ld. Regd. 1884. Business was acquired by Ripanji Quicksilver & Silver Mines Ld. in 1887. Vol. liq. Mar. 1889. Final meeting return regd. 25 July 1889 .... **1891**

Ripanji Quicksilver & Silver Mines Ld. Regd. 1887. Vol. liq. 29 July 1891. Final meeting return regd. 19 Nov. 1891 .... **1899**

Ripanji Quicksilver & Silver Mines Co. Ld. Regd. 1891. Vol. liq. 2 July 1895. Reconstructed as company of same name. Shareholders were entitled to 1 share of £1 (credited with 16s. paid) in new company for each share of £1 held. Final meeting return regd. 7 Nov. 1896 .... **1899**

Ripanji Quicksilver & Silver Mines Co. Ld. Regd. 1895. Vol. liq. 4 Jan. 1899. Final meeting return regd. 19 Jan. 1900 .... **1899**

Riparbella Ld. Regd. 1907 as South Italy Copper Mines Ld.; name changed Mar. 1909. Vol. liq. 22 Dec. 1913. Final meeting return regd. 12 Mar. 1914 .... **1914**

Ripley Gas Co. Ld. Regd.1863 as Ripley Water Works & Gas Light & Coke Co. Ld.; name changed 1912. Dissolved 1 May 1949, undertaking being vested in East Midland Area Gas Board under Gas Act 1948. Holders of securities were entitled to receive, in respect of each £5 unit held, British Gas 3% guaranteed stock 1990–95 as follows:

	£	s.	d.
Orig. ord. shares (10% stand.)	14	10	0
Orig. 5% pref. shares	5	14	6
6% pref. shares	6	14	0

.... **1952**

Rippingille (Frank) Stove Co. Ld. Regd. 1896. Removed from Register 1906 .... **1904**

Rippingille's Albion Lamp Co. Ld. *See* Rippingille's (Holdings) Ld.

Rippingilles (Holdings) Ld. Regd. 1897 as Rippingille's Albion Lamp Co. Ld.; name changed July 1937. Undertaking acquired by Rippingilles Ld. for £95,000 in cash, 60,000 fully-paid ordinary shares of 5s. and 25,000 fully-paid preference shares of 10s. Vol. liq. (members') Aug. 1937. Final meeting return regd. 17 Jan. 1939 .... **1938**

Rippingilles Ld. Regd. 15 July 1937. Winding-up order made on 17 Jan. 1972 .... **1983–4**

Ripponden Commercial Co. Ld. Regd. 1856. Vol. liq. (members') Feb. 1961. Pref. shares repaid in full. Capital returned to contributories £18·91 per ordinary share (of £10) £6,384 was paid into Companies' Liquidation Account in respect of unclaimed distribution. Final meeting return regd. 1 Oct. 1975 .... **1976-7**

Risca Investment Co. Ld. Regd. 1881. Vol. liq. 29 Apr. 1892. Final meeting return regd. 7 Sept. 1893 ...... ***1892**

Rishworth, Ingleby & Lofthouse Ld. Regd. 1898. Vol. liq. 31 Jan. 1927. Direct controlling interest held by Spillers Milling & Associated Industries Ld. (later Spillers Ld.). Final meeting return regd. 23 Jan. 1928 .... **1927**

Risk (M.) & Sons Ld. Regd. Edinburgh 1894 as Moses Risk & Sons Ld.; name changed Dec. 1907. Vol. liq. Feb. 1920. Final meeting return regd. 20 Nov. 1924 **1921**

Rist (A.) (1927) Ld. Regd. 1927. Vol. liq. (members') 12 June 1935. Capital returned to contributories—10s. 3¾d. per preferred ordinary share of 10s.; no payment made to deferred shareholders. Final meeting return regd. 13 Jan. 1936 .... **1936**

Ritsons (Burnhope Collieries) Ld. Regd. 1936. Undertaking was acquired by Bearpark Coal & Coke Co. Ld. in 1939. Struck off Register 17 Sept.1946 ...... **1946**

Ritz Hotels (Egypt) Ld. Regd. 1906. Vol. liq. 28 Mar. 1921. Final meeting return regd. 16 July 1923 ..... **1922**

River Diamonds Syndicate Ld. Regd. 1906. Vol. liq. July 1909. Undertaking and assets were acquired by New Vaal River Diamond & Exploration Co. Ld. [now New Vaal Farms Ld., in which company shareholders were entitled to 1 share of £1 (credited as fully-paid) for every 2 shares of £1 held. Removed from Register 1910 .... **1910**

River Gambia Trading Co. Ld. Regd. 1881. Court Orders: to wind up June 1885; to dissolve Aug. 1888 **1886**

River Plate, British & Continental Meat Co. Ld. Regd. 1925. Struck off Register 11 Aug. 1961. .... **1950**

See Stock Exchange Year-Book.

VOL. FOR

River Plate Electric Light & Traction Co. Ld. Regd. 1896. Undertaking and certain assets were acquired by River Plate Electricity Co. Ld. Debenture stockholders received £100,000 debenture stock and 50,000 preference shares in purchasing company. Holders of 2nd debentures were entitled to 50,000 preference shares. Holders of share and debenture capital were entitled to subscribe for debenture stock in purchasing company and to receive a bonus of 75 ordinary shares for every £100 stock subscribed for. The remaining assets were sold to Rosario Electric Co. Ld. for £22,000 in ordinary shares. Removed from Register 1905 1903

River Plate Electricity & Other Securities Corpn. Ld. *See* Plate Investment Trust Ld.

River Plate Electricity Co. Ld. Business was acquired in 1896 by River Plate Electric Lint & Traction Co. Ld. for £139,960 in ordinary shares and £25,000 in cash 1902

River Plate Electricity Co. Ld. Regd. 1902. Vol. liq. (members') 15 Apr. 1937. Undertaking was acquired by River Plate Electricity & Other Securities Corporation Ld. (later Plate Investment Trust Ld.) in which company shareholders were entitled to 1 6% preference share of £1 for each £1 preference stock held or 3 4¼% preferred ordinary shares of 10s. and 3 ordinary shares of 10s. for every £2 ordinary stock. £44 5s. 6d. was paid into Companies' Liquidation Account for unclaimed dividends. Final meeting return regd. 10 Jan. 1938.............. 1938

River Plate Fresh Meat Co. Ld. Regd. 1882. Vol. liq. 11 Oct. 1889. Reconstructed as company of same name. Shareholders received equivalent interest in new company. Final meeting return regd. 4 Jan. 1904 1903

River Plate Fresh Meat Co. Ld. Regd. 1889 as River Plate Fresh Meat New Co. Ld.; name changed Dec. 1889. Vol. liq. 6 May 1914. Shareholders were entitled to 105 6% preference and 20 ordinary shares of £1 in James Nelson & Sons Ld. (later British & Argentine Meat Co. Ld., for every 100 preference shares of £1 held or 48 6% preference and 100 ordinary shares of £1 in that company for every 100 ordinary shares of £1 held. Final meeting return regd. 4 Oct. 1915 1915

River Plate Gas Co. Ld. Regd. 1897. Vol. liq. Dec. 1909. Undertaking and assets were acquired by Primitiva Gas & Electric Lighting Co. of Buenos Aires Ld. later Primitiva Gas Co. of Buenos Aires Ld. Shareholders were entitled to 1 ordinary and 2 preference shares of £5 for each share of £10 held. The purchasing company assumed liability for debenture stock. Removed from Register 1910 1910

River Plate Land and Farming Co. Ld. Regd. 1863. Vol. liq. 17 Aug. 1928. Capital returned to contributories—£8 per share of £5 at Jan. 1929; further payments (expected at approximately £2 10s. per share) not known. Final meeting return regd. 28 Oct. 1929 1929

River Plate Pressure Meat Preserving Co. Ld. Regd. 1871. Court Orders: to wind up 4 Feb. 1878; to dissolve 11 Aug. 1886 .... *1878

River Plate Telegraph Co. Ld. Regd. Edinburgh. Vol. liq. (members') 25 Feb. 1936. All shares owned by Western Telegraph Co. Ld. Final meeting return regd. 30 Nov. 1936 1937

River Plate Telephone & Electric Light Co. Ld. Regd. 1882. Vol. liq. Dec. 1886. Reconstructed as United River Plate Telephone Co. Ld. for £20,000 7% debentures £40,000 in fully-paid shares of £5 and £85,000 in cash. Final meeting return regd. 5 Sept. 1889 1890

River Plate Water & Drainage Trust. Trust Certificates were issued in 1887. The trust has been dissolved and the assets divided among certificate holders .. 1890

River Thames Steamboat Co. Ld. Regd. 1884. Removed from Register 1906 1888

River Tyne Dry Docks, Engineering and Boilermaking Co. Ld. *See* Tyne Pontoons & Dry Docks Co. Ld.

Riverside Cold Storage & Ice Co. Ld. Regd. 1898. Receiver appointed 1 Feb. 1907; ceased to act 15 June 1909. Vol. liq. 31 Dec. 1907. Final meeting return regd. 2 Sept. 1909 .... *1909

Riverside Gold Mines Ld. Regd. 1896. Removed from Register 1903 1903

Riverside Orange Co. Ld. Regd. 1890. Vol. liq. 1 July 1913. Shareholders were entitled to 12½ shares of £1 (credited with 16s. paid) in Riverside Trust & Orange Co. Ld. (later Riverside Orange Co. Ld.) for every share of £10 held; debenture stockholders were entitled to an equal amount of debenture stock in new company. Final meeting return regd. 30 Nov. 1915 1914

Riverside Orange Co. Ld. Regd. 1913 as Riverside Trust & Orange Co. Ld.; name changed Dec. 1913. Vol.

VOL. FOR

liq. 6 Nov. 1928. Capital returned to contributories—5s. per share of £1 at Nov. 1928; further payments (if any) not known. Final meeting return regd. 8 Apr. 1931 1929

Riverside (Selangor) Rubber Co. Ld. Regd. Edinburgh 1909. Vol. liq. Mar. 1920. Struck off Register 4 June 1937 1938

Riverside (Selangor) Rubber Co. Ld. Regd. Edinburgh 1920. Vol. liq. (members') July 1935. Undertaking and assets were acquired by Scottish Malayan Estates Ld., in which company shareholders were entitled to 3 shares of £1 (credited as fully-paid) for every 8 shares of £1 held. Struck off Register 4 June 1937 1936

Riverside Trust and Orange Co. Ld. *See* Riverside Orange Co. Ld.

Riverside Trust Co. Ld. Regd. 1899. Vol. liq. 1 July 1913. Shareholders were entitled to 62½ shares of £1 (credited with 16s. paid) in Riverside Trust & Orange Co. Ld. (later Riverside Orange Co. Ld.) for each A share of £50 held or 25 shares of £1 (credited with 16s. paid) in that company for each B share of £1 held. Debenture stockholders were entitled to an equal amount of debenture stock in new company. Final meeting return regd. 30 Nov. 1915 1914

Rixon's Iron & Brick Co. Ld. Regd. 1883. Vol. liq. 30 June 1887. Removed from Register 1906 1888

Rizine Food Co. Ld. Regd. 1889. Removed from Register 1906 1895

Road Block Gold Mines of India Ld. Regd. 1903. Vol. liq. Dec.1907. Removed from Register 1911 1908

Road Block Gold Mining Co. Ld. Regd. 1896. Vol. liq. 23 Aug. 1900. Reconstructed as Road Block Gold Mining Co. of India Ld., in which company shareholders were entitled to 1 share of £1 (credited with 13s. 4d. paid) for each share of £1 held. Final meeting return regd. 23 Oct. 1901 1903

Road Block Gold Mining Co. of India Ld. Regd. 1900. Reconstructed 1903 as Road Block Gold Mines of India Ld., in which company shareholders were entitled to 1 share of £1 (credited with 16s. 6d. paid) for each share of £1 held. Removed from Register 1904 1907

Roadrails Ld. Regd. 1921. Vol. liq. 16 Aug. 1927. Final meeting return regd. 14 Nov. 1929................... 1928

Roads Reconstruction Ld. Regd. 1910 as Teign Valley Granite Co. Ld.; name changed Jan. 1924. Vol. liq. (members') 5 Feb. 1934. Undertaking and assets were aquired by Roads Reconstruction (1934) Ld. (later Roads Reconstruction Ld.) (Regd. 1960), in which company shareholders were entitled to 5 preference shares of £1 (credited as fully-paid) for every 4 preference shares of £1 held or 1 fully-paid ordinary share of 10s. for every 2 ordinary shares of 8s. held. Final meeting return regd. 29 Aug. 1936 1935

Roadway Time Tables, Bookings & Publications Ld. Regd. 1929 as Roadway Time Tables Ld.; name changed Sept. 1929. Vol. liq. Sept. 1931. Struck off Register 4 Oct. 1938 1939

Roadway Time Tables Ld. *See* Roadway Time Tables, Bookings & Publications Ld.

Roadways (Preliminary) Ld. Regd. 1928. Undertaking and assets were acquired by Roadway Time Tables, Bookings & Publications Ld. Struck off Register 1933 1930

Roadways Transport Development Ld. Regd. 1922. Vol.liq. (members') 30 June 1948 for the purpose of amalgamating undertaking with Olds Discount Co. Ld., which owned all ordinary and preference shares. Ordinary shareholders received 21s. 7·813d. per share of £1. Final meeting return regd. 1 Mar. 1956 1957

Roan Antelope Copper Mines Ld. Regd. 1927. Registration transferred to Northern Rhodesia (now Zambia) 1 July 1954, control of company having been transferred 1 July 1953. Vol. liq. (members') 14 Feb. 1962. Undertaking, property and assets transferred to Rhodesian Selection Tr. Ld. (now Roan Selection Tr. Ld.) for 8,088,920 fully-paid shares (of £1) of that company. Shareholders received 1 share for every 8 shares (of 5s.) held. Final meeting held 21 Sept. 1976. Struck off Register 15 Feb. 1977 1977–8

Roartey's Luck Mining & Developing Syndicate Ld. Regd. 1888. Vol. liq. 3 June 1897. Reconstructed as company of same name. Shareholders were entitled to 1 share of 2s. (credited with 3d. paid) for each share of £1 held. Struck off Register 24 May 1910 1898

Roartey's Luck Mining & Development Syndicate Ld. Regd. 1897. Vol. liq. 6 June 1906. Struck off Register 21 June 1912 1925

Robarts G. Tarran & Son Ld. *See* Dorran Construction Ld.

Robert's Lubbock & Co. Amalgamated with Coutts & Co. in 1914 1915

VOL. FOR

Roberts Brewery Ld. Regd. 1935. Vol. liq. (members') 24 Oct. 1941. Undertaking and assets acquired by David Roberts & Sons Ld., in which company shareholders were entitled to 1 fully-paid 5½% preference share of £1 for each preference share of £1 held and 1 fully-paid ordinary share of 2*s.* 6*d.* for each ordinary share of 5*s.* held. £22 12*s.* was paid into Companies' Liquidation Account in respect of unclaimed dividends. Final meeting return regd. 28 Dec. 1943 .... **1942**

Roberts Brothers Ld. Regd. 1905. Court Order to wind up 1907. Removed from Register 1911 .... **1908**

Roberts (Charles) & Co. Ld. Regd. 1899. Vol. liq. 24 Sept. 1927 for reconstruction as Charles Roberts & Co. (1927) Ld. (later Charles Roberts & Co. Ld.). Shareholders were entitled to (*a*) £3 4*s.* 7·721*d.* in fully-paid shares in new company *plus* £5 11*s.* 4·1544*d.* in cash for every 5 fully-paid shares of £1 held, (*b*) £3 4*s.* 7·721*d.* in fully-paid shares in new company *plus* £2 11*s.* 4·1544*d.* in cash for each share of £5 (£2 paid), and (*c*) £3 4*s.* 7·721*d.* in fully-paid shares of new company *plus* £1 11*s.* 4·1544*d.* in cash for each share of £5, (£1 paid). Final meeting return regd. 16 June 1928 .... **1928**

Roberts (Ebenezer) & Sons Ld. Regd. 1897. Reconstructed as Ebenezer Roberts Ld., in which company shareholders were entitled to 1 ordinary share of £1 (credited with 14*s.* paid) for each ordinary share of £1 held or 1 preference share of £1 (credited with 14*s.* paid) for each preference share of £1 held. Removed from Register 1906 .... **1908**

Roberts (Ebenezer) Ld. Regd. 1899. Vol. liq. May 1908. Removed from Register 1912 .... **1909**

Roberts (Robt.) & Co. Ld. Regd. 1888. Vol. liq. Sept. 1916. Struck off Register July 1929 .... **1930**

Roberts (William) Ld. Properties were acquired in 1925 by Eley's Stafford Brewery Ld., for £112,500 in cash and £30,000 in fully-paid A shares of £10 .... **1927**

Roberts (William) (Tipton) Ld. Regd.1899. Vol. liq. (members') 15 Oct 1937. Capital returned to contributories—£5 per preference share of £5; £1 2*s.* 8*d.* per ordinary share of £1. Final meeting return regd. 13 Aug. 1938 .... **1938**

Robertsbridge & Pevensey Light Railway Co. Inc. (under the Light Railways Act 1896) in 1900 .... **1910**

Robertsbridge & Salehurst Water Co. Ld. *See below.*

Robertsbridge, Salehurst & Hurst Green Water & Gas Co. Ld. Regd.1905 as Robertsbridge & Salehurst Water Co. Ld.; name changed July 1905. Receiver appointed on behalf of debenture holders 4 Oct. 1909. Removed from Register 24 Mar. 1914 .... ***1910**

Robertson Automatic Variable Speed Gear Co. Ld. Regd. 1928. Court Order to wind up June 1933. Struck off Register 16 Aug. 1938 .... **1939**

Robertson Electric Lamps Ld. Regd. 1893. Vol. liq. Mar. 1919. Struck off Register 2 Apr. 1943 .... **1945**

Robertson Engineering Co. Ld. Regd. 1939. Vol. liq. (creditors') 18 Mar. 1946 .... **1943**

Robertson, Sanderson & Co. Ld. Regd. Edinburgh 1895. Vol. liq. Dec. 1915. Court Orders: to continue winding up under supervision June 1916; to dissolve 7 Nov. 1923 .... **1916**

Robertson (Thomas) & Co. Ld. Inc. Quebec 1897. Glasgow office discontinued July 1915 .... **1916**

Robertson's Film Service Ld. Producing and distributing organisation was acquired in 1928 by British & Foreign Films Ld. **1929**

Robey and Co. Ld. Regd. 1893. Vol. liq. (members') 31 July 1969. Capital returned to contributories—6½*p.* per share of 5*p.* £496·99 was paid into Companies' Liquidation Account in respect of unclaimed dividends and £10,791·46 in respect of unclaimed distributions. Final meeting return regd. 29 Mar. 1972 .... **1972**

Robin & Houston Ld. Regd. 1896. Vol. liq. (members') 20 Dec. 1950. Final meeting return regd. 17 Aug. 1951 .... **1909**

Robins (E.) and Son Ld. Regd. 1894. Vol. liq. (members') 29 Jan. 1945. All shares were held by Findlater, Mackie & Co. Ld. (later Findlater Prentis & Co. Ld.). Final meeting return regd. 1 Jan. 1946. **1946**

Robinson & Co. (Hull) Ld. *See* Cadora Ld.

Robinson & Price Ld. Regd. 1896. Vol. liq. 28 Dec. 1904. Final meeting return regd. 31 Mar. 1908 .... **1905**

Robinson Brothers (Carlisle) Ld. Regd. 1911. Vol. liq. (members') 22 Jan. 1934. Holders of 1,070 preference shares were repaid at par: holders of the remaining preference shares were entitled to an equal number of 7½% preference shares of £1 in H. Binns Son & Co. Ld. (later Binns Ld.); holders of ordinary shares were entitled to £1 3*s.* per ordinary share of £1 held. Final meeting return regd. 29 Mar. 1934 .... **1934**

VOL. FOR

Robinson Central Deep Ld. Inc. Transvaal 1898. Properties were sold to Crown Mines Ld., in which company shareholders were entitled to 7 shares of 10*s.* (credited as fully-paid) for every 10 shares of £1 held **1910**

Robinson Deep Gold Mining Co. Ld. Inc. Transvaal 1899. Vol. liq. Dec. 1915. Assets were acquired by Robinson Deep Ld. for 500,000 A shares of 1*s.* ... **1917**

Robinson Deep Ld. Inc. South Africa 1894. Reconstructed in 1899 as Robinson Deep Gold Mining Co. Ld., in which company shareholders were entitled to 2 shares of £1 for each share of £1 held **1899**

Robinson Diamond Mining Co. Ld. *See* Orange Free State & Transvaal Diamond Mines Ld.

Robinson, Fleming & Co. Ld. Regd. 1935. Vol. liq. (members') 22 Jan. 1959. Final meeting return regd. 26 Apr. 1960 .... **1961**

Robinson Gold Mines Ld. Regd. 1900. Vol. liq. 16 Jan. 1902. A receiver was appointed on behalf of debenture holders. Final meeting return regd. 31 Aug. 1903 .... **1903**

Robinson Gold Mining Co. Ld. Inc. Transvaal 1887. Resolution to wind up passed May 1926. Capital returned to contributories—16*s.* per share of £5. Company dissolved 16 Feb. 1932 .... **1927**

Robinson (J. A.) & Sons Ld. Undertaking and assets were acquired by Cauldon Potteries Ld. **1924**

Robinson (Joseph) & Co. Ld. Regd. 1888. Vol. liq. 20 Apr. 1912. Reconstructed as Carlisle Plaster & Cement Co. Ld. Final meeting return regd. 3 Aug. 1915 .... **1913**

Robinson (Peter) Ld. Regd. 1896. Vol. liq. (members') 18 Mar. 1949. The assets (less cash and Government bonds) were transferred to Peter Robinson Ld. (regd. 1949). 4% 1st mortgage debenture stock was repaid at 102% in Mar. 1949 and preference and preferred ordinary stocks were repaid at 21*s.* per £1 stock and par respectively. Final meeting return regd. 24 Mar. 1959 .... **1961**

Robinson Printing Co. Ld. Regd. 1898. Receiver was appointed 24 July 1908. Removed from Register 1913 .... **1909**

Robinson Randfontein Gold Mining Co. Ld. *See* Randfontein South Gold Mining Co. Ld.

Robinson River Co. Ld. Regd. 1917. Vol. liq. (members') 16 Mar. 1936. Capital returned to contributories—12*s.* 5·058*d.* per share of £1. Final meeting return regd. 30 Sept. 1936 .... **1937**

Robinson South African Banking Co. Ld. Regd. 1902 as Robinson South African Banking Co. (1902) Ld.; name changed Jan. 1903. Vol. liq. 8 Feb. 1905. Capital returned to contributories—20*s.* per share of £1; further payments (if any) not known. Removed from Register 1905 .... **1906**

Robinson's Brewery Ld. Regd. 1896. Vol. liq. 24 Apr. 1929. Undertaking and assets were acquired by Ind Coope & Co. Ld. (later Ind Coope Ld.), which company held all ordinary shares. Preference shareholders were entitled to either £10 in cash or 10 fully-paid preference shares of £1 for each preference share of £10 held. The debenture stockholders were entitled to an equal amount of consolidated mortgage debenture stock in acquiring company. Final meeting return regd. 24 Sept. 1929 .... **1930**

Robinson's Motors Ld. Regd. 1914. Vol. liq. (members') 24 Feb. 1933. Capital returned to contributories—£14,169 14*s.* 10*d.* Final meeting return regd. 21 June 1933 .... **1934**

Robinson (Thomas) Sons & Co. Ld. Regd. 1922. All capital acquired by Oriel Foods Ld. Vol. liq. 28 Dec. 1979. Company dissolved 15 July 1980 .... **1975–6**

Robson & Sons Ld. Regd. 1885. Vol. liq. 26 Oct. 1893. Amalgamated with Wyman & Sons Ld. (later Wyman & Marshall Ld.). Final meeting return regd. 4 Apr. 1894 .... **1894**

Roburite Explosives Co. Ld. Regd. 1887. Vol. liq. 30 June 1891. Reconstructed as company of same name. Shareholders were entitled to an equal number of shares of £5 in new company. Final meeting return regd. 8 Mar. 1899 .... **1908**

Rochdale & Oldham Brewery Co. Ld. Regd. 1887. Vol. liq. 12 Aug. 1895. Reconstructed as Rochdale & Manor Brewery Ld. Final meeting return regd. 6 Dec. 1895.......... **1896**

Rochdale Joint Stock Bank Ld. Regd. 1872. Vol. liq. June 1882. Taken over by Oldham Joint Stock Bank Ld. Final meeting return regd. 24 Jan. 1884 .... **1883**

Rochdale Rhea Fibre Spinning Co. Ld. Regd. 1896. Vol. liq. 14 Sept. 1901. Final meeting return regd. 17 June 1904 .... ***1901**

Roehes Stores, Dublin Ld. Regd. Dublin 1878 as Hazleton, Connor & Co. Ld.; name changed to Henry Street Warehouse Co. Ld. in 1882 and as

**See Stock Exchange Year-Book.*

VOL. FOR

above in Aug. 1929. Vol. liq. Jan. 1934. Assets sold to Roches Stores Ld. for £61,875 1934

Rochester, Chatham & Gillingham Gas Co. Inc. by Special Act 1825 as Rochester, Chatham & Strood Gaslight Co.; name changed 1906. Dissolved 1 May 1949, undertaking being vested in South Eastern Area Gas Board under Gas Act 1948. Holders of securities were entitled to receive, in respect of each £100 unit held, British Gas 3% guaranteed stock 1990—95 as follows:

	£	s.	d.
Cons. ord. stock (5% stand.)	155	0	0
5½% irred. pref. stock	130	0	0
5% red. deb. stock	108	0	0
4% irred. deb. stock	103	0	0

1952

Rock Brewery, Brighton, Ld. Regd. 1901. Vol. liq. (members') 30 June 1960. Directly controlled by Portsmouth & Brighton United Breweries Ld. Preference stock repaid at par 30 June 1960. Final meeting return regd. 2 Dec. 1960 1962

Rock Brewery Co. Ld. Regd. 1897. Vol. liq. 14 May 1910. Final meeting return regd. 14 Oct. 1915 1911

Rock Island Company. Organised in New Jersey 1902. Court Order to wind up Apr. 1916 1917

Rock Life Assurance Co. Established under Deed of Settlement 1806. Business was transferred to Law Union & Crown Insurance Co. (later Law Union & Rock Insurance Co. Ld.), in which company shareholders were entitled to 3 shares of £1 (credited as fully-paid) for every 4 shares of £5 (10*s.* paid) held. The share annuity was repaid at 1*s.* 4*d.* or 8*d.* per share instead of 1*s.* or 6*d.* per share 1910

Rocket & Schneider Ld. Regd. 1905. Vol. liq. 21 Dec. 1907. Final meeting return regd. 17 Aug. 1909 .... *1909

Rockwell Silver Mines Ld. Regd. 1888. Vol. liq. 24 Aug. 1893. Final meeting return regd. 22 June 1898 1895

Rocky Bar Wide West Gold Ld. Regd. 1888. Vol. liq. June 1889. Reconstructed as company of same name. Shareholders were entitled to 1 share of £1 (credited with 18*s.* paid) for each share of £1 held. Final meeting return regd. 15 Apr. 1890 1890

Rocky Bar Wide West Gold Ld. Regd. 1889. Vol. liq. Feb. 1890. Final meeting return regd. 22 Aug. 1890 1890

Rocky Mountain Milling Co. Ld. Regd. 1895. Removed from Register 1906 1901

Rocky Point Gold Mines Ld. Regd. 1906. Reconstructed 1907 as Lake Kerford Gold Mines Ld. in which company shareholders were entitled to 1 share of 1*s.* (credited with 10*d.* paid) for each share of 1*s.* held. Removed from Register 1908 1908

Rodez Coal Co. Ld. Regd. 1911. Struck off Register 1919 1915

Rodmell Works Ld. Regd. 1931 as Cement Industries Ld.; name changed to Alpha Cement Co. Ld. in Sept. 1933 and as above in June 1934. Vol. liq. (members') 31 Oct. 1935. All shares were owned by Alpha Cement Ld. Final meeting return regd. 16 Oct. 1936 1936

Rodocanachi, Sons & Co. Established 1830. Receiving order made on 23 Nov. 1929 on debtors' petition 1930

Roebourne Copper Mines Ld. Regd. 1913. Vol. liq. 6 Jan. 1922 for reconstruction as United Copper Mines (Pilbarra) Ld. in which company shareholders were entitled to 2 shares of 5*s.* (credited with 3*s.* 9*d.* paid) for each share of £1 held. Final meeting return regd. 5 July 1924 1922

Roebourne Finance & Investment Co. Ld. Regd. 1911. Vol. liq. (members') 23 May 1932. Shareholders were entitled to subscribe for shares at par in Peradin Rubber & Finance Ld. (later Peradin Ld.). Final meeting return regd. 29 May 1933 1933

Rogers' Golden Gate Ld. Regd. 1901. Vol. liq. Apr. 1906. Removed from Register 1906 1907

Rogers' (J. B.) Electric Light & Power Co. Ld. Regd. 1882. Court Orders: to wind up June 1884; to dissolve Mar. 1887 1885

Rogers (W. J.) Ld. Regd. 1894. All share capital was owned by H. & G. Simonds Ld., which company acquired the undertaking. Holders of 4% A and B mortgage debentures were offered £106 19*s.* in 3½% debenture stock in acquiring company for every £100 debentures held or repayment at par. Vol. liq. (members') 1 Oct. 1938. Final meeting return regd. 20 June 1939 1939

Rohilkund & Kumson Railway Co. Ld. Regd. 1882. Vol. liq. (members') 31 Dec. 1942. Capital returned to contributories—preference stock 100%; £399 17*s.* 3*d.* per £100 ordinary stock held. Final meeting return regd. 25 Jan. 1946 1946

Rohren Ld. Regd. 1890 as Elmore's Austro-Hungarian Patent Copper Depositing Co. Ld.; name changed to Elmore's German & Austro-Hungarian Metal Co. Ld. Mar. 1891; to Elmore's Metal Co. Ld. Oct. 1919; and to present title Oct. 1962. Vol. liq. (members') 22 Oct. 1962. 6½% convertible unsecured loan stock was repaid at par Nov. 1962. Capital returned to contributories—£1 11*s.* ½*d.* per ordinary share of 10*s.* £38,179 16*s.* 1*d.* was paid into Companies' Liquidation Account. Final meeting return regd. 9 Apr. 1964 1965
To contributories—£1 11*s.* ½*d.* per ordinary share of 10*s.* £38,179 16*s.* 1*d:* was paid into Companies' Liquidation Account. Final meeting return regd. 9 Apr. 1964 1965

Rolez (Jules) Ld. Regd. 1895. Vol. liq. July 1908. Removed from Register 1912 1909

Rolinson (John) & Son Ld. Regd. 1899. Vol. liq. 5 Mar. 1925. Undertaking was acquired by Wolverhampton & Dudley Breweries Ld. Final meeting return regd. 2 Dec. 1925 1926

Rolled Steel Axle Box & Forge Co. Ld. Regd. Edinburgh 1902. Vol. liq. Mar. 1904. Final meeting return regd. 1 June 1909 1905

Roller-Bearings Co. Ld. Regd. 1896. Vol. liq. 30 Aug. 1900. Final meeting return regd. 5 May 1902 1901

Rolleston Water Co. Ld. Regd. 1925. Undertaking was acquired in 1932 by South Staffordshire Waterworks Co. Vol. liq. (members') 18 Jan. 1933. Capital returned to contributories—4*s.* 10·8*d.* per share of 1*s.* Final meeting return regd. 25 Oct. 1933 1934

Rolling Stock Corporation Ld. Regd. 1904. Vol. liq. 20 Jan. 1915. Final meeting return regd. 10 Mar. 1915 *1916

Rollo (David) & Sons Ld. Regd. 1920. Vol. liq. (members') 5 Feb. 1932. All shares owned by Grayson, Rollo & Clover Docks Ld. Final meeting return regd. 5 Oct. 1932 1932

Rolls (J.) & Sons Ld. Regd. 1886. Vol. liq. 7 Nov. 1890. Court Order to continue winding up under supervision Dec. 1890. Final meeting return regd. 31 Dec. 1901 1891

Rolls Razor Ld. Regd. 1927 as Rolls Razor (1927) Ld.; name changed May 1929. Vol. liq. (creditors') 27 Aug. 1964. Final meeting return regd. 18 Nov. 1981 1981–2

Rolls Razor Ld. Undertaking and assets were acquired by Rolls Razor (1927) Ld. (later Rolls Razor Ld.) 1928

Rolls Razor Ld. *See* Rolls Razor Ld.

Rolls-Royce Ld. *See* R. R. Realisations Ld.

Rom Tyre & Rubber Co. Ld. Regd. 1909. Struck off Register 1928 1928

Roman Gravels Boundary Mining Co. Ld. Regd. 1881. Vol. liq. 21 May 1883. Court Order to continue winding up under supervision 12 Sept. 1883. Final meeting return regd. 23 Mar. 1889 .... *1884

Roman Gravels Co. Ld. Regd. 1891. Vol. liq. 26 Oct. 1892. Final meeting return regd. 31 Aug. 1894 1893

Romana Petroleum Co. Ld. Regd. 1910 as Anglo-Galician Naphtha Syndicate Ld.; name changed Mar. 1913. Struck off Register 28 Feb. 1939 1940

Romanera Copper Co. Ld. Regd. 1908. Vol. liq. 7 Nov. 1913. Final meeting return regd. 15 Jan. 1914 ...... *1914

Romano Carpathian Oil Co. Ld. Regd. 1912. Vol. liq. 1913. Struck off Register 1914 1914

Romano's Ld. Regd. 1902. Winding-up order 16 June 1941. Capital returned to contributories—4*s.* 6*d.* per share (of £1). Liquidator released on 10 Nov. 1953. Struck off Register 15 May 1956 1954

Rome Consolidated Gold Mines Ld. 1896. Vol. liq. 28 July 1898. Reconstructed as Boulder Junction Mines Ld., in which company shareholders were entitled to 2 shares of £1 (credited with 17*s.* paid) for each share of £1 held. Final meeting return regd. 22 June 1900 1900

Rome International Amusement & Construction Co. Ld. Regd. 1910. Vol. liq. June 1911. Court Order to continue winding up under supervision Feb. 1912. Removed from Register 1914 1912

Romford Gas Co. Estd. by Deed of Settlement 1847 as Romford Gas & Coke Co. Regd. 1856 as unlimited and as limited in 1874; inc. by Special Act 1929 as above. Dissolved 1 May 1949, undertaking being vested in North Thames Area Gas Board under Gas Act 1948. Holders of securities were entitled to receive, in respect of each £100 unit held, British Gas 3% guaranteed stock 1990—95 as follows:

	£	s.	d.
Ord. stock (5% basic)	121	0	0
5½% pref. stock	126	0	0
4% red. pref. stock (1958)	100	0	0
4% red. pref. stock (1963)	100	0	0
3¾% red. pref stock	98	0	0
5% irred. deb. stock	125	0	0
4% irred. deb. stock	102	10	0
2% red. deb. stock	97	5	0
5% debs. (1950)	103	10	0
5% debs. (1951)	104	0	0

A distribution on ord. stock of 33·77703% out of reserves was made in Nov. 1953 1952

Romsey Gas & Coke Co. Ld. Regd. 1878. Dissolved 1 May 1949, undertaking being vested in Southern

**See Stock Exchange Year-Book.*

Area Gas Board under Gas Act 1948. Holders of ordinary shares (both denominations) were entitled to receive, in respect of each £5 unit held, £12 British Gas 3% guaranteed stock 1990–95 .... **1952**

Ronacher Ld. Regd. 1889. Struck off Register 1925 ... **1917**

Ronaldson (Thomas) & Co. Ld. Regd. 1899. Removed from Register 24 Mar. 1914 .... ***1908**

Roodeklip Gold Mining Co. Ld. Inc. Transvaal 1902. Voluntary liquidation (creditors') 1937 .... **1938**

Roodeplaats (De Beer) Diamond Mines Ld. Regd. 1913. Struck off Register 1928 .... ***1915**

Roodepoort Central Deep Ld. Inc. Transvaal 1895. Wound up 1911. Undertaking and assets were sold to Princess Estates & Gold Mining Co. Ld. for 108,333 shares of £1 and the payment of the debentures and other liabilities. Shareholders were entitled to 1 share of £1 for every 3 shares of £1 held **1911**

Roodepoort Deep Level Gold Mining Co. Ld. Regd. 1892. Vol. liq. 6 Dec. 1897 for reconstruction as Roodepoort Deep Ld. Final meeting return regd. 13 Aug. 1898 .... **1898**

Roodepoort Deep Ld. Inc. South African Republic 1898. In liquidation, the property was sold to Roodepoort United Main Reef Gold Mining Co. Ld., in which company shareholders were entitled to 2 shares of £1 for every 3 shares held **1899**

Roodepoort Gold Mining Co. Ld. Inc. Cape Colony and South African Republic 1887. Reconstructed as company of same name 1893 .... **1909**

Roodepoort Gold Mining Co. Ld. Inc. Transvaal 1893. Vol. liq. 1909. Undertaking and assets were sold to Roodepoort United Main Reef Gold Mining Co. Ld., in which company shareholders were entitled to 1 share of £1 for every 5 shares of £1 held **1909**

Roodepoort United Main Reef Gold Mining Co. Ld. Assets were acquired in Sept. 1933 by New Steyn Estate Gold Mines Ld. for £200,000 cash, which was insufficient to meet claims of creditors **1934**

Rooderand Gold Mining Co. Ld. Inc. Transvaal 1895. Vol. liq. Aug. 1913. A dividend of 1s. per share of £1 was paid in Dec. 1913. Further payments (if any) not known **1914**

Rooderand Main Reef Gold Mining Co. Ld. Regd. 1896. Struck off Register 29 Nov. 1907 .... **1908**

Rookhope Lead Mining Co. Ld. Regd. 1876. Vol. liq. 17 July 1879. Final meeting return regd. 3 June 1881 ***1879**

Roots Oil Motor & Motor Car Ld. Regd. 1897. Vol. liq. 1907. Removed from Register 1911 .... **1908**

Roper River Land and Minerals Co. Ld. Regd. 1906. Vol. liq. (creditors') 10 June 1930. Assets were not realisable. Final meeting return regd. 3 Nov. 1931 **1931**

Ropner & Sons Ld. Regd. 1907. Vol. liq. 3 Sept. 1919. Undertaking acquired by Ropner Shipbuilding & Repairing Co. (Stockton) Ld. Final meeting return regd. 11 Aug. 1920 .... ***1920**

Ropner Shipbuilding & Repairing Co. (Stockton) Ld. Regd. 1919. Vol. liq. 7 Dec. 1922. Reconstructed as company of same name. Shareholders were entitled to 2 fully-paid preferred shares of 5s. in new company plus 10s. in cash for each preference share of £1 held or 1 fully-paid deferred share of 5s. plus 5% in cash for each ordinary share of 5s. held. Final meeting return regd. 8 Dec. 1923 .... **1923**

Ropner Shipbuilding & Repairing Co. (Stockton) Ld. Regd. 1922. Vol. liq. 7 June 1928. Capital returned to contributories—2s. per share of 5s.; further payments (if any) not known. Final meeting return regd. 21 Nov. 1928 .... **1929**

Ropp Tin Ld. Regd. 1911. Vol. liq. Aug. 1929. Amalgamated with London Tin Corporation Ld., in which company shareholders were entitled to 1 fully-paid share of 10s. for every 6 shares of 4s. held. Struck off Register Mar. 1933 .... **1934**

Rorke's Roodepoort Ld. Regd. 1895. Shareholders' subscriptions were returned. Removed from Register 1898 .... **1896**

Rosar (E.) & Co. Ld. Regd. 1936 as L. Simonson & Co. Ld., name changed 2 May 1928. Vol. liq. (members') 4 Jan. 1930. Struck off Register 13 May 1960 ...... **1954**

Rosario City Improvements Co. Ld. Regd. 1888. Vol. liq. 1 June 1898. Undertaking was acquired by Rosario Drainage Co. Ld. Debenture holders were entitled to £66 in debenture stock, £80 in preferred shares of £5 and £15 in ordinary share of £5 for every £100 debenture held. No return of capital to contributories. Final meeting return regd. 17 Dec. 1898 .... **1908**

Rosario Drainage Co. Ld. Regd. 1897. Undertaking (excluding certain assets) sold to Argentine Govt. as from 1 July 1948. Vol. liq. (members') 28 Oct. 1948. Capital returned to contributories (per £1 stock)— preference, £1; ordinary, £1 10s. 3d. Final meeting return regd. 2 Jan. 1956 .... **1956**

Rosario Electric Co. Ld. Regd. 1902. Removed from Register 1911 .... **1911**

Rosario Nitrate Co. Ld. Regd. 1889. Vol. liq. (members') 20 Mar. 1931. Undertaking and assets acquired by Nitrate Corporation of Chile, in which corporation shareholders were entitled to receive 23 fully-paid series B shares of 100 pesos (either ordinary or 7% cumulative preferred) for every 100 shares of £1 held. £1,320 3s. 10d. was paid into Companies' Liquidation Account in respect of unclaimed dividends and £141 9s. 4d. in respect of sale of unclaimed shares. Final meeting return regd. 18 Dec. 1934. Court Order to declare dissolution void 8 Jan. 1935. Final meeting return regd. 16 Mar. 1939 .... **1932**

Rosario Water Works Co. Ld. Regd. 1886. Vol. liq. 17 Oct. 1896. Undertaking rights and obligations were acquired by Consolidated Water Works Co. of Rosario Ld. Debenture holders were entitled to 50% of holding in 4% debenture stock in new company and 50% in fully-paid preference shares of £10. Final meeting return regd. 16 June 1897 .... **1908**

Rosario Waterworks (New) Co. Ld. Regd. 1889. Vol. liq. 22 May 1896. Undertaking rights and obligations were acquired by Consolidated Water Works Co. of Rosario Ld. 1st preference shareholders were entitled to 15,000 ordinary shares of £10 in new company. Final meeting return regd. 16 June 1897 **1908**

Rosbach Springs Ld. Regd. 1895. Removed from Register 1903 .... **1901**

Rose Automatic Target Co. Ld. Regd. 1912. Vol. liq. 30 Apr. 1914. Final meeting return regd. 28 Aug. 1917 **1915**

Rose-Hill United Gold Mines Ld. Regd. Dec. 1896. Vol. liq. 8 Aug. 1898. Final meeting return regd. 17 Jan. 1899 .... **1899**

Rose (Klerksdorp) Gold Co. Ld. Regd. 1889. Removed from Register 1907 .... **1893**

Rose (L. J.) & Co. Ld. Regd. 1886. Vol. liq. 30 Apr. 1890. Reconstructed as company of same name. Preference shareholders were entitled to 8 shares of £1 (15s. paid) for each preference share of £10 held. Final meeting return regd. 1 Mar.1891 .... **1906**

Rose (L. J.) & Co. Ld. Regd. 1890. Struck off Register 8 Aug. 1905 .... **1906**

Rose of England Gold Mine Ld. Regd. 1895. Vol. liq. 26 May 1897. Final meeting return regd. 21 Mar. 1898 **1898**

Rose of Sharon & Shamrock Gold Mines Ld. Regd. 1900. Vol. liq. 20 Sept. 1911. The undertaking and assets were sold to Rose of Sharon & Shamrock Gold Mines (1911) Ld., in which company shareholders were entitled to 1 share of £1 (credited with 16s. 3d. paid) for each share of £1 held. Final meeting return regd. 5 June 1918 .... **1912**

Rose of Sharon & Shamrock Gold Mines (1911) Ld. Regd. 1911. Vol. liq. 18 Jan. 1917. Final meeting return regd. 22 Mar 1922 .... **1917**

Rose Patent Fuel Co. Ld. Regd. 1920. Vol. liq. (members') 4 Sept. 1930. Debenture stockholders received 1 fully-paid preference share in British Briquettes Ld. for each £1 stock held; shareholders received 115 preference shares of £1 and 185 ordinary shares of £1 in British Briquettes Ld. for every 300 shares of 10s. held plus 1·274d. per share in cash. Final meeting return regd. 29 July 1931 ...... **1931**

Rose-Pearl Group Gold Mines Ld. Regd. 1895. Removed from Register 1901 .... **1899**

Rose Reef Gold and Platinum Ld. Regd. 1925. Vol. liq. 14 Jan. 1929. Final meeting return regd. 25 May 1929 .... **1929**

Rose, Smith & Co. Ld. Regd. 1918. Vol. liq. (members') 28 nov. 1947. Capital returned to contributories— 20s. per £1 preference stock and 2s. 6‍⁷⁄₈d. per 1s. ordinary stock; ordinary stockholders were also entitled to receive 1 fully-paid ordinary share of £1 of Rose, Smith & Co. (Fuel) Ld. for every £2 ordinary stock held. £46 was paid into Companies' Liquidation Account. Final meeting return regd. 30 Aug. 1949 .... **1950**

Rose Tube Co. Ld. Regd. 1896. Vol. liq. 4 May 1904. Struck off Register 10 Oct. 1916 .... **1906**

Rose, Van Cutsem & Co. Established 1903. Dissolved in Apr. 1937. The business was acquired by Metropolitan Canadian Corporation Ld. **1938**

Rosebank Distillery Ld. Regd. Edinburgh 1894. Vol. liq. Aug. 1914. Undertaking and assets sold to Scottish Malt Distillers Ld. Shareholders were entitled to 1 ordinary share of £1 for each ordinary share of £10 held or 8 preference shares of £1 for each preference share of £10 held. Final meeting return regd. 27 Apr. 1916 .... **1915**

Rosebush & Fishguard Railway Co. See North Pembrokeshire & Fishguard Railway Co.

Rosedale Estates (Canada) Ld. Regd. 1912. Vol. liq. 10 Dec. 1914. Reconstructed as company of same name. Shareholders were entitled to 1 share of £1 (credited with 10s. paid) in new company for each share of £1 held. Third mortgage debenture holders were entitled to an equal amount of third mortgage debentures. Final meeting return regd. 20 June 1916 **1915**

Rosedale Estates (Canada) Ld. Regd. 1915. Vol. liq. 12 Apr. 1917. Final meeting return regd. 12 Sept. 1918 **1917**

Rosedale Mining Co. Ld. Regd. 1900. Removed from Register 1909 **1908**

Rosehaugh Tea & Rubber Co. Ld. Regd. 1907. Vol. liq. Feb. 1920. Reconstructed as Rosehaugh Co. Ld., in which company shareholders were entitled to £90 in 6% preference shares of £10 (credited as fully-paid) or £105 in cash for every £100 preference capital held. Ordinary shareholders were entitled to 16⅞% in cash, 100% in preference shares of £10 and 200% in ordinary shares of £1. Struck off Register 9 Apr. 1937 **1938**

Rosemont Lydenburg Estates Co. Ld. Regd. 1895. Removed from Register 1911 **1908**

Rosenblock Twin Reef Gold Mining Co. Ld. Regd. 1895. Property was sold on behalf of debenture holders who received £5 2s. 6d. per bond of £10; further payments (if any) not known. Removed from Register 1904 **1900**

Rosenkrantz Estate & Gold Mining Co. Ld. Regd. 1889. Reconstructed 1912 as Kobolondo Development Syndicate Ld., in which company shareholders were entitled to 1 share of £1 (credited as fully-paid) for every 5 shares of 8s. held. Removed from Register 1912 **1900**

Rosevale Rubber Co. Ld. Regd. 1912. All capital was owned by Seafield Amalgamated Rubber Co. Ld. Vol. liq. (members') 13 Jan. 1961. Final meeting return regd. 9 Nov. 1963 **1960**

Rosevear Clays Ld. Regd. 1922. Vol. liq. (members') 28 June 1933. All shares owned by English China Clays Ld. Final meeting return regd. 7 Feb. 1935 **1934**

Rosewell Gas Coal Co. Ld. Regd. Edinburgh 1885. Vol. liq. Mar. 1906. Capital returned to contributories— £1 2s. 6d. per preference share of £10; further payments (if any) not known. Final meeting return regd. 29 Jan. 1907 **1907**

Rosey Cross Asbestos Mines of Rhodesia Ld. Regd. 1929. Vol. liq. May 1931. Court Order to wind up July 1931. Struck off Register 24 Oct. 1939 **1940**

Rosling & Fynn Ld. Regd. 1900 as Rosling, Appleby & Fynn Ld.; name changed 1901. Removed from Register 1903 **1903**

Rosling, Appleby & Fynn Ld. See Rosling & Fynn Ld.

Ross & Ledbury Railway Co. Inc. by Special Act 1873. Under Great Western Railway Act 1892 undertaking was vested in that company **1893**

Ross and Monmouth Railway Co. Inc. by Special Act 1865. In 1922 the undertaking was merged into the Great Western Railway Co., in which company stockholders were entitled to stock as follows:

For each £100 held	G. W.
6% Preference	£120 5% Cons. Pref.
Ordinary	£35 5% Cons. Pref.

The liability in respect of the £47,300 Debentures was assumed by the Great Western Company **1924**

Ross & Walpole Ld. Inc. Dublin 1898. In voluntary liquidation in 1931 **1932**

Ross Gas Co. Ld. Regd. 1889. Dissolved 1 May 1949, undertaking being vested in South Western Area Gas Board under Gas Act 1948. Holders of ordinary shares (10% max.—of £1) were entitled to receive £2 1s. British Gas 3% guaranteed stock 1990—95. Liability in respect of certain mortgage loans assumed by the Board **1952**

Ross (James) & Co. Philpstoun Oil Works Ld. Regd. Edinburgh 1918. Vol. liq. (members') 24 Feb. 1936. Direct controlling interest held Scottish Oils Ld. [later B. P. Refinery (Grangemouth) Ld.]. Certain assets were distributed in specie. Final meeting return regd. 25 May 1936 **1937**

Ross Steam Trawl Fishing Co. Ld. Regd. Edinburgh 1901. Vol. liq. May 1920. Final meeting return regd. 27 Apr. 1921 **1921**

Rossa Grande Gold Mining Co. Ld. Regd. 1864. Vol. liq. 13 June 1894. Final meeting return regd. 2 Oct. 1897 ***1885**

Rossell (Henry) & Co. Ld. See Meadow Hall Steel Co. Ld.

Rossendale Union Gas Co. Inc. by Special Act 1854. Dissolved 1 May 1949, undertaking being vested in North Western Area Gas Board under Gas Act 1948. Holders of securities were entitled to receive, in respect of each £10 unit, unless otherwise stated, of security held, British Gas 3% guaranteed stock 1990—95 as follows:

	£	s.	d.
Ord. shares (10% max.)	20	10	0
Prefd. ord. shares (10% max.)	21	0	0
Ord. shares (7% max.)	14	10	0
Ord. shares (7½% max.)	15	10	0

	VOL.	FOR
5% pref. shares	11	4	0
4½% deb. stock (per £100)	104	5	0

Liability in respect of certain mortgage loans assumed by the Board **1952**

Rossendale Valley Tramways Co. Ld. Regd. 1909. Vol. liq. Mar. 1909. Removed from Register 1910 **1910**

Rosser Cycle & Vehicle Brake Co. Ld. Regd. 1896. Vol. liq. 31 Mar. 1898. Final meeting return regd. 7 Jan. 1899 **1899**

Rossington Main Colliery Co. Ld. Regd. 1911. Vol. liq. (members') 30 Mar. 1949. Final meeting return regd. 28 Dec. 1949 **1940**

Rossland Great Western Mines Ld. Regd. 1900. Removed from Register 1914 **1908**

Rossland-Kootenay Mining Co. Ld. Regd. 1902. Vol. liq. 21 Apr. 1928. Capital returned to contributories— 2d. per share of £1. Final meeting return regd. 25 Apr. 1929 **1929**

Rossleigh Cycle Co. Ld. Regd. Edinburgh 1896. Vol. liq. 25 May 1898. Business was acquired in 1898 by New Rossleigh Cycle & Motor Co. Ld. (later Rossleigh Ld.) for £19,750 in shares of £1 and £18,250 in cash. Final meeting return regd. 19 Dec. 1899 **1898**

Ross-shire Electric Supply Co. Ld. Regd. Edinburgh 1 Oct. 1926. Vol. liq. (members') 30 Mar. 1944. All shares were owned by Scottish Power Co. Ld. **1945**

Rota Anna Mines Ld. Regd. 1899. Vol. liq. 19 Dec. 1904. The property was sold for £10,000. No capital was expected to be returned to contributories. Removed from Register 1910 **1905**

Rotary Photographic Co. Ld. Regd. 1898. Vol. liq. 19 Apr. 1916. Struck off Register 24 July 1923 **1916**

Rotax Ld. Regd. 1896 as Newton Electrical Works Ld.; name changed to Newtons Ld. in Jan. 1904; to Rotax (Motor Accessories) Ld. in Apr. 1921 and as above in June 1931. Vol. liq. 5 Apr. 1933. All shares held by Joseph Lucas Industries Ld. Final meeting return regd. 15 Feb. 1934 **1934**

Rotax (Motor Accessories) Ld. See Rotax Ld.

Rother Vale Collieries Ld. Regd. 1875. Vol. liq. 10 Feb. 1919. Direct controlling interest held by United Steel Companies Ld. Final meeting return regd. 30 Apr. 1921 **1927**

Rother Valley (Light) Railway Co. See Kent & East Sussex Light Railway Co.

Rotherham & Bawtrey Railway Co. Inc. by Special Act 1881. Undertaking abandoned by Act of 1888 **1889**

Rotherham, Blyth & Sutton Railway Co. See Retford, Rotherham & Barnsley Railway Co.

Rotherham Investment Trust Ld. See Brandts (Wm.) Investment Trust Ld.

Rotherham, Maltby & Laughton Railway Co. Inc. by Special Act 1905. Powers transferred to Great Central Railway Co. by Act of 1906 **1907**

Rotherham, Masbro' and Holmes Colliery Co. Ld. Regd. 1856. Vol. liq. Sept. 1881. Court Order to continue winding up Sept. 1881. Final meeting return regd. 17 Jan. 1885 **1882**

Rothery Block Gold Mine Ld. Regd. 1895. Vol. liq. 18 Feb. 1898. Final meeting return regd. 15 Feb. 1899 **1899**

Rothesay Tramways Co. Ld. Regd. Edinburgh 1879. Vol. liq. (members') 31 Oct. 1949. Final meeting return regd. 4 Dec. 1950 **1940**

Rothmans (Ceylon) Ld. Regd. 1936. Vol. liq. (members') 1 Nov. 1940. Capital returned to contributories— £21,367 8s. 2d. Final meeting return regd. 10 June 1942 **1941**

Rothschilds' Gold Mines Ld. See Heidelberg Gold Mines Ld.

Rothwell Gas-Light Co. Inc. by Special Act 1882. Dissolved 1 May 1949, undertaking being vested in North Eastern Area Gas Board under Gas Act 1948. Holders of securities were entitled to receive, in respect of each £10 unit held, British Gas 3% guaranteed stock 1990—95 as follows: £ s. d.

Orig. shares (10% max.)	21	0	0
Addit. shares (7% max.)	15	0	0

Liability in respect of certain mortgage loans assumed by the Corporation **1952**

Rothwell Hosiery Co. Ld. Regd. 1886. Removed from Register 1901 ***1895**

Rotterdam-Deli Heavea Ld. Regd. 1911. Vol. liq. 17 Feb. 1920. The undertaking and assets were acquired by Amalgamated Rubber Estates Ld. (later Amalgamated Rubber & General Estates Ld.) in which company shareholders were entitled to 1 share of 2s. (credited as fully-paid) for each share of 2s. held and an option (since expired) over further shares at par. Final meeting return regd. 2 Feb. 1921 **1920**

Rotulo Ld. Regd. 1895. Struck off Register 1915 **1912**

Roumanian Anthracite Coal Co. Ld. Regd. 1895. Removed from Register 1908 **1901**

Roumanian Consolidated Oilfields Ld. Regd. 1910 as Bitter Creek Prospectors Ld.; name changed Oct.

VOL. FOR

1910. Vol. liq. Apr. 1912. Reconstructed as company of same name. Shareholders entitled to 1 fully-paid share of £1 for each ordinary share of £1 or every 3 deferred shares of 1s. held. Removed from Register 1913 .... **1913**

Roumanian Consolidated Oilfields Ld. Regd. 1912. In 1923 all shares and debentures were acquired by Phoenix Oil & Transport Co. Ld. in exchange for shares (1 Phoenix share for every 2 held and 300 Phoenix shares for every £400 debentures held), holders being entitled also to bearer certificates for deferred payments out of compensation for destruction of property when received. Holders of (green) bearer certificates in respect of debentures were entitled to 2s. 8d. cash per Phoenix share received plus 2 months' interest at 10% p.a. on debentures exchanged; payments—6d. in Oct. 1932, 5d. in May 1934, 5d. in Feb. 1937, 4d. in Feb. 1939, 4d. in Feb. 1946 and final 8d. plus the 2 months' interest in July 1957. Struck off the Register 9 Jan. 1953 .... **1924**

Roumanian Hotel Co. Ld. Regd. 1881. Struck off Register Feb. 1933 .... **1933**

Roumanian Oil Trust Ld. Regd. 1898. Undertaking and assets were acquired by Steaua Romana S. A. pour l'Industrie du Pétrole. Shareholders were entitled to 50% of their holdings in shares of purchasing company in respect of preference shares held or 10% in respect of ordinary shares held. Debenture holders were entitled to 6% 1st mortgage bonds of purchasing company. Removed from Register 1905 **1904**

Roumanian Oilfields Ld. Regd. 1910. Vol. liq. Apr. 1912. Undertaking was acquired by Roumanian Consolidated Oilfields Ld., in which company shareholders were entitled to 2 fully-paid shares of £1 for every 3 shares of £1 held. Struck off Register Feb. 1930 .... **1931**

Roumanian Pipeline & Trading Co. Ld. Regd. 1911. Vol. liq. 8 Sept. 1914. Final meeting return regd. 27 Sept. 1919 .... **1915**

Roumanian Road Transport Co. Ld. Regd. 1919. Vol. liq. 24 July 1922. Final meeting return regd. 28 Sept. 1922 .... **1923**

Round (John) and Son, Ld. Regd. 1874. Vol. liq. 19 Dec. 1962. Final meeting return regd. 17 Apr. 1965....... **1947**

Roundhill Textiles Ld. Regd. 1904 as Knowles Ld.; name changed 1953. Vol. liq. (members') 28 July 1960. Capital returned to contributories—47s. 2¼d. per share of £1. £402 6s. 11d. was paid into Companies' Liquidation Account in respect of unclaimed distributions. Final meeting return regd. 20 July 1962 .... **1963**

Roundwood & Dalton Colliery Co. Ld. Regd. 1898. Undertaking was acquired in 1899 by Dalton Main Collieries Ld. Removed from Register 1901.......... **1940**

Routledge (George) & Sons Ld. Regd. 1889. Business was acquired in 1902 by company of same name (later Routledge & Kegan Paul Ld.). Removed from Register 1907 .... **1908**

Roweka Rubber Co. Ld. Regd. 1911. Vol. liq. 2 Apr. 1924. Final meeting return regd. 15 Aug. 1928 ..... **1925**

Rowell (John) & Son, Ld. Regd. 1894. Vol. liq. (members') 2 Sept. 1960. All ordinary and preference capital owned by The Newcastle Breweries Ld. The outstanding £127,500 debentures were redeemed on 30 Sept. 1960 at par. Capital returned to contributories—£1,074,091. Final meeting return regd. 4 May 1961.. **1962**

Rowley Regis & Blackheath Gas Co. Estd. 1862; inc. by Special Act 1886. Dissolved 1 May 1949, undertaking being vested in West Midland Area Gas Board under Gas Act 1948. Holders of securities were entitled to receive British Gas 3% guaranteed stock 1990—95 as follows in respect of each £10 unit, unless otherwise stated, of security held:

	£	s.	d.
Orig. ord. A shares (10% max.).........	20	10	0
Ord. B shares (7% max.)..................	14	12	0
4% deb. stock (per £100)................	100	5	0
4% tax-free deb. stock (per £100)......	101	5	0
5% deb. stock (per £100)................	100	15	0

.... **1952**

Rowrah & Kelton Fell (Mineral) Railway Co. Inc. by Special Act 1874... **1931**

Roy Mill (1919) Ld. Regd. 1919. Vol. liq. 31 Mar. 1953. The undertaking and assets were acquired by Shiloh Spinners Ld., in which company shareholders were entitled to receive £41 18s. 3d. in preference shares and £97 15s. 10d. in ordinary shares for each £100 capital stock held. Final meeting return regd. 21 Dec. 1953... **1954**

Royal Aquarium & Summer & Winter Garden Society Ld. Regd. 1874. Removed from Register 1904...... **1903**

Royal Bank of Australia Ld. Established Victoria 1888. The business was acquired by English Scottish &

VOL. FOR

Australian Bank Ld. Shareholders received repayment of capital in full *plus* 1 share of £5 (credited with £3 paid) in purchasing company for every £6 paid-up capital held **1928**

Royal Bank of Bohemia. See Zemska Banks Pro Cechy

Royal Bank of Queensland Ld. Inc. Queensland 1885. Vol. liq. 1918, the business having been acquired by the Bank of Queensland Ld. **1918**

Royal Carl Rosa Opera Co. Ld. Regd. 1887 as Carl Rosa Opera Co. Ld.; name changed Apr. 1893. Vol. liq. 30 June 1898. Final meeting return regd. 4 July 1900 **1899**

Royal Consolidated Mines (California) Co. Ld. Regd. 1898. Receiver for debenture stockholders appointed Aug. 1905. Struck off Register 1927 .... **1909**

Royal Courts of Justice Chambers Co. Ld. Regd. 1881. Vol. liq. 31 Jan. 1894. Final meeting return regd. 28 May 1894 .... **1895**

Royal Exchange Bank Ld. Established 1879. Business was taken over in 1889 by Metropolitan Bank of England & Wales Ld. **1909**

Royal Exchange, Glasgow, Ld. Regd. in Edinburgh as unlimited as Royal Exchange Buildings. Glasgow (Society of Proprietors of the) 1869; regd. as limited 1911; name changed 1924. Vol. liq. (members') 7 Aug. 1950. Capital returned to contributories—£12 11s. 3d. per share (of £10). Final meeting return regd. 7 Nov. 1955 .... **1956**

Royal Exchange Buildings, Glasgow. See above.

Royal Exchange Shipping Co. Ld. Regd. 1874. Court Orders; to wind up 15 Jan. 1887; to dissolve 7 Feb. 1893 .... **1888**

Royal Farmers and General Insurance Co. Established 1840 as Farmers and General Fire and Life Insurance and Loan and Annuity Co.; name changed on registration as unlimited company in Mar. 1883. Business was transferred in 1888 to Alliance Assurance Co. **1888**

Royal Financial Corporation Ld. Inc. British Columbia 1910. A petition in bankruptcy was presented against the corporation in Oct. 1931 .... **1933**

Royal Holborn Theatre of Varieties Ld. Regd. 1891. Removed from Register 11 June 1895 .... ***1893**

Royal Hotel Co. (Scarborough) Ld. Regd. 1870. Vol. liq. 20 Jan. 1893. Final meeting return regd. 17 Jan. 1894 .... ***1882**

Royal Hotel, Edinburgh, Co. Ld. Regd. Edinburgh 1897. Vol. liq. (members') 31 May 1950. Capital returned to contributories (shares of £1)—preference £1; ordinary £5·304 (approx.) Final meeting return regd. 30 Apr. 1970 .... **1970**

Royal Italian Opera. Covent Garden Ld. Regd. 1881. Receiver appointed 7 Aug. 1884. Removed from Register 1906 .... **1885**

Royal London Auxiliary Insurance Co. Ld. Regd. 1910. Vol. liq. 14 June 1922. Undertaking and assets were acquired by Royal London Mutual Insurance Society Ld. Capital returned to contributories—15s. 1d. per share of £1 (10s. paid); 15s. per fully-paid share of 10s. Final meeting return regd. 22 June 1923 **1923**

Royal Machine Manufacturing Co. Ld. Regd. 1877 as Royal Sewing-Machine Co. Ld.; name changed 9 Jan. 1882. Vol. liq. 16 Dec. 1887. Final meeting return regd. 19 June 1889 .... ***1881**

Royal Mail Steam Packet Co. Inc. by Royal Charter 1839. A scheme of arrangement of 1932 provided (inter alia) for transfer of fleet to Royal Mail Lines Ld. for 880,000 fully-paid shares and for a moratorium under control of the creditors. Under a scheme of arrangement of Jan. 1935 it was provided (inter alia) as follows-(a) R. M. Realisation Co. Ld. was formed to acquire and realise the assets. (b) The outstanding 4½% 1st debenture stock held by the public was repaid by the Realisation company in cash at par (*plus* accrued interest) or exchanged for an equal amount of 4% 1st debenture stock of the Realisation company; and the stock held by bankers as security for loans was cancelled on repayment of the loans by the Realisation company in cash. (c) The outstanding 5% debenture stock was satisfied by the issue of £50 income debenture stock and 15 fully-paid shares of £1 each of the Realisation company for each £100 stock held, all accrued interest being cancelled. Court Order to wind up 10 Feb. 1936 .... **1936**

Royal Oak of Hauraki Ld. Regd. 1895. Reconstructed 1900 as company of same name. Shareholders were entitled to 1 share of 2s. 6d. (credited with 2s. 3d. paid) in new company for each share of 5s. held. Removed from Register 1901 .... **1906**

Royal Oak of Hauraki Ld. Regd. 1900. Reconstructed 1906 as North Mount Boppy Ld., in which company shareholders were entitled to 1 share of 2s. 6d. (credited with 2s. 3d. paid) for each share of 2s. 6d. held. Removed from Register 1909 .... **1908**

Royal Sardinian Railway Co. Constituted by Act of Italian Government 1863. In 1929 the company was acquired by Compagnia Fondiaria Regionale. The purchasing company assumed all liability for outstanding bonds; the ordinary and preference shareholders were entitled to (a) exchange their holdings for an equal number of privileged shares Series A of purchasing company, or (b) repayment at £3 15s. per share. Jouissance shareholders were offered 1 privileged share Series A for every 4 shares held ... 1930

Royal Sewing-Machine Co. Ld. See Royal Machine Manufacturing Co. Ld.

Royal Sheba Ld. Regd. 1895. Vol. liq. 13 Apr. 1898. Reconstructed 1898 as company of same name. Shareholders were entitled to 1 share of £1 (credited with 15s. paid) in new company for each share of £1 held. Final meeting return regd. 13 Mar. 1924 1904

Royal Sheba Ld. Regd. 1898. Vol. liq. 8 July 1904. Reconstructed as company of same name. Shareholders were entitled to 1 share of £1 (credited with 15s. paid) in new company for every 3 shares of £1 held. Debenture holders were entitled to an equal nominal amount of shares in new company for their holdings. Final meeting return regd. 13 Mar. 1924 ... 1908

Royal Sheba Ld. Regd. 1904. Vol. liq. 22 Nov. 1923. Final meeting return regd. 13 Mar. 1924 1924

Royal Silver Mines of Potosi, Bolivia Ld. Regd. 1884. Receiver for debenture holders was appointed. Struck off Register 1915 1910

Royal Sovereign Gold Mining Co. Ld. Regd. 1895. Removed from Register 1908 1902

Royal Sovereign Steamship Co. Ld. Regd. 1919. Court Order to wind up Mar. 1925. Undertaking was acquired by R. S. Steamship Co. Ld. Struck off Register 16 Aug. 1938 1939

Royal Standard Gold Mines Ld. Regd. 1896. Assets realised insufficient to satisfy claims of debenture holders. Removed from Register 1909. 1900

Royal Swedish Railway. Inc. by Royal Charter Sweden 1852. In 1897 the property was sold to Graugesberg-Oxelosund Traffic Co. for £683,333 1898

Royal Trans-African Railway Co. See Companhia de Ambaca.

Royal York Palace of Varieties Ld. Regd. 1897. Removed from Register 1910 1901

Royalberg Copper Mines Ld. Regd. 1903. Vol. liq. Mar. 1912. Removed from Register 1913 1913

Royalton Tin Mine Co. Ld. Regd. 1881. Removed from Register 1888 1883

Royce Ld. See Factory Holdings Ld.

Royston & Brodsworth Gas Co. Inc. by Special Act 1931. Dissolved 1 May 1949, undertaking being vested in North Eastern Area Gas Board under Gas Act 1948. Holders of securities were entitled to receive, in respect of each £100 unit held, British Gas 3% guaranteed stock 1990—95 as follows:

	£	s.	d.
Ord. stock (6% stand.)	130	0	0
6% pref. stock	133	0	0
4% red. deb. stock	101	15	0

Liability in respect of certain mortgage loans assumed by the Board 1952

Royston & Hitchin Railway Co. Inc. by Special Act 1846. Under Great Northern Railway Act 1897 the undertaking was amalgamated with that company in which holders of £100 Royston, Hitchin and Shepreth consolidated stock received £146 13s. 4d. 4% guaranteed stock 1898

Royston Cement Co. Ld. Regd. 1899. Removed from Register 1906 1902

Royston Gas Co. Ld. Regd. 1860. Dissolved 1 May 1949, undertaking being vested in Eastern Area Gas Board under Gas Act 1948. Holders of securities were entitled to receive British Gas 3% guaranteed stock 1990—95 as follows:

	£	s.	d.
Ord. shares (of £10)	20	0	0
4% red. mort. deb. bonds (of £100)	101	10	0

1952

Royston Industries Ld. Regd. 1936 as British Emulsifiers Ld.; name changed Jan. 1957. Vol. liq. 21 June 1968. Debenture stock redeemed at par 31 Aug. 1968. Unsecured loan stockholders received 43·24p per £1 stock on account of principal. No return made to ordinary shareholders. Final meeting return regd. 16 Sept. 1975. Company dissolved 14 Dec. 1975. 1975-6

Royston Water Co. Ld. Regd. 1859. Undertaking vested in Lee Valley Water Co. on 1 Apr. 1960 under Lee Valley Water Act 1959. Vol. liq. (members') 1 Apr. 1960. Final meeting return regd. 8 Apr. 1963 1911

Royton Ring Mill Ld. Regd. 1907. Struck off Register 25 Mar. 1938 1939

Royton Spinning Co. Ld. Regd. 1871. Vol. liq. (members') 31 Mar. 1953. Undertaking and assets

acquired by Shiloh Spinners Ld. Stockholders were entitled to receive, in respect of every £100 held, £91 13s. 4d. preference and £213 17s. 9d. ordinary capital of Shiloh Spinners Ld. Final meeting return regd. 23 Dec. 1953 1954

Rubana Rubber Estates Ld. Regd. 1910. All capital acquired by Straits Rubber Co. Ld. Vol. liq. (members') 30 June 1961. Final meeting return regd. 26 Sept. 1962 1961

Rubastic Ld. Regd. 1913. Vol. liq. 26 May 1920. Final meeting return regd. 13 Jan. 1923 1921

Rubber & General Trust Co. Ld. Regd. 1910. Vol. liq. 5 Apr. 1916. Final meeting return regd. 3 Sept. 1918 ... 1916

Rubber & Industrial Trust Ld. Regd. 1910. Vol. liq. 16 Dec. 1914. Final meeting return regd. 18 Apr. 1916 ... 1915

Rubber & Industrial Trust Ld. See Sterling & Overseas Investments Ld.

Rubber & Mercantile Corporation Ld. Regd. 1912 as London, Singapore & Java Bank Ld.; name changed to London & General Trade Bank Ld. in June 1920 and as above in Feb. 1922. Vol. liq. June 1924. Struck off Register 15 Oct. 1935 1936

Rubber & Oil Consolidated Investment Ld. Regd. 1910. Vol. liq. Jan. 1913. Struck off Register Jan. 1933 . 1933

Rubber and Produce Investment Trust Ld. Regd. 1910. Vol. liq. 5 Mar. 1913. Court Order to wind up 8 July 1913. Liquidator released 24 Oct. 1917. Struck off Register 1 July 1921 1914

Rubber and Tea Investors' Trust Ld. Regd. 1910. Vol. liq. 15 Mar. 1916. Final meeting return regd. 22 May 1917 1916

Rubber & Tropical Trust Ld. See T. Y. T. Ld.

Rubber & Tyre Publicity Ld. Regd. 1923. Vol. liq. (members') 27 May 1931. Direct controlling interest was held by North British Rubber Co. Ld. (later Uniroyal Ld.). Final meeting return regd. 27 July 1931 1932

Rubber Co. of Malay Ld. Regd. 1905. Vol. liq. 6 Oct. 1927. Shareholders were entitled to 5 shares of 2s. in Kepong (Malay) Rubber Estates Ld. for every 21 shares of 2s. held plus 1⅝d. per share in cash. Final meeting return regd. 29 May 1928 1928

Rubber Corporation of Brazil Ld. Regd. 1910. Vol. liq. 12 June 1911. Final meeting return regd. 22 Oct. 1915 1912

Rubber Curing Patents Syndicate Ld. Regd. 1912. Vol. liq. 28 Feb. 1921. Final meeting return regd. 4 Oct. 1921 1922

Rubber Estates & General Development Co. Ld. Regd. 1910. Vol. liq. July 1911. Removed from Register 1912 1912

Rubber Estates of Johore Ld. Regd. 1906. Vol. liq. (members') 15 Oct. 1947. Undertaking and assets acquired by Lanadron Rubber Estates Ld. in which company stockholders were entitled to receive 46 £1 units of stock for each 100 held. £43 17s. was paid into Companies' Liquidation Account. Final meeting return regd. 13 Sept. 1948 1949

Rubber Estates of Kedah Ld. See below.

Rubber Estates of Krian Ld. Regd. Oct. 1909 as Rubber Estates of Kedah Ld.; name changed Dec. 1909. Vol. liq. (members') 29 Dec. 1950. Capital returned to contributories—1s. 9·87d. per share of 2s. £5,334 was paid into Companies' Liquidation Account. Final meeting return regd. 17 Dec. 1951 1953

Rubber Estates of Mexico Ld. Regd. 1919. Vol. liq. 16 Aug. 1922. Shareholders were entitled to 2 participating preference shares of 1s. (credited as fully-paid) in Central Petroleum & General Corporation Ld. for every 3 shares of 1s. held and an option (since expired) over further shares. The note holders were entitled to an equal amount of notes in new company. Final meeting return regd. 22 Aug. 1924 ... 1924

Rubber Estates of Pará Ld. Regd. 1898. Removed from Register 1903 1902

Rubber Estates Trust & Investment Cosporation Ld. Regd. 1909. Vol. liq. 23 Jan. 1913. Struck off Register 18 Jan. 1921 .... *1911

Rubber Exploration Co. Ld. Regd. 1896. Vol. liq. 27 June 1912. Court Order to continue winding up under supervision 26 Nov. 1912. Final meeting return regd. 20 Dec. 1916 1913

Rubber Improvement Ld. Regd. 1946. Vol. liq. (creditors') 17 Dec. 1962. No capital returned to contributories, unsecured creditors received 8s. 9½d. in the £1. Final meeting return regd. 29 Jan. 1969 1969

Rubber, Oil & General Promotions Ld. Regd. 1910. Vol. liq. 20 May 1914. Final meeting return regd. 21 Dec. 1916 1915

Rubber Plantations Ld. See Dangan Rubber Co. Ld.

Rubber Planters, Oil & Investment Trust Ld. Regd. 1910. Vol. liq. 18 Oct. 1910. Final meeting return regd. 14 Sept. 1911 .... *1911

*See Stock Exchange Year-Book.

VOL. FOR

Rubber Processes Ld. Regd. 1929. Court Order to wind up Nov. 1929. Struck off Register Dec. 1934 .... **1935**

Rubber Promotions Ld. Regd. 1910. Vol. liq. 17 May 1918. Final meeting return regd. 9 Aug. 1919........ **1919**

Rubber Roadways Ld. Regd. 1915. Vol. liq. (members') 14 Dec. 1956. Capital returned to contributories—£3 1*s*. 9*d*. per preference share of £1, 2*s*. per ordinary share of £1 and 7*s*. 11½*d*. per deferred share of £1. Final meeting return regd. 2 Apr. 1958 .... **1959**

Rubber Share Trust & Finance Co. Ld. Regd. 1910. Vol. liq. 15 Apr. 1915. Reconstructed as Culloden Consolidated Co. Ld. in which company shareholders were entitled to 1 share of £1 (credited as fully-paid) for every 5 shares of 10*s*. held. Final meeting return regd. 1 Feb. 1918 .... **1916**

Rubber Tanned Leather Co. Ld. Regd. 1909. Vol. liq. 2 July 1913. Final meeting return regd. 6 Sept. 1915 **1914**

Rubber Tyre Manufacturing Co. Ld. Regd. 1896. Vol. liq. 25 Apr. 1901. Business was acquired by Dunlop Rubber Co. Ld., (later Dunlop Co. Ld.) in which company shareholders were entitled to £1 debenture stock for each share of £1 held. Final meeting return regd. 9 Nov. 1901 .... **1902**

Rubber Ventures Ld. Regd. 1910. Vol. liq. 22 June 1914. The undertaking and assets were sold to Securities & Finance Syndicate Ld. for 13,309 shares of 5*s*. in Blue Bells Gold Mines Ld. Final meeting return regd. 16 Oct. 1916.. **1915**

Rubberine Ld. Regd. 1914. Vol. liq. 17 Dec. 1920. Final meeting return regd. 31 May 1922 .... **1921**

Rubel Bronze & Metal Co. Ld. Regd. 1915 as Rubel Bronze (1915) Ld.; name changed July 1915. Vol. liq. 12 Sept. 1919. Final meeting return regd. 29 Jan. 1920 .... **1920**

Rubens-Rembrandt Associated Hotels Ld. Regd. 1928. Vol. liq. (members') 17 Dec. 1962. Capital returned to contributories—17*s*. 6*d*. per 8*s*. ordinary stock. Paid into Companies' Liquidation Account—unclaimed dividends £149 8*s*. 2*d*.; distributions: £3,961 5*s*. Final meeting return regd. 29 Oct. 1964 **1965**

Rubinat-Condal Co. Ld. Regd. 1900 as Condal Water (1900) Ld.; name changed 1909. Removed from Register 1913 .... **1911**

Ruby and Dunderberg Consolidated Mining Co. Ld. Regd. 1879. Reconstructed 1885 as company of same name. Shareholders were entitled to subscribe for shares of £1 (credited with 15*s*. paid). Debenture holders were entitled to debentures in new company in respect of capital and fully-paid shares in respect of interest **1890**

Ruby & Dunderberg Consolidated Mining Co., 1885, Ld. Regd. 1885. Vol. liq. Jan 1890. Reconstructed as Ruby Mining Co. Ld. in which company shareholders were entitled to 2 shares of 5*s*. (credited with 4*s*. paid) for each fully-paid share of £1 held. Holders of 10% debentures were entitled to an equal amount of debentures or fully-paid shares in new company. Holders of 2nd debentures were entitled to 2 fully-paid shares of 5*s*. for each £1 debenture held. Final meeting return regd. 9 Mar. 1891......................... **1890**

Ruby Mining Co. Ld. Regd. 1890. Vol. liq. 7 Dec. 1893. Final meeting return regd. 11 Mar. 1896 .... **1894**

Rudge Cycle Co. Ld. Amalgamated in 1894 with Whitworth Cycle Co. Ld. to form Rudge Whitworth Ld. Debenture holders received an equal amount of 5% registered debentures in the new company. Shareholders received shares in new company **1896**

Rudge (E.) & Co. Ld. Regd. 1918. Vol. liq. 19 June 1920. Undertaking acquired by Victoria Enterprises Ld. Final meeting return regd. 18 Aug. 1921............. **1940**

Rudge, Wedge & Co. Ld. Regd. 1896. Receiver was appointed 7 Jan. 1901. Struck off Register 18 Nov. 1902 .... **1903**

Rudge-Whitworth (Foreign) Ld. Regd. 1897. Struck off Register 18 Nov. 1902 .... **1903**

Rudge Whitworth Ld. Regd. 1894. Vol. liq. (creditors') 9 Apr. 1934. Assets realised insufficient to pay unsecured creditors in full. Final meeting return regd. 25 Sept. 1935 .... **1935**

Ruffer (A.) & Sons Ld. Regd. 1923. Vol. liq. 29 Jan. 1941. Capital returned to contributories—14*s*. 3·8*d*. per ordinary share of £1. Final meeting return regd. 1 Sept. 1964 .... **1965**

Ruffy, Arnell & Baumann Aviation Co. Ld. Regd. 1916. Struck off Register 3 Nov. 1939 .... ***1924**

Rugby Gas Co. Estd. 1838; inc. by Special Act 1882. Dissolved 1 May 1949, undertaking being vested in West Midland Area Gas Board under Gas Act 1948. Holders of securities were entitled to receive, in respect of each £100 unit held, British Gas 3% guaranteed stock 1990—95 as follows:

	£	s.	d.
Sliding scale stock (3½% stand.).........	167	0	0
5% max. div. stock...........................	120	0	0
4½% pref. stock..................................	110	0	0
5½% pref. stock..................................	128	0	0
6% red. pref. stock	105	0	0
4½% perp. deb. stock	114	0	0
5½% perp. deb. stock	137	10	0
3½% red. deb. stock (issued before 1 Jan. 1946	100	0	0
3½% red. deb. stock (issued since 31 Dec. 1945).....................................	100	0	0

1952

Rugby, Tennessee Co. Ld. Regd. 1892. Vol. liq. 14 July 1915. Capital returned to contributories—7*d*. per preference share of £5 in Oct. 1915; further payments (if any) not known. Final meeting return regd. 10 Nov. 1915.. **1916**

Rugeley Gas Co. Inc. by Special Act 1900. Dissolved 1 May 1949, undertaking being vested in West Midland Area Gas Board under Gas Act 1948. Holders of securities were entitled to receive British Gas 3% guaranteed stock 1990–95 as follows in respect of each £100 unit, unless otherwise stated, of security held:

	£	s.	d.
A ord. stock (5% stand.)...................	145	0	0
B ord. stock (5% stand.)...................	145	0	0
4% red. pref. stock (per £1)..............	1	0	2
4½% perp. deb. stock	113	10	0

1952

Ruislip Manor, Ld. Regd. 1910. Vol. liq. (members') 15 Dec. 1954. Capital returned to contributories—preference (of £1), 20*s*. per share (with arrears of dividend); ordinary (of £1), 18*s*. 10·361*d*. per share. Amounts paid into Companies' Liquidation Account in respect of unclaimed dividends or distributions £299 4*s*. 9*d*. for preference and £2,236 1*s*. 1*d*. for ordinary. Final meeting return regd. 27 Aug. 1957... **1958**

Rukuba (Nigeria) Tin Mining Co. Ld. Regd. 1912. Vol. liq. 12 May 1924. Reconstructed as Rukuba Tin Mines Ld. (later Brayhead Ld.) in which company shareholders were entitled to 1 share of 2*s*. (credited as fully-paid) for each share of £1 held. Final meeting return regd. 1 Aug. 1925......................... **1925**

Rumney Steamship Co. Ld. Regd. 1919. Vol. liq. 11 Feb. 1924. Final meeting return regd. 17 June 1924 ..... **1925**

Rumney (William) & Co. Ld. Regd. 1894. Business was transferred in 1899 to Calico Printers' Association Ld. Removed from Register 1902 .... **1900**

Runcorn & District Gas Co. Inc. by Special Acts 1847 & 1885 as Runcorn Gas Co.; name changed 1938. Dissolved 1 May 1949, undertaking being vested in North Western Area Gas Board under Gas Act 1948. Holders of securities were entitled to receive, in respect of £100 unit held, British Gas 3% guaranteed stock 1990—95 as follows:

	£	s.	d.
Cons. stock (5% basic)	111	0	0
4% perp. deb. stock..........................	102	0	0

Liability in respect of certain mortgage loans assumed by the Board. A distribution on cons. stock of 0·40213% out of reserves was made in Apr. 1951 **1952**

Runcorn Soap and Alkali Co. Ld. Regd. 1865. Vol. liq. 30 Jan. 1891. Taken over by United Alkali Co. Ld. [later I.C.I. (General Chemicals) Ld.] Final meeting return regd. 3 May 1893... **1892**

Rural Districts Water Co. Ld. Regd. 1924. Dissolved as from 22 Jan. 1951 under Bucks. Water Order 1950. The 4% debenture stock and 4% debentures were redeemed at par on 2 Oct. 1950; the preference shares were repaid at 25*s*. per share (of £1) on 1 Oct. 1950 and the A and B ordinary shares were repaid at £2 18*s*. 4*d*. per share (of £1) on 1 Oct. 1950.......... **1952**

Rushden & District Electric Supply Co. Ld. Regd. 1912. Dissolved 1 Apr. 1948, undertaking being vested in British (later Central) Electricity Authority and East Midlands Area Board under British Electricity Act 1947. Holders of ordinary shares were entitled to receive £2 7*s*. 6*d*. British Electricity 3% guaranteed stock (1968—73) in respect of each share (of £1) held **1949**

Rushden District Gas Co. Regd. as Rushden & Higham Ferrers District Gas Co. 1892; inc. by Special Act 1899; name changed 1947. Dissolved 1 May 1949, undertaking being vested in East Midland Area Gas Board under Gas Act 1948. Holders of securities were entitled to receive, in respect of each £100 unit held, British Gas 3% guaranteed stock 1990—95 as follows:

	£	s.	d.
Orig. ord. stock (10% stand.)............	264	0	0
Addit. ord. stock (7% stand.)	185	0	0
A ord. stock (5% max.)	100	0	0
4% red. pref. stock (1971)	100	8	8
4% red. pref. stock (1976)	101	14	11
5% red. pref. stock	112	0	0
7% perp. deb. stock..........................	155	0	0

**See Stock Exchange Year-Book*.

VOL. FOR

3¼% red. deb. stock (1971)................ 102 10 0

3½% red. deb. stock (1976)................ 102 10 0   **1952**

Rushton Tractor Co. (1929) Ld. Regd. 1929. Vol. liq. (creditors') 29 Dec. 1930. No capital returned to contributories. Final meeting return regd. 20 Sept. 1932 ....   ***1931**

Russell (Andrew) Ld. Regd. 1913. Vol. liq. (members') 1 Apr. 1931. Capital returned to contributories—£2,414 7s. 5d. Undertaking and assets were acquired by Thornton-Smith Ld. (later Investment & Property Trust Ld.). Final meeting return regd. 4 Apr. 1932   **1931**

Russell Copper Mine Ld. Regd. 1883. Court Orders: to wind up 28 Dec. 1883; to dissolve 23 Mar. 1888 ..   ***1885**

Russell, Edwards & Co. Ld. See Bamber Bridge Engineers Ld.

Russell Gold Mining Co. Ld. Regd. 1884. Vol. liq. 10 Nov. 1887. Reconstructed as New Russell Gold Mining Co. Ld. in which company shareholders were entitled to 1 share of £1 (credited with 18s. paid) for each share held. Final meeting return regd. 8 Aug. 1892 ....   **1890**

Russell Investment Trust Ld. See Sanctuary Buildings Ld.

Russell Mines Co. Ld. Regd. 1889. Vol. liq. 25 Aug. 1891. Reconstructed as Russell Mines Ld. in which company shareholders were entitled to 1 share of 5s. (credited with 4s. 6d. paid) for each share of 5s. held. Final meeting return regd. 26 May 1892 ....   **1893**

Russell Mines Ld. Regd. 1891. Vol. liq. 25 July 1893. Final meeting return regd. 14 Apr. 1896 ....   **1894**

Russell United Mines Ld. Regd. 1881. Vol. liq. Sept. 1889. Reconstructed as Russell Mines Co. Ld. in which company shareholders were entitled to 1 fully-paid share of 5s. for each share of £1 held. Final meeting return regd. 14 Jan. 1890 ....   **1891**

Russia Copper Co. Ld. Regd. 1871. Vol. liq. 3 Aug. 1871. Removed from Register 30 Sept. 1884 ....   ***1884**

Russian & Eastern Agency Ld. Regd. 1912. Vol. liq. (creditors') 25 Apr. 1932. Capital returned to contributories—1⅜d. per share of £1. £99 18s. 10d. was paid into Companies' Liquidation Account. Final meeting return regd. 22 Apr. 1933 ....   **1933**

Russian & English Bank. Inc. Russia 1910. Court Order to wind up Mar. 1932 ....   **1933**

Russian Bank for Foreign Trade. Inc. Russia 1871. Court Order to wind up Feb. 1933 ....   **1933**

Russian Collieries Co. Ld. Regd. 1899 as Russian Collieries & Railway Co. Ld.; name changed May 1899. The property was sold in 1912 to provide payment of 95% of principal and arrears of interest to the prior lien bondholders, 90% of principal and arrears of interest to profit sharing debenture stockholders and about 12% of principal to 1st mortgage debenture holders. Struck off Register 3 Aug. 1928 ....   **1913**

Russian Commercial & Industrial Bank. Inc. Russia 1889. Court Order to wind up Oct. 1922 ....   **1923**

Russian Engineering Co. Ld. Regd. 1897. Vol. liq. Aug. 1910. Removed from Register 1912 ....   **1911**

Russian Estates & Mines Ld. Regd. 1907. Vol. liq. Sept. 1910 for reconstruction as Russian Ventures Ld. in which company shareholders were entitled to 1 share of 5s. (credited with 3s. paid) for each share of £1 held. Removed from Register 1911 ....   **1911**

Russian General Oil Corpn. (Sociéte Général Napthifére Russe), Ld. Regd. 1912. Vol. liq. (members') 27 Apr. 1949. Capital returned to contributories—3s. 11·82d. per share of £1. Court Order to wind up 28 July 1952. Liquidator released 17 July 1963. Struck off Register 1 Sept. 1967 ....   **1965**

Russian Goldfields Ld. Regd. 1912. Struck off Register 11 Sept. 1953 ....   **1935**

Russian Industrial & Mining Co. (1901) Ld. Regd. 1901. Vol. liq. 31 Oct. 1904. Removed from Register 1906   **1905**

Russian Kuban Industrial & Petroleum Co. Ld. Regd. 1910. Properties were in hands of Soviet Government. Struck off Register 31 Dec. 1940 ....   **1941**

Russian Mining Corporation Ld. Regd. 1906. Vol. liq. Jan. 1911. Reconstructed as company of same name. Shareholders were entitled to 5 shares of £1 (credited as fully-paid) in new company for every 4 ordinary shares of £1 (10s. paid) or 4 deferred shares of 1s. held. Removed from Register 1911 ....   **1911**

Russian Mining Corporation Ld. Regd. 1911. Vol. liq. 29 Dec. 1926. Reconstructed as Peregrine Investment Co. Ld., in which company shareholders were entitled to 4 shares of 5s. (credited with 3s. 9d. paid) for each share of £1 held. Final meeting return regd. 27 July 1942..   **1928**

Russian Oil Lands Ld. Regd. 1910. Vol. liq. 15 Jan. 1914. Shareholders were entitled to 1 share of £1 (credited with 16s. paid) in International Oil Lands Ld. for each share of £1 held. Final meeting return regd. 19 July 1916 ....   **1915**

Russian Petroleum and Liquid Fuel Co. Ld. Regd. 1897. Vol. liq. 15 June 1910. Final meeting return regd. 29 Dec. 1920 ....   **1911**

Russian Petroleum Co. Ld. Regd. 1910. A resolution to wind up was passed on 1 Sept. 1919, the undertaking and assets having been acquired by Baku Consolidated Oilfields Ld. Debenture holders received 25% of nominal value of their holdings in fully-paid A preferred ordinary shares of £1 and 50% in fully-paid B ordinary shares of £1. Shareholders were entitled to receive 1 fully-paid B ordinary share for every 20 shares of 10s. held and right to subscribe for 1 A preferred ordinary share (credited with 2s. 6d. paid) for every 8 shares held. Holders of profit-sharing notes received 1 fully-paid B ordinary share for every 100 notes of 5s. held. Struck off Register 13 Dec. 1955...   **1954**

Russian Produce Co. Ld. Regd. 1882. Vol. liq. Oct. 1883. Court Order to continue winding up under supervision Nov. 1883. Final meeting return regd. 12 Apr. 1886 ....   **1884**

Russian (Smieloff) Chain, Anchor & Testing Works Ld. Regd. 1909. Vol. liq. 23 Mar. 1917. No capital was returned to contributories. Struck off Register 21 Feb. 1958 ....   **1959**

Russian Spratt's Patent Ld. Regd. 1891. Vol. liq. 21 Apr. 1896. Removed from Register 1902 ....   **1897**

Russian Tobacco Co. (Societe De Tabacs Russe) Ld. Regd. 1913. Struck off register 28 May 1965 ......   **1961**

Russian Ventures Ld. Regd. 1910. Removed from Register 1913 ....   **1912**

Russo-Asiatic Bank. See Banque Russo-Asiatique.

Russo-Asiatic Consolidated Ld. Regd. 1919. Vol. liq. 20 June 1929. Reconstructed as company of same name. Non-Russian assets were acquired by Mining Trust Ld. Shareholders were entitled to 1 fully-paid share of 2s. 6d. in new company for each share held and 1 fully-paid share of £1 in Mining Trust Ld. for every 8 shares of 2s. 6d. held. Final meeting return regd. 14 Aug. 1931 ....   **1930**

Russo-Asiatic Consolidated Ld. Regd. 1929. Vol. liq. (members') 21 Nov. 1957. Capital returned to contributories—0·3648d. per share (of 2s. 6d.). Final meeting return regd. 10 Oct. 1963 ....   **1964**

Russo-Asiatic Corporation Ld. Regd. 1912. Vol. liq. 19 Dec. 1919. The 816,641 fully-paid shares of Irtysh Corporation Ld. which formed parts of the assets, were distributed in specie to shareholders. Final meeting return regd. 22 Dec. 1920 ....   **1920**

Russo-Canadian Development Corporation Ld. Inc. Canada 1917. Vol. liq. Dec. 1919 for reconstruction as Russo-Asiatic Consolidated Ld. Holders of preferred and ordinary shares of $5 were entitled to 1·05042 and 0·52521 shares of £1 respectively; shareholders who subscribed for shares in Sept. 1918 received an additional 6·642% on the pro rata distribution. **1920**

Rushton-Lister Marine Ld. Regd. 1931. Vol. liq. (members') 29 June 1934. All shares owned by R. A. Lister & Co. Ld. Final meeting return regd. 26 July 1940 ....   **1935**

Ruth Mines Ld. Regd. 1897. Vol. liq. 13 Mar. 1918. Final meeting return regd. 17 Sept. 1919 ....   **1918**

Ruthin & Cerrig-y-Druidion Railway Co. Inc. 1876. Abandoned by Act of 1884 ....   **1885**

Ruthin Castle Ld. Regd. 1913. Vol. liq. (members') 12 Aug. 1954. The undertaking and assets were transferred to Ruthin Castle (Holdings) Ld. Capital returned to contributories—8s. 2¼d. per preference share and 1s. 11¼d. per ordinary share of £1. Final meeting return regd. 12 Mar. 1956........................   **1957**

Ruthin Electric Supply Co. Ld. Regd. 1914. Vol. liq. (members') 16 Mar. 1936. Capital returned to contributories—£5 5s. 0d. per preference share of £5; £2 3s. 7d. per preferred ordinary or ordinary share of £1. Final meeting return regd. 26 Aug. 1936   **1937**

Ryan Nigel Gold Mining & Estate Co. Ld. Inc. Transvaal 1895. London office closed in June 1913   **1914**

Ryde & Newport Railway Co. Inc. by Special Act 1872. By Act of 1887 undertaking was amalgamated into Isle of Wight Central Railway Co. Ordinary and 5% 1st preference shares were converted into ordinary and 5% 1st preference stocks respectively at par; 5% 2nd and 3rd preference shares were converted at par into 5% 2nd preference stock; 5% 4th preference shares were converted into ordinary stock; 5% debentures and temporary debentures received 4% debenture stock (C) **1888**

Ryde Gaslight Co. Inc. by Special Act 1866. Dissolved 1 May 1949, undertaking being vested in Southern Area Gas Board under Gas Act 1948. Holders of securities were entitled to receive, in respect of each £100 unit held, British Gas 3% guaranteed stock 1990—95 as follows:

See Stock Exchange Year-Book.

VOL. FOR

	£	s.	d.	
Ord. stock (5% stand.)	150	0	0	
4% per .deb. stock	102	0	0	1952

Ryde Pier Co. Inc. by Special Act 1812. In 1924 the undertaking and assets were transferred to the Southern Railway Co. Stockholders received £60 5% preferred ordinary and £57 10*s*. deferred ordinary stock of the Railway Company in exchange for every £100 stock held. The Railway Company assumed all liability in respect of this company's £16,000 mortgage debenture bonds **1925**

Ryder (William), Ld. Regd. 1902. Vol. liq. 22 Jan. 1959. Final meeting return regd. 30 Mar. 1962 ..... **1955**

Rye Gas & Coke Co. Ld. Regd. 1954. Dissolved 1 May 1949, undertaking being vested in South Eastern Area Gas Board under Gas Act 1948. Holders of securities were entitled to receive British Gas 3% guaranteed stock 1990—95 as follows:

	£	s.	d.	
Ord. shares (of £1)	2	0	0	
Ord. shares (of £5)	10	0	0	
4½% debs. (of £100)	100	10	0	1952

Ryecroft Mills Co. Ld. Regd. 1920. Vol. liq. (members') 12 Oct. 1939. Capital returned to contributories—14*s*. 6½*d*. per share of £1 (17*s*. 6*d*. paid). Final meeting return regd. 12 Apr. 1940 ..... **1940**

Ryland (Dan) Ld. *See* Rylands Glass & Engineering Co. Ld.

Rylands Concession Ld. Regd. 1889. Vol. liq. 8 Oct. 1914. Final meeting return regd. 13 Jan. 1920 ..... **1915**

Ryland's Electro-Plating Co. Ld. Regd. 1873. Vol. liq. (members') 15 Sept. 1933. Capital returned to contributories—£2 19*s*. 5⅛*d*. per share of £10. £14 17*s*. 1*d*. was paid into Companies' Liquidation Account. Final meeting return regd. 8 Dec. 1933 **1934**

Rylands' Glass & Engineering Co. Ld. Regd. 1888 as Dan Ryland Ld.; name changed 1897. Receiver appointed 13 Feb. 1926. Struck off Register Jan. 1931 ..... **1931**

Rymer (C. F.) Ld. Regd. 1912. Receiver for 1st debenture holders appointed 10 July 1924; ceased to act 11 Oct. 1927. Assets realised insufficient to pay claims of debenture holders. Struck off Register Dec. 1931 ..... **1932**

S

S. A. I. (Leith) Ld. Regd. Edinburgh 1896 as J. & J. Cunningham Ld.; name changed June 1943. Vol. liq. (members') 30 June 1951. Final meeting return regd. 28 May 1953 ..... **1950**

S. A. M. Mining Syndicate Ld. Regd. 1926. Struck off Register Apr. 1938 ..... **1939**

S. A. Minerals Syndicate Ld. Regd. 1905. Vol. liq. Mar. 1909. Removed from Register 1910 ..... **1910**

S. A. Minerals Syndicate Ld. Regd. 1905. Removed from Register 1910 ..... **1910**

S. A. Proprietary Ld. Regd. 1903. Vol. liq. 14 Jan. 1925. Undertaking was acquired by South American Proprietary Ld. Final meeting return regd. 14 June 1927 ..... **1916**

S. A. Prospecting & Concessions Syndicate Ld. Regd. 1905. Vol. liq. 28 Feb. 1919. Court Order to continue winding up under supervision 8 Apr. 1919. Final meeting return regd. 2 Mar. 1922 ..... **1919**

S. & M. Ld. Regd. 1918 as Maxsons Ld.; name changed Apr. 1923. Vol. liq. 28 Nov. 1928. Final meeting return regd. 26 Nov. 1931 ..... **1934**

S. & M. (1928) Ld. Regd. 1928. Vol. liq. (members') 16 Apr. 1934. Undertaking and assets were acquired by Swears & Wells Ld. in which company shareholders were entitled to 1 ordinary share of £1 (credited as fully-paid) for every 20 ordinary shares of 1*s*. held or 1 preference of £1 for every 2 preference shares of 10*s*. held. Final meeting return regd. 1 Aug. 1935 **1935**

S. B. A. Properties Ld. Regd. 1929 as South Bukeru Areas Ld.; name changed July 1959. Winding-up Order 25 Apr. 1967. Struck off Register 20 June 1975 ..... **1962**

S. C. T. Ld. Regd. 1888 as Sun Investment & Trust Ld.; name changed to Sun Investment Trust Ld., in July, 1888, to Stock Conversion & Investment Trust Ld., in Feb. 1889, and as above in Jan. 1932. Vol. liq. (members') 26 Jan. 1932. Undertaking and assets were acquired by Stock Conversion & Investment Trust Ld. Holders of stock and shares were entitled to shares in the new company as follows—5 fully-paid ordinary shares for each £3 preference stock held; 2 fully-paid ordinary shares for every 9 annuity shares held; 9 fully-paid ordinary shares for each £10 ordinary stock held; and 1 fully-paid 2nd preference share for every £1 paid up by ordinary shareholders in the winding up of the company *plus* 1 fully-paid ordinary share for every £10 so paid up. Holders of debenture stock were entitled to £100 4% debenture stock for each £100 stock held *plus* 50 1st preference and 50 ordinary shares for each £100 5½% participating convertible 15-year debenture stock held, 25 1st preference shares for each £100 5% debenture stock held, 31 1st preference shares for each £100 5¼% debenture stock held and 37 1st preference shares for each £100 5¼% debenture stock held. Final meeting return regd. 31 May 1934 ..... **1932**

S. D. H. Pianos Ld. Regd. 1928. Vol. liq. (creditors') 21 Apr. 1933. Assets realised insufficient to pay creditors in full. Final meeting return regd. 25 July 1935 ..... **1934**

S. Gibson & Sons Ld. *See* Gibson (S.) & Sons Ld.

S. G. Minerals Syndicate Ld. Regd. 1906. Struck off Register 3 Oct. 1941 ..... **1942**

S. I. Holdings Ld. *See* Midland Holdings Ld.

S. R. Anthracite Collieries Ld. Regd. 1914. Vol. liq. (creditors') 16 Mar. 1933. Undertaking was acquired in 1932 by New Blaenhirwaun Anthracite Collieries Ld. No funds were available for debenture holders, unsecured creditors or shareholders. Final meeting return regd. 25 Feb. 1935 ..... **1940**

S. T. D. Motors Ld. Regd. 1905 as A. Darracq & Co. (1905) Ld.; name changed 30 Aug. 1920. Vol. liq. (members') 15 May 1936. Capital returned to contributories—11·0375*d*. in the £ to holders of 8% non-cumulative participating preference stock. £169 14*s*. 5*d*. was paid into Companies' Liquidation Account. Final meeting return regd. 17 Feb. 1938 **1937**

S. W. & S. Development Co. Ld. Regd. 1909 as Halesowen Lighting & Traction Co. Ld.; name changed to Shropshire, Worcestershire & Staffordshire Electric Power Development Co. Ld. in Aug. 1929 and as above in Oct. 1930. Vol. liq. (members') 23 Nov. 1951. Final meeting return regd. 21 Aug. 1952 ..... **1937**

S. X. B. Motors Ld. Regd. 1905 as Sunbeam Motor Car Co. Ld.; name changed 17 Apr. 1936. Undertaking and assets were acquired by Motor Industries Ld. (later Sunbeam Motors Ld.). 5% debenture holders were entitled to 17*s*. 5*d*. in £ in full discharge. Struck off Register 23 Sept. 1938 ..... **1939**

Sabaki Cotton & Rubber Co. Ld. Regd. 1906 as Sabaki Syndicate Ld.; name changed Nov. 1908. Struck off Register 8 Mar. 1935 ..... **1936**

Sabi Ophir Mining Co. Ld. Regd. 1889. Vol. liq. 3 Oct. 1899. The property was sold in 1899 to Bartisol Gold Mining Co. Ld. for £10,000 in cash and £100,000 in fully-paid shares. Final meeting return regd. 16 Apr. 1902 ..... **1900**

Sabi (Rhodesia) Gold Mining Co. Ld. Regd. 1899. Undertaking and assets were acquired by Rhodesia Consolidated Ld. in which company shareholders were entitled to 1 share of 10*s*. (credited with 7*s*. paid) for each share of £1 held. Removed from Register 1906 ..... **1904**

Sabie Transvaal Gold Mining Co. Ld. Inc. Transvaal 1923. Vol. liq. Dec. 1930 ..... **1931**

Sabiwa Central Gold Mining Co. Ld. Regd. 1902. Vol. liq. 9 Jan. 1905. Undertaking and assets were acquired by Rice-Hamilton Exploration Syndicate Ld. in which company shareholders were entitled to 1 share of £1 for every 3 shares of £1 held. Removed from Register 1907 ..... **1905**

Sabiwa Gold Mines Ld. Regd. 1924. Vol. liq. 10 Jan. 1929. Final meeting return regd. 15 July 1931 ..... **1929**

Sabiwa Proprietary Mines Ld. Regd. 1901. Vol. liq. Jan. 1905. Undertaking and assets were acquired by Rice-Hamilton Exploration Syndicate Ld. in which company shareholders were entitled to 1 share of £1 for every 4 shares of £1 held. Removed from Register 1907 ..... **1905**

Sablas-North Borneo-Rubber Ld. Regd. 1910. Vol. liq. 18 Jan. 1937. Undertaking was acquired by Kimanis Rubber Ld. in which company shareholders were entitled to 1·24 shares of 2*s*. (credited as fully-paid) for each share of £1 held. The debenture stock was repaid at 102½% in Jan. 1937. £198 2*s*. 1*d*. was paid into Companies' Liquidation Account in respect of unclaimed dividends and fractional warrants. Final meeting return regd. 15 Dec. 1937 **1937**

Sabrang Rubber Estates Ld. Regd. 1920. All capital acquired by Straits Rubber Co. Ld. Vol. liq. (members') 30 June 1961. Final meeting return regd. 26 Sept. 1962 ..... **1961**

Saccharin Corporation Ld. Regd. 1897. Vol. liq. Jan. 1909 for reconstruction as company of same name. Holders of 6% debenture stock received £40,000 debentures, 15,678 ordinary shares of £1 and 62,712 preference shares of £1 in new company. Holders of shares of £5 were entitled to an equal number of

**See Stock Exchange Year-Book.*

VOL. FOR

shares of £1 in new company. Removed from Register 1913 1909

Sacke Estates & Mining Co. Ld. Inc. Transvaal 1895. Vol. liq. Apr. 1924. Shareholders received a first and final distribution of 6s. 5¼d. per share of £1 in June 1924. Assets were acquired by General Mining & Finance Corporation Ld. 1925

Sadler & Barnes Ld. Regd. 1930 as Stevensons Ld.; name changed Jan. 1937. Vol. liq. (members') 9 June 1937. Undertaking was acquired by Thomas Blackburn & Sons Ld. Capital returned to contributories—£68 14s. Final meeting return regd. 1 Dec. 1939 1946

Safetex Safety Glass Ld. Regd. 1928. Court Order to wind up 15 Dec. 1930. Struck off Register 15 June 1937 1938

Safety Automatic Railway Couplings Co. Ld. Regd. 1886. Removed from Register 1906 1890

Safety Bioscope Supplies Co. Ld. Regd. 1910. Vol. liq. 11 June 1913. Reconstructed as company of same name. Shareholders were entitled to 1 share of 1s. (credited with 6d. paid) for every 2 shares of 5s. held. Original shareholders were entitled to 1 fully-paid share of 1s. for every 2 shares held in satisfaction of guaranteed dividend. Final meeting return regd. 31 Mar. 1915 1914

Safety Blasting Powder Co. Ld. Regd. 1881. Struck off Register 20 Mar. 1906 1887

Safety Explosives Ld. Regd. 1901. Court Order to wind up 5 Aug. 1902. Removed from Register 1910 1903

Saffell & Martin Ld. Regd. 1926. Vol. liq. 2 Mar. 1934. Final meeting return regd. 18 Dec. 1942 1935

Sagar (W. & J.) (Holdings) Ld. Regd. 1919 as W. & J. Sagar Ld.; name changed 1961. Om 3 July 1970 it was stated that the main operating subsidiary was being placed in liquidation and that it was unlikely that there would be any residue on the shares. Dissolved 20 Jan. 1983 1975–6

Sagga Rubber Co. Ld. Regd. 1904. Vol. liq. 8 Apr. 1981. Final meeting return regd. 5 Nov. 1981 1972

Saguenay Pulp & Power Co. Undertaking and assets were acquired in 1925 by Quebec Pulp & Paper Mills Ld. 1927

Sahang Rubber Estates Ld. Regd. 1909. Vol. liq. 17 June 1915. Reconstructed as company of same name. Shareholders were entitled to 1 share of £1 (credited with 16s. paid) in new company for each share of £1 held. Final meeting return regd. 17 Jan. 1916 1916

Sahang Rubber Estates Ld. Regd. 1915. Vol. liq. 17 Oct. 1918. Reconstructed as company of same name. Shareholders were entitled to 1 share of £1 (credited with 10s. paid) in new company for each share of £1 held. The debenture holders were entitled to an equal amount of debentures in new company. Final meeting return regd. 21 Mar. 1919 1919

Sahang Rubber Estates Ld. Regd. 1918. The claims of the debenture holders were satisfied. Struck off Register 1924 1924

Sahang Rubber Selections, Ld. Regd. 1935. Vol. liq. (members') 29 Dec. 1947. Undertaking and assets acquired by Kapoewas Rubber Co. Ld. [later Pritchard Cleaners (Holdings) Ld.] Shareholders entitled to 1 fully-paid share in that company for each share held. Final meeting return regd. 17 Feb. 1949 1950

Saikowah (Assam) Tea Co. Ld. Regd. 1926. Vol. liq. (members') 22 Jan. 1943. Capital returned to contributories—preference—£1 per share (of £1); ordinary—31s. 2d. per share (of £1). £340 9s. 7d. was paid into Companies' Liquidation Account. Final meeting return regd. 20 Apr. 1951 1952

St. Abb's Whaling Ld. Regd. Edinburgh 1914. Court Order to wind up Oct. 1915. Final meeting return regd. Mar. 1930 1916

St. Agnes Consolidated Mines Ld. Regd. 1909. Court Order to wind up 30 Jan. 1917. Struck off Register 1 July 1921 1917

St. Agnes Gold Reefs Ld. Regd. 1895. Vol. liq. 23 Sept. 1898. Final meeting return regd. 23 June 1904 1899

St. Albans Gas Co. Established 1852; inc. by Special Act 1870. Under Special Order of 1929 the undertaking was acquired by Watford & St. Albans Gas Co. in which company holders of consolidated stock were entitled to £133 B consolidated stock for each £100 held; holders of 5% debenture stock were entitled to an equivalent amount of 5% debenture stock in the acquiring company, and the liability in respect of the mortgage bonds was taken over by the acquiring company 1930

St. Albans Waterworks Co. Inc. by Special Act 1865. Under provisions of the Colne Valley Water Order 1959 the undertaking vested in the Colne Valley Water Co. from 1 July 1959. Contributories received stock in the Colne Valley Company in exchange for

VOL. FOR

their holdings at the following rates—£10 5% redeemable preference stock 1972 per £10 5% redeemable preference stock 1972; £10 4% redeemable preference stock 1979 per £10 4% redeemable preference stock 1979; £12 10s. 4% consolidated preference stock per £10 5% new preference stock; £25 4% consolidated preference stock per 10% original ordinary share of £10, and £17 10s. 4% consolidated preference stock per 7% new ordinary share of £10. The outstanding debenture stocks became debenture stocks of the Colne Valley Company. Company was Dissolved on 26 Oct. 1959 1960

St. Andrews Gas Co. Ld. Regd. in Edinburgh 1910. Dissolved 1 May 1949, undertaking being vested in Scottish Area Gas Board under Gas Act 1948. Holders of ordinary shares (of £1) were entitled to receive £1 13s. 6d. British Gas 3% guaranteed stock 1990–95 for each share held 1952

St. Anne's-on-Sea Palace Cinema & Cafes Ld. Regd. 1922. Vol. liq. 27 Oct. 1925. Undertaking was acquired by Blackpool Tower Co. Ld. Final meeting return regd. 25 Feb. 1926 1926

St. Anne's-on-the-Sea Gas Co. Regd. as limited 1875. Inc. by Special Act 1898. Undertaking transferred to St. Anne's-on-the-Sea U.D.C. on 13 Dec. 1920 for £4,000 cash, the assumption of the mortgage debt and the issue of mortgages of the council in exchange for shares as follows—for each 10% preference share of £10, £20; each 7% preference share of £10, £14; each 15% ordinary share of £10, £23; and each 5% ordinary share of £10, £11 10s. 1923

St. Anne's Well Brewery Co. Ld. Regd. 1889. Vol. liq. (members') 1 Apr. 1960. Undertaking and assets were taken over by Norman & Pring Ld. from 31 Mar. 1960. Preference shareholders received 11 6% preference shares of £1 in Norman & Pring Ld. for every share held and debenture stockholders received a like amount of 5% redeemable debenture stock of Norman, & Pring Ld. £85 2s. 4d. was paid into Companies' Liquidation Account in respect of unclaimed preference dividends and interest on debenture stock. Final meeting return regd. 23 May 1960 1961

St. Antonio (Para) Rubber Estates Ld. Regd. 1910. Vol. liq. 3 Oct. 1912. Final meeting return regd. 3 Jan. 1914 1913

St. Asaph Gas Co. Ld. Regd. 1859. Dissolved 1 May 1949, undertaking being vested in Wales Area Gas Board under Gas Act 1948. Holders of securities were entitled to receive British Gas 3% guaranteed stock 1990–95 as follows:

	£	s.	d.
Ord. shares (of £2 10s.)	2	15	0
Ord. shares (of £5)	5	10	0	1952

St. Asaph Zinc, Lead & Baryta Co. Ld. Regd. 1890 as St. Asaph Iron, Lead & Baryta Co. Ld. Struck off Register 3 Feb. 1933 1933

St. Augustine Diamond Mining Co. Ld. Regd. 1896. Vol. liq. 20 Mar. 1899. The machinery sold by receiver for debenture holders realised insufficient to meet their claims. Final meeting return regd. 1 July 1921 1900

St. Augustine Ld. Regd. 1889. Vol. liq. 29 Oct. 1891. Reconstructed as St. Augustine Mine Ld. in which company shareholders were entitled to 1 share of £1 (credited with 18s. paid) for each share of £1 held. Final meeting return regd. 1 Sept. 1892 1894

St. Augustine Mine Ld. Regd. 1891. Removed from Register 1907 1896

St. Augustine's Diamond Mine Ld. Regd. 1885. Vol. liq. Oct. 1889. Reconstructed as St. Austine Ld. in which company shareholders were entitled to 1 share of £1 (credited with 17s. paid) for each share of £1 held. Final meeting return regd. 17 June 1890 1891

St. Augustine's Parade Hippodrome, Bristol Ld. See Bristol Hippodrome Ld.

St. Austell & District Electric Lighting & Power Co. Ld. Regd. 1900. Dissolved 1 Apr. 1948. undertaking being vested in British (later Central) Electricity Authority and South Western Area Board under Electricity Act 1947. Holders of securities were entitled to receive British Electricity 3% guaranteed stock (1968—73) as follows in respect of each £1 unit of capital held:

	£	s.	d.
7% preference stock	1	14	3
4½% preference stock	1	4	0
Ordinary stock	2	10	9	1949

St. Austell China-Clay Works Ld. Regd. 1910. Receiver appointed in Nov. 1921. Struck off Register 1927. 1924

St. Austell Gas Co. Ld. Regd. 1870. Dissolved 1 May 1949, undertaking being vested in South Western Area Gas Board under Gas Act 1948. Holders of securities were entitled to receive British Gas 3% guaranteed stock 1990—95 as follows in respect of

VOL. FOR

each £2 unit, unless otherwise stated, of security held:

	£	s.	d.	
Old ord. shares	3	8	0	
New ord. shares	2	16	0	
4½% red. pref. shares	2	0	1	
4% red. debs. (1958) (of £100)	101	10	0	
4% red. debs. (of £100)	100	0	0	1952

St. Austell Valleys Railway & Dock Co. Inc. by Special Act 1887. Undertaking abandoned 1892 ... 1893

St. Benet Property Co. Ld. Regd. 1927. Vol. liq. (members') 3 Nov. 1937. All shares owned by Waddon Investments Ld. Final meeting return regd. 7 Mar. 1938 ... 1938

St. Blazey Gas Co. Ld. Regd. 1892. Dissolved 1 May 1949, undertaking being vested in South Western Area Gas Board under Gas Act 1948. Holders of securities were entitled to receive British Gas 3% guaranteed stock 1990—95 as follows in respect of each £1 unit, unless otherwise stated, of security held:

	£	s.	d.	
Ord. shares	1	12	3	
6% pref. shares	1	6	8	
4½% red. debs. (of £100)	100	0	0	
3½% debs. (of £100)	100	0	0	1952

St. Breward Syndicate Ld. Regd. 1908. Struck off Register 1921. ... 1911

St. Christopher Insurance Co. Ld. Regd. 1924. Vol. liq. Feb. 1929. Capital returned to contributories—19*s.* 1*d.* per share of £1 at Dec. 1929; further payments (if any) not known. Final meeting return regd. 14 Mar. 1930 ... 1930

St. Clement Investment Trust (Jersey) Ld. Inc. in Jersey 1922 as St. Clement's Housing Association Ld.; name changed 1965. Company was merged with Jersey General Investment Trust Ld. in 1968, ordinary shareholders receiving 23 ordinary shares of £1 of that company for every 25 ordinary shares held and preference shareholders 1 5¼% preference share of £1 for every preference share held. Vol. liq. (members') 3 Mar. 1969 ... 1971

St. Clement's House, Ld. Regd. 1910. Vol. liq. (members') 27 July 1965. Final meeting return regd. 27 Apr. 1966 ... 1911

St. Clement's Housing Association Ld. *See* Clement Investment Trust (Jersey) Ld.

St. Clements Investment Trust Ld. Regd. 1963. Vol. liq. (members') 14 Jan. 1966. Capital returned to contributories—5*s.* 5·76*d.* per share of 5*s.* £12 was paid into Companies' Liquidation Account in respect of unclaimed dividends. Final meeting return regd. 27 Sept. 1972 ... 1973-4

St. Cue Development Co. Ld. Regd. 1894 Vol. liq. 3 Oct. 1895. Final meeting return regd. 5 Jan. 1898 ... 1896

St. Cuthbert's Paper Works Ld. Regd. 1896 as Pirie, Wyatt & Co. Ld.; name changed June 1923. Vol. liq. Mar. 1931. Dissolved before 1938 ... 1932

St. David's Gold & Copper Mines Ld. Regd. 1898. Reconstructed as St. David's Gold Mines (1903) Ld. in which company shareholders were entitled to 1 share of 5*s.* (credited with 4*s.* paid) for each share of 5*s.* held. Removed from Register 1905 ... 1908

St. David's Gold & Copper Mines Ld. Regd. 1903. Removed from Register 1905 ... 1908

St. David's Gold Mines (1903) Ld. Regd. 1903. Struck off Register 1916 ... 1912

St. David's Mining Development Co. Ld. Regd. 1898. Removed from Register 1909 ... 1908

St. David's Railway Co. Inc. by Special Act 1898. Authorised to be abandoned by Act of 1900 ... 1901

St. David's Water & Gas Co. Inc. by Special Act 1899. A receiver was appointed on behalf of debenture holders in Aug. 1910 ... 1911

St. Denis Gold Mine Ld. Regd. 1895. Vol. liq. 5 Jan. 1897. Final meeting return regd. 25 Apr. 1898 ... 1897

St. Dennis Mining Co. Ld. Regd. 1902. Vol. liq. Mar. 1907. Removed from Register 1909 ... 1908

St. Ermins Hotel Ld. Regd. 1903. Vol. liq. 12 Feb. 1920. Capital returned to contributories—£2 5*s.* per share of £1; further payments (if any) not known. Final meeting return regd. 8 June 1926 ... 1921

St. Etienne Brewery Co. Ld. Regd. 1890. Court Order to continue winding up under supervision 20 Feb. 1893. Removed from Register 1907 ... 1894

St. George & Moonstone Gold Mines Ld. Inc. Queensland 1913. Vol. liq. Aug. 1918 ... 1919

St. George (Coolgardie) Proprietary Gold Mines Ld. Regd. Edinburgh 1895. Vol. liq. Dec. 1896. Final meeting return regd. 29 July 1899 ... 1897

St. George Gold Mining Co. Ld. Regd. 1886. Vol. liq. 28 June 1894. Reconstructed as company of same name. Shareholders were entitled to 1 fully-paid share of 5*s.* and 4 shares of 5*s.* (credited with 3*s.* 9*d.* paid) for each ordinary or preference share of £1 held. Final meeting return regd. 13 Aug. 1900 ... 1897

St. George Gold Mining Co. Ld. Regd. 1894. Vol. liq. 1 Feb. 1897. Final meeting return regd. 1 May 1903 ... 1907

St. George (Queensland) Gold Mining Co. Ld. Regd. 1890. Vol. liq. 20 Aug. 1891. Final meeting return regd. 13 Jan. 1895 ... 1892

St. George's Coal & Estate Co. Ld. Inc. Natal 1897. Vol. liq. Apr. 1913. Assets were transferred to Dundee Coal Co. Ld. (later Coal By-Products & Investments Ld.) in which company shareholders were entitled to 1 share of £1 (credited as fully-paid) for every 2 shares of £1 held ... 1914

St. George's Engineering Co. Ld. Regd. 1894. Vol. liq. 3 June 1897. Taken over by New Rapid Cycle Co. Ld. Final meeting return regd. 6 Oct. 1897 ... *1898

St. George's Hall Co. Ld. Regd. 1857. Vol. liq. 27 Nov. 1925. Final meeting return regd. 26 July 1926 ... *1926

St. Gerera Development Co. Ld. Regd. 1899. Removed from Register 1905 ... 1904

St. Helens & District Tramways Co. Inc. 1879. In liquidation in 1890 ... 1890

St. Helens & Wigan Railway Co. *See* Liverpool, St. Helens & South Lancashire Railway Co.

St. Helens Bulawayo Association Ld. Regd. 1894. Reconstructed 1904 as Bulawayo Commonage Claims Ld. in which company shareholders were entitled to 1 share of £1 (credited with 15*s.* paid) for each share of £1 held. Removed from Register 1905 ... 1905

St. Helens Cable Co. Ld. Regd. 1899. Vol. liq. 21 Dec. 1905. Final meeting return regd. 7 Dec. 1908 ... *1907

St. Helens Coal & Clay Co. Ld. Regd. 1884. Court Orders: to wind up 24 May 1886; to dissolve 13 June 1894 ... *1887

Saint Helen's Colliery & Brickworks Co. Ld. Regd. 1876. Properties vested in National Coal Board 1 Jan. 1947. A subsidiary of United Steel Companies Ld. Vol. liq. (members') 6 Aug. 1954. Final meeting return regd. 10 Oct. 1955 ... 1953

St. Helens Copper Co. Ld. Regd. 1866. Removed from Register 1905 ... *1905

St. Helen's Development Syndicate Ld. Regd. 1894. Removed from Register 1904 ... 1903

St. Helens Electric Lighting Co. Ld. Regd. 1900. Vol. liq. 12 Nov. 1926. Final meeting return regd. 26 Mar. 1927 ... 1927

St. Helen's Petroleum Co. Ld. Regd. 1913. Vol. liq. (members') 1 May 1939. All shares held by Kern Oil Co. Ld. Final meeting return regd. 15 July 1939 ... 1940

St. Helens Theatre, Ld. Regd. 1900. Vol. liq. (members') 26 Apr. 1961. Final meeting return regd. 20 May 1963 ... 1911

St. Ivel Ld. *See* Investments (Yeovil) Ld.

St. Ives (Banket) Exploration Co. Ld. Regd. 1909. Vol. liq. 6 Nov. 1914. Final meeting return regd. 22 May 1915 ... 1915

St. Ives Consolidated Mines Ld. Regd. 1908. Vol. liq. 16 Mar. 1915. Liquidator released 31 Jan. 1921. Struck off Register 20 Mar. 1925 ... 1915

St. Ives (Hunts) Gas Co. Ld. Regd. 1878; statutory powers 1889 and subsequently. Dissolved 1 May 1949, undertaking being vested in Eastern Area Gas Board under Gas Act 1948. Holders of securities were entitled to receive British Gas 3% guaranteed stock 1990—95 as follows in respect of each £10 unit, unless otherwise stated, of security held:

	£	s.	d.	
Orig. ord. shares (10% stand.)	9	0	0	
Ord. shares (7% stand.)	6	10	0	
5% pref. shares	11	4	0	
6% pref. shares	13	4	0	
7% pref. shares	15	0	0	
4½% debs. (of £100)	100	10	0	1952

St. Ives Rubber Estates Ld. Regd. 1926. Vol. liq. 26 Oct. 1928. Undertaking and assets were acquired by Amherst Estates (Selangor) Rubber Co. Ld. in which company shareholders were entitled to 1 share of 2*s.* (credited as fully-paid) for every 2 shares of 2*s.* held. Final meeting return regd. 26 July 1929 ... 1929

St. Jacobs Oil Ld. Regd. 1901. Vol. liq. 30 Aug. 1913. Capital returned to contributories—3*s.* 9*d.* per share; further payments (if any) not known. Final meeting return regd. 28 May 1914 ... 1914

St. James & Pall Mall Electric Light Co. Ld. Regd. 1888. Undertaking was acquired in 1937 by Central London Electricity Ld. Holders of preference shares and ordinary stock (London Associated Electricity Undertaking Ld.) received 116,667 6% preference and 770,500 ordinary fully-paid shares in purchasing company of £1 respectively. Dissolved under Sec. 154 of Companies Act 1929 ... 1938

St. James (Bristol) Trust Ld. *See* Mendip Investment Co. Ld.

**See Stock Exchange Year-Book.*

VOL. FOR

St. James' Court Estate Ld. Regd. 2 Dec. 1927.
Dissolved 8 Apr. 1979 .... **1969**

St. James's Hall Co. Ld. Regd. 1881. Undertaking and assets were acquired by P. & R. Syndicate Ld. Capital returned to contributories—£5 per preference share of £10; 5s. per ordinary share of £10; further payments (if any) not known. Removed from Register 1904 .... **1904**

St. James's Investment Trust Ld. *See* Michalinos and General Investment Co. Ld.

St. James's Restaurant Ld. Regd. 1896. The properties and goodwill were sold to P. & R. Syndicate Ld. for £75,801. Capital returned to contributories—£5 per preference share; 7s. 8¼d. per ordinary share; further payments (if any) not known. Removed from Register 1906 .... **1906**

St. John & Maine Railway Co. Inc. 1878. Undertaking acquired by Canadian Pacific Railway Co. in 1892. Shareholders were entitled to £40 New Brunswick Railway 4% consolidated debenture stock for each £100 share held. Debenture stock was exchanged at par for that of the New Brunswick Railway **1893**

St. John & Quebec Railway Co. Inc. New Brunswick by Special Act 1910. By Act of 1930 the undertaking was acquired by Canadian National Railways from the Province of New Brunswick for $6,000,000; of this, $2,727,977 was paid by the assumption by the purchasing company of the liability in respect of the 4% debenture stock, and the balance ($3,272,023) was to be applied in repaying the debentures (forming the remaining funded debt of the company) falling due from time to time up to 1958 .... **1931**

St. John del Rey Mining Co. Ld. Est. 1830. Regd. 1858. Vol. liq. 9 Feb. 1887 for reconstruction under same name. Stockholders were entitled to 1 share of £1 (credited 15s. paid) in new company for every £1 stock held. The 7% debentures were taken over by the new company. Struck off Register 29 July 1902 **1888**

St. John D'el Rey Mining Company p.l.c. Regd. 24 July 1888 and re-registered as public limited company 1982. Dissolved 27 Dec. 1988. Management and control transferred to USA in May 1960. Following 1971 merger of interests with Companhia Auxiliar de Empresas de Mineracao CAEMI, assets consisted principally of shares of Mineracoes Brasileiras Reunidas SA-MBR. Acquired by offer of Sept. 1986 of $27 cash for each ordinary share by CAEMI Overseas Ld. **1987–8**

St. John Mines (Colorado) Ld. Regd. 1913. Struck off Register Apr. 1930. .... **1931**

St. John's Gas Co. Ld. Regd. 1879. Struck off Register 1925 .... **1904**

St. Kew Prospecting Syndicate Ld. Regd. 1894. Vol. liq. 3 June 1898. Final meeting return regd. 22 June 1900 **1899**

St. Kitts (London) Sugar Factory Ld. Regd. 1925. Dissolved 22 Jan. 1983 ....**1979–80**

St. Lawrence Timber (Pulp and Steamship) Co. Ld. Regd. 1916. Vol. liq. (members') 28 May 1943. Capital returned to contributories—16s. 5⅜d. per preference share of £1. Final meeting return regd. 27 Dec. 1944. .... **1945**

St. Louis & San Francisco Railroad Co. Organised Missouri 1896. Reorganised 1916 as St. Louis-San Francisco Railway Co. Holders of securities were entitled to securities in new company as follows:
For every $100 held

*1st prefd. ....{ $50 5% prior lien mort. bds. / $100 common stock

*2nd prefd. ....{ $50 5% prior lien mort. bds. / $90 common stock

*Common ....{ $50 5% prior lien mort. bds. / $82 common stock

Refdg. mort. bds.{ $75 4% p. lien mort. bds. A / $25 6% Adj. mort. bds. A

Gen. lien bds. {$25 4% p. lien mort. bds. A / $25 6% Adj. mort. bds. A / $50 6% Inc. mort. bds. / $3·3 Adj. mort. bds.

6% 1st. mort { $125 4% prior lien bds. A / gold bds. ....{ $12·5 cash

* After payment of $50 per share of $100. The remaining funded debt was taken over by new company **1917**

St. Louis, Arkansas & Texas Railway Co. Inc. Texas 1886. Reorganised 1891 as St. Louis Southwestern Railway Co. Holders of capital stock were entitled to common stock; holders of 6% 1st mortgage gold certificates were entitled to 1st mortgage certificates in respect of capital and preferred stock in respect of arrears of interest; holders of 6% 2nd mortgage gold certificates were entitled to preferred stock **1891**

St. Louis Fur Trading Co. Ld. Regd. 1929. Vol. liq. (members') 25 Apr. 1932. Direct controlling interest

VOL. FOR

owned by Bernstein (Wm.) (Furriers) Ld. Capital returned to contributories—10s. per share of £1. Final meeting return regd. 26 June 1933 .... **1932**

St. Louis, Iron Mountain & Southern Railway Co. Properties acquired in 1917 by Missouri Pacific Railroad Co. which took over the funded debt except equipment obligations, which were repaid in cash, and $4,715,000 6% 1st and refunding mortgage bonds in hands of the public, who were entitled to $4,383,750 5% 1st and refunding mortgage bonds of that company in exchange **1917**

St. Louis Merchants Bridge Terminal Railway Co. Organised Missouri 1887. The 1st mortgage 5% gold bonds were redeemed at par on 1 Oct. 1930 ...... **1930**

St. Louis, Springfield & Peoria Railroad. Inc. Illinois 1909. Undertaking was acquired in 1923 by Illinois Traction Co. [later Liquidating Railway Corporation] which company assumed liability for 1st and refunding mortgage bonds. These bonds were redeemed 1 Dec. 1939 by Illinois Terminal Rail Road Co. **1923**

St Louis Terminal Cupples Station & Property Co. Organised Missouri 1897. The outstanding 4½% 1st mortgage gold bonds were redeemed at par on 1 June 1917. .... **1916**

St. Louis Watkins & Gulf Rail Road Co. Organised Louisiana 1902. Practically all the shares (of $20) and bonds held in England were repaid in cash in 1905—the former at $4 per share and the latter at par **1905**

St. Lucia Central Sugar Factory Co. Ld. Regd. 1874. Property was foreclosed in Dec. 1894 and subsequently sold by mortgagees. Removed from Register 1897 .... **1898**

St. Margarets Gas Co. Ld. Regd. 1898. Dissolved 1 May 1949, undertaking being vested in Eastern Area Gas Board under Gas Act 1948. Holders of 4½% red. debs. were entitled to receive, in respect of each £100 unit held, £100 10s. British Gas 3% guaranteed stock 1990—95 .... **1952**

St. Martin Preserving Co. Ld. Regd. 1927 as Brauston Artificial Silk Co. Ld.; name changed Nov. 1937. Receiver discharged Dec. 1974. As at 30 July 1975 debenture holder not repaid in full **1976-7**

St. Mary Abbots Investments Ld. Regd. 1956. Vol. liq. (creditors') 17 Mar. 1977. The outstanding 7% 1st mortgage debenture stock 1988–93 was redeemed on 29 June 1979. No capital returned to contributories. Final meeting return regd. 14 Aug. 1980 .... **1980–1**

St. Mary Steamship Co. Ld. Regd. 1919. Struck off Register Feb. 1935. .... **1935**

St. Mary's Lead Works Ld. Regd. 1899. Vol. liq. 6 June 1908. Final meeting return regd. 28 Jan. 1928 ...... **1909**

St. Maurice Power Co. Ld. Inc. Canada 1921. Business and assets were acquired by Shawinigan Water & Power Co. Shareholders were entitled to 2 shares of no par value in acquiring company for each share of $100 held or $175 per share. The 1st mortgage 30-year 6½% sinking fund debenture stock and 1st mortgage 30-year 6½% sinking fund gold bonds were repaid at 107¾% on 1 Aug. 1928 .... **1929**

St. Maurice Valley Corporation. Inc. Quebec 1925. Undertaking and assets were acquired by Consolidated Paper Corporation Ld., in which company shareholders were entitled to 1½ shares of no par value for each preference share of $100, or every 20 preference shares of $5 or 6 common shares of no par value held. Holders of registered debenture stock were entitled to £20 1st mortgage sterling debenture stock and 1 share of no par value in the acquiring company for every £20 stock held; holders of bonds were entitled to $100 1st mortgage bonds and 1 share for every $100 bond (Series A or B) held **1932**

St. Michael's Gas Co. Ld. Regd. 1881. Removed from Register 1905 .... **1886**

St. Neots Gas & Coke Co. Inc. by Deed of Settlement 1846; statutory powers 1883 and subsequently. Dissolved 1 May 1949, undertaking being vested in Eastern Area Gas Board under Gas Act 1948. Holders of securities were entitled to receive, in respect of each £10 unit held, British Gas 3% guaranteed stock 1990—95 as follows:

	£	s.	d.
Orig. shares (10% stand.)	22	0	0
New ord. shares (7% stand.)	16	0	0

.... **1952**

St. Neots Paper Mill Co., Ld. *See* N.P.M. Co., Ld.

St. Neots Water Co. Inc. 1897. Court Order to wind up 25 Apr. 1906. .... **1907**

St. Pancras Garage Co. Ld. Regd. 1910. Receiver appointed 31 Jan. 1914; ceased to act 31 Aug. 1915. Vol. liq. 11 Mar. 1914. Final meeting return regd. 30 June 1917 .... ***1915**

St. Patrick Gold Mine Ld. Regd. Edinburgh 1904. Struck off Register 22 Dec. 1908 .... **1908**

See Stock Exchange Year-Book.

VOL. FOR

St. Paul, Minneapolis & Manitoba Railway Co. Organised Minnesota 1897. 98% of capital stock was owned by Great Northern Railway Co. The funded debt was taken over by acquiring company and redeemed on the following dates—2nd mortgage gold bonds—Oct. 1909; 1st mortgage Dakota Extension gold bonds—Nov. 1910; consolidated mortgage gold bonds—1 July 1933; Montana Extension bonds—July 1937; Pacific Extension bonds—1 July 1940 .... **1908**

St. Pauli Breweries Co. Ld. Regd. 1888. Court Order to wind up 22 Jan. 1918. Struck off Register 1928 ... **1918**

St. Paul's River Tin Ld. Regd. 1928. Vol. liq. (members') 22 Sept. 1930. Capital returned to contributories—£5,427 10s. 7d. Final meeting return regd. 1 Jan. 1936 .... **1931**

St. Petersburg Land & Mortgage Co. Ld. Regd. 18 Aug. 1911. Struck off Register 23 Aug. 1949 .... **1949**

Saint-Phalle Ld. Regd. 1924. Vol. liq. (creditors') 3 May 1932. Assets reslised insufficient to pay creditors in full. Final meeting return regd. 6 May 1939 .... **1933**

St. Piran Ld. See Saint Piran Ld.

St. Piran Mining Co. Ld. See Saint Piran Ld.

Saint Piran Ld. Regd. 1970 as St. Piran Mining Co. Ld.; name changed Aug. 1974. All shares owned by Gasco Investments N.V. Winding-up order (London) 10 June 1986 .... **1982–3**

St. Thomas Dock Co. Ld. Regd. 1869. Vol. liq. Apr. 1878. Final meeting return regd. 20 Dec. 1878 .... ***1879**

St. Thomas Dock, Engineering & Coaling Co. Ld. Regd. 1909. Vol. liq. 12 May 1924. Capital returned to contributories—20s. per ordinary or preference share of £1; further payments (if any) not known. Final meeting return regd. 12 Mar. 1925 .... **1925**

Ste. Madeleine Sugar Co. Ld. Regd. 1913. Vol. liq. 10 Mar. 1920. Reconstructed as company of same name. Shareholders were entitled to 4 shares of £1 (credited as fully-paid) in new company for each share of £1 held and 1 fully-paid share in an oil company (unspecified) for every 2 shares held. Holders of fully-paid shares of £1 were entitled to 10s. per share in cash; the liability on the shares of £1 (10s. paid) was offset by this payment. Final meeting return regd. 6 Apr. 1922 .... **1921**

Ste. Madeleine Sugar Co. Ld. Regd. 1920. Vol. liq. (members') 1 July 1963. A subsidiary of Tate & Lyle Ld. £97 3s. 1d. paid into Companies' Liquidation Account in respect of unclaimed dividends. Final meeting return regd. 3 Apr. 1968 .... **1969**

Saker (D. H.) & Co. Ld. Inc. South Africa. In liquidation. All capital was owned by Saker, Bartle (South Africa) Ld. (later Saker's Motor Corpn. Ld.) **1938**

Sakhalin Oil Fields Ld. Regd. 1912. Struck off Register 18 Aug. 1953 .... **1939**

Salak Syndicate Ld. Rcgd. 1903. Removed from Register 1905 .... **1905**

Salamanca Tin Co. Ld. Regd. 1887. Vol. liq. 12 Aug. 1890. Removed from Register 1906 .... **1891**

Salar del Carmen Nitrate Syndicate Ld. Regd. 1896. Vol. liq. 17 June 1929. Undertaking and assets were transferred to Liverpool Nitrate Co. Ld. in which company shareholders were entitled to 4 shares of £1 for every 5 shares of £1 held. Final meeting return regd. 14 Mar. 1931 .... **1930**

Salcombe Gas & Electricity Co. Ld. Regd. 1865 as Salcombe Gas & Coke Co. Ld. name changed 1924. Dissolved 1 Apr. 1948, undertaking being vested in the British (later Central) Electricity Authority and South-Western Area Board under the Electricity Act 1947. Ordinary shareholders were entitled to receive £3 British Electricity 3% guaranteed stock (1968–73), for each share (of £1) held **1949**

Saldanha Bay Harbour & Railway Co. Ld. Regd. 1907. Vol. liq. (creditors') 12 Aug. 1932. No capital returned to contributories. Final meeting return regd. 11 Nov. 1936 .... **1933**

Sale & Co. Established 1908. The partnership was sold to Sale Continuation Ld which company continued to trade under title of Sale & Co. until placed in liquidation on 28 Sept. 1965. .... **1966**

Sale (F. G.) & Sons Ld. Regd. 1921. Vol. liq. 1 May 1933. Capital returned to contributories—£60 12s. 5d. per share of £100. Final meeting return regd. 15 June 1933. .... **1934**

Salerni Coupling Ld. Regd. 1929. Court Order to wind up 17 Oct. 1938. Liquidator released 3 July 1940. Struck off Register 14 May 1943 .... **1939**

Salinas of Mexico, Ld. Regd. 1906. Vol. liq. (creditors') 13 Oct. 1944. 5% debenture and 5¼% income debenture stockholders received 75% and 25% respectively of principal in full satisfaction of principal and arrears of interest. Capital returned to contributories—5·7075d. per share of 4s. £12,194 1s.

6d. was paid into Companies' Liquidation Account. Final meeting return regd. 7 Oct. 1946 .... **1947**

Salisbury & District Merchants & Development Co. Ld. Regd. 1899 as Salisbury & District Merchants & Estates Co. Ld. Reconstructed 1905 as company of same name. Shareholders were entitled to 1 share of £1 (credited with 15s. paid) in new company for each share of £1 held. Removed from Register 1910 ... **1905**

Salisbury & District Merchants & Development Co. Ld. Regd. 1905. Vol. liq. Mar. 1910 for reconstruction as Salisbury (Rhodesia) Estates Ld. in which company shareholders were entitled to 1½ shares of 5s. (credited as fully-paid) for each share of £1 held. Removed from Register 1912 .... **1911**

Salisbury & Dorset Junction Raiiway Co. Inc. by Special Act 1861. Amalgamated with London & South Western Railway in 1883 by exchange of securities **1884**

Salisbury & Harvey Railway Co. Inc. in New Brunswick 1889. Stated in 1891 to be wound up **1891**

Salisbury Building and Estates Co. Ld. Regd. 1902. Vol. liq. Mar. 1910 for reconstruction as Salisbury (Rhodesia) Estates Ld. in which company shareholders were entitled so 3 fully-paid shares of 5s. for each share of £1 held. Removed from Register 1912 **1911**

Salisbury Consolidated Estates Co. Ld. Regd. 1897. Properties were sold to Salisbury Building & Estates Co. Ld. Removed from Register 1903 .... **1903**

Salisbury Electric Light & Supply Co. Ld. Regd. 1894. Dissolved 1 Apr. 1948, undertaking being vested in British (later Central) Electricity Authority and Southern Area Board under Electricity Act 1947. Holders of ordinary shares and 4½% debentures were entitled to receive British Electricity 3% guaranteed stock (1968—73) as follows—£2 9s. 6d. stock for each share (of £1) held and £106 10s. stock for each £100 debentures held **1949**

Salisbury Gas Co. Inc. by Special Act 1864 as Salisbury Gas Light & Coke Co.; name changed 1921. Dissolved 1 May 1949 undertaking being vested in Southern Ares Gas Board under Gas Act 1948. Holders of securities were entitled to receive British Gas 3% guaranteed stock 1990 95 as follows in respect of each £12 10s. unit, unless otherwise stated, of security held:

	£	s.	d.
Orig. shares (10% max.)	25	14	7
New ord. shares (8% max.)	20	15	7
New ord. shares (7% max.)	18	5	0
New ord. shares (5% max.)	13	18	9
New ord. shares (6% max.)	16	0	0
6% pref. shares	16	12	6
5% pref. shares	14	1	3
5% irred. deb. stock (per £100)	125	0	0
4% irred. deb. stock	102	0	0

.... **1952**

Salisbury Gold Mining Co. Ld. Inc. in Natal and Transvaal 1886. Wound up Aug. 1913 .... **1914**

Salisbury Hotel (London) Ld. Regd. 1913. Vol. liq. 28 Sept. 1923. Final meeting return regd. 25 Oct. 1924 **1917**

Salisbury House Estate Ld. Regd. 1902. Vol. liq. (members') 8 Nov. 1953. 4% debentures repaid at 103% 27 Nov. 1953. Capital returned to contributories—18s. 0½d. per share (of £1). Final meeting return regd. 18 May 1955 .... **1956**

Salisbury Land Corporation Ld. Regd. 1902. Vol. liq. June 1909. Removed from Register 1910 .... **1910**

Salisbury-Murchison Gold Mine Ld. Regd. 1895. Vol. liq. 31 Mar. 1897. Reconstructed as Agamemnon Ld. in which company shareholders were entitled to 47 shares of £1 for every 100 shares of £1 held. Final meeting return regd. 14 May 1898 .... **1899**

Salisbury Railway & Market House Co. Ld. Inc. by Special Act 1856 as Salisbury Railway & Market House Co. regd. as limited company and name changed 5 May 1965. Vol. liq. (members') 31 Dec. 1965. Capital returned to contributories—£199 15s. per ordinary and preference share of £25. Final meeting return regd. 2 Oct. 1970 .... **1971**

Salisbury Reef Gold Mining Co. Ld. Regd. 1894. Removed from Register 1909 .... **1904**

Salisbury (Rhodesia) Estates Ld. Regd. 1910. Vol. liq. Aug. 1911. The undertaking and assets were sold to Transvaal & Rhodesian Estates Ld. in which company shareholders were entitled to 1 share of 5s. (credited as fully-paid) for each share of 5s. held. Removed from Register 1913 .... **1912**

Salisbury (Rhodesia) Goldfields Ld. Regd. 1936. Vol. liq. (creditors') 14 July 1937. Contributories received options (since expired) on shares of South American Exploration Co. Ld. Final meeting return regd. 6 Feb. 1939 .... **1938**

Salisbury, Semley and Gillingham Dairies Ld. See United Dairies (Wholesale) Ld.

Salisbury Services Co. Ld. Regd. 1925 as Mermac Ld.; name changed to Chic Clothing Co. Ld. in Jan. 1926

VOL. FOR

and as above in June 1927. Vol. liq. (members') 25 July 1930. Capital returned to contributories—£203 11s. 4d. Final meeting return regd. 29 Jan. 1931 — **1928**

Salisbury Trust Ld. Regd. 1927. Vol. liq. (members') 2 July 1931. Capital returned to contributories—8s. 4·9d. per ordinary share of £1. Final meeting return regd. 16 Jan. 1932 — **1932**

Salmon Gold Syndicate of Tasmania Ld. Regd. 1898. Removed from Register 1904 — **1904**

Salocin Patent Carriage-Wheel Co. Ld. Regd. 1896. Removed from Register 1908 — **1898**

Salonica Gas Works Ld. Regd. 1887. Undertaking was acquired by a French company and capital was returned in full. Removed from Register 1892 — **1890**

Salop Fire Office. Established 1780. Inc. by Special Act 1864. Business was acquired in 1889 by Alliance Assurance Co. — **1889**

Salpine Ld. Regd. Edinburgh 1918. Vol. liq. (members') 18 Aug. 1931. Capital returned to contributories—20s. per share of £1. Direct controlling interest held by Fairy Dyes Ld. Final meeting return regd. 20 Oct. 1931 — **1931**

Salsadella Lithographic Stone Quarry Ld. Regd. 1898. Removed from Register 1909 — **1901**

Salt Lake and Ogden Gas and Electric Light Co. Ld. Regd. 1893. Vol. liq. 10 Dec. 1897. Reconstructed as Union Light & Power Co. of Utah. Final meeting return regd. 3 Sept. 1918 — **1900**

Salt (Thomas) & Co. Ld. Regd. 1893. Vol. liq. 15 Jan. 1906. Court Order staying proceedings 7 Sept. 1908. Vol. liq. 10 May 1928. Undertaking and assets were acquired by Bass Ratcliff & Gretton Ld. Preference and preferred ordinary stockholders were entitled to £2 per £1 stock held. The debenture stocks were repaid as follows—4½% 1st—110%; 4% B—115%; 4% Albion—105%; 4% Bell A—110%; 4% Bell B—100%; 4% income stock was repaid at 100%. Final meeting return regd. 29 Mar. 1932 — **1929**

Salt Union Ld. See I.C.I. (Salt) Ld.

Saltash Gas & Coke Co. Ld. Regd. 1863. Dissolved 1 May 1949, undertaking being vested in South Western Area Gas Board under Gas Act 1948. Holders of securities were entitled to receive British Gas 3% guaranteed stock 1990—95 as follows in respect of each £5 unit, unless otherwise stated, of security held:

	£	s.	d.
Ord. shares	9	10	0
5% pref. shares	5	13	0
5% B pref. shares (issued before 1 Jan.1946)	5	12	0
5% B pref. shares (issued since 31 Dec. 1945)	5	0	0
4½% red. debs. (of £50)	50	5	0
4½% B debs. (issued before 1 Jan. 1946) of £25	25	2	6
4½% B debs. (issued since 31 Dec. 1945) of £25	25	0	0

— **1952**

Saltcoats Gas Co. Ld. Regd. in Edinburgh 1836. Dissolved 1 May 1949, undertaking being vested in Scottish Area Gas Board under Gas Act 1948. Holders of ordinary shares (of £1) were entitled to receive £2 10s. British Gas 3% guaranteed stock 1990—95 for each share held — **1952**

Salter & Salter (1900) Ld. Regd. 1900. Vol. liq. (members') 5 Dec. 1962. Capital returned to contributories (per share of £1)—preference; £1; ordinary 13s. 9d. Amount paid into Companies' Liquidation Account—on account of unclaimed preference dividends and distributions £1,044 16s. 5d.; unclaimed ordinary distributions £247 10s. Final meeting return regd. 27 Aug. 1965 — **1966**

Salter (Samuel) & Co. Ld. Regd. 1896. Struck off Register 1915 — **1898**

Salterns Ld. Regd. 1919. Receiver appointed 10 Sept. 1923. Struck off Register July 1931 — **1932**

Salvador Railway Company Limited (The). Regd. Aug. 1895 as Salvador Central Railway Co. Ld.; name changed Mar. 1897. Vol. liq. (creditors) Mar. 1977. Final meeting return registered 25 July 1977. Dissolved 25 Oct. 1977 — **1978-9**

Salvador Railway Construction Co. Ld. Regd 1883. Vol. liq. Feb. 1890. Final meeting return regd. 5 Apr. 1890 — **1891**

Salviati, Jersurum & Co. Ld. Regd. 1898. Vol. liq. 14 Nov. 1946. The assets were sold in 1906. Final meeting return regd. 31 July 1947 — **1948**

Sam Christian Gold Hydraulic Ld. Regd. 1887. Vol. liq. 26 Sept. 1892. Final meeting return regd. 3 Sept. 1894 — **1893**

Samaná and Santiago Railway Co. Ld. Regd. Edinburgh 1888. Court Order to wind up 27 Feb. 1942. 2s. 1·6649d. in the £ was paid on account of principal of

debentures. Liquidator released and company dissolved by Court Order 20 June 1944 — **1945**

Samara Sugar Estate & Refining Co. Ld. Regd. 1874. Removed from Register 1890 — ***1885**

Sambas Exploration Co. Ld. Regd. 1889. Removed from Register 1907 — **1893**

Sambas Rubber & Gutta-Percha Co. Ld. Regd. 1907. Vol. liq. Feb. 1908. Removed from Register 1910 — **1909**

Sambre & Meuse Railway. Inc. in Belgium 1854. Purchased by Belgian Government for about Fcs. 29,000,000. Dissolved 1 Jan. 1896 — **1899**

Samdang Tea Co. Ld. Regd. 1876. Vol. liq. 10 Aug. 1891. Tea estate was acquired by Doom Dooma Tea Co. Ld. Final meeting return regd. 2 Feb.1892 — **1892**

Sammel Brothers Ld. Regd. 1909. Vol. liq. 3 Apr. 1925. Capital returned to contributories—20s. per preference share of £1; further payments (if any) not known. Final meeting return regd. 19 Dec. 1930 — **1926**

Sam's Wealth Mines Development Co. Ld. Regd. 1896. Vol. liq. 12 Apr. 1898. Reconstructed as Australian Gold Leases Development Co. Ld. in which company shareholders were entitled to 1 share of £1 (credited with 17s. 9d. paid) for each share of £1 held. Final meeting return regd. 29 Mar. 1900 — **1900**

Sam's Wealth of Nations Gold & Exploration Ld. Regd. 1895. Vol. liq. 11 Dec. 1896. Reconstructed as Sam's Wealth Mines Development Co. Ld. in which company shareholders were entitled to 1 share of £1 (credited with 17s. paid) for each share of £1 held. Final meeting return regd. 31 Jan. 1898 — **1898**

Samuda Brothers Ld. Regd. 1885. Vol. liq. 21 Dec. 1892. Final meeting return regd. 15 Oct. 1901 — **1893**

Samuda (J.) Ld. Regd. 1908. Struck off Register 3 Mar. 1944 — **1944**

Samuel Brothers Ld. Regd. 1897. Vol. liq. Mar. 1927. £1,502 and £90,762 was paid to A and B shareholders respectively. Final meeting return regd. 28 Nov. 1950. Struck off Register 31 July 1953 — **1951**

Samuelson Transport Co. Ld. Regd. 1921. Vol. liq. 25 Sept. 1922. Final meeting return regd. 25 Feb. 1924 — **1923**

San Albino Gold Mines Ld. Regd. 1899. Removed from Register 1911 — **1908**

San Antonio de Esquilache (Peru) Mines Ld. Regd. 1914. Vol. liq. June 1922 for reconstruction as Southern Peruvian Mines Ld. in which company shareholders were entitled to 1 share of 5s. (credited with 4s. paid) for each share held. Struck off Register 7 Aug. 1945 — **1923**

San Antonio Land & Irrigation Co. Ld. In Sept. 1924 the property was sold under foreclosure and bought in on behalf of the bondholders. The property was transferred to trustees, who were to realise it and distribute the proceeds; for the purpose of such distribution trust participation certificates were issued. A holding company was organised in Canada (San Antonio Realisations Ld.) and trust participation certificates exchanged for shares of that company. In their report of 6 Oct. 1933 the trustees stated, in their opinion the trust had become worthless and certificate holders would therefore receive no dividend or distribution whatsoever from the property — **1934**

San Antonio Mining & Smelting Co. Ld. Regd. 1920. Vol. liq. (creditors') 12 Aug. 1930. No capital returned to contributories. Final meeting return regd. 27 Oct. 1932 — **1931**

San Bernardo Mining Co. Ld. Regd. 1892. Removed from Register 1910 — **1909**

San Bernardo Silver Mines Ld. Regd. 1890. Vol. liq. 12 Nov. 1892. Reconstructed as San Bernardo Mining Co. Ld. Ordinary shareholders were entitled to 1 preference share of 5s. (credited with 2s. 6d. paid) or 4 ordinary shares of 5s. (credited with 4s. 6d. paid) for every 2 ordinary shares of £1 held. Deferred shareholders were entitled to 1 preference share of 5s. (credited with 4s. 6d. paid) in new company for each deferred share of 1s. held. Final meeting return regd. 13 Dec. 1893 — **1909**

San Buena Ventura Road Co. See Cúcuta Railway Co.

San Carlos Brewery Co. Ld. Regd. 1908. Vol. liq. 19 Dec. 1913. Undertaking and assets were sold to Sociedad Anonima Cerveceria Argentine San Carlos (Inc. Argentine). Final meeting return regd. 10 Dec. 1914 — **1914**

San Carlos Gold Mine Ld. Regd. 1906. Vol. liq. Oct. 1909 for reconstruction as San Carlos Gold Mining Co. Ld. in which company shareholders were entitled to 1 share of 5s. (credited with 3s. paid) for each share of 5s. held. Removed from Register 1912 — **1910**

San Carlos Gold Mining Co. Ld. Regd. 1909. Vol. liq. 18 Dec. 1916. Final meeting return regd. 27 Mar. 1917 — **1917**

San Cebrian Ld. Regd. 1890. Struck off Register 11 June 1895 — **1900**

San Cebrian Railway & Collieries Co. Ld. Regd. 1885. Reconstructed 1890 as San Cebrian Ld. for 100,360

VOL. FOR

fully-paid shares of £1 and £64,770 in debentures. Removed from Register 1901 .... **1899**

San Christobal (Mexico) Rubber, Tobacco and Estates Co. Ld. Regd. 1909. Vol. liq. 24 Feb. 1915. Final meeting return regd. 29 Dec. 1917 .... **1915**

San Donato Nitrate Co. Ld. Regd. 1889. Vol. liq. Jan. 1909. Shareholders were entitled to 1 fully-paid share of £2 in Liverpool Nitrate Co. Ld. plus £7 10*s*. in cash for every 5 shares of £5 held. Removed from Register 1910 .... **1909**

San Finx Tin Mines Ld. Regd. 1897. Vol. liq. Feb. 1912. Removed from Register 1912 .... **1913**

San Finx Tin Mines Ld. Regd. 1926. Receiver appointed 27 May 1932; ceased to act 30 Sept. 1936. Vol. liq. (creditors') 29 Dec. 1932. Undertaking was acquired by San Finx Tin Mines (1933) Ld. Final meeting return regd. 17 June 1941 .... ***1933**

San Finx Tin Mines (1933) Ld. Regd. 1933. Vol. liq. (members') 19 Sept. 1940. Capital returned to contributories—8*d*. per share. Final meeting return regd. 17 Oct. 1941 .... **1942**

San Francisco Breweries Ld. Regd. 1890. Vol. liq. 1 May 1899. Reconstructed as company of same name. Shareholders were entitled to 2 ordinary shares of £1 in new company for each ordinary share of £10 held or 3 preference shares of £1 for each preference share of £10 held. Final meeting return regd. 12 Dec. 1899 .... **1900**

San Francisco Breweries Ld. Regd. 1899. Vol. liq. 27 Nov. 1922. Struck off Register 23 May 1930 .... **1923**

San Francisco Del Oro Mines Ld. Regd. 1903. Vol. liq. Oct. 1908 for reconstruction as San Francisco del Oro Mining Co. Ld. in which company shareholders were entitled to 1 share of £1 (credited with 15*s*. paid) for each share of £1 held. Removed from Register 1910 .... **1909**

San Francisco Del Oro Mining Co. Ld. Regd. 1908. Vol. liq. 18 Apr. 1921. Shareholders were entitled to 1 share of 10*s*. in San Francisco Mines of Mexico Ld. for every 2 shares held. Final meeting return regd. 28 Feb. 1922 .... **1922**

San Francisco Mines of Mexico Ld. Regd. 1913. Dissolved 20 Nov. 1981 .... **1968**

San Jacinto Land Co. Ld. Regd. 1894. Vol. liq. (members') 2 Feb. 1945. Capital returned to contributories—£3 7*s*. 3·4957*d*. per preference share (of 1*d*.) and £1 10*s*. 2·9157*d*. per ordinary share (of 15*s*. 9*d*.). Final meeting return regd. 18 June 1948 **1949**

San Jorge Nitrate Co. Ld. Regd. 1888. Vol. liq. July 1910. Capital returned to contributories—9*s*. per share of £4 in Aug. 1910; further payments (if any) not known. Removed from Register 1913 .... **1911**

San Juan Gold Mines Ld. Regd. 1896. Removed from Register 4 Oct. 1898 .... ***1897**

San Lorenzo Nitrate Co. Ld. Regd. 1902. Vol. liq. 1 Sept. 1920. The assets and liabilities were acquired by Liverpool Nitrate Co. Ld. in which company shareholders were entitled to 1 share of 5*s*. (credited as fully-paid) for each share of £1 held. Final meeting return regd. 10 Sept. 1921 .... **1921**

San Luis Gold & Silver Mines Ld. Regd. 1889. Removed from Register 1903 .... **1903**

San Luis (Mexico) Tramways Ld. Regd. 1911. Vol. liq. (members') 5 Oct. 1931. No capital returned to contributories. Final meeting return regd. 2 Dec. 1952 .... **1954**

San Miguel Copper Mines Ld. Regd. 1904. Vol. liq. 17 Sept. 1919. Final meeting return regd. 27 June 1935 **1920**

San Miguel de Colquechaca Ld. Formed 1884. Reconstructed 1892 as San Miguel Silver Mines Ld. in which company shareholders were entitled to subscribe for shares of £1 (credited with 15*s*. paid) **1898**

San Miguel Proprietary Ld. Regd. 1904. Vol. liq. June 1908. Removed from Register 1909 .... **1909**

San Miguel Silver Mines Ld. Regd. 1892. Removed from Register 1903 .... **1899**

San Nicolas Gold Mines Ld. Regd. 1934. Vol. liq. (members') 18 Sept. 1944. Assets realised sufficient to pay debenture stockholders 8*s*. 1½d. per £. Final meeting return regd. 14 Sept. 1945 .... **1946**

San Pablo Nitrate Co. Ld. Regd. 1888. Capital returned to contributories—£2 15*s*. 9*d*. per share at Feb. 1906; further payments (if any) not known. Removed from Register 1906 .... **1907**

San Patricio Nitrate Co. Ld. Regd. 1904. Vol. liq. 10 Sept. 1925. The undertaking and assets were acquired by Santa Rita Nitrate Co. Ld. in which company shareholders were entitled to 1 fully-paid share of £1 for every 4 shares of £1 held, or a cash payment of 7*s*. 6*d*. per share of £1. Final meeting return regd. 1 July 1926 .... **1926**

San Patricio United Nitrate Co. Ld. Regd. 1894. Vol. liq. 5 June 1895. Capital was returned in full *plus* 6*d*. per share bonus. Final meeting return regd. 4 Nov. 1895 **1896**

San Paulo and Minas Railway Co. Ld. Regd. 1907. Receiver appointed in June 1914. Struck off Register 26 Apr. 1929 .... **1920**

San Paulo & Rio de Janeiro Railway Co. Established 1874. The Government exercised its option to purchase on 25 Apr. 1891. Both series of bonds were repaid at par in sterling on 1 Apr.1891 .... **1892**

San Paulo Central Sugar Factory of Brazil Ld. Regd. 1882. Vol. liq. 25 Feb. 1886. Final meeting return regd. 1 Mar. 1899 .... **1887**

San Paulo Coffee Estates Co. Ld. Regd. 1897. Vol. liq. (creditors') 14 Oct. 1938. Assets realised insufficient to pay unsecured creditors in full. Final meeting return regd. 18 Oct. 1939 .... **1939**

San Paulo Land Co. Ld. Regd. 1911. Vol. liq. 20 Jan. 1921. Capital returned to contributories—21*s*. 11½*d*. per ordinary share of £1 and 1*s*. 5·34*d*. per deferred share of 1*s*. Struck off Register 30 July 1971 .... **1971**

San Paulo Match Factory Ld. Regd. 1906. Receiver for debenture holders appointed 8 Mar. 1912. Assets were realised and proceeds distributed by Court to debenture holders. Struck off Register 1915 .... **1914**

San Paulo Mortgage and Finance Co. Ld. Regd. 1921. Vol. liq. (members') 2 Apr. 1942. Holders of 8% 1st debenture stock accepted £102 10*s*. City of San Paulo Improvements & Freehold Land Co. Ld. 7½% 1st debenture stock in exchange for every £100 stock held. Capital returned to contributories—9*s*. 3·65*d*. per share of £1. Final meeting return regd. 26 Feb. 1943 .... **1945**

San Pedro (Chili) Copper Mining Co. Ld. Regd. 1880. Vol. liq. May 1883. Final meeting return regd. 26 Jan. 1887 .... **1884**

San Quintin Milling Co. Ld. Regd. 1893. Vol. liq. (members') 26 Apr. 1940. Capital returned to contributories—1*s*. per share. Final meeting return regd. 18 Jan. 1941 .... **1942**

San Ramon Gold Ld. Regd. 1900. Vol. liq. 10 July 1906. Removed from Register 1907 .... **1907**

San Salvador Spanish Iron Ore Co. Ld. Regd. 1889. Vol. liq. 29 Aug. 1919. Reconstructed as San Salvador Spanish Iron Ore Co. (1919) Ld. Shareholders were entitled to 1 share of £1 (credited with 15*s*. paid) in new company for every 2 ordinary shares of £1 held or 3 shares of £1 (credited with 15*s*. paid) for every 2 preference shares of £1 held or 2 shares of £1 (credited with 15*s*. paid) for each "Pier" share of £1 held. The A and B debenture holders were entitled to an equal amount of debentures in new company. Final meeting return regd. 13 May 1921 .... **1920**

San Salvador Spanish Iron Ore Co. (1919) Ld. Regd. 1919. Vol. liq. 5 May 1921. Capital returned to contributories—16*s*. per share of £1 in May 1921; further payments (if any) not known. Final meeting return regd. 9 May 1922 .... **1922**

San Sebastian Nitrate Co. Ld. Regd. 1889. Vol. liq. (members') 23 Apr. 1931. Undertaking and assets acquired by Nitrate Corporation of Chile in which shareholders were entitled to 23 fully-paid series B shares of 100 pesos (either ordinary or 7% cumulative preferred) for every 100 shares of £1 held. Final meeting return regd. 18 Dec. 1934 .... **1932**

Sanctuary Buildings Ld. Regd. 1919 as Russell Investment Trust Ld.; name changed Mar. 1926. All capital was owned by Land Securities Investment Trust Ld. Dissolved under section 208 of Companies Act, 1948 on 28 July 1955 .... **1953**

Sandac Rubber Estates Ld. Regd. 1935. Vol. liq. (members') 19 Sept. 1969. Amount returned to contributories—28¼*p* (5*s*. 3*d*. and 2*p*). £1,223 5*s*. 10*d*. paid into Companies' Liquidation Account in respect of unclaimed dividends. Final meeting return regd. 19 Feb. 1971 .... **1971**

Sandakan Bay Coal Field Ld. Regd. 1898. The undertaking and concession were acquired by Cowie Harbour Coal Co. Ld. in which company shareholders were entitled to 13½ fully-paid shares of £1 for each share of £10 held. A cash distribution was anticipated. Removed from Register 1907 .... **1907**

Sandakan (British North Borneo) Tobacco Co. Ld. Regd. 1889. Vol. liq. 3 Feb. 1891. Final meeting return regd. 30 July 1895 .... **1892**

Sandbach Gas Co. Inc. by Special Act 1884. Dissolved 1 May 1949, undertaking being vested in North Western Area Gas Board under Gas 1948. Holders of securities were entitled to receive, in respect of each £100 unit held, British Gas 3% guaranteed stock 1990—95 as follows:

	£	s.	d.	
Orig. stock (10% stand.)	207	0	0	
New stock (7% stand.)	150	0	0	**1952**

Sandeman (Frank Stewart) & Sons Ld. Regd. Edinburgh 1915. Vol. liq. (members') 3 Oct. 1932. All shares were owned by Jute Industries Ld. [later Jute

*See *Stock Exchange Year-Book*.

VOL. FOR

Industries (Holdings) Ld.]. Final meeting return regd. 1 Apr. 1933 .... **1933**

Sanders Bros. (Stores) Ld. Regd. 1925. Vol. liq. (members') 27 July 1953. Capital returned to contributories—7s. 0·28d. per ordinary share (of £1). £442 was paid into Companies' Liquidation Account. Final meeting return regd. 27 Nov. 1956 .. **1957**

Sanderson (William) & Son Ld. Regd. Edinburgh 1925. Vol. liq. Dec. 1933. Undertaking was acquired by Booth's Distilleries Ld. Final meeting return regd. 28 Feb. 1935 .... **1934**

Sandown Gas & Coke Co. Ld. Regd. 1862. Undertaking was acquired in 1937 by East Wight Gas Co. Vol. liq. (members') 30 Sept. 1937. Shareholders were entitled to stock in acquiring company as follows— for each 10% standard share of £10 held—£20 consolidated stock; for each 7% standard share of £10 held—£14 consolidated stock; for each preference share of £10 held—£12 5% preference stock. The acquiring company assumed liability for the redeemable debenture bonds. Final meeting return regd. 12 Sept. 1938 .... **1938**

Sandow's Cocoa & Chocolate Co. Ld. Regd. 1912. Court Order to wind up 16 Apr. 1918. Struck off Register Apr. 1929 .... **1930**

Sandret (G.) Ld. Regd. 1917. All capital was held by Fortnum & Mason Ld. Struck off Register Nov. 1946 .... **1938**

Sandwell Park Colliery Co. Ld. Regd. 1870. Vol. liq. 18 Mar. 1914. Reconstructed as company of same name. Shareholders were entitled to 7 preferred ordinary shares of £1 (credited with 15s. paid) in new company for every 5 preferred ordinary shares of £1 held or 1 ordinary share of £5 (credited with £4 paid) for each ordinary share of £10 held or 1 fully-paid preference of £1 for each pref. share of £1 held. Final meeting return regd. 10 Mar. 1915 .... **1915**

Sandwell Park Colliery Co. Ld. Regd. 1914. Vol. liq. (members') 26 Apr. 1935. Capital returned to contributories—9s. 10½d. per share of £1. Final meeting return regd. 27 Oct. 1936 .... **1936**

Sandy Gas Co. Ld. Regd. 1888. Dissolved 1 May 1949, undertaking being vested in Eastern Area Gas Board under Gas Act 1948. Holders of securities were entitled to receive British Gas 3% guaranteed stock 1990—95 as follows:

	£ s. d.
Ord. shares (of £5)	5 0 0
4% red. debs (both red. dates) (of £100)	100 0 0

1952

Sanella Outcrop Reefs Co. Ld. Inc. Transvaal 1905. Vol. liq. Apr. 1908 .... **1909**

Sanger [Lord George] (The Original) Ld. Regd. 1897. Assets realised insufficient to pay creditors in full. Removed from Register 1905 .... **1940**

Sangli Gold Mines Ld. Regd. 1903. Reconstructed 1906 as Sangli Gold Mining Co. Ld. in which company shareholders were entitled to 1 share of £1 (credited with 14s. paid) for each share of £1 held. Removed from Register 1907 .... **1907**

Sangli Gold Mining Co. Ld. Regd. 1906. Reconstructed as Sangli Mines Ld. in which company shareholders were entitled to 1 share of £1 (credited with 10s. paid) for each share of £1 (19s. paid) held. Removed from Register 1909 .... **1908**

Sangli Mines Ld. Regd. 1907. Vol. liq. Nov. 1910. Removed from Register 1913 .... **1911**

Sanitary Block & Tile Pavement Co. Ld. Regd. 1903. Vol. liq. 25 June 1912. Final meeting return regd. 21 Dec. 1914 .... **1913**

Sanitary Supply Corporation Ld. See Webb's Engineering Co. Ld.

"Sanitas" Co. Ld. Regd. 1878. Vol. liq. 1 July 1898. Reconstructed as company of same name. Shareholders were entitled to 2 fully-paid shares of £1 in new company for each share of £1 held. Final meeting return regd. 29 Mar. 1899 .... **1898**

Sankey & Co. Ld. Regd. 1919. Vol. liq. (members') 25 Feb. 1930. All shares owned by Wiggins & Co. (Hammersmith) Ld. Final meeting return regd. 27 June 1930 .... **1931**

"Sanogen" Ventilating Appliance Co. Ld. Regd. 1889. Removed from Register 1906 .... **1893**

Sanspareil Cycle Co. Ld. Regd. 1896. Removed from Register 1901 .... **1902**

Sansu Mine Ld. Regd. 1905. Vol. liq. Feb. 1910. The undertaking and assets were sold to Ashanti Goldfields Corporation Ld. in which company shareholders were entitled to 1 share of 4s. (credited as fully-paid) for every 10 shares of 10s. held. Removed from Register 1910 .... **1910**

Santa Ana Central Coffee Co. Ld. Regd. 1900. Vol. liq. Mar. 1909. Removed from Register 1910 .... **1910**

VOL. FOR

Santa Anna Gold Mining Co. Ld. Regd. 1896. Removed from Register 1901 .... **1908**

Santa-Barbara (California) Oil Co. Ld. Regd. 1907. Vol. liq. 20 Jan. 1916. Final meeting return regd. 10 Oct. 1916 .... **1916**

Santa Barbara Gold Mining Co. Ld. Regd. 1867. Removed from Register 1912 .... **1898**

Santa Catalina Nitrate Co. Ld. Regd. 1900. Vol. liq. (members') 23 Apr. 1931. Undertaking and assets acquired by Nitrate Corporation of Chile in which company shareholders were entitled to 1 fully-paid series B share of 100 pesos (either ordinary or 7% cumulative preferred) for every 8 shares of £1 held plus 12s. 4d. per share in cash. £121 5s. 10d. was paid into Companies' Liquidation Account. Final meeting return regd. 2 Dec. 1936 .... **1932**

Santa Cruz Coffee Co. Ld. Regd. 1911. Vol. liq. 15 Aug. 1946. Capital returned to contributories—11s. 8½d. per share (of £1). £1,780 was paid into Companies' Liquidation Account. Final meeting return regd. 2 June 1949 .... **1950**

Santa-Cruz Sulphur & Copper Co. Ld. Regd. 1881. Vol. liq. Feb. 1882. Final meeting return regd. 6 Oct. 1887 .... **1883**

Santa Elena Nitrate Co. Ld. Regd. 1889. Vol. liq. July 1906. Capital returned to contributories—£1 per share of £5 at Aug. 1906; further payments (if any) not known. Removed from Register 1907 .... **1907**

Santa Fé & Cordova Great Southern Land Co. Ld. Regd. 1888. Vol. liq. 25 Apr. 1913. Undertaking and assets were sold to Cordova Land Co. Ld., in which company shareholders were entitled to 4 shares of £1 and £3 in 5% mortgage debenture stock for each share of £1 held. Final meeting return regd. 13 Nov. 1913 .... **1914**

Santa Fé & Cordova Great Southern Construction Co. Ld. See Santa Fé & Cordova Great Southern Railway Co. Ld.

Santa Fé & Cordova Great Southern Railway Co. Ld. Regd. 1888 as Santa Fé & Cordova Great Southern Construction Co. Ld. name changed 1893. In May 1900, the undertaking was acquired by the Buenos Aires & Rosario Railway Co. Ld. (later Central Argentine Railway Ld.) Holders of 4% prior lien bonds were entitled to cash or 4% debenture stock in purchasing company at par. Holders of 6% 1st debenture stock were entitled to £100 4% debenture stock and £30 7% Sunchales preference shares in purchasing company for every £100 stock held. Holders of 4% 1st funding bonds were entitled to 4% debenture stock in purchasing company at par. Holders of 5% 2nd debentures and 6% 2nd funding bonds were entitled to £50 7% Sunchales preference shares, and £35 ordinary stock in purchasing company for every £100 stock held. Holders of ordinary shares were entitled to an equal amount of ordinary stock in purchasing company. Removed from Register 1901 .... **1901**

Santa Fé & Cordova Southern Extension Railway Ld. Regd. 1898. Undertaking acquired in 1900 by Buenos Aires and Rosario Railway Co. Ld. (later Central Argentine Railway Ld.). Holders of 6% 4% debenture stock were entitled to an equal amount of 4% debenture stock plus 10% of holding in ordinary stock of purchasing company. Removed from Register 1901 .... **1901**

Santa Fé Compagnie Financière Française pour la République Argentine et l'Etranger. See French Railways Co. of the Province of Santa Fé.

Santa Fé Land Co. Ld. Regd. 1883. Vol. liq. 24 Mar. 1914. Properties sold to Forestal Land, Timber & Railways Co. Ld. in which company shareholders received 1 preference and 1 ordinary share (of £1) for every two shares (of £1) held. The 5% debentures were repaid at 105%. Final meeting return regd. 22 Apr. 1918 .... **1915**

Santa Fé Territorial and Agricultural Bank. See Banquede Crédit Foncieret Agricole de Santa Fé

Santa Francisca Gold Estates Ld. Regd. 1907. Receiver appointed in July 1913. Struck off Register 1920 . **1914**

Santa Gertrudis Co. Ld. Regd. 1909. Vol. liq. (members') 24 Aug. 1934. Undertaking and assets were acquired by Camp Bird Ld. in which company shareholders were entitled to 5 shares of 1s. (credited as fully-paid) for each share of £1 held. Final meeting return regd. 2 May 1936 .... **1935**

Santa Gertrudis Jute Mill Co. Ld. Regd. 1893. Vol. liq. (members') 13 Apr. 1954. Final meeting return regd. 20 Dec. 1971 .... **1947**

Santa Gertrudis Mines Ld. Regd. 1902. Vol. liq. 20 Mar. 1905. Struck off Register 3 Sept. 1918 .... **1906**

Santa Gertrudis South Ld. Regd. 1910. Vol. liq. Apr. 1912 for reconstruction as Aabada Trust Ld. in which company shareholders were entitled to 4

VOL. FOR

shares of 5s. (credited with 4s. paid) for each share of £1 held. Removed from Register 1913.... **1913**

Santa Isabel United Gold Mines Ld. Regd. 1905. Vol. liq. 18 Dec. 1912. Struck off Register 7 Aug. 1945 **1946**

Santa Luisa Nitrate Co. Ld. Regd. 1888. Vol. liq. 11 Apr. 1892. Taken over by Lautaro Nitrate Co. Ld. Final meeting return regd. 8 Apr. 1893.............. **1893**

Santa Maria Consolidated Oil Fields Ld. Regd. 1919. Vol. liq. 25 July 1924. Final meeting return regd. 29 July 1925.. **1925**

Santa Maria Mining Co. Ld. Regd. 1901. Vol. liq. Dec. 1911. Removed from Register 1913.......... **1912**

Santa Maria Oil Fields Inc. Inc. Arizona 1916. Direct controlling interest was held by Santa Maria Consolidated Oil Fields Ld. In liquidation in 1925 **1925**

Santa Maria Oil Fields of California Ld. Regd. 1911. Vol. liq. 8 Jan. 1917. Reconstructed 1919 as Santa Maria Consolidated Oil Fields Ld. in which company shareholders were entitled to 160 fully-paid ordinary shares of 8s. for every 500 ordinary shares of 10s. or 100 preference shares of £1 held. Final meeting return regd. 18 May 1921............... **1920**

Santa Maria Silver Mines Ld. Regd. 1885. Removed from Register 1895................................ **1891**

Santa Marta Railway Co. Ld. Regd. 1887. Vol. liq. (members') 31 July 1945. The assets were distributed to the holders of the preferred stock in partial liquidation thereof. Final meeting return regd. 20 Dec. 1945.................................. **1947**

Santa Rita Nitrate Co. Ld. Regd. 1889. Vol. liq. Apr. 1931. Undertaking and assets acquired by Nitrate Corporation of Chile in which company shareholders received 1 fully-paid series B share of 100 pesos (either ordinary or 7% cumulative preferred) for every 4 shares of £1 held *plus* 5s. 8·815d. per share of £1 held. Final meeting return regd. 15 Sept. 1933 **1932**

Santa Rosa Milling Co. Ld. Regd. 1913. Vol. liq. (members') 1 July 1968. Capital returned to contributories—5s. 10¼d. per share of 10s. £40·14 was paid into Companies' Liquidation Account in respect of unclaimed distributions. Final meeting return regd. Apr. 1975.................................. **1975-6**

Santa Rosa Mining Co. Ld. Regd. 1896. Vol. liq. 25 May 1905. Removed from Register 1906.......... **1906**

Santa Rosa Mining Co. Ld. Regd. 1910. Vol. liq. (creditors') 14 Feb. 1934. The prior lien debenture held by Exploration Co. Ld. was not repaid in full. No capital returned to contributories. Final meeting return regd. 6 Sept. 1934.................. **1935**

Santa Rosa Nitrate Co. Ld. Regd. 1901. Vol. liq. Aug. 1912. Removed from Register 1913............ **1918**

Santa Rosalia del Carmen (Mexico) Copper Co. Ld. Regd. 1891. Removed from Register 1905.......... **1897**

Santa Teresa Copper Co. Ld. Regd. 1887. Removed from Register 1892.............................. ***1890**

Santana Mines Ld. Regd. 1910. Struck off Register 1929 ***1924**

Santiago Nitrate Co. Ld. Regd. 1899. Vol. liq. 24 Oct. 1929. Undertaking and assets were acquired by Liverpool Nitrate Co. Capital returned to contributories—30s. 6d. per share of £4 at Dec. 1929; further payments (if any) not known. Final meeting return regd. 14 Jan. 1930............................ **1930**

Sao Bento Gold Estates Ld. Regd. 1897. Reconstructed 1903 as company of same name. Shareholders were entitled to 1 share of £1 (credited with 17s. paid) in new company for each share of £1 held. Removed from Register 1901.......................... **1904**

Sao Bento Gold Estates Ld. Regd. 1900. Reconstructed 1905 as company of same name. Shareholders were entitled to 1 share of £1 (credited with 15s. paid) in new company for each share of £1 held. Removed from Register 1906.......................... **1907**

Sao Bento Gold Estates Ld. Regd. 1905. Vol. liq. 12 Apr.1907. Removed from Register 1913.......... **1908**

São José (Brazil) Diamonds & Carbons Ld. Regd. 1903. Vol. liq. Nov. 1911. Struck off Register 1926...... **1914**

Sao Pedro Brazil Gas Co. Ld. Regd. 1871. Vol. liq. 26 Sept. 1876. Removed from Register 29 July 1902 . ***1877**

Sapon Ld. Regd. 1900. Vol. liq. 27 Aug. 1917. Reconstructed as Sapon Soaps Ld. Final meeting return regd. 27 Sept. 1918............................ ***1918**

Sapon Soaps Ld. Regd. 1917. Receiver appointed 21 June 1922. Court Order to wind up 21 Nov. 1922. Struck off Register Apr. 1929.................... **1930**

Sapphire & Ruby Co. of Montana Ld. Regd. 1891. Company was taken over by El Dorado Gold & Gem Co. of Montana in exchange for 425,000 ordinary and 400 deferred shares of $2. Removed from Register 1901.............................. **1898**

Sapphire Gold & Silver Co. Ld. Regd. 1886. Struck off Register 31 Dec. 1895........................ **1900**

Sapphires & Rubies of Siam Ld. Regd. 1890. Vol. liq. 29 Jan. 1895. Concession was acquired by Siam

VOL. FOR

Exploring Co. Ld. for 55,000 fully-paid shares of £1. Final meeting return regd. 10 Aug. 1896.......... **1895**

Sapumalkande Rubber Co. Ld. Regd. 1909. Vol. liq. 14 June 1926. Undertaking and certain assets were acquired by Lunuva (Ceylon) Tea & Rubber Estates Ld., in which company shareholders were entitled to 3 shares of £1 (credited as fully-paid) for every 5 shares of £1 held and an option (since expired) over further shares. Final meeting return regd. 13 Apr. 1927 .... **1927**

Saragossa & Mediterranean Railway Co. (La Compania de los Ferro-Carilles de Zaragoza al Mediterráneo). Established as Val de Zafán to San Carlos de la Rapita Railway Co. to acquire a concession dated 17 Oct. 1882; name changed in 1887. In 1890 the Aragon & Catalonia Railway Co. Ld., (later Construction & Investment Co. Ld.) was formed to take over the construction of the railway. Shareholders received 1 ordinary share (of £10) in new company for each share (of £20 with £10 paid) and 3% obligation holders received 1 preference share (of £10) for each bond (of £20) *plus* £2 10s. cash per bond **1895**

Sarapiqui Estates Co. Ld. Regd. 1896. Vol. liq. Mar. 1909. Struck off Register 1926................ **1910**

Saratov Water Works Co. Ld. Regd. Mar. 1874. Vol. liq. Apr. 1874. Struck off Register 28 Apr. 1885... **1899**

Saratov Water Works Co. Ld. Regd. Apr. 1874. Vol. liq. 27 Sept. 1898. The works were transferred in 1898 to the Municipality for about £65,000. Final meeting return regd. 28 Sept. 1899.................... **1899**

Sarawak Rubber Estates Ld. See Clinical and General Industries Ld.

Sarum Fine Woollen Mills Ld. Regd. 1950. Vol. liq. (members') 30 Jan. 1970. Capital returned to contributories—22s. 6d. per preference share (of £1) and 115·3p per ordinary share (of £1). Final meeting return filed 2 July 1975.................... **1975-6**

Sassoon (E. D.) & Co. Ld. Inc. India 1920. Vol. liq. 29 Dec. 1948................................ **1968**

Sauce Holdings Ld. Regd. 1897 as Birmingham Vinegar Brewery Co., 1897, Ld.; name changed in 1898 to Birmingham Vinegar Brewery Co. Ld., in 1900 to Holbrooks Ld. and as above in 1954. Vol. liq. (members') 29 Dec. 1955. Capital returned to contributories—9s. 10·65d. per stock unit of 2s. 6d. Final meeting return regd. 1 Oct. 1958........ **1959**

Saunders Garage & Motor Car Co. Ld. See Saunders Motors Ld.

Saunders Motors Ld. Regd. 1920 as Saunders Garage & Motor Car Co. Ld.; name changed Aug 1924. Vol. liq. Feb. 1926. Struck off Register Jan. 1934 .... **1934**

Saunderson (H. P.) & Co. Ld. Regd. 1899. Vol. liq. 1 Jan. 1910. Final meeting return regd. 4 July 1919 **1910**

Savage (F.) & Co. Ld. Regd. 1906. Court Order to wind up 26 Sept. 1906. Liquidator released 7 Dec. 1914. Struck off Register 14 Feb. 1919.............. **1907**

Savannah, Florida & Western Railway Co. Inc. Georgia and Florida 1879. Acquired by Atlantic Coast Line Railroad Co. The St. John's River Division 4% 1st mortgage gold coupon bonds and 1st guaranteed gold bonds 1928 (Alabama Midland Railway) were included in the funded debt of the acquiring company **1902**

Savill Brothers Ld. Regd. 1893. Vol. liq. (members') 4 Apr. 1932. Undertaking was acquired by Charrington and Co. Ld., which company owned all shares. Final meeting return regd. 14 Oct. 1932............ **1933**

Savings and Economic Bank of Bihor Ld. Inc. in Transylvania 1872 as Savings Bank of Bihar; name changed in 1918. In Oct. 1952 it was stated (by Banque de la Republique Populaire Roumania) "that the Bank is completely liquidated since 25 Mar. 1952".................................. **1953**

Savings Bank of Bihar. See above.

Savoy Café (Brighton) Ld. Regd. 1935. Struck off Register 30 June 1944.......................... **1945**

Savoy Cinemas Ld. Regd. 1924. Undertaking and assets acquired by Associated British Cinemas Ld. in Nov. 1928. Vol. liq. 28 Feb. 1929. Final meeting return regd. 4 Apr. 1932............................ **1929**

Savoy Palace of Varieties, Dublin Ld. Regd. 1896. Struck off Register 26 Oct. 1900................ **1901**

Savoy Theatre (Glasgow) Ld. Regd. Edinburgh 1910. Vol. liq. May 1912. Undertaking and assets were acquired by Savoy Theatre (Glasgow 1912) Ld. Court Order to dissolve 15 Dec. 1913............ **1913**

Savoy Theatre (Glasgow, 1912) Ld. Regd. Edinburgh 1913. Court Orders: to wind up 3 July 1915; to dissolve 22 Dec. 1916............................ **1916**

Sawhee Gold Mines (West Africa) Ld. Regd. 1910. Vol. liq. 4 Sept. 1922. Reconstructed as Colonial Mines Development Ld. in which company shareholders were entitled to 3 shares of 2s. (credited with 1s. 6d.

paid) for each share of 5s. held. Final meeting return regd. 11 Nov. 1924 .... **1923**

Saxmundham Gas Co. Ld. Regd. 1906. Dissolved 1 May 1949, undertaking being vested in Eastern Area Gas Board under Gas Act 1948. Holders of securities were entitled to receive British Gas 3% guaranteed stock 1990—95 as follows in respect of each £1 unit, unless otherwise stated, of security held:

	£	s.	d.
Ord. shares	2	2	0
5% pref. shares	1	2	6
4% red. deb. stock (per £100).........	101	0	0
5% 2nd debs. (of £100).................	100	10	0

1952

Saxon Gold Mines Ld. Inc. Transvaal 1902. Vol. liq. May 1908 .... **1909**

Saxon Portland Cement Co. Ld. Regd. 1899. Vol. liq. 19 Jan. 1912. Undertaking acquired by British Portland Cement Manufacturers Ld. Final meeting return regd. 6 Mar. 1913 .... *****1913**

Saxon Securities (Amalgamated) Ld. Regd. 1930. Struck off Register 16 July 1937 .... **1938**

Saxon Securities Trust Ld. Regd. 1925. Vol. liq. Dec. 1929. Undertaking and assets were acquired by Saxon Securities (Amalgamated) Ld. in which company shareholders were entitled to 1 preference share of £1 for each preference share of £1 held or 1 ordinary share of £1 for every 4 ordinary shares of £1 held or 1 ordinary share for every 8 Notes of £1 held. Struck off Register 3 Oct. 1897 .... **1942**

Saxon Tin & Wolfram Mining Co. Ld. Regd. 1913. Wound up under Trading with Enemy Amendment Act (1918) on 3 Mar. 1919. Liquidator released 16 Dec. 1926. Struck off Register under Trading with Enemy Amendment Act (1918) on 18 Dec. 1926 **1920**

Scala (Birkenhead) Ld. Regd. 1920. Vol. liq. (members') 1 Mar. 1937. Capital returned to contributories—7s. 4d. per share of £1. Final meeting return regd. 12 July 1938 .... **1938**

Scala (Leeds) Ld. Regd. 1919 a subsidiary of Denman Picture Houses Ld. Vol. liq. (members') 2 May 1956. Final meeting return regd. 1 Aug. 1970 .... **1951**

Scan Data International p.l.c. Regd. as private company 18 Nov. 1969; converted to public company 3 Nov. 1980. All capital acquired by Audiotronic Holdings p.l.c. in Feb. 1984. Winding-up order 31 Oct. 1986 **1984–5**

Scandinavian Exploration Co. Ld. Regd. 1890. Vol. liq. 29 Sept. 1892. Final meeting return regd. 25 Mar. 1896 .... **1893**

Scandinavian Moss Litter Co. Ld. Regd. 1894. Struck off Register 22 Oct. 1897 .... **1899**

Scandinvest Trust Co. Ld. *See* Trans-America Investment Trust Ld.

Scarab Co. Ld. Regd. 1919 as Scarab Oil Burning Co. Ld.; name changed Apr. 1928. Vol. liq. (creditors') 28 Sept. 1933. No capital returned to contributories. Final meeting return regd. 11 Feb. 1935 .... **1934**

Scarab Oil Burning Co. Ld. *See* Scarab Co. Ld.

Scarborough & Whitby Railway Co. Inc. by Special Act 1871. Undertaking acquired by North Eastern Railway Co. on 1 July 1898. Holders of 5% debenture stock received £100 3% debenture stock for each £100; 5% 1st preference shares of £10 received £20 4% preference stock for every 10 shares; 5% C preference shares of £10 received £10 4% preference stock for every 10 shares; ordinary B stock received £5 4% preference stock for each £100; ordinary A shares of £10 received £3 4% preference stock for every 10 shares and the £124,792 bond debts were paid off by £78,130 4% preference stock **1899**

Scarborough, Bridlington & West Riding Junction Railway Co. Inc. by Special Act 1885. Undertaking acquired by North Eastern Railway Co. on 1 July 1914. Debenture stockholders received £150 3% debenture stock for each £100 held and ordinary stockholders £46 North Eastern Consols for every £100 held **1915**

Scarborough Cliff Bridge Co. Inc. under Deed of Settlement 1837. Vol. liq. June 1920. Undertaking was acquired by Spa (Scarborough) Ld. **1921**

Scarborough Electric Supply Co. Ld. Regd. 1892. The undertaking was sold to the Corporation from 31 Dec. 1925. Vol. liq. 14 Aug. 1926. 6% 1st mortgage debenture stock was repaid. Capital returned to contributories—£1 per ordinary share of £1; further payments (if any) not known. Final meeting return regd. 14 Jan. 1929 .... **1927**

Scarborough Gas Co. Estd. 1834; inc. by Special Act 1851. Dissolved 1 May 1949, undertaking being vested in North Eastern Area Gas Board under Gas Act 1948. Holders of securities were entitled to receive, in respect of each £100 unit held, British Gas 3% guaranteed stock 1990—95 as follows:

	£	s.	d.
Cons. ord. stock (5% basic)............	120	0	0

	£	s.	d.
1895 ord. stock (5% basic)...............	120	0	0
5% 1867 pref. stock.........................	112	10	0
4½% red. pref. stock........................	102	10	0
4½% red. pref. stock........................	103	5	0
5% new red. pref. stock....................	102	13	4

Liability in respect of certain mortgage loans assumed by the Board **1952**

Scarborough Promenade Pier Co. Ld. Regd. 1865. Vol. liq. Feb. 1889. Final meeting return regd. 22 July 1889 .... **1890**

Scarborough South Cliff Tramway Co. Ld. Regd. 1873. Vol. liq. 28 Mar. 1966. Final meeting return regd. 30 Oct. 1968 .... **1911**

Sceptre Life Association Ld. Regd. 1864. Vol. liq. 23 Aug. 1917. Undertaking and assets were acquired by Eagle & British Dominions Insurance Co. Ld. (later Eagle Star Insurance Co. Ld.), in which company shareholders were entitled to 1 ordinary share of £3 (credited as fully-paid) for each share held. Shareholders were also entitled to £6 5s. per partly-paid share or £12 5s. per fully-paid share. Final meeting return regd. 26 Sept. 1921 .... **1921**

Schanschieff Electric Battery Syndicate Ld. Regd. 1887. Vol. liq. 21 Jan. 1890. Final meeting return regd. 18 July 1895 .... **1891**

Schattner Electricity Meter Co. Ld. *See* Engineering Instruments Ld.

Schibaieff Petroleum Co. Ld. Regd. 1898. Vol. liq. 11 Apr. 1913. Reconstructed as New Schibaieff Petroleum Co. Ld., in which company shareholders were entitled to 4 ordinary shares of £1 (credited with 14s. paid) for each preference share of £5 held or 2 ordinary shares of £1 (credited with 14s. paid) for every 5 ordinary shares of £1 held. Final meeting return regd. 16 Jan. 1914 .... **1914**

Schmidt (Conrad Wm.) (F. A. Glaeser) Ld. *See* London Varnish & Enamel Co. Ld.

Schmidt Locomotive Engine Co. Ld. *See* Schmidt's Superheating Co. Ld.

Scull (Arthur) & Son Ld. Regd. 1928. Vol. liq. (members') 17 Mar. 1966. All capital was owned by Drake & Scull Engineering Co. Ld. Final meeting return regd. 13 Apr. 1969 .... **1969**

Schmidt's Superheating Co. Ld. Regd. 1899 as Schmidt Locomotive Engine Co. Ld. Vol. liq. July 1910. Removed from Register 1911 .... **1911**

Schmidt's Superheating (1910) Ld. *See* Marine & Locomotive Superheaters Ld.

Schodnica (Galicia) Oil Co. Ld. Regd. 1912. Vol. liq. 6 Aug. 1914. Final meeting return regd. 22 Aug. 1924 **1916**

Schoen Steel Wheel Co. Ld. *See* Newlay Wheel Co. Ld.

Schoenhofen (Peter) Brewing Co. Ld. Regd. 1889. Removed from Register 1907 .... **1901**

Schofield Brothers (Stocksbridge) Ld. Regd. 1920. Vol. liq. 27 June 1923. Final meeting return regd. 4 June 1925 .... *****1924**

Schofield (Frank) Ld. Regd. 1906. Vol. liq. 22 Mar. 1907. Final meeting return regd. 20 Sept. 1910 .... *****1909**

Schofield (J. K.) & Co. Ld. Regd. 1874. Struck off Register 26 Jan. 1940 .... **1940**

Scholefield Steamshipping Co. Ld. Regd. 1905. Vol. liq. 5 Feb. 1917. Final meeting return regd. 21 Oct. 1918 *****1918**

Schröder (J. F.) Bank Kommanditgesselschaft auf Aktien. *See* Norddeutsche Kreditbank A. G.

Schull and Skibbereen Tramway and Light Railway Co. (West Carbery Tramways and Light Railways Co. Ld.). Inc. 1883 under the Tramways and Public Companies (Ireland) Act 1883, as West Carbery Tramways & Light Railways Co. Ld.; name changed 1892. In 1925 the undertaking was merged into the Great Southern Railways Co. The scheme provided that the shareholders should receive £125 4% preference stock for every £100 shares held **1925**

Schuller Diamond Mines Ld. Inc. Transvaal 1898. Vol. liq. 19 Oct. 1905 .... **1906**

Schultze Co. Ld. *See* Schultze Gunpowder Co. Ld. (Regd. 1911).

Schultze Gunpowder Co. Ld. Regd. 1868. Vol. liq. 4 Apr. 1892. Final meeting return regd. 14 July 1893 ...... **1899**

Schultze Gunpowder Co. Ld. Regd. 1892. *See* Smokeless Powder & Ammunition Co. Ld.

Schultze Gunpowder Co. Ld. Regd. 1898 as New Schultze Gunpowder Co. Ld.; name changed 1899. Vol. liq. Mar. 1911. After repayment of debenture stock a return of 25s. per preference share of £5 was anticipated. Removed from Register 1913............. **1911**

Schultze Gunpowder Co. Ld. Regd. 1911 as Schultze Co. Ld.; name changed 4 Jan. 1916. Vol. liq. 25 June 1923. Final meeting return regd. 4 July 1927 .... *****1924**

Schwabacher (Leopold) Ld. *See* Edwards & Co. (Bread Street) Ld.

Schwabe (S.) & Co. Ld. Regd. 1894. Undertaking sold to Calico Printer's Association Ld. Removed from Register 1903 .... **1901**

VOL. FOR

Schweizerische Discontobank. *See* Banque d'Escompte Suisse.

Schweppe (J.) & Co. Ld. Regd. 1886. Vol. liq. 22 Dec. 1892. Reconstructed as company of same name. Shareholders were entitled to 2 ordinary shares and 1 preference share of £5, all fully-paid, for each share of £13 held. Final meeting return regd. 30 Apr. 1894 .... **1897**

Schweppe (J.) and Co. Ld. Regd. 1893. Vol. liq. 26 Apr. 1897. Business was acquired by Schweppes Ld. Preference shareholders were entitled to 5 fully-paid preference shares of £1 in new company *plus* £1 5s. in cash for each preference share of £5 held. Ordinary shareholders were entitled to £12 in cash per ordinary share of £5 held; further payments (if any) not known. Debenture holders were entitled to £105 in cash or an equal amount of 4% perpetual debenture stock in new company. Final meeting return regd. 26 Apr. 1898 .... **1897**

Scinde, Punjaub & Delhi Railway Co. Inc. by Special Act 1869. The line was purchased by the Secretary of State for India in 1885. Stockholders were entitled to £126 10s. India 3½% Stock for every £100 stock held. Stockholders not so converting were entitled to Annuities A or B which terminated on 31 Dec. 1958; holders of Class B received £21 8s. 10·89d. per £1 annuity on division of sinking fund **1886**

Scotch Whisky Distillers Ld. Regd. 1887. Court Orders: to wind up 20 May 1889; to dissolve 9 May 1894 **1890**

Scotgate Ash Stone Co. Ld. Regd. 1872. Vol. liq. 2 July 1912. Final meeting return regd. 23 June 1914 .... **1913**

Scotia Development Co. Ld. Regd. 1903. Struck off Register 1915 .... **1908**

Scotsman Matabele Gold Reefs Ld. Regd. 1898. Struck off Register 29 Nov. 1897 .... **1908**

Scotswood Bridge Co. Inc. Special Act 1829. Undertaking acquired by Newcastle Corporation. Shareholders received £91 8s. 8·58d. per share of £50 .... **1907**

Scotswood, Newburn & Wylam Railway Co. Inc. by Special Act 1871. Amalgamated with North Eastern Railway Co. in 1883. Holders of ordinary shares received an equal amount of preference stock; holders of 4% preference shares received 4% preference stock **1884**

Scott (Ernest) & Mountain Ld. Regd. 1890. Vol. liq. 29 Dec. 1911. Struck off Register 10 Oct. 1916 .... **1940**

Scott Motor Cycle Co. Ld. Regd. 1924. Struck off Register Jan. 1935 .... **1935**

Scott, Son & Co. Ld. Regd. 1899. Vol. liq. (members') 27 July 1936. Capital returned to contributories—7s. 3¼d. per share of £1. Final meeting return regd. 14 Aug. 1939 .... **1940**

Scott (Thomas) & Sons (Bakers) Ld. Regd. 1903 as John H. Lunt & Co. Ld.; name changed 28 Mar. 1942. All shares owned by Allied Bakeries Ld. (later Associated British Foods Ld.). Vol. liq. (members') 28 Mar. 1942. Final meeting return regd. 21 Oct. 1942 ..... **1943**

Scott (Walter) Ld. Regd. 1900. Receiver appointed in July 1934. Struck off Register 26 Jan. 1940 .... **1941**

Scottish Africa Ld. Regd. 1897. Reconstructed 1902 as Scottish African Trust Ld. in which company shareholders were entitled to 1 share of 10s (credited with 7s. paid) for each share of £1 held. Removed from Register 1909 .... **1906**

Scottish African Corporation Ld. Regd. Edinburgh 1895. Amalgamated with Scottish Rhodesia Ld. under title of Scottish Africa Ld. Vol. liq. July 1897. Final meeting return regd. 11 May 1906 .... **1902**

Scottish African Trust Ld. Regd. 1902. Vol. liq. 28 May 1906. The fully-paid shares in French South African Development Co. Ld. were distributed in specie. In Nov. 1906 other investments were in liquidators' hands. Final meeting return regd. 22 Sept 1927.... **1907**

Scottish Alliance Insurance Co. Ld. Regd. Edinburgh 1888. Vol. liq. Feb. 1904. Undertaking and assets acquired by Union Assurance Society. Final meeting return regd. 4 Oct. 1907 .... **1904**

Scottish Allied Investors Ld. Regd. Edinburgh 1928. On 5 Apr. 1961 the undertaking was acquired by Scottish United Investors Ld. Ordinary stockholders received £22 10s. ordinary stock of that company for every £25 ordinary stock held; 5% preference and debenture stockholders received a like amount of a similar security of that company in exchange for their holding. Company was dissolved on 29 Dec. 1961 under Section 208 of The Companies Act, 1948 .... **1963**

Scottish Aluminium Ld. Regd. Edinburgh 1898. Vol. liq. July 1901. Final meeting return regd. 14 Jan. 1904 **1902**

Scottish Amalgamated Silks Ld. Regd. Edinburgh 1928. Vol. liq. (members') 7 Sept. 1930. Capital returned to contributories—£96,216 13s. 11d. Final meeting return regd. 1 Mar. 1939 .... **1931**

VOL. FOR

Scottish-American Land Co. Ld. Regd. Edinburgh 1880. Vol. liq. Apr. 1892. Capital returned to contributories—£3 per share of £7; further payments (if any) not known. Final meeting return regd. 17 Oct. 1899 **1893**

Scottish American Mortgage Co. Ld. Regd. Edinburgh 1874. Undertaking was merged with Scottish Eastern Investment Trust Ld. and Second Scottish Eastern Investment Trust Ld. in July 1966. Ordinary shareholders and preference stockholders were entitled to receive shares of Scottish Eastern Investment Trust Ld. as follows: 8 deferred shares (of 5s.) for every 5 ordinary shares (of 5s.); 1 4½% preferred share (of £1) for every £1 A preference stock; 10 4½% preferred shares (of £1) for every £9 B preference stock. Debenture stockholders were entitled to receive a like amount of stock of Scottish Eastern Investment Trust Ld. Dissolved under Sect. 208 of Companies Act, 1948, 11 Oct. 1966 .... **1967**

Scottish-American Oil & Transport Co. Ld. Regd. 1919. Vol. liq. 29 Dec. 1927. Shareholders were entitled to 1 fully-paid ordinary share of 1s. in Tankers Ld. for each share of 5s. held. Final meeting return regd. 3 Dec. 1928 .... **1928**

Scottish Amicable Heritable Securities Association Ld. Regd. Edinburgh 1875. Vol. liq. Dec. 1883. Struck off Register 27 Sept. 1932 .... **1885**

Scottish & Foreign Trust Ld. Regd. Edinburgh 1914. Vol. liq. July 1927. Final meeting return regd. 22 June 1928.................. **1928**

Scottish and New Zealand Investment Co. Ld. Regd. Edinburgh 1877. Vol. liq. Dec. 1906. Capital returned to contributories—15s. 6d. per share of £1 prior to liquidation and 3s. per share on 31 Dec. 1906; further payments (if any) not known. Final meeting return regd. 1 Aug. 1907 .... **1907**

Scottish & Southern Counties Investment Trust Ld. *See* Scottish Stockholders Invest. Trust Ld.

Scottish Artificial Silks Ld. Regd. Edinburgh 1927. Vol. liq. (creditors') 9 Sept. 1930. Assets realised insufficient to pay creditors in full. Final meeting return regd. 1 Mar. 1939 .... **1931**

Scottish Australian Mining Co. Ld. Regd. 1859. Vol. liq. (members') 28 Dec. 1956. Capital returned to contributories—6s. 5d. per unit of 4s. Final meeting return regd. 20 Mar. 1959 .... **1960**

Scottish Canadian Fruit & Land Co. Ld. Regd. Edinburgh 1910. Vol. liq. June 1924. Struck off Register 15 Oct. 1937 .... **1938**

Scottish Canadian Mortgage Co. Ld. *See* Second Scottish Mortgage & Trust Co. Ld.

Scottish Capital Investment Co. Ld. Regd. in Edinburgh 1925. Undertaking transferred to Scottish, Mortgage & Trust Co. Ld. in Nov. 1969. Ordinary stockholders' received 123 ordinary shares for each £25 stock held and preference stockholders a like amount of similar stock. Debenture stock liability was assumed by Scottish & Mortgage Trust Co. Ld. Company dissolved by Order of the Court on 28 Mar. 1970 .... **1970**

Scottish Carolina Timber & Land Co. Ld. Regd. Edinburgh 1884. Vol. liq. May 1889. Final meeting return regd. 16 May 1898 .... **1890**

Scottish Central Electric Power Co. Inc. by Special Act 1903. All capital was owned by Scottish Power Co. Ld. Dissolved 1 Apr. 1948 under Electricity Act 1947 .... **1940**

Scottish Central Investment Trust Ld. (The). *See* Edinburgh and Dundee Investment Co. Ld. (The)

Scottish Cinema & Variety Theatres Ld. Regd. Edinburgh. 1916. Vol. liq. (members') 30 Mar. 1938. Capital returned to contributories—20s. per share of £1. All shares owned by Associated British Cinemas Ld. Final meeting return regd. 3 Mar. 1944.......... **1939**

Scottish Coal Products Ld. Regd. 1928. Receiver appointed in Apr. 1932. Court Order to wind up Dec. 1932. Struck off Register 14 Oct. 1938 .... **1939**

Scottish Cold Storage & Ice Co. Ld. Regd. Edinburgh 1896. Vol. liq. Sept. 1906. Premises, machinery and plant acquired by Union Cold Storage Co. Ld. Capital returned to contributories—10s. per preference share of £5; further payments (if any) not known. No return made to holders of ordinary shares of £5. Final meeting return regd. 15 Jan. 1908 **1941**

Scottish Colonial Gold Fields Ld. Regd. Edinburgh 1896. Vol. liq. Nov. 1911. Final meeting return regd. 27 Nov. 1912 .... **1912**

Scottish Consolidated Trust Ld. Regd. Edinburgh 1927. On 5 Apr. 1961 the undertaking was acquired by Scottish United Investors Ld. Ordinary stockholders received £23 10s. ordinary stock of that company for every £25 ordinary stock held; 5% preference and debenture stockholders received a like amount of a similar security of that company in

VOL. FOR

exchange for their holdings. Dissolved on 29 Dec. 1961 under Sec. 208 of Companies Act, 1948 ...... **1963**

Scottish County & Mercantile Insurance Co. Ld. Regd. Edinburgh 1895 as Farmers' & Landowners' Insurance Co. Ld.; name changed 1897 to Farmers', Landowners' and Mercantile Insurance Co. Ld., and as above in 1899. Vol. liq. Feb. 1907. Undertaking and assets were acquired by Commercial Union Assurance Co. Ld. Capital returned to contributories—£1 11s. in cash per share of £5 (£1 paid); further payments (if any) not known. Struck off Register 10 Mar. 1936 .... **1907**

Scottish Cyanide Co. Ld. Regd. Edinburgh 1905. Vol. liq. Sept. 1907. Final meeting return regd. 7 Feb. 1910 ...... **1908**

Scottish Deposit and Investment Co. Ld. Regd. Edinburgh 1885. At 30 Sept. 1896 all assets had been realised and liabilities discharged. Vol. liq. Dec. 1896; it was stated that funds would permit a return of 2s. per share (of £10 with £2 paid). Final meeting return regd. 9 Apr. 1897 .... **1897**

Scottish Drainage & Improvement Co. Inc. by Special Acts 1846 and 1860. Wound up. Interim payment of £4 per share (of £20 with £4 paid) **1935**

Scottish Drapery Corporation Ld. Regd. Edinburgh 1926. Vol. liq. (members') 30 Jan. 1953. All ordinary capital was owned by House of Fraser Ld. to whom all trading assets were transferred. Preference shares repaid at par. Final meeting return regd. 15 Mar. 1965 .... **1966**

Scottish Dyes Ld. Regd. Edinburgh 1918. Vol. liq. (members') 31 Mar. 1942. Direct controlling interest held by Imperial Chemical Industries Ld. Final meeting return regd. 30 Aug. 1947 .... **1943**

Scottish Economic Life Assurance Society Ld. Regd. Edinburgh 1885. Business acquired by Scottish Metropolitan Life Assurance Co. (later Scottish Metropolitan Assurance Co. Ld.). Vol. liq. May 1892. Final meeting return regd. 12 July 1893 ..... **1909**

Scottish Employers' Liability & Accident Assurance Co. Ld. See Scottish Employers' Liability & General Insurance Co. Ld.

Scottish Employers' Liability & General Insurance Co. Ld. Regd. 1881 as Scottish Employers' Liability & Accident Assurance Co. Ld.; name changed Dec. 1896. Vol. liq. Undertaking and assets transferred to London & Lancashire Fire Insurance Co. Ld. (later London & Lancashire Insurance Co.). Shareholders were entitled to 1 share of £10 (£2 paid) in purchasing company plus £10 5s. in cash for every 10 shares of £5 (15s. paid); holders of less than 10 shares were paid off in cash at £3 5s. per share. Removed from Register 1906 .... **1905**

Scottish General Fire Assurance Corporation Ld. Regd. Edinburgh 1895. Vol. liq. June 1900. Business acquired by General Accident Assurance Corporation Ld. (later General Accident Fire & Life Assurance Corporation Ld.) in which corporation shareholders were entitled to 5 shares of £1 (credited with 5s. paid) for every 2 shares of £5 (£1 paid) held or repayment in cash at par. Final meeting return regd. 13 Dec. 1901 .... **1901**

Scottish General Omnibus Co. Ld. Regd. Edinburgh 1919. Vol. liq. 5 June 1934. All shares were owned by Fife Tramway, Light & Power Co. Ld. Final meeting return regd. 16 May 1935 .... **1930**

Scottish Gympie Consols Co. Ld. Regd. Edinburgh 1902. Vol. liq. May 1905. Struck off Register 5 Feb. 1937 **1937**

Scottish Gympie Freehold Mining Co. (1900) Ld. Regd. Edinburgh 1900. Vol. liq. Dec. 1917. Final meeting return regd. 17 Feb. 1921 .... **1918**

Scottish Gympie Gold Mines Ld. Regd. Edinburgh 1895 as Gympie Gold Mines Ld.; name changed Feb. 1897. Vol. liq. June 1902 for reconstruction as company of same name. Shareholders were entitled to 20 fully-paid shares of £1 in new company for each share of £1 held. Struck off Register 27 Sept. 1932 .... **1908**

Scottish Gympie Gold Mines Ld. Regd. Edinburgh 1902. Vol. liq. July 1923. Final meeting return regd. 21 Dec. 1926 .... **1924**

Scottish Heritages Co. Ld. Regd. Edinburgh 1874. Vol. liq. 14 May 1891. Court Order to continue winding up under supervision 16 May 1891. Final meeting return regd. 7 Jan. 1901 .... **1892**

Scottish House-to-House Electricity Co. Ld. Regd. 1889. Business acquired in 1906 by Coatbridge & Airdrie Electric Supply Co. Ld. Removed from Register 1907 .... **1909**

Scottish Imperial Insurance Co. Regd. Edinburgh as unlimited 1866. Undertaking and assets were acquired in 1906 by Norwich Union Life Insurance Society. A return of £2 2s. per share of £10 (£1 paid) was anticipated. Removed from Register 1906...... **1906**

VOL. FOR

Scottish Live Stock Insurance Co. Ld. Regd. Edinburgh 1899. Vol. liq. Oct. 1909. Undertaking and assets acquired by General Accident Fire Life Assurance Corporation Ld. in which Corporation shareholders were entitled to 1 share of £5 (£1 5s. paid) plus 2s. 3d. in cash for every 3 shares of £5 (15s. paid) held, or 15s. per share in cash. Final meeting return regd. 2 Apr. 1910 .... **1910**

Scottish-Maikop Oil Wells Ld. See Scottish-Trinidad Oil Fields Ld.

Scottish Malay Rubber Co. Ld. Regd. Edinburgh 1906. Vol. liq. Mar. 1920. Struck off Register 9 Apr. 1937 **1938**

Scottish Malay Rubber Co. Ld. Regd. Edinburgh 1920. Vol. liq. (members') July 1935. Undertaking and assets were acquired by Scottish Malayan Estates Ld. in which company shareholders were entitled to 1 share of £1 (credited as fully-paid) plus 8d. in cash for every 2 shares of £1 held. Final meeting return regd. 17 July 1936 .... **1936**

Scottish Manitoba Co. Ld. Regd. Edinburgh 1881 as Scottish Manitoba & North West Real Estate Co. Ld.; name changed Aug. 1911. Vol. liq. (creditors') 30 June 1941. Debenture holders received 9s. 9d. in £. Final meeting return regd. 2 Mar. 1944 .... **1942**

Scottish Manufacturing Co. Ld. Regd. Edinburgh 1896. Vol. liq. Sept. 1899. Final meeting return regd. 26 Dec. 1903 .... **1900**

Scottish Mashonaland Gold Mining Co Ld. Regd. 1900. Vol. liq. 8 Nov. 1920. Final meeting return regd. 6 July 1923 .... **1921**

Scottish Metal-Edged Box Co. Ld. Regd. Edinburgh 1887. Vol. liq. June 1888. Final meeting return regd. 25 June 1896 .... **1889**

Scottish Metropolitan Fire Assurance Co. Regd. as unlimited in 1880. Business transferred to Caledonian Fire & Life Insurance Co. in 1883 .... **1884**

Scottish Midlands Electricity Supply Ld. Regd. Edinburgh 1913. All capital was owned by Scottish Power Co. Ld. Dissolved 1 Apr. 1948 under Electricity Act 1947 .... **1963**

Scottish Mortgage and Land Investment Co. of New Mexico Ld. Regd. Edinburgh 1882. Vol. liq. 16 Mar. 1906. Capital returned to contributories—£1 15s. 7d. per share of £1 10s. Final meeting return regd. 22 June 1944...................... **1907**

Scottish Motor Engineering Co. Ld. Regd. Edinburgh 1905. Vol. liq. Apr. 1907. Court Orders: to continue winding up under supervision; to dissolve 19 Dec. 1908 .... **1908**

Scottish Motor Traction Co. Ld. Regd. Edinburgh 1905. Vol. liq. July 1929. Reconstructed as company of same name. Shareholders were entitled to 3 preference shares and 1 ordinary share of £1 for every 2 shares of £1 held. Struck off Register 9 Apr. 1937 **1930**

Scottish Mutual Fire Insurance Co. Ld. See Scottish Standard Fire Insurance Co. Ld.

Scottish National Housing Co. Ld. Regd. Edinburgh 1914. Vol. liq. (members') 19 Feb. 1964. Final meeting return regd. 11 Feb. 1970 .... **1970**

Scottish-National Key Registry & Assurance Association Ld. Regd. 1897. Vol. liq. (members') 14 Mar. 1962. All capital was owned by Scottish Union and National Insurance Co. Final meeting return regd. 13 June 1963 .... **1960**

Scottish National Securities Corpn. Ld. Regd. 1907. Vol. liq. (members') 26 May 1961. Final meeting return regd. 26 Apr. 1962 .... **1947**

Scottish North Queensland Exploration Co. Ld. Regd. Edinburgh 1907. Vol. liq. May 1911. Properties sold to Mammoth Copper Mine Ld. for 5,500 ordinary shares of £1 and £350 in cash. Struck off Register 2 Apr. 1935 .... **1912**

Scottish Oil Agency Ld. Regd. Edinburgh 1918. Vol. liq. (members') 28 June 1933. The petroleum-distributing business was acquired in 1932 by Shell-Mex & B. P. Ld. Capital returned to contributories—£286,178 18s. 11d. including certain assets distributed in specie. Final meeting return regd. 6 Dec. 1933 ..... **1934**

Scottish Ontario Investment Co. p.l.c. Regd. in Edinburgh Dec. 1879 as Scottish Ontario & Manitoba Land Co. Ld.; name changed 1960. Vol. liq. (members') 22 Aug. 1983. Assets transferred to 4 units Trusts: Scottish Pacific Fund; Scottish North American Fund; Scottish World Growth Fund and Scottish Income Fund. Holders of ordinary shares received units in one or more funds as elected based on value of net assets transferred to relevant fund. First and final distribution of 0·01925p per ordinary share of 25p made on 28 Feb. 1985. 5% preference shares repaid at par. Amount which was deposited with the Accountant of Court was £2,068·22 in respect of unclaimed distributions. Final meeting held on 20 Aug. 1985 .... **1986–7**

*See Stock Exchange Year-Book.

VOL. FOR

Scottish Ontario & Manitoba Land Co. Ld. *See* Scottish Ontario Investment Co. p.l.c.

Scottish, Overseas & Commonwealth Investment Trust Ld. Regd. 1908 as Lena Goldfields Ld.; name changed to Lena Investment Trust Ld. Mar. 1950 and to above 18 Dec. 1964. On 21 July 1975 capital was cancelled, holders being entitled to 88 ordinary shares of 25p and 1 5·04% preference shares of £1 of Estates House Investment Trust Ld. for every 100 ordinary shares and 1 6% preference share respectively. Company dissolved without winding up on 31 Dec. 1976 .... **1977-8**

Scottish Pacific Coast Mining Co. Ld. Regd. Edinburgh 1881. Vol. liq. Feb. 1885. Court Order to dissolve 17 Nov. 1899 .... **1886**

Scottish Pacific Mortgage Co. Ld. Regd. Edinburgh 1887 as Edinburgh Lombard Investment Co. Ld.; name changed Feb. 1914. Vol. liq. Mar. 1917. Final meeting return regd. 8 Feb. 1919 .... **1917**

Scottish Power Co. Ld. Regd. in Edinburgh 1909. Dissolved 1 Apr. 1948, undertaking being vested in British (later Central) Electricity Authority under Electricity Act 1947. Holders of securities were entitled to receive British Electricity 3% guaranteed stock (1968—73) as follows in respect of each £1 unit of capital held:

	£	s.	d.
6% preference stock	1	11	4
4% preference stock	1	2	4
Ordinary stock	2	6	2

1949

Scottish Provident Investment Co. Ld. Regd. Edinburgh 1874. Vol. liq. Dec. 1895. Final meeting return regd. 30 Apr. 1896 .... **1890**

Scottish Provincial Assurance Co. Established 1825. Inc. 1852. In 1890 business was acquired by North British & Mercantile Insurance Co. in which company shareholders were entitled to 1 share of £25 (£6 5s. paid) for every 2 shares of £50 (£3 paid) held **1894**

Scottish Queensland Mortgage Co. Ld. Regd. Edinburgh 1886. Vol. liq. Nov. 1920. Final meeting return regd. 11 Jan. 1924 .... **1921**

Scottish Re-insurance Co. Ld. Regd. Edinburgh 1894. Vol. liq. (members') 8 Apr. 1938. All shares were owned by Commercial Union Assurance Co. Ld. which company acquired undertaking. Final meeting return regd. 25 Feb. 1939 .... **1939**

Scottish Reversionary Co. Ld. Regd.in Edinburgh Dec. 1877. Vol. liq. (members') 28 Dec. 1951. The 3½% debenture stock was repaid at apr in Jan–May 1952. Amount of distributions was £1,484,506. Return of final meeting regd. 23 Dec. 1987 .... **1988-9**

Scottish Rhodesia Ld. Regd. Edinburgh 1895. Amalgamated with Scottish African Corporation Ld. under title of Scottish Africa Ld. Vol. liq. July 1897. Final meeting return regd. 11 May 1906 .... **1902**

Scottish Sea-Fishing & Curing Co. Ld. Regd. Edinburgh 1884. Vol. liq. Jan. 1886. Final meeting return regd. 31 Jan. 1887 .... **1886**

Scottish Ship and Ship-Share Investment Co. Ld. Regd. Edinburgh 1893. Vol. liq. Nov. 1911. Final meeting return regd. 21 May 1913 .... **1912**

Scottish Sickness & Accident Insurance Co. Ld. Regd. Edinburgh 1907. Vol. liq. (creditors') 6 Jan. 1930. No capital returned to contributories. Final meeting return regd. 17 Jan. 1933 .... **1930**

Scottish Spitsbergen Syndicate Ld. Regd. Edinburgh 1919; Vol. liq. (members') 29 June 1910; ceased to act was acquired by Scottish Spitsbergen (Development) Ld. in which company shareholders were entitled to 1 fully-paid founders' share of 3d. for each £1 share held; a return of capital of 6d. per share was also made. Final meeting return regd. 26 June 1953; £734 was paid to Accountant to the Court **1954**

Scottish Standard Fire Insurance Co. Ld. Regd. Edinburgh 1885 as Scottish Mutual Fire Insurance Co. Ld.; name changed Jan. 1886. Vol. liq. Aug. 1887. Business taken over by National Assurance Co. of Ireland. Final meeting return regd. 27 Aug. 1889 **1888**

Scottish Standard Reversionary Co. Ld. Regd. Edinburgh 1904. Vol. liq. (members') 15 Oct. 1934. Capital returned to contributories—£8 1s. 2·8d. per share of £5. Final meeting return regd. 12 Dec. 1936 **1935**

Scottish Steam Drifter & Insurance Co. Ld. Regd. Edinburgh 1907. Vol. liq. Oct. 1910. Undertaking and assets sold to Herring Drifter Insurance Co. Ld. in which company shareholders were entitled to 1 share of £1 (credited with 2s. paid) for every 4½ shares of £1 (2s. paid) held or to be paid off in cash at 2s. 1d. per share *plus* interest. Final meeting return regd. 8 Oct. 1913 .... **1911**

Scottish Steam Herring Fishing Co. Ld. Regd. Edinburgh 1899. Vol. liq. (members') 25 Sept. 1956.

VOL. FOR

Capital returned to contributories—30s. 10½d. per share of 10s. Final meeting return regd. 1 May 1957 **1958**

Scottish Stockholders Investment Trust Ld. Regd. 1926 as Scottish & Southern Counties Invest. Trust Ld.; name changed Jan. 1929. On 29 June 1962 undertaking acquired by Stockholders Invest. Trust Ld. Holders of preference and ordinary capital and debenture stocks received a corresponding nominal amount of similar capital of that company in exchange for their holdings. Company was dissolved 13 Nov. 1962 under Section 208 of Companies Act 1948 .... **1963**

Scottish-Trinidad Oil Fields Ld. Regd. 1910 as Scottish-Maikop Oil Wells Ld.; name changed Oct. 1922. Struck off Register 11 May 1951 .... **1952**

Scottish United Investors p.l.c. Regd. in Edinburgh 12 Sept. 1924; re-regd. as p.l.c. in Nov. 1981. Vol. liq. (members') 25 Nov. 1983 .... **1984-5**

Scottish Vacuum Cleaner Co. Ld. Regd. 1903. Vol. liq. Nov. 1917. Struck off Register 5 Feb. 1937 .... **1937**

Scottish Waggon Co. Ld. Regd. Edinburgh 1861. Vol. liq. Jan. 1904 for reconstruction under same name, in which company shareholders were entitled to 1 fully-paid share of £10 for each fully-paid share of £10 held or 1 share of £10 (credited with £4 paid) for each share of £10 (£4 paid). Struck off Register 27 Sept. 1932 .... **1904**

Scottish Waggon Co. Ld. Regd. Edinburgh 1904. Vol. liq. (members') 28 Feb. 1941. Capital returned to contributories—£2 1s. 11 7/10. per share of £1. Final meeting return regd. 6 May 1942 .... **1945**

Scottish Westralia Ld. Regd. 1895. Vol. liq. 23 July 1898. The assets were sold to English & Scottish Finance Corporation Ld. in which company shareholders were entitled to 4 fully-paid ordinary shares of £1 and 2 preference shares of £1 (credited with 10s. paid) for every 5 preference shares of £1 held. Final meeting return regd. 19 Sept. 1900 .... **1899**

Scottish Wharf Co. Ld. Regd. Edinburgh 1868. Vol. liq. Aug. 1899. Final meeting return regd. 28 July 1900 **1900**

Scottish Wood Haskinizing Co. Ld. Regd. Edinburgh 1903. Vol. liq. May 1911. Final meeting return regd. 4 Nov. 1912 .... **1912**

Scotts (Garments) Ld. *See* Kalbur Coats Ld.

Scott's Standard Pneumatic Tyre Co. Ld. Regd. 1896. Vol. liq. 10 Nov. 1897. Business acquired by Amalgamated Pneumatic Tyre Companies Ld. Final meeting return regd. 7 June 1900 .... **1898**

Scotts the West End Tailors Ld. Regd. 1928. All capital was owned by Lockwood & Bradley Ld. Struck off Register 1940 .... **1940**

Scotty's Gold Mines Ld. Regd. 1897. Removed from Register 1901 .... **1902**

"Scotty's" Hauraki Gold Mining Co Ld. Regd. 1895. Vol. liq. 10 Aug. 1897. Reconstructed 1897 as Scotty's Gold Mine Ld. in which company shareholders were entitled to 1 share of 5s. (credited with 4s. paid) for each share of 5s. held. Final meeting return regd. 16 Mar. 1898 .... **1901**

Scragg (Ernest) & Sons (Holdings) Ld. Regd. 1919 as private company as Ernest Scragg & Sons Ld.; converted public company 1956; name changed 1965. Vol. liq. 18 Mar. 1982. Dissolved 30 Jan. 1986 **1976-7**

Scrase's Brewery Ld. Regd. 1889. Vol. liq. (members') 15 May 1947. Undertaking and assets taken over by controlling company, Strong & Co. of Romsey Ld. Final meeting return regd. 23 Mar.1948 .... **1948**

Scratcherd & Co. Ld. Regd. 1900. Receiver appointed 7 May 1911; ceased to act 6 Sept. 1918. Struck off Register 18 July 1919 .... ***1916**

Scull (Arthur) & Son Ld. Regd. 1928. All capital owned by Drake & Scull Engineering. Co. Ld. Vol. liq. (members') 17 Mar. 1966. Final meeting return regd. 13 Apr. 1969 .... **1969**

Sea Salvage Co. Ld. Regd. 1908. Vol. liq. 6 June 1913. Final meeting return regd. 2 July 1918 .... **1914**

Seaboard Air Line Railway. Organised Virginia 1900. Reorganised as company of same name. Holders of common stock were entitled to an equal amount of common stock in new company; holders of preferred to an equal amount of preferred stock; the 4% refunding mortgage gold bonds, 5% adjustment mortgage gold bonds and Georgia, Carolina & Northern Railway 1st mortgage 5% gold bonds were taken over by new company **1916**

Seabrook Estate Co. Ld. Regd. 1872. Vol. liq. (members') 7 Sept. 1948. Company's holding of £985 ordinary stock of Imperial Tobacco Co. (of Gt. Britain & Ireland) Ld. was distributed to shareholders at rate of £1 of stock for each share (of £31 10s.) held. Capital returned to contributories—£20 8s. 6d. Final meeting return regd. 22 June 1950 .... **1951**

Seabrooke & Sons Ld. Regd. 1891. Vol. liq. (members') Apr. 1934. Undertaking and assets were acquired by

VOL. FOR

Charrington & Co. Ld. which company owned all shares. The 5½% 1st mortgage deb. stock was repaid at par. Final meeting return regd. 20 Mar. 1935 **1935**

Seacombe, Hoylake & Deeside Railway Co. Inc. by Special Act 1863 as Hoylake Railway Co. Undertaking sold to Hoylake & Birkenhead Rail & Tramway Co. in 1872; name changed 1881. All ordinary shares were held by Wirral Railways Co. Ld. in 1891 **1891**

Seacombe Phospho Guano Co. Ld. See Phospho Guano Co. Ld.

Seafield Dock & Railway Co. *See* Kirkcaldy & District Railway Co.

Seafield Rubber Co. Ld. Regd. 1907. Vol. liq. 4 Mar. 1920. Reconstructed as company of same name. Shareholders were entitled to 4 shares of £1 (credited as fully-paid) in new company for each share of £1 held. Final meeting return regd. 30 Sept. 1921 .... **1920**

Seafield Rubber Co. Ld. Regd. 1920. Vol. liq. (members') 7 Aug. 1958. Undertaking and assets acquired by Seafield Amalgamated Rubber Co. Ld. stockholders receiving 17 fully-paid shares (of 2*s.*) in that company *plus* 10*s.* cash for every £1 stock held. £358 5*s.* 2*d.* paid into Companies' Liquidation Account. Final meeting return regd. 1 Nov. 1961 .... **1963**

Seafield Shipping Co. Ld. Regd. 1896. Vol. liq. 18 Feb. 1908. Undertaking and assets were acquired by Nitrate Producers' Steamship Co. Ld. in which company shareholders were entitled to 5 preference and 3 ordinary shares of £5 for every 8 shares of £5 held. Final meeting return regd. 20 Apr.1909 ...... **1908**

Seaforth and Sefton Junction Railway Co. Inc. by Special Act 1903. In 1923 the undertaking was merged into the London & North Eastern Railway Co. No part of the capital was in the hands of the public **1924**

Seaham Gas & Lighting Co. Regd. as unlimited 1897. Inc. by Special Act 1905. Undertaking was acquired in 1936 by Sunderland Gas Co. which company assumed the liability for the mortgages. Holders of A ordinary stock (8% maximum) and B shares (8% maximum) of £25 were entitled to an equal amount of ordinary stock (6% basic) in purchasing company. Holders of 4½% preference and C (6% maximum) stocks were entitled to £75 ordinary (6% basic) stock for every £100 stock held **1937**

Sealcones Ld. Regd. 1931. Vol. liq. (members') 31 Dec. 1948. Capital returned to contributories—5·587*d.* per participating preference share of 1*s.* £233 7*s.* 10*d.* was paid into Companies' Liquidation Account. Final meeting return regd. 6 Jan. 1950 ..... **1950**

Seaport (Selangor) Rubber Estate, Ld. Regd. 1910. Vol. liq. (members') 30 Nov. 1965. Amount returned to contributories (per £1 stock)—£6 13*s.* 6·25*d.* £526 10*s.* 2*d.* paid into Companies' Liquidation Account in respect of unclaimed dividends and £1,487 15*s.* 6*d.* in respect of unclaimed distributions. Final meeting return regd. 28 Oct. 1970......................... **1970**

Search Syndicate Ld. Regd. 1906. Vol. liq. 24 June 1914. Capital returned to contributories—23*s.* 9¼*d.* per ordinary share of £1; 20*s.* 7*d.* per deferred share of 1*s.*; further payments (if any) not known. Final meeting return regd. 18 June 1915 .... **1915**

Searcy, Tansley & Co. Ld. Regd. 1898. Vol. liq. 14 Jan.1916. Struck off Register 8 July 1926 .... **1916**

Searle & Herring Ld. Regd 1889. Vol. liq. 6 June 1898. Business was acquired by Lloyd & Yorath Ld. (later Lloyds (Newport) Ld.). Final meeting return regd. 21 Feb. 1899 .... **1899**

Searle (H. J.) & Son Ld. Regd. 1887. Vol. liq. 5 Mar. 1926 for reconstruction as H. J. Searle & Son (1926) Ld. (later H. J. Searle & Son Ld.). Capital returned to contributories—£5 10*s.* per preference share of £1; £4 7*s.* 3*d.* per ordinary share of £1. Final meeting return regd. 27 Mar. 1928 .... **1927**

Searle Unburstable Inner Tube Co. Ld. Regd. 1913. Receivers for debenture holders appointed in Oct. 1917. Struck off Register 1921 .... **1920**

Seascale Gas Co. (1929) Ld. Regd. 1929. Dissolved 1 May 1949, undertaking being vested in Northern Area Gas Board under Gas Act 1948. Holders of ordinary shares (of £1) were entitled to receive £1 British Gas 3% guaranteed stock 199#5 for each share held **1952**

Seascale Mineral Exploration Co. Ld. Regd. 1906. Vol. liq. 21 Dec. 1914. Final meeting return regd. 1 July 1915.. **1915**

Seaside Hotels Ld. Regd. 1902. Court Order to wind up 1904. Liquidator released 18 June 1907. Struck off Register 20 Jan. 1931 .... **1931**

Seaside Resorts & Developments Co. Ld. Regd. 1921. Struck off Register 27 June 1961 .... **1940**

Seaton & Beer Railway Co. Inc. by Special Act 1863. Holders of ordinary shares of £10 and £100 5% preference stock received £1 13*s.* 4*d.* and £75 London & South Western Railway 4% preference stock respectively. Company was dissolved on 1 Jan. 1888 .... **1889**

Seaton & District Electric Light Co. Ld. Regd. 1923. Dissolved 1 Apr. 1948, undertaking being vested in the British (later Central) Electricity Authority and South-Western Area Board under the Electricity Act 1947. Ordinary shareholders were entitled to receive £1 6*s.* 6*d.* British Electricity 3% guaranteed stock (1968—73), for every share (of £1) held **1949**

Seaton, Axminster & District Gas Co. Ld. Regd. 1863 as Seaton Gas & Coke Co. Ld.; name subsequently changed. Dissolved 1 May 1949, undertaking being vested in South Western Area Gas Board under Gas Act 1948. Holders of securities were entitled to receive British Gas 3% guaranteed stock 1990—95 as follows in respect of each £100 unit, unless otherwise stated of security held:

	£	s.	d.	
Ord. shares (of £1)...........................	1	8	0	
3½% red. mort. deb. bonds (1952)......	100	0	0	
3½% red. mort. deb. bonds (1966)......	100	0	0	
4% red. mort. deb. bonds..................	101	10	0	**1952**

Seaton Brick & Tile Co. Ld. Regd. Edinburgh 1884. Vol. liq. July 1924. Final meeting return regd. 28 July 1928.. **1925**

Seaton Gas & Coke Co. Ld. *See* Seaton, Axminster & District Gas Co. Ld.

Seattle National Bank. Inc. Seattle 1890. In 1929 the assets and liabilities were merged into those of the First National Bank of Seattle and the Dexter Horton National Bank under the name of the First-Seattle-Dexter Horton National Bank **1930**

Sebakwe & District Mines Ld. Inc. Southern Rhodesia 1901. Vol. liq. (members') 31 Mar. 1936. A first distribution of 1 share in Silbak Premier Mines Ld. for every 8 shares of 2*s.* 6*d.* held was made in Dec. 1936 .... **1937**

Secco Films (British and Colonial) Ld. Regd. 1899. Court Order to wind up 6 Mar. 1901. Removed from Register 1910 .... **1902**

Second American Trust Co. Ld. Regd. Edinburgh 1926. On 31 Oct. 1961 the assets and liabilities were acquired by American Trust Co. Ld. Ordinary shareholders received 7 ordinary shares of 5*s.* in that company for every 6 shares (of 5*s.*) held and preference stockholders £110 preference stock for every £10 held; liability for the debenture stocks and terminal debentures was assumed by that company. Company was dissolved under Section 208 of Companies Act 1948 on 5 July 1962 .... **1963**

Second Anglo-Celtic Trust Ld. Regd 1929. All capital was owned by Anglo Celtic Trust Co. Vol. liq. (members') 31 Mar. 1960. Final return regd. 17 Dec. 1963.. **1960**

Second Austrian Incandescent Share Co. Ld. Regd. 1896. Vol. liq. 29 Mar. 1898. The business was sold to Welsbach Incandescent Gas Light Co. Ld. in 1897. Holders of shares of £1 received £1 payable two-thirds in cash and one-third in shares in purchasing company. Final meeting return regd. 17 Mar. 1899 **1899**

Second Bartholomew Investment Trust Ld. *See* Second General & Provincial Investment Trust Ld.

Second Broadmount Trust Ld. Regd. 1928. Vol. liq. (members') 14 Apr. 1978 for purpose of merging with Target Growth Fund. The 7% preference shares were redeemed at par and ordinary shareholders received 1·2579 units of target Growth Fund per share (of 5p) **1980–1**

Second Caledonian Trust Co. Ld. Regd. Edinburgh 1927. On 3 Jan. 1961 the undertaking and assets were acquired by The Clydesdale Investment Co. Ld. Stockholders received securities of that company in exchange for their holdings as follows—85 fully-paid ordinary shares of 5*s.* for every 100 stock units of 5*s.*; 110 fully-paid 4¾% preference shares of £1 for every £100 preference stock; debenture stockholders received a like amount of a similar security of Clydesdale and the liability for the £90,000 outstanding terminal debentures was assumed by the company. Dissolved on 2 May 1961 under Sec. 208 of Companies Act 1948................ **1962**

Second Clydesdale Investment Co. Ld. Regd. Edinburgh 1930. The undertaking and assets were acquired from 2 June 1960 by The Caledonian Trust Co. Ld. in which company ordinary stockholders were entitled to receive 35*s.* ordinary capital for every 30*s.* held and preference stockholders £21 preference capital for every £20 held: holders of 4% and 3½% debenture stocks and terminal debentures received the same nominal amounts of identical securities. Dissolved on 6 Oct. 1960 under Sec. 208 of Companies Act, 1948 .... **1961**

**See Stock Exchange Year-Book.*

VOL. FOR

Second Continental & Industrial Trust Ld. Regd. 1927. Vol. liq. (members') 22 Nov. 1929. All capital owned by Continental & Industrial Trust Ld. Final meeting return regd. 14 May 1930 .... **1930**

Second Conversion Investment Trust Ld. Regd. 1937. Vol. liq. (members') 20 Dec. 1945 for amalgamation with First Conversion Investment Trust Ld. (later Hambros Investment Trust Ld.) in which company shareholders were entitled to 1 fully-paid share of £1 and 3·738*d*. cash for every 2 shares of 9*s*. held. Final meeting return regd. 18 Mar. 1947 .... **1947**

Second Edinburgh & Dundee Investment Co. Ld. Regd. in Edinburgh 1927. Undertaking was transferred to Edinburgh & Dundee Investment Co. Ld. in Nov. 1969; ordinary stockholders received 124 ordinary shares for every £25 stock held and preference stockholders a like amount of similar stock. Liability for debenture stock was assumed by Edinburgh & Dundee Investment Co. Ld. Company finally dissolved by Order of the Court on 14 Mar. 1970 **1970**

Second General & Provincial Investment Trust Ld. Regd. 1925 as Second Bartholomew Investment Trust Ld.; name changed May 1928. Vol. liq. (members') 20 Mar. 1936. Undertaking was acquired by General Funds Investment Trust Ld. in which company shareholders were entitled to £7 ordinary and £7 preference stocks *plus* 12*s*. in cash for every 10 shares of £1 held. Final meeting return regd. 10 Sept. 1936 .... **1937**

Second Hampstead Tenants Ld. *See* Co-Partnership Tenants Ld. (regd. 1930).

Second Industrial Trust Ld. Regd. 1911. Undertaking acquired as from 1 Oct. 1961 by Industrial & General Trust Ld. Ordinary and preference shareholders and debenture stockholders received an equivalent amount of ordinary and preference shares and debenture stock respectively in that company. Dissolved under section 208 of Companies Act 1948 on 30 Sept. 1962 .... **1963**

Second Investors Mortgage Security Co. Ld. Regd. in Edinburgh 1914. All capital was acquired by Investors Mortgage Security Co. Ld. at the rate of: 9 ordinary shares (of 5*s*.) for every £2 ordinary stock and 1 5½% preference share (of £1) for every £1 5% preference stock; the outstanding £404,997 3½% debenture stock 1965—75, £907,400 3½% debenture stock 1974–80 and £51,905 terminable debentures were cancelled in consideration for a like amount of stocks of Investors' Mortgage Security Co. Ld. Vol. liq. (members') 4 Aug. 1965. Final meeting return regd. 30 Dec. 1965 .... **1967**

Second Keystone Fixed Trust Ld. Regd. 1935. A subsidiary of British Industrial Corpn. Ld. Vol. liq. (members') 8 May 1957. Final meeting return regd. 25 Apr. 1958 .... **1940**

Second Lincolnshire Beet Sugar Co. Ld. See Second Lincolnshire Sugar Co. Ld.

Second Lincolnshire Sugar Co. Ld. Regd. 1928 as Second Lincolnshire Beet Sugar Co. Ld.; name changed Dec. 1929. Vol. liq. (members') 15 Sept. 1936. Undertaking was acquired by British Sugar Corporation Ld. for 303,555 fully-paid shares. Shareholders received 249,683 fully-paid shares and £2,859 3*s*. 5*d*. in cash. Final meeting return regd. 17 Jan. 1940 **1937**

Second Mercantile Trust Ld. Regd. 1923. Under scheme of 1 Feb. 1960 the undertaking and assets were acquired by Mercantile Investment Trust Ld. in which company contributories were entitled to receive fully-paid capital as follows—112 ordinary shares of 5*s*. for every 100 ordinary shares of 5*s*. held and 215 preference shares of £1 for every £200 preference stock held. The outstanding £500,000 5% and £250,000 3½% redeemable debenture stocks were cancelled, holders receiving a like amount of 5% stock 1960—78 and 3½% stock 1960–95 respectively, in exchange. Dissolved on 1 June 1960 under Sec. 208 of Companies Act, 1948 .... **1961**

Second Moorside Trust Ld. Regd. 1960. Vol. liq. (members') 6 Jan. 1976. Assets transferred to Moorside Trust Ld. in Jan. 1976. The 8½% Debenture Stock 1997–2002 was cancelled, holders receiving a like amount of 9% Debenture Stock of Moorside Trust Ld. No returns of capital. Final meeting return regd. 26 Jan. 1977 .... **1977-8**

Second Sakhalin Syndicate Ld. Regd. 1910. Struck off Register 18 Aug. 1953 .... **1937**

Second Saxon Securities Trust Ld. Regd. 1926. Vol. liq. Dec. 1929. Undertaking and assets were acquired by Saxon Securities (Amalgamated) Ld. in which company shareholders were entitled to 1 ordinary share of £1 for every two shares of £1 held. Struck off Register 3 Oct. 1941 .... **1942**

Second Scottish American Trust Co. Ld. (The). Regd. in Edinburgh 1879. On 28 Jan. 1970 undertaking merged with First Scottish American Trust Co. Ld. in which company ordinary shareholders received 212 ordinary shares for 200 ordinary shares; and preference shareholders a like amount of 5% preference stock. That company also assumed liability for debenture stock and U. S. $ loans. Dissolved by Order of Court 28 Apr. 1970 .... **1970**

Second Scottish Eastern Investment Trust Ld. Regd. Edinburgh 1927. Undertaking was merged with Scottish Eastern Investment Trust Ld. (all shares already owned) and Scottish American Mortgage Co. Ld. in July 1966. Debenture stockholders were entitled to receive a like amount of stock of Scottish Eastern Investment Trust Ld. Dissolved under Sect. 201 of Companies Act 1948, 11 Oct. 1966 .... **1967**

Second Scottish Investment Trust Co. Ld. Regd. 1889. On 1 Nov. 1976 undertaking and assets transferred to The Scottish Investment Trust Co. Ld., holders receiving 19 ordinary stock units for 20 ordinary stock units; £1 3·5% preferred stock for £1 5% preferred stock; £1 4·55% A preference stock for £1 6½% A preference stock. Holders of 4% perpetual debenture stock, 5% perpetual debenture stock and 5% redeemable debenture stock 1975–80 received a like amount of 4% perpetual debenture stock, 5% perpetual debenture stock and 5% redeemable debenture stock 1975–80 respectively. Company was dissolved under Section 208 of Companies Act 1948 without winding up on 1 Mar. 1977 .... **1977-8**

Second Scottish Mortgage & Trust Co. Ld. (The). Regd. in Edinburgh 1912 as Scottish Canadian, Mortgage Co. Ld.; name changed 1927. On 28 Nov. 1969 undertaking transferred to Scottish Mortgage & Trust Co. Ld. in which company ordinary stockholders received 103 ordinary shares per £25 stock; and preference stockholders a like amount of a similar preference stock. Obligations for 5% and 4½% debenture stocks were assured also by that company. Dissolved by Order of Court 28 Mar. 1970 **1970**

Second Scottish Northern Investment Trust Ld. (The). Regd. in Edinburgh 1910. On 16 Dec. 1968 undertaking transferred to Scottish Northern Investment Trust Ld. in which company ordinary shareholders received 3 ordinary shares for every 4 held; and preference stockholders 1 4¾% preference share for every £1 stock held. Obligations for 3%, 4% and 5½% debenture stocks were assumed also by that company. Dissolved by Order of Court 16 Dec. 1968 **1970**

Second Scottish United Investors Ld. Regd. Edinburgh 1928. On 5 Apr. 1961 the undertaking was acquired by Scottish United Investors Ld. Ordinary stockholders received £27 ordinary stock of that company for every £25 ordinary stock held; 5% preference and debenture stockholders received a like amount of a similar security of that company in exchange for their holdings. Dissolved on 29 Dec. 1961 under Sec. 208 of Companies Act, 1948 .... **1963**

Second Securities Trust of Scotland Ld. Regd. Edinburgh 1927. On 28 Feb. 1961 undertaking was acquired by Securities Trust of Scotland Ld. Ordinary stockholders received £190 ordinary and 5% preference stockholders £115 4½% preference capital of that company per £100 held. The 4% debenture stock was amalgamated with a similar security of Securities Trust and the 5% debenture stock and the terminable debentures became the liability of that company. Dissolved on 31 Oct. 1961 under Section 208 of Companies Act 1948 .... **1963**

Securities Co. Inc. New York 1899. The outstanding 4% sterling debentures (consols A) were redeemed at 105% on 1 Mar. 1950 .... **1950**

Securities Investment Co. Ld. Regd. 1896. Vol. liq. 21 Jan. 1905. Final meeting return regd. 20 June 1912. Court Order to dissolve 20 Sept. 1912 .... **1905**

Securities of America Ld. Regd. 1964. Vol. liq. (members') 5 Mar. 1968. Outstanding assets transferred to Securities of America Unit Trust under scheme of reconstruction of Feb. 1968 and 1 unit of the trust was issued for each share held. £35 6*s*. 6*d*. was paid into Companies' Liquidation Account. Final meeting return regd. 3 June 1969 .... **1970**

Securities Trust of Jersey Ld. Inc. in Jersey 1962. Vol. liq. (members') 29 June 1971. Capital returned to contributories—£1·56 per share of £1 .... **1977–8**

Security Co. Ld. Regd. 1889. Business acquired in 1899 by Ocean Accident & Guarantee Corporation Ld. Removed from Register 1907. .... **1908**

Sedburgh Electricity Supply Co. Regd. 1935. Dissolved 1 Apr. 1948, undertaking being vested in the British (later Central) Electricity Authority and North Western Area Board under the Electricity Act 1947. Ordinary shareholders were entitled to receive £2 15*s*. British Electricity 3% guaranteed stock (1968–73), for every share (of £1) held **1949**

**See Stock Exchange Year-Book.*

VOL. FOR

Sedburgh New Gas Co. Ld. Regd.1896. Dissolved 1 May 1949, undertaking being vested in North Western Area Gas Board under Gas Act 1948. Holders of securities were entitled to receive, in respect of each £5 unit held, British Gas 3% guaranteed stock 1990–95 as follows:

	£	s.	d.
Ord. shares (7% max)	7	10	0
4½% pref. shares	5	10	0

1952

Seddon's Pneumatic Tyre Co. (French Patents) Ld. Regd. 1893. Vol. liq. 3 Nov. 1894. Amalgamated with International Pneumatic Tyre Co. Ld. Final meeting return regd. 18 Dec. 1915 .... *1895

Seddon's Pneumatic Tyre Co. Ld. Regd. Dublin 1892. Amalgamated with International Pneumatic Tyre Co. Ld. 1952

Seddon's Pneumatic Tyre (Continental) Co. Ld. Regd. 1893. Vol. liq. 3 Nov. 1894. Amalgamated with International Pneumatic Tyre Co. Ld. Removed from Register 24 Dec. 1907 .... *1895

Sedenak Rubber Estates Ld. Regd. 1909. Dissolved 7 Feb. 1982. 1960

Sedgeley (F. M. S.) Rubber Co. Ld. Regd. 1911. All capital owned by Kuala Lumpur Rubber Co. Ld. (later Kuala Lumpur-Kepong Amalgamated Ld.). Vol. liq. (members') 25 May 1954. Final meeting return regd. 19 July 1956 1951

Sedgwick Gunpowder Co. Ld. Regd. 1896. Vol. liq. (members') 31 Dec. 1936. Capital returned to contributories—£46 12s. 5d. per share of £10. Final meeting return regd. 7 Jan. 1938. 1937

Seed (Richard) & Co. Ld. Regd. 1896. Vol. liq. (members') 12 Jan. 1939. Undertaking and assets were acquired by Dutton's Lancashire & Yorkshire Brewery Corporation Ld. in which company shareholders were entitled to 11 5½% preference shares of £1 for every 2 preference shares of £5 held. Ordinary shareholders received securities in acquiring company *plus* cash. Final meeting return regd. 17 Apr. 1941 1939

Seed's Syndicate Ld. Regd. 1901. Struck off Register 1928 1910

Sefwi & Wassau Gold Syndicate Ld. Regd. 1900. Removed from Register 1904 1903

Sefwi (Gold Coast) Concessions Ld. *See* Pafu Concessions Ld.

Sefwi Goldfields Ld. Regd. 1910. Vol. liq. (creditors') 16 Jan. 1933. Undertaking and assets sold to Anglo African Goldfields Ld. in which company shareholders were entitled to apply for 2 shares of 5s. (credited with 3s. 9d. paid) for each preference share of 5s. held and 1 such share for each ordinary share of 5s. held. Final meeting return regd. 16 July 1938   1933

Segaliud (Borneo) Tobacco Co. Ld. Regd. 1889. Vol. liq. 24 Sept. 1890. Amalgamated with British Borneo Trading & Planting Co. Ld. Final meeting return regd. 4 May 1891 1891

Segamat (Johore) Rubber Estates Ld. Regd. 1910. Vol. liq. 6 Sept. 1920. Capital returned to contributories—£3 4s. 1d. per share of £1 in Sept. 1920; further payments (if any) not known. Final meeting return regd. 27 Apr. 1921 1921

Segovia Gold Mines Ld. Regd. 1893. Removed from Register 1901 1899

Seine River (Ontario) Gold Mines Ld. Regd. 1896. Removed from Register 1903 1903

Seine River Syndicate Ld. Regd. Edinburgh 1898. Struck off Register 19 Dec. 1913 1909

Sekampong (Sumatra) Rubber Estates Ld. *See* Eastern & General Trust & Development Co. Ld.

Sekenke Gold Mining Co. Ld. *See* Tanganyika Central Gold Mines Ld.

Sekondi & Tarkwa Co. Ld. Regd. 1898. Reconstructed 1900 as company of same name. Shareholders were entitled to 5 fully-paid shares of £1 for each share of £1 held. Removed from Register 1910 1908

Sekondi & Tarkwa Co. Ld. Regd. 1900. Vol. liq. Aug. 1909. Reconstructed as company of same name. Shareholders were entitled to 1 fully-paid share of 5s. in new company for each share of £1 held. Removed from Register 1910 1910

Sekondi & Tarkwa Co. Ld. Regd. 1909. Vol. liq. 15 Jan. 1914. Reconstructed as company of same name. Shareholders were entitled to 1 share of 4s. (credited with 3s. paid) in new company for each share of 5s. held. Final meeting return regd. 3 Apr. 1917 1914

Sekondi & Tarkwa Co. Ld. Regd. 1914. Vol. liq. 28 Jan. 1916. Final meeting return regd. 3 Apr. 1917 1916

Sekong Rubber Co. Ld. Regd. 1908. All capital owned by Madjedie Investments Ld. Vol. liq. 8 Apr. 1981. Final meeting return regd. 5 Nov. 1981 1980–1

Selaba Rubber Estates Ld. Regd. 1909. Vol. liq. 8 Aug. 1928. Undertaking and assets were acquired by Golden Hope Rubber Estate Ld., (now Golden

VOL. FOR

Hope Plantations Ld.) in which company shareholders were entitled to 3 shares of £1 for every 4 shares of £1 held. Final meeting return regd. 4 Dec. 1928   1929

Selangor Coffee Co. Ld. Regd. 1892. Removed from Register 1905 1905

Selangor Oil Palm Co. Ld. Regd. Edinburgh 1924. A subsidiary of Scottish Malayan Estates Ld. Vol. liq. 30 Nov. 1962. Final meeting return regd. 30 Oct. 1963 1951

Selangor River Rubber Estate Co. Ld. Regd. 1906. Vol. liq. 23 Feb. 1920. Shareholders were entitled to 5 fully-paid shares of £1 in Selangor River Rubber Estates Ld. for each share of £1 held. The debentures were to be repaid. Final meeting return regd. 25 Feb. 1921 1920

Selangor River Rubber Estates Ld. Regd. 1920. Vol. liq. (members') 30 Sept. 1932. Undertaking and assets were acquired by company of same name. Shareholders were entitled to 1 share of £1 (credited with 18s. paid) in new company for each share of £1 held. £10 7s. 8d. was paid into Companies' Liquidation Account in respect of sale of unclaimed shares. Final meeting return regd. 5 May 1934 1933

Selangor Rubber Co. Ld. Regd. in Edinburgh 1899. All capital was owned by Highlands & Lowlands Para Rubber Co. Ld. Vol. liq. 5 Nov. 1963. Final meeting return regd. 23 Mar. 1965 1960

Selangor United Rubber Estates Ld. Regd. 1911. Winding-up Order 5 June 1961. Capital returned to contributories—28·3p per share. Struck off Register 24 June 1980 1982–3

Selbourne Rubber Estates Ld. Regd. 1925. Court Order to wind up 16 Dec. 1929. Struck off Register Aug. 1934 1935

Selby & Mid-Yorkshire Union Railway Co. Inc. by Special Act 1879 as Church Fenton, Cawood & Wistow Railway; name changed by Act of 1883. Undertaking abandoned by Acts of 1889 and 1890   1891

Selby Brewing & Wine Co. Ld. Regd. 1882. Vol. liq. 1 Oct. 1889. Final meeting return regd. 1 Jan. 1891   *1887

Selby Manufacturing Co. Ld. Regd. 1920 as Coverings Ld.; name changed Oct. 1924. Vol. liq. 11 Jan. 1933. Capital returned to contributories—£4,250. Final meeting return regd. 5 Aug. 1941 1933

Selby Picture Houses Ld. Regd. 1920. Vol. liq. 7 June 1924. Final meeting return regd. 4 Apr. 1928 .... *1925

Selby Shipbuilding and Engineering Co. Ld. Regd. 1898. Removed from Register 1908 1904

Selecta Gramophones Ld. Regd. 1928. Vol. liq. (members') 28 Feb. 1941, undertaking acquired by company of same name. Capital returned to contributories—2s. 8·56d. per share of 2s. 6d. £285 3s. 11d. was paid into Companies' Liquidation Account. Final meeting return regd. 31 May 1954   1955

Selected Gold Mines of Australia Ld. Regd. 1904. Court Order to wind up 20 Feb. 1906. Liquidator released 10 May 1910. Struck off Register 19 Nov. 1946.... 1906

Selected Investments Trust Ld. Regd. 1925. Vol. liq. (members') 12 Dec. 1938. Capital returned to contributories—3s. 8·55d. per share of £1. £438 was paid into Companies' Liquidation Account. Final meeting return regd. 20 Apr. 1944 1945

Selected Options Ld. Regd. 1910. Vol. liq. 14 Apr. 1924. Final meeting return regd. 25 June 1925 .... *1925

Selection Secretariat, Ld. Regd. 1930. A subsidiary of Selection Trust Ld. Vol. liq. (members') 31 Dec. 1953. Final meeting return regd. 9 Mar. 1955 1940

Selection Trust Ld. Regd. 1914. Vol. liq. 30 Mar. 1926. Reconstructed as company of same name. Shareholders were entitled to 3 ordinary shares of £1 for every 2 ordinary shares of 2s. 6d. held or 4 preference shares of £1 for every 3 shares of £1 held. Final meeting return regd. 22 Dec. 1926 1927

Selection Trust Ld. Regd. 1926. Vol. liq. (members') 25 Sept. 1930. All ordinary shares of 5s. were acquired by Canadian Selection Co. Ld. by exchanging 1 share of no par value for every 2½ shares of 5s. held. Vol. liq. (members') 25 Sept. 1930. Debenture stock was repaid at 103%; an option to apply for debenture stock in the Canadian company has since expired. Preference shares were repaid at 21s. per share of £1. Final meeting return regd. 6 July 1932   1931

Selective Fixed Investments Ld. Regd. 1935. Vol. liq. (members') 30 Jan. 1939. All shares owned by Investment Managers & Secretaries Ld. Final meeting return regd. 15 Sept. 1939 1939

Seletar Rubber Estates Ld. Regd. 1910. Vol. liq. 31 Oct. 1921. Reconstructed as Seletar Plantations Ld. [later Seletar Industrial Holdings Ld., now Electronic Rentals & General Holdings Ld.] in which company shareholders were entitled to 10 shares of 2s. (credited with 1s. 3d. paid) for each share of £1 held. Final meeting return regd. 20 Dec. 1921 1922

See Stock Exchange Year-Book.

VOL. FOR

Self-Acting Pneumatic Tyre Pump Syndicate Ld. Regd. 1898. Removed from Register 1910 .... **1900**

Self-Controlled Air Cushion Co. Ld. Regd. 1922. Vol. liq. (members') 6 Aug. 1941. Capital returned to contributories—8s. 7$\frac{7}{12}$d. per preferred ordinary share of 10s. Final meeting return regd. 9 Mar. 1944 **1943**

Self-Developing Plate Co. Ld. Regd. 1906. Vol. liq. Dec. 1910. Removed from Register 1912 .... **1911**

Self-Opening Tin Box Co. Ld. Regd 1890. Final meeting return regd. 5 Nov. 1976 .... **1940**

Self-Winding & Synchronising Clock Co. Ld. Regd. 1886. Court Orders: to wind up 29 June 1889; to dissolve 23 Apr. 1891 .... **1890**

Selfridge (Gordon) Trust Ld. Regd. 1926. Dissolved under Section 154 of the Companies Act 1929 on 12 Aug. 1946. Under a scheme of arrangement with Selfridge (Holdings) Ld. (later Selfridges Ld.) preference and ordinary stockholders were entitled to receive £1 ordinary stock of that company for every £4 preference or £20 ordinary stock held **1947**

Selfridges Ld. Regd. 1941. Vol. liq. (members') 3 July 1958. The undertaking and assets transferred to parent company [Selfridges Ld.-formerly Selfridge (Holdings) Ld.] 3$\frac{1}{2}$% 1st mortgage debenture stock exchanged for a like amount of 3$\frac{3}{4}$% stock of that company. Final meeting return regd. 31 July 1959 **1960**

Seligman Brothers. Established 1864; converted into limited company 1928; re-established as a partnership 1935. Business merged with S. G. Warburg & Co. Ld. as from May 1957 .... **1958**

Selkirk Gas Co. Ld. Regd. in Edinburgh 1936. Dissolved 1 May 1949. undertaking being vested in Scottish Area Gas Board under Gas Act 1948. Holders of ordinary shares (of £1) were entitled to receive £2 5s. British Gas 3% guaranteed stock 1990—95 .... **1952**

Selkirk (J. H.) Ld. Regd. 1905. Court Order to wind up 1906. Removed from Register 1911 .... **1907**

Sell's Advertising Agency Ld. Regd. 1886. Vol. liq. 1 Nov. 1897. Reconstructed as company of same name. Final meeting return regd. 30 Mar. 1898 .. **1898**

Selmer (Henri) & Co. Ld. Regd. 1937. Vol. liq. (members') 28 Nov. 1940. Capital returned to contributories—1s. 2·07d. per share of 2s. Final meeting return regd. 10 Jan. 1947 .... **1947**

Selsey Water Co. Inc. by Special Act 1907. Under provisions of Portsmouth & Gosport Water Order 1963 undertaking was vested in Portsmouth Water Co. on 1 Oct. 1963 and shareholders received capital stock in that company in exchange for their holdings at following rates (per share of £10): 10% ordinary—£20 5% ordinary stock and £3 15s. cash; 8% ordinary—£16 5% ordinary stock and 7s. 6d. cash; 4$\frac{1}{2}$% preference—£10 4$\frac{1}{2}$% redeemable preference stock 1970. The outstanding debenture stocks of this company became debenture stocks of Portsmouth Water Co. Company is being wound up and will be dissolved upon a declaration by the directors that the winding up has been completed **1973-4**

Selson Engineering Co. Ld. Regd. 1909. Receiver appointed 1 Dec. 1931; ceased to act 15 Dec. 1933. Struck off Register 4 Oct. 1935 ' .... *__1912**

Selukwe Columbia Gold Mine Ld. Regd. 1900 as New Selukwe Gold Mine Ld.; name changed 1901. Vol. liq. 12 May 1908 for reconstruction as company of same name. Shareholders were entitled to 1 share of £1 in new company for every 6 shares of £1 held. Struck off Register 18 Jan. 1921 .... **1909**

Selukwe Columbia Gold Mine Ld. Regd. 1908. Vol. liq. 31 July 1919. Final meeting return regd. 1 Nov. 1920 **1920**

Selukwe Consolidated Ld. Regd. 1895. Vol. liq. 17 Nov. 1898. The undertaking and assets were transferred to Buluwayo Syndicate Ld. in which company shareholders were entitled to 1 share of £1 (credited as fully-paid) for every 3 shares of £1 held. Final meeting return regd. 6 Feb. 1900 .... **1899**

Selukwe Development Syndicate Ld. Regd. 1895. Vol. liq. 20 Mar. 1896. Undertaking acquired by Selukwe Gold Mining Co. Ld. for £200,000 in shares. Final meeting return regd. 11 Dec. 1896 .... **1909**

Selukwe Exmouth Ld. Regd. 1910. Struck off Register 1916 .... **1915**

Selukwe Gold Mining Co. Ld. Regd. 1896. Vol. liq. Mar. 1910 for reconstruction as company of same name (later Selukwe Gold Mining & Finance Co. Ld.). Shareholders were entitled to 1 fully-paid share of 5s. for each share of £1 held. Removed from Register 1911 .... **1911**

Semenyih Rubber Estate Ld. Regd. 1910. Vol. liq. 11 Feb. 1914. Reconstructed as company of same name. Struck off Register 24 July 1923 .... **1914**

Semon (Charles) & Co. Ld. Regd. 1920. Vol. liq. (creditors') 19 Aug. 1931. Goodwill was acquired by A. & S. Henry & Co. Ld. Unsecured creditors

VOL. FOR

received 13s. 2$\frac{1}{4}$d. in the £. Final meeting return regd. 4 Dec. 1939 .... **1932**

Sempah Rubber Estates Ld. Regd. 1909. Vol. liq. (members') 11 Nov. 1931. Undertaking and assets were acquired by company of same name [later Sempah (Holdings) Ld.]. Shareholders were entitled to 5 shares of 2s. (credited with 1s. 6d. paid) in new company for each share of £1 held. Final meeting return regd. 10 Nov. 1932 .... **1932**

Sempam Tin Mines Ld. Regd. 1907. Vol. liq. 9 Dec. 1914. Final meeting return regd. 29 May 1926 .... **1915**

Semple, M'Lean & Reid (Belfast) Ld. Regd. Dublin 1908. Vol. liq. Oct. 1928 .... **1929**

Sena Sugar Factory Ld. Regd. 1910. Vol. liq. 11 Mar. 1920. Reconstructed as Sena Sugar Estates Ld. Holders of debentures were entitled to an equal amount of 6$\frac{1}{2}$% 1st mortgage debenture stock in new company; holders of preference shares were entitled to an equal amount of 7% 2nd mortgage debenture stock; holders of ordinary shares were entitled to 12 fully-paid ordinary shares of £1 for each ordinary share of £5 held, ordinary shareholders also received cash distributions. Struck off Register 23 Apr. 1929 **1930**

Senaar Syndicate Ld. Regd. 1900. Vol. liq. Jan. 1909. Removed from Register 1914 .... **1909**

Sendayan (F.M.S.) Rubber Co. Ld. Regd. 1909. Vol. liq. (members') 30 Sept. 1959. All capital was acquired by Port Dickson-Lukut Rubber Estates Ld. in which company shareholders were entitled to receive 5 shares of 2s. plus 6s. cash for every £1 stock held. Amount paid into Companies' Liquidation Account in respect of unclaimed dividends—£107 14s. 10d. Final meeting return regd. 31 May 1968 .... **1969**

Sengon (Java) Co. Ld. Regd. 1907. Vol. liq. 27 Apr. 1910. The undertaking and assets were acquired by East Java Rubber Co. Ld. in which company shareholders were entitled to 1 share of £1 (credited as fully-paid) plus 3s. in cash for each share of £1 held. Final meeting return regd. 7 Jan. 1916........ **1911**

Sensible Heat Distillation Ld. Regd. 1924. Court Order to wind up 23 Jan. 1933. Liquidator released 6 Dec. 1935. Struck off Register 30 Apr. 1954 .... **1933**

Sentein Mining Co. Ld. Regd. 1871. Removed from Register 1903 .... **1885**

Sentinel Waggon Works Ld. Regd. 1918. Vol. liq. 24 Mar. 1920. Final meeting return regd. 2 Jan. 1925 **1936**

Sentinel Waggon Works Ld. Regd. 1920 as Sentinel Waggon Works (1920) Ld.; name changed 9 Mar. 1925. Undertaking was transferred to Sentinel Waggon Works (1936) Ld. [later Sentinel (Shrewsbury) Ld.]. Shareholders were entitled to apply for 1 preference share of 6s. (credited with 5s. 6d. paid) conditional on applying for 1 ordinary share of 2s. (credited with 1s. paid) for each preference share of £1 held or 1 ordinary share of 2s. (credited with 1s. paid) for each ordinary share of 15s. held. Dissolved under Sec. 154 of Companies Act 1929 on 28 May 1936 .... **1937**

Sepang Selangor Rubber Estate Ld. Regd. 1923. Vol. liq. (members') 22 May 1931. Undertaking and assets were acquired by London Asiatic Rubber & Produce Co. Ld. in which company shareholders were entitled to 4$\frac{1}{2}$ shares of 2s. (credited with 1s. 6d. paid) for each share of £1 held. Final meeting return regd. 12 Feb. 1932 .... **1932**

Sequah Ld. Regd. 1890. Vol. liq. 28 Oct. 1895. Final meeting return regd. 15 June 1898 .... **1896**

Serajgunge Jute Co. Ld. Inc. Calcutta 1894. In liquidation in 1898 .... **1898**

Seranamu Diamond Syndicate Ld. Regd. 1903. Vol. liq. Nov. 1907. Removed from Register 1909 .... **1908**

Serangoon Rubber Co. Ld. Regd. 1910. Assets were taken over by the receiver for debenture holders. Struck off Register 1917 .... **1916**

Serdang Central Plantations Ld. Regd. 1909. Vol. liq. (members') 30 Aug. 1932. Undertaking and assets were acquired by company of same name. Shareholders were entitled yo 1 share of £1 (credited with 17s. 6d. paid) in new company for each share of £1 held. Final meeting return regd. 25 Aug. 1933 .... **1933**

Serdang Central Plantations Ld. Regd. 1932. Vol. liq. (members') 30 Aug. 1955. Capital returned to contributories—2·912d. per share of 2s. £503 9s. 2d. was paid into Companies' Liquidation Account. Final meeting return regd. 6 Dec. 1960 .... **1962**

Serdang (Sumatra) Rubber & Produce Estates Ld. Regd. 1910. Vol. liq. 19 Mar. 1913. The estates were sold to United Serdang (Sumatra) Rubber Plantations Ld. for £7,727 in shares and £2,322 in cash. Final meeting return regd. 29 Dec. 1913 .... **1913**

Seremban Rubber Estate Co. Ld. Regd. 1909. Vol. liq. 24 Mar. 1920. Reconstructed as Seremban Rubber Estates Ld. in which company shareholders were

entitled to 2 fully-paid shares of £1 for each share of
£1 held. Final meeting return regd. 8 Apr. 1921 ..   **1921**

Seremban Rubber Estates, Ld. Regd. 1920. Vol. liq.
(members') 9 Jan. 1959. Undertaking and assets
acquired by Anglo Oriental Plantations Ld. in
which company shareholders were entitled to
receive (per £1 stock) 7 fully-paid shares (of 2s.) plus
2s. 6d. cash. Final meeting return regd. 18 Nov. 1965   **1967**

Seremban Tin Mining Co. Ld. Regd. 1897. Vol. liq. 2
July 1921. Reconstructed as Seremban Ld. (later
Century Electric Holdings Ld., later Century Securities Ld.) in which company shareholders were
entitled to 7 shares of 2s. (credited with 1s. 3d. paid)
for each share of £1 held. Final meeting return regd.
11 Mar. 1924   **1922**

Serendah Tin Ld. Inc. Federated Malay States 1926.
Vol. liq. Aug. 1929. Undertaking and assets were
acquired by Rawang Tin Fields Ld. in which
company shareholders were entitled to 12 shares of
10s. (credited as fully-paid) for every 5 shares of £1
held   **1931**

Serendib Tea Estates Co. Ld. *See* Korale Tea Estates Ld.

Serenje Concessions Ld. Regd. 1926. Vol. liq. 23 Feb.
1928. The undertaking and assets were acquired by
Loangara Concessions (Northern Rhodesia) Ld. in
which company shareholders were entitled to 3
fully-paid shares of 5s. for each share of £1 held.
Final meeting return regd. 12 Sept. 1928 ....   **1928**

Series Electrical Traction Syndicate Ld. Regd. 1888.
Vol. liq. 17 June 1889. Final meeting return regd. 7
Sept. 1891   ***1891**

Serinha Rubber Estate Ld. Regd. 1910. Vol. liq. Apr.
1916. Struck off Register 1927 ....   **1916**

Seroeway Rubber Estates Ld. Regd. 1926. Vol. liq.
(creditors') 19 May 1965. 9s. 10½d. in the £1 was paid
to creditors from U. K. assets. E. B. Ridsdel & Co.
Ld. was appointed trustee in respect of compensation monies which may be received in the future
from Indonesian assets. Final meeting return regd.
31 Dec. 1965   **1967**

Serre-Alliott Associated Patents Ld. Regd. 1927. Vol.
liq. (members) 13 July 1936. Capital returned to
contributories—2s. 3¼d. per share of £1. Final
meeting return regd. 31 Mar. 1937 ....   **1937**

Servian Bacon-Curing Co. Ld. Regd. 1891. Removed
from Register 1901   **1892**

Servian Dredging and Mining Syndicate Ld. Regd. 1903.
Property and undertaking were acquired by Société
d'Exploration Minieré en Serbie, in which company
shareholders were entitled to 1 share of Fr. 100
(credited as fully-paid) for every 8 preference shares
of £1 held or every 20 ordinary shares of £1 held.
Removed from Register 1907 ....   **1906**

Service Flats Ld. Regd. 1918. Vol. liq. 26 Apr. 1929.
Capital returned to contributories—20s. per preference share of £1; payments (if any) to ordinary
shareholders not known. Final meeting return regd.
21 Aug. 1930. ....   **1930**

Service Petroleum Co. Ld. Regd. 1927. Winding-up
order 18 Nov. 1940. No capital returned to
contributories. Liquidator released 25 Mar. 1958.
Struck off Register 20 June 1975 ....   **1959**

Services' Canadian Lands Ld. Regd. 1912. Struck off
Register 1916 ....   **1915**

Sesan Syndicate Ld. Regd. 1906. Vol. liq. Feb. 1908.
Undertaking was sold to West Altai Gold Claims
Ld. with exception of Kaneika United Gold Fields
Shares. Removed from Register 1909 ....   **1908**

Setalite Ld. Regd. 1928. Controlling interest held by
Sphinx Electric Ld. Struck off Register 1931 ....   **1930**

Settle Gas Co. Ld. Regd. 1856; statutory powers 1896
and subsequently. Dissolved 1 May 1949, undertaking being vested in North Eastern Area Gas Board
under Gas Act 1948. Holders of securities were
entitled to receive in respect of each £5 unit held,
British Gas 3% guaranteed stock 1990–95 as
follows:

	£	s.	d.
Orig. shares (10% max.)	10	5	0
Addit shares (7% max.)	7	5	0
4% Pref. shares	5	2	0	**1952**

Seven Seas Shipping Co. Ld. Regd.1924. Struck off
Register 22 Nov. 1940   **1941**

Sevenoaks & District Electricity Co. Ld. Regd. 1912.
Dissolved 1 Apr. 1948, undertaking being vested in
British (later Central) Electricity Authority and
South-Eastern Area Board under Electricity Act
1947. Holders of securities were entitled to receive
British Electricity 3% guaranteed stock (1968–73) as
follows in respect of each £1 unit of capital held:

	£	s.	d.
8% preference shares	2	1	6

Ordinary shares (fully-paid)...................1	15	0	
Ordinary shares (15s. paid) 1	6	3	**1949**

Sevenoaks Gas Co. Inc. by Special Act 1876. By Act of
1932 the undertaking was acquired by South
Suburban Gas Co. in which company holders of A
shares were entitled to £214 4s. 5% preference stock
for every 10 shares held; holders of B shares were
entitled to £15 5% preference stock for each share
held; holders of debenture stock were entitled to an
equal amount of 5% Perpetual Debenture Stock ..   **1933**

Sevenoaks, Maidstone & Tunbridge Rly. Co. (formerly
Sevenoaks) **1882**

Severn Bridge & Forest of Dean Central Railway Co. Inc.
by Special Act 1873. Dissolved by Act of 1884 ...   **1885**

Severn Commissioners. Inc. by Severn Navigation Act
1842. Undertaking vested from 1 Jan. 1948 in
British Transport Commission under Transport Act
1947. Holders of 5% mortgage (1890 Act) were
entitled to receive £111 13s. 9d. British Transport
3% guaranteed stock 1978–88 for every £100
mortgages held   **1949**

Severn Dry Docks Co. Ld. Regd. 1900 as Barry New Dry
Docks Co. Ld.; name changed June 1902. The
undertaking and properties were acquired in May
1905 by Cardiff Channel Dry Docks Pontoon Co.
Ld. for £65,000 in cash. Vol. liq. 6 Sept. 1906. Final
meeting return regd. 18 July 1910 ....   **1903**

Severn Valley Gas Corpn. Ld Regd. 1934. Dissolved 1
May 1949, undertaking being vested in Gas Council
under Gas Act 1948. Holders of securities were
entitled to receive in respect of each £1 unit held,
British Gas 3% guaranteed stock 1990–95 as
follows:

	£	s.	d.
4½% pref. stock	1	1	11
Ord. stock...	1	3	8
Defd. stock	1	14	0	**1952**

Sevier Gold Mines Ld. *See* Utah Consolidated Gold
Mines Ld.

Seville and United Kingdom Carrying Co. Ld. Regd.
1897. Vol. liq. 14 June 1919. Final meeting return
regd. 20 Jan. 1920   **1920**

Seville Tramways Co. Ld. Regd. 1886. Vol. liq. June
1908. Undertaking and assets were acquired by a
Spanish company. Removed from Register 1909 .   **1909**

Sewell (C. A.) Ld. Regd. 1895. "The properties were sold
on behalf of the debenture holders." Removed from
Register 16 Nov. 1906 ....   ***1904**

Seychelles Produce Co. Ld. Regd. 1910 as Seychelles
Rubber & Cocoanut Estates Ld.; name changed
Apr. 1925. Vol. liq. (members') 5 June 1939.
Undertaking sold to Seychelles Government. Outstanding debentures were repaid at 110%. Capital
returned to contributories—11·6406d. per share of
2s. Final meeting return regd. 4 Sept. 1939 ....   **1940**

Seychelles Rubber & Cocoanut Estates Ld. *See* Seychelles Produce Co. Ld.

Seyidie Rubber & Cotton Estates Ld. Regd. 1917. Vol.
liq. 19 June 1924. Final meeting return regd. 9 Feb.
1925 ....   **1925**

Sha Falls (Nigeria) Tin Fields Ld. Regd. 1912. Vol. liq.
(creditors') 28 Feb 1930. No capital returned to
contributories. Final meeting return regd. 17 Feb.
1931 ....   **1931**

Shabani Railway Co. Ld. Regd. 1926. A subsidiary of
Rhodesia Railways Trust Ld. Vol. liq. (members')
21 Nov. 1956. Final meeting return regd. 14 May
1957   **1940**

Shackleford Ford & Co. Ld. *See* Swansea Wagon Co.
Ld.

Shackleton (Roger) & Sons Ld. The flour milling
properties and goodwill were acquired in 1928 by
Spillers Ld. for cash **1929**

Shaerf (R.) Ld. *See* Shaerf (Recenia R.) Ld.

Shaerf (Recenia R.) Ld. Regd. 1924 as R. Shaerf Ld.
Name changed Mar. 1928. Vol. liq. (creditors') 19
May 1933. No capital returned to contributories.
Final meeting return regd. 30 Dec. 1938 ....   **1934**

Shaftesbury Gas & Coke Co. Ld. *See below.*

Shaftesbury, Gillingham & District Gas Co. Ld. Regd.
1909. Dissolved 1 May 1949, undertaking being
vested in Southern Area Gas Board under Gas Act
1948. Holders of securities were entitled to receive
British Gas 3% guaranteed stock 1990–95 as follows
in respect of each £5 unit, unless otherwise stated, of
security held:

	£	s.	d.
Ord. shares (both denominations)	9	15	0
Prefd. ord. shares (both denomina-			
tions)..	9	15	0
4½% red. debs. (per £100)	105	0	0
3½% red. debs. (of £100)	100	0	0	**1952**

Shagirt (Cheleken) Oil Co. Ld. Regd. 1911. Struck off
Register 30 Mar. 1951 ....   **1952**

VOL. FOR

Shahdara (Delhi)—Saharanpur Light Railway Co. Ld. Inc. India 1905. Vol. liq. (members') 10 Dec. 1970. Debenture stock was repaid at par 31 Aug. 1974.. **1975-6**

Shahzada Mines Ld. Regd. 1895. Removed from Register 1911 .... **1900**

Shalders Textiles Ld. Regd. 1919. Vol. liq. (creditors') 9 June 1932. Assets realised insufficient to pay creditors in full. Final meeting return regd. 25 Aug. 1936 .... **1933**

Shamokin, Sunbury & Lewisburg Railroad Co. Organised Pennsylvania 1882. Undertaking was acquired in 1924 by Reading Company. All capital stock was owned by acquiring company, which took over the 1st and 2nd mortgage bonds. The 1st mortgage bonds were redeemed in July 1925 and the 2nd mortgage bonds were extended to July 1945 and redeemed at maturity **1924**

Shamrock Gold Mining Co. Ld. Regd. 1896. Removed from Register 1903 .... **1903**

Shamva East Ld. Inc. Southern Rhodesia 1910. In Feb. 1933 it was stated that company had no assets of any description, and application had been made to have the company struck off the Register **1933**

Shamva Mines Ld. Regd. 1910. Vol. liq. (members') 4 Apr. 1930. Capital returned to contributories—3s. 4·63d. per share of £1. Final meeting return regd. 5 July 1950 .... **1951**

Shamva (Rhodesia) Options Corporation Ld. Regd. 1910. Vol. liq. 18 Mar. 1912. Struck off Register 30 Jan. 1923 .... **1913**

Shan States Silver-Lead Corporation Ld. Inc. India 1923. Operations ceased 1930. London office closed in 1936.. **1938**

Shandon Candle Co. Ld. Regd. Dublin. In liquidation. All capital was owned by Irish American Oil Co. Ld. [later Esso Petroleum Co. (Ireland) Ld.] **1933**

Shandon Hydropathic Co. Ld. Regd. Edinburgh 1877. Vol. liq. Feb 1919. Property sold to Admiralty for £48,000. Final meeting return regd. 3 Oct. 1919 .. **1919**

Shanghai Water Works Fittings Co. Ld. Inc. in Shanghai 1926; transferred to Hong Kong register 1946. Vol. liq. (members') 22 Dec. 1947. Distributions (per share of Hong Kong $1·50) 4s. in Oct. 1948 and 2¼d. (final) in Aug. 1951. Final meeting 15 Oct. 1952 .... **1953**

Shanklin & Chale Railway Co. *See* Newport, Godshill & St. Lawrence Railway Co.

Shanklin & Ventnor Gas Co. *See* East Wight Gas Co.

Shanklin Gas Co. Ld. See East Wight Gas Co.

Shanks (J.) & Co. Ld. Regd. Dublin 1897. Removed from Register 1912 .... **1911**

Shanks (Thomas) & Co. Ld. In 1928 the machine tool business was acquired by Craven Bros., Manchester Ld **1929**

Shannon (John) & Son Ld. Regd. 1898. Vol. liq. 3 Mar. 1926. Business was acquired by company of same name for £120,000 in cash. Final meeting return regd. 15 July 1927 .... **1927**

Shannon Water & Electrical Power Co. Inc. by Special Act 1901. In July 1906, the chairman stated that the company had ceased to exist **1907**

Shap Granite & Patent Concrete Co. Ld. Regd. 1890. Vol. liq. Apr. 1907. Removed from Register 1908 **1908**

Share and General Investment Trust Ld. Regd. 1888. All capital was owned by Anglo-American Securities Corpn. Ld. Vol. liq. (members') 14 June 1963. Final meeting return regd. 22 Jan. 1965 .... **1961**

Sharegrant Ld. *See* Océ-Van Der Grintern Finance Ld.

Share Registers Ld. Regd. 1910 as Share Registers and Publishing Co. Ld.; name changed May 1911. Vol. liq. 26 May 1913. Final meeting return regd. 26 May 1914 .... **1914**

Sharman (Joseph) & Sons Ld. Regd. 1896. All capital owned by Northwestern Brewery Investments Ld. Vol. liq. (members') 30 Sept. 1955. Final meeting return regd. 18 Feb. 1959 .... **1936**

Sharp (James & M. S.) & Co. Ld. Regd. 1897. Vol. liq. 25 Jan. 1899. Final meeting return regd. 1 Jan. 1901 **1899**

Sharp (John) & Sons, Ld. Regd. Edinburgh 1904. Vol. liq. June 1951. Final meeting return regd. 1 Aug. 1952 .... **1947**

Sharp (Jonas) & Son Ld. Regd. 1896. Vol. liq. 29 June 1917. Final meeting return regd. 22 Feb. 1918...... **1918**

Sharp, Stewart & Co. Ld. Regd. 1863. Vol. liq. 15 Dec. 1887 for amalgamation with Clyde Locomotive Co. Ld. and reconstruction under same name. Shareholders received 35·7149% of their holding in securities of new company and 30% in cash; further payments (if any) not known. Final meeting return regd. 3 Dec. 1897 .... **1891**

Sharp, Stewart & Co. Ld. Regd. Edinburgh 1887. Vol. liq. July 1903. Amalgamated with Neilson, Reid & Co. and Dubs & Co. under title of North British

VOL. FOR

Locomotive Co. Ld. Capital returned to contributories—preference shares were repaid at par; ordinary shareholders were entitled to an equal number of ordinary shares in new company *plus* £6 per share of £10 in cash. Final meeting return regd. 29 Dec. 1906 .... **1905**

Sharpe (William) & Son Ld. Regd. 1907. Vol. liq. May 1908. Removed from Register 1909 .... **1909**

Sharpness Docks & Gloucester & Birmingham Navigation Co. Inc. by Special Act 1793 as Gloucester & Berkeley Canal Co.; practically reconstituted in 1870; name changed to Sharpness New Docks & Gloucester & Birmingham Navigation Co. in 1874 and to above title in 1935. Dissolved 23 Dec. 1949; undertaking vested from 1 Jan. 1948 in British Transport Commission under Transport Act 1947. Holders of securities were entitled to receive British Transport 3% guaranteed stock 1978–88 as follows in respect of every £100 of old security held:

	£	s.	d.
5% preference stock A	94	10	0
5½% preference stock B	79	10	0
5% preference stock C	65	0	0
Ordinary consolidated stock	30	0	0
4% debenture stock	96	10	0

The liability for the Sharpness Dock perpetual annuities and Sharpness Dock 1952 annuities was assumed by British Transport Commission on 1 Jan. 1948; the 1952 annuities ceased to exist on 25 Feb. 1952 .... **1949**

Sharrer's Zambesi Traffic Co. Ld. Regd. 1895. Vol. liq. 6 Aug. 1903. Undertaking and assets were acquired by British Central Africa Co. Ld. in which company shareholders were entitled to 5 shares of £1 (credited as fully-paid) for every 4 shares of £1 held. Final meeting return regd. 3 July 1917 .... **1904**

Shashi & Macloutsie Exploration & Mining Co. Ld. Regd. 1894. Vol. liq. (creditors') 31 Dec. 1934. No capital returned to contributories. Final meeting return regd. 22 July 1935 .... **1935**

Shaw (George) & Co Ld. Regd. 1866 as Bedlord Brewing & Malting Co. Ld.; name changed 1902. All capital owned by Northwestern Brewery Investments Ld. Vol. liq. (members') 30 Sept. 1955. Final meeting return regd. 18 Feb. 1959 .... **1950**

Shaw (Henry) & Co. Ld. Regd. 1897. Vol. liq. (members') 20 Oct. 1936. The undertaking was acquired by Daniel Thwaites & Co. Ld which company owned all shares. Final meeting return regd. 21 Aug. 1937 .... **1937**

Shaw (John) & Sons Ld. Regd. 1880. Vol. liq. (creditors') 11 Sept. 1930. Capital returned to contributories—10¾d. per share of £1. A payment was made into Companies' Liquidation Account. Final meeting return regd. 2 Aug. 1941 .... **1931**

Shaw Motors Ld. Regd. 1920. Vol. liq. 10 June 1925. Final meeting return regd. 2 Dec. 1926 .... **1926**

Shawlands Estates Co. of Ceylon Ld. Regd. 1909. Vol. liq. 27 June 1924. Final meeting return regd. 19 Dec. 1924 .... **1925**

Shaws, Bryant & Co. Ld. Regd. 1896. Vol. iiq. 22 Mar. 1900. Final meeting return regd. 8 Apr. 1902 .... **1901**

Shawsrigg Fire-Clay & Enamelling Co. Ld. Regd. Edinburgh 1895. Vol. liq. Apr. 1910. Undertaking and assets sold to Southhook Fire Clay Co. Ld. Final meeting return regd. 15 Dec. 1910 .... **1911**

Shearer (William) Ld. Regd. 1914. Vol. liq. (members') 3 July 1933. Capital returned to contributories—4s. 4½d. per share of £1. Final meeting return regd. 29 July 1935 .... **1935**

Sheba Crown Ld. Regd. 1902. Vol. liq. Dec. 1911. Removed from Register 1913 .... **1912**

Sheba Gold Mining Co. Ld. Regd. 1887. Vol. liq. 11 Aug. 1904. Reconstructed as company of same name. Shareholders were entitled to 1 share of £1 (credited with 14s. paid) for each share of £1 held. Final meeting return regd. 10 Feb. 1914 .... **1908**

Sheba Gold Mining Co. Ld. Inc. Transvaal 1904. Vol. liq. 1919 for reconstruction under same name. Shareholders were entitled to equal number of shares of 5s. (with 4s. paid) in new company **1920**

Sheba Gold Mining Co. Ld. Regd. 1920. Vol. liq. 23 Feb. 1922. Reconstructed as company of same name. Shareholders were entitled to 11 shares of 5s. (credited with 2s. 6d. paid) for each share of 5s. held. Final meeting return regd. 25 Nov. 1924 .... **1922**

Sheba Gold Mining Co. Ld. Regd. 1922. Vol. liq. 14 Apr. 1924. Reconstructed as company of same name. Shareholders were entitled to 1 share of 4s. (credited with 2s. 6d. paid) for each share of 5s. held. Final meeting return regd. 21 Nov. 1929 .... **1925**

Sheba Gold Mining Co. Ld. Regd. 1924. Vol. liq. 16 May 1927. Final meeting return regd. 21 Nov. 1929 .... **1928**

VOL. FOR

Sheba Hill Ld. Regd. 1896. Amalgamated with East Rand Consolidated Ld. Removed from Register 1905 .... **1904**

Sheba Lode Exploration Ld. Regd. 1893. Reconstructed 1896 as Sheba Hill Ld., in which company shareholders were entitled to 1 fully-paid share of 5s. and 8 shares of 5s. (credited with 4s. 4d. paid) for each share of £1 held. Removed from Register 1905 ... **1903**

Sheba Queen Gold & Exploration Ld. Regd. 1895. Vol. liq. 27 July 1897. Reconstructed as company of same name. Shareholders were entitled to 1 share of 10s. (credited with 7s. paid) in new company for each share of £1 held. Final meeting return regd. 21 Jan. 1899 .... **1905**

Sheba Queen Gold & Exploration Ld. Regd. 1897. Vol. liq. 8 May 1905. Reconstructed as company of same name, in which company shareholders were entitled to 1 ordinary share of 10s. (credited with 8s. 6d. paid) for each ordinary share of 10s. held or 1 preference share of 10s. (credited with 9s. paid) for each preference share of 10s. held. Final meeting return regd. 20 Feb. 1912 .... **1908**

Sheba Queen Gold & Exploration Ld. Regd. 1905. Vol. liq. June 1909. Removed from Register 1912 .... **1910**

Sheba Reef Extension Gold Mining Co. Ld. Regd. 1888. Court Orders: to wind up 11 Nov. 1889; to dissolve 5 July 1895 .... **1890**

Sheepshed Gas & Coke Co. Ld. Regd. 1857. Undertaking and assets were acquired by Sheepshed Urban District Council. Removed from Register 1905 .... **1904**

Sheerness & District Electric Supply Co. Ld. Regd. 1900 as County of Kent Electrical Power Distribution Co. Ld.; name changed to Sheerness & District Electric Power & Traction Co. Ld. in 1903 and to present title in 1922. Dissolved 1 Apr. 1948, undertaking being vested in the British (later Central) Electricity Authority and South-Eastern Area Board under the Electricity Act 1947. Ordinary shareholders were entitled to receive £2 15s. British Electricity 3% guaranteed stock (1968–73), for each share (of £1) held **1949**

Sheet Anchor Investment Co. Ld. Regd. 1947 as Langbourn Investment Trust Ld.; name changed 9 Mar. 1964. Vol. liq. (members) 10 Feb. 1965. 6% debenture stock redeemed at par in Feb. 1965. Capital returned to contributories—29s. 10½d. per share of £1. Final meeting return regd. 1 Dec. 1966 **1968**

Sheffield & District Cinematograph Theatres Ld. Regd. 1910. Majority of capital was owned by Mappin & Webb Ld. Vol. liq. 21 May 1963. Final meeting return regd. 9 May 1965 .... **1961**

Sheffield & District Gas Co. Estd. 1844 as Sheffield United Gas-Light Co.; inc. by Special Act 1855; name changed 1917 to Sheffield Gas Co. and in 1938 as above. Dissolved 1 May 1949, undertaking being vested in East Midland Area Gas Board under Gas Act 1948. Holders of securities were entitled to receive, in respect of each £100 unit held, British Gas 3% guaranteed stock 1990–95 as follows:

	£	s.	d.
Cons. stock (5% basic)	149	16	8
Perp. 4% deb. stock	103	0	0
4½% red. deb.stock	108	10	0
3½% red. deb. stock	99	12	6
5⅜% perp. deb. stock (Barnsley Gas Co.)	140	0	0
4% red. deb. stock	101	0	0

A distribution (being additional dividend) on consolidated stock of 5·454187% out of reserves was made in Sept. 1955 .... **1952**

Sheffield & Hallamshire Bank Ld. Inc. 1836. Regd. 1893. Vol. liq. June 1913. Undertaking and assets were acquired by London City & Midland Bank Ld. (later Midland Bank Ld.), in which company shareholders were entitled to 3 shares of £60 (credited with £12 10s. paid) for every 11 shares of £20 (£5 paid) held *plus* 1s. 8d. per share in cash .. **1914**

Sheffield & Midland Railway Companies Committee. *See* Great Central & Midland Joint Committee.

Sheffield & Rotherham Joint Stock Banking Co. Ld. Established 1836. Regd. 1880. Vol. liq. 27 Dec. 1906. Undertaking and assets were acquired by Williams Deacon's Bank Ld., in which company shareholders were entitled to 1 share of £50 (credited with £8 paid) for each share of £50 (£8 paid) held. Struck off Register 27 Oct. 1942 .... **1945**

Sheffield & South Yorkshire Navigation Co. Inc. by Special Act 1889. Dissolved 3 June 1949; undertaking vested from 1 Jan. 1948 in British Transport Commission under Transport Act 1947. Holders of securities were entitled to receive British Transport 3% guaranteed stock 1978–88 as follows—11s. and 4s. 4½d. British Transport stock for every ordinary share of £10 (fully-paid) and ordinary share of £10 (£4 paid) respectively; and £22 and £85 British

Transport Stock for every £100 4½% preference stock and 3% debenture stock held respectively **1949**

Sheffield Banking Co. Ld. Regd. 1880. Amalgamated 1918 as National Provincial & Union Bank of England Ld. (later National Provincial Bank Ld.). Vol. liq. 6 Nov. 1919, in which company shareholders were entitled to 6 shares of £20 (credited with £4 paid) for each share of £50 (£17 10s. paid) held .. **1920**

Sheffield Bath Co. Ld. Regd. 1876. Removed from Register 1891 .... **1892**

Sheffield Cafe Co. Ld. Regd. 1877. Vol. liq. 15 June 1922. Capital returned to contributories—£2 per share; further payments (if any) not known. Undertaking was acquired by Sheffield Refreshment Houses Ld. Final meeting return regd. 15 Sept. 1923 .... **1923**

Sheffield Canal Co. By Special Act 1848 the canal was vested in Manchester, Sheffield & Lincolnshire Railway Co.; the original capital of £70,400 was converted into 704 perpetual annuities of £2 10s. **1885**

Sheffield Coal Co. Ld. Regd 1876. A subsidiary of United Steel Companies Ld. Vol. liq. (members) 24 Aug. 1955. Final meeting return regd. 25 Mar. 1958 **1940**

Sheffield Cutlery Manufacturers Ld. Regd. 1919. Receiver appointed 30 July 1931. Struck off Register 7 Mar. 1939 .... **1940**

Sheffield District Railway Co. Inc. by Special Act 1896. In 1923 the undertaking was merged into the London & North Eastern Railway Co., in which company stockholders were entitled to stock as follows:

For each £100 held		L. & N. E.
4% Perm. Deb.	£100	4% Debenture
4% Perm. 2nd Deb.	£100	4% Debenture
5% Preference	£125	4% 2nd Gtd.
Ordinary	£87¼	4% 2nd Gtd.

The Company also received £10,520 cash for the discharge of capital and other liabilities shown in table No. 4 of its accounts to 31st Dec. 1922 .... **1924**

Sheffield Electric Light and Power Co. Ld. Regd. 1892. Vol. liq. 4 Jan. 1899. Undertaking and assets were acquired by Sheffield Corporation in 1898. Capital returned to contributories—£17 10s. per share of £7 at Jan. 1899; further payments (if any) not known. Final meeting return regd. 28 Dec. 1899 .... **1899**

Sheffield Empire Palace Ld. Regd. Edinburgh 1894. Reconstructed 1899 as Moss Empires Ld. (later M. E. Theatres Ld.), in which company shareholders were entitled either to 6 fully-paid preference and 6 fully-paid ordinary shares of £5 for every 10 shares of £5 held, subject to payment of £5 10s. or to 11 fully-paid preference and 11 fully-paid ordinary shares of £5 and £1 10s. in cash for every 20 shares of £5 held. Debenture holders were entitled to repayment or £105 debenture stock in new company for every £100 bonds held. Removed from Register 1909 .... **1900**

Sheffield Gas Co. *See* Sheffield & District Gas Co.

Sheffield Insurance Co. Ld. Regd. 1922. All shares were owned by Lancashire & General Assurance Co. Ld. Struck off Register 1929 .... **1927**

Sheffield Mineral Water Syndicate Ld. Regd. 1898. Receiver appointed 1905 for debenture holders. Removed from Register 1909 .... **1908**

Sheffield Music Hall Co. Ld. Regd. 1867. Vol. liq. (members) 10 Jan. 1941. Capital returned to contributories—£88 14s. 6d. per ordinary share of £30. Final meeting return regd. 22 Aug. 1941 .... **1941**

Sheffield Olympia & Provincial Rinks Ld. Regd. 1909. Vol. liq. 25 May 1917. Final meeting return regd. 14 Nov. 1917 .... ***1918**

Sheffield Scissors, Razor & Tool Co. Ld. Regd. 1917. Vol. liq. 3 Feb. 1921. Undertaking acquired by Sheffield Steel Products Ld. Final meeting return regd. 9 Nov. 1921'.... ***1921**

Sheffield Sports Stadium Ld. Regd. 1931. Vol. liq. (members) 4 Oct. 1961. Capital returned to contributories—£1 5s. 9d. per share of 5s. Final meeting return regd. 4 Jan. 1963 .... **1963**

Sheffield Steel & Manufacturing Co. Ld. Regd. 1873. Vol. liq. 24 Feb. 1887. Final meeting return regd. 4 Nov. 1887 .... ***1882**

Sheffield Steel Products (Stores) Ld. Regd. 1921. Vol. liq. 14 Nov. 1927. Capital returned to contributories—4s. per preference share of £1 at Dec. 1927; further payments (if any) not known. Final meeting return regd. 20 Dec. 1928 .... **1928**

Sheffield Tramways Co. Inc. by Special Act 1872. Lease expired and assets sold to Sheffield Corporation. Resolutions to wind up were passed in 1897 .... **1897**

Sheffield Union Banking Co. Regd. 1883. Vol. liq. 9 Aug. 1901. Business was acquired by London City & Midland Bank Ld. (later Midand Bank Ld.), in which company shareholders were entitled to 1

See Stock Exchange Year-Book.

VOL. FOR

share of £60 (credited with £12 10s. paid) for every 2 shares of £40 (£10 paid) held **1902**

Sheffield United Gas-Light Co. See Sheffield & District Gas Co.

Sheffield Wagon Co. Ld. Regd. 1868. Vol. liq. Apr. 1884. Final meeting return regd. 20 Aug. 1890 .... **1886**

Sheffield Water Works. Inc. 1830. The undertaking was acquired by Sheffield Corporation from 1 Jan. 1888 **1890**

Shelf Waterworks Co. Ld. Regd. 1878. Vol. liq. 12 July 1920. Final meeting return regd. 4 Oct. 1920....... **1921**

Shell Mex Ld. Regd. 1920. Vol. liq. Dec. 1934. Distributing business was acquired by Shell-Mex and B. P. Ld. Final meeting return regd. ll June 1935 **1935**

Shelley & Shepley Gas Light Co. Ld. Regd. 1859. Vol. liq. (members') 31 Dec. 1936. Company amalgamated with Kirkburton Gas Light Co. Ld. under title of Kirkburton, Shelley & Shepley Gas Co. Ld., in which company shareholders received 10 ordinary (5% standard) shares of £1 for each original share of £5 held or 7 ordinary (5% standard) shares of £1 for each additional share of £5 held. Final meeting return regd. 5 Apr. 1938.................................... **1937**

Shenango Railway & Mercer Coal Co. Ld. Regd. 1880. Vol. liq. 25 Aug. 1898. Final meeting return regd. 26 June 1900 .... **1899**

Shepherd & Blackburn Ld. Regd. 1921. Vol. liq. (creditors') 10 Nov. 1937. Assets realised insufficient to pay unsecured creditors in full. Final meeting return regd. 14 Dec. 1939 .... **1938**

Shepherd & Blackburn's Cotton Spinning Co. Ld. Regd. 1875. Vol. liq. 28 Jan. 1921. Struck off Register 20 Mar. 1925 .... **1937**

Shepherd (Philip) & Co. Ld. Regd. 1916. Court Order to wind up Mar. 1926. Struck off Register June 1931 **1932**

Shepherd (William) & Sons Ld. Regd. 1922. Vol. liq. (creditors') 8 Mar. 1933. Struck off Register 29 Dec. 1942 .... **1934**

Shepherd (William L.) & Co. Ld. Regd. 1926. Receiver appointed 15 July 1932. Vol. liq. (creditors') 22 July 1932. Direct controlling interest held by Shepherd (William) & Sons Ld. Struck off Register 7 Aug. 1945 .... **1933**

Shepherds (Acton) Ld. Regd. 1926. Vol. liq. (members') 23 Feb. 1932. Direct controlling interest held by Shepherd (William) & Sons Ld. Final meeting return regd. 12 Dec. 1936 .... **1933**

Shepherds Ld. Regd. 1910. Vol. liq. 9 Sept. 1913. A return of 3s. to 4s. in the £ to shareholders was anticipated. Final meeting return regd. 2 Sept. 1914 **1914**

Shepherds (Materials) Ld. Regd. 1928. Vol. liq. (members') 23 Feb. 1932. Direct controlling interest held by Shepherd (William) & Sons Ld. Final meeting return regd. 12 Dec. 1936 .... **1933**

Shepherds Parging Block Co. Ld. Regd. 1919. Direct controlling interest was owned by Shepherd (William) & Sons Ld. Struck off Register 1937 .... **1933**

Shepherds United Ld. Regd. 1885. Court Orders: to wind up 6 Oct. 1886; to dissolve 26 Jan. 1892 ..... **1887**

Shepperson Fertilizers Ld. Regd. 1931. Vol. liq. (members') 8 June 1944. All capital was owned by Fisons Ld. Final meeting return regd. 29 Sept. 1944 ...... **1945**

Sheppy Gas Co. Regd. as Sheppy Gas Consumer Co. Ld. in 1857; inc. as above by Special Act 1871. Dissolved 1 May 1949, undertaking being vested in South Eastern Area Gas Board under Gas Act 1948. Holders of securities were entitled to receive, in respect of each £100 unit held. British Gas 3% guaranteed stock 1990–95 as follows:

	£	s.	d.
Cons. ord. stock (5% stand.)	90	0	0
4% pref. stock	103	0	0
4% pref. A shares (of £10)	10	6	0
6% pref. stock	134	0	0
5% perp. deb. stock...........................	125	0	0
3½% deb. stock (1955)	100	0	0

1952

Sheppey Light Railway Co. Inc. (under Light Railways Act 1896) by order of Light Railway Commissioners confirmed by Board of Trade 3 May 1899. Under Act of 1905 undertaking was purchased by South Eastern & Chatham Railway Co.'s Managing Committee for £65,000 .... **1906**

Sheppey Water & Lighting Co. Ld. Regd. 1902. Under Act of 1937 the undertaking was acquired by Sheppey Water Co., in which company ordinary or preference shareholders received £1 ordinary or preference stock respectively for each share of £1 held. Dissolved 1 Jan. 1938 .... **1939**

Sheppey Water Co. Inc. by Special Act 1937 on 1 Jan. 1938. Under provisions of the Kent Water Act 1955 the undertaking vested in the Sheppey Water Board as from 1 Apr. 1956. Distributions of £1 1s. 9d. per £1 10% ordinary stock and £1 0s. 9d. per £1 7% preference stock were made on 1 Feb. 1960; in addition thereto interest was paid on these amounts

VOL. FOR

at 4% p.a. for period from 1 Apr. 1956 to 30 Sept. 1959 and 300% p.a. from 1 Oct. 1959 to 1 Feb. 1960. £508 14s. unclaimed distributions was paid into Court and the company was dissolved on 11 Apr. 1961 .... **1962**

Shepton Mallet Gas Co. Inc. by Special Act 1902. Dissolved 1 May 1949, undertaking being vested in South Western Area Gas Board under Gas Act 1948. Holders of preference shares (of £10) were entitled to receive £11 9s. 6d. British Gas 3% guaranteed stock 1990–95 for each share held. Liability in respect of certain mortgage loans assumed by the Board **1952**

Shepton Mallet Water Works Co. Inc. by Special Act 1859 .... **1910**

Sherborne Gas & Coke Co. Ld. Regd. 1875. Dissolved 1 May 1949, undertaking being vested in Southern Area Gas Board under Gas Act 1948. Holders of securities were entitled to receive British Gas 3% guaranteed stock 1990–95 as follows in respect of each £5 unit, unless otherwise stated, of security held:

	£	s.	d.
Ord. shares (7% stand.)	6	7	6
5% pref. shares.................................	5	12	6
4½% red. deb. stock (per £100) 100	10	0

1952

Sherbro Palm Oil Co. Ld. Regd. 1920. Vol. liq. 26 July 1921. Final meeting return regd. 22 Feb. 1926 .... **1922**

Sheringham Gas & Water Co Regd. as limited 1887; Inc. by Special Act 1898. Dissolved 1 May 1949, undertaking being vested in Eastern Area Gas Board under Gas Act 1948. Holders of securities were entitled to receive in respect of each £100 unit held, British Gas 3% guaranteed stock 1990–95 as follows:

	£	s.	d.
Orig. gas stock (10% max.)	130	0	0
Addit. gas stock (7% max.)	92	0	0
6% pref. gas stock............................	133	0	0
5% pref. water stock.........................	125	0	0
5% perp. deb. stock (gas)..................	125	0	0
5% perp. deb. stock (water)..............	130	0	0

1952

Sherlaw's Gold Mine Ld. Regd. 1895. Reconstructed 1899 as Sherlaw's Gold Mining Co. Ld. Shareholders were entitled to 1 share of 10s. (credited with 6s. paid) in new company for each share of 10s. held. Removed from Register 1901 .... **1902**

Sherlaw's Gold Mining Co. Ld. Regd. 1899. Reconstructed 1902 as Perseverance Gold Mines Ld., in which company shareholders were entitled to 1 share of 10s. (credited with 7s. 6d. paid) for each share of 10s. held. Removed from Register 1905 **1902**

Sherley (A. F.) & Co. Ld. Regd. July 1928 as A. F. Sherley & Co. (1928) Ld.; name changed Oct. 1928. A subsidiary of Macleans Ld. Vol. liq. (members') 17 May 1954. Preferred ordinary shares of £1 were repaid at par. Final meeting return regd. 13 Dec. 1955 .... **1956**

Sherrards Wood Properties Ld. Undertaking and assets were acquired by Welwyn Public Utility Society Ld. **1929**

Sherwood Billposting Co. Ld. Regd. 1920. Vol. liq. (members') 18 July 1933. Capital returned to contributories—£8,710 8s. 6d. Final meeting return regd. 18 Oct. 1933 .... **1934**

Shields (John) & Co. Ld. Regd. Edinburgh 1897. Vol. liq. (creditors') 17 Apr. 1936. Capital returned to contributories—£1 11s. per preference share of £10. Final meeting return regd. 28 Dec. 1937............. **1937**

Shifnal Gas Light & Coke Co. Ld. Regd. 1936. Dissolved 1 May 1949, undertaking being vested in West Midland Area Gas Board under Gas Act 1948. Holders of securities were entitled to receive, British Gas 3% guaranteed stock 1990–95 as follows:

	£	s.	d.
Ord. shares (of £1)...........................	9	9	0
5% red. debs. (of £100)..................... 100	0	0

1952

Shillelagh & Newtonbarry Light Railway Co. Ld. Powers conferred by order of Privy Council under Tramways and Light Railways Act (1883) expired **1891**

Shillingford Engineering Co. Ld. Regd. 1899 as Trusty Engine Works Ld.; name changed Oct. 1899. Removed from Register 1910 .... **1909**

Shillitoe & Minter Ld. Regd. 1919. Vol. liq. (members') 27 Jan. 1936. All capital was owned by Proprietors of Hay's Wharf Ld. Final meeting return regd. 14 Apr. 1936.. **1929**

Shiloh Mills Ld. Regd. 1920. Vol. liq. (members') 31 Mar. 1953, the undertaking and assets being transferred to Shiloh Spinners Ld. Stockholders received, in respect of every £100 held, £170 13s. ordinary and £73 2s. 9d. preference capital of Shiloh Spinners Ld. Final meeting return regd. 23 Dec. 1953 .... **1954**

See Stock Exchange Year-Book.

VOL. FOR

Ship & Turtle (Painter's) Ld. Regd. 1898. Removed from Register 1901 .... **1900**

Ship Canal Lock Co. Ld. Regd. 1888. Removed from Register 1904 .... ***1901**

Ship Canal Portland Cement Manufacturers Ld. *See* Allied Cement Manufacturers Ld.

Ship Cleaning Co. (operating Macdonald's Patents) Ld. *See* Submersible Motors Ld.

Ship Salvage Corporation Ld. Regd. 1919. Vol. liq. 28 May 1924. Final meeting return regd. 23 June 1926 **1925**

Shipbuilders' Investment Co. Ld. Regd. 1926. Vol. liq. (members') 1 Mar. 1937. Capital returned to contributories—15s. 4·065d. per share of £1. Final meeting return regd. 29 Sept. 1937 .... **1938**

Shipley Collieries Ld. Regd. 1922. Vol. liq. (members') 30 July 1952. Capital returned to contributories—42s. 6·6d. per ordinary share of 2s. 6d. Final meeting return regd. 20 Sept. 1956 .... **1957**

Shipley Gas Light Co. Undertaking purchased by Shipley Urban District Council June 1899 .... **1902**

Shippey Brothers Ld. Regd. 1887. Removed from Register 1911 .... **1905**

Shipston-on-Stour Gas Light, Coke & Coal Co. (1921) Ld. Regd. 1921. Dissolved 1 May 1949, undertaking being vested in West Midland Area Gas Board under Gas Act 1948. Holders of ordinary shares (of £1) were entitled to receive £1 14s. British Gas 3% guaranteed stock 1990–95 for each share held **1952**

Shipton Automation Ld. Regd. 1954 as E. Shipton & Co. (Holdings); name changed 1962. Dissolved 6 Jan. 1983 .... **1974–5**

Shipton (E.) & Co. Ld. Regd. 15 July 1925. Vol. liq. (members') 26 Apr. 1965. Undertaking and assets acquired by Singapore Traction Co. (1964) Ld., in which company shareholders received 15 shares *plus* 7·2d. cash per £1 stock held. Final meeting return regd. 6 Feb. 1981. £2,859·80 was paid into Companys' Liquidation Account **1981–2**

Shire Highlands Railway Nyasaland Ld. Regd. 1895. Vol. liq. (members') 27 Feb. 1931. Undertaking and assets were acquired by Nyasaland Railways Ld. (later Malawi Railways Ld.) for £536,750 5% A debenture stock and 243,375 fully-paid ordinary shares of £1 in exchange for £536,750 5% debenture stock. All capital and 2nd debentures were owned by British Central Africa Co. Ld. Final meeting return regd. 27 Aug. 1940 .... **1931**

Shirebrook & District Gas Co. Inc. by Special Act 1899. Dissolved 1 May 1949, undertaking being vested in East Midland Area Gas Board under Gas Act 1948. Holders of ordinary shares (10% stand.—of £10) were entitled to receive £21 10s. British Gas 3% guaranteed stock 1990–95 for each share held **1952**

Shirebrook Colliery Ld. Regd. 1895. Vol. liq. (members') 4 May 1951. Capital returned to contributories—£4 0s. 3·1017d. per share (of 5s.). £7,019 0s. 7d. was paid into Companies' Liquidation Account. Final meeting return regd. 13 Aug. 1956 .... **1957**

Shireoakes, Laughton & Maltby Railway Co. Inc. by Special Act 1901. By Great Central Railway Co. and Midland Railway Co. Act 1902 the powers were transferred to those two companies jointly **1903**

Shirland Gas Co. Ld. Regd. 1928. Dissolved 1 May 1949, undertaking being vested in East Midland Area Gas Board under Gas Act 1948. Holders of ordinary shares (of £1) were entitled to receive £2 6s. British Gas 3% guaranteed stock 1990–95 for each share held **1952**

Shirley Syndicate Ld. Regd. 1897. Vol. liq. 3 Dec. 1917. Final meeting return regd. 20 July 1918 .... **1918**

Shoolbred (James) & Co. Ld. Regd. 1913. Vol. liq. (creditors') July 1930. Assets realised insufficient to meet claims of unsecured creditors in full. No capital returned to contributories. Final meeting return regd. 5 Mar. 1946 .... **1947**

Shoreditch Property Disposals Ld. Regd. 1897 as Hill's Ld.; name changed to R. & J. Hill Ld. in 1897 and to present title in 1953. Vol. liq. (members') 1 July 1953. Undertaking and assets of company and subsidiaries (except cash, book debts and claims, investments and certain properties) were sold to Carreras Ld. for £520,000. 4% 1st mort. deb. stock repaid at 120% 30 Apr. 1953, and preference stock at par 30 Sept. 1953. Capital returned to ordinary stockholders—19s. 0·1d. per £1 stock. £3,660 19s. was paid into Companies' Liquidation Account. Final meeting return regd. 12 Jan. 1957 .... **1957**

Shoreham Portland Cement Co. Ld. Regd. 1883. Vol. liq. 31 Dec. 1890. Final meeting return regd. 6 Dec.1893 **1891**

Shorthorn Dairy Co. Ld. Regd. 1881. Removed from Register 1905 .... **1887**

Shortlands & Nunhead Railway Co. Inc. by Special Act 1889. Amalgamated with London Chatham & Dover Railway Co. under Act of 1896 .... **1897**

VOL. FOR

Shotley Bridge & Consett District Gas Co. Regd. as Shotley Bridge Gas Co. Ld. 1856; reinc. as above by Special Act 1869. Dissolved 1 May 1949. undertaking being vested in Northern Area Gas Board under Gas Act 1948. Holders of securities were entitled to receive, in respect of each £100 unit held, British Gas 3% guaranteed stock 1990–95 as follows:

	£	s.	d.	
Cons. stock (5% max.)......................	104	0	0	
5½% perp. deb. stock	134	0	0	
4% red. deb. stock	101	0	0	
3½% red. deb. stock	100	0	0	**1952**

Shotts Iron Co. Inc. by Special Act 1871. Reconstructed as Shotts Iron Co. Ld. Contributories were entitled to 3 ordinary shares of £5 in new company for every £100 ordinary stock held or to 4 ordinary shares of £5 for every £100 preference stock held. Mortgage holders were entitled to an equal amount of 4% debenture stock in new company **1897**

Shotts Iron Co. Ld. Regd. Edinburgh 1897. Vol. liq. (members') 5 Mar. 1952. Capital returned to contributories—54s. 1·5868d. per share of 10s. Final meeting return regd. 3 Feb. 1958 .... **1959**

Showell (Walter) & Sons Ld. *See* Ind Coope (South Midlands) Ld.

Showells Stockport Brewery Ld. Regd. 1896. Vol. liq. Oct. 1910. Undertaking was acquired by Walker & Homfrays Ld., in which company shareholders were entitled to 2 ordinary shares of £1 (credited as fully-paid) for each ordinary share of £10 held or 4 preference shares of £1 (credited as fully-paid) for each preference share of £10 held. Debenture holders were entitled to an equal amount of 4% debentures in acquiring company. Removed from Register 1911 .... **1911**

Shrewsbury & Challiner Tyre Co. Ld. Regd. 1900 as Shrewsbury S. T. & Challiner Tyre Co. Ld.; name changed Nov. 1924. Vol. liq. 16 Nov. 1926. The business was acquired in 1925 by Chas. Macintosh & Co. Ld. Final meeting return regd. 19 Oct. 1927. Court Order deferred dissolution until 30 Apr. 1928 **1928**

Shrewsbury & Hereford Railway Co. Inc. by Special Act 1846. Dissolved 2 Apr. 1949; undertaking vested 1 Jan. 1948 in British Transport Commission under Transport Act 1947. Holders of securities were entitled to receive British Transport 3% guaranteed stock 1978–88 as follows in respect of each £100 of capital stock held:

	£	s.	d.	
6% rent-charge stock	159	10	0	
4½% rent-charge stock.......................	120	0	0	**1949**

Shrewsbury & Talbot S. T. Cab & Noiseless Tyre Co. Ld. Regd. 1888. Vol. liq. 30 Apr. 1901. Reconstructed as Shrewsbury S. T. & Challiner Tyre Co. Ld. (later Shrewsbury & Challiner Tyre Co. Ld.). Final meeting return regd. 10 Jan. 1902 .... **1925**

Shrewsbury Empires Ld. Regd. 1921. Vol. liq. (members') 13 Feb. 1956. Capital returned to contributories (per share of £1)—preference: £1 *plus* arrears of dividend; ordinary: £5 5s. 8d. £58 9s. 11d. was paid into Companies' Liquidation Account. Final meeting return regd. 11 Jan. 1957 .... **1957**

Shrewsbury Gaslight Co. Inc. by Special Act 1820. Dissolved 1 May 1949, undertaking being vested in West Midland Area Gas Board under Gas Act 1948. Holders of securities were entitled to receive, in respect of each £100 unit held, British Gas 3% guaranteed stock 1990–95 as follows:

	£	s.	d.	
Conv. add. ord. stock (5% stand.).....	162	10	0	
4% red. pref. stock	100	0	3	
Liability in respect of certain mortgage loans assumed by the Board				**1952**

Shrewsbury S. T. & Challiner Tyre Co. Ld. *See* Shrewsbury & Challiner Tyre Co. Ld.

Shropshire & Montgomeryshire Light Railway Co. Inc. by Special Act 11 Feb. 1909 under Light Railways Act 1896; Amendment Order 1910. Dissolved 23 Dec. 1949; undertaking vested 1 Jan. 1948 in British Transport Commission under Transport Act 1947. Holders of ordinary shares (of £10) were entitled to receive 6d. British Transport 3% guaranteed stock 1978–88 for each share held **1949**

Shropshire & North Wales Assurance Co. Ld. Regd. 1889. Undertaking was acquired by Alliance Assurance Co. Ld. Struck off Register Mar. 1929 .... **1930**

Shropshire & Worcestershire Electric Power Co. *See* Shropshire, Worcestershire & Staffordshire Electric Power Co.

Shropshire Beet Sugar Co. Ld. Regd. 1927. Vol. liq. (members') 5 Aug. 1936. Undertaking was transferred to British Sugar Corporation Ld. for 242,015 fully-paid shares. In addition to participation in distribution of these shares, preferred ordinary

VOL. FOR

shareholders were entitled to 3*s.* 10⅕*d.* per share in cash. Final meeting return regd. 18 Aug. 1939 .... **1937**

Shropshire Electric Light & Power Co. Regd. 1891. Undertaking sold to local authority for £21,500. Vol. liq. 17 Apr. 1899. Final meeting return regd. 6 Dec. 1899 .... **1899**

Shropshire Mineral Light Railway Co. Inc. 1891. No capital had been issued at 31 Dec. 1895 .... **1898**

Shropshire Mines Ld. Regd. 1916 as Shropshire Mines (1916) Ld.; name changed Mar. 1917. Vol. liq. 11 Sept. 1925. Final meeting return regd. 22 Aug. 1931 **1926**

Shropshire Railways Co. Inc. by Special Act 1888. Undertaking vested 1 Jan. 1948 in British Transport Commission under Transport Act 1947. Dissolved 11 Dec. 1950; holders of securities were entitled to receive British Transport 3% guaranteed stock 1978–88 as follows in respect of each £100 of capital stock held:

	£	s.	d.	
Ordinary Stock		5	0	
4½% prior charge deb. stock	5	0	0	
5% 1st deb. stock		5	0	
5% 2nd deb. stock		5	0	
5% deb. bonds	50	0	0	**1949**

Shropshire Union Railways and Canal Co. Inc. by Special Acts 1846 and 1854. In 1923 the undertaking was merged into the London & North Western Railway Co. £330,154 Shropshire Union Stock held by the North Western Company was cancelled, and holders of the remaining Shropshire Union Stock received £50 of London & North Western Consolidated Stock for every £100 held by them **1924**

Shropshire, Worcestershire & Staffordshire Electric Power Co. Inc. by Special Act 1903 as Shropshire & Worcestershire Electric Power Co.; name changed 1905. Dissolved 1 Apr. 1948, undertaking being vested in British (later Central) Electricity Authority and Midlands Area Board under Electricity Act 1947. Holders of securities were entitled to receive British Electricity 3% guaranteed stock (1968–73), as follows in respect of each £1 unit of capital held:

	£	s.	d.	
6% preference shares	1	12	0	
A ordinary shares	2	2	6	
B ordinary shares	1	7	6	
5% debenture stock	1	1	10⅘	**1949**

Shropshire Worcestershire & Staffordshire Electric Power Development Co. Ld. See S. W. S. Development Co. Ld.

Shuman Engine Syndicate Ld. Regd. 1910. Struck off Register 1924 .... **1924**

Shuniah Weachu Mine Co. Ld. Regd. 1886. Vol. liq. 28 Nov. 1893. Final meeting return regd. 1 Aug. 1902 **1894**

Shuswap & Okanagon Railway Co. Inc. in Canada by Special Act 1886. The then outstanding 4% sterling bonds were redeemed in 1915; holders were entitled to repayment in cash at par, or £107 of Canadian Pacific 4% debenture stock for every £100 held ... **1915**

Shuters, Chippindale and Colyers Ld. Regd. 1891 as Chippindales Ld.; name changed to Shuters and Chippindales Ld. in Feb. 1894; and as above in Nov. 1894. Struck off Register 24 Mar. 1914 ...... **1894**

Shwegyin (Burma) Rubber Estate Ld. Regd 1906 as Mergui Rubber Co. Ld.; name changed Jan. 1912. Vol. liq. 22 Dec. 1925. Estates were sold to Sittang Valley Rubber Estate Ld. Capital returned to contributories—£2 (approx.) per share of £1; further payments (if any) not known. Final meeting return regd. 28 Apr. 1926 .... **1926**

Siak Rubber Estates Ld. Regd. 1932. Vol. liq. (members') 11 Dec. 1953. Capital returned to contributories—3½*d.* per share (of 2*s.*). £471 15s. 7*d.* was paid into Companies' Liquidation Account. Final meeting return regd. 12 Dec. 1955 .... **1957**

Siak (Sumatra) Rubber Estates Ld. Regd. 1910. Vol. liq (members') 31 Oct. 1932. Undertaking and assets were acquired by Siak Rubber Estates Ld., in which company shareholders were entitled to 1 fully-paid share and 1 share of £1 (credited with 18*s.* paid) for each preference share of £1 held or 1 share of £1 (credited with 18*s.* paid) for each ordinary share of £1 held. £6 17*s.* 10*d.* was paid into Companies' Liquidation Account. Final meeting return regd. 21 June 1934 .... **1933**

Siak Tin & Land Co. Ld. Established under Dutch Law 1888. Wound up 1898 .... **1899**

Siam Exploring Co. Ld. Regd 1895. Shareholders were entitled to 1 share of £1 (credited with 17*s.* 6*d.* paid) of New Kabin Gold Mines of Siam Ld. for each share of £1 held. Removed from Register 1901..... **1901**

Siamese Trading Corporation Ld. Regd. 1905. Vol. liq. 24 June 1925. Capital returned to contributories—£1 19*s.* 8*d.* per ordinary share; £2 15*s.* 11*d.* per deferred share; further payments (if any) not known. Final meeting return regd. 17 Oct. 1925 .. **1926**

Siberian Estates Ld. Regd. 1906. Struck off Register 1931 .... ***1912**

Siberian Gold Dredging Co. Ld. Regd. 1900. Struck off Register 1916 .... **1910**

Siberian Mines Ld. Regd. 1906. Vol. liq. May 1908. Removed from Register 1913 .... **1909**

Siberian Proprietary Mines, Ld. Regd. 1905. Vol. liq. (members') 13 Dec. 1938. Capital returned to contributories—4*s.* per share of £1. £1,962 9*s.* 6*d.* was paid into Companies' Liquidation Account. Final meeting return regd. 21 Apr. 1955 .... **1956**

Siberian Syndicate Ld. Regd 1902. Undertaking and assets were acquired by company of same name for £85,900 in shares. Removed from Register 1905... **1905**

Siberian Syndicate Ld. Regd. 1903. Reconstructed 1905 as company of same name. Shareholders were entitled to 1 share of £1 (credited as fully-paid) and 1 fully-paid share in Spassky Copper Mine Ld for every 20 shares of £1 held. Removed from Register 1905 .... **1908**

Siberian Syndicate Ld. Regd. 1905. Vol. liq 31 July 1913. Reconstructed as company of same name. Shareholders were entitled to 1 share of £1 (credited as fully-paid) in new company for each share of £1 held and 4 fully-paid shares of £1 in Spassky Copper Mine Ld. for every 5 shares of £1 held. Final meeting return regd. 24 Apr. 1914 .... **1914**

Siberian Timber Ld. Regd. 1905. Vol. liq. 8 Jan. 1907. Final meeting return regd. 26 Feb. 1907 .... ***1908**

Siberian Trust Ld. Regd. 1906. Vol. liq. 28 Nov. 1912. Final meeting return regd. 16 Oct. 1913 .... **1913**

Sibunion Textiles Ld. Regd. 1919. Struck off Register Sept. 1933 .... **1934**

Sich & Co. Ld. The business was acquired by Isleworth Brewery Ld. **1921**

Sicilian Railways Co. Ld. Regd. 1885. Undertaking sold 1901. Holders of debentures received £7 10*s.* for each £100 held; further payments (if any) not known. Struck off Register 9 Jan. 1953 .... **1908**

Sicilian United Copper Mines Ld. Regd. 1888. Removed from Register 1906 .... **1892**

Sidebottoms (Rochdale & Oldham) Ld. Regd 1898. Vol. liq. Feb. 1907. Removed from Register 1908 .... **1908**

Sidebottoms (Rochdale) Ld. Regd. 1907. Vol. liq. Nov. 1952. Final meeting return regd. 23 Jan. 1953 ..... **1938**

Sidi Salem Estates of Egypt Ld. Regd. 1906 as Cotton Lands of Egypt Ld; name changed Nov. 1906. Vol. liq. Mar. 1909. Undertaking and assets were acquired by Sidi Salem Co. of Egypt (an Egyptian company) in which company shareholders were entitled to 1 share of £4 (credited as fully-paid) for each founders' share of 1*s.* held. Ordinary shareholders were entitled to 92½% of their holding in fully-paid ordinary shares of £4 in new company. Removed from Register 1912 .... **1910**

Sidmouth Gas & Electricity Co. Inc. by Special Act 1911. Undertaking acquired by Sidmouth Urban Distnct Council by Act of 1912 for £34,684. A and B preference shares were repaid at par. and the ordinary shares at about 250% **1914**

Sidmouth Knowle Hotel Co. Ld. Regd. 1882. Debenture holders took possession of property Mar. 1891. Removed from Register 1894 .... **1892**

Sidmouth Railway Co. Inc. by Special Act 1871. In 1923 the undertaking was merged into the London & South Western Railway in which company stockholders were entitled to stock as follows:

For each £100 held		*L & S. W.*	
5% Debenture	£166⅔	3% Deb. Cons.	
Ordinary Share	£100	4% Cons. Gtd.	**1924**

Sidmouth Water Co. Inc. by Special Act 1886. Undertaking was acquired by Sidmouth Urban District Council in Sept. 1933 for £48,250. Capital returned to contributories—£21 10*s.* per share on account; further returns (if any) not known.......... **1934**

Siemens' Patent Gas Light Co. Ld. Regd. 1881 as Siemens (F.) Patent Gas Light Co. Ld.; name changed Nov. 1881. Vol. liq. Nov. 1886. Final meeting return regd. 25 Mar. 1887 .... **1887**

Sierra Buttes Gold Mining Co. Ld. Regd. 1870. Vol. liq 24 May 1906. Capital returned to contributories—2*s.* per Sierra Buttes Share of £2; 2*s.* 5¼*d.* per Plimas Eureka 1872 share of £2; further payments (if any) not known. Removed from Register 1907 .... **1907**

Sierra Co. Ld. Regd. 1898. Vol. liq. 25 Mar. 1920. Final meeting return regd. 16 Sept. 1920 .... ***1920**

Sierra Guaranty Syndicate Ld. See Babilonia Gold Mines, Ld.

Sierra Leone Exploration Syndicate Ld. Regd. 1900. Removed from Register 1903 .... **1903**

Sierra Madre Exploration Ld. Regd. 1900. Struck off Register 1921 .... **1914**

**See Stock Exchange Year-Book.*

VOL. FOR

Sierra Morena Copper Mines Ld. Regd. 1900. Court Order to wind up July 1913. Struck off Register Apr. 1929 ...... **1930**

Siginting (Negri Sembilan) Rubber Estate Ld. Regd. 1910. Winding-up order 6 May 1963. Dissolved 30 June 1978 ...... **1962**

Sika (Africa) Ld. Regd. 1929. Vol. liq. (members') 27 Mar. 1931. Undertaking and assets transferred to Sika Dominion Ld. (later Cement Waterproofing Co. Ld.), in which company shareholders were entitled to 5 ordinary shares of 1s. for every 8 ordinary shares of 1s. held or 5 preference shares of 10s. for every 8 preference shares of 10s. held. Final meeting return regd. 29 Mar. 1933 ...... **1934**

Sika (Australasia) Ld. Regd. 1928. Vol. liq. (members') 27 Mar. 1931. Undertaking and assets transferred to Sika Dominion Ld. (later Cement Waterproofing Co. Ld.), in which company shareholders were entitled to 7 preference shares of 10s. and 27 ordinary shares of 1s. for every 125 ordinary shares of 1s. held or 8 preference shares of 10s. for every 5 preference shares of £1 held. Final meeting return regd. 29 Mar. 1933 ...... **1934**

Sika (Canada) Ld. Regd. 1928. Vol. liq. (members') 27 Mar. 1931. Undertaking and assets transferred to Sika Dominion Ld. (later Cement Waterproofing Co. Ld.), in which company shareholders were entitled to 1 ordinary share of 1s. for every 2 ordinary shares of 1s. held or 1 preference share of 10s. for every 2 preference shares of 10s. held. Final meeting return regd. 29 Mar. 1933 ...... **1934**

Sika Dominion Ld. *See* Cement Waterproofing Ld.

Sika (India) Ld. Regd. 1928: Vol. liq. (members') 27 Mar. 1931. Undertaking transferred to Sika Dominion Ld. (later Cement Waterproofing Co. Ld.), in which company shareholders were entitled to 3 ordinary shares of 1s. for every 4 ordinary shares of 1s. or 3 preference shares of 10s. for every 4 preference shares of 10s. held. Final meeting return regd. 29 Mar.1933 ...... **1934**

Sikassoo Rubber Estates Ld. Regd. 1910. Struck off Register 1915 ...... **1912**

Silati Co. Ld. Regd. 1921. Struck off Register Oct. 1933 **1934**

Silati Gold Mining Co. Ld. Regd. 1894. Vol. liq. 6 Oct. 1921. Ordinary shareholders were entitled to 2 shares of 5s. (credited with 2s. 6d. per share paid) in Silati Co. Ld. for each ordinary share of £1 held. Deferred shareholders were entitled to option (since expired) over surplus shares partly-paid. Final meeting return regd. 12 Oct. 1936 ...... **1922**

Silati River Gold Mining & Prospecting Co. Ld. Regd. 1889. Vol. liq. 29 Dec. 1893. Reconstructed as Silati Gold Mining Co. Ld., in which company shareholders were entitled to 1 share of £1 (credited with 15s. paid) for every 5 ordinary shares of £1 held or 1 deferred share for each founders' share held. Final meeting return regd. 10 nov. 1894 ...... **1894**

Sileby Gas Light & Coke Co. Ld. Regd. 1866. Dissolved 1 May 1949, undertaking being vested in East Midland Area Gas Board under Gas Act 1948. Holders of ordinary shares (of 10s.) were entitled to receive £1 British Gas 3% guaranteed stock 1990–95 for each share held **1952**

Silberhütte Supply Co. Ld. Regd. 1899. Vol. liq. 6 Jan. 1910. Final meeting return regd. 13 May 1924 .... **1910**

Silencio Gold Mines Ld. Regd. 1885. Properties were acquired by Colombian Gold Mines Ld. Removed from Register 1906 ...... ***1891**

Silensing Gold Mining Co. Ld. Regd. 1898. Removed from Register 1903 ...... **1903**

Silent Sales Ld. Regd. 1929. Vol. liq. (creditors') 25 Oct. 1930. No capital returned to contributories. Final meeting return regd. 21 Jan. 1932 ...... **1931**

Silindi Co. Ld. Regd. 1895. Vol. liq. 14 Jan. 1898. Certain assets were acquired by Panga Co. Ld. (later Panga & Silindi United Ld.), in which company shareholders were entitled to 1 share of £1 for each share of £1 held. Removed from Register 1907 ...... **1898**

Silk & Goodman Ld. Regd. 1925. Vol. liq. (members') 10 Feb. 1938. Capital returned to contributories—10s. 6½d. per ordinary share of £1. Final meeting return regd. 14 Dec. 1938 ...... **1939**

Silkstone & Dodworth Coal & Iron Co. Ld. Regd. 1873. Wound up by Order of Court 19 Nov. 1890 ...... ***1882**

Silva, Berras Pinto & Co. *See* Banco Espirito Santo.

Silver & Steelcrafts Ld. Regd. 1935. Receiver appointed 9 Dec. 1938. Struck off Register 3 Mar. 1944 ...... **1945**

Silver Bell Mining and Smelting Co. Ld. Regd. 1890. Vol. liq. 18 Apr. 1895. Final meeting return regd. 26 June 1897 ...... **1896**

Silver City Steam Trawling Co. Ld. Regd. in Edinburgh 1899. Vol. liq. Mar. 1929. Distributions amounting to 14s. per share of 6s. 6d. had been made in July 1929. Struck off Register 8 June 1948 ...... **1949**

VOL. FOR

Silver Fox Electrical Co. Ld. Regd. 1919 as Belcher Ld.; name changed Sept. 1934. Vol. liq. (members') 4 Nov. 1935. Capital returned to contributories—£1,359 14s. 6d. Final meeting return regd. 8 Jan. 1936 ...... **1936**

Silver Hill Mining Co. Ld. Regd. 1881. Court Orders: to wind up Mar. 1883; to dissolve 19 Aug. 1886. ..... **1885**

Silver King Mining Co. Ld. Regd. 1888. Struck off Register 28 July 1899 ...... **1901**

Silver Ledge Syndicate Ld. Regd. 1890. Vol. liq. 12 Mar. 1892. Removed from Register 20 Mar. 1906 ...... ***1893**

Silver Mines of La Luz Ld. Regd. 1890. Vol. liq. 5 Apr. 1893. Reconstructed as La Yesca Gold & Silver Mines Ld., in which company shareholders were entitled to 1 share of £1 (credited with 17s. 6d. paid) for each share of £1 held. Debenture holders were entitled to an equal amount of debentures in new company. Final meeting return regd. 13 Nov. 1897 **1899**

Silver Peak Mining Co. Ld. Regd. 1880. Court Orders: to wind up 26 May 1884; to dissolve 17 July 1891 **1885**

Silver Queen United Ld. Regd. 1885. Removed from Register 1906 ...... ***1888**

Silver Spring Brewery Co. Ld. Regd. 1900. Vol. liq. 31 Dec. 1928. The assets were transferred to a Canadian company, in which shareholders were entitled to receive shares. Final meeting return regd. 26 Oct. 1929 ...... **1929**

Silver Wolverine Ld. Regd. 1888. Removed from Register 1906 ...... **1892**

Silverton Mines Ld. Regd. 1887. Vol. liq. 5 July 1892. Final meeting return regd. 5 July 1893 ...... **1893**

Silverton Mines Ld. Regd. 1909. Struck off Register 1923 ...... **1921**

Silvertown, Canning Town and Victoria Dock Freehold Land & Building Co. Ld. Regd. 1879. Vol. liq. Mar. 1902. After repayment of capital the directors were entitled to surplus assets. Removed from Register 1903 ...... **1903**

Simmer & Jack East Ld. Inc Transvaal 1895. Placed in liquidation, and finally dissolved in 1913. Sale of the properties realised insufficient to meet the 1st debenture debt **1912**

Simmer & Jack Gold Mining Co. Ld. *See* Simmer & Jack Proprietary Mines Ld.

Simmer & Jack Proprietary Mines Ld. Inc. Transvaal 1887 as Simmer & Jack Gold Mining Co. Ld.; name changed 1896. Vol. liq. May 1924. Undertaking and assets were acquired by Simmer & Jack Mines Ld., in which company shareholders were entitled to 1 share of 2s. 6d. (credited as fully-paid) for each share of £1 held **1925**

Simmer & Jack West Ld. Inc. Transvaal 1895. Vol. liq. 1907. Undertaking and assets were acquired by Jupiter Gold Mining Co. Ld., in which company shareholders were entitled to 6 shares of £1 for every 5 shares of £1 held **1908**

Simmer Deep Ld. Inc. Transvaal 1906. Vol. liq. Dec. 1920 ...... **1922**

Simmer East Deep Ld. Inc. Transvaal 1902. In liquidation in 1914 ...... **1914**

Simmers Gold Mines Ld. Regd. 1895. Struck off Register 1916 ...... **1912**

Simmonds Aircraft Ld. Regd. 1928. Vol. liq. (members') 5 May 1931. Direct controlling interest owned by Whitehall Securities Corporation Ld. The assets were distributed in specie. Final meeting return regd. 3 July 1931 ...... **1932**

Simmonds Brothers Ld. Regd. 1889. Vol. liq. 14 Dec. 1923. Final meeting return regd. 17 July **1924**

Simo Rubber Estates Ld. Regd. 1907. Vol. liq. (members') 21 May 1935. Reconstructed as Simo Rubber Co. Ld. (later Simo Properties Ld.) in which company shareholders were entitled to 4 shares of 2s. (credited as fully-paid) for each share of 2s. held. Final meeting return regd. 14 Dec. 1935 ...... **1936**

Simonds Steel & Iron Forging Co. Ld. Regd. 1886. Vol. liq. 13 Dec. 1890. Final meeting return regd. 28 May 1894 ...... **1892**

Simons' Reef Consolidated Gold Mining Corporation Ld. Regd. 1881. Vol. liq. 31 Oct. 1882. Court Order to continue winding up under supervision Jan. 1883. Final meeting return regd. 21 Aug. 1891 ...... **1883**

Simonson (L.) & Co. Ld. *See* Rosar (E.) & Co. Ld.

Simoona Development Co. Ld. Regd. 1899. Vol. liq. 30 Mar. 1915. Final meeting return regd. 29 Oct. 1915 **1916**

Simpa Reefs Ld. Regd. 1920. Struck off Register 7 Dec. 1937 ...... **1938**

Simpah (Tarkwa) Gold Mining Syndicate Ld. Regd. 1900. Removed from Register 1910 ...... **1909**

Simpang Sumatra Rubber Co. Ld. Regd. 1909. Vol. liq. 17 Oct. 1913. Reconstructed as Ampat (Sumatra) Rubber Estate Ld., in which company shareholders were entitled to 1 share of 10s. (credited with 6s. 6d. paid) for each share of £1 held. The debentures were

VOL. FOR

exchanged at par for debentures in new company. Final meeting return regd. 20 Apr. 1914 .... **1914**

Simpkin, Marshall, Hamilton, Kent & Co. Ld. *See below.*

Simpkin Marshall Ld. Regd. 1889 as Simpkin, Marshall, Hamilton, Kent & Co. Ld.; name changed Feb. 1928. Vol. liq. (members') 17 Feb. 1941. Capital returned to contributories (per £1 stock)—preference 24s.; ordinary 36s. (subject to adjustment in accordance with a Scheme of Distribution & Adjustment of Rights). Final meeting return regd. 24 July 1957 .... **1958**

Simplex Automatic Machine Co. Ld. Regd. 1887. Vol. liq. Apr. 1890. Final meeting return regd. 17 Nov. 1890 .... **1891**

Simplex Construction Co. Ld. Regd. 1919. Court Order to wind up Mar. 1921. Struck off Register 1925.... **1922**

Simplex Copper Extraction Co. Ld. Regd. 1903. Vol. liq. June 1907. Removed from Register 1908 .... **1908**

Simplex Electrical Syndicate Ld. Regd. 1886. Vol. liq. 7 May 1891. Final meeting return regd. 17 Feb. 1891 **1892**

Simplex Ld. Regd. 1926. Vol. liq. 16 Aug. 1929. Undertaking and assets were transferred to Universal & General Securities Ld., in which company shareholders were entitled to 3 fully-paid ordinary shares of 1s. and 1 deferred share of 1s. for every 20 ordinary shares of 1s. held or 1 fully-paid deferred share of 1s. for every 20 deferred shares of 1s. held. Final meeting return regd. 21 Jan. 1931................. **1930**

Simpson & Jackson Ld. Regd. 1901. Vol. liq. (members') 5 Oct. 1944. A direct controlling interest was held by Bleachers' Association Ld. (later Whitecroft Industrial Holdings Ld.). Final meeting return regd. 6 Jan. 1945 .... **1945**

Simpson's Lever Chain & Cycle Co. Ld. Regd. 1895 as Simpson's Lever Chain Ld.; name changed May 1897. Court Order to wind up 8 July 1898. Liquidator released 23 June 1915. Struck off Register 14 Feb. 1919.................................... **1899**

Simpson's Lever Chain (Foreign & Canadian) Ld. Regd. 1895. Removed from Register 1911 .... **1899**

Simpson's Ld. Regd. 1865. Removed from Register 1903 **1903**

Sim's Ships' Compositions Co. Ld. Regd. 1885. Vol. liq. 29 Oct. 1892. Final meeting return regd. 11 Dec. 1893 .... **1893**

Simson & McPherson Ld. Regd. 1896. A subsidiary of Robert Deuchar Ld. Vol. liq. (members') 11 May 1959. Final meeting return regd. 14 Feb. 1961...... **1950**

Simson & Mason Ld. Regd. 1886. Removed from Register 1906 .... **1892**

Sinai Petroleum Syndicate Ld. Regd. 1909. Vol. liq. 24 July 1914. Final meeting return regd. 28 June 1915 **1915**

Sinaloa Mining Syndicate Ld. Regd. 1888. Removed from Register 1907 .... **1895**

Sinanombi Development Co. Ld. Regd. 1896. Vol. liq. 14 Apr. 1898. Final meeting return regd. 24 Oct. 1898 **1899**

Sinclair Iron Co. Ld. Regd. 1928; all capital owned by Allied Ironfounders Ld. Vol. liq. (members') 24 June 1963. Final meeting return regd. 23 Mar. 1964...... **1940**

Singapore Electric Tramways Ld. Regd. 1905. Vol. liq. Apr. 1925. Reconstructed as Singapore Traction Co. Ld., in which company shareholders were entitled to 1 ordinary share of £1 (credited as fully-paid) for every 8 shares of 5s. held. Holders of £257,500 5% debentures were entitled to 180,250 fully-paid preference and 103,000 fully-paid ordinary shares of £1 in new company. Struck off Register Jan. 1934 **1934**

Singapore Gas Co. Ld. Regd. 1862. The undertaking was sold to the Municipality for £41,420. Removed from Register 1904 .... **1902**

Singapore Traction Co. Ltd. Regd. 15 Jul 1925. Vol. liq. (members') 26 Apr 1965. Undertaking and assets acquired by Singapore Traction Co. (1964) Ld. in which company shareholders received 15 shares *plus* 7·2d cash per £1 stock held. Final meeting return regd. 6 Feb 1981. £2,859·80 was paid into Companies' Liquidation Account **1981–82**

Singer & Co. Ld. Regd. 1903. Vol. liq. Aug. 1909. The undertaking and assets were acquired by Singer & Co. (1909) Ld. (later Singer & Co. Ld) in which company debenture holders were entitled to 25 ordinary shares of £1 and 1 debenture of £21 for every £80 debenture held. No capital returned to contributories. Removed from Register 1911 .... **1910**

Singer & Co. Ld. Regd. 1909 as Singer & Co. (1909) Ld.; name changed June 1912. Undertaking transferred to Singer Motors Ld. under a Scheme of Arrangement. Ordinary stockholders were entitled to 1 ordinary share of 5s. (credited with 2s. 6d. paid) for every 5s. stock held; preference stockholders received 1 fully-paid preference share of 8s. for every £1 stock held; debenture stockholders received a like amount of debenture stock. Dissolved on 24 Mar. 1937 under Sec. 154 of Companies Act 1929 **1937**

Singer Cycle Co. Ld. Regd. 1896. Undertaking was acquired by Singer & Co. Ld. Removed from Register 1911 .... **1904**

VOL. FOR

Singla Tea Co. Ld. Regd. 1879. Removed from Register 1905 .... ***1888**

Single Rose China Clay Co. Ld. Regd. 1881. Struck off Register 22 June 1894 .... **1892**

Sinjaul (Holdings) Ld. Regd. 1891 as Raine and Co. Ld; name subsequently changed. Vol. liq. (members') 24 Dec. 1964. Final meeting return regd. 23 Nov. 1965 **1958**

Sinti Reefs Ld. Regd 1909. Vol. liq. 30 Dec. 1919. Final meeting return regd. 1 June 1920 .... **1920**

Siput Tin Co. Ld. Regd. 1927. Vol. liq. (creditors') 30 July 1931. Assets were sold on behalf of debenture holders, who were not repaid in full. Final meeting return regd. 1 Feb. 1935 .... **1932**

Siputeh Tin Mines Ld. Regd. 1907. Vol. liq. 4 July 1919. Undertaking and assets were acquired by Pusing Rubber & Tin Ld. (later Commodity & Associated Investments Ld. later London Wall Investment Trust Ld.) in which company shareholders were entitled to 266 shares of 2s. (credited as fully-paid) for every 100 shares of £1 held. Final meeting return regd. 25 May 1921 .... **1920**

Sir Walter Raleigh Mining Co. Ld. Regd. 1895. Removed from Register 1901 .... **1899**

Sisal Estates Ld. Regd. 1936. Vol. liq. 31 Mar. 1952. Preference shares (of £1) were repaid at 24s. 10·2d. per share and ordinary shareholders were entitled to receive 3 fully-paid stock units of 5s. each of Bird & Co. (Africa) Ld. plus a capital cash distribution of 4s. 6d. per share (of 5s.) for each share held. £1,041 0s. 9d. was paid into Companies' Liquidation Account. Final meeting return regd. 19 Jan. 1953 **1955**

Siskol Machines Ld. Regd. 1913 as International Channelling Machines (1913) Ld.; name changed to International Channelling Machines Ld. 1915 and as above Dec. 1935. Vol. liq. (members') 8 Oct. 1963. Final meeting return regd. 9 Oct. 1964 .... **1938**

Sissert Co. Ld. Regd. 1912. Struck off Register 22 Sept. 1939 .... **1940**

Sissert Mining District Co. Ld. Inc. Russia. All capital owned by Sissert Co. Ld. In 1918 property was under control of the Siberian Government **1937**

Sittang Valley Rubber Estate Ld. Regd. 1925. Vol. liq. (members') 28 Feb. 1934. Undertaking and assets were acquired by company of same name. Shareholders were entitled to 1 share of 2s. (credited with 1s. 10d. paid) in new company for each share of 2s. held. Final meeting return regd. 2 Jan. 1936......... **1935**

Sittingbourne District Gas Co. Inc. by Special Act 1877. Dissolved 1 May 1949, undertaking being vested in South Eastern Area Gas Board under Gas Act 1948. Holders of securities were entitled to receive British Gas 3% guaranteed stock 1990–95 as follows in respect of each £20 unit, unless otherwise stated, of security held:

	£	s.	d.
Ord. shares (10% max.)	33	8	0	
Ord. shares (7% max.)	23	8	0	
4¼% red. pref. stock (per £100).........	102	10	0	**1952**

Sizaire-Berwick Ld. Regd. 1913. The 8% prior lien debentures were repaid in full with accrued interest. Holders of the 6½% debentures received a return of approx. 9d. in the £; further payments (if any) not known. Struck off Register 1928 .... **1928**

Sjalati Gold Mines Ld. Regd. 1890. Wound up. Final meeting return regd. 17 Dec. 1895 .... **1896**

Skegness Gas Co. Regd. 1877. Inc. 1914 by Special Act. Liquidated by Act of 1915 .... **1918**

Skela (Roumanian) Coal Syndicate Ld. Regd. 1897. Removed from Register 1912 .... **1905**

Skelmanthorpe Gas Co. Ld. Regd. 1934. Dissolved 1 May 1949, undertaking being vested in North Eastern Area Gas Board under Gas Act 1948. Holders of ordinary shares (of 10s.) were entitled to receive 10s. British Gas 3% guaranteed stock 1990–95 for each share held **1952**

Skelmorlie & Wemyss Bay Gas & Electric Supply Co. Ld. Regd. in Edinburgh 1876. Dissolved 1 May 1949, undertaking being vested in Scottish Area Gas Board, under Gas Act 1948. Holders of shares (of £5, with £2 10s. paid) were entitled to receive £3 10s. British Gas 3% guaranteed stock 1990–95 for each share held **1952**

Skelmorlie Electric Supply Co. Ld. Regd. in Edinburgh 1911. Dissolved 1 Apr. 1948, undertaking being vested in the British (later Central) Electricity Authority and South-West Scotland Ares Board under the Electricity Act 1947. Ordinary shareholders were entitled to receive £5 British Electricity 3% guaranteed stock (1968–73), for each share (of £10) held **1949**

Skerne Ironworks Co. Ld. Regd. 1873. Vol. liq. 1879. Struck off Register 27 Apr. 1894 .... **1902**

Skerne Steel & Wire Co. Ld. Regd. 1893. Vol. liq. 3 Oct. 1894. Final meeting return regd. 7 Oct. 1902 .... **1902**

Skinner and Holford Ld. Regd 1884. Vol. liq (members') 10 Nov. 1955. Returns to contributories—£0·35927 ord. stock of Thomas Tilling Ld., 10·46 ordinary shares of Skinner & Holford (Hldgs.) Ld. and 10·333p cash per share of 5p. 80p in respect of unclaimed distribution and £11·92 in respect of unclaimed dividends paid into Companies' Liquidation Account. Final meeting return regd. 20 Dec. 1975. .... **1976-7**

Skipthwaite Ld. *See* Slater, Walker Australian Investment Trust Ld.

Skipton & Kettlewell Railway Co. Inc. by Special Act 1880 .... **1886**

Skylark Motor Coach Co. Ld. See London General Omnibus Co. Ld.

Slack Mills (Holdings) Ld. Regd. 1919 as Slack Mills Co. Ld.; name changed Mar. 1953. Vol. liq. (members') 23 Mar. 1960. Capital returned to contributories—13s. 0·31d. per 10s. stock. £1,165 paid into Companies' Liquidation Account in respect of unclaimed dividends. Final meeting return regd. 14 Mar. 1962 .... **1963**

Slade & Bullock Ld. Regd. 1891 as B. Bullock Ld.; name changed Aug. 1911. Vol. liq. 16 Nov. 1928. Final meeting return regd. 25 Jan. 1934 .... **1929**

Slag & Tarmacadam Co. Ld. Regd. 1909. Vol. liq. (members') 23 Nov. 1936. Capital returned to contributories—£4,327 14s. 4d. Final meeting return regd. 7 Apr. 1937 .... **1937**

Slag Power Ld. Regd. 1910. Struck off Register 9 Dec. 1930. .... **1931**

Slaithwaite Gas Co. Est. 1855. Inc. 1876 by Special Act. By Act of 1914 undertaking was acquired by Longwood Gas Co. (later Longwood & Slaithwaite Gas Co.) from 1 Jan. 1915. Holders of 10% maximum old ordinary shares were entitled to £20 5% consolidated ordinary stock for every £10 fully-paid share held and to £4 of such stock for every £10 share (with £2 paid) held. Holders of 3½% pref. shares were entitled so £10 4% consolidated pref. stock for every £10 fully-paid share held. The Longwood Co. assumed liability for the outstanding £3,600 bonds. **1915**

Slaithwaite Land & Building Co. Ld. *See* Slaithwaite Spinning Co. Ld.

Slaithwaite Spinning Co. Ld. Regd. 1876 as Slaithwaite Land & Building Co. Ld.; name changed Feb. 1877. Vol. liq. (creditors') 26 Oct. 1937. Assets realised insufficient to pay unsecured creditors in full. Final meeting return regd. 1 Apr. 1939 .... **1938**

Slater Ld. Regd. 1889. Vol. liq. 10 Dec. 1894. Reconstructed as Slaters Ld. [later Slaters & Bodega Ld.; later Forte's (Holdings) Ld.], in which company shareholders were entitled to 7½ ordinary shares of £1 (credited as fully-paid) for each ordinary share of £5 held. The 200 founders' shares of £5 were exchanged for 26,500 ordinary shares of £1. Final meeting return regd. 19 Oct. 1896 .... **1894**

Slater, Walker Australian Investment Trust Ld. Regd. 1971 as Skipthwaite Ld.; name changed 1972. Vol. liq. (members') 8 Apr. 1974 for purpose of reconstruction as Slater, Walker Minerals Trust, a unit trust, in which shareholders were to receive 1 unit for every share held; terminal dividend of 0·5897p per share paid in Aug. 1974. Final meeting return regd. 25 July 1978 .... **1979-80**

Slater (William) & Co. Ld. Regd. 1887. Struck off Register 1915 .... **1895**

Sleaford Brick Co. Ld. Regd. 1919. Court Order to wind up 23 May 1922. Struck off Register 1928 .... **1923**

Sleaford Gas Co. Ld. Regd. 1866. Dissolved 1 May 1949, undertaking being vested in East Midland Area Gas Board under Gas Act 1948. Holders of securities were entitled to receive British Gas 3% guaranteed stock 1990–95 as follows:

	£	s.	d.
Ord. shares (of £1)	2	2	6
4% red. mort. debs. (of £100)	101	0	0	**1952**

Sleaths Ld. Regd. 1896. Vol. liq. (members') 20 June 1942. Capital returned to contributories—5s. 7½d. per share. £133 12s. was paid into Companies' Liquidation Account on account of unclaimed capital. Final meeting return regd. 3 Jan. 1947 ... **1947**

Slide & Spur Gold Mines Ld. Regd. 1887. Vol. liq. 28 Feb. 1898. Final meeting return regd. 2 June 1898 .... **1899**

Sligo & Arigna Railway Co. Inc. 1908. No capital had been raised at 31 Dec. 1911 .... **1913**

Sligo, Leitrim and Northern Counties Railway Co. Ld. Inc. by Special Act, 1875; regd. as limited under Northern Ireland Companies Act, 1932. 17 Dec. 1957. Winding-up Order 3 May 1958. Holders of 3½% A Debenture Stock received 13s. 11·51d. per £1 stock. Dissolved 30 June 1966 .... **1967**

Sloane Avenue Mansions Ld. Regd. 1932. Vol. liq. (members') 8 Mar. 1935. Debenture holders were repaid at 105%. Capital returned to contributories— £36,000. £267 17s. 5d. was paid into Companies'

Liquidation Account. Final meeting return regd. 22 June 1938 .... **1936**

Sloane Gardens House Ld. *See below.*

Sloane Securities Ld. Regd. 1888 as Ladies Dwellings Co. Ld.; name changed in 1934 to Sloane Gardens House, Ld. and subsequently as above. Vol. liq. 16 Jan. 1959. Final meeting return regd. 20 Oct. 1959 .... **1954**

Slocan Prospecting Syndicate Ld. Regd. 1899. Struck off Register 26 Dec. 1902 .... **1902**

Slot Machines Sales Ld. Regd. 1928. Vol. liq. (members') 24 Apr. 1931. Shareholders were repaid in full in June 1931. £37 18s. 4d. was paid into Companies' Liquidation Account. Final meeting return regd. 23 Apr. 1932 .... **1932**

Slough & Datchet Electric Supply Co. Ld. Regd. 1902. Dissolved 1 Apr. 1948, undertaking being vested in British (later Central) Electricity Authority and Southern Area Board under Electricity Act 1947 .... **1949**

Slough & Langley Brick Co. (1935) Ld. Regd. 1935. Vol. liq. (members') 20 Jan. 1942. Capital returned to contributories—20s. per preference share of £1; 3s. 4⅜d. per ordinary share of 10s. Final meeting return regd. 17 July 1944 .... **1942**

Slough Creek Gravel Gold Ld. Regd. 1905. Vol. liq. 1906. Reconstructed as Slough Creek Ld., in which company shareholders were entitled to 1 share of 4s. (credited with 3s. paid) for each share held. Removed from Register 1910. .... **1908**

Slough Creek Ld. Regd. 1900. Reconstructed 1903 as company of same name. Shareholders were entitled to 1 share of £1 (credited with 17s. paid) in new company for each share of £1 held. Removed from Register 1907 .... **1904**

Slough Creek Ld. Regd. 1903. Vol. liq. 22 Dec. 1904. Removed from Register 1908 .... **1908**

Slough Creek Ld. Regd. 1906. Struck off Register 1916 .... **1917**

Slough Gas & Coke Co. Inc. by Special Act 1866. Dissolved 1 May 1949 undertaking being vested in North Thames Area Board under Gas Act 1948. Holders of securities were entitled to receive, in respect of each £100 unit held, British Gas 3% guaranteed stock 1990–95 as follows:

	£	s.	d.
Ord. stock (5% stand.)	163	0	0
5% pref. stock	115	0	0
4% red. pref. stock	100	10	0
5% perp. deb. stock	125	0	0
4% perp. deb. stock	103	0	0
4% red. deb. stock	101	0	0	**1952**

Slug Hill (Pride of the Hill) Gold Mining Co. Ld. Regd. 1895. Removed from Register 1905 .... **1908**

Slyth (F.) & Co. Ld. Regd. 1924. Vol. liq. (members') 27 Nov. 1930. Capital returned to contributories— £5,466 11s. 5d. to preference shareholders. Final meeting return regd. 25 Jan. 1940 .... **1941**

Smailes (Thomas) & Son's Steamship Co. Ld. Regd. 1904. Vol. liq. 24 Jan. 1918. Final meeting return regd. 16 Aug. 1920 .... **1918**

Smaldeel Development Syndicate Ld. Regd. 1903. Removed from Register 1909 .... **1908**

Smale (Josiah) & Son Ld. Regd. 1918. Vol. liq. (members') 22 July 1937. Undertaking and assets were acquired by company of same name. Shareholders were entitled to 1 share of 7s. 6d. (credited as fully-paid) in new company *plus* 2s. 6d. in cash for each share of £1 held. £128 15s. was paid into Companies' Liquidation Account in respect of unclaimed distributions. Final meeting return regd. 13 Dec. 1928. .... **1938**

Small Farm & Labourers' Land Co. Ld. Regd. 1885. Removed from Register 1905 .... **1902**

Smallbrook Mill Ld. Regd. 1919. Vol. liq. (creditors') 6 Mar. 1931. Assets realised insufficient to pay creditors in full. Final meeting return regd. 16 May 1941 .... **1923**

Smallbrook Spinning Co. Ld. Regd. 1875. Vol. liq. 28 Nov. 1919. Final meeting return regd. 23 Jan. 1922 .... **1902**

Smart & Brown Ld. Regd. 1898. Vol. liq. (members') 10 July 1947, undertaking acquired by Henry Barker Ld. (now Henry Barker, Smart & Brown Ld.). Final meeting return regd. 10 Apr. 1948 .... **1949**

Smart & Parker Ld. Regd. 1897. Vol. liq. 3 Aug. 1906. Final meeting return regd. 10 Dec. 1914 .... **1907**

Smart Brothers Ld. Regd. 1927. All capital acquired by Great Universal Stores Ld. Vol. liq. (members') 17 May 1961. Final meeting return regd. 19 Feb. 1964 .... **1960**

Smedley's Hydropathic Co. Ld. Regd. 1875. Vol. liq. (members') 10 Jan. 1956. Capital returned to contributories (per share of £1)—preference: 24s.; ordinary; 24s. 6d. Final meeting return regd. 10 Jan. 1957 .... **1957**

Smelting & Refining Co. of Australia (1901) Ld. Regd. 1901. Vol. liq. 24 July 1905. Debenture stock in Australian Smelting Corporation Ld. was issued in

VOL. FOR

Société Sucrière Anonyme de Marle. Inc. France 1890. Vol. liq. Apr. 1929. Undertaking and assets were acquired by Compagnie Sucrière. Shareholders were entitled to 1 share for each share held. After payment of capitalised bonus of 150% **1930**

Société Turque du Chemin de Fer Smyrne—Cassaba et Prolongement. *See* Ottoman Smyrna & Cassaba & Extension Railway Co.

Society Islands Co. Ld. Regd. 1912. Vol. liq. 29 June 1917. Final meeting return regd. 14 Dec. 1917 .... **1918**

Society of Proprietors of the Royal Exchange Buildings. *See* Royal Exchange, Glasgow, Ld.

Soconusco Rubber Plantations Ld. Regd. 1910. Vol. liq. 16 June 1919. Reconstructed as Rubber Estates of Mexico Ld., in which company shareholders were entitled to 1 share of 1*s.* (credited with 9*d.* paid) for each share of 2*s.* held. The new company took over the debenture stock. Final meeting return regd. 19 Aug. 1924 .... **1920**

Socorro Gold & Silver Mine Ld. Regd. 1912. Struck off Register 9 Dec. 1930 .... **1917**

Socorro Gold Mines Ld. Regd. 1886. Removed from Register 1895 .... **1891**

Soda Fountains Ld. Regd. 1921. Vol. liq. (creditors') 21 Feb. 1935. No capital returned to contributories. Final meeting return regd. 24 Feb. 1936 .... **1936**

Sodax (1929) Ld. Regd. 1929. Vol. liq. (members') 17 July 1941. Capital returned to contributories—5*d.* per share of 5*s*; £416 0*s.* 5*d.* was paid into Companies' Liquidation Account. Final meeting return regd. 1 Nov. 1946 .... **1947**

Soekapoera Tea Estate Ld. Regd. 1912. Vol. liq 30 Dec. 1918. Final meeting return regd. 24 Sept. 1919..... **1919**

Soember Ajoe Rubber Estates Ld. Regd. 1910. Company dissolved 30 Aug. 1980 .... **1960**

Soengei Parit Rubber Co. Ld. Regd. 1924 as Pita Fibre & Rubber Estates Ld.; name changed Aug. 1926. Vol. liq. (members') 19 Aug. 1930. Debentures were redeemed at 105%. Shareholders were entitled to 219 shares of $1 in Indragiri Rubber Ld for every 1,000 shares of 2*s.* held. £330 12*s.* 8*d.* was paid into Companies' Liquidation Account. Final meeting return regd. 3 May 1933 .... **1931**

Sofala Gold Dredging Co. Ld. Regd. Edinburgh 1899. Final meeting return regd. 3 Sept 1912 .... **1903**

Soham & District Gas Co. Ld. Regd. 1884. Dissolved 1 May 1949, undertaking being vested in Eastern Area Gas Board under Gas Act 1948. Holders of securities were entitled to receive British Gas 3% guaranteed stack 1990–95 as follows in respect of each £100 unit, unless otherwise stated, of security held:

	£	s.	d.	
Ord. shares (of £10)	24	0	0	
5½% red. pref. stock	105	0	0	
4½% red. debs.	105	0	0	**1952**

Soho Automatic Machine Co. Ld. Regd. 1929. Vol. liq. (members') 30 Dec. 1952. Final meeting return regd. 18 Mar. 1953 .... **1951**

Solderless Tin Co. Ld. Regd. 1901 as Maconochie's Solderless Tinning Syndicate Ld.; name changed Jan. 1905. Vol. liq. 6 Nov. 1907. Final meeting return regd. 28 July 1931 .... **1908**

Solicitors' Government Stock Investment Trust Ld. Regd 1890. Court Order to wind up 11 Mar. 1893. Removed from Register 1907 .... **1894**

Solidified Petroleum Co. Ld. Regd 1910 as Upper Acre Rubber Estates (Brazil) Ld; name changed Nov. 1910. Struck off Register 1915 .... **1913**

Solidol Chemical (France) Ld. Regd. 1928. Vol. liq. (members') 2 Feb. 1932. Undertaking was acquired by Solidal Chemical Ld. [later Ashe Chemical Ld.] for 827,915 shares of 1*s.* Final meeting return regd. 11 July 1934 .... **1932**

Solihull Gas Co. Inc. by Special Act 1886. Dissolved 1 May 1949, undertaking being vested in West Midland Area Gas Board under Gas Act 1948. Holders of securities were entitled to receive British Gas 3% guaranteed stock 1990–95 as follows in respect of each £1 unit, unless otherwise stated, of security held:

	£	s.	d.	
Cons. shares (5% basic)	1	3	9	
5% pref. shares	1	2	6	
4½% red. pref. shares	1	0	8	
4% perp. deb stock (per £100)	102	10	0	
4½% perp. deb. stock (per £100)	112	10	0	
5% perp. deb. stock (per £100)	123	0	0	**1952**

Solomon's Temple Tin Mines Ld. Inc. Transvaal 1909. Court Order to wind up Oct. 1913 .... **1914**

Solric Fabrics Ld. Regd. 1923 as Solric-D'fysun Fabrics Ld.; name changed Mar. 1931. Vol. liq (creditors') 21 Mar. 1938. Assets realised insufficient to pay unsecured creditors in full. Final meeting return regd. 28 Apr. 1939 .... **1939**

Solway Junction Railway Co. Inc. by Special Act 1864. In 1923 the undertaking was merged into the London Midland & Scottish Railway Co., in which company stockholders were entitled to £75 4% guaranteed stock for every £100 Solway Railway (Caledonian Guaranteed) 3% annuities stock held **1924**

Somaliland Petroleum Co. Ld. Regd. 1928. Vol. liq. (members') 18 Mar 1932. Direct controlling interest held by Anglo-Egyptian Oilfields Ld. (later Al Nasr Oilfields Co.) Final meeting return regd. 26 July 1932 .... **1933**

Somera Gold Mining Co. Ld. Regd. 1905. Vol. liq. Feb. 1908. Undertaking was acquired by El Oro Mining and Railway Co. Ld., in which company shareholders were entitled to 5 shares of £1 (credited as fully-paid) for every 16 shares of £1 (5*s.* paid) held. Removed from Resister 1911 .... **1908**

Somerset & District Electric Power Co. Inc. by Special Act 1903 .... **1911**

Somerdale Investments Ld. Regd. 1942. Vol. liq. (members') 16 Sept. 1963. Capital returned to contributories—8*s.* 8*d.* per share (of £1) plus 481·227 ordinary shares in British Cocoa and Chocolate Co. Ld (approx 1·9249 shares per share held). Final meeting return regd. 25 Apr. 1964 .... **1965**

Somerset and Dorset Railway Co. Inc. by Special Act 1862. By Act of 1889 the following amounts of Midland Railway 2½% debenture stock were offered in exchange for Somerset and Dorset securities—No. 1 debenture stock, No. 2 debenture stock (Somerset Central), No. 2 debenture stock (Dorset Central) and extension debenture stocks, 1871 and 1874, 192%; No. 2 debenture stock (Somerset and Dorset), 96%; No. 3 Somerset and Dorset debenture stock, with contingency, 140⅗%; 1st preference stock (5%), 36%; 1st preference stock (4½%), 24%; 2nd preference stock (5%) 24%; extension ordinary stock, 144%; other ordinary stocks, 18%. In 1923 the undertaking was vested in the Southern Railway Co. and the London Midland & Scottish Railway Co., "jointly in equal undivided moieties". Holders of the unexchanged stocks (viz. £2,010 ordinary stock, £100 ordinary stock A, and £440 ordinary stock B) were entitled to £11¼ of 4% debenture stock of the London Midland & Scottish Railway Co. for every £100 of such unexchanged stock held **1924**

Somerset & Dorset Railway Joint Committee. Dissolved 2 Apr. 1949; undertaking vested 1 Jan. 1948 in British Transport Commission under Transport Act 1947 .... **1949**

Somerset Collieries Ld. Regd. 1935. Vol. liq. (members') 12 Feb. 1954. Final meeting return regd. 27 June 1959 .... **1952**

Somerset Egg & Poultry Co. Ld. Regd. 1928. Vol. liq. (members') 30 Aug. 1935. All shares held by Taunton Cold Storage & Ice Co. Ld. Final meeting return regd. 23 Dec. 1935 .... **1936**

Somerset (Matabele) Development Co. Ld. Regd. 1899. Vol. liq. 30 Mar. 1904. Removed from Register 1906 **1905**

Somersetshire Tramways Co. Ld. Regd. 1891 as Somerton, Keinton, Manderville, Castle Cary and Evercreech Tramway Syndicate Ld.; name changed Oct. 1894. Vol. liq 17 May 1898. Final meeting return regd. 12 Nov. 1901 .... **1899**

Somerton Gas Co. Ld. Regd. 1857. Dissolved 1 May 1949, undertaking being vested in South Western Area Gas Board under Gas Act 1948. Holders of securities were entitled to receive British Gas 3% guaranteed stock 1990–95 as follows:

	£	s.	d.	
Ord. shares (of £10)	10	0	0	
4% red. debs. (of £100)	100	0	0	**1952**

Somerton, Keinton, Manderville, Castle Cary and Evercreech Tramway Syndicate Ld. *See* Somersetshire Tramways Co. Ld.

Somerville (John) & Co. Ld. Regd. Edinburgh 1897. Vol. liq. Feb. 1922. Capital returned to contributories—£10 per preference share of £10; £2 per ordinary share of £2; further payments (if any) not known. Final meeting return regd 13 May 1924. Court Order declared dissolution void July 1926. Final meeting return regd. 3 Sept 1926 .... **1923**

Somondoco Emeralds Ld. Regd. 1899. Court Order to wind up 15 Dec. 1904. Assets realised insufficient to pay creditors in full. Removed from Register 1910 **1905**

Sonoma Mines of Mexico Ld. Regd. 1899. Removed from Register 1909 .... **1908**

Sonora Mexican Silver Mines Ld. Regd. 1919. Vol. liq. 24 Oct. 1921. Final meeting return regd. 11 Aug. 1924 .... **1922**

**See Stock Exchange Year-Book.*

Sonora (Mexico) Land & Timber Co. Ld Regd. 1911. Vol. liq 26 Nov. 1951, the company having no assets. Final meeting return regd 31 Jan. 1952 .... **1953**

Sonora Silver Mining Co. Ld. Regd. 1886. Vol. liq. Jan. 1889. Final meeting return regd. 13 Mar. 1890 .... **1889**

Sonosekar Planting Co. Ld. Regd. 1912. Vol. liq. (members') 30 Oct. 1933. Undertaking and assets were acquired by company of same name. Shareholders were entitled to 1 share of £1 (credited with 17s. paid) for each share of £1 held. £55 6s. 1d. was paid into Companies' Liquidation Account. Final meeting return regd. 26 June 1934 **1934**

Sonosekar Planting Co. Ld. Regd. 1933. Vol. liq. (members') 30 Sept. 1952. Capital returned to contributories—7s. 0$\frac{7}{16}$d. per share of £1. £81 7s. 5d. was paid into Companies' Liquidation Account. Final meeting return regd. 23 Oct. 1953 **1955**

Sons of Gwalia Ld. Regd. 1898. Receiver and Manager appointed by the Western Australian Government on 1 Jan. 1964. Assets realised insufficient to discharge the outstanding debenture holder's debt in full. No capital returned to contributories. Receiver ceased to act 2 Nov. 1969. **1970**

Sons of Gwalia South Gold Mines Ld. Inc. W. Australia 1905. The London office was closed in Sept. 1911 **1912**

Soowin Concessions Ld. Regd. 1901. Vol. liq. 25 Apr. 1914. Reconstructed as Glen May (Rhodesia) Mines Ld., in which company shareholders were entitled to 5 shares of 5s. (credited with 4s. paid) for each share of £1 held. Final meeting return regd. 7 Dec. 1915 **1915**

Sopa Diamond Mine Ld. Regd. 1911. Vol. liq. 29 June 1914. Capital returned to contributories—1s. 3d. per share of £1 in Oct 1914; further payments (if any) not known. Final meeting return regd. 7 Dec. 1915 **1915**

Sopwith Aviation & Engineering Co. Ld. Regd. 1913 as Sopwith Aviation Co. Ld.; name changed Apr. 1919. Vol. liq. 16 Sept. 1920. Final meeting return regd. 7 Feb. 1924 ***1921**

Sorbo Rubber Sponge Products Ld. Regd. 1918. Vol. liq. (creditors') 17 Mar. 1933. 1st debenture holders received £28,575 in settlement. 2nd debenture holders received £31,091 2s. 5d.; other creditors were not paid in full. Final meeting return regd. 1 Nov. 1934 **1934**

Soria Mining Co. Ld. Regd. 1898. Vol. liq. 5 Dec. 1923. Final meeting return regd. 13 Mar. 1924 **1924**

Sorocabana Railway Co. Established Brazil 1871. In 1892 the company was amalgamated with Ituana Railway Co. to form Uniao Soracabana e Ytuana. In Sept. 1903 the line was sold and notice of redemption of 6% debentures at par was given..... **1905**

Sorocabana Railway Co. Inc. in Maine 1907. In Sept. 1948 it was announced that arrangements were being made to file a final return with the U.S.A. federal authorities; and for the resignation of the board of directors and the discontinuance of business. In Oct. 1944 1st debenture holders surrendered their bonds on payment of £36 1s. 6d. % following a settlement with the Government; a final distribution of £4 3s. 3d. was subsequently made **1950**

Sorosis Shoe Co. Ld. Regd. 1905. Vol. liq. (members') 18 June 1942. Direct controlling interest was held by Saxone Shoe Co. Ld. (later Saxone Lilley & Skinner (Holdings) Ld.). Final meeting return regd. 10 Dec. 1942 **1943**

Sortridge Copper Mining Co. Ld. Regd. 1881. Removed from Register 1905 **1885**

Sosa-y-Mendez Gold Mining Co. Ld. Regd. 1881. Undertaking was acquired by Callao Bis Gold Mining Co. Ld. in which company shareholders were entitled to 1 fully-paid share of £1 for each share held. Removed from Register 1888 **1883**

Sospiro Oilfields Ld. Regd. 1923. Vol. liq (creditors') 13 Mar. 1934. Assets realised insufficient to pay creditors in full. Final meeting return regd. 11 June 1934 **1935**

Sotheby Parke Barnet Group p.l.c. Regd. Oct. 1970; re-registered 1981. Vol. liq. 13 Mar. 1986. All capital acquired by Taubman U.K. Investments Inc. **1984-5**

Souback & Catir Alan Mining Co. Ld. Regd. 1881. Removed from Register 1905 **1885**

Soudan Development & Exploration Co. Ld. Regd. 1900. Vol. liq. 16 Dec. 1912. Capital returned to contributories—16s. 8d. per ordinary share of £1 in Dec. 1912; further payments (if any) not known. Final meeting return regd. 31 Dec. 1913 **1913**

Soudan Mill Co. (Holdings) Ld. Regd. 1903 as Soudan Mill Co. Ld.; name changed as above 1953. All capital owned by Cyril Lord Ld.; stockholders were entitled (under offer of 1953) to receive 18s. cash per 5s. stock held. Vol. liq. 1 Apr. 1966. Final meeting return regd. 24 May 1967 **1954**

Soulby, Sons & Winch Ld. Regd. 1896. Vol. liq. (members') 28 June 1957. Final meeting return regd. 6 June 1958 **1959**

South A1 Group Gold Mines Syndicate Ld. Regd. 1904. Vol. liq. June 1908. Property was sold to Victorian Mining Co. Ld. for 10,000 fully-paid ordinary shares of £1. Removed from Register 1909 **1909**

South African Agricultural & Ostrich Farms Ld. See Namaqua River Lands Ld.

South African & Australasian Supply & Cold Storage Co. Ld. Regd. 1902. The undertaking was acquired in 1902 by Imperial Cold Storage and Supply Co. Ld., in which company shareholders were entitled to 1 share of £1 (credited as fully-paid) for each share of £1 held. Debenture holders were entitled to be repaid in cash at premium to be settled by Court or to exchange holdings at par for debentures in purchasing company. Removed from Register 1904 **1904**

South African & General Agency Ld. See Colonial & General Agency Ld.

South African Argonauts Ld. Regd. 1889. Vol. liq. 19 Dec. 1892. Final meeting return regd. 17 July 1895 ***1894**

South African "Brush" Electric Light & Power Co. Ld. Regd. 1882. Vol. liq. Feb. 1885. Capital returned to contributories—13s. 9½d. per share of £2 10s. at 4 Mar. 1886; further payments (if any) not known. Final meeting return regd. 21 Dec. 1886 **1887**

South African Carbide & By-Products Co. Ld. Regd. 1919. Vol. liq. 15 June 1927. The undertaking and assets were sold to company of same name (inc. Transvaal). Prior lien debenture stock was exchanged for an equal amount of 8% debenture stock in new company. Holders of 1st mortgage debenture stock were entitled to 1 fully-paid preference share of £1 for every £2 stock held. Preference shareholders were expected to receive new ordinary shares and the ordinary shareholders were expected to receive no return. Final meeting return regd. 27 Nov. 1930 **1928**

South African Colonies Exploration Co. Ld. Regd. 1900. Capital returned to contributories—20s. per share of £1; further payments (if any) not known. Removed from Register 1906 **1904**

South African Co. Ld. Regd. 1886. Vol. liq 20 Sept. 1889. Property was transferred to De Beers Consolidated Mines Ld. Capital returned to contributories—£1 2s. per share of £1 at Nov. 1889; further payments (if any) not known. Purchase money could be applied in purchasing shares in Consolidated Co. Bultfontein Mine Ld. at £1 4s. per share. Final meeting return regd. 28 June 1892 **1889**

South African Co. Ld. Regd. 1896. Vol liq. (members') 17 Jan. 1961. Final meeting return regd. 30 June 1961 **1940**

South African Concessions Ld. Regd. 1924. Struck off Register 18 Feb. 1936 **1936**

South African Copper Trust Ld. Regd. 1910. Vol. liq. 22 Oct. 1915. Final meeting return regd. 21 Mar. 1922 **1925**

South African Cotton & Tobacco Estates Ld. Regd. 1917. Vol. liq. 11 Nov. 1921 for reconstruction as South African Lands & Produce Ld. in which company shareholders were entitled to 2 shares of 5s. (credited with 4s. paid) for each share of 5s. held. Struck off Register 7 June 1932 **1925**

South African Diamond Corporation Ld. Inc. Transvaal 1913. Wound up 1925 **1926**

South African Diamond Exploration Corporation Ld. Inc. Guernsey 1902. In 1907 the Secretary stated that company had ceased to do business **1907**

South African Estates and Mining Co. Ld. See African Estates and Mining Co. Ld.

South African Exploring Co. Ld. Regd. 1895. Undertaking was acquired in 1899 by De Beers Consolidated Mines Ld. Vol. liq. 9 Jan. 1901. Final meeting return regd 28 May 1902 **1901**

South African Export Co. Ld. Regd. 1904. Vol. liq. 16 Dec. 1925. Final meeting return regd. 13 July 1927 **1926**

South African Finance Corporation Ld. Regd. 1902. Vol. liq. 3 Feb. 1913. Final meeting return regd. 19 Nov. 1913 **1913**

South African Gas Co. Ld. Regd. 1887. Undertaking was acquired in 1890 by Cape Town and District Gas Light and Coke Co. Ld. Vol. liq. 30 June 1891. Final meeting return regd. 19 Oct. 1893 **1890**

South African General Development Syndicate Ld. Regd. 1895. Vol. liq. 29 Dec. 1904. Final meeting return regd. 10 Apr. 1926 **1905**

South African General Syndicate Ld. Regd. 1892. Vol. liq. 16 Feb. 1921. Final meeting return regd. 8 Feb. 1922 **1922**

South African Gold & Copper Syndicate Ld. Regd. 1903. Removed from Register 1910 **1909**

South African Gold Dredging Co. Ld. Regd. 1901. Vol. liq. 19 Feb. 1906. Removed from Register 1907 ... **1906**

VOL. FOR

South African Gold Mines Ld. Inc. Transvaal 1897. Undertaking and assets were acquired in Dec. 1919 by South African Townships Mining and Finance Corporation Ld., in which company shareholders were entitled to 1 share of 10s. (credited as fully-paid) for each share of £1 held 1920

South African Gold Properties Ld. Regd. 1905. Removed from Register 25 Feb. 1910 .... *1908

South African Gold-Quartz Crushing Mills & Mining Exploration Co. Ld. Regd. 1888. Struck off Register 3 Aug. 1894 1901

South African Gold Trust Ld. Regd. 1894. Vol. liq. (members') 11 June 1930. Undertaking and assets were acquired by Consolidated Gold Fields of South Africa Ld., (later Consolidated Gold Fields Ld.) in which company shareholders were entitled to 3 ordinary shares of £1 (credited as fully-paid) for every 4 ordinary shares of £1 held or one 1st preference share of £1 for each preference share of £1 held. Certain unclaimed balances in respect of fractions, warrants and coupons were paid to New Consolidated Gold Fields Ld. Final meeting return regd. 27 June 1931 1931

South African Goldfields Ld. Regd. 1903. Vol. liq. Feb. 1907. Removed from Register 1907 1907

South African Hotels Ld. Regd. 1901. Vol. liq. (members') 28 June 1951. Capital returned to contributories (per share of £1)—preference; 22s. 6d.; ordinary; £5 3s 8·96d. £301 6s. 6d. was paid into Companies' Liquidation Account. Final meeting return regd. 21 Dec. 1953 1954

South African Investment & Trust Co. Ld. Inc. Transvaal 1895. Wound up Jan. 1909 for sale of property and assets to South African & General Investment & Trust Co. Ld., in which company shareholders were entitled to receive 3 shares of £1 for every 2 shares of £1 held 1909

South African Lands & Produce Ld. Regd. 1921. Struck off Register 18 Feb. 1936 1936

South African Loan, Mortgage & Mercantile Agency Ld. Regd. 1880. Removed from Register 1912 1898

South African Marble Co. Ld. Regd 1923. Vol. liq. 2 Dec. 1926. Final meeting return regd. 21 May 1929 1927

South African Mining Syndicate Ld. Regd. 1894. Vol. liq. 22 July 1897. Reconstructed as company of same name. Shareholders were entitled to 1 share of £1 (credited with 17s. paid) in new company for each share of £1 held. Final meeting return regd 20 July 1898 1908

South African Mining Syndicate Ld. Regd. 1897. Vol. liq. June 1924. Reconstructed as South African Concessions Ld., in which company shareholders were entitled to 4 shares of 2s. (credited with 1s. 6d. paid) for each share of 5s. held. Struck off Register Dec. 1932 1933

South African Oil Co. Ld. Regd. 1910. Vol. liq. 12 June 1913. Final meeting return regd. 12 Oct. 1915 1914

South African Option Syndicate Ld. Regd. 1903. Court Order to wind up 13 Jan. 1925. Struck off Register 20 Mar. 1936 1937

South African Prospecting & Mortgage Corporation Ld. Regd. 1888. Vol. liq. 29 June 1892. Business was acquired by South African Trust & Finance Co. Ld. for 60,000 ordinary shares of £1 (credited with 7s. 6d. paid) and £10,670 in 5% registered debentures (later repaid). Final meeting return regd. 28 July 1898 1895

South African Super-Aeration Ld. Regd. 1901. Removed from Register 1913 1905

South African Supply & Cold Storage Co. Ld. Regd. 1899. Certain assets were sold in 1903 to Cold Storage Trust Ld, in which company shareholders were entitled to 2 ordinary shares of £1 for each ordinary share of £1 held, or 1 preference share of £1 for each preference share of £1 held. Removed from Register 1908 1904

South African Territories Ld. Regd. 1895. Reconstructed 1900 as company of same name. Shareholders were entitled to 1 share of £1 (credited with 17s. paid) in new company for each share of £1 held. Debenture holders were entitled to £15 in cash and £62 10s. in fully-paid shares in new company for each bond of £50 held. Removed from Register 1901 1908

South African Territories Ld. Regd. 1900. Vol. liq. 21 Aug. 1924. Final meeting return regd. 22 June 1937 1925

South African Trust & Finance Co. Ld. Regd. 1890. Vol. liq. 7 Mar. 1895. Assets, goodwill and undertaking were acquired by Johannesburg Consolidated Investment Co. Ld. for £345,000 in cash. Final meeting return regd. 6 May 1898 1896

South African Union Wattle Bark Estates Ld. Regd. 1909. Receiver for debenture holders appointed in Dec. 1915. Struck off Register 1924 1917

VOL. FOR

South African United Breweries. Regd. 1892. Vol. liq 24 May 1895. Reconstructed as South African Breweries Ld., in which company shareholders were entitled to 1 fully-paid preference and 1½ fully-paid ordinary shares of £1 plus 10s. in cash for each share of £1 held. Final meeting return regd. 15 Sept. 1896 1895

South African Venture Syndicate Ld. Regd. 1897. Reconstructed 1901 as company of same name. Shareholders were entitled to 10 fully-paid shares of £1 for each deferred share of £1 held or 1 fully-paid share of £1 for each ordinary share of £1 held. Removed from Register 1903 1908

South African Venture Syndicate Ld. Regd. 1901. Vol. liq. Dec. 1910. Strnck off Register Apr. 1929........ 1930

South American & Mexican Co. Ld. Regd. 1890. Court Order to wind up 2 Aug. 1893. Removed from Register 1911 1894

South American Bank of Buenos Aires. See Banco Sud Americana de Buenos Aires.

South American Cable Co. Ld. Regd. 1891. Vol. liq. 27 July 1915. Final meeting return regd. 26 Apr. 1916 1916

South American Copper Co. Ld. Regd. 1928. Vol. liq. (creditors') 19 Dec. 1940. No capital returned to contributories. £47 15s. was paid into Companies' Liquidation Account. Final meeting return regd. 22 Dec. 1955 1956

South American Copper Syndicate Ld. Regd. 1907. Vol. liq. (members') 6 Jan. 1928. No capital returned to contributories. £19 8s. 2d. was paid into Companies' Liquidation Account. Final meeting return regd. 7 Jan. 1956. Struck off Register 14 Aug. 1958.......... 1958

South American Gold Areas Ld. Regd. 1921. Struck off Register 8 Feb. 1957.................... 1958

South American Goldfields Ld. Regd. 1904. Vol. liq. Jan. 1908. Assets were sold to Compagnie Miniéré et de dragages de Guyane for Frs. 4,550,000 in shares of Frs. 100. Removed from Register 1908 1908

South American Land Co. Ld. Regd. 1881. Vol. liq. May 1909. Removed from Register 1912 1910

South American Light & Power Co. Ld. Regd 1902. The electric light and power undertaking was sold to an Argentine company. The 5% registered debentures were repaid at 102% on 30 June 1928. Vol. liq. 9 Aug. 1928. Certain assets were acquired by Argentine Industrial Co. Ld. (later Outwich Investment Trust Ld.) for £180,000 in fully-paid shares of £1. Final meeting return regd. 30 July 1929 1929

South American Manganese Co. Ld. Regd. 1928. Vol. liq. (members') 10 Oct. 1930. Assets realised insufficient to pay creditors in full. Final meeting return regd. 20 July 1933 1931

South American Metal Syndicate Ld. Regd. 1906. Vol. liq. 31 Mar. 1922. Capital returned to contributories—15s. 6d. % to ordinary shareholders; 8s. 4d. to A shareholders. Final meeting return regd. 3 July 1925 1923

South American Public Utilities Trust Ld. Regd. 1927. Vol. liq. (members') 18 Feb. 1935. Compagnie Générale de Tramways de Buenos Aires held all ordinary shares and Société Financiere de Transport et d'Enterprises Industrielles held all preference shares. Final meeting return regd. 5 July 1925 1936

South & North Alabama Railroad. Organised Alabama 1858. Acquired in 1913 by Louisville and Nashville Railroad Co. The 5% consolidated mortgage gold bonds were taken over by acquiring company and were redeemed in Aug. 1936.................... 1913

South Australian Co. Established 1836. Inc. by Royal Charter 1855. Wound up in accordance with resolutions passed July 1922. Charter surrendered in Dec. 1950. Capital returned to contributories-£122 15s. 11d. per share (of £4) 1951

South Australian Electric Light & Motive Power Co. Ld. Undertaking acquired in 1900 by Melbourne Electric Supply Co. Ld. 1937

South Australian Insurance Co. Ld. Established Australia 1846. In liquidation in 1899 1899

South Australian Land Mortgage & Agency Co. Ld. Regd. 1880. Vol. liq. 4 Jan. 1924. Final meeting return regd. 3 Aug. 1926 1924

South Australian Mining & Smelting Co. Ld. Regd. 1885. Vol. liq. 9 Mar. 1891. Final meeting return regd. 9 Nov. 1894 1892

South Australian Petroleum Fields Ld. Regd. 1888. Struck off Register 26 Oct. 1900 1901

South Bank & Normanby Gas Light & Coke Co. Ld. Regd. 1866; statutory powers 1871 and subsequently. Dissolved 1 May 1949, undertaking being vested in Northern Area Gas Board under Gas Act 1948. Holders of securities were entitled to receive British Gas 3% guaranteed stock 1990–95 as follows in respect of each £5 unit, unless otherwise stated, of security held:

	£	s.	d.
Orig. shares (10% stand.)	7	15	0

*See Stock Exchange Year-Book.

	VOL. FOR
New shares (7% stand.) 7 10 0	
6% pref. shares 6 0 0	
4½% pref. shares 5 5 0	
4% red. mort. debs. of (£100) 101 0 0	1952

South Banket Areas Ld. Regd. 1934. Vol. liq. (members') 28 Feb. 1950. Undertaking and assets acquired by Amalgamated Banket Areas Ld. in which company shareholders received 3 shares (of 3*s.*) for every 10 shares (of 1*s.*) held. Final meeting return regd. 28 Sept. 1962 1963

South Barracas (Buenos Aires) Gas & Coke Co. Ld. Regd. 1890. Vol. liq. 20 Dec. 1928. Undertaking and assets were acquired by Primitiva Gas Co. of Buenos Aires Ld. for £5,000 ordinary shares of £1, which were to be distributed among the prior lien debenture stockholders. Final meeting return regd 2 Oct. 1929 1929

South Behar Railway Co. Ld. Regd. 1895. Railway transferred to State 30 June 1939. Vol. liq (members') 20 July 1939. Debenture stock was redeemed at par on 1 June 1939. Capital returned to stockholders—104$\frac{13}{20}$% Final meeting return regd. 6 Aug. 1940 1941

South Bendigo Gold Mines Ld. Regd. 1895. Struck off Register 17 Nov. 1899. Restored 1900. Removed from Register 1902 1900

South Berks Brewery Co. Ld. Regd. 1897 as Hawkins & Parfitt South Berks Brewery Co. Ld.; name changed Apr. 1913. Vol. liq. (members') 1 Oct. 1936. Undertaking was acquired by H. & G. Simonds Ld., in which company shareholders were entitled to £6 preference stock for each preference share of £5 held. Holders of 4½% 1st. 4½% B and 4½% Reading debenture stocks were entitled to either repayment at 110% on 7 Nov. 1936 or 110% in 3½% debenture stock in purchasing company *plus* 1% of amount issued in cash. Final meeting return regd. 22 June 1937 1937

South Brazilian Railways Co. Ld. Regd. 1910. Vol. liq. (members') 10 July 1930. Undertaking and assets transferred to Companhia Forca e Luz do Parana, which held 74,975 (out of 75,000) shares. £93 3*s.* 2*d.* was paid into Companies' Liquidation Account (*see preface*). Final meeting return regd. 1 Oct. 1930. Court Order declared dissolution void 20 Apr. 1931. Final meeting return regd. 20 Jan. 1932 1931

South British Investment Trust Ld. Regd. 1926. Vol. liq. (members') 30 Apr. 1945. Capital returned to contributories—12*s.* 11*d.* per share (of 10*s.*). £1,597 14*s.* 7*d.* paid into Companies' Liquidation Account in respect of unclaimed dividends or distributions. Final meeting return regd. 18 May 1954 1955

South Bukeru Areas Ld. *See* S.B.A. Properties Ld.

South Bukeru (Nigeria) Tin Co. Ld. Regd. 1910. Vol. liq. 14 Aug. 1929. Reconstructed as South Bukeru Areas Ld. [later S.B.A. Properties Ld.] in which company shareholders were entitled to 5 shares of 2*s.* (credited as fully-paid) for every 4 shares of 5*s.* held. Final meeting return regd. 21 July 1930 1930

South Burma Tin Mines Ld. Regd. 1905. Vol. liq. Jan 1908. Removed from Register 1908 1908

South Caradon Mine Ld. Regd. Truro 1883. Vol. liq. 11 Nov. 1885. Final meeting return regd. 11 May 1887 1886

South Caucasian Syndicate Ld. Regd. 1912. Vol. liq. 1928. Struck off Register 15 Aug. 1944 1945

South Chilian Syndicate Ld. Regd. 1898. Vol. liq. 17 July 1905. Removed from Register 1906 1906

South Cinderella Deep Ld. Inc. Transvaal 1902. Wound up June 1910 for sale of property to Cinderella Consolidated Mines Ld. for 35,700 shares of £1 .. 1911

South City Ld. Inc. Transvaal 1899. Vol. liq. Mar. 1908. Undertaking and assets were acquired by City Deep Ld., in which company shareholders were entitled to 1 share of £1 (credited as fully-paid) for every 2 shares of £1 held 1909

South Clare Railways Co. Ld. Regd. 1884. Inc. by Special Act 1890. In 1925 the undertaking was merged into the Great Southern Railways Co. The scheme provided that the holders of the Baronial Guaranteed Share capital should receive an equal amount of Great Southern Railways 4% Preference Stock, and that the other shares should be cancelled 1925

South Cleveland Ironworks Co. Ld. Regd. 1872. Removed from Register 1884 .... *1876

South Coast Land & Resort Co. Ld. Regd. 1917. Vol. liq. (members') 9 Aug. 1939. Private company. Final meeting return regd. 22 May 1940 1940

South Coast Mutosope Co. Ld. Regd. 1899. Vol. liq. 3 Feb. 1902. Final meeting return regd. 22 Dec. 1914 *1903

South Condurrow Mine Ld. Regd. 1902. Removed from Register 1904 1904

South Darren Mining Co. Ld. Reconstructed in 1887 as South Darren Silver-Lead Co. Ld. in which company shareholders were entitled to 2 shares of £1 (credited with 17*s.* paid) for every share of £1 10*s.* held 1890

South Darren Silver-Lead Co. Ld. Regd. 1887. Vol. liq. 15 Sept. 1890. Reconstructed as company of same name. Final meeting return regd. 13 July 1894 1891

South Devon Railway Company. Undertaking acquired by Great Western Railway Company, under Act of 1878 1949

South Devon United Copper Mines Ld. Regd. Truro 1878, Vol. liq. 20 Nov. 1884. Final meeting return regd. 21 May 1887 1885

South Durham Steel & Iron Co. Ld. Regd. 1898. Undertaking was vested in British Steel Corpn. as from 28 July 1967. Holders of securities were entitled to receive 6½% Treasury Stock 1971 at an issue price of 99⅝% at the following compensation values per £100:

	£ s. d.
5¼% Debenture stock 1976–81	79 12 8
6% Convertible 2nd debenture stock 1978—83	84 17 5

Struck off Register 31 Mar. 1970 1969

South East Africa Ld. Regd. 1898 as Dr. Carl Peters' Estates & Exploration Co. Ld.; name changed Sept. 1903. Vol. liq. 15 Oct. 1910 for reconstruction as South East Africa (1910) Ld., in which company shareholders were entitled to 1 fully-paid share of 10s. for each share of £1 held. Final meeting return regd. 12 Dec. 1911 1911

South East Africa (1910) Ld. Regd. 1910. Vol. liq. 26 Nov. 1913. Reconstructed as Anglo-German Exploration Co. Ld. (later Minerals Exploration Co. Ld.), in which company shareholders were entitled to 1 share of 2*s.* 6*d.* (credited with 1*s.* 3*d.* paid) for each share of 10*s.* held. Final meeting return regd. 6 Sept. 1917 1914

South East African Transport Co. Ld. Regd. 1895. Vol. liq. 29 Dec. 1899. Final meeting return regd. 19 Feb. 1900 1898

South East Borneo Rubber Plantations Ld. Regd. 1909. Vol liq. 22 Mar. 1917. Reconstructed as Martapoera Rubber Estates Ld., in which company shareholders were entitled to 12 shares of 2*s.* (credited with 1*s.* 6*d.* paid) for each share of £1 held. Debenture holders were entitled to an equal amount of similar debentures in new company. Final meeting return regd. 20 Dec. 1917 1918

South-East Essex Gas & Water Co. Ld. Regd. 1890. Vol. liq. 29 Nov. 1894. Final meeting return regd.27 July 1896 .... *1894

South East Kent Electric Power Co. Ld. Regd. 1911. Dissolved 1 Apr. 1948, undertaking being vested in the British (later Central) Electricity Authority and South-Eastern Area Board under the Electricity Act 1947. Ordinary shareholders were entitled to receive £1 15*s.* British Electricity 3% guaranteed stock (1968—73) for esch share (of £1) held 1949

South East Lancashire Mutual Fire Insurance Co. Ld. Capital assets and liabilities were acquired by National Union Society Ld., in 1903 1907

South East Mysore Gold Co. Ld. Regd. 1886. Vol. liq. 19 Nov. 1891. Reconstructed as company of same name. Shareholders were entitled to 1 share of 4*s.* (credited with 1*s.* paid) in new company for each preference share held or for every 10 ordinary shares held. Final meeting return regd. 15 Dec. 1892 1894

South East Mysore Gold Co. Ld. Regd. 1891. Vol. liq. 10 Nov. 1894; reconstructed as Yarrakonda Gold Mining Co. Ld. Final meeting return regd. 1 May 1896 1903

South East Rand Deep Ld. Inc. in Transvaal 1896. In liquidation in 1907 1907

South East Rand Investment Co. Ld. Regd. 1918. Vol. liq. 13 Oct. 1924. Reconstructed as East Rand Consolidated Ld., in which company shareholders were entitled to 3 shares of 1*s.* (credited with 9*d.* paid) for each ordinary share of 5*s.* held or 2 fully-paid shares of 1*s.* for each preference share of 2*s.* held. Final meeting return regd. 11 Nov. 1930 1925

South-East Wynaad Estates & Gold Mining Co. Ld. Regd. 1880. Court Orders: to wind up 3 Nov. 1883; to dissolve 17 Jan. 1891. Properties were transferred to New South East Wynaad Estates Co. Ld. 1884

South Eastern and Chatham Railway Companies Managing Committee. Inc. under Special Act 1899. The undertakings of this committee, the London & South Western Railway, the London, Brighton & South Coast Railway, the London, Chatham & Dover Railway Co., and the South Eastern Railway Co. were amalgamated to form the Southern Railway Co. 1924

South-Eastern Brush Electric Light & Power Co. Ld. Regd. 1882. Vol. liq. Aug. 1885. Final meeting return regd. 31 July 1888 1886

**See Stock Exchange Year-Book.*

VOL. FOR

South Eastern Coalfield Extension Ld. Regd. 1907. Repayment amounting to £7 17*s*. 6*d*. per £10 1st mortgage debenture were made. No capital was returned to contributories. Struck off Register 25 Nov. 1958 .... **1960**

South-Eastern (Deal) Hotel Co. Ld. Regd. 1892. Removed from Register 1906 .... **1897**

South Eastern Development Syndicate Ld. Regd. 1907. Vol. liq. 27 July 1909. Final meeting return regd. 10 Nov. 1910 .... ***1910**

South Eastern Gas Corp. Ld. Regd. 1932. Dissolved 1 May 1949, undertaking being vested in Gas Council under Gas Act 1948. Holders of securities were entitled to receive British Gas 3% guaranteed stock 1990–95 as follows in respect of each £100 unit unless otherwise stated, held:

	£	s.	d.
Ord. stock (per £1)	1	8	3
4½%red.pref. stock (per £1)	1	2	8
4% irred. pref. stock (per £1)	1	0	7½
4% deb. stock	103	0	0
3¾% deb. stock	102	0	0
3½% deb. stock	100	0	0

1952

South Eastern Metropolitan Tramways Co. Ld. Inc. by Special Act 1888. Regd. 1902. Vol. liq. Undertaking sold to London County Council on 1 Apr. 1902 for £50,000 .... **1903**

South Eastern Railway Co. Inc. by Special Act 1836. In 1923 the undertaking was merged into the Southern Railway Co. in which company stockholders were entitled to stock as follows:

For each £100 *held*		*S. R.*
5½% Annuity*	£128½	4% Debenture
3% Debenture	£75	4% Debenture
3¼% Debenture	£81¼	4% Debenture
3½% Debenture	£87½	4% Debenture
4% Debenture	£100	4% Debenture
4½% Debenture	£112½	4% Debenture
5% Debenture	£125	4% Debenture
4% Vested Companies'	£80	5% Gtd. Pref.
4½% Cons. Gtd.	£90	5% Gtd. Pref.
4½% Cons. Pref.	£90	5% Preference
5% Cons. Pref.	£100	5% Preference
4% Pref. (1891)	£80	5% Preference
3½% Preference	£70	5% Preference
3% Preference	£60	5% Preference
4% Preference (1900)	£80	5% Preference
4% Conv. Pref. (1903)	£80	5% Preference
	£10	Ordinary B §
5% Preference (1914)	£100	5% Preference
5% Redeemable Pref.	£100	5% Red. Pref. (1926)
Undivided Ordinary	£60	Prefd. Ord.
	£43⅓	Defd. Ord.
Preferred Ordinary	£120	Prefd. Ord.
Deferred Ordinary	£86⅔	Defd. Ord.

* Instead of taking Debenture Stock of the Amalgamated Company (as shown above) each Annuity-holder was given the right until 31st Jan. 1923. to require that Company to assume the obligations of the South Eastern Railway Company in respect of his Annuities.

§ In exchange for conversion rights **1924**

South Elmsall & District Gas Co. Inc. by Special Act 1923. Under Royston and Brodsworth Gas Act 1931 the undertaking was amalgamated with those of Brodsworth & District Gas Co. and Royston (Yorks.) & District Gas Co. Ld. to form Royston & Brodsworth Gas Co. Shareholders were entitled to stock in new company as follows—for each original (10% maximum) ordinary share of £5 held—£6 15*s*. 5*d*. ordinary (6% standard) stock; for each original (8% maximum) ordinary share of £5 held—£5 8*s*. 4*d*. ordinary (6% standard) stock; for each 7% preference share of £5—£5 16*s*. 8*d*. 6% preference stock **1932**

South End Spinning Co. Ld. Regd. 1902. Receiver appointed 18 Dec. 1916; ceased to act 12 Sept. 1919. Vol. liq. 29 Jan. 1917. Final meeting return regd. 19 Mar. 1920 .... ***1919**

South Europe Mining Co. Ld. Regd. 1858. Court Orders: to wind up 21 Oct. 1885; to dissolve Aug. 1890.... **1886**

South Fingall Ld. Regd. 1901. Removed from Register 1905 .... **1905**

South Fleetwood Fishing Co. Ld. Regd. 1918. Court Order to wind up 1 Nov. 1921. Struck off Register 15 Oct. 1935 .... **1936**

South Frances United Mines. Inc. 1892 under cost book system. Amalgamated in 1896 with Wheal Basset Mines Ld. to form Basset Mines Ld. in which company shareholders were entitled to 2 new fully-paid shares of £1 for every share held **1908**

South Geldenhuis Deep Ld. Inc. Transvaal 1898. Wound up 16 Nov. 1906 to effect amalgamation with three other companies under title of Simmer Deep Ld., in which company shareholders were entitled to 1 share of £1 for each share of £1 held. Debentures were to be exchanged pro rata for debentures of the new company **1907**

South Halkyn & Rhydymwyn Mining Co. Ld. Regd. 1890. Vol. liq. June 1929. Mining rights were acquired by Halkyn District United Mines Ld. Struck off Register July 1933 .... **1934**

South Hampshire Railways & Pier Co. Inc. by Special Act 1886. Powers expired through non-completion **1896**

South Hants Steam Laundry Co. Ld. Regd. 1879. Vol. liq. (members') 23 Feb. 1934. Capital returned to contributories—£1,575. Final meeting return regd. 2 Jan. 1935 .... **1935**

South Hants Waterworks Co. Inc. by Special Act 1876. Undertaking acquired by Southampton Corporation on 29 Sept. 1921. Ordinary and preference shareholders received sufficient 6% Corporation stock to give them the amount of their prescribed maximum dividends. viz. (for each £10) 4% preference shares £6 13*s*. 4*d*.; 5% preference £8 6*s*. 8*d*.; 10% ordinary £13 16*s*. 4*d*.; 7% ordinary £11 13*s*. 4*d*.; 5% ordinary £8 6*s*. 8*d*.; in addition, the 10% and 7% maximum shares participated in a further £7,500 stock as a contribution towards back dividends. The £6,500 4% debenture stock was assumed by the Corporation **1922**

South Hayling Water Co. Ld. Regd. 1895. Vol. liq. 19 Nov. 1925. Final meeting return regd. 18 Aug. 1926 **1926**

South Hetton Coal Co. Ld. Regd. 1874. Vol. liq. 24 Mar. 1898. Reconstructed as company of same name. Stockholders were entitled to 10 ordinary and 6 preference shares of £10 for every £100 stock held. Final meeting return regd. 25 Oct. 1898 .... **1898**

South Hetton Coal Co. Ld. Regd. 1898. Vol. liq. (members') 7 Aug. 1953. Capital returned to contributories—20*s*. 7*d*. per 6*d*. ordinary stock and 19*s*. 7*d*. per 6*d*. preference stock. £215 4*s*. 11*d*. was paid into Companies' Liquidation Account. Final meeting return regd. 15 Nov. 1955 .... **1957**

South Hill Park Estate Co. Ld. Regd 1896. Vol. liq. 18 Apr. 1912. Final meeting return regd. 7 Oct. 1912 ***1909**

South Hylton Iron & Steel Co. Ld. Regd. 1882. Removed from Register 1903 .... ***1884**

South Indian Gold Mining Co. Ld. Regd. 1879. Property was acquired in Feb. 1882 by Indian Glenrock Gold Mining Co. Ld. for 100,000 fully-paid shares of £1. Removed from Register 1905 .... **1883**

South Indian Railway Co. Inc. by Special Act 1874. The railway was taken over by the Secretary of State for India and worked by South Indian Railway Co. Ld. **1944**

South Indian Railway Co. Ld. Regd. 1890. Vol. liq. (members') 4 Apr. 1944. Capital returned to contributories—£119 19*s*. 3*d*. per £100 stock. £7,095 was paid into Companies' Liquidation Account. Final meeting return regd. 24 Sept. 1948 .... **1949**

South Italy Copper Mines Ld. *See* Riparbella Ld.

South Kalgurli Consolidated Ld. Regd. 1913. Vol. liq. (members') 10 May 1955. All shares owned by Gold Mines of Kalgoorlie (Aust.) Ld. Struck off Register 28 May 1963 .... **1959**

South Kalgurli Gold Mines Ld. Regd. 1895. Vol. liq. 7 Mar. 1913. Reconstructed as South Kalgurli Consolidated Ld., in which company shareholders were entitled to 1 share of 10*s*. (credited as fully-paid) *plus* 6*s*. 8*d*. in cash for each share of £1 held. Final meeting return regd. 26 Nov. 1913 .... **1914**

South Kent Water Co. Inc. by Special Act 1889. Undertaking amalgamated with Mid-Kent Water Co. from 1 Apr. 1949. Share and debenture holders entitled to equal amount of capital and debentures in Mid-Kent Co. **1951**

South Kirkby Colliery Co. Ld. *See below.*

South Kirkby, Featherstone & Hemsworth Collieries Ld. Regd. 1882 as South Kirkby Colliery Co. Ld.; name changed 1906. Collieries, &c. vested in National Coal Board as from 1 Jan. 1947. Vol. liq. (members') 3 Mar. 1952. Final meeting return regd. 4 Oct. 1960 **1962**

South Knights Ld. Inc. Transvaal 1902. Wound up March 1908 for sale of undertaking to Knight Central Ld., in which company shareholders were entitled to £3 in shares (of £1) or shares and cash for each £1 of shares (of £1) held **1909**

South Lancashire Electric Traction & Power Co. Ld. Regd. 1900. Reconstructed 1905 as Lancashire United Tramways Ld. (later Lancashire United Transport Ld.) for £192,871 in ordinary shares of £1 and £296,500 in 2nd mortgage debenture stock. 148,247 shares and £296,500 2nd mortgage debenture stock were allotted to debenture stockholders and 25,580 shares to preference shareholders. Removed from Register 1906 .... **1906**

South Lancashire Theatre Co. Ld. Regd. 1920. Vol. liq. (creditors') 3 Apr. 1930. Assets realised insufficient

VOL. FOR

to pay unsecured creditors in full. Final meeting return regd. 7 Mar. 1931 1931

South Leeds Junction Railway Co. Inc. by Special Act 1893. Under East and West Yorkshire Union Railways Act 1896, the undertaking was purchased by that company 1897

South Llanfair Silver Lead Mining Co. Ld. Regd. 1882. Removed from Register 1889 .... *1885

South Llanharran Colliery Co. Ld. Regd. 1873. Removed from Register 1885 .... *1876

South London Dwellings Co. Ld. Regd 1879. Vol. liq. (members') 27 July 1950. Capital returned to contributories—21s. 2*d.* per £1 of issued capital (shares of £50 and £1). Final meeting return regd. 26 July 1952 1953

South London Electric Supply Corpn. Ld. Regd. 1896. Dissolved 1 Apr. 1948, undertaking being vested in British (later Central) Electricity Authority and London Area Board under Electricity Act 1947. Holders of securities were entitled to receive British Electricity 3% guaranteed stock (1968–73) as follows in respect of each £1 unit of capital held:

	£	s.	d.
6% preference shares	1	14	6
Ordinary shares	1	13	0
4½% debenture stock	1	1	7½

1949

South London Homesteads Ld. Regd. 1920. Vol. liq. 10 July 1924. Final meeting return regd. 2 Jan. 1925 1925

South London Music Hall Ld. Regd. 1893. Vol. liq. 28 Jan. 1896. Final meeting return regd. 7 Jan. 1898 1896

South London Tramways Co. Ld. Inc. by Special Act 1879. Regd. 1902. Vol. liq. 20 Feb. 1903. Undertaking sold to London County Council on 21 Nov. 1902 for £226,560. Final meeting return regd. 16 Nov. 1903 1903

South Londonderry Gold & Exploration Ld. Regd. 1895. Vol. liq. 1 Sept. 1896. Reconstructed as First Find Consolidated Gold Mines (Bulla Bulling) Ld., in which company shareholders were entitled to 1 share of 10*s.* (credited with 9*s.* paid) for each share of £1 held. Final meeting return regd. 24 Mar. 1898 1897

South Luipaard's Vlei Gold Mines Ld. Regd. 1895. Court Order to wind up 5 May 1897. Removed from Register 1908 1898

South Malay Rubber Plantations Ld. Regd. 1913. Vol. liq. (members') 11 July 1932. Undertaking and assets were acquired by South Malay Rubber Plantations (1932) Ld. in which company shareholders were entitled to 1 share of 2*s.* (credited with 1*s.* 9*d.* paid) for each share of 2*s.* held. Final meeting return regd. 12 June 1934 1933

South Malay Rubber Plantations (1932) Ld. Regd. 1932. Vol. liq. (members') 8 Oct. 1952. Capital returned to contributories—3*s.* $1\frac{13}{16}$*d.* per share of 2*s.* £537 16*s.* 6*d.* was paid into Companies' Liquidation Account. Final meeting return regd. 17 July 1956 1957

South Manchurian Railway Co. Ld. Inc. Tokyo 1906. Under Japanese Law of 1920 the 5% and 4½% sterling bonds became a direct liability of the Japanese Government 1922

South Manchurian Syndicate Ld. Regd. 1912. Vol. liq. 10 Nov. 1922. Final meeting return regd. 20 Feb. 1924 1923

South Medomsley Colliery Co. Ld. Regd. 1931. Vol. liq. (members') 24 Sept. 1952. Capital returned to contributories—£20 19*s.* 5*d.* cash and £25 3½% Treasury Stock 1977–80 per share of £6. Final meeting return regd. 15 Oct. 1956 1958

South Metropolitan Electric Light & Power Co. Ld. Regd. 1896 as Blackheath & Greenwich District Electric Light Co. Ld.; name changed 1904. Dissolved 1 Apr. 1948, undertaking being vested in British (later Central) Electricity Authority and London Area Board under Electricity Act 1947. Holders of securities were entitled to receive British Electricity 3% guaranteed stock (1968–73) as follows in respect of each £1 unit of capital held:

	£	s.	d.
7% 1st preference shares	1	13	9
6% 2nd preference shares	1	9	10
4% 3rd preference shares	1	2	4
Ordinary preference shares	1	16	0
4½% debenture stock	1	1	8⅖
3½% debenture stock	1	0	6
3¼% debenture stock	1	0	0

1949

South Metropolitan Electric Supply Co. Ld. *See* Metropolitan Electric Supply Co. Ld.

South Metropolitan Electric Tramways & Lighting Co. Ld. Regd. 1899 as County of Surrey Electrical Power Distribution Co. Ld.; name changed Aug. 1904. Vol. liq. (members') 30 June 1933. The electricity supply undertaking of the company was acquired by the London & Home Counties Joint Electricity Authority and the tramway and light railway undertaking (including all lands, works and other property, assets, powers, &c. in connexion therewith) was, by the London Passenger Transport Act 1933, transferred to the London Passenger Transport Board for £75,000 C stock. Ordinary and preference shareholders were entitled to £12 10*s.* C stock *plus* £110 0*s.* 10·9*d.* in cash for every £100 shares held. Holders of the outstanding 4% debenture stock were repaid at par in July 1933. Final meeting return regd. 18 Dec. 1934 1934

South Metropolitan Gas Co. Founded 1829; inc. by Special Act 1842. Dissolved 1 May 1949, undertaking being vested in South Eastern Area Gas Board under Gas Act 1948. Holders of securities were entitled to receive, in respect of each £100 unit held, British Gas 3% guaranteed stock 1990–95 as follows:

	£	s.	d.
Ord. stock (5% basic)	118	0	0
6% pref. stock	134	0	0
4% pref. stock	102	15	0
Perp. 3% deb. stock	88	0	0
5% red. deb. stock	105	6	8
3¾% red. deb. stock	102	5	0

A distribution on ord. stock of 4·94% out of reserves was made in Mar. 1955 1952

South Midland Gas Corporation Ld. Regd. 1933. Vol. liq. Nov.-Dec. 1950. Gas interests (including Eynsham) undertaking vested in accordance with Gas Act 1948. Capital returned to contributories—£1 per preference share (of £1) and £1 15*s.* per ordinary share (of £1). Final meeting return regd. 30 Aug. 1951 1952

South Minnesota Land Co. Ld. Regd. 1885. Vol. liq. 14 Dec. 1900. Final meeting return regd. 5 July 1902 1901

South Moor Colliery Co. Ld. *See* Holmside & South Moor Collieries Ld.

South Mount Boppy Gold Mining Co. Ld. Regd. 1906. Vol. liq. 26 May 1916. Final meeting return reg. 23 Feb. 1917 1917

South Naparima (Trinidad) Oil Co. Ld. Regd. 1910. Vol. liq. 29 Dec. 1916. The undertaking and assets were sold to Trinidad Oil & Transport Co. Ld. for 66,000 fully-paid shares of 5*s.* Final meeting return regd. 12 July 1917 1917

South Nigel Gold Mining Co. Ld. Regd. 1895. Court Order to wind up 12 May 1897. Removed from Register 1913 1898

South Nigel Reef Estates & Development Co. Ld. Regd. 1927. Struck off Register Feb. 1935 1925

South Norfolk Light Railway Co. Inc. (under Light Railways Act 1896) by order of Light Railway Commissioners confirmed by Board of Trade 13 Feb. 1899. Powers expired 1907 1907

South Normanton & Blackwell Gas Co. Ld. Regd. 1891. Dissolved 1 May 1949, undertaking being vested in East Midland Area Gas Board under Gas Act 1948. Holders of securities were entitled to receive British Gas 3% guaranteed stock 1990–95 as follows:

	£	s.	d.
Ord. shares (10% stand.) of £5	10	10	0
4½% red. deb. stock (per £100)	100	0	0

1952

South Norway Copper Co. Ld. Regd. 1882. Removed from Register 1909 1887

South Nourse Ld. Inc. Transvaal 1899. Vol. liq. Mar. 1909. Undertaking and assets were acquired by Nourse Mines Ld. in which company shareholders were entitled to 3 shares of £1 for every 10 shares of £1 held 1909

South of England Telephone Co. Ld. Regd. 1885. Vol. liq. 13 Apr. 1891. Business was transferred to National Telephone Co. Ld., in which company shareholders were entitled to 1 fully-paid share of £5 for every 25 ordinary shares of £1 held or £1 debenture stock for each £1 paid-up preference share held. Final meeting return regd. 10 June 1892 1892

South Orion Gold Mines Ld. Inc. in South African Republic 1895. In liquidation in 1898 1898

South Orofu Ld. Regd. 1912. Vol. liq. 1 June 1928. Capital returned to contributories—5*s.* per share of 10*s.* at Nov. 1928; further payments (if any) not known. Final meeting return regd. 26 Sept. 1930 1929

South Oxfordshire Water & Gas Co. *See* South Oxfordshire Water Co.

South Oxfordshire Water Co. Regd. 1888 as Goring & Streatley District Gas & Water Co. Ld.; name changed to Thames Valley & Goring Water & Gas Co. in 1903; inc. by Special Act 1905 as South Oxfordshire Water & Gas Co.; name changed to above title 30 Apr. 1948. Under provisions of Reading & Berkshire Water, Act 1959, undertaking vested in Thames Valley Water Board from 1 Apr. 1960. Consideration distributed in Aug. 1960 as follows (per £100): 5% irredeemable and 4½%

*See Stock Exchange Year-Book.

VOL. FOR

redeemable debenture stocks. £100; 4½% preference stock £78 15*s*.; 8% ordinary stock, £136 15*s*.; 5% ordinary stock £85 5*s*., *plus* interest at 6% from 1 Apr. 1960 in each case. Company was dissolved 7 Sept. 1963 .... **1964**

South Pensgruthal Mining Co. Formed in 1880. In liquidation in 1888 .... **1888**

South Perak Rubber Syndicate Ld. Regd. 1912. Vol. liq. (members') 31 May 1932. Undertaking and assets were acquired by company of same name (later Mitre Trust Ld.). Shareholders were entitled to 1 share of £1 (credited with 17*s*. 6*d*. paid) in new company for each share of £1 held. Final meeting return regd. 20 Mar. 1934 .... **1933**

South Perak Rubber Syndicate Ld. *See* Mitre Trust Ld.

South Phoenix & Caradon Mine Ld. Regd. 1883. Vol. liq. Aug. 1886. Final meeting return regd. 18 Apr. 1887 .... **1887**

South Preanger Rubber Co. Ld. Regd. 1912. Vol. liq. 18 Oct. 1917. Final meeting return regd. 21 May 1919 **1918**

South Rand Exploration Co. Ld. Regd. 1902. Vol. liq. 18 Apr. 1906. Undertaking acquired by South Rand Gold Exploration (1906) Ld. (later South Rand Gold Exploration Ld.), in Vol. liq. 18 Apr. 1906. Undertaking acquired by South Rand Gold Exploration (1906) Ld. in which company shareholders were entitled to 1 share of £1 for every 5 shares of £1 held. Final meeting return regd. 25 Apr. 1907 ...... **1907**

South Rand Exploration Co. Ld. Regd. Mar. 1906 as South Rand Exploration Co. (1906) Ld.; name changed May 1906. Vol. liq. (members') 7 Aug. 1941. Capital returned to contributories-£1 7*s*. per share of £1. Final meeting return regd. 18 July 1942 **1942**

South Rand Gold Corporation Ld. Regd. 1896. Mining properties were acquired by South Rand Exploration Co. Ld., in which company shareholders were entitled to 1 share of £1 (credited as fully-paid) for every 2 shares of £1 held. Removed from Register 1905 .... **1906**

South Rand Gold Mining Co. Ld. Inc. Transvaal 1893. Vol. liq. Apr. 1909. Undertaking and assets were acquired by Crown Mines Ld., in which company shareholders were entitled to 22 shares of 10*s*. (credited as fully-paid) for every 25 shares of £1 held **1910**

South Rand Proprietary Co. Ld. Regd. 1895. Court Order to wind up 8 Dec. 1 897. Removed from Register 1908 .... **1898**

South Randfontein Deep Ld. Regd. 1895. Vol. liq. Oct. 1909. Reconstructed as company of same name. Shareholders were entitled to 1 share of 10*s*. in new company for each share of £1 held, and option (since expired) to subscribe for further shares at par. Removed from Register 1913 .... **1910**

South Randfontein Deep Ld. Regd. 1909. Vol. liq. 24 July 1912. Certain assets were sold to Randfontein Central Gold Mining Co. Ld., in which company shareholders were entitled to 1 fully-paid share of £1 for every 6 shares of 10*s*. held. Final meeting return regd. 23 Jan. 1914 .... **1913**

South Randfontein Gold Mining Co. Ld. Inc. Transvaal 1897. Vol. liq. 1909. Undertaking and assets sold to Randfontein South Gold Mining Co. Ld., in which company shareholders were entitled to 86 new shares of £1 for every 100 shares of £1 held.......... **1910**

South Rhodesia Gold Fields Ld. Regd. 1897. Vol. liq. Aug. 1907. Removed from Register 1911 .... **1925**

South Rhodesia Land and Mining Co. Ld. Regd. 1905. Vol. liq. Dec. 1911. Removed from Register 1912 **1912**

South Rhondda Colliery Co. Ld. Regd. 1898. Vol. liq. 2 Feb. 1928. Direct controlling interest held by Meiros Collieries Ld. Final meeting return regd. 10 Oct. 1929 .... **1929**

South Rose Deep Ld. Inc. Transvaal 1898. Vol. liq 16 Nov. 1906 to effect an amalgamation with 3 other companies under title of Simmer Deep Ld. Shareholders were entitled to 1 share in new company for every 4 shares of £1 held. Debentures were exchanged pro rata for debentures in new company **1907**

South Russia Banking Agency Ld. Regd. 1919. Vol. liq. 23 Feb. 1925. Final meeting return regd. 28 Apr. 1925 .... **1926**

South Rnssian Oil Co. Ld. Regd. 1898. Struck off Register 19 Aug. 1960 .... **1949**

South Shields Gas Co. Established 1824. Inc. by Special Act 1857. Undertaking was acquired by Newcastle-upon-Tyne & Gateshead Gas Co. in which company stockholders were entitled to £158 2*s*. 9*d*. 5% ordinary stock for every £100 consolidated stock held or £106 19*s*. 6*d*. 5% ordinary stock for every £100 5% ordinary stock held. The liability for the mortgages was assumed by purchasing company **1938**

South Shields Greyhound Stadium Ld. *See* South Shields Sports Stadium Ld.

South Shields Sports Stadium Ld. Regd. 1932 as South Shields Greyhound Stadium Ld.; name changed 1963. Vol. liq. 27 Oct. 1967. Dissolved 8 Aug. 1977 **1982–3**

South Shields Steam Shipping Co. Ld. *See* Moor Line Ld.

South Shields Tramway & Carriage Co. Ld. Regd. 1887. Vol. liq. 23 Apr. 1906. Final meeting return regd. 15 Oct. 1906 .... ***1890**

South Shore Hotel Co. Ld. Regd. 1896. Removed from Register 1909 .... **1904**

South Simmer & Jack Deep Level Gold Mining Co. Ld. Regd. 1892. The property was acquired by Consolidated Gold Fields of South Africa Ld. (later Consolidated Gold Fields Ld.) Struck off Register Apr. 1929 .... **1930**

South Staffordshire & Birmingham District Steam Tramways Co. Ld. *See* South Staffordshire Tramways Co. Ld.

South Staffordshire Blue Brick Co. Ld. Regd. 1887. Receiver for 1st mortgage debenture holders appointed in July 1907. Struck off Register 1928...... **1911**

South Staffordshire Brewery Co. Ld. Regd. 1886. Vol. liq. 27 Jan. 1899. Business was acquired by J. & J. Yardley & Co. Ld. Final meeting return regd. 21 Oct. 1899 .... **1899**

South Staffordshire Mines Drainage Commissioners. Constituted by Special Act 1873. Receiver appointed 2 Nov. 1888 .... **1922**

South Staffordshire Mond Gas Co. Inc. by Special Act 1901 as South Staffordshire Mond Gas (Power & Heating) Co.; name changed 1923. Dissolved 1 May 1949, undertaking being vested in West Midland Area Gas Board under Gas Act 1948. Holders of securities were entitled to receive British Gas 3% guaranteed stock 1990–95 as follows in respect of each £1 unit, unless otherwise stated, of security held:

	£	s.	d.
6% pref. shares	1	3	4
Ord. shares		10	1
B shares		4	0
6½% prior lien irred. deb. stock (per £100)	127	0	0
5% deb. stock (perp.) per £100	99	10	0

1952

South Staffordshire Tramways Co. Ld. Inc. by Special Act 1882 as South Staffordshire & Birmingham District Steam Tramways Co. Ld.; name changed by Act of 1889. Regd. as limited Aug. 1930. Vol. liq. (members') 23 Oct. 1930. Capital returned to contributories—£6 2*s*. 6*d*. per preference share of £10. £291 5*s*. 6*d*. was paid into Companies' Liquidation Account in respect of unclaimed dividends and £520 12*s*. 6*d*. in respect of unclaimed capital returns. Final meeting return regd. 16 Dec. 1931 .... **1931**

South Staffordshire Tramways (Lessee) Co. Ld. Regd. 1899. Vol. liq. (members') 22 Dec. 1930. Capital returned to contributories—£3 4*s*. 1½*d*. per preference or ordinary share of £5. £195 10*s*. 6*d*. was paid into Companies' Liquidation Account. Final meeting return regd. 24 Dec. 1931 .... **1931**

South Standard (Witwatersrand) Gold Mine Ld. Regd. 1889. Properties were sold and mortgages were repaid. Capital returned to contributories—4*s*. per share of £1 at 30 Sept. 1902; further payments (if any) not known. Removed from Register 1903 .... **1903**

South Suburban Gas Co. Estd. 1854; inc. as Crystal Palace District Gas Co. by Special Act 1858; name changed 1904. Dissolved 1 May 1949, undertaking being vested in South Eastern Area Gas Board under Gas Act 1948. Holders of securities were entitled to receive in respect of each £100 unit held, British Gas 3% guaranteed stock 1990–95 as follows:

	£	s.	d.
Ord. stock (5% basic)	122	6	8
5% perp. pref. stock	115	0	0
4% per. pref. stock	102	15	0
3½% red. pref. stock	101	10	0
4% perp. deb. stock	102	10	0
5% perp. deb. stock	125	3	4
5% red. deb. stock	105	0	0
3½% red. deb. stock	100	0	0

1952

South Sumatra Rubber Estates Ld. Regd. 1910. Vol. liq. 30 Nov. 1911. Court Order to wind up Dec. 1911. Struck off Register 1 July 1921 .... **1912**

South Swaziland Gold & Exploration Co. Ld. Regd. 1895. Vol. liq. 10 May 1897. Final meeting return regd. 17 Aug. 1899 .... **1898**

South Sweden Forest & Saw-mill Co. Ld. Regd. 1883. In liquidation in 1886. Removed from Register 1891 **1886**

South Transvaal Syndicate Ld. Regd. 1889. Vol. liq. 20 June 1894. Final meeting return regd. 6 Aug. 1895 **1895**

South Travancore Tea Co. Ld. Regd. 1896. Vol. liq. Apr. 1910. The properties were acquired by Rubber

**See Stock Exchange Year-Book.*

VOL. FOR

Plantations Investment Trust Ld. The debentures were repaid at par. Capital returned to contributories—£10 1*s.* 2*d.* per ordinary or preference share of £10; further payments (if any) not known. Removed from Register 1911 1911

South Utah Mines & Smelters. Inc. Maine 1909. London agency closed in 1914 1915

South Village Deep Ld. Inc. Transvaal 1899. Vol. liq. Aug. 1924. Capital returned to contributories—1*s.* 8½*d.* per share of £1; further payments (if any) not known 1925

South Wales Colliery Co. Ld. Regd. 1864. Vol. liq. 15 Mar. 1916. Agreement for sale of assets to Lancaster's Steam Coal Collieries Ld. provided for repayment of capital at par. Final meeting return regd. 29 Mar. 1917 1916

South Wales Concrete Brick Co. Ld. Regd. 1909. Vol. liq. 30 Nov. 1928. Undertaking was acquired by Baldwins Ld. [later Baldwins (Holdings) Ld.]. Final meeting return regd. 3 Dec. 1929 1929

South Wales Electric Power Co. Inc. by Special Act 1900 as South Wales Electrical Power Distribution Co.; name changed 1932. Dissolved 1 Apr. 1948. undertaking being vested in British (later Central) Electricity Authority and South Wales Area Board under Electricity Act 1947. Holders of securities were entitled to receive British Electricity 3% guaranteed stock (1968—73) as follows in respect of each £1 unit of capital held:

	£	s.	d.	
Ordinary stock	1	12	0	
5% debenture stock	1	7	0	
3½% debenture stock	1	0	6	1949

South Wales Electrical Power Distribution Co. Ld. *See* British Power Co. Ld.

South Wales Fuel Co. Ld. Regd. 1919. Vol. liq. 23 Jan. 1923. Final meeting return regd. 21 May 1925 1924

South Wales Gas Corpn. Ld. Regd. 1935. Dissolved 1 May 1949, undertaking being vested in Gas Council under Gas Act 1948. Holders of securities were entitled to receive British Gas 3% guaranteed stock 1990–95 as follows in respect of each £1 unit, unless otherwise stated, of security held:

	£	s.	d.	
4½% cum. pref. shares	1	1	8	
5% prefd. ord. shares		13	0	
Defd. ord. shares (of 5*s.*)			1	1952

South Wales Mineral Railway Co. Inc. by Special Act 1853. In 1923 the undertaking was merged into the Great Western Railway Co. in which company stockholders were entitled to stock as follows:

For each £100 held		*G.W.*	
3% A Debenture	£75	4% Debenture	
3% B Debenture	£75	4% Debenture	
Consolidated 3% Pref.	£25	cash	
Ordinary	£10	cash	1924

South Wales, Post Newspaper Co. Ld. Regd. 1894. Vol. liq. (members') 16 June 1930. Direct controlling interest held by Northcliffe Newspapers Ld. Final meeting return regd. 29 Nov. 1930 1931

South Wales Power Co. Ld. Regd. 1907 as Treforest Electrical Consumers Co. Ld.; name changed May 1923. Vol. liq. (members') 25 Sept. 1931. All assets acquired by Shropshire, Worcestershire & Staffordshire Electric Power Co. The outstanding 1st mortgage debenture stock was redeemed at 103%. Capital returned to contributories—preference shares at par; ordinary stockholders 72·675%. An unspecified amount was paid into Companies' Liquidation Account. Final meeting return regd. 21 Mar. 1932 1932

South Wales Power Station Co. Ld. Regd. 1942. Dissolved 1 Apr. 1948, undertaking being vested in British (later Central) Electricity Authority under Electricity Act 1947. Holders of 3½% 1st mortgage debenture stock were entitled to receive £1 0*s.* 1½*d.* British Electricity 3% guaranteed stock (1968–73) for each £1 stock held 1949

South Wales Primrose Coal Co. Ld. Regd. 1894. Vol. liq. June 1929. Undertaking was acquired by Tareni Colliery Co. Ld. Struck off Register 12 Mar. 1935 1936

South Wales Public House Trust Co. Ld. Regd. 1902 as Glamorgan Public House Trust Co. Ld.; name changed 21 Feb. 1914. Vol. liq. (members') 21 Jan. 1938. Capital returned to contributories—£1 per ordinary share of £1: £238 6*s.* 3*d.* to deferred shareholders. Final meeting return regd. 21 Jan. 1938 1938

South Wales Refractories Ld. Regd. 1935 as Welsh Refractories Ld.; name changed Sept. 1937. Vol. liq. (members') 2 Jan. 1939. Undertaking and assets were acquired by N. B. Allen & South Wales Refractories Ld. in which company shareholders were entitled to 1 fully-paid share of £1 for every share of £1 held. Final meeting return regd. 3 Jan. 1940 1939

South Wales Union Bank Ld. Regd. 1872 as Swansea Bank Ld.; name changed Aug. 1888. Vol. liq. 12 Apr. 1892. Final meeting return regd. 22 Oct. 1895 1894

South Weld Hercules Gold Mining Co. Ld. Regd. 1896 as Burbank Gold Mining Co. Ld.; name changed May 1898. Absorbed May 1900 by Weld-Hercules Gold Mines Ld. for 89,500 fully-paid shares of £1. Removed from Register 1905 1901

South-West Randt Mines Ld. Regd. 1894. Vol. liq. Sept. 1908. Removed from Register 1911 1909

South-West Suburban Water Co. Ld. *See* Waterworks Construction Co. Ld.

South Western & Isle of Wight Junction Railway Co. Inc. by Special Act 1901. Period for completion of railway and pier expired 16 Aug. 1924 1924

South Western Brewery Co. Ld. Regd. Edinburgh 1898. Vol. liq. Dec. 1925. Undertaking was acquired by Archibald Campbell Hope and King Ld. in 1926. Final meeting return regd. 19 June 1926 1926

South Western Exploration Co. Ld. Inc. Transvaal 1909. London office closed Apr. 1912 1913

South Western Gas & Water Corpn. Ld. *See below.*

South Western Gas Corpn. Ld. *See below.*

South Western Industrial Corporation Ld. Regd. 1934 as South Western Gas Corpn. Ld.; name changed to South Western Gas & Water Corpn. Ld. in Dec. 1949 and as above in Dec. 1951. Vol. liq. (members') 6 Jan. 1955, the company's holdings were transferred to two new holding companies, viz. Midland Aluminium Ld. and Staffordshire Potteries (Holdings) Ld. Holders of preference stock and ordinary shares were entitled to receive-(a) in respect of every 5 ordinary shares of 5*s.*—2 ordinary shares of 5*s.* in Midland Aluminium Ld. and 1 ordinary share of 5*s.* in Staffordshire Potteries (Holdings) Ld., and (b) in respect of every £5 preference stock—15 6% preference shares of 5*s.* and 1 ordinary share of 5*s.* in Midland Aluminium Ld. and 5 6% preference shares of 5*s.* and 1 ordinary share of 5*s.* in Staffordshire Potteries (Holdings) Ld. £47 was paid into Companies' Liquidation Account. Final meeting return regd. 21 Jan. 1958 1958

South Western of Venezuela (Barquisimeto) Railway Co. Ld. Regd. 1888. In Mar. 1901 the undertaking was acquired by Bolivar Railway Co. Ld. Holders of each 3½% bond of £100 were entitled to £25 6% debenture stock, £36 5% preferred shares and £35 10*s.* ordinary shares in acquiring company; holders of every £100 2nd debenture stock were entitled to £37 ordinary shares: holders of every £100 ordinary shares were entitled to £7 16*s.* 6*d.* ordinary shares. Removed from Register 1910 1902

South Western Vacuum Cleaner Co. Ld. Regd. 1903. Struck off Register 1922 1910

South Wheal Crebor Ld. Regd. 1879. Property acquired by Russell Copper Mine Ld. Removed from Register 1905 .... *1884

South Wheal Crofty. Worked on cost book system. Reorganised 1906 as South Crofty Ld., in which company shareholders were entitled to $3\frac{41}{133}$ shares of £1 (credited with 15*s.* paid) for each share held 1906

South Wheal Frances Mine. Amalgamated in 1892 with West Basset Mine to form South Frances United Mines 1896

South Winnipeg Ld. Inc. Manitoba 1912. Vol. liq. May 1923. Reconstructed as South Winnipeg (1923) Ld. Debenture stockholders were entitled to 1 fully-paid share of $5 in new company for every £20 stock held and 1 share of $5 (credited with $3.75 paid) for each £1 debenture stock held 1924

South Wolhuter Ld. Inc. Transvaal 1899. Vol. liq. Mar. 1908. Undertaking and assets were sold to City Deep Ld., in which company shareholders were entitled to 9 shares of £1 for every 20 shares of £1 held 1909

South Yorkshire & Derbyshire Gas Co. Inc. by Special Act 1931. Dissolved 1 May 1949, undertaking being vested in East Midland Area Gas Board under Gas Act 1948. Holders of ordinary stock (6% stand.—orig. and addit.) were entitled to receive, in respect of each £100 unit held, £157 British Gas 3% guaranteed stock 1990–95 1952

South Yorkshire Gas Grid Co. Ld. Regd. 1930. Dissolved 1 May 1949. undertaking being vested in East Midland Area Gas Board under Gas Act 1948. Holders of ordinary shares (of 10s. with 9*s.* paid) were entitled to receive 13*s.* 6*d.* British Gas 3% guaranteed stock 1990–95 for each share held 1952

South Yorkshire Joint Line Committee. Dissolved 2 Apr. 1949; undertaking vested 1 Jan. 1948 in British Transport Commission under Transport Act 1947 1949

**See Stock Exchange Year-Book.*

VOL. FOR

South Yorkshire Junction Railway Co. Inc. by Special Act 1890. In 1923 the undertaking was merged into the London & North Eastern Railway Co. Holders of every £100 Consolidated Stock were entitled to (1) £87 10*s*. London and North Eastern 4% First Guaranteed Stock, (2) £50 London and North Eastern 4% Second Preference Stock, and (3) a certificate of Contingent Rights ... **1925**

South Zambesi Development Co. Ld. Regd. 1896. Court Order to wind up 12 May 1897. Liquidator released 27 Mar. 1899. Removed from Register 3 Nov. 1908 ***1898**

Southall Investment Trust Ld. Regd. 1897 as Crown Cork Co. Ld.; name changed May 1935. Vol. liq. (members') 2 Dec. 1935. Undertaking and assets were acquired by Crown Cork Co. Ld., in which company shareholders were entitled to 2 ordinary shares of 5*s*. (credited as fully-paid) *plus* 15s. 4½*d*. in cash for each preference share of 10*s*. held or 2 ordinary shares *plus* 10*s*. 4½*d*. in cash for each ordinary share of 5*s*. held. Final meeting return regd. 26 Apr. 1941 ... **1936**

Southampton & Winchester Great Western Junction Railway Co. Inc. by Special Act 1901. Abandoned by Act of 1905 ... **1906**

Southampton Cold Storage & Lairage Co. Ld. Regd. 1899. Removed from Register 1905 ... **1908**

Southampton Dock Co. Inc. by Special Acts 1836 and 1871. Under Act of 1892 the undertaking was sold to London and South Western Railway. The mortgage debentures were assumed by purchasing company. Holders of stocks were entitled to cash or stock, at the following rates: 4½% debenture 4% debenture, consolidated preference, second preference and ordinary stocks at 120%, 105%, 75%, 80% and 45% respectively ... **1893**

Southampton Electric Light & Power Co. Ld. Regd. 1888. Vol. liq. 12 Oct. 1896. Capital returned to contributories—£6 5*s*. per ordinary and preference share of £5; further payments (if any) not known. Final meeting return regd. 19 Mar. 1897 ... **1897**

Southampton Gaslight & Coke Co. Inc. by Special Act 1848. Dissolved 1 May 1949, undertaking being vested in Southern Area Gas Board under Gas Act 1948. Holders of securities were entitled to receive, in respect of each £100 unit held, British Gas 3% guaranteed stock 1990–95 as follows:

	£	s.	d.
Ord. stock (5% basic)	120	0	0
5½% pref. stock	124	0	0
5% pref. stock	112	10	0
4% pref. stock	101	0	0
4% perp. deb. stock	102	10	0
5% perp. deb. stock	125	0	0
5% red. deb. stock (1967)	111	0	0
5% red. deb. stock (1961)	110	0	0
3½% red. deb. stock	99	10	0

A distribution on ordinary stock of 5·6375% out of reserves was made in June 1955 ... **1952**

Southampton Harbour & Pier Board. *See below.*

Southampton Harbour Board. Constituted by Special Act 1863 as Southampton Harbour & Pier Board; inc. under present title 1877. On 1 Aug. 1968 the undertaking was transferred to the British Transport Docks Board and the Harbour Board dissolved **1969**

Southampton Insurance Co. Ld. Regd. 1922. All shares were owned by Lancashire & General Assurance Co. Ld. Struck off Register 1929 ... **1927**

Southampton Naval Works Ld. Regd. 1889. Removed from Register 1907 ... **1892**

Southampton Oxygen Co. Ld. *See* Oxygen Contracts Ld.

Southampton Tramways Co. Inc. by Special Act 1877. Company dissolved, undertaking was acquired by the Corporation on and from 30 June 1898 ... **1901**

Southdown & East Grinstead Breweries Ld. Regd. 1895. Vol. liq. 25 Apr. 1924. Undertaking and properties were acquired by Tamplin & Son's Brewery, Brighton Ld. (later Tamplins Brewery Ld.). Capital returned to contributories—£17 10*s*. per ordinary share of £10 in May 1924; further payments (if any) not known. Final meeting return regd. 19 Dec. 1925 **1925**

Southeastern Power & Light Co. Inc. Maine, 1924. In Feb. 1930 the undertaking was acquired by Commonwealth & Southern Corpn. The liability for 6% gold debentures was assumed by Commonwealth & Southern Corpn. Holders of shares and option warrants received the following securities of Commonwealth & Southern Corpn.—1⅓ $6 dividend preferred shares for each $7 dividend preferred share held; 1 $6 dividend preferred share for each $6 dividend preferred or participating preferred share held; 4½ common shares and 2¼ option warrants for each common share held; 2 common shares and 1 option warrant for each option warrant held ... **1931**

VOL. FOR

Southend Hotel Co. Ld. Regd. 1883. Vol. liq. 2 Oct. 1899. Final meeting return regd. 16 May 1902 ... **1900**

Southend-on-Sea & District Gas Co. Established 1854 as Southend Gas Co.; inc. by Special Act 1877; name changed 1923. Under Act of 1931 the undertaking was acquired by Gas Light & Coke Co. Stockholders were entitled to stock in acquiring company as follows—for every £100 original consolidated stock or new ordinary stock held—£130 ordinary stock *plus* £7 13*s*. in cash; for every £100 new ordinary B stock held—£123 6*s*. 8*d*. ordinary stock *plus* £7 5*s*. 6*d*. in cash; for every £100 5½% irredeemable preference stock held—£137 10*s*. 4% consolidated preference stock; for every £100 6% irredeemable preference stock held—£150 4% consolidated preference stock; for every £100 4% perpetual debenture stock held—£133 6*s*. 8*d*. 3% consolidated debenture stock for every £100 5% perpetual debenture stock held—£166 13*s*. 4*d*. 3% consolidated debenture stock ... **1932**

Southend-on-Sea Tower & Marine Park Co. Ld. *See* Margate & Southend Kursaals Ld.

Southend Palace Hotel Co. Ld. Regd. 1905. Removed from Register 26 Sept. 1912 ... ***1907**

Southend Waterworks Co. Regd. as limited 1970 Inc. by Special Act 1879. Under provisions of Essex Water Order 1970 undertaking was vested in Essex Water Co. 1 July 1970. Original and new ordinary shareholders received the following: £20 consolidated ordinary stock of Essex Water Co. per 10% original £10 share; £14 consolidated ordinary stock per 7% new ordinary £10 share and £10 consolidated ordinary stock per 5% new ordinary £10 share. Ordinary stockholders received similar amounts of 5% new ordinary stock of Essex Water Co. and preference stockholders received like amounts of similar or comparable stocks of Essex Water Co. and that company assumed liability for this company's debenture stocks. Company is being wound up and will be dissolved upon a declaration by the directors that the winding up has been completed **1973-4**

Southern Alberta Land Co. Ld. Regd. 1906. Vol. liq. 29 June 1917 for reconstruction as Canada Land & Irrigation Co. Ld. in which company shareholders were entitled to 5 ordinary shares of £1 (credited with 16*s*. paid) for every 4 shares of £1 held; holders of 5% debenture stock were entitled to 50% of holding in 6% debenture stock and 50% in ordinary shares of new company. The holders of 6% A debenture stock were entitled to nominal value of holding in fully-paid ordinary shares. Final meeting return regd. 15 Jan. 1919 ... **1918**

Southern Asbestos Mines Ld. *See* Universal Holdings Ld.

Southern Brazil Electric Co. Ld. Regd. 1913. Struck off Register 30 Jan. 1960 ... **1957**

Southern Brazilian Rio Grande do Sul Railway Co. Ld. Regd. 1882. Vol. liq. Jan. 1905. Railway and assets in Brazil were sold to Brazilian Government who undertook to pay off the French obligations. 6% debenture stockholders were entitled either to repayment in cash at par or Brazilian Government Railway Guarantees Rescission 4% Bonds at 83%. Shareholders were entitled to £21 13*s*. 4*d*. in Rescission Bonds and £2 10*s*. in cash per share of £20 held. Removed from Register 1906 ... **1906**

Southern Brick & Tile Co. Ld. Regd. 1927. Vol. liq. (members') 30 Dec. 1937. Capital returned to contributories—2·55*d*. per ordinary share of £1. Final meeting return regd. 8 Mar. 1943 ... **1938**

Southern British Columbia Land Co. Ld. *See* Baynes Lake Land Co. Ld.

Southern Canine Racing Stadium (Founders' Syndicate) Ld. Regd. 1927. Vol. liq. 7 Jan. 1928. Final meeting return regd. 24 Mar. 1933 ... **1928**

Southern Coal Co. of New South Wales Ld. Regd. 1887. The assets were sold and proceeds were to be distributed by Court to debenture holders. Struck off Register 1914 ... **1912**

Southern Coalfields of France Ld. Regd. 1915. Court Order to wind up July 1921. Struck off Register 1928 **1922**

Southern Counties Contract Co. Ld. Regd. 1883. Removed from Register 1903 ... **1886**

Southern Counties Guarantee Trust Ld. Regd. 1919. Struck off Register 24 May 1938 ... **1939**

Southern Cross Copper Mine Co, Ld. Inc. Victoria, British Columbia 1906. London office closed in 1909 **1909**

Southern Cross Explorers Ld. Regd. 1896. Struck off Register 23 July 1901 ... **1902**

Southern Cross Gold Development Ld. Regd. 1934. Vol. liq. (creditors') 3 Nov. 1938. Court Order to wind up 24 Feb. 1947. No capital returned to contributories. Liquidator released 14 Jan. 1950. Struck off Register 2 Oct. 1953 ... **1950**

**See Stock Exchange Year-Book.*

Southern Cross Gold Mines Development Co. Ld. Regd. 1896. Struck off Register 18 Nov. 1902 .... **1903**

Southern Development Co. Ld. Regd. 1895. Vol. liq. 7 Dec. 1914. Final meeting return regd. 4 Dec. 1915 **1899**

Southern Forbes Reef Co. Ld. Regd. 1889. Vol. liq. 18 Nov. 1890. Shareholders were entitled to 1 fully-paid share of £1 in Forbes Reef Gold Mining Co. Ld. for every 2 shares of 10s. held. Final meeting return regd. 24 Apr. 1891 .... **1891**

Southern Gas & Power Corporation. See Central Public Service Corporation.

Southern Geldenhus Ld. Regd. 1892. Vol. liq. 20 Jan. 1896. Reconstructed as Elandsfontein No. 2 Gold Mining Co. Ld., in which company shareholders were entitled to 1 share of £1 (credited with 18s. paid) for each share of £1 held. Final meeting return regd. 9 May 1898 .... **1903**

Southern Gold Trust Ld. Regd. 1898. Vol. liq. 25 May 1911. Reconstructed as Bahia Proprietary Mines Ld., in which company shareholders were entitled to 3 fully-paid ordinary shares for each £4 share of £1 or 2 fully-paid ordinary shares for every 5 ordinary shares of £1 held. Final meeting return regd. 16 Feb. 1916 .... **1925**

Southern Hotels Ld. Regd. Dublin 1894. Undertaking acquired by Great Southern & Western Railway Co. Ireland. Shareholders were paid off at £4 10s. per preference share of £5; holders of debenture stock at 105% **1902**

Southern India Alpha Gold Mining Co. Ld. Inc. India 1874. In liquidation in 1897 .... **1897**

Southern India Plantations Agency Ld. Regd. 1930. Vol. liq. (members') 3 Apr. 1939. The undertaking was sold as a going concern. Capital returned to contributories—20s. per share of £1. Final meeting return regd. 22 Nov. 1939 .... **1940**

Southern India Rubber Co. Ld. Regd. 1910. Vol. liq. 4 Nov. 1921. Final meeting return regd. 11 Apr. 1922 **1922**

Southern Iron & Steel Co. Inc. New Jersey 1909. Under plan of reorganisation carried through in 1912 properties were transferred to Standard Steel Co.. **1914**

Southern Jumpers Ld. Regd. 1892. Removed from Register 1904 .... **1900**

Southern Kampar Tin Dredging Ld. Inc. Federated Malay States 1932. Undertaking and assets were acquired by Southern Kinta Consolidated Ld., in which company shareholders were entitled to 13 shares of 5s. (credited as fully-paid) for every 5 shares of £1 held **1935**

Southern Land Co. Ld. Regd. 1889. Vol. liq. 6 June 1912. Reconstructed as Southern Lands Corporation Ld., in which company shareholders were entitled to 2 shares of 5s. (credited with 2s. 6d. paid) for each share of £1 held. Final meeting return regd. 2 Dec. 1919 .... **1913**

Southern Lands Corpn. Ld. Regd. 1912. Vol. liq. (members') 16 Sept. 1948. Capital returned to contributories—4s. 3⅜d. per share of 3s. 3d. (1s. 3d. paid up). £1,637 9s. 10d. was paid into Companies' Liquidation Account. Final meeting return regd. 26 Apr. 1951 .... **1952**

Southern Mahratta Railway Co. Ld. See Madras & Southern Mahratta Railway Co. Ld.

Southern New Chum Gold Mines Ld. Regd. 1895. Vol. liq. 10 Apr. 1899. Amalgamated with Goldfields of Victoria Ld., in which company shareholders were entitled to 1 share of 10s. (credited with 8s. 6d. paid) for every 2 shares of 10s. held. Final meeting return regd. 23 Apr. 1900 .... **1900**

Southern Oil & Transport Corporation. In liquidation. Controlling interest held by Tankers Ld. **1928**

Southern Oregon Goldfields Ld. Regd. 1914. Struck off Register Dec.1931 .... **1932**

Southern Patagonia Sheep Farming Co. Ld. Regd. 1912. Vol. liq. 19 Sept. 1919. Final meeting return regd. 4 Nov. 1920 .... **1920**

Southern Perak Dredging Ld. Regd. 1919. Vol. liq. (members') 31 Oct. 1935. Undertaking and assets were acquired by Southern Malayan Tin Dredging Ld., in which company shareholders were entitled to 9 shares of 5s. (credited as fully-paid) for every 5 shares of £1 held. £6 6s. 7d. was paid into Companies' Liquidation Account. Final meeting return regd. 2 July 1936 .... **1936**

Southern Peruvian Mines Ld. Regd. 1922. Vol. liq. (members') 19 June 1950. Capital returned to contributories—2s. 5½d. per share of 5s. £339 was paid into Companies' Liquidation Account. Final meeting return regd. 27 Oct. 1953 .... **1954**

Southern Punjab Railway Co. Ld. Regd. 1895. Vol. liq. (members') 5 Mar. 1930. Lines acquired by Secretary of State for India. Capital returned to contributories—preference shares at par; ordinary stockholders received £217 18s. 5·47d.%. £3,456 6s. 11d.

was paid into Companies' Liquidation Account. Final meeting return regd. 3 Dec. 1930 .... **1931**

Southern Railway Co. Inc. 1 Jan. 1923 as an amalgamated company under provisions of Railways Act 1921. Dissolved 3 June 1949; undertaking vested 1 Jan. 1948 in British Transport Commission under Transport Act 1947. Holders of securities were entitled to receive British Transport 3% guaranteed stock 1978–88 as follows in respect of each £100 of capital stock held:

	£	s.	d.
Def. ord. stock	24	0	0
Prefd. ord. stock......................	77	12	6
5% guaranteed pref. stock	137	0	0
5% red. guaranteed pref. stock (1957)	115	7	6
5% pref. stock	124	8	9
5% red. pref. stock (1964)	115	7	6
4% deb. stock	128	3	9
5% deb. stock	139	10	0
4% red. deb. stock (1962–7)	113	10	0
4% red. deb. stock (1970–80)....	115	3	9
Perp. annuities of £1 0s. 6d. p.a.......	31	15	0

.... **1949**

Southern Railway (Ireland). Inc. by Special Act 1865. Undertaking was merged into Great Southern Railways Co. All the stocks and shares were cancelled **1926**

Southern Rand Proprietary Ld. Regd. 1902. Vol. liq. 2 Mar. 1906. Removed from Register 1913.......... **1907**

Southern Rhodesia Base Metals Corporation Ld. Regd. 1925. Vol. liq. (creditors') 13 Dec. 1934. Assets realised insufficient to pay debenture holders in full. Final meeting return regd. 27 June 1935 .... **1935**

Southern Rhodesian Goldfields Ld. Regd. 1923 as Rhozambia Mines Ld., name changed 1934. Vol. liq. (members') 21 Dec. 1949. Capital returned to contributories—1·2d. per share of 5s. Final meeting return regd. 4 Jan. 1951 .... **1951**

Southern San Paulo Railway Co. Ld. Regd. 1911. Vol. liq. (creditors') 3 Sept. 1945. Holders of 5% debenture stock were entitled to £83 6s. 6d. per £100 stocks held. £4 12s. 5d. was paid into Companies' Liquidation Account in respect of unclaimed dividends. Final meeting return regd. 13 June 1946 .. **1947**

Southern Shan States Syndicate (1909) Ld. Regd. 1909. Assets realised sufficient to pay 7d. in £ to debenture holders. Struck off Register 27 July 1937 .... **1938**

Southern Siamese Tin Dredging Ld. Regd. 1933. Vol. liq. (members') 6 Jan. 1941. Shareholders were entitled to receive 2 shares (of 5s. of Tongkah Harbour Tin Dredging Ld.) for every 5 shares (of 5s.) held. Final meeting return regd. 6 June 1950 .... **1951**

Southern Silica Ld. Regd. 1924. Receiver and manager appointed by debenture holders in Aug. 1941, sold the business in Jan. 1944 to Charmouth Trust Ld. and ceased to act in Nov. 1944. Struck off Register 21 Dec. 1945 .... **1946**

Southern Star Gold Mines Ld. Regd. 1895. Vol. liq. 13 Apr. 1898. Final meeting return regd. 24 Aug. 1898 **1899**

Southern States Coal, Iron & Land Co. Ld. Regd. 1875. Properties sold in 1881 to an American company. Vol. liq. Aug. 1882. Court Order to continue winding up under supervision 12 Sept. 1882. Final meeting return regd. 20 Dec. 1886 .... **1883**

Southern States Land & Timber Co. Ld. Regd. 1889. Reconstructed 1896 as Southern States Lumber Co., in which company debenture holders were entitled to securities after payment of $200 assessment per bond of £100. Removed from Register 1906 .... **1898**

Southern States Lumber Co. Inc. United States 1898 **1900**

Southern Trinidad Oil Syndicate Ld. Regd. 1918. Vol. liq. (members') 30 May 1935. Capital returned to contributories—8s. 11·6813d. per share of £1. Final meeting return regd. 27 Jan. 1936........................ **1936**

Southern Union General Insurance Co. of Australasia. See Union Investment Co. Ld.

Southern Union Marine & General Insurance Co. Ld. Regd. 1897 as Provincial Homes Investment Co. Ld.; name changed Feb. 1920. Vol. liq. (members') 4 Oct. 1935. Capital returned to contributories—12s. 6d. per share of £1, fully-paid; 2s. 6d. per share of £1, 10s. paid. £148 was paid into Companies' Liquidation Account in respect of unclaimed dividends and £26 5s. in respect of unclaimed distributions. Final meeting return regd. 10 May 1938 .... **1936**

Southern United Investment Co. Ld. Regd. Edinburgh 1925. Vol. liq. (members') 6 Apr. 1951. Capital returned to contributories—£2 2s. 3d. per share of £1. Final meeting return regd. 1 Apr. 1953.......... **1954**

Southern Wassau Syndicate Ld. Regd. 1900. Removed from Register 1903 .... **1903**

Southgate & District Gas Co. Established 1858. Inc. by Special Act 1866 as Colney Hatch Gas Co.; name changed 1904. Undertaking was transferred to

See Stock Exchange Year-Book.

VOL. FOR

Tottenham & District Gas Co., in which company stockholders were entitled to £140 or £100 5% preference stock for every £100 consolidated 7% stock or 5% preference stock respectively held. Debenture stockholders were entitled to £100 or £125 4% debenture stock in purchasing company for every £100 4% or 5% perpetual debenture stock held **1939**

Southleigh Mines Ld. Inc. Transvaal 1895. London Office was closed Mar. 1897 **1903**

Southport & Cheshire Lines Extension Railway Co. Inc. by Special Act. 1881. Dissolved 3 June 1949; undertaking vested 1 Jan. 1948 in British Transport Commission under Transport Act 1947. Holders of securities were entitled to receive British Transport 3% guaranteed stock 1978–88 as follows in respect of each £100 of capital stock held:

	£	s.	d.
Ordinary stock	7	0	0
2½% perp. pref. stock	67	0	0
3% guaranteed deb. stock	97	0	0

1949

Southport & Churchtown Botanic Gardens & Museum Co. Ld. Regd. 1874. Vol. liq. (members') 31 July 1933. Capital returned to contributories—£4,442 10*s.* £432 10*s.* was paid into Companies' Liquidation Account. Final meeting return regd. 21 Oct. 1936 **1934**

Southport & Lytham Tramroad Co. Inc. by Special Act 1899 as Southport District Tramroad Co. Wound up and dissolved under Act of 1909 **1910**

Southport & West Lancashire Banking Co. Ld. Regd. 1881. Vol. liq. 20 Aug. 1884. Business sold to Manchester & Liverpool District Banking Co. Ld. (later District Bank Ld.) in 1884. Final meeting return regd. 15 Nov. 1894 **1885**

Southport Baths Co. Ld. Regd. 1869 as Southport Baths and Assembly Rooms Co. Ld.; name changed 28 May 1872. Vol. liq. 6 Mar. 1920. Final meeting return regd. 18 May 1920 **1921**

Southport District Tramroad Co. *See* Southport & Lytham Tramroad Co.

Southport Opera House & Winter Gardens (1905) Ld. *See* Southport Winter Gardens Ld.

Southport Pavilion & Winter Gardens Co. Ld. Regd. 1872. Vol. liq. Apr. 1898. Removed from Register 1901 **1899**

Southport Pier Co. Ld. Regd. 1893. Vol. liq. (members') 11 Feb. 1937. Undertaking acquired by Southport Corporation. Capital returned to contributories—8*s.* 3*d.* per share of £1. Final meeting return regd. 1 Sept. 1937 **1937**

Southport Tramways Co. Ld. Regd. 1871. Vol. liq. 22 May 1918. Final meeting return regd. 4 Dec.1922 **1919**

Southport Waterworks Co. Inc. 1854. Undertaking was transferred in 1902 to Southport, Birkdale and West Lancashire Water Board for £756,000; the Board assumed liability for the 5% debenture stock **1902**

Southport Winter Gardens Ld. Regd. 1905 as Southport Opera House & Winter Gardens (1905) Ld.; name changed in Jan. 1927 to Southport Opera House & Winter Gardens Ld., and as above in Mar. 1929. Vol. liq. (members') 15 Oct. 1948. Capital returned to contributories—28*s.* per share. £20 4*s.* was paid into Companies' Liquidation Account. Final meeting return regd. 16 Feb. 1949 **1950**

Southsea Railway Co. Inc. by Special Act 1880. Under London and South Western (Various Powers) Act (1883) the line was jointly purchased by London and South Western Railway and London, Brighton and South Coast Railway in Jan. 1886 **1886**

Southwark & Deptford Tramways Co. *See* London, Deptford & Greenwich Tramways Ld.

Southwark & Vauxhall Water Co. Inc. by Special Act 1845. Undertaking acquired by Metropolitan Water Board on and from 24 June 1904 **1905**

Southwell District Gas Co. Regd. as limited 1906; inc. by Special Act 1908. Dissolved 1 May 1949, undertaking being vested in East Midland Area Gas Board under Gas Act 1948. Holders of securities were entitled to receive, in respect of each £100 unit held, British Gas 3% guaranteed stock 1990–95 as follows:

	£	s.	d.
Orig. ord. stock (10% stand.)	50	0	0
Addit. ord. stock (7% stand.)	35	0	0
Orig. 5% pref. stock	102	12	6
Addit. 5% pref. stock	102	4	0

1952

Southwell (H. & M.) Ld. Regd. 1890. Vol. liq. (members') 29 Dec. 1949, undertaking having been acquired by Carpet Manufacturing Co. Ld. Capital returned to contributories (per £1 share): preference £1, ordinary £2 16*s.* 3½*d.* £466 was paid into Companies' Liquidation Account. Final meeting return regd. 22 Sept. 1950 **1951**

Southwold Gas Light Co. Ld. Regd. 1848. Dissolved 1 May 1949, undertaking being vested in Eastern Area Gas Board under Gas Act 1948. Holders of securities were entitled to receive British Gas 3% guaranteed stock 1990–95 as follows in respect of each £10 unit, unless otherwise stated, of security held:

	£	s.	d.
Ord. shares (of £5)	10	0	0
6% pref. shares (of £5)	6	15	0
4½% 1st mort. debs. (issued before 1 Jan. 1946)	10	2	6
4½% 1st mort. debs. (issued since 31 Dec. 1945)	10	0	0

1952

Southwold Waterworks Co. Ld. Regd. 1886. Undertaking acquired by East Anglian Water Co. in 1965. in which company shareholders were entitled to receive stocks in exchange as follows (per share of £10): ordinary (10% maximum), £20 5% Consolidated ordinary; new ordinary (7% maximum), £14 5% consolidated ordinary preference, £10 5% redeemable debenture stock 1970. Holders of debentures were entitled to receive equivalent amount of debenture stock 1970. Company was dissolved 27 June 1966 **1967**

Sovereign Life Assurance Co. Regd. as unlimited 1845. Regd. as limited 1862. Court Order to wind up 30 July 1889. Undertaking was acquired by Sun Life Assurance Society. A call of £5 10*s.* per share of £10 (£4 10*s.* paid) *plus* £1 10*s.* per share liquidation expenses was made. Court Order to dissolve 25 May 1900 **1892**

Sovereign Shipping Co. Ld. Regd. 1916. Court Order to wind up 13 Oct. 1926. Liquidator released 9 Jan. 1932. Struck off Register 17 Aug. 1934 **1927**

Sowler (Thos.) & Sons Ld. Regd. 1897. Undertaking was to be sold to Manchester Courier Ld., in which company shareholders were entitled to £2 in shares for every 2 preference shares of £5 held, or £1 in shares for every 10 ordinary shares of £1 held. Removed from Register 1906 **1905**

Spa Hotel Co. Ld. Regd. Edinburgh 1895. Vol. liq. Feb. 1923. Final meeting return regd. 26 Feb. 1924 **1924**

Spa (Scarborough) Ld. Regd. 1920. Vol. liq. (members') 2 Nov. 1957. Capital returned to contributories—16*s.* 4·125*d.* per share (of £1). £56 3*s.* was paid into Companies' Liquidation Account. Final meeting return regd. 14 May 1959 **1960**

Spain & Albury Ld. Regd. 1931. Direct controlling interest was held by Findlater Mackie & Co. Ld. (later Findlater Prentis & Co. Ld.). Vol. liq. (members') 30 Oct. 1944. Final meeting return regd. 27 Aug. 1945 **1946**

Spanish and General Wireless Trust Ld. Regd. 1912. Vol. liq. 13 Apr. 1920. Reconstructed as Spanish and General Corporation Ld. (later Giltspur Investment & Finance Ld.) in which company shareholders were entitled to 1 share of £1 (credited as fully-paid) for each share of £1 held. Final meeting return regd. 1 Mar.1927 **1921**

Spanish Antimony Co. Ld. Regd. 1891. Removed from Register 1896 **1899**

Spanish Copper Co. Ld. Regd. 1883. Vol. liq. 6 Aug. 1919. Final meeting return regd. 16 Apr. 1920 **1920**

Spanish Corporarion Ld. Regd. 1890. Removed from Register 1903 **1899**

Spanish Goldfields Ld. Regd. 1912. Struck off Register 1915 **1915**

Spanish Industries Ld. Regd. 1900. Struck off Register 1922 **1912**

Spanish Lead Syndicate Ld. Regd. 1902. Struck off Register July 1929 **1930**

Spanish Minerals Development Ld. Regd. 1900. Vol. liq. 27 June 1906. Removed from Register 1907 **1907**

Spanish Mines Consolidated Ld. Regd. 1909. Struck off Register 1917 **1912**

Spanish Mines General Syndicate Ld. Regd. 1900. Removed from Register 1909 **1908**

Spanish Mining Properties Ld. Regd. 1900. Removed from Register 1905 **1904**

Spanish National Submarine Telegraph Co. Ld. Regd. 1883. Vol. liq. 25 Mar. 1915. Final meeting return regd. 17 Sept. 1915 **1916**

Spanish Petroleum Co. Ld. Regd. 1909. Struck off Register 1916 **1915**

Spanish Prospecting Co. Ld. Regd. 1901. Vol. liq. 16 Feb. 1909. Final meeting return regd. 24 Feb. 1925 **1909**

Spanish River Pulp & Paper Mills Ld. Inc. Ontario 1910. Undertaking was acquired by Abitibi Power & Paper Co. Ld. Stockholders received—for each share of common stock (of $100) 2 shares (of no par value) of Abitibi Power, and for each preferred share of $100 (*a*) 1½ shares of 6% preferred stock, or (*b*) 1⅙ shares of 6% preferred stock and ¼ share of common stock, or (*c*) 1 share of 6% preferred stock and ½ share of common stock of Abitibi Co. **1929**

VOL. FOR

Spanish Shale Oil Syndicate Ld. Regd. 1910. Vol. liq. Aug. 1911. Removed from Register 1913 .... **1912**

Spanish Telephone Co. Ld. Regd. 1894. Vol. liq. (members') 16 May 1935. Capital returned to contributories—£20 per preference share of £20; £8 0s. 9-6d. per share of £10. Final meeting return regd. 14 Nov. 1936 .... **1936**

Spanish Tin Mines Co. Ld. Regd. 1912. Vol. liq. 31 May 1921. Final meeting return regd. 13 Dec. 1922 ..... **1922**

Spanish Tin Mining Corporation Ld. Regd. 1900. Removed from Register 29 Aug. 1911 .... ***1909**

Spare Motor Wheel of America Ld. Regd. 1907. Vol. liq. 8 Feb. 1910. The undertaking and assets were sold to United States Wheel & Rim Co. Ld. for £32,000 fully-paid ordinary shares (for old debenture holders) and £18,750 in fully-paid deferred shares (for the shareholders). Struck off Register 3 Sept. 1918 .... **1910**

Spark Alloys Ld. See Heenan Spark Ld.

Spark Holdings Ld. See Heenan Spark Ld.

Sparre Patents Co. Ld. Regd. 1888. Removed from Register 1910 .... **1895**

Sparth Mills (1919) Ld. Regd. 1919. Vol. liq. June 1929. Undertaking and assets acquired by Combined Egyptian Mills Ld., [later Combined English Mills (Spinners) Ld.] in which company shareholders were entitled to 1 ordinary share of £1 (credited as fully-paid) for every £2 12s. paid up capital held. Loanholders were entitled to 11s. income debenture stock in new company *plus* 9s. in cash for each £1 owing to them. Struck off Register 31 Aug. 1937.. **1938**

Spassky Copper Mine Ld. Regd. 1904. The properties were nationalised by U.S.S.R. Struck off Register 9 Feb.1951................................. **1951**

Speakman's Mount Callion Ld. Regd. 1897. Debenture holders foreclosed. Removed from Register 1909 .. **1906**

Special Areas Reconstruction Association Ld. Regd. 1936. Vol. liq. (members') 13 July 1945. Capital returned to contributories—11s. 3·41638d. per preference share of £1 (11s. paid); £1 per ordinary of £1. Final meeting return regd. 16 July 1952 .... **1953**

Specialised Unit Trusts Ld. Regd. 1937. Vol. liq. (members') 30 Oct. 1947. Final meeting return regd. 1 Apr. 1948......................... **1940**

Speeding and Marshall Steam Shipping Co. Ld. Regd. 1894. Vol. liq. 7 Feb. 1916. Final meeting return regd. 29 Sept. 1917 .... ***1917**

Speedways Trust Ld. Regd. 1928. Court Order to wind up July 1933. Struck off Register 21 Sept. 1927 ... **1938**

Spelonk (Zoutpansberg) Land & Gold Co. Ld. Regd. 1889. Vol. liq. 30 June 1916. Final meeting return regd. 5 July 1919 .... **1917**

Spencer & Co. Ld. Regd. 1894. Vol. liq. 6 Apr. 1923; the undertaking and assets were acquired by Spencer (Melksham) Ld.† The debenture holders and preference shareholders were repaid at par on 16 Apr. 1923. The ordinary shareholders received 207$\frac{5}{10}$% at Jan. 1924; further payments (if any) not known. Struck off Register 22 July 1927 .... **1924**

Spencer (J. E. & S.) Ld. Regd. 1918. Vol. liq. (members') 10 Dec. 1936. Shares privately held. Final meeting return regd. 7 Dec. 1937 .... **1937**

Spencer (John) & Sons Ld. Regd. 1888. Vol. liq. 23 Jan. 1925. All the assets were sold and the proceeds applied in repaying the debentures and a "substantial" amount of accrued interest. Final meeting return regd. 27 Mar. 1929 .... **1930**

Spencer (John) & Sons (1928) Ld. Regd. 1928. Vol. liq. 6 Apr. 1961. Final meeting return regd. 14 Aug. 1968 **1938**

Spencer, Santo & Co. Ld. Regd. 1898. Vol. liq. 23 Jan. 1911. Final meeting return regd. 4 Nov. 1916...... **1911**

Spencer's (G. & T.) Brewery Ld. Regd. 1889. Vol. liq. 14 Jan. 1914. Undertaking was sold to Ushers' Wiltshire Brewery Ld. in which company shareholders were entitled to 1 5% preference share of £5 (credited as fully-paid) for every 10 ordinary or 5 preference shares of £10 held. Final meeting return regd. 10 July 1915................. **1914**

Spence's Metal Manufacturing Co. Ld. Regd. 1881. Court Orders: to wind up 26 Dec. 1882; to stay proceedings Feb. 1890. Vol. liq. 15 Mar. 1892. Final meeting return regd. 4 May 1893 .... **1883**

Spencer, Turner and Boldero p.l.c. Regd. 2 May 1894; all owned by Dewhurst Dent Ld. Vol. liq. (members') 16 July 1986 .... **1977–8**

Spennymoor & Tudhoe Gas Co. Inc. by Special Act 1876. Dissolved 1 May 1949, undertaking being vested in Northern Area Gas Board under Gas Act 1948. Holders of securities were entitled to receive, in respect of each £10 unit held, British Gas 3% guaranteed stock 1990–95 as follows:

	£	s.	d.
Orig. shares (10% max.)	20	2	0
Addit. shares (7% max.)	14	2	0	**1952**

VOL. FOR

Sperling & Co. Established 1878. Company ceased business as from 30 Nov. 1945 .... **1946**

Spes Bona Bultifontein Diamond Mining Co. Ld. Regd. 1887. Vol. liq. Jan. 1890. Property was acquired by De Beers Consolidated Mines Ld. for 60,000 fully-paid shares of £1 and redemption of debenture debt. Final meeting return regd. 8 Apr. 1892 .... **1889**

Spes Bona Gold Mining Co. Ld. Reconstructed as New Spes Bona Gold Mining Co. Ld., in which company shareholders were entitled to 1 share of £1 (credited with 12s. 6d. paid) for each share of £1 held **1894**

Speyer Brothers. Dissolved on and from 1 Apr. 1922. **1922**

Sphere & Tatler Ld. Regd. 1903. Vol. liq. 25 Apr. 1927. Final meeting return regd. 23 Sept. 1927 .... **1928**

Sphincter Grip Armoured Hose Co. Ld. See Sphincter Hose and Engineering Co. Ld.

Sphincter Hose and Engineering Co. Ld. Regd. 1888 as Sphincter Grip Armoured Hose Co. Ld.; name changed Jan. 1893. Vol. liq. 6. June 1895. Final meeting return regd. Sept. 1895 .... **1899**

Sphinx Electric Ld. Regd. 1929. Court Order to wind up 10 Sept. 1930. Struck off Register 20 Mar. 1936 .. **1937**

Sphinx Electric Supplies (Ireland) Ld. Regd. Dublin 1923. All shares were acquired by Sphinx Electric Ld. **1930**

Sphinx Petroleum Co. Ld. Regd. 1913. Vol. liq. (creditors') 3 Oct. 1935. No capital returned to contributories. Final meeting return regd. 9 June 1936 .... **1936**

Spicer (H.) & Co. Ld. Regd. 1888. Receiver for debenture holders appointed in Mar. 1908. Removed from Register 1912 .... **1911**

Spiel's Patent Petroleum Engine Co. Ld. Regd. 1886. Struck off Register 31 Dec. 1895 .... **1901**

Spies Petroleum Co. Ld. Regd. 1900. Struck off Register 25 July 1952.............................. **1953**

Spillers & Bakers Ld. Regd. 1919. Vol. liq. 31 Jan. 1927. Direct controlling interest held by Spillers Milling & Associated Industries Ld. (later Spillers Ld.). Final meeting return regd. 23 Jan. 1928 .... **1937**

Spillers Grain Co. Ld. Regd. 1913. Vol. liq. 31 Jan. 1927. Direct controlling interest held by Spillers Milling & Associated Industries Ld. (later Spillers Ld.). Final meeting return regd. 23 Jan. 1928 .... **1937**

Spillers' Nephews Biscuit Co. Ld. Regd. 1894. Vol. liq. 19 May. 1900. Reconstructed as Spillers Nephews Ld., in which company shareholders were entitled to 10 ordinary A and 1 ordinary B share of £1 (credited with 10s. paid) for each ordinary share of £10 (£9 paid) held or 10 preference shares of £1 (credited as fully-paid) for every preference share of £10 held. Final meeting return regd. 7 Jan. 1902 .... **1908**

Spillers Nephews Ld. Regd. 1900. Vol. liq. 31 Jan. 1927. Final meeting return regd. 23 Jan. 1928 .... **1927**

Spillers Overseas Industries Ld. Regd. 1924. Vol. liq. (members') 18 Dec. 1929. Assets were acquired by Spillers Ld. which company owned all shares. Final meeting return regd. 14 May 1930...................... **1930**

Spillers Steamship Co. Ld. Regd. 1913. Vol. liq. 31 Jan. 1927. Direct controlling interest held by Spillers Milling & Associated Industries Ld. (later Spillers Ld.). Final meeting return regd. 23 Jan. 1928....... **1927**

Spillers Victoria Foods Ld. Regd. 1913. Vol. liq. 31 Jan. 1927, direct controlling interest held by Spillers Milling & Associated Industries Ld. (later Spillers Ld.). Final meeting return regd. 23 Jan. 1928....... **1927**

Spilsby & Firsby Railway Co. Inc. by Special Act 1865. Under Great Northern Railway (Various Powers) Act 1890 the undertaking was purchased by that company for £20,000; the 4% debentures were taken over by purchasing company. Holders of ordinary shares of £10 received £8 (approx.) for each share held **1891**

Spilsby Gas Co. Ld. Regd. 1856. Dissolved in May 1949, undertaking being vested in East Midland Area Gas Board under Gas Act 1948. Holders of ordinary shares (of £10) were entitled to receive British Gas 3% guaranteed stock 1990–95 for each share held (amount not yet fixed) **1952**

Spink (Joseph) & Sons Ld. Regd. 1889. Vol. liq. (members') 20 Aug. 1934. Undertaking and assets were acquired by J. Hey & Co. Ld., which company owned all shares. The 4% 1st mortgage debentures were redeemed on 26 June 1934. Final meeting return regd. 11 Sept. 1935. .... **1935**

Spiral Globe Ld. Regd. 1897. Removed from Register 1905 .... **1902**

Spitzkop Farm Gold Co. Ld. Regd. 1893. Vol. liq. 8 Jan. 1926. Final meeting return regd. 29 July 1927 ... **1926**

Spitzkop Ld. Regd. 1889. Vol. liq. 29 Aug 1893. Reconstructed as Spitzkop Farm Gold Co. Ld., in which company shareholders were entitled to 1 share of £1 (credited with 19s. paid) for each share of £1 held. Final meeting return regd. 10 Nov. 1896 **1908**

*See Stock Exchange Year-Book.

VOL. FOR

Spikoptz (Lydenburg) Gold Mining Co. Ld. Regd. 1883. Vol. liq. Sept. 1887. Reconstructed as New Spitzkop Ld., in which company shareholders were entitled to 1 share of £1 (credited with 17*s*. 6*d*. paid) for each share of £1 held. Final meeting return regd. 2 Dec. 1889 1889

Splintex Safety Glass (Continental) Ld. Regd. 1929. Vol. liq. (creditors') 10 Dec. 1931. Assets realised insufficient to meet claims of creditors in full. Final meeting return regd. 30 Aug. 1935 ..... *1932

Sponge Rubber Seat Co. Ld. Regd. 1925. Undertaking and assets acquired by Sorbo Rubber Sponge Products Ld. for £15,000 in fully-paid shares. Struck off Register 10 Mar. 1939 1930

Sport & Play Ld. Regd. 1897. Vol. liq. (members') 31 Oct. 1930. Capital returned to contributories—2*s*. per share of £1. £60 was paid into Companies' Liquidation Account. Final meeting return regd. 7 Nov. 1932 1931

Sporting Times (1928) Ld. Regd. 1928. Court Order to wind up 3 Nov. 1930. Struck off Register 16 Aug. 1938 1939

Spratt's Patent (Russia) Ld. Regd. 1886. Vol. liq. 19 Aug. 1891. Reconstructed as Russian Spratt's Patent Ld., in which company shareholders were entitled to 5 ordinary shares of £1 (credited with 15*s*. paid) for each share of £5 held. Final meeting return regd. 14 Feb. 1893 1896

Spread Eagle Restaurants Co. Ld. Regd. 1895. Undertaking and assets were acquired by Callard Stewart and Watt Ld. Capital returned to contributories—12*s*. per share of £1; further payments (if any) not known. Removed from Register 1901 1901

Spreckley Brothers Ld. Regd. 1897. Vol. liq. (members') 30 Sept. 1960. Capital returned to contributories—preference capital repaid at par; ordinary shareholders received £42 9*s*. 11½*d*. per share of £10. Final meeting return regd. 25 May 1962 1963

Spring (Alf.) & Co. Ld. Regd. 1900. Vol. liq. 21 Nov. 1923. Final meeting return regd. 18 July 1929 ..... *1924

Springdale Gold Mines Ld. Regd. 1901. Vol. liq. Dec. 1908. Removed from Register 1909 1909

Springdale Gold Mining & Milling Co. of Denver, Colorado, U.S.A. Inc. Colorado 1892. Reconstructed as Springdale Gold Mining Co. Ld. in which company shareholders were entitled to 1 share of 2*s*. 6*d*. (credited with 2*s*. 3*d*. paid) for each share of $1 held 1897

Springdale Gold Mining Co. Ld. Regd. 1897. Reconstructed 1900 as Springdale Gold Mines Ld., in which company shareholders were entitled to 2 shares of 5*s*. (credited with 4*s*. 6*d*. paid) for every 5 shares of 2*s*. 6*d*. held. Removed from Register 1910 1908

Springfield Breweries Ld. Regd. 1890. Vol. liq. 31 Mar. 1922. Final meeting return regd. 29 Mar. 1923 1923

Springfield Pastoral and Estates Co. Ld. Regd. 1897. Vol. liq. Oct. 1907. Removed from Register 1908 1908

Springs Mines Ld. Inc. in the Transvaal 1909. Final capital repayment of 0·86 cents per share (of R0·02½) in Feb. 1969. Struck off the Register 13 June 1969 1970

Springwell Brewery Co. Ld. Regd. 1888. Vol. liq. (members') 16 July 1951, the undertaking and assets were transferred to Hammonds United Breweries Ld. which company owned practically all shares. The outstanding £105,000 4½% perpetual A debenture stock and £60,000 5¾% perpetual B debenture stock were called for redemption on 16 July 1951 at 105% and par respectively, but under an offer made in June 1951 by Hammonds United Breweries Ld. holders were invited to convert their holdings as from 12 July 1951 into 4% mortgage debenture stock 1981 of Hammonds at the rate of £105 and £110 10*s*. 4% stock for each £100 stock held respectively. £49 was paid into Companies' Liquidation Account on account of unclaimed dividends. Final meeting return regd. 1 Aug. 1952 1953

Sprinkler Fire Office Ld. Regd. 1894. Vol. liq. 15 Oct. 1896. Absorbed by Manchester Fire Assurance Co. Final meeting return regd. 23 Feb. 1898 ..... *1897

Spurgeon (Richard) Ld. Regd. 1895. Court Order to wind up 3 Nov. 1897. Liquidator released 15 Oct. 1901. Removed from Register 10 July 1908 ..... *1898

Square Drilling Machine Co. Ld. Regd. 1890. Vol. liq. 20 Sept. 1893. Final meeting return regd. 17 Dec. 1897 1894

Stabell Gold Mines Ld. (N.P.L.). *See* Greene Stabell Mines Ld.

Stableford & Co. Ld. Regd. 1900. Vol. liq. 26 Mar. 1928. Struck off Register 13 Dec. 1932 1929

Stafford Ld. Regd. 1887. Removed from Register 1906 *1891

Stafford Northcote & Co. Ld. *See* Northcote (Stafford) & Co. Ld.

Stafford Syndicate Ld. Regd. 1895. Vol. liq. 14 Feb. 1905. Removed from Register 1906 1906

VOL. FOR

Staffordshire & Worcestershire Canal Co. Inc. by Special Act 1766 as Co. of Proprietors of the Staffordshire & Worcestershire Canal Navigation; name changed in 1933. Dissolved 3 June 1949; undertaking vested from 1 Jan. 1948 in British Transport Commission under Transport Act 1947. Holders of consolidated stock and 4½% debenture stock were entitled to receive £50 and £103 British Transport 3% guaranteed stock 1978–88 in respect of every £100 held respectively 1949

Staffordshire Financial Co. Ld. Regd. 1864. Court Order to wind up Apr. 1911; capital returned to contributories—4*s*. per share of £2 at Nov. 1911: further payments (if any) not known. Struck off Register 1927; restored to Register 16 Jan. 1939. Struck off Register 9 Feb. 1954 1912

Staffordshire Fire Insurance Co. Ld. *See* London & Staffordshire Fire Insurance Co. Ld.

Staffordshire Gas & Coke Co. Ld. Regd. 1889 as Staffordshire Water-Gas Co. Ld.; name changed Oct. 1889. Court Orders: to wind up Nov. 1889; to dissolve 10 July 1894 1891

Staffordshire Housing Co. Ld. Regd. 1928. Vol. liq. 30 Oct. 1943. All shares owned by Goodyear Tyre & Rubber Co. (Gt. Britain) Ld. Final meeting return regd. 17 Jan. 1944 1944

Staffordshire Joint Stock Bank Ld. Regd. 1863. Vol. liq. 15 Jan. 1889. Final meeting return regd. 1 July 1891 1889

Staffordshire Potteries Waterworks Co. Inc. by Special Act 1847. Undertaking was acquired in 1924 by Staffordshire Potteries Water Board for £840,000 in cash. The Water Board took over the perpetual debenture stocks. The preference stock was repaid at 105%. It was estimated that 200% and 140% would be paid to holders of ordinary 10% and new ordinary 7% stocks 1925

Staffordsbire Rolling Stock Co. Ld. Regd. 1880. Court Orders: to wind up 3 Nov. 1883; to dissolve 23 Sept. 1889 1884

Staffordshire Steel & Ingot Iron Co. Ld. *See* Alfred Hickman Ld.

Staffordshire Union Bank Co. Ld. Regd. 1881. Amalgamated with Cheshire Banking Co. Ld. Removed from Register 1906 1883

Staffordshire Water-Gas Co. Ld. *See* Staffordshire Gas & Coke Ld.

Stagbrook Rubber & Tea Estates, Ld. Regd. 1908. Vol. liq. (members') 8 Nov. 1955, Capital returned to contributories—44*s*. per 5*s*. stock. £204 was paid into Companies' Liquidation Account in respect of unclaimed dividends. Final meeting return regd. 27 May 1964 1965

Stagg & Mantle Ld. *See below.*

Stagg & Russell Ld. Regd. 1907 as Stagg & Mantle Ld.; name changed 7 June 1926. Vol. liq. (members') 14 Dec. 1949, the premises and business having been sold to Montague Burton Ld. Capital returned to contributories—£1 2*s*. 10*d*. per ordinary share of 10*s*. £244 was paid into Companies' Liquidation Account. Final meeting return regd. 17 Dec. 1952 1953

Staines & Egham District Gas & Coke Co. Ld. Established 1833, regd. 1870. By Act of 1914 the undertaking was acquired by Brentford Gas Co. from 1 Jan. 1915. Holders of 10% ordinary shares of £25 were entitled to £264 A consolidated stock in Brentford Gas Co. for every 4 shares held, holders of 7% ordinary shares of £25 were entitled to £214 B consolidated stock of Brentford Gas Co. for every 4 held, holders of 5% preference of £25 to £100 5% preference stock of Brentford Gas Co. for every 4 shares held and holders of 5% debentures to £125 4% debenture stock of Brentford Gas Co. for every £100 held 1915

Staines & West Drayton Railway Co. Inc. by Special Act 1873. Under Great Western Railway Act (1900) the undertaking was transferred to that company, in which holders of 4½% debenture stock received an equal amount of 4½% debenture stock. Holders of preference shares and ordinary shares received £3 and £2 respectively in cash 1901

Staines Greyhound Racecourse Ld. Regd. 1927 Receiver for debenture holders appointed in Apr. 1930. Assets realised insufficient to satisfy claims of mortgagee and debenture holders. Struck off Register 16 July 1937 1938

Staines Reservoirs Joint Committee. Inc. by Special Act 1896. Under Metropolis Water Act 1902 the undertaking was transferred to the Metropolitan Water Board. The 3% guaranteed debenture stock was assumed by the Board 1905

Stakehill & Co. Ld. Regd. 1897 as Barlows Ld.; name changed to Samuel Barlow & Co. Ld. in 1898 and as above July 1929. Vol. liq. 2 Aug. 1929. Undertaking and assets were acquired by Bradford Dyers'

VOL. FOR

Association Ld. Capital returned to contributories—£5 per preference share of £5; it was estimated that 34s. 6d. per ordinary share of £1 would be paid. Final meeting return regd. 19 Apr. 1930 .... **1930**

Stallard (Josiah) & Sons Ld. Regd. 1883. Vol. liq. 31 May 1912. Final meeting return regd. 26 Oct. 1915 ***1913**

Stalybridge Cotton Mill Co. (1919) Ld. Regd. 1919. Vol. liq. (members') 22 Sept. 1931. Undertaking acquired by Lancashire Cotton Corporation Ld. Final meeting return regd. 1 Sept. 1936...................... **1932**

Stamford and Essendine Railway Co. Inc. by Special Act 1853. In 1923 the undertaking was merged into the London & North Eastern Railway Co., in which company stockholders were entitled to stock, as follows:

For each £100 held		L.&N. E.	
5% Debenture	£112 7s. 2d.	4% Deb.	
4% Debenture	£112 7s. 2d.	4% Deb.	
4% Preference	£100	4% Deb.	
5% Preference	£100	cash.	
Stam. & Ess. Ord.	£98 9s. 0d.	4% Deb.	
Sibson Ext. Ord.	£21 1s. 11d.	4%Deb.	**1924**

Stamford & St. Martin's (Stamford Baron) Gas Light & Coke Co. Inc. by Special Act 1892. Dissolved 1 May 1949, undertaking being vested in East Midland Area Gas Board under Gas Act 1948. Holders of securities were entitled to receive, in respect of each £100 unit held, British Gas 3% guaranteed stock 1990–95 as follows:

	£ s. d.
Orig. stock (8% stand.)	275 0 0
5% pref. stock	112 0 0
7% pref. stock	150 0 0	**1952**

Stamford, Spalding & Boston Banking Co. Ld. Established 1832. Regd. 1880. Vol. liq. 1 Sept. 1911. Undertaking and assets were acquired by Barclay & Co. Ld. (later Barclays Bank Ld.). Final meeting return regd. 5 Oct. 1927 .... **1941**

Stamp Distribution (Parent) Co. Ld. Regd. 1892. Court Order to wind up 13 Mar. 1895. Removed from Register 1907 .... **1896**

Stanbridge (S.) & Co. Ld. Regd. 1887. Removed from Register 1906 .... ***1888**

Stancliffe Estates Co. Ld. Regd. 1897. Vol. liq. (members') 24 Feb. 1949. Final meeting return regd. 17 June 1949 .... **1946**

Standard Accident Insurance Co. Ld. Regd. 1888. Vol. liq. 13 Mar. 1893. Undertaking transferred to Scottish Metropolitan Life Assurance Co. (later Scottish Metropolitan Assurance Co. Ld.). Final meeting return regd. 12 Aug. 1897 .... ***1894**

Standard Bank of Australia Ld. Inc. Victoria 1893. In liquidation in 1901 .... **1901**

Standard Bank of Canada. Inc. Toronto 1873. Undertaking and assets were acquired by Canadian Bank of Commerce, in which company shareholders were entitled to 1 share of $100 (credited as fully-paid) for each share of $100 held **1929**

Standard Bank of London Ld. Regd. 1880. In liquidation. Capital returned to contributories—£3 per share (£5 paid) of £20; further payments (if any) not known **1883**

Standard Brick Co. Ld. Regd. 1900. Vol. liq. Nov. 1908. Removed from Register 1911 .... **1909**

Standard Calico Printers Ld. Regd. 1910. Struck off Register 1917 .... **1911**

Standard Carburettor and Gaserator Co. Ld. Regd. 1912 as Standard Petroleum Carburettor (Parent) Co. Ld.; name changed Sept. 1920. Struck off Register 11 Oct. 1927 .... **1916**

Standard Carpet Co. Foreign Ld. Regd. 1928 as Standard Carpet Co. Foreign (1928) Ld.; name changed Sept. 1929. Vol. liq. (members') 11 Mar. 1931. All capital owned by Standard Carpet Co. Ld. Final meeting return regd. 25 Aug. 1935 .... **1931**

Standard Carpet Co. Ld. Regd. 1923. Business was acquired in 1928 by Standard Carpet Co. (1928) Ld. (later Standard Carpet Co. Ld.). **1929**

Standard Carpet Co. Ld. Regd. 1928 as Standard Carpet Co. (1928) Ld.; name changed July 1929. Vol. liq. Sept. 1931. Struck off Register 31 Aug. 1937 .... **1938**

Standard Cash Register Co. Ld. Regd. 1890. Vol. liq. 31 July 1893. Final meeting return regd. 21 Apr. 1896 **1894**

Standard Cement Syndicate Ld. Regd. 1899. Removed from Register 1904 .... **1905**

Standard Chemical & Iron Lumber Co. of Canada Ld. See below.

Standard Chemical Co. Ld. Inc. Canada 1911 as Standard Chemical & Iron Lumber Co. of Canada Ld.; name changed 1919. All assets sold as from 30 Apr. 1951 to Dominion Tar & Chemical Co. Ld. in which holders of common shares of no par value were entitled to receive ⅞ths of a common share plus 58·4 cents per share held **1954**

VOL. FOR

Standard Chemical Co. of Toronto Ld. Inc. Ontario 1897. Vol. liq. Mar. 1911. Undertaking and assets were acquired by Standard Chemical, Iron and Lumber Co. of Canada Ld. (later Standard Chemical Co. Ld.), in which company shareholders were entitled to 1 1/10 preference and 1 1/10 ordinary shares of $100 for each share of $100 held **1911**

Standard Commercial Co. Ld. Regd. 1900. Vol. liq. May 1918. Struck off Register Mar. 1929 .... **1930**

Standard Consolidated Tin Mines Ld. Regd. 1911. Vol. liq. 11 May 1915. Final meeting return regd. 15 May 1916 .... **1916**

Standard Construction Corporation Ld. Regd. 1902. Vol. liq. 19 Aug. 1909. Final meeting return regd. 10 Dec. 1914 .... **1910**

Standard Copper Mines. Inc. Arizona. The London office was closed in 1905..................................... **1906**

Standard Electric Theatres Ld. Regd. 1910. Struck off Register 1919 .... **1911**

Standard Exploration Co. Ld. Regd. 1898. Court Order to wind up 16 Jan. 1901. Removed from Register 1910 .... **1901**

Standard Finance Corporation of South Africa Ld. Inc. S. Africa 1944. Provisional liq. 2 Oct. 1961 and final liq. 24 Oct. 1961. No returns of capital made to contributories **1975-6**

Standard Financial Association Ld. Regd. 1892. Vol. liq. 22 Mar. 1913. Court Order to wind up 8 Apr. 1913. Liquidator released 7 Mar. 1918. Struck off Register 24 July 1923 .... **1914**

Standard Fire Office Ld. Regd. 1879. Vol. liq. Apr. 1884. Court Order to continue winding up under supervision 17 May 1884. Final meeting return regd. 27 July 1893... **1885**

Standard Gold Mining Co. Ld. Regd. 1888. Removed from Register 1906 .... **1892**

Standard Housing Co. Ld. Regd. 1920. Court Order to wind up 7 Mar. 1922. Struck off Register June 1931 **1932**

Standard Insurance Co. Ld. Inc. in New Zealand 27 Jan. 1874; reincorporated as limited 11 Feb. 1908 as Standard Fire & Marine Insurance Co. of New Zealand Ld.; name changed Apr. 1922. Winding-up order by Supreme Courty of New Zealand made 24 May 1961. A first dividend of 7s. in the £ was paid to unsecured creditors on 9 June 1967, a second of 3s. in the £ on 25 June 1969, a third of 65 cents in the $ 16 July 1971, a fourth of 20 cents in the $ on 1 Nov. 1972, a fifth of 5 cents in the $ on 16 Apr. 1975 and a final of 6·82 cents in the $ on 25 Aept. 1978. In Mar. 1979 the liquidator stated that the company was in the process of being finbally wound-up and dissolved **1986-7**

Standard Investment Co. Ld. Regd. 1882. Court Orders: to wind up 27 Mar. 1884; to dissolve 20 Aug. 1886 ***1884**

Standard Manufacturing Co. (1920) Ld. Regd. 1920. Vol. liq. 10 Oct. 1928. Final meeting return regd. 17 July 1930 .... ***1930**

Standard Mining Co. Ld. See Emerald Mines of Columbia Ld.

Standard Newspapers Ld. Regd. 1904. Vol. liq. May 1915. Court Order to continue winding up under supervision 15 June 1915. Struck off Register 1927 **1916**

Standard Oil Co. of Canada Ld. Regd. 1910. Vol. liq. 8 Dec. 1913. Final meeting return regd. 26 Nov. 1917 **1914**

Standard Oil Co. of England Ld. Regd. 1910. Vol. liq. 30 Dec. 1914. Final meeting return regd. 14 Aug. 1915 **1912**

Standard Oil Co. of Galicia Ld. Regd. July 1896. Vol. liq. 15 Dec. 1896. Final meeting return regd. 1 Dec. 1898 **1897**

Standard Oil Co. of Maikop (Schirvanski) Ld. Regd. 1910. Vol. liq. 21 July 1914. Final meeting return regd. 26 Feb. 1921 .... **1915**

Standard Oil Co. of Mexico Ld. Regd. 1909. Vol. liq. 30 Nov. 1922. Reconstructed as Standard Oil Co. of Mexico (1922) Ld., in which company shareholders were entitled to 4 fully-paid participating preference shares of 2s. for each preference share of 5s. held, or 3 such shares for every 5 A shares of 2s. held, or 1 such share for each B share of 1s. held. Final meeting return regd. 8 Mar. 1927 .... **1923**

Standard Oil Co. of Mexico (1922) Ld. Regd. 1922. Vol. liq. 1 Apr. 1926 for reconstruction as Second Saxon Securities Trust Ld., in which company shareholders were entitled to 1 share of £1 (credited with 10s. paid) for every 7 preference shares of 2s. or 15 ordinary shares of 1s. held. Final meeting return regd. 14 June 1927 .... **1928**

Standard Oil Export Corporation. Inc. Delaware 1928. The preferred stock was redeemed at 110% on 30 June 1936 and the company was dissolved on that date. Undertaking was acquired by Standard Oil Co. (New Jersey), which owned all the common stock **1937**

VOL. FOR

Standard Oil-Refinery of Roumania Ld. Regd. 1912. Vol. liq. 3 Mar. 1916. Final meeting return regd. 8 July 1916 .... **1916**

Standard Petroleum Carburettor (Parent) Co. Ld. *See* Standard Carburettor and Gaserator Co. Ld.

Standard Petroleum Exploration Co. Ld. Regd. 1899. Vol. liq. 18 July 1928. Final meeting return regd. 24 Dec. 1930 .... **1929**

Standard Portland Cement Co. Ld. Regd. 1887 as Natural Portland Cement Co. Ld.; name changed Sept. 1888. Vol. liq. Jan. 1890. Final meeting return regd. 26 Nov. 1890 .... **1891**

Standard Rubber Corporation of Mexico Ld. Regd. 1910. Struck off Register 1927 .... **1911**

Standard Screw Co. Ld. Regd. 1922. Receiver appointed 4 Nov. 1929. Assets realised insufficient to meet claims of debenture holders. Struck off Register June 1931 .... **1933**

Standard Shipbuilding & Engineering Co. Ld. Regd. 1916. Vol. liq. 6 May 1921. Final meeting return regd. 28 Mar. 1927 .... ***1922**

Standard Time Co. Ld. Regd. 1896. Vol. liq. 20 Feb. 1912. Final meeting return regd. 18 July 1912 ...... **1897**

Standard Tyre & Rubber Manufacturers Ld. Regd. 1919. Vol. liq. 12 Nov. 1924. Final meeting return regd. 14 Nov. 1927 .... **1925**

Standard Union Trust Ld. Regd. 1911. Vol. liq. 2 July 1913. Final meeting return regd. 3 Mar. 1917 ...... **1914**

Standard Wagon & Carriage Co. Ld. Regd. 1899. Vol. liq. 11 Feb. 1901. Removed from Register 24 July 1923 .... ***1902**

Standard Weldless Tube & Cycle Components Co. Ld. Regd. 1897. Removed from Register 1903 .... **1899**

Standard Wood Pulp Co. Ld. Regd. 1928. Vol. liq. (members') 17 July 1939. No capital returned to contributories. Final meeting return regd. 4 Sept. 1940 .... **1941**

Standardised China Clay Co. Ld. Regd. 1912. Receiver appointed 9 May 1924. Struck off Register Dec. 1931 .... **1932**

Standering & Burton Ld. Regd. 1882. Vol. liq. 19 Sept. 1889. Final meeting return regd. 1 Jan. 1891 ...... ***1885**

Standerton-Ermelo Gold Fields Ld. Regd. 1903. Vol. liq. 7 May 1906. Removed from Register 1906 .... **1907**

Stanhill Ring Spinning Co. (1920) Ld. Regd. 1920. Vol. liq. (members') 4 July 1955. Final meeting return regd. 15 Sept. 1955 .... **1941**

Stanhope Gas & Water Co. Ld. Regd. 1866. Dissolved 1 May 1949, undertaking being vested in Northern Area Gas Board under Gas Act 1948. Holders of ordinary shares (of £5) were entitled to receive £1 10s. British Gas 3% guaranteed stock 1990–95 for each share held **1952**

Stanhope Gold Mining Co. Ld. Inc. Natal 1887. Vol. liq. 1903. A capital return of 20% was made in Feb. 1904; further returns (if any) not known **1904**

Stanhope Steamship Co. Ld. Regd. 1934. Vol. liq. (members') 7 Feb. 1952. Vessels and certain other assets transferred to Stanhope Steamship Co. Ld. in which company stockholders were entitled to 1 fully-paid share of £1 per 5s. stock held and also received £2 1s. 8·94d. cash per 5s. stock held; £3,719 16s. 10d. was paid into Companies' Liquidation Account in respect of unclaimed distributions. Final meeting return regd. 9 June 1960 .... **1961**

Stanislaus Gold & Hydraulic Co. Ld. Regd. 1895. Vol. liq. Feb. 1899. Removed from Register 1912 ...... **1900**

Stanley (Alexander) Linings (Manchester) Ld. *See below.*

Stanley Linings Ld. Regd. 1931 as Alexander Stanley Linings (Manchester) Ld.; name changed 13 Jan. 1949. Vol. liq. (members') 17 Mar. 1953. Capital repaid at par. Final meeting return regd. 18 Feb. 1956 .... **1956**

Stanlow Works Estate Ld. *See* Allied Cement Manufacturers Ld.

Stanly Freehold Gold Mines Ld. Regd. 1887. Vol. liq. 11 Mar. 1890. Reconstructed as Parker Gold Mines Ld. in which company shareholders were entitled to 3 preference shares of 5s. (credited with 4s. 3d. paid) for each preference share of 5s. held or 2 ordinary shares of 10s. (credited with 9s. 6d. paid) and 1 preference share of 5s. (credited with 4s. 3d. paid) for each ordinary share of £1 held. Final meeting return regd. 31 Aug. 1892 .... **1892**

Stanmore Estates Ld. Regd. 1909. Vol. liq. 21 June 1916. Reconstructed as company of same name. Final meeting return regd. 18 Dec. 1916 .... **1927**

Stapleton National Bank. Acquired in Apr. 1918 by Corn Exchange Bank **1929**

Stapley & Smith, Ld. Regd. 1920. Vol. liq. (members') 25 Mar. 1963. Final meeting return regd. 4 July 1963 **1956**

Stapp's Water-Gas Patents Ld. Regd. 1889. Vol. liq. 10 Mar. 1891. Final meeting return regd. 14 Mar. 1894 **1892**

VOL. FOR

Star Assurance Society. Constituted by Deed of Settlement 1843 as Star Life Assurance Society; inc. by Special Act and name changed 1911. Vol. liq. Dec. 1917 for amalgamation with Eagle and British Dominion Insurance Co. Ld. (later Eagle Star Insurance Co. Ld.). The 100,000 shares of £1 were exchanged for £200,000 5% War Loan Stock and 10,000 fully-paid ordinary shares of £3 of the purchasing company **1918**

Star Cycle Co. Ld. *See* Star Motor Co. Ld.

Star Cycle Co. (Sharratt & Lisle) Ld. Regd. 1895. Vol. liq. 17 Dec. 1896. Taken over by Star Cycle Co. Ld. Final meeting return regd. 24 Mar. 1897 .... ***1898**

Star Development Mines Ld. Regd. 1911 as Star of Egypt Mines Ld.; name changed Apr. 1920. Struck off Register 22 Nov. 1940 .... **1941**

Star Emerald Mining Syndicate Ld. Regd. 1910 as Star Mining Syndicate Ld.; name changed Feb. 1927. Vol. liq. (creditors') 18 June 1936. Assets realised insufficient to pay unsecured creditors in full. Final meeting return regd. 29 Apr. 1940 .... **1937**

Star Engineering Co. Ld. *See* Star Motor Co. Ld.

Star Explorations Ld. Regd. 1910. All capital was owned by Exploration Co. Ld. Vol. liq. (members') 14 Mar. 1966. Final meeting return regd. 2 July 1974 **1956**

Star Life Assurance Society. *See* Star Assurance Society

Star Mining Syndicate Ld. *See* Star Emerald Mining Syndicate Ld.

Star Motor Co. Ld. Regd. 1896 as Star Cycle Co. Ld.: name changed to Star Engineering Co. Ld. in 1909 and as above in Aug. 1928. Court Order to wind up 21 Mar. 1932. Struck off Register 15 June 1937 .. **1938**

Star of Egypt Mines Ld. *See* Star Development Mines Ld.

Star of Gwalia Ld. *See* Gwalia Consolidated Ld.—regd. 1898.

Star of Normanby Gold Mining Co. Ld. Regd. 1888. Vol. liq. 24 Mar. 1892. Struck off Register 1926 .... **1893**

Star of the East Gold Mining Co. Ld. Regd. 1895. Vol. liq. 28 Oct. 1898. Reconstructed as Star of the East Ld., in which company shareholders were entitled to 2 shares of £1 (credited with 17s. paid) for every 3 shares of £1 held. Final meeting return regd. 21 June 1899 .... **1901**

Star of the East Gold Mining Co. Ld. Regd. 1907. Vol. liq. 2 Oct. 1913. Final meeting return regd. 12 May 1918 .... **1914**

Star of the East Ld. Regd. 1898. Reconstructed 1901 as company of same name. Shareholders were entitled to 1 share of £1 (credited with 17s. 6d. paid) in new company for each share of £1 held. Removed from Register 1907 .... **1903**

Star of the East Ld. Regd. 1901. Vol. liq. 31 Mar. 1903. Reconstructed as Star of the East (1903) Ld., in which company, 285,000 shares of 10s. (7s. 6d. paid) were allotted. Final meeting return regd. 16 Apr. 1907 .... **1907**

Star of the East (1903) Ld. Regd. 1903. Reconstructed 1907 as Star of the East Gold Mining Co. Ld., in which company shareholders were entitled to 1 share of 2s. (credited as fully-paid) for every 7 shares of 10s. held. Removed from Register 1909 .... **1908**

Star Omnibus Co., London Ld. Regd. 1899. Vol. liq. 6 Mar. 1908. Final meeting return regd. 24 Oct. 1925 **1916**

Star Paper Mill Co. Ld. Regd. 1875. Vol. liq. 15 May 1920. Reconstructed as Star Paper Mill Co. (1920) Ld. (later Star Paper Mills Ld.). Final meeting return regd. 28 Sept. 1921 .... **1921**

Star Patent Fuel Co. Ld. Regd. 1909. Vol. liq. (members') 2 July 1930. Capital returned to contributories—£1 1s. 10½d. per fully-paid share of £1; 2s. 10½d. per share of £1 (1s. paid). Final meeting return regd. 21 Feb. 1934 .... **1939**

Star Tea Co. Ld. Regd. 1892. Under scheme of arrangement sanctioned by Court Nov. 1929 the undertaking and assets were transferred to International Tea Co.'s Stores Ld., in which company shareholders received approx. 7¼ or 10 fully-paid A preference shares of £1 for every 7 preference or 7 preferred ordinary shares of £1 respectively held; deferred ordinary shareholders received 1 fully-paid ordinary share of 5s. plus 9d. in cash for each deferred ordinary share of 1s. held. Dissolved under Sec. 154 of Companies Act 1929 on 24 Dec. 1930 **1930**

Star Tube Co. Ld. Regd. 1896. Vol. liq. 14 July 1897. Undertaking acquired by Tubes Ld. Final meeting return regd. 24 Apr. 1901 .... ***1898**

Starbuck Car & Wagon Co. Ld. Regd. 1872. Vol. liq. Apr. 1886. Court Order to continue winding up under supervision June 1886. Final meeting return regd. 20 Dec. 1889 .... **1887**

Starey's Carriage Works & Horse Repository Co. Ld. *See* Starey's Ld.

See Stock Exchange Year-Book.

VOL. FOR

Starey's Ld. Regd. 1898 as Starey's Carriage Works & Horse Repository Co. Ld.; name changed 4 Apr. 1907 to Starey's Ld.; 2 July 1908 to Starey's & Woolleys, Ld. and as above 8 Apr. 1916. Receiver appointed 25 Jan. 1918; ceased to act 24 Aug. 1920. Struck off Register 3 June 1921 .... ***1914**

Starley Brothers & Westwood Manufacturing Co. Ld. Regd. 1896. Vol. liq. 12 Jan. 1899. Final meeting return regd. 15 Mar. 1902 .... **1899**

Starley (Russia) Ld. Regd. 1897. Vol. liq. 16 Dec. 1898. Final meeting return regd. 16 Jan. 1900 .... **1899**

State of Bahia Cocoa Estates Ld. Regd. 1919. Vol. liq. 29 Sept. 1920. Undertaking was acquired in 1920 by Mucambo Cocoa Estates Ld. Final meeting return regd. 14 Mar. 1922 .... **1943**

State of Bahia South Western Railway Co. Ld. Regd. 1908. Vol. liq. 25 Apr. 1963 the Government having taken over the system as from 30 Apr. 1949. The prior lien debenture stock was repaid, with interest, on 22 Dec. 1960 and under a scheme of arrangement of 25 Mar. 1963 holders of mortgage bonds who claimed within 3 years of 29 Mar. 1963 received a 1st distribution of £2 5*s*. per bond (of £10) and final distribution, to holders who claimed the first distribution of (*a*) £1 11*s*. 8*d*. per 1st mortgage bond of £20; (b) £1 per 1st mortgage bond of £10; (*c*) 6*s*. 8*d*. per participating bond of £10; (*d*) 13*s*. 4*d*. per income bond of £10; (*e*) 1*s*. 4*d*. per $\frac{1}{15}$th voucher representing $\frac{1}{15}$th of a £10 mortgage bond; (*f*) 8*d*. per $\frac{1}{30}$th voucher representing $\frac{1}{30}$th per £10 mortgage bond; (*g*) 4*d*. per $\frac{1}{40}$ voucher representing $\frac{1}{60}$th per £10 mortgage bond; (*h*) 1*s*. 4*d*. coupons No. 12 and 13 ex £20 mortgage bonds; (*i*) 8*d*. coupons No. 1 to 5 and 7 ex £10 participating bonds; (*j*) 4*d*. coupons No. 14, 15 and 17 ex £10 1st mortgage bonds. Shareholders who lodged claims within 6 months of 29 Mar. 1963 received 2*s*. per share (of £1). Final meeting return regd. 21 Aug. 1969 .... **1970**

State Savings Bank of Western Australia. Acquired in Oct. 1931 by Commonwealth Bank of Australia. **1932**

State Steamship Co. Ld. Regd. Edinburgh 1876. Vol. liq. 4 Mar. 1891. Final meeting return regd. 21 Apr. 1898 .... **1892**

Staten Chemical Co. Ld. Regd. 1882. Vol. liq. 23 July 1897. Final meeting return regd. 25 Apr. 1899...... **1898**

Status Investment Trust Ld. Regd. 1912. Vol. liq. 5 Oct. 1925. Reconstructed as Anglo-Scottish Amalgamated Corporation Ld., in which company shareholders were entitled to 1 ordinary share of £1 and $1\frac{1}{2}$ deferred shares of 1*s*. (credited as fully-paid) for every 2 shares of £1 held. Final meeting return regd. 23 July 1927 .... **1126**

Staveley Investment Trust Ld. Regd. 1942. Under provisions of a Scheme of Arrangement effective 9 July 1969 undertaking and assets acquired by Anglo-Scottish Investment Trust Ld. in which company ordinary stockholders received £41 5*s*. ordinary stock per £50 ordinary stock; and preference stockholders £1 $6\frac{1}{4}$% debenture stock for every £1 preference stock. Holders of debenture stock received a like amount of 4% debenture stock. Dissolved by Order of Court 22 Aug. 1970 .... **1970**

Stavropoleo Moreni (Roumania) Oil Properties Ld. Regd. 1912. Vol. liq. (members') 14 June 1935. 73,253 (out of 134,257) shares of £1 were held by Phoenix Oil and Transport Co. Ld. Final meeting return regd. 17 Sept. 1935 .... **1936**

Steam Boiler Assurance Co. Ld. Regd. 1862. Business was acquired by Vulcan Boiler & General Insurance Co. Ld. Removed from Register 1882 .... **1897**

Steam Herring Fleet Ld. Regd. Edinburgh 1899. Vol. liq. May 1921. Shareholders received 1 fully-paid share of £1 and 13*s*. 9*d*. in 10% 2nd mortgage debentures of Fish Traders Ld. *plus* £2 10*s*. in cash for every 5 shares of 5*s*. held. Final meeting return regd. 30 Dec. 1924 .... **1922**

"Steam Loop" Co. Ld. Regd. 1890. Removed from Register 1907........................ **1894**

Steam Tramway Traction Co. Ld. Regd. 1883. Removed from Register 1891 .... ***1885**

Steamship Co. Ld. *See* National Steam Ship Co. Ld.

Steegman (Edward) & Co. Ld. Regd. 1879. Removed from Register 1905 .... ***1886**

Steel & Garland Ld. Regd. 1894. Removed from Register 1905........................ **1905**

Steel Balls Ld. Regd. 1899. Removed from Register 1906........................ **1905**

Steel Brand & Cement Factories Ld. Regd. 1895. Removed from Register 4 Oct. 1898 .... ***1896**

Steel Co. of Canada Ld. Regd. 1874. Removed from Register 1904........................ **1885**

Steel Corporation of Bengal Ld. Inc. in India 20 Apr. 1937. Dissolved as from 1 Jan. 1953, undertaking having been vested in The Indian Iron & Steel Co. Ld. Shareholders received 1 fully-paid preference share (of R.100) of that company for each preference share (of R.100) and 4 fully-paid ordinary shares (of R.10) for each 5 ordinary shares (of R.10) held........................ **1954**

Steel Developments, Ld. Regd. 1913. Vol. liq. (members') 14 May 1948. Capital returned to contributories—9*s*. $5\frac{1}{8}$*d*. per share of 6*s*. Final meeting return regd. 9 Aug. 1949 .... **1950**

Steel Industries of Great Britain Ld. Regd. 1929. Vol. liq. (members') 8 June 1934. Capital returned to contributories—£1 7*s*. 7·4598*d*. per preference share of £1; 13s. 4·3802*d*. per A ordinary share of £1. An unspecified amount was paid into Companies' Liquidation Account. Final meeting return regd. 24 Sept. 1935 .... **1935**

Steel, Peech & Tozer Ld. Regd. 1875 as Steel, Tozer & Hampton Ld.; name changed Dec. 1883. Vol. liq. (members') 31 Dec. 1930. Assets and liabilities were acquired by United Steel Cos. Ld. Final meeting return regd. 14 Nov. 1931 .... **1931**

Steele, Lockhart & Co. Ld. Regd. 1908. Vol. liq. 23 Feb. 1911. Struck off Register 10 Oct. 1916 .... **1911**

Steelite Explosives Ld. Regd. 1908. Vol. liq. Apr. 1912. Removed from Register 1913 .... **1913**

Steep Grade Tramways and Works Co. Ld. Regd. 1881. Court Orders: to wind up 5 June 1886; to dissolve 12 Aug. 1891 .... **1887**

Steiner (F.) & Co. Ld. Regd. 1897. Vol. liq. (members') 15 Dec. 1955. Debenture stock was repaid at 105% (plus interest to 15 Dec. 1955) in June 1956. Capital returned to contributories—9*s*. $1\frac{3}{4}$*d*. per 10*s*. ordinary stock. £1,625 was paid into Companies' Liquidation Account in respect of unclaimed distributions. Final meeting return regd. 27 July 1964.. **1965**

Stein's Bakery & Patent Oven Co. Ld. Regd. 1886. Removed from Register 1906 .... **1890**

Stelastic Tyres Ld. Regd. 1913. Vol. liq. 4 July 1923. Final meeting return regd. 14 Jan. 1925 .... **1924**

Stella Gill Coke & Bye-Products Co. Ld. Regd. 1920. Receiver appointed in Dec. 1927. Works were acquired by Mid Durham Carbonization Co. Ld. Struck off Register 19 Dec. 1930 .... **1940**

Stella Shipping Co. Ld. Regd. 1915. Vol. liq. 19 Dec. 1921. Final meeting return regd. 1 Apr. 1924 ...... **1922**

Stephenson Clarke & Co. Ld. Regd. 1922. Vol. liq. 1 May 1928. Reconstructed as Stephenson Clarke and Associated Companies Ld. (later Stephenson Clarke Ld.). Final meeting return regd. 3 Aug. 1928 ...... **1929**

Stephenson (Richard) Ld. Regd. 1896. Removed from Register 1903 .... **1900**

Stephenson (Robert) & Co. Ld. Regd. 1899. Receiver was appointed July 1909. Certain assets at Hebburn were sold to Palmers Hebburn Co. Ld. for £200,000 4% debenture stock. Certain assets at Darlington were sold to Robert Stephenson & Co. (1914) Ld., in which company debenture stockholders were entitled to 11 fully-paid shares of £1 for every £10 stock held. Holders of 5% A debenture stock were not to receive any return. Final meeting return regd. 24 Oct. 1916 .... **1915**

Stepney Spare Motor Wheel Ld. *See* Stepney Tyres Ld.

Stepney Tyre & Rubber Co. Ld. Regd. 1932. All capital was owned by British Tyre & Rubber Co. Ld. (later B. T. R. Industries Ld.). Vol. liq. (members') 26 July 1963. Final meeting return regd. 6 Jan. 1965 .... **1940**

Stepney Tyres Ld. Regd. 1906 as Stepney Spare Motor Wheel Ld.; name changed Jan. 1923. Vol. liq. (creditors') 8 Dec. 1931. No capital returned to contributories. Final meeting return regd. 14 July 1934........................ **1940**

Stepper Point Quarry Ld. Regd. 1931. Undertaking was acquired in 1932 by Padstow Granite Quarry Co. Ld. Vol. liq. (members') 3 May 1934. Final meeting return regd. 22 Oct. 1934 .... **1935**

Steralis Ld. *See* Steralis Mineral Waters Ld.

Steralis Mineral Waters Ld. Regd. 1904 as Steralis Ld. Vol. liq. Sept. 1906. Removed from Register 1908 **1907**

Sterax Co. Ld. Regd. 1900. Vol. liq. 5 Feb. 1909. Final meeting return regd. 5 Apr. 1917 .... **1910**

Sterkfontein Gold Estates Ld. Regd. 1895. Vol. liq. Aug. 1909 for reconstruction as Sterkfontein Gold Estates (1909) Ld., in which company shareholders were entitled to 3 shares of £1 (credited with 17*s*. paid) for each share of £1 held. Removed from Register 1913 **1910**

Sterkfontein Gold Estates (1909) Ld. Regd. 1909. Vol. liq. 10 July 1913. Undertaking and assets were acquired by Montrose Exploration Co. Ld. in which company shareholders were entitled to 1 share of 10*s*. (credited as fully-paid) for every 5 shares of £1 (19*s*. paid) held. Final meeting return regd. 1 Aug. 1919 .... **1914**

Sterkfontein Proprietary Gold Fields Ld. Regd. 1896. Removed from Register 1908 .... **1899**

**See Stock Exchange Year-Book.*

Sterling & Overseas Investments Ld. Regd. 1922 as Rubber & Industrial Trust Ld.; name changed 21 June 1960. On 21 July 1975 ordinary and debenture capital cancelled, holders being entitled to 45 ordinary shares of 25p and £1 7·2% debenture stock of Estates House Investment Trust Ld. for every 400 ordinary shares and £1 6% debenture stock respectively. Company dissolved without winding up on 31 Dec. 1976 .... **1977-8**

Sterling Gold Mines (Montana) Ld. Regd. 1886. Removed from Register 1906 .... **1892**

Sterte Manufacturing Co. Ld. Undertaking and assets were acquired in 1928 by Phantestra (Renn's Gramophone & Wireless) Ld. **1929**

Stevens (A. J.) & Co. (1914) Ld. Regd. 1914. Vol. liq. (members') 2 Oct. 1931. Capital returned to contributories—3s. 4½d. per preference of £1. £11 9s. was paid into Companies' Liquidation Account. Final meeting return regd. 6 Jan. 1937 .... **1932**

Stevens (William) Ld. Regd. 1891. Vol. liq. (members') 16 July 1931. Undertaking was acquired by William Stevens (1931) Ld. Final meeting return regd. 10 Mar. 1932 .... ***1932**

Stevensons Ld. See Sadlar & Barnes Ld.

Stevenston Gas Co. Ld. Regd. in Edinburgh 1898. Dissolved 1 May 1949, undertaking being vested in Scottish Area Gas Board under Gas Act 1948. Holders of ordinary shares (of £1) were entitled to receive £1 17s. 6d. British Gas 3% guaranteed stock 1990–95 for each share held **1952**

Stewart & Macdonald Ld. See Argyll Assets Co. Ld.

Stewart & Young Ld. Regd. Edinburgh 1923. Vol. liq. (members') 29 Jan. 1937. Capital returned to contributories—£15,108. Final meeting return regd. 22 July 1940 .... **1937**

Stewarton Gas Co. Ld. Regd. in Edinburgh 1940. Dissolved 1 May 1949, undertaking being vested in Scottish Area Gas Board under Gas Act 1948. Holders of ordinary shares (of £1) were entitled to receive £1 1s. British Gas 3% guaranteed stock 1990–95 for each share held **1952**

Stewarts Ld. Regd. Dublin 1897. Removed from Register 1901 .... **1901**

Stewiacke Valley & Lansdowne Railway Co. Inc. by Special Act Nova Scotia 1886. The property which was sold on behalf of the sterling 6% bondholders realised insufficient to pay costs of liquidation and trustees proceeded against shareholders for uncalled capital **1897**

Steyning & District Waterworks Co. Ld. Regd. 1897. Undertaking and assets transferred to North West Sussex Water Board from 1 Apr. 1960 for £22,548, distributed to contributories (per share of £10) as follows—4% preference, £7; ordinary (10% maximum), £16 6s.; and ordinary (7% maximum), £11 6s. The 4% debentures were exchanged for a like amount of a similar mortgage of the Board. Vol. liq. (members') 16 May 1960. Final meeting return regd. 8 June 1962 .... **1963**

Stiefel's Weldless Tube Patents (Foreign) Ld. Regd. 1896. Removed from Register 1906 .... **1901**

Still Engine Co. Ld. See Diesel-Steam Locomotives Ld.

Stilwell & Sons. The undertaking and assets were acquired by Westminster Bank Ld. from 7 Apr. 1923 .... **1924**

Stinnes (Hugo) Ld. Regd. Edinburgh 1925. Vol. liq. (members') July 1950. Final meeting return regd. 20 Apr. 1967 .... **1938**

Stirling and Bridge of Allan Tramways Co. Ld. Regd. Edinburgh 1872. Vol. liq. July 1921. Final meeting return regd. 21 Dec. 1921 .... **1922**

Stirling Gas Light Co. Inc. by Special Act 1898. Dissolved 1 May 1949, undertaking being vested in Scottish Area Gas Board under Gas Act 1948. Holders of securities were entitled to receive British Gas 3% guaranteed stock 1990–95 as follows:

	£	s.	d.
Cons. ord. stock (5% stand.) (per £1)	1	16	0
4% cons. pref. stock (per £100)	102	0	0	**1952**

Stobart (Henry) & Co. Ld. Regd. 1893. Vol. liq. (members') 15 June 1951. Distribution to sole shareholder £1,011,721. Final meeting return regd. 29 Mar. 1955 .... **1956**

Stocal Enamelled Tile & Iron Co. Ld. See below.

Stocal Enamels Ld. Regd. 1914 as Stocal Enamelled Tile & Iron Co. Ld.; name changed 1926. Vol. liq. (members') 22 Dec. 1955. Final meeting return regd. 31 Dec. 1957 .... **1939**

Stock & Bond Trust Corporation Ld. See Dental & Druggists Holdings Ld.

Stock & Debenture Corporation Ld. Regd. 1898. Vol. liq. 26 Jan. 1905. Final meeting return regd. 30 Sept. 1907. Court Order dissolved company on 18 Oct. 1907 .... **1905**

Stock & Share Auction Co. Ld. Regd. 1880. Vol. liq. 9 Dec. 1882. Reconstructed as Stock & Share Auction & Banking Co. Ld. Removed from Register 19 Aug. 1887 .... ***1891**

Stock & Share Auction & Banking Co. Ld. Regd. 1886. Removed from Register 1906 .... ***1892**

Stock Conversion & Investment Trust Ld. See S.C.T. Ld.

Stockbrokers' Banking Corporation Ld. Regd. 1891. Vol. liq. 2 Jan. 1894. Final meeting return regd. 2 May 1895 .... **1894**

Stockport & Hazel Grove Carriage & Tramway Co. Ld. Regd. 1888. Vol. liq. Dec. 1904. The undertaking was sold to Stockport Corporation for £24,000. Removed from Register 1905 .... **1905**

Stockport District Waterworks Co. Undertaking transferred to Stockport Corporation on 29 Sept. 1899 **1900**

Stockport Doubling Co. Ld. See Halifax Doubling Co. Ld.

Stockport Rolling Mills Ld. Regd. 1919 as Stockport Ring Mills (1919) Ld.; name changed Feb. 1946. Vol. liq. (members') 29 July 1960. Capital returned to contributories—5s. 2¾d. per share of 5s. Final meeting return regd. 10 Sept. 1962 .... **1963**

Stocksbridge Gas Co. Inc. by Special Act 1919. Dissolved 1 May 1949, undertaking being vested in East Midland Area Gas Board under Gas Act 1948. Holders of securities were entitled to receive, in respect of each £10 unit held, British Gas 3% guaranteed stock 1990–95 as follows:

	£	s.	d.
Ord. shares (10% max.)	22	0	0
Addit. ord. shares (7½% max.)	17	0	0	**1952**

Stockton & Darlington Steam Tramways Co. Ld. Regd. 1880. Vol. liq. June 1888. Undertaking was acquired in 1897 by Imperial Tramways Co. Ld. for £9,000. Removed from Register 1905 .... **1898**

Stockton-on-Tees Chemical Works Ld. Regd. 1915. Direct controlling interest was held by Pease & Partners Ld. (later Pease Realisation Ld.). Struck off Register 1935 .... **1932**

Stokvis (R. S.) & Zonen, Ld. Regd. 1920. A subsidiary of Handelmaatschappij R. S. Stokvis & Zonen. Vol. liq. (members') 28 Feb. 1949. Final meeting return regd. 28 Mar. 1950 .... **1953**

Stoll Film Co. Ld. Regd. 1918. Vol. liq. 30 Dec. 1925. Properties and certain assets were acquired by Stoll Picture Productions Ld., in which company shareholders were entitled to 3 B preference shares of £1 (credited as fully-paid) for every 4 preference shares of £1 held. Final meeting return regd. 16 Mar. 1927 **1926**

Stoll Picture Productions Ld. Regd. 1920. Vol. liq. (members') 25 Aug. 1948. Capital returned to contributories: 3s. 1¾d. per 8% participating preference share of £1. Final meeting return regd. 30 May 1950. £41 was paid into Companies' Liquidation Account **1951**

Stoll Picture Theatre (Kingsway) Ld. See below.

Stoll Theatre Kingsway, Ld. Regd. 1919 as Stoll Picture Theatre (Kingsway) Ld.; name changed. 1942. Vol. liq. (members') 6 Nov. 1957. Capital returned to contributories—£1 per preference share (of £1) and 13s. 6d. per ordinary share (of 5s.). Final meeting return regd. 11 Dec. 1959 .... **1960**

Stoll Theatres (South) Ld. Regd. 1911 as Chatham Empire Theatre of Varieties Ld.; name changed to Chatham Empire Ld. in 1942 and as above 21 Sept. 1946. A subsidiary of Stoll Theatres Corpn. Ld. Vol. liq. (members') 30 July 1954. Final meeting return regd. 3 Dec. 1954 .... **1950**

Stolz Electrophone Co. (1913) Ld. Regd. 1913. Court Order to wind up 17 Feb. 1914. Struck off Register 1921 .... **1914**

Stone Gas Light & Coke Co. Ld. Regd. 1877 as Stone Gas Light & Coke Co. Ld. name changed to Stone Gas & Electricity Co. Ld. in 1914 and as above in 1939. Dissolved 1 May 1949 under Gas Act 1948 and undertaking vested in West Midland Gas Board **1949**

Stonehall Colliery, Ld. Regd. 1913. Vol. liq. 27 May 1924. Final meeting return regd. 1 Dec. 1925 ...... ***1925**

Stonehams (Hove) Ld. Regd. 1929. In 1937 the business was acquired by Mansfields Ld. Struck off Register 1943 .... **1943**

Stonehaven Gas Co. Ld. Regd. in Edinburgh 1912. Dissolved 1 May 1949, undertaking being vested in Scottish Area Gas Board under Gas Act 1948. Holders of ordinary shares (of £1) were entitled to receive £1 12s. British Gas 3% guaranteed stock 1990–95 for each share held **1952**

Stonehouse & Nailsworth Railway Co. Inc. by Special Act 1863. Under Midland Railway (Additional Powers) Act of 1878, the undertaking became vested in that company **1886**

Stonehouse Pool Improvement Co. Inc. by Special Act 1876. By Act of 1909 the undertaking was acquired

VOL. FOR

by the London & South Western Railway, in which company shareholders received £57 2s. 10d. 3½% preference stock for every 10 shares held, fractions of £1 were paid in cash 1910

Stones Mills Co. Ld. Regd. 1904. Vol. liq. (members') 3 Apr. 1959. Final meeting return regd. 21 Nov. 1959 1909

Stoneware Ld. See Grafton (Management) Ld.

Stoneware (1928) Ld. See Grafton (Management) Ld.

Store Properties Ld. Regd. 1934. Vol. liq. (members') 10 July 1947. Undertaking acquired by Property Holding & Investment Trust Ld.; shareholders were entitled to 4 fully-paid preference shares of £1 and 19 fully-paid ordinary shares of 10s. in that company for every 10 ordinary shares of £1 held. Final meeting return regd. 22 Nov. 1948 1949

Stornoway Electric Supply Co. Ld. Regd. in Edinburgh 1932. Dissolved 1 Apr. 1948, undertaking being vested in the North of Scotland Hydro Electric Board under the Electricity Act 1947. Ordinary shareholders were entitled to receive £1 12s. 6d. British Electricity 3% guaranteed stock (1968–73), for each share (of £1) held 1949

Stornoway Gas Light Co. Ld. Regd. in Edinburgh 1888. Dissolved 1 May 1949, undertaking being vested in Scottish Area Gas Board under Gas Act 1948. Holders of securities were entitled to receive in respect of each £1 unit held, British Gas 3% guaranteed stock 1990–95 as follows:

	£	s.	d.
Ord. shares	2	0	0
5% pref. shares	1	0	0	1952

Stottesdon, Kinlet & Billingsley Light Railway Co. Inc. (under Light Railways Act 1896) by order of Light Railway Commissioners confirmed by Board of Trade 1908. No capital was in issue in 1910 1912

Stoughton (Perak) Rubber Plantations Ld. Regd. 1919. Vol. liq. (members') 25 Jan. 1937. Reconstructed as Padang Senang Rubber Ld., in which company shareholders were entitled to 8·89 shares of 2s. (credited as fully-paid) for every 13 shares of 2s. held. Final meeting return regd. 6 July 1937 1937

Stourbridge & District Water Board. Inc. by Special Act 1909. Dissolved and undertaking vested in the North West Worcestershire Water Board on 1 Oct. 1962 1964

Stourbridge Central Theatre Ld. Regd. 1928. Vol. liq. (members') 29 Dec. 1937. Undertaking sold to Odeon Theatres Ld. (later The Rank Organisation Ld.). Capital returned to contributories—preference shares were repaid at par; £1 0s. 10½d. per ordinary share of £1. Final meeting return regd. 11 July 1939 1938

Stourbridge Navigation (Co. Of Proprietors Of The). Inc. by Special Act 1776. Dissolved 23 Dec. 1949; undertaking vested from 1 Jan. 1948 in British Transport Commission under Transport Act 1947. Holders of ordinary shares were entitled to receive £8 6s. British Transport 3% guaranteed stock 1978–88 for each share (of £10) held 1949

Stourbridge Waterworks Co. Ld. Inc. by Special Act 1854. Regd. 1856. By Act of 1909 undertaking was acquired by Stourbridge and District Water Board. Shareholders were entitled to Water Board redeemable stock sufficient to yield a dividend equal to maximum dividend payable on shares held. Dissolved by Act in Nov. 1909 1910

Stourport Gas Co. Regd. 1865 as Stourport Gas, Coal & Coke Ld.; inc. as above by Special Act 1919. Dissolved 1 May 1949. undertaking being vested in West Midland Area Gas Board under Gas Act 1948. Holders of securities were entitled to receive, in respect of each £100 unit held, British Gas 3% guaranteed stock 1990–95 as follows.

	£	s.	d.
Ord. stock (5% stand.)	106	0	0
New ord. stock (7% stand.)	145	10	0
4½% pref. stock	110	0	0
3½% red. deb. stock (1962)	99	10	0	1952

Stourvale Gas Co. Ld. Regd. 1937. Dissolved 1 May 1949. undertaking being vested in West Midland Area Gas Board under Gas Act 1948. Holders of securities were entitled to receive, in respect of each £1 unit held, British Gas 3% guaranteed stock 1990–95 as follows:

	£	s.	d.
Ord. shares	1	3	0
4½% pref. shares	1	2	0	1952

Stow-on-the-Wold Gas & Coke Co. Ld. Regd. 1860. Dissolved 1 May 1949, undertaking being vested in South Western Area Gas Board under Gas Act 1948. Holders of ordinary shares (of £1) were entitled to receive 11s. British Gas 3% guaranteed stock 1990–95 for each share held 1952

Stowmarket Gas Light & Coke Co. Ld. Regd. 1907. Dissolved 1 May 1949, undertaking being vested in Eastern Area Gas Board under Gas Act 1948.

VOL. FOR

Holders of securities were entitled to receive British Gas 3% guaranteed stock 1990–95 as follows in respect of each £1 unit, unless otherwise stated, of security held:

	£	s.	d.
Ord. shares	1	0	0
5½% pref. shares	1	4	6
5% pref. shares	1	2	3
4% red. debs. (of £100)	100	10	0	1952

Strabane & Letterkenny Railway Co. The Transport (Miscellaneous Provisions) Bill 1971 provided for the dissolution of the company and the transfer of its assets to Coras Iompair Eireann 1971

Straffontein Syndicate Ld. Regd. 1902. Struck off Register 20 Nov. 1925. Restored to Register 5 July 1927. Vol. liq. 10 Feb. 1928. Final meeting return regd. 12 Apr. 1928. 1929

Strafford Collieries Ld. Regd. 1891. Vol. liq. (members') 12 Jan. 1940. Colliery properties acquired by Amalgamated Denaby Collieries ld. for 34,120 fully-paid shares of £1. All capital owned by Maltby Main Colliery Co. Ld. Final meeting return regd. 19 Aug. 1940 1940

Straits & China Textile Co. Ld. Regd. 1916. Vol. liq. (members') 16 jan. 1932. Capital returned to contributories—£27,477 17s. 6d. Final meeting return regd. 26 June 1932 1933

Straits & General Development Co. Ld. Regd. 1902. Vol. liq. (members') 30 Dec. 1930. Reconstructed as Straits & General Development Co. (1931) Ld., in which company shareholders were entitled to 1 share of 2s. (credited with 1s. 6d. paid) for each share of 2s. held. Final meeting return regd. 27 May 1933 1931

Straits Development Co. Ld. Regd. 1894. Reconstructed 1902 as Straits and General Development Co. Ld in which company shareholders were entitled to 1 share of £1 (credited with 14s. paid) for each share of £1 held. Removed from Register 1904 1908

Straits Fire Insurance Co. Ld. Established 1866. Undertaking was acquired in 1894 by Commercial Union Assurance Co. Ld. 1894

Straits Insurance Co. Ld. Inc. India 1883. In liquidation in 1900 1900

Straits Prospecting Syndicate Ld. Regd. 1888. Removed from Register 1905 1894

Straits Rubber Co. Ld. Regd. 1909. Vol. liq. 29 Dec. 1919. Reconstructed as company of same name. Shareholders were entitled to 3 shares of £1 (credited as fully-paid) in new company for each share of £1 held. Final meeting return regd. 24 Sept.1921....... 1920

Straker-Squire Ld. Regd. 1913 as Straker-Squire (1913) Ld.; name changed June 1917. Vol. liq. 12 May 1925. Reconstructed as company of same name. The 8% mortgage debenture stock was exchanged for an equal amount of similar stock in new company. No return was made to 10% 2nd mortgage debenture stockholders or shareholders. Final meeting return regd. 9 Oct. 1926 1926

Straker-Squire Ld. Regd. 1925. Receiver appointed 16 July 1926. Proceeds from assets were expected to provide only for prior charges ranking before debenture stock. Struck off Register 20 Jan. 1931 1931

Strakers & Love Ld. Regd. 1925. Vol. liq. (members') 4 Jan. 1950. Capital returned to contributories—£81 12s. cash and £10 17s. 7·46d. Treasury stock 1977–80 per share of £50. Final meeting return regd. 23 Oct. 1964 1966

Stranaghan & Stephens Stores, Ld. Regd. 1895. Vol. liq. (members') 12 Apr. 1943. Final meeting return regd. 8 July 1948 1949

Strand & Interchangeable Signs Ld. Regd. 1926. Vol. liq. (members') 31 Dec. 1940. All shares owned by Strand Electric & Engineering Co. Ld. Final meeting return regd. 2 Jan. 1942 1941

Stranraer Gas Co. Ld. Regd. in Edinburgh 1916. Dissolved 1 May 1949, undertaking being vested in Scottish Area Gas Board under Gas Act 1948. Holders of ordinary shares (of £1) were entitled to receive £1 15s. 6d. British Gas 3% guaranteed stock 1990–95 for each share held 1952

Stratford-upon-Avon and Midland Junction Railway Co. Inc. by Special Act 1908. In 1923 the undertaking was merged into the London Midland & Scottish Railway Co. The 6% Bonds were to be repaid on 1st July 1923 at par. Holders of every £100 of Consolidated Ordinary Stock were entitled to £39 5s. in cash 1924

Stratford upon Avon Investment Co. Ld. Regd,. 1895 as Stratford upon Avon Labourers Dwellings Co. Ld. Dissolved 5 Jan. 1983 1910

Stratford upon Avon Labourers Dwellings Co. Ld. See Stratford upon Avon Investment Co. Ld.

VOL. FOR

Stratford-upon-Avon Railway Co. Inc. by Special Act. Amalgamated with Great Western Railway Co. in 1883. Holders of £100 debenture stock, preference shares (1861 or 1874) or ordinary shares received £100 4% debenture, 5% preference or ordinary stock in the purchasing company respectively **1884**

Stratford-upon-Avon, Towcester & Midland Junction Railway Co. Inc. by Special Act 1879 as Easton Neston Mineral and Towcester, Roade and Olney Junction Railway Co.; name changed by Act of 1882. Amalgamated as Stratford-upon Avon and Midland Junction Railway Co. by Act of 1908. Holders of £100 debenture stock (1887), 5% perpetual rent-charge interest guaranteed shares or 5% preference shares received £100, £60 or £60 consolidated stock in the new company respectively **1909**

Stratharlie Rubber Co. Ld. Regd. Edinburgh 1922. Vol. liq. Dec. 1926. Undertaking acquired by Kenny (Selangor) Rubber Co. Ld., in which company shareholders were entitled to 4⅕ shares of £1 for each share of £1 held. Struck off Register 10 June 1938 **1939**

Strathclyde Electricity Supply Co. Ld. Regd. 1905. All capital owned by Clyde Valley Electrical Power Co. Dissolved 1 Apr. 1948 under Electricity Act 1947 **1938**

Strathendrick & Aberfoyle Railway Co. Inc. by Special Act 1880. Under North British Railway Act of 1891 the undertaking was amalgamated with that company. Holders of ordinary shares were repaid at par in cash; 4% loans and feu duties were taken over by purchasing company **1892**

Strathida (Perak) Rubber Estates Ld. Regd. 1910. Vol. liq. (members') 2 Nov. 1959. All capital acquired by Pataling Rubber Estates Ld. Final meeting return regd. 6 Aug. 1960 .... **1961**

Strathmiglo Gas Co. Ld. Regd. in Edinburgh 1910; Dissolved 1 May 1949, undertaking being vested in Scottish Area Gas Board under Gas Act 1948. Holders of ordinary shares (of £1) were entitled to recieve £1 13*s*. 4*d*. British Gas 3% guaranteed stock 1990–95 for each share held **1952**

Strathmore Rubber Co. Ld. Regd. Edinburgh 1907. Vol. liq. Mar. 1920. Reconstructed as company of same name. Shareholders were entitled to 3½ shares of £1 (credited as fully-paid) in new company for each share of £1 held. Struck off Register 9 Apr. 1937. **1938**

Strathmore Rubber Co. Ld. Regd. Edinburgh 1920. A subsidiary of Scottish Malayan Estates Ld. Vol. liq. (members') 1 Apr. 1959. Final meeting return regd. 10 Feb. 1961 .... **1951**

Strathpeffer & Dingwall Electric Co. Ld. Regd. Edinburgh 1909. Vol. liq. 13 Dec. 1926. All creditors were to be paid in full. Undertaking was acquired by Ross-shire Electric Supply Co. Ld. Struck off Register 27 Sept. 1932 .... **1938**

Stratton Trust Ld. Regd. 1924. Vol. liq. (members') 21 Apr. 1933. Holders of 6½% 1st mortgage debenture stock were repaid in cash at 102½%. Capital returned to contributories—3*s*. 3·70758*d*. per share of £1 7*s*. 6*d*. paid, *plus* a distribution in specie. Final meeting return regd. 22 Nov. 1934 .... **1948**

Stratton's Independence Ld. Regd. 1899. Vol. liq. Aug. 1908 for reconstruction as company of same name. Shareholders were entitled to 1 share of 2*s*. 6*d*. (credited with 1*s*. 6*d*. paid) in new company for each share of £1 held. Removed from Register 1910..... **1909**

Stratton's Independence Ld. Regd. 1908. Court Order to wind up 20 Feb. 1917. Liquidator released 3 Sept. 1918. Struck off Register 20 Mar. 1925 .... **1917**

Strawsons Ld. Regd. 1889. Vol. liq. 6 May 1897. Final meeting return regd. 18 Apr. 1898 .... **1898**

Stray Shot & Excelsior Gold Mines Ld. Regd. 1895. Court Order to wind up 6 Mar. 1899. Removed from Register 1908 .... **1900**

Strazza & Co. Ld. Regd. 1897. Removed from Register 1909 .... **1901**

Streatham & General Estates Co. Ld. Regd. 1881 as Streatham Hill & General Estates Development Co. Ld.; name changed May 1886. Vol. liq. Aug. 1890. Court Order to continue winding up under supervision Sept. 1890. Final meeting return regd. 17 Feb. 1896. .... **1891**

Streatham Hill & General Estates Development Co. Ld. *See* Streatham & General Estates Co. Ld.

Streatham Recreations Ld. Regd. 1924. Struck off Register 1927. .... ***1925**

Street Brothers Ld. Regd. Edinburgh 1899. Vol. liq. June 1906. Court Orders: to wind up June 1906; to dissolve 10 June 1908 .... **1907**

Streeter & Co. Ld. Regd. 1895. Vol. liq. Mar. 1905. Capital returned to contributories—20*s*. per preference share of £1; 12*s*. 6*d*. per ordinary or management share of £1. Removed from Register 1906 .. **1907**

Stretford & District Gas Board. Inc. by Special Act 1922. Dissolved 1 May 1949, undertaking being vested in North-Western Area Gas Board undr Gas Act 1948. Liability in respect of certain mortgage loans assumed by the area Board **1952**

Stretford Gas Co. Established 1852. Inc. by Special Act 1862. Under Act of 1921 the undertaking was purchased by Manchester Corporation for £285,000 in cash. The Corporation assumed liability for debenture stock.. **1922**

Strichen Electrical Supply Co. Ld. Regd. Edinburgh. Vol. liq. (members') 17 Dec. 1936. All shares owned by Scottish Power Co. Ld. Final meeting return regd. 3 Nov. 1937.. **1937**

Strick Line Ld. Regd. 1896 as Anglo-Algerian Steamship Co. (1896) Ld.; name changed Jan. 1913. Vol. liq. 6 Jan. 1922. Final meeting return regd. 27 Aug. 1929.. **1922**

Stringertype Manufacturing Co. Ld. Regd. 1900 as Stringertype Manufacturing Co. (1900) Ld.; name changed Mar. 1911. Struck off Register 4 Oct. 1935 **1936**

Stroud & Painswick (Light) Railway Co. Inc. by Special Act 1896. No steps were taken to construct line; time for acquisition of land expired Nov. 1900..... **1901**

Stroud Brewery Co. Ld. Regd. 1888. All capital was owned by West Country Brewery Holdings Ld. Vol. liq. (members') 1 May 1961. Final meeting return regd.7 Jan. 1964 .... **1961**

Stroud Electric Supply Co. Ld. Regd. 1914. Dissolved 1 Apr. 1948, undertaking being vested in the British (later Central) Electricity Authority and Midlands Area Board under the Electricity Act 1947. Holders of ordinary and preference shares were entitled to receive British Electricity 3% guaranteed stock (1968–73) as follows—£2 10*s*. for each ordinary share (of £1) held and £8 for each preference share (of £5) held **1949**

Stroud Gas Light & Coke Co. Ld. Estd. 1833; inc. by Special Act 1864. Dissolved 1 May 1949, undertaking being vested in South Western Area Gas Board under Gas Act 1948. Holders of securities were entitled to receive, in respect of each £100 unit held, British Gas 3% guaranteed stock 1990–95 as follows

	£	s.	d.
Cons. ord. stock (5% basic)..............	122	10	0
3½% red. deb. stock	100	0	0

A distribution on cons. ord. stock of 4·2387% out of reserves was made in Oct. 1953 .... **1952**

Stroud Water Co. Inc. by Special Act 1882. By the Stroud District Water Board, &c. Act of 1939 the undertaking was transferred to Stroud District Water Board. A ordinary stock was repaid at 205%, B ordinary at 175%, preference at 125%, 6% debenture at 103%, 5% debenture at 130% and 4% debenture at 102½% **1940**

Strout's Brewery Co. Ld. Regd. 1889. Vol. liq. 18 Apr. 1918. Undertaking was acquired by Tennant Brothers Ld. Final meeting return regd. 31 Aug. 1921 **1919**

Stuart (A.A.) & Sons (Contractors) Ld. Regd in Edinburgh 4 May 1948 as A. A. Stuart (Carmyle) Ld.; name changed to A. A. Stuart & Sons (Glasgow) Ld. in Feb. 1951 and to current title in June 1960. Winding-up order 14 Apr. 1967. Dissolved by order of Court of Sessions 19 Sept. 1984. Total dividend of 26·53p in £1 paid to ordinary creditors. No distribution made to any class of shareholder. £25,914 in respect of unclaimed distributions consigned to Accountant of Court **1986–7**

Stuart & Sons (Housing) Ld. *See* Stuart Construction Ld.

Stuart Construction Ld. Regd. 1937 as Stuart & Sons (Housing) Ld.; name changed Sept. 1955. Vol. liq. (members') 24 June 1959. Preference capital repaid at par on 31 Jan. 1961. Capital returned to contributories—13*s*. 9⅛*d*. per ordinary share of 5*s*. Final meeting return regd. 11 Jan. 1965 .... **1965**

Stubbs Randfontein Gold Mining Co. Ld. Inc.Transvaal 1899. Vol. liq. July 1909, the undertaking and assets were sold to the Randfontein South Gold Mining Co. Ld. for 174,000 shares of £1 .... **1910**

Stuckey's Banking Co. Ld. Inc. 1806, regd. as limited 1892. Vol. liq. 1909. The undertaking and assets were acquired by Parr's Bank Ld., in which company shareholders were entitled to 5 shares of £50 (£10 paid) for every 4 shares of £60 (£12 paid) held **1910**

Stutchbury's Ld. Regd. 1906. Struck off Register Apr. 1929 .... **1930**

Suakin Mining Syndicate Ld. Regd. 1904. Vol. liq. Nov. 1909. Removed from Register 1910......................... **1910**

Suanlambah (Borneo) Tobacco Co. Ld. Regd. 1889. Vol. liq. 29 June 1891. Amalgamated with British Borneo Trading & Planting Co. Ld. in which company shareholders were entitled to 2 fully-paid shares of

*See Stock Exchange Year-Book.

VOL. FOR

£1 *plus* 10*s*. in cash for each share of £5 (2 10*s*. paid) held. Final meeting return regd. 9 Apr. 1895 .... **1892**

Sub-Target Co. Ld. Regd. 1906. Vol. liq. 27 June 1919. Final meeting return regd. 7 Oct. 1920 .... **1920**

Subil Gold Mines Ld. Regd. 1901. Vol. liq. Sept. 1905. Amalgamated with six other companies under the title of African Mines Ld. in which company shareholders were entitled to 2 shares of 10*s*. (credited with 8*s*. paid) for each share of £1 held. Removed from Register 1906 .... **1906**

Submarine Cables' Trust. Established by trust deed 1871. The outstanding certificates of £100 were redeemed at 120% in Nov. 1926. Holders of the 3,381 outstanding Coupons of Reversion received a total distribution of £153 2*s*. 6*d*. per coupon **1927**

Submarine Mining & Torpedo Explosives Co. Ld. Regd. 1888. Vol. liq. 24 June 1892. Final meeting return regd. 4 Oct. 1895 .... **1893**

Submarine Telegraph Co. Inc. 1852. Vol. liq. 19 June 1889. According to a report presented in Apr. 1890 the capital was returned in full and certain further monies were in the hands of the liquidators **1892**

Submersible & J. L. Motors Ld. *See* Submersible Motors Ld.

Submersible Motors Ld. Regd. 1907 as Ship Cleaning Co. (operating Macdonald's Patents) Ld.; name changed Apr. 1911 to Submersible Motors Ld.; name changed to Submersible & J. L. Motors Ld. in Feb. 1912 and as above in Aug. 1918. Vol. liq. (members') 20 Mar. 1930. No capital returned to contributories. Final meeting return regd. 22 Nov. 1932 .... **1931**

Subur Rubber Estates Ld. Regd. 1925. Vol. liq. 28 Aug. 1928. Undertaking and assets were transferred to North Malay Rubber Estates Ld., in which company shareholders were entitled to 5 fully-paid shares of 2*s*. for every 11 shares of 2*s*. held. Final meeting return regd. 19 Oct. 1929 .... **1929**

Suburban Land & Cottage Co. Ld. Regd. 1880. Removed from Register 1911 .... **1897**

Suburban Laundries Ld. Undertaking and assets were acquired by Advance Laundries Ld. **1929**

Success and Ressouvenir Co. Ld. Regd. 1900. Vol. liq. 3 Feb. 1914. Final meeting return regd. 23 Apr. 1915 **1914**

Suchi Timber Co. Ld. Regd. 1908. Vol. liq. (members') 31 Oct. 1938. Cia. Maderera de Durago S.A. of Mexico City was beneficial owner of all shares. Final meeting return regd. 2 May 1939 .... **1939**

Sucre Mine Ld. Regd. 1882. Vol. liq. (members') 26 Mar. 1935. Capital returned to contributories—2*s*. $1\frac{11}{16}$*d*. per preference or ordinary share of £1. Final meeting return regd. 22 Aug. 1935 .... **1936**

Sudan Building & Agricultural Co. Ld. Inc. Sudan 1925. Vol. liq. Mar. 1929. The undertaking and assets were sold to Contomichalos, Darke & Co. (1929) Ld., in which company shareholders received 17 preference shares of £1 for every 20 preference shares of £1 held and 15 preference shares for every 40 ordinary shares of £1 held **1930**

Sudan Construction and Equipment Co. Ld. Regd. 1924. Outstanding $4\frac{1}{2}$% guaranteed debenture stock was redeemed on 1 Feb. 1945 at par. Vol. liq. (members') 6 June 1945. All shares were owned by Sudan Government. Final meeting return regd. 25 July 1945 .... **1946**

Sudan Experimental Plantation Syndicate Ld. *See* Sudan Plantations Syndicate Ld.

Sudan Exploration Ld. Regd. 1903. Receiver appointed 3 May 1915. Struck off Register Apr. 1929 .... **1930**

Sudan Gold Field Co. Ld. Regd. 1908. Vol. liq. 3 Mar. 1925. Capital returned to contributories—4*d*. per share of 10*s*. at Apr. 1925; further payments (if any) not known. Final meeting return regd. 18 Feb. 1931 **1926**

Sudan Gold Field Ld. Regd. 1904. Vol. liq. 1908 for reconstruction as Sudan Gold Field Co. Ld., in which company shareholders were entitled to 1 share of 10*s*. (credited with 6*s*. paid) for each share of £1 held. Removed from Register 1911 .... **1909**

Sudan Gold Mines Ld. *See* Gabait Gold Mines Ld.

Sudan Light & Power Co. Ld. Regd. 1925. Capital purchased by Sudan Government and debenture stocks redeemed. Control of company removed to Sudan in 1952. Vol. liq. (members') 31 Mar. 1959. Struck off Register 8 Feb. 1963 .... **1952**

Sudan Mines Ld. Regd. 1904. Vol. liq. Nov. 1910. Removed from Register 1911 .... **1911**

Sudan Plantations Syndicate Ld. Regd. 1904 as Sudan Experimental Plantation Syndicate Ld.; name changed 1907. Vol. liq. (members') 4 Apr. 1951. Capital returned to contributoties—£3 17*s*. 6*d*. per share (of £1). Final meeting return regd. 21 Apr. 1953 .... **1954**

Sudan Salt Ld. Regd. 1929. Vol. liq. (members') 4 Apr. 1952. Capital returned to contributories—1*s*. 6*d*. per 1*s*. stock. £1,239 was paid into Companies' Liquidation Account. Final meeting return regd. 21 Apr. 1953 .... **1954**

Sudbury (C. & F.) (1922) Ld. Regd. 1922. Receiver appointed in Aug. 1931. Assets were acquired by F. A. Sudbury Ld. A distribution of 5*s*. 6*d*. in £ to debenture holders was made in Feb. 1934. Struck off Register 19 Mar. 1937 .... **1934**

Sudbury (F. A.) Ld. Regd. 1933. Receiver appointed 9 Dec. 1936. Struck off Register 18 Apr. 1947 .... **1938**

Sudbury Gas & Coke Co. Ld. Regd. 1937. Dissolved 1 May 1949, undertaking being vested in Eastern Area Gas Board under Gas Act 1948. Holders of securities were entitled to receive, in respect of each £1 unit held, British Gas 3% guaranteed stock 1990–95 as follows:

	£ s. d.	
Ord. shares ($8\frac{1}{2}$% max.)	1 15 6	
$6\frac{1}{2}$% pref. shares	1 7 6	**1952**

Sudbury Syndicate Ld. Regd. 1914. Vol. liq. 5 Sept. 1919 for reconstruction as Kirkland Lake Proprietary (1919) Ld, in which company shareholders were entitled to 5 shares of £1 for every 4 shares of £1 held. Final meeting return regd. 1 July 1920 .... **1920**

Sudd Fuel (Suddite) Ld. Regd. 1912. Receiver for debenture holders appointed 23 July 1915. Struck off Register Jan. 1932 .... **1932**

Suddia Road Tea Co. Ld. Regd. 1892. Vol. liq. Dec. 1911. The undertaking and assets were sold to Assam Frontier Tea Co. Ld. for 3,000 ordinary and 3,000 preferred shares of £10 (credited as fully-paid). Removed from Register 1913 .... **1912**

Suez Oil Co. Ld. Regd. 1910. Vol. liq. Nov. 1915 for reconstruction as Suez Oil Co. (1915) Ld., in which company shareholders were entitled to 1 share of 10*s*. (credited with 9*s*. paid) for each share of £1 held. Removed from Register 1911 .... **1916**

Suez Oil Co. (1915) Ld. Regd. 1916. Vol. liq. 6 Nov. 1922. Reconstructed as Suez Oil Co. Ld., in which company shareholders were entitled to 5 shares of 2*s*. (credited with 1*s*. 6*d*. paid) for each share of 10*s*. held. Final meeting return regd. 21 Aug. 1924...... **1923**

Suez Oil Co. Ld. Regd. 1922. Struck off Register 7 Mar. 1939 .... **1940**

Suffolk Steamship Co. Ld. Regd. 1881. Vol. liq. Mar. 1890. Capital returned to contributories—£4 11*s*. 5*d*. per share of £50. Final meeting return regd. 27 June 1890 .... **1891**

Suffolk Trust Co. Ld. Regd. 1896. Vol. liq. 21 Dec. 1909. Final meeting return regd. 29 Dec. 1916 .... **1910**

Sugar & Malt Products Ld. Regd. 1906. Vol. liq. 19 Aug. 1919. Undertaking and assets were acquired by Manbre Sugar and Malt Ld. (later Manbre & Garton Ld.). Final meeting return regd. 29 May 1920 .... **1920**

Sugar Beet & Crop Driers Ld. Regd. 1926. Receiver appointed 31 Dec. 1930; ceased to act 7 Nov. 1939. Court Order to wind up 13 Oct. 1931. Liquidator released 22 Aug. 1940. Court Order to dissolve 11 Oct. 1940 .... ***1932**

Sugar Refiners' Appliances Co. Ld. Regd. Edinburgh 1882. Vol. liq. July 1888. Final meeting return regd. 14 July 1891 .... **1889**

Sugarloaf "25-Mile" Cement Leases Ld. Regd. 1896. Removed from Register 1901 .... **1904**

Sugg (Frank) Ld. Regd 1906. Receiver appointed 6 Dec. 1923. Court Order to wind up 18 Dec. 1923 .... ***1924**

Sukkoria Goldfields Ld. Regd. 1910. Vol. liq. 13 Aug. 1913. Final meeting return regd. 8 Nov. 1918 ..... **1914**

Suloh Rubber Estates Ld. Inc. in Federated Malay States 1925. Vol. liq. (members') 22 Oct. 1960. Capital returned to contributories—$1·375 per share of $0·50. $61,322·95 paid into Companies' Liquidation Account. Final meeting return regd. 4 May 1962 .... **1963**

Sulphate of Ammonia Co. Ld. Regd. 1908. Vol. liq. 19 Sept. 1910. Final meeting return regd. 10 Dec. 1916 **1911**

Sulphide Corporation Ld. Regd. 1895 as Sulphide Corpn. (Ashcroft's Process) Ld. Vol. liq. (members') 23 Jan. 1950, business transferred to Sulphide Corpn. Pty. Ld. (inc. in New South Wales). Final meeting return regd. 1 Aug. 1951 .... **1952**

Sulphides Reduction (New Process) Ld. Regd. 1902. Court Order to wind up 7 Nov. 1905. Removed from Register 1910 .... **1906**

Sultana Mine of Canada Ld. Regd. 1899. Removed from Register 1906 .... **1904**

Sulymah & Sherboro' Trading Co. Ld. Regd. 1882. Vol. liq. 19 Mar. 1886. Court Orders: to wind up Apr. 1886; to dissolve 10 Apr. 1891 .... **1887**

Sumatra Consolidated (Extended) Rubber Plantations Ld. Regd. 1925. Vol. liq. (members') 22 Dec. 1932. Undertaking acquired by Padang Langkat Rubber Estates Ld. for 628,390 fully-paid shares of 2*s*. which

**See Stock Exchange Year-Book.*

VOL. FOR

were distributed in specie. Final meeting return regd. 13 Jan. 1936 .... *1933

Sumatra-Deli Rubber Estates Ld. Regd. 1907. Vol. liq. Apr. 1910. The estates were sold for £50,000 in cash. Removed from Register 1912 .... **1911**

Sumatra Gold Mines Development Co. Ld. Regd. 1937. Struck off Register 3 Oct. 1939 .... **1940**

Sumatra Petroleum Co. Ld. Regd. 1910. Vol. liq. 6 Aug. 1914. Undertaking and assets were sold to Algemeene Exploratie Maatschappij. Shareholders received 1s. cash per share of £1. Final meeting return regd. 3 Nov. 1914 .... **1915**

Sumatra Planting Syndicate Ld. Regd. 1916. Vol. liq. (members') 25 May 1934. Capital returned to contributories—7·986d. in cash and 5 fully-paid shares of 2s. in Eastern Sumatra Rubber Estates Ld. for each share of £1 held. £56 11s. 4d. was paid into Companies' Liquidation Account. Final meeting return regd. 12 Dec. 1935 .... **1935**

Sumatra Proprietary Rubber Plantations Ld. Regd. 1909. Vol. liq. (members') 22 Dec. 1932. Undertaking and assets were acquired by Padang Langkat Rubber Estates Ld in which company shareholders were entitled to 11 shares of 2s. (credited as fully-paid) for every 4 shares of £1 held. Final meeting return regd. 13 Jan. 1934. .... **1933**

Sumatra Syndicate Ld. Regd. Feb. 1904 as Java Syndicate Ld.; name changed Sept. 1904. Vol. liq 28 June 1906. Removed from Register 1912 .... **1907**

Sumatra Tea Estates Ld. Regd. 1925. Vol. liq. (members') 27 Feb. 1953. No capital returned to contributories. Final meeting return regd. 16 Nov. 1953 .. **1955**

Sumatra Tobacco Plantations Co. Ld. Regd. 1888. Capital returned to contributories—4s. 0½d. per share of 6s. 8d. at 17 Oct. 1904; further payments (if any) not known. Removed from Register 1905 .... **1950**

Summerlee & Mossend Iron & Steel Co. Ld. See below.

Summerlee Iron Co. Ld. Regd. Edinburgh 1896 as Summerlee & Mossend Iron & Steel Co. Ld.; name changed 1906. Collieries, &c. vested in National Coal Board as from 1 Jan. 1947. Vol. liq. (members') 7 July 1954. Capital returned to contributories—£5 6s. 10½d. per share of 12s. (1s. paid). £68 19s. 11d. paid into Companies' Liquidation Account. Final meeting return regd. 26 Jan. 1961 .... **1962**

Summerscales Ld. Regd. 1898 as Summerscales (W.) & Sons (1898) Ld.; name changed July 1911. Vol. liq. 21 Jan. 1920. Final meeting return regd. 28 Apr. 1924 .... **1920**

Summerscales (W.) & Sons (1898) Ld. See Summerscales Ld.

Summit Flat Gold Mines Ld. Regd. 1896. Struck off Register 18 Nov. 1902 .... **1903**

Summit Motor Engineering & Transport Co. Ld. Regd. 1919. Struck off Register Mar. 1930 .... **1931**

Sumner Leivesley & Kennedy Ld. Regd. 1920. Vol. liq. 24 Apr. 1923. Final meeting return regd. 3 Dec. 1924 **1924**

Sun Fuel Co. Ld. Regd. 1919. Vol. liq. June 1922. Struck off Register 1929 .... **1923**

Sun Gas Co. Ld. See Alby United Carbide Factories Ld.

Sun Investment & Trust Ld. See S.C.T. Ld.

Sun Investment Trust Ld. See S.C.T. Ld.

Sun Life Assurance Co. of India Ld. Regd. 1891. Vol. liq. 13 May 1897. Business was transferred to Sun Life Assurance Society; shareholders received back their paid-up capital plus 10% bonus. Final meeting return regd. 18 Apr. 1898 .... **1898**

Sun Mill Co. Ld. Regd. 13 Jan. 1858 as Oldham Building & Manufacturing Co. Ld.; name changed July 1867. Vol. liq. (members') 8 Mar. 1960. Capital returned to contributories—£1 10s. 8½d. per share of 10s. £155 11s. paid into Companies' Liquidation Account in respect of unclaimed dividends. Final meeting return regd. 21 Sept. 1962 .... **1963**

Sun Power Co. (Eastern Hemisphere) Ld. Regd. 1908. Vol. liq. Oct. 1913 for reconstruction as Sun Power Co. Ld. in which company shareholders were entitled to 1 fully-paid ordinary share of £1 for each ordinary share of £1 held or 100 fully-paid ordinary shares of £1 for each founders' share of 1s. held. Struck off Register Aug. 1929 .... **1930**

Sun Power Co. Ld. Regd. 1913. Struck off Register 1925 **1916**

Sun Ray & Health Institutes (West London) Ld. Regd. 1928. All shares were owned by National Sun Ray & Health Centres Ld. Struck off Register 1934 .... **1932**

Sun Ray Treatment Centre (Glasgow) Ld. Regd. Edinburgh 1927. All shares were owned by National Sun Ray & Health Centre Ld. Struck off Register 18 Nov. 1930 .... **1932**

Sun Ray Treatment Centre Ld. Regd. 1927. All shares were owned by National Sun Ray & Health Centres Ld. Struck off Register 1934 .... **1932**

Sun Syndicate Ld. Regd. 1897. Vol. liq. Aug. 1908. Removed from Register 1912 .... **1909**

VOL. FOR

Sunbeam & Twilight Gold Mines Ld. Regd. 1895. Vol. liq. 16 May 1898. Final meeting return regd. 8 Feb. 1899 .... **1899**

Sunbeam & Vigilant Gold Mines Ld. Regd. 1896. Vol. liq. 21 Oct. 1896. Final meeting return regd. 2 Mar. 1898 .... **1897**

Sunbeam Art Silk Ld. See Sunbeam Holdings Ld.

Sunbeam Gold Mining Co. Ld. Read 1889. Vol. liq. 8 Dec. 1892. Final meeting return regd. 21 Sept. 1893 **1893**

Sunbeam Gramophone & Record Co. Ld. See Sunbeam Presswork & Conveyors Ld.

Sunbeam Holdings Ld. Regd. 1928 as Sunbeam Art Silk Ld.; name changed July 1929. Struck off Register 27 Jan. 1942 .... **1924**

Sunbeam Lamp Co. Ld. Regd. 1887. Vol. liq. May 1912. Receiver appointed 14 May 1912. Struck off Register Mar. 1929 .... **1930**

Sunbeam Presswork & Conveyors Ld. Regd. 1928 as Sunbeam Gramophone & Record Co. Ld.; name changed 23 Jan. 1920. Receiver appointed 6 June 1930. Assets realised insufficient to meet claims of debenture holders. Struck off Register 8 Dec. 1936 **1937**

Sunburst Gold Mining Co. Ld. Regd. 1893. Vol. liq. 31 July 1899. Reconstructed as Union Jack Consolidated Mines Ld. in which company shareholders were entitled to 2 shares of 5s. (credited with 3s. 6d. paid) for each share of 10s. held. Final meeting return regd. 14 Aug. 1901 .... **1900**

Sunbury Gas Consumers' Co. Ld. Regd. 1862. Act dissolved 4 Sept. 1914 .... **1915**

Sunday Times Ld. See United Publications Ld.

Sunderland District Electric Tramways Ld. See Sunderland District Transport Co. Ld.

Sunderland District Transport Co. Ld. Regd. 1903 as Sunderland District Electric Tramways Ld.; name changed Feb. 1925. Receiver for 1st mortgage debenture holders appointed in June 1926; ceased to act Nov. 1927. Undertaking and assets were acquired by Sunderland District Omnibus Co. Ld. Prior lien bondholders were repaid at par. 1st mortgage debenture holders were entitled to 1 fully-paid share of 5s. in acquiring company for each £1 debenture held. Holders of income bonds and shares were entitled to subscribe for shares at par. Struck off Register Jan. 1931 .... **1931**

Sunderland Gas Co. Inc. by Special Act 1857. Dissolved 1 May 1949, undertaking being vested in Northern Area Gas Board under Gas Act 1948. Holders of ordinary stock (6% basic) were entitled to receive, in respect of each £100 unit held, £140 British Gas 3% guaranteed stock 1990–95 .... **1952**

Sunderland Theatres Ld. Regd. 1895. Vol. liq. Aug. 1907. Removed from Register 1908 .... **1908**

Sunderland Tramways Co. Ld. Regd. 1877. The undertaking was sold in 1900 to Sunderland Corporation for £35,000. Capital returned to contributories—£6 3s. 9d. per share of £10 at 20 Dec. 1900; further payments (if any) not known. Removed from Register 1901 .... **1901**

Sunfruit Products Ld. Regd. 1929. A winding-up order was made on 8 June 1931. Liquidator released 24 June 1949. Struck off Register 1 Sept. 1953 .... **1953**

Sungei Bahru Rubber Estates Ld. Regd. 1909. Vol. liq. (members') 2 Mar. 1932. Undertaking and assets were acquired by company of same name. Shareholders were entitled to 10 fully-paid shares of 2s. in new company for each preference share of £1 held or 6 shares of 2s. (credited with 1s. 4d. paid) for each ordinary share of £1 held. Final meeting return regd. 13 Feb. 1933 .... **1933**

Sungei Batu (Malaya) Rubber Estates Ld. Regd. 1912. Vol. liq. (members') 1 June 1962. Capital returned to contributories—£4 17s. 10½d. per share of £1. Final meeting return regd. 28 Oct. 1965 .... **1967**

Sungei Buaya (Sumatra) Rubber Co. Ld. Regd. 13 Aug. 1909. Dissolved 7 Mar. 1974 .... **1970**

Sungei Chermang Rubber Co. Ld. Regd. 1929. Vol. liq. (members') 2 Mar. 1959. All capital owned by Kuala Lumpur-Kepong Amalgamated Ld. Final meeting return regd. 4 Oct. 1961 .... **1963**

Sungei Chinoh Rubber Co. Ld. Regd. 1914. Vol. liq. 12 Mar. 1920. Reconstructed as company of same name. Shareholders were entitled to 4 shares of £1 (credited as fully-paid) for each share of £1 held. Final meeting return regd. 18 Oct. 1921................. **1921**

Sungei Chinoh Rubber Estate Co. Ld. Regd. 1920 Dissolved 15 Mar. 1981 .... **1962**

Sungei Choh Rubber Estate Co. Ld. Regd. 1907. Vol. liq. 29 Mar. 1920. Reconstructed as Sungei Choh Rubber Co. Ld., in which company shareholders were entitled to 4 shares of £1 (credited as fully-paid) for each share of £1 held. Final meeting return regd. 8 Apr. 1921 .... **1921**

Sungei Choh Rubber Co. Ld. Regd. 1920. Vol. liq. (members') 9 Jan. 1959. Undertaking and assets acquired by Anglo Oriental Plantations Ld. in which company stockholders were entitled to receive 8 fully-paid shares of 2s. plus 4s. cash for every £1 stock held. Final meeting return regd. 3 June 1960 ...... **1961**

Sungei Dangar (Malay) Rubber Co. Ld. Regd. 1911. Vol. liq. 8 Mar. 1927. Undertaking and assets were acquired by Tai Tak Plantations Ld., in which company shareholders were entitled to 636 shares of 2s. (credited as fully-paid) for every 100 shares of £1 held. Final meeting return regd. 20 Sept. 1927 .... **1927**

Sungei Engun Rubber Estate Ld. Regd. 1926. Vol. liq. (members') 24 Nov. 1933. Undertaking and assets were acquired by company of same name (later Cannon Street Investments Ld.). Shareholders were entitled to 3 ordinary shares of 2s. (credited with 1s. 1d. paid) in new company for every 4 shares of 2s. held. Debenture holders were entitled to 800 fully-paid preference shares of 2s. and 201 fully-paid ordinary shares of 2s. for every £100 held. Final meeting return regd. 31 May 1935 ...... **1934**

Sungei Gettah Rubber Estates Ld. Regd. 1925. Vol. liq. 18 Dec. 1950. Undertaking and assets acquired by Aberfoyle Plantations Ld. Shareholders were entitled to receive 31·542 fully-paid shares of 2s. for every 100 shares of 2s. held. Final meeting return regd. 26 Mar. 1954 ...... **1955**

Sungei Kechil Cocoanut & Rubber Co. Ld. Regd. Edinburgh 1912. Vol. liq. May 1914 for reconstruction under title of Pitchikawa Rubber Estate Ld., in which company shareholders were entitled to 1 share of 15s. fully-paid, for each share of £1 held. Final meeting return regd. 18 Sept. 1915 ...... **1915**

Sungei Krian Rubber Estate Ld. Regd. 26 July 1909; voluntary winding-up 26 Nov. 1985. All capital owned by Barlow Holdings p.l.c. Dissolved 17 May 1986 ...... **1980–1**

Sungei Liang Rubber Co. Ld. Regd. 1909. Receiver appointed in Oct. 1913. Assets were sold in 1915 to Raub Rubber Estates Ld.; debenture stockholders were entitled to 1 share of £1 (credited with 18s. paid) in new company for every £1 stock held. Struck off Register 1917 ...... **1916**

Sungei Matang Rubber Co. Ld. Regd. 1910. Vol. liq. 27 Nov. 1914. Reconstructed as Sungei Matang Rubber Estate Ld., in which company shareholders were entitled to 1 share of 2s. (credited with 1s. paid) for each share of 2s. held. Debenture stockholders were entitled to an equal amount of 7½% debenture stock in new company. Final meeting return regd. 22 Sept. 1919 ...... **1915**

Sungei Matang Rubber Estate, Ld. Regd. 1914. Vol. liq. (members') 1 June 1962. Capital returned to contributories (per share of 2s.)—5s. 2d. £402 6s. 2d. was paid into Companies' Liquidation Account in respect of unclaimed distributions. Final meeting return regd. 28 Oct. 1965 ...... **1967**

Sungei Nipah Estate Ld. Regd. 1915. Struck off Register 9 Jan. 1931 ...... **1931**

Sungei Pari Hydraulic Tin Ld. Regd. 1929. Assets were sold to Meru Tin Ld., in May 1934 for £14,100 in cash and 92,000 fully-paid shares of 1s. Vol. liq. (creditors') 11 Dec. 1934. Final meeting return regd. 27 Dec. 1935 ...... **1935**

Sungei Purun (F. M. S.) Rubber Co. Ld. Regd. 1911. All capital was owned by Bedong (Malaya) Rubber Ld. Vol. liq. (members') 1 June 1962. Final meeting return regd. 28 Oct. 1965 ...... **1960**

Sungei Raya Rubber Estate Ld. Regd. 1925. Vol. liq. 28 Aug. 1928. Undertaking and assets were transferred to Rambutan Rubber Estates Ld. in which company shareholders were entitled to 1 share of 2s. for every 2 shares of 2s. held. Final meeting return regd. 19 Oct. 1929 ...... **1926**

Sungei Reyla (F. M. S.) Rubber Estate Ld. Regd. 1910. Vol. liq. (members') 25 Jan. 1937. Reconstructed as Padang Senang Rubber Ld., in which company shareholders were entitled to 3 shares of 2s. (credited as fully-paid) for every 5 shares of 2s. held. Final meeting return regd. 3 July 1937 ...... **1937**

Sungei Rinching Rubber Co. Ld. Regd. 1910. Vol. liq. 28 Jan. 1920. Reconstructed as Sungei Rinching Rubber Estates Ld. in which company shareholders were entitled to 4 shares of £1 (credited as fully-paid) plus 3s. in cash for each share of £1 held. Final meeting return regd. 7 June 1920 ...... **1920**

Sungei Salak Rubber Co. Ld. Regd. 1907. Vol. liq. (members') 25 Mar. 1953. Undertaking and assets were acquired by Consolidated Salak Rubber Estates Ld. Stockholders were entitled to receive 1 share of 2s. of that company for each 2s. stock held plus a cash distribution (not subject to tax) of 1½d. per

2s. stock (in Apr. 1953). Final meeting return regd. 20 July 1960 ...... **1961**

Sungei Sayong Rubber Co. Ld. Regd. 1910. Estate was acquired by North Labis (Johore) Rubber & Produce Co. Ld. for 20,091 fully-paid shares of £1. Struck off Register Feb. 1935 ...... **1935**

Sungei Sekah (F. M. S.) Rubber Co. Ld. Regd. 1920. Vol. liq. 23 July 1924. Final meeting return regd. 28 Sept. 1925 ...... **1925**

Sungei Tabo (F. M. S.) Rubber Estate Ld. Regd. 1920. Vol. liq. 9 Jan. 1922. Undertaking and assets were acquired by Narborough (F. M. S.) Rubber Estate Ld. in which company shareholders were entitled to 1 share of 2s. (credited as fully-paid) for every 2½ shares of 2s. held. Final meeting return regd. 31 Oct. 1923 ...... **1922**

Sungei Tamu Rubber Co. Ld. Regd. 1912. Vol. liq. (members') June 1952. Capital returned to contributories—1s. 1·447d. per share (of 2s.). Final meeting return regd. 7 Dec. 1956 ...... **1958**

Sungei Telor (Malaya) Rubber Estate Ld. Regd. 1925. Vol. liq. (members') 1 July 1952. Preference shares were repaid at par on 19 Sept. 1952. Capital returned to contributories—1s. 4·5650d. per ordinary share (of 1s.). £1,961 19s. was paid into Companies' Liquidation Account. Final meeting return regd. 6 July 1956 ...... **1957**

Sungei Tukong Rubber Plantations Ld. Regd. 1925. Vol. liq. 27 Apr. 1961. Undertaking and assets acquired by Anglo-Asian Rubber Plantations Ld. Final meeting return regd. 13 Sept. 1961 ...... **1962**

Sungei Ujong (Malay Peninsular) Railway Co. Ld. Regd. 1888. Vol. liq. Aug 1908. The Government of Negri Semblian took over the railway. The directors stated that purchase consideration would do little more than pay 1st mortgage debenture holders. Removed from Register 1909 ...... **1909**

Sungei Way (Selangor) Rubber Co. Ld. Regd. Edinburgh 1904. Vol. liq. Jan. 1920. Reconstructed as company of same name. Shareholders were entitled to 4 shares of £1 (credited as fully-paid) in new company for each share of £1 held. Final meeting return regd. 30 Dec. 1922 ...... **1920**

Sungkai-Chumor Estates Ld. Regd. 1906. Vol. liq. (members') 28 Dec. 1933. Undertaking and assets were acquired by Bikan Rubber Estate Ld., in which company shareholders were entitled to 53 shares of 2s. (credited as fully-paid) for every 40 shares of 2s. held. Final meeting return regd. 2 July 1934 ...... **1934**

Sungkap Para Plantations Ld. Regd. 1925. All capital was owned by Kulim Rubber Plantations Ld. Vol. liq. (members') 29 Dec. 1961. Final meeting return regd. 5 Aug. 1964 ...... **1961**

Sunja Syndicate Ld. Regd. 1914. Vol. liq. (members') 24 Aug. 1965. Final meeting return regd. 9 Dec. 1965 ...... **1956**

Sunnygama (Ceylon) Tea Estates Co. Ld. See Sunnygama Co. Ld.

Sunnygama Co. Ld. Regd. 1893 as Sunnygama (Ceylon) Tea Estates Co. Ld.; name changed 1912. All capital owned by J. H. Vavasseur & Co. Ld. Vol. liq. (members') 5 Aug. 1960. Capital returned to contributories—£1 per preference share (of £1) and 27s. 1d. per ordinary share (of £1). Final meeting return regd. 16 Dec. 1972 ...... **1969**

Sunnyside Iron Co. Ld. Regd. Edinburgh 1895. Vol. liq. 7 Mar. 1898. Undertaking acquired by Forth & Clyde & Sunnyside Iron Cos. Ld. Final meeting return regd. 12 Jan. 1899 ...... **1940**

Sunsheen Ld. Regd. 1925 as Raysheen Ld.; name changed May 1927. Receiver appointed 8 Mar. 1929. Struck off Register Jan. 1933 ...... **1933**

Sunshine Ld. Regd. 1897. Capital returned to contributories—16s. per preference share of £1 on 12 Dec. 1902; further payments (if any) not known. Removed from Register 1903 ...... **1903**

Super-Aeration, France Ld. Regd. 1901. Removed from Register 1906 ...... **1908**

Super-Aëration (1901) Ld. Regd. 1901. Undertaking and assets were acquired by London Super-Aëration Ld. in which company shareholders were entitled to 3 shares of £1 (credited as fully-paid) for every 5 shares of £1 held. Removed from Register 1905 .. **1903**

Super Automatic Machine Co. Ld. Regd. 1925. Vol. liq. 26 Aug. 1930. All capital owned by Super Automatic Machines (1928) Ld. Final meeeting return regd. 28 June 1932 ...... **1931**

Super Automatic Machines (1928) Ld. Regd. 1928. Vol. liq. (creditors') 8 Aug. 1931. Final meeting return regd. 31 Dec. 1932 ...... **1933**

Super Kinema & Restaurant Ld. Regd. 1921 as Super Kinema & Restaurant (S. E. Barnes) Ld.; name changed Dec. 1924. Struck off Register 24 Jan. 1936 **1936**

See Stock Exchange Year-Book.

VOL. FOR

Superheater Co. Ld. Regd. 1938. Dissolved 25 Nov. 1981 .... **1962**

Superheaters Ld. *See* Marine & Locomotive Superheaters Ld.

Supersites Ld. Regd. by Deed of Settlement as Nottingham Church Cemetery Co. Ld., re-registered as limited 1 June 1954; name changed to Central Shops & Offices Ld. 1958; and as above 1962. Vol. liq. (members') 7 Mar. 1962. Final meeting return regd. 21 Nov. 1962 .... **1959**

Suppliers' Construction Co. Regd. 1900 as Charing Cross and City Electric Co. Ld.; name changed Mar. 1905. Vol. liq. (members') 23 Jan. 1941. Central London Electricity Ld. was sole beneficial contributory. Final meeting return regd. 11 Apr. 1941 .... **1941**

Surinam Gold Concessions Ld. Regd. 1903. Vol. liq. 29 May 1908. Final meeting return regd. 31 Oct. 1910. Struck off Register 1911 .... **1909**

Surrey & General Land Co. Ld. Regd. 1891. Court Order to wind up 11 Jan. 1894. Removed from Register 1907 .... **1894**

Surrey & Hampshire Canal Corporation. In liquidation in 1883. Properties transferred to London & Hampshire Canal & Water Co. Ld. **1883**

Surrey Commercial Dock Co. Inc. Special Act 1865. Undertaking transferred to Port of London Authority by Act 1908. 4½% debenture stockholders received 150% 3% A stock; A preference stockholders received 112½% 4% B stock; and ordinary stockholders received 95% 4% B stock **1909**

Surrey Dairy Farmers Association Ld. *See* J. Trigg & Son (Dairy Farmers) Ld.

Surrey Estates Co. Ld. Regd. 1889. Vol. liq. 5 Jan. 1897. Final meeting return regd. 10 July 1897. .... **1897**

Susanna Mines Ld. Inc. Rhodesia 1911. In liquidation in 1918 .... **1918**

Sussex Brick & Estates Co. Ld. Regd. 1903. Vol. liq. 14 Dec. 1927. Undertaking and assets were acquired by Sussex Brick Co. Ld. Capital returned to contributories—£2 per share of £1 at Jan. 1928; further payments (if any) not known. Final meeting return regd. 20 Feb. 1929 .... **1928**

Sussex Brick Co. Ld. Regd. 1899. Undertaking and assets were acquired by Sussex Brick and Estates Ld. Removed from Register 1910 .... **1904**

Sussex Electricity Supply Co. Ld. Regd. 1921. Dissolved 1 Apr 1948, undertaking being vested in the British (later Central) Electricity Authority and South-Eastern Area Board under the Electricity Act 1947. Ordinary shareholders were entitled to receive £1 5*s*. British Electricity 3% guaranteed stock (1968-73), for each share (of £1) held **1949**

Sussex Motors Ld. Regd. 1904 as Wilbury Stables Co. Ld.; name changed June 1913 to Wilbury Co. Ld. and as above in Jan. 1925. Vol. liq. 18 Aug. 1925. Final meeting return regd. 22 Dec. 1926 .... **1926**

Sussex Portland Cement Co. Ld. Regd. 1884. Vol. liq. Feb. 1912. The undertaking was sold to British Portland Cement Manufacturers Ld., in which company shareholders were entitled to 1 6% preference share of £10 for every 10 preference shares of £1 held *plus* 2*s*. per share in cash or 1 fully-paid ordinary share of £1 for each ordinary share of £1 held *plus* participation in surplus assets (if any). Removed from Register 1913 .... **1913**

Sussex Steamship Co. Ld. Regd. 1883. Vol. liq. Mar. 1886. Final meeting return regd. 30 June 1887 .... **1887**

Sussmann Electric Miners' Lamp Co. Ld. Regd. 1900. Removed from Register 1903 .... **1903**

Sutherland & Caithness Railway Co. Inc. 1871. Amalgamated with Highland Railway Co. on 1 Sept. 1884. Ordinary stockholders received 50% Highland ordinary stock; debentures and temporary loans were taken over or paid off **1885**

Sutherland Gas Meter Co. Ld. *See* Sutherland Meter Co. Ld.

Sutherland Gold Mines Ld. Regd. 1910. Vol. liq. 1913. Struck off Register 1 Feb. 1944 .... **1944**

Sutherland Meter Co. Ld. Regd. 1904 as Sutherland Gas Meter Co. Ld.; name changed 1905. Vol. liq. 7 Nov. 1961. Final meeting return regd. 27 Mar. 1962 .... **1940**

Sutherland Railway Co. Inc. 1865. Dissolved and amalgamated with Highland Railway Co. on 1 Sept. 1884. Ordinary stockholders received 60% Highland ordinary stock; debentures and temporary loans were taken over or paid off **1885**

Sutherland Reef Ld. Regd. 1889. Vol. liq. 18 July 1893. Reconstructed as company of same name. Shareholders were entitled to 1 share of £1 (credited with 17*s*. paid) in new company for each share of £1 held. Final meeting return regd. 18 July 1894 .... **1896**

VOL. FOR

Sutherland Reef Ld. Regd. 1893. Vol. liq. 21 Aug. 1896. Reconstructed as company of same name. Shareholders were entitled to 1 share of £1 (credited with 15*s*. paid) in new company for each share of £1 held. Final meeting return regd. 29 Dec. 1898 .... **1904**

Sutherland Reef Ld. Regd. 1896. Vol. liq. for reconstruction under same name. Ordinary shareholders were entitled to 1 ordinary share of £1 (credited with 16*s*. paid) in new company for each fully-paid ordinary share of £1 held; preference shareholders received 1 preference share of 4*s*. for each preference share of 4*s*. held. Struck off Register 1 Feb. 1944 .... **1944**

Sutherland Reef Ld. Regd. 1904. Vol. liq. 11 July 1906. Reconstructed as Sutherland Reefs Proprietary Gold Mines Ld. Struck off Register 3 Oct.1941 ... **1942**

Sutherland Reefs Proprietary Gold Mines Ld. Regd. 1906. Vol. liq. 15 Sept. 1910. Reconstructed as Sutherland Gold Mines Ld. in which company shareholders were entitled to 1 share of 2*s*. 6*d*. (credited with 1*s*. 6*d*. paid) for each share of 2*s*. 6*d*. held. Holders of 10% debentures were entitled to debentures in new company at par. Final meeting return regd. 6 Jan. 1915 .... **1911**

Sutherland Steamship Co. Ld. Regd. 1898 as Isles Steam Shipping Co. Ld.; name changed May 1922. Vol. liq. (members') 10 Jan. 1934. Capital returned to contributories—8*s*. 2¾*d*. per share of £1. Final meeting return regd. 28 June 1934 .... **1934**

Sutton & Willoughby Railway Co. Inc. by Special Act 1884. Under Great Northern Railway Act of 1902, undertaking was purchased for £40,500. The 4½% debentures were repaid at par **1903**

Sutton, Carden & Co. Ld. Regd. 1886. Vol. liq. 27 Jan. 1925. Direct controlling interest held by Distillers Co. Ld. Final meeting return regd. 31 May 1927 **1926**

Sutton Gas Co. Inc. by Special Act 1876. Under Special Order of 1931, undertaking was acquired by Wandsworth & District Gas Co. Holders of debenture stock were entitled to an equal amount of 5% debenture stock in acquiring company: holders of ordinary stock were entitled to £165 preference stock in acquiring company for every £100 ordinary stock held **1932**

Sutton Heath & Lea Green Collieries Ld. Regd. 1920. Collieries vested in the National Coal Board as from 1 Jan. 1947. Vol. liq. (members') 25 July 1951 for purposes of reconstruction as Roughdales Brickworks Ld. Shareholders entitled to receive 3 shares of 5*s*. of new company for every ordinary share of £1 held. Capital returned to contributories—£1 2*s*. 5*d*. per share of £1. Final meeting return regd. 10 Feb. 1961 .... **1962**

Sutton, Southcoates & Drypool Gas Co. *See* East Hull Gas Co.

Suvoroff Taman Oilfields Ld. Regd. 1911. Vol. liq. 20 Feb. 1922. Final meeting return regd. 1 June 1939 **1938**

Suvretta Ld. Regd. 1928. Vol. liq. (members') 15 July 1948. Capital returned to contributories—1*s*. 10*d*. per ordinary share of 10*s*. and £1 8*s*. 5*d*. per management deferred share of 10*s*.; a distribution of ordinary shares of Trust Houses Ld. (valued for this purpose at 33*s*. per share) was also made, giving a return of capital at the rate of 15*s*. 6·42*d*. per ordinary share and £4 15*s*. 9·9*d*. per management deferred share. Final meeting return regd. 12 Jan. 1950 .... **1950**

Suyapa Silver Concessions Ld. Regd. 1890. Vol. liq. 3 July 1894. Final meeting return regd. 8 Jan. 1896 **1895**

Swaledale & Wensleydale Banking Co. Ld. Established 1836. Regd. as limited in July 1881. Business transferred to Barclay & Co. Ld. (later Barclays Bank Ld.), in which company shareholders received 1 share for every share held. **1900**

Swan & Edgar Ld. Regd. 1886 as Waterloo House & Swan & Edgar Ld.; name changed 1896. Vol. liq. 6 May 1927. Undertaking and assets were acquired by Swan & Edgar (1927) Ld. (later Swan & Edgar Ld.), for £1,052,902 in cash. Final meeting return regd. 25 Feb. 1929 .... **1928**

Swan Brewery (Leatherhead) Ld. Regd. 1903. Vol. liq. 2 Nov. 1921. Undertaking was acquired by Mellersh and Neale Ld., for 1,780 fully-paid ordinary and 3,108 fully-paid preference shares of £10, £35,700 5% debenture stock, £10,000 in cash and £6,300 to repay debentures at par. Final meeting return regd. 2 Nov. 1922 .... **1922**

Swan Co. Inc. in Delaware U.S.A. in 1926. Placed in liquidation 27 Nov. 1950. Capital returned to contributories—$13·55 per share of $10. Finally dissolved in 1952 .... **1953**

Swan Cotton Spinning Co. Ld. Regd. 1875. Vol. liq. 20 Nov. 1919. Final meeting return regd. 4 May 1923 ***1884**

Swan Estates Ld. Regd. 1933. Vol. liq. (members') 10 July 1947. Undertaking acquired by Property

**See Stock Exchange Year-Book.*

Holding & Investment Trust Ld.; shareholders were entitled to 8 fully-paid preference shares of £1 in that company for every 25 ordinary shares of £1 and 3 fully-paid ordinary shares of 10s. in that company for every 2 ordinary shares of £1 held. Final meeting return regd. 22 Nov. 1948 .... **1949**

Swan Hunter Group p.l.c. Regd. 15 June 1903 as Swan, Hunter & Wigham Richardson, Ld.; name changed to Associated Shipbuilders Ld. on 12 July 1966 and to present title 28 Dec. 1966. Vol. liq. (members') 12 Jan. 1979. Following the settlement of the amount of compensation now received from H.M. Government in respect of the nationalisation of the shipbuilding interests, the remaining activities and certain assets and obligations were transferred by way of scheme of reconstruction effective 12 Jan. 1979 to Gosforth Industrial Hldgs Ld., in which company ordinary shareholders received one ordinary share of 10p for each share held, a 1st distribution (per share of £1) (to non-dissenters) of 139p was paid 6 Apr. 1979, a second distribution of 5½p was paid 3 Dec. 1979, a third distribution of 3·5p was paid 24 Oct. 1980 and a fourth and final distribution of 2·4776p was paid 14 May 1982. The share register was finally closed 23 Apr. 1982. £44,576 was paid into the Insolvency Services Account in respect of unclaimed distributions. Final meeting held 29 June 1982 .... **1984–5**

Swan, Hunter & Wigham Richardson, Ld. *See* Swan Hunter Group p.l.c.

Swan Investment Trust Ld. Regd. 1942. All capital was owned by Discount & General Investment Co. Ld. Vol. liq. (members') 1 Mar. 1967. Final meeting return regd. 9 June 1967 .... **1965**

Swan (John) & Sons Ld. Regd. Edinburgh 1894. Vol. liq. Dec. 1911. Undertaking and assets were acquired by Swan & Sons Ld. (later John Swan & Sons Ld.). Struck off Register 10 Mar. 1936........................... **1937**

Swan Land & Cattle Co. Ld. Regd. Edinburgh 1883. Vol. liq. Mar. 1926. Undertaking and assets were acquired by The Swan Co. (inc. Delaware), in which company shareholders were entitled to 1 share of $10 (credited as fully-paid) and $8 in 2nd bearer bonds for each share of 2s. held or $5 1st bearer bonds for each £1 stock held. Final meeting return regd. 10 Mar. 1927 .... **1927**

Swan Mill Holdings (Middleton Junction) Ld. Regd. 1919 as Swan Mill Ld.; name subsequently changed. Vol. liq. (members') 24 Feb. 1960. Final meeting return regd. 13 Aug. 1964 .... **1941**

Swan Mills Ld. Regd. 1903. Vol. liq. 15 May 1912. Final meeting return regd. 28 Dec. 1912 .... **1909**

Swan Sonnenschein & Co. Ld. Regd. 1895. Struck off Register 31 Oct. 1916 .... ***1912**

Swan Syndicate Ld. Regd. 1894. Vol. liq. 20 Aug. 1906. Undertaking and assets were acquired by Bowers Randfontein Ld., in which company shareholders were entitled to 2 fully-paid shares of £1 for every 5 shares of £1 held. Struck off Register 1926 .... **1907**

Swan United Electric Light Co. Ld. Regd. 1882. Vol. liq. 3 July 1894 for reconstruction as Edison Swan Electric Co. Ld. Final meeting return regd. 20 Dec. 1895 .... **1940**

Swanage Gas & Electricity Co. Inc. as Swanage Gas & Water Co. by Special Act 1901; name changed in 1914 to Swanage Gas Co. and in 1923 as above. Dissolved 1 May 1949, undertaking being vested in Southern Area Gas Board under Gas Act 1948. Holders of securities were entitled to receive, in respect of each £100 unit held, British Gas 3% guaranteed stock 1990–95 as follows:

	£	s.	d.
A ord. stock (10% max.)	125	0	0
B ord. stock (7% max.)	85	0	0
4½% pref. stock	105	0	0
7% pref. stock	130	0	0 **1952**

Swanage Railway Co. Inc. by Special Act 1881. Under Act of 1886 holders were offered (a) repayment at 105% or (b) conversion of £100 stock into £95 perpetual preference stock (1884) **1888**

Swans Departmental Stores Ld. Regd. 1933 as Peacock's Stores Ld.; name changed Aug. 1962. All ordinary owned by Walfrin Investments Ld. Winding-up order 29 July 1963. Struck off Register 8 Aug. 1975 **1973-4**

Swansea & Mumbles Railway Co. Ld. Regd. 1879. Vol. liq. 1 July 1893 for reconstruction as company of same name. Final meeting return regd. 8 June 1896 **1893**

Swansea & Mumbles Railways Ld. Regd. 1893. Under provisions of the South Wales Transport Act 1959 the company was dissolved and the undertaking vested in the South Wales Transport Co. Ld. (which company owned nearly all capital) on 31 Dec. 1959 **1959**

Swansea Bank Ld. *See* South Wales Union Bank Ld.

Swansea Central Dry Docks Ld. Regd. 1903. Vol. liq. Mar. 1904. Removed from Register 1905............. **1905**

Swansea Coal Trust Ld. Regd. 1903. Vol. liq. July 1906. Removed from Register 1907 .... **1907**

Swansea Gas Light Co. Inc. 1830; reinc. by Special Act 1861. Dissolved 1 May 1949, undertaking being vested in Wales Area Gas Board under Gas Act 1948. Holders of Securities were entitled to receive, in respect of each £100 unit held, British Gas 3% guaranteed stock 1990–95 as follows:

	£	s.	d.
Ord. stock (5% basic)	92	10	0
5½% red. pref. stock.........................	107	6	8
3½% perp. deb. stock	98	0	0
4% perp. deb. stock	102	0	0
3½% red. deb. stock (1955)...............	100	0	0
3½% deb. bonds (all red. dates)........	100	0	0
3½% deb. bonds (all red. dates)........	100	2	6

A distribution on ord. stock of 11·14583% out of reserves (plus 0·5% final adjustment of dividend) was made in Oct. 1953 .... **1952**

Swansea Harbour Trust. Inc. by Special Act 1854. The undertaking was acquired in July 1923 by Great Western Railway Co. which company assumed liability for mortgages. Holders of 4% stocks were entitled to £80 in 5% consolidated preference stock for every £100 stock held **1924**

Swansea Hotel Co. Ld. Regd. 1896. Vol. liq. (members') 25 June 1947. Capital returned to contributories (per share of £5)—preference: £5; ordinary: £2 6s. £4 12s. was paid into Companies' Liquidation Account. Final meeting return regd. 9 June 1953 ..... **1954**

Swansea Improvements & Tramways Co. Inc. by Special Act 1874. Dissolved 30 Sept. 1953 .... **1954**

Swansea Old Brewery & Davies' (Cardigan) Bonded Stores Ld. *See* Swansea Old Brewery Ld.

Swansea Old Brewery Ld. Regd. 1896 as Swansea Old Brewery & Davies' (Cardigan) Bonded Stores Ld.; name changed Apr. 1921. Vol. liq. 5 Apr. 1928. Undertaking was acquired by William Hancock & Co. Ld. Capital returned to contributories—15s. per ordinary share of £1; a further return of 4s. 6d. per share was anticipated. Final meeting return regd. 11 Mar. 1929 .... **1929**

Swansea Shipping Co. Ld. Regd. 1873. Vol. liq. 22 Dec. 1896. Final meeting return regd. 19 July 1898 ...... **1897**

Swansea Steamers Ld. Regd. 1907. Vol. liq. 26 Oct. 1917. Final meeting return regd. 18 Aug. 1919 ...... ***1918**

Swansea Telephonic Exchange Co. Ld. Regd. 1880. Vol. liq. June 1887. Taken over by Western Counties & South Wales Telephone Co. Ld. for £6,000. Final meeting return regd. 4 Aug. 1888...................... **1888**

Swansea United Breweries Ld. Regd. 1890. Vol. liq. 15 Dec. 1926. The 4½% 1st mortgage debentures were redeemed at 110% in Feb. 1927. Undertaking was acquired by Truman, Hanbury, Buxton and Co. Ld. Final meeting return regd. 3 June 1929 .... **1927**

Swansea Wagon Co. Ld. Regd. 1866 as Shackleford Ford & Co. Ld.; name changed Feb. 1868 to Cheltenham & Swansea Railway Carriage & Wagon Co. Ld.; name changed Oct. 1922 as above. Vol. liq. 2 Dec. 1927. Final meeting return regd. 27 Nov. 1928 .... **1928**

Swansea Zinc Ore Co. Ld. Regd. 1878. Court Order to wind up Mar. 1884. Struck off Register 27 Apr. 1894. .... **1887**

Swanson Bay Forests, Wood Pulp & Lumber Mills Ld. Inc. by Charter in Canada 1910. Property sold in 1917 to Empire Pulp & Paper Mills Ld. (later amalgamated with 2 other companies to form Whalen Pulp and Paper Mills Ld.), for 625,000 fully-paid 7% cumulative preference shares of $1 which were to belong to the bondholders **1918**

Swansons Stores Ld. Regd. 1919. Vol. liq. (members') 4 Apr. 1934. Directly controlled by Joseph Burton & Sons, Ld. Final meeting return regd. 18 July 1934 **1934**

Swanzy (F. & A.) Ld. Regd. 1904. Vol. liq. 4 Apr. 1929. All shares owned by United Africa Co. Ld. Struck off Register 7 Aug. 1945 .... **1930**

Swavesey & General Farming & Dairy Co. Ld. Regd. 1882. Vol. liq. Jan. 1888. Final meeting return regd. 24 Jan 1889 .... **1888**

Swazi Goldfields Ld. Regd. 1889. Vol. liq. (members') 15 Jan. 1932. No capital returned to contributories. Final meeting return regd. 18 Mar. 1932 .... **1932**

Swazieland Corporation Ld. Inc. Transvaal 1898. Vol. liq. Nov. 1924. Reconstructed as company of same name. Shareholders were entitled to 1 share of 5s. (credited with 3s. 9d. paid) in new company for each share of 10s. held **1925**

Swazieland Gold Exploration & Land Co. Ld. Regd. 1889. Vol. liq. 12 Feb. 1897. Reconstructed as company of same name. Shareholders were entitled to subscribe at par for 1 share of £1 in new company

VOL. FOR

for every 100 shares of £1 held. Final meeting return regd. 1 July 1897 .... **1903**

Swazieland Gold Exploration & Land Co. Ld. Regd. 1897. Vol. liq. 5 Aug. 1903. Reconstructed as company of same name. Shareholders were entitled to subscribe for shares at par. Final meeting return regd. 30 Dec. 1903 .... **1908**

Swazieland Gold Exploration & Land Co. Ld. Regd. 1903. Struck off Register 1920 .... **1908**

Swaziland (African) Gold Estates Ld. Regd. 1889. Vol. liq. 5 May 1890. Final meeting return regd. 5 Sept. 1893 .... **1891**

Swaziland Corporation (1924) Ld. Inc in the Transvaal on 4 Dec. 1924. Vol. liq. (members') 14 Sept. 1945. The first and final liquidation account was confirmed by the master of the Supreme Court, Pretoria, on 28 Mar. 1947, and the company was struck off the South African Register on that date **1948**

Swears & Wells Ld. Regd. 1897. Vol. liq. 31 Dec. 1920. Undertaking was acquired by Swears & Wells (1926) Ld. (later Swears & Wells Ld.), for fully-paid ordinary shares. Final meeting return regd. 14 Nov. 1924 .... **1921**

Swedish & Norwegian Railway Co. Ld. Regd. 1838. Court Order to wind up 22 Apr. 1893. Payments totalling 5*s.* in £ were paid to debenture stockholders; further payments (if any) not known. Removed from Register 1906 .... **1894**

Swedish Association Ld. Regd. 1875. Vol. liq. 22 Mar. 1900. Final meeting return regd. 11 June 1902 ..... ***1901**

Swedish Central Railway Co. Ld. Regd. Dec. 1870. Vol. liq. 16 Dec. 1925. Final meeting return regd. 14 Aug. 1927 .... **1927**

Swedish Ice Co. Ld. Regd. 1885. Vol. liq. 15 Jan. 1891. Final meeting return regd. 2 June 1891 .... **1891**

Swedish Iron Rolling Stock & Implement Works Ld. Regd. 1873. Vol. liq. 18 Oct. 1880. Final meeting return regd. 28 July 1882 .... ***1877**

Swedish Match Co. Ld. Regd. 1887. Court Orders: to wind up 2 Nov. 1889; to dissolve 10 Feb. 1910.... **1890**

Swedish Match Co. Ld. Regd. 1908. Vol. liq. 2 Nov. 1914. In 1914 the assets in Sweden were sold to Aktirbolaget Forenade Svenska Tandsticksfabriken for 2,554 fully-paid ordinary shares of kr. 100 and £16,926 in cash. Final meeting return regd. 16 Dec. 1915 .... **1915**

Swedish Metals Extraction Co. Ld. Regd. 1907 as Naversberg Falun Copper Mines & Works Ld.; name changed Dec. 1910. Vol. liq. (creditors') 30 July 1934. Assets realised insufficient to pay unsecured creditors in full. Final meeting return regd. 10 Jan. 1935 .... **1935**

Swedish Railway Equipment Co. Ld. Regd. 1877. Vol. liq. 5 June 1893. Final meeting return regd. 23 Mar. 1900 .... **1894**

Sweetland Creek Gold Mines Ld. Regd. 1870. Vol. liq. 3 Apr. 1877. Final meeting return regd. 18 July 1877 ***1877**

Swift Beef Co. Ld. Regd. 1891. Vol. liq. (members') 3 Dec. 1927. Capital returned to contributories—£10 0*s.* 3·708*d.* per share of £10. Final meeting return regd. 20 Jan. 1938 .... **1938**

Swift Cycle Co. Ld. Regd. 1896. Reconstructed 1901 as company of same name (later Swift of Coventry Ld.). Shareholders were entitled to 1 fully-paid ordinary share of £1 in new company for every 5 ordinary shares of £1 held or 1 preference share of £1 for each preference share of £1 held. Removed from Register 1903 .... **1908**

Swift Cycle Co. Ld. Regd. 1901. *See* Swift of Coventry Ld.

Swift of Coventry Ld. Regd. 1901 as Swift Cycle Co. Ld.; name changed 1918. Court Order to wind up 27 July 1931. Struck off Register 14 Oct. 1938 .... **1939**

Swindon Junction Hotel Co. Ld. Regd. 1886. Vol. liq. 6 Dec. 1895. Business was purchased by Great Western Railway Co. for £100,000. Final meeting return regd. 19 May 1896 .... **1896**

Swindon New Gas Co. *See* Swindon United Gas Co.

Swindon United Gas Co. Regd. 1862 as Swindon New Gas Co. Ld.; inc. by Special Act 1893 as New Swindon Gas Co.; name changed 1902. Dissolved 1 May 1949, undertaking being vested in South Western Area Gas Board under Gas Act 1948. Holders of securities were entitled to receive British Gas 3% guaranteed stock 1990–95 as follows in respect of each £100 unit, unless otherwise stated, of security held:

	£	s.	d.
Cons. ord. stock (5% stand.)	142	0	0
5½% pref. stock	127	0	0
4% red. pref. stock (1965)	100	10	0
4½% pref. shares (of £10)	10	18	0
4% red. pref. shares (1955–65) (of £10)	10	0	0
4½% red. pref. shares (1955) (of £1)..	1	0	8
4% red. pref. stock (1962)	100	4	5
4% red. pref. shares (1970) (of £10)..	10	1	6
5% perp. deb. stock	126	0	0
3½ red. mort. deb. stock (1969)	100	0	0
3½% red. deb. stock (1960) 96,000	96	10	0
3½% red. deb. stock (1960) £4,000	100	5	0

Liability in respect of certain mortgage loans assumed by the Board **1952**

Swindon Waterworks Co. Ld. Regd. 1857. By Act of Parliament company was vested in Swindon Water Board as from 1 Jan. 1895 .... ***1896**

Swinton & Mexbrough Gas Light Co. Inc. Special Act 1908. Undertaking acquired by Swinton & Mexbrough Gas Board under Act of 1909 .... **1912**

Swire (Robert) & Sons Ld. Regd. 1920. Vol. liq. 18 Sept. 1920. Final meeting return regd. 15 June 1921 .... **1936**

Swiss Discount Bank. *See* Banque d'Escompte Suisse.

Swiss Milkpowder Co. Ld. Regd. 1889. Court Orders; to wind up 17 Dec. 1890; to dissolve 2 Dec.1896...... **1892**

Swonnell (S) & Son, Ld. Regd. 1898. Vol. liq. (members') 31 Aug. 1965. Final meeting return regd. 18 Jan. 1968 .... **1954**

Sybu Syndicate Ld. Regd. 1910. Vol. liq. 18 Dec. 1922. Final meeting return regd. 15 July 1925 .... **1923**

Sydney & Louisburg Coal & Railway Co. Ld. Regd. 1880. Vol. liq. 14 Feb. 1894. Final meeting return regd. 23 Dec. 1895 .... **1895**

Sydney Godolphin Tin Mine Ld. Regd. 1888. Vol. liq. Mar. 1890. Final meeting return regd. 12 Oct. 1899 **1891**

Sydney Harbour Collieries Ld. Regd. 1894. Vol. liq. 4 May 1903. Reconstructed as company of same name. Shareholders were entitled to 12 shares of £1 (credited with 15*s.* paid) in new company for each preference share of £10 held or 10 shares of £1 (credited with 15*s.* paid) for each ordinary share of £10 held. Struck off Register 18 Jan. 1921 .... **1908**

Sydney Harbour Collieries Ld. Inc. New South Wales 1903. Vol. liq. Mar. 1909 .... **1910**

Sydney Harbour Colliery Ld. Regd. 1910. Vol. liq. 21 Aug. 1917. Struck off Register 24 July 1923 .... **1918**

Sydney Harbour Colliery Ld. Inc. New South Wales 1914. Property offered for sale 1916–17 .... **1920**

Sydney Pneumatic Cycle Tyre Co. Ld. Regd. 1893. Removed from Register 1907 .... **1895**

Sykes (Daniel) & Co. Ld. Regd. 1889. Business was sold to Bristol United Breweries Ld. for £7,500 in cash, 6,000 fully-paid preference and 2,500 ordinary shares of £10 and assumption of liability for debenture stocks. Removed from Register 1903 ... **1898**

Sykes (R. H.) & Co. Ld. Regd. 1896. Vol. liq. 14 Apr. 1898. Reconstructed as Leeds and Batley Breweries Ld. [later Leeds & Batley Properties Ld.]. Final meeting return regd. 14 Dec. 1898 .... **1899**

Sykes's Brewery Co. Ld. Regd. 1889. Vol. liq. 10 Mar. 1892. Court Order to continue winding up under supervision 29 Mar. 1892. Final meeting return regd. 1 June 1896 .... **1893**

Sylvanite Gold Mines Limited. Inc. in Ontario 1913. Capital returned to contributories (shares of $0.35)—$2·12 ($0·65 as shares in Alminex Ld., Delmite Mines Ld. and cash and $1·47 cash). Charter surrendered 20 May 1964 .... **1965**

Sylverlyte (1909) Ld. Regd. 1909. Vol. liq. 11 July 1912. Final meeting return regd. 26 Aug. 1916............ **1913**

Symington (Wm.) & Co. Ld. *See* General Rubber Co. Ld.

Symonds London Stores Ld. Regd. 1904. Court Order to wind up 1905. Removed from Register 1910 .... **1906**

Symons (S.) & Co. Ld. Regd. 1918. Vol. liq. 16 Apr. 1929. Undertaking and assets were acquired in Jan. 1929 by company of same name for £66,000 in fully-paid shares of 1*s.* Final meeting return regd. 5 July 1930 .... **1930**

Symphony Gramophone & Radio Co. Ld. Regd. 1928. Court Order to wind up 17 Mar. 1930. Liquidator released 18 Feb. 1935. Struck off Register 21 Sept. 1937 .... **1938**

Symphony Gramophone & Radio (Foreign) Ld. Regd. 1928. Vol. liq. (creditors') 3 Sept. 1930. Assets realised insufficient to pay unsecured creditors in full. Final meeting return regd. 13 Sept. 1935 ...... **1931**

Synchronome Syndicate Ld. Regd. 1897. Removed from Register 1903 .... **1903**

Syndicat du Yunnan Ld. Regd. 1899 as Anglo-French Syndicate Ld.; name changed 22 Nov. 1900. Vol. liq. 4 Apr. 1921. Final meeting return regd. 28 Apr. 1922 .... **1922**

Syndicat Francais des Brevets E. M. Bowden Ld. Regd. 1902. A subsidiary of Bowden (Engineers) Ld. Vol. liq. (members') 26 June 1957. Final meeting return regd. 14 July 1959 .... **1942**

Synoloids Ld. Regd. 1907. Vol. liq. 30 Dec. 1921. Final meeting return regd. 10 Mar. 1922 .... ***1922**

*_See Stock Exchange Year-Book._

VOL. FOR

Synthetic Ammonia & Nitrates Ld. *See* I.C.I. (Fertilizer & Synthetic Products) Ld.

Synthetic Marble Co. Ld. Regd. 1924. Vol. liq. (members') 29 Mar. 1935. Properties, *plus* £42 13*s*. cash were conveyed to Metropolitan United Estates Ld. which company owned all shares. Final meeting return regd. 1935 .... **1935**

Synthetic Products Co. Ld. Regd. 1912. Vol. liq. May 1926. Struck off Register Mar. 1933 .... **1934**

Synthol Ld. Regd. 1913. Struck off Register 1933 ..... *1930

Syracuse Brewing Union Ld. Regd. 1889. Vol. liq. Mar. 1890. Final meeting return regd. 16 Oct. 1891 ..... **1892**

Syrian Exploration Co. Ld. Regd. Vol. liq. (creditors') 20 June 1930. No capital returned to contributories. Final meeting return regd. 25 Feb. 1931 .... **1931**

Syrolit Ld. Regd. 1911. Vol. liq. 10 Nov. 1915. Reconstructed as Erinoid Ld. in which company shareholders were entitled to 1 share of 5*s*. (credited as fully-paid) for each preference share of 2*s*. held or each ordinary share of £1 held or every 4 deferred shares of £1 held. Final meeting return regd. 10 July 1916 .... **1916**

T

T. & S. Investments Syndicate Ld. Regd. 1899. Vol. liq. 7 June 1905. Final meeting return regd. 23 Jan. 1923 **1906**

T. & T. Assets Ld. Regd. 1935. Vol. liq. (members') 7 Mar. 1938. Undertaking was acquired by Armstrong Whitworth Securities Co. Ld., which company owned all shares. Certain investments were distributed in specie *plus* £808 8*s*. 6*d*. in cash. Final meeting returned regd. 15 Feb. 1939 .... **1943**

T. B. & Co. (Holdings) Ld. Regd. 1884 as T. Beynon & Co. Ld.; name subsequently changed. Vol. liq. (members') 22 May 1958. Final meeting return regd. 15 Dec. 1961 .... **1949**

T. B. Syndicate Ld. Regd. 1903. Vol. liq. 15 Dec. 1904. Removed from Register 1905 .... **1905**

T. C. E. T. Ld. *See* Trans Europe Investment Trust Ld.

T. D. C. Syndicate Ld. Regd. 1897. Struck off Register 17 Nov. 1899. Restored to Register 14 July 1900. Vol. liq. 5 May 1905. Final meeting return regd. 16 Oct. 1907 .... **1906**

T. H. S. Syndicate Ld. *See* Rhodesia Asbestos Co. Ld.

T. P. Realisation Ld. Regd. 1954. Vol. liq. (members') 31 Mar. 1955. Capital returned to contributories—£6 6*s*. per share of £1. Final meeting return regd. 23 July 1956 .... **1957**

T. Y. T. Ld. Regd. 1925 as Rubber & Tropical Trust Ld.; name changed to Yeoman Trust Ld. Aug. 1954 and subsequently as above. All capital was owned by Investment Loan & Agency Ld. Vol. liq. (members') 13 Dec. 1960. Final meeting return regd. 20 July 1962 .... **1960**

'Tabacus'' (Naamlooze Vennootschap Maatschappij Voor Tabakhandel) Voorheen M. L. Herzog & Co., **Cavalla** [Joint Stock Company for Trading in Tobacco ("Tabacus"), formerly M. L. Herzog & Co., Cavalla]. Inc. Amsterdam 1923. Wound up Apr. 1928 .... **1929**

Tacquah Gold Mines Co. Ld. Regd. 1881. Court Orders: to wind up Mar. 1886; to dissolve 9 July 1890...... **1887**

Tadcaster Tower Brewery Co. Ld. Regd. 1894. Debenture stock and mortgage loan was exchanged for a like amount of 5½% debenture stock of Hammonds United Breweries Ld. which company owned all capital. Vol. liq. (members') 12 Apr. 1961. Final meeting return regd. 12 Sept. 1961 .... **1961**

Taf Fechan Water Supply Board. Inc. by Special Act 1921. Under provisions of Taf Fechan Water Board Order 1964 undertaking was transferred to Taf Fechan Water Board on 1 Apr. 1966 and the board dissolved **1968**

Taff Rhondda Navigation Steam Coal Co. Ld. Regd. 1920 as Taylor's Navigation Steam Coal Co. Ld.; name changed Dec. 1924. Vol. liq. 26 Aug. 1927. Direct controlling interest held by Baldwins Ld. [later Baldwins (Holdings) Ld.]. Final meeting return regd. 31 Aug. 1929 .... **1928**

Taff Vale Railway Co. Inc. by Special Act 1836. In 1922 the undertaking was merged into the Great Western Railway Co. in which company stockholders were entitled to stock as follows:

For each £100 held		G. W.	
3% Debenture	£75	4% Debenture	
4% Preference	£80	5% Cons. Pref.	
Ordinary	£60	Cons. Ordinary	**1924**

Tai Tak (Johore) Rubber Estates Ld. Regd. 1920. Vol. liq. 25 Jan. 1922. Reconstructed as Tai Tak Plantations Ld., in which company shareholders were entitled to 1 share of 10*s*. (credited with 7*s*.

VOL. FOR

paid) for each share of £1 held. Final meeting return regd. 21 Sept. 1923 .... **1922**

Tai Tak Plantations Ld. Regd. 1922. Vol. liq. 30 Oct. 1950. Undertaking and assets acquired by Golden Hope Rubber Estate Ld., now Golden Hope Plantations Ld. in which company shareholders were entitled to receive 1 fully-paid share of £1 for each £2 stock held. £98 was paid into Companies' Liquidation Account. Final meeting return regd. 18 July 1951 .... **1952**

Taikoo Dockyard & Engineering Co. of Hong Kong Ld. Regd. 1908. Vol. liq. (members') 15 Feb. 1940. Shareholders were given one share of £10 in new company of same name for each share of £10 held. Final meeting return regd. 16 July 1941 .... **1914**

Taiping (Hydraulic) Tin Properties Ld. Regd. 1912. Vol. liq. 3 Oct. 1917. Struck off Register 20 Mar. 1925 **1918**

Taiping Tin Dredging Co. Ld. Inc. Straits Settlements 1 Mar. 1918. Vol. liq. (members') 19 Mar 1937. Undertaking and assets were acquired by Taiping Consolidated Ld., in which company shareholders were entitled to 1 share of $1 (credited as fully-paid) for every 2 shares of $1 held............................ **1938**

Taitapu Gold Estates Ld. Regd. 1895. Reconstructed 1899 as company of same name. Shareholders were entitled to 1 share of £1 (credited with 17*s*. paid) in new company for each share of £1 held. Removed from Register 1907 .... **1908**

Taitapu Gold Estates Ld. Regd. 1899. Vol. liq. 11 Mar. 1920. Final meeting return regd. 15 Nov. 1928..... **1921**

Takau (F. M. S.) Rubber Estates Ld. Regd. 1923. Vol. liq. (members') 8 Jan. 1948, undertaking and assets having been acquired by Takau Rubber Plantations Ld. in which company stockholders were entitled to 1 2*s*. share credited with 1*s*. 6*d*. paid for every 2*s*. stock held. Outstanding debenture stock redeemed on 8 Mar. 1948, arrears of interest from 1 May 1944 being cancelled. Final meeting return regd. 21 Oct. 1949 .... **1950**

Takau Rubber Plantations Ld. Regd. 1948. Vol. liq. (members') 9 Apr. 1952. Capital returned to contributories—1*s*. 4⅚₀₀*d*. per 2*s*. stock. £271 13*s*. 4*d*. was paid into Companies' Liquidation Account. Final meeting return regd. 30 Apr. 1956.............. **1957**

Takinta Oil Co. Ld. Regd. 1910. Court Order to wind up 14 Oct. 1913. Liquidator released 22 Nov. 1918. Struck off Register 1 July 1921 .... **1914**

Takoradi Coaling & Lighterage Co. Ld. Regd. 1926. Vol. liq. (members') 20 Feb. 1931. Direct controlling interest held by United Africa Co. Ld. Capital returned to contributories—£21,915 2*s*. 8*d*. Final meeting return regd. 2 Mar. 1933 .... **1931**

Takush Harbour Timber Co. Ld. Regd. 1895. Vol. liq. 24 Sept. 1897. Final meeting return regd. 4 Oct. 1898 **1898**

Talacre & Gronant Mining Co. Ld. Regd. 1880. Removed from Register 1905 .... **1887**

Talacre District Mining & Drainage Co. Ld. Regd. 1892. Vol. liq. Dec. 1910. Removed from Register 1912 **1911**

Talana Collieries Ld. Inc. Southern Rhodesia 1907. Vol. liq. 1910 for reconstruction as company of same name. Shareholders were entitled to 1 share of £1 (with 17*s*. credited as paid) in new company for each share of £1 held **1911**

Talana Collieries Ld. Regd. 1910. Vol. liq. 8 Feb. 1912. Removed from Register 1913 .... **1912**

Talana (Natal) Collieries Ld. Regd. 1904. Vol. liq. Aug. 1907. Undertaking and assets were acquired by Talana Collieries Ld. (inc. Southern Rhodesia), in which company shareholders were entitled to 1 share of £1 (credited with 17*s*. paid) for each share of £1 held. Removed from Register 1913 .... **1908**

Talawakelle Estates Co. Ld. Regd. 1897. Vol. liq. (members') 15 Nov. 1949. Reconstructed as company of same name, in which company shareholders were entitled to receive 1 preference share per preference share held and 1 ordinary share plus proportion of £90,000 cash per ordinary share held. Final meeting return regd.9 June 1955............. **1956**

Talbot Alluvials Ld. Regd. 1914. Vol. liq. 15 May 1925. Reconstructed as Platinum Areas Ld., in which company shareholders were entitled to 3 ordinary shares of 2*s*. (credited with 1*s*. 6*d*. paid) for each preference share of 4*s*. held, or 2 ordinary shares of 2*s*. (credited with 1*s*. 6*d*. paid) for each ordinary share of 4*s*. held. Final meeting return regd. 6 Oct. 1928 .... **1926**

Talbot Alluvials, Ld. Inc. in Victoria 1931. Vol. liq. (members') 31 Mar. 1949. Capital returned to contributories—1*s*. 2·457*d*. (Australian currency) per share (of A5*s*.) £A2,028 7*s*. was paid to Receiver of Revenue, Melbourne, Dissolved 20 Dec. 1952.. **1953**

Talbot Continuous Steel Process Ld. Regd. 1900. Vol. liq. 29 Apr. 1913. Reconstructed as Steel Developments Ld. in which company shareholders were

VOL. FOR

entitled to 1 share of 6*s.* (credited as fully-paid) for each share of £1 held. Final meeting return regd. 25 Feb. 1919 .... **1914**

Talbot Hotel (Bristol) Ld. Regd. 1890. Vol. liq. 28 Aug. 1919. Final meeting return regd. 12 June 1920 ..... **1920**

Talbot Spinning & Weaving Co. Ld. Regd. 1905. Dissolved before 1951 .... **1950**

Talering Tin Dredging, Ld. Regd. 1927. Vol. liq. (members') 12 Oct. 1956. Company was a subsidiary of London Tin Corpn. Ld. Properties were sold to Tongkah Harbour Tin Dredging Ld. Shareholders were entitled to receive 1 fully-paid share of 5*s.* of the latter company for every 2 shares held, plus 8*d.* per share cash. £73 15*s.* was paid into Companies' Liquidation Account. Final meeting return regd. 20 Dec. 1957 .... **1959**

Talisman Consolidated Ld. Regd. 1899. Reconstructed 1904 as Talisman Consolidated (1904) Ld. (later Talisman Consolidated Ld.), in which company shareholders were entitled to 1 share of £1 (credited with 17*s.* paid) for each share of £1 held. Removed from Register 1905 .... **1905**

Talisman Consolidated Ld. Regd. 1904 as Talisman Consolidated (1904) Ld.; name changed Mar. 1904. Vol. liq. Mar. 1916. Reconstructed as company of same name, in which company shareholders were entitled to 1 fully-paid share of £1 for each share of £1 held. Final meeting return regd. 16 Nov. 1917 **1921**

Talisman Consolidated Ld. Regd. 1916. Vol. liq. 21 July 1921. Capital returned to contributories—5*s.* per share of £1 in Oct. 1921; further payments (if any) not known. Final meeting return regd. 26 Jan. 1923 **1922**

"Talisman" Gold Mines Ld. Regd. 1895. Vol. liq. 27 Nov. 1896. Reconstructed as Talisman Mines Ld., in which company shareholders were entitled to 6 shares of £1 (credited with 17*s.* paid) for every 5 shares of £1 held. Final meeting return regd. 6 June 1899 .... **1897**

Talisman Mines Ld. Regd. 1896. Vol. liq. 16 Sept. 1897. Court Order to continue winding up under supervision 20 Dec. 1897. Final meeting return regd. 21 Nov. 1899 .... **1898**

Talk o' th' Hill Colliery Co. Ld. Regd. 1885. Vol. liq. (members') 22 May 1931. Capital returned to contributories—£117,917 16*s.* 3*d.* Final meeting return regd. 27 June 1932 .... **1932**

Talliar Estates Ld. Regd. 30 Nov. 1936. Vol. liq. (members') 24 July 1945. Capital returned to contributories—£2 10*s.* 8½*d.* per share (of £1). Final meeting return regd. 15 Apr. 1954 .... **1955**

Taltal (Chile) Nitrate Co. Ld. Regd. 1888. Undertaking acquired by Julia Nitrate Co. Ld. Removed from Register 1901 .... **1896**

Talunga Gold Fields Development Co. Ld. Regd. 1897. Undertaking and assets were acquired by Talunga Consolidated Ld in which company shareholders were entitled to 1 share of 10*s.* (credited with 7*s.* 6*d.* paid) for every 3 shares of £1 held. Removed from Register 1909 .... **1901**

Talysarn Copper Mines Ld. Regd. 1907. Vol. liq. 30 Oct. 1914. Final meeting return regd. 18 Feb. 1915...... **1915**

Taman Consolidated Oilfields Ld. Regd. 1913. Vol. liq. 21 Feb. 1916. Final meeting return regd. 30 Dec. 1916 .... **1916**

Tamarugal Nitrate Co. Ld. Regd. 1889. Vol. liq. 28 July 1890. Reconstructed as New Tamarugal Nitrate Co. Ld., in which company shareholders were entitled to 5 fully-paid preference and 5 ordinary shares of £1 10*s.* *plus* £10 debenture for every 5 shares of £5 held. Final meeting return regd. 29 May 1895 .... **1908**

Tambaroora Creek Gold Mine Ld. Regd. 1895. Removed from Register 1901 .... **1900**

Tambracherry Coffee Estates Co. Ld. Regd. 1874. Undertaking acquired by Tambracherry Estates Co. Ld. **1894**

Tambracherry Estates and Wynaad Gold Mining Co. Ld. See Tambracherry Estates Co. Ld.

Tambracherry Estates Co. Ld. Regd. 1881 as Tambracherry Estates and Wynaad Gold Mining Co. Ld.; name changed Jan. 1884. Vol. liq. 18 Jan. 1894. Fully-paid ordinary shares of £1 in new company were allotted to shareholders who subscribed for 1 preference share of £1 in respect of every 10 shares of 12*s.* 6*d.* held. Final meeting return regd. 13 Apr. 1908 .... **1907**

Tamiang Planting Syndicate Ld. *See* Boekit Boendar Rubber Co. Ld.

Tampico Electric Light, Power and Traction Ld. Regd. 1912. Vol. liq. 29 Dec. 1921. Undertaking and assets were acquired by Compania Electrica de Tampico S.A. Final meeting return regd. 18 May 1932....... **1927**

Tampico Oil Ld. Regd. 1919. Vol. liq. (creditors') 3 Jan. 1945. 1st debenture holders were repaid to the extent of 3·7%. No capital returned to contributories. Final meeting return regd. 20 Oct. 1949 .... **1950**

Tampico-Panuco Oil Fields Ld. Regd. 1911. Vol. liq. 30 Jan. 1929. Final meeting return regd. 15 Jan. 1931 **1929**

Tampico-Panuco Valley Railway Co. Ld. Regd. 1913. Vol. liq. (members') 11 Nov. 1930. Capital returned to contributories—£4,006 17*s.* 8*d.* Final meeting return regd. 21 Mar. 1931 .... **1919**

Tamsoo (Wassaw) Gold Mining Co. Ld. Regd. 1898. Vol. liq. 26 Feb. 1901. Undertaking and assets were acquired by United Gold Coast Mining Properties Ld., in which company shareholders were entitled to 1 share of £1 (credited as fully-paid) for each share of £1 held. Final meeting return regd. 26 Sept. 1902 **1901**

Tamworth District Electric Supply Co. Ld. Regd. 1930. Dissolved 1 Apr. 1948, undertaking being vested in British (later Central) Electricity Authority and East Midlands Area Board under Electricity Act 1947. Holders of securities were entitled to receive British Electricity 3% guaranteed stock (1968–73), as follows in respect of each £1 unit of capital held:

	£	s.	d.	
6% preference shares	1	9	0	
4% preference shares	1	4	0	
4¼% debentures	1	0	9⅗	
4% debentures	1	0	9⅗	**1949**

Tamworth Gaslight & Coke Co. Inc. by Special Act 1872. Dissolved 1 May 1949, undertaking being vested in West Midland Area Gas Board under Gas Act 1948. Holders of securities were entitled to receive British Gas 3% guaranteed stock 1990–95 as follows in respect of each £100 unit, unless otherwise stated, of security held:

	£	s.	d.	
Old shares (10% max.) of £20	33	0	0	
New Shares (7% max.) of £20	24	4	0	
New shares (7% max.) of £2	2	8	5	
4½% red. pref. stock	105	0	0	
4% (tax-free) deb. stock	137	10	0	
5% deb. stock	105	0	0	**1952**

Tamworth Gold Mining Co. Ld. Regd. 1895. Vol. liq. 15 Jan. 1897. Reconstructed as company of same name. Shareholders were entitled to 4 shares of 5*s.* (credited with 4*s.* 6*d.* paid) in new company for each share of £1 held. Final meeting return regd. 29 Dec. 1898 .... **1897**

Tamworth Gold Mining Co. Ld. Regd. 1897. Vol. liq. 9 Feb. 1899. Reconstructed as Associated Tamworth Mines Ld., in which company shareholders were entitled to 1 share of 5*s.* (credited with 4*s.* paid) for each share of 5*s.* held. Final meeting return regd. 27 Mar. 1906 .... **1908**

Tan Bark, Timber, Balata & Produce Co. Ld. Regd. 1911. Court Order to wind up 12 Mar. 1912. A first and final dividend of 20*s.* in the £ was announced in Sept. 1912. Struck off Register 1919 .... **1913**

Tanah Brunei Rubber Co. Ld. Regd. 1910 Vol. liq. 1 Aug. 1912. Final meeting return regd. 30 Oct. 1913 **1913**

Tanah Estates Ld. Regd. 1930. Vol. liq. (members') 23 Sept. 1931. Undertaking and assets were acquired by Tanah Estates (1921) Ld., in which company shareholders were entitled to 1 share of 2*s.* (credited with 1*s.* 8*d.* paid) for each share of 2*s.* held. Final meeting return regd. 2 Nov. 1933 .... **1932**

Tanah Gemok Rubber Estates Ld. Regd. 1917. Undertaking acquired in 1920 by Bekoh Consolidated Rubber Estates Ld. Struck off Register 30 Apr. 1946 **1946**

Tanalyk Corporation Ld. Regd. 1912. Vol. liq. 30 Dec. 1919. Reconstructed as Russo-Asiastic Consolidated Ld., in which company shareholders were entitled to 2 shares of £1 (credited as fully-paid) for each share of £1 held. Debenture stockholders were entitled to an equal amount of debenture stock in new company. Final meeting return regd. 23 Jan. 1922 .... **1920**

Tanat Valley Light Railway Co. Inc. (under Light Railways Act 1896) by order of Light Railway Commissioners confirmed by Board of Trade 4 Jan.1899 .... **1922**

Tanfield Steamship Co. Ld. Regd. 1919. Vol. liq. (members') 30 Mar. 1954. Capital returned to contributories—£2 3*s.* 1·4252*d.* per share of £1. Final meeting return regd. 7 Dec. 1955 .... **1957**

Tanganyika Central Gold Mines Ld. Inc. in South Africa 1927 as Sekenke Gold Mining Co. Ld.; name changed 1928. Vol. liq. (members') 15 Nov. 1961. Shareholders were entitled to 1 share of R0·50 in Afrikander Lease Ld. for every 8 shares held plus R0·043072636 cash per share. Liquidators released 25 May 1962 .... **1963**

Tanganyika Cordage Co. Ld. Regd. 1933. Vol. liq. (members') 8 Jan. 1937. Assets realised insufficient to pay unsecured creditors in full. Final meeting return regd. 19 Jan. 1940 .... **1937**

**See Stock Exchange Year-Book.*

VOL. FOR

Tanganyika Development Co. Ld. Regd. 1921. Vol. liq. (members') 18 Dec. 1929. Shareholders received 1 share of £1 in Bird & Co. (Africa) Ld. for each share of £1 held. Final meeting return regd. 9 July 1930 — **1930**

Tanganyika Exploration Ld. Undertaking and assets were acquired in 1927 by Tanganyika Goldfields Ld. for £17,580 in fully-paid shares .... — **1928**

Tanganyika Goldfields Ld. Regd. 1925. Vol. liq. (creditors') 17 Mar. 1931. 1st debenture holders received £6,000; 2nd debenture holders received £522 4s. 3d. Final meeting return regd. 28 June 1932 .... — **1932**

Tanganyika Minerals Ld. Regd. 1935. Vol. liq. (creditors') 21 July 1941. No capital returned to contributories. Final meeting return regd. 28 Nov. 1946 .. — **1947**

Tanganyika Sisal & Produce Co. Ld. Regd. 1923. Vol. liq. (members') 26 Aug. 1936. Capital returned to contributories—1$\frac{7}{10}$d. per share of 2s. Final meeting return regd. 13 May 1937 .... — **1937**

Tangent Wheels Ld. Regd. 1905. Vol. liq. 15 Jan. 1908. Final meeting return regd. 24 May 1909 .... — ***1909**

Tangga Batu Rubber Co. Ld. Regd. in Edinburgh 1909. Vol. liq. (members') 3 Apr. 1952. Capital returned to contributories—2s. 4$\frac{3}{4}$d. per share of 2s. £320 12s. 10d. was paid into Companies' Liquidation Account. Final meeting return regd. 25 July 1956 ..... — **1957**

Tangier Mine Ld. Regd. 1897. Vol. liq. 28 May 1900 for amalgamation with two other companies under title of Empire Gold Fields Ld. in which company shareholders were entitled to 1 share of £1 (credited with 19s. paid) for each share of £1 held. Final meeting return regd. 10 Mar. 1915 .... — **1901**

Tangkah Rubber Estate Ld Regd. 1909. Vol. liq. 14 June 1923. Estate and equipment were transferred to London Asiatic Rubber & Produce Co. Ld., in which company shareholders were entitled to 44 shares of 2s. (credited as fully-paid) for every 100 shares of 2s. held. Final meeting return regd. 22 Dec. 1923 .... — **1924**

Tangkok Rubber Plantations Ld. Regd. 1925. Vol. liq. (members') 27 Mar. 1956. Final meeting return regd. 6 Sept. 1958 .... — **1951**

Taniong Labu Rubber Plantations Ld. Regd. 1925. Vol. liq. (members') 24 Apr. 1956. Final meeting return regd. 16 Oct. 1958 .... — **1951**

Taniong Pagar Dock Co. Ld. Inc. Singapore 1899. The undertaking was expropriated on 30 June 1905 for $27,929,177. Capital returned to contributories— $761·76 per share of $100 in 1907; further payments (if any) not known .... — **1909**

Tankers Ld. Regd. 1920. Vol. liq. (members') 3 Dec. 1957. Capital returned to contributories—£1 10s. 1·68d. (approx.) per preference share of 10s. and 1s. 10·385d. per ordinary share of 1s. Final meeting return regd. 10 Sept. 1959 .... — **1960**

Tankerville Great Consols Co. Ld. Established 1880. In liquidation 1884 .... — **1885**

Tankerville Mining Co. Ld. Regd. 1870. Vol. liq. 23 Oct. 1880. Taken over by Tankerville Great Consols Co. Ld. Final meeting return regd. 9 June 1881 .... — **1883**

Tannadine Co. Ld. Regd. 1903. Vol. liq. 5 Mar. 1912. Final meeting return regd. 17 July 1914 .... — **1913**

Tanners & Leather Trades Insurance Co. Ld. See North-Western Insurance Co. Ld.

Tannett-Walker & Co. Ld. Regd. 1898. Court Order to wind up Oct. 1914. Struck off Register Mar. 1932 — **1933**

Tannic Black Co. Ld. Regd. 1882. Removed from Register 1906 .... — ***1885**

Tano Bippo Gold Mines Ld. Regd. 1902. Property acquired by Tarkwa Proprietary Ld., in which company shareholders were entitled to 1 share of 10s. (credited as fully-paid) for every 2 shares of 5s. held. Removed from Register 1907 .... — **1905**

Tano Consolidated Mines Ld. Regd. 1932. Vol. liq. (members') 10 Sept. 1936. Undertaking and assets were acquired by West African Mines & Estates Ld., in which company shareholders were entitled to 4 fully-paid ordinary shares of 2s. 6d. and 4 fully-paid shares and 3 shares of 5s. (credited with 2s. 6d. paid) in Bramansu Gold Corporation Ld. for every 12 shares of 2s. 6d. held. Final meeting return regd. 14 Apr. 1938 .... — **1937**

Tano Gold Dredging Ld. Regd 1934. Vol. liq. (members') 4 Nov. 1942. Certain assets were acquired by Bremang Gold Dredging Co. Ld in which company shareholders received 7 shares of 5s. for every 45 shares held. Shareholders also received 1s. 0·1d. per share in cash. £168 7s. was paid into Companies' Liquidation Account. Final meeting return regd. 27 Dec. 1944 .... — **1945**

Tansan Mineral Water Co. Ld. Regd. 1910. Receiver for debenture holders appointed 2 June 1913; ceased to act 22 Nov. 1913. Struck off Register 1915 .... — **1914**

Tapscott Steamship Co. Ld. Regd. 1883. Removed from Register 1906 .... — ***1898**

VOL. FOR

Taquah & Abosso Consolidated Ld. Regd. 1923. Vol. liq. 6 May 1927. Reconstructed as Taquah & Abosso Mines Ld., in which company shareholders were entitled to 1 share of 5s. (credited with 3s. 6d. paid) for each share of 5s. held. Final meeting return regd. 25 May 1928 .... — **1928**

Taquah & Abosso Gold Mining Co. Ld. Regd. 1888. Vol. liq. 31 Dec. 1898. Reconstructed as company of same name. Shareholders were entitled to 1 preferred ordinary and 1 ordinary share of £1 in new company for each ordinary share of £1 held, or 1 preference and 2 preferred ordinary shares of £1 for each preference share of £1 held. Final meeting return regd. 22 Feb. 1900 .... — **1900**

Taquah & Abosso Gold Mining Co. Ld. Regd. 1899. Vol. liq. 8 Feb. 1901. Reconstructed as Taquah and Abosso Gold Mining Co., (1900) Ld. (later Taquah Mining and Exploration Co. Ld.), in which company shareholders were entitled to 1 fully-paid share of £1 for each preference share of £1 held, or 75 fully-paid shares for every 100 preferred ordinary shares of £1 held, or 10 fully-paid shares for every 100 ordinary shares of £1 held. Holders of 1st debentures were entitled to an equal amount of 1st debentures (later converted into shares) in new company together with income bonds giving dividend rights equivalent to one ordinary share for £2 debentures and an option (since expired) over ordinary shares at par. Holders of 2nd debentures were entitled to an equal amount of 2nd debentures (later converted into shares) and 5,878 fully-paid shares in lieu of arrears of interest. Final meeting return regd. 12 Dec. 1901 .... — **1908**

Taquah and Abosso Gold Mining Co. (1900) Ld. See Taquah Mining and Exploration Co. Ld.

Taquah & Abosso Mines, Ld. Regd. 1927 in reconstruction of Taquah & Abosso Consolidated Ld. Vol. liq. (members') 30 Oct. 1956. Capital returned to contributories: 3s. 5$\frac{1}{4}$d. per share of 4s. Final meeting return regd. 28 Apr. 1961 .... — **1962**

Taquah Central Mines Ld. Regd. 1909. Vol. liq. (members') 29 Nov. 1929. No capital returned to contributories. Final meeting return regd. 16 Apr. 1930 .... — **1930**

Taquah Mining and Exploration Co. Ld. Regd. 1900 as Taquah and Abosso Gold Mining Co. (1900) Ld.; name changed Jan. 1908. Vol. liq. 13 Mar. 1923. Reconstructed as company of same name. Shareholders were entitled to 1 fully-paid share in new company for each share of £1 held; holders of income bonds were entitled to shares in new company. Final meeting return regd. 13 Mar. 1924 — **1924**

Tar (Patents) Solidifying & Distilling Co. Ld. See Patent Block Tar Motor Oil Co. Ld.

Taranki (New Zealand) Oil Wells Ld. Regd. 1911. Vol. liq. 12 Feb. 1920. Final meeting return regd. 11 July 1923 .... — **1921**

Tarapaca & Antofagasta Nitrate Co. See Compania Salitrera de Tarapaca y Antofagasta.

Tarapaca & Tocopilla Nitrate Co. Ld. See Taratoco Investment Ld.

Tarapaca Copper Quarries Ld. Regd. 1912. Struck off Register 27 Jan. 1942 .... — **1942**

Tarapaca Nitrate Co. Ld. Regd. 1889. Vol. liq. 21 Aug. 1891. The shares held in Paccha & Jazpampa Nitrate Co. Ld. were distributed to shareholders. Final meeting return regd. 8 Sept. 1894 .... — **1892**

Tarapaca Water Works Co. Ld. Regd. 1888. Vol. liq. (members') 22 Feb. 1956, the installations and springs were sold to the Chilian Government. Capital returned to contributories—2s. 7$\frac{1}{4}$d. per share of £2 5s. £261 7s. 3d. was paid into Companies Liquidation Account on account of unclaimed dividends and distributions. Final meeting return regd. 20 Aug. 1957 .... — **1958**

Tararu Creek Gold Mining Co. Ld. Regd. 1899. Removed from Register 1903 .... — **1903**

Taratoco Investment Ld. Regd. 1906 as Tarapaca & Tocopilla Nitrate Co. Ld.; name changed Oct. 1931. Struck off Register 19 Feb. 1965. .... — **1965**

Tarbrax Oil Co. Ld. Regd. Edinburgh 1904. Vol. liq. Dec. 1912. Undertaking acquired by Pumpherston Oil Co. Ld., in which company shareholders were entitled to 3 ordinary shares of £1 fully-paid, for every 10 ordinary shares of £1 held. Preference shares were repaid at par. Final meeting return regd. 12 June 1913 .... — **1913**

Tarbuck's Brewery Co. Ld. Regd. 1889. Vol. liq. 3 Nov. 1913. The undertaking and assets were sold to Peter Walker & Son, Warrington & Burton Ld. [later Peter Walker (Warrington) Ld.] Final meeting return regd. 12 July 1916 .... — **1914**

Tarfroid Ld. Regd. 1927. Vol. liq. (members') 26 Nov. 1931. Undertaking and assets were acquired by

VOL. FOR

Tarfroid (1931) Ld. (later Thames Tar Products & Contractors Ld.), in which company shareholders were entitled to 3 fully-paid shares and 8 shares of 1s. (credited with 9d. paid) for each preference share of 10s. held or 4 shares of 1s. (credited with 9d. paid) for every 5 ordinary shares of 1s. held. Final meeting return regd. 22 Nov. 1932 .... **1932**

Tarkoid Ld. Undertaking and assets were acquired in 1927 by Tarfroid Ld., for £23,195 in cash, £2,925 in fully-paid ordinary and £4,250 in fully-paid preference shares **1928**

Tarkwa & Ashanti Mines Ld. Regd. 1909. Vol. liq. Oct. 1911. Removed from Register 1913 .... **1912**

Tarkwa Banket Mining Syndicate Ld. Regd. 1900. Vol. liq. 2 Jan. 1918. Final meeting return regd. 5 Oct. 1918 .... **1918**

Tarkwa Banket West Ld. Regd. 1909. Vol. liq. (members') 22 June 1938. Undertaking and assets were acquired by London & African Mining Trust Ld. (later London & Associated Investment Trust Ld.) in which company shareholders were entitled to 1 fully-paid share of 1s. for each share of 1s. held. Final meeting return regd. 3 May 1941 .... **1939**

Tarkwa Consols Ld. Regd. 1901. Reconstructed 1907 as Cornish Adventurers Ld. (later Tarkwa Consols Ld. *see below*), in which company shareholders were entitled to 1 share of 5s. (credited as fully-paid) for each share of £1 held. Removed from Register 1912 **1908**

Tarkwa Consols Ld. Regd. 1907 as Cornish Adventurers Ld.; name changed 1909. Vol. liq. Dec. 1912. Struck off Register 1922 .... **1913**

Tarkwa District Exploration Co. Ld. Regd. 1901. Vol. liq. 29 June 1902. Final meeting return regd. 19 Apr. 1904 .... **1904**

Tarkwa, Dixcove & Sekondi Syndicate Ld. Regd. 1901. Struck off Register 19 Mar. 1907 .... **1908**

Tarkwa Gold Mines Ld. Regd. 1934. Vol. liq. (members') 23 June 1938. Undertaking and assets were acquired by London & African Mining Trust Ld. (later London & Associated Investment Trust Ld.) in which company shareholders were entitled to 1 share of 1s. (credited as fully-paid) for each share of 5s. held. Final meeting return regd. 1 May 1941 . **1939**

Tarkwa Insoryim Gold Syndicate Ld. Regd. 1901. Struck off Register 19 Mar. 1907 .... **1908**

Tarkwa Main Reef Ld. Regd. 1901. Vol. liq. Dec. 1909 for sale of properties to Tarquah Central Mines Ld., in which company shareholders were entitled to 1 share of £5 (credited as fully-paid) for every 3 shares of £1 held. Removed from Register 1910 .... **1910**

Tarkwa Mansu Gold Syndicate Ld. Regd. 1901. Removed from Register 1905 .... **1905**

Tarkwa Proprietary Ld. Regd. 1901. Vol. liq. Dec. 1906. The West African property was sold to Claremont Trust Ld. for 100,000 shares of £1 (credited with 15s. paid) and £500 in cash. Removed from Register 1907 .... **1907**

Tarkwa-Tomento Concession Ld. Regd. 1901. Vol. liq. 26 Sept. 1901. Final meeting return regd. 17 July 1902 .... **1902**

Tarkwa Whin Gold Syndicate Ld. Regd. 1901. Removed from Register 1905 .... **1905**

Tarless Fuel Syndicate Ld. Regd. 1907. Struck off Register 1928 .... **1927**

Tarnagulia Consols Gold Mine Ld. Regd. 1897. Reconstructed 1900 as Mines Development Co. of Victoria Ld in which company shareholders were entitled to 1 share of 10s. (credited with 8s. 6d. paid) for each share of £1 held. Removed from Register 1901..... **1901**

Tarpoley Light Railway Co. Inc. 1906 under the Light Railways Act 1896. Board of Trade Order to wind up 1916 .... **1918**

Tarquah Trading Co. Ld. Regd. 1911. Vol. liq 4 Apr. 1929. All shares owned by United Africa Co. Ld. Struck off Register 2 Apr. 1943 .... **1930**

Tarran (Robert G.) & Son Ld. *See* Dorran Construction Ld.

Tarryall Creek Gold Co. Ld. Regd. 1887 as Nouveau Monde Gold Mining Co. Ld.; name changed July 1889. Court Order to wind up 8 Nov. 1893. Liquidator released 27 Sept. 1895. Struck off Register 10 July 1906 .... **1894**

Tarstow, Denver & Co. Ld. Regd. 1889 as Authors' Co-operative Publishing Co. Ld. Struck off Register 28 July 1899 .... **1900**

Tasman & Crown Lyell Extended Mining Corporation. No Liability. Inc. Victoria 1907. London office closed during 1913 .... **1914**

Tasman & Crown Lyell Extended Mining Corporation. No Liability. Inc. Victoria 1906. Reconstructed as Tasman & Crown Lyell Extended Mines. No Liability, in which company shareholders were entitled to 2 fully-paid shares of 5s. for each fully-

VOL. FOR

paid share of 5s. held, and 2 shares credited with 4s. paid up for every share (with 7d. paid up) held ... **1908**

Tasman Lyell Copper Co. Ld. Regd. 1900. Vol. liq. 22 Oct. 1903. Undertaking acquired by Lyell Comstock Consolidated Copper Co. Ld. Final meeting return regd. 26 Jan. 1905 .... ***1904**

Tasman Lyall Prospecting Association. Inc. Victoria. Interest in copper mine acquired by Mount Lyell Comstock Copper Co. Ld. (later Lyell Comstock Consolidated Copper Co. Ld.). **1902**

Tasmania Crown Silver Mining Co. Ld. Regd. 1891. The property was sold to Zeehan Montana Mine Ld. for £5,000. Removed from Register 1901 .... **1900**

Tasmania Gold Mine Ld. Regd. 1910. Vol. liq. 17 Mar. 1915. Final meeting return regd. 20 May 1932...... **1915**

Tasmania Gold Mining Co. Ld. Regd. 1903. Vol. liq. 4 Oct. 1910 for reconstruction as Tasmania Gold Mine Ld., in which company shareholders were entitled to 1 share of 10s. (credited with 7s. 6d. paid) for each share of £1 held. Final meeting return regd. 28 July 1911 .... **1911**

Tasmanian Consols Ld. Regd. 1902. Vol. liq. 17 Aug. 1908. Properties and assets were to be sold to Mount Arthur Properties Ld. Struck off Register 7 Dec. 1926 .... **1909**

Tasmanian Copper Co. Ld. Regd. 1897. Vol. liq. 18 July 1918. Final meeting return regd. 27 Sept. 1923 ..... **1919**

Tasmanian Exploration Co. Ld. Inc. Tasmania 1895. Vol. liq. 1904 for reconstruction under same name. Shareholders were entitled to 2 shares of 10s. (credited with 9s. paid) in new company for each share of £1 held **1908**

Tasmanian Exploration Co. Ld. Inc. Guernsey 1904. Wound up 1912 .... **1913**

Tasmanian Gold Estates Co. Ld. Inc. Guernsey 1904 **1909**

Tasmanian Golden Gate Mine Ld. Regd. 1895. Vol. liq. July 1907. Capital returned to contributories—2s. 7½d. per share of £1 at Dec. 1907; further payments (if any) not known. Removed from Register 1909 **1908**

Tasmanian Hardwood Corporation Ld. Regd. 1906. Removed from Register 1912 .... **1909**

Tasmanian Investment and Trust Co. Ld. Regd. 1905. Vol. liq. 30 Nov. 1912. Final meeting return regd. 10 Aug. 1917 .... **1913**

Tasmanian Land & Exploration Co. Ld. Regd. 1889. Removed from Register 1906 .... **1895**

Tasmanian Main Line Railway Co. Ld. Formed with direct sanction of Tasmanian Government under provisions of the Acts of 1869 & 1870. Vol. liq. 1890, and the line transferred to Tasmanian Government **1891**

Tasmanian Metals Extraction Co. Ld. Inc. Tasmania 1908. 113,992 of the shares were held by Metals Extraction Corporation Ld. **1932**

Tasmanian New Golden Gate Extended Mines Ld. Regd. 1897. Removed from Register 1904 .... **1908**

Tasmanian Properties Ld. Regd. 1917. Struck off Register 1927.. **1925**

Tasmanian Silver Mining Co. Ld. Regd. 1889. Vol. liq. 2 May 1892. Reconstructed as New Tasmanian Silver Mining Co. Ld., in which company shareholders were entitled to 1 share of £1 (credited with 17s. paid) for each share of £1 held. Final meeting return regd. 15 Mar. 1893 .... **1893**

Tasmanian Smelting Co. Ld. Regd. 1898. Vol. liq. 2 June 1914. Struck off Register 14 Feb. 1922 .... **1915**

Tasmanian Tin Dredging Co. Ld. Regd. 1897. Removed from Register 1904 .... **1905**

Tata Industrial Bank Ld. Inc. British India 1917. Undertaking and assets were acquired in 1923 by Central Bank of India Ld. in which company shareholders were entitled to 1 share of Rs.50 (credited with Rs.25 paid) for every 2 shares of Rs.75 (Rs.22½ paid) held **1924**

Tata Power Co. Ld. Inc. India 1919. The outstanding 2% guaranteed A mortgage debenture stock was redeemed at par on 15 May 1948 .... **1949**

Tate Brothers' Agency & Trading Co. Ld. Inc. New South Wales 1887. Vol. liq. 1889 .... **1890**

Tate Steamers Ld. Regd. 1899. Vol. liq. 16 Nov. 1903. Final meeting return regd. 7 Apr. 1914 .... ***1905**

Tatem Steam Navigation Co. Ld. Regd. 1909. Vol. liq. (members') 6 Mar. 1945. Shareholders were entitled to 1 share of £1 of Atlantic Shipping & Trading Co. Ld. for each share of £1 held. Capital returned to contributories—£9 15s. 7d. per share of £1. Final meeting return regd. 27 Dec. 1946 .... **1947**

Tatham (John) & Sons Ld. Regd. 1888. Removed from Register 1901 .... **1891**

Tati Blue Jacket Syndicate Ld. Regd. 1893. Vol. liq. 10 Aug. 1908. Final meeting return regd. 18 June 1912 **1909**

Tati Concessions Ld. Regd. 1895. Vol. liq. 6 Mar. 1914. Reconstructed as Tati Co. Ld in which company shareholders were entitled to 1 share of £1 (credited

VOL. FOR

with 15s. paid) for each share of £1 held. Final
meeting return regd. 3 May 1916 .... **1914**

Tattersall (James) & Sons Ld. Regd. 1882. Vol. liq. 16
Mar. 1920. Final meeting return regd. 8 June 1920 *****1887**

Tattersall's (of Chicago) Ld. Regd. 1891. Vol. liq. 19
May 1898. Final meeting return regd. 2 Dec. 1898 **1899**

Tattersall's (of New York) Ld. Regd. 1890. Vol. liq. 19
May 1898. Final meeting return regd. 2 Dec. 1898 **1899**

Taunton & District Gas Co. Inc. by Special Act 1845 as
Taunton Gas Light & Coke Co.; name changed
1936. Dissolved 1 May 1949. undertaking being
vested in South Western Area Gas Board under Gas
Act 1948. Holders of securities were entitled to
receive British Gas 3% guaranteed stock 1990–95 as
follows in respect of each £100 unit, unless otherwise
stated, of security held:

	£	s.	d.
Cons. A stock (8% stand.)	167	0	0
New yellow shares (7% stand.) (of £5)	7	5	0
Ord. (1897) stock	145	0	0
5% perp. pref. stock	114	0	0
4% red. pref. stock	102	10	0
4% pref. stock	102	10	0
5% red. pref. stock	105	0	0
5% irred. deb. stock	125	0	0
4% red. deb. stock (1956)	102	0	0
4% red. deb. stock	100	5	0

1952

Taunton Cold Storage and Ice Co. Ld. Regd. 1927.
Majority of capital was owned by Western Ice &
Cold Storage Co. Ld. Vol. liq. (members') 25 Nov.
1963. Final meeting return regd. 25 Jan. 1964 .... **1955**

Taunton, Delmard, Lane & Co. Ld. Regd. 1889. Vol. liq.
5 Dec. 1890. Final meeting return regd. 14 Sept.
1893 .... **1892**

Taunton Electric Traction Co. Ld. Regd. 1903. Vol. liq.
25 July 1923. Final meeting return regd. 1 Aug. 1924 **1924**

Taunton Gas Light & Coke Co. See Taunton & District
Gas Co.

Taunus Silver-Lead & Copper Mining Co. Ld. Regd.
1881. Removed from Register 1888 .... *****1885**

Tavistock Great Consols Ld. Regd. 1881. Removed from
Register 1888 .... **1883**

Tavistock Hotel Co. Ld. Regd. 1886. Vol. liq. 12 Apr.
1928. Capital returned to contributories—£10 13s.
6d. per share of £10. Final meeting return regd. 27
Oct. 1928 .... **1929**

Tavistock Lighting, Coal & Coke Co. Ld. Regd. 1904.
Dissolved 1 May 1949, undertaking being vested in
South Western Area Gas Board under Gas Act
1948. Holders of securities were entitled to receive,
British Gas 3% guaranteed stock 1990–95 as follows
in respect of each £5 unit. unless otherwise stated, of
security held:

	£	s.	d.
Orig. shares	10	5	0
Addit. shares		7	5	0
4½% pref. shares (of £1)	1	0	0

1952

Tavoy Prospectors Ld. Regd. 1924. Vol. liq. (members')
28 Nov. 1958. All capital was owned by Tavoy Tin
Dredging Corpn. Ld. Final meeting return regd. 18
Mar. 1960 .... **1950**

Tavoy Rubber Co. Ld. Regd. 1917. Vol. liq. (creditors')
24 Nov. 1930. No capital returned to contributories.
Final meeting return regd. 27 Oct. 1931 .... **1931**

Tavoy Tin Dredging Corporation Ld. Regd. 20 Dec.
1923. Vol. loq. (members') 28 Nov. 1958. Winding-
up order 18 Nov. 1987. Final meeting held 22 Feb.
1988. Dissolved 22 May 1988. First distribution of
11p per share was made 28 Feb. 1959. In Jan. 1988
the liquidator stated that there is no indication that a
further remittance is likely to be effected in a
reasonable time. Should the funds in Burma
subsequently be received they would be "Bona
Vacantia" (ie property of the Crown). In these
circumstances it would, however, be open to any
shareholder or other interested party to applty to the
Court to have the company restored to the Register
in order that the funds might be recovered for
distribution to the shareholders. Amount paid into
Companies' Liquidation Account at 1 Apr. 1967
was £8,191·10 in respect of unclaimed distributions
and £1,523·36 in respect of unclaimed dividends **1988–9**

Tawar Rubber Estates Ld. Regd. 1923. Vol. liq. 28 Aug.
1928. Undertaking and assets were transferred to
Rambutan Rubber Estates Ld. in which company
shareholders were entitled to 1 share of 2s. for each
share of 2s. held. Final meeting return regd. 19 Oct.
1929 .... **1929**

Tawe Valley Gas Co. Inc. by Special Act 1908.
Dissolved 1 May 1949. undertaking being vested in
Wales Area Gas Board under Gas Act 1948. Holders
of securities were entitled to receive British Gas 3%
guaranteed stock 1990–95 as follows in respect of
each £10 unit, unless otherwise stated, of security

held:

VOL. FOR

	£	s.	d.
Orig. shares (10% stand.)	8	10	0
Addit. shares (7% stand.)	6	0	0
5% red. pref. shares	10	0	0
4½% irred. deb. stock (per £100)	110	0	0

1952

Taxco Mines of Mexico Ld. Regd. 1910. Vol. liq. 4 Oct.
1918. Final meeting return regd. 7 June 1921 .... **1919**

Taxicab & Motor Supply Co. Ld. Regd. 1919. Vol. liq.
July 1926. Struck off Register Mar. 1930 .... **1931**

Taylor & Sanderson Steam Shipping Co. Ld. Regd. 1899.
Vol. liq. 6 Jan. 1917. Final meeting return regd. 12
Oct. 1922 .... *****1918**

Taylor (Ernest) Ld. Regd. 1897 as Liverpool Tin
Canister Co. Ld.; name changed May 1918. Vol. liq.
26 Feb. 1930. Undertaking acquired by British Can
Co. Ld. Final meeting return regd. 26 Apr. 1933 **1940**

Taylor (John) & Co. Ld. Regd 1895. Vol. liq. (members')
7 July 1943. All shares owned by Walker &
Homfrays Ld. Final meeting return regd. 31 Oct.
1944 .... **1945**

Taylor (John) & Son, Edinburgh Ld. Regd. Edinburgh
1898. Vol. liq. (members') 25 Oct. 1945. Capital
returned to contributories—20s. 9d. per preference
share of £1. £27 17s. 5d. was paid into Companies'
Liquidation Account. Final meeting return regd. 29
Sept. 1947 .... **1948**

Taylor, Tunnicliff (Electrical Industries) Ld. Regd. 1938.
Vol. liq. (members') 17 June 1959 for amalgamation
with Bullers Ld.; the operating subsidiaries were
sold to Allied Insulators Ld. in which company
shareholders were entitled to receive 12 fully-paid
preference shares of £1 for every 1 preference
shares of £1 held and 1 fully-paid ordinary share of
5s. plus 5s. 10d. cash for every ordinary share of 5s.
held. Final meeting return regd. 4 Apr. 1960 .... **1960**

Taylor, Usher & Young Ld. Regd. 1923 as Vickers &
International Combustion Engineering Ld.; name
changed to International Combustion Ld. in May
1925 and as above July 1934. Vol. liq. (members')
Aug. 1934. Undertaking and assets acquired by
International Combustion Ld. now International
Combustion Holdings Ld. Final meeting return
regd. 5 Mar. 1937 .... **1935**

Taylor's Hygienic Service Ld. Regd. 1912. Vol. liq.
(members') 15 Apr. 1932. Undertaking and assets
were acquired by Mono Containers Ld. Shareholders were entitled to £5 7s. 1d. in cash and 172 fully-
paid shares of £1 in acquiring company for every 100
shares of £1 held. Final meeting return regd. 3 Apr.
1934 .... **1933**

Taylor's Matabele Gold Fields Ld. Regd. 1895. Vol. liq.
27 Sept. 1897. Reconstructed as company of same
name. Shareholders were entitled to 4 shares of £1
(credited with 16s. paid) for every 3 fully-paid
ordinary shares of £1 held. The peference shares
were repaid at par. Final meeting return regd. 7 Apr.
1898. .... **1902**

Taylor's Matabele Gold Fields Ld. Regd. 1897. Vol. liq.
14 Apr. 1902. Reconstructed as Estates and Mining
Co. of Rhodesia Ld., in which company shareholders were entitled to 2 shares of 5s. (credited with 3s.
6d. paid) for each share of £1 held. Final meeting
return regd. 30 Dec. 1905 .... **1908**

Taylor's Patent Shunting Lever Ld. Regd. 1904. Court
Order to wind up 21 July 1908. Capital returned to
conttibutories—4s. 2½d. in the £ in Aug. 1909;
further payments (if any) not known. Removed
from Register 1912 .... **1910**

Taymouth Castle Hotel Ld. Regd. Edinburgh 1922 as
Taymouth Castle Hydro Hotel Ld. Vol. liq. Mar.
1926. Court Order to continue winding up under
supervision 14 June 1926. Final meeting return regd.
15 July 1931. Court Order to dissolve 7 Dec. 1931 **1927**

Tcharken Cheleken Oil Co. Ld. Regd. 1911. Properties
were in hands of Soviet Government. Struck off
Register Apr. 1929 .... **1930**

Tchengelek Proprietary Co. Ld. Regd. 1911. Struck off
the Register 22 June 1956 .... **1957**

Tea & Rubber Plantations (Ceylon) Ld. Regd. 1914. Vol.
liq. 10 Nov. 1927. Capital returned to contributories—9d. per share of 1s. at Dec. 1927; further
payments (if any) not known. Final meeting return
regd. 9 Aug. 1928 .... **1928**

Tea Corporation Ld. Regd. 1903. Vol. liq. 3 Feb 1921.
Reconstructed as Tea Corporation (1921) Ld. (later
Tea Corporation Ld.) in which company shareholders were entitled to 1 share of £1 (credited with 10s.
paid) for each share of £1 held. Final meeting return
regd. 1 Oct. 1927 .... **1921**

Teakwood Steamship Co. (1926) Ld. Regd. 1926. Vol.
liq. (members') 31 Mar. 1930. Capital returned to
contributories—£1 9s. 0½d. per share of £1. Final
meeting return regd. 31 Jan. 1931 .... **1931**

VOL. FOR

Teall, Simpson & Co. Ld. Regd. 1872. Vol. liq. 21 Apr. 1887. Final meeting return regd. 26 Nov. 1892..... **1888**

Team By-Product Coke Co. Ld. Regd. 1912. Vol. liq. 24 May 1930. Assets realised insufficient to pay secured creditors in full. Final meeting return regd. 10 July 1935 .... **1931**

Tebing Rubber Estates Ld. Regd. 1919. Vol. liq. (members') 15 July 1931. Undertaking and assets were acquired by Tebing Rubber Estates (1931) Ld. in which company shareholders were entitled to 1 share of 2s. (credited with 1s. 6d. paid) for each share of 2s. held. Final meeting return regd. 13 June 1936 .... **1932**

Tebing Rubber Estates (1931) Ld. Regd. 1931. Vol. liq. (creditors) 19 May 1965, the estates having been expropriated by the Indonesian Govt. 14s. 10d. in the £1 was returned to creditors and E. B. Riddel & Co. Ld. was appointed as trustee to the company in respect of distribution of any compensation monies receivable in future from Indonesian Govt. £299 1s. 4d. was paid into Companies' Liquidation Account in respect of unclaimed dividends. Final meeting return regd. 31 Dec. 1965 .... **1967**

Tebolang Rubber Estate Ld. Regd. 1914. Vol. liq. (members') 20 May 1935. Reconstructed as Bikam Rubber Estate Ld., in which company shareholders were entitled to 6 shares of 2s. (credited as fully-paid) for each share of £1 held. Final meeting return regd. 9 Nov. 1935 .... **1936**

Tebrau (Johore) Rubber Syndicate Ld. Regd. Edinburgh 1907. Vol. liq. June 1909. Undertaking and assets sold to Tebrau Rubber Estates Ld., in which company shareholders received 6 shares of £1 for every 5 shares of £1 held. Final meeting return regd. 15 Dec. 1910 .... **1910**

Technology Investments Ld. Regd. 1963. Undertaking and assets acquired by Technological Investment Trust Ld., in which company A and B shareholders received 66 ordinary shares and 66 B shares respectively per 100 shares and 5½% debenture stockholders received a like amount of 5½% debenture stock. Company to be dissolved under Section 208 of Companies Act 1948 .... **1973-4**

Teck-Lebel (Kirkland) Syndicate Ld. Regd. 1914. Vol. liq. (members') 11 June 1940. No capital returned to contributories. Final meeting return regd. 24 Sept. 1940 .... **1943**

Tecla Ld. Regd. 1912. Vol. liq. 23 Apr. 1926. Final meeting return regd. 14 Jan. 1927 .... **1927**

Tecoma Silver Mining Co. Ld. Regd. 1873. Removed from Register 1885 .... ***1885**

Tedcastle, McCormick & Co. Ld. Regd. Dublin 1897. Vol. liq. Nov. 1919. Property and assets sold to British and Irish Steam Packet Co. Ld. Capital returned to contributories—£12 15s. per ordinary share of £5 held **1920**

Tee (J.) & Co. Ld. (See Pettigrew & Merriman) **1931**

Teekoy Rubber Estate Ld. Regd. 1910. Vol. liq. (members') 5 June 1944. The estate having been sold for £150,000. Capital returned to contributories—£2 6s. 0¾d. per £1 stock. £735 12s. 10d. was paid into Companies' Liquidation Account. Final meeting return regd. 30 Apr. 1947 .... **1948**

Tees Conservancy Commissioners. Constituted by Tees Conservancy Acts 1852 to 1964. Under provisions of Tees and Hartlepools Port Authority Act 1967 the undertaking was transferred to that authority on 1 Jan. 1967 and the board dissolved on that date ... **1968**

Tees Furnace Co. Ld. Regd. 1896. Vol. liq. 12 May 1924. Final meeting return regd. 14 May 1927 .... ***1925**

Tees Power Station Co. Ld. Regd. 1918. Under Act of 1932 the assets were transferred to North Eastern Electric Supply Co. Ld. which owned all shares of this company. Dissolved under Act on 30 Sept. 1932 **1933**

Tees Salt Co. Ld. Regd. 1890. Vol. liq. (members') 23 July 1931. Direct controlling interest held by Imperial Chemical Industries Ld. Final meeting return regd. 19 Sept. 1932 .... **1932**

Tees Side Iron and Engine Works Co. Ld. Regd. 1889. Vol. liq. 17 Apr. 1896. Final meeting return regd. 9 Oct. 1902 .... **1897**

Tees Valley Railway Co. Inc. 1865 .... **1882**

Teesdale Lead & Zinc Mines Ld. Regd. 1906. Vol. liq. 3 Oct. 1910. Final meeting return regd. 24 Dec. 1913 **1911**

Teesdale Mining Co. Ld. Regd. 1874. Removed from Register 1904 .... **1883**

Teetgen & Co. Ld. Regd. 1895. Vol. liq. (creditors') 5 Oct. 1966. No capital returned to contributories. Final meeting return regd. 9 June 1972 .... **1972**

Tehuantepec Exploration & Development Co. Ld. Regd. 1895. Vol. liq. Apr. 1908. Removed from Register 1912 .... **1909**

Teign Valley Granite Co. Ld. See Roads Reconstruction Ld.

VOL. FOR

Teign Valley Mining Co. Ld. Regd. 1896. Vol. liq. 14 Jan. 1901. Reconstructed 1901 as New Teign Valley Mining Co. Ld in which company shareholders were entitled to 4 shares of 5s. (credited with 4s. paid) for each share of 5s. held. Struck off Register 7 June 1932 .... **1904**

Teign Valley Railway Co. Inc. by Special Act 1863. In 1923 the undertaking was merged into the Great Western Railway Co. in which company stockholders were entitled to stock as follows:

For each £100 held	G. W.
A 4% Deb. ....£100 4% Debenture	
1884 4% Deb. ....£100 4% Debenture	
B 4% Deb. .... { £80 5% Cons. Pref.	£50 cash
C 4% Deb. .... £80 5% Cons. Pref.	
No. 1 5% Pref. .... £14 cash	
No. 2 5% Pref. .... £9 cash	
No. 3 5% Pref. .... £6 cash	
Ordinary.......................... £5 5s. cash	**1924**

Teja Malaya Tin Dredging Co. Ld. Regd. 1925. Vol. liq. (creditors') 21 Dec. 1931. Debenture stockholders received £647 0s. 4d. No capital returned to contributories. Final meeting return regd. 1 Feb. 1935 .... **1932**

Tekka Ld. Regd. 1907. Vol. liq. 2 Mar. 1920. Reconstructed as company of same name†. Shareholders were entitled to 4 shares of £1 in new company for each share of £1 held. Final meeting return regd. 31 May 1922 .... **1920**

Tekka-Taiping Ld. Regd. 1913. Vol. liq. 10 Oct. 1919. Reconstructed as company of same name. Shareholders were entitled to 5 shares of £1 (credited as fully-paid) in new company for each share of £1 held. Final meeting return regd. 10 June 1922..... **1920**

Tekka-Taiping Ld. Regd. 1919. Vol. liq. (members') 2 June 1958. Capital returned to contributories—12s. 6·3d. per share (of 15s.). Final meeting return regd. 23 Feb. 1963 .... **1964**

Telaga Oil Co. Ld. Regd. 1901. Vol. liq. 16 Mar. 1908. Final meeting return regd. 29 July 1908 .... **1909**

Telegraph Manufacturing Co. Ld. Regd. 1898. Vol. liq. 1 July 1902. Undertaking and assets were acquired by British Insulated and Helsby Cables Ld. (later British Insulated Cables Ld.). in which company shareholders were entitled to 6 ordinary shares of £5 for every 5 ordinary shares of £5 held or 1 preference share of £5 for each preference share of £5 held. Final meeting return regd. 27 Jan. 1903 .... **1903**

Telemarken Copper Mining & Smelting Co. Ld. Regd. 1906. Receiver appointed in June 1910. Struck off Register 1915 .... **1911**

Telephone Co. of Austria Ld. Regd. 1883. Vol. liq. 16 Feb. 1893. Final meeting return regd. 7 May 1895 **1893**

Telephone Co. of Egypt Ld. Regd. 1883. Vol. liq. 20 Nov. 1918. Business was sold to Egyptian Government. Struck off Register 20 Mar. 1925 .... **1919**

Telephone Co. of Ireland Ld. Regd. Dublin 1882. Business acquired by National Telephone Co. Ld. for £81,300 in cash **1894**

Telephone Development Co. Ld. Regd. 1912 as Telephone Development Co. (1912) Ld.; name changed Aug. 1914. Vol. liq. 15 Feb. 1917. Shareholders were entitled to 100 shares of £1 in Anglo-Portuguese Telephone Co. Ld. and 9 common shares of $100 in Brazilian Traction, Light & Power Co. Ld. (later Brazilian Light & Power) for every 50 shares of £5 held. Final meeting return regd. 23 Oct. 1918 ...... **1917**

Telephone Manufacturing Co. Ld. Regd. 1920 as Telephone Manufacturing Co. (1920) Ld.; name changed Jan. 1922. Vol. liq. 25 Nov. 1929. Part of the assets were transferred to Telephone Manufacturing (1929) Ld. (later Telephone Manufacturing Co. Ld.), and the remainder to Telephone Rentals Ld. Shareholders were entitled to 1 fully-paid share of 5s. in new company and 2 fully-paid shares of 5s. in Telephone Rentals Ld. for every 2 shares of 10s. held. £531 10s. 3d. was paid into Companies' Liquidation Account in respect of sale of unclaimed shares. Final meeting return regd. 29 Oct. 1931 .. **1930**

Telephone Properties Ld. See Temple Bar Investment Trust (Realisations) Ld.

Telfer & Co. Ld. Regd. in Edinburgh 1947. Vol. liq. 24 Feb. 1975. Capital returned to contributories— 11·14p per share (of 10p). The winding-up had been completed by 12 Feb. 1 980 .... **1982-3**

Telogoredjo United Plantations Ld. Regd. 1910. Vol. liq. (members') 7 June 1933. Undertaking and assets were acquired by company of same name. Shareholders were entitled to 1 share of £1 (credited with 17s. paid) in new company for each share of £1 held. Debenture stockholders were entitled to an equal amount of similar stock in new company. Final meeting return regd. 25 Apr. 1934 .... **1934**

*See Stock Exchange Year-Book.

VOL. FOR

Telogoredjo United Plantations Ld. Regd. 1933. The holders of the 5% Debenture stock, except Anglo-Indonesian Plantations Ld., were paid in full **1975-76**

Telok (F.M.S.) Rubber Co. Ld. Regd. 1912. Vol. liq. (members') 29 Dec. 1959. Capital returned to contributories—2*s*. per share of 2*s*. £11 13*s*. 11*d*. was paid into Companies' Liquidation Account. Final meeting return regd. 13 Mar 1961 .... **1962**

Telpherage Co. Ld. Regd. 1883. Vol. liq. 10 June 1890. Final meeting return regd. 6 Mar. 1895 .... **1891**

Telsen Electric Co. Ld. Regd. 1932. Court Order to wind up Dec. 1934. Assets realised insufficient to pay creditors in full. Liquidator released 14 Mar. 1939. Struck off Register 28 Jan. 1949 .... **1945**

Teluk Gong Rubber Co. Ld. Regd. Edinburgh 1922. Vol. liq. (members') 25 Nov. 1936. Undertaking was acquired by Scottish Malayan Estates Ld., in which company shareholders were entitled to 1 share of £1 (credited as fully-paid) and 1*s*. 6*d*. in cash for every 2 shares of £1 held. Final meeting return regd. 24 Nov. 1939 .... **1937**

Teluk Piah Rubber Estate Ld. Regd. 1910. Vol. liq. 6 Feb. 1914. Reconstructed as Teluk Piah Rubber Estate (1914) Ld., in which company shareholders were entitled to 4 shares of 2*s*. (credited with 1*s*. 3*d*. paid) for every 3 shares of 2*s*. held. Final meeting return regd. 11 Apr. 1916 .... **1914**

Teluk Piah Rubber Estate (1914) Ld. Regd 1914. All capital was owned by Seafield Amalgamated Rubber Co. Ld. Vol. liq. (members') 13 Jan 1961. Final meeting return regd. 6 Apr. 1963 .... **1960**

Temengor Tin Mining Co. Ld. Regd. 1926. Receiver appointed in Nov. 1931; ceased to Act 27 Nov. 1933. Assets realised insufficient to meet claims of debenture holders. Struck off Register 17 Dec. 1935 **1936**

Temiscouata Railway Bondholders' Committee Ld. Regd. 1898. Struck off Register 27 May 1955 .... **1952**

Temiscouata Railway Co. Inc. in Canada 1885. The undertaking was acquired by Canadian Government as from 1 Jan. 1949. Holders of provisional certificates issued by Temiscouata Railway Bondholders' Committee Ld. (in lieu of 5% consid. mortgage income bonds deposited with them) were entitled to a first and final repayment of 24½% per provisional certificate **1952**

Temma Tin Ld. Regd. 1912. Vol. liq. 11 July 1913. Final meeting return regd. 4 Nov. 1916 .... **1914**

Temperance Billiard Halls Ld. Regd. 1903 as Manchester & District Billiard Halls Ld.; name changed 9 June 1906. Vol. liq. 26 Oct. 1964. Capital returned to contributories (per share of 2*s*.)—8*s*. 3*d*. up to 1966 and 1·8129p thereafter. Final meeting held 23 Aug. 1979 .... **1983-3**

Temperley Steam Shipping Co. Ld. Regd. 1889. Vol. liq. 8 Dec. 1924. Final meeting return regd. 16 Sept. 1927 .... ***1925**

Temple Bar Investment Trust (Realisation) Ld. Regd. 1931 as Telephone Properties Ld.; name changed 1955 to Temple Bar Investment Trust Ld. and to present title 1977. Undertaking and assets acquired by Temple Bar Investment Trust Ld. 19 Aug 1977, stockholders received 5 ordinary stock units in acquiring company for every 7 ordinary units held, preference and 5¾% loan holders received like amounts of 4·2% preference and 5¾% loan stock respectively. Dissolved under Section 208 of Companies Act 1948 on 21 July 1978 .... **1979-80**

Temple Shipping Co. Ld. Regd. 1919. Vol. liq. 1 Dec. 1919. Final meeting return regd. 10 June 1920 .... ***1921**

Templeton Asbestos Mining Co. Ld. Regd. 1891. Vol. liq. 18 Aug. 1893. Final meeting return regd. 1 June 1898 .... ***1894**

Tempus Shipping Co. Ld. Regd. 1904. Vol. liq. (members') 3 June 1964. Final meeting return regd. 13 Aug. 1966 .... **1967**

Tenant Co. Ld. Regd. 1917. Vol. liq. 21 Oct. 1920. Final meeting return regd. 22 Aug. 1924 .... **1921**

Tenasserim Hevea Plantation Ld. Regd. 1910. Vol. liq. (members') 3 Aug. 1932. Undertaking and assets were acquired by Tenasserim Plantations Ld., in which company shareholders were entitied to 1 share of 2*s*. (credited with 1*s*. 10*d*. paid) for each share of 2*s*. held, £155 8*s*. 1*d*. was paid into Companies' Liquidation Account in respect of unclaimed shares and £135 14*s*. 8*d*. in respect of unclaimed dividends. Final meeting return regd. 2 Aug. 1933 .... **1933**

Tenasserim Plantations Ld. Regd. 1932. Vol. liq. (members') 5 Mar. 1953. Estates were sold to King Island Rubber Estates Ld., in which company stockholders received Kyats 2 stock for every 6*s*. stock held. Capital returned to contributories—1*s*. 4·15*d*. per 2*s*. stock. £9,267 4*s*. 6*d*. paid into Companies' Liquidation Account. Final meeting return regd. 31 July 1962 .... **1963**

Tenbury Railway Co. Inc. by Special Act 1859. Dissolved 2 Apr. 1949: undertaking vested 1 Jan. 1948 in British Transport Commission under Transport Act 1947. Holders of 4½% guaranteed shares were entitled to receive, in respect of each share of £10 held, £12 6*s*. British Transport 3% guaranteed stock 1978-88 .... **1949**

Tenby Gas Consumer Co. Ld. Regd. 1877. Dissolved 1 May 1949, undertaking being vested in Wales Area Gas Board under Gas Act 1948. Holders of ordinary shares (of £1) were entitled to receive £1 6*s*. British Gas 3% guaranteed stock 1990-95 for each share held **1952**

Tendring Hundred Railway Co. Inc. by Special Act in 1859. By Act of 1883 the undertaking was amalgamated with Great Eastern Railway, Co., in which company ordinary shareholders received £70 ordinary stock for every £100 shares held. Holders of A (4½%) debenture or B (3%) debenture stocks received 112½% or 87½% debenture stock respectively **1884**

Tennamaram Palm Oil Co. Ld. Regd. 1923. Vol. liq. 5 Mar. 1979. Final meeting return regd. 28 May 1981 **1974-5**

Tennant (Charles) & Partners Ld. Regd. 1884. Vol. liq. 4 May 1891. Salt mines and works acquired by I. C. I. (General Chemicals) Ld. Final meeting return regd. 16 June 1892 .... **1940**

Tennant's Estates Ld. Regd. 1909. Vol. liq. 6 Sept. 1928 for reconstruction as Tennant's Estates (1928) Ld. Struck off Register 8 Apr. 1938 .... **1939**

Tenom (Borneo) Rubber Co. Ld. Regd. Edinburgh 1906. Vol. liq. Apr. 1920 for reconstruction as Tenom Rubber Estates Ld., in which company shareholders were entitled to $3\frac{1}{5}$ or $37\frac{9}{100}$ shares of £1 for each ordinary or deferred share respectively held. Final meeting return regd. 5 Mar. 1921 .... **1921**

Tenom (Borneo) Rubber Co. Ld. Regd. Edinburgh 1920. Vol. liq. Aug. 1931. Undertaking and assets were acquired by Tenom Rubber Estates Ld., in which company shareholders were entitled to 3 shares of 2*s*. (credited with 1*s*. 6*d*. paid) for each share of £1 held. Final meeting return regd. 11 June 1932 ..... **1932**

Tenom Rubber Estates Ld. Regd. Edinburgh 1931. Vol. liq. (members') 28 Nov. 1960. Capital returned to contributories—6*s*. 6·44*d*. per share of 2*s*. £1,785 18*s*. 7*d*. paid into Companies' Liquidation Account. Final meeting return regd. 7 Dec. 1961 .... **1963**

Tenterden Brewery Co. Ld. Regd. 1922. Vol. liq. (members') 6 May 1937. Undertaking was acquired by Jude, Hanbury & Co. Ld. Capital returned to contributories—£25,784 3*s*. 7*d*. Final meeting return regd. 21 Oct. 1937 .... **1940**

Tenterden Railway Co. Inc. by Special Act 1895. Construction abandoned by South Eastern and London, Chatham and Dover Railways Act 1906 **1907**

Teofani & Co. Ld. Regd. 1908. Vol. liq. (members') 27 Aug. 1946. Undertaking acquired by company of similar title. Capital returned to contributories—preference shares repaid at par; 10*s*. 10*d*. per ordinary share of £1. Final meeting return regd. 8 Jan. 1955 .... **1951**

Terek General Oil Co. Ld. Regd. 9 Jan. 1914. Struck off Register 23 Apr. 1954 .... **1955**

Teria Tin Mines Ld. Regd. 1911. Vol. liq. 21 May 1914. Final meeting return regd. 7 Sept. 1917 .... **1915**

Terminal Cities of Canada Ld. Inc. Canada 1912. Vol. liq. Apr. 1926 .... **1927**

Terry (Henry K.) & Co. Ld. Regd. 1888. Vol. liq. 31 Dec. 1890. Final meeting return regd. 19 Jan. 1892 ..... **1891**

Terry (Herbert) & Sons Ld. *See* H.T. Investments Ld.

Tesoro Gold Mines Ld. Regd. 1889. Vol. liq. 14 Dec. 1893. Reconstructed as Segovia Gold Mines Ld., in which company shareholders were entitled to 1 share of 5*s*. (credited with 2*s*. 6*d*. paid) for each share of £1 held. Final meeting return regd. 18 Jan. 1896 .... **1898**

Tetbury Electric Supply Co. Ld. Regd. 1924. Vol. liq. (members') 3 Oct. 1933. Electric supply undertakings acquired by Wessex Electricity Co. Ld. Capital returned to contributories-£5 per preference share of £5; £1 7*s*. 3½*d*. per ordinary share of £1. Final meeting return regd. 22 Feb. 1934 .... **1934**

Tete Concessions Syndicate Ld. Regd. 1900. Vol. liq. May 1908. Removed from Register 1912. .... **1909**

Tetela Mining Co. Ld. Regd. 1904. Struck off Register 31 Oct. 1916 .... ***1915**

Tetiuhe Mining Corporation Ld. Regd. 1925. Vol. liq. (members') 16 Oct. 1936. Capital returned to contributories—2*s*. 0·014*d*. per share of 5*s*. £1,158 16*s*. 9*d*. was paid into Companies' Liquidation Account. Final meeting return regd. 14 Apr. 1938 **1937**

Tetley (Joseph) & Co. Ld. *See* Worship Street Realisations Ld.

**See Stock Exchange Year-Book.*

VOL. FOR

Tetuan Gold Mines Ld. Regd. 1888. Removed from Register 1895 .... *1892

Texas Land & Cattle Co. Ld. Regd. Edinburgh 1881. Vol. liq. Jan. 1908. Capital returned to contributories—£3 per share of £10 (£2 10s. paid); further payments (if any) not known. Final meeting return regd. 29 Oct. 1908 1908

Texas Oilfields Ld. Regd. June 1901. Vol. liq. 31 July 1913. The undertaking and assets were acquired by Fremont Oil Co. Ld., in which company shareholders were entitled to 1 share of £1 (credited with 15s. paid) for every 5 shares of £1 held. Final meeting return regd. 2 June 1921 1915

Textile Appliances Ld. Regd. Edinburgh 1902. Vol. liq. Sept. 1915. Final meeting return regd. 16 June 1925 1916

Textile Corporation Ld. Regd. 1920. Vol. liq. 6 Mar. 1923. Final meeting return regd. 9 June 1925 1924

Textile Industrial Trust Co. Ld. Regd. 1928. Holders of 6% debenture stock were entitled to 5% in cash and 1 share of 5s. in Kirklees Ld. for every £3 stock held in 1935. Receiver appointed in Apr. 1930; ceased to act Mar. 1939. Struck off Register 26 Apr. 1940 .. 1940

Textile Machinery Association Ld. Regd. 1899. Assets were realised and proceeds distributed to debenture holders. Struck off Register Apr. 1929 1930

Textile Manufacturing Co. (Stourport) Ld. Regd. 1894. Vol. liq. (members') 30 June 1931. Direct controlling interest held by Carpet Manufacturing Co. Ld. Final meeting return regd. 23 Apr. 1932 1932

Textile Patent Printing Co. (of England) Ld. Regd. 1902. Vol. liq. Mar. 1905. Removed from Register 1907 1906

Textile Securities Ld. Regd. 1916. Vol. liq. 28 Apr. 1919. Final meeting return regd. 21 Oct. 1919 .... *1920

Textile Trades Corporation, Berlin. Est. in Berlin in 1919. In liquidation 1940

Textorial Holdings Ld. Regd. 1949. Vol. liq. (members') 12 July 1961. All capital was owned by Whitworth & Mitchell Textorial Ld. Final meeting return regd. 23 Mar. 1962 1956

Thabawleik Tin Dredging Ld. Inc. Federated Malay States 13 Aug. 1923. Vol. liq. (members') 1 Oct. 1957. Distribution 16s. 8d per share (of 10s.). 1977 8

Thame Gas & Coke Co. Ld. Regd. 1856. Dissolved 1 May 1949. undertaking being vested in Southern Area Gas Board under Gas Act 1948. Holders of securities were entitled to receive British Gas 3% guaranteed stock 1990–95 as follows in respect of each £1 unit, unless otherwise stated, of security held:

	£	s.	d.
Orig. ord. shares	1	16	0
New ord. shares	1	8	0
3½% red. mort. debs. (of £50)	50	0	0

1952

Thames Association Football Club Ld. Regd. 1928. Vol. liq. (creditors') 13 Nov. 1935. Direct controlling interest held by West Ham Stadium Ld. Final meeting return regd. 16 Jan. 1936 1936

Thames Bank Wharf Motor Works Ld. Regd. 1907. Vol. liq. 6 Mar. 1911. Final meeting return regd. 19 July 1913 .... *1912

Thames Barge Co. Ld. Regd. 1879. Vol. liq. 1 Oct. 1887. Struck off Register 11 Aug. 1905. Restored to Register 22 Feb. 1908. Final meeting return regd. 30 Mar. 1911 1888

Thames Colour Plate Ld. Regd. 1909. Struck off Register 1916 1911

Thames Export Packing Co. Ld. Regd. 1916. Vol. liq. 19 Jan. 1926. Controlled by W. V. Bowater & Son Ld. Final meeting return regd. 14 Apr. 1927 1926

Thames Hauraki Goldfields Ld. Regd. 1896. Property was sold in 1898 to Standard Exploration Co. Ld. for 137,500 shares. Removed from Register 1903 1899

Thames Iron Works & Shipbuilding Co. Ld. Regd. 1872. Vol. liq. 13 July 1899. Business was acquired by Thames Iron Works Shipbuilding and Engineering Co. Ld. for 300,000 ordinary shares of £1; 70,357 preference shares of £1 and £379,643 in cash. Final meeting return regd. 24 Feb. 1902 1909

Thames Iron Works Shipbuilding & Engineering Co. Ld. Regd. 1899. Receiver appointed in Nov. 1911. A distribution to debenture holders was anticipated. Struck off Register 1928 1914

Thames (New Zealand) Exploring Syndicate Ld. Regd. 1897. Vol. liq. 3 Jan. 1899. Final meeting return regd. 26 July 1899 1899

Thames Steamboat Co. (1897) Ld. Regd. 1897. Struck off Register 1917 1902

Thames Storage (Explosives) Co. Ld. Regd. 1892. Vol. liq. July 1907. Removed from Register 1908 1908

Thames Valley & Goring Water & Gas Co. Ld. See South Oxfordshire Water Co.

Thames Valley Electric Supply Co. Ld. Regd. 1900. Vol. liq. 3 Dec. 1906. Removed from Register 1907 1907

VOL. FOR

Thanet Investment Trust Ld. Regd. 1933. Vol. liq. (members') 1 Nov. 1977. Capital returned to contributories—83·821p per ordinary share of 50p. Final meeting return regd. 8 Aug. 1978 1979–80

Thanet Super-Aëration Ld. See Kent Super Aëration Ld.

Thatched House (Sheffield) Ld. Regd. 1897. Vol. liq. 14 May 1928. Final meeting return regd. 16 Nov. 1928 1929

Thatchers' Breweries Ld. See Welton Breweries Ld.

Thawpit Exports Ld. Regd. 1929. Vol. liq. (creditors') 22 Oct. 1934. No capital returned to contributories. Final meeting return regd. 25 Aug. 1936 1935

Thawpit Ld. Regd. 1927. Vol. liq. (members') 24 Nov. 1932. Undertaking and assets transferred to Thawpit (1932) Ld., in which company shareholders were entitled to 1 share of 1s. (credited with 9d. paid) for each share of 1s. held. Final meeting return regd. 14 Aug. 1934 1933

Thawpit (1932) Ld. Regd. 1932. Vol. liq. (creditors') 20 July 1934. Assets were insufficient to pay unsecured creditors in full. Final meeting return regd. 13 Feb. 1939 1935

"The Adelphi" (London) Ld. Regd. 1946. All capital was owned by United City Property Trust Ld. Dissolved under section 208 of Companies Act, 1948 on 28 July 1955 1955

Theale & Great Western Sand & Gravel Co. Ld. Regd. 1928. Vol. liq. (members') 3 Sept. 1936. Undertaking was acquired by Wraysbury Sand & Gravel Co. Ld. in which company shareholders were entitled to 1 share of 2s. (credited as fully-paid) for each share of 2s. held. Final meeting return regd. 8 Sept. 1937 1937

Theatre Buildings Ld. Regd. 1915. Vol. liq. (members') 13 Oct. 1931. All shares owned by United Theatres Co. Ld. Final meeting return regd. 22 Mar. 1932 1932

Theatre Cinema (Cambridge) Ld. Regd. 1933. Vol. liq. 31 Mar. 1938. Indirect controlling interest held by Cambridge Holdings Ld. Final meeting return regd. 23 Nov. 1940 1939

Theatre Grimsby Ld. Regd. 1924. Vol. liq. (members') 26 Mar. 1940. All issued shares owned by Gaumont British Picture Corporation Ld. Final meeting return regd. 24 Mar. 1941 1941

Theatre Royal, Birmingham Ld. Regd. 1903. Vol. liq. 1 June 1929. Lease and equipment were sold to Moss' Empires Ld. (later M. E. Theatres Ld.). Capital returned to contributories—£2 7s. 6d. per share of 10s. plus 1 share in Prince of Wales Theatre (Birmingham) Ld. for each share of 10s. held. Final meeting return regd. 26 Feb. 1930 1930

Theatre Royal Cinema (Manchester) Ld. Regd. 1922. Court Order to wind up 13 Mar. 1923. Struck off Register Apr. 1929 1930

Theatre Royal Co., Manchester Ld. Regd. 1875. Vol. liq. 21 June 1920. Capital returned to contributories—£23 per share of £10 at Sept. 1920; further payments (if any) not known. Final meeting return regd. 4 Apr. 1921 1921

Theatre Securities Ld. Regd. 1928. Struck off Register 6 Aug. 1943 1944

Theindaw Tin Dredging Co. Ld. Regd. 1925. Vol. liq. (creditors') 27 Aug. 1930. Undertaking and assets were acquired by Tavoy Tin Dredging Corporation Ld., in which company shareholders were entitled to 1 share of 4s. (credited as fully-paid) for every 2 shares of £1 held. Final meeting return regd. 18 July 1931 1931

Theresie Safety Coaches Ld. Regd. 1928. Vol. liq. (members') 14 July 1933. Direct controlling interest held by Maidstone & District Motor Services Ld. Capital returned to contributories—£22 7s. 6d. Final meeting return regd. 27 Sept. 1933........................ 1934

Thermo Electric Ld. Regd. 1912 as Thermo-Electric Ore Reduction Corporation Ld.; name changed Aug. 1918. Receiver appointed 29 Apr. 1920. Assets realised insufficient to repay debentures. Struck off Register 12 Jan. 1932 1932

Thermos Ld. Regd. 1907. Vol. liq. 28 Aug. 1925. Reconstructed as Thermos (1925) Ld in which company shareholders were entitled to 1 fully-paid ordinary share of 1s. for each share of £1 held. Final meeting return regd. 26 May 1926 1926

Theta Gold Mining Co. Ld. Regd. 1904. Vol. liq. July 1908. The undertaking was acquired by Empress (Rhodesia) Mines Ld., in which company shareholders were entitled to 1 fully-paid share of £1 for each share of £1 held. Removed from Register 1909 1909

Thetford & Watton Railway Co. Inc. by Special Act 1866. Under Great Eastern Railway Act of 1887 the undertaking was amalgamated with that company. Holders of £100 debenture, preference or ordinary stocks received £93, £90 8s. 3d., or £19 4% debenture stock respectively 1898

Thetis Marine Insurance Co. Ld. Regd. 1870. Vol. liq. 9 Dec. 1875. Final meeting return regd. 16 Nov. 1882 *1876

VOL. FOR

Thew, Hooker & Gilbey Ld. Regd. 1884 as Condensed Peptonised Milk Co. Ld.; name changed Mar. 1909. Vol. liq. (members') 22 Dec. 1933. All capital held by United Dairies Ld. Final meeting return regd. 2 Oct. 1937 1934

Thingandon Tin Dredging Co. Ld. Regd. 1926. Vol. liq. (creditors') 27 Aug. 1930. Undertaking and assets were acquired by Tavoy Tin Dredging Corporation Ld., in which company shareholders were entitled to 1 share of 4s. (credited as fully-paid) for every 2 shares of 5s. held. Final meeting return regd. 18 July 1931 1931

Third Caledonian Trust Co. Ld. Regd. Edinburgh 1928. On 3 Jan. 1961. the undertaking and assets were acquired by The Clydesdale Investment Co. Ld. Stockholders received securities of that company in exchange for their holdings as follows—77 fully-paid ordinary shares of 5s. for every 100 stock units of 5s.; 110 fully-paid 4¾% preference shares of £1 for every £100 preference stock; debenture stockholders received a like amount of a similar security of Clydesdale and the liability for the £220,000 outstanding terminal debentures was assumed by that company. Dissolved on 2 May 1961 under Sec. 208 of Companies Act, 1948 1962

Third Conversion Investment Trust Ld. Regd. 1937. Vol. liq. (members') 20 Dec. 1945 for amalgamation with First Conversion Investment Trust Ld. (later Hambros Investment Trust Ld.) in which company shareholders were entitled to 3 fully-paid shares of £1 and 10s. 7·364d. cash for every 4 shares of 15s. held. Final meeting return regd. 18 Mar. 1947 1947

Third Scottish American Trust Co. Ld. Regd. in Edinburgh 1879. Undertaking merged with First Scottish American Trust Co. Ld. in Jan. 1970;. ordinary shareholders received 221 ordinary shares for every 200 shares held and preference stockholders a like amount of 5% preference stock. Liability for debenture stocks and dollar loan was assumed by First Scottish American Trust Co. Ld. Dissolved on 28 Apr. 1970 by Order of the Court 1970

Third Scottish Northern Investment Trust Ld. Regd. in Edinburgh 1925. Undertaking was merged with Scottish Northern Investment Trust Ld.; ordinary shareholders received 43 ordinary shares for every 40 held and 5% preference stockholders received 11 4¾% preference shares for every £10 held; liability for debenture stocks was assumed by Scottish Northern Investment Trust Ld. Dissolved by Order of the Court on 16 Dec. 1968 1970

Third Scottish Western Investment Co. Ld. Regd. Edinburgh 1926. On 3 Jan. 1961 the undertaking and assets were acquired by The Clydesdale Investment Co. Ld. Stockholders received securities of that company in exchange for their holdings as follows—80 fully-paid ordinary shares of 5s. for every 100 stock units of 5s.; 110 4¾% preference shares of £1 for every £100 preference stock; debenture stockholders received a like amount of a similar security of Clydesdale and the liability for the £90,000 outstanding terminal debentures was assumed by that company. Dissolved on 2 May 1961 under Sec. 108 of Companies Act, 1948 1962

Thirsk District Water Co. Ld. Regd. 1878. On 1 Jan. 1965 the undertaking was vested in the Ryedale Joint Water Board. Vol. liq. (members') 2 Nov. 1967. Capital returned to contributories—£1 6s. 4d. per share of £5. Final meeting return regd. 27 Mar 1969 1970

Thirsk Gas Co. Inc. by Special Act 1871. Dissolved 1 May 1949, undertaking being vested In North Eastern Area Gas Board under Gas Act 1948. Holders of securities were entitled to receive British Gas 3% guaranteed stock 1990–95 as follows in respect of each £10 unit unless otherwise stated, of security held:

	£	s.	d.
Orig. shares (10% max.)	11	0	0
Addit. shares (7% max.)	11	0	0
5% irred. debs. (of £100)	125	0	0

.... 1952

Thistle Consolidated Mines Ld. Regd. 1896. Reconstructed 1904 as company of same name. Shareholders were entitled to 6 shares of 5s. (credited with 4s paid) in new company for every 5 preference shares of 5s. or every 5 ordinary shares of 5s. held. Removed from Register 1907 1908

Thistle Consolidated Mines Ld. Inc. Transvaal 1904. In liquidation in 1915 1925

Thistle-Etna Gold Mines Ld. Regd. 1908. Vol. liq. 6 June 1918. Capital returned to contributories—5s. per share of £1 in Oct. 1918; further payments (if any) not known. Final meeting return regd. 1 Aug. 1919 1919

Thistle-Etna Gold Mines Ld. Regd. 1934. Vol. liq. (members') 8 Apr. 1952. Capital returned to contributories—1s. 9½d. per share (of 4s.). Final meeting return regd. 2 Nov. 1956 1958

Thistle Reef Gold Mining Co. Ld. Regd. 1888 as New Eberhardt Co. Ld.; name changed 1894. Reconstructed 1896 as Thistle Consolidated Mines Ld., in which company shareholders were entitled to 1 preference share of 5s. (credited as fully-paid) for each preference share of 5s. held, or 6 ordinary shares of 5s. (credited with 3s. 3d. paid) for every 5 ordinary shares of 5s. held. Removed from Register 1903 1904

Thistle Syndicate Ld. Regd. 1901. Reconstructed 1904 as Amalgamated Mining and Exploration Co. Ld., in which company shareholders were entitled to 2 shares of 5s. (credited with 3s. 6d. paid) and 3 fully-paid shares for each share of £1 held. Removed from Register 1905 1905

Thom (Alexander) & Co. Ld. Regd. Dublin 1887 as Printing & Publishing Co. Ld.; name changed Nov. 1887. Undertaking acquired by company of same name (later Hely Thom Ld.) in 1890 1890

Thom (David) & Co. Ld. Regd 1905. Vol. liq. (members') 18 June 1965. No capital returned to contributories. Final meeting return regd. 9 Sept. 1966 1967

Thom (David), Dornier & Co. Ld. Regd. 1898. Reconstructed 1905 as David Thom and Co. Ld. in which company shareholders were entitled to 4 preference shares of £1 (credited as fully-paid) for each preference share of £5 held or 1 ordinary share of £1 (credited as fully-paid) for each ordinary share of £5 held. Removed from Register 1906 1905

Thomas & Appleton Shipping Co. Ld. Regd. 1911. Vol. liq. 31 Dec. 1917. Final meeting return regd. 16 Mar. 1920 .... *1919

Thomas & Davey Ld. Regd. 1920. Vol. liq. (members') 12 May 1950. Struck off Register 17 Dec. 1954 ... 1938

Thomas & Evans and John Dyer, Ld. Regd. 1899. All capital was owned by Weaver & Co. Ld. Vol. liq. (members') 11 June 1964. Final meeting return regd. 21 Aug. 1964 1940

Thomas Bond Worth & Sons Ld. See Worth (Bond) Hldgs Ld.

Thomas Brothers Shipping Co. Ld. Regd. 1920. Vol. liq. 2 May 1929. Final meeting return regd. 13 Mar. 1931 .... *1930

Thomas Danks & Co. Ld. See Town and Commercial Properties Ld.

Thomas (J.) & Co. (Cardiff) Ld. Regd. 1908. Vol. liq. 30 Oct. 1929. Direct controlling interest held by R. E. Jones Ld. Struck off Register 13 July 1934 1930

Thomas' Reef Gold Mining Co. Ld. Established 1886 and Inc. as limited in Natal, Transvaal and Cape Colony. In liquidation in 1891 1892

Thomasson (John) & Son Ld. Regd. 1905. Vol. liq. 25 Oct. 1922. The undertaking and assets were acquired by Crosses and Heaton's Associated Mills Ld. Final meeting return regd. 1 Jan. 1926 1923

Thomasson (John) & Son Ld. Regd. 1922. Vol. liq. (members') 31 Aug. 1944. All capital was owned by Crosses & Heaton Ld. Final meeting return regd. 17 July 1945 1946

Thompson Alpine & Co. Ld. See Mann, Little & Co. Ld.

Thompson & Collins' Enterprises Ld. Regd. 1923. Vol. liq. 10 Sept. 1928. Properties acquired by Denman Picture Houses Ld. Struck off Register 3 Oct. 1941 1940

Thompson & Shackell Ld. Regd. 1886. Vol. liq. (members') 22 Nov. 1930. Capital returned to contributories—20s. per preference share of £1; 11s. per ordinary share of £1. Final meeting return regd. 13 Mar. 1945 1931

Thompson & Southwick Ld. Regd. 1897. Vol. liq. Dec. 1912. Reconstructed as company of same name. Removed from Register 1913 1913

Thompson (Geo.) & Co. Ld. Regd. 1905. In July 1932 the 5 vessels, goodwill and business were sold to Shaw, Savill and Albion Co. Ld., for £350,000. Debenture stockholders were expected to receive about 15% cash, 42% in scrip, and 43% in deferred creditors' certificates of Oceanic Steam Navigation Co. Ld. Vol. liq. (creditors') 4 Jan. 1933. No capital returned to contributories. Final meeting return regd. 12 Mar. 1937 1933

Thompson (Henry) & Sons Ld. Regd. 1895. Vol. liq. (members') 25 Aug. 1950. Capital returned to contributories—£3 11s. 3d. per preference share of £5. £442 was paid into Companies' Liquidation Account. Final meeting return regd. 1 Jan. 1952 1952

Thompson (L. A.) Scenic Railways, Continental Ld. Regd. 1908. Court Order to wind up 23 Nov. 1915. Liquidator released 19 Feb. 1921. Struck off Register 1 July 1921 1916

Thompson, McKay & Co. Ld. Regd. 1897. Business was absorbed by London & North Eastern Railway Co. who held all shares. Dissolved by Act of 1939 1940

*See Stock Exchange Year-Book.

VOL. FOR

Thompson Steamshipping Co. Ld. Regd. 1892. Vol. liq. (members') 31 Mar. 1954 undertaking and assets (excluding certain shareholdings and cash) being transferred to Scottish Tanker Co. Ld. for 600,012 fully-paid ordinary shares of £1 of that company. Preference shares were repaid at par and ordinary shareholders were entitled to receive £2 cash plus 42 ordinary shares of £1 of Scottish Tanker Co. Ld. for each share of £6 held. £36 5s. 11d. was paid into Companies' Liquidation Account. Final meeting return regd. 26 July 1955 .... **1956**

Thompson (Stephen) & Co. Ld. Regd. 1888. Vol. liq. 17 Jan. 1905. Final meeting return regd. 29 June 1905 **1940**

Thompson (W. B.) & Co. Ld. Regd. Edinburgh 1886. Vol. liq. 13 Feb. 1896. Undertaking acquired by Caledon Shipbuilding and Engineering Co. Ld. Final meeting return regd. 6 Jan. 1897 .... **1897**

Thomson (I.) T. Bonar & Co. Dissolved 1923 .... **1922**

Thomson (James and George) Ld. *See* Clydebank Engineering & Shipbuilding Co. Ld.

Thomson (J. G.) and Co. Ld. Regd. Edinburgh 1904. Vol. liq. Mar. 1921. Undertaking and assets were acquired by company of same name. Preference shares were repaid in cash at par. Final meeting return regd. 18 Feb. 1924 .... **1922**

Thomson, Marshall & Co. Ld. Regd. Edinburgh 1890. Vol. liq. Feb. 1902. Final meeting return regd. 16 May 1907 .... **1902**

Thomson (Patrick) Ld. Regd. Edinburgh 1907. Vol. liq. (members') 30 Jan. 1953. Struck off Register 1 May 1962 .... **1951**

Thomson (W. B.) Ld. Regd. Edinburgh 1898. Vol. liq. Mar. 1915. Court Order to dissolve 3 Sept. 1918 **1916**

Thorley (Joseph) Ld. Regd. 1898. Vol. liq. (members') 30 Dec. 1957. Final meeting return regd. 16 Oct. 1958 .... **1947**

Thorn & Hoddle Ld. Regd. 1900 as Thorn & Hoddle Acetylene Co. Ld.; name changed Aug. 1923. Vol. liq. (members') 3 Oct. 1960. Capital returned to contributories—preference repaid at par; ordinary £4 6s. per share of £1. Final meeting return regd. 20 June 1962 .... **1963**

Thornbury Gas Light & Coke Co. Ld. Regd. 1856. Dissolved 1 May 1949, undertaking being vested in South Western Area Gas Board under Gas Act 1948. Holders of securities were entitled to receive British Gas 3% guaranteed stock 1990–95 as follows:

	£	s.	d.
Ord. stock (per £100)...........................	105	0	0
New ord. shares (of £1)	1	1	0

1952

Thorncliffe Coal Distillation Ld. Regd. 1920. Vol. liq. (members') 8 Oct. 1953. Capital returned to contributories—24s. per preference share of £1; 22s. 8·85d. per ordinary share of 1s. Final meeting return regd. 10 June 1954 .... **1955**

Thorne (R.) & Sons Ld. Regd. Edinburgh 1892. Vol. liq. Feb. 1920. Final meeting return regd. 22 Dec. 1925 **1921**

Thorneburry Miners' Safety Lamp Co. Ld. Regd. 1890. Vol. liq. 18 July 1893. Final meeting return regd. 20 Apr. 1894 .... **1894**

Thornewill & Warham (1919) Ld. Regd. 1919. Vol. liq. 14 May 1929. Final meeting return regd. 15 July 1931 .... **1930**

Thornham Spinning Co. Ld. Regd. 1920. Vol. liq. (creditors') 22 May 1962. Final meeting held 7 May 1976 .... **1976–77**

Thorns, Son & Co. Ld. Regd. 1898. Vol. liq. 7 Mar. 1925. Final meeting return regd. 14 Sept. 1926 .... **1926**

Thornthwaite Mines Ld. Regd. 1901. Vol. liq. 19 Jan. 1923. Final meeting return regd. 21 Apr. 1927 ..... **1924**

Thornton-Norris Products Ld. Regd. 1928. Controlling interest held by Sphinx Electric Ld. Struck off Register 1932 .... **1930**

Thornton-Scarth Automatic Lighting Syndicate Ld. Regd. 1897. Removed from Register 1901 .... **1901**

Thornton-Smith Ld. *See* Investment & Property Trust Ld

Thorougood (T. W.) Ld. *See* Thorougood's Breweries Ld.

Thorougood's Breweries Ld. Regd. 1896 as T. W. Thorougood Ld.; name changed in Feb. 1898. Vol. liq. 15 Jan. 1925. Undertaking was acquired by Threlfall's Brewery Co. Ld. (later Threlfalls Chesters Ld.). Final meeting return regd. 24 Sept. 1926 **1926**

Thorpe Bros. & Co. Ld. Regd. 1896. Removed from Register 1903 .... **1901**

Thorp's Gawber Hall Collleries Ld. Regd. 1872. Wound up by Order of Court 28 Apr. 1881. .... ***1882**

Thrapston Gas Co. Ld. Regd. 1857. Dissolved 1 May 1949, undertaking being vested in East Midland Ares Gas Board under Gas Act 1948. Holders of ordinary shares (of £10) were entitled to receive £23

VOL. FOR

British Gas 3% guaranteed stock 1990–95 for each share held **1952**

3 North Smithfield Gold Mining Co. Ld. Inc. Queensland 1895. Reconstructed as company of same name.... **1906**

3 North Smithfield Gold Mining Co. Ld. Inc. Queensland 1898. In 1905 the London agents stated that no accounts had been issued and no work done by company **1906**

Three Towns Banking Co. Ld. Established 1856. Regd. 1863 as Three Towns Loan and Banking Co. Ld.; name changed May 1866. Vol. liq. 27 Feb. 1890. Taken over by Devon & Cornwall Banking Co. Ld. Final meeting return regd. 2 June 1893 .... **1906**

Threikeld Lead Mines Ld. Regd. 1913. Receiver appointed 21 Mar. 1917; ceased to act 21 Nov. 1919. Struck off Register 21 June 1921 .... ***1919**

Thrutchley Brothers Ld. Regd. 1889. Vol. liq. 3 Apr. 1895. Court Orders: to continue winding up under supervision 10 Apr. 1895; to dissolve 14 Feb. 1900 **1896**

Thunder & Little Ld. Regd. 1895. Vol. liq. 27 Mar. 1899. Undertaking acquired by Mitcham & Cheam Brewery Co. Ld. Final meeting return regd. 11 Nov. 1899 .... **1939**

Thwaites Brothers Ld. Regd. 1886. Receiver appointed 17 Sept. 1923; ceased to act 25 Oct. 1929. Goodwill and patterns were acquired by Alldays & Onions Ld. Struck off Register 20 Jan. 1931 .... **1940**

Thwaites (R.) & Co. Ld. Regd. 1898. Receiver appointed 5 Oct. 1915. Struck off Register 1921 .... **1916**

Ticehurst & District Water & Gas Co. Inc. by Special Act 1904. Receiver for debenture holders sold the water undertaking to Heathfield and District Water Co. for £9,000 and the gas undertaking to Wadhurst and District Gas and Coke Co. for £2,700 .... **1915**

Ticehurst and Robertsbridge Water Co. Inc. by Special Act 1902. Amalgamated in 1905 with Wadhurst, Ticehurst and District Gas Light and Coke Co. to form Ticehurst and District Water and Gas Co.... **1908**

Ticehurst Gas Light and Coke Co. Undertaking acquired in 1902 by Wadhurst Ticehurst and District Gas, Light and Coke Co. **1904**

Tickhill Light Railway Co. Inc. (under Light Railways Act 1896) by order of Light Railway Commissioners, confirmed by Board of Trade 1901. Powers to construct purchased on behalf of Great Northern Railway Co. by Order of 1907 .... **1908**

Tide Water Oil Co. (England) Ld. Regd. 1923 as British Mineral Oil Products Ld.; name changed 29 Sept. 1927. Vol. liq. (members') 27 May 1930. Final meeting return 12 Aug. 1931. .... ***1931**

Tideswell Gas Light & Coke Co. Ld. Regd. 1861. Dissolved 1 May 1949. undertaking being vested in East Midland Area Gas Board under Gas Act 1948. Holders of securities were entitled to receive British Gas 3% guaranteed stock 1990–95 as follows:

	£	s.	d.
Ord. shares (of £1)...........................		17	6
4% red. debs. (of £100)......................	100	0	0

1952

Tidewater Railway Co. *See* Virginia Railway Co.

Tierra del Fuego Development Co. Inc. Chile 1892. The outstanding 6% debentures were repaid on 30 Nov. 1915 .... **1916**

Tiger (Masse Kesse) Gold Co. Ld. Regd. 1895. Vol. liq. 18 Dec. 1902. Removed from Register 1908 .... **1903**

Tigerfontein Gold Mines Ld. Regd. 1895. Vol. liq. 26 Nov. 1897. Undertaking was acquired by Rooder- and Gold Mining Co. Ld., in which company shareholders were entitled to 5 fully-paid shares of £1 for every 6 shares of £1 held. Final meeting return regd. 8 June 1898 .... **1898**

Tigon Mining & Finance Corpn. Ld. Regd. 1913 as Anatolia Copper Co. Ld., name changed 12 Apr. 1926. Struck off Register 2 June 1944 .... **1945**

Tikam Batu Rubber Co. Ld. Regd. 1910. Vol. liq. 12 June 1919. Reconstructed as company of same name. Shareholders were entitled to 5 fully-paid shares of 2s. for each A share of 2s. held or 3 shares of 2s. (credited with 1s. paid) for every 2 ordinary shares of 2s. held. Debenture stocks were entitled to an equal amount of similar stock in new company. Final meeting return regd. 9 Dec. 1920 .... **1919**

Tikam Batu Rubber Co. Ld. Regd. 1919. Vol. liq. 31 May 1932. Final meeting return regd. 23 Feb. 1934 **1933**

Tilbury & Gravesend Tunnel Junction Railway Co. Inc. by Special Act 1882. Abandoned by Act of 1884 **1886**

Tilbury Contracting and Dredging Co. Ld. Regd. 1884 as London & Tilbury Lighterage Co. Ld.; name changed to London & Tilbury Lighterage, Contracting & Dredging Co. Ld. in Jan. 1896 and as above Aug. 1904. Undertaking and assets were acquired by Tilbury Contracting and Dredging Co. (1906) Ld. (later Tilbury Contracting Group Ld.) in which company shareholders were entitled to 10 shares of

See Stock Exchange Year-Book.

VOL. FOR

£1 for each share of £10 held. Removed from Register 1908.. **1906**

Tilbury Dock Ship & Engine Repairing Co. Ld. Regd. 1885. Vol. liq. 3 Dec. 1888. Final meeting return regd. 24 July 1891 .... **1889**

Tilling and British Automobile Traction Ld. Regd. 1905 as British Automobile Development Co. Ld.; name changed in 1912 to British Automobile Traction Co. Ld. and as above in May 1928. Vol. liq. (members') 28 Sept. 1942. Shareholders received 1 fully-paid ordinary share of 10s. and 1 fully-paid preference share of 10s. in each of B. E. T. Omnibus Services Ld. and Tilling Motor Services Ld., in exchange for each ordinary or preference share of £1 held respectively. Final meeting return regd. 20 Dec. 1943 .... **1945**

Tilling Motor Services Ld. Regd. 1942. Vol. liq. (members') 31 Dec. 1949, the undertaking was acquired by British Transport Commission who owned all capital. Final meeting return regd. 21 Sept. 1950 .... **1951**

Tillyfour Rubber Co. Ld. Regd. 25 Sept. 1909. Vol. liq. (members) 4 July 1951. Capital returned to contributories—1s. 0·98d. per 2s. stock. £848 18s. 9d. was paid into Companies' Liquidation Account. Final meeting return regd. 10 June 1953 .... **1954**

Tilmanstone Investment Trust Ld. Regd. 1925 as Tilmanstone (Kent) Collieries Ld.; name changed to Tilmanstone Holdings Ld. in 1947 and as above 17 July 1961. In Apr. 1968 the undertaking was transferred to Union Commercial Investment Co. Ld. in which company shareholders were entitled to receive 7 ordinary shares of 5s. per 25 shares of 2s. held. Company is to be dissolved under Section 208 of Companies Act 1948 .... **1970**

Tilmanstone (Kent) Collieries Ld., later Tilmanstone Holdings Ld. *See above.*

Tilt Cove Copper Co. Ld. Regd. 1888. Vol. liq. 11 Dec. 1913. Final meeting return regd. 12 Dec. 1914 .... **1914**

Timachevo Estate Co. Ld. Regd. 1881. Removed from Register 1888 .... *****1885**

Timar Mining Syndicate Ld. Regd. 1900. Removed from Register 1911 .... **1905**

Timber Corporation Ld. Regd. 1902. The assets were acquired by Millars Timber & Trading Co. Ld. which company owned over 98% of the capital. Struck off Register 16 Feb. 1951 .... **1951**

Timberlake & Co. Ld. Regd. 1896. Court Order to wind up 2 May 1898. Liquidator released 21 Aug. 1899. Removed from Register 19 Mar. 1909 .... *****1898**

Timbiqui Gold Mines Co. Ld. Regd. 1899. Removed from Register 1908 .... **1941**

Times Insurance Co. Ld. Regd. 1902. Court Order to wind up 1905. Removed from Register 1911 .... **1906**

Times Mutual Insurance Co. Ld. Regd. 1892. Vol. liq. 18 Aug. 1896. Undertaking absorbed by Manchester Fire Assurance Co. Final meeting return regd. 9 Feb. 1898 .... *****1897**

Times Shipping Co. Ld. Regd. 1919. Vol. liq. July 1925. Final meeting return regd. 4 Oct. 1926 .... **1926**

Times (The) S. A. (Paris). Wound up 30 June 1946. Controlling interest was held by Times Publishing Co. Ld. **1946**

Timoleague and Courtmacsherry Extension Light Railway Co. Ld. Regd. 1888. In 1925 the undertaking was merged into the Great Southern Railways Co. under a scheme which provided that the shareholders should receive £125 Great Southern Railways 4% Preference Stock for every £100 held **1925**

Tin & Amblygonite Mines Ld. Regd. 1905. Removed from Register 1908 .... **1908**

Tin & Trading Co. of Nigeria Ld. Regd. 1910 as Malay & Foreign Contract Syndicate Ld.; name changed June 1911. Vol. liq. 17 Jan. 1916. Final meeting return regd. 27 Feb. 1926 .... **1916**

Tin Areas of Cornwall Ld. Regd. 1913. Struck off Register 11 Oct. 1927 .... **1927**

Tin Areas of Nigeria Ld. *See* British West African Trading Co. Ld.

Tin Electro Smelting (Zinnoxyd) Co. Ld. Regd. 1900. The assets were transferred to a French company. Removed from Register 1906 .... **1906**

Tin Era Mines Ld. Regd. 1887. Struck off Register Jan. 1896 .... **1899**

Tin Fields of Northern Nigeria Ld. Regd. 1909. Vol. liq. 5 Apr. 1928. Reconstructed as Tin Fields of Nigeria Ld., in which company shareholders were entitled to 1 share of 2s. (credited as fully-paid) for each share of 5s. held. Final meeting return regd. 10 June 1929 **1929**

Tin Holdings Ld. Regd. 1932. Vol. liq. (members') 19 Dec. 1933. Capital returned to contributories—£1 16s. 8$\frac{7}{16}$d. per preference share of £1 (2s. paid); 9$\frac{1}{2}$d. per ordinary share of 1s. Final meeting return regd. 4 Apr. 1935 .... **1935**

VOL. FOR

Tin Properties Ld. Regd. 1912. Vol. liq. (creditors') 13 Nov. 1935. Assets realised insufficient to pay unsecured creditors in full. Final meeting return regd. 19 Jan. 1937 .... **1936**

Tin Selection Trust Ld. Regd. 1924. Vol. liq. (members') 13 Jan. 1930. Undertaking and assets were acquired by London Tin Syndicate Ld. (later London Tin Corporation Ld.), in which company shareholders were entitled to 7 shares of £1 (credited as fully-paid) for every 16 shares of £1 held. Final meeting return regd. 28 Jan. 1931 .... **1930**

Tin Trust Ld. Regd. 1912. Vol. liq. Oct. 1917. Struck off Register 1925 .... **1918**

Tincroft Mines. Established under cost book system. In 1896 the undertaking was acquired by Carn Brea and Tincroft Mines Ld., in which company shareholders were entitled to 6 shares of £1 (credited with 10s. paid) for each share held **1897**

Tincroft Mines Ld. Regd. 1900 as Carn Brea & Tincroft Mines Ld.; name changed Oct. 1916. Receiver appointed 15 Jan. 1921. Struck off Register 1925 **1925**

Tindal's Gold Mines Development Co. Ld. Regd. 1896. Vol. liq. Dec. 1908. Removed from Register 1912 **1909**

Tindals Gold Mines Ld. Regd. 1935. Struck off the Register 15 Sept. 1961 .... **1962**

Tingha Consolidated Tin Mines. No Liability. Inc. Victoria 1906. London office closed in 1915 and company wound up. No capital returned to contributories **1916**

Tingha (N. S. W.) Hydraulic Tin Mines Ld. Regd. 1924. Vol. liq. (creditors') 14 Apr. 1931. No capital returned to contributories. Final meeting return regd. 18 July 1931 .... **1932**

Tingri Holdings Ld. Regd. 1960. All capital was owned by Williamson Tea Holdings Ld. Vol. liq. (members') 16 Nov. 1966. Final meeting return regd. 24 Mar. 1972 .... **1966**

Tinkers Ld. Regd. 1922. Direct controlling interest held by Vickers Ld. Struck off Register 1935 .... **1927**

Tinsley Park Colliery Co. Ld. Regd. 1898. Vol. liq. (members') 5 Dec. 1945. Capital returned to contributories—11s. per £1 stock; certain assets were distributed in specie. £755 11s. 6d. was paid into Companies' Liquidation Account. Final meeting return regd. 8 Aug. 1946 .... **1947**

Tinsley Rolling Mills Co. Ld. Regd. 1874. Vol. liq. 29 Jan. 1897. Reconstructed as company of same name. Final meeting return regd. 4 Jan. 1898 ..... **1908**

Tiphook Tea Co. Ld. Regd. 1869. The undertaking and property were sold to Naga Ali Tea Co. Ld. for £3,500 in cash and payment of 2 bills of exchange of £500 each. Removed from Register 1903 .... **1908**

Tipperary Gold Mine Ld. Regd. 1891. Reconstructed 1896 as Westralia and New Zealand Gold Explorers Ld. Removed from Register 1907 .... **1901**

Tirdonkin Collieries Ld. Regd. 1895 as Cefn Gyfelach Colliery Co. Ld.; name changed Aug. 1903. Vol. liq. 23 Oct. 1920. Final meeting return regd. 1 Aug. 1922 **1921**

Tirucalli Rubber Concessions Ld. Regd. 1911. Vol. liq. 10 Dec. 1913. Final meeting return regd. 7 Feb. 1919 *****1915**

Tismoda Estates Co. Ld. Regd. 1910. Vol. liq. (members') 31 Jan. 1951. Capital returned to contributories—£3 13s. 9d. per share (of £1). Final meeting return regd. 29 Mar. 1954 .... **1955**

Tissus Michels Holdings Ld. *See* Monument Securities Ld.

Titan Soap Ld. Regd. 1899. Vol. liq. Nov. 1907. Removed from Register 1910 .... **1908**

Titancrete Co. Ld. Regd. 1888. Vol. liq. 30 Nov. 1891. Final meeting regd. 31 Dec. 1892 .... *****1892**

Titchfield District Gas Co. Inc. by Special Act 1913. Dissolved 1 May 1949, undertaking being vested in Southern Area Gas Board under Gas Act 1948. Holders of securities were entitled to receive British Gas 3% guaranteed stock 1990–95 as follows in respect of each £1 unit, unless otherwise stated, of security held:

	£	s.	d.
Orig. ord. shares (9% stand.).............	2	6	
6% pref. shares..................................		5	0
4$\frac{1}{2}$% perm. deb. stock (per £100) 100	0	0	**1951**

Tiverton & North Devon Railway Co. Inc. by Special Act 1875. Under Great Western Railway Act of 1894 the undertaking was merged into that company which held all the issued share and loan capitals **1895**

Tivoli (Aberdeen) Ld. Regd. Edinburgh 1909. Vol. liq. (members') 10 May 1938. Theatre sold for £9,000 cash. Capital returned to contributories—20s. per preference share of £1; £1 16s. 6d. per ordinary share of £1. Final meeting return regd. 15 July 1939 .... **1939**

Tivoli, Leicester Ld. Regd. 1895. Vol. liq. 9 Mar. 1898. Court Order to continue winding up under supervision 17 Mar. 1898. Final meeting return regd. 5 Sept. 1900 .... **1899**

See Stock Exchange Year-Book.

VOL. FOR

"Tivoli" Ld. Regd. 1888. Certain properties were sold in 1891 to New Tivoli Ld. for £85,000 (subject to mortgage of £70,000, later repaid) in £9,000 in shares, £18,450 in debentures and £57,550 in cash. Removed from Register 1906 .... **1908**

Tivoli, Manchester Ld. Regd. 1896. Vol. liq. 17 Aug. 1915. Final meeting return regd. 23 Mar. 1917 .... **1916**

Tivoli Palace Ld. Regd. 1920. Vol. liq. (members') 2 Dec. 1948. Final meeting return regd. 13 May 1963 **1940**

Tivoli Restaurant and Buffet Co. Ld. Regd. 1897. Removed from Register 1909 .... **1899**

Tjisadea Tea Co. Ld. Regd. 1909. Vol. liq. 5 Mar. 1923. Capital returned to contributories—20s. per preference share of £1; 16s. 2½d. per ordinary share of £1; further payments (if any) not known. Undertaking was acquired by Pandan Tea Co. Ld. Final meeting return regd. 10 Dec. 1923 .... **1924**

Tjoekoel Tea & Cinchona Co. Ld. Regd. Edinburgh 1910. Vol. liq. Feb. 1923. Capital returned to contributories—£1 5s. per share of £1; further payments (if any) not known. Undertaking was acquired by Anglo-Dutch Plantations of Java Ld. (later Anglo. Indonesian Plantations Ld.). Final meeting return regd. 28 June 1927 .... **1924**

Tobacco Co. of British North Borneo Ld. *See* Borneo Proprietary Estates Ld.

Tobacco Co. of Rhodesia & South Africa Ld. Regd. 1910. Vol. liq. (members') 6 Oct. 1960. Capital returned to contributories—5s. 3d. per stock unit of 2s. 6d. Amount paid into Companies' Liquidation Account—£1,069 13s. 9d. in respect of unclaimed distributions and £158 19s. 10d. in respect of unclaimed dividends. Final meeting return regd. 9 Dec. 1961 .... **1962**

Tocopilla Copper Mining & Smelting Co. Ld. Regd. 1881. Vol. liq. 2 June 1890. Final meeting return regd. 29 June 1891 .... **1891**

Tocuyo Oilfields of Venezuela Ld. Regd. 1928. Vol. liq. (members') 30 Aug. 1940. Capital returned to contributories—1s. 2·768d. per share of £1. Final meeting return regd. 1 July 1943 .... **1943**

Tod (John & James) & Sons Limited. Regd. in Edinburgh 1916; a subsidiary of Beecham Group Ld. Vol. liq. 25 Sept. 1954. Preference shares repaid at par. Final meeting return regd. 22 Aug. 1955 .. **1956**

Tod (William) Junior & Co. Ld. Regd. Edinburgh 1898. Vol. liq. June 1923. Reconstructed as Wiliam Tod, Junior and Co. (1923) Ld. (later William Tod, Junior & Co. Ld.). Preference shareholders were entitled to £16,950 in cash and 13,050 preference shares of £1; ordinary shareholders were entitled to £10,000 in cash, 5,000 preference and 45,000 ordinary shares of £1. Final meeting return regd. 29 Mar. 1924 ...... **1924**

Toegoesari Rubber & Coffee Estates Ld. Regd. 1925. Vol. liq. 27 Mar. 1928. Undertaking and assets were acquired by British Rubber Estates of Java Ld., in which company shareholders were entitled to 8 fully-paid shares of 2s. for each share of £1 held. Final meeting return regd. 1 Jan. 1929 .... **1928**

Toho Electric Power Co. Ld. [Toho Denryoku Kabushiki Kaisha]. Inc. in Japan 1905 as Kansai Water Power Co. Ld.; name changed to Kansai Electric Light Co. Ld. in 1921 on merger with Nagoya Electric Light Co. Ld., and to Toho Electric Power Co. Ld. in 1922 on merger with Kyushu Electric Light & Traction Co. Ld. Liquidated 1 Apr. 1942 under orders from Japanese Electric Supply Control Ordinance issued under National Mobilisation Act **1948**

Tokai Bank Ld. Absorbed in 1927 by Dai Ichi Ginko Ld. **1928**

Tokar (Sudan) Prospecting Syndicate Ld. Regd. 1904. Vol. liq. Aug. 1906. Capital returned to contributories—7s. per share of £1; further payments (if any) not known. Removed from Register 1907 .... **1907**

Tokatea Consolidated Ld. Regd. 1903. Vol. liq. Dec. 1907. Undertaking and assets were acquired by West Mount Lyell Ld., in which company shareholders were entitled to 1 share of £1 (credited with 15s. paid) for every 4 shares of 10s. held. Removed from Register 1908 .... **1908**

Tokatea Consols Gold Mines Ld. Regd. 1896. Removed from Register 1906 .... **1901**

Tokatea Ld. Regd. 1922. Vol. liq. 3 July 1928 for reconstruction as company of same name. Shareholders were entitled to 1 fully-paid share of 2s. in new company for each preferred ordinary share of 1s. held, or 1 share of 2s. (credited with 1s. 4d. paid) for every 2 ordinary shares of 1s. held. Final meeting return regd. 6 Mar. 1929 .... **1929**

Tokatea Ld. Regd. 1928. Vol. liq. (members') 11 Mar. 1931. Undertaking and assets were acquired by Gold Coast Consolidated Lands Ld., in which company shareholders were entitled to 1 share of 2s.

VOL. FOR

6d. (credited with 2s. 2d. paid) for each share of 2s. held. Final meeting return regd. 28 Oct. 1931 ..... **1932**

Tokatea of Hauraki Ld. Regd. 1895. Vol. liq. 15 July 1897. Undertaking and assets were acquired by Royal Oak of Hauraki Ld. Final meeting return regd. 16 Mar. 1898 .... **1898**

Tokatea Trust Ld. Regd. 1899. Vol. liq. 21 July 1914. Reconstructed as company of same name. Shareholders were entitled to 1 share of 5s. (credited with 3s. 6d. paid) in new company for each deferred ordinary share of 5s. held, or 1 share of 5s. (credited as fully-paid) for each preferred ordinary share of 5s. held. Final meeting return regd. 14 Mar. 1916...... **1915**

Tokatea Trust Ld. Regd. 1914. Vol. liq. 19 Oct. 1922. Reconstructed as Tokatea Ld., in which company shareholders were entitled to 3 shares of 1s. (credited with 8d. paid) for every 2 shares of 1s. held. Final meeting return regd. 26 Nov. 1923 .... **1923**

Tokengate Investment Co. Ld. Regd. 4 Nov. 1912 as Guatrache Land Co. Ld.; name changed to Argentine Lands & Industries Ld. in Aug. 1929 and to present title 13 Mar 1964. Vol. liq. (members') 26 July 1976. Final meeting return held 4 July 1984. Distributions per ordinary share (of 10p): 99·6p on 26 July 1976, 0·7p on 1 Mar. 1978, 4·0p on 15 Apr. 1980 and 0·09p on 25 May 1984. £8,562·41 paid into Insolvency Services Account on 9 Aug. 1977 which included £6,830·12 in respect of unclaimed dividends **1985–6**

Tokyo Electric Light Co Ld. [Tokyo Dento Kabushiki Kaisha]. Established in Japan Feb. 1883; terms of existence unlimited. In accordance with an Imperial Ordinance of 30 Aug. 1941 company was merged, with 3 other companies, to form Kanto Electric Supply Co. Ld., to which company was transferred all remaining assets of this company not previously taken over by Japan Electric Generation & Transmission Co. Ld. Company's 6% 1st mortgage bonds became, under Japanese law, a direct unsecured obligation of the Japanese Government **1948**

Tokyo Savings Bank. Absorbed in 1936 by One Hundredth Bank............................ **1942**

Toledo & Cincinnati Railroad Co. *See* Cincinnati Hamilton & Dayton Railway Co.

Toledo, St. Louis & Western Railroad Co. Organised Indiana 1900. Consolidated with 4 other companies to form New York Chicago and St. Louis Railroad Co. (later reconstructed as company of same name) **1909**

Toledo, Walhonding Valley & Ohio Railroad Co. Organised Ohio 1891. All capital stock held by Pennsylvania Company. Reorganised as Toledo, Columbus & Ohio River Railroad Co. (later reorganised as Pennsylvania Ohio & Detroit Railroad Co.). The 40-year 1st mortgage gold bonds Series A, B and C were taken over by acquiring companies; these bonds were redeemed at maturity **1911**

Tolgullow United Mines Co. Ld. Regd. Truro 1886. Vol. liq. 4 Feb. 1889. Final meeting return regd. 17 Apr. 1890 .... **1890**

Tolgus Mines Ld. Regd. 1919. Vol. liq. 26 Apr. 1927. Undertaking and assets were transferred to Tolgus Mines (1927) Ld., in which company shareholders were entitled to 1 share of 5s. (credited with 2s. paid) for each share of 5s. held. Final meeting return regd. 8 Dec. 1927 .... **1928**

Tolgus Mines (1927) Ld. Regd. 1927. Vol. liq. (members') 3 Jan. 1930. Undertaking and assets were acquired by East Pool & Agar Ld., in which company shareholders were entitled to 1 ordinary share of 5s. (credited as fully-paid) for every 3 shares of 5s. held. Final meeting return regd. 23 Sept. 1930 **1930**

Tolima El Dorado Mines Ld. Regd. 1899. Removed from Register 9 Dec. 1902 .... ***1904**

Tolima Mining Co. Ld. Regd. 1871. Reconstructed as company of same name. Shareholders were entitled to 5 shares of £1 (credited with 17s. paid) for each A share of £5 held, or 5 shares of £1 (credited with 16s. paid) for each B share of £5 held. Removed from Register 1905............................ **1908**

Tolima Mining Co. Ld. Regd. 1904. Vol. liq. June 1909. Reconstructed as company of same name. Shareholders were entitled to 1 share of £1 (credited with 17s. paid) in new company for each share of £1 held. Removed from Register 1910 .... **1910**

Tolima Mining Co. Ld. Regd. 1909. Vol. liq. 15 June 1922. Reconstructed as company of same name. Shareholders were entitled to 1 share of 5s. (credited with 3s. paid) for each share of £1 held. Struck off Register 7 Dec. 1926 .... **1923**

Tolima Mining Co. Ld. Regd. 1922. Vol. liq. (creditors') 31 May 1932. Final meeting return registered 19 May 1948............................ **1949**

Tolteca Portland Cement Co. Inc. Mexico 1912. Holders of 6% 1st mortgage debenture bonds agreed to

VOL. FOR

accept in exchange 6% registered Tolteca debentures of Associated Portland Cement Manufacturers (1900) Ld. **1929**

Tom Norton Ld. *See* Nortons (Cardiff) Ld.

Tomboy Gold Mines Co. Ld. Regd. 1899. Vol. liq. Feb. 1927. Final meeting return regd. 24 Apr. 1929 .... **1927**

Tomingley Gold Mines Ld. Regd. 1896. Removed from Register 1903 **1901**

Tominil-Española Proprietary Co. Ld. Regd. 1920. Vol. liq. 26 Feb. 1925. Shareholders were entitled to 1 share of 10s. (credited with 8s. paid) in Española Proprietary Co. Ld. for each share of 10s. held. Noteholders were entitled to an equal amount of 10 year secured notes in new company. Final meeting return regd. 28 Aug. 1929............... **1926**

Tominil (Mexican) Mining Co. Ld. Regd. 1906. Vol. liq. Aug. 1910. Reconstructed as Tominil (Mexican) Mining Co. (1910) Ld. Shareholders were entitled to 11 shares of 10s. (credited as fully-paid) in new company for every 10 preference shares of £1 held, or 1 share of 10s. (credited with 8s. paid) for each ordinary share of £1 held; ordinary shareholders were also entitled to 1 fully-paid share of 10s. for every 5 subscribed. Debenture holders were entitled to an equal amount of debentures in new company and an option (since expired) over 10,000 shares at par. Removed from Register 1912 ...... **1911**

Tominil (Mexican) Mining Co. (1910) Ld. Regd. 1910. Vol. liq. 16 Aug. 1920. Reconstructed as Tominil-Espanola Proprietary Co. Ld., in which company shareholders were entitled to 3 shares of 10s. (credited with 6s. 8d. paid) for every 10 ordinary or preference shares of 10s. held. The debenture holders were entitled to 25,600 shares in new company. Final meeting return regd. 22 Aug. 1923 **1921**

Tominil Mines Ld. Regd. 1891. Court Order to wind up 2 Aug. 1893. Removed from Register 1907............. **1894**

Tominil Syndicate Ld. Regd. 1906. Vol. liq. Apr. 1910. Removed from Register 1911 .... **1911**

Tomler Productions Ld. Regd. 1910 as Co-operative Cinematograph Co. Ld.; name subsequently changed as above. Vol. liq. (members') 13 Nov. 1963. Final meeting return regd. 5 Aug. 1964 ...... **1946**

Tomlinson (Henry) Ld. Regd. 1894. Vol. liq. (members') 19 May 1942. Undertaking acquired by Hope & Anchor Breweries Ld., in which company shareholders received in exchange fully-paid ordinary and preference shares (of £1) pro rata at par and debenture stockholders received 4½% debenture stock in equal amount to their holding of 4% debenture stock. Final meeting return regd. 18 Apr. 1947 ...... **1943**

Tonbridge Gas Co. Established 1836; inc. by Special Act 1872. By Act of 1932 the undertaking was acquired by South Suburban Gas Co., in which company holders of A stock were entitled to £280 5% preference stock for each £100 held; holders of B, D & E stocks were entitled to £220 5% preference stock for each £100 held; holders of C stock were entitled to £100 5% preference stock for each £100 held; holders of 4% perpetual debenture stock were entitled to £80 5% perpetual debenture stock for each £100 held; holders of 5% redeemable debenture stock were entitled to an equal nominal amount of 5% redeemable debenture stock subject to the same terms and conditions **1933**

Tonbridge Waterworks Co. Ld. Regd. 4 Oct. 1856; parliamentary powers later. Vol. liq. (members') 30 Sept. 1948, undertaking having been amalgamated with Sevenoaks & Tonbridge Water Co. Holders of £5 ordinary shares were entitled to consolidated ordinary stock in Sevenoaks Co.—£10 for each original share and £7 for each additional or C share, and holders of 4½% preference shares to 1 Sevenoaks Co. 4½% redeemable preference share for each share held. Liability for £21,000 mortgage loans was assumed by Sevenoaks Co. Final meeting return regd. 31 Aug. 1949 .... **1951**

Tongaat Sugar Co. Ld. Regd. 1899. Vol. liq. 13 Aug. 1918. Reconstructed as company of same name (inc. Natal). Shareholders were entitled to 10 preference shares of £1 in new company for each preference share of £10 held or 25 ordinary shares of £1 for each ordinary share of £10 held. Final meeting return regd. 8 May 1919 .... **1919**

Tonge Valley Spinning Co. Ld. Regd. 1875. Vol. liq. 15 Sept. 1927. Struck off Register 21 Mar. 1933 .... ***1885**

Tonghurst Rubber Estate Ld. Regd. 1925. Vol. liq. (creditors') 14 Sept. 1932. Undertaking and assets were acquired by Tonghurst Rubber Estates (1932) Ld. in which company shareholders were entitled to 1 share of 2s. (credited with 1s. 6d. paid) for every 2 shares of 2s. held. Debenture principal and interest

VOL. FOR

were satisfied by allotment of fully-paid shares at par. Final meeting return regd. 3 Nov. 1933 ...... **1933**

Tonghurst Rubber Estates (1932) Ld. Regd. 1932. Vol. liq. 18 Dec. 1950. Undertaking and assets acquired by Aberfoyle Plantations Ld. in which shareholders were entitled to receive 43·071 fully-paid shares of 2s. for every 100 shares of 2s. held. Final meeting return regd. 26 Mar. 1954 .... **1955**

Tongkah, Harbour Tin Dredging Co., N.L. Inc. Tasmania 1906. Undertaking and assets sold to Tongkah Harbour Tin Dredging Ld., in which company shareholders were entitled to receive 2 fully-paid shares (of 5s.) for each share (of £A1 5s.) held **1939**

Tongoy Railway Co. Inc. 1865. Liquidated 30 Aug. 1900 **1902**

Tonicity Laboratories Ld. Regd. 1933. Vol. liq. (creditors') 30 June 1952. No capital was returned to contributories. Final meeting return regd. 29 Feb. 1956 .... **1957**

Tonkin Exploration Co. Ld. Regd. 1895. Removed from Register 1910 .... **1903**

Tonopah and Tidewater Railroad Co. Inc. New Jersey 1904. In Nov. 1946 it was stated that steps had been taken in the United States with a view to the final dissolution of the company **1947**

Toora Proprietory Tin Fields Ld. Regd. 1912. Vol. liq. 24 Mar. 1914. Reconstructed as company of same name. Shareholders were entitled to 1 share of 5s. (credited with 4s. paid) in new company for each share of 5s. held. The debentures were paid off in full. Final meeting return regd. 12 Jan. 1916 .... **1915**

Toora Proprietary Tin Fields Ld. Regd. 1914. Vol. liq. 17 Mar. 1915. Final meeting return regd. 5 Nov. 1929 **1916**

Toorah Gold Mines Ld. Regd. 1900. Struck off Register 19 Mar. 1907 .... **1909**

Topham, Jones & Railton Ld. Regd. 1926 as Topham, Jones & Railton (1926) Ld.; name changed May 1930. Vol. liq. (members) 29 Jan. 1951. Capital returned to contributories:—ordinary shares (of £10)—fully-paid, £24 13s. 5·0815d.; £5 paid, £12 6s. 8·5407d.; 2nd preference shares (of £100), £10 paid—£10. Final meeting return regd. 10 Nov. 1959 **1960**

Topham, Jones & Railton (1926) Ld. *See* above.

Topuldodi (Nizam's) Gold Mines Ld. Regd. 1905. Vol. liq. May 1909. The undertaking and assets were sold to Hutti (Nizam's) Gold Mines Ld., in which company shareholders were entitled to 1 share of £1 for every 4 shares of £1 held. Removed from Register 1911 .... **1910**

Tor Tin Mines Ld. Regd. 1925. Struck off Register Feb. 1935 .... **1935**

Torbay Brewery & Cyder Co. Ld. Regd. 1890. Vol. liq. 21 June 1893. Final meeting return regd. 23 Jan. 1895 .... **1894**

Torbay Paint Co. Ld. Regd. 1925. Vol. liq. (members') 31 Dec. 1946, undertaking having been acquired by Pinchin, Johnson and Associates Ld. Final meeting return regd. 13 Apr. 1951 .... **1952**

Torkington Tires Ld. Regd. 1908. Vol. liq. May 1911. Undertaking and assets were acquired by company of same name for £4,482 2s. in fully-paid shares of 2s., 67,694 shares of 2s. (credited with 1s. paid) and £50 19s. 10d. in cash. Removed from Register 1912 **1912**

Torkington Tires Ld. Regd. 1911. Vol. liq. 5 Jan. 1916. Final meeting return regd. 12 Sept. 1916 .... **1912**

Toro Tin Co. Ld. Regd. 1912. Vol. liq. 11 Nov. 1920 for reconstruction as Keffi Consolidated Tin Co. Ld., in which company shareholders were entitled to 11 fully-paid shares of 5s. for every 10 shares of 5s. held and an option (since expired) over further shares at par. Final meeting return regd. 9 Aug. 1921 .... **1921**

Toronto & Mimico Electric Railway & Light Co. Ld. *See* Toronto Power Co. Ld.

Toronto Mortgage Co. Inc. in Ontario 1899. Undertaking acquired by Canada Permanent Mortgage Corpn. in 1959. Capital returned to contributories—$152·03 per share of $50. Finally wound up June 1960 .... **1961**

Toronto Power Co. Ld. Inc. Ontario 1890 as Toronto & Mimico Electric Railway & Light Co. Ld.; name changed Mar. 1908 .... **1933**

Toronto Railway Co. Inc. Ontario 1892. Undertaking acquired by City of Toronto. Bonds of the company were redeemed in 1922 .... **1925**

Toronto (Rhodesia) Syndicate Ld. Regd. 1912. Vol. liq. (creditors') 15 Feb. 1943. Assets realised insufficient to make distribution to debenture holders or shareholders. Final meeting return regd. 23 May 1946 .... **1947**

Toronto Savings & Loan Co. Inc. Ontario 1884. The outstanding sterling and dollar debentures were redeemed on 11 Nov. 1938 .... **1939**

Toronto Suburban Railway Co. Inc. by Special Act of Province of Ontario as Toronto Suburban Street Railway Co.; name changed 1900. Amalgamated by

VOL. FOR

Order of Council 17 Dec. 1923 with Toronto Eastern Railway Co. to form Canadian National Electric Railways. ... **1935**

Toronto Suburban Street Railway Co. *See* Toronto Suburban Railway Co.

Torpoint Coal & Gas Co. Ld. Regd. 1905. Dissolved 1 May 1949, undertaking being vested in South Western Area Gas Board under Gas Act 1948. Holders of ordinary shares (of £1) were entitled to receive £1 British Gas 3% guaranteed stock 1990–95 for each share held ... **1952**

Torpoint Electric Supply Co. Ld. *See* East Cornwall Electricity Supply Co. Ld.

Torquay and District Motor Omnibus Co. Ld. Regd. 1903. Vol. liq. 1907. Removed from Register 1908 ... **1908**

Torquay & Paignton Gas Co. Inc. by Special Act 1860 as Torquay Gas Co.; name changed 1923. Dissolved 1 May 1949, undertaking being vested in South Western Area Gas Board under Gas Act 1948. Holders of securities were entitled to receive, in respect of each £100 unit held. British Gas 3% guaranteed stock 1990–95 as follows:

	£	s.	d.
Ord. stock (6% basic)	139	0	0
5% pref. stock	114	10	0
4% red. pref. stock (1963–8)	101	0	0
4% red. pref. stock (1969)	100	0	4
4% red. pref. stock (1971)	103	10	0
3½% red. deb. stock (1975)	100	18	3
3½% red. deb. stock (1972)	103	0	0
3½% red. deb. stock (1964)	100	0	0
3½% red. deb. stock (1976)	103	7	10
4% irred. deb. stock	102	10	0
4½% red. deb. stock (1964)	105	10	0

A distribution on ordinary stock of 11·6129% out of reserves was made in Nov. 1955 ... **1952**

Torquay Tramways Co. Ld. Regd. 1907. Vol. liq. (members') 19 Apr. 1934. Tramway undertaking was abandoned in Jan. 1934. Transport undertaking was sold to Devon General Omnibus & Touring Co. Ld. and all investments were acquired by National Electric Construction Co. Ld. for £152,716 in cash. The debentures were redeemed. Shareholders were entitled to 1 share of £1 in Devon General Omnibus & Touring Co. Ld. or £1 10s. in cash for every 3 shares of £1 held. £27 12s. 9d. was paid into Companies' Liquidation Account. Final meeting return regd. 21 Oct. 1935 ... **1935**

Torquay Tramways Construction Syndicate Ld. Regd. 1905. Vol. liq. 17 Nov. 1911. Final meeting return regd. 14 July 1920 ... **1912**

Torres Mines Ld. Regd. 1906. Vol. liq. 18 Aug. 1911. Reconstructed as Ceniza Gold Mines Ld., in which company shareholders were entitled to 1 share of 2s. (credited with 1s. 6d. paid) for every 5 A shares of 1s. or 1 ordinary share of 2s. held. The debentures were exchanged at par for bonds of new company. Final meeting return regd. 13 Dec. 1915 ... **1912**

Torrington & Okehampton Railway Co. *See* Plymouth & North Devon Direct Railway Co.

Torva Exploring Syndicate Ld. Regd. 1894. Reconstructed 1900 as Matabele Proprietary Mines Ld., in which company shareholders were entitled to 3 shares of £1 (credited as fully-paid) for every 4 shares of £1 held. Removed from Register 1904 .. **1901**

Total Gold Extraction Co. Ld. Regd. 1895. Vol. liq. 21 Jan. 1898. Removed from Register 10 July 1908... **1898**

Totland Bay Pier & Hotel Co. Ld. Regd. 1878. Vol. liq. 13 May 1895. Court Order to continue winding up under supervision 5 June 1895. Final meeting return regd. 10 May 1898 ... **1896**

Totland Water Works Co. Ld. Regd. 1883. Property vested in statutory company by Act of 1899 ... **1910**

Totnes Electricity Supply Co. Ld. Regd. 1899. Vol. liq. Oct. 1907. The undertaking was sold to Electric Supply Corporation Ld. Removed from Register 1908 ... **1908**

Totnes, Paignton & Torquay Direct Railway Co. Inc. by Special Act 1880. Abandoned by Act of 1884 ... **1885**

Totoral Mining Co. Ld. Regd. 1901. Vol. liq. Nov. 1906. Removed from Register 1907 ... **1907**

Tottenham & District Gas Co. Estd. 1847; inc. as Tottenham & Edmonton Gas Light & Coke Co. by Special Act 1859; name changed to Tottenham District Light, Heat & Power Co. in 1913 and as above in 1929. Dissolved 1 May 1949, undertaking being vested in Eastern Area Gas Board under Gas Act 1948. Holders of securities were entitled to receive, in respect of each £100 unit held, British Gas 3% guaranteed stock 1990–95 as follows:

	£	s.	d.
Ord. stock (5% basic)	122	6	8
5% pref. stock	114	16	8
5½% pref. stock	128	10	0

VOL. FOR

4% perp. deb. stock	102	3	4
3½% red. deb. stock	101	15	0
4½% red. deb. stock	102	10	0

A distribution on ord. stock of 8·543976% out of reserves was made in Feb. 1954 ... **1952**

Tottenham & Edmonton Gas Light & Coke Co. *See* Tottenham & District Gas Co.

Tottenham and Forest Gate Railway Co. Inc. by Special Act 1890. In 1923 the undertaking was merged into the London Midland & Scottish Railway Co. in which company stockholders were entitled to stock as follows:

For each £100 *held*		*L.M. & S.*	
4% Debenture	£100	4%	Debenture
3% Gtd. Preference	£75	4%	Guaranteed

The Preferred and Deferred Ordinary Shares were held by the London Midland & Scottish Company and were cancelled ... **1924**

Tottenham & Hampstead Joint Committee. Dissolved 2 Apr. 1949; undertaking vested 1 Jan. 1948 in British Transport Commission under Transport Act 1947 ... **1949**

Tottenham & Hampstead Junction Railway Co. Inc. by Special Act 1862. Under Midland Railway Act of 1902 the undertaking was vested in Midland Railway Co. and Great Eastern Railway Co. Holders of each 5% preference, 4% preference or ordinary share of £10 received £20, £16 or £32 Midland Railway 2½% consolidated perpetual guaranteed preferential stock respectively ... **1904**

Tottenham Cinema & Entertainment Co., Ld. Regd. 1920. Vol. liq. (members') 28 Aug. 1964. Final meeting return regd. 26 Apr. 1967 ... **1961**

Tottenham District Light, Heat & Power Co. *See* Tottenham & District Gas Co.

Tottenham Lager Beer Brewery & Ice Factory Ld. Regd. 1886. Vol. liq. 5 Mar. 1895. Final meeting return regd. 19 Dec. 1895 ... **1896**

Totton, Hythe & Fawley Light Railway Company. Undertaking acquired by Southern Railway Company in 1923 ... **1947**

Totumo Alluvial Gold Co. Ld. Regd. Edinburgh 1896. Vol. liq. May 1901. Struck off Register 2 Apr. 1935 ... **1902**

Tough-Oakes Burnside Gold Mines Ld. Inc. Canada 1913 as Tough-Oakes Gold Mines Ld.; name changed Sept. 1923. All assets were disposed of and bondholders received 9s. 6d. in the £ in July 1932; further payments (if any) not known ... **1933**

Tough-Oakes Gold Mines Ld. Regd. 1914. Vol. liq. 5 Sept. 1919. Reconstructed as Kirkland Lake Proprietary (1919) Ld. in which company shareholders were entitled to 1 share of £1 for every 2 shares of £1 held. Final meeting return regd. 4 Sept. 1920 ... **1920**

Toughened Glass Co. Ld. Regd. 1883. Removed from Register 1890 ... ***1885**

Tournai to Jurbise & Landen to Hasselt Railway Co. *See* Société Anonyme des Chemins de Fer de Tournai a Jurbise et de Landen à Hasselt

Towcester & Buckingham Railway Co. Inc. by Special Act 1889. Undertaking abandoned by Act of 1893 ... **1894**

Toweli South African Estates Ld. Regd. 1889 as Toweli (Swaziland) Estate & Gold Exploration Ld. Vol. liq. Dec. 1910. Removed from Register 1912 ... **1911**

Tower Cinema Ld. Regd. 1928. Vol. liq. 24 Apr. 1931. Assets realised insufficient to pay unsecured creditors in full. Final meeting return regd. 16 June 1933 ***1932**

Tower Co. Ld. *See* Wembley Park Estate Co. Ld.

Tower Estates Ld. Regd. 1924. Vol. liq. (members') 25 Mar. 1935. Capital returned to contributories—£1 3s. 3·87d. per share of £1 *plus* certain investments distributed in specie. Final meeting return regd. 18 July 1942 ... **1936**

Tower House Retreat and Sanatorium Ld. Regd. 1886. Removed from Register 1905 ... **1904**

Tower Securities Trust Ld. Regd. 1928. Struck off Register 8 June 1951 ... **1938**

Towers Hill Gold Mine Ld. Regd. 1893. Struck off Register 14 Jan. 1897 ... **1899**

Towles Ld. Regd. 1923. Vol. liq. 14 Aug. 1929. Undertaking and assets were acquired by Towles (1928) Ld. (later Towles Ld.) for £140,000 in cash and 465,000 fully-paid ordinary shares of 2s. Final meeting return regd. 4 May 1929 ... **1929**

Town and Central Holdings (Leeds) Ld. Regd. 3 Feb. 1897 as Hart & Levy Ld.; name changed Hart, Levy & John Barran Ld. 20 Aug. 1963, to John Barran Ld. 10 Sept. 1965 and to present title 20 Dec. 1972. Winding-up order 23 Feb. 1976 ... **1986–7**

Town and Commercial Properties Ld. Regd. 17 Dec. 1881 as Thomas Danks & Co. Ld.; name changed 13 Mar. 1959. Vol. liq. (members') 6 Dec. 1976. Final meeting held 11 Sept. 1987 ... **1988–9**

Town & County Bank Ld. Established 1825 as Aberdeen Town & County Banking Co.; regd. as unlimited 1862 and regd. as limited Edinburgh and name

VOL. FOR

changed Apr. 1882. Wound up Apr. 1908. Undertaking acquired by North of Scotland Bank Ld. (later Clydesdale Bank Ld.) in which company shareholders received 1¾ ordinary shares of £20 (credited with £4 paid) for each share of £35 (credited with £7 paid). Final meeting return regd. 27 Feb. 1922 .... **1909**

Town & County of Poole Gas and Coke Co. Ld. Regd. 1876. Undertaking and assets were acquired in 1902 by Bournemouth Gas and Water Co. [later Bournemouth & District Water Co.] for 2,181 B and 320 6% preference shares of £10, credited as fully-paid. The purchasing company also assumed liability in respect of £10,000 4% debentures. Removed from Register 1903 .... **1903**

Town & General Estates Ld. Regd. 1900. Court Order to wind up 1905. Removed from Register 1913........ **1906**

Town & Gown Association Ld. Regd. in Edinburgh 1896. Vol. liq. (members') 22 Mar. 1948. Capital returned to contributories—£8 7s. 3d. per ordinary share (of £5 fully-paid); £5 17s. 3d. per ordinary share (of £5 with £2 10s. paid); £8 7s. 3d. per preference share (of £5). £4,558 8s. was paid to the Accountant of the Court in respect of unclaimed dividends and distributions. Final meeting return regd. 23 May 1951 .... **1952**

Town (Joseph) & Sons Ld. Regd. 1906. Vol. liq. (members') 30 June 1932. All shares held by Wiggins, Teape & Alex, Pirie (Merchants) Ld. but in 1932 undertaking and assets transferred to Allied Paper Merchants (W. T. & Co.) Ld. Final meeting return regd. 30 Oct. 1933....................... **1933**

Town Line (London) Ld. Regd. 1906 as Duffryn Shipping Co. Ld.; name changed in Dec. 1914. Court Order to wind up Jan. 1931. Struck off Register 13 Dec. 1938 .... **1939**

Town of Dudley Gas Light Co. See Dudley, Brierly Hill & District Gas Co.

Town Properties of Bulawayo Ld. Regd. 1897. Receiver appointed 26 Apr. 1920; ceased to act 8 Mar. 1923. Vol. liq. 18 Apr. 1921. Certain assets were purchased by Town Properties of Bulawayo (South Africa) Ld. Final meeting return regd. 8 June 1922 ... ***1922***

Town Properties of Bulawayo (South Africa) Ld. Inc. Southern Rhodesia 1921. Vol. liq. May 1934. Undertaking and assets were acquired by London & Rhodesian Mining & Land Co. Ld. (later Lonrho Ld.) in which company shareholders were entitled to 2 shares of 5s. (credited as fully-paid) for each share of 10s. held **1935**

Town Properties of West Australia Ld. Regd. 1894. Reconstructed 1905 as Town Properties of West Australia (1905) Ld., in which company shareholders were entitled to 1 share of 1s. and 10s. 1st mortgage debentures for each share of £1 held. Removed from Register 1907 .... **1909**

Town Properties of West Australia (1905) Ld. Regd. 1905. Vol. liq. 19 Oct. 1922. Capital returned to contributories—2s. 1d. per ordinary share of 1s. Final meeting return regd. 17 Jan. 1929 .... **1923**

Townhill Colliery Co. Ld. Regd. Edinburgh 1897. Vol. liq. Aug. 1900. Final meeting return regd. 10 June 1902 .... **1901**

Townsend Trust Ld. Regd. 1929. Vol. liq. (members') 23 Sept. 1931. Capital returned to contributories—£3,366 19s. 10d. Final meeting return regd. 16 June 1932 .... **1932**

Townshend's Art Metal Co. Ld. Regd. 1897. Vol. liq. Apr. 1907. Removed from Register 1910 .... **1908**

Townsite Extension Silver Mines of Cobalt Ld. Regd. 1912. Vol. liq. 30 Sept. 1918. Shareholders were entitled to 10 shares in New Extension Mines Ld. and 2 shares in Mining Corporation of Canada Ld. for every 5 shares of £1 held plus an unspecified amount in cash. Final meeting return regd. 1 Mar. 1921 .... **1919**

Towranna Gold Mines of Western Australia Ld. Regd. 1896. Removed from Register 1906 .... **1908**

Towyn & Aberdovey Gas Co. Ld. Regd. 1868 as Dysynni Gas Co. Ld.; name changed 1945. Dissolved 1 May 1949, undertaking being vested in Wales Area Gas Board under Gas Act 1948. Holders of securities were entitled to receive, in respect of each £10 unit held, British Gas 3% guaranteed stock 1990–95 as follows:

	£	s.	d.
Ord. shares (10% max.)	25	0	0
Ord. shares (7% max.)	16	0	0	**1952**

Towyn, Aberdovey & District Electricity Co. Ld. Regd. 1934. Dissolved 1 Apr. 1948, undertaking being vested in the British (later Central) Electricity Authority and Merseyside & North Wales Area Board under the Electricity Act 1947. Ordinary shareholders were entitled to receive £1 16s. British

VOL. FOR

Electrcity 3% guaranteed stock (1968–73). for each £1 ordinary capital held **1949**

Toyo Tin Ld. Regd. 1927. Vol. liq. (members') 12 Jan. 1940. Capital returned to contributories—£90,747 5s. 8d. £29 14s. 6d. was paid into Companies' Liquidation Account in respect of unclaimed dividends. Final meeting return regd. 18 Apr. 1940 .. **1941**

Traction Insurance Association Ld. Regd. 1903. Struck off Register 17 Dec. 1918 .... ***1908***

Trade Facilities Corporation Ld. See B.G.I. Consolidated Ld.

Traders & General Insurance Association Ld. Regd. 1907. Vol. liq. May 1922. Struck off Register 12 Mar. 1935 .... **1936**

Traders Deposit Co. See Equitable Trust Co. of New York.

Trades Lane Callendering Co. of Dundee Ld. Regd. Edinburgh 1874. Vol. liq. (members') 13 Mar. 1941. Capital returned to contributories—£1 7s. 6d. per share of £10. £38 17s. was lodged with Accountant of Court in respect of unclaimed dividends. Final meeting return regd. 26 June 1948 .... **1949**

Trading & Exploring Co. Ld. Regd. 1898. Vol. liq. Apr. 1905. Struck off Register Apr. 1929 .... **1930**

Trading Co. of England Ld. Regd. 1884. Removed from Register 1911 .... **1907**

Trading Steamship Co. Ld. Regd. 1879. Removed from Register 1911 .... **1886**

Trafalgar Colliery Co. Ld. Regd. 1883. Vol. liq. Feb. 1919. Struck off Register 1927 .... **1919**

Trafalgar Film Producing Co. Ld. Regd. 1920. Vol. liq. 12 Sept. 1921. Final meeting return regd. 2 May 1922 .... ***1922***

Trafalgar Gold Mine (W.A.) Ld. Regd. 1897. Reconstructed 1899 as company of same name. Shareholders were entitled to 1 share of £1 (credited with 17s. paid) for each share of £1 held. Removed from Register 1901 .... **1900**

Trafalgar Gold Mine (W.A.) Ld. Regd. 1899. Undertaking and assets were acquired by Hannan's Trust Ld., in which company shareholders were entitled to 1 share of £1 (credited as fully-paid) for every 20 shares of £1 held. Removed from Register 1905 ... **1905**

Trafford Brick Co. Ld. Regd. 1897. Vol. liq. 19 Jan. 1900. Final meeting return regd. 7 Apr. 1900 ...... **1900**

Trafford Chemical Co. Ld. Regd. 1938. Vol. liq. (members') 31 May 1941. All shares held by I.C.I. (Dyestuffs) Ld. Final meeting return regd. 24 Jan. 1942 .... **1942**

Trafford Park Bacon Factory Ld. Regd. 1923. Vol. liq. 12 Jan. 1928. Final meeting return regd. 10 Aug. 1929 .... **1929**

Trafford Picture House Ld. Regd. 1920. Vol. liq. (members') 24 Mar. 1938. Capital returned to contributories—£15,174 6s. 11d. Final meeting return regd. 21 Mar. 1940 .... **1939**

Trafford Power & Light Supply (1902) Ld. Regd. 1902. Vol. liq. 10 Mar. 1920. The undertaking and assets were sold to Stretford Urban District Council. 1st debenture stockholders were repaid at 105%. Capital returned to contributories—20s. per preference share of £1; £1 14s. per ordinary share of £1 at 31 Dec. 1920; further payments (if any) not known. Final meeting return regd. 17 Mar. 1921 .... **1921**

Trajan Roumanian Oil Co. Ld. Regd. 1913. Vol. liq. (members') 15 Nov. 1935. Capital returned to contributories—3·805d. per share of £1. Final meeting return regd. 29 Feb. 1936 .... **1936**

Trail Creek Mining Co. Ld. Regd. 1899. Struck off Register 1912 .... **1906**

Tralee and Dingle Light Railway Co. Ld. Inc. 1884. under the Tramways and Public Companies (Ireland) Act 1883. In 1925 the undertaking was merged Into the Great Southern Railways Co. The scheme provided that the holders of the Baronial Guaranteed Share capital should receive an equal amount of Great Southern Railways 4% Preference Stock, and that the other Shares should be cancelled **1925**

Tralee and Fenit Railway Co. Inc. by Special Act 1880. In 1925 the undertaking was merged into the Great Southern Railways Co., in which company shareholders were entitled to stock as follows:

For each £100 held	Gt. Sthn. Rly.
5% Mort. Deb.	£125 4% Deb.
5% Preference	£58 12s. 8d. 4% Pref.
Ordinary	£10 Ordinary

In payment of arrears of interest the debenture-holders received 4% Debenture Stock equal to 64·62% of such sum and cash equal to 40·25%.... **1925**

Tramway Traction Co. Ld. Regd. 1879. Vol. liq. Dec. 1882. Final meeting return regd. 23 June 1883 .... **1883**

Tramways and General Works Co. Ld. Regd. 1877. Vol. liq. 3 Apr. 1919. Capital returned to contributories—£1 per share of 6s. in Apr. 1919; further

VOL. FOR

payments (if any) not known. Final meeting return regd. 4 Oct. 1920 — **1919**

Tramways & Light Railways Estates Co. Ld. Regd. 1900. Vol. liq. (members') 2 Aug. 1934. Capital returned to contributories—£3 4s. 7d. per share of £10 (£3 paid). £8 0s. 2d. was paid into Companies' Liquidation Account. Final meeting return regd. 17 Mar. 1936 — **1935**

Tramways Capital Guarantee Co. Ld. Regd. 1884. Vol. liq. (members') 4 Mar. 1932. No capital returned to contributories. Final meeting return regd. 18 June 1932 — **1933**

Tramways Co. of France Ld. Regd. 1879. Vol. liq. 11 Mar. 1895. Shareholders were entitled to apply for preference shares and to receive an equal number of fully-paid ordinary shares of 30s. in Tramways Electrical Traction Co. Ld. or 30s. per share in cash. Final meeting return regd. 5 Mar. 1897 — **1896**

Tramways Co. of Germany Ld. Regd. 1879. Vol. liq. 14 July 1894. Undertaking was acquired by Dresden Strasoenbahn in which company shareholders were entitled to 1 share of 1,000 marks for every 5 shares of £10 held. Final meeting return regd. 30 Oct. 1896 — **1895**

Tramways Electrical Traction Co. Ld. Regd. 1895. Vol. liq. 24 Apr. 1896. Final meeting return regd. 14 Dec. 1898 — **1897**

Tramways Light & Power Co. Ld. *See* Midland Counties Electric Supply Co. Ld.

Tramways (M.E.T.) Omnibus Co. Ld. Regd. 1912. Vol. liq. 1 July 1930. Undertaking (including all lands, works and other property, assets and powers) was transferred by London Passenger Transport Act 1933 to that Board. As consideration for such transfer and part consideration of transfer of Overground Ld., the Transport Board issued £182,635 4½% A stock, £101,545 5% B stock and £348,014 C stock. Final meeting return regd. 6 Apr. 1934 — **1934**

Tramways Trust Co. Ld. Regd. 1879. Court Orders: to wind up 12 Dec. 1885; to dissolve 10 June 1897 — **1886**

Tramways Union Co. Ld. Regd. 1874. Vol. liq. Debentures were paid off. Capital returned to contributories—£2 per share of £5 on 1 Nov. 1899; further payments (if any) not known. Removed from Register 1901 — **1900**

Tranent Gas Co. Ld. Regd. in Edinburgh 1884. Dissolved 1 May 1949, undertaking being vested in Scottish Area Gas Board under Gas Act 1948. Holders of ordinary shares (of £1) were entitled to receive £6 British Gas 3% guaranteed stock 1990–95 for each share held — **1952**

Trans-African Railway Co. (Cia. dos Caminhos de Ferro Atravez d'Africa). *See* Companhia de Ambaca.

Trans-America Investment Trust Ld. Regd. 1963 as Scandinvest Trust Co. Ld.; name changed Mar. 1968. All capital was owned by Hambros Investment Trust Ld. Vol. liq. (members') 5 Mar. 1970. Capital returned to contributories—4s. 8·1d. and 0·0327p. per share of 4s. Final meeting return regd. 7 Sept. 1971 — **1972**

Transatlantic and General Investments p.l.c. Regd. 4 Aug. 1959 as Anglo-Israel Securities Ld.; name changed 26 June 1968. Vol. liq. (members') 22 July 1983. Final meeting regd. 18 Dec. 1985. By Scheme of Unitisation, all net assets were transferred to M&G American Smaller Companies Fund in which unit trust holder received 4·8814 Income Units for each share held. After settlement of all liabilities and the costs of the liquidation the residual balance amounting to £29,968 was paid to the trustee of the M&G American Smaller Companies Fund in accordance with the provisions of the unitisation scheme — **1986–7**

Trans Australia Investment Trust Ld. *See* Australian and International Trust Ld.

Trans-Continental Transportation & Mining Co. Inc. Colorado 1903. In liquidation in 1909 — **1909**

Trans Europe Investment Trust Ld. Regd. 1962 as T.C.E.T. Ld.; name changed May 1962. Vol. liq. (members') 2 Apr. 1971. Assets were transferred to Schroder Europe Fund, shareholders receiving 1 unit (either accumulation or income) for each ordinary share of 4s. Final meeting return regd. 4 Apr. 1973 — **1974-5**

Trans-Oceanic Finance Subsidiary Ld. Regd. 1928. Vol. liq. (members') 2 Apr. 1931. All capital owned by Trans-Oceanic Trust. Final meeting return regd. 30 Oct. 1931 — **1932**

Transito Co. Ld. Regd. 1893. Vol. liq. June 1908. Removed from Register 1903 — **1904**

Transito Gold Mines Ld. Regd. 1904. Vol. liq. 29 June 1908. Final meeting return regd. 29 Jan. 1926 — **1909**

VOL. FOR

Transmutograph Ld. Regd. 1929. Vol. liq. (creditors') 31 July 1930. No capital returned to contributories. Final meeting return regd. 27 Oct. 1933 — **1931**

Transparent Paper (Canada) Ld. Inc. Canada. A direct controlling interest was held by Transparent Paper Ld. Liquidation was completed in 1944 — **1945**

Transport Co. *See* Compania de Trasportes "Expreso Villalonga."

Transport Hotels Ld. Regd. 1932. Vol. liq. (members') 14 Dec. 1936. Capital returned to contributories—£1 7s. 3d. per share of £1. Final meeting return regd. 5 Jan. 1938 — **1937**

Transport Services Ld. Regd. 1936. Vol. liq. (members') 8 Sept. 1949. Headquarters organisation and ownership and management of the transport interests passed into the control of British Transport Commission on and from 1 Jan. 1948. Capital returned to contributories—36s. 5·875d. per ordinary share of 5s. The preference shares (of £1) were repaid at 23s. per share in Sept. 1949. £1,310 12s. 2d. was paid into Companies' Liquidation Account in respect of unclaimed distributions. Final meeting return regd. 12 Sept. 1952 — **1953**

Transport, Trading & Agency Co. of West Australia Ld. Regd. 1896. Vol. liq. Aug. 1912. Court Order to wind up 4 Sept. 1912. Liquidator released 12 Feb. 1920. Struck off Register 20 Mar. 1925 — **1913**

Transvaal Agency Ld. Regd. 1902. Vol. liq. 31 May 1929. Final meeting return regd. 5 Jan. 1932 — **1930**

Transvaal Agency Ld. Regd. 1929. Vol. liq. (members') 24 May 1934. Capital returned to contributories—3s. 4·896d. per share of £1 *plus* a distribution in specie. Final meeting return regd. 6 Apr. 1935 — **1935**

Transvaal Agency Ld. Regd. 1934. Vol. liq. (members') 6 Mar. 1951. Final meeting return regd. 15 Mar. 1955 — **1947**

Transvaal & General Association Ld. Regd. 1894. Removed from Register 1905 — **1904**

Transvaal & Mashonaland Investment Co. Ld. Regd. 1892. Removed from Register 1909 — **1906**

Transvaal & Mexican Estates Ld. Regd. 1927. Struck off Register 18 Feb. 1936 — **1936**

Transvaal & Natal Collieries Ld. Regd. 1909 to Vaalbank Coal Co. Ld.; name changed as Uitkyk Collieries Ld. in Mar. 1913 and as above in Dec. 1919. Vol. liq. 3 Nov. 1924. Final meeting return regd. 6 Nov. 1935 — **1925**

Transvaal & Rhodesian Estates Ld. Regd. 1911. Undertaking and assets were acquired in Dec. 1927 by Rhodesian Corporation Ld., in which company shareholders were entitled to 2 shares of 5s. (credited as fully-paid) for each share of 10s. held. Vol. liq. 2 Apr. 1928. Final meeting return regd. 19 Feb. 1937 — **1929**

Transvaal & Rhodesian Farms & Mines Ld. Inc. Transvaal 1910. Vol. liq. 1911. Undertaking acquired by Amalgamated Properties of Rhodesia Ld — **1912**

Transvaal & South African Land Trust Ld. Regd. 1874. Vol. liq. 14 Aug. 1928. Capital returned to contributories—£1 per share of 4s. in Oct. 1928; further payments (if any) not known. Final meeting return regd. 13 Dec. 1928 — **1929**

Transvaal Associated Gold Mines Ld. Regd. 1902. Removed from Register 1909 — **1908**

Transvaal Banket Ld. Inc. Transvaal 1904. London office closed — **1908**

Transvaal Bischoff Ld. Inc. Transvaal 1907. London office closed in Mar. 1911 — **1911**

Transvaal Chemical Co. Ld. Regd. Edinburgh 1891. Undertaking acquired by New Transvaal Chemical Co. Ld. Vol. liq. June 1896. Final meeting return regd. 30 Aug. 1897 — **1940**

Transvaal Coal & Oil Shale Corporation Ld. Inc. Orange Free State 1921. Wound up 1926 — **1927**

Transvaal Commercial Bank (Transvaalsche Bank-en Handels-Vereeniging). *See* Transvaal Commercial Bank (Transvaalsche Handelsbank).

Transvaal Commercial Bank. (Transvaalsche Handelsbank). Inc. Netherlands 1898 as Transvaal Commercial Bank (Transvaalsche Bank-en Handels-Vereeniging); name changed Aug. 1923. Amalgamated with Netherlands Bank of South Africa on 4 May 1925 — **1926**

Transvaal Consolidated Coal Mines Ld. Inc. Transvaal 1895. Wound up Dec. 1909 — **1910**

Transvaal Copper Mines Ld. Inc. Transvaal 1905. In liquidation in 1908 — **1908**

Transvaal Diamond Development Syndicate Ld. Inc. Transvaal 1902. Wound up Dec. 1919. Undertaking acquired by Kameelfontein Diamond Development Syndicate Ld. for £35,035 in fully-paid shares of 5s. — **1920**

Transvaal Diamond Mines Ld. *See* Montrose Diamond Mining Co. Ld.

Transvaal Estates & Development Co. Ld. Regd. 1889. Vol. liq. 26 July 1929. Undertaking and assets were acquired by African & European Investment Co.

VOL. FOR

Ld., in which company shareholders were entitled to 3 shares of £1 (credited as fully-paid) for each 5 shares of £1 held. Final meeting return regd. 4 Oct. 1938 1930

Transvaal Exploration Co. Ld. Regd. 1902. Struck off Register 1915 1914

Transvaal Exploring Co. Ld. Regd. 1895. Vol. liq. 14 Nov. 1898. Reconstructed as Transvaal Exploring Land and Minerals Co. Ld. in which company shareholders were entitled to 1 share of £1 (credited with 16s. paid) for each share of £1 held. Debenture holders were entitled to 3 fully-paid shares of £1 for each £1 due in respect of principal or interest. Final meeting return regd. 16 May 1900 1908

Transvaal Exploring Land & Minerals Co. Ld. Regd. 1899. Vol. liq. 7 Aug. 1928 for reconstruction as company of same name (inc. South Africa) in which company shareholders were entitled to 1 share of 1s. for each share of 2s. held. Final meeting return regd. 8 Jan. 1930 1929

Transvaal Exploring Land & Minerals Co. Ld. Inc. Union of South Africa 1928. Vol. liq. July 1933. Undertaking and assets were acquired by South African Townships, Mining & Finance Corporation Ld., in which company shareholders were entitled to 1 fully-paid share of 10s. for every 10 shares of 1s. held 1934

Transvaal Farms & Finance Co. Ld. Regd. 1902. Vol. liq. (members) 28 Dec. 1936. Capital returned to contributories—£1 2s. 11·622d. per share of £1. Final meeting return regd. 27 Feb. 1937 1937

Transvaal Gold Consols Ld. Regd. 1902. Amalgamated with East Rand Consolidated Ld. in which company shareholders were entitled to 1 fully-paid share of 10s. for every 5 shares held. Removed from Register 1905 1905

Transvaal Gold Exploration and Land Co. Ld. Regd. 1882. Vol. liq. May 1885. Final meeting return regd. 8 Dec. 1886 1896

Transvaal Gold Exploration and Land Co. Ld. Regd. 1885. Reconstructed 1895 as Transvaal Gold Mining Estates Ld. Vol. liq. 31 Mar 1896. Final meeting return regd. 1 Dec. 1898 1896

Transvaal Gold Fields Ld. Regd. 1894. Vol. liq. 25 May 1908. Shareholders were entitled to 1 share in Transvaal & Delagoa Bay Investment Co. Ld. for every 4 shares of £1 held. plus 13s. 10¼d. per share in cash. Final meeting return regd. 20 Nov. 1913 1910

Transvaal Gold Trust Ld. Regd. 1905. Vol. liq. 17 May 1916. Final meeting return regd. 17 Apr. 1917...... 1916

Transvaal Land & Minerals Corporation Ld. Regd. Guernsey 1902. Dissolved before 1949 1903

Transvaal Ld. Regd. 1902. Removed from Register 1913 1911

Transvaal Minerals Ld. Regd. 1889. Vol. liq. 24 June 1897. Final meeting return regd. 8 May 1902 1898

Transvaal Mines Ld. Inc. Transvaal 1905. Wound up May 1910. Capital returned to contributories—5s. 4¾d. per share of £1 at Oct. 1910; further payments (if any) not known 1911

Transvaal Navigation Coal Estates Ld. Inc. Transvaal 1897 as Anglo French Transvaal Navigation Coal Estates Ld.; name changed Sept. 1920. Vol. liq. Feb. 1921. Undertaking and assets were acquired by South African Coal Estates (Witbank) Ld., in which company shareholders were entitled to 1 share of £1 (credited as fully-paid) for each ordinary share of £1 held and 8 fully-paid shares of £1 for every 5 preference shares of £1 held 1922

Transvaal Nigel Ld. Inc. Transvaal 1895. London office closed. Placed in liquidation in Dec. 1954. Preference shareholders received 1st and final liquidation dividend of 8s. 9·35136d. per share and ordinary shareholders received a 1st liquidation distribution of 3s. per share in Aug. 1955; further distributions (if any) not known 1910

Transvaal (North) Gold Mining Co. Ld. See Carabobo Venezuela Gold Mines Ld.

Transvaal Northern Estates Co. Ld. Regd. 1897. Vol. liq. 17 Jan. 1927 for amalgamation with Transvaal Exploring Lands & Minerals Co. Ld. Final meeting return regd. 29 Aug. 1928 1927

Transvaal Oil Shale Syndicate Ld. Regd. 1912. Vol. liq. 6 Jan. 1922. Final meeting return regd. 29 Dec. 1922 1922

Transvaal Platinum Ld. Inc. Orange Free State 1923. Wound up Apr. 1927 1928

Transvaal Proprietary Ld. Regd. 1900 as New Buffels Land & Mining Co. Ld.; name changed Feb. 1902. Vol. liq. June 1907. Assets and property were sold to African and European Investment Co. Ld., in which company shareholders were entitled to 1 share of £1 (credited as fully-paid) for every 2 shares of £1 held. Struck off Register 7 Oct. 1936 1937

Transvaal Prospecting Co. Ld. Regd. 1887. Vol. liq. 22 May 1895. Reconstructed as Gold Explorers Ld., in

VOL. FOR

which company shareholders were entitled to 2 shares of 5s. (credited with 2s. 6d. paid) for each share of £1 held. Final meeting return regd. 20 July 1898 1898

Transvaal Prospecting Syndicate Ld. Inc. Transvaal 1903. In liquidation in 1907 1907

Transvaal Silver & Base Metals Ld. Inc. Transvaal 1919. Wound up Nov. 1926. First and final return of 10s. 6d. per share (of £1) 1927

Transvaal Silver Mines Ld. Inc. Transvaal 1889. Mine closed in Mar. 1895 1903

Transvaal Trading Co. Ld. Regd. 1887. Vol. liq. Apr. 1907. Removed from Register 1913 1908

Transvaal United Trust & Finance Co. Ld. Regd. 1898 as Nigel Extension Ld.; name changed 1902. Vol. liq. Oct. 1927. Reconstructed as company of same name (inc. Union of South Africa). Struck off Register 8 Apr. 1938 1939

Transvaal-Westralian Gold Concessions Ld. Regd. 1895. Removed from Register 1909 1899

Transvaal-Zambesi Co. Ld. Regd. 1899. Vol. liq. 27 Aug. 1915. Struck off Register 30 Jan. 1923 1916

Transvaalsche Banken Handels-Vereeniging. See Transvaal Commercial Bank.

Transvaalsche Handelsbank. See Transvaal Commercial Bank.

Transworld Corporation. Inc. 1978 in Delaware as Trans World Corpn.; name changed 1984. Under a Plan of Liquidation effective 30 Dec. 1986, all assets transferred to Transworld Corpn. Liquidating Trust holders received common shares in TW Services Inc. on a 1 for 1 basis 1987–8

Transylvanian Gold Mining Co. Ld. Regd. 1886. Struck off Register 3 Aug. 1894 1899

Trápeza tes Anatoles (Banque d'Orient). Inc. Athens by Royal Decree 1904. Absorbed in Sept. 1932 by Ethniki Trápeza tes Ellados (National Mortgage Bank of Greece)† 1933

Travancore Rubber Co. Ld. Regd. Edinburgh 1907. Vol. liq. 12 Sept. 1944. Capital returned to conttibutories—£3 8s. 6½d. (per £1 Stock). £287 2s. 5d. was paid into Companies' Liquidation Account. Final meeting return regd. 30 Nov. 1950 1952

Travellers' Accident Insurance Co. Ld. Regd. 1890. Business transferred to Crown Accident Insurance Co. Ld. Vol. liq. 11 Apr. 1893. Removed from Register 21 June 1907 .... *1894

Traversella Mines Ld. Regd. 1899. Vol. liq. 29 Dec. 1902. Removed from Register 1903 1903

Treadwell Yukon Co. Ld. Inc. Delaware 1924. Undertaking acquired by Treadwell Yukon Corporation Ld. Shareholders received 1 share of $1 for every 8·718 shares of $1 1938

Treasury Gold Mines Ld. Inc. Transvaal 1891 as Treasury Gold Mining; name changed 1895. Vol. liq. Feb. 1914 1914

Treburgett Consolidated Mines Ld. Regd. 1919. Receiver for debenture holders appointed 19 Dec. 1921; ceased to act 4 Apr. 1923. Struck off Register 1928 1927

Treburland Wolfram & Tin Co. Ld. Regd. 1913. Vol. liq. 16 July 1919. Final meeting return regd. 1 Apr. 1920 1920

Trechmann, Weekes & Co. Ld. Regd. 1892. In 1900 business was acquired by Associated Portland Cement Manufacturers Ld. Vol. liq. 9 Feb. 1920. Final meeting return regd. 1 Nov. 1920 1940

Tredegar & Hereford Brewery Co. Ld. See Hereford & Tredegar Brewery Ld

Tredegar Iron & Coal Co. Ld. Regd. 1873. Vol. liq. (members') 25 June 1953. Capital returned to contributories—11s. 3·32d. per share of 10s. £4,299 was paid into Companies' Liquidation Account. Final meeting return regd. 16 Apr. 1957 1958

Treferig Valley Railway Co. Inc. by Special Act 1879. Under Taff Vale Railway Act 1889 the undertaking was acquired by that company. Holders of each ordinary share received £10 preference stock; holders of every £100 debenture stock received £133 6s. 8d. 3% debenture stock in purchasing company 1890

Treforest Electrical Consumers Co. Ld. See South Wales Power Co. Ld.

Tregeagle Mine Ld. Regd. 1906. Struck off Register 1921 1909

Tregembo Mining Co. Established on cost-book system. In liquidation in 1890 1890

Tregontrees & Old Polgooth Consols Mining Co. Ld. Regd. 1883, subsequently placed in liquidation. Final meeting return regd. 13 July 1886 .... *1886

Tregurtha Downs Mines Ld. Regd. 1885. Vol. liq. 10 Oct. 1891. Removed from Register 1906 1892

Tremelbye (Selangor) Rubber Co. Ld. Regd. 1906. Vol. liq. 17 Mar. 1920. Reconstructed as company of same name. Shareholders were entitled to 4 shares of £1 (credited as fully-paid) in new company for each

VOL. FOR

share of £1 held. Final meeting return regd. 17 Dec. 1921 ... **1921**

Tremelbye (Selangor) Rubber Co. Ld. Regd. 18 Mar. 1920. Winding-up order made 21 May 1962. Distributions to unsecured creditors—10s. in £1 on 27 Aug. 1966; 5s. in £1 on 25 Sept. 1968; 5s. in £1 on 2 Dec. 1971. First and final return of capital of £1·755 per £1 was declared on 24 Mar. 1976. Struck off Registger 2 Aug. 1983 ... **1983–4**

Trench Tubeless Tyre Co. Ld. Regd. 1897. Removed from Register 1909 ... **1901**

Trencherfield Mills Ld. Regd. 1920. Vol. liq. (creditors') 2 Nov. 1932. Shareholders were entitled to 13·104 fully-paid ordinary and 13·106 fully-paid deferred shares of Lancashire Cotton Corporation Ld. for every £100 capital paid up, together with 1 fully-paid deferred share for every 2s. 6d. of the half of the capital called but not paid. Final meeting return regd. 19 Oct. 1938 ... **1933**

Trencherfield Spinning Co. Ld. Regd. 1906 as William Woods & Son Ld.; name changed June 1914. Vol. liq. 29 Apr. 1920. Final meeting return regd. 30 Mar. 1929 ... **1921**

Trent Cycle Co. Ld. Regd. 1896. Vol. liq. 31 Jan. 1900. Final meeting return regd. 27 June 1903 ... **1901**

Trent Iron Co. Ld. Regd. 1907. Vol. liq. (members') 27 Feb. 1933. Capital returned to contributories—3½d. per share of £1. Final meeting return regd. 12 May 1933 ... **1934**

Trent Navigation Co. Inc. by Special Act 1887 as Trent (Burton-upon-Trent & Humber) Navigation Co.; name changed 1892. Undertaking vesting from 1 Jan. 1948 in British Transport Commission under Transport Act 1947. Dissolved 11 Dec. 1950; holders of securities were entitled to receive British Transport 3% guaranteed stock (1978–88) as follows:—£5 10s. and £9 British Transport stock for every ordinary and 5% preference share of £10 held respectively; and £100 and £110 British Transport stock for every £100 of 3½% debenture stock and 6% debenture stock held respectively ... **1949**

Trenton Gold Mines Ld. Regd 1895. Vol. liq. 3 Jan. 1896. Capital returned to contributories—14s. 7d. per share with 15s. paid. Final meeting return regd. 25 Sept. 1896 ... **1897**

Trepca Mines Ld. Regd. 1927. Vol. liq. (members') 3 June 1957. Capital returned to contributories: 6s. 4·3d. per 5s. stock. Final meeting return regd. 2 Sept. 1961 ... **1962**

Tresavean Mines Ld. Regd. 1881. Vol. liq. Aug. 1885. Reconstructed as Shepherds United Ld., in which company shareholders were entitled to an equal number of shares. Final meeting return regd. 2 June 1886 ... **1886**

Tresavean Mines Ld. Regd. Edinburgh 1907. Vol. liq. (members') 19 Nov. 1930. No capital returned to contributories. Final meeting return regd. 21 Feb. 1931 ... **1931**

Treselca Ld. Regd. 1957. All capital was owned by Selection Trust Ld. Vol. liq. (members') 31 Jan. 1966. Final meeting return regd. 30 Mar. 1966 .... **1962**

Treskillard Minerals Ld. Regd. 1913 as Lancarrow Tin Alluvials Ld.; name changed 11 July 1924. Vol. liq. (members') 28 Aug. 1946. Capital returned to contributories—3s. 5·4342d. per share of 5s. Final meeting return regd. 16 June 1947 ... **1948**

Trevaunance United Mines Co. Established 1882. Taken over in 1892 by Polberro Mine Co., in which company shareholders received 1 share with £3 3s. 3d. paid for each share with £1 17s. 9d. paid **1893**

Treveddoe Mining Co. Ld. Regd. 1900. Vol. liq. 1 Nov. 1920. Final meeting return regd. 13 Jan. 1921 ..... **1921**

Trevethoe Co. Ld. Regd. 1901 as D.C.D. Syndicate Ld.; name changed Aug. 1903. Vol. liq. 18 Apr. 1905. Final meeting return regd. 22 Mar. 1906 .... **1906**

Trevor's Rhodesian Exploration Ld. Regd. 1899. Re-moved from Register 1909 .... **1905**

Trewitten Mining Co. Ld. Regd. 1881. Vol. liq. 25 Apr. 1884. Final meeting return regd. 25 Nov. 1884 .... *1885

Tri-Chrome Photos & Films Ld. Regd. 1928. Vol. liq. (members') 22 July 1930. Undertaking and assets (except cash) transferred to Art Photogravure Co. Ld., in which company shareholders received 1 fully-paid share of 4s. for every 5 shares of 4s. held; a cash payment of 6d. per share of 4s. was made in Aug. 1930. Final meeting return regd. 24 Apr. 1931 **1931**

Tricity Restaurants Ld. Regd. 1926. Receiver appointed 16 June 1934; ceased to act 28 Nov. 1934. Vol. liq. 28 Nov. 1934. Directly controlled by British Electric Transformer Co. Ld. Final meeting return regd. 27 June 1936 .... **1935**

Trickett Bailey & Co. Ld. See Coventry Repetition Co. Ld.

VOL. FOR

Tricolor Nitrate Co. Ld. Regd. 1905. Vol. liq. Jan. 1909. Property and assets were acquired by Britannia Nitrate Co. Ld., in which company shareholders were entitled to an equal amount of shares; debentures were exchanged at par. Removed from Register 1910 ... **1909**

Tri-Continental Allied Co. Inc. Consolidated with Tri-Continental Corporation in 1929 to form Tri-Continental Corporation (inc. Maryland) **1931**

Trident Marine Insurance Co. Ld. Regd. 1872. Removed from Register 1904 .... *1876

Tri-Metallic Syndicate Ld. Inc. in Tasmania 1908. Struck off Register 1910 ... **1917**

Trigg (J.) & Son (Dairy Farmers) Ld. Regd. 1908 as Trigg's Dairies Ld.; name changed Oct. 1909 to Surrey Dairy Farmers Association Ld. and as above in Apr. 1919. Vol. liq. (members') 28 Jan. 1931. Capital returned to contributories—£29,626 13s. 4d. Final meeting return regd. 25 Jan. 1934 .... **1931**

Trigg's Dairies Ld. See J. Trigg & Son (Dairy Farmers) Ld.

Trigwell & Co. Ld. Regd. 1893. Removed from Register 1901 .... **1901**

Trincomalee Estates Ld. Regd. 1914. Vol. liq. May 1922 for reconstruction as Western Petroleum & General Corporation Ld., in which company shareholders were entitled to shares as follows—1 fully-paid participating preference share of 2s. and right to apply for 4 ordinary shares of 1s. (with 6d. paid) for each preference share of 2s. held and 2 fully-paid participating preference shares of 2s. and right to apply for 3 ordinary shares of 1s. (with 6d. paid) for each ordinary share of 2s. held. Struck off Register 21 Mar. 1947 ... **1947**

Tring Gas Co. Inc. by Special Act 1936. Dissolved 1 May 1949, undertaking being vested in Southern Area Gas Board under Gas Act 1948. Holders of securities were entitled to receive, in respect of each £100 unit held. British Gas 3% guaranteed stock 1990–95 as follows:

	£	s.	d.
Orig. ord. stock (10% stand.)............	170	0	0
4½% red. pref. stock........................	103	0	0	**1952**

Trinidad & British Maikop Oil Ld. Regd. 1923. Vol. liq. (members') in Mar. 1929 for reconstruction as Trinidad & General Holdings Ld. (later British Colonial & Foreign Holdings Ld.) in which company shareholders were entitled to 1 fully-paid ordinary share of 1s. for each share of 2s. (1s. 6d. paid) held. Struck off Register 9 Feb. 1954.......... **1947**

Trinidad & General Holdings Ld. See British Colonial & Foreign Holdings Ld.

Trinidad-Cedros Oil Co. Ld. Regd. 1910. Vol. liq. 16 Dec. 1915. Final meeting return regd. 14 Nov. 1916 **1916**

Trinidad Central Oilfields Ld. Regd. 1911. Vol. liq. 29 Dec. 1916. Undertaking was acquired by company of same name. Shareholders were entitled to 2 fully-paid shares of £1 in new company for each fully-paid share of £1 held or 2 shares of £1 (credited with 12s. paid) for each share of £1 (15s. paid) held. Final meeting return regd. 24 Jan. 1919 ... **1917**

Trinidad Consolidated Oilfields Ld. Regd. 1919. Vol. liq. 16 Aug. 1921. The undertaking, property and assets were acquired by General Petroleum Co. of Trinidad Ld. in which company shareholders were entitled to 1 share of £1 (credited as fully-paid) for each share of £1 held. Final meeting return regd. 21 Mar. 1925 ... **1922**

Trinidad Consolidated Oilfields Ld. Regd. 1936. Vol. liq. (members') 7 Feb. 1951. Stockholders were entitled to receive 3 fully-paid shares of 1s. of Premier Consolidated Oilfields Ld. for every 2 stock units of 4s. held. Final meeting returned regd. 7 Feb. 1953 **1954**

Trinidad Dock and Engineering Co. Ld. Regd. 1906. Vol. liq. Dec. 1910. Removed from Register 1912........ **1911**

Trinidad Dominion Oil Ld. Regd. 1912. Vol. liq. 3 Feb. 1922. Undertaking and assets were acquired by Trinidad Oil Lands Ld. Final meeting return regd. 16 June 1928 ... **1923**

Trinidad Esmeralda Estate Ld. Regd. 1919. Vol. liq. 30 May 1927. Undertaking acquired by African Investment Trust Ld. Final meeting return regd. 29 Aug. 1928 ... **1937**

Trinidad Estates Co. Ld. Regd. Edinburgh 1902. Vol. liq. May 1924. Capital returned to contributories—£13 15s. per share during 1924; further distributions (if any) not known. Final meeting return regd. 22 Feb. 1928 ... **1925**

Trinidad Forest Reserve Oil Co. Ld. Regd. 1910. Vol. liq. July 1913. Properties were sold to Trinidad Lease-holds Ld. (later Trinidad Oil Co. Ld.) in which company shareholders were entitled to 1 share of £1 (credited as fully-paid) for every 6 fully-paid shares of £1 held or 1 share of £1 (credited as fully-paid) for

*See Stock Exchange Year-Book.

VOL. FOR

every 8 shares of £1 (12s. 6d. paid) held. Struck off Register 1914 .... **1915**

Trinidad Friendship Petroleum Co. Ld. See Venezuelan Consolidated Oilfields Ld.

Trinidad Grand River Oil Co. Ld. Regd. Edinburgh 1914. Vol. liq. Sept. 1915. Struck off Register 25 Jan. 1938 .... **1938**

Trinidad Lands Reclamation Ld. Regd. 1921. Vol. liq. (creditors') 30 Dec. 1931. No capital returned to contributories. Final meeting return regd. 5 Nov. 1936 .... **1932**

Trinidad National Petroleum Co. Ld. Regd. 1917. Vol. liq. 4 Jan. 1928. Reconstructed as Trinidad National Petroleum Co. (1928) Ld., in which company shareholders were entitled to 1 share (credited with 2s. 6d. paid) for each ordinary share of £1 held, or 1 fully-paid share and 1 share (credited with 2s. 6d. paid) for every 5 preference shares of 2s. held. Final meeting return regd. 3 Oct. 1928 .... **1928**

Trinidad Oil & Fuel Co. Ld. Regd. 1910. Court Order to wind up 15 July 1913. Liquidator released 6 Apr. 1921. Struck off Register 20 Mar. 1925 .... **1914**

Trinidad Oil Co. Ld. Regd. 1913 as Trinidad Leaseholds Ld.; name changed 4 May 1956. All capital was acquired by The Texas Co. in 1956. Final meeting return regd. 12 Aug. 1971 .... **1957**

Trinidad Oil Lands Ld. Regd. 1923. Struck off Register 17 Sept. 1946 .... **1947**

Trinidad Oilfields Ld. Regd. 1910. Vol. liq. 10 Dec. 1919. Property was acquired by United British Oilfields of Trinidad Ld., in which company shareholders were entitled to 2 ordinary shares of £1 (credited as fully-paid) for every 3 shares of £1 held. Final meeting return regd. 5 Mar. 1921 .... **1920**

Trinidad Petroleum Developments Ld. Regd. 1912. Vol. liq. 8 Aug. 1914. Final meeting return regd. 12 July 1915 .... ***1915**

Trinidad Produce Co. Ld. Regd. 1912. Receiver appointed 28 Oct. 1921; ceased to act 7 July 1924. Struck off Register 1925 .... **1925**

Trinidad Shipping & Trading Co. Ld. Regd. Edinburgh 1895. Vol. liq. Nov. 1920. Final meeting return regd. 22 Dec. 1923 .... **1921**

Trinidad Silverstream Oilfields Ld. Regd. 1912. Vol. liq. 3 Aug. 1917. Final meeting return regd. 15 Mar. 1918 .... **1918**

Trinidad Southern Oilfields Ld. Regd. 1910. Vol. liq. 16 Dec. 1912. Final meeting return regd. 21 Apr. 1914 **1913**

Trinidad Spies Oil Co. Ld. Regd. 1922. Formed to acquire certain lands; purchase of properties was not completed at 28 Dec. 1938. Struck off Register 2 Mar. 1943 .... **1944**

Trinidad United Oilfields Ld. Regd. 1910. Struck off Register Dec. 1931 .... **1932**

Trinidad Western Oilfields Ld. Regd. 1910 Vol. liq. Dec. 1911. Removed from Register 1913 .... **1912**

Trinidad Western Oilfields Ld. Regd. 1919. Court-Order to wind up Jan. 1923. Struck off Register June 1931 **1932**

Triplex (Continental) Ld. Regd. 1929, Vol. liq. (members') 20 May 1946. Final meeting return regd. 25 June 1946 .... **1946**

Triplex Safety Glass Co. Ld. Regd. 1912. Court Order to wind up 12 May 1921. Certain assets were acquired by company of the same name (later Triplex Holdings Ld.). Struck off Register Mar. 1932 .... **1933**

Tri-State Railway & Electric Co. Inc. in Ohio 1911. The $68,000 1st mortgage and collateral trust 50-year 6% gold bonds sold in London in 1911 at 95% were redeemed at that price in 1913 .... **1914**

Triticine Ld. Regd. 1896. Removed from Register 1911 **1900**

Triton Gold Mines No Liability. Inc. in Victoria 1933. Vol. liq. 3 Feb. 1949. Capital returned to contributories—11·4d. (Australian currency) per share of A10s. **1952**

Triumph Auto Pianos Ld. (Regd. 1917). See Triumphauto Ld.

Triumph Auto Pianos Ld. Regd. 1929. Vol. liq. (members') 10 Aug. 1931. Final meeting return regd. 9 Jan. 1950 .... **1950**

Triumph Co. Ld. Regd. 1897 as New Triumph Cycle Co. Ld.; name changed July 1897 to Triumph Cycle Co. Ld. and as above in Dec. 1930. In Oct. 1939 it was stated that receiver had disposed of the assets and no funds were available for winding up the company **1940**

Triumph Cycle Co. Ld. See Triumph Co. Ld.

Triumph Hauraki Gold Mines Ld. Regd. 1895. Vol. liq. 2 Nov. 1897. Reconstructed as Triumph Komata Gold Mine Ld., in which company shareholders were entitled to 1 share of £1 (credited with 16s. paid) for every 4 shares of 5s. held. Final meeting return regd. 30 Aug. 1898 .... **1898**

Triumph Komata Gold Mine Ld. Regd. 1897. Vol. liq. 29 Sept. 1898. Undertaking and assets were acquired by West Tokatea Gold Mine Ld. for £500 in cash,

VOL. FOR

£31,293 in fully-paid shares and £14,025 in 18,700 shares of £1 (credited with 15s. paid). Final meeting return regd. 12 June 1899 .... **1899**

Triumph Leases Ld. Regd. 1896. Vol. liq. 2 Nov. 1898. Final meeting return regd. 31 Mar. 1900 .... **1899**

Triumph Oil & Transport Co. Ld. Regd. 1911. Struck off Register 12 July 1935 .... ***1913**

Triumphauto Ld. Regd. 1917 as Triumph Auto Pianos Ld., name changed Oct. 1917. Vol. liq. (creditors') 19 Dec. 1930. Undertaking and assets were acquired by Triumph Auto Pianos Ld. for 187,500 fully-paid ordinary shares of 2s. and 11,250 fully-paid preference shares of £1. Final meeting return regd. 20 Mar. 1940 .... **1920**

Trocadero Cinema (Leeds) Ld. Regd. 1920. Vol. liq. 8 Nov. 1923. Final meeting return regd. 30 May 1924 ***1924**

Trocadero Super-Cinema (Liverpool) Ld. Regd. 1921. Vol. liq. (members') 2 May 1956; undertaking was sold to Provincial Cinematograph Theatres Ld. for £164,250. Capital returned to contributories—£1 15s. per share of £1. £13 15s. was paid into Companies' Liquidation Account in respect of unclaimed distributions. Final meeting return regd. 1 Aug. 1970 .... **1970**

Troedyrhiw Coal Co. Ld. Regd 1919. Vol. liq. (members') 21 July 1936. Undertaking was acquired by Powell Duffryn Associated Collieries Ld. (later Powell Duffryn Ld.), which company owned all the shares. Final meeting return regd. 18 Feb. 1937 .. **1937**

Troesan Estates Ld. Regd. 1910 as Troesan Rubber Estate Ld.; name changed 1912. Court Order to wind up Oct. 1914. Struck off Register 1927 .... **1915**

Troitzk Goldfields Ld. Regd. 1906. Vol. liq. 20 Dec. 1916. Final meeting return regd. 18 Apr. 1918 .... **1917**

Trolak Plantations Ld. Regd. Edinburgh 1906. Vol. liq. Jan. 1920. Undertaking and assets were acquired by Trolak Estates Ld., in which company shareholders were entitled to 4 shares of £1 (credited as fully-paid) for each share of £1 held. Final meeting return regd. 11 Sept. 1922 .... **1920**

Tronoh South Ld. Regd. 1911. Vol. liq. 31 Aug. 1922. Reconstructed as Pari Tin Ld. in which company shareholders were entitled to 1 share of 5s. (credited as fully-paid) plus 1s. in cash for each share of £1 held. Final meeting return regd. 29 May 1923 .... **1923**

Tropical Trading and Transport Co. Ld. Regd. 1894. Removed from Register 1901 .... **1901**

Trouville Pier Steamboat Co. Ld. Regd. 1888. Court Orders: to wind up under supervision 6 Dec. 1890; to dissolve 30 June 1893. Debenture holders received preference shares in Trouville Pier Co. (La Jetée de Trouville) Ld. equal to their holding and arrears of interest. Shareholders received an equal number of fully-paid shares of £1 in the new company. **1908**

Trouville Pier Co. (La Jetée de Trouville) Ld. Regd. 1891. Vol. liq. Apr. 1908. Removed from Register 1912 .... **1909**

Trowbridge Tyre & Rubber Co. Ld. Regd. 1929 as Trowbridge Tyre & Rubber Co. (1929) Ld.; name changed 27 Oct. 1933. Court Order to wind up 14 Oct. 1935. Struck off Register 20 Feb. 1942 .... **1942**

Trowbridge Water Co. Inc. by Special Act 1873. By Act of 1931 the undertaking was acquired by Trowbridge, Melksham and District Water Board. Stockholders were entitled to Water Board Stock as follows—for each £100 10% maximum consolidated stock 1873 held—£160 5% stock; for each 7% maximum consolidated stock 1878 held—£112 5% stock. The liability for mortgages and debenture stocks was assumed by the Water Board **1932**

Troys Exploration Co. Ld. Regd. 1895. Vol. liq. 7 Oct. 1902. Undertaking and assets in South Africa were acquired by Johannesburg Consolidated Investment Co. Ld. for 27,500 fully-paid shares of £1 and £16,000 in cash. Shareholders were entitled to 1 fully-paid share of £1 in purchasing company for every 8 shares of £1 held. Struck off Register 1927 **1903**

True Blue Block Gold Mining Co. Ld. Inc. Queensland 1891. Wound up 1898; assets were sold to Croydon Goldfields Ld. **1898**

True Blue (Hannan's) Gold Mine Ld. Regd. 1895. Vol. liq. 19 Apr. 1899. Reconstructed as company of same name. Final meeting return regd. 2 Jan. 1900 **1900**

True Blue (Hannan's) Gold Mine Ld. Regd. Apr. 1899. Vol. liq. 25 Sept. 1899. Undertaking and assets were acquired by Hannan's Brownhill Gold Mining Co. Ld. (later Oroyd Brownhill Co. Ld.) for 30,000 fully-paid shares and £3,500 in cash. Final meeting return regd. 25 Mar. 1902 .... **1908**

Truefitt (H. P.) Ld. Regd. 1880. Vol. liq. 27 Feb. 1923. Capital returned to contributories—£3 per share of £6 in Apr. 1923; further payments (if any) not known. Final meeting return regd. 6 Mar. 1924 .. **1924**

See Stock Exchange Year-Book.

VOL. FOR

Truer River Gold Mining Co. Ld. Regd. 1896. Vol. liq. 1 Feb. 1899. Final meeting return regd. 8 July 1899 ... **1899**

Truffault Cycle and Tube Manufacturing Co. Ld. Regd. 1896 as Dunlop-Truffault Cycle and Tube Manufacturing Co. Ld.; name changed July 1896. Vol. liq. 29 June 1898. Final meeting return regd. 2 Dec. 1905 **1900**

Truphonic Ld. Regd. 1928. Vol. liq. 28 Jan. 1929. Undertaking and assets together with certain patent rights were acquired by Truphonic Radio Ld. for 225,000 fully-paid shares of 2*s*. Struck off Register 24 July 1930 ... **1930**

Truphonic Radio Ld. Regd. 1929. Court Order to wind up July 1930. Struck off Register 15 June 1937 ... **1938**

Truro Electricity Supply Co. Ld. Regd. 1926. Vol. liq. (members') 24 Jan. 1938. Undertaking acquired by Cornwall Electric Power Co. Capital returned to contributories—£23,092 19*s*. 10*d*. Final meeting return regd. 12 May 1938 ... **1938**

Truro Gas Co. Regd. as limited 1895; inc. by Special Act 1906. Dissolved 1 May 1949, undertaking being vested in South Western Area Gas Board under Gas Act 1948. Holders of securities were entitled to receive, in respect of each £100 unit held, British Gas 3% guaranteed stock 1990–95 as follows:

	£	s.	d.	
Ord. stock (5% stand.)	125	0	0	
5% pref. stock	112	10	0	
4% perp. deb. stock	102	10	0	
3½% red. deb. stock (1966)	100	0	0	
3½% red. deb. stock (1956)	100	0	0	
3¼% red. deb. stock	99	0	0	**1952**

Truro Water Co. Ld. Inc. by Special Act 1875 as The Truro Water Co., regd. as limited company and name changed 30 June 1966. Vol. liq. (members') 2 Apr. 1968. Undertaking transferred to South Cornwall Water Board on 1 Apr. 1968. Contributories were entitled to receive stock in the Board as follows—£19 6% stock per ordinary share of £10; £1 3*s*. 4*d*. 6% stock per £1 ordinary stock; £1 4½% stock per £1 4% and 4½% preference stock respectively; £1 5½% stock per £1 5½% preference stock; £1 4½% stock per £1 3% irredeemable debenture stock. Final meeting return regd. 15 Aug. 1968 ... **1969**

Truscott (Jas.) & Son Ld. Regd. 1902. Vol. liq. (members') 12 Jan. 1937. Undertaking and assets were transferred to Brown, Knight & Truscott Ld. for 22,000 C preference shares of £1, 39,000 D shares of £1, 90,614 ordinary shares of £1 and assumption of debts. Final meeting return regd. 7 Dec. 1937 **1937**

Trust & Agency Assets Ld. Regd. 1907. Vol. liq. (creditors') 9 Jan. 1953. Mortgage debenture stockholders received total distributions of 17*s*. 5¼*d*. per £1 unit. Final meeting return regd. 25 Sept. 1953 **1945**

Trust & Investment Corporation of South Africa Ld. Regd. 1890. Removed from Register 1907 ... **1893**

Trust & Loan Co. of China, Japan & the Straits Ld. *See* Bank of China, Japan and the Straits Ld.

Trust Association Ld. Regd. 1874. Court Orders to wind up 9 Apr. 1877; to dissolve 12 Jan. 1883 ... ***1877**

Trust Company of America. Constituted 1905. In Feb. 1912 amalgamated with Equitable Trust Co. of New York ... **1913**

Trust Financier de Transports et d'Enterprises Industrielles. *See* Société Financiere de Transports et D'Enterprises Industrielles (Sofina) S. A.

Trust Français Ld. Regd. 1896. Vol. liq. 17 July 1900. Undertaking and assets were acquired by South African Gold Trust Ld., in which company shareholders were entitled to 2 fully-paid ordinary shares of £1 for every 25 ordinary shares of 1*s*. held or 1 preference and ½ ordinary share *plus* 2*s*. 1*d*. in cash for each preference share of £4 held. Final meeting return regd. 30 Nov. 1920 ... **1901**

Trust Loan & Agency Co. of Mexico Ld. Regd. 1889. In liquidation in 1898. Capital returned to contributories—4*s*. 2*d*. per share of £10 (£2 paid) in May 1898; further payments (if any) not known. Removed from Register 1901 ... **1899**

Trust of Transport Shares Ld. Regd. 1936. Vol. liq. (members') 30 Jan. 1939. 99% of shares were held by Investment Managers & Secretaries Ld. Final meeting return regd. 15 Sept. 1939 ... **1939**

Trustee Assets and Investment Insurance Co. Ld. Regd. 1889. In liquidation in 1900. Capital returned to contributories—9*s*. per share; further payments (if any) not known. Removed from Register 1901 ... **1901**

Trustee, Industrial & Investment Corporation Ld. Regd. 1891. Vol. liq. 10 June 1904. Final meeting return regd. 20 Oct. 1905 ... **1892**

Trustees & Bankers Securities Co. Ld. Regd. 1890. Removed from Register 1909 ... **1892**

Trusty Engine Works Ld. *See* Shillingford Engineering Co. Ld.

VOL. FOR

Tubeless Pneumatic Tire & Capon Heaton Ld. Regd. 1896. Removed from Register 1903 ... **1902**

Tubes (America) Ld. Regd. 1897. Removed from Register 1899 ... **1898**

Tubes Ld. Regd. 1897. as Weldless Tubes Ld.; name changed June 1897. Removed from Register 1908 **1907**

Tucker (James) Ld. *See* Cardiff Milling Co. Ld.

Tucker (Wm. Duncan) & Sons Ld. Regd. 1906. Vol. liq. 15 Oct. 1928. Undertaking and assets were acquired in Jan. 1928 by Tucker (Duncan) (Tottenham) Ld. for £25,000 fully-paid preference shares of £1, £23,749 13*s*. in fully-paid ordinary shares of 1*s*. and £121,250 in cash. Final meeting return regd. 8 Jan. 1930 ... **1929**

Tucson Mining & Smelting Co. Ld. Regd. 1894. Struck off Register 26 Oct. 1900 ... **1901**

Tucuman Sugar Co. Formed in Argentine 1895. The outstanding 5% 1st mortgage debentures were redeemed at par on 1 May 1930 ... **1931**

Tucuman Tramways, Light & Power Co. Ld. Regd. 1914. Vol. liq. (members') 28 Feb. 1935. Undertaking acquired by Cia. de Electricidad del Norte Argentine S.A. Capital returned to contributories—20*s*. per 6% cumulative preferred share of £1; 20*s*. per participating second preferred share of £1; £1 per deferred share of 10*s*. £500 was paid into Companies' Liquidation Account. Final meeting return regd. 14 Nov. 1935 ... **1936**

Tudhoe & Sunderland Bridge Gas Co. Inc. by Special Act 1877. Dissolved 1 May 1949, undertaking being vested in Northern Area Gas Board under Gas Act 1948. Holders of capital A stock were entitled to receive, in respect of each £100 unit held, £180 British Gas 3% guaranteed stock 1990–95 ... **1952**

Tudor Gold Mining Co. Ld. Inc. Transvaal 1899. Wound up Jan. 1925. Capital returned to contributories—$\frac{7}{10}$*d*. per share of £1 in May 1925; further payments (if any) not known ... **1926**

Tui Gold Mines Ld. Regd. 1896. Removed from Register 1903 ... **1900**

Tully Gas Plants Ld. Regd. 1921. Vol. liq. 9 May 1924. Amalgamated with Gas & Fuel Plants Ld., in which company shareholders were entitled to 64,880 ordinary shares of 1*s*., 107,645 8% participating preference shares of £1 and £207,973 income debenture stock. Final meeting return regd. 13 Sept. 1927 ... **1925**

Tully Gas Plants (1927) Ld. Regd. 1927. Vol. liq. 6 Mar. 1929. Final meeting return regd. 4 Oct. 1932 ... ***1929**

Tulsa Oil Co. Ld. Regd. 1912. Assets realised insufficient to satisfy claims of debenture holders. Struck off Register 1921 ... **1921**

Tunbridge Wells Gas Co. Estd. 1843; inc. by Special Act 1864. Dissolved 1 May 1949, undertaking being vested in South Eastern Area Gas Board under Gas Act 1948. Holders of securities were entitled to receive, in respect of each £100 unit held, British Gas 3% guaranteed stock 1990–95 as follows:

	£	s.	d.	
Sliding scale stock (4% stand.)	131	5	0	
5% max. stock	111	0	0	
4½% perp. deb. stock	114	0	0	
5½% perp. deb. stock	135	0	0	**1952**

Tungsten & Rare Metals Co. Ld. Regd. 1900. Vol. liq. 21 Sept. 1906. Struck off Register 24 July 1923 ... **1907**

Tungsten Manufacturing Co. Ld. Regd. 1919. Vol. liq. (creditors') 10 July 1958. No capital returned to contributories. Final meeting return regd. 28 June 1965 ... **1966**

Tunnel Asbestos Cement Co. Ld. Regd. 1935. Vol. liq. (members') 20 Jan. 1958. Undertaking acquired by Tunnel Cement Ld. in 1958 for £1,375,000. Distributions—per ordinary share (of 10*s*.) £2 1*s*. 8*d*.; per deferred share (of 1*s*.) 4*s*. 2*d*. Amount paid into Companies' Liquidation Account—£14 11*s*. 10*d*. in respect of unclaimed dividends. Final meeting return regd. 18 Feb. 1969 ... **1969**

Tunnel Driving Co. Ld. Regd. 1886. Vol. liq. 20 Dec. 1889. Final meeting return regd. 1 Apr. 1892 ... **1890**

Tunnicliffe & Hampson (1920) Ld. Regd. 1920. Vol. liq. 1929. Undertaking and assets acquired by Combined Egyptian Mills Ld. (later Combined English Mills (Spinners) Ld.) Struck off Register 1 Feb. 1944 **1944**

Tunstall Coal & Iron Co. Ld. Regd. 1900. Removed from Register 1905 ... **1904**

Turbine Corporation Ld. Regd. 1907. Vol. liq. Dec. 1910. Removed from Register 1912 ... **1911**

Turf Mines Ld. Inc. Transvaal 1902. Wound up Sept. 1908. Undertaking was transferred to Village Deep Ld., in which company shareholders were entitled to 3 shares of £1 for every 10 shares of £1 held ... **1909**

Turffontein Estates Ld. Regd. 1893. Vol. liq. 15 Jan. 1919. Assets were acquired by Robinson Deep Ld. Final meeting return regd. 17 June 1927 ... **1919**

**See Stock Exchange Year-Book.*

VOL. FOR

Turkish Régie Export Co. Ld. Regd. 1893. Undertaking and assets were acquired by Société de la Régie Cointéressée des Tabacs de l'Empire Ottoman (later Société de la Régie Cointéressée des Tabacs de Turquie). Capital returned to contributories—4s. per A share of 4s.; 16s. 4d. per B share or founders' share of £1; further payments (if any) not known. Removed from Register 1904 .... **1903**

Turler & Co. Ld. Regd. 1906 as Messrs. Turler & Co. Ld.; name changed July 1907. Court Order to wind up 28 Aug. 1907. Liquidator released 23 Sept. 1910. Struck off Register 6 June 1913 .... **1908**

Turn of the Tide Development Syndicate Ld. Regd. 1899. Removed from Register 1910 .... **1906**

Turnbull (Alev.) & Co. Ld. Regd. Edinburgh 1891. Vol. liq. (creditors') 6 Mar. 1936. Assets realised insufficient to pay creditors in full. Final meeting return regd. 9 Oct. 1937. .... **1937**

Turnbull Coal & Shipping Co. Ld. Regd. 1924. Struck off Register 8 Mar. 1935 .... **1936**

Turnbull (George) & Co. Ld. Regd. 1919. Vol. liq. (members') 3 Jan. 1939. Undertaking and assets were acquired by Glenboig Union Fire Clay Co. Ld., in which company shareholders were entitled to 1 fully-paid preferred share of £1 for each preferred ordinary share of £1 held. £347 3s. 5d. was paid into Companies' Liquidation Account. Final meeting return regd. 29 Dec. 1939 .... **1940**

Turner (Albert) & Son Ld. Regd. 1919. Vol. liq. 11 Dec. 1957 for reconstruction as Albert Turner & Son (Subsidiary) Ld. (name changed to Albert Turner & Son Ld.). Shareholders received £1 cash and one share of 10s. in new company for each ordinary share of £1 held. Final meeting return regd. 3 May 1961 .... **1962**

Turner & Hudson Ld. Regd. 1898. Vol. liq. Mar. 1905. Capital returned to contributories—2s. per share of £1; further payments (if any) not known. Removed from Register 1906 .... **1907**

Turner & Wainwright Ld. Regd. 1933 as Turner & Wainwright (1933) Ld.; name changed Nov. 1940. Vol. liq. (creditors') 22 Dec. 1938. Assets realised insufficient to pay creditors in full. Final meeting return regd. 15 Nov. 1940 .... **1939**

Turner & Wainwright (1919) Ld. Regd. 1919. Vol. liq. (members') 19 Sept. 1932. Capital returned to contributories—12s. 5⅓d. per preference share of £1. Final meeting return regd. 13 Mar. 1935........ **1938**

Turner Automatic Machines Ld. Regd. 1928. Vol. liq. (members') 26 Feb. 1930. Shareholders received 1 fully-paid share of 1s. in Turner Automatic Machines (1931) Ld. for each share of 5s. held. Final meeting return regd. 5 Nov. 1931 .... **1932**

Turner Automatic Machines (1931) Ld. Regd. 1931. Vol. liq. (members') 22 Nov. 1932. Capital returned to contributories—⅞₀d. per share of 1s. Final meeting return regd. 22 Aug. 1933 .... **1933**

Turner Brothers Asbestos Co. Ld. Regd. 1899 as Turner Brothers Ld.; name changed Nov. 1916. Vol. liq. 24 Mar. 1920. Undertaking acquired by Turner & Newall Ld. Final meeting return regd. 1 Dec. 1920 **1941**

Turner Gas Engine Co. Ld. Regd. 1881. Vol. liq. 8 May, 1885. Final meeting return regd. 27 June 1891 .... ***1886**

Turner (G. R.) (Realisation) Ld. Regd. 1903 as G. R. Turner Ld. Vol. liq. (members') 28 May 1962. Final meeting return regd. 20 Aug. 1964 .... **1938**

Turner (Harry) (Macclesfield) Ld. Regd. 1928. Vol. liq. (members') 8 Jan. 1937. Capital returned to contributories—8s. 6·414d. per share of £1. Final meeting return regd. 25 Oct. 1937 .... **1937**

Turner, Nott & Co. Ld. Regd. 1897. Vol. liq. (members') 18 July 1934. Capital returned to contributories—£3 5s. 8d. per preference share of £10. Final meeting return regd. 29 June 1935 .... **1935**

Turner Pneumatic Tyre Co. Ld. Regd. 1893. Court Orders: to wind up 19 Dec. 1894; to stay proceedings 18 July 1896. Vol. liq. 16 Dec. 1897. Business was acquired by Amalgamated Pneumatic Tyre Companies Ld., in which company shareholders were entitled to 4 fully-paid ordinary shares of £1 and £1 debenture for each share of £1 held. Final meeting return regd. 27 July 1899 .... **1898**

Turner Steam Navigation Co. Ld. Regd. 1920. Vol. liq. 31 Mar. 1922. Struck off Register 1926 .... ***1923**

Turner (Thomas) & Co. (Sheffield) Ld. Regd. 1918. Court Order to wind up Oct. 1932. Struck off Register 15 June 1937 .... **1938**

Turner (Thomas) Ld. Regd. 1887. Removed from Register 1905 .... **1904**

Turners Garages (Cardiff) Ld. Regd. 1919. Vol. liq. 30 Oct. 1929. Direct controlling interest held by R. E. Jones Ld. Struck off Register 1934 .... **1930**

Turners Ld. Regd. Edinburgh 1895. Vol. liq. Mar. 1909. Court Order to dissolve Nov. 1913 .... **1910**

VOL. FOR

Turnpenny Bros. Ld. Undertaking and assets were acquired by Hackney Furnishing Co. (1928) Ld ... **1929**

Turog Brown Flour Co. Ld. Regd. 1909. Vol. liq. 31 Jan. 1927. Controlling interest held by Spillers Milling & Associated Industries Ld. (later Spillers Ld.). Final meeting return regd. 23 Jan. 1928 .... **1927**

Turon Mines Ld. Regd. 1897. Removed from Register 1904 .... **1899**

Turriff Gas Co. Ld. Regd. in Edinburgh 1906. Dissolved 1 May, 1949, undertaking being vested in Scottish Area Gas Board under Gas Act 1948. Holders of ordinary shares (of £1) were entitled to receive £1 15s. British Gas 3% guaranteed stock 1990–95 for each share held **1952**

Turtle Cup (1911) Ld. Regd. 1911. Vol. liq. 14 Feb. 1921. Final meeting return regd. 9 Mar. 1922 .... **1922**

Tuscan Gas Co. Ld. Regd. 1876. In accordance with Law of 5 Mar. 1942 company was merged with Soc. Italiana per il Gas which took over all assets and liabilities. The 97 shares held by the public were exchanged for 2,425 fully-paid shares of Soc. Italiana per il Gas and the 18,141 shares owned by that company were cancelled **1947**

Tustanowise Oil Development Syndicate Ld. Regd. 1911. Vol. liq. 30 Jan. 1911. Final meeting return regd. 11 June 1912 .... ***1913**

Tuxford & District Gas Light & Coke Co. Inc. by Special Act 1897 .... **1911**

Tweefontein Gold Mining Co. Ld. Regd. 1890 as Great Stan Anton Gold Mining Co. Ld.; name changed 2 June 1894. Vol liq. 17 Mar. 1896. Final meeting return regd. 29 June 1896 .... ***1893**

Tweefontein Platinum Ld. Inc. Transvaal 1925. Vol. liq. 11 Nov. 1941. Capital returned to contributories— 0·8725d. per share of 2s. In Dec. 1944 it was stated that company was non-existent **1945**

Twentieth Century-Fox Film Corpn. Inc. in State of New York 1 Feb. 1915 as Fox Film Corpn., name changed Aug. 1935. A plan of reorganisation which became effective 27 Sept. 1952 provided for dissolution of this corporation and transfer of its assets to two new corporations, viz. Twentieth Century-Fox Film Corpn. and National Theatres Inc. (both inc. in Delaware) **1953**

20th Century Investment Co. Ld. Regd. 1904. Vol. liq. (members') 9 Dec. 1948. Shareholders were entitled to 30s. for each preference share of £1 held, and 26s. 4d. plus 1 fully-paid ordinary share of £1 in Waterloo Investment Trust Ld. for each ordinary share of £1 held. £3 14s. 7d. was paid into Companies' Liquidation Account. Final meeting return regd. 14 Dec. 1949 .... **1950**

Twigge & Crosfield Ld. Regd. 1916. Vol. liq. 5 June 1925. Final meeting return regd. 18 Aug. 1926 ... ***1926**

Twin Bobbin Sewing Machine Co. Ld. Regd. 1913. Receiver appointed in Dec. 1926. Struck off Register Dec. 1929 .... **1930**

Twin Lakes Hydraulic Gold Mining Syndicate Ld. Regd. 1883. Vol. liq. 22 July 1892. Reconstructed as Twin Lakes Placers Ld. Final meeting return regd. 22 July 1893 .... **1894**

Twin Lakes Placers Ld. Regd. 1892. Vol. liq. 11 Apr. 1899. Reconstructed as company of same name. Shareholders were entitled to 4 shares of 10s. (credited with 7s. paid) in new company for each share of £1 held. Final meeting return regd. 4 Aug. 1899 .... **1908**

Twin Lakes Placers Ld. Regd. 1899. Vol. liq. 18 June 1913. Final meeting return regd. 26 July 1918 ..... **1914**

Twining (Richard) & Co. Business acquired in 1892 by Lloyds Bank Ld **1897**

Twisted Steel Bar Co. Ld. Regd. 1919 as Improved Twisted Steel Bar Co. (1919) Ld.; name changed Aug. 1920. Struck off Register Apr. 1929 .... **1930**

Two-Reel Lock-Stitch Sewing Machine Co. Ld. Regd. 1891. Vol. liq. 3 Dec. 1896. Final meeting return regd. 30 Dec. 1897 .... **1898**

Tybar (Java) Plantations Ld. Regd. 1925. Vol. liq. 27 Mar. 1928. Undertaking and assets were acquired by British Rubber Estates of Java Ld. in which company shareholders were entitled to 7 fully-paid shares of 2s. for every 10 shares of 2s. held. Final meeting return regd. 1 Jan. 1929 .... **1928**

Tyddynmawr & North Wales Exploration Gold Mining Co. Ld. Regd. 1888. Vol. liq. 10 Mar. 1890. Final meeting return regd. 13 Nov. 1901 .... ***1891**

Tyee Copper Ld. Regd. 1900. Vol. liq. 17 Feb. 1922. Capital returned to contributories—5s. 3½d. per share of £1 at Jan. 1923; further payments (if any) not known. Final meeting return regd. 17 Feb. 1923 **1923**

Tyldesley Coal Co. Ld. Regd. 1870. Vol. liq. (members') 16 Oct. 1951. Capital returned to contributories— 28s. 8·96d. per ordinary share of £1 and £71 17s. 4d. per preference share of £50. £101 9s. 2d. was paid

VOL. FOR

into Companies' Liquidation Account. Final meeting return regd. 16 Aug. 1956 .... **1957**

Tyler Industries (Parent Co.) Ld. Regd. 1913. Receiver appointed in Oct. 1916. Struck off Register Jan. 1932 .... **1932**

Tyler, Johnson & Co. Ld. Regd. 1909. Vol. liq. 10 Mar. 1911. The undertaking and assets were acquired by Johnson, Tyler & Co. Ld. Struck off Register 3 Sept. 1918 .... **1912**

Tylor (J.) & Sons Ld. Regd. 1898. Court Order to wind up May 1921. Struck off Register Apr. 1929 .... **1930**

Tyne & Blyth Steamship Owning Co Ld. Regd. 1885. Vol. liq. 19 Nov. 1915. Final meeting return regd. 26 Jan. 1922 .... **1916**

Tyne & Wear Steam Ship Owning Co. Ld. Regd. 1882. Vol. liq. 29 Oct. 1885. Final meeting return regd. 29 Oct. 1886 .... ***1885**

Tyne Boiler Works Co. Ld. Regd. 1882. Struck off Register 22 June 1894 .... **1899**

Tyne Forge Co. Ld. Regd. 1881. Vol. liq. 10 June 1887. Final meeting return regd. 14 June 1894 .... **1889**

Tyne Improvement Commission. Constituted by Act of 1850; inc. by Act of 1857. On 1 Aug. 1968 the undertaking was transferred to the Port of Tyne Authority and the commission dissolved **1969**

Tyne Pontoons & Dry Docks Co. Ld. Regd. 1883 as River Tyne Dry Docks Engineering and Boiler Making Co. Ld.; name changed Oct. 1885. Vol. liq. 19 Dec. 1900. Reconstructed as company of same name. Shareholders were entitled to 7½ fully-paid ordinary and 7½ fully-paid preference shares of £1 in new company for each ordinary or preference share of £1 held. Final meeting return regd. 15 July 1901. Removed from Register 1901 .... **1903**

Tyne Pontoons and Dry Docks Co. Ld. Regd. 1900. Vol. liq. 31 Dec. 1903. The undertaking was acquired by Swan Hunter & Wigham Richardson Ld., in which company shareholders were entitled to 1 fully-paid ordinary share of £1 for each ordinary share of £1 held, or 1 preference share of £1 (credited as fully-paid) for each preference share of £1 held. Final meeting return regd. 6 Jan. 1905 .... **1904**

Tyne Steam Shipping Co. Ld. Regd. 1864. Reconstructed 1903 as Tyne-Tees Steam Shipping Co. Ld., in which company shareholders were entitled to £6 in shares and £6 in 4½% debenture stock for each share of £20 (£14 paid) held. Removed from Register 1906 **1904**

Tyne Valley Colliery Ld. Regd. 1894. Vol. liq. Nov. 1908. Removed from Register 1909 .... **1909**

Tyne Wherry Co. Ld. Regd. 1872. Vol. liq. (members') 16 Jan 1967. Final meeting return regd. 1 May 1968 **1939**

Tynemouth Gas Co. Established 1820. Inc. by Special Act 1867. Under Order of 1928 the undertaking was acquired by Newcastle-upon Tyne & Gateshead Gas Co., in which company stockholders were entitled to £125 or £100 4% preference stock for every £100 ordinary or preference stock respectively held. The acquiring company took over all the mortgages **1929**

Tynemouth Palace Co. Ld. Regd. 1909. Vol. liq. Aug. 1922. Struck off Register 12 Mar. 1935 .... **1936**

Tyneside Electrical Development Co. Ld. See Tyneside Investment Trust Ld.

Tyneside Investment Trust Ld. Regd. as Tyneside Electrical Development Co. Ld.; name changed 1929. Vol. liq. 12 June 1980. The company was unitised and ordinary shareholders received a total of 3·64964 units of Target Income and Growth Fund for each share held. Final meeting held 15 Feb. 1982 **1982–3**

Type Trust Ld. Regd. 1901. Vol. liq. 22 Feb. 1904. Final meeting return regd. 10 May 1905 .... ***1905**

Typewriting Telegraph Corporation Ld. Regd. 1900. Vol. liq. May 1910. Removed from Register 1913 .... **1911**

Tyspane Tea Holdings Ld. Regd. 1960. All capital was owned by Robertson Bois & Co. Ld. Vol. liq. (members') 18 Mar. 1963. Final meeting return regd. 19 Mar. 1965 .... **1963**

Tywarnhaile Mine Ld. Regd. 1903. Assets were sold to Tywarnhaile Syndicate Ld. for £7,500 in fully-paid shares. Removed from Register 1907 .... **1906**

Tywarnhaile Mining Co. Ld. Regd. 1907. Vol. liq. Jan. 1909. Removed from Register 1912 .... **1909**

Tywarnhaile Syndicate Ld. Regd. 1905. Reconstructed 1907 as Tywarnhaile Mining Co. Ld., in which company shareholders were entitled to 1 share of £1 (credited with 10s. paid) for each share of £1 held. Removed from Register 1909 .... **1908**

Tysack & Branfort Sieam Shipping Co. Ld. See Well Line Ld.

U

Ubique Investment Trust Ld. See Ubique Trust Ld.

Ubique Trust Ld. Regd. 1921 as Ubique Investment Trust Ld.; name changed Jan. 1925. Vol. liq.

VOL. FOR

(members') 9 July 1934. Undertaking and assets were acquired by Mining Securities Ld., in which company holders of debentures and preference shares were entitled to fully-paid shares equal to nominal amount of their holdings, together with 1 share of 2s. (credited with 1s. 6d. paid) for each 1s. 6d. arrears of interest or dividend; ordinary shareholders were entitled to 1 share of 2s. (credited with 1s. 6d. paid) for each share of 2s. held. Final meeting return regd. 10 Sept. 1937 .... **1935**

Uckfield Gas & Electricity Co. Regd. 1858 as Uckfield Gas Co. and as Uckfield Gas Co. Ld. in 1882; inc. under present title by Special Act 1925. Dissolved 1 Apr. 1948, undertaking being vested in British (later Central) Electricity Authority and South-Eastern Area Board under Electricity Act 1947. Holders of gas ordinary stock were entitled to receive an equal amount of British Electricity 3% guaranteed stock (1968–73) **1949**

Uckfield Water Co. Inc. by Special Act 1888. Winding-up order 31 May 1948, the undertaking having been sold to Uckfield Rural District Council. Capital returned to contributories (per share of £10)—£14 per preference share and £14 5s. 4d. per ordinary share. Liquidator released 17 Nov. 1950 .... **1952**

Udston Colliery Co. Ld. Regd. Edinburgh 1901. Vol. liq. Sept. 1927. Final meeting return regd. 8 May 1933 **1928**

Uganda & East Africa Exploration Synd. Ld. Regd. 1928. Vol. liq. (members') 24 Feb. 1948. Capital returned to contributories—£1 10s. 11d. per ordinary share (of £1) and 8s. 2d. per deferred share (of 1s.), satisfied by cash payment and allotment of 14,641 fully-paid shares (of £1) of Kyagwe Planting Co. Ld. (at valuation of 29s. per share). £385 14s. 6d. was paid into Companies' Liquidation Account. Final meeting return regd. 24 Mar. 1950 .... **1951**

Uganda Plantations Ld. Inc. Dublin 1913. Vol. liq. (members') 22 Nov. 1948. Capital returned to contributories—12s. 2½d. per share of £1. £429 2s. 11d. was paid into Court on account of unclaimed dividends or distributions. Final meeting return regd. 14 Dec. 1953 .... **1955**

Uganda Tin Fields Ld. Regd. 1927. Receiver appointed in Oct. 1930. Vol. liq. Nov. 1932. Assets realised insufficient to pay debenture holders. Struck off Register 12 Mar. 1935 .... **1936**

Uitkyk Collieries Ld. See Transvaal & Natal Collieries Ld.

Ukaranga Syndicate Ld. Regd. 1933. Struck off Register 17 July 1942 .... **1943**

Ukraine Corporation Ld. Regd. 1922. Vol. liq. (creditors') 14 Mar. 1934. No capital returned to contributories. Final meeting return regd. 18 Dec. 1934 ... **1935**

Ukuwela Estates Co. Ld. Regd 1899. Vol. liq. (members') 4 Jan. 1952. Capital returned to contributories (per share of £25)—preference: £26 5s.; ordinary: £295 7s. 9d. Final meeting return regd. 29 Mar. 1954 **1955**

Ulster & Connaught Light Railways Co. See Newry, Keady & Tynan Railway Co.

Ulster Land, Building & Investment Co. Ld. Regd. Dublin 1868. In liquidation in 1887 .... **1887**

Ulster Spinning Co. Ld. Regd. in Dublin 1887; transferred to Belfast under Government of Ireland Act 1920. Vol. liq. (members') 27 Sept. 1957. A majority of the ordinary capital was owned by Lindustries Ld. Capital returned to contributories; £1 2s. per preference share (of £1) and 5s. 7½d. per ordinary share (of 1s.) £13 6s. 3d. was paid into Companies' Liquidation Account in respect of unclaimed dividends. Final meeting return regd. 21 Apr. 1964 .... **1965**

Ulster Steamship Co. Ld. Regd. Dublin 1877. All shares were sold in 1920 to Amalgamated Industrials Ld. at £45 per share of £10, payable as to £30 15s. in cash or £14 5s. in cash and £15 in 7% debentures **1933**

Ulu Buloh (Selangor) Rubber Co. Ld. Regd. Edinburgh 1909. Vol. liq. Aug. 1914. Struck off Register 4 June 1937 .... **1938**

Ulu Klang Tin Ld. Inc. in the Federation of Malaya 20 Feb. 1928. Vol. liq. (members') 27 Sept. 1957. Capital returned to contributories—$0·3145 per share (of $0·60). Final meeting return regd. 25 Aug. 1958 .... **1959**

Ulu Selangor Rubber Plantations Ld. Regd. 1926. Vol. liq. (members') 3 Feb. 1933. No capital returned to contributories. Final meeting return regd. 11 May 1934 .... **1933**

Ulu Yam Tin Dredging Ld. Inc. Federated Malay States 1919. Vol. liq. 11 Feb. 1939. Undertaking was acquired by Austral Amalgamated Tin Ld., in which company shareholders were entitled to 280 fully-paid shares of 5s. for every 100 shares of £1 held **1940**

VOL. FOR

Ulundi Gold Mining Co. Ld. Regd. 1904. Vol. liq. Aug. 1908 for reconstruction as company of same name. Shareholders were entitled to 120 ordinary shares of 2s. (credited with 1s. 6d. paid) for every 100 ordinary shares of 2s. held. Preference shareholders were entitled to an equal amount of preference shares in the new company. Removed from Register 1911   **1909**

Ulundi Gold Mining Co. Ld. Regd. 1908. Vol. liq. Apr. 1911. Reconstructed as company of same name. Shareholders were entitled to 1 fully-paid share of 5s. for every 20 ordinary shares of 5s. held, or 2 fully-paid shares of 5s. for every 5 preference shares of 2s. held. Debentures were exchanged at par for bonds in new company. Removed from Register 1913 ...   **1912**

Ulundi Gold Mining Co. Ld. Regd. 1911. Vol. liq. 15 May 1913. Reconstructed as company of same name. Shareholders were entitled to 4 shares of 2s. (credited with 1s. 6d. paid) in new company for each share of 5s. held. Debenture holders were entitled to an equal amount of debentures in the new company. Final meeting return regd. 27 May 1915   **1914**

Ulundi Gold Mining Co. Ld. Regd. 1913. Struck off Register 1920   **1915**

Ulverston Gold Mining Co. Ld. Regd. 1873. Court Orders; to wind up Mar. 1884. to dissolve 22 Aug. 1889 ......   **1885**

Um Rus Gold Mines of Egypt Ld. Regd. 1903. Reconstructed 1906 as company of same name. Shareholders were entitled to 1 share of £1 (credited with 15s. paid) for each share of £1 held. Removed from Register 1907   **1907**

Um Rus Gold Mines of Egypt Ld. Regd. 1906. Vol. liq. Jan. 1908. Removed from Register 1909 ....   **1908**

Umbandine Swazieland Concessions Syndicate Ld. Regd. 1891. Vol. liq. 1 Sept. 1898. Undertaking was transferred to Swazieland Corporation Ld. for 143,333 fully-paid shares of £1; 99,863 shares were distributed to debenture holders. Final meeting return regd. 25 Apr. 1899   **1899**

Umeari Gold Ld. Inc. New South Wales 1912 ....   **1916**

Umniati Development Co. Ld. Regd. 1896. Vol. liq. Oct. 1908. Removed from Register 1909   **1909**

Umtali Exploration Co. Ld. Regd. 1899. Vol. liq. 14 Dec. 1908. Final meeting return regd. 18 Dec. 1919   **1909**

Underfeed Stoker Co. Ld. Regd. 1900. Undertaking and assets were acquired in 1934 by International Combustion Ld., now International Combustion Holdings Ld. in which company shareholders were entitled to 1 ordinary share of £1 (credited as fully-paid) for each share of £1 held. Dissolved under Sec. 154 of Companies Act 1929 on 28 Jan. 1937 ....   **1935**

Underground Electric Railways Co. of London Ld. Regd. 1902. Vol. liq. (members') 28 July 1933. Holders of 5% 1st mortgage debenture stock were entitled to an equal amount of B stock in London Passenger Transport Board, holders of 6% 1st cumulative income debenture stock were entitled to £60 B stock, £55 C stock and 10s. in cash for every £100 income debenture stock held. Shareholders were entitled to £117 C stock 4¹⁄₁₆ shares in North Metropolitan Electric Power Supply Co. (later Northmet Power Co.) and 13½ shares of £1 in Associated Equipment Co. Ld. for every 100 shares of £1 held; shareholders were also entitled to 9·3137d. per share in cash. Final meeting return regd. 28 June 1935 ....   **1934**

Undertakers of the Navigation of the Rivers of Aire and Calder in the West Riding of the County of York. See Aire & Calder Navigation (The Undertakers of the)

Underwood (E.) & Son Ld. Regd. 1888. Court Order to wind up 1906. Removed from Register 1912 ....   **1907**

Underwriters' Association Ld. Regd. 1877. Vol. liq. 18 Mar. 1884. Business transferred to Equitable Guarantee & Accident Co. Ld. Struck off Register 11 Aug. 1905   **1921**

Underwriters' Association Ld. Regd. 1912. Struck off Register 3 Jan. 1919   **1921**

Underwriters' Association Ld. Regd. 1919. Vol. liq. 29 June 1920. Final meeting return regd. 10 Aug. 1921   **1921**

Underwriters' Trust Ld. Regd. 1929. Vol. liq. (members') 28 Nov. 1933. Capital returned to contributories—16s. 4½d. per share of £1. Final meeting return regd. 14 June 1934   **1934**

Ungarisch Bulgarische Bank. Inc. Sofia 1912. Business discontinued 29 Nov. 1926   **1928**

Ungarische Agrar & Rentenbank A. G. See Hungarian Land Mortgage Bank.

Ungarische Allgemeine Sparcassa A. G. See Hungarian General Savings Bank Ld.

Ungarisches Bodenkroditinstitut. See Hungarian Land Mortgage Institute.

União Sorocabana e Ytuana. Established Brazil 1892. In Sept. 1902 the Sorocabana railway was sold and notice of redemption of debentures at par was given. In 1904 the Brazilian Government paid £128 10s. for

VOL. FOR

each £100 6% 1st mortgage debentures (Ituana Railway Co.) and in respect of principal and arrears of interest. Compulsory liquidation 5 Aug. 1904. Undertaking was purchased by Brazilian Government for £3,000,000   **1905**

Unilever, Ld. Regd. 1927 as Margarine Union Ld.; name changed Mar. 1930. Under a scheme of amalgamation the undertaking and assets were transferred to Lever Brothers Ld. (later Lever Brothers & Unilever Ld. and later Unilever Ld.). Holders of 7% preferred, 5% preferred ordinary or deferred stock were entitled to an equal amount of 7% preference, 5% preference, ordinary or deferred stock respectively in Lever Brothers Ld. Dissolved under Sec. 154 of Companies Act 1929 ....   **1938**

Union Acid Ld. Regd. 1910. Vol. liq. (members') 31 Mar. 1932. Direct controlling interest held by Imperial Chemical Industries Ld. Capital returned to contributories—£37,789 5s. Final meeting return regd. 16 Dec. 1932   **1933**

Union Advance Co. Ld. See Union Finance Co. Ld.

Union Advance Deposit & Discount Co. Ld. See Union Finance Co. Ld.

Union & Rhodesian Trust Ld. Regd. 1912. Vol. liq. 7 Apr. 1920. South African assets were acquired by Anglo-Trsnsvaal Rhodesian Trust Ld. Final meeting return regd. 30 June 1930   **1925**

Union Assurance Society. Established by Deed of Settlement 1714. Regd. 1903. Vol. liq. 24 July 1907. Business acquired by Union Assurance Society Ld.   **1908**

Union Bank. In 1927 amalgamated with Allgemeine Osterreichische Boden-Credit-Anstalt, in which company shareholders were entitled to 1 share of 50 schillings for every 18 shares held   **1928**

Union Bank of Birmingham Ld. Regd. 1878. Vol. liq. Oct. 1883. Absorbed by Birmingham & Midland Bank Ld. (later Midland Bank Ld.). Final meeting return regd. 2 May 1885   **1883**

Union Bank of Canada. Inc. Canada by Special Act 1865 as Union Bank of Lower Canada; name changed 1885. Undertaking and assets were acquired by Royal Bank of Canada, in which company shareholders were entitled to 1 share of $100 (credited as fully-paid) for every 2 shares of $100 held; odd shares were repaid at $115 per share **1926**

Union Bank of London Ld. See Union of London & Smiths Bank.

Union Bank of Lower Canada. See Union Bank of Canada.

Union Bank of Manchester Ld. Established 1836. Regd. 1862. Vol. liq. (members') 30 Dec. 1939. All shares were owned by Barclays Bank Ld., who acquired the business   **1940**

Union Bank of Scotland Ld. Est. 1830 as Glasgow Union Banking Co.; name changed 1843. Regd. Edinburgh as unlimited 1862 and as limited 1882. Dissolved 1 Mar. 1955 all capital having been previously acquired by Bank of Scotland **1956**

Union Bank of Spain & England Ld. Established 1881. Vol.liquidation in 1897   **1897**

Union Bank of Warsaw. Inc. Warsaw 1921. In liquidation Dec. 1925   **1926**

Union Boot & Shoe Machine Co. Ld. Regd. 1899. Vol. liq. 11 Oct. 1901. Undertaking and assets were acquired by British United Shoe Machinery Co. Ld. Final meeting return regd. 12 Dec. 1901 ....   **1902**

Union Carriage & Horse Insurance Co. Ld. See Protector Carriage & Horse Insurance Co. Ld.

Union Cement Co. Ld. Regd. 1888. Vol. liq. 6 Sept. 1910. Final meeting return regd. 20 Nov. 1911   **1911**

Union Cinema Co. Ld. Regd. 1928. Vol. liq. (members') 16 Dec. 1936. Reconstructed as Union Cinemas Ld. in which company shareholders were entitled to 37 A ordinary and 12 ordinary shares of 5s. (credited as fully-paid) for each ordinary share of £1 held or 5 1st preference and 5 2nd preference shares of £1 for every 6 preference shares of £1 held. Final meeting return regd. 16 Oct. 1942   **1937**

Union Cinema Subsidiary Properties Ld. Regd. 1937. Vol. liq. (members') 13 Feb. 1941. Cinema properties were acquired by Union Cinemas Investments Ld., in which company shareholders were entitled to £1 6% mortgage debenture stock for each preference share of £1 held. Ordinary shareholders were entitled to approximately 1s. 10d. per ordinary share of 4s. plus participation in certain assets distributed in specie. Final meeting return regd. 20 July 1944   **1945**

Union Cinemas Investments Ld. Regd. 1940. Vol. liq. (members') 19 Feb. 1964. All capital was owned by Union Cinemas Ld. Final meeting return regd. 17 Apr. 1964   **1951**

Union Cold Storage of Blackfriars Ld. See Alliance Cold Storage Co. Ld.

VOL. FOR

Union Cold Storage Co. of Riga. Undertaking acquired in 1903 by Union Cold Storage Co. Ld. **1941**

Union Co. (Aktieselskapet Union). Inc. Norway 1873. The outstanding 5½% 1st mortgage debentures were redeemed at 130% on 15 Jan. 1948 .... **1948**

Union Consolidated Copper Mines (1911) Ld. Regd. 1911. Vol. liq. 11 Mar. 1914 for reconstruction as Flinders Copper Co. Ld. Final meeting return regd. 22 July 1915 .... **1915**

Union Consolidated Copper Mines, No Liability. Inc. Victoria 1904. Vol. liq. Nov. 1912 for purpose of amalgamation with Lyndhurst (South Australia) Copper Co. Ld. under title of Union Consolidated Copper Mines (1911) Ld. in which company shareholders were entitled to 1 share of 5s. (with 3s. 6d. paid) for each share of £1 held **1913**

Union Consolidated Drift Mines Ld. Regd. 1887. Vol. liq. 22 Aug. 1899. Final meeting return regd. 21 Mar. 1902 .... **1903**

Union Consolidated Trust Ld. Regd. 1906. Vol. liq. 3 May 1909. The assets were sold to African Mines Ld., in which company shareholders were entitled to 1 share of 5s. for every 2 shares of 5s. held. Final meeting return regd. 15 Oct. 1913 .... **1910**

Union Construction & Finance Co. Ld. Regd. 1901 as Union Construction Co. Ld.; name changed Feb. 1929. Vol. liq. (members') 1 July 1933. Undertaking was transferred to London Passenger Transport Board for £365 C stock which was distributed to shareholders. Final meeting return regd. 6 Apr. 1934 **1934**

Union Construction Co. Ld. *See* Union Construction & Finance Co. Ld.

Union Corporation of Egypt Ld. Regd. 1907 as H. de Vries & Boutigny Ld.; name changed Nov. 1908. Vol. liq. 18 June 1912. Final meeting return regd. 30 Sept. 1914 .... **1914**

Union Credit Bank Ld. *See* Union Credit Corporation Ld.

Union Credit Corporation Ld. Regd. 1885 as Union Loan & Discount Co. Ld.; name changed in 1897 to Union Credit Bank Ld.; and to above title in 1912. Vol. liq. (members') 3 Sept. 1945. Capital returned to contributors: 10s. 11¼d. per preference share of £1. £1,000 was paid into Companies' Liquidation Account. Final meeting return regd. 11 Sept. 1952 **1954**

Union Debenture Co. Ld. Regd. 1887. Removed from Register 1901 .... **1894**

Union Finance Co Ld. Regd. 1861 as Union Advance Deposit & Discount Co. Ld.; name changed to Union Advance Co. Ld. in Apr. 1863 and as above in June 1865. Vol. liq. Apr. 1874. Struck off Register 7 Mar. 1882 .... **1893**

Union Financial Syndicate Ld. Regd. 1897. Removed from Register 1904 .... **1904**

Union Financiere de Genève. Established 1890. Reconstructed 1931 as Banque d'Escompte Suisse **1934**

L'Union Fonciere d'Egypte (S. A). Est. in Egypt by Khedivial Decree 1905. Vol. liq. from 16 Apr. 1955. Distributions totalling £E3,025 had been made by 1965, the nominal value of the shares being reduced to £E1·85; no later information received. By Decree Law No. 111 of 1961 of the United Arab Republic the bearer shares had to be converted to registered form **1969**

Union Free State Coal & Gold Mines Ld. Regd. in Union of S. A. 1947. Vol. liq. (members') 14 Jan. 1953. Shareholders received a 1st distribution of 2 shares (of 5s.) in Harmony Gold Mining Co. Ld. for every 5 shares (of 5s.) held plus a total in cash distributions amounting to 1s. 5·274593389d. per share (of 5s.). £3,168 9s. 10d. was paid to The Master of the Supreme Court, Pretoria in respect to unclaimed Liquidation distributions. Final meeting return regd. 28 Jan. 1958 .... **1959**

Union Gold Co. Ld. Regd 1886. Removed from Register 1906 .... **1890**

Union Investment Co. Ld. Inc. Australia 1920 as Southern Union General Insurance Co. of Australasia Ld.; name changed Apr. 1931 .... **1932**

Union Jack Consolidated Mines Ld. Regd. 1899. Reconstructed 1903 as company of same name. Shareholders were entitled to 1 share of 5s. (credited with 3s. 6d. paid) in new company for each share of 5s. held. Removed from Register 1906 .... **1908**

Union Jack Consolidated Mines Ld. Regd. 1903. Struck off Register 1914 .... **1911**

Union Jack Gold Mining Co. Ld. Regd. 1895. Reconstructed 1899 as Union Jack Consolidated Mines Ld., in which company shareholders were entitled to 4 shares of 5s. (credited with 3s. 6d. paid) for every share of £1 held. Removed from Register 1901 ... **1903**

Union Jack of Rhodesia Ld. Regd. 1909. Vol. liq. 11 Apr. 1912. The properties and assets were sold to Golden Kopje Proprietary Mines Ld., in which

VOL. FOR

company shareholders were entitled to 1·38375 shares of £1 for each share held. Final meeting return regd. 20 Apr. 1914 .... **1913**

Union Land Co. of New York. In liquidation. All capital was owned by K. C. M. & O. R. Land Syndicate Ld **1931**

Union Loan & Discount Co. Ld. *See* Union Credit Corporation Ld.

Union Loan & Savings Co. Inc. Canada. 1865. Reconstructed 1899 as Toronto Mortgage Co. **1901**

Union Mining & Smelting Co. Ld. Regd. 1919. Struck off Register Jan. 1932 .... **1932**

Union Mortgage & Agency Co. of Australia Ld. Regd. 1886. Certain properties were acquired in 1894 by Australian Estates and Mortgage Co. Ld. (later Australian Estates Ld.) for £999,930 in fully-paid shares, £1,200,000 1st mortgage debenture stock. £500,000 5% 2nd mortgage debenture stock and £70 in cash. In 1896 further properties were acquired for £250,000 in fully-paid shares, £300,000 in 1st mortgage debenture stock and £150,000 in B debenture stock. The undertaking was acquired in 1899 for £200,000 B debenture stock. Removed from Register 1909 .... **1903**

Union Mortgage, Banking & Trust Co. Ld. Regd. 1888. Removed from Register 1905 .... **1903**

Union of London & Smiths Bank Ld. Regd. 1882 as Union Bank of London Ld., name changed 1902. Vol. liq. Mar. 1918. Amalgamated with National Provincial Bank of England Ld. (later National Provincial Bank Ld.), in which company shareholders were entitled to 9 shares of £60 (credited with £12 paid) for every 10 shares of £100 (£15 10s. paid) held **1918**

Union Oil Co. of Roumania Ld. Regd. 1910 as British Oil and General Securities Corporation Ld.; name changed Jan. 1914. Vol. liq. (creditors') 30 May 1930. £90 was paid into Companies' Liquidation Account. Final meeting return regd. 10 Sept. 1932 **1931**

Union Oil Trust Ld. Regd. 1914 as Union Oil Co. of South Africa Ld.; name changed Nov. 1922. Struck off Register Feb. 1933 .... **1933**

Union Petroleum Products Ld. *See* Redline Glico Ld.

Union Plate Glass Co. Ld. Regd. 1864. Vol. liq. 13 Mar. 1913. Struck off Register Mar. 1929 .... **1930**

Union Plate Glass Insurance Co. Ld. Regd. 1882. Removed from Register 1889 .... **1886**

Union Radiator Co. Ld. Regd. 1914. Vol. liq. (members') 22 Dec. 1936. Capital returned to contributories—£1 12s. 9d. per share of £1. Final meeting return regd. 30 Apr. 1937 .... **1937**

Union Railway Carriage & Wagon Co. Ld. Regd. 1874. Vol. liq. 18 Dec. 1878. Court Order to continue winding up under supervision 26 Mar. 1879. Final meeting return regd. 30 Sept. 1890 .... *****1877**

Union Rolling Stock Co. Ld. Regd. 1875. In liquidation in 1902. On 3 Oct. 1902 the paid up capital was returned in full; further payments (if any) not known. Removed from Register 1908 .... **1903**

Union Steam Ship Co. Ld. Regd. 1856. Business was acquired in 1900 by Castle Mail Packets Co. Ld. (later Union-Castle Mail Steamship Co. Ld.). Removed from Register 1908 .... **1901**

Union Steam Ship Co. of New Zealand Ld. Inc. under Colonial Act (1860) in 1875. Vol. liq. Sept. 1913. Reconstructed as company of same name. Shareholders were entitled to 1 ordinary and 1 preference share of £1 (both credited as fully-paid) in new company for each share of £1 held. Debenture stockholders were entitled to repayment at 105% or £105 in 4½% debenture stock for every £100 stock held **1914**

Union Surplus Lands Co. Ld. Regd. 1914. Vol. liq. 1 July 1933. Undertaking was transferred to London Passenger Transport Board for £88,889 4½% A stock and £238,936 C stock. Final meeting return regd. 25 Sept. 1934 .... **1934**

Union Trust Co. Ld. Inc. Canada 1901. Assets purchased by Trust & Guarantee Co. Ld. from 31 Dec. 1933 .... **1935**

Union-Waihi Gold Mining Co. Ld. Regd. 1895. Vol. liq. 11 Feb. 1902. Undertaking acquired by Waihi Gold Mining Co. Ld., in which company shareholders were entitled to 1 share of £1 (credited as fully-paid) for every 20 shares of £1 held. Removed from Register 1906 .... **1920**

Unit Investments Ld. Regd. 1938. Struck off Register 6 Oct. 1950 .... **1939**

Unit Trusts Ld. *See* Property Units Ld.

United Africa Trading Co. Ld. Regd. 1910. Vol. liq. 16 Oct 1913. Final meeting return regd. 3 June 1915 **1914**

United African Collieries Ld. Regd. 1895. Vol. liq. 18 Dec. 1900. Assets were acquired by United African Lands Ld. Final meeting return regd. 1 Jan. 1902 **1901**

United African Lands Ld. Regd. 1892. Removed from Register 1907 .... **1901**

VOL. FOR

United African Lands Ld. Regd. 1900. Vol. liq. 4 Apr. 1924. Capital returned to contributories—6d. per share of 10s. at June 1924; further payments (if any) not known. Final meeting return regd. 21 June 1930 ... 1925

United African Syndicate Ld. Regd. 1888. Vol. liq. 5 Jan. 1905. Removed from Register 1913 1905

United Albion Gold Mines Ld. Regd. 1897. Removed from Register 1904 1905

United Alkali Co. Ld. *See* I. C. I. (General Chemicals) Ld.

United Anglo-Continental Ice Co. Ld. Regd. 1887. Vol. liq. 31 Dec. 1890. Final meeting return regd. 13 Mar. 1900 1892

United Anthracite Collieries Ld. Regd. 1927. All shares owned by Amalgamated Anthracite Collieries Ld. Struck off Register 10 Mar. 1939 1939

United Arizona Copper Co. Ld. Regd. 1902. Struck off Register 1916 1912

United Asbestos Co. Ld. Regd. 1880. Vol. liq. Mar. 1910. The undertaking and assets were acquired by Bell's Asbestos Co. Ld. (later Bell's United Asbestos Co. Ld.). Every 10 10% non-cumulative preference shares of £10 were entitled to 1 debenture of £100 of the new company; every 20 6% cumulative preference shares of £5 were entitled to 1 debenture of £100, and for every complete 3 shares 2 new ordinary £1 shares, the latter being in satisfaction of arrears of dividend; every complete 7 ordinary A shares of £5 were entitled to 8 ordinary £1 shares; and every 10 deferred B shares of £5 were entitled to 1 ordinary £1 share. Debenture holders (both classes) were entitled to 75% of holding in debentures and 25% in cash. Removed from Register 1911 ... 1911

United Australian Exploration Ld. Regd. 1896. Removed from Register 1905 1901

United Bacon Curing Co. Ld. Regd. 1889. Vol. liq. Mar. 1890. Final meeting return regd. 11 July 1891 1891

United Batang Rubber Estates Ld. Regd. 1910. Receiver appointed in Feb. 1912. Struck off Register 1928 ... 1925

United Breweries Co., Liverpool Ld. Regd. 1887 as City of Liverpool & District Brewery Ld.; name changed Aug. 1888. Vol. liq. 25 July 1892. Struck off Register 1922 1893

United Brewing & Malting Co. Ld. Regd. 1892. Removed from Register 1903 1904

United British & Russian Commerce Ld. Regd. 1909. Vol. liq. Jan. 1911. Removed from Register 1911 ... 1911

United British Castor Oil Co. Ld. Regd. 1896. Vol. liq. 12 Mar. 1902. Business was sold to British Indian Oil Mills Ld., in which company shareholders were entitled to 5 deferred shares of £1 (credited as fully-paid) for each ordinary share of £10 held, or 5 ordinary shares of £1 (credited as fully-paid) for each preference share of £10 held. Final meeting return regd. 4 Sept. 1902 1903

United British Mineral Oil Co. Ld. Regd. 1918. Vol. liq. 19 Dec. 1924. ⅔rds of the shares were held by United British Oilfields of Trinidad Ld. Final meeting return regd. 9 July 1925 1924

United British Pipelines Ld. Regd. 1919. Vol. liq. (members') 23 Dec. 1932. All shares were held by United British West Indies Petroleum Syndicate Ld. Final meeting return regd. 13 June 1934 1934

United British Producing Co. Ld. Regd. 1916. Vol. liq. 30 Oct. 1925. Final meeting return regd. 1 Apr. 1932 ... 1926

United British Refineries Ld. Regd. 1915. Vol. liq. (members') 23 Dec. 1932. All shares owned by United British Oilfields of Trinidad Ld. Final meeting return regd. 13 June 1934 1933

United British Steamship Co. Ld. *See* Court Line Ld.

United British West Indies Petroleum Syndicate Ld. Regd. 1912. Vol. liq. 23 Dec. 1932. All shares owned by United British Oilfields of Trinidad Ld. Final meeting return regd. 13 June 1933 1933

United Buffelsdoorn Mines Ld. Inc. Transvaal 1895. London office closed 31 Mar. 1907 1908

United Butter Companies of France Ld. Regd. 1906 as Nantes Butter & Refrigerating Co. Ld.; name changed Dec. 1908. Vol. liq. July 1909. Removed from Register 1911 1910

United Capitals Investment Trust Ld. Regd. as private company 4 Dec. 1964; converted into a public company 9 Dec. 1964. Vol. liq. (members') 21 May 1980. Distributions on ordinary shares (of 25p): 20p on 18 June 1980; 4p on 22 Dec. 1980; shares in Parkfield Foundries Ld. equivalent to 4·486p cash in Jan. 1981; 0·8p on 28 July 1981 and 0·35p on 1 Sept. 1982. Final meeting held 24 Sept. 1982 and regd. 6 Oct. 1982 1983–4

United Capitol National Bank & Trust of New York. Inc. New York 1922 as Capitol National Bank of New York; name changed 15 Jan. 1927 to Capitol National Bank & Trust of New York and as above 12 Mar. 1928 1929

VOL. FOR

United Caucasian Oil Co. Ld. *See* United Oil Importers Co. Ld.

United Cellulo Silk Spinners Ld. Regd. 1907. Vol. liq. Mar. 1912. Removed from Register 1913 1913

United Chemical Corporation Ld. Regd. 1919. Struck off Register 1925 1925

United Cigarette Machine Co. Ld. Regd. 1899. Vol. liq. 27 Feb. 1917. The business was sold to United Cigarette Machine Co. Inc. (of Virginia, U. S. A.). in which company shareholders were entitled to 1 share of $5 (credited as fully-paid) for each share of £1 held. Final meeting return regd. 9 June 1925 .. 1917

United Citizens' Investment Trust Ld. Regd. 1927 under Industrial & Provident Societies' Acts. Vol. liq. Apr. 1930 1931

United City Property Trust Ld. Regd. 1934. All capital was owned by Land Securities Investment Trust Ld. Dissolved under section 208 of Companies Act, 1948 on 28 July 1955 1955

United Coal Fields of British Columbia Ld. Regd. 1900 as United Gold Fields of British Columbia Ld.; name changed Apr. 1903. The assets and liabilities were acquired in 1904 by West Canadian Collieries Ld., in which company shareholders were entitled to 1 share of £1 for each share of £1 held. Removed from Register 1906 1905

United Collieries Ld. Regd. Edinburgh 1898. Vol. liq. (members') 22 Mar. 1957. Capital returned to contributories—preference repaid at par; ordinary 8$\frac{7}{32}$d. per 2s. 6d. stock. Final meeting return regd. 22 Mar. 1962 1963

United Colonial Exploration Ld. Regd. 1896. Vol. liq. 25 May 1899. Final meeting return regd. 14 Aug. 1902 ... 1900

United Concessions Co. Ld. Regd. 1890. Vol. liq. 3 Jan. 1894. Final meeting return regd. 4 Jan. 1895 1894

United Contract & Investment Co. Ld. Regd. 1919. Court Order to wind up July 1929. Struck off Register Apr. 1934 1935

United Contract Corporation Ld. Reg. 1896. Removed from Register 18 Nov. 1902 .... *1905

United Copper Mines Ld. Regd. 1928. Struck off Register 8 Apr. 1938 1939

United Copper Mines (Pilbarra) Ld. Regd. 1922. Vol. liq. 23 July 1928 for reconstruction as United Copper Mines Ld., in which company shareholders were entitled to 5 shares of 2s. (credited with 1s. 6d. paid) for every 2 shares of 5s. held. Final meeting return regd. 7 Apr. 1932 1929

United Counties Bank Ld. Established 1836. Regd. 1881 as Birmingham, Dudley and District Banking Co. Ld.; name changed to Birmingham District and Counties Banking Co. Ld., in 1889 and as above in Jan. 1907. Vol. liq. Feb. 1916. Amalgamated with Barclay & Co. Ld. (later Barclay's Bank Ld.), in which company shareholders were entitled to 3 B shares of £4 (credited with £1 paid) for each share of £20 (£4 paid) held *plus* 1 fully-paid A share of £4 for every 12 shares held. Struck off Register 27 Jan. 1956 1916

United Counties Insurance Co. Ld. Regd. 1909. In 1911 the Property Insurance Co. Ld. acquired practically all the shares. Vol. liq. 29 May 1913. Final meeting return regd. 23 Feb. 1923 1914

United Dairies (Wholesale) Ld. Regd. 1890 as Salisbury, Semley and Gillingham Dairies, Ld.; name subsequently changed. Vol. liq. (members') 15 Mar. 1966. Final meeting return regd. 8 Mar. 1968 1919

United Diamond Fields of British Guiana Ld. Regd. 1926. Vol. liq. (members') 13 June 1930. Capital returned to contributories—12s. 4·576d. per share of £1. £1,460 11s. 3d. was paid into Companies' Liquidation Account. Final meeting return regd. 12 Mar. 1931 1931

United Discount & Securities Co. Ld. Regd. 1889. Vol. liq. (members') 9 Jan. 1935. Undertaking and assets were acquired by London General Investment Trust Ld. The preference capital was repaid with accrued interest 134,360 preferred shares and 73,190 deferred shares of £1 in acquiring company were distributed among contributories. £52 19s. 9d. was paid into Companies' Liquidation Account. Final meeting return regd. 14 Feb. 1936 1935

United Discount Corporation Ld. Regd. 1866. Vol. liq. May 1885. Reconstructed as Union Discount Co. of London Ld., in which company shareholders were entitled to 4 shares of £10 (credited with £5 paid) for every 5 shares of £15 (£6 paid) held *plus* £2 per share in cash at Nov. 1885; further payments (if any) not known. Final meeting return regd. 13 Aug. 1886 1885

United District Gas Co. Regd. as Counties Gas Co. Ld. 1911; reinc. as above by Special Act 1913. Dissolved 1 May 1949, undertaking being vested in Southern Area Gas Board under Gas Act 1948. Holders of securities were entitled to receive British Gas 3%

See Stock Exchange Year-Book.

VOL. FOR

guaranteed stock 1990–95 as follows in respect of each £10 unit, uuless otherwise stated, of security held:

	£	s.	d.
Orig. ord. shares (9% stand.)	16	10	0
Addit. ord. shares (7% stand.)	12	16	0
6% pref. shares	13	0	0
Addit. 6% pref. shares	13	0	0

1952

United Dominions Insurance Co. Ld. Regd. 1897 as Credit Assurance and Guarantee Corporation Ld.; name changed to British Dominions Insurance Co. Ld. in May 1902 and as above in Feb. 1911. Vol. liq. 23 Sept. 1915. Undertaking was acquired by British Dominions General Insurance Co. Ld. (later Eagle Star Insurance Co. Ld.) for 62,092 ordinary shares of £3 (credited with 10s. paid), 2,246 ordinary shares of £3 (credited with £1 paid) and 666 ordinary shares of £3 (credited as fully-paid). Final meeting return regd. 12 Mar. 1920 1916

United Dutch Oyster Co. Ld. Regd. 1891. Vol. liq. 10 Mar. 1892. Final meeting return regd. 6 June 1893 .... *1893

United Egyptian Lands Ld. Regd. 1906. Vol. liq. 17 Apr. 1919. Undertaking was acquired by Egyptian Consolidated Lands Ld., in which company shareholders were entitled to 2 shares of 5s. (credited with 3s. 9d. paid) for each ordinary share of 10s. held or 1 share of 5s. (credited with 3s. 9d. paid) for each deferred share of 1s. held. Final meeting return regd. 3 Jan. 1921 1943

United Electric Car Co. Ld. Regd. 1898 as Electric Railway and Tramway Carriage Works Ld.; name changed June 1905. Vol. liq. 22 June 1921. Final meeting return regd. 2 July 1927 1922

United Electric Theatres Ld. Regd. 1910. Vol. liq. July 1911 for reconstruction as company of same name. Removed from Register 1913 1912

United Electric Theatres Ld. Regd. 1911. Vol. liq. July 1914. Reconstructed as company of same name. Shareholders were entitled to 5 shares of £1 (credited with 15s. paid) in new company for every 6 shares of 12s. 6d. held. Struck off Register 1929 1915

United Electric Theatres Ld. Regd. 1914. Receiver for debenture holders appointed in June 1919. Struck off Register 1923 1920

United Electric Tramways Co. of Caracas, Ld. Regd. 1906. Vol. liq. (creditors') 31 July 1946. No capital returned to contributories. Final meeting return regd. 26 July 1947 1948

United Electrical Engineering Co. Ld. Regd. 1885 as Jablochkoff & General Electricity Co. Ld.; name changed 1 Apr. 1887. Vol. liq. 20 June 1890. Final meeting return regd. 5 Apr. 1893 .... *1890

United Estates & Investment Trust Ld. Regd. 1926. Vol. liq. (members') 15 Oct. 1941. Capital returned to contributories—£1 per £1 preference stock; 24s. 1·5954d. per £1 ordinary stock. Final meeting return regd. 14 May 1947 1948

United Excelsior Mines Ld. Regd. 1898. Vol. liq. (creditors') 2 Apr. 1931. Undertaking and assets acquired by New Albion Transvaal Gold Mines Ld., in which company shareholders were entitled to 1 ordinary share of 1s. (credited with 6d. paid) for each share of 5s. held. Final meeting return regd. 26 Sept. 1933 1932

United Exploration Co. Ld. (The). Regd. 19 July 1909. Vol. liq. (members') 20 Aug. 1942. Amalgamated with Charterland & General Ld.; stockholders received 2 ord. shares or stock units (of 5s) in that company for every 4 stock units (of 5s) held. Dissolved 7 Nov. 1944 1977-8

United Fire & Marine Insurance Co. Ld. Regd. 1919. Struck off Register 1937 .... *1928

United Fire Insurance Co. Ld. Regd. 1877 as United Fire Re-insurance Co. Ld.; name changed May 1891. Business was acquired in 1899 by Palatine Insurance Co. Ld. Removed from Register 1901 1900

United Fire Re-Insurance Co. Ld. See United Fire Insurance Co. Ld.

United Footwear Services Ld. Regd. 1936. Vol. liq. (creditors') 14 July 1938. Assets realised insufficient to pay creditors in full. Final meeting return regd. 5 Aug. 1939 1941

United Founders & Investment Trust Ld. Regd. 1890. Vol. liq. 23 Nov. 1891. Final meeting return regd. 21 Feb. 1893 .... *1892

United General Commercial Insurance Corporation Ld. Regd. 1919. Court Order to wind up June 1923. Struck off Register Aug. 1934 1935

United Gold Coast Mining Properties Ld. Regd. 1900. Vol. liq. 14 Apr. 1915. Final meeting return regd. 28 Feb. 1918 1916

United Gold Fields of British Columbia Ld. See United Coal Fields of British Columbia Ld.

VOL. FOR

United Goldfields Exploration & Investment Co. Ld. See London United Investment Co. Ld.

United Goldfields of Manica Ld. Regd. 1892. Vol. liq. 16 Feb. 1898. Reconstructed as Rezende Ld., in which company shareholders were entitled to 1 share of £1 (credited with 14s. paid) for each share of £1 held. Final meeting return regd. 11 May 1900 1905

United Gold Mines of West Africa Ld. Regd. 1902. Vol. liq. Dec. 1906 for reconstruction as Union Consolidated Trust Ld., in which company shareholders were entitled to 1 share of 5s. (credited with 3s. 9d. paid) for every share held. Removed from Register 1909 1908

United Gold Reefs Ld. Regd. 1895. Removed from Register 1905 1899

United Horse Nail Co. Ld. Regd. 1881. Vol. liq. Aug. 1883. Court Order to continue winding up under supervision Sept. 1883. Final meeting return regd. 5 Mar. 1885 1909

United Horse Shoe & Nail Co. Ld. Regd. 1883. Receivers were appointed in Oct. 1908 on behalf of the debenture holders. Vol. liq. July 1909. Removed from Register 1911 1910

United Industrial Corporation Ld. Regd. Edinburgh 1897. Vol. liq. June 1898. Final meeting return regd. 16 Jan. 1900 1899

United Investment and Agency Trust Ld. Regd. 1899. Removed from Register 1912 1905

United Ivy Extension Gold Mining Co. Ld. Inc. South African Republic 1888. Taken over by United Ivy Reef Gold Mining Co. Ld., in which company shareholders were entitled to 3 shares of £1 for every 5 of £1 held 1896

United Ivy Reef Gold Mining Co. Ld. Inc. Natal and Transvaal 1888. Liquidated Feb. 1911. Properties abandoned to lessors 1911

United Jewish People's Bank Ld. Regd. 1923. Struck off Register 1931 .... *1928

United Kent Life Assurance & Annuity Institution or Co. Ld. Regd. 1874. Vol. liq. 1 May 1901. Undertaking was acquired by Royal Insurance Co. Final meeting return regd. 3 Mar. 1902 1901

United Kingdom & Argentine 1933 Convention Trust. Constituted by trust deed 1933. Liquidation commenced 1 May 1948, the outstanding B certificates were redeemed on that date. Holders of outstanding C certificates were entitled to receive (per £100 certificate)—a distribution of about £58·87 in Argentine Govt. 4% sterling bonds of 1933 and £66 15s. 9d. in cash 1949

United Kingdom & Foreign Investment & Finance Co. Ld. Regd. 1889. Vol. liq. 17 July 1896. Preference shareholders agreed to accept £8 10s. (per share of £10) in full settlement of claims. Final meeting return regd. 8 Apr. 1897 1897

United Kingdom & Overseas Investment Co. Ld. Regd. 1963. On 21 July 1975 capital was cancelled holders being entitled to 52 ordinary shares of 25p and 1 6·72% preference share of £1 of Estates House Investment Trust Ld. for every 100 ordinary and 1 8% preference share respectively. Company dissolved without winding up on 31 Dec. 1976 1977-8

United Kingdom Assurance Corporation Ld. Regd. 1866. Vol. liq. 27 May 1890. Business was transferred to London Edinburgh and Glasgow Assurance Co. Ld. Final meeting return regd. 30 Mar. 1892 1890

United Kingdom Commercial Corporation Ld. Regd. 1940. Vol. liq. (members') 31 July 1946; all shares owned by H. M. Treasury. Final meeting return regd. 15 Oct. 1958 1949

United Kingdom Debenture Bank Ld. Regd. 1888 as United Kingdom Ground Rents and Mortgage Investment Society Ld.; name changed 11 July 1894. Court Orders: to wind up 25 May 1910; staying proceedings 30 July 1912. Struck off Register 24 Feb. 1922 1916

United Kingdom Gas Corpn. Ld. Regd. 1935. Dissolved 1 May 1949, undertaking being vested in Gas Council under Gas Act 1948. Holders of securities were entitled to receive British Gas 3% guaranteed stock 1990–95 as follows in respect of each £1 unit, unless otherwise stated, of security held:

	£	s.	d.
4½% 1st pref. stock	1	3	6
4½% 1st. red. pref. stock	1	0	1
4½% 2nd pref. stock	1	0	8
Ord. stock	1	3	8
3½% deb. stock (per £100)	100	11	0

1952

United Kingdom Ground Rents and Mortgage Investment Society Ld. See United Kingdom Debenture Bank Ld.

United Kingdom Lighting Trust Ld. Regd. 1902. Receiver appointed 13 Nov. 1922; ceased to act 11 May 1923. Struck off Register 1927 1924

VOL. FOR

United Kingdom Metal-Edged Box Co. Ld. Regd. 1886. Court Orders: to wind up 21 June 1888; to dissolve 28 Apr. 1892 ... **1889**

United Kingdom Property Trust Ld. Regd. 1890. Court Order to wind up 31 Oct. 1891. Liquidator released 7 Mar. 1897. Removed from Register 21 June 1907 ... ***1893**

United Kingdom Terra Cotta Fire- & Sound-Proof Brick Co. Ld. Regd. 1889. In liquidation in 1900. Capital returned to contributories—2s. per share in Nov. 1900; further payments (if any) not known. Removed from Register 1901 ... **1901**

United Kingdom Trades Ld. Regd. 1929 as United Kingdom Trust Ld.; name changed July 1929. Struck off Register 24 Dec. 1943 ... **1944**

United Kingdom Trust Ld. See United Kingdom Trades Ld.

United Land Co. Ld. Regd. 1867. Vol. liq. 19 Mar. 1889. Struck off Register 1927 ... **1890**

United Langlaagte Gold Mining Co. Ld. Inc. South Africa 1888. In liquidation in 1897 ... **1897**

United Limmer & Vorwohle Rock Asphalte Co. Ld. Regd. 1871. Vol. liq. 29 May 1959. Final meeting return regd. 23 July 1959 ... **1951**

United London & Scottish Insurance Co. Ld. Regd. 1907. Court Order to wind up 18 June 1912. A considerable portion of the business was taken over by London & Lancashire Fire Insurance Co. (later London & Lancashire Insurance Co.). Struck off Register 1927 ... **1931**

United Lubricants Ld. Regd. 1924. Vol. liq. (members') 17 Mar. 1930. Undertaking and assets were acquired by company of same name (later United Guarantee Holdings Ld.). Shareholders were entitled to 1 preference share of 10s. (credited as fully-paid) for each preference share of £1 held or 1 ordinary share of 6d. for each ordinary share of 1s. held. Final meeting return regd. 13 Nov. 1930 .... **1931**

United Malaysian Rubber Co. Ld. Regd. 1910. Court Order to wind up Dec. 1920. Struck off Register 1927 ... **1921**

United Matabele Claims Development Co. Ld. Regd. 1894. Undertaking and assets were acquired by Matabele Proprietary Mines Ld., in which company shareholders were entitled to 2 shares of £1 (credited as fully-paid) for every 5 shares of £1 held. Removed from Register 1901 ... **1901**

United Match Industries Ld. Regd. 1928. Vol. liq. (creditors') 13 Feb. 1970. Assets realised insufficient to pay creditors in full. Final meeting return regd. 30 July 1974 ... **1974-5**

United May Lundy Gold Co. Ld. Regd. 1886, subsequently placed in vol. liq. Final meeting return regd. 7 May 1888 ... ***1887**

United Mercury Mines of Granada Ld. Regd. 1903. Vol. liq. June 1908. Removed from Register 1910 ... **1909**

United Mexican Mines Association Ld. Regd. 1898. Vol. liq. Aug. 1907. Removed from Register 1913 ... **1908**

United Mexican Mines Ld. Regd. 1895. Removed from Register 1908 ... **1897**

United Mexican Mining Co. Ld. Regd. 1862. Vol. liq. 28 Feb. 1895. Reconstructed as United Mexican Mines Ld., in which company shareholders were entitled to 1 share of 2s. 6d. (credited with 2s. paid) for each share of £1 held. Debenture holders were entitled to an equal number of debentures in new company. Struck off Register 29 July 1902 ... **1896**

United Mexican Oilfields Ld. Regd. 1918. Struck off Register 11 May 1951 ... **1940**

United Minera Mining Co. Ld. Regd. 1897. Vol. liq. 19 Feb. 1916. Final meeting return regd. 22 June 1916 ... **1916**

United Mines Ore Reduction Co. Ld. Regd. 1894. Removed from Register 1903 ... **1899**

United Mining & General Trust Ld. Regd. 1911 as Brazilian Mining & General Trust Ld., name changed 1927. Vol. liq. (creditors'—subject to supervision of Court) 17 Mar. 1930. Struck off Register 29 Jan. 1952 ... **1953**

United Motion Picture Producers Ld. See British International Pictures Ld.

United Motor & General Insurance Co. Ld. Regd. 1917. Court Order to wind up July 1924. Struck off Register 10 May 1935 ... **1936**

United Motor Cab Co. Ld. Regd. 1907. Vol. liq. July 1908. The undertaking and assets were acquired by General Motor Cab Co. Ld., in which company shareholders were entitled to 1 fully-paid deferred or preferred share for each deferred or preferred share held respectively. Removed from Register 1910 ... **1909**

United Motor Finance Corpn. Ld. Regd. 1921. All capital acquired by Mercantile Credit Co. Ld. Dissolved 19 Nov. 1980 ... **1959**

United New Jersey Railroad & Canal Co. Inc. New Jersey 1872. The outstanding 4% general mortgage gold bonds were redeemed at par on 1 Mar. 1944 ... **1944**

VOL. FOR

United New Zealand Exploration Ld. Regd. 1896. Vol. liq. 18 Jan. 1900. Final meeting return regd. 9 July 1902 ... **1900**

United Newry Granite Co. Ld. Regd. 1900. Vol. liq. Nov. 1907. Removed from Register 1909 ... **1908**

United Nicol Gold Mines of Western Australia Ld. In 1895 the undertaking was acquired by Consolidated Gold Mines of Western Australia Ld. for 60,007 fully-paid shares of £1 and 9,993 shares of £1 (credited with 10s. paid) ... **1897**

United Nigerian Tin Ld. Regd. 1912. Vol. liq. 27 July 1914. Final meeting return regd. 9 July 1919 ... **1915**

United Oil & Coal Corporation Ld. See Industrial Appliances & Oil & Coal Corporation Ld.

United Oil & Refinery Co. Ld. Regd. 1920. Vol. liq. 12 May 1926. Final meeting return regd. 21 Dec. 1927 ... **1927**

United Oil Importers Ld. Regd. 1923 as United Caucasian Oil Co. Ld.; name changed Dec. 1925. Vol. liq. (creditors') 5 Nov. 1931. Assets realised insufficient to pay unsecured creditors in full. Final meeting return regd. 1 Feb. 1935 ... **1932**

United Ordnance & Engineering Co. Ld. Regd. 1898. Vol. liq. 14 Nov. 1898. The subscriptions for debenture stock were repaid. Final meeting return regd. 12 Oct. 1914 ... **1899**

United Paper Mills Co. Ld. Regd. 1920. Vol. liq. (members') 30 June 1932. All shares held by Wiggins, Teape & Alex. Pirie (Merchants) Ld. Undertaking and assets transferred to Allied Paper Merchants (W. T. & Co.) Ld. Final meeting return regd. 30 Oct. 1933 ... **1933**

United Patani (Malaya) Rubber Estates, Ld. Regd. 1920. Vol. liq. (members') 30 Mar. 1960. Distributions per £1 share—20s. on 12 Apr.1960 and final 1½p on 12 Nov. 1973. Final meeting return regd. 7 Feb. 1974 ... **1976-7**

United Picture Theatres Ld. Regd. 1928. Vol. liq. (members') 14 Apr. 1955. Participating preferred ordinary shareholders received 1s. per share (of £1). Amount paid into Companies' Liquidation Account-£3,201·80 in respect of unclaimed distributions and £21·43 in respect of unclaimed dividends. Final meeting return regd. 16 June 1971 ... **1971**

United Pioneer Gold Mining Co. Ld. Regd. 1894. Vol. liq. 20 July 1896. The property was sold to Barberton Consolidated Goldfields Ld. Removed from Register 1905 ... **1897**

United Pioneer (Moodie's) Gold Mining Co. Ld. Inc. Cape of Good Hope 1888. Reconstructed as Moodie's Pioneer Gold Mining Co. Ld. ... **1893**

United Plymouth Hotels Ld. Regd. 1903. Court Order to wind up 8 Dec. 1908. Removed from Register 1914 ... **1909**

United Press Ld. Regd. 1922. Struck off Register 1928 ... ***1923**

United Producing Corporation Ld. Regd. 1928. Vol. liq. (members') 27 Oct. 1932. Capital returned to contributories—5·125d. per share of £1. Final meeting return regd. 28 Nov. 1933 ... **1934**

United Properties Ld. Regd. Queensland 1908. Struck off Register 16 Dec. 1949 ... **1916**

United Property Insurance Co. Ld. Regd. 1910. Struck off Register Apr. 1930 ... **1931**

United Provident Assurance Co. Ld. Regd. 1900. Vol. liq. 4 Jan. 1910. The undertaking and assets were sold to British Legal Life Assurance Co. Ld. Ordinary shareholders were entitled to 1 share credited with the same amount paid up for each ordinary share held. Deferred shareholders were entitled to 5 fully-paid ordinary shares for each share held. Final meeting return regd. 13 Jan. 1914 ... **1910**

United Publications Ld. Regd. 1912 as Sunday Times Ld.; name changed Aug. 1924. Vol. liq. 26 Mar. 1925. Final meeting return regd. 23 Aug. 1927 .... **1926**

United Railway & Trading Co. Ld. Regd. 1900. Vol. liq. 28 July 1926. Final meeting return regd. 20 June 1927 ... **1927**

United Railways of the Havanas and Regla Warehouses Ld. Regd. 8 Feb. 1898. Vol. liq. (members') 4 Mar. 1954 ... **1986-7**

United Realization Co. Ld. Regd. 1895. Vol. liq. (members') 11 June 1931. Capital returned to contributories—6s. 2d. per share of £1. Final meeting return regd. 9 Mar. 1932 ... **1932**

United Reefs (Sheba) Ld. Regd. 1897. Reconstructed 1898 as company of same name. Shareholders were entitled to 2 shares of £1 (credited with 15s. paid) in new company for sach share of £1 held. Removed from Register 1905 ... **1903**

United Reefs (Sheba) Ld. Regd. 1898. Reconstructed 1903 as company of same name. Shareholders were entitled to 3 shares of 10s. (credited with 7s. 6d. paid) in new company for each fully-paid share of £1 held. Removed from Register 1905 ... **1908**

United Reefs (Sheba) Ld. Regd. 1903. Vol. liq. 21 Dec. 1908. Undertaking and assets were acquired by

*See Stock Exchange Year-Book.

VOL. FOR

New United Reefs (Sheba) Ld. for a sum (£13,702) sufficient to satisfy all liabilities. Final meeting return regd. 13 Apr. 1922 1909

United Rhodesia Gold Fields Ld. Regd. 1894. Vol. liq. 31 Dec. 1919 for amalgamation with Mayo (Rhodesia) Development Co. (1908) Ld., in which company shareholders were entitled to 1 share of £1 (credited as fully-paid) for every 5 shares of 7s. 6d. held. Debenture holders were entitled to an equal amount of debentures in new company carrying conversion rights (since expired). Final meeting return regd. 24 Oct. 1923. Court Order deferred dissolution until 22 Jan. 1924 1930

United River Plate Telephone Co. Ld. Regd. 1886. Vol. liq. 27 Dec. 1946. Undertaking and assets sold to Empress Mixta Telefonica Argentina for U. S. $94,991,364 plus an adjusting sum of about $m/n.2,802,500, purchasing company assuming responsibility for outstanding liabilities. The 5½% redeemable 1st preference (sterling) shares (of £1) were repaid at 21s. per share. Capital returned to ordinary shareholders-£2 16s. 5d. per share (of £1). Final meeting return regd. 14 Apr. 1948 1948

United Roumanian Oilfields Ld. Regd. 1912. Vol. liq. 12 Jan. 1927. Final meeting return regd. 19 July 1948 1949

United Rubber & Coffee Plantations Ld. Regd. 1919. Vol. liq. (members') 2 Feb. 1932. Undertaking and assets were acquired by United Rubber & Coffee Plantations (1932) Ld., in which company shareholders were entitled to 1 share of 1s. (credited with 8d. paid) for each share of 2s. held. Final meeting return regd. 15 Oct. 1935 1933

United Securities Ld. Inc. in Quebec 1924. The outstanding collateral trust bonds were redeemed at 100½% in July 1951 1952

United Sewing Machine Co. Ld. Regd. 1886 as Moldacot (Colonial & Foreign) Pocket Sewing Machine Co. Ld.; name changed Jan. 1888. Court Orders: to wind up 3 Nov. 1888; to dissolve 8 Jan. 1895 1889

United Shoe Machinery Co. Inc. New Jersey 1899. Reorganised 1905 as United Shoe Machinery Corporation, in which company shareholders were entitled to 1½ ordinary shares of $25 for each ordinary share of $25 held or 1 preference share of $25 for each preference share of $25 held 1905

United Silica & Minerals Ld. Regd. 1913. Vol. liq. 4 Mar. 1915. Final meeting return regd. 14 May 1915 1915

United Small Arms Ld. Regd. 1918. Vol. liq. Mar. 7 1921. Final meeting return regd. 7 Oct. 1924 1922

United Smelters, Railway & Copper Co. Ld. Regd. Wyoming 1909. Dissolved in 1918, the properties having been sold under foreclosure 1912

United South Africa Association Ld. Regd. 1902. Reconstructed 1907 as company of same name. Shareholders were entitled to 1 fully-paid share of 10s. in new company for each share of £1 held. Removed from Register 1908 1908

United South Africa Association Ld. Regd. 1907. Vol. liq. Mar. 1911. Removed from Register 1913 1911

United Spanish Copper Mines Ld. Regd. 1899. Removed from Register 1905 1901

United Spinning Co. Ld. Regd. 1874. Vol. liq. 20 Jan. 1920. Reconstructed as company of same name. Final meeting return regd. 27 Sept. 1920 1920

United Spinning Co. Ld. Regd. 1920. Vol. liq. (members') 1 Apr. 1960. Final meeting return regd. 15 Jan. 1963 1951

United States and General Trust Corporation p.l.c. Regd. Feb. 1890 as United States Trust & Guarantee Corpn. Ld.; name changed 1911 to United States Trust Corporation Ld. and in 1920 to United States and General Trust Corporation Ld.; re-regd. 1981. Vol. liq. (members') 9 Nov. 1982. Company unitised by Scheme of Arrangement and holders of ordinary shares received in exchange units in Save & Prosper United States Growth Fund, Save & Prosper South East Asia Growth Fund and Save & Prosper Special Situations Fund according to their holdings and after taking into account the holders election, based on a net asset value per ordinary share of 399·93414p; preference stock repaid in accordance with rights. First and final distribution of 8·79p per share made 11 Mar. 1985. Final meeting held 17 June 1985. Amounts paid into Companies' Liquidation Account: £2,509 in respect of unclaimed dividends (pre-liquidation); £7,208 in respect of distributions (post liquidation) 1986–7

United States & Mercantile Investment Trust Ld. Regd. 1886 as United States & South American Investment Trust Co. Ld.; name changed 18 June 1954. Under scheme of 1 Feb. 1960 the undertaking and assets were acquired by Mercantile Investment Trust Ld., in which company contributories were entitled to receive fully-paid capital as follows—112

ordinary shares of 5s. for every 100 ordinary shares of 5s. held and 215 preference shares of £1 for every £200 preference stock held, The outstanding £450,000 4% and £400,000 4½% perpetual debenture stocks were cancelled, holders receiving a like amount of 4½% perpetual debenture stock in exchange. Company was dissolved on 1 June 1960 under Section 208 of the Companies' Act, 1948.... 1961

United States & Mexican Trust Co. Inc. Alabama 1901. London office closed in 1913 1914

United States & South American Investment Trust Ld. See United States & Mercantile Investment Trust Ld.

United States Brewing Co. Inc. in New Jersey 1908. In liquidation in July 1922. Preferred shareholders received full par value of their shares ($48·50) and common shareholders received a first dividend of 100% per share of $48·50 in Aug. 1923. 1st mortgage sinking fund gold debentures were redeemed at 105% on 1 July 1923 1924

United States Brewing Co. Ld. Regd. 1889. Vol. liq. Sept. 1909. Undertaking and assets were sold to United States Brewing Co. (see above). Holders of each preference share of £10 were entitled to 1 fully-paid preference share of $48·50 in the new company. Holders of every 2 ordinary shares of £10 were entitled to 1 fully-paid ordinary share of $48·50 in the new company. Holders of each debenture of £100 received $500 gold debentures. Removed from Register 1909 1909

United States Car Co. Inc. New Jersey 1892. Reorganised 1897 as Illinois Car and Equipment Co. Holders of 6% Real Estate bonds of $1,000 were entitled to an equal amount of 1st mortgage bonds in the new company. Holders of 1st mortgage 5% bonds of $500 were required to pay an assessment of £25 15s. 7½d. per bond and received $225 in 1st mortgage bonds and $325 in shares. Holders of 2nd mortgage bonds of $500 were required to pay an assessment of £15 9s. 4½d. per bond and received $75 in 1st mortgage bonds and $200 in shares. Shareholders (ordinary and preference) were required to pay an assessment of 6s. 5½d. per share and received $1·56 in 1s. mortgage bonds and $3·75 in shares 1898

United States Cattle Ranche Co. Ld. Regd. 1882. Vol. liq. Apr. 1883. Shareholders' subscriptions were returned. Final meeting return regd. 26 Aug. 1884 1896

United States Cheque Bank Ld. Regd. 1896. Vol. liq. 28 Dec. 1897. Final meeting return regd. 30 May 1899 1899

United States Dolement Co. Ld. Regd. 1907. Vol. liq. Apr. 1910. Removed from Register 1912 1911

United States Gold Placers (New Co.) Ld. Regd. 1889. Court Orders: to wind up 13 Dec. 1890; to dissolve 18 Mar. 1896 1891

United States Investment Corpn., Ld. (The). Regd. Edinburgh 1890. On 4 June 1968 the undertaking was merged with that of St. Andrew Trust Ld. Ordinary shareholders received 47 ordinary shares of 5s. in that company for every £12 10s. ordinary stock held and preference stockholders received an equal amount of preference stock to that held; liability for the debenture stocks was assumed by that company. Company was dissolved under Section 208 of the Companies Act 1948 on 4 Sept. 1968 1969

United States Land & Colonization Co. Ld. Regd. 1874. Vol. liq. 8 July 1901. Final meeting return regd. 28 Aug. 1902 .... *1877

United States Lumber & Cotton Co. Inc. Mains 1907. Property sold by Court decree of 5 Nov. 1940, holders of 5% 1st mortgage bonds being entitled to proceeds. Trustee stated in 1947 that company had no property or funds and that no investor need expect anything from company 1948

United States Mortgage Co. of Scotland Ld. See United States Trust Co. of Scotland Ld.

United States Packing Co. See Mexican National Packing Co.—Inc. 1902.

United States Rolling Stock Co. Inc. New York 1871. Reorganised 1892 as United States Car Co. After payment of an assessment of £2 per share of $50 holders were entitled to $10 2nd mortgage bonds, $25 5% preference shares, and $25 ordinary shares in new company. The old Real Estate bonds remained in force. The old consolidated 1st mortgage bonds of £100 were exchanged for $533·33 in new 1st mortgage bonds; each old £100 6% debenture for $552·50 in new 2nd mortgage bonds; and the Collateral Car Trust debentures for similar Car Trust bonds 1897

United States Trust Co. of Scotland Ld. Regd. Edinburgh 1884 as United States Mortgage Co. of Scotland Ld. name changed 15 May 1928. Under scheme of 18 Sept. 1962 the undertaking was

VOL. FOR

acquired by Second Scottish Investment Trust Co., Ld., in which company preferred stockholders received a corresponding nominal amount of preferred stock in exchange for their holdings, and holders of debenture stock and terminable debentures became holders of same nominal amounts of similar stocks in that company. Holders of deferred stock (other than Second Scottish Investment Trust Co. Ld.) received £25 6s. 1d. cash per £1 stock. Dissolved under Section 208 of Companies Act 1948 on 16 Jan. 1963 .... **1963**

United States Wheel & Rim Co. Ld. Regd. 1910. Vol. liq. Nov. 1911. Struck off Register 1922 .... **1912**

United Steam Fishing Co. of Aberdeen Ld. Regd. Edinburgh 1901. Vol. liq. Feb. 1921. Capital returned to contributories—£2 10s. 4½d. per share of £1 (10s. paid); further payments (if any) not known. Final meeting return regd. 9 May 1921 .... **1922**

United Steel Companies Ld. Regd. 1918. Undertaking and assets were acquired by company of same name. Share and debenture holders were entitled to fully-paid share of the new Company as follows—for every £100 A debenture held—75 shares; £100 B debenture stock held—80 shares; £100 C debenture stock held—97½ shares; £100 unsecured obligations held—50 shares; and for every 3 preference or 5 ordinary shares held—1 share. Court Order to dissolve 16 Nov. 1930 .... **1931**

United Stone Firms Ld. Regd. 1909. Vol. liq. 4 July 1913. Final meeting return regd. 22 Oct. 1920 .... ***1915**

United Stores Delivery Co. Ld. Regd. 1917. Vol. liq. (members') 25 Oct. 1932. Direct controlling interest held by Civil Service Co-operative Society Ld. Final meeting return regd. 20 July 1934 .... **1933**

United Strip & Bar Mills Ld. Regd. 1920. Undertaking and assets were acquired by United Steel Companies Ld., in which company shareholders were entitled to 3 fully-paid shares of £1 for every 8 preference shares of £1 held. Dissolved by Court Order 16 Nov. 1930 .... **1931**

United Sugar Co. Ld. Regd. 1925. Vol. liq. (members') 6 Aug. 1936. Undertaking was transferred to British Sugar Corporation Ld. Shareholders were entitled to 490,000 fully-paid shares of £1 in that company plus £127,842 10s. 3d. in cash. Final meeting return regd. 12 Feb. 1941 .... **1937**

United Telephone Co. Ld. Regd. 1880. Taken over by National Telephone Co. Ld. Removed from Register 1901 .... **1890**

United Telephone Co. of the River Plate Ld. Regd. 1882. Vol. liq. Dec. 1886. Reconstructed as United River Plate Telephone Co. Ld., for £20,000 7% debentures and £40,000 in fully-paid shares of £5 and £85,000 in cash. Final meeting return regd. 15 July 1891 ..... **1888**

United Theatres Co. Ld. Regd. 1898. Vol. liq. (members') 2 Apr. 1936. Capital returned to contributories—£2 10s. 6½d. per share of £1. Final meeting return regd. 5 Aug. 1936 .... **1937**

United Tile Manufacturers Ld. Regd. 1935. Vol. liq. (creditors') 10 Apr. 1951. No capital was returned to contributories. Final meeting return regd. 31 May 1954 .... **1955**

United Tobacco Companies Ld. Regd. 1904. Vol. liq. 17 Jan. 1922. Preference shares were to be repaid at par. Ordinary shareholders were entitled to 3 fully-paid shares of £1 and 1 fully-paid deferred share of £1 in United Tobacco Cos. (South) Ld. for each ordinary share of £1 held. Final meeting return regd. 29 Sept. 1923 .... **1926**

United Tools and Instruments Co. Ld. Regd. 1921. Vol. liq. (creditors') 12 July 1933. All capital owned by Oliver Typewriter Manufacturing Co. Ld. (later Oliver Industries Ld.). Final meeting return regd. 27 Nov. 1935 .... **1934**

United Trust Ld. Regd. 1888 as United Trust Co. Ld.; name changed 17 May 1889. Vol. liq. 4 July 1905, at Nov. 1905 all preferred and preference capital had been repaid. Final meeting return regd. 1 Apr. 1926 **1906**

United Trustees & General Investments Ld. Regd. 1928. Vol. liq. (members') 4 Aug. 1933. Reconstructed as United Trustees Investment Co. Ld., in which company shareholders were entitled to 1 share of 1s. (credited as fully-paid) for every 5 A shares of 10s. or 5 ordinary shares of £1 held or £14 10s. in debenture stock for every 100 preference shares of £1 held. Final meeting return regd. 4 Mar. 1935 .... **1934**

United Trustees Investment Co. Ld. Regd. 1933. Vol. liq. (members') 24 Aug. 1949. Capital returned to contributories—11s. 1d. per share (of 1s.). Final meeting return regd. 7 Nov. 1953 .... **1954**

United Van Consols & Glyn Lead & Barytes Mining Co. Ld. Regd. 1874. Reconstructed 1882 as New Van Consols & Glyn Mining Co. Ld. Removed from Register 1904 .... **1883**

VOL. FOR

United Venezuelan Oilfields Ld. Regd. 1927. Struck off Register 27 Jan. 1942 .... **1942**

United Westminster & Wrexham Collieries Ld. Regd. 1905. Vol. liq. (members') 24 Jan. 1951. Capital returned to contributories—23s. 1d. per share of £1. Final meeting return regd. 26 July 1958 .... **1959**

Unity Assurance Co. Ld. Regd. 1909. Court Order to wind up Nov. 1914. Struck off Register Apr. 1929 **1930**

Unity Gold Mining Co. Ld. Regd. 1888. Removed from Register 1906 .... **1892**

Unity Investment Trust Ld. Regd. 1914. Vol. liq. (members') 6 Mar. 1947. Final meeting return regd. 9 Oct. 1947 .... **1948**

Unity Ring Mill (Holdings) Ld. Regd 1907. Vol. liq. (members') 31 Mar. 1960. Final meeting return regd. 30 Mar. 1962 .... **1941**

Unity Rubber Co. Ld. Regd. 1905. Vol. liq. 19 Sept. 1911. Final meeting return regd. 11 Sept. 1914 .... **1912**

Unity Shipping & Trading Co. Ld. Regd. 1921. Vol. liq. 28 Oct. 1929. Capital returned to contributories—12s. 11d. per share of £1 at Jan. 1930; further payments (if any) not known. Final meeting return regd. 18 Feb. 1930 .... **1930**

Universal & General Securities Ld. Regd. 1929. Struck off Register 16 July 1937 .... **1938**

Universal Automatic Machines Co. Ld. Regd. 1887. Court Orders: to wind up 24 Sept. 1890; to dissolve 15 July 1899 .... ***1891**

Universal Automatic Shuttle Changer Ld. Regd. 1910. Vol. liq. 9 July 1914. Final meeting return regd. 1 Sept. 1915 .... **1915**

Universal Automobile Insurance Co. Ld. See Universal Insurance Co. Ld.

Universal Brazing Hearth Co. Ld. Regd. 1896. Vol. liq. 14 Dec. 1898. Final meeting return regd. 5 Oct. 1901 **1899**

Universal Cheap Cables Ld. Regd. 1911. Vol. liq. 26 Apr. 1916. Final meeting return regd. 17 June 1919 **1916**

Universal Corporation Ld. Regd. 1895. Vol. liq. 4 Jan. 1910. Final meeting return regd. 8 Dec. 1910 ...... **1910**

Universal Corporation of Western Australia Ld. Regd. 1896. Reconstructed 1898 as company of same name. Shareholders were entitled to 1 ordinary share of £1 (credited with 15s. paid) in new company for every share of £1 held **1908**

Universal Corporation of Western Australia Ld. Regd. 1898. Reconstructed 1901 as Universal Mining Co. Ld. Removed from Register 1906 .... **1909**

Universal Gas Light & Fuel Syndicate Ld. Regd. 1895. Removed from Register 4 Oct. 1898 .... ***1898**

Universal Gas Methane & "Buisson Hella" Co. Ld. Regd. 1908. Vol. liq. Nov. 1909. The undertaking and assets were acquired by Société Industrielle du Gaz Méthane, in which company shareholders were entitled to 2 participating shares, series A and 1 participating share series B for every 10 preference shares held or 1 participating share, series A and 1 participating share, series B, for every 10 ordinary shares held. Removed from Register 1912 .... **1910**

Universal Gramophone & Radio Co. Ld. Regd. 1928. Vol. liq. (members') 5 Feb. 1931. Assets realised insufficient to repay outstanding debentures. Final meeting return regd. 12 Nov. 1937 .... **1931**

Universal Grinding Wheel Co. Ld. Regd. 1918 as Vitrified Grinding Wheel Ld.; name changed July 1926. Vol. liq. (members') 8 Mar. 1935. Undertaking acquired by company of same name (later Universal Grinding Wheel Group Holdings, Ld.). Capital returned to contributories—£270,000. Final meeting return regd. 2 Mar. 1937 .... **1936**

Universal Holdings Ld. Regd. 1929 as Southern Asbestos Mines Ld.; name changed 1930. Vol. liq. (creditors') 10 July 1931. Struck off Register 31 Aug. 1937 .... **1935**

Universal Insurance Co. Ld. Regd. 1908 as Universal Automobile Insurance Co. Ld.; name changed 15 Mar. 1934. Vol. liq. (members') 17 May 1944. Final meeting return regd. 2 Jan. 1947 .... **1947**

Universal Insurance, Loan & Investment Co. Ld. Regd. 1866. Vol. liq. Jan. 1912. Struck off Register June 1932 .... **1933**

Universal Life Assurance Society. Established 1834. In liquidation in 1902. Undertaking acquired by North British & Mercantile Insurance Co **1902**

Universal Manifold Co. Ld. Regd. 1901. Vol. liq. Apr. 1905. Removed from Register 1912 .... **1906**

Universal Marine Insurance Co. Ld. Established 1860. Undertaking acquired by British and Foreign Marine Insurance Co. Ld. for 17,000 shares of £20 (credited with £4 paid). Dissolved before 1931 .... **1892**

Universal Metal Corporation Ld. Regd. 1906. Court Order to wind up 1907. Removed from Register 1912 .... **1908**

Universal Mineral Water Machine Co. Ld. Regd. 1901. Vol. liq. May 1905. Removed from Register 1906 **1906**

See Stock Exchange Year-Book.

VOL. FOR

Universal Mining Co. Ld. Regd. 1901. Vol. liq. Sept. 1909. Removed from Register 1911 .... **1910**

Universal Motor Cab Co. Ld. Regd. 1908. Struck off Register 1913 .... ***1913**

Universal Motor Carriage & Cycle Co. Ld. Regd. 1896 as British Motor Carriage & Cycle Co. Ld.; name subsequently changed. Removed from Register 1903 .... **1901**

Universal Music Co. Ld. Regd. 1909. Vol. liq. (members') 28 Nov. 1947. Final meeting return regd. 30 Mar. 1949 .... ***1933**

Universal Patent Fuel Machine & Manufacturing Co. Ld. Regd. 1888. Vol. liq. 25 Jan. 1895. Final meeting return regd. 3 Aug. 1897 .... ***1896**

Universal Plate Glass Insurance Co. Ld. Regd. 1884. Business was transferred to London Plate Glass Insurance Co. Ld. Removed from Register 1894 .. ***1887**

Universal Radio Syndicate Ld. Regd. 1912. Vol. liq. 19 Jan. 1915. Final meeting return regd. 16 Mar. 1927 ***1916**

Universal Refrigerators Ld. Regd. 1928. Struck off Register 4 Aug. 1939 .... **1940**

Universal Ring Spindle Co. Ld. Regd. 1922. Struck off Register 20 July 1937 .... **1938**

Universal Rubber Paviors Ld. Regd. 1928. Vol. liq. (members') 30 May 1935 for reconstruction as company of same name (later Shockstop Rubber Products Ld.) in which company ordinary shareholders were entitled to 4 fully-paid shares of £1 for every 5 ordinary shares of £1 held and preference shareholders 1 fully-paid share of £1 for every 2 shares of £1 held. Final meeting return regd. 27 Aug. 1947 .... **1943**

Universal Rubber Paviors (Manchester 1923) Ld. Regd. 1923. Vol. liq. 12 May 1928. Final meeting return regd. 11 sept. 1929 .... **1935**

Universal Simplex Type-Writer Ld. Regd. 1887. Vol. liq. 8 Mar. 1889. Final meeting return regd. 9 May 1891 **1890**

Universal Steam Coal Co. Ld. Regd. 1889. Vol. liq. 10 June 1905. Final meeting return regd. 1 Mar. 1907 **1906**

Universal Steam Navigation Co. Ld. Regd. 1907 as Nora Steamship Co. Ld.; name changed Dec. 1913. Struck off Register Mar. 1934 .... **1935**

Universal Steam Shipping Co. Ld. Regd. 1882. Vol. liq. 9 July 1886. Court Order to continue winding up under supervision 10 Aug. 1886. Final meeting return regd. 29 July 1893 .... **1887**

Universal Steam Tram-Car Construction Co. Ld. Regd. 1879. Vol. liq. 29 July 1882. Court Order to continue winding up under supervision 3 July 1882 .... ***1882**

Universal Sterlization Co. Ld. Regd. 1907. Court Order to wind up 1 Mar. 1910. Removed from Register 1914 .... **1911**

Universal Weldless Steel Tubes Co. (Ehrhardt's Process) Ld. Regd. 1897. Wound up under supervision of Court. Removed from Register 1904 .... **1902**

Universe Fire Insurance Association Ld. *See* Capital Fire Insurance Association Ld.

Universe Insurance Co. Ld. Regd. 1920. Vol. liq. 26 June 1922. Final meeting return regd. 26 Jan. 1934 ...... **1923**

University & City Association of London Ld. Regd. 1908. Vol. liq. 8 June 1928. The capital was repaid in full. Final meeting return regd. 1 Nov. 1928 .... **1929**

Uphall Oil Co. Ld. Regd. Edinburgh 1876. Vol. liq. Dec. 1883. Undertaking purchased by Young's Paraffin Mineral Oil Co. Ld. Final meeting return regd. 3 Jan. 1885 .... **1884**

Upolu Rubber & Cacao Estates Ld. Regd. 1910. Vol. liq. 8 Jan. 1920. Final meeting return regd. 29 July 1939 **1920**

Upolu Rubber Co. Ld. Regd. Edinburgh 1905. Vol. liq. May 1910. Undertaking and assets acquired by Upolu Rubber and Cacao Estates Ld., in which company shareholders were entitled to 1 share of £1 held or 1 share of £1 for each ordinary share of £1 held and 2s. in cash for each preferred ordinary share of £1 held. Final meeting return regd. 25 May 1912 .... **1911**

Upper Acre Rubber Estates (Brazil) Ld. *See* Solidified Petroleum Co. Ld.

Upper Ankobra Dredging Syndicate Ld. Regd. 1903. Vol. liq. June 1908. Removed from Register 1909 **1909**

Upper Burma Oil Co. Ld. Regd. 1911. Struck off Register May 1929 .... **1930**

Upper Burmah Ruby Exploration & Trading Co. Ld. Regd. 1889. Court Order to wind up 23 July 1892. Removed from Register 1906 .... **1893**

Upper Forest and Worcester Steel and Tin Plate Works Ld. Regd. 1905. All capital was owned by Richard Thomas & Baldwins Ld. Vol. liq. (members') 26 June 1963. Final meeting return regd. 24 Dec. 1965 **1959**

Upper Fraser River (British Columbia) Lumber Co. Ld. Inc. Canada 1911 .... **1916**

Upper Nile Co. Ld. Regd. 1898. Vol. liq. 1 Oct. 1900. Final meeting return regd. 9 Aug. 1922 .... **1901**

VOL. FOR

Upper Roodepoort Gold Mining Co. Ld. Regd. 1889. Vol. liq. 16 Feb. 1891. Final meeting return regd. 9 Aug. 1892 .... **1892**

Upper Wassau Gold Mines Ld. Regd. 1900. Reconstructed as African Mines Ld., in which company shareholders were entitled to 2 shares of 10s. (credited with 8s. paid) for each share of £1 held. Removed from Register 1906 .... **1906**

Upper Yangtse Syndicate Ld. Regd. 1899. Vol. liq. 9 Jan. 1901. Reconstructed 1900 as Yangtse Valley Co. Ld., in which company shareholders were entitled to 1 priority share of £1 (credited with 10s. paid) for each ordinary share of £1 (10s. paid) held, or 1 deferred share of 1s. for each deferred share of 1s. held. Final meeting return regd. 19 Oct. 1901 **1901**

Upton Colliery Co. Ld. Regd. 1923. Vol. liq. (members') 31 Mar. 1939. Undertaking acquired by Dorman Long & Co. Ld. Final meeting return regd. 9 May 1940 .... **1940**

Upton-on-Severn Gas Co. Ld. Regd. 1892. Dissolved 1 May 1949, undertaking being vested in West Midland Area Gas Board under Gas Act 1948. Holders of securities were entitled to receive, in respect of each £5 unit held, British Gas 3% guaranteed stock 1990–95 as follows:

	£	s.	d.
Ord. shares	2	0	0
Ord. shares (£4 paid)	1	12	0
Pref. shares	2	2	6

1952

Upwell, Outwell & Wisbech Railway Co. Abandoned by Act of 1884 .... **1885**

Ural Emba Oilfields Ld. Regd. 1913. Vol. liq. 28 Nov. 1915. Final meeting return regd. 16 Mar. 1916..... **1916**

Ural Gold Fields of Western Siberia Ld. Regd. 1899. Struck off Register 7 May 1907 .... **1908**

Uranium Mines Ld. Regd. 1889. Vol. liq. 28 July 1891. Final meeting return regd. 23 Mar. 1900 .... **1892**

Urban Electric Supply Co. Ld. Regd. 1898. Dissolved 1 Apr. 1948, undertaking being vested in British (later Central) Electricity Authority and East Midlands Area Board under Electricity Act 1947. Holders of ordinary and 6% preference shares were entitled to receive British Electricity 3% guaranteed stock (1968–73) as follows—10s. 6d. stock for each ordinary share held (of 5s.) and £1 12s. stock for each preference share (of £1) held **1949**

Urban Fire Insurance Co. Ld. Regd. 1905. Vol. liq. (members') 5 Jan. 1931. Capital returned to contributories—£5,819 19s. 8d. Final meeting return regd. 17 Mar. 1934 .... ***1931**

Urban Railway Co. of Lima. Inc. Peru 1887. Undertaking and assets transferred to Lima Light Power & Tramways Co. (later Lima Light & Power Co.). The 6% bonds were repaid on 1 Jan. 1911 .... **1911**

Uroz Co. Ld. Regd. 1925. Vol. liq. 26 Oct. 1928 for reconstruction as Uroz Ld., in which company shareholders were entitled to 1 fully-paid share of 1s. for each share of 5s. held. Final meeting return regd. 6 June 1935 .... **1929**

Uroz Ld. Regd. 1928. Vol. liq. (creditors') July 1930. Undertaking and assets were acquired by Consolidated Mines & Minerals Development Corporation Ld., in which company shareholders received 1 fully-paid share of 5s. for every 5 shares of 1s. held. Final meeting return regd. 24 July 1940............... **1931**

Uroz Oilfields Ld. Regd. 1912. Vol. liq. 1 July 1925. Reconstructed as Uroz Co. Ld., in which company shareholders were entitled to 1 share of 5s. (credited with 3s. 6d. paid) for each share of 10s. held. Final meeting return regd. 9 Dec. 1931 .... **1926**

Uruguay Central & Hygueritas Railway of Montevideo Ld. Regd. 1873. Undertaking was sold to Central Uruguay Railway Co. of Montevideo Ld., on and from 1 July 1885 for 11,000 fully-paid shares of £10. Removed from Register 1904 .... **1887**

Uruguay Consolidated Gold Mines Ld. Regd. 1909. Vol. liq. 16 Feb. 1914. Final meeting return regd. 2 Nov. 1914 .... **1914**

Uruguay Development Co. Ld. Regd. 1897. A receiver and manager was appointed 3 July 1900 on behalf of debenture holders amongst whom property was distributed. Removed from Register 1907 .... **1903**

Uruguay East Coast Railway Co. Ld. Regd. 1908. Vol. liq. 31 Mar. 1921. Final meeting return regd. 10 Jan. 1922 .... **1922**

Uruguay Goldfields Ld. Regd. 1909. Vol. liq. 14 Aug. 1913. Final meeting return regd. 2 Nov. 1914 ..... **1914**

Uruguay Great Eastern Railway Co. Ld. Regd. 1889. Vol. liq. Feb. 1908. Reconstructed as Uruguay East Coast Railway Co. Ld. Debenture stockholders were entitled to £60 income debenture stock and £40 in shares in the new company for each £100 debentures held. Removed from Register 1911 .... **1909**

VOL. FOR

Uruguay Land and Development Co. Ld. Regd. 1888. Reconstructed 1897 as Uruguay Development Co. Ld. Removed from Register 1903 1902

Uruguay Land Co. Ld. Regd. 1911. Vol. liq. 2 Dec. 1913. Final meeting return regd. 17 Dec. 1915 1914

Uruguay Northern Railway Co. Ld. Regd. 1887. Vol. liq. (members') 24 Feb. 1949, undertaking having been sold to Uruguayan Govt. 5% prior lien debenture stock was redeemed at 105%, with interest to 31 July 1948 (47½%). 5% income debenture stock was redeemed at 34%, no interest payment being made. Holders of preferred stock and ordinary shares received distributions of 10·956% and 2·739% respectively, all arrears of preferred dividend being cancelled. £802 was paid into Companies' Liquidation Account. Final meeting return regd. 9 Aug. 1951 1953

Uruguay Pastoral Association Ld. Regd. 1864. Vol. liq. 14 Aug. 1890. Final meeting return regd. 31 Dec. 1890 1891

Uruguay United Estancias Ld. Regd. 1905. Vol. liq. (members') 10 May 1937. Capital returned to contributories—£8 12s. 6d. per share of £5. Final meeting return regd. 21 July 1938 1938

Uruwira Goldfields Ld. See Uruwira Minerals Ld.

Uruwira Minerals Ld. Inc. 1936 in Tanganyika as Uruwira Goldfields Ld.; name changed as above 1946. Winding up Order 6 June 1960. Liquidator released 18 April 1968 1969

Usambara Sisal Co. Ld. Regd. 1925. Vol. liq. (members') 24 Sept. 1936. Undertaking was acquired by Sisal Estates Ld. Capital returned to contributories—20s. per preference share of £1; 6s. 10d. per ordinary share of 1s. ordinary shareholders were also entitled to ·3826 fully-paid share of 5s. in Sisal Estates Ld. for each share held. Final meeting return regd. 26 Jan. 1942 1937

Usher (J. & T.) Ld. Regd. 1896. Vol. liq. (members') 29 July 1959. Final meeting return regd. 21 Dec. 1960 1958

Usico Ld. Regd. Edinburgh 1930. Vol. liq. (members') 4 Nov. 1943. All capital owned by United States Investment Corporation Ld. Final meeting return regd. 17 Dec. 1943 1945

Usk & Towy Railway Co. Inc. by Special Act 1871. Undertaking abandoned 1888

Usumbara Plantations Ld. Regd. 1927. Receiver appointed in June 1930. Struck off Register 18 Nov. 1938 1939

Usumbara Rubber Estates Ld. Regd. 1925. Vol. liq. 5 Sept. 1927. Reconstructed as Usumbara Plantations Ld., in which company shareholders were entitled to 1 share of 2s. (credited with 1s. paid) for every 2 shares of 2s. held. Struck off Register 21 Mar. 1933 1928

Utah Apex Mining Co. See National Tunnel & Mines Co.

Utah Bingham Mining Co. Inc. Maine 1906. Certain assets were sold in Apr. 1912 to New Utah Bingham Mining Co., in which company shareholders were entitled to 1 share of $2·50 (credited with $2·15 paid for each share of $5 held) 1913

Utah Consolidated Gold Mines Ld. Regd. 1896 as Sevier Gold Mines Ld.; name changed Oct. 1896. Undertaking and assets were acquired by Utah Consolidated Mining Co., in which company shareholders were entitled to 1 fully-paid share of $5 for each share of £1 held. Removed from Register 1904 ... 1904

Utah Consolidated Mining Co. Inc. New Jersey 1903. Property was purchased under foreclosure sale by International Smelting Co. for $1,000,000 in Apr. 1924 1926

Utah Copper Co. Inc. New Jersey 1904. In 1936 merged with Copper Corporation of Utah, in which company shareholders were entitled to 3 shares for each share of $10 held. These shares were thereupon exchanged for an equal number of shares of no par value in Kennecott Copper Corporation 1937

Utah Development Co. Inc. Maine 1904. Company was absorbed by the North Utah Mining Company of Bingham, in which company shareholders were entitled to 1 share of $5 for every 4 shares of $5 held 1910

Utah Light & Power Co. Inc. Utah 1899. Undertaking transferred to Utah Light & Railway Company in Dec. 1903 for $2,000,000 1908

Ute & Ulay Mines Ld. Regd. 1889. Vol. liq. 7 Dec. 1894. Final meeting return regd. 22 Mar. 1902 1895

Utilities & General Trust Ld. Regd. Edinburgh 1913. Vol. liq. 8 Nov. 1951. 5% debenture stock repaid at par 11 Feb. 1952. Capital returned to contributories—preference: 107¼%; ordinary 219¾%. Final meeting return regd. 17 July 1952 1953

Utilities Corporation (Poland) Ld. Regd. 1928. Vol. liq. (members') 24 June 1964. Final meeting return regd. 2 June 1964 1958

VOL. FOR

Utilities Improvement Co. Inc. Delaware 1912. The assets were acquired in 1913 by Cities Service Company, in which company preferred stockholders were entitled to an equal amount of preferred stock; the holders of common stock were entitled to 1 share of $100 for every 2 shares held 1916

Utopia Bakery Ld. Undertaking and assets acquired in 1925 by Lunt (George), Sons & Co. Ld. (later Wright's Cakes Ld.) 1928

Uttoxeter Brewery Ld. Regd. 1888. Receiver for debenture holders appointed in 1889. Court Orders: to wind up 29 Mar. 1890; to dissolve 18 July 1898 1892

Uttoxeter Gas Works Ld. Regd. 1893. Dissolved 1 May 1949, undertaking being vested in West Midland Area Gas Board under Gas Act 1948. Holders of securities were entitled to receive British Gas 3% guaranteed stock 1990–95 as follows in respect of each £5 unit held:

	£	s.	d.
Ord. shares (10% stand.)	11	0	0
6% cum. pref. shares...........................	6	14	0	1952

Uva Ceylon Rubber Estates Ld. See Hingrakadua Rubber Estates Ld.

Uveco Cereals Ld. Regd. 1902. Vol. liq. 31 June 1927. Controlling interest held by Spillers Milling & Associated Industries Ld. (later Spillers Ld.). Final meeting return regd. 23 Jan. 1928 1927

Uxbridge & District Electric Supply Co. Ld. Regd. 1899 as Uxbridge & District Development Synd. Ld.; name changed 1901. Dissolved 1 Apr. 1948, undertaking being vested in British (later Central) Electricity Authority and Southern Area Board under Electricity Act 1947. Ordinary shareholders were entitled to receive £2 British Electricity 3% guaranteed stock(1968–73) for each share (of £1) held. 1949

Uxbridge & Hillingdon Gas Consumers' Co. See Uxbridge, Maidenhead, Wycombe & District Gas Co.

Uxbridge & Rickmansworth Railway Co. Inc. by Special Act 1881. Undertaking abandoned by Act of 1888 1889

Uxbridge Gas Co. See Uxbridge, Maidenhead, Wycombe & District Gas Co.

Uxbridge, Maidenhead, Wycombe & District Gas Co. Estd. as Uxbridge & Hillingdon Gas Consumers' Co. 1854; inc. by Special Act 1861; name changed to Uxbridge Gas Co. 1907, to Uxbridge, Wycombe & District Gas Co. 1920 and as above 1924. Dissolved 1 May 1949, undertaking being vested in North Thames Area Gas Board under Gas Act 1948. Holders of securities were entitled to receive, in respect of each £100 unit held, British Gas 3% guaranteed stock 1990–95 as follows:

	£	s.	d.
Cap, stock (5% stand.)	147	0	0
5% pref. stock	116	0	0
5½% pref. stock	128	0	0
4% red. pref. stock	100	10	0
4% perp. deb. stock	103	0	0
4½% perp. deb. stock	114	0	0
5% perp. deb. stock.........................	125	0	0	1952

Uxbridge, Wycombe & District Gas Co. See Uxbridge, Maidenhead, Wycombe & District Gas Co.

V

V. B. Co. Ld. Regd. 1910. Vol. liq. 27 Feb. 1925. Final meeting return regd. 5 Dec. 1925 1926

V. C. (De Bernier Patent) Motor Co. Ld. Regd. 1913 as V. C. (Variable Compression de Bernier Patent) Oil Engine Ld.; name changed 18 June 1914. Struck off Register 30 Oct. 1919 .... *1915

V. C. [Variable Compression de Bernier Patent] Oil Engine Ld. See above.

V. M. Syndicate Ld. Regd. 1902. Vol. liq. 14 Mar. 1913. Final meeting return regd. 26 Sept. 1914 ....

V. O. C. Holding Co. Ld. Regd. 1921. Vol. liq. (members') 24 Mar. 1930. Undertaking and assets were acquired by Venezualan Oil Concessions Ld. (later Shell Venezuelan Oil Ld.) in which company shareholders were entitled to 1 ordinary share of £1 (credited as fully-paid) for each ordinary share of £1 held or 1 preference share of £1 for each preference share of £1 held. Final meeting return regd. 12 Dec. 1930 1931

V. P. Produce Ld. See Vacuum Packed Produce Ld.

V. V. (Gwanda) Syndicate Ld. Regd. 1895. Vol. liq. 4 May 1905 for reconstruction as New Rhodesia Mines Ld., in which company shareholders were entitled to 1 share of £1 (credited as fully-paid) for every 2 shares of £1 held. Removed from Register 1906 1906

VOL. FOR

"V.V." (Vis Vitæ) Bread Co. Ld. Regd. 1897. Business was sold to Joy's Ld. for 45,000 fully-paid shares. Struck off Register 16 Dec. 1938 **1939**

Vaal River Diamond Co. Ld. Regd. 1889. Vol. liq. (members') 2 May 1939. Shareholders entitled to 10 shares of 2s. (credited with 1s. paid) in company of same name (regd. 1939) for each share of £1 held. Final meeting return regd. 8 Dec. 1939 **1940**

Vaal River (Droogveld) Diamonds Ld. Regd. 1907. Vol. liq. Feb. 1910. Removed from Register 1912 **1911**

Vaal River Gold Estates Ld. Regd. 1915. Vol. liq. 20 Feb. 1919. Final meeting return regd. 15 Apr. 1926 ***1920**

Vaal River Gold Fields Ld. Inc. Transvaal 1907. Vol. liq. 1910. For reconstruction under same name. Shareholders were entitled to 1 share of 2s. 6d. in new company for each share of 5s. held, and to subscribe pro rata for further shares credited with 1s. 9d. paid up **1911**

Vaal River Gold Fields Ld. Regd. 1910. Vol. liq. 8 Feb. 1915. The assets were sold to Orion Development Co. Ld., in which company shareholders were entitled to subscribe for shares at par. Debenture holders were entitled to an equal amount of similar debentures in new company. Final meeting return regd. 14 Nov. 1919 **1920**

Vaal River Minerals Syndicate Ld. Regd. 1896. Vol. liq. (members') 5 Sept. 1935. Undertaking acquired by Afric Gold Corporation Ld. Final meeting return regd. 18 Dec. 1936 **1936**

Vaalbank Coal Co. Ld. See Transvaal & Natal Collieries Ld.

Vaalbank (Transvaal) Colliery Ld. Regd. 1917. Court Order to wind up 17 Jan. 1922. Struck off Register 1928 **1922**

Vactric Ld. Regd. 1934. Court Order to wind up 14 Nov. 1960. No capital returned to contributories. £5,202 was paid into Companies' Liquidation Account in respect of unclaimed dividends. Liquidator released 9 Jan. 1974. Dissolved 12 Nov. 1976 **1974–5**

Vacuum Drying Co. Ld. Regd. 1892. Vol. liq. 31 May 1894. Final meeting return regd. 2 Dec. 1899 **1895**

Vacuum Oil Co. Inc. New York 1866. Undertaking was acquired in 1931 by Socony-Vacuum Corporation [later Socony-Vacuum Oil Co. Inc.—later Socony Mobil Oil Co. Inc.] **1934**

Vacuum Packed Produce Ld. Regd. 1934 as V. P. Produce Ld.; name changed Nov. 1934. Vol. liq. (creditors') 21 Apr. 1938. Assets realised insufficient to pay unsecured creditors in full. Final meeting return regd. 10 July 1940 **1939**

Vagliano Anthracite Collieries Ld. Regd. 1908. Vol. liq. 1 Jan. 1913. Liquidator released 30 June 1916. Struck off Register 14 Feb. 1919 **1940**

Val de Zafan to San Carlos de la Rapita Railway Co. See Saragossa & Mediterranean Railway Co.

Val D'or Rubber Estates, Ld. Regd. 1909. Winding-up Order 2 Mar. 1964 **1962**

Val Parnell Investment Ld. See Parnell Electric Industries Ld.

Vale of Clyde Tramways Co. Inc. by Special Act 1871. Vol. liq. under supervision of the Court in 1895 **1895**

Vale of Coolgardie Gold Mines Ld. Regd. 1896. Removed from Register 1911 **1904**

Vale of Glamorgan Railway Co. Inc. by Special Act 1889. In 1922 the undertaking was merged into the Great Western Railway Co., in which company stockholders were entitled to stock as follows:

For each £100 held		G.W.R.
3% Debenture	£75	4% Debenture
Ordinary	£100	5% Cons. Gtd.	**1924**

Vale of Leven Gas Co. Ld. Regd. in Edinburgh 1907. Dissolved 1 May 1949, undertaking being vested in Scottish Area Gas Board under Gas Act 1948. Holders of ordinary shares (of £1) were entitled to receive £2 8s. British Gas 3% guaranteed stock 1990–95 for each share held **1952**

Vale of Llangollen Railway Co. Inc. by Special Act 1859. Under Great Western Railway Act of 1896 the undertaking was amalgamated with that company. Holders of 41% debenture stock received an equal amount of debenture stock in the purchasing company. Holders of £100 5% preference stock or shares. 4% 3rd preference stock or ordinary stock received £100, £80 or £145 5% consolidated guaranteed stock in purchasing company **1897**

Vale of Neath Colliery Co. Ld. Regd. 1920. Undertaking and assets were acquired by Amalgamated Anthracite Collieries Ld. Vol. liq. (members') 24 Dec. 1931. Capital returned to contributories—£63,774 plus certain investments which were distributed in specie. Final meeting return regd. 2 Dec. 1932 **1932**

Vale of Rheidol Light Railway Co. Inc. by Special Act 1897. Placed under Light Railways Act (1896) in Aug. 1902 **1914**

VOL. FOR

Valencia & Liria Railway Co. Ld. Regd. 1887. Removed from Register 1894 **1893**

Valencia & North Eastern of Spain Railway Co. Ld. Regd. 1889. Receiver for debenture holders appointed in Jan. 1896. Struck off Register 1916 **1899**

Valley Combing Co. Ld. See Valley Woolcombers Ld.

Valley Gold Ld. Regd. 1890. Vol. liq. 29 Aug. 1892. Reconstructed as Holcomb Valley Co. Ld., in which company shareholders were entitled to 1 share of 5s. (credited with 4s. 6d. paid) for each ordinary share of 5s. held or 1 fully-paid share of 5s. for each preference share of 5s. held of 40 fully-paid shares of 5s. for each debenture of £10 held. Final meeting return regd. 24 Feb. 1896 **1897**

Valley Ring Mill Ld. Regd. 1920. Vol. liq. (members') 14 Aug. 1944. Capital returned to contributories—17s. 3d. per share of £1. Final meeting return regd. 12 May 1945 **1946**

Valley Woolcombers Ld. Regd. 1926 as Valley Combing Co. Ld.; name changed Nov. 1926. Vol. liq. (members') 30 Aug. 1933. Certain assets were sold to Woolcombers' Mutual Association Ld., for £105,000. Capital returned to contributories—9s. 7·9d. per preference share of £1 at Nov. 1933. £58 13s. was paid into Companies' Liquidation Account. Final meeting return regd. 18 Apr. 1935 **1934**

Vallongo Antimony Co. Ld. Regd. 1906. Struck off Register 1922 **1912**

Valophone Ld. Regd. 1931. Struck off Register 14 Jan. 1936 **1936**

Valor Co. Ld. Regd. 1897. Vol. liq. (members') 12 Feb. 1936. Undertaking and certain assets were acquired by Rolav Ld. (later Valor Co. Ld.) for £320,815 in cash. Final meeting return regd. 18 Jan. 1938 **1936**

Valour Rubber Extracting Machine Ld. Regd. 1910. Vol. liq. 17 Aug. 1925. Final meeting return regd. 20 Nov. 1925 **1926**

Valparaiso Drainage Co. Ld. Regd. 1880. Concession was acquired in 1905 by Valparaiso (Chile) Drainage Co. Ld., for £150,000 in shares. Removed from Register 1907 **1907**

Valve Gears Ld. See Caprotti Valve Gears, Ld.

Van Consols Lead & Barytes Mining Co. Ld. Regd. 1869. Court Orders: to wind up 30 Aug. 1877: to dissolve 19 May 1881 ***1877**

Van den Bergh (Arnold I.) Ld. Regd. 22 Dec. 1897. Vol. liq. 1 Apr. 1921. Final meeting return regd. 20 June 1929 **1922**

Van den Bergh (Arnold I.) N.V. Inc. by Royal Decree 1920 as Arnold I. Van den Bergh's Emballage-Fabrieken; name changed Apr. 1930. Undertaking and assets were acquired by Emballagefabrieken en Houthandel, N.V. Holders of the outstanding debentures were entitled to an equal amount of 4½% debentures of the acquiring company, preference shareholders were entitled to repayment at par plus dividend to 30 Sept. 1934 and ordinary shareholders were entitled to 3 fully-paid shares of Fl. 300 of the acquiring company and Fl. 22·70 cash for each share of Fl. 1,200 held, sub-shares being dealt with in the same way in proportion to their value **1940**

Van den Bergh's (Arnold I.) Emballage-Fabrieken. See Van den Bergh (Arnold I.) N.V.

Van der Lugt (W.) & Zoon, N.V. Undertaking was acquired in 1929 by Emballagefabrieken en Houthandel, N.V. **1940**

Van Diemen's Land Minerals Co. Ld. Regd. 1882. Vol. liq. 2 Mar. 1892. Final meeting return regd. 30 Nov. 1892 **1893**

Van Dyk Consolidated Mines Ld. Inc. in South Africa 1934. Vol. liq. (members') 1 Aug. 1969. Capital returned to contributories: 12·93186641 cents (1s. 6·105d) per share of R0·02½. Final meeting return regd. 18 Nov. 1970 **1972**

Van Dyk Proprietary Mines Ld. Inc. Transvaal 1904. Undertaking and assets were acquired by Van Dyk Consolidated Mines Ld., in which company shareholders were entitled to 1 share of 10s. (credited as fully-paid) for each share of £1 held **1935**

Van Emden (Dutch Guiana) Gold Mines, Ld. Regd. 1912. Receiver appointed 6 May 1941 and ceased to act 31 Dec. 1946. Vol. liq. (members') 2 Jan. 1947 when it was stated that all realisable assets had been sold by the receiver and there was little likelihood of the liquidator realising sufficient to pay the costs of liquidation. Final meeting return regd. 22 Dec. 1947 **1948**

Van Hulsteyn Randfontein Gold Mining Co. Ld. Inc. Transvaal 1899. Vol. liq. 1909; the undertaking and assets were sold to Randfontein Central Gold Mining Co. Ld. for 139,583 shares of £1 **1910**

Van Mines Ld. Regd. 1902. Vol. liq. 20 July 1908. Struck off Register 10 Oct. 1916 **1909**

Van Mining Co. Ld. Regd. 1891. Vol. liq. 19 Dec. 1891. Court Order to wind up 30 Jan. 1892. Liquidator

VOL. FOR

released 6 Dec. 1895. Removed from Register 21 June 1907 .... *1893

Van Railway Co. Regd. 1870 as Van Railway Co. Ld. Inc. by Board of Trade Certificate 1873. In 1923 the undertaking was merged into the Great Western Railway Co. Holders of £100 of Debenture Stock were entitled to £27 4s. 5d. in cash. The shares were cancelled 1924

Van-Roi Mining Co. Ld. Regd. 1908. Vol. liq. 7 July 1921. Final meeting return regd. 26 Feb. 1923..... 1922

Van Ryn Deep, Ld. Inc. in Transvaal 1902. Vol. liq. (members') 31 Oct. 1945. Capital returned to contributories—9s. 6·249d. per share of £1. Finally dissolved 30 June 1952 1953

Van Ryn Estate & Gold Mining Co. Ld. Regd. 1891. Vol. liq. 14 June 1894. Reconstructed as Van Ryn Gold Mines Estate Ld. for £70,000 fully-paid shares of £1. Final meeting return regd. 28 June 1895 1894

Van Ryn Gold Mines Estate, Ld. Regd 1894. Vol. liq. (members') 19 Nov. 1957. Company's holdings of stock in General Exploration Orange Free State Ld. (later Sentrust Beperk) and shares in Riebeeck Gold Mining Co. Ld. were distributed in June 1958 to shareholders as follows:
1 2s. 6d. unit of stock for every 4 shares (of 1s.) and 3 shares (of 1s.) for every 20 shares (of 1s.). Bearer shares of this company lodged for conversion into registered shares after 19 Nov. 1968 were exchanged for shares of Loraine Gold Mines Ld. instead of shares of Riebeeck Gold Mining Co. Ld. in proportion of 9 Loraine shares of 10s. for every .7 Riebeeck shares into which they would have been exchanged. Capital returned to contributories: 11s. 10½d, per share (of 1s.). £5,297 8s. 7d. was paid into Companies' Liquidation Account. Final meeting return regd. 1 Nov. 1963 1965

Van Ryn North Exploration & Mining Co. Ld. Regd. 1895. Vol. liq. 24 June 1897. Property was acquired by Van Ryn Gold Mines Estate Ld. Final meeting return regd. 23 Nov. 1897 1897

Van Ryn West Mining Co. Ld. Regd. 1894. Vol. liq. 15 Jan. 1898. Undertaking was acquired by Van Ryn West Mining Co. Ld. in which company shareholders were entitled to 1 share of £1 (credited as fully-paid) for every 2 shares of £1 held. The purchasing company assumed liability for the debentures. Final meeting return regd. 12 Sept. 1898 1898

Vancouver & British Columbia General Exploration Co. Ld. Regd. 1896. Removed from Register 1906 1903

Vancouver Coal Mining & Land Co. Ld. Regd. 1962. Vol. liq. 28 Feb. 1889. Reconstructed as New Vancouver Coal Mining & Land Co. Ld., in which company shareholders were entitled to 10 fully-paid shares of £1 for each share of £10 held. Final meeting return regd. 28 Apr. 1892 1903

Vancouver Copper Co. Ld. Regd. 1907. Vol. liq. Apr. 1912. Removed from Register 1913 1913

Vancouver Island Mining & Development Co. Ld. Regd. 1902. Vol. liq. Jan. 1918. Struck off Register 1927 1918

Vancouver Land and Securities Corporation Ld. Regd. 1890. Vol. liq. 18 Feb. 1903. Capital returned to contributories—1s. 2s. 6d. per share of 1s. at Nov. 1903; further payments (if any) not known. Final meeting return regd. 3 June 1926 1904

Vandalia Railroad Co. Organised Indiana and Illinois 1904. Reorganised 1916 as Pittsburgh, Cincinnati Chicago & St. Louis Railroad Co. Shareholders were entitled to $85 stock in new company for each share of $100 held. The consolidated mortgage 4% bonds were taken over by acquiring company 1917

Vanguard Cycle Co. Ld. Regd. 1897 as New Vanguard Cycle Co. Ld.; name changed July 1898. Vol. liq. 3 July 1900. Final meeting return regd. 13 May 1901 1901

Vanguard Motorbus Co. Ld. Regd. 1907. Vol. liq. Sept. 1908. Undertaking and assets were sold on and from 1 July 1908 to London General Omnibus Co. Ld. Court Order to continue winding up under supervision Feb. 1909. Debenture stockholders were entitled to an equal amount of C debenture stock in purchasing company. Shareholders were entitled to fully-paid ordinary shares of £10 in purchasing company at the rate of 1s. 9·217d. per ordinary share of £1 held or 4s. 6·1919d. per preference share of £1 held. Struck off Register May 1929 1930

Vannan (A. & R.) Ld. Regd. Edinburgh 1897. Vol. liq. Mar. 1915. Final meeting return regd. 2 Nov.1918 1915

Var Mines Ld. Regd. 1909. Vol. liq. 25 Apr. 1913. Final meeting return regd. 14 Aug. 1918 1914

Var Oil & Coal Co. Ld. Regd. 1920. Vol. liq. 20 Jan. 1925. Reconstructed as Var Oil Co. Ld., in which company shareholders were entitled to 1 share of 5s. (credited with 2s. paid) for each share of £1 held. The debenture stock was to be redeemed. Final meeting return regd. 28 Nov. 1925 1925

VOL. FOR

Var Oil Co. Ld. Regd. 1925. Vol. liq. 6 Dec. 1927. Struck off Register 3 Oct. 1941 1942

Varcoe (William) & Sons Ld. Regd. 1909. Vol. liq. (members') 25 July 1933. All shares owned by English China Clays Ld. Final meeting return regd. 7 Feb. 1935 1934

"Varieties" Ld. Regd. 1892. Court Order to wind up 7 Feb. 1893. Capital returned to contributories—£1 per share of £2. Removed from Register 1907 1894

Variety Automatic Supply Stores Ld. Regd. 1889. Removed from Register 1906 .... *1895

Variety Theatres, Birmingham Ld. Regd. 1920. Vol. liq. (members') 9 Aug. 1937. Final meeting return regd. 7 Feb. 1938 1938

Variety Theatres Controlling Co. Ld. Regd. 1910. Vol. liq. 29 Mar. 1928. Subsidiary of London Theatres of Varieties Ld. Final meeting return regd. 13 June 1931 1929

Varsseveld & Co. N.V. Undertaking was acquired in 1929 by Emballagefabrieken en Houthandel, N.V. 1940

Vasa Murrhina Glass Co. Ld. Regd. 1880. Court Orders: to wind up 15 July 1882; to dissolve 10 Dec. 1891 1883

Vaudeville Theatre (Reading) Ld. Regd. 1920. Vol. liq. 18 Oct. 1929. Final meeting return regd. 30 Apr. 1930 1930

Vaughan-Williams Rhodesia Development Co. Ld. Regd. 1895. Removed from Register 1910 1904

Vauxhall Glass Manufacturing Co. Ld. Regd. 1919. Vol. liq. 28 Sept. 1921. Final meeting return regd. 30 Dec. 1922 1922

Vayles (1924) Ld. Regd. 1924. Directly controlled by Fortnum & Mason Ld. Struck off Register 25 Mar. 1938 1938

Vectis Engineering Co. Ld. Regd. 1919. Vol. liq. 15 Apr. 1920. Certain patents were acquired by Industrial Appliances & Oil Corporation Ld. Final meeting return regd. 7 Dec. 1920. Court Orders deferring dissolution until 4 Mar. 1921; deferring dissolution until 1 June 1922 1934

Vedrine (A.) & Co. Ld. Regd. 1905. Vol. liq. June 1909. Removed from Register 1913 1910

Vegetable Oil & Lard Compound Refiners Ld. Regd. 1920. Vol. liq. 20 Apr. 1922. Reconstructed as Vegetable Oils & Margarine Ld., in which company shareholders were entitled to 1 ordinary share of 1s. (credited with 6d. paid) for each ordinary share of 1s. held, or 1 preference share of £1 (credited with 15s. paid) for each preference share of £1 held. Final meeting return regd. 30 July 1926 1923

Vegetable Oils & Margarine Ld. Regd. 1922. Receiver appointed in June 1927; ceased to act 31 July 1930. Struck off Register Jan. 1932 1932

Veitsch (G. Haswell) & Co. Ld. Regd. 1924. Struck off Register 18 Aug. 1953 .... *1933

Vejos Ld. Regd. 1897. Removed from Register 1901 1900

Vellani Tea Estates Ld. Regd. in Edinburgh 1926. Vol. liq. 1 May 1945. Capital returned to contributories—30s. 0·6594d. per share (of £1). Final meeting return regd. 18 Apr. 1949 1950

Vellikellie Tea Co. of Ceylon, Ld. Regd. 1897. Vol. liq. (members') 3 Feb. 1955. Capital returned to contributories—£10 per preference share of £10 and £45 10s. 3d. per ordinary share of £10. Final meeting return regd. 2 May 1957 1958

Velocium Ld. See Middleton & Payne Ld.

Velocium Ld. Regd. 1928. Vol. liq. 9 May 1929. Final meeting return regd. 26 June 1931 1930

Veloplastic Co. Ld. Regd. 1883. Vol. liq. Dec. 1884. Final meeting return regd. 9 Aug. 1888 1885

Velox Motor Co. Ld. Regd. 1902. Court Order to wind up 3 Nov. 1903. Removed from Register 1910 1904

Velvet Mines Ld. Regd. 1898. Reconstructed 1900 as Velvet (Rossland) Mine Ld., in which company shareholders were entitled to 1⅞₀ shares of £1 (credited as fully-paid) for each share of £1 held. The debentures were repaid at par. Removed from Register 1901 1902

Velvet Portland Mine Ld. Regd. 1904. Undertaking was acquired by New Velvet Portland Mine Ld. for £3,000 in cash. Removed from Register 1906........ 1908

Velvet (Rossland) Mine Ld. Regd. 1900. Reconstructed 1902 as Velvet Rossland Mine Ld., in which company shareholders were entitled to 1 share of £1 (credited with 17s. 6d paid) for each share of £1 held. Removed from Register 1905 1904

Velvet Rossland Mine Ld. Regd. 1902. Vol. liq. 4 Mar. 1904. Reconstructed as Velvet Portland Mine Ld., in which company shareholders were entitled to 1 share of 10s. (credited with 7s. 6d. paid) for each share of £1 held. Final meeting return regd. 20 Sept. 1905 1905

Velvril-Bonnaud Ld. Regd. 1906. Vol. liq. Nov. 1909. Undertaking was acquired by F. Reddaway and Co. Ld., in 1910. Removed from Register 1912 1910

Venesta International Ld. Regd. 1898 as Venesta Ld.; name changed 30 May 1969. Winding-up order 10 Apr. 1978. Liquidator stated no return to contributories anticipated **1978-9**

Venesta Ld. *See* Venesta International Ld.

Venezuela Central Area Oilfields Ld. Regd. 1925. Vol. liq. 19 July 1927. Direct controlling interest held by Anglo-Venezuelan Oil Trust Ld. Final meeting return regd. 25 Oct. 1928 .... **1928**

Venezuela Central Railway Co. Ld. Regd. 1885. Assets and liabilities were transferred to Electric Equipment and Securities Co. Ld. (later Reid, Evans & Co. Ld.) for bonds of Venezuelan Government Loan 1896. Removed from Register 1906 .... **1904**

Venezuela Central Railway Co. Ld. Regd. 1905. Struck off Register 28 Feb. 1939 .... **1940**

Venezuela-Panama Gold Mine Co. Ld. Regd. 1882. Vol. liq. 29 Sept. 1894. Removed from Register 1905 . **1887**

Venezuela Public Works & Credit Co. Ld. Regd. 1890. Struck off Register 28 July 1899 .... **1900**

Venezuela Telephone Electrical Appliances Co. Ld. Regd. 1890. Vol. liq. (members') 31 July 1931. Undertaking and assets were acquired by Telephone Properties Ld. (later Temple Bar Investment Ld.). in which company shareholders were entitled to 4 preference and 2 ordinary shares of £1 (credited as fully-paid) for every 4 preference shares of £1 held or 5 fully-paid ordinary shares of £1 for every 4 ordinary or A ordinary shares of £1 held. The outstanding 1st and 2nd mortgage debentures were to be redeemed at 105% and par respectively on 30 Apr. 1931. £36 was paid into Companies' Liquidation Account. Final meeting return regd. 30 Dec. 1931 .... **1932**

Venezuelan Austin Gold Mining Co. Ld. Regd. 1886. Vol. liq. 16 Nov. 1891. Final meeting return regd. 15 Jan. 1897 .... **1892**

Venezuelan Consolidated Oilfields Ld. Regd. 1919 as Trinidad Friendship Petroleum Co. Ld.; name changed Feb. 1927. Court Order to wind up Apr. 1932. Struck off Register 17 July 1942 .... **1943**

Venezuelan Match Monopoly Ld. *See* National Match Factory of Venezuela Ld.

Venezuelan Oilfields Exploration Co. Ld. Regd. 1911. Vol. liq. Dec. 1919, the undertaking and assets sold to Oilfields Finance Corporation Ld., in which company shareholders were entitled to 2½ shares of 4s. for each participating preference share of £1 held, or for every 10 deferred shares of 1s. held. Final meeting return regd. 17 Nov. 1920 .... **1920**

Venezuelan Salt Monopoly Ld. *See* National Salt Co. of Venezuela Ld.

Venice Hotels Ld. Regd. 1898. Vol. liq. Apr. 1906. Undertaking transferred to an Italian company. Removed from Register 1907 .... **1907**

Venner Ld. *See* Cloxwiches Ld.

Venner Time Switches Ld. *See* Cloxwiches Ld.

Venner's Cigarette Machine Co. Ld. Regd. 1898. Reconstructed as company of same name. Removed from Register 1909 .... **1902**

Venner's Cigarette Machine Co. Ld. Regd. 1902. Vol. liq. 13 Jan. 1909. Final meeting return regd. 12 July 1909. Court Order to postpone dissolution for 6 months (12 Oct. 1909) and 12 months (8 Apr. 1910) ***1910**

Veno Drug Co. Ld. Regd. 1908. Vol. liq. Jan. 1925. Proprietary medicine business was acquired by Veno Drug Co. (1925) Ld. (later Veno Drug Co. Ld.) for cash. Struck off Register Mar. 1929 .... **1930**

Veno Drug Co. Ld. Regd. 1925 as Veno Drug Co. (1925) Ld.; name changed 1932. Vol. liq. (members') 17 May 1954. Preference and preferred ordinary shares (of £1) repaid at par together with ex-gratia payments of 4s. and 9s. 6d. per share respectively. £1,319 was paid into Companies' Liquidation Account. Final meeting return regd. 2 Feb. 1956 **1956**

Veno Drug Co. (1925) Ld. *See above.*

Veno Trust Ld. Reg. 1925. Vol. liq. (members') 18 Oct. 1963. Final meeting return regd. 19 Aug. 1964 .... **1947**

Ventanas Mining & Exploration Co. Ld. Regd. 1907. Vol. liq. 20 Apr. 1911. Liquidation stayed by Court Order 8 July 1925. Vol. liq. 18 Nov. 1927 for reconstruction as New Ventanas Mining & Exploration Co. Ld. Struck off Register 8 Apr. 1938 .... ***1912**

Ventersdorp Gold Estates Ld. Regd. 1925. Reconstructed 1900 as Ventersdorp Proprietary Co. Ld., in which company shareholders were entitled to 1 share of 10s. (credited with 7s. 6d. paid) for each share of £1 held. Removed from Register 1906 ..... **1908**

Ventersdorp Proprietary Co. Ld. Regd. 1900. Vol. liq. 27 Aug. 1914. Final meeting return regd. 5 Aug. 1916 **1915**

Ventiheta (United Kingdom) Ld. Regd. 1919. Vol. liq. Feb. 1925. Struck off Register Mar. 1930 .... **1931**

Ventnor Electric Light & Power Co, Ld. *See* Isle of Wight Electric Light & Power Co. Ld.

Ventnor Gas & Water Co. Inc. by Special Act 1866. By Act of 1931, the water undertaking was acquired by Ventnor Urban District Council for £21,500; out of this amount mortgage bonds for £9,150 were repaid, and distributions were made of £6 per share to holders of original (10% maximum) shares and £5 per share to holders of new ordinary (7% maximum) shares and preference shares; the nominal and paid-up amount of each of the original, new ordinary and preference shares was reduced from £20 to £15. By Order of 1932, the gas undertaking was acquired by Shanklin Gas Co. (later East Wight Gas Co.), in which company holders of original 10% shares were entitled to £15 consolidated ordinary stock for each share held; holders of new ordinary 7% shares and preference shares were entitled to £10 10s. consolidated ordinary stock for each share held **1930**

Ventnor Inclined (Light) Railway Co. Ld. Regd. 1898. Struck off Register 22 Dec. 1903 .... **1907**

Venture Corporation Ld. Regd. 1897. In 1908 shareholders were offered 23 fully-paid shares of 4s. and 100 shares of 4s. (credited with 2s. paid) in London Venture Corporation Ld. for every 100 shares of £1 held. Vol. liq. Oct. 1909. Removed from Register 1913 .... **1910**

Venture Trust Ld. Regd. 1913. Vol. liq. 19 Nov. 1919. Reconstructed as company of same name. Shareholders were entitled to 1 share of 10s. (credited as fully-paid) in new company for every 10 shares of 4s. held. Final meeting return regd. 21 July 1921 ...... **1920**

Venture Trust, Ld. Regd. 1917. Vol. liq. (members') 21 July 1950. Capital returned to contributories—6s. 3·375d. per stock unit of 6s. 8d. £4,901 7s. 10d. was paid into Companies' Liquidation Account. Final meeting return regd. 3 Dec. 1951 .... **1952**

Vera Cruz & Pacific Railroad Co. *See* Vera Cruz to Isthmus Railroad.

Vera Cruz Electric Light, Power & Traction Ld. Regd. 1906. A majority of the capital was owned by American & Foreign Power Co. Inc. In 1956 the undertaking was transferred to a Mexican company, Compania Electrica Mexicana del Sureste, S.A. in exchange for securities of that company. Struck off Register 9 Sept. 1960 .... **1959**

Vera Cruz Mexican Oil Co. Ld. Regd. 1914. Vol. liq. 30 Nov. 1915. Final meeting return regd. 6 Jan. ***1917**

Vera Cruz Terminal Co. Ld. Regd. 1907. Holders received £54 8s. 5d. in final satisfaction of each 44% debenture of £100. Struck off Register 15 Nov. 1957 **1951**

Vera Cruz to Isthmus Railroad. Inc. West Virginia 1898 as Vera Cruz & Pacific Railroad Co.; reincorporated under Laws of Mexico 1908. All capital held by Mexican Government. The 4½% 1st mortgage Guaranteed Gold Bonds of 1934 were taken over by National Railways of Mexico **1918**

Veredas Lead Mining Co. Ld. Regd. 1907. Vol. liq. Dec. 1910. Removed from Register 1912 .... **1911**

Vereingte Kunstseide-Fabriken A.G. Undertaking acquired in 1928 by Vereingte Glanzstoff Fabriken . **1937**

Veritys Founders' Ld. Regd. 1917. Vol. liq. 22 July 1919. Final meeting return regd. 11 Dec. 1919 .... ***1920**

Veritys, Ld. Regd. 1896. Vol. liq. (creditors') 9 Mar. 1959. No capital returned to contributories. Final meeting return regd. 28 Mar. 1961 .... **1962**

Vermilion Forks Mining & Development Co. Ld. Regd. 1898. Vol. liq. 11 Feb. 1910 for sale of assets to Princeton Coal & Land Co. Ld. in which company shareholders were entitled to 1¾ shares of £1 (credited as fully-paid) for each ordinary share of £1 held, or 10½ shares of £1 (credited as fully-paid) for each A share of £1 held. Final meeting return regd. 21 May 1917 .... **1911**

Vernco Steamship Co. Ld. Regd. 1919. Vol. liq. 5 Oct. 1921. Final meeting return regd. 30 Aug. 1924 ..... **1922**

Vernon Lockwood Manufacturing Co. Ld. *See* Goldring Ld.

Vernon & Nelson Telephone Co. *See* British Columbia Telephone Co.

Vernon (W.) & Sons Ld. Regd. 1920. Vol. liq. 31 Jan. 1927. Controlling interest held by Spillers Milling & Associated Industries Ld. (later Spillers Ld.). Final meeting return regd. 23 Jan. 1928 .... **1927**

Veteripont Estates Ld. Regd. 1925. Vol. liq. (members') 3 June 1949. Certain assets distributed in specie. Capital returned to contributories—20s. per preference share of £1 and 22s. 9d. per ordinary share of £1. Final meeting return regd. 31 Aug. 1950 .... **1951**

Vesta Gold Mining Co. Ld. Inc. South African Republic 1892. In liquidation in 1899 .... **1899**

Vestfold Shipping Co. Ld. Regd. 1934 as Vestfold Whaling Co. Ld., name changed 1 Feb. 1949. Nearly all capital was owned by Viking International Corpn. Ld. Vol. liq. (members') 29 July 1960. Final meeting return regd. 5 July 1961 .... **1957**

VOL. FOR

Vestfold Whaling Co. Ld. *See above.*

Vette (H.) (Dutch Oysters) Ld. Regd. 1911. Vol. liq. Aug. 1912. Removed from Register 1914 .... **1913**

Veuve Monnier et ses Fils Ld. Regd. 1890. Court Order to wind up 16 Jan. 1895. Removed from Register 1909 .... **1896**

Viborita Gold Mines Ld. Regd. 1929. Vol. liq. (members') 17 Apr. 1945. Assets did not realise sufficient to repay debenture holders in full. Final meeting return regd. 9 May 1950. .... **1951**

Vickerman (B.) & Sons Ld. *See* Hillbrigg Textiles Ld.

Vickers & International Combustion Engineering Ld. *See* Taylor, Usher & Young Ld.

Vickers (Crayford) Ld. Regd. 1928. Vol. liq. (members') 25 Nov. 1931. All shares owned by Vickers Ld. Final meeting return regd. 23 Nov. 1932 .... **1932**

Vickers-Petters Ld. *See* Petters (Ipswich) Ld.

Vickers (Thomas) & Sons Ld. Regd. 1908. Vol. liq. (members') 8 June 1944. All shares held by National Fertilizers Ld. Final meeting return regd. 29 Sept. 1944 .... **1945**

Victor Cycle Co. Ld. Regd. 1896. Vol. liq. 10 Feb. 1898. Final meeting return regd. 25 July 1908 .... ***1898**

Victor Gas Engine Co. Ld. Regd. 1883. Court Orders: to wind up 14 June 1884; to dissolve 13 Feb. 1893... ***1884**

Victor Mill Ld. Regd. 1903. Vol. liq. 7 Feb. 1929. Final meeting return regd. 1 Oct. 1931 .... **1930**

Victor Talking Machine Co. Inc. New Jersey 1901. All common stock acquired in 1929 by Radio Corporation of America and substantially all business and assets transferred to R.C.A. Victor Co. Inc. In Jan. 1935 the secretary stated that company was in process of dissolution **1935**

Victor (Transvaal) Exploration Co. Ld. Regd. 1897. Vol. liq. 12 July 1906. Removed from Register 1907.... **1907**

Victor Tyre Co. Ld. Regd. 1910 as Challenge Reinforced Tube Co. Ld.; name changed Feb. 1913. Vol. liq. Jan. 1921. Struck off Register 1929 .... **1921**

Victor Waihou Gold Mining Co. Ld. Regd. 1895. Vol. liq. 30 Dec. 1897. Final meeting return regd. 24 Aug. 1898 .... **1899**

Victoria and Albert Hotel Co. Ld. Regd. 1870. Vol. liq. (members') 29 May 1947. Capital returned to contributories—£4 5*s*. 6*d*. per share of £1. Final meeting return regd. 7 Jan. 1949 .... **1949**

Victoria & Altamira Ld. Regd. 1893. Vol. liq. 20 Dec. 1895. Reconstructed as Victory Gold Mining Co. Ld., in which company shareholders were entitled to 1 share of 5*s*. (credited with 4*s*. paid) for each share of 5*s*. held. Final meeting return regd. 17 June 1897 **1896**

Victoria & Queen Gold Mining Co. Ld. Inc. Queensland 1891. Reconstructed under same name. Shareholders were entitled to receive 1 share of £1 (credited 16*s*. paid) in new company for each share of £1 held **1908**

Victoria & Queen Gold Mining Co. Ld. Inc. Queensland 1901. Wound up June 1912. Capital returned to contributories—5*s*. 6*d*. per 100 shares of 10*s*. in Dec. 1912; further distributions (if any) not known **1914**

Victoria & Sidney Railway Co. Inc. under Act of British Columbia 1892. In July 1920 the secretary of the bondholders' committee announced that the receiver had sold bulk of company's assets. Holders received £43 17*s*. 2*d*. per $1,000 bond; further payments (if any) not known **1921**

Victoria Bread & Biscuit Co. Ld. Regd. 1886. Vol. liq. 18 Feb. 1889. Final meeting return regd. 21 May 1891 **1890**

Victoria Copper Co. Ld. *See* West Australian Mining Co. Ld.

Victoria Cycle Co. Ld. *See* Victoria Motor & Cycle Co. Ld.

Victoria District (Mashonaland) Gold Mining Co. Ld. Regd. 1893. Vol. liq. 18 Nov. 1898. Final meeting return regd. 22 Sept. 1900 .... **1899**

Victoria Docks Gas Co. Under Act of 1857 the undertaking was acquired by Gas Light and Coke Co. **1888**

Victoria Dry Docks Co. (Swansea) Ld. Regd. 1897. Undertaking was sold to Swansea Central Dry Docks Ld. Vol. liq. 23 Oct. 1907. Final meeting return regd. 14 Dec. 1907 .... **1904**

Victoria Electric Railway & Lighting Co. Ld. Inc. British Columbia 1889. Absorbed in 1896 by Consolidated Railway Co. of Vancouver **1898**

Victoria Enterprises Ld. Regd. 1920. Vol. liq. (members') 7 June 1956. Final meeting return regd. 9 Sept. 1957 .... **1940**

Victoria Exploration & Land Co. of Swazieland, South Africa, Ld. Regd. 1889. Removed from Register 1895 .... ***1890**

Victoria Falls & Transvaal Power Co. Ld. Inc. in Southern Rhodesia 1906 as Victoria Falls Power Co. Ld.; name changed Feb. 1909. Vol. liq. 31 Mar. 1949. Capital returned to contributories—preference stock at par; ordinary £9 1*s*. 4*d*. per £1 stock. Return of final meeting was lodged with the Master of the High Court in Salisbury on 26 June 1959 .. **1960**

Victoria Falls Power Co. Ld. *See above.*

Victoria Gold Co. Ld. Regd. 1882. Vol. liq. 29 Dec. 1885. Final meeting return regd. 6 Sept. 1893 .... **1886**

Victoria Gold Dredging Company No. Liability. Inc. Victoria 1963. Vol. liq. (members') 10 Sept. 1957. Capital returned to contributories —125,000 shares (of 10*s*.) in Central Victoria Dredging Co. N.L. in proportion to the number of shares held (9,000 £1 shares were fully-paid and 241,000 £1 shares were 10*s*. paid) plus 2*d*. in cash for every share held. £44 0*s*. 11*d*. was paid into Companies' Liquidation Account. Struck off register 13 Nov. 1963 .... **1965**

Victoria Gramophones Ld. *See* Victoria Woodworking Ld.

Victoria Hall Co. Ld. Regd. 1869. Vol. liq. 18 July 1917. Final meeting return regd. 27 Dec. 1918 .... **1918**

"Victoria-Hansom" Cab Co. Ld. Regd. 1887. Vol. liq. 16 Apr. 1888. Court Order to continue winding up under supervision May 1888. Final meeting return regd. 23 Sept. 1891 .... **1889**

Victoria Investment Corporation Ld. Regd. 1899. Vol. liq. 6 Nov. 1907. Final meeting return regd. 18 Dec. 1919 .... **1908**

Victoria (London) Mining Co. Ld. Regd. 1860. Vol. liq. 7 July 1896. Final meeting return regd. 14 July 1897 **1897**

Victoria (London) Property & Commercial Trust Ld. Regd. 1920 as Grosvenor Property & Commercial Trust Ld.; name changed Nov. 1921. Vol. liq. Mar. 1931. Court Order to wind up Apr. 1931. Struck off Register 27 Jan. 1942 .... **1942**

Victoria (Malaya) Rubber Estates Ld. Regd. 1910. Vol. liq. 16 May 1927. Undertaking and assets were acquired by Bikam Rubber Estate Ld., for 1,085,000 fully-paid shares of 2*s*. Final meeting return regd. 23 Nov. 1927 .... **1928**

Victoria Mineral Concession Ld. Regd. 1892. Removed from Register 1904 .... **1897**

Victoria Motor & Cycle Co. Ld. Regd. in Edinburgh 1899 as Victoria Cycle Co. Ld. name changed 1906. Vol. liq. 28 Nov. 1947. Capital returned to contributories—£1 per preference share of £1; 3*s*. 0½*d*. per ordinary share of 5*s*. £165 10*s*. 1*d*. was paid to the Accountant of the Court. Final meeting return regd. 14 Oct. 1948 .... **1949**

Victoria Mutual Assurance Society Ld. Inc. by Act of 1860 and regd. 1882. Vol. liq. Dec. 1909. Undertaking was amalgamated with Norwich Union Life Insurance Society. Removed from Register 1910 .. **1910**

Victoria Newmarket Gas Light & Coke Co. Ld. *See* Newmarket Gas Co.

Victoria Nyanza Sugar Co. Ld. Inc. Victoria 1921. Liquidation of company, which began in Dec. 1947, was completed in Dec. 1948. Capital returned to contributories—28*s*. per share of £1 .... **1949**

Victoria Oil & Refining Co. Ld. Regd. 1924. Vol. liq. (creditors') 5 Nov. 1930. Undertaking and assets were acquired by British National Petroleum Refineries Ld. for 600,000 fully-paid shares of 1*s*. Final meeting return regd. 7 Mar. 1939 .... **1930**

Victoria Palace Ld. Regd. 1910. Vol. liq. (members') 28 July 1955. Capital returned to contributories—12*s*. 7·7327*d*. per share of 3*s*. 4*d*. Final meeting return regd. 19 Apr. 1956 .... **1957**

Victoria Picture Theatres Ld. Regd. 1910. Vol. liq. 27 Aug. 1917. Final meeting return regd. 5 Sept. 1918 **1911**

Victoria Plastering Co. Ld. Regd. 1933 as Carbo Plastering Co. Ld.; name changed in Jan. 1935. All shares held by Carbo Plaster Ld., which company acquired undertaking. Vol. liq. (members') 2 Apr. 1935. Final meeting return regd. 31 Mar. 1936 .... **1940**

Victoria Proprietary Ld. Regd. 1902. Vol. liq. 8 June 1903. Reconstructed as Victoria Proprietary (1903) Ld. Final meeting return regd. 28 Apr. 1914 .... ***1904**

Victoria Proprietary (1903) Ld. Regd. 1903. Vol. liq. 26 Mar. 1913. Final meeting return regd. 1 Mar. 1921 **1914**

Victoria Proprietary (1913) Ld. Regd. 1913. Vol. liq. 24 Nov. 1916. Final meeting return regd. 30 May 1923 ***1917**

Victoria Reef Gold Mine Ld. Regd. 1896. Vol. liq. 15 Feb. 1898. Final meeting return regd. 24 Oct. 1901 **1899**

Victoria Spinning Co. (Rochdale) Ld. Regd. 1920. Vol. liq. (members') 31 Mar. 1960. Final meeting return regd. 13 Oct. 1961 .... **1947**

Victoria Standard Gold Mines Ld. Regd. 1903. Struck off Register 4 Oct. 1907 .... **1908**

Victoria Station and Pimlico Railway Co. Inc. by Special Act 1858. In 1923 the undertaking was merged into the Southern Railway Co. in which company stockholders were entitled to stock as follows:

For each £100 held	*S. R.*
4½% Debenture	£113½ 4% Debenture
4½% Preference	£113 4% Debenture
Ordinary	£230¾ 4% Debenture

1924

**See Stock Exchange Year-Book.*

VOL. FOR

Victoria Steamboat Association Ld. Regd. 1888. Removed from Register 1906 1896

Victoria Woodworking Ld. Regd. 1928 as Victoria Gramophones Ld.; name changed Dec. 1929. Vol. liq. (members') 18 Dec. 1930. Undertaking and assets transferred to Dependable Upholstery Ld., in which company shareholders were entitled to 1 share of 1s. (credited with 6d. paid) for every 3 shares of 1s. held. Final meeting return regd. 30 May 1932 1931

Victoria A1 Gold Mines Ld. Regd. 1901. Vol. liq. Dec. 1905. Undertaking and assets were acquired by Victorian Mining Co. Ld. Removed from Register 1912 1907

Victorian Consolidated Goldfields Ld. Regd. 1905. Removed from Register 1910 1908

Victorian Cornish Gold Mines Ld. Regd. 1903. Vol. liq. May 1910. Removed from Register 1911 1911

Victorian Deep Leads Ld. Regd. 1898. Reconstructed under same name in 1903. Shareholders were entitled to 1 share of £1 (credited with 18s. paid) in new company for each share of £1 held. Removed from Register 1908 1906

Victorian Deep Leads Ld. Inc. New South Wales 1903. Reconstructed as Victorian Deep Leads (1906) Ld., in which company shareholders were entitled to receive 5 shares of £1 for every 8 shares of £1 held ... 1908

Victorian Deep Leads (1906) Ld. Inc. New South Wales 1906. Vol. liq. May 1911. Undertaking and assets were acquired by Malkop Orient Oil Co. Ld., in which company shareholders were entitled to 1 share of 2s. (credited as fully-paid) for each share of £1 held 1912

Victorian Freehold Bank Ld. See British Bank of Australia Ld.

Victorian Gold Estates Ld. Regd. 1896. Vol. liq. Feb. 1901. Removed from Register 1906 1901

Victorian Goldfields Ld. Regd. 1895. Removed from Register 1904 1907

Victorian Mining Co. Ld. Regd. 1901. Vol. liq. Oct. 1910. Removed from Register 1912 1911

Victorian Mount Morgan Mining & Ore Treatment Co. Ld. Regd. 1901. Removed from Register 1906 1905

Victorian Star Gold Mines Ld. Regd. 1906. Vol. liq. Feb. 1911. Removed from Register 1913 1911

Victorine Gold Mining Co. Ld. Regd. 1881. Vol. liq. 21 Feb. 1883. Court Order to continue winding up under supervision Mar. 1883. Struck off Register 11 Aug. 1905 1884

Victors (Hosiery) Ld. Regd. 1931. Vol. liq. (members') 15 Nov. 1935. Undertaking was acquired by Victors Stores Ld. Final meeting return regd. 15 Dec. 1945 ... 1940

Victors Stores Ld. Regd. 1935. Vol. liq. (creditors') 13 June 1940. No capital returned to contributories. Final meeting return regd. 30 Jan. 1946 1946

Victory (Charters Towers) Gold Mining Co. Ld. Inc. New South Wales 1893. Wound up June 1918 1919

Victory Gold Mining Co. Ld. Regd. 1888. Vol. liq. 9 June 1892. Reconstructed as Altamira Ld. Final meeting return regd. 7 Apr. 1894 1893

Victory Gold Mining Co. Ld. Regd. 1895. Vol. liq. 27 Dec. 1900. Reconstructed as Victory-Lydenburg Gold Co. Ld., in which company shareholders were entitled to 1 share of 5s. (credited with 4s. paid) for each fully-paid share of 5s. held. Final meeting return regd. 4 Mar. 1902 1901

Victory Hill Consolidated Gold Mining Co. Ld. Regd. 1889. Absorbed by Barberton Estates and Gold Mining Co. Ld. Removed from Register 1901 1896

"Victory" Ld. Regd. 1886. Court Orders: to wind up 26 Nov. 1887; to dissolve 31 Aug. 1893 1888

Victory-Lydenburg Gold Co. Ld. Regd. 1900. Vol. liq. Dec. 1906 for amalgamation with Mayblossom Mining Co. Ld., in which company shareholders were entitled to 1 share of £1 (credited with 16s. paid) for every 4 ordinary or preference shares of 5s. held. Removed from Register 1908 1907

Victory Oil & Cake Mills Ld. Regd. 1919. Vol. liq. 6 June 1922. Final meeting return regd. 7 May 1924 ... 1924

Victory Real Estate Co. Ld. Regd. 1919. Vol. liq. 26 Oct. 1964. Capital returned to contributories (per 1s. stock)—6d. in 1966; 11¾d. in 1968 and 0·05p in 1975. Final meeting return regd. 6 Oct. 1979. £1,750·19 was paid into Companies' Liquidation Account .1981—2

Victory Warehouse Co. Ld. Regd. 1919. Vol. liq. (members') 15 July 1931. Capital returned to contributories—2s. 6d. per share of 5s. Final meeting return regd. 18 July 1933 1932

Viella Copper Co. Ld. Regd. 1901. Court Order to wind up 13 Jan. 1903. Removed from Register 1916 1903

Vienna General Omnibus Co. Ld. Regd. 1881. A receiver for debenture holders was appointed in Dec. 1903. The Vienna City Council agreed to pay £58,350 for buildings and stock. Struck off Register 1915 1909

VOL. FOR

Vienna Ice Co. Ld. Regd. 1882. Vol. liq. 8 Aug. 1913. Capital returned to contributories—4s. 6d. per share of £1 at Oct. 1913; further payments (if any) not known. Final meeting return regd. 18 Jan. 1923 ... 1914

Vienna Motor Cab Co. Ld. Regd. 1909. Vol. liq. 26 June 1928. Capital returned to contributories—20 Belgian francs per preferred share of £1; further payments (if any) not known. Final meeting return regd. 20 May 1930 1929

Vienna Works Ld. Regd. 1912. Struck off Register 1917 1915

View Forth Investment Trust Ld. Regd. in Edinburgh as a private company 28 Dec. 1962; converted into a public company 1 Mar. 1963. Vol. liq. (members') 3 Aug. 1979. 4,823,494 units in Crescent Reserve Fund issued to holders on basis of 1·60 units per share. First and final distribution of 1·719p per share made in Mar. 1980. Final meeting held 7 Jan. 1981 .... 1984—5

Viking Gold Mines Ld. Inc. Rhodesia 1910. Wound up Sept. 1914 1915

Viking Investment Trust Ld. Regd. 1928 as Bouvet Whaling Co. Ld.; name changed to Viking Whaling Co. Ld. in 1928 and as above in 1940. Vol. liq. (members') 15 Oct. 1953. Capital returned to contributories—preference shares of 10s. were repaid at par; ordinary shareholders were entitled to receive 1 share of £1 in Viking Tanker Co. Ld. (later Viking International Corpn. Ld.) for every 2 shares held and a cash payment of £3 9s. 2·71d. per ordinary share of 10s. Final meeting return regd. 12 July 1954 1955

Viking Manufacturing Co. Ld. Regd. 1912. Receiver for debenture holders appointed May 1914. Vol. liq. June 1914. Struck off Register 1918 1915

Viking Syndicate Ld. Regd. 1902. Removed from Register 1910 1908

Viking Whaling Co. Ld. See Viking Investment Trust Ld.

Vilaque Bolivian Tin Mines Ld. Regd. 1913. Struck off Register 1922 1921

Villa Maria & Rufino Railway Co. Ld. Regd. 1888. Vol. liq. (members) 1 April 1948. The undertaking was acquired by the Argentine Government as from 1 July 1946. The 4% debenture stock was repaid at par on 19 May 1948 and repayment of £60 per £100 guaranteed stock, in full and final satisfaction was made on 4 Oct. 1948. £629 12s. 4d. was paid into Companies' Liquidation Account. Final meeting return regd.7 Apr.1954 1955

Villa Nova Rubber Estates & Trading Co. Ld. Regd. 1911. Vol. liq. 19 Nov. 1913. Final meeting return regd. 8 Feb. 1923 1914

Village Deep Ld. Inc. Transvaal 1898. Vol. liq. (members') 2 May 1935. Certain assets were acquired by Robinson Deep Ld. 1936

Village Main Reef Gold Mining Co. Ld. Regd. 1890. Vol. liq. 11 Feb. 1921. Final meeting return regd. 6 June 1924 1921

Villamartin & Gibraltar Oil Co. Ld. Regd. 1910. Struck off Register 1916 1915

Villier's Hotel Co. Ld. Inc. Isle of Man 1880. In liquidation in 1908 1908

Villier's Hotel Ld. Inc. Isle of Man. 1896 1910

Viloro Syndicate Ld. Regd. 1904. Vol. liq. 26 Sept. 1916. Final meeting return regd. 1 Feb. 1917 1917

Vimax Machinery Co. Ld. Regd. 1929. Court Order to wind up Nov. 1931. Struck off Register 18 Feb. 1938 1929

Vimbos Ld. Regd. 1897. In liquidation. Undertaking sold to Bovril Ld. for £27,500. Liquidator stated (27 Sept. 1899) that amount realised after paying debenture holders would be hardly sufficient to meet claims of unsecured creditors. Removed from Register 1906 1900

Vincent (25-mile Coolgardie) Ld. Regd. 1896. The property was sold to Emperor Gold Mines Ld. Removed from Register 1901 1899

Vincent's Rhodesia Ld. Regd. 1897. Removed from Register 1910 1904

Vincent's Rhodesian Development Co. Ld. Regd. 1895. Reconstructed 1897 as Vincent's Rhodesia Ld., in which company shareholders were entitled to 1 share of £1 (credited with 17s. 6d. paid) for each share of £1 held. Removed from Register 1908 1901

Vince's Dry Batteries Ld. Regd. 1930. Vol. liq. (members') 1 Dec. 1948. A subsidiary of Ever Ready Co. (Great Britain) Ld. Final meeting return regd. 1 Mar. 1949 1940

Vine & General Rubber Trust Ld. See Plantations Trust Ld.

Vine Mill (Royton) Ld. Regd. 1920. Dissolved under Section 208 of Companies' Act 1948, on 25 Nov. 1949 undertaking and assets having been acquired by Royton Textile Corpn. Ld., in which company

See Stock Exchange Year-Book.

VOL. FOR

Vymo Cork Stopper Co, Ld. Regd. 1906. Court Order to wind up 1907. Removed from Register 1911 .... **1908**

W

W. A. G. Assets Co. Ld. Regd. 1910. Vol. liq. (creditors') 14 Sept. 1931. No capital returned to contributories. Final meeting return regd. 14 Dec. 1931 .... **1932**

W. & J. Sagar Ld. *See* Sagar (W. & J.) (Holdings) Ld.

W. A. P. Co. Ld. Regd. 1910. Vol. liq. 8 Dec. 1913. Final meeting return regd. 9 Feb. 1916 .... **1914**

W. C. B. (Holdings) Ld. *See* Welwyn Commercial Buldings Ld.

W. G. Frityh & Co. Ld. *See* Frith (W. G.) & Co. Ld.

W. H. Chaplin & Co. Ld. *See* Chaplin Holdings Ld.

W. J. Nine Silver Mines Ld. (*See* Huronian Belt).

W. L. Co. Ld. Regd. 1922 as Whittaker Loucks Co. Ld.; name changed Apr. 1929. Vol. liq. (members') 28 Dec. 1932. Capital returned to contributories–£41 9s. 3d. Final meeting return regd. 21 Apr. 1936 .. **1932**

W. W. Diamond Syndicate Ld. Regd. 1907. Vol. liq. July 1909. Undertaking and assets were acquired by New Vaal River Diamond Exploration Co. Ld. [later New Vaal Farms Ld.] in which company shareholders were entitled to 1 share of £1 (credited as fully-paid) for every 4 shares of £1 held. Removed from Register 1910 .... **1910**

Wa Syndicate Ld. Regd. 1901. Vol. liq. 24 June 1907. Final meeting return regd. 9 July 1908 .... **1908**

Wabash Railroad Co. Organised Michigan in 1889. Reorganised 22 Oct. 1915 as Wabash Railway Co **1915**

Wabash Railway Co. Organised Indiana 1915. The properties and assets were acquired by Wabash Railroad Co. The shares of capital stock were determined by Court to be of no par value, but holders of profit sharing preferred stock A and common stock were entitled to purchase common no par value stock in new company at $12·75 per share. Holders of 1st mortgage 5% gold bonds were entitled to £850 1st mortgage 4% bonds and $283·33 general mortgage 4% income bonds series A in new company and $25 in cash for every $1,000 bond held. Holders of 6% debenture bonds series B were entitled to £868 general mortgage 4½% income bonds series B and $372 preferred stock in new company for every $1,000 bond held **1943**

Wackrill & Co. Ld. Regd. 1896. Vol. liq. 15 Apr. 1910. The preference capital had been repaid at 27 Oct. 1910; further payments (if any) not known. Final meeting return regd. 8 May 1915 .... **1911**

Wad Medani Light & Power Co. Ld. Regd. 1930. Capital purchased by Sudan Government and debenture stocks redeemed. Vol. liq. 31 Mar. 1959. Struck off Register 1 Feb. 1963 .... **1952**

Wadebridge & District Electric Supply Co. Ld. Regd. 1914. Vol. liq. (members') 30 Nov. 1931. Undertaking was acquired by Urban Electric Supply Co. Ld. Capital returned to contributories–20s. per preference share of £1; £2 10s. 4d. per ordinary share of £1. Final meeting return regd. 26 May 1932 .... **1932**

Wadebridge Gas Co. Ld. Regd. 1914. Dissolved 1 May 1949, undertaking being vested in South Western Area Gas Board under Gas Act 1948. Holders of securities were entitled to receive, British Gas 3% guaranteed stock 1990–95 as follows:

	£	s.	d.
Ord. shares (of £1)	4	9	0
5½% red. debs. (of £50)	50	10	0

1952

Wadhurst & District Gas & Coke Co. Inc. by Special Act 1914. Dissolved 1 May 1949 under Gas Act 1948 and undertaking vested in South Eastern Gas Board .. **1949**

Wadhurst, Ticehurst and District Gas Light & Coke Co. Inc. by Special Act 1902. Amalgamated in 1905 with Ticehurst and Robertsbridge Water Co. to form Ticehurst and District Water and Gas Co **1908**

Waihi Consolidated Gold Mines Ld. Regd. 1898. Vol. liq. 4 Aug. 1899. Final meeting return regd. 8 Mar. 1901 .... **1900**

Waihi Gladstone Gold Mining Co. Ld. Regd. 1896. Removed from Register 1903 .... **1901**

Waihi Gold Mining Co. Ld. Regd. 1897. Vol. liq. (members') 26 Sept. 1935. Certain investments were acquired by Martha Gold Mining Co. (Waihi) Ld. and the remaining assets were acquired by Waihi Investments & Exploration Ld. Shareholders were entitled to 1 fully-paid share of 5s. in each of the acquiring companies *plus* 3s. in cash for each share of 5s. held. Final meeting return regd. 24 June 1936 **1936**

Waihi Grand Junction Gold Co. Ld. Regd. 1897. Vol. liq. (members') 1 Mar. 1939. Capital returned to contributories–3s. 1¾d. per share of £1. £262 15s.

VOL. FOR

7d. was paid into Companies' Liquidation Account in respect of unclaimed dividends. Final meeting return regd. 20 Feb. 1940 .... **1940**

Waihi Grand Junction Syndicate Ld. Regd. 1894. Vol. liq. 3 Oct. 1895. Final meeting return regd. 22 May 1896 .... **1896**

Waihi Proprietary Co. Ld. Regd. 1895. Vol. liq. 28 Feb. 1896. Final meeting return regd. 16 June 1896 .... **1897**

Waihi Silverton Extended Gold Mining Co. Ld. Regd. 1895. Vol. liq. 24 Mar. 1898. Reconstructed as Waihi Silverton Gold Mines Ld., in which company shareholders were entitled to 1 share of £1 (credited with 15s. paid) for each share of £1 held. Final meeting return regd. 22 Nov. 1899 .... **1900**

Waihi Silverton Gold Mines Ld. Regd. 1898. Removed from Register 1901 .... **1902**

Waikato Land Association Ld. *See* New Zealand Land Association Ld.

Wainfleet & Firsby (Extension to Skegness) Railway Co. Inc. by Special Act 1872. Under Great Northern Railway Act of 1895 the undertaking was absorbed into that company. Shareholders received £17 per share in cash **1896**

Wainfleet & Firsby Railway Co. Inc. by Special Act 1869. Under Great Northern Railway Act of 1895 the undertaking was absorbed into that company. Shareholders received £17 per share in cash. The purchasing company assumed the debenture debt **1896**

Waitahu (New Zealand) Colliery Co. Ld. Regd. 1917. Struck off Register 25 Mar. 1938 .... **1939**

Waitaia Gold Mines Ld. Regd. 1896. Vol. liq. Sept. 1909. Removed from Register 1909 .... **1909**

Waitekauri Central Gold Mine Ld. Regd. 1895. Vol. liq. 2 Dec. 1896. Taken over by Waitekauri Extended. Final meeting return regd. 4 May 1897 .... ***1898**

Waitekauri Consolidated Gold Mines Ld. Regd. 1896. Removed from Register 1911 .... **1899**

Waitekauri Cross Gold Mining Co. Ld. Regd. 1896. In liquidation in 1902. Capital returned to contributories–3d. per share of £1 at July 1902; further payments (if any) not known. Removed from Register 1904 .... **1903**

Waitekauri Extended Ld. Regd. 1895. Vol. liq. 30 Dec. 1897. Reconstructed 1898 as company of same name. Shareholders were entitled to 1 share of 10s. (credited with 8s. 6d. paid) in new company for each share of 10s. held. Final meeting return regd. 24 Aug. 1898 .... **1901**

Waitekauri Extended Ld. Regd. 1898. Vol. liq. 7 June 1901. Undertaking and assets were acquired by (New) Waitekauri Extended Mines Ld. for £14,579 and repayment of debentures. The priority shares of 10s. were repaid. Final meeting return regd. 16 Apr. 1903 .... **1902**

Waitekauri Gold Mining Co. Ld. Regd. 1895. Certain assets were acquired by Sudan Exploration Ld., in which company shareholders were entitled to 1 fully-paid share of 10s. and 5 shares of 5s. in Komata Reefs Company for every 5 shares of £1 held. Removed from Register 1906 .... **1905**

Waitekauri Union Claims Ld. Regd. 1896. Vol. liq. 14 July 1899. Final meeting return regd. 1 Mar. 1900 **1900**

Waitekauri United Gold Mining Co. Ld. Regd. 1896. Removed from Register 1910 .... **1901**

Wakefield & Barnsley Union Bank Ld. Established 1832 as Wakefield Banking Co.; name changed 1840. Regd. as unlimited 1875 and as limited 1884. Vol. liq. 16 Oct. 1906. Undertaking was acquired by Birmingham District and Counties Banking Co. Ld. (later United Counties Bank Ld.), in which company shareholders were entitled to 1½ shares of £20 (credited with £4 per share paid) for every share of £50 (£13 10s. paid) held **1907**

Wakefield Gaslight Co. Estd. 1822; Inc. by Special Act 1847. Dissolved 1 May 1949, undertaking being vested in North Eastern Area Gas Board under Gas Act 1948. Holders of securities were entitled to receive, in respect of each £100 unit held, British Gas 3% guaranteed stock 1990–95 as follows:

	£	s.	d.
Ord. stock (5% stand.)	120	0	0
5% max. stock	111	5	0
4½% pref. stock	110	0	0
Liability in respect of certain mortgage loans assumed by the Board			**1952**

Wakefield Mines Ld. Regd. Edinburgh 1898. Vol. liq. Jan. 1909. Final meeting return regd. 20 Apr. 1915 **1909**

Wakefield Rolling Stock Co. Ld. Regd. 1872. Vol. liq. 31 Mar. 1872. Taken over by Yorkshire Railway Waggon Co. Ld. Final meeting return regd. 9 Dec. 1892 .... **1893**

Wala-Wynaad Indian Gold Mining Co. Ld. Regd. 1880. Court Orders: to wind up Aug. 1882; to dissolve 2 Jan. 1891 .... **1883**

*See Stock Exchange Year-Book.

VOL. FOR

Walbrook Trust Ld. Regd. 1918 as Covent Garden Estate Co. Ld.; name changed July 1924. Vol. liq. (members') 5 Nov. 1936. Assets were distributed in specie among contributories. Final meeting return regd. 13 July 1937. Court Orders deferred dissolution to 12 July 1938 1937

Waldon's Find Gold Mines Ld. Regd. 1895. Vol. liq. 1 Dec. 1897. Reconstructed as company of same name. Shareholders were entitled to 1 share of 10s. (credited with 9s. paid) in new company for each share of 10s. held. Final meeting return regd. 26 June 1899 1899

Waldon's Find Gold Mines Ld. Regd. 1897. Vol. liq. 30 Nov. 1899. Reconstructed as Kanowna Consolidated Gold Mines Ld., in which company shareholders were entitled to 1 share of 10s. (8s. paid) for each share of 10s. (9s. 9d. paid) held. Final meeting return regd. 31 May 1900 1902

Waldorf Palais de Danse Ld. Regd. Edinburgh 1926. Vol. liq. (members') 14 Mar. 1930. Undertaking and assets acquired by Scottish Cinema and Variety Theatres Ld. for 40,000 fully-paid ordinary shares. Final meeting return regd. 15 Feb. 1932 1931

Waldorf Theatre Syndicate Ld. Regd. 1903. Removed from Register 29 Aug. 1913 .... *1911

Walduck (H.) Properties Ld. Regd. 1911 as Imperial London Hotels Ld.; name subsequently changed. Vol. liq. (members') 24 Apr. 1951. Final meeting return regd. 11 Apr. 1956. *See under* Imperial London Hotels Ld. 1940

Walery Ld. Regd. 1890. In liquidation in 1900. Capital returned to contributories—6d. per share; further payments (if any) not known. Removed from Register 1907 1901

Wales & Laughton Light Railway Co. Inc. (under Light Railways Act 1896) by order of Light Railway Commissioners confirmed by Board of Trade 1901 1903

Walford (Leopold) Transports Ld. Regd. 1918. Vol. liq. (members') 29 Dec. 1933. Capital returned to contributories—5s. 0½d. per share of 10s. plus distribution of shares in new company of same name. Dissolved before 1938 1934

Walford Lines Ld. *See* Angola Holdings Ld.

Walker (Alexander) & Co. Ld. Regd. Edinburgh 1906. Vol. liq. (members') 30 June 1939. Capital returned to contributories—£1 14s. 7⅞d. per share of £1. Final meeting return regd. 6 July 1940 1940

Walker & Homfrays Ld. Regd 1896. Vol. liq. Nov. 1956. Undertaking acquired by Wilson's Brewery Ld. in 1953. All capital was owned by Wilson & Walker Breweries Ld. Final meeting return regd. 14 Mar. 1957 1955

Walker & Meimarachi Ld. Regd. 1897. Vol. liq. 17 July 1913. Final meeting return regd. 27 Apr. 1921 1914

Walker & Son Ld. Regd. 1896. Undertaking was acquired in 1904 by Charrington and Co. Ld. Removed from Register 1907 1902

Walker & Wallsend Union Gas Co. Inc. by Special Act 1866. Undertaking was acquired in 1924 by Newcastle-upon-Tyne & Gateshead Gas Co., in which company stockholders were entitled to £100 or £153 in 3½% ordinary stock for every £100 ordinary 3½% or ordinary 5% respectively held or £125 4% preference stock for every £100 5% preference stock held 1925

Walker (C. H.) & Co. Ld. Regd. 1898. Vol. liq. (members') 29 June 1948. Final meeting return regd. 10 Sept. 1959 1940

Walker (Edwin) & Co. Ld. Regd. 1897. Vol. liq. (members') 14 Oct. 1947. Final meeting returned regd. 19 Feb. 1949 1939

Walker (Edwin) & Co. Ld. Regd. 1947. Vol. liq. (creditors') 30 June 1960. Creditors received 10s. 6d. in the £1. Final meeting return regd. 28 Aug. 1964 1965

Walker (Hiram) & Sons (Scotland) Ld. Regd. Edinburgh 1936. Vol. liq. (members') 1 Nov. 1937. Capital returned to contributories—£14,842 16s. 4d. in cash plus certain assets distributed in specie. Final meeting return regd. 8 Oct. 1938 1938

Walker (J. & G.) (1920) Ld. Regd. 1920. Vol. liq. (members') 23 July 1947. Capital returned to contributories—5s. 6·2d. per share of 2s. 6d. £14 3s. 4d. was paid into Companies' Liquidation Account. Final meeting return regd. 17 Mar. 1948 1949

Walker (J. B.) & Co. Ld. Regd. 1905. Vol. liq. 15 Feb. 1926. Controlling interest held by Vegetable Oils & Margarine Ld. Final meeting return regd. 23 Dec. 1926 1927

Walker (J. R.) Ld. Regd. 1931. Vol. liq. (creditors') 10 Aug. 1934. Assets realised insufficient to repay unsecured creditors in full. Final meeting return regd. 25 Feb. 1936 1935

Walker, Kempson & Stevens Ld. Regd. 1896. Vol. liq. (members') 26 Nov. 1935. Capital returned to

VOL. FOR

contributories—17s. per 6% preference share of £1. Final meeting return regd. 11 Aug. 1937 1936

Walker, Maynard & Co. Ld. Regd. Dec. 1900. Vol. liq. 2 Mar. 1916. The undertaking and properties were sold to Dorman Long & Co. Ld. Final meeting return regd. 16 Oct. 1918 1916

Walker (Peter) & Son Property Corporation (No. 2) Ld. Regd. 1905. Vol. liq. (members') 18 Sept. 1934. Undertaking was acquired by Peter Walker & Son Warrington and Burton Ld. The preference and ordinary shares were repaid at par; the ordinary received the surplus amounting to £10,814. Final meeting return regd. 7 Nov. 1934 1935

Walkham United Mines Ld. Regd. Truro 1881. Order of Stannaries Court to wind up 4 Aug. 1882. Struck off Register 7 Mar. 1913 1883

Walkinshaw Oil Co. Ld. Regd. Edinburgh 1880. Vol. liq. Mar. 1890 for reconstruction as Hemand Oil Co. Ld. Final meeting return regd. 19 Mar. 1892 1892

Wall (George) & Co. Regd. 1897. Undertaking and assets were acquired in 1906 by Lovell and Christmas Ld. Preference shareholders received an equal amount of preference shares of £5 in acquiring company. Ordinary shareholders received 8,000 ordinary shares of £5 and £50,000 in debenture stock. Removed from Register 1907 1907

Wallace (Glasgow) Ld. Regd. Edinburgh 1920. Vol. liq. June 1924. Court Orders: to continue winding up under supervision July 1924; to dissolve 7 Apr. 1945 1925

Wallace (William) & Co. Ld. Regd. 1899 as William Wallace and Co. (1899) Ld. Vol. liq. May 1908. Removed from Register 1910 1909

Wallardie Tea Estates Ld. Regd. 1913. Vol. liq. 27 Apr. 1923. Estates and equipment were acquired by Malayalam Plantations Ld., in which company shareholders were entitled to 1 share of £1 (credited as fully-paid) for every 100 shares of 2s. held. Final meeting return regd. 12 June 1926 1929

Waller & Hartley Ld. Undertaking and assets were acquired by Waller & Hartley (1927) Ld. (later Waller & Hartley Ld.), for £80,000 in cash 1928

Waller & Son Ld. Regd. 1887. Vol. liq. 25 Aug. 1925. Undertaking was acquired by Waller's Bradford Brewery Ld. Final meeting return regd. 27 Nov. 1926 1926

Waller Housing Corporation Ld. Regd. 1919. Court Order to wind up 3 Aug. 1921. Liquidator released 28 Mar. 1928. Struck off Register 16 June 1931 .. 1922

Waller's Bradford Brewery Ld. Regd. 1925. Vol. liq. (members') 24 May 1935. Undertaking and assets were acquired by Leeds & Wakefield Breweries Ld. [later Melbourne Brewery (Leeds) Ld.]. Stockholders were entitled to 16⅔ preference shares of £1 in Brownsea Haven Properties Ld. plus £80 in cash for every £100 ordinary stock held. Final meeting return regd. 3 June 1936 1936

Wallis Company Ld. Regd. 1910. Vol. liq. 13 June 1918. Final meeting return regd. 13 Dec. 1921 1919

Wallis (John) & Sons Ld. Undertaking acquired by Great Southern Railway Co. in Jan. 1934 1945

Wallis Tin Stamping Co. Ld. Regd. 1936. All capital was owned by Metal Box Co. Ld. to which company all assets were transferred under agreement of 30 Mar. 1963 that all liabilities and costs would be satisfied. Final meeting return regd. 25 Aug. 1967 1968

Walls & Highley Ld. *See* Walls (Tom) & Reginald Highley Ld.

Walls & Highley Theatres Ld. Regd. 1929. Vol. liq. (creditors') 21 Dec. 1933. No capital returned to contributories. Final meeting return regd. 2 Aug. 1957 1958

Walls (Tom) & Leslie Henson Ld. *See* Walls (Tom) & Reginald Highley Ld.

Walls (Tom) & Reginald Highley Ld. Regd. 1919 as Walls & Highley Ld.; name changed to Tom Walls & Leslie Henson Ld. in Aug. 1920 and as above in Oct. 1927. Vol. liq. (creditors') 18 July 1933. All shares were owned by Walls & Highley Theatres Ld. Assets realised insufficient to meet claims of unsecured creditors in full. Final meeting return regd. 19 Sept. 1934 1933

Wallsend & Hebburn Coal Co. Ld. Regd. 1892. Vol. liq. 30 Sept. 1952. Final meeting return regd. 14 Aug. 1962 1940

Wallsend Ld. Regd. 1906. Vol. liq. 1 Apr. 1919. Final meeting return regd. 30 June 1921 1919

Wallsend Pontoon Co. Ld. Regd. 1886. Vol. liq. 23 Dec. 1895. Final meeting return regd. 22 Sept. 1896 1896

Walmer Estates Co. Ld. Regd. 1896. Vol. liq. 15 Oct. 1912. Final meeting return regd. 24 Jan. 1913 ..... *1909

Walmsley (Bury) Group Ld. Regd. 1933 as Walmsleys (Bury) Ld.; name changed 1954. All capital owned by Beloit Corpn. Vol. liq. 2 Jan. 1980. Final meeting return regd. 9 Oct. 1980 1976–7

See Stock Exchange Year-Book.

VOL. FOR

Walmsley (Charles) & Co. Regd. 1922. Vol. liq. (members') 27 July 1933. Undertaking and assets were acquired by Walmsleys (Bury) Ld. (later Walmsley (Bury) Group Ld.) for £455,000 which was distributed to contributories. Final meeting return regd. 16 Oct. 1934 .... **1934**

Walsall Wood Colliery Co. Ld. Regd. 1875. Vol. liq. (members') 14 Dec. 1951. Capital returned to contributories—£15 per preference share of £10 and £26 8s. 5d. per ordinary share of £10. Final meeting return regd. 3 Apr. 1957 .... **1958**

Waltham Abbey and Cheshunt Gas and Coke Co. See Waltham & Cheshunt Gas Co.

Waltham & Cheshunt Gas Co. Inc. by Special Act 1869 as Waltham Abbey and Cheshunt Gas and Coke Co.; name changed 1921. By Act of 1928 the undertaking was acquired by Tottenham & District Gas Co., in which company shareholders were entitled to B consolidated ordinary stock (3¼% standard) as follows—for every 10 original ordinary (10% standard) shares of £10 held—£156 17s. 3d.; for every 10 additional ordinary (7% standard) shares of £10 held—£109 16s. 1d. Holders of 4% debenture and 7½% redeemable debenture stocks were entitled to an equal amount of similar stock in acquiring company **1929**

Walthamstow Palace Ld. Regd. 1903. Reconstructed 1904 as Variety Theatres Consolidated Ld. in which company shareholders were entitled to 1 share of £1 (credited as fully-paid) for each share of £1 held. Removed from Register 1907 .... **1905**

Walton (G. E.) Ld. Regd. 1899. Vol. liq. 15 May 1913. Final meeting return regd. 28 Apr. 1914. .... **1914**

Walton Motors Ld. Regd. 1917. Vol. liq. Dec. 1924. Final meeting return regd. 18 May 1948 .... **1949**

Walton-on-Thames and Weybridge Gas Co. Inc. by Special Act 1869. Under Special Order of 1936 the undertaking was acquired by Wandsworth & District Gas Co. Holders of A ordinary shares received for each share held £13 of 5% preference stock and £5 of consolidated stock of the Wandsworth company plus £57 2s. 10d. of consolidated stock for each £100 arrears of dividends. Holders of B ordinary shares received for each share held £15 of 5% preference stock of the Wandsworth company. Holders of 6% preference stock received for each £100 held £120 of 5% preference stock of the Wandsworth company. Holders of 4% and 5% debenture stock received equal amounts of 4% or 5% debenture stock respectively of the Wandsworth company **1937**

Walton's (Frederick) Continental Co. Ld. Regd. 1904. Vol. liq. Dec. 1911. Removed from Register 1912 **1912**

Walton's (Frederick) Continental Inlaid Linoleum Co. Ld. Regd. 1901. Reconstructed as Walton's (Frederick) Continental Co. Ld. Shareholders were entitled to £38 in cash and 7·142 shares in F. W. Syndicate Ld. for every 100 shares of £1 held. Removed from Register 1905 .... **1909**

Walturdaw Cinema Supply Co. Ld. Regd. 1925. Vol. liq. 12 Oct. 1951. Final meeting return regd. 1 Aug. 1957 **1938**

Walturdaw Co. Ld. Regd. 1904. Vol. liq. 17 June 1925. Undertaking was acquired by Walturdaw Cinema Supply Co. Ld. Final meeting return regd. 2 Sept. 1927 .... **1926**

Walworth Gold Mine Ld. Regd. 1895. Removed from Register 1899 .... **1899**

Wampach's Hotel Ld. Regd. 1897. Vol. liq. 18 Mar. 1920. Struck off Register 9 July 1926 .... **1921**

Wampoe Tobacco & Rubber Estates Ld. Regd. 1910. Vol. liq. (members') 16 Dec. 1938. Stockholders were entitled to 2 fully-paid shares of £1 in Bah Lias Rubber Estates Ld. for every £5 stock held. Final meeting return regd. 1 Aug. 1939 .... **1939**

Wanderer Consolidated Gold Mines, Ld. Regd. 13 June 1928. Vol. liq. (members') 27 Nov. 1951. Capital returned to contributories: 5s. 1d. per share of £1). £961 was paid into Companies' Liquidation Account. Final meeting return regd. 13 May 1955 ... **1956**

Wanderer (Selukwe) Gold Mines Ld. Regd. 1899. Vol. liq. July 1909. Reconstructed as company of same name. Shareholders were entitled to 1⅔ shares of 5s. in new company for each share of £1 held. Removed from Register 1910 .... **1910**

Wanderer (Selukwe) Gold Mines Ld. Regd. 1909. Vol. liq. 26 Jan. 1920. Final meeting return regd. 24 Mar. 1921 .... **1920**

Wandsworth & District Gas Co. Inc. by Special Act 1912 as Wandsworth Wimbledon & Epsom District Gas Co.; name changed 1931. Dissolved 1 May 1949, undertaking being vested in South Eastern Area Gas Board under Gas Act 1948. Holders of securities were entitled to receive, in respect of each £100 unit held, British Gas 3% guaranteed stock

1990–95 as follows:

VOL. FOR

	£	s.	d.	
Cons. stock (5% basic)	123	16	8	
4% pref. stock	103	6	8	
5% irred. deb. stock	128	13	4	
4% irred. deb. stock	102	10	0	
3⅞% red. deb. stock	102	5	0	**1952**

Wandsworth and Putney Gas Light and Coke Co. Established 1834. Inc. by Special Act 1856. Reconstructed as Wandsworth, Wimbledon and Epsom District Gas Co. (later Wandsworth & District Gas Co.) which company assumed liability for debenture stocks. Holders of A, B or C stocks were entitled to an equal amount of 5% standard Wandsworth A, 3½% standard Wandsworth B, or 3¼% standard Wandsworth C stock respectively **1913**

Wandsworth, Wimbledon & Epsom District Gas Co. See Wandsworth & District Gas Co.

Wankie Colliery Co. Ld. Regd. 1909. Vol. liq. 23 Dec. 1914. Reconstructed as company of same name. Shareholders were entitled to 2 shares of 10s. (credited as fully-paid) in new company for each share of 10s. held; debenture holders were entitled to an equal amount of debentures in new company. Final meeting return regd. 18 Oct. 1915 .... **1915**

Wankie Colliery Co. Ld. Regd. 1914. Vol. liq. 24 Oct. 1923. Reconstructed as company of same name. Shareholders were entitled to 3 fully-paid shares of 10s. for every 2 shares of 10s. held plus 9d. per share in cash. Final meeting return regd. 16 Jan. 1926 **1924**

Wankie (Rhodesia) Coal, Railway & Exploration Co. Ld. Regd. 1899. Vol. liq. Aug. 1909 for reconstruction as Wankie Colliery Co. Ld., In which company shareholders were entitled to 1 share of 10s. (credited as fully-paid) for each share of £1 held and an option (since expired) over further shares at par. Debenture holders agreed to accept 25% of holdings in cash and 75% in 6% 1st mortgage debentures of new company. Removed from Register 1910 ...... **1910**

Wankowa Brelikow Ld. Regd. 1894. Vol. liq. 17 June 1914. Final meeting return regd. 4 Nov. 1914 ..... **1915**

Wansbrough Paper Co. Ld. Regd. 1897. Removed from Register 1904 .... **1902**

Wantage Electric Supply Co. Ld. Regd. 1924. Vol. liq. (members') 15 Feb. 1938. Capital returned to contributories-£5 per preference share of £5; £2 1s. 4d. per ordinary share of £1. Final meeting return regd. 4 Aug. 1938 .... **1939**

Wanzer Ld. Regd. 1888. Court Orders; to wind up 27 Aug. 1890; to dissolve 30 June 1896 .... **1891**

Waratah Gold Mines Ld. Regd. 1894. Vol. liq. 6 Oct. 1897. Reconstructed as company of same name. Shareholders were entitled to 1 share of 10s. (credited with 7s. paid) in new company for each share of 10s. held. Final meeting return regd. 5 May 1898 .... **1899**

Waratah Gold Mines Ld. Regd. 1899. Vol. liq. 31 Jan. 1899. Reconstructed as Federation United Gold Mines Ld., in which company shareholders were entitled to 1 share of 10s. (credited with 7s. paid) for each share of 10s. held. Final meeting return regd. 4 July 1899 .... **1900**

Ward (Albany) Theatres Ld. Regd. 1920. Vol. liq. (members') 2 Dec. 1948. Final meeting return regd. 13 May 1963 .... **1940**

Ward & Walker Ld. Regd. 1920. Vol. liq. (members') 31 Aug. 1944. All capital was owned by Crosses & Heaton Ld. Final meeting return regd. 17 July 1945 **1945**

Ward Lock & Bowden Ld. See Locks Ld.

Ward Lock & Co. Ld. See Locks Ld.

Ward (Marcus) & Co. Ld. Regd. Dublin 1883. Undertaking was acquired in 1899 by McCaw Stevenson and Orr Ld. Removed from Register 1901 .... **1900**

Ward (S.) Ld. Regd. 1891. Vol. liq. (members') 28 June 1955. Capital returned to contributories—£4 2s. 6d. per ordinary or preference share of £5. £183 6s. was paid into Companies' Liquidation Account. Final meeting return regd. 27 June 1956 .... **1957**

Warden, Ld. Inc. Dublin 1895; transferred to Belfast 1920. Vol. liq. (members') 22 Dec. 1961. Capital returned to contributories—£2 19s. 2·4333d. per 5s. ordinary stock. Amounts paid into Companies' Liquidation Account—£106 15s. 6d. in respect of unclaimed dividends, £80 in respect of unclaimed capital repayment (1958) and £532 16s. 6d. unclaimed distributions. Final meeting return regd. 7 Jan. 1966 .... **1966**

Wardman (C. B.) & Co. Ld. Regd. 1919. Vol. liq. 26 May 1930. Assets were taken over by Vulcan Motor Services Ld. Final meeting return regd. 1 Sept. 1932 **1931**

Wardour Films Ld. Regd. 1916 as Bolton's Mutual Films Ld.; name changed Sept. 1919. Vol. liq. (members') 30 Mar. 1937. All shares owned by

See Stock Exchange Year-Book.

See Stock Exchange Year-Book.

VOL. FOR

Wassau Central Banket Gold Reef Ld. Regd. 1900. Vol. liq. Dec. 1909. The properties were sold to Taquah Central Mines Ld., In which company shareholders were entitled to 5 shares of £1 for every 13 shares of £1 held. Removed from Register 1911 1910

Wassau Consolidated Goldfields Ld. Regd. 1901. Undertaking and assets were acquired by Akinas Syndicate (Ashanti) Ld., in which company shareholders were entitled to 2 shares of £1 (credited with 18s. paid) for every 5 shares of £1 held. Removed from Register 1904 1904

Wassau Extended Gold Mines Ld. Regd. 1900. Vol. liq. Apr. 1909. The undertaking and assets were sold to Wassau Central Banket Gold Reef. Ld., in which company shareholders were entitled to 1 share of £1 for every 4 shares of £1 held. Removed from Register 1910 1910

Wassau (Gold Coast) Mining Co. Ld. Regd. 1882. Vol. liq. Apr. 1909. Reconstructed as company of same name. Shareholders were entitled to 1 share of 10s. in new company for each share of £1 held. Removed from Register 1911 1910

Wassau (Gold Coast) Mining Co. Ld. Regd. 1909. Vol. liq. Nov. 1911. Reconstructed as company of same name. Shareholders were entitled to 1 share of 5s. (credited with 3s.) paid) in new company for each share of 10s. held. Removed from Register 1913 ... 1912

Wassau (Gold Coast) Mining Co. Ld. Regd. 1911. Court Order to wind up 6 July 1920. Liquidator released 14 Mar. 1922. Struck off Register 20 Mar. 1925 1921

Wassau Gold Concessions Ld. Regd. 1900. Reconstructed 1904 as Amalgamated Mining and Exploration Co. Ld., in which company shareholders were entitled to 2 shares of 5s. (credited with 3s. 6d. paid) and 1 fully-paid share for every 2 shares of 5s. held. Removed from Register 1905 1905

Wassau Gold Reefs Ld. Regd. 1895 as Golden Reefs Ld.; name changed Feb. 1901. Removed from Register 1911 1905

Wassau Prospecting Syndicate Ld. Regd. 1901. Assets were taken by debenture holders. Removed from Register 1903 1904

Wassau (Western) Mines Ld. Regd. 1901. Removed from Register 29 Oct. 1909 .... *1906

Wassaushanti Mines Ld. Regd. 1901. Vol. liq. 26 July 1906. Final meeting return regd. 14 Mar. 1919 .... *1907

Wassaw & Ahanta Co. Ld. Regd. 1894. Removed from Register 1903 1902

Wassaw & Ashanti Gold Mines Syndicate Ld. Regd. 1882. Vol. liq. 8 Nov. 1893. Final meeting return regd. 29 Apr. 1902 1894

Wassaw West Amalgamated Mines Ld. Regd. 1901. Vol. liq. 4 Jan. 1909 for reconstruction under same name. Shareholders were entitled to an equal amount of shares in the new company. Final meeting return regd. 7 July 1909 1909

Wassaw West Amalgamated Mines Ld. Regd. 1909. Vol. liq. 25 July 1917. Final meeting return regd. 22 Aug. 1919 1918

Waste Food Products Ld. Regd. 1928. Court Order to wind up Dec. 1929. Struck off Register 18 Feb. 1938 1939

Waste Fuel Recovery Briquette Co. Ld. Regd. 1920. Vol. liq. 29 July 1921. Final meeting return regd. 7 Feb. 1922 1922

Waste Heat & Gas E;ectrical Generation Stations Ld. See Carliol Investments Trust Ld.

Watchet & Williton Gas Light & Coke Co. Ld. Regd. 1866. Dissolved 1 May 1949, undertaking being vested in the South Western Area Gas Board under Gas Act 1948. Holders of ordinary shares (both denominations) were entitled to receive, in respect of each £1 unit held, £2 12s. British Gas 3% guaranteed stock 1990–95 1952

Watchmakers' Alliance & Ernest Goode's Stores Ld. Regd. 1897. Removed from Register 1904 1904

Watende Ld. Regd. 1934 as Watende Mines (Kenya) Ld.; name changed 4 Sept. 1936. Struck off Register 1 Feb. 1952 1952

Water & Gas Debenture & Share Investment Trust Ld. Regd. 1905. Removed from Register 1911 1910

Water Reform Co. Ld. See Atkins Water Softening & Purifying Co. Ld.

Water Softeners (France) Ld. Regd. 1911. Vol. liq. 7 Mar. 1928. Final meeting return regd. 31 Dec. 1929 1929

Water Softeners Ld. Regd. 1911. Vol. liq. July 1923. Goodwill and assets were acquired by United Water Softeners Ld. (later Permutit Co. Ld.), in which company shareholders were entitled to 1 A share of £1 for every 5 shares of £1 held. Struck off Register Mar. 1930 1931

Water Trust, Mining and Public Crushing Co. of Western Australia Ld. Regd. 1895. Vol. liq. 16 Dec. 1897. Reconstructed as Northam Milling and Mining Co. Ld., In which company shareholders were entitled

VOL. FOR

to 1 share of £1 (credited with 16s. 6d. paid) for each share of £1 held. Final meeting return regd. 16 Dec. 1898 1901

Waterberg (Transvaal) Land, Trading and Prospecting Co, Ld. Undertaking acquired 1892 by United African Lands Ld., in which company shareholders were entitled to 6 fully-paid shares of £1 for every 5 shares held 1900

Waterfall (Anamalai) Tea Estates Ld. Regd. 1925. Vol. liq. (members') 20 Dec. 1943. Capital returned to contributories-£2 9s. 8½d. per share of 5s. £34 15s. 11d. was paid into Companies' Liquidation Account. Final meeting return regd. 20 Dec. 1946 ... 1947

Waterfall Estate & Gold Mines Ld. Regd. 1895. Vol. liq. Dec. 1924. Struck off Register Feb. 1932 1932

Waterfall Prospecting Co. Ld. Regd. 1895. Vol. liq. 25 Oct. 1897. Final meeting return regd. 24 Mar. 1898 1898

Waterford & Central Ireland Railway Co. Inc. by Special Act 1845 as Waterford & Kilkenny Railway Co.; name changed by Act of 1868. Under Great Southern and Western and Waterford and Central Ireland Railway Cos. Amalgamation Act of 1900 the undertaking was vested in the Great Southern and Western Railway Co. Ireland. Holders of £100 consolidated 3% debenture stock, new preference 6% stock or original stock received £75 4% debenture stock, £100 4% preference stock of £17 10s. in cash respectively 1901

Waterford & Kilkenny Railway Co. See Waterford & Central Ireland Railway Co.

Waterford & Limerick Railway Co. See Waterford, Limerick & Western Railway Co.

Waterford and Tramore Railway Co, Inc. by Special Act 1851. In 1924 the undertaking was transferred to the Great Southern Railway Co. in which company stockholders were entitled to stock as follows:

For each £10 held   G. S. R.
  5% Pref. Share ... £12 10s.   4% Gtd. Pref. Stock
  Ordinary Share .. £12 10s.   4% Preference Stock
The liability for the £5,000 6% Loans and the £4,200 7½% Loans was to be assumed by the Great Southern Railway Co. 1952

Waterford & Wexford Railway Co. Inc. by Special Act 1864. Undertaking purchased by Fishguard and Rosslare Railways and Harbour Co. 1895

Waterford, Dungarvan & Lismore Railway Co. Inc. by Special Act 1872. Acquired by Fishguard & Rosslare Railways & Harbours Co. on 1 July 1898. Ordinary shareholders received £7 12s. 6d. cash per share of £10 1899

Waterford, Limerick & Western Railway Co. Inc. by Special Act 1845 as Waterford & Limerick Railway Co.; name changed by Act of 1895. Under Great Southern and Western and Waterford, Limerick and Western Railway Cos. Amalgamation Act of 1900, the undertaking was vested in the Great Southern and Western Railway Co. Ireland 1901

Waterford Wexford, Wicklow & Dublin Railway Co. See Dublin and South Eastern Railway Co.

Waterloo & City Railway Co. Inc. by Special Act 1893. Undertaking purchased in 1907 by London and South Western Railway. Holders were entitled to either (a) £67 ordinary stock, (b) £105 3½% preference stock, or (c) £110 3% debenture stock for every £100 ordinary stock held 1907

Waterloo Feed Mills Ld. Regd. 1879 as Waterloo Mills, Cake and Warehousing Co. Ld.; name changed 14 Oct. 1965. Vol. liq. (members') 27 Mar. 1968. Capital returned to contributories: 13s. 4d. and 31·54p. (per share of £1). Final meeting return regd. 24 June 1972 1972

Waterloo Mills, Cake and Warehousing Co. Ld. See Waterloo Feed Mills Ld. as above.

Waterloo House & Swan & Edgar Ld. See Swan & Edgar Ld.

Waterloo Investment Trust Ld. Regd. 1919. Vol. liq. (members') 31 July 1961. Capital returned to contributories—£10 5s. per share of £1. Final meeting return regd. 15 Dec. 1962 1964

Waterloo Place (West Side) Estates Ld. Regd. 1916. Vol. liq. (members') 14 May 1934. Private company. Final meeting return regd. 27 Feb. 1936 1935

Waterloo Sugar Estates (Trinidad) Ld. Regd. 1937. Vol. liq. (members') 30 Nov. 1937. Undertaking and assets were acquired by Caroni Co. Ld., in which company shareholders were entitled to 1 preference share of £1 (credited as fully-paid) for each preference share of £1 held or 105 ordinary shares of 2s. for every 26 ordinary shares of 5s. held. Final meeting return regd. 2 Dec. 1938 1938

Waterlow & Sons Ld. Regd. 1876. Reconstructed 1889 as company of same name. Final meeting return regd. 16 Oct. 1890 1897

VOL. FOR

Waterlow & Sons Ld. Regd. 1889. Vol. liq. 4 Oct. 1897. Reconstructed as company of same name. Shareholders were entitled to 2 fully-paid preference shares of £10 for each 6% preference share of £10 held or 2 6% preferred ordinary shares and 1 deferred share of £10, all fully-paid, for each ordinary share of £10 held. Final meeting return regd. 14 Sept. 1898 .... **1897**

Waterlow Brothers & Layton Ld. Regd. 1887. Vol. liq. 31 July 1893. Reconstructed as company of same name. Shareholders were entitled to 1 fully-paid ordinary share and 1 fully-paid preference share of £10 in new company for each share of £10 held. Final meeting return regd. 12 Feb. 1895 .... **1908**

Waterlow Brothers & Layton Ld. Regd. 1893. Vol. liq. 15 Apr. 1920. Undertaking and assets were acquired by Waterlow & Sons Ld. Shareholders were entitled to either £10 in War Loan 1929–47 or cash payment of £9 per preference share of £10; ordinary shareholders were entitled to £5 in cash and 3 fully-paid deferred ordinary shares of £10 in purchasing company for every 2 ordinary shares of £10 held. The debentures were repaid at par. Final meeting return regd. 26 Oct. 1920 .... **1921**

Waterpan Estate & Gold Mining Co. Ld. Regd. 1904. Struck off Register 1915 .... **1910**

Waterson Gold Ld. Regd. 1902. Reconstructed as Waterson Gold Mining Co. Ld., in which company shareholders were entitled to 1 share of 10*s*. (credited with 8*s*. paid) for each share of £1 held. Removed from Register 1908 .... **1908**

Waterson Gold Mining Co. Ld. Regd. 1905. Vol. liq. 11 Dec. 1923. Final meeting return regd. 21 Oct. 1925 **1924**

Waterworks Construction Co. Ld. Regd. 1893 as South West Suburban Water Co. Ld.; name changed Sept. 1895. Vol. liq. 17 Dec. 1900. Final meeting return regd. 7 Mar. 1901 .... **1896**

Watford & St. Albans Gas Co. Estd. 1834; Inc. by Special Act 1871 as Watford Gas & Coke Co.; name changed 1930. Dissolved 1 May 1949, undertaking being vested in Eastern Area Gas Board under Gas Act 1948. Holders of securities were entitled to receive, in respect of each £100 unit held, British Gas 3% guaranteed stock 1990–95 as follows:

	£	s.	d.
Ord. stock (3½% stand.)	123	0	0
5½% pref. stock	129	3	4
5% pref. stock	115	0	0
6% red. pref. stock (1955)	110	0	0
4% red. pref. stock (1973—8)	101	10	0
4% red. pref. stock (1959)	100	10	0
4% red. pref. stock (1967)	100	4	9
5% irred. deb. stock	127	10	0
4% red. deb. stock	102	0	0
3½% red. deb. stock	99	10	0

1952

Watford Gas & Coke Co. *See* Watford & St. Albans Gas Co.

Watford Manufacturing Co. Ld. Regd. 1898 as Dr. Tibbles' Vi-Cocoa Ld.; (1898) name changed to Dr. Tibbles' Vi-Cocoa Ld. in 1899 and as above in 1906. Vol. liq. 19 Sept. 1922. Assets realised sufficient to pay creditors in full but not sufficient to make any return to contributories. Final meeting return regd. 8 Feb. 1923 .... **1923**

Wath Main Colliery Co. Ld. Regd. 1900. Vol. liq. (members') 5 Mar. 1953. Capital returned to contributories—6*s*. per preference share of 5*s*. and 64*s*. 7½*d*. per ordinary share of 5*s*. £67 12*s*. 1*d*. was paid into Companies' Liquidation Account. Final meeting return regd. 16 Aug. 1957 .... **1958**

Wath-upon-Dearne & District Gas Co. Ld. Regd. 1879 as Wath-upon-Dearne Gas and Lighting Co. Ld.; name changed 26 Jan. 1900. By Act of 1908, the undertaking was purchased by Wath and Bolton Gas Board on payment of £11,250 to A preference shareholders, £49,901 to ordinary shareholders and £7,800 to debenture holders. The Act also provided for dissolution **1909**

Watkins & Doncaster & Westminster Garage Ld. Regd. 1913 as Watkins & Doncaster Ld.; name changed 18 Apr. 1935. Vol. liq. (members') 8 Apr. 1946. Capital returned to contributories—15*s*. 4·0625*d*. per share of 5*s*. Final meeting return regd. 21 Mar. 1947 ... **1947**

Watkins & Doncaster Ld. *See* Watkins & Doncaster & Westminster Garage Ld.

Watkin's (J. B.) Land Mortgage Co. Inc. America 1883. Liquidated by English and American Committees of Creditors **1899**

Watkinson (George) & Sons Ld. Regd. 1872. Vol. liq. 18 June 1920. Final meeting return regd. 23 Apr. 1923 ***1921**

Watlington & Princes Risborough Railway Co. Inc. by Special Act 1869. Under Great Western Railway Act 1883 the undertaking was purchased by that company for £1,500 in cash and £21,500 bonds **1884**

Watney & Co. Ld. Regd. 1885. Reconstructed 1898 as Watney Combe Reid & Co. Ld. (later Watney Mann Ld.), in which company shareholders were entitled to £120 in preference shares of £1 *plus* £6 in cash for every £100 preference stock held or £449 8*s*. in ordinary shares for every £100 ordinary shares held. Holders of 4½% debenture stock were entitled to £114 either in debenture stock or in cash for every £100 stock held; holders of 5% debenture stock to either £119 in debenture stock or £117·833 in cash for every £100 stock held; holders of 3½% debenture stock to either £100 in debenture stock or £103 in cash for every £100 stock held. Removed from Register 1906 .... **1899**

Watney (D.) & Son Ld. Regd. 1895. Vol. liq. (members') 13 Nov. 1947. The assets were acquired by Brandon's Putney Brewery Ld. which company owned all ordinary shares. The 4½% mortgage debenture stock was redeemed at 110% and the preference shares (of £10) were repaid at £12 per share. £192 was paid into Companies' Liquidation Account. Final meeting return regd. 14 Oct. 1948 **1950**

Watson & Woodhead Ld. *See* Watson, Woodhead & Wagstaffe Ld.

Watson, Laidlaw & Co. Ld. Regd. 1907. Vol. liq. (creditors') 21 Oct 1966. £1,571·06 was paid into Companies' Liquidation Account in respect of unclaimed dividends. Final meeting return regd. 1 Aug. 1972 .... **1972**

Watson Steamship Co. Ld. Regd. 1902. Vol. liq. 31 July 1916. Final meeting return regd. 17 July 1918 ..... **1917**

Watson, Todd & Co. (Millers) Ld. Regd. 1918. Vol. liq. 31 Jan. 1927. Controlling interest held by Spillers Milling & Associated Industries Ld. (later Spillers Ld.). Final meeting return regd. 23 Jan. 1928 ...... **1927**

Watson, Woodhead & Wagstaffe Ld. Regd. 1895 as Watson and Woodhead Ld.; name changed 1898. Vol. liq. Dec. 1911. Undertaking and assets were acquired by Walker & Homfrays Ld., in which company shareholders were entited to 3 ordinary shares of £1 (credited with 3*s*. 4*d*. paid) for each ordinary share of £5 (£2 10*s*. paid) held or 2 fully-paid preference shares of £1 for each preference share of £5 held. Debenture stockholders were entitled to an equal amount of 4% debenture stock in purchasing company. Removed from Register 1913 **1912**

Watt & Grant Ld. Regd. Edinburgh 1927. Vol. liq. (members') 30 Jan. 1953. Final meeting return regd. 1 May 1962 .... **1940**

Watton & Swaffham Railway Co. Inc. by Special Act 1869. Under Great Eastern Railway Act of 1897 the undertaking was amalgamated with that company. Holders of £100 debenture stock, preference stock or ordinary stock received £93, £83 or £10 2*s*. 1*d*. 4% debenture stock in purchasing company respectively **1898**

Waverley Block Gold Mines Ld. Regd. 1900. Vol. liq. Jan. 1908. Removed from Register 1913 .... **1908**

Waverley Hotel (Whitley Bay) Co. Ld. *See* Rex Hotel Co. Ld.

Waverley Mine Ld. Regd. 1897. Vol. liq. 9 May 1900. Reconstructed as Empire Goldfields Ld., in which company shareholders were entitled to 1 share of £1 (credited with 19*s*. paid) for every 4 shares of £1 held. Final meeting return regd. 21 Jan. 1915 ..... **1901**

Waverley Picture House (1920) Ld. Regd. Edinburgh 1920. Vol. liq. (members') 14 Mar. 1930. Undertaking and assets acquired by Scottish Cinema & Variety Theatres Ld. for £5,000. Capital returned to contributories—3*s*. 4*d*. per share of £1. £20 16*s*. 8*d*. was paid to Accountant of the Court. Final meeting return regd. 26 Mar. 1936 .... **1931**

Waverley Plantations Ld. Regd. 1914. Vol. liq. 27 Mar. 1928. Undertaking and assets were acquired by British Rubber Estates of Java Ld., in which company shareholders were entitled to 12 fully-paid shares of 2*s*. for every 10 shares of 2*s*. held. Final meeting return regd. 1 Jan. 1929 .... **1928**

Waverley Rubber & Produce Estates of Java Ld. Regd. 1910. Vol. liq. 18 June 1914. Reconstructed as company of Waverley Plantations Ld. Shareholders were entitled to 5 shares of 5*s*. (credited with 4*s*. paid) in new company for each share of £1 held. Final meeting return regd. 31 Oct. 1916 .... **1915**

Waverley Rubber Co. Ld. Regd. Edinburgh 1907. Vol. liq. (members') 21 Mar. 1956. Capital returned to contributories per ordinary or preference share of £1—£2 8*s*. 6½*d*. £221 15*s*. 7*d*. was paid into Companies' Liquidation Account in respect of unclaimed dividends and distributions. Final meeting return regd. 17 Apr. 1957 .... **1958**

Way Halim (Sumatra) Rubber & Coffee Estates Ld. Regd. 1910. Vol. liq. 19 Feb. 1914. Reconstructed as Way-Halim (Sumatra) Estates Ld. (later Way

**See Stock Exchange Year-Book.*

VOL. FOR

Holdings Ld.). Shareholders were entitled to 1 share of 2s. (credited with 1s. 4d. paid) in new company for every 2 shares of 2s. held. Final meeting return regd. 24 Mar. 1915 ... **1914**

Wayne's Merthyr Steam Coal & Iron Works Ld. Regd. 1874. Court Orders: to wind up 18 Apr. 1877; to dissolve 15 Dec. 1880 ... ***1877**

Weald Electricity Supply Co. Ld. Regd. 1925. All capital was owned by County of London Electric Supply Co. Ld. Dissolved 1 Apr. 1948 under Electricity Act 1947 ... **1937**

Wealth of Nations Extended Ld. Regd. 1895. Undertaking acquired by Standard Exploration Co. Ld. Removed from Register 1903 ... **1899**

Wealth of Nations Ld. Regd. 1895. Undertaking acquired by Standard Exploration Co. Ld. Removed from Register 1903 ... **1899**

Wear Rolling Mills Co. Ld. Regd. 1880. Removed from Register 1905 ... **1883**

Wear Steel Co. Ld. Regd. 1888. Vol. liq. 13 Sept. 1894. Final meeting return regd. 30 Mar. 1897 ... **1895**

Wear Valley Extension Railway Co. Inc. by Special Act 1892. Under North Eastern Railway Act 1894 powers were vested in that company ... **1895**

Weardale & Consett Water Co. Inc. by Special Act 1866 as Weardale & Shildon District Waterworks Co.; name changed 1902. Undertaking was transferred to Durham County Water Board in 1920. Stockholders were entitled to 6% stock of the Water Board as follows—for each £100 4% preference stock—£75; for each £100 10% maximum ordinary stock—£115; for each £100 7% maximum stock—£114. The mortgage debt stock was assumed by the Water Board ... **1921**

Weardale & Shildon District Waterworks Co. See Weardale & Consett Water Co.

Weardale Iron & Coal Co. Ld. Regd. 1863. Business was acquired in 1899 by Weardale Steel, Coal and Coke Co. Ld. Vol. liq. 23 Aug. 1900. Capital returned to contributories—£15 per share of £10. The debentures were repaid at par. Final meeting return regd. 19 Dec. 1901 ... **1900**

Weardale Lead Co. Ld. Regd. 1883. Reconstructed 1900 as company of same name. Shareholders were entitled to 2 shares of £1 (credited with 15s. paid) for each share of £4 (£2 5s. paid). Removed from Register 1901 ... **1900**

Weardale Steel, Coal & Coke Co. Ld. Regd. 1899. Vol. liq. (members') 12 June 1953. Capital returned to contributories—56s. 4¾d. per £1 deferred and 36s. 4½d. per £1 preferred stock. Final meeting return regd. 27 Feb. 1957 ... **1958**

Wearmouth Coal Co. Ld. Regd. 1896. Vol. liq. (members') 30 Oct. 1952. Capital returned to contributories-£4 7s. 1·42d. per share of 1s. £307 14s. 6d. was paid into Companies' Liquidation Account. Final meeting return regd. 5 Mar. 1956 ... **1957**

Wearwell Cycle Co. Ld. Regd. 1896. Vol. liq. 2 June 1910. Court Order to wind up 14 June 1910. Struck off Register 10 Oct. 1916 ... **1911**

Webb & Ellen Ld. Regd. 1898. Removed from Register 1906 ... **1905**

Webb (Edward) & Sons (Stourbridge) Ld. Regd. 1914. All capital acquired by Cornwall Property (Holdings) Ld. Company dissolved 7 Sept. 1980 ... **1971**

Webb (James H.) & Co. Ld. Inc. Dublin 1876. Court Order to wind up June 1932 ... **1933**

Webb (Jubal) Ld. Regd. 1896. Court Order to wind up 21 Nov. 1900. Removed from Register 1909 ... **1901**

Webb (R. F.) & Co. Ld. Regd. 1920. Vol. liq. Oct. 1927. Struck off Register Feb. 1932 ... **1932**

Webb (R. W.) Ld. Regd. 1895. Vol. liq. 9 Aug. 1898. Final meeting return regd. 1 Jan. 1899 ... **1900**

Webb (Thos.) & Sons Ld. Regd. 1886. Court Orders: to wind up Mar. 1887; to dissolve Aug. 1888 ... **1888**

Webb (Thomas) & Sons Ld. Regd. 1887. Vol. liq. 26 Mar. 1920. Undertaking and assets were acquired by Webb's Crystal Glass Co. Ld. Final meeting return regd. 27 Dec. 1922. Court Order declared dissolution void Mar. 1925. Final meeting return regd. 26 Mar. 1927 ... **1921**

Webb's Engineering Co. Ld. Regd. 1896 as Sanitary Supply Corporation Ld.; name changed 1898. Removed from Register 1901 ... **1901**

Weber, Smith & Hoare Ld. Regd. 1923. All ordinary capital was owned by Wm. Cory & Son Ld. Vol. liq. (members') 20 Feb. 1964. Final meeting return regd. 31 Mar. 1964 ... **1965**

Webster (Charles) (1899) Ld. Regd. 1899 Vol. liq. 3 Feb. 1913. Final meeting return regd. 29 Nov. 1913 .... **1913**

Webster (Charles) Ld. Regd. 1913. Vol. liq. (members') 12 Jan. 1931. Capital returned to contributories— £26,681 5s. 7d. Final meeting return regd. 11 Sept. 1931 ... **1931**

VOL. FOR

Webster's Brickworks Ld. Regd. 1897. Struck off Register 16 Nov. 1906 ... **1907**

Webster's Find Ld. Regd. 1896. Reconstructed 1900 as Webster's Gold Mining Co. Ld., In which company shareholders were entitled to 1 share of 10s. (credited with 6s. paid) for each share of 10s. held. Removed from Register 1908 ... **1902**

Webster's Gold Mining Co. Ld. Regd. 1900. Reconstructed 1902 as Perseverance Gold Mines Ld. Removed from Register 1905 ... **1905**

Weiners Ld. Regd. 1895. Undertaking was acquired by Weiners Lithographic Printing and Advertising Co. Ld. Removed from Register 1910 ... **1906**

Weiner's Lithographic Printing & Advertising Co. Ld. Regd. 1904. Court Order to wind up 12 July 1910. Liquidator released 31 May 1912. Struck off Register 10 Oct. 1916 ... **1911**

Weis (Charles) & Co. Ld. Regd. 1912. Vol. liq. 24 July 1922. Final meeting return regd. 28 Oct. 1927 ..... ***1923**

Welch Ale Brewery Ld. Regd. 1897 as Chelsea Brewery Co. Ld.; name changed 1900. Vol. liq. 25 Sept. 1921. Undertaking acquired by Watney Combe Reid & Co. Ld. (later Watney Mann Ld.) in 1920. Final meeting return regd. 10 May 1922 ... **1922**

Welch & Sons Ld. Regd. 1895. Vol. liq. (members') 20 Feb. 1935. Capital returned to contributories—10s. 6d. per preference share of £10; ordinary, nil. Final meeting return regd. 25 July 1935 ... **1935**

Welcome Gold Mining Co. Ld. Regd. 1898. Undertaking and assets were acquired in 1903 by Consolidated Gold Fields of New Zealand Ld., in which company shareholders were entitled to 1 share of £1 (credited as fully-paid) for every 8 shares of £1 held. Removed from Register 1905 ... **1904**

Weld Hercules Gold Mines Ld. Regd. 1895. Reconstructed 1899 as company of same name. Shareholders were entitled to 1 fully-paid share and 1 share of £1 (credited with 13s. paid) for every 2 shares of £1 held. Removed from Register 1906 ... **1902**

Weld Hercules Gold Mines Ld. Regd. 1899. Vol. liq. 19 Apr. 1902. Reconstructed as New Weld-Hercules Gold Mines Ld., in which company shareholders were entitled to 1 share of 5s. (credited with 3s. 9d. paid) for each share of 10s. held. Struck off Register 19 Oct. 1906 ... **1903**

Weldless Tubes Ld. See Tubes Ld.

Weldons Ld. Regd. 1898. Vol. liq. (members') 9 Apr. 1941. The undertaking was acquired by Amalgamated Press Ld., later Fleetway Publications Ld. ... **1942**

Welford & Co, Dairy Farmers Ld. See Welfords & Premier Dairies Ld.

Welfords & Premier Dairies Ld. Regd. 1903 as Welford & Co. Dairy Farmers Ld.; name changed Apr. 1923. Vol. liq. (members') 19 Mar. 1931. Capital returned to contributories—£35,951 0s. 3d. Final meeting return regd. 20 Mar. 1934 ... **1932**

Welfords Surrey Dairies Ld. Regd. 1897. In Nov. 1917 shareholders were offered 1 preference share of £1 and 7 ordinary shares of £1 in United Dairies Ld. for every 6 ordinary shares of £1 held or 1 preference share of £1 in that company for each preference share of £1 held. Vol. liq. (members') 19 Mar. 1931. £101 5s. was paid into Companies' Liquidation Account. Final meeting return regd. 20 Mar. 1934 ... **1932**

Welgelegen Diamond Mining Co. Ld. Inc. Transvaal 1906. Vol. liq. Oct 1911. Undertaking was acquired by Frank Smith Diamond Vanises & Exploration Co. Ld. Holders of shares Nos. 1—100000 were entitled to 55 shares (of 7s. 6d.) in new company for every 100 shares (of £1) held ... **1912**

Well Line Ld. Regd. 1894 as Tyzack and Branfoot Steam Shipping Co. Ld.; name changed June 1911. Vol. liq. 3 Apr. 1919. All capital owned by Thos. & Jno. Brocklebank Ld. Final meeting return regd. 4 Apr. 1927 ... **1928**

Welland (Canada) Railway Co. Inc. Canada 1858. Under Act (Canada) of 1884 the line was purchased by Grand Trunk Railway Co. of Canada for £141,267 4% consolidated debenture stock ... **1910**

Wellaway Plantations Ld. Regd. 1924. Vol. liq. (members') 23 Mar. 1949. Capital returned to contributories—⅜d. per share of 2s. Final meeting return regd. 17 June 1952 ... **1953**

Wellesley-Brown Aircraft Ld. See Navarro Wellesley Aviation Ld.

Wellesley (Penang) Estates Ld. Regd. 1904. Receiver appointed on behalf of debenture holders who received £4 1s. 5d. per £20 bond. Removed from Register 1909 ... **1908**

Wellfield Galvanising Co. Ld. Regd. 1908. Vol. liq. (members') 29 Aug. 1940. Undertaking acquired by Gravesend Steel & Tinplate Co. Ld. which company is discharging all debts. Final meeting return regd. 21 Apr. 1941 ... **1946**

VOL. FOR

Wellingborough Electric Supply Co. Ld. Regd. 1900 as County of Northampton Electric Power & Traction Co. Ld.; name changed 1910. Dissolved 1 Apr. 1948, undertaking being vested in the British (later Central) Electricity Authority and East Midlands Area Board under the Electricity Act 1947. Ordinary shareholders were entitled to receive £23 15s. British Electricity 3% guaranteed stock (1968–73), for each share (of £10) held **1949**

Wellingborough Gas Light Co. Ld. Estd. 1833 regd. as limited 1871; Parliamentary Powers 1879 and subsequently. Dissolved 1 May 1949, undertaking being vested in East Midland Area Gas Board under Gas Act 1948. Holders of securities were entitled to receive British Gas 3% guaranteed stock 1990–95 as follows in respect of each £100 unit, unless otherwise stated, of security held:

	£	s.	d.
Orig. shares (10% stand.) (of £5)	16	14	0
Addit. shares (7% stand.) (of £1)	2	18	6
3½% red. debs.	101	10	0
4% red. debs. (1961)	103	0	0
4% red. debs. (1953)	101	15	0	**1952**

Wellington & Manawatu Railway Co. Ld. Inc. New Zealand 1881 & 1883. Line taken over by Government on 7 Dec. 1908. In liquidation 28 Feb. 1909. Debenture holders were repaid and a return of about 55s. per share was expected **1909**

Wellington & Severn Junction Railway Co. Inc. by Special Act 1853. Under Great Western Railway Act of 1892 the undertaking was acquired by that company. Holders of every 10 shares of £10 received £100 consolidated guaranteed stock in purchasing company **1893**

Wellington Coal & Gaslight Co. *See* Wellington (Salop) Gas Co.

Wellington District Electricity Co. Ld. Regd. 1926. All capital was owned by West of England Electric Investments Ld. Dissolved 1 Apr. 1941 under Electricity Act 1947 **1936**

Wellington Gas Co. Ld. Inc. New Zealand 1869. 5% mortgage debentures repaid 1912 **1912**

Wellington Gas & Coal Co. *See* Wellington (Somerset) Gas Co.

Wellington, Grey & Bruce Railway. Inc. Canada 1869. Amalgamated with Grand Trunk Railway Co. of Canada in 1893. Holders of ordinary stock were entitled to an equal amount of consolidated ordinary stock in acquiring company. The 7% 1st mortgage bonds were acquired in Jan. 1942. by H. M. Treasury at £125 9s. 8d. for every £100 bonds held **1893**

Wellington Hotel (Tunbridge Wells) Co. Ld. Regd. 1896. Vol. liq. 3 May 1927. Final meeting return regd. 29 July 1927 **1928**

Wellington House Ld. Regd. 1909. Court Order to wind up 19 Dec. 1911. Liquidator released 13 Feb. 1914. Struck off Register 3 Sept.1918 **1913**

Wellington Iron & Coal Co. Ld. Regd. 1873. Court Orders: to wind up 23 Aug. 1877; to dissolve 2 Mar. 1880 ***1877**

Wellington (Salop) Gas Co. Estd. as Wellington Coal & Gaslight Co. by Deed of Settlement 1851; inc. as above by Special Act 1903. Dissolved 1 May 1949, undertaking being vested in West Midland Area Gas Board under Gas Act 1948. Holders of securities were entitled to receive, in respect of each £100 unit held, British Gas 3% guaranteed stock 1990–95 as follows:

	£	s.	d.
Ord. stock (5% stand.)	162	10	0
4% red. pref. stock (1967)	102	0	0
4% red. pref. stock (1968)	100	0	0
5% perp. deb. stock	127	0	0	**1952**

Wellington (Somerset) Gas Co. Estd. as Wellington Gas & Coal Co. by Deed of Settlement 1834; regd. as Wellington (Somerset) Gas, Coke & Light Co. Ld. 1898; inc. as above by Special Act 1904. Dissolved 1 May 1949, undertaking being vested in South Western Area Gas Board under Gas Act 1948. Holders of securities were entitled to receive, in respect of each £100 unit held. British Gas 3 guaranteed stock 1990–95 as follows:

	£	s.	d.
6% irred. deb. stock	145	0	0
4% irred. deb. stock	102	10	0
4½% red. debs	104	0	0	**1952**

Wellington Water Co. Undertaking was purchased by Wellington (Salop) Improvement Commissioners **1886**

Wells & Co. Ld. Regd. 1882. Removed from Register 1906 **1885**

Wells, Birch Ryde & Co. Ld. *See* Hoyland Silkstone Colliery Co. Ld.

Wells, Gas Light Co. Inc. by Special Act 1832. Dissolved 1 May 1949, undertaking being vested in

VOL. FOR

South Western Area Gas Board under Gas Act 1948. Holders of securities were entitled to receive, in respect of each £100 unit held, British Gas 3% guaranteed stock 1990–95 as follows:

	£	s.	d.
Cons. ord. stock (5% max.)	110	0	0
5% cons. pref. stock	112	10	0
6½% pref. stock	145	0	0
4½% red. deb. stock	102	10	0
3½% red. deb. stock	100	0	0	**1952**

Wells (J. & G.) Ld. Regd. 1876. A subsidiary of United Steel Companies Ld. Vol. liq. (members') 24 Aug. 1955. Final meeting return regd. 24 Aug. 1956 .... **1942**

Wells Water Co. Ld. Regd 1870 as Wells Water Works Co. Ld. Under Act of 1901, the undertaking was sold to Wells Corporation for £19,176. Removed from Register 1903 **1904**

Wells Watford Brewery Ld. Regd. 1925. All capital owned by Benskin's Watford Brewery Ld. Vol. liq. (members') 9 June 1955. Final meeting return regd. 4 Oct. 1955 **1953**

Welsbach Incandescent Gas Light Co. Ld. Regd. 1897. Vol. liq. 31 Mar. 1911. Undertaking was acquired by Welsbach Light Co. Ld., in which company shareholders were entitled to 2s. 8d. in shares of £1 for each ordinary share of £1 held or 8s. in 4½% debentures in new company and 3s. 4d. in cash per preference share of £1. Final meeting return regd. 30 May 1912. Court Order deferred dissolution. Dissolved 19 Oct. 1923 **1940**

Welsbach Light Co. Ld. Regd. 1911. Vol. liq. (members') 29 Feb. 1944. Almost all shares were held indirectly by Imperial Chemical Industries Ld. Final meeting return regd. 10 Sept. 1945 **1946**

Welsford (J. H.) & Co. Ld. Regd. 1902. Vol. liq. (members') 18 June 1931. Capital returned to contributories—£19 12s. 6d. per share of £10, plus certain investments in specie. Final meeting return regd. 19 July 1933 **1932**

Welsh Anthracite Collieries Ld. Regd. 1926. In 1940 debenture stockholders were allotted 20 fully-paid ordinary shares of 4s. of Abercrave & International Collieries Ld. for each £100 held; and subsequently received 6s. 11½d. (approx.) in the £. Struck off Register 15 Sept. 1961 **1962**

Welsh Associated Collieries Ld. Regd. 1930. Vol. liq. (members') 1 Mar. 1944. Holders of 5½% preference stock were entitled either to repayment at par in cash or 1 ordinary share of £1 in Powell Duffryn Ld., for each £1 preference stock held. All preferred ordinary and ordinary stocks were held by Powell Duffryn Steam Coal Co. Ld. £1,435 6s. 7d. was paid into Companies' Liquidation Account. Final meeting return regd. 3 Mar. 1945 **1946**

Welsh Cold Stores & Ice Co. Ld. (*See* Pellet Street Cold Store Ld.)

Welsh Copper Mining Syndicate Ld. Regd. 1902. Vol. liq. Aug. 1909. No capital returned to contributories. Removed from Register 1910 **1910**

Welsh Crown Spelter Co. Ld. Regd. 1899. Vol. liq. 7 Feb. 1905. Removed from Register 1908 **1905**

Welsh Greyhound Association Ld. Regd. 1927. Vol. liq. 7 May 1928. Final meeting return regd. 28 Aug. 1930 ***1929**

Welsh Insurance Corporation Ld. Regd. 1909. Vol. liq. 11 Aug. 1911. Business was acquired by company of same name. Final meeting return regd. 14 Aug. 1912 **1912**

Welsh Mines Corporation Ld. Regd. 1919. Vol. liq. 7 Mar. 1922. for reconstruction as Cambrian Electrolytic Zinc Co. Ld., in which company shareholders were entitled to 4 15% preference shares of 5s. (credited with 3s. paid) for each preference share of £1 held, or 1 ordinary share of 1s. (credited with 10d. paid) for each ordinary share of 1s. held. Debenture holders received an equal amount of debentures in new company. Final meeting return regd. 17 Mar. 1923 **1923**

Welsh Navigation Steam Coal Co. Ld. Regd. 1906. Vol. liq. (members') 15 Dec. 1952. Capital returned to contributories—2s. 6·55d. per 1s. ordinary share and 15s. 6½d. per 1d. preference stock. £3,710 4s. 9d. was paid into Companies' Liquidation Account. Final meeting return regd. 15 July 1957 **1958**

Welsh, Pearson & Co. Ld. Films, film rights contracts and other assets were acquired by Welsh Pearson-Elder Films Ld. (later Welsh-Pearson Films Ld.-*see below*) for £40,000 in cash and 380,000 fully-paid ordinary shares of 1s. **1929**

Welsh-Pearson Films Ld. Regd. 1928 as Welsh Pearson-Elder Films Ld.; name changed Dec. 1930. Vol. liq. (members') 12 Aug. 1932. Assets realised insufficient to pay unsecured creditors in full. Final meeting return regd. 13 Nov. 1937 **1933**

*See Stock Exchange Year-Book.

VOL. FOR

Welsh-Pearson Films (1932) Ld. Regd. 1932. Vol. liq. (members') 19 Sept. 1932. Final meeting return regd. 2 Nov. 1933 1933

Welsh Refractories Ld. *See* South Wales Refractories Ld.

Welsh Whisky Distillery Co. Ld. Regd. 1889. Removed from Register 1904 1900

Welsh Woollen Manufacturing Co. Ld. Regd. 1874. Removed from Register 1903 1883

Welshpool and Llanfair Light Railway Co. Inc. (under Light Railways Act 1895) by order of Light Railway Commissioners confirmed by Board of Trade 1899. In 1923 the undertaking was merged into the Great Western Railway Co., in which company stockholders were entitled to cash as follows:

For each £100 *held*

3½% Mortgages	£81 cash
3¼% Mortgages	£80 cash
3⅜% Mortgages	£80 cash
3¾% Mortgages	£80 cash
4½% Debenture stock	£90 cash
Ordinary Capital	£24 11*s.* 8*d.* cash

1924

Welshpool & Llanfair Railway Co. Inc. by Special Act 1887. Undertaking abandoned by Act of 1892 1893

Weltevreden Estate & Diamond Mining Co. Ld. Regd. 1897. Mine was sold to New Weltevreden Estate and Diamond Mining Co. Ld., in which company shareholders were entitled to 7 shares for every 10 shares held *plus* 1*s.* 6*d.* per share in cash. Removed from Register 1905 1904

Weltevreden Estate and Gold Mining Co. Ld. Regd. 1888. Vol. liq. 28 June 1905. Removed from Register 1907 1906

Welton Breweries Ld. Regd. 1896 as Thatcher's Breweries Ld.; name changed 1906. Vol. liq. 12 Mar. 1919. Final meeting return regd. 6 May 1920 1919

Welwyn & Hatfield Gas Co. Ld. Regd. 1911 as Welwyn, Knebworth & District Gas Co. Ld.; name changed in 1925. Vol. liq. 19 July 1932. By Special Order of 1933 the undertaking was acquired by Watford & St. Albans Gas Co., in which company contributories were entitled to stock as follows—for each ordinary (10% standard) share of £5 held—£7 8*s.* ordinary stock; for each ordinary (7% standard) share of £5 held—£5 3*s.* 9*d.* ordinary stock; for each 6½% preference share of £5 held—£6 10*s.* 5% preference stock; for every £100 6% preference stock held—£120 5% preference stock; for every £100 7½% redeemable preference stock held—£100 7½% redeemable preference stock. The acquiring company assumed liability for the redeemable mortgages and debentures. Final meeting return regd. 18 May 1933 1934

Welwyn Commercial Buildings Ld. Regd. 1926 under Industrial & Provident Societies Act as Factory Buildings Ld.; name changed to Welwyn Commercial Buildings Ld. 1929; registered under Companies' Act as W. C. B. (Holdings) Ld. 1937; name changed 1938. Vol. liq. (members') 12 May 1949. Preference shares (of £1) were repaid at 21*s.* 6*d.* per share. Capital returned to ordinary contributories—60*s.* 9·447*d.* per share of 10*s.* £248 14*s.* 11*d.* was paid into Companies' Liquidation Account. Final meeting return regd. 14 Dec. 1950 1951

Welwyn Garden City Electricity Supply Co. Ld. Regd. 1922. Dissolved 1 Apr. 1948, undertaking being vested in British (later Central) Electricity Authority and Eastern Area Board under Electricity Act 1947. Holders of ordinary and 7% preference shares were entitled to receive British Electricity 3% guaranteed stock (1968–73), as follows—2*s.* 1½*d.* stock for each ordinary share (of 1*s.*) held and £1 12*s.* 6*d.* stock for each preference share (of £1) held ... 1949

Welwyn Garden City Ld. Regd. 1920. Vol. liq. (members') 12 May 1949. Shareholders received (per share of £1) 24*s.* 8·71*d.* cash and shares of a nominal value of approx. 37*s.* 3½*d.* in Howardsgate Trust Ld. £6,091 19*s.* 1*d.* was paid into Companies' Liquidation Account. Final meeting return regd. 21 Mar. 1952 1953

Welwyn, Knebworth & District Gas Co. Ld. *See* Welwyn and Hatfield Gas Co. Ld.

Welwyn Restaurants Ld. Regd. 1920. Vol. liq. (members') 28 Oct. 1957. Final meeting return regd. 29 July 1958 1951

Wem Gas Light & Coke Co. Ld. Regd. 1860. Dissolved 1 May 1949, undertaking being vested in West Midland Area Gas Board under Gas Act 1948. Holders of ordinary shares (of £5) were entitled to receive £10 2*s.* 6*d.* British Gas 3% guaranteed stock 1990–95 for each share held 1952

Wembley Motors Ld. Regd. 1906 as Fiat Motors Ld.; name changed Aug. 1919. Vol. liq. 12 Feb. 1926. Undertaking and assets were acquired by Fiat (England) Ld. Final meeting return regd. 19 Dec. 1928 1927

Wembley Park Estate Co. Ld. Regd. 1889 as Tower Co. Ld.; name changed 1906. Vol. liq. (members') 24 Sept. 1930. Capital returned to contributories—£1 7*s.* 9*d.* per share of £1. £536 10*s.* 11*d.* was paid into Companies' Liquidation Account in respect of repayments and a further £303 13*s.* 3*d.* in respect of unclaimed dividends. Final meeting return regd. 26 Sept. 1931 1931

Wemmer Gold Mining Co. Ld. Inc. Transvaal 1891. Vol. liq. 29 Mar. 1906. Acquired by Village Main Reef Gold Mining Co. Ld., in which company shareholders received 6 shares of £1 for every 5 shares of £1 held 1907

Wemyss & Buckhaven Railway Co. Authorised by Board of Trade Certificate in 1879. Under North British Railway Act 1889 the undertaking was amalgamated with that company 1890

Wemyss and District Tramways Co. Ld. Regd. Edinburgh 1905. Vol. liq. (members') 6 Apr. 1937. Capital returned to contributories—20*s.* per preference share of £1; £3 9*s.* 6*d.* per ordinary share of £1. £13 4*s.* 11*d.* was paid to Accountant of the Court in respect of shares acquired under Sec. 152 of Companies Act 1929 by W. Alexander & Sons Ld. and £11 12*s.* 4*d.* in respect of unclaimed dividends. Final meeting return regd. 29 July 1938 1938

Wendigo Copper Co. Ld. *See* Isle Royale Land Corporation Ld.

Wenham Co. Ld. Regd. 1885 as Anglo-Continental Gas-Lamp Co. Ld.; name changed Mar. 1886. Vol. liq. May 1888. Final meeting return regd. 11 Dec. 1890 1894

Wenham Patent Gas Lamp Co. Ld. Regd. 1884. Vol. liq. 10 May 1886. Business acquired by Wenham Co. Ld. Final meeting return regd. 15 Aug. 1889 1893

Wenlock Railway Co. Inc. by Special Act 1861. Under Great Western Railway Act of 1896 the undertaking was amalgamated with that company. Holders of 3½% debenture stock received 4% debenture stock on basis of equal income. Holders of £100 5% preference shares or ordinary shares received £100 or £70 consolidated preference stock respectively 1897

Wensley Line Co., Ld. Regd. 1920. Vol. liq. (members') 27 Apr. 1953. Final meeting return regd. 2 Sept. 1953 1940

Wentworth Extension Ld. Regd. 1893. Reconstructed 1898 as company of same name. Shareholders were entitled to 1 share of 5*s.* (credited with 4*s.* paid) in new company for each share of 5*s.* held. Removed from Register 1903 1900

Wentworth Extension Ld. Regd. 1898. Amalgamated 1900 with D'Arcy Wentworth Gold Mines Ld., in which company shareholders were entitled to 3 shares of £1 (credited as fully-paid) for every 16 shares of 5*s.* held. Removed from Register 1903 1901

Wentworth Gold Mining & Indian Estates Co. Ld. Regd. 1881. Vol. liq. 18 Jan. 1895. Final meeting return regd. 14 Jan. 1896 1895

Wentworth Goldfields Property Co. Ld. Regd. 1890. Amalgamated 1900 with D'Arcy Wentworth Gold Mines Ld., in which company shareholders were entitled to 1 fully-paid share of £1 for every 4 shares of £1 held. Removed from Register 1903 1901

Werneth Investment Trust Ld. Regd. 1934. Vol. liq. (members') 22 Jan. 1947. Assets were transferred to Platt Bros. & Co. (Holdings) Ld. (later Stone Platt Industries Ld.). Final meeting return regd. 10 June 1947 1939

Wessex Aircraft & Shipbuilding Co. Ld. *See* Wessex Shipbuilding & Manufacturing Co. Ld.

Wessex Electricity Co. Inc. by Special Act 1927. Dissolved 1 Apr. 1948, undertaking being vested in British (later Central) Electricity Authority and Southern Area Board under Electricity Act 1947. Holders of 3½% debenture stock were entitled to receive £1 0*s.* 10*d.* British Electricity 3% guaranteed stock (1968–73), for each £1 stock held 1946

Wessex Flax Factories Ld. Regd. 1920. Receiver appointed 2 Feb. 1923; ceased to act 28 Jan. 1926. Assets were distributed among debenture holders. Struck off Register Dec. 1931 1932

Wessex Shipbuilding & Manufacturing Co. Ld. Regd. 1917 as Wessex Aircraft & Shipbuilding Co. Ld.; name changed July 1919. Receiver appointed 21 Oct. 1920. Vol. liq. 26 Oct. 1920. Court Order to continue winding up under supervision 23 Nov. 1920. Receiver ceased to act 7 Aug. 1923. Struck off Register 26 Mar. 1929 .... *1921

West Africa Buildings Ld. Regd. 1913. Vol. liq. (members') 30 June 1943. All shares were held by Bank of West Africa Ld. (later Standard Bank of West Africa Ld.). Final meeting return regd. 28 Feb. 1944 1944

**See Stock Exchange Year-Book.*

VOL. FOR

West African Co. Ld. Regd. 1877. Vol. liq. 31 Mar. 1879. Final meeting return regd. 30 Dec. 1881 .... ***1880**

West Africa Corporation Ld. Regd. 1900. The properties were acquired by Himan Central Gold Mines Ld. Removed from Register 1910 .... **1908**

West African Consolidated Gold Mines Ld. Regd. 1895. Vol. liq. 8 Dec. 1899. Final meeting return regd. 25 May 1938 .... **1900**

West African Development Co. Ld. Regd. 1909. Vol. liq. 2 Feb. 1914. Final meeting return regd. 14 July 1915 **1914**

West African Development Trust Ld. Regd. 1925. Court Order to wind-up 8 Feb. 1954. No capital returned to contributories. Liquidator released 11 Jan. 1957. Struck off Register 25 Aug. 1959 .... **1958**

West African Diamond Syndicate Ld. Regd. 1923. Vol. liq. (members') 8 Sept. 1948 for construction as Akim Concessions Ld. in which company shareholders were entitled to receive 1 fully-paid deferred share (of 1s.) for every 10 shares (of 5s.) held. Final meeting return regd. 17 May 1949 .... **1950**

West African Diamonds Ld. *See* Kwahu Mining Co. Ld.

West African Enterprise Syndicate, Ld. Regd. 1909. Vol. liq. (creditors') 9 Dec. 1929. Struck off Register 1 Oct. 1946 .... **1946**

West African Estates, Agency and Development Ld. Regd. 1901. Struck off Register 29 Nov. 1907 ..... **1908**

West African Estates and Development Co. Ld. Regd. 1895. Court Order to wind up 2 Aug. 1897. Removed from Register 1908 .... **1898**

West African Exploring Co. Ld. Regd. 1895. Struck off Register 15 Aug. 1952 .... **1911**

West African (Gold Coast) Mining Corporation Ld. Regd. 1900. Vol. liq. July 1909. Removed from Register 1913 .... **1910**

West African Gold Concessions Ld. *See* Liberian Development Co. Chartered and Limited.

West African Gold Mines & Estates Ld. *See* West African Mines & Estates Ld.

West African Gold Trust Ld. Regd. 1900. Vol. liq. 7 June 1906. Reconstructed as West African Gold Trust (1906) Ld., in which company shareholders were entitled to 1 share of 5s. (credited with 3s. paid) for each share of £1 held. Final meeting return regd. 26 Feb. 1907 .... **1908**

West African Gold Trust (1906) Ld. Regd. 1906. Vol. liq. 13 May 1915. Final meeting return regd. 2 Mar. 1916 .... **1916**

West African Hinterland Consolidated Ld. Regd. 1901. Vol. liq. 18 July 1906. Removed from Register 1907 **1907**

West African Lands Ld. Regd. 1901. Struck off Register 1911 .... **1909**

West African Mahogany & Petroleum Co. Ld. Regd. 1895. Removed from Register 1904 .... **1899**

West African Mahogany & Petroleum Co. Ld. See West African Mahogany, Petroleum and Gold Co. Ld.— regd. 1899.

West African Mahogany, Petroleum and Gold Co. Ld. Regd. 1899 as West African Mahogany and Petroleum Co. Ld.; name changed Jan. 1900. Vol. liq. 5 June 1923. Reconstructed as West African Mahogany Co. Ld., in which company shareholders were entitled to 2 shares of 5s. (credited with 3s. paid) for each share of £1 held. Holders of income bonds and debentures were entitled to fully-paid shares in new company to nominal value of holding. Holders of outstanding and former income bonds were entitled to profit sharing certificate of same nominal value of bonds held. Final meeting return regd. 16 July 1926 **1924**

West African Mines & Estates Ld. Regd. 1900 as West African Gold Mines & Estates Ld.; name changed July 1926. Vol. liq. 17 July 1929 for reconstruction as company of same name. Shareholders were entitled to 1 fully-paid preference share of 4s. for every 2 preferred ordinary shares of 2s. held or 3 ordinary shares of 4s. (credited with 2s. 6d. paid) for every 8 ordinary shares of 2s. held, or 1 ordinary share of 4s. (credited with 2s. 6d. paid) for every 2 deferred shares of 2s. held. Final meeting return regd. 28 Mar. 1930 .... **1930**

West African Mines & Estates Ld. Regd. 1929. Vol. liq. (members') 12 Apr. 1932. Reconstructed as company of same name. Shareholders were entitled to 2 preference shares of 2s. 6d. (credited with 2s. paid) for each preference share of 4s. held or 3 ordinary shares of 2s. 6d. (credited with 2s. paid) for every 2 ordinary shares of 4s. held. Final meeting return regd. 8 Oct. 1932 .... **1933**

West African Mines Ld. Regd. 1900. Vol. liq. 2 July 1903. The properties were sold to Nanwa Gold Mines Ld., in which company shareholders were entitled to 18 shares of £1 (credited as fully-paid) for every 5 shares of £1 (5s. paid) held. Struck off Register 7 Dec. 1926 .... **1904**

VOL. FOR

West African Mines Ld. Regd. 1910. Vol. liq. 7 Nov. 1917. Final meeting return regd. 14 Mar. 1921 ..... **1918**

West African Mines Selection Syndicate Ld. Regd. 1910. Vol. liq. 13 Mar. 1919. Final meeting return regd. 5 Nov. 1921 .... **1919**

West African Motors Ld. Regd. 1926. Vol. liq. (members') 19 Feb. 1931. Capital returned to contributories—£2,160 14s. 1d. Final meeting return regd. 4 Apr. 1942 .... **1931**

West African, Nigerian & General Trust Ld. Regd. 1920. Vol. liq. (members') 12 Nov. 1930. Reconstructed as Swithin's Investment Co. Ld., in which company shareholders were entitled to 3 shares of £1 for every 5 shares of £1 held. Final meeting return regd. 7 Aug. 1931 .... **1931**

West African Properties Ld. Regd. 1900. Removed from Register 1911 .... **1908**

West African Proprietary Ld. Regd. 1909. Vol. liq. 23 Sept. 1915. Final meeting return regd. 1 Sept. 1916 **1916**

West African Prospectors Ld. Regd. 1900. Vol. liq. 22 Nov. 1926. Final meeting return regd. 5 July 1927 **1927**

West African Rubber & Produce Association Ld. *See* Nigerian & Colonial Corporation Ld.

West African Rubber, Oil, Gold & Stores Syndicate Ld. Regd. 1910. Vol. liq. 29 Jan. 1915. Final meeting return regd. 9 Feb. 1916 .... **1915**

West African Rubber Plantations Ld. Regd. 1905. Vol liq. Oct. 1920. Struck off Register 3 June 1955 ..... **1956**

West African Securities Co. Ld. Regd. 1902 as London & Liverpool Ashanti Ld.; name changed Mar. 1905. Vol. liq. Mar. 1908. Removed from Register 1909 **1909**

West African Trust Ld. Regd. 1910. Vol. liq. 22 June 1914. Undertaking and assets were acquired by Colonial Proprietary Co. Ld., in which company shareholders were entitled to 1 share of 5s. (credited as fully-paid) for each share of £1 held. Final meeting return regd. 4 Mar. 1915 .... **1915**

West African Union Mines Ld. Regd. 1910. Vol. liq. 4 May 1915. Final meeting return regd. 30 Nov. 1921 **1916**

West Argentine Extensions Ld. Regd. 1888. Struck off Register 18 Nov. 1902 .... **1903**

West Argentine Gold Co. Ld. Regd. 1883. Vol. liq. 18 June 1889. Reconstructed 1892 as West Argentine Ld., in which company shareholders were entitled to 1 share of £1 (credited with 17s. 6d. paid) for each share of £1 held. Final meeting return regd. 28 Mar. 1893 .... **1895**

West Argentine Ld. Regd. 1892. Vol. liq. 20 Sept. 1895. Reconstructed as Phoenix Ld., in which company shareholders were entitled to 2 shares of 10s. (credited with 7s. 6d. paid) for each share of £1 held. Struck off Register 27 Aug. 1907........................ **1903**

West Assheton Mining Co. Ld. Regd. 1875. Vol. liq. Aug. 1881. Property purchased by Assheton United Mining Co. Ld. Final meeting return regd. 7 June 1882 .... **1883**

West Australian & General Association Ld. Regd. 1896. Vol. liq. 16 June 1896. Reconstructed as Exploration Co. Ld. Shareholders were entitled (inter alia) to preference shares in Sulphide Corporation (Ashcroft's Process) Ld. Final meeting return regd. 9 May 1898 .... **1904**

West Australian and New Zealand Market Trust Ld. *See* West Australian Market Trust Ld.

West Australian Collieries & Fireclay Co. Ld. Regd. 1899. Vol. liq. June 1908. Removed from Register 1909 .... **1909**

West Australian El Dorado Syndicate Ld. Regd. 1895. Removed from Register 1912 .... **1899**

West Australian Exploration Co. Ld. Regd. 1889. Vol. liq. 28 Sept. 1893. Final meeting return regd. 26 Mar. 1895 .... **1894**

West Australian Exploring and Finance Corporation Ld. Regd. 1894. Reconstructed 1897 as London and Globe Finance Corporation Ld. Deferred shareholders were entitled to 61 fully-paid shares of £1 in new company for each deferred share of £1 held; ordinary shareholders were entitled to 5 fully-paid shares of £1 for every 2 shares of £1 held *plus* 9½d. per share in cash. Removed from Register 1906 .... **1901**

West Australian Gold Concessions Ld. Regd. 1894. Vol. liq. 7 Jan. 1897. Reconstructed as company of same name. Shareholders were entitled to 2 shares of £1 (credited with 17s. 6d. paid) for each share of £1 held. Final meeting return regd. 9 June 1898 ...... **1903**

West Australian Gold Concessions Ld. Regd. 1897. Struck off Register 22 Dec. 1903 .... **1904**

West Australian (Gold District) Trading Corporation Ld. Regd. July 1896. Court Order to wind up; 25 Jan. 1897. Removed from Register 1909 .... **1897**

West Australian (Gold District) Trading Syndicate Ld. Regd. Feb. 1896. Undertaking was sold July 1896 to West Australian (Gold District) Trading Corporation Ld. for 340,000 fully-paid ordinary shares of 5s.

VOL. FOR

and 1,200 fully-paid founders' shares of £1. Removed from Register 1908 1897

West Australian Gold Fields Ld. Regd. 1893. Vol. liq. May 1907. Capital returned to contributories—4s. per preference share of £1. Removed from Register 1911 1909

West Australian Gold Properties Development Ld. See General Property Development Ld.

West Australian Goldfields Water Supply Co. Ld. Inc. Australia 1890. In liquidation in 1899 1899

West Australian Joint Stock Trust & Finance Corporation Ld. Regd. 1895. Vol. liq. 18 Oct. 1898. Undertaking was transferred to Westralian Joint Stock Loan & Finance Corporation Ld. Final meeting return regd. 13 June 1900 1899

West Australian Land Co. Ld. Regd. 1885. Vol. liq. 4 July 1894. Court Order to stay proceedings 19 Dec. 1894. Vol. liq. 28 Jan. 1897. The debentures were redeemed on 31 Jan. 1897. Capital returned to contributories—£11 per share of £10; further payments (if any) not known. Final meeting return regd. 19 Apr. 1898 1898

West Australian Loan & General Finance Corporation Ld. Regd. 1894. Vol. liq. 18 Oct. 1898. Undertaking was transferred to Westralian Joint Stock Loan and Finance Corporation Ld., in which company shareholders were entitled to 1 share of £1 (credited as fully-paid) for each ordinary share of £1 held, or 25 fully-paid shares of £1 for each founders' share of £1 held. Final meeting return regd. 13 June 1900 1899

West Australian Market Trust Ld. Regd. Jan. 1897 as West Australian and New Zealand Market Trust Ld.; name changed Aug. 1897. Vol. liq. 18 June 1898. Reconstructed as Westralian Market Trust Ld., in which company shareholders were entitled to 1 share of £1 (credited with 15s. paid) for each share of £1 held. Final meeting return regd. 15 June 1900 1899

West Australian Mine Owners' Exploration Syndicate Ld. Regd. 1894. Removed from Register 1906 1901

West Australian Minerals & Finance Co. Ld. Regd. 1893. Removed from Register 1905 1904

West Australian Mines Development Syndicate Ld. Regd. 1895. Reconstructed 1897 as Venture Corporation Ld., in which company shareholders were entitled to 2 shares of £1 (credited with 17s. 6d. paid) for each share of £1 held. Final meeting return regd. 9 June 1898 1903

West Australian Mining Co. Ld. Regd. 1892 as Victoria Copper Co. Ld.; name changed Jan. 1893. Vol. liq. 18 June 1895. Reconstructed as company of same name. Shareholders were entitled to 1 fully-paid share of 5s. in new company for each share held. Final meeting return regd. 3 Sept. 1896 1902

West Australian Mining Co. Ld. Regd. 1895. Vol. liq. 6 Aug. 1897. Reconstructed as company of same name. Shareholders entitled to 1 share of 2s. (credited as fully-paid) for each share of 5s. held. Final meeting return regd. 3 Apr. 1900 1902

West Australian Mining Co. Ld. Regd. 1897. Vol. liq. 17 Mar. 1902. Reconstructed as African and Australian Co. Ld., in which company shareholders were entitled to 1 share of 2s. (credited with 1s. paid) for each share of 2s. held. Final meeting return regd. 15 Feb. 1906 1908

West Australian Mortgage & Agency Corporation Ld. Regd. Edinburgh 1887. Vol. liq. June 1904. Final meeting return regd. 18 July 1905 1905

West Australian Pastoral & Colonization Co. Ld. Regd. 1890. Removed from Register 1910 1901

West Australian Pioneers Ld. Regd. 1895. Vol. liq. 14 Dec. 1898. Undertaking and assets were transferred to Colonial Consolidated Finance Corporation Ld., in which company shareholders were entitled to 1 fully-paid share of £1 for each fully-paid share of £1 held or 1 share of £1 (15s. paid) for each share of £1 (15s. paid) held. Final meeting return regd. 28 July 1902 1899

West Australian Proprietary Cement Leases Ld. Regd. 1896. Removed from Register 1901 1900

West Australian Share Corporation Ld. Regd. 1895. Vol. liq. 4 Oct. 1897. Amalgamated with West Australian Gold Fields Ld., in which company shareholders were entitled to 3 ordinary shares of £1 (credited as fully-paid) for every 3 shares of £1 held. Final meeting return regd. 21 Mar. 1900 1907

West Australian Timber & Saw Mills Co. Ld. Regd. 1895. Application money was returned. Removed from Register 1898 1897

West Australian Tin Syndicate Ld. Vol. liq. 4 Apr. 1902. Final meeting return regd. 30 Apr. 1908 .... *1901

West Australian Trading and Exploration Co. Ld. Regd. 1895. Vol. liq. 3 Aug. 1898. Final meeting return regd. 13 Sept. 1899 1899

West Australian Trust Ld. Regd. 1895. Removed from Register 1905 1904

West Australian Venture Syndicate Ld. Regd. 1895. Reconstructed 1897 as Venture Corporation Ld., in which company shareholders were entitled to 93 fully-paid shares of £1 for every 100 ordinary shares of £1 (17s. 6d. paid) held or 92½ fully-paid shares of £1 for each founders' share of £1 held. Removed from Register 1901 1903

West Basset Mine. Amalgamated with South Wheal Frances Mine in 1892 to form South Frances United Mines 1896

West Battery Reef Gold Mining Co. Ld. Regd. 1889. Vol. liq. 30 July 1891. Final meeting return regd. 5 July 1893 1892

West Boulder Gold Mines (W. A.) Ld. Regd. 1895. Vol. liq. 4 May 1898. Reconstructed as Central and West Boulder Gold Mines (W. A.) Ld., in which company shareholders were entitled to 2 shares of £1 (credited with 17s. paid) for every 3 shares of £1 held. Final meeting return regd. 24 Feb. 1899 1899

West Brighton Estate Co. Ld. Regd. 1872. Final meeting return regd. 25 July 1977 1951

West British Development Syndicate Ld. Regd. 1905. Vol. liq. 20 Mar. 1912. Final meeting return regd. 26 Nov. 1918 1913

West (Butchers) Ld. See West (Food Stores) Ld.

West Calder Gas Co. Ld. Regd. in Edinburgh 1871. Dissolved 1 May 1949, undertaking being vested in Scottish Area Gas Board† under Gas Act 1948. Holders of ordinary shares (of £1) were entitled to receive 10s. British Gas 3% guaranteed stock 1990–95 for each share held 1952

West Callao Gold Mining Co. Ld. Regd. 1882. Removed from Register 1905 1886

West Canadian Collieries, Ld. Regd. 1903. Vol. liq. (members') 22 Dec. 1964. Capital returned to contributories (per share of 10s.); C$5·19 plus 1 share of C$·10 of West Canadian Mineral Holdings Ld. Final meeting return regd. 12 Feb. 1972 1972

West Canadian Deep Leads Ld. Regd. 1908. Receiver for debenture holders appointed in Nov. 1915. Struck off Register Jan. 1932 1932

West Canadian Placer Ld. Regd. 1909. Struck off Register Apr. 1929 1930

West Carbury Tramways & Light Railways Co. Ld. See Schull and Skibbereen Tramways & Light Railways Co. Ld.

West Carclaze China Clay Co. Ld. Regd. 1913. Vol liq. 13 Oct. 1930. All capital was owned by Lovering China Clays Ld. Final meeting return regd. 12 Sept. 1931 1933

West Carzise Mine. Formed 1887 under cost-book system. Company was being wound up in 1892 ... 1892

West Caucasian Oilfields Ld. Regd. 1913. Properties were in hand of Soviet Government. Struck off Register Feb. 1930 1930

West Central Wagon Co. Ld. Regd. 1872. Vol. liq. 15 May 1875. Court Order to continue winding up under supervision 11 Sept. 1878. Final meeting return regd. 17 July 1886 .... *1876

West Cheshire Water Co. Inc. by Special Act. All issued capital was held by West Cheshire Water Co. Ld ... 1926

West Cheshire Water Co. Ld. Regd. 1884. Vol. liq. 17 Feb. 1926. Undertaking was acquired by West Cheshire Water Board for £44,000 in cash and £150,000 5% Water Board stock. Final meeting return regd. 11 Jan. 1927 1926

West Chiverton Mine. Formed under cost-book system. Company was being wound up 1883 1883

West Clare Railway Co. Ld. Regd. 1883. Inc. by Special Act 1884. In 1925 the undertaking was merged into the Great Southern Railways Co. The scheme provided that the holders of the Baronial Guaranteed Share capital should receive an equal amount of Great Southern Railways 4% Preference Stock, and that the other shares should be cancelled 1925

West Coast Associated Tanneries Ld. Regd. 2 Mar. 1949. Vol. liq. (creditors') 26 May 1977. Return of final meeting filed Aug. 1985. Distribution of 20p in £1 per preference share made 18 Apr. 1980 and 2nd & final distribution of 19·591p per preference share made 9 July 1985. £1,850·15 paid into Companies' Liquidation Account in respect of unclaimed dividend 1986–7

West Coast Consols Ld. Regd. 1901. Struck off Register 20 Nov. 1908 1909

West Coast Explorers Parent Syndicate Ld. Regd. 1900. Removed from Register 1909 1905

West Coast Gold Fields Ld. Regd. 1901. Removed from Register 1906 1905

West Coast Mines Ld. Regd. 1925. Vol. liq. 10 Dec. 1926. Interest in Gold Coast and Nigeria were sold to West African Mines & Estates Ld., in which

VOL. FOR

company shareholders were entitled to 1 fully-paid ordinary share of 2s. and 9 fully-paid deferred shares of 2s. for every 10 fully-paid shares of 2s. held and an option (since expired) over further shares. Final meeting return regd. 23 Apr. 1927 .... **1927**

West Coast of Africa Oil & Fuel Co. Ld. Regd. 1901. Vol. liq. May 1910. Removed from Register 1911 ... **1911**

West Combe Park Estate Ld. Regd. 1877. Removed from Register 1906 .... ***1886**

West Condurrow Mine. Formed under cost-book system 1886. In liquidation in 1889 .... **1889**

West Cornwall Electricity Supply Co. Ld. Regd. 1926. Vol. liq. (members') 24 Jan. 1938. Undertaking acquired by Cornwall Electric Power Co. Capital returned to contributories—£139,171 2s. 9d. Final meeting return regd. 12 May 1938 .... **1938**

West Cornwall Railway Co. Inc. by Special Act 1846. Dissolved 2 Apr. 1948, undertaking vested 1 Jan. 1948 in British Transport Commission under Transport Act 1947. Holders of securities were entitled to receive British Transport 3% guaranteed stock 1978–88 in respect of each £100 of capital stock held:

	£	s.	d.
Great Western, Bristol & Exeter & South Devon 4½% joint rent-charge stock..................	115	10	0
West Cornwall gtd. 5% stock	130	0	0

1949

West Cornwall Steamship Co. Ld. Regd. 1870. Vol. liq. 27 June 1907. Final meeting return regd. 26 Feb. 1908 .... ***1886**

West Country Brewery Holdings Ld. Regd. 1956 as Cheltenham Brewery Holdings Ld.; name changed Mar. 1959. All capital was owned by Whitbread & Co. Ld. Vol. liq. (members') 7 Aug 1964. Final meeting return regd. 28 Nov. 1967 .... **1969**

West Crebor Mine. In liquidation in 1886 .... **1886**

West Cumberland Electric Tramways Co. Inc. 1901 by Special Act. Company had not started operations at 4 Feb. 1907. An agreement of 4 May 1906 provided for transfer of all issued shares to Cumberland Electricity & Power Gas Co. **1908**

West Cumberland Iron and Steel Co. Ld. Regd. 1872. Vol. liq. 19 Dec. 1888. Court Order to continue winding up under supervision 17 Jan. 1889. Proceedings were stayed. Vol. liq. 21 May 1892. Final meeting return regd. 5 Dec. 1899 .... **1893**

West Devon Electric Supply Co. Ld. Regd. 1931. Dissolved 1 Apr. 1948, undertaking being vested in British (later Central) Electricity Authority and South-Western Area Board under Electricity Act 1947. Holders of ordinary and 6% preference stock were entitled to receive, in respect of each £1 unit of capital held, £1 8s. and £1 7s. British Electricity 3% guaranteed stock (1968–73) respectively **1949**

West Drayton Millboard Co. Ld. Regd. 1905. Vol. liq. 22 Feb. 1909. Struck off Register 18 Jan. 1921 .... **1910**

West End Brick Works Ld. Regd. 1925. Vol. liq. 4 Oct. 1927. Final meeting return regd. 5 Dec. 1927 .... **1937**

West End Clothiers Co. Ld. Regd. 1902 as West End Clothiers (1902) Ld.; name changed 1903. Receiver for debenture stockholders appointed 26 Mar. 1915. Struck off Register 1924 .... **1917**

West End Diamonds, Ld. Inc. in the Orange Free State 25 Oct. 1919. Vol. liq. 22 Dec. 1941 .... **1948**

West End Playhouse Ld. Regd. Edinburgh 1911. Vol. liq. (members') 15 July 1960. Final meeting return regd. 7 Nov. 1962 .... **1947**

West End Ranching Co. Ld. Inc. Transvaal 1921. In liquidation July 1923 .... **1924**

West End Wine Co. Ld. Regd. 1925. Direct controlling interest was held by Findlater Mackie & Co. Ld. (later Findlater Prentis & Co. Ld.). Vol. liq. (members') 29 Jan. 1945. Final meeting return regd. 1 Jan. 1946 .... **1946**

West Fingall Ld. Regd. 1900. Undertaking and assets were acquired by Great Fingall Consolidated Ld. Capital returned to contributories—10s. per share of £1; further payments (if any) not known. Removed from Register 1904 .... **1904**

West Flanders Railways Co. See Société Anonyme des Chemins de Fer de la Flandre Occidental.

West (Food Stores) Ld. Regd. 1918 as West (Butchers) Ld.; name subsequently changed. All capital was owned by Fitch Lovell Ld. Vol. liq. (members') 24 May 1965. Final meeting return regd. 12 May 1966 **1960**

West Galicia Railway Co. Ld. Regd. 1886 as Coruna, Santiago & Peninsular Railway Co. Ld.; name changed Feb. 1896. Vol. liq. 29 Feb. 1928. Final meeting return regd. 12 Oct. 1928 .... **1929**

West Gloucestershire Power Co. Ld. Regd. 1922 as Norchard Synd. Ld.; name changed 1922. Dissolved 1 Apr. 1948, undertaking being vested in British (later Central) Electricity Authority and Midlands

VOL. FOR

Area Board under Electricity Act 1947. Holders of securities were entitled to receive British Electricity 3% guaranteed stock (1968–73) as follows in respect of each £1 unit of capital held:

6½% participating preference stock.....	1	11	8
Ordinary stock.......................................	1	12	9
4% 1st mortgage debenture stock	1	0	7½

1949

West Gloucestershire Water Co. Inc. by Special Act 1884. Under provisions of The Bristol Waterworks (West-Gloucestershire) Order 1959 the undertaking vested in the Bristol Waterworks Co. from 1 July 1959. Stockholders received in exchange for their holdings, a like amount of Bristol company stocks carrying similar rights in each case to those of the stock exchanged. The outstanding debenture stocks became debenture stocks of the Bristol company. charged upon the undertaking and assets thereof, Company was dissolved by resolution of the directors passed on 22 Oct. 1959 .... **1961**

West Godolphin Mining Co. Established 1880. Liquidated. Capital returned to contributories—1s. 3d. per share **1891**

West Hallam Colliery Co. Ld. Regd. 1895. Vol. liq. (creditors') 30 June 1947. No capital was returned to contributories. Final meeting return regd. 28 July 1952 .... **1953**

West Ham Gas Co. Formed by Deed of Settlement 1846; inc. by Special Act 1856. Undertaking was transferred in 1910 to Gas Light and Coke Co. Stockholders were entitled to £121 ordinary, £125 4% consolidated preference and £133½ 3% consolidated debenture stocks in purchasing company for every £100 ordinary, preference and debenture stocks respectively held **1910**

West Highland Railway Co. Inc. by Special Act 1889. Under North British Railway (General Powers) Act of 1902 the ordinary and 3% debenture stocks were exchanged for an equal amount of 3% debenture stock in that company. Under North British Railway Act of 1908 the undertaking was transferred to that company **1909**

West Holway Lead Co. Ld. Regd. 1879. Property acquired by Holywell District Lead Co. Ld. Court Orders: to wind up 5 June 1884; to dissolve 12 Aug. 1886 .... ***1885**

West India & Pacific Steam Ship Co. Ld. Regd. 1863. Business was acquired in 1899 by Frederick Leyland & Co. Ld. Capital returned to contributories—£62 per share of £25 (£20 paid). Removed from Register 1901 .... **1901**

West Indian Aerial Transport Co. Ld. Regd. 1924. Struck off Register 1927 .... ***1926**

West Indian and British Guiana Ice Co. Ld. Regd. 1891. A first return of capital was made to debenture holders out of sale of assets realised by the receiver. Removed from Register 1907 .... **1900**

West Indian Copra and Produce Estates Ld. Regd. 1913. Vol. liq. June 1915. Struck off Register 1921 .... **1916**

West Indian Estates Ld. Group of sugar estates was acquired in 1923 by Trinidad Sugar Estates Ld. for £140,000 cash and £10,000 fully-paid deferred shares of 1s. **1924**

West Indian Exploration Co. Ld. Regd. 1892. Struck off Register 2 Aug. 1904 .... **1905**

West Indian Gold Mining Corporation Ld. Regd. 1887. Reconstructed 1890 as West Indian New Gold Mining Corporation Ld., in which company shareholders were entitled to 1 share of 5s. (credited with 2s. 6d. paid) for each share of £1 held. Removed from Register 1904 .... **1891**

West Indian New Gold Mining Corporation Ld. Regd. 1890. Court Order to wind up 16 Jan. 1892. Reconstructed as West Indian Exploration Co. Ld., in which company shareholders were entitled to 1 share of 5s. (credited with 4s. paid) for each share of 5s. held. Debenture holders were entitled to 145,200 fully-paid shares of 5s. Liquidator released 18 Jan. 1904. Struck off Register 17 May 1929 .... **1900**

West Indian Oil Co. Ld. Regd. 1896 as West Indian Oil Syndicate Ld.; name subsequently changed. Removed from Register 1904 .... ***1901**

West Indian Petroleum Co. Ld. Regd. 1900. Struck off Register 24 Feb. 1922 .... **1915**

West Jequié Rubber Estates Ld. Regd. 1910. Vol. liq. 2 July 1913. Shareholders were entitled to 1 preference share of 1s. (credited as fully-paid) in Jequié Rubber Syndicate Ld. for every 3 shares of 2s. held; fractions were exchanged at par for fully-paid ordinary shares of 2s. in that company. Final meeting return regd. 31 Mar. 1914 .... **1914**

West Kalgurlie Gold Mines Ld. Regd. 1895. Vol. liq. 23 Sept. 1898. Removed from Register 19 Oct. 1906 ***1899**

West Kensington Estates Co. Ld. Regd. 1882 as Gibbs & Flew Ld.; name changed June 1885. Court Order to

VOL. FOR

wind up June 1886. Liquidator released 1 Nov. 1893. Struck off Register 17 June 1904 ... **1886**

West Kent Electric Co. Ld. Regd. 1908. Dissolved 1 Apr. 1948, undertaking being vested in British (later Central) Electricity Authority and South-Eastern Area Board under Electricity Act 1947. Holders of ordinary and 4½% preference shares were entitled to receive, in respect of each share (of £1) held, £2 9*s*. 5*d*. and £1 3*s*. 5*d*. British Electricity 3% guaranteed stock (1968—73) respectively ... **1949**

West Kent Gas Co. Inc. by Special Act 1867. By Act of 1912 the undertaking was acquired by South Suburban Gas Co. Shareholders were entitled to £20 or £14 West Kent Co. ordinary stock (standard dividend 5%) for each 10% original share of 7% maximum share of £10 respectively held ... **1913**

West Kent Gault Brick & Portland Cement Co. Ld. *See* West Kent Portland Cement Co. Ld.

West Kent Portland Cement Co. Ld. Regd. 1872 as West Kent Gault Brick & Portland Cement Co. Ld.; name changed 4 Jan. 1894. Business acquired in 1900 by Associated Portland Cement Manufacturers Ld. Vol. liq. 25 Jan. 1912. Final meeting return regd. 26 Mar. 1912 ... **1940**

West Kerry Light Railway or Tramroad Co. Ld. Inc. 1889 under Tramways & Public Cos. (Ireland) Act (1883). The undertaking was abandoned in pursuance of an Order in Council dated 17 Feb. 1891 ... **1892**

West Kilbride Gas Light Co. Ld. Regd. in Edinburgh 1895. Dissolved 1 May 1949, undertaking being vested in Scottish Area Gas Board under Gas Act 1948. Holders of ordinary shares (of £1) were entitled to receive £2 10s. British Gas 3% guaranteed stock 1990–95 for each share held ... **1952**

West Kitty Mine Co. Established 1879. In liquidation in 1911 ... **1911**

West Kitty Mines Ld. Regd. 1910. Struck off Register 1921 ... **1905**

West Kootenay Mining Corporation Ld. Regd. 1910. Struck off Register 3 June 1921 ... ***1917**

West Lancashire Railway. Inc. by Special Act 1871 .. **1918**

West Lancashire Wagon Co. Ld. Regd. 1874. Vol. liq. 1 Apr. 1920. Final meeting return regd. 17 June 1922 **1921**

West London & Provincial Electric & General Investment Co. Ld. Regd. 1889 as London & Westminster Game Supply Assn. Ld.; name changed to London & Westminster Stores Ld., and later to above. Vol. liq. 12 Apr. 1957. Final meeting return regd. 28 June 1957 ... **1902**

West London & Provincial Electric Supply Co. Ld., later West London & Provincial Electric & General Trust Ld. *See*-London & Westminster Investment Trust Ld

West London Commercial Bank Ld. Regd. 1866. Business was transferred to London & South Western Bank Ld. Court Orders: to wind up 19 Feb. 1887; to dissolve 10 Aug.1894 ... **1888**

West London Dairy Co. Ld. *See* Bennett's Dairies Ld.

West London Extension Railway Co. Inc. by Special Act 1859. Dissolved 2 Apr. 1949; undertaking vested 1 Jan. 1948 in British Transport Commission under Transport Act 1947 ... **1949**

West London Railway Co. Inc. by Special Act 1836 as Birmingham Bristol & Thames Junction Railway Co.; name changed by Act 1840. Dissolved 2 Apr. 1949; undertaking vested 1 Jan. 1948 in British Transport Commission under Transport Act 1947. Holders of ordinary and preference shares were entitled to receive British Transport 3% guaranteed stock 1971–88 as follows in respect of each share of £20 held:

	£	s.	d.	
2% Ord. (class C) shares ...	13	0	0	
3½% 1st class pref. (class A) shares	20	4	0	
6% 2nd class pref. (class B) shares....	31	8	0	**1949**

West Lothian Oil Co. Ld. Regd. Edinburgh 1883. Court Orders: to wind up 24 Feb. 1892; to dissolve 23 Nov. 1895 ... **1894**

West Mallina Gold Mine Ld. The undertaking was acquired in 1895 by Consolidated Gold Mines of Western Australia Ld. for 20,405 fully-paid shares of £1 and 9,595 shares of £1 (credited with 12*s*. paid) **1901**

West Manchester Light Railways Co. Inc. (under Light Railways Act 1896) by order of Light Railway Commissioners confirmed by Board of Trade 1899. Under Trafford Park Act of 1904 the powers were transferred to that company, in which shareholders were entitled to an equal number of shares in exchange for their holdings ... **1905**

West Metropolitan Railway Co. Inc. by Special Act 1899. Construction abandoned by Act of 1904...... **1905**

West Metropolitan Tramways Co. Under an order of Court of Chancery the undertaking was sold in 1894 to London United Tramways Ld. for cash ... **1900**

VOL. FOR

West Mexican Mines Ld. Regd. 1910. Vol. liq. (members') 21 Dec. 1939. No capital returned to contributories. Final meeting return regd. 28 Dec. 1943 ... **1945**

West Middlesex Water Works Co, [Company of Proprietors of the]. Inc. 1806. Undertaking acquired by Metropolitan Water Board as from 24 June 1904 by Act of 1902 ... **1905**

West Midland Sugar Co. Ld. Regd. 1924. Vol. liq. (members') 27 Aug. 1936. Undertaking was acquired by British Sugar Corporation Ld:, for 188,377 fully-paid shares of £1. Shareholders were entitled to 1 such share for each share of £1 held *plus* 10·65*d*. per share in cash. Final meeting return regd. 29 Oct. 1940 ... **1937**

West Midlands Joint Electricity Authority. Inc. by West Midlands Electricity District Order 1925. Dissolved 1 Apr. 1948, undertaking vested in British (later Central) Electricity Authority and Midlands Area Board under the Electricity Act 1947. Holders of 5% stock (1948—68) were entitled to receive £106 10*s*.British Electricity 3% guaranteed stock (1968–73) for every £100 stock held ... **1949**

West Moodie's Gold & Exploration Co. Ld. Regd. 1887. Vol. liq. 28 Feb. 1889. Court Order to continue winding up under supervision Mar. 1889. Final meeting return regd. 3 Mar. 1897 ... **1890**

West Mount Lyell Copper, Gold & Silver Mining Co. (Tasmania) Ld. Regd. 1894. Vol. liq. 7 Mar. 1895. Final meeting return regd. 31 Oct. 1895 ... **1897**

West Mount Lyell Copper, Gold & Silver Mining (Tasmania) Ld. Regd. 1895. Vol. liq. 20 Jan. 1898. Final meeting return regd. 5 May 1899 ... **1897**

West Mount Lyell Ld. Regd. 1907. Struck off Register 1915 ... **1911**

West Mountain Mining Co. Ld. Regd. 1888. Vol. liq. 13 Apr. 1892. Capital returned to contributories—5⅜d. per share of £1. Final meeting return regd. 14 June 1892 ... **1893**

West Nicholson Gold Mining Co. Ld. Regd. 1898. Reconstructed 1905 as East Gwanda Mines Ld., in which company shareholders were entitled to 1½ shares of £1 (credited with 14*s*. paid) for every 5 shares of £1 held. Removed from Register 1908 .. **1905**

West of England Electric Investments Ld. Regd. 1932. Dissolved 1 Apr. 1948, undertaking being vested in British Electricity Authority under Electricity Act 1947. Holders of ordinary shares and 3½% debenture stock were entitled to receive British Electricity 3% guaranteed stock (1968—73) as follows—£2 4*s*. stock for each ordinary share held and £1 0*s*. 7⅛*d*. stock for each £1 debenture stock held ... **1949**

West of England Fire & Life Insurance Co. Established 1807. Undertaking was acquired in 1894 by Commercial Union Assurance Co. Ld., in which company shareholders were entitled to £50 debenture stock for each share of £100 (£35 paid) held **1894**

West of England Fire-clay, Bitumen & Chemical Co. Ld. *See* Cornwall Chemical Co. Ld.

West of England Iron Ore Co. Ld. Regd. 1880. Removed from Register 1905 ... ***1882**

West of England Manganese Mining Co. Ld. Regd. 1881. Vol. liq. 22 Jan. 1883. Final meeting return regd. 21 Sept. 1883 ... **1885**

West of Fife Coal Co. Ld. Regd. Edinburgh 1900. Vol. liq. Nov. 1910. Final meeting return regd. 23 July 1912 ... **1911**

West of India Portuguese Guaranteed Railway Co. Ld. Regd. 1881. Vol. liq. (members') 25 Oct. 1961. Capital stock repaid at par *plus* distribution of 59·29%. Final meeting return regd. 28 Sept. 1968 **1969**

West of Ireland Distillery Co. Ld. Regd. Dublin 1897. In liquidation in 1899 ... **1899**

West of Scotland American Investment Co. Ld. Regd. in Edinburgh 1896. Vol. liq. (creditors') 24 Oct. 1951. Debenture holders received £94 7*s*. 3*d*. per £100. £261 4*s*. 6*d*. was paid to the Accountant of the Court. Final meeting return regd. 26 July 1952 ... **1953**

West of Scotland Gympie Gold Mine Ld. Regd. Edinburgh 1898. Vol. liq. Dec. 1903 for reconstruction under same name. Final meeting return regd. 2 Oct. 1919 ... **1906**

West of Scotland Gympie Gold Mine Ld. Regd. Edinburgh 1903. Vol. liq. 17 Apr. 1907. Struck off Register 5 Feb. 1937 ... **1908**

West of Scotland Investment Trust Ld. Regd. Edinburgh 1912. Vol. liq. (members') 25 Feb. 1935. All shares held by Great Northern Investment Trust Ld. Bulk of assets were distributed in specie. Final meeting return regd. 7 Aug.1936... **1936**

West of Scotland Mines Trust Ld. Regd. Edinburgh 1903. Vol. liq. Mar. 1924. Final meeting return regd. 28 Aug. 1925 ... **1925**

**See Stock Exchange Year-Book.*

VOL. FOR

West Pateley Bridge Lead Mines Ld. Regd. 1876. Vol. liq. Mar. 1885. Final meeting return regd. 9 June 1886 .... **1885**

West Peevor (or West Wheal Peevor). Winding up Order 21 May 1897.......... **1898**

West Polbreen MIne Co. Established 1881. In liquidation in 1891 .... **1891**

West Prussian Mining Co. Ld. Regd. 1875. Vol. liq. 19 Dec. 1910. Final meeting return regd. 12 Oct. 1928 **1911**

West Rand Central Gold Mining Co. Ld. Regd. 1897. Court Order to wind up 15 May 1917. Liquidator released 13 Apr. 1920. Struck off Register 20 Mar. 1925.......... **1918**

West Rand Mines Ld. Inc. Transvaal 1893. Vol. liq. Apr. 1907. Undertaking and assets were acquired by West Rand Consolidated Mines Ld., in which company shareholders were entitled to 1 ordinary share of £1 (credited as fully-paid) for each share of £1 held **1908**

West Randfontein Gold Mining Co. Ld. Inc. Transvaal 1899. Vol. liq. in Mar. 1907, to effect amalgamation with 2 other companies under title of Randfontein Central Gold Mining Co. Ld., in which company shareholders were offered 1 share of £1 for every 2 shares of £1 held.......... **1908**

West Randt Development Syndicate Ld. Regd. 1896. Removed from Register 26 Feb. 1909 .... ***1900**

West Randt Estates and Land Co. Ld. Regd. 1889. Vol. liq. 10 Dec. 1895. Freehold mineral land was acquired by Sterkfontein Gold Estates Ld. for £21,116 in fully-paid shares. Final meeting return regd. 8 Mar. 1898 .... **1896**

West Rhodesian Banket Co. Ld. Regd. 1905. Vol. liq. 10 June 1909. Reconstructed as Amalgamated Properties of Rhodesia Ld. in which company shareholders were entitled to 1 share of 5*s*. for each share of £1 held. Final meeting return regd. 17 June 1910 ..... **1910**

West Riding A. B. C. Publishing Co. Ld. Regd. 1909. Vol. liq. (creditors') 25 Aug. 1938. Assets were acquired by Jackson (J. C.) & Co. Ld. for £22,000 (£12,000 cash and £10,000 in fully-paid shares of 1*s*.) but realisation was insufficient to pay unsecured creditors in full. Final meeting return regd. 2 Sept. 1939 .... **1938**

West Riding Automobile Co. Ld. Regd. 1923. Vol. liq. (members') 20 Mar. 1935. Undertaking was acquired by Yorkshire (West Riding) Electric Tramways Co. Ld. (later West Riding Automobile Co. Ld.). Capital returned to contributories—£180,072 13s. 6*d*. Final meeting return regd. 13 July 1935 . **1936**

West Riding Brickworks Ld. Regd. 1919. Receiver appointed 28 Aug. 1922; ceased to act 9 Oct. 1923. Vol. liq. Oct. 1922. Struck off Register 1930 .... **1925**

West Riding Insurance Co. Ld. Regd. 1897. Vol. liq. 22 Feb. 1908. Final meeting return regd. 3 June 1908 **1909**

West Riding Railway Committee. Inc. by Special Act 1866. In 1923 the undertaking was merged into the London & North Eastern Railway Co., in which company shareholders were entitled to £156¼ 4% first guaranteed stock for each £100 West Riding & Grimsby Railway (Wakefield Station) shares held **1924**

West Riding Union Banking Co. Ld. Established 1832. Inc. 1874. Regd. as limited 1881. Amalgamated Sept. 1902 with Lancashire & Yorkshire Bank Ld., in which company shareholders were entitled to 4 shares of £20 (£10 paid) *plus* cash payment of 21*s*. for every 7 shares of £50 (£10 paid) held **1903**

West Roodepoort Deep Ld. Inc. Transvaal 1895. Vol. liq. in Apr. 1911. Undertaking sold to Princess Estate & Gold Mining Co. Ld., in which company shareholders were entitled to 1 share of £1 for every 5 shares of £1 held and to subscribe for further shares pro rata at 27*s*. 6*d*. per share **1911**

West Somerset Minera Railway Co. Inc. by Special Act 1857. Act of 1923 provided for the abandonment of the railway and winding up of the company **1924**

West Somerset Railway Co. Inc. by Special Act 1857. In 1922 the undertaking was merged into the Great Western Railway Co., in which company stockholders were entitled to stock as follows:

For each £100 held	*G. W.*	
4% Debenture..........	£100 4% Debenture	
4% Irred. Pref	£80 5% Rent Charge	
Ordinary..........	£55 5% Rent Charge	**1924**

West Springs Ld. Inc. Transvaal 1918. Vol. liq. (members') 6 Aug. 1948. Undertaking and assets were sold to Springs Mines Ld., in which company shareholders were entitled to 2 shares (of 5*s*.) for each share of £1 held **1954**

West Staffordshire Gas Co. Ld. Regd. 1913. Dissolved 1 May 1949, undertaking being vested in West Midland Area Gas Board under Gas Act 1948. Holders of securities were entitled to receive British Gas 3% guaranteed stock 1990–95 as follows in respect of each £100 unit, unless otherwise stated, of security held:

	£	s.	d.	
Ord. shares (of £1)..........		11	0	
6% red. debs	100	5	0	
5% red. debs..........	100	5	0	**1952**

West Suburban Gas Light and Coke Co. Ld. Regd. 1905. Vol. liq. 15 Oct. 1906. Undertaking and assets were acquired by Uxbridge Gas Co. Final meeting return regd. 16 Nov. 1918 .... **1907**

West Surrey Water Co. Inc. by Special Act 1869. Undertaking vested in Woking & District Water Co. from 1 Jan. 1960. Holders of capital received capital in the Woking company in exchange as follows—£14 6*s*. 7% ordinary stock per 10% ordinary share; £10 7% ordinary stock per 7% ordinary share; £1 5% ordinary stock per £1 5% ordinary stock; £12 5% preference stock per 6% preference share; £11 5% preference stock per 5½% preference share; £10 5% preference stock per 5% preference share; £1 4½% redeemable preference stock per £1 redeemable preference stock. Outstanding debenture stocks became debenture stocks of the Woking company from 1 Jan. 1960. Company was dissolved 30 June 1962.......... **1963**

West Tokatea Gold Mine Ld. Regd. 1900. Vol. liq. 14 Sept. 1903. Final meeting return regd. 3 May 1904 **1904**

West Ural Petroleum Co. Ld. Regd. 1912. Properties in hands of Soviet Government. Struck off Register 15 Aug. 1952 .... **1953**

West Virginia & Pittsburgh Railroad Co. Organised Virginia 1890. Properties acquired by Baltimore and Ohio Railroad Co., which company owned all capital stock. The 1st mortgage 100-year gold bonds were taken over by acquiring company.......... **1902**

West Wheal Frances. Winding-up Order 21 Jan. 1898 **1898**

West Wheal Grenville Mine Ld. Regd. 1888. Vol. liq. 30 July 1891. Final meeting return regd. 23 Feb. 1892 **1892**

West Wheal Peevor (or West Peevor). Winding-up Order 21 May 1897.......... **1898**

West Wheal Seton. Mine abandoned in 1891 .... **1892**

West Wheal Tolgus. Being wound up in 1885 .... **1885**

West Wilts Electric Light & Power Co. Ld. Regd. 1924. Vol. liq. (members') 15 Feb. 1938. Undertaking acquired by Wessex Electricity Co. Capital returned to contributories—£5 per preference share of £5; £1 6*s*. 7½*d*. per ordinary share of £1. Final meeting return regd. 5 July 1938.......... **1939**

West Wye Valley Lead Mining Co. Ld. Regd. 1875. Vol. liq. 24 July 1880. Final meeting return regd. 24 July 1884 .... ***1880**

West Yorkshire Bank Ld. Regd. 1880 as Halifax Joint Stock Banking Co. Ld.; name changed July 1911. Vol. liq. 5 Nov. 1919. Amalgamated with Lloyds Bank Ld., in which company shareholders were entitled to 5 shares of £50 (credited with £8 paid) for every 4 shares of £25 (£10 paid) held *plus* £5 per share in cash.......... **1920**

West Yorkshire Gas Distribution Co. Inc. by Special Act 1938. Dissolved 1 May 1949, undertaking being vested in North Eastern Area Gas Board under Gas Act 1948. Holders of securities were entitled to receive, British Gas 3% guaranteed stock 1990–95 as follows in respect of each £100 unit of security held:

	£	s.	d.
4½% red. pref. stock..........	106	0	0
4% deb. stock	103	10	0
4½% deb. stock..........	105	10	0

Liability in respect of certain mortgage loans assumed by the Board **1952**

West Yorkshire Tramways Co. Inc. by Special Act 1906 **1911**

Westbourne Grove Drapery & Furnishing Co. Ld. Regd. 1874. Vol. liq. 16 Oct. 1876. Final meeting return regd. 25 Sept. 1877 .... ***1876**

Westbury Gas & Coke Co. Ld. Regd. 1868; statutory powers 1897. Dissolved 1 May 1949, undertaking being vested in South Western Area Gas Board under Gas Act 1948. Holders of securities were entitled to receive, British Gas 3% guaranteed stock 1990–95 as follows in respect of each £10 unit, unless otherwise stated, of security held:

	£	s.	d.	
Orig. ord. shares (10% max.)..........	20	10	0	
New ord. shares (7% max.)..........	14	10	0	
4½% red. pref. shares (of £1)..........	1	0	11	
3½% red. deb. stock (30 Sept. 1952) (per £100)..........	100	0	0	
3½% red. debs. (1952) (issued 29 Sept. 1947) (per £100)..........	100	0	0	
3½% red. deb. stock (1957) (per £100)..........	100	0	0	**1952**

Western Alliance Reinsurance Co. Ld. Regd. 1919. Vol. liq. 1 Apr. 1925. The undertaking and assets were acquired by the Consolidated Assurance Co. Ld., in

VOL. FOR

which company shareholders were entitled to 1 share of £1 (credited as fully-paid) *plus* 3s. in cash for every 3 shares of £1 (10s. paid) held. Final meeting return regd.2 June 1928 .... **1926**

Western American Cattle Co. Ld. Regd. Edinburgh 1882. Vol. liq. Mar. 1883 for reconstruction as Western Ranches Ld. Final meeting return regd. 7 Feb. 1884 .... **1884**

Western & Brazilian Telegraph Co. Established 1873. Undertaking was merged in 1899 into Brazilian Submarine Telegraph Co. Ld. (later Western Telegraph Co. Ld.), in which company shareholders were entitled to 5 shares of £10 for every 6 ordinary shares of £15 held or every 6 preferred and 6 deferred shares of £7 10s. held. Removed from Register 1901 .... **1900**

Western and Mersey Estates Ld. Regd. 1934. Vol. liq. (members') 7 June 1946. Capital returned to contributories; preference shares (of £1)—21s. per share. Ordinary shares (of £1)—17s. per share. £115 1s. was paid into Companies' Liquidation Aecount. Final meeting return regd. 21 May 1963 .... **1964**

Western Andes Mining Co. Ld. Regd. 1872. Struck off Register 22 Aug. 1947 .... **1948**

Western Australia Proprietary Gold Mines Ld. Regd. 1894. Struck off Register 18 Nov. 1902 .... **1903**

Western Australian Bank. Inc. Western Australia 1879. The assets and liabilities were transferred to Bank of New South Wales, in which company shareholders were entitled to 1 share of £20 (credited as fully-paid) for every 16 shares of £1 held **1928**

Western Australian Development Corporation Ld. Regd. 1895. Court Order to wind up 16 Feb. 1898. Liquidator released 19 June 1905. Struck off Register 10 July 1908 .... **1899**

Western Australian Smelting Co. Ld. Regd. 1897. Undertaking and assets were acquired by Fremantle Smelting Works Ld. for £140,000 in shares. Removed from Register 1903 .... **1902**

Western Australian Steam Packet & Transport Co. Ld. Regd. 1895. Vol. liq. 17 Jan. 1898. Final meeting return regd. 23 Sept. 1898 .... **1898**

Western Automatic Machines Ld. Regd. 1929. Vol. liq. (creditors') 8 July 1930. Undertaking and assets transferred to National Distributors Ld., in which company shareholders were entitled to 1 share of 2s. 6d. (credited with 2s. paid) for every 2 shares of 1s. held. Assets realised insufficient to pay creditors in full. Final meeting return regd. 1 Jan. 1931 .... **1931**

Western Bank Ld. Regd. 1919. Vol. liq. 15 Dec. 1925. Final meeting return regd. 18 July 1936.............. **1926**

Western Canada Cement & Coal Co. Ld. Inc. Canada 1905. In liquidation in 1911. Assets and properties purchased by Canada Cement Co. Ld. **1911**

Western Canada Flour Mills Co. Ld. Inc. Ontario 1905. The outstanding 6% 1st mortgage sterling bonds were redeemed at 105% on 1 Sept. 1926 .... **1927**

Western Canada Land Co. Ld. Regd. 1906. Struck off the Register 4 June 1954 .... **1955**

Western Canada Loan & Savings Co. Established Canada 1863 as Western Canada Permanent Building and Savings Society; name changed Aug. 1874. Reconstructed 1899 as Canada Permanent and Western Canada Mortgage Corporation (later Canada Permanent Mortgage Corporation) **1900**

Western Canada Mortgage Co. Inc. Alberta 1911. In July 1945 holders of 5% 20-year 1st mortgage bonds agreed to accept £135 10s. 11d.% in satisfaction of principal, premium and interest accrued from 1 Feb. 1940 .... **1946**

Western Canada Permanent Building and Savings Society. See Western Canada Loan & Savings Co.

Western Canada Power Co. Ld. Inc. Canada 1909. Reconstructed 1916 as Western Power Co. of Canada Ld **1940**

Western Canada Pulp & Paper Co. Ld. Regd. 1905. Vol. liq. 11 July 1906. Final meeting return regd. 4 Nov. 1914 .... **1907**

Western Canada Timber Co. Ld. Regd. 1907. Vol. liq. (creditors') 23 Apr. 1934. No capital returned to contributories. Final meeting return regd. 24 Apr. 1935 .... **1935**

Western Canada Trust Ld. See Equitable Trust of London Ld.

Western Canadian City & Town Lands Ld. Regd. 1912. Struck off Register Oct. 1934 .... **1935**

Western Canadian Ranching Co. Ld. Regd. 1891. Vol. liq. 28 Feb. 1950. Capital returned to contributories—£8 2s. 9d. per share of £5. Final meeting return regd. 22 May 1952 .... **1953**

Western Coconut Estates Ld. Regd. 1914. Struck off Register 1929 .... ***1917**

Western Counties & London Mutual Life Assurance Co. Established 1861. In liquidation in 1890. Business

VOL. FOR

transferred to British Empire Mutal Life Assurance Co.. **1890**

Western Counties and South Wales Telephone Co. Ld. Regd. 1884. Vol. liq. 8 July 1892. Business was acquired by National Telephone Co: Ld. for 28,284 fully-paid 3rd preference shares of £5 and 6,378 fully-paid ordinary shares of £5. Final meeting return regd. 21 July 1893 .... **1894**

Western Counties Bank Ld. Regd. 1885. Vol. liq. 20 May 1890. Business acquired by Capital and Counties Bank Ld. Final meeting return regd. 21 June 1897 **1891**

Western Counties Railway (Nova Scotia). See Yarmouth and Annapolis Railway Co.

Western Counties Shipping Co. Ld. Regd. 1915. Court Order to wind up 25 Apr. 1922. Liquidator released 20 Sept. 1928. Struck off Register 16 June 1931 .. **1923**

Western Counties Steam Bakeries & Milling Co Ld. Regd. 1888. Reconstructed 1891 as Phoenix Flour Mills & Bread Factory Ld. Removed from Register 1906 .... **1893**

Western Debenture Trust, Ld. Regd. 1901 as Share Investments Ld.; name changed Dec. 1901. Vol. liq. (members') 4 Apr. 1945. Final meeting return regd. 3 Aug. 1948 .... **1939**

Western District Bank Ld. Regd. 1875. Removed from Register 1905 .... ***1880**

Western Dominion Collieries Ld. Regd. 1906. Receiver appointed in Apr. 1932. Proceeds from sale of assets were expected to be absorbed in payment of loans raised by receiver. Struck off Register 27 Jan. 1942 **1942**

Western Electric Distributing Corporation Ld. See Western Electricity Supply Co. Ld.

Western Electricity Supply Co. Ld. Regd. 1903 as Western Electric Distributing Corporation Ld. name changed Dec. 1927. Vol. liq. (members') 10 Mar. 1938. Capital returned to contributories—21s. per preference share of £1; £3 1s. 2d. per ordinary share of £1. Final meeting return regd. 30 Dec. 1938 **1939**

Western Exploration (Proprietary) Ld. In liquidation. All capital owned by Eastern Transvaal Consolidated Mines Ld. **1939**

Western Explorers Ld. See Manica Consolidated.

Western Farm Mortgage Trust Co. Inc. Kansas 1880. In liquidation in 1894 .... **1894**

Western Frontier Goldfields Ld. Regd. 1914. Struck off Register May 1930 .... **1931**

Western Gas Co. Ld. Undertaking acquired by Gas Light and Coke Co **1888**

Western Gold Mines No Liability. Inc. Victoria 1933. Vol. liq. 15 May 1945. Shareholders were entitled to 2 fully-paid shares of 10s. in Triton Gold Mines N. L. for each share of 10s. held **1946**

Western Insurance Co. Ld. Regd. Edinburgh 1899. Business acquired by West of Scotland Fire Office Ld. Capital returned to contributories at par; further payments (if any) not known. Vol. liq. Dec. 1901. Final meeting return regd. 30 May 1903........ **1902**

Western Kleinfontein Ld. Inc. Transvaal 1895. Vol. liq. Nov. 1907 .... **1908**

Western Land & Cattle Co. Ld. Regd. 1882. Removed from Register 1901 .... **1893**

Western Langlaagte Gold Mining Co. Ld. Inc. South Africa 1889. Amalgamated in 1893 with New Crœsus Gold Mining Co. Ld. **1894**

Western Mansions Ld. Regd. 1888 as Middle Class Dwellings Co. Ld.; name changed Jan. 1905. Vol. liq. (members') 14 Mar. 1934. Undertaking and assets were acquired by London County Freehold & Leasehold Properties Ld. Holders of 5% mortgage debentures were entitled to repayment at par *plus* accrued interest or to an equal amount of 4% 1st mortgage debenture stock *plus* £5 5s.% in cash. Final meeting return regd. 24 Nov. 1934 .... **1935**

Western Maskeliya (Ceylon) Tea Co. Ld. Regd. 1924. Vol. liq. 30 Mar. 1927. Capital returned to contributories—20s. 8½d. per share of £1 at Nov. 1927; further payments (if any) not known. Final meeting return regd. 11 Nov. 1927 .... **1928**

Western Molyneux Mines Ld. Inc. South Africa 1895. In liquidation in 1899 .... **1899**

Western Mortgage and Investment Co. Ld. Regd. 1883. Vol. liq. 15 Feb. 1906. Final meeting return regd. 20 Mar. 1919 .... **1907**

Western New South Wales Electric Power Proprietary Ld. Inc. Victoria 1930. The outstanding 8% 1st mortgage debentures were redeemed at par on 15 Mar. 1946 .... **1946**

Western Nigerian Tin Mines Ld. Regd. 1926. Vol. liq. 11 Apr. 1928. Undertaking acquired by Associated Tin Mines of Nigeria Ld. Final meeting return regd. 5 Feb. 1929 .... **1939**

Western of Canada Oil, Lands & Works Co. Ld. Regd. 1871. Vol. liq. 11 May 1891. Reconstructed as Ontario Lands and Oil Co. Ld., in which company shareholders were entitled to 2 deferred shares of £2 10s. (credited as fully-paid) for each A share of £100 held or 1 deferred share for each B share of £50 held. Holders of A debentures were entitled to 3 ordinary or preference shares of £10 (credited as fully-paid) for each bond of £100 held. Final meeting return regd. 1 June 1894 1892

Western of France Railway Co. Authorised from 1855. Undertaking sold to state from 1 Jan. 1909 and company placed in liquidation. Outstanding 3% obligations 1st series redeemed at par 1 July 1951 1953

Western of Minas Railway. The outstanding 5% Bonds were repaid at par on 17 May 1910 1910

Western Orufu Mines Ld. Regd. 1912. Vol. liq. 10 Nov. 1913. Final meeting return regd. 10 Nov. 1914..... 1914

Western Pennsylvania Railroad Co. Organised Pennsylvania 1864. The line was acquired in 1903 by Pennsylvania Railroad Co. 1927

Western Petroleum & General Corporation Ld. Regd. 1922. Vol. liq. (creditors') 4 Oct. 1932. No capital returned to contributories, but a bonus was made of 1 share in Normont Gold Mine Ld. (inc. in Canada) for every 50 shares held. Final meeting return regd. 4 Jan. 1934 1933

Western Railway of Havana Ld. Regd. 1892. Undertaking was acquired in July 1920 by United Railways of the Havana & Regla Warehouse Ld. Holders of shares of £10 were entitled to an equal amount of ordinary shares of £1 in acquiring company. The 4½% debenture stock was guaranteed by the acquiring company as the 4¾% Western debenture stock. Vol. liq. 29 Jan. 1921. Final meeting return regd. 1 Apr. 1924 1921

Western Railway of Santa Fé Ld. Regd. 1899. In Nov. 1900, £1,107,000 consolidated scrip, representing the original 7% bonds of the Oeste Santefacino, were sold for £768,750 in ordinary shares of the Central Argentine Railway Co. Holders of every £100 debenture stock, preference shares, and ordinary shares, were entitled to £95, £83 6s. 8d., and £39 17s. 2d. respectively in Central Argentine Railway ordinary shares; fractions of £5 ordinary share of the Central Argentine Railway Co. being paid in cash at par. The remaining assets were to be distributed amongst the ordinary shareholders. Removed from Register 1901 1901

Western Railway Co. of San Paulo. See Companhia Paulista de Estrados de Ferro.

Western Ranches and Investment Co. Ld. Regd. Edinburgh 1910. Vol. liq. Dec. 1919. Capital returned to contributories—£9 per share of £5; further payments (if any) not known. Final meeting return regd. 20 Jan. 1921 1920

Western Ranches Ld. Regd. Edinburgh 1883. Vol. liq. Mar. 1910 for reconstruction as Western Ranches and Investment Co. Ld., in which company shareholders were entitled to 1 share of £5, fully-paid, for each share of £3 10s. held. Final meeting return regd. 12 May 1911 1911

Western Rand Estates Ld. Inc. Transvaal 1902. Winding-up Order made in 1926 1927

Western Rand Exploration Ld. Inc. Transvaal 1903.... 1909

Western Rand Prospectors Ld. Inc. Transvaal 1896. London agency closed 31 Dec. 1906 1907

Western Samoa Estates Ld. Regd. 1924. Court Order to wind up 6 July 1926. Struck off Register June 1931 1932

Western Stockholders Investment Trust, Ld. Regd. 1929 as Non Ferrous Metal Products Ld.; name changed Apr. 1955. Undertaking and assets acquired by Border & Southern Stockholders Trust Ld. in which company shareholders received 1 ordinary share for every 6 shares held (or 57p. cash per share of 200 or less shares held). 3½% and 4½% debenture stockholders received like amounts of 3½% and 4½% debenture stock respectively. Company to be dissolved under Section 208 of Companies Act 1948 1973-4

Western Transport Co. Ld. Regd. 1901 as Wrexham & District Electric Tramways Ld.; name changed to Wrexham & District Transport Co. Ld. in Mar. 1914 and as above in Nov. 1930. Vol. liq. (members') 25 May 1933. Undertaking and assets were acquired by Crosville Motor Services Ld., in which company shareholders were entitled to 1 share of £1 (credited as fully-paid) for each share of £1 held. Final meeting return regd. 3 Jan. 1934 1934

Western Transvaal Development Co. Ld. Regd. 1895. Struck off Register 1920 1920

Western Viscose Silk Mills Ld. Regd. 1925. Vol. liq. July 1929. Struck off Register 31 Aug. 1937 1938

Western Wagon & Property Co. Ld. Regd. 1881. Vol. liq. (members') 8 Apr. 1935. Capital returned to contributories—£19 16s. 3d. per share of £6, fully-paid; £6 12s. 1d. per share of £6, £2 paid. Final meeting return regd. 10 June 1937 1936

Western Wheat Lands & Timber Co. Ld. Inc. Ontario 1906 1910

Western Witwatersrand Exploration Co. Ld. Regd. 1895. Undertaking and assets were acquired by Africa Trust Consolidated and General Exploration Co. Ld., in which company shareholders were entitled to 40 shares of £1 (credited as fully-paid) for every 100 shares of £1 held. Removed from Register 1908 1899

Westfield Oil Co. Ld. Regd. Edinburgh 1883. Court Orders: to wind up Feb. 1886; to dissolve 28 Mar. 1889 1887

Westgate & Birchington Gas & Electricity Co. Inc. as Westgate & Birchington Gas Co. by Special Act 1881; name changed 1913. Dissolved 1 May 1949, undertaking being vested in South Eastern Area Gas Board under Gas Act 1948. Holders of 10% max. shares (of £10) were entitled to receive £15 British Gas 3% guaranteed stock 1990–95 for each share held 1952

Westhead (J. P.) & Co. Ld. Regd. 1875. Vol. liq. 14 Aug. 1891. Business was acquired by Rylands & Sons Ld. Final meeting return regd. 23 Nov. 1895 1892

Westhoughton Consumers' Gas Co. Inc. by Special Act 1871. Dissolved 1 May 1949, undertaking being vested in North Western Area Gas Board under Gas Act 1948. Holders of securities were entitled to receive, in respect of each £10 unit held, British Gas 3% guaranteed stock 1990–95 as follows:

	£	s.	d.
A shares (10% max.)	1	0	0
B shares (7% max.)	1	0	0
New B shares (£4 paid)		8	0
New B shares (£2 paid)		4	0	1952

Westinghouse Brake Subsidiaries Ld. Regd. 1920. Vol. liq. (members') 15 June 1933. Certain assets were acquired by Westinghouse Brake & Saxby Signal Co. Ld. (later Westinghouse Brake & Signal Co. Ld.). Capital returned to contributories—8s. 6½d. per share of £1. £11 7s. 2d. was paid into Companies' Liquidation Account in respect of dividends; £18 6s. 5d. in respect of capital. Final meeting return regd. 12 Mar. 1934 1934

Westlake's Brewery Ld. Regd. 1889. Struck off Register 2 Apr. 1939. 1940

Westland Dredging & Sluicing Co. Ld. Regd. 1900. Removed from Register 1911 1909

Westleigh Mines Ld. Inc. South African Republic 1895 1899

Westminster & General Life Assurance Association. Established by Deed of Settlement 1836. Business was acquired in 1906 by Guardian Assurance Co. Ld 1907

Westminster Bank Ld. Established as London & County Banking Co. by Deed of Settlement 1836; regd. as unlimited 1874 and as limited 1880; name changed to London County & Westminster Bank Ld. 1909, to London County Westminster & Parrs' Bank Ld. in 1918 and as above in 1923. From 1 Jan. 1970 the undertaking vested in National Westminster Bank Ld. under provisions of National Westminster Bank Act 1969 which also provided for eventual dissolution of this bank 1971

Westminster Chambers Association Ld. Regd. 1863 as Mutual Tontine Westminster Chambers Assn.; name changed 1927. Vol. liq. (members') 8 Apr. 1952. Capital returned to contributories; £66 13s. per share (of £10). £50 was paid into Companies' Liquidation Account. Final meeting return regd. 10 Aug. 1953 1954

Westminster City Properties Ld. Regd. 1928. Vol. liq. (creditors') 19 July 1932. No capital returned to contributories. Final meeting return regd. 29 Nov. 1934 1933

Westminster Electric Supply Corporation Ld. Regd. 1888. Undertaking was acquired in 1937 by Central London Electricity Ld. Holders of preference and ordinary stocks were entitled to 550,000 4½% preference and 1,450,000 ordinary fully-paid shares of £1 respectively in purchasing company. Dissolved under Sec. 154 of the Companies Act 1929 1938

Westminster Fire Office. Est. 1717. Regd. as unlimited 1905. Vol. liq. 29 Jan. 1906. Undertaking transferred to Alliance Assurance Co. Ld., for £340,000 in cash plus interest at 3½% p.a. from 1 May 1905 1906

Westminster Garage Ld. Regd. 1928. Vol. liq. (members') 29 Mar. 1935. Undertaking and certain assets were acquired by Watkins & Doncaster & Westminster Garage Ld., in which company shareholders were entitled to 1 ordinary share of 5s. (credited as fully-paid) for each share of £1 held. Final meeting return regd. 2 Jan.1936 1936

Westminster Gazette Ld. See Westminster Press Ld.

Westminster Investment Group Ld. See Anglowest Ld.

VOL. FOR

Westminster Oil Syndicate Ld. Regd. 1912. Vol. liq. 18 July 1928. Final meeting return regd. 24 Dec. 1930 — 1929

Westminster Palace Hotel Co. Ld. Regd. 1857. Vol. liq. 23 Oct. 1916. Capital returned to contributories—£5 per share of £10 (out of an anticipated return of £10 per share) was made in Feb. 1917. Final meeting return regd. 20 July 1917 — 1917

Westminster Press Ld. Regd. 1908 as Westminster Gazette Ld.; name changed Apr. 1937. Vol. liq. (members') 6 Apr. 1938 for amalgamation with Westminster Press Provincial Newspapers Ld. Each ordinary or preference share of £1 was exchanged for one ordinary or preference share of £1 respectively. Final meeting meeting return regd. 12 May 1939 — 1939

Westminster Trust (Realizations) Ld. (The). Regd. 1886 as The Westminster Trust Ld.; name changed Apr. 1965. Vol. liq. (members') 5 Apr. 1965. All assets other than shares in William Willett Ld. (later Westminster Trust Ld.) were sold to that company and its subsidiaries for £2,810,128 non-interest bearing loan notes of 8s. and 525,320 fully-paid ordinary shares of 4s. of William Willett Ld. Capital returned to contributories—1 fully-paid share of 4s. and 1 unsecured loan note of 8s. of William Willett Ld. per share of 4s. held. £506 3s. 4d. was paid into Companies' Liquidation Account in respect of unclaimed distributions. Final meeting return regd. 14 Aug. 1967 — 1968

Westmorland & District Electricity Supply Co. Ld. Regd. 1933. Dissolved 1 Apr. 1948, undertaking being vested in the British (later Central) Electricity Authority and North-Western Area Board under the Electricity Act 1947. Ordinary shareholders were entitled to receive £1 8s. 9d. British Electricity 3% guaranteed stock (1968–73), for each share (of £1) held. — 1949

Westoe Breweries Ld. Regd. 1917 as Joseph Johnson (Durham) Ld.; name changed 24 Nov. 1938. All capital was owned by Keg Investment Co. Ld. Vol. liq. (members') 30 Sept. 1961. Final meeting return regd. 27 Aug. 1963 — 1961

Weston & Westall Ld. Regd. 1894. Vol. liq. (members') 30 June 1939. Undertaking acquired by I. C. I. (Salt) Ld. Capital returned to contributories—£1 17s. 1¾d. per share of £10. Final meeting return regd. 26 June 1940 — 1943

Weston, Clevedon & Portishead Docks Railway Co. Ld. Regd. 1904. Receiver appointed 1912; ceased to act Oct. 1925 after having no receipts or payments. Struck off Register Apr. 1929 — 1930

Weston, Clevedon & Portishead Light Railways Co. Inc. by Special Act 1885 as Weston-Super-Mare, Clevedon & Portishead (Steam) Tramways Co.; name changed by Act of 1899. Receiver was appointed in 1909 and ceased to act by Order of Court 1941 .... — 1951

Weston-Super-Mare & District Electric Supply Co. Ld. Regd. 1899. Dissolved 1 Apr. 1948, undertaking being vested in British (later Central) Electricity Authority and South Western Area Gas Board under Gas Act 1947. Holders of ordinary and 6% preference shares were entitled to receive, in respect of each share (of £1) held, £3 17s. 6d. and £1 13s. British Electricity 3% guaranteed stock (1968–73) respectively — 1949

Weston-Super-Mare & District Gas Co. Inc. by Special Act 1855 as Weston-Super-Mare Gaslight Co.; name changed 1934. Dissolved 1 May 1949, undertaking being vested in South Western Area Gas Board under Gas Act 1948. Holders of securities were entitled to receive, in respect of each £100 unit held, British Gas 3% guaranteed stock 1990–95 as follows:

	£	s.	d.
Cons. ord. stock (5% basic)	113	0	0
5% irred. pref. stock	112	0	0
4% pref. stock	99	10	0
4½% red. pref. stock	101	0	0
4% red. pref. stock	101	14	2
4% perp. deb. stock	101	0	0
5% irred. deb. stock	124	0	0
7½% perp. deb. stock	160	0	0
3½% red. deb. stock (1961)	98	10	0
3½% red. deb. stock (1963)	97	10	0

A distribution on consolidated ordinary stock of 10·42% out of reserves was made in Apr. 1955 ..... — 1952

Weston-Super-Mare, Clevedon & Portishead (Steam) Tramways Co. See Weston, Clevedon & Portishead Light Railways Co.

Weston-Super-Mare Grand Pier Co. Inc. by Special Act 1893. Winding-up Order made 1 Dec. 1914 .... — 1915

Weston's Music Hall Co. Ld. Regd. 1886. Vol. liq. 25 July 1890. Final meeting return regd. 16 Jan. 1892 — 1891

VOL. FOR

Westport Twin Gold Mines Ld. Regd. 1897. Struck off Register 9 Dec. 1902 .... — 1903

Westport-Wallsend Coal Co. Ld. Regd. 1889. Vol. liq. 5 May 1893. Final meeting return regd. 22 Apr. 1895 — 1894

Westralia and East Extension Mines Ld. Regd. 1895. Vol. liq. 12 Nov. 1918. Final meeting return regd. 25 Oct. 1919 — 1919

Westralia & New Zealand Gold Explorers Ld. Regd. 1896. Removed from Register 1905 .... — 1901

Westralia & Randt Ld. Regd. 1895. Vol. liq. 13 Mar. 1899. Final meeting return regd. 26 May 1902 .... — 1901

Westralia & West Africa Ld. Regd. 1898 as Westralia Ld.; name changed Feb. 1901. Struck off Register 1914 — 1909

Westralia Mount Morgans Gold Mines Co. Ld. Regd. 1899. Vol. liq. Oct. 1909. Reconstructed as company of same name. Shareholders were entitled to 1 share of 5s. (credited with 3s. 9d. paid) in new company for each ordinary or preference share of 5s. held. Removed from Register 1913 — 1910

Westralia Mount Morgans Gold Mines Co. Ld. Regd. 1909. Vol. liq. Feb. 1911. Removed from Register 1913 — 1911

Westralia United Goldfields Ld. Regd. 1911. Vol. liq. 13 Jan. 1914. Struck off Register 24 July 1923 .... — 1914

Westralian Consolidated Investment Co. Ld. Regd. 1899. Vol. liq. Nov. 1910. Removed from Register 1912 — 1911

Westralian Copper Mine Ld. See Balla Balla Copper Mines Ld.

Westralian De Kaap Ld. See Consolidated Finance Corporation Ld.

Westralian Electric Lighting and Supply Co. Ld. Regd. 1897. Vol. liq. 19 Mar. 1902. Business was taken over by Electric Supply Co. of Western Australia Ld. Final meeting return regd. 10 Jan. 1903 ...... — 1899

Westralian Estates & Timber Co. Ld. Regd 1904. Vol. liq. 31 July 1908. Final meeting return regd. 20 July 1923 .... — 1910

Westralian Gold Extracting Co. Ld. Regd. 1900. Removed from Register 1903 .... — 1903

Westralian Jarrah Forests Ld. Regd. 1899. Business and undertaking was acquired by Timber Corporation Ld. for £15,500 in cash, £24,000 in preference shares of £1 and £20,500 in ordinary shares. Removed from Register 1903 .... — 1903

Westralian Joint Stock Founders Ld. Regd. 1897. Reconstructed as Westralian Joint Stock Loan and Finance Corporation Ld., in which company shareholders were entitled to 1 fully paid share of £1 for every 2 shares of £1 held. Removed from Register 1901 .... — 1899

Westralian Joint Stock Loan & Finance Corporation Ld. Regd. 1898. Reconstructed 1899 as Associated Financial Corporation Ld., in which company shareholders were entitled to 1 fully paid B share of 10s. and 1 A share of 10s. (credited with 8s. 6d. paid) for each share of £1 held. Removed from Register 1903 .... — 1900

Westralian, London & Johannesburg Co. Ld. Regd. 1896. Court Order to wind up 11 Jan. 1900. Removed from Register 1903 .... — 1900

Westralian Market Trust Ld. Regd. 1898. Vol. liq. 1899 for reconstruction as Associated Financial Corporation Ld., in which company shareholders were entitled to 2 A shares of 10s. for each preference share of £1 held, or 1 A share of 10s. (with 8s. 6d. paid) and 1 B share of 10s. for each ordinary share of £1 held. Shareholders were entitled to rank ratably for the shares of Westralian Joint Stock & Finance Corporation Ld. Removed from Register 1903 .... — 1900

Westralian Mines Development Syndicate Ld. Regd. 1915. Vol. liq. 28 Dec. 1928. Undertaking and assets were transferred to Orion Development Co. Ld., in which company shareholders were entitled to 1 share of 2s. (credited with 1s. paid) for each ordinary share of 2s. or 5 deferred shares of 3s. held. Final meeting return regd. 19 Dec. 1930 .... — 1929

Westralian Premier Gold Mines Ld. Regd. 1895. Vol. liq. 30 Aug. 1898. Final meeting return regd. 1 Mar. 1900 .... — 1900

Westralian Properties Ld. Regd. 1895. Vol. liq. 3 Jan. 1899. Final meeting return regd. 16 Oct. 1899 ...... — 1899

Westrumite Ld. Regd. 1903. Vol. liq. Mar. 1905. Removed from Register 1907 .... — 1906

West's Brewery Co. Ld. Regd. 1895. Vol. liq. (members') 5 Aug. 1930. Undertaking acquired by Hoare & Co. Ld. Capital returned to contributories—£100 per preference share of £100; £963 18s. 10d. per fully-paid ordinary share of £100. Final meeting return regd. 21 May 1932 .... — 1939

Westville Shipping Co. Ld. Regd. 1919. Vol. liq. 1 Nov. 1922. Final meeting return regd. 8 Dec. 1925 .... — *1923

Westwood (Joseph) and Co. Ld. Regd. 1897. Vol. liq. (members') 9 Nov. 1971. Capital returned to

VOL. FOR

conttibutories—102·6p. per ordinary share of 25p. and 108·125p. per preference share of £1. Final meeting return regd. 16 July 1974 .... **1974–5**

Westwood Manor Coal & Iron Co. Ld. Regd. 1906. Vol. liq. Jan. 1911. Removed from Register 1913 .... **1911**

Westwood Trust Ld. Regd. 1928. Vol. liq. (members') 17 July 1930. Final meeting return regd. 21 June 1932 ***1931**

Wetcarbonizing Ld. Regd. 1912. Vol. liq. 2 Dec. 1920. Final meeting return regd. 1 Sept. 1921 .... **1921**

Wetherall Steamship Co. Ld. Regd. 1900. Vol. liq. 31 Mar. 1917. Final meeting return regd. 26 Aug. 1919 **1917**

Wetherby District Water Co. Ld. Inc. by Special Act 1899; regd. as limited 1954. Vol. liq. (members') 2 Apr. 1954. the undertaking having been compulsorily acquired by the Rural District Council as from Apr. 1950. Capital returned to contributories—£4 13s. 4d. per ordinary and preference share of £5. Final meeting return regd. 27 Nov. 1954 .... **1956**

Wey Valley Water Co. Under the provisions of the Mid Southern Water Order, 1969 the undertaking was vested in the Mid Southern Water Co. (formerly Mid-Wessex Water Co.) on 1 Jan. 1970. Preference stockholders received in exchange a like amount of similar of Mid Southern Water Co. and original and ordinary shares were converted and consolidated into ordinary stock of Mid Southern Water Co. on the following basis—for each 10% original share of £10, £20 consolidated ordinary stock; for each 7% additional ordinary share of £10, £14 consolidated ordinary stock; for each 5% ordinary share of £10, £10 consolidated ordinary stock. The outstanding debenture stocks of the company became debenture stocks of the Mid Southern Water Co. Company was dissolved upon a declaration by the directors on 30 Jan. 1970 .... **1970**

Weymann Motor Bodies Inc. Inc. Delaware 1927 as Weyman Patents Corpn.; name changed Jan. 1928. Dissolved 26 May 1933 .... **1933**

Weyman Patents Corpn. *See above.*

Weymouth & Channel Islands Steam Packet Co. Ld. Regd. 1857. Vol. liq. 15 Aug. 1889. Final meeting return regd. 18 July 1891 .... **1890**

Weymouth & Portland Railway Co. Inc. by Special Act 1862. Dissolved 3 June 1949; undertaking vested 1 Jan. 1948 in British Transport Commission under Transport Act 1947. Holders of securities were entitled to receive British Transport 3% guaranteed stock 1978–88 as follows in respect of each £100 of capital held:

	£	s.	d.	
Con. stock	110	0	0	
4% deb. stock	112	10	0	
4½% deb. stock.......................	125	0	0	**1949**

Weymouth Consumers Gas Co. Inc. by Special Act 1867. Dissolved 1 May 1949, undertaking being vested in Southern Area Gas Board under Gas Act 1948. Holders of securities were entitled to receive, in respect of each £100 unit held, British Gas 3% guaranteed stock 1990–95 as follows:

	£	s.	d.
Ord. stock (5% basic)	117	10	0
5½% red. pref. stock...........................	106	0	0
3½% perp. deb. stock	95	0	0
4% perp. deb. stock...........................	101	10	0

A distribution on ordinary stock of 5·85885% out of reserves was made in June 1955 .... **1952**

Weymouth Waterworks Co. Under the provisions of the Dorset Water Order 1968 the undertaking was transferred to the Dorset Water Board on 1 Apr. 1969. Share and stockholders received stock in the Board in exchange for their holdings as follows—(1) £20 ordinary 10% maximum shares, £39 7s. 6d. 5¾% stock for each share numbered 1–1529; £35 5¾% stock for each share numbered 1530–2000; plus for each share numbered 1530–1704, cash payment equal to arrears of dividend to the appointed day; (2) £20 ordinary 5% maximum shares, £20 5% stock; (3) 4% preference stock, £1 4½% stock per £1 stock; and (4) 3½% debenture stock, £1 4% stock per £1 stock held. Company was dissolved upon a declaration by tbe directors on 4 Feb. 1970. .... **1970**

Whalen Pulp & Paper Mills Co. Ld. *See* Swanson Bay Forests, Wood-Pulp and Lumber Mills Ld.

Whangamata Gold Corporation Ld. Regd. 1898. The mortgages foreclosed and the properties were sold. Removed from Register 1905 .... **1906**

Whangamata Proprietary Ld. Regd. 1896. Vol. liq. 2 Dec. 1898. Reconstructed as Whangamata Gold Corporation Ld., in which company shareholders were entitled to 1 share of £1 (credited with 17s. 6d. paid) for each share of £1 held. Final meeting return regd. 8 Mar 1900 .... **1906**

Wharncliffe Silkstone Colliery Co. Ld. Regd. 1879. Vol. liq. (members') 16 Mar. 1953. Capital returned to

VOL. FOR

contributories—preference: 1s. 6d. per share of 1s.; ordinary; 13s. 10·375d. per share of 1s. Final meeting return regd. 19 Mar. 1956.................... **1957**

Wharncliffe Wood-Moor Colliery Co. Ld. *See below.*

Wharncliffe Woodmoor Colliery Co. Ld. Regd. 1883 as Wharncliffe Wood-Moor Colliery Co. Ld.; name changed 1901. Vol. liq. (members') 18 Dec. 1952. Preference capital repaid at par. Capital returned to ordinary shareholders 25s. 10½d. per share of £1 .. **1970**

Whatley (Spenser) Ld. Regd. 1905. Court Order to wind up 14 Oct. 1930. Struck off Register 10 May 1935 **1936**

Wheal Agar Mine. Established under cost-book system. In 1897 the mine was acquired by East Pool and Agar United Mines **1908**

Wheal Basset Mines Ld. Constituted under costbook system 1832; regd. as unlimited 1895. Amalgamated in 1896 with South Frances United Mines to form Basset Mines Ld., in which company shareholders were entitled to 3 fully-paid shares of £1 for each share held **1908**

Wheal Benny Mining Co. Ld. Regd. 1883. Vol. liq. 1 Feb. 1886. Final meeting return regd. 21 May 1886 ***1884**

Wheal Breage Tin Ld. Regd. 1934. Vol. liq. (members') 20 Apr. 1936. Undertaking was acquired by Wheal Reeth Tin Ld., in which company shareholders were entitled to 1 share of 1s. (credited as fully-paid) for every 2 shares of 1s. held. Final meeting return regd. 12 Feb. 1938.. **1937**

Wheal Buller Ld. Regd. 1928. Vol. liq. (members') 31 Dec. 1930. No capital returned to contributors. Final meeting return regd. 9 Sept. 1936 .... **1931**

Wheal Castle Mines Ld. Regd. 1882. Removed from Register 1890 .... ***1887**

Wheal Coates Mine Co. Established 1882. In course of dissolution in 1888 .... **1888**

Wheal Commerce Tin Mine Ld. Regd. 1906. Vol. liq. May 1910 for reconstruction as "Lane" Rubber & Finance Ld., in which company shareholders were entitled to 1 fully-paid share of 2s. for every 2 shares of £1 held, and an option (since expired) to subscribe at par for further shares. Removed from Register 1911 .... **1911**

Wheal Crebor Co. Formed under cost-book system. In liquidation in 1893 .... **1893**

Wheal Eliza Consol Mining Co. Formed under cost-book system **1899**

Wheal Friendly Mine Co. Established 1890. In liquidation in 1897 .... **1897**

Wheal George Lead Mining Co. Ld. Regd. 1880. Removed from Register 1905 .... ***1884**

Wheal Grenville Mining Co. Worked on the cost-book system. Reorganised 1906 as Grenville United Mines Ld. Shareholders were entitled to 10 fully-paid shares of £1 for every share held, conditional upon taking 5 further shares of £1 (credited with 5s. paid) for every share held..................................... **1908**

Wheal Hampton Ld. Regd. 1903. Removed from Register 1910.. **1906**

Wheal Hony & Trelawney United Silver Lead Mining Co. Ld. Regd. 1880. Reconstructed 1884 as Hony United Mining Co. Ld., in which company shareholders were entitled to 1 share of £1 (credited with 17s. 6d. paid) for each share held. Removed from Register 1905 .... **1890**

Wheal Kitty & Penhalls United Ld. Regd. 1906. Receiver appointed in July 1916. Assets were acquired by Wheal Kitty Tin Ld. Struck off Register May 1929 .... **1930**

Wheal Kitty Tin Ld. Regd. 1925. Vol. liq. (creditors') 8 June 1936. Assets realised insufficient to pay unsecured creditors in full. Final meeting return regd. 13 Nov. 1937 .... **1937**

Wheal Metal & Flow Ld. Regd. 1895. Removed from Register 1903 .... **1903**

Wheal Nut Ld. Inc. Guernsey 1907. Vol. liq. June 1914 **1915**

Wheal Peevor. Formed under cost-book system. Winding-up Order 21 May 1897 .... **1898**

Wheal Rashleigh & Criggan China Clay Co. Ld. Regd. 1912. Vol. liq. 24 Oct. 1918. Final meeting return regd. 26 Apr. 1919 .... **1919**

Wheal Reeth Tin Ld. Regd. 1927. Vol. liq. (members') 21 Sept. 1949. Debenture stockholders received 3s. 9d. per £1 stock held. No capital returned to contributories. Final meeting return regd. 11 Nov. 1949 .... **1950**

Wheal Uny. Formed under cost-book system. In liquidation in 1894.. **1894**

Wheal Vor Ld. Regd. 1906. Vol. liq. 6 Nov. 1925. Final meeting return regd. 24 Apr. 1936 .... **1926**

Wheatley & Bates, Ld. Regd. 1893. All capital was owed by Hope & Anchor Breweries Ld. Vol. liq. (members') 28 Mar. 1965. Final meeting return regd. 7 Jan. 1966 .... **1956**

See Stock Exchange Year-Book.

VOL. FOR

Wheatman & Smith Ld. Regd. 1871. Vol. liq. 12 June 1914. Final meeting return regd. 18 Jan. 1916 ...... **1915**

Wheel & Wings Assurance Association Ld. Regd. 1917. Struck off Register 1931 .... ***1925**

Wheel of Fortune Ld. Regd. 1898. The property was seized by debenture holders and sold on their behalf in 1904. Removed from Register 1908 .... **1905**

Wheeler Hill Ld. Regd. 1895. Struck off Register 16 Nov. 1906 .... **1907**

Wheeler's Wycombe Breweries Ld. Regd. 1898. Vol. liq. (members') Mar. 1950, the undertaking and assets having been acquired by H. & G. Simonds Ld **1952**

Wheeling & Lake Erie Railroad Co. Organised Ohio 1899. Reorganised 1917 as Wheeling and Lake Erie *Railway* Co. Holders of securities were entitled to securities in new company as follows:

For every £100 *held*	
4% 1st cons, mort. bds.	$100 Refdg. mort. bds.
* 1st prefd. stk	$27 preferred stock $100 common stock
* 2nd prefd. stk	$27 preferred stock $90 common stock
* Common stk	$27 preferred stock $87½% common stock

* After payment of $27 per share of $100. Holders of 3-year gold bonds were allotted $11,882,600 prior lien stock **1917**

Wheelwright (J. W.) & Son, Ld. Regd. 1907. Vol. liq, (members') 11 Nov. 1949. Final meeting return regd. 28 Mar. 1952 .... **1938**

Wheen (Richard) & Sons Ld. Regd. 1898. Vol. liq. (members') 24 Jan. 1955. Capital returned to contributories—£1 per preference share of £1. All ordinary capital privately held. Final meeting return regd. 20 Jan. 1956 .... **1956**

Wheway (Job) & Son Ld. *See below.*

Wheway, Watson & McLean Ld. Regd. 1917 as Job. Wheway & Son Ld.; name changed 31 Dec. 1959. Vol. liq. (members') 29 Sept. 1965 under scheme of reorganisation. Preference shares (of £1) were repaid at 22*s.* per share on 29 Sept. 1965, and ordinary shareholders were entitled to receive 1 fully-paid ordinary share (of 1*s.*) of Job. Wheway & Son Ld. (later Wheway, Watson Ld.) per ordinary share (of 1*s.*) held. £85 12s. 9*d.* was paid into Companies' Liquidation Account on account of unclaimed dividends. Final meeting return regd. 1 Mar. 1967 .... **1967**

While (Samuel) & Son Ld. Regd. 1933. Dissolved 1 May 1949, the Callington and Gunnislake gas undertakings being vested in South Western Area Gas Board under Gas Act 1948. Holders of ordinary shares (of £1) were entitled to receive £1 2*s.* British Gas 3% guaranteed stock 1990–95 for each share held **1952**

Whim Well Copper Mines Ld. Regd. 1906. Vol. liq. 7 Apr. 1915. Struck off Register 30 Jan. 1923 .... **1917**

Whinanarfu Ld. Regd. 1901. Undertaking and assets were acquired by Gold Coast and Ashanti Explorers Ld., in which company shareholders were entitled to 5 fully-paid ordinary and 3 fully-paid deferred shares of £1 for every 10 shares of £1 held, and 1 fully-paid deferred share of £1 for every 5 vendors' shares of £1 held. Removed from Register 1907 .. **1905**

Whitaker (G.) & Co. Ld. Regd. 1925. Vol. liq. 31 Mar. 1954. Final meeting return regd. 18 Apr. 1955; dissolution deferred till 27 Jan. 1956 .... **1947**

Whitbread's Properties Ld. Regd. 1885 as Forest Hill Brewery Co. Ld., name subsequently changed. Directly controlled by Whitbread & Co. Ld. Vol. liq. (members') 31 Dec. 1953. Final meeting return regd. 8 Dec. 1954 .... **1924**

Whitby & London Steam Shipping Co. Ld. Regd. 1875. Vol. liq. 23 June 1881. Final meeting return regd. 1 Dec. 1881 .... ***1882**

Whitby Brothers Ld. Regd. 1894. Vol. liq. (members') 19 Aug. 1965. Final meeting return regd. 20 Nov. 1967 **1910**

Whitby Gas Co, Inc. by Special Act 1871. Dissolved 1 May 1949, undertaking being vested in North Eastern Area Gas Board under Gas Act 1948. Holders of securities were entitled to receive British Gas 3% guaranteed stock 1990–95 as follows in respect of each £100 unit, unless otherwise stated, of security held:

	£	s.	d.
Orig. shares (10% stand.) (of £10)	11	16	0
Addit. shares (7% stand.) (of £10)	8	8	0
4% red. pref stock (1951)	100	0	0
4½% red. pref. stock (1960–5)	104	0	0
4% red. pref. stock (1957)	101	10	0
3% deb. stock	90	0	0
3½% deb. stock	99	0	0
3¾% deb. stock	100	10	0

Liability in respect of certain mortgage loans assumed by the Board **1952**

Whitby, Redcar & Middlesbrough United Railway Co. Inc. by Special Act 1866. Under North Eastern Railway Act 1889 the undertaking was purchased by that company. Holders of ordinary stock received £10 (approx.) in cash for every £100 held. The 4% and 4½% debentures were assumed by purchasing company **1890**

Whitby Steam Shipping Co. Ld. Regd. 1902. Vol. liq. 9 July 1920. Final meeting return regd. 19 Dec. 1921 **1921**

Whitby Waterworks Co. Inc. by Special Act 1864. Under provisions of Scarborough Water Order 1961 undertaking vested in Borough of Scarborough from 25 June 1961 for £85,000. Holders of 5% debenture stock received Corpn. annuities in exchange (to yield same income). Original (10% max.) and new (7% max.) shares of £10 and 3½% and 6% preference stock were all repaid at par *plus* £25 per £100 capital (all classes). Company was dissolved 5 Oct. 1962 **1965**

Whitchurch & Ellesmere Banking Co. Ld. Regd. 1880. Court Orders: to wind up 26 July 1881; to dissolve 18 June 1888 .... ***1882**

Whitchurch and Pangbourne Electric Supply Co. Ld. Regd. 1902. Vol. liq. (members') 14 Dec. 1932. Capital returned to contributories—£6 10*s.* 6*d.* per ordinary share of £5. Final meeting return regd. 26 Apr. 1933 .... **1933**

Whitchurch (Hants.) Gas & Electricity Co. Ld. Regd. 1884. The electricity undertaking was vested on 1 Apr. 1948 in the British (later Central) Electricity Authority and Southern Area Electricity Board. Dissolved 1 May 1949, the remaining undertaking being vested in Southern Area Gas Board under Gas Act 1948. Holders of securities were entitled to receive in respect of each £100 unit held, British Gas 3% guaranteed stock 1990–95 as follows:

	£	s.	d.
Ord. stock	137	10	0
4½% red. deb. stock	106	0	0

1952

Whitechurch (Salop) Gas Co. Ld. Regd. 1896. Dissolved 1 May 1949, undertaking being vested in North Western Area Gas Board under Gas Act 1948. Holders of securities were entitled to receive British Gas 3% guaranteed stock 1990–95 as follows:

	£	s.	d.
Ord. shares (10% max.) (of £5)	8	0	0
3½% red. 1st mort. debs. (of £50)	50	0	0

1952

White (A. J.) Ld. Regd. 1884. Vol. liq. 13 Apr. 1897. Business was acquired by company of same name, for £166,666 ordinary shares, £166,666 preference shares and £626,668 in cash. Final meeting return regd. 7 Apr. 1898 .... **1908**

White & Pike Ld. Regd. 1891. Wound up under supervision of Court. Removed from Register 1905 **1901**

White & Poppe Ld. Regd. 1899. Vol. liq. (members') 28 Mar. 1933. Capital returned to contributories—£147,908 19*s.* 10*d. plus* certain assets distributed in specie. Final meeting return regd. 23 Feb. 1934 .. **1934**

White Cliffs Opal Mines Ld. Regd. 1896. Vol. liq. Jan. 1909. Removed from Register 1910 .... **1909**

White Drummond & Co. Ld. Regd. 1900 as J. G. White & Co. Ld.; name changed 1933. Vol. liq. (members') 24 July 1959. Reconstructed as company of same name. Shareholders received 1 fully-paid share (of 10*s.*) plus £2 15*s.* 11½*d.* cash for every share (of 10*s.*) held. £54 5*s.* 1*d.* in respect of unclaimed dividends and £25 3*s.* 8*d.* in respect of distributions paid into Companies' Liquidation Account. Final meeting return regd. 19 July 1960 .... **1961**

White Feather Extended Ld. Regd. 1895. Vol. liq. 9 Jan. 1899. Final meeting return regd. 1 July 1900 .... **1902**

White Feather Main Reef Gold Mining Co. Ld. Regd. 1894. Vol. liq. 28 Jan. 1898. Reconstructed as White Feather Main Reefs Ld., in which company shareholders were entitled to 1 share of £1 (credited with 18*s.* paid) for each share of £1 held. Final meeting return regd. 29 June 1900 .... **1906**

White Feather Main Reefs Ld. Regd. 1898. Vol. liq. Jan. 1906 for reconstruction as White Feather Main Reefs (1906) Ld., in which company shareholders were entitled to 1 share of 5*s.* (credited with 3*s.* 6*d.* paid) for each share of £1 held. Removed from Register 1908 .... **1906**

White Feather Main Reefs (1906) Ld. Regd. 1906. Vol. liq. Apr. 1911. Certain assets were sold to North White Feather Gold Mines Ld., in which company shareholders were entitled to 1 fully-paid share of 10*s*, for every 4 shares of 5*s.* held. A small cash payment was expected. Removed from Register 1912 .... **1912**

White Feather Reward Claim Ld. Regd. 1894. Vol. liq. 15 Nov. 1900. Reconstructed as White Feather "Reward" Ld., in which company shareholders

**See Stock Exchange Year-Book.*

VOL. FOR

were entitled to 1 share of £1 (credited with 17s. 6d. paid) for each share of £1 held. Final meeting return regd. 18 July 1902 .... **1906**

White Feather "Reward" Ld. Regd. 1900. Vol. liq. Jan. 1906. Reconstructed as White Feather Main Reefs (1906) Ld., in which company shareholders were entitled to 1 share of 5s. (credited with 3s. 6d. paid) for each share of £1 held. Removed from Register 1908 .... **1906**

White Feather United Gold Mines Ld. Regd. 1894. Vol. liq. 16 Dec. 1896. Final meeting return regd. 11 Jan. 1899 .... **1897**

White Flag Consols Gold Mines Ld. Regd. 1896. Vol. liq. 8 Feb. 1897. Final meeting return regd. 12 Jan. 1898 .... **1898**

White (George) & Co. Ld. Regd. 1896. Vol. liq. (members') 20 Jan. 1937. All shares owned by Younger (George) & Son Ld. Final meeting return regd. 11 Feb. 1938 .... **1937**

White Hope Gold Mines (No Liability). Inc. South Australia 1920. Vol. liq. 1921 .... **1922**

White Horse Gold Mining Co. Ld. Regd. 1899. Removed from Register 1903 .... **1902**

White House Investment Co. Ld. Regd. 1896. Vol. liq. 12 May 1899. Final meeting return regd. 6 Sept. 1899 .... *1900

White Lead Co. Ld. Regd. 1889. Vol. liq. 23 Nov. 1898. Final meeting return regd. 11 July 1900 .... **1899**

White Mule (Abercorn) Development Co. Ld. Regd. 1910. Struck off Register 3 Dec. 1915 .... *1914

White Oak Colliery Co. Ld. Regd. 1874. Removed from Register 1905 .... *1882

White Pass & Yukon Railway Co., Ld. Regd. 1898. Vol. liq. (members') 24 Oct. 1951 for purpose of reconstruction as White Pass & Yukon Corpn., Ld. Holders of 5% cons. mtg. deb. stock were repaid at par together with arrears of interest, holders of 6% Income stock at par without interest and A and ordinary shareholders received common shares of the new company as follows—37½ shares per A share and ⅞th of a share per ordinary share. Final meeting return regd. 2 Jan. 1956 .... **1956**

White Petrol Ld. Regd. 1914. Struck off Register 1927 *1919

White Rock Silver Mine Ld. Regd. 1896. Removed from Register 1908 .... **1904**

White Rose Gold Mining Co. Ld. Regd. 1895. Vol. liq. 3 June 1897. Reconstructed as West Rand Central Gold Mining Co. Ld., in which company shareholders were entitled to 1 share of £1 (credited with 15s. paid) for each share of £1 held. Final meeting return regd. 7 June 1900 .... **1908**

White Star Consolidated Mining Co. Ld. Regd. 1882. Removed from Register 1906 .... *1884

White Star Line Ld. Regd. 1927. Court Order to wind up 8 Apr. 1935. On liquidation of Royal Mail Steam Packet Co. preference shareholders of this company received payments totalling 1s. 4·845d. in the £ as guaranteed creditors. Liquidator released 9 Nov. 1942. Struck off Register 16 Mar. 1945 .... **1945**

White Star Steam Fishing Co. of Aberdeen Ld. Regd. Edinburgh 1902. Vol. liq. (members') 22 May 1939. Capital returned to contributories—12s. 3d. per share of £1 (with 10s. paid) Final meeting return regd. 4 Dec. 1939 .... **1940**

White (T. H.) & Co. Ld. Regd. 1893. Vol. liq. 6 Aug. 1896. Business was acquired by White Tomkins and Courage Ld. Final meeting return regd. 5 Nov. 1896 .... **1896**

White (W. N.) & Co. Ld. Regd. 1897. Vol. liq. 1 Feb. 1900. Court Order to wind up 21 Feb. 1900. Liquidator released 30 June 1903. Struck off Register 27 Aug. 1909 .... **1901**

White Water Alluvials Ld. Regd. 1912. Struck off Register 1921 .... **1917**

Whiteabbey Flax Spinning Co. Ld. Regd. Dublin 1866. Reconstructed under same name **1908**

Whiteabbey Flax Spinning Co. Ld. Regd. Dublin 1891; transferred to Belfast under Government of Ireland Act 1920. Vol. liq. June 1932 .... **1933**

Whitechapel & Bow Railway Co. Inc. by Special Act 1897. Dissolved 3 June 1949; undertaking vested 1 Jan. 1948 in British Transport Commission under Transport Act 1947. Holders of 4% debenture stock were entitled to receive, in respect of every £100 stock held, £112 10s. British Transport 3% guaranteed stock 1978–88 .... **1949**

Whitechurch (George) Ld. Regd. 1897. Vol. liq. (creditors') 12 Dec. 1935. No capital returned to contributories. Final meeting return regd. 15 Mar. 1938.... **1936**

Whitecross Wire and Iron Co. Ld. Regd. 1872. Vol. liq. July 1886. Final meeting return regd. 2 May 1887 **1940**

Whitefield Breweries Ld. Regd. 1899 as Breweries Ld.; name changed Mar. 1901. Struck off Register 15 June 1937 .... **1938**

Whitehall Films Ld. Regd. 1927. Court Order to wind up 4 Nov. 1929. Liquidator released 3 Oct. 1933. Struck off Register 20 Mar. 1936 .... *1930

VOL. FOR

Whitehall Steam Navigation Co. Ld. Regd. 1915. Vol. liq. 18 Mar. 1918. Final meeting return regd. 14 Apr. 1919 .... *1919

Whitehaven Colliery Co. Ld. Regd. 1914. Vol. liq. (creditors') 18 Aug. 1933. Final meeting return regd. 29 Sept. 1948 .... **1949**

Whitehaven Hematite Iron & Steel Co. Ld. Regd. 1888. Vol. liq. (creditors') 11 Sept. 1942. No return of capital to contributories was anticipated. Final meeting return regd. 7 July 1944 .... **1945**

Whitehaven Iron Mines Ld. Regd. 1871. Court Orders; to wind up Apr. 1882; to dissolve 29 June 1900 ... **1883**

Whitehaven Joint Stock Banking Co. Ld. Established 1829. Regd. as limited 1888. Vol. liq. 29 Oct. 1908; goodwill, business and bank premises acquired by Parr's Bank Ld., in which company shareholders were entitled to receive (a) 1 share of £100 with £20 paid in respect of every 2½ shares of £25 with £7 10s. paid held and (b) £1 per share in cash **1909**

Whitehaven Shipbuilding Co. Ld. Regd. 1880. Vol. liq. 11 Feb. 1890. Final meeting return regd. 24 Nov. 1893 .... *1885

Whitehaven United Gas Co. Ld. Regd. 1884. Dissolved 1 May 1949, undertaking being vested in Northern Area Gas Board under Gas Act 1948. Holders of ordinary shares (of £1) were entitled to receive 19s. 9d. British Gas 3% guaranteed stock 1990–95 for each share held **1952**

Whitehead Aircraft (1917) Ld. Regd. 1917. Assets were realised by Receiver. Struck off Register 1928 .... **1925**

Whitehead & Sultan Gold Mines Ld. See Hauraki Golden Age Mines Ld.

Whitehead Torpedo Works (Weymouth) Ld. Regd. 1907. Vol. liq. 15 Mar. 1921. Final meeting return regd. 17 Mar. 1927 .... *1922

White's Asbestos Ld. Regd. 1889. Vol. liq. 2 Feb. 1891. Final meeting return regd. 21 Oct. 1901 .... **1891**

White's Carriage Co. Ld. Regd. 1898. Vol. liq. Dec. 1906. Undertaking and assets were acquired by Liverpool Carriage Co. Ld. for £53,880. Removed from Register 1909 .... **1907**

White's Consolidated Co. Ld. Regd. 1896. Vol. liq. June 1907. Removed from Register 1911 .... **1908**

Whiteside (H. S.) & Co. Ld. Regd. 1925 as Gilbart Ld. name changed 1927. Winding-up Order 6 Nov. 1967. No capital returned to contributories. Liquidator released 24 Apr. 1975 .... **1975-6**

Whitewater Mines Ld. Regd. 1898. Vol. liq. 5 July 1912. Final meeting return regd. 18 Feb. 1920 .... **1913**

Whiteway (Henry) & Co. Ld. Regd. 1904. Vol. liq. (members') 7 July 1934. Undertaking and assets were acquired by Whiteways Cyder Co. Ld., for £200,000 in cash and 150,000 fully-paid ordinary shares of £1. All shares were privately held. Final meeting return regd. 8 Mar. 1937 .... **1935**

Whitfield Aviation Ld. Regd. 1918. Struck off Register 1926 .... **1922**

Whitford Steel Sheet & Galvanising Co. Ld. Regd. 1909. Vol. liq. (members') 1 Apr. 1939. Undertaking acquired by Gravesend Steel & Tinplate Co. Ld., which company discharged all debts. Final meeting return regd. 14 Dec. 1939 .... **1946**

Whiting Manufacturing Co. Inc. Tennessee 1904. In Feb. 1926 the chief assets were sold for $984,000, of which $130,000 was paid and the balance was payable by annual instalments of $70,000 (plus accrued interest) up to and including 1936 .... *1933

Whitland & Cardigan Railway Co. (formerly Whitland & Taf Vale) **1891**

Whitland, Cronware & Pendine Railway Co. Inc. by Special Act 1877. Undertaking abandoned by Act of 1892 .... **1893**

Whitmarsh, Watson & Co. Ld. Regd. 1895. Undertaking and assets were acquired by Duncan Gilmour & Co. Ld. in which company shareholders were entitled to 1 2nd preference share of £10 (credited as fully-paid) for every 6 ordinary shares of £1 held or 11 1st preference shares of £10 (credited as fully-paid) for every 120 preference shares of £1 held. Debenture stockholders were entitled to sufficient 4½% debenture stock to yield same income. Removed from Register 1908 .... **1907**

Whitstable and Canterbury Coalfields Ld. Regd. 1913. Vol. liq. 5 Jan. 1925. Final meeting return regd. 14 July 1925 .... **1925**

Whitstable Electric Co. Ld. Regd. 1913. Dissolved 1 Apr. 1948, undertaking being vested in the British (later Central) Electricity Authority and South-Eastern Area Board under the Electricity Act 1947. Holders of ordinary and preference shares were entitled to receive British Electricity 3% guaranteed stock (1968–73), as follows:—£2 6s. 6d. stock for each ordinary share (of £1) held and £1 14s. stock for each preference share (of £1) held. **1949**

VOL. FOR

Whitstable Gas & Coke Co. Ld. Regd. 1869; statutory powers 1938. Dissolved 1 May 1949, undertaking being vested in South Eastern Area Gas Board under Gas Act 1948. Holders of original shares (both denominations) were entitled to receive, in respect of each £10 unit held, £20 16s. British Gas 3% guaranteed stock 1990–95 1952

Whittaker Automatic Looms Ld. Regd. 1928. Vol. liq. (members') 5 Aug. 1932. Assets realised insufficient to pay creditors in full. Final meeting return regd. 21 Apr. 1936.. 1933

Whittaker (C.) & Co. Ld. Regd. 1897. Removed from Register 1901 1940

Whittaker Loom Co. Ld. (*See* W. L. Co. Ld.)

Whittaker (Samuel) Ld. Regd. 1899 as S. Whittaker, Sons & Purdy Ld.; name changed Oct. 1914. Court Order to wind up 17 Jan. 1938. Struck off Register 14 May 1943 1945

Whittakers Ld. Regd. 1895. Vol. liq. (creditors') 30 Dec. 1929. Assets realised insufficient to pay creditors in full. Final meeting return regd.8 Nov. 1932.......... 1930

Whittingham (W. B.) & Co. Ld. Regd. 1891. Receiver for debenture holders was appointed. Removed from Register 1903 1902

Whittington & Sheepbridge Colliery Co. Ld. Regd. 1873. Court Orders: to wind up July 1878. Final meeting return regd. 1 Dec. 1883 .... *1878

Whittington Life Assurance Co. Established 1855. The business was acquired by the National Life Assurance Society, in 1893 1893

Whittington Silkstone Colliery Co. Ld. Regd. 1874. Vol. liq. May 1882. Final meeting return regd. 25 Sept. 1886 1883

Whittle Springs Brewery Ld. Undertaking and assets were acquired by Nuttall's Breweries Ld. for £665,000 in cash 1928

Whittle Superheater Co. Ld. Regd. 1933. Vol. liq. (members') 30 Oct. 1935. Capital returned to contributories—9s. per share of £1. Final meeting return regd. 6 Nov. 1936 1936

Whittlesey Gas Co. Ld. Regd. 1911. Dissolved 1 May 1949, undertaking being vested in Eastern Area Gas Board under Gas Act 1949. Holders of securities were entitled to receive British Gas 3% guaranteed stock 1990–95 as follows in respect of each £10 unit, unless otherwise stated, of security held:

	£	s.	d.
Ord. shares	20	0	0
5% pref. shares	11	4	0
5% debs. (of £100).................	124	0	0	1952

Whitwick Colliery Co. Ld. Regd. 1873. Vol. liq. (members') 31 Dec. 1948. Capital returned to contributories—£7 0s. 4¾d. per share of 5s. Final meeting return regd. 8 Jan. 1958 1959

Whitworth & Co. Ld. Regd. 1874. Vol. liq. 29 May 1919. Final meeting return regd. 25 Feb. 1920 .... *1882

Whitworth & Co. of Openshaw Ld. *See* Whitworth (Sir Jos.) & Co. Ld.

Whitworth Cycle Co. Ld. Amalgamated in 1894 with Rudge Cycle Co. Ld. to form Rudge Whitworth Ld 1896

Whitworth Collieries Ld. Regd. 1905. Foreclosure by mortgaged holders was made absolute by Court Order on 29 Jan. 1913. Struck off Register 1915... 1913

Whitworth Finance & Mining Corporation Ld. Regd. 1927 as Alaska Whitworth Ld.; name changed Apr. 1928. Vol. liq. Oct. 1931. Struck off Register 31 Aug. 1937 1938

Whitworth (Sir Jos.) & Co. Ld. Regd. 1888 as Whitworth & Co. of Openshaw Ld.; name changed June 1888. Vol. liq. 12 Mar. 1897. Final meeting return regd. 10 Mar. 1898 1898

Whybrow (George) Ld. Regd. 1897. Removed from Register 1912 1900

Whyte (Brice) & Sons Ld. Regd. Edinburgh 1900. Vol. liq. (members') 30 Apr. 1946. £21,977 7s. 4d. was returned to contributories. Final meeting return regd. 7 Mar. 1947 1930

Wick and Lybster Light Railway Co. Inc. (under Light Railways Act 1896) by order of Light Railway Commissioners confirmed by Board of Trade 1899. In 1923 the undertaking was merged into the London Midland & Scottish Railway Co. which company assumed all liability for the Treasury Loan of £2,000 and agreed to provide 2s. 6d. in cash for every share of £1 (the holders of which also received a sum of 2s. 6d. per share out of assets that were not transferred to the London Midland Co.) 1924

Wick Gas Co. Ld. Regd. in Edinburgh 1921. Dissolved 1 May 1949, undertaking being vested in Scottish Area Gas Board under Gas Act 1948. Holders of ordinary shares (of £1) were entitled to receive £1 10s. British Gas 3% guaranteed stock 1990–95 for each share held 1952

Wickham & Co. (Tunbridge Wells) Ld. Undertaking and assets were acquired by Hackney Furnishing Co. (1928) Ld 1929

Wickham Hard Cure (Rubber) Patents Ld. Regd. 1913. Vol. liq. 10 Nov. 1915. Final meeting return regd. 6 Sept. 1917 1916

Wickhams (C. Barker) Ld. Regd. 1919. All capital was owned through Alexander Sloan & Co. Ld. by Great Universal Stores Ld. Vol. liq. (members') 29 Dec. 1964. Final meeting return regd. 9 Mar. 1965 1960

Wicklow Copper Mine Co. *See* Arklow Manure Co. Ld.

Wicklow District Gas Co. Ld. Regd. Dublin 1907 1911

Wicks Rotary Type Casting Co. Ld. Regd. 1897. Removed from Register 1909 1906

Widin Copper Syndicate Ld. Regd. 1907. Vol. liq. 1 Aug. 1912. Final meeting return regd. 15 July 1914 1913

Widnes & Runcorn Bridge Co. Inc. by Special Act 1900. By Act of 1911 the undertaking was transferred to the Widnes Corporation. 1912

Widnes Foundry Co. Ld. Regd. 1905. Vol. liq. 6 Aug. 1924. Final meeting return regd. 2 Dec.1927 .... *1925

Widnes Foundry (1925) Ld. Regd. 1925. Court Order to wind up 22 July 1935. Struck off Register 27 Jan. 1942 1942

Wiener Bank-Verein. Inc. Vienna 1869. In 1934 this bank was amalgamated with the Oesterreichische Credit-Anstalt für Handel und Gewerbe under the title of Oesterreichische Credit-Anstalt und Wiener Bank-Verein (later Creditanstalt Bankverein) in which company shareholders were entitled to 1 share of Sch. 100 for every 100 B shares (1933 issue) or 2,500 B shares (1932 issue) held 1935

Wienholt Estates Co. of Australia Ld. Regd. 1899. Vol. liq. 13 Apr. 1911. Capital returned to contributories—£9 10s. per preference share of £10 at 1 Jan. 1912; further payments (if any) not known. Final meeting return regd. 14 Aug. 1922 1912

Wigan & District Tramway Co. Ld. Regd. 1893. Vol. liq. 3 Oct. 1902. Undertaking was acquired in 1902 by Wigan Corporation for £45,000. Final meeting return regd. 1 July 1904 1903

Wigan Coal & Iron Co. Ld. Regd. 1865. Vol. liq. (members') 30 Dec. 1952. Capital returned to contributories—8s. 3·2837d. per share of 3d. £4,174 10s. 2d. was paid into Companies' Liquidation Account. Final meeting return regd. 24 July 1956 1957

Wigan Coal Corpn. Ld. Regd. 1930. Vol. liq. (members') 10 Nov. 1952. Capital returned to contributories—preference: 2s. per share of 6d.; A and B ordinary: £1 1s. 8·587d. per share of 6d. Final meeting return regd. 12 July 1956 1957

Wigan Junction Railway Co. Inc. by Special Act 1874. Under Great Central Railway Act 1905 the undertaking was acquired by that company. Holders of 4% debenture stock received 3¼% 2nd debenture stock on basis of equal income. Holders of £100 ordinary shares received £40 2nd debenture (or £40 cash), £30 preferred ordinary, and £30 deferred ordinary stocks in purchasing company 1906

Wigan Picturedromes Ld. Regd. 1920. Vol. liq. 9 May 1922. Final meeting return regd. 5 July 1923 .... *1924

Wigan Tramways Co. Ld. Regd. 1878. Line was sold in Sept. 1891 for £4,500. Struck off Register 27 Apr. 1894 1892

Wiggins (P.) Ld. Regd. 1921. Vol. liq. (members') 29 Nov. 1933. Capital returned to contributories—£724 11s. 8d. Final meeting return regd. 10 Aug. 1934 1934

Wiggins, Teape & Alex. Pirie (Merchants) Ld. Regd. 1928. A subsidiary of Wiggins Teape & Co. (1910) Ld. (later Wiggins Teape & Co. Ld.). Vol. liq. (members') 20 Apr. 1953. Final meeting return regd. 5 Dec. 1955 1956

Wigham Richardson & Co. Ld. Regd. 1899. Reconstructed 1903 as Swan Hunter & Wigham Richardson Ld in which company shareholders were entitled to 43 preference shares of £1 for every 40 preference shares of £1 held or 14 ordinary shares of £1 for every 10 ordinary shares of £1 held. Removed from Register 1905 1904

Wigram (Money) & Sons Ld. Regd. 1881. Vol. liq. 19 May 1893. Final meeting return regd. 29 Dec. 1893 1894

Wigton Gas Light & Coke Co. Ld. Regd. 1884. Dissolved 1 May 1949, undertaking being vested in Northern Area Gas Board under Gas Act 1948. Holders of securities were entitled to receive British Gas 3% guaranteed stock 1990–95 as follows in respect of each £100 unit, unless otherwise stated, of security held:

	£	s.	d.
Ord. shares (of £10).................	6	0	0
4% mort. deb. bonds	100	0	0
4% 2nd mort. deb. bonds	100	0	0	1952

See Stock Exchange Year-Book.

VOL. FOR

Wigtownshire Railway Co. Inc. by Special Act 1872. Under Portpatrick and Wigtownshire Railways (Sale and Transfer) Act 1885, Portpatrick and Wigtownshire guaranteed stock was issued to holders of ordinary shares at 50% **1886**

Wilbury Co. Ld. *See* Sussex Motors Ld.

Wilbury Stables Co. Ld. *See* Sussex Motors Ld.

Wilfley Co. Ld. Regd. 1898 as Wilfley Ore Concentrator Syndicate Ld.; name changed to Wifley Mining Machinery Co. Ld., in June 1907 and as above in Mar. 1915. Court Order to wind up 13 Nov. 1923. Liquidator released 22 Nov. 1929. Struck off Register 13 Apr. 1934 .... **1924**

Wilfley Mining Machinery Co. Ld. *See* Wilfley Co. Ld.

Wilfley Ore Concentrator Syndicate Ld. *See* Wilfley Co. Ld.

Wilkes' Metallic Flooring & Eureka Concrete Co. Ld. Regd. 1883. Court Orders: to wind up 12 May 1888; to dissolve 29 Jan. 1891 .... **1889**

Wilkins (Oliver) & Co. Ld. Regd. 1908. Vol. liq. (members') 31 Mar. 1939. Capital returned to contributories—£2 11*s.* 4*d.* per ordinary share of £1. Final meeting return registered 22 Nov. 1940 .... **1940**

Wilkinson Exploration Syndicate Ld. Regd. 1895. Capital returned to contributories—£16 per share of £50 (£40 paid); further payments (if any) not known. Removed from Register 1911 .... **1904**

Wilkinson (Henry) & Co. Ld. Regd. 1872. Vol. liq. 14 Jan. 1892. Final meeting return regd. 14 Aug. 1896 **1892**

Wilkinson, Heywood & Clark Ld. Undertaking was acquired in 1923 by Pinchin Johnson & Co. Ld. (later Pinchin Johnson & Associates Ld.). **1924**

Wilkinson (John) (Manchester & Nelson) Ld. Regd. 1924. Vol. liq. (creditors) 3 Nov. 1932. No capital returned to contributories. Final meeting return regd. 23 Nov. 1935 .... ***1933**

Wilkinsons (Producer to Consumer) Ld. Regd. 1920. Vol. liq. Oct. 1926. Struck off Register 27 Oct. 1942 **1943**

Willans & Robinson Ld. Regd. 1894. Vol. liq. (members') 29 July 1935. The works were purchased by English Electric Co. Ld., on terms sufficient to pay all debts and liabilities, repay A and B preference capital and provide a surplus of £45,000 for the ordinary shareholders. The outstanding 4% 1st mortgage debenture stock was redeemed at 105% on 11 Sept. 1935. £98 0*s.* 7*d.* was paid into Companies' Liquidation Account in respect of unclaimed dividends and capital. Final meeting return regd. 30 June 1936 .... **1936**

Willenhall Gas Co. Estd. 1837; inc. by Special Act 1857. Dissolved 1 May 1949, undertaking being vested in West Midland Area Gas Board under Gas Act 1948. Holders of securities were entitled to receive British Gas 3% guaranteed stock 1990–95 as follows:

	£	s.	d.
A shares (10% stand.) (of £5)	13	12	6
B 5% pref. shares (of £2 14*s.*)	3	0	9
C shares (7½% stand.) (of £5)	11	7	6
D shares (7% stand.) (of £10)	21	15	0
E shares (7% stand.) (of £5)	10	17	6
4% perp. deb. stock (per £100)	102	10	0

1952

Willer & Riley Ld. Regd. 1897. Business was acquired in 1901 by company of same name, for £33,333 in ordinary shares, £96,000 in preference shares and £66,667 in cash. Removed from Register 1903 .... **1908**

Willer & Riley Ld. Regd. 1901. Vol. liq. 19 Oct. 1908. Court Order to continue winding up under supervision Nov. 1908. Final meeting return regd. 8 Jan. 1914. Court Order deferred dissolution until 26 Apr. 1914 .... **1909**

Willesden Glass Co. Ld. Regd. 1918. Vol. liq. (creditors') 23 July 1935. No capital returned to contributories. Final meeting return regd. 8 Nov. 1935 .... **1936**

Willet Works Ld. Regd. 1923. Vol. liq. (members') 12 Apr. 1944. All capital held by Turner & Newall Ld. Final meeting return regd. 18 Aug. 1944 .... **1931**

Willett Investments Ld. Regd. 1960. Vol. liq. (members') 11 Oct. 1966. Capital returned to contributories—8*d.* and ½*d.* per share of £1. Distribution in specie was made of 3 British Cocoa & Chocolate Co. Ld. ordinary shares for every 2 shares held. Final meeting return regd.5 Oct.1972 .... **1973-4**

Willey & Co. Holding Trust Ld. Regd. 1903 as Willey & Co. Ld.; name changed Dec. 1929. Vol. liq. (members') 25 Apr. 1933. Preference shareholders received 13 preference shares of £1 in United Gas Industries Ld for every 12 shares of £1 held and two months' dividend in cash. Ordinary shareholders received 79 preference, 81 ordinary and 65 deferred shares of United Gas Industries Ld. for every 100 shares of £1 held; a cash payment of 8*d.* per ordinary share was made in Nov. 1933; further payments (if any) not known. Final meeting return regd. 21 Apr. 1934 .... **1934**

VOL. FOR

Willey & Co. Ld. *See* Willey & Co. Holding Trust Ld.

Willey & Pearson Ld. Regd. 1895. Vol. liq. (members') 5 Feb. 1930. £17,321 5*s.* 1*d.* was paid to holders of 5% mortgage debentures. No capital returned to contributories. Final meeting return regd. 23 Dec. 1931 **1930**

Willey (Francis) & Co. Ld. controlled by Willey Investment Co. Ld. Regd. 1919. Vol. liq. (creditors') 21 Feb. 1935. Final meeting return regd. 12 May 1948 .... **1949**

Wm. Brandts Investment Trust Ld. *See* Brandts (Wm.) Investment Trust Ld.

Williams (Birmingham) Ld. Regd. 1937. Vol. liq. (members') 13 June 1946, undertaking having been acquired by former subsidiary (London Aluminium Co. Ld.) whose issued ordinary capital (800,000 shares) was distributed to members of this company. Final meeting return regd. 10 Mar. 1948 .... **1949**

Williams, Foster & Co. & Pascoe Grenfell & Sons Ld. Regd. 1838 as Williams. Foster & Co. Ld.; name changed Dec. 1892. Vol. liq. 2 July 1928. Final meeting return regd. 12 Dec. 1928 .... **1940**

Williams Hudson Group Ld. Regd. 30 Sept. 1936 as King's Motors (Oxford) Ld.; name changed to Adepton Ld. on 4 Jan. 1971 and to present title 22 Nov. 1971. Winding-up order made 1 Mar. 1982 **1984–5**

Williams, Jowett & Co., Ld. Regd. 1908. Vol. liq. (members') 15 Mar. 1943. Capital returned to contributories: £1 9*s.* 6¾*d.* per ordinary share of £1 and £1 0*s.* 4*d.* per preference share of £1. Final meeting return regd. 11 Aug. 1951 .... **1952**

Williams (Thomas) & Co. (Skewen Ld.) *See* Blue Bird. Coaches (Skewen) Ld.

Williams West Africa Ld. Regd. Feb. 1901. Undertaking and assets were acquired in 1901 by Akim Corporation Ld., in which company shareholders were entitled to 3 fully-paid shares of £1 for each share held. Removed from Register 1909 .... **1903**

Williams (William) & Sons Ld. *See* Macdonald, Greenlees & Williams (Distillers) Ld.

Williamson (G. H.) & Sons Ld. Regd. 1899. Vol. liq. (members') 3 Apr. 1944. Undertaking acquired by Metal Box Co. Ld. Final meeting return regd. 15 Jan. 1946 .... **1939**

Williamson (H.) Ld. Regd. 1898. Receiver for debenture holders distributed 6*s.* 4½*d.* in the £, after selling all assets. Struck off Register 21 Apr. 1944 .... **1945**

Williamson's Pioneer & Development Co. Ld. Regd. 1895. Vol. liq. 28 Feb. 1917. Final meeting return regd. 15 Sept. 1917 .... **1917**

Williamstown Gas Co. Ld. Undertaking acquired in 1924 by Colonial Gas Association Ld. for 51,750 fully-paid ordinary shares of £1 .... **1925**

Willis (J.F.) (Cinderella Shoes) Ld. Regd. 1937. Dissolved 3 Dec. 1982 .... **1961**

Willis's Rooms Ld. Regd. 1886. Vol. liq. 12 Feb. 1890. Removed from Register 1906 .... **1891**

Willmar & Sioux Falls Railway Co. Organised Minnesota 1886. All capital stock was owned by Great Northern Railway Co. The 1st mortgage 50-year gold bonds were taken over by acquiring company and redeemed Jan. 1938 .... **1908**

Willow Bank Mills (Holdings) Ld. Regd. 1922 as Willow Bank Mills Ld.; name changed 1953. A subsidiary of Lancashire Cotton Corpn. Ld. Vol. liq. 31 Mar. 1959. Final meeting return regd. 5 Oct. 1959 .... **1958**

Willow Bank Mills Ld. *See above.*

Willows, Holt & Willows Ld. Regd. 1897. Vol. liq. 22 Dec. 1899. The business was transferred to British Oil and Cake Mills Ld., in which company shareholders were entitled to 10 preference shares of £1 for each preference share of £10 held. Holders of 4% debenture stock were entitled to an equal amount of 4½% debenture stock in purchasing company. Final meeting return regd. 24 May 1900 **1900**

Wills Consolidated Gold Mining Co. Ld. Regd. 1895. Vol. liq. 18 Feb. 1899. Reconstructed as Phoenix Gold Mines Ld., in which company shareholders were entitled to 2 shares of 10*s.* (credited with 8*s.* paid) for every share of £1 held. Final meeting return regd. 25 July 1900 .... **1903**

Wills (Geo.) & Co. Ld. Regd. 1927. Vol. liq. (members') 14 Apr. 1930. Capital returned to contributories—20*s.* per share of £1. Final meeting return regd. 1 Sept. 1930 .... **1931**

Willys Overland Crossley (Irish Free State) Ld. In liquidation. Direct controlling interest was owned by Willys Overland Crossley, Ld. **1932**

Willys Overland Crossley, Ld. Regd. 1919. Vol. liq. (members') 14 Dec. 1933. Capital returned to contributories—5*s.* 6·356*d.* per preferred ordinary share of 6*s.* Final meeting return regd. 21 Feb. 1936 **1934**

Wilmot (S. M.) & Co. Ld. Regd. 20 Mar. 1923. Winding-up order 18 Mar. 1963. Struck off register 7 Apr. 1972 .... **1940**

**See Stock Exchange Year-Book.*

VOL. FOR

Wilmslow & Alderley Edge Gas Co. Inc. by Special Act 1872. Dissolved 1 May 1949, undertaking being vested in North Western Area Gas Board under Gas Act 1948. Holders of securities were entitled to receive, in respect of each £10 unit held, British Gas 3% guaranteed stock 1990–95 as follows: £ s. d.
Orig. shares (10% max.) 23 0 0
New shares (7% max.) 16 0 0
Liability in respect of certain mortgage loans assumed by the Board **1952**

Wilson & Strain Ld. Regd. Dublin 1895. Vol. liq. Jan. 1909. Undertaking and assets acquired by Bloomfield Bakery Ld., in which company shareholders were entitled to 1 fully-paid share (ordinary or preference) of £2 5s. for each preference share of £5 held or fully-paid shares (ordinary or preference) equal to 5s. per share on the ordinary shares **1909**

Wilson Brothers' Bedstead Co. Ld. Regd. 1896. Removed from Register 1907 .... **1905**

Wilson Brothers Bobbin Co. Ld. Regd. 1897. Undertaking and assets were acquired in 1900 by Wilson Brothers Bobbin Co. (1900) Ld. (later Wilson Brothers Bobbin Co. Ld.), for £70,000 in shares of £1, £80,000 in debenture stock and £182,042 in cash. Removed from Register 1904 .... **1900**

Wilson Brothers Bobbin Co., Ld. Regd. 1900 as Wilson Brothers Bobbin Co. (1900) Ld.; name changed as above 1904. Vol. liq. (creditors') 7 Oct. 1965. No capital was returned to contributories. Final meeting return regd. 31 Jan. 1967. .... **1967**

Wilson Bros.' Parkside Brewery Ld. Regd. 1897. The brewery and other properties and assets were acquired in 1900 by Whitmarsh, Watson & Co. Ld. Removed from Register 1901 .... **1901**

Wilson (George) & Co., Leicester Ld. Regd. 1897. Vol. liq. Sept. 1909. Removed from Register 1913 ...... **1910**

Wilson (John) & Son (Belfast) Ld. Regd. Dublin 1896; transferred to Belfast under Government of Ireland Act 1920 .... **1940**

Wilson (John K.) & Co. Ld. Regd. Dublin 1898. Vol. liq. Mar. 1922. .... **1923**

Wilson Lovatt & Sons Ld. Regd. as private company 21 Jan. 1914; converted into public company 15 Dec. 1952. Winding-up order made 4 Oct. 1971 .... **1986–7**

Wilsons & Clyde Coal Co. Ld. Regd. Edinburgh 1876 as Clyde Coal Co. Ld.; name changed Feb. 1892. Vol. liq. (members') 8 Jan. 1952. A repayment of 7s. 6d. per 10s. ordinary stock was made in Mar. 1952. Capital returned to contributories—17s. 5d. per stock unit of 2s. 6d. Final meeting return regd. 21 Mar. 1961 .... **1962**

Wilsons & Furness-Leyland Line Ld. Regd. 1896. Vol. liq. 18 Feb. 1915. Final meeting return regd. 19 May 1916 .... **1916**

Wilsons & Union Tube Co. Ld. Regd. Edinburgh 1898. Vol. liq. July 1912. Undertaking and assets sold to Scottish Tube Co. Ld. for 56,167 ordinary and 100,000 preference shares of £1 fully-paid, and £62,000 in cash. Final meeting return regd. 14 May 1921 .... **1940**

Wilson's (D. M.) Komatie Reefs Ld. *See* Komatie Reefs Ld.

Wilson's (D. M.) Options Ld. Regd. 1902. Struck off Register 1914. .... **1909**

Wilton (George), Son & Co. Ld. Regd. 1887. Vol. liq. May 1912. Removed from Register 1913 .... **1913**

Wilton Road Properties Ld. Regd. 1921. Vol. liq. 5 Mar. 1928. Final meeting return regd. 3 Oct. 1929 .... **1929**

Wilton Tea Co. of Assam Ld. Regd. 1871. Vol. liq. 25 Feb. 1892. Undertaking was acquired by Jokai (Assam) Tea Co. Ld., for 2,100 fully-paid shares of £10 and £3,150 in cash. Final meeting return regd. 18 Oct. 1892 .... **1893**

Wilts & Dorset Banking Co. Ld. Established 1835. Regd. as unlimited 1874 and as limited 1883. Vol. liq. 21 May 1914 for amalgamation with Lloyds Bank Ld., in which company shareholders were entitled to 10 shares of £50 (credited with £8 paid) for every 7 shares of £50 (£10 paid) held *plus* £2 per share in cash **1915**

Wiltshire Bacon Curing Co. Ld. Regd. 1890. Vol. liq. 30 Sept. 1920. Final meeting return regd. 11 Dec. 1923 **1892**

Wiltshire Brewery Co. Ld. Regd. 1888. Court Orders: to wind up 20 July 1889; to dissolve 5 Mar. 1895 ..... **1890**

Wiltshire Development Co. Ld. Regd. 1896. Undertaking and assets were acquired by Exploring Land and Minerals Co. Ld. for £500. Removed from Register 1904 .... **1903**

Wiluna Gold Corporation Ld. Regd. 1926. Vol. liq. (members') 20 Dec. 1951. Capital returned to contributories—14s. 5d. per share of £1. £9,506 was paid into Companies' Liquidation Account. Final meeting return regd. 24 June 1954 .... **1955**

VOL. FOR

Wimbledon and Sutton Railway Co. Inc. by Special Act 1910. Under Act of 1924 the Southern Railway Co. acquired the undertaking and unexercised capital powers. Shareholders were entitled to £10 per share in cash **1925**

Wimbledon & West Metropolitan Junction Railway Co. Inc. by Special Act 1882. Under London and South Western Railway Act 1886 the undertaking was acquired by that company **1887**

Wincanton Coal Gas Co. Ld. Regd. 1877. Dissolved 1 May 1949, undertaking being vested in South Western Area Gas Board under Gas Act 1948. Holders of securities were entitled to receive, British Gas 3% guaranteed stock 1990–95 as follows in respect of each. £1 unit, unless otherwise stated, of security held:
                                                          £ s. d.
Ord. shares 2 18 6
6% pref. shares (issued before 1 Jan. 1946) 1 6 5
6% pref. shares (issued since 31 Dec. 1945) 1 2 0
4% red. debs. (of £100) 102 15 0   **1952**

Winchester Electric Light and Power Co. Ld. Regd. 1897. Vol. liq. Sept. 1911. The undertaking was acquired by Winchester Corporation. The 5% debentures were repaid at 105%. Capital returned to contributories—£6 per share of £5 at 25 Jan. 1912; a further 10s. per share was expected. Removed from Register 1912 .... **1912**

Winchester Gas, Light & Coke Co. Regd. 1856. Reconstructed 1865 as Winchester Water & Gas Co. Dissolved by Act of 1865 .... **1937**

Winchester Gold Mining Co. Ld. Regd. 1895 as North Coolgardie Co. Ld.; name changed Apr. 1903. Vol. liq. Oct. 1906. Removed from Register 1912 .... **1907**

Winchester House Co. Ld. Regd. 1883. Vol. liq. 25 Jan. 1888. Final meeting return regd. 5 Feb. 1891 ...... **1889**

Winchester Syndicate Ld. Regd. 1896. Removed from Register 1904 .... **1898**

Winchester Water and Gas Co. Inc. by Special Act 1865 as consolidation of Winchester Waterworks Co. and Winchester Gas Light & Coke Co. Under Act of 1936 the water undertaking was acquired by Winchester Corporation and under Order of 1936 the gas undertaking was acquired by Southampton Gas Light & Coke Co. On acquisition of water undertaking stockholders were entitled to stock in Winchester Corporation as follows—for every £100 consolidated ordinary stock held—45 2s. redeemable 5% stock; for every £100 4%, 5% or 5½% preference stock held—£41 redeemable stock bearing a like rate of interest; for every £100 4% or 5% irredeemable stock held—£41 irredeemable stock bearing a like rate of interest. On acquisition of gas undertaking, stockholders were entitled to stock in acquiring company as follows—for every £100 consolidated ordinary stock held—£64 18s. ordinary stock; for every £100 4%, 5% or 5½% preference stock held—£59 preference stock bearing a like rate of dividend; for every £100 4% or 5% irredeemable debenture stock held—£59 irredeemable debenture stock bearing a like rate of interest **1937**

Winchester Waterworks Co. Regd. 1856. Reconstructed 1865 as Winchester Water & Gas Co. Dissolved by Act of 1865 .... **1937**

Windermere & District Electricity Supply Co. Ld. Regd. 1894. Dissolved 1 Apr. 1948. undertaking being vested in British (later Central) Electricity Authority and North-Western Area Board under Electricity Act 1947. Holders of securities were entitled to receive British Electricity 3% guaranteed stock (1968–73), as follows in respect of each £5 unit of capital held:
                                                          £ s. d.
7½% preference shares 8 2 6
6% preference shares 7 10 0
Ordinary shares 19 0 0   **1949**

Windermere District Gas & Water Co. Inc. by Special Act 1862 as Windermere District Gas Co.; name changed 1869. By Act of 1929 the undertaking was acquired by Urban District Council of Windermere for £74,000. The mortgages were repaid at par. The preference and ordinary shares were repaid at par in Oct. 1929; a further distribution was to be made to ordinary shareholders on ascertainment of surplus assets **1930**

Windermere District Gas Co. *See* Windermere District Gas & Water Co.

Winding Creek Gold Mining Co. Ld. Regd. 1898. Removed from Register 1904 .... **1903**

Windover (Charles S.) & Co. Ld. Regd. 1885. Vol. liq. Sept. 1908. Removed from Register 1910 .... **1909**

VOL. FOR

Windsor & Annapolis Railway Co. Ld. Inc. Nova Scotia by Special Act 1867. In 1894 the company was reconstructed as Dominion Atlantic Railway Co., when the Yarmouth and Annapolis Railway Co. was purchased **1908**

Windsor & Ascot Railway Co. Inc. by Special Act 1898. Powers acquired by Great Western Railway Co. under Act of 1901 .... **1900**

Windsor Castle Gold Mines Ld. Regd. 1896. Removed from Register 1901 .... **1902**

Windsor Consolidated (W. A.) Gold Mines Ld. Regd. 1899. Removed from Register 1905 .... **1905**

Windsor Diamond Mining Co. Ld. Inc. Cape of Good Hope 1903. Undertaking and assets acquired by Welgelegan Diamond Mining Co. Ld. **1907**

Windsor Electrical Installation Co. Ld. Regd. 1895. Dissolved 1 Apr. 1948, undertaking being vested in British (later Central) Electricity Authority and Southern Area Board under Electricity Act 1947 .. **1949**

Windsor (F.M.S.) Rubber Estate Ld. Regd, 1910. Dissolved 20 Oct. 1981 .... **1971**

Windsor Gold Mines Ld. Inc. Transvaal 1902. Vol. liq. Apr. 1909. Undertaking and assets were acquired by Luipaard's Vlei Estate and Gold Mining Co. Ld., in which company shareholders were entitled to 1 share of £1 (credited as fully-paid) for every 4 shares of £1 held **1910**

Windsor Gold Mining Co. Ld. Inc. Transvaal 1894. In 1902 amalgamated with Eton Gold Mining Co. Ld. under title of Windsor Gold Mines Ld., in which company shareholders were entitled to 16 shares of £1 for every 10 shares of £1 held **1908**

Windsor Royal Gaslight Co. Estd. 1827; inc. by Special Act 1867. Dissolved 1 May 1949. undertaking being vested in North Thames Area Gas Board under Gas Act 1948. Holders of securities were entitled to receive British Gas 3% guaranteed stock 1990–95 as follows:

	£	s.	d.
Orig. shares (10% basic) (of £20).....	46	0	0
New Shares (7% basic) (of £20)	32	8	0
5% pref. shares (of £8)	9	4	0
5% pref. shares (of £10).................	11	10	0
4% perp. deb. stock (per £100).........	103	0	0
3½% red. deb. stock (per £100)	100	0	0

1952

Windsor Slipways, Dry Docks & Engineering Co. Ld. Regd. 1883. Vol. liq. 30 May 1895. Works were acquired by Mordey Carney & Co. Ld in which company shareholders were entitled to 2,459 fully-paid shares of £10 plus £10,410 in cash. Final meeting return regd. 20 May 1899 .... **1899**

Windsor Steam Coal Co. (1901) Ld. Regd. 1901. Vol. liq. 1 Jan. 1926. The property and undertaking were acquired by Powell Duffryn Steam Coal Co. Ld. for £250,000 in cash. The debentures were redeemed at 105% in July 1925. Final meeting return regd. 9 July 1930 .... **1944**

Windsor Trust Ld. Regd. 1911. Vol. liq. (members') 15 Feb. 1937. Investments were sold to British Empire Land Mortgage & Loan Co. Ld. for £20,000 5% convertible debenture stock and 280,000 fully-paid shares of 1s. £1 10s. 6d. was paid into Companies' Liquidation Account in respect of unclaimed dividends. Final meeting return regd. 5 Apr. 1938 .... **1937**

Winfields Ld. Regd. 1887. Removed from Register 1904 **1898**

Wingello Coal Co. Ld. Regd. 1888. Vol. liq. 5 Jan. 1891. Struck off Register 1921 .... **1891**

Wingham and Stour Valley Collieries Ld. Regd. 1911. Vol. liq. 24 May 1927. Reconstructed as Wingham Holding Co. Ld., in which company shareholders were entitled to 1 fully-paid share of 6d. for every 4 deferred shares of 1s. held, or 1 fully-paid share of 6d. plus 1s. in cash for each preference share of 10s. held. Final meeting return regd. 28 Nov. 1928 .... **1928**

Wingham Holding Co. Ld. Regd. 1927. Vol. liq. (members') 1 Dec. 1942. Capital returned to contributories—9d. per share of 6d. £244 was paid into Companies' Liquidation Account. Final meeting return regd. 15 Feb. 1944 .... **1945**

Winnebah Tinfields Ld. Regd. 1919. Vol. liq. (members') 13 Apr. 1938. Undertaking and assets were acquired by Offin River Gold Estates Ld. (later Offin River Estates Ld.), in which company shareholders were entitled to 2 shares of 5s. (credited as fully-paid) for every 5 shares of 5s. held. Final meeting return regd. 29 May 1941 .... **1939**

Winnipeg Paint & Glass Co. Ld. Inc. Manitoba 1903. Wound up Feb. 1928 .... **1929**

Winnipeg Waterworks Co. Inc. by Special Act of Manitoba 1881. Property sold in 1899 to Corporation of Winnipeg for $237,500. Preferred bondholders were repaid in full and ordinary bondholders received £36 10s. per bond **1900**

VOL. FOR

Winox Ld. Regd. 1912. Vol. liq. 12 Apr. 1927. The undertaking and assets were sold to F. Anderson & Co. Ld. Final meeting return regd. 15 Aug. 1928 . **1928**

Winser's (Tunbridge Wells) Ld. Regd. 1920. Receiver appointed 10 Oct. 1922; ceased to act 10 Nov. 1924. Vol. liq. 12 Oct. 1922. Final meeting return regd. 6 May 1925 .... ***1923**

Winsford Gas Co. Ld. Regd. 1936. Dissolved 1 May 1949, undertaking being vested in North Western Area Gas Board under Gas Act 1948. Holders of 3½% red. 1st mort. debentures were entitled to receive, in respect of each £100 unit held £100 5s. British Gas 3% guaranteed stock 1990–95............. **1952**

Winsley Press Agency Ld. Regd. 1924. Vol. liq. (creditors') 16 Feb. 1934. Waring & Gillow Ld. (later Waring & Gillow Holdings Ld.) held a direct controlling interest. Asset realised insufficient to pay unsecured creditors in full. Final meeting return regd. 8 Mar. 1935 .... **1931**

Winslow New Gas Co. Ld. Regd. 1880. Dissolved 1 May 1949, undertaking being vested in Southern Area Gas Board under Gas Act 1948. Holders of ordinary shares (of £10) were entitled to receive £11 British Gas 3% guaranteed stock 1990–95 for each share held **1952**

Winter Gardens Theatre (London) Ld. Regd. 1928. Vol. liq. (members') 4 Dec. 1961. Amount returned to contributories—5½d. per share of 10s. Paid into Companies' Liquidation Account—£84·60 in respect of unclaimed distributions. Final meeting return regd. 30 Nov. 1970 .... **1971**

Winter's Gold Mine Ld. Regd. 1897. Removed from Register 1903 .... **1901**

Winterton Gas Co. Ld. Estd. 1855; regd. as limited 1857. Dissolved 1 May 1949, undertaking being vested in East Midland Area Gas Board under Gas Act 1948. Holders of securities were entitled to receive, British Gas 3% guaranteed stock 1990–95 as follows in respect of each £100 unit, unless otherwise stated, of security held:

	£	s.	d.
Ord. shares (of £10).......................	17	10	0
3½% mort. debs.............................	100	0	0
5% mort. debs.	100	0	0

1952

Wireless Pictures (1928) Ld. Regd. 1928. Vol. liq. July 1930. Struck off Register 12 July 1935 .... **1936**

Wirksworth Gas Light & Coke Co. Regd. 1864. Dissolved 1 May 1949, undertaking being vested in East Midland Area Gas Board under Gas Act 1948. Holders of securities were entitled to receive, British Gas 3% guaranteed stock 1990–95 as follows:

	£	s.	d.
Orig. ord. shares (10% stand.) (of £10).	14	5	0
4% red. mort. debs. (of £100)...............	101	0	0

1952

Wirral Railway Co. Inc. by Special Act 1891. In 1923 the undertaking was merged into the London Midland & Scottish Railway Co. in which company stockholders were entitled to stock as follows:

For each £100 held		L. M. & S.
Debenture......................	£75	4% Debenture
Preference	£100	4% Pref.(1923)
4½% preference	£112½	4% Pref. (1923)
Ordinary.......................	£50	cash

The £70,920 Loans were taken over by the London Midland & Scottish Co. **1924**

Wirral Railways Co. Ld. Regd. 1884. Vol. liq. 27 Mar. 1929. Final meeting return regd. 8 Sept. 1937....... **1930**

Wirral Transport Co. Ld. Regd. 1911. Vol. liq. (members') 13 Dec. 1934. Capital returned to contributories—3s. 5·78d. per share of £1. Final meeting return regd. 3 May 1935 .... **1935**

Wirrall Waterworks Co. Inc. by Special Act. Part of undertaking was acquired by Birkenhead Corporation for £80,000 in cash and part of the undertaking was acquired by West Cheshire Water Board for £20,000 payable in cash or in stock.................. **1926**

Wisbech Electric Light & Power Co. Ld. Regd. 1907. Dissolved 1 Apr. 1948. undertaking being vested in the British (later Central) Electrcity Authority and Eastern Area Board under the Electricity Act 1947. Preference shareholders were entitled to receive £1 11s. 6d. British Electricity 3% guaranteed stock (1968–73) for each share (of £1) held **1949**

Wisbech Lighting Co. Inc. by Special Act 1879. Dissolved 1 May 1949, undertaking being vested in Eastern Area Gas Board under Gas Act 1948. Holders of securities were entitled to receive British Gas 3% guaranteed stock 1990–95 as follows:

	£	s.	d.
Ord. stock (10% stand.) (per £3).........	7	10	0
Ord. shares (7% stand.) (of £5)...........	10	10	0
6% pref. shares (of £10)......................	14	0	0
4½% debs. (of £100)	100	5	0

1952

VOL. FOR

Wisconsin Central Railway Co. Inc. in Wisconsin 1897. Placed in bankruptcy as from 1 Mar. 1954 under a reorganisation plan, which vested all the properties in a new company (Wisconsin Central Railroad Co.). The plan made no provision for holders of common stock and only contingent provision for holders of preferred stock. Holders of 4% 1st and refunding mtg. gold bonds (which were known in London) received, in respect of every $1,000 bond held, $150 4% 1st mtg. bonds, $1,000 4½% gen. mtg. bonds and $500 common stock (at $100 per share) of the new company 1956

Wisconsin, Minnesota & Pacific Railroad Co. Inc. Minnesota 1894. All capital stock was held by Chicago Great Western Railroad Co. Majority of 1st mortgage 4% 50-year gold bonds were exchanged for $500 in 1st mortgage 50-year 4% gold bonds and $500 preferred stock of controlling company for each bond of $1,000 held 1914

Witham Gas Light & Coke Co. Ld. Regd. 1860. Dissolved 1 May 1949, undertaking being vested in Eastern Area Gas Board under Gas Act 1948. Holders of ordinary shares were entitled to receive, in respect of each £1 unit held, £1 British Gas 3% guaranteed stock 1990–95 1952

Witkopje Gold Mines Ld. Inc. Transvaal 1896. Reconstructed 1904 under same name. Shareholders received 1 share of £1 (credited 16s. 6d. paid) in new company for each share of £1 held 1909

Witney, Burford & Andoversford Light Railway Co. Inc. 1904. Powers expired 1908 1908

Witney Gas & Coke Co. Ld. Regd. 1899; statutory powers 1911 and subsequently. Dissolved 1 May 1949, undertaking being vested in Southern Area Gas Board under Gas Act 1948. Holders of securities were entitled to receive British Gas 3% guaranteed stock 1990–95 as follows:

	£	s.	d.
Ord. shares (7% max.) (of £5)	7	5	0
5% pref. shares (both denominations—per £1)	1	2	6
0% red. mort. debs. (of £100)	100	5	0	1952

Witney Railway Co. Inc. by Special Act 1859. Under Great Western Railway Act of 1890 the undertaking was purchased by that company. Holders of ordinary and preference shares of £10 received an equal amount of 5% preference stock in the purchasing company 1891

Witpoort Gold Areas Ld. Inc. Transvaal 1895 as Rand Collieries Ld.; name changed Oct. 1928. Assets were sold to Brakpan Mines Ld., for £200,000. Vol.liq. Sept. 1932 1933

Witpoortje Gold Mines Ld. See Paris (Transvaal) Gold Mines Ld.

Witu Rubber Estates Ld. Regd. 1910. Vol. liq. 23 Dec. 1915. Final meeting return regd. 27 June 1917 1916

Witwatersrand & General Development Co. Ld. Regd. 1895. Vol. liq. 4 Aug. 1897. Final meeting return regd. 5 May 1898 .... *1898

Witwatersrandt "Venture Syndicate" Gold Mining Co. Ld. Reconstructed in 1890 as New Venture Witwatersrandt Gold Mining Co. Ld., in which company shareholders were entitled to 4 shares of 5s. (credited with 3s. 6d. paid) for each share of £1 held. Dissolved before 1931 1892

Wivenhoe & Brightlingsea Railway Co. Inc. Special Act 1861. Undertaking acquired by Great Eastern Railway Co. by Act 1893 for £31,000 in cash 1894

Woah Hawp (Ballarat, Victoria) Gold Mine Ld. Regd. 1902. Vol. liq. 26 Apr. 1905. Final meeting return regd. 17 July 1906 .... *1906

Woburn Gas Light & Coke Co. Ld. Regd. 1857. Dissolved 1 May 1949, undertaking being vested in Eastern Area Gas Board under Gas Act 1948. Holders of ordinary shares (of £10) were entitled to receive £24 British Gas 3% guaranteed stock 1990–95 for each share held 1952

Wohlfahrt Lead Mines Ld. Regd. 1881. Vol. liq. 20 Nov. 1919. Final meeting return regd. 19 Mar. 1920 1920

Woking & District Water Co. Inc. by Special Act 1881 as Woking Water & Gas Co. name changed 14 Dec. 1949. Under provisions of North Surrey Water Order 1973 undertakings and assets vested in North Surrey Water Co. on 1 Oct. 1973, shareholders receiving stock in that company as follows—£10 7% ordinary stock for each 10% ordinary share; £10 4·9% "A" ordinary stock for each 7% ordinary share; £4·9% "B" ordinary stock for each £1 7% ordinary stock; £3·5% ordinary stock for each £1 5% ordinary stock; £10 3·15% preference stock for each 5½% irredeemable preference share; £10 3·15% preference stock for each 4½% irredeemable preference share; £1 3·5% preference stock for each £1 5%

irredeemable preference stock. Redeemable preference stockholders received like amounts of comparable stocks of North Surrey Water Co. and the debenture stocks became stocks of that company. Company dissolved 21 Oct. 1974. 1975-6

Woking District Gas Co. Regd. as limited 1890; reinc. by Special Act 1912. Dissolved 1 May 1949, undertaking being vested in South Eastern Area Gas Board under Gas Act 1948. Holders of securities were entitled to receive, in respect of each £100 unit held, British Gas 3% guaranteed stock 1990–95 as follows:

	£	s.	d.
A ord. stock (10% stand.).................	210	0	0
B ord. stock (7% stand.)	146	0	0
5% C pref. stock	114	0	0
4% perp. pref. stock	102	6	8
4% 1st mort. debs.	102	0	0
4% 2nd mort. debs.	100	0	0
5% red. deb. stock	105	0	0
3½% red. deb. stock	100	0	0	1952

Woking Electric Supply Co. Ld. Regd. 1895. Dissolved 1 Apr. 1948. undertaking being vested in British (later Central) Electricity Authority and South-Eastern Area Board under Electricity Act 1947. Holders of securities were entitled to receive British Electricity 3% guaranteed stock (1968–73), as follows in respect of each £1 unit, unless otherwise stated, of capital held:

	£	s.	d.
10% C preference shares	2	10	0
7% B preference shares	1	16	0
6% preference shares......................	1	11	6
Ordinary shares..............................	4	0	0
4½% debenture stock	1	1	1½
4½% bearer debenture bonds (per £50)	50	10	0
4½% registered debenture bonds (per £50) 50	10	0		1949

Wokingham District Water Co. Ld. Regd. 1877. By Special Order of 1933 the undertaking was acquired by Frimley & Farnborough District Water Co. later Mid-Wessex Water Co., in which company shareholders were entitled to shares as follows—for every 7 original (10% maximum) shares of £10 held—10 7% additional ordinary shares of £10; for each additional ordinary (7% maximum) share of £10 held—1 7% additional ordinary share of £10. The liability for the 5% 1st debentures was assumed by the acquiring company 1934

Wolfhill Collieries Ld. Inc. Dublin 1921. Court Order to wind up 1926 1927

Wolfram Mining & Smelting Co. Ld. Regd. 1909. Vol. liq. 27 Oct. 1924. Reconstructed as company of same name. Shareholders were entitled to 1 share of £1 (credited with 16s. paid) for each share of £1 held. Final meeting return regd. 27 Feb. 1929 1925

Wolfram Mining & Smelting Co. Ld. Regd. 1924. Vol. liq. 9 Mar. 1927. Reconstructed as Beralt Tin & Wolfram Ld., in which company shareholders were entitled to 4 shares of 5s. (credited with 3s. paid) for each ordinary share of £1 held, or 4 fully-paid shares of 5s. for each preference share of £1 held. Final meeting return regd. 27 Feb. 1929 1928

Wolhuter Deep Ld. Inc. Transvaal 1899. Vol. liq. Mar. 1908. Undertaking and assets were acquired by City Deep Ld., in which company shareholders were entitled to 11 fully-paid shares of £1 for every 20 shares of £1 held 1909

Wolluter Gold Mines Ld. Inc. Transvaal 1895 Wound up Mar. 1930 1930

Wolhuter Gold Mining Co. Ld. Inc. Cape Colony 1887. Reconstructed 1895 as Wolhuter Gold Mines Ld. Shareholders received 1 share of £4 in new company for each share of £1 held 1908

Wolseley Motors Ld. Regd. 1901 as Wolseley Tool and Motor Car. Co. Ld.; name changed 14 July 1914. Court Orders: to appoint receiver 29 Oct. 1926; to wind up 16 Nov. 1926. Receiver ceased to act 18 July 1927. Liquidator released 2 Dec. 1929. Struck off Register 30 Aug. 1932 .... *1915

Wolseley Tool & Motor Car. Ld. See Wolseley Motors Ld.

Wolstanton Ld. Regd. 1917. Vol. liq. Jan. 1953. Final meeting return regd. 29 Sept. 1961 1950

Wolumla Goldfield Ld. Regd. 1900. Removed from Register 1905 1903

Wolverand Gold Estate & Mining Corporation Ld. Inc. South African Republic 1895. Undertaking and assets acquired in 1898 by Swaziland Corporation Ld. for fully-paid shares 1899

Wolverand Gold Mines Ld. Regd. 1893. Vol. liq. 25 Sept. 1895. Reconstructed as Wolverand Gold Estate & Mining Corporation Ld., in which company shareholders were entitled to 3 fully-paid shares of £1 for

VOL. FOR

every 5 shares of £1 held. Final meeting return regd. 17 June 1896.   **1898**

Wolverhampton & Cannock Chase Railway Co. Inc. by Special Act 1901. Powers transferred to London & North Western Railway Co. by order of 1913 .....   **1914**

Wolverhampton & Staffordshire Banking Co. Ld. In 1889 the business was acquired by Birmingham District and Counties Banking Co. Ld. (later United Counties Bank Ld.). Shareholders were entitled to either £13 in cash or 7 shares of £10 (credited with £4 paid) in acquiring company for every 4 shares held   **1890**

Wolverhampton District Brewery Ld. Regd. 1898. Removed from Register 18 Nov. 1902 ....   ***1901**

Wolverhampton District Electric Tramways Ld. *See* Black Country Tramways Estates Ld.

Wolverhampton Empire Palace Co. Ld. Regd. 1899. Court Order to wind up 23 May 1911. Liquidator released 30 Mar. 1912. Struck off Register 1 July 1921 ....   **1912**

Wolverhampton Gas Co. Estd. 1820; inc. by Special Act 1852. Dissolved 1 May 1949, undertaking being vested in West Midland Area Gas Board under Gas Act 1948. Holders of securities were entitled to receive, in respect of each £100 unit held, British Gas 3% guaranteed stock 1990–95 as follows:

	£	s.	d.
Cons. ord. stock (6% stand.)	160	0	0
6% pref. stock	134	0	0
5% pref. stock	112	0	0
3½% perp. deb. stock	98	0	0
5½% red. deb. stock	105	0	0
3½% red. deb. stock	102	10	0	**1952**

Wolverhampton New Waterworks Co. Inc. by Special Act 1855. Waterworks were leased in perpetuity to Wolverhampton Corporation but under the Wolverhampton Corporation Act 1950 the rents were redeemed on 5 Jan. 1951 on which date shareholders were entitled to British Government 2½% consolidated stock as follows— £8 stock per ordinary share (of £5) and £10 stock per preference share (of £5). Winding-up completed 22 May 1952 and company dissolved **1954**

Wolverhampton Tramways Co. Ld. Regd. 1876. Vol. liq. 9 Apr. 1901. The lines within the borough were purchased by Wolverhampton Corporation for £22,500 and the remainder were purchased by British Electric Traction Co. Ld. for £10,200. Final meeting return regd. 19 Nov. 1901 ....   **1920**

Wolverhampton Union Flour & Bread Co. *See* Wolverhampton Union Mill Co. Ld.

Wolverhampton Union Mill Co. Ld. Regd. 1856 as Wolverhampton Union Flour & Bread Co.; regd. as limited June 1907; name changed Aug. 1907. Vol. liq. 22 Mar. 1909. Final meeting return regd. 2 Sept. 1915 ....   **1910**

Wolverton, Stony Stratford & District Tramway Co. Ld. Inc. as a light railway 1886. Undertaking was placed in hands of official liquidator 17 Dec. 1889..........   **1892**

Women's Printing Society Ld. Regd. 1876. Vol. liq. (members') 4 May 1955. Final meeting return regd. 3 Oct. 1956 ....   **1906**

Wondalli (Deccan) Gold Mine Ld. Regd. 1895. Struck off Register 13 Oct. 1908 ....   **1909**

Wood (John) & Brothers (1920) Ld. Regd. 1920. Receiver appointed 11 Apr. 1924. Property was acquired by Wood Brothers (Glossop) Ld. The 1st debenture holders were entitled to repayment in full and 2nd debenture holders to 17s. 6d. in £. Struck off Register Feb. 1930   **1931**

Wood (W.) & Son Ld. Regd. 1909. Vol. liq. (creditors') 12 Aug. 1976. Final meeting held 2 Mar. 1981 .... **1981–2**

Wood Pulp Vessels Ld. In 1921 the business was acquired by Taylor's Hygienic Service Ld. for 7,000 fully-paid shares of £1   **1923**

Woodbine Gold Mining Co. Ld. Inc. Transvaal 1885. Stated to be in liquidation in 1905 ....   **1905**

Woodbridge & Bawdsey Light Railway Co. Ld. Inc. 1904 under Light Railways Act 1896. Powers expired 1909................   **1909**

Woodbyrne Ayrshire Development Co. Ld. Regd. 1895. Undertaking and assets were acquired by Lomagunda Development Co. Ld. in 1899 for 49,628 fully-paid shares of £1. Removed from Register 1901 ..   **1908**

Woodall-Duckham (1920) Ld. Regd. 1920 as Woodall Duckham & Jones (1920) Ld. Vol. liq. (members') 13 Aug. 1948. Undertaking and assets acquired by Woodall-Duckham Ld. Final meeting return regd. 14 Nov. 1951 ....   **1952**

Woodend (Kelani Valley, Ceylon) Rubber & Tea Co. Ld. Regd. 1905. Vol. liq. 27 Feb. 1920. Reconstructed as company of same name. Shareholders were entitled to 3 shares of £1 (credited as fully-paid) in new company for each share of £1 held. Final meeting return regd. 15 May 1922 ....   **1920**

VOL. FOR

Woodfield Steam Shipping Co. Ld. Regd. 1903. Vol. liq. (members') 13 June 1933. Capital returned to contributories—10s. per preference share of 10s.; £1 3s. 9·58d. per ordinary share of £1. £176 11s. was paid into Companies' Liquidation Account in respect of unclaimed dividends and a further £130 4s. 8d. in respect of unclaimed capital. Final meeting return regd. 23 Dec. 1933 ....   **1934**

Woodhall Spa Gas Co. Inc. by Special Act 1904. Dissolved 1 May 1949, undertaking being vested in East Midfand Area Gas Board under Gas Act 1948. Holders of securities were entitled to receive British Gas 3% guaranteed stock 1990–95 as follows:

	£	s.	d.
Ord shares (of £10)........................	11	13	4
5% red. mort. debs. (of £100)..........	103	0	0	**1952**

Woodham's & Co. Ld. Regd. 1895. Vol. liq. 25 May 1927. Controlling interest held by Style & Winch Ld. Final meeting return regd. 24 Nov. 1927 ....   **1928**

Woodhouse & Baillie Riviera Electricity Co. Ld. Regd. 1899. Struck off Register 1927 ....   **1914**

Woodhouse & Conisbrough Railway Co. Inc. by Special Act 1897. Construction abandoned by Act of 1899   **1900**

Woudhouse & Rawson Electrical Manufacturing Co. Ld. Regd. 1885. Vol. liq. 9 Feb. 1891. Business was acquired by Woodhouse & Rawson United Ld. Final meeting return regd. 16 Dec. 1893 ....   **1892**

Woodhouse & Rawson Ld. Regd. 1887. Vol. liq. 26 Sept. 1889. Business was acquired by Woodhouse & Rawson United Ld. Final meeting return regd. 27 Feb. 1894 ....   **1892**

Woodhouse & Rawson United Ld. Regd. 1889. Court Order to wind up 17 May 1893. Removed from Register 1907 ....   **1894**

"Woodite" Co. Ld. Regd. 1888. Removed from Register 1906 ....   **1893**

Woodlands Chemists, Ld. Regd. 1934. Vol. liq. (creditors') 11 Aug. 1943. No capital returned to contributories. Final meeting return regd. 12 Apr. 1946 ....   **1947**

Woodley Co. Ld. Regd. 1896. Removed from Register 1904 ....   **1903**

Woodley's Gold Mines Ld. Regd. 1899. Removed from Register 1904 ....   **1902**

Woodley's Reward Gold Mines Ld. Regd. 1896. Reconstructed 1899 as Woodley's Gold Mines Ld., in which company shareholders were entitled to 1 share of £1 (credited with 18s. paid) for each share of £1 held. Removed from Register 1901................   **1901**

Wood-Milne Ld. Regd. 1907. Vol. liq. 4 Apr. 1927. All shares owned by Federated Rubber Growers & Manufacturers Ld. Final meeting return regd. 10 Mar. 1931 ....   **1928**

Woods-Gilbert Rail Remodelling Co. Ld. Regd. 1918. Vol. liq. (members') 25 Nov. 1929. Capital returned to contributories—15s. per preference share of £1 at 21 Jan. 1930. Final meeting return regd. 30 June 1932 ....   **1930**

Woods (William) & Son Ld. *See* Trencherfield Spinning Co. Ld.

Woodstock & District Electrical Distribution Co. Ld. Regd. 1930. Dissolved 1 Apr. 1948, undertaking being vested in the British (later Central) Electricity Authority and Southern Area Board under the Electricity Act 1947. Holders of ordinary shares and 4% debentures were entitled to receive British Electricity 3% guaranteed stock (1968–73), as follows–£4 10s. for each ordinary share (of £1) held and £1,005 for every £1,000 of debenture capital held   **1949**

Woodstock Gold Mining Co. Ld. Regd. 1902. Vol. liq. Dec. 1903. Removed from Register 1908 ....   **1904**

Woodstock Main Reef Ld. Regd. 1896. Vol. liq. 13 Mar. 1899. Final meeting return regd. 8 Nov. 1899 .....   **1900**

Woodstock Power Syndicate Ld. Regd. 1926. Dissolved 1 May 1949, undertaking being vested in Southern Area Gas Board under Gas Act 1948. Holders of securities were entitled to receive British Gas 3% guaranteed stock 1990–95 as follows:

	£	s.	d.
Ord. shares (of £1)............................	2	18	0
4% red. debs. (of £100).....................	100	0	0	**1952**

Woodstock Railway Co. Inc. by Special Act 1886. Under Great Western Railway Act of 1897 the undertaking was amalgamated with that company for £15,000 ....   **1898**

Woodstock (Transvaal) Gold Mine Ld. Regd. 1895. Reconstructed 1898 as company of same name. Shareholders were entitled to 1 share of £1 (credited with 17s. 6d. paid) in new company for each share of £1 held. Removed from Register 1904 ....   **1903**

Woodstock (Transvaal) Gold Mine Ld. Regd. 1898. Reconstructed 1903 as Woodstock Transvaal Gold Mine Ld., in which company shareholders were entitled to 1 share of 10s. (credited with 7s. 6d. paid)

VOL. FOR

for each share of £1 held. Removed from Register 1909 .... **1908**

Woodstock Transvaal Gold Mine Ld. Regd. 1903. Vol. liq. June 1912. Removed from Register 1913 .... **1913**

Woodward & Walker's Gold Mine Ld. Regd. 1887. Vol. liq. 13 June 1889. Final meeting return regd. 20 Jan. 1894 .... **1891**

Wool Industries Employers' Insurance Association Ld. Regd. 1898. The business was acquired by Manchester Assurance Co. Removed from Register 1901 .. **1901**

Wool Textile Finance Co. Ld. Regd. 1922. Struck off Register; 1931 .... ***1925**

Wooler Gas Co. Ld. Regd. 1925. Dissolved 1 May 1949, undertaking being vested in Northern Area Gas Board under Gas Act 1948. Holders of ordinary shares (of £1) were entitled to receive £2 2*s*. British Gas 3% guaranteed stock 1990–95 for each share held **1952**

Wooler Motor-Cycle Co. (1919) Ld. Regd. 1919. Vol. liq. 14 Oct. 1921. Final meeting return regd. 11 Dec. 1923 .... **1922**

Woolley & Arnfield Ld. *See* B. D. H. (Woolley & Arnfield) Ld.

Woolley (James) Sons & Co. Ld. *See* B. D. H. (Woolley & Arnfield) Ld.

Woolpit Brick Co. Ld. Regd. 1899. Removed from Register 1911 .... **1905**

Woolwich and South East London Tramways Co. Ld. Regd. 1880. Vol. liq. 19 Oct. 1905. Capital returned to contributories—£1 10*s*. per ordinary share of £4; £1 17*s*. 6*d*. per preference share of £5; further payments (if any) not known. Removed from Register 1906 .... **1906**

Woolwich District Electric Light Co. Ld. Regd. 1890. Undertaking sold to Borough Council of Woolwich. Removed from Register 1903 .... **1904**

Woolwich Equitable Gas Co. Amalgamated with South Metropolitan Gas Co. 1 Jan. 1885. The 10% original shares received an equal amount of C stock and the 7½% shares received 75% of their holding in C stock of the South Metropolitan Gas Co **1885**

Woolwich (Old Barge House) Steam Ferry Ld. Regd. 1886. Court Orders: to wind up Mar. 1888; to dissolve 24 Dec. 1889 .... **1888**

Woolwich, Plumstead & Charlton Consumers' Gas Co. Inc. 1855. Amalgamated with South Metropolitan Gas Co. 1 Jan. 1885. The 10% original shares received an equal amount of C stock, the 7½% shares 75% of their holding and the 7% shares 70% of their holding in South Metropolitan C stock **1885**

Worcester & Broom Railway Co. Inc. by Special Act 1885. Undertaking abandoned by Act of 1894 .... **1895**

Worcester, Bromyard & Leominster Railway Co. Inc. by Special Act 1861. Under Great Western Railway Act 1888 the undertaking was transferred to that company. Holders of ordinary shares of £10 received 10*s*. per share in cash; holders of preference stock received £95 in cash for every £100 held; holders of 5% debenture stock received 5% debenture stock in the purchasing company **1889**

Worcester City & County Banking Co. Ld. Established 1840. Regd. as limited 1865. Business was acquired in 1889 by Lloyds Bank Ld. for 15,150 shares of £50 (credited with £8 paid) and an unspecified amount of cash **1897**

Worcester Electric Traction Co. Ld. Regd. 1902. Vol. liq. (members') 17 Sept. 1934. Capital returned to contributories—£4 12*s*. 7¼*d*. per share of £5 *plus* a distribution of investments in specie. £8 17*s*. 2*d*. was paid into Companies' Liquidation Account. Undertaking was acquired by the Worcester Corporation. Final meeting return regd. 11 June 1936 .... **1935**

Worcester Exploration & Gold Mining Co. Ld. Inc. Cape of Good Hope and Transvaal 1887. Wound up Jan. 1916 .... **1916**

Worcester New Gas Light Co. Inc. by Special Act 1846. Dissolved 1 May 1949, undertaking being vested in West Midland Area Gas Board under Gas Act 1948. Holders of securities were entitled to receive, in respect of each £100 unit held, British Gas 3% guaranteed stock 1990–95 as follows:

	£	s.	d.	
Cons. ord. stock (10% max.)	240	0	0	
4½% deb. stock	112	10	0	**1952**

Worcester Properties Ld. Regd. 1900 as Hill, Evans & Co. Ld.; name changed 1964. Vol. liq. (members') 29 Sept. 1967. Final meeting return regd. 28 Dec. 1973 .... **1966**

Worcester Royal Porcelain Co. Ld. Regd. 1862. Vol. liq. (creditors') 11 Dec. 1934. Business sold to Worcester China Co. Ld. £34,011 17*s*. 11*d*. was paid to debenture holders. No capital returned to contributories. Final meeting return regd. 27 Mar. 1935 .. **1935**

Worcester Tramways Ld. Regd. 1893. Undertaking and assets were acquired in 1902 by Worcester Electric Traction Co. Ld. Removed from Register 1906 ... **1903**

Worcestershire Brewing & Malting Co. Ld. Regd. 1896. Vol. liq. July 1905. Undertaking and assets were acquired by Kidderminster Brewery Co. Ld. Holders of 4½% 1st mortgage debenture stock were entitled to £27 in 4% debenture stock and £27 in fully-paid shares in new company for every £100 stock held. No return of capital to contributories. Removed from Register 1910 .... **1906**

Worcestershire Malting Co. Ld. Regd. 1922. Vol. liq. (members') 6 Aug. 1936. Capital returned to contributories—19*s*. 10·536*d*. per share of £1. Final meeting return regd. 9 Sept. 1937 .... **1937**

Worcestershire Motor Transport Co. Ld. Regd. 1913 as Kidderminster, Stourport & Bewdley Motor Omnibus Co. Ld.; name changed 1914. Vol. liq. (members') 30 Sept. 1946. Final meeting return regd. 7 Oct. 1947 .... **1940**

Workington Blackstone Slag Ld. Regd. 1924. Vol. liq. (members') 9 Dec. 1930. All shares held by United Steel Cos. Ld. Final meeting return regd. 10 Sept. 1934 .... **1931**

Workington Iron & Steel Co. Ld. Regd. 1909. In 1918 United Steel Companies Ld. acquired 99% of ordinary and preference shares. Vol. liq. 22 Aug. 1919. Final meeting return regd. 14 Sept. 1922 .... **1920**

Workington Iron Co. Ld. Regd. 1900. Vol. liq. July 1909. The undertaking was amalgamated with three other companies to form Workington Iron & Steel Co. Ld., in which company shareholders were entitled to 6 preference shares of £1 for every 5 preference shares of £1 held, or 7 ordinary shares of £1 for every 4 ordinary shares of £1 held. Removed from Register 1911 .... **1910**

Workington Railways & Docks Co. Inc. by Special Act 1900. No capital in issue at 31 Dec. 1906 .... **1908**

Workman, Clark (1928) Ld. Regd. Belfast 1928. Vol. liq. (members') 14 Aug. 1935. Shipyard and undertaking acquired by National Shipbuilders' Security Ld. .. **1936**

Worksop Gas Co. Inc. by Special Act 1856. Dissolved 1 May 1949, undertaking being vested in East Midland Area Gas Board under Gas Act 1948. Holders of securities were entitled to receive, British Gas 3% guaranteed stock 1990–95 as follows in respect of each £100 unit held:

	£	s.	d.	
Cons. ord. stock (6% stand.)	215	0	0	
5% cons. pref. stock A	115	0	0	
5% cons. pref. stock B	115	0	0	
4½% red. deb. stock (1943)	100	15	0	
4½% red. deb. stock (red. 1947)	101	10	0	**1952**

World Echo Records Ld. Regd. 1928. Vol. liq. (creditors') 3 June 1930. Assets realised insufficient to pay unsecured creditors in full. Final meeting return regd. 6 June 1933 .... **1931**

World's Treasure Ld. Regd. 1895. Vol. liq. 15 Dec. 1896. Final meeting return regd. 21 Dec. 1898 .... **1897**

Worsbroughdale & Worsbrough Gas Light & Coke Co. Ld. Regd. 1860. Vol. liq. in 1947, when undertaking was acquired by Sheffield & District Gas Co. **1907**

Worship Street Realisations Ld. Regd. 1907 as Joseph Tetley & Co. Ld.; name changed Nov. 1961. Vol. liq. (members') 30 Nov. 1961. Capital returned to contributories—21*s*. (plus accrued dividend) per 5½% redeemable preference share of £1. 20*s*. (plus accrued dividend) per 6½% preference share of £1, and 28*s*. per ordinary share of 5*s*. £5 15*s*. paid into Companies' Liquidation Account in respect of unclaimed dividends. Final meeting return regd. 10 Jan. 1963 .... **1963**

Worsleys Ld. Regd. 1896. Removed from Register 1909 **1899**

Worsnop & Co. Ld. Regd. 1896. Vol. liq. (creditors') 31 Mar. 1931. No capital returned to contributories. Final meeting return regd. 14 May 1934 .... **1932**

Worth (Bond) Holdings Ld. Regd. as private company 28 Apr. 1896 as Thomas Bond Worth & Sons Ld.; converted into public company 12 Aug. 1952; name changed 17 Feb. 1969. Winding-up order made by High Court on 15 Oct. 1979 and completed 18 Jan. 1983 .... **1978–9**

Worthing Gas Light & Coke Co. Established 1835. Inc. by Special Act 1868. By Special Order of 1931 the undertaking was acquired by Brighton and Hove General Gas Co. (later Brighton Hove and Worthing Gas Co.). Stockholders were entitled to stock in acquiring company as follows—for every £100 ordinary stock held—£110 5% standard consolidated stock; for every £100 5½% preference stock held—£91 13*s*. 4*d*. 6% B preference consolidated stock; for every £100 4% perpetual debenture stock held—£80 5% perpetual debenture stock. The liability for the

**See Stock Exchange Year-Book.*

VOL. FOR

5½% and 7% mortgages was assumed by acquiring company **1932**

Worthing Pier Co. Ld. Regd. 1888. Vol. liq. 2 June 1921. The undertaking and assets were sold to Worthing Corporation. Capital returned to contributories— 5s. per share; further payments (if any) not known. Final meeting return regd. 6 Juiy 1922 .... **1922**

Worthington Pump and Machinery Corporation. Inc. Virginia 1916. Succeeded by corporation of same name 1937. .... **1937**

Wotton-under-Edge & District Gas Co. Ld. Regd. 1912. Dissolved 1 May 1949, undertaking being vested in South Western Area Gas Board under Gas Act 1948. Holders of ordinary shares (of £1) were entitled to receive £1 18s. British Gas 3% guaranteed stock 1990–95 for each share held **1952**

Wotton-under-Edge Light Railway Co. Inc. (under Light Railways Act 1896) by order of Light Railways Commissioners confirmed by Board of Trade 1900 **1902**

Wouldham Cement Co. Ld. Regd. 1900 as Wouldham Cement Co. (1900) Ld.; name changed June 1906. Vol. liq. 24 June 1925. All ordinary and 2nd preference shares were held by British Portland Cement Manufacturers Ld., which company acquired all the assets. Holders of 1st preference shares were entitled to repayment at par in cash. Holders of debentures were entitled to an equal amount of Wouldham and Martin Earle debenture stock in acquiring company. Final meeting return regd. 19 Oct. 1926 .... **1926**

Woven Leather Machine-Belting Co. Ld. Regd. 1898. Vol. liq. 29 Oct. 1900. Final meeting return regd. 9 Jan. 1902 .... **1901**

Wraight, Dumbrill & Co. Ld. See Curtis Bros. & Dumbrill Co.

Wrexham & Acton Collieries Co. Ld. Regd. 1863. Vol. liq. 27 May 1921. Reconstructed as Wrexham Colliery Co. Ld. Final meeting return regd. 13 June 1924 .... ***1922**

Wrexham & District Electric Tramways Ld. See Western Transport Co. Ld.

Wrexham & District Transport Co. Ld. See Western Transport Co. Ld.

Wrexham and Ellesmere Railway Co. Inc. by Special Act 1885. In 1922 the undertaking was merged into the Great Western Railway Co., in which company stockholders were entitled to stock as follows:

For each £100 held   G. W.
  4% Debenture................. £100   4% Debenture
  4% Preference................. £80   5% Cons. Pref.
  Ordinary......................... £70   5% Cons. Pref.   **1924**

Wrexham Colliery Co. Ld. Regd. 1921. Vol. liq. 30 Oct. 1924. Final meeting return regd. 16 Dec. 1926 .... ***1925**

Wrexham Gas Co. Inc. by Special Act 1870 as Wrexham Gas Light Co.; name changed 1905. Dissolved 1 May 1949, undertaking being vested in Wales Area Gas Board under Gas Act 1948. Holders of securities were entitled to receive, in respect of each £100 unit held, British Gas 3% guaranteed stock 1990–95 as follows:

                              £   s.   d.
  Ord. stock (5% stand.)........... 108 15 0
  5%, red. pref. stock 100 5 0   **1952**

Wrexham, Mold & Connah's Quay Railway Co. Inc. by Special Act 1862. Under Great Central Railway Act of 1904, the undertaking was sold to that company **1905**

Wright & Greig Ld. Regd. Edinburgh 1890. Vol. liq. Feb. 1918. Final meeting return regd. 28 May 1919 **1918**

Wright (E. J.) Ld. Regd. 1885. Court Orders: to wind up Feb. 1889; to dissolve Aug. 1889. .... **1887**

Wright Hamer Textiles Ld. Regd. 1949. Winding-up order 20 Oct. 1958. Liquidator released 7 Dec. 1964. No capital returned to contributories. Company dissolved and struck off Register 6 Mar. 1965 ...... **1965**

Wright, Layman & Umney Ld. Regd. 1909 as Wright, Layman & Umney (1909) Ld.; name changed Feb. 1914. Vol. liq. (members') 30 May 1932. Undertaking and assets were acquired by Wright, Layman & Umney (1932) Ld. (later Wright, Layman & Umney Ld.). Preference shareholders were repaid at par. Ordinary shareholders were entitled to 2 fully-paid ordinary shares in acquiring company for every 3 shares of £1 held, to participate in distribution of 10,667 preference shares and 12,500 ordinary shares in Savory & Moore Ld., and to £2 1s. 1¼d. per ordinary share in cash. Final meeting return regd. 23 May 1934 .... **1933**

Wright's (Frank) Pre-payment Gas Meter Corporation Ld. Regd. 1895. Reconstructed 1900 as Metropolitan Gas Meters Ld., in which company shareholders were entitled to 3 shares of 10s. for every 2 ordinary shares of 10s. held or 5 shares of 10s. (credited with 8s. paid) for every 2 preference shares of £1 held. Removed from Register 1901 .... **1901**

VOL. FOR

Wright's Taper-Roller Bearings Syndicate Ld. Regd. 1899. Removed from Register 1906 .... **1905**

Wrigley (E. G.) & Co. Ld. Regd. 1898. Vol. liq. Jan. 1924. Undertaking was acquired by Morris Commercial Cars Ld. Struck off Register June 1932 ... **1933**

Wycombe (Borough) Electric Light & Power Co. Ld. Regd. 1897. Vol. liq. (members') 18 Nov. 1940. Undertaking acquired by the local authority 25 Dec. 1939. Capital returned to contributories—20s. per preference share of £1; £1 15s. 8⅝d. per ordinary share of £1. Final meeting return regd. 23 Oct. 1941 **1941**

Wye Shipping Co. Ld. Regd. 1919. Struck off Register 1928 .... **1926**

Wye Valley Railway Co. Inc. by Special Act 1866. By Great Western Railway Act 1905 the undertaking was acquired by that company. Holders of 5% debenture stock received an equal amount of 4½% debenture stock; holders of preference stock received £12 10s. in cash for every £100 held; holders of ordinary shares of £10 received 10s. in cash for each share held **1906**

Wykeham Trust Ld. Regd. 1929. Vol. liq. (members') 15 May 1934. Capital returned to contributories—£10 per preference share of £10; 5s. per ordinary share of £1. Final meeting return regd. 12 Feb. 1935 .... **1935**

Wyldsdale Gold Exploration & Development Co. Ld. Regd. 1889. Vol. liq. 20 Feb. 1893. Final meeting return regd. 26 Feb. 1895 .... **1894**

Wynaad District Gold Mining Co. Ld. Regd. 1881. Vol. liq. June 1882. Court Order to continue winding up under supervision June 1882. Final meeting return regd. 10 Aug. 1885 .... **1883**

Wynaad Perserverance Estate and Gold Mining Co. Ld. Regd. 1880. Removed from Register 1903 .... **1891**

Wynaad Tea Co. Ld. Regd. 1894. Vol liq. Oct. 1907. Undertaking and assets were acquired by East India Tea and Produce Co. Ld. for £29,000 in cash. Removed from Register 1909 .... **1908**

Wyndham's Marine Patents Ld. Undertaking and assets were acquired by Wyndham's Marine Patents (1928) Ld. (later Wyndham Engineering Ld.) for £60,000 in cash and 20,000 fully-paid shares of £1 **1929**

Wynnstay Collieries Ld. Regd. 1889. Receiver appointed in Apr. 1924. All assets were sold. 1st mortgage debenture holders received 8s. 8d. in £ at 28 Jan. 1930; further payments (if any) not known. Struck off Register 24 Nov. 1931 .... **1930**

Wyoming Cattle Ranche Co. Ld. Regd. Edinburgh 1882. Vol. liq. Mar. 1894. Final meeting return regd. 9 Apr. 1897 .... **1895**

Wyvenhoe Gas Co. Ld. Regd. 1901. Dissolved 1 May 1949, undertaking being vested in Eastern Area Gas Board under Gas Act 1948. Holders of securities were entitled to receive, in respect of each £5 unit held, British Gas 3% guaranteed stock 1990–95 as follows:

                              £   s.   d.
  Ord. shares................................. 5 0 0
  5% pref. shares....................... 5 12 0   **1952**

X

Xetal Safety Glass Ld. Regd. 1928. Vol. liq. (members') 23 Nov. 1932. Capital returned to contributories— 2s. per preferred ordinary share of 10s. £122 6s. 4d. was paid into Companies' Liquidation Account. Final meeting return regd. 16 Feb. 1935 .... **1933**

Y

"Y" Syndicate Ld. Regd. 1909. Vol. liq. July 1911. Capital returned to contributories—13s. 6d. in £; further payments (if any) not known. Removed from Register 1912 .... **1913**

Yagerphone Ld. Regd. 1928. Vol. liq. (creditors') 31 Mar. 1933. No capital returned to contributories. Final meeting return regd. 13 Dec. 1935 .... **1934**

Yakutsk Explorers Ld. Regd. 1906. Vol. liq. Feb. 1909. Removed from Register 1910 .... **1910**

Yalgoo Proprietary Gold Mines Ld. Regd. 1896. Vol. liq. 4 Jan. 1899. Reconstructed as company of same name. Final meeting return regd. 19 Mar. 1900 .. **1900**

Yalgoo Proprietary Gold Mines Ld. Regd. 1899 .... **1900**

Yalgoo Public Battery & Gold Mining Co. Ld. Regd. 1895. Removed from Register 1908 .... **1898**

Yan & Axim Exploration Syndicate Ld. Regd. 1901. Struck off Register 1916 .... **1913**

Yana (Wassau) Mines Ld. Regd. 1901. Amalgamated 1904 with Abbassi (Wassau) Gold Mines Ld., in which company shareholders were entitled to 12

See Stock Exchange Year-Book.

VOL. FOR

fully-paid shares of 5s. for every 5 shares of £1 held. Removed from Register 1908 .... **1905**

Yangtse Valley Co. Ld. Regd. 1900. Vol. liq. (members') 18 Dec. 1939. Capital returned to contributories—7½d. per priority share of 6d.; 1½d. per ordinary share of 6d.; 2½d. per deferred share of 1s. £875 13s. 5d. was paid into Companies' Liquidation Account in respect of unclaimed capital (£542 9s. relating to repayment effected prior to liquidation). Final meeting return regd. 20 June 1944 .... **1940**

Yangtse Valley Syndicate Ld. Regd. 1899. Vol. liq. 16 Jan. 1901. Reconstructed 1900 as Yangtse Valley Co. Ld., in which company shareholders were entitled to 1 fully-paid priority share of £1 for each ordinary share of £1 held or 1 deferred share of 1s. for each deferred share of 1s. held. Final meeting return regd. 15 Oct. 1901 .... **1901**

Yankee Doodle Development Co. Ld. Regd. 1899. Reconstructed 1900 as New Selukwe Gold Mine Ld. (later Selukwe Columbia Gold Mine Ld.) for £125,000 in fully-paid shares of £1. Removed from Register 1905 .... **1902**

"Yankee Girl" Silver Mines Ld. Regd. 1890. Vol. liq. 16 Aug. 1893. Final meeting return regd. 13 Apr. 1897 **1894**

Yarde Kerri Group Tin Mines Ld. Regd. 1920. Vol. liq. (members') 6 Mar. 1933. Undertaking acquired by Nigerian Tin & Exploration Co. Ld. Debenture holders were satisfied. Final meeting return regd. 5 Dec. 1933 .... **1934**

Yardley (J. & J.) & Co. Ld. Regd. 1897. Vol. liq. June 1909. The undertaking was acquired by Old Wolverhampton Breweries Ld. The 1st mortgage debenture stockholders received 47% of holding in B debenture stock and 11% in shares of new company; the A mortgage debenture stockholders were entitled to 52% of holding in B debenture stock and 13% in shares of new company. No return was made to ordinary and preference shareholders. Removed from Register 1913 .... **1911**

Yarmouth and Annapolis Railway Co. Inc. Nova Scotia by Special Act 1870 as Western Counties Railway. In 1894 the undertaking was acquired by Windsor & Annapolis Railway Co. Ld. for £130,000 4% debenture stock, £50,000 preference shares and £85,000 ordinary shares of £20 .... **1894**

Yates & Co. Ld. Regd. 1889. Receiver for debenture holders appointed. A dividend (amount unspecified) was paid in Nov. 1905 on account of debenture stock. Removed from Register 1906 .... **1906**

Yates and Thom Ld. Regd. 1905.Vol. liq. 15 June 1927. Capital returned to contributories—20s. per preference share of £1; 10s per ordinary share of £1; further payments (if any) not known. Final meeting return regd. 23 Mar. 1929 .... **1928**

Yates, Haywood & Co. and the Rotherham Foundry Co. Ld. Regd. 1900. Vol. liq. 4 Nov. 1908. Final meeting return regd. 4 Dec. 1923 .... **1909**

Ye Olde Bell & Wardrobe Chambers Ld. Regd. 1902. Vol. liq. 13 Jan. 1921. Capital returned to contributories—10s. 2d. per share; further payments (if any) not known. Final meeting return regd. 13 Aug. 1921 **1922**

Yeadon & Guiseley Gas Co. Inc. by Special Act 1868 as Yeadon & Guiseley Gaslight & Coke Co.; name changed 1925. Dissolved 1 May 1949, undertaking being vested in North Eastern Area Gas Board under Gas Act 1948. Holders of securities were entitled to receive, in respect of each £100 unit held, British Gas 3% guaranteed stock 1990–95 as follows:

	£	s.	d.
Cons. A stock (10% stand.)	230	0	0
New B stock (7% stand.)	165	0	0

Liability in respect of certain mortgage loans assumed by the Board **1952**

Yeadon Waterworks Co. Inc. by Special Acts 1870 & 1889. The undertaking was transferred to the Rombalds Water Board in 1962. Winding up order 29 July 1964. Capital returned to contributories (per £1 stock)—4½% redeemable preference stock, £1; 10% consold. A ordinary stock, £1 13s. 8d.; 7% new B ordinary stock, £1 3s. 7d. The 4½%, 6% and 5½% mortgage were repaid at par in Dec. 1963, Liquidator released 19 Oct. 1972................................ **1973–4**

Yelnut Syndicate Ld. Regd. 1931. Vol. liq. (members') 3 Aug. 1934. Directly controlled by North Ashanti Mining Co. Ld. Final meeting return regd. 31 Jan. 1935 .... **1935**

Yenisei Copper Co. Ld. Regd. 1902. Court Order to wind up Mar. 1913. Struck off Register 20 Feb. 1942 ... **1943**

Yeoland Consols Ld. Regd. 1881. Wound up by Order of Court 15 Mar. 1888 .... ***1889**

Yeoman Trust Ld. See T. Y. T. Ld.

Yeovil Electric Light & Power Co. Ld. Regd. 1922. Undertaking was acquired by Wessex Electricity

VOL. FOR

Co. as from 1 July 1937. Dissolved 1 Apr. 1948 under Electricity Act 1947 .... **1937**

Yerilla Claims Ld. Regd. 1896. Vol. liq. 21 Sept. 1900. Final meeting return regd. 8 Oct. 1901 .... **1901**

Yerrakonda Gold Mining Co. Ld. Regd. 1894. Reconstructed 1903 as Indian Mines Development Syndicate Ld., in which company shareholders were entitled to 1 share of 4s. (credited with 2s. 6d. paid) for every 4 shares of 4s. held. Removed from Register 1904 .... **1904**

Yerua Estancia Co. Ld. Regd. 1878. Vol. liq. 2 Feb. 1889. Final meeting return regd. 12 Mar. 1890 .... ***1890**

Yilgarn Exploring Co. Ld. Regd. 1895. Removed from Register 1912 .... **1905**

Yilgarn Gold Mines Ld. Regd. Dublin 1894. Amalgamated with Carlyle Gold Mines Ld. as Carlyle Consolidated Gold Mines Ld. Removed from Register 1908 .... **1901**

Ymir Gold Mines Ld. Regd. 1898. Reconstructed 1902 as company of same name, Shareholders were entitled to 1 share of £1 (credited with 17s. paid) in new company for each share of £1 held. Removed from Register 1909 .... **1907**

Ymir Gold Mines Ld. Regd 1902. Reconstructed 1907 as company of same name. Shareholders were entitled to 1 share of 5s. (credited with 4s. paid) in new company for each share of £1 held. Removed from Register 1909 .... **1908**

Ymir Gold Mines Ld. Regd. 1907. Vol. liq. 29 Dec. 1913. Final meeting return regd. 14 Dec. 1928 .... **1914**

Yoker Distillery Ld. Regd. Edinburgh 1913. Vol. liq. Jan. 1927. Creditors were to be paid in full. Direct controlling interest held by Distillers Co. Ld. Final meeting return regd. 1 July 1927 .... **1928**

Yokohama Shokin Ginko. Established Japan 1880. On 21 Jan. 1942 Board of Trade ordered London branch to be wound up under Trading with the Enemy Act 1939 and Defence Regulations **1943**

Yokohama Specie Bank (See Yokohama Shokin Ginko) **1943**

Yolland, Husson & Birkett Ld. Regd. 1903. Court Order to wind up 1906. Removed from Register 1912 ... **1907**

Yomah Oil Co. Ld. Regd. 1913. Receiver appointed 15 Dec. 1916. Struck off Register 1923 .... **1920**

York City County Banking Co. Ld. Established 1830. Vol. liq. Jan. 1909. Business acquired by London Joint Stock Bank Ld., in which company shareholders were entitled to 3 shares of £100 (credited with £15 paid) in the London Joint Stock Bank Ld. and £5 in cash for every 10 shares of £10 held **1909**

York District & East Riding Public House Trust Co. Ld. Regd. 1902. Vol. liq. Oct. 1911. Removed from Register 1912 .... **1912**

York Gas Co. Inc. as York Gas Light Co. by Special Act 1823; reinc. as York United Gas Light Co. by Special Act 1844; name changed 1912. Dissolved 1 May 1949, undertaking being vested in North Eastern Area Gas Board under Gas Act 1948. Holders of securities were entitled to receive, in respect of each £100 unit held, British Gas 3% guaranteed stock 1990–95 as follows:

	£	s.	d.
Cons. ord. stock (4% stand.)	115	0	0
4% A pref. stock	102	0	0
3¾% perp. deb. stock	100	0	0
5% red. deb. stock	104	0	0

Liability in respect of certain mortgage loans assumed by the Board **1952**

York Gold Mining Co. Ld. Inc. Transvaal 1895; reconstructed 1898. Vol. liq. Oct. 1906 .... **1907**

York Investment Co. Ld. Regd. 1877 as County Loan Co. Ld.; name changed to Provincial Discount and Credit Co. Ld. in May 1883, to Provincial Discount Co. Ld. in Aug. 1891 and as above in Feb. 1898. Vol. liq. 12 June 1899. Reconstructed as Ebor Investment and Trading Co. Ld in which company shareholders were entitled to 1 share of £1 (credited as fully-paid) for each share of £1 held. Final meeting return regd.6 Apr. 1900 .... **1900**

York Street Flax Spinning Co., Ld. Regd. in Dublin 1888; transferred to Belfast under Government of Ireland Act 1920. Vol. liq. (members') 18 May 1961, Debenture stock was repaid at par in Dec. 1961 and preference stock at par in Jan. 1962. Capital returned to contributories—£4 15s. per £1 ordinary stock. Final meeting return regd. 8 Mar. 1968 ..... **1968**

York Town & Blackwater Gas & Coke Co. Ld. (later York Town & Blackwater Gas Co.) See Yorktown (Camberley) & District Gas & District Gas & Electricity Co.

York Tramways Co. Ld. Regd. 1878. Vol. liq. Feb. 1884. Court Order to continue winding up under supervision Feb. 1884. Final meeting 1885 return regd. 20 July 1886 .... **1885**

VOL. FOR

York Union Banking Co. Ld. Regd. 1883. Removed from Register 1912 1941

York United Gas Light Co. *See* York Gas Co.

Yorke Peninsula Mining Co. Ld. Regd. 1864. Vol. liq. Apr. 1885. Final meeting return regd. 26 Apr. 1888 1886

Yorke, Stoneham & Jones, Ld. Regd. 1910. Vol. liq. 5 Apr. 1928. Final meeting return regd. 3 Oct. 1947 1948

Yorkshire Aërated Bread & Restaurant Co. Ld. Regd. 1888. Vol. liq. 19 Aug. 1890. Final meeting return regd. 22 July 1891 1891

Yorkshire Aeroplane Club Ld. Regd. 1925. Vol. liq. (members') 3 Aug. 1934. Direct controlling interest was held by National Flying Services Ld. Final meeting return regd. 4 Apr. 1936 1934

Yorkshire Amalgamated Collieries Ld. Regd. 1927. Vol. liq. (members') 29 Apr. 1953. Capital returned to contributories—preference; 6s. 1·041d. per share of 5s.; ordinary: 25s. 2d. per share of 5s.; deferred 5s. 0·4d. per share of 1s. £1,278 was paid into Companies' Liquidation Account. Final meeting return regd. 2 Feb. 1956. Dissolution declared void 28 Apr. 1958 and restored to register. Final meeting return regd. 31 May 1961 1962

Yorkshire & Derbyshire Coal & Iron Co. Ld. *See* Carlton Main Colliery Co. Ld.

Yorkshire & Lancashire Water-Gas Co. Ld. Regd. 1889. Reconstructed 1893 as Amalgamated Water Gas Companies Ld in which company acquired the assets for 25,000 fully-paid shares of £1. Removed from Register 1904 1897

Yorkshire & Rhodesia Development Co. Ld. *See* Anglo-Rhodesia Development Co. Ld.

Yorkshire Artificial Silk Co. Ld. Regd. 1928. Court Order to wind up 1 July 1929. Struck off Register 27 Jan. 1942 1942

Yorkshire Bacon Curing Co. Ld. Regd. 1897. Removed from Register 1903 1902

Yorkshire Banking Co. Ld. Established 1843. Regd. 1880. Vol. liq. Dec. 1901. Business was acquired by London City and Midland Bank Ld. (later Midland Bank Ld.), in which company shareholders were entitled to 1½ shares of £60 (credited with 12s. 6d. paid) *plus* 12s. in cash for every 6 shares of £10 (£2 10s. paid) held 1902

Yorkshire Boiler Insurance & Steam Users Co. Ld. Regd. 1873. In 1896 the business was acquired by Vulcan Boiler and General Insurance Co. Ld. Dissolved before 1931 1909

Yorkshire "Brush" Electric Light & Power Co. Ld. Regd. 1882. Vol. liq. Jan. 1884. Absorbed by Hammond Electric Light & Power Supply Co. Ld., in which company shareholders were entitled to 1 fully-paid share of £5 for every 6 shares of £2 held. Final meeting return regd. 7 July 1884 1884

Yorkshire Coking & Chemical Co. Ld. Regd. 1913. Vol. liq. (members') 3 Feb. 1953. Final meeting return regd. 22 May 1954 1940

Yorkshire Dales Railway Co. (Skipton to Grassington). Inc. by Special Act 1897. In 1922 the undertaking was merged into the Midland Railway Co., in which company stockholders were entitled to stock as follows:

For each share of £10 held   *Midland Rly.*
4½% Preference ...... £18 2¼% Prefd. Conv. Ord.
Ordinary .... £16 2¼% Prefd. Conv. Ord.
The loans owing by the Company to the Midland Railway Co. and the 500 Yorkshire Dales Ordinary Shares owned by that Company were cancelled.... 1924

Yorkshire Discount Co. Ld. Regd. 1872. Vol. liq. 12 June 1899. Reconstructed as Ebor Investment and Trading Co. Ld., in which company shareholders were entitled to 2 shares of £1 (credited as fully-paid) for each share of £2 held, or 1 share of £1 for each share of £1 held. Final meeting return regd. 6 Apr. 1900 1900

Yorkshire Electric Power Co. Inc. by Special Act 1901. Dissolved 1 Apr. 1948, undertaking being vested in British (later Central) Electricity Authority and Yorkshire Area Board under Electricity Act 1947. Holders of securities were entitled to receive British Electricity 3% guaranteed stock (1968–73), as follows in respect of each £1 unit of capital held:

	£	s.	d.
6% preference stock	1	11	10
Ordinary stock	2	10	10
3¼% redeemable debenture stock	1	0	8¾
3½% redeemable debenture stock	1	0	6	1949

Yorkshire Electric Tramways Construction Syndicate Ld. Regd. 1903. Vol. liq. 16 May 1905. Control of the system was transferred to Yorkshire (West Riding) Electric Tramways Co. Ld. (later West Riding Automobile Co. Ld.). Removed from Register 1906 1906

Yorkshire House-to-House Electricity Co. Ld. Regd. 1889. Vol. liq. 10 Feb. 1899. Business was acquired

VOL. FOR

by Corporation of Leeds for £217,421 5% irredeemable stock and £774 in cash. Final meeting return regd. 24 Feb. 1902 1899

Yorkshire Indigo, Scarlet and Colour Dyers, Ld. Regd. 1899. Vol. liq. 22 Mar. 1963. Capital returned to contributories—3d. per preference share of 10s. £113 19s. 9d. was paid into Companies' Liquidation Account. Final meeting return regd. 17 Aug. 1967 1968

Yorkshire Investment & American Mortgage Co Ld. Regd. 1886. Vol. liq. 12 Apr. 1897. Court Order to continue winding up under supervision 14 Apr. 1897. Final meeting return regd. 22 Feb. 1927 1898

Yorkshire Iron & Coal Co. Ld. Regd. 1901. Assets realised insufficient to satisfy claims of debenture holders. Struck off Register 21 Apr. 1944.............. 1945

Yorkshire Laundries Ld. Regd. 1898. Vol. liq. 9 May 1921. Final meeting return regd. 5 Feb. 1924 1922

Yorkshire Liberal Newspaper & Publishing Co. Ld. Regd. 1905. Vol. liq. 7 Feb. 1929. Undertaking and assets were acquired by Provincial Newspapers Ld. (later United Newspapers Publications Ld.) in which company shareholders were entitled to 1 1st preference share of £1 for each preference share of £1 held or 6 1st preference shares for every 5 A preference shares of £1 held or 8 1st preference shares for every 5 preferred ordinary shares of £1 held. Final meeting return regd. 7 Apr. 1931 1930

Yorkshire Main Colliery (1923) Ld. Regd. 1923. Undertaking amalgamated with Doncaster Amalgamated Collieries Ld 1938

Yorkshire Paper Mills Ld. Regd. 1925. Vol. liq. (creditors') 8 Oct. 1930. Assets realised insufficient to pay unsecured creditors in full. Final meeting return regd. 21 July 1934 1931

Yorkshire Provident Life Assurance Co. Ld. Regd. 1870. Vol. liq. Aug. 1906. Undertaking and assets were acquired by United Provident Assurance Co. Ld., in which company shareholders were entitled to shares or debentures paid up to extent of their holdings. Holders of debenture stock were entitled to cash or an equal amount of 2nd mortgage debentures in new company. Removed from Register 1908 1907

Yorkshire Railway Waggon Co. Ld. Regd. 1889. Vol. liq. (members') 5 Oct. 1931. Wagon hire business was acquired by North Central Wagon Co. Ld. (later North Central Finance Ld.). Capital returned to contributories—£3 15s. 5·495d. per share of £10 (£2 paid). Final meeting return regd. 13 Sept. 1935 ... 1932

Yorkshire Railway Waggon Co., Ld. Regd. 1932. Vol. liq. (members') 2 Jan. 1947. Capital returned to contributories—£1 6s. 11·505d. per share of £1. Final meeting return regd. 22 Oct. 1947 1948

Yorkshire Sugar Co. Ld. Regd. 1927. Vol. liq. (members') 30 July 1936. Undertaking was transferred to British Sugar Corporation Ld., in which company shareholders were entitled to 6 shares of £1 (credited as fully-paid) for every 5 shares of £1 held *plus* approximately 4s. 10d. per share. Final meeting return regd. 12 Aug. 1939 1937

Yorkshire Trust Ld. Regd. 1892. Removed from Register 1907 1896

Yorkshire Waste Heat Co. Ld. Regd. 1912. Vol. liq. (members') 18 July 1938. Capital returned to contributories—£56,095 6s. 5d. *plus* benefits and obligations of two agreements for right of way over property of London, Midland & Scottish Railway Co. Final meeting return regd. 21 Dec. 1928 1939

Yorkshire Wool Combers Association Ld. Regd. 1899. Undertaking (except certain items) and goodwill were acquired in 1904 by Woolcombers Ld., (later Woolcombers Holdings Ld.) for £75,000 in cash and £325,000 in debenture stock. Removed from Register 1907 1907

Yorktown (Camberley) & District Gas & Electricity Co. Regd. 1859 as York Town & Blackwater Gas & Coke Co. Ld.; inc. by Special Act 1904 as York Town & Blackwater Gas Co.; name changed 1928. The electricity undertaking was vested on 1 Apr. 1948 in British (later Central) Electricity Authority and Southern Area Electricity Board. Dissolved 1 May 1949, the remaining undertaking being vested in Southern Area Gas Board under Gas Act 1948. Holders of securities were entitled to receive, in respect of each £100 unit held, British Gas 3% guaranteed stock 1990–95 as follows:

	£	s.	d.
Cons. ord. stock (5% stand.)	121	0	0
5% cons. pref. stock	113	0	0
4% red. pref. stock	101	0	0
5½% red. deb. bonds	105	0	0
6% red. deb. bonds	107	0	0
5½% perp. deb. stock	133	10	0
5% red. deb. stock	108	0	0
3½% red. deb. stock (issued before			

See Stock Exchange Year-Book.

VOL. FOR

1 Jan. 1946) 103 0 0
3½% red. deb. stock (issued since
31 Dec. 1945). 104 0 0   1952

Yoruba Exploration Ld. Regd. 1900. Vol. liq. 12 Mar.
1902. Final meeting return regd. 13 June 1902 ....   *1903

Yost Typewriter Co. Ld. Regd. 1891. Vol. liq. 19 Dec.
1923. Struck off Register 24 July 1936.   1925

Youanmi Gold Mines Ld. Regd. 1934. Winding-up order
26 Mar. 1945. Capital returned to contributories—
3s. 2¾d. per share of 10s. Liquidator released Feb.
1956. Struck off Register 22 Apr. 1958   1956

Youlten Openers Ld. Regd. 1922. Struck off Register
Jan. 1932   1932

Young & Son Ld. Regd. 1922. Vol. liq. 26 Nov. 1928.
Final meeting return regd. 9 Mar. 1933   1930

Young (Charles L.) & Co. Ld. Regd. 1896. Removed
from Register 1905   1904

Young (David) Rubber Estates (British Guiana) Ld.
Regd. 1910. Court Order to wind up 18 June 1912.
Liquidator released 14 Nov. 1914. Struck off
Register 14 Feb. 1919   1913

Young (H. D.) & Sons Ld. Regd. Edinburgh 1898. Vol.
liq. (creditors') 17 Nov. 1930. No capital returned to
contributories. Final meeting return regd. 16 Nov.
1931   1931

Young (John) [of Radcliffe] Ld. Regd. 1894. Receiver
appointed 4 Aug. 1925; ceased to act 18 May 1929.
Struck off Register Dec. 1930   1931

Young, King & Co. Ld. Regd. Dublin 1885; transferred
to Belfast under Government of Ireland Act 1920.
Vol. liq. (members') 30 Sept. 1944. Assets and
liabilities were taken over by Distillers Co. (Northern Ireland) Ld. which company was the sole
shareholder. Final meeting return regd. 28 May
1946   1947

Young's Collieries Ld. Regd. Edinburgh 1898. Vol. liq.
Sept 1908. Collieries taken over by Banknock Coal
Co. Ld. Final meeting return regd. 30 June 1911   1909

Youngs, Crawshay and Youngs, Ld. Regd. 1897. Vol. liq.
(members') 1 Oct. 1958. Preference shares (of £1)
were repaid at par and the surplus assets distributed
in specie to ordinary shareholders. Final meeting
return regd. 23 Sept. 1961   1963

Young's Reversible Nut Lock Syndicate Ld. Regd. 1892.
Removed from Register 2 Aug. 1904 ....   *1894

Ystradgunlais & Swansea Colliery Co. Ld. Regd. 1874.
Vol. liq. 8 June 1893; Court order dated 21 June
1893 to continue under supervision. Capital returned to contributories—£33 7s. 4d. per share.
Final meeting return regd. 1 June 1949.............   1950

Ystwith Lead Mining Co. Ld. Regd. 1880. Vol. liq. July
1884. Final meeting return regd. 20 Nov. 1885   1885

Ytterően Mining Co. Ld. Regd. 1863. Vol. liq. 3 July
1888. Final meeting return regd. 9 Apr. 1891 ......   *1889

Yuanmi Gold Mines Ld. Regd 1911. Vol. liq. 16 Jan.
1924. Final meeting return regd. 20 Jan. 1930   1924

Yuba River Gold Washing Co. Ld. Regd. 1881. Vol. liq.
Nov. 1883. Final meeting return regd.7 June 1890   1885

Yuca Films Ld. See N. F. X. Ld.

Yukon Corporation Ld. Regd. 1898. Vol. liq. 26 June
1906. Removed from Register 1913   1907

Yukon Goldfields Ld. Regd. 1897. Vol. liq. 10 Oct. 1899:
Reconstructed as company of same name. Shareholders were entitled to 8 ordinary shares of £1 in
new company for each deferred share of £1 held or 1
ordinary share of £1 for each ordinary share of £1
held. Final meeting return regd. 11 Dec. 1900   1908

Yukon Goldfields Ld. Regd. 1899. Vol. liq. June 1908.
Removed from Register 1910   1909

Yunnan Rubber Estates, Ld. Regd. 27 Oct. 1925. Vol.
liq. (members') 22 Sept. 1950. Capital returned to
contributories—6s. 4¼d. per share of 2s. £2,039 19s.
2d. was paid into Companies' Liquidation Account.
Final meeting return regd.1 Apr. 1953   1954

Yuruari Co. Ld. Regd. 1888. Vol. liq. 21 Nov. 1891.
Court Order to continue winding up under supervision 23 Jan. 1892. Reconstructed as Caratal Mining
Co. Ld., in which company shareholders were
entitled to 1 share of 2s. 6d. (credited with 2s. paid)
for each share of 2s. 6d. held. Final meeting return
regd. 25 Feb. 1897   1896

Z

"Z" Electric Lamp Manufacturing Co. Ld. Regd. 1908.
Vol. liq. 13 Aug. 1920. Final meeting return regd. 15
Nov. 1923   1921

Zafra & Huelva Railway Co. [Compania del Ferrocarril
de Zafra a Huelva]. Inc. in Spain 1884. Taken over
by Spanish Government, holders of bonds and

VOL. FOR

shares being offered exchange into Spanish Government 3½% redeemable bonds (Deuda Amortizable)
as follows—for each 3% 1st mtg. bond of £20. Ptas
85·018 3½% government stock; for each 3% 2nd mtg.
bond of £20. Ptas 10 3½% government stock; for each
share of Ptas 500 (£20). Ptas 2 3½% government
stock. Winding-up order made 17 Jan. 1949;
liquidator released 15 June 1954 having made a
return of 25s. per bond to 1st. mtge. bondholders   1955

Zalamea Copper Co. Ld. Regd. 1906. The properties
were sold. No return to Noteholders was anticipated. Struck off Register Mar. 1934   1935

Zambesi (Gaza) Concessions Co. Ld. Regd. 1889. Vol.
liq. 14 Jan. 1892. Reconstructed as company of same
name. Shareholders were entitled to 1 share of £1
(credited with 17s. 6d. paid) in new company for
each share of £1 held or 4 fully-paid shares for each
founders' share of £1 held. Struck off Register 21
Feb. 1911   1894

Zambesi (Sofala) Concessions Co. Ld. Regd. 1889. Vol.
liq. 14 Jan. 1892. Reconstructed as company of same
name. Shareholders were entitled to 1 share of £1
(credited with 17s. 6d. paid) in new company for
each share of £1 held or 4 fully-paid shares for each
founders' share of £1 held. Struck off Register 21
Feb. 1911   1894

Zambesia Mining Development Ld. Regd. 1911. Vol. liq.
(creditors') 15 Mar. 1949. Final meeting return regd.
3 May 1952   1953

Zambesia-Rand Investment Co. Ld. Regd. 1895. Vol. liq.
13 June 1898. Undertaking and asset were acquired
by Zambesia Exploring Co. Ld., for 44,865 fully-
paid shares of £1. Final meeting return regd. 3 Nov.
1898   1899

Zambia Broken Hill Development Co. Ld. Regd. 1910 as
Rhodesia Broken Hill Development Co. Ld.; name
changed Apr. 1965. Under scheme of arrangement
of June 1971 mining assets, undertaking and
liabilities were transferred to Nchanga Consolidated Copper Mines Ld.; all other assets to Zambia
Copper Investments Ld. Shareholders were entitled
to receive 1 share in Zambia Copper Investments
Ld. for every 5 shares held. Company was dissolved
28 June 1971   1972

Zante Oilfields Ld. Regd. 1931. Struck off Register 25
Apr. 1939   1940

Zapiga Nitrate Co. Ld. Regd. 1906. Vol. liq. 5 Apr.
1923. Final meeting return regd. 27 July 1923   1924

Zapopan Mines Ld. Regd. 1889. Vol. liq. 16 Sept. 1896.
Reconstructed as Brock's Gold Fields of the
Northern Territories of Australia Ld., in which
company shareholders were entitled to 1 share of £1
(credited with 18s. paid) for each share of £1 held.
Final meeting return regd. 11 May 1898   1897

Zaruma Gold Mining Co. Ld. Regd. 1892. Vol. liq. 26
Feb. 1894. Struck off Register 20 Mar. 1906   1895

Zaruma Mining Corporation Ld. Regd. 1913. Vol. liq. 10
Feb. 1926. Final meeting return regd. 2 Aug. 1932   1926

Zavaleta Ld. Regd. 1896. Vol. liq. 2 Aug. 1899. Final
meeting return regd. 29 June 1900   1900

Zebril Food Co. Ld. Regd. 1899. Removed from
Register 1903 ....   *1902

Zeehan Dundas Mines Ld. Regd. 1910. Vol. liq. 10 Mar.
1921. Final meeting return regd. 23 May 1924   1922

Zeehan-Montana Mine Ld. Regd. 1892. Vol. liq. 26 Feb.
1920. Capital returned to contributories—5s. 1d. per
share of £1; further payments (if any) not known.
Final meeting return regd. 16 Nov. 1923   1921

Zeehan-Queen Ld. Regd. 1902. Vol. liq. 9 June 1921.
Final meeting return regd. 23 May 1924   1922

Zeehan South Comstock Ld. Regd. 1901. Reconstructed
1906 as company of same name. Removed from
Register 1909   1908

Zeehan South Comstock Ld. Regd. 1906. Court Orders:
to wind up 8 Dec. 1908; to stay proceedings 30 Dec.
1908; to wind up 16 Aug. 1911. Liquidator released 6
Dec. 1913. Struck off Register 3 Sept. 1918   1912

Zeehan-Western Ld. Regd. 1903. Vol. liq. 28 June 1918.
Final meeting return regd. 17 Sept. 1920   1919

Zemská Banka Pro Cechy. [Central Bank of the Savings
Banks of Bohemia and Moravia.] Inc. in Prague in
1889 as Royal Bank of Bohemia; name changed to
Zemska Banka in 1922 and to above title in Aug.
1943. Under Decree 183 of 20 July 1948 the rights
and commitments of the bank were transferred
without liquidation, as from 1 Oct. 1948 to Inves-
ticni Banka   1949

Zenebi Tin Mines Ld. Regd. 1925. Vol. liq. 11 Apr. 1928.
Undertaking acquired by Associated Tin Mines of
Nigeria Ld. Final meeting return regd. 5 Feb. 1929   1939

Zeta Shipping Co. Ld. Regd. 1920. Vol. liq. 15 July 1924.
Final meeting return regd. 14 Jan. 1925................   *1925

See Stock Exchange Year-Book.

VOL. FOR

Ziervogel Gold Mining Co. Ld. Regd. 1889. Vol. liq. 28 Oct. 1890. Property was taken over by Johannesburg Gold Fields Ld. for £135,000 in fully-paid shares of £1. Final meeting return regd. 8 Dec. 1894 — 1891

Zimbo Products (1929) Ld. Regd. 1929. Vol. liq. (creditors') 12 June 1933. Assets realised insufficient to pay creditors in full. Final meeting return regd. 11 Mar. 1936 1934

Zinc Corporation Ld. Inc. Victoria 1905. Vol. liq. July 1911. Reconstructed as company of same name. Shareholders (ordinary and preference) were entitled to an equal number of shares of same class in new company 1912

Zinc Investments Ld. Inc. Victoria 1936 as Zinc Investments Proprietary Ld.; name changed 1937. Vol. liq. (members') 9 Dec. 1955. Shareholders received 18 shares of Associated Pulp & Paper Mills Ld. for every 100 shares held. Company dissolved 17 Sept. 1960 1962

Zinc Manufacturing Co. Ld. Regd. 1929. Vol. liq. (members') 17 June 1935. Undertaking acquired by Amalgamated Oxides Ld., in which company shareholders were entitled to 1 share of 10s., fully-paid, for every 20 A ordinary or 6 B ordinary shares of 10s. held. Final meeting return regd. 10 Apr. 1940 — 1936

Zietovo Mines Ld. Regd. 1929. Vol. liq. (members') 16 Aug. 1938. Undertaking acquired by Trepca Mines Ld., in which company shareholders were entitled to 2 fully-paid shares of 5s. for every 5 shares of 5s. held. Final meeting return regd. 25 July 1947 1948

Zoedone Co. Ld. Regd. 1886. Vol. liq. 29 Nov 1889. Reconstructed as Aërated Beverage & Buffet Co. Ld., in which company shareholders were entitled to 1 share of £1 10s. (credited with £1 5s. paid) for each fully-paid share and 1 share of £1 10s. (credited with £1 3s. paid) for each share (£1 8s. paid) held. Final meeting return regd. 31 July 1896 1891

Zog Ld. Regd. 1910. Vol. liq. 21 Dec. 1923. Controlling interest held by Hargreaves Bros. & Co. Ld. Final meeting return regd. 11 Sept. 1924 1923

Zongo Rubber Estate Ld. Regd. 1910. Vol. liq 4 Aug. 1917. Final meeting return regd. 31 July 1920 1918

Zoroastrian Gold Estates Ld. Regd. 1900. Reconstructed as Zoroastrian Ld., in which company shareholders were entitled to 1 fully-paid share of 5s. and 3 shares of 5s. (credited with 4s. paid) for each share of £1 held. Removed from Register 1905 1906

Zoroastrian Gold Mines Ld. Regd. 1897. Reconstructed 1900 as Zoroastrian Gold Estates Ld., in which

VOL. FOR

company shareholders were entitled to 1 share of £1 (credited with 17s. paid) for each share of £1 held. Removed from Register 1903 1900

Zoroastrian Ld. Inc. Guernsey 1902. Vol. liq. Dec. 1906. Undertaking and assets acquired by Cardigan Mines Ld. Shareholders were entitled to receive 1 share of 2s. 6d. credited with 1s. 6d. paid for each share of 5s. held 1907

Zoutpansberg Consolidated Mines Ld. Regd. 1899. Vol. liq. 8 Nov. 1905. Removed from Register 1906 ... 1906

Zoutpansberg Exploration & Gold Mining Co. Ld. Regd. 1888. Vol. liq. 12 Apr. 1892. Undertaking and property were acquired by Central African & Zoutpansberg Exploration Co. Ld., in which company shareholders were entitled to 6 ordinary shares of 5s. (credited with 2s. 6d. paid) for each preference share of £1 held or 1 fully-paid ordinary share of 5s. for each ordinary share of £1 held. Final meeting return regd. 26 May 1893 1893

Zoutpansberg Mines Development Syndicate Ld. Regd. 1902. Removed from Register 1905 1905

Zoutpansberg Prospecting Co. Ld. Regd. 1889. Court Order to wind up 20 Dec. 1890. Removed from Register 1906 1891

Zuid African Syndicate Ld. Regd. 1903. Removed from Register 4 Oct. 1907 1908

Zuma Tin Areas (Nigeria) Ld. Regd. 1911. Vol. liq. (members') 31 July 1947. Direct controlling interest was owned by Gold & Base Metal Mines of Nigeria Ld. Final meeting return regd. 10 Dec. 1947 1917

Zungon Tin Syndicate Ld. Regd. 1914. Vol. liq. (members') 11 Mar. 1931. Undertaking and assets were acquired by Gold Coast Consolidated Lands Ld., in which company shareholders were entitled to 1 share of 2s. 6d. (credited with 2s. 2d. paid) for every 2 shares of 1s. held. Final meeting return regd. 28 Oct. 1931 1932

Zwanenberg Ld. Regd. 1911. Vol. liq. (members') 17 June 1948. Preference shareholders (both classes) were entitled to 5 shares in Zwanenberg-Organon Ld. (later Zwanenberg Associated Food Companies Ld.) for every 4 held and deferred shareholders were allotted 290,000 ordinary and 300,000 deferred shares in the new company. Final meeting return regd. 5 Oct. 1953 1954

Zwartland (Transvaal) Land Co. Ld. Regd. 1889. Vol. liq. 4 Feb. 1927. Undertaking was acquired by Transvaal Exploring Land & Minerals Co. Ld. Final meeting return regd. 29 Aug. 1928 1927